P9-ECY-118

PRESENTED TO

____

BY ______________________________

____

____

____

DATE ______________________________

THIS CERTIFIES THAT

and

were united in

on the day of

in the year of our LORD 19

at

by

WITNESS

WITNESS

WIFE'S FAMILY TREE

WIFE

BROTHERS & SISTERS

MOTHER

BROTHERS & SISTERS

GRANDFATHER

BROTHERS & SISTERS

GRANDMOTHER

BROTHERS & SISTERS

GREAT GRANDFATHER

GREAT GRANDMOTHER

GREAT GRANDMOTHER

GREAT GRANDFATHER

FATHER

BROTHERS & SISTERS

GRANDFATHER

BROTHERS & SISTERS

GRANDMOTHER

BROTHERS & SISTERS

GREAT GRANDFATHER

GREAT GRANDMOTHER

GREAT GRANDFATHER

GREAT GRANDMOTHER

HUSBAND

BROTHERS & SISTERS

MOTHER

BROTHERS & SISTERS

FATHER

BROTHERS & SISTERS

GRANDFATHER

BROTHERS & SISTERS

GRANDFATHER

BROTHERS & SISTERS

GRANDMOTHER

BROTHERS & SISTERS

GRANDMOTHER

BROTHERS & SISTERS

GREAT GRANDFATHER

GREAT GRANDMOTHER

GREAT GRANDFATHER

GREAT GRANDMOTHER

GREAT GRANDFATHER

GREAT GRANDMOTHER

GREAT GRANDFATHER

GREAT GRANDMOTHER

NAME	DATE

BIRTHS

NAME	DATE

NAME DATE

NEW AMERICAN STANDARD BIBLE

with
Read-Along References
Read-Along Translations

Illustrated
DICTIONARY-CONCORDANCE

Words of Christ in Red

THOMAS NELSON PUBLISHERS
Nashville

Printed in the Republic of Korea

7 8 9 10 11 12 13 14 15 16 17 18 19 20—86 87 88 89 92 93

The grass withers, the flower fades, but the word of our God stands forever. (Isaiah 40:8)

Foreword

The New American Standard Bible has been produced with the conviction that the words of Scripture as originally penned in the Hebrew and Greek were inspired by God. Since they are the eternal Word of God, the Holy Scriptures speak with fresh power to each generation, to give wisdom that leads to salvation, that men may serve Christ to the glory of God.

The Editorial Board had a twofold purpose in making this translation: to adhere as closely as possible to the original languages of the Holy Scriptures, and to make the translation in a fluent and readable style according to current English usage.

THE FOURFOLD AIM
OF
THE LOCKMAN FOUNDATION

1. These publications shall be true to the original Hebrew, Aramaic, and Greek.
2. They shall be grammatically correct.
3. They shall be understandable to the masses.
4. They shall give the Lord Jesus Christ His proper place, the place which the Word gives Him; therefore, no translation work will ever be personalized.

Preface To The New American Standard Bible

In the history of English Bible translations, the King James Version is the most prestigious. This time-honored version of 1611, itself a revision of the Bishops' Bible of 1568, became the basis for the English Revised Version appearing in 1881 (New Testament) and 1885 (Old Testament). The American counterpart of this last work was published in 1901 as the American Standard Version. Recognizing the values of the American Standard Version, the Lockman Foundation felt an urgency to update it by incorporating recent discoveries of Hebrew and Greek textual sources and by rendering it into more current English. Therefore, in 1959 a new translation project was launched, based on the ASV. The result is the New American Standard Bible.

The American Standard Version (1901) has been highly regarded for its scholarship and accuracy. A product of both British and American scholarship, it has frequently been used as a standard for other translations. It is still recognized as a valuable tool for study of the Scriptures. The New American Standard Bible has sought to preserve these and other lasting values of the ASV.

Furthermore, in the preparation of this work numerous other translations have been consulted along with the linguistic tools and literature of biblical scholarship. Decisions about English renderings were made by consensus of a team composed of educators and pastors. Subsequently, review and evaluation by other Hebrew and Greek scholars outside the Editorial Board were sought and carefully considered.

The Editorial Board has continued to function since publication of the complete Bible in 1971. Minor revisions and refinements, recommended over the last five years, are presented in this edition.

Principles of Translation

Modern English Usage: The attempt has been made to render the grammar and terminology in contemporary English. When it was felt that the word-for-word literalness was unacceptable to the modern reader, a change was made in the direction of a more current English idiom. In the instances where this has been done, the more literal rendering has been indicated in the notes.

Alternative Readings: In addition to the more literal renderings, notations have been made to include alternate translations, readings of variant manuscripts and explanatory equivalents of the text. Only such notations have been used as have been felt justified in assisting the reader's comprehension of the terms used by the original author.

Hebrew Text: In the present translation the latest edition of Rudolph Kittel's BIBLIA HEBRAICA has been employed together with the most recent light from lexicography, cognate languages, and the Dead Sea Scrolls.

Hebrew Tenses: Consecution of tenses in Hebrew remains a puzzling factor in translation. The translators have been guided by the requirements of a literal translation, the sequence of tenses, and the immediate and broad contexts.

The Proper Name of God in the Old Testament: In the Scriptures, the name of God is most significant and understandably so. It is inconceivable to think of spiritual matters without a proper designation for the Supreme Deity. Thus the most common name for deity is God, a translation of the original Elohim. The normal word for Master is Lord, a rendering of Adonai. There is yet another name which is particularly assigned to God as His special or proper name, that is, the four letters YHWH (Exodus 3:14 and Isaiah 42:8). This name has not been pronounced by the Jews because of reverence for the great sacredness of the divine name. Therefore, it was consistently pronounced and translated LORD. The only exception to this translation of YHWH is when it occurs in immediate proximity to the word Lord, that is, Adonai. In that case it is regularly translated GOD in order to avoid confusion.

It is known that for many years YHWH has been transliterated as Yahweh, however no complete certainty attaches to this pronunciation.

Greek Text: Consideration was given to the latest available manuscripts with a view to determining the best Greek text. In most instances the 23rd edition of the Nestle Greek New Testament was followed.

Greek Tenses: A careful distinction has been made in the treatment of the Greek aorist tense (usually translated as the English past, "He did") and the Greek imperfect tense (rendered either as English past progressive, "He was doing"; or, if inceptive, as "He *began* to do" or "He started to do"; or else if customary past, as "He used to do"). "Began" is italicized if it renders an imperfect tense, in order to distinguish it from the Greek verb for "begin."

On the other hand, not all aorists have been rendered as English pasts ("He did"), for some of them are clearly to be rendered as English perfects ("He has done"), or even as past perfects ("He had done"), judging from the context in which they occur. Such aorists have been rendered as perfects or past perfects in this translation.

As for the distinction between aorist and present imperatives, the translators have usually rendered these imperatives in the customary manner, rather than attempting any such fine distinction as "Begin to do!" (for the aorist imperative), or, "Continually do!" (for the present imperative).

As for sequence of tenses, the translators took care to follow English rules rather than Greek in translating Greek presents, imperfects and aorists. Thus, where English says, "We knew that he was doing," Greek puts it, "We knew that he does"; similarly, "We knew that he had done" is the Greek, "We knew that he did." Likewise, the English, "When he had come, they met him," is represented in Greek by: "When he came, they met him." In all cases a consistent transfer has been made from the Greek tense in the subordinate clause to the appropriate tense in English.

In the rendering of negative questions introduced by the particle **mē** (which always expects the answer, "No") the wording has been altered from a mere, "Will he not do this?" to a more accurate, "He will not do this, will he?"

Editorial Board
THE LOCKMAN FOUNDATION

Special Features of Your

NEW AMERICAN STANDARD BIBLE

The helps and educational features found in this Bible have been prepared by eminent scholars. They are strictly non-sectarian. The New American Standard text is used.

In this edition Read-A-Long References© and Read-A-Long Translations© are used to help you understand the text. The symbol "R" beside a word denotes a Read-A-Long Reference© which lists at the end of the verse other passages which have similar meanings or further bearing on the word or phrase indicated. This exciting cross-reference method of Bible study ties the magnificent truths of Scripture together.

The symbol "T" beside a word or phrase indicates a Read-A-Long Translation©, an easy-to-understand literal meaning at the end of the verse.

When the symbol "A" is used, an alternate translation is given at the end of the verse. Such word clarifications built right into the text eliminate the need for constant referral to a Bible dictionary or other volumes.

When more than one reference or translation follows a verse, a center point "•" is used for division. When space does not allow the symbol letter (R, T or A) to precede the word or phrase referenced, then the symbol follows immediately at the end of the word or first word of the phrase referenced.

Explanation of General Format

FOOTNOTES are used only where the text especially requires them for clarification. Marginal notes and cross references have been deleted from this edition.

PARAGRAPHS are designated by bold face numbers or letters.

QUOTATION MARKS are used in the text in accordance with modern English usage.

"THOU," "THEE" AND "THY" are not used in this translation except in the language of prayer when addressing Diety.

PERSONAL PRONOUNS are capitalized when pertaining to Diety.

ITALICS are used in the text to indicate words which are not found in the original Hebrew or Greek but implied by it. Italics are used in the footnotes to signify alternate readings for the text.

SMALL CAPS in the New Testament are used in the text to indicate Old Testament quotations or obvious allusions to Old Testament texts. Variations of Old Testament wording are found in New Testament citations depending on whether the New Testament writer translated from a Hebrew text, used existing Greek or Aramaic translations, or paraphrased the material. It should be noted that modern rules for the indication of direct quotation were not used in biblical times thus allowing freedom for omissions or insertions without specific indication of these.

ASTERISK—In regard to the use in Greek of the historical present, the translators recognized that in some contexts the present tense seems more unexpected and unjustified to the English reader than a past tense would have been. But Greek authors frequently used the present tense for the sake of heightened vividness, thereby transporting their readers in imagination to the actual scene at the time of occurrence. However, the translators felt that it would be wise to change these historical presents to English past tenses. Therefore verbs marked with an asterisk (*) represent historical presents in the Greek which have been translated with an English past tense in order to conform to modern usage.

DSS = Dead Sea Scrolls

Gr. = Greek translation of O.T. (Septuagint or LXX) or Greek text of N.T.

Heb. = Hebrew text, usually Masoretic

M.T. = Masoretic text

Lit. = A literal translation

Or = An alternate translation justified by the Hebrew or Greek

[ ] = Brackets in the text are around words probably not in the original writings

[?] = After some references indicates a similar name, place or thing not necessarily identical with that in the text

f., ff. = following verse or verses

ms., mss. = manuscript, manuscripts

v., vv. = verse, verses

BOOKS OF THE OLD TESTAMENT

BOOKS OF THE NEW TESTAMENT

THE

OLD TESTAMENT

THE BOOK OF

GENESIS

IN the beginning[r]God created the
heavens and the earth. Ps. 89:11
2 And the earth was [1]formless
and void, and darkness was over
the [t]surface of the deep; and the
Spirit of God was [2]moving over
the surface of the waters. *face of*
3 Then[r]God said, "Let there be
light"; and there was light. Ps. 33:6
4 And God saw that the light
was good; and God[r]separated the
light from the darkness. Is. 45:7
5 And[r]God called the light day,
and the darkness He called night.
And there was evening and there
was morning, one day. Ps. 74:16
6 Then God said, "Let there be
[a]an expanse in the midst of the waters, and let it separate the waters
from the waters." *firmament*
7 And God made the [3]expanse,
and separated the waters which
were below the expanse from the
waters which were above the expanse; and it was so.
8 And God called the expanse
heaven. And there was evening
and there was morning, a second
day.
9 Then God said, "Let the waters below the heavens be gathered into one place, and let the dry
land appear"; and it was so.
10 And God called the dry land
earth, and the [r]gathering of the
waters He called seas; and God
saw that it was good. Ps. 33:7; 95:5
11 Then God said, "Let the
earth sprout [a]vegetation, [a]plants
yielding seed, *and* fruit trees bearing fruit after their kind,[t]with seed
in them, on the earth"; and it was
so. *herbs • grass • in which is its seed*
12 And the earth brought forth
[a]vegetation, [a]plants yielding seed
after their kind, and trees bearing
fruit,[t]with seed in them, after their
kind; and God saw that it was
good. *grass • herbs • in which is its seed*
13 And there was evening and
there was morning, a third day.
14 Then God said, "Let there be
[a]lights in the expanse of the heavens to separate the day from the
night, and let them be for signs,
and for seasons, and for days and
years; *luminaries, light-bearers*
15 and let them be for lights in
the expanse of the heavens to give
light on the earth"; and it was so.
16 And God made the two great
lights, the greater light to govern
the day, and the lesser light [t]to
govern the night; *He made* the
stars also. *for the dominion of*
17 [r]And God placed them in the
expanse of the heavens to give
light on the earth, Jer. 33:20, 25
18 and [t]to govern the day and
the night, and to separate the light
from the darkness; and God saw
that it was good. *for the dominion of*
19 And there was evening and
there was morning, a fourth day.
20 Then God said, "Let the waters[a]teem with swarms of living
creatures, and let birds fly above
the earth[t]in the open expanse of
the heavens." *swarm • on the face*
21 And God created[r]the great

[1]Or, *a waste and emptiness* [2]Or, *hovering*
[3]Or, *firmament*

sea monsters, and every living
creature that moves, with which
the waters swarmed after their
kind, and every winged bird after
its kind; and God saw that it was
good. Ps. 104:25-28
22 And God blessed them, saying, "Be fruitful and multiply, and
fill the waters in the seas, and let
birds multiply on the earth."
23 And there was evening and
there was morning, a fifth day.
24 Then God said, "Let the
earth bring forth living creatures
after their kind: cattle and creeping things and beasts of the earth
after their kind"; and it was so.
25 And God made the[r]beasts of
the earth after[t]their kind, and the
cattle after[t]their kind, and everything that creeps on the ground
after its kind; and God saw that it
was good. Jer. 27:5 • *its*
26 Then God said, "Let Us make
man in Our image, according to
Our likeness; and let them rule
over the fish of the sea and over
the birds of the[t]sky and over the
cattle and over all the earth, and
over every creeping thing that
creeps on the earth." *heavens*
27 And God created man[r]in His
own image, in the image of God
He created him; male and female
He created them. Gen. 5:1f.
28 And God blessed them; and
God said to them, "Be fruitful and
multiply, and fill the earth, and
subdue it; and rule over the fish of
the sea and over the birds of the
sky, and over every living thing
that[a]moves on the earth." *creeps*
29 Then God said, "Behold, [r]I
have given you every plant yielding seed that is on the[t]surface of
all the earth, and every tree which
has fruit yielding seed; it shall be
food for you; Ps. 104:14 • *face of*
30 and to every beast of the
earth and to every bird of the sky
and to every thing that moves on
the earth[t]which has life, *I have
given* every green plant for food";
and it was so. *in which is a living soul*
31 And God saw all that He had
made, and behold, it was very
good. And there was evening and
there was morning, the sixth day.

CHAPTER 2

THUS the heavens and the earth
were completed, and all [r]their
hosts. Deut. 4:19; 17:3
2 And by the seventh day God
completed His work which He
had done; and[r]He rested on the
seventh day from all His work
which He had done. Heb. 4:4, 10
3 Then God blessed the seventh day and sanctified it, because
in it He rested from all His work
which God had created and made.
4 This is the account of the
heavens and the earth when they
were created, in the day that the
LORD God made earth and heaven.
5 Now no shrub of the field
was yet in the earth, and no plant
of the field had yet sprouted, for
the LORD God had not sent rain
upon the earth; and there was no
man to cultivate the ground.
6 But a[a]mist used to rise from
the earth and water the whole[t]sur-
face of the ground. *flow • face of*
7 Then the LORD God formed
man of[r]dust from the ground, and
breathed into his nostrils the

breath of life; and man became a
living[t]being. Gen. 3:19 • *soul*
8 And the LORD God planted a
[r]garden toward the east, in Eden;
and there He placed the man
whom He had formed. Is. 51:3
9 And out of the ground the
LORD God caused to grow [r]every
tree that is pleasing to the sight
and good for food; the tree of life
also in the midst of the garden,
and the tree of the knowledge of
good and evil. Ezek. 47:12
10 Now a river [t]flowed out of
Eden to water the garden; and
from there it divided and became
four [t]rivers. *was going out* • *heads*
11 The name of the first is Pishon; it [t]flows around the whole
land of [r]Havilah, where there is
gold. *surrounds* • Gen. 25:18
12 And the gold of that land is
good; the bdellium and the onyx
stone are there.
13 And the name of the second
river is Gihon; it flows around the
whole land of Cush.
14 And the name of the third
river is Tigris; it[t]flows east of Assyria. And the fourth river is the
Euphrates. *is the one going*
15 Then the LORD God took the
man and put him into the garden
of Eden to cultivate it and keep it.
16 And the LORD God [r]com-
manded the man, saying, "From
any tree of the garden you may
eat freely; Gen. 3:2, 3
17 but from the tree of the
knowledge of good and evil you
shall not [t]eat, for in the day that
you eat from it [r]you shall surely
die." *eat from it* • Rom. 6:23
18 Then the LORD God said, "It
is not good for the man to be
alone; [r]I will make him a helper
[4]suitable for him." 1 Cor. 11:9
19 And out of the ground the
LORD God formed every beast of
the field and every bird of the sky,
and brought *them* to the man to
see what he would call them; and
whatever the man called a living
creature, that was its name.
20 And the man gave names to
all the cattle, and to the birds of
the sky, and to every beast of the
field, but for [5]Adam there was not
found a helper suitable for him.
21 So the LORD God caused a
[r]deep sleep to fall upon the man,
and he slept; then He took one of
his ribs, and closed up the flesh at
that place. Gen. 15:12
22 And the LORD God [6]fashioned
into a woman the rib which He
had taken from the man, and
brought her to the man.
23 And the man said,
"This is now bone of my
bones,
And flesh of my flesh;
[t]She shall be called Woman,
Because she was taken out
of Man." *This one*
24 For this cause a man shall
leave his father and his mother,
and shall cleave to his wife; and
they shall become one flesh.
25 [r]And the man and his wife
were both naked and were not
ashamed. Gen. 3:7, 10, 11

CHAPTER 3

NOW [r]the serpent was more
crafty than any beast of the field
which the LORD God had made.
And he said to the woman, "Indeed, has God said, 'You shall not

[4]Lit., *corresponding to* [5]Or, *man* [6]Lit., *built*

eat from [a]any tree of the garden'?" 2 Cor. 11:3 · *every*
2 And the woman said to the
serpent, "From the fruit of the
trees of the garden we may eat;
3 but from the fruit of the tree
which is in the middle of the garden, God has said, 'You shall not
eat from it or touch it, lest you
die.'"
4 And the serpent said to the
woman, "You surely shall not die!
5 "For God knows that in the
day you eat from it your eyes will
be opened, and you will be like
God, knowing good and evil."
6 When the woman saw that
the tree was good for food, and
that it was a delight to the eyes,
and that the tree was desirable to
make *one* wise, she took from its
fruit and ate; and she gave also to
her husband with her, and he ate.
7 Then the eyes of both of
them were opened, and they knew
that they were naked; and they
sewed fig leaves together and
made themselves loin coverings.
8 And they heard the sound of
[r]the LORD God walking in the garden in the [t]cool of the day, and the
man and his wife hid themselves
from the presence of the LORD
God among the trees of the garden. Gen. 18:33 · *wind, breeze*
9 Then the LORD God called to
the man, and said to him, "Where[r]
are you?" Gen. 4:9; 18:9
10 And he said, "I[r] heard the
sound of Thee in the garden, and I
was afraid because I was naked;
so I hid myself." [r]Ex. 20:18, 19
11 And He said, "Who told you
that you were naked? Have you
eaten from the tree of which I
commanded you not to eat?"
12 [r]And the man said, "The
woman whom Thou gavest *to be*
with me, she gave me from the
tree, and I ate." Job 31:33; Prov. 28:13
13 Then the LORD God said to
the woman, "What is this you
have done?" And the woman said,
"The[r] serpent deceived me, and I
ate." 2 Cor. 11:3; 1 Tim. 2:14
14 And the LORD God said to the
serpent,
"Because[r] you have done
this, Deut. 28:15-20
Cursed are you more than
all cattle,
And more than every beast
of the field;
On your belly shall you go,
And dust shall you eat
All the days of your life;
15 And I will put [r]enmity
Between you and the
woman, Rev. 12:17
And between your seed and
her seed;
[r]He shall [a]bruise you on the
head, Rom. 16:20
And you shall bruise him on
the heel." *crush*
16 To the woman He said,
"I will greatly multiply
Your pain in childbirth,
In pain you shall bring forth
children;
Yet your desire shall be for
your husband,
And he shall rule over you."
17 Then to Adam He said, "Because you have listened to the
voice of your wife, and have eaten
from the tree about which I commanded you, saying, 'You shall
not eat from it';

Cursed is the ground be-
cause of you;
In toil you shall eat of it
All the days of your life.
18 "Both thorns and thistles it
shall grow for you;
And you shall eat the [t]plants
of the field; *plant*
19 By the sweat of your face
You shall eat bread,
Till you [r]return to the
ground,
Because [r]from it you were
taken; Ps. 90:3 • Gen. 2:7
For you are dust,
And to dust you shall re-
turn."

20 Now the man called his
wife's name [7]Eve, because she was
the mother of all *the* living.
21 And the LORD God made garments of skin for Adam and his
wife, and clothed them.
22 Then the LORD God said,
"Behold, the man has become like
one of [r]Us, knowing good and evil;
and now, lest he stretch out his
hand, and take also from [r]the tree
of life, and eat, and live forever"— Gen. 1:26 • Rev. 22:14
23 therefore the LORD God sent
him out from the garden of Eden,
to cultivate the ground from
which he was taken.
24 So He drove the man out;
and at the [r]east of the garden of
Eden He stationed the cherubim,
and the flaming sword which
turned every direction, to guard
the way to the tree of life. Gen. 2:8

CHAPTER 4

NOW the man [t]had relations with
his wife Eve, and she conceived
and gave birth to Cain, and she
said, "I have gotten a manchild
with *the help of* the LORD." *knew*
2 And again, she gave birth to
his brother Abel. And [r]Abel was a
keeper of flocks, but Cain was a
tiller of the ground. Luke 11:50, 51
3 So it came about [t]in the
course of time that Cain brought
an offering to the LORD of the fruit
of the ground. *at the end of days*
4 And Abel, on his part also
brought of the firstlings of his
flock and of their fat portions.
And [r]the LORD had regard for Abel
and for his offering; 1 Sam. 15:22
5 but [r]for Cain and for his offering He had no regard. So [r]Cain became very angry and his countenance fell. 1 Sam. 16:7 • Jude 11
6 Then the LORD said to Cain,
"Why are you angry? And why
has your countenance fallen?
7 "If you do well, will not *your
countenance* be lifted up? And if
you do not do well, sin is crouch-
ing at the door; and its desire is
for you, but you must master it."
8 And Cain [t]told Abel his
brother. And it came about when
they were in the field, that Cain
rose up against Abel his brother
and killed him. *said to*
9 Then the LORD said to Cain,
[r]"Where is Abel your brother?"
And he said, "I do not know. Am I
my brother's keeper?" Gen. 3:9
10 And He said, "What have
you done? [r]The voice of your
brother's blood is crying to Me
from the ground. Num. 35:33
11 "And now you are cursed
from the ground, which has
opened its mouth to receive your
brother's blood from your hand.

[7]I.e., living or life

12 "When you cultivate the
ground, it shall no longer yield its
strength to you; [r]you shall be a vagrant and a wanderer on the
earth." Lev. 26:17, 36
13 And Cain said to the LORD,
"My punishment is too great to
bear!
14 "Behold, Thou hast [r]driven me
this day from the face of the
ground; and from Thy face I shall
be hidden, and I shall be a vagrant
and a wanderer on the earth, and
it will come about that whoever
finds me will kill me." Gen. 3:24
15 So the LORD said to him,
"Therefore whoever kills Cain,
vengeance will be taken on him
sevenfold." And the LORD appointed a sign for Cain, lest anyone finding him should slay him.
16 Then Cain went out from the
presence of the LORD, and settled
in the land of Nod, east of Eden.
17 And Cain [t]had relations with
his wife and she conceived, and
gave birth to Enoch; and he built a
city, and called the name of the
city Enoch, after the name of his
son. *knew*
18 Now to Enoch was born Irad;
and Irad [t]became the father of Mehujael; and Mehujael became the
father of Methushael; and Methushael became the father of Lamech. *begot*
19 And Lamech took to himself
[r]two wives: the name of the one
was Adah, and the name of the
other, Zillah. Gen. 2:24
20 And Adah gave birth to Ja-
bal; he was the father of those
who dwell in tents and *have* livestock.
21 And his brother's name was
Jubal; he was the father of all
those who play the lyre and pipe.
22 As for Zillah, she also gave
birth to Tubal-cain, the forger of
all implements of bronze and iron;
and the sister of Tubal-cain was
Naamah.
23 And Lamech said to his
wives,

"Adah and Zillah,
Listen to my voice,
You wives of Lamech,
Give heed to my speech,
For I [a]have killed a man for
wounding me; *kill*
And a boy for striking me;
24 If Cain is avenged [r]seven-
fold, Gen. 4:15
Then Lamech seventy-
sevenfold."

25 And Adam [t]had relations
with his wife again; and she gave
birth to a son, and named him
Seth, for, *she said,* "God has appointed me another [t]offspring in
place of Abel; [r]for Cain killed
him." *knew* · *seed* · Gen. 4:8
26 And to Seth, to him also a
son was born; and he called his
name Enosh. Then *men* began to
call upon the name of the LORD.

CHAPTER 5

THIS is the book of the generations of Adam. In the day when
God created man, He made him [r]in
the likeness of God. Col. 3:10
2 He created them male and
female, and He [r]blessed them and
named them [8]Man in the day when
they were created. Gen. 1:28
3 When Adam had lived one
hundred and thirty years, he [9]be-
came the father of *a son* in his

[8] Lit., *Adam*
[9] Lit., *begot,* and so throughout this context

own likeness, according to his
image, and named him Seth.
4 Then the days of Adam after
he became the father of Seth were
eight hundred years, and he had
other sons and daughters.
5 So all the days that Adam
lived were nine hundred and
thirty years, and he died.
6 And Seth lived one hundred
and five years, and became the father of Enosh.
7 Then Seth lived eight hundred and seven years after he became the father of Enosh, and he
had *other* sons and daughters.
8 So all the days of Seth were
nine hundred and twelve years,
and he died.
9 And Enosh lived ninety
years, and became the father of
Kenan.
10 Then Enosh lived eight hundred and fifteen years after he became the father of Kenan, and he
had *other* sons and daughters.
11 So all the days of Enosh were
nine hundred and five years, and
he died.
12 And Kenan lived seventy
years, and became the father of
Mahalalel.
13 Then Kenan lived eight hundred and forty years after he became the father of Mahalalel, and
he had *other* sons and daughters.
14 So all the days of Kenan
were nine hundred and ten years,
and he died.
15 And Mahalalel lived sixty-
five years, and became the father
of Jared.
16 Then Mahalalel lived eight
hundred and thirty years after he
became the father of Jared, and he
had *other* sons and daughters.
17 So all the days of Mahalalel
were eight hundred and ninety-
five years, and he died.
18 And Jared lived one hundred
and sixty-two years, and became
the father of Enoch.
19 Then Jared lived eight hundred years after he became the father of Enoch, and he had *other*
sons and daughters.
20 So all the days of Jared were
nine hundred and sixty-two years,
and he died.
21 And Enoch lived sixty-five
years, and became the father of
Methuselah.
22 Then Enoch [r]walked with
God three hundred years after he
became the father of Methuselah,
and he had *other* sons and daughters. Gen. 6:9; 17:1; 24:40
23 So all the days of Enoch were
three hundred and sixty-five
years.
24 And Enoch walked with God;
and he was not, for God took him.
25 And Methuselah lived one
hundred and eighty-seven years,
and became the father of Lamech.
26 Then Methuselah lived seven
hundred and eighty-two years after he became the father of Lamech, and he had *other* sons and
daughters.
27 So all the days of Methuselah
were nine hundred and sixty-nine
years, and he died.
28 And Lamech lived one hundred and eighty-two years, and
became the father of a son.
29 Now he called his name
Noah, saying, "This one shall [t]give
us rest from our work and from

the toil of our hands *arising from*
the ground which the LORD has
cursed." *comfort us in*
30 Then Lamech lived five hundred and ninety-five years after he
became the father of Noah, and he
had *other* sons and daughters.
31 So all the days of Lamech
were seven hundred and seventy-
seven years, and he died.
32 And Noah was[r]five hundred
years old, and Noah became the
father of Shem, Ham, and Japheth. Gen. 7:6

CHAPTER 6

NOW it came about, when men
began to multiply on the face of
the land, and daughters were born
to them,
2 that the sons of God saw that
the daughters of men were[t]beauti-
ful; and they took wives for themselves, whomever they chose. *good*
3 Then the LORD said, "My
Spirit shall not strive with man
forever, because he also is flesh;
nevertheless his days shall be one
hundred and twenty years."
4 The [r][10]Nephilim were on the
earth in those days, and also afterward, when the sons of God came
in to the daughters of men, and
they bore *children* to them. Those
were the mighty men who *were* of
old, men of renown. Num. 13:33
5 Then the LORD saw that the
wickedness of man was great on
the earth, and that[r]every intent of
the thoughts of his heart was only
evil continually. Rom. 1:28-32
6 And the LORD was sorry that
He had made man on the earth,
and He was grieved in His heart.

[10]Or, *giants*

7 And the LORD said, "I will
blot out man whom I have created
from the face of the land, from
man to animals to creeping things
and to birds of the sky; for I am
sorry that I have made them."
8 But[r]Noah found favor in the
eyes of the LORD. Matt. 24:37
9 These are *the records of* the
generations of Noah. Noah was a
righteous man, blameless in his
time; Noah walked with God.
10 And Noah[t]became the father
of three sons: Shem, Ham, and Japheth. *begot*
11 Now the earth was corrupt in
the sight of God, and the earth
was[r]filled with violence. Ezek. 8:17
12 And God looked on the earth,
and behold, it was corrupt; for[r]all
flesh had corrupted their way
upon the earth. Ps. 14:1-3
13 Then God said to Noah, "The[r]
end of all flesh has come before
Me; for the earth is filled with violence because of them; and behold, I am about to destroy them
with the earth. Is. 34:1-4; 1 Pet. 4:7
14 "Make for yourself an ark of
gopher wood; you shall make the
ark with rooms, and shall[a]cover it
inside and out with pitch. *pitch*
15 "And this is how you shall
make it: the length of the ark
three hundred [11]cubits, its breadth
fifty cubits, and its height thirty
cubits.
16 "You shall make a[a]window for
the ark, and finish it to a cubit
from[t]the top; and set the door of
the ark in the side of it; you shall
make it with lower, second, and
third decks. *roof* • *above*
17 "And behold, [r]I, even I am
bringing the flood of water upon

[11]I.e., One cubit equals approx. 18 in.

kind, and every bird after its kind, all sorts of birds. *its*

15 So they went into the ark to Noah, by twos of all flesh in which was the breath of life.

16 And those that entered, male and female of all flesh, entered as God had commanded him; and the LORD closed *it* behind him.

17 Then the flood [t]came upon the earth for [r]forty days; and the water increased and lifted up the ark, so that it rose above the earth. *was* • Gen. 7:4

18 And the water prevailed and increased greatly upon the earth; and the ark [t]floated on the [t]surface of the water. *went* • *face*

19 And the water prevailed more and more upon the earth, so that all the high mountains everywhere under the heavens were covered.

20 The water prevailed fifteen cubits higher, [r]and the mountains were covered. Gen. 8:4

21 And all flesh that [a]moved on the earth perished, birds and cattle and beasts and every swarming thing that swarms upon the earth, and all mankind; *crept*

22 of all that was on the dry land, all in whose nostrils was the breath of the spirit of life, died.

23 Thus He blotted out [t]every living thing that was upon the face of the land, from man to animals to creeping things and to birds of the [t]sky, and they were blotted out from the earth; and only Noah was left, together with those that were with him in the ark. *all existence* • *heavens*

24 [r]And the water prevailed upon the earth one hundred and fifty days. Gen. 8:3

CHAPTER 8

BUT God remembered Noah and all the beasts and all the cattle that were with him in the ark; and God caused a wind to pass over the earth, and the water subsided.

2 Also the fountains of the deep and the floodgates of the sky were closed, and [r]the rain from the sky was restrained; Gen. 7:4, 12

3 and the water receded steadily from the earth, and at the end [r]of one hundred and fifty days the water decreased. Gen. 7:24

4 And in the seventh month, on the seventeenth day of the month, [r]the ark rested upon the mountains of Ararat. Gen. 7:20

5 And the water decreased steadily until the tenth month; in the tenth month, on the first day of the month, the tops of the mountains became visible.

6 Then it came about at the end of forty days, that Noah opened the [r]window of the ark which he had made; Gen. 6:16

7 and he sent out a raven, and it flew here and there until the water was dried up from the earth.

8 Then he sent out a dove from him, to see if the water was abated from the face of the land;

9 but the dove found no resting place for the sole of her foot, so she returned to him into the ark; for the water was on the [t]surface of all the earth. Then he put out his hand and took her, and brought her into the ark to himself. *face*

the earth, to destroy all flesh in which is the breath of life, from under heaven; everything that is on the earth shall perish. 2 Pet. 2:5

18 "But I will establish [r]My covenant with you; and you shall enter the ark—you and your sons and your wife, and your sons' wives with you. Gen. 9:9-16; 17:7

19 "And [r]of every living thing of all flesh, you shall bring two of every *kind* into the ark, to keep *them* alive with you; they shall be male and female. Gen. 7:2, 14, 15

20 "Of [r]the birds after their kind, and of the animals after their kind, of every creeping thing of the ground after its kind, two of every *kind* shall come to you to keep *them* alive. Gen. 7:3

21 "And as for you, take for yourself some of all [r]food which is edible, and gather *it* to yourself; and it shall be for food for you and for them." Gen. 1:29, 30

22 [r]Thus Noah did; according to all that God had commanded him, so he did. Gen. 7:5; Heb. 11:7

CHAPTER 7

THEN the LORD said to Noah, "Enter the ark, you and all your household; for you *alone* I have seen *to be* [r]righteous before Me in this [t]time. Gen. 6:9 • *generation*

2 "You shall take with you of every clean animal [t]by sevens, a male and his female; and of the animals that are not clean two, a male and his female; *seven seven*

3 also of the birds of the [t]sky, by sevens, male and female, to keep [t]offspring alive on the face of all the earth. *heavens* • *seed*

4 "For after [r]seven more days, I will send rain on the earth [r]forty days and forty nights; and I will blot out from the face of the land every living thing that I have made." Gen. 7:10 • Gen. 7:12, 17

5 [r]And Noah did according to all that the LORD had commanded him. Gen. 6:22

6 Now Noah was six hundred years old when the flood of water [t]came upon the earth. *was*

7 Then Noah and his sons and his wife and his sons' wives with him entered the ark because of the water of the flood.

8 [r]Of clean animals and animals that are not clean and birds and everything that creeps on the ground, Gen. 6:19, 20; 7:2, 3

9 there went into the ark to Noah by twos, male and female, as God had commanded Noah.

10 And it came about after the seven days, that the water of the flood [t]came upon the earth. *were*

11 In the six hundredth year of Noah's life, in the second month, on the seventeenth day of the month, on the same day all [r]the fountains of the great deep burst open, and the floodgates of the sky were opened. Gen. 8:2

12 And [r]the rain [t]fell upon the earth for forty days and forty nights. Gen. 7:4, 17 • *was*

13 On the very same day Noah and Shem and Ham and Japheth, the sons of Noah, and Noah's wife and the three wives of his sons with them, entered the ark,

14 they and every beast after its kind, and all the cattle after [t]their kind, and every creeping thing that creeps on the earth after its

10 So he waited yet another
seven days; and again he sent out
the dove from the ark.
11 And the dove came to him
toward evening; and behold, in
her beak was a freshly picked olive leaf. So Noah knew that the
water was abated from the earth.
12 Then he waited yet another
seven days, and sent out[r]the dove;
but she did not return to him
again. Jer. 48:28
13 Now it came about in the six
hundred and first year, in the first
month, on the first of the month,
the water was dried up[t]from the
earth. Then Noah removed the
covering of the ark, and looked,
and behold, the surface of the
ground was dried up. *from upon*
14 And in the second month, on
the twenty-seventh day of the
month, the earth was dry.
15 Then God spoke to Noah,
saying,
16 "Go out of the ark, you and
your wife and your sons and your
sons' wives with you.
17 "Bring out with you every living thing of all flesh that is with
you, birds and animals and every
creeping thing that creeps on the
earth, that they may[a]breed abundantly on the earth, and be fruitful
and multiply on the earth." *swarm*
18 So Noah went out, and his
sons and his wife and his sons'
wives with him.
19 Every beast, every creeping
thing, and every bird, everything
that moves on the earth, went out
by their families from the ark.
20 Then Noah built [r]an altar to
the LORD, and took of every [r]clean
animal and of every clean bird
and offered burnt offerings on the
altar. Gen. 12:7, 8 • Lev. 11:1-47
21 And the LORD smelled the
soothing aroma; and the LORD
said to Himself, "I will never
again curse the ground on account
of man, for the intent of man's
heart is evil from his youth; and I
will never again [t]destroy every living thing, as I have done. *smite*
22 "While the earth remains,
Seedtime and harvest,
And cold and heat,
And [r]summer and winter,
And day and night
Shall not cease." Ps. 74:17

CHAPTER 9

AND God blessed Noah and his
sons and said to them, "Be fruitful
and multiply, and fill the earth.
2 "And the fear of you and the
terror of you shall be on every
beast of the earth and on every
bird of the [t]sky; with everything
that creeps on the ground, and all
the fish of the sea, into your hand
they are given. *heavens*
3 "Every moving thing that is
alive shall be food for you; I give
all to you, [r]as *I gave* the green
plant. Gen. 1:29
4 "Only you shall not eat flesh
with its life, *that is,* its blood.
5 "And surely I will require
your lifeblood; from every beast I
will require it. And from *every*
man, from every man's brother I
will require the life of man.
6 "Whoever[r] sheds man's
blood, Matt. 26:52
By man his blood shall be
shed,
For in the image of God
He made man.

7 "And as for you, be fruitful
and multiply;
[t]Populate the earth abundantly and multiply in it." *Swarm in the earth*

8 Then God spoke to Noah and
to his sons with him, saying,
9 "Now behold, [r]I Myself do establish My covenant with you, and with your [t]descendants after you; Gen. 6:18 • *seed*
10 and with every living creature that is with you, the birds, the cattle, and every beast of the earth with you; of all that comes out of the ark, even every beast of the earth.
11 "And I establish My covenant with you; and all flesh shall never again be cut off by the water of the flood, neither shall there again be a flood to destroy the earth."
12 And God said, "This is the sign of the covenant which I am making between Me and you and every living creature that is with you, for [a]all successive generations; *everlasting generations*
13 I set My bow in the cloud, and it shall be for a sign of a covenant between Me and the earth.
14 "And it shall come about, when I bring a cloud over the earth, that the bow shall be seen in the cloud,
15 and [r]I will remember My covenant, which is between Me and you and every living creature of all flesh; and [r]never again shall the water become a flood to destroy all flesh. Ezek. 16:60 • Gen. 9:11
16 "When the bow is in the cloud, then I will look upon it, to remember the [r]everlasting covenant between God and every living creature of all flesh that is on the earth." 2 Sam. 23:5
17 And God said to Noah, "This is the sign of the covenant which I have established between Me and all flesh that is on the earth."

18 Now the sons of Noah who came out of the ark were Shem and Ham and Japheth; and Ham was the father of Canaan.
19 These three *were* the sons of Noah; and from these the whole earth was [t]populated. *scattered*

20 Then Noah began farming and planted a vineyard.
21 And he drank of the wine and [r]became drunk, and uncovered himself inside his tent. Prov. 20:1
22 And Ham, the father of Canaan, [r]saw the nakedness of his father, and told his two brothers outside. Hab. 2:15
23 But Shem and Japheth took a garment and laid it upon both their shoulders and walked backward and covered the nakedness of their father; and their faces were [t]turned away, so that they did not see their father's nakedness. *backward*
24 When Noah awoke from his wine, he knew what his youngest son had done to him.
25 So he said,
"Cursed be Canaan;
[12]A servant of servants
He shall be to his brothers."
26 He also said,
"Blessed [r]be the LORD,
The God of Shem;
And let Canaan be [a]his servant. Gen. 14:20 • *their*

[12] I.e., The lowest of servants

27 "May [r]God enlarge Japheth,
And let him dwell in the tents of Shem;
And let Canaan be [a]his servant." Is. 66:19 • *their*
28 And Noah lived three hundred and fifty years after the flood.
29 So all the days of Noah were nine hundred and fifty years, and he died.

CHAPTER 10

NOW these are *the records of* the generations of Shem, Ham, and Japheth, the sons of Noah; and sons were born to them after the flood.
2 The sons of Japheth *were* [r]Gomer and Magog and Madai and [r]Javan and Tubal and Meshech and Tiras. Ezek. 38:2, 6 • Is. 66:19
3 And the sons of Gomer *were* [r]Ashkenaz and Riphath and [r]Togarmah. Jer. 51:27 • Ezek. 27:14
4 And the sons of Javan *were* Elishah and [r]Tarshish, Kittim and Dodanim. Ezek. 27:12, 25
5 From these the coastlands of the nations were separated into their lands, every one according to his language, according to their families, into their nations.
6 [r]And the sons of Ham *were* Cush and Mizraim and Put and Canaan. 1 Chr. 1:8-10
7 And the sons of Cush *were* [r]Seba and Havilah and Sabtah and [r]Raamah and Sabteca; and the sons of Raamah *were* [r]Sheba and Dedan. Is. 43:3 • Ezek. 27:22
8 Now Cush [t]became the father of Nimrod; he became a mighty one on the earth. *begot*
9 He was a mighty hunter before the LORD; therefore it is said, "Like Nimrod a mighty hunter before the LORD."
10 And the beginning of his kingdom was [13]Babel and Erech and Accad and Calneh, in the land of [r]Shinar. Gen. 11:2; 14:1
11 From that land he went forth into Assyria, and built Nineveh and Rehoboth-Ir and Calah,
12 and Resen between Nineveh and Calah; that is the great city.
13 And Mizraim [t]became the father of Ludim and Anamim and Lehabim and Naphtuhim *begot*
14 and [r]Pathrusim and Casluhim (from which came the Philistines) and Caphtorim. 1 Chr. 1:12
15 And Canaan [t]became the father of [r]Sidon, his first-born, and [r]Heth *begot* • 1 Chr. 1:13 • Gen. 23:3
16 and the Jebusite and the Amorite and the Girgashite
17 and the Hivite and the Arkite and the Sinite
18 and the Arvadite and the Zemarite and the Hamathite; and afterward the families of the Canaanite were spread abroad.
19 And the territory of the Canaanite [t]extended from Sidon as you go toward Gerar, as far as Gaza; as you go toward Sodom and Gomorrah and Admah and Zeboiim, as far as Lasha. *was*
20 These are the sons of Ham, according to their families, according to their languages, by their lands, by their nations.
21 And also to Shem, the father of all the children of Eber, *and* the older brother of Japheth, children were born.
22 The sons of Shem *were* Elam

[13]Or, *Babylon*

and Asshur and Arpachshad and
Lud and Aram.
23 And the sons of Aram *were*
Uz and Hul and Gether and Mash.
24 And Arpachshad [t]became the
father of Shelah; and Shelah became the father of Eber. *begot*
25 And two sons were born to
Eber; the name of the one *was* Peleg, for in his days the earth was
divided; and his brother's name
was Joktan.
26 And Joktan [t]became the father of Almodad and Sheleph and
Hazarmaveth and Jerah *begot*
27 and Hadoram and Uzal and
Diklah
28 and Obal and Abimael and
Sheba
29 and Ophir and Havilah and
Jobab; all these were the sons of
Joktan.
30 Now their [t]settlement [t]ex-
tended from Mesha as you go
toward Sephar, the hill country of
the east. *dwelling • was*
31 These are the sons of Shem,
according to their families, according to their languages, by
their lands, according to their nations.
32 These are the families of the
sons of Noah, according to their
genealogies, by their nations; and
[r]out of these the nations were
separated on the earth after the
flood. Gen. 9:19

CHAPTER 11

NOW the whole earth [t]used the
same language and the same
words. *was one lip*
2 And it came about as they
journeyed east, that they found a
plain in the land [r]of Shinar and [t]set-
tled there. Dan. 1:2 • *dwelt*
3 And they said to one another,
"Come, let us make bricks and
burn *them* thoroughly." And they
used brick for stone, and they
used [r]tar for mortar. Gen. 14:10
4 And they said, "Come, let us
build for ourselves a city, and a
tower whose top [r]*will reach* into
heaven, and let us make for ourselves a name; lest we [r]be scattered abroad over the face of the
whole earth." Ps. 107:26 • Deut. 4:27
5 And the LORD came down to
see the city and the tower which
the sons of men had built.
6 And the LORD said, "Behold,
they are one people, and they all
have [t]the same language. And this
is what they began to do, and now
nothing which they purpose to do
will be impossible for them. *one lip*
7 "Come, let Us go down and
there [r]confuse their language, that
they may not understand one another's [t]speech." Is. 33:19 • *lip*
8 So the LORD [r]scattered them
abroad from there over the face of
the whole earth; and they stopped
building the city. Luke 1:51
9 Therefore its name was
called [14]Babel, because there the
LORD confused the language of
the whole earth; and from there
the LORD scattered them abroad
over the face of the whole earth.
10 These are *the records of* the
generations of Shem. Shem was
one hundred years old, and [t]be-
came the father of Arpachshad
two years after the flood; *begot*
11 and Shem lived five hundred
years after he became the father

[14]Or, *Babylon*

of Arpachshad, and he had *other*
sons and daughters.
12 And Arpachshad lived thirty-
five years, and became the father
of Shelah;
13 and Arpachshad lived four
hundred and three years after he
became the father of Shelah, and
he had *other* sons and daughters.
14 And Shelah lived thirty
years, and became the father of
Eber;
15 and Shelah lived four hundred and three years after he became the father of Eber, and he
had *other* sons and daughters.
16 And Eber lived thirty-four
years, and became the father of
Peleg;
17 and Eber lived four hundred
and thirty years after he became
the father of Peleg, and he had
other sons and daughters.
18 And Peleg lived thirty years,
and became the father of Reu;
19 and Peleg lived two hundred
and nine years after he became
the father of Reu, and he had *other* sons and daughters.
20 And Reu lived thirty-two
years, and became the father of
Serug;
21 and Reu lived two hundred
and seven years after he became
the father of Serug, and he had
other sons and daughters.
22 And Serug lived thirty years,
and became the father of Nahor;
23 and Serug lived two hundred
years after he became the father
of Nahor, and he had *other* sons
and daughters.
24 And Nahor lived twenty-nine
years, and became the father of
[r]Terah; Josh. 24:2
25 and Nahor lived one hundred
and nineteen years after he became the father of Terah, and he
had *other* sons and daughters.
26 And Terah lived seventy
years, and became[r] the father of A-
bram, Nahor and Haran. Josh. 24:2
27 Now these are *the records of*
the generations of Terah. Terah
became the father of Abram, Nahor and Haran; and Haran became
the father of[r] Lot. Gen. 13:10; 14:12
28 And Haran died[a] in the presence of his father Terah in the
land of his birth, in Ur of the Chaldeans. *during the lifetime of*
29 And Abram and Nahor took
wives for themselves. The name
of Abram's wife was Sarai; and
the name of Nahor's wife was Milcah, the daughter of Haran, the father of Milcah and Iscah.
30 And [r]Sarai was barren; she
had no child. Gen. 16:1
31 And Terah took Abram his
son, and Lot the son of Haran, his
grandson, and Sarai his daughter-
in-law, his son Abram's wife; and
they went out together from Ur of
the Chaldeans in order to enter
the land of Canaan; and they went
as far as Haran, and settled there.
32 And the days of Terah were
two hundred and five years; and
Terah died in Haran.

CHAPTER 12

NOW the LORD said to Abram,
"Go[t] forth from your country,
And from your relatives
And from your father's
house, *Go for yourself*
To the land which I will
show you;

2 And I will make you a great
nation,
And I will bless you,
And make your name great;
And so[t]you shall be a blessing; *be a blessing*
3 And I will bless those who
bless you,
And the one who [a]curses
you I will curse. *reviles*
And in you all the families
of the earth shall be
blessed."
4 So Abram went forth as the
LORD had spoken to him; and[r]Lot
went with him. Now Abram was
seventy-five years old when he departed from Haran. Gen. 11:27, 31
5 And Abram took Sarai his
wife and Lot his nephew, and all
their possessions which they had
accumulated, and the persons
which they had acquired in Haran,
and they [t]set out for the land of
Canaan; thus they came to the
land of Canaan. *went forth to go to*
6 And Abram passed through
the land as far as the site of[r]She-
chem, to the[a]oak of Moreh. Now
the Canaanite *was* then in the
land. Deut. 11:30 · *terebinth*
7 And the LORD appeared to A-
bram and said, "To your[t]descend-
ants I will give this land." So he
built an altar there to the LORD
who had appeared to him. *seed*
8 Then he proceeded from
there to the mountain on the east
of Bethel, and pitched his tent,
with[r]Bethel on the west and Ai on
the east; and there he built an altar to the LORD and called upon
the name of the LORD. Josh. 8:9, 12
9 And Abram journeyed on,
continuing toward the [15]Negev.

[15]I.e., South country

10 Now there was a famine in
the land; so Abram went down to
Egypt to sojourn there, for the
famine was severe in the land.
11 And it came about when he
[t]came near to Egypt, that he said
to Sarai his wife, "See now, I
know that you are a beautiful
woman; *drew near to enter*
12 [r]and it will come about when
the Egyptians see you, that they
will say, 'This is his wife'; and
they will kill me, but they will let
you live. Gen. 20:11
13 "Please say that you are my
sister so that it may go well with
me because of you, and that[t]I may
live on account of you." *my soul*
14 And it came about when A-
bram came into Egypt, the Egyptians saw that the woman was
very beautiful.
15 And Pharaoh's officials saw
her and praised her to Pharaoh;
and [r]the woman was taken into
Pharaoh's house. Gen. 20:2
16 Therefore he treated Abram
well for her sake; and [t]gave him
sheep and oxen and donkeys and
male and female servants and female donkeys and camels. *he had*
17 But the LORD struck Pharaoh
and his house with great plagues
because of Sarai, Abram's wife.
18 Then Pharaoh called Abram
and said, "What is this you have
done to me? Why did you not tell
me that she was your wife?
19 "Why did you say, 'She is my
sister,' so that I took her for my
wife? Now then,[a]here is your wife,
take her and go." *behold*
20 And Pharaoh commanded
his men concerning him; and they

[t]escorted him away, with his wife
and all that belonged to him. *sent*

CHAPTER 13

SO Abram went up from Egypt to
[r]the [15]Negev, he and his wife and
all that belonged to him; and Lot
with him. Gen. 12:9
2 Now Abram was very rich in
livestock, in silver and in gold.
3 And he went [t]on his journeys
from the [16]Negev as far as Bethel,
to the place where his tent had
been at the beginning, between
Bethel and Ai, *by his stages*
4 to the place of the [r]altar,
which he had made there formerly; and there Abram called on
the name of the LORD. Gen. 12:7, 8
5 Now [r]Lot, who went with A-
bram, also had flocks and herds
and tents. Gen. 12:5
6 And the land could not [t]sus-
tain them [t]while dwelling together;
for their possessions were so
great that they were not able to
remain together. *bear · to dwell*
7 [r]And there was strife between
the herdsmen of Abram's livestock and the herdsmen of Lot's
livestock. Now the Canaanite and
the Perizzite were dwelling then
in the land. Gen. 26:20
8 Then Abram said to Lot,
"Please let there be no strife between you and me, nor between
my herdsmen and your herdsmen,
for we are brothers.
9 "Is not the whole land before
you? Please separate from me: if
to the left, then I will go to the
right; or if *to* the right, then I will
go to the left."
10 And Lot lifted up his eyes
and saw all the [t]valley of the Jordan, that it was well watered
everywhere—*this was* before the
LORD destroyed Sodom and Gomorrah—like the garden of the
LORD, like the land of Egypt as
you go to Zoar. *circle*
11 So Lot chose for himself all
the [t]valley of the Jordan; and Lot
journeyed eastward. Thus they
separated from each other. *circle*
12 Abram [t]settled in the land of
Canaan, while Lot settled in the
cities of the valley, and moved his
tents as far as Sodom. *dwelt*
13 Now [r]the men of Sodom were
wicked exceedingly and sinners
against the LORD. Ezek. 16:49
14 And the LORD said to Abram,
after Lot had separated from him,
"Now lift up your eyes and look
from the place where you are,
northward and southward and
eastward and westward;
15 for all the land which you
see, I will give it to you and to
your [t]descendants forever. *seed*
16 "And I will make your descendants as the dust of the earth;
so that if anyone can number the
dust of the earth, then your descendants can also be numbered.
17 "Arise, walk about the land
through its length and breadth; for
I will give it to you."
18 Then Abram moved his tent
and came and dwelt by the [a]oaks
of Mamre, which are in Hebron,
and there he built [r]an altar to the
LORD. *terebinths* · Gen. 8:20

CHAPTER 14

AND it came about in the days of
Amraphel king of Shinar, Arioch
king of Ellasar, Chedorlaomer

[15]I.e., South country [16]I.e., South country

king of [r]Elam, and Tidal king of
[a]Goiim, Is. 11:11 • *nations*
2 *that* they made war with
Bera king of Sodom, and with Birsha king of Gomorrah, Shinab
king of Admah, and Shemeber
king of [r]Zeboiim, and the king of
Bela (that is, Zoar). Deut. 29:23
3 All these [t]came as allies to
the valley of Siddim (that is, the
Salt Sea). *joined together*
4 Twelve years they had
served Chedorlaomer, but the
thirteenth year they rebelled.
5 And in the fourteenth year
Chedorlaomer and the kings that
were with him, came and defeated
the Rephaim in Ashteroth-karnaim and the Zuzim in Ham and
the Emim in Shaveh-kiriathaim,
6 and the Horites in their
Mount Seir, as far as El-paran,
which is by the wilderness.
7 Then they turned back and
came to En-mishpat (that is, [r]Kadesh), and [t]conquered all the country of the Amalekites, and also the
Amorites, who lived in Hazazon-tamar. Num. 13:26 • *smote*
8 And the king of Sodom and
the king of Gomorrah and the
king of Admah and the king of Zeboiim and the king of Bela (that is,
Zoar) came out; and they arrayed
for battle against them in [r]the valley of Siddim, Gen. 14:3
9 against Chedorlaomer king
of Elam and Tidal king of [a]Goiim
and Amraphel king of Shinar and
Arioch king of Ellasar—four kings
against five. *nations*
10 Now the valley of Siddim
was full of tar pits; and the kings
of Sodom and Gomorrah fled, and
they fell into them. But those who
survived fled to the hill country.
11 Then they took all the goods
of Sodom and Gomorrah and all
their food supply, and departed.
12 And they also took Lot, [r]Abram's nephew, and his possessions and departed, for he was living in Sodom. Gen. 11:27
13 Then a fugitive came and
told Abram the Hebrew. Now he
was [t]living by the oaks of Mamre
the Amorite, brother of Eshcol
and brother of Aner, and these
were allies with Abram. *abiding*
14 And when Abram heard that
his [t]relative had been taken captive, he [a]led out his trained men,
born in his house, three hundred
and eighteen, and went in pursuit
as far as Dan. *brother* • *mustered*
15 And he divided his forces
against them by night, he and his
servants, and [t]defeated them, and
pursued them as far as Hobah,
which is north of Damascus. *smote*
16 And he [r]brought back all the
goods, and also brought back his
[t]relative Lot with his possessions,
and also the women, and the people. 1 Sam. 30:8, 18, 19 • *brother*
17 Then after his return from
the [t]defeat of Chedorlaomer and
the kings who were with him, the
king of Sodom went out to meet
him at the valley of Shaveh (that
is, the King's Valley). *smiting*
18 And [r]Melchizedek king of Salem brought out bread and wine;
now he was a [r]priest of God Most
High. Heb. 7:1-10 • Heb. 5:6, 10
19 And he blessed him and said,

> "Blessed be Abram of God
> Most High,
> [a]Possessor of heaven and
> earth; *Creator*

20 And blessed be God Most
High,
Who has delivered your enemies into your hand."
And he gave him a tenth of all.
21 And the king of Sodom said
to Abram, "Give the people to me
and take the goods for yourself."
22 And Abram said to the king
of Sodom, "I have sworn to the
LORD God Most High,[a]possessor
of heaven and earth, *Creator*
23 that I will not take a thread
or a sandal thong or anything that
is yours, lest you should say, 'I
have made Abram rich.'
24 "I[t] will take nothing except
what the young men have eaten,
and the share of the men who
went with me, Aner, Eshcol, and
Mamre; let them take their
share." *Not to me except*

CHAPTER 15

AFTER these things[r]the word of
the LORD came to Abram in a vision, saying, 1 Sam. 15:10
"Do not fear, Abram,
I am a shield to you;
Your reward shall be very
great."
2 And Abram said, "O Lord
GOD, what wilt Thou give me,
since I[t]am childless, and the[t]heir
of my house is Eliezer of Damascus?" *go* • *son of acquisition*
3 And Abram said, "Since[t]
Thou hast given no[t]offspring to
me, one[r]born in my house is my
heir." *Behold* • *seed* • Gen. 14:14
4 Then behold, the word of the
LORD came to him, saying, "This
man will not be your heir; but one
who shall come forth from your
own body, he shall be your heir."
5 And He took him outside and
said, "Now look toward the heavens, and count the stars, if you are
able to count them." And He said
to him,[r]"So shall your[t]descend-
ants be." Rom. 4:18 • *seed*
6 [r]Then he believed in the
LORD; and He reckoned it to him
as righteousness. Rom. 4:3, 20-22
7 And He said to him, "I am
the LORD who brought you out of
Ur of the Chaldeans, to give you
this land to[a]possess it." *inherit*
8 And he said, "O Lord GOD,
[r]how may I know that I shall[a]pos-
sess it?" Luke 1:18 • *inherit*
9 So He said to him, "Bring[t]Me
a three year old heifer, and a three
year old female goat, and a three
year old ram, and a turtledove,
and a young pigeon." *Take*
10 Then he brought all these to
Him and cut them[t]in two, and laid
each half opposite the other; but
he did not cut the birds. *in the midst*
11 And the birds of prey came
down upon the carcasses, and A-
bram drove them away.
12 Now when the sun was going
down, a deep sleep fell upon A-
bram; and behold, terror *and*
great darkness fell upon him.
13 And *God* said to Abram,
"Know for certain that your[t]de-
scendants will be strangers in a
land that is not theirs, where they
will be enslaved and oppressed
four hundred years. *seed*
14 "But I will also judge the nation whom they will serve; and afterward they will come out with
[t]many possessions. *great*
15 "And as for you, you shall go

to your fathers in peace; you shall
be buried at a good old age.
16 "Then in ʳthe fourth generation
they shall return here, for ʳthe iniquity of the Amorite is not yet complete." Gen. 15:13 • Lev. 18:24-28
17 And it came about when the
sun had set, that it was very dark,
and behold, *there appeared* a
smoking oven and a flaming torch
which ʳpassed between these
pieces. Jer. 34:18, 19
18 On that day the LORD made a
covenant with Abram, saying,

"To your ᵗdescendants I have
given this land, *seed*
From the river of Egypt as
far as the great river, the
river Euphrates:

19 ʳthe Kenite and the Kenizzite
and the Kadmonite Josh. 24:11
20 and the Hittite and the Perizzite and the Rephaim
21 and the Amorite and the Canaanite and the Girgashite and the
Jebusite."

CHAPTER 16

NOW ʳSarai, Abram's wife had
borne him no *children*, and she
had an Egyptian maid whose
name was Hagar. Gen. 11:30
2 So Sarai said to Abram,
"Now behold, the LORD has prevented me from bearing *children*.
Please go in to my maid; perhaps I
shall ᵗobtain children through
her." And Abram listened to the
voice of Sarai. *be built from her*
3 And after Abram had ᵗlived
ʳten years in the land of Canaan,
Abram's wife Sarai took Hagar
the Egyptian, her maid, and gave
her to her husband Abram as his
wife. *dwelt* • Gen. 12:4
4 And he went in to Hagar, and
she conceived; and when she saw
that she had conceived, her mistress was despised in her sight.
5 And Sarai said to Abram,
"May the wrong done me be upon
you. I gave my maid into your
ᵗarms; but when she saw that she
had conceived, I was despised in
her ᵗsight. May the LORD judge between you and me." *bosom* • *eyes*
6 But Abram said to Sarai,
"Behold, your maid is in your
ᵗpower; do to her what is good in
your ᵗsight." So Sarai treated her
harshly, and she fled from her
presence. *hand* • *eyes*
7 Now ʳthe angel of the LORD
found her by a spring of water in
the wilderness, by the spring on
the way to Shur. Gen. 21:17, 18
8 And he said, "Hagar, Sarai's
maid, where have you come from
and where are you going?" And
she said, "I am fleeing from the
presence of my mistress Sarai."
9 Then the angel of the LORD
said to her, "Return to your mistress, and submit yourself ᵗto her
authority." *under her hands*
10 Moreover, the angel of the
LORD said to her, "I will greatly
multiply your descendants so that
they shall be too many to count."
11 The angel of the LORD said to
her further,

"Behold, you are with child,
And you shall bear a son;
And you shall call his name
[17]Ishmael,
Because the LORD has given
heed to your affliction.

[17]I.e., God hears

12 "And he will be a wild donkey of a man,
His hand *will be* against
everyone,
And everyone's hand *will*
be against him;
And he will[t]live to the east
of all his brothers." *dwell*
13 Then she called the name of
the LORD who spoke to her, "Thou
art a God who sees"; for she said,
"Have[r] I even remained alive here
after seeing Him?" Ps. 139:1-12
14 Therefore the well was called
[18]Beer-lahai-roi; behold, it is between Kadesh and Bered.
15 So Hagar bore Abram a son;
and Abram called the name of his
son, whom Hagar bore, Ishmael.
16 And Abram was [r]eighty-six
years old when Hagar bore Ishmael to[t]him. Gen. 12:4 • *Abram*

CHAPTER 17

NOW when Abram was ninety-
nine years old, the LORD appeared
to Abram and said to him,
"I am God Almighty;
Walk before Me, and be
[t]blameless. *complete, perfect*
2 "And I will[t]establish My covenant between Me and
you, *give*
And I will multiply you exceedingly."
3 And Abram fell on his face,
and God talked with him, saying,
4 "As for Me, behold, My covenant is with you,
And you shall be the father
of a multitude of nations.
5 "No longer shall your name
be called [19]Abram,
But your name shall be
[20]Abraham;
For I will make you the father of a multitude of nations.
6 "And I will make you exceedingly fruitful, and I will make nations of you, and[r]kings shall come
forth from you. Gen. 17:16
7 "And I will establish My covenant between Me and you and
your [t]descendants after you
throughout their generations for
an [r]everlasting covenant, to be
God to you and to your descendants after you. *seed* • Luke 1:55
8 "And I will give to you and to
your [t]descendants after you, the
land of your sojournings, all the
land of Canaan, for an everlasting
possession; and [r]I will be their
God." *seed* • Rev. 21:7
9 God said further to Abraham, "Now as for you, [r]you shall
keep My covenant, you and your
[t]descendants after you throughout
their generations. Ex. 19:5 • *seed*
10 "This[r] is My covenant, which
you shall keep, between Me and
you and your [t]descendants after
you: every male among you shall
be circumcised. Rom. 4:11 • *seed*
11 "And[r]you shall be circumcised
in the flesh of your foreskin; and it
shall be the sign of the covenant
between Me and you. Acts 7:8
12 "And every male among you
who is eight days old shall be circumcised throughout your generations, a *servant* who is born in
the house or who is bought with
money from any foreigner, who is
not of your[t]descendants. *seed*
13 "A *servant* who is born in
your house or[r]who is bought with

[18]I.e., the well of the living one who sees me
[19]I.e., exalted father
[20]I.e., father of a multitude

your money shall surely be circumcised; thus shall My covenant
be in your flesh for an everlasting
covenant. Ex. 12:44
14 "But an uncircumcised male
who is not circumcised in the flesh
of his foreskin, that person shall
be [r]cut off from his people; he has
broken My covenant." Ex. 4:24-26
15 Then God said to Abraham,
"As for Sarai your wife, you shall
not call her name Sarai, but [21]Sar-
ah *shall be* her name.
16 "And I will bless her, and indeed I will give you a son by her.
Then I will bless her, and she shall
be *a mother of* nations; kings of
peoples shall [t]come from her." *be*
17 Then Abraham fell on his
face and laughed, and said in his
heart, "Will a child be born to a
man one hundred years old? And
[r]will Sarah, who is ninety years
old, bear *a child?*" Gen. 21:7
18 And Abraham said to God,
"Oh that Ishmael might live before Thee!"
19 But God said, "No, but Sarah
your wife shall bear you [r]a son,
and you shall call his name [22]Isaac;
and I will establish My covenant
with him for an everlasting covenant for his [t]descendants after
him. Gen. 17:16 · *seed*
20 "And as for Ishmael, I have
heard you; behold, I will bless
him, and will make him fruitful,
and will multiply him exceedingly. [r]He shall become the father
of twelve princes, and I will make
him a great nation. Gen. 25:12-16
21 "But My covenant I will establish with [r]Isaac, whom Sarah will
bear to you at this season next
year." Gen. 17:19

[21] I.e., princess [22] I.e., he laughs

22 And when He finished talking with him, [r]God went up from
Abraham. Gen. 18:33
23 Then Abraham took Ishmael
his son, and all *the servants* who
were [r]born in his house and all
who were bought with his money,
every male among the men of
Abraham's household, and circumcised the flesh of their foreskin in the very same day, as God
had said to him. Gen. 14:14
24 Now Abraham was ninety-
nine years old when [r]he was circumcised in the flesh of his foreskin. Rom. 4:11
25 And [r]Ishmael his son was
thirteen years old when he was
circumcised in the flesh of his
foreskin. Gen. 16:16
26 In the very same day Abraham was circumcised, and Ishmael his son.
27 And all the men of his household, who were [r]born in the house
or bought with money from a foreigner, were circumcised with
him. Gen. 14:14

CHAPTER 18

NOW the LORD appeared to him
by the [a]oaks of Mamre, while he
was sitting at the tent door in the
heat of the day. *terebinths*
2 And when he lifted up his
eyes and looked, behold, three
men were standing opposite him;
and when he saw *them*, he ran
from the tent door to meet them,
and bowed himself to the earth,
3 and said, "My lord, if now I
have found favor in [a]your sight,
please do not [t]pass [a]your servant
by. *Thy · pass away from your servant*

4 "Please let a little water be
brought and wash your feet, and
rest yourselves under the tree;
5 and I will [t]bring a piece of
bread, that you may refresh yourselves; after that you may go on,
since you have [t]visited your servant." And they said, "So do, as
you have said." *take · come to*
6 So Abraham hurried into the
tent to Sarah, and said, "Quickly[t]
prepare three measures of fine
flour, knead *it,* and make bread
cakes." *Hasten three measures*
7 Abraham also ran to the
herd, and took a tender and [t]choice
calf, and gave *it* to the servant;
and he hurried to prepare it. *good*
8 And he took curds and milk
and the calf which he had prepared, and placed *it* before them;
and he was standing by them under the tree [t]as they ate. *and*
9 Then they said to him,
"Where is Sarah your wife?" And
he said, "Behold, in the tent."
10 And he said, "I will surely return to you [t]at this time next year;
and behold, Sarah your wife shall
have a son." And Sarah was listening at the tent door, which was
behind him. *when the time revives*
11 Now [r]Abraham and Sarah
were old, advanced in age; Sarah
was past childbearing. Rom. 4:19
12 And Sarah laughed [t]to herself, saying, "After [r]I have become
old, shall I have pleasure, my lord
being old also?" *within* · Luke 1:18
13 And the LORD said to Abraham, "Why did Sarah laugh, saying, 'Shall I indeed [t]bear *a child,*
when I am so old?' *surely bear*
14 "Is anything too [a]difficult for
the LORD? At the appointed time I
will return to you, [t]at this time
next year, and Sarah shall have a
son." *wonderful · when the time revives*
15 Sarah denied *it* however,
saying, "I did not laugh"; for she
was afraid. And He said, "No, but
you did laugh."
16 Then the men rose up from
there, and looked down toward
Sodom; and Abraham was walking with them to send them off.
17 And [r]the LORD said, "Shall I
hide from Abraham what I am
about to do, Amos 3:7
18 since Abraham will surely
become a great and [a]mighty nation, and in him all the nations of
the earth will be blessed? *populous*
19 "For I have [t]chosen him, in order that he may command his
children and his household after
him to keep the way of the LORD
by doing righteousness and justice; in order that the LORD may
bring upon Abraham what He has
spoken about him." *known*
20 And the LORD said, "The [r]out-
cry of Sodom and Gomorrah is indeed great, and their sin is exceedingly grave. Gen. 19:13
21 "I will go down now, and see
if they have done entirely according to its outcry, which has come
to Me; and if not, I will know."
22 Then the men turned away
from there and went toward Sodom, while Abraham was still
standing before the LORD.
23 And Abraham came near and
said, "Wilt [r] Thou indeed sweep
away the righteous with the
wicked? 2 Sam. 24:17
24 "Suppose there are fifty righteous within the city; wilt Thou indeed sweep *it* away and not [a]spare

the place for the sake of the fifty
righteous who are in it? *forgive*
25 "Far be it from Thee to do
[t]such a thing, to slay the righteous
with the wicked, so that the righteous and the wicked are *treated*
alike. Far be it from Thee! Shall
not the Judge of all the earth [t]deal
justly?" *after this manner · do justice*
26 So the LORD said, "If I find in
Sodom fifty righteous within the
city, then I will [a]spare the whole
place on their account." *forgive*
27 And Abraham answered and
said, "Now behold, I have ventured to speak to the Lord, although I am *but* dust and ashes.
28 "Suppose the fifty righteous
are lacking five, wilt Thou destroy
the whole city because of five?"
And He said, "I will not destroy *it*
if I find forty-five there."
29 And he spoke to Him yet
again and said, "Suppose forty are
found there?" And He said, "I will
not do *it* on account of the forty."
30 Then he said, "Oh may the
Lord not be angry, and I shall
speak; suppose thirty are found
there?" And He said, "I will not do
it if I find thirty there."
31 And he said, "Now behold, I
have [t]ventured to speak to the
Lord; suppose twenty are found
there?" And He said, "I will not
destroy *it* on account of the
twenty." *undertaken*
32 Then he said, "Oh [r]may the
Lord not be angry, and I shall
speak only this once; suppose ten
are found there?" And He said, "I
will not destroy *it* on account of
the ten." Judg. 6:39
33 And as soon as He had finished speaking to Abraham [r]the
LORD departed; and Abraham returned to his place. Gen. 17:22

CHAPTER 19

NOW the two angels came to
Sodom in the evening as Lot was
sitting in the gate of Sodom.
When Lot saw *them*, he rose to
meet them and bowed down *with
his* face to the ground.
2 And he said, "Now behold,
my lords, please turn aside into
your servant's house, and spend
the night, and wash your feet;
then you may rise early and go on
your way." They said however,
"No, but we shall spend the night
in the square."
3 Yet he urged them strongly,
so they turned aside to him and
entered his house; and he prepared a feast for them, and baked
unleavened bread, and they ate.
4 Before they lay down, the
men of the city, the men of Sodom, surrounded the house, both
young and old, all the people [t]from
every quarter; *from every end*
5 and they called to Lot and
said to him, "Where [r]are the men
who came to you tonight? Bring
them out to us that we may have
relations with them." Lev. 18:22
6 But Lot went out to them at
the doorway, and shut the door
behind him,
7 and said, "Please, my brothers, do not act wickedly.
8 "Now behold, I have two
daughters who have not had relations with man; please let me
bring them out to you, and do to
them whatever you like; only do
nothing to these men, inasmuch

as they have come under the[t]shel-
ter of my roof." *shadow*
9 But they said, "Stand aside."
Furthermore, they said, "This one
came in as an alien, and already
he is acting like a judge; now we
will treat you worse than them."
So they pressed hard against Lot
and came near to break the door.
10 But [r]the men reached out
their[t]hands and brought Lot into
the house[t]with them, and shut the
door. Gen. 19:1 · *hand* · *to*
11 And [r]they [t]struck the men
who were at the doorway of the
house with blindness, both small
and great, so that they wearied
themselves trying to find the doorway. Acts 13:11 · *smote*
12 Then the men said to Lot,
"Whom else have you here? A
son-in-law, and your sons, and
your daughters, and whomever
you have in the city, bring *them*
out of the place;
13 for we are about to destroy
this place, because [r]their outcry
has become so great before the
LORD that the LORD has sent us to
destroy it." Gen. 18:20
14 And Lot went out and spoke
to his sons-in-law, who [t]were to
marry his daughters, and said,
"Up, [r]get out of this place, for the
LORD will destroy the city." But he
appeared to his sons-in-law to be
jesting. *were taking* · Rev. 18:4
15 And when morning dawned,
the angels urged Lot, saying, "Up,
take your wife and your two
daughters, who are here, lest you
be swept away in the[a]punishment
of the city." *iniquity*
16 But he hesitated. So the men
seized his hand and the hand of
his wife and the [t]hands of his
daughters, for the compassion of
the LORD *was* upon him; and they
brought him out, and put him outside the city. *hand*
17 And it came about when they
had brought them outside, that
[t]one said, "Escape for your life! Do
not look behind you, and do not
stay [t]anywhere in the valley; escape to the mountains, lest you be
swept away." *he* · *in all the circle*
18 But Lot said to them, "Oh no,
my lords!
19 "Now behold, your servant
has found favor in your sight, and
you have magnified your lovingkindness, which you have shown
me by saving my life; but I cannot
escape to the mountains, lest the
disaster overtake me and I die;
20 now behold, this town is near
enough to flee to, and it is small.
Please, let me escape there (is it
not small?) [t]that my life may be
saved." *and my soul will live*
21 And he said to him, "Behold,
I grant you this[t]request also, not
to overthrow the town of which
you have spoken. *thing*
22 "Hurry, escape there, for I
cannot do anything until you arrive there." Therefore the name of
the town was called [23]Zoar.
23 The sun had risen over the
earth when Lot came to Zoar.
24 Then the LORD [r]rained on
Sodom and Gomorrah brimstone
and fire from the LORD out of
heaven, Ps. 11:6; Jude 7
25 and He overthrew those
cities, and all the [t]valley, and all
the inhabitants of the cities, and
what grew on the ground. *circle*
26 But his wife, from behind

[23]I.e., small

him,[r]looked *back;* and she became
a pillar of salt. Luke 17:32
27 Now Abraham arose early in
the morning *and went* to[r]the place
where he had stood before the
LORD; Gen. 18:22
28 and he looked down toward
Sodom and Gomorrah, and
toward all the land of the valley,
and he saw, and behold, the
smoke of the land ascended like
the smoke of a[t]furnace. *kiln*
29 Thus it came about, when
God destroyed the cities of the
[t]valley, that God remembered
Abraham, and[r]sent Lot out of the
midst of the overthrow, when He
overthrew the cities in which Lot
lived. *circle* • 2 Pet. 2:7
30 And Lot went up from Zoar,
and[t]stayed in the[t]mountains, and
his two daughters with him; for he
was afraid to stay in Zoar; and he
stayed in a cave, he and his two
daughters. *dwelt* • *mountain*
31 Then the first-born said to
the younger, "Our father is old,
and there is not a man[a]on earth to
come in to us after the manner of
the earth. *in the land*
32 "Come,[r]let us make our father
drink wine, and let us lie with him,
that we may preserve our family
through our father." Luke 21:34
33 So they made their father
drink wine that night, and the
first-born went in and lay with her
father; and he did not know when
she lay down or when she arose.
34 And it came about on the
morrow, that the first-born said to
the younger, "Behold, I lay last
night with my father; let us make
him drink wine tonight also; then
you go in and lie with him, that we
may preserve[t]our family through
our father." *seed from our father*
35 So they made their father
drink wine that night also, and the
younger arose and lay with him;
and he did not know when she lay
down or when she arose.
36 Thus both the daughters of
Lot were with child by their father.
37 And the first-born bore a son,
and called his name[r]Moab; he is
the father of the Moabites to this
day. Deut. 2:9
38 And as for the younger, she
also bore a son, and called his
name Ben-ammi; he is the father
of the sons of Ammon to this day.

CHAPTER 20

NOW Abraham journeyed from
[r]there toward the land of the [24]Neg-
ev, and [t]settled between Kadesh
and Shur; then he sojourned in
Gerar. Gen. 18:1 • *dwelt*
2 And Abraham said of Sarah
his wife,[r]"She is my sister." So
Abimelech king of Gerar sent and
took Sarah. Gen. 12:11-13
3 But God came to Abimelech
in a dream of the night, and said
to him, "Behold, you are a dead
man because of the woman whom
you have taken, for she is [t]mar-
ried." *married to a husband*
4 Now Abimelech had not
come near her; and he said, "Lord,
wilt Thou slay a nation, even
though[t]blameless? *righteous*
5 "Did he not himself say to me,
'She is my sister'? And she herself
said, 'He is my brother.' In[r]the integrity of my heart and the inno-

[24]I.e., South country

cence of my [t]hands I have done
this." Ps. 7:8 • *palms*
6 Then God said to him in the
dream, "Yes, I know that in the integrity of your heart you have
done this, and I also kept you
from sinning against Me; therefore I did not let you touch her.
7 "Now therefore, restore the
man's wife, for he is a prophet,
and he will pray for you, and you
will live. But if you do not restore
her, know that you shall surely
die, you and all who are yours."
8 So Abimelech arose early in
the morning and called all his servants and told all these things in
their hearing; and the men were
greatly frightened.
9 [r]Then Abimelech called Abraham and said to him, "What have
you done to us? And [t]how have I
sinned against you, that you have
brought on me and on my kingdom a great sin? You have done to
me [t]things that ought not to be
done." Gen. 12:18 • *what* • *deeds*
10 And Abimelech said to Abraham, "What have you [t]encoun-
tered, that you have done this
thing?" *seen*
11 And Abraham said, "Be-
cause I thought, surely there is no
fear of God in this place; and they
will kill me because of my wife.
12 "Besides, she actually is my
sister, the daughter of my father,
but not the daughter of my
mother, and she became my wife;
13 and it came about, when God
caused me to wander from my father's house, that I said to her,
'This is the kindness which you
will show to me: [t]everywhere
we go, say of me, "He is my
brother." ' " *at every place where*
14 [r]Abimelech then took sheep
and oxen and male and female
servants, and gave them to Abraham, and restored his wife Sarah
to him. Gen. 12:16
15 And Abimelech said, "Be-
hold, my land is before you; [t]settle
wherever you please." *dwell*
16 And to Sarah he said, "Behold, I have given your [r]brother a
thousand pieces of silver; behold,
it is your vindication before all
who are with you, and before all
men you are cleared." Gen. 20:5
17 And [r]Abraham prayed to
God; and God healed Abimelech
and his wife and his maids, so that
they bore *children.* James 5:16
18 [r]For the LORD had closed fast
all the wombs of the household of
Abimelech because of Sarah,
Abraham's wife. Gen. 12:17

CHAPTER 21

THEN the LORD took note of Sarah as He had said, and the LORD
did for Sarah as He had promised.
2 [r]So Sarah conceived and bore
a son to Abraham in his old age, at
the appointed time of which God
had spoken to him. Gal. 4:22
3 And Abraham called the
name of his son who was born to
him, whom Sarah bore to him,
[r]Isaac. Gen. 17:19, 21
4 Then Abraham circumcised
his son Isaac when he was [r]eight
days old, as God had commanded
him. Gen. 17:12; Acts 7:8
5 Now Abraham was [r]one hundred years old when his son Isaac
was born to him. Gen. 17:17

6 And Sarah said, "God has made laughter for me; everyone who hears will laugh with me."

7 And she said, "Who would have said to Abraham that Sarah would nurse children? Yet I have borne him a son in his old age."

8 And the child grew and was weaned, and Abraham made a great feast on the day that Isaac was weaned.

9 Now Sarah saw the son of Hagar the Egyptian, whom she had borne to Abraham, mocking.

10 Therefore she said to Abraham, "Drive out this maid and her son, for the son of this maid shall not be an heir with my son Isaac."

11 And the matter [t]distressed Abraham greatly because of his son. *was very grievous in Abraham's sight*

12 But God said to Abraham, "Do not be distressed because of the lad and your maid; whatever Sarah tells you, listen to her, for [r]through Isaac your descendants shall be named. Rom. 9:7

13 "And of the son of the maid I will make a nation also, because he is your [t]descendant." *seed*

14 So Abraham rose early in the morning, and took bread and a skin of water, and gave *them* to Hagar, putting *them* on her shoulder, and *gave her* the boy, and sent her away. And she departed, and wandered about in the wilderness of Beersheba.

15 And the water in the skin was used up, and she [t]left the boy under one of the bushes. *cast*

16 Then she went and sat down opposite him, about a bowshot away, for she said, "Do not let me see the boy die." And she sat opposite him, and [r]lifted up her voice and wept. Jer. 6:26

17 And God [r]heard the lad crying; and the angel of God called to Hagar from heaven, and said to her, "What is the matter with you, Hagar? [r]Do not fear, for God has heard the voice of the lad where he is. Ex. 3:7; Ps. 6:8 • Gen. 26:24

18 "Arise, lift up the lad, and hold him by [t]the hand; for I will make a great nation of him." *your*

19 Then God opened her eyes and she saw a well of water; and she went and filled the skin with water, and gave the lad a drink.

20 And [r]God was with the lad, and he grew; and he [t]lived in the wilderness, and became an archer. Gen. 28:15 • *dwelt*

21 And [r]he [t]lived in the wilderness of Paran; and his mother took a wife for him from the land of Egypt. Gen. 25:18 • *dwelt*

22 Now it came about at that time, that Abimelech and Phicol, the commander of his army, spoke to Abraham, saying, "God is with you in all that you do;

23 now therefore, swear to me here by God that you will not deal falsely with me, or with my offspring, or with my posterity; but according to the kindness that I have shown to you, you shall show to me, and to the land in which you have sojourned."

24 And Abraham said, "I swear it."

25 But Abraham [t]complained to Abimelech because of the well of water which the servants of Abimelech had seized. *reproved*

26 And Abimelech said, "I do not know who has done this thing;

neither did you tell me, nor did I
hear of it [t]until today." *except*
27 And Abraham took sheep
and oxen, and gave them to Abimelech; and [r]the two of them made a
covenant. Gen. 26:31
28 Then Abraham set seven ewe
lambs of the flock by themselves.
29 And Abimelech said to Abraham, "What do these seven ewe
lambs mean, which you have set
by themselves?"
30 And he said, "You shall take
these seven ewe lambs from my
hand in order that it may be a witness to me, that I dug this well."
31 Therefore he called that
place Beersheba; because there
the two of them took an oath.
32 So they made a covenant at
Beersheba; and Abimelech and
Phicol, the commander of his
army, arose and returned to the
land of the Philistines.
33 And *Abraham* planted a
tamarisk tree at Beersheba, and
there he called on the name of the
LORD, the Everlasting God.
34 And Abraham sojourned [r]in
the land of the Philistines for
many days. Gen. 22:19

CHAPTER 22

NOW it came about after these
things, that [r]God tested Abraham,
and said to him, "Abraham!" And
he said, "Here I am." Heb. 11:17
2 And He said, "Take now
[r]your son, your only son, whom
you love, Isaac, and go to the land
of Moriah; and offer him there as
a burnt offering on one of the
mountains of which I will tell
you." John 3:16; 1 John 4:9
3 So Abraham rose early in the
morning and saddled his donkey,
and took two of his young men
with him and Isaac his son; and he
split wood for the burnt offering,
and arose and went to the place of
which God had told him.
4 On the third day Abraham
raised his eyes and saw the place
from a distance.
5 And Abraham said to his
young men, "Stay here with the
donkey, and I and the lad will go
yonder; and we will worship and
return to you."
6 And Abraham took the wood
of the burnt offering and laid it on
Isaac his son, and he took in his
hand the fire and the knife. So the
two of them walked on together.
7 And Isaac spoke to Abraham
his father and said, "My father!"
And he said, "Here I am, my son."
And he said, "Behold, the fire and
the wood, but where is the [r]lamb
for the burnt offering?" Rev. 13:8
8 And Abraham said, "God
will [t]provide for Himself the lamb
for the burnt offering, my son." So
the two of them walked on together. *see*
9 Then they came to [r]the place
of which God had told him; and
Abraham built the altar there, and
arranged the wood, and bound his
son Isaac, and laid him on the altar on top of the wood. Gen. 22:2
10 And Abraham stretched out
his hand, and took the knife to
slay his son.
11 But [r]the angel of the LORD
called to him from heaven, and
said, "Abraham, Abraham!" And
he said, "Here I am." Gen. 16:7-11
12 And he said, "Do not stretch

out your hand against the lad, and
do nothing to him; for now I know
that you[t]fear God, since you have
not withheld your son, your only
son, from Me." *are a fearer of God*
13 Then Abraham raised his
eyes and looked, and behold, behind *him* a ram caught in the
thicket by his horns; and Abraham went and took the ram, and
offered him up for a burnt offering
in the place of his son.
14 And Abraham called the
name of that place The LORD Will
Provide, as it is said to this day,
"In the mount of the LORD it will
[t]be provided." *be seen*
15 Then the angel of the LORD
called to Abraham a second time
from heaven,
16 and said, "By[r]Myself I have
sworn, declares the LORD, because
you have done this thing, and
have not withheld your son, your
only son, Heb. 6:13, 14
17 indeed I will greatly bless
you, and I will greatly multiply
your seed as the stars of the heavens, and as the sand which is on
the seashore; and your seed shall
possess the gate of their enemies.
18 "And in your seed all the nations of the earth shall[a]be blessed,
because you have obeyed My
voice." *bless themselves*
19 So Abraham returned to his
young men, and they arose and
went together to Beersheba; and
Abraham lived at Beersheba.
20 Now it came about after
these things, that it was told
Abraham, saying, "Behold, Milcah
[t]also has borne children to your
brother Nahor: *she also*
21 Uz his first-born and Buz his
brother and Kemuel the father of
Aram
22 and Chesed and Hazo and
Pildash and Jidlaph and Bethuel."
23 And Bethuel[t]became the father of[r]Rebekah: these eight Milcah bore to Nahor, Abraham's
brother. *begot* · Gen. 24:15
24 And his concubine, whose
name was Reumah, [t]also bore Te-
bah and Gaham and Tahash and
Maacah. *she also*

CHAPTER 23

NOW Sarah lived one hundred
and twenty-seven years; *these*
were the years of the life of Sarah.
2 And Sarah died in Kiriath-
arba (that is, Hebron) in the land
of Canaan; and Abraham[a]went in
to mourn for Sarah and to weep
for her. *proceeded*
3 Then Abraham rose from before his dead, and spoke to the
[r]sons of Heth, saying, Gen. 10:15
4 "I am a stranger and a sojourner among you; give me a
burial site among you, that I may
bury my dead out of my sight."
5 And the sons of Heth answered Abraham, saying to him,
6 "Hear us, my lord, you are a
mighty prince among us; bury
your dead in the choicest of our
graves; none of us will refuse you
his grave for burying your dead."
7 So Abraham rose and bowed
to the people of the land, the sons
of Heth.
8 And he spoke with them,
saying, "If it is your[t]wish *for me*
to bury my dead out of my sight,
hear me, and approach Ephron
the son of Zohar for me, *soul*

9 that he may give me the cave
of Machpelah which he owns,
which is at the end of his field; for
the full price let him give it to me
in your presence for a burial site."
10 Now Ephron was sitting
among the sons of Heth; and
Ephron the Hittite answered
Abraham in the hearing of the
sons of Heth; *even* of all who went
in at the gate of his city, saying,
11 "No, my lord, hear me; I give
you the field, and I give you the
cave that is in it. In the presence
of the sons of my people I give it
to you; bury your dead."
12 And Abraham bowed before
the people of the land.
13 And he spoke to Ephron in
the hearing of the people of the
land, saying, "If you will only
please listen to me; I will give the
price of the field, accept *it* from
me, that I may bury my dead
there."
14 Then Ephron answered
Abraham, saying to him,
15 "My lord, listen to me; a piece
of land worth four hundred shekels of silver, what is that between
me and you? So bury your dead."
16 And Abraham listened to
Ephron; and Abraham weighed
out for Ephron the silver which he
had named in the hearing of the
sons of Heth, four hundred shekels of silver, commercial standard.
17 So Ephron's field, which was
in Machpelah, which faced
Mamre, the field and cave which
was in it, and all the trees which
were in the field, that were[t]within
all the confines of its border, were
deeded over *in all its border around*
18 to Abraham for a possession
[r]in the presence of the sons of
Heth, before all who went in at
the gate of his city. Gen. 23:10
19 And after this, Abraham buried Sarah his wife in the cave of
the field at Machpelah facing
Mamre (that is, Hebron) in the
land of Canaan.
20 So the field, and the cave
that is in it,[a]were deeded over to
Abraham for a burial site by the
sons of Heth. *were ratified*

CHAPTER 24

NOW Abraham was old, ad-
vanced in age; and the LORD had
blessed Abraham in every way.
2 And Abraham said to his servant, the oldest of his household,
who had [r]charge of all that he
owned, "Please place your hand
under my thigh, Gen. 39:4-6
3 and I will make you swear by
the LORD, the God of heaven and
the God of earth, that you [r]shall
not take a wife for my son from
the daughters of the Canaanites,
among whom I live, 2 Cor. 6:14-17
4 but you shall go to [r]my country and to my relatives, and take a
wife for my son Isaac." Heb. 11:15
5 And the servant said to him,
"Suppose the woman will not be
willing to follow me to this land;
should I take your son back to the
land from where you came?"
6 Then Abraham said to him,
"Beware[r] lest you take my son
back there! Gen. 24:8
7 "The LORD, the God of
heaven, who took me from my father's house and from the land of
my birth, and who spoke to me,
and who swore to me, saying, 'To

your [t]descendants I will give this
land,' He will send His angel before you, and you will take a wife
for my son from there. *seed*
8 "But if the woman is not willing to follow you, then you will be
free from this my oath; only do
not take my son back there."
9 So the servant [r]placed his
hand under the thigh of Abraham
his master, and swore to him concerning this matter. Gen. 24:2
10 Then the servant took ten
camels from the camels of his
master, and set out with a variety
of [r]good things of his master's in
his hand; and he arose, and went
to Mesopotamia, to [r]the city of Nahor. Gen. 24:22, 53 • Gen. 11:31, 32
11 And he made the camels
kneel down outside the city by [r]the
well of water at evening time, [r]the
time when women go out to draw
water. Gen. 24:42 • Ex. 2:16
12 And he said, "O LORD, the
God of my master Abraham,
please [r]grant me success today,
and show lovingkindness to my
master Abraham. Gen. 27:20
13 "Behold, I am standing by the
[t]spring, and the daughters of the
men of the city are coming out to
draw water; *fountain of water*
14 now may it be that the girl to
whom I say, 'Please let down your
jar so that I may drink,' and [t]who
answers, 'Drink, and I will water
your camels also';—*may* she *be*
the one whom Thou hast appointed for Thy servant Isaac; and
by this I shall know that Thou
hast shown lovingkindness to my
master." *she will say*
15 And it came about [r]before he
had finished speaking, that behold, Rebekah who was born to
Bethuel the son of Milcah, the
wife of Abraham's brother Nahor,
came out with her jar on her
shoulder. Gen. 24:45
16 And the girl was very beautiful, a virgin, and no man had [t]had
relations with her; and she went
down to the spring and filled her
jar, and came up. *known*
17 Then the servant ran to meet
her, and said, "Please let me drink
a little water from your jar."
18 And [r]she said, "Drink, my
lord"; and she quickly lowered her
jar to her hand, and gave him a
drink. Gen. 24:14, 46
19 Now when she had finished
giving him a drink, she said, "I
will draw also for your camels until they have finished drinking."
20 So she quickly emptied her
jar into the trough, and ran back
to the well to draw, and she drew
for all his camels.
21 Meanwhile, the man was
gazing at her in silence, to know
whether the LORD had made his
journey successful or not.
22 Then it came about, when
the camels had finished drinking,
that the man took a gold ring
weighing a half-shekel and two
bracelets for her [t]wrists weighing
ten shekels in gold, *hands*
23 and said, "Whose daughter
are you? Please tell me, is there
room for us to lodge in your father's house?"
24 And she said to him, "I am
the daughter of Bethuel, the son of
Milcah, whom she bore to Nahor."
25 Again she said to him, "We
have plenty of both straw and
feed, and room to lodge in."

26 Then the man ʳbowed low and
worshiped the LORD. Ex. 4:31
27 And he said, "Blessed ʳbe the
LORD, the God of my master Abraham, who has not forsaken ʳHis
lovingkindness and His truth
toward my master; as for me, the
LORD has guided me in the way to
the house of my master's brothers." Ruth 4:14 • Ps. 98:3
28 Then ʳthe girl ran and told her
mother's household about these
things. Gen. 29:12
29 Now Rebekah had a brother
whose name was ʳLaban; and Laban ran outside to the man at the
spring. Gen. 29:5, 13
30 And it came about that when
he saw the ring, and the bracelets
on his sister's ᵗwrists, and when he
heard the words of Rebekah his
sister, saying, "This is what the
man said to me," he went to the
man; and behold, he was standing
by the camels at the spring. *hands*
31 And he said, "Come in,
ʳblessed of the LORD! Why do you
stand outside since I have prepared the house, and a place for
the camels?" Ruth 3:10
32 So the man entered the
house. Then ᵗLaban unloaded the
camels, and he gave straw and
feed to the camels, and water to
wash his feet and the feet of the
men who were with him. *he*
33 But when *food* was set before him to eat, he said, "I will not
eat until I have told my business."
And he said, "Speak on."
34 So he said, "I am ʳAbraham's
servant. Gen. 24:2
35 "And the LORD has greatly
blessed my master, so that he has
become ᵗrich; and He has given
him flocks and herds, and silver
and gold, and servants and maids,
and camels and donkeys. *great*
36 "Now Sarah my master's wife
bore a son to my master ᵗin her old
age; and he has given him all that
he has. *after she was old*
37 "And ʳ my master made me
swear, saying, 'You shall not take
a wife for my son from the daughters of the Canaanites, in whose
land I ᵗlive; Gen. 24:2-4 • *dwell*
38 but you shall go to my father's house, and to my relatives,
and take a wife for my son.'
39 "And ʳ I said to my master,
'Suppose the woman does not follow me.' Gen. 24:5
40 "And he said to me, ʳ'The
LORD, before whom I have
walked, will send His angel with
you to make your journey successful, and you will take a wife
for my son from my relatives, and
from my father's house; Gen. 24:7
41 ʳthen you will be free from
my oath, when you come to my
relatives; and if they do not give
her to you, you will be free from
my oath.' Gen. 24:8
42 "So I came today to the
spring, and said, 'O LORD, the God
of my master Abraham, if now
Thou wilt make my journey on
which I go ʳsuccessful; Neh. 1:11
43 behold, I am standing by the
spring, and may it be that the
maiden who comes out to draw,
and to whom I say, "Please let me
drink a little water from your jar";
44 and she will say to me, "You
drink, and I will draw for your
camels also"; let her be the
woman whom the LORD has appointed for my master's son.'

45 "Before I had finished [r]speak-
ing in my heart, behold, Rebekah
came out with her jar on her
shoulder, and went down to the
spring and drew; and I said to her,
'Please let me drink.' 1 Sam. 1:13
46 "And she quickly lowered her
jar from her *shoulder*, and said,
'Drink, and I will water your camels also'; so I drank, and she watered the camels also.
47 "Then I asked her, and said,
'Whose daughter are you?' And
she said, 'The daughter of Bethuel,
Nahor's son, whom Milcah bore to
him'; and I put the [r]ring on her
nose, and the bracelets on her
[t]wrists. Ezek. 16:11, 12 • *hands*
48 "And I bowed low and worshiped the LORD, and blessed the
LORD, the God of my master Abraham, who had guided me in the
right way to take the daughter of
my master's kinsman for his son.
49 "So now if you are going to
[25]deal kindly and truly with my
master, tell me; and if not, let me
know, that I may turn to the right
hand or the left."
50 Then Laban and Bethuel answered and said, "The matter
comes from the LORD; so we cannot speak to you bad or good.
51 "Behold, Rebekah is before
you, take *her* and go, and let her
be the wife of your master's son,
as the LORD has spoken."
52 And it came about when
Abraham's servant heard their
words, that he bowed himself to
the ground [t]before the LORD. *to*
53 And the servant brought out
[r]articles of silver and articles of
gold, and garments, and gave
them to Rebekah; he also gave
precious things to her brother and
to her mother. Ex. 3:22
54 Then he and the men who
were with him ate and drank and
spent the night. When they arose
in the morning, he said, "Send [r]me
away to my master." Gen. 30:25
55 But her brother and her
mother said, "Let [r] the girl stay
with us *a few* days, say ten; afterward she may go." Judg. 19:4
56 And he said to them, "Do not
delay me, since the LORD has
prospered my way. Send me away
that I may go to my master."
57 And they said, "We will call
the girl and consult her wishes."
58 Then they called Rebekah
and said to her, "Will you go with
this man?" And she said, "I will
go."
59 Thus they sent away their
sister Rebekah and her nurse with
Abraham's servant and his men.
60 And they blessed Rebekah
and said to her,

"May you, our sister,
Become thousands of ten
thousands,
And may your [t]descendants
possess *seed*
The gate of those who hate
them."

61 Then Rebekah arose with her
maids, and they mounted the
camels and followed the man. So
the servant took Rebekah and departed.
62 Now Isaac had come from
going to Beer-lahai-roi; for he [t]was
living in the Negev. *was dwelling*
63 And Isaac went out [r]to [a]medi-
tate in the field toward evening;
and he lifted up his eyes and

[25]Lit., *show lovingkindness and truth*

looked, and behold, camels were
coming. Ps. 1:2 · *stroll*
64 And Rebekah lifted up her
eyes, and when she saw Isaac she
dismounted from the camel.
65 And she said to the servant,
"Who is that man walking in the
field to meet us?" And the servant
said, "He is my master." Then she
took her veil and covered herself.
66 And the servant told Isaac all
the things that he had done.
67 Then Isaac brought her into
his mother Sarah's tent, and[r]he
took Rebekah, and she became his
wife; and he loved her; thus Isaac
was comforted after his mother's
death. Gen. 25:20

CHAPTER 25

NOW Abraham took another
wife, whose name was Keturah.
2 And she bore to him Zimran
and Jokshan and Medan and Midian and Ishbak and Shuah.
3 And Jokshan[t]became the father of Sheba and Dedan. And the
sons of Dedan were Asshurim and
Letushim and Leummim. *begot*
4 And the sons of Midian *were*
Ephah and Epher and Hanoch and
Abida and Eldaah. All these *were*
the sons of Keturah.
5 [r]Now Abraham gave all that
he had to Isaac; Gen. 24:35, 36
6 but to the sons of his concubines, Abraham gave gifts while
he was still living, and[r]sent them
away from his son Isaac eastward,
to the land of the east. Gen. 21:14
7 And these are all the years of
Abraham's life that he lived, one
hundred and seventy-five years.
8 And Abraham breathed his
last and died in a ripe old age, an
old man and satisfied *with life;*
and he was gathered to his people.
9 Then his sons Isaac and Ishmael buried him in[r]the cave of
Machpelah, in the field of Ephron
the son of Zohar the Hittite, facing Mamre, Gen. 23:17, 18
10 [r]the field which Abraham
purchased from the sons of Heth;
there Abraham was buried with
Sarah his wife. Gen. 23:3-16
11 And it came about after the
death of Abraham, that God
blessed his son Isaac; and Isaac
[t]lived by Beer-lahai-roi. *dwelt*
12 Now these are *the records of*
the generations of[r]Ishmael, Abraham's son, whom Hagar the Egyptian, Sarah's maid, bore to Abraham; Gen. 16:15
13 and these are the names of
the sons of Ishmael, by their
names,[t]in the order of their birth:
Nebaioth, the first-born of Ishmael, and Kedar and Adbeel and
Mibsam *in regard to their generations*
14 and Mishma and Dumah and
Massa,
15 Hadad and Tema, Jetur, Naphish and Kedemah.
16 These are the sons of Ishmael and these are their names,
by their villages, and by their
camps; twelve princes according
to their[a]tribes. *peoples*
17 And these are the years of
the life of Ishmael, one hundred
and thirty-seven years; and he
breathed his last and died, and
was gathered to his people.
18 And they[t]settled from Havilah to Shur which is[t]east of Egypt
[t]as one goes toward Assyria; he

settled in defiance of all his relatives. *dwelt* • *before* • *as you go*
19 Now these are *the records of*
[r]the generations of Isaac, Abraham's son: Abraham [t]became the
father of Isaac; Matt. 1:2 • *begot*
20 and Isaac was forty years old
when he took Rebekah, the
daughter of Bethuel the Aramean
of Paddan-aram, the sister of Laban the Aramean, to be his wife.
21 And Isaac prayed to the
LORD on behalf of his wife, because she was barren; and the
LORD answered him and Rebekah
his wife [r]conceived. Rom. 9:10
22 But the children struggled together within her; and she said,
"If it is so, why then am I *this*
way?" So she went to [r]inquire of
the LORD. 1 Sam. 9:9; 10:22
23 And the LORD said to her,
"Two[r] nations are in your
womb; Num. 20:14
And two peoples shall be
separated from your
body;
And one people shall be
stronger than the other;
And the older shall serve
the younger."
24 When her days to be delivered were fulfilled, behold, there
were twins in her womb.
25 Now the first came forth red,
[r]all over like a hairy garment; and
they named him Esau. Gen. 27:11
26 And afterward his brother
came forth with [r]his hand holding
on to Esau's heel, so [r]his name was
called [26]Jacob; and Isaac was sixty
years old when she gave birth to
them. Hos. 12:3 • Gen. 27:36
27 When the boys grew up,
Esau became a skillful hunter, a
man of the field; but Jacob was a
peaceful man, living in tents.
28 Now Isaac loved Esau, because he had [r]a taste for game; but
Rebekah loved Jacob. Gen. 27:19
29 And when Jacob had cooked
stew, Esau came in from the field
and he was [t]famished; *weary*
30 and Esau said to Jacob,
"Please let me have a swallow of
[t]that red stuff there, for I am famished." Therefore his name was
called [27]Edom. *the red, this red*
31 But Jacob said, "First[t] sell me
your birthright." *Today*
32 And Esau said, "Behold, I am
about to die; so of what *use* then is
the birthright to me?"
33 And Jacob said, "First[t] swear
to me"; so he swore to him, and
sold his birthright to Jacob. *Today*
34 Then Jacob gave Esau bread
and lentil stew; and he ate and
drank, and rose and went on his
way. Thus Esau despised his
birthright.

CHAPTER 26

NOW there was [r]a famine in the
land, besides the previous famine
that had occurred in the days of
Abraham. So Isaac went to Gerar,
to [r]Abimelech king of the Philistines. Gen. 12:10 • Gen. 20:1, 2
2 And the LORD appeared to
him and said, "Do not go down to
Egypt; [t]stay[r] in the land of which I
shall tell you. *dwell* • Gen. 12:1
3 "Sojourn in this land and I
will be with you and bless you, for
to you and to your [t]descendants I
will give all these lands, and I will
establish the oath which I swore
to your father Abraham. *seed*

[26] I.e., one who takes by the heel, or supplants

[27] I.e., red

4 "And I will multiply your descendants as the stars of heaven,
and will give your [t]descendants all
these lands; and [r]by your descendants all the nations of the earth
shall be blessed; *seed* · Gal. 3:8
5 because Abraham [t]obeyed
Me and kept My charge, My commandments, My statutes and My
laws." *hearkened to My voice*
6 So Isaac [t]lived in Gerar. *dwelt*
7 When the men of the place
asked about his wife, he said,
"She is my sister," for he was
afraid to say, "my wife," *thinking,*
"the[t] men of the place might kill
me on account of Rebekah, for
she is beautiful." *lest . . . place*
8 And it came about, when he
had been there a long time, that
Abimelech king of the Philistines
looked out through a window, and
saw, and behold, Isaac was ca-
ressing his wife Rebekah.
9 Then Abimelech called Isaac
and said, "Behold, certainly she is
your wife! How then did you say,
'She is my sister'?" And Isaac said
to him, "Because I said, 'Lest I die
on account of her.' "
10 And Abimelech said, "What
is this you have done to us? One of
the people might easily have lain
with your wife, and you would
have brought guilt upon us."
11 So Abimelech charged all the
people, saying, "He who [r]touches
this man or his wife shall surely
be put to death." Ps. 105:15
12 Now Isaac sowed in that
land, and [t]reaped in the same year
a hundredfold. And [r]the LORD
blessed him, *found* · Prov. 10:22
13 and the man became rich,
and continued to grow [t]richer until
he became very wealthy; *great*
14 for he had possessions of
flocks [t]and herds and a great
household, so that the Philistines
envied him. *and possessions of herds*
15 Now all the wells which his
father's servants had dug in the
days of Abraham his father, the
Philistines stopped up [t]by filling
them with earth. *and filled them*
16 Then Abimelech said to
Isaac, "Go away from us, for you
are [r]too powerful for us." Ex. 1:9
17 And Isaac departed from
there and camped in the valley of
Gerar, and [t]settled there. *dwelt*
18 Then Isaac dug again the
wells of water which [t]had been
dug in the days of his father Abraham, for the Philistines had
stopped them up after the death
of Abraham; and he gave them the
same names which his father had
[t]given them. *they had dug* · *called*
19 But when Isaac's servants
dug in the valley and found there
a well of [t]flowing water, *living*
20 the herdsmen of Gerar quarreled with the herdsmen of Isaac,
saying, "The water is ours!" So he
named the well Esek, because
they contended with him.
21 Then they dug another well,
and they quarreled over it too, so
he named it Sitnah.
22 And he moved away from
there and dug another well, and
they did not quarrel over it; so he
named it Rehoboth, for he said,
[t]"At last the LORD has made [a]room
for us, and we shall be [r]fruitful in
the land." *Truly now* · *broad* · Ex. 1:7
23 Then he went up from there
to [r]Beersheba. Gen. 22:19

24 And the LORD appeared to
him the same night and said,
"I am the God of your father
Abraham;
Do not fear, for I am with
you.
I will bless you, and multi-
ply your [t]descendants,
For the sake of My servant
Abraham." *seed*

25 So he built an [r]altar there,
and called upon the name of the
LORD, and pitched his tent there;
and there Isaac's servants dug a
well. Gen. 12:7, 8; Ps. 116:17

26 Then [r]Abimelech came to him
from Gerar with his adviser Ahuz-
zath, and Phicol the commander
of his army. Gen. 21:22

27 And Isaac said to them,
"Why [r]have you come to me, since
you hate me, and have sent me
away from you?" Judg. 11:7

28 And they said, "We see
plainly that the LORD has been
with you; so we said, 'Let there
now be an oath between us, *even*
between you and us, and let us
make a covenant with you,

29 that you will do us no harm,
just as we have not touched you
[t]and have done to you nothing but
good, and have sent you away in
peace. You are now the blessed of
the LORD.'" *and just as we*

30 Then [r]he made them a feast,
and they ate and drank. Gen. 19:3

31 And in the morning they
arose early and exchanged oaths;
then Isaac sent them away and
they departed from him in peace.

32 Now it came about on the
same day, that Isaac's servants
came in and told him about the
well which they had dug, and said
to him, "We have found water."

33 So he called it Shibah; therefore the name of the city is [r]Beer-
sheba to this day. Gen. 21:31

34 And when Esau was forty
years old he [t]married Judith the
daughter of Beeri the Hittite, and
Basemath the daughter of Elon
the Hittite; *took as wife*

35 and they [28]brought grief to
Isaac and Rebekah.

CHAPTER 27

NOW it came about, when Isaac
was old, and [r]his eyes were too
dim to see, that he called his older
son Esau and said to him, "My
son." And he said to him, "Here I
am." 1 Sam. 3:2

2 [r]And [t]Isaac said, "Behold now,
I am old *and* I do not know the
day of my death. Gen. 47:29 • *he*

3 "Now then, please take your
gear, your quiver and your bow,
and go out to the field and [r]hunt
game for me; Gen. 25:28

4 and prepare a savory dish for
me such as I love, and bring it to
me that I may eat, so that my soul
may bless you before I die."

5 And Rebekah was listening
while Isaac spoke to his son Esau.
So when Esau went to the field to
hunt for game to bring *home*,

6 [r]Rebekah said to her son Jacob, "Behold, I heard your father
speak to your brother Esau, saying, Gen. 25:28

7 'Bring me *some* game and
prepare a savory dish for me, that
I may eat, and bless you in the
presence of the LORD before my
death.'

[28]Lit., *were a bitterness of spirit to*

8 "Now therefore, my son, listen to me as I command you.
9 "Go now to the flock and
[t]bring me two choice [t]kids from
there, that I may prepare them *as*
a savory dish for your father, such
as he loves. *take* • *kids of goats*
10 "Then you shall bring *it* to
your father, that he may eat, so
that he may bless you before his
death."
11 And Jacob [t]answered his
mother Rebekah, "Behold, Esau
my brother is a hairy man and I
am a smooth man. *said to*
12 "Perhaps[r] my father will feel
me, then I shall be as a [t]deceiver in
his sight; and I shall bring upon
myself a curse and not a blessing." Gen. 27:21, 22 • *mocker*
13 But his mother said to him,
"Your curse be on me, my son;
only [r]obey my voice, and go, get
them for me." Gen. 27:8
14 So he went and got *them*,
and brought *them* to his mother;
and his mother made savory food
such as his father loved.
15 Then Rebekah took the [t]best
garments of Esau her elder son,
which were with her in the house,
and put them on Jacob her younger son. *desirable;* or, *choice*
16 And she put the skins of the
kids on his hands and on the
smooth part of his neck.
17 She also gave the savory
food and the bread, which she had
made, to her son Jacob.
18 Then he came to his father
and said, "My father." And he
said, "Here I am. Who are you,
my son?"
19 And Jacob said to his father,
"I am Esau your first-born; I have
done as you told me. Get up,
please, sit and eat of my game,
that [t]you may bless me." *your soul*
20 And Isaac said to his son,
"How is it that you have *it* so
quickly, my son?" And he said,
"Because the LORD your God
caused *it* to happen to me."
21 Then Isaac said to Jacob,
"Please come close, that I may
feel you, my son, whether you are
really my son Esau or not."
22 So Jacob came close to Isaac
his father, and he felt him and
said, "The voice is the voice of Jacob, but the hands are the hands
of Esau."
23 And he did not recognize
him, because his hands were [r]hairy
like his brother Esau's hands; so
he blessed him. Gen. 27:16
24 And he said, "Are you really
my son Esau?" And he said, "I
am."
25 So he said, "Bring *it* to me,
and I will eat of my son's game,
that [t]I[r] may bless you." And he
brought *it* to him, and he ate; he
also brought him wine and he
drank. *my soul* • Gen. 27:4
26 Then his father Isaac said to
him, "Please come close and kiss
me, my son."
27 So he came close and kissed
him; and when he smelled the
smell of his garments, he [r]blessed
him and said, Heb. 11:20

"See, the smell of my son
Is like the smell of a field
which the LORD has
blessed;
28 Now may [r]God give you of
the dew of heaven,
And of the fatness of the
earth, Prov. 3:20

And an abundance of grain
and new wine;
29 [r]May peoples serve you,
And nations bow down to
you; Gen. 25:23
Be master of your brothers,
And may your mother's
sons bow down to you.
Cursed be those who curse
you,
And blessed be those who
bless you."

30 Now it came about, as soon
as Isaac had finished blessing Jacob, and Jacob had hardly gone
out from the presence of Isaac his
father, that Esau his brother came
in from his hunting.
31 Then he also made savory
food, and brought it to his father;
and he said to his father, "Let my
father arise, and eat of his son's
game, that you may bless me."
32 And Isaac his father said to
him, "Who[r] are you?" And he said,
"I am your son, your first-born,
Esau." Gen. 27:18
33 Then Isaac trembled violently, and said, [r]"Who was he
then that hunted game and
brought *it* to me, so that I ate of
all *of it* before you came, and
blessed him?[r]Yes, and he shall be
blessed." Gen. 27:35 • Num. 23:20
34 When Esau heard the words
of his father, he cried out with an
exceedingly great and bitter cry,
and said to his father, "Bless me,
even me also, O my father!"
35 And he said, "Your[r] brother
came deceitfully, and has taken
away your blessing." Gen. 27:19
36 Then he said, "Is he not
rightly named [r]Jacob, for he has
supplanted me these two times?
He took away my birthright, and
behold, now he has taken away
my blessing." And he said, "Have
you not reserved a blessing for
me?" Gen. 25:26, 32-34
37 But Isaac answered and said
to Esau, "Behold, I have made him
your master, and all his relatives I
have given to him as servants; and
with grain and new wine I have
sustained him. Now as for you
then, what can I do, my son?"
38 And Esau said to his father,
"Do you have only one blessing,
my father? Bless me, *even* me
also, O my father." So Esau lifted
his voice and[r] wept. Heb. 12:17
39 Then Isaac his father answered and said to him,
"Behold,[a] away from the fertility of the earth shall be
your dwelling, *of*
And away from the dew of
heaven from above.
40 "And by your sword you
shall live,
And your brother you shall
serve;
But it shall come about
when you become rest-
less,
That you shall break his
yoke from your neck."
41 So Esau bore a grudge
against Jacob because of the
blessing with which his father had
blessed him; and Esau said[r] to himself, "The days of mourning for
my father are near; then I will kill
my brother Jacob." *in his heart*
42 Now when the words of her
elder son Esau were reported to
Rebekah, she sent and called her
younger son Jacob, and said to
him, "Behold your brother Esau is

consoling himself concerning you, *by planning* to kill you.

43 "Now therefore, my son, obey my voice, and arise, flee to [r]Haran, to my brother Laban! Gen. 11:31

44 "And stay with him [r]a few days, until your brother's fury [t]subsides, Gen. 31:41 • *turns away*

45 until your brother's anger against you subsides, and he forgets what you did to him. Then I shall send and get you from there. Why should I be bereaved of you both in one day?"

46 And Rebekah said to Isaac, "I am tired of [t]living because of the daughters of Heth; if Jacob takes a wife from the daughters of Heth, like these, from the daughters of the land, what good will my life be to me?" *my life*

CHAPTER 28

SO Isaac called Jacob and blessed him and charged him, and said to him, "You shall not take a wife from the daughters of Canaan.

2 "Arise, go to Paddan-aram, to the house of [r]Bethuel your mother's father; and from there take to yourself a wife from the daughters of Laban your mother's brother. Gen. 25:20

3 "And may God Almighty bless you and make you fruitful and multiply you, that you may become a company of peoples.

4 "May He also give you the blessing of Abraham, to you and to your [t]descendants with you; that you may possess the land of your [r]sojournings, which God gave to Abraham." *seed* • Ps. 39:12

5 Then Isaac sent Jacob away, and he went to Paddan-aram to Laban, son of Bethuel the Aramean, the brother of Rebekah, the mother of Jacob and Esau.

6 Now Esau saw that Isaac had blessed Jacob and sent him away to Paddan-aram, to take to himself a wife from there, *and that* when he blessed him he charged him, saying, "You [r]shall not take a wife from the daughters of Canaan," Gen. 28:1

7 and that Jacob had obeyed his father and his mother and had gone to Paddan-aram.

8 So Esau saw that the daughters of Canaan displeased [t]his father Isaac; *in the eyes of his*

9 and Esau went to Ishmael, and [t]married, besides the wives that he had, Mahalath the daughter of Ishmael, Abraham's son, the sister of Nebaioth. *took for his wife*

10 Then Jacob departed from [r]Beersheba and went toward [r]Haran. Gen. 26:23 • Gen. 12:4, 5

11 And he [t]came to a certain place and spent the night there, because the sun had set; and he took one of the stones of the place and put it under his head, and lay down in that place. *lighted on*

12 And [r]he had a dream, and behold, a ladder was set on the earth with its top reaching to heaven; and behold, [r]the angels of God were ascending and descending on it. Gen. 41:1 • John 1:51

13 And behold, the LORD stood above it and said, "I am the LORD, the God of your father Abraham and the God of Isaac; the land on which you lie, I will give it to you and to your [t]descendants. *seed*

14 "Your descendants shall also be like the dust of the earth, and you shall spread out to the west and to the east and to the north and to the south; and in you and in your descendants shall all the families of the earth be blessed.

15 "And behold, I am with you, and [r]will keep you wherever you go, and will bring you back to this land; for I will not leave you until I have done what I have [t]promised you." Num. 6:24 · *spoken to*

16 Then Jacob [r]awoke from his sleep and said, "Surely [r]the LORD is in this place, and I did not know it." 1 Kin. 3:15 · Josh. 5:13-15

17 And he was afraid and said, "How [r]awesome is this place! This is none other than the house of God, and this is the gate of heaven." Ps. 68:35

18 So Jacob rose early in the morning, and took the stone that he had put [t]under his head and set it up as a pillar, and poured oil on its top. *at his head-place*

19 And he called the name of that place [29]Bethel; however, [t]previously the name of the city had been Luz. *at the first*

20 Then Jacob made a vow, saying, "If God will be with me and will keep me on this journey that I [t]take, and will give me [t]food to eat and garments to wear, *go* · *bread*

21 and [r]I return to my father's house in [t]safety, then the LORD will be my God. Judg. 11:31 · *peace*

22 "And this stone, which I have set up as a pillar, [r]will be God's house; and [r]of all that Thou dost give me I will surely give a tenth to Thee." Gen. 35:7 · Lev. 27:30

[29]I.e., the house of God

CHAPTER 29

THEN Jacob [30]went on his journey, and came to the land of the sons of the east.

2 And he looked, and [t]saw [r]a well in the field, and behold, three flocks of sheep were lying there beside it, for from that well they watered the flocks. Now the stone on the mouth of the well was large. *behold* · Ex. 2:15, 16

3 When all the flocks were gathered there, they would then roll the stone from the mouth of the well, and water the sheep, and put the stone back in its place on the mouth of the well.

4 And Jacob said to them, "My brothers, where are you from?" And they said, "We are from [r]Haran." Gen. 28:10

5 And he said to them, "Do you know Laban the [r]son of Nahor?" And they said, "We know *him.*" Gen. 24:24, 29

6 And he said to them, "Is it well with him?" And they said, "It is well, and behold, [r]Rachel his daughter is coming with the sheep." Ex. 2:16

7 And he said, "Behold, it is still high day; it is not time for the livestock to be gathered. Water the sheep, and go, pasture them."

8 But they said, "We cannot, until all the flocks are gathered, and they roll the stone from the mouth of the well; then we water the sheep."

9 While he was still speaking with them, Rachel came with her father's sheep, for she was a shepherdess.

10 And it came about, when Ja-

[30]Lit., *lifted up his feet*

cob saw Rachel the daughter of
Laban his mother's brother, and
the sheep of Laban his mother's
brother, that Jacob went up, and
rolled the stone from the mouth of
the well, and watered the flock of
Laban his mother's brother.
11 Then Jacob kissed Rachel,
and lifted his voice and wept.
12 And Jacob told Rachel that
he was a relative of her father and
that he was Rebekah's son, and
she ran and told her father.
13 So it came about, when Laban heard the news of Jacob his
sister's son, that he ran to meet
him, and [r]embraced him and
kissed him, and brought him to
his house. Then he related to Laban all these things. Gen. 33:4
14 And Laban said to him,
"Surely you are [r]my bone and my
flesh." And he stayed with him a
month. Gen. 2:23; Judg. 9:2
15 Then Laban said to Jacob,
"Because you are my [t]relative,
should you therefore serve me for
nothing? Tell me, what shall [r]your
wages be?" *brother* • Gen. 31:41
16 Now Laban had two daughters; the name of the older was
Leah, and the name of the younger was Rachel.
17 And Leah's eyes were weak,
but Rachel was beautiful of form
and [t]face. *beautiful of appearance*
18 Now Jacob [r]loved Rachel, so
he said, "I [r] will serve you seven
years for your younger daughter
Rachel." Gen. 24:67 • Hos. 12:12
19 And Laban said, "It is better
that I give her to you than that I
should give her to another man;
stay with me."
20 So Jacob served seven years
for Rachel and they seemed to
him but a few days [r]because of his
love for her. Song 8:7
21 Then Jacob said to Laban,
"Give *me* my wife, for my [t]time is
completed, that I may [r]go in to
her." *days are* • Judg. 15:1
22 And Laban gathered all the
men of the place, and made a
feast.
23 Now it came about in the
evening that he took his daughter
Leah, and brought her to him; and
Jacob went in to her.
24 Laban also gave his maid Zilpah to his daughter Leah as a
maid.
25 So it came about in the
morning that, behold, it was Leah!
And he said to Laban, "What [r] is
this you have done to me? Was it
not for Rachel that I served with
you? Why then have you [r]deceived
me?" Gen. 12:18 • 1 Sam. 28:12
26 But Laban said, "It is not the
practice in our place, to marry off
the younger before the first-born.
27 "Complete the week of this
one, and we will give you the other also for the service which [r]you
shall serve with me for another
seven years." Gen. 31:41
28 And Jacob did so and completed her week, and he gave him
his daughter Rachel as his wife.
29 Laban also gave his maid Bilhah to his daughter Rachel as her
maid.
30 So *Jacob* went in to Rachel
also, and indeed [r]he loved Rachel
more than Leah, and he served
with [t]Laban for another seven
years. Gen. 29:17, 18 • *him*
31 Now the LORD saw that Leah

was unloved, and He opened her womb, but Rachel was barren.

32 And Leah conceived and bore a son and named him Reuben, for she said, "Because the LORD has [t]seen[r] my affliction; surely now my husband will love me." *looked upon* • Ps. 25:18

33 Then she conceived again and bore a son and said, "Because[r] the LORD has heard that I am [t]unloved, He has therefore given me this *son* also." So she named him Simeon. Deut. 21:15 • *hated*

34 And she conceived again and bore a son and said, "Now this time my husband will become attached to me, because I have borne him three sons." Therefore he was named [r]Levi. Gen. 49:5

35 And she conceived again and bore a son and said, "This time I will praise the LORD." Therefore she named him [r]Judah. Then she stopped bearing. Matt. 1:2

CHAPTER 30

NOW when Rachel saw that she bore Jacob no children, [t]she became jealous of her sister; and she said to Jacob, "Give me children, or else I die." *Rachel*

2 Then Jacob's anger burned against Rachel, and he said, "Am I in the place of God, who has [r]withheld from you the fruit of the womb?" Gen. 20:18; 29:31

3 And she said, "Here is my maid Bilhah, go in to her, that she may bear on my knees, that [t]through her I too may have children." *from her I too may be built*

4 So [r]she gave him her maid Bilhah as a wife, and Jacob went in to her. Gen. 16:3, 4

5 And Bilhah conceived and bore Jacob a son.

6 Then Rachel said, "God has [t]vindicated[r] me, and has indeed heard my voice and has given me a son." Therefore she named him Dan. *judged* • Ps. 35:24

7 And Rachel's maid Bilhah conceived again and bore Jacob a second son.

8 So Rachel said, "With [t]mighty wrestlings I have wrestled with my sister, *and* I have indeed prevailed." And she named him Naphtali. *wrestlings of God*

9 When Leah saw that she had stopped bearing, she took her maid Zilpah and gave her to Jacob as a wife.

10 And Leah's maid Zilpah bore Jacob a son.

11 Then Leah said, "How fortunate!" So she named him Gad.

12 And Leah's maid Zilpah bore Jacob a second son.

13 Then Leah said, "Happy am I! For women will call me happy." So she named him Asher.

14 Now in the days of wheat harvest Reuben went and found [r]mandrakes in the field, and brought them to his mother Leah. Then Rachel said to Leah, "Please give me some of your son's mandrakes." Song 7:13

15 But she said to her, "Is it a small matter for you to take my husband? And would you take my son's mandrakes also?" So Rachel said, "Therefore he may lie with you tonight in return for your son's mandrakes."

16 When Jacob came in from

the field in the evening, then Leah
went out to meet him and said,
"You must come in to me, for I
have surely hired you with my
son's mandrakes." So he lay with
her that night.
17 And God gave heed to Leah,
and she conceived and bore Jacob
a fifth son.
18 Then Leah said, "God has
given me my wages, because I
gave my maid to my husband." So
she named him Issachar.
19 And Leah conceived again
and bore a sixth son to Jacob.
20 Then Leah said, "God has endowed me with a good gift; now
my husband will dwell with me,
because I have borne him six
sons." So she named him Zebulun.
21 And afterward she bore a
daughter and named her Dinah.
22 Then God remembered Rachel, and God gave heed to her
and [r]opened her womb. Gen. 29:31
23 So she conceived and bore a
son and said, "God has [r]taken
away my reproach." Luke 1:25
24 And she named him Joseph,
saying, "May the LORD [t]give me
another son." *add to me*
25 Now it came about when Rachel had borne Joseph, that Jacob
said to Laban, "Send[r] me away,
that I may go to my own place and
to my own country. Gen. 24:54, 56
26 "Give *me* my wives and my
children for whom I have served
you, and let me depart; for you
yourself know my service which I
have [t]rendered you." *served*
27 But Laban said to him, "If
now [31]it pleases you, *stay with me;*

[31] Lit., *I have found favor in your eyes*

I have divined that the LORD has
blessed me on your account."
28 And he continued, "Name
me your wages, and I will give it."
29 But he said to him, "You[r]
yourself know how I have served
you and how your cattle have
[t]fared with me. Gen. 31:6 • *been*
30 "For you had little before [t]I
came, and it has increased to a
multitude; and the LORD has
blessed you wherever I turned.
But now, when shall I provide for
my own household also?" *me*
31 So he said, "What shall I give
you?" And Jacob said, "You shall
not give me anything. If you will
do this *one* thing for me, I will
again pasture *and* keep your
flock:
32 let me pass through your entire flock today, removing from
there every [r]speckled and spotted
sheep, and every black one among
the lambs, and the spotted and
speckled among the goats; and
such shall be my wages. Gen. 31:8
33 "So my [t]honesty will answer
for me later, when you come concerning my wages. Every one that
is not speckled and spotted
among the goats and black among
the lambs, *if found* with me, will
be considered stolen." *righteousness*
34 And Laban said, "Good, let it
be according to your word."
35 So he removed on that day
the striped and spotted male goats
and all the speckled and spotted
female goats, every one with
white in it, and all the black ones
among the sheep, and gave them
into the [t]care of his sons. *hand*
36 And he put *a distance of*
three days' journey between him-

self and Jacob, and Jacob fed the
rest of Laban's flocks.
37 Then Jacob [t]took fresh rods
of poplar and almond and plane
trees, and peeled white stripes in
them, exposing the white which
was in the rods. *took to himself*
38 And he set the rods which he
had peeled in front of the flocks in
the gutters, *even* in the watering
troughs, where the flocks came to
drink; and they[a]mated when they
came to drink. *conceived*
39 So the flocks mated by the
rods, and the flocks brought forth
striped, speckled, and spotted.
40 And Jacob separated the
lambs, and made the flocks face
toward the striped and all the
black in the flock of Laban; and he
put his own herds apart, and did
not put them with Laban's flock.
41 Moreover, it came about
whenever the stronger of the flock
[a]were mating, that Jacob would
place the rods in the sight of the
flock in the gutters, so that they
might mate by the rods; *conceived*
42 but when the flock was feeble, he did not put *them* in; so the
feebler were Laban's and the
[t]stronger Jacob's. *bound ones*
43 So the man became exceedingly prosperous, and had large
flocks and female and male servants and camels and donkeys.

CHAPTER 31

NOW [t]Jacob heard the words of
Laban's sons, saying, "Jacob has
taken away all that was our father's, and from what belonged to
our father he has made all this
[t]wealth." *he • glory*
2 And Jacob saw the [32]attitude
of Laban, and behold, it was not
friendly toward him as formerly.
3 Then the LORD said to Jacob,
"Return[r] to the land of your fathers and to your relatives, and I
will be with you." Gen. 32:9
4 So Jacob sent and called Rachel and Leah to his flock in the
field,
5 and said to them, "I see your
father's [t]attitude, that it is not
friendly toward me as formerly,
but[r]the God of my father has been
with me. *face* • Heb. 13:5
6 "And [r]you know that I have
served your father with all my
strength. Gen. 30:29
7 "Yet your father has [r]cheated
me and changed my wages ten
times; however, God did not allow
him to hurt me. Gen. 29:25
8 "If [r]he spoke thus, 'The
speckled shall be your wages,'
then all the flock brought forth
speckled; and if he spoke thus,
'The striped shall be your wages,'
then all the flock brought forth
striped. Gen. 30:32
9 "Thus God has [r]taken away
your father's livestock and given
them to me. Gen. 31:1, 16
10 "And it came about at the
time when the flock were mating
that I lifted up my eyes and saw in
a dream, and behold, the male
goats which were mating *were*
striped, speckled, and mottled.
11 "Then[r]the angel of God said to
me in the dream, 'Jacob,' and I
said, 'Here I am.' Gen. 16:7-11
12 "And he said, 'Lift up, now,
your eyes and see *that* all the male
goats which are mating are
striped, speckled, and mottled; for

[32]Lit., *face*

[r]I have seen all that Laban has
been doing to you. Ex. 3:7
13 'I am the God *of* Bethel,
where you anointed a pillar,
where you made a vow to Me;
now arise, leave this land, and return to the land of your birth.' "
14 And Rachel and Leah answered and said to him, "Do we
still have any portion or inheritance in our father's house?
15 "Are we not reckoned by him
as foreigners? For he has sold us,
and has also entirely consumed
[t]our purchase price. *our money*
16 "Surely all the wealth which
God has taken away from our father belongs to us and our children; now then, do whatever God
has said to you."
17 Then Jacob arose and put his
children and his wives upon camels;
18 and he drove away all his
livestock and all his property
which he had gathered, his acquired livestock which he had
gathered in Paddan-aram, [r]to go to
the land of Canaan to his father
Isaac. Gen. 35:27
19 When Laban had gone to
shear his flock, then Rachel stole
the [r]household idols that were her
father's. 1 Sam. 19:13; Hos. 3:4
20 And Jacob [t]deceived Laban
the Aramean, by not telling him
that he was fleeing. *stole the heart of*
21 So he fled with all that he
had; and he arose and crossed the
Euphrates River, and set his face
toward the hill country of Gilead.
22 When it was told Laban on
the third day that Jacob had fled,
23 then he took his [t]kinsmen
with him, and pursued him *a dis-*
tance of seven days' journey; and
he overtook him in the hill country of Gilead. *brothers*
24 And God came to Laban the
Aramean in a dream of the night,
and said to him, "Be[t] careful that
you do not speak to Jacob either
good or bad." *Take heed to yourself*
25 And Laban caught up with
Jacob. Now Jacob had pitched his
tent in the hill country, and Laban
with his [t]kinsmen camped in the
hill country of Gilead. *brothers*
26 Then Laban said to Jacob,
"What have you done by deceiving me and carrying away my
daughters like captives of the
sword?
27 "Why did you flee secretly
and deceive me, and did not tell
me, so that I might have sent you
away with joy and with songs,
with timbrel and with lyre;
28 and did not allow me [r]to kiss
my sons and my daughters? Now
you have done foolishly. Gen. 31:55
29 "It is in [t]my power to do you
harm, but the God of your father
spoke to me last night, saying, 'Be
careful not to speak either good or
bad to Jacob.' *the power of my hand*
30 "And now you have indeed
gone away because you longed
greatly for your father's house;
but why did you steal my gods?"
31 Then Jacob answered and
said to Laban, "Because I was
afraid, for I said, 'Lest you would
take your daughters from me by
force.'
32 "The one with whom you find
your gods shall not live; in the
presence of our kinsmen [t]point out
what is yours among my belong-
ings and take *it* for yourself." For

Jacob did not know that Rachel
had stolen them. *recognize*
33 So Laban went into Jacob's
tent, and into Leah's tent, and into
the tent of the two maids, but he
did not find *them*. Then he went
out of Leah's tent and entered Rachel's tent.
34 Now Rachel had taken the
household idols and put them in
the camel's saddle, and she sat on
them. And Laban felt through all
the tent, but did not find *them*.
35 And she said to her father,
"Let not my lord be angry that I
cannot [r]rise before you, for the
manner of women is upon me." So
he searched, but did not find the
household idols. Lev. 19:32
36 Then Jacob became angry
and contended with Laban; and
Jacob answered and said to Laban, "What is my transgression?
What is my sin, that you have hotly pursued me?
37 "Though you have felt
through all my goods, what have
you found of all your household
goods? Set *it* here before my kinsmen and your kinsmen, that they
may decide between us two.
38 "These twenty years I *have
been* with you; your ewes and
your female goats have not miscarried, nor have I eaten the rams
of your flocks.
39 "That which was torn *of
beasts* I did not bring to you; I
bore the loss of it myself. You required it of my hand *whether* stolen by day or stolen by night.
40 "*Thus* I was: by day the [a]heat
consumed me, and the frost by
night, and my sleep fled from my
eyes. *drought*
41 "These twenty years I have
been in your house; [r]I served you
fourteen years for your two
daughters, and six years for your
flock, and you changed my wages
ten times. Gen. 29:27, 30
42 "If [r]the God of my father, the
God of Abraham, and the fear of
Isaac, had not been for me, surely
now you would have sent me
away empty-handed. God has
seen my affliction and the toil of
my hands, so He rendered judgment last night." Gen. 31:5, 29, 53
43 Then Laban answered and
said to Jacob, "The daughters are
my daughters, and the children
are my children, and the flocks are
my flocks, and all that you see is
mine. But what can I do this day
to these my daughters or to their
children whom they have borne?
44 "So now come, let us make a
covenant, you and I, and let it be a
witness between you and me."
45 Then Jacob took [r]a stone and
set it up *as* a pillar. Josh. 24:26, 27
46 And Jacob said to his kinsmen, "Gather stones." So they
took stones and made a heap, and
they ate there by the heap.
47 Now Laban [r]called it [33]Jegar-
sahadutha, but Jacob called it
[34]Galeed. Josh. 22:34
48 And Laban said, "This [r]heap
is a witness between [t]you and me
this day." Therefore it was named
Galeed; Josh. 24:27 • *me and you*
49 and [35]Mizpah, for he said,
"May the LORD watch between
you and me when we are [t]absent
one from the other. *hidden*
50 "If you mistreat my daughters, or if you take wives besides

[33] I.e., the heap of witness, in Aramaic
[34] I.e., the heap of witness, in Hebrew
[35] I.e., the watchtower

my daughters, *although* no man is
with us, see, God is witness between[t]you and me." *me and you*
51 And Laban said to Jacob,
"Behold this heap and behold the
pillar which I have set between
[t]you and me. *me and you*
52 "This heap is a witness, and
the pillar is a witness, that I will
not pass by this heap to you for
harm, and you will not pass by
this heap and this pillar to me, for
harm.
53 "The[r]God of Abraham and the
God of Nahor, the God of their father,[r]judge between us." So Jacob
swore by the fear of his father
Isaac. Gen. 28:13 • Gen. 16:5
54 Then Jacob offered a sacrifice on the mountain, and called
his kinsmen to[t]the meal; and they
ate[t]the meal and spent the night
on the mountain. *eat bread • bread*
55 And early in the morning Laban arose, and[r]kissed his sons and
his daughters and blessed them.
Then Laban departed and returned to his place. Gen. 31:28, 43

CHAPTER 32

NOW as Jacob went on his way,
the angels of God met him.
2 And Jacob said when he saw
them, "This is God's [36]camp." So
he named that place [37]Mahanaim.
3 Then Jacob[r]sent messengers
before him to his brother Esau in
the land of Seir, the[t]country of
Edom. Gen. 27:41, 42 • *field*
4 He also commanded them
saying, "Thus you shall say to my
lord Esau: 'Thus says your servant
Jacob, "I have sojourned with Laban, and stayed until now;

[36]Or, *company*
[37]I.e., Two Camps, or, Two Companies

5 and[r]I have oxen and donkeys
and flocks and male and female
servants; and I have sent to tell
my lord, that I may find favor in
your sight."'" Gen. 30:43
6 And the messengers re-
turned to Jacob, saying, "We
came to your brother Esau, and
furthermore[r]he is coming to meet
you, and four hundred men are
with him." Gen. 33:1
7 Then Jacob was[r]greatly
afraid and distressed; and he divided the people who were with
him, and the flocks and the herds
and the camels, into two companies; Gen. 32:11
8 for he said, "If Esau comes to
the one company and[t]attacks it,
then the company which is left
will escape." *smites*
9 And Jacob said, "O God of
my father Abraham and God of
my father Isaac, O LORD, who
didst say to me, 'Return to your
country and to your relatives, and
I will[t]prosper you,' *do good with you*
10 [t]I am unworthy of all the
lovingkindness and of all the
[a]faithfulness which Thou hast
shown to Thy servant; for with my
staff *only* I crossed this Jordan,
and now I have become two companies. *I am less than all • truth*
11 "Deliver me, I pray, from the
hand of my brother, from the
hand of Esau; for I fear him, lest
he come and[t]attack me, the mothers with the children. *smite*
12 "For Thou didst say, 'I will
surely[t]prosper you, and make
your descendants as the sand of
the sea, which cannot be numbered for multitude.'" *do good with*
13 So he spent the night there.
Then he[t]selected from what he

had with him a [r]present for his brother Esau: *took* • Gen. 43:11

14 two hundred female goats and twenty male goats, two hundred ewes and twenty rams,

15 thirty milking camels and their colts, forty cows and ten bulls, twenty female donkeys and ten male donkeys.

16 And he delivered *them* into the hand of his servants, every drove by itself, and said to his servants, "Pass on before me, and put a space between droves."

17 And he commanded the [t]one in front, saying, "When my brother Esau meets you and asks you, saying, 'To whom do you belong, and where are you going, and to whom do these *animals* in front of you belong?' *first*

18 then you shall say, '*These* belong to your servant Jacob; it is a present sent to my lord Esau. And behold, he also is behind us.' "

19 Then he commanded also the second and the third, and all those who followed the droves, saying, "After this manner you shall speak to Esau when you find him;

20 and you shall say, 'Behold, your servant Jacob also is behind us.' " For he said, "I will appease him with the present that goes before me. Then afterward I will see his face; perhaps he will accept me."

21 So the present passed on before him, while he himself spent that night in the camp.

22 Now he arose that same night and took his two wives and his two maids and his eleven children, and crossed the ford of the [r]Jabbok. Deut. 3:16; Josh. 12:2

23 And he took them and sent them across the stream. And he sent across whatever he had.

24 Then Jacob was left alone, and a man [r]wrestled with him until daybreak. Hos. 12:3, 4

25 And when he saw that he had not prevailed against him, he touched the socket of his thigh; so the socket of Jacob's thigh was dislocated while he wrestled with him.

26 Then he said, "Let me go, for the dawn is breaking." But he said, "I [r]will not let you go unless you bless me." Hos. 12:4

27 So he said to him, "What is your name?" And he said, "Jacob."

28 And [r]he said, "Your name shall no longer be Jacob, but [38]Israel; for you have striven with God and with men and have prevailed." Gen. 35:10; 1 Kin. 18:31

29 Then [r]Jacob asked him and said, "Please tell me your name." But he said, "Why is it that you ask my name?" And he blessed him there. Judg. 13:17, 18

30 So Jacob named the place [39]Peniel, for *he said,* "I [r]have seen God face to face, yet my life has been preserved." Ex. 24:10, 11

31 Now the sun rose upon him just as he crossed over Penuel, and he was limping on his thigh.

32 Therefore, to this day the sons of Israel do not eat the sinew of the hip which is on the socket of the thigh, because he touched the socket of Jacob's thigh in the sinew of the hip.

[38] I.e., he who strives with God, or, God strives [39] I.e., the face of God

CHAPTER 33

THEN Jacob lifted his eyes and looked, and behold, [r]Esau was coming, and four hundred men with him. So he divided the children[a] among Leah and Rachel and the two maids. Gen. 32:6 • *to*

2 And he put the maids and their children [t]in front, and Leah and her children [t]next, and Rachel and Joseph last. *first* • *behind*

3 But he himself passed on ahead of them and [r]bowed down to the ground seven times, until he came near to his brother. Gen. 42:6

4 Then Esau ran to meet him and embraced him, and [r]fell on his neck and kissed him, and they wept. Gen. 45:14, 15

5 And he lifted his eyes and saw the women and the children, and said, "Who are these with you?" So he said, "The[r] children whom God has graciously given your servant." Ps. 127:3

6 Then the maids came near [t]with their children, and they bowed down. *they and*

7 And Leah likewise came near with her children, and they bowed down; and afterward Joseph came near with Rachel, and they bowed down.

8 And he said, "What do you mean by all this company which I have met?" And he said, "To find favor in the sight of my lord."

9 But Esau said, "I[r] have plenty, my brother; let what you have be your own." Gen. 27:39, 40

10 And Jacob said, "No, please, if now I have found favor in your sight, then take my present from my hand, for I see your face as one sees the face of God, and you have received me favorably.

11 "Please take my gift which has been brought to you, because God has dealt graciously with me, and because I have plenty." Thus he urged him and he took *it*.

12 Then [t]Esau said, "Let us take our journey and go, and I will go before you." *he*

13 But he said to him, "My lord knows that the children are frail and that the flocks and herds which are nursing are a care to me. And if they are driven hard one day, all the flocks will die.

14 "Please let my lord pass on before his servant; and I will proceed at my leisure, according to the pace of the cattle that are before me and according to the pace of the children, until I come to my lord at [r]Seir." Gen. 32:3

15 And Esau said, "Please let me leave with you some of the people who are with me." But he said, "[40]What need is there? [r]Let me find favor in the sight of my lord." Ruth 2:13

16 So Esau returned that day on his way to Seir.

17 And Jacob journeyed to [41]Succoth; and built for himself a house, and made booths for his livestock, therefore the place is named Succoth.

18 Now Jacob came safely to the city of [r]Shechem, which is in the land of Canaan, when he came from Paddan-aram, and camped before the city. Josh. 24:1; Judg. 9:1

19 And [r]he bought the piece of land where he had pitched his tent from the hand of the sons of Ha-

[40] Lit., *"Why this?"* [41] I.e., booths

mor, Shechem's father, for one
hundred pieces of money. John 4:5
20 Then he erected there an altar, and called it [42]El-Elohe-Israel.

CHAPTER 34

NOW [r]Dinah the daughter of
Leah, whom she had borne to Jacob, went out to [t]visit the daughters of the land. Gen. 30:21 · *see*
2 And when Shechem the son
of Hamor [r]the Hivite, the prince of
the land, saw her, he took her and
lay with her by force. Gen. 34:30
3 And [t]he was deeply attracted
to Dinah the daughter of Jacob,
and he loved the girl and spoke
tenderly to her. *his soul clung*
4 So Shechem [r]spoke to his father Hamor, saying, "Get me this
young girl for a wife." Judg. 14:2
5 Now Jacob heard that he had
defiled Dinah his daughter; but his
sons were with his livestock in the
field, so Jacob kept silent until
they came in.
6 Then Hamor the father of
Shechem went out to Jacob to
speak with him.
7 Now the sons of Jacob came
in from the field when they heard
it; and the men were grieved, and
they were very angry because he
had done a [t]disgraceful thing in Israel [t]by lying with Jacob's daughter, for such a thing ought not to
be done. *senseless · to lie*
8 But Hamor spoke with them,
saying, "The soul of my son Shechem longs for your daughter;
please give her to him [t]in marriage. *for a wife*
9 "And intermarry with us; give
your daughters to us, and take our
daughters for yourselves.
10 "Thus you shall live with us,
and the land shall be *open* before
you; [t]live and trade in it, and acquire property in it." *dwell*
11 Shechem also said to her father and to her brothers, "If I find
favor in your sight, then I will give
whatever you say to me.
12 "Ask me ever so much bridal
payment and gift, and I will give
according as you say to me; but
give me the girl in marriage."
13 But Jacob's sons answered
Shechem and his father Hamor,
with deceit, and spoke to them,
because he had defiled Dinah their
sister.
14 And they said to them, "We
cannot do this thing, to give our
sister to [r]one who is uncircumcised, for that would be a disgrace
to us. Gen. 17:14
15 "Only on this *condition* will
we consent to you: if you will become like us, in that every male of
you be circumcised,
16 then we will give our daughters to you, and we will take your
daughters for ourselves; and we
will [t]live with you and become one
people. *dwell*
17 "But if you will not listen to us
to be circumcised, then we will
take our daughter and go."
18 Now their words seemed
[t]reasonable to Hamor and Shechem, Hamor's son. *good*
19 And the young man did not
delay to do the thing, because he
was delighted with Jacob's daughter. Now he was more respected
than all the household of his father.

[42] I.e., God, the God of Israel

20 So Hamor and his son Shechem came to the [r]gate of their
city, and spoke to the men of their
city, saying, Ruth 4:1; 2 Sam. 15:2
21 "These men are [t]friendly with
us; therefore let them live in the
land and trade in it, for behold,
the land is large enough for them.
Let us take their daughters [t]in
marriage, and give our daughters
to them. *peaceful • to us for wives*
22 "Only on this *condition* will
the men consent to us to live with
us, to become one people: that every male among us be circumcised as they are circumcised.
23 "Will not their livestock and
their property and all their animals be ours? Only let us consent
to them, and they will [t]live with
us." *dwell*
24 And all who went out of the
gate of his city listened to Hamor
and to his son Shechem, and every male was circumcised, all who
went out of the gate of his city.
25 Now it came about on the
third day, when they were in pain,
that two of Jacob's sons, [r]Simeon
and Levi, Dinah's brothers, each
took his sword and came upon the
city unawares, and killed every
male. Gen. 49:5-7
26 And they killed Hamor and
his son Shechem with the edge of
the sword, and took Dinah from
Shechem's house, and went forth.
27 Jacob's sons came upon the
slain and looted the city, because
they had defiled their sister.
28 They took their flocks and
their herds and their donkeys, and
that which was in the city and
that which was in the field;
29 and they captured and looted
all their wealth and all their little
ones and their wives, even all that
was in the houses.
30 Then Jacob said to Simeon
and Levi, "You have brought trouble on me, by making me odious
among the inhabitants of the land,
among the Canaanites and the
Perizzites; and [t]my men being few
in number, they will gather together against me and [t]attack me
and I shall be destroyed, I and my
household." *I, few in number • smite*
31 But they said, "Should he
[a]treat our sister as a harlot?" *make*

CHAPTER 35

THEN God said to Jacob, "Arise,
go up to Bethel, and live there;
and make an altar there to God,
who appeared to you when you
fled from your brother Esau."
2 So Jacob said to his [r]house-
hold and to all who were with
him, "Put away the foreign gods
which are among you, and purify
yourselves, and change your garments; Gen. 18:19; Josh. 24:15
3 and let us arise and go up to
Bethel; and I will make an altar
there to God, [r]who answered me in
the day of my distress, and has
been with me [t]wherever I have
gone." Ps. 107:6 • *in the way which*
4 So they gave to Jacob all the
foreign gods which they had, and
the rings which were in their ears;
and Jacob hid them under the oak
which was near Shechem.
5 As they journeyed, there was
[a]a[r] great terror upon the cities
which were around them, and
they did not pursue the sons of Jacob. *a terror of God* • Deut. 2:25
6 So Jacob came to [r]Luz (that

is, Bethel), which is in the land of
Canaan, he and all the people who
were with him. Gen. 28:19; 48:3
7 And he built an altar there,
and called the place [t]El-bethel, because there God had revealed
Himself to him, when he fled from
his brother. *from the face of*
8 Now [r]Deborah, Rebekah's
nurse, died, and she was buried
below Bethel under the oak; it was
named [43]Allon-bacuth. Gen. 24:59
9 Then God appeared to Jacob
again when he came from Paddan-aram, and He blessed him.
10 And God said to him,
"Your name is Jacob;
You shall no longer be
called Jacob,
But Israel shall be your
name."
Thus He called him Israel.
11 God also said to him,
"I am God Almighty;
Be fruitful and multiply;
A nation and a company of
nations shall come from
you,
And kings shall come forth
from [t]you. *your loins*
12 "And [r]the land which I gave
to Abraham and Isaac,
I will give it to you,
And I will give the land to
your [t]descendants after
you." Gen. 12:7 • *seed*
13 Then [r]God went up from him
in the place where He had spoken
with him. Gen. 17:22; 18:33
14 And Jacob set up a pillar in
the place where He had spoken
with him, a pillar of stone, and he
poured out a [a]libation on it; he also
poured oil on it. *drink offering*
15 So Jacob named the place

[43]I.e., oak of weeping

where God had spoken with him,
[44]Bethel.
16 Then they journeyed from
Bethel; and when there was still
some distance to go to [r]Ephrath,
Rachel began to give birth and she
suffered severe labor. Ruth 4:11
17 And it came about when she
was in severe labor that the midwife said to her, "Do not fear, for
now you have *another* son."
18 And it came about as her
soul was departing (for she died),
that she named him [45]Ben-oni; but
his father called him [46]Benjamin.
19 So Rachel died and was buried on the way to [r]Ephrath (that is,
Bethlehem). Ruth 1:2; 4:11
20 And Jacob set up a pillar
over her grave; that is the pillar of
Rachel's grave to this day.
21 Then Israel journeyed on and
pitched his tent beyond the [r]tower
of [a]Eder. Mic. 4:8 • *flock*
22 And it came about while Israel was dwelling in that land,
that [r]Reuben went and lay with
Bilhah his father's concubine; and
Israel heard *of it.* 1 Chr. 5:1
Now there were twelve sons of
Jacob—
23 [r]the sons of Leah: Reuben, Jacob's first-born, then Simeon and
Levi and Judah and Issachar and
Zebulun; Gen. 29:31-35
24 [r]the sons of Rachel: Joseph
and Benjamin; Gen. 30:22-24
25 and the sons of Bilhah, Rachel's maid: Dan and Naphtali;
26 and the sons of Zilpah,
Leah's maid: Gad and Asher.
These are the sons of Jacob who
were born to him in Paddan-aram.

[44]I.e., the house of God
[45]I.e., the son of my sorrow
[46]I.e., the son of the right hand

27 And Jacob came to his father Isaac at Mamre of Kiriath-arba (that is, Hebron), where Abraham and Isaac had sojourned.

28 Now the days of Isaac were one hundred and eighty years.

29 And Isaac breathed his last and died, and was gathered to his people, an old man [t]of ripe age; and his sons Esau and Jacob buried him. *and satisfied with days*

CHAPTER 36

NOW these are *the records of* the generations of [r]Esau (that is, Edom). Gen. 25:30

2 Esau [r]took his wives from the daughters of Canaan: Adah the daughter of Elon the Hittite, and [r]Oholibamah the daughter of Anah and the granddaughter of Zibeon the Hivite; Gen. 28:9 • Gen. 36:25

3 also Basemath, Ishmael's daughter, the sister of Nebaioth.

4 And Adah bore Eliphaz to Esau, and Basemath bore Reuel,

5 and Oholibamah bore Jeush and Jalam and Korah. These are the sons of Esau who were born to him in the land of Canaan.

6 Then Esau took his wives and his sons and his daughters and all [t]his household, and his livestock and all his cattle and all his goods which he had acquired in the land of Canaan, and went to *another* land away from his brother Jacob. *the souls of his house*

7 For their property had become too great for them to [t]live together, and the land where they sojourned could not sustain them because of their livestock. *dwell*

8 So Esau lived in the hill country of Seir; Esau is Edom.

9 These then are *the records of* the generations of Esau the father of [t]the Edomites in the hill country of Seir. *Edom*

10 These are the names of Esau's sons: Eliphaz the son of Esau's wife Adah, Reuel the son of Esau's wife Basemath.

11 And the sons of Eliphaz were Teman, Omar, Zepho and Gatam and Kenaz.

12 And Timna was a concubine of Esau's son Eliphaz and she bore Amalek to Eliphaz. These are the sons of Esau's wife Adah.

13 And these are the sons of Reuel: Nahath and Zerah, Shammah and Mizzah. These were the sons of Esau's wife Basemath.

14 And these were the sons of Esau's wife Oholibamah, the daughter of Anah and the granddaughter of Zibeon: she bore to Esau, Jeush and Jalam and Korah.

15 These are the chiefs of the sons of Esau. The sons of Eliphaz, the first-born of Esau, are chief Teman, chief Omar, chief Zepho, chief Kenaz,

16 chief Korah, chief Gatam, chief Amalek. These are the chiefs [t]descended from Eliphaz in the land of Edom; these are the sons of Adah. *of Eliphaz*

17 And these are the sons of Reuel, Esau's son: chief Nahath, chief Zerah, chief Shammah, chief Mizzah. These are the chiefs [t]descended from Reuel in the land of Edom; these are the sons of Esau's wife Basemath. *of Reuel*

18 And these are the sons of Esau's wife Oholibamah: chief Jeush, chief Jalam, chief Korah. These are the chiefs descended

from Esau's wife Oholibamah, the
daughter of Anah.
19 These are the sons of Esau
(that is, Edom), and these are
their chiefs.
20 These are the sons of Seir[r] the
Horite, the inhabitants of the land:
Lotan and Shobal and Zibeon and
Anah, 1 Chr. 1:38-42
21 and Dishon and Ezer and Dishan. These are the chiefs descended from the Horites, the
sons of Seir in the land of Edom.
22 And the sons of Lotan were
Hori and Hemam; and Lotan's sister was Timna.
23 And these are the sons of
Shobal: Alvan and Manahath and
Ebal, Shepho and Onam.
24 And these are the sons of
Zibeon: Aiah and Anah—he is the
Anah who found the hot springs
in the wilderness when he was
pasturing the donkeys of his father Zibeon.
25 And these are the children of
Anah: Dishon, and Oholibamah,
the daughter of Anah.
26 And these are the sons of [r]Di-
shon: Hemdan and Eshban and
Ithran and Cheran. 1 Chr. 1:41
27 These are the sons of Ezer:
Bilhan and Zaavan and Akan.
28 These are the sons of Dishan:
Uz and Aran.
29 These are the chiefs [t]de-
scended from the Horites: chief
Lotan, chief Shobal, chief Zibeon,
chief Anah, *of the Horites*
30 chief Dishon, chief Ezer,
chief Dishan. These are the chiefs
[t]descended from the Horites, according to their *various* chiefs in
the land of Seir. *of the Horites*
31 Now these are the kings who
reigned in the land of Edom before any [r]king reigned over the
sons of Israel. Gen. 17:6, 16; 35:11
32 [t]Bela the son of Beor reigned
in Edom, and the name of his city
was Dinhabah. *And Bela*
33 Then Bela died, and Jobab
the son of Zerah of Bozrah became king in his place.
34 Then Jobab died, and Husham of the land of the Temanites
became king in his place.
35 Then Husham died, and Hadad the son of Bedad, who [a]de-
feated Midian in the field of Moab,
became king in his place; and the
name of his city was Avith. *smote*
36 Then Hadad died, and Samlah of Masrekah became king in
his place.
37 Then Samlah died, and Shaul
of Rehoboth on the *Euphrates*
River became king in his place.
38 Then Shaul died, and Baal-
hanan the son of Achbor became
king in his place.
39 Then Baal-hanan the son of
Achbor died, and Hadar became
king in his place; and the name of
his city was Pau; and his wife's
name was Mehetabel, the daughter of Matred, daughter of Mezahab.
40 Now these are the names of
the chiefs [t]descended from Esau,
according to their families *and*
their localities, by their names:
chief Timna, chief Alvah, chief Jetheth, *of Esau*
41 chief Oholibamah, chief
Elah, chief Pinon,
42 chief Kenaz, chief Teman,
chief Mibzar,
43 chief Magdiel, chief Iram.
These are the chiefs of Edom (that
is, Esau, the father of the Edom-

ites), according to their habitations in the land of their possession.

CHAPTER 37

NOW Jacob lived in [r]the land where his father had sojourned, in the land of Canaan. Gen. 17:8; 28:4

2 These are *the records of* the generations of Jacob.

Joseph, when [r]seventeen years of age, was pasturing the flock with his brothers while he was *still* a youth, along with the sons of Bilhah and the sons of Zilpah, his father's wives. And Joseph brought back a bad report about them to their father. Gen. 41:46

3 Now Israel loved Joseph more than all his sons, because he was the son of his old age; and he made him a [47]varicolored tunic.

4 And his brothers saw that their father loved him more than all his brothers; and *so* they [r]hated him and could not speak to him [48]on friendly terms. 1 Sam. 17:28

5 Then Joseph had a dream, and when he told it to his brothers, they hated him even more.

6 And he said to them, "Please listen to this dream which I have [t]had; *dreamed*

7 for behold, we were binding sheaves in the field, and lo, my sheaf rose up and also stood erect; and behold, your sheaves gathered around and [r]bowed down to my sheaf." Gen. 42:6, 9; 43:26

8 Then his brothers said to him, "Are you actually going to reign over us? Or are you really going to rule over us?" So they hated him even more for his dreams and for his words.

9 Now he had still another dream, and related it to his brothers, and said, "Lo, I have had still another dream; and behold, the sun and the moon and eleven stars were bowing down to me."

10 And he related *it* to his father and to his brothers; and his father rebuked him and said to him, "What is this dream that you have [t]had? Shall I and your mother and [r]your brothers actually come to bow ourselves down before you to the ground?" *dreamed* • Gen. 27:29

11 And [r]his brothers were jealous of him, but his father [r]kept the saying *in mind.* Acts 7:9 • Dan. 7:28

12 Then his brothers went to pasture their father's flock in Shechem.

13 And Israel said to Joseph, "Are not your brothers pasturing *the flock* in Shechem? Come, and I will send you to them." And he said to him, "I[t] will go." *Behold me*

14 Then he said to him, "Go now and see about the welfare of your brothers and the welfare of the flock; and bring word back to me." So he sent him from the valley of [r]Hebron, and he came to Shechem. Gen. 13:18; 23:2

15 And a man found him, and behold, he was wandering in the field; and the man asked him, "What are you looking for?"

16 And he said, "I am looking for my brothers; please tell me where they are pasturing *the flock.*"

17 Then the man said, "They have moved from here; for I heard *them* say, 'Let us go to Dothan.' "

[47]Or, *full-length robe* [48]Lit., *in peace*

So Joseph went after his brothers
and found them at Dothan.
18 [a]When they saw him from a
distance and before he came close
to them, they plotted against him
to put him to death. *And*
19 And they said to one another,
"Here comes this dreamer!
20 "Now then, come and let us
kill him and throw him into one of
the pits; and [r]we will say, 'A wild
beast devoured him.' Then let us
see what will become of his
dreams!" Gen. 37:32, 33
21 But Reuben heard *this* and
rescued him out of their hands
and said, "Let us not take his life."
22 Reuben further said to them,
"Shed no blood. Throw him into
this pit that is in the wilderness,
but do not lay hands on him"—
that he might rescue him out of
their hands, to restore him to his
father.
23 So it came about, when
Joseph [t]reached his brothers, that
they stripped Joseph of his [a]tunic,
the varicolored tunic that was on
him; *came to* · *full-length robe*
24 and they took him and threw
him into the pit. Now the pit was
empty, without any water in it.
25 Then they sat down to eat [t]a
meal. And as they raised their
eyes and looked, behold, a caravan of Ishmaelites was coming
from Gilead, with their camels
bearing aromatic gum and balm
and myrrh, on their way to bring
them down to Egypt. *bread*
26 And Judah said to his brothers, "What profit is it for us to kill
our brother and [r]cover up his
blood? Gen. 37:20
27 "Come and let us sell him to
the Ishmaelites and not lay our
hands on him; for he is our
brother, our *own* flesh." And his
brothers listened *to him.*
28 Then some Midianite traders
passed by, so they pulled *him* up
and lifted Joseph out of the pit,
and sold him to the Ishmaelites
for twenty *shekels* of silver. Thus
they brought Joseph into Egypt.
29 Now Reuben returned to the
pit, and behold, Joseph was not in
the pit; so he tore his garments.
30 And he returned to his brothers and said, "The [r]boy is not
there; as for me, where am I to
go?" Gen. 42:13, 36
31 So they took Joseph's tunic,
and slaughtered a male goat, and
dipped the tunic in the blood;
32 and they sent the varicolored
tunic and brought it to their father
and said, "We found this; please
[a]examine *it* to *see* whether it is
your son's tunic or not." *recognize*
33 Then he examined it and
said, "It is my son's tunic. A wild
beast has devoured him; Joseph
has surely been torn to pieces!"
34 So Jacob tore his clothes,
and put sackcloth on his loins, and
mourned for his son many days.
35 Then all his sons and all his
daughters arose to comfort him,
but he refused to be comforted.
And he said, "Surely I will go
down to Sheol in mourning for my
son." So his father wept for him.
36 Meanwhile, the [t]Midianites
sold him in Egypt to Potiphar,
Pharaoh's officer, the captain of
the bodyguard. *Medanites*

CHAPTER 38

AND it came about at that time,
that Judah [t]departed from his
brothers, and [t]visited a certain
Adullamite, whose name was Hirah. *went down · turned aside to*
2 And Judah saw there a
daughter of a certain Canaanite
whose name was Shua; and he
took her and went in to her.
3 So she conceived and bore a
son and he named him Er.
4 Then she conceived again
and bore a son and named him
[r]Onan. Gen. 46:12
5 And she bore still another
son and named him Shelah; and it
was at Chezib that she bore him.
6 Now Judah took a wife for
Er his first-born, and her name
was Tamar.
7 But Er, Judah's first-born,
was evil in the sight of the LORD,
so the LORD took his life.
8 Then Judah said to Onan,
"Go in to your brother's wife, and
perform your duty as a brother-in-
law to her, and raise up [t]offspring
for your brother." *seed*
9 And Onan knew that the [t]off-
spring would not be his; so it
came about that when he went in
to his brother's wife, he [t]wasted
his seed on the ground, in order
not to give offspring to his
brother. *seed · spilled on the ground*
10 But what he did was displeasing in the sight of the LORD;
so He took his life also.
11 Then Judah said to his
daughter-in-law Tamar, "Remain[r]
a widow in your father's house
until my son Shelah grows up";
for he [t]thought, "*I am afraid* that
he too may die like his brothers."
So Tamar went and lived in her father's house. Ruth 1:12, 13 · *said*
12 Now after a considerable
time Shua's daughter, the wife of
Judah, died; and when [t]the time of
mourning was ended, Judah went
up to his sheepshearers at Timnah, he and his friend Hirah the
Adullamite. *Judah was comforted, he*
13 And it was told to Tamar,
"Behold,[t] your father-in-law is
going up to Timnah to shear his
sheep." *saying, Behold*
14 So she removed her widow's
garments and covered *herself*
with a [49]veil, and wrapped herself,
and sat in the gateway of Enaim,
which is on the road to Timnah;
for she saw that Shelah had
grown up, and she had not been
given to him as a wife.
15 When Judah saw her, he
thought she *was* a harlot, for she
had covered her face.
16 So he turned aside to her by
the road, and said, "Here[a] now, let
me come in to you"; for he did not
know that she was his daughter-
in-law. And she said, "What will
you give me, that you may come
in to me?" *Come, now*
17 He said, therefore, "I will
send you a kid from the flock."
She said, moreover, "Will you
give a pledge until you send *it?*"
18 And he said, "What pledge
shall I give you?" And she said,
"Your seal and your cord, and
your staff that is in your hand." So
he gave *them* to her, and went in
to her, and she conceived by him.
19 Then she arose and departed,
and removed her [a]veil and put on
her widow's garments. *shawl*

[49]Or, *shawl*

20 When Judah sent the kid by
his friend the Adullamite, to receive the pledge from the woman's hand, he did not find her.
21 And he asked the men of her
place, saying, "Where is the temple prostitute who was by the
road at Enaim?" But they said,
"There has been no temple prostitute here."
22 So he returned to Judah, and
said, "I did not find her; and furthermore, the men of the place
said, 'There has been no temple
prostitute here.'"
23 Then Judah said, "Let her
keep them, lest we become a
laughingstock. After all, I sent this
kid, but you did not find her."
24 Now it was about three
months later that Judah was informed, "Your[t] daughter-in-law
Tamar has played the harlot, and
behold, she is also with child by
harlotry." Then Judah said,
"Bring her out and [r]let her be
burned!" *saying, Your* • Lev. 21:9
25 It was while she was being
brought out that she sent to her
father-in-law, saying, "I am with
child by the man to whom these
things belong." And she said,
"Please[r] examine and see, whose
signet ring and cords and staff are
these?" Gen. 37:32
26 And Judah recognized *them*,
and said, "She is more righteous
than I, inasmuch as I did not give
her to my son Shelah." And he did
not have relations with her again.
27 And it came about at the
time she was giving birth, that behold, there were [r]twins in her
womb. Gen. 25:24-26
28 Moreover, it took place while
she was giving birth, one put out a
hand, and the midwife took and
tied a scarlet *thread* on his hand,
saying, "This one came out first."
29 But it came about as he drew
back his hand, that behold, his
brother came out. Then she said,
"What a breach you have made
for yourself!" So he was named
[50]Perez.
30 And afterward his brother
came out who had the scarlet
thread on his hand; and he was
named [51]Zerah.

CHAPTER 39

NOW Joseph had been taken
down to Egypt; and Potiphar, an
Egyptian officer of Pharaoh, the
captain of the bodyguard, bought
him from the Ishmaelites, who
had taken him down there.
2 And the LORD was with
Joseph, so he became a successful
man. And he was in the house of
his master, the Egyptian.
3 Now his master saw that the
LORD was with him and *how* the
LORD [r]caused all that he did to
prosper in his hand. Ps. 1:3
4 So Joseph found favor in his
sight, and became his personal
servant; and he made him overseer over his house, and all that he
owned he put in his charge.
5 And it came about that from
the time he made him overseer in
his house, and over all that he
owned, the LORD [r]blessed the
Egyptian's house on account of
Joseph; thus the LORD's blessing
was upon all that he owned, in the
house and in the field. Gen. 30:27
6 So he left everything he

[50]I.e., a breach
[51]I.e., a dawning or brightness

owned in Joseph's [t]charge; and
with him *there* he did not [t]concern
himself with anything except the
[t]food which he ate. Now Joseph
was handsome in form and appearance. *hand • know • bread*
7 And it came about after
these events that his master's wife
looked with desire at Joseph, and
she said, "Lie with me."
8 But he refused and said to his
master's wife, "Behold, with me
here, my master does not concern
himself with anything in the
house, and he has put all that he
owns in my [t]charge. *hand*
9 "There[a] is no one greater in
this house than I, and he has withheld nothing from me except you,
because you are his wife. How
then could I do this great evil, and
sin against God?" *He is not greater*
10 And it came about as she
spoke to Joseph day after day,
that he did not listen to her to lie
beside her, *or* be with her.
11 Now it happened one day
that he went into the house to do
his work, and none of the men of
the household was there inside.
12 And she caught him by his
garment, saying, "Lie with me!"
And he left his garment in her
hand and fled, and went outside.
13 When she saw that he had
left his garment in her hand, and
had fled outside,
14 she called to the men of her
household, and said to them,
"See, he has brought in a [t]Hebrew
to us to make sport of us; he came
in to me to lie with me, and I
screamed. *Hebrew man*
15 "And it came about when he
heard that I raised my voice and
[52]screamed, that he left his garment beside me and fled, and
went outside."
16 So she [t]left his garment beside her until his master came
home. *let . . . lie beside*
17 Then she spoke to him with
these words, "The Hebrew slave,
whom you brought to us, came in
to me to make sport of me;
18 and it happened as I raised
my voice and [t]screamed, that he
left his garment beside me and
fled outside." *called out*
19 Now it came about when his
master heard the words of his
wife, which she spoke to him, saying, "This is what your slave did
to me," that his anger burned.
20 So Joseph's master took him
and [r]put him into the jail, the place
where the king's prisoners were
confined; and he was there in the
jail. Gen. 40:3; Ps. 105:18
21 But [r]the LORD was with
Joseph and extended kindness to
him, and gave him favor in the
sight of the chief jailer. Acts 7:9
22 And the chief jailer committed to Joseph's [t]charge all the prisoners who were in the jail; so that
whatever was done there, he was
[t]responsible *for it.* *hand • the doer*
23 The chief jailer did not supervise anything under Joseph's
charge because the LORD was
with him; and whatever he did,
the LORD made to prosper.

CHAPTER 40

THEN it came about after these
things the cupbearer and the baker for the king of Egypt offended
their lord, the king of Egypt.

[52] Lit., *called out*

2 And Pharaoh was furious
with his two officials, the chief
cupbearer and the chief baker.
3 So he put them in confinement in the house of the [r]captain
of the bodyguard, in the jail, the
same place where Joseph was imprisoned. Gen. 39:1, 20
4 And the captain of the bodyguard put Joseph in charge of
them, and he [t]took care of them;
and they were in confinement for
[t]some time. *ministered to* • *days*
5 Then the cupbearer and the
baker for the king of Egypt, who
were confined in jail, both had a
dream the same night, each man
with his *own* dream *and* each
dream with its *own* interpretation.
6 When Joseph came to them
in the morning and observed
them, behold, they were dejected.
7 And he asked Pharaoh's officials who were with him in confinement in his master's house,
"Why [tr]are your faces so sad today?" *saying, Why* • Neh. 2:2
8 Then they said to him, "We[r]
have [t]had a dream and there is no
one to interpret it." Then Joseph
said to them, "Do not interpretations belong to God? Tell *it* to me,
please." Gen. 41:15 • *dreamed*
9 So the chief cupbearer told
his dream to Joseph, and said to
him, "In my dream, behold, *there*
was a vine in front of me;
10 and on the vine *were* three
branches. And as it was budding,
its blossoms came out, *and* its
clusters produced ripe grapes.
11 "Now Pharaoh's cup was in
my hand; so I took the grapes and
squeezed them into Pharaoh's
cup, and I put the cup into Pharaoh's [t]hand." *palm*
12 Then Joseph said to him,
"This is the interpretation of it:
the three branches are three days;
13 within three more days Pharaoh will [53]lift up your head and restore you to your [t]office; and you
will put Pharaoh's cup into his
hand according to your former
custom when you were his cupbearer. *place*
14 "Only keep me in mind when
it goes well with you, and please
do me a kindness [t]by mentioning
me to Pharaoh, and get me out of
this house. *and mention*
15 "For [r]I was in fact kidnapped
from the land of the Hebrews, and
even here I have done nothing
that they should have put me into
the [a]dungeon." Gen. 37:26-28 • *pit*
16 When the chief baker saw
that he had interpreted favorably,
he said to Joseph, "I also *saw* in
my dream, and behold, *there were*
three baskets of white bread on
my head;
17 and in the top basket *there*
were some of all sorts of baked
food for Pharaoh, and the birds
were eating them out of the basket on my head."
18 Then Joseph answered and
said, "This is its interpretation:
the three baskets are three days;
19 within three more days Pharaoh will lift up your head from
you and will hang you on a tree;
and the birds will eat your flesh
off you."
20 Thus it came about on the
third day, *which was* [r]Pharaoh's
birthday, that he made a feast for
all his servants; and he lifted up

[53]Or possibly, *forgive you*

the head of the chief cupbearer
and the head of the chief baker
among his servants. Matt. 14:6
21 And he restored the chief
cupbearer to his office, and he put
the cup into Pharaoh's hand;
22 but [r]he hanged the chief baker, just as Joseph had interpreted
to them. Gen. 40:19; Esth. 7:10
23 Yet the chief cupbearer did
not remember Joseph, but [r]forgot
him. Job 19:14; Ps. 31:12

CHAPTER 41

NOW it happened at the end of
two full years that Pharaoh had a
dream, and behold, he was standing by the Nile.
2 And lo, from the Nile there
came up seven cows, sleek and
[t]fat; and they grazed in the [r]marsh
grass. *fat of flesh* • Job 8:11
3 Then behold, seven other
cows came up after them from the
Nile, ugly and [t]gaunt, and they
stood by the *other* cows on the
bank of the Nile. *lean of flesh*
4 And the ugly and gaunt cows
ate up the seven sleek and fat
cows. Then Pharaoh awoke.
5 And he fell asleep and
dreamed a second time; and behold, seven ears of grain came up
on a single stalk, plump and good.
6 Then behold, seven ears, thin
and scorched by the east wind,
sprouted up after them.
7 And the thin ears swallowed
up the seven plump and full ears.
Then Pharaoh awoke, and behold,
it was a dream.
8 Now it came about in the
morning that his spirit was troubled, so he sent and called for all
the [a]magicians of Egypt, and all its
wise men. And Pharaoh told them
his [t]dreams, but there was no one
who could interpret them to Pharaoh. *soothsayer priests* • *dream*
9 Then the chief cupbearer
spoke to Pharaoh, saying, "I
would make mention today of [r]my
own [a]offenses. Gen. 40:14, 23 • *sins*
10 "Pharaoh was [r]furious with his
servants, and he put me in confinement in the house of the captain of the bodyguard, *both* me
and the chief baker. Gen. 40:2, 3
11 "And we had a dream on the
same night, he and I; each of us
dreamed according to the interpretation of his *own* dream.
12 "Now a Hebrew youth *was*
with us there, a [r]servant of the
captain of the bodyguard, and we
related *them* to him, and he interpreted our dreams for us. To each
one he interpreted according to
his *own* dream. Gen. 37:36
13 "And it came about that just
as he interpreted for us, so it happened; he restored me in my [t]of-
fice, but he hanged him." *place*
14 Then Pharaoh sent and
called for Joseph, and they [r]hur-
riedly brought him out of the dungeon; and when he had shaved
himself and changed his clothes,
he came to Pharaoh. Dan. 2:25
15 And Pharaoh said to Joseph,
"I have had a dream, but no one
can interpret it; and [r]I have heard
[t]it said about you, that when you
hear a dream you can interpret
it." Dan. 5:16 • *about you, saying*
16 Joseph then answered Pharaoh, saying, "It is not in me; God
will [t]give Pharaoh a favorable answer." *answer the peace of Pharaoh*

17 So Pharaoh spoke to Joseph, "In my dream, behold, I was standing on the bank of the Nile;

18 and behold, seven cows, [t]fat and sleek came up out of the Nile; and they grazed in the marsh grass. *fat of flesh*

19 "And lo, seven other cows came up after them, poor and very ugly and [t]gaunt, such as I had never seen for [t]ugliness in all the land of Egypt; *lean of flesh • badness*

20 and the lean and ugly cows ate up the first seven fat cows.

21 "Yet when they had [t]devoured them, it could not be detected that they had devoured them; [t]for they were just as ugly as before. Then I awoke. *entered their inward parts • and*

22 "I saw also in my dream, and behold, seven ears, full and good, came up on a single stalk;

23 and lo, seven ears, withered, thin, *and* scorched by the east wind, sprouted up after them;

24 and the thin ears swallowed the seven good ears. Then I told it to the magicians, but there was no one who could explain it to me."

25 Now Joseph said to Pharaoh, "Pharaoh's [t]dreams are one *and the same;* God has told to Pharaoh what He is about to do. *dream is*

26 "The seven good cows are seven years; and the seven good ears are seven years; the [t]dreams are one *and the same.* *dream is*

27 "And the seven lean and ugly cows that came up after them are seven years, and the seven thin ears scorched by the east wind shall be seven years of famine.

28 "It is as I have spoken to Pharaoh: God has shown to Pharaoh what He is about to do.

29 "Behold, [r]seven years of great abundance are coming in all the land of Egypt; Gen. 41:47

30 and after them seven years of famine will [t]come, and all the abundance will be forgotten in the land of Egypt; and the famine will [t]ravage the land. *arise • destroy*

31 "So the abundance will be unknown in the land because of that subsequent famine; for it *will be* very severe.

32 "Now as for the repeating of the dream to Pharaoh twice, *it means* that the matter is determined by God, and God will quickly bring it about.

33 "And now let Pharaoh look for a man [r]discerning and wise, and set him over the land of Egypt. Gen. 41:39

34 "Let Pharaoh take action to appoint overseers in charge of the land, and let him exact a fifth *of the produce* of the land of Egypt in the seven years of abundance.

35 "Then let them gather all the food of these good years that are coming, and store up the grain for food in the cities under Pharaoh's authority, and let them guard *it.*

36 "And let the food become as a reserve for the land for the seven years of famine which will occur in the land of Egypt, so that the land may not perish during the famine."

37 Now the [t]proposal seemed good [t]to Pharaoh and to all his servants. *word • in the sight of*

38 Then Pharaoh said to his servants, "Can we find a man like this, in whom is a divine spirit?"

39 So Pharaoh said to Joseph, "Since God has informed you of all this, there is no one so [r]discerning and wise as you are. Gen. 41:33

40 "You shall be over my house, and according to your [t]command all my people shall [t]do homage; only in the throne I will be greater than you." *mouth · kiss*

41 And Pharaoh said to Joseph, "See I have set you [r]over all the land of Egypt." Gen. 42:6; Acts 7:10

42 Then Pharaoh [r]took off his signet ring from his hand, and put it on Joseph's hand, and clothed him in garments of fine linen, and put the gold necklace around his neck. Esth. 3:10; 8:2

43 And he had him ride in his second chariot; and they proclaimed before him, "Bow the knee!" And he set him over all the land of Egypt.

44 Moreover, Pharaoh said to Joseph, "*Though* I am Pharaoh, yet without [t]your permission no one shall raise his hand or foot in all the land of Egypt." *you no one*

45 Then Pharaoh named Joseph [54]Zaphenath-paneah; and he gave him Asenath, the daughter of Potiphera priest of [r]On, as his wife. And Joseph went forth over the land of Egypt. Jer. 43:13; Ezek. 30:17

46 Now Joseph was thirty years old when he [55]stood before Pharaoh, king of Egypt. And Joseph went out from the presence of Pharaoh, and went through all the land of Egypt.

47 And during the seven years of plenty the land brought forth [t]abundantly. *by handfuls*

48 So he gathered all the food of *these* seven years which occurred in the land of Egypt, and placed the food in the cities; he placed in every city the food from its own surrounding fields.

49 Thus Joseph stored up grain [t]in great abundance like the sand of the sea, until he stopped [t]measuring *it*, for it was beyond measure. *very much · numbering*

50 Now before the year of famine came, two sons were born to Joseph, whom Asenath, the daughter of Potiphera priest of [56]On, bore to him.

51 And Joseph named the firstborn [57]Manasseh, "For," *he said*, "God has made me forget all my trouble and all my father's household."

52 And he named the second [58]Ephraim, "For," *he said*, "God[r] has made me fruitful in the land of my affliction." Gen. 17:6; 28:3

53 When the seven years of plenty which had been in the land of Egypt came to an end,

54 and [r]the seven years of famine began to come, just as Joseph had said, then there was famine in all the lands; but in all the land of Egypt there was bread. Ps. 105:16

55 So when all the land of Egypt was famished, the people cried out to Pharaoh for bread; and Pharaoh said to all the Egyptians, "Go to Joseph; [r]whatever he says to you, you shall do." John 2:5

56 When the famine was *spread* over all the face of the earth, then Joseph opened all [t]the storehouses, and sold to the Egyptians; and the famine was severe in the land of Egypt. *that which was in them*

57 And *the people of* all the earth came to Egypt to buy grain

[54]Probably Egyptian for "God speaks; he lives" [55]Or, *entered the service of*

[56]Or, *Heliopolis* [57]I.e., making to forget
[58]I.e., fruitfulness

from Joseph, because the famine
was severe in all the earth.

CHAPTER 42

NOW [r]Jacob saw that there was
grain in Egypt, and Jacob said to
his sons, "Why are you staring at
one another?" Acts 7:12
2 And he said, "Behold, I have
heard that there is grain in Egypt;
go down there and buy *some* for
us[t]from that place, so that we may
live and not die." *from there*
3 Then ten brothers of Joseph
went down to buy grain from
Egypt.
4 But Jacob did not send Joseph's brother Benjamin with his
brothers, for he said, "I am afraid
that harm may befall him."
5 So the sons of Israel came to
buy grain among those who were
coming, [r]for the famine was in the
land of Canaan *also.* Acts 7:11
6 Now [r]Joseph was the ruler
over the land; he was the one who
sold to all the people of the land.
And Joseph's brothers came and
bowed down to him with *their*
faces to the ground. Gen. 41:41, 55
7 When Joseph saw his brothers he recognized them, but he
disguised himself to them and
[r]spoke to them harshly. And he
said to them, "Where have you
come from?" And they said,
"From the land of Canaan, to buy
food." Gen. 42:30
8 But Joseph had recognized
his brothers, although [r]they did not
recognize him. Gen. 37:2; 41:46
9 And Joseph remembered the
dreams which he had about them,
and said to them, "You are spies;
you have come to look at the un-
defended parts of our land."
10 Then they said to him, "No,
[r]my lord, but your servants have
come to buy food. Gen. 37:8
11 "We are all sons of one man;
we are honest men, your servants
are not spies."
12 Yet he said to them, "No, but
you have come to look at the un-
defended parts of our land!"
13 But they said, "Your servants are twelve brothers *in all,*
the sons of one man in the land of
Canaan; and behold, the youngest
is with [r]our father today, and [r]one
is no more." Gen. 43:7 • Gen. 37:30
14 And Joseph said to them, "It
is as I said to you, you are spies;
15 by this you will be tested: by
the life of Pharaoh, you shall not
go from this place unless your
youngest brother comes here!
16 "Send one of you that he may
get your brother, while you remain confined, that your words
may be tested, whether there is
truth in you. But if not, by the life
of Pharaoh, surely you are spies."
17 So he put them all together
in [r]prison for three days. Gen. 40:4, 7
18 Now Joseph said to them on
the third day, "Do this and live,
for [r]I fear God: Gen. 39:9; Lev. 25:43
19 if you are honest men, let one
of your brothers be confined in
your prison; but as for *the rest of*
you, go, carry grain for the famine
of your households,
20 and [r]bring your youngest
brother to me, so your words may
be verified, and you will not die."
And they did so. Gen. 42:34
21 Then they said to one another, "Truly [r]we are guilty concerning our brother, because we

saw the distress of his soul when
he pleaded with us, yet we would
not listen; therefore this distress
has come upon us." Gen. 37:26-28
22 And Reuben answered them,
saying, "Did I not tell you, 'Do not
sin against the boy'; and you
would not listen? Now comes the
reckoning for his blood."
23 They did not know, however,
that Joseph understood, for there
was an interpreter between them.
24 And he turned away from
them and wept. But when he returned to them and spoke to them,
he took Simeon from them and
bound him before their eyes.
25 [r]Then Joseph gave orders to
fill their bags with grain and to restore every man's money in his
sack, and to give them provisions
for the journey. And thus it was
done for them. 1 Pet. 3:9
26 So they loaded their donkeys
with their grain, and departed
from there.
27 And as one *of them* opened
his sack to give his donkey fodder
at the lodging place, he saw his
[r]money; and behold, it was in the
mouth of his sack. Gen. 43:21, 22
28 Then he said to his brothers,
"My money has been returned,
and behold, it is even in my sack."
And their hearts [t]sank, and they
turned [t]trembling to one another,
saying, "What is this that God has
done to us?" *went out* · *trembled*
29 When they came to their father Jacob in the land of Canaan,
they told him all that had happened to them, saying,
30 "The man, the lord of the land,
spoke harshly with us, and took
us for spies of the country.
31 "But we said to him, 'We are
honest men; we are not spies.
32 'We are twelve brothers, sons
of our father; one is no more, and
the youngest is with our father today in the land of Canaan.'
33 "And the man, the lord of the
land, said to us, 'By this I shall
know that you are honest men:
leave one of your brothers with
me and take *grain for* the famine
of your households, and go.
34 'But bring your youngest
brother to me that I may know
that you are not spies, but [t]honest
men. I will give your brother to
you, and you may [r]trade in the
land.' " *you are honest* · Gen. 34:10
35 Now it came about as they
were emptying their sacks, that
behold, [r]every man's bundle of
money *was* in his sack; and when
they and their father saw their
bundles of money, they were dismayed. Gen. 43:12, 15, 21
36 And their father Jacob said
to them, "You have [r]bereaved me
of my children: Joseph is no more,
and Simeon is no more, and you
would take Benjamin; all these
things are against me." Gen. 43:14
37 Then Reuben spoke to his father, saying, "You may put my
two sons to death if I do not bring
him *back* to you; put him in my
[t]care, and I will return him to
you." *hand*
38 But [t]Jacob said, "My son
shall not go down with you; for his
brother is dead, and he alone is
left. If harm should befall him on
the journey you are taking, then
you will bring my gray hair down
to Sheol in sorrow." *he*

CHAPTER 43

NOW the famine was severe in
the land.
2 So it came about when they
had finished eating the grain
which they had brought from
Egypt, that their father said to
them, "Go back, buy us a little
food."
3 Judah spoke to him, however, saying, "The[r] man solemnly
warned[t] us, 'You shall not see my
face unless your brother is with
you.' Gen. 43:5 • *us, saying*
4 "If you send our brother with
us, we will go down and buy you
food.
5 "But if you do not send *him*,
we will not go down; for the man
said to us, 'You shall not see my
face unless your brother is with
you.' "
6 Then Israel said, "Why did
you treat me so badly[t] by telling
the man whether you still had *another* brother?" *to tell*
7 But they said, "The man
questioned particularly about us
and our relatives, saying, 'Is[r] your
father still alive? Have you *another* brother?' So we answered
his questions. Could we possibly
know that he would say, 'Bring
your brother down'?" Gen. 42:13
8 And Judah said to his father
Israel, "Send the lad with me, and
we will arise and go,[r] that we may
live and not die, we as well as you
and our little ones. Gen. 42:2
9 "I[r] myself will be surety for
him; you may hold me responsible
for him. If I do not bring him *back*
to you and set him before you,
then let me bear the blame before
you forever. Philem. 18, 19
10 "For if we had not delayed,
surely by now we could have returned twice."
11 Then their father Israel said
to them, "If *it must be* so, then do
this: take some of the best products of the land in your[a] bags, and
carry down to the man as a present, a little balm and a little honey, aromatic gum and myrrh, pis-
tachio nuts and almonds. *vessels*
12 "And take double *the* money
in your hand, and take back in
your hand the money that was returned in the mouth of your sacks;
perhaps it was a mistake.
13 "Take your brother also, and
arise, return to the man;
14 and may God Almighty grant
you compassion in the sight of the
man, that he may release to you
your other brother and Benjamin.
And as for me, if I am bereaved of
my children, I am bereaved."
15 So the men took this present,
and they took double *the* money
in their hand, and Benjamin; then
they arose and went down to
Egypt and stood before Joseph.
16 When Joseph saw Benjamin
with them, he said to his[r] house
steward, "Bring the men into the
house, and slay *an animal* and
make ready; for the men are to
dine with me at noon." Gen. 44:1
17 So the man did as Joseph
said, and[t] brought the men to Joseph's house. *the man brought*
18 Now the men were afraid,
because they were brought to Joseph's house; and they said, "*It is*
because of the money that was returned in our sacks the first time

that we are being brought in, that
he may seek occasion against us
and fall upon us, and take us for
slaves with our donkeys."
19 So they came near to Joseph's house steward, and spoke
to him at the entrance of the
house,
20 and said, "Oh, my lord, we
indeed came down the first time
to buy food,
21 and it came about when we
came to the lodging place, that we
opened our sacks, and behold,
each man's money was in the
mouth of his sack, our money in
[t]full. So we have brought it back in
our hand. *its weight*
22 "We have also brought down
other money in our hand to buy
food; we do not know who put our
money in our sacks."
23 And he said, "[59]Be at ease, do
not be afraid. [r]Your God and the
God of your father has given you
treasure in your sacks; I had your
money." Then he brought Simeon
out to them. Gen. 42:28
24 Then the man brought the
men into Joseph's house and gave
them water, and they [r]washed
their feet; and he gave their donkeys fodder. John 13:5; 1 Tim. 5:10
25 So they prepared the present
[t]for Joseph's coming at noon; for
they had heard that they were to
eat [t]a meal there. *until* · *bread*
26 When Joseph came home,
they brought into the house to
him the present which was in
their hand and [r]bowed to the
ground before him. Gen. 37:7, 10
27 Then he asked them about
their welfare, and said, "Is your
old father well, of whom you
spoke? Is he still alive?"
28 And they said, "Your servant
our father is well; he is still alive."
And they bowed down in homage.
29 As he lifted his eyes and saw
his brother Benjamin, his mother's son, he said, "Is this your
youngest brother, of whom you
spoke to me?" And he said, "May
God be gracious to you, my son."
30 And Joseph hurried *out* for
[r]he was deeply stirred over his
brother, and he sought *a place* to
weep; and he entered his chamber
and wept there. 1 Kin. 3:26
31 Then he washed his face, and
came out; and he controlled himself and said, "Serve the meal."
32 So they served him by himself, and them by themselves, and
the Egyptians, who ate with him,
by themselves; because the Egyptians could not eat bread with the
Hebrews, for that is [t]loathsome to
the Egyptians. *an abomination*
33 Now they [t]were seated before
him, [r]the first-born according to
his birthright and the youngest according to his youth, and the men
looked at one another in astonishment. *sat* · Gen. 42:7
34 And he took portions to them
from his own table; but Benjamin's portion was five times as
much as any of theirs. So they
feasted and drank freely with him.

CHAPTER 44

THEN he commanded his house
steward, saying, "Fill the men's
sacks with food, as much as they
can carry, and put each man's
money in the mouth of his sack.

[59]Lit., *Peace be to you*

2 "And put my cup, the silver
cup, in the mouth of the sack of
the youngest, and his money for
the grain." And he did[a] as Joseph
had told *him*. *according to the word*
3 [t]As soon as it was light, the
men were sent away, they with
their donkeys. *The morning was light*
4 They had *just* gone out of [r]the
city, *and* were not far off, when
Joseph said to his house steward,
"Up, follow the men; and when
you overtake them, say to them,
'Why have you repaid evil for
good? Gen. 44:13
5 'Is not this the one from
which my lord drinks, and which
he indeed uses for divination? You
have done wrong in doing this.' "
6 So he overtook them and
spoke these words to them.
7 And they said to him, "Why
does my lord speak such words as
these? Far be it from your servants to do such a thing.
8 "Behold, [r]the money which we
found in the mouth of our sacks
we have brought back to you from
the land of Canaan. How then
could we steal silver or gold from
your lord's house? Gen. 43:21
9 "With whomever of your servants it is found, let him die, and
we also will be my lord's slaves."
10 So he said, "Now let it also
be according to your words; he
with whom it is found shall be my
slave, and *the rest of* you shall be
innocent."
11 Then they hurried, each man
lowered his sack to the ground,
and each man opened his sack.
12 And he searched, beginning
with the oldest and ending with
the youngest, and the cup was
found in Benjamin's sack.
13 Then they tore their clothes,
and when each man loaded his
donkey, they returned to the city.
14 When Judah and his brothers came to Joseph's house, he
was still there, and [r]they fell to the
ground before him. Gen. 37:7, 10
15 And Joseph said to them,
"What is this deed that you have
done? Do you not know that such
a man as I can indeed practice
[r]divination?" Gen. 44:5
16 So Judah said, "What can we
say to my lord? What can we
speak? And how can we justify
ourselves? God has found out the
iniquity of your servants; behold,
we are my lord's slaves, both we
and the one in whose [t]possession
the cup has been found." *hand*
17 But he said, "Far be it from
me to do this. The man in whose
[t]possession the cup has been
found, he shall be my slave; but as
for you, go up in peace to your father." *hand*
18 Then Judah approached him,
and said, "Oh my lord, may your
servant please speak a word in my
lord's ears, and [r]do not be angry
with your servant; for you are
equal to Pharaoh. Gen. 18:30, 32
19 "My [r]lord asked his servants,
saying, 'Have you a father or a
brother?' Gen. 43:7
20 "And we said to my lord, 'We
have an old father and [r]a little
child of *his* old age. Now [r]his
brother is dead, so he alone is left
of his mother, and his father loves
him.' Gen. 37:3 • Gen. 37:33
21 "Then you said to your servants, 'Bring him down to me,

that I may set my eyes on him.'
22 "But we said to my lord, 'The
lad cannot leave his father, for if
he should leave his father, his father would die.'
23 "You said to your servants,
however, 'Unless your youngest
brother comes down with you,
you shall not see my face again.'
24 "Thus it came about when we
went up to your servant my father, we told him the words of my
lord.
25 "And our father said, 'Go
back, buy us a little food.'
26 "But we said, 'We cannot go
down. If our youngest brother is
with us, then we will go down; for
we cannot see the man's face unless our youngest brother is with
us.'
27 "And your servant my father
said to us, 'You know that [r]my
wife bore me two sons; Gen. 46:19
28 and the one went out from
me, and [r]I said, "Surely he is torn
in pieces," and I have not seen
him since. Gen. 37:31-35
29 'And if you take this one also
from [t]me, and harm befalls him,
you will bring my gray hair down
to Sheol in [t]sorrow.' *my face* · *evil*
30 "Now, therefore, when I come
to your servant my father, and the
lad is not with us, since his life is
bound up in the lad's life,
31 it will come about when he
sees that the lad is not *with us*,
that he will die. Thus your servants will bring the gray hair of
your servant our father down to
Sheol in sorrow.
32 "For your servant became
surety for the lad to my father,
saying, 'If I do not bring him *back*
to you, then let me bear the blame
before my father forever.'
33 "Now, therefore, please let
your servant remain instead of the
lad a slave to my lord, and let the
lad go up with his brothers.
34 "For how shall I go up to my
father if the lad is not with me,
lest I see the evil that would [t]over-
take my father?" *find*

CHAPTER 45

THEN Joseph could not control
himself before all those who stood
by him, and he cried, "Have
everyone go out from me." So
there [t]was no man with him [r]when
Joseph made himself known to his
brothers. *stood* · Acts 7:13
2 And he wept so loudly that
the Egyptians heard *it*, and the
household of Pharaoh heard *of it*.
3 Then Joseph said to his
brothers, "I am Joseph! Is my father still alive?" But his brothers
could not answer him, for they
were dismayed at his presence.
4 Then Joseph said to his
brothers, "Please come [t]closer to
me." And they came [t]closer. And
he said, "I am your brother
Joseph, whom you [r]sold into
Egypt. *near* · Gen. 37:28
5 "And now do not be grieved
or angry with yourselves, because
you sold me here; for God sent me
before you to preserve life.
6 "For the famine *has been* in
the land [r]these two years, and
there are still five years in which
there will be neither plowing nor
harvesting. Gen. 37:2; 41:46, 53
7 "And God sent me before you
to preserve for you a remnant in

the earth, and to keep you alive by
a great [t]deliverance. *escaped company*
8 "Now, therefore, it was not
you who sent me here, but God;
and He has made me a [r]father to
Pharaoh and lord of all his household and ruler over all the land of
Egypt. Judg. 17:10
9 "Hurry and go up to my father, and [r]say to him, 'Thus says
your son Joseph, "God has made
me lord of all Egypt; come down
to me, do not delay. Acts 7:14
10 "And you shall [t]live in the land
of [r]Goshen, and you shall be near
me, you and your children and
your children's children and your
flocks and your herds and all that
you have. *dwell* • Gen. 46:28
11 "There I will also [r]provide for
you, for there are still five years of
famine *to come*, lest you and your
household and all that you have
be impoverished." ' Gen. 47:12
12 "And behold, your eyes see,
and the eyes of my brother Benjamin *see*, that it is my mouth which
is speaking to you.
13 "Now you must tell my father
of all my splendor in Egypt, and
all that you have seen; and you
must hurry and [r]bring my father
down here." Acts 7:14
14 Then he fell on his brother
Benjamin's neck and wept; and
Benjamin wept on his neck.
15 And he kissed all his brothers and wept on them, and afterward his brothers talked with
him.
16 Now when the news was
heard in Pharaoh's house that Joseph's brothers had come, it
pleased Pharaoh and his servants.
17 Then Pharaoh said to Joseph,
"Say to your brothers, 'Do this:
load your beasts and [t]go to the
land of Canaan, *come, go*
18 and take your father and
your households and come to me,
and I will give you the [t]best of the
land of Egypt and you shall eat
the fat of the land.' *good*
19 "Now you are ordered, 'Do
this: [t]take wagons from the land of
Egypt for your little ones and for
your wives, and bring your father
and come. *take for yourselves*
20 'And do not concern yourselves with your goods, for the
[t]best of all the land of Egypt is
yours.' " *good*
21 Then the sons of Israel did
so; and Joseph gave them wagons
according to the [t]command of Pharaoh, and gave them provisions
for the journey. *mouth*
22 To each of them he gave
[r]changes of garments, but to Benjamin he gave three hundred
pieces of silver and five changes
of garments. 2 Kin. 5:5
23 And to his father he sent [t]as
follows: ten donkeys loaded with
the best things of Egypt, and ten
female donkeys loaded with grain
and bread and sustenance for his
father on the journey. *like this*
24 So he sent his brothers away,
and [t]as they departed, he said to
them, "Do not quarrel on the journey." *they departed; and he said*
25 Then they went up from
Egypt, and came to the land of Canaan to their father Jacob.
26 And they told him, saying,
"Joseph is still alive, and indeed
he is ruler over all the land of
Egypt." But he was stunned, for
he did not believe them.

27 When they told him all the words of Joseph that he had spoken to them, and when he saw the [r]wagons that Joseph had sent to carry him, the spirit of their father Jacob revived. Gen. 45:19

28 Then Israel said, "It is enough; my son Joseph is still alive. I will go and see him before I die."

CHAPTER 46

SO Israel set out with all that he had, and came to [r]Beersheba, and offered sacrifices to the God of his father Isaac. Gen. 21:31

2 And God spoke to Israel [t]in visions of the night and said, "Jacob, Jacob." And he said, "Here I am." *in the visions*

3 And He said, "I [r]am God, the God of your father; do not be afraid to go down to Egypt, for I will make you a great nation there. Gen. 17:1; 28:13

4 "I will go down with you to Egypt, and I will also surely bring you up again; and Joseph will [t]close your eyes." *put his hand on*

5 Then Jacob arose from Beersheba; and the sons of Israel carried their father Jacob and their little ones and their wives, in the [r]wagons which Pharaoh had sent to carry him. Gen. 45:21

6 And they took their livestock and their property, which they had acquired in the land of Canaan, and came to Egypt, Jacob and all his descendants with him:

7 his sons and his grandsons with him, his daughters and his granddaughters, and all his [t]descendants he brought with him to Egypt. *seed*

8 Now these are the [r]names of the sons of Israel, Jacob and his sons, who went to Egypt: Reuben, Jacob's first-born. Ex. 1:1-4

9 And the sons of Reuben: Hanoch and Pallu and Hezron and Carmi.

10 And the [r]sons of Simeon: Jemuel and Jamin and Ohad and Jachin and Zohar and Shaul the son of a Canaanite woman. Ex. 6:15

11 And the sons of Levi: Gershon, Kohath, and Merari.

12 And the sons of Judah: Er and Onan and Shelah and Perez and Zerah (but Er and Onan died in the land of Canaan). And the [r]sons of Perez were Hezron and Hamul. 1 Chr. 2:5

13 And the sons of Issachar: Tola and Puvvah and Iob and Shimron.

14 And the sons of Zebulun: Sered and Elon and Jahleel.

15 These are the sons of Leah, whom she bore to Jacob in Paddan-aram, with his daughter Dinah; all his sons and his daughters *numbered* thirty-three.

16 And the [r]sons of Gad: Ziphion and Haggi, Shuni and Ezbon, Eri and Arodi and Areli. Num. 26:15-18

17 And the [r]sons of Asher: Imnah and Ishvah and Ishvi and Beriah and their sister Serah. And the sons of Beriah: Heber and Malchiel. 1 Chr. 7:30

18 These are the sons of Zilpah, whom Laban gave to his daughter Leah; and she bore to Jacob these sixteen persons.

19 The sons of Jacob's wife Rachel: Joseph and Benjamin.

20 [r]Now to Joseph in the land of
Egypt were born Manasseh and E-
phraim, whom Asenath, the
daughter of Potiphera, priest of
On, bore to him. Gen. 41:50-52
21 And the sons of Benjamin:
Bela and Becher and Ashbel, Gera
and Naaman, Ehi and Rosh, Mup-
pim and Huppim and Ard.
22 These are the sons of Rachel,
who were born to Jacob; *there*
were fourteen persons in all.
23 And the sons of Dan: Hushim.
24 And the sons of Naphtali:
Jahzeel and Guni and Jezer and
Shillem.
25 These are the [r]sons of Bilhah,
whom [r]Laban gave to his daughter
Rachel, and she bore these to Jacob; *there were* seven persons in
all. Gen. 30:5, 7 · Gen. 29:29
26 [r]All the persons belonging to
Jacob, who came to Egypt, his direct descendants, not including
the wives of Jacob's sons, *were*
sixty-six persons in all, Ex. 1:5
27 and the sons of Joseph, who
were born to him in Egypt were
[t]two; all the persons of the house
of Jacob, who came to Egypt,
were seventy. *two souls*
28 Now he sent Judah before
him to Joseph, to point out *the*
way before him to [r]Goshen; and
they came into the land of Goshen. Gen. 45:10
29 And Joseph [t]prepared his
chariot and went up to Goshen to
meet his father Israel; as soon as
he appeared [t]before him, he fell on
his neck and wept on his neck a
long time. *tied, harnessed · to*
30 Then Israel said to Joseph,
"Now let me die, since I have seen
your face, that you are still alive."
31 And Joseph said to his brothers and to his father's household,
"I [r]will go up and tell Pharaoh, and
will say to him, 'My brothers and
my father's household, who *were*
in the land of Canaan, have come
to me; Gen. 47:1
32 and the men are shepherds,
for they have been [t]keepers of livestock; and they have brought their
flocks and their herds and all that
they have.' *men*
33 "And it shall come about
when Pharaoh calls you and says,
'What is your occupation?'
34 that you shall say, 'Your servants have been [t]keepers of livestock from our youth even until
now, both we and our fathers,'
that you may live in the land of
Goshen; for every shepherd is
loathsome to the Egyptians." *men*

CHAPTER 47

THEN [r]Joseph went in and told
Pharaoh, and said, "My father and
my brothers and their flocks and
their herds and all that they have,
have come out of the land of Canaan; and behold, they are in the
land of Goshen." Gen. 46:31
2 And he took five men from
among his brothers, and presented them to Pharaoh.
3 Then Pharaoh said to his
brothers, "What is your occupation?" So they said to Pharaoh,
"Your servants are shepherds,
both we and our fathers."
4 And they said to Pharaoh,
"We [r]have come to sojourn in the
land, for there is no pasture for
your servants' flocks, for the fam-

ine is severe in the land of Canaan. Now, therefore, please let
your servants [t]live in the land of
Goshen." Gen. 15:13 • *dwell*
5 Then Pharaoh said to [t]Joseph,
"Your father and your brothers
have come to you. *Joseph, saying*
6 "The land of Egypt is [60]at your
disposal; settle your father and
your brothers in the best of the
land, let them live in the land of
Goshen; and if you know any capable men among them, then put
them in charge of my livestock."
7 Then Joseph brought his father Jacob and [t]presented him to
Pharaoh; and Jacob [r]blessed Pharaoh. *set him before* • Gen. 47:10
8 And Pharaoh said to Jacob,
"How many years have you
lived?"
9 So Jacob said to Pharaoh,
"The years of my sojourning are
one hundred and thirty; few and
unpleasant have been the years of
my life, nor have they attained the
years that my fathers lived during
the days of their sojourning."
10 And Jacob blessed Pharaoh,
and went out from his presence.
11 So Joseph settled his father
and his brothers, and gave them a
possession in the land of Egypt, in
the best of the land, in the land of
Rameses, as Pharaoh had ordered.
12 And Joseph provided his father and his brothers and all his
father's household with food, according to their little ones.
13 Now there was no food in all
the land, because the famine was
very severe, so that the land of
Egypt and the land of Canaan languished because of the famine.
14 And Joseph gathered all the
money that was found in the land
of Egypt and in the land of Canaan for the grain which they
bought, and Joseph brought the
money into Pharaoh's house.
15 And when the money was all
spent in the land of Egypt and in
the land of Canaan, all the Egyptians came to Joseph [t]and said,
"Give us food, for why should we
die in your presence? For *our*
money [t]is gone." *saying* • *ceases*
16 Then Joseph said, "Give up
your livestock, and I will give you
food for your livestock, since *your*
money [t]is gone." *ceases*
17 So they brought their livestock to Joseph, and Joseph gave
them [a]food in exchange for the
horses and the flocks and the
herds and the donkeys; and he fed
them with food in exchange for all
their livestock that year. *bread*
18 And when that year was
ended, they came to him the [t]next
year and said to him, "We will not
hide from my lord that our money
is all spent, and the cattle are my
lord's. There is nothing left [t]for my
lord except our bodies and our
lands. *second* • *in the presence of*
19 "Why should we die before
your eyes, both we and our land?
Buy us and our land for [a]food, and
we and our land will be slaves to
Pharaoh. So give us seed, that we
may live and not die, and that the
land may not be desolate." *bread*
20 So Joseph bought all the land
of Egypt for Pharaoh, for every
Egyptian sold his field, because
the famine was severe upon them.
Thus the land became Pharaoh's.
21 And as for the people, he removed them to the cities from one

[60] Lit., *before you*

end of Egypt's border to the other.
22 Only the land of the priests
he did not buy, for the priests had
an allotment from Pharaoh, and
they lived off the allotment which
Pharaoh gave them. Therefore,
they did not sell their land.
23 Then Joseph said to the people, "Behold, I have today bought
you and your land for Pharaoh;
now, *here* is seed for you, and you
may sow the land.
24 "And at the harvest you shall
give a fifth to Pharaoh, and four-
fifths shall be your own for seed of
the field and for your food and for
those of your households and as
food for your little ones."
25 So they said, "You have
saved our lives! Let us find favor
in the sight of my lord, and we
will be Pharaoh's slaves."
26 And Joseph made it a statute
concerning the land of Egypt *valid*
to this day, that Pharaoh should
have the fifth; only the land of the
priests did not become Pharaoh's.
27 Now Israel [t]lived in the land
of Egypt, in [t]Goshen, and they acquired property in it and were
fruitful and became very numerous. *dwelt • in the land of Goshen*
28 And Jacob lived in the land
of Egypt seventeen years; so the
length of Jacob's life was one hundred and forty-seven years.
29 When the time for Israel to
die drew near, he called his son
Joseph and said to him, "Please, if
I have found favor in your sight,
place now your hand under my
thigh and deal with me in kindness and [61]faithfulness. Please do
not bury me in Egypt,

[61] Lit., *truth*

30 but when I [r]lie down with my
fathers, you shall carry me out of
Egypt and bury me in their burial
place." And he said, "I will do as
you have said." Gen. 15:15
31 And he said, "Swear [r]to me."
So he swore to him. Then Israel
bowed *in worship* at the head of
the bed. Gen. 21:23, 24; 24:3

CHAPTER 48

NOW it came about after these
things that Joseph was told, "Behold, your father is sick." So he
took his two sons [r]Manasseh and
Ephraim with him. Josh. 14:4
2 When it was told to Jacob,
"Behold, your son Joseph has
come to you," Israel collected his
strength and sat up in the bed.
3 Then Jacob said to Joseph,
"God [r]Almighty appeared to me at
Luz in the land of Canaan and
blessed me, Gen. 28:13f.; 35:9-12
4 and He said to me, 'Behold, I
will make you fruitful and numerous, and I will make you a company of peoples, and will give this
land to your descendants after
you for an everlasting possession.'
5 "And now your two sons, who
were born to you in the land of
Egypt before I came to you in
Egypt, are mine; [r]Ephraim and Manasseh shall be mine, as Reuben
and Simeon are. Gen. 41:50-52
6 "But your offspring that [t]have
been born after them shall be
yours; they shall be called by the
[t]names of their brothers in their inheritance. *you have begotten • name*
7 "Now as for me, when I came
from Paddan, Rachel died, to my

sorrow, in the land of Canaan on
the journey, when there was still
some distance to go to Ephrath;
and I buried her there on the way
to Ephrath (that is, Bethlehem)."
8 When Israel saw Joseph's
sons, he said, "Who are these?"
9 And Joseph said to his father, "They[r] are my sons, whom
God has given me here." So he
said, "Bring them to me, please,
that I may bless them." Gen. 33:5
10 Now the eyes of Israel were
so dim from age *that* he could not
see. Then [t]Joseph brought them
close to him, and he kissed them
and embraced them. *he*
11 And Israel said to Joseph, "I
never expected to see your face,
and behold, God has let me see
your [t]children as well." *seed*
12 Then Joseph took them from
his knees, and [r]bowed with his
face to the ground. Gen. 42:6
13 And Joseph took them both,
Ephraim with his right hand
toward Israel's left, and Manasseh
with his left hand toward Israel's
right, and brought them close to
him.
14 But Israel stretched out his
right hand and laid it on the head
of Ephraim, who was the younger,
and his left hand on Manasseh's
head, crossing his hands, although
Manasseh was the first-born.
15 And he blessed Joseph, and
said,

"The[r] God before whom my
fathers Abraham and
Isaac walked,
The God who has been my
shepherd all my life to
this day, Gen. 17:1
16 The angel who has re-
deemed me from all evil,
Bless the lads;
And may my name [t]live on
in them,
And the names of my fa-
thers Abraham and Isaac;
And may they grow into a
multitude in the midst of
the earth." *be called*

17 When Joseph saw that his father [r]laid his right hand on Ephraim's head, it displeased him; and
he grasped his father's hand to remove it from Ephraim's head to
Manasseh's head. Gen. 48:14
18 And Joseph said to his father, "Not so, my father, for this
one is the first-born. Place your
right hand on his head."
19 But his father refused and
said, "I know, my son, I know; he
also shall become a people and he
also shall be great. However, his
younger brother shall be greater
than he, and his descendants shall
become a multitude of nations."
20 And [r]he blessed them that
day, saying,

"By you Israel shall pro-
nounce blessing, saying,
'May God make you like E-
phraim and Manasseh!' "

Thus he put Ephraim before Manasseh. Heb. 11:21
21 Then Israel said to Joseph,
"Behold, I am about to die, but
[r]God will be with you, and [r]bring
you back to the land of your fathers. Gen. 26:3 • Gen. 28:15
22 "And I give you one portion
more than your brothers, which I
took from the hand of the Amorite
with my sword and my bow."

CHAPTER 49

THEN Jacob summoned his sons and said, "Assemble yourselves that I may tell you what shall befall you in the days to come.

2 "Gather together and hear, O sons of Jacob;
And[r] listen to Israel your father. Ps. 34:11

3 "Reuben, you are my firstborn;
My might and the beginning of my strength,
Preeminent in dignity and preeminent in power.
4 "Uncontrolled as water, you shall not have preeminence,
Because you went up to your father's bed;
Then you defiled *it*—he went up to my couch.

5 "Simeon and Levi are brothers;
Their swords are implements of violence.
6 "Let my soul not enter into their council;
Let not my glory be united with their assembly;
Because in their anger they slew[t] men,
And in their self-will they lamed oxen. *a man*
7 "Cursed be their anger, for it is fierce;
And their wrath, for it is cruel.
I will disperse them in Jacob,
And scatter them in Israel.

8 "Judah, your brothers shall praise you;
Your hand shall be on the neck of your enemies;
Your father's sons shall bow down to you.
9 "Judah is a lion's whelp;
From the prey, my son, you have gone up.
He[t] couches, he lies down as a lion,
And as a lion, who dares rouse him up? *bows down*
10 "The scepter shall not depart from Judah,
Nor the ruler's staff from between his feet,
[62]Until Shiloh comes,
And to him *shall be* the obedience of the peoples.
11 "He[t] ties *his* foal to the vine,
And his donkey's colt to the choice vine;
He washes his garments in wine,
And his robes in the blood of grapes. *Binding of*
12 "His eyes are [63]dull from wine,
And his teeth [64]white from milk.

13 "Zebulun shall dwell at the seashore;
And he *shall be* a haven for ships,
And his flank *shall be* toward Sidon.

14 "Issachar is[t] a strong donkey,
Lying down between the sheepfolds. *a donkey of bone*
15 "When he saw that a resting place was good
And that the land was pleasant,

[62] Or, *Until he comes to Shiloh*
[63] Or, *darker than* [64] Or, *whiter than*

He bowed his shoulder to
bear *burdens*,
And became a slave at
forced labor.

16 "Dan[r] shall judge his people,
As one of the tribes of Israel. Deut. 33:22
17 "Dan shall be a serpent in
the way,
A horned snake in the path,
That bites the horse's heels,
So that his rider falls backward.
18 "For[r] Thy salvation I wait, O
LORD. Ex. 15:2
19 "As for Gad, [t]raiders shall
raid him,
But he shall raid *at* their
heels. *a raiding band*
20 "As[t] for Asher, his food shall
be[t] rich,
And he shall yield royal
dainties. *From • fat*
21 "Naphtali is a doe let loose,
He gives beautiful words.
22 "Joseph[r] is a fruitful [65]bough,
A fruitful bough by a
spring;
Its [66]branches run over a
wall. Deut. 33:13-17
23 "The archers bitterly attacked him,
And shot *at him* and harassed him;
24 But his bow remained firm,
And his arms were agile,
From the hands of the
Mighty One of Jacob
(From there is the Shepherd, the Stone of Israel),
25 From the God of your father who helps you,
And[a] by the Almighty who
blesses you
With blessings of heaven
above,
Blessings of the deep that
lies beneath,
Blessings of the breasts and
of the womb. *with*
26 "The blessings of your father
Have surpassed the blessings of my ancestors
Up to the [t]utmost bound of
the everlasting hills;
May they be on the head of
Joseph,
And on the crown of the
head of the one distinguished among his brothers. *limit*
27 "Benjamin is a ravenous
wolf;
In the morning he devours
the prey,
And in the evening he divides the spoil."

28 All these are the twelve
tribes of Israel, and this is what
their father said to them [t]when he
blessed them. He blessed them,
every one with the blessing appropriate to him. *and*
29 Then he charged them and
said to them, "I am about to be
gathered to my people; bury me
with my fathers in the cave that is
in the field of Ephron the Hittite,
30 in the cave that is in the field
of Machpelah, which is before
Mamre, in the land of Canaan,
which Abraham bought along
with the field from Ephron the
Hittite for a burial site.
31 "There they buried Abraham
and his wife Sarah, there they
buried Isaac and his wife Re-

[65]Lit., *son* [66]Lit., *daughters*

bekah, and there I buried Leah—
32 the field and the cave that is
in it, purchased from the sons of
Heth."
33 When Jacob finished charging his sons, he drew his feet into
the bed and breathed his last, and
was gathered to his people.

CHAPTER 50

THEN Joseph fell on his father's
face, and wept over him and
kissed him.
2 And Joseph commanded his
servants the physicians to em-
balm his father. So the physicians
[r]embalmed Israel. Gen. 50:26
3 Now forty days were [t]re-
quired for[a] it, for such is the period
required for embalming. And the
Egyptians wept for him seventy
days. *fulfilled • him*
4 And when the days of
[t]mourning for him were past,
Joseph spoke to the household of
Pharaoh, saying, "If now I have
found favor in your sight, please
speak to Pharaoh, saying, *weeping*
5 'My father made me swear,
saying, "Behold, I am about to die;
in my grave which I dug for myself in the land of Canaan, there
you shall bury me." Now therefore, please let me go up and bury
my father; then I will return.' "
6 And Pharaoh said, "Go up
and bury your father, as he made
you swear."
7 So Joseph went up to bury
his father, and with him went up
all the servants of Pharaoh, the elders of his household and all the
elders of the land of Egypt,
8 and all the household of
Joseph and his brothers and his
father's household; they left only
their little ones and their flocks
and their herds in the land of Goshen.
9 There also went up with him
both chariots and horsemen; and
it was a very great company.
10 When they came to the
threshing floor of Atad, which is
beyond the Jordan, they[r] lamented
there with a very great and [t]sor-
rowful lamentation; and he observed seven days mourning for
his father. Acts 8:2 • *heavy*
11 Now when the inhabitants of
the land, the Canaanites, saw the
mourning at the threshing floor of
Atad, they said, "This is a grievous mourning for the Egyptians."
Therefore it was named Abel-miz-
raim, which is beyond the Jordan.
12 And thus his sons did for him
as he had charged them;
13 for his sons carried him to
the land of Canaan, and buried
him in [r]the cave of the field of
Machpelah before Mamre, which
Abraham had bought along with
the field for a burial site from
Ephron the Hittite. Acts 7:16
14 And after he had buried his
father, Joseph returned to Egypt,
he and his brothers, and all who
had gone up with him to bury his
father.
15 When Joseph's brothers saw
that their father was dead, they
said, "What[r] if Joseph should bear
a grudge against us and pay us
back in full for all the wrong
which we did to him!" Gen. 37:28
16 So they sent *a message* to
Joseph, saying, "Your father
charged before he died, saying,
17 'Thus you shall say to Joseph,

"Please forgive, I beg you, the
transgression of your brothers
and their sin, for they did you
wrong." ' And now, please forgive
the transgression of the servants
of the God of your father." And
Joseph wept when they spoke to
him.
18 Then his brothers also came
and fell down before him and said,
"Behold, we are your servants."
19 But Joseph said to them, "Do
not be afraid, for am I in God's
place?
20 "And as for you, you meant
evil against me, *but* God meant it
for good in order to bring about
[t]this present result, to preserve
many people alive. *as it is this day*
21 "So therefore, do not be
afraid; I will provide for you and
your little ones." So he comforted
them and spoke kindly to them.
22 Now Joseph stayed in Egypt,
he and his father's household, and
Joseph lived one hundred and ten
years.
23 And Joseph saw the third
generation of Ephraim's sons; also
the sons of Machir, the son of Manasseh, were [r]born on Joseph's
knees. Gen. 30:3
24 And Joseph said to his brothers, "I am about to die, but God
will surely[a]take care of you, and
bring you up from this land to the
land which He[t]promised on oath
to Abraham, to Isaac and to Jacob." *visit • swore*
25 Then Joseph made the sons
of Israel swear, saying, "God will
surely[a]take care of you, and[r]you
shall carry my bones up from
here." *visit* • Heb. 11:22
26 So Joseph died at the age of
one hundred and ten years; and[t]he
was embalmed and placed in a
coffin in Egypt. *they embalmed him*

THE BOOK OF

EXODUS

NOW these are the[r]names of the
sons of Israel who came to Egypt
with Jacob; they came each one
with his household: Gen. 46:8-27
2 Reuben, Simeon, Levi and
Judah;
3 Issachar, Zebulun and Benjamin;
4 Dan and Naphtali, Gad and
Asher.
5 And all the [t]persons who
came from the loins of Jacob were
seventy in number, but Joseph
was *already* in Egypt. *souls*
6 And Joseph died, and all his
brothers and all that generation.
7 But the sons of Israel were
fruitful and[t]increased greatly, and
multiplied, and became exceedingly mighty, so that the land was
filled with them. *swarmed*
8 Now a new king arose over
Egypt, who did not know Joseph.
9 And he said to his people,

"Behold, the people of the sons of
Israel are[a]more and mightier than
we. *too many and too mighty for us*
10 "Come, let us[r]deal wisely with
them, lest they multiply and in the
event of war, they also join themselves to those who hate us, and
fight against us, and [t]depart from
the land." Acts 7:19 • *go up from*
11 So they appointed taskmasters over them to afflict them with
[t]hard labor. And they built for Pharaoh storage cities, Pithom and
Raamses. *their burdens*
12 But the more they afflicted
them, the more they multiplied
and the more they[t]spread out, so
that they were in dread of the
sons of Israel. *broke forth*
13 And the Egyptians com-
pelled the sons of Israel[r]to labor
rigorously; Gen. 15:13; Deut. 4:20
14 and they made their lives bitter with hard labor in mortar and
bricks and at *all kinds* of labor in
the field, all their labors which
they rigorously imposed on them.
15 Then the king of Egypt spoke
to the Hebrew midwives, one of
whom was named Shiphrah, and
the other was named Puah;
16 and he said, "When you are
helping the Hebrew women to
give birth and see *them* upon the
birthstool, if it is a son, then you
shall put him to death; but if it is a
daughter, then she shall live."
17 But the midwives feared
God, and did not do as the king of
Egypt had [t]commanded them, but
let the boys live. *spoken to*
18 So the king of Egypt called
for the midwives, and said to
them, "Why have you done this
thing, and let the boys live?"
19 And the midwives said to
Pharaoh, "Because the Hebrew
women are not as the Egyptian
women; for they are vigorous, and
they give birth before the midwife
[t]can get to them." *comes to*
20 So God was good to the midwives, and the people multiplied,
and became very mighty.
21 And it came about because
the midwives feared God, that He
established households for them.
22 Then Pharaoh commanded
all his people, saying, "Every[r]son
who is born [1]you are to cast into
the Nile, and every daughter you
are to keep alive." Acts 7:19

CHAPTER 2

NOW a man from [r]the house of
Levi went and[t]married a daughter
of Levi. Ex. 6:16, 18, 20 • *took*
2 And the woman conceived
and bore a son; and when she saw
[t]that he was[t]beautiful, she hid him
for three months. *him that* • *good*
3 But when she could hide him
no longer, she got him a [2]wicker
basket and covered it over with
tar and pitch. Then she put the
child into it, and set *it* among the
reeds by the bank of the Nile.
4 And his sister stood at a distance to[t]find out what would[t]hap-
pen to him. *know* • *be done*
5 Then the daughter of Pharaoh came down [r]to bathe at the
Nile, with her maidens walking
alongside the Nile; and she saw
the[a]basket among the reeds and
sent her maid, and she brought it
to her. Ex. 7:15; 8:20 • *chest*
6 When she opened *it*, she saw
the child, and behold, *the*[a]boy was

[1] Some versions insert, *to the Hebrews*
[2] I.e., papyrus reeds

crying. And she had pity on him
and said, "This is one of the Hebrews' children." *lad*
7 Then his sister said to Pharaoh's daughter, "Shall I go and
call a nurse for you from the Hebrew women, that she may nurse
the child for you?"
8 And Pharaoh's daughter said
to her, "Go *ahead.*" So the girl
went and called the child's
mother.
9 Then Pharaoh's daughter
said to her, "Take this child away
and nurse him for me and I shall
give *you* your wages." So the
woman took the child and nursed
him.
10 And the child grew, and she
brought him to Pharaoh's daughter, and [r]he became her son. And
she named him Moses, and said,
"Because I drew him out of the
water." Acts 7:21
11 Now it came about in those
days, when Moses had grown up,
that he went out to his brethren
and looked on their hard labors;
and he saw an Egyptian beating a
Hebrew, one of his brethren.
12 So he [t]looked this way and
that, and when he saw there was
no one *around,* he [r]struck down
the Egyptian and hid him in the
sand. *turned* • Acts 7:24, 25
13 And he went out the next
day, and behold, two Hebrews
were fighting with each other; and
he said to the offender, "Why are
you striking your companion?"
14 But he said, "Who made you
a prince or a judge over us? Are
you intending to kill me, as you
killed the Egyptian?" Then Moses
was afraid, and said, "Surely the
matter has become known."
15 When Pharaoh heard of this
matter, he tried to kill Moses. But
[r]Moses fled from the presence of
Pharaoh and [t]settled in the land of
Midian; and he sat down by a
well. Acts 7:29; Heb. 11:27 • *dwelt*
16 Now [r]the priest of Midian had
seven daughters; and they came
to draw water, and filled the
troughs to water their father's
flock. Ex. 3:1; 18:12
17 Then the shepherds came
and drove them away, but [r]Moses
stood up and helped them, and
watered their flock. Gen. 29:3, 10
18 When they came to Reuel
their father, he said, "Why have
you come *back* so soon today?"
19 So they said, "An Egyptian
delivered us from the hand of the
shepherds; and what is more, he
even drew the water for us and
watered the flock."
20 And he said to his daughters,
"Where is he then? Why is it that
you have left the man behind? Invite him [t]to have something to
eat." *that he may eat bread*
21 And Moses was willing to
dwell with the man, and he gave
his daughter Zipporah to Moses.
22 Then she gave birth to a son,
and he named him Gershom, for
he said, "I have been [r]a sojourner
in a foreign land." Heb. 11:13, 14
23 Now it came about in *the
course of* those many days that
the king of Egypt died. And the
sons of Israel sighed because of
the bondage, and they cried out;
and their cry for help because of
their bondage rose up to God.
24 So [r]God heard their groaning;

and God remembered His covenant with Abraham, Isaac, and
Jacob. Ex. 6:5; Acts 7:34
25 And God saw the sons of Israel, and God took notice *of them.*

CHAPTER 3

NOW Moses was pasturing the
flock of Jethro his father-in-law,
the priest of Midian; and he led
the flock to the [a]west side of the
wilderness, and came to Horeb,
the mountain of God. *rear part*
2 And the angel of the LORD
appeared to him in a blazing fire
from the midst of [t]a [r]bush; and he
looked, and behold, the bush was
burning with fire, yet the bush
was not consumed. *the* • Acts 7:30
3 So Moses said, "I [t]must turn
aside now, and see this [t]marvelous
sight, why the bush is not burned
up." *Let me turn* • *great*
4 When the LORD saw that he
turned aside to look, [r]God called to
him from the midst of the bush,
and said, "Moses, Moses!" And he
said, "Here I am." Ex. 4:5
5 Then He said, "Do not come
near here; [r]remove your sandals
from your feet, for the place on
which you are standing is holy
ground." Josh. 5:15; Acts 7:33
6 He said also, "I [r]am the God
of your father, the God of Abraham, the God of Isaac, and the
God of Jacob." Then Moses hid
his face, for he was [r]afraid to look
at God. Mark 12:26 • Rev. 1:17
7 And the LORD said, "I have
surely [r]seen the affliction of My
people who are in Egypt, and have
given heed to their cry because of
their taskmasters, for I am aware
of their sufferings. Is. 63:9
8 "So I have come down to deliver them from the [t]power of the
Egyptians, and to bring them up
from that land to a good and spacious land, to a land flowing with
milk and honey, to the place of the
Canaanite and the Hittite and the
Amorite and the Perizzite and the
Hivite and the Jebusite. *hand*
9 "And now, behold, [r]the cry of
the sons of Israel has come to Me;
furthermore, I have seen the oppression with which the Egyptians
are oppressing them. Ex. 2:23
10 "Therefore, come now, and I
will send you to Pharaoh, so that
you may bring My people, the
sons of Israel, out of Egypt."
11 But Moses said to God,
"Who am I, that I should go to
Pharaoh, and that I should bring
the sons of Israel out of Egypt?"
12 And He said, "Certainly I
will be with you, and this shall be
the sign to you that it is I who
have sent you: when you have
brought the people out of Egypt,
[r]you shall [a]worship God at this
mountain." Acts 7:7 • *serve*
13 Then Moses said to God,
"Behold, I am going to the sons of
Israel, and I shall say to them,
'The God of your fathers has sent
me to you.' Now they may say to
me, 'What is His name?' What
shall I say to them?"
14 And God said to Moses, "[3]I
AM WHO [3]I AM"; and He said,
"Thus you shall say to the sons of
Israel, '[3]I AM has sent me to
you.'"

[3]Related to the name of God, *YHWH,* rendered *LORD,* which is derived from the verb *HAYAH, to be*

15 And God, furthermore, said
to Moses, "Thus you shall say to
the sons of Israel, 'The LORD, the
God of your fathers, the God of
Abraham, the God of Isaac, and
the God of Jacob, has sent me to
you.' This is My name forever, and
this is My [r]memorial-name to all
generations. Ps. 30:4; 97:12
16 "Go and [r]gather the elders of
Israel together, and say to them,
'The LORD, the God of your fathers, the God of Abraham, Isaac
and Jacob, has appeared to me,
saying, "I am indeed concerned
about you and what has been
done to you in Egypt. Ex. 4:29
17 "So [r]I said, I will bring you up
out of the affliction of Egypt to the
land of the Canaanite and the Hittite and the Amorite and the Perizzite and the Hivite and the Jebusite, to a land flowing with milk
and honey." ' Gen. 15:13-21
18 "And they will [t]pay heed to
what you say; and you with the elders of Israel will come to the king
of Egypt, and you will say to him,
'The LORD, the God of the Hebrews, has met with us. So now,
please, let us go a three days' journey into the wilderness, that we
may sacrifice to the LORD our
God.' *hear your voice*
19 "But I know that the king of
Egypt [r]will not permit you to go,
except under compulsion. Ex. 5:2
20 "So I will stretch out [r]My
hand, and strike Egypt with all My
[r]miracles which I shall do in the
midst of it; and after that he will
let you go. Ex. 6:1 • Acts 7:36
21 "And I will grant this people
favor in the sight of the Egyptians;
and it shall be that when you go,
you will not go empty-handed.
22 "But every woman shall ask
of her neighbor and the woman
who lives in her house, articles of
silver and articles of gold, and
clothing; and you will put them on
your sons and daughters. Thus
you will plunder the Egyptians."

CHAPTER 4

THEN Moses answered and said,
"What if they will not believe me,
or listen [t]to what I say? For they
may say, 'The LORD has not appeared to you.' " *to my voice*
2 And the LORD said to him,
"What is that in your hand?" And
he said, "A [r]staff." Ex. 4:17, 20
3 Then He said, "Throw it on
the ground." So he threw it on the
ground, and [r]it became a serpent;
and Moses fled from it. Ex. 7:10-12
4 But the LORD said to Moses,
"Stretch out your hand and grasp
it by its tail"—so he stretched out
his hand and caught it, and it became a staff in his [t]hand— *palm*
5 "that [r]they may believe that
the LORD, the God of their fathers,
the God of Abraham, the God of
Isaac, and the God of Jacob, has
appeared to you." Ex. 4:31
6 And the LORD furthermore
said to him, "Now put your hand
into your bosom." So he put his
hand into his bosom, and when he
took it out, behold, his hand was
[r]leprous like snow. Num. 12:10
7 Then He said, "Put your
hand into your bosom again." So
he put his hand into his bosom
again; and when he took it out of
his bosom, behold, [r]it was restored
like *the rest of* his flesh. Matt. 8:3
8 "And it shall come about that
if they will not believe you or [t]heed

the [t]witness of the first sign, they may believe the [t]witness of the last sign. *listen to • voice*

9 "But it shall be that if they will not believe even these two signs or heed what you say, then you shall take some water from the Nile and pour it on the dry ground; and the water which you take from the Nile will become blood on the dry ground."

10 Then Moses said to the LORD, "Please, Lord, I have never been [t]eloquent, neither recently nor in time past, nor since Thou hast spoken to Thy servant; for I am [t]slow of speech and slow of tongue." *a man of words • heavy*

11 And the LORD said to him, "Who has made man's mouth? Or [r]who makes *him* dumb or deaf, or seeing or blind? Is it not I, the LORD? Ps. 94:9; Matt. 11:5

12 "Now then go, and I, even I, will be with your mouth, and teach you what you are to say."

13 But he said, "Please, Lord, now send *the message* by whomever Thou wilt."

14 Then the anger of the LORD burned against Moses, and He said, "Is there not your brother Aaron the Levite? I know that [t]he speaks fluently. And moreover, behold, he is coming out to meet you; when he sees you, he will be glad in his heart. *speaking he speaks*

15 "And you are to speak to him and put the words in his mouth; and I, even I, will be with your mouth and his mouth, and I will teach you what you are to do.

16 "Moreover, [r]he shall speak for you to the people; and it shall come about that he shall be as a mouth for you, and you shall be as God to him. Ex. 7:1, 2

17 "And you shall take in your hand this staff, with which you shall perform the signs."

18 Then Moses departed and returned to Jethro his father-in-law, and said to him, "Please, let me go, that I may return to my brethren who are in Egypt, and see if they are still alive." And Jethro said to Moses, "Go in peace."

19 Now the LORD said to Moses in Midian, "Go [t]back to Egypt, for all the men who were seeking your life are dead." *return*

20 So Moses took his wife and his [r]sons and mounted them on a donkey, and he returned to the land of Egypt. Moses also took the staff of God in his hand. Acts 7:29

21 And the LORD said to Moses, "When you go [t]back to Egypt see that you perform before Pharaoh all the wonders which I have put in your [t]power; but I will harden his heart so that he will not let the people go. *to return • hand*

22 "Then you shall say to Pharaoh, 'Thus says the LORD, "Israel[r] is My son, My first-born. Rom. 9:4

23 "So I said to you, 'Let [r]My son go, that he may serve Me'; but you have refused to let him go. Behold, I will kill your son, your first-born." ' " Ex. 5:1; 6:11

24 Now it came about at the lodging place on the way that the LORD met him and [r]sought to put him to death. Num. 22:22

25 Then Zipporah took [r]a flint and cut off her son's foreskin and threw *it* at Moses' feet, and she said, "You are indeed a bridegroom of blood to me." Josh. 5:2, 3

26 So He let him alone. At that time she said, "*You are* a bridegroom of blood"—[t]because of the circumcision. *with reference to*

27 [r]Now the LORD said to Aaron, "Go to meet Moses in the wilderness." So he went and met him at the [r]mountain of God, and he kissed him. Ex. 4:14 • Ex. 3:1

28 And [r]Moses told Aaron all the words of the LORD with which He had sent him, and [r]all the signs that He had commanded him *to do.* Ex. 4:15f. • Ex. 4:8f.

29 Then Moses and Aaron went and [r]assembled all the elders of the sons of Israel; Ex. 3:16

30 and Aaron spoke all the words which the LORD had spoken to Moses. He then performed the signs in the sight of the people.

31 So the people believed; and when they heard that the LORD [t]was concerned about the sons of Israel and that He had seen their affliction, then they bowed low and worshiped. *had visited*

CHAPTER 5

AND afterward Moses and Aaron came and said to Pharaoh, "Thus[r] says the LORD, the God of Israel, 'Let [r]My people go that they may celebrate a feast to Me in the wilderness.' " Ex. 3:18 • Ex. 4:23

2 But Pharaoh said, "Who[r] is the LORD that I should obey His voice to let Israel go? I do not know the LORD, and besides, I will not let Israel go." 2 Kin. 18:35

3 Then they said, "The God of the Hebrews has met with us. Please, let us go a three days' journey into the wilderness that we may sacrifice to the LORD our God, lest He fall upon us with pestilence or with the sword."

4 But the king of Egypt said to them, "Moses and Aaron, why do you [t]draw the people away from their [t]work? Get *back* to your [t]labors!" *loose • works • burdens*

5 Again Pharaoh said, "Look, [r]the people of the land are now many, and you would have them cease from their labors!" Ex. 1:7, 9

6 So the same day Pharaoh commanded [r]the taskmasters over the people and their foremen, saying, Ex. 1:11; 3:7

7 "You are no longer to give the people straw to make brick as previously; let them go and gather straw for themselves.

8 "But the quota of bricks which they were making previously, you shall impose on them; you are not to reduce any of it. Because they are [r]lazy, therefore they cry out, 'Let [t]us go and sacrifice to our God.' Ex. 5:17 • *saying, 'Let*

9 "Let the labor be heavier on the men, and let them work at it that they may pay no attention to false words."

10 So the taskmasters of the people and their foremen went out and spoke to the people, saying, "Thus says Pharaoh, 'I am not going to give you *any* straw.

11 'You go *and* get straw for yourselves wherever you can find *it;* but none of your labor will be reduced.' "

12 So the people scattered through all the land of Egypt to gather stubble for straw.

13 And the taskmasters pressed them, saying, "Complete your

work quota, *your* daily amount, just as when you had straw."

14 Moreover,[r]the foremen of the sons of Israel, whom Pharaoh's taskmasters had set over them, were beaten [t]and were asked, "Why have you not completed your required amount either yesterday or today in making brick as previously?" Ex. 5:6 · *saying*

15 Then the foremen of the sons of Israel came and cried out to Pharaoh, saying, "Why do you deal this way with your servants?

16 "There is no straw given to your servants, yet they keep saying to us, 'Make bricks!' And behold, your servants are being beaten; but it is the fault of your *own* people."

17 But he said, "You are lazy, *very* lazy; therefore you say, 'Let us go *and* sacrifice to the LORD.'

18 "So go now *and* work; for you shall be given no straw, yet you must deliver the quota of bricks."

19 And the foremen of the sons of Israel saw that they were in trouble [t]because they were told, "You must not reduce *your* daily amount of bricks." *saying*

20 When they left Pharaoh's presence, they met Moses and Aaron as they were[t]waiting for them. *standing to meet*

21 And[r]they said to them, "May the LORD look upon you and judge *you*, for you have made [4]us odious in Pharaoh's sight and in the sight of his servants, to put a sword in their hand to kill us." Ex. 14:11

22 Then Moses returned to the LORD and said, "O Lord, why hast Thou brought harm to this people? Why didst Thou ever send me?

[4]Lit., *our savor to stink*

23 "Ever since I came to Pharaoh to speak in Thy name, he has done harm to this people; [r]and Thou hast not delivered Thy people at all." Ex. 3:8

CHAPTER 6

THEN the LORD said to Moses, "Now you shall see what I will do to Pharaoh; for[t]under compulsion he shall let them go, and [t]under compulsion he shall drive them out of his land." *by a strong hand*

2 God spoke further to Moses and said to him, "I am the LORD;

3 and I appeared to Abraham, Isaac, and Jacob, as God Almighty, but *by*[r]My name, [5]LORD, I did not make Myself known to them. Is. 52:6; Jer. 16:21

4 "And I also established [r]My covenant with them, to give them the land of Canaan, the land in which they sojourned. Gen. 12:7

5 "And furthermore I have heard the groaning of the sons of Israel, because the Egyptians are holding them in bondage; and I have remembered My covenant.

6 "Say, therefore, to the sons of Israel, 'I[r]am the LORD, and I will bring you out from under the burdens of the Egyptians, and I will deliver you from their bondage. I will also redeem you with an outstretched arm and with great judgments. Ex. 13:3, 14

7 'Then I will take you[t]for My people, and I will be your God; and you shall know that I am the LORD your God, who brought you out from under the burdens of the Egyptians. *to Me for a people*

8 'And I will bring you to the

[5]Heb., *YHWH*, usually rendered *LORD*

land which I [t]swore to give to
Abraham, Isaac, and Jacob, and I
will give it to you *for* a possession;
I am the LORD.' " *lifted up My hand*
9 So Moses spoke thus to the
sons of Israel, but they did not listen to Moses on account of *their*
despondency and cruel bondage.
10 Now the LORD spoke to
Moses, saying,
11 "Go, [t]tell Pharaoh king of
Egypt to let the sons of Israel go
out of his land." *speak to*
12 But Moses spoke before the
LORD, saying, "Behold, the sons of
Israel have not listened to me;
how then will Pharaoh listen to
me, for I am unskilled in speech?"
13 Then the LORD spoke to
Moses and to Aaron, and gave
them a charge to the sons of Israel
and to Pharaoh king of Egypt, to
bring the sons of Israel out of the
land of Egypt.
14 These are the heads of their
fathers' households. [r]The sons of
Reuben, Israel's first-born: Hanoch and Pallu, Hezron and Carmi; these are the families of Reuben. Gen. 46:9; Num. 26:5-11
15 And the [r]sons of Simeon: Jemuel and Jamin and Ohad and Jachin and Zohar and Shaul the son
of a Canaanite woman; these are
the families of Simeon. Gen. 46:10
16 And these are the names of
[r]the sons of Levi according to their
generations: Gershon and Kohath
and Merari; and the [t]length of Levi's life was one hundred and
thirty-seven years. Gen. 46:11 • *years*
17 [r]The sons of Gershon: Libni
and Shimei, according to their
families. Num. 3:18-20
18 And [r]the sons of Kohath: Amram and Izhar and Hebron and
Uzziel; and the [t]length of Kohath's
life was one hundred and thirty-
three years. Num. 3:19 • *years*
19 And [r]the sons of Merari:
Mahli and Mushi. These are the
families of the Levites according
to their generations. Num. 3:20
20 And Amram [t]married his father's sister Jochebed, and she
bore him Aaron and Moses; and
the [t]length of Amram's life was
one hundred and thirty-seven
years. *took to him to wife • years*
21 And the sons of Izhar: Korah
and Nepheg and Zichri.
22 And the sons of Uzziel: Mishael and Elzaphan and Sithri.
23 And Aaron [t]married Elisheba,
the daughter of Amminadab, the
sister of Nahshon, and she bore
him Nadab and Abihu, Eleazar
and Ithamar. *took to him to wife*
24 And the sons of Korah: Assir
and Elkanah and Abiasaph; these
are the families of the Korahites.
25 And Aaron's son [r]Eleazar
married one of the daughters of
Putiel, and she bore him Phinehas.
These are the heads of the fathers'
households of the Levites according to their families. Josh. 24:33
26 It was *the same* Aaron and
Moses to whom the LORD said,
"Bring [r]out the sons of Israel from
the land of Egypt according to
their hosts." Ex. 3:10; 6:13
27 They were the ones who
spoke to Pharaoh king of Egypt
[t]about bringing out the sons of Israel from Egypt; it was *the same*
Moses and Aaron. *to bring out*
28 Now it came about on the
day when the LORD spoke to
Moses in the land of Egypt,

29 that the LORD spoke to Moses, saying, "I am the LORD; [r]speak to Pharaoh king of Egypt all that I speak to you." Ex. 6:11

30 But Moses said before the LORD, "Behold, I am [t]unskilled in speech; how then will Pharaoh listen to me?" *uncircumcised of lips*

CHAPTER 7

THEN the LORD said to Moses, "See,[r] I make you *as* God to Pharaoh, and your brother Aaron shall be your prophet. Ex. 4:16

2 "You shall speak all that I command you, and your brother [r]Aaron shall speak to Pharaoh that he let the sons of Israel go out of his land. Ex. 4:15

3 "But [r]I will harden Pharaoh's heart that I may [r]multiply My signs and My wonders in the land of Egypt. Ex. 4:21 • Ex. 11:9

4 "When [r]Pharaoh will not listen to you, then I will lay My hand on Egypt, and [r]bring out My hosts, My people the sons of Israel, from the land of Egypt by great judgments. Ex. 3:19, 20 • Ex. 12:51

5 "And [r]the Egyptians shall know that I am the LORD, when I [r]stretch out My hand on Egypt and bring out the sons of Israel from their midst." Ex. 7:17 • Ex. 3:20

6 So Moses and Aaron did *it;* [r]as the LORD commanded them, thus they did. Gen. 6:22; 7:5

7 And Moses was eighty years old and Aaron eighty-three, when they spoke to Pharaoh.

8 Now the LORD spoke to Moses and Aaron, saying,

9 "When Pharaoh speaks to you, saying, 'Work[r] a miracle,' then you shall say to Aaron, 'Take your staff and throw *it* down before Pharaoh, *that* it may become a serpent.' " Is. 7:11; John 2:18

10 So Moses and Aaron came to Pharaoh, and thus they did just as the LORD had commanded; and Aaron threw his staff down before Pharaoh and [t]his servants, and it became a serpent. *before his*

11 Then Pharaoh also called for *the* wise men and *the* sorcerers, and they also, the [a]magicians of Egypt, did [t]the same with their secret arts. *soothsayer priests • thus*

12 For each one threw down his staff and they turned into serpents. But Aaron's staff swallowed up their staffs.

13 Yet Pharaoh's heart was hardened, and he did not listen to them, as the LORD had said.

14 Then the LORD said to Moses, "Pharaoh's heart is [a]stubborn; he refuses to let the people go. *hard*

15 "Go to Pharaoh in the morning as he is going out to the water, and station yourself to meet him on the bank of the Nile; and you shall take in your hand the staff that was turned into a serpent.

16 "And you will say to him, 'The LORD, the God of the Hebrews, sent me to you, saying, "Let My people go, that they may serve Me in the wilderness. But behold, you have not listened until now."

17 'Thus says the LORD, "By this you shall know that I am the LORD: behold, I will strike [t]the water that is in the Nile with the staff that is in my hand, and it shall be turned to blood. *upon the waters*

18 "And the fish that are in the
Nile will die, and the Nile will become foul; and the Egyptians will
[a]find difficulty in drinking water
from the Nile." ' " *be weary of*
19 Then the LORD said to Moses,
"Say to Aaron, 'Take your staff
and stretch out your hand over
the waters of Egypt, over their rivers, over their [a]streams, and over
their pools, and over all their res-
ervoirs of water, that they may
become blood; and there shall be
blood throughout all the land of
Egypt, both in *vessels of* wood and
in *vessels of* stone.' " *canals*
20 So Moses and Aaron did
even as the LORD had com-
manded. And he lifted up [r]the staff
and struck the water that *was* in
the Nile, in the sight of Pharaoh
and in the sight of his servants,
and all the water that *was* in the
Nile was turned to blood. Ex. 17:5
21 And the fish that *were* in the
Nile died, and the Nile became
foul, so that the Egyptians could
not drink water from the Nile.
And the blood was through all the
land of Egypt.
22 But the magicians of Egypt
did the same with their secret
arts; and Pharaoh's heart was
hardened, and he did not listen to
them, as the LORD had said.
23 Then Pharaoh turned and
went into his house with no concern even for this.
24 So all the Egyptians dug
around the Nile for water to drink,
for they could not drink of the water of the Nile.
25 And seven days passed after
the LORD had struck the Nile.

CHAPTER 8

THEN the LORD said to Moses,
"Go to Pharaoh and say to him,
'Thus says the LORD, "Let My people go, that they may serve Me.
2 "But if you refuse to let *them*
go, behold, I will smite your whole
territory with frogs.
3 "And the Nile will swarm with
frogs, which will come up and go
into your house and into your bedroom and on your bed, and into
the houses of your servants and
on your people, and into your ovens and into your kneading bowls.
4 "So the frogs will come up on
you and your people and all your
servants." ' "
5 Then the LORD said to Moses,
"Say to Aaron, 'Stretch out your
hand with your staff over the rivers, over the [a]streams and over the
pools, and make frogs come up on
the land of Egypt.' " *canals*
6 So Aaron stretched out his
hand over the waters of Egypt,
and the [t]frogs came up and covered the land of Egypt. *frog*
7 And the [a]magicians did the
same with their secret arts, [t]mak-
ing frogs come up on the land of
Egypt. *soothsayer priests • and made*
8 Then Pharaoh [r]called for
Moses and Aaron and said, "Entreat [r]the LORD that He remove the
frogs from me and from my people; and I will let the people go,
that they may sacrifice to the
LORD." Ex. 8:25 • Num. 21:7
9 And Moses said to Pharaoh,
"The honor is yours to tell me:
when shall I entreat for you and
your servants and your people,
that the frogs be destroyed from

you and your houses, *that* they
may be left only in the Nile?"
10 Then he said, "Tomorrow."
So he said, "*May it be* according
to your word, that you may know
that there is [r]no one like the LORD
our God. Ex. 9:14; Ps. 86:8
11 "And the frogs will depart
from you and your houses and
your servants and your people;
they will be left only in the Nile."
12 Then Moses and Aaron went
out from Pharaoh, and [r]Moses
cried to the LORD concerning the
frogs which He had [t]inflicted upon
Pharaoh. Ex. 8:30 • *placed*
13 And the LORD did according
to the word of Moses, and the
frogs died out of the houses, the
courts, and the fields.
14 So they piled them in heaps,
and the land became foul.
15 But when Pharaoh saw that
there was relief, he [t]hardened his
heart and did not listen to them,
as the LORD had said. *made heavy*
16 Then the LORD said to Moses,
"Say to Aaron, 'Stretch out your
staff and strike the dust of the
earth, that it may become [6]gnats
through all the land of Egypt.' "
17 And they did so; and Aaron
stretched out his hand with his
staff, and struck the dust of the
earth, and there were gnats on
man and beast. All the dust of the
earth became [a]gnats[r] through all
the land of Egypt. *lice* • Ps. 105:31
18 And the magicians tried with
their secret arts to bring forth
gnats, but they could not; so there
were gnats on man and beast.
19 Then the magicians said to
Pharaoh, "This is the finger of
God." But Pharaoh's heart was
hardened, and he did not listen to
them, as the LORD had said.
20 Now the LORD said to Moses,
"Rise[r] early in the morning and
present yourself before Pharaoh,
[t]as he comes out to the water, and
say to him, 'Thus says the LORD,
"Let My people go, that they may
serve Me. Ex. 7:15 • *behold*
21 "For if you will not let My
people go, behold, I will send
swarms of insects on you and on
your servants and on your people
and into your houses; and the
houses of the Egyptians shall be
full of swarms of insects, and also
the ground on which they *dwell.*
22 "But[r] on that day I will set
apart the land of Goshen, where
My people are [t]living, so that no
swarms of insects will be there, in
order that you may know that [r]I,
the LORD, am in the midst of the
land. Ex. 9:4 • *standing* • Ex. 9:29
23 "And I will [7]put a division between My people and your people.
Tomorrow this sign shall occur." ' "
24 Then the LORD did so. And
there came [t]great swarms of insects into the house of Pharaoh
and the houses of his servants and
the land was [r]laid waste because of
the swarms of insects in all the
land of Egypt. *heavy* • Ps. 78:45
25 And Pharaoh [r]called for
Moses and Aaron and said, "Go,[r]
sacrifice to your God within the
land." Ex. 8:8 • Ex. 9:28
26 But Moses said, "It is not
right to do so, for we shall sacrifice to the LORD our God what is
an abomination to the Egyptians.
If we sacrifice [t]what is an abomination to the Egyptians before

[6] Or, *lice*

[7] Lit., *set a ransom*

their eyes, will they not then stone
us? *the abomination of Egypt*

27 "We must go a three days'
journey into the wilderness and
sacrifice to the LORD our God as
He [t]commands us." *says to us*

28 And Pharaoh said, "I [r]will let
you go, that you may sacrifice to
the LORD your God in the wilderness; only you shall not go very
far away. [r]Make supplication for
me." Ex. 8:8 • 1 Kin. 13:6

29 Then Moses said, "Behold, I
am going out from you, and I shall
make supplication to the LORD
that the swarms of insects may
depart from Pharaoh, from his
servants, and from his people tomorrow; only do not let Pharaoh
[r]deal deceitfully again in not letting the people go to sacrifice to
the LORD." Ex. 8:8, 15

30 So [r]Moses went out from
Pharaoh and made supplication to
the LORD. Ex. 8:12

31 And the LORD did as Moses
asked, and removed the swarms
of insects from Pharaoh, from his
servants and from his people; not
one remained.

32 But Pharaoh [t]hardened his
heart this time also, and he did not
let the people go. *made heavy*

CHAPTER 9

THEN the LORD said to Moses,
"Go to Pharaoh and speak to him,
'Thus says the LORD, the God of
the Hebrews, "Let [r]My people go,
that they may serve Me. Ex. 4:23

2 "For if you refuse to let *them*
go, and continue to hold them,

3 behold, the hand of the LORD
[t]will come *with* a very severe pestilence on your livestock which
are in the field, on the horses, on
the donkeys, on the camels, on the
herds, and on the flocks. *will be*

4 "But the LORD will make a distinction between the livestock of
Israel and the livestock of Egypt,
so that nothing will die of all that
belongs to the sons of Israel." ' "

5 And the LORD set a definite
time, saying, "Tomorrow the
LORD will do this thing in the
land."

6 So the LORD did this thing on
the morrow, and all the livestock
of Egypt died; but of the livestock
of the sons of Israel, not one died.

7 And Pharaoh sent, and behold, there was not even one of
the livestock of Israel dead. But
[r]the heart of Pharaoh was [t]hard-
ened, and he did not let the people
go. Ex. 7:14; 8:32 • *heavy*

8 Then the LORD said to Moses
and Aaron, "Take for yourselves
handfuls of soot from a kiln, and
let Moses throw it toward the sky
in the sight of Pharaoh.

9 "And it will become fine dust
over all the land of Egypt, and will
become [r]boils breaking out with
sores on man and beast through
all the land of Egypt." Rev. 16:2

10 So they took soot from a
kiln, and stood before Pharaoh;
and Moses threw it toward the
sky, and it became boils breaking
out with sores on man and beast.

11 And the [a]magicians could not
stand before Moses because of the
boils, for the boils were on the
magicians as well as on all the
Egyptians. *soothsayer priests*

12 And the LORD [t]hardened Pharaoh's heart, and he did not listen

to them, just as the LORD had spoken to Moses. *made strong*
13 Then the LORD said to Moses,
"Rise up early in the morning and
stand before Pharaoh and say to
him, 'Thus says the LORD, the God
of the Hebrews, "Let My people
go, that they may serve Me.
14 "For this time I will send all
My plagues [t]on you and your servants and your people, so that you
may know that there is no one like
Me in all the earth. *to your heart*
15 "For *if by* now I had put forth
My hand and struck you and your
people with pestilence, you would
then have been cut off from the
earth.
16 "But, indeed, for this cause I
have allowed you to [t]remain, in order to show you My power, and in
order to proclaim My name
through all the earth. *stand*
17 "Still you exalt yourself
against My people [t]by not letting
them go. *so as not to let*
18 "Behold, about this time tomorrow, I will send a very heavy
hail, such as has not been *seen* in
Egypt from the day it was
founded until now. *cause to rain*
19 "Now therefore send, bring
[r]your livestock and whatever you
have in the field to safety. Every
man and beast that is found in the
field and is not brought home,
when the hail comes down on
them, will die." ' " Ex. 9:6
20 The one among the servants
of Pharaoh who feared the word
of the LORD made his servants and
his livestock flee into the houses;
21 but he who paid no regard to
the word of the LORD left his servants and his livestock in the field.
22 Now the LORD said to Moses,
"Stretch out your hand toward
the sky, that [t]hail may fall on all
the land of Egypt, on man and on
beast and on every plant of the
field, throughout the land of
Egypt." *there may be hail*
23 And Moses stretched out his
staff toward the sky, and the LORD
sent thunder and hail, and fire ran
down to the earth. And the LORD
rained hail on the land of Egypt.
24 So there was hail, and fire
flashing continually in the midst
of the hail, very severe, such as
had not been in all the land of
Egypt since it became a nation.
25 And [r]the hail struck all that
was in the field through all the
land of Egypt, both man and
beast; the hail also struck every
plant of the field and shattered every tree of the field. Ex. 9:19
26 [r]Only in the land of Goshen,
where the sons of Israel *were*,
there was no hail. Ex. 8:22
27 Then Pharaoh sent for Moses
and Aaron, and said to them, "I
have sinned this time; the LORD is
the righteous one, and I and my
people are the wicked ones.
28 "Make supplication to the
LORD, for there has been enough
of God's [t]thunder and hail; and I
will let you go, and you shall stay
no longer." *sounds*
29 And Moses said to him, "As
soon as I go out of the city, I will
spread out my [t]hands to the LORD;
the [t]thunder will cease, and there
will be hail no longer, that you
may know that the earth is the
LORD'S. *palms • sounds*
30 "But as for you and your ser-

vants, I know that you do not yet [a]fear the LORD God." *reverence*

31 (Now the flax and the barley were ruined, for the barley was in the ear and the flax was in bud.

32 But the wheat and the spelt were not [t]ruined, for they *ripen* late.) *smitten*

33 So Moses went out of the city from Pharaoh, and spread out his [t]hands to the LORD; and the [t]thunder and the hail ceased, and rain no longer poured on the earth. *palms* · *sounds*

34 But when Pharaoh saw that the rain and the hail and the [t]thunder had ceased, he sinned again and [t]hardened his heart, he and his servants. *sounds* · *made heavy*

35 And Pharaoh's heart was [t]hardened, and he did not let the sons of Israel go, just as the LORD had spoken through Moses. *strong*

CHAPTER 10

THEN the LORD said to Moses, "Go to Pharaoh, for I have [8]hardened his heart and the heart of his servants, that I may perform these signs of Mine among them,

2 and [r]that you may tell in the [t]hearing of your son, and of your grandson, how I made a mockery of the Egyptians, and how I [t]performed My signs among them; that you may know that I am the LORD." Ps. 44:1 · *ears* · *put*

3 And Moses and Aaron went to Pharaoh and said to him, "Thus says the LORD, the God of the Hebrews, 'How long will you refuse to [r]humble yourself before Me? [r]Let My people go, that they may serve Me. James 4:10; 1 Pet. 5:6 · Ex. 4:23

[8]Lit., *made heavy*

4 'For if you refuse to let My people go, behold, tomorrow I will bring locusts into your territory.

5 'And they shall cover the surface of the land, so that no one shall be able to see the land. [r]They shall also eat the rest of what has escaped—what is left to you from the hail—and they shall eat every tree which sprouts for you out of the field. Joel 1:4; 2:25

6 'Then your houses shall be filled, and the houses of all your servants and the houses of all the Egyptians, *something* which neither your fathers nor your grandfathers have seen, from the day that they [t]came upon the earth until this day.' " And he turned and went out from Pharaoh. *were*

7 And Pharaoh's servants said to him, "How long will this man be a snare to us? Let the men go, that they may serve the LORD their God. Do you not [t]realize that Egypt is destroyed?" *know*

8 So Moses and Aaron were brought back to Pharaoh, and he said to them, "Go, serve the LORD your God! [t]Who are the ones that are going?" *Who and who are*

9 And Moses said, "We shall go with our young and our old; with our sons and our daughters, with our flocks and our herds we will go, for we [t]must hold a feast to the LORD." *have a feast*

10 Then he said to them, "Thus may the LORD be with you, [t]if ever I let you and your little ones go! Take heed, for evil is [t]in your mind. *when I* · *before your face*

11 "Not so! Go now, the men *among you*, and serve the LORD, for [t]that is what you desire." So

they were driven out from Pharaoh's presence. *you desire it*
12 Then the LORD said to Moses,
"Stretch[r] out your hand over the
land of Egypt for the locusts, that
they may come up on the land of
Egypt, and [r]eat every plant of the
land, *even* all that the hail has
left." Ex. 7:19 • Ex. 10:5, 15
13 So Moses stretched out his
staff over the land of Egypt, and
the LORD directed an east wind on
the land all that day and all that
night; and when it was morning,
the east wind brought the locusts.
14 And the locusts came up
over all the land of Egypt and settled in all the territory of Egypt;
they were very numerous. There
had never been so *many* locusts,
nor would there be so *many* again.
15 For they covered the surface
of the whole land, so that the land
was darkened; and they [r]ate every
plant of the land and all the fruit
of the trees that the hail had left.
Thus nothing green was left on
tree or plant of the field through
all the land of Egypt. Ps. 105:34f.
16 Then Pharaoh hurriedly
called for Moses and Aaron, and
he said, "I have sinned against the
LORD your God and against you.
17 "Now therefore, please forgive my sin only this once, and
make supplication to the LORD
your God, that He would only remove this death from me."
18 And [r]he went out from Pharaoh and made supplication to the
LORD. Ex. 8:30
19 So the LORD shifted *the wind*
to a very strong west wind which
took up the locusts and drove
them into the [9]Red Sea; not one locust was left in all the territory of
Egypt.
20 But the LORD [t]hardened Pharaoh's heart, and he did not let the
sons of Israel go. *made strong*
21 Then the LORD said to Moses,
"Stretch out your hand toward
the sky, that there may be darkness over the land of Egypt, even
a darkness which may be felt."
22 So Moses stretched out his
hand toward the sky, and there
was [r]thick darkness in all the land
of Egypt for three days. Ps. 105:28
23 They did not see one another,
nor did anyone rise from his place
for three days, but all the sons of
Israel had light in their dwellings.
24 Then Pharaoh called to
Moses, and said, "Go, serve the
LORD; only let your flocks and
your herds be detained. Even your
little ones may go with you."
25 But Moses said, "You must
also let us have sacrifices and
burnt offerings, that we may sacrifice *them* to the LORD our God.
26 "Therefore,[r] our livestock, too,
will go with us; not a hoof will be
left behind, for we shall take some
of them to serve the LORD our
God. And until we arrive there, we
ourselves do not know with what
we shall serve the LORD." Ex. 10:9
27 But the LORD [t]hardened Pharaoh's heart, and he was not willing to let them go. *made strong*
28 Then Pharaoh said to him,
"Get away from me! [t]Beware, do
not see my face again, for in the
day you see my face you shall
die!" *Take heed to yourself*
29 And Moses said, "You are
right; [r]I shall never see your face
again!" Ex. 11:8; Heb. 11:27

[9]Lit., *Sea of Reeds*

CHAPTER 11

NOW the LORD said to Moses, "One more plague I will bring on Pharaoh and on Egypt; after that he will let you go from here. When he lets you go, he will surely drive you out from here completely.

2 "Speak now in the hearing of the people that each man ask from his neighbor and each woman from her neighbor for articles of silver and articles of gold."

3 And the LORD gave the people favor in the sight of the Egyptians. Furthermore, the man Moses *himself* was greatly esteemed in the land of Egypt, *both* in the sight of Pharaoh's servants and in the sight of the people.

4 And Moses said, "Thus says the LORD, 'About midnight I am going out into the midst of Egypt,

5 and all the first-born in the land of Egypt shall die, from the first-born of the Pharaoh who sits on his throne, even to the first-born of the slave girl who is behind the millstones; all the first-born of the cattle as well.

6 'Moreover, there shall be a great cry in all the land of Egypt, such as there has not been *before* and such as shall never be again.

7 'But against any of the sons of Israel a dog shall not *even* [t]bark, whether against man or beast, that you may understand how the LORD makes a distinction between Egypt and Israel.' *sharpen his tongue*

8 "And all these your servants will come down to me and bow themselves before me, saying, 'Go out, you and all the people who [t]follow you,' and after that I will go out." And he went out from Pharaoh in hot anger. *are at your feet*

9 Then the LORD said to Moses, "Pharaoh will not listen to you, so that My wonders will be multiplied in the land of Egypt."

10 And Moses and Aaron performed all these wonders before Pharaoh; yet [r]the LORD [t]hardened Pharaoh's heart, and he did not let the sons of Israel go out of his land. John 12:40 • *made strong*

CHAPTER 12

NOW the LORD said to Moses and Aaron in the land of Egypt,

2 "This[r] month shall be the beginning of months for you; it is to be the first month of the year to you. Ex. 13:4; 23:15;34:18

3 "Speak to all the congregation of Israel, saying, 'On the tenth of this month they are each one to take a lamb for themselves, according to their fathers' households, a lamb for each household.

4 'Now if the household is too small for a [a]lamb, then he and his neighbor nearest to his house are to take one according to the number of persons *in them;* according to what each man should eat, you are to divide the lamb. *kid*

5 'Your [a]lamb shall be [r]an unblemished male a year old; you may take it from the sheep or from the goats. *kid* • Heb. 9:14

6 'And you shall keep it until the [r]fourteenth day of the same month, then the whole assembly of the congregation of Israel is to kill it at twilight. Ex. 12:14, 17

7 'Moreover,[r] they shall take some of the blood and put it on

the two doorposts and on the lintel[t] of the houses in which they eat
it. Ex. 12:22 · *upon*
8 'And they shall eat the flesh
that *same* night, roasted with fire,
and they shall eat it with unleavened bread and bitter herbs.
9 'Do not eat any of it raw or
boiled at all with water, but rather
roasted with fire, *both* its head
and its legs along with its entrails.
10 'And[r] you shall not leave any
of it over until morning, but whatever is left of it until morning, you
shall burn with fire. Ex. 16:19
11 'Now you shall eat it in this
manner: *with* your loins girded,
your sandals on your feet, and
your staff in your hand; and you
shall eat it in haste—it is the
LORD's Passover.
12 'For[r] I will go through the land
of Egypt on that night, and will
strike down all the first-born in
the land of Egypt, both man and
beast; and against all the gods of
Egypt I will execute judgments—I
am the LORD. Ex. 11:4, 5
13 'And the blood shall be a sign
for you on the houses where you
live; and when I see the blood I
will pass over you, and no plague
will befall you to destroy *you*
when I strike the land of Egypt.
14 'Now this day will be a memorial to you, and you shall celebrate it *as* a feast to the LORD;
throughout your generations you
are to celebrate it *as*[a] a permanent
ordinance. *an eternal*
15 'Seven days you shall eat unleavened bread, but on the first
day you shall remove leaven from
your houses; for whoever eats
anything leavened from the first
day until the seventh day, that
person shall be cut off from Israel.
16 'And on the first day you shall
have a holy assembly, and *an-*
other holy assembly on the seventh day; no work at all shall be
done on them, except what must
be eaten by every person, that
alone may be prepared by you.
17 'You shall also observe the
Feast of Unleavened Bread, for on
this very day I brought your hosts
out of the land of Egypt; therefore
you shall observe this day
throughout your generations as a
[a]permanent ordinance. *eternal*
18 'In[r] the first *month*, on the
fourteenth day of the month at
evening, you shall eat unleavened
bread, until the twenty-first day of
the month at evening. Ex. 12:2
19 'Seven[r] days there shall be no
leaven found in your houses; for
whoever eats what is leavened,
that[t] person shall be cut off from
the congregation of Israel,
whether *he is* an alien or a native
of the land. Ex. 12:15 · *soul*
20 'You shall not eat anything
leavened; in all your dwellings
you shall eat unleavened bread.' "
21 Then Moses called for all the
elders of Israel, and said to them,
"Go and take for yourselves
lambs according to your families,
and slay the Passover *lamb*.
22 "And you shall take a bunch
of hyssop and dip it in the blood
which is in the basin, and [t]apply
some of the blood that is in the basin to the lintel and the two doorposts; and none of you shall go
outside the door of his house until
morning. *cause to touch*
23 "For the LORD will pass

through to smite the Egyptians;
and when He sees the blood on
the lintel and on the two doorposts, the LORD will pass over the
door and will [r]not allow the destroyer to come in to your houses
to smite *you*. Rev. 7:3; 9:4
24 "And [r]you shall observe this
event as an ordinance for you and
your children forever. Ex. 12:14
25 "And it will come about when
you enter the land which the LORD
will give you, as He has promised,
that you shall observe this rite.
26 "And it will come about when
your children will say to you,
'What does this rite mean to you?'
27 that you shall say, 'It is a
Passover sacrifice to the LORD
who passed over the houses of the
sons of Israel in Egypt when He
smote the Egyptians, but spared
our homes.' " And the people
bowed low and worshiped.
28 Then the sons of Israel went
and did *so;* just as the LORD had
commanded Moses and Aaron, so
they did.
29 Now it came about at [r]mid-
night that [r]the LORD struck all the
first-born in the land of Egypt,
from the first-born of Pharaoh
who sat on his throne to the first-
born of the captive who was in the
dungeon, and all the first born of
cattle. Ex. 11:4, 5 • Num. 8:17
30 And Pharaoh arose in the
night, he and all his servants and
all the Egyptians; and there was [r]a
great cry in Egypt, for there was
no home where there was not
someone dead. Ex. 11:6
31 Then [r]he called for Moses and
Aaron at night and said, "Rise up,
get out from among my people,
both you and the sons of Israel;
and go, [a]worship the LORD, as you
have said. Ex. 8:8 • *serve*
32 "Take both your flocks and
your herds, as you have said, and
go, and bless me also."
33 And [r]the Egyptians urged the
people, to send them out of the
land in haste, for they said, "We
shall all be dead." Ex. 10:7
34 So the people took [r]their
dough before it was leavened,
with their kneading bowls bound
up in the clothes on their shoulders. Ex. 12:39
35 [r]Now the sons of Israel had
done according to the word of
Moses, for they had requested
from the Egyptians articles of silver and articles of gold, and clothing; Ex. 3:21, 22; Ps. 105:37
36 and the LORD had given the
people favor in the sight of the
Egyptians, so that they let them
have their request. Thus they
[r]plundered the Egyptians. Ex. 3:22
37 Now the sons of Israel journeyed from Rameses to Succoth,
about six hundred thousand men
on foot, aside from children.
38 And a mixed multitude also
went up with them, [t]along with
flocks and herds, a very large
number of livestock. *and*
39 And they baked the dough
which they had brought out of
Egypt into cakes of unleavened
bread. For it had not become leavened, since they were [r]driven out
of Egypt and could not delay, nor
had they [t]prepared any provisions
for themselves. Ex. 6:1 • *made*
40 Now the time that the sons
of Israel lived in Egypt was four
hundred and thirty years.

41 And it came about at the end of four hundred and thirty years, to[r] the very day, that[r] all the hosts of the LORD went out from the land of Egypt. Ex. 12:17 • Ex. 3:8

42 It is a night to be observed for the LORD for having brought them out from the land of Egypt; this night is for the LORD, to be observed by all the sons of Israel throughout their generations.

43 And the LORD said to Moses and Aaron, "This is the ordinance of[r] the Passover: no [10]foreigner is to eat of it; Ex. 12:11; Num. 9:14

44 but every man's[r] slave purchased with money, after you have circumcised him, then he may eat of it. Lev. 22:11

45 "A[r] sojourner or a hired servant shall not eat of it. Lev. 22:10

46 "It is to be eaten in a single house; you are not to bring forth any of the flesh outside of the house,[r] nor are you to break any bone of it. Num. 9:12; Ps. 34:20

47 "All the congregation of Israel are to[t] celebrate this. *do*

48 "But if a[t] stranger sojourns with you, and[t] celebrates the Passover to the LORD, let all his males be circumcised, and then let him come near to[t] celebrate it; and he shall be like a native of the land. But no uncircumcised person may eat of it. *sojourner • does • do*

49 "The[t] same law shall apply to the native as to the stranger who sojourns among you." *One law*

50 Then all the sons of Israel did *so;* they did just as the LORD had commanded Moses and Aaron.

51 And it came about on that same day that[r] the LORD brought the sons of Israel out of the land of Egypt by their hosts. Ex. 12:41

[10]Lit., *son of a stranger*

CHAPTER 13

THEN the LORD spoke to Moses, saying,

2 "Sanctify[r] to Me every firstborn, the first[t] offspring of every womb among the sons of Israel, both of man and beast; it belongs to Me." Num. 3:13 • *opening*

3 And Moses said to the people, "Remember this day in which you went out from Egypt, from the house of[t] slavery; for by a powerful hand the LORD brought you out from this place. And nothing leavened shall be eaten. *slaves*

4 "On this day in the month of Abib, you are about to go forth.

5 "And it shall be when the LORD[r] brings you to the land of the Canaanite, the Hittite, the Amorite, the Hivite and the Jebusite, which He swore to your fathers to give you, a land flowing with milk and honey, that you shall observe this rite in this month. Ex. 3:8, 17

6 "For[r] seven days you shall eat unleavened bread, and on the seventh day there shall be a feast to the LORD. Ex. 12:15-20

7 "Unleavened bread shall be eaten throughout the seven days; and[r] nothing leavened shall be seen among you, nor shall any leaven be seen[t] among you in all your borders. Ex. 12:19 • *to*

8 "And[r] you shall tell your son on that day, saying, 'It is because of what the LORD did for me when I came out of Egypt.' Ex. 10:2

9 "And it shall[t] serve as a sign to you on your hand, and as a re-

minder[t] on your forehead, that the
law of the LORD may be in your
mouth; for with a powerful hand
the LORD brought you out of
Egypt. *be for · between your eyes*
10 "Therefore, you shall [r]keep
this ordinance at its appointed
time from year to year. Ex. 13:5
11 "Now it shall come about
when [r]the LORD brings you to the
land of the Canaanite, as He
swore to you and to your fathers,
and gives it to you, Ex. 13:5
12 that you shall devote to the
LORD the first offspring of every
womb, and the first offspring of
every beast that you own; the
males belong to the LORD.
13 "But every first offspring of a
donkey you shall redeem with a
lamb, but if you do not redeem *it*,
then you shall break its neck; and
every first-born of man among
your sons you shall redeem.
14 "And it shall be when your
son asks you in time to come, saying, 'What is this?' then you shall
say to him, 'With a powerful hand
the LORD brought us out of Egypt,
from the house of [t]slavery. *slaves*
15 'And it came about, when
Pharaoh was stubborn about letting us go, that the [r]LORD killed every first-born in the land of Egypt,
both the first-born of man and the
first-born of beast. Therefore, I
sacrifice to the LORD the males,
the first [t]offspring of every womb,
but every first-born of my sons I
redeem.' Ex. 12:29 · *opening*
16 "So it shall [t]serve as a sign on
your hand, and as phylacteries on
your forehead, for with a [t]powerful
hand the LORD brought us out of
Egypt." *be for · strength of hand*
17 Now it came about when
Pharaoh had let the people go,
that God did not lead them by the
way of the land of the Philistines,
even though it was near; for God
said, "Lest the people change
their minds when they see war,
and they return to Egypt."
18 Hence God led the people
around by the way of the wilderness to the Red Sea; and the sons
of Israel went up in martial array
from the land of Egypt.
19 And Moses took the bones of
Joseph with him, for he had made
the sons of Israel solemnly swear,
saying, "God shall surely take
care of you; and you shall carry
my bones from here with you."
20 Then they set out from [r]Suc-
coth and camped in Etham on the
edge of the wilderness. Ex. 12:37
21 And the LORD was going before them in a pillar of cloud by
day to lead them on the way, and
in a pillar of fire by night to give
them light, that they might [t]travel
by day and by night. *go*
22 He [r]did not take away the pillar of cloud by day, nor the pillar
of fire by night, from before the
people. Neh. 9:19

CHAPTER 14

NOW the LORD spoke to Moses,
saying,
2 "Tell the sons of Israel to turn
back and camp before Pi-hahiroth, between Migdol and the sea;
you shall camp in front of Baal-
zephon, opposite it, by the sea.
3 "For Pharaoh will say of the
sons of Israel, 'They are wander-

ing aimlessly in the land; the wilderness has shut them in.'
4 "Thus I will harden Pharaoh's
heart, and he will chase after
them; and I will be honored
through Pharaoh and all his army,
and the Egyptians will know that I
am the LORD." And they did so.
5 When the king of Egypt was
told that the people had fled, Pharaoh and his servants had a
change of heart toward the people, and they said, "What is this
we have done, that we have let Israel go from serving us?"
6 So he made his chariot ready
and took his people with him;
7 and he took six hundred select chariots, and all the *other*
chariots of Egypt with officers
over all of them.
8 And the LORD[t] hardened the
heart of Pharaoh, king of Egypt,
and he chased after the sons of Israel as the sons of Israel were
going out boldly. *made strong*
9 Then[r] the Egyptians chased
after them *with* all the horses *and*
chariots of Pharaoh, his horsemen
and his army, and they overtook
them camping by the sea, beside
Pi-hahiroth, in front of Baal-zephon. Ex. 15:9; Josh. 24:6
10 And as Pharaoh drew near,
the sons of Israel looked, and behold, the Egyptians were marching after them, and they became
very frightened; so the sons of Israel cried out to the LORD.
11 Then[r] they said to Moses, "Is
it because there were no graves in
Egypt that you have taken us
away to die in the wilderness?
Why have you dealt with us in
this way,[t] bringing us out of
Egypt? Ex. 5:21 · *so as to bring*
12 "Is[r] this not the word that we
spoke to you in Egypt, saying,
'Leave[t] us alone that we may serve
the Egyptians'? For it would have
been better for us to serve the
Egyptians than to die in the wilderness." Ex. 6:9 · *Cease from us*
13 But Moses said to the people,
"Do not fear![a] Stand by and see the
salvation of the LORD which He
will accomplish for you today; for
the Egyptians whom you have
seen today, you will never see
them again forever. *Take your stand*
14 "The[r] LORD will fight for you
while you keep silent." Ex. 14:25
15 Then the LORD said to Moses,
"Why are you crying out to Me?
Tell the sons of Israel to go forward.
16 "And as for you, lift up your
staff and stretch out your hand
over the sea and divide it, and the
sons of Israel shall go through the
midst of the sea on dry land.
17 "And as for Me, behold, I will
harden the hearts of the Egyptians
so that they will go in after them;
and I will be honored through
Pharaoh and all his army, through
his chariots and his horsemen.
18 "Then[r] the Egyptians will
know that I am the LORD, when I
am honored through Pharaoh,
through his chariots and his
horsemen." Ex. 14:25
19 And[r] the angel of God, who
had been going before the camp of
Israel, moved and went behind
them; and the pillar of cloud
moved from before them and
stood behind them. Ex. 13:21, 22
20 So it came between the camp

of Egypt and the camp of Israel;
and there was the cloud along
with the darkness, yet it gave light
at night. Thus the one did not
come near the other all night.
21 Then Moses stretched out his
hand over the sea; and the LORD
[t]swept the sea *back* by a strong
east wind all night, and turned the
sea into dry land, so the waters
were divided. *caused to go*
22 And the sons of Israel [t]went
through the midst of the sea on
the dry land, and the waters *were*
like a wall to them on their right
hand and on their left. *entered the*
23 Then [r]the Egyptians took up
the pursuit, and all Pharaoh's
horses, his chariots and his horsemen went in after them into the
midst of the sea. Ex. 14:4, 17
24 And it came about at the
morning watch, that [r]the LORD
looked down on the [t]army of the
Egyptians[a] through the pillar of
fire and cloud and brought the
army of the Egyptians into confusion. Ex. 13:21 · *camp* · *in*
25 And He caused their chariot
wheels to swerve, and He made
them drive with difficulty; so the
Egyptians said, "Let us flee from
Israel, for the LORD is fighting for
them against the Egyptians."
26 Then the LORD said to Moses,
"Stretch [r]out your hand over the
sea so that the waters may come
back over the Egyptians, over
their chariots and their horsemen." Ex. 14:16
27 So Moses stretched out his
hand over the sea, and the sea returned to its normal state at daybreak, while the Egyptians were
fleeing [t]right into it; then the LORD
overthrew the Egyptians in the
midst of the sea. *to meet it*
28 And the waters returned and
covered the chariots and the
horsemen,[t] even Pharaoh's entire
army that had gone into the sea
after them; [r]not even one of them
remained. *in respect to* · Ps. 78:53
29 But the sons of Israel walked
on [r]dry land through the midst of
the sea, and the waters *were like* a
wall to them on their right hand
and on their left. Ex. 14:22; Ps. 66:6
30 Thus the LORD saved Israel
that day from the hand of the
Egyptians, and Israel saw the
Egyptians dead on the seashore.
31 And when Israel saw the
great [t]power which the LORD had
[t]used against the Egyptians, the
people feared the LORD, and they
believed in the LORD and in His
servant Moses. *hand* · *done*

CHAPTER 15

THEN Moses and the sons of Israel sang this song to the LORD,
and said,

"I will sing to the LORD, for
He is highly exalted;
The horse and its rider He
has hurled into the sea.
2 "The [r]LORD is my strength
and song, Ps. 18:1, 2
And He has become my sal-
vation;
This is my God, and I will
praise Him;
My father's God, and I will
extol Him.
3 "The LORD is a warrior;
The LORD is His name.
4 "Pharaoh's chariots and his

army He has cast into the sea;
And the choicest of his officers are [t]drowned in the [11]Red Sea. *sunk*
5 "The deeps cover them;
They went down into the depths like a stone.
6 "Thy right hand, O LORD, is majestic in power,
Thy right hand, O LORD, shatters the enemy.
7 "And in the greatness of Thine excellence Thou dost overthrow those who rise up against Thee;
Thou dost send forth Thy burning anger, *and* it consumes them as chaff.
8 "And at the blast of Thy nostrils the waters were piled up,
The flowing waters stood up like a heap;
The deeps were congealed in the heart of the sea.
9 "The enemy said, 'I will pursue, I will overtake, I will divide the spoil;
My [t]desire shall be gratified against them; *soul*
I will draw out my sword, my hand shall destroy them.'
10 "Thou didst blow with Thy wind, the sea covered them;
They sank like lead in the [a]mighty waters. *majestic*
11 "Who [r]is like Thee among the gods, O LORD? Ex. 8:10
Who is like Thee, majestic in holiness,
Awesome in praises, working wonders?
12 "Thou didst stretch out Thy right hand,
The earth swallowed them.
13 "In Thy lovingkindness Thou hast [r]led the people whom Thou hast redeemed;
In Thy strength Thou hast guided *them* to Thy holy habitation. Ps. 77:20
14 "The peoples have heard, they tremble;
Anguish has gripped the inhabitants of Philistia.
15 "Then the chiefs of Edom were dismayed;
The leaders of Moab, trembling grips them;
All the inhabitants of Canaan have melted away.
16 "Terror and dread fall upon them;
By the greatness of Thine arm they are motionless as stone;
Until Thy people pass over, O LORD,
Until the people pass over whom Thou [r]hast purchased. Titus 2:14
17 "Thou wilt bring them and [r]plant them in the mountain of Thine inheritance,
The place, O LORD, which Thou hast made for Thy dwelling, Ps. 44:2
The sanctuary, O Lord, which Thy hands have established.
18 "The [r]LORD shall reign forever and ever." Ps. 10:16

19 [r]For the horses of Pharaoh
with his chariots and his horsemen went into the sea, and the
LORD brought back the waters of
the sea on them; but the sons of

[11]Lit., *Sea of Reeds*

Israel walked on dry land through
the midst of the sea. Ex. 14:23, 28
20 And [r]Miriam the prophetess,
Aaron's sister, took the timbrel in
her hand, and all the women went
out after her with timbrels and
with [t]dancing. Ex. 2:4 • *dances*
21 And Miriam answered them,
"Sing to the LORD, for He is
highly exalted;
The horse and his rider He
has hurled into the sea."
22 Then Moses led Israel from
the Red Sea, and they went out
into the wilderness of Shur; and
they went three days in the wilderness and found no water.
23 And when they came to [r]Ma-
rah, they could not drink the waters [t]of Marah, for they were bitter; therefore it was named
[12]Marah. Ruth 1:20 • *from*
24 So the people [r]grumbled at
Moses, saying, "What shall we
drink?" Ex. 14:11; Ps. 106:13
25 Then he [r]cried out to the
LORD, and the LORD showed him a
tree; and he threw *it* into the waters, and the waters became
sweet. There He made for them a
statute and regulation, and there
He tested them. Ex. 14:10
26 And He said, [r]"If you will give
earnest heed to the voice of the
LORD your God, and do what is
right in His sight, and give ear to
His commandments, and keep all
His statutes, I will put none of the
diseases on you which I have put
on the Egyptians; for I, the LORD,
am your healer." Ex. 19:5, 6
27 Then they came to [r]Elim
where there *were* twelve springs
of water and seventy date palms,
and they camped there beside the
waters. Num. 33:9

CHAPTER 16

THEN they set out from Elim,
and all the congregation of the
sons of Israel came to the wilderness of Sin, which is between Elim
and Sinai, on the fifteenth day of
the second month after their departure from the land of Egypt.
2 And the whole congregation
of the sons of Israel [r]grumbled
against Moses and Aaron in the
wilderness. Ex. 14:11; 15:24
3 And the sons of Israel said to
them, "Would that we had died by
the LORD's hand in the land of
Egypt, when we sat by the pots of
meat, when we ate bread to the
full; for you have brought us out
into this wilderness to kill this
whole assembly with hunger."
4 Then the LORD said to Moses,
"Behold, I will rain bread from
heaven for you; and the people
shall go out and gather a day's
portion every day, that I may test
them, whether or not they will
walk in My [13]instruction.
5 "And it will come about on
the sixth day, when they prepare
what they bring in, it will be twice
as much as they gather daily."
6 So Moses and Aaron said to
all the sons of Israel, "At evening
[t]you [r]will know that the LORD has
brought you out of the land of
Egypt; *and you* • Ex. 6:7
7 and in the morning [t]you will
see the glory of the LORD, for He
hears your grumblings against the
LORD; and what are we, that you
grumble against us?" *and you*

[12]I.e., bitterness

[13]Or, *law*

8 And Moses said, "*This will happen* when the LORD gives you [a]meat to eat in the evening, and bread to the full in the morning; for the LORD hears your grumblings which you grumble against Him. And what are we? Your grumblings are not against us but against the LORD." *flesh*

9 Then Moses said to Aaron, "Say to all the congregation of the sons of Israel,[r] 'Come near before the LORD, for He has heard your grumblings.' " Num. 16:16

10 And it came about as Aaron spoke to the whole congregation of the sons of Israel, that they [t]looked toward the wilderness, and behold, the glory of the LORD appeared in the cloud. *turned*

11 And the LORD spoke to Moses, saying,

12 "I have heard the grumblings of the sons of Israel; speak to them, saying, 'At[t] twilight you shall eat meat, and in the morning you shall be filled with bread; and you shall know that I am the LORD your God.' " *Between the two evenings*

13 So it came about at evening that[r] the quails came up and covered the camp, and in the morning there was a layer of dew around the camp. Num. 11:31

14 When the layer of dew[t] evaporated, behold, on the surface of the wilderness there was a fine flake-like thing, fine as the frost on the ground. *had gone up*

15 When the sons of Israel saw *it*, they said to one another, "What is it?" For they did not know what it was. And Moses said to them, "It[r] is the bread which the LORD has given you to eat. John 6:31; 1 Cor. 10:3

16 "This is what the LORD has commanded, 'Gather of it every man as much as he should eat; you shall take an omer apiece according to the number of persons each of you has in his tent.' "

17 And the sons of Israel did so, and *some* gathered much and *some* little.

18 When they measured it with an omer, he who had gathered much had no excess, and he who had gathered little had no lack; every man gathered[t] as much as he should eat. *according to his eating*

19 And Moses said to them, "Let[r] no man leave any of it until morning." Ex. 12:10; 16:23

20 But they did not listen to Moses, and some left part of it until morning, and it bred worms and became foul; and Moses was angry with them.

21 And they gathered it morning by morning, every man as much as he should eat; but when the sun grew hot, it would melt.

22 [r]Now it came about on the sixth day they gathered twice as much bread, two omers for each one. When all the[r] leaders of the congregation came and told Moses, Ex. 16:5 • Ex. 34:31

23 then he said to them, "This is what the LORD[t] meant: Tomorrow is a sabbath observance, a holy sabbath to the LORD. Bake what you will bake and boil what you will boil, and all that is left over [t]put aside to be kept until morning." *spoke • lay up for you*

24 So they put it aside until morning, as Moses had ordered,

and it did not become foul, nor
was there any worm in it.
25 And Moses said, "Eat it today, for today is a sabbath to the
LORD; today you will not find it in
the field.
26 "Six days you shall gather it,
but on the seventh day, *the* sabbath, there will be none."
27 And it came about on the
seventh day that some of the people went out to gather, but they
found none.
28 Then the LORD said to Moses,
"How[r] long do you refuse to keep
My commandments and My [14]in-
structions? 2 Kin. 17:14; Ps. 78:10
29 "See, the LORD has given you
the sabbath; therefore He gives
you bread for two days on the
sixth day. Remain every man in
his place; let no man go out of his
place on the seventh day."
30 So the people rested on the
seventh day.
31 And the house of Israel
named it manna, and it was like
coriander seed, white; and its
taste was like wafers with honey.
32 Then Moses said, "This is
[t]what the LORD has commanded,
'Let an omerful of it be kept
throughout your generations, that
they may see the bread that I fed
you in the wilderness, when I
brought you out of the land of
Egypt.'" *the thing which*
33 And Moses said to Aaron,
"Take[r] a jar and put an omerful of
manna in it, and place it before
the LORD, to be kept throughout
your generations." Heb. 9:4
34 As the LORD commanded
Moses, so Aaron placed it before
the Testimony, to be kept.
35 And the sons of Israel ate the
manna forty years, until they
came to an inhabited land; they
ate the manna until they came to
the border of the land of Canaan.
36 (Now an omer is a tenth of
an ephah.)

CHAPTER 17

THEN all the congregation of the
sons of Israel journeyed by[t] stages
from the wilderness of Sin, according to the command of the
LORD, and camped at Rephidim,
and there was no water for the
people to drink. *their journeyings*
2 Therefore the people [r]quar-
reled with Moses and said, "Give
us water that we may drink." And
Moses said to them, "Why do you
quarrel with me?[r] Why do you test
the LORD?" Ex. 14:11 • 1 Cor. 10:9
3 But the people thirsted there
for water; and they grumbled
against Moses and said, "Why,
now, have you brought us up from
Egypt, to kill us and our children
and our livestock with thirst?"
4 So Moses cried out to the
LORD, saying, "What shall I do to
this people? A[r] little more and they
will stone me." Num. 14:10
5 Then the LORD said to Moses,
"Pass before the people and take
with you some of[r] the elders of Israel; and take in your hand your
staff with which you struck the
Nile, and go. Ex. 3:16, 18
6 "Behold, I will stand before
you there on the rock at[r] Horeb;
and[r] you shall strike the rock, and
water will come out of it, that the
people may drink." And Moses

[14]Or, *laws*

did so in the sight of the elders of Israel. Ex. 3:1 • 1 Cor. 10:4

7 And he named the place [15]Massah and [16]Meribah because of the quarrel of the sons of Israel, and because they[r]tested the LORD, saying, "Is the LORD among us, or not?" Num. 14:22; Deut. 33:8

8 Then Amalek came and fought against Israel at Rephidim.

9 So Moses said to [r]Joshua, "Choose men for us, and go out, fight against Amalek. Tomorrow I will station myself on the top of the hill with[r]the staff of God in my hand." Ex. 24:13 • Ex. 4:20

10 And Joshua did as Moses told him, and fought against Amalek; and Moses, Aaron, and Hur went up to the top of the hill.

11 So it came about when Moses held his hand up, that Israel prevailed, and when he let his hand down, Amalek prevailed.

12 But Moses' hands were heavy. Then they took a stone and put it under him, and he sat on it; and Aaron and Hur[r]supported his hands, one on one side and one on the other. Thus his hands were steady until the sun set. Is. 35:3

13 So Joshua [t]overwhelmed Amalek and his people with the edge of the sword. *weakened*

14 Then the LORD said to Moses, "Write this in a book as a memorial, and recite it to Joshua, that I will utterly blot out the memory of Amalek from under heaven."

15 And Moses built an altar, and named it The LORD is My Banner;

16 and he said, "The[r]LORD has sworn; the LORD will have war against Amalek from generation to generation." Gen. 22:16

[15]I.e., test [16]I.e., quarrel

CHAPTER 18

NOW [r]Jethro, the priest of Midian, Moses' father-in-law, heard of all that God had done for Moses and for Israel His people, how the LORD had brought Israel out of Egypt. Ex. 2:16, 18; 3:1

2 And Jethro, Moses' father-in-law, took Moses' wife Zipporah, after he had sent her away,

3 and her[r]two sons, of whom one was named Gershom, for he said, "I have been[r]a sojourner in a foreign land." Acts 7:29 • Ex. 2:22

4 And [t]the other was named Eliezer, for *he said,* "The God of my father was my help, and delivered me from the sword of Pharaoh." *the name of the other was*

5 Then Jethro, Moses' father-in-law, came with his sons and his wife to Moses[t]in the wilderness where he was camped, at [r]the mount of God. *unto* • Ex. 4:27

6 And he[t]sent word to Moses, "I, your father-in-law Jethro, am coming to you with your wife and her two sons with her." *said*

7 Then Moses went out to meet his father-in-law, and he bowed down and kissed him; and they asked each other of their welfare, and went into the tent.

8 And Moses told his father-in-law all that the LORD had done to Pharaoh and to the Egyptians[r]for Israel's sake, all the hardship that had befallen them on the journey, and *how* the LORD had delivered them. Ex. 4:23; 7:4, 5

9 And Jethro rejoiced over all the goodness which the LORD had done to Israel, in delivering them from the hand of the Egyptians.

10 So Jethro said, "Blessed be the LORD who delivered you from the hand of the Egyptians and from the hand of Pharaoh, *and* who delivered the people from under the hand of the Egyptians.

11 "Now I know that the LORD is greater than all the gods; indeed, it was proven when they dealt proudly against the people."

12 Then Jethro, Moses' father-in-law, took a burnt offering and sacrifices for God, and Aaron came with all the elders of Israel to eat[t]a meal with Moses' father-in-law before God. *bread*

13 And it came about the next day that Moses sat to judge the people, and the people stood about Moses from the morning until the evening.

14 Now when Moses' father-in-law saw all that he was doing for the people, he said, "What is this thing that you are doing for the people? Why do you alone sit *as judge* and all the people stand about you from morning until evening?"

15 And Moses said to his father-in-law, "Because the people come to me to inquire of God.

16 "When they have a [t]dispute,[r] it comes to me, and I judge between a man and his neighbor, and make known the statutes of God and His laws." *matter* • Ex. 24:14

17 And Moses' father-in-law said to him, "The thing that you are doing is not good.

18 "You will surely wear out, both yourself and [t]these people who are with you, for the[t]task is too heavy for you; you cannot do it alone. *this* • *matter*

19 "Now listen to[t]me: I shall give you counsel, and God be with you. You be the people's representative before God, and you bring the [t]disputes to God, *my voice* • *matters*

20 then teach them the statutes and the laws, and make known to them the way in which they are to walk, and the work they are to do.

21 "Furthermore, you shall[t]select out of all the people able men who fear God, men of truth, those who hate dishonest gain; and you shall place *these* over them, *as* leaders of thousands, [t]of hundreds, [t]of fifties and [t]of tens. *see* • *leaders of*

22 "And let them judge the people at all times; and let it be[r]that every major [t]dispute they will bring to you, but every minor dispute they themselves will judge. So it will be easier for you, and they will bear *the burden* with you. Deut. 1:17, 18 • *matter*

23 "If you do this thing and God *so* commands you, then you will be able to[t]endure, and all[t]these people also will go to[t]their place in peace." *stand* • *this* • *his*

24 So Moses listened[t]to his father-in-law, and did all that he had said. *to the voice of*

25 And Moses chose able men out of all Israel, and made them heads over the people, leaders of thousands, [t]of hundreds, [t]of fifties and [t]of tens. *leaders of*

26 And they judged the people at all times; the difficult[t]dispute they would bring to Moses, but every minor [t]dispute they themselves would judge. *matter*

27 Then Moses bade his father-in-law farewell, and he went his way into his own land.

CHAPTER 19

IN the third month after the sons
of Israel had gone out of the land
of Egypt, on that very day they
came into the wilderness of Sinai.
2 When they set out from
Rephidim, they came to the wilderness of Sinai, and camped in
the wilderness; and there Israel
camped in front of the mountain.
3 And Moses went up to God,
and[r] the LORD called to him from
the mountain, saying, "Thus you
shall say to the house of Jacob
and tell the sons of Israel: Ex. 3:4
4 'You yourselves have seen
what I did to the Egyptians, and
how I bore you on eagles' wings,
and brought you to Myself.
5 'Now then, if you will indeed
obey My voice and keep My covenant, then you shall be My [17]own
possession among all the peoples,
for all the earth is Mine;
6 and you shall be to Me[r] a
kingdom of priests and a holy nation.' These are the words that
you shall speak to the sons of Israel." 1 Pet. 2:5, 9; Rev. 1:6; 5:10
7 So Moses came and called
the elders of the people, and set
before them all these words which
the LORD had commanded him.
8 [r]And all the people answered
together and said, "All that the
LORD has spoken we will do!" And
Moses brought back the words of
the people to the LORD. Ex. 4:31
9 And the LORD said to Moses,
"Behold, I shall come to you in a
thick cloud, in order that the people may hear when I speak with
you, and may also believe in you
forever." Then Moses told the
words of the people to the LORD.
10 The LORD also said to Moses,
"Go to the people and consecrate
them today and tomorrow, and let
them wash their garments;
11 and let them be ready for the
third day, for on the third day the
LORD will come down on Mount
Sinai in the sight of all the people.
12 "And you shall set bounds for
the people all around, saying, 'Beware that you do not go up on the
mountain or touch the border of
it; whoever touches the mountain
shall surely be put to death.
13 'No hand shall touch him, but
he shall surely be stoned or [18]shot
through; whether beast or man, he
shall not live.' When the ram's
horn sounds a long blast, they
shall come up to the mountain."
14 So Moses went down from
the mountain to the people and
consecrated the people, and they
washed their garments.
15 And he said to the people,
"Be ready for the third day; do not
go near a woman."
16 So it came about on the third
day, when it was morning, that
there were thunder and lightning
flashes and a thick cloud upon the
mountain and a very loud trumpet
sound, so that all the people who
were in the camp trembled.
17 And Moses brought the people out of the camp to meet God,
and they stood at the[t] foot of the
mountain. *lower part*
18 Now Mount Sinai *was* all in
smoke because the LORD descended upon it in fire; and its
smoke ascended like the smoke of
a furnace, and the whole mountain[a] quaked violently. *trembled*

[17]Or, *special treasure*

[18]I.e., with arrows

19 When the sound of the trumpet grew louder and louder,
Moses spoke and God answered
him with[t]thunder. *a sound*
20 [r]And the LORD came down on
Mount Sinai, to the top of the
mountain; and the LORD called
Moses to the top of the mountain,
and Moses went up. Neh. 9:13
21 Then the LORD spoke to
Moses, "Go down,[t] warn the people, lest they break through to the
LORD to gaze, and many of them
[t]perish. ***testify to • fall***
22 "And also let the[r]priests who
come near to the LORD consecrate
themselves, lest the LORD break
out against them." Ex. 19:24
23 And Moses said to the LORD,
"The people cannot come up to
Mount Sinai, for Thou didst warn
us, saying, 'Set bounds about the
mountain and consecrate it.' "
24 Then the LORD said to him,
"Go[t] down and come up *again*,
you and Aaron with you; but do
not let the[r]priests and the people
break through to come up to the
LORD, lest He break forth upon
them." *Go, descend* • Ex. 19:22
25 So Moses went down to the
people and told them.

CHAPTER 20

THEN God spoke all these
words, saying,
2 "I am the LORD your God, who
brought you out of the land of
Egypt, out of the house of slavery.
3 "You[r]shall have no other gods
[19]before Me. Deut. 6:14
4 "You shall not make for yourself [20]an idol, or any likeness of
what is in heaven above or on the
earth beneath or in the water under the earth.
5 "You[r] shall not worship them
or serve them; for I, the LORD your
God, am a[r]jealous God, visiting
the iniquity of the fathers on the
children, on the third and the
fourth generations of those who
hate Me, Josh. 23:7 • Nah. 1:2
6 but showing lovingkindness
to thousands, to those who love
Me and keep My commandments.
7 "You[r]shall not take the name
of the LORD your God in vain, for
the LORD will not[a]leave him unpunished who takes His name in
vain. Lev. 19:12 • *hold him guiltless*
8 "Remember[r]the sabbath day,
to keep it holy. Ex. 23:12
9 "Six[r]days you shall labor and
do all your work, Ex. 34:21
10 but the seventh day is a sabbath of the LORD your God; *in it*
you shall not do any work, you or
your son or your daughter, your
male or your female servant or
your cattle or your sojourner who
[t]stays with you. *is in your gates*
11 "For[r] in six days the LORD
made the heavens and the earth,
the sea and all that is in them, and
rested on the seventh day; therefore the LORD blessed the sabbath
day and made it holy. Gen. 2:2, 3
12 "Honor[r]your father and your
mother, that your days may be
prolonged in the land which the
LORD your God gives you. Lev. 19:3
13 "You shall not murder.
14 "You[r]shall not commit adultery. Lev. 20:10; Deut. 5:18
15 "You shall not steal.
16 "You shall not bear false witness against your neighbor.
17 "You[r] shall not covet your

[19]Or, *besides Me* [20]Or, *a graven image*

neighbor's house; you shall not covet your neighbor's wife or his male servant or his female servant or his ox or his donkey or anything that belongs to your neighbor." Rom. 7:7; Eph. 5:3, 5

18 And all the people perceived the thunder and the lightning flashes and the sound of the trumpet and the mountain smoking; and when the people saw *it,* they trembled and stood at a distance.

19 [r]Then they said to Moses, "Speak[t] to us yourself and we will listen; but let not God speak to us, lest we die." Gal. 3:19 • *with*

20 And Moses said to the people, "Do[r] not be afraid; for God has come in order to test you, and in order that the fear of Him may[t] remain with you, so that you may not sin." Ex. 14:13 • *be before*

21 So the people stood at a distance, while Moses approached the thick cloud where God *was.*

22 Then the LORD said to Moses, "Thus you shall say to the sons of Israel, 'You yourselves have seen that[r] I have spoken[t] to you from heaven. Deut. 4:36; 5:24 • *with*

23 'You[r] shall not make *other gods* besides Me; gods of silver or gods of gold, you shall not make for yourselves. Ex. 20:3

24 'You shall make[r] an altar of earth for Me, and you shall sacrifice on it your burnt offerings and your peace offerings, your sheep and your oxen; in every place where I cause My name to be remembered, I will come to you and bless you. Ex. 20:25; 27:1-8

25 'And if you make an altar of stone for Me, you shall not build it of cut stones, for if you wield your tool on it, you will profane it.

26 'And you shall not go up by steps to My altar, that[r] your nakedness may not be exposed on it.' Ex. 28:42, 43

CHAPTER 21

"NOW these are the ordinances which you are to set before them.

2 "If you buy a Hebrew slave, he shall serve for six years; but on the seventh he shall go out as a free man without payment.

3 "If he comes[t] alone, he shall go out alone; if he is the husband of a wife, then his wife shall go out with him. *by himself*

4 "If his master gives him a wife, and she bears him sons or daughters, the wife and her children shall belong to her master, and he shall go out alone.

5 "But[r] if the slave plainly says, 'I love my master, my wife and my children; I will not go out as a free man,' Deut. 15:16, 17

6 then his master shall bring him to [21]God, then he shall bring him to the door or the doorpost. And his master shall pierce his ear with an awl; and he shall serve him permanently.

7 "And if a man sells his daughter as a female slave, she is not to go free as the male slaves do.

8 "If she is[t] displeasing in the eyes of her master who designated her for himself, then he shall let her be redeemed. He does not have authority to sell her to a foreign people because of his unfairness to her. *bad*

9 "And if he designates her for

[21] Or, *the judges who acted in God's name*

his son, he shall deal with her according to the custom of daughters.
10 "If he takes to himself another
woman, he may not reduce her
[t]food, her clothing, or[r] her conjugal
rights. *flesh* • 1 Cor. 7:3, 5
11 "And if he will not do these
three *things* for her, then she shall
go out for nothing, without *payment of* money.
12 "He[r] who strikes a man so that
he dies shall surely be put to
death. Gen. 9:6; Lev. 24:17
13 "But if he did not lie in wait
for him, but God let *him* fall into
his hand, then I will appoint you a
place to which he may flee.
14 "If,[r] however, a man acts presumptuously toward his neighbor,
so as to kill him craftily, you are
to take him *even* from My altar,
that he may die. Deut. 19:11, 12
15 "And he who strikes his father or his mother shall surely be
put to death.
16 "And he who [t]kidnaps a man,
whether he sells him or he is
found in his possession, shall
surely be put to death. *steals*
17 "And[r] he who curses his father
or his mother shall surely be put
to death. Lev. 20:9; Prov. 20:20
18 "And if men have a quarrel
and one strikes the other with a
stone or with *his* fist, and he does
not die but remains in bed;
19 if he gets up and walks
around outside on his staff, then
he who struck him shall go unpunished; he shall only pay for his
loss of time, and shall take care of
him until he is completely healed.
20 "And if a man strikes his male
or female slave with a rod and he
dies [t]at his hand, he shall [t]be punished. *under* • *suffer vengeance*
21 "If, however, he survives a
day or two, no vengeance shall be
taken; for he is his property.
22 "And *if* men struggle with
each other and strike a woman
with child so that she has a miscarriage, yet there is no *further* injury, he shall surely be fined as
the woman's husband [t]may demand of him; and he shall pay as
the judges *decide.* *lays on him*
23 "But if there is *any further* injury,[r] then you shall appoint *as a
penalty* life for life, Lev. 24:19
24 eye for eye, tooth for tooth,
hand for hand, foot for foot,
25 burn for burn, wound for
wound,[t] bruise for bruise. *welt*
26 "And if a man strikes the eye
of his male or female slave, and
destroys it, he shall let him go free
on account of his eye.
27 "And if he[t] knocks out a tooth
of his male or female slave, he
shall let him go free on account of
his tooth. *causes to fall*
28 "And if an ox gores a man or a
woman to death, [r]the ox shall
surely be stoned and its flesh shall
not be eaten; but the owner of the
ox shall go unpunished. Gen. 9:5
29 "If, however, an ox was previously in the habit of goring, and
its owner has been warned, yet he
does not confine it, and it kills a
man or a woman, the ox shall be
stoned and its owner also shall be
put to death.
30 "If a ransom is [t]demanded of
him, then he shall give for the redemption of his life whatever is
demanded of him. *laid on him*
31 "Whether it gores a son or a

daughter, it shall be done to him
according to the same rule.
32"If the ox gores a male or female slave, the owner shall give
his *or her* master thirty shekels of
silver, and the ox shall be stoned.
33"And if a man opens a pit, or
[t]digs a pit and does not cover it
over, and an ox or a donkey falls
into it, *if a man digs*
34 the owner of the pit shall
make restitution; he shall [t]give
money to its owner, and the dead
animal shall become his. *give back*
35"And if one man's ox hurts
another's so that it dies, then they
shall sell the live ox and divide its
price equally; and also they shall
divide the dead *ox.*
36"Or *if* it is known that the ox
was previously in the habit of goring, yet its owner has not confined
it, he shall surely pay ox for ox,
and the dead *animal* shall become
his.

CHAPTER 22

"IF a man steals an ox or a
sheep, and slaughters it or sells it,
he shall pay five oxen for the ox
and four sheep for the sheep.
2"If the thief is caught while
breaking in, and is struck so that
he dies, there will be no bloodguiltiness on his account.
3"*But* if the sun has risen on
him, there will be bloodguiltiness
on his account. He shall surely
make restitution; if he owns nothing, then he shall be [r]sold for his
theft. Matt. 18:25
4"If what he stole is actually
found alive in his [t] possession,
whether an ox or a donkey or a
sheep, he shall pay double. *hand*
5"If a man lets a field or vineyard be grazed *bare* and lets his
animal loose so that it grazes in
another man's field, he shall make
restitution from the best of his
own field and the best of his own
vineyard.
6"If a fire breaks out and
spreads to thorn bushes, so that
stacked grain or the standing
grain or the field *itself* is consumed, he who started the fire
shall surely make restitution.
7"If [r]a man gives his neighbor
money or goods to keep *for him,*
and it is stolen from the man's
house, if the thief is [t]caught, he
shall pay double. Lev. 6:1-7 • *found*
8"If the thief is not [t] caught,
then the owner of the house shall
appear before the judges, *to* determine whether he laid his hands on
his neighbor's property. *found*
9"For every breach of trust,
whether it is for ox, for donkey,
for sheep, for clothing, *or* for any
lost thing about which one says,
'This is it,' the case of both parties
shall come before the judges; he
whom the judges condemn shall
pay double to his neighbor.
10"If a man gives his neighbor a
donkey, an ox, a sheep, or any animal to keep *for him,* and it dies or
is hurt or is driven away while no
one is looking,
11 an [r]oath before the LORD shall
be made by the two of them, [t]that
he has not laid hands on his neighbor's property; and its owner shall
accept *it,* and he shall not make
restitution. Heb. 6:16 • *whether*
12"But if it is actually stolen

from him, he shall make restitution to its owner.
13 "If it is all torn to pieces, let
him bring it as evidence; he shall
not make restitution for what has
been torn to pieces.
14 "And if a man[t] borrows *anything* from his neighbor, and it is
injured or dies while its owner is
not with it, he shall make full restitution. *asks*
15 "If its owner is with it, he shall
not make restitution; if it is hired,
it came for its hire.
16 "And[r] if a man seduces a virgin who is not engaged, and lies
with her, he must pay a dowry for
her *to be* his wife. Deut. 22:28, 29
17 "If her father absolutely refuses to give her to him, he shall
[t]pay money equal to the dowry for
virgins. *weigh out silver*
18 "You shall not allow a[r] sorcer-
ess to live. Lev. 19:31; 20:6, 27
19 "Whoever lies with an animal
shall surely be put to death.
20 "He who sacrifices to[t] any god,
other than to the LORD alone, shall
be utterly destroyed. *the gods*
21 "And[r] you shall not wrong a
stranger or oppress him, for you
were strangers in the land of
Egypt. Ex. 23:9; Lev. 19:33, 34
22 "You[r] shall not afflict any
widow or orphan. Jer. 7:6, 7
23 "If you afflict him at all, *and* if
he does cry out to Me,[r] I will surely
hear his cry; James 5:4
24 and My anger will be kindled, and I will kill you with the
sword;[r] and your wives shall become widows and your children
fatherless. Ps. 109:2, 9
25 "If you lend money to My people, to the poor among you, you
are not to act as a creditor to him;
you shall not charge him interest.
26 "If you ever take your neighbor's cloak[r] as a pledge, you are to
return it to him before the sun
sets, Deut. 24:6, 10-13
27 for that is his only covering;
it is his cloak for his[t] body. What
else shall he sleep in? And it shall
come about that[r] when he cries out
to Me, I will hear *him*, for I am
gracious. *skin* • Ex. 22:23
28 "You shall not curse God, nor
curse a ruler of your people.
29 "You shall not delay *the offering from* your harvest and your
vintage. The first-born of your
sons you shall give to Me.
30 "You[r] shall do the same with
your oxen *and* with your sheep. It
shall be with its mother seven
days; on the eighth day you shall
give it to Me. Deut. 15:19
31 "And[r] you shall be holy men to
Me, therefore you shall not eat
any flesh torn to pieces in the
field; you shall throw it to the
dogs. Ex. 19:6; Lev. 11:44

CHAPTER 23

"YOU shall not bear a false report; do not join your hand with a
wicked man to be a[r] malicious witness. Prov. 19:5; Acts 6:11
2 "You shall not follow[t] a multitude in doing evil, nor shall you
[a]testify in a dispute so as to turn
aside after a multitude in order to
pervert *justice*; *many men* • *answer*
3 nor shall you[t] be partial to a
poor man in his dispute. *honor*
4 "If you meet your enemy's ox
or his donkey wandering away,
you shall surely return it to him.

5 "If [r]you see the donkey of one
who hates you lying *helpless* under its load, you shall refrain from
leaving it to him, you shall surely
release *it* with him. Deut. 22:4
6 "You [r]shall not pervert the justice *due* to your needy *brother* in
his dispute. Ex. 23,2, 3; Lev. 19:15
7 "Keep [r]far from a false charge,
and do not kill the innocent or the
righteous, for I will not acquit the
guilty. Ex. 20:16; Ps. 119:29
8 "And you shall not take a
bribe, for a bribe blinds the clear-
sighted and [a]subverts the cause of
the just. *distorts the words*
9 "And you shall not oppress a
[a]stranger, since you yourselves
know the [t]feelings of a [a]stranger,
for you *also* were [a]strangers in the
land of Egypt. *sojourner(s) • soul*
10 "And [r]you shall sow your land
for six years and gather in its
yield, Lev. 25:1-7
11 but *on* the seventh year you
shall let it [t]rest and lie fallow, so
that the needy of your people may
eat; and whatever they leave the
beast of the field may eat. You are
to do the same with your vineyard
and your olive grove. *drop*
12 "Six days you are to do your
work, but on the seventh day you
shall cease *from labor* in order
that your ox and your donkey may
rest, and the son of your female
slave, as well as your stranger,
may refresh themselves.
13 "Now concerning everything
which I have said to you, be on
your guard; and do not mention
the name of other gods, nor let
them be heard from your mouth.
14 "Three times a year you shall
celebrate a feast to Me.
15 "You shall observe the Feast
of Unleavened Bread; for seven
days you are to eat unleavened
bread, as I commanded you, at the
appointed time in the month Abib,
for in it you came out of Egypt.
And [t]none shall appear before Me
empty-handed. *they . . . not*
16 "Also *you shall observe* the
Feast of the Harvest *of* the first
fruits of your labors *from* what
you sow in the field; also the Feast
of the Ingathering at the end of
the year when you gather in *the
fruit of* your labors from the field.
17 "Three [r]times a year all your
males shall appear before the
Lord GOD. Ex. 23:14; 34:23
18 "You shall not offer the blood
of My sacrifice with leavened
bread; nor is the fat of My feast to
remain overnight until morning.
19 "You shall bring [r]the choice
first fruits of your soil into the
house of the LORD your God. You
are not to boil a kid in the milk of
its mother. Neh. 10:35; Prov. 3:9
20 "Behold, I am going to send
[r]an angel before you to guard you
along the way, and to bring you
into the place which I have prepared. Ex. 3:2; 14:19; 23:23
21 "Be on your guard before him
and obey his voice; [r]do not be rebellious toward him, for he will
not pardon your transgression,
since My name is in him. Deut. 9:7
22 "But if you will truly obey his
voice and do all that I say, then [r]I
will be an enemy to your enemies
and an adversary to your adversaries. Gen. 12:3; Num. 24:9
23 "For My angel will go before
you and bring you in to *the* land of
the Amorites, the Hittites, the Per-

izzites, the Canaanites, the Hivites and the Jebusites; and I will
completely destroy them.
24 "You shall not worship their
gods, nor serve them, nor do according to their deeds;[r] but you
shall utterly overthrow them, and
break their [r]*sacred* pillars in
pieces. 2 Kin. 18:4 • 2 Kin. 3:2
25 "But you shall serve the LORD
your God, and He will bless your
bread and your water; and I will
remove sickness from your midst.
26 "There shall be no one miscarrying or barren in your land; I will
fulfill the number of your days.
27 "I will send My terror ahead
of you, and throw into confusion
all the people among whom you
come, and I will make all your enemies turn *their* backs to you.
28 "And I will send hornets
ahead of you, that they may drive
out the Hivites, the Canaanites,
and the Hittites before you.
29 "I [r]will not drive them out before you in a single year, that the
land may not become desolate,
and the beasts of the field become
too numerous for you. Deut. 7:22
30 "I will drive them out before
you[r] little by little, until you become fruitful and take possession
of the land. Deut. 7:22
31 "And I will fix your boundary
from the Red Sea to the sea of the
Philistines, and from the wilderness to the River *Euphrates;* for I
will deliver the inhabitants of the
land into your hand, and you will
drive them out before you.
32 "You shall make no covenant
with them or with their gods.
33 "They shall not live in your
land, lest they make you sin
against Me; for *if* you serve their
gods,[r] it will surely be a snare to
you." Josh. 23:13; Ps. 106:36

CHAPTER 24

THEN He said to Moses, "Come
up to the LORD, you and Aaron,
Nadab and Abihu and seventy of
the elders of Israel, and you shall
worship at a distance.
2 "Moses alone, however, shall
come near to the LORD, but they
shall not come near, nor shall the
people come up with him."
3 Then Moses came and re-
counted to the people all the
words of the LORD and all the ordinances; and all the people answered with one voice, and said,
"All the words which the LORD
has spoken we will do!"
4 And Moses wrote down all
the words of the LORD. Then he
arose early in the morning, and
built an altar [t]at the foot of the
mountain with twelve pillars for
the twelve tribes of Israel. *under*
5 And he sent young men of
the sons of Israel,[r] and they offered
burnt offerings and sacrificed
young bulls as peace offerings to
the LORD. Ex. 18:12
6 And[r] Moses took half of the
blood and put *it* in basins, and the
other half of the blood he sprinkled on the altar. Heb. 9:18
7 Then he took the book of the
covenant and read *it* in the hearing of the people; and they said,
"All that the LORD has spoken we
will do, and we will be obedient!"
8 So Moses took the blood and
sprinkled *it* on the people, and
said, "Behold the blood of the cov-

enant, which the LORD has [t]made
with you [t]in accordance with all
these words." *cut • on all*
9 Then Moses went up [t]with
Aaron, Nadab and Abihu, and seventy of the elders of Israel, *and*
10 and they saw the God of Israel; and under His feet there appeared to be a pavement of sapphire, as clear as the sky itself.
11 Yet He did not stretch out
His hand against the nobles of the
sons of Israel; and they beheld
God, and they ate and drank.
12 Now the LORD said to Moses,
"Come up to Me on the mountain
and [t]remain there, and [r]I will give
you the stone tablets [t]with the law
and the commandment which I
have written for their instruction." *be* • Deut. 5:22 • *and*
13 So Moses arose [t]with Joshua
his servant, and Moses went up to
the mountain of God. *and*
14 But to the elders he said,
"Wait here for us until we return
to you. And behold, Aaron and
Hur are with you; whoever [t]has a
legal matter, let him approach
them." *is a master of matters*
15 Then Moses went up to the
mountain, and [r]the cloud covered
the mountain. Ex. 19:9
16 And the glory of the LORD
[t]rested on Mount Sinai, and the
cloud covered it for six days; and
on the seventh day He [r]called to
Moses from the midst of the
cloud. *dwelt* • Ps. 99:7
17 [r]And to the eyes of the sons of
Israel the appearance of the glory
of the LORD was like a consuming
fire on the mountain top. Ex. 3:2
18 And Moses entered the midst
of the cloud [t]as he went up to the
mountain; and Moses was on the
mountain [r]forty days and forty
nights. *and* • Deut. 9:9

CHAPTER 25

THEN the LORD spoke to Moses,
saying,
2 "Tell the sons of Israel to [t]raise
a contribution for Me; from every
man whose heart moves him you
shall raise My contribution. *take*
3 "And this is the contribution
which you are to [t]raise from them:
gold, silver and bronze, *take*
4 [a]blue, purple and scarlet *material,* fine linen, goat *hair,* *violet*
5 rams' skins dyed red, por-
poise skins, acacia wood,
6 [r]oil for lighting, [r]spices for the
anointing oil and for the fragrant
incense, Ex. 27:20 • Ex. 30:23f.
7 onyx stones and setting
stones, for the [r]ephod and for the
[a]breastpiece. Ex. 28:4 • *pouch*
8 "And let them construct a
sanctuary for Me, [r]that I may
dwell among them. Rev. 21:3
9 "According [r]to all that I am
going to show you, *as* the pattern
of the tabernacle and the pattern
of all its furniture, just so you
shall construct *it.* Heb. 8:2, 5
10 "And they shall construct an
ark of acacia wood two and a half
cubits [t]long, and one and a half cubits [t]wide, and one and a half cubits high. *its length • its width*
11 "And you shall [r]overlay it with
pure gold, inside and out you shall
overlay it, and you shall make a
gold molding around it. Heb. 9:4
12 "And you shall cast four gold
rings for it, and [a]fasten them on its
four feet, and two rings shall be

on one side of it and two rings on
the other side of it. *put*
13 "And you shall make poles of
acacia wood and overlay them
with gold.
14 "And you shall put the poles
into the rings on the sides of the
ark, to carry the ark with them.
15 "The[r] poles shall[t] remain in the
rings of the ark; they shall not be
removed from it. 1 Kin. 8:8 • *be*
16 "And you shall[r] put into the
ark the testimony which I shall
give you. Deut. 10:2; 1 Kin. 8:9
17 "And you shall make a [22]mercy
seat of pure gold, two and a half
cubits[t] long and one and a half cubits[t] wide. *its length* • *its width*
18 "And you shall make two
cherubim of gold, make them of
hammered work[t] at the two ends
of the mercy seat. *from*
19 "And make one cherub[t] at one
end and one cherub[t] at the other
end; you shall make the cherubim
of one piece with the mercy seat
at its two ends. *from*
20 "And the cherubim shall have
their wings spread upward, covering the mercy seat with their
wings and facing one another; the
faces of the cherubim are to be
turned toward the mercy seat.
21 "And you shall put the mercy
seat on top of the ark, and in the
ark you shall put the testimony
which I shall give to you.
22 "And there I will meet with
you; and from above the mercy
seat, from[r] between the two cherubim which are upon the ark of the
testimony, I will speak to you
about all that I will give you in
commandment for the sons of Israel. Ps. 80:1; Is. 37:16

[22] Lit., *propitiatory;* and so through v. 22

23 "And you shall make a table
of acacia wood, two cubits long
and one cubit wide and one and a
half cubits[t] high. *its height*
24 "And you shall overlay it with
pure gold and make a gold[r] border
around it. Ex. 25:11
25 "And you shall make for it a
rim of a handbreadth around *it;*
and you shall make a gold border
for the rim around it.
26 "And you shall make four
gold rings for it and put rings on
the four corners which are on its
four feet.
27 "The rings shall be close to
the rim as holders for the poles to
carry the table.
28 "And you shall make the poles
of acacia wood and overlay them
with gold, so that with them the
table may be carried.
29 "And you shall make its
[a]dishes and its pans and its jars
and its[t] bowls, with which to pour
libations; you shall make them of
pure gold. *platters* • *libation bowls*
30 "And you shall set the bread
of the[t] Presence on the table before Me at all times. *Face*
31 "Then you shall make a lampstand of pure gold. The lampstand
and its base and its shaft are to be
made of hammered work; its
cups, its bulbs and its flowers
shall be *of one piece* with it.
32 "And six branches shall go
out from its sides; three branches
of the lampstand from its one
side, and three branches of the
lampstand from its other side.
33 "Three[r] cups *shall be* shaped
like almond *blossoms* in the one
branch, a [23]bulb and a flower, and
three cups shaped like almond

[23] Or, *calyx*

blossoms in the [t]other branch, a
bulb and a flower—so for six
branches going out from the
lampstand; Ex. 37:19 • *one branch*
34 and in the lampstand four
cups shaped like almond *blos-*
soms, its bulbs and its flowers.
35 "And [r]a [a]bulb shall be under the
first pair of branches *coming* out
of it, and a [a]bulb under the *second*
pair of branches *coming* out of it,
and a [a]bulb under the *third* pair of
branches *coming* out of it, for the
six branches coming out of the
lampstand. Ex. 37:21 • *calyx*
36 "Their bulbs and their
branches *shall be of one piece*
with it; all of it shall be one piece
of hammered work of pure gold.
37 "Then you shall make its
lamps seven *in number;* and [r]they
shall [t]mount its lamps so as to
shed light on the space in front of
it. Num. 8:2 • *raise up*
38 "And its snuffers and their
trays *shall be* of pure gold.
39 "It shall be made from a talent
of pure gold, with all these utensils.
40 "And [r]see that you make *them*
[r]after the pattern for them, which
was shown to you on the mountain. Heb. 8:5 • Acts 7:44

CHAPTER 26

"MOREOVER you shall make
the tabernacle with ten curtains of
fine twisted linen and [24]blue and
purple and scarlet *material;* you
shall make them with cherubim,
the work of a skillful workman.
2 "The length of each curtain
shall be twenty-eight cubits, and
the width of each curtain four cubits; all the curtains shall have [t]the
same measurements. *one measure*
3 "Five curtains shall be [a]joined
to one another; and *the other* five
curtains *shall be* [a]joined to one another. *coupled*
4 "And you shall make loops of
blue on the edge of the outermost
curtain in the *first* set, and likewise you shall make *them* on the
edge of the curtain that is outermost in the second [t]set. *coupling*
5 "You shall make fifty loops in
the one curtain, and you shall
make fifty loops on the [t]edge of the
curtain that is in the second [t]set;
the loops shall be opposite each
other. *end* • *coupling*
6 "And you shall make fifty
clasps of gold, and [a]join the curtains to one another with the
clasps, that the [25]tabernacle may
be a unit. *couple*
7 "Then [r]you shall make curtains of goats' *hair* for a tent over
the tabernacle; you shall make
eleven curtains in all. Ex. 36:14
8 "The length of each curtain
shall be thirty cubits, and the
width of each curtain four cubits;
the eleven curtains shall have [t]the
same measurements. *one measure*
9 "And you shall join five curtains by themselves, and the *other*
six curtains by themselves, and
you shall double over the sixth
curtain at the front of the tent.
10 "And you shall make fifty
loops on the edge of the [t]curtain
that is outermost in the *first* [t]set,
and fifty loops on the edge of the
curtain *that is outermost in* the
second [t]set. *one curtain* • *coupling*
11 "And you shall make fifty

[24]Or, *violet,* and so throughout this context

[25]Or, *dwelling place,* and so throughout the ch.

clasps of [26]bronze, and you shall put the clasps into the loops and [a]join the tent together, that it may be[t]a unit. *couple · one*

12 "And the [t] overlapping part that is left over in the curtains of the tent, the half curtain that is left over, shall lap over the back of the tabernacle. *excess*

13 "And the cubit on one side and the cubit on the other, of what is left over in the length of the curtains of the tent, shall lap over the sides of the tabernacle on one side and on the other, to cover it.

14 "And you shall make a covering for the tent of rams' skins [a]dyed red, and a covering of porpoise skins above. *tanned*

15 "Then you shall make the boards for the tabernacle of acacia wood, standing upright.

16 "Ten cubits *shall be* the length of each board, and one and a half cubits the width of each board.

17 "There *shall be* two tenons for each board,[t] fitted to one another; thus you shall do for all the boards of the tabernacle. *bound*

18 "And you shall make the boards for the tabernacle: twenty boards for the south side.

19 "And you shall make forty [27]sockets of silver under the twenty boards, two sockets under one board for its two tenons and two sockets under another board for its two tenons;

20 and for the second side of the tabernacle, on the north side, twenty boards,

21 and their forty sockets of silver; two sockets under one board and two sockets under another board.

22 "And for the[t]rear of the tabernacle, to the west, you shall make six boards. *extreme parts*

23 "And you shall make two boards for the corners of the tabernacle at the[t]rear. *extreme parts*

24 "And they shall be double beneath, and together they shall be complete[a] to its top[a] to the first ring; thus it shall be with both of them: they shall form the two corners. *at its head · with reference to*

25 "And there shall be eight boards with their sockets of silver, sixteen sockets; two sockets under one board and two sockets under another board.

26 "Then you shall make bars of acacia wood, five for the boards of one side of the tabernacle,

27 and five bars for the boards of the[t]other side of the tabernacle, and five bars for the boards of the side of the tabernacle for the rear *side* to the west. *second*

28 "And the middle bar in the [t]center of the boards shall pass through from end to end. *midst*

29 "And you shall overlay the boards with gold and make their rings of gold *as* holders for the bars; and you shall overlay the bars with gold.

30 "Then you shall erect the tabernacle [r]according to its plan which you have been shown in the mountain. Ex. 25:9, 40

31 "And you shall make[r]a veil of blue and purple and scarlet *material* and fine twisted linen; it shall be made with cherubim, the work of a skillful workman. Matt. 27:51

32 "And you shall hang it on four pillars of acacia overlaid with

[26]Or, *copper*
[27]Or, *bases,* and so throughout this context

gold, their hooks *also being of*
gold, on four sockets of silver.
33 "And you shall hang up the
veil under the clasps, and shall
bring in the ark of the testimony
there within the veil; and the veil
shall serve for you as a partition
[r]between the holy place and the
holy of holies. Heb. 9:2f.
34 "And[r]you shall put the mercy
seat on the ark of the testimony in
the holy of holies. Ex. 25:21
35 "And[r]you shall set the table
outside the veil, and the lampstand opposite the table on the
side of the tabernacle toward the
south; and you shall put the table
on the north side. Ex. 40:22
36 "And[r]you shall make a screen
for the doorway of the tent of blue
and purple and scarlet *material*
and fine twisted linen, the work of
a weaver. Ex. 36:37
37 "And[r]you shall make five pillars of acacia for the screen, and
overlay them with gold, their
hooks *also being of* gold; and you
shall cast five sockets of bronze
for them. Ex. 36:38

CHAPTER 27

"AND you shall make[r]the altar
of acacia wood, five cubits long
and five cubits wide; the altar
shall be square, and its height
shall be three cubits. Ex. 38:1-7
2 "And you shall make its horns
on its four corners; its horns shall
be of one piece with it, and you
shall overlay it with[a]bronze. *copper*
3 "And you shall make its pails
for removing its ashes, and its
shovels and its basins and its
forks and its firepans; you shall
make all its utensils of bronze.
4 "And you shall make for it a
grating of network of bronze, and
on the net you shall make four
bronze rings at its four corners.
5 "And you shall put it beneath,
under the ledge of the altar, that
the net may reach halfway up the
altar.
6 "And you shall make poles for
the altar, poles of acacia wood,
and overlay them with bronze.
7 "And its poles shall be inserted into the rings, so that the
poles shall be on the two sides of
the altar when it is carried.
8 "You shall make it hollow
with planks;[r]as it was shown to
you in the mountain, so they shall
make *it*. Acts 7:44; Heb. 8:5
9 "And you shall make [r] the
court of the[a]tabernacle. On the
south side *there shall be* hangings
for the court of fine twisted linen
one hundred cubits long for one
side; Ex. 38:9-20 • *dwelling place*
10 and its pillars *shall be*
twenty, with their twenty sockets
of bronze; the hooks of the pillars
and their bands *shall be* of silver.
11 "And likewise for the north
side in length *there shall be* hangings one hundred *cubits* long, and
its twenty pillars with their
twenty sockets of bronze; the
hooks of the pillars and their
bands *shall be* of silver.
12 "And *for* the width of the
court on the west side *shall be*
hangings of fifty cubits *with* their
ten pillars and their ten sockets.
13 "And the width of the court
on the[t]east side *shall be* fifty cubits. *east side eastward*
14 "The hangings for the *one*[t]side
of the gate shall be fifteen cubits

with their three pillars and their
three sockets. *shoulder*
15"And for the[t] other[t] side *shall*
be hangings of fifteen cubits *with*
their three pillars and their three
sockets. *second · shoulder*
16"And for the gate of the court
there *shall be* a screen of twenty
cubits, of[a] blue and purple and
scarlet *material* and fine twisted
linen, the work of a[t] weaver, *with*
their four pillars and their four
sockets. *violet · variegator*
17"All the pillars around the
court shall be furnished with silver bands *with* their hooks of silver and their sockets of bronze.
18"The length of the court *shall*
be one hundred cubits, and the
width fifty throughout, and the
height five cubits of fine twisted
linen, and their sockets of bronze.
19"All the utensils of the tabernacle *used* in all its service, and all
its pegs, and all the pegs of the
court, *shall be* of bronze.
20"And you shall charge the
sons of Israel, that they bring you
clear oil of beaten olives for the
[a]light, to make a lamp[t] burn continually. *luminary · ascend*
21"In the tent of meeting, outside the veil which is before the
testimony, Aaron and his sons
shall keep it in order from evening
to morning before the LORD; *it*
shall be a perpetual statute
throughout their generations[t] for
the sons of Israel. *from*

CHAPTER 28

"THEN[r] bring near to yourself
Aaron your brother, and his sons
with him, from among the sons of
Israel, to minister as priest to
Me—Aaron, Nadab and Abihu,
Eleazar and Ithamar, Aaron's
sons. Num. 18:7; Ps. 99:6
2"And you shall make[r] holy garments for Aaron your brother, for
glory and for beauty. Ex. 29:5, 29
3"And you shall speak to all the
skillful persons whom I have endowed with the spirit of wisdom,
that they make Aaron's garments
to consecrate him, that he may
minister as priest to Me.
4"And these are the garments
which they shall make: a [28]breast-
piece and an ephod and a robe and
a tunic of checkered work, a turban and a sash, and they shall
make holy garments for Aaron
your brother and his sons, that he
may minister as priest to Me.
5"And they shall take the[r] gold
and the[a] blue and the purple and
the scarlet *material* and the fine
linen. Ex. 25:3 · *violet*
6"They shall also make[r] the
ephod of gold, of[a] blue and purple
and scarlet *material* and fine
twisted linen, the work of the
skillful workman. Lev. 8:7 · *violet*
7"It shall have two shoulder
pieces joined to its two ends, that
it may be joined.
8"And the skillfully woven
band, which is on it, shall be like
its workmanship,[t] of the same material: of gold, of[a] blue and purple
and scarlet *material* and fine
twisted linen. *from it · violet*
9"And you shall take two onyx
stones and engrave on them the
names of the sons of Israel,
10 six of their names on the one
stone, and the names of the re-

[28]Or, *pouch*

maining six on the[t]other stone, according to their birth. *second*
11"As a jeweler engraves a signet, you shall engrave the two
stones according to the names of
the sons of Israel; you shall set
them in filigree *settings* of gold.
12"And you shall put the two
stones on the shoulder pieces of
the ephod, *as* stones of memorial
for the sons of Israel, and Aaron
shall bear their names before the
LORD on his two shoulders[r]for a
memorial. Num. 31:54
13"And[r]you shall make filigree
settings of gold, Ex. 39:16-18
14 and two chains of pure gold;
you shall make them of twisted
cordage work, and you shall put
the corded chains on the filigree
settings.
15"And you shall make a[a]breast-
piece of judgment, the work of a
skillful workman; like the work of
the ephod you shall make it: of
gold, of[a]blue and purple and scarlet *material* and fine twisted linen
you shall make it. *pouch • violet*
16"It shall be square *and* folded
double, a span[t] in length and a
span in width. *its*
17"And you shall mount on it
four rows of stones; the first row
shall be a row of ruby, topaz and
emerald;
18 and the second row a turquoise, a sapphire and a diamond;
19 and the third row a jacinth,
an agate and an amethyst;
20 and the fourth row a beryl
and an onyx and a jasper; they
shall be set in gold filigree.
21"And the stones shall be according to the names of the sons
of Israel: twelve, according to
their names; they shall be *like* the
engravings of a seal, each[r]accord-
ing to his name for the twelve
tribes. Rev. 7:4-8; 21:12
22"And you shall make on the
breastpiece chains of twisted
cordage work in pure gold.
23"And you shall make on the
breastpiece two rings of gold, and
shall put the two rings on the two
ends of the breastpiece.
24"And you shall put the two
cords of gold on the two rings at
the ends of the breastpiece.
25"And you shall put the *other*
two ends of the two cords on the
two filigree *settings*, and put them
on the shoulder pieces of the
ephod, at the front of it.
26"And you shall make two
rings of gold and shall place them
on the two ends of the breastpiece, on the edge of it, which is
toward the inner side of the
ephod.
27"And you shall make two
rings of gold and put them on the
bottom of the two shoulder pieces
of the ephod, on the front of it
close to the place where it is
joined, above the skillfully woven
band of the ephod.
28"And they shall bind the
breastpiece by its rings to the
rings of the ephod with a blue
cord, that it may be on the skillfully woven band of the ephod,
and that the breastpiece may not
come loose from the ephod.
29"And Aaron shall carry the
names of the sons of Israel in the
breastpiece of judgment over his
heart when he enters the holy
place, for a memorial before the
LORD continually.

30"And you shall put in the
breastpiece of judgment the
[29]Urim and the Thummim, and
they shall be over Aaron's heart
when he goes in before the LORD;
and Aaron shall carry the judgment of the sons of Israel over his
heart before the LORD continually.
31"And you shall make the robe
of the ephod all of [a]blue. *violet*
32"And there shall be an opening [a]at its top in the middle of it;
around its opening there shall be a
binding of woven work, as *it were*
the opening of a coat of mail, that
it may not be torn. *for his head*
33"And you shall make on its
hem pomegranates of blue and
purple and scarlet *material,* all
around on its hem, and bells of
gold between them all around:
34 a golden bell and a pomegranate, a golden bell and a pomegranate, all around on the hem of
the robe.
35"And it shall be on Aaron
when he ministers; and its tinkling
may be heard when he enters and
leaves the holy place before the
LORD, that he may not die.
36"You shall also make a plate
of pure gold and shall engrave on
it, like the engravings of a seal,
'Holy [r]to the LORD.' Zech. 14:20
37"And you shall [t]fasten it on a
[a]blue cord, and it shall be on the
turban; it shall be at the front of
the turban. *place • violet*
38"And it shall be on Aaron's
forehead, and Aaron shall [a]take
away the iniquity of the holy
things which the sons of Israel
consecrate, with regard to all their
holy gifts; and it shall always be
on his forehead, that they may be
accepted before the LORD. *bear*
39"And you shall weave the tunic of checkered work of fine lin-
en, and shall make a turban of fine
linen, and you shall make a sash,
the work of a [t]weaver. *variegator*
40"And for Aaron's sons you
shall make tunics; you shall also
make sashes for them, and you
shall make [t]caps for them, for glory and for beauty. *headgear*
41"And you shall put them on
Aaron your brother and on his
sons with him; and you shall
anoint them and [t]ordain them and
consecrate them, that they may
serve Me as priests. *fill their hand*
42"And you shall make for them
linen breeches to cover *their* bare
flesh; they shall [t]reach from the
loins even to the thighs. *be*
43"And they shall be on Aaron
and on his sons when they enter
the tent of meeting, or when they
approach the altar to minister in
the holy place, so that they do not
incur guilt and die. It *shall be* a
statute forever to him and to his
[t]descendants after him. *seed*

CHAPTER 29

"NOW this is [t]what you shall do
to them to consecrate them to
minister as priests to Me: take one
young bull and two rams without
blemish, *the thing which*
2 and unleavened bread and
unleavened cakes mixed with oil,
and unleavened wafers [a]spread
with oil; you shall make them of
fine wheat flour. *anointed*
3"And you shall put them in
one basket, and present them in

[29]I.e., lights and perfections

the basket along with the bull and the two rams.

4 "Then [r]you shall bring Aaron and his sons to the doorway of the tent of meeting, and wash them with water. Ex. 40:12; Lev. 8:6

5 "And you shall take the garments, and put on Aaron the tunic and the robe of the ephod and the ephod and the [a]breastpiece, and gird him with the skillfully woven band of the ephod; *pouch*

6 and you shall set the turban on his head, and put [r]the holy crown on the turban. Lev. 8:9

7 "Then you shall take [r]the anointing oil, and pour it on his head and anoint him. Num. 35:25

8 "And you shall bring his sons and put [r]tunics on them. Lev. 8:13

9 "And you shall gird them with sashes, Aaron and his sons, and bind [t]caps on them, and they shall have the priesthood by a perpetual statute. So you shall ordain Aaron and his sons. *headgear*

10 "Then you shall bring the bull before the tent of meeting, and Aaron and his sons shall lay their hands on the head of the bull.

11 "And you shall slaughter the bull before the LORD at the doorway of the tent of meeting.

12 "And you shall take some of the blood of the bull and put *it* on the horns of the altar with your finger; and you shall pour out all the blood at the base of the altar.

13 "And you shall take all the fat that covers the entrails and the [a]lobe of the liver, and the two kidneys and the fat that is on them, and offer them up in smoke on the altar. *appendage on*

14 "But [r]the flesh of the bull and its hide and its refuse, you shall burn with fire outside the camp; it is a sin offering. Heb. 13:11

15 "You [r]shall also take the one ram, and Aaron and his sons shall lay their hands on the head of the ram; Lev. 8:18

16 and you shall slaughter the ram and shall take its blood and sprinkle it around on the altar.

17 "Then you shall cut the ram into its pieces, and wash its entrails and its legs, and put *them* [t]with its pieces and its head. *on*

18 "And you shall offer up in smoke the whole ram on the altar; it is a burnt offering to the LORD: [r]it is a soothing aroma, an offering by fire to the LORD. Gen. 8:21

19 "Then [r]you shall take the [t]other ram, and Aaron and his sons shall lay their hands on the head of the ram. Lev. 8:22f. • *second*

20 "And you shall slaughter the ram, and take some of its blood and put *it* on the lobe of Aaron's right ear and on the lobes of his sons' right ears and on the thumbs of their right hands and on the big toes of their right feet, and sprinkle the *rest of the* blood around on the altar.

21 "Then you shall take some of the blood that is on the altar and some of the [r]anointing oil, and sprinkle *it* on Aaron and on his garments, and on his sons and on his sons' garments with him; so he and his garments shall be consecrated, as well as his sons and his sons' garments with him. Lev. 8:30

22 "You shall also take the fat from the ram and the fat tail, and the fat that covers the entrails and the lobe of the liver, and the two

kidneys and the fat that is on
them and the right thigh (for it is a
ram of [t]ordination), *filling*
23 and one cake of bread and
[r]one cake of bread *mixed with* oil
and one wafer from the basket of
unleavened bread which is *set* before the LORD; Lev. 8:26
24 and you shall put [t]all these [t]in
the [t]hands of Aaron and in the
[t]hands of his sons, and shall wave
them as a wave offering before
the LORD. *the whole • on • palms*
25 "And [r]you shall take them
from their hands, and offer them
up in smoke on the altar on the
burnt offering for a soothing aroma before the LORD; it is an offering by fire to the LORD. Lev. 8:28
26 "Then you shall take the
breast of Aaron's ram of [t]ordina-
tion, and wave it as a wave offering before the LORD; and it shall
be your portion. *filling*
27 "And you shall consecrate the
breast of the wave offering and
the thigh of the heave offering
which was waved and which was
[t]offered from the ram of [t]ordina-
tion, from the one which was for
Aaron and from the one which
was for his sons. *heaved • filling*
28 "And it shall be for Aaron and
his sons as *their* portion forever
from the sons of Israel, for it is a
heave offering; and it shall be a
heave offering from the sons of Israel from the sacrifices of their
peace offerings, *even* their heave
offering to the LORD.
29 "And the holy garments of
Aaron shall be for his sons after
him, that in them they may be
anointed and ordained.
30 "For seven days the one of his
sons who is priest in his stead
shall put them on when he enters
the tent of meeting to minister in
the holy place.
31 "And you shall take the ram
of [t]ordination and boil its flesh in a
holy place. *filling*
32 "And Aaron and his sons shall
eat the flesh of the ram, and the
bread that is in the basket, at the
doorway of the tent of meeting.
33 "Thus they shall eat those
things by which atonement was
made at their ordination *and* consecration; but a layman shall not
eat *them*, because they are holy.
34 "And [r]if any of the flesh of [t]or-
dination or any of the bread remains until morning, then you
shall burn the remainder with fire;
it shall not be eaten, because it is
holy. Ex. 12:10 • *filling*
35 "And thus you shall do to Aaron and to his sons, according to all
that I have commanded you; you
shall [t]ordain them through seven
days. *fill their hand*
36 "And [r]each day you shall offer
a bull as a sin offering for atonement, and you shall purify the altar when you make atonement [t]for
it; and you shall anoint it to consecrate it. **Heb. 10:11** • ***upon***
37 "For seven days you shall
make atonement for the altar and
consecrate it; then the altar shall
be most holy, *and* whatever
touches the altar shall be holy.
38 "Now this is what you shall
offer on the altar: two one year old
lambs each day, continuously.
39 "The one lamb you shall offer
in the morning, and the other
lamb you shall offer at twilight;
40 and there *shall be* one-tenth

of an ephah of fine flour mixed with one-fourth of a hin of beaten oil, and one-fourth of a hin of wine for a libation with one lamb.

41 "And the[t]other lamb you shall offer at twilight, and shall offer with it the same grain offering as the morning and the same libation, for a soothing aroma, an offering by fire to the LORD. *second*

42 "It shall be a continual burnt offering throughout your generations at the doorway of the tent of meeting before the LORD,[r]where I will meet with you, to speak to you there. Ex. 25:22; Num. 17:4

43 "And I will meet there with the sons of Israel, and it shall be consecrated by My glory.

44 "And I will consecrate the tent of meeting and the altar; I will also consecrate Aaron and his sons to minister as priests to Me.

45 "And[r]I will dwell among the sons of Israel and will be their God. 2 Cor. 6:16; Rev. 21:3

46 "And they shall know that I am the LORD their God who brought them out of the land of Egypt, that I might dwell among them; I am the LORD their God.

CHAPTER 30

"MOREOVER, you shall make [r]an altar as a place for burning incense; you shall make it of acacia wood. Ex. 37:25-29

2 "Its length *shall be* a cubit, and its width a cubit, it shall be square, and its height *shall be* two cubits; its horns *shall be*[t]of one piece with it. *from itself*

3 "And you shall overlay it with pure gold, its top and its[t]sides all around, and its horns; and you shall make a gold molding all around for it. *walls*

4 "And you shall make two gold rings for it under its molding; you shall make *them* on its two side walls—on [t]opposite sides—and [t]they shall be holders for poles with which to carry it. *its two • it*

5 "And you shall make the poles of acacia wood and overlay them with gold.

6 "And you shall put[t]this altar in front of the veil that is near the ark of the testimony, in front of the[t]mercy seat that is over *the ark of* the testimony, where I will meet with you. *it • propitiatory*

7 "And Aaron shall burn fragrant incense on it; he shall burn it every morning when he trims the lamps.

8 "And when Aaron [t]trims the lamps at twilight, he shall burn incense. *There shall be* perpetual incense before the LORD throughout your generations. *causes to ascend*

9 "You shall not offer any strange incense on[t]this altar, or burnt offering or meal offering; and you shall not pour out a libation on it. *it*

10 "And Aaron shall[r]make atonement on its horns once a year; he shall make atonement on it with the blood of the sin offering of atonement once a year throughout your generations. It is most holy to the LORD." Lev. 16:18

11 The LORD also spoke to Moses, saying,

12 "When you take a census of the sons of Israel to number them, then each one of them shall give a ransom for himself to the LORD,

when you number them, that there may be no plague among them when you number them.

13 "This is what everyone who is numbered shall give: half a shekel according to the shekel of the sanctuary (the shekel is twenty gerahs), half a shekel as a [t]contribution to the LORD. *heave offering*

14 "Everyone who is numbered, from twenty years old and over, shall give the [t]contribution to the LORD. *heave offering of the* LORD

15 "The rich shall not pay more, and the poor shall not pay less than the half shekel, when you give the contribution to the LORD to make atonement for [t] yourselves. *your souls*

16 "And you shall take the atonement money from the sons of Israel, and shall give it for the service of the tent of meeting, that it may be a memorial for the sons of Israel before the LORD, to make atonement for yourselves."

17 And the LORD spoke to Moses, saying,

18 "You shall also make [r]a laver of [a]bronze, with its base of bronze, for washing; and you shall [r]put it between the tent of meeting and the altar, and you shall put water in it. Ex. 38:8 • *copper* • Ex. 40:30

19 "And Aaron and his sons shall [r]wash their hands and their feet from it; Ex. 40:31f.; Is. 52:11

20 when they enter the tent of meeting, they shall wash with water, that they may not die; or when they approach the altar to minister, by offering up in smoke a fire *sacrifice* to the LORD.

21 "So they shall wash their hands and their feet, that they may not die; and it shall be a perpetual statute for them, for [t]Aaron and his [t]descendants throughout their generations." *him* • *seed*

22 Moreover, the LORD spoke to Moses, saying,

23 "Take also for yourself the finest of spices: of flowing myrrh five hundred *shekels*, and of fragrant cinnamon half as much, two hundred and fifty, and of fragrant cane two hundred and fifty,

24 and of cassia five hundred, according to the shekel of the sanctuary, and of olive oil a hin.

25 "And you shall make of these a holy anointing oil, a perfume mixture, the work of a perfumer; it shall be a holy anointing oil.

26 "And with it [r]you shall anoint the tent of meeting and the ark of the testimony, Ex. 40:9; Lev. 8:10

27 and the table and all its utensils, and the lampstand and its utensils, and the altar of incense,

28 and the altar of burnt offering and all its utensils, and the laver and its stand.

29 "You shall also consecrate them, that they may be most holy; whatever touches them shall be holy.

30 "And [r]you shall anoint Aaron and his sons, and consecrate them, that they may minister as priests to Me. Ex. 29:7; Lev. 8:12

31 "And you shall speak to the sons of Israel, saying, 'This shall be a holy anointing oil to Me throughout your generations.

32 'It shall not be poured on [t]anyone's body, nor shall you make *any* like it, in the same proportions; it is holy, *and* it shall be holy to you. *the flesh of man*

33 'Whoever shall mix *any* like it, or whoever puts any of it on a [t]layman,[t] shall be cut off from his people.' " *stranger • even he shall*

34 Then the LORD said to Moses, "Take for yourself spices, stacte and onycha and galbanum, spices with pure frankincense; there shall be an equal part of each.

35 "And with it you shall make incense, a perfume, the work of a perfumer, salted, pure, *and* holy.

36 "And you shall beat some of it very fine, and put part of it before the testimony in the tent of meeting, where I shall meet with you; it shall be most holy to you.

37 "And the incense which you shall make, you shall not make in [t]the same proportions for yourselves; it shall be holy to you for the LORD. *its proportion*

38 "Whoever shall make *any* like it, to[t]use as perfume, shall be cut off from his people." *smell of it*

CHAPTER 31

NOW the LORD spoke to Moses, saying,

2 "See, I have called by name Bezalel, the son of Uri, the son of Hur, of the tribe of Judah.

3 "And I have filled him with the Spirit of God in wisdom, in understanding, in knowledge, and in all *kinds of* craftsmanship,

4 to[t]make artistic designs for work in gold, in silver, and in [a]bronze, *devise devices • copper*

5 and in the cutting of stones for settings, and in the carving of wood, that he may work in all *kinds of* craftsmanship.

6 "And behold, I Myself have [t]appointed with him Oholiab, the son of Ahisamach, of the tribe of Dan; and in the hearts of all who are skillful I have put[t]skill, that they may make all that I have commanded you: *given • wisdom*

7 the tent of meeting, and the ark of testimony, and the[t]mercy seat upon it, and all the furniture of the tent, *propitiatory*

8 the table also and its[a]utensils, and the[r]pure *gold* lampstand with all its utensils, and the altar of incense, *vessels* • Lev. 24:4

9 the altar of burnt offering also with all its[a]utensils, and the laver and its stand, *vessels*

10 the woven garments as well, and the holy garments for Aaron the priest, and the garments of his sons, *with which* to[t]carry on their priesthood; *minister as priests*

11 [r]the anointing oil also, and the fragrant incense for the holy place, they are to make *them* according to all that I have commanded you." Ex. 30:23-32

12 And the LORD spoke to Moses, saying,

13 "But as for you, speak to the sons of Israel, saying, 'You[r] shall surely observe My sabbaths; for *this* is a sign between Me and you throughout your generations, that you may know that I am the LORD who sanctifies you. Ex. 20:8

14 'Therefore you are to observe the sabbath, for it is holy to you. [r]Everyone who profanes it shall surely be put to death; for whoever does any work on it, that person shall be cut off from among his people. Ex. 31:15; John 7:23

15 'For six days work may be done, but on the seventh day there

is a sabbath of complete rest, holy
to the LORD; [r]whoever does any
work on the sabbath day shall
surely be put to death. Ex. 31:14
16 'So the sons of Israel shall observe the sabbath, to [t]celebrate the
sabbath throughout their generations as a perpetual covenant.' *do*
17 "It [r]is a sign between Me and
the sons of Israel forever; for in
six days the LORD made heaven
and earth, but on the seventh day
He ceased *from labor,* and was refreshed." Ex. 31:13; Ezek. 20:12
18 And when He had finished
speaking with him upon Mount
Sinai, He gave Moses [r]the two tablets of the testimony, tablets of
stone, [r]written by the finger of
God. Ex. 24:12 • Deut. 9:10

CHAPTER 32

NOW when the people saw that
Moses [r]delayed to come down
from the mountain, the people assembled about Aaron, and said to
him, "Come, make us [a]a god who
will go before us; as for this
Moses, the man who brought us
up from the land of Egypt, we do
not know what has become of
him." Deut. 9:11, 12 • *gods*
2 And Aaron said to them,
"Tear [r]off the gold rings which are
in the ears of your wives, your
sons, and your daughters, and
bring *them* to me." Ex. 35:22
3 Then all the people tore off
the gold rings which were in their
ears, and brought *them* to Aaron.
4 And he took *this* from their
hand, and fashioned it with a
graving tool, and made it into a
molten calf; and they said, "This is
your god, O Israel, who brought
you up from the land of Egypt."
5 Now when Aaron saw *this,*
he built an altar before it; and
Aaron made a proclamation and
said, "Tomorrow *shall be* a feast
to the LORD."
6 So the next day they rose
early and offered burnt offerings,
and brought peace offerings; and
the people sat down to eat and to
drink, and rose up to play.
7 Then the LORD spoke to
Moses, "Go [t]down at once, for
your people, whom you brought
up from the land of Egypt, have
corrupted *themselves.* *go down*
8 "They have quickly turned
aside from the way which I commanded them. They have made
for themselves a molten calf, and
have worshiped it, and have sacrificed to it, and said, 'This is your
god, O Israel, who brought you up
from the land of Egypt!' "
9 And the LORD said to Moses,
"I have seen this people, and behold, they are an obstinate people.
10 "Now then let Me alone, that
My anger may burn against them,
and that I may destroy them; and I
will make of you a great nation."
11 Then [r]Moses entreated the
LORD his God, and said, "O LORD,
why doth Thine anger burn
against Thy people whom Thou
hast brought out from the land of
Egypt with great power and with
a mighty hand? Deut. 9:18, 26
12 "Why should [r]the Egyptians
speak, saying, 'With evil *intent* He
brought them out to kill them in
the mountains and to destroy
them from the face of the earth'?
Turn from Thy burning anger and

change Thy mind about *doing* harm to Thy people. Josh. 7:9

13 "Remember Abraham, Isaac, and Israel, Thy servants to whom Thou didst swear by Thyself, and didst say to them, 'I will multiply your[t] descendants as the stars of the heavens, and all this land of which I have spoken I will give to your[t] descendants, and they shall inherit *it* forever.' " *seed*

14 So the LORD changed His mind about the harm which He said He would do to His people.

15 Then Moses turned and went down from the mountain with the two tablets of the testimony in his hand, tablets which were written on both sides; they were written on one *side* and the other.

16 And the tablets were God's work, and the writing was God's writing engraved on the tablets.

17 Now when Joshua heard the sound of the people as they shouted, he said to Moses, "There is a sound of war in the camp."

18 But he said,

"It is not the sound of the cry
of triumph,
Nor is it the sound of the
cry of defeat;
But the sound of singing I
hear."

19 And it came about, as soon as[t] Moses came near the camp, that he saw the calf and *the* dancing; and Moses' anger burned, and he threw the tablets from his hands and shattered them[t] at the foot of the mountain. *he · beneath*

20 [r]And he took the calf which they had made and burned *it* with fire, and ground it to powder, and scattered it over the surface of the water, and made the sons of Israel drink *it*. Deut. 9:21

21 Then Moses said to Aaron, "What did this people do to you, that you have brought *such* great sin upon them?"

22 And Aaron said, "Do not let the anger of my lord burn; you know the people yourself, that they are[t] prone to evil. *in evil*

23 "For[r] they said to me, 'Make[a] a god for us who will go before us; for this Moses, the man who brought us up from the land of Egypt, we do not know what has become of him.' Ex. 32:1-4 · *gods*

24 "And I said to them, 'Whoever has any gold, let them tear it off.' So they gave *it* to me, and[r] I threw it into the fire, and out came this calf." Ex. 32:4

25 Now when Moses saw that the people were[t] out of control—for Aaron had let them[t] get out of control to be a derision among their enemies— *let loose · go loose*

26 then Moses stood in the gate of the camp, and said, "Whoever is for the LORD, *come* to me!" And all the sons of Levi gathered together to him.

27 And he said to them, "Thus says the LORD, the God of Israel, 'Every man *of you* put his sword upon his thigh, and go back and forth from gate to gate in the camp, and kill every man his brother, and every man his friend, and every man his neighbor.' "

28 So the sons of Levi did[t] as Moses instructed, and about three thousand men of the people fell that day. *according to Moses' word*

29 Then Moses said, "Dedicate[t] yourselves today to the LORD—for

every man has been against his
son and against his brother—in
order that He may bestow a blessing upon you today." *Fill your hand*
30 And it came about on the
next day that Moses said to the
people, "You[r] yourselves have
[t]committed a great sin; and now I
am going up to the LORD, perhaps
I can make atonement for your
sin." 1 Sam. 12:20, 23 • *sinned*
31 Then Moses returned to the
LORD, and said, "Alas, this people
has[t]committed a great sin, and
they have made[a]a god of gold for
themselves. *sinned • gods*
32"But now, if Thou wilt, forgive
their sin—and if not, please blot
me out from Thy[r]book which
Thou hast written!" Dan. 12:1
33 And the LORD said to Moses,
"Whoever has sinned against Me,
I will blot him out of My book.
34"But go now, lead the people
where I told you. Behold, My angel shall go before you; nevertheless in the day when I punish, I
will punish them for their sin."
35[r]Then the LORD smote the
people, because of[r]what they did
with the calf which Aaron had
made. Ex. 32:28 • Ex. 32:4, 24

CHAPTER 33

THEN the LORD spoke to Moses,
"Depart, go up from here, you and
the people whom you have
brought up from the land of
Egypt, to the land of which I
swore to Abraham, Isaac, and Jacob, saying, 'To your[t]descendants
I will give it.' *seed*
2"And I will send[r]an angel before you and[r]I will drive out the
Canaanite, the Amorite, the Hittite, the Perizzite, the Hivite and
the Jebusite. Ex. 32:34 • Josh. 24:11
3"*Go up* to a land flowing with
milk and honey; for I will not go
up in your midst, because you are
[t]an obstinate people, lest I destroy
you on the way." *a stiff-necked*
4 When the people heard this
[t]sad word,[r]they went into mourning, and none of them put on his
ornaments. *evil* • Num. 14:1, 39
5 For the LORD had said to
Moses, "Say to the sons of Israel,
'You are an obstinate people;
should I go up in your midst for
one moment, I would destroy you.
Now therefore, put off your ornaments from you, that I may know
what I will do with you.'"
6 So the sons of Israel stripped
themselves of their ornaments
from Mount Horeb *onward.*
7 Now Moses used to take the
tent and pitch it outside the camp,
a good distance from the camp,
and he called it the tent of meeting. And it came about, that
everyone who sought the LORD
would go out to the tent of meeting which was outside the camp.
8 And it came about, whenever
Moses went out to the tent, that
all the people would arise and
stand, each at the entrance of his
tent, and gaze after Moses until he
entered the tent.
9 And it came about, whenever
Moses entered the tent, the pillar
of cloud would descend and stand
at the entrance of the tent; and the
LORD would speak with Moses.
10 When all the people saw the
pillar of cloud standing at the entrance of the tent, all the people

would arise and worship, each at
the entrance of his tent.
11 Thus[r] the LORD used to speak
to Moses face to face, just as a
man speaks to his friend. When
[t]Moses returned to the camp, his
servant Joshua, the son of Nun, a
young man, would not depart
from the tent. Num. 12:8 • *he*
12 Then Moses said to the LORD,
"See, Thou dost say to me, 'Bring[r]
up this people!' But Thou Thyself
hast not let me know whom Thou
wilt send with me. Moreover,
Thou hast said, 'I have known you
by name, and you have also found
favor in My sight.' Ex. 3:10
13 "Now therefore, I pray Thee,
if I have found favor in Thy sight,
let me know Thy ways, that I may
know Thee, so that I may find favor in Thy sight. Consider too,
that this nation is Thy people."
14 And He said, "My[r] presence
shall go *with you,* and I will give
you rest." Deut. 4:37; Is. 63:9
15 Then he said to Him, "If Thy
presence does not go *with us,* do
not lead us up from here.
16 "For how then can it be
known that I have found favor in
Thy sight, I and Thy people? Is it
not by Thy going with us, so that
[r]we, I and Thy people, may be distinguished from all the *other* people who are upon the face of the
[t]earth?" Lev. 20:24, 26 • *ground*
17 And the LORD said to Moses,
"I will also do this thing of which
you have spoken; for you have
found favor in My sight, and I
have known you by name."
18 Then [t]Moses said, "I pray
Thee, show me Thy glory!" *he*
19 And He said, "I[r] Myself will
make all My goodness pass before
you, and will proclaim the name
of the LORD before you; and[r] I will
be gracious to whom I will be gracious, and will show compassion
on whom I will show compassion." Ex. 34:6, 7 • Rom. 9:15
20 But He said, "You cannot see
My face,[r] for no man can see Me
and live!" Is. 6:5; 1 Tim. 6:16
21 Then the LORD said, "Behold,
there is a place by Me, and you
shall stand *there* on the rock;
22 and it will come about, while
My glory is passing by, that I will
put you in the cleft of the rock and
[r]cover you with My hand until I
have passed by. Ps. 91:1, 4
23 "Then I will take My hand
away and you shall see My back,
but My face shall not be seen."

CHAPTER 34

NOW the LORD said to Moses,
"Cut out for yourself two stone
tablets like the former ones, and[r] I
will write on the tablets the words
that were on the former tablets
which you shattered. Deut. 10:2, 4
2 "So be ready by morning, and
come up in the morning to Mount
Sinai, and present yourself there
to Me on the top of the mountain.
3 "And no man is to come up
with you, nor let any man be seen
anywhere on the mountain; even
the flocks and the herds may not
graze in front of that mountain."
4 So he cut out[r] two stone tablets like the former ones, and
Moses rose up early in the morning and went up to Mount Sinai,
as the LORD had commanded him,

and he took two stone tablets in
his hand. Ex. 34:1
5 And[r] the LORD descended in
the cloud and stood there with
him as he called upon the name of
the LORD. Ex. 19:9; 33:9
6 Then the LORD passed by in
front of him and proclaimed, "The
LORD, the LORD God, compassionate and gracious, slow to anger,
and abounding in lovingkindness
and[a] truth; *faithfulness*
7 who [r] keeps lovingkindness
for thousands, who forgives iniquity, transgression and sin; yet He
will by no means leave *the guilty*
unpunished, visiting the iniquity
of fathers on the children and on
the grandchildren to the third and
fourth generations." Ps. 103:3
8 And Moses made haste [t] to
bow low toward the earth and
worship. *and bowed ... worshiped*
9 And he said, "If now I have
found favor in Thy sight, O Lord, I
pray, let the Lord go along in our
midst, even though the people are
so obstinate; and do Thou pardon
our iniquity and our sin, and take
us as Thine own possession."
10 Then[t] God said, "Behold, I am
going to make a covenant. Before
all your people I will perform miracles which have not been[t] produced in all the earth, nor among
any of the nations; and all the people among whom you live will see
the working of the LORD, for it is a
fearful thing that I am going to
perform with you. *He • created*
11 "Be sure to observe what I am
commanding you this day: behold,
[r] I am going to drive out the Amorite before you, and the Canaanite, the Hittite, the Perizzite, the
Hivite and the Jebusite. Ex. 33:2
12 "Watch[r] yourself that you
make no covenant with the inhabitants of the land into which
you are going, lest it become a
snare in your midst. Ex. 23:32, 33
13 "But[r] *rather*, you are to tear
down their altars and smash their
sacred pillars and cut down their
[30] Asherim Ex. 23:24; Deut. 12:3
14 —for[r] you shall not worship
any other god, for the LORD,
whose name is Jealous, is a jealous God— Ex. 20:3, 5; Deut. 4:24
15 lest you make a covenant
with the inhabitants of the land
and they play the harlot with their
gods, and sacrifice to their gods,
and someone invite you[t] to eat of
his sacrifice; *and you eat*
16 and[r] you take some of his
daughters for your sons, and his
daughters play the harlot with
their gods, and cause your sons
also to play the harlot with their
gods. Deut. 7:3; 1 Kin. 11:1-4
17 "You[r] shall make for yourself
no molten gods. Deut. 5:8
18 "You shall observe the Feast
of Unleavened Bread. For seven
days you are to eat unleavened
bread,[a] as I commanded you, at the
appointed time in the month of
Abib, for in the month of Abib you
came out of Egypt. *which*
19 "The first offspring from every womb belongs to Me, and all
your male livestock, the first offspring from cattle and sheep.
20 "And you shall redeem with a
lamb the first offspring from a
donkey; and if you do not redeem
it, then you shall break its neck.
You shall redeem all the first-born

[30] I.e., wooden symbols of a female deity

of your sons. And none shall appear before Me empty-handed.
21 "You shall work[r] six days, but
on the seventh day you shall rest;
even during plowing time and harvest you shall rest. Ex. 20:9f.
22 "And you shall celebrate[r] the
Feast of Weeks, *that is,* the first
fruits of the wheat harvest, and
the Feast of Ingathering at the
turn of the year. Num. 28:26
23 "Three times a year all your
males are to appear before the
Lord GOD, the God of Israel.
24 "For I will [a]drive[r] out nations
before you and enlarge your borders, and no man shall covet your
land when you go up three times a
year to appear before the LORD
your God. *dispossess* • Ps. 78:55
25 "You shall not[t] offer the blood
of My sacrifice with leavened
bread, nor is the sacrifice of the
Feast of the Passover to be left
over until morning. *slaughter*
26 "You shall bring[r] the very first
of the first fruits of your soil into
the house of the LORD your God.
You shall not boil a kid in its
mother's milk." Ex. 23:19
27 Then the LORD said to Moses,
"Write[t] down these words, for in
accordance with these words I
have made a covenant with you
and with Israel." *for yourself*
28 So he was there with the
LORD forty days and forty nights;
he did not eat bread or drink water. And he wrote on the tablets
the words of the covenant, the
Ten[t] Commandments. *Words*
29 And it came about when
Moses was coming down from
Mount Sinai (and the two tablets
of the testimony *were* in Moses'
hand as he was coming down
from the mountain), that Moses
did not know that[r] the skin of his
face shone because of his speaking with Him. 2 Cor. 3:7
30 So when Aaron and all the
sons of Israel saw Moses, behold,
the skin of his face shone, and
[r]they were afraid to come near
him. 2 Cor. 3:7
31 Then Moses called to them,
and Aaron and all the rulers in the
congregation returned to him; and
Moses spoke to them.
32 And afterward all the sons of
Israel came near, and he commanded them *to do* everything
that the LORD had spoken[t] to him
on Mount Sinai. *with*
33 When Moses had finished
speaking with them,[r] he put a veil
over his face. 2 Cor. 3:13
34 But whenever Moses went in
before the LORD to speak with
Him,[r] he would take off the veil until he came out; and whenever he
came out and spoke to the sons of
Israel what he had been commanded, 2 Cor. 3:16
35 [r]the sons of Israel would see
the face of Moses, that the skin of
Moses' face shone. So Moses
would replace the veil over his
face until he went in to speak with
Him. 2 Cor. 3:13

CHAPTER 35

THEN Moses assembled all the
congregation of the sons of Israel,
and said to them, "These are the
things that the LORD has commanded *you* to[t] do. *do them*
2 "For[r] six days work may be
done, but on the seventh day you

shall have a holy *day*, a sabbath of complete rest to the LORD; whoever does any work on it shall be put to death. Ex. 20:9,10

3 "You[r] shall not kindle a fire in any of your dwellings on the sabbath day." Ex. 12:16; 16:23

4 And Moses spoke to all the congregation of the sons of Israel, saying, "This is the thing which the LORD has commanded, saying,

5 'Take from among you a[a] contribution to the LORD; whoever is of a willing heart, let him bring it as the LORD's[a] contribution: gold, silver, and bronze, *heave offering*

6 and blue, purple and scarlet *material*, fine linen, goats' *hair*,

7 and rams' skins [a]dyed red, and porpoise skins, and acacia wood, *tanned*

8 and oil for lighting, and spices for the anointing oil, and for the fragrant incense,

9 and onyx stones and setting stones, for the ephod and for the [a]breastpiece. *pouch*

10 'And let every skillful man among you come, and make all that the LORD has commanded:

11 the [t]tabernacle, its tent and its covering, its hooks and its boards, its bars, its pillars, and its sockets; *dwelling place*

12 the ark and its poles, the [t]mercy seat, and the curtain of the screen; *propitiatory*

13 the table and its poles, and all its[a] utensils, and the bread of the [31]Presence; *vessels*

14 the [r]lampstand also for the light and its utensils and its lamps and the oil for the light; Ex. 25:31ff.

15 and the altar of incense and its poles, and the anointing oil and the fragrant incense, and the screen for the doorway at the[a] entrance of the tabernacle; *doorway*

16 the altar of burnt offering with its[a] bronze grating, its poles, and all its[a] utensils, the[a] basin and its stand; *copper • vessels • laver*

17 the hangings of the court, its pillars and its sockets, and the screen for the gate of the court;

18 the pegs of the tabernacle and the pegs of the court and their cords;

19 the woven garments, for ministering in the holy place, the holy garments for Aaron the priest, and the garments of his sons, to minister as priests.'"

20 Then all the congregation of the sons of Israel departed from Moses' presence.

21 And everyone whose heart [t]stirred him and everyone whose spirit moved him came *and* brought the LORD's contribution for the work of the tent of meeting and for all its service and for the holy garments. *lifted up*

22 Then all whose hearts moved them, both men and women, came *and* brought brooches and earrings and signet rings and bracelets, all articles of gold; so *did* every man who presented an offering of gold to the LORD.

23 And every man,[t] who had in his possession blue and purple and scarlet *material* and fine linen and goats' *hair* and rams' skins dyed red and porpoise skins, brought them. *with whom was found*

24 Everyone who could make a contribution of silver and bronze brought the LORD's contribution;

[31] Lit., *Face*

and every man, who had in his possession acacia wood for any work of the service, brought it.

25 And all the skilled women spun with their hands, and brought what they had spun, *in* [a]blue and purple *and* scarlet *material* and *in* fine linen. *violet*

26 And all the women whose heart stirred with a skill spun the goats' *hair.*

27 And the rulers brought the onyx stones and the stones for setting for the ephod and for the [a]breastpiece; *pouch*

28 and the spice and the oil for the light and for the anointing oil and for the fragrant incense.

29 The Israelites, all the men and women, whose heart [t]moved them to bring *material* for all the work, which the LORD had commanded through Moses to be done, brought a freewill offering to the LORD. *made them willing*

30[r] Then Moses said to the sons of Israel, "See, the LORD has called by name Bezalel the son of Uri, the son of Hur, of the tribe of Judah. Ex. 31:1-6

31 "And He has filled him with the Spirit of God, in wisdom, in understanding and in knowledge and in all [t]craftsmanship; *work*

32 to make designs for working in gold and in silver and in bronze,

33 and in the cutting of stones for settings, and in the carving of wood, so as to perform in every inventive work.

34 "He also has put in his heart to teach, both he and [r]Oholiab, the son of Ahisamach, of the tribe of Dan. Ex. 31:6

35 "He has filled them with [t]skill to perform every work of an engraver and of a designer and of an embroiderer, in blue and in purple *and* in scarlet *material,* and in fine linen, and of a weaver, as performers of every work and makers of designs. *wisdom of heart*

CHAPTER 36

"NOW Bezalel and Oholiab, and every skillful person in whom the LORD has put [t]skill and understanding to know how to perform all the work in the construction of the sanctuary, shall perform in accordance with all that the LORD has commanded." *wisdom*

2 Then Moses called Bezalel and Oholiab and every [t]skillful person in whom the LORD had put skill, everyone whose heart stirred him, to come to the work to perform it. *man wise of heart*

3 And they received from Moses all the contributions which the sons of Israel had brought to perform the work in the construction of the sanctuary. And they still *continued* bringing to him freewill offerings every morning.

4 And all the [t]skillful men who were performing all the work of the sanctuary came, each from [t]the work which [t]he was performing, *wise · his · they were*

5 and they said to Moses, "The people are bringing much more than enough for the [t]construction work which the LORD commanded *us* to perform." *service for the work*

6 So Moses issued a command, and a [t]proclamation was circulated throughout the camp, saying, "Let neither man nor woman any

longer perform work for the contributions of the sanctuary." Thus
the people were restrained from
bringing *any more.* *voice*
7 [r]For the [t]material they had
was sufficient and more than
enough for all the work, to perform it. 1 Kin. 8:64 • *work*
8 And all the [t] skillful men
among those who were performing the work made the tabernacle
with ten curtains; of fine twisted
linen and blue and purple and
scarlet *material,* with cherubim,
the work of a skillful workman,
Bezalel made them. *wise of heart*
9 The length of each curtain
was twenty-eight cubits, and the
width of each curtain four cubits;
all the curtains had [t]the same measurements. *one measure*
10 And he joined five curtains
to one another, and *the other* five
curtains he joined to one another.
11 And he made loops of blue
on the edge of the outermost curtain in the first set; he did likewise
on the edge of the curtain that
was outermost in the second set.
12 He made fifty loops in the
one curtain and he made fifty
loops on the edge of the curtain
that was in the second set; the
loops were opposite each other.
13 And he made fifty clasps of
gold, and joined the curtains to
one another with the clasps, so
the tabernacle was [t]a unit. *one*
14 Then [r]he made curtains of
goats' *hair* for a tent over the tabernacle; he made eleven curtains
[t]in all. Ex. 26:7-14 • *in number*
15 The length of each curtain
was thirty cubits, and four cubits
the width of each curtain; the
eleven curtains had [t]the same
measurements. *one measure*
16 And he [a]joined five curtains
by themselves, and *the other* six
curtains by themselves. *coupled*
17 Moreover, he made fifty
loops on the edge of the curtain
that was outermost in the *first* set,
and he made fifty loops on the
edge of the curtain *that was outermost in* the second set.
18 And he made fifty clasps of
bronze to join the tent together,
that it might be [t]a unit. *one*
19 And he made a covering for
the tent of rams' skins [a]dyed red,
and a covering of porpoise skins
above. *tanned*
20 [r]Then he made the boards for
the tabernacle of acacia wood,
standing upright. Ex. 26:15-29
21 Ten cubits was the length of
[t]each board, and one and a half cubits the width of each board. *the*
22 There were two tenons for
each board,[t] fitted to one another;
thus he did for all the boards of
the tabernacle. *bound*
23 And he made the boards for
the tabernacle: twenty boards for
the south side;
24 and he made forty [a]sockets of
silver under the twenty boards;
two sockets under one board for
its two tenons and two sockets
under another board for its two
tenons. *bases*
25 Then for the second side of
the tabernacle, on the north side,
he made twenty boards,
26 and their forty [a]sockets of silver; two sockets under one board
and two sockets under another
board. *bases*
27 And for the [t]rear of the taber-

nacle, to the west, he made six boards. *extreme parts*

28 And he made two boards for the corners of the [t]tabernacle at the rear. *dwelling place*

29 And they were double beneath, and together they were complete to its [a]top to the first ring; thus he did with both of them for the two corners. *head*

30 And there were eight boards with their [a]sockets of silver, sixteen [a]sockets, [t]two under every board. *bases · two sockets*

31 Then he made [r]bars of acacia wood, five for the boards of one side of the tabernacle, Ex. 26:26-29

32 and five bars for the boards of the [a]other side of the tabernacle, and five bars for the boards of the tabernacle for the [t]rear *side* to the west. *second · extreme parts*

33 And he made the middle bar to pass through in the [t]center of the boards from end to end. *midst*

34 And he overlaid the boards with gold and made their rings of gold *as* holders for the bars, and overlaid the bars with gold.

35 Moreover, he made the veil of [a]blue and purple and scarlet *material,* and fine twisted linen; he made it with cherubim, the work of a skillful workman. *violet*

36 And he made four pillars of acacia for it, and overlaid them with gold, with their hooks of gold; and he cast four [a]sockets of silver for them. *bases*

37 And he made a screen for the doorway of the tent, of [a]blue and purple and scarlet *material,* and fine twisted linen, the work of a [t]weaver; *violet · variegator*

38 and *he made* its five pillars with their hooks, and he overlaid their tops and their [a]bands with gold; but their five [a]sockets were of [a]bronze. *fillets, rings · bases · copper*

CHAPTER 37

NOW Bezalel made the ark of acacia wood; its length was two and a half cubits, and its width one and a half cubits, and its height one and a half cubits;

2 and he overlaid it with pure gold inside and out, and made a gold molding for it all around.

3 And he cast four rings of gold for it on its four feet; even two rings on one side of it, and two rings on the other side of it.

4 And he made poles of acacia wood and overlaid them with gold.

5 And he put the poles into the rings on the sides of the ark, to carry [t]it. *the ark*

6 And he made a [t]mercy seat of pure gold, two and a half cubits [t]long, and one and a half cubits wide. *propitiatory · its length*

7 And he made two cherubim of gold; he made them of hammered work, [t]at the two ends of the mercy seat; *from*

8 one cherub [t]at the one end, and one cherub [t]at the other end; he made the cherubim *of one piece* with the mercy seat [t]at the two ends. *from*

9 And the cherubim had *their* wings spread upward, covering the [t]mercy seat with their wings, with their faces toward each other; the faces of the cherubim were toward the mercy seat. *propitiatory*

10 Then he made the table of

acacia wood, two cubits long and a cubit [t]wide and one and a half cubits[t]high. *its width · its height*

11 And he overlaid it with pure gold, and made a gold molding for it all around.

12 And he made a rim for it of a handbreadth all around, and made a gold molding for its rim all around.

13 And he cast four gold rings for it and put the rings on the four corners that were on its four feet.

14 Close by the rim were the rings, the holders for the poles to carry the table.

15 And he made the poles of acacia wood and overlaid them with gold, to carry the table.

16 And he made the utensils which were on the table, its[t]dishes and its pans and its bowls and its jars, with which to pour out libations, of pure gold. *libation bowls*

17 [r]Then he made the lampstand of pure gold. He made the lampstand of hammered work, its base and its shaft; its cups, its[a]bulbs and its flowers were *of one piece* with it. Ex. 25:31-39 · *calyxes*

18 And there were six branches going out of its sides; three branches of the lampstand from the one side of it, and three branches of the lampstand from the[t]other side of it; *second*

19 three cups shaped like almond *blossoms,* a[a]bulb and a flower in one branch, and three cups shaped like almond *blossoms,* a[a]bulb and a flower in the other branch—so for the six branches going out of the lampstand. *calyx*

20 And in the lampstand *there were* four cups shaped like almond *blossoms,* its[a]bulbs and its flowers; *calyxes*

21 and a[a]bulb was under the *first* pair of branches *coming* out of it, and a[a]bulb under the *second* pair of branches *coming* out of it, and a[a]bulb under the *third* pair of branches *coming* out of it, for the six branches coming out of the lampstand. *calyx*

22 Their bulbs and their branches were *of one piece* with it; the whole of it *was* a single hammered work of pure gold.

23 And he made its seven lamps with its snuffers and its[t]trays of pure gold. *snuff dishes*

24 He made it and all its utensils from a talent of pure gold.

25 Then he made the altar of incense of acacia wood: a cubit long and a cubit wide, square, and two cubits high; its horns were *of one piece* with it.

26 And he overlaid it with pure gold, its top and its [t]sides all around, and its horns; and he made a gold molding for it all around. *walls*

27 And he made two golden rings for it under its molding, on its two sides—on opposite sides—as holders for poles with which to carry it.

28 And he made the poles of acacia wood and overlaid them with gold.

29 [r]And he made the holy anointing oil and the pure, fragrant incense of spices, the work of a perfumer. Ex. 30:23-25, 34, 35

CHAPTER 38

THEN he made the altar of burnt offering of acacia wood, five cubits long, and five cubits wide, square, and three cubits high.

2 And he made its horns on its four corners, its horns[t] being *of one piece* with it, and he overlaid it with[a] bronze. *were · copper*

3 And he made all the utensils of the altar, the pails and the shovels and the basins, the flesh hooks and the firepans; he made all its utensils of bronze.

4 And he made for the altar a grating of bronze network beneath, under its ledge, reaching halfway up.

5 And he cast four rings on the four ends of the bronze grating *as* holders for the poles.

6 And he made the poles of acacia wood and overlaid them with bronze.

7 And he inserted the poles into the rings on the sides of the altar, with which to carry it. He made it hollow with planks.

8 Moreover, he made the laver of bronze with its base of bronze, [t]from the mirrors of the serving women who served at the doorway of the tent of meeting. *with*

9 [r]Then he made the court: for the south side the hangings of the court were of fine twisted linen, one hundred cubits; Ex. 27:9-19

10 their twenty pillars, and their twenty[a] sockets, *made* of bronze; the hooks of the pillars and their bands *were* of silver. *bases*

11 And for the north side *there were* one hundred cubits; their twenty pillars and their twenty sockets *were* of bronze, the hooks of the pillars and their[a] bands *were* of silver. *fillets, rings*

12 And for the west side *there were* hangings of fifty cubits *with* their ten pillars and their ten sockets; the hooks of the pillars and their bands *were* of silver.

13 And for the[t] east side fifty cubits. *east side, eastward*

14 The hangings for the *one*[t] side *of the gate were* fifteen cubits, *with* their three pillars and their three[a] sockets, *shoulder · bases*

15 and so for the [t]other [t]side. On both sides of the gate of the court *were* hangings of fifteen cubits, *with* their three pillars and their three sockets. *second · shoulder*

16 All the hangings of the court all around *were* of fine twisted linen.

17 And the[a] sockets for the pillars *were* of[a] bronze, the hooks of the pillars and their bands, of silver; and the overlaying of their tops, of silver, and all the pillars of the court were furnished with silver bands. *bases · copper*

18 And the screen of the gate of the court was the work of the [t]weaver, of blue and purple and scarlet *material*, and fine twisted linen. And the length was twenty cubits and the height was five cubits, corresponding to the hangings of the court. *variegator*

19 And their four pillars and their four[a] sockets *were* of bronze; their hooks *were* of silver, and the overlaying of their tops and their bands *were* of silver. *bases*

20 And all the pegs of the[t] tabernacle and of the court all around *were* of bronze. *dwelling place*

21 This is the number of *the*
things for the[t]tabernacle, the[t]tab-
ernacle of the testimony, as they
were[t]numbered according to the
command of Moses, for the service of the Levites, by the hand of
Ithamar, the son of Aaron the
priest. *dwelling place • appointed*
22 Now[r]Bezalel, the son of Uri
the son of Hur, of the tribe of Judah, made all that the LORD had
commanded Moses. Ex. 31:2
23 And with him was Oholiab,
the son of Ahisamach, of the tribe
of Dan, an engraver and a skillful
workman and a [t]weaver in blue
and in purple and in scarlet *mate-*
rial, and fine linen. *variegator*
24 All the gold that was used
for the work, in all the work of the
sanctuary, even the gold of the
wave offering, was 29 talents and
730 shekels, according to [r]the
shekel of the sanctuary. Ex. 30:13
25 [r]And the silver of those of the
congregation who were[t]numbered
was 100 talents and 1,775 shekels,
according to the shekel of the
sanctuary; Ex. 30:11-16 • *mustered*
26 a beka a head (*that is,* half a
shekel according to the shekel of
the sanctuary), for each one who
passed over to those who were
numbered, from twenty years old
and upward, for 603,550 men.
27 And the hundred talents of
silver were for casting the[a]sockets
of the sanctuary and the[a]sockets
of the veil; one hundred[a]sockets
for the hundred talents, a talent
for a[a]socket. *bases*
28 And of the 1,775 *shekels,* he
made hooks for the pillars and
overlaid their tops and made
[a]bands for them. *fillets, rings*
29 And the bronze of the wave
offering was 70 talents, and 2,400
shekels.
30 And with it he made the
[a]sockets to the doorway of the tent
of meeting, and the bronze altar
and its bronze grating, and all the
utensils of the altar, *bases*
31 and the sockets of the court
all around and the sockets of the
gate of the court, and all the pegs
of the tabernacle and all the pegs
of the court all around.

CHAPTER 39

MOREOVER, from the[a]blue and
purple and scarlet *material,* they
made finely woven garments for
ministering in the holy place, as
well as the holy garments which
were for Aaron, just as the LORD
had commanded Moses. *violet*
2 [r]And he made the ephod of
gold, *and* of[a]blue and purple and
scarlet *material,* and fine twisted
linen. Ex. 28:6-12 • *violet*
3 Then they hammered out
gold sheets and cut *them* into
threads to be woven in *with* the
blue and the purple and the scarlet *material,* and the fine linen, the
work of a skillful workman.
4 They made attaching shoul-
der pieces for[t]the ephod; it was attached at its two *upper* ends. *it*
5 And the skillfully woven
band which was on it was like its
workmanship, [t]of the same material: of gold *and* of blue and purple and scarlet *material,* and fine
twisted linen, just as the LORD had
commanded Moses. *from it*
6 And they made the onyx
stones, set in gold filigree *settings;*

they were engraved *like* the engravings of a signet, according to
the names of the sons of Israel.
7 And[r] he placed them on the
shoulder pieces of the ephod, *as*
memorial stones for the sons of Israel, just as the LORD had commanded Moses. Ex. 28:12
8 And he made the breastpiece, the work of a skillful workman, like the workmanship of the
ephod: of gold *and* of[a] blue and
purple and scarlet *material* and
fine twisted linen. *violet*
9 It was square; they made the
breastpiece folded double, a span
[t]long and a span[t] wide when folded
double. *its length · its width*
10 And they mounted four rows
of stones on it. The first row *was* a
row of ruby, topaz, and emerald;
11 and the second row, a turquoise, a sapphire and a diamond;
12 and the third row, a jacinth,
an agate, and an amethyst;
13 and the fourth row, a beryl,
an onyx, and a jasper. They were
set in gold filigree *settings* when
they were[t] mounted. *filled*
14 And the stones were corresponding to the names of the sons
of Israel; they were twelve, corresponding to their names, *engraved*
with the engravings of a signet,
each with its name for the twelve
tribes.
15 And they made on the
breastpiece chains like cords, of
twisted cordage work in pure
gold.
16 And they made two gold filigree *settings* and two gold rings,
and put the two rings on the two
ends of the breastpiece.
17 Then they put the two gold
cords in the two rings at the ends
of the breastpiece.
18 And they put the *other* two
ends of the two cords on the two
filigree *settings,* and put them on
the shoulder pieces of the ephod
at the front of it.
19 And they made two gold
rings and placed *them* on the two
ends of the breastpiece, on its inner edge which was next to the
ephod.
20 Furthermore, they made two
gold rings and placed them on the
bottom of the two shoulder pieces
of the ephod, on the front of it,
close to the place where it joined,
above the woven band of the
ephod.
21 And they bound the breastpiece by its rings to the rings of
the ephod with a[a] blue cord, that it
might be on the woven band of
the ephod, and that the breastpiece might not come loose from
the ephod, just as the LORD had
commanded Moses. *violet*
22 Then he made the robe of the
ephod of woven work, all of blue;
23 [r]and the opening of the robe
was *at the top* in the center, as the
opening of a coat of mail, with a
binding all around its opening,
that it might not be torn. Ex. 28:32
24 And they made pomegran-
ates of blue[a] and purple and scarlet
material and twisted *linen* on the
hem of the robe. *violet*
25 They also made bells of pure
gold, and put the bells between
the pomegranates all around on
the hem of the robe,
26 alternating a bell and a
pomegranate all around on the
hem of the robe, for the service,

just as the LORD had commanded
Moses.
27 [r]And they made the tunics of
finely woven linen for Aaron and
his sons, Ex. 28:39, 40, 42
28 and the turban of fine linen,
and the decorated [t]caps of fine lin-
en, and the linen breeches of fine
twisted linen, *headgear*
29 and the sash of fine twisted
linen, and blue and purple and
scarlet *material,* the work of the
[t]weaver, just as the LORD had commanded Moses. *variegator*
30 And they made the plate of
the holy crown of pure gold, and
inscribed it like the engravings of
a signet, "Holy to the LORD."
31 And they [t]fastened a blue
cord to it, to fasten it on the turban above, just as the LORD had
commanded Moses. *put*
32 Thus all the work of the [t]tab-
ernacle of the tent of meeting was
completed; and the sons of Israel
did according to all that the LORD
had commanded Moses; so they
did. *dwelling place*
33 And they brought the tabernacle to Moses, the tent and all its
[32]furnishings: its clasps, its boards,
its bars, and its pillars and its
[a]sockets; *bases*
34 and the covering of rams'
skins [a]dyed red, and the covering
of porpoise skins, and the screen-
ing veil; *tanned*
35 the ark of the testimony and
its poles and the mercy seat;
36 the table, all its utensils, and
the bread of the [t]Presence; *Face*
37 the pure *gold* lampstand,
[t]with its arrangement of lamps and
all its utensils, and the oil for the
light; *its lamps, the lamps set in order*

[32]Or, *utensils,* and so throughout this context

38 and the gold altar, and the
anointing oil and the fragrant incense, and the veil for the doorway of the tent;
39 the bronze altar and its
bronze grating, its poles and all its
utensils, the laver and its stand;
40 the hangings for the court, its
pillars and its [a]sockets, and the
screen for the gate of the court, its
cords and its pegs and all the
equipment for the service of the
tabernacle, for the tent of meeting; *bases*
41 the woven garments for ministering in the holy place and the
holy garments for Aaron the
priest and the garments of his
sons, to minister as priests.
42 So the sons of Israel did all
the work according to all that the
LORD had commanded Moses.
43 And Moses [t]examined all the
work and behold, they had done
it; just as the LORD had commanded, this they had done. So
Moses blessed them. *saw*

CHAPTER 40

THEN the LORD spoke to Moses,
saying,
2 "On the first day of the first
month you shall set up the tabernacle of the tent of meeting.
3 "And you shall place the ark
of the testimony there, and you
shall screen the ark with the veil.
4 "And you shall bring in the table and arrange what belongs on
it; and you shall bring in the lampstand and [a]mount its lamps. *light*
5 "Moreover, you shall [r]set the
gold altar of incense before the
ark of the testimony, and set up

the veil for the doorway to the tabernacle. Ex. 40:26

6 "And you shall set the altar of burnt offering in front of the doorway of the tabernacle of the tent of meeting.

7 "And you shall set the laver between the tent of meeting and the altar, and put water[t] in it. *there*

8 "And you shall set up the court all around and hang up the veil for the gateway of the court.

9 "Then you shall take the anointing oil and anoint the tabernacle and all that is in it, and shall consecrate it and all its furnishings; and it shall be holy.

10 "And you shall anoint the altar of burnt offering and all its utensils, and consecrate the altar; and the altar shall be most holy.

11 "And you shall anoint the laver and its stand, and consecrate it.

12 "Then you shall[r] bring Aaron and his sons to the doorway of the tent of meeting and wash them with water. Lev. 8:1-6

13 "And you shall put the holy garments on Aaron and anoint him and consecrate him, that he may minister as a priest to Me.

14 "And you shall bring his sons and put tunics on them;

15 and you shall anoint them even as you have anointed their father, that they may minister as priests to Me; and their anointing shall[t] qualify them for a perpetual priesthood throughout their generations." *be for them*

16 Thus Moses did; according to all that the LORD had commanded him, so he did.

17 Now it came about in the first month[t] of the second year, on the first day of the month, that the tabernacle was erected. *in*

18 And Moses erected the tabernacle and[t] laid its sockets, and set up its boards, and inserted its bars and erected its pillars. *put*

19 And he spread the tent over the tabernacle and put the covering of the tent on top of it, just as the LORD had commanded Moses.

20 Then he took the testimony and put *it* into the ark, and[t] attached the poles to the ark, and put the mercy seat[t] on top of the ark. *set · over the ark above*

21 And he brought the ark into the tabernacle, and set up a veil for the screen, and screened off the ark of the testimony, just as the LORD had commanded Moses.

22 Then he put the table in the tent of meeting, on the north side of the tabernacle, outside the veil.

23 And he set the arrangement of[r] bread in order on it before the LORD, just as the LORD had commanded Moses. Ex. 25:30

24 Then he placed the [t]lampstand in the tent of meeting, opposite the table, on the south side of the tabernacle.

25 And he[r] lighted the lamps before the LORD, just as the LORD had commanded Moses. Ex. 25:37

26 Then he[r] placed the gold altar in the tent of meeting in front of the veil; Ex. 30:6; 40:5

27 and he[r] burned fragrant incense on it, just as the LORD had commanded Moses. Ex. 30:7

28 Then he set up the veil for the doorway of the tabernacle.

29 And he set the altar of burnt

offering *before* the doorway of the
tabernacle of the tent of meeting,
and offered on it the burnt offering and the meal offering, just as
the LORD had commanded Moses.
30 And he placed the laver between the tent of meeting and the
altar, and put water in it for washing.
31 [r]And from it Moses and Aaron and his sons washed their
hands and their feet. Ex. 30:19, 20
32 When they entered the tent
of meeting, and when they approached the altar, they washed,
just as the LORD had commanded
Moses.
33 And he erected the court all
around the tabernacle and the altar, and [t]hung up the veil for the
gateway of the court. Thus Moses
finished the work. *put the screen*
34 Then the cloud covered the
tent of meeting, and the glory of
the LORD filled the tabernacle.
35 And Moses [r]was not able to
enter the tent of meeting because
the cloud had settled on it, and the
glory of the LORD filled the tabernacle. 1 Kin. 8:11; 2 Chr. 5:13, 14
36 And throughout all their
journeys [r]whenever the cloud was
taken up from over the tabernacle, the sons of Israel would set
out; Num. 9:17; Neh. 9:19
37 but [r]if the cloud was not
taken up, then they did not set out
until the day when it was taken
up. Num. 9:19-22
38 For throughout all their journeys, the cloud of the LORD was
on the tabernacle by day, and
there was fire in it by night, in the
sight of all the house of Israel.

THE BOOK OF

LEVITICUS

THEN [r]the LORD called to Moses
and spoke to him from the tent of
meeting, saying, Ex. 19:3; 25:22
2 "Speak to the sons of Israel
and say to them, 'When any man
of you brings an [r]offering to the
LORD, you shall bring your offering of animals from [r]the herd or
the flock. Mark 7:11 • Lev. 22:18f.
3 'If his offering is a [r]burnt offering from the herd, he shall offer it,
a male without defect; he shall offer it at the doorway of the tent of
meeting, that he may be accepted
before the LORD. Lev. 6:8-13
4 'And he shall lay his hand on
the head of the burnt offering, that
it may be accepted for him to
make atonement on his behalf.
5 'And he shall slay the young
bull before the LORD; and Aaron's
sons, the priests, shall offer up the
blood and sprinkle the blood
around on the altar that is at the
doorway of the tent of meeting.
6 'He shall then skin the burnt
offering and cut it into its pieces.
7 'And the sons of Aaron the
priest shall put fire on the altar
and arrange wood on the fire.

8 'Then Aaron's sons, the priests, shall arrange the pieces, the head, and the[r] suet over the wood which is on the fire that is on the altar. Lev. 1:12; 3:3, 4

9 'Its entrails, however, and its legs he shall wash with water. And the priest shall offer up in smoke all of it on the altar for a burnt offering, an offering by fire of a soothing aroma to the LORD.

10 'But if his offering is from the flock, of the sheep or of the goats, for a burnt offering, he shall offer it a[r] male without defect. Lev. 1:3

11 'And[r] he shall slay it on the side of the altar northward before the LORD, and Aaron's sons, the priests, shall sprinkle its blood around on the altar. Ex. 24:6

12 'He shall then cut it into its pieces with its head and its[r] suet, and the priest shall arrange them on the wood which is on the fire that is on the altar. Lev. 3:3, 4

13 'The entrails, however, and the legs he shall wash with water. And[r] the priest shall offer all of it, and offer it up in smoke on the altar; it is a burnt offering, an offering by fire of a soothing aroma to the LORD. Num. 15:4-7; 28:11-14

14 'But if his offering to the LORD is a burnt offering of birds, then he shall bring his offering from the [r] turtledoves or from young pigeons. Luke 2:24

15 'And the priest shall bring it to the altar and wring off its head, and offer it up in smoke on the altar; and its blood is to be drained out on the side of the altar.

16 'He shall also take away its crop with its feathers, and cast it beside the altar eastward, to the place of the[a] ashes. *fat ashes*

17 'Then he shall tear it by its wings, *but* shall not sever *it*. And the priest shall offer it up in smoke on the altar on the wood which is on the fire; it is a burnt offering, an offering by fire of a soothing aroma to the LORD.

CHAPTER 2

'NOW when anyone presents a grain offering as an offering to the LORD, his offering shall be of fine flour, and he shall pour oil on it and put frankincense on it.

2 'He shall then bring it to Aaron's sons, the priests; and shall take from it[r] his handful of its fine flour and of its oil with all of its frankincense. And the priest shall offer *it* up in smoke *as* its[r] memorial portion on the altar, an offering by fire of a soothing aroma to the LORD. Lev. 5:12 • Acts 10:4

3 'And the remainder of the grain offering belongs to Aaron and his sons: a thing most holy, of the offerings to the LORD by fire.

4 'Now when you bring an offering of a grain offering baked in an oven, *it shall be* [r] unleavened cakes of fine flour mixed with oil, or unleavened wafers[t] spread with oil. Ex. 29:2 • *anointed*

5 'And if your offering is a grain offering *made* [r] on the griddle, *it shall be* of fine flour, unleavened, mixed with oil; Lev. 6:21; 7:9

6 you shall break it into bits, and pour oil on it; it is a grain offering.

7 'Now if your offering is a grain offering *made* in a pan, it

shall be made of fine flour with oil.
8 'When you bring in the grain
offering which is made of these
things to the LORD, it shall be presented to the priest and he shall
bring it to the altar.
9 'The priest then shall take up
from the grain offering[r] its memorial portion, and shall offer *it* up in
smoke on the altar *as* an offering
by fire of a soothing aroma to the
LORD. Lev. 2:2, 16; 5:12
10 'And the remainder of the
grain offering belongs to Aaron
and his sons: a thing most holy, of
the offerings to the LORD by fire.
11 'No grain offering, which you
bring to the LORD, shall be made
with leaven, for you shall not offer
[t]up in smoke any leaven or any
honey as an[r] offering by fire to the
LORD. *up from it* • Lev. 1:13
12 'As an offering of first fruits,
you shall bring them to the LORD,
but they shall not ascend for a
soothing aroma on the altar.
13 'Every grain offering of yours,
moreover, you shall season with
salt, so that[r] the salt of the covenant of your God shall not be
lacking from your grain offering;
with all your offerings you shall
offer salt. Num. 18:19; 2 Chr. 13:5
14 'Also if you bring a grain offering of early ripened things to
the LORD, you shall bring[r] fresh
heads of grain roasted in the fire,
grits of new growth, for the grain
offering of your early ripened
things. Lev. 23:14
15 'You shall then put oil on it
and lay incense on it; it is a grain
offering.
16 'And the priest shall offer up
in smoke[r] its memorial portion,
part of its grits and its oil with all
its incense as an offering by fire to
the LORD. Lev. 2:2

CHAPTER 3

'NOW if his offering is a sacrifice
of peace offerings, if he is going to
offer out of the herd, whether
male or female, he shall offer it
without defect before the LORD.
2 'And[r] he shall lay his hand on
the head of his offering and slay it
at the doorway of the tent of
meeting, and Aaron's sons, the
priests, shall sprinkle the blood
around on the altar. Lev. 1:4
3 'And from the sacrifice of the
peace offerings, he shall present
an offering by fire to the LORD, the
fat that covers the entrails and all
the fat that is on the entrails,
4 and the two kidneys with the
fat that is on them, which is on the
loins, and the[a] lobe of the liver,
which he shall remove with the
kidneys. *appendage on*
5 'Then Aaron's sons shall offer
it up in smoke on the altar on the
burnt offering, which is on the
wood that is on the fire;[r] it is an
offering by fire of a soothing aroma to the LORD. Num. 15:8-10
6 'But if his offering for a sacrifice of peace offerings to the LORD
is from the flock, he shall offer it,
male or female, without defect.
7 'If he is going to offer[r] a lamb
for his offering, then he shall offer
it before the LORD, Num. 15:4, 5
8 and he shall lay his hand on
the head of his offering, and slay it
before the tent of meeting; and

Aaron's sons shall sprinkle its blood around on the altar.

9 'And from the sacrifice of peace offerings he shall bring as an offering by fire to the LORD, its fat,[t] the entire fat tail which he shall remove close to the backbone, and the fat that covers the entrails and all the fat that is on the entrails, *the fat tail, entire*

10 and the two kidneys with the fat that is on them, which is on the loins, and the[a] lobe of the liver, which he shall remove[r] with the kidneys. *appendage on* • Lev. 3:4, 15

11 'Then the priest shall offer *it* up in smoke on the altar, *as* food, an offering by fire to the LORD.

12 'Moreover, if his offering is[r] a goat, then he shall offer it before the LORD, Num. 15:6-11

13 and he shall lay his hand on its head and slay it before the tent of meeting; and the sons of Aaron shall sprinkle its blood around on the altar.

14 'And from it he shall present his offering as an offering by fire to the LORD, the fat that covers the entrails and all the fat that is on the entrails,

15 and the two kidneys with the fat that is on them, which is on the loins, and the[a] lobe of the liver, which he shall remove[r] with the kidneys. *appendage on* • Lev. 3:4

16 'And the priest shall offer them up in smoke on the altar *as* food, an offering by fire for a soothing aroma;[r] all fat is the LORD'S. Lev. 7:23-25

17 'It is a [r]perpetual statute throughout your generations in all your dwellings: you shall not eat any fat or any blood.' " Lev. 7:34

CHAPTER 4

THEN the LORD spoke to Moses, saying,

2 "Speak to the sons of Israel, saying, 'If a person sins[r] unintentionally in any of the things which the LORD has commanded not to be done, and commits any of them, Lev. 4:22, 27; 5:15-18

3 if the anointed priest sins so as to bring guilt on the people, then let him offer to the LORD a bull without defect as a sin offering for the sin he has committed.

4 'And he shall bring the bull to the doorway of the tent of meeting before the LORD, and[r] he shall lay his hand on the head of the bull, and slay the bull before the LORD. Lev. 1:4; 4:15; Num. 8:12

5 'Then the anointed priest is to take some of the blood of the bull and bring it to the tent of meeting,

6 and the priest shall dip his finger in the blood, and sprinkle some of the blood seven times before the LORD, in front of[r] the veil of the sanctuary. Ex. 40:21, 26

7 'The priest shall also put some of the blood on the horns of [r]the altar of fragrant incense which is before the LORD in the tent of meeting; and all the blood of the bull he shall pour out at the base of the altar of burnt offering which is at the doorway of the tent of meeting. Lev. 8:15

8 'And[r] he shall remove from it all the fat of the bull of the sin offering: the fat that covers the entrails, and all the fat which is on the entrails, Lev. 3:3, 4

9 and the two kidneys with the fat that is on them, which is on the

loins, and the[a] lobe of the liver,
which he shall remove with the
kidneys *appendage on*
10 (just as it is removed from
the ox of the sacrifice of peace offerings), and the priest is to offer
them up in smoke on the altar of
burnt offering.
11 'But the hide of the bull and
all its flesh with its head and its
legs and its entrails and its refuse,
12 that is, all *the rest of* the bull,
he is to bring out to a clean place
outside the camp where the ashes
are poured out, and burn it on
wood with fire; where the ashes
are poured out it shall be burned.
13 'Now if the whole congregation of Israel commits error, and
the matter escapes the notice of
the assembly, and they commit
any of the things which the LORD
has commanded not to be done,
and they become guilty;
14 when the sin [t]which they
have[t] committed becomes known,
then the assembly shall offer a
bull of the herd for a sin offering,
and bring it before the tent of
meeting. *concerning which · sinned*
15 'Then the elders of the congregation shall lay their hands on
the head of the bull before the
LORD, and the bull shall be slain
[r]before the LORD. Lev. 1:3
16 'Then the anointed priest is to
bring some of the blood of the bull
to the tent of meeting;
17 and[r] the priest shall dip his
finger in the blood, and sprinkle *it*
seven times before the LORD, in
front of the veil. Lev. 4:6
18 'And he shall put some of the
blood on the horns of the altar
which is before the LORD[t] in the
tent of meeting; and all the blood
he shall pour out at the base of the
altar of burnt offering which is at
the doorway of the tent of meeting. *which is in*
19 'And[r] he shall remove all its
fat from it and offer it up in smoke
on the altar. Lev. 4:8
20 'He shall also do with the bull
just as he did with[r] the bull of the
sin offering; thus he shall do with
it. So the priest shall make atonement for them, and they shall be
forgiven. Lev. 4:8, 21
21 'Then he is to bring out the
bull to *a place* outside the camp,
and burn it as he burned the first
bull; it is[r] the sin offering for the
assembly. Lev. 4:13f.
22 'When a leader[r] sins and unintentionally does any one of all the
things which the LORD God has
commanded not to be done, and
he becomes guilty, Lev. 4:2, 27
23 [t]if his sin which he has committed is made known to him, he
shall bring for his offering a goat,
a male without defect. *or*
24 'And he shall lay his hand on
the head of the male goat, and
slay it in the place where[t] they slay
the burnt offering before the
LORD; it is a sin offering. *one slays*
25 'Then the priest is to take
some of the blood of the sin offering with his finger, and put it on
the horns of the altar of burnt offering; and *the rest of* its blood he
shall pour out at the base of the
altar of burnt offering.
26 'And[r] all its fat he shall offer
up in smoke on the altar as *in the
case of* the fat of the sacrifice of
peace offerings. Thus[r] the priest
shall make atonement for him in

regard to his sin, and he shall be
forgiven. Lev. 4:19 • Lev. 6:7
27 'Now if anyone of the common people sins unintentionally in
doing any of the things which the
LORD has commanded not to be
done, and becomes guilty,
28 [t]if his sin, which he has[t]com-
mitted is made known to him,
then he shall bring for his offering
a [a]goat, a female without defect,
for his sin which he has committed. *or • sinned • female goat*
29 'And[r]he shall lay his hand on
the head of the sin offering, and
slay the sin offering at the place of
the burnt offering. Lev. 1:4
30 'And the priest shall take
some of its blood with his finger
and put it on the horns of the altar
of burnt offering; and[r]all *the rest*
of its blood he shall pour out at
the base of the altar. Lev. 4:7
31 'Then he shall remove all its
fat, just as the fat was removed
from the sacrifice of peace offerings; and the priest shall offer it
up in smoke on the altar for a
soothing aroma to the LORD. Thus
the priest shall make atonement
for him, and he shall be forgiven.
32 'But if he brings a lamb as his
offering for a sin offering, he shall
bring it, a female without defect.
33 'And he shall lay his hand on
the head of the sin offering, and
slay it for a sin offering[r]in the
place where[t]they slay the burnt
offering. Lev. 4:29 • *one slays*
34 'And the priest is to take
some of the blood of the sin offering with his finger and put it on
the horns of[r]the altar of burnt offering; and all *the rest of* its blood
he shall pour out at the base of the
altar. Lev. 4:7, 18, 25, 30
35 'Then he shall remove all its
fat, just as the fat of the lamb is
removed from the sacrifice of the
peace offerings, and the priest
shall offer them up in smoke on
the altar, on the offerings by fire
to the LORD. Thus the priest shall
make atonement for him in regard
to his sin which he has committed, and he shall be forgiven.

CHAPTER 5

'NOW if a person sins, after he
hears a public adjuration *to tes-*
tify, when he is a witness,
whether he has seen or *otherwise*
known, if he does not tell *it*, then
he will bear his guilt.
2 'Or if a person touches any
unclean thing, whether a carcass
of an unclean beast, or the carcass
of unclean cattle, or a carcass of
unclean swarming things, though
it is hidden from him, and he is
unclean, then he will be guilty.
3 'Or if he touches human uncleanness, of whatever *sort* his
uncleanness *may* be with which
he becomes unclean, and it is hidden from him, and then he comes
to know *it*, he will be guilty.
4 'Or if a person [r]swears
thoughtlessly with his lips to do
evil or to do good, in whatever
matter a man may speak thoughtlessly with an oath, and it is hidden from him, and then he comes
to know *it*, he will be guilty in one
of these. Num. 30:6, 8; Ps. 106:33
5 'So it shall be when he becomes guilty in one of these, that

he shall [r]confess that in which he
has sinned. Lev. 16:21
6 'He shall also bring his guilt
offering to the LORD for his sin
which he has [t]committed, a female
from the flock, a lamb or a [t]goat as
a sin offering. So the priest shall
make atonement on his behalf for
his sin. *sinned* • *female goat*
7 'But if he cannot afford a
lamb, then he shall bring to the
LORD his guilt offering for that in
which he has sinned, two turtledoves or two young pigeons,[r] one
for a sin offering and the other for
a burnt offering. Lev. 12:6, 8
8 'And he shall bring them to
the priest, who shall offer first
that which is for the sin offering
and shall nip its head at the front
of its neck, but he [r]shall not sever
it. Lev. 1:17
9 'He shall also sprinkle some
of the blood of the sin offering [r]on
the side of the altar, while the rest
of the blood shall be drained out
[r]at the base of the altar: it is a sin
offering. Lev. 1:15 • Lev. 4:7, 18
10 'The second he shall then prepare as a burnt offering [r]according
to the ordinance. So the priest
shall make atonement on his behalf for his sin which he has [t]com-
mitted, and it shall be forgiven
him. Lev. 1:14-17 • *sinned*
11 'But if his [t]means are insufficient for two turtledoves or two
young pigeons, then for his offering for that which he has sinned,
he shall bring the tenth of an [1]e-
phah of fine flour for a sin offering; he shall not put oil on it or
place incense on it, for it is a sin
offering. *hand does not reach*
12 'And he shall bring it to the
priest, and the priest shall take his
handful of it as its memorial portion and offer *it* up in smoke on
the altar, with the offerings of the
LORD by fire: it is a sin offering.
13 'So the priest shall make
atonement for him concerning his
sin which he has [t]committed from
one of these, and it shall be forgiven him; then [r]*the rest* shall become the priest's, like the grain
offering.' " *sinned* • Lev. 2:3
14 Then the LORD spoke to
Moses, saying,
15 "If [r]a person acts unfaithfully
and sins unintentionally against
the LORD's holy things, then he
shall bring his guilt offering to the
LORD: a ram without defect from
the flock, according to your valuation in silver by shekels, in *terms*
of the shekel of the sanctuary, for
a guilt offering. Num. 5:5-8
16 "And he shall make restitution for that which he has sinned
against the holy thing, and shall
add to it a fifth part of it, and give
it to the priest. The priest shall
then make atonement for him
with the ram of the guilt offering,
and it shall be forgiven him.
17 "Now if a person sins and
does any of the things which the
LORD has commanded not to be
done, [r]though he was unaware,
still he is guilty, and shall bear his
punishment. Lev. 4:2; 5:19
18 "He is then to bring to the
priest [r]a ram without defect from
the flock, according to your valuation, for a guilt offering. So the
priest shall make atonement for
him concerning his error in which
he sinned unintentionally and did

[1]I.e., Approx. one bushel

not know *it*, and it shall be forgiven him. Lev. 5:15

19 "It is a guilt offering; he was certainly guilty before the LORD."

CHAPTER 6

THEN the LORD spoke to Moses, saying,

2 "When[r] a person sins and acts unfaithfully against the LORD, and deceives his companion in regard to a deposit or a security entrusted *to him*, or through robbery, or *if* he has extorted from his companion, Ex. 22:7-15

3 or[r] has found what was lost and lied about it and sworn falsely, so that he sins in regard to any one of the things a man may do; Ex. 23:4; Deut. 22:1-4

4 then it shall be, when he sins and becomes guilty, that he shall restore what he took by robbery, or what he got by extortion, or the deposit which was[a] entrusted to him, or the lost thing which he found, *deposited with*

5 or anything about which he swore falsely; he shall make restitution for it in full, and add to it one-fifth more. He shall give it to the one to whom it belongs on the day *he presents* his guilt offering.

6 "Then he shall bring to the priest his guilt offering to the LORD, [r]a ram without defect from the flock, according to your valuation, for a guilt offering, Lev. 5:15

7 and the priest shall make atonement for him before the LORD; and he shall be forgiven for any one of the things which he may have done to incur guilt."

8 Then the LORD spoke to Moses, saying,

9 "Command Aaron and his sons, saying, 'This is the law for the burnt offering: the burnt offering itself *shall remain* on the hearth on the altar all night until the morning, and the fire on the altar is to be kept burning on it.

10 'And the priest is to put on his linen robe, and he shall put on undergarments next to his flesh; and he shall take up the ashes *to* which the fire[t] reduces the burnt offering on the altar, and place them beside the altar. *consumes*

11 'Then he shall take off his garments and put on other garments, and carry the[a] ashes outside the camp to a clean place. *fat ashes*

12 'And the fire on the altar shall be kept burning on it. It shall not go out, but the priest shall burn wood on it every morning; and he shall lay out the burnt offering on it, and offer up in smoke the fat portions of the peace offerings[r] on it. Lev. 3:5

13 'Fire shall be kept burning continually on the altar; it is not to go out.

14 'Now this is the law of the grain offering: the sons of Aaron shall present it before the LORD in front of the altar.

15 'Then one *of them* shall lift up from it a handful of the fine flour of the grain offering, [t]with its oil and all the incense that is on the grain offering, and he shall offer *it* up in smoke on the altar, a soothing aroma, as its memorial offering to the LORD. *and some of*

16 'And what is left of it Aaron and his sons are to eat. It shall be

eaten as unleavened cakes in a holy place; they are to eat it in the court of the tent of meeting.

17 'It[r] shall not be baked with leaven. I have given it as their share from My offerings by fire; it is most holy, like the sin offering and the guilt offering. Lev. 2:11

18 'Every male among the sons of Aaron may eat it; it is a permanent ordinance throughout your generations, from the offerings by fire to the LORD. Whoever touches them shall become consecrated.' "

19 Then the LORD spoke to Moses, saying,

20 "This is the offering which Aaron and his sons are to present to the LORD on the day when he is anointed; the tenth of an[r] ephah of fine flour as a regular grain offering, half of it in the morning and half of it in the evening. Lev. 5:11

21 "It shall be prepared with oil on a[r] griddle. When it is *well* stirred, you shall bring it. You shall present the grain offering in baked pieces as a soothing aroma to the LORD. Lev. 2:5

22 "And the anointed priest who will be in his place among his sons shall[t] offer it. By a permanent ordinance it shall be entirely offered up in smoke to the LORD. *do*

23 "So every grain offering of the priest shall be burned entirely. It shall not be eaten."

24 Then the LORD spoke to Moses, saying,

25 "Speak to Aaron and to his sons, saying, 'This is the law of the sin offering:[r] in the place where the burnt offering is slain the sin offering shall be slain before the LORD; it is most holy. Lev. 1:11

26 'The[r] priest who offers it for sin shall eat it. It shall be eaten in a holy place, in the court of the tent of meeting. Lev. 6:29

27 'Anyone who touches its flesh shall become consecrated; and when any of its blood splashes on a garment, in a holy place[r] you shall wash what was splashed on.

28 'Also the earthenware vessel in which it was boiled shall be broken; and if it was boiled in a bronze vessel, then it shall be scoured and rinsed in water.

29 'Every[r] male among the priests may eat of it;[r] it is most holy. Lev. 6:18 • Lev. 6:17, 25

30 'But no sin offering of which any of the blood is brought into the tent of meeting to make atonement in the holy place shall be eaten; it shall be burned with fire.

CHAPTER 7

'NOW this is the law of the guilt offering; it is most holy.

2 'In[r] the place where they slay the burnt offering they are to slay the guilt offering, and he shall sprinkle its blood around on the altar. Lev. 1:11

3 'Then he shall offer from it all its fat: the[r] fat tail and the fat that covers the entrails, Lev. 3:9

4 and the two kidneys with the fat that is on them, which is on the loins, and the lobe on the liver he shall remove with the kidneys.

5 'And the priest shall offer them up in smoke on the altar as an offering by fire to the LORD; it is a guilt offering.

6 'Every[r] male among the priests may eat of it. It shall be

eaten in a holy place; it is most
holy. Lev. 6:18, 29; Num. 18:9
7 'The guilt offering is like the
sin offering, there is one law for
them; the priest who makes
atonement with it shall have it.
8 'Also the priest who presents
any man's burnt offering, that
priest shall have for himself the
skin of the burnt offering which
he has presented.
9 'Likewise, every grain offering that is baked in the oven, and
everything prepared in a[t]pan or on
a griddle, shall belong to the priest
who presents it. *lidded cooking pan*
10 'And every grain offering
mixed with oil, or dry, shall[t]be-
long to all the sons of Aaron,[t]to all
alike. *be • a man as his brother*
11 'Now this is the law of the
sacrifice of peace offerings which
shall be presented to the LORD.
12 'If he offers it by way of
thanksgiving, then along with the
sacrifice of thanksgiving he shall
offer unleavened cakes mixed
with oil, and unleavened wafers
spread with oil, and cakes *of well*
stirred fine flour mixed with oil.
13 'With the sacrifice of his
peace offerings for thanksgiving,
he shall present his offering with
cakes of[r]leavened bread. Amos 4:5
14 'And of this he shall present
one of every offering as a contribution to the LORD; it shall belong
to the priest who sprinkles the
blood of the peace offerings.
15 'Now *as for* the flesh of the
sacrifice of his thanksgiving peace
offerings, it shall be eaten on the
day of his offering; he shall not
leave any of it over until morning.
16 'But if the sacrifice of his offering is a votive or a freewill offering, it shall be eaten on the day
that he offers his sacrifice; and on
the[t]next day what is left of it may
be eaten; *morrow and what*
17 but what is left over from the
flesh of the sacrifice on the third
day shall be burned with fire.
18 'So if any of the flesh of the
sacrifice of his peace offerings
should *ever* be eaten on the third
day, he who offers it shall not be
accepted, *and* it shall not be reckoned to his *benefit*. It shall be an
[r]offensive thing, and the person
who eats of it shall bear his *own*
iniquity. Lev. 19:7; Prov. 15:8
19 'Also the flesh that touches
anything unclean shall not be eat-
en; it shall be burned with fire. As
for *other* flesh, anyone who is
clean may eat *such* flesh.
20 'But the person who eats the
flesh of the sacrifice of peace offerings which belong to the LORD,
in his uncleanness, that person
shall be cut off from his people.
21 'And when anyone touches
anything unclean, whether human
uncleanness, or an unclean animal, or any unclean [2]detestable
thing, and eats of the flesh of the
sacrifice of peace offerings which
belong to the LORD, that person
shall be cut off from his people.' "
22 Then the LORD spoke to
Moses, saying,
23 "Speak to the sons of Israel,
saying, 'You shall not eat any fat
from an ox, a sheep, or a goat.
24 'Also the fat of *an animal*
which dies, and the fat of an animal[r]torn *by beasts*, may be put to
any other use, but you must certainly not eat it. Ex. 22:31

[2] Some mss. read *swarming thing*

25 'For whoever eats the fat of
the animal from which an offering
by fire is offered to the LORD, even
the person who eats shall be cut
off from his people.
26 'And[r] you are not to eat any
blood, either of bird or animal, in
any of your dwellings. Gen. 9:4
27 'Any person who eats any
blood, even that person shall be
cut off from his people.' "
28 Then the LORD spoke to
Moses, saying,
29 "Speak to the sons of Israel,
saying, 'He who offers[r] the sacrifice of his peace offerings to the
LORD shall bring his offering to
the LORD from the sacrifice of his
peace offerings. Lev. 3:1
30 'His own hands are to bring
offerings by fire to the LORD. He
shall bring the fat with the breast,
that the[r] breast may be[t] presented
as a wave offering before the
LORD. Lev. 8:29 • *waved*
31 'And the priest shall offer up
the fat in smoke on the altar; but
[r] the breast shall belong to Aaron
and his sons. Num. 18:11
32 'And you shall give the right
thigh to the priest as a[a] contribution from the sacrifices of your
peace offerings. *heave offering*
33 'The one among the sons of
Aaron who offers the blood of the
peace offerings and the fat, the
right thigh shall be his as *his* portion.
34 'For I have taken the breast of
the wave offering and the thigh of
the[a] contribution from the sons of
Israel from the sacrifices of their
peace offerings, and have given
them to Aaron the priest and to
his sons as *their* due forever from
the sons of Israel. *heave offering*
35 'This is that which is consecrated to Aaron and that which is
consecrated to his sons from the
offerings by fire to the LORD, in
that day when he presented them
to serve as priests to the LORD.
36 'These[t] the LORD had commanded to be given them from the
sons of Israel in the day that He
[r] anointed them. It is *their* due forever throughout their generations.' " *which* • Lev. 8:12, 30
37 This is the law of the burnt
offering, the grain offering and the
sin offering and the guilt offering
and the ordination offering and
the sacrifice of peace offerings,
38 [r] which the LORD commanded
Moses at Mount Sinai in the day
that He commanded the sons of
Israel to[a] present their offerings to
the LORD in the wilderness of Sinai. Lev. 1:1 • *offer*

CHAPTER 8

THEN the LORD spoke to Moses,
saying,
2 "Take[r] Aaron and his sons
with him, and the[r] garments and
the anointing oil and the bull of
the sin offering, and the two rams
and the basket of unleavened
bread; Ex. 28:1 • Lev. 6:10
3 and assemble all the congregation at the doorway of the tent
of meeting."
4 So Moses did just as the
LORD commanded him. When the
congregation was assembled at
the doorway of the tent of meeting,
5 Moses said to the congrega-

tion, “This is the thing which the LORD has commanded to do.”

6 Then[r]Moses had Aaron and his sons come near, and washed them with water. Ex. 29:4-6

7 And he[r]put the tunic on him and girded him with the sash, and clothed him with the robe, and put the ephod on him; and he girded him with the artistic band of the ephod,[t]with which he tied *it* to him. Ex. 28:4 • *and with it*

8 He then placed the[t]breastpiece on him, and in the breastpiece he put [3]the Urim and the Thummim. *pouch*

9 He also placed the turban on his head, and on the turban, at its front, he placed[r]the golden plate, the holy crown, just as the LORD had commanded Moses. Ex. 28:36

10 Moses then took the anointing oil and anointed the[a]tabernacle and all that was in it, and consecrated them. *dwelling place*

11 And he sprinkled some of it on the altar seven times and anointed the altar and all its utensils, and the basin and its stand, to [r]consecrate them. Ex. 30:29

12 Then he poured some of the anointing oil on Aaron's head and anointed him, to consecrate him.

13[r]Next Moses had Aaron's sons come near and clothed them with tunics, and girded them with sashes, and bound[t]caps on them, just as the LORD had commanded Moses. Ex. 29:8, 9 • *headgear*

14 Then he brought the bull of the sin offering, and Aaron and his sons laid their hands on the head of the bull of the sin offering.

15 Next Moses slaughtered *it* and took the blood and with his finger[r]put *some of it* around on the horns of the altar, and purified the altar. Then he poured out *the rest of* the blood at the base of the altar and consecrated it, to make atonement for it. Ezek. 43:20

16 He also[r]took all the fat that was on the entrails and the lobe of the liver, and the two kidneys and their fat; and Moses offered it up in smoke on the altar. Ex. 29:13

17[r]But the bull and its hide and its flesh and its refuse, he burned in the fire outside the camp, just as the LORD had commanded Moses. Lev. 4:11, 12

18 Then he presented[r]the ram of the burnt offering, and Aaron and his sons laid their hands on the head of the ram. Ex. 29:15

19 And Moses slaughtered *it* and sprinkled the blood around on the altar.

20 When he had cut the ram into its pieces, Moses[r]offered up the head and the pieces and the suet in smoke. Lev. 1:8

21 After he had washed the entrails and the legs with water, Moses[r]offered up the whole ram in smoke on the altar. It was a burnt offering for a soothing aroma; it was an offering by fire to the LORD, just as the LORD had commanded Moses. Ex. 29:18

22 Then he presented the second ram, the ram of [4]ordination; and Aaron and his sons laid their hands on the head of the ram.

23 And Moses slaughtered *it* and took some of its blood and[r]put it on the lobe of Aaron's right ear, and on the thumb of his right hand, and on the big toe of his right foot. Ex. 29:20, 21

[3]I.e., the lights and perfections

[4]Lit., *filling*, and so throughout this context

24 He also had Aaron's sons
come near; and Moses put some
of the blood on the lobe of their
right ear, and on the thumb of
their right hand, and on the big
toe of their right foot. Moses then
[r]sprinkled *the rest of* the blood
around on the altar. Heb. 9:18-22
25 And he took the fat, and the
fat tail, and all the fat that was on
the entrails, and the lobe of the
liver and the two kidneys and
their fat and the right thigh.
26 And[r] from the basket of unleavened bread that was before
the LORD, he took one unleavened
cake and one cake of bread *mixed*
with oil and one wafer, and placed
them on the portions of fat and on
the right thigh. Ex. 29:23
27 He then put all *these* on the
hands of Aaron and on the hands
of his sons, and presented them as
a wave offering before the LORD.
28 Then Moses[r] took them from
their hands and offered them up in
smoke on the altar with the burnt
offering. They were an ordination
offering for [r]a soothing aroma; it
was an offering by fire to the
LORD. Ex. 29:25 • Gen. 8:21
29 Moses also took[r] the breast
and presented it for a wave offering before the LORD; it was Moses'
portion of the ram of ordination,
just as the LORD had commanded
Moses. Lev. 7:31-34
30 So Moses[r] took some of the
anointing oil and some of the
blood which was on the altar, and
sprinkled it on Aaron, on his garments, on his sons, and on the garments of his sons with him; and he
consecrated Aaron, his garments,
and his sons, and the garments of
his sons with him. Ex. 29:21
31 Then Moses said to Aaron
and to his sons, "Boil[r] the flesh at
the doorway of the tent of meeting, and eat it there together with
the bread which is in the basket of
the ordination offering, just as I
commanded, saying, 'Aaron and
his sons shall eat it.' Ex. 29:31
32 "And [r]the remainder of the
flesh and of the bread you shall
burn in the fire. Ex. 29:34
33 "And you shall not go outside
the doorway of the tent of meeting for seven days, until the day
that the period of your ordination
is fulfilled; for he will[t] ordain you
through seven days. *fill your hands*
34 "The LORD has commanded to
do as has been done this day, to
make atonement on your behalf.
35 "At the doorway of the tent of
meeting, moreover, you shall remain day and night for seven
days, and keep the charge of the
LORD, that you may not die, for so
I have been commanded."
36 Thus Aaron and his sons did
all the things which the LORD had
commanded through Moses.

CHAPTER 9

NOW it came about [r]on the
eighth day that Moses called Aaron and his sons and the elders of
Israel; Ezek. 43:27
2 and he said to Aaron, "Take
for yourself a calf, a bull, for a sin
offering and a ram for a burnt offering, *both* without defect, and
offer *them* before the LORD.
3 "Then to the sons of Israel you
shall speak, saying, 'Take a male

goat for a sin offering, and a calf and a lamb, both one year old, without defect, for a burnt offering,

4 and an ox and a ram for peace offerings, to sacrifice before the LORD, and a grain offering mixed with oil; for today[r]the LORD shall appear to you.' " Ex. 29:43

5 So they took what Moses had commanded to the front of the tent of meeting, and the whole congregation came near and stood before the LORD.

6 And Moses said, "This is the thing which the LORD has commanded you to do, that the glory of the LORD may appear to you."

7 Moses then said to Aaron, "Come near to the altar and[t]offer your sin offering and your burnt offering, that you may make atonement for yourself and for the people; then make the offering for the people, that you may make atonement for them, just as the LORD has commanded." *make*

8 [r]So Aaron came near to the altar and slaughtered the calf of the sin offering which was for himself. Lev. 4:1-12

9 And Aaron's sons presented the blood to him; and he dipped his finger in the blood, and put *some* on the horns of the altar, and poured out *the rest of* the blood at the base of the altar.

10 The fat and the kidneys and the lobe of the liver of the sin offering, he then offered up in smoke on the altar just as the LORD had commanded Moses.

11[r]The flesh and the skin, however, he burned with fire outside the camp. Lev. 4:11, 12; 8:17

12 Then he slaughtered the burnt offering; and Aaron's sons handed the blood to him and he sprinkled it around on the altar.

13 And they handed the burnt offering to him in[t]pieces with the head, and he offered *them* up in smoke on the altar. *its pieces*

14 He also washed the entrails and the legs, and offered *them* up in smoke with the burnt offering on the altar.

15 Then he presented the people's offering, and took the goat of the sin offering which was for the people, and slaughtered it and offered it for sin, like the first.

16 He also presented the burnt offering, and[t]offered it according to the ordinance. *made*

17 Next he presented the grain offering, and filled his hand with some of it and offered *it* up in smoke on the altar, besides the burnt offering of the morning.

18 Then[r]he slaughtered the ox and the ram, the sacrifice of peace offerings which was for the people; and Aaron's sons handed the blood to him and he sprinkled it around on the altar. Lev. 3:1-11

19 As for the portions of fat from the ox and from the ram, the fat tail, and the *fat*[r]covering, and the kidneys and the[a]lobe of the liver, Lev. 3:9 • *appendage on*

20 they now placed the portions of fat on the breasts; and he offered[t]them up in smoke on the altar. *the portions of fat*

21 But the breasts and the right thigh Aaron[t]presented as a wave offering before the LORD, just as Moses had commanded. *waved*

22 Then Aaron lifted up his

hands toward the people and [r]blessed them, and he stepped down after making the sin offering and the burnt offering and the peace offerings. Num. 6:22-26

23 And Moses and Aaron went into the tent of meeting. When they came out and blessed the people,[r]the glory of the LORD appeared to all the people. Lev. 9:6

24 [r]Then fire came out from before the LORD and consumed the burnt offering and the portions of fat on the altar; and when all the people saw *it*, they shouted and fell on their faces. 2 Chr. 7:1

CHAPTER 10

NOW[r]Nadab and Abihu, the sons of Aaron, took their respective [r]firepans, and after putting fire in them, placed incense on it and offered strange fire before the LORD, which He had not commanded them. Ex. 24:1, 9 • Lev. 16:12

2 [r]And fire came out from the presence of the LORD and consumed them, and they died before the LORD. Num. 3:4; 16:35

3 Then Moses said to Aaron, "It is what the LORD spoke, saying,

'By those who come near Me
I will be treated as holy,
And before all the people I
will be honored.'"

So Aaron, therefore, kept silent.

4 Moses called also to[r]Mishael and Elzaphan, the sons of Aaron's uncle Uzziel, and said to them, "Come forward, carry your[t]relatives away from the front of the sanctuary to the outside of the camp." Ex. 6:22 • *brothers*

5 So they came forward and carried them still in their[r]tunics to the outside of the camp, as Moses had said. Ex. 29:5; Lev. 8:13

6 Then Moses said to Aaron and to his sons Eleazar and Ithamar, "Do not [5]uncover your heads nor tear your clothes, so that you may not die, and that He may not become wrathful against all the congregation. But your kinsmen, the whole house of Israel, shall bewail the burning which the LORD has[t]brought about. *burned*

7 "You shall not even go out from the doorway of the tent of meeting, lest you die; for [r]the LORD's anointing oil is upon you." So they did according to the word of Moses. Lev. 21:12

8 The LORD then spoke to Aaron, saying,

9 "Do not drink wine or strong drink, neither you nor your sons with you, when you come into the tent of meeting, so that you may not die—it is a perpetual statute throughout your generations—

10 and[r]so as to make a distinction between the holy and the profane, and between the unclean and the clean, Lev. 11:47; 20:25

11 and[r]so as to teach the sons of Israel all the statutes which the LORD has spoken to them through Moses." Deut. 17:10, 11

12 Then Moses spoke to Aaron, and to his surviving sons,[r]Eleazar and Ithamar, "Take[r] the grain offering that is left over from the LORD's offerings by fire and eat it unleavened beside the altar, for it is most holy. Ex. 6:23 • Lev. 6:14-18

13 "You shall eat it, moreover, in a holy place, because it is your

[5]Lit., *unbind*

due and your sons' due out of the
LORD's offerings by fire; for thus I
have been commanded.
14 "The[r] breast of the wave offering, however, and the thigh of the
offering you may eat in a clean
place, you and your sons and your
daughters with you; for they have
been given as your due and your
sons' due out of the sacrifices of
the peace offerings of the sons of
Israel. Lev. 7:30-34; Num. 18:11
15 "The thigh offered by lifting
up and the breast offered by waving, they shall bring along with
the offerings by fire of the portions of fat, to present as a wave
offering before the LORD; so it
shall be a thing perpetually due
you and your sons with you, just
as the LORD has commanded."
16 But Moses searched carefully for the[r] goat of the sin offering, and behold, it had been
burned up! So he was angry with
Aaron's surviving sons Eleazar
and Ithamar, saying, Lev. 9:3, 15
17 "Why did you not eat the sin
offering at the holy place? For it is
most holy, and[a] He gave it to you
to bear away the guilt of the congregation, to make atonement for
them before the LORD. *was given*
18 "Behold, [r]since its blood had
not been brought inside, into the
sanctuary, you should certainly
have eaten it in the sanctuary, just
as I commanded." Lev. 6:30
19 But Aaron spoke to Moses,
"Behold, this very day they presented their sin offering and their
burnt offering before the LORD.
When things like these happened
to me, if I had eaten a sin offering
today, would it have been good in
the sight of the LORD?"
20 And when Moses heard *that*,
it seemed good in his sight.

CHAPTER 11

THE LORD spoke again to Moses
and to Aaron, saying to them,
2 "Speak to the sons of Israel,
saying, 'These are the creatures
which you may eat from all the
animals that are on the earth.
3 'Whatever divides a hoof,
thus making split hoofs, *and*
chews the cud, among the animals, that you may eat.
4 'Nevertheless,[r] you are not to
eat of these, among those which
chew the cud, or among those
which divide the hoof: the camel,
for though it chews cud, it does
not divide the hoof, it is unclean to
you. Acts 10:14
5 'Likewise, the rock badger,
for though it chews cud, it does
not divide the hoof, it is unclean to
you;
6 the[a] rabbit also, for though it
chews cud, it does not divide the
hoof, it is unclean to you; *hare*
7 and the pig, for though it divides the hoof, thus making a split
hoof, it does not chew cud, it is
unclean to you.
8 'You shall not eat of their
flesh nor touch their carcasses;
they are unclean to you.
9 'These[r] you may eat, whatever
is in the water: all that have fins
and scales, those in the water, in
the seas or in the rivers, you may
eat. Deut. 14:9
10 'But[r] whatever is in the seas
and in the rivers, that do not have

fins and scales among all the
teeming life of the water, and
among all the living creatures that
are in the water, they are detestable things to you, Deut. 14:10
11 and they shall be [6]abhorrent
to you; you may not eat of their
flesh, and their carcasses you
shall detest.
12 'Whatever in the water does
not have fins and scales is abhorrent to you.
13 'These, moreover, you shall
detest among the birds; they are
abhorrent, not to be eaten: the
[a]eagle and the vulture and the [a]buz-
zard, *vulture • black vulture*
14 and the kite and the falcon in
its kind,
15 every raven in its kind,
16 and the ostrich and the owl
and the sea gull and the hawk in
its kind,
17 and the little owl and the cormorant and the great owl,
18 and the white owl and the
pelican and the carrion vulture,
19 and the stork, the heron in its
kinds, and the hoopoe, and the
bat.
20 'All the [t]winged insects that
walk on *all* fours are detestable to
you. *swarming things with wings*
21 'Yet these you may eat
among all the winged insects
which walk on *all* fours: those
which have above their feet
jointed legs with which to jump
on the earth.
22 'These of them you may eat:
the locust in its kinds, and the
devastating locust in its kinds,
and the cricket in its kinds, and
the grasshopper in its kinds.
23 'But all other winged insects
which are four-footed are detestable to you.
24 'By these, moreover, you will
be made unclean: whoever
touches their carcasses becomes
unclean until evening,
25 and [r]whoever picks up any of
their carcasses shall wash his
clothes and be unclean until evening. Lev. 11:40
26 'Concerning all the animals
which divide the hoof, but do not
make a split *hoof*, or which do not
chew cud, they are unclean to
you: whoever touches them becomes unclean.
27 'Also whatever walks on its
paws, among all the creatures that
walk on *all* fours, are unclean to
you; whoever touches their carcasses becomes unclean until evening,
28 and the one who picks up
their carcasses shall wash his
clothes and be unclean until evening; they are unclean to you.
29 'Now these are to you the unclean among the swarming things
which swarm on the earth: the
mole, and the mouse, and the
great lizard in its kinds,
30 and the gecko, and the crocodile, and the lizard, and the sand
reptile, and the chameleon.
31 'These are to you the unclean
among all the swarming things;
whoever touches them when they
are dead becomes unclean until
evening.
32 'Also anything on which one
of them may fall when they are
dead, becomes unclean, including
any wooden article, or clothing, or
a skin, or a sack—any article of
which use is made—it shall be put

[6]Lit., *detestable things*

in the water and be unclean until
evening, then it becomes clean.
33 'As for any[r] earthenware vessel into which one of them may
fall, whatever is in it becomes unclean and you shall break[t] the vessel. Lev. 6:28; 15:12 • *it*
34 'Any of the food which may
be eaten, on which water comes,
shall become unclean; and any liquid which may be drunk in every
vessel shall become unclean.
35 'Everything, moreover, on
which part of their carcass may
fall becomes unclean; an oven or a
[7]stove shall be smashed; they are
unclean and shall continue as unclean to you.
36 'Nevertheless a spring or a
cistern [t]collecting water shall be
clean, though the one who
touches their carcass shall be unclean. *of a gathering of*
37 'And if a part of their carcass
falls on any seed for sowing which
is to be sown, it is clean.
38 'Though if water is put on the
seed, and a part of their carcass
falls on it, it is unclean to you.
39 'Also if one of the animals
dies which you have for food, the
one who touches its carcass becomes unclean until evening.
40 'He[r] too, who eats some of its
carcass shall wash his clothes and
be unclean until evening; and the
one who picks up its carcass shall
wash his clothes and be unclean
until evening. Lev. 17:15
41 'Now every swarming thing
that swarms on the earth is detestable, not to be eaten.
42 'Whatever crawls on its belly,
and whatever walks on *all* fours,
whatever has many feet, in re-

[7]Lit., *hearth for supporting (two) pots*

spect to every swarming thing
that swarms on the earth, you
shall not eat them, for they are detestable.
43 'Do not render[t] yourselves detestable through any of the
swarming things that swarm; and
you shall not make yourselves unclean with them so that you become unclean. *your souls*
44 'For I am the LORD your God.
Consecrate yourselves therefore,
and be holy; for I am holy. And
you shall not make yourselves unclean with any of the swarming
things that swarm on the earth.
45 'For I am the LORD, who
brought you up from the land of
Egypt, to be your God; thus you
shall be holy for I am holy.' "
46 This is the law regarding the
animal, and the bird, and every
living thing that moves in the waters, and everything that swarms
on the earth,
47 [r]to make a distinction between the unclean and the clean,
and between the edible creature
and the creature which is not to
be eaten. Lev. 10:10

CHAPTER 12

THEN the LORD spoke to Moses,
saying,
2 "Speak to the sons of Israel,
saying, 'When a woman gives
birth and bears a male *child*, then
she shall be unclean for seven
days, as in the days of her menstruation she shall be unclean.
3 'And on [r]the eighth day the
flesh of his foreskin shall be circumcised. Gen. 17:12; Luke 1:59
4 'Then she shall remain in the

blood of *her* purification for thirty-three days; she shall not touch any consecrated thing, nor enter the sanctuary, until the days of her purification are completed.

5 'But if she bears a female *child,* then she shall be unclean for two weeks, as in her [t]menstruation; and she shall remain in the blood of *her* purification for sixty-six days. *impurity*

6 'And [r]when the days of her purification are completed, for a son or for a daughter, she shall bring to the priest at the doorway of the tent of meeting, a one year old lamb for a burnt offering, and a young pigeon or a turtledove[r] for a sin offering. Luke 2:22 • Lev. 5:7

7 'Then he shall offer it before the LORD and make atonement for her; and she shall be cleansed from the flow of her blood. This is the law for her who bears *a child, whether* a male or a female.

8 'But if she cannot afford a lamb, then she shall take two turtledoves or two young pigeons, the one for a burnt offering and the other for a sin offering; and the priest shall make atonement for her, and she shall be clean.' "

CHAPTER 13

THEN the LORD spoke to Moses and to Aaron, saying,

2 "When a man has on the skin of his [t]body a swelling or a scab or a bright spot, and it becomes [8]an infection of leprosy on the skin of his body, then he shall be brought to Aaron the priest, or to one of his sons the priests. *flesh*

[8]Lit., *a mark, stroke,* and so throughout this context

3 "And the priest shall look at the mark on the skin of the [t]body, and if the hair in the infection has turned white and the infection appears to be deeper than the skin of his body, it is an infection of leprosy; when the priest has looked at him, he shall pronounce him unclean. *flesh*

4 "But if the bright spot is white on the skin of his [t]body, and it does not appear to be deeper than the skin, and the hair on it has not turned white, then the priest shall [t]isolate *him who has* the infection for seven days. *flesh • shut up*

5 "And the priest shall look at him on the seventh day, and if in his eyes the infection [t]has not changed, *and* the infection has not spread on the skin, then the priest shall [t]isolate him for seven more days. *has stood • shut up*

6 "And the priest shall look at him again on the seventh day; and if the infection has faded, and the mark has not spread on the skin, then the priest shall pronounce him clean; it is *only* a scab. And he shall [r]wash his clothes and be clean. Lev. 11:25; 14:8

7 "But if the scab spreads farther on the skin, after he has shown himself to the priest for his cleansing, he shall appear again to the priest.

8 "And the priest shall look, and if the scab has spread on the skin, then the priest shall pronounce him unclean; it is leprosy.

9 "When the infection of leprosy is on a man, then he shall be brought to the priest.

10 "The priest shall then look, and if there is a [r]white swelling in the skin, and it has turned the hair

white, and there is quick raw flesh in the swelling, Num. 12:10

11 it is[t]a chronic leprosy on the skin of his[t]body, and the priest shall pronounce him unclean; he shall not isolate him, for he is unclean. *an old • flesh*

12 "And if the leprosy breaks out farther on the skin, and the leprosy covers all the skin of *him who has* the infection from his head even to his feet, as far as the priest can see,

13 then the priest shall look, and behold, *if* the leprosy has covered all his[t]body, he shall pronounce clean *him who has* the infection; it has all turned white *and* he is clean. *flesh*

14 "But whenever raw flesh appears on him, he shall be unclean.

15 "And the priest shall look at the raw flesh, and he shall pronounce him unclean; the raw flesh is unclean, it is leprosy.

16 "Or if the raw flesh turns again and is changed to white, then he shall come to the priest,

17 and the priest shall look at him, and behold, *if* the infection has turned to white, then the priest shall pronounce clean *him who has* the infection; he is clean.

18 "And when the body has a boil on its skin, and it is healed,

19 and in the place of the boil there is a white swelling or a reddish-white, bright spot, then it shall be shown to the priest;

20 and the priest shall look, and behold, *if* it appears to be lower than the skin, and the hair on it has turned white, then the priest shall pronounce him unclean; it is the infection of leprosy, it has broken out in the boil.

21 "But if the priest looks at it, and behold, there are no white hairs in it and it is not lower than the skin and is faded, then the priest shall[t]isolate him for seven days; *shut up*

22 and if it spreads farther on the skin, then the priest shall pronounce him unclean; it is an infection.

23 "But if the bright spot remains in its place, and does not spread, it is *only* the scar of the boil; and the priest shall pronounce him clean.

24 "Or if the body sustains in its skin a burn by fire, and the raw *flesh* of the burn becomes a bright spot, reddish-white, or white,

25 then the priest shall look at it. And if the hair in the bright spot has[r]turned white, and it appears to be deeper than the skin, it is leprosy; it has broken out in the burn. Therefore, the priest shall pronounce him unclean; it is an infection of leprosy. Ex. 4:6

26 "But if the priest looks at it, and indeed, there is no white hair in the bright spot, and it is no [t]deeper than the skin, but is dim, then the priest shall[t]isolate him for seven days; *lower • shut up*

27 and the priest shall look at him on the seventh day. If it spreads farther in the skin, then the priest shall pronounce him unclean; it is an infection of leprosy.

28 "But if the bright spot remains in its place, and has not spread in the skin, but is dim, it is the swelling from the burn; and the priest shall pronounce him clean, for it is *only* the scar of the burn.

29 "Now if a man or woman has an infection on the head or on the beard,

30 then the priest shall look at the infection, and if it appears to be deeper than the skin, and there is thin yellowish hair in it, then the priest shall pronounce him unclean; it is a scale, it is leprosy of the head or of the beard.

31 "But if the priest looks at the infection of the scale, and indeed, it appears to be no deeper than the skin, and there is no black hair in it, then the priest shall [t]isolate *the person* with the scaly infection for seven days. *shut up*

32 "And on the seventh day the priest shall look at the infection, and if the scale has not spread, and no yellowish hair has grown in it, and the appearance of the scale is no deeper than the skin,

33 then he shall shave himself, but he shall not shave the scale; and the priest shall [t]isolate *the person* with the scale seven more days. *shut up*

34 "Then on the seventh day the priest shall look at the scale, and if the scale has not spread in the skin, and it appears to be no deeper than the skin, the priest shall pronounce him clean; and he shall wash his clothes and be clean.

35 "But if the scale spreads farther in the skin after his cleansing,

36 then the priest shall look at him, and if the scale has spread in the skin, the priest need not seek for the yellowish hair; he is unclean.

37 "If in his sight the scale has remained, however, and black hair has grown in it, the scale has healed, he is clean; and the priest shall pronounce him clean.

38 "And when a man or a woman has bright spots on the skin of the body, *even* white bright spots,

39 then the priest shall look, and if the bright spots on the skin of their bodies are a faint white, it is [t]eczema that has broken out on the skin; he is clean. *tetter*

40 "Now if a man loses the hair of his head, he is bald; he is clean.

41 "And if his head becomes bald at the front and sides, he is bald on the forehead; he is clean.

42 "But if on the bald head or the bald forehead, there occurs a reddish-white infection, it is leprosy breaking out on his bald head or on his bald forehead.

43 "Then the priest shall look at him; and if the swelling of the infection is reddish-white on his bald head or on his bald forehead, like the appearance of leprosy in the skin of the [t]body, *flesh*

44 he is a leprous man, he is unclean. The priest shall surely pronounce him unclean; his infection is on his head.

45 "As for the leper who has the infection, his clothes shall be torn, and the hair of his head shall be [a]uncovered, and he shall [r]cover his mustache and cry, 'Unclean! Unclean!' *disheveled* • Mic. 3:7

46 "He shall remain unclean all the days during which he has the infection; he is unclean. He shall live alone; his dwelling shall be [r]outside the camp. Num. 5:1-4

47 "When a garment has a mark of leprosy in it, whether it is a wool garment or a linen garment,

48 whether in[a]warp or woof, of
linen or of wool, whether in
leather or in any article made of
leather, *weaving or texture*
49 if the mark is greenish or
reddish in the garment or in the
leather, or in the warp or in the
woof, or in any article of leather,
it is a leprous mark and shall be
shown to the priest.
50"Then[r]the priest shall look at
the mark, and shall[t]quarantine the
article with the mark for seven
days. Ezek. 44:23 • *shut up*
51"He shall then look at the
mark on the seventh day; if the
mark has spread in the garment,
whether in the warp or in the
woof, or in the leather, whatever
the purpose for which the leather
is used, the mark is a leprous malignancy, it is unclean.
52"So he shall burn the garment,
whether the warp or the woof, in
wool or in linen, or any article of
leather in which the mark occurs,
for it is a leprous malignancy; it
shall be burned in the fire.
53"But if the priest shall look,
and indeed, the mark has not
spread in the garment, either in
the warp or in the woof, or in any
article of leather,
54 then the priest shall order
them to wash the thing in which
the mark occurs, and he shall
quarantine it for seven more days.
55"After the article with the
mark has been washed, the priest
shall again look, and if the mark
has not changed its appearance,
even though the mark has not
spread, it is unclean; you shall
burn it in the fire, whether an eating away has produced bareness
on the top or on the front of it.
56"Then if the priest shall look,
and if the mark has faded after it
has been washed, then he shall
tear it out of the garment or out of
the leather, whether from the
warp or from the woof;
57 and if it appears again in the
garment, whether in the warp or
in the woof, or in any article of
leather, it is an outbreak; the article with the mark shall be burned
in the fire.
58"And the garment, whether
the warp or the woof, or any article of leather from which the
mark has departed when you
washed it, it shall then be washed
a second time and shall be clean."
59 This is the law for the mark
of leprosy in a garment of wool or
linen, whether in the warp or in
the woof, or in any article of
leather, for pronouncing it clean
or unclean.

CHAPTER 14

THEN the LORD spoke to Moses,
saying,
2 "This shall be the law of the
leper in the day of his cleansing.
[r]Now he shall be brought to the
priest, Matt. 8:4; Mark 1:44
3 and the priest shall go out to
the outside of the camp. Thus the
priest shall look, and if the[t]infec-
tion of leprosy has been healed in
the leper, *mark, stroke*
4 then the priest shall give orders to take two live clean birds
and cedar wood and a [t]scarlet
string and hyssop for the one who
is to be cleansed. *scarlet color and*

5"The priest shall also give orders to slay the one bird in an earthenware vessel over [t]running water. *living*

6"*As for* the live bird, he shall take it, together with the cedar wood and the [t]scarlet string and the hyssop, and shall dip them and the live bird in the blood of the bird that was slain over the running water. *scarlet color and*

7"He [r]shall then sprinkle seven times the one who is to be cleansed from the leprosy, and shall pronounce him clean, and shall let the live bird go free over the open field. Ezek. 36:25

8"The [r]one to be cleansed shall then wash his clothes and shave off all his hair, and bathe in water and be clean. Now afterward, he may enter the camp, but he [r]shall stay outside his tent for seven days. Lev. 11:25 • 2 Chr. 26:21

9"And it will be on the seventh day that he shall shave off all his hair: he shall shave his head and his beard and his eyebrows, even all his hair. He shall then wash his clothes and bathe his [t]body in water and be clean. *flesh*

10"Now on the eighth day he is to take two male lambs without defect, and a yearling ewe lamb without defect, and three-tenths *of an ephah* of fine flour mixed with oil for a grain offering, and one [9]log of oil;

11 and the priest who pronounces him clean shall present the man to be cleansed and the aforesaid before the LORD at the doorway of the tent of meeting.

12"Then the priest shall take the one male lamb and bring it for a [r]guilt offering, with the log of oil, and present them as a wave offering before the LORD. Lev. 5:6, 18

13"Next he shall slaughter the male lamb in [r]the place where they slaughter the sin offering and the burnt offering, at the place of the sanctuary—for the guilt offering, like the sin offering, belongs to the priest; it is most holy. Ex. 29:11

14"The priest shall then take some of the blood of the guilt offering, and the priest shall put *it* on the lobe of the right ear of the one to be cleansed, and on the thumb of his right hand, and on the big toe of his right foot.

15"The priest shall also take some of the log of oil, and pour *it* into his left palm;

16 the priest shall then dip his right-hand finger into the oil that is in his left palm, and with his finger sprinkle some of the oil seven times before the LORD.

17"And of the remaining oil which is in his palm, the priest shall put some on the right ear lobe of the one to be cleansed, and on the thumb of his right hand, and on the big toe of his right foot, on the blood of the guilt offering;

18 while the rest of the oil that is in the priest's palm, he shall put on the head of the one to be cleansed. So the priest shall make [r]atonement on his behalf before the LORD. Lev. 4:26; Heb. 2:17

19"The priest shall next offer the sin offering and make atonement for the one to be cleansed from his uncleanness. Then afterward, he shall slaughter the burnt offering.

20"And the priest shall offer up the burnt offering and the grain

[9]I.e., Approx. one pint, and so through v. 24

offering on the altar. Thus the
priest shall make atonement for
him, and he shall be clean.
21 "But if he is poor, and his
[t]means are insufficient, then he is
to take one male lamb for a guilt
offering as a wave offering to
make atonement for him, and one-
tenth *of an ephah* of fine flour
mixed with oil for a grain offering,
and a log of oil, *hand is not reaching*
22 and two turtledoves or two
young pigeons which [t]are within
his means, the one shall be a sin
offering and the other a burnt offering. *his hand reaches*
23 "Then the eighth day he shall
bring them for his cleansing to the
priest, at the doorway of the tent
of meeting, before the LORD.
24 "And the priest shall take the
lamb of the guilt offering, and [r]the
log of oil, and the priest shall offer
them for a wave offering before
the LORD. Lev. 14:10
25 "Next he shall slaughter the
lamb of the guilt offering; and the
priest is to take some of the blood
of the guilt offering and put *it* on
[r]the lobe of the right ear of the one
to be cleansed and on the thumb
of his right hand, and on the big
toe of his right foot. Lev. 14:14
26 "The priest shall also pour
some of the oil into his left palm;
27 and with his right-hand finger the priest shall sprinkle some
of the oil that is in his left palm
seven times before the LORD.
28 "The priest shall then put
some of the oil that is in his palm
on the lobe of the right ear of the
one to be cleansed, and on the
thumb of his right hand, and on
the big toe of his right foot, on the
place of the blood of the guilt offering.
29 "Moreover, the rest of the oil
that is in the priest's palm he shall
put on the head of the one to be
cleansed, to make atonement on
his behalf before the LORD.
30 "He shall then offer one of the
turtledoves or young pigeons,
which are within his means.
31 "*He shall offer* what he can afford, the one for a sin offering,
and the other for a burnt offering,
together with the grain offering.
So the priest shall make atonement before the LORD on behalf of
the one to be cleansed.
32 "This is the law *for him* in
whom there is an infection of leprosy, whose [t]means are limited for
his cleansing." *hand does not reach*
33 The LORD further spoke to
Moses and to Aaron, saying,
34 "When [r]you enter the land of
Canaan, which I give you for a
possession, and I put a mark of
leprosy on a house in the land of
your possession, Gen. 17:8
35 then the one who owns the
house shall come and tell the
priest, saying, '*Something* like [r]a
mark *of leprosy* has become visible to me in the house.' Ps. 91:10
36 "The priest shall then order
that they empty the house before
the priest goes in to look at the
mark, so that everything in the
house need not become unclean;
and afterward the priest shall go
in to look at the house.
37 "So he shall look at the mark,
and if the mark on the walls of the
house has greenish or reddish de-

pressions, and appears deeper
than the[t]surface; *wall*
38 then the priest shall come
out of the house, to the[t]doorway,
and quarantine the house for
seven days. *doorway of the house*
39 "And the priest shall return on
the seventh day and make an inspection. If the mark has indeed
spread in the walls of the house,
40 then the priest shall order
them to tear out the stones with
the mark in them and throw them
away[t]at an unclean place outside
the city. *to*
41 "And he shall have the house
scraped all around inside, and
they shall dump the plaster that
they scrape off at an unclean
place outside the city.
42 "Then they shall take other
stones and replace *those* stones;
and he shall take other plaster and
replaster the house.
43 "If, however, the mark breaks
out again in the house, after he
has torn out the stones and
scraped the house, and after it has
been replastered,
44 then the priest shall come in
and make an inspection. If he sees
that the mark has indeed spread
in the house, it is a malignant
mark in the house; it is unclean.
45 "He shall therefore tear down
the house, its stones, and its timbers, and all the plaster of the
house, and he shall take *them* outside the city to an unclean place.
46 "Moreover, whoever goes into
the house during the time that he
has [t]quarantined it, becomes unclean until evening. *shut up*
47 "Likewise, whoever lies down
in the house shall wash his
clothes, and whoever eats in the
house shall wash his clothes.
48 "If, on the other hand, the
priest comes in and[t]makes an inspection, and the mark has not indeed spread in the house after the
house has been replastered, then
the priest shall pronounce the
house clean because the mark has
[t]not reappeared. *looks • healed*
49 "To cleanse the house then, he
shall take[r]two birds and cedar
wood and a[t]scarlet string and hyssop, Lev. 14:4 • *scarlet color*
50 and he shall slaughter the
one bird in an earthenware vessel
over[t]running water. *living*
51 "Then he shall take the cedar
wood and the hyssop and the
[t]scarlet string, with the live bird,
and dip them in the blood of the
slain bird, as well as in the[t]run-
ning water, and sprinkle the house
seven times. *scarlet color • living*
52 "He shall thus cleanse the
house with the blood of the bird
and with the[t]running water, along
with the live bird and with the cedar wood and with the hyssop and
with the scarlet string. *living*
53 "However, he shall let the live
bird go free outside the city into
the open field. So he shall make
atonement for the house, and it
shall be clean."
54 This is the law for any mark
of leprosy—even for a scale,
55 and for the[r]leprous garment
or house, Lev. 13:47-52
56 and for a swelling, and for a
scab, and for a bright spot—
57 to teach when they are unclean, and when they are clean.
This is the law of leprosy.

CHAPTER 15

THE LORD also spoke to Moses and to Aaron, saying,

2 "Speak to the sons of Israel, and say to them, 'When any man has a discharge from his [t]body, his discharge is unclean. *flesh*

3 'This, moreover, shall be his uncleanness in his discharge: it is his uncleanness whether his body allows its discharge to flow, or whether his body obstructs its discharge.

4 'Every bed on which the person with the discharge lies becomes unclean, and everything on which he sits becomes unclean.

5 'Anyone, moreover, who touches his bed shall wash his clothes and bathe in water and be unclean until evening;

6 and whoever sits on the thing on which the man with the discharge has been sitting, shall wash his clothes and bathe in water and be unclean until evening.

7 'Also whoever touches the person with the discharge shall wash his clothes and bathe in water and be unclean until evening.

8 'Or if the man with the discharge spits on one who is clean, he too shall wash his clothes and bathe in water and be unclean until evening.

9 'And every saddle on which the person with the discharge rides becomes unclean.

10 'Whoever then touches any of the things which were under him shall be unclean until evening, and he who carries them shall wash his clothes and bathe in water and be unclean until evening.

11 'Likewise, whomever the one with the discharge touches without having rinsed his hands in water shall wash his clothes and bathe in water and be unclean until evening.

12 'However, an [r]earthenware vessel which the person with the discharge touches shall be broken, and every wooden vessel shall be rinsed in water. Lev. 6:28; 11:33

13 'Now when the man with the discharge becomes cleansed from his discharge, then he [r]shall count off for himself seven days for his cleansing; he shall then wash his clothes and bathe his body in [t]running water and shall become clean. Lev. 8:33 • *living*

14 'Then on the eighth day he shall take for himself two turtledoves or two young pigeons, and come before the LORD to the doorway of the tent of meeting, and give them to the priest;

15 and the priest shall offer them, [r]one for a sin offering, and the other for a burnt offering. So the priest shall make atonement on his behalf before the LORD because of his discharge. Lev. 5:7

16 'Now [r]if a man has a seminal emission, he shall bathe all his body in water and be unclean until evening. Deut. 23:10, 11

17 'As for any garment or any leather on which there is seminal emission, it shall be washed with water and be unclean until evening.

18 'If a man lies with a woman *so that* there is a seminal emission, they shall both bathe in water and be unclean until evening.

19 'When a woman has a discharge, *if* her discharge in her body is blood, she shall continue in her menstrual impurity for seven days; and whoever touches her shall be unclean until evening.

20 'Everything also on which she lies during her menstrual impurity shall be unclean, and everything on which she sits shall be unclean.

21 'And anyone who touches her bed shall wash his clothes and bathe in water and be unclean until evening.

22 'And whoever touches any thing on which she sits shall wash his clothes and bathe in water and be unclean until evening.

23 'Whether it be on the bed or on the thing on which she is sitting, when he touches it, he shall be unclean until evening.

24 'And if a man actually lies with her, so that her menstrual impurity is on him, he shall be unclean seven days, and every bed on which he lies shall be unclean.

25 'Now if a woman has a discharge of her blood many days, not at the period of her menstrual impurity, or if she has a discharge beyond that period, all the days of her impure discharge she shall continue as though in her menstrual impurity; she is unclean.

26 'Any bed on which she lies all the days of her discharge shall be to her like her bed at menstruation; and every thing on which she sits shall be unclean, like her uncleanness at that time.

27 'Likewise, whoever touches them shall be unclean and shall wash his clothes and bathe in water and be unclean until evening.

28 'When she becomes clean from her discharge, she shall count off for herself seven days; and afterward she shall be clean.

29 'Then on the eighth day she shall take for herself two turtledoves or two young pigeons, and bring them in to the priest, to the doorway of the tent of meeting.

30 'And the priest shall offer the [r]one for a sin offering and the other for a burnt offering. So the priest shall make atonement on her behalf before the LORD because of her impure discharge.' Lev. 5:7

31 "Thus you shall keep the sons of Israel separated from their uncleanness, lest they die in their uncleanness by their defiling My tabernacle that is among them."

32 This is the law for the one with a discharge, and for the man who has a seminal emission so that he is unclean by it,

33 and for the woman who is ill because of menstrual impurity, and for the one who has a discharge, whether a male or a female, or a man who lies with an unclean woman.

CHAPTER 16

NOW the LORD spoke to Moses after the death of the two sons of Aaron, when they had approached the presence of the LORD and died.

2 And the LORD said to Moses, "Tell your brother Aaron that he shall not enter at any time into the holy place inside the veil, before the [10]mercy seat which is on the ark, lest he die; for I will appear in the cloud over the mercy seat.

3 "Aaron shall enter the holy place with this: with a [a]bull for a

[10] Lit., *propitiatory*

sin offering and a ram for a burnt offering. *bull of the herd*

4"He shall put on the holy linen tunic, and the linen undergarments shall be next to his[t] body, and he shall be girded with the linen sash, and attired with the linen turban (these are holy garments). Then he shall bathe his[t] body in water and put them on. *flesh*

5"And he shall take from the congregation of the sons of Israel two male goats for a sin offering and one ram for a burnt offering.

6"Then [r]Aaron shall offer the bull for the sin offering which is for himself, that he may make atonement for himself and for his household. Heb. 5:3

7"And he shall take the two goats and present them before the LORD at the doorway of the tent of meeting.

8"And Aaron shall cast lots for the two goats, one lot for the LORD and the other lot for the [11]scapegoat.

9"Then Aaron shall offer the goat on which the lot for the LORD fell, and make it a sin offering.

10"But the goat on which the lot for the scapegoat fell, shall be presented alive before the LORD, to make[r] atonement upon it, to send it into the wilderness as the scapegoat. Is. 53:4-10; Rom. 3:25

11"Then Aaron shall offer the bull of the sin offering which is for himself, and make atonement for himself and for his household, and he shall slaughter the bull of the sin offering which is for himself.

12"And he shall take a firepan full of coals of fire from upon the altar before the LORD, and[t] two handfuls of finely ground sweet incense, and bring *it* inside the veil. *the filling of the hollow of his hands*

13"And he shall put the incense on the fire before the LORD, that the cloud of incense may cover the mercy seat that is on *the ark of* the testimony, lest he die.

14"Moreover,[r] he shall take some of the blood of the bull and sprinkle *it* with his finger on the[t] mercy seat on the east *side*; also in front of the mercy seat he shall sprinkle some of the blood with his finger seven times. Heb. 9:25 • *propitiatory*

15"Then he shall slaughter the goat of the sin offering[r] which is for the people, and bring its blood inside the veil, and do with its blood as he did with the blood of the bull, and sprinkle it on the [t]mercy seat and in front of the [t]mercy seat. Heb. 7:27 • *propitiatory*

16"And[r] he shall make atonement for the holy place, because of the impurities of the sons of Israel, and because of their transgressions, in regard to all their sins; and thus he shall do for the tent of meeting which abides with them in the midst of their impurities. Ex. 30:10; Heb. 2:17

17"When he goes in to make atonement in the holy place, no one shall be in the tent of meeting until he comes out, that he may make atonement for himself and for his household and for all the assembly of Israel.

18"Then he shall go out to the altar that is before the LORD and make atonement for it, and shall take some of the blood of the bull and of the blood of the goat, and

[11]Lit., *goat of removal*, or else a name: *Azazel*

[r]put it on the horns of the altar on all sides. Ezek. 43:20, 22

19 "And [r]with his finger he shall sprinkle some of the blood on it seven times, and cleanse it, and from the impurities of the sons of Israel consecrate it. Lev. 16:14

20 "When he finishes atoning for the holy place, and the tent of meeting and the altar, he shall offer the live goat.

21 "Then Aaron shall lay both of his hands on the head of the live goat, and confess over it all the iniquities of the sons of Israel, and all their transgressions [t]in regard to all their sins; and he shall lay them on the head of the goat and send *it* away into the wilderness by the hand of a man who *stands* in readiness. *in addition to*

22 "And the goat shall bear on itself all their iniquities to a solitary land; and he shall release the goat in the wilderness.

23 "Then Aaron shall come into the tent of meeting, and take off the linen garments which he put on when he went into the holy place, and shall leave them there.

24 "And [r]he shall bathe his [t]body with water in a holy place and put on his clothes, and come forth and offer his burnt offering and the burnt offering of the people, and make atonement for himself and for the people. Lev. 16:4 · *flesh*

25 "Then he shall offer up in smoke the fat of the sin offering on the altar.

26 "And the one who released the goat as the scapegoat shall wash his clothes and bathe his body with water; then afterward he shall come into the camp.

27 "But the bull of the sin offering and the goat of the sin offering, [r]whose blood was brought in to make atonement in the holy place, shall be taken outside the camp, and they shall burn their hides, their flesh, and their refuse in the fire. Lev. 6:30; Heb. 13:11

28 "Then the [r]one who burns them shall wash his clothes and bathe his body with water, then afterward he shall come into the camp. Num. 19:8

29 "And *this* shall be a permanent statute for you: in the seventh month, on the tenth day of the month, you shall humble your souls, and not do any work, whether the native, or the alien who sojourns among you;

30 for it is on this day that [t]atonement shall be made for you to cleanse you; you shall be clean from all your sins before the LORD. *he shall make atonement*

31 "It is to be a sabbath of solemn rest for you, that you may [r]humble your souls; it is a permanent statute. Ezra 8:21; Dan. 10:12

32 "So the priest who is anointed and [t]ordained to serve as priest in his father's place shall make atonement: he shall thus put on the linen garments, the holy garments, *whose hand is filled*

33 and make atonement for the holy sanctuary; and he shall make atonement for the tent of meeting and for the altar. He shall also make atonement for [r]the priests and for all the people of the assembly. Lev. 16:11

34 "Now you shall have this as a permanent statute, to [r]make atonement for the sons of Israel for all

their sins once every year." And just as the LORD had commanded Moses, *so* he did. Heb. 9:7

CHAPTER 17

THEN the LORD spoke to Moses, saying,

2 "Speak to Aaron and to his sons, and to all the sons of Israel, and say to them, 'This is what the LORD has commanded, saying,

3 "Any man from the house of Israel who slaughters an ox, or a lamb, or a goat in the camp, or who slaughters it outside the camp,

4 and has not brought it to the doorway of the tent of meeting to present *it* as an offering to the LORD before the tabernacle of the LORD, bloodguiltiness is to be reckoned to that man. He has shed blood and that man shall be cut off from among his people.

5 "The[t] reason is so that the sons of Israel may bring their sacrifices which they were sacrificing in the open field, that they may bring them in to the LORD, at the doorway of the tent of meeting to the priest, and sacrifice them as sacrifices of peace offerings to the LORD. *In order that*

6 "And the priest shall sprinkle the blood on the altar of the LORD at the doorway of the tent of meeting, and[r] offer up the fat in smoke as a soothing aroma to the LORD. Num. 18:17

7 "And they shall no longer sacrifice their sacrifices to the[a] goat demons with which they play the harlot. This shall be a permanent statute to them throughout their generations." ' *goat-idols*

8 "Then you shall say to them, 'Any man from the house of Israel, or from the aliens who sojourn among them, who offers a burnt offering or sacrifice,

9 and does not bring it to the doorway of the tent of meeting to offer it to the LORD, that man also shall be cut off from his people.

10 'And[r] any man from the house of Israel, or from the aliens who sojourn among them, who eats any blood, I will set My face against that person who eats blood, and will cut him off from among his people. 1 Sam. 14:33

11 'For the[t] life of the flesh is in the blood, and I have given it to you on the altar to make atonement for your souls; for it is the blood by reason of the life that makes atonement.' *soul*

12 "Therefore I said to the sons of Israel, 'No person among you may eat blood, nor may any alien who sojourns among you eat blood.'

13 "So when any man from the sons of Israel, or from the aliens who sojourn among them, [t] in hunting catches a beast or a bird which may be eaten,[r] he shall pour out its blood and cover it with earth. *who in hunting* • Deut. 12:16

14 "For[r] *as for the*[t] life of all flesh, its blood is *identified* with its life. Therefore I said to the sons of Israel, 'You are not to eat the blood of any flesh, for the life of all flesh is its blood; whoever eats it shall be cut off.' Gen. 9:4 • *soul*

15 "And when any person eats *an animal* which dies, or is torn

by beasts, whether he is a native or an alien, he shall wash his clothes and bathe in water, and remain unclean until evening; then he will become clean.

16 "But if he does not wash *them* or bathe his body, then he shall bear his[a]guilt." *iniquity*

CHAPTER 18

THEN the LORD spoke to Moses, saying,

2 "Speak to the sons of Israel and say to them,[r] 'I am the LORD your God. Ex. 6:7; Lev. 11:44

3 'You shall not do what is done in the land of Egypt where you lived, nor are you to do what is done in the land of Canaan where I am bringing you; you shall not walk in their statutes.

4 'You are to perform My judgments and keep My statutes,[t] to live in accord with them; I am the LORD your God. *to walk in them*

5 'So you shall keep My statutes and My judgments,[r] by which a man may live if he does them; I am the LORD. Neh. 9:29; Rom. 10:5

6 'None of you shall approach any blood relative of his to uncover nakedness; I am the LORD.

7 'You[r] shall not uncover the nakedness of your father, that is, the nakedness of your mother. She is your mother; you are not to uncover her nakedness. Deut. 27:20

8 'You[r] shall not uncover the nakedness of your father's wife; it is your father's nakedness. 1 Cor. 5:1

9 'The[r] nakedness of your sister, *either* your father's daughter or your mother's daughter, whether born at home or born outside, their nakedness you shall not uncover. Lev. 18:11; 20:17

10 'The nakedness of your son's daughter or your daughter's daughter, their nakedness you shall not uncover; for[t] their nakedness is yours. *they are your nakedness*

11 'The nakedness of your father's wife's daughter, born to your father, she is your sister, you shall not uncover her nakedness.

12 'You shall not uncover the nakedness of your father's sister; she is your father's blood relative.

13 'You shall not uncover the nakedness of your mother's sister, for she is your mother's blood relative.

14 'You[r] shall not uncover the nakedness of your father's brother; you shall not approach his wife, she is your aunt. Lev. 20:20

15 'You shall not uncover the nakedness of your daughter-in-law; she is your son's wife, you shall not uncover her nakedness.

16 'You shall not uncover the nakedness of your brother's wife; it is your brother's nakedness.

17 'You[r] shall not uncover the nakedness of a woman and of her daughter, nor shall you take her son's daughter or her daughter's daughter, to uncover her nakedness; they are blood relatives. It is [a]lewdness. Lev. 20:14 · *wickedness*

18 'And you shall not [t]marry a woman in addition to her sister as a rival while she is alive, to uncover her nakedness. *take a wife*

19 'Also[r] you shall not approach a woman to uncover her nakedness during her menstrual impurity. Lev. 15:24; 20:18

20 'And[r] you shall not have inter-

course with your neighbor's wife,
to be defiled with her. 1 Cor. 6:9
21 'Neither shall you give any of
your offspring to offer them to
Molech, nor shall you profane the
name of your God; I am the LORD.
22 'You shall not lie with a male
as[t] one lies with a female; it is an
abomination. *those who lie*
23 'Also you shall not have intercourse with any animal to be defiled with it, nor shall any woman
stand before an animal to mate
with it; it is a perversion.
24 'Do not defile yourselves by
any of these things; for by all
these[r] the nations which I am casting out before you have become
defiled. Lev. 18:3; Deut. 18:12
25 'For the land has become defiled, therefore I have visited its
punishment upon it, so the land
has spewed out its inhabitants.
26 'But as for you, you are to
keep My statutes and My judgments, and shall not do any of
these abominations, *neither* the
native, nor the alien who sojourns
among you
27 (for the men of the land who
have been before you have done
all these abominations, and the
land has become defiled);
28 so that the land may not
spew you out, should you defile it,
as it has spewed out the nation
which has been before you.
29 'For whoever does any of
these abominations,[a] those persons
who do *so* shall be cut off from
among their people. *and the*
30 'Thus you are to keep[r] My
charge, that you do not practice
any of the abominable customs
which have been practiced before
you, so as not to defile yourselves
with them; I am the LORD your
God.' " Lev. 22:9; Deut. 11:1

CHAPTER 19

THEN the LORD spoke to Moses,
saying,
2 "Speak to all the congregation
of the sons of Israel and say to
them,[r] 'You shall be holy, for I the
LORD your God am holy. Eph. 1:4
3 'Every one of you[r] shall reverence his mother and his father,
and you shall keep My sabbaths; I
am the LORD your God. Ex. 20:12
4 'Do not turn to[r] idols or make
for yourselves molten gods; I am
the LORD your God. Ps. 96:5
5 'Now when you offer a sacrifice of peace offerings to the
LORD, you shall offer it so that you
may be accepted.
6 'It shall be eaten the same
day you offer *it*, and the next day;
but what remains until the third
day shall be burned with fire.
7 'So if it is eaten at all on the
third day, it is an offense; it will
not be accepted.
8 'And everyone who eats it
will bear his iniquity, for he has
profaned the holy thing of the
LORD; and that person shall be cut
off from his people.
9 'Now when you reap the harvest of your land, you shall not
reap to the very corners of your
field, neither shall you gather the
gleanings of your harvest.
10 'Nor shall you glean your
vineyard, nor shall you gather the
fallen fruit of your vineyard; you
shall leave them for the needy and

for the stranger. I am the LORD
your God.
11 'You shall not steal, nor deal
falsely, nor lie to one another.
12 'And[r] you shall not swear
falsely by My name, so as to profane the name of your God; I am
the LORD. Deut. 5:11; Matt. 5:33
13 'You shall not oppress your
neighbor, nor rob *him*. The wages
of a hired man are not to remain
with you all night until morning.
14 'You shall not curse a deaf
man, nor place a stumbling block
before the blind, but you shall revere your God; I am the LORD.
15 'You[r] shall do no injustice in
judgment; you shall not be partial
to the poor nor defer to the great,
but you are to judge your neighbor fairly. Ex. 23:3, 6; Deut. 1:17
16 'You shall not go about as a
slanderer among your people, and
you are not to act against the life
of your neighbor; I am the LORD.
17 'You shall not hate your[t] fellow countryman in your heart;
you may surely reprove your
neighbor, but shall not incur sin
because of him. *brother*
18 'You shall not take vengeance, nor bear any grudge
against the sons of your people,
but you shall love your neighbor
as yourself; I am the LORD.
19 'You are to keep My statutes.
You shall not breed together two
kinds of your cattle;[r] you shall not
sow your field with two kinds of
seed, nor wear a garment upon
you of two kinds of material
mixed together. Deut. 22:9, 11
20 'Now[r] if a man lies carnally
with a woman who is a slave acquired for *another* man, but who
has in no way been redeemed, nor
given her freedom, there shall be
punishment; they shall not, *however*, be put to death, because she
was not free. Deut. 22:23-27
21 'And he shall bring his guilt
offering to the LORD to the doorway of the tent of meeting,[r] a ram
for a guilt offering. Lev. 6:1-7
22 'The priest shall also make
atonement for him with the ram
of the guilt offering before the
LORD for his sin which he has
committed, and the sin which he
has committed shall be forgiven
him.
23 'And when you enter the land
and plant all kinds of trees for
food, then you shall count their
fruit as[t] forbidden. Three years it
shall be[t] forbidden to you; *it* shall
not be eaten. *uncircumcised*
24 'But in the fourth year all its
fruit shall be holy, an offering of
praise to the LORD.
25 'And in the fifth year you are
to eat of its fruit, that its yield
may increase for you; I am the
LORD your God.
26 'You shall not eat *anything*
[r]with the blood, nor practice divination or soothsaying. Gen. 9:4
27 'You shall not round off the
side-growth of your heads, nor
harm the edges of your beard.
28 'You shall not make any cuts
in your[t] body for the dead, nor
make any tattoo marks on yourselves: I am the LORD. *flesh*
29 'Do[r] not[a] profane your daughter by making her a harlot, so that
the land may not fall to harlotry,
and the land become full of lewdness. Lev. 21:9 • *degrade*
30 'You shall[r] keep My sabbaths

and[r]revere My sanctuary; I am the
LORD. Lev. 19:3 • Lev. 26:2
31 'Do not turn to[a]mediums or
spiritists; do not seek them out to
be defiled by them. I am the LORD
your God. *ghosts or spirits*
32 'You shall rise up before the
grayheaded, and honor the[t]aged,
and you shall revere your God; I
am the LORD. *face of the aged*
33 'When[r]a stranger resides with
you in your land, you shall not do
him wrong. Deut. 24:17, 18
34 'The stranger who resides
with you shall be to you as the native among you, and[r]you shall
love him as yourself; for you were
aliens in the land of Egypt: I am
the LORD your God. Lev. 19:18
35 'You[r] shall do no wrong in
judgment, in measurement of
weight, or capacity. Ezek. 45:10
36 'You shall have just balances,
just weights, a just [12]ephah, and a
just [13]hin: I am the LORD your God,
who brought you out from the
land of Egypt.
37 'You shall thus observe all
My statutes, and all My ordinances, and do them: I am the
LORD.' "

CHAPTER 20

THEN the LORD spoke to Moses,
saying,
2 "You shall also say to the sons
of Israel, 'Any man from the sons
of Israel or from the aliens sojourning in Israel, who gives any
of his[t]offspring to Molech, shall
surely be put to death;[r]the people
of the land shall stone him with
stones. *seed* • Num. 15:35, 36

[12]I.e., Approx. one bushel
[13]I.e., Approx. one gallon

3 'I will also set My face
against that man and will cut him
off from among his people, because he has given some of his[t]off-
spring to Molech,[r] so as to defile
My sanctuary and to profane My
holy name. *seed* • Lev. 15:31
4 'If the people of the land,
however, should ever disregard
that man when he gives any of his
[t]offspring to Molech, so as not to
put him to death, *seed*
5 then I Myself will set My
face against that man and against
his family; and I will cut off from
among their people both him and
all those who play the harlot after
him, by playing the harlot after
Molech.
6 'As for the person who turns
to[a]mediums and to spiritists, to
play the harlot after them, I will
also set My face against that person and will cut him off from
among his people. *ghosts and spirits*
7 'You shall consecrate yourselves therefore and[r]be holy, for I
am the LORD your God. Eph. 1:4
8 'And you shall keep My statutes and practice them; I am the
LORD who sanctifies you.
9 'If *there is* anyone who curses
his father or his mother, he shall
surely be put to death; he has
cursed his father or his mother,
his bloodguiltiness is upon him.
10 'If[r]*there is* a man who commits adultery with another man's
wife, one who commits adultery
with his friend's wife, the adulterer and the adulteress shall surely
be put to death. Ex. 20:14
11 'If[r]*there is* a man who lies
with his father's wife, he has uncovered his father's nakedness;
both of them shall surely be put to

death, their bloodguiltiness is upon them. Lev. 18:7, 8

12 'If *there is* a man who lies with his daughter-in-law, both of them shall surely be put to death; they have committed incest, their bloodguiltiness is upon them.

13 'If *there is* a man who lies with a male as those who lie with a woman, both of them have committed a detestable act; they shall surely be put to death. Their bloodguiltiness is upon them.

14 'If [r]*there is* a man who [t]marries a woman and her mother, it is immorality; both he and they shall be burned with fire, that there may be no immorality in your midst. Lev. 18:17 • *takes*

15 'If [r]*there is* a man who lies with an animal, he shall surely be put to death; you shall also kill the animal. Lev. 18:23; Deut. 27:21

16 'If *there is* a woman who approaches any animal to [t]mate with it, you shall kill the woman and the animal; they shall surely be put to death. Their bloodguiltiness is upon them. *lie*

17 'If [r]*there is* a man who takes his sister, his father's daughter or his mother's daughter, so that he sees her nakedness and she sees his nakedness, it is a disgrace; and they shall be cut off in the sight of the sons of their people. He has uncovered his sister's nakedness; he bears his guilt. Deut. 27:22

18 'If *there is* a man who lies with a [t]menstruous woman and uncovers her nakedness, he has laid bare her flow, and she has exposed the flow of her blood; thus both of them shall be cut off from among their people. *sick*

19 'You [r]shall also not uncover the nakedness of your mother's sister or of your father's sister, for such a one has made naked his [t]blood relative; they shall bear their guilt. Lev. 18:12, 13 • *flesh*

20 'If [r]*there is* a man who lies with his uncle's wife he has uncovered his uncle's nakedness; they shall bear their sin. They shall die childless. Lev. 18:14

21 'If *there is* a man who takes his brother's wife, it is abhorrent; he has uncovered his brother's nakedness. They shall be childless.

22 'You are therefore to keep all My statutes and all My ordinances and do them, so that the land to which I am bringing you to [t]live will not spew you out. *dwell in it*

23 'Moreover, you shall not follow the customs of the nation which I shall drive out before you, for they did all these things, and therefore I have abhorred them.

24 'Hence I have said to you, "You are to possess their land, and I Myself will give it to you to possess it, a land flowing with milk and honey." I am the LORD your God, who has [r]separated you from the peoples. Ex. 33:16

25 'You are therefore to make a distinction between the clean animal and the unclean, and between the unclean bird and the clean; and you shall not make [t]yourselves detestable by animal or by bird or by anything that creeps on the ground, which I have separated for you as unclean. *your souls*

26 'Thus you are to be holy to Me, for I the LORD am holy; and I [r]have set you apart from the peoples to be Mine. Lev. 20:24

27 'Now a man or a woman who is a medium or a spiritist shall surely be put to death. They shall be stoned with stones, their bloodguiltiness is upon them.' "

CHAPTER 21

THEN the LORD said to Moses, "Speak to the priests, the sons of Aaron, and say to them,[r] 'No one shall defile himself for a *dead* person among his people, Ezek. 44:25

2 [r]except for his relatives who are nearest to him, his mother and his father and his son and his daughter and his brother, Lev. 21:11

3 also for his virgin sister, who is near to him[a]because she has had no husband; for her he may defile himself. *whom no man has had*

4 'He shall not defile himself as a relative by marriage among his people, and so profane himself.

5 'They shall not make any baldness on their heads, nor shave off the edges of their beards, nor make any cuts in their flesh.

6 'They shall be holy to their God and not profane the name of their God, for they present the offerings by fire[t] to the LORD,[r] the bread of their God; so they shall be holy. *of* • Lev. 3:11

7 'They[r]shall not take a woman who is profaned by harlotry, nor shall they take a woman divorced from her husband; for he is holy to his God. Lev. 21:13, 14

8 'You shall consecrate him, therefore, for he offers[r]the bread of your God; he shall be holy to you; for I the LORD, who sanctifies you, am holy. Lev. 21:6

9 'Also the daughter of any priest, if she profanes herself by harlotry, she profanes her father; she shall be burned with fire.

10 'And the priest who is the highest among his brothers, on whose head the anointing oil has been poured, and who has been consecrated to wear the garments, shall not[t]uncover his head, nor tear his clothes; *unbind*

11 nor shall he approach any dead person, nor defile himself *even* for his father or his mother;

12 nor shall he go out of the sanctuary, nor profane the sanctuary of his God; for the consecration of the anointing oil of his God is on him: I am the LORD.

13 'And he shall take a wife in her virginity.

14 'A widow, or a divorced woman, or one who is profaned by harlotry, these he may not take; but rather he is to[t]marry a virgin of his own people; *take as wife*

15 that he may not profane his [t]offspring among his people: for I am the LORD who sanctifies him.' " *seed*

16 Then the LORD spoke to Moses, saying,

17 "Speak to Aaron, saying, 'No man of your[t]offspring throughout their generations who has a defect shall approach to offer the[r]bread of his God. *seed* • Lev. 21:6

18 'For no one who has a defect shall approach: a blind man, or a lame man, or he who has a disfigured *face*, or any deformed *limb*,

19 or a man who has a broken foot or broken hand,

20 or a hunchback or a dwarf, or *one who has* a defect in his eye

or eczema or scabs or[t]crushed testicles. *obscurity*

21 'No man among the descendants of Aaron the priest, who has a defect, is to come near to offer the LORD's offerings by fire; *since* he has a defect, he shall not come near to offer the bread of his God.

22 'He may eat[r]the bread of his God, *both* of the most holy and of the holy, 1 Cor. 9:13

23 only he shall not go in to the veil or come near the altar because he has a defect, that he may not profane My sanctuaries. For I am the LORD who sanctifies them.'"

24 So Moses spoke to Aaron and to his sons and to all the sons of Israel.

CHAPTER 22

THEN the LORD spoke to Moses, saying,

2 "Tell Aaron and his sons to be careful with the holy *gifts* of the sons of Israel, which they dedicate to Me, so as not to profane My holy name; I am the LORD.

3 "Say to them, 'If any man among all your descendants throughout your generations approaches the holy *gifts* which the sons of Israel dedicate to the LORD, while he has an uncleanness, that person shall be cut off from before Me. I am the LORD.

4 'No man, of the[t]descendants of Aaron, who is a leper or who has a discharge, may eat of the holy *gifts* until he is clean. And if one touches anything made unclean by a corpse or if a man has a seminal emission, *seed*

5 or if a man touches any teeming things, by which he is made unclean, or any man by whom he is made unclean, whatever his uncleanness;

6 a[t] person who touches any such shall be unclean until evening, and shall not eat of the holy *gifts*, unless he has bathed his [t]body in water. *soul · flesh*

7 'But when the sun sets, he shall be clean, and afterward he shall eat of the holy *gifts*, for[r]it is his[t]food. Num. 18:11 · *bread*

8 'He shall not eat [r]*an animal* which dies or is torn *by beasts*, becoming unclean by it; I am the LORD. Lev. 7:24; 11:39, 40; 17:15

9 'They shall therefore keep My charge, so that they may not bear sin because of it, and die thereby because they profane it; I am the LORD who sanctifies them.

10 'No [14]layman, however, is to eat the holy *gift*; a sojourner with the priest or a hired man shall not eat of the holy *gift*.

11 'But if a priest buys a[t]slave as *his* property with his money,[t]that one may eat of it, and those who are born in his house may eat of his[t]food. *soul · he may · bread*

12 'And if a priest's daughter is married to a layman, she shall not eat of the offering of the *gifts*.

13 'But if a priest's daughter becomes a widow or divorced, and has no child and returns to her father's house as in her youth, she shall eat of her father's[t]food; but no layman shall eat of it. *bread*

14 'But if a man eats a holy *gift* unintentionally, then he shall add to it a fifth of it and shall give the holy *gift* to the priest.

[14]Lit., *stranger*

15 'And they shall not profane
the holy *gifts* of the sons of Israel
which they offer to the LORD,
16 and *so* cause them [r]to bear
punishment for guilt by eating
their holy *gifts*; for I am the LORD
who sanctifies them.' " Lev. 22:9
17 Then the LORD spoke to
Moses, saying,
18 "Speak to Aaron and to his
sons and to all the sons of Israel,
and say to them, 'Any man of the
house of Israel or of the aliens in
Israel who presents his offering,
whether it is any of their [t]votive or
any of their freewill offerings,
which they present to the LORD
for a burnt offering— *vows*
19 [r]for you to be accepted—*it
must be* a male without defect
from the cattle, the sheep, or the
goats. Lev. 21:18-21; Deut. 15:21
20 'Whatever [r]has a defect, you
shall not offer, for it will not be
accepted for you. 1 Pet. 1:19
21 'And when a man offers a
sacrifice of peace offerings to the
LORD [r]to fulfill a special vow, or for
a freewill offering, of the herd or
of the flock, it must be perfect to
be accepted; there shall be no defect in it. Num. 15:3, 8
22 'Those *that are* blind or frac-
tured or maimed or having a running sore or eczema or scabs, you
shall not offer to the LORD, nor
make of them an offering by fire
on the altar to the LORD.
23 'In respect to an ox or a lamb
which has an overgrown or
stunted *member*, you may present
it for a freewill offering, but for a
vow it shall not be accepted.
24 'Also anything *with its testicles* bruised or crushed or torn or
cut, you shall not offer to the
LORD, or sacrifice in your land,
25 nor shall you accept any
such from the hand of a foreigner
for offering as the food of your
God; for their corruption is in
them, they have a defect, they
shall not be accepted for you.' "
26 Then the LORD spoke to
Moses, saying,
27 "When an ox or a sheep or a
goat is born, it shall [t]remain seven
days [t] with its mother, and from
the eighth day on it shall be accepted as a sacrifice of an offering
by fire to the LORD. *be · under*
28 "But, *whether* it is an ox or a
sheep, you shall not kill *both* it
and its young in one day.
29 "And when you sacrifice [r] a
sacrifice of thanksgiving to the
LORD, you shall sacrifice it so that
you may be accepted. Lev. 7:12
30 "It shall be eaten on the same
day, you shall leave none of it until morning: I am the LORD.
31 "So [r] you shall keep My commandments, and do them: I am
the LORD. Lev. 19:37; Num. 15:40
32 "And you shall not profane
My holy name, but I will be sanctified among the sons of Israel: I
am the LORD who sanctifies you,
33 [r] who brought you out from
the land of Egypt, to be your God:
I am the LORD." Lev. 11:45

CHAPTER 23

THE LORD spoke again to Moses,
saying,
2 "Speak to the sons of Israel,
and say to them, 'The LORD's appointed times which you shall

proclaim as holy convocations—
My appointed times are these:
3 'For six days work may be
done; but on the seventh day there
is a sabbath of complete rest, a
holy convocation. You shall not
do any work; it is a sabbath to the
LORD in all your dwellings.
4 'These are the appointed
times of the LORD, holy convocations which you shall proclaim at
the times appointed for them.
5 'In the first month, on the
fourteenth day of the month at
twilight is the LORD's Passover.
6 'Then on the fifteenth day of
the same month there is the[r]Feast
of Unleavened Bread to the LORD;
for seven days you shall eat unleavened bread. Deut. 16:3-8
7 'On the first day you shall
have a holy convocation; you shall
not do any laborious work.
8 'But for seven days you shall
present an offering by fire to the
LORD. On the seventh day is a holy
convocation; you shall not do any
laborious work.' "
9 Then the LORD spoke to
Moses, saying,
10 "Speak to the sons of Israel,
and say to them, 'When you enter
the land which I am going to give
to you and[r]reap its harvest, then
you shall bring in the sheaf of the
first fruits of your harvest to the
priest. Ex. 23:19; 34:26
11 'And he shall wave the sheaf
before the LORD for you to be accepted; on the day after the sabbath the priest shall wave it.
12 'Now on the day when you
wave the sheaf, you shall offer a
male lamb one year old without
defect for a burnt offering to the
LORD.
13 'Its[r]grain offering shall then
be two-tenths *of an ephah* of fine
flour mixed with oil, an offering
by fire to the LORD *for* a soothing
aroma, with its libation, a fourth
of a [15]hin of wine. Lev. 6:20
14 'Until this same day, until you
have brought in the offering of
your God, you shall eat neither
bread nor roasted grain nor new
growth. It is to be a perpetual statute throughout your generations
in all your dwelling places.
15 'You[r] shall also count for
yourselves from the day after the
sabbath, from the day when you
brought in the sheaf of the wave
offering; there shall be seven complete sabbaths. Num. 28:26-31
16 'You shall count fifty days to
the day after the seventh sabbath;
then you shall present a[r]new grain
offering to the LORD. Num. 28:26
17 'You shall bring in from your
dwelling places two *loaves* of
bread for a wave offering, made of
two-tenths *of an ephah*; they shall
be of a fine flour, baked with
leaven as first fruits to the LORD.
18 'Along with the bread, you
shall present seven one year old
male lambs without defect, and a
bull of the herd, and two rams;
they are to be a burnt offering to
the LORD, with their grain offering
and their libations, an offering by
fire of a soothing aroma to the
LORD.
19 'You shall also offer[r]one male
goat for a sin offering and two
male lambs one year old for a sacrifice of peace offerings. Lev. 4:23
20 'The priest shall then wave

[15]I.e., Approx. one gallon

them with the bread of the first
fruits for a wave offering with two
lambs before the LORD; they are to
be holy to the LORD for the priest.
21 'On this same day you shall
[r]make a proclamation as well; you
are to have a holy convocation.
You shall do no laborious work. It
is to be a perpetual statute in all
your dwelling places throughout
your generations. Lev. 23:2, 4
22 'When you reap the harvest
of your land, moreover, you shall
not reap to the very corners of
your field, nor gather the gleaning
of your harvest; you are to leave
them for the needy and the alien. I
am the LORD your God.' "
23 Again the LORD spoke to
Moses, saying,
24 "Speak to the sons of Israel,
saying,[r] 'In the seventh month on
the first of the month, you shall
have a [t]rest, a reminder by blowing *of trumpets*, a holy convocation. Num. 29:1 • *sabbath rest*
25 'You shall not do any laborious work, but you shall present an
offering by fire to the LORD.' "
26 And the LORD spoke to
Moses, saying,
27 "On exactly the tenth day of
this seventh month is the day of
atonement; it shall be a holy convocation for you, and you shall
humble your souls and present an
offering by fire to the LORD.
28 "Neither shall you do any
work on this same day, for it is a
[r]day of atonement, to make atonement on your behalf before the
LORD your God. Lev. 23:27
29 "If there is any [t]person who
will not humble himself on this
same day, he shall be cut off from
his people. *soul*
30 "As for any person who does
any work on this same day, that
person I will destroy from among
his people.
31 "You shall do no work at all. It
is to be a perpetual statute
throughout your generations in all
your dwelling places.
32 "It is to be a sabbath of complete rest to you, and you shall
humble your souls; on the ninth of
the month at evening, from evening until evening you shall keep
your sabbath."
33 Again the LORD spoke to
Moses, saying,
34 "Speak to the sons of Israel,
saying, 'On the fifteenth of this
seventh month is the [r]Feast of
Booths for seven days to the
LORD. Neh. 8:14; John 7:2
35 'On the first day is a holy convocation; you shall do [r]no laborious work of any kind. Lev. 23:25
36 'For seven days you shall present an offering by fire to the
LORD. On the eighth day you shall
have a holy convocation and present an offering by fire to the
LORD; it is an assembly. You shall
do no laborious work.
37 'These are the appointed
times of the LORD which you shall
proclaim as holy convocations, to
present offerings by fire to the
LORD—burnt offerings and grain
offerings, sacrifices and libations,
[r]*each* day's matter on its own
day— Num. 28:1-29:38
38 besides *those of* the sabbaths
of the LORD, and besides your
gifts, and besides all your votive

and freewill offerings, which you
give to the LORD.
39 'On exactly the fifteenth day
of the seventh month, when you
have gathered in the crops of the
land, you shall celebrate the feast
of the LORD for seven days, with a
rest on the first day and a[t]rest on
the eighth day. *sabbath rest*
40 'Now on the first day you
shall take for yourselves the foliage of beautiful trees, palm
branches and boughs of leafy
trees and willows of the brook;
and you shall rejoice before the
LORD your God for seven days.
41 'You shall thus celebrate it *as*
a feast to the LORD for seven days
in the year. It *shall be* a perpetual
statute throughout your generations; you shall celebrate it in the
seventh month.
42 'You shall[t] live in booths for
seven days; all the native-born in
Israel shall live in booths, *dwell*
43 so that your generations may
know that I had the sons of Israel
live in booths when I brought
them out from the land of Egypt. I
am the LORD your God.' "
44 So Moses declared to the
sons of Israel[r]the appointed times
of the LORD. Lev. 23:37

CHAPTER 24

THEN the LORD spoke to Moses,
saying,
2 "Command the sons of Israel
that they bring to you clear oil
from beaten olives for the light, to
make a lamp burn continually.
3 "Outside the veil of testimony
in the tent of meeting, Aaron shall
keep it in order from evening to
morning before the LORD continually; *it shall be* a perpetual statute
throughout your generations.
4 "He shall keep the lamps in
order on the pure *gold* lampstand
before the LORD continually.
5 "Then[r]you shall take fine flour
and bake twelve cakes with it;
two-tenths *of an ephah* shall be *in*
each cake. Ex. 25:30; 39:36
6 "And you shall set them *in*
two rows, six *to* a row, on the
pure *gold* table before the LORD.
7 "And you shall put pure
frankincense on each row, that it
may be[r]a memorial portion for the
bread, *even* an offering by fire to
the LORD. Lev. 2:2, 9, 16
8 "Every sabbath day he shall
set it in order before the LORD
continually; it is an everlasting
covenant for the sons of Israel.
9 "And it shall be for Aaron and
his sons, and they shall eat it in a
holy place; for it is most holy to
him from the LORD's offerings by
fire, *his* portion forever."
10 Now the son of an Israelite
woman, whose father was an
Egyptian, went out among the
sons of Israel; and the Israelite
woman's son and a man of Israel
struggled with each other in the
camp.
11 And the son of the Israelite
woman blasphemed the Name
and cursed. So they brought him
to Moses. (Now his mother's
name was Shelomith, the daughter of Dibri, of the tribe of Dan.)
12 And they put him in custody
so that the command of the LORD
might be made clear to them.
13 Then the LORD spoke to
Moses, saying,

14 "Bring the one who has
cursed outside the camp, and let
all who heard him [r]lay their hands
on his head; then let all the congregation stone him. Deut. 13:9
15 "And you shall speak to the
sons of Israel, saying, [r]'If anyone
curses his God, then he shall bear
his sin. Ex. 22:28
16 'Moreover, the one who blasphemes the name of the LORD
shall surely be put to death; all the
congregation shall certainly stone
him. The alien as well as the native, when he blasphemes the
Name, shall be put to death.
17 'And [r]if a man [t]takes the life of
any human being, he shall surely
be put to death. Gen. 9:6 · *smites*
18 'And the one who [t]takes the
life of an animal shall make it
good, life for life. Lev. 24:21 · *smites*
19 'And if a man injures his
neighbor, just as he has done, so it
shall be done to him:
20 fracture for fracture, eye for
eye, tooth for tooth; just as he has
[t]injured a man, so it shall be inflicted on him. *given a blemish*
21 'Thus the one who [t]kills an
animal shall make it good, but [r]the
one who [t]kills a man shall be put to
death. *smites* · Lev. 24:17
22 'There shall be one [t]standard
for you; it shall be for the stranger
as well as the native, for I am the
LORD your God.' " *judgment*
23 Then Moses spoke to the
sons of Israel, and they brought
the one who had cursed outside
the camp and stoned him with
stones. Thus the sons of Israel did,
just as the LORD had commanded
Moses.

CHAPTER 25

THE LORD then spoke to Moses
[a]at Mount Sinai, saying, *on*
2 "Speak to the sons of Israel,
and say to them, 'When you come
into the land which I shall give
you, then the land shall have a
sabbath to the LORD.
3 'Six [r]years you shall sow your
field, and six years you shall
prune your vineyard and gather in
its crop, Ex. 23:10, 11
4 but during [r]the seventh year
the land shall have a sabbath rest,
a sabbath to the LORD; you shall
not sow your field nor prune your
vineyard. Lev. 25:20
5 'Your harvest's [16]aftergrowth
you shall not reap, and your
grapes of untrimmed vines you
shall not gather; the land shall
have a sabbatical year.
6 'And all of you shall have the
sabbath *products* of the land for
food; yourself, and your male and
female slaves, and your hired man
and your foreign resident, those
who live as aliens with you.
7 'Even your cattle and the animals that are in your land shall
have all its crops to eat.
8 'You are also to count off
seven sabbaths of years for yourself, seven times seven years, so
that you have the time of the
seven sabbaths of years, *namely*,
forty-nine years.
9 'You shall then sound a ram's
horn abroad on [r]the tenth day of
the seventh month; on the day of
atonement you shall sound a horn
all through your land. Lev. 23:27
10 'You shall thus consecrate the
fiftieth year and proclaim [17]a re-

[16] Lit., *growth from spilled kernels*
[17] Or, *liberty*

lease through the land to all its inhabitants. It shall be a jubilee for you, and each of you shall return to his own property, and each of you shall return to his family.

11 'You shall have the fiftieth year as a jubilee; you shall not sow, nor reap its aftergrowth, nor gather in *from* its untrimmed vines.

12 'For it is a jubilee; it shall be holy to you. You shall eat its crops out of the field.

13 'On[r] this year of jubilee each of you shall return to his own property. Lev. 25:10; 27:24

14 'If you make a sale, moreover, to your friend, or buy from your friend's hand, [r]you shall not wrong one another. Lev. 25:17

15 'Corresponding to the number of years after the jubilee, you shall buy from your[t] friend; he is to sell to you according to the number of years of crops. *friend's hands*

16 'In proportion to the extent of the years you shall increase its price, and in proportion to the fewness of the years, you shall diminish its price; for *it is* a number of crops he is selling to you.

17 'So you shall not wrong one another, but you shall fear your God; for I am the LORD your God.

18 'You shall thus observe My statutes, and keep My judgments, so as to carry them out, that you may live securely on the land.

19 'Then the land will yield its produce, so that you can eat your fill and live securely on it.

20 'But if you say, "What[r] are we going to eat on the seventh year[a] if we do not sow or gather in our crops?" Lev. 25:4 • *behold*

21 then[r] I will so order My blessing for you in the sixth year that it will bring forth the crop for three years. Deut. 28:8

22 'When you are sowing the eighth year, you can still eat[r] old things from the crop, eating *the old* until the ninth year when its crop comes in. Lev. 26:10

23 'The land, moreover, shall not be sold permanently, for the land is Mine; for[r] you are *but* aliens and sojourners with Me. Heb. 11:13

24 'Thus for every[t] piece of your property, you are to provide for the redemption of the land. *land*

25 'If[r] a[t] fellow countryman of yours becomes so poor he has to sell part of his property, then his nearest kinsman is to come and buy back what his[t] relative has sold. Ruth 2:20; 4:4, 6 • *brother*

26 'Or in case a man has no kinsman, but so[t] recovers his means as to find sufficient for its redemption, *his hand reaches*

27 [r]then he shall calculate the years since its sale and refund the balance to the man to whom he sold it, and so return to his property. Lev. 25:16

28 'But if he has not found sufficient means to get it back for himself, then what he has sold shall remain in the hands of its purchaser until the year of jubilee; but at the jubilee it shall[t] revert, that[r] he may return to his property. *go out* • Lev. 25:10, 13

29 'Likewise, if a man sells a dwelling house in a walled city, then his redemption right remains valid until a full year from its sale; his right of redemption lasts a full year.

30 'But if it is not bought back for him within the space of a full year, then the house that is in the walled city passes permanently to its purchaser throughout his generations; it does not [t]revert in the jubilee. *go out*

31 'The houses of the villages, however, which have no surrounding wall shall be considered [t]as open fields; they have redemption rights and [t]revert in the jubilee. *according to • go out*

32 'As for [r]cities of the Levites, the Levites have a permanent right of redemption for the houses of the cities which are their possession. Num. 35:1-8; Josh. 21:2

33 'What, therefore, [t]belongs to the Levites may be redeemed and a house sale [t]in the city of this possession [t]reverts in the jubilee, for the houses of the cities of the Levites are their possession among the sons of Israel. *is from • and • goes out*

34 'But pasture fields of their cities shall not be sold, for that is their perpetual possession.

35 'Now in case a [t]countryman of yours becomes poor and his [t]means with regard to you falter, then you are to sustain him, like a stranger or a sojourner, that he may live with you. *brother • hand*

36 'Do not take [t]usurious interest from him, but revere your God, that your [t]countryman may live with you. *interest and usury • brother*

37 'You shall not give him your silver at interest, nor your food for gain.

38 'I am the LORD your God, who brought you out of the land of Egypt to give you the land of Canaan *and* to be your God.

39 'And if a [t]countryman of yours becomes so poor with regard to you that he sells himself to you, you shall not subject him to a slave's service. *brother*

40 'He shall be with you as a hired man, as [r]if he were a sojourner; he shall serve with you until the year of jubilee. Ex. 21:2

41 'He shall then go out from you, he and his sons with him, and shall go back to his family, that he may return to the property of his forefathers.

42 'For they are My servants whom I brought out from the land of Egypt; they are not to be sold *in* a slave sale.

43 'You [r]shall not rule over him with severity, but are to revere your God. Ezek. 34:4; Col. 4:1

44 'As for your male and female slaves whom you may have—you may acquire male and female slaves from the pagan nations that are around you.

45 'Then, too, *it is* out of the sons of the sojourners who live as aliens among you that you may gain acquisition, and out of their families who are with you, whom they will have [t]produced in your land; they also may become your possession. *begotten*

46 'You may even bequeath them to your sons after you, to receive as a possession; you can use them as permanent slaves. But in respect to your countrymen, the sons of Israel, you shall not rule with severity over one another.

47 'Now if the means of a stranger or of a sojourner with you becomes sufficient, and a countryman of yours becomes so poor with regard to him as to sell himself to a stranger who is sojourning with you, or to the descendants of a stranger's family,

48 then he shall have redemption right after he has been sold. One of his brothers may redeem him,

49 or his uncle, or his uncle's son, may redeem him, or one of his blood relatives from his family may redeem him; or if he prospers, he may redeem himself.

50 'He then with his purchaser shall calculate from the year when he sold himself to him up to the year of jubilee; and the price of his sale shall correspond to the number of years. *It is* like the days of a hired man *that* he shall be with him.

51 'If there are still many years, [r]he shall refund part of his purchase price in proportion to them for his own redemption; Lev. 25:16

52 and if few years remain until the year of jubilee, he shall so calculate with him. In proportion to his years he is to refund *the amount for* his redemption.

53 'Like a man hired year by year he shall be with him;[r]he shall not rule over him with severity in your sight. Lev. 25:43

54 'Even if he is not redeemed by [a]these *means*, he shall still go out in the year of jubilee, he and his sons with him. *these years*

55 'For the sons of Israel are My servants; they are My servants whom I brought out from the land of Egypt. I am the LORD your God.

CHAPTER 26

'YOU shall not make for yourselves[a]idols, nor shall you set up for yourselves an image or a *sacred* pillar, nor shall you place a figured stone in your land to bow down[t]to it; for I am the LORD your God. *graven images • over*

2 'You[r]shall keep My sabbaths and reverence My sanctuary; I am the LORD. Lev. 19:30

3 'If[r]you walk in My statutes and keep My commandments so as to carry them out, Deut. 7:12-26

4 then I shall give you rains in their season, so that the land will yield its produce and the trees of the field will bear their fruit.

5 'Indeed, your threshing will last for you until grape gathering, and grape gathering will last until sowing time. You will thus eat your[t]food to the full and live securely in your land. *bread*

6 'I[r]shall also grant peace in the land, so that [r]you may lie down with no one making *you* tremble. I shall also eliminate harmful beasts from the land, and no sword will pass through your land. Ps. 29:11 • Zeph. 3:13

7 'But you will chase your enemies, and they will fall before you by the sword;

8 [r]five of you will chase a hundred, and a hundred of you will chase ten thousand, and your enemies will fall before you by the sword. Deut. 32:30

9 'So I will turn toward you and [r]make you fruitful and multiply you, and I will confirm My covenant with you. Gen. 17:6

10 'And[r]you will eat the old sup-

ply and clear out the old because
of the new. Lev. 25:22
11 'Moreover, I will make My
dwelling among you, and My soul
will not[t]reject you. *abhor*
12 'I[r]will also walk among you
and be your God, and you shall be
My people. Gen. 3:8; 2 Cor. 6:16
13 'I[r]am the LORD your God, who
brought you out of the land of
Egypt so that *you* should not be
their slaves, and[r]I broke the bars
of your yoke and made you walk
erect. Ex. 20:2 • Ezek. 34:27
14 'But[r]if you do not obey Me
and do not carry out all these
commandments, Josh. 23:15
15 if, instead, you reject My
statutes, and if your soul abhors
My ordinances so as not to carry
out all My commandments, *and*
so[r]break My covenant, Lev. 26:9
16 I, in turn, will do this to you:
I will appoint over you a[r]sudden
terror, consumption and fever
that shall waste away the eyes
and cause the soul to pine away;
also, you shall sow your seed uselessly, for your enemies shall eat it
up. Deut. 28:22; Ps. 78:33
17 'And I will set My face
against you so that you shall be
struck down before your enemies;
and those who hate you shall rule
over you, and[r]you shall flee when
no one is pursuing you. Prov. 28:1
18 'If also after these things, you
do not obey Me, then I will punish
you[r]seven times more for your
sins. Lev. 26:21, 24, 28
19 'And I will also[r]break down
your pride of power; I will also
make your sky like iron and your
earth like bronze. Is. 28:1-3
20 'And[r]your strength shall be
spent uselessly, for your land shall
not yield its produce and the trees
of the land shall not yield their
fruit. Is. 17:10, 11; Jer. 12:13
21 'If then, you[t]act with hostility
against Me and are unwilling to
obey Me, I will increase the
plague on you seven times according to your sins. *walk*
22 'And I will let loose among
you the beasts of the field, which
shall bereave you of your children
and destroy your cattle and reduce your number so that[r]your
roads lie deserted. Judg. 5:6
23 'And[r]if by these things you
are not turned to Me, but act with
hostility against Me, Jer. 5:3
24 then I will[r]act with hostility
against you; and I, even I, will
strike you[r]seven times for your
sins. Lev. 26:28, 41 • Lev. 26:21
25 'I will also bring upon you a
sword which will execute vengeance for the covenant; and
when you gather together into
your cities, I will send pestilence
among you, so that you shall be
delivered into enemy hands.
26 'When I break your staff of
bread, ten women will bake your
bread in one oven, and they will
bring back your bread [18]in ra-
tioned amounts, so that you will
eat and not be satisfied.
27 'Yet if in spite of this, you do
not obey Me, but act with hostility
against Me,
28 then[r]I will act with wrathful
hostility against you; and I, even I,
will punish you seven times for
your sins. Lev. 26:24, 41; Is. 59:18
29 'Further, you shall eat the
flesh of your sons and the flesh of
your daughters you shall eat.

[18]Lit., *by weight*

30 'I then will destroy your high
places, and cut down your incense
altars, and heap your[t]remains on
the[t]remains of your idols; for My
soul shall abhor you. *corpses*
31 'I will lay[r]waste your cities as
well, and will make your sanctuaries desolate; and I will not smell
your soothing aromas. Neh. 2:3
32 'And I will make [r]the land
desolate so that your enemies who
settle in it shall be appalled over
it. Jer. 9:11; 12:11; 25:11
33 'You, however, I[r]will scatter
among the nations and will draw
out a sword after you, as your
land becomes desolate and your
cities become waste. Deut. 4:27
34 'Then the land will[t]enjoy its
sabbaths all the days of the desolation, while you are in your enemies' land; then the land will rest
and enjoy its sabbaths. *satisfy*
35 'All the days of *its* desolation
it will observe the rest which it
did not observe on your sabbaths,
while you were living on it.
36 'As for those of you who may
be left, I will also bring[r]weakness
into their hearts in the lands of
their enemies. And the sound of a
driven leaf will chase them and
even when no one is pursuing,
they will flee as though from the
sword, and they will fall. Is. 30:17
37 'They[r]will therefore stumble
over each other as if *running* from
the sword, although no one is pursuing; and you will have *no
strength*[t]to stand up before your
enemies. Nah. 3:3 • *you will stand*
38 'But[r]you will perish among
the nations, and your enemies'
land will consume you. Deut. 4:26
39 'So those of you who may be
left will rot away because of their
iniquity in the lands of your enemies; and also because of the iniquities of their forefathers they
will rot away with them.
40 'If they confess their iniquity
and the iniquity of their forefathers, in their unfaithfulness
which they committed against
Me, and also in their acting with
hostility against Me—
41 I also was acting with hostility against them, to bring them
into the land of their enemies—or
if their uncircumcised heart becomes humbled so that they then
make amends for their iniquity,
42 then I will remember My
covenant with Jacob, and I will remember also[r]My covenant with
Isaac, and My covenant with
Abraham as well, and I will remember the land. Gen. 26:2-5
43 'For the land shall be abandoned by them, and shall make up
for its sabbaths while it is made
desolate without them. They,
meanwhile, shall be making
amends for their iniquity, because
they rejected My ordinances and
their soul abhorred My statutes.
44 'Yet in spite of this, when
they are in the land of their enemies, I will not reject them, nor
will I so abhor them as to destroy
them, breaking My covenant with
them; for I am the LORD their God.
45 'But I will remember for them
the[r]covenant with their ancestors,
whom I brought out of the land of
Egypt in the sight of the nations,
that[r]I might be their God. I am the
LORD.' " Ex. 6:6-8 • Gen. 17:7
46 [r]These are the statutes and
ordinances and laws which the

LORD established between Himself and the sons of Israel through
Moses at Mount Sinai. Deut. 4:5

CHAPTER 27

AGAIN, the LORD spoke to
Moses, saying,
2 "Speak to the sons of Israel,
and say to them, 'When[r] a man
makes a difficult vow, he *shall be*
valued according to your valuation of persons belonging to the
LORD. Num. 6:2; Deut. 23:21-23
3 'If your valuation is of the
male from twenty years even to
sixty years old, then your valuation shall be fifty shekels of silver, after[r] the shekel of the sanctuary. Ex. 30:13; Lev. 27:25
4 'Or if it is a female, then your
valuation shall be thirty shekels.
5 'And if it be from five years
even to twenty years old then
your valuation for the male shall
be twenty shekels, and for the female ten shekels.
6 'But if *they are* from a month
even up to five years old, then
your valuation shall be[r] five shekels of silver for the male, and for
the female your valuation shall be
three shekels of silver. Num. 18:16
7 'And if *they are* from sixty
years old and upward, if it is a
male, then your valuation shall be
fifteen shekels, and for the female
ten shekels.
8 'But if he is poorer than your
valuation, then he shall be placed
before the priest, and the priest
shall value him;[r] according to the
means of the one who vowed, the
priest shall value him. Lev. 5:11
9 'Now if it is an animal of the
kind which[t] men can present as an
offering to the LORD, any such
that one gives to the LORD shall be
holy. *they*
10 'He[r] shall not replace it or exchange it, a good for a bad, or a
bad for a good; or if he does exchange animal for animal, then
both it and its substitute shall become holy. Lev. 27:33
11 'If, however, it is any unclean
animal of the kind which[t] men do
not present as an offering to the
LORD, then he shall place the animal before the priest. *they*
12 'And the priest shall value it
as either good or bad; as you, the
priest, value it, so it shall be.
13 'But if he should ever *wish to*
redeem it, then he shall add one-
fifth of it to your valuation.
14 'Now if a man consecrates his
house as holy to the LORD, then
the priest shall value it[t] as either
good or bad; as the priest values
it, so it shall stand. *between good*
15 'Yet if the one who consecrates it should *wish to* redeem
his house, then he shall add one-
fifth of your valuation price to it,
so that it may be his.
16 'Again, if a man consecrates
to the LORD part of the fields of his
own property, then your valuation
shall be proportionate to the seed
needed for it: a homer of barley
seed at fifty shekels of silver.
17 'If he consecrates his field as
of the year of jubilee, according to
your valuation it shall stand.
18 'If he consecrates his field after the jubilee, however, then the
priest shall calculate the price for
[a] him proportionate to the years
that are left until the year of jubi-

lee; and it shall be deducted from
your valuation. *it*
19 'And if the one who consecrates it should ever wish to redeem the field, then he shall add
one-fifth of your valuation price to
it, so that it may pass to him.
20 'Yet if he will not redeem the
field,[a] but has sold the field to another man, it may no longer be redeemed; *if he*
21 and when it reverts in the jubilee, the field shall be holy to the
LORD, like a field set apart; it shall
be for the priest as his property.
22 'Or if he consecrates to the
LORD a field which he has bought,
which is not a part of the field of
his own[t]property, *possession*
23 then the priest shall calculate
for him the amount of your valuation up to the year of jubilee; and
he shall on that day give your
valuation as holy to the LORD.
24 'In the year of jubilee the field
shall return to the one from whom
he bought it, to whom the possession of the land belongs.
25 'Every valuation of yours,
moreover, shall be after[r]the shekel
of the sanctuary. The shekel shall
be twenty gerahs. Ex. 30:13
26 'However,[r] a first-born among
animals, which as a first-born belongs to the LORD, no man may
consecrate it; whether ox or
sheep, it is the LORD'S. Ex. 13:2
27 'But if *it is* among the unclean
animals, then he shall redeem it
according to your valuation, and
add to it one-fifth of it; and if it is
not redeemed, then it shall be sold
according to your valuation.
28 'Nevertheless, anything
which a man [19]sets apart to the
LORD out of all that he has, of man
or animal or of the fields of his
own property, shall not be sold or
redeemed. Anything[a] devoted to
destruction is most holy to the
LORD. *puts under the ban*
29 'No one who may have been
[t]set apart among men shall be ransomed; he shall surely be put to
death. *one devoted;* or, *banned*
30 'Thus[r]all the tithe of the land,
of the seed of the land or of the
fruit of the tree, is the LORD'S; it is
holy to the LORD. Neh. 13:12
31 'If, therefore, a man wishes to
redeem part of his tithe, he shall
add to it one-fifth of it.
32 'And for every tenth part of
herd or flock, whatever[r]passes under the rod, the tenth one shall be
holy to the LORD. Jer. 33:13
33 'He is not to be concerned
whether *it is* good or bad, nor
shall he exchange it; or if he does
exchange it, then both it and its
substitute shall become holy. It
shall not be redeemed.' "
34[r]These are the commandments which the LORD com-
manded Moses for the sons of Israel at Mount Sinai. Deut. 4:5

[19]Or, *puts under the ban*

THE BOOK OF

NUMBERS

THEN the LORD spoke to Moses
in the wilderness of Sinai, in the
tent of meeting, on [r]the first of the
second month, in the second year
after they had come out of the
land of Egypt, saying, Ex. 40:2, 17
2 "Take a [1]census of all the congregation of the sons of Israel, by
their families, by their fathers'
households, according to the number of names, every male, head by
head
3 from [r]twenty years old and
upward, whoever *is able to* go out
to war in Israel, you and Aaron
shall [2]number them by their
armies. Ex. 30:14; 38:26
4 "With you, moreover, there
shall be a man of each tribe, [r]each
one head of his father's household. Num. 1:16; Deut. 1:15
5 "These then are the names of
the men who shall stand with you:
[r]of Reuben, Elizur the son of Shedeur; Ex. 1:2; Rev. 7:5
6 of Simeon, Shelumiel the son
of Zurishaddai;
7 of Judah, [r]Nahshon the son of
Amminadab; Ruth 4:20
8 of Issachar, Nethanel the son
of Zuar;
9 of Zebulun, Eliab the son of
Helon;
10 of the sons of Joseph: of E-
phraim, Elishama the son of Ammihud; of Manasseh, Gamaliel the
son of Pedahzur;
11 of Benjamin, Abidan the son
of Gideoni;

[1] Lit., *sum*
[2] Lit., *muster*, and so throughout this context

12 of Dan, Ahiezer the son of
Ammishaddai;
13 of Asher, Pagiel the son of
Ochran;
14 of Gad, Eliasaph the son of
[r]Deuel; Num. 2:14
15 of Naphtali, Ahira the son of
Enan.
16 "These are they who were
[r]called of the congregation, the
leaders of their fathers' tribes;
they were the heads of [3]divisions
of Israel." Ex. 18:21
17 So Moses and Aaron took
these men who had been designated by name,
18 and they assembled all the
congregation together on the first
of the second month. Then they
registered by [r]ancestry in their
families, by their fathers' households, according to the number of
names, from twenty years old and
upward, head by head, Heb. 7:3
19 just as the LORD had commanded Moses. So he numbered
them in the wilderness of Sinai.
20 Now the sons of Reuben, Israel's first-born, their genealogical
registration by their families, by
their fathers' households, according to the number of names, head
by head, every male from twenty
years old and upward, whoever
was able to go out to war,
21 their numbered men, of the
tribe of Reuben, *were* 46,500.
22 Of the sons of Simeon, their
genealogical registration by their
families, by their fathers' house-

[3] Lit., *thousands*, or, *clans*

holds, their numbered men, according to the number of names,
head by head, every male from
twenty years old and upward,
[r]whoever *was able to* go out to
war, Ps. 144:1
23 their numbered men, of the
tribe of Simeon, *were* 59,300.
24 [r]Of the sons of Gad, their genealogical registration by their
families, by their fathers' households, according to the number of
names, from twenty years old and
upward, whoever *was able to* go
out to war, Jer. 49:1
25 their numbered men, of the
tribe of Gad, *were* 45,650.
26 [r]Of the sons of Judah, their
genealogical registration by their
families, by their fathers' households, according to the number of
names, from twenty years old and
upward, whoever *was able to* go
out to war, Ps. 78:68; Matt. 1:2
27 their numbered men, of the
tribe of Judah, *were* 74,600.
28 [r]Of the sons of Issachar, their
genealogical registration by their
families, by their fathers' households, according to the number of
names, from twenty years old and
upward, whoever *was able to* go
out to war, Num. 26:23-25
29 their numbered men, of the
tribe of Issachar, *were* 54,400.
30 [r]Of the sons of Zebulun, their
genealogical registration by their
families, by their fathers' households, according to the number of
names, from twenty years old and
upward, whoever *was able to* go
out to war, Num. 26:26, 27
31 their numbered men, of the
tribe of Zebulun, *were* 57,400.
32 [r]Of the sons of Joseph,
namely, of the sons of Ephraim,
their genealogical registration by
their families, by their fathers'
households, according to the number of names, from twenty years
old and upward, whoever *was
able to* go out to war, Obad. 19
33 their numbered men, of the
tribe of Ephraim, *were* 40,500.
34 Of the sons of Manasseh,
their genealogical registration by
their families, by their fathers'
households, according to the number of names, from twenty years
old and upward, whoever *was
able to* go out to war,
35 their numbered men, of the
tribe of Manasseh, *were* 32,200.
36 [r]Of the sons of Benjamin,
their genealogical registration by
their families, by their fathers'
households, according to the number of names, from twenty years
old and upward, whoever *was
able to* go out to war, Rev. 7:8
37 their numbered men, of the
tribe of Benjamin, *were* 35,400.
38 [r]Of the sons of Dan, their genealogical registration by their
families, by their fathers' households, according to the number of
names, from twenty years old and
upward, whoever *was able to* go
out to war, Gen. 30:6; 46:23
39 their numbered men, of the
tribe of Dan, *were* 62,700.
40 [r]Of the sons of Asher, their
genealogical registration by their
families, by their fathers' households, according to the number of
names, from twenty years old and
upward, whoever *was able to* go
out to war, Num. 26:44-47
41 their numbered men, of the
tribe of Asher, *were* 41,500.

42 [r]Of the sons of Naphtali, their genealogical registration by their families, by their fathers' households, according to the number of names, from twenty years old and upward, whoever *was able to* go out to war, Num. 26:48-50

43 their numbered men, of the tribe of Naphtali, *were* 53,400.

44 These are the ones who were numbered, whom Moses and Aaron numbered, with the leaders of Israel, twelve men, each of whom was of his father's household.

45 So all the numbered men of the sons of Israel by their fathers' households, from twenty years old and upward, whoever *was able to* go out to war in Israel,

46 even all the numbered men were [r]603,550. Ex. 12:37; 38:26

47 [r]The Levites, however, were not numbered among them by their fathers' tribe. Num. 2:33

48 For the LORD had spoken to Moses, saying,

49 "Only the tribe of Levi [r]you shall not number, nor shall you take their [t]census among the sons of Israel. Num. 26:62 • *sum*

50 "But you shall appoint the Levites over the [4]tabernacle of the testimony, and over all its furnishings and over all that belongs to it. They shall carry the tabernacle and all its furnishings, and they shall take care of it; they shall also camp around the tabernacle.

51 "So when the tabernacle is to set out, the Levites shall take it down; and when the tabernacle encamps, the Levites shall set it up. But the [5]layman who comes near shall be put to death.

[4]Lit., *dwelling place,* and so throughout this context [5]Lit., *stranger*

52 "And the sons of Israel shall camp, each man by his own camp, and each man by his own standard, according to their armies.

53 "But the Levites shall camp around the tabernacle of the testimony, that there may be [r]no wrath on the congregation of the sons of Israel. So the Levites shall keep charge of the tabernacle of the testimony." Num. 16:46; 18:5

54 Thus the sons of Israel did; according to all which the LORD had commanded Moses, so they did.

CHAPTER 2

NOW the LORD spoke to Moses and to Aaron, saying,

2 "The sons of Israel shall camp, each by his own standard, with the [t]banners of their fathers' households; they shall camp around the tent of meeting [a]at a distance. *signs* • *facing it*

3 "Now those who camp on the east side toward the sunrise *shall be* of the standard of the camp of Judah, by their armies, and the leader of the sons of Judah: Nahshon the son of Amminadab,

4 and his army, even their numbered men, 74,600.

5 "And those who camp next to him *shall be* the tribe of Issachar, and the leader of the sons of Issachar: Nethanel the son of Zuar,

6 and his army, even their numbered men, 54,400.

7 "Then *comes* the tribe of Zebulun, and the leader of the sons of Zebulun: [r]Eliab the son of Helon, Num. 1:9

8 and his army, even his numbered men, 57,400.

9 "The total of the numbered
men of the camp of Judah:
186,400, by their armies. They
shall set out first. Num. 10:14
10 "On the south side *shall be*
the standard of the camp of Reuben by their armies, and the
leader of the sons of Reuben: Elizur the son of Shedeur, Num. 1:5
11 and his army, even their
numbered men, 46,500.
12 "And those who camp next to
him *shall be* the tribe of Simeon,
and the leader of the sons of Simeon: Shelumiel the son of Zurishaddai, Num. 1:6
13 and his army, even their
numbered men, 59,300.
14 "Then *comes* the tribe of Gad,
and the leader of the sons of Gad:
Eliasaph the son of Deuel,
15 and his army, even their
numbered men, 45,650.
16 "The total of the numbered
men of the camp of Reuben:
151,450 by their armies. And they
shall set out second. Num. 10:18
17 "Then the tent of meeting
shall set out *with* the camp of the
Levites in the midst of the camps;
just as they camp, so they shall
set out, every man in his place, by
their standards. Num. 1:53
18 "On the west side *shall be* the
standard of the camp of Ephraim
by their armies, and the leader of
the sons of Ephraim *shall be*
Elishama the son of Ammihud,
19 and his army, even their
numbered men, 40,500.
20 "And next to him *shall be* the
tribe of Manasseh, and the leader
of the sons of Manasseh: Gamaliel
the son of Pedahzur, Num. 1:10
21 and his army, even their
numbered men, 32,200.
22 "Then *comes* the tribe of Benjamin, and the leader of the sons
of Benjamin: Abidan the son of
Gideoni, Ps. 68:27 • Num. 1:11
23 and his army, even their
numbered men, 35,400.
24 "The total of the numbered
men of the camp of Ephraim:
108,100, by their armies. And they
shall set out third. Num. 10:22
25 "On the north side *shall be* the
standard of the camp of Dan by
their armies, and the leader of the
sons of Dan: Ahiezer the son of
Ammishaddai, Num. 1:12
26 and his army, even their
numbered men, 62,700.
27 "And those who camp next to
him *shall be* the tribe of Asher,
and the leader of the sons of
Asher: Pagiel the son of Ochran,
28 and his army, even their
numbered men, 41,500.
29 "Then *comes* the tribe of
Naphtali, and the leader of the
sons of Naphtali: Ahira the son of
Enan, Gen. 30:8 • Num. 1:15
30 and his army, even their
numbered men, 53,400.
31 "The total of the numbered
men of the camp of Dan, *was*
157,600. They shall set out last by
their standards." Num. 10:25
32 These are the numbered men
of the sons of Israel by their fathers' households; the total of the
numbered men of the camps by
their armies, 603,550. Ex. 38:26
33 The Levites, however, were
not numbered among the sons of
Israel, just as the LORD had commanded Moses. Num. 1:47
34 Thus the sons of Israel did;
according to all that the LORD
commanded Moses, so they

camped by their standards, and so
they set out, every one by his family, according to his father's
household.

CHAPTER 3

NOW these are *the records of* the
generations of Aaron and Moses
at the time when the LORD spoke
with Moses on Mount Sinai.
2 [r]These then are the names of
the sons of Aaron: Nadab the first-
born, and Abihu, Eleazar and Ithamar. Ex. 6:23; Num. 26:60
3 These are the names of the
sons of Aaron, the anointed
priests, whom he [t]ordained to
serve as priests. *filled their hand*
4 But Nadab and Abihu died
before the LORD when they offered strange fire before the LORD
in the wilderness of Sinai; and
they had no children. So Eleazar
and Ithamar served as priests in
the lifetime of their father Aaron.
5 Then the LORD spoke to
Moses, saying,
6 "Bring the tribe of Levi near
and set them before Aaron the
priest, that they may serve him.
7 "And they shall perform the
duties for him and for the whole
congregation before the tent of
meeting, to do the [r]service of the
tabernacle. Num. 1:50
8 "They shall also keep all the
furnishings of the tent of meeting,
along with the duties of the sons
of Israel, to do the service of the
tabernacle.
9 "You shall thus [r]give the Levites to Aaron and to his sons;
they are wholly given to him from
among the sons of Israel. Num. 18:6
10 "So you shall appoint Aaron
and his sons that [r]they may keep
their priesthood, but the [t]layman
who comes near shall be put to
death." Ex. 29:9 • *stranger*
11 Again the LORD spoke to
Moses, saying,
12 "Now, behold, I have taken
the Levites from among the sons
of Israel instead of every [r]first-
born, the first issue of the womb
among the sons of Israel. So the
Levites shall be Mine. Ex. 13:2
13 "For [r]all the first-born are
Mine; on the day that I struck
down all the first-born in the land
of Egypt, I sanctified to Myself all
the first-born in Israel, from man
to beast. They shall be Mine; I am
the LORD." Ex. 13:2; Lev. 27:26
14 Then the LORD spoke to
Moses [r]in the wilderness of Sinai,
saying, Ex. 19:1
15 "Number [t][r]the sons of Levi by
their fathers' households, by their
families; every male from a month
old and upward you shall number." *muster* • Num. 1:47
16 So Moses numbered them
according to the [t]word of the
LORD, just as he had been commanded. *mouth*
17 [r]These then are the sons of
Levi by their names: Gershon and
Kohath and Merari. Ex. 6:16-22
18 And these are the names of
the [r]sons of Gershon by their families: Libni and Shimei; Ex. 6:17
19 and the sons of Kohath by
their families: Amram and Izhar,
Hebron and Uzziel;
20 and the sons of Merari by
their families: Mahli and Mushi.
These are the families of the Levites according to their fathers'
households.

21 Of Gershon *was* the family of
the Libnites and the family of the
Shimeites; these *were* the families
of the Gershonites.
22 Their numbered men, in the
numbering of every male from a
month old and upward, *even* their
numbered men *were* 7,500.
23 The families of the Gershonites were to camp behind the [t]tab-
ernacle westward, *dwelling place*
24 and the leader of the fathers'
households of the Gershonites
was Eliasaph the son of Lael.
25 Now [r]the duties of the sons of
Gershon in the tent of meeting *involved* the tabernacle and the
tent, its covering, and the screen
for the doorway of the tent of
meeting, Num. 4:24-26
26 and the hangings of the
court, and the screen for the doorway of the court, which is around
the tabernacle and the altar, and
its cords, according to all the service [t]concerning them. *of it*
27 And of Kohath *was* the family of the Amramites and the family of the Izharites and the family
of the Hebronites and the family
of the Uzzielites; these were the
families of the Kohathites.
28 In the numbering of every
male from a month old and upward, *there were* 8,600, performing the duties of the sanctuary.
29 The families of the sons of
Kohath were to camp on the
southward side of the tabernacle,
30 and the leader of the fathers'
households of the Kohathite families was Elizaphan the son of Uzziel.
31 Now their duties *involved*
the ark, the table, the lampstand,
the altars, and the utensils of the
sanctuary with which they minister, and the screen, and all the service [t]concerning them; *of it*
32 and Eleazar the son of Aaron
the priest *was* the chief of the
leaders of Levi, *and had* the oversight of those who perform the
duties of the sanctuary.
33 Of Merari *was* the family of
the Mahlites and the family of the
Mushites; these *were* the families
of Merari.
34 Their numbered men in the
numbering of every male from a
month old and upward, *were*
6,200.
35 And the leader of the fathers'
households of the families of Merari *was* Zuriel the son of Abihail.
They *were* to camp on the northward side of the tabernacle.
36 Now the appointed duties of
the sons of Merari *involved* the
frames of the tabernacle, its bars,
its pillars, its sockets, all its equipment, and the service concerning
them,
37 and the pillars around the
court with their sockets and their
pegs and their cords.
38 Now those who were to
camp before the tabernacle eastward, before the tent of meeting
toward the sunrise, are Moses and
Aaron and his sons, performing
the duties of the sanctuary for the
obligation of the sons of Israel;
but the [t]layman coming near was
to be put to death. *stranger*
39 All the numbered men of the
Levites, whom Moses and Aaron
numbered at the [t]command of the
LORD by their families, every male

from a month old and upward,
were 22,000. *word*
40 Then the LORD said to Moses,
"Number every first-born male of
the sons of Israel from a month
old and upward, and [t]make a list of
their names. *take the number*
41 "And you [r]shall take the Levites for Me, I am the LORD, instead of all the first-born among
the sons of Israel, and the cattle of
the Levites instead of all the first-
born among the cattle of the sons
of Israel." Num. 3:12, 45
42 So Moses numbered all the
first-born among the sons of Israel, just as the LORD had commanded him;
43 and all the first-born males
by the number of names from a
month old and upward, for their
numbered men were 22,273.
44 Then the LORD spoke to
Moses, saying,
45 "Take[r] the Levites instead of
all the first-born among the sons
of Israel and the cattle of the Levites. And the Levites shall be
Mine; I am the LORD. Num. 3:12
46 "And[r] for the ransom of the
273 of the first-born of the sons of
Israel who are in excess beyond
the Levites, Ex. 13:13, 15
47 you shall take [r]five shekels
apiece, per head; you shall take
them in terms of the shekel of the
sanctuary (the shekel is twenty
[6]gerahs), Num. 18:16
48 and give the money, the ransom of those who are in excess
among them, to Aaron and to his
sons."
49 So Moses took the ransom
money from those who were in
excess, beyond those ransomed
by the Levites;
50 from the first-born of the
sons of Israel he took the money
in terms of the shekel of the sanctuary, 1,365.
51 Then Moses gave the ransom
money to Aaron and to his sons,
at the [t]command of the LORD, just
as the LORD had commanded
Moses. *mouth*

CHAPTER 4

THEN the LORD spoke to Moses
and to Aaron, saying,
2 "Take a census of the [t]de-
scendants of Kohath from among
the sons of Levi, by their families,
by their fathers' households, *sons*
3 from thirty years and upward, even to fifty years old, all
who enter the service to do the
work in the tent of meeting.
4 "This is the work of the [t]de-
scendants of Kohath in the tent of
meeting, *concerning* the most
holy things. *sons*
5 "When the camp sets out,
Aaron and his sons shall go in and
they shall take down [r]the veil of
the screen and cover the ark of
the testimony with it; Ex. 40:5
6 and they shall lay a covering
of porpoise skin on it, and shall
spread over *it* a cloth of pure [a]blue,
and shall insert its poles. *violet*
7 "Over the table of the bread of
the Presence they shall also
spread a cloth of [a]blue and put on
it the dishes and the pans and the
sacrificial bowls and the jars for
the libation, and the continual
bread shall be on it. *violet*
8 "And they shall spread over
them a cloth of scarlet *material*,

[6]I.e., A gerah equals approx. one-fortieth ounce

and cover the same with a covering of porpoise skin, and they
shall insert its poles.
9"Then they shall take a [a]blue
cloth and cover the lampstand for
the light, along with its lamps and
its snuffers, and its [t]trays and all
its oil vessels, by which they serve
it; *violet* • *snuff dishes*
10 and they shall put it and all
its utensils in a covering of porpoise skin, and shall put it on the
carrying bars.
11"And over the golden altar
they shall spread a [a]blue cloth and
cover it with a covering of porpoise skin, and shall insert its
poles; *violet*
12 and they shall take all the
utensils of service, with which
they serve in the sanctuary, and
put them in a [a]blue cloth and cover
them with a covering of porpoise
skin, and put them on the carrying
bars. *violet*
13"Then they shall take away
the ashes from the altar, and
spread a purple cloth over it.
14"They shall also put on it all
its utensils by which they serve in
connection with it: the firepans,
the forks and shovels and the basins, all the utensils of the altar;
and they shall spread a cover of
porpoise skin over it and insert its
poles.
15"And when Aaron and his
sons have finished covering the
holy *objects* and all the furnishings of the sanctuary, when the
camp is to set out, after that the
sons of Kohath shall come to carry *them,* so that they may not
touch the holy *objects* and die.
These are the things in the tent of
meeting which the sons of Kohath
are to carry.
16"And the responsibility of Eleazar the son of Aaron the priest
is the oil for the light and the fragrant incense and [r]the continual
grain offering and the anointing
oil—the responsibility of all [r] the
[t]tabernacle and of all that is in it,
with the sanctuary and its furnishings." Lev. 6:20 • *dwelling place*
17 Then the LORD spoke to
Moses and to Aaron, saying,
18"Do not let the tribe of the
families of the Kohathites be cut
off from among the Levites.
19"But do this to them that they
may live and [r]not die when they
approach the most holy *objects*:
Aaron and his sons shall go in and
assign each of them to his work
and to his load; Num. 4:15
20 but [r]they shall not go in to see
the holy *objects* even for a moment, lest they die." 1 Sam. 6:19
21 Then the LORD spoke to
Moses, saying,
22"Take a census of the sons of
Gershon also, by their fathers'
households, by their families;
23 from thirty years and upward to fifty years old, you shall
number them; all who enter to
perform the service to do the
work in the tent of meeting.
24"This is the service of the families of the Gershonites, in serving
and in carrying:
25 they shall carry the curtains
of the tabernacle and the tent of
meeting *with* its covering and the
covering of porpoise skin that is
on top of it, and the screen for the
doorway of the tent of meeting,
26 and the hangings of the

court, and the screen for the doorway of the gate of the court which is around the tabernacle and the altar, and their cords and all the equipment for their service; and all that is to be done, [t]they shall perform. *so they shall serve*

27 "All the service of the sons of the Gershonites, in all their loads and in all their work, shall be *performed* at the command of Aaron and his sons; and you shall assign to them as a duty all their loads.

28 "This is the service of the families of the sons of the Gershonites in the tent of meeting, and their duties *shall be* [t]under the direction of Ithamar the son of Aaron the priest. *in the hand*

29 "*As for* the sons of Merari, you shall number them by their families, by their fathers' households;

30 from [r]thirty years and upward even to fifty years old, you shall number them, everyone who enters the service to do the work of the tent of meeting. Num. 4:3

31 "Now this is the duty of their loads, for all their service in the tent of meeting: the boards of the tabernacle and its bars and its pillars and its [a]sockets, *bases*

32 and the pillars around the court and their sockets and their pegs and their cords, with all their equipment and with all their service; and you shall assign *each man* by name the items [t]he is to carry. *of the duty of their loads*

33 "This is the service of the families of the sons of Merari, according to all their service in the tent of meeting, [t]under the direction of Ithamar the son of Aaron the priest." *in the hand*

34 So Moses and Aaron and the leaders of the congregation numbered the sons of the Kohathites by their families, and by their fathers' households,

35 from thirty years and upward even to fifty years old, everyone who entered the service for work in the tent of meeting.

36 And their numbered men by their families were 2,750.

37 These are the numbered men of the Kohathite families, everyone who was serving in the tent of meeting, whom Moses and Aaron numbered according to the [t]commandment of the LORD [t]through Moses. *mouth • by the hand of*

38 And the numbered men of the sons of Gershon by their families, and by their fathers' households,

39 from thirty years and upward even to fifty years old, everyone who entered the service for work in the tent of meeting.

40 And their numbered men by their families, by their fathers' households, were 2,630.

41 These are the numbered men of the families of the sons of Gershon, everyone who was serving in the tent of meeting, whom Moses and Aaron numbered according to the [t]commandment of the LORD. *mouth*

42 And the numbered men of the families of the sons of Merari by their families, by their fathers' households,

43 from thirty years and upward even to fifty years old,

everyone who entered the service
for work in the tent of meeting.
44 And their numbered men by
their families were 3,200.
45 These are the numbered men
of the families of the sons of Merari, whom Moses and Aaron
numbered according to the [t]com-
mandment of the LORD [t]through
Moses. *mouth • by the hand of*
46 All the numbered men of the
Levites, whom Moses and Aaron
and the leaders of Israel numbered, by their families and by
their fathers' households,
47 from thirty years and upward even to fifty years old,
everyone who could enter to do
the work of service and the work
of carrying in the tent of meeting.
48 And their numbered men
were [r]8,580. Num. 3:39
49 According to the commandment of the LORD through Moses,
they were numbered, everyone by
his serving or carrying; thus these
were his numbered men, just as
the LORD had commanded Moses.

CHAPTER 5

THEN the LORD spoke to Moses,
saying,
2 "Command the sons of Israel
that they [r]send away from the
camp every leper and everyone
having a discharge and everyone
who is unclean because of a *dead*
person. Lev. 13:8, 46; Num. 12:10
3 "You shall send away both
male and female; you shall send
them outside the camp so that
they will not defile their camp
where I dwell in their midst."
4 And the sons of Israel did so
and sent them outside the camp;
just as the LORD had spoken to
Moses, thus the sons of Israel did.
5 Then the LORD spoke to
Moses, saying,
6 "Speak to the sons of Israel,
'When [r]a man or woman commits
any of the sins of mankind, acting
unfaithfully against the LORD, and
that person is guilty, Lev. 5:14-6:7
7 then [t]he shall confess [t]his sins
which he has committed, and he
shall make restitution in full for
his wrong, and add to it one-fifth
of it, and give *it* to him whom he
has wronged. *they • their*
8 'But if the man has no [7]rela-
tive to whom restitution may be
made for the wrong, the restitution which is made for the wrong
must go to the LORD for the priest,
besides the ram of atonement, by
which atonement is made for him.
9 'Also every contribution pertaining to all the holy *gifts* of the
sons of Israel, which they offer to
the priest, shall be his.
10 'So every man's holy *gifts*
shall be his; whatever any man
gives to the priest, it [r]becomes
his.'" Lev. 10:13
11 Then the LORD spoke to
Moses, saying,
12 "Speak to the sons of Israel,
and say to them, 'If any man's
wife [r]goes astray and is unfaithful
to him, Num. 5:19-21, 29
13 and a man has intercourse
with her and it is hidden from the
eyes of her husband and she is [t]un-
detected, although she has defiled
herself, and there is no witness
against her and she has not been
caught in the act, *concealed*
14 [t]if a spirit of [r]jealousy comes

[7]Lit., *redeemer*

over him and he is jealous of his
wife when she has defiled herself,
or if a spirit of jealousy comes
over him and he is jealous of his
wife when she has not defiled herself, *and* • Prov. 6:34; Song 8:6
15 the man shall then bring his
wife to the priest, and shall bring
as an offering for her one-tenth of
an ephah of barley meal; he shall
not pour oil on it, nor put frankincense on it, for it is a grain offering of jealousy, a grain offering of
memorial, a reminder of iniquity.
16 'Then the priest shall bring
her near and have her stand before the LORD,
17 and the priest shall take holy
water in an earthenware vessel;
and he shall take some of the dust
that is on the floor of the tabernacle and put *it* into the water.
18 'The priest shall then have the
woman stand before the LORD and
let *the hair of* the woman's head
go loose, and place the grain offering of memorial [t]in her hands,
which is the grain offering of jealousy, and in the hand of the priest
is to be the water of bitterness
that brings a curse. *on her palms*
19 'And the priest shall have her
take an oath and shall say to the
woman, "If no man has lain with
you and if you have not gone
astray into uncleanness, *being* under *the authority of* your husband,
be immune to this water of bitterness that brings a curse;
20 if you, however, have [r]gone
astray, *being* under *the authority
of* your husband, and if you have
defiled yourself and a man other
than your husband has had intercourse with you" Num. 5:12

21 (then the priest shall have
the woman swear with the oath of
the curse, and the priest shall say
to the woman), "the LORD make
you a curse and an oath among
your people by the LORD's making
your thigh [t]waste away and your
abdomen swell; *fall*
22 and this water that brings a
curse shall go into your [a]stomach,
and make your abdomen swell
and your thigh [t]waste away." And
the woman shall say, "Amen.
Amen." *inward parts* • *fall*
23 'The priest shall then write
these curses on a scroll, and he
shall [t]wash them off into the water
of bitterness. *wipe*
24 'Then he shall make the
woman drink the water of bitterness that brings a curse, so that
the water which brings a curse
will go into her [t]and *cause* bitterness. *to*
25 'And the priest shall take the
grain offering of jealousy from the
woman's hand, and he shall wave
the grain offering before the LORD
and bring it to the altar;
26 and [r]the priest shall take a
handful of the grain offering as its
memorial offering and offer *it* up
in smoke on the altar, and afterward he shall make the woman
drink the water. Lev. 2:2, 9
27 'When he has made her drink
the water, then it shall come
about, if she has defiled herself
and has been unfaithful to her
husband, that the water which
brings a curse shall go into her
[t]and *cause* bitterness, and her abdomen will swell and her thigh
will [t]waste away, and the woman

will become a curse among her
people. *to·fall*
28 'But if the woman has not defiled herself and is clean, she will
then be free and conceive [t]chil-
dren. *seed*
29 'This is the law of jealousy:
when a wife, *being* under *the authority of* her husband, goes
astray and defiles herself,
30 or when a spirit of jealousy
comes over a man and he is jealous of his wife, he shall then make
the woman stand before the LORD,
and the priest shall apply all this
law to her.
31 'Moreover, the man shall be
free from [a]guilt, but that woman
shall bear her [a]guilt.' " *iniquity*

CHAPTER 6

AGAIN the LORD spoke to Moses,
saying,
2 "Speak to the sons of Israel,
and say to them, 'When a man or
woman makes a [a]special vow, the
vow of a [8]Nazirite, to dedicate
himself to the LORD, *difficult*
3 he shall [r]abstain from wine
and strong drink; he shall drink no
vinegar, whether made from wine
or strong drink, neither shall he
drink any grape juice, nor eat
fresh or dried grapes. Luke 1:15
4 'All the days of his [9]separa-
tion he shall not eat anything that
is produced by the grape vine,
from *the* seeds even to *the* skin.
5 'All the days of his vow of
separation [r]no razor shall pass
over his head. He shall be holy until the days are fulfilled for which
he separated himself to the LORD;
he shall let the locks of hair on his
head grow long. 1 Sam. 1:11
6 'All [r]the days of his separation
to the LORD he shall not go near to
a dead person. Num. 19:11-22
7 'He shall not make himself
unclean for his father or for his
mother, for his brother or for his
sister, when they die, because his
separation to God is on his head.
8 'All the days of his separation
he is holy to the LORD.
9 'But if a man dies very suddenly beside him and he defiles
his dedicated head *of hair*, then he
shall shave his head on the day
when he becomes clean; he shall
shave it on the seventh day.
10 'Then on the eighth day he
shall bring two turtledoves or two
young pigeons to the priest, to the
doorway of the tent of meeting.
11 'And the priest shall offer [r]one
for a sin offering and *the* other for
a burnt offering, and make atonement for him concerning his sin
because of the *dead* person. And
that same day he shall consecrate
his head, Lev. 5:7
12 and shall dedicate to the
LORD his days as a Nazirite, and
shall bring a male lamb a year old
for a guilt offering; but the former
days shall be void because his
separation was defiled.
13 'Now this is the law of the
Nazirite when the days of his
separation are fulfilled, he shall
bring [t]the offering to the doorway
of the tent of meeting. *it*
14 'And he shall present his offering to the LORD: one male lamb
a year old without defect for a
burnt offering and one ewe-lamb a
year old without defect for a sin

[8] I.e., one separated
[9] Or, *living as a Nazirite*, and so through v. 21

offering and one ram without defect for a peace offering,
15 and a basket of unleavened
cakes of fine flour mixed with oil
and unleavened wafers spread
with oil, along with their grain offering and their libations.
16 'Then the priest shall present
them before the LORD and shall offer his sin offering and his burnt
offering.
17 'He shall also offer the ram
for a sacrifice of peace offerings to
the LORD, together with the basket of unleavened cakes; the
priest shall likewise offer its grain
offering and its libation.
18 'The [r]Nazirite shall then shave
his dedicated head *of hair* at the
doorway of the tent of meeting,
and take the dedicated hair of his
head and put *it* on the fire which is
under the sacrifice of peace offerings. Acts 21:23, 24
19 'And the priest shall take the
ram's shoulder *when it has been*
boiled, and one unleavened cake
out of the basket, and one unleavened wafer, and shall put *them* on
the hands of the Nazirite after he
has shaved his dedicated *hair*.
20 'Then the priest shall wave
them for a wave offering before
the LORD. It is holy for the priest,
together with the breast offered
by waving and the thigh offered
by lifting up; and afterward the
Nazirite may drink wine.'
21 "This is the law of the Nazirite
who vows his offering to the LORD
according to his separation, in addition to what *else* he can afford;
according to his vow which he
takes, so he shall do according to
the law of his separation."

22 Then the LORD spoke to
Moses, saying,
23 "Speak to Aaron and to his
sons, saying, 'Thus [r]you shall bless
the sons of Israel. You shall say to
them: 1 Chr. 23:13

24 The LORD bless you, and
keep you;
25 The LORD make His face
shine on you,
And be gracious to you;
26 The LORD lift up His countenance on you,
And give you peace.'

27 "So they shall [t]invoke My
name on the sons of Israel, and I
then will bless them." *put*

CHAPTER 7

NOW it came about on [r]the day
that Moses had finished setting up
the tabernacle, he anointed it and
consecrated it with all its furnishings and the altar and all its utensils; he anointed them and consecrated them also. Ex. 40:17
2 Then the leaders of Israel,
the heads of their fathers' households, made an offering (they
were the leaders of the tribes;
they were the ones who [t]were over
the numbered men). *stood*
3 When they brought their offering before the LORD, six [r]cov-
ered carts and twelve oxen, a cart
for *every* two of the leaders and an
ox for each one, then they presented them before the tabernacle. Is. 66:20
4 Then the LORD spoke to
Moses, saying,
5 "Accept *these things* from
them, that they may be [t]used in the
service of the tent of meeting, and
you shall give them to the Levites,

to each man according to his service." *for serving*

6 So Moses took the carts and the oxen, and gave them to the Levites.

7 Two carts and four oxen he gave to the sons of Gershon, according to their service,

8 and four carts and eight oxen he gave to the sons of Merari, according to their service, under the [t]direction of Ithamar the son of Aaron the priest. *hand*

9 But he did not give *any* to the sons of Kohath because theirs *was* [r]the service of the holy *objects, which* they carried on the shoulder. Num. 4:5-15

10 And the leaders offered the dedication *offering* [t]for the altar [t]when it was anointed, so the leaders offered their offering before the altar. *of · in the day that*

11 Then the LORD said to Moses, "Let them present their offering, one leader each day, for the dedication of the altar."

12 Now the one who presented his offering on the first day *was* Nahshon the son of Amminadab, of the tribe of Judah;

13 and his offering *was* one silver [10]dish whose weight *was* one hundred and thirty *shekels,* one silver bowl of seventy shekels, [r]according to [11]the shekel of the sanctuary, both of them full of fine flour mixed with oil for a grain offering; Num. 3:47

14 one gold pan of ten *shekels,* full of incense;

15 one [a]bull, one ram, one male lamb one year old, for a burnt offering; *bull of the herd*

16 [r]one male goat for a sin offering; Lev. 4:23

17 and for the sacrifice of peace offerings, two oxen, five rams, five male goats, five male lambs one year old. This *was* the offering of Nahshon the son of Amminadab.

18 On the second day Nethanel the son of Zuar, leader of Issachar, presented *an offering;*

19 he presented as his offering one silver dish whose weight *was* one hundred and thirty *shekels,* one silver bowl of seventy shekels, according to the shekel of the sanctuary, both of them full of fine flour mixed with oil for a grain offering;

20 one gold pan of ten *shekels,* full of incense;

21 one bull, one ram, one male lamb one year old, for a burnt offering;

22 one male goat for a sin offering;

23 and for the sacrifice of peace offerings, two oxen, five rams, five male goats, five male lambs one year old. This *was* the offering of Nethanel the son of Zuar.

24 On the third day *it was* Eliab the son of Helon, leader of the sons of Zebulun;

25 his offering *was* one silver dish whose weight *was* one hundred and thirty *shekels,* one silver bowl of seventy shekels, according to the shekel of the sanctuary, both of them full of fine flour mixed with oil for a grain offering;

26 one gold pan of ten *shekels,* full of incense;

27 one young bull, one ram, one

[10]Or, *platter,* and so through v. 85
[11]I.e., Approx. one-half ounce, and so through v. 86

ʳmale lamb one year old, for a
burnt offering; John 1:29
28 one male goat for a sin offering;
29 and for the sacrifice of peace
offerings, two oxen, five rams, five
male goats, five male lambs one
year old. This *was* the offering of
Eliab the son of Helon.
30 On the fourth day *it was* Elizur the son of Shedeur, leader of
the sons of Reuben;
31 his offering *was* one silver
dish whose weight *was* one hundred and thirty *shekels,* one silver
bowl of seventy shekels, according to the shekel of the sanctuary,
both of them full of fine flour
mixed with oil for a grain offering;
32 one gold pan of ten *shekels,*
full of incense;
33 one bull, one ram, one ʳmale
lamb one year old, for a burnt offering; Heb. 9:28
34 one male goat for a sin offering;
35 and for the sacrifice of peace
offerings, two oxen, five rams, five
male goats, five male lambs one
year old. This *was* the offering of
Elizur the son of Shedeur.
36 On the fifth day *it was* Shelumiel the son of Zurishaddai,
leader of the children of Simeon;
37 his offering *was* one silver
dish whose weight *was* one hundred and thirty *shekels,* one silver
bowl of seventy shekels, according to the shekel of the sanctuary,
both of them full of fine flour
mixed with oil for a grain offering;
38 one gold pan of ten *shekels,*
full of incense;
39 one bull, one ram, one male
lamb one year old, for a burnt offering;
40 one male goat for a sin offering;
41 and for the sacrifice of peace
offerings, two oxen, five rams, five
male goats, five male lambs one
year old. This *was* the offering of
Shelumiel the son of Zurishaddai.
42 On the sixth day *it was* ʳElia-
saph the son of Deuel, leader of
the sons of Gad; Num. 1:14
43 his offering *was* one silver
dish whose weight *was* one hundred and thirty *shekels,* one silver
bowl of seventy shekels, according to the shekel of the sanctuary,
both of them full of fine flour
mixed with oil for a grain offering;
44 one gold pan of ten *shekels,*
full of incense;
45 ʳone bull, one ram, one male
lamb one year old, for a burnt offering; Ps. 50:8-14; Is. 1:11
46 one male goat for a sin offering;
47 and for the sacrifice of peace
offerings, two oxen, five rams, five
male goats, five male lambs one
year old. This *was* the offering of
Eliasaph the son of Deuel.
48 On the seventh day *it was*
Elishama the son of Ammihud,
leader of the sons of Ephraim;
49 his offering *was* one silver
dish whose weight *was* one hundred and thirty *shekels,* one silver
bowl of seventy shekels, according to the shekel of the sanctuary,
both of them full of fine flour
mixed with oil for a grain offering;
50 one gold pan of ten *shekels,*
full of ʳincense; Luke 1:10
51 ʳone bull, one ram, one male

lamb one year old, for a burnt offering; Mic. 6:6-8
52 one male goat for a sin offering;
53 and for the sacrifice of peace
offerings, two oxen, five rams, five
male goats, five male lambs one
year old. This *was* the offering of
Elishama the son of Ammihud.
54 On the eighth day *it was* Gamaliel the son of Pedahzur, leader
of the sons of Manasseh;
55 his offering *was* one silver
dish whose weight *was* one hundred and thirty *shekels,* one silver
bowl of seventy shekels, according to the shekel of the sanctuary,
both of them full of fine flour
mixed with oil for a grain offering;
56 one gold pan of ten *shekels,*
full of [r]incense; Ex. 30:7
57 one bull, one ram, one [r]male
lamb one year old, for a burnt offering; Ex. 12:5; Acts 8:32
58 one male goat for a sin offering;
59 and for the sacrifice of peace
offerings, two oxen, five rams, five
male goats, five male lambs one
year old. This *was* the offering of
Gamaliel the son of Pedahzur.
60 On the ninth day *it was* [r]Abi-
dan the son of Gideoni, leader of
the sons of Benjamin; Num. 1:11
61 his offering *was* one silver
dish whose weight *was* one hundred and thirty *shekels,* one silver
bowl of seventy shekels, according to the shekel of the sanctuary,
both of them full of fine flour
mixed with oil for a grain offering;
62 one gold pan of ten *shekels,*
full of [r]incense; Rev. 5:8
63 one bull, one ram, one male
lamb one year old, for a burnt offering;
64 one male goat for a [r]sin offering; 2 Cor. 5:21
65 and for the sacrifice of peace
offerings, two oxen, five rams, five
male goats, five male lambs one
year old. This *was* the offering of
Abidan the son of Gideoni.
66 On the tenth day *it was* Ahiezer the son of Ammishaddai,
leader of the sons of Dan;
67 his offering *was* one silver
dish whose weight *was* one hundred and thirty *shekels,* one silver
bowl of seventy shekels, according to the shekel of the sanctuary,
both of them full of fine flour
mixed with oil for a grain offering;
68 one gold pan of ten *shekels,*
full of [r]incense; Ps. 141:2
69 one bull, one ram, one male
lamb one year old, for a burnt offering;
70 one male goat for a sin offering;
71 and for the sacrifice of peace
offerings, two oxen, five rams, five
male goats, five male lambs one
year old. This *was* the offering of
Ahiezer the son of Ammishaddai.
72 On the eleventh day *it was*
[r]Pagiel the son of Ochran, leader of
the sons of Asher; Num. 1:13
73 his offering *was* one silver
dish whose weight *was* one hundred and thirty *shekels,* one silver
bowl of seventy shekels, according to the shekel of the sanctuary,
both of them full of fine flour
mixed with oil for a grain offering;
74 one gold pan of ten *shekels,*
full of [r]incense; Mal. 1:11
75 one bull, one ram, one male

lamb one year old, for a burnt offering;
76 one male goat for a sin offering;
77 and for the sacrifice of peace
offerings, two oxen, five rams, five
male goats, five male lambs one
year old. This *was* the offering of
Pagiel the son of Ochran.
78 On the twelfth day *it was*
Ahira the son of Enan, leader of
the sons of Naphtali; **Num. 1:15**
79 his offering *was* one silver
dish whose weight *was* one hundred and thirty *shekels,* one silver
bowl of seventy shekels, according to the shekel of the sanctuary,
both of them full of fine flour
mixed with oil for a grain offering;
80 one gold pan of ten *shekels,*
full of incense;
81 one bull, one ram, one male
lamb one year old, for a burnt offering;
82 one male goat for a sin offering;
83 and for the sacrifice of peace
offerings, two oxen, five rams, five
male goats, five male lambs one
year old. This *was* the offering of
Ahira the son of Enan.
84 This *was* the dedication *of-*
fering for the altar from the leaders of Israel when it was anointed:
twelve silver dishes, twelve silver
bowls, twelve gold pans, ***of***
85 each silver dish *weighing* one
hundred and thirty *shekels* and
each bowl seventy; all the silver of
the utensils *was* 2,400 *shekels,* according to the shekel of the sanctuary;
86 the twelve gold pans, full of
incense, *weighing* ten *shekels*
apiece, according to the shekel of
the sanctuary, all the gold of the
pans 120 *shekels;* **Ex. 30:13**
87 all the oxen for the burnt offering twelve bulls, *all* the rams
twelve, the male lambs one year
old with their grain offering
twelve, and the male goats for a
sin offering twelve;
88 and all the oxen for the sacrifice of peace offerings 24 bulls, *all*
the rams 60, the male goats 60,
the male lambs one year old 60.
This *was* the dedication *offering*
for the altar after it was anointed.
89 Now when Moses went into
the tent of meeting to speak with
Him, he heard the voice speaking
to him from above the mercy seat
that was on the ark of the testimony, from between the two
cherubim, so He spoke to him.

CHAPTER 8

THEN the LORD spoke to Moses,
saying,
2 "Speak to Aaron and say to
him, 'When you mount the lamps,
the seven lamps will give light in
the front of the lampstand.' "
3 Aaron therefore did so; he
mounted its lamps at the front of
the lampstand, just as the LORD
had commanded Moses. ***raised up***
4 Now this was the workmanship of the lampstand, hammered
work of gold; from its base to its
flowers, it was hammered work;
according to the pattern which the
LORD had showed Moses, so he
made the lampstand.
5 Again the LORD spoke to
Moses, saying,
6 "Take the Levites from among
the sons of Israel and cleanse
them. **Is. 52:11**

7 "And thus you shall do to
them, for their cleansing: *sprinkle*
[t]purifying water on them, and let
them use a razor over their whole
body, and wash their clothes, and
they shall be clean. *water of sin*
8 "Then let them take a bull
with its grain offering, fine flour
mixed with oil; and a second bull
you shall take for a sin offering.
9 "So you shall present the Levites before the tent of meeting.
You shall also assemble the whole
congregation of the sons of Israel,
10 and present the Levites before the LORD; and the sons of Israel [r]shall lay their hands on the
Levites. Lev. 1:4
11 "Aaron then shall [t]present the
Levites before the LORD as a wave
offering from the sons of Israel,
that they may qualify to perform
the service of the LORD. *wave*
12 "Now the Levites shall lay
their hands on the heads of the
bulls; then offer the one for a sin
offering and the other for a burnt
offering to the LORD, to make
atonement for the Levites.
13 "And you shall have the Levites stand before Aaron and before his sons so as to present them
as a wave offering to the LORD.
14 "Thus you shall separate the
Levites from among the sons of
Israel, and [r]the Levites shall be
Mine. Num. 3:12; 16:9
15 "Then after that the Levites
may go in to serve the tent of
meeting. But you shall cleanse
them and [r]present them as a wave
offering; Ex. 29:24
16 for they are [r]wholly given to
Me from among the sons of Israel.
I have taken them for Myself instead of every first issue of the
womb, the first-born of all the
sons of Israel. Num. 3:9
17 "For every first-born among
the sons of Israel is Mine, among
the men and among the animals;
on the day that I struck down all
the first-born in the land of Egypt
I sanctified them for Myself.
18 "But I have taken the Levites
instead of every first-born among
the sons of Israel.
19 "And [r]I have given the Levites
as [t]a gift to Aaron and to his sons
from among the sons of Israel, to
perform the service of the sons of
Israel at the tent of meeting, and
to make atonement on behalf of
the sons of Israel, that there may
be no plague among the sons of
Israel by their coming near to the
sanctuary." Num. 3:9 • *given ones*
20 Thus did Moses and Aaron
and all the congregation of the
sons of Israel to the Levites; according to all that the LORD had
commanded Moses concerning
the Levites, so the sons of Israel
did to them.
21 [r]The Levites, too, purified
themselves from sin and washed
their clothes; and Aaron presented them as a wave offering
before the LORD. Aaron also made
atonement for them to cleanse
them. Num. 8:7
22 Then after that the Levites
went in to perform their service in
the tent of meeting before Aaron
and before his sons; just as the
LORD had commanded Moses concerning the Levites, so they did to
them.
23 Now the LORD spoke to
Moses, saying,

24 "This is what *applies* to the
Levites: from [r]twenty-five years
old and upward[t]they shall enter to
perform service in the work of the
tent of meeting. Num. 4:3 • *he*
25 "But at the age of fifty years
they shall retire from service in
the work and not work any more.
26 "They may, however, [t]assist
their brothers in the tent of meeting, [r]to keep an obligation; but
they *themselves* shall do no work.
Thus you shall deal with the Levites concerning their obligations." *serve* • Num. 1:53

CHAPTER 9

THUS the LORD spoke to Moses
in the wilderness of Sinai, in [r]the
first month of the second year after they had come out of the land
of Egypt, saying, Ex. 40:2, 17
2 "Now, let the sons of Israel
observe the Passover at [r]its appointed time. Ex. 12:6; Lev. 23:5
3 "On the fourteenth day of this
month, at twilight, you shall observe it at its appointed time; you
shall observe it according to all its
statutes and according to all its
ordinances."
4 So Moses told the sons of Israel to observe the Passover.
5 And [r]they observed the Passover in the first *month*, on the
fourteenth day of the month, at
twilight, in the wilderness of Sinai; according to all that the LORD
had commanded Moses, so the
sons of Israel did. Josh. 5:10
6 But there were *some* men
who were unclean because of *the*
[t]dead person, so that they could
not observe Passover on that day;
so they came before Moses and
Aaron on that day. *soul of man*
7 And those men said to him,
"*Though* we are unclean because
of *the* dead person, why are we restrained from presenting the offering of the LORD at its appointed
time among the sons of Israel?"
8 Moses therefore said to
them, "Wait,[t][r] and I will listen to
what the LORD will command concerning you." *Stand* • Ps. 85:8
9 Then the LORD spoke to
Moses, saying,
10 "Speak to the sons of Israel,
saying, 'If any one of you or of
your generations becomes unclean because of a *dead*[t]person, or
is on a distant journey, he may,
however, observe the Passover to
the LORD. *soul*
11 'In the second month on the
[r]fourteenth day at twilight, they
shall observe it; they shall eat it
with unleavened bread and bitter
herbs. 2 Chr. 30:2, 15
12 'They shall leave none of it
until morning, nor break a bone of
it; according to all the statute of
the Passover they shall observe it.
13 'But the man who is clean and
is not on a journey, and yet [a]ne-
glects to observe the Passover,
that [t]person shall then be cut off
from his people, for he did not
present the offering of the LORD at
its appointed time. That man shall
bear his sin. *ceases* • *soul*
14 'And if an alien sojourns
among you and [a]observes the Passover to the LORD, according to the
statute of the Passover and according to its ordinance, so he

shall do; you shall have one statute, both for the alien and for the native of the land.'" *would observe*
15 Now on [r]the day that the tabernacle was erected [r]the cloud covered the tabernacle, the tent of the testimony, and in the evening it was like the appearance of fire over the tabernacle, until morning. Ex. 40:2, 17 • Ex. 40:34
16 So it was continuously; the cloud would cover it *by day*, and the appearance of fire by night.
17 And whenever the cloud was lifted from over the tent, afterward the sons of Israel would then set out; and in the place where the cloud settled down, there the sons of Israel would camp.
18 At the [t]command of the LORD the sons of Israel would set out, and at the [t]command of the LORD they would camp; as long as the cloud settled over the tabernacle, they remained camped. *mouth*
19 Even when the cloud lingered over the tabernacle for many days, [t]the sons of Israel would keep the LORD's charge and not set out. *and the*
20 If [t]sometimes the cloud remained a few days over the tabernacle, according to the [t]command of the LORD they remained camped. Then according to the [t]command of the LORD they set out. *it was that • mouth*
21 If [t]sometimes the cloud [t]remained from evening until morning, when the cloud was lifted in the morning, they would move out; or *if it remained* in the daytime and at night, whenever the cloud was lifted, they would set out. *its was that • was*
22 Whether it was two days or a month or a year that the cloud lingered over the tabernacle, staying above it, the sons of Israel remained camped and did not set out; but [r]when it was lifted, they did set out. Ex. 40:36, 37
23 [r]At the [t]command of the LORD they camped, and at the command of the LORD they set out; they kept the LORD's charge, according to the command of the LORD through Moses. Ps. 73:24 • *mouth*

CHAPTER 10

THE LORD spoke further to Moses, saying,
2 "Make yourself two trumpets of silver, of hammered work you shall make them; and you shall use them for [r]summoning the congregation and for having the camps set out. Is. 1:13
3 "And [r]when both are blown, all the congregation shall gather themselves to you at the doorway of the tent of meeting. Joel 2:15
4 "Yet if *only* one is blown, then the leaders, the heads of the [t]divisions of Israel, shall assemble before you. *thousands;* or, *clans*
5 "But when you blow an alarm, the camps that are pitched [r]on the east side shall set out. Num. 10:14
6 "And when you blow an alarm the second time, the camps that are pitched on [r]the south side shall set out; an alarm is to be blown for them to set out. Num. 10:18
7 "When convening the assembly, however, you shall blow without [r]sounding an alarm. Joel 2:1
8 "The[r] priestly sons of Aaron,

moreover, shall blow the trumpets; and [t]this shall be for you a
perpetual statute throughout your
generations. Josh. 6:4 • *it*
9 "And when you go to war in
your land against the adversary
who attacks you, then you shall
sound an alarm with the trumpets,
that you may be remembered before the LORD your God, and be
saved from your enemies.
10 "Also in the day of your gladness and in your appointed feasts,
and on the first *days* of your
months, you shall blow the trumpets over your burnt offerings,
and over the sacrifices of your
peace offerings; and they shall be
as a reminder of you before your
God. I am the LORD your God."
11 Now it came about in the
second year, in the second month,
on the twentieth of the month,
that the cloud was lifted from
over the [t]tabernacle of the testimony; *dwelling place*
12 and the sons of Israel set out
on [r]their journeys from the wilderness of Sinai. Then the cloud settled down in the [r]wilderness of Paran. Ex. 40:36 • Gen. 21:21
13 [r]So they moved out for the
first time according to the [t]com-
mandment of the LORD through
Moses. Deut. 1:6 • *mouth*
14 And the standard of the
camp of the sons of Judah, according to their armies, set out
first, with Nahshon the son of Amminadab, over its army,
15 and Nethanel the son of
Zuar, over the tribal army of the
sons of Issachar;
16 and Eliab the son of Helon
over the tribal army of the sons of
Zebulun.
17 [r]Then the tabernacle was
taken down; and the sons of Gershon and the sons of Merari, who
were carrying the tabernacle, set
out. Num. 4:21-32
18 Next the standard of the
camp of Reuben, according to
their armies, set out with Elizur
the son of Shedeur, over its army,
19 and Shelumiel the son of Zurishaddai over the tribal army of
the sons of Simeon,
20 and Eliasaph the son of
Deuel was over the tribal army of
the sons of Gad.
21 [r]Then the Kohathites set out,
carrying the holy *objects;* and the
tabernacle was set up before their
arrival. Num. 4:4-20
22 [r]Next the standard of the
camp of the sons of Ephraim, according to their armies, was set
out, with Elishama the son of Ammihud over its army, Num. 2:18-24
23 and Gamaliel the son of Pedahzur over the tribal army of the
sons of Manasseh;
24 and Abidan the son of Gideoni over the tribal army of the
sons of Benjamin.
25 Then the standard of the
camp of the sons of Dan, according to their armies, *which formed*
the rear guard for all the camps,
set out, with Ahiezer the son of
Ammishaddai over its army,
26 and Pagiel the son of Ochran
over the tribal army of the sons of
Asher;
27 and Ahira the son of Enan
over the tribal army of the sons of
Naphtali.

28 This was the order of march of the sons of Israel by their armies as they set out.

29 Then Moses said to Hobab the son of Reuel the Midianite, Moses' father-in-law, "We are setting out to the place of which the LORD said, 'I will give it to you'; come with us and we will do you good, for the LORD has [t]promised good concerning Israel." *spoken*

30 But he said to him, "I will not come, but rather will go to my *own* land and relatives."

31 Then he said, "Please do not leave us, inasmuch as you know where we should camp in the wilderness, and you [r]will be as eyes for us. Job 29:15

32 "So it will be, if you go with us, it will come about that whatever good the LORD [t]does for us, we will do for you." *does good*

33 Thus they set out from the mount of the LORD three days' journey, with the ark of the covenant of the LORD journeying in front of them for the [t]three days, to seek out a resting place for them. *three days' journey*

34 And the cloud of the LORD was over them by day, when they set out from the camp.

35 Then it came about when the ark set out that Moses said,

"Rise up, O LORD!
And let Thine enemies be scattered,
And let those who hate Thee flee [12]before Thee."

36 And when it came to rest, he said,

"Return[r] Thou, O LORD
To the myriad thousands of Israel." Is. 63:17

[12]Or, *from Thy presence*

CHAPTER 11

NOW the people became like [r]those who complain of adversity in the hearing of the LORD; and when the LORD heard *it,* His anger was kindled, and the fire of the LORD burned among them and consumed *some* of the outskirts of the camp. Num. 14:2; 16:11

2 The people therefore cried out to Moses, and Moses prayed to the LORD, and the fire died out.

3 So the name of that place was called [13]Taberah, because the fire of the LORD burned among them.

4 And the rabble who were among them [t]had greedy desires; and also the sons of Israel wept again and said, "Who will give us meat to eat? *desired a desire*

5 "We[r] remember the fish which we used to eat free in Egypt, the cucumbers and the melons and the leeks and the onions and the garlic, Ex. 16:3

6 but now our [14]appetite is gone. There is nothing at all to look at except this manna."

7 Now the manna was like coriander seed, and its appearance like that of [r]bdellium. Gen. 2:12

8 The people would go about and gather *it* and grind *it* [t]between two millstones or beat *it* in the mortar, and boil *it* in the pot and make cakes with it; and its taste was as the taste of [t]cakes baked with oil. *with • juice of oil*

9 [r]And when the dew fell on the camp at night, the manna would fall [t]with it. Ex. 16:13, 14 • *on*

10 Now Moses heard the people weeping throughout their fam-

[13]I.e., burning [14]Lit., *soul is dried up*

ilies, each man at the doorway of
his tent; and the anger of the LORD
was kindled greatly, and Moses
was displeased.
11 So Moses said to the LORD,
"Why hast Thou [15]been so hard on
Thy servant? And why have I not
found favor in Thy sight, that
Thou hast laid the burden of all
this people on me?
12 "Was it I who conceived all
this people? Was it I who brought
them forth, that Thou shouldest
say to me, 'Carry them in your
bosom as a nurse carries a nursing
infant, to the land which Thou
didst swear to their fathers'?
13 "Where am I to get meat to
give to all this people? For they
weep before me, saying, 'Give us
meat that we may eat!'
14 "I alone am not able to carry
all this people, because it is too
[t]burdensome for me. *heavy*
15 "So[r] if Thou art going to deal
thus with me, please kill me at
once, if I have found favor in Thy
sight, and do not let me see my
wretchedness." Ex. 32:32
16 The LORD therefore said to
Moses, "Gather for Me seventy
men from the elders of Israel,
[r]whom you know to be the elders
of the people and their officers
and bring them to the tent of
meeting, and let them take their
stand there with you. Ex. 18:25
17 "Then I will come down and
speak with you there, and I will
take of [r]the Spirit who is upon you,
and will put *Him* upon them; and
they shall bear the burden of the
people with you, so that you shall
not bear *it* all alone. Joel 2:28
18 "And say to the people, 'Consecrate[r] yourselves for tomorrow,
and you shall eat meat; for you
have wept in the ears of the LORD,
saying, "Oh that someone would
give us meat to eat! For we were
well-off in Egypt." Therefore the
LORD will give you meat and you
shall eat. Ex. 19:10, 22
19 'You shall eat, not one day,
nor two days, nor five days, nor
ten days, nor twenty days,
20 [t]but a whole month, until it
comes out of your nostrils and becomes loathsome to you; because
you have rejected the LORD who is
among you and have wept before
Him, saying, "Why did we ever
leave Egypt?" ' " *until*
21 But Moses said, "The people,
among whom I am, are 600,000 on
foot; yet Thou hast said, 'I will
give them meat in order that they
may eat for a whole month.'
22 "Should flocks and herds be
slaughtered for them, to be sufficient for them? Or should all the
fish of the sea be gathered together for them, to be sufficient
for them?"
23 And the LORD said to Moses,
"Is the LORD's [t]power limited?
Now you shall see whether My
word will [t]come true for you or
not." *hand short • befall you*
24 So Moses went out and told
the people the words of the LORD.
Also, he gathered seventy men of
the elders of the people, and stationed them around the tent.
25 Then the LORD came down in
the cloud and spoke to him; and
He took of the Spirit who was
upon him and placed *Him* upon
the seventy elders. And it came
about that when the Spirit rested

[15]Lit., *dealt ill with*

upon them, they prophesied. But they did not do *it* again.

26 But two men had remained in the camp; the name of one was Eldad and the name of the other Medad. And the Spirit rested upon them (now they were among those who had been registered, but had not gone out to the tent), and they prophesied in the camp.

27 So a young man ran and told Moses and said, "Eldad and Medad are prophesying in the camp."

28 Then Joshua the son of Nun, the attendant of Moses from his youth, answered and said, "Moses, my lord, restrain them."

29 But Moses said to him, "Are you jealous for my sake? [r]Would that all the LORD's people were prophets, that the LORD would put His Spirit upon them!" 1 Cor. 14:5

30 Then Moses [t]returned to the camp, *both* he and the elders of Israel. *removed himself*

31 Now there went forth a wind from the LORD, and it brought quail from the sea, and let *them* fall beside the camp, about a day's journey on this side and a day's journey on the other side, all around the camp, and [a]about two cubits *deep* on the surface of the ground. *from about two cubits above*

32 And the people [t]spent all day and all night and all the next day, and gathered the quail (he who gathered least gathered ten [r]homers) and they spread *them* out for themselves all around the camp. *rose* • Ezek. 45:11

33 While the meat was still between their teeth, before it was chewed, the anger of the LORD was kindled against the people, and the LORD struck the people with a very severe plague.

34 So the name of that place was called [16]Kibroth-hattaavah, because there they buried the people who had been greedy.

35 From Kibroth-hattaavah the people set out for Hazeroth, and they remained at Hazeroth.

CHAPTER 12

THEN Miriam and Aaron spoke against Moses because of the Cushite woman whom he had married (for he had married a [r]Cushite woman); Ex. 2:21

2 [r]and they said, "Has the LORD indeed spoken only through Moses? Has He not spoken through us as well?" And the LORD heard it. Num. 16:3

3 (Now the man Moses was very humble, more than any man who was on the face of the earth.)

4 And suddenly the LORD said to Moses and Aaron and to Miriam, "You three come out to the tent of meeting." So the three of them came out.

5 Then the LORD came down in a pillar of cloud and stood at the doorway of the tent, and He called Aaron and Miriam. When they had both come forward,

6 He said,

"Hear now My words:
If there is a prophet among you,
I, the LORD, shall make Myself known to him in a vision.
I shall speak with him in a [r]dream. Gen. 31:11

7 "Not so, with [r]My servant Moses, Josh. 1:1

[16]I.e., the graves of greediness

He is faithful in all My
household;
8 With him I speak mouth to
mouth,
Even openly, and not in
dark sayings,
And he beholds the form of
the LORD.
Why then were you not
afraid
To speak against My ser-
vant, against Moses?"
9 So the anger of the LORD
burned against them and [r]He departed. Gen. 17:22; 18:33
10 But when the cloud had withdrawn from over the tent, behold,
Miriam *was* leprous, as *white as*
snow. As Aaron turned toward
Miriam, behold, she *was* leprous.
11 Then Aaron said to Moses,
"Oh, my lord, I beg you, [r]do not
account *this* sin to us, in which we
have acted foolishly and in which
we have sinned. 2 Sam. 19:19
12 "Oh, do not let her be like one
dead, whose flesh is half eaten
away when he comes from his
mother's womb!"
13 And Moses cried out to the
LORD, saying, "O God, [r]heal her, I
pray!" Ps. 30:2; Is. 30:26
14 But the LORD said to Moses,
"If her father had but [r]spit in her
face, would she not bear her
shame for seven days? Let her be
shut up for seven days outside the
camp, and afterward she may be
received again." Job 17:6
15 So Miriam was shut up outside the camp for seven days, and
the people did not move on until
Miriam was received again.
16 Afterward, however, the
people moved out from Hazeroth
and camped in the wilderness of
Paran.

CHAPTER 13

THEN [r]the LORD spoke to Moses
saying, Deut. 1:22, 23
2 "Send [r]out for yourself men so
that they may spy out the land of
Canaan, which I am going to give
to the sons of Israel; you shall
send a man from each of their fathers' tribes, every one a leader
among them." Deut. 1:22; 9:23
3 So Moses sent them from the
wilderness of Paran at the [t]com-
mand of the LORD, all of them men
who were heads of the sons of Israel. *mouth*
4 These then *were* their names:
from the tribe of Reuben, Shammua the son of Zaccur;
5 from the tribe of Simeon,
Shaphat the son of Hori;
6 from the tribe of Judah, Caleb the son of Jephunneh;
7 from the tribe of Issachar,
Igal the son of Joseph;
8 from the tribe of Ephraim,
Hoshea the son of Nun;
9 from the tribe of Benjamin,
Palti the son of Raphu;
10 from the tribe of Zebulun,
Gaddiel the son of Sodi;
11 from the tribe of Joseph,
from the tribe of Manasseh, Gaddi
the son of Susi;
12 from the tribe of Dan, Ammiel the son of Gemalli;
13 from the tribe of Asher, Se-
thur the son of Michael;
14 from the tribe of Naphtali,
Nahbi the son of Vophsi;
15 from the tribe of Gad, Geuel
the son of Machi.

16 These are the names of the
men whom Moses sent to spy out
the land; but Moses called Hoshea
the son of Nun, Joshua.
17 When Moses sent them to
spy out the land of Canaan, he
said to them, "Go up [t]there into
[r]the [17]Negev; then go up into the
hill country. *here* • Gen. 12:9
18 "And see what the land is like,
and whether the people who live
in it are strong *or* weak, whether
they are few or many.
19 "And how is the land in which
they live, is it good or bad? And
how are the cities in which they
live, are *they* [t]like *open* camps or
with fortifications? *in*
20 "And how is the land, is it fat
or lean? Are there trees in it or
not? [t]Make an effort then to get
some of the fruit of the land."
Now the time was the time of the
first ripe grapes. *Use your strength*
21 So they went up and spied
out the land from the wilderness
of Zin as far as Rehob, [a]at Lebo-
hamath. *to the entrance of Hamath*
22 When they had gone up into
the Negev, [t]they came to Hebron
where Ahiman, Sheshai and Talmai, the [t]descendants of Anak
were. (Now Hebron was built
seven years before Zoan in
Egypt.) *one came • children*
23 Then they came to the [t]valley
of [18]Eshcol and from there cut
down a branch with a single cluster of grapes; and they carried it
on a pole between two *men,* with
some of the pomegranates and the
figs. *wadi*
24 That place was called the
valley of Eshcol, because of the
cluster which the sons of Israel
cut down from there.
25 When they returned from
spying out the land, at the end of
forty days,
26 they proceeded to come to
Moses and Aaron and to all the
congregation of the sons of Israel
[t]in the wilderness of Paran, at [r]Ka-
desh; and they brought back word
to them and to all the congregation and showed them the fruit of
the land. *to* • Num. 20:1, 14
27 Thus they told him, and said,
"We went in to the land where
you sent us; and [r]it certainly does
flow with milk and honey, and this
is its fruit. Ex. 3:8, 17
28 "Nevertheless, the people who
live in the land are strong, and the
cities are fortified *and* very large;
and moreover, we saw the [t]de-
scendants of Anak there. *born ones*
29 "Amalek is living in the land
of the Negev and the Hittites and
the Jebusites and the Amorites
are living in the hill country, and
the Canaanites are living by the
sea and by the side of the Jordan."
30 Then Caleb quieted the people [t]before Moses, and said, "We
should by all means go up and
take possession of it, for we shall
surely overcome it." *toward*
31 But the men who had gone
up with him said, "We are not
able to go up against the people,
for they are too strong for us."
32 So they gave out to the sons
of Israel a bad report of the land
which they had spied out, saying,
"The land through which we have
gone, in spying it out, is a land
that devours its [a]inhabitants; and

[17]I.e., South country, and so throughout this context [18]I.e., cluster

all the people whom we saw in it
are men of *great* size. *settlers*
33 "There also we saw the [r]Neph-
ilim (the sons of Anak are part of
the Nephilim); and [r]we became
like grasshoppers in our own
sight, and so we were in their
sight." Gen. 6:4 • Deut. 1:28

CHAPTER 14

THEN all the congregation lifted
up their voices and cried, and the
people wept [t]that night. *in that*
2 And all the sons of Israel
grumbled against Moses and Aaron; and the whole congregation
said to them, "Would [r]that we had
died in the land of Egypt! Or
would that we had died in this wilderness! Num. 11:5; 16:13
3 "And why is the LORD bring-
ing us into this land, [r]to fall by the
sword? Our wives and our little
ones will become plunder; would
it not be better for us to return to
Egypt?" Ex. 5:21; 16:3
4 So they said to one another,
"Let [r]us appoint a leader and return to Egypt." Neh. 9:17
5 Then Moses and Aaron fell
on their faces in the presence of
all the assembly of the congregation of the sons of Israel.
6 And Joshua the son of Nun
and Caleb the son of Jephunneh,
of those who had spied out the
land, tore their clothes;
7 and they spoke to all the congregation of the sons of Israel,
saying, "The [r] land which we
passed through to spy out is an
exceedingly good land. Deut. 1:25
8 "If the LORD is pleased with
us, then He will bring us into this
land, and give it to us—a land
which flows with milk and honey.
9 "Only do not rebel against the
LORD; and do not fear the people
of the land, for they shall be our
[t]prey. Their protection has been removed from them, and the LORD is
with us; do not fear them." *food*
10 [r]But all the congregation said
to stone them with stones. Then
[r]the glory of the LORD appeared in
the tent of meeting to all the sons
of Israel. Ex. 17:4 • Ex. 16:10
11 [r]And the LORD said to Moses,
"How long will this people spurn
Me? And how long will [r]they not
believe in Me, despite all the signs
which I have performed in their
midst? Ex. 32:9-13 • Ps. 106:24
12 "I will smite them with pestilence and dispossess them, and I
will make you into a nation
greater and mightier than they."
13 [r]But Moses said to the LORD,
"Then the Egyptians will hear of
it, for by Thy strength Thou didst
bring up this people from their
midst, Ex. 32:11-14
14 and they will tell *it* to the inhabitants of this land. They have
heard that Thou, O LORD, art in
the midst of this people, for [r]Thou,
O LORD, art seen eye to eye, while
Thy cloud stands over them; and
Thou dost go before them in a pillar of cloud by day and in a pillar
of fire by night. Ex. 13:21
15 "Now if Thou dost slay this
people as one man, then the nations who have heard of Thy fame
will [t]say, *speak, saying*
16 'Because the LORD [r]could not
bring this people into the land
which He promised them by oath,

therefore He slaughtered them in
the wilderness.' Josh. 7:7
17 "But now, I pray, let the
power of the Lord be great, just as
Thou hast [t]declared, *spoken, saying*
18 'The[r] LORD is slow to anger
and abundant in lovingkindness,
forgiving iniquity and transgression; but He will by no means
clear *the guilty,* visiting the iniquity of the fathers on the children
[t]to the third and the fourth *generations.'* Ps. 103:8; 145:8 • *on*
19 "Pardon[r], I pray, the iniquity of
this people according to the greatness of Thy lovingkindness, just
as Thou also hast forgiven this
people, from Egypt even until
now." Ex. 32:32; 34:9
20 So the LORD said, "I[r] have
pardoned *them* according to your
word; Mic. 7:18-20
21 but indeed, [r]as I live, [t]all the
earth will be filled with the glory
of the LORD. Is. 49:18 • *and all*
22 "Surely all the men who have
seen My glory and My signs,
which I performed in Egypt and in
the wilderness, yet have put Me to
the test these ten times and have
not listened to My voice,
23 [r]shall by no means see the
land which I swore to their fathers, nor shall any of those who
spurned Me see it. Heb. 3:18
24 "But My servant Caleb, because he has had a different spirit
and has followed Me fully, [t]I will
bring into the land which he entered, and his descendants shall
take possession of it. *him I*
25 "Now the Amalekites and the
Canaanites live in the valleys; turn
tomorrow and set out to the wilderness by the way of the [t]Red
Sea." *Sea of Reeds*
26 And the LORD spoke to
Moses and Aaron, saying,
27 "How long *shall I bear* with
this evil congregation who are
grumbling against Me? I have
heard the complaints of the sons
of Israel, which they are [t]making
against Me. *complaining*
28 "Say to them, 'As[r] I live,' says
the LORD, 'just as you have spoken in My hearing, so I will surely
do to you; Num. 14:21
29 your corpses shall fall in this
wilderness, even all your [t]num-
bered men, according to your
complete number from twenty
years old and upward, who have
grumbled against Me. *mustered*
30 'Surely you shall not come
into the land in which I [t]swore to
settle you, except Caleb the son of
Jephunneh and Joshua the son of
Nun. *raised My hand*
31 'Your[r] children, however,
whom you said would become a
prey—I will bring them in, and
they shall know the land which
you have rejected. Num. 14:3
32 'But as for you, your corpses
shall fall in this wilderness.
33 'And your sons shall be shepherds for forty years in the wilderness, and they shall [t]suffer *for* your
unfaithfulness, until your corpses
lie in the wilderness. *bear*
34 'According to the [r]number of
days which you spied out the land,
forty days, for every day you shall
bear your [a]guilt a year, *even* forty
years, and you shall know My opposition. Num. 13:25 • *iniquities*
35 'I[r], the LORD, have spoken,
surely this I will do to all this evil

congregation who are gathered together against Me. In this wilderness they shall be destroyed, and there they shall die.' " Num. 23:19

36 [r]As for the men whom Moses sent to spy out the land and who returned and made all the congregation grumble against him by bringing out a bad report concerning the land, Num. 13:4-16, 32

37 even those men who brought out the very bad report of the land died by a plague before the LORD.

38 But Joshua the son of Nun and Caleb the son of Jephunneh remained alive out of those men who went to spy out the land.

39 And when Moses spoke these words to all the sons of Israel, the people mourned greatly.

40 In the morning, however, they rose up early and went up to the [a]ridge of the hill country, saying, "Here we are; we have indeed sinned, but we will go up to the place which the LORD has promised." *top of the mountain*

41 But Moses said, "Why then are you transgressing the [t]commandment of the LORD, when it will not succeed? *mouth*

42 "Do not go up, lest you be struck down before your enemies, for the LORD is not among you.

43 "For the Amalekites and the Canaanites will be there in front of you, and you will fall by the sword, inasmuch as you have turned back from following the LORD. And the LORD will not be with you."

44 But they went up heedlessly to the ridge of the hill country; neither the ark of the covenant of the LORD nor Moses left the camp.

45 Then the Amalekites and the Canaanites who lived in that hill country came down, and struck them and beat them down as far as [r]Hormah. Num. 21:3

CHAPTER 15

NOW the LORD spoke to Moses, saying,

2 "Speak[r] to the sons of Israel, and say to them, 'When you enter the land where you are to live, which I am giving you, Lev. 23:10

3 then make [r]an offering by fire to the LORD, a burnt offering or a sacrifice to fulfill a special vow, or as a freewill offering or in your appointed times, to make a soothing aroma to the LORD, from the herd or from the flock. Lev. 1:2, 3

4 'And the one who presents his offering shall present to the LORD a grain offering of one-tenth *of an ephah* of fine flour mixed with one-fourth of a [19]hin of oil,

5 and you shall prepare wine for the libation, one-fourth of a hin, with the burnt offering or for the sacrifice, for each lamb.

6 'Or for a ram you shall prepare as a grain offering two-tenths *of an ephah* of fine flour mixed with one-third of a hin of oil;

7 and for the libation you shall offer one-third of a hin of wine as a soothing aroma to the LORD.

8 'And when you prepare a bull as a burnt offering or a sacrifice, to fulfill a special vow, or for peace offerings to the LORD,

9 then you shall offer with the bull a grain offering of three-tenths *of an ephah* of fine flour mixed with one-half a hin of oil;

[19] I.e., Approx. one gallon, and so through v. 10

10 and you shall offer as the libation one-half a hin of wine as an offering by fire, as a soothing aroma to the LORD.

11 'Thus it shall be done for each ox, or for each ram, or for each of the male lambs, or of the goats.

12 'According to the number that you prepare, so you shall do for everyone according to their number.

13 'All who are native shall do these things in this manner, in presenting an offering by fire, as a soothing aroma to the LORD.

14 'And if an alien sojourns with you, or one who may be among you throughout your generations, and he *wishes to* make an offering by fire, as a soothing aroma to the LORD, just as you do, so he shall do.

15 '*As for* the assembly, there shall be [r]one statute for you and for the alien who sojourns *with you*, a perpetual statute throughout your generations; as you are, so shall the alien be before the LORD. Num. 9:14; 15:29

16 'There is to be one law and one ordinance for you and for the alien who sojourns with you.' "

17 Then the LORD spoke to Moses, saying,

18 "Speak to the sons of Israel, and say to them, 'When you enter the land where I bring you,

19 then it shall be, that when you eat of the [t]food of the land, you shall lift up [a]an offering to the LORD. *bread • a heave offering*

20 'Of the first of your [20]dough you shall lift up a cake as an offering; as the offering of the threshing floor, so you shall lift it up.

[20]Or, *coarse meal*

21 'From the first of your [20]dough you shall give to the LORD an [a]offering throughout your generations. *offering lifted up*

22 'But when you [r]unwittingly fail and do not observe all these commandments, which the LORD has spoken to Moses, Lev. 4:2

23 *even* all that the LORD has commanded you through Moses, from the day when the LORD gave commandment and onward throughout your generations,

24 then it shall be, if it is done unintentionally, [t]without the knowledge of the congregation, that all the congregation shall offer one bull for a burnt offering, as a soothing aroma to the LORD, with its grain offering, and its libation, according to the ordinance, and one male goat for a sin offering. *from the eyes of the congregation*

25 'Then [r]the priest shall make atonement for all the congregation of the sons of Israel, and they shall be forgiven; for it was an error, and they have brought their offering, an offering by fire to the LORD, and their sin offering before the LORD, for their error. Heb. 2:17

26 'So all the congregation of the sons of Israel will be forgiven, with the alien who sojourns among them, for *it happened* to all the people through error.

27 'Also if one person sins [r]unintentionally, then he shall offer a one year old female goat for a sin offering. Luke 12:48

28 'And the priest shall make atonement before the LORD for the person who goes astray when he sins unintentionally, making

[20]Or, *coarse meal*

atonement for him[a]that he may be
forgiven. *and he shall*
29 'You shall have one law for
him who does *anything* unintentionally, for him who is native
among the sons of Israel and for
the alien who sojourns among
them.
30 'But the person who does
anything [r]defiantly, whether he is
native or an alien, that one is blaspheming the LORD; and that person shall be cut off from among
his people. Num. 14:40-44
31 'Because he has despised the
word of the LORD and has broken
His commandment, that person
shall be completely cut off; his
[a]guilt *shall be* on him.' " *iniquity*
32 Now while the sons of Israel
were in the wilderness, they found
a man [r]gathering wood on the sabbath day. Ex. 31:14, 15
33 And those who found him
gathering wood brought him to
Moses and Aaron, and to all the
congregation;
34 and they put him in custody
because it had not been declared
what should be done to him.
35 Then the LORD said to Moses,
"The man shall surely be put to
death; [r]all the congregation shall
stone him with stones outside the
camp." Lev. 20:2, 27
36 So all the congregation
brought him outside the camp,
and stoned him to death with
stones, just as the LORD had commanded Moses.
37 The LORD also spoke to
Moses, saying,
38 "Speak to the sons of Israel,
and tell them that they shall make
for themselves [r]tassels on the corners of their garments throughout
their generations, and that they
shall put on the tassel of each corner a cord of blue. Matt. 23:5
39 "And it shall be a tassel for
you [t]to look at and remember all
the commandments of the LORD,
so as to do them and not follow
after your own heart and your
own eyes, after which you played
the harlot, *and you shall look at it*
40 in order that you may remember to do all My commandments, and be holy to your God.
41 "I am the LORD your God who
brought you out from the land of
Egypt to be your God; I am the
LORD your God."

CHAPTER 16

NOW Korah the son of Izhar, the
son of Kohath, the son of Levi,
with Dathan and Abiram, the sons
of Eliab, and On the son of Peleth,
sons of Reuben, took *action*,
2 and they rose up before
Moses, [t]together with some of the
sons of Israel, two hundred and
fifty leaders of the congregation,
[t]chosen in the assembly, men of renown. *and men from • called ones of*
3 And they assembled together
against Moses and Aaron, and
said to them, "You have gone far
enough, for all the congregation
are holy, every one of them, and
the LORD is in their midst; so why
do you exalt yourselves above the
assembly of the LORD?"
4 When Moses heard *this*, [r]he
fell on his face; Num. 14:5
5 and he spoke to Korah and
all his company, saying, "Tomorrow morning the LORD will show

who is His, and [r]who is holy, and
will bring *him* near to Himself;
even the one whom He will
choose, He will bring near to Himself. Lev. 10:3; Ps. 65:4
6 "Do this: take censers for
yourselves, Korah and all [t]your
company, *his*
7 and put fire in them, and lay
incense upon them in the presence
of the LORD tomorrow; and the
man whom the LORD chooses
shall be the one who is holy. [t]You
have gone far enough, you sons of
Levi!" *It is much for you*
8 Then Moses said to Korah,
"Hear now, you sons of Levi,
9 is it [a]not enough for you that
the God of Israel has separated
you from the *rest of* the congregation of Israel, to bring you near to
Himself, to do the service of the
tabernacle of the LORD, and to
stand before the congregation to
minister to them; *too little for you*
10 and that He has brought you
near, *Korah,* and all your brothers, sons of Levi, with you? And
are you [r]seeking for the priesthood
also? Num. 3:10; 18:1-7
11 "Therefore you and all your
company are gathered together
against the LORD; but as for Aaron, [t]who is he that you grumble
against him?" *what*
12 Then Moses sent [t]a summons
to Dathan and Abiram, the sons of
Eliab; but they said, "We will not
come up. *to call*
13 "Is it not enough that you
have brought us up out of a land
flowing with milk and honey to
have us die in the wilderness, but
you would also lord it over us?
14 "Indeed, you have not brought
us into a land flowing with milk
and honey, nor have you given us
an inheritance of fields and vineyards. Would you [t]put out the eyes
of [t]these men? We will not come
up!" *bore out • those*
15 Then Moses became very angry and said to the LORD, "Do [r]not
regard their offering! [r]I have not
taken a single donkey from them,
nor have I done harm to any of
them." Gen. 4:4, 5 • 1 Sam. 12:3
16 And Moses said to Korah,
"You and all your company be
present before the LORD tomorrow, both you and they along with
Aaron.
17 "And each of you take his firepan and put incense on it, and
each of you bring his censer before the LORD, two hundred and
fifty firepans; also you and Aaron
shall each *bring* his firepan."
18 So they each took his *own*
censer and put fire on it, and laid
incense on it; and they stood at
the doorway of the tent of meeting, with Moses and Aaron.
19 Thus Korah assembled all
the congregation against them at
the doorway of the tent of meeting. And the glory of the LORD appeared to all the congregation.
20 Then the LORD spoke to
Moses and Aaron, saying,
21 "Separate yourselves from
among this congregation, that I
may consume them instantly."
22 But they fell on their faces,
and said, "O God, Thou God of the
spirits of all flesh, [r]when one man
sins, wilt Thou be angry with the
entire congregation?" Lev. 4:3
23 Then the LORD spoke to
Moses, saying,

24 "Speak to the congregation,
saying, 'Get[r] back from around the
dwellings of Korah, Dathan and
Abiram.'" Num. 16:45
25 Then Moses arose and went
to Dathan and Abiram, with the
elders of Israel following him,
26 and he spoke to the congregation, saying, "Depart now from
the tents of these wicked men,
and touch nothing that belongs to
them, [r]lest you be swept away in
all their sin." Gen. 19:15, 17
27 So they got back from
around the dwellings of Korah,
Dathan and Abiram; and Dathan
and Abiram came out *and* stood
at the doorway of their tents,
along with their wives and their
sons and their little ones.
28 And Moses said, "By this you
shall know that the LORD has sent
me to do all these deeds; for this is
not [t]my doing. *from my heart*
29 "If these men die [t]the death of
all men, or if they suffer the [r]fate
of all men, *then* the LORD has not
sent me. *like the death* • Eccl. 3:19
30 "But if the LORD [t]brings about
an entirely new thing and the
ground opens its mouth and swallows them up with all that is
theirs, and they descend alive into
Sheol, then you will understand
that these men have spurned the
LORD." *creates a new creation*
31 Then it came about as he finished speaking all these words,
that the ground that was under
them split open;
32 and [r]the earth opened its
mouth and swallowed them up,
and their households, and all the
men who belonged to Korah, with
their possessions. Num. 26:10
33 So they and all that belonged
to them went down alive to Sheol;
and the earth closed over them,
and they perished from the midst
of the assembly.
34 And all Israel who *were*
around them fled at their outcry,
for they said, "The[t] earth may
swallow us up!" *Lest the earth*
35 Fire also came forth from the
LORD and consumed the [r]two hundred and fifty men who were offering the incense. Num. 16:2
36 Then the LORD spoke to
Moses, saying,
37 "Say to Eleazar, the son of
Aaron the priest, that he shall
take up the censers out of the
midst of the blaze, for they are
holy; and you scatter the [t]burning
coals abroad. *the fire*
38 "As for the censers of these
men who have sinned at the cost
of their lives, let them be made
into hammered sheets for a plating of the altar, since they did present them before the LORD and
they are holy; and they shall be for
a sign to the sons of Israel."
39 So Eleazar the priest took
the bronze censers which the men
who were burned had offered; and
they hammered them out as a
plating for the altar,
40 as a reminder to the sons of
Israel that no layman who is not
of the descendants of Aaron
should come near to burn incense
before the LORD; that he might not
become like Korah and his company—just as the LORD had spoken to him through Moses.
41 But on the next day all the
congregation of the sons of Israel

[r]grumbled against Moses and Aaron, saying, "You are the ones who
have caused the death of the
LORD's people." Num. 16:3
42 It came about, however,
when the congregation had assembled against Moses and Aaron, that they turned toward the
tent of meeting, and behold, the
cloud covered it and [r]the glory of
the LORD appeared. Num. 16:19
43 Then Moses and Aaron came
to the front of the tent of meeting,
44 and the LORD spoke to
Moses, saying,
45 "Get[ar]away from among this
congregation, that I may consume
them instantly." Then they fell on
their faces. *Arise* • Num. 16:21, 24
46 And Moses said to Aaron,
"Take your censer and put in it
fire from the altar, and lay incense
on it; then bring it quickly to the
congregation and [r]make atonement for them, for wrath has gone
forth from the LORD, the plague
has begun!" Num. 25:13
47 Then Aaron took *it* as Moses
had spoken, and ran into the
midst of the assembly, for behold,
the plague had begun among the
people. [r]So he put *on* the incense
and made atonement for the people. Num. 25:6-8, 13
48 And he took his stand between the dead and the living, so
that the plague was checked.
49 But those who died by the
plague were 14,700, besides those
who died on account of Korah.
50 Then Aaron returned to
Moses at the doorway of the tent
of meeting, for the plague had
been checked.

CHAPTER 17

THEN the LORD spoke to Moses,
saying,
2 "Speak to the sons of Israel,
and get from them a rod for each
father's household: twelve rods,
from all their leaders according to
their fathers' households. You
shall write each name on his rod,
3 and write Aaron's name on
the rod of Levi; for there is one
rod for the head *of each* of their
fathers' households.
4 "You shall then deposit them
in the tent of meeting in front of
[r]the testimony, where I meet with
you. Ex. 25:16, 21, 22
5 "And it will come about that
the rod of the man whom I choose
will sprout. Thus I shall lessen
from upon Myself the grumblings
of the sons of Israel, who are
grumbling against you."
6 Moses therefore spoke to the
sons of Israel, and all their leaders
gave him a rod apiece, for each
leader according to their fathers'
households, twelve rods, with the
rod of Aaron among their rods.
7 So Moses deposited the rods
before the LORD in [r]the tent of the
testimony. Num. 1:50, 53
8 Now it came about on the
next day that Moses went into the
tent of the testimony; and behold,
[r]the rod of Aaron for the house of
Levi had sprouted and put forth
buds and produced blossoms, and
it bore ripe almonds. Heb. 9:4
9 Moses then brought out all
the rods from the presence of the
LORD to all the sons of Israel; and
they looked, and each man took
his rod.

10 But the LORD said to Moses,
"Put back the rod of Aaron before
the testimony[t] to be kept as a sign
against the rebels, that you may
put an end to their grumblings
against Me, so that they should
not die." *for preserving*
11 Thus Moses did; just as the
LORD had commanded him, so he
did.
12 Then the sons of Israel spoke
to Moses, saying, "Behold,[r] we
perish, we are dying, we are all
dying! Is. 6:5
13 "Everyone[r] who comes near,
who comes near to the tabernacle
of the LORD, must die. Are we to
perish completely?" Num. 1:51

CHAPTER 18

SO the LORD said to Aaron, "You
and your sons and your father's
household with you shall bear the
guilt in connection with the sanctuary; and you and your sons with
you shall bear the guilt in connection with your priesthood.
2 "But bring with you also your
brothers, the tribe of Levi, the
tribe of your father, that they may
be[r] joined with you and serve you,
while you and your sons with you
are before the tent of the testimony. Num. 3:5-10
3 "And they shall thus attend to
your obligation and the obligation
of all the tent, but they shall not
come near to the furnishings of
the sanctuary and [r]the altar, lest
both they and you die. Num. 1:51
4 "And they shall be joined with
you and attend to the obligations
of the tent of meeting, for all the
service of the tent; but an outsider
may not come near you.
5 "So you shall attend to the [r]ob-
ligations of the sanctuary and the
obligations of the altar, that there
may no longer be wrath on the
sons of Israel. Ex. 27:21; Lev. 24:3
6 "And behold, I Myself have
taken your [t]fellow Levites from
among the sons of Israel; they are
a gift to you, dedicated to the
LORD, to perform the service for
the tent of meeting. *brethren the*
7 "But you and your sons with
you shall attend to your priesthood for everything concerning
the altar and inside the veil, and
you are to perform service. I am
giving you the priesthood as a [t]be-
stowed service, but the [t]outsider
who comes near shall be put to
death." *service of gift • stranger*
8 Then the LORD spoke to Aaron, "Now behold, I Myself have
given you charge of My [t]offerings,
even all the holy gifts of the sons
of Israel, I have given them to you
as a portion, and to your sons as a
perpetual allotment. *heave offerings*
9 "This shall be yours from the
most holy *gifts, reserved* from the
fire; every offering of theirs, even
[r]every grain offering and every [r]sin
offering and every guilt offering,
which they shall render to Me,
shall be most holy for you and for
your sons. Lev. 2:1-16 • Lev. 6:30
10 "As the most holy *gifts* you
shall eat it; every male shall eat it.
It shall be holy to you.
11 "This also is yours, [r]the offering of their gift, even all the wave
offerings of the sons of Israel; I
have given them to you and to
your sons and daughters with you,

as a perpetual allotment. Everyone of your household who is clean may eat it. Num. 18:1

12 "All the [t]best of the fresh oil and all the best of the fresh wine and of the grain, the first fruits of those which they give to the LORD, I give them to you. *fat*

13 "The [r]first ripe fruits of all that is in their land, which they bring to the LORD, shall be yours; everyone of your household who is clean may eat it. Ex. 22:29

14 "Every [r]devoted thing in Israel shall be yours. Lev. 27:1-33

15 "Every first issue of the womb of all flesh, whether man or animal, which they offer to the LORD, shall be yours; nevertheless the first-born of man you shall surely redeem, and the first-born of unclean animals you shall redeem.

16 "And as to their redemption price, from a month old you shall redeem them, by your valuation, five [21]shekels in silver, according to the shekel of the sanctuary, which is twenty gerahs.

17 "But the first-born of an ox or the first-born of a sheep or the first-born of a goat, you shall not redeem; they are holy. You shall sprinkle their blood on the altar and shall offer up their fat in smoke *as* an offering by fire, for a soothing aroma to the LORD.

18 "And their [t]meat shall be yours; it shall be yours like the [r]breast of a wave offering and like the right thigh. *flesh* • Lev. 7:31

19 "All the offerings of the holy *gifts*, which the sons of Israel offer to the LORD, I have given to you and your sons and your daughters with you, as a perpetual allotment. It is an everlasting covenant of salt before the LORD to you and your [t]descendants with you." *seed*

20 Then the LORD said to Aaron, "You [r]shall have no inheritance in their land, nor own any portion among them; I am your portion and your inheritance among the sons of Israel. Deut. 10:9; 12:12

21 "And to the sons of Levi, behold, I have given all the [r]tithe in Israel for an inheritance, in return for their service which they perform, the service of the tent of meeting. Lev. 27:30-33

22 "And the sons of Israel shall not come near the tent of meeting again, lest they bear sin and die.

23 "Only the Levites shall perform the service of the tent of meeting, and they shall [r]bear their iniquity; it shall be a perpetual statute throughout your generations, and among the sons of Israel [r]they shall have no inheritance. Num. 18:1 • Num. 18:20

24 "For the tithe of the sons of Israel, which they offer as an offering to the LORD, I have given to the Levites for an inheritance; therefore I have said concerning them, 'They shall have no inheritance among the sons of Israel.' "

25 Then the LORD spoke to Moses, saying,

26 "Moreover, you shall speak to the Levites and say to them, 'When you take from the sons of Israel [r]the tithe which I have given you from them for your inheritance, then you shall present an offering from it to the LORD, a tithe of the tithe. Num. 18:21

27 'And your offering shall be reckoned to you as the grain from

[21] I.e., A shekel equals approx. one-half ounce

the threshing floor or the full produce from the wine vat.

28 'So you shall also present an offering to the LORD from your tithes, which you receive from the sons of Israel; and from it you shall give the LORD's offering to Aaron the priest.

29 'Out of all your gifts you shall present every offering due to the LORD, from all the [t]best of them, the sacred part from them.' *fat*

30 "And you shall say to them, 'When you have offered from it the best of it, then *the rest* shall be reckoned to the Levites as the product of the threshing floor, and as the product of the wine vat.

31 'And you may eat it anywhere, you and your households, for it is your compensation in return for your service in the tent of meeting.

32 'And you shall bear no sin by reason of it, when you have offered the [t]best of it. But you shall not profane the sacred gifts of the sons of Israel, lest you die.' " *fat*

CHAPTER 19

THEN the LORD spoke to Moses and Aaron, saying,

2 "This is the statute of the law which the LORD has commanded, saying, 'Speak to the sons of Israel that they bring you an unblemished red heifer in which is no defect, *and* on which a yoke has never [t]been placed. *come up*

3 'And you shall give it to Eleazar the priest, and it shall be brought outside the camp and be slaughtered in his presence.

4 'Next Eleazar the priest shall take some of its blood with his finger, and [r]sprinkle some of its blood toward the front of the tent of meeting seven times. Lev. 4:6, 17

5 'Then the heifer shall be burned in his sight; [r]its hide and its flesh and its blood, with its refuse, shall be burned. Ex. 29:14

6 'And the priest shall take cedar wood and hyssop and scarlet *material,* and cast it into the midst of the burning heifer.

7 'The priest shall then wash his clothes and bathe his [t]body in water, and afterward come into the camp, but the priest shall be unclean until evening. *flesh*

8 'The one who burns it shall also wash his clothes in water and bathe his [t]body in water, and shall be unclean until evening. *flesh*

9 'Now a man who is clean shall gather up the ashes of the heifer and deposit them outside the camp in a clean place, and the congregation of the sons of Israel shall keep it as [r]water to remove impurity; it is [a]purification from sin. Num. 8:7 • *a sin offering*

10 'And the one who gathers the ashes of the heifer [r]shall wash his clothes and be unclean until evening; and it shall be a perpetual statute to the sons of Israel and to the alien who sojourns among them. Num. 19:7

11 'The one who touches the corpse of any [t]person shall be unclean for seven days. *soul of man*

12 'That one shall [r]purify himself from uncleanness with [t]the water on the third day and on the seventh day, *and then* he shall be clean; but if he does not purify himself on the third day and on

the seventh day, he shall not be clean. Num. 19:19; 31:19 • *it*

13 'Anyone who touches a corpse, the [t]body of a man who has died, and does not purify himself, defiles the tabernacle of the LORD; and that person shall be cut off from Israel. Because the water for impurity was not sprinkled on him, he shall be unclean; his uncleanness is still on him. *soul*

14 'This is the law when a man dies in a tent: everyone who comes into the tent and everyone who is in the tent shall be unclean for seven days.

15 'And every open vessel, which has no covering [t]tied down on it, shall be unclean. *cord*

16 'Also[r], anyone who in the open field touches one who has been slain with a sword or who has died *naturally*, or a human bone or a grave, shall be unclean for seven days. Num. 31:19

17 'Then for the unclean *person* they shall take some of the [t]ashes of the burnt purification from sin and flowing water shall be [t]added to them in a vessel. *dust* • *put*

18 'And a clean person shall take hyssop and dip *it* in the water, and sprinkle *it* on the tent and on all the furnishings and on the persons who were there, and on the one who touched the bone or the one slain or the one dying *naturally* or the grave.

19 'Then the clean *person* [r]shall sprinkle on the unclean on the third day and on the seventh day; and on the seventh day he shall purify him from uncleanness, and he shall wash his clothes and bathe *himself* in water and shall be clean by evening. Heb. 10:22

20 'But the man who is unclean and does not purify himself from uncleanness, that person shall be cut off from the midst of the assembly, because he has defiled the sanctuary of the LORD; the water for impurity has not been sprinkled on him, he is unclean.

21 'So it shall be a perpetual statute for them. And he who sprinkles the water for impurity shall wash his clothes, and he who touches the water for impurity shall be unclean until evening.

22 'Furthermore[r], anything that the unclean *person* touches shall be unclean; and the person who touches *it* shall be unclean until evening.' " Lev. 5:2, 3; 7:21

CHAPTER 20

THEN the sons of Israel, the whole congregation, came to the [r]wilderness of Zin in the first month; and the people stayed at Kadesh. Now Miriam died there and was buried there. Num. 13:21

2 And there was no water for the congregation; [r]and they assembled themselves against Moses and Aaron. Num. 16:19, 42

3 The people thus contended with Moses and spoke, saying, "If only we had perished [r]when our brothers perished before the LORD! Num. 16:31-35

4 "Why[r] then have you brought the LORD's assembly into this wilderness, for us and our beasts to die [t]here? Ex. 17:3 • *there*

5 "And why have you made us come up from Egypt, to bring us

in to this wretched place?[r]It is not
a place of[t]grain or figs or vines or
pomegranates, nor is there water
to drink." Num. 16:14 • *seed*
6 Then Moses and Aaron came
in from the presence of the assembly to the doorway of the tent of
meeting, and[r]fell on their faces.
Then the glory of the LORD appeared to them; Num. 14:5
7 and the LORD spoke to
Moses, saying,
8 "Take the rod; and you and
your brother Aaron assemble the
congregation and speak to the
rock before their eyes, that it may
yield its water. You shall thus
bring forth water for them out of
the rock and let the congregation
and their beasts drink."
9 So Moses took the rod[r]from
before the LORD, just as He had
commanded him; Num. 17:10
10 and Moses and Aaron gathered the assembly before the rock.
And he said to them, "Listen now,
you rebels; shall we bring forth
water for you out of this rock?"
11 Then Moses lifted up his
hand and struck the rock twice
with his rod; and water came
forth abundantly, and the congregation and their beasts drank.
12 But the LORD said to Moses
and Aaron, "Because[r] you have
not believed Me, to treat Me as
holy in the sight of the sons of Israel, therefore you shall not bring
this assembly into the land which
I have given them." Num. 20:24
13 Those *were* the waters of
[22]Meribah,[a]because the sons of Israel contended with the LORD, and
He proved Himself holy among
them. *where*

[22]I.e., contention

14 From Kadesh Moses then
sent messengers to the king of
Edom: "Thus your brother Israel
has said, 'You know all the hardship that has befallen us;
15 that our fathers went down
to Egypt, and we stayed in Egypt
a long time, and the Egyptians
treated us and our fathers badly.
16 'But[r]when we cried out to the
LORD, He heard our voice and sent
an angel and brought us out from
Egypt; now behold, we are at Kadesh, a town on the edge of your
territory. Ex. 2:23; 3:7
17 'Please[r]let us pass through
your land. We shall not pass
through field or through vineyard;
we shall not even drink water
from a well. We shall go along the
king's highway, not turning to the
right or left, until we pass through
your territory.'" Num. 21:22
18[r]Edom, however, said to him,
"You shall not pass through[t]us,
lest I come out with the sword
against you." Num. 24:18 • *me*
19 Again, the sons of Israel said
to him, "We shall go up by the
highway, and if I and my livestock
do drink any of your water, then I
will pay its price. Let me only pass
through on my feet, nothing *else*."
20 But he said, "You shall not
pass through." And Edom came
out against him with a heavy
force, and with a strong hand.
21[r]Thus Edom refused to allow
Israel to pass through his territory;[r]so Israel turned away from
him. Judg. 11:17 • Deut. 2:8
22 Now when they set out from
[r]Kadesh, the sons of Israel, the
whole congregation, came to
Mount Hor. Num. 20:1, 14

23 Then the LORD spoke to
Moses and Aaron at [r]Mount Hor
by the border of the land of Edom,
saying, Num. 33:37
24 "Aaron shall be gathered to
his people; for he shall not enter
the land which I have given to the
sons of Israel, because you rebelled against My [t]command at the
waters of Meribah. *mouth*
25 "Take Aaron and his son [r]Elea-
zar, and bring them up to Mount
Hor; Num. 3:4
26 and strip Aaron of his garments and put them on his son Eleazar. So Aaron will be gathered
to his people, and will die there."
27 So Moses did just as the
LORD had commanded, and they
went up to Mount Hor in the sight
of all the congregation.
28 And after Moses had
stripped Aaron of his garments
and put them on his son Eleazar,
Aaron died there on the mountain
top. Then Moses and Eleazar
came down from the mountain.
29 And when all the congregation saw that Aaron had died, all
the house of Israel wept for Aaron
thirty [r]days. Gen. 1:5; 50:3, 10

CHAPTER 21

WHEN the Canaanite, the king
of Arad, who lived in the [23]Negev,
heard that Israel was coming by
the way of [24]Atharim, then he
fought against Israel, and took
some of them captive.
2 So Israel made a vow to the
LORD, and said, "If Thou wilt indeed deliver this people into my
hand, then I will [t]utterly destroy
their cities." *devote to destruction*

[23] I.e., South country [24] Or, *the spies*

3 And the LORD heard the
voice of Israel, and delivered up
the Canaanites; then they utterly
destroyed them and their cities.
Thus the name of the place was
called [25]Hormah.
4 Then they set out from
Mount Hor by the way of the Red
Sea, to go around the land of
Edom; and the people became impatient because of the journey.
5 And the people spoke against
God and Moses, "Why have you
brought us up out of Egypt to die
in the wilderness? For there is no
[t]food and no water, and we loathe
this miserable food." *bread*
6 [r]And the LORD sent fiery serpents among the people and they
bit the people, so that many people of Israel died. Deut. 8:15
7 So the people came to Moses
and said, "We have sinned, because we have spoken against the
LORD and you; intercede with the
LORD, that He may remove the
serpents from us." And Moses interceded for the people.
8 Then the LORD said to Moses,
"Make[t] a [r]fiery *serpent,* and set it
on a standard; and it shall come
about, that everyone who is bit-
ten, when he looks at it, he shall
live." *Make for yourself* • John 3:14
9 And Moses made a bronze
serpent and set it on the standard;
and it came about, that if a serpent bit any man, when he looked
to the bronze serpent, he lived.
10 Now the sons of Israel
moved out and camped in Oboth.
11 And they journeyed from
Oboth, and camped at Iyeabarim,
in the wilderness which is opposite Moab, to the [t]east. *sunrise*

[25] I.e., a devoted thing; or, Destruction

12 From there they set out and
camped in [26]Wadi Zered.
13 From there they journeyed
and camped on the other side of
the Arnon, which is in the wilderness that comes out of the border
of the Amorites, for the Arnon is
the border of Moab, between
Moab and the Amorites.
14 Therefore it is said in the
Book of the Wars of the LORD,
"Waheb in Suphah,
And the wadis of the Ar-
non,
15 And the slope of the wadis
That extends to the site of
ʳAr,
And leans to the border of
Moab." Num. 21:28
16 ʳAnd from there *they continued* to Beer, that is the well where
the LORD said to Moses, "Assemble the people, that I may give
them water." Num. 33:46-49
17 ʳThen Israel sang this song:
"Spring up, O well! Sing to
it! Ex. 15:1; Ps. 105:2
18 "The well, which the leaders
sank,
Which the nobles of the
people dug,
With the scepter *and* with
their staffs."
And from the wilderness *they
continued* to Mattanah,
19 and from Mattanah to Nahaliel, and from Nahaliel to Bamoth,
20 and from Bamoth to the valley that is in the land of Moab, at
the top of Pisgah which overlooks
the [a]wasteland. *Jeshimon*
21 ʳThen Israel sent messengers
to Sihon, king of the Amorites,
saying, Deut. 2:26-37
22 "Let me pass through your
land. We will not turn off into field
or vineyard; we will not drink water from wells. We will go by the
king's highway until we have
passed through your border."
23 But Sihon would not permit
Israel to pass through his border.
So Sihon gathered all his people
and went out against Israel in the
wilderness, and came to Jahaz
and fought against Israel.
24 Then Israel struck him with
the edge of the sword, and took
possession of his land from the
Arnon to the Jabbok, as far as the
sons of Ammon; for the border of
the sons of Ammon *was* Jazer.
25 And Israel took all these
cities and Israel lived in all the
cities of the Amorites, in Heshbon, and in all her villages.
26 For Heshbon was the city of
Sihon, king of the Amorites, who
had fought against the former
king of Moab and had taken all his
land out of his hand, as far as the
Arnon.
27 Therefore those who use
proverbs say,
"Come to Heshbon! Let it be
built!
So let the city of Sihon be
established.
28 "For a fire went forth from
Heshbon,
A flame from the town of
Sihon;
It devoured Ar of Moab,
The [t]dominant heights of the
Arnon. *lords of the*
29 "Woe to you, O Moab!
You are ruined, O people of
Chemosh!
He has given his sons as fu-
gitives,

[26]I.e., a dry ravine except during rainy season

And his daughters into captivity,
To an Amorite king, Sihon.
30 "But we have cast them
down,
Heshbon is ruined as far as
Dibon,
Then we have laid waste
even to Nophah,
Which *reaches* to Medeba."
31 Thus Israel lived in the land
of the Amorites.
32 And Moses sent to spy out
[r]Jazer, and they captured its villages and dispossessed the Amorites who *were* there. Jer. 48:32
33 Then they turned and went
up by the way of Bashan, and Og
the king of Bashan went out with
all his people, for battle at Edrei.
34 But the LORD said to Moses,
"Do[r] not fear him, for I have given
him into your hand, and all his
people and his land; and you shall
do to him as you did to Sihon,
king of the Amorites, who lived at
Heshbon." Deut. 3:2
35 So they [t]killed him and his
sons and all his people, until there
was no remnant left him; and they
possessed his land. *smote*

CHAPTER 22

THEN the sons of Israel journeyed, and camped in the plains
of Moab beyond the Jordan *opposite* Jericho.
2 Now [r]Balak the son of Zippor
saw all that Israel had done to the
Amorites. Judg. 11:25
3 So Moab was in great fear
because of the people, for they
were numerous; and Moab was in
dread of the sons of Israel.
4 And Moab said to the elders
of Midian, "Now this horde will
lick up all that is around us, as the
ox licks up the grass of the field."
And Balak the son of Zippor was
king of Moab at that time.
5 So he sent messengers to Balaam the son of Beor, at Pethor,
which is near the [27]River, *in* the
land of the sons of his people, to
call him, saying, "Behold, a people
came out of Egypt; behold, they
cover the surface of the land, and
they are living opposite me.
6 "Now, therefore, please come,
curse this people for me since
they are too mighty for me; perhaps I may be able to [t]defeat them
and drive them out of the land.
For I know that he whom you
bless is blessed, and he whom you
curse is cursed." *smite*
7 So the elders of Moab and
the elders of Midian departed with
the *fees for* [r]divination in their
hand; and they came to Balaam
and [t]repeated Balak's words to
him. Josh. 13:22 • *spoke*
8 And he said to them, "Spend
the night here, and I will bring
word back to you as the LORD
may speak to me." And the leaders of Moab stayed with Balaam.
9 Then [r]God came to Balaam
and said, "Who are these men
with you?" Gen. 20:3
10 And Balaam said to God,
"Balak the son of Zippor, king of
Moab, has sent *word* to me,
11 'Behold, there is a people who
came out of Egypt and they cover
the surface of the land; now come,
curse them for me; perhaps I may
be able to fight against them, and
drive them out.' "

[27] I.e., Euphrates

12 And God said to Balaam, "Do not go with them; [r]you shall not curse the people; for they are blessed." Num. 23:8; 24:9

13 So Balaam arose in the morning and said to Balak's leaders, "Go back to your land, for the LORD has refused to let me go with you."

14 And the leaders of Moab arose and went to Balak, and said, "Balaam refused to come with us."

15 Then Balak again sent leaders, more numerous and more distinguished than [t]the former. *these*

16 And they came to Balaam and said to him, "Thus says Balak the son of Zippor, 'Let nothing, I beg you, hinder you from coming to me;

17 for I will indeed honor you richly, and I will do whatever you say to me. Please come then, curse this people for me.' "

18 And Balaam answered and said to the servants of Balak, "Though Balak were to give me his house full of silver and gold, I could not do anything, either small or great, contrary to the command of the LORD my God.

19 "And now please, you also stay here tonight, and I will find out what else the LORD will speak to me."

20 And God came to Balaam at night and said to him, "If the men have come to call you, rise up *and* go with them; but [r]only the word which I speak to you shall you do." Num. 22:35; 24:13

21 [r]So Balaam arose in the morning, and saddled his donkey, and went with the leaders of Moab. 2 Pet. 2:15

22 But God was angry because he was going, and the angel of the LORD took his stand in the way as an adversary against him. Now he was riding on his donkey and his two servants were with him.

23 When the donkey saw the angel of the LORD standing in the way with his drawn sword in his hand, the donkey turned off from the way and went into the field; but Balaam struck the donkey to turn her back into the way.

24 Then the angel of the LORD stood in a narrow path of the vineyards, *with* a wall on this side and a wall on that side.

25 When the donkey saw the angel of the LORD, she pressed herself to the wall and pressed Balaam's foot against the wall, so he struck her again.

26 And the angel of the LORD went further, and stood in a narrow place where there was no way to turn to the right hand or the left.

27 When the donkey saw the angel of the LORD, she lay down under Balaam; so [r]Balaam was angry and struck the donkey with his stick. James 1:19

28 And [r]the LORD opened the mouth of the donkey, and she said to Balaam, "What have I done to you, that you have struck me these three times?" 2 Pet. 2:16

29 Then Balaam said to the donkey, "Because you have made a mockery of me! If there had been a sword in my hand, [r]I would have killed you by now." Matt. 15:19

30 And the donkey said to Ba-

laam, "Am I not your donkey on which you have ridden all your life to this day? Have I ever been accustomed to do so to you?" And he said, "No."

31 Then the LORD opened the eyes of Balaam, and he saw [r]the angel of the LORD standing in the way with his drawn sword in his hand; and he bowed all the way to the ground. Josh. 5:13-15

32 And the angel of the LORD said to him, "Why have you struck your donkey these three times? Behold, I have come out as an adversary, because your way was [t]contrary to me. *reckless*

33 "But the donkey saw me and turned aside from me these three times. If she had not turned aside from me, I would surely have killed you just now, and let her live."

34 And Balaam said to the angel of the LORD, "I [r]have sinned, for I did not know that you were standing in the way against me. Now then, if it is displeasing to you, I will turn back." Num. 14:40

35 But the angel of the LORD said to Balaam, "Go with the men, but [r]you shall speak only the word which I shall [a]tell you." So Balaam went along with the leaders of Balak. Num. 22:20 • *speak to*

36 When Balak heard that Balaam was coming, he went out to meet him at the city of Moab, which is on the Arnon border, at the extreme end of the border.

37 Then Balak said to Balaam, "Did I not urgently send to you to call you? Why did you not come to me? Am I really unable to honor you?"

38 So Balaam said to Balak, "Behold, I have come now to you! Am I able to speak anything at all? The word that God puts in my mouth, that I shall speak."

39 And Balaam went with Balak, and they came to Kiriath-huzoth.

40 And Balak sacrificed oxen and sheep, and sent *some* to Balaam and the leaders who were with him.

41 Then it came about in the morning that Balak took Balaam, and brought him up to the high places of Baal; and he saw from there a portion of the people.

CHAPTER 23

THEN Balaam said to Balak, "Build seven altars for me here, and prepare seven bulls and seven rams for me here."

2 And Balak did just as Balaam had spoken, and Balak and Balaam offered up a bull and a ram on each altar.

3 Then Balaam said to Balak, "Stand beside your burnt offering, and I will go; perhaps the LORD will come to me, and whatever He shows me I will tell you." So he went to a bare hill.

4 Now God met Balaam, and he said to Him, "I have set up the seven altars, and I have offered up a bull and a ram on each altar."

5 Then the LORD [r]put a word in Balaam's mouth and said, "Return to Balak, and you shall speak thus." Num. 22:20; Jer. 1:9

6 So he returned to him, and behold, he was standing beside his

burnt offering, he and all the leaders of Moab.

7 And he took up his [28]discourse and said,

"From Aram Balak has
brought me,
Moab's king from the
mountains of the East,
'Come curse Jacob for me,
And come, denounce Israel!'

8 "How[r] shall I curse, whom
God has not cursed?
And how can I denounce,
whom the LORD has not
denounced? Num. 22:12

9 "As I see him from the top of
the rocks,
And I look at him from the
hills;
Behold, a people *who*
dwells apart,
And shall not be reckoned
among the nations.

10 "Who can count the dust of
Jacob,
Or number the fourth part
of Israel?
Let me die the death of the
upright,
And let my end be like his!"

11 Then Balak said to Balaam, "What have you done to me? [r]I took you to curse my enemies, but behold, you have actually blessed them!" Neh. 13:2

12 And he answered and said, "Must I not be careful to speak [r]what the LORD puts in my mouth?" Num. 22:20

13 Then Balak said to him, "Please come with me to another place from where you may see them, although you will only see the extreme end of them, and will

[28]Lit., *parable,* and so throughout this context

not see all of them; and curse them for me from there."

14 So he took him to the field of Zophim, to the top of Pisgah, and built seven altars and offered a bull and a ram on *each* altar.

15 And he said to Balak, "Stand here beside your burnt offering, while I myself meet *the LORD* yonder."

16 Then the LORD met Balaam and [r]put a word in his mouth and said, "Return to Balak, and thus you shall speak." Num. 22:20

17 And he came to him, and behold, he was standing beside his burnt offering, and the leaders of Moab with him. And Balak said to him, "What has the LORD spoken?"

18 Then he took up his [28]discourse and said,

"Arise, O Balak, and hear;
Give ear to me, O son of
Zippor!

19 "God is not a man, that He
should lie,
Nor a son of man, that He
should repent;
Has He said, and will He
not do it?
Or has He spoken, and will
He not make it good?

20 "Behold, I have received *a*
command to bless;
When He has blessed, then
I cannot revoke it.

21 "He has not observed [a]misfortune in Jacob; *iniquity*
Nor has He seen trouble in
Israel;
The LORD his God is with
him,
And the shout of a king is
among them.

[28]Lit., *parable,* and so throughout this context

22 "God brings them out of
Egypt,
He is for them like the
horns of the wild ox.
23 "For[r] there is no omen
against Jacob,
Nor is there any divination
against Israel;
At the proper time it shall
be said to Jacob
And to Israel, what God has
done. Num. 22:7; 24:1
24 "Behold,[r] a people rises like a
lioness,
And as a lion it lifts itself;
It shall not lie down until it
devours the prey,
And drinks the blood of the
slain." Nah. 2:11, 12
25 Then Balak said to Balaam,
"Do not curse them at all nor
bless them at all!"
26 But Balaam answered and
said to Balak, "Did I not tell you,
'Whatever[t] the LORD speaks, that I
must do'?" *saying, Whatever*
27 Then Balak said to Balaam,
"Please come, I will take you to
another place; perhaps it will be
agreeable with God that you curse
them for me from there."
28 So Balak took Balaam to the
top of Peor which overlooks the
[a]wasteland. *Jeshimon*
29 And Balaam said to Balak,
"Build seven altars for me here
and prepare seven bulls and seven
rams for me here."
30 And Balak did just as Balaam had said, and offered up a
bull and a ram on *each* altar.

CHAPTER 24

WHEN Balaam saw that it
pleased the LORD to bless Israel,
he did not go as at other times to
[t]seek omens but he set his face
toward the wilderness. *encounter*
2 And Balaam lifted up his
eyes and saw Israel [t]camping tribe
by tribe; and the Spirit of God
came upon him. *dwelling*
3 And he took up his discourse
and said,
"The oracle of Balaam the
son of Beor,
And the oracle of the man
whose eye is opened;
4 The oracle of him who
hears the words of God,
Who sees the vision of the
Almighty,
Falling down, yet having
his eyes uncovered,
5 How fair are your tents, O
Jacob,
Your dwellings, O Israel!
6 "Like [a]valleys that stretch
out,
Like gardens beside the
river,
Like aloes planted by the
LORD,
Like cedars beside the waters. *palm trees*
7 "Water shall flow from his
buckets,
And his seed *shall be* by
many waters,
And his king shall be higher
than Agag,
And[r] his kingdom shall be
exalted. Ps. 145:11-13
8 "God[r] brings him out of
Egypt, Num. 23:22
He is for him like the horns
of the wild ox.
He shall devour the nations
who are his adversaries,

And shall crush their bones
in pieces,
And shatter *them* with his
arrows.
9 "He couches, he lies down as
a lion,
And as a lion, who [t]dares
rouse him?
Blessed is everyone who
blesses you,
And cursed is everyone
who curses you." *shall*
10 Then Balak's anger burned
against Balaam, and he struck his
[t]hands together; and Balak said to
Balaam, "I called you to curse my
enemies, but behold, you have
persisted in blessing them these
three times! *palms*
11 "Therefore, flee to your place
now. I said I would honor you
greatly, but behold, the LORD has
held you back from honor."
12 And Balaam said to Balak,
"Did I not tell your messengers
whom you had sent to me, saying,
13 'Though Balak were to give
me his house full of silver and
gold, I could not do anything contrary to the [t]command of the LORD,
either good or bad, of my own [t]ac-
cord. What the LORD speaks, that
I will speak'? *mouth* • *heart*
14 "And now behold, I am going
to my people; come, *and* I will advise you what this people will do
to your people in the [t]days to
come." *end of the days*
15 And he took up his discourse
and said,
"The oracle of Balaam the
son of Beor,
And the oracle of the man
whose eye is opened,
16 The oracle of him who
hears the words of God,
And knows the knowledge
of the Most High,
Who sees the vision of the
Almighty,
Falling down, yet having
his eyes uncovered.
17 "I see him, but not now;
I behold him, but not near;
A star shall come forth
from Jacob,
And a scepter shall rise
from Israel,
And shall crush through the
[t]forehead of Moab,
And tear down all the sons
of [29]Sheth. *corners*
18 "And [r]Edom shall be a possession,
Seir, its enemies, also shall
be a possession,
While Israel performs valiantly. Amos 9:11, 12
19 "One from Jacob shall have
dominion,
And shall destroy the remnant from the city."
20 And he looked at Amalek
and took up his discourse and
said,
"Amalek was the first of the
nations,
But his end *shall be* [t]de-
struction." *to destroying*
21 And he looked at the [r]Kenite,
and took up his discourse and
said,
"Your dwelling place is enduring,
And your nest is set in the
cliff. Gen. 15:19
22 "Nevertheless Kain shall be
consumed;

[29] I.e., tumult

How long shall Asshur[t]keep
you captive?" *take*
23 And he took up his discourse
and said,
"Alas, who can live except
God has ordained it?
24 "But ships *shall come* from
the coast of[r]Kittim,
And they shall afflict Asshur and shall afflict
Eber;
So they also *shall come* to
destruction." Ezek. 27:6
25 Then Balaam arose and departed and returned to his place,
and Balak also went his way.

CHAPTER 25

WHILE Israel remained at Shittim, the people began[r]to play the
harlot with the daughters of
Moab. 1 Cor. 10:8; Rev. 2:14
2 For[r]they invited the people to
the sacrifices of their gods, and
the people ate and bowed down to
their gods. Ex. 34:15; Deut. 32:38
3 So Israel joined themselves
to[a]Baal of Peor, and the LORD was
angry against Israel. *Baal-peor*
4 And the LORD said to Moses,
"Take all the leaders of the people
and execute them in broad daylight before the LORD, [r]so that the
fierce anger of the LORD may turn
away from Israel." Deut. 13:17
5 So Moses said to the judges
of Israel, "Each of you slay his
men who have joined themselves
to[a]Baal of Peor." *Baal-peor*
6 Then behold, one of the sons
of Israel came and brought to his
[t]relatives a Midianite woman, in
the sight of Moses and in the sight
of all the congregation of the sons
of Israel, [r]while they were weeping
at the doorway of the tent of
meeting. *brothers* • Joel 2:17
7 [r]When Phinehas the son of Eleazar, the son of Aaron the priest,
saw it, he arose from the midst of
the congregation, and took a
spear in his hand; Ps. 106:30
8 and he went after the man of
Israel into the tent, and pierced
both of them through, the man of
Israel and the woman, through the
[a]body. So the plague on the sons of
Israel was checked. *belly*
9 And those who died by the
plague were 24,000.
10 Then the LORD spoke to
Moses, saying,
11 "Phinehas the son of Eleazar,
the son of Aaron the priest, has
turned away My wrath from the
sons of Israel, in that he was jealous with My jealousy among
them, so that I did not destroy the
sons of Israel in My jealousy.
12 "Therefore say, 'Behold, I give
him My covenant of peace;
13 and it shall be for him and
his [t]descendants after him, a covenant of a perpetual priesthood,
because he was jealous for his
God, and made atonement for the
sons of Israel.' " *seed*
14 Now the name of the [t]slain
man of Israel who was [t]slain with
the Midianite woman, was Zimri
the son of Salu, a leader of a father's household among the Simeonites. *smitten*
15 And the name of the Midianite woman who was slain was
Cozbi the daughter of Zur, [t]who

was head of the people of a father's household in Midian. *he*
16 Then the LORD spoke to
Moses, saying,
17 "Be[r] hostile to the Midianites
and strike them; Num. 25:1
18 for they have been hostile to
you with their tricks, with which
they have deceived you in the affair of Peor, and in the affair of
Cozbi, the daughter of the leader
of Midian, their sister who was
slain on the day of the plague because of Peor."

CHAPTER 26

THEN it came about after the
plague, that the LORD spoke to
Moses and to Eleazar the son of
Aaron the priest, saying,
2 "Take[r] a [t]census of all the congregation of the sons of Israel
from twenty years old and upward, by their fathers' households, whoever is able to go out to
war in Israel." Num. 1:2 · *sum*
3 So Moses and Eleazar the
priest spoke with them [r]in the
plains of Moab by the Jordan at
Jericho, saying, Num. 22:1
4 "*Take a census of the people*
from twenty years old and upward, as the LORD has commanded Moses."
Now the sons of Israel who
came out of the land of Egypt
were:
5 Reuben, Israel's first-born,
the sons of Reuben: *of* Hanoch,
the family of the Hanochites; of
Pallu, the family of the Palluites;
6 of Hezron, the family of the
Hezronites; of Carmi, the family
of the Carmites.
7 These are the families of the
Reubenites, and those who were
numbered of them were 43,730.
8 And the son of Pallu: Eliab.
9 And the sons of Eliab: Nemuel and Dathan and Abiram. These
are the Dathan and Abiram who
were [r]called by the congregation,
who contended against Moses and
against Aaron in the company of
Korah, when they contended
against the LORD, Num. 1:16
10 and [r]the earth opened its
mouth and swallowed them up
along with Korah, when that company died, when the fire devoured
250 men, so that they became a
[t]warning. Num. 16:32 · *sign*
11 [r]The sons of Korah, however,
did not die. Num. 16:27, 33
12 The sons of Simeon according to their families: of Nemuel,
the family of the Nemuelites; of
Jamin, the family of the Jaminites;
of Jachin, the family of the Jachinites;
13 of Zerah, the family of the
Zerahites; of Shaul, the family of
the Shaulites.
14 These are the families of the
Simeonites, [r]22,200. Num. 1:23
15 The sons of Gad according to
their families: of Zephon, the family of the Zephonites; of Haggi,
the family of the Haggites; of Shuni, the family of the Shunites;
16 of Ozni, the family of the Oz-
nites; of Eri, the family of the
Erites;
17 of Arod, the family of the
Arodites; of Areli, the family of
the Arelites.
18 These are the families of the
sons of Gad according to those

who were numbered of them, [r]40,500. Num. 1:25

19 The [r]sons of Judah *were* Er and Onan, but Er and Onan died in the land of Canaan. Gen. 38:2

20 And the [r]sons of Judah according to their families were: of Shelah, the family of the Shelanites; of Perez, the family of the Perezites; of Zerah, the family of the Zerahites. 1 Chr. 2:3; Rev. 7:5

21 And the sons of Perez were: of Hezron, the family of the Hezronites; of Hamul, the family of the Hamulites.

22 These are the families of Judah according to those who were numbered of them, 76,500.

23 The sons of Issachar according to their families: *of* Tola, the family of the Tolaites; of Puvah, the family of the Punites;

24 of Jashub, the family of the Jashubites; of Shimron, the family of the Shimronites.

25 These are the families of Issachar according to those who were numbered of them, 64,300.

26 The sons of Zebulun according to their families: of Sered, the family of the Seredites; of Elon, the family of the Elonites; of Jahleel, the family of the Jahleelites.

27 These are the families of the Zebulunites according to those who were numbered of them, [r]60,500. Num. 1:31

28 The [r]sons of Joseph according to their families: Manasseh and Ephraim. Deut. 33:16f.

29 The sons of Manasseh: of Machir, the family of the Machirites; and Machir [r]became the father of Gilead: of Gilead, the family of the Gileadites. *begot*

30 These are the sons of Gilead: *of* Iezer, the family of the Iezerites; of Helek, the family of the Helekites;

31 and *of* Asriel, the family of the Asrielites; and *of* Shechem, the family of the Shechemites;

32 and *of* Shemida, the family of the Shemidaites; and *of* Hepher, the family of the Hepherites.

33 Now Zelophehad the son of Hepher had no sons, but only daughters; and [r]the names of the daughters of Zelophehad were Mahlah, Noah, Hoglah, Milcah and Tirzah. Num. 27:1

34 These are the families of Manasseh; and those who were numbered of them were 52,700.

35 These are the sons of Ephraim according to their families: of Shuthelah, the family of the Shuthelahites; of Becher, the family of the Becherites; of Tahan, the family of the Tahanites.

36 And these are the sons of Shuthelah: of Eran, the family of the Eranites.

37 These are the families of the sons of Ephraim according to those who were numbered of them, [r]32,500. These are the sons of Joseph according to their families. Num. 1:33

38 The sons of Benjamin according to their families: of Bela, the family of the Belaites; of Ashbel, the family of the Ashbelites; of Ahiram, the family of the Ahiramites;

39 of Shephupham, the family of the Shuphamites; of Hupham, the family of the Huphamites.

40 And the sons of Bela were Ard and Naaman: *of Ard*, the fam-

ily of the Ardites; of Naaman, the family of the Naamites.

41 These are the sons of Benjamin according to their families; and those who were numbered of them were [r]45,600. Num. 1:37

42 These are the sons of Dan according to their families: of Shuham, the family of the Shuhamites. These are the families of Dan according to their families.

43 All the families of the Shuhamites, according to those who were numbered of them, were [r]64,400. Num. 1:39

44 The sons of Asher according to their families: of Imnah, the family of the Imnites; of Ishvi, the family of the Ishvites; of Beriah, the family of the Beriites.

45 Of the sons of Beriah: of Heber, the family of the Heberites; of Malchiel, the family of the Malchielites.

46 And the name of the daughter of Asher *was* Serah.

47 These are the families of the sons of Asher according to those who were numbered of them, [r]53,400. Num. 1:41

48 The sons of Naphtali according to their families: of Jahzeel, the family of the Jahzeelites; of Guni, the family of the Gunites;

49 of Jezer, the family of the Jezerites; of [r]Shillem, the family of the Shillemites. 1 Chr. 7:13

50 These are the families of Naphtali according to their families; and those who were numbered of them were 45,400.

51 These are those who were numbered of the sons of Israel, [r]601,730. Ex. 12:37; 38:26

52 Then the LORD spoke to Moses, saying,

53 "Among these the land shall be divided for an inheritance according to the number of names.

54 "To [r]the larger *group* you shall increase their inheritance, and to the smaller *group* you shall diminish their inheritance; each shall be given their inheritance according to those who were numbered of them. Num. 33:54

55 "But the land shall be divided by lot. They shall receive their inheritance according to the names of the tribes of their fathers.

56 "According to the selection by lot, their inheritance shall be divided between the larger and the smaller *groups*."

57 And [r]these are those who were numbered of the Levites according to their families: of Gershon, the family of the Gershonites; of Kohath, the family of the Kohathites; of Merari, the family of the Merarites. Gen. 46:11

58 These are the families of Levi: the family of the Libnites, the family of the Hebronites, the family of the Mahlites, the family of the Mushites, the family of the Korahites. And Kohath [t]became the father of Amram. *begot*

59 And the name of Amram's wife [r]was Jochebed, the daughter of Levi, who was born to Levi in Egypt; and she bore to Amram: Aaron and Moses and their sister Miriam. Ex. 2:1, 2; 6:20

60 [r]And to Aaron were born Nadab and Abihu, Eleazar and Ithamar. Num. 3:2

61 [r]But Nadab and Abihu died

when they offered strange fire before the LORD. Lev. 10:1, 2
62 And those who were numbered of them were 23,000, every
male from a month old and upward, for they were not numbered
among the sons of Israel since no
inheritance was given to them
among the sons of Israel.
63 These are those who were
numbered by Moses and Eleazar
the priest, who numbered the sons
of Israel in the plains of Moab by
the Jordan at Jericho.
64 But among these there was
not a man of those who were
numbered by Moses and Aaron
the priest, who numbered the sons
of Israel in the wilderness of Sinai.
65 For the LORD had said [a]of
them, "They[r] shall surely die in the
wilderness." And not a man was
left of them, except Caleb the son
of Jephunneh, and Joshua the son
of Nun. *to* • Ps. 90:3-10

CHAPTER 27

THEN the daughters of Zelophehad, the son of Hepher, the son of
Gilead, the son of Machir, the son
of Manasseh, of the families of
Manasseh the son of Joseph, came
near; and these are the names of
his daughters: Mahlah, Noah and
Hoglah and Milcah and Tirzah.
2 And they stood before Moses
and before Eleazar the priest and
before the leaders and all the congregation, at the doorway of the
tent of meeting, saying,
3 "Our father [r]died in the wilderness, yet he was not among the
company of those who gathered
themselves together against the
LORD in the company of Korah;
but he died in his own sin, and he
had no sons. Num. 26:64, 65
4 "Why should the name of our
father be withdrawn from among
his family because he had no son?
Give us a possession among our
father's brothers."
5 [r]And Moses brought their
case before the LORD. Num. 9:8
6 Then the LORD spoke to
Moses, saying,
7 "The[r] daughters of Zelophehad
are right in *their* statements. You
shall surely give them a heredi-
tary possession among their father's brothers, and you shall
transfer the inheritance of their
father to them. Josh. 17:4
8 "Further, you shall speak to
the sons of Israel, saying, 'If a
man dies and has no son, then you
shall transfer his inheritance to
his daughter.
9 'And if he has no daughter,
then you shall give his inheritance
to his brothers.
10 'And if he has no brothers,
then you shall give his inheritance
to his father's brothers.
11 'And if his father has no
brothers, then you shall give his
inheritance to his nearest relative
in his own family, and he shall
possess it; and it shall be a [r]statu-
tory ordinance to the sons of Israel, just as the LORD commanded
Moses.'" Num. 35:29
12 Then the LORD said to Moses,
"Go up to this mountain of Abarim, and see the land which I have
given to the sons of Israel.
13 "And when you have seen it,
you too shall be gathered to your

people, [r]as Aaron your brother
[t]was; Deut. 10:6 • *was gathered*
14 for in the wilderness of Zin,
during the strife of the congregation, you rebelled against My
[t]command [t]to treat Me as holy before their eyes at the water."
(These are the waters of Meribah
of Kadesh in the wilderness of
Zin.) *mouth • for My sanctity*
15 Then Moses spoke to the
LORD, saying,
16 "May [r]the LORD, the God of the
spirits of all flesh, appoint a man
over the congregation, Num. 16:22
17 who will go out and come in
before them, and who will lead
them out and [t]bring them in, that
the congregation of the LORD may
not be like sheep which have no
shepherd." *who will bring*
18 So the LORD said to Moses,
"Take Joshua the son of Nun, a
man [r]in whom is the Spirit, and lay
your hand on him; Deut. 34:9
19 and have him stand before
Eleazar the priest and before all
the congregation; and [r]commission
him in their sight. Deut. 3:28
20 "And you shall put some of
your authority on him, in order
that all the congregation of the
sons of Israel may obey *him*.
21 "Moreover, he shall stand before Eleazar the priest, who shall
inquire for him [r]by the judgment
of the Urim before the LORD. At
his [t]command they shall go out
and at his [t]command they shall
come in, *both* he and the sons of
Israel with him, even all the congregation." 1 Sam. 28:6 • *mouth*
22 And Moses did just as the
LORD commanded him; and he
took Joshua and set him before
Eleazar the priest, and before all
the congregation.
23 Then he laid his hands on
him and commissioned him, just
as the LORD had spoken [t]through
Moses. *by the hand of*

CHAPTER 28

THEN the LORD spoke to Moses,
saying,
2 "Command the sons of Israel
and say to them, 'You shall [t]be
careful to present My offering, My
[r]food for My offerings by fire, of a
soothing aroma to Me, at their appointed time.' *watch* • Lev. 3:11
3 "And [r]you shall say to them,
'This is the offering by fire which
you shall offer to the LORD; two
male lambs one year old without
defect *as* a continual burnt offering every day. Ex. 29:38-42
4 'You shall offer the one lamb
in the morning, and the other
lamb you shall offer at twilight;
5 also [r]a tenth of an ephah of
fine flour for a grain offering,
mixed with a fourth of a hin of
beaten oil. Ex. 16:36; Num. 15:4
6 'It is a continual burnt offering which was ordained in Mount
Sinai as a soothing aroma, an offering by fire to the LORD.
7 'Then the libation with it *shall
be* a fourth of a hin for each lamb,
[r]in the holy place you shall pour
out a libation of strong drink to
the LORD. Ex. 29:42
8 'And the other lamb you shall
offer [t]at twilight; as the grain offering of the morning and as its libation, you shall offer it, an offering
by fire, a soothing aroma to the
LORD. *between the two evenings*

9 'Then on the sabbath day two
male lambs one year old without
defect, and two-tenths *of an e-
phah* of fine flour mixed with oil
as a grain offering, and its libation:
10 *This is* the burnt offering of
every sabbath in addition to the
[r]continual burnt offering and its libation. Num. 28:3
11 'Then at the beginning of
each of your months you shall
present a burnt offering to the
LORD; two [t]bulls and one ram,
seven male lambs one year old
without defect, *bulls of the herd*
12 [r]and three-tenths *of an ephah*
of fine flour for a grain offering,
mixed with oil, for each bull; and
two-tenths of fine flour for a grain
offering, mixed with oil, for the
one ram; Num. 15:4-12
13 and a tenth *of an ephah* of
fine flour mixed with oil for a
grain offering for each lamb, for a
burnt offering of a soothing aroma, an offering by fire to the
LORD.
14 'And their libations shall be
half a hin of wine for a bull and a
third of a hin for the ram and a
fourth of a hin for a lamb; this is
the burnt offering of each month
throughout the months of the
year.
15 'And one male goat for a sin
offering to the LORD; it shall be offered with its libation in addition
to the continual burnt offering.
16 'Then[r] on the fourteenth day
of the first month shall be the
LORD's Passover. Ex. 12:1-20
17 'And[r] on the fifteenth day of
this month *shall be* a feast, unleavened bread *shall be* eaten for
seven days. Lev. 23:6
18 'On the [r]first day *shall be* a
holy convocation; you shall do no
laborious work. Lev. 23:7
19 'And you shall present an offering by fire, a burnt offering to
the LORD: two bulls and one ram
and seven male lambs one year
old, having them without defect.
20 'And for their grain offering,
you shall offer fine flour mixed
with oil: three-tenths *of an ephah*
for a bull and two-tenths for the
ram.
21 'A tenth *of an ephah* you
shall offer for [t]each of the seven
lambs, *each lamb*
22 and one male goat for a [r]sin
offering, to make atonement for
you. Lev. 16:18; Rom. 8:3
23 'You shall present these besides [r]the burnt offering of the
morning, which is for a continual
burnt offering. Num. 28:3
24 'After this manner you shall
present daily, for seven days, [r]the
food of the offering by fire, of a
soothing aroma to the LORD; it
shall be presented with its libation
in addition to the [r]continual burnt
offering. Lev. 3:11 • Num. 28:3
25 'And on the seventh day you
shall have a holy convocation; you
shall do no laborious work.
26 'Also on the day of the first
fruits, when you present a new
grain offering to the LORD in your
Feast of Weeks, you shall have a
holy convocation; you shall do no
laborious work.
27 'And you shall offer a burnt
offering for a soothing aroma to
the LORD, two young bulls, one

ram, seven male lambs one year
old,
28 and their grain offering, fine
flour mixed with oil, three-tenths
of an ephah for each bull, two-
tenths for the one ram,
29 a tenth for [t]each of the seven
lambs, *each lamb*
30 one male goat to make
atonement for you.
31 'Besides the continual burnt
offering and its grain offering, you
shall present *them* with their libations. They shall be [t]without defect. *without defect to you*

CHAPTER 29

'NOW in the seventh month, on
the first day of the month, you
shall also have a holy convocation; [r]you shall do no laborious
work. It will be to you a day for
blowing trumpets. Num. 28:26
2 'And you shall offer a burnt
offering as a soothing aroma to
the LORD: one [a]bull, one ram, *and*
seven male lambs one year old
without defect; *bull of a herd*
3 also their grain offering, fine
flour mixed with oil, three-tenths
of an ephah for the bull, two-
tenths for the ram,
4 and one-tenth for [t]each of the
seven lambs. *each lamb*
5 'And *offer* one male goat for a
sin offering, to make atonement
for you,
6 besides the burnt offering of
the new moon, and its grain offering, and the continual burnt offering and its grain offering, and
their libations, according to their
ordinance, for a soothing aroma,
an offering by fire to the LORD.

7 'Then on [r]the tenth day of this
seventh month you shall have a
holy convocation, and you shall
humble yourselves; you shall not
do any work. Lev. 16:29-34
8 'And you shall present a
burnt offering to the LORD *as* a
soothing aroma: one bull, one
ram, seven male lambs one year
old, having them without defect;
9 and their grain offering, fine
flour mixed with oil, three-tenths
of an ephah for the bull, two-
tenths for the one ram,
10 a tenth for each of the seven
lambs;
11 one male goat for a sin offering, besides the sin offering of
atonement and [r]the continual
burnt offering and its grain offering, and their libations. Num. 28:3
12 'Then on [r]the fifteenth day of
the seventh month you shall have
a holy convocation; you shall do
no laborious work, and you shall
observe a feast to the LORD for
seven days. Lev. 23:33-35
13 'And you shall present a
burnt offering, an offering by fire
as a soothing aroma to the LORD:
thirteen bulls, two rams, fourteen
male lambs one year old, which
are without defect,
14 and their grain offering, fine
flour mixed with oil, three-tenths
of an ephah for [t]each of the thirteen bulls, two-tenths for [t]each of
the two rams, *each bull · each ram*
15 and a tenth for each of the
fourteen lambs;
16 and one male goat for a sin
offering, [r]besides the continual
burnt offering, its grain offering
and its libation. Num. 28:3
17 'Then on [r]the second day:

twelve bulls, two rams, fourteen
male lambs one year old without
defect; Lev. 23:36
18 and their grain offering and
their libations for the bulls, for the
rams and for the lambs, by their
number according to the ordinance; Lev. 2:1-16
19 and one male goat for a sin
offering, besides the continual
burnt offering and its grain offering, and their libations.
20 'Then on the third day: eleven
bulls, two rams, fourteen male
lambs one year old without defect;
21 and their grain offering and
their libations for the bulls, for the
rams and for the lambs, by their
number according to the ordinance;
22 and one male goat for a sin
offering, besides the continual
burnt offering and its grain offering and its libation.
23 'Then on the fourth day: ten
bulls, two rams, fourteen male
lambs one year old without defect;
24 their grain offering and their
libations for the bulls, for the
rams and for the lambs, by their
number according to the ordinance;
25 and one male goat for a sin
offering, besides the continual
burnt offering, its grain offering
and its libation.
26 'Then on the fifth day: nine
bulls, two rams, fourteen male
lambs one year old without defect; Heb. 7:26
27 and their grain offering and
their libations for the bulls, for the
rams and for the lambs, by their
number according to the ordinance;
28 and one male goat for a sin
offering, besides the continual
burnt offering and its grain offering and its libation.
29 'Then on the sixth day: eight
bulls, two rams, fourteen male
lambs one year old without defect;
30 and their grain offering and
their libations for the bulls, for the
rams and for the lambs, by their
number according to the ordinance;
31 and one male goat for a sin
offering, besides the continual
burnt offering, its grain offering
and its libations.
32 'Then on the seventh day:
seven bulls, two rams, fourteen
male lambs one year old without
defect;
33 and their grain offering and
their libations for the bulls, for the
rams and for the lambs, by their
number according to the ordinance;
34 and one male goat for a sin
offering, besides the continual
burnt offering, its grain offering
and its libation.
35 'On the eighth day you shall
have a solemn assembly; you shall
do no laborious work. Lev. 23:36
36 'But you shall present a burnt
offering, an offering by fire, as a
soothing aroma to the LORD: one
bull, one ram, seven male lambs
one year old without defect;
37 their grain offering and their
libations for the bull, for the ram
and for the lambs, by their number according to the ordinance;
38 and one male goat for a sin

offering, besides the continual
burnt offering and its grain offering and its libation.
39 'You shall present these to
the LORD at your appointed times,
besides your votive offerings and
your freewill offerings, for your
burnt offerings and for your grain
offerings and for your libations
and for your peace offerings.' "
40 And Moses spoke to the sons
of Israel in accordance with all
that the LORD had commanded
Moses.

CHAPTER 30

THEN Moses spoke to the heads
of the tribes of the sons of Israel,
saying, "This is the word which
the LORD has commanded.
2 "If a man makes a vow to the
LORD, or takes an oath to bind
himself with a binding obligation,
he shall not violate his word; he
shall do according to all that proceeds out of his mouth.
3 "Also if a woman makes a
vow to the LORD, and binds herself by an obligation in her father's house in her youth,
4 and her father hears her vow
and her obligation by which she
has bound herself, and her father
[t]says nothing to her, then all her
vows shall stand, and every obligation by which she has bound
herself shall stand. *is silent to her*
5 "But if her father should forbid her on the day he hears *of it,*
none of her vows or her obligations by which she has bound herself shall stand; and the LORD will
forgive her because her father had
forbidden her.
6 "However, if she should marry while under her vows or the
rash statement of her lips by
which she has bound herself,
7 and her husband hears of it
and says nothing to her on the day
he hears *it,* then her vows shall
stand and her obligations by
which she has bound herself shall
stand.
8 "But if on the day her husband
hears *of it,* he forbids her, then he
shall annul her vow which [t]she is
under and the rash statement of
her lips by which she has bound
herself; and the LORD will forgive
her. *is on her*
9 "But the vow of a widow or of
a divorced woman, everything by
which she has bound herself, shall
stand against her.
10 "However, if she vowed in her
husband's house, or bound herself
by an obligation with an oath,
11 and her husband heard *it,* but
said nothing to her *and* did not
forbid her, then all her vows shall
stand, and every obligation by
which she bound herself shall
stand.
12 "But if her husband indeed annuls them on the day he hears
them, then whatever proceeds out
of her lips concerning her vows or
concerning the obligation of herself, shall not stand; her husband
has annulled them, and the LORD
will forgive her.
13 "Every vow and every binding
oath to humble herself, her husband may confirm it or her husband may annul it.
14 "But if her husband indeed
says nothing to her from day to
day, then he confirms all her vows

or all her obligations which are on
her; he has confirmed them, because he said nothing to her on
the day he heard them.
15 "But if he indeed annuls them
after he has heard them, then he
shall bear her guilt."
16 These are the statutes which
the LORD commanded Moses, *as*
between a man and his wife, *and*
as between a father and his
daughter, *while she is* in her youth
in her father's house.

CHAPTER 31

THEN the LORD spoke to Moses,
saying,
2 "Take full vengeance for the
sons of Israel on the Midianites;
afterward you will be ʳgathered to
your people." Num. 20:24, 26
3 And Moses spoke to the people, saying, "Arm men from
among you for the war, that they
may go against Midian, to execute
the LORD's vengeance on Midian.
4 "A thousand from each tribe
of all the tribes of Israel you shall
send to the war."
5 So there were ᵗfurnished from
the thousands of Israel, a thousand from each tribe, twelve thousand armed for war. *delivered*
6 And Moses sent them, a
thousand from each tribe, to the
war, and Phinehas the son of Eleazar the priest, to the war with
them, ʳand the holy vessels and ʳthe
trumpets for the alarm in his
hand. Num. 14:44 • Num. 10:8, 9
7 So they made war against
Midian, just as the LORD had commanded Moses, and ʳthey killed
every male. 1 Kin. 11:15, 16
8 And they killed the kings of
Midian along with the *rest of* their
slain: Evi and Rekem and Zur and
Hur and Reba, the five kings of
Midian; they also killed Balaam
the son of Beor with the sword.
9 And the sons of Israel captured the women of Midian and
their little ones; and all their cattle
and all their flocks and all their
goods, they plundered.
10 Then they burned all their
cities where they lived and all
their camps with fire.
11 And ʳthey took all the spoil
and all the prey, both of man and
of beast. Deut. 20:14
12 And they brought the captives and the prey and the spoil to
Moses, and to Eleazar the priest
and to the congregation of the
sons of Israel, to the camp at the
plains of Moab, which are by the
Jordan opposite Jericho.
13 And Moses and Eleazar the
priest and all the leaders of the
congregation went out to meet
them outside the camp.
14 And Moses was angry with
the officers of the army, the captains of thousands and the captains of hundreds, who had come
from service in the war.
15 And Moses said to them,
"Have you spared all the women?
16 "Behold, these ᵗcaused the
sons of Israel, through the counsel
of Balaam, to trespass against the
LORD in the matter of Peor, so the
plague was among the congregation of the LORD. *were to*
17 "Now therefore, kill every
male among the little ones, and
kill every woman who has known
man ᵗintimately. *by lying with a man*

18 "But all the [t]girls who have not known man intimately, spare for yourselves. *female children*

19 "And [r]you, camp outside the camp seven days; whoever has killed any person, and whoever has touched any slain, purify yourselves, you and your captives, on the third day and on the seventh day. Num. 19:11-22

20 "And you shall purify for yourselves every garment and every article of [a]leather and all the work of goats' *hair,* and all articles of wood." *skin*

21 Then Eleazar the priest said to the men of war who had gone to battle, "This is the statute of the law which the LORD has commanded Moses:

22 only the gold and the silver, the bronze, the iron, the tin and the lead,

23 everything that can stand the fire, you shall pass through the fire, and it shall be clean, but it shall be purified with [r]water for impurity. But whatever cannot stand the fire you shall pass through the water. Num. 19:9, 17

24 "And you shall wash your clothes on the seventh day and be clean, and afterward you may enter the camp."

25 Then the LORD spoke to Moses, saying,

26 "You and Eleazar the priest and the heads of the fathers' *households* of the congregation, take a count of the booty [t]that was captured, both of man and of animal; *of captives*

27 and divide the booty between the warriors who went out to battle and all the congregation.

28 "And [r]levy a tax for the LORD from the men of war who went out to battle, one [t]in five hundred of the persons and of the cattle and of the donkeys and of the sheep; Num. 18:21-30 • *soul from*

29 take it from their half and give it to Eleazar the priest, as an [t]offering to the LORD. *heave offering*

30 "And from the sons of Israel's half, you shall take one drawn out of every fifty of the persons, of the cattle, of the donkeys and of the sheep, from all the animals, and give them to the Levites who [r]keep charge of the tabernacle of the LORD." Num. 18:3, 4

31 And Moses and Eleazar the priest did just as the LORD had commanded Moses.

32 Now the booty that remained from the spoil which the [t]men of war had plundered was 675,000 sheep, *people*

33 and 72,000 cattle,

34 and 61,000 donkeys,

35 and of human beings, of the women who had not known man [t]intimately, all the persons were 32,000. *by lying with a man*

36 And the half, the portion of those who went out to war, was *as follows:* the number of sheep was 337,500,

37 and the LORD's levy of the sheep was 675,

38 and the cattle were 36,000, from which the LORD's levy was 72.

39 And the donkeys were 30,500, from which the LORD's levy was 61.

40 And the human beings were 16,000, from whom the LORD's levy was 32 persons.

41 And Moses gave the levy
which was the LORD's offering to
Eleazar the priest, just as the
LORD had commanded Moses.
42 As for the sons of Israel's
half, which Moses separated from
the men who had gone to war—
43 now the congregation's half
was 337,500 sheep,
44 and 36,000 cattle,
45 and 30,500 donkeys,
46 and the human beings were
16,000—
47 and from the sons of Israel's
half, Moses took one drawn out of
every fifty, both of man and of
animals, and gave them to the Levites, who kept charge of the tabernacle of the LORD, just as the
LORD had commanded Moses.
48 Then the officers who were
over the thousands of the army,
the captains of thousands and the
captains of hundreds, approached
Moses;
49 and they said to Moses,
"Your servants have taken a census of men of war who are in our
charge, and no man of us is missing.
50 "So we have brought as an offering to the LORD what each man
found, articles of gold, armlets
and bracelets, signet rings, earrings and necklaces, to make
atonement for ourselves before
the LORD." Ex. 30:12-16
51 And Moses and Eleazar the
priest took the gold from them, all
kinds of wrought articles.
52 And all the gold of the offering which they offered up to the
LORD, from the captains of thousands and the captains of hundreds, was 16,750 shekels.
53 The men of war had taken
booty, every man for himself.
54 So Moses and Eleazar the
priest took the gold from the captains of thousands and of hundreds, and brought it to the tent of
meeting as a memorial for the
sons of Israel before the LORD.

CHAPTER 32

NOW the sons of Reuben and the
sons of Gad had an exceedingly
large number of livestock. So
when they saw the land of Jazer
and the land of Gilead, that it was
indeed a place suitable for livestock, *behold, the place, a place for*
2 the sons of Gad and the sons
of Reuben came and spoke to
Moses and to Eleazar the priest
and to the leaders of the congregation, saying,
3 "Ataroth, Dibon, Jazer, Nim-
rah, Heshbon, Elealeh, Sebam,
Nebo and Beon, Num. 32:34-38
4 the land which the LORD conquered before the congregation of
Israel, is a land for livestock; and
your servants have livestock."
5 And they said, "If we have
found favor in your sight, let this
land be given to your servants as a
possession; do not take us across
the Jordan."
6 But Moses said to the sons of
Gad and to the sons of Reuben,
"Shall your brothers go to war
while you yourselves sit here?
7 "Now why are you discourag-
ing the sons of Israel from crossing over into the land which the
LORD has given them?
8 "This is what your fathers did

when I sent them from Kadesh-
barnea to see the land.
9 "For when they went up to the
valley of Eshcol and saw the land,
they [t]discouraged the sons of Israel so that they did not go into
the land which the LORD had giv-
en them. *restrained the hearts of*
10 "So the LORD's anger burned
in that day, and He swore, saying,
11 'None of the men who came
up from Egypt, from twenty years
old and upward, shall see the land
which I swore to Abraham, to
Isaac and to Jacob; for they did
not follow Me fully,
12 except Caleb the son of Jephunneh the Kenizzite and Joshua
the son of Nun, for they have followed the LORD fully.'
13 "So the LORD's anger burned
against Israel, and He made them
wander in the wilderness forty
years, until the entire generation
of those who had done evil in the
sight of the LORD was destroyed.
14 "Now behold, you have risen
up in your fathers' place, a brood
of sinful men, to add still more to
the burning [r]anger of the LORD
against Israel. Deut. 1:34f.
15 "For if you [r]turn away from
following Him, He will once more
abandon them in the wilderness;
and you will destroy all these people." Deut. 30:17, 18
16 Then they came near to him
and said, "We will build here
sheepfolds for our livestock and
cities for our little ones;
17 [r]but we ourselves will be
armed ready *to* go before the sons
of Israel, until we have brought
them to their place, while our little ones live in the fortified cities
because of the inhabitants of the
land. Josh. 4:12, 13
18 "We[r] will not return to our
homes until every one of the sons
of Israel has possessed his inheritance. Josh. 22:1-4
19 "For we will not have an inheritance with them on the other
side of the Jordan and beyond, because our inheritance has fallen to
us [r]on this side of the Jordan
toward the east." Josh. 12:1
20 [r]So Moses said to them, "If
you will do [t]this, if you will arm
yourselves before the LORD for the
war, Deut. 3:18 • *this thing*
21 and all of you armed men
cross over the Jordan before the
LORD until He has driven His enemies out from before Him,
22 and the land is subdued before the LORD, then afterward you
shall return and be free of obligation toward the LORD and toward
Israel, and this land shall be yours
for a possession before the LORD.
23 "But if you will not do so, behold, you have sinned against the
LORD, and be sure [r]your sin will
find you out. Gen. 4:7; 44:16
24 "Build yourselves cities for
your little ones, and sheepfolds
for your sheep; and [r]do what you
have promised." Num. 30:2
25 And the sons of Gad and the
sons of Reuben spoke to Moses,
saying, "Your servants will do
just as my lord commands.
26 "Our[r] little ones, our wives,
our livestock and all our cattle
shall [t]remain there in the cities of
Gilead; Josh. 1:14 • *be*
27 while your servants, everyone who is armed for war, will
[r]cross over in the presence of the

LORD to battle, just as my lord
says." Josh. 4:12
28 So Moses gave command
concerning them to Eleazar the
priest, and to Joshua the son of
Nun, and to the heads of the fathers' *households* of the tribes of
the sons of Israel.
29 And Moses said to them, "If
the sons of Gad and the sons of
Reuben, everyone who is armed
for battle, will cross with you over
the Jordan in the presence of the
LORD, and the land will be subdued before you, then you shall
give them the land of Gilead for a
possession;
30 but if they will not cross over
with you armed, they shall have
possessions among you in the
land of Canaan."
31 And the sons of Gad and the
sons of Reuben answered, saying,
"As the LORD has said to your servants, so we will do.
32 "We ourselves will cross over
armed in the presence of the LORD
into the land of Canaan, and the
possession of our inheritance
shall remain with us across the
Jordan."
33 So Moses gave to them, to
the sons of Gad and to the sons of
Reuben and to the half-tribe of Joseph's son Manasseh, the kingdom of Sihon, king of the Amorites and the kingdom of Og, the
king of Bashan, the land with its
cities with *their* territories, the
cities of the surrounding land.
34 And the sons of Gad built Dibon and Ataroth and Aroer,
35 and Atroth-shophan and Jazer and Jogbehah,
36 and Beth-nimrah and Beth-
haran as fortified cities, and
sheepfolds for sheep.
37 And the sons of Reuben built
Heshbon and Elealeh and Kiriathaim,
38 and [r]Nebo and Baal-meon—
their names being changed—and
Sibmah, and they gave *other*
names to the cities which they
built. Is. 46:1
39 And the sons of Machir the
son of Manasseh went to Gilead
and took it, and dispossessed the
Amorites who were in it.
40 So Moses gave [r]Gilead to Machir the son of Manasseh, and he
lived in it. Deut. 3:12, 13, 15
41 And Jair the son of Manasseh went and took its towns, and
called them Havvoth-jair.
42 And Nobah went and took
Kenath and its villages, and called
it Nobah after his own name.

CHAPTER 33

THESE are the journeys of the
sons of Israel, by which they came
out from the land of Egypt by
their armies, under the [t]leadership
of Moses and Aaron. *hand*
2 And Moses recorded their
starting places according to their
journeys by the command of the
LORD, and these are their journeys
according to their starting places.
3 And they journeyed from
Rameses in the first month, on the
fifteenth day of the first month; on
the [t]next day after the Passover
the sons of Israel started out
[t]boldly in the sight of all the Egyptians, *morrow • with a high hand*
4 while the Egyptians were
burying all their first-born whom

the LORD had struck down among
them. The LORD had also executed
judgments on their gods.
5 Then [r]the sons of Israel journeyed from Rameses, and camped
in Succoth. Ex. 12:37
6 [r]And they journeyed from
Succoth, and camped in Etham,
which is on the edge of the wilderness. Ex. 13:20
7 And they journeyed from E-
tham, and turned back to Pi-hahiroth, which faces Baal-zephon;
and they camped before Migdol.
8 And they journeyed from before Hahiroth, and passed through
the midst of the sea into the wilderness; and they went three
days' journey in the wilderness of
Etham, and camped at Marah.
9 [r]And they journeyed from
Marah, and came to Elim; and in
Elim there were twelve springs of
water and seventy palm trees; and
they camped there. Ex. 15:27
10 And they journeyed from
Elim, and camped by the Red Sea.
11 And they journeyed from the
[t]Red Sea, and camped in the wilderness of Sin. *Sea of Reeds*
12 And they journeyed from the
wilderness of Sin, and camped at
Dophkah.
13 And they journeyed from
Dophkah, and camped at Alush.
14 And they journeyed from
Alush, and camped [r]at Rephidim;
now it was there that the people
had no water to drink. Ex. 17:1
15 And they journeyed from
Rephidim, and camped in [r]the wilderness of Sinai. Ex. 19:1
16 And they journeyed from the
wilderness of Sinai, and camped
at [r]Kibroth-hattaavah. Num. 11:34
17 And they journeyed from
Kibroth-hattaavah, and camped at
[r]Hazeroth. Num. 11:35
18 And they journeyed from
Hazeroth, and camped at Rithmah.
19 And they journeyed from
Rithmah, and camped at Rimmon-
perez.
20 And they journeyed from
Rimmon-perez, and camped at
[r]Libnah. Deut. 1:1
21 And they journeyed from
Libnah, and camped at Rissah.
22 And they journeyed from
Rissah, and camped in Kehela-
thah.
23 And they journeyed from Ke-
helathah, and camped at Mount
Shepher.
24 And they journeyed from
Mount Shepher, and camped at
Haradah.
25 And they journeyed from
Haradah, and camped at Makheloth.
26 And they journeyed from
Makheloth, and camped at Tahath.
27 And they journeyed from Tahath, and camped at Terah.
28 And they journeyed from Terah, and camped at Mithkah.
29 And they journeyed from
Mithkah, and camped at Hashmonah.
30 And they journeyed from
Hashmonah, and camped at [r]Mo-
seroth. Deut. 10:6
31 And they journeyed from
Moseroth, and camped at Bene-jaakan.
32 And they journeyed from
[r]Bene-jaakan, and camped at Hor-
haggidgad. Gen. 36:27

33 And they journeyed from
Hor-haggidgad, and camped at
Jotbathah. Deut. 10:7
34 And they journeyed from
Jotbathah, and camped at Abro-
nah.
35 And they journeyed from A-
bronah, and camped at Ezion-geber. Deut. 2:8
36 And they journeyed from
Ezion-geber, and camped in the
wilderness of Zin, that is, Kadesh.
37 And they journeyed from
Kadesh, and camped at Mount
Hor, at the edge of the land of
Edom. Num. 20:22 • Num. 20:16
38 Then Aaron the priest went
up to Mount Hor at the command
of the LORD, and died there, in the
fortieth year after the sons of Israel had come from the land of
Egypt on the first *day* in the fifth
month. Num. 20:28 • *mouth*
39 And Aaron was one hundred
twenty-three years old when he
died on Mount Hor.
40 Now the Canaanite, the king
of Arad who lived in the Negev in
the land of Canaan, heard of the
coming of the sons of Israel.
41 Then they journeyed from
Mount Hor, and camped at Zalmonah.
42 And they journeyed from
Zalmonah, and camped at Punon.
43 And they journeyed from Punon, and camped at Oboth.
44 And they journeyed from
Oboth, and camped at Iye-abarim,
at the border of Moab.
45 And they journeyed from
Iyim, and camped at Dibon-gad.
46 And they journeyed from Dibon-gad, and camped at Almon-
diblathaim.
47 And they journeyed from Al-
mon-diblathaim, and camped in
the mountains of Abarim, before
Nebo. Num. 27:12
48 And they journeyed from the
mountains of Abarim, and
camped in the plains of Moab by
the Jordan *opposite* Jericho.
49 And they camped by the Jordan, from Beth-jeshimoth as far
as Abel-shittim in the plains of
Moab. Num. 25:1
50 Then the LORD spoke to
Moses in the plains of Moab by
the Jordan *opposite* Jericho, saying,
51 "Speak to the sons of Israel
and say to them, 'When you cross
over the Jordan into the land of
Canaan, Josh. 3:17
52 then you shall drive out all
the inhabitants of the land from
before you, and destroy all their
figured stones, and destroy all
their molten images and demolish
all their high places; Ex. 23:24
53 and you shall take possession of the land and live in it, for I
have given the land to you to possess it. Deut. 11:31; 17:14
54 'And you shall inherit the
land by lot according to your families; to the larger you shall give
more inheritance, and to the
smaller you shall give less inheritance. Wherever the lot falls to
anyone, that shall be his. You
shall inherit according to the
tribes of your fathers.
55 'But if you do not drive out
the inhabitants of the land from
before you, then it shall come
about that those whom you let remain of them *will become* as
pricks in your eyes and as thorns
in your sides, and they shall trou-

ble you in the land in which you live.

56 'And it shall come about that as I plan to do to them, so I will do to you.' "

CHAPTER 34

THEN the LORD spoke to Moses, saying,

2 "Command the sons of Israel and say to them, 'When you enter the land of Canaan, this is the land that shall fall to you as an inheritance, *even the* land of Canaan according to its borders.

3 'Your southern sector shall extend from the wilderness of Zin along the side of Edom, and your southern border shall extend from the end of the Salt Sea eastward.

4 'Then your border shall turn *direction* from the south to the ascent of Akrabbim, and [t]continue to Zin, and its [30]termination shall be to the south of Kadesh-barnea; and it shall reach Hazaraddar, and continue to Azmon. *pass along*

5 'And the border shall turn *direction* from Azmon to the brook of Egypt, and its termination shall be at [r]the sea. Josh. 15:4

6 'As for the western border, you shall have the Great Sea, that is, *its* [t]coastline; this shall be your west border. *border*

7 'And [r]this shall be your north border: you shall draw your *border* line from the Great Sea to Mount Hor. Ezek. 47:15-17

8 'You shall draw a line from Mount Hor to [r]the Lebo-hamath, and the termination of the border shall be at Zedad; Josh. 13:5

9 and the border shall proceed to Ziphron, and its termination shall be at Hazar-enan. This shall be your north border.

10 'For your eastern border you shall also draw a line from Hazar-enan to Shepham,

11 and the border shall go down from Shepham to Riblah on the east side of Ain; and the border shall go down and reach to the [31]slope on the east side of the Sea of Chinnereth.

12 'And the border shall go down to the Jordan and its termination shall be at the Salt Sea. This shall be your land according to its borders all around.' "

13 So Moses commanded the sons of Israel, saying, "This [r]is the land that you are to apportion by lot among you as a possession, which the LORD has commanded to give to the nine and a half tribes. Gen. 15:18; Josh. 14:1-5

14 "For [r]the tribe of the sons of Reuben have received *theirs* according to their fathers' households, and the tribe of the sons of Gad according to their fathers' households, and the half-tribe of Manasseh have received their possession. Num. 32:33

15 "The two and a half tribes have received their possession across the Jordan opposite Jericho, eastward toward the sunrising."

16 Then the LORD spoke to Moses, saying,

17 "These are the names of the men who shall apportion the land to you for inheritance: Eleazar the priest and Joshua the son of Nun.

18 "And you shall take one

[30] Lit., *goings out*, and so throughout this context

[31] Lit., *shoulder*

leader of every tribe to apportion
the land for inheritance.
19 "And these are the names of
the men: of the tribe of Judah, Caleb the son of Jephunneh.
20 "And of the tribe of the sons
of [r]Simeon, Samuel the son of Ammihud. Gen. 29:33; 49:5
21 "Of the tribe of Benjamin, Eli-
dad the son of Chislon.
22 "And of the tribe of the sons
of Dan a leader, Bukki the son of
Jogli.
23 "Of the sons of Joseph: of the
tribe of the sons of Manasseh a
leader, Hanniel the son of Ephod.
24 "And of the tribe of the sons
of Ephraim a leader, Kemuel the
son of Shiphtan.
25 "And of the tribe of the sons
of Zebulun a leader, Elizaphan the
son of Parnach.
26 "And of the tribe of the sons
of Issachar a leader, Paltiel the
son of Azzan.
27 "And of the tribe of the sons
of Asher a leader, Ahihud the son
of Shelomi.
28 "And of the tribe of the sons
of Naphtali a leader, Pedahel the
son of Ammihud."
29 These are those whom the
LORD commanded to apportion
the inheritance to the sons of Israel in the land of Canaan.

CHAPTER 35

NOW the LORD spoke to Moses
in the plains of Moab by the Jordan opposite Jericho, saying,
2 "Command the sons of Israel
that they give to the Levites from
the inheritance of their possession, cities to live in; and you shall
give to the Levites pasture lands
around the cities.
3 "And the cities shall be theirs
to live in; and their pasture lands
shall be for their cattle and for
their herds and for all their beasts.
4 "And the pasture lands of the
cities which you shall give to the
Levites *shall extend* from the wall
of the city [t]outward a thousand cubits around. *and outward*
5 "You shall also measure outside the city on the east side two
thousand cubits, and on the south
side two thousand cubits, and on
the west side two thousand cubits,
and on the north side two thousand cubits, with the city in the
center. This shall become theirs as
pasture lands for the cities.
6 "And the cities which you
shall give to the Levites *shall be*
the six cities of refuge, which you
shall give for the manslayer to flee
to; and in addition to them you
shall give forty-two cities.
7 "All the cities which you shall
give to the Levites *shall be* [r]forty-
eight cities, [t]together with their
pasture lands. Josh. 21:41 • *them*
8 "As for the cities which you
shall give from the possession of
the sons of Israel, you shall take
more from the larger and you
shall take less from the smaller;
each shall give some of his cities
to the Levites in proportion to his
possession which he inherits."
9 Then the LORD spoke to
Moses, saying,
10 "Speak [r]to the sons of Israel
and say to them, 'When you cross
the Jordan into the land of Canaan, Josh. 20:1-9
11 then you shall select for

yourselves cities to be your cities of refuge, that the manslayer who has[t]killed any person unintentionally may flee there. *smote*

12 'And the cities shall be to you as a refuge from the avenger, so that the manslayer may not die until he stands before the congregation for[t]trial. *judgment*

13 'And the cities which you are to give shall be your six cities of refuge.

14 'You shall give three cities across the Jordan and three cities [t]in the land of Canaan; they are to be cities of refuge. *you shall give in*

15 'These six cities shall be for refuge for the sons of Israel, and for the alien and for the sojourner among them; that anyone who [t]kills a person[r]unintentionally may flee there. *smites* • Num. 35:11

16 'But if he struck him down with an iron object, so that he died, he is a murderer; the murderer shall surely be put to death.

17 'And if he struck him down with a stone in the hand, by which he may die, and *as a result* he died, he is a murderer; the murderer shall surely be put to death.

18 'Or if he struck him with a wooden object in the hand, by which he may die, and *as a result* he died, he is a murderer; the murderer shall surely be put to death.

19 'The blood avenger himself shall put the murderer to death; he shall put him to death when he meets him.

20 'And if he pushed him of hatred, or threw something at him lying in wait and *as a result* he died,

21 or if he struck him down with his hand in enmity, and *as a result* he died, the one who struck him shall surely be put to death, he is a murderer; the blood avenger shall put the murderer to death when he meets him.

22 'But[r] if he pushed him suddenly without enmity, or threw something at him without lying in wait, Num. 35:11

23 or with any deadly object of stone, and without seeing it dropped on him so that he died, while he was not his enemy nor seeking his injury,

24 then [r]the congregation shall judge between the slayer and the blood avenger according to these ordinances. Josh. 20:6

25 'And the congregation shall deliver the manslayer from the hand of the blood avenger, and the congregation shall restore him to his city of refuge to which he fled; and he shall live in it until the death of the high priest who was anointed with the holy oil.

26 'But if the manslayer shall at any time go beyond the border of his city of refuge to which he may flee,

27 and the blood avenger finds him outside the border of his city of refuge, and the blood avenger kills the manslayer, he shall not be guilty of blood

28 because he should have remained in his city of refuge until the death of the high priest. But after the death of the high priest the manslayer shall return to the land of his possession.

29 'And these things shall be for a [r]statutory ordinance to you throughout your generations in all your dwellings. Num. 27:11

30 'If anyone kills a person, the murderer shall be put to death at the [t]evidence of witnesses, but no person shall be put to death on the testimony of one witness. *mouth*

31 'Moreover, you shall not take ransom for the life of a murderer who is guilty of death, but he shall surely be put to death.

32 'And you shall not take ransom for him who has fled to his city of refuge, that he may return to live in the land[a]before the death of the priest. *until*

33 'So you shall not pollute the land in which you are; for blood pollutes the land and no expiation can be made for the land for the blood that is shed on it, except by the blood of him who shed it.

34 'And you shall not defile the land in which you live, in the midst of which [r]I dwell; for I the LORD am dwelling in the midst of the sons of Israel.' " Num. 5:3

CHAPTER 36

AND the heads of the fathers' *households* of the family of the sons of Gilead, the son of Machir, the son of Manasseh, of the families of the sons of Joseph, came near and spoke before Moses and before the leaders, the heads of the fathers' *households* of the sons of Israel,

2 and they said, "The LORD commanded my lord to give the land by lot to the sons of Israel as an inheritance, and my lord was commanded by the LORD to give the inheritance of Zelophehad our brother to his daughters.

3 "But if they [t]marry one of the sons of the *other* tribes of the sons of Israel, their inheritance will be withdrawn from the inheritance of our fathers and will be added to the inheritance of the tribe to which they belong; thus it will be withdrawn from our allotted inheritance. *become wives to*

4 "And when the jubilee of the sons of Israel comes, then their inheritance will be added to the inheritance of the tribe to which they belong; so their inheritance will be withdrawn from the inheritance of the tribe of our fathers."

5 Then Moses commanded the sons of Israel according to the [t]word of the LORD, saying, "The tribe of the sons of Joseph are right in *their* statements. *mouth*

6 "This is what the LORD has commanded concerning the daughters of Zelophehad, saying, 'Let them marry whom they wish; only they must marry within the family of the tribe of their father.'

7 "Thus no inheritance of the sons of Israel shall be transferred from tribe to tribe, for the sons of Israel shall each hold to the inheritance of the tribe of his fathers.

8 "And[r] every daughter who comes into possession of an inheritance of any tribe of the sons of Israel, shall be wife to one of the family of the tribe of her father, so that the sons of Israel each may possess the inheritance of his fathers. 1 Chr. 23:22

9 "Thus no inheritance shall [t]be transferred from one tribe to another tribe, for the tribes of the

sons of Israel shall each hold to his own inheritance." *turn about*

10 Just as the LORD had commanded Moses, so the daughters of Zelophehad did:

11 [r]Mahlah, Tirzah, Hoglah, Milcah and Noah, the daughters of Zelophehad married their uncles' sons. Num. 26:33

12 They married *those* from the families of the sons of Manasseh the son of Joseph, and their inheritance [t]remained with the tribe of the family of their father. *was*

13 These are the commandments and the ordinances which the LORD commanded to the sons of Israel through Moses in the plains of Moab by the Jordan *opposite* Jericho.

THE BOOK OF

DEUTERONOMY

THESE are the words which Moses spoke to all Israel across the Jordan in the wilderness, in the Arabah opposite Suph, between Paran and Tophel and Laban and Hazeroth and Dizahab.

2 It is eleven days' *journey* from [r]Horeb by the way of Mount Seir to Kadesh-barnea. Ex. 3:1

3 And it came about in the fortieth year, on the first day of the eleventh month, that Moses spoke to the children of Israel, according to all that the LORD had commanded him *to give* to them,

4 after he had [t]defeated Sihon the king of the Amorites, who lived in Heshbon, and Og the king of Bashan, who lived in Ashtaroth and Edrei. *smitten*

5 Across the Jordan in the land of Moab, Moses undertook to expound this law, saying,

6 "The LORD our God [r]spoke to us at Horeb, saying, 'You have [t]stayed long enough at this mountain. Num. 10:11-13 • *dwelt*

7 'Turn and set your journey, and go to the hill country of the Amorites, and to all their neighbors in the Arabah, in the hill country and in the lowland and in the [1]Negev and by the seacoast, the land of the Canaanites, and Lebanon, as far as the great river, the river Euphrates.

8 'See, I have placed the land before you; go in and possess the land which the LORD swore to give to your fathers, to Abraham, to Isaac, and to Jacob, to them and their descendants after them.'

9 "And I spoke to you at that time, saying, 'I am not able to bear *the burden* of you alone.

10 'The LORD your God has [r]multiplied you, and behold, you are this day as the stars of heaven for multitude. Gen. 15:5; 22:17

11 'May the LORD, the God of your fathers, increase you a thousand-fold more than you are, and bless you, [r]just as He has [t]promised you! Deut. 1:8, 10 • *spoken to*

[1]I.e., South country

12 'How can I alone bear the load and burden of you and your strife?

13 'Choose[t] wise and discerning and experienced men from your tribes, and I will appoint them as your heads.' *Give for yourselves*

14 "And you answered me and said, 'The thing which you have said to do is good.'

15 "So I took the heads of your tribes, wise and experienced men, and [t]appointed them heads over you, leaders of thousands, and of hundreds, of fifties and of tens, and officers for your tribes. *gave*

16 "Then I charged your judges at that time, saying, 'Hear *the cases* between your [t]fellow countrymen, and judge righteously between a man and his [t]fellow countryman, or the alien who is with him. *brothers • brother*

17 'You shall not show partiality in judgment; you shall hear the small and the great alike. You shall not fear man, for the judgment is God's. And the case that is too hard for you, you shall bring to me, and I will hear it.'

18 "And[r] I commanded you at that time all the things that you should do. Ex. 18:20

19 "Then we set out from Horeb, and went through all that great and terrible wilderness which you saw, on the way to the hill country of the Amorites, just as the LORD our God had commanded us; and we came to Kadesh-barnea.

20 "And I said to you, 'You have come to the hill country of the Amorites which the LORD our God is about to give us.

21 'See, the LORD your God has placed the land before you; go up, take possession, as the LORD, the God of your fathers, has spoken to you. Do not fear or be dismayed.'

22 "Then[r] all of you approached me and said, 'Let us send men before us, that they may search out the land for us, and bring back to us word of the way by which we should go up, and the cities which we shall enter.' Num. 13:1-3

23 "And the thing pleased me and I took twelve of your men, one man for each tribe.

24 "And[r] they turned and went up into the hill country, and came to the valley of Eshcol, and spied it out. Num. 13:21-25

25 "Then they took *some* of the fruit of the land in their hands and brought it down to us; and they brought us back a report and said, 'It is a good land which the LORD our God is about to give us.'

26 "Yet you were not willing to go up, but rebelled against the command of the LORD your God;

27 and [r]you grumbled in your tents and said, 'Because the LORD hates us, He has brought us out of the land of Egypt to deliver us into the hand of the Amorites to destroy us. Deut. 9:28; Ps. 106:25

28 'Where can we go up? Our brethren have made our hearts melt, saying, "The people are bigger and taller than we; the cities are large and fortified to heaven. And besides, we saw [r]the sons of the Anakim there." ' Deut. 9:2

29 "Then I said to you, 'Do not be shocked, nor fear them.

30 'The LORD your God who goes before you will Himself fight on

your behalf, just as He did for you
in Egypt before your eyes,
31 and in the wilderness where
you saw how [r]the LORD your God
carried you, just as a man carries
his son, in all the way which you
have walked, until you came to
this place.' Deut. 32:10-12
32 "But for all this, you did not
trust the LORD your God,
33 [r]who goes before you on *your*
way, to seek out a place for you to
encamp, in fire by night and cloud
by day, to show you the way in
which you should go. Ex. 13:21
34 "Then the LORD heard the
sound of your words, and He was
angry and took an oath, saying,
35 'Not[r] one of these men, this
evil generation, shall see the good
land which I swore to give your
fathers, 1 Cor. 10:5; Heb. 3:14-19
36 except Caleb the son of Jephunneh; he shall see it, and [r]to
him and to his sons I will give the
land on which he has set foot, because he has followed the LORD
fully.' Num. 14:24; Josh. 14:9
37 "The LORD was angry with me
also on your account, saying, 'Not
even you shall enter there.
38 'Joshua the son of Nun, who
stands before you, he shall enter
there; encourage him, for he shall
cause Israel to inherit it.
39 'Moreover, your little ones
who you said would become a
prey, and your sons, who this day
have [r]no knowledge of good or
evil, shall enter there, and I will
give it to them, and they shall possess it. Is. 7:15, 16
40 'But as for you, turn around
and set out for the wilderness by
the way to the Red Sea.'
41 "Then you answered and said
to me, 'We have sinned against
the LORD; we will indeed go up
and fight, just as the LORD our
God commanded us.' And every
man of you girded on his weapons
of war, and regarded it as easy to
go up into the hill country.
42 "And[r] the LORD said to me,
'Say to them, "Do not go up, nor
fight, for I am not among you; lest
you be [t]defeated before your enemies." ' Num. 14:41-43 • *smitten*
43 "So I spoke to you, but you
would not listen. Instead you rebelled against the command of the
LORD, and acted presumptuously
and went up into the hill country.
44 "And the Amorites who [t]lived
in that hill country came out
against you, and chased you as
bees do, and crushed you from
Seir to Hormah. *dwelt*
45 "Then you returned and wept
before the LORD; but the [r]LORD did
not listen to your voice, nor give
ear to you. Job 27:8, 9
46 "So you remained in Kadesh
many days, [t]the days that you
spent *there*. *as the days*

CHAPTER 2

"THEN we turned and set out
for the wilderness by the way to
the [t]Red Sea, as the LORD spoke to
me, and circled Mount Seir for
many days. *Sea of Reeds*
2 "And the LORD spoke to me,
saying,
3 'You have circled this mountain long enough. Now turn north,
4 [r]and command the people,
saying, "You will pass through the
territory of your brothers the sons

of Esau who live in Seir; and they
will be afraid of you. So be very
careful; Num. 20:14-21
5 do not provoke them, for I
will not give you any of their land,
even *as little as* a footstep because I have given Mount Seir to
Esau as a possession.
6 "You shall buy food from
them with money so that you may
eat, and you shall also purchase
water from them with money so
that you may drink.
7 "For the LORD your God has
blessed you in all that you have
done; He has known your wanderings through this great wilderness. These forty years the LORD
your God has been with you; you
have not lacked a thing." '
8 "So we passed beyond our
brothers the sons of Esau, who
live in Seir, away from the Arabah
road, away from Elath and from
Ezion-geber. And we turned and
passed through by the way of the
wilderness of Moab. Deut. 1:1
9 "Then the LORD said to me,
'Do not harass Moab, nor provoke
them to war, for I will not give
you any of their land as a possession, because I have given Ar to
the sons of Lot as a possession.
10 (The Emim lived there formerly, a people as great, numerous, and tall as the Anakim.
11 Like the Anakim, they are
also regarded as Rephaim, but the
Moabites call them Emim.
12 The Horites formerly lived in
Seir, but the sons of Esau dispossessed them and destroyed them
from before them and settled in
their place, just as Israel did to the
land of their possession which the
LORD gave to them.)
13 'Now arise and cross over the
brook Zered yourselves.' So we
crossed over the brook Zered.
14 "Now the time that it took for
us to come from Kadesh-barnea,
until we crossed over the brook
Zered, was thirty-eight years; until all the generation of the men of
war perished from within the
camp, as the LORD had sworn to
them. *days in which we went*
15 "Moreover the hand of the
LORD was against them, to destroy them from within the camp,
until they all perished. Jude 5
16 "So it came about when all
the men of war had finally perished from among the people,
17 that the LORD spoke to me,
saying,
18 'You shall cross over Ar, the
border of Moab, today. Deut. 2:9
19 'And when you come opposite the sons of Ammon, do not
harass them nor provoke them,
for I will not give you any of the
land of the sons of Ammon as a
possession, because I have given
it to the sons of Lot as a possession.' Gen. 19:38 • Deut. 2:9
20 (It is also regarded as the
land of the Rephaim, *for* Rephaim
formerly lived in it, but the Ammonites call them Zamzummin,
21 a people as great, numerous,
and tall as the Anakim, but the
LORD destroyed them before
them. And they dispossessed
them and settled in their place,
22 just as He did for the sons of
Esau, who live in Seir, when He
destroyed the Horites from before
them; and they dispossessed

them, and settled in their place
even to this day. Gen. 36:8
23 And the [r]Avvim, who lived in
villages as far as Gaza, the [2]Caph-
torim who came from [3]Caphtor,
destroyed them and lived in their
place.) Josh. 13:3
24 'Arise, set out, and pass
through the [a]valley[r] of Arnon.
Look! I have given Sihon the Amorite, king of Heshbon, and his
land into your hand; begin to take
possession and contend with him
in battle. *wadi* • Judg. 11:18
25 'This day I will begin to put
the dread and fear of you upon the
peoples everywhere under the
heavens, who, when they hear the
report of you, shall tremble and be
in anguish because of you.'
26 "So[r] I sent messengers from
the wilderness of Kedemoth to Sihon king of Heshbon with words
of peace, saying, Deut. 1:4
27 'Let me pass through your
land, I will [t]travel only on the highway; I will not turn aside to the
right or to the left. *go by the way*
28 'You will sell me food for
money so that I may eat, and give
me water for money so that I may
drink, [r]only let me pass through on
[t]foot, Num. 20:19 • *my feet*
29 just as the sons of Esau who
live in Seir and the Moabites who
live in [r]Ar did for me, until I cross
over the Jordan into the land
which the LORD our God is giving
to us.' Deut. 2:9
30 "But Sihon king of Heshbon
was not willing for us to pass
[t]through his land; for the [r]LORD
your God hardened his spirit and
made his heart obstinate, in order
to deliver him into your hand, as
he is today. *by him* • Ex. 4:21
31 "And the LORD said to me,
'See, I have begun to deliver Sihon
and his land [t]over to you. Begin to
[t]occupy, that you may possess his
land.' *before you* • *possess*
32 "Then Sihon [t]with all his people came out to meet us in battle
at Jahaz. *he and*
33 "And the LORD our God delivered him [t]over to us; and we [t]de-
feated him with his sons and all
his people. *before us* • *smote*
34 "So we captured all his cities
at that time, and utterly destroyed
the men, women and children of
every city. We left no survivor.
35 "We took only the animals as
our booty and the spoil of the
cities which we had captured.
36 "From Aroer which is on the
edge of the [a]valley of Arnon and
from the city which is in the [a]val-
ley, even to Gilead, there was no
city that was too high for us; the
LORD our God delivered all [t]over to
us. *wadi* • *before us*
37 "Only you did not go near to
the land of the sons of Ammon, all
along the [a]river Jabbok and the
cities of the hill country, and
wherever the LORD our God had
commanded us. *wadi*

CHAPTER 3

"THEN we turned and went up
the road to Bashan, and Og, king
of Bashan, [t]with all his people
came out to meet us in battle at
Edrei. *he and*
2 "But the LORD said to me, 'Do
not fear him, for I have delivered
him and all his people and his land

[2]I.e., Philistines [3]I.e., Crete

into your hand; and you shall do to him just as you did to Sihon king of the Amorites, who lived at Heshbon.'

3 "So the LORD our God delivered Og also, king of Bashan, with all his people into our hand, and we smote [t]them until no survivor was [t]left. *him • left to him*

4 "And we captured all his cities at that time; there was not a city which we did not take from them: sixty cities, all the region of [r]Argob, the kingdom of Og in Bashan. Deut. 3:13, 14; 1 Kin. 4:13

5 "All these were cities fortified with high walls, gates and bars, besides a great many [a]unwalled towns. *rural*

6 "And we utterly destroyed them, as we did to Sihon king of Heshbon, utterly destroying [t]the men, women and children of every city. *every city of men . . .*

7 "But[r] all the animals and the spoil of the cities we took as our booty. Deut. 2:35

8 "Thus we took the land at that time from the hand of the two kings of the Amorites who were beyond the Jordan, from the valley of Arnon to Mount Hermon

9 (Sidonians [r]call Hermon Sirion, and the Amorites call it Senir): Deut. 4:48; Josh. 11:17

10 all the cities of the tableland and all Gilead and all Bashan, as far as Salecah and Edrei, cities of the kingdom of Og in Bashan.

11 (For only Og king of Bashan was left of the remnant of the Rephaim. Behold, his [a]bedstead was an iron [a]bedstead; it is in Rabbah of the sons of Ammon. Its length was nine cubits and its width four cubits [t]by ordinary cubit.) *couch • by a man's forearm*

12 "So we took possession of this land at that time. From Aroer, which is by the valley of Arnon, and half the hill country of Gilead and its cities, I gave to the Reubenites and to the Gadites.

13 "And the rest of Gilead, and all Bashan, the kingdom of Og, I gave to the half-tribe of Manasseh, all the region of Argob (concerning all Bashan, it is called the land of Rephaim.

14 [r]Jair the son of Manasseh took all the region of Argob as far as the border of the Geshurites and the Maacathites, and called [t]it, *that is*, Bashan, after his own name, Havvoth-jair, *as it is* to this day.) Num. 32:41 • *them*

15 "And to Machir I gave Gilead.

16 "And to the Reubenites and to the Gadites, I gave from Gilead even as far as the valley of Arnon, the middle of the valley as *a* border and as far as the river Jabbok, the border of the sons of Ammon;

17 the Arabah also, with the Jordan as *a* border, from [4]Chinnereth even as far as the sea of the Arabah, the Salt Sea, at the foot of the slopes of Pisgah on the east.

18 "Then I commanded you at that time, saying, 'The LORD your God has given you this land to possess it; all you valiant men shall cross over armed before your brothers, the sons of Israel.

19 'But your wives and your little ones and your livestock (I know that you have much livestock), shall remain in your cities which I have given you,

20 [r]until the LORD gives rest to

[4] I.e., the Sea of Galilee

your fellow countrymen as to you,
and they also possess the land
which the LORD your God will
give them beyond the Jordan.
[r]Then you may return every man
to his possession, which I have
given you.' Josh. 1:15 • Josh. 22:4
21 "And I commanded Joshua at
that time, saying, 'Your eyes have
seen all that the LORD your God
has done to these two kings; so
the LORD shall do to all the kingdoms into which you are about to
cross.
22 'Do not fear them, for the
LORD your God [r]is the one fighting
for you.' Ex. 14:14; Deut. 1:30
23 "I also pleaded with the LORD
at that time, saying,
24 'O Lord GOD, Thou hast begun to show Thy servant Thy
greatness and Thy strong hand;
for what god is there in heaven or
on earth who can do such works
and mighty acts as Thine?
25 'Let me, I pray, cross over
and see the fair land that is beyond the Jordan, [t]that good hill
country and Lebanon.' *this*
26 "But the LORD was angry with
me on your account, and would
not listen to me; and the LORD said
to me, 'Enough![t] Speak to Me no
more of this matter. *Enough for you*
27 'Go up to the top of Pisgah
and lift up your eyes to the west
and north and south and east, and
see *it* with your eyes, for you shall
not cross over this Jordan.
28 'But[r] charge Joshua and encourage him and strengthen him;
for he shall go across at the head
of this people, and he shall give
them as an inheritance the land
which you will see.' Num. 27:18
29 "So we remained in the valley
opposite Beth-peor.

CHAPTER 4

"AND now, O Israel, listen to the
statutes and the judgments which
[r]I am teaching you to perform, in
order that you may live and go in
and take possession of the land
which the LORD, the God of your
fathers, is giving you. Deut. 1:3
2 "You[r] shall not add to the
word which I am commanding
you, nor take away from it, that
you may keep the commandments
of the LORD your God which I
command you. Deut. 12:32
3 "Your[r] eyes have seen what
the LORD has done in the case of
Baal-peor, for all the men who followed Baal-peor, the LORD your
God has destroyed [t]them from
among you. Num. 25:1-9 • *him*
4 "But you who held fast to the
LORD your God are alive today,
every one of you.
5 "See, I have taught you statutes and judgments [r]just as the
LORD my God commanded me,
that you should do thus in the
land where you are entering to
possess it. Lev. 26:46; 27:34
6 "So keep and do *them*, [r]for
that is your wisdom and your understanding in the sight of the
peoples who will hear all these
statutes and say, 'Surely this great
nation is a wise and understanding people.' Prov. 1:7; 2 Tim. 3:15
7 "For what great nation is
there that has a god [r]so near to it
as is the LORD our God whenever
we call on Him? Is. 55:6
8 "Or what great nation is there

that has statutes and judgments as righteous as this whole law which I am setting before you today? Ps. 89:14; 97:2

9 "Only give heed to yourself and keep your soul diligently, lest you forget the things which your eyes have seen, and lest they depart from your heart all the days of your life; but make them known to your sons and your grandsons. Prov. 4:23; 23:19

10 "*Remember* the day you stood before the LORD your God at Horeb, when the LORD said to me, 'Assemble the people to Me, that I may let them hear My words so they may learn to [5]fear Me all the days they live on the earth, and that they may teach their children.' Deut. 14:23; 17:19

11 "And you came near and stood at the foot of the mountain, and the mountain burned with fire to the *very* heart of the heavens: darkness, cloud and thick gloom.

12 "Then the LORD spoke to you from the midst of the fire; you heard the sound of words, but you saw no form—only a voice.

13 "So He declared to you His covenant which He commanded you to perform, *that is,* the ten commandments; and He wrote them on two tablets of stone.

14 "And the LORD commanded me at that time to teach you statutes and judgments, that you might perform them in the land where you are going over to possess it.

15 "So watch yourselves carefully, since you did not see any form on the day the LORD spoke to you at Horeb from the midst of the fire, Josh. 23:11 • Is. 40:18

16 lest you act corruptly and make a graven image for yourselves in the form of any figure, the likeness of male or female,

17 the likeness of any animal that is on the earth, the likeness of any winged bird that flies in the sky, Rom. 1:23

18 the likeness of anything that creeps on the ground, the likeness of any fish that is in the water below the earth.

19 "And *beware,* lest you lift up your eyes to heaven and see the sun and the moon and the stars, all the host of heaven, and be drawn away and worship them and serve them, those which the LORD your God has allotted to all the peoples under the whole heaven. 2 Kin. 17:16; 21:3

20 "But the LORD has taken you and brought you out of the iron furnace, from Egypt, to be a people for His own possession, as today. 1 Kin. 8:51; Jer. 11:4

21 "Now the LORD was angry with me on your account, and swore that I should not cross the Jordan, and that I should not enter the good land which the LORD your God is giving you as an inheritance. Num. 20:12; Deut. 1:37

22 "For I shall die in this land, I shall not cross the Jordan, but you shall cross and take possession of this good land. Num. 27:13, 14

23 "So watch yourselves, lest you forget the covenant of the LORD your God, which He made with you, and make for yourselves a graven image in the form of any-

[5]Or, *reverence*

thing *against* which the LORD
your God has commanded you.
24 "For the LORD your God is a
consuming fire, a jealous God.
25 "When you[t] become the father
of children and children's children
and have remained long in the
land, and act corruptly, and make
an idol in the form of anything,
and do that which is evil in the
sight of the LORD your God *so as*
to provoke Him to anger, *beget*
26 I [r]call heaven and earth to
witness against you today, that
you shall surely perish quickly
from the land where you are going
over the Jordan to possess it. You
shall not live long on it, but shall
be utterly destroyed. Deut. 30:19
27 "And the LORD will [r]scatter
you among the peoples, and you
shall be left few in number among
the nations, where the LORD shall
drive you. Lev. 26:33; Deut. 28:64
28 "And there you will serve
gods, the work of man's hands,
wood and stone, which neither see
nor hear nor eat nor smell.
29 "But[r] from there you will seek
the LORD your God, and you will
find *Him* if you search for Him
with all your heart and all your
soul. Is. 55:6; Jer. 29:13
30 "When you [r]are in distress and
all these things have come upon
you, in the latter days, you will return to the LORD your God and listen to His voice. Ps. 18:6; 59:16
31 "For the LORD your God is a
compassionate God; He will not
fail you nor destroy you nor forget
the covenant with your fathers
which He swore to them.
32 "Indeed, ask now concerning
the former days which were before you, since the day that God
created man on the earth, and *inquire* from one end of the heavens
to the other. Has *anything* been
done like this great thing, or has
anything been heard like it?
33 "Has[r] *any* people heard the
voice of God speaking from the
midst of the fire, as you have
heard *it*, and survived? Ex. 20:22
34 "Or has a god tried to go to
take for himself a nation from
within *another* nation by trials, by
signs and wonders and by war
and by a mighty hand and by an
outstretched arm and by great terrors, as the LORD your God did for
you in Egypt before your eyes?
35 "To you it was shown that you
might know that the LORD, He is
God; [r]there is no other besides
Him. Is. 44:6-8; 45:5-7; Mark 12:32
36 "Out of the heavens He let
you hear His voice to discipline
you; and on earth He let you see
His great fire, and you heard His
words from the midst of the fire.
37 "Because He loved your fathers, therefore He chose[t] their descendants after them. And He personally brought you from Egypt
by His great power, *his seed*
38 driving out from before you
nations greater and mightier than
you, to bring you in *and* [r]to give
you their land for an inheritance,
as it is today. Num. 32:4
39 "Know therefore today, and
take it to your heart, that [r]the
LORD, He is God in heaven above
and on the earth below; there is no
other. Deut. 4:35; Josh. 2:11
40 "So you shall keep His statutes and His commandments
which I am [t]giving you today, that

it may go well with you and with
your children after you, and that
you may live long on the land
which the LORD your God is giving
you for all time." *commanding*
41 [r]Then Moses set apart three
cities across the Jordan to the
[t]east, Num. 35:6 • *sunrise*
42 that a manslayer might flee
there, who unintentionally slew
his neighbor without having enmity toward him in time past; and
by fleeing to one of these cities he
might live:
43 [r]Bezer in the wilderness on
the plateau for the Reubenites,
and Ramoth in Gilead for the Gadites, and Golan in Bashan for the
Manassites. Josh. 20:8
44 Now this is the law which
Moses set before the sons of Israel;
45 these are the testimonies and
the statutes and the ordinances
which Moses spoke to the sons of
Israel, when they came out from
Egypt,
46 across the Jordan, in the valley opposite Beth-peor, in the land
of Sihon king of the Amorites who
lived at Heshbon, whom Moses
and the sons of Israel defeated
when they came out from Egypt.
47 And they took possession of
his land and the land of [r]Og king of
Bashan, the two kings of the Amorites, *who were* across the Jordan
to the [t]east, Deut. 1:4 • *sunrise*
48 from Aroer, which is on the
edge of the [a]valley of Arnon, even
as far as [r]Mount Sion (that is, Hermon), *wadi* • Deut. 3:9; Ps. 133:3
49 with all the Arabah across
the Jordan to the east, even as far
as the sea of the Arabah, at the
foot of the slopes of Pisgah.

CHAPTER 5

THEN Moses summoned all Israel, and said to them, "Hear, O
Israel, the statutes and the ordinances which I am speaking today
in your [t]hearing, that you may
learn them and observe [t]them
carefully. *ears* • *to do them*
2 "The LORD our God made a
covenant with us at Horeb.
3 "The [r] LORD did not make this
covenant with our fathers, but
with us, *with* all those of [t]us alive
here today. Heb. 8:9 • *us ourselves*
4 "The LORD spoke to you [r]face
to face at the mountain from the
midst of the fire, Num. 14:14
5 *while* I was standing between the LORD and you at that
time, to declare to you the word of
the LORD; for you were afraid because of the fire and did not go up
the mountain. [t]He said, *saying*
6 'I am the LORD your God, who
brought you out of the land of
Egypt, out of the house of slavery.
7 'You [r]shall have no other gods
[a]before Me. Ex. 20:3 • *besides*
8 'You shall not make for yourself [t]an idol, *or* any likeness *of*
what is in heaven above or on the
earth beneath or in the water under the earth. *or what is*
9 'You shall not worship them
or serve them; for I, the LORD your
God, am a jealous God, [r]visiting
the iniquity of the fathers on the
children, and on the third and the
fourth *generations* of those who
hate Me, Ex. 34:7; Num. 14:18
10 but showing lovingkindness

to thousands, to those who love
Me and keep My commandments.
11 'You shall not take the name
of the LORD your God in vain, for
the LORD will not[a] leave him unpunished who takes His name in
vain. *hold him guiltless*
12 'Observe[r] the sabbath day to
keep it holy, as the LORD your God
commanded you. Ex. 16:23-30
13 'Six days you shall labor and
do all your work,
14 but[r] the seventh day is a sabbath of the LORD your God; *in it*
you shall not do any work, you or
your son or your daughter or your
male servant or your female servant or your ox or your donkey or
any of your cattle or your sojourner who[t] stays with you, so
that your male servant and your
female servant may rest as well as
you. Heb. 4:4 • *is in your gates*
15 'And[r] you shall remember that
you were a slave in the land of
Egypt, and the LORD your God
brought you out of there by a
mighty hand and by an outstretched arm; therefore the LORD
your God commanded you to observe the sabbath day. Ex. 20:11
16 'Honor[r] your father and your
mother, as the LORD your God has
commanded you, that your days
may be prolonged, and that it may
go well with you on the land
which the LORD your God gives
you. Eph. 6:2, 3; Col. 3:20
17 'You shall not murder.
18 'You[r] shall not commit adultery. Luke 18:20; Rom. 13:9
19 'You[r] shall not steal. Ex. 20:15
20 'You shall not bear false witness against your neighbor.
21 'You shall not covet your
neighbor's wife, and you shall not
desire your neighbor's house, his
field or his male servant or his female servant, his ox or his donkey
or anything that belongs to your
neighbor.'
22 "These words the LORD spoke
to all your assembly at the mountain from the midst of the fire, *of*
the cloud and *of* the thick gloom,
with a great voice, and He added
no more. And[r] He wrote them on
two tablets of stone and gave
them to me. Ex. 24:12; 31:18
23 "And it came about, when you
heard the voice from the midst of
the darkness, while the mountain
was burning with fire, that you
came near to me, all the heads of
your tribes and your elders.
24 "And you said, 'Behold, the
LORD our God has shown us His
glory and His greatness, and we
have heard His voice from the
midst of the fire; we have seen today that God speaks with man,
yet he lives.
25 'Now[r] then why should we
die? For this great fire will consume us; if we hear the voice of
the LORD our God any longer, then
we shall die. Ex. 20:18, 19
26 'For who is there of all flesh,
who has heard the voice of the living God speaking from the midst
of the fire, as we *have*, and lived?
27 'Go[t] near and hear all that the
LORD our God says; then speak to
us all that the LORD our God will
speak to you, and we will hear and
do *it*.' *Go yourself*
28 "And the LORD heard the
voice of your words when you
spoke to me, [r] and the LORD said to
me, 'I have heard the voice of the

words of this people which they
have spoken to you. They have
done well in all that they have
spoken. Deut. 18:17
29 'Oh[r] that they had such a
heart in them, that they would
fear Me, and keep all My commandments always, that it may be
well with them and with their
sons forever! Ps. 81:13
30 'Go, say to them, "Return to
your tents."
31 'But[r] as for you, stand here by
Me, that I may speak to you all the
commandments and the statutes
and the judgments which you
shall teach them, that they may
observe *them* in the land which I
give them to possess.' Ex. 24:12
32 "So you shall observe to do
just as the LORD your God has
commanded you; [r]you shall not
turn aside to the right or to the
left. Deut. 17:20; 28:14
33 "You[r] shall walk in all the way
which the LORD your God has
commanded you, that you may
live, and that it may be well with
you, and that you may prolong
your days in the land which you
shall possess. Deut. 10:12; Jer. 7:23

CHAPTER 6

"NOW this is the command-
ment, the statutes and the judgments which the LORD your God
has commanded *me* to teach you,
that you might do *them* in the land
where you are going over to possess it,
2 so that you and your son and
your grandson might fear the
LORD your God, to keep all His
statutes and His commandments,
which I command you, all the
days of your life, and that your
days may be prolonged.
3 "O Israel, you should listen
and[t] be careful to do *it*, that it may
be well with you and that you may
multiply greatly, just as the LORD,
the God of your fathers, has promised you, *in* a land flowing with
milk and honey. *keep*
4 "Hear, O Israel! The LORD is
our God, the LORD is one!
5 "And [r]you shall love the LORD
your God with all your heart and
with all your soul and with all
your might. Matt. 22:37
6 "And[r] these words, which I am
commanding you today, shall be
on your heart; Deut. 11:18
7 and[r] you shall teach them diligently to your sons and shall talk
of them when you sit in your
house and when you walk by the
way and when you lie down and
when you rise up. Eph. 6:4
8 "And you shall bind them as a
sign on your hand and they shall
be as frontals on your forehead.
9 "And[r] you shall write them on
the doorposts of your house and
on your gates. Deut. 11:20
10 "Then it shall come about
when the LORD your God brings
you into the land which He swore
to your fathers, Abraham, Isaac
and Jacob, to give you, [r]great and
splendid cities which you did not
build, Deut. 9:1; 19:1
11 and houses full of all good
things which you did not fill, and
hewn cisterns which you did not
dig, vineyards and olive trees
which you did not plant, and you
shall eat and be satisfied,
12 then watch yourself, lest you

forget the LORD who brought you from the land of Egypt, out of the house of [t]slavery. *slaves*

13 "You shall [6]fear *only* the LORD your God; and you shall worship Him, and swear by His name.

14 "You[r] shall not follow other gods, any of the gods of the peoples who surround you, Jer. 25:6

15 for the LORD your God in the midst of you is a [r]jealous God; otherwise the anger of the LORD your God will be kindled against you, and He will [t]wipe you off the face of the earth. Deut. 4:24 • *destroy*

16 "You[r] shall not put the LORD your God to the test, as you tested *Him* at Massah. Matt. 4:7

17 "You[r] should diligently keep the commandments of the LORD your God, and His testimonies and His statutes which He has commanded you. Ps. 119:4

18 "And you shall do what is right and good in the sight of the LORD, that it may be well with you and that you may go in and possess the good land which the LORD swore to *give* your fathers,

19 by driving out all your enemies from before you, as the LORD has spoken.

20 "When your son asks you in time to come, saying, 'What *do* the testimonies and the statutes and the judgments *mean* which the LORD commanded you?'

21 then you shall say to your son, 'We were slaves to Pharaoh in Egypt; and the LORD brought us from Egypt with a mighty hand.

22 'Moreover, the LORD showed great and distressing signs and wonders before our eyes against Egypt, Pharaoh and all his household;

23 and He brought us out from there in order to bring us in, to give us the land which He had sworn to our fathers.'

24 "So the LORD commanded us to observe all these statutes, to fear the LORD our God for our good always and for our survival, as *it is* today.

25 "And [r]it will be righteousness for us if we [t]are careful to observe all this commandment before the LORD our God, just as He commanded us. Rom. 10:3 • *keep*

CHAPTER 7

"WHEN the LORD your God shall bring you into the land where you are entering to possess it, and shall clear away many nations before you, the Hittites and the Girgashites and the Amorites and the Canaanites and the Perizzites and the Hivites and the Jebusites, seven nations greater and stronger than you,

2 and when the LORD your God shall deliver them before you, and you shall [t]defeat them, then you shall utterly destroy them. You shall make no covenant with them and show no favor to them. *smite*

3 "Furthermore, you shall not intermarry with them; you shall not give your daughters to their sons, nor shall you take their daughters for your sons.

4 "For they will turn your sons away from following Me to serve other gods; then the anger of the LORD will be kindled against you, and He will quickly destroy you.

[6]Or, *reverence*

5 "But thus you shall do to them: [r]you shall tear down their altars, and smash their *sacred* pillars, and hew down their [7]Asherim, and burn their graven images with fire. Ex. 23:24; 34:13

6 "For you are a holy people to the LORD your God; the LORD your God has chosen you to be a people for His [a]own possession out of all the peoples who are on the face of the [t]earth. *special treasure • ground*

7 "The LORD did not set His love on you nor choose you because you were more in number than any of the peoples, for you were the fewest of all peoples,

8 but because the LORD loved you and kept the oath which He swore to your forefathers, the LORD brought you out by a mighty hand, and redeemed you from the house of [t]slavery, from the hand of Pharaoh king of Egypt. *slaves*

9 "Know therefore that the LORD your God, [r]He is God, the faithful God, who keeps [t]His covenant and [t]His lovingkindness to a thousandth generation with those who love Him and keep His commandments; 1 Cor. 1:9 • *the*

10 but repays those who hate Him to [t]their faces, to destroy [t]them; He will not delay [t]with him who hates Him, He will repay him to his face. *his face • him • to*

11 "Therefore, you shall keep the commandment and the statutes and the judgments which I am commanding you today, to do them.

12 "Then it shall come about, because you listen to these judgments and keep and do them, that the LORD your God will keep with you [t]His covenant and [t]His lovingkindness which He swore to your forefathers. *the*

[7]I.e., wooden symbols of a female deity

13 "And He will love you and bless you and multiply you; He will also bless the fruit of your womb and the fruit of your ground, your grain and your new wine and your oil, the increase of your herd and the young of your flock, in the land which He swore to your forefathers to give you.

14 "You shall be blessed above all peoples; there shall be no male or female [r]barren among you or among your cattle. Ex. 23:26

15 "And [r]the LORD will remove from you all sickness; and He will not put on you any of the harmful diseases of Egypt which you have known, but He will lay them on all who hate you. Ex. 15:26

16 "And you shall consume all the peoples whom the LORD your God will deliver to you; your eye shall not pity them, neither shall you serve their gods, for that *would be* a snare to you.

17 "If you should say in your heart, 'These nations are greater than I; how can I [r]dispossess them?' Num. 33:53

18 you shall not be afraid of them; you shall well remember what the LORD your God did to Pharaoh and to all Egypt:

19 [r]the great trials which your eyes saw and the signs and the wonders and the mighty hand and the outstretched arm by which the LORD your God brought you out. So shall the LORD your God do to all the peoples of whom you are afraid. Deut. 4:34

20 "Moreover, the LORD your

God will send the hornet against
them, until those who are left and
hide themselves from you perish.
21"You shall not dread them, for
the LORD your God is in your
midst, a great and awesome God.
22"And the LORD your God will
clear away these nations before
you little by little; you will not be
able to put an end to them
quickly, lest the wild beasts grow
too numerous for you.
23"But the LORD your God shall
deliver them before you, and will
throw them into great confusion
until they are destroyed.
24"And[r] He will deliver their
kings into your hand so that you
shall make their name perish from
under heaven; no man will be able
to stand before you until you have
destroyed them. Josh. 6:2
25"The graven images of their
gods you are to [r]burn with fire; you
shall not covet the silver or the
gold that is on them, nor take it
for yourselves, lest you be snared
by it, for it is an abomination to
the LORD your God. Ex. 32:20
26"And you shall not bring an
abomination into your house, and
like it come under the [r]ban; you
shall utterly detest it and you shall
utterly abhor it, for it is something
banned. Lev. 27:28f.

CHAPTER 8

"ALL the commandments that I
am commanding you today you
shall be careful to do, that you
[r]may live and multiply, and go in
and possess the land which the
LORD swore *to give* to your forefathers. Deut. 4:1
2"And you shall remember all
the way which the LORD your God
has [r]led you in the wilderness
these forty years, that He might
humble you, testing you, to know
what was in your heart, whether
you would keep His commandments or not. Ps. 136:16
3"And He humbled you and let
you be hungry, and fed you with
manna which you did not know,
nor did your fathers know, that
He might make you [t]understand
that [r]man does not live by bread
alone, but man lives by everything
that proceeds out of the mouth of
the LORD. *know* • Luke 4:4
4"Your[r] clothing did not wear
out on you, nor did your foot swell
these forty years. Neh. 9:21
5"Thus[r] you are to know in your
heart that the LORD your God was
disciplining you just as a man disciplines his son. Heb. 12:6
6"Therefore, you shall keep the
commandments of the LORD your
God, to walk in His ways and to
[a]fear Him. *reverence*
7"For [r]the LORD your God is
bringing you into a good land, a
land of brooks of water, of fountains and springs, flowing forth in
valleys and hills; Jer. 2:7
8 a land of wheat and barley,
of vines and fig trees and pomegranates, a land of olive oil and
honey;
9 a land where you shall eat
food without scarcity, in which
you shall not lack anything; a land
whose stones are iron, and out of
whose hills you can dig copper.
10"When you have eaten and
are satisfied, you shall bless the

LORD your God for the good land
which He has given you.
11"Beware lest you forget the
LORD your God by not keeping His
commandments and His ordinances and His statutes which I
am commanding you today;
12 lest, when you have eaten
and are satisfied, and have built
good houses and lived *in them,*
13 and when your herds and
your flocks multiply, and your silver and gold multiply, and all that
you have multiplies,
14 then your heart becomes
[t]proud, and you forget the LORD
your God who brought you out
from the land of Egypt, out of the
house of [t]slavery. *lifted up • slaves*
15"He led you through the great
and terrible wilderness, *with its* fiery serpents and scorpions and
thirsty ground where there was no
water; He [r]brought water for you
out of the rock of flint. Ex. 17:6
16"In the wilderness He fed you
manna which your fathers did not
know, that He might humble you
and that He might test you, to do
good for you in the end.
17"Otherwise, [r]you may say in
your heart, 'My power and the
strength of my hand made me this
wealth.' Deut. 9:4
18"But you shall remember the
LORD your God, for [r]it is He who is
giving you power to make wealth,
that He may confirm His covenant
which He swore to your fathers,
as *it is* this day. Prov. 10:22
19"And it shall come about if
you ever forget the LORD your
God, and go after other gods and
serve them and worship them, [r]I
testify against you today that you
shall surely perish. Deut. 4:26
20"Like the nations that the
LORD makes to perish before you,
so [r]you shall perish; because you
would not listen to the voice of the
LORD your God. Ezek. 5:5-17

CHAPTER 9

"HEAR, O Israel! You are crossing over the Jordan today to go in
to dispossess nations greater and
mightier than you, great cities
[t]fortified to heaven, *and fortified*
2 a people great and tall, the
sons of the Anakim, whom you
know and of whom you have
heard *it said,* 'Who can stand before the sons of Anak?'
3"Know therefore today that it
is the LORD your God who is
crossing over before you as a consuming fire. He will destroy them
and He will subdue them before
you, so that you may drive them
out and destroy them quickly, just
as the LORD has spoken to you.
4"Do not say in your heart
when the LORD your God has
driven them out before [t]you, 'Because of my righteousness the
LORD has brought me in to possess this land,' but *it is* because of
the wickedness of these nations
that the LORD is dispossessing
them before you. *you saying*
5"It is not for your righteousness or for the uprightness of your
heart that you are going to possess their land, but *it is* because of
the wickedness of these nations
that the LORD your God is driving
them out before you, in order to
confirm the [t]oath which the LORD

swore to your fathers, to Abraham, Isaac and Jacob. *word*

6 "Know, then, *it is* not because of your righteousness *that* the LORD your God is giving you this good land to possess, for you are a [a]stubborn people. *stiff-necked*

7 "Remember, do not forget how you provoked the LORD your God to wrath in the wilderness; [r]from the day that you left the land of Egypt until you arrived at this place, you have been rebellious against the LORD. Ex. 14:10f.

8 "Even at Horeb you provoked the LORD to wrath, and the LORD was so angry with you that He would have destroyed you.

9 "When I went up to the mountain to receive the tablets of stone, the tablets of the covenant which the LORD had made with you, then I remained on the mountain forty days and nights; [r]I neither ate bread nor drank water. Ex. 24:18

10 "And the LORD gave me the two tablets of stone [r]written by the finger of God; and on them *were* all the words which the LORD had spoken with you at the mountain from the midst of the fire on the day of the assembly. Deut. 4:13

11 "And it came about at the end of forty days and nights that the LORD gave me the two tablets of stone, the tablets of the covenant.

12 "Then[r] the LORD said to me, 'Arise, go down from here quickly, for your people whom you brought out of Egypt have acted corruptly. They have quickly turned aside from the way which I commanded them; they have made a molten image for themselves.' Ex. 32:7, 8

13 "The LORD spoke further to me, saying, 'I have seen this people, and indeed, it is a [a]stubborn people. *stiff-necked*

14 'Let[r] Me alone, that I may destroy them and blot out their name from under heaven; and I will make of you a nation mightier and greater than they.' Ex. 32:10

15 "So I turned and came down from the mountain while the mountain was burning with fire, and the two tablets of the covenant were in my two hands.

16 "And I saw that you had indeed sinned against the LORD your God. You had made for yourselves a molten calf; you had turned aside quickly from the way which the LORD had commanded you.

17 "And I took hold of the two tablets and threw them from my hands, and smashed them before your eyes.

18 "And[r] I fell down before the LORD, [r]as at the first, forty days and nights; I neither ate bread nor drank water, because of all your sin which you had committed in doing what was evil in the sight of the LORD to provoke Him to anger. Ex. 34:28 • Deut. 10:10

19 "For[r] I was afraid of the anger and hot displeasure with which the LORD was wrathful against you in order to destroy you, but the LORD listened to me that time also. Ex. 32:10f.; Heb. 12:21

20 "And the LORD was angry enough with Aaron to destroy him; so I also prayed for Aaron at the same time.

21 "And I took your [t]sinful *thing*, the calf which you had made, and

burned it with fire and crushed it, grinding it very small until it was as fine as dust; and I threw its dust into the brook that came down from the mountain. *sin*

22 "Again at Taberah and at Massah and at Kibroth-hattaavah you provoked the LORD to wrath.

23 "And when the LORD sent you from Kadesh-barnea, saying, 'Go up and possess the land which I have given you,' then you rebelled against the command of the LORD your God; you neither believed Him nor listened to His voice.

24 "You[r] have been rebellious against the LORD from the day I knew you. Deut. 9:7; 31:27

25 "So I fell down before the LORD the forty days and nights, which I did because the LORD had said He would destroy you.

26 "And I prayed to the LORD, and said, 'O Lord GOD, do not destroy Thy people, even Thine inheritance, whom Thou hast redeemed through Thy greatness, whom Thou hast brought out of Egypt with a mighty hand.

27 'Remember Thy servants, Abraham, Isaac, and Jacob; do not look at the stubbornness of this people or at their wickedness or their sin.

28 'Otherwise the land from which Thou didst bring us may say, "Because the LORD was not able to bring them into the land which He had [t]promised them and because He hated them He has brought them out to slay them in the wilderness." *spoken to*

29 'Yet they are Thy people, even [r]Thine inheritance, whom Thou hast brought out by Thy great power and Thine outstretched arm.' Deut. 4:20

CHAPTER 10

"AT that time the LORD said to me, 'Cut[r] out for yourself two tablets of stone like the former ones, and come up to Me on the mountain, and [r]make an ark of wood for yourself. Ex. 34:1 • Ex. 25:10

2 'And [r]I will write on the tablets the words that were on the former tablets which you shattered, and [r]you shall put them in the ark.' Deut. 4:13 • Ex. 25:16

3 "So I made an ark of acacia wood and [r]cut out two tablets of stone like the former ones, and went up on the mountain with the two tablets in my hand. Ex. 34:4

4 "And He wrote on the tablets, like the former writing, the Ten [t]Commandments which the LORD had spoken to you on the mountain from the midst of the fire on the day of the assembly; and the LORD gave them to me. *Words*

5 "Then I turned and came down from the mountain, and [r]put the tablets in the ark which I had made; and there they are, as the LORD commanded me." Ex. 40:20

6 (Now the sons of Israel set out from [a]Beeroth Bene-jaakan to Moserah. There Aaron died and there he was buried and Eleazar his son ministered as priest in his place. *the wells of the sons of Jaakan*

7 [r]From there they set out to Gudgodah; and from Gudgodah to Jotbathah, a land of brooks of water. Num. 33:33, 34

8 [r]At that time the LORD set apart the tribe of Levi to carry the

ark of the covenant of the LORD, to stand before the LORD to serve Him and to bless in His name until this day. Num. 3:6; 18:1-7

9 [r]Therefore, Levi does not have a portion or inheritance with his brothers; the LORD is his inheritance, just as the LORD your God spoke to him.) Num. 18:20, 24

10 "I,[r] moreover, stayed on the mountain forty days and forty nights like the first time, and the LORD listened to me that time also; the LORD was not willing to destroy you. Ex. 34:28; Deut. 9:18

11 "Then the LORD said to me, 'Arise, proceed on your journey ahead of the people, that they may go in and possess the land which I swore to their fathers to give them.'

12 "And now, Israel, what does the LORD your God require from you, but to [a]fear the LORD your God, to walk in all His ways and love Him, and to serve the LORD your God with all your heart and with all your soul, *reverence*

13 *and* to keep the LORD's commandments and His statutes which I am commanding you today for your good?

14 "Behold, to the LORD your God belong heaven and the [t]highest heavens, the earth and all that is in it. *heaven of heavens*

15 "Yet on your fathers did the LORD set His affection to love them, and He chose their descendants after them, *even* you above all peoples, as *it is* this day.

16 "Circumcise then your heart, and stiffen your neck no more.

17 "For the LORD your God is the God of gods and the Lord of lords, the great, the mighty, and the awesome God who does not show partiality, nor take a bribe.

18 "He executes justice for [r]the orphan and the widow, and shows His love for the alien by giving him food and clothing. Ps. 68:5

19 "So[r] show your love for the alien, for you were aliens in the land of Egypt. Lev. 19:34

20 "You shall fear the LORD your God; you shall serve Him and [r]cling to Him, and you shall swear by His name. Deut. 11:22; 13:4

21 "He is your praise and He is your God, who has done these great and awesome things for you which your eyes have seen.

22 "Your[r] fathers went down to Egypt seventy persons *in all*, [r]and now the LORD your God has made you as numerous as the stars of heaven. Gen. 46:27 • Gen. 15:5

CHAPTER 11

"YOU shall therefore love the LORD your God, and always keep His charge, His statutes, His ordinances, and His commandments.

2 "And know this day that I *am* not *speaking* with your sons who have not known and who have not seen the [8]discipline of the LORD your God—His greatness, His mighty hand, and His outstretched arm,

3 and His signs and His works which He did in the midst of Egypt to Pharaoh the king of Egypt and to all his land;

4 and what He did to Egypt's army, to its horses and its chariots, when He made the water of the Red Sea to engulf them while they were pursuing you, and the

[8]Or, *instruction*

LORD completely destroyed them;
5 and what He did to you in the
wilderness until you came to this
place;
6 and what He did to Dathan
and Abiram, the sons of Eliab, the
son of Reuben, when the earth
opened its mouth and swallowed
them, their households, their
tents, and every living thing that
followed them, among all Israel—
7 but your own eyes have seen
all the great work of the LORD
which He did.
8 "You shall therefore keep every commandment which I am
commanding you today, so that
you may be strong and go in and
possess the land into which you
are about to cross to possess it;
9 so that you may prolong *your*
days on the land which the LORD
swore to your fathers to give to
them and to their descendants, a
land flowing with milk and honey.
10 "For the land, into which you
are entering to possess it, is not
like the land of Egypt from which
you came, where you used to sow
your seed and water it with your
[9]foot like a vegetable garden.
11 "But the land into which you
are about to cross to possess it, a
land of hills and valleys, drinks
water from the rain of heaven,
12 a land for which the LORD
your God cares; [r]the eyes of the
LORD your God are always on it,
from the beginning even to the
end of the year. 1 Kin. 9:3
13 "And it shall come about, [r]if
you listen obediently to my commandments which I am com-
manding you today, to love the
LORD your God and to serve Him
with all your heart and all your
soul, Lev. 26:3; Deut. 7:12
14 that He[r] will give the rain for
your land in its season, the [10]early
and late rain, that you may gather
in your grain and your new wine
and your oil. Deut. 28:12
15 "And He will give grass in
your fields for your cattle, and you
shall eat and be satisfied.
16 "Beware[t], lest your hearts be
deceived and you turn away and
serve other gods and worship
them. *Watch yourselves*
17 "Or [r]the anger of the LORD will
be kindled against you, and He
will shut up the heavens so that
there will be no rain and the
ground will not yield its fruit; and
you will perish quickly from the
good land which the LORD is giving you. Deut. 6:15; 9:19
18 "You shall therefore impress
these words of mine on your heart
and on your soul; and you shall
bind them as a sign on your hand,
and they shall be as [t]frontals on
your forehead. *frontlet bands*
19 "And [r]you shall teach them to
your sons, talking of them when
you sit in your house and when
you walk along the road and when
you lie down and when you rise
up. Deut. 4:9, 10; 6:7; Prov. 22:6
20 "And [r]you shall write them on
the doorposts of your house and
on your gates, Deut. 6:9
21 so that your days and the
days of your sons may be multiplied on the land which the LORD
swore to your fathers to give
them, as [r]long as the heavens *re-*
main above the earth. Ps. 72:5
22 "For if you are careful to keep
all this commandment which I am

[9]I.e., probably a treadmill

[10]I.e., autumn and spring rain

commanding you, to do it, to love
the LORD your God, to walk in all
His ways and hold fast to Him;
23 then the LORD will drive out
all these nations from before you,
and you will dispossess nations
greater and mightier than you.
24 "Every[r] place on which the
sole of your foot shall tread shall
be yours; your border shall be
from the wilderness to Lebanon,
and from the river, the river Euphrates, as far as [11]the western
sea. Josh. 1:3; 14:9
25 "There[r] shall no man be able to
stand before you; the LORD your
God shall lay the dread of you and
the fear of you on all the land on
which you set foot, as He has spoken to you. Ex. 23:27; Deut. 7:24
26 "See, I am setting before you
today a blessing and a curse:
27 the [r]blessing, if you listen to
the commandments of the LORD
your God, which I am commanding you today; Deut. 28:1-14
28 and the [r]curse, if you do not
listen to the commandments of
the LORD your God, but turn aside
from the way which I am commanding you today, [t]by following
other gods which you have not
known. Deut. 28:15-68 • *to follow*
29 "And it shall come about,
when the LORD your God brings
you into the land where you are
entering to possess it, [r]that you
shall place the blessing on Mount
Gerizim and the curse on Mount
Ebal. Deut. 27:12; Josh. 8:33
30 "Are they not across the Jordan, west of the way toward the
sunset, in the land of the Canaanites who live in the Arabah, opposite [r]Gilgal, beside the [t]oaks of Moreh? Josh. 4:19 • *terebinths*
31 "For you are about to cross
the Jordan to go in to possess the
land which the LORD your God is
giving you, and [r]you shall possess
it and live in it, Deut. 17:14
32 and you shall be careful to do
all the statutes and the judgments
which I am setting before you today.

CHAPTER 12

"THESE are the statutes and the
judgments which you shall carefully observe in the land which the
LORD, the God of your fathers, has
given you to possess [t]as long as
you live on the earth. *all the days*
2 "You shall utterly destroy all
the places where the nations
whom you shall dispossess serve
their gods, on the [r]high mountains
and on the hills and under every
green tree. 2 Kin. 16:4
3 "And you shall tear down
their altars and smash their *sacred* pillars and burn their [12]Ashe-
rim with fire, and you shall cut
down the engraved images of
their gods, and you shall obliter-
ate their name from that place.
4 "You shall not act like this
toward the LORD your God.
5 "But[r] you shall seek *the LORD*
at the place which the LORD your
God shall choose from all your
tribes, to establish His name there
for His dwelling, and there you
shall come. 2 Chr. 7:12; Ps. 78:68
6 "And there you shall bring
your burnt offerings, your sacrifices, your tithes, the [a]contribution
of your hand, your votive offer-

[11] I.e., the Mediterranean

[12] I.e., wooden symbols of a female deity

ings, your freewill offerings, and the first-born of your herd and of your flock. *heave offering*

7 "There also you and your households shall eat before the LORD your God, and rejoice in all your undertakings in which the LORD your God has blessed you.

8 "You shall not do at all what we are doing here today, every man *doing* whatever is right in his own eyes;

9 for you have not as yet come to [r]the resting place and the inheritance which the LORD your God is giving you. Deut. 3:20; 25:19

10 "When you cross the Jordan and live in the land which the LORD your God is giving you to inherit, and He gives you rest from all your enemies around *you* so that you live in security,

11 [r]then it shall come about that the place in which the LORD your God shall choose for His name to dwell, there you shall bring all that I command you: your burnt offerings and your sacrifices, your tithes and the [a]contribution of your hand, and all your choice votive offerings which you will vow to the LORD. Deut. 12:5 • *heave offering*

12 "And you shall [r]rejoice before the LORD your God, you and your sons and daughters, your male and female servants, and the Levite who is within your gates, since he has no portion or inheritance with you. Deut. 12:7

13 "Be careful that you do not offer your burnt offerings in every *cultic* place you see,

14 but in the place which the LORD chooses in one of your tribes, there you shall offer your burnt offerings, and there you shall do all that I command you.

15 "However, you may slaughter and eat meat within any of your gates, [t]whatever you desire, according to the blessing of the LORD your God which He has given you; the unclean and the clean may eat of it, as of the gazelle and the deer. *in every desire of your soul*

16 "Only [r] you shall not eat the blood; you are to pour it out on the ground like water. Gen. 9:4

17 "You [r] are not allowed to eat within your gates the tithe of your grain, or new wine, or oil, or the first-born of your herd or flock, or any of your votive offerings which you vow, or your freewill offerings, or the [t]contribution of your hand. Deut. 12:26 • *heave offering*

18 "But you shall eat them before the LORD your God in the place which the LORD your God will choose, you and your son and daughter, and your male and female servants, and the Levite who is within your gates; and you shall rejoice before the LORD your God in all your undertakings.

19 "Be [r] careful that you do not forsake the Levite as long as you live in your land. Deut. 14:27

20 "When the LORD your God extends your border [r]as He has promised you, and you say, 'I will eat meat,' because you desire to eat meat, *then* you may eat meat, whatever you desire. Gen. 15:18

21 "If the place which the LORD your God chooses to put His name is too far from you, then you may slaughter of your herd and flock which the LORD has given you, as I have commanded you; and you

may eat within your gates whatever you desire.
22 "Just as a gazelle or a deer is
eaten, so you shall eat it; the unclean and the clean alike may eat
of it.
23 "Only be sure [r]not to eat the
blood, for the blood is the [t]life, and
you shall not eat the [t]life with the
flesh. Lev. 17:10-14 • *soul*
24 "You shall not eat it; you shall
pour it out on the ground like water.
25 "You shall not eat it, in order
that [r]it may be well with you and
your sons after you, for you will
be doing what is right in the sight
of the LORD. Deut. 4:40; Is. 3:10
26 "Only your holy things which
you may have and your votive offerings, you shall take and go to
the place which the LORD chooses.
27 "And you shall offer your
burnt offerings, the flesh and the
blood, on the altar of the LORD
your God; and the blood of your
sacrifices shall be poured out on
the altar of the LORD your God,
and you shall eat the flesh.
28 "Be careful to listen to all
these words which I command
you, in order that [r]it may be well
with you and your sons after you
forever, for you will be doing
what is good and right in the sight
of the LORD your God. Eccl. 8:12
29 "When [r]the LORD your God
cuts off before you the nations
which you are going in to dispossess, and you dispossess them and
dwell in their land, Josh. 23:4
30 beware that you are not ensnared [t]to follow them, after they
are destroyed before you, and that
you do not inquire after their
gods, saying, 'How do these nations serve their gods, that I also
may do likewise?' *after them*
31 "You[r] shall not behave thus
toward the LORD your God, for every abominable act which the
LORD hates they have done for
their gods; for they even burn
their sons and daughters in the
fire to their gods. Deut. 9:5
32 "Whatever[t] I command you,
you shall be careful to do; you
shall not add to nor take away
from it. *Everything that*

CHAPTER 13

"IF a prophet or a dreamer of
dreams arises among you and
gives you a sign or a wonder,
2 and the sign or the wonder
comes true, concerning which he
spoke to you, saying, 'Let us go after other gods (whom you have
not known) and let us serve them,'
3 you shall not listen to the
words of that prophet or that
dreamer of dreams; for the LORD
your God is [r]testing you to find out
if you love the LORD your God
with all your heart and with all
your soul. Ex. 20:20; Deut. 8:2, 16
4 "You[r] shall follow the LORD
your God and fear Him; and you
shall keep His commandments,
listen to His voice, serve Him, and
cling to Him. 2 Kin. 23:3
5 "But that prophet or that
dreamer of dreams shall be put to
death, because he has [t]counseled
rebellion against the LORD your
God who brought you from the
land of Egypt and redeemed you
from the house of slavery, to se-
duce you from the way in which

the LORD your God commanded
you to walk. So you shall purge
the evil from among you. *spoken*
6 "If your brother, your mother's son, or your son or daughter,
or the wife [t]you cherish, or your
friend who is as your own soul,
entice you secretly, saying, 'Let[r] us
go and serve other gods' (whom
neither you nor your fathers have
known, *of your bosom* • Deut. 13:2
7 of the gods of the peoples
who are around you, near you or
far from you, from one end of the
earth to the other end),
8 [r]you shall not yield to him or
listen to him; and your eye shall
not pity him, nor shall you spare
or conceal him. Prov. 1:10
9 "But you shall surely kill him;
your hand shall be first against
him to put him to death, and afterwards the hand of all the people.
10 "So you shall stone him [t]to
death because he has sought to se-
duce you from the LORD your God
who brought you out from the
land of Egypt, out of the house of
slavery. *with stones so that he dies*
11 "Then all Israel will hear and
be afraid, and will never again do
such a wicked thing among you.
12 "If you hear in one of your
cities, which the LORD your God is
giving you to live in, *anyone* saying *that*
13 some worthless men have
gone out from among you and
have seduced the inhabitants of
their city, saying, 'Let[r] us go and
serve other gods' (whom you have
not known), Deut. 13:2
14 then you shall investigate
and search out and inquire thoroughly. And if it is true *and* the
matter established that this
abomination has been done
among you,
15 you shall surely strike the inhabitants of that city with the
edge of the sword, utterly destroying it and all that is in it and its
cattle with the edge of the sword.
16 "Then you shall gather all its
booty into the middle of its open
square and burn the city and all
its booty with fire as a whole
burnt offering to the LORD your
God; and it shall be a [t]ruin forever.
It shall never be rebuilt. *mound*
17 "And nothing from that which
is put under the ban shall cling to
your hand, in order that the LORD
may turn from [r]His burning anger
and show mercy to you, and have
compassion on you and make you
increase, just as He has sworn to
your fathers, Ex. 32:12; Num. 25:4
18 if you will listen to the voice
of the LORD your God, [t]keeping all
His commandments which I am
commanding you today, and
doing what is right in the sight of
the LORD your God. *to keep*

CHAPTER 14

"YOU are [r]the sons of the LORD
your God; you shall not cut yourselves nor shave your forehead for
the sake of the dead. Gal. 3:26
2 "For you are [r]a holy people to
the LORD your God; and the LORD
has chosen you to be a people for
His [a]own possession out of all the
peoples who are on the face of the
earth. Rom. 12:1 • *special treasure*
3 "You[r] shall not eat any detestable thing. Ezek. 4:14
4 "These[r] are the animals which

you may eat: the ox, the sheep,
the goat, Acts 10:14
5 the deer, the gazelle, the roe-
buck, the wild goat, the ibex, the
antelope and the mountain sheep.
6 "And any animal that divides
the hoof and has the hoof split in
two *and* chews the cud, among
the animals, that you may eat.
7 "Nevertheless, you are not to
eat of these among those which
[t]chew the cud, or among those that
divide the hoof in two: the camel
and the rabbit and the rock-bad-
ger, for though they [t]chew the cud,
they do not divide the hoof; they
are unclean for you. *brings up*
8 "And the pig, because it divides the hoof but *does* not *chew*
the cud, it is unclean for you. You
shall not eat any of their flesh nor
touch their carcasses.
9 "These you may eat of all that
are in water: anything that has
fins and scales you may eat,
10 but anything that does not
have fins and scales you shall not
eat; it is unclean for you.
11 "You may eat any clean bird.
12 "But these are the ones which
you shall not eat: the eagle and
the vulture and the buzzard,
13 and the red kite, the falcon,
and the kite in their kinds,
14 and every raven in its kind,
15 and the ostrich, the owl, the
sea gull, and the hawk in their
kinds,
16 the little owl, the [a]great owl,
the white owl, *great horned owl*
17 the pelican, the carrion vulture, the cormorant,
18 the stork, and the heron in
their kinds, and the hoopoe and
the bat.

19 "And all the teeming life with
wings are unclean to you; they
shall not be eaten.
20 "You may eat any clean bird.
21 "You[r] shall not eat anything
which dies *of itself*. You may give
it to the alien who is in your [t]town,
so that he may eat it, or you may
sell it to a foreigner, for you are a
holy people to the LORD your God.
You shall not boil a kid in its
mother's milk. Ezek. 4:14 • *gates*
22 "You [r]shall surely tithe all the
produce from [t]what you sow,
which comes out of the field every
year. Neh. 10:37 • *your seed*
23 "And you shall eat in the presence of the LORD your God, [r]at the
place where He chooses to establish His name, the tithe of your
grain, your new wine, your oil,
and the first-born of your herd
and your flock, in order that you
may learn to fear the LORD your
God always. Deut. 12:5
24 "And if the [t]distance is so
great for you that you are not able
to [t]bring *the tithe*, since the place
where the LORD your God chooses
to set His name is too far away
from you when the LORD your
God blesses you, *way • carry it*
25 then you shall [t]exchange *it*
for money, and bind the money in
your hand and go to the place
which the LORD your God
chooses. *give in money*
26 "And you may spend the money for whatever your [t]heart desires, for oxen, or sheep, or wine,
or strong drink, or whatever your
[t]heart [t]desires; and there you shall
eat in the presence of the LORD
your God and rejoice, you and
your household. *soul • asks of you*

27"Also you shall not neglect
[r]the Levite who is in your[t]town, for
he has no portion or inheritance
among you. Deut. 12:12 • *gates*
28"At the end of every third
year you shall bring out all the
tithe of your produce in that year,
and shall deposit *it* in your town.
29"And the Levite, because he
has no portion or inheritance
among you, and the alien, the orphan and the widow who are in
your town, shall come and eat and
be satisfied, in order that the LORD
your God may bless you in all the
work of your hand which you do.

CHAPTER 15

"AT the end of *every* seven years
you shall [13]grant a remission *of
debts*.
2"And this is the manner of remission: every creditor shall release what he has loaned to his
neighbor; he shall not exact it of
his neighbor and his brother, because the LORD's remission has
been proclaimed.
3"From[r] a foreigner you may
exact *it*, but your hand shall release whatever of yours is with
your brother. Deut. 23:20
4"However, there shall be no
poor among you, since the LORD
will surely bless you in the land
which the LORD your God is giving
you as an inheritance to possess,
5 if only you listen obediently
to the voice of the LORD your God,
to observe carefully all this commandment which I am commanding you today.
6"For the LORD your God shall
bless you as He has promised you,
and you will lend to many nations,
but you will not borrow; and you
will rule over many nations, but
they will not rule over you.
7"If there is [r]a poor man with
you, one of your brothers, in any
of your[t]towns in your land which
the LORD your God is giving you,
you shall not harden your heart,
nor close your hand from your
poor brother; Lev. 25:35 • *gates*
8 but you shall freely open
your hand to him, and shall generously lend him sufficient for his
need *in* whatever he lacks.
9"Beware, lest there is a base
[t]thought in your heart, saying, 'The
seventh year, the year of remission, is near,' and your eye is hostile toward your poor brother, and
you give him nothing; then he
may cry to the LORD against you,
and it will be a sin in you. *word*
10"You shall generously give to
him, and your heart shall not be
grieved when you give to him, because for this thing the LORD your
God will bless you in all your
work and in all your undertakings.
11"For the poor will never cease
to be[t]in the land; therefore I command you, saying, 'You shall
freely open your hand to your
brother, to your needy and poor in
your land.' *in the midst of*
12"If your [t]kinsman, a Hebrew
man or woman, is sold to you,
then he shall serve you six years,
but in the seventh year you shall
set him free. *brother*
13"And when you set him [t]free,
you shall not send him away empty-handed. *free from you*
14"You shall furnish him liber-
ally from your flock and from

[13]Lit., *make a release*

your threshing floor and from
your wine vat; you shall give to
him as the LORD your God has
blessed you.
15 "And you shall remember that
you were a slave in the land of
Egypt, and the LORD your God redeemed you; therefore I command
you [t]this today. *this thing*
16 "And it shall come about [r]if he
says to you, 'I will not go out from
you,' because he loves you and
your household, since he fares
well with you; Ex. 21:5, 6
17 then you shall take an awl
and pierce it through his ear into
the door, and he shall be your servant forever. And also you shall
do likewise to your maidservant.
18 "It shall not seem hard to you
when you set him free, for he has
given you six years *with* [t]double
the service of a hired man; so the
LORD your God will bless you in
whatever you do. *double the amount*
19 "You[r] shall consecrate to the
LORD your God all the first-born
males that are born of your herd
and of your flock; you shall not
work with the first-born of your
herd, nor shear the first-born of
your flock. Ex. 13:2, 12
20 "You[r] and your household
shall eat it every year before the
LORD your God in the place which
the LORD chooses. Lev. 7:15-18
21 "But if it has any defect, *such
as* lameness or blindness, *or* any
serious defect, you shall not sacrifice it to the LORD your God.
22 "You shall eat it within your
gates; [r]the unclean and the clean
alike *may eat it,* as [r]a gazelle or a
deer. Deut. 12:15, 16, 22
23 "Only [r]you shall not eat its
blood; you are to pour it out on
the ground like water. Gen. 9:4

CHAPTER 16

"OBSERVE the month of Abib
and celebrate the Passover to the
LORD your God, for in the month
of Abib the LORD your God
brought you out of Egypt by night.
2 "And you shall sacrifice the
Passover to the LORD your God
from the flock and the herd, in the
place where the LORD chooses to
establish His name.
3 "You[r] shall not eat leavened
bread with it; seven days you shall
eat with it unleavened bread, the
bread of affliction (for you came
out of the land of Egypt in haste),
in order that you may remember
all the days of your life the day
when you came out of the land of
Egypt. Ex. 12:8, 15, 19, 39
4 "For seven days no leaven
shall be seen with you in all your
territory, and [r]none of the flesh
which you sacrifice on the evening
of the first day shall remain overnight until morning. Ex. 12:8, 10
5 "You are not allowed to sacrifice the Passover in any of your
[t]towns which the LORD your God is
giving you; *gates*
6 but [r]at the place where the
LORD your God chooses to establish His name, you shall sacrifice
the Passover in the evening at
sunset, at the time that you came
out of Egypt. Deut. 12:5
7 "And you shall cook and eat *it*
in the place which the LORD your
God chooses. And in the morning
you are to return to your tents.
8 "Six days you shall eat un-

leavened bread, and on the seventh day there shall be a solemn
assembly to the LORD your God;
you shall do no work *on it.*
9 "You[r] shall count seven weeks
for yourself; you shall begin to
count seven weeks from the time
you begin to put the sickle to the
standing grain. Ex. 23:16; 34:22
10 "Then you shall [t]celebrate the
Feast of Weeks to the LORD your
God with a tribute of a freewill offering of your hand, which you
shall give just as the LORD your
God blesses you; *perform*
11 and you shall rejoice before
the LORD your God, you and your
son and your daughter and your
male and female servants and the
Levite who is in your [t]town, and
the stranger and the [a]orphan and
the widow who are in your midst,
in the place where the LORD your
God chooses to establish His
name. *gates • fatherless*
12 "And [r]you shall remember that
you were a slave in Egypt, and
you shall be careful to observe
these statutes. Deut. 15:15
13 "You shall celebrate the Feast
of Booths seven days after you
have gathered in from your
threshing floor and your wine vat;
14 and you shall rejoice in your
feast, you and your son and your
daughter and your male and female servants and the Levite and
the stranger and the orphan and
the widow who are in your towns.
15 "Seven days you shall celebrate a feast to the LORD your God
in the place which the LORD
chooses, because the LORD your
God will bless you in all your produce and in all the work of your
hands, so that you shall be altogether joyful.
16 "Three times in a year all your
males shall appear before the
LORD your God in the place which
He chooses, at the Feast of Unleavened Bread and at the Feast of
Weeks and at the Feast of Booths,
and they shall not appear before
the LORD empty-handed.
17 "Every man shall give as he is
able, according to the blessing of
the LORD your God which He has
given you.
18 "You shall appoint for yourself judges and officers in all your
towns which the LORD your God is
giving you, according to your
tribes, and they shall judge the
people with righteous judgment.
19 "You[r] shall not distort justice;
you shall not [t]be partial, and you
shall not take a bribe, for a bribe
blinds the eyes of the wise and
perverts the words of the righteous. Ex. 23:2 • *regard persons*
20 "Justice, *and only* justice, you
shall pursue, that you may live
and possess the land which the
LORD your God is giving you.
21 "You[r] shall not plant for yourself an Asherah of any kind of tree
beside the altar of the LORD your
God, which you shall make for
yourself. 2 Kin. 17:16; 21:3
22 "Neither shall you set up for
yourself a *sacred* pillar which the
LORD your God hates.

CHAPTER 17

"YOU shall not sacrifice to the
LORD your God an ox or a sheep
which has a blemish or any [t]defect,

for that is a detestable thing to the
LORD your God. *evil thing*
2"If[r] there is found in your
midst, in any of your [t]towns,
which the LORD your God is giving
you, a man or a woman who does
what is evil in the sight of the
LORD your God, by transgressing
His covenant, Deut. 13:6-11 • *gates*
3 and has gone and served other gods and worshiped them, [r]or
the sun or the moon or any of the
heavenly host, which I have not
commanded, Job 31:26-28
4 and if it is told you and you
have heard of it, then you shall inquire thoroughly. And behold, if it
is true and the thing certain that
this detestable thing has been
done in Israel,
5 then you shall bring out that
man or that woman who has done
this evil deed, to your gates, *that
is*, the man or the woman, and you
shall stone them to death.
6"On the [t]evidence of two witnesses or three witnesses, he who
is to die shall be put to death; he
shall not be put to death on the
[t]evidence of one witness. *mouth*
7"The[r] hand of the witnesses
shall be first against him to put
him to death, and afterward the
hand of all the people. [r]So you
shall purge the evil from your
midst. Lev. 24:14 • 1 Cor. 5:13
8"If any case is too difficult for
you to decide, between one kind
of homicide or another, between
one kind of lawsuit or another,
and between one kind of assault
or another, being cases of dispute
in your [t]courts, then you shall arise
and go up to the place which the
LORD your God chooses. *gates*
9"So you shall come to [r]the Levitical priest or the judge who is
in office in those days, and you
shall inquire *of them*, and they
will declare to you the verdict in
the case. Deut. 19:17
10"And you shall do according
to the [t]terms of the verdict which
they declare to you from that
place which the LORD chooses;
and you shall be careful to observe according to all that they
teach you. *mouth*
11"According[r] to the [t]terms of the
law which they teach you, and according to the verdict which they
tell you, you shall do; you shall
not turn aside from the word
which they declare to you, to the
right or the left. Deut. 25:1 • *mouth*
12"And the man who acts [r]pre-
sumptuously by not listening to
the priest who stands there to
serve the LORD your God, nor to
the judge, that man shall die; thus
you shall purge the evil from Israel. Num. 15:30; Deut. 1:43
13"Then all the people will hear
and be afraid, and will not act [r]pre-
sumptuously again. Deut. 17:12
14"When you enter the land
which the LORD your God gives
you, and you [r]possess it and live in
it, and you say, 'I will set a king
over me like all the nations who
are around me,' Deut. 11:31
15 you shall surely set a king
over you whom the LORD your
God chooses, *one* from among
your countrymen you shall set as
king over yourselves; you may not
put a foreigner over yourselves
who is not your countryman.
16"Moreover, he shall not multiply horses for himself, nor shall he

cause the people to return to
Egypt to multiply horses, since
the LORD has said to you, 'You
shall never again return that way.'
17"Neither shall he multiply
wives for himself, lest his heart
turn away; nor shall he greatly increase silver and gold for himself.
18"Now it shall come about
when he sits on the throne of his
kingdom, he shall write for himself a copy of this law on a scroll
[t]in the presence of the Levitical
priests. *from before*
19"And it shall be with him, and
he shall read it [r]all the days of his
life, that he may learn to fear the
LORD his God, by carefully observing all the words of this law
and these statutes, Deut. 4:9, 10
20 that his heart may not be
lifted up above his countrymen
and that he may not turn aside
from the commandment, to the
right or the left; in order that he
and his sons may continue long in
his kingdom in the midst of Israel.

CHAPTER 18

"THE Levitical priests, the
whole tribe of Levi, shall have no
portion or inheritance with Israel;
they shall eat the LORD's offerings
by fire and His portion.
2"And they shall have no inheritance among their [t]countrymen;
the LORD is their inheritance, as
He promised them. *brothers*
3"Now this shall be the priests'
due from the people, from those
who offer a sacrifice, either an ox
or a sheep, of which they shall
give to the priest the shoulder and
the two cheeks and the stomach.
4"You shall give him the first
fruits of your grain, your new
wine, and your oil, and the first
shearing of your sheep.
5"For the LORD your God has
chosen him and his sons from all
your tribes, to stand and serve in
the name of the LORD forever.
6"Now if a Levite comes from
any of your [t]towns throughout Israel where he resides, and comes
whenever he desires to the place
which the LORD chooses, *gates*
7 then he shall serve in the
name of the LORD his God, like all
his fellow Levites who stand there
before the LORD.
8"They shall eat equal portions,
except *what they receive* from the
sale of their fathers' *estates*.
9"When you enter the land
which the LORD your God gives
you, you shall not learn to [t]imitate[r]
the detestable things of those nations. *do according to* • Deut. 9:5
10"There shall not be found
among you anyone who makes his
son or his daughter pass through
the fire, one who uses divination,
one [r]who practices witchcraft, or
one who interprets omens, or a
sorcerer, Lev. 19:26, 31; 20:6
11 or one who casts a spell, [r]or a
medium, or a spiritist, or one who
calls up the dead. Lev. 19:31
12"For whoever does these
things is detestable to the LORD;
and because of these detestable
things the LORD your God will
drive them out before you.
13"You[r] shall be blameless before the LORD your God. Gen. 6:9
14"For those nations, which you
shall dispossess, listen to those

who [r]practice witchcraft and to diviners, but as for you, the LORD
your God has not allowed you *to*
do so. 2 Kin. 21:6
15 "The LORD your God will raise
up for you a prophet like me from
among you, from your countrymen, you shall listen to him.
16 "This is [r]according to all that
you asked of the LORD your God
in Horeb on the day of the assembly, saying, 'Let me not hear again
the voice of the LORD my God, let
me not see this great fire anymore, lest I die.' Ex. 20:18, 19
17 "And the LORD said to me,
'They have spoken well.
18 'I will raise up a prophet from
among their [t]countrymen like you,
and I will put My words in his
mouth, and he shall speak to them
all that I command him. *brothers*
19 'And [r]it shall come about that
whoever will not listen to My
words which he shall speak in My
name, I Myself will require *it* of
him. Acts 3:23; Heb. 12:25
20 'But the prophet who shall
speak a word presumptuously in
My name which I have not commanded him to speak, or which he
shall speak in the name of other
gods, that prophet shall die.'
21 "And [t]you may say in your
heart, 'How shall we know the
word which the LORD has not spoken?' *if you say*
22 "When a prophet speaks in
the name of the LORD, if the thing
does not come about or come
true, that is the thing which the
LORD has not spoken. The prophet
has spoken it presumptuously;
you shall not be afraid of him.

CHAPTER 19

"WHEN the LORD your God cuts
off the nations, whose land the
LORD your God gives you, and you
dispossess them and settle in their
cities and in their houses,
2 you shall set aside three
cities for yourself in the midst of
your land, which the LORD your
God gives you to possess.
3 "You shall prepare the roads
for yourself, and divide into three
parts the territory of your land,
which the LORD your God will
give you as a possession, so that
any manslayer may flee there.
4 "Now this is the case of the
manslayer who may flee there and
live: when he [t]kills his friend [t]unin-
tentionally, not hating him previously— *smites • without knowledge*
5 as when *a man* goes into the
forest with his friend to cut wood,
and his hand swings the axe to cut
down the tree, and the iron *head*
slips off the handle and strikes his
friend so that he dies—he may
flee to one of these cities and live;
6 lest the avenger of blood pursue the manslayer [t]in the heat of
his anger, and overtake him, because the way is long, and take his
life, though he was not deserving
of death, since he had not hated
him previously. *while his heart is hot*
7 "Therefore, I command you,
saying, 'You shall set aside three
cities for yourself.'
8 "And if the LORD your God enlarges your territory, just as He
has sworn to your fathers, and
gives you all the land which He
promised to give your fathers—

9 if you [t]carefully observe all this commandment, which I command you today, to love the LORD your God, and to walk in His ways always—then you shall add three more cities for yourself, besides these three. *keep . . . to do it*

10 "So innocent blood will not be shed in the midst of your land which the LORD your God gives you as an inheritance, and [r]bloodguiltiness be on you. Num. 35:33

11 "But if there is a man who hates his neighbor and lies in wait for him and rises up against him and strikes him so that he dies, and he flees to one of these cities,

12 then the elders of his city shall send and take him from there and deliver him into the hand of the avenger of blood, that he may die.

13 "You[t] shall not pity him, but you shall purge the blood of the innocent from Israel, that it may go well with you. *Your eye*

14 "You shall not move your neighbor's boundary mark, which the ancestors have set, in your inheritance which you shall inherit in the land that the LORD your God gives you to possess.

15 "A[r] single witness shall not rise up against a man on account of any iniquity or any sin which he has committed; on the evidence of two or three witnesses a matter shall be confirmed. Num. 35:30

16 "If a malicious witness rises up against a man to [t]accuse him of wrongdoing, *testify against*

17 then both the men who have the dispute shall stand [r]before the LORD, before the priests and the judges who will be *in office* in those days. Deut. 17:9

18 "And the judges shall investigate thoroughly; and if the witness is a false witness *and* he has accused his brother falsely,

19 then [r]you shall do to him just as he had intended to do to his brother. Thus you shall purge the evil from among you. Prov. 19:5

20 "And the rest will hear and be afraid, and will never again do such an evil thing among you.

21 "Thus you shall not show pity: life for life, eye for eye, tooth for tooth, hand for hand, foot for foot.

CHAPTER 20

"WHEN you go out to battle against your enemies and see [r]horses and chariots *and* people more numerous than you, do not be afraid of them; for the LORD your God, who brought you up from the land of Egypt, is with you. Deut. 3:22; 7:18; 31:6, 8

2 "Now it shall come about that when you are approaching the battle, the priest shall come near and speak to the people.

3 "And he shall say to them, 'Hear, O Israel, you are approaching the battle against your enemies today. Do not be fainthearted. Do not be afraid, or panic, or tremble before them,

4 for the LORD your God [r]is the one who goes with you, to fight for you against your enemies, to save you.' Deut. 1:30; 3:22

5 "The officers also shall speak to the people, saying, 'Who is the man that has built a new house and has not [r]dedicated it? Let him

depart and return to his house,
lest he die in the battle and another man dedicate it. Neh. 12:27
6 'And who is the man that has
planted a vineyard and has not begun to use its fruit? Let him depart
and return to his house, lest he die
in the battle and another man begin to use its fruit.
7 'And[r] who is the man that is
engaged to a woman and has not
[t]married her? Let him depart and
return to his house, lest he die in
the battle and another man[t]marry
her.' Deut. 24:5 • *taken* • *take*
8 "Then the officers shall speak
further to the people, and they
shall say, 'Who is the man that is
afraid and fainthearted? Let him
depart and return to his house, so
that he might not make his brothers' hearts melt like his heart.'
9 "And it shall come about that
when the officers have finished
speaking to the people, they shall
appoint commanders of armies at
the head of the people.
10 "When you approach a city to
fight against it, you shall [t]offer it
terms of peace. *call to it for peace*
11 "And it shall come about, if it
agrees to make peace with you
and opens to you, then it shall be
that all the people who are found
in it shall become your forced labor and shall serve you.
12 "However, if it does not make
peace with you, but makes war
against you, then you shall besiege it.
13 "When the LORD your God
gives it into your hand, you shall
strike all the [t]men in it with the
edge of the sword. *males*
14 "Only the women and the children and [r]the animals and all that
is in the city, all its spoil, you shall
take as booty for yourself; and
you shall [t]use the spoil of your enemies which the LORD your God
has given you. Josh. 8:2 • *eat*
15 "Thus you shall do to all the
cities that are very far from you,
which are not of the cities of these
nations [t]nearby. *here*
16 "Only[r] in the cities of these
peoples that the LORD your God is
giving you as an inheritance, you
shall not leave alive anything that
breathes. Deut. 7:1-5; Josh. 11:14
17 "But you shall[a]utterly destroy
them, the Hittite and the Amorite,
the Canaanite and the Perizzite,
the Hivite and the Jebusite, as the
LORD your God has commanded
you, *put them under the ban*
18 in order that they may not
teach you to do [r]according to all
their detestable things which they
have done for their gods, so that
you would sin against the LORD
your God. Ex. 34:12-16
19 "When you besiege a city a
long time, to make war against it
in order to capture it, you shall
not destroy its trees by swinging
an axe against them; for you may
eat from them, and you shall not
cut them down. For is the tree of
the field a man, that it should be
besieged by you?
20 "Only the trees which you
know are not fruit trees you shall
destroy and cut down, that you
may construct siegeworks against
the city that is making war with
you until it falls.

CHAPTER 21

"IF a slain person is found lying
in the open country in the land

which the LORD your God gives
you to possess, *and* it is not
known who has struck him,
2 then your elders and your
judges shall go out and measure
the distance to the cities which
are around the slain one.
3 "And it shall be that the city
which is nearest to the slain man,
that is, the elders of that city, shall
take a heifer of the herd, which
has not been worked and which
has not pulled in a yoke;
4 and the elders of that city
shall bring the heifer down to a
valley with running water, which
has not been plowed or sown, and
shall break the heifer's neck there
in the valley.
5 "Then the priests, the sons of
Levi, shall come near, for the
LORD your God has chosen them
to serve Him and to bless in the
name of the LORD; and every dispute and every [t]assault shall be
settled by them. *stroke*
6 "And all the elders of that city
[t]which is nearest to the slain man
shall [r]wash their hands over the
heifer whose neck was broken in
the valley; *who are* • Matt. 27:24
7 and they shall answer and
say, 'Our hands have not shed this
blood, nor did our eyes see *it*.
8 '[14]Forgive Thy people Israel
whom Thou hast redeemed, O
LORD, and do not place the guilt of
innocent blood in the midst of Thy
people Israel.' And the bloodguiltiness shall be forgiven them.
9 "So you shall remove the guilt
of innocent blood from your
midst, when you do what is right
in the eyes of the LORD.

[14] Lit., *Cover over, atone for*

10 "When you go out to battle
against your enemies, and [r]the
LORD your God delivers them into
your hands, and you take them
away captive, Josh. 21:44
11 and see among the captives a
beautiful woman, and have a desire for her and would take her as
a wife for yourself,
12 then you shall bring her
home to your house, and she shall
shave her head and trim her nails.
13 "She shall also remove the
clothes of her captivity and shall
remain in your house, and [r]mourn
her father and mother a full
month; and after that you may go
in to her and be her husband and
she shall be your wife. Ps. 45:10
14 "And it shall be, if you are not
pleased with her, then you shall
let her go [t]wherever she wishes;
but you shall certainly not sell her
for money, you shall not [a]mistreat
her, because you have humbled
her. *according to her soul* • *enslave*
15 "If a man has two wives, the
one loved and [r]the other [t]unloved,
and *both* the loved and the [t]un-
loved have borne him sons, if the
first-born son belongs to the [t]un-
loved, Gen. 29:33 • *hated*
16 then it shall be in the day he
wills what he has to his sons, he
cannot make the son of the loved
the first-born before the son of the
unloved, who is the first-born.
17 "But he shall acknowledge the
first-born, the son of the unloved,
by giving him a double portion of
all that he has, for he is the beginning of his strength; to him belongs the right of the first-born.
18 "If any man has a stubborn

and rebellious son who will [r]not
obey his father or his mother, and
when they chastise him, he will
not even listen to them, Ex. 20:12
19 then his father and mother
shall seize him, and bring him out
to the elders of his city at the gateway of his home town.
20"And they shall say to the elders of his city, 'This son of ours is
stubborn and rebellious, he will
not obey us, he is a glutton and a
drunkard.'
21"Then[r] all the men of his city
shall stone him to death; so you
shall remove the evil from your
midst, and all Israel shall hear *of*
it and fear. Lev. 20:2, 27
22"And if a man has committed
a sin [r]worthy of death, and he is
put to death, and you hang him on
a tree, Deut. 22:26; Matt. 26:66
23 his corpse shall not hang all
night on the tree, but you shall
surely bury him on the same day
(for he who is hanged is accursed
of God), so that you do not defile
your land which the LORD your
God gives you as an inheritance.

CHAPTER 22

"YOU shall not see your countryman's ox or his sheep straying
away, and pay no attention to
them; you shall certainly bring
them back to your countryman.
2"And if your countryman is
not near you, or if you do not
know him, then you shall bring it
home to your house, and it shall
remain with you until your countryman looks for it; then you shall
restore it to him.
3"And thus you shall do with
his donkey, and you shall do the
same with his garment, and you
shall do likewise with anything
lost by your countryman, which
he has lost and you have found.
You are not allowed to [t]neglect
them. *hide yourself*
4"You shall not see your countryman's donkey or his ox fallen
down on the way, and pay no attention to them; you shall certainly help him to raise *them* up.
5"A woman shall not wear
man's clothing, nor shall a man
put on a woman's clothing; for
whoever does these things is an
abomination to the LORD your
God.
6"If you happen to come upon
a bird's nest along the way, in any
tree or on the ground, with young
ones or eggs, and the mother sitting on the young or on the eggs,
[r]you shall not take the mother with
the young; Lev. 22:28
7 you shall certainly let the
mother go, but the young you may
take for yourself, in order that it
may be well with you, and that
you may prolong your days.
8"When you build a new
house, you shall make a parapet
for your roof, that you may not
bring bloodguilt on your house if
anyone falls from it.
9"You shall not sow your vineyard with two kinds of seed, lest
all the produce of the seed which
you have sown, and the increase
of the vineyard become defiled.
10"You shall not plow with an
ox and a donkey together.
11"You shall not wear a material
mixed of wool and linen together.

12"You[r] shall make yourself tassels on the four corners of your
garment with which you cover
yourself. Num. 15:37-41; Matt. 23:5
13"If[r] any man takes a wife and
goes in to her and *then* [t]turns
against her, Gen. 29:21 • *hates her*
14 and charges her with shameful deeds and publicly defames
her, and says, 'I took this woman,
but when I came near her, I did
not find her a virgin,'
15 then the girl's father and her
mother shall take and bring out
the *evidence* of the girl's virginity
to the elders of the city at the
gate.
16"And the girl's father shall say
to the elders, 'I gave my daughter
to this man for a wife, but he
[t]turned against her; *hated her*
17 and behold, he has charged
her with shameful deeds, saying,
"I did not find your daughter a virgin." But [t]this is the *evidence* of
my daughter's virginity.' And they
shall spread the garment before
the elders of the city. *these are*
18"So [r]the elders of that city
shall take the man and chastise
him, Ex. 18:21; Deut. 1:9-18
19 and they shall fine him a hundred *shekels* of silver and give it
to the girl's father, because he
publicly defamed a virgin of Israel. And she shall remain his
wife; he cannot [t]divorce her all his
days. *send her away*
20"But if this charge is true, that
the girl was not found a virgin,
21 then they shall bring out the
girl to the doorway of her father's
house, and the men of her city
shall stone her to death because
she has committed an act of folly
in Israel, by playing the harlot in
her father's house; thus you shall
purge the evil from among you.
22"If[r] a man is found lying with a
married woman, then both of
them shall die, the man who lay
with the woman, and the woman;
thus you shall purge the evil from
Israel. 1 Cor. 6:9; Heb. 13:4
23"If[r] there is a girl who is a virgin engaged to a man, and *another* man finds her in the city and
lies with her, Matt. 1:18, 19
24 then you shall bring them
both out to the gate of that city
and you shall stone them to death;
the girl, because she did not cry
out in the city, and the man, because he has violated his neighbor's wife. Thus you shall purge
the evil from among you.
25"But if in the field the man
finds the girl who is engaged, and
the man forces her and lies with
her, then only the man who lies
with her shall die.
26"But you shall do nothing to
the girl; there is no sin in the girl
worthy of death, for just as a man
rises against his neighbor and
murders him, so is this case.
27"When he found her in the
field, the engaged girl cried out,
but there was no one to save her.
28"If[r] a man finds a girl who is a
virgin, who is not engaged, and
seizes her and lies with her and
they are discovered, Ex. 22:16
29 then the man who lay with
her shall give to the girl's father
fifty *shekels* of silver, and she
shall become his wife because he
has violated her; he cannot divorce her all his days.

30"A man shall not take his father's wife so that he shall not uncover his father's skirt.

CHAPTER 23

"NO one who is emasculated, or has his male organ cut off, shall enter the assembly of the LORD.

2"No one of illegitimate birth shall enter the assembly of the LORD; none of his *descendants,* even to the tenth generation, shall enter the assembly of the LORD.

3"No[r] Ammonite or Moabite shall enter the assembly of the LORD; none of their *descendants,* even to the tenth generation, shall ever enter the assembly of the LORD, Neh. 13:1, 2

4 [r]because they did not meet you with [t]food and water on the way when you came out of Egypt, and because they hired against you Balaam the son of Beor from Pethor of Mesopotamia, to curse you. Neh. 13:2 • *bread*

5"Nevertheless, the LORD your God was not willing to listen to Balaam, but the LORD your God [r]turned the curse into a blessing for you because the LORD your God loves you. Prov. 26:2

6"You[r] shall never seek their peace or their prosperity all your days. Ezra 9:12

7"You shall not detest an Edomite, for [r]he is your brother; you shall not detest an Egyptian, because you were an alien in his land. Gen. 25:24-26; Obad. 10, 12

8"The sons of the third generation who are born to them may enter the assembly of the LORD.

9"When you go out as [a]an army against your enemies, then you shall keep yourself from every evil thing. *a camp*

10"If[r] there is among you any man who is unclean because of a nocturnal emission, then he must go outside the camp; he may not reenter the camp. Lev. 15:16

11"But it shall be when evening approaches, he shall bathe himself with water, and at sundown he may reenter the camp.

12"You shall also have a place outside the camp and go out there,

13 and you shall have a [t]spade among your tools, and it shall be when you sit down outside, you shall dig with it and shall turn to cover up your excrement. *peg*

14"Since the LORD your God walks in the midst of your camp to deliver you and to [t]defeat your enemies before you, therefore your camp must be holy; and He must not see anything indecent among you [t]lest He turn away from you. *give* • *and*

15"You shall not hand over to his master a slave who has escaped from his master to you.

16"He shall live with you in your midst, in the place which he shall choose in one of your [t]towns where it pleases him; [r]you shall not mistreat him. *gates* • Ex. 22:21

17"None[r] of the daughters of Israel shall be a cult prostitute, nor shall any of the sons of Israel be a cult prostitute. Lev. 19:29

18"You shall not bring the hire of a harlot or the wages of a [15]dog into the house of the LORD your

[15]I.e., male prostitute, sodomite

God for any votive offering, for
both of these are an abomination
to the LORD your God.
19 "You shall not charge interest
to your countrymen: interest on
money, food, *or* anything that
may be loaned at interest.
20 "You may charge interest to a
foreigner, but to your [t]countryman
you shall not charge interest, so
that the LORD your God may bless
you in all that you undertake in
the land which you are about to
enter to possess. *brother*
21 "When you make a vow to the
LORD your God, you shall not delay to pay it, for it would be sin in
you, [t]and the LORD your God will
surely require it of you. *for*
22 "However, if you refrain from
vowing, it would not be sin in you.
23 "You shall be careful to perform what goes out from your
lips, just as you have voluntarily
vowed to the LORD your God,
what you have promised.
24 "When you enter your neighbor's vineyard, then you may eat
grapes until you are fully satisfied,
but you shall not put any in your
[a]basket. *vessel*
25 "When[r] you enter your neighbor's standing grain, then you
may pluck the heads with your
hand, but you shall not wield a
sickle in your neighbor's standing
grain. Matt. 12:1; Mark 2:23

CHAPTER 24

"WHEN a man takes a wife and
marries her, and it happens [t]that
she finds no favor in his eyes because he has found some inde-
cency in her, and [r]he writes her a
certificate of divorce and puts *it* in
her hand and sends her out from
his house, *if* • Matt. 5:31
2 and she leaves his house and
goes and becomes another man's
wife,
3 and if the latter husband
turns against her and writes her a
certificate of divorce and puts *it* in
her hand and sends her out of his
house, or if the latter husband dies
who took her to be his wife,
4 *then* her former husband
who sent her away is not allowed
to take her again to be his wife,
since she has been defiled; for that
is an abomination before the
LORD, and you shall not bring sin
on the land which the LORD your
God gives you as an inheritance.
5 "When a man takes a new
wife, he shall not go out with the
army, nor be charged with any
duty; he shall be free at home one
year and shall give happiness to
his wife whom he has taken.
6 "No one shall take a handmill
or an upper millstone in pledge,
for he would be taking a life in
pledge.
7 "If a man is caught kidnap-
ping any of his countrymen of the
sons of Israel, and he deals with
him violently, or sells him, then
that thief shall die; so you shall
purge the evil from among you.
8 "Be careful against [t]an infection of leprosy, that you diligently
observe and do according to all
that the Levitical priests shall
teach you; as I have commanded
them, so you shall be careful to
do. *a mark or stroke*
9 "Remember what the LORD

your God did to Miriam on the
way as you came out of Egypt.
10"When[r] you make your neighbor a loan of any sort, you shall
not enter his house to take his
pledge. Ex. 22:26, 27
11"You shall remain outside,
and the man to whom you make
the loan shall bring the pledge out
to you.
12"And if he is a poor man, you
shall not sleep with his pledge.
13"When the sun goes down you
shall surely return the pledge to
him, that he may sleep in his cloak
and bless you; and[r] it will be righteousness for you before the LORD
your God. Ps. 106:31; Dan. 4:27
14"You shall not oppress a hired
servant *who is* poor and needy,
whether *he is* one of your countrymen or one of your aliens who is
in your land in your towns.
15"You[r] shall give him his wages
on his day before the sun sets, for
he is poor and sets his[t] heart on it;
so that he may not cry against you
to the LORD and it become sin in
you. Jer. 22:13 • *soul*
16"Fathers[r] shall not be put to
death[a] for *their* sons, nor shall sons
be put to death[a] for *their* fathers;
everyone shall be put to death for
his own sin. 2 Chr. 25:4 • *with*
17"You[r] shall not pervert the justice[t] due an alien *or* [16]an orphan,
nor take a widow's garment in
pledge. Deut. 1:17; 10:17 • *of*
18"But you shall remember that
you were a slave in Egypt, and
that the LORD your God redeemed
you from there; therefore I am
commanding you to do this thing.
19"When[r] you reap your harvest
in your field and have forgotten a
sheaf in the field, you shall not go
back to get it; it shall be for the
alien, for the orphan, and for the
widow, in order that the LORD
your God may bless you in all the
work of your hands. Lev. 19:9, 10
20"When[r] you beat your olive
tree, you shall not go over the
boughs[t] again; it shall be for the
alien, for the orphan, and for the
widow. Lev. 19:10 • *after yourself*
21"When you gather the grapes
of your vineyard, you shall not[t] go
over it again; it shall be for the
alien, for the orphan, and for the
widow. *glean it after yourself*
22"And you shall remember that
you were a slave in the land of
Egypt; therefore I am commanding you to do this thing.

CHAPTER 25

"IF there is a dispute between
men and they go to[t] court, and the
judges decide their case, and they
justify the righteous and condemn
the wicked, *the judgment*
2 then it shall be if the wicked
man deserves to be beaten, the
judge shall then make him lie
down and be beaten in his presence with the number of stripes
according to his[a] guilt. *wickedness*
3"He[r] may beat him forty times
but no more, lest he beat him with
many more stripes than these, and
your brother be[r] degraded in your
eyes. 2 Cor. 11:24 • Job 18:3
4"You[r] shall not muzzle the ox
while he is threshing. 1 Cor. 9:9
5"When brothers live together
and one of them dies and has no
son, the wife of the deceased shall
not be *married* outside *the family*

[16]Or, *the fatherless,* and so throughout this context

to a strange man. [r]Her husband's brother shall go in to her and take her to himself as wife and perform the duty of a husband's brother to her. Matt. 22:24; Mark 12:19

6 "And it shall be that the firstborn whom she bears shall [t]assume the name of his dead brother, that his name may not be blotted out from Israel. *stand on*

7 "But[r] if the man does not desire to take his brother's wife, then his brother's wife shall go up to the gate to the elders and say, 'My husband's brother refuses to establish a name for his brother in Israel; he is not willing to perform the duty of a husband's brother to me.' Ruth 4:5, 6

8 "Then the elders of his city shall summon him and speak to him. And *if* he persists and says, 'I do not desire to take her,'

9 then his brother's wife shall come to him in the sight of the elders, and pull his sandal off his foot and spit in his face; and she shall [t]declare, 'Thus it is done to the man who does not build up his brother's house.' *answer and say*

10 "And in Israel his name shall be called, 'The house of him whose sandal is removed.'

11 "If *two* men, a man and his [t]countryman, are struggling together, and the wife of one comes near to deliver her husband from the hand of the one who is striking him, and puts out her hand and seizes his genitals, *brother*

12 then you shall cut off her hand; you shall not show pity.

13 "You shall not have in your bag [t]differing weights, a large and a small. *a stone and a stone*

14 "You shall not have in your house [t]differing measures, a large and a small. *an ephah and an ephah*

15 "You shall have a full and just weight; you shall have a full and just measure, that your days may be prolonged in the land which the LORD your God gives you.

16 "For [r]everyone who does these things, everyone who acts unjustly is an abomination to the LORD your God. Prov. 11:1

17 "Remember[r] what Amalek did to you along the way when you came out from Egypt, Ex. 17:8-16

18 how he met you along the way and attacked among you all the stragglers at your rear when you were faint and weary; and he did not [17]fear God.

19 "Therefore it shall come about when the LORD your God has given you rest from all your surrounding enemies, in the land which the LORD your God gives you as an inheritance to [t]possess, you shall blot out the memory of Amalek from under heaven; you must not forget. *possess it*

CHAPTER 26

"THEN it shall be, when you enter the land which the LORD your God gives you as an inheritance, and you possess it and live in it,

2 that you shall take some of the first of all the produce of the ground which you shall bring in from your land that the LORD your God gives you, and you shall put *it* in a basket and [r]go to the place where the LORD your God chooses to establish His name. Deut. 12:5

3 "And you shall go to the priest who is in office at that time, and

[17]Or, *reverence*

say to him, 'I declare this day to
the LORD my God that I have entered the land which the LORD
swore to our fathers to give us.'
4 "Then the priest shall take the
basket from your hand and set it
down before the altar of the LORD
your God.
5 "And you shall answer and
say before the LORD your God,
'My father was a wandering Aramean, and he went down to Egypt
and sojourned there, few in number; but there he became a great,
mighty and populous nation.
6 'And the Egyptians treated us
harshly and afflicted us, and imposed hard labor on us.
7 'Then [r]we cried to the LORD,
the God of our fathers, and the
LORD heard our voice and saw our
affliction and our toil and our oppression; Ex. 2:23-25; 3:9
8 [r]and the LORD brought us out
of Egypt with a mighty hand and
an outstretched arm and with
great terror and with signs and
wonders; Deut. 4:34; 34:11, 12
9 and He has brought us to this
place, and has given us this land, a
land flowing with milk and honey.
10 'And now behold, I have
brought the first of the produce of
the ground [r]which Thou, O LORD
hast given me.' And you shall set
it down before the LORD your
God, and worship before the LORD
your God; Deut. 8:18; Prov. 10:22
11 and you and [r]the Levite and
the alien who is among you shall
rejoice in all the good which the
LORD your God has given you and
your household. Deut. 12:12
12 "When you have finished paying all the tithe of your increase in
the third year, the year of tithing,
then you shall give it to the Levite,
to the stranger, to the orphan and
to the widow, that they may eat in
your towns, and be satisfied.
13 "And you shall say before the
LORD your God, 'I have removed
the sacred *portion* from *my* house,
and also have given it to the Levite and the alien, the [a]orphan and
the widow, according to all Thy
commandments which Thou hast
commanded me; I have not transgressed or forgotten any of Thy
commandments. *fatherless*
14 'I have not eaten of it [t]while
mourning, nor have I removed
any of it while I was unclean, nor
offered any of it to the dead. I
have listened to the voice of the
LORD my God; I have done according to all that Thou hast commanded me. *while in my*
15 'Look down from Thy holy
habitation, from heaven, and bless
Thy people Israel, and the ground
which Thou hast given us, a land
flowing with milk and honey, as
Thou didst swear to our fathers.'
16 "This day the LORD your God
commands you to do these statutes and ordinances. You shall
therefore be careful to do them
[r]with all your heart and with all
your soul. Deut. 4:29
17 "You[r] have today declared the
LORD to be your God, and [t]that you
would walk in His ways and keep
His statutes, His commandments
and His ordinances, and listen to
His voice. Ps. 48:14 • *to walk in*
18 "And the LORD has today declared you to be His people, a
treasured possession, as He prom-

ised you, and that you should
keep all His commandments;
19 and that He shall set you
high above all nations which He
has made, for praise, fame, and
honor; and that you shall be a consecrated people to the LORD your
God, as He has spoken."

CHAPTER 27

THEN Moses and the elders of Israel charged the people, saying,
"Keep all the commandments
which I command you today.
2"So[r] it shall be on the day
when you shall cross the Jordan
to the land which the LORD your
God gives you, that you shall set
up for yourself large stones, and
coat them with lime *Josh. 8:30-32*
3 and write on them all the
words of this law, when you cross
over, in order that you may enter
the land which the LORD your God
gives you, [r]'a land flowing with
milk and honey, as the LORD, the
God of your fathers, [t]promised
you. *Deut. 26:9 • spoke to*
4"So it shall be when you cross
the Jordan, you shall set up on
Mount Ebal, these stones, [t]as I am
commanding you today, and you
shall coat them with lime. *which*
5"Moreover, you shall build
there an altar to the LORD your
God, an altar of stones; you shall
not wield an iron *tool* on them.
6"You shall build the altar of
the LORD your God of [t]uncut
stones; and you shall offer on it
burnt offerings to the LORD your
God; *whole*
7 and you shall sacrifice peace
offerings and eat there, and you
shall [r]rejoice before the LORD your
God. *Deut. 26:11*
8"And you shall write on the
stones all the words of this law
very distinctly."
9 Then Moses and the Levitical
priests spoke to all Israel, saying,
"Be silent and listen, O Israel!
This day you have become a people for the LORD your God.
10"You shall therefore obey the
LORD your God, and do His commandments and His statutes
which I command you today."
11 Moses also charged the people on that day, saying,
12"When you cross the Jordan,
these shall stand on Mount Gerizim to bless the people: [r]Simeon,
Levi, Judah, Issachar, Joseph, and
Benjamin. *Josh. 8:33-35*
13"And for the curse, these shall
stand on Mount Ebal: Reuben,
Gad, Asher, Zebulun, Dan, and
Naphtali.
14"The Levites shall then answer and say to all the men of Israel with a loud voice,
15 'Cursed is the man who
makes [a]an idol or a molten image,
an abomination to the LORD, the
work of the hands of the craftsman, and sets *it* up in secret.' And
all the people shall answer and
say, 'Amen.' *a graven image*
16 'Cursed is he who dishonors
his father or mother.' And all the
people shall say, 'Amen.'
17 'Cursed is he who moves his
neighbor's boundary mark.' And
all the people shall say, 'Amen.'
18 'Cursed is he who misleads a
blind *person* on the road.' And all
the people shall say, 'Amen.'
19 'Cursed[r] is he who distorts the

justice due an alien, [a]orphan, and
widow.' And all the people shall
say, 'Amen.' Ex. 22:21 • *fatherless*
20 'Cursed is he who lies with
his father's wife, because he has
uncovered his father's skirt.' And
all the people shall say, 'Amen.'
21 'Cursed[r] is he who lies with
any animal.' And all the people
shall say, 'Amen.' Ex. 22:19
22 'Cursed is he who lies with
his sister, the daughter of his father or of his mother.' And all the
people shall say, 'Amen.'
23 'Cursed is he who lies with
his mother-in-law.' And all the
people shall say, 'Amen.'
24 'Cursed is he who strikes his
neighbor in secret.' And all the
people shall say, 'Amen.'
25 'Cursed[r] is he who accepts a
bribe to strike down an innocent
person.' And all the people shall
say, 'Amen.' Deut. 10:17
26 'Cursed[r] is he who does not
confirm the words of this law by
doing them.' And all the people
shall say, 'Amen.' Ps. 119:21

CHAPTER 28

"NOW it shall be, if you will diligently [t]obey the LORD your God,
being careful to do all His commandments which I command
you today, the LORD your God will
set you high above all the nations
of the earth. *listen to the voice of*
2"And all these blessings shall
come upon you and overtake you,
if you will [t]obey the LORD your
God. *listen to the voice of*
3"Blessed *shall* you *be* in the
city, and blessed *shall* you *be* [r]in
the [a]country. Gen. 39:5 • *field*
4"Blessed *shall be* the offspring
of your body and the produce of
your ground and the offspring of
your beasts, the increase of your
herd and the young of your flock.
5"Blessed *shall be* your basket
and your kneading bowl.
6"Blessed *shall* you *be* [r]when
you come in, and blessed *shall*
you *be* when you go out. Ps. 121:8
7"The LORD will cause your enemies who rise up against you to
be defeated before you; they shall
come out against you one way and
shall flee before you seven ways.
8"The LORD will command the
blessing upon you in your barns
and in [r]all that you put your hand
to, and He will bless you in the
land which the LORD your God
gives you. Deut. 15:10
9"The LORD will establish you
as a holy people to Himself, as He
swore to you, if you will keep the
commandments of the LORD your
God, and walk in His ways.
10"So all the peoples of the
earth shall see that [r]you are called
by the name of the LORD; and they
shall be afraid of you. 2 Chr. 7:14
11"And the LORD will make you
abound in prosperity, in the [t]off-
spring of your body and in the [t]off-
spring of your beast and in the
[t]produce of your ground, in the
land which the LORD swore to
your fathers to give you. *fruit*
12"The LORD will open for you
His good storehouse, the heavens,
to give rain to your land in its season and to bless all the work of
your hand; and [r]you shall lend to
many nations, but you shall not
borrow. Deut. 23:20
13"And [r]the LORD shall make you

the head and not the tail, and you
only shall be above, and you shall
not be underneath, if you will listen to the commandments of the
LORD your God, which I charge
you today, to [t]observe *them* carefully, Deut. 28:1, 44 • *keep and do*
14 and [r]do not turn aside from
any of the words which I command you today, to the right or to
the left, to go after other gods to
serve them. Deut. 5:32; Josh. 1:7
15 "But[r] it shall come about, if
you will not obey the LORD your
God, to observe to do all His commandments and His statutes with
which I charge you today, that all
these curses shall come upon you
and overtake you. Josh. 23:15
16 "Cursed *shall* you *be* in the
city, and cursed *shall* you *be* in
the [a]country. *field*
17 "Cursed *shall be* your basket
and your kneading bowl.
18 "Cursed *shall be* the offspring
of your body and the produce of
your ground, the increase of your
herd and the young of your flock.
19 "Cursed[r] *shall* you *be* when
you come in, and cursed *shall* you
be when you go out. Deut. 28:6
20 "The[r] LORD will send upon you
curses, confusion, and rebuke, in
all you undertake to do, until you
are destroyed and until you perish
quickly, on account of the evil of
your deeds, because you have forsaken Me. Deut. 28:8; Mal. 2:2
21 "The[r] LORD will make the pestilence cling to you until He has
consumed you from the land,
where you are entering to possess
it. Lev. 26:25; Num. 14:12
22 "The LORD will smite you with
consumption and with fever and
with inflammation and with fiery
heat and with [18]the sword and with
blight and with mildew, and they
shall pursue you until you perish.
23 "And [t]the heaven which is
over your head shall be bronze,
and the earth which is under you,
iron. *your*
24 "The LORD will make the rain
of your land powder and dust;
from heaven it shall come down
on you until you are destroyed.
25 "The LORD will cause you to
be [t]defeated before your enemies;
you shall go out one way against
them, but you shall flee seven
ways before them, and you shall
be *an example of* terror to all the
kingdoms of the earth. *smitten*
26 "And[r] your carcasses shall be
food to all birds of the sky and to
the beasts of the earth, and there
shall be no one to frighten *them*
away. Jer. 7:33; 16:4; 19:7; 34:20
27 "The[r] LORD will smite you with
the boils of Egypt and with tumors and with the scab and with
the itch, from which you cannot
be healed. Ex. 9:9; Deut. 7:15
28 "The LORD will smite you with
madness and with blindness and
with bewilderment of heart;
29 and you shall grope at noon,
as the blind man gropes in darkness, and you shall not prosper in
your ways; but you shall only be
oppressed and robbed continually,
with none to save you.
30 "You[r] shall betroth a wife, but
another man shall violate her; you
shall build a house, but you shall
not live in it; you shall plant a
vineyard, but you shall not [t]use its
fruit. Job 31:10 • *begin it*
31 "Your ox shall be slaughtered

[18]Another reading is *drought*

before your eyes, but you shall not
eat of it; your donkey shall be torn
away from you, and shall not be
restored to you; your sheep shall
be given to your enemies, and you
shall have none to save you.
32 "Your sons and your daughters shall be given to another people, while your eyes shall look on
and yearn for them continually;
but there shall be nothing [t]you can
do. *in the power of your hand*
33 "A[r] people whom you do not
know shall eat up the produce of
your ground and all your labors,
and you shall never be anything
but oppressed and crushed continually. Jer. 5:15, 17
34 "And you shall be driven mad
by the sight of what you see.
35 "The[r] LORD will strike you on
the knees and legs with sore boils,
from which you cannot be healed,
from the sole of your foot to the
crown of your head. Deut. 28:27
36 "The LORD will bring you and
your king, whom you shall set
over you, to a nation which neither you nor your fathers have
known, and there you shall serve
other gods, wood and stone.
37 "And [r]you shall become a horror, a proverb, and a taunt among
all the people where the LORD will
drive you. 1 Kin. 9:7, 8; Jer. 19:8
38 "You[r] shall bring out much
seed to the field but you shall
gather in little, for the locust shall
consume it. Is. 5:10; Mic. 6:15
39 "You[r] shall plant and cultivate
vineyards, but you shall neither
drink of the wine nor gather *the
grapes*, for the worm shall devour
them. Is. 5:10; 17:10, 11
40 "You shall have olive trees
throughout your territory but you
shall not anoint yourself with the
oil, for your olives shall drop off.
41 "You[r] shall [t]have sons and
daughters but they shall not be
yours, for they shall go into captivity. Deut. 28:32 • *beget*
42 "The[r] cricket shall possess all
your trees and the produce of
your ground. Deut. 28:38
43 "The[r] alien who is among you
shall rise above you higher and
higher, but you shall go down lower and lower. Deut. 28:13
44 "He shall lend to you, but you
shall not lend to him; he shall be
the head, and you shall be the tail.
45 "So all these curses shall
come on you and pursue you and
overtake you until you are destroyed, because you would not
[t]obey the LORD your God by keeping His commandments and His
statutes which He commanded
you. *listen to the voice of*
46 "And they shall become a sign
and a wonder on you and your [t]de-
scendants forever. *seed*
47 "Because[r] you did not serve
the LORD your God with joy and a
glad heart, for the abundance of
all things; Neh. 9:35-37
48 therefore you shall serve
your enemies whom the LORD
shall send against you, [r]in hunger,
in thirst, in nakedness, and in the
lack of all things; and He will put
an iron yoke on your neck until He
has destroyed you. Lam. 4:4-6
49 "The LORD will bring a nation
against you from afar, from the
end of the earth, as the eagle
swoops down, a nation whose language you shall not understand,
50 a nation of fierce counte-

nance who shall [r]have no respect
for the old, nor show favor to the
young. Is. 47:6
51 "Moreover, it shall eat the [t]off-
spring of your herd and the produce of your ground until you are
destroyed, who also leaves you no
grain, new wine, or oil, nor the increase of your herd or the young
of your flock until they have
caused you to perish. *fruit*
52 "And [r]it shall besiege you in all
your [t]towns until your high and
fortified walls in which you
trusted come down throughout
your land, and it shall besiege you
in all your [t]towns throughout your
land which the LORD your God has
given you. Jer. 10:17, 18 • *gates*
53 "Then you shall eat the [t]off-
spring of your own body, the flesh
of your sons and of your daughters whom the LORD your God has
given you, during the siege and
the distress by which your enemy
shall [a]oppress you. *fruit • distress*
54 "The man who is [t]refined and
very delicate among you shall be
hostile toward his brother and
toward the wife [t]he cherishes and
toward the rest of his children
who remain, *tender • of his bosom*
55 so that he will not give *even*
one of them any of the flesh of his
children which he shall eat, since
he has nothing *else* left, during the
siege and the distress by which
your enemy shall [a]oppress you in
all your [t]towns. *distress • gates*
56 "The [t]refined and delicate
woman among you, who would
not venture to set the sole of her
foot on the ground for delicate-
ness and [t]refinement, shall be hostile toward the husband she cherishes and toward her son and
daughter, *tender • tenderness*
57 and toward her afterbirth
which issues from between her
legs and toward her children
whom she bears; for she shall eat
them secretly for lack of anything
else, during the siege and the distress by which your enemy shall
oppress you in your towns.
58 "If you are not careful to observe all the words of this law
which are written in this book, to
fear this honored and awesome
name, the LORD your God,
59 then the LORD will bring
extraordinary plagues on you and
your descendants, even [t]severe
and lasting plagues, and miserable
and chronic sicknesses. *great*
60 "And [r]He will bring back on
you all the diseases of Egypt of
which you were afraid, and they
shall cling to you. Deut. 28:27
61 "Also every sickness and every plague which, not written in
the book of this law, the LORD will
bring on you [r]until you are destroyed. Deut. 4:25, 26
62 "Then you shall be left few in
number, whereas you were as the
stars of heaven for multitude, because you did not [t]obey the LORD
your God. *listen to the voice of*
63 "And it shall come about that
as the LORD [r]delighted over you to
prosper you, and multiply you, so
the LORD will [r]delight over you to
make you perish and destroy you;
and you shall be torn from the
land where you are entering to
possess it. Jer. 32:41 • Prov. 1:26
64 "Moreover, the LORD will
[r]scatter you among all peoples,
from one end of the earth to the

other end of the earth; and there
you shall serve other gods, wood
and stone, which you or your fathers have not known. Lev. 26:33
65"And [r]among those nations
you shall find no rest, and there
shall be no resting place for the
sole of your foot; but there [r]the
LORD will give you a trembling
heart, failing of eyes, and despair
of soul. Lam. 1:3 • Lev. 26:36
66"So your life shall hang in
doubt before you; and you shall be
in dread night and day, and shall
have no assurance of your life.
67"In[r] the morning you shall say,
'Would that it were evening!' And
at evening you shall say, 'Would
that it were morning!' because of
the dread of your heart which you
dread, and for the sight of your
eyes which you shall see. Job 7:4
68"And the LORD will bring you
back to Egypt in ships, by the way
about which I spoke to you, 'You
will never see it again!' And there
you shall offer yourselves for sale
to your enemies as male and female slaves, but there will be no
buyer."

CHAPTER 29

THESE are the words of the covenant which the LORD com-
manded Moses to make with the
sons of Israel in the land of Moab,
besides the covenant which He
had made with them at Horeb.
2 And Moses summoned all Israel and said to them, "You have
seen all that the LORD did before
your eyes in the land of Egypt to
Pharaoh and all his servants and
all his land;
3 [r]the great trials which your
eyes have seen, those great signs
and wonders. Deut. 4:34; 7:19
4"Yet to this day the LORD has
not given you a heart to know, nor
eyes to see, nor ears to hear.
5"And I have led you forty
years in the wilderness; [r]your
clothes have not worn out on you,
and your sandal has not worn out
on your foot. Deut. 8:4
6"You[r] have not eaten bread,
nor have you drunk wine or
strong drink, in order that you
might know that I am the LORD
your God. Deut. 8:3
7"When you [t]reached this
place, Sihon the king of Heshbon
and Og the king of Bashan came
out to meet us for battle, but we
[t]defeated them; *came to • smote*
8 and we took their land and
gave it as an inheritance to the
Reubenites, the Gadites, and the
half-tribe of the Manassites.
9"So keep the words of this
covenant to do them, that you
may prosper in all that you do.
10"You stand today, all of you,
before the LORD your God: your
chiefs, your tribes, your elders
and your officers, *even* all the men
of Israel,
11 your little ones, your wives,
and the alien who is within your
camps, from [r]the one who chops
your wood to the one who draws
your water, Josh. 9:21, 23, 27
12 that you may enter into the
covenant with the LORD your God,
and into His oath which the LORD
your God is making with you today,
13 in order that He may establish you today as His people and

that ʳHe may be your God, just as
He spoke to you and as He swore
to your fathers, to Abraham,
Isaac, and Jacob. Gen. 17:7
14 "Now not with you alone am I
ʳmaking this covenant and this
oath, Jer. 31:31; Heb. 8:7, 8
15 ʳbut both with those who
stand here with us today in the
presence of the LORD our God and
with those who are not with us
here today Acts 2:39
16 (for you know how we lived
in the land of Egypt, and how we
came through the midst of the nations through which you passed.
17 "Moreover, you have seen
their abominations and their idols
of wood, stone, silver, and gold,
which *they had* with them);
18 ʳlest there shall be among you
a man or woman, or family or
tribe, whose heart turns away today from the LORD our God, to go
and serve the gods of those nations; lest there shall be among
you a root bearing poisonous fruit
and wormwood. Deut. 13:6
19 "And it shall be when he hears
the words of this curse, that he
will boast, saying, 'I have peace
though I walk in the stubbornness
of my heart in order to destroy the
watered *land* with the dry.'
20 "The LORD shall never be willing to forgive him, but rather the
anger of the LORD and His jealousy will ᵗburn against that man,
and every curse which is written
in this book will rest on him, and
the LORD will blot out his name
from under heaven. *smoke*
21 "Then the LORD will single
him out for adversity from all the
tribes of Israel, according to all
the curses of the covenant which
are written in this book of the law.
22 "Now the generation to come,
your sons who rise up after you
and the foreigner who comes from
a distant land, when they see the
plagues of the land and the diseases with which the LORD has ᵗaf-
flicted it, will say, *made it sick*
23 'All its land is brimstone and
salt, a burning waste, unsown and
unproductive, and no grass grows
in it, like the overthrow of Sodom
and Gomorrah, Admah and Zeboiim, which the LORD overthrew in
His anger and in His wrath.'
24 "And all the nations shall say,
'Why ʳhas the LORD done thus to
this land? Why this great ᵗoutburst
of anger?' Jer. 22:8 • *heat*
25 "Then *men* shall say, 'Because ʳ
they forsook the covenant of the
LORD, the God of their fathers,
which He made with them when
He brought them out of the land
of Egypt. 2 Kin. 17:9-23
26 'And they went and served
other gods and worshiped them,
gods whom they have not known
and whom He had not ᵗallotted to
them. *portioned*
27 'Therefore, the anger of the
LORD burned against that land, ʳto
bring upon it every curse which is
written in this book; Dan. 9:11
28 and ʳthe LORD uprooted them
from their land in anger and in
fury and in great wrath, and cast
them into another land, as *it is*
this day.' 2 Chr. 7:20; Ps. 52:5
29 "The secret things belong to
the LORD our God, but the things
revealed belong to us and to our
sons forever, that we may observe
all the words of this law.

CHAPTER 30

"SO it shall be when all of these
things have come upon you, the
blessing and the curse which I
have set before you, and you [t]call
them to mind in all nations where
the LORD your God has banished
you, *cause them to return to your heart*
2 and you return to the LORD
your God and [t]obey Him with all
your heart and soul according to
all that I command you today, you
and your sons, *listen to His voice*
3 then the LORD your God will
restore [t]you from captivity, and
have compassion on you, and will
gather you again from all the peoples where the LORD your God has
scattered you. *your captivity*
4 "If your outcasts are at the
ends of the [t]earth, from there the
LORD your God will gather you,
and from there He will [t]bring you
back. *sky • take you*
5 "And [r]the LORD your God will
bring you into the land which your
fathers possessed, and you shall
possess it; and He will prosper
you and multiply you more than
your fathers. Jer. 29:14; 30:3
6 "Moreover the LORD your God
will circumcise your heart and the
heart of your [t]descendants, to love
the LORD your God with all your
heart and with all your soul, in order that you may live. *seed*
7 "And the LORD your God will
[t]inflict all these curses on your enemies and on those who hate you,
who persecuted you. *put*
8 "And you shall again [t]obey the
LORD, and observe all His commandments which I command
you today. *listen to the voice of*
9 "Then the LORD your God will
prosper you abundantly in all the
work of your hand, in the [t]off-
spring of your [t]body and in the [t]off-
spring of your cattle and in the
[t]produce of your ground, for the
LORD will again rejoice over you
for good, just as He rejoiced over
your fathers; *fruit • womb*
10 [a]if you obey the LORD your
God to keep His commandments
and His statutes which are written
in this book of the law, if you turn
to the LORD your God with all
your heart and soul. *for you will*
11 "For this commandment
which I command you today is not
too difficult for you, nor is it [t]out of
reach. *far off*
12 "It is not in heaven, [t]that you
should say, 'Who[r] will go up to
heaven for us to get it for us and
make us hear it, that we may observe it?' *to say* • Rom. 10:6-8
13 "Nor is it beyond the sea, [t]that
you should say, 'Who will cross
the sea for us to get it for us and
make us hear it, that we may observe it?' *to say*
14 "But the word is very near
you, in your mouth and in your
heart, that you may observe it.
15 "See, I have set before you today life and [t]prosperity, and death
and [t]adversity; *good • evil*
16 in that I command you today
[r]to love the LORD your God, to
walk in His ways and to keep His
commandments and His statutes
and His judgments, that you [r]may
live and multiply, and that the
LORD your God may bless you in
the land where you are entering to
possess it. Deut. 6:5 • Deut. 4:1
17 "But if your heart turns away

and you will not obey, but are
drawn away and worship other
gods and serve them,
18 I declare to you today that
you shall surely perish. You shall
not prolong *your* days in the land
where you are crossing the Jordan
to enter [t]and possess it. *to*
19 "I call heaven and earth to
witness against you today, that I
have set before you life and death,
the blessing and the curse. So
choose life in order that you may
live, you and your descendants,
20 by loving the LORD your God,
by obeying His voice, and by holding fast to Him; for [t]this is your life
and the length of your days, [t]that
you may live in the land which the
LORD swore to your fathers, to
Abraham, Isaac, and Jacob, to
give them." *that • to dwell*

CHAPTER 31

SO Moses went and spoke these
words to all Israel.
2 And he said to them, "I am [r]a
hundred and twenty years old today; [r]I am no longer able to come
and go, and the LORD has said to
me, 'You shall not cross this Jordan.' Deut. 34:7 • Num. 27:17
3 "It [r]is the LORD your God who
will cross ahead of you; He will
destroy these nations before you,
and you shall dispossess them.
[r]Joshua is the one who will cross
ahead of you, just as the LORD has
spoken. Deut. 9:3 • Num. 27:18
4 "And the LORD will do to them
just as He did to Sihon and Og,
the kings of the Amorites, and to
their land, when He destroyed
them.
5 "And [r]the LORD will deliver
them up before you, and you shall
do to them according to all the
commandments which I have
commanded you. Deut. 7:2
6 "Be strong and courageous,
do not be afraid or tremble at
them, for the LORD your God is
the one who goes with you. He
will not fail you or forsake you."
7 Then Moses called to Joshua
and said to him in the sight of all
Israel, "Be [r]strong and courageous,
for you shall go with this people
into the land which the LORD has
sworn to their fathers to give
them, and you shall give it to them
as an inheritance. Deut. 1:38
8 "And [r]the LORD is the one who
goes ahead of you; He will be with
you. He will not fail you or forsake you. Do not fear, or be dismayed." Ex. 13:21; 33:14
9 So Moses wrote this law and
gave it to the priests, the sons of
Levi [r]who carried the ark of the
covenant of the LORD, and to all
the elders of Israel. Josh. 3:3
10 Then Moses commanded
them, saying, "At the end of *every*
seven years, at the time of the
year of remission of debts, at the
[r]Feast of Booths, Lev. 23:34
11 when all Israel comes to appear before the LORD your God at
the place which He will choose,
you shall read this law in front of
all Israel in their hearing.
12 "Assemble the people, the
men and the women and children
and [t]the alien who is in your town,
in order that they may hear and
learn and fear the LORD your God,
and be careful to observe all the
words of this law. *your alien*

13 "And their children, who have not known, will hear and learn to fear the LORD your God, as long as you live on the land[t] which you are about to cross the Jordan to [t]possess." *where · possess it*

14 Then the LORD said to Moses, "Behold, [t]the time for you to die is near; call Joshua, and present yourselves at the tent of meeting, that I may commission him." So Moses and Joshua went and presented themselves at the tent of meeting. *your days to die are*

15 [r]And the LORD appeared in the tent in a pillar of cloud, and the pillar of cloud stood at the doorway of the tent. Ex. 33:9

16 And the LORD said to Moses, "Behold, [r]you are about to lie down with your fathers; and this people will arise and play the harlot with the strange gods of the land, into the midst of which they are going, and will forsake Me and break My covenant which I have made with them. Gen. 15:15

17 "Then[r] My anger will be kindled against them in that day, and I will forsake them and hide My face from them, and they shall be consumed, and many evils and troubles shall come upon them; so that they will say in that day, 'Is it not because our God is not among us that these evils have come upon us?' Judg. 2:14; 6:13

18 "But I will surely hide My face in that day because of all the evil which they will do, for they will turn to other gods.

19 "Now therefore, write this song for yourselves, and teach it to the sons of Israel; put it [t]on their lips, in order that this song may be a witness for Me against the sons of Israel. *in their mouths*

20 "For when I bring them into the land flowing with milk and honey, which I swore to their fathers, and they have eaten and are satisfied and become [t]prosperous, then they will turn to other gods and serve them, and spurn Me and break My covenant. *fat*

21 "Then it shall come about, when many evils and troubles have come upon them, that this song will testify before them as a witness (for it shall not be forgotten from the lips of their descendants); for I know their intent which they are [t]developing today, before I have brought them into the land which I swore." *making*

22 [r]So Moses wrote this song the same day, and taught it to the sons of Israel. Deut. 31:19

23 Then He commissioned Joshua the son of Nun, and said, "Be strong and courageous, for you shall bring the sons of Israel into the land which I swore to them, and I will be with you."

24 And it came about, when Moses finished writing the words of this law in a book until they were complete,

25 that Moses commanded the Levites who carried the ark of the covenant of the LORD, saying,

26 "Take this book of the law and place it beside the ark of the covenant of the LORD your God, that it may [t]remain there as a witness against you. *be*

27 "For I know your rebellion and your stubbornness; behold, while I am still alive with you today, you have been rebellious

against the LORD; how much more, then, after my death?

28 "Assemble to me all the elders of your tribes and your officers, that I may speak these words in their hearing and [r]call the heavens and the earth to witness against them. Deut. 4:26; 30:19; 32:1

29 "For I know that after my death you will [r]act corruptly and turn from the way which I have commanded you; and evil will befall you in the latter days, for you will do that which is evil in the sight of the LORD, provoking Him to anger with the work of your hands." Judg. 2:19

30 Then Moses spoke in the hearing of all the assembly of Israel the words of this song, until they were complete:

CHAPTER 32

"GIVE ear, O heavens, and let me speak;
And let the earth hear the words of my mouth.
2 "Let[r] my teaching drop as the rain,
My speech distill as the dew,
As the droplets on the fresh grass
And as the showers on the herb. Is. 55:10, 11
3 "For[r] I proclaim the name of the LORD;
Ascribe greatness to our God! Ex. 33:19
4 "The Rock! His work is perfect,
For all His ways are just;
A God of faithfulness and without injustice,
Righteous and upright is He.
5 "They have acted corruptly toward Him,
They are not His children, because of their defect;
But are a perverse and crooked generation.
6 "Do you thus [r]repay the LORD,
O foolish and unwise people?
Is not He your Father who has bought you?
He has made you and established you. Ps. 116:12
7 "Remember the days of old,
Consider the years of all generations.
Ask[r] your father, and he will inform you,
Your elders, and they will tell you. Ex. 12:26; Ps. 78:5-8
8 "When the Most High gave the nations their inheritance,
When He separated the sons of [a]man,
He set the boundaries of the peoples
According to the number of the sons of Israel. *Adam*
9 "For[r] the LORD's portion is His people;
Jacob is the allotment of His inheritance. 1 Sam. 10:1
10 "He found him in a desert land,
And in the howling waste of a wilderness;
He encircled him, He cared for him,
He guarded him as [r]the pupil of His eye. Ps. 17:8
11 "Like an eagle that stirs up its nest,
That hovers over its young,
[r]He spread His wings and caught them,

He carried them on His pinions. Ps. 18:10-18
12 "The LORD alone guided him,
ʳAnd there was no foreign god with him. Is. 43:12
13 "He made him ride on the high places of the earth,
And he ate the produce of the field;
And He made him suck honey from the rock,
And oil from the flinty rock,
14 Curds of cows, and milk of the flock,
With fat of lambs,
And rams, the breed of Bashan, and goats,
ʳWith the finest of the wheat—
And of the blood of grapes you drank wine. Ps. 81:16

15 "Butʳ [19]Jeshurun grew fat and kicked—
You are grown fat, thick, and sleek—
Then he forsook God who made him,
And scorned the Rock of his salvation. Deut. 31:20
16 "They made Him jealous with strange *gods;*
With abominations they provoked Him to anger.
17 "Theyʳ sacrificed to demons who were not God,
To gods whom they have not known,
New *gods* who came lately,
Whom your fathers did not dread. 1 Cor. 10:20
18 "You neglected the Rock who begot you,
ʳAnd forgot the God who gave you birth. Ps. 106:21

[19]Le., Israel

19 "Andʳ the LORD saw *this,* and spurned *them*
Because of the provocation of His sons and daughters. Ps. 106:40
20 "Then He said, 'I will hide My face from them,
ʳI will see what their end *shall be;*
For they are a perverse generation,
Sons in whom is no faithfulness. Deut. 31:29
21 'They have made Me jealous with *what* is not God;
They have provoked Me to anger with their idols.
So I will make them jealous with *those who* are not a people;
I will provoke them to anger with a foolish nation,
22 For a fire is kindled in My anger,
And burns to the lowest part of Sheol,
And consumes the earth with its yield,
And sets on fire the foundations of the mountains.

23 'I will heap misfortunes on them;
ʳI will use My arrows on them. Ps. 18:14; 45:5
24 '*They shall be* wasted by famine, and consumed by plague
And bitter destruction;
And the teeth of beasts I will send upon them,
With the venom of crawling things of the dust.
25 'Outside the sword shall bereave,

And inside terror—
[r]Both young man and virgin,
The nursling with the man of
gray hair. 2 Chr. 36:17
26 'I would have said, "I will cut
them to pieces,
I will remove the memory of
them from men,"
27 Had I not feared the provocation by the enemy,
Lest their adversaries should
misjudge,
Lest they should say, "Our
hand is [t]triumphant,
And the LORD has not done
all this." ' *high*

28 "For they are a nation [t]lacking
in counsel,
And there is no understanding in them. *perishing*
29 "Would that they were wise,
that they understood this,
That they would discern
their [a]future! *latter end*
30 "How [r]could one chase a thousand,
And two put ten thousand to
flight,
Unless their Rock had sold
them,
And the LORD had given
them up? Lev. 26:7, 8
31 "Indeed their rock is not like
our Rock,
Even our enemies them-
selves judge this.
32 "For their vine is from the
vine of Sodom,
And from the fields of Gomorrah;
Their grapes are grapes of
poison,
Their clusters, bitter.
33 "Their wine is the venom of
[t]serpents,
And the [t]deadly poison of cobras. *dragons · cruel*

34 'Is it not laid up in store with
Me,
Sealed up in My treasuries?
35 'Vengeance [r]is Mine, and retribution,
In due time their foot will
slip;
For the day of their calamity
is near,
And the impending things
are hastening upon
them.' Ps. 94:1; Rom. 12:19
36 "For the LORD will vindicate
His people,
And will have compassion on
His servants;
When He sees that *their*
[t]strength is gone,
And there is none *remaining,*
bond or free. *hand*
37 "And He will say, 'Where [r]are
their gods,
The rock in which they
sought refuge? Jer. 2:28
38 'Who [r]ate the fat of their sacrifices,
And drank the wine of their
libation?
Let them rise up and help
you,
Let them be your hiding
place! Num. 25:1, 2
39 'See now that I, I am He,
And there is no god besides
Me;
It is I who put to death and
give life.
I have wounded, and it is I
who heal;

And there is no one who can
deliver from My hand.
40 'Indeed, I lift up My hand to
heaven,
And say, as I live forever,
41 If I sharpen My [a]flashing
sword,
And My hand takes hold on
justice,
I will render vengeance on
My adversaries,
And I will repay those who
hate Me. *lightning*
42 'I will make My arrows drunk
with blood,
And My sword shall devour
flesh,
With the blood of the slain
and the captives,
From the long-haired [t]leaders
of the enemy.' *head*
43 "Rejoice, O nations, *with* His
people;
For He will avenge the blood
of His servants,
And will render vengeance
on His adversaries,
And will atone for His land
and His people."
44 Then Moses came and spoke
all the words of this song in the
hearing of the people, he, with
[t]Joshua the son of Nun. *Hoshea*
45 When Moses had finished
speaking all these words to all Israel,
46 he said to them, "Take to
your heart all the words with
which I am warning you today,
which you shall command your
sons to observe [t]carefully, *even* all
the words of this law. *to do*
47 "For it is not an idle word for
you; indeed it is your life. And by
this word you shall prolong your
days in the land, [t]which you are
about to cross the Jordan to [t]pos-
sess." *where • possess it*
48 And the LORD spoke to
Moses that very same day, saying,
49 "Go up to this mountain of the
Abarim, Mount Nebo, which is in
the land of Moab opposite Jericho,
and look at the land of Canaan,
which I am giving to the sons of
Israel for a possession.
50 "Then die on the mountain
where you ascend, and be gathered to your people, as Aaron
your brother died on Mount Hor
and was gathered to his people,
51 because you broke faith with
Me in the midst of the sons of Israel at the waters of Meribah-ka-
desh, in the wilderness of Zin, because you did not treat Me as holy
in the midst of the sons of Israel.
52 "For you shall see the land at
a distance, but you shall not go
there, into the land which I am
giving the sons of Israel."

CHAPTER 33

NOW this is the blessing with
which Moses [r]the man of God
blessed the sons of Israel before
his death. Josh. 14:6
2 And he said,
"The LORD came from Sinai,
And [t]dawned on them from
Seir;
He shone forth from Mount
Paran,
And He came from the
midst of ten thousand
holy ones;
At His right hand there was
[a]flashing lightning for
them. *rose to • a fiery law*

3 "Indeed, He loves [t]the people;
All [t]Thy holy ones are in Thy hand,
And they followed in Thy steps;
Everyone receives of Thy words. *peoples* · *His*
4 "Moses[r] charged us with a law,
A possession for the assembly of Jacob. John 7:19
5 "And [r]He was king in Jeshurun,
When the heads of the people were gathered,
The tribes of Israel together. Num. 23:21

6 "May Reuben live and not die,
Nor his men be few."

7 And this regarding Judah; so
he said,
"Hear, O LORD, the voice of Judah,
And bring him to his people.
With his hands he contended for them;
And mayest Thou be a help against his adversaries."

8 And of Levi he said,
"*Let* Thy [r]Thummim and Thy Urim *belong* to [t]Thy godly man,
Whom Thou didst prove at Massah,
With whom Thou didst contend at the waters of Meribah; Ex. 28:30 · *him*
9 Who said of his father and his mother,
'I did not consider them';
And he did not acknowledge his brothers,
Nor did he regard his own sons,
For they observed Thy word,
And kept Thy covenant.
10 "They [r]shall teach Thine ordinances to Jacob,
And Thy law to Israel.
They shall put incense before Thee,
And whole burnt offerings on Thine altar. Lev. 10:11
11 "O LORD, bless his substance,
And accept the work of his hands;
Shatter the loins of those who rise up against him,
And those who hate him, so that they may not rise *again*."

12 Of Benjamin he said,
"May[r] the beloved of the LORD dwell in security by Him,
Who shields him all the day,
And he dwells between His shoulders." Deut. 4:37f.

13 And of Joseph he said,
"Blessed[r] of the LORD *be* his land,
With the choice things of heaven, with the dew,
And from the deep lying beneath, Gen. 27:27, 28
14 And with the choice yield of the sun,
And with the choice produce of the months.
15 "And with the best things of the ancient mountains,

And with the choice things
of the everlasting hills,
16 And with the choice things
of the earth and its fulness,
And the favor [r]of Him who
dwelt in the bush.
Let it come to the head of
Joseph,
And to the crown of the
head of the one distinguished among his brothers. Ex. 2:2-6; 3:2, 4
17 "As the first-born of his ox,
majesty is his,
And his horns are the horns
of the wild ox;
With them he shall push the
peoples,
All at once, *to* the ends of
the earth.
And those are the ten thousands of Ephraim,
And those are the thousands of Manasseh."

18 [r]And of Zebulun he said,
"Rejoice, Zebulun, in your
going forth,
And, Issachar, in your
tents. Gen. 49:13-15
19 "They shall call peoples *to*
the mountain;
There they shall offer [r]righteous sacrifices;
For they shall [t]draw out the
abundance of the seas,
And the hidden treasures of
the sand." Ps. 4:5 • *suck*

20 And of Gad he said,
"Blessed is the one who enlarges Gad;
He lies down as a [a]lion,
And tears the arm, also the
crown of the head. *lioness*

21 "Then he [t]provided the first
part for himself,
For there the ruler's portion
was [a]reserved;
And he came *with* the leaders of the people;
He executed the justice of
the LORD,
And His ordinances with Israel." *saw • covered up*

22 And of Dan he said,
"Dan is [r]a lion's whelp,
That leaps forth from Bashan." Ezek. 19:2, 3

23 And of Naphtali he said,
"O[r] Naphtali, satisfied with
favor,
And full of the blessing of
the LORD,
Take possession of the sea
and the south." Gen. 49:21

24 [r]And of Asher he said,
"More blessed than sons is
Asher;
May he be favored by his
brothers,
[r]And may he dip his foot in
oil. Gen. 49:20 • Job 29:6
25 "Your locks shall be iron and
bronze,
[r]And according to your
days, so shall your leisurely walk be. Deut. 4:40

26 "There is none like the God
of [20]Jeshurun,
Who rides the heavens [t]to
your help,
And through the skies in
His majesty. *in*
27 "The eternal God is a [a]dwelling place,

[20]I.e., Israel

And underneath are the
everlasting arms;
And He drove out the enemy
from before you,
And said, 'Destroy!' *refuge*
28 "So[r] Israel dwells in security,
[r]The fountain of Jacob secluded,
Deut. 33:12
In a land of grain and new
wine; Deut. 32:8
[r]His heavens also drop down
dew. Deut. 33:13
29 "Blessed are you, O Israel;
Who is like you, a people
saved by the LORD,
[r]Who is the shield of your
help, Gen. 15:1
And the sword of your majesty!
So your enemies shall
cringe before you,
And you shall tread upon
their high places."

CHAPTER 34

NOW Moses went up from the
plains of Moab to Mount Nebo, to
the top of Pisgah, which is opposite
Jericho. And the LORD
[r]showed him all the land, Gilead as
far as Dan, Deut. 32:52
2 and all Naphtali and the land
of Ephraim and Manasseh, and all
the land of Judah as far as the
[21]western sea,
3 and the Negev and the plain
in the valley of Jericho, the city of
palm trees, as far as Zoar.
4 Then the LORD said to him,
"This is the land which[r] I swore to
Abraham, Isaac, and Jacob, saying,
'I will give it to your [t]descendants';
I have let you see *it* with
your eyes, but you shall not go
over there." Gen. 12:7 • *seed*
5 So Moses [r]the servant of the
LORD died there in the land of
Moab, according to the [t]word of
the LORD. Num. 12:7 • *mouth*
6 And He buried him in the
valley in the land of Moab, opposite
Beth-peor; but [r]no man knows
his burial place to this day. Jude 9
7 Although Moses was one
hundred and twenty years old
when he died, [r]his eye was not
dim, nor his vigor abated. Gen. 27:1
8 So the sons of Israel wept for
Moses in the plains of Moab thirty
days; then the days of weeping
and mourning for Moses came to
an end.
9 Now Joshua the son of Nun
was [r]filled with the spirit of wisdom,
for Moses had laid his hands
on him; and the sons of Israel listened
to him and did as the LORD
had commanded Moses. Is. 11:2
10 Since then no prophet has
risen in Israel like Moses, whom
the LORD knew face to face,
11 for all the signs and wonders
which the LORD sent him to perform
in the land of Egypt against
Pharaoh, all his servants, and all
his land,
12 and for all the mighty [t]power
and for all the great terror which
Moses performed in the sight of
all Israel. *hand*

[21] I.e., Mediterranean Sea

THE BOOK OF

JOSHUA

NOW it came about after the
death of Moses the servant of the
LORD that the LORD spoke to
Joshua the son of Nun, Moses'
[1]servant, saying,
2 "Moses My servant is dead;
now therefore arise, cross this
Jordan, you and all this people, to
the land which I am giving to
them, to the sons of Israel.
3 "Every[r] place on which the
sole of your foot treads, I have
given it to you, just as I spoke to
Moses. Deut. 11:24
4 "From the wilderness and this
Lebanon, even as far as the great
river, the river Euphrates, all the
land of the Hittites, and as far as
the Great Sea toward the setting
of the sun, will be your territory.
5 "No man will *be able to* stand
before you all the days of your
life. Just as I have been with
Moses, I will be with you; I will
not fail you or forsake you.
6 "Be strong and courageous,
for you shall give this people possession of the land which I swore
to their fathers to give them.
7 "Only be strong and very courageous;[t]be careful to do according to all the law which Moses My
servant commanded you; do not
turn from it to the right or to the
left, so that you may have success
wherever you go. *observe*
8 "This book of the law shall not
depart from your mouth, but you
shall meditate on it day and night,
so that you may[t]be careful to do
according to all that is written in
it; for then you will make your
way prosperous, and then you will
[a]have success. *observe · act wisely*
9 "Have I not commanded you?
[r]Be strong and courageous![r]Do not
tremble or be dismayed, for the
LORD your God is with you wherever you go." Josh. 1:7 · Deut. 31:8
10 Then Joshua commanded the
officers of the people, saying,
11 "Pass through the midst of the
camp and command the people,
saying, 'Prepare provisions for
yourselves, for within [r]three days
you are to cross this Jordan, to go
in to possess the land which the
LORD your God is giving you, to
possess it.' " Josh. 3:2
12 And to the Reubenites and to
the Gadites and to the half-tribe of
Manasseh, Joshua[t]said, *said, saying*
13 "Remember the word which
Moses the servant of the LORD
commanded you, saying, 'The
LORD your God gives you rest, and
will give you this land.'
14 "Your wives, your little ones,
and your cattle shall remain in the
land which Moses gave you beyond the Jordan, but you shall
cross before your brothers in battle array, all your valiant warriors,
and shall help them,
15 until the LORD gives your
brothers rest, as *He gives* you, and
they also possess the land which
the LORD your God is giving them.
Then you shall return to your own
land, and possess [t]that which

[1]Or, *minister*

Moses [r]the servant of the LORD
gave you beyond the Jordan
toward the sunrise." *it* • Josh. 1:1
16 And they answered Joshua,
saying, "All that you have commanded us we will do, and wherever you send us we will go.
17 "Just as we obeyed Moses in
all things, so we will obey you;
only may the LORD your God be
with you, as He was with Moses.
18 "Anyone who rebels against
your command and does not obey
your words in all that you command him, shall be put to death;
only be strong and courageous."

CHAPTER 2

THEN Joshua the son of Nun
sent two men as spies secretly
from Shittim, saying, "Go, view
the land, especially Jericho." So
they went and came into the
house of a harlot whose name was
Rahab, and [t]lodged there. *lay down*
2 And it was told the king of
Jericho, saying, "Behold, men
from the sons of Israel have come
here tonight to search out the
land."
3 And the king of Jericho sent
word to Rahab, saying, "Bring out
the men who have come to you,
who have entered your house, for
they have come to search out all
the land."
4 But the [r]woman had taken the
two men and hidden them, and
she said, "Yes, the men came to
me, but I did not know where they
were from. 2 Sam. 17:19
5 "And it came about when *it
was time* to shut the gate, at dark,
that the men went out; I do not
know where the men went. Pursue them quickly, for you will
overtake them."
6 But [r]she had brought them up
to the roof and hidden them in the
stalks of flax which she had laid in
order on the roof. James 2:25
7 So the men pursued them on
the road to the Jordan to the
fords; and as soon as those who
were pursuing them had gone out,
they shut the gate.
8 Now before they lay down,
she came up to them on the roof,
9 and said to the men, "I know
that the LORD has given you the
land, and that the terror of you
has fallen on us, and that all the
inhabitants of the land have
melted away before you.
10 "For we have heard how the
LORD dried up the water of the
[t]Red Sea before you when you
came out of Egypt, and what you
did to the two kings of the Amorites who were beyond the Jordan,
to Sihon and Og, whom you utterly destroyed. *Sea of Reeds*
11 "And when we heard *it*, our
hearts melted and no [t]courage remained in any man any longer because of you; for the LORD your
God, He is God in heaven above
and on earth beneath. *spirit arose*
12 "Now therefore, please swear
to me by the LORD, since I have
dealt kindly with you, that you
also will deal kindly with my father's household, and give me a
pledge of [a]truth, *faithfulness*
13 and [t]spare my father and my
mother and my brothers and my
sisters, with all who belong to
them, and deliver our [2]lives from
death." *let live*

[2] Lit., *souls*

14 So the men said to her, "Our
'life for yours if you do not tell this
business of ours; and it shall come
about when the LORD gives us the
land that we will deal kindly and
[a]faithfully with you." *soul* · *truly*
15 Then she let them down by a
rope through the window, for her
house was on the city wall, so that
she was living on the wall.
16 And she said to them, "Go to
the hill country, lest the pursuers
happen upon you, and hide yourselves there for three days, until
the pursuers return. Then afterward you may go on your way."
17 And the men said to her,
"We[r] *shall be* free from this oath
[t]to you which you have made us
swear, Gen. 24:8 · *of yours*
18 [t]unless, when we come into
the land, you tie this cord of scarlet thread in the window through
which you let us down, and [r]gather
to yourself into the house your father and your mother and your
brothers and all your father's
household. *behold* · Josh. 2:12
19 "And it shall come about that
anyone who goes out of the doors
of your house into the street, his
blood *shall be* on his own head,
and we *shall be* free; but anyone
who is with you in the house, [r]his
blood *shall be* on our head, if a
hand is *laid* on him. Matt. 27:25
20 "But if you tell this business
of ours, then we shall be free from
the oath which you have made us
swear."
21 And she said, "According to
your words, so be it." So she sent
them away, and they departed;
and she tied the scarlet cord in the
window.
22 And they departed and came
to the hill country, and remained
there for three days until the pursuers returned. Now the pursuers
had sought *them* all along the
road, but had not found *them*.
23 Then the two men returned
and came down from the hill
country and crossed over and
came to Joshua the son of Nun,
and they related to him all that
had happened to them.
24 And they said to Joshua,
"Surely the LORD has given all the
land into our hands, and all the inhabitants of the land, moreover,
have melted away before us."

CHAPTER 3

THEN Joshua rose early in the
morning; and he and all the sons
of Israel set out from Shittim and
came to the Jordan, and they
lodged there before they crossed.
2 And it came about [r]at the end
of three days that the officers
went through the midst of the
camp; Josh. 1:11
3 and they commanded the
people, saying, "When you see the
[r]ark of the covenant of the LORD
your God with the Levitical
priests carrying it, then you shall
set out from your place and go after it. Deut. 31:9
4 "However, there shall be between you and it a distance of
about 2,000 cubits by measure. Do
not come near it, that you may
know the way by which you shall
go, for you have not passed this
way before."
5 Then Joshua said to the peo-

ple, "Consecrate[r] yourselves, for
tomorrow the LORD will do wonders among you." Ex. 19:10, 11
6 And Joshua spoke to the
priests, saying, "Take up the ark
of the covenant and cross over
ahead of the people." So they took
up the ark of the covenant and
went ahead of the people.
7 Now the LORD said to
Joshua, "This day I will begin to
[r]exalt you in the sight of all Israel,
that they may know that just as I
have been with Moses, I will be
with you. Josh. 4:14
8 "You shall, moreover, command the priests who are carrying
the ark of the covenant, saying,
'When you come to the edge of
the waters of the Jordan, you shall
stand *still* in the Jordan.' "
9 Then Joshua said to the sons
of Israel, "Come here, and hear
the words of the LORD your God."
10 And Joshua said, "By this
you shall know that[r] the living God
is among you, and that He will assuredly [r]dispossess from before
you the Canaanite, the Hittite, the
Hivite, the Perizzite, the Girgashite, the Amorite, and the Jebusite. Deut. 5:26 • Ex. 33:2; Deut. 7:1
11 "Behold, the ark of the covenant of[r] the Lord of all the earth is
crossing over ahead of you into
the Jordan. Job 41:11; Ps. 24:1
12 "Now then, take for yourselves twelve men from the tribes
of Israel, one man for each tribe.
13 "And it shall come about
when the soles of the feet of the
priests who carry the ark of the
LORD, the Lord of all the earth,
shall rest in the waters of the Jordan, the waters of the Jordan shall
be cut off, *and* the waters which
are [t]flowing down from above
shall stand in one heap." *going*
14 So it came about when the
people set out from their tents to
cross the Jordan with the priests
carrying[r] the ark of the covenant
before the people, Ps. 132:8
15 and when those who carried
the ark came into the Jordan, and
the feet of the priests carrying the
ark were dipped in the edge of the
water (for the [r]Jordan overflows
all its banks all the days of harvest), 1 Chr. 12:15; Jer. 12:5; 49:19
16 [r]that the waters which were
[t]flowing down from above stood
and rose up in one heap, a great
distance away at Adam, the city
that is beside Zarethan; and those
which were flowing down toward
the sea of the [r]Arabah, the Salt
Sea, were completely cut off. So
the people crossed opposite Jericho. Ps. 66:6 • *going* • Deut. 1:1
17 And the priests who carried
the ark of the covenant of the
LORD stood firm[r] on dry ground in
the middle of the Jordan while all
Israel crossed on dry ground, until
all the nation had finished crossing the Jordan. Ex. 14:21, 22, 29

CHAPTER 4

NOW it came about when all the
nation had finished crossing the
[r]Jordan, that the LORD spoke to
Joshua, saying, Deut. 27:2
2 "Take[r] for yourselves twelve
men from the people, one man
from each tribe, Josh. 3:12
3 and command them, saying,
'Take up for yourselves twelve

stones from here out of the middle of the Jordan, from the place where the priests' feet are standing firm, and carry them over with you, and lay them down in [r]the lodging place where you will lodge tonight.' " Josh. 4:20

4 So Joshua called the twelve men whom he had appointed from the sons of Israel, one man from each tribe;

5 and Joshua said to them, "Cross again to the ark of the LORD your God into the middle of the Jordan, and each of you take up a stone on his shoulder, according to the number of the tribes of the sons of Israel.

6 "Let this be a sign among you, so that when your children ask [t]later, saying, 'What do these stones mean to you?' *tomorrow*

7 then you shall say to them, 'Because the waters of the Jordan were cut off before the ark of the covenant of the LORD; when it crossed the Jordan, the waters of the Jordan were cut off.' So these stones shall become a memorial to the sons of Israel forever."

8 And thus the sons of Israel did, as Joshua commanded, and took up twelve stones from the middle of the Jordan, just as the LORD spoke to Joshua, according to the number of the tribes of the sons of Israel; and they carried them over with them to [r]the lodging place, and put them down there. Josh. 4:20

9 Then Joshua set up twelve [r]stones in the middle of the Jordan at the place where the feet of the priests who carried the ark of the covenant were standing, and they are there to this day. Gen. 28:18

10 For the priests who carried the ark were standing in the middle of the Jordan until everything was completed that the LORD had commanded Joshua to speak to the people, according to all that Moses had commanded Joshua. And the people hurried and crossed;

11 and it came about when all the people had finished crossing, that the ark of the LORD and the priests crossed before the people.

12 And the sons of Reuben and the sons of Gad and the half-tribe of Manasseh crossed over in battle array before the sons of Israel, just as Moses had spoken to them;

13 about 40,000, equipped for war, crossed for battle before the LORD to the desert plains of Jericho.

14 [r]On that day the LORD exalted Joshua in the sight of all Israel; so that they [3]revered him, just as they had revered Moses all the days of his life. Josh. 3:7

15 Now the LORD said to [t]Joshua, *Joshua, saying*

16 "Command the priests who carry the ark of the testimony that they come up from the Jordan."

17 So Joshua commanded the priests, saying, "Come up from the Jordan."

18 And it came about when the priests who carried the ark of the covenant of the LORD had come up from the middle of the Jordan, and the soles of the priests' feet were lifted up to the dry ground, that the waters of the Jordan re-

[3]Or, *feared*

turned to their place, and went over all its banks as before.

19 Now the people came up from the Jordan on the tenth of the first month and camped at Gilgal on the eastern edge of Jericho.

20 And those twelve stones which they had taken from the Jordan, Joshua set up at Gilgal.

21 And he said to the sons of Israel, "When your children ask their fathers in time to come, saying, 'What are these stones?'

22 then you shall inform your children, saying, 'Israel crossed this Jordan on dry ground.'

23 "For the LORD your God dried up the waters of the Jordan before you until you had crossed, just as the LORD your God had done to the Red Sea, which He dried up before us until we had crossed;

24 that all the peoples of the earth may know that the hand of the LORD is mighty, so that you may [a]fear the LORD your God [t]forever." *reverence · all the days*

CHAPTER 5

NOW it came about when all the kings of the Amorites who *were* beyond the Jordan to the west, and all the kings of the Canaanites who *were* by the sea, heard how the LORD had dried up the waters of the Jordan before the sons of Israel until they had crossed, that their hearts melted, and there was no spirit in them any longer, because of the sons of Israel.

2 At that time the LORD said to Joshua, "Make for yourself flint knives and circumcise again the sons of Israel the second time."

3 So Joshua made himself flint knives and circumcised the sons of Israel at [4]Gibeath-haaraloth.

4 And this is the reason why Joshua circumcised them: [r]all the people who came out of Egypt who were males, all the men of war, died in the wilderness along the way, after they came out of Egypt. Deut. 2:14

5 For all the people who came out were circumcised, but all the people who were born in the wilderness along the way as they came out of Egypt had not been circumcised.

6 For the sons of Israel walked forty years in the wilderness, until all the nation, *that is,* the men of war who came out of Egypt, [t]perished because they did not listen to the voice of the LORD, to whom the LORD had sworn that He would not let them see the land which the LORD had sworn to their fathers to give us, a land flowing with milk and honey. *were finished*

7 And their children whom He raised up in their place, Joshua circumcised; for they were uncircumcised, because they had not circumcised them along the way.

8 Now it came about when they had finished circumcising all the nation, that they remained in their places in the camp until they were [t]healed. *revived*

9 Then the LORD said to Joshua, "Today I have rolled away [r]the reproach of Egypt from you." So the name of that place is called [5]Gilgal to this day. Zeph. 2:8

10 While the sons of Israel camped at Gilgal, they observed the Passover on the evening of the

[4]I.e., the hill of the foreskins [5]I.e., rolling

fourteenth day of the month on
the desert plains of Jericho.
11 And on the [t]day after the
Passover, on [t]that very day, they
ate some of the produce of the
land, unleavened cakes and
parched grain. *morrow* • *this*
12 And [r]the manna ceased on
the [t]day after they had eaten some
of the produce of the land, so that
the sons of Israel no longer had
manna, but they ate some of the
yield of the land of Canaan during
that year. Ex. 16:35 • *morrow*
13 Now it came about when
Joshua was by Jericho, that he
lifted up his eyes and looked, and
behold, a man was standing opposite him with his sword drawn in
his hand, and Joshua went to him
and said to him, "Are you for us
or for our adversaries?"
14 And he said, "No, rather I indeed come now *as* captain of the
host of the LORD." And Joshua [r]fell
on his face to the earth, and
bowed down, and said to him,
"What has my lord to say to his
servant?" Gen. 17:3
15 And the captain of the
LORD's host said to Joshua, "Remove your sandals from your feet,
for the place where you are standing is holy." And Joshua did so.

CHAPTER 6

NOW Jericho was tightly shut
because of the sons of Israel; no
one went out and no one came in.
2 And the LORD said to Joshua,
"See, I have given Jericho into
your hand, with [r]its king *and* the
valiant warriors. Deut. 7:24
3 "And you shall march around
the city, all the men of war circling the city once. You shall do
so for six days.
4 "Also seven priests shall carry
seven [r]trumpets of rams' horns before the ark; then on the seventh
day you shall march around the
city seven times, and the priests
shall blow the trumpets. Lev. 25:9
5 "And it shall be that when
they make a long blast with the
ram's horn, and when you hear
the sound of the trumpet, all the
people shall shout with a great
shout; and the wall of the city will
fall down flat, and the people will
go up every man straight ahead."
6 So Joshua the son of Nun
called the priests and said to
them, "Take up the ark of the covenant, and let seven priests carry
seven trumpets of rams' horns before the ark of the LORD."
7 Then he said to the people,
"Go forward, and march around
the city, and let the armed men go
on before the ark of the LORD."
8 And it was *so*, that when
Joshua had spoken to the people,
the seven priests carrying the
seven trumpets of rams' horns before the LORD went forward and
blew the trumpets; and the ark of
the covenant of the LORD followed
them.
9 And the armed men went before the priests who blew the
trumpets, and the rear guard
came after the ark, while they
continued to blow the trumpets.
10 But Joshua commanded the
people, saying, "You shall not
shout nor let your voice be heard,
nor let a word proceed out of your

mouth, until the day I tell you, 'Shout!' Then you shall shout!"

11 So he had the ark of the LORD [t]taken around the city, circling *it* once; then they came into the camp and spent the night in the camp. *to go around*

12 Now Joshua rose early in the morning, and the priests took up the ark of the LORD.

13 And [r]the seven priests carrying the seven trumpets of rams' horns before the ark of the LORD went on continually, and blew the trumpets; and the armed men went before them, and the rear guard came after the ark of the LORD, while they continued to blow the trumpets. Josh. 6:4

14 Thus the second day they marched around the city once and returned to the camp; they did so for six days.

15 Then it came about on the seventh day that they rose early at the dawning of the day and marched around the city in the same manner seven times; only on that day they marched around the city seven times.

16 And it came about at the seventh time, when the priests blew the trumpets, Joshua said to the people, "Shout! [r]For the LORD has given you the city. 2 Chr. 13:14f.

17 "And the city shall be [r]under the ban, it and all that is in it belongs to the LORD; only Rahab the harlot [t]and all who are with her in the house shall live, because she hid the messengers whom we sent. Lev. 27:28 • *she and all*

18 "But as for you, only keep yourselves from the things under the ban, lest you [t]covet *them* and [r]take some of the things under the ban, so you would make the camp of Israel accursed and bring trouble on it. *devote* • Josh. 7:1

19 "But all the silver and gold and articles of bronze and iron are holy to the LORD; they shall go into the treasury of the LORD."

20 So the people shouted, and *priests* blew the trumpets; and it came about, when the people heard the sound of the trumpet, that the people shouted with a great shout and the wall fell down flat, so that the people went up into the city, every man straight ahead, and they took the city.

21 [r]And they utterly destroyed everything in the city, both man and woman, young and old, and ox and sheep and donkey, with the edge of the sword. Deut. 20:16

22 And Joshua said to the two men who had spied out the land, "Go[r] into the harlot's house and bring the woman and all she has out of there, as you have sworn to her." Josh. 2:12-19

23 So the young men who were spies went in and [r]brought out Rahab and her father and her mother and her brothers and all she had; they also brought out all her relatives, and placed them outside the camp of Israel. Heb. 11:31

24 [r]And they burned the city with fire, and all that was in it. Only the silver and gold and articles of bronze and iron, they put into the treasury of the [6]house of the LORD. Deut. 20:16-18

25 However, [r]Rahab the harlot and her father's household and all she had, Joshua [t]spared; and she has lived in the midst of Israel to

[6]I.e., tabernacle

this day, for she hid the messengers whom Joshua sent to spy out
Jericho. Heb. 11:31 • *let live*
26 Then Joshua made them take
an oath at that time, saying,
"Cursed before the LORD is the
man who rises up and builds this
city Jericho; with *the loss of* his
first-born he shall lay its foundation, and with *the loss of* his youngest son he shall set up its gates."
27 So the LORD was with
Joshua, and his fame was in all
the land.

CHAPTER 7

[r]BUT the sons of Israel acted unfaithfully in regard to the things
under the ban, for Achan, the son
of Carmi, the son of Zabdi, the son
of Zerah, from the tribe of Judah,
took some of the things under the
ban, therefore the anger of the
LORD burned against the sons of
Israel. Josh. 6:17-19
2 Now Joshua sent men from
Jericho to Ai, which is near Beth-
aven, east of Bethel, and said to
them, "Go[t] up and spy out the
land." So the men went up and
spied out Ai. *saying, Go*
3 And they returned to Joshua
and said to him, "Do not let all the
people go up; *only* about two or
three thousand men need go up to
Ai; do not make all the people toil
up there, for they are few."
4 So about three thousand men
from the people went up there,
but they fled from the men of Ai.
5 And the men of Ai struck
down about thirty-six of their
men, and pursued them[a] from the
gate as far as Shebarim, and
struck them down on the descent,
so the hearts of the people melted
and became as water. *before*
6 Then Joshua[r] tore his clothes
and fell to the earth on his face before the ark of the LORD until the
evening, *both* he and the elders of
Israel; and[r] they put dust on their
heads. Job 2:12 • Job 42:6
7 And Joshua said, "Alas, O
Lord GOD, why didst Thou ever
bring this people over the Jordan,
only to deliver us into the hand of
the Amorites, to destroy us? If
only we had been willing[t] to dwell
beyond the Jordan! *and had dwelt*
8 "O Lord, what can I say since
Israel has turned *their*[t] back before
their enemies? *neck*
9 "For[r] the Canaanites and all
the inhabitants of the land will
hear of it, and they will surround
us and cut off our name from the
earth. And what wilt Thou do for
Thy great name?" Ex. 32:12
10 So the LORD said to Joshua,
"Rise up! Why is it that you have
fallen on your face?
11 "Israel has sinned, and they
have also transgressed My covenant which I commanded them.
And they have even taken some of
the things under the ban and have
both stolen and deceived. Moreover, they have also put *them*
among their own things.
12 "Therefore the[r] sons of Israel
cannot stand before their enemies; they turn *their*[t] backs before their enemies, for they have
become accursed. I will not be
with you anymore unless you destroy the things under the ban
from your midst. Judg. 2:14 • *necks*
13 "Rise up! Consecrate the peo-

ple and say, 'Consecrate yourselves for tomorrow, for thus the LORD, the God of Israel, has said, "There are things under the ban in your midst, O Israel. You cannot stand before your enemies until you have removed the things under the ban from your midst."

14 'In the morning then you shall come near by your tribes. And it shall be that the tribe which [r]the LORD takes *by lot* shall come near by families, and the family which the LORD takes shall come near by households, and the household which the LORD takes shall come near man by man. Prov. 16:33

15 'And it shall be that the one who is taken with the things under the ban shall be burned with fire, he and all that belongs to him, because he has transgressed the covenant of the LORD, and because he has committed a disgraceful thing in Israel.' "

16 So Joshua arose early in the morning and brought Israel near by [t]tribes, and the tribe of Judah was taken. *its tribes*

17 And he brought the family of Judah near, and he took the family of the Zerahites; and he brought the family of the Zerahites near man by man, and Zabdi was taken.

18 And he brought his household near man by man; and [r]Achan, son of Carmi, son of Zabdi, son of Zerah, from the tribe of Judah, was taken. Num. 32:23

19 Then Joshua said to Achan, "My son, I implore you, [r]give glory to the LORD, the God of Israel, and give praise to Him; and tell me now what you have done. Do not hide it from me." 1 Sam. 6:5

20 So Achan answered Joshua and said, "Truly, I have sinned against the LORD, the God of Israel, and this is what I did:

21 when I saw among the spoil a beautiful mantle from Shinar and two hundred shekels of silver and a bar of gold fifty shekels in weight, then I [r]coveted them and took them; and behold, they are concealed in the earth inside my tent with the silver underneath it." Eph. 5:5; 1 Tim. 6:10

22 So Joshua sent messengers, and they ran to the tent; and behold, it was concealed in his tent with the silver underneath it.

23 And they took them from inside the tent and brought them to Joshua and to all the sons of Israel, and they poured them out before the LORD.

24 Then Joshua and all Israel with him, took Achan the son of Zerah, the silver, the mantle, the bar of gold, his sons, his daughters, his oxen, his donkeys, his sheep, his tent and all that belonged to him; and they brought them up to the valley of [7]Achor.

25 And Joshua said, "Why have you troubled us? The LORD will trouble you this day." And all Israel stoned them with stones; and they burned them with fire after they had stoned them with stones.

26 And they raised over him a great heap of stones that stands to this day, and the LORD turned from the fierceness of His anger. Therefore the name of that place has been called [r]the valley of [7]Achor to this day. Is. 65:10

[7]I.e., trouble

CHAPTER 8

NOW the LORD said to Joshua,
"Do not fear or be dismayed. Take
all the people of war with you and
arise, go up to Ai; see, I have giv-
en into your hand the king of Ai,
his people, his city, and his land.
2 "And you shall do to Ai and
its king just as you did to Jericho
and its king; you shall take only
its spoil and its cattle as plunder
for yourselves. [t]Set an ambush for
the city behind it." *Set for yourself*
3 So Joshua rose with all the
people of war to go up to Ai; and
Joshua chose 30,000 men, valiant
warriors, and sent them out at
night.
4 And he commanded them,
saying, "See, you are going to ambush the city from behind [t]it. Do
not go very far from the city, but
all of you be ready. *the city*
5 "Then I and all the people who
are with me will approach the
city. And it will come about when
they come out to meet us as at the
first, that we will flee before them.
6 "And they will come out after
us until we have drawn them
away from the city, for they will
say, '*They* are fleeing before us as
at the first.' So we will flee before
them.
7 "And you shall rise from *your*
ambush and take possession of
the city, for the LORD your God
will deliver it into your hand.
8 "Then it will be when you
have seized the city, that you shall
set the city on fire. You shall do *it*
[r]according to the word of the
LORD. See, I have commanded
you." Deut. 20:16-18; Josh. 8:2
9 So Joshua sent them away,
and they went to the place of ambush and remained between
Bethel and Ai, on the west side of
Ai; but Joshua spent that night
among the people.
10 Now Joshua rose early in the
morning and mustered the people,
and he went up with the elders of
Israel before the people to Ai.
11 Then all the people of war
who *were* with him went up and
drew near and arrived in front of
the city, and camped on the north
side of Ai. Now *there was* a valley
between him and Ai.
12 And he took about 5,000 men
and set them in ambush between
[r]Bethel and Ai, on the west side of
the city. Gen. 12:8; 28:19; Judg. 1:22
13 So they stationed the people,
all the army that was on the north
side of the city, and its rear guard
on the west side of the city, and
Joshua spent that night in the
midst of the valley.
14 And it came about when the
king of Ai saw *it,* that the men of
the city hurried and rose up early
and went out to meet Israel in battle, he and all his people at the appointed place before the desert
plain. But he did not know that
there was an ambush against him
behind the city.
15 And Joshua and all Israel
pretended to be beaten before
them, and fled [r]by the way of the
wilderness. Josh. 15:61; 16:1; 18:12
16 And all the people who were
in the city were called together to
pursue them, and they pursued
Joshua, and [r]were drawn away
from the city. Judg. 20:31
17 So not a man was left in Ai

or Bethel who had not gone out after Israel, and they left the city
unguarded and pursued Israel.
18 Then the LORD said to
Joshua, "Stretch[r] out the javelin
that is in your hand toward Ai, for
I will give it into your hand." So
Joshua stretched out the javelin
that was in his hand toward the
city. Ex. 14:16; 17:9-13; Josh. 8:26
19 And the *men in* ambush rose
quickly from their place, and
when he had stretched out his
hand, they ran and entered the
city and captured it; and they
quickly set the city on fire.
20 When the men of Ai turned
[t]back and looked, behold, the
smoke of the city ascended to the
sky, and they had no place to flee
this way or that, for the people
who had been fleeing to the wilderness turned against the pursuers. *behind them*
21 When Joshua and all Israel
saw that the *men in* ambush had
captured the city and that the
smoke of the city ascended, they
turned back and [t]slew the men of
Ai. *smote*
22 And the others came out
from the city to encounter them,
so that they were *trapped* in the
midst of Israel, some on this side
and some on that side; and they
slew them until no one was left of
those who survived or escaped.
23 But they took alive the king
of Ai and brought him to Joshua.
24 Now it came about when Israel had finished killing all the inhabitants of Ai in the field in the
wilderness where they pursued
them, and all of them were fallen
by the edge of the sword until
they were destroyed, then all Israel returned to Ai and struck it
with the edge of the sword.
25 And all who fell that day,
both men and women, were
12,000—all the[t]people of Ai. *men*
26 For Joshua [r]did not withdraw
his hand with which he stretched
out the javelin until he had[a]utterly
destroyed all the inhabitants of
Ai. Ex. 17:11, 12 • *put under the ban*
27 [r]Israel took only the cattle
and the spoil of that city as plunder for themselves, according to
the word of the LORD which He
had commanded Joshua. Josh. 8:2
28 So Joshua burned Ai and
made it [r]a heap forever, a desolation until this day. Deut. 13:16
29 [r]And he hanged the king of Ai
on a tree until evening; and at sunset Joshua gave command and
they took his body down from the
tree, and threw it at the entrance
of the city gate, and raised over it
a great heap of stones *that stands*
to this day. Deut. 21:22, 23
30 Then Joshua built an altar to
the LORD, the God of Israel, in
[r]Mount Ebal, Deut. 27:2-8
31 just as Moses the servant of
the LORD had commanded the
sons of Israel, as it is written in
the book of the law of Moses, [r]an
altar of uncut stones, on which no
man had wielded an iron *tool;* and
they offered burnt offerings on it
to the LORD, and sacrificed peace
offerings. Ex. 20:25
32 And he wrote there on the
stones a copy of the law of Moses,
which he had written, in the presence of the sons of Israel.
33 And all Israel with their elders and officers and their judges

were standing on both sides of the
ark before the Levitical priests
who carried the ark of the covenant of the LORD, the stranger as
well as the native. Half of them
stood in front of Mount Gerizim
and half of them in front of Mount
Ebal, just as Moses the servant of
the LORD had given command at
first to bless the people of Israel.
34 Then afterward he read all
the words of the law, the blessing
and the curse, according to all
that is written in [r]the book of the
law. Josh. 1:8
35 There was not a word of all
that Moses had commanded
which Joshua did not read before
all the assembly of Israel [r]with the
women and the little ones and the
strangers who were [t]living among
them. Ex. 12:38 • *walking*

CHAPTER 9

NOW it came about when all the
kings who were beyond the Jordan, in the hill country and in the
lowland and on all the coast of the
Great Sea toward Lebanon, the
Hittite and the Amorite, the Canaanite, the Perizzite, the Hivite
and the Jebusite, heard of it,
2 that they gathered themselves together with one accord to
fight with Joshua and with Israel.
3 When the inhabitants of [r]Gib-
eon heard what Joshua had done
to Jericho and to Ai, Josh. 9:17, 22
4 they also acted craftily and
[t]set out as envoys, and took worn-
out sacks on their donkeys, and
wineskins, worn-out and torn and
mended, *went and traveled as envoys*
5 and worn-out and patched
sandals on their feet, and worn-
out clothes on themselves; and all
the bread of their provision was
dry *and* had become crumbled.
6 And they went to Joshua to
the [r]camp at Gilgal, and said to
him and to the men of Israel, "We
have come from a far country;
now therefore, make a covenant
with us." Josh. 5:10
7 And the men of Israel said to
the [r]Hivites, "Perhaps you are living [t]within our land; how then
shall we make a covenant with
you?" Josh. 9:1; 11:19 • *among us*
8 But they said to Joshua, "We
are your servants." Then Joshua
said to them, "Who are you, and
where do you come from?"
9 And they said to him, "Your
servants have come from a very
far country because of the [a]fame of
the LORD your God; for we have
heard the report of Him and all
that He did in Egypt, *name*
10 and all that He did to the two
kings of the Amorites who were
beyond the Jordan, to Sihon king
of Heshbon and to Og king of Bashan who was at Ashtaroth.
11 "So our elders and all the inhabitants of our country spoke to
us, saying, 'Take provisions in
your hand for the journey, and go
to meet them and say to them,
"We are your servants; now then,
make a covenant with us." '
12 "This our bread *was* warm
when we took it for our provisions
out of our houses on the day that
we left to come to you; but now
behold, it is dry and has become
crumbled.
13 "And these wineskins which
we filled were new, and behold,

they are torn; and these our
clothes and our sandals are worn
out because of the very long journey."
14 So the men *of Israel* took
some of their provisions, and did
not ask for the [t]counsel of the
LORD. Num. 27:21 · *mouth*
15 [r]And Joshua made peace with
them and made a covenant with
them, to let them live; and the
leaders of the congregation swore
an oath to them. Ex. 23:32
16 And it came about at the end
of three days after they had made
a covenant with them, that they
heard that they were neighbors
and that they were living [t]within
their land. *among them*
17 Then the sons of Israel set
out and came to their cities on the
third day. Now their cities *were*
Gibeon and Chephirah and Beeroth and Kiriath-jearim.
18 And the sons of Israel did not
strike them because the leaders of
the congregation had sworn to
them by the LORD the God of Israel. And the whole congregation
grumbled against the leaders.
19 But all the leaders said to the
whole congregation, "We have
sworn to them by the LORD, the
God of Israel, and now we cannot
touch them.
20 "This we will do to them, even
let them live, lest wrath be upon
us for the oath which we swore to
them."
21 And the leaders said to them,
"Let them live." So they became
[r]hewers of wood and drawers of
water for the whole congregation,
just as the leaders had spoken to
them. Deut. 29:11
22 Then Joshua called for them
and spoke to them, saying, "Why
have you deceived us, saying, 'We
are very far from you,' when you
are living within our land?
23 "Now therefore, you are
[r]cursed, and you shall never cease
being slaves, both hewers of wood
and drawers of water for the
house of my God." Gen. 9:25
24 So they answered Joshua
and said, "Because[r] it was certainly told your servants that the
LORD your God had commanded
His servant Moses to give you all
the land, and to destroy all the inhabitants of the land before you;
therefore we feared greatly for
our lives because of you, and have
done this thing. Josh. 9:9
25 "And now behold, [r]we are in
your hands; do as it seems good
and right in your sight to do to
us." Gen. 16:6
26 Thus he did to them, and delivered them from the hands of
the sons of Israel, and they did not
kill them.
27 But Joshua made them that
day hewers of wood and drawers
of water for the congregation and
for the altar of the LORD, to this
day, [r]in the place which He would
choose. Deut. 12:5

CHAPTER 10

NOW it came about when Adoni-
zedek king of Jerusalem heard
that Joshua had captured Ai, and
had utterly destroyed it (just as he
had done to Jericho and its king,
so he had done to Ai and its king),
and that the inhabitants of Gibeon

had [r]made peace with Israel and
were within their land, Josh. 9:15
2 that [t]he feared greatly, because Gibeon *was* a great city,
like one of the royal cities, and because it was greater than Ai, and
all its men *were* mighty. *they*
3 Therefore Adoni-zedek of Jerusalem sent *word* [r]to Hoham king
of Hebron and to Piram king of
Jarmuth and to Japhia king of Lachish and to Debir king of Eglon,
saying, Josh. 10:23
4 "Come up to me and help me,
and let us [t]attack Gibeon, for it has
made peace with Joshua and with
the sons of Israel." *smite*
5 So the five kings of [r]the Amorites, the king of Jerusalem, the
king of Hebron, the king of Jarmuth, the king of Lachish, *and* the
king of Eglon, gathered together
and went up, they with all their
armies, and camped by Gibeon
and fought against it. Num. 13:29
6 Then the men of Gibeon sent
word to Joshua to the camp at Gilgal, saying, "Do not [t]abandon your
servants; come up to us quickly
and save us and help us, for all the
kings of the Amorites that live in
the hill country have assembled
against us." *slacken your hands from*
7 So Joshua went up from Gilgal, he and [r]all the people of war
with him and all the valiant warriors. Josh. 8:1
8 And the LORD said to Joshua,
"Do not fear them, for I have giv-
en them into your hands; not one
of them shall stand before you."
9 So Joshua came upon them
suddenly [t]by marching all night
from Gilgal. *he went up*
10 [r]And the LORD confounded
them before Israel, and He [t]slew
them with a great slaughter at
Gibeon, and pursued them by the
way of the ascent of Beth-horon,
and struck them as far as Azekah
and Makkedah. Deut. 7:23 • *struck*
11 And it came about as they
fled from before Israel, *while* they
were at the descent of Beth-horon,
that the LORD threw large stones
from heaven on them as far as
Azekah, and they died; *there were*
more who died from the hailstones than those whom the sons
of Israel killed with the sword.
12 Then Joshua spoke to the
LORD in the day when the LORD
delivered up the Amorites before
the sons of Israel, and he said in
the sight of Israel,

"O [r]sun, stand still at Gibeon,
And O moon in the valley of
Aijalon." Hab. 3:11
13 [r]So the sun stood still, and
the moon stopped,
Until the nation avenged
themselves of their en-
emies.

Is it not written in [r]the book of Jashar? And the sun stopped in the
middle of the sky, and did not hasten to go *down* for about a whole
day. Hab. 3:11 • 2 Sam. 1:18
14 And there was no day like
that before it or after it, when the
LORD listened to the voice of a
man; for [r]the LORD fought for Israel. Ex. 14:14; Deut. 1:30
15 Then Joshua and all Israel
with him returned to the camp to
Gilgal.
16 Now these [r]five kings had fled
and hidden themselves in the cave
at Makkedah. Josh. 10:5
17 And it was told Joshua, say-

ing, "The five kings have been found hidden in the cave at Makkedah."

18 And Joshua said, "Roll large stones against the mouth of the cave, and assign men by it to guard them,

19 but do not stay *there* yourselves; pursue your enemies and attack them in the rear. Do not allow them to enter their cities, for the LORD your God has delivered them into your hand."

20 And it came about when Joshua and the sons of Israel had finished [t]slaying them with a very great slaughter, until they were destroyed, and the survivors *who* remained of them [t]had entered the fortified cities, *striking · and had*

21 that all the people returned to the camp to Joshua at Makkedah in peace. No one [t]uttered a word against any of the sons of Israel. *sharpened his tongue*

22 Then Joshua said, "Open the mouth of the cave and bring these five kings out to me from the cave."

23 And they did so, and [r]brought these five kings out to him from the cave: the king of Jerusalem, the king of Hebron, the king of Jarmuth, the king of Lachish, *and* the king of Eglon. Deut. 7:24

24 And it came about when they brought these kings out to Joshua, that Joshua called for all the men of Israel, and said to the chiefs of the men of war who had gone with him, "Come near, put your feet on the necks of these kings." So they came near and put their feet on their necks.

25 Joshua then said to them, "Do not fear or be dismayed! Be strong and courageous, for thus the LORD will do to all your enemies with whom you fight."

26 So afterward Joshua struck them and put them to death, and he [r]hanged them on five trees; and they hung on the trees until evening. Josh. 8:29

27 And it came about at [t]sunset that Joshua commanded, and they took them down from the trees and threw them into the cave where they had hidden themselves, and put large stones over the mouth of the cave, to this very day. *the time of the going of the sun*

28 Now Joshua captured Makkedah on that day, and struck it and its king with the edge of the sword; he utterly destroyed it and every [8]person who was in it. He left no survivor. Thus he did to the king of Makkedah just as he had done to the king of Jericho.

29 Then Joshua and all Israel with him passed on from Makkedah to [r]Libnah, and fought against Libnah. Josh. 15:42; 21:13

30 And the LORD gave it also with its king into the hands of Israel, and he struck it and every person who *was* in it with the edge of the sword. He left no survivor in it. Thus he did to its king just as he had done to the king of Jericho.

31 And Joshua and all Israel with him passed on from Libnah to Lachish, and they camped by it and fought against it.

32 And the LORD gave Lachish into the hands of Israel; and he captured it on the second day, and struck it and every person who

[8]Lit., *soul*, and so throughout this context

was in it with the edge of the
sword, according to all that he
had done to Libnah.
33 Then Horam king of [r]Gezer
came up to help Lachish, and
Joshua [t]defeated him and his people until he had left him no survivor. Josh. 16:3, 10 • *smote*
34 And Joshua and all Israel
with him passed on from Lachish
to Eglon, and they camped by it
and fought against it.
35 And they captured it on that
day and struck it with the edge of
the sword; and he utterly destroyed that day every person
who *was* in it, according to all that
he had done to Lachish.
36 Then Joshua and all Israel
with him went up from Eglon to
[r]Hebron, and they fought against
it. Num. 13:22; Judg. 1:10, 20
37 And they captured it and
struck it and its king and all its
cities and all the persons who
were in it with the edge of the
sword. He left no survivor, according to all that he had done to
Eglon. And he utterly destroyed it
and every person who *was* in it.
38 Then Joshua and all Israel
with him returned to [r]Debir, and
they fought against it. Josh. 15:15
39 And he captured it and its
king and all its cities, and they
struck them with the edge of the
sword, and utterly destroyed every person *who was* in it. He left
no survivor. Just as he had done
to Hebron, so he did to Debir and
its king, as he had also done to
Libnah and its king.
40 Thus Joshua struck all the
land, the hill country and the
[9]Negev and the lowland and the
slopes and all their kings. He left
no survivor, but he [a]utterly destroyed all who breathed, just as
the LORD, the God of Israel, had
commanded. *put it under the ban*
41 And Joshua struck them
from Kadesh-barnea even as far
as Gaza, and all the country of
Goshen even as far as Gibeon.
42 And Joshua captured all
these kings and their lands at one
time, because the LORD, the God
of Israel, fought for Israel.
43 So Joshua and all Israel with
him returned to the camp at Gilgal.

CHAPTER 11

THEN it came about, when Jabin
king of [r]Hazor heard *of it,* that he
sent to Jobab king of Madon and
to the king of Shimron and to the
king of Achshaph, Josh. 11:10
2 and to the kings who were of
the north in the hill country, and
in the Arabah—south of [10]Chin-
neroth and in the lowland and on
the heights of Dor on the west—
3 to the Canaanite on the east
and on the west, and the Amorite
and the Hittite and the Perizzite
and the Jebusite in the hill country, and the Hivite at the foot of
Hermon in the land of Mizpeh.
4 And they came out, they and
all their armies with them, [r]*as*
many people *as* the sand that is on
the seashore, with very many
horses and chariots. Judg. 7:12
5 So all of these kings having
agreed to meet, came and encamped together at the waters of
Merom, to fight against Israel.
6 Then the LORD said to

[9]I.e., South country

[10]I.e., Sea of Galilee

Joshua, "Do[r] not be afraid because of them, for tomorrow at this time I will deliver all of them slain before Israel; you shall hamstring their horses and burn their chariots with fire." Josh. 10:8

7 So Joshua and all the people of war with him came upon them suddenly by the waters of Merom, and attacked them.

8 And the LORD delivered them into the hand of Israel, so that they [t]defeated them, and pursued them as far as Great Sidon and [r]Misrephoth-maim and the valley of Mizpeh to the east; and they struck them until no survivor was left to them. *smote* • Josh. 13:6

9 And Joshua did to them as the LORD had told him; he [r]hamstrung their horses, and burned their chariots with fire. Josh. 11:6

10 Then Joshua turned back at that time, and captured [r]Hazor and struck its king with the sword; for Hazor formerly was the head of all these kingdoms. Josh. 11:1

11 And they struck every person who was in it with the edge of the sword, [a]utterly destroying *them;* there was no one left who breathed. And he burned Hazor with fire. *putting them under the ban*

12 And Joshua captured all the cities of these kings, and all their kings, and he struck them with the edge of the sword, *and* utterly destroyed them; just [r]as Moses the servant of the LORD had commanded. Num. 33:50-52; Deut. 7:2

13 However, Israel did not burn any cities that stood on their mounds, except Hazor alone, *which* Joshua burned.

14 [r]And all the spoil of these cities and the cattle, the sons of Israel took as their plunder; but they struck every man with the edge of the sword, until they had destroyed them. They left no one who breathed. Num. 31:11, 12

15 Just as the LORD had commanded Moses his servant, so Moses commanded Joshua, and so Joshua did; he left nothing undone of all that the LORD had commanded Moses.

16 Thus Joshua took all that land: the hill country and all the Negev, all that land of Goshen, the lowland, the Arabah, the hill country of Israel and its lowland

17 from Mount Halak, that rises toward Seir, even as far as Baal-gad in the valley of Lebanon at the foot of Mount Hermon. And he captured all their kings and struck them down and put them to death.

18 Joshua waged war a long time with all these kings.

19 There was not a city which made peace with the sons of Israel except the Hivites living in Gibeon; they took them all in battle.

20 For it was of the LORD to harden their hearts, to meet Israel in battle in order that he might utterly destroy them, that they might receive no mercy, but that he might destroy them, just as the LORD had commanded Moses.

21 Then Joshua came at that time and cut off [r]the Anakim from the hill country, from Hebron, from Debir, from Anab and from all the hill country of Judah and from all the hill country of Israel. Joshua utterly destroyed them with their cities. Num. 13:33

22 There were no Anakim left in

the land of the sons of Israel; only
in Gaza, in [r]Gath, and in Ashdod
some remained. 1 Sam. 17:4
23 So Joshua took the whole
land, according to all that the
LORD had spoken to Moses, and
[r]Joshua gave it for an inheritance
to Israel according to their divisions by their tribes. Thus the land
had rest from war. Deut. 1:38

CHAPTER 12

NOW these are the kings of the
land whom the sons of Israel defeated, and whose land they possessed beyond the Jordan toward
the sunrise, from the valley of the
Arnon as far as Mount Hermon,
and all the Arabah to the east:
2 Sihon king of the Amorites,
who lived in Heshbon, *and* ruled
[r]from Aroer, which is on the edge
of the valley of the Arnon, both
the middle of the valley and half
of Gilead, even as far as the brook
Jabbok, the border of the sons of
Ammon; Deut. 2:36
3 and the Arabah as far as the
Sea of [‖]Chinneroth toward the
east, and as far as the sea of the
Arabah, *even* the Salt Sea, eastward [t]toward Beth-jeshimoth, and
on the south, [t]at the foot of the
slopes of Pisgah; *the way of* · *under*
4 and the territory of Og king
of Bashan, one of [r]the remnant of
Rephaim, who lived at [r]Ashtaroth
and at Edrei, Deut. 3:11 · Deut. 1:4
5 and ruled over Mount Hermon and Salecah and all Bashan,
as far as the border of the Geshurites and the Maacathites, and
half of Gilead, *as far as* the border
of Sihon king of Heshbon.
6 Moses the servant of the
LORD and the sons of Israel [t]de-
feated them; and [r]Moses the servant of the LORD gave it to the
Reubenites and the Gadites, and
the half-tribe of Manasseh as a
possession. *smote* · Num. 32:33
7 Now these are the kings of
the land whom Joshua and the
sons of Israel [t]defeated beyond the
Jordan toward the west, from
Baal-gad in the valley of Lebanon
even as far as [r]Mount Halak,
which rises toward Seir; and
Joshua gave it to the tribes of Israel as a possession according to
their divisions, *smote* · Josh. 11:17
8 in the hill country, in the lowland, in the Arabah, on the slopes,
and in the wilderness, and in the
Negev; the Hittite, the Amorite
and the Canaanite, the Perizzite,
the Hivite and the Jebusite:
9 the [r]king of Jericho, one; the
[r]king of Ai, which is beside Bethel,
one; Josh. 6:2 · Josh. 8:29
10 the king of Jerusalem, one;
the king of Hebron, one;
11 the king of Jarmuth, one; the
king of Lachish, one;
12 the king of Eglon, one; the
king of Gezer, one;
13 the king of Debir, one; the
king of Geder, one;
14 the king of Hormah, one; the
king of [r]Arad, one; Num. 21:1
15 the king of Libnah, one; the
king of Adullam, one;
16 the king of Makkedah, one;
the king of Bethel, one;
17 the king of Tappuah, one; the
[r]king of Hepher, one; 1 Kin. 4:10

[‖]I.e., Galilee

18 the king of [r]Aphek, one; the
king of Lasharon, one; Josh. 13:4
19 the king of Madon, one; the
king of Hazor, one;
20 the king of Shimron-meron,
one; the king of Achshaph, one;
21 the king of Taanach, one; the
king of Megiddo, one;
22 the king of Kedesh, one; the
king of Jokneam in Carmel, one;
23 the king of Dor in the [a]heights
of Dor, one; the king of [r]Goiim in
Gilgal, one; *Naphath-dor* • Gen. 4:1
24 the king of Tirzah, one: [r]in all,
thirty-one kings. Deut. 7:24

CHAPTER 13

NOW Joshua was old *and* advanced in years when the LORD
said to him, "You are old *and* advanced in years, and very much of
the land remains to be possessed.
2 "This is the land that remains:
all the regions *of* the Philistines
and all *those of* the Geshurites;
3 from the Shihor which is [t]east
of Egypt, even as far as the border
of Ekron to the north (it is
counted as Canaanite); the [r]five
lords of the Philistines: the Gazite,
the Ashdodite, the Ashkelonite,
the Gittite, the Ekronite; and the
Avvite *on the face of* • 1 Sam. 6:4, 16
4 [a]to the south, all the land of
the Canaanite, and Mearah that
belongs to the Sidonians, as far as
[r]Aphek, to the border of the Amorite; *from the Teman* • Josh. 12:18
5 and the land of the Gebalite,
and all of Lebanon, toward the
east, from Baal-gad below Mount
Hermon as far as Lebo-hamath.
6 "All the inhabitants of the hill
country from Lebanon as far as
Misrephoth-maim, all the Sidonians, I will [a]drive them out from before the sons of Israel; only allot it
to Israel for an inheritance as I
have commanded you. *dispossess*
7 "Now therefore, apportion
this land for an inheritance to the
nine tribes, and the half-tribe of
Manasseh."
8 With the other half-tribe, the
Reubenites and the Gadites received their inheritance which
Moses gave them beyond the Jordan to the east, just as Moses the
servant of the LORD gave to them;
9 from Aroer, which is on the
edge of the valley of the Arnon,
with the city which is in the middle of the valley, and all the plain
of Medeba, as far as Dibon;
10 and all the cities of Sihon
king of the Amorites, who reigned
in Heshbon, as far as the border of
the sons of Ammon;
11 and Gilead, and the territory
of the Geshurites and Maacathites, and all Mount Hermon, and
all Bashan as far as Salecah;
12 all the kingdom of [r]Og in Bashan, who reigned in Ashtaroth
and in Edrei (he alone was left of
the remnant of the Rephaim); for
Moses struck them and dispossessed them. Deut. 3:11
13 But the sons of Israel did not
dispossess the Geshurites or the
Maacathites; for Geshur and Maa-
cath live among Israel until this
day.
14 Only to the tribe of Levi he
did not give an inheritance; the offerings by fire to the LORD, the
God of Israel, are [t]their inheritance, as He spoke to him. *his*

15 So Moses gave *an inheritance* to the tribe of the sons of Reuben according to their families.

16 And their territory was from Aroer, which is on the edge of the valley of the Arnon, with the city which is in the middle of the valley and all the plain by Medeba;

17 Heshbon, and all its cities which are on the plain: Dibon and Bamoth-baal and Beth-baal-meon,

18 and [r]Jahaz and Kedemoth and Mephaath, Num. 21:23; Is. 15:4

19 and [r]Kiriathaim and Sibmah and Zereth-shahar on the hill of the valley, Num. 32:37; Jer. 48:1, 23

20 and Beth-peor and the slopes of Pisgah and Beth-jeshimoth,

21 even all the cities of the plain and all the kingdom of Sihon king of the Amorites who reigned in Heshbon, whom Moses struck with the chiefs of Midian, [r]Evi and Rekem and Zur and Hur and Reba, the princes of Sihon, who lived in the land. Num. 31:8

22 The sons of Israel also killed [r]Balaam the son of Beor, the diviner, with the sword among *the rest of* their slain. Num. 31:8

23 And the border of the sons of Reuben was the Jordan. This was the inheritance of the sons of Reuben according to their families, the cities and their villages.

24 Moses also gave *an inheritance* to the tribe of Gad, to the sons of Gad, according to their families.

25 And their territory was [r]Jazer, and all the cities of Gilead, and half the land of the sons of Ammon, as far as Aroer which is before Rabbah; Num. 21:32

26 and from Heshbon as far as Ramath-mizpeh and Betonim, and from Mahanaim as far as the border of [a]Debir; *Lidebir*

27 and in the valley, Beth-haram and Beth-nimrah and Succoth and Zaphon, the rest of the kingdom of Sihon king of Heshbon, with the Jordan [t]as a border, as far as the *lower* end of the Sea of [r]Chinnereth beyond the Jordan to the east. *and border* • Num. 34:11

28 This is the inheritance of the sons of Gad according to their families, the cities and their villages.

29 Moses also gave *an inheritance* to the half-tribe of Manasseh; and it was for the half-tribe of the sons of Manasseh according to their families.

30 And their territory was from Mahanaim, all Bashan, all the kingdom of Og king of Bashan, and all the towns of Jair, which are in Bashan, sixty cities;

31 also half of Gilead, with [r]Ashtaroth and Edrei, the cities of the kingdom of Og in Bashan, *were* for the sons of Machir the son of Manasseh, for half of the sons of Machir according to their families. Josh. 9:10; 12:4; 13:12

32 These are *the territories* which Moses apportioned for an inheritance in the plains of Moab, beyond the Jordan at Jericho to the east.

33 But to the tribe of Levi, Moses did not give an inheritance; the LORD, the God of Israel, is their inheritance, as He had [t]promised to them. *spoken to*

CHAPTER 14

NOW these are *the territories* which the sons of Israel inherited in the land of Canaan, which Eleazar the priest, and Joshua the son of Nun, and the heads of the [t]households of the tribes of the sons of Israel apportioned to them for an inheritance, *fathers'*

2 by the lot of their inheritance, as the LORD commanded [t]through Moses, for the nine tribes and the half-tribe. *by the hand of*

3 For Moses had given the inheritance of the two tribes and the half-tribe beyond the Jordan; but he did not give an inheritance to the Levites among them.

4 For the sons of Joseph were two tribes, [r]Manasseh and Ephraim, and they did not give a portion to the Levites in the land, except cities to live in, with their pasture lands for their livestock and for their property. Gen. 41:51f.; 46:20

5 Thus the sons of Israel did just as the LORD had commanded Moses, and they divided the land.

6 Then the sons of Judah drew near to Joshua in Gilgal, and Caleb the son of Jephunneh the Kenizzite said to him, "You know the word which the LORD spoke to Moses the man of God concerning you and me in Kadesh-barnea.

7 "I was forty years old when [r]Moses the servant of the LORD sent me from Kadesh-barnea to spy out the land, and I brought word back to him as *it was* in my heart. Num. 13:1-31

8 "Nevertheless my brethren who went up with me made the heart of the people [t]melt with fear; but I followed the LORD my God fully. *become demoralized*

9 "So Moses swore on that day, saying, 'Surely [r]the land on which your foot has trodden shall be an inheritance to you and to your children forever, because you have followed the LORD my God fully.' Deut. 1:36

10 "And now behold, the LORD has let me live, just as He spoke, these forty-five years, from the time that the LORD spoke this word to Moses, when Israel walked in the wilderness; and now behold, I am eighty-five years old today.

11 "I am still as strong today as I was in the day Moses sent me; as my strength was then, so my strength is now, for war and for going out and coming in.

12 "Now then, give me this hill country about which the LORD spoke on that day, for you heard on that day that Anakim *were* there, with great fortified cities; perhaps the LORD will be with me, and I shall [a]drive them out as the LORD has spoken." *dispossess*

13 So Joshua blessed him, and gave Hebron to Caleb the son of Jephunneh for an inheritance.

14 Therefore, Hebron became the inheritance of Caleb the son of Jephunneh the Kenizzite until this day, because he followed the LORD God of Israel fully.

15 Now the name of Hebron was formerly Kiriath-arba; *for Arba* was the greatest man among the Anakim. [r]Then the land had rest from war. Josh. 11:23

CHAPTER 15

NOW the lot for the tribe of the sons of Judah according to their families reached the border of Edom, southward to the wilderness of Zin at the extreme south.

2 And their south border was from the lower end of the Salt Sea, from the bay that turns to the south.

3 Then it proceeded southward to the ascent of Akrabbim and continued to Zin, then went up by the south of Kadesh-barnea and continued to Hezron, and went up to Addar and turned about to Karka.

4 And it continued to Azmon and proceeded to the brook of Egypt; and the [t]border ended at the sea. This shall be your south border. *goings out of the border were*

5 And the east border *was* the Salt Sea, as far as the mouth of the Jordan. And the border of the north side was from the bay of the sea at the mouth of the Jordan.

6 Then the border went up to Beth-hoglah, and continued on the north of Beth-arabah, and the border went up to the stone of Bohan the son of Reuben.

7 And the border went up to Debir from the valley of Achor, and turned northward toward Gilgal which is opposite the ascent of Adummim, which is on the south of the valley; and the border continued to the waters of En-shemesh, and it ended at En-rogel.

8 Then the border went up the valley of Ben-hinnom to the slope of the [r]Jebusite on the south (that is, Jerusalem); and the border went up to the top of the mountain which is before the valley of Hinnom to the west, which is at the end of the valley of Rephaim toward the north. Josh. 15:63

9 And from the top of the mountain the border curved to the spring of the waters of Nephtoah and proceeded to the cities of Mount Ephron, then the border curved to [r]Baalah (that is, [r]Kiriath-jearim). 1 Chr. 13:6 • Judg. 18:12

10 And the border turned about from Baalah westward to Mount Seir, and continued to the slope of Mount Jearim on the north (that is, Chesalon), and went down to Beth-shemesh and continued through [r]Timnah. Gen. 38:13

11 And the border proceeded to the side of Ekron northward. Then the border curved to Shikkeron and continued to Mount Baalah and proceeded to Jabneel, and the border ended at the sea.

12 And the west border *was* [r]at the Great Sea, even *its* [t]coastline. This is the border around the sons of Judah according to their families. Num. 34:6 • *border*

13 Now he gave to Caleb the son of Jephunneh a portion among the sons of Judah, according to the [t]command of the LORD to Joshua, *namely,* Kiriath-arba, *Arba being* the father of Anak (that is, Hebron). *mouth*

14 And Caleb [a]drove out from there the three sons of Anak: Sheshai and Ahiman and Talmai, the children of Anak. *dispossessed*

15 Then [r]he went up from there against the inhabitants of Debir; now the name of Debir formerly was Kiriath-sepher. Josh. 10:38

16 And Caleb said, "The one
who [t]attacks Kiriath-sepher and
captures it, I will give him Achsah
my daughter as a wife." *smites*
17 And [r]Othniel the son of Kenaz, the brother of Caleb, captured it; so he gave him Achsah
his daughter as a wife. Judg. 1:13
18 [r]And it came about that when
she came *to him,* she persuaded
him to ask her father for a field.
So she alighted from the donkey,
and Caleb said to her, "What do
you want?" Judg. 1:14
19 Then she said, "Give me a
blessing; since you have given me
the land of the Negev, give me
also springs of water." So he gave
her the upper springs and the lower springs.
20 This is the inheritance of the
tribe of the sons of Judah according to their families.
21 Now the cities at the extremity of the tribe of the sons of Judah toward the border of Edom in
the south were Kabzeel and [r]Eder
and Jagur, Gen. 35:21
22 and Kinah and Dimonah and
Adadah,
23 and Kedesh and Hazor and
Ithnan,
24 Ziph and Telem and Bealoth,
25 and Hazor-hadattah and Ke-
rioth-hezron (that is, Hazor),
26 Amam and Shema and Moladah,
27 and Hazar-gaddah and Hesh-
mon and Beth-pelet,
28 and Hazar-shual and [r]Beer-
sheba and Biziothiah, Gen. 21:31
29 Baalah and Iim and Ezem,
30 and Eltolad and Chesil and
Hormah,
31 and [r]Ziklag and Madmannah
and Sansannah, 1 Sam. 27:6; 30:1
32 and Lebaoth and Shilhim and
Ain and Rimmon; in all, twenty-
nine cities with their villages.
33 In the lowland: [r]Eshtaol and
Zorah and Ashnah, Judg. 13:25
34 and Zanoah and En-gannim,
Tappuah and Enam,
35 Jarmuth and [r]Adullam, Socoh
and Azekah, 1 Sam. 22:1
36 and Shaaraim and Adithaim
and Gederah and Gederothaim;
fourteen cities with their villages.
37 Zenan and Hadashah and
Migdal-gad,
38 and Dilean and Mizpeh and
Joktheel,
39 [r]Lachish and Bozkath and Eglon, Josh. 10:3; 2 Kin. 14:19
40 and Cabbon and Lahmas and
Chitlish,
41 and Gederoth, Beth-dagon
and Naamah and Makkedah; sixteen cities with their villages.
42 Libnah and Ether and Ashan,
43 and Iphtah and Ashnah and
Nezib,
44 and Keilah and Achzib and
Mareshah; nine cities with their
villages.
45 Ekron, with its towns and its
villages;
46 from Ekron even to the sea,
all that were by the [t]side of Ashdod, with their villages. *hand*
47 Ashdod, its towns and its villages; Gaza, its towns and its villages; as far as [r]the [a]brook of Egypt
and the Great Sea, even *its* [t]coast-
line. Josh. 15:4 • *wadi* • *border*
48 And in the hill country: Shamir and Jattir and Socoh,
49 and Dannah and Kiriath-san-
nah (that is, Debir),

50 and Anab and Eshtemoh and
Anim,
51 and Goshen and Holon and
Giloh; eleven cities with their villages.
52 Arab and Dumah and Eshan,
53 and Janum and Beth-tappu-
ah and Aphekah,
54 and Humtah and Kiriath-
arba (that is, Hebron), and Zior;
nine cities with their villages.
55 Maon, Carmel and Ziph and
Juttah,
56 and Jezreel and Jokdeam
and Zanoah,
57 Kain, Gibeah and Timnah;
ten cities with their villages.
58 Halhul, Beth-zur and Gedor,
59 and Maarath and Beth-anoth
and Eltekon; six cities with their
villages.
60 Kiriath-baal (that is, Kiriath-
jearim), and Rabbah; two cities
with their villages.
61 In the wilderness: Beth-arabah, Middin and Secacah,
62 and Nibshan and the City of
Salt and Engedi; six cities with
their villages.
63 Now as for the [r]Jebusites, the
inhabitants of Jerusalem, the sons
of Judah could not [a]drive them out;
so the Jebusites live with the sons
of Judah at Jerusalem until this
day. Judg. 1:21 • *dispossess them*

CHAPTER 16

THEN the lot for the sons of
Joseph went from the Jordan at
Jericho to the waters of Jericho on
the east into [r]the wilderness, going
up from Jericho through the hill
country to Bethel. Josh. 8:15
2 And it went from Bethel to
Luz, and continued to the border
of the Archites at Ataroth.
3 And it went down westward
to the territory of the Japhletites,
as far as the territory of lower
[r]Beth-horon even to Gezer, and it
ended at the sea. Josh. 18:13
4 And the [r]sons of Joseph, Manasseh and Ephraim, received
their inheritance. Josh. 17:14
5 Now *this* was the territory of
the sons of Ephraim according to
their families: the border of their
inheritance eastward was [r]Ata-
roth-addar, as far as upper Beth-
horon. Josh. 18:13
6 Then the border went westward at [r]Michmethath on the
north, and the border turned
about eastward to Taanath-shiloh,
and continued *beyond* it to the
east of Janoah. Josh. 17:7
7 And it went down from Janoah to Ataroth and to [r]Naarah, then
reached Jericho and came out at
the Jordan. 1 Chr. 7:28
8 From [r]Tappuah the border
continued westward to the [a]brook
of Kanah, and it ended at the sea.
This is the inheritance of the tribe
of the sons of Ephraim according
to their families, Josh. 17:8 • *wadi*
9 *together* with the cities
which were set apart for the sons
of Ephraim in the midst of the inheritance of the sons of Manasseh, all the cities with their villages.
10 But they did not [a]drive out the
Canaanites who lived in Gezer, so
the Canaanites live in the midst of
Ephraim to this day, and they became forced laborers. *dispossess*

CHAPTER 17

NOW *this* was the lot for the tribe of Manasseh, for he was the first-born of Joseph. To Machir the first-born of Manasseh, the father of Gilead,[t]was allotted Gilead and Bashan, because he was a man of war. *and there was to him*

2 So *the lot* was *made* for the rest of the sons of Manasseh according to their families: for the sons of Abiezer and for the sons of Helek and for the sons of Asriel and for the sons of Shechem and for the sons of Hepher and for the sons of Shemida; these *were* the male *descendants* of Manasseh the son of Joseph according to their families.

3 However, Zelophehad, the son of Hepher, the son of Gilead, the son of Machir, the son of Manasseh, had no sons, only daughters; and these are the names of his daughters: Mahlah and Noah, Hoglah, Milcah and Tirzah.

4 And they came near before Eleazar the priest and before Joshua the son of Nun and before the leaders, saying, "The LORD commanded Moses to give us an inheritance among our brothers." So[r]according to the[t]command of the LORD he gave them an inheritance among their father's brothers. Num. 27:5-7 · *mouth*

5 Thus there fell ten portions to Manasseh, besides the land of Gilead and Bashan, which is beyond the Jordan,

6 because the daughters of Manasseh received an inheritance among his sons. And the[r]land of Gilead belonged to the rest of the sons of Manasseh. Josh. 13:30, 31

7 And the border of Manasseh [t]ran from Asher to Michmethath which was east of Shechem; then the border went southward to the inhabitants of En-tappuah. *was*

8 The land of Tappuah[r] belonged to Manasseh, but Tappuah on the border of Manasseh *belonged* to the sons of Ephraim.

9 And the border went down to the brook of Kanah, southward of the brook (these cities *belonged* to Ephraim among the cities of Manasseh), and the border of Manasseh *was* on the north side of the brook, and it ended at the sea.

10 The south side *belonged* to Ephraim and the north side to Manasseh, and the sea was[t]their border; and they reached to Asher on the north and to Issachar on the east. *its*

11 And in Issachar and in Asher,[r]Manasseh had Beth-shean and its towns and Ibleam and its towns, and the inhabitants of Dor and its towns, and the inhabitants of En-dor and its towns, and the inhabitants of Taanach and its towns, and the inhabitants of Megiddo and its towns, the third is [r]Napheth. 1 Chr. 7:29 · Josh. 11:2

12 But the sons of Manasseh could not take possession of these cities, because the Canaanites persisted in living in that land.

13 And it came about when the sons of Israel became strong, they put the Canaanites to forced labor, but they did not[a]drive them out completely. *dispossess*

14 Then the[r]sons of Joseph spoke to Joshua, saying, "Why

have you given me only one lot
and one portion for an inheritance, since I am a numerous people whom the LORD has thus far
blessed?" Num. 13:7
15 And Joshua said to them, "If
you are a numerous people, go up
to the forest and [t]clear a place for
yourself there in the land of the
Perizzites and of the Rephaim,
since the hill country of Ephraim
is too narrow for you." *cut down*
16 And the sons of Joseph said,
"The hill country is not enough for
us, and all the Canaanites who
live in the valley land have [r]chari-
ots of iron, both those who are in
Beth-shean and its towns, and
those who are in the valley of Jezreel." Josh. 17:18; Judg. 1:19; 4:3, 13
17 And Joshua spoke to the
house of Joseph, to Ephraim and
Manasseh, saying, "You are a numerous people and have great
power; you shall not have one lot
only,
18 but the hill country shall be
yours. For though it is a forest,
you shall [t]clear it, and to its [t]far-
thest borders it shall be yours; for
you shall drive out the Canaanites, even though they have chariots of iron *and* though they are
strong." *cut it down • goings out*

CHAPTER 18

THEN the whole congregation of
the sons of Israel assembled
themselves at Shiloh, and set up
the tent of meeting there; and the
land was subdued before them.
2 And there remained among
the sons of Israel seven tribes who
had not divided their inheritance.
3 So Joshua said to the sons of
Israel, "How long will you put off
entering to take possession of the
land which the LORD, the God of
your fathers, has given you?
4 "Provide for yourselves three
men from [t]each tribe that I may
send them, and that they may
arise and walk through the land
and write a description of it according to their inheritance; then
they shall [t]return to me. *the • come*
5 "And they shall divide it into
seven portions; [r]Judah shall stay in
its territory on the south, and the
house of Joseph shall stay in their
territory on the north. Josh. 15:1
6 "And you shall describe the
land in seven divisions, and bring
the description here to me. [r]And I
will cast lots for you here before
the LORD our God. Josh. 14:2
7 "For the Levites have no portion among you, because the
priesthood of the LORD is [t]their inheritance. Gad and Reuben and
the half-tribe of Manasseh also
have received their inheritance
eastward beyond the Jordan,
which Moses the servant of the
LORD gave them." *his*
8 Then the men arose and
went, and Joshua commanded
those who went to describe the
land, saying, "Go and walk
through the land and describe it,
and return to me; then I will cast
lots for you here before the LORD
in [r]Shiloh." Josh. 18:1
9 So the men went and passed
through the land, and described it
by cities in seven divisions in a
book; and they came to Joshua to
the camp at Shiloh.
10 And [r]Joshua cast lots for

them in Shiloh before the LORD,
and there Joshua divided the land
to the sons of Israel according to
their divisions. Num. 34:16-29
11 Now the lot of the tribe of
the sons of Benjamin came up according to their families, and the
territory of their lot [t]lay between
the sons of Judah and the sons of
Joseph. *went out*
12 And [r]their border on the
north side was from the Jordan,
then the border went up to the
side of Jericho on the north, and
went up through the hill country
westward; and [12]it ended at the
wilderness of Beth-aven. Josh. 16:1
13 And from there the border
continued to Luz, to the side of
Luz (that is, Bethel) southward;
and the border went down to Ata-
roth-addar, near the hill which *lies*
on the south of lower Beth-horon.
14 And the border extended
from there, and turned round on
the west side southward, from the
hill which *lies* before Beth-horon
southward; and [12]it ended at Kiriath-baal (that is, Kiriath-jearim), a
city of the sons of Judah. This *was*
the west side.
15 Then the [r]south side *was* from
the edge of Kiriath-jearim, and
the border went westward and
went to the fountain of the waters
of Nephtoah. Josh. 15:5-9
16 And the border went down to
the edge of the hill which is in the
[r]valley of Ben-hinnom, which is in
the valley of Rephaim northward;
and it went down to the valley of
Hinnom, to the slope of the Jebusite southward, and went down to
En-rogel. 2 Kin. 23:10

[12]Lit., *goings out of it were*

17 And it extended northward
and went to En-shemesh and went
to Geliloth, which is opposite the
ascent of Adummim, and it went
down to the [r]stone of Bohan the
son of Reuben. Josh. 15:6
18 And it continued to the side
in front of the Arabah northward,
and went down to the Arabah.
19 And the border continued to
the side of Beth-hoglah northward; and the [12]border ended at
the north bay of the Salt Sea, at
the south end of the Jordan. This
was the south border.
20 Moreover, the Jordan was its
border on the east side. This *was*
the inheritance of the sons of Benjamin, according to their families
and according to its borders all
around.
21 Now the cities of the tribe of
the sons of Benjamin according to
their families were Jericho and
Beth-hoglah and Emek-keziz,
22 and Beth-arabah and Zema-
raim and Bethel,
23 and Avvim and Parah and
Ophrah,
24 and Chephar-ammoni and
Ophni and [r]Geba; twelve cities
with their villages. Ezra 2:26
25 Gibeon and Ramah and Beeroth,
26 and Mizpeh and Chephirah
and Mozah,
27 and Rekem and Irpeel and
Taralah,
28 and Zelah, Haeleph and the
Jebusite (that is, Jerusalem), Gibeah, Kiriath; fourteen cities with
their villages. This is the inheritance of the sons of Benjamin according to their families.

[12]Lit., *goings out of it were*

CHAPTER 19

THEN the second lot [t]fell to Simeon, to the tribe of the sons of Simeon according to their families, and their inheritance was in the midst of the inheritance of the sons of Judah. *came out*

2 So they had as their inheritance Beersheba and Sheba and Moladah,

3 and Hazar-shual and Balah and Ezem,

4 and Eltolad and Bethul and Hormah,

5 and Ziklag and Beth-marcaboth and Hazar-susah,

6 and Beth-lebaoth and Sharuhen, thirteen cities with their villages;

7 Ain, Rimmon and Ether and Ashan, four cities with their villages;

8 and all the villages which *were* around these cities as far as Baalath-beer, Ramah of the Negev. This *was* the inheritance of the tribe of the sons of Simeon according to their families.

9 The inheritance of the sons of Simeon *was taken* from the portion of the sons of Judah, for the share of the sons of Judah was too large for them; so the sons of Simeon received *an* inheritance in the midst of Judah's inheritance.

10 Now the third lot came up for the sons of Zebulun according to their families. And the territory of their inheritance was as far as Sarid.

11 Then their border went up to the west and to Maralah, it then [a]touched Dabbesheth, and reached to the [a]brook that is before Jokneam. *reached to • wadi*

12 Then it turned from Sarid to the east toward the sunrise as far as the border of Chisloth-tabor, and it proceeded to Daberath and [t]up to Japhia. *went up*

13 And from there it continued eastward toward the sunrise to Gath-hepher, to Eth-kazin, and it proceeded to Rimmon which stretches to Neah.

14 And the border circled around it on the north to Hannathon, and it ended at the valley of Iphtahel.

15 *Included* also *were* Kattah and Nahalal and Shimron and Idalah and Bethlehem; twelve cities with their villages.

16 This *was* the inheritance of the sons of Zebulun according to their families, these cities with their villages.

17 The fourth lot [t]fell to Issachar, to the sons of Issachar according to their families. *came out*

18 And their territory was to Jezreel and *included* Chesulloth and [r]Shunem, 1 Sam. 28:4; 2 Kin. 4:8

19 and Hapharaim and Shion and Anaharath,

20 and Rabbith and Kishion and Ebez,

21 and Remeth and En-gannim and En-haddah and Beth-pazzez.

22 And the border reached to [r]Tabor and Shahazumah and Beth-shemesh, and their border ended at the Jordan; sixteen cities with their villages. Judg. 4:6; Ps. 89:12

23 This *was* the inheritance of the tribe of the sons of Issachar according to their families, the cities with their villages.

24 Now the fifth lot [t]fell to the
tribe of the sons of Asher according to their families. *came out*
25 And their territory was Helkath and Hali and Beten and Achshaph,
26 and Allammelech and Amad
and Mishal; and it reached to Carmel on the west and to Shihor-lib-
nath.
27 And it turned toward the
[t]east to Beth-dagon, and reached
to Zebulun, and to the valley of
Iphtahel northward to Beth-emek
and Neiel; then it proceeded on
north to [r]Cabul, *sunrise* • 1 Kin. 9:13
28 and Ebron and Rehob and
Hammon and Kanah, as far as
Great [r]Sidon. Gen. 10:19; Judg. 1:31
29 And the border turned to Ramah, and to the fortified city of
Tyre; then the border turned to
Hosah, and it ended at the sea by
the region of [r]Achzib. Judg. 1:31
30 *Included* also *were* Ummah,
and Aphek and Rehob; twenty-
two cities with their villages.
31 This *was* the inheritance of
the tribe of the sons of Asher according to their families, these
cities with their villages.
32 The sixth lot fell to the sons
of Naphtali; to the sons of Naphtali according to their families.
33 And their border was from
Heleph, from the oak in Zaanannim and Adami-nekeb and Jabneel, as far as Lakkum; and it
ended at the Jordan.
34 Then the border turned westward to Aznoth-tabor, and proceeded from there to Hukkok; and
it reached to Zebulun on the south
and [a]touched Asher on the west,
and to Judah at the Jordan toward
the [t]east. *reached to* • *sunrise*
35 And the fortified cities *were*
Ziddim, Zer and [r]Hammath, Rak-
kath and Chinnereth, Gen. 10:18
36 and Adamah and Ramah and
Hazor,
37 and Kedesh and Edrei and
En-hazor,
38 and Yiron and Migdal-el, Ho-
rem and Beth-anath and Beth-shemesh; nineteen cities with their
villages.
39 This *was* the inheritance of
the tribe of the sons of Naphtali
according to their families, the
cities with their villages.
40 The seventh lot [t]fell to the
tribe of the sons of Dan according
to their families. *came out*
41 And the territory of their inheritance was Zorah and Eshtaol
and Ir-shemesh,
42 and Shaalabbin and Aijalon
and Ithlah,
43 and Elon and Timnah and
Ekron,
44 and Eltekeh and Gibbethon
and Baalath,
45 and Jehud and Bene-berak
and Gath-rimmon,
46 and Me-jarkon and Rakkon,
with the territory over against
Joppa.
47 And the territory of the sons
of Dan proceeded [t]beyond them;
for the sons of Dan went up and
fought with Leshem and captured
it. Then they struck it with the
edge of the sword and possessed
it and [t]settled in it; and they called
Leshem Dan after the name of
Dan their father. *from* • *dwelt*
48 This *was* the inheritance of
the tribe of the sons of Dan ac-

cording to their families, these cities with their villages.

49 When they finished apportioning the land for inheritance by its borders, the sons of Israel gave an inheritance in their midst to Joshua the son of Nun.

50 In accordance with the [t]command of the LORD they gave him the city for which he asked, Timnath-serah in the hill country of Ephraim. So he built the city and [t]settled in it. *mouth* • *dwelt*

51 [r]These are the inheritances which Eleazar the priest and Joshua the son of Nun and the heads of the [t]households of the tribes of the sons of Israel distributed by lot in Shiloh before the LORD, at the doorway of the tent of meeting. So they finished dividing the land. Josh. 18:10 • *fathers*

CHAPTER 20

THEN the LORD spoke to Joshua, saying,

2 "Speak to the sons of Israel, saying, 'Designate[t] the cities of refuge, of which I spoke to you through Moses, *Set for yourselves*

3 that the manslayer who [t]kills any person unintentionally, without premeditation, may flee there, and they shall become your refuge from the avenger of blood. *smites*

4 'And he shall flee to one of these cities, and shall stand at the entrance of the gate of the city and state his case in the hearing of the elders of that city; and they shall [t]take him into the city to them and give him a place, so that he may dwell among them. *gather*

5 'Now if the avenger of blood pursues him, then they shall not deliver the manslayer into his hand, because he struck his neighbor without premeditation and did not hate him beforehand.

6 'And he shall dwell in that city until he stands before the congregation for judgment, until the death of the one who is high priest in those days. Then the manslayer shall return to his own city and to his own house, to the city from which he fled.' "

7 So they [t]set apart Kedesh in Galilee in the hill country of Naphtali and Shechem in the hill country of Ephraim, and Kiriath-arba (that is, Hebron) in the hill country of Judah. *sanctified*

8 And beyond the Jordan east of Jericho, they [t]designated Bezer in the wilderness on the plain from the tribe of Reuben, and Ramoth in Gilead from the tribe of Gad, and Golan in Bashan from the tribe of Manasseh. *set*

9 These were the appointed cities for all the sons of Israel and for the stranger who sojourns among them, that whoever kills any person unintentionally may flee there, and not die by the hand of the avenger of blood until he stands before the congregation.

CHAPTER 21

THEN the heads of households of the Levites approached Eleazar the priest and Joshua the son of Nun and the heads of households of the tribes of the sons of Israel.

2 And they spoke to them at Shiloh in the land of Canaan, saying, "The LORD commanded

[t]through Moses to give us cities to live in, with their pasture lands for our cattle." *by the hand of*

3 So the sons of Israel gave the Levites from their inheritance these cities with their pasture lands, according to the [t]command of the LORD. *mouth*

4 Then the lot came out for the families of the Kohathites. And the sons of Aaron the priest, who were of the Levites, [t]received thirteen cities by lot from the tribe of Judah and from the tribe of the Simeonites and from the tribe of Benjamin. *had*

5 And the rest of the sons of Kohath [t]received ten cities by lot from the families of the tribe of Ephraim and from the tribe of Dan and from the half-tribe of Manasseh. *had*

6 And the sons of Gershon [t]received thirteen cities by lot from the families of the tribe of Issachar and from the tribe of Asher and from the tribe of Naphtali and from the half-tribe of Manasseh in Bashan. *had*

7 The sons of Merari according to their families [t]received twelve cities from the tribe of Reuben and from the tribe of Gad and from the tribe of Zebulun. *had*

8 Now the [r]sons of Israel gave by lot to the Levites these cities with their pasture lands, as the LORD had commanded [t]through Moses. Gen. 49:5ff. • *by the hand of*

9 And they gave these cities which are *here* mentioned by name from the tribe of the sons of Judah and from the tribe of the sons of Simeon;

10 and they were for the sons of Aaron, one of the families of the Kohathites, of the sons of Levi, for the lot was theirs first.

11 Thus [r]they gave them Kiriath-arba, *Arba being* the father of Anak (that is, Hebron), in the hill country of Judah, with its surrounding pasture lands. 1 Chr. 6:55

12 But the fields of the city and its villages, they gave to Caleb the son of Jephunneh as his possession.

13 So [r]to the sons of Aaron the priest they gave Hebron, the city of refuge for the manslayer, with its pasture lands, and Libnah with its pasture lands, 1 Chr. 6:57

14 and [r]Jattir with its pasture lands and [r]Eshtemoa with its pasture lands, Josh. 15:48 • Josh. 15:50

15 and Holon with its pasture lands and [r]Debir with its pasture lands, Josh. 15:49

16 and Ain with its pasture lands and [r]Juttah with its pasture lands *and* Beth-shemesh with its pasture lands; nine cities from these two tribes. Josh. 15:55

17 And from the tribe of Benjamin, Gibeon with its pasture lands, Geba with its pasture lands,

18 Anathoth with its pasture lands and Almon with its pasture lands; four cities.

19 All the cities of the sons of Aaron, the priests, were thirteen cities with their pasture lands.

20 Then the cities from the tribe of Ephraim were allotted to the [r]families of the sons of Kohath, the Levites, *even to* the rest of the sons of Kohath. 1 Chr. 6:66

21 And they gave them Shechem, the city of refuge for the manslayer, with its pasture lands,

in the hill country of Ephraim, and
Gezer with its pasture lands,
22 and Kibzaim with its pasture
lands and Beth-horon with its pasture lands; four cities.
23 And from the tribe of Dan,
Elteke with its pasture lands, Gibbethon with its pasture lands,
24 Aijalon with its pasture
lands, Gath-rimmon with its pasture lands; four cities.
25 And from the half-tribe of
Manasseh, *they allotted* Taanach
with its pasture lands and Gath-
rimmon with its pasture lands;
two cities.
26 All the cities with their pasture lands for the families of the
rest of the sons of Kohath were
ten.
27 And[r]to the sons of Gershon,
one of the families of the Levites,
from the half-tribe of Manasseh,
they gave Golan in Bashan, the
city of refuge for the manslayer,
with its pasture lands, and Be-esh-
terah with its pasture lands; two
cities. 1 Chr. 6:71
28 And from the tribe of Issachar, *they gave* Kishion with its
pasture lands, Daberath with its
pasture lands,
29 Jarmuth with its pasture
lands, En-gannim with its pasture
lands; four cities.
30 And from the tribe of Asher,
they gave Mishal with its pasture
lands, Abdon with its pasture
lands,
31 Helkath with its pasture
lands and Rehob with its pasture
lands; four cities.
32 And from the tribe of Naphtali, *they gave*[r]Kedesh in Galilee,
the city of refuge for the manslayer, with its pasture lands and
Hammoth-dor with its pasture
lands and Kartan with its pasture
lands; three cities. Josh. 20:7
33 All the cities of the Gershonites according to their families
were thirteen cities with their pasture lands.
34 And to the families of [r]the
sons of Merari, the rest of the Levites, *they gave* from the tribe of
Zebulun, Jokneam with its pasture lands and Kartah with its
pasture lands. 1 Chr. 6:77
35 Dimnah with its pasture
lands, Nahalal with its pasture
lands; four cities.
36 And from the tribe of Reuben, *they gave*[r]Bezer with its pasture lands and Jahaz with its pasture lands, Deut. 4:43; Josh. 20:8
37 Kedemoth with its pasture
lands and Mephaath with its pasture lands; four cities.
38 And from the tribe of Gad,
they gave Ramoth in Gilead, the
city of refuge for the manslayer,
with its pasture lands and Mahanaim with its pasture lands,
39 Heshbon with its pasture
lands, Jazer with its pasture lands;
four cities in all.
40 All *these were* the cities of
the sons of Merari according to
their families, the rest of the families of the Levites; and their lot
was twelve cities.
41 All the cities of the Levites in
the midst of the possession of the
sons of Israel were forty-eight
cities with their pasture lands.
42 These cities each had its surrounding pasture lands; thus *it
was* with all these cities.
43 [r]So the LORD gave Israel all

the land which He had sworn to give to their fathers, and they possessed it and lived in it. Deut. 34:4

44 And the LORD gave them rest on every side, according to all that He had sworn to their fathers, and no one of all their enemies stood before them; the LORD gave all their enemies into their hand.

45 Not[t] one of the good[t] promises which the LORD had[t] made to the house of Israel failed; all came to pass. *a word • words • spoken*

CHAPTER 22

THEN Joshua summoned the Reubenites and the Gadites and the half-tribe of Manasseh,

2 and said to them, "You have kept all that Moses the servant of the LORD commanded you, and have listened to my voice in all that I commanded you.

3 "You have not forsaken your brothers these many days to this day, but have kept the charge of the commandment of the LORD your God.

4 "And now the LORD your God has given rest to your brothers, as He spoke to them; therefore turn now and go to your tents, to the land of your possession, which Moses the servant of the LORD gave you beyond the Jordan.

5 "Only be very careful to observe the commandment and the law which Moses the servant of the LORD commanded you, to[r] love the LORD your God and walk in all His ways and keep His commandments and hold fast to Him and serve Him with all your heart and with all your soul." Deut. 5:10

6 So Joshua[r] blessed them and sent them away, and they went to their tents. Gen. 47:7; Josh. 14:13

7 Now[r] to the one half-tribe of Manasseh Moses had given *a possession* in Bashan, but to the other half Joshua gave *a possession* among their brothers westward beyond the Jordan. So when Joshua sent them away to their tents, he blessed them, Num. 32:33

8 and said to[t] them, "Return to your tents with great riches and with very much livestock, with silver, gold, bronze, iron, and with very many clothes; divide the spoil of your enemies with your brothers." *them, saying, "Return*

9 And the sons of Reuben and the sons of Gad and the half-tribe of Manasseh returned *home* and departed from the sons of Israel at Shiloh which is in the land of Canaan, to go to the land of Gilead, to the land of their possession which they had possessed, according to the[t] command of the LORD through Moses. *mouth*

10 And when they came to the region of the Jordan which is in the land of Canaan, the sons of Reuben and the sons of Gad and the half-tribe of Manasseh built an altar there by the Jordan, a large altar in appearance.

11 And the sons of Israel heard *it*[t] said, "Behold, the sons of Reuben and the sons of Gad and the half-tribe of Manasseh have built an altar at the[t] frontier of the land of Canaan, in the region of the Jordan, on the side *belonging to* the sons of Israel." *saying • front*

12 And when the sons of Israel heard *of it*, the whole congrega-

tion of the sons of Israel gathered
themselves at [r]Shiloh, to go up
against them in war. Josh. 18:1
13 Then the sons of Israel sent
to the sons of Reuben and to the
sons of Gad and to the half-tribe
of Manasseh, into the land of Gilead, [r]Phinehas the son of Eleazar
the priest, Num. 25:7, 11; 31:6
14 and with him ten chiefs, one
chief for each father's household
from each of the tribes of Israel;
and each one of them *was* the
head of his father's household
among the thousands of Israel.
15 And they came to the sons of
Reuben and to the sons of Gad
and to the half-tribe of Manasseh,
to the land of Gilead, and they
spoke with them saying,
16 "Thus says the whole congregation of the LORD, 'What is this
unfaithful act which you have
committed against the God of Israel, turning away from following
the LORD this day, by building
yourselves an altar, to rebel
against the LORD this day?
17 'Is not the iniquity of Peor
enough for us, from which we
have not cleansed ourselves to
this day, although a plague came
on the congregation of the LORD,
18 that you must turn away this
day from following the LORD? And
it will come about if you rebel
against the LORD today, that He
will be angry with the whole congregation of Israel tomorrow.
19 'If, however, the land of your
possession is unclean, then [t]cross
into the land of the possession of
the LORD, where the LORD's tabernacle stands, and take possession
among us. Only do not rebel
against the LORD, or rebel against
us by building an altar for yourselves, besides the altar of the
LORD our God. *cross for yourselves*
20 'Did not [r]Achan the son of Zerah act unfaithfully in the things
under the ban, and wrath fall on
all the congregation of Israel? And
that man did not perish alone in
his iniquity.' " Josh. 7:1-26
21 Then the sons of Reuben and
the sons of Gad and the half-tribe
of Manasseh answered, and spoke
to the heads of the [t]families of Israel. *thousands*
22 "The [r]Mighty One, God, the
LORD, the Mighty One, God, the
LORD! [r]He knows, and may Israel
itself know. If *it was* in rebellion,
or if in an unfaithful act against
the LORD do not Thou save us this
day! Deut. 10:17 • 1 Kin. 8:39
23 "If we have built us an altar to
turn away from following the
LORD, or if to offer a burnt offering
or grain offering on it, or if to offer
sacrifices of peace offerings on it,
may the LORD Himself require it.
24 "But truly we have done this
out of concern, [t]for a reason, saying, 'In time to come your sons
may say to our [t]sons, "What have
you to do with the LORD, the God
of Israel? *from • sons, saying*
25 "For the LORD has made the
Jordan a border between us and
you, *you* sons of Reuben and sons
of Gad; you have no portion in the
LORD." So your sons may make
our sons stop fearing the LORD.'
26 "Therefore we said, 'Let us
build an altar, not for burnt offering or for sacrifice;
27 rather it shall be [r]a witness
between us and you and between

our generations after us, that we are to perform the service of the LORD before Him with our burnt offerings, and with our sacrifices and with our peace offerings, that your sons may not say to our sons in time to come, "You have no portion in the LORD." ' Gen. 31:48

28 "Therefore we said, 'It shall also come about if they say *this* to us or to our generations in time to come, then we shall say, "See the copy of the altar of the LORD which our fathers made, not for burnt offering or for sacrifice; rather it is a witness between us and you." '

29 "Far be it from us that we should rebel against the LORD and turn away from following the LORD this day, by building an altar for burnt offering, for grain offering or for sacrifice, besides the altar of the LORD our God which is before His [13]tabernacle."

30 So when Phinehas the priest and the leaders of the congregation, even the heads of the [t]families of Israel who *were* with him, heard the words which the sons of Reuben and the sons of Gad and the sons of Manasseh spoke, it pleased them. *thousands*

31 And Phinehas the son of Eleazar the priest said to the sons of Reuben and to the sons of Gad and to the sons of Manasseh, "Today we know that the [r]LORD is in our midst, because you have not committed this unfaithful act against the LORD; now you have delivered the sons of Israel from the hand of the LORD." Ex. 25:8

32 Then Phinehas the son of Eleazar the priest and the leaders returned from the sons of Reuben and from the sons of Gad, from the land of Gilead, to the land of Canaan, to the sons of Israel, and brought back word to them.

33 And the word pleased the sons of Israel, and the sons of Israel [r]blessed God; and they did not speak of going up against them in war, to destroy the land in which the sons of Reuben and the sons of Gad were living. 1 Chr. 29:20

34 And the sons of Reuben and the sons of Gad [r]called the altar *Witness;* "For," *they said,* "it is a witness between us that the LORD is God." Gen. 31:47-49

[13]Lit., *dwelling place*

CHAPTER 23

NOW it came about after many days, when the LORD had given rest to Israel from all their enemies on every side, and Joshua was old, advanced in years,

2 that [r]Joshua called for all Israel, for their elders and their heads and their judges and their officers, and said to them, "I am old, advanced in years. Josh. 24:1

3 "And you have seen all that the LORD your God has done to all these nations because of you, for [r]the LORD your God is He who has been fighting for you. Deut. 1:30

4 "See, [r]I have apportioned to you these nations which remain as an inheritance for your tribes, with all the nations which I have cut off, from the Jordan even to the Great Sea toward the setting of the sun. Ex. 23:30

5 "And the LORD your God, He shall thrust them out from before you and [a]drive them from before

you; and you shall possess their
land, just as the LORD your God
[t]promised you. *dispossess • spoke to*
6 "Be very firm, then, to keep
and do all that is written in the
book of the law of Moses, so that
you may not turn aside from it to
the right hand or to the left,
7 in order that you may not associate with these nations, these
which remain among you, or mention the name of their gods, or
make *anyone* swear *by them,* or
serve them, or bow down to them.
8 "But you are to cling to the
LORD your God, as you have done
to this day.
9 "For the LORD has driven out
great and strong nations from before you; and as for you, no man
has stood before you to this day.
10 "One of your men puts to
flight a thousand, for the LORD
your God is He who fights for you,
just as He[t]promised you. *spoke to*
11 "So take diligent heed to yourselves to love the LORD your God.
12 "For if you ever go back and
[r]cling to the rest of these nations,
these which remain among you,
and intermarry with them, so that
you [t]associate with them and they
with you, Ex. 34:15, 16 • *go among*
13 know with certainty that the
LORD your God will not continue
to[a]drive these nations out from before you; but they shall be a snare
and a trap to you, and a whip on
your sides and thorns in your
eyes, until you perish from off this
good land which the LORD your
God has given you. *dispossess*
14 "Now behold, today [r]I am
going the way of all the earth, and
you know in all your hearts and in
all your souls that not one word of
all the good words which the
LORD your God spoke concerning
you has failed; all have [t]been fulfilled for you, not [t]one of them has
failed. 1 Kin. 2:2 • *come • one word*
15 "And it shall come about that
just as all the good words which
the LORD your God spoke to you
have come upon you, so the LORD
will bring upon you all the threats,
until He has destroyed you from
off this good land which the LORD
your God has given you.
16 "When[r] you transgress the
covenant of the LORD your God,
which He commanded you, and
go and serve other gods, and bow
down to them, then the anger of
the LORD will burn against you,
and you shall perish quickly from
off the good land which He has
given you." Deut. 4:25, 26

CHAPTER 24

THEN Joshua gathered all the
tribes of Israel to Shechem, and
called for the elders of Israel and
for their heads and their judges
and their officers; and they presented themselves before God.
2 And Joshua said to all the
people, "Thus says the LORD, the
God of Israel, 'From ancient times
your fathers lived beyond the
[14]River, *namely,* Terah, the father
of Abraham and the father of Nahor, and they served other gods.
3 'Then I took your father
Abraham from beyond the [14]River,
and led him through all the land of
Canaan, and multiplied his descendants and gave him Isaac.
4 'And to Isaac I gave [r]Jacob

[14] I.e., Euphrates

and Esau, and [r]to Esau I gave
Mount Seir, to possess it; but Jacob and his sons went down to
Egypt. Gen. 25:25, 26 • Gen. 36:8
5 'Then I sent Moses and Aaron, and I plagued Egypt [t]by what I
did in its midst; and afterward I
brought you out. *according to*
6 'And I brought your fathers
out of Egypt, and you came to the
sea; and Egypt pursued your fathers with chariots and horsemen
to the [t]Red Sea. *Sea of Reeds*
7 'But when they cried out to
the LORD, He put darkness between you and the Egyptians, and
brought the sea upon them and
covered them; and your own eyes
saw what I did in Egypt. And [r]you
lived in the wilderness for a long
time. Deut. 1:46; 2:14
8 'Then I brought you into the
land of the Amorites who lived beyond the Jordan, and they fought
with you; and I gave them into
your hand, and you took possession of their land when I destroyed them before you.
9 'Then [r]Balak the son of Zippor, king of Moab, arose and
fought against Israel, and he sent
and summoned Balaam the son of
Beor to curse you. Num. 22:2-6
10 'But I was not willing to listen
to Balaam. So he had to bless you,
and I delivered you from his hand.
11 'And [r]you crossed the Jordan
and came to Jericho; and the citizens of Jericho fought against
you, *and* the Amorite and the Perizzite and the Canaanite and the
Hittite and the Girgashite, the Hivite and the Jebusite. Thus I gave
them into your hand. Josh. 3:14-17
12 'Then I [r]sent the hornet before
you and it [t]drove out the two kings
of the Amorites from before you,
but not by your sword or your
bow. Ex. 23:28 • *drove them out*
13 'And I gave you a land on
which you had not labored, and
cities which you had not built, and
you have lived in them; you are
eating of vineyards and olive
groves which you did not plant.'
14 "Now, therefore, [a]fear the
LORD and serve Him in sincerity
and [a]truth; and put away the gods
which your fathers served beyond
the River and in Egypt, and serve
the LORD. *reverence • faithfulness*
15 "And if it is disagreeable in
your sight to serve the LORD,
choose for yourselves today
whom you will serve: whether the
gods which your fathers served
which were beyond the River, or
[r]the gods of the Amorites in whose
land you are living; but as for me
and my house, we will serve the
LORD." Judg. 6:10
16 And the people answered
and said, "Far be it from us that
we should forsake the LORD to
serve other gods;
17 for the LORD our God is He
who brought us and our fathers
up out of the land of Egypt, from
the house of [t]bondage, and who
did these great signs in our sight
and preserved us through all the
way in which we went and among
all the peoples through whose
midst we passed. *bondmen*
18 "And the LORD drove out from
before us all the peoples, even the
Amorites who lived in the land.
We also will serve the LORD, for
He is our God."
19 Then Joshua said to the peo-

ple, "You will not be able to serve
the LORD,[r]for He is a holy God. He
is a jealous God;[r]He will not forgive your transgression or your
sins. Lev. 19:2; 20:7, 26 • Ex. 23:21
20 "If[r]you forsake the LORD and
serve foreign gods, then He will
turn and do you harm and consume you after He has done good
to you." Deut. 4:25, 26
21 And the people said to
Joshua, "No, but we will serve the
LORD."
22 And Joshua said to the people, "You are witnesses against
yourselves that[r]you have chosen
for yourselves the LORD, to serve
Him." And they said, "We are witnesses." Ps. 119:173
23 "Now therefore, put away the
foreign gods which are in your
midst, and incline your hearts to
the LORD, the God of Israel."
24 [r]And the people said to
Joshua, "We will serve the LORD
our God and we will [t]obey His
voice." Ex. 19:8; 24:3, 7 • *listen to*
25 [r]So Joshua made a covenant
with the people that day, and
made for them a statute and an
ordinance in Shechem. Ex. 24:8
26 And Joshua [r]wrote these
words in the book of the law of
God; and he took a large stone
and set it up there under the oak
that was by the sanctuary of the
LORD. Deut. 31:24
27 And Joshua said to all the
people, "Behold, this stone shall
be for a witness against us, for it
has heard all the words of the
LORD which He spoke to us; thus
it shall be for a witness against
you, lest you deny your God."
28 Then Joshua dismissed the
people, each to his inheritance.
29 And it came about after
these things that Joshua the son
of Nun, the servant of the LORD,
died, being one hundred and ten
years old.
30 And they buried him in the
territory of his inheritance in[r]Tim-
nath-serah, which is in the hill
country of Ephraim, on the north
of Mount Gaash. Josh. 19:50
31 And Israel served the LORD
all the days of Joshua and all the
days of the elders who [t]survived
Joshua, and had known all the
deeds of the LORD which He had
done for Israel. *prolonged days after*
32 Now they buried the bones
of Joseph, which the sons of Israel
brought up from Egypt, at Shechem, in the piece of ground
which Jacob had bought from the
sons of Hamor the father of Shechem for one hundred pieces of
money; and they became the inheritance of Joseph's sons.
33 And Eleazar the son of Aaron died; and they buried him [a]at
Gibeah of[r]Phinehas his son, which
was given him in the hill country
of Ephraim. *on the hill* • Josh. 22:13

THE BOOK OF

JUDGES

NOW it came about after the
death of Joshua that the sons of
Israel [r]inquired of the LORD, saying, "Who shall go up first for us
against the Canaanites, to fight
against them?" Num. 27:21
2 And the LORD said, "Judah[r]
shall go up; behold, I have given
the land into his hand." Gen. 49:8
3 Then Judah said to Simeon
his brother, "Come up with me
into the territory allotted me, that
we may fight against the Canaanites; and I in turn will go with you
into the territory allotted you." So
Simeon went with him.
4 And Judah went up, and [r]the
LORD gave the Canaanites and the
Perizzites into their hands; and
they [t]defeated ten thousand men
at Bezek. Ps. 44:2 • *smote them*
5 And they found Adoni-bezek
in Bezek and fought against him
and they [t]defeated the Canaanites
and the Perizzites. *smote*
6 But Adoni-bezek fled; and
they pursued him and caught him
and cut off his [t]thumbs and big
toes. *thumbs of his hands and his feet*
7 And Adoni-bezek said, "Seventy kings with their thumbs and
their big toes cut off used to
gather up *scraps* under my table;
as I have done, so God has repaid
me." So they brought him to Jerusalem and he died there.
8 Then the sons of Judah
fought against [r]Jerusalem and captured it and struck it with the
edge of the sword and set the city
on fire. Josh. 15:63; Judg. 1:21

9 And afterward the sons of
Judah went down to fight against
the Canaanites living in the hill
country and in the [1]Negev and in
the lowland.
10 [r]So Judah went against the
Canaanites who lived in Hebron
(now the name of Hebron formerly *was* Kiriath-arba); and they
struck Sheshai and Ahiman and
Talmai. Josh. 15:13-19
11 Then [r]from there he went
against the inhabitants of Debir
(now the name of Debir formerly
was Kiriath-sepher). Josh. 15:15
12 And Caleb said, "The one
who attacks Kiriath-sepher and
captures it, I will even give him
my daughter Achsah for a wife."
13 And [r]Othniel the son of Kenaz, Caleb's younger brother, captured it; so he gave him his daughter Achsah for a wife. Judg. 3:9
14 Then it came about when she
came *to him*, that she persuaded
him to ask her father for a field.
Then she alighted from [t]her donkey, and Caleb said to her, "What
[t]do you want?" *the • for yourself*
15 And she said to him, "Give
me a blessing, since you have giv-
en me the land of the [1]Negev, give
me also springs of water." So Caleb gave her the upper springs and
the lower springs.
16 And the [t]descendants of the
Kenite, Moses' father-in-law,
went up from the city of palms
with the sons of Judah, to the wilderness of Judah which is in the

[1] I.e., South country

south of Arad; and they went and
lived with the people. *sons*
17 Then Judah went with Simeon his brother, and they struck the
Canaanites living in Zephath, and
utterly destroyed it. So the name
of the city was called Hormah.
18 And Judah took [r]Gaza with
its territory and Ashkelon with its
territory and Ekron with its territory. Josh. 11:22
19 Now the LORD was with Judah, and they took possession of
the hill country; but they could
not [a]drive out the inhabitants of
the valley because they had [r]iron
chariots. *dispossess* • Josh. 17:16
20 Then they gave Hebron to
Caleb, as Moses had [t]promised;
and he drove out from there the
three sons of Anak. *spoken*
21 [r]But the sons of Benjamin did
not drive out the [r]Jebusites who
lived in Jerusalem; so the Jebusites have lived with the sons of
Benjamin in Jerusalem to this
day. Josh. 15:63 • 1 Chr. 11:4
22 Likewise the house of Joseph
went up against Bethel, and the
LORD was with them.
23 And the house of Joseph
spied out Bethel (now the name of
the city was formerly Luz).
24 And the spies saw a man
coming out of the city, and they
said to him, "Please show us the
entrance to the city and [r]we will
treat you kindly." Josh. 2:12
25 So he showed them the entrance to the city, and they struck
the city with the edge of the
sword, [r]but they let the man and
all his family go free. Josh. 6:25
26 And the man went into the
land of the Hittites and built a city
and named it Luz [t]which is its
name to this day. *it*
27 But Manasseh did not take
possession of Beth-shean and its
villages, or Taanach and its villages, or the inhabitants of Dor
and its villages, or the inhabitants
of Ibleam and its villages, or the
inhabitants of Megiddo and its villages; so [r]the Canaanites persisted
in living in that land. Judg. 1:1
28 And it came about when Israel became strong, that they put
the Canaanites to forced labor,
but they did not drive them out
completely.
29 Neither did Ephraim drive
out the Canaanites who were living in Gezer; so the Canaanites
lived in Gezer among them.
30 Zebulun did not drive out the
inhabitants of Kitron, or the inhabitants of Nahalol; so the Canaanites lived among them and
became subject to forced labor.
31 Asher did not drive out the
inhabitants of Acco, or the inhabitants of Sidon, or of Ahlab, or of
Achzib, or of Helbah, or of Aphik,
or of Rehob.
32 So the Asherites lived among
the Canaanites, the inhabitants of
the land; for they did not drive
them out.
33 Naphtali did not drive out
the inhabitants of Beth-shemesh,
or the inhabitants of Beth-anath,
but lived among the Canaanites,
the inhabitants of the land; and
the inhabitants of Beth-shemesh
and Beth-anath became forced labor for them.
34 Then the Amorites [t]forced
the sons of Dan into the hill coun-

try, for they did not allow them to
come down to the valley; *pressed*
35 yet the Amorites persisted in
[t]living in Mount Heres, in Aijalon
and in Shaalbim; but when the
[t]power of the house of Joseph
[t]grew strong, they became forced
labor. *dwelling • hand • was heavy*
36 And the border of the Amorites ran from the ascent of Akrabbim, from Sela and upward.

CHAPTER 2

NOW the angel of the LORD came
up from Gilgal to Bochim. And he
said, "I brought you up out of
Egypt and led you into the land
which I have sworn to your fathers; and I said, 'I will never
break My covenant with you,
2 and as for you, you shall
make no covenant with the inhabitants of this land; you shall
tear down their altars.' But you
have not [t]obeyed Me; what is this
you have done? *listened to My voice*
3 "Therefore I also said, 'I will
not drive them out before you; but
they shall [2]become *as thorns* in
your sides, and their gods shall be
a snare to you.'"
4 And it came about when the
angel of the LORD spoke these
words to all the sons of Israel, that
the people lifted up their voices
and wept.
5 So they named that place
[3]Bochim; and there they sacrificed
to the LORD.
6 [r]When Joshua had dismissed
the people, the sons of Israel went
each to his inheritance to possess
the land. Josh. 24:28-31

[2]Some ancient mss. read *be adversaries, and*
[3]I.e., weepers

7 And the people served the
LORD all the days of Joshua, and
all the days of the elders who survived Joshua, who had seen all the
great work of the LORD which He
had done for Israel.
8 Then Joshua the son of Nun,
the servant of the LORD, died at
the age of one hundred and ten.
9 And they buried him in the
territory of his inheritance in Tim-
nath-heres, in the hill country of
Ephraim, north of Mount Gaash.
10 And all that generation also
were gathered to their fathers;
and there arose another generation after them who [r]did not know
the LORD, nor yet the work which
He had done for Israel. Ex. 5:2
11 Then the sons of Israel did
[r]evil in the sight of the LORD, and
[4]served the Baals, Judg. 3:7, 12
12 and [r]they forsook the LORD,
the God of their fathers, who had
brought them out of the land of
Egypt, and followed other gods
from *among* the gods of the peoples who were around them, and
bowed themselves down to them;
thus they provoked the LORD to
anger. Deut. 31:16
13 So they forsook the LORD
and [r]served Baal and the Ashtaroth. Judg. 10:6
14 And the anger of the LORD
burned against Israel, and He
gave them into the hands of plunderers who plundered them; and
[r]He sold them into the hands of
their enemies around *them*, so
that they could no longer stand
before their enemies. Deut. 28:25
15 Wherever they went, the
hand of the LORD was against
them for evil, as the LORD had

[4]Or, *worshiped*

spoken and [r]as the LORD had
sworn to them, so that they were
severely distressed. Lev. 26:14-39
16 [r]Then the LORD raised up
judges [t]who delivered them from
the hands of those who plundered
them. Ps. 106:43-45 • *and they*
17 And yet they did not listen to
their judges, for they played the
harlot after other gods and bowed
themselves down to them. They
turned aside quickly from the way
[r]in which their fathers had walked
in obeying the commandments of
the LORD; they did not do as *their*
fathers. Judg. 2:7
18 And when the LORD raised
up judges for them, the LORD was
with the judge and delivered them
from the hand of their enemies all
the days of the judge; for the LORD
was moved to pity by their groaning because of those who oppressed and afflicted them.
19 But it came about when the
judge died, that they would turn
back and act more corruptly than
their fathers, in following other
gods to serve them and bow down
to them; they did not abandon
their practices or their stubborn
ways.
20 So the anger of the LORD
burned against Israel, and He
said, "Because this nation has
transgressed My covenant which I
commanded their fathers, and has
not listened to My voice,
21 I also will no longer drive out
before them any of the nations
which Joshua left when he died,
22 in order to test Israel by
them, whether they will keep the
way of the LORD to walk in it as
their fathers [t]did, or not." *kept*
23 So the LORD allowed those
nations to remain, not driving
them out quickly; and He did not
give them into the hand of Joshua.

CHAPTER 3

[r]NOW these are the nations
which the LORD left, to test Israel
by them (*that is,* all who had not
[t]experienced any of the wars of
Canaan; Judg. 1:1; 2:21, 22 • *known*
2 only in order that the generations of the sons of Israel might be
taught war, [t]those who had not experienced it formerly). *only*
3 *These nations are:* the five
lords of the Philistines and all the
Canaanites and the Sidonians and
the Hivites who lived in Mount
Lebanon, from Mount Baal-hermon as far as Lebo-hamath.
4 And they were for testing Israel, to find out if they would [t]obey
the commandments of the LORD,
which He had commanded their
fathers through Moses. *hear*
5 And the sons of Israel lived
among the Canaanites, the Hittites, the Amorites, the Perizzites,
the Hivites, and the Jebusites;
6 and they took their daughters for themselves as wives, and
gave their own daughters to their
sons, and served their gods.
7 And the sons of Israel did
[r]what was evil in the sight of the
LORD, and [r]forgot the LORD their
God, and served the Baals and the
[5]Asheroth. Judg. 2:11 • Deut. 4:9
8 Then the anger of the LORD
was kindled against Israel, so that
He sold them into the hands of
Cushan-rishathaim king of Mesopotamia; and the sons of Israel

[5]I.e., wooden symbol of a female deity

served Cushan-rishathaim eight
years.
9 And when the sons of Israel
cried to the LORD, the LORD raised
up a deliverer for the sons of Israel to deliver them, [r]Othniel the
son of Kenaz, Caleb's younger
brother. Judg. 1:13
10 And [r]the Spirit of the LORD
came upon him, and he judged Israel. When he went out to war,
the LORD gave Cushan-rishathaim
king of Mesopotamia into his
hand, so that he prevailed over
Cushan-rishathaim. Num. 11:25-29
11 Then the land had rest forty
years. And Othniel the son of Kenaz died.
12 Now the sons of Israel again
[r]did evil in the sight of the LORD.
So the LORD strengthened Eglon
the king of Moab against Israel,
because they had done evil in the
sight of the LORD. Judg. 2:11
13 And he gathered to himself
the sons of Ammon and Amalek;
and he went and [t]defeated Israel,
and they possessed [r]the city of the
palm trees. *smote* • Deut. 34:3
14 And the sons of Israel served
Eglon the king of Moab eighteen
years.
15 But when the sons of Israel
cried to the LORD, the LORD raised
up a deliverer for them, Ehud the
son of Gera, the Benjamite, a left-
handed man. And the sons of Israel sent tribute by [t]him to Eglon
the king of Moab. *his hand*
16 And Ehud made himself a
sword which had two edges, a cubit in length; and he bound it on
his right thigh under his cloak.
17 And he presented the tribute
to Eglon king of Moab. Now Eglon
was a very fat man.
18 And it came about when he
had finished presenting the tribute, that he sent away the people
who had carried the tribute.
19 But he himself turned back
from the idols which were at Gilgal, and said, "I have a secret
message for you, O king." And he
said, "Keep silence." And all who
attended him left him.
20 And Ehud came to him while
he was sitting alone in his cool
roof chamber. And Ehud said, "I
have a message from God for
you." And he arose from his seat.
21 And Ehud stretched out his
left hand, took the sword from his
right thigh and thrust it into his
belly.
22 The handle also went in after
the blade, and the fat closed over
the blade, for he did not draw the
sword out of his belly; and the refuse came out.
23 Then Ehud went out into the
vestibule and shut the doors of the
roof chamber behind him, and
locked *them*.
24 When he had gone out, his
servants came and looked, and behold, the doors of the roof chamber were locked; and they said,
"He is only [t]relieving himself in
the cool room." *covering his feet*
25 And they waited until they
[t]became anxious; but behold, he
did not open the doors of the roof
chamber. Therefore they took the
key and opened them, and behold,
their master had fallen to the [t]floor
dead. *were ashamed* • *earth*
26 Now Ehud escaped while
they were delaying, and he passed

by the idols and escaped to Sei-
rah.
27 And it came about when he
had arrived, that [r]he blew the
trumpet in the hill country of E-
phraim; and the sons of Israel
went down with him from the hill
country, and he *was* in front of
them. Judg. 6:34; 1 Sam. 13:3
28 And he said to them, "Pursue
them, for the LORD has given your
enemies the Moabites into your
hands." So they went down after
him and seized the fords of the
Jordan opposite Moab, and did
not allow anyone to cross.
29 And they struck down at that
time about ten thousand Moabites, all robust and valiant men;
and no one escaped.
30 So Moab was subdued that
day under the hand of Israel. And
the land was undisturbed for
eighty years.
31 And after him came [r]Sham-
gar the son of Anath, who struck
down six hundred Philistines with
an oxgoad; and he also saved Israel. Judg. 5:6

CHAPTER 4

THEN [r]the sons of Israel again
did evil in the sight of the LORD,
after Ehud died. Judg. 2:19
2 And the LORD sold them into
the hand of [r]Jabin king of Canaan,
who reigned in Hazor; and the
commander of his army was Sisera, who lived in [r]Harosheth-ha-
goyim. Josh. 11:1, 10 • Judg. 4:13, 16
3 And the sons of Israel cried
to the LORD; for he had nine hundred [r]iron chariots, and he oppressed the sons of Israel severely
for twenty years. Judg. 1:19
4 Now Deborah, a prophetess,
the wife of Lappidoth, was judging Israel at that time.
5 And she used to [a]sit under the
palm tree of Deborah between Ramah and Bethel in the hill country
of Ephraim; and the sons of Israel
came up to her for judgment. *live*
6 Now she sent and summoned
[r]Barak the son of Abinoam from
Kedesh-naphtali, and said to him,
"Behold, the LORD, the God of Israel, has commanded, 'Go and
march to Mount Tabor, and take
with you ten thousand men from
the sons of Naphtali and from the
sons of Zebulun. Heb. 11:32
7 'And I will draw out to you
Sisera, the commander of Jabin's
army, with his chariots and his
[t]many *troops* to the river Kishon;
and [r]I will give him into your
hand.' " *multitude* • Ps. 83:9
8 Then Barak said to her, "If
you will go with me, then I will go;
but if you will not go with me, I
will not go."
9 And she said, "I will surely
go with you; nevertheless, the
honor shall not be yours on the
journey that you are about to
take, [r]for the LORD will sell Sisera
into the hands of a woman." Then
Deborah arose and went with Barak to Kedesh. Judg. 4:21
10 And Barak called [r]Zebulun
and Naphtali together to Kedesh,
and ten thousand men went up
[t]with him; Deborah also went up
with him. Judg. 5:18 • *at his feet*
11 Now Heber [r]the Kenite had
separated himself from the Kenites, from the sons of Hobab the

father-in-law of Moses, and had pitched his tent as far away as the [a]oak in Zaanannim, which is near Kedesh. Judg. 1:16 • *terebinth*

12 Then they told Sisera that Barak the son of Abinoam had gone up to Mount Tabor.

13 And Sisera called together all his chariots, nine hundred iron chariots, and all the people who *were* with him, from Harosheth-hagoyim to the river Kishon.

14 And Deborah said to Barak, "Arise! For this is the day in which the LORD has given Sisera into your hands; [6]behold, [r]the LORD has gone out before you." So Barak went down from Mount Tabor with ten thousand men following him. Deut. 9:3; 2 Sam. 5:24; Ps. 68:7

15 [r]And the LORD [t]routed Sisera and all *his* chariots and all *his* army, with the edge of the sword before Barak; and Sisera alighted from *his* chariot and fled away on foot. Deut. 7:23 • *confused*

16 But Barak pursued the chariots and the army as far as Harosheth-hagoyim, and all the army of Sisera fell by the edge of the sword; not even one was left.

17 Now Sisera fled away on foot to the tent of Jael the wife of Heber the Kenite, for *there was* peace between Jabin the king of Hazor and the house of Heber the Kenite.

18 And Jael went out to meet Sisera, and said to him, "Turn aside, my master, turn aside to me! Do not be afraid." And he turned aside to her into the tent, and she covered him with a rug.

19 And he said to her, "Please give me a little water to drink, for I am thirsty." So she opened a [7]bottle of milk and gave him a drink; then she covered him.

20 And he said to her, "Stand in the doorway of the tent, and it shall be if anyone comes and inquires of you, and says, 'Is there anyone here?' that you shall say, 'No.' "

21 But Jael, Heber's wife, took a tent peg and seized a hammer in her hand, and went secretly to him and drove the peg into his temple, and it went through into the ground; for he was sound asleep and exhausted. So he died.

22 And behold, as Barak pursued Sisera, Jael came out to meet him and said to him, "Come, and I will show you the man whom you are seeking." And he entered [t]with her, and behold Sisera was lying dead with the tent peg in his temple. *to*

23 So [r]God subdued on that day Jabin the king of Canaan before the sons of Israel. Neh. 9:24

24 And the hand of the sons of Israel pressed heavier and heavier upon Jabin the king of Canaan, until they had [t]destroyed Jabin the king of Canaan. *cut off*

CHAPTER 5

[r]THEN Deborah and Barak the son of Abinoam sang on that day, saying, Ex. 15:1

2 "That the leaders led in Israel,
That [r]the people volunteered,
Bless the LORD! Ps. 110:3

3 "Hear, O kings; give ear, O rulers!

[6]Or, *has not the LORD gone . . . ?*

[7]I.e., skin container

I—to the LORD, I will sing,
I will sing praise to the LORD, the God of Israel.
4 "LORD, when Thou didst go out from Seir,
When Thou didst march from the field of Edom,
[r]The earth quaked, the heavens also dripped,
Even the clouds dripped water. Ps. 68:8, 9
5 "The mountains [t]quaked at the presence of the LORD,
[r]This Sinai, at the presence of the LORD, the God of Israel. *flowed* • Ps. 68:8
6 "In the days of Shamgar the son of Anath,
In the days of Jael, the highways were deserted,
And travelers [t]went by roundabout ways. *walked*
7 "The peasantry ceased, they ceased in Israel,
Until I, Deborah, arose,
Until I arose, a mother in Israel.
8 "New[r] gods were chosen;
Then war *was* in the gates.
Not a shield or a spear was seen
Among forty thousand in Israel. Deut. 32:17
9 "My heart *goes out* to [r]the commanders of Israel,
The volunteers among the people;
Bless the LORD! Judg. 5:2
10 "You who ride on [a]white donkeys,
You who sit on *rich* carpets,
And you who travel on the road—sing! *tawny*
11 "At the sound of those who divide *flocks* among the watering places,
There they shall recount the righteous deeds of the LORD,
The righteous deeds for His peasantry in Israel.
Then the people of the LORD went down to the gates.
12 "Awake, awake, Deborah;
Awake, awake, [a]sing a song!
Arise, Barak, and take away your captives, O son of Abinoam. *utter*
13 "Then survivors came down to the nobles;
The people of the LORD came down to me as warriors.
14 "From Ephraim those whose root is [r]in Amalek *came down,*
Following you, Benjamin, with your peoples;
From Machir commanders came down,
And from Zebulun those who wield the staff of [t]office. Judg. 12:15 • *the scribe*
15 "And the princes of Issachar *were* with Deborah;
As *was* Issachar, so *was* Barak;
Into the valley they rushed [r]at his [t]heels;
Among the divisions of Reuben
There were great resolves of heart. Judg. 4:10 • *feet*
16 "Why did you sit among [r]the [8]sheepfolds,
To hear the piping for the flocks? Num. 32:1, 2, 24, 36

[8]Or, *saddlebags*

Among the divisions of Reuben
There were great searchings of heart.
17 "Gilead[r] remained[a] across the Jordan;
And why did Dan stay in ships?
Asher sat at the seashore,
And[a] remained by its landings. Josh. 22:9 • *dwelt*
18 "Zebulun *was* a people who despised their lives *even* to death,
And Naphtali also, on the high places of the field.

19 "The kings came *and* fought;
Then fought the kings of Canaan
[r]At Taanach near the waters of Megiddo;
[r]They took no plunder in silver. Judg. 1:27 • Judg. 5:30
20 "The stars fought from heaven,
From their courses they fought against Sisera.
21 "The torrent of Kishon swept them away,
The ancient torrent, the torrent Kishon.
[r]O my soul, march on with strength. Ex. 15:2; Ps. 44:5
22 "Then the horses' hoofs beat
From the dashing, the dashing of his valiant steeds.
23 'Curse Meroz,' said the angel of the LORD,
'Utterly curse its inhabitants;
Because they did not come to the help of the LORD,
To the help of the LORD against the warriors.'

24 "Most blessed of women is Jael,
The wife of Heber the Kenite;
Most blessed is she of women in the tent.
25 "He asked for water *and* she gave him milk;
In a magnificent bowl she brought him curds.
26 "She reached out her hand for the tent peg,
And her right hand for the workmen's hammer.
Then she struck Sisera, she smashed his head;
And she shattered and pierced his temple.
27 "Between her feet he bowed, he fell, he lay;
Between her feet he bowed, he fell;
Where he bowed, there he fell [t]dead. *devastated*

28 "Out of the window she looked and lamented,
The mother of Sisera through the[a] lattice,
'Why does his chariot delay in coming?
Why do the hoofbeats of his chariots tarry?' *window*
29 "Her wise princesses would answer her,
Indeed she repeats her words to herself,
30 'Are[r] they not finding, are they not dividing the spoil?
A maiden, two maidens for every warrior;
To Sisera a spoil of dyed work, Ex. 15:9

A spoil of dyed work em-
broidered,
Dyed work of double em-
broidery on the neck of
the spoiler?'
31 "Thus let all Thine enemies
perish, O LORD;
But let those who love Him
be like the rising of the
sun in its might."
And the land was undisturbed for
forty years.

CHAPTER 6

THEN the sons of Israel did what
was evil in the sight of the LORD;
and the LORD gave them into the
hands of Midian seven years.
2 And the [t]power of Midian
prevailed against Israel. Because
of Midian the sons of Israel made
for themselves the dens which
were in the mountains and the
caves and the strongholds. *hand*
3 For it was when Israel had
sown, that the Midianites would
come up with the Amalekites and
the sons of the east and [t]go against
them. *go up*
4 So they would camp against
them and [r]destroy the produce of
the earth as far as Gaza, and leave
no sustenance in Israel as well as
no sheep, ox, or donkey. Lev. 26:16
5 For they would come up with
their livestock and their tents,
they would come in [r]like locusts
for number, both they and their
camels were innumerable; and
they came into the land to devastate it. Judg. 7:12; 8:10
6 So Israel was brought very
low because of Midian, and the
sons of Israel cried to the LORD.
7 Now it came about when the
sons of Israel cried to the LORD on
account of Midian,
8 that the LORD sent a prophet
to the sons of Israel, and [r]he said to
them, "Thus says the LORD, the
God of Israel, 'It was I who
brought you up from Egypt, and
brought you out from the house of
[t]slavery. Judg. 2:1, 2 • *slaves*
9 'And I delivered you from the
hands of the Egyptians and from
the hands of all your oppressors,
and dispossessed them before you
and gave you their land,
10 and I said to you, "I am the
LORD your God; you shall not fear
the gods of the Amorites in whose
land you live. But you have not
[t]obeyed Me."'" *listened to My voice*
11 Then [r]the angel of the LORD
came and sat under the [a]oak that
was in Ophrah, which belonged to
Joash the Abiezrite as his son Gideon was beating out wheat in the
wine press in order to save *it* from
the Midianites. Judg. 2:1 • *terebinth*
12 And the angel of the LORD
appeared to him and said to him,
"The LORD is with you, O valiant
warrior."
13 Then Gideon said to him, "O
my lord, if the LORD is with us,
why then has all this happened to
us? And where are all His miracles which our fathers told us
about, saying, 'Did not the LORD
bring us up from Egypt?' But now
the LORD has abandoned us and
given us into the hand of Midian."
14 And the LORD looked at him
and said, "Go in this your strength
and deliver Israel from the hand
of Midian. Have I not sent you?"
15 And he said to Him, "O Lord,

[t]how shall I deliver Israel? Behold, my family is the least in Manasseh, and I am the youngest in my father's house." *with what*

16 [r]But the LORD said to him, "Surely I will be with you, and you shall [t]defeat Midian as one man." Ex. 3:12; Josh. 1:5 • *smite*

17 So [t]Gideon said to Him, "If now I have found favor in Thy sight, then show me a sign that it is Thou who speakest with me. *he*

18 "Please do not depart from here, until I come *back* to Thee, and bring out my offering and lay it before Thee." And He said, "I will remain until you return."

19 Then Gideon went in and prepared a kid and unleavened bread from an [9]ephah of flour; he put the meat in a basket [t]and the broth in a pot, and brought *them* out to him under the [a]oak, and presented *them*. *and he put* • *terebinth*

20 And the angel of God said to him, "Take the meat and the unleavened bread and lay them on this rock, and pour out the broth." And he did so.

21 Then the angel of the LORD put out the end of the staff that was in his hand and touched the meat and the unleavened bread; and [r]fire sprang up from the rock and consumed the meat and the unleavened bread. Then the angel of the LORD [a]vanished from his sight. Lev. 9:24 • *departed*

22 [r]When Gideon saw that he was the angel of the LORD, [t]he said, "Alas, O Lord GOD! For now I have seen the angel of the LORD face to face." Gen. 32:30 • *Gideon*

23 And the LORD said to him, "Peace to you, do not fear; you shall not die."

24 Then Gideon built an altar there to the LORD and named it The LORD is Peace. To this day it is still in Ophrah of the Abiezrites.

25 Now the same night it came about that the LORD said to him, "Take your father's bull and a second bull seven years old, and pull down the altar of Baal which belongs to your father, and cut down the [10]Asherah that is beside it;

26 and build an altar to the LORD your God on the top of this stronghold in an orderly manner, and take a second bull and offer a burnt offering with the wood of the Asherah which you shall cut down."

27 Then Gideon took ten men of his servants and did as the LORD had spoken to him; and it came about, because he was too afraid of his father's household and the men of the city to do it by day, that he did it by night.

28 When the men of the city arose early in the morning, behold, the altar of Baal was torn down, and the Asherah which was beside it was cut down, and the second bull was offered on the altar which had been built.

29 And they said to one another, "Who did this thing?" And when they searched about and inquired, they said, "Gideon the son of Joash did this thing."

30 Then the men of the city said to Joash, "Bring out your son, that he may die, for he has torn down the altar of Baal, and indeed, he has cut down the Asherah which was beside it."

[9]I.e., Approx. one bushel

[10]I.e., wooden symbol of a female deity

31 But Joash said to all who stood against him, "Will you contend for Baal, or will you deliver him? Whoever will [a]plead for him shall be put to death by morning. If he is a god, let him contend for himself, because someone has torn down his altar." *contend*

32 Therefore on that day he named him [r]Jerubbaal, that is to say, "Let Baal contend against him," because he had torn down his altar. Judg. 7:1

33 Then all the Midianites and the Amalekites and the sons of the east assembled themselves; and they crossed over and camped in the valley of Jezreel.

34 So the Spirit of the LORD came upon Gideon; and he blew a trumpet, and the Abiezrites were called together to follow him.

35 And he sent messengers throughout Manasseh, and they also were called together to follow him; and he sent messengers to Asher, Zebulun, and Naphtali, and they came up to meet them.

36 Then Gideon said to God, "If Thou wilt deliver Israel through me, as Thou hast spoken,

37 behold, I will put a fleece of wool on the threshing floor. If there is dew on the fleece only, and it is dry on all the ground, then I will know that Thou wilt deliver Israel [t]through me, as Thou hast spoken." *by my hand*

38 And it was so. When he arose early the next morning and squeezed the fleece, he drained the dew from the fleece, a bowl full of water.

39 Then Gideon said to God, "Do[r] not let Thine anger burn against me that I may speak once more; please let me make a test once more with the fleece, let it now be dry only on the fleece, and let there be dew on all the ground." Gen. 18:32

40 And God did so that night; for it was dry only on the fleece, and dew was on all the ground.

CHAPTER 7

THEN Jerubbaal (that is, Gideon) and all the people who were with him, rose early and camped beside [a]the spring of Harod; and the camp of Midian was on the north side of [t]them by the hill of Moreh in the valley. *En-Harod • him*

2 And the LORD said to Gideon, "The people who are with you are too many for Me to give Midian into their hands, lest Israel become boastful, saying, 'My own [t]power has delivered me.' *hand*

3 "Now therefore [a]come, proclaim in the hearing of the people, saying, 'Whoever[r] is afraid and trembling, let him return and depart from Mount Gilead.'" So 22,000 people returned, but 10,000 remained. *please* • Deut. 20:8

4 [r]Then the LORD said to Gideon, "The people are still too many; bring them down to the water and I will test them for you there. Therefore it shall be that he of whom I say to you, 'This one shall go with you,' he shall go with you; but everyone of whom I say to you, 'This one shall not go with you,' he shall not go." 1 Sam. 14:6

5 So he brought the people down to the water. And the LORD said to Gideon, "You shall sepa-

rate everyone who laps the water with his tongue, as a dog laps, as well as everyone who kneels to drink."

6 Now the number of those who lapped, putting their hand to their mouth, was 300 men; but all the rest of the people kneeled to drink water.

7 And the LORD said to Gideon, "I will deliver you [r]with the 300 men who lapped and will give the Midianites into your hands; so let all the *other* people go, each man to his [t]home." 1 Sam. 14:6 • *place*

8 So [t]the 300 men took the people's provisions and their trumpets into their hands. And Gideon sent all the *other* men of Israel, each to his tent, but retained the 300 men; and the camp of Midian was below him in the valley. *they*

9 Now the same night it came about that the LORD said to him, "Arise, go down against the camp, for I have given it into your hands.

10 "But if you are afraid to go down, go with Purah your servant down to the camp,

11 and you will hear what they say; and [r]afterward your hands will be strengthened that you may go down against the camp." So he went with Purah his servant down to the outposts of the army that was in the camp. Judg. 7:15

12 Now the Midianites and the Amalekites and all the sons of the east were lying in the valley [r]as numerous as locusts; and their camels were without number, as numerous as the sand on the seashore. Judg. 6:5; 8:10

13 When Gideon came, behold, a man was relating a dream to his friend. And he said, "Behold, I [t]had a dream; a loaf of barley bread was tumbling into the camp of Midian, and it came to the tent and struck it so that it fell, and turned it [t]upside down so that the tent lay flat." *dreamed* • *upwards*

14 And his friend answered and said, "This is nothing less than the sword of Gideon the son of Joash, a man of Israel; God has given Midian and all the camp [r]into his hand." Josh. 2:9

15 And it came about when Gideon heard the account of the dream and its interpretation, that he bowed in worship. He returned to the camp of Israel and said, "Arise, for the LORD has given the camp of Midian into your hands."

16 And he divided the 300 men into three [t]companies, and he put trumpets and empty pitchers into the hands of all of them, with torches inside the pitchers. *heads*

17 And he said to them, "Look at me, and do likewise. And behold, when I come to the outskirts of the camp, do as I do.

18 "When I and all who are with me blow the trumpet, then you also blow the trumpets all around the camp, and say, 'For the LORD and for Gideon.' "

19 So Gideon and the hundred men who were with him came to the outskirts of the camp at the beginning of the middle watch, when they had just posted the watch; and they blew the trumpets and smashed the pitchers that were in their hands.

20 When the three [t]companies blew the trumpets and broke the pitchers, they held the torches in

their left hands and the trumpets
in their right hands for blowing,
and cried, "A sword for the LORD
and for Gideon!" *heads*
21 And each stood in his place
around the camp; and all the
[11]army ran, crying out as they fled.
22 And when they blew 300
trumpets, the[r]LORD set the sword
of one against another even
throughout the whole[a]army; and
the[a]army fled as far as Beth-shit-
tah toward Zererah, as far as the
edge of Abel-meholah, by Tab-
bath. 1 Sam. 14:20 · *camp*
23 And the men of Israel were
summoned from [r]Naphtali and
Asher and all Manasseh, and they
pursued Midian. Judg. 6:35
24 And Gideon sent messengers
throughout all the hill country of
Ephraim, saying, "Come down
against Midian and take the waters before them, as far as Beth-
barah and the Jordan." So all the
men of Ephraim were summoned,
and they took the waters as far as
Beth-barah and the Jordan.
25 And they captured the two
leaders of Midian, Oreb and Zeeb,
and they killed Oreb at the rock of
Oreb, and they killed Zeeb at the
wine press of Zeeb, while they
pursued Midian; and they brought
the heads of Oreb and Zeeb to
Gideon from across the Jordan.

CHAPTER 8

THEN the men of Ephraim said
to him, "What[r] is this thing you
have done to us, not calling us
when you went to fight against
Midian?" And they contended
with him vigorously. Judg. 12:1

[11]Or, *camp*

2 But he said to them, "What
have I done now in comparison
with you? Is not the gleaning *of
the grapes* of Ephraim better than
the vintage of Abiezer?
3"God has given the leaders of
Midian, Oreb and Zeeb into your
hands; and what was I able to do
in comparison with you?" Then
their [t]anger toward him subsided
when he said that. *spirit*
4 Then Gideon and the 300
men who were with him came to
the Jordan *and* crossed over,
weary yet pursuing.
5 And he said to the men of
Succoth, "Please give loaves of
bread to the people who are following me, for they are weary,
and I am pursuing Zebah and Zalmunna, the kings of Midian."
6 And the leaders of Succoth
said, "Are[t] the hands of Zebah and
Zalmunna already in your hands,
that we should give bread to your
army?" *Is the palm*
7 And Gideon said, "All[t] right,
when the LORD has given Zebah
and Zalmunna into my hand, then
I will[a]thrash your[t]bodies with the
thorns of the wilderness and with
briers." *For thus* · *trample* · *flesh*
8 And he went up from there
to Penuel, and spoke similarly to
them; and the men of Penuel answered him just as the men of
Succoth had answered.
9 So he spoke also to the men
of Penuel, saying, "When I return
safely, [r]I will tear down this
tower." Judg. 8:17
10 Now Zebah and Zalmunna
were in Karkor, and their armies
with them, about 15,000 men, all
who were left of the entire army

of the sons of the east; for the
fallen were 120,000 swordsmen.
11 And Gideon went up by the
way of those who lived in tents on
the east of Nobah and Jogbehah,
and [t]attacked the camp, when the
camp was unsuspecting. *smote*
12 When Zebah and Zalmunna
fled, he pursued them and captured the two kings of Midian, Zebah and Zalmunna, and routed the
whole [a]army. *camp*
13 Then Gideon the son of
Joash returned from the battle [a]by
the ascent of Heres. *from*
14 And he captured a youth
from Succoth and questioned him.
Then *the youth* wrote down for
him the princes of Succoth and its
elders, seventy-seven men.
15 And he came to the men of
Succoth and said, "Behold Zebah
and Zalmunna, concerning whom
you taunted me, saying, 'Are[t] the
hands of Zebah and Zalmunna already in your hand, that we
should give bread to your men
who are weary?' " *Is the palm*
16 And he took the elders of the
city, and thorns of the wilderness
and briers, and he disciplined the
men of Succoth with them.
17 [r]And he tore down the tower
of Penuel and killed the men of
the city. Judg. 8:9
18 Then he said to Zebah and
Zalmunna, "What kind of men
were they whom you killed at Tabor?" And they said, "They were
like you, each one resembling the
son of a king."
19 And he said, "They *were* my
brothers, the sons of my mother.
As the LORD lives, if only you had
let them live, I would not kill
you."
20 So he said to Jether his first-
born, "Rise, kill them." But the
youth did not draw his sword, for
he was afraid, because he was still
a youth.
21 Then Zebah and Zalmunna
said, "Rise up yourself, and fall on
us; for as the man, so is his
strength." [r]So Gideon arose and
killed Zebah and Zalmunna, and
[r]took the crescent ornaments
which were on their camels'
necks. Ps. 83:11 • Judg. 8:26
22 Then the men of Israel said
to Gideon, "Rule over us, both you
and your son, also your son's son,
for you have delivered us from the
hand of Midian."
23 But Gideon said to them, "I
will not rule over you, nor shall
my son rule over you; [r]the LORD
shall rule over you." 1 Sam. 8:7
24 Yet Gideon said to them, "I
would [t]request of you, that each of
you give me [a]an earring from his
spoil." (For they had gold earrings, because they were Ishmaelites.) *request a request • a nose ring*
25 And they said, "We will
surely give *them*." So they spread
out a garment, and every one of
them threw an earring there from
his spoil.
26 And the weight of the gold
earrings that he requested was
1,700 *shekels* of gold, besides the
crescent ornaments and the pen-
dants and the purple robes which
were on the kings of Midian, and
besides the neck bands that *were*
on their camels' necks.
27 And Gideon made it into [r]an
ephod, and placed it in his city,

Ophrah, and all Israel played the
harlot with it there, so that it became a snare to Gideon and his
household. Ex. 28:6-35; Judg. 17:5
28 So Midian was subdued before the sons of Israel, and they
did not lift up their heads anymore. And the land was undisturbed for forty years in the days
of Gideon.
29 Then [r]Jerubbaal the son of
Joash went and lived in his own
house. Judg. 7:1
30 Now Gideon had seventy
sons who were his direct descendants, for he had many wives.
31 And his concubine who was
in Shechem also bore him a son,
and he named him Abimelech.
32 And Gideon the son of Joash
died at a ripe old age and was buried in the tomb of his father Joash,
in Ophrah of the Abiezrites.
33 Then it came about, as soon
as Gideon was dead, [r]that the sons
of Israel again played the harlot
with the Baals, and made Baal-
berith their god. Judg. 2:11, 12
34 Thus the sons of Israel [r]did
not remember the LORD their God,
who had delivered them from the
hands of all their enemies on every side; Deut. 4:9; Judg. 3:7
35 [r]nor did they show kindness
to the household of Jerubbaal
(*that is,* Gideon), in accord with
all the good that he had done to
Israel. Judg. 9:16-18

CHAPTER 9

AND [r]Abimelech the son of Jerubbaal went to Shechem to his
mother's [t]relatives, and spoke to
them and to the whole clan of the
household of his mother's father,
saying, Judg. 8:31, 35 • *brothers*
2 "Speak, now, in the hearing of
all the leaders of Shechem,
'Which is better for you, that [r]sev-
enty men, all the sons of Jerubbaal, rule over you, or that one man
rule over you?' Also, remember
that I am your bone and your
flesh." Judg. 8:30; 9:5, 18
3 And his mother's relatives
spoke all these words on his behalf in the hearing of all the leaders of Shechem; and they were inclined to follow Abimelech, for
they said, "He is our relative."
4 And they gave him seventy
pieces of silver from the house of
Baal-berith with which Abimelech
hired worthless and reckless fellows, and they followed him.
5 Then he went to his father's
house at Ophrah, and killed his
brothers the sons of Jerubbaal,
seventy men, on one stone. But
Jotham the youngest son of Jerubbaal was left, for he hid himself.
6 And all the men of Shechem
and all [12]Beth-millo assembled together, and they went and made
Abimelech king, by the oak of the
pillar which was in Shechem.
7 Now when they told Jotham,
he went and stood on the top of
[r]Mount Gerizim, and lifted his
voice and called out. Thus he said
to them, "Listen to me, O men of
Shechem, that God may listen to
you. Deut. 11:29, 30
8 "Once the trees went forth to
anoint a king over them, and they
said to the olive tree, 'Reign over
us!'
9 "But the olive tree said to
them, 'Shall I leave my fatness

[12]Or, *the house of Millo*

with[t]which God and men are honored, and go to wave over the
trees?' *which by me*
10 "Then the trees said to the fig
tree, 'You come, reign over us!'
11 "But the fig tree said to them,
'Shall I leave my sweetness and
my good [a]fruit, and go to wave
over the trees?' *produce*
12 "Then the trees said to the
vine, 'You come, reign over us!'
13 "But the vine said to them,
'Shall I leave my new wine, which
cheers God and men, and go to
wave over the trees?'
14 "Finally all the trees said to
the bramble, 'You come, reign
over us!'
15 "And the bramble said to the
trees, 'If in [a]truth you are anointing
me as king over you, come and
take refuge in my shade; but if
not, may fire come out from the
bramble and consume the cedars
of Lebanon.' *sincerity*
16 "Now therefore, if you have
dealt in truth and integrity in
making Abimelech king, and if
you have dealt well with Jerubbaal and his house, and have dealt
with him as he deserved—
17 for my father fought for you
and risked his life and delivered
you from the hand of Midian;
18 but you have risen against
my father's house today and have
killed his sons, seventy men, on
one stone, and have made Abimelech, the son of his maidservant,
king over the men of Shechem,
because he is your relative—
19 if then you have dealt in
[a]truth and integrity with Jerubbaal
and his house this day, rejoice in
Abimelech, and let him also rejoice in you. *sincerity*
20 "But if not, let fire come out
from Abimelech and consume the
men of Shechem and Beth-millo;
and let fire come out from the
men of Shechem and from Beth-
millo, and consume Abimelech."
21 Then Jotham escaped and
fled, and went to Beer and remained there because of Abimelech his brother.
22 Now Abimelech ruled over
Israel three years.
23 [r]Then God sent an evil spirit
between Abimelech and the men
of Shechem; and the men of Shechem [r]dealt treacherously with
Abimelech, 1 Sam. 16:14 • Is. 33:1
24 in order that the violence
[t]done to the seventy sons of Jerubbaal might come, and their blood
might be laid on Abimelech their
brother, who killed them, and on
the men of Shechem, who
strengthened his hands to kill his
brothers. *of the seventy*
25 And the men of Shechem set
[t]men in ambush against him on the
tops of the mountains, and they
robbed all who might pass by
them along the road; and it was
told to Abimelech. *liers-in-wait for*
26 Now Gaal the son of Ebed
came with his [t]relatives, and
crossed over into Shechem; and
the men of Shechem put their
trust in him. *brothers*
27 And they went out into the
field and gathered *the grapes of*
their vineyards and trod *them,*
and held a [t]festival; and they went
into the house of [r]their god, and
ate and drank and cursed Abimelech. *rejoicing* • Judg. 8:33; 9:46

28 Then Gaal the son of Ebed said, "Who is Abimelech, and who is Shechem, that we should serve him? Is he not the son of Jerubbaal, and *is* Zebul *not* his [t]lieutenant? Serve the men of Hamor the father of Shechem; but why should we serve him? *overseer*

29 "Would, therefore, that this people were under my authority! Then I would remove Abimelech." And he said to Abimelech, "Increase your army, and come out."

30 And when Zebul the ruler of the city heard the words of Gaal the son of Ebed, his anger burned.

31 And he sent messengers to Abimelech deceitfully, saying, "Behold, Gaal the son of Ebed and his relatives have come to Shechem; and behold, they are stirring up the city against you.

32 "Now therefore, arise by night, you and the people who are with you, and lie in wait in the field.

33 "And it shall come about in the morning, as soon as the sun is up, that you shall rise early and rush upon the city; and behold, when he and the people who are with him come out against you, you shall do to them [t]whatever you can." *as your hand can find*

34 So Abimelech and all the people who *were* with him arose by night and lay in wait against Shechem in four companies.

35 Now Gaal the son of Ebed went out and stood in the entrance of the city gate; and Abimelech and the people who *were* with him arose from the ambush.

36 And when Gaal saw the people, he said to Zebul, "Look,[t] people are coming down from the tops of the mountains." But Zebul said to him, "You are seeing the shadow of the mountains as *if they were* men." *Behold*

37 And Gaal spoke again and said, "Behold, people are coming down from the highest part of the land, and one company comes by the way of the diviners' oak."

38 Then Zebul said to him, "Where is your [t]boasting now with which you said, 'Who is Abimelech that we should serve him?' Is this not the people whom you despised? Go out now and fight with them!" *mouth*

39 So Gaal went out before the leaders of Shechem and fought with Abimelech.

40 And Abimelech chased him, and he fled before him; and many fell wounded up to the entrance of the gate.

41 Then Abimelech remained at Arumah, but Zebul drove out Gaal and his relatives so that they could not remain in Shechem.

42 Now it came about the next day, that the people went out to the field, and it was told to Abimelech.

43 So he took [t]his people and divided them into three companies, and lay in wait in the field; when he looked and saw the people coming out from the city, he arose against them and slew them. *the*

44 Then Abimelech and the company who was with him dashed forward and stood in the entrance of the city gate; the other two [t]companies then dashed against all who *were* in the field and [t]slew them. *heads • smote*

45 And Abimelech fought against the city all that day, and he captured the city and killed the people who *were* in it; then he [r]razed the city and sowed it with salt. 2 Kin. 3:25

46 When all the leaders of the tower of Shechem heard of *it,* they entered the inner chamber of the [t]temple of El-berith. *house*

47 And it was told Abimelech that all the leaders of the tower of Shechem were gathered together.

48 So Abimelech went up to Mount Zalmon, he and all the people who *were* with him; and Abimelech took [t]an axe in his hand and cut down a branch from the trees, and lifted it and laid *it* on his shoulder. Then he said to the people who *were* with him, "What you have seen me do, hurry *and* do [t]likewise." *the axes • like me*

49 And all the people also cut down each one his branch and followed Abimelech, and put *them* on the inner chamber and set the inner chamber on fire over those *inside,* so that all the men of the tower of Shechem also died, about a thousand men and women.

50 Then Abimelech went to Thebez, and he camped against Thebez and captured it.

51 But there was a strong tower in the center of the city, and all the men and women with all the leaders of the city fled there and shut themselves in; and they went up on the roof of the tower.

52 So Abimelech came to the tower and fought against it, and approached the entrance of the tower to burn it with fire.

53 But a certain woman threw an upper millstone on Abimelech's head, crushing his skull.

54 Then [r]he called quickly to the young man, his armor bearer, and said to him, "Draw your sword and kill me, lest it be said of me, 'A woman slew him.' " So [t]the young man pierced him through, and he died. 1 Sam. 31:4 • *his*

55 And when the men of Israel saw that Abimelech was dead, each departed to his home.

56 Thus [r]God repaid the wickedness of Abimelech, which he had done to his father, in killing his seventy brothers. Gen. 9:5, 6

57 Also God returned all the wickedness of the men of Shechem on their heads, and the curse of Jotham the son of Jerubbaal came [t]upon them. *to*

CHAPTER 10

NOW after Abimelech died, Tola the son of Puah, the son of Dodo, a man of Issachar, arose to save Israel; and he lived in Shamir in the hill country of Ephraim.

2 And he judged Israel twenty-three years. Then he died and was buried in Shamir.

3 And after him, Jair the Gileadite arose, and judged Israel twenty-two years.

4 And he had thirty sons who rode on thirty donkeys, and they had thirty cities [t]in the land of Gilead that are called Havvoth-jair to this day. *which are in*

5 And Jair died and was buried in Kamon.

6 Then the sons of Israel again did evil in the sight of the LORD, [r]served the Baals and the Ashta-

roth, the gods of Aram, the gods
of Sidon, the gods of Moab, the
gods of the sons of Ammon, and
the gods of the Philistines; thus
they forsook the LORD and did not
serve Him. Judg. 2:13
7 And the anger of the LORD
burned against Israel, and He [r]sold
them into the hands of the Philistines, and into the hands of the
sons of Ammon. 1 Sam. 12:9
8 And they afflicted and
crushed the sons of Israel that
year; for eighteen years they *afflicted* all the sons of Israel who
were beyond the Jordan in Gilead
in the land of the Amorites.
9 And the sons of Ammon
crossed the Jordan to fight also
against Judah, Benjamin, and the
house of Ephraim, so that Israel
was greatly distressed.
10 Then the [r]sons of Israel cried
out to the LORD, saying, "We have
sinned against Thee, for indeed,
we have forsaken our God and
served the Baals." 1 Sam. 12:10
11 And the LORD said to the
sons of Israel, "*Did I* not *deliver
you* [r]from the Egyptians, the Amorites, [r]the sons of Ammon, and the
Philistines? Judg. 2:12 • Judg. 3:13
12 "Also when the Sidonians, the
Amalekites and the Maonites [r]op-
pressed you, you cried out to Me,
and I delivered you from their
hands. Ps. 106:42
13 "Yet you have forsaken Me
and served other gods; therefore I
will deliver you no more.
14 "Go[r] and cry out to the gods
which you have chosen; let them
deliver you in the time of your distress." Deut. 32:37
15 And the sons of Israel said to
the LORD, "We have sinned, do to
us whatever seems good to Thee;
only please deliver us this day."
16 [r]So they put away the foreign
gods from among them, and
served the LORD; and [r]He could
bear the misery of Israel no
longer. Josh. 24:23 • Deut. 32:36
17 Then the sons of Ammon
were summoned, and they
camped in Gilead. And the sons of
Israel gathered together, and
camped in [r]Mizpah. Judg. 11:29
18 And the people, the leaders
of Gilead, said to one another,
"Who is the man who will begin
to fight against the sons of Ammon? He shall become head over
all the inhabitants of Gilead."

CHAPTER 11

NOW Jephthah the Gileadite was
a valiant warrior, but he was the
son of a harlot. And Gilead [t]was
the father of Jephthah. *begat*
2 And Gilead's wife bore him
sons; and when his wife's sons
grew up, they drove Jephthah out
and said to him, "You shall not
have an inheritance in our father's
house, for you are the son of another woman."
3 So Jephthah fled from his
brothers and lived in the land of
Tob; and worthless fellows gathered themselves [t]about Jephthah,
and they went out with him. *to*
4 And it came about after a
while that the sons of Ammon
fought against Israel.
5 And it happened when the
sons of Ammon fought against Israel that the elders of Gilead went

to get Jephthah from the land of Tob;

6 and they said to Jephthah, "Come and be our chief that we may fight against the sons of Ammon."

7 Then Jephthah said to the elders of Gilead, "Did you not hate me and drive me from my father's house? So why have you come to me now when you are in trouble?"

8 And the elders of Gilead said to Jephthah, "For this reason we have now returned to you, that you may go with us and fight with the sons of Ammon and [r]become head over all the inhabitants of Gilead." Judg. 10:18

9 So Jephthah said to the elders of Gilead, "If you take me back to fight against the sons of Ammon and the LORD gives them up [t]to me, will I become your head?" *before*

10 And the elders of Gilead said to Jephthah, "The[r] LORD is[t]witness between us; surely we will do as you have said." Mic. 1:2 • *hearer*

11 Then Jephthah went with the elders of Gilead, and the people made him head and chief over them; and Jephthah spoke all his words before the LORD at Mizpah.

12 Now Jephthah sent messengers to the king of the sons of Ammon, saying, "What is between you and me, that you have come to me to fight against my land?"

13 And the king of the sons of Ammon said to the messengers of Jephthah, "Because Israel [r]took away my land when they came up from Egypt, from the Arnon as far as the [r]Jabbok and the Jordan; therefore, return them peaceably now." Num. 21:24 • Gen. 32:22

14 But Jephthah sent messengers again to the king of the sons of Ammon,

15 and they said to him, "Thus says Jephthah, 'Israel did not take away the land of Moab, nor the land of the sons of Ammon.

16 'For when they came up from Egypt, and Israel went through the wilderness to the [t]Red Sea and came to Kadesh, *Sea of Reeds*

17 then Israel [r]sent messengers to the king of Edom, saying, "Please let us pass through your land," but the king of Edom would not listen. And they also sent to the king of Moab, but he would not consent. So Israel remained at Kadesh. Num. 20:14-21

18 'Then they went through the wilderness and around the land of Edom and the land of Moab, and came to the east side of the land of Moab, and they camped beyond the Arnon; but they did not enter the territory of Moab, for the Arnon *was* the border of Moab.

19 'And Israel sent messengers to Sihon king of the Amorites, the king of Heshbon, and Israel said to him, "Please let us pass through your land to our place."

20 'But Sihon did not trust Israel to pass through his territory; so Sihon gathered all his people and camped in Jahaz, and fought with Israel.

21 'And the LORD, the God of Israel, gave Sihon and all his people into the hand of Israel, and they defeated them; so Israel possessed all the land of the Amorites, the inhabitants of that country.

22 'So[r] they possessed all the territory of the Amorites, from the
Arnon as far as the Jabbok, and
from the wilderness as far as the
Jordan. Deut. 2:36, 37
23 'Since now the LORD, the God
of Israel, drove out the Amorites
from before His people Israel, are
you then to possess it?
24 'Do you not possess what
[r]Chemosh your god gives you to
possess? So whatever the LORD
our God has driven out before us,
we will possess it. Num. 21:29
25 'And now are you any better
than [r]Balak the son of Zippor, king
of Moab? Did he ever strive with
Israel, or did he ever fight against
them? Num. 22:2; Josh. 24:9
26 'While[r] Israel lived in Heshbon and its villages, and in Aroer
and its villages, and in all the
cities that are on the banks of the
Arnon, three hundred years, why
did you not recover them within
that time? Num. 21:25, 26
27 'I therefore have not sinned
against you, but you are doing me
wrong by making war against me;
may the LORD, the Judge, judge
today between the sons of Israel
and the sons of Ammon.' "
28 But the king of the sons of
Ammon disregarded the message
which Jephthah sent him.
29 Now [r]the Spirit of the LORD
came upon Jephthah, so that he
passed through Gilead and Manasseh; then he passed through
Mizpah of Gilead, and from Mizpah of Gilead he went on to the
sons of Ammon. Judg. 3:10
30 And Jephthah made a vow to
the LORD and said, "If Thou wilt
indeed give the sons of Ammon
into my hand,
31 then it shall be that whatever
comes out of the doors of my
house to meet me when I return in
peace from the sons of Ammon, it
shall be the LORD's, and I will offer it up as a burnt offering."
32 So Jephthah crossed over to
the sons of Ammon to fight
against them; and the LORD gave
them into his hand.
33 And he struck them with a
very great slaughter from Aroer
to the entrance of Minnith, twenty
cities, and as far as Abel-kera-
mim. So the sons of Ammon were
subdued before the sons of Israel.
34 When Jephthah came to his
house at Mizpah, behold, his
daughter was coming out to meet
him [r]with tambourines and with
dancing. Now she was his one *and*
only child; besides her he had neither son nor daughter. Ex. 15:20
35 And it came about when he
saw her, that he tore his clothes
and said, "Alas, my daughter! You
have brought me very low, and
you are among those who trouble
me; for I have [t]given my word to
the LORD, and I cannot take *it*
back." *opened my mouth*
36 So she said to him, "My father, you have [t]given your word to
the LORD; do to me as you have
said, since the LORD has avenged
you of your enemies, the sons of
Ammon." *opened your mouth*
37 And she said to her father,
"Let this thing be done for me; let
me alone two months, that I may
[t]go to the mountains and weep because of my virginity, I and my
companions." *go and go down on*

38 Then he said, "Go." So he
sent her away for two months;
and she left with her companions,
and wept on the mountains because of her virginity.
39 And it came about at the end
of two months that she returned
to her father, who did to her according to the vow which he had
made; and she [t]had no relations
with a man. Thus it became a custom in Israel, *knew no man*
40 that the daughters of Israel
went yearly to [t]commemorate the
daughter of Jephthah the Gileadite four days in the year. *recount*

CHAPTER 12

THEN the men of Ephraim were
summoned, and they crossed [a]to
Zaphon and [r]said to Jephthah,
"Why did you cross over to fight
against the sons of Ammon without calling us to go with you? We
will burn your house down on
you." *northward* · Judg. 8:1
2 And Jephthah said to them,
"I and my people were at great
strife with the sons of Ammon;
when I called you, you did not deliver me from their hand.
3 "And when I saw that you
would not deliver *me,* I took my
life in my hands and crossed over
against the sons of Ammon, and
the LORD gave them into my hand.
Why then have you come up to
me this day, to fight against me?"
4 Then Jephthah gathered all
the men of Gilead and fought E-
phraim; and the men of Gilead [t]de-
feated Ephraim, because they
said, "You are fugitives of Ephraim, O Gileadites, in the midst of
Ephraim *and* in the midst of Manasseh." *smote*
5 And the Gileadites [r]captured
the fords of the Jordan opposite E-
phraim. And it happened when
any of the fugitives of Ephraim
said, "Let me cross over," the men
of Gilead would say to him, "Are
you an Ephraimite?" If he said,
"No," Judg. 3:28
6 then they would say to him,
"Say now, 'Shibboleth.'" But he
said, "Sibboleth," for he could not
pronounce it correctly. Then they
seized him and slew him at the
fords of the Jordan. Thus there fell
at that time 42,000 of Ephraim.
7 And Jephthah judged Israel
six years. Then Jephthah the Gileadite died and was buried in *one
of* the cities of Gilead.
8 Now Ibzan of Bethlehem
judged Israel after him.
9 And he had thirty sons, and
thirty daughters *whom* he gave in
marriage outside *the family,* and
he brought in thirty daughters
from outside for his sons. And he
judged Israel seven years.
10 Then Ibzan died and was
buried in Bethlehem.
11 Now Elon the Zebulunite
judged Israel after him; and he
judged Israel ten years.
12 Then Elon the Zebulunite
died and was buried at Aijalon in
the land of Zebulun.
13 Now Abdon the son of Hillel
the Pirathonite judged Israel after
him.
14 And he had forty sons and
thirty grandsons who rode on seventy donkeys; and he judged Israel eight years.
15 Then Abdon the son of Hillel

the Pirathonite died and was buried at Pirathon in the land of E-
phraim, in the hill country of the
Amalekites.

CHAPTER 13

NOW the sons of Israel [r]again did
evil in the sight of the LORD, so
that the LORD gave them into the
hands of the Philistines forty
years. Judg. 2:11
2 And there was a certain man
of [r]Zorah, of the family of the Danites, whose name was Manoah;
and his wife was barren and had
borne no *children*. Josh. 19:41
3 [r]Then the angel of the LORD
appeared to the woman, and said
to her, "Behold now, you are barren and have borne no *children*,
but you shall conceive and give
birth to a son. Judg. 6:11, 14
4 "Now therefore, be careful
not to drink wine or strong drink,
nor eat any unclean thing.
5 "For behold, you shall conceive and give birth to a son, and
no razor shall come upon his
head, for the boy shall be a Nazirite to God from the womb; and he
shall begin to deliver Israel from
the hands of the Philistines."
6 Then the woman came and
told her husband, saying, "A [r]man
of God came to me and his appearance was like the appearance
of the angel of God, very awesome. And I did not ask him
where he *came* from, nor did he
tell me his name. Judg. 6:11
7 "But he said to me, 'Behold,
you shall conceive and give birth
to a son, and now you shall not
drink wine or strong drink nor eat
any unclean thing, for the boy
shall be a Nazirite to God from the
womb to the day of his death.' "
8 Then Manoah entreated the
LORD and said, "O Lord, please let
[r]the man of God whom Thou hast
sent come to us again that he may
teach us what to do for the boy
who is to be born." Judg. 13:3, 7
9 And God listened to the
voice of Manoah; and [r]the angel of
God came again to the woman as
she was sitting in the field, but
Manoah her husband was not
with her. Judg. 13:8
10 So the woman ran quickly
and told her husband, "Behold,
the man who [t]came the *other* day
has appeared to me." *came to me*
11 Then Manoah arose and followed his wife, and when he came
to the man he said to him, "Are
you the man who spoke to the
woman?" And he said, "I am."
12 And Manoah said, "Now
when your words come *to pass*,
what shall be the boy's mode of
life and his vocation?"
13 So the angel of the LORD said
to Manoah, "Let the woman pay
attention [t]to all that I said. *from*
14 "She should not eat anything
that comes from the [r]vine nor
drink wine or strong drink, nor eat
any unclean thing; let her observe
all that I commanded." Num. 6:4
15 Then Manoah said to [r]the angel of the LORD, "Please let us de-
tain you so that we may prepare a
kid for you." Judg. 13:3
16 And the angel of the LORD
said to Manoah, "Though you de-
tain me, I will not eat your [t]food,
but if you prepare a burnt offering, *then* offer it to the LORD." For

Manoah did not know that he was
the angel of the LORD. *bread*
17 And Manoah said to the angel of the LORD, "What[r] is your
name, so that when your words
come *to pass,* we may honor
you?" Gen. 32:29
18 But the angel of the LORD
said to him, "Why do you ask my
name, seeing it is [13]wonderful?"
19 So Manoah took the kid with
the grain offering and offered it on
the rock to the LORD, and He performed wonders while Manoah
and his wife looked on.
20 For it came about when the
flame went up from the altar
toward heaven, that the angel of
the LORD ascended in the flame of
the altar. When Manoah and his
wife saw *this,* they [r]fell on their
faces to the ground. Lev. 9:24
21 Now the angel of the LORD
appeared no more to Manoah or
his wife. Then Manoah knew that
he was the angel of the LORD.
22 So Manoah said to his wife,
"We[r] shall surely die, for we have
seen God." Gen. 32:30; Deut. 5:26
23 But his wife said to him, "If
the LORD had desired to kill us, He
would not have accepted a burnt
offering and a grain offering from
our hands, nor would He have
[r]shown us all these things, nor
would He have let us hear *things*
like this at this time." Ps. 25:14
24 Then the woman gave birth
to a son and named him Samson;
and the [r]child grew up and the
LORD blessed him. 1 Sam. 3:19
25 And the Spirit of the LORD
began to stir him in [14]Mahaneh-
dan, between Zorah and Eshtaol.

[13] I.e., incomprehensible
[14] I.e., the camp of Dan

CHAPTER 14

THEN Samson went down to
Timnah and saw a woman in Timnah, *one* of the daughters of the
Philistines.
2 So he came[t] back and told his
father and [t]mother, "I saw a
woman in Timnah, *one* of the
daughters of the Philistines; now
therefore, get her for me as a
wife." *up • mother, saying,*
3 Then his father and his
mother said to him, "Is there no
woman among the daughters of
your [t]relatives, or among all [t]our
people, that you go to take a wife
from the uncircumcised Philistines?" But Samson said to his father, "Get her for me, for she
looks good to me." *brothers • my*
4 However, his father and
mother did not know that it was
of the LORD, for He was seeking
an occasion against the Philistines. Now at that time the Philistines were ruling over Israel.
5 Then Samson went down to
Timnah with his father and
mother, and came as far as the
vineyards of Timnah; and behold,
a young lion *came* roaring toward
him.
6 And the Spirit of the LORD
came upon him mightily, so that
he tore him as one tears a kid
though he had nothing in his
hand; but he did not tell his father
or mother what he had done.
7 So he went down and talked
to the woman; and she looked
good to Samson.
8 When he returned later to
take her, he turned aside to look
at the carcass of the lion; and be-

hold, a swarm of bees and honey
were in the body of the lion.
9 So he scraped[t]the honey into
his[t]hands and went on, eating as
he went. When he came to his father and mother, he gave *some* to
them and they ate *it;* but he did
not tell them that he had scraped
the honey out of the body of the
lion. *it* • *palms*
10 Then his father went down to
the woman; and Samson made a
feast there, for the young men
customarily did this.
11 And it came about when they
saw him that they brought thirty
companions to be with him.
12 Then Samson said to them,
"Let me now[r]propound a riddle to
you; if you will indeed tell it to me
within the seven days of the feast,
and find it out, then I will give you
thirty linen wraps and thirty
changes of clothes. Ezek. 17:2
13 "But if you are unable to tell
me, then you shall give me thirty
linen wraps and thirty changes of
clothes." And they said to him,
"Propound your riddle, that we
may hear it."
14 So he said to them,

"Out of the eater came
something to eat,
And out of the strong came
something sweet."

But they could not tell the riddle
in three days.
15 Then it came about on the
fourth day that they said to Samson's wife, "Entice[r]your husband,
that he may tell us the riddle,[r]lest
we burn you and your father's
house with fire. Have you invited
us to impoverish us? Is this not
so?" Judg. 16:5 • Judg. 15:6
16 And Samson's wife wept before him and said, "You[r]only hate
me, and you do not love me; you
have propounded a riddle to the
sons of my people, and have not
told *it* to me." And he said to her,
"Behold, I have not told *it* to my
father or mother; so should I tell
you?" Judg. 16:15
17 However she wept before
him seven days while their feast
lasted. And it came about on the
seventh day that he told her because she pressed him so hard.
She then told the riddle to the
sons of her people.
18 So the men of the city said to
him on the seventh day before the
sun went down,

"What is sweeter than honey?
And what is stronger than a
lion?"

And he said to them,

"If you had not plowed with
my heifer,
You would not have found
out my riddle."

19 Then the Spirit of the LORD
[t]came upon him mightily, and he
went down to Ashkelon and killed
thirty of them and took their spoil,
and gave the changes *of clothes* to
those who told the riddle. And his
anger burned, and he went up to
his father's house. *rushed upon*
20 But Samson's wife was[r]*given*
to his companion who had been
his[a]friend. Judg. 15:2 • *best man*

CHAPTER 15

BUT after a while, in the time of
wheat harvest, it came about that
Samson visited his wife with a

young goat, and said, "I will go in
to my wife in *her* room." But her
father did not let him enter.
2 And her father said, "I really
thought that you hated her intensely; so I gave her to your companion. Is not her younger sister
[t]more beautiful than she? Please
let her be yours instead." *better*
3 Samson then said to them,
"This time I shall be blameless in
regard to the Philistines when I do
them harm."
4 And Samson went and
caught three hundred foxes, and
took torches, and turned *the foxes*
tail to tail, and put one torch in the
middle between two tails.
5 When he had set fire to the
torches, he released[t]the foxes into
the standing grain of the Philistines, thus burning up both the
shocks and the standing grain,
along with the vineyards *and*
groves. *them*
6 Then the Philistines said,
"Who did this?" And they said,
"Samson, the son-in-law of the
Timnite, because he took his wife
and gave her to his companion."
So the Philistines came up and
[r]burned her and her father with
fire. Judg. 14:15
7 And Samson said to them,
"Since you act like this, I will
surely take revenge on you, but
after that I will quit."
8 And he struck them ruthlessly with a great slaughter; and
he went down and lived in the
cleft of the rock of Etam.
9 Then the Philistines went up
and camped in Judah, and spread
out in Lehi.
10 And the men of Judah said,
"Why have you come up against
us?" And they said, "We have
come up to bind Samson in order
to do to him as he did to us."
11 Then 3,000 men of Judah
went down to the cleft of the rock
of Etam and said to Samson, "Do
you not know that the Philistines
are rulers over us? What then is
this that you have done to us?"
And he said to them, "As they did
to me, so I have done to them."
12 And they said to him, "We
have come down to bind you so
that we may give you into the
hands of the Philistines." And
Samson said to them, "Swear to
me that you will not kill me."
13 So they said to him, "No, but
we will bind you fast and give you
into their hands; yet surely we will
not kill you." Then they bound
him with two new ropes and
brought him up from the rock.
14 When he came to Lehi, the
Philistines shouted as they met
him. And the Spirit of the LORD
[t]came upon him mightily so that
the ropes that were on his arms
were as flax that is burned with
fire, and his bonds dropped from
his hands. *rushed upon*
15 And he found a fresh jawbone of a donkey, so he reached
out and took it and[t]killed a thousand men with it. *smote*
16 Then Samson said,
"With the jawbone of a donkey,
Heaps upon heaps,
With the jawbone of a donkey
I have [t]killed a thousand
men." *smitten*
17 And it came about when he

had finished speaking, that he
threw the jawbone from his hand;
and he named that place [15]Ra-
math-lehi.
18 Then he became very thirsty,
and he [r]called to the LORD and
said, "Thou hast given this great
deliverance by the hand of Thy
servant, and now shall I die of
thirst [a]and fall into the hands of the
uncircumcised?" Judg. 16:28 • *or*
19 But God split the hollow
place that is in Lehi so that water
came out of it. When he drank, his
strength returned and he revived.
Therefore, he named it En-hak-
kore, which is in Lehi to this day.
20 So [r]he judged Israel twenty
years in [r]the days of the Philistines. Judg. 16:31 • Judg. 13:1

CHAPTER 16

NOW Samson went to [r]Gaza and
saw a harlot there, and went in to
her. Josh. 15:47
2 *When it was told* to the Ga-
zites, saying, "Samson has come
here," they [r]surrounded *the place*
and lay in wait for him all night at
the gate of the city. And they kept
silent all night, saying, "*Let us
wait* until the morning light, then
we will kill him." 1 Sam. 23:26
3 Now Samson lay until midnight, and at midnight he arose
and took hold of the doors of the
city gate and the two posts and
pulled them up along with the
bars; then he put them on his
shoulders and carried them up to
the top of the mountain which is
opposite Hebron.
4 After this it came about that
he loved a woman in the valley of
Sorek, whose name was Delilah.
5 And the lords of the Philistines came up to her, and said to
her, "Entice him, and see where
his great strength *lies* and [t]how we
may overpower him that we may
bind him to afflict him. Then we
will each give you eleven hundred
pieces of silver." *by what*
6 So Delilah said to Samson,
"Please tell me where your great
strength is and [t]how you may be
bound to afflict you." *by what*
7 And Samson said to her, "If
they bind me with seven fresh
cords that have not been dried,
then I shall become weak and be
like any *other* man."
8 Then the lords of the Philistines brought up to her seven
fresh cords that had not been
dried, and she bound him with
them.
9 Now she had *men* lying in
wait in an inner room. And she
said to him, "The Philistines are
upon you, Samson!" But he
snapped the cords as a string of
tow snaps when it touches fire. So
his strength was not discovered.
10 Then Delilah said to Samson,
"Behold, you have deceived me
and told me lies; now please tell
me, how you may be bound."
11 And he said to her, "If they
bind me tightly with new ropes
which have not been used, then I
shall become weak and be like
any *other* man."
12 So Delilah took new ropes
and bound him with them and
said to him, "The Philistines are
upon you, Samson!" For the *men*
were lying in wait in the inner

[15]I.e., the high place of the jawbone

room. But he snapped the ropes from his arms like a thread.

13 Then Delilah said to Samson, "Up to now you have deceived me and told me lies; tell me [t]how you may be bound." And he said to her, "If you weave the seven locks of my [t]hair with the web [16][and fasten it with a pin, then I shall become weak and be like any other man." *by what • head*

14 So while he slept, Delilah took the seven locks of his hair and wove them into the web]. And she fastened *it* with the pin, and said to him, "The Philistines are upon you, Samson!" But he awoke from his sleep and pulled out the pin of the loom and the web.

15 Then she said to him, "How can you say, 'I love you,' when your heart is not with me? You have deceived me these three times and have not told me where your great strength is."

16 And it came about when she pressed him daily with her words and urged him, that his soul was annoyed to death.

17 So he told her all *that was* in his heart and said to her, "A razor has never come on my head, for I have been a Nazirite to God from my mother's womb. If I am shaved, then my strength will leave me and I shall become weak and be like any *other* man."

18 When Delilah saw that he had told her all *that was* in his heart, she sent and called the lords of the Philistines, saying, "Come up once more, for he has told me all *that is* in his heart." Then the lords of the Philistines came up to her, and brought the money in their hands.

[16]The passage in brackets is found in Gr. but not in any Heb. mss.

19 And she made him sleep on her knees, and called for a man and had him shave off the seven locks of his [t]hair. Then she began to afflict him, and his strength left him. *head*

20 And she said, "The Philistines are upon you, Samson!" And he awoke from his sleep and said, "I will go out as at other times and shake myself free." But he did not know that [r]the LORD had departed from him. Num. 14:42, 43

21 Then the Philistines seized him and gouged out his eyes; and they brought him down to Gaza and bound him with bronze chains, and he was a grinder in the prison.

22 However, the hair of his head began to grow again after it was shaved off.

23 Now the lords of the Philistines assembled to offer a great sacrifice to [r]Dagon their god, and to rejoice, for they said,

"Our god has given Samson
our enemy into our
hands." 1 Sam. 5:2

24 When the people saw him, they praised their god, for they said,

"Our god has given our enemy into our hands,
Even the destroyer of our country,
Who has slain many of us."

25 It so happened when they were in high spirits, that they said, "Call for Samson, that he may amuse us." So they called for Samson from the prison, and he

entertained them. And they made
him stand between the pillars.
26 Then Samson said to the boy
who was holding his hand, "Let
me feel the pillars on which the
house rests, that I may lean
against them."
27 Now the house was full of
men and women, and all the lords
of the Philistines were there. And
about 3,000 men and women were
on the roof looking on while Samson was amusing *them*.
28 Then Samson called to the
LORD and said, "O Lord GOD,
please remember me and please
strengthen me just this time, O
God, that I may at once [r]be
avenged of the Philistines for my
two eyes." Jer. 15:15
29 And Samson grasped the two
middle pillars on which the house
rested, and braced himself against
them, the one with his right hand
and the other with his left.
30 And Samson said, "Let me
die with the Philistines!" And he
bent with [t]all his might so that the
house fell on the lords and all the
people who were in it. So the dead
whom he killed at his death were
more than those whom he killed
in his life. *strength*
31 Then his brothers and all his
father's household came down,
took him, brought him up, and
buried him between Zorah and
Eshtaol in the tomb of Manoah his
father. [r]Thus he had judged Israel
twenty years. Judg. 15:20

CHAPTER 17

NOW there was a man of the hill
country of Ephraim whose name
was Micah.
2 And he said to his mother,
"The eleven hundred *pieces* of silver which were taken from you,
about which you uttered a curse
in my hearing, behold, the silver is
with me; I took it." And his
mother said, "Blessed be my son
by the LORD."
3 He then returned the eleven
hundred *pieces* of silver to his
mother, and his mother said, "I
wholly dedicate the silver from
my hand to the LORD for my son
to make a graven image and a
molten image; now therefore, I
will return [t]them to you." *it*
4 So when he returned the silver to his mother, his mother took
two hundred *pieces* of silver and
gave them to the silversmith who
made [t]them into a graven image
and a molten image, and they
were in the house of Micah. *it*
5 And the man Micah had a
[17]shrine and he made an ephod and
household idols and [t]consecrated
one of his sons, that he might become his priest. *filled the hand of*
6 In those days there was no
king in Israel; every man did what
was right in his own eyes.
7 Now there was a young man
from Bethlehem in Judah, of the
family of Judah, who was a Levite; and he was staying there.
8 Then the man departed from
the city, from Bethlehem in Judah,
to stay wherever he might find *a
place;* and as he made his journey,
he came to the hill country of E-
phraim to the house of Micah.
9 And Micah said to him,
"Where do you come from?" And
he said to him, "I am a Levite
from Bethlehem in Judah, and I

[17]Lit., *house of gods*

am going to [a]stay wherever I may
find *a place.*" *sojourn*
10 Micah then said to him,
"Dwell with me and be a father
and a priest to me, and I will give
you ten *pieces* of silver a year, a
suit of clothes, and your mainte-
nance." So the Levite went *in.*
11 And the Levite agreed to live
with the man; and the young man
became to him like one of his
sons.
12 So Micah [t]consecrated the
Levite, and the young man became his priest and lived in the
house of Micah. *filled the hand of*
13 Then Micah said, "Now I
know that the LORD will prosper
me, seeing I have a Levite as
priest."

CHAPTER 18

IN those days there was no king
of Israel; and in those days the
tribe of the Danites was seeking
an inheritance for themselves to
live in, for until that day [t]an inheritance had not [t]been allotted to
them as a possession among the
tribes of Israel. *it · fallen*
2 So the sons of Dan sent from
their family five men out of their
whole number, valiant men from
Zorah and Eshtaol, to spy out the
land and to search it; and they
said to them, "Go, search the
land." And they came to the hill
country of Ephraim, to the house
of Micah, and lodged there.
3 When they were near the
house of Micah, they recognized
the voice of the young man, the
Levite; and they turned aside
there, and said to him, "Who
brought you here? And what are
you doing in this *place?* And what
do you have here?"
4 And he said to them, "Thus
and so has Micah done to me, and
he has hired me, and [r]I have become his priest." Judg. 17:12
5 And they said to him, "Inquire of God, please, that we may
know whether our way on which
we are going will be prosperous."
6 And the priest said to them,
"Go in peace; your way in which
you are going [t]has the LORD's approval." *is before the LORD*
7 Then the five men departed
and came to Laish and saw the
people who were in it living in security, after the manner of the Sidonians, quiet and secure; for
there was no ruler humiliating
them for anything in the land, and
they were far from the Sidonians
and had no dealings with anyone.
8 When they came back to
their brothers at Zorah and Eshtaol, their brothers said to them,
"What *do* you *report?*"
9 And they said, "Arise, and let
us go up against them; for we
have seen the land, and behold, it
is very good. And will you [t]sit still?
Do not delay to go, to enter, to
possess the land. *be*
10 "When you enter, you shall
come to a secure people with a
spacious land; for God has given it
into your hand, [r]a place where
there is no lack of anything that is
on the earth." Deut. 8:9
11 Then from the family of the
Danites, from Zorah and from
Eshtaol, six hundred men armed
with weapons of war set out.
12 And they went up and
camped at Kiriath-jearim in Ju-

dah. Therefore they called that
place [18]Mahaneh-dan[r] to this day;
behold, it is [t]west of Kiriath-jearim. Judg. 13:25 • *behind*
13 And they passed from there
to the hill country of Ephraim and
came to the house of Micah.
14 Then the five men who went
to spy out the country of Laish answered and said to their kinsmen,
"Do you know that there are in
these houses [r]an ephod and
[19]household idols and a graven
image and a molten image? Now
therefore, consider what you
should do." Judg. 17:5
15 And they turned aside there
and came to the house of the
young man, the Levite, to the
house of Micah, and asked him of
his welfare.
16 And the six hundred men
armed with their weapons of war,
who were of the sons of Dan,
stood by the entrance of the gate.
17 Now the five men who went
to spy out the land went up *and*
entered there, *and* took [r]the
graven image and the ephod and
household idols and the molten
image, while the priest stood by
the entrance of the gate with the
six hundred men armed with
weapons of war. Gen. 31:19, 30
18 And when these went into
Micah's house and took the
graven image, the ephod and
household idols and the molten
image, the priest said to them,
"What are you doing?"
19 And they said to him, "Be silent, put your hand over your
mouth and come with us, and be
to us a father and a priest. Is it
better for you to be a priest to the
house of one man, or to be priest
to a tribe and a family in Israel?"
20 And the priest's heart was
glad, and he took the ephod and
household idols and the graven
image, and went among the people.
21 Then they turned and departed, and put the little ones and
the livestock and the valuables in
front of them.
22 When they had gone some
distance from the house of Micah,
the men who *were* in the houses
near Micah's house assembled
and overtook the sons of Dan.
23 And they cried to the sons of
Dan, who turned [t]around and said
to Micah, "What is *the matter*
with you, that you have assembled together?" *their faces*
24 And he said, "You have
taken away my gods which I
made, and the priest, and have
gone away, and what do I have
besides? So how can you say to
me, 'What is *the matter* with
you?' "
25 And the sons of Dan said to
him, "Do not let your voice be
heard among us, lest [t]fierce men
fall upon you and you [t]lose your
life, with the lives of your household." *bitter of soul* • *gather*
26 So the sons of Dan went on
their way; and when Micah saw
that they were too strong for him,
he turned and went back to his
house.
27 Then they took what Micah
had made and the priest who had
belonged to him, and came to
Laish, to a people quiet and se-

[18] I.e., the camp of Dan
[19] Heb., *teraphim*, and so throughout this context

cure, and struck them with the
edge of the sword; and they
burned the city with fire.
28 And there was no one to deliver *them,* because it was far
from Sidon and they had no dealings with anyone, and it was in
the valley which is near [r]Beth-re-
hob. And they rebuilt the city and
lived in it. 2 Sam. 10:6
29 And they called the name of
the city Dan, after the name of
Dan their father who was born in
Israel; however, the name of the
city formerly was Laish.
30 And the sons of Dan set up
for themselves the graven image;
and Jonathan, the son of Gershom, the son of [20]Manasseh, he
and his sons were priests to the
tribe of the Danites until the day
of the captivity of the land.
31 So they set up for themselves
Micah's graven image which he
had made, all the time that the
house of God was at Shiloh.

CHAPTER 19

Now it came about in those
days, when there was no king in
Israel, that there was a certain Levite [a]staying in the remote part of
the hill country of Ephraim, who
took a concubine for himself from
Bethlehem in Judah. *sojourning*
2 But his concubine played the
harlot against him, and she went
away from him to her father's
house in Bethlehem in Judah, and
was there for a period of four
months.
3 Then her husband arose and
went after her to speak tenderly
to her in order to bring her back,
[t]taking with him his servant and a

[20]Some ancient versions read *Moses*

pair of donkeys. So she brought
him into her father's house, and
when the girl's father saw him, he
was glad to meet him. *and*
4 And his father-in-law, the
girl's father, detained him; and he
remained with him three days. So
they ate and drank and lodged
there.
5 Now it came about on the
fourth day that they got up early
in the morning, and he [t]prepared
to go; and the girl's father said to
his son-in-law, "Sustain yourself
with a piece of bread, and afterward you may go." *arose*
6 So both of them sat down
and ate and drank together; and
the girl's father said to the man,
"Please be willing to spend the
night, and [r]let your heart be merry." Judg. 16:25; 19:9, 22; Ruth 3:7
7 Then the man arose to go,
but his father-in-law urged him so
that he spent the night there
again.
8 And on the fifth day he arose
to go early in the morning, and the
girl's father said, "Please sustain
yourself, and wait until after-
noon"; so both of them ate.
9 When the man arose to go
along with his concubine and servant, his father-in-law, the girl's
father, said to him, "Behold now,
the day has drawn to a close;
please spend the night. Lo, the
day is coming to an end; spend the
night here that your heart may be
merry. Then tomorrow you may
arise early for your journey so
that you may go home."
10 But the man was not willing
to spend the night, so he arose and
departed and came to *a place* op-

posite [r]Jebus (that is, Jerusalem).
And there were with him a pair of
saddled donkeys; his concubine
also was with him. 1 Chr. 11:4, 5
11 When they *were* near Jebus,
the day was almost gone; and the
servant said to his master, "Please
come, and let us turn aside into
this city of the Jebusites and
spend the night in it."
12 However, his master said to
him, "We will not turn aside into
the city of foreigners who are not
of the sons of Israel; but we will
go on as far as Gibeah."
13 And he said to his servant,
"Come and let us approach one of
these places; and we will spend
the night in Gibeah or Ramah."
14 So they passed along and
went their way, and the sun set on
them near Gibeah which belongs
to Benjamin.
15 And they turned aside there
in order to enter *and* lodge in Gibeah. When they entered, they sat
down in the open square of the
city, for no one took them into *his*
house to spend the night.
16 Then behold, an old man was
coming out of the field from his
work at evening. Now the man
was from the hill country of E-
phraim, and he was [a]staying in
Gibeah, but the men of the place
were Benjamites. *sojourning*
17 And he lifted up his eyes and
saw the traveler in the open
square of the city; and the old
man said, "Where are you going,
and where do you come from?"
18 And he said to him, "We are
passing from Bethlehem in Judah
to the remote part of the hill country of Ephraim, *for* I am from
there, and I went to Bethlehem in
Judah. But I am *now* going to my
house, and no man will take me
into his house.
19 "Yet there is both straw and
fodder for our donkeys, and also
bread and wine for me, your
maidservant, and [r]the young man
who is with your servants; there is
no lack of anything." Judg. 19:11
20 And the old man said, "Peace[r]
to you. Only let me *take care of* all
your needs; however, do not
spend the night in the open
square." Gen. 43:23; Judg. 6:23
21 [r]So he took him into his house
and gave the donkeys fodder, and
they washed their feet and ate and
drank. Gen. 24:32, 33
22 While they were making
merry, behold, the men of the city,
certain [t]worthless fellows, surrounded the house, pounding the
door; and they spoke to the owner
of the house, the old man, saying,
"Bring out the man who came into
your house that we may have relations with him." *sons of Belial*
23 Then the man, the owner of
the house, went out to them and
said to them, "No, my fellows,
please do not act so wickedly;
since this man has come into my
house, [r]do not commit this act of
folly. Gen. 34:7; Deut. 22:21
24 "Here is my virgin daughter
and his concubine. Please let me
bring them out that you may rav-
ish them and do to them whatever
you wish. But do not commit such
an act of folly against this man."
25 But the men would not listen
to him, so the man seized his concubine and brought *her* out to
them. And they raped her and

abused her all night until morning, then let her go at the approach of dawn.

26 As the day began to dawn, the woman came and fell down at the doorway of the man's house where her master was, until *full* daylight.

27 When her master arose in the morning and opened the doors of the house and went out to go on his way, then behold, his concubine was lying at the doorway of the house, with her hands on the threshold.

28 And he said to her, "Get up and let us go," but there was no answer. Then he placed her on the donkey; and the man arose and went to his [t]home. *place*

29 When he entered his house, he took a knife and laid hold of his concubine and cut her in twelve pieces, limb by limb, and sent her throughout the territory of Israel.

30 And it came about that all who saw *it* said, "Nothing like this has *ever* happened or been seen from the day when the sons of Israel came up from the land of Egypt to this day. Consider it, take counsel and speak up!"

CHAPTER 20

THEN all the sons of Israel from Dan to Beersheba, including the land of Gilead, came out, and the congregation assembled as one man to the LORD at Mizpah.

2 And the chiefs of all the people, *even* of all the tribes of Israel, took their stand in the assembly of the people of God, 400,000 foot soldiers who drew the sword.

3 (Now the sons of Benjamin heard that the sons of Israel had gone up to Mizpah.) And the sons of Israel said, "Tell *us*, how did this wickedness take place?"

4 So the Levite, the husband of the woman who was murdered, answered and said, "I came with my concubine to spend the night at Gibeah which belongs to Benjamin.

5 "But the [r]men of Gibeah rose up against me and surrounded the house at night because of me. They intended to kill me; instead, they ravished my concubine so that she died. Judg. 19:22

6 "And I [r]took hold of my concubine and cut her in pieces and sent her throughout the land of Israel's inheritance; for [r]they have committed a lewd and disgraceful act in Israel. Judg. 19:29 • Gen. 34:7

7 "Behold, all you sons of Israel, [r]give your advice and counsel here." Judg. 19:30

8 Then all the people arose as one man, saying, "Not one of us will go to his tent, nor will any of us return to his house.

9 "But now this is the thing which we will do to Gibeah; *we will go up* against it by lot.

10 "And we will take 10 men out of 100 throughout the tribes of Israel, and 100 out of 1,000, and 1,000 out of 10,000 to [t]supply food for the people, that when they come to Gibeah of Benjamin, they may [t]punish *them* for all the disgraceful acts that they have committed in Israel." *take • do*

11 Thus all the men of Israel were gathered against the city, united as one man.

12 Then the tribes of Israel sent
men through the entire [t]tribe of
Benjamin, saying, "What is this
wickedness that has taken place
among you? *tribes*
13 "Now then, deliver up the
men, the [21]worthless fellows in
Gibeah, that we may put them to
death and [r]remove *this* wickedness
from Israel." But the sons of Benjamin would not listen to the
voice of their brothers, the sons of
Israel. Deut. 13:5; 17:12
14 And the sons of Benjamin
gathered from the cities to Gibeah, to go out to battle against the
sons of Israel.
15 And from the cities on that
day the sons of Benjamin were
[a]numbered, 26,000 men who draw
the sword, besides the inhabitants
of Gibeah who were [a]numbered,
700 choice men. *mustered*
16 Out of all these people 700
[r]choice men were left-handed;
each one could sling a stone at a
hair and not miss. Judg. 3:15
17 Then the men of Israel besides Benjamin were numbered,
400,000 men who draw the sword;
all these were men of war.
18 Now the sons of Israel arose,
went up to Bethel, and [r]inquired of
God, and said, "Who shall go up
first for us to battle against the
sons of Benjamin?" Then the
LORD said, "Judah *shall* go *up*
first." Num. 27:21; Judg. 20:23, 27
19 So the sons of Israel arose in
the morning and camped against
Gibeah.
20 And the men of Israel went
out to battle against Benjamin,
and the men of Israel arrayed for
battle against them at Gibeah.

[21]Lit., *sons of Belial*

21 Then the sons of Benjamin
came out of Gibeah and [t]felled to
the ground on that day 22,000
men of Israel. *destroyed*
22 But the people, the men of Israel, encouraged themselves and
arrayed for battle again in the
place where they had arrayed
themselves the first day.
23 And the sons of Israel went
up and wept before the LORD until
evening, and inquired of the LORD,
saying, "Shall we again draw near
for battle against the sons of my
brother Benjamin?" And the LORD
said, "Go up against him."
24 Then the sons of Israel [t]came
against the sons of Benjamin the
second day. *approached*
25 And Benjamin went out
against them from Gibeah the second day and felled to the ground
again 18,000 men of the sons of Israel; all these drew the sword.
26 Then [r]all the sons of Israel
and all the people went up and
came to Bethel and wept; thus
they remained there before the
LORD and fasted that day until
evening. And they offered burnt
offerings and peace offerings before the LORD. Judg. 20:23; 21:2
27 And the sons of Israel [r]in-
quired of the LORD (for the ark of
the covenant of God *was* there in
those days, Judg. 20:18
28 and Phinehas the son of Eleazar, Aaron's son, stood before it to
minister in those days), saying,
"Shall I yet again go out to battle
against the sons of my brother
Benjamin, or shall I cease?" And
the LORD said, "Go up, [r]for tomorrow I will deliver them into your
hand." Judg. 7:9

29 [r]So Israel set men in ambush
around Gibeah. Josh. 8:4
30 And the sons of Israel went
up against the sons of Benjamin
on the third day and arrayed
themselves against Gibeah, as at
other times.
31 And the sons of Benjamin
went out against the people and
were drawn away from the city,
and they began to strike and kill
some of the people, as at other
times, on the highways, one of
which goes up to Bethel and the
other to Gibeah, *and* in the field,
about thirty men of Israel.
32 And the sons of Benjamin
said, "They are struck down before us, as at the first." But the
sons of Israel said, "Let us flee
that we may draw them away
from the city to the highways."
33 Then all the men of Israel
arose from their place and arrayed themselves at Baal-tamar;
[r]and the men of Israel in ambush
broke out of their place, even out
of Maareh-geba. Josh. 8:19
34 When ten thousand choice
men from all Israel came against
Gibeah, the battle became fierce;
but [t]Benjamin did not know that
disaster was close to them. *they*
35 And the LORD struck Benjamin before Israel, so that the sons
of Israel destroyed 25,100 men of
Benjamin that day, all [t]who draw
the sword. *these*
36 So the sons of Benjamin saw
that they were [t]defeated. When
the men of Israel gave ground to
Benjamin because they relied on
the men in ambush whom they
had set against Gibeah, *smitten*
37 [r]the men in ambush hurried
and rushed against Gibeah; the
men in ambush also deployed and
struck all the city with the edge of
the sword. Josh. 8:19
38 Now the appointed sign between the men of Israel and the
men in ambush was that they
should make a great cloud of
smoke rise from the city.
39 Then the men of Israel
turned in the battle, and Benjamin
began to strike and kill about
thirty men of Israel, for they said,
"Surely they are [t]defeated before
us, as in the first battle." *smitten*
40 But when the cloud began to
rise from the city in a column of
smoke, Benjamin looked behind
them; and behold, the whole city
was going up *in smoke* to heaven.
41 Then the men of Israel
turned, and the men of Benjamin
were terrified; for they saw that
[t]disaster was close to them. *evil*
42 Therefore, they turned their
backs before the men of Israel
[r]toward the direction of the wilderness, but the battle overtook them
while those who came out of the
cities destroyed them in the midst
of them. Josh. 8:15, 24
43 They surrounded Benjamin,
pursued them without rest *and*
trod them down opposite Gibeah
toward the [t]east. *sunrise*
44 Thus 18,000 men of Benjamin fell; all these were valiant
warriors.
45 The rest turned and fled
toward the wilderness to the rock
of Rimmon, but they [t]caught 5,000
of them on the highways and
overtook them at Gidom and
killed 2,000 of them. *gleaned*
46 So all of Benjamin who fell

that day were 25,000 men who draw the sword; all these were valiant warriors.

47 But 600 men turned and fled toward the wilderness to the rock of Rimmon, and they remained at the rock of Rimmon four months.

48 The men of Israel then turned back against the sons of Benjamin and struck them with the edge of the sword, both the entire city with the cattle and all that they found; they also set on fire all the cities which they found.

CHAPTER 21

NOW the men of Israel had sworn in Mizpah, saying, "None of us shall give his daughter to Benjamin [t]in marriage." *for a wife*

2 [r]So the people came to Bethel and sat there before God until evening, and lifted up their voices and wept bitterly. Judg. 20:26

3 And they said, "Why, O LORD, God of Israel, has this come about in Israel, so that one tribe should be *missing* today in Israel?"

4 And it came about the next day that the people arose early and built [r]an altar there, and offered burnt offerings and peace offerings. Deut. 12:5; 2 Sam. 24:25

5 Then the sons of Israel said, "Who is there among all the tribes of Israel who did not come up in the assembly to the LORD?" For they had taken a great oath concerning him who did not come up to the LORD at Mizpah, saying, "He shall surely be put to death."

6 And the sons of Israel were sorry for their brother Benjamin and said, "One tribe is cut off from Israel today.

7 "What shall we do for wives for those who are left, since we have [r]sworn by the LORD not to give them any of our daughters in marriage?" Judg. 21:1

8 And they said, "What one is there of the tribes of Israel who did not come up to the LORD at Mizpah?" And behold, no one had come to the camp from Jabesh-gilead to the assembly.

9 For when the people were [a]numbered, behold, not one of the inhabitants of Jabesh-gilead was there. *mustered*

10 And the congregation sent 12,000 of the valiant warriors there, and commanded them, saying, "Go and [r]strike the inhabitants of Jabesh-gilead with the edge of the sword, with the women and the little ones. Num. 31:17

11 "And this is the thing that you shall do: you [r]shall utterly destroy every man and every woman who has lain with a man." Num. 31:17

12 And they found among the inhabitants of Jabesh-gilead 400 young virgins who had not known a man by lying with [t]him; and they brought them to the camp at Shiloh, which is in the land of Canaan. *a male*

13 Then the whole congregation sent *word* and spoke to the sons of Benjamin who were [r]at the rock of Rimmon, and [r]proclaimed peace to them. Judg. 20:47 • Deut. 20:10

14 And Benjamin returned at that time, and they gave them the women whom they had kept alive

from the women of Jabesh-gilead;
yet they [t]were not enough for
them. *did not find it so*
15 And the people were sorry
for Benjamin because the LORD
had made a breach in the tribes of
Israel.
16 Then the elders of the congregation said, "What shall we do
for wives for those who are left,
since the women are destroyed
out of Benjamin?"
17 And they said, "*There must*
be an inheritance for the survivors
of Benjamin, that a tribe may not
be blotted out from Israel.
18 "But we cannot give them
wives of our daughters." For the
sons of Israel [r]had sworn, saying,
"Cursed is he who gives a wife to
Benjamin." Judg. 21:1
19 So they said, "Behold, there
is a feast of the LORD from year to
year in Shiloh, which is on the
north side of Bethel, on the east
side of the highway that goes up
from Bethel to Shechem, and on
the south side of Lebonah."
20 And they commanded the
sons of Benjamin, saying, "Go and
lie in wait in the vineyards,
21 and watch; and behold, if the
daughters of Shiloh come out to
take part in the dances, then you
shall come out of the vineyards
and each of you shall catch his
wife from the daughters of Shiloh,
and go to the land of Benjamin.
22 "And it shall come about,
when their fathers or their brothers come to complain to us, that
we shall say to them, 'Give them
to us voluntarily, because we did
not take for each man *of Benja-*
min [t]a wife in battle, [t]nor did you
give *them* to them, *else* you would
now be guilty.' " *his · because*
23 And the sons of Benjamin
did so, and took wives according
to their number from those who
danced, whom they carried away.
And they went and returned to
their inheritance, and rebuilt the
cities and lived in them.
24 And the sons of Israel departed from there at that time, every man to his tribe and family,
and each one of them went out
from there to his inheritance.
25 In those days there was no
king in Israel; everyone did what
was right in his own eyes.

THE BOOK OF

RUTH

NOW it came about in the days
when the judges [a]governed, that
there was a famine in the land.
And a certain man of Bethlehem
in Judah went to sojourn in the
land of Moab [t]with his wife and his
two sons. *judged · he, and*
2 And the name of the man
was Elimelech, and the name of
his wife, Naomi; and the names of
his two sons *were* Mahlon and
Chilion, Ephrathites of Bethlehem
in Judah. Now they entered the
land of Moab and remained there.

3 Then Elimelech, Naomi's
husband, died; and she was left
with her two sons.
4 And they took for them-
selves Moabite women *as* wives;
the name of the one was Orpah
and the name of the other Ruth.
And they lived there about ten
years.
5 Then [t]both Mahlon and Chilion also died; and the woman was
bereft of her two children and her
husband. *both of them*
6 Then she arose with her
daughters-in-law that she might
return from the land of Moab, for
she had heard in the land of Moab
that the LORD had visited His people in giving them food.
7 So she departed from the
place where she was, and her two
daughters-in-law with her; and
they went on the way to return to
the land of Judah.
8 And Naomi said to her two
daughters-in-law, "Go, return
each of you to her mother's house.
[r]May the LORD deal kindly with
you as you have dealt with the
dead and with me. 2 Tim. 1:16
9 "May the LORD grant that you
may find rest, each in the house of
her husband." Then she kissed
them, and they lifted up their
voices and wept.
10 And they said to her, "*No*,
but we will surely return with you
to your people."
11 But Naomi said, "Return, my
daughters. Why should you go
with me? Have I yet sons in my
womb, that [r]they may be your husbands? Gen. 38:11; Deut. 25:5
12 "Return, my daughters! Go,
for I am too old to have a husband. If I said I have hope, if I
should even have a husband tonight and also bear sons,
13 would you therefore wait until they were grown? Would you
therefore refrain from marrying?
No, my daughters; for it is [t]harder
for me than for you, for [r]the hand
of the LORD has gone forth against
me." *more bitter* • Judg. 2:15
14 And they lifted up their
voices and wept again; and Orpah
kissed her mother-in-law, but
Ruth clung to her.
15 Then she said, "Behold, your
sister-in-law has gone back to her
people and her [r]gods; return after
your sister-in-law." Josh. 24:15
16 But Ruth said, "Do not urge
me to leave you *or* turn back from
following you; for where you go, I
will go, and where you lodge, I
will lodge. Your people *shall be*
my people, and your God, my
God.
17 "Where you die, I will die, and
there I will be buried. Thus may
[r]the LORD do to me, and worse, if
anything but death parts you and
me." 1 Sam. 3:17; 2 Kin. 6:31
18 When [r]she saw that she was
determined to go with her, she
said no more to her. Acts 21:14
19 So they both went until they
came to Bethlehem. And it came
about when they had come to
Bethlehem, that all the city was
stirred because of them, and the
women said, "Is this Naomi?"
20 And she said to them, "Do
not call me [1]Naomi; call me [2]Mara,
for [r]the Almighty has dealt very
bitterly with me. Ex. 6:3; Job 6:4
21 "I went out full, but [r]the LORD

[1]I.e., pleasant [2]I.e., bitter

has brought me back empty. Why
do you call me Naomi, since the
LORD has witnessed against me
and the Almighty has afflicted
me?" Job 1:21
22 So Naomi returned, and with
her Ruth the Moabitess, her
daughter-in-law, who returned
from the land of Moab. And they
came to Bethlehem at [r]the beginning of barley harvest. Ex. 9:31

CHAPTER 2

NOW Naomi had a kinsman of
her husband, a man of great
wealth, of the family of [r]Elimelech,
whose name was Boaz. Ruth 1:2
2 And Ruth the Moabitess said
to Naomi, "Please let me go to the
field and glean among the ears of
grain after one in whose sight I
may find favor." And she said to
her, "Go, my daughter."
3 So she departed and went
and gleaned in the field after the
reapers; and she happened to
come to the portion of the field belonging to Boaz, who was of the
family of Elimelech.
4 Now behold, Boaz came
from Bethlehem and said to the
reapers, "May [r]the LORD be with
you." And they said to him, "May
the LORD bless you." Judg. 6:12
5 Then Boaz said to his servant
who was in charge of the reapers,
"Whose young woman is this?"
6 And the servant in charge of
the reapers answered and said,
"She is the young Moabite woman
who returned with Naomi from
the land of Moab.
7 "And she said, 'Please let me
glean and gather after the reapers
among the sheaves.' Thus she
came and has remained from the
morning until now; she has been
sitting in the house for a little
while."
8 Then Boaz said to Ruth, "Listen carefully, my daughter. Do not
go to glean in another field; furthermore, do not go on from this
one, but stay here with my maids.
9 "Let your eyes be on the field
which they reap, and go after
them. Indeed, I have commanded
the servants not to touch you.
When you are thirsty, go to the
[t]water jars and drink from what
the servants draw." *vessels*
10 Then she [r]fell on her face,
bowing to the ground and said to
him, "Why have I found favor in
your sight that you should take
notice of me, since I am a foreigner?" 1 Sam. 25:23
11 And Boaz answered and said
to her, "All that you have done for
your mother-in-law after the
death of your husband has been
fully reported to me, and how you
left your father and your mother
and the land of your birth, and
came to a people that you did not
previously know.
12 "May the LORD reward your
work, and your wages be full from
the LORD, the God of Israel, [r]under
whose wings you have come to
seek refuge." Ruth 1:16; Ps. 17:8
13 Then she said, "I have found
favor in your sight, my lord, for
you have comforted me and indeed have spoken kindly to your
maidservant, though I am not like
one of your maidservants."

14 And at mealtime Boaz said to her, "Come[t] here, that you may eat of the bread and dip your piece of bread in the vinegar." So she sat beside the reapers; and he [t]served her roasted grain, and she ate and was satisfied and had some left. *Draw near • held out to*

15 When she rose to glean, Boaz commanded his servants, saying, "Let her glean even among the sheaves, and do not insult her.

16 "And also you shall purposely pull out for her *some grain* from the bundles and leave *it* that she may glean, and do not rebuke her."

17 So she gleaned in the field until evening. Then she beat out what she had gleaned, and it was about an ephah of barley.

18 And she took *it* up and went into the city, and her mother-in-law saw what she had gleaned. She also took *it* out and gave [t]Naomi what she had left after [t]she was satisfied. *her • her satiety*

19 Her mother-in-law then said to her, "Where did you glean today and where did you work? May he who [r]took notice of you be blessed." So she told her mother-in-law with whom she had worked and said, "The name of the man with whom I worked today is Boaz." Ps. 41:1

20 And Naomi said to her daughter-in-law, "May he be blessed of the LORD who has not withdrawn his kindness to the living and to the dead." Again Naomi said to her, "The man is [t]our relative, he is one of our [t]closest relatives." *near to us • redeemers*

21 Then Ruth the Moabitess said, "Furthermore[t] he said to me, 'You should stay close to my servants until they have finished all my harvest.' " *Also that*

22 And Naomi said to Ruth her daughter-in-law, "It is good, my daughter, that you go out with his maids, lest *others* fall upon you in another field."

23 So she stayed close by the maids of Boaz in order to glean until the end of the barley harvest and the wheat harvest. And she lived with her mother-in-law.

CHAPTER 3

THEN Naomi her mother-in-law said to her, "My daughter, shall I not seek [t]security for you, that it may be well with you? *rest*

2 "And now is not Boaz our kinsman, with whose maids you were? Behold, he winnows barley at the threshing floor tonight.

3 "Wash yourself therefore, and anoint yourself and put on your *best* clothes, and go down to the threshing floor; *but* do not make yourself known to the man until he has finished eating and drinking.

4 "And it shall be when he lies down, that you shall [t]notice the place where he lies, and you shall go and uncover his feet and lie down; then he will tell you what you shall do." *know*

5 And she said to her, "All[r] that you say I will do." Eph. 6:1

6 So she went down to the threshing floor and did according to all that her mother-in-law had commanded her.

7 When Boaz had eaten and
drunk and[r] his heart was merry, he
went to lie down at the end of the
heap of grain; and she came secretly, and uncovered his feet and
lay down. Judg. 19:6, 9
8 And it happened in the middle of the night that the man was
startled and[t] bent forward; and behold, a woman was lying at his
feet. *twisted himself*
9 And he said, "Who are you?"
And she answered, "I am Ruth
your maid. So spread your covering over your maid, for you are a
[3]close relative."
10 Then he said, "May[r] you be
blessed of the LORD, my daughter.
You have shown your last kindness to be better than the first by
not going after young men,
whether poor or rich. Ruth 2:20
11 "And now, my daughter, do
not fear. I will do for you whatever you[t] ask, for all my people in
the [t]city know that you are a
woman of excellence. *say* · *gate*
12 "And now it is true I am a
[a]close relative; however, there is a
[a]relative closer than I. *redeemer*
13 "Remain this night, and when
morning comes, if he will[a] redeem
you, good; let him redeem you.
But if he does not wish to[a] redeem
you, then I will redeem you, as the
LORD lives. Lie down until morning." *act as close relative to*
14 So she lay at his feet until
morning and rose before one
could recognize another; and he
said, "Let[r] it not be known that the
woman came to the threshing
floor." Rom. 14:16; 2 Cor. 8:21
15 Again he said, "Give me the
cloak that is on you and hold it."
So she held it, and he measured
six *measures* of barley and laid *it*
on her. Then she went into the
city.
16 And when she came to her
mother-in-law, she said, "How[t] did
it go, my daughter?" And she told
her all that the man had done for
her. *Who* are you?
17 And she said, "These six
measures of barley he gave to me,
for he said, 'Do not go to your
mother-in-law empty-handed.' "
18 Then she said, "Wait, my
daughter, until you know how the
matter[t] turns out; for the man will
not rest until he has [t]settled it today." *falls* · *finished the matter*

CHAPTER 4

NOW Boaz went up to the gate
and sat down there, and behold,
the[a] close relative of whom Boaz
spoke was passing by, so he said,
"Turn aside, [t]friend, sit down
here." And he turned aside and
sat down. *redeemer* · *a certain one*
2 And he took ten men of the
elders of the city and said, "Sit
down here." So they sat down.
3 Then he said to the closest
relative, "Naomi, who has come
back from the land of Moab, has
to sell the piece of land which belonged to our brother Elimelech.
4 "So I thought to [t]inform you,
saying, 'Buy *it* before those who
are sitting *here,* and before the elders of my people. If you will redeem *it,* redeem *it;* but if not, tell
me that I may know; for there is
no one but you to redeem *it,* and I
am after you.' " And he said, "I
will redeem *it.*" *uncover your ear*

[3]Or, *redeemer,* and so throughout this context

5 Then Boaz said, "On the day you buy the field from the hand of Naomi, you must also acquire Ruth the Moabitess, the widow of the deceased, in order[r] to raise up the name of the deceased on his inheritance." Gen. 38:8

6 And the[t] closest relative said, "I cannot redeem *it* for myself, lest I jeopardize my own inheritance. Redeem *it* for yourself; you *may have* my right of redemption, for I cannot redeem *it*." *redeemer*

7 Now this was *the custom* in former times in Israel concerning the redemption and the exchange *of land* to confirm any matter: a man removed his sandal and gave it to another; and this was the *manner of* attestation in Israel.

8 So the[t] closest relative said to Boaz, "Buy *it* for yourself." And he removed his sandal. *redeemer*

9 Then Boaz said to the elders and all the people, "You are witnesses today that I have bought from the hand of Naomi all that belonged to Elimelech and all that belonged to Chilion and Mahlon.

10 "Moreover, I have acquired Ruth the Moabitess, the widow of Mahlon, to be my wife in order to raise up the name of the deceased on his inheritance, so that the name of the deceased may not be cut off from his brothers or from the[t] court of his *birth* place; you are witnesses today." *gate*

11 And all the people who were in the court, and the elders, said, "*We are* witnesses. May the LORD make the woman who is coming into your home like Rachel and Leah, both of whom built the house of Israel; and may you achieve wealth in Ephrathah and become famous in Bethlehem.

12 "Moreover, may your house be like the house of Perez whom Tamar bore to Judah, through the offspring which the LORD shall give you by this young woman."

13 So Boaz took Ruth, and she became his wife, and he went in to her. And the LORD[t] enabled her to conceive, and she gave birth to a son. *gave her conception*

14 Then the women said to Naomi, "Blessed is the LORD who has not left you without a[a] redeemer today, and may his name become famous in Israel. *closest relative*

15 "May he also be to you a restorer of life and a sustainer of your old age; for your daughter-in-law, who loves you[t] and is better to you than seven sons, has given birth to him." *who*

16 Then Naomi took the child and laid him in her lap, and became his nurse.

17 And the neighbor women gave him a name, saying, "A son has been born to Naomi!" So they named him Obed. He is the father of Jesse, the father of David.

18 Now these are the generations of Perez:[r] to Perez[t] was born Hezron, Matt. 1:3-6 • *begot*

19 and to Hezron was born Ram, and to Ram, Amminadab,

20 and to Amminadab was born Nahshon, and to Nahshon, Salmon,

21 and to Salmon was born Boaz, and to Boaz, Obed,

22 and to Obed was born Jesse, and to Jesse, David.

THE FIRST BOOK OF

SAMUEL

NOW there was a certain man from [r] Ramathaim-zophim from the hill country of Ephraim, and his name was Elkanah the son of Jeroham, the son of Elihu, the son of Tohu, the son of Zuph, an Ephraimite. 1 Sam. 1:19

2 And he had two wives: the name of one was[r] Hannah and the name of the other Peninnah; and Peninnah had children, but Hannah had no children. Luke 2:36

3 Now this man would go up from his city yearly to worship and to sacrifice to the LORD of hosts in Shiloh. And the two sons of Eli, Hophni and Phinehas were priests to the LORD there.

4 And when the day came that Elkanah sacrificed, he would give portions to Peninnah his wife and to all her sons and her daughters;

5 but to Hannah he would give a double portion, for he loved Hannah,[r] but the LORD had closed her womb. Gen. 16:1; 30:1

6 Her rival, however, [r] would provoke her bitterly to irritate her, because the LORD had closed her womb. Job 24:21

7 And it happened year after year, as often as she went up to the house of the LORD, she would provoke her, so she wept and would not eat.

8 Then Elkanah her husband said to her, "Hannah, why do you weep and why do you not eat and why is your heart sad? Am I not better to you than ten sons?"

9 Then Hannah rose after eating and drinking in Shiloh. Now Eli the priest was sitting on the seat by the doorpost of[r] the temple of the LORD. 1 Sam. 3:3

10 And she,[t] greatly distressed, prayed to the LORD and wept bitterly. *bitter of soul*

11 And she made a vow and said, "O LORD of hosts, if Thou wilt indeed look on the affliction of Thy maidservant and remember me, and not forget Thy maidservant, but wilt give Thy maidservant a[t] son, then I will give him to the LORD all the days of his life, and [r]a razor shall never come on his head." *seed of men* • Num. 6:5

12 Now it came about, as she [t]continued praying before the LORD, that Eli was watching her mouth. *multiplied*

13 As for Hannah, [r]she was speaking in her heart, only her lips were moving, but her voice was not heard. So Eli thought she was drunk. Gen. 24:42-45

14 Then Eli said to her, "How[r] long will you make yourself drunk? Put away your wine from you." Acts 2:4, 13

15 But Hannah answered and said, "No, my lord, I am a woman [t]oppressed in spirit; I have drunk neither wine nor strong drink, but I[r] have poured out my soul before the LORD. *severe* • Job 30:16

16 "Do not consider your maidservant as a worthless woman; for

I have spoken until now out of my
great concern and provocation."
17 Then Eli answered and said,
"Go[r] in peace; and may the God of
Israel grant your petition that you
have asked of Him." Judg. 18:6
18 And she said, "Let[r] your
maidservant find favor in your
sight." So the woman went her
way and ate, and her face was no
longer *sad*. Gen. 33:15; Ruth 2:13
19 Then they arose early in the
morning and worshiped before
the LORD, and returned again to
their house in[r] Ramah. And Elkanah[t] had relations with Hannah his
wife, and the LORD remembered
her. 1 Sam. 1:1; 2:11 • *knew*
20 And it came about[t] in due
time, after Hannah had conceived,
that she gave birth to a son; and
she named him Samuel, *saying*,
"Because I have asked him of the
LORD." *at the circuit of the days*
21 Then the man Elkanah[r] went
up with all his household to offer
to the LORD the yearly sacrifice
and *pay* his vow. Deut. 12:11
22 But Hannah did not go up,
for she said to her husband, "*I will
not go up* until the child is
weaned; then I will bring him, that
he may appear before the LORD
and stay there forever."
23 And Elkanah her husband
said to her, "Do what seems best
[t] to you. Remain until you have
weaned him; only may the LORD
confirm His word." So the woman
remained and nursed her son until
she weaned him. *in your eyes*
24 Now when she had weaned
him, [r] she took him up with her,
with a three-year-old bull and one
ephah of flour and a jug of wine,
and brought him to the house of
the LORD in Shiloh, although the
child was young. Num. 15:9, 10
25 Then they slaughtered the
bull, and brought the boy to Eli.
26 And she said, "Oh, my lord!
As your soul lives, my lord, I am
the woman who stood here beside
you, praying to the LORD.
27 "For[r] this boy I prayed, and the
LORD has given me my petition
which I asked of Him. Ps. 6:9
28 "So I have also [1] dedicated him
to the LORD; as long as he lives he
is [1] dedicated to the LORD." And he
worshiped the LORD there.

CHAPTER 2

THEN Hannah prayed and said,
"My heart exults in the
LORD;
My horn is exalted in the
LORD,
My mouth [t] speaks boldly
against my enemies,
Because I rejoice in Thy salvation. *is enlarged*
2 "There is no one holy like the
LORD,
Indeed,[r] there is no one besides Thee,
Nor is there any rock like
our God. 2 Sam. 22:32
3 "Boast[t] no more so very
proudly,
Do not let arrogance come
out of your mouth;
For the LORD is a God of
knowledge,
And with Him actions are
weighed. *Talk much*
4 "The bows of the mighty are
shattered,

[1] Lit., *lent*

[r]But the feeble gird on
strength. Ps. 18:39
5 "Those who were full hire
themselves out for bread,
But those who were hungry
cease *to hunger.*
Even the barren gives birth
to seven,
But she who has many children languishes.
6 "The LORD kills and makes
alive;
[r]He brings down to Sheol
and raises up. Is. 26:19
7 "The LORD makes poor and
rich;
[r]He brings low, He also exalts. Job 5:11; Ps. 75:7
8 "He raises the poor from the
dust,
[r]He lifts the needy from the
ash heap
[r]To make them sit with
nobles,
And inherit a seat of honor;
For the pillars of the earth
are the LORD's,
And He set the world on
them. 2 Sam. 7:8 • Job 36:7
9 "He keeps the feet of His
godly ones,
[r]But the wicked ones are silenced in darkness;
For not by might shall a
man prevail. Matt. 8:12
10 "Those who contend with
the LORD will be shat-
tered;
Against them He will thunder in the heavens,
[r]The LORD will judge the
ends of the earth;
And He will give strength
to His king,
And will exalt the horn of
His anointed." Ps. 96:13

11 Then Elkanah went to his
home at [r]Ramah. [r]But the boy ministered to the LORD before Eli the
priest. 1 Sam. 1:1, 19 • 1 Sam. 1:28
12 Now the sons of Eli were
[2]worthless [r]men; they did not know
the LORD Jer. 2:8; 9:3, 6; 2 Cor. 6:15
13 and the custom of the priests
with the people. When any man
was offering a sacrifice, the
priest's servant would come while
the meat was boiling, with a
three-pronged fork in his hand.
14 Then he would thrust it into
the pan, or kettle, or caldron, or
pot; all that the fork brought up
the priest would take for himself.
Thus they did in Shiloh to all the
Israelites who came there.
15 Also, before they burned the
fat, the priest's servant would
come and say to the man who was
sacrificing, "Give the priest meat
for roasting, as he will not take
boiled meat from you, only raw."
16 And if the man said to him,
"They must surely [t]burn the fat
first, and then take as much as
[t]you desire," then he would say,
"No, but you shall give *it to me*
now; and if not, I will take it by
force." *offer up in smoke • your soul*
17 Thus the sin of the young
men was very great before the
LORD, for the men [r]despised the offering of the LORD. Mal. 2:7-9
18 Now Samuel was ministering before the LORD, *as* a boy
wearing a linen ephod.
19 And his mother would make
him a little robe and bring it to
him from year to year when she

[2]Lit., *sons of Belial*

would come up with her husband
to offer the yearly sacrifice.
20 Then Eli would bless Elkanah
and his wife and say, "May the
LORD give you [t]children from this
woman in place of the one she
dedicated to the LORD." And they
went to their own home. *seed*
21 And [r]the LORD visited Hannah; and she conceived and gave
birth to three sons and two daughters. And the boy Samuel grew
before the LORD. Gen. 21:1
22 Now Eli was very old; and he
heard all that his sons were doing
to all Israel, and how they lay with
the women who served at the
doorway of the tent of meeting.
23 And he said to them, "Why
do you do such things, the evil
things that I hear from all these
people?
24 "No, my sons; for the report is
not good [r]which I hear the LORD's
people circulating. 1 Kin. 15:26
25 "If one man sins against another, God will mediate for him;
but if a man sins against the LORD,
who can intercede for him?" But
they would not listen to the voice
of their father, for the LORD desired to put them to death.
26 Now the boy Samuel was
growing in stature and in favor
both with the LORD and with men.
27 Then a man of God came to
Eli and said to him, "Thus says the
LORD, 'Did I *not* indeed reveal Myself to the house of your father
when they were in Egypt *in bondage* to Pharaoh's house?
28 'And did I *not* choose them
from all the tribes of Israel to be
My priests, to go up to My altar,
to burn incense, to carry an ephod
before Me; and did I *not* give to
the house of your father all the
fire *offerings* of the sons of Israel?
29 'Why do you kick at My sacrifice and at My offering which I
have commanded *in My* [r]dwelling,
and honor your sons above Me, by
making yourselves fat with the
[a]choicest of every offering of My
people Israel?' Ps. 26:8 • *first*
30 "Therefore the LORD God of
Israel declares, 'I [r] did indeed say
that your house and the house of
your father should walk before
Me forever'; but now the LORD declares, 'Far be it from Me—for
those who honor Me I will honor,
and those [r]who despise Me will be
lightly esteemed. Ex. 29:9 • Mal. 2:9
31 'Behold, the days are coming
when I will break your [a]strength
and the [a]strength of your father's
house so that there will not be an
old man in your house. *arm*
32 'And you will see [r]the distress
of *My* dwelling, in *spite of* all that
[t]I do good for Israel; and an old
man will not be in your house forever. 1 Kin. 2:26, 27 • *He does*
33 'Yet I will not cut off every
man of yours from My altar that
your eyes may fail *from weeping*
and your soul grieve, and all the
increase of your house will die [t]in
the prime of life. *as men*
34 'And this will be [r]the sign to
you which shall come concerning
your two sons, Hophni and Phinehas: on the same day both of them
shall die. 1 Sam. 10:7-9; 1 Kin. 13:3
35 'But I will raise up for Myself
a faithful priest who will do according to what is in My heart and
in My soul; and I will build him an

enduring house, and he will walk
before My anointed always.
36 'And it shall come about that
everyone who is left in your house
shall come and bow down to him
for a[a]piece of silver or a loaf of
bread, and say, "Please[t]assign me
to one of the priest's offices so
that I may eat a piece of
bread."' "
payment · attach

CHAPTER 3

NOW the boy Samuel was ministering to the LORD before Eli. And
word from the LORD was rare in
those days, [t]visions were infre-
quent.
no vision spread abroad
2 And it happened at that time
as Eli was lying down in his place
(now[r]his eyesight had begun to
grow dim *and* he could not see
well),
Gen. 27:1; 48:10
3 and the lamp of God had not
yet gone out, and Samuel was
lying down in the temple of the
LORD where the ark of God *was*,
4 that the LORD called Samuel;
and he said, "Here[r]I am."
Is. 6:8
5 Then he ran to Eli and said,
"Here I am, for you called me."
But he said, "I did not call, lie
down again." So he went and lay
down.
6 And the LORD called yet
again, "Samuel!" So Samuel arose
and went to Eli, and said, "Here I
am, for you called me." But he[t]an-
swered, "I did not call, my son, lie
down again."
said
7[r]Now Samuel did not yet
know the LORD, nor had the word
of the LORD yet been revealed to
him.
Acts 19:2; 1 Cor. 13:11
8 So the LORD called Samuel
again for the third time. And he
arose and went to Eli, and said,
"Here I am, for you called me."
Then Eli discerned that the LORD
was calling the boy.
9 And Eli said to Samuel, "Go
lie down, and it shall be if He calls
you, that you shall say, 'Speak,
LORD, for Thy servant is listening.' " So Samuel went and lay
down in his place.
10 Then the LORD came and
stood and called as at other times,
"Samuel! Samuel!" And Samuel
said, "Speak, for Thy servant is
listening."
11 And the LORD said to Samuel, "Behold,[r]I am about to do a
thing in Israel at which both ears
of everyone who hears it will
tingle.
2 Kin. 21:12; Jer. 19:3
12 "In that day[r]I will carry out
against Eli all that I have spoken
concerning his house, from beginning to end.
1 Sam. 2:27-36
13 "For[r]I have told him that I am
about to judge his house forever
for the iniquity which he knew,
because his sons brought a curse
on themselves and he did not rebuke them.
1 Sam. 2:29-31
14 "And therefore I have sworn
to the house of Eli that[r]the iniquity of Eli's house shall not be
atoned for by sacrifice or offering
forever."
Lev. 15:31; Is. 22:14
15 So Samuel lay down until
morning. Then he [r]opened the
doors of the house of the LORD.
But Samuel was afraid to tell the
vision to Eli.
1 Chr. 15:23
16 Then Eli called Samuel and
said, "Samuel, my son." And he
said, "Here I am."
17 And he said, "What is the

word that He spoke to you? Please do not hide it from me. May God do so to you, and more also, if you hide anything from me of all the words that He spoke to you."

18 So Samuel told him everything and hid nothing from him. And he said, "It is the LORD; let Him do what seems good to Him."

19 Thus Samuel grew and the LORD was with him and let none of his words[t] fail. *fall to the ground*

20 And all Israel[r] from Dan even to Beersheba knew that Samuel was confirmed as a prophet of the LORD. Judg. 20:1

21 And the LORD appeared again at Shiloh, because the LORD revealed Himself to Samuel at Shiloh by the word of the LORD.

CHAPTER 4

THUS the word of Samuel came to all Israel. Now Israel went out to meet the Philistines in battle and camped beside [r]Ebenezer while the Philistines camped in [r]Aphek. 1 Sam. 7:12 • Josh. 12:18

2 And the Philistines drew up in battle array to meet Israel. When the battle spread, Israel was defeated before the Philistines who killed about four thousand men on the battlefield.

3 When the people came into the camp, the elders of Israel said, "Why[r] has the LORD defeated us today before the Philistines? Let us take to ourselves from Shiloh the ark of the covenant of the LORD, that[a] it may come among us and deliver us from the power of our enemies." Josh. 7:7, 8 • *he*

4 So the people sent to Shiloh, and from there they carried the ark of the covenant of the LORD of hosts[r] who sits *above* the cherubim; and the two sons of Eli, Hophni and Phinehas, *were* there with the ark of the covenant of God. Ex. 25:22; 2 Sam. 6:2; Ps. 80:1

5 And it happened as the ark of the covenant of the LORD came into the camp, that all Israel shouted with a great shout, so that the earth resounded.

6 And when the Philistines heard the noise of the shout, they said, "What *does* the noise of this great shout in the camp of the Hebrews *mean?*" Then they understood that the ark of the LORD had come into the camp.

7 And the Philistines were afraid, for they said, "God has come into the camp." And they said, "Woe to us! For nothing like this has happened before.

8 "Woe to us! Who shall deliver us from the hand of these mighty gods? These are the gods who smote the Egyptians with all *kinds of* plagues in the wilderness.

9 "Take courage and be men, O Philistines, lest you become slaves to the Hebrews,[r] as they have been slaves to you; therefore, be men and fight." Judg. 13:1; 1 Sam. 14:21

10 So the Philistines fought and [r]Israel was [t]defeated, and every man fled to his tent, and the slaughter was very great; for there fell of Israel thirty thousand foot soldiers. Deut. 28:15, 25 • *smitten*

11 And the ark of God was taken; and the two sons of Eli, Hophni and Phinehas, died.

12 Now a man of Benjamin ran from the battle line and came to

Shiloh the same day with his
clothes torn and dust on his head.
13 When he came, behold, Eli
was sitting on *his* seat by the road
eagerly watching, because his
heart was trembling for the ark of
God. So the man came to tell *it* in
the city, and all the city cried out.
14 When Eli heard the noise of
the outcry, he said, "What *does*
the noise of this commotion
mean?" Then the man came hurriedly and told Eli.
15 Now Eli was ninety-eight
years old, and[r]his eyes were set so
that he could not see. 1 Sam. 3:2
16 And the man said to Eli, "I
am the one who came from the
battle line. Indeed, I escaped from
the battle line today." And he
said, "How[r] did things go, my
son?" 2 Sam. 1:4
17 Then the one who brought
the news answered and said, "Israel has fled before the Philistines
and there has also been a great
slaughter among the people, and
your two sons also, Hophni and
Phinehas, are dead, and the ark of
God has been taken."
18 And it came about when he
mentioned the ark of God that[t]Eli
fell off the seat backward beside
the gate, and his neck was broken
and he died, for[t]he was old and
heavy. Thus he judged Israel forty
years. *he • the man*
19 Now his daughter-in-law,
Phinehas' wife, was pregnant and
about to give birth; and when she
heard the news that the ark of
God was taken and that her father-in-law and her husband had
died, she kneeled down and gave
birth, for her pains came upon
her.
20 And about the time of her
death the women who stood by
her said to her, "Do[r]not be afraid,
for you have given birth to a son."
But she did not answer or pay attention. Gen. 35:16-19
21 And she called the boy [3]Icha-
bod, saying, "The[r] glory has departed from Israel," because[r]the
ark of God was taken and because
of her father-in-law and her husband. Ps. 26:8 • 1 Sam. 4:11
22 And she said, "The glory has
departed from Israel, for the ark
of God was taken."

CHAPTER 5

NOW the Philistines took the ark
of God and[r]brought it from Eben-
ezer to Ashdod. 1 Sam. 4:1; 7:12
2 Then the Philistines took the
ark of God and brought it to[r]the
house of Dagon, and set it by Dagon. Judg. 16:23-30; 1 Chr. 10:8-10
3 When the Ashdodites arose
early the next morning, behold,
[r]Dagon had fallen on his face to
the ground before the ark of the
LORD. So they took Dagon and set
him in his place again. Is. 19:1
4 But when they arose early
the next morning, behold, Dagon
had fallen on his face to the
ground before the ark of the LORD.
And the head of Dagon and both
the palms of his hands *were* cut
off on the threshold; only the
trunk of Dagon was left to him.
5 Therefore neither the priests
of Dagon nor all who enter Dagon's house tread on the threshold
of Dagon in Ashdod to this day.

[3]I.e., no glory

6 Now [r]the hand of the LORD was heavy on the Ashdodites, and [r]He ravaged them and smote them with tumors, both Ashdod and its territories. Ex. 9:3 • 1 Sam. 6:5

7 When the men of Ashdod saw that it was so, they said, "The ark of the God of Israel must not remain with us, for His hand is severe on us and on Dagon our god."

8 So they sent and gathered all the lords of the Philistines to them and said, "What shall we do with the ark of the God of Israel?" And they said, "Let the ark of the God of Israel be brought around to Gath." And they brought the ark of the God of Israel *around.*

9 And it came about that after they had brought it around, the hand of the LORD was against the city with very great confusion; and He smote the men of the city, both young and old, so that tumors broke out on them.

10 So they sent the ark of God to Ekron. And it happened as the ark of God came to Ekron that the Ekronites cried out, saying, "They have brought the ark of the God of Israel around to [t]us, to kill [t]us and [t]our people." *me • my*

11 They sent therefore and gathered all the lords of the Philistines and said, "Send away the ark of the God of Israel, and let it return to its own place, that it may not kill [t]us and our people." For there was a deadly confusion throughout the city; the hand of God was very heavy there. *me*

12 And the men who did not die were smitten with tumors and the cry of the city went up to heaven.

CHAPTER 6

NOW the ark of the LORD had been in the [t]country of the Philistines seven months. *field*

2 And [r]the Philistines called for the priests and the diviners, saying, "What shall we do with the ark of the LORD? Tell us how we shall send it to its place." Is. 2:6

3 And they said, "If you send away the ark of the God of Israel, do not send it empty; but you shall surely return to Him a guilt offering. Then you shall be healed and it shall be known to you why His hand is not removed from you."

4 Then they said, "What shall be the guilt offering which we shall return to Him?" And they said, "Five golden tumors and five golden mice *according to* the number of the lords of the Philistines, for one plague was on all of [t]you and on your lords. *them*

5 "So you shall make likenesses of your tumors and likenesses of your mice that ravage the land, and [r]you shall give glory to the God of Israel; perhaps He will ease His hand from you, your gods, and your land. Josh. 7:19

6 "Why then do you harden your hearts as the Egyptians and Pharaoh hardened their hearts? When He had severely dealt with them, did they not allow the people to go, and they departed?

7 "Now therefore take and prepare a new cart and two milch cows on which there has never been a yoke; and hitch the cows to the cart and take their calves home, away from them.

8 "And take the ark of the LORD

and place it on the cart; and put
[r]the articles of gold which you return to Him as a guilt offering in a
box by its side. Then send it away
that it may go. 1 Sam. 6:4, 5
9 "And watch, if it goes up by
the way of its own territory to
[r]Beth-shemesh, then He has done
us this great evil. But if not, then
we shall know that it was not His
hand that struck us; it happened
to us by chance." Josh. 15:10
10 Then the men did so, and
took two milch cows and hitched
them to the cart, and shut up their
calves at home.
11 And they put the ark of the
LORD on the cart, and the box with
the golden mice and the likenesses of their tumors.
12 And the cows took the
straight way in the [t]direction of
Beth-shemesh; they went along
the highway, lowing as they went,
and did not turn aside to the right
or to the left. And the lords of the
Philistines followed them to the
border of Beth-shemesh. *way*
13 Now *the people of* Beth-shemesh were reaping their wheat
harvest in the valley, and they
raised their eyes and saw the ark
and were glad to see *it*.
14 And the cart came into the
field of Joshua the Beth-shemite
and stood there where there *was* a
large stone; and they split the
wood of the cart and [r]offered the
cows as a burnt offering to the
LORD. 2 Sam. 24:22; 1 Kin. 19:21
15 And [r]the Levites took down
the ark of the LORD and the box
that was with it, in which were the
articles of gold, and put them on
the large stone; and the men of
Beth-shemesh offered burnt offerings and sacrificed sacrifices that
day to the LORD. Josh. 3:3
16 And when the five lords of
the Philistines saw it, they returned to Ekron that day.
17 And [r]these are the golden tumors which the Philistines returned for a guilt offering to the
LORD: one for Ashdod, one for
Gaza, one for Ashkelon, one for
Gath, one for Ekron; 1 Sam. 6:4
18 and the golden mice, *according* to the number of all the cities
of the Philistines belonging to the
five lords,[r] both of fortified cities
and of country villages. The large
stone on which they set the ark of
the LORD *is a witness* to this day
in the field of Joshua the Beth-
shemite. Deut. 3:5
19 And [r]He struck down some of
the men of Beth-shemesh because
they had looked into the ark of the
LORD. He struck down of all the
people, 50,070 men, and the people mourned because the LORD
had struck the people with a great
slaughter. Ex. 19:21; Num. 4:5, 15
20 And the men of Beth-shemesh said, "Who [r]is able to stand
before the LORD, this holy God?
And to whom shall He go up from
us?" Lev. 11:44, 45; 2 Sam. 6:9
21 So they sent messengers to
the inhabitants of Kiriath-jearim,
saying, "The Philistines have
brought back the ark of the LORD;
come down and take it up to you."

CHAPTER 7

AND the men of Kiriath-jearim
came and took the ark of the LORD
and [r]brought it into the house of

Abinadab on the hill, and consecrated Eleazar his son to keep the
ark of the LORD. 2 Sam. 6:3, 4
2 And it came about from the
day that the ark remained at Kiriath-jearim that the time was long,
for it was twenty years; and all the
house of Israel lamented after the
LORD.
3 Then Samuel spoke to all the
house of Israel, saying, "If [r]you return to the LORD with all your
heart, remove the foreign gods
and the Ashtaroth from among
you and direct your hearts to the
LORD and serve Him alone; and
He will deliver you from the hand
of the Philistines." 1 Kin. 8:48
4 So the sons of Israel removed the Baals and the Ashtaroth and served the LORD alone.
5 Then Samuel said, "Gather
all Israel to Mizpah, and I will
pray to the LORD for you."
6 And they gathered to Mizpah, and drew water and [r]poured it
out before the LORD, and fasted on
that day, and said there, "We
have sinned against the LORD."
And Samuel judged the sons of Israel at Mizpah. 1 Sam. 1:15
7 Now when the Philistines
heard that the sons of Israel had
gathered to Mizpah, the lords of
the Philistines went up against Israel. And when the sons of Israel
heard it, [r]they were afraid of the
Philistines. 1 Sam. 13:6; 17:11
8 Then the sons of Israel said
to Samuel, "Do [r]not cease to cry to
the LORD our God for us, that He
may save us from the hand of the
Philistines." 1 Sam. 12:19-24
9 And Samuel took a suckling
lamb and offered it for a whole
burnt offering to the LORD; and
Samuel cried to the LORD for Israel and the LORD answered him.
10 Now Samuel was offering up
the burnt offering, and the Philistines drew near to battle against
Israel. But the LORD thundered
with a great [t]thunder on that day
against the Philistines and confused them, so that they were
routed before Israel. *voice*
11 And the men of Israel went
out of Mizpah and pursued the
Philistines, and struck them down
as far as below Beth-car.
12 Then Samuel [r]took a stone
and set it between Mizpah and
Shen, and named it [4]Ebenezer,
saying, "Thus far the LORD has
helped us." Gen. 35:14; Josh. 4:9
13 So the Philistines were subdued and [r]they did not come anymore within the border of Israel.
And the hand of the LORD was
against the Philistines all the days
of Samuel. 1 Sam. 13:5
14 And the cities which the Philistines had taken from Israel
were restored to Israel, from Ekron even to Gath; and Israel delivered their territory from the hand
of the Philistines. So there was
peace between Israel and [r]the Amorites. Num. 13:29; Josh. 10:5-10
15 Now Samuel [r]judged Israel
all the days of his life. 1 Sam. 7:6
16 And he used to go annually
on circuit to [r]Bethel and Gilgal and
Mizpah, and he judged Israel in all
these places. Gen. 28:19; 35:6
17 Then his return *was* to Ramah, for his house *was* there, and
there he judged Israel; and he
built there an altar to the LORD.

[4]I.e., the stone of help

CHAPTER 8

AND it came about when Samuel
was old that[r]he appointed his sons
judges over Israel. Deut. 16:18,19
2 Now the name of his first-
born was Joel, and the name of his
second, Abijah; *they* were judging
in[r]Beersheba. Gen. 22:19; Amos 5:5
3 His sons, however, did not
walk in his ways, but turned aside
after dishonest gain and took
bribes and perverted justice.
4 Then all the elders of Israel
gathered together and came to
Samuel at[r]Ramah; 1 Sam. 7:17
5 and they said to him, "Behold, you have grown old, and
your sons do not walk in your
ways. Now appoint a king for us
to judge us like all the nations."
6 But the thing was displeasing
in the sight of Samuel when they
said, "Give us a king to judge us."
And Samuel prayed to the LORD.
7 And the LORD said to Samuel, "Listen to the voice of the
people in regard to all that they
say to you, for they have not rejected you, but they have rejected
Me from being king over them.
8 "Like all the deeds which they
have done since the day that I
brought them up from Egypt even
to this day—in that they have forsaken Me and served other
gods—so they are doing to you
also.
9 "Now then, listen to their
voice; however, you shall solemnly[t]warn them and tell them of
the [5]procedure of the king who
will reign over them." *testify to*
10 So Samuel spoke all the
words of the LORD to the people
who had asked of him a king.
11 And he said, "This[r]will be the
[t]procedure of the king who will
reign over you: he will take your
sons and place *them* for himself in
his chariots and among his horsemen and they will run before his
chariots. Deut. 17:14-20 • *custom*
12 "And he will appoint for himself commanders of thousands
and of fifties, and *some* to do his
plowing and to reap his harvest
and to make his weapons of war
and equipment for his chariots.
13 "He will also take your daughters for perfumers and cooks and
bakers.
14 "And[r]he will take the best of
your fields and your vineyards
and your olive groves, and give
them to his servants. 1 Kin. 21:7
15 "And he will take a tenth of
your seed and of your vineyards,
and give to his officers and to his
servants.
16 "He will also take your male
servants and your female servants
and your best young men and
your donkeys, and[t]use *them* for
his work. *make*
17 "He will take a tenth of your
flocks, and you yourselves will become his servants.
18 "Then[r]you will cry out in that
day because of your king whom
you have chosen for yourselves,
but[r]the LORD will not answer you
in that day." Is. 8:21 • Mic. 3:4
19 Nevertheless, the people refused to listen to the voice of
Samuel, and they said, "No, but
there shall be a king over us,
20 [r]that we also may be like all
the nations, that our king may

[5]Lit., *custom*

judge us and go out before us and
fight our battles." 1 Sam. 8:5
21 Now after Samuel had heard
all the words of the people,[r] he repeated them in the LORD's hearing. Judg. 11:11
22 And the LORD said to Sam-
uel, "Listen[r] to their voice, and appoint them a king." So Samuel
said to the men of Israel, "Go every man to his city." 1 Sam. 8:7

CHAPTER 9

NOW there was a man of Benjamin whose name was Kish the son
of Abiel, the son of Zeror, the son
of Becorath, the son of Aphiah,
the son of a Benjamite, a mighty
man of[a] valor. *wealth* or *influence*
2 And he had a son whose
name was Saul, a choice and
handsome *man*, and there was not
a more handsome person than he
among the sons of Israel; from his
shoulders and up he was taller
than any of the people.
3 Now the donkeys of Kish,
Saul's father, were lost. So Kish
said to his son Saul, "Take now
with you one of the servants, and
arise, go search for the donkeys."
4 And he passed through [r]the
hill country of Ephraim and
passed through the land of Shalishah, but they did not find *them*.
Then they passed through the
land of Shaalim, but *they were* not
there. Then he passed through the
land of the Benjamites, but they
did not find *them*. Josh. 24:33
5 When they came to the land
of Zuph, Saul said to his servant
who was with him, "Come, and let
us return, lest my father cease *to*
be concerned about the donkeys
and become anxious for us."
6 And he said to him, "Behold
now, there is a man of God in this
city, and the man is held in honor;
all that he says surely comes true.
Now let us go there, perhaps he
can tell us about our journey on
which we have set out."
7 Then Saul said to his servant,
"But behold, if we go, what shall
we bring the man? For the bread
is gone from our sack and there is
no present to bring to the man of
God. What do we have?"
8 And the servant answered
Saul again and said, "Behold, I
have in my hand a fourth of a
shekel of silver; I will give *it* to the
man of God and he will[r] tell us our
way." 1 Sam. 9:6
9 (Formerly in Israel, when a
man went to inquire of God, he
used to say, "Come, and let us go
to the seer"; for *he who is called* a
prophet now was formerly called
[r]a seer.) 2 Sam. 24:11; 2 Kin. 17:13
10 Then Saul said to his servant,
"Well said; come, let us go." So
they went to the city where the
man of God was.
11 As they went up the slope to
the city, they found young women
going out to draw water, and said
to them, "Is the seer here?"
12 And they answered them and
said, "He is;[a] see, *he is* ahead of
you. Hurry now, for he has come
into the city today, for[r] the people
have a sacrifice on the high place
today. *behold* • Gen. 31:54
13 "As soon as you enter the city
you will find him before he goes
up to the high place to eat, for the
people will not eat until he comes,

because he must bless the sacrifice; afterward those who are invited will eat. Now therefore, go
up for you will find him at once."
14 So they went up to the city.
As they came into the city, behold, Samuel was coming out
toward them to go up to the high
place.
15 Now a day before Saul's
coming,[r] the LORD had revealed
this to Samuel saying, Acts 13:21
16"About this time tomorrow I
will send you a man from the land
of Benjamin, and[r]you shall anoint
him to be prince over My people
Israel; and he shall deliver My
people from the hand of the Philistines. For[r]I have regarded My people, because their cry has come to
Me." 1 Sam. 10:1 • Ex. 3:7, 9
17 When Samuel saw Saul, the
LORD said to him, "Behold, the
man of whom I spoke to you! This
one shall rule over My people."
18 Then Saul approached Samuel in the gate, and said, "Please
tell me where the seer's house is."
19 And Samuel answered Saul
and said, "I am the seer. Go up before me to the high place, for you
shall eat with me today; and in the
morning I will let you go, and will
tell you all that is on your mind.
20"And as for your donkeys
which were lost three days ago,
do not set your mind on them, for
they have been found. And for
whom is all that is desirable in Israel? Is it not for you and for all
your father's household?"
21 And Saul answered and said,
"Am[r] I not a Benjamite, of the
smallest of the tribes of Israel, and
my family the least of all the families of the tribe of Benjamin?
Why then do you speak to me in
this way?" 1 Sam. 15:17
22 Then Samuel took Saul and
his servant and brought them into
the hall, and gave them a place at
the head of those who were invited, who were about thirty men.
23 And Samuel said to the cook,
"Bring[t]the portion that I gave you,
concerning which I said to you,
'Set it[t]aside.'" *Give • with you*
24 Then the cook took up the
leg with what was on it and set *it*
before Saul. And *Samuel* said,
"Here is what has been reserved!
Set *it* before you *and* eat, because
it has been kept for you until the
appointed time,[t] since I said I have
invited the people." So Saul ate
with Samuel that day. *saying*
25 When they came down from
the high place into the city, *Samuel* spoke with Saul on the roof.[6]
26 And they arose early; and it
came about at daybreak that Samuel called to Saul on the roof, saying, "Get up, that I may send you
away." So Saul arose, and both he
and Samuel went out into the
street.
27 As they were going down to
the edge of the city, Samuel said
to Saul, "Say to the servant that
he might go ahead of us and pass
on, but you remain standing now,
that I may proclaim the word of
God to you."

CHAPTER 10

THEN[r]Samuel took the flask of
oil, poured it on his head,[r]kissed
him and said, "Has not the LORD

[6]Gr. adds *and they spread a bed for Saul on the roof and he slept.*

anointed you a ruler over His inheritance? Ex. 30:23-33 • Ps. 2:12
2 "When you go from me today,
then you will find two men close
to[r] Rachel's tomb in the territory
of Benjamin at Zelzah; and they
will say to you, 'The donkeys
which you went to look for have
been found. Now behold, your father has ceased to be concerned
about the donkeys and is anxious
for you, saying, "What shall I do
about my son?"' Gen. 35:16-20
3 "Then you will go on further
from there, and you will come as
far as the[a] oak of Tabor, and there
three men going up to God at
Bethel will meet you, one carrying
three kids, another carrying three
loaves of bread, and another carrying a jug of wine; *terebinth*
4 and they will greet you and
give you two *loaves* of bread,
which you will accept from their
hand.
5 "Afterward you will come to
[a]the hill of God where the Philistine garrison is; and it shall be as
soon as you have come there to
the city, that you will meet a
group of prophets coming down
from the high place with harp,
tambourine, flute, and a lyre before them, and they will be prophesying. *Gibeath-haelohim*
6 "Then the Spirit of the LORD
will come upon you mightily, and
you shall prophesy with them and
be changed into another man.
7 "And it shall be when these
signs come to you, do for yourself
what[t] the occasion requires; for
God is with you. *your hand finds*
8 "And you shall go down before me to Gilgal; and behold, I
will come down to you to offer
burnt offerings and sacrifice peace
offerings. You shall wait seven
days until I come to you and show
you what you should do."
9 Then it happened when he
turned his back to leave Samuel,
God changed[t] his heart; and all
those signs came about on that
day. *for him another heart*
10 When they came to the hill
there, behold, a group of prophets
met him; and the Spirit of God
came upon him mightily, so that
he prophesied among them.
11 And it came about, when all
who knew him previously saw
that he prophesied now with the
prophets, that the people said to
one another, "What has happened
to the son of Kish?[r] Is Saul also
among the prophets?" John 7:15
12 And a man there answered
and said, "Now, who is their father?" Therefore it became a proverb: "Is[r] Saul also among the
prophets?" 1 Sam. 19:23, 24
13 When he had finished prophesying, he came to the high place.
14 Now[r] Saul's uncle said to him
and his servant, "Where did you
go?" And he said, "To look for the
donkeys. When we saw that they
could not be found, we went to
Samuel." 1 Sam. 14:50
15 And Saul's uncle said,
"Please tell me what Samuel said
to you."
16 So Saul said to his uncle, "He[r]
told us plainly that the donkeys
had been found." But he did not
tell him about the matter of the
kingdom which Samuel had mentioned. 1 Sam. 9:20
17 Thereafter Samuel called the

[r]people together to the LORD at
Mizpah; Judg. 20:1; 1 Sam. 7:5
18 and he said to the sons of Israel, "Thus[r] says the LORD, the
God of Israel, 'I brought Israel up
from Egypt, and I delivered you
from the hand of the Egyptians,
and from the [t]power of all the
kingdoms that were oppressing
you.' Judg. 6:8, 9 • *hand*
19 "But you[r] today rejected your
God, who delivers you from all
your calamities and your distresses; yet you have said, 'No,
but set a king over us!' Now therefore, present yourselves before
the LORD by your tribes and by
your clans." 1 Sam. 8:6, 7; 12:12
20 Thus Samuel brought all the
tribes of Israel near, and the tribe
of Benjamin was taken by lot.
21 Then he brought the tribe of
Benjamin near by its families, and
the Matrite family was taken. And
Saul the son of Kish was taken;
but when they looked for him, he
could not be found.
22 Therefore[r] they inquired further of the LORD, "Has the man
come here yet?" So the LORD said,
"Behold, he is hiding himself by
the baggage." 1 Sam. 23:2, 4
23 So they ran and took him
from there, and when he stood
among the people, [r]he was taller
than any of the people from his
shoulders upward. 1 Sam. 9:2
24 And Samuel said to all the
people, "Do you see him whom
the LORD has chosen? Surely there
is no one like him among all the
people." So all the people shouted
and said, "Long live the king!"
25 Then Samuel told the people
the ordinances of the kingdom,
and wrote *them* in the book and
placed *it* before the LORD. And
Samuel sent all the people away,
each one to his house.
26 And Saul also went to his
house at Gibeah; and the valiant
men whose hearts God had
touched went with him.
27 But certain [t]worthless men
said, "How can this one deliver
us?" And they despised him and
did not bring him any present. But
he kept silent. *sons of Belial,* cf.

CHAPTER 11

NOW Nahash the Ammonite
came up and besieged Jabesh-gilead; and all the men of Jabesh
said to Nahash, "Make a covenant
with us and we will serve you."
2 But Nahash the Ammonite
said to them, "I will make *it* with
you on this condition, that I will
gouge out the right eye of every
one of you, thus I will make it[r] a
reproach on all Israel." Ps. 44:13
3 And the elders of Jabesh said
to him, "Let us alone for seven
days, that we may send messengers throughout the territory of Israel. Then, if there is no one to deliver us, we will come out to you."
4 Then the messengers came
to Gibeah of Saul and spoke these
words in the hearing of the people, and all the people[r] lifted up
their voices and wept. Judg. 2:4
5 Now behold, Saul was coming from the field behind the oxen;
and [t]he said, "What is *the matter*
with the people that they weep?"
So they related to him the words
of the men of Jabesh. *Saul*
6 Then the Spirit of God came

upon Saul mightily when he heard
these words, and[t]he became very
angry. *his anger burned exceedingly*
7 And he took a yoke of oxen
and[r]cut them in pieces, and sent
them throughout the territory of
Israel by the hand of messengers,
saying, "Whoever does not come
out after Saul and after Samuel,
so shall it be done to his oxen."
Then the dread of the LORD fell on
the people, and they came out[r]as
one man. Judg. 19:29 • Judg. 20:1
8 And he[t] numbered them in
[r]Bezek; and the sons of Israel were
300,000, and the men of Judah
30,000. *mustered* • Judg. 1:5
9 And they said to the messengers who had come, "Thus you
shall say to the men of Jabesh-gilead, 'Tomorrow, by the time the
sun is hot, you shall have deliverance.' " So the messengers went
and told the men of Jabesh; and
they were glad.
10 Then the men of Jabesh said,
"Tomorrow we will come out to
you, and you may do to us whatever seems good to you."
11 And it happened the next
morning that Saul put the people
[r]in three companies; and they
came into the midst of the camp
at the morning watch, and struck
down the Ammonites until the
heat of the day. And it came about
that those who survived were
scattered, so that no two of them
were left together. Judg. 7:16, 20
12 Then the people said to Samuel, "Who[r] is he that said, 'Shall
Saul reign over us?' [t]Bring the
men, that we may put them to
death." 1 Sam. 10:27 • *Give*
13 But Saul said, "Not a man
shall be put to death this day, for
today[r]the LORD has accomplished
deliverance in Israel." 1 Sam. 19:5
14 Then Samuel said to the people, "Come and let us go to Gilgal
and renew the kingdom there."
15 So all the people went to Gilgal, and there they made Saul
king before the LORD in Gilgal.
There they also offered sacrifices
of peace offerings before the
LORD; and there Saul and all the
men of Israel rejoiced greatly.

CHAPTER 12

THEN Samuel said to all Israel,
"Behold,[r]I have listened to your
voice in all that you said to me,
and I have[t]appointed a king over
you. 1 Sam. 8:7, 9, 22 • *made*
2 "And now, [r]here is the king
walking before you, but[r]I am old
and gray, and behold my sons are
with you. And I have walked before you from my youth even to
this day. 1 Sam. 8:20 • 1 Sam. 8:1, 5
3 "Here I am; bear witness
against me before the LORD and
[r]His anointed. Whose ox have I
taken, or whose donkey have I
taken, or whom have I defrauded?
Whom have I oppressed, or from
whose hand have I taken a bribe
to blind my eyes with it? I will restore *it* to you." 1 Sam. 10:1
4 And they said, "You have not
defrauded us, or oppressed us, or
taken anything from any man's
hand."
5 And he said to them, "The
LORD is witness against you, and
His anointed is witness this day
that[r]you have found nothing[r]in my

hand." And they said, "*He is* witness." Acts 23:9; 24:20 • Ex. 22:4
6 Then Samuel said to the people, "It is the LORD who[t]appointed
Moses and Aaron and who
brought your fathers up from the
land of Egypt. *made*
7 "So now, take your stand,[r]that
I may plead with you before the
LORD concerning all the righteous
acts of the LORD which He did for
you and your fathers. Ezek. 20:35
8 "When Jacob went into Egypt
and[r]your fathers cried out to the
LORD, then the LORD sent Moses
and Aaron who brought your fathers out of Egypt and settled
them in this place. Ex. 2:23-25
9 "But they forgot the LORD
their God, so He sold them into
the hand of Sisera, captain of the
army of Hazor, and into the hand
of the Philistines and into the
hand of the king of Moab, and
they fought against them.
10 "And they cried out to the
LORD and said, 'We have sinned
because we have forsaken the
LORD and have served the Baals
and the Ashtaroth; but now deliver us from the hands of our enemies, and we will serve Thee.'
11 "Then the LORD sent[r]Jerubba-
al and [7]Bedan and[r]Jephthah and
Samuel, and delivered you from
the hands of your enemies all
around, so that you lived in security. Judg. 6:31, 32 • Judg. 11:29
12 "When you saw[r]that Nahash
the king of the sons of Ammon
came against you, you said to me,
'No, but a king shall reign over
us,' although the LORD your God
was your king. 1 Sam. 11:1, 2
13 "Now therefore,[r]here is the
king whom you have chosen,
[r]whom you have asked for, and behold, the LORD has set a king over
you. 1 Sam. 10:24 • 1 Sam. 8:5
14 "If[r]you will fear the LORD and
serve Him, and listen to His voice
and not rebel against the[t]com-
mand of the LORD, then both you
and also the king who reigns over
you will follow the LORD your
God. Josh. 24:14 • *mouth*
15 "And[r]if you will not listen to
the voice of the LORD, but rebel
against the[t]command of the LORD,
then the hand of the LORD will be
against you, *as it was* against your
fathers. Lev. 26:14, 15 • *mouth*
16 "Even now, take your stand
and see this great thing which the
LORD will do before your eyes.
17 "Is it not the wheat harvest today?[r]I will call to the LORD, that
He may send[t]thunder and rain.
Then you will know and see that
your wickedness is great which
you have done in the sight of the
LORD by asking for yourselves a
king." 1 Sam. 7:9, 10 • *sounds*
18 So Samuel called to the
LORD, and the LORD sent[t]thunder
and rain that day; and[r]all the people greatly feared the LORD and
Samuel. *sounds* • Ex. 14:31
19 Then all the people said to
Samuel, "Pray[r]for your servants
to the LORD your God, so that we
may not die, for we have added to
all our sins *this* evil by asking for
ourselves a king." Ex. 9:28
20 And Samuel said to the people, "Do not fear. You have committed all this evil, yet[r]do not turn
aside from following the LORD,
but serve the LORD with all your
heart. Deut. 11:16

[7]Gr. and Syr. read *Barak*

21 "And you must not turn aside,
for *then you would* go after futile
things which can not profit or deliver, because they are futile.
22 "For [r]the LORD will not abandon His people on account of His
great name, because the LORD has
been pleased to make you a people for Himself. Deut. 31:6
23 "Moreover, as for me, [r]far be it
from me that I should sin against
the LORD by ceasing to pray for
you; but I will instruct you in the
good and right way. Rom. 1:9
24 "Only [8]fear the LORD and
serve Him in truth with all your
heart; for consider what great
things He has done for you.
25 "But if you still do wickedly,
[r]both you and your king shall be
swept away." Josh. 24:20

CHAPTER 13

SAUL was *forty* years old when
he began to reign, and he reigned
thirty-two years over Israel.
2 Now Saul chose for himself
3,000 men of Israel, of which 2,000
were with Saul in [r]Michmash and
in the hill country of Bethel, while
1,000 were with Jonathan at Gibeah of Benjamin. But he sent
away the rest of the people, each
to his tent. 1 Sam. 13:5; 14:31
3 And Jonathan smote [r]the garrison of the Philistines that was in
Geba, and the Philistines heard of
it. Then Saul blew the trumpet
throughout the land, saying, "Let
the Hebrews hear." 1 Sam. 10:5
4 And all Israel heard the news
that Saul had smitten the garrison
of the Philistines, and also that Israel had become odious to the Philistines. The people were then
summoned to Saul at Gilgal.
5 Now the Philistines assembled to fight with Israel, 30,000
chariots and 6,000 horsemen, and
people like the sand which is on
the seashore in abundance; and
they came up and camped in
Michmash, east of Beth-aven.
6 When the men of Israel saw
that they were in a strait (for the
people were hard-pressed), then
[r]the people hid themselves in
caves, in thickets, in cliffs, in cellars, and in pits. Judg. 6:2
7 Also *some of* the Hebrews
crossed the Jordan into the land of
Gad and Gilead. But as for Saul,
he *was* still in Gilgal, and all the
people followed him trembling.
8 Now he waited seven days,
according to the appointed time
set by Samuel, but Samuel did not
come to Gilgal; and the people
were scattering from him.
9 So Saul said, "Bring to me
the burnt offering and the peace
offerings." And [r]he offered the
burnt offering. Deut. 12:5-14
10 And it came about as soon as
he finished offering the burnt offering, that behold, Samuel came;
and Saul went out to meet him
and to [t]greet him. *bless*
11 But Samuel said, "What
have you done?" And Saul said,
"Because I saw that the people
were scattering from me, and that
you did not come within the appointed days, and that [r]the Philistines were assembling at Michmash, 1 Sam. 13:2, 5, 16, 23
12 therefore I said, 'Now the
Philistines will come down
against me at Gilgal, and I have

[8]Or, *reverence*

not asked the favor of the LORD.'
So I forced myself and offered the
burnt offering."
13 And Samuel said to Saul,
"You have acted foolishly; you
have not kept the commandment
of the LORD your God, which He
commanded you, for now the
LORD would have established your
kingdom [t]over Israel forever. *to*
14 "But now your kingdom shall
not endure. The LORD has sought
out for Himself a man after His
own heart, and the LORD has appointed him as ruler over His people, because you have not kept
what the LORD commanded you."
15 Then Samuel arose and went
up from Gilgal to Gibeah of Benjamin. And Saul numbered the people who were present with him,
about six hundred men.
16 Now Saul and his son Jonathan and the people who were
present with them were staying in
Geba of Benjamin while the Philistines camped at Michmash.
17 And the [t]raiders came from
the camp of the Philistines in
three [t] companies: one [t] company
turned toward Ophrah, to the land
of Shual, *destroyers • heads • head*
18 and another company turned
toward Beth-horon, and another
company turned toward the border which overlooks the valley of
Zeboim toward the wilderness.
19 Now no blacksmith could be
found in all the land of Israel, for
the Philistines said, "Lest the Hebrews make swords or spears."
20 So all Israel went down to
the Philistines, each to sharpen
his plowshare, his mattock, his
axe, and his hoe.
21 And the charge was two-
thirds of a shekel for the plowshares, the mattocks, the forks,
and the axes, and to fix the hoes.
22 So it came about on the day
of battle that [r]neither sword nor
spear was found in the hands of
any of the people who *were* with
Saul and Jonathan, but they were
found with Saul and his son Jonathan. Judg. 5:8
23 And [r]the garrison of the Philistines went out to [r]the pass of
Michmash. 1 Sam. 14:1 • Is. 10:28

CHAPTER 14

NOW the day came that Jonathan, the son of Saul, said to the
young man who was carrying his
armor, "Come and let us cross
over to the Philistines' garrison
that is on yonder side." But he did
not tell his father.
2 And Saul was staying in the
outskirts of [r]Gibeah under the
pomegranate tree which is in [r]Mig-
ron. And the people who *were*
with him *were* about six hundred
men, 1 Sam. 13:15, 16 • Is. 10:28
3 and Ahijah, the son of Ahitub, Ichabod's brother, the son of
Phinehas, the son of Eli, the priest
of the LORD at Shiloh, was wearing an ephod. And the people did
not know that Jonathan had gone.
4 And [r]between the passes by
which Jonathan sought to cross
over to the Philistines' garrison,
there was a sharp crag on the one
side, and a sharp crag on the other
side, and the name of the one was
Bozez, and the name of the other
Seneh. 1 Sam. 13:23
5 The one crag rose on the

north opposite Michmash, and the
other on the south opposite Geba.
6 Then Jonathan said to the
young man who was carrying his
armor, "Come and let us cross
over to the garrison of [r]these uncircumcised; perhaps the LORD
will work for us, for the LORD is
not restrained to save by many or
by few." 1 Sam. 17:26, 36
7 And his armor bearer said to
him, "Do all that is in your heart;
turn yourself, *and* here I am with
you according to your desire."
8 Then Jonathan said, "Behold,
we will cross over to the men and
reveal ourselves to them.
9 "If they [t]say to us, 'Wait until
we come to you'; then we will
stand in our place and not go up to
them. *say thus*
10 "But if they [t]say, 'Come up to
us,' then we will go up, for the
LORD has given them into our
hands; and [r]this shall be the sign to
us." *say thus* • Gen. 24:14
11 And when both of them revealed themselves to the garrison
of the Philistines, the Philistines
said, "Behold, Hebrews are coming out of the holes where they
have hidden themselves."
12 So the men of the garrison
[t]hailed Jonathan and his armor
bearer and said, "Come up to us
and we will tell you something."
And Jonathan said to his armor
bearer, "Come up after me, for the
LORD has given them into the
hands of Israel." *answered*
13 Then Jonathan climbed up
on his hands and feet, with his armor bearer behind him; and they
fell before Jonathan, and his armor bearer put some to death after him.
14 And that first slaughter
which Jonathan and his armor
bearer made was about twenty
men within about half a furrow in
an acre of land.
15 And there was a trembling in
the camp, in the field, and among
all the people. Even the garrison
and [r]the raiders trembled, and the
earth quaked so that it became a
[9]great trembling. 1 Sam. 13:17, 18
16 Now Saul's watchmen in
Gibeah of Benjamin looked, and
behold, the multitude melted
away; and they went here and
there.
17 And Saul said to the people
who *were* with him, "Number
now and see who has gone from
us." And when they had numbered, behold, Jonathan and his
armor bearer were not *there.*
18 Then Saul said to Ahijah,
"Bring the ark of God here." For
the ark of God was at that time
with the sons of Israel.
19 And it happened [r]while Saul
talked to the priest, that the commotion in the camp of the Philistines continued and increased; so
Saul said to the priest, "Withdraw
your hand." Num. 27:21
20 Then Saul and all the people
who *were* with him rallied and
came to the battle; and behold, [r]ev-
ery man's sword was against his
fellow, *and there was* very great
confusion. Judg. 7:22; 2 Chr. 20:23
21 Now the Hebrews *who* were
with the Philistines previously,
who went up with them all around
in the camp, even they also *turned*

[9]Lit., *trembling of God*

to be with the Israelites who *were*
with Saul and Jonathan.
22 When all the [r]men of Israel
who had hidden themselves in the
hill country of Ephraim heard that
the Philistines had fled, even they
also pursued them closely in the
battle. 1 Sam. 13:6
23 So the LORD delivered Israel
that day, and the battle [t]spread beyond Beth-aven. *passed over*
24 Now the men of Israel were
hard-pressed on that day, for Saul
had [r]put the people under oath,
saying, "Cursed be the man who
eats food [t]before evening, and until I have avenged myself on my
enemies." So none of the people
tasted food. Josh. 6:26 • *until*
25 And all *the people of* the land
entered the forest, and there was
honey on the ground.
26 When the people entered the
forest, behold, [r]*there was* a flow of
honey; but no man put his hand to
his mouth, for the people feared
the oath. Matt. 3:4
27 But Jonathan had not heard
when his father put the people under oath; therefore, he put out the
end of the staff that *was* in his
hand and dipped it in the honeycomb, and put his hand to his
mouth, and his eyes brightened.
28 Then one of the people answered and said, "Your father
strictly put the people under oath,
saying, 'Cursed be the man who
eats food today.'" And the people
were weary.
29 Then Jonathan said, "My [r]fa-
ther has troubled the land. See
now, how my eyes have brightened because I tasted a little of
this honey. Josh. 7:25; 1 Kin. 18:18
30 "How much more, if only the
people had eaten freely today of
the spoil of their enemies which
they found! For now the slaughter
among the Philistines has not
been great."
31 And they struck among the
Philistines that day from [r]Mich-
mash to Aijalon. And the people
were very weary. 1 Sam. 14:5
32 And the people rushed
greedily upon the spoil, and took
sheep and oxen and calves, and
slew *them* on the ground; and the
people ate *them* with the blood.
33 Then they told Saul, saying,
"Behold, the people are sinning
against the LORD by eating with
the blood." And he said, "You
have acted treacherously; roll a
great stone to me today."
34 And Saul said, "Disperse
yourselves among the people and
say to them, 'Each one of you
bring me his ox or his sheep, and
slaughter *it* here and eat; and do
not sin against the LORD by eating
with the blood.'" So all the people
that night brought each one his ox
with him, and slaughtered *it* there.
35 And [r]Saul built an altar to the
LORD; it was the first altar that he
built to the LORD. 1 Sam. 7:12, 17
36 Then Saul said, "Let us go
down after the Philistines by night
and take spoil among them until
the morning light, and let us not
leave a man of them." And they
said, "Do whatever seems good to
you." So the priest said, "Let us
draw near to God here."
37 And Saul inquired of God,
"Shall I go down after the Philistines? Wilt Thou give them into

the hand of Israel?" But He did
not answer him on that day.
38 And Saul said, "Draw near
here, all you[t] chiefs of the people,
and investigate and see how this
sin has happened today. *corners*
39 "For [r]as the LORD lives, who
delivers Israel, though it is in
Jonathan my son, he shall surely
die." But not one of all the people
answered him. 1 Sam. 14:24, 44
40 Then he said to all Israel,
"You shall be on one side and I
and Jonathan my son will be on
the other side." And the people
said to Saul, "Do what seems
good[t] to you." *in your eyes*
41 Therefore, Saul said to the
LORD, the God of Israel, "Give[r] a
perfect *lot*." And Jonathan and
Saul were taken, but the people
escaped. Acts 1:24
42 And Saul said, "Cast *lots* between me and Jonathan my son."
And Jonathan was taken.
43 Then Saul said to Jonathan,
"Tell me what you have done." So
Jonathan told him and said, "I indeed tasted a little honey with the
end of the staff that was in my
hand. Here I am, I must die!"
44 And Saul said, "May God do
[t]this *to me* and more also, for you
shall surely die, Jonathan." *thus*
45 But the people said to Saul,
"Must Jonathan die, who has
[t]brought about this great deliverance in Israel? Far from it! As the
LORD lives, there shall not one
hair of his head fall to the ground,
for he has worked with God this
day." So the people rescued Jonathan and he did not die. *worked*
46 Then Saul went up from pursuing the Philistines, and the Philistines went to their own place.
47 Now when Saul had taken
the kingdom over Israel, he fought
against all his enemies on every
side, against Moab, the sons of
Ammon, Edom, the kings of Zobah, and [r]the Philistines; and wherever he turned, he [a]inflicted punishment. 1 Sam. 14:52 • *condemned*
48 And he acted valiantly and
[t]defeated the Amalekites, and delivered Israel from the hands of
those who plundered them. *smote*
49 Now the sons of Saul were
Jonathan and Ishvi and Malchi-
shua; and the names of his two
daughters *were these:* the name of
the first-born Merab and the name
of the younger Michal.
50 And the name of Saul's wife
was Ahinoam the daughter of
Ahimaaz. And the name of the
captain of his army was Abner the
son of Ner, Saul's uncle.
51 [r]And Kish *was* the father of
Saul, and Ner the father of Abner
was the son of Abiel. 1 Sam. 9:1, 21
52 Now the war against the Philistines was severe all the days of
Saul; and when Saul saw any
mighty man or any valiant man,
he attached him to his staff.

CHAPTER 15

THEN Samuel said to Saul, "The
LORD sent me to anoint you as
king over His people, over Israel;
now therefore, listen to the [t]words
of the LORD. *sound of the words*
2 "Thus says the LORD of hosts,
'I will [a]punish Amalek *for* what he
did to Israel, how he set himself

against him on the way while he
was coming up from Egypt. *visit*
3 'Now go and strike Amalek
and [r]utterly destroy all that he has,
and do not spare him; but put to
death both man and woman, child
and infant, ox and sheep, camel
and donkey.' " Num. 24:20
4 Then Saul summoned the
people and [t]numbered them in Te-
laim, 200,000 foot soldiers and
10,000 men of Judah. *mustered*
5 And Saul came to the city of
Amalek, and set an ambush in the
valley.
6 And Saul said to [r]the Kenites,
"Go, depart, go down from among
the Amalekites, lest I destroy you
with them; for you showed kindness to all the sons of Israel when
they came up from Egypt." So the
Kenites departed from among the
Amalekites. Num. 24:21
7 So Saul defeated the Amalekites, from Havilah as you go to
Shur, which is east of Egypt.
8 And he captured Agag the
king of the Amalekites alive, and
utterly destroyed all the people
with the edge of the sword.
9 But Saul and the people
[r]spared Agag and the best of the
sheep, the oxen, the fatlings, the
lambs, and all that was good, and
were not willing to destroy them
utterly; but everything despised
and worthless, that they utterly
destroyed. 1 Sam. 15:3, 15, 19
10 Then the word of the LORD
came to Samuel, saying,
11 "I regret that I have made
Saul king, for he has turned back
from [t]following Me, and has not
carried out My commands." And
Samuel was distressed and cried
out to the LORD all night. *after*
12 And Samuel rose early in the
morning to meet Saul; and it was
told Samuel, saying, "Saul came
to Carmel, and behold, he set up a
monument for himself, then
turned and proceeded on [t]down to
Gilgal." *and went down*
13 And Samuel came to Saul,
and Saul said to him, "Blessed are
you of the LORD! I have carried
out the command of the LORD."
14 But Samuel said, "What then
is this [t]bleating of the sheep in my
ears, and the lowing of the oxen
which I hear?" *sound*
15 And Saul said, "They have
brought them from the Amalekites, for the people spared the best
of the sheep and oxen, to sacrifice
to the LORD your God; but the rest
we have utterly destroyed."
16 Then Samuel said to Saul,
"Wait, and let me tell you what
the LORD said to me last night."
And he said to him, "Speak!"
17 And Samuel said, "Is it not
true, [r]though you were little in
your own eyes, you were *made*
the head of the tribes of Israel?
And the LORD anointed you king
over Israel, 1 Sam. 9:21; 10:22
18 and the LORD sent you on a
[t]mission, and said, 'Go and utterly
destroy the sinners, the Amalekites, and fight against them until
they are exterminated.' *way*
19 "Why then did you not obey
the voice of the LORD, but rushed
upon the spoil and did what was
evil in the sight of the LORD?"
20 Then Saul said to Samuel, "I
did obey the voice of the LORD,
and went on the [t]mission on which

the LORD sent me, and have
brought back Agag the king of
Amalek, and have utterly destroyed the Amalekites. *way*
21 "But the people took *some* of
the spoil, sheep and oxen, the
choicest of the things devoted to
destruction, to sacrifice to the
LORD your God at Gilgal."
22 And Samuel said,
"Has[r] the LORD as much delight in burnt offerings
and sacrifices
As in obeying the voice of
the LORD?
Behold, [r]to obey is better
than sacrifice,
And to heed than the fat of
rams. Ps. 40:6-8 • Hos. 6:6
23 "For rebellion is as the sin of
divination,
And insubordination is as
iniquity and idolatry.
Because you have rejected
the word of the LORD,
He has also rejected you
from *being* king."
24 Then Saul said to Samuel, "I[r]
have sinned; I have indeed transgressed the[t]command of the LORD
and your words, because I feared
the people and listened to their
voice. Num. 22:34 • *mouth*
25 "Now therefore, please pardon my sin and return with me,
that I may worship the LORD."
26 But Samuel said to Saul, "I
will not return with you; for you
have rejected the word of the
LORD, and the LORD has rejected
you from being king over Israel."
27 And as Samuel turned to go,
[r]*Saul* seized the edge of his robe,
and it tore. 1 Kin. 11:30, 31
28 So Samuel said to him, "The[r]
LORD has torn the kingdom of Israel from you today, and has giv-
en it to your neighbor who is better than you. 1 Sam. 28:17, 18
29 "And also the[a]Glory of Israel
will not lie or change His mind;
for He is not a man that He should
change His mind." *Eminence*
30 Then he said, "I have sinned;
but please honor me now before
the elders of my people and before
Israel, and go back with me, that I
may worship the LORD your God."
31 So Samuel went back following Saul, and Saul worshiped the
LORD.
32 Then Samuel said, "Bring me
Agag, the king of the Amalekites." And Agag came to him
[a]cheerfully. And Agag said,
"Surely the bitterness of death is
past." *in bonds*
33 But Samuel said, "As[r] your
sword has made women childless,
so shall your mother be childless
among women." And Samuel
hewed Agag to pieces before the
LORD at Gilgal. Gen. 9:6; Judg. 1:7
34 Then Samuel went to Ramah, but Saul went up to his
house at Gibeah of Saul.
35 And Samuel did not see Saul
again until the day of his death;
for Samuel grieved over Saul. And
the LORD regretted that He had
made Saul king over Israel.

CHAPTER 16

NOW the LORD said to Samuel,
"How long will you grieve over
Saul, since I have rejected him
from being king over Israel? Fill
your horn with oil, and go; I will
send you to Jesse the Bethlehem-

ite, for I have selected a king for Myself among his sons."

2 But Samuel said, "How can I go? When Saul hears *of it*, he will kill me." And the LORD said, "Take[r] a heifer with you, and say, 'I have come to sacrifice to the LORD.' 1 Sam. 20:29

3 "And you shall invite Jesse to the sacrifice, and I will show you what you shall do; and you shall anoint for Me the one whom I[t] designate to you." *say to you*

4 So Samuel did what the LORD said, and came to Bethlehem. And the elders of the city came trembling to meet him and said, "Do you come in peace?"

5 And he said, "In peace; I have come to sacrifice to the LORD. [r]Consecrate yourselves and come with me to the sacrifice." He also consecrated Jesse and his sons, and invited them to the sacrifice. Gen. 35:2; Ex. 19:10

6 Then it came about when they entered, that he looked at Eliab and thought, "Surely the LORD's anointed is before Him."

7 But the LORD said to Samuel, "Do not look at his appearance or at the height of his stature, because I have rejected him; for God *sees* not as man sees, for man looks at the outward appearance, but the LORD looks at the heart."

8 Then Jesse called Abinadab, and made him pass before Samuel. And he said, "Neither has the LORD chosen this one."

9 Next Jesse made Shammah pass by. And he said, "Neither has the LORD chosen this one."

10 Thus Jesse made seven of his sons pass before Samuel. But Samuel said to Jesse, "The LORD has not chosen these."

11 And Samuel said to Jesse, "Are these all the children?" And he said, "There[r] remains yet the youngest, and behold, he is tending the sheep." Then Samuel said to Jesse, "Send and[t] bring him; for we will not sit down until he comes here." 1 Sam. 17:12 • *take*

12 So he sent and brought him in. Now he was ruddy, with beautiful eyes and a handsome appearance. And the LORD said, "Arise, anoint him; for this is he."

13 Then Samuel took the horn of oil and [r]anointed him in the midst of his brothers; and the Spirit of the LORD came mightily upon David from that day forward. And Samuel arose and went to Ramah. 1 Sam. 10:1

14 Now the Spirit of the LORD departed from Saul, and [r]an evil spirit from the LORD terrorized him. Judg. 9:23; 1 Sam. 16:15, 16

15 Saul's servants then said to him, "Behold now, an evil spirit from God is terrorizing you.

16 "Let our lord now command your servants who are before you. Let them seek a man who is a skillful player on the harp; and it shall come about when the evil spirit from God is on you, that he shall play *the harp* with his hand, and you will be well."

17 So Saul said to his servants, "Provide for me now a man who can play well, and bring *him* to me."

18 Then one of the young men answered and said, "Behold, I have seen a son of Jesse the Bethlehemite who is a skillful musi-

cian, a mighty man of valor, a
warrior, one prudent in speech,
and a handsome man; and [r]the
LORD is with him." 1 Sam. 3:19
19 So Saul sent messengers to
Jesse, and said, "Send me your
son David who is with the flock."
20 And Jesse took a donkey
loaded with bread and a jug of
wine and a young goat, and sent
them to Saul by David his son.
21 Then David came to Saul and
[t]attended him, and [t]Saul loved him
greatly; and he became his armor
bearer. *stood before him* • *he*
22 And Saul sent to Jesse, saying,
"Let David now stand before
me; for he has found favor in my
sight."
23 So it came about whenever
[r]the *evil* spirit from God came to
Saul, David would take the harp
and play *it* with his hand; and Saul
would be refreshed and be well,
and the evil spirit would depart
from him. 1 Sam. 16:14-16

CHAPTER 17

NOW [r]the Philistines gathered
their armies for battle; and they
were gathered at Socoh which belongs
to Judah, and they camped
between Socoh and Azekah, in
Ephes-dammim. 1 Sam. 13:5
2 And Saul and the men of Israel
were gathered, and camped in
[r]the valley of Elah, and drew up in
battle array to encounter the Philistines.
1 Sam. 21:9
3 And the Philistines stood on
the mountain on one side while Israel
stood on the mountain on the
other side, with the valley between
them.
4 Then a champion came out
from the armies of the Philistines
named Goliath, from Gath, whose
height was six [10]cubits and a span.
5 And *he had* a bronze helmet
on his head, and he was clothed
with scale-armor which weighed
five thousand shekels of bronze.
6 *He* also *had* bronze [11]greaves
on his legs and a bronze javelin
slung between his shoulders.
7 And the shaft of his spear
was like a weaver's beam, and the
head of his spear *weighed* six hundred
shekels of iron; his shield-carrier
also walked before him.
8 And he stood and shouted to
the ranks of Israel, and said to
them, "Why do you come out to
draw up in battle array? Am I not
the Philistine and you [r]servants of
Saul? Choose a man for yourselves
and let him come down to
me. 1 Sam. 8:17
9 "If [r]he is able to fight with me
and [t]kill me, then we will become
your servants; but if I prevail
against him and [t]kill him, then you
shall become our servants and
serve us." 2 Sam. 2:12-16 • *smite*
10 Again the Philistine said, "I [r]
defy the ranks of Israel this day;
give me a man that we may fight
together." 1 Sam. 17:26, 36, 45
11 When Saul and all Israel
heard these words of the Philistine,
they were dismayed and
greatly afraid.
12 Now David was the son of
[t]the Ephrathite of Bethlehem in Judah,
whose name was Jesse, and
he had eight sons. And Jesse was
old in the days of Saul, advanced
in years among men. *this*

[10]I.e., One cubit equals approx. 18 in.
[11]Or, *shin guards*

13 And the three older sons of
Jesse had[t]gone after Saul to the
battle. And the names of his three
sons who went to the battle were
Eliab the first-born, and the second to him Abinadab, and the
third Shammah. *gone; they went*
14 And[r]David was the youngest.
Now the three oldest followed
Saul, 1 Sam. 16:11
15 but David went back and
forth from Saul to tend his father's flock at Bethlehem.
16 And the Philistine came forward morning and evening for
forty days, and took his stand.
17 Then Jesse said to David his
son, "Take now for your brothers
an ephah of this roasted grain and
these ten loaves, and run to the
camp to your brothers.
18 "Bring also these ten cuts of
cheese to the commander of *their*
thousand, and look into the welfare of your brothers, and bring
back[t]news of them. *their pledge*
19 "For Saul and they and all the
men of Israel are in the valley of
Elah, fighting with the Philistines."
20 So David arose early in the
morning and left the flock with a
keeper and took *the supplies* and
went as Jesse had commanded
him. And he came to the[r]circle of
the camp while the army was
going out in battle array shouting
the war cry. 1 Sam. 26:5, 7
21 And Israel and the Philistines
drew up in battle array, army
against army.
22 Then David left his[r]baggage
in the[t]care of the baggage keeper,
and ran to the battle line and entered in order to greet his brothers. Judg. 18:21; Is. 10:28 • *hand*

23 As he was talking with them,
behold, the champion, the Philistine from Gath named Goliath,
was coming up from the army of
the Philistines, and he spoke[r]these
same words; and David heard
them. 1 Sam. 17:8-10
24 When all the men of Israel
saw the man, they fled from him
and were greatly afraid.
25 And the men of Israel said,
"Have you seen this man who is
coming up? Surely he is coming
up to defy Israel. And it will be
that the king will enrich the man
who kills him with great riches
and[r]will give him his daughter and
make his father's house [12]free in
Israel." Josh. 15:16
26 Then David spoke to the men
who were standing by him, saying, "What will be done for the
man who kills this Philistine, and
takes away[r]the reproach from Israel? For who is this[r]uncircum-
cised Philistine, that he should
taunt the armies of the living
God?" 1 Sam. 11:2 • 1 Sam. 14:6
27 And the people [t]answered
him in accord with this word, saying, "Thus it will be done for the
man who kills him." *said to*
28 Now Eliab his oldest brother
heard when he spoke to the men;
and Eliab's anger burned against
David and he said, "Why have
you come down? And with whom
have you left those few sheep in
the wilderness? I know your insolence and the wickedness of your
heart; for you have come down in
order to see the battle."
29 But David said, "What have I
done now? Was it not just a[t]ques-
tion?" *word*

[12]I.e., free from taxes and public service

30 Then he turned away from
him to another and said the same
thing; and the people answered
the same thing as before.
31 When the words which David spoke were heard, they told
them to Saul, and he sent for him.
32 And David said to Saul, "Let[r]
no man's heart fail on account of
him; your servant will go and fight
with this Philistine." Deut. 20:1-4
33 Then Saul said to David,
"You[r] are not able to go against
this Philistine to fight with him;
for you are *but* a youth while he
has been a warrior from his
youth." Num. 13:31
34 But David said to Saul,
"Your servant was tending his father's sheep. When a lion or a
bear came and took a lamb from
the flock,
35 I went out after him and [t]at-
tacked him, and [r]rescued *it* from
his mouth; and when he rose up
against me, I seized *him* by his
beard and struck him and killed
him. *smote* • Amos 3:12
36 "Your servant has killed both
the lion and the bear; and this uncircumcised Philistine will be like
one of them, since he has taunted
the armies of the living God."
37 And David said, "The[r] LORD
who delivered me from the paw of
the lion and from the paw of the
bear, He will deliver me from the
hand of this Philistine." And Saul
said to David, "Go, and may the
LORD be with you." 2 Cor. 1:10
38 Then Saul clothed David
with his garments and put a
bronze helmet on his head, and he
clothed him with armor.
39 And David girded his sword
over his armor and tried to walk,
for he had not tested *them*. So David said to Saul, "I cannot go with
these, for I have not tested *them*."
And David took them off.
40 And he took his stick in his
hand and chose for himself five
smooth stones from the brook,
and put them in the shepherd's
bag which he had, even in *his*
pouch, and [r]his sling was in his
hand; and he approached the Philistine. Judg. 20:16
41 Then the Philistine came on
and approached David, with the
shield-bearer in front of him.
42 When the Philistine looked
and saw David, he disdained him;
for he was *but* a youth, and ruddy,
with a handsome appearance.
43 And the Philistine said to David, "Am I a dog, that you come to
me with sticks?" And the Philistine cursed David by his gods.
44 The Philistine also said to
David, "Come to me, and I will
give your flesh to the birds of the
sky and the beasts of the field."
45 Then David said to the Philistine, "You come to me with a
sword, a spear, and a javelin,[r] but I
come to you in the name of the
LORD of hosts, the God of the
armies of Israel, whom you have
taunted. 2 Sam. 22:35; 2 Chr. 32:8
46 "This day the LORD will deliver you up into my hands, and I
will strike you down and remove
your head from you. And I will
give the [r]dead bodies of the army
of the Philistines this day to the
birds of the sky and the wild
beasts of the earth, that all the
earth may know that there is a
God in Israel, Deut. 28:26

47 and that all this assembly
may know that the LORD does not
deliver by sword or by spear; for
the battle is the LORD's and He
will give you into our hands."
48 Then it happened when the
Philistine rose and came and drew
near to meet David, that [r]David
ran quickly toward the battle line
to meet the Philistine. Ps. 27:3
49 And David put his hand into
his bag and took from it a stone
and slung *it*, and struck the Philistine on his forehead. And the
stone sank into his forehead, so
that he fell on his face to the
ground.
50 Thus David prevailed over
the Philistine with a sling and a
stone, and he struck the Philistine
and killed him; but there was no
sword in David's hand.
51 Then David ran and stood
over the Philistine and [r]took his
sword and drew it out of its
sheath and killed him, and cut off
his head with it. When the Philistines saw that their champion was
dead, they fled. 1 Sam. 21:9
52 And the men of Israel and
Judah arose and shouted and pursued the Philistines as far as the
valley, and to the gates of Ekron.
And the slain Philistines [r]lay along
the way to Shaaraim, even to
Gath and Ekron. *fell*
53 And the sons of Israel returned from chasing the Philistines and plundered their camps.
54 Then David took the Philistine's head and brought it to Jerusalem, but he put his weapons in
his tent.
55 Now when Saul saw David
going out against the Philistine, he
said to Abner the commander of
the army, "Abner, whose son is
[r]this young man?" And Abner said,
"By your life, O king, I do not
know." 1 Sam. 16:12, 21, 22
56 And the king said, "You inquire whose son the youth is."
57 So when David returned
from killing the Philistine, Abner
took him and [r]brought him before
Saul with the Philistine's head in
his hand. 1 Sam. 17:54
58 And Saul said to him,
"Whose son are you, young
man?" And David answered, "*I*[r]
am the son of your servant Jesse
the Bethlehemite." 1 Sam. 17:12

CHAPTER 18

NOW it came about when he had
finished speaking to Saul, that [r]the
soul of Jonathan was knit to the
soul of David, and Jonathan loved
him as himself. Gen. 44:30
2 And Saul took him that day
and [r]did not let him return to his
father's house. 1 Sam. 17:15
3 Then Jonathan made a covenant with David because he
loved him as himself.
4 And [r]Jonathan stripped himself of the robe that was on him
and gave it to David, with his armor, including his sword and his
bow and his belt. Gen. 41:42
5 So David went out wherever
Saul sent him, *and* [a]prospered; and
Saul set him over the men of war.
And it was pleasing in the sight of
all the people and also in the sight
of Saul's servants. *acted wisely*
6 And it happened as they
were coming, when David returned from killing the Philistine,

that[r] the women came out of all
the cities of Israel, singing and
dancing, to meet King Saul, with
tambourines, with joy and with
[13]musical instruments. Ps. 68:25
7 And the women sang as they
[a]played, and said,
"Saul has slain his thou-
sands,
And David his ten thou-
sands." *danced*
8 Then Saul became very angry, for this saying displeased
him; and he said, "They have ascribed to David ten thousands, but
to me they have ascribed thousands. Now what more can he
have but the kingdom?"
9 And Saul looked at David
with suspicion from that day on.
10 Now it came about on the
next day that an evil spirit from
God came mightily upon Saul, and
he raved in the midst of the house,
while David was playing *the harp*
with his hand, as usual; and [t]a
spear *was* in Saul's hand. *the*
11 And Saul hurled the spear
for he thought, "I will pin David to
the wall." But David[t] escaped from
his presence twice. *turned about*
12 Now Saul was afraid of David, for the LORD was with him
but had departed from Saul.
13 Therefore Saul removed him
from[t] his presence, and appointed
him as his commander of a thousand; and he went out and came in
before the people. *with him*
14 And David was[a] prospering in
all his ways for[r] the LORD *was* with
him. *acting wisely* • Gen. 39:2, 3, 23
15 When Saul saw that he was
[a]prospering greatly, he dreaded
him. *acting very wisely*

[13]I.e., triangles, or three-stringed instruments

16 But [r] all Israel and Judah
loved David, and he went out and
came in before them. 1 Sam. 18:5
17 Then Saul said to David,
"Here is my older daughter Merab; I will give her to you as a
wife, only be a valiant man for me
and fight the LORD's battles." For
Saul thought, "My hand shall not
be against him, but let the hand of
the Philistines be against him."
18 But David said to Saul, "Who
am I, and what is my life *or* my
father's family in Israel, that I
should be the king's son-in-law?"
19 So it came about at the time
when Merab, Saul's daughter,
should have been given to David,
that she was given to Adriel[r] the
Meholathite for a wife. Judg. 7:22
20 Now[r] Michal, Saul's daughter, loved David. When they told
Saul, the thing was agreeable [t]to
him. 1 Sam. 18:28 • *in his sight*
21 And Saul thought, "I will
give her to him that she may become a snare to him, and that the
hand of the Philistines may be
against him." Therefore Saul said
to David, "For a second time you
may be my son-in-law today."
22 Then Saul commanded his
servants, "Speak to David secretly, saying, 'Behold, the king
delights in you, and all his servants love you; now therefore, become the king's son-in-law.' "
23 So Saul's servants spoke
these words [t]to David. But David
said, "Is it trivial in your sight to
become the king's son-in-law,
since I am a poor man and lightly
esteemed?" *in the ears of*
24 And the servants of Saul re-

ported to him according to these
words *which* David spoke.
25 Saul then said, "Thus you
shall say to David, 'The king does
not desire any [r]dowry except a
hundred foreskins of the Philistines, to take vengeance on the
king's enemies.'" Now Saul
planned to make David fall by the
hand of the Philistines. Ex. 22:17
26 When his servants told David these words, it pleased David
to become the king's son-in-law.
Before the days had expired
27 David rose up and went, [r]he
and his men, and struck down two
hundred men among the Philistines. Then David brought their
foreskins, and they gave them in
full number to the king, that he
might become the king's son-in-
law. So Saul gave him Michal his
daughter for a wife. 1 Sam. 18:17
28 When Saul saw and knew
that the LORD was with David,
and *that* Michal, Saul's daughter,
loved him,
29 then Saul was even more
afraid of David. Thus Saul was
David's enemy continually.
30 Then the commanders of the
Philistines [r]went out *to battle*, and
it happened as often as they went
out, that David behaved himself
more wisely than all the servants
of Saul. So his name was highly
esteemed. 2 Sam. 11:1

CHAPTER 19

NOW Saul told Jonathan his son
and all his servants to put David
to death. But Jonathan, Saul's son,
greatly delighted in David.
2 So Jonathan told David saying, "Saul my father is seeking to
put you to death. Now therefore,
please be on guard in the morning,
and stay in a secret place and hide
yourself.
3 "And I will go out and stand
beside my father in the field
where you are, and I will speak
with my father about you; [r]if I [t]find
out anything, then I shall tell
you." 1 Sam. 20:9, 13 • *see*
4 Then Jonathan spoke well of
David to Saul his father, and said
to him, "Do not let the king sin
against his servant David, since
he has not sinned against you, and
since his deeds *have been* very
[t]beneficial to you. *good*
5 "For [r]he took his life in his
hand and struck the Philistine,
and the LORD brought about a
great deliverance for all Israel;
you saw *it* and rejoiced. Why then
will you sin against innocent
blood, by putting David to death
without a cause?" Judg. 9:17
6 And Saul listened to the
voice of Jonathan, and Saul
vowed, "As the LORD lives, he
shall not be put to death."
7 Then Jonathan called David,
and Jonathan told him all these
words. And Jonathan brought David to Saul, and he was in his presence as [r]formerly. 1 Sam. 16:21
8 When there was war again,
David went out and fought with
the Philistines, and [t]defeated them
with great slaughter, so that they
fled before him. *smote*
9 Now there was an evil spirit
from the LORD on Saul as he was
sitting in his house with his spear
in his hand, and David was playing *the harp* with *his* hand.

10 [r]And Saul tried to pin David
to the wall with the spear, but he
slipped away out of Saul's presence, so that he struck the spear
into the wall. And David fled and
escaped that night. 1 Sam. 18:11
11 Then Saul sent messengers
to David's house to watch him, in
order to put him to death in the
morning. But Michal, David's
wife, told him, saying, "If you do
not save your life tonight, tomorrow you will be put to death."
12 So Michal let David down
through a window, and he went
out and fled and escaped.
13 And Michal took the household idol and laid *it* on the bed,
and put a quilt of goats' *hair* at its
head, and covered *it* with clothes.
14 When Saul sent messengers
to take David, she said, "He[r] is
sick." Josh. 2:5
15 Then Saul sent messengers
to see David, saying, "Bring him
up to me on[t] his bed, that I may
put him to death." *the*
16 When the messengers entered, behold, the household idol
was on the bed with the quilt of
goats' *hair* at its head.
17 So Saul said to Michal, "Why
have you deceived me like this
and let my enemy go, so that he
has escaped?" And Michal said to
Saul, "He said to me, 'Let me go!
Why should I put you to death?' "
18 Now David fled and escaped
and came to Samuel at Ramah,
and told him all that Saul had
done to him. And he and Samuel
went and stayed in Naioth.
19 And it was told Saul, saying,
"Behold, David is at Naioth in Ramah."
20 Then [r]Saul sent messengers
to take David, but when they saw
the company of the prophets
prophesying, with Samuel standing *and* presiding over them, the
Spirit of God came upon the messengers of Saul; and they also
prophesied. 1 Sam. 19:11, 14
21 And when it was told Saul,
he sent other messengers, and
they also prophesied. So Saul sent
messengers again the third time,
and they also prophesied.
22 Then he himself went to Ramah, and came as far as the large
well that is in Secu; and he asked
and said, "Where are Samuel and
David?" And *someone* said, "Behold, they are at Naioth in Ramah."
23 And he [t]proceeded there to
Naioth in Ramah; and [r]the Spirit of
God came upon him also, so that
he went along prophesying continually until he came to Naioth in
Ramah. *went* • 1 Sam. 10:10
24 And he also stripped off his
clothes, and he too prophesied before Samuel and [t]lay down naked
all that day and all that night.
Therefore they say, "Is Saul also
among the prophets?" *fell*

CHAPTER 20

THEN David fled from Naioth in
Ramah, and came and said [t]to
Jonathan, "What have I done?
What is my iniquity? And what is
my sin before your father, that he
is seeking my life?" *before*
2 And he said to him, "Far
from it, you shall not die. Behold,
my father does nothing either
great or small [t]without disclosing

it to me. So why should my father
hide this thing from me? It is not
so!" *and he does not uncover my ear*
3 Yet David vowed again,[t] saying, "Your father knows well that
I have found favor in your sight,
and he has said, 'Do not let Jonathan know this, lest he be
grieved.' But truly as the LORD
lives and as your soul lives, there
is[t] hardly a step between me and
death." *and said • about*
4 Then Jonathan said to David,
"Whatever[t] you say, I will do for
you." *your soul says*
5 So David said to Jonathan,
"Behold, tomorrow is [r]the new
moon, and I ought to sit down to
eat with the king. But let me go,
that I may hide myself in the field
until the third evening. Amos 8:5
6 "If your father misses me at
all, then say, 'David earnestly
asked *leave* of me to run to[r] Bethlehem his city, because it is the
yearly sacrifice there for the
whole family.' 1 Sam. 17:58
7 "If he [t]says, 'It is good,' your
servant *shall be* safe; but if he is
very angry, know that he has decided on evil. *says thus*
8 "Therefore deal kindly with
your servant, for [r]you have
brought your servant into a covenant of the LORD with you. But[r] if
there is iniquity in me, put me to
death yourself; for why then
should you bring me to your father?" 1 Sam. 18:3 • 2 Sam. 14:32
9 And Jonathan said, "Far be it
from you! For if I should indeed
learn that evil has been decided
by my father to come upon you,
then would I not tell you about
it?"
10 Then David said to Jonathan,
"Who will tell me[t] if your father
answers you harshly?" *or what*
11 And Jonathan said to David,
"Come, and let us go out into the
field." So both of them went out
to the field.
12 Then Jonathan said to David,
"The LORD, the God of Israel, *be
witness*! When I have sounded out
my father about this time tomorrow, *or* the third day, behold, if
there is good *feeling* toward David, shall I not then send to you
and make it known to you?
13 "If it please my father to do
you harm, may the LORD do so to
Jonathan and more also, if I do
not[t] make it known to you and
send you away, that you may go
in safety. And may the LORD be
with you as He has been with my
father. *uncover your ear*
14 "And if I am still alive, will
you not show me the lovingkindness of the LORD, that I may not
die?
15 "And [r]you shall not cut off
your lovingkindness from my
house forever, not even when the
LORD cuts off every one of the enemies of David from the face of
the earth." 2 Sam. 9:1, 3
16 So Jonathan made a *covenant* with the house of David,
saying, "May the LORD require *it*
at the hands of David's enemies."
17 And Jonathan made David
vow again because of his love for
him, because[r] he loved him as he
loved his own life. 1 Sam. 18:1
18 Then Jonathan said to him,
"Tomorrow is the new moon, and
you will be missed because your
seat will be empty.

19 "When you have stayed for
three days, you shall go down
quickly and come to the place
where you hid yourself on that
eventful day, and you shall remain
by the stone Ezel.
20 "And I will shoot three arrows
to the side, as though I shot at a
target.
21 "And behold, I will send the
lad, *saying,* 'Go, find the arrows.'
If I specifically say to the lad, 'Behold, the arrows are on this side of
you, get them,' then come; for
there is safety for you and no
harm, as the LORD lives.
22 "But if I [t]say to the youth, 'Behold,[r] the arrows are beyond you,'
go, for the LORD has sent you
away. *say thus* • 1 Sam. 20:37
23 "As for the [t]agreement of
which you and I have spoken, behold,[r] the LORD is between you and
me forever." *word* • Gen. 31:49, 53
24 So David hid in the field; and
when the new moon came, the
king sat down to eat food.
25 And the king sat on his seat
as usual, the seat by the wall; then
Jonathan rose up and Abner sat
down by Saul's side, but [r]David's
place was empty. 1 Sam. 20:18
26 Nevertheless Saul did not
speak anything that day, for he
thought, "It is an accident, he is
not clean, surely *he is* not clean."
27 And it came about the next
day, the second *day* of the new
moon, that David's place was
empty; so Saul said to Jonathan
his son, "Why has the son of Jesse
not come to the meal, either yesterday or today?"
28 Jonathan then answered
Saul, "David earnestly asked
leave of me *to* go to Bethlehem,
29 for he said, 'Please [t]let me go,
since our family has a sacrifice in
the city, and my brother has commanded me to attend. And now, if
I have found favor in your sight,
please let me get away that I may
see my brothers.' For this reason
he has not come to the king's table." *send me away*
30 Then Saul's anger burned
against Jonathan and he said to
him, "You son of a perverse, rebellious woman! Do I not know
that you are choosing the son of
Jesse to your own shame and to
the shame of your mother's nakedness?
31 "For [t]as long as the son of
Jesse lives on the earth, neither
you nor your kingdom will be established. Therefore now, send
and bring him to me, for he must
surely die." *all the days which*
32 But Jonathan answered Saul
his father and said to him, "Why[r]
should he be put to death? What
has he done?" Gen. 31:36
33 Then Saul hurled his spear at
him to strike him down; so Jonathan knew that his father had decided to put David to death.
34 Then Jonathan arose from
the table in fierce anger, and did
not eat food on the second day of
the new moon, for he was grieved
over David because his father had
dishonored him.
35 Now it came about in the
morning that Jonathan went out
into the field for the appointment
with David, and a little lad *was*
with him.
36 And he said to his lad, "Run,[r]
find now the arrows which I am

about to shoot." As the lad was
running, he shot [t]an arrow past
him. 1 Sam. 20:20, 21 • *the*
37 When the lad reached the
place of the arrow which Jonathan had shot, Jonathan called after the lad, and said, "Is [r]not the
arrow beyond you?" 1 Sam. 20:22
38 And Jonathan called after
the lad, "Hurry, be quick, do not
stay!" And Jonathan's lad picked
up the arrow and came to his master.
39 But the lad was not aware of
anything; only Jonathan and David knew about the matter.
40 Then Jonathan gave his
weapons to his lad and said to
him, "Go, bring *them* to the city."
41 When the lad was gone, David rose from the south side and
fell on his face to the ground, and
bowed three times. And they
kissed each other and wept together, but David more.
42 And Jonathan said to David,
"Go in safety, inasmuch as we
have sworn to each other in the
name of the LORD, saying, 'The
LORD will be between me and you,
and between my [t]descendants and
your descendants forever.' " Then
he rose and departed, while Jonathan went into the city. *seed*

CHAPTER 21

THEN David came to Nob to
Ahimelech the priest; and Ahimelech came trembling to meet David, and said to him, "Why are
you alone and no one with you?"
2 And David said to Ahimelech
the priest, "The king has commissioned me with a matter, and has
said to me, 'Let [r]no one know anything about the matter on which I
am sending you and with which
I have commissioned you; and I
have directed the young men to a
certain place.' Ps. 141:3
3 "Now therefore, what [t]do you
have on hand? Give me five loaves
of bread, or whatever can be
found." *is under your hand?*
4 And the priest answered David and said, "There is no ordinary
bread [t]on hand, but there is consecrated bread; if only the young
men have kept themselves from
women." *under my hand*
5 And David answered the
priest and said to him, "Surely
women have been kept from us as
previously when I set out and the
vessels of the young men were
holy, though it was an ordinary
journey; how much more then today will their vessels *be holy*?"
6 So [r]the priest gave him consecrated *bread*; for there was no
bread there but the bread of the
Presence which was removed
from before the LORD, in order to
put hot bread *in its place* when it
was taken away. Matt. 12:3, 4
7 Now one of the servants of
Saul was there that day, detained
before the LORD; and his name
was [r]Doeg the Edomite, the chief
of Saul's shepherds. 1 Sam. 14:47
8 And David said to Ahimelech, "Now is there not a spear or
a sword on hand? For I brought
neither my sword nor my weapons [t]with me, because the king's
matter was urgent." *in my hand*
9 Then the priest said, "The
sword of Goliath the Philistine,
whom you [t]killed in the valley of

Elah, behold, it is wrapped in a
cloth behind the ephod; if you
would take it for yourself, take *it*.
For there is no other except it
here." And David said, "There is
none like it; give it to me." *smote*
10 Then David arose and fled
that day from Saul, and went to
Achish king of Gath.
11 But the servants of Achish
said to him, "Is this not David the
king of the land? ʳDid they not sing
of this one as they danced, saying,

'Saul has slain his thousands,
And David his ten thousands'?" 1 Sam. 18:7

12 And David took these words
ᵗto heart, and greatly feared Achish king of Gath. *in his*
13 So he disguised his sanity before them, and acted insanely in
their hands, and scribbled on the
doors of the gate, and let his saliva run down into his beard.
14 Then Achish said to his servants, "Behold, you see the man
behaving as a madman. Why do
you bring him to me?
15 "Do I lack madmen, that you
have brought this one to act the
madman in my presence? Shall
this one come into my house?"

CHAPTER 22

So David departed from there
and escaped to the cave of Adullam; and when his brothers and all
his father's household heard *of it*,
they went down there to him.
2 And everyone who was in
distress, and everyone who ᵗwas in
debt, and everyone who was discontented, gathered to him; and
he became captain over them.
Now there were about four hundred men with him. *had a creditor*
3 And David went from there
to Mizpah of Moab; and he said to
the king of Moab, "Please let my
father and my mother come *and
stay* with you until I know what
God will do for me."
4 Then he left them with the
king of Moab; and they stayed
with him all the time that David
was in the stronghold.
5 And the prophet Gad said to
David, "Do not stay in the stronghold; depart, and go into the land
of Judah." So David departed and
went into the forest of Hereth.
6 Then Saul heard that David
and the men who were with him
had been discovered. Now ʳSaul
was sitting in Gibeah, under the
tamarisk tree on the height with
his spear in his hand, and all his
servants were standing around
him. Judg. 4:5; 1 Sam. 14:2
7 And Saul said to his servants
who stood around him, "Hear
now, O Benjamites! Will the son
of Jesse also give to all of you
fields and vineyards? ʳWill he
make you all commanders of
thousands and commanders of
hundreds? 1 Sam. 8:12
8 "For all of you have conspired
against me so that there is no one
who discloses to me when my son
makes *a covenant* with the son of
Jesse, and there is none of you
who is sorry for me or discloses to
me that my son has stirred up my
servant against me to lie in ambush, as *it is* this day."
9 Then Doeg the Edomite, who
was standing by the servants of

Saul, answered and said, "I saw
the son of Jesse coming to Nob, to
Ahimelech the son of Ahitub.
10 "And [r]he inquired of the LORD
for him, gave him provisions, and
gave him the sword of Goliath the
Philistine." Num. 27:21
11 Then the king sent someone
to summon Ahimelech the priest,
the son of Ahitub, and all his father's household, the priests who
were in Nob; and all of them came
to the king.
12 And Saul said, "Listen now,
son of Ahitub." And he [t]answered,
"Here I am, my lord." *said*
13 Saul then said to him, "Why
have you and the son of Jesse conspired against me, in that you
have given him bread and a sword
and have inquired of God for him,
that he should rise up against me
[r]by lying in ambush as *it is* this
day?" 1 Sam. 22:8
14 [r]Then Ahimelech answered
the king and said, "And who
among all your servants is as
faithful as David, even the king's
son-in-law, who is captain over
your guard, and is honored in your
house? 1 Sam. 19:4, 5; 20:32
15 "Did I *just* begin to inquire of
God for him today? Far be it from
me! Do not let the king impute
anything to his servant *or* to any
of the household of my father, for
your servant knows nothing at all
of this whole affair."
16 But the king said, "You shall
surely die, Ahimelech, you and all
your father's household!"
17 And the king said to the
[t]guards who were attending him,
"Turn around and put the priests
of the LORD to death, because
their hand also is with David and
because they knew that he was
fleeing and did not [t]reveal it to
me." But the servants of the king
were not willing to put forth their
hands to attack the priests of the
LORD. *runners* • *uncover my ear*
18 Then the king said to Doeg,
"You turn around and [t]attack the
priests." And Doeg the Edomite
turned around and [t]attacked the
priests, and he killed that day
eighty-five men who wore the lin-
en ephod. *smite* • *smote*
19 And he struck Nob the city
of the priests with the edge of the
sword, both men and women,
children and infants; also oxen,
donkeys, and sheep, *he struck*
with the edge of the sword.
20 But [r]one son of Ahimelech
the son of Ahitub, named Abiathar, [r]escaped and fled after David. 1 Sam. 23:6, 9 • 1 Sam. 23:6
21 And Abiathar told David that
Saul had killed the priests of the
LORD.
22 Then David said to Abiathar,
"I knew on that day, when Doeg
the Edomite was there, that he
would surely tell Saul. I have
brought about *the death* of every
person in your father's household.
23 "Stay with me, do not be
afraid, for [r]he who seeks my life
seeks your life; for you are [t]safe
with me." 1 Kin. 2:26 • *a charge*

CHAPTER 23

THEN they told David, saying,
"Behold, the Philistines are fighting against Keilah, and are plundering the threshing floors."
2 So David [r]inquired of the

LORD, saying, "Shall I go and [t]at-
tack these Philistines?" And the
LORD said to David, "Go and attack the Philistines, and deliver
Keilah." 2 Sam. 5:19, 23 • *smite*
3 But David's men said to him,
"Behold, we are afraid here in Judah. How much more then if we
go to Keilah against the ranks of
the Philistines?"
4 Then David inquired of the
LORD once more. And the LORD
answered him and said, "Arise, go
down to Keilah, for I will give the
Philistines into your hand."
5 So David and his men went
to Keilah and fought with the Philistines; and he led away their
livestock and struck them with a
great slaughter. Thus David delivered the inhabitants of Keilah.
6 Now it came about, when
Abiathar the son of Ahimelech
[r]fled to David at Keilah, *that* he
came down *with* an ephod in his
hand. 1 Sam. 22:20
7 When it was told Saul that
David had come to Keilah, Saul
said, "God has [t]delivered him into
my hand, for he shut himself in by
entering a city with double gates
and bars." *alienated*
8 So Saul summoned all the
people for war, to go down to Keilah to besiege David and his men.
9 Now David knew that Saul
was plotting evil against him; so
he said to Abiathar the priest,
"Bring the ephod here."
10 Then David said, "O LORD
God of Israel, Thy servant has
heard for certain that Saul is seeking to come to Keilah to destroy
the city on my account.
11 "Will the men of Keilah surrender me into his hand? Will Saul
come down just as Thy servant
has heard? O LORD God of Israel, I
pray, tell Thy servant." And the
LORD said, "He will come down."
12 Then David said, "Will the
men of Keilah surrender me and
my men into the hand of Saul?"
And the LORD said, "They [r]will surrender you." Judg. 15:10-13
13 Then David and his men,
about six hundred, arose and departed from Keilah, and they went
wherever they could go. When it
was told Saul that David had escaped from Keilah, he [t]gave up the
pursuit. *ceased going out*
14 And David stayed in the wilderness in the strongholds, and remained in the hill country in the
wilderness of Ziph. And Saul
sought him every day, but God did
not deliver him into his hand.
15 Now David [t]became aware
that Saul had come out to seek his
life while David was in the wilderness of Ziph at Horesh. *saw*
16 And Jonathan, Saul's son,
arose and went to David at Horesh, and [14]encouraged him in
God.
17 Thus he said to him, "Do not
be afraid, because the hand of
Saul my father shall not find you,
and you will be king over Israel
and I will be next to you; and Saul
my father knows that also."
18 So the two of them made a
covenant before the LORD; and
David stayed at Horesh while
Jonathan went to his house.
19 Then Ziphites came up to
Saul at Gibeah, saying, "Is David
not hiding with us in the strongholds at Horesh, on the hill of

[14] Lit., *strengthened his hand*

Hachilah, which is on the [t]south of [15]Jeshimon? *right side*

20 "Now then, O king, come down according to all the desire of your soul to [t]do so; and our part *shall be* to surrender him into the king's hand." *come down*

21 And Saul said, "May you be blessed of the LORD; for you have had compassion on me.

22 "Go now, make more sure, and investigate and see his place where his [t]haunt is, *and* who has seen him there; for I am told that he is very cunning. *foot*

23 "So look, and learn about all the hiding places where he hides himself, and return to me with certainty, and I will go with you; and it shall come about if he is in the land that I will search him out among all the thousands of Judah."

24 Then they arose and went to Ziph before Saul. Now David and his men were in the wilderness of Maon, in the Arabah to the [t]south of Jeshimon. *right side*

25 When Saul and his men went to seek *him,* they told David, and he came down to the rock and stayed in the wilderness of Maon. And when Saul heard *it,* he pursued David in the wilderness of Maon.

26 And Saul went on one side of the mountain, and David and his men on the other side of the mountain; and David was hurrying to get away from Saul, for Saul and his men [r]were surrounding David and his men to seize them. Ps. 17:9

27 But a messenger came to Saul, saying, "Hurry and come, for the Philistines have made a raid on the land."

28 So Saul returned from pursuing David, and went to meet the Philistines; therefore they called that place the Rock of Escape.

29 And David went up from there and stayed in the strongholds of [r]Engedi. Josh. 15:62

CHAPTER 24

NOW it came about [r]when Saul returned from pursuing the Philistines, he was told, saying, "Behold, David is in the wilderness of Engedi." 1 Sam. 23:28, 29

2 Then [r]Saul took three thousand chosen men from all Israel, and went to seek David and his men in front of the Rocks of the Wild Goats. 1 Sam. 26:2

3 And he came to the sheepfolds on the way, where there *was* a cave; and Saul went in to [t]relieve himself. Now David and his men were sitting in the inner recesses of the cave. *cover his feet*

4 And the men of David said to him, "Behold, [r]*this is* the day of which the LORD said to you, 'Behold; I am about to give your enemy into your hand, and you shall do to him as it seems good [t]to you.' " Then David arose and cut off the edge of Saul's robe secretly. 1 Sam. 23:17 • *in your sight*

5 And it came about afterward that David's [t]conscience bothered him because he had cut off the edge of Saul's *robe.* *heart struck*

6 So he said to his men, "Far be it from me because of the LORD that I should do this thing to my lord, the LORD's anointed, to

[15]Or, *the desert*

stretch out my hand against him,
since he is the LORD's anointed."
7 And David [t]persuaded his
men with *these* words and did not
allow them to rise up against Saul.
And Saul arose, left the cave, and
went on *his* way. *tore apart*
8 Now afterward David arose
and went out of the cave and
called after Saul, saying, "My lord
the king!" And when Saul looked
behind him, [r]David bowed with his
face to the ground and prostrated
himself. 1 Sam. 25:23, 24
9 And David said to Saul,
"Why do you listen to the words
of men, saying, 'Behold, David
seeks [t]to harm you'? *your hurt*
10 "Behold, this day your eyes
have seen that the LORD had given
you today into my hand in the
cave, and [r]some said to kill you,
but *my eye* had pity on you; and I
said, 'I will not stretch out my
hand against my lord, for he is the
LORD's anointed.' 1 Sam. 24:4
11 "Now, my father, see! Indeed,
see the edge of your robe in my
hand! For in that I cut off the edge
of your robe and did not kill you,
know and perceive that there is no
evil or [t]rebellion in my hands, and
I have not sinned against you,
though you are lying in wait for
my life to take it. *transgression*
12 "May the LORD judge between
you and me, and may the LORD
avenge me on you; but my hand
shall not be against you.
13 "As the proverb of the ancients says, 'Out of the wicked
comes forth wickedness'; but my
hand shall not be against you.
14 "After whom has the king of
Israel come out? Whom are you
pursuing? [r]A dead dog, [r]a single
flea? 2 Sam. 9:8 • 1 Sam. 26:20
15 "The LORD therefore be
judge and decide between [t]you
and me; and may He see and
plead my cause, and deliver me
from your hand." *me and you*
16 Now it came about when David had finished speaking these
words to Saul, that Saul said, "Is[r]
this your voice, my son David?"
Then Saul lifted up his voice and
wept. 1 Sam. 26:17
17 And he said to David, "You
are more righteous than I; for you
have dealt well with me, while I
have dealt wickedly with you.
18 "And you have declared today
that you have done good to me,
that [r]the LORD delivered me into
your hand and *yet* you did not kill
me. 1 Sam. 26:23
19 "For if a man finds his enemy,
will he let him go away safely?
May the LORD therefore reward
you with good in return for what
you have done to me this day.
20 "And now, behold, I know
that you shall surely be king, and
that the kingdom of Israel shall be
established in your hand.
21 "So now swear to me by the
LORD that you will not cut off my
descendants after me, and that
you will not destroy my name
from my father's household."
22 And David swore to Saul.
And Saul went to his home, but
David and his men went up to [r]the
stronghold. 1 Sam. 23:29

CHAPTER 25

THEN Samuel died; and all Israel
gathered together and [r]mourned
for him, and [r]buried him at his

house in Ramah. And David arose
and went down to the wilderness
of Paran. Deut. 34:8 • 2 Kin. 21:18
2 Now *there was* a man in
Maon whose business was in Carmel; and the man was very [t]rich,
and he had three thousand sheep
and a thousand goats. And it came
about while he was shearing his
sheep in Carmel *great*
3 (now the man's name was
Nabal, and his wife's name was
Abigail. And the woman was [t]in-
telligent and beautiful in appearance, but the man was harsh and
evil in *his* dealings, and he was a
Calebite), *of good understanding*
4 that David heard in the wilderness that Nabal was shearing
his sheep.
5 So David sent ten young
men, and David said to the young
men, "Go up to Carmel, visit Nabal and greet him in my name;
6 and thus you shall say, 'Have[t]
a long life, peace be to you, and
peace be to your house, and peace
be to all that you have. *To life*
7 'And now I have heard that
you have shearers; now your
shepherds have been with us and
we have not insulted them, nor
have they missed anything all the
days they were in Carmel.
8 'Ask your young men and
they will tell you. Therefore let *my*
young men find favor in your
eyes, for we have come on a [t]fes-
tive day. Please give whatever you
find at hand to your servants and
to your son David.' " *good*
9 When David's young men
came, they spoke to Nabal according to all these words in David's name; then they waited.
10 But Nabal answered David's
servants, and said, "Who[r] is David? And who is the son of Jesse?
There are many servants today
who are each breaking away from
his master. Judg. 9:28
11 "Shall I then take my bread
and my water and my meat that I
have slaughtered for my shearers,
and give it to men [t]whose origin I
do not know?" *from where they are*
12 So David's young men re-
traced their way and went back;
and they came and told him according to all these words.
13 And David said to his men,
"Each *of you* gird on his sword."
So each man girded on his sword.
And David also girded on his
sword, and about [r]four hundred
men went up behind David while
two hundred [r]stayed with the baggage. 1 Sam. 23:13 • 1 Sam. 30:24
14 But one of the young men
told Abigail, Nabal's wife, saying,
"Behold, David sent messengers
from the wilderness to greet our
master, and he scorned them.
15 "Yet the men were very good
to us, and we were not insulted,
nor did we miss anything as long
as we went about with them,
while we were in the fields.
16 "They[r] were a wall to us both
by night and by day, all the time
we were with them tending the
sheep. Ex. 14:22; Job 1:10
17 "Now therefore, know and
[t]consider what you should do, for
evil is plotted against our master
and against all his household; and
he is such a worthless man that no
one can speak to him." *see*
18 Then Abigail hurried and
took two hundred *loaves* of bread

and two jugs of wine and five
sheep already prepared and five
measures of roasted grain and a
hundred clusters of raisins and
two hundred cakes of figs, and
loaded *them* on donkeys.
19 And she said to her young
men, "Go on before me; behold, I
am coming after you." But she did
not tell her husband Nabal.
20 And it came about as she
was riding on her donkey and
coming down by the hidden part
of the mountain, that behold, David and his men were coming
down toward her; so she met
them.
21 Now David had said, "Surely
in vain I have guarded all that this
man has in the wilderness, so that
nothing was missed of all that belonged to him; and he has returned me evil for good.
22 "May God do so to the enemies of David, and more also, if
by morning I leave *as much as*
one [t]male of any who belong to
him." *who urinates against the wall*
23 When Abigail saw David,
she hurried and dismounted from
her donkey, and fell on her face
before David, [r]and bowed herself
to the ground. 1 Sam. 20:41
24 And she fell at his feet and
said, "On me [t]alone, my lord, be
the blame. And please let your
maidservant speak [t]to you, and listen to the words of your maidservant. *even me • in your ears*
25 "Please do not let my lord [t]pay
attention to this worthless man,
Nabal, for as his name is, so is he.
Nabal is his name and folly is with
him; but I your maidservant did
not see the young men of my lord
whom you sent. *set his heart to*
26 "Now therefore, my lord, as
the LORD lives, and as your soul
lives, since the LORD has restrained you from shedding blood,
and from avenging yourself by
your own hand, now then let your
enemies, and those who seek evil
against my lord, be as Nabal.
27 "And now let this gift which
your maidservant has brought to
my lord be given to the young
men who accompany my lord.
28 "Please forgive the transgression of your maidservant; for the
LORD will certainly make for my
lord an enduring house, because
my lord is fighting the battles of
the LORD, and evil shall not be
found in you all your days.
29 "And should anyone rise up to
pursue you and to seek your life,
then the life of my lord shall be
bound in the bundle of the living
with the LORD your God; but the
lives of your enemies He will sling
out as from the hollow of a sling.
30 "And it shall come about
when the LORD shall do for my
lord according to all the good that
He has spoken concerning you,
and [r]shall appoint you ruler over
Israel, 1 Sam. 13:14
31 that this will not cause grief
or a troubled heart to my lord,
both by having shed blood without cause and by my lord having
avenged himself. When the LORD
shall deal well with my lord, then
remember your maidservant."
32 Then David said to Abigail,
"Blessed [r]be the LORD God of Israel, who sent you this day to
meet me, Ex. 18:10; 1 Kin. 1:48

33 and blessed be your discernment, and blessed be you, who have kept me this day from bloodshed, and from [t]avenging myself by my own hand. *saving*
34 "Nevertheless, as the LORD God of Israel lives, who has restrained me from harming you, unless you had come quickly to meet me, surely there would not have been left to Nabal until the morning light *as much as* one [t]male." *who urinates against the wall*
35 So David received from her hand what she had brought him, and he said to her, "Go up to your house in peace. See, I have listened to [t]you and [r]granted your request." *your voice* • Gen. 19:21
36 Then Abigail came to Nabal, and behold, he was holding a feast in his house, like the feast of a king. And Nabal's heart was merry within him, for he was very drunk; so she did not tell him anything at all until the morning light.
37 But it came about in the morning, when the wine had gone out of Nabal, that his wife told him these things, and his heart died within him so that he became *as* a stone.
38 And about ten days later, it happened that [r]the LORD struck Nabal, and he died. 1 Sam. 26:10
39 When David heard that Nabal was dead, he said, "Blessed be the LORD, who has pleaded the cause of my reproach from the hand of Nabal, and has kept back His servant from evil. The LORD has also returned the evildoing of Nabal on his own head." Then David sent [t]a proposal to Abigail, to take her as his wife. *and spoke*
40 When the servants of David came to Abigail at Carmel, they spoke to her, saying, "David has sent us to you, to take you as his wife."
41 And she arose [r]and bowed with her face to the ground and said, "Behold, your maidservant is a maid to wash the feet of my lord's servants." 1 Sam. 25:23
42 Then Abigail quickly arose, and rode on a donkey, with her five maidens who attended her; and she followed the messengers of David, and became his wife.
43 David had also taken Ahinoam of [r]Jezreel, and they both became his wives. Josh. 15:56
44 Now Saul had given [r]Michal his daughter, David's wife, to Palti the son of Laish, who was from [r]Gallim. 1 Sam. 18:27 • Is. 10:30

CHAPTER 26

THEN the Ziphites came to Saul at Gibeah, saying, "Is not David hiding on the hill of Hachilah, *which is* before [16]Jeshimon?"
2 So Saul arose and went down to the wilderness of Ziph, having with him three thousand chosen men of Israel, to search for David in the wilderness of Ziph.
3 And Saul camped in the hill of Hachilah, which is before [16]Jeshimon, beside the road, and David was staying in the wilderness. When he saw that Saul came after him into the wilderness,
4 David sent out spies, and he knew that Saul was definitely coming.
5 David then arose and came to the place where Saul had

[16]Or, *the desert*

camped. And David saw the place where Saul lay, and Abner the son of Ner, the commander of his army; and Saul was lying in the circle of the camp, and the people were camped around him.

6 Then David answered and said to Ahimelech [r]the Hittite and to Abishai the son of Zeruiah, Joab's brother, saying, "Who will go down with me to Saul in the camp?" And Abishai said, "I will go down with you." Gen. 23:3

7 So David and Abishai came to the people by night, and behold, Saul lay sleeping inside the circle of the camp, with his spear stuck in the ground at his head; and Abner and the people were lying around him.

8 Then Abishai said to David, "Today God has delivered your enemy into your hand; now therefore, please let me strike him with the spear [t]to the ground with one stroke, and I will not strike him the second time." *even into*

9 But David said to Abishai, "Do not destroy him, for [r]who can stretch out his hand against the LORD's anointed and be without guilt?" 1 Sam. 24:6, 7

10 David also said, "As the LORD lives, surely the LORD will strike him, or [r]his day will come that he dies, or he will go down into battle and perish. Ps. 37:13

11 "The [r]LORD forbid that I should stretch out my hand against the LORD's anointed; but now please take the spear that is at his head and the jug of water, and let us go." 1 Sam. 24:6, 12; 1 Pet. 3:9

12 So David took the spear and the jug of water from *beside* Saul's head, and they went away, but no one saw or knew *it*, nor did any awake, for they were all asleep, because a sound sleep from the LORD had fallen on them.

13 Then David crossed over to the other side, and stood on top of the mountain at a distance *with* a large area between them.

14 And David called to the people and to Abner the son of Ner, saying, "Will you not answer, Abner?" Then Abner answered and said, "Who are you who calls to the king?"

15 So David said to Abner, "Are you not a man? And who is like you in Israel? Why then have you not guarded your lord the king? For one of the people came to destroy the king your lord.

16 "This thing that you have done is not good. As the LORD lives, *all* of you [t]must surely die, because you did not guard your lord, the LORD's anointed. And now, see where the king's spear is, and the jug of water that was at his head." *are surely sons of death*

17 Then Saul recognized David's voice and said, "Is [r]this your voice, my son David?" And David said, "It is my voice, my lord the king." 1 Sam. 24:16

18 He also said, "Why [r]then is my lord pursuing his servant? For what have I done? Or what evil is in my hand? 1 Sam. 24:9, 11-14

19 "Now therefore, please let my lord the king listen to the words of his servant. If the LORD has stirred you up against me, let Him [t]accept an offering; but if it is men, cursed are they before the LORD, for they have driven me out today that I

should have no attachment with the inheritance of the LORD, saying, 'Go, serve other gods.' *smell*
20 "Now then, do not let my blood fall to the ground away from the presence of the LORD; for the king of Israel has come out to search for ʳa single flea, just as one hunts a partridge in the mountains." 1 Sam. 24:14
21 Then Saul said, "Iʳ have sinned. Return, my son David, for I will not harm you again because my life was precious in your sight this day. Behold, I have played the fool and have committed a serious error." Ex. 9:27; 1 Sam. 15:24, 30
22 And David answered and said, "Behold the spear of the king! Now let one of the young men come over and take it.
23 "And the LORD will repay each man *for* his righteousness and his faithfulness; for the LORD delivered you into *my* hand today, but I refused to stretch out my hand against the LORD's anointed.
24 "Now behold, as your life was highly valued in my sight this day, so may my life be highly valued in the sight of the LORD, and may He deliver me from all distress."
25 Then Saul said to David, "Blessedʳ are you, my son David; you will both accomplish much and surely prevail." So David went on his way, and Saul returned to his place. 1 Sam. 24:19

CHAPTER 27

THEN David said ᵗto himself, "Now I will perish one day by the hand of Saul.ʳThere is nothing better for me than to escape into the land of the Philistines. Saul then will despair of searching for me anymore in all the territory of Israel, and I will escape from his hand." *in his heart* • 1 Sam. 26:19
2 So David arose and crossed over, he and the six hundred men who were with him, to Achish the son of Maoch, king of Gath.
3 And David lived with Achish at Gath, he and his men, each with his household, *even* David with his two wives, Ahinoam the Jezreelitess, and Abigail the Carmelitess, Nabal'sᵗwidow. *wife*
4 Now it was told Saul that David had fled to Gath, so he no longer searched for him.
5 Then David said to Achish, "If now I have found favor in your sight, let them give me a place in one of the cities in the country, that I may live there; for why should your servant live in the royal city with you?"
6 So Achish gave him Ziklag that day; thereforeʳZiklag has belonged to the kings of Judah to this day. Josh. 15:31; 19:5
7 And the number of days that David lived in the country of the Philistines was ʳa year and four months. 1 Sam. 29:3
8 Now David and his men went up and raidedʳthe Geshurites and the Girzites and the Amalekites; for they were the inhabitants of the land from ancient times, as you come to Shur even as far as the land of Egypt. Josh. 13:2, 13
9 And David attacked the land and did not leave a man or a woman alive, and he took away the sheep, the cattle, the donkeys, the camels, and the clothing. Then

he returned and came to Achish.

10 Now Achish said, "Where have you made a raid today?" And David said, "Against the [17]Negev of Judah and against the Negev of the Jerahmeelites and against the Negev of the Kenites."

11 And David did not leave a man or a woman alive, to bring to Gath, saying, "Lest they should tell about us, saying, 'So has David done and so *has been* his practice all the time he has lived in the country of the Philistines.' "

12 So Achish believed David, saying, "He has surely made himself odious among his people Israel; therefore he will become my servant forever."

CHAPTER 28

NOW it came about in those days that the Philistines gathered their armed camps for war, to fight against Israel. And Achish said to David, "Know assuredly that you will go out with me in the camp, you and your men."

2 And David said to Achish, "Very well, you shall know what your servant can do." So Achish said to David, "Very well, I will make you my bodyguard for life."

3 Now [r]Samuel was dead, and all Israel had lamented him and buried him in Ramah his own city. And Saul had removed from the land those who were mediums and spiritists. 1 Sam. 25:1

4 So the Philistines gathered together and came and camped [r]in Shunem; and Saul gathered all Israel together and they camped in [r]Gilboa. Josh. 19:18 • 1 Sam. 31:1

5 When Saul saw the camp of the Philistines, he was afraid and his heart trembled greatly.

6 When Saul inquired of the LORD, [r]the LORD did not answer him, either by dreams or by Urim or by prophets. Prov. 1:24-31

7 Then Saul said to his servants, "Seek for me a woman who is a medium, that I may go to her and inquire of her." And his servants said to him, "Behold, [r]there is a woman who is a medium at [r]En-dor." Acts 16:16 • Josh. 17:11

8 Then Saul disguised himself by putting on other clothes, and went, he and two men with him, and they came to the woman by night; and he said, "Conjure up for me, please, and bring up for me whom I shall name to you."

9 But the woman said to him, "Behold, you know [r]what Saul has done, how he has cut off those who are mediums and spiritists from the land. Why are you then laying a snare for my life to bring about my death?" 1 Sam. 28:3

10 And Saul vowed to her by the LORD, saying, "As the LORD lives, there shall no punishment come upon you for this thing."

11 Then the woman said, "Whom shall I bring up for you?" And he said, "Bring up Samuel for me."

12 When the woman saw Samuel, she cried out with a loud voice; and the woman spoke to Saul, saying, "Why have you deceived me? For you are Saul."

13 And the king said to her, "Do not be afraid; but what do you see?" And the woman said to

[17]I.e., South country

Saul, "I see a[a]divine being coming
up out of the earth." *god*
14 And he said to her, "What is
his form?" And she said, "An old
man is coming up, and [r]he is
wrapped with a robe." And Saul
knew that it was Samuel, and he
bowed with his face to the ground
and did homage. 1 Sam. 15:27
15 Then Samuel said to Saul,
"Why have you disturbed me by
bringing me up?" And Saul answered, "I am greatly distressed;
for the Philistines are waging war
against me, and God has departed
from me and answers me no
more, either through prophets or
by dreams; therefore I have called
you, that you may make known to
me what I should do."
16 And Samuel said, "Why then
do you ask me, since the LORD has
departed from you and has become your adversary?
17"And the LORD has done [t]ac-
cordingly [r]as He spoke through
me; for the LORD has torn the
kingdom out of your hand and
given it to your neighbor, to David. *for himself* • 1 Sam. 15:28
18"As you did not obey the LORD
and did not execute His fierce
wrath on Amalek, so the LORD has
done this thing to you this day.
19"Moreover the LORD will also
give over Israel along with you
into the hands of the Philistines,
therefore tomorrow [r]you and your
sons will be with me. Indeed the
LORD will give over the army of
Israel into the hands of the Philistines!" 1 Sam. 31:2; Job 3:17-19
20 Then Saul immediately fell
full length upon the ground and
was very afraid because of the
words of Samuel; also there was
no strength in him, for he had eat-
en no food all day and all night.
21 And the woman came to Saul
and saw that he was terrified, and
said to him, "Behold, your maidservant has obeyed you, and I
have [t]taken my life in my hand,
and have listened to your words
which you spoke to me. *put*
22"So now also, please listen to
the voice of your maidservant,
and let me set a piece of bread before you that *you may* eat and
have strength when you go on
your way."
23 But he refused and said, "I
will not eat." However, his servants together with the woman
urged him, and he listened to
them. So he arose from the
ground and sat on the bed.
24 And the woman had a fattened calf in the house, and she
quickly slaughtered it; and she
took flour, kneaded it, and baked
unleavened bread from it.
25 And she brought *it* before
Saul and his servants, and they
ate. Then they arose and went
away that night.

CHAPTER 29

NOW the Philistines gathered together all their armies to Aphek,
while the Israelites were camping
by the spring which is in Jezreel.
2 And the lords of the Philistines were proceeding on by hundreds and by thousands, and David and his men were proceeding
on in the rear with Achish.
3 Then the commanders of the
Philistines said, "What *are* these

Hebrews *doing here*?" And Achish
said to the commanders of the
Philistines, "Is this not David, the
servant of Saul the king of Israel,
who has been with me these days,
or *rather* these years, and I have
found no fault in him from the day
he deserted *to me* to this day?"
4 But the commanders of the
Philistines were angry with him,
and the commanders of the Philistines said to him, "Make the man
go back, that he may return[r] to his
place where you have assigned
him, and do not let him go down
to battle with us, lest in the battle
he become an adversary to us. For
with what could this *man* make
himself acceptable to his lord?
Would it not *be* with the heads of
[t]these men? 1 Sam. 27:6 · *those*
5 "Is this not David, [r]of whom
they sing in the dances, saying,

'Saul has slain his thou-
sands,
And David his ten thou-
sands'?" 1 Sam. 18:7

6 Then Achish called David
and said to him, "*As* the LORD
lives, you *have been* upright, and
[r]your going out and your coming in
with me in the army are pleasing
in my sight; for I have not found
evil in you from the day of your
coming to me to this day. Nevertheless, you are not pleasing in the
sight of the lords. 2 Sam. 3:25
7 "Now therefore return, and go
in peace, that you may not dis-
please the lords of the Philistines."
8 And David said to Achish,
"But what have I done? And what
have you found in your servant
from the day when I came before
you to this day, that I may not go
and fight against the enemies of
my lord the king?"
9 But Achish answered and
said to David, "I know that you
are pleasing in my sight, like an
angel of God; nevertheless [r]the
commanders of the Philistines
have said, 'He must not go up
with us to the battle.' 1 Sam. 29:4
10 "Now then arise early in the
morning[r] with the servants of your
lord who have come with you, and
as soon as you have arisen early in
the morning and have light, depart." 1 Chr. 12:19, 22
11 So David arose early, he and
his men, to depart in the morning,
to return to the land of the Philistines. And the Philistines went up
to Jezreel.

CHAPTER 30

THEN it happened when David
and his men came to Ziklag on the
third day, that the Amalekites had
made a raid on the Negev and on
Ziklag, and had [t]overthrown Ziklag and burned it with fire; *smote*
2 and they took captive the
women *and all* who were in it,
both small and great, [r]without killing anyone, and carried *them* off
and went their way. 1 Sam. 27:11
3 And when David and his men
came to the city, behold, it was
burned with fire, and their wives
and their sons and their daughters
had been taken captive.
4 Then David and the people
who were with him lifted their
voices and wept until there was
no strength in them to weep.
5 Now David's two wives had

been taken captive, Ahinoam the
Jezreelitess and Abigail the
widow of Nabal the Carmelite.
6 Moreover David was greatly
distressed because the people
spoke of stoning him, for all the
people were embittered, each one
because of his sons and his daughters. But [r]David strengthened himself in the LORD his God. Ps. 18:2
7 Then [r]David said to Abiathar
the priest, the son of Ahimelech,
"Please bring me the ephod." So
Abiathar brought the ephod to
David. 1 Sam. 23:6, 9
8 And David inquired of the
LORD, saying, "Shall I pursue this
band? Shall I overtake them?"
And He said to him, "Pursue, for
you shall surely overtake them,
and you shall surely rescue *all*."
9 So David went, he and the
six hundred men who were with
him, and came to the brook Besor,
where those left behind remained.
10 But David pursued, he and
four hundred men, for [r]two hundred who were too exhausted to
cross the brook Besor, remained
behind. 1 Sam. 30:9, 21
11 Now they found an Egyptian
in the field and brought him to David, and gave him bread and he
ate, and they provided him water
to drink.
12 And they gave him a piece of
fig cake and two clusters of raisins, and he ate; then his spirit [t]re-
vived. For he had not eaten bread
or drunk water for three days and
three nights. *returned to him*
13 And David said to him, "To
whom do you belong? And where
are you from?" And he said, "I am
a young man of Egypt, a servant
of an Amalekite; and my master
left me behind when I fell sick
three days ago.
14 "We made a raid on the Negev of the Cherethites, and on that
which belongs to Judah, and on
the Negev of Caleb, and we
burned Ziklag with fire."
15 Then David said to him,
"Will you bring me down to this
band?" And he said, "Swear to me
by God that you will not kill me or
deliver me into the hands of my
master, and I will bring you down
to this band."
16 And when he had brought
him down, behold, they were
spread over all the land, eating
and drinking and dancing because
of all the great spoil that they had
taken from the land of the Philistines and from the land of Judah.
17 And David [t]slaughtered them
from the twilight until the evening
of [t]the next day; and not a man of
them escaped, except four hundred young men who rode on
camels and fled. *smote • their*
18 So David recovered all that
the Amalekites had taken, and
rescued his two wives.
19 But nothing of theirs was
missing, whether small or great,
sons or daughters, spoil or anything that they had taken for
themselves; [r]David brought *it* all
back. 1 Sam. 30:8
20 So David had [t]captured all
the sheep and the cattle *which the*
people drove ahead of the *other*
livestock, and they said, "This is
David's spoil." *taken*
21 When David came to the two
hundred men who were too exhausted to follow David, who had

also been left at the brook Besor, and they went out to meet David and to meet the people who were with him, then David approached the people and greeted them.

22 Then all the wicked and worthless men among those who went with David answered and said, "Because they did not go with [t]us, we will not give them any of the spoil that we have recovered, except to every man his wife and his children, that they may lead *them* away and depart." *me*

23 Then David said, "You must not do so, my brothers, with what the LORD has given us, who has kept us and delivered into our hand the band that came against us.

24 "And who will listen to you in this matter? For as his share is who goes down to the battle, so shall his share be who stays by the baggage; they shall share alike."

25 And so it has been from that day forward, that he made it a statute and an ordinance for Israel to this day.

26 Now when David came to Ziklag, he sent *some* of the spoil to the elders of Judah, to his friends, saying, "Behold, a [t]gift for you from the spoil of the enemies of the LORD: *blessing*

27 to those who were in [r]Bethel, and to those who were in [r]Ramoth of the Negev, and to those who were in Jattir, Gen. 12:8 • Josh. 19:8

28 and to those who were in [r]Aroer, and to those who were in Siphmoth, and to those who were in Eshtemoa, Josh. 13:16

29 and to those who were in Racal, and to those who were in the cities of [r]the Jerahmeelites, and to those who were in the cities of [r]the Kenites, 1 Sam. 27:10 • Judg. 1:16

30 and to those who were in [r]Hormah, and to those who were in Bor-ashan, and to those who were in Athach, Num. 14:45; 21:3

31 and to those who were in [r]Hebron, and to all the places where David himself and his men were accustomed to go." Num. 13:22

CHAPTER 31

[r]NOW the Philistines were fighting against Israel, and the men of Israel fled from before the Philistines and fell slain [r]on Mount Gilboa. 1 Chr. 10:1-12 • 1 Sam. 28:4

2 And the Philistines overtook Saul and his sons; and the Philistines [t]killed [r]Jonathan and Abinadab and Malchi-shua the sons of Saul. *smote* • 1 Chr. 8:33f.

3 And [r]the battle went heavily against Saul, and the archers [t]hit him; and he was badly wounded by the archers. 2 Sam. 1:6 • *found*

4 [r]Then Saul said to his armor bearer, "Draw your sword and pierce me through with it, lest [r]these uncircumcised come and pierce me through and make sport of me." But his armor bearer would not, for he was greatly afraid. So Saul took his sword and fell on it. Judg. 9:54 • Judg. 14:3

5 And when his armor bearer saw that Saul was dead, he also fell on his sword and died with him.

6 Thus Saul died with his three sons, his armor bearer, and all his men on that day together.

7 And when the men of Israel who were on the other side of the valley, with those who were be-

yond the Jordan, saw that the men
of Israel had fled and that Saul
and his sons were dead, they
abandoned the cities and fled;
then the Philistines came and
lived in them.
8 And it came about on the
[t]next day when the Philistines
came to strip the slain, that they
found Saul and his three sons
fallen on Mount Gilboa. *morrow*
9 And they cut off his head,
and stripped off his weapons, and
sent *them*[t]throughout the land of
the Philistines, to carry the good
news to the house of their idols
and to the people. *into . . . around*
10 And they put his weapons in
the[t]temple of[r]Ashtaroth, and they
fastened his body to the wall of
Beth-shan. *house* • Judg. 2:13
11 Now when the inhabitants of
Jabesh-gilead heard what the Philistines had done to Saul,
12 all the valiant men rose and
walked all night, and took the
body of Saul and the bodies of his
sons from the wall of Beth-shan,
and they came to Jabesh, and
[r]burned them there. 2 Chr. 16:14
13 And they took their bones
and[r]buried them under the tamarisk tree at Jabesh, and fasted
seven days. 2 Sam. 21:12-14

THE SECOND BOOK OF

SAMUEL

NOW it came about after[r]the
death of Saul, when David had returned from the slaughter of the
Amalekites, that David remained
two days in Ziklag. 1 Sam. 31:6
2 And it happened on the third
day, that behold, a man came out
of the camp from Saul, with his
clothes torn and[t]dust on his head.
And it came about when he came
to David that he fell to the ground
and prostrated himself. *ground*
3 Then David said to him,
"From where do you come?" And
he said to him, "I have escaped
from the camp of Israel."
4 And David said to him,
"How did things go? Please tell
me." And he said, "The people
have fled from the battle, and also
many of the people have fallen
and are dead; and Saul and Jonathan his son are dead also."
5 So David said to the young
man who told him, "How do you
know that Saul and his son Jonathan are dead?"
6 And the young man who told
him said, "By chance I happened
to be on[r]Mount Gilboa, and behold, [r]Saul was leaning on his
spear. And behold, the chariots
and the horsemen pursued him
closely. 1 Sam 28:4 • 1 Sam. 31:2-4
7 "And when he looked behind

him, he saw me and called to me.
And I said, 'Here I am.'
8 "And he said to me, 'Who are
you?' And I [t]answered him, 'I am
an Amalekite.' *said to*
9 "Then he said to me, 'Please
stand beside me and kill me; for
agony has seized me because my
life still lingers in me.'
10 "So I stood beside him and
killed him, because I knew that he
could not live after he had fallen.
And I took the crown which *was*
on his head and the bracelet
which *was* on his arm, and I have
brought them here to my lord."
11 Then [r]David took hold of his
clothes and tore them, and *so* also
did all the men who *were* with
him. Gen. 37:29, 34; Josh. 7:6
12 And they mourned and wept
and [r]fasted until evening for Saul
and his son Jonathan and for the
people of the LORD and the house
of Israel, because they had fallen
by the sword. 2 Sam. 3:35
13 And David said to the young
man who told him, "Where are
you from?" And he [t]answered, "I [r]
am the son of an alien, an Amalekite." *said* • 2 Sam. 1:8
14 Then David said to him,
"How is it you were not afraid to
stretch out your hand to destroy
the LORD's anointed?"
15 And David called one of the
young men and said, "Go, [t]cut him
down." So he struck him and he
died. *fall upon him*
16 And David said to him,
"Your [r]blood is on your head, for
your mouth has testified against
you, saying, 'I have killed the
LORD's anointed.'" 1 Sam. 26:9

17 Then David [r]chanted with
this lament over Saul and Jonathan his son, 2 Chr. 35:25
18 and he told *them* to teach the
sons of Judah *the song of* the bow;
behold, it is written in [r]the book of
Jashar. Josh. 10:13

19 "Your[t] beauty, O Israel, is
slain on your high places!
How have the mighty
fallen! *The*
20 "Tell *it* not in Gath,
Proclaim it not in the
streets of Ashkelon;
Lest the daughters of the
Philistines rejoice,
Lest the daughters of the
uncircumcised exult.
21 "O mountains of Gilboa,
Let not dew or rain be on
you, nor fields of offer-
ings;
For there the shield of the
mighty was defiled,
The shield of Saul, not
anointed with oil.
22 "From the blood of the slain,
from the fat of the
mighty,
The bow of Jonathan did
not turn back,
And the sword of Saul did
not return empty.
23 "Saul and Jonathan, beloved
and pleasant in their life,
And in their death they
were not parted;
[r]They were swifter than eagles,
They were stronger than
lions. Jer. 4:13
24 "O daughters of Israel, weep
over Saul,
Who clothed you luxuriously in scarlet,

Who put ornaments of gold
on your apparel.
25 "How[r] have the mighty fallen
in the midst of the battle!
Jonathan is slain on your
high places. 2 Sam. 1:19
26 "I am distressed for you, my
brother Jonathan;
You have been very pleas-
ant to me.
Your love to me was more
wonderful
Than the love of women.
27 "How have the mighty
fallen,
And [r]the weapons of war
perished!" Is. 13:5

CHAPTER 2

THEN it came about afterwards
that David inquired of the LORD,
saying, "Shall I go up to one of the
cities of Judah?" And the LORD
said to him, "Go up." So David
said, "Where shall I go up?" And
He said, "To[r] Hebron." Josh. 14:13
2 So David went up there, and
his two wives also, Ahinoam the
Jezreelitess and Abigail the
widow of Nabal the Carmelite.
3 And David brought up his
men who *were* with him, each
with his household; and they lived
in the cities of Hebron.
4 Then the men of Judah came
and there [r]anointed David king
over the house of Judah.
And they told David, saying, "It
was the men of Jabesh-gilead who
buried Saul." 1 Sam. 16:13
5 And David sent messengers
to the men of Jabesh-gilead, and
said to them, "May you be blessed
of the LORD because you have
[t]shown this kindness to Saul your
lord, and have buried him. *done*
6 "And now [r]may the LORD [t]show
lovingkindness and truth to you;
and I also will [t]show this goodness
to you, because you have done
this thing. Ex. 34:6 • *do*
7 "Now therefore, let your
hands be strong, and be valiant;
for Saul your lord is dead, and
also the house of Judah has
anointed me king over them."
8 But [r]Abner the son of Ner,
commander of Saul's army, had
taken [1]Ish-bosheth the son of Saul,
and brought him over to [r]Maha-
naim. 1 Sam. 14:50 • Gen. 32:2
9 And he made him king over
Gilead, over the Ashurites, over
Jezreel, over Ephraim, and over
Benjamin, even over all Israel.
10 Ish-bosheth, Saul's son, was
forty years old when he became
king over Israel, and he was king
for two years. The house of Judah,
however, followed David.
11 And the [t]time that David was
king in Hebron over the house of
Judah was seven years and six
months. *number of days*
12 Now Abner the son of Ner,
went out from Mahanaim to Gibeon with the servants of Ish-bosheth the son of Saul.
13 And Joab the son of Zeruiah
and the servants of David went
out and met them by the pool of
Gibeon; and they sat down, one on
the one side of the pool and the
other on the other side of the pool.
14 Then Abner said to Joab,
"Now let the young men arise and
[2]hold a contest before us." And
Joab said, "Let them arise."
15 So they arose and went over

[1] I.e., man of shame [2] Lit., *make sport*

by count, twelve for Benjamin and
Ish-bosheth the son of Saul, and
twelve of the servants of David.
16 And each one of them seized
his [t]opponent by the head, and
thrust his sword in his [t]opponent's
side; so they fell down together.
Therefore that place was called
[3]Helkath-hazzurim, which is in
Gibeon. *fellow • fellow's*
17 And that day the battle was
very severe, and [r]Abner and the
men of Israel were beaten before
the servants of David. 2 Sam. 3:1
18 Now the three sons of
Zeruiah were there, Joab and Abishai and Asahel; and Asahel *was*
as swift-footed as one of the gazelles which is in the field.
19 And Asahel pursued Abner
and did not turn to the right or to
the left from following Abner.
20 Then Abner looked behind
him and said, "Is that you, Asahel?" And he answered, "It is I."
21 So Abner said to him, "Turn[t]
to your right or to your left, and
take hold of one of the young men
for yourself, and take for yourself
his spoil." But Asahel was not
willing to turn aside from following him. *Turn for yourself*
22 And Abner repeated again to
Asahel, "Turn aside from following me. Why should I strike you to
the ground? How then could I lift
up my face to your brother Joab?"
23 However, he refused to turn
aside; therefore Abner struck him
in the belly with the butt end of
the spear, so that the spear came
out at his back. And he fell there
and died on the spot. And it came
about that all who came to the
place where [r]Asahel had fallen and
died, stood still. 2 Sam. 20:12
24 But Joab and Abishai pursued Abner, and when the sun
was going down, they came to the
hill of Ammah, which is in front of
Giah by the way of the wilderness
of Gibeon.
25 And the sons of Benjamin
gathered together behind Abner
and became one band, and they
stood on the top of a certain hill.
26 Then Abner called to Joab
and said, "Shall the sword devour
forever? Do you not know that it
will be bitter in the end? How long
will you refrain from telling the
people to turn back from following their brothers?"
27 And Joab said, "As God
lives, if you had not spoken,
surely then the people would have
gone away in the morning, each
from following his brother."
28 So Joab blew the trumpet;
and all the people halted and pursued Israel no longer, nor did they
continue to fight anymore.
29 Abner and his men then went
through the Arabah all that night;
so they crossed the Jordan,
walked all morning, and came to
[r]Mahanaim. 2 Sam. 2:8
30 Then Joab returned from following Abner; when he had gathered all the people together, [t]nine-
teen of David's servants besides
Asahel were missing. *nineteen men*
31 But the servants of David
had struck down many of Benjamin and Abner's men, *so that*
three hundred and sixty men died.
32 And they took up Asahel and
buried him in his father's tomb
which was in Bethlehem. Then

[3]I.e., the field of sword-edges

Joab and his men went all night
until the day dawned at Hebron.

CHAPTER 3

NOW there was a long war between the house of Saul and the
house of David; and David grew
steadily stronger, but the house of
Saul grew weaker continually.
2 Sons were born to David at
Hebron: his first-born was Amnon, by Ahinoam the Jezreelitess;
3 and his second, Chileab, by
Abigail the [t]widow of Nabal the
Carmelite; and the third, Absalom
the son of Maacah, the daughter
of Talmai, king of Geshur; *wife*
4 and the fourth, Adonijah the
son of Haggith; and the fifth,
Shephatiah the son of Abital;
5 and the sixth, Ithream, by
David's wife Eglah. These were
born to David at Hebron.
6 And it came about while
there was war between the house
of Saul and the house of David
that Abner was making himself
strong in the house of Saul.
7 Now Saul had a concubine
whose name was [r]Rizpah, the
daughter of Aiah; and Ish-bosheth
said to Abner, "Why have you
gone in to my father's concubine?" 2 Sam. 21:8-11
8 Then Abner was very angry
over the words of Ish-bosheth and
said, "Am I a dog's head that belongs to Judah? Today I show
kindness to the house of Saul your
father, to his brothers and to his
friends, and have not delivered
you into the hands of David; and
yet today you charge me with a
guilt concerning the woman.
9 "May God do so to Abner, and
more also, if [r]as the LORD has
sworn to David, I do not accomplish this for him, 1 Sam. 15:28
10 to transfer the kingdom from
the house of Saul, and to establish
the throne of David over Israel
and over Judah, [r]from Dan even to
Beersheba." 1 Sam. 3:20
11 And he could no longer answer Abner a word, because he
was afraid of him.
12 Then Abner sent messengers
to David in his place, saying,
"Whose is the land? Make your
covenant with me, and behold, my
hand shall be with you to bring all
Israel over to you."
13 And he said, "Good! I will
make a covenant with you, but I
demand one thing of you, [t]namely,
[r]you shall not see my face unless
you first bring Michal, Saul's
daughter, when you come to see
[t]me." *saying* • Gen. 43:3 • *my face*
14 So David sent messengers to
Ish-bosheth, Saul's son, saying,
"Give me my wife Michal, to
whom I was betrothed for a hundred foreskins of the Philistines."
15 And Ish-bosheth sent and
took her from *her* husband, from
Paltiel the son of Laish.
16 But her husband went with
her, weeping as he went, and followed her as far as [r]Bahurim. Then
Abner said to him, "Go, return."
So he returned. 2 Sam. 16:5
17 Now Abner had consultation
with the elders of Israel, saying,
"In times past you were seeking
for David to be king over you.
18 "Now then, do *it*! For the
LORD has spoken of David, saying,

'By ʳthe hand of My servant David
I will save My people Israel from
the hand of the Philistines and
from the hand of all their enemies.' " 1 Sam. 9:16; 15:28
19 And Abner also spoke in the
hearing of Benjamin; and in addition Abner went to speak in the
hearing of David in Hebron all
that seemed good to Israel and to
the whole house of Benjamin.
20 Then Abner and twenty men
with him came to David at Hebron. And David made a feast for
Abner and the men who were
with him.
21 And Abner said to David,
"Let me arise and go, and ʳgather
all Israel to my lord the king that
they may make a covenant with
you, and that you may be king
over all that your soul desires." So
David sent Abner away, and he
went in peace. 2 Sam. 3:10, 12
22 And behold, the servants of
David and Joab came from a raid
and brought much spoil with
them; but Abner was not with David in Hebron, for he had sent him
away, and he had gone in peace.
23 When Joab and all the army
that was with him arrived, they
told Joab, saying, "Abner the son
of Ner came to the king, and he
has sent him away, and he has
gone in peace."
24 Then Joab came to the king
and said, "What have you done?
Behold, Abner came to you; why
then have you sent him away and
he is already gone?
25 "You know Abner the son of
Ner, that he came to deceive you
and to learn of ʳyour going out and
coming in, and to find out all that
you are doing." Deut. 28:6
26 When Joab came out from
David, he sent messengers after
Abner, and they brought him back
from the well of Sirah; but David
did not know *it*.
27 So when Abner returned to
Hebron, Joab took him aside into
the middle of the gate to speak
with him privately, and there ʳhe
struck him in the belly so that he
died on account of the blood of
Asahel his brother. 2 Sam. 2:23
28 And afterward when David
heard it, he said, "I and my kingdom are innocent before the LORD
forever of the blood of Abner the
son of Ner.
29 "May it ᵗfall on the head of
Joab and on all his father's house;
and may there not fail from the
house of Joab ʳone who has a discharge, or who is a leper, or who
takes hold of a distaff, or who falls
by the sword, or who lacks
bread." *whirl* • Lev. 13:46
30 So Joab and Abishai his
brother killed Abner because he
had put their brother Asahel to
death in the battle at Gibeon.
31 Then David said to Joab and
to all the people who were with
him, "Tear ʳyour clothes and gird
on sackcloth and lament before
Abner." And King David walked
behind the bier. Gen. 37:34
32 Thus they buried Abner in
Hebron; and the king lifted up his
voice and wept at the grave of Abner, and all the people wept.
33 And ʳthe king chanted a *lament* for Abner and said,
"Should Abner die as a fool
dies? 2 Sam. 1:17

34 "Your hands were not
bound, nor your feet put
in fetters;
As one falls before the
[t]wicked, you have fallen."
And all the people wept again
over him. *sons of wickedness*
35 Then all the people came [r]to
[t]persuade David to eat bread while
it was still day; but David vowed,
saying, "May God do so to me,
and more also, if I taste bread or
anything else before the sun goes
down." 2 Sam. 12:17 • *cause*
36 Now all the people took note
of it, and it [t]pleased them, just as
everything the king did pleased all
the people. *was good in their eyes*
37 So all the people and all Israel understood that day that it
had not been *the will* of the king
to put Abner the son of Ner to
death.
38 Then the king said to his servants, "Do you not know that a
prince and a great man has fallen
this day in Israel?
39 "And I am [r]weak today,
though anointed king; and these
men [r]the sons of Zeruiah are too
difficult for me. May the LORD repay the evildoer according to his
evil." 1 Chr. 29:1 • 2 Sam. 19:5-7

CHAPTER 4

NOW when Ish-bosheth, Saul's
son, heard that [r]Abner had died in
Hebron, he lost courage, and all
Israel was disturbed. 2 Sam. 3:27
2 And Saul's son *had* two men
who were commanders of bands:
the name of the one was Baanah
and the name of the other Rechab,
sons of Rimmon the Beerothite, of
the sons of Benjamin (for [r]Beeroth
is also considered [r]*part* of Benjamin, Josh. 9:17 • Josh. 18:25
3 and the Beerothites fled to
[r]Gittaim, and have been aliens
there until this day). Neh. 11:33
4 Now [r]Jonathan, Saul's son,
had a son crippled in his feet. He
was five years old when the report
of Saul and Jonathan came from
Jezreel, and his nurse took him up
and fled. And it happened that in
her hurry to flee, he fell and became lame. And his name was
Mephibosheth. 2 Sam. 9:3, 6
5 So the sons of Rimmon the
Beerothite, Rechab and Baanah,
departed and came to the house of
[r]Ish-bosheth in the heat of the day
while he was taking his midday
rest. 2 Sam. 2:8
6 And they came to the middle
of the house as [t]if to get wheat,
and they struck him in the belly;
and Rechab and Baanah his
brother escaped. *takers of wheat*
7 Now when they came into
the house, as he was lying on his
bed in his bedroom, they struck
him and killed him and beheaded
him. And they took his head and
[t]traveled by way of the Arabah all
night. *went*
8 Then they brought the head
of Ish-bosheth to David at Hebron, and said to the king, "Behold, the head of Ish-bosheth, [r]the
son of Saul, your enemy, who
sought your life; thus the LORD
has given my lord the king vengeance this day on Saul and his
[t]descendants." 1 Sam. 24:4 • *seed*
9 And David answered Rechab
and Baanah his brother, sons of
Rimmon the Beerothite, and said
to them, "As the LORD lives, [r]who

has redeemed my life from all distress, Gen. 48:16; 1 Kin. 1:29

10 when one told me, saying, 'Behold, Saul is dead,' and thought he was bringing good news, I seized him and killed him in Ziklag, which was the reward I gave him for *his* news.

11 "How much more, when wicked men have killed a righteous man in his own house on his bed, shall I not now require his blood from your hand, and [t]destroy you from the earth?" *burn*

12 Then David commanded the young men, and they killed them and cut off their hands and feet, and hung them up beside the pool in Hebron. But they took the head of Ish-bosheth and buried it in the grave of Abner in Hebron.

CHAPTER 5

THEN all the tribes of Israel came to David at Hebron and [t]said, "Behold, we are your bone and your flesh. *said, saying*

2 "Previously, when Saul was king over us, you were the one who led Israel out and in. And the LORD said to you, 'You will shepherd My people Israel, and you will be a ruler over Israel.' "

3 So all the elders of Israel came to the king at Hebron, and King David [r]made a covenant with them before the LORD at Hebron; then they anointed David king over Israel. 2 Sam. 3:21

4 David was [r]thirty years old when he became king, *and* he reigned forty years. Gen. 41:46

5 At Hebron [r]he reigned over Judah seven years and six months, and in Jerusalem he reigned thirty-three years over all Israel and Judah. 2 Sam. 2:11

6 Now the king and his men went to Jerusalem against the Jebusites, the inhabitants of the land, and they said to [t]David, "You shall not come in here, but the blind and lame shall turn you away"; thinking, "David cannot enter here." *David, saying*

7 Nevertheless, David captured the stronghold of Zion, that is [r]the city of David. 1 Kin. 2:10

8 And David said on that day, "Whoever would strike the Jebusites, let him reach the lame and the blind, who are hated by David's soul, through the water tunnel." Therefore they say, "The blind or the lame shall not come into the house."

9 So David lived in the stronghold, and called it the city of David. And David built all around from the [4]Millo and inward.

10 And [r]David became greater and greater, for the LORD God of hosts was with him. 2 Sam. 3:1

11 [r]Then Hiram king of Tyre sent messengers to David with cedar trees and carpenters and stonemasons; and they built a house for David. 1 Chr. 14:1

12 And David realized that the LORD had established him as king over Israel, and that He had exalted his kingdom for the sake of His people Israel.

13 Meanwhile David took more concubines and wives from Jerusalem, after he came from Hebron; and more sons and daughters were born to David.

14 Now [r]these are the names of

[4] I.e., citadel

those who were born to him in Jerusalem: Shammua, Shobab, Nathan, Solomon, 1 Chr. 3:5-8
15 Ibhar, Elishua, Nepheg, Japhia,
16 Elishama, Eliada and Eliphelet.
17 When the Philistines heard
that they had anointed David king
over Israel,[r]all the Philistines went
up to seek out David; and when
David heard *of it,* he went down
to the stronghold. 1 Sam. 29:1
18 Now the Philistines came
and spread themselves out in[r]the
valley of Rephaim. Gen. 14:5
19 Then [r]David inquired of the
LORD, saying, "Shall I go up
against the Philistines? Wilt Thou
give them into my hand?" And the
LORD said to David, "Go up, for I
will certainly give the Philistines
into your hand." 1 Sam. 23:2
20 So David came to Baal-perazim, and[t]defeated them there; and
he said, "The LORD has broken
through my enemies before me
like the breakthrough of waters."
Therefore he named that place
[5]Baal-perazim. *David smote*
21 And they abandoned their
idols there, so[r]David and his men
carried them away. 1 Chr. 14:12
22 Now the Philistines came up
once again and spread themselves
out in the valley of Rephaim.
23 And when David inquired of
the LORD, He said, "You shall not
go *directly* up; circle around behind them and come at them in
front of the [6]balsam trees.
24 "And it shall be, when [r]you
hear the sound of marching in the
tops of the [6]balsam trees, then you
shall act promptly, for then [r]the
LORD will have gone out before
you to strike the army of the Philistines." 2 Kin. 7:6 • Judg. 4:14
25 Then David did so, just as
the LORD had commanded him,
and struck down the Philistines
from Geba as far as Gezer.

CHAPTER 6

[r]NOW David again gathered all
the chosen men of Israel, thirty
thousand. 1 Chr. 13:5-14
2 And David arose and went
with all the people who were with
him to Baale-judah, to bring up
from there the ark of God which is
called by the Name, the very
name of the LORD of hosts who is
enthroned *above* the cherubim.
3 And they placed the ark of
God on a new cart that they might
bring it from the house of Abinadab which was on the hill; and Uzzah and Ahio, the sons of Abinadab, were leading the new cart.
4 So [r]they brought it with the
ark of God from the house of
Abinadab, which was on the hill;
and Ahio was walking ahead of
the ark. 1 Sam. 7:1; 1 Chr. 13:7
5 Meanwhile, David and all the
house of Israel were celebrating
before the LORD with all kinds of
instruments made of fir[a]wood, and
with lyres, harps, tambourines,
castanets and cymbals. *cypress*
6 But when they came to the
[r]threshing floor of Nacon, Uzzah
reached out toward the ark of God
and took hold of it, for the oxen
nearly upset *it.* 1 Chr. 13:9
7 And the anger of the LORD
burned against Uzzah, and [r]God
struck him down there for[t]his ir-

[5]I.e., the master of breakthrough
[6]Or, *baka-shrubs*

reverence; and he died there by
the ark of God. 1 Sam. 6:19 • *the*
8 And David became angry because of the LORD's outburst
against Uzzah, and that place is
called [7]Perez-uzzah to this day.
9 So [r]David was afraid of the
LORD that day; and he said, "How
can the ark of the LORD come to
me?" Ps. 119:120; Luke 5:8
10 And David was unwilling to
move the ark of the LORD into the
city of David with him; but David
took it aside to the house of [r]Obed-
edom the Gittite. 1 Chr. 26:4-8
11 Thus the ark of the LORD remained in the house of Obed-
edom the Gittite three months,
and the LORD [r]blessed Obed-edom
and all his household. Gen. 30:27
12 Now it was told King David,
saying, "The LORD has blessed the
house of Obed-edom and all that
belongs to him, on account of the
ark of God." And David went and
brought up the ark of God from
the house of Obed-edom into the
city of David with gladness.
13 And so it was, that when the
[r]bearers of the ark of the LORD had
gone six paces, he sacrificed an ox
and a fatling. Num. 4:15
14 And [r]David was dancing before the LORD with all *his* might,
and David was [t]wearing a linen
ephod. Ex. 15:20, 21 • *girded with*
15 So David and all the house of
Israel were bringing up the ark of
the LORD with shouting and the
sound of the trumpet.
16 Then it happened *as* the ark
of the LORD came into the city of
David that Michal the daughter of
Saul looked out of the window
and saw King David leaping and
dancing before the LORD; and she
despised him in her heart.
17 So they brought in the ark of
the LORD and set it [r]in its place inside the tent which David had
pitched for it; and David offered
burnt offerings and peace offerings before the LORD. 2 Chr. 1:4
18 And when David had finished offering the burnt offering
and the peace offering, [r]he blessed
the people in the name of the
LORD of hosts. 1 Kin. 8:14, 15
19 Further, he distributed to all
the people, to all the multitude of
Israel, both to men and women, a
cake of bread and one of dates
and one of raisins to each one.
Then all the people departed each
to his house.
20 But when David returned to
bless his household, Michal the
daughter of Saul came out to meet
David and said, "How the king of
Israel distinguished himself today!
[r]He uncovered himself today in the
eyes of his servants' maids as one
of the foolish ones shamelessly
uncovers himself!" Eccl. 7:17
21 So David said to Michal, "*It*[r]
was before the LORD, who chose
me above your father and above
all his house, to appoint me ruler
over the people of the LORD, over
Israel; therefore I will celebrate
before the LORD. 1 Sam. 13:14
22 "And I will be more lightly esteemed than this and will be humble in my own eyes, but with the
maids of whom you have spoken,
with them I will be distinguished."
23 And Michal the daughter of
Saul had no child to the day of her
death.

[7]I.e., the breakthrough of Uzzah

CHAPTER 7

NOW it came about when the
king lived in his house, and the
LORD had given him rest on every
side from all his enemies,
2 that the king said to Nathan
the prophet, "See now, I dwell in a
house of cedar, but the ark of God
dwells within tent curtains."
3 And Nathan said to the king,
"Go, do all that is in your mind,
for the LORD is with you."
4 But it came about in the
same night that the word of the
LORD came to Nathan, saying,
5 "Go and say to My servant
David, 'Thus says the LORD, "Are[r]
you the one who should build Me
a house to dwell in? 1 Kin. 5:3, 4
6 "For I have not dwelt in a
house since the day I brought up
the sons of Israel from Egypt,
even to this day; but I have been
moving about in a tent, even in a
[t]tabernacle. *dwelling place*
7 "Wherever I have gone with
all the sons of Israel, did I speak a
word with one of the tribes of Israel,[r]which I commanded to shepherd My people Israel, saying,
'Why have you not built Me a
house of cedar?' " ' 2 Sam. 5:2
8 "Now therefore, thus you
shall say to My servant David,
'Thus says the LORD of hosts, "I[r]
took you from the pasture, from
following the sheep, that you
should be ruler over My people Israel. 1 Sam. 16:11, 12; Ps. 78:70, 71
9 "And I have been with you
wherever you have gone and have
cut off all your enemies from before you; and I will make you a
great name, like the names of the
great men who are on the earth.
10 "I will also appoint a place for
My people Israel and will plant
them, that they may live in their
own place and not be disturbed
again, nor will the wicked afflict
them any more as formerly,
11 even from the day that I
commanded judges to be over My
people Israel; and I will give you
rest from all your enemies. The
LORD also declares to you that the
LORD will make a house for you.
12 "When your days are complete and you lie down with your
fathers, I will raise up your [t]de-
scendant after you, who will come
forth from you, and I will establish his kingdom. *seed*
13 "He shall build a house for My
name, and I will establish the
throne of his kingdom forever.
14 "I will be a father to him and
he will be a son to Me; when he
commits iniquity, I will correct
him with the rod of men and the
strokes of the sons of men,
15 but My lovingkindness shall
not depart from him, [r]as I took *it*
away from Saul, whom I removed
from before you. 1 Sam. 15:23
16 "And your house and your
kingdom shall endure before Me
forever; your throne shall be established forever." ' "
17 In accordance with all these
words and all this vision, so Nathan spoke to David.
18 Then David the king went in
and sat before the LORD, and he
said, "Who[r]am I, O Lord GOD, and
what is my house, that Thou hast
brought me this far? Ex. 3:11
19 "And yet this was insignificant in Thine eyes, O Lord GOD,

for Thou hast spoken also of the
house of Thy servant concerning
the distant future. And this is the
custom of man, O Lord GOD.
20 "And again what more can
David say to Thee? For [r]Thou
knowest Thy servant, O Lord
GOD! 1 Sam. 16:7; John 21:17
21 "For the sake of Thy word,
and according to Thine own heart,
Thou hast done all this greatness
to let Thy servant know.
22 "For this reason Thou art
great, O Lord GOD; for there is
none like Thee, and there is no
God besides Thee, according to all
that we have heard with our ears.
23 "And what one nation on the
earth is like Thy people Israel,
whom God went to redeem for
Himself as a people and to make a
name for Himself, and to do a
great thing for Thee and awesome
things for Thy land, before Thy
people whom Thou hast redeemed
for Thyself from Egypt, *from* nations and their gods?
24 "For Thou hast established for
Thyself Thy people Israel as Thine
own people forever, and Thou, O
LORD, hast become their God.
25 "Now therefore, O LORD God,
the word that Thou hast spoken
concerning Thy servant and his
house, confirm *it* forever, and do
as Thou hast spoken,
26 that Thy name may be magnified forever, by saying, 'The
LORD of hosts is God over Israel';
and may the house of Thy servant
David be established before Thee.
27 "For Thou, O LORD of hosts,
the God of Israel, hast made a revelation to Thy servant, saying, 'I
will build you a house'; therefore
Thy servant has found courage to
pray this prayer to Thee.
28 "And now, O Lord GOD, Thou
art God, and Thy words are truth,
and Thou hast [a]promised this good
thing to Thy servant. *spoken*
29 "Now therefore, may it please
Thee to bless the house of Thy servant, that it may continue forever
before Thee. For Thou, O Lord
GOD, hast spoken; and with Thy
blessing may the house of Thy
servant be blessed forever."

CHAPTER 8

NOW after this it came about
that David defeated the Philistines
and subdued them; and David
took control of the chief city from
the hand of the Philistines.
2 And he [t]defeated Moab, and
measured them with the line,
making them lie down on the
ground; and he measured two
lines to put to death and one full
line to keep alive. And the Moabites became servants to David,
bringing tribute. *smote*
3 Then David [t]defeated Hadadezer, the son of Rehob king of Zobah, as he went to restore his [t]rule
at the [8]River. *smote • hand*
4 And David captured from
him 1,700 horsemen and 20,000
foot soldiers; and David [r]ham-
strung the chariot horses, but reserved *enough* of them for 100
chariots. Josh. 11:6, 9
5 And when the Arameans of
Damascus came to help Hadadezer, king of Zobah, David [t]killed
22,000 Arameans. *smote*
6 Then David put garrisons
among the Arameans of Damas-

[8]I.e., Euphrates

cus, and [r]the Arameans became
servants to David, bringing tribute. And the LORD helped David
wherever he went. 2 Sam. 8:2
7 And David took the shields
of gold which were [t]carried by the
servants of Hadadezer, and
brought them to Jerusalem. *on*
8 And from Betah and from
[r]Berothai, cities of Hadadezer,
King David took a very large
amount of bronze. Ezek. 47:16
9 Now when Toi king of Hamath heard that David had defeated all the army of Hadadezer,
10 Toi sent Joram his son to
King David to greet him and bless
him, because he had fought
against Hadadezer and defeated
him; for Hadadezer [t]had been at
war with Toi. And *Joram* brought
with him articles of silver, of gold
and of bronze. *was a man of wars*
11 King David also [r]dedicated
these to the LORD, with the silver
and gold that he had dedicated
from all the nations which he had
subdued: 1 Kin. 7:51
12 from [9]Aram and [r]Moab and
the sons of Ammon and the Philistines and Amalek, and from the
spoil of Hadadezer, son of Rehob,
king of Zobah. 2 Sam. 8:2
13 So David made a name *for
himself* when he returned from
[t]killing 18,000 [9]Arameans in the
Valley of Salt. *smiting*
14 And he put garrisons in
Edom. In all Edom he put garrisons, and all the Edomites became
servants to David. And the LORD
helped David wherever he went.
15 So David reigned over all Israel; and David [t]administered justice and righteousness for all his
people. *was doing*
16 And [r]Joab the son of Zeruiah
was over the army, and [r]Jehosha-
phat the son of Ahilud *was* recorder. 1 Chr. 11:6 • 1 Kin. 4:3
17 And [r]Zadok the son of Ahitub
and Ahimelech the son of Abiathar *were* priests, and Seraiah
was secretary. 1 Chr. 6:4-8
18 And Benaiah the son of Jehoiada was over the Cherethites
and the Pelethites; and David's
sons were chief ministers.

CHAPTER 9

THEN David said, "Is there yet
[t]anyone left of the house of Saul,
that I may show him kindness for
Jonathan's sake?" *he who is*
2 Now there was a servant of
the house of Saul whose name
was Ziba, and they called him to
David; and the king said to him,
"Are you [r]Ziba?" And he said, "*I
am* your servant." 2 Sam. 16:1-4
3 And the king said, "Is there
not yet anyone of the house of
Saul to whom I may show the
[r]kindness of God?" And Ziba said
to the king, "There [r]is still a son of
Jonathan who is crippled in both
feet." 1 Sam. 20:14 • 2 Sam. 4:4
4 So the king said to him,
"Where is he?" And Ziba said to
the king, "Behold, he is [r]in the
house of Machir the son of Ammiel in Lo-debar." 2 Sam. 17:27-29
5 Then King David sent and
brought him from the house of
Machir the son of Ammiel, from
Lo-debar.
6 And Mephibosheth, the son
of Jonathan the son of Saul, came

[9]Some mss. read *Edom(ites)*

to David and fell on his face and prostrated himself. And David said, "Mephibosheth." And he said, "Here is your servant!"

7 And David said to him, "Do not fear, for I will surely show kindness to you for the sake of your father Jonathan, and will restore to you all the [t]land of your grandfather Saul; and you shall eat at my table regularly." *field*

8 Again he prostrated himself and said, "What is your servant, that you should regard [r]a dead dog like me?" 2 Sam. 16:9; 24:14

9 Then the king called Saul's servant Ziba, and said to him, "All that belonged to Saul and to all his house I have given to your master's [t]grandson. *son*

10 "And you and your sons and your servants shall cultivate the land for him, and you shall bring in *the produce* so that your master's grandson may have food; nevertheless Mephibosheth your master's grandson shall eat at my table regularly." Now Ziba had fifteen sons and twenty servants.

11 Then Ziba said to the king, "According to all that my lord the king commands his servant so your servant will do." So Mephibosheth ate at [t]David's table as one of the king's sons. *my*

12 And Mephibosheth had a young son whose name was Mica. And all who lived in the house of Ziba were servants to Mephibosheth.

13 So Mephibosheth lived in Jerusalem, for [r]he ate at the king's table regularly. Now he was lame in both feet. 2 Sam. 9:7, 11

CHAPTER 10

NOW it happened afterwards that [r]the king of the Ammonites died, and Hanun his son became king in his place. 1 Sam. 11:1

2 Then David said, "I will show kindness to Hanun the son of Nahash, just as his father showed kindness to me." So David sent some of his servants to console him concerning his father. But when David's servants came to the land of the Ammonites,

3 the princes of the Ammonites said to Hanun their lord, "Do you think that David is honoring your father because he has sent consolers to you? [r]Has David not sent his servants to you in order to search the city, to spy it out and overthrow it?" Gen. 42:9, 16

4 So Hanun took David's servants and [r]shaved off half of their beards, and cut off their garments in the middle as far as their hips, and sent them away. Is. 15:2

5 When they told *it* to David, he sent to meet them, for the men were greatly humiliated. And the king said, "Stay[t] at Jericho until your beards grow, and then return." *Return to*

6 Now when the sons of Ammon saw that [r]they had become odious to David, the sons of Ammon sent and hired the Arameans of Beth-rehob and the Arameans of Zobah, 20,000 foot soldiers, and the king of Maacah with 1,000 men, and the men of Tob with 12,000 men. Gen. 34:30

7 When David heard *of it,* he sent Joab and all the army, the mighty men.

8 And the sons of Ammon
came out and drew up in battle array [r]at the entrance of the [t]city,
while the Arameans of Zobah and
of Rehob and the men of Tob and
Maacah *were* by themselves in the
field. 1 Chr. 19:9 • *gate*
9 Now when Joab saw that the
battle was set against him in front
and in the rear, he selected from
all the choice men of Israel, and
arrayed *them* against the Arameans.
10 But the remainder of the people he placed in the hand of A-
bishai his brother, and he arrayed
them against the sons of Ammon.
11 And he said, "If the Arameans are too strong for me, then
you shall help me, but if the sons
of Ammon are too strong for you,
then I will come to help you.
12 "Be strong, and let us show
ourselves courageous for the sake
of our people and for the cities of
our God; and may the LORD do
what is good in His sight."
13 So Joab and the people who
were with him drew near to the
battle against the Arameans, and
they fled before him.
14 When the sons of Ammon
saw that the Arameans fled, they
also fled before Abishai and entered the city. Then Joab returned
from *fighting* against the sons of
Ammon and came to Jerusalem.
15 When the Arameans saw
that they had been [t]defeated by Israel, they gathered themselves together. *smitten before*
16 And Hadadezer sent and
brought out the Arameans who
were beyond the [10]River, and they
came to Helam; and Shobach the
commander of the army of Hadadezer [t]led them. *before*
17 Now when it was told David,
he gathered all Israel together and
crossed the Jordan, and came to
Helam. And the Arameans arrayed themselves to meet David
and fought against him.
18 But the Arameans fled before
Israel, and David killed 700 charioteers of the Arameans and
40,000 horsemen and struck down
Shobach the commander of their
army, and he died there.
19 When all the kings, servants
of Hadadezer, saw that they were
defeated by Israel, they made
peace with Israel and served
them. So the Arameans feared to
help the sons of Ammon anymore.

CHAPTER 11

THEN it happened in the spring,
at the time when kings go out *to
battle*, that David sent Joab and
his servants with him and all Israel, and they destroyed the sons
of Ammon and besieged Rabbah.
But David stayed at Jerusalem.
2 Now when evening came David arose from his bed and walked
around on the roof of the king's
house, and from the roof he saw a
woman bathing; and the woman
was very beautiful in appearance.
3 So David sent and inquired
about the woman. And one said,
"Is this not [r]Bathsheba, the daughter of Eliam, the wife of [r]Uriah the
Hittite?" 1 Chr. 3:5 • 2 Sam. 23:39
4 And David sent messengers
and took her, and when she came
to him, [r]he lay with her; [r]and when
she had purified herself from her

[10] I.e., Euphrates

uncleanness, she returned to her
house. James 1:14, 15 • Lev. 12:2-5
5 And the woman conceived;
and she sent and told David, and
said, "I[r]am pregnant." Lev. 20:10
6 Then David sent to Joab,
saying, "Send me Uriah the Hittite." So Joab sent Uriah to David.
7 When Uriah came to him,
David asked concerning the welfare of Joab and [t]the people and
the state of the war. *welfare of*
8 Then David said to Uriah,
"Go down to your house, and
[r]wash your feet." And Uriah went
out of the king's house, and a
present from the king [t]was sent
out after him. Gen. 43:24 • *went out*
9 But Uriah slept at the door of
the king's house with all the servants of his lord, and did not go
down to his house.
10 Now when they told David,
saying, "Uriah did not go down to
his house," David said to Uriah,
"Have you not come from a journey? Why did you not go down to
your house?"
11 And Uriah said to David,
"The[r]ark and Israel and Judah are
staying in[a]temporary shelters, and
my lord Joab and the servants of
my lord are camping in the open
field. Shall I then go to my house
to eat and to drink and to lie with
my wife? By your life and the life
of your soul, I will not do this
thing." 2 Sam. 7:2, 6 • *booths*
12 Then David said to Uriah,
"Stay here today also, and tomorrow I will let you go." So Uriah
remained in Jerusalem that day
and the[t]next. *morrow*
13 Now David called him, and
he ate and drank before him, and
he made him drunk; and in the
evening he went out to lie on his
bed with his lord's servants, but
he did not go down to his house.
14 Now it came about in the
morning that David[r]wrote a letter
to Joab, and sent *it* by the hand of
Uriah. 1 Kin. 21:8-10
15 And he had written in the letter, saying, "Place Uriah in the
front line of the fiercest battle and
withdraw from him, so that he
may be struck down and die."
16 So it was as Joab kept watch
on the city, that he put Uriah at
the place where he knew there
were valiant men.
17 And the men of the city went
out and fought against Joab, and
some of the people among David's
servants fell; and[r]Uriah the Hittite
also died. 2 Sam. 11:21
18 Then Joab sent and reported
to David all the events of the war.
19 And he charged the messenger, saying, "When you have finished telling all the events of the
war to the king,
20 and if it happens that the
king's wrath rises and he says to
you, 'Why did you go so near to
the city to fight? Did you not
know that they would shoot from
the wall?
21 'Who[r]struck down Abimelech
the son of Jerubbesheth? Did not a
woman throw an upper millstone
on him from the wall so that he
died at Thebez? Why did you go
so near the wall?'—then you shall
say, 'Your servant Uriah the Hittite is dead also.'" Judg. 9:50-54
22 So the messenger departed
and came and reported to David
all that Joab had sent him *to tell*.

23 And the messenger said to
David, "The men prevailed
against us and came out against
us in the field, but we [t]pressed
them as far as the entrance of the
gate. *were upon*
24 "Moreover, the archers shot
at your servants from the wall; so
some of the king's servants are
dead, and your servant Uriah the
Hittite is also dead."
25 Then David said to the messenger, "Thus you shall say to
Joab, 'Do not let this thing [t]dis-
please you, for the sword devours
one as well as another; make your
battle against the city stronger
and overthrow it;' and *so* encourage him." *be evil in your sight*
26 Now when the wife of Uriah
heard that Uriah her husband was
dead, [r]she mourned for her husband. Gen. 50:10; Deut. 34:8
27 When the *time of* mourning
was over, David sent and brought
her to his house and she became
his wife; then she bore him a son.
But the thing that David had done
was evil in the sight of the LORD.

CHAPTER 12

THEN the LORD sent [r]Nathan to
David. And he came to him, and
[t]said, 2 Sam. 7:2, 4 • *said to him*

"There were two men in one city, the one rich and the other poor.
2 "The rich man had a great many flocks and herds.
3 "But the poor man had nothing except [r]one little ewe lamb
Which he bought and nourished;
And it grew up together with him and his children.
It would eat of his [t]bread and drink of his cup and lie in his bosom,
And was like a daughter to him. 2 Sam. 11:3 • *morsel*
4 "Now a traveler came to the rich man,
And he [t]was unwilling to take from his own flock or his own herd,
To prepare for the wayfarer who had come to him;
Rather he took the poor man's ewe lamb and prepared it for the man who had come to him." *spared*

5 Then David's anger burned
greatly against the man, and he
said to Nathan, "As the LORD
lives, surely the man who has
done this deserves to die.
6 "And he must make restitution for the lamb [r]fourfold, because he did this thing and had no
compassion." Ex. 22:1; Luke 19:8
7 Nathan then said to David,
"You [r]are the man! Thus says the
LORD God of Israel, 'It is I who
anointed you king over Israel and
it is I who delivered you from the
hand of Saul. 1 Kin. 20:42
8 'I also gave you your master's
house and your master's wives
into your [t]care, and I gave you the
house of Israel and Judah; and if
that had been too little, I would
have added to you many more
things like these! *bosom*
9 'Why have you despised the
word of the LORD by doing evil in
His sight? You have struck down
Uriah the Hittite with the sword,

have taken his wife to be your
wife, and have killed him with the
sword of the sons of Ammon.
10 'Now therefore, the sword
shall never depart from your
house, because you have despised
Me and have taken the wife of
Uriah the Hittite to be your wife.'
11 "Thus says the LORD, 'Behold,
I will raise up evil against you
from your own household; I will
even take your wives before your
eyes, and give *them* to your companion, and he shall lie with your
wives in broad daylight.
12 'Indeed you did it secretly,
but I will do this thing before all
Israel, and under the sun.' "
13 Then David said to Nathan,
"I have sinned against the LORD."
And Nathan said to David, "The
LORD also has [r]taken away your
sin; you shall not die. Mic. 7:18
14 "However, because by this
deed you have [r]given occasion to
the enemies of the LORD to blaspheme, the child also that is born
to you shall surely die." Is. 52:5
15 So Nathan went to his house.
Then the LORD struck the child
that Uriah's [t]widow bore to David,
so that he was *very* sick. *wife*
16 David therefore inquired of
God for the child; and David
[r]fasted and went and lay all night
on the ground. Neh. 1:4
17 And [r]the elders of his household stood beside him in order to
raise him up from the ground, but
he was unwilling and would not
eat food with them. Gen. 24:2
18 Then it happened on the seventh day that the child died. And
the servants of David were afraid
to tell him that the child was dead,
for they said, "Behold, while the
child was *still* alive, we spoke to
him and he did not listen to our
voice. How then can we tell him
that the child is dead, since he
might do *himself* harm!"
19 But when David saw that his
servants were whispering together, David perceived that the
child was dead; so David said to
his servants, "Is the child dead?"
And they said, "He is dead."
20 So David arose from the
ground, [r]washed, anointed *himself*,
and changed his clothes; and he
came into the house of the LORD
and [r]worshiped. Then he came to
his own house, and when he requested, they set food before him
and he ate. Ruth 3:3 • Ps. 95:6-8
21 Then his servants said to
him, "What is this thing that you
have done? [t]While the child was
alive, you fasted and wept; but
when the child died, you arose
and ate food." *On account of*
22 And he said, "While the child
was *still* alive, [r]I fasted and wept;
for I said, 'Who knows, the LORD
may be gracious to me, that the
child may live.' Is. 38:1-3
23 "But now he has died; why
should I fast? Can I bring him
back again? I shall go to him, but
he will not return to me."
24 Then David comforted his
wife Bathsheba, and went in to
her and lay with her; and she gave
birth to a son, and [r]he named him
Solomon. Now the LORD loved
him 1 Chr. 22:9; Matt. 1:6
25 and sent *word* through Nathan the prophet, and he named
him [11]Jedidiah for the LORD's sake.
26 Now Joab fought against

[11]I.e., beloved of the LORD

Rabbah of the sons of Ammon,
and captured the royal city.
27 And Joab sent messengers to
David and said, "I have fought
against Rabbah, I have even captured the city of waters.
28 "Now therefore, gather the
rest of the people together and
camp against the city and capture
it, lest I capture the city myself
and it be named after me."
29 So David gathered all the
people and went to Rabbah,
fought against it, and captured it.
30 Then he took the crown of
[a]their king from his head; and its
weight *was* a talent of gold, and *in
it was* a precious stone; and it was
placed on David's head. And he
brought out the spoil of the city in
great amounts. *Malcam*
31 He also brought out the people who were in it, and [r]set *them*
under saws, sharp iron instruments, and iron axes, and made
them pass through the brickkiln.
And thus he did to all the cities of
the sons of Ammon. Then David
and all the people returned *to* Jerusalem. 1 Chr. 20:3; Heb. 11:37

CHAPTER 13

NOW it was after this that [r]Absa-
lom the son of David had a beautiful sister whose name was Tamar,
and Amnon the son of David
loved her. 2 Sam. 3:2, 3
2 And Amnon was so frus-
trated because of his sister Tamar
that he made himself ill, for she
was a virgin, and it seemed hard
to Amnon to do anything to her.
3 But Amnon had a friend
whose name was Jonadab, the son
of Shimeah, David's brother; and
Jonadab was a very shrewd man.
4 And he said to him, "O son of
the king, why are you so de-
pressed morning after morning?
Will you not tell me?" Then Amnon said to him, "I am in love with
Tamar, the sister of my brother
Absalom."
5 Jonadab then said to him,
"Lie down on your bed and pretend to be ill; when your father
comes to see you, say to him,
'Please let my sister Tamar come
and give me *some* food to eat, and
let her prepare the food in my
sight, that I may see *it* and eat
from her hand.' "
6 So Amnon lay down and pretended to be ill; when the king
came to see him, Amnon said to
the king, "Please let my sister Tamar come and [r]make me a couple
of cakes in my sight, that I may
eat from her hand." Gen. 18:6
7 Then David sent to the house
for Tamar, saying, "Go now to
your brother Amnon's house, and
prepare food for him."
8 So Tamar went to her
brother Amnon's house, and he
was lying down. And she took
dough, kneaded *it*, made cakes in
his sight, and baked the cakes.
9 And she took the pan and
[t]dished *them* out before him, but
he refused to eat. And Amnon
said, "Have [r]everyone go out from
me." So everyone went out from
him. *poured* • Gen. 45:1
10 Then Amnon said to Tamar,
"Bring the food into the [a]bedroom,
that I may eat from your hand."
So Tamar took the cakes which
she had made and brought them

into the bedroom to her brother
Amnon. *inner room*
11 When she brought *them* to
him to eat, he[r] took hold of her and
said to her, "Come, lie with me,
my sister." Gen. 39:12
12 But she answered him, "No,
my brother, do not violate me, for
such a thing is not done in Israel;
do not do this disgraceful thing!
13 "As for me, where could I get
rid of my reproach? And as for
you, you will be like one of the
fools in Israel. Now therefore,
please speak to the king, for he
will not withhold me from you."
14 However, he would not listen
to[t] her; since he was stronger than
she, he[r] violated her and lay with
her. *her voice* • Lev. 18:9
15 Then Amnon hated her with
a very great hatred; for the hatred
with which he hated her was
greater than the love with which
he had loved her. And Amnon said
to her, "Get up, go away!"
16 But she said to him, "No, because this wrong in sending me
away is greater than the other
that you have done to me!" Yet he
would not listen to her.
17 Then he called his young
man who attended him and said,
"Now throw this woman out of
my *presence,* and lock the door
behind her."
18 Now she had on a long-
sleeved garment; for in this manner the virgin daughters of the
king dressed themselves in robes.
Then his attendant took her out
and locked the door behind her.
19 And Tamar put[a] ashes on her
head, and tore her[t] long-sleeved
garment which *was* on her; and
she put her hand on her head and
went away, crying aloud as she
went. *dust* • *varicolored tunic*
20 Then Absalom her brother
said to her, "Has Amnon your
brother been with you? But now
keep silent, my sister, he is your
brother; do not take this matter to
heart." So Tamar remained and
was desolate in her brother Absalom's house.
21 Now when King David heard
of all these matters, he was very
angry.
22 But Absalom did not speak
to Amnon either good or bad; for
Absalom hated Amnon because
he had violated his sister Tamar.
23 Now it came about after two
full years that Absalom had
sheepshearers in Baal-hazor,
which is near Ephraim, and Absalom invited all the king's sons.
24 And Absalom came to the
king and said, "Behold now, your
servant has sheepshearers; please
let the king and his servants go
with your servant."
25 But the king said to Absalom, "No, my son, we should not
all go, lest we be burdensome to
you." Although he urged him, he
would not go, but blessed him.
26 Then[r] Absalom said, "If not,
please let my brother Amnon go
with us." And the king said to
him, "Why should he go with
you?" 2 Sam. 3:27; 11:13-15
27 But when Absalom urged
him, he let Amnon and all the
king's sons go with him.
28 And Absalom commanded
his servants, saying, "See now,
when Amnon's heart is merry
with wine, and when I say to you,

'Strike Amnon,' then put him to
death. Do not fear; have not I myself commanded you? Be courageous and be valiant."
29 And the servants of Absalom
did to Amnon just as Absalom
had commanded. Then all the
king's sons arose and each
mounted his mule and fled.
30 Now it was while they were
on the way that the report came to
David, saying, "Absalom has
struck down all the king's sons,
and not one of them is left."
31 Then the king arose,[r]tore his
clothes and lay on the ground; and
all his servants were standing by
with clothes torn. 2 Sam. 1:11
32 And Jonadab, the son of
Shimeah, David's brother, responded, "Do not let my lord suppose they have put to death all the
young men, the king's sons, for
Amnon alone is dead; because by
the intent of Absalom this has
been determined since the day
that he violated his sister Tamar.
33 "Now therefore, do not let my
lord the king [r]take the report to
[t]heart, namely, 'all the king's sons
are dead,' for only Amnon is
dead." 2 Sam. 19:19 • *his heart*
34 Now [r]Absalom had fled. And
the young man who was the
watchman raised his eyes and
looked, and behold, many people
were coming from the road behind him by the side of the mountain. 2 Sam. 13:37, 38
35 And Jonadab said to the
king, "Behold, the king's sons
have come; according to your servant's word, so it happened."
36 And it came about as soon as
he had finished speaking, that behold, the king's sons came and
lifted their voices and wept; and
also the king and all his servants
wept very bitterly.
37 Now Absalom fled and went
to Talmai the son of Ammihud,
the king of Geshur. And *David*
mourned for his son every day.
38 [r]So Absalom had fled and
gone to Geshur, and was there
three years. 2 Sam. 13:34
39 And *the heart of* King David
longed to go out to Absalom; for
he was comforted concerning
Amnon, since he was dead.

CHAPTER 14

NOW Joab the son of Zeruiah
perceived that the king's heart
was inclined toward Absalom.
2 So Joab sent to Tekoa and
[t]brought a wise woman from there
and said to her, "Please pretend to
be a mourner, and put on mourning garments now, and do not
anoint yourself with oil, but like a
woman who has been mourning
for the dead many days; *took*
3 then go to the king and speak
to him in this manner." So Joab
put the words in her mouth.
4 Now when the woman of Tekoa [12]spoke to the king, she fell on
her face to the ground and [r]pros-
trated herself and said, "Help, O
king." 1 Sam. 25:23
5 And the king said to her,
"What is your trouble?" And she
[t]answered, "Truly I am a widow,
for my husband is dead. *said*
6 "And your maidservant had
two sons, but the two of them
struggled together in the field, and
there was no [13]one to separate

[12] Many mss. and ancient versions read *came*
[13] Lit., *deliverer between*

them, so one struck the other and
killed him.
7 "Now behold, the whole family has risen against your maidservant, and they say, 'Hand over the
one who struck his brother, that
we may put him to death for the
life of his brother whom he killed,
and destroy the heir also.' Thus
they will extinguish my coal
which is left, so as to leave my
husband neither name nor remnant on the face of the earth."
8 Then the king said to the
woman, "Go to your house, and I
will give orders concerning you."
9 And the woman of Tekoa
said to the king, "O my lord, the
king, the iniquity is on me and my
father's house, but the king and
his throne are guiltless."
10 So the king said, "Whoever
speaks to you, bring him to me,
and he will not touch you anymore."
11 Then she said, "Please let the
king remember the LORD your
God, [r]*so that* the avenger of blood
may not continue to destroy, lest
they destroy my son." And he
said, "As the LORD lives, not one
hair of your son shall fall to the
ground." Num. 35:19, 21
12 Then the woman said,
"Please let your maidservant
speak a word to my lord the
king." And he said, "Speak."
13 And the woman said, "Why[r]
then have you planned such a
thing against the people of God?
For in speaking this word the king
is as one who is guilty, *in that* the
king does not bring back his banished one. 2 Sam. 12:7
14 "For [r]we shall surely die and
are like water spilled on the
ground which cannot be gathered
up again. Yet God does not take
away life, but plans [t]ways so that
the banished one may not be cast
out from him. Job 30:23 • *devices*
15 "Now [t]the reason I have come
to speak this word to my lord the
king is because the people have
made me afraid; so your maidservant said, 'Let me now speak to
the king, perhaps the king will
perform the [t]request of his maidservant. *that* • *word*
16 'For the king will hear [t]and deliver his maidservant from the
hand of the man who would destroy both me and my son from
the inheritance of God.' *to*
17 "Then your maidservant said,
'Please let the word of my lord the
king be comforting, for as the angel of God, so is my lord the king
to discern good and evil. And may
the LORD your God be with you.' "
18 Then the king answered and
said to the woman, "Please do not
hide anything from me that I am
about to ask you." And the
woman said, "Let my lord the
king please speak."
19 So the king said, "Is the hand
of Joab with you in all this?" And
the woman answered and said,
"As your soul lives, my lord the
king, no one can turn to the right
or to the left from anything that
my lord the king has spoken. Indeed, it was your servant Joab
who commanded me, and it was
he who put all these words in the
mouth of your maidservant;
20 in order to change the appearance of things your servant
Joab has done this thing. But my

lord is wise, [r]like the wisdom of
the angel of God, to know all that
is in the earth." 2 Sam. 14:17
21 Then the king said to Joab,
"Behold now, I will surely do this
thing; go therefore, bring back the
young man Absalom."
22 And Joab fell on his face to
the ground, prostrated himself
and blessed the king; then Joab
said, "Today your servant knows
that I have found favor in your
sight, O my lord, the king, in that
the king has performed the [t]re-
quest of his servant." *word*
23 So Joab arose and went to
[r]Geshur, and brought Absalom to
Jerusalem. Deut. 3:14
24 However the king said, "Let
him turn to his own house, and let
him not see my face." So Absalom
turned to his own house and did
not see the king's face.
25 Now in all Israel was no one
as handsome as Absalom, so
highly praised; [r]from the sole of his
foot to the crown of his head there
was no defect in him. Job 2:7
26 And when he cut the hair of
his head (and it was at the end of
every year that he cut *it*, for it was
heavy on him so he cut it), he
weighed the hair of his head at
200 shekels by the king's weight.
27 And to Absalom there were
born three sons, and one daughter
whose name was Tamar; she was
a woman of beautiful appearance.
28 Now Absalom lived two full
years in Jerusalem, [r]and did not
see the king's face. 2 Sam. 14:24
29 Then Absalom sent for Joab,
to send him to the king, but he
would not come to him. So he sent
again a second time, but he would
not come.
30 Therefore he said to his servants, "See, Joab's [14]field is next to
mine, and he has barley there; go
and set it on fire." So Absalom's
servants set the field on fire.
31 Then Joab arose, came to
Absalom at his house and said to
him, "Why have your servants set
my [14]field on fire?"
32 And Absalom answered
Joab, "Behold, I sent for you, saying, 'Come here, that I may send
you to the king, to say, "Why have
I come from Geshur? It would be
better for me still to be there."'
Now therefore, let me see the
king's face; and if there is iniquity
in me, let him put me to death."
33 So when Joab came to the
king and told him, he called for
Absalom. Thus he came to the
king and prostrated himself on his
face to the ground before the king,
and the king kissed Absalom.

CHAPTER 15

NOW it came about after this
that Absalom provided for himself
a chariot and horses, and fifty
men as runners before him.
2 And Absalom used to rise
early and [r]stand beside the way to
the gate; and it happened that
when any man had a suit to come
to the king for judgment, Absalom
would call to him and say, "From
what city are you?" And he would
say, "Your servant is from one of
the tribes of Israel." Ruth 4:1
3 Then Absalom would say to
him, "See, your claims are good

[14] Lit., *portion*

and right, but no man listens to
you on the part of the king."
4 Moreover, Absalom would
say, "Oh[r] that one would appoint
me judge in the land, then every
man who has any suit or cause
could come to me, and I would
give him justice." Judg. 9:29
5 And it happened that when a
man came near to prostrate himself before him, he would put out
his hand and take hold of him and
[r]kiss him. 2 Sam. 14:33; 20:9
6 And in this manner Absalom
dealt with all Israel who came to
the king for judgment; [r]so Absalom stole away the hearts of the
men of Israel. Rom. 16:18
7 Now it came about at the
end of [15]forty years that Absalom
said to the king, "Please let me go
and pay my vow which I have
vowed to the LORD, in Hebron.
8 "For your servant vowed a
vow while I was living at Geshur
in Aram, saying, 'If the LORD shall
indeed bring me back to Jerusalem, then I will serve the LORD.' "
9 And the king said to him,
"Go in peace." So he arose and
went to Hebron.
10 But Absalom sent spies
throughout all the tribes of Israel,
saying, "As soon as you hear the
sound of the trumpet, then you
shall say, 'Absalom[r] is king in Hebron.' " 1 Kin. 1:34; 2 Kin. 9:13
11 Then two hundred men went
with Absalom from Jerusalem,
who were invited and went [t]inno-
cently, and they did not know
anything. *in their integrity*
12 And Absalom sent for
Ahithophel the Gilonite, David's
counselor, from his city Giloh,
while he was offering the sacrifices. And the conspiracy was
strong, for the people increased
continually with Absalom.
13 Then a messenger came to
David, saying, "The hearts of the
men of Israel are with Absalom."
14 And David said to all his servants who were with him at Jerusalem, "Arise[r] and let us flee, for
otherwise none of us shall escape
from Absalom. Go in haste, lest he
overtake us quickly and bring
down calamity on us and strike
the city with the edge of the
sword." 2 Sam. 12:11
15 Then the king's servants said
to the king, "Behold, your servants *are ready to do* whatever
my lord the king chooses."
16 So the king went out and all
his household [t]with him. But the
king left ten concubines to keep
the house. *at his feet*
17 And the king went out and
all the people with him, and they
stopped at the last house.
18 Now all his servants passed
on beside him, all the Cherethites,
all the Pelethites, and all the Git-
tites, six hundred men who had
come [t]with him from Gath, passed
on before the king. *at his feet*
19 Then the king said to [r]Ittai
the Gittite, "Why will you also go
with us? Return and remain with
the king, for you are a foreigner
and also an exile; *return* to your
own place. 2 Sam. 18:2
20 "You came *only* yesterday,
and shall I today make you wander with us, while [r]I go where I
will? Return and take back your

[15]Some ancient versions render *four*

brothers; mercy and[a]truth be with
you." 1 Sam. 23:13 • *faithfulness*
21 But Ittai answered the king
and said, "As the LORD lives, and
as my lord the king lives, surely
wherever my lord the king may
be, whether for death or for life,
there also your servant will be."
22 Therefore David said to Ittai,
"Go and pass over." So Ittai the
Gittite passed over with all his
men and all the little ones who
were with him.
23 While all the country was
weeping with a loud voice, all the
people passed over. The king also
passed over the brook Kidron, and
all the people passed over toward
the way of the wilderness.
24 Now behold, [r]Zadok also
came, and all the Levites with him
carrying the ark of the covenant
of God. And they set down the ark
of God, and Abiathar came up until all the people had finished passing from the city. 2 Sam. 8:17
25 And the king said to Zadok,
"Return the ark of God to the city.
If I find favor in the sight of the
LORD, then[r]He will bring me back
again, and show me both it and
His habitation. Ps. 43:3
26"But if He should say thus, 'I
have no delight in you,' behold,
here I am, let Him do to me as
seems good[t]to Him." *in His sight*
27 The king said also to Zadok
the priest, "Are you *not* [r]a seer?
Return to the city in peace and
your two sons with you, your son
Ahimaaz and Jonathan the son of
Abiathar. 1 Sam. 9:6-9
28"See, I am going to wait at the
fords of the wilderness until word
comes from you to inform me."

29 Therefore Zadok and Abiathar returned the ark of God to
Jerusalem and remained there.
30 And David went up the ascent of the *Mount of* Olives, and
wept as he went, and his head was
covered and he walked barefoot.
Then all the people who were with
him each covered his head and
went up weeping as they went.
31 Now someone told David,
saying, "Ahithophel[r]is among the
conspirators with Absalom." And
David said, "O LORD, I pray, make
the counsel of Ahithophel foolishness." 2 Sam. 15:12
32 It happened as David was
coming to the summit, where God
was worshiped, that behold, Hushai the Archite met him with his
coat torn, and dust on his head.
33 And David said to him, "If
you pass over with me, then you
will be a burden to me.
34"But if you return to the city,
and say to Absalom, 'I will be
your servant, O king; as I have
been your father's servant in time
past, so I will now be your servant,' then you can thwart the
counsel of Ahithophel for me.
35"And are not Zadok and Abiathar the priests with you there?
So it shall be that [r]whatever you
hear from the king's house, you
shall report to Zadok and Abiathar the priests. 2 Sam. 17:15, 16
36"Behold [r]their two sons are
with them there, Ahimaaz, Zadok's son and Jonathan, Abiathar's son; and by them you shall
send me everything that you
hear." 2 Sam. 15:27
37 So Hushai, David's friend,

came into the city, and Absalom
came into Jerusalem.

CHAPTER 16

NOW when David had passed a
little beyond the summit, behold,
Ziba the servant of Mephibosheth
met him with a couple of saddled
donkeys, and on them *were* two
hundred loaves of bread, a hundred clusters of raisins, a hundred
summer fruits, and a jug of wine.
2 And the king said to Ziba,
"Why do you have these?" And
Ziba said, "The[r] donkeys are for
the king's household to ride, and
the bread and summer fruit for
the young men to eat, and the
wine, for whoever is faint in the
wilderness to drink." Judg. 10:4
3 Then the king said, "And
where is [r]your master's son?" And
Ziba said to the king, "Behold, he
is staying in Jerusalem, for he
said, 'Today the house of Israel
will restore the kingdom of my father to me.'" 2 Sam. 9:9, 10
4 So the king said to Ziba, "Behold, all that belongs to Mephibosheth is yours." And Ziba said, "I
prostrate myself; let me find favor
in your sight, O my lord, the
king!"
5 When King David came to
[r]Bahurim, behold, there came out
from there a man of the family of
the house of Saul whose name
was Shimei, the son of Gera; he
came out [r]cursing continually as
he came. 2 Sam. 3:16 • Ex. 22:28
6 And he threw stones at David and at all the servants of King
David; and all the people and all
the mighty men were at his right
hand and at his left.
7 And thus Shimei said when
he cursed, "Get out, get out, [r]you
man of bloodshed, and worthless
fellow! 2 Sam. 12:9
8 "The LORD has returned upon
you all the bloodshed of the house
of Saul, in whose place you have
reigned; and the LORD has given
the kingdom into the hand of your
son Absalom. And behold, you are
taken in your own evil, for you are
a man of bloodshed!"
9 Then Abishai the son of
Zeruiah said to the king, "Why
should this dead dog curse my
lord the king? Let me go over
now, and cut off his head."
10 But the king said, "What[r]
have I to do with you, O sons of
Zeruiah? If he curses, and if the
LORD has told him, 'Curse David,'
then who shall say, 'Why have
you done so?'" 2 Sam. 3:39
11 Then David said to Abishai
and to all his servants, "Behold,
my son who came out from [t]me
seeks my life; how much more
now this Benjamite? Let him
alone and let him curse, for the
LORD has told him. *my body*
12 "Perhaps the LORD will look
on my affliction and [t]return good
to me instead of his cursing this
day." *the LORD will return*
13 So David and his men went
on the way; and Shimei went
along on the hillside parallel with
him and as he went he cursed, and
cast stones and threw dust at him.
14 And the king and all the people who were with him arrived
weary and he refreshed himself
there.

15 [r]Then Absalom and all the
people, the men of Israel, entered
Jerusalem, and Ahithophel with
him. 2 Sam. 15:12, 37
16 Now it came about when Hushai the Archite, David's friend,
came to Absalom, that Hushai
said to Absalom, "*Long* live the
king! *Long* live the king!"
17 And Absalom said to Hushai,
"Is this your [a]loyalty to your
friend? Why did you not go with
your friend?" *kindness*
18 Then Hushai said to Absalom, "No! For whom the LORD,
this people, and all the men of Israel have chosen, his will I be, and
with him I will remain.
19 "And besides, whom should I
serve? *Should I* not *serve* in the
presence of his son? As I have
served in your father's presence,
so I will be in your presence."
20 Then Absalom said to
Ahithophel, "Give your advice.
What shall we do?"
21 And Ahithophel said to Absalom, "Go [r]in to your father's concubines, whom he has left to keep
the house; then all Israel will hear
that you have made yourself odious to your father. The hands of
all who are with you will also be
strengthened." 2 Sam. 15:16
22 So they pitched a tent for
Absalom on the roof, and Absalom went in to his father's concubines in the sight of all Israel.
23 And the advice of Ahithophel, which he [t]gave in those days,
was as if one inquired of the word
of God; so was all the advice of
Ahithophel *regarded* by both David and Absalom. *advised*

CHAPTER 17

FURTHERMORE, Ahithophel
said to Absalom, "Please let me
choose 12,000 men that I may
arise and pursue David tonight.
2 "And I will come upon him
while he is weary and [t]exhausted
and will terrify him so that all the
people who are with him will flee.
Then I will strike down the king
alone, *slack of hands*
3 and I will bring back all the
people to you. The return of
everyone depends on the man you
seek; *then* all the people shall be
at [r]peace." Jer. 6:14
4 So the plan pleased Absalom
and all the elders of Israel.
5 Then Absalom said, "Now
call Hushai the Archite also, and
let us hear what he has to say."
6 When Hushai had come to
Absalom, Absalom said to [t]him,
"Ahithophel has spoken thus.
Shall we carry out his plan? If not,
you speak." *him, saying*
7 So Hushai said to Absalom,
"This time the advice that Ahithophel has given is not good."
8 Moreover, Hushai said, "You
know your father and his men,
that they are mighty men and they
are [t]fierce, like a bear robbed of
her cubs in the field. And your father is an [t]expert in warfare, and
will not spend the night with the
people. *bitter of soul • man of war*
9 "Behold, he has now hidden
himself in one of the [t]caves or in
another place; and it will be when
he falls on them at the first attack,
that whoever hears *it* will say,
'There has been a slaughter
among the people who follow Absalom.' *pits*

10 "And even the one who is valiant, whose heart is like the heart
of a lion, [r]will completely [t]lose
heart; for all Israel knows that
your father is a mighty man and
those who are with him are valiant men. Josh. 2:9-11 • *melt*
11 "But I counsel that all Israel
be surely gathered to you, from
Dan even to Beersheba, as the
sand that is by the sea in abundance, and that [t]you personally go
into battle. *your face go*
12 "So we shall come to him in
one of the places where he can be
found, and we will fall on him as
the dew falls on the ground; and
of him and of all the men who are
with him, not even one will be left.
13 "And if he withdraws into a
city, then all Israel shall bring
ropes to that city, and we will
drag it into the valley until not
even a small stone is found there."
14 Then Absalom and all the
men of Israel said, "The counsel
of Hushai the Archite is better
than the counsel of Ahithophel."
For the LORD had ordained to
thwart the good counsel of
Ahithophel, in order that the LORD
might bring calamity on Absalom.
15 Then Hushai said to Zadok
and to Abiathar the priests, "This
is what Ahithophel counseled Absalom and the elders of Israel, and
this is what I have counseled.
16 "Now therefore, send quickly
and tell David, saying, 'Do not
spend the night at the fords of the
wilderness, but by all means cross
over, lest the king and all the people who are with him be [t]de-
stroyed.'" *swallowed up*

17 Now Jonathan and Ahimaaz
were staying at [r]En-rogel, and a
maidservant would go and tell
them, and they would go and tell
King David, for they could not be
seen entering the city. Josh. 15:7
18 But a lad did see them, and
told Absalom; so the two of them
departed quickly and came to the
house of a man in Bahurim, who
had a well in his courtyard, and
they went down [t]into it. *there*
19 And the woman took a covering and spread it over the well's
mouth and scattered grain on it,
so that nothing was known.
20 Then Absalom's servants
came to the woman at the house
and said, "Where are Ahimaaz
and Jonathan?" And the woman
said to them, "They have crossed
the brook of water." And when
they searched and could not find
them, they returned to Jerusalem.
21 And it came about after they
had departed that they came up
out of the well and went and told
King David; and they said to David, "Arise and cross over the water quickly for thus Ahithophel
has counseled against you."
22 Then David and all the people who *were* with him arose and
crossed the Jordan; and by dawn
not even one remained who had
not crossed the Jordan.
23 Now when Ahithophel saw
that his counsel was not [t]followed,
he [t]saddled *his* donkey and arose
and went to his home, to his city,
and set his house in order, and
[r]strangled himself; thus he died
and was buried in the grave of his
father. *done* • *bound* • Matt. 27:5

24 Then David came to ʳMaha-
naim. And Absalom crossed the
Jordan, he and all the men of Israel with him. Gen. 32:2, 10
25 And Absalom set Amasa
over the army in place of Joab.
Now Amasa was the son of a man
whose name was Ithra the Israelite, who went in to Abigail the
daughter of Nahash, sister of
Zeruiah, Joab's mother.
26 And Israel and Absalom
camped in the land of Gilead.
27 Now when David had come
to Mahanaim, Shobi the son of
Nahash from Rabbah of the sons
of Ammon, Machir the son of Ammiel from Lo-debar, and Barzillai
the Gileadite from Rogelim,
28 brought ʳbeds, basins, pottery, wheat, barley, flour, parched
grain, beans, lentils, parched
seeds, Prov. 11:25; Matt. 5:7
29 honey, curds, sheep, and
cheese of the herd, for David and
for the people who *were* with him,
ʳto eat; for they said, "The people
are hungry and weary and thirsty
in the wilderness." Eccl. 11:1

CHAPTER 18

THEN David ᵗnumbered the people who were with him and ʳset
over them commanders of thousands and commanders of hundreds. *mustered* • Ex. 18:25
2 And David sent the people
out, one third under the ᵗcommand
of Joab, one third under the ᵗcommand of Abishai the son of
Zeruiah, Joab's brother, and one
third under the ᵗcommand of Ittai
the Gittite. And the king said to
the people, "I myself will surely
go out with you also." *hand*
3 But the people said, "You
should not go out; for if we indeed
flee, they will not care about us,
even if half of us die, they will not
care about us. But you are worth
ten thousand of us; therefore now
it is better that you *be ready* to
help us from the city."
4 Then the king said to them,
"Whatever seems best to you I
will do." So the king stood beside
the gate, and all the people went
out by hundreds and thousands.
5 And the king charged Joab
and Abishai and Ittai, saying,
"*Deal* gently for my sake with the
young man Absalom." And ʳall the
people heard when the king
charged all the commanders concerning Absalom. 2 Sam. 18:12
6 Then the people went out
into the field against Israel, and
the battle took place in ʳthe forest
of Ephraim. Josh. 17:15, 18
7 And the people of Israel were
defeated there before the servants
of David, and the slaughter there
that day was great, 20,000 men.
8 For the battle there was
spread over the whole countryside, and the forest devoured
more people that day than the
sword devoured.
9 Now Absalom happened to
meet the servants of David. For
Absalom was riding on *his* mule,
and the mule went under the thick
branches of a great oak. And his
head caught fast in the oak, so he
was ᵗleft hanging between heaven
and earth, while the mule that was
under him kept going. *placed*

10 When a certain man saw *it*,
he told Joab and said, "Behold, I
saw Absalom hanging in an oak."
11 Then Joab said to the man
who had told him, "Now behold,
you saw *him!* Why then did you
not strike him there to the
ground? And I would have given
you ten *pieces* of silver and a
belt."
12 And the man said to Joab,
"Even if I should receive a thousand *pieces of* silver in my hand, I
would not put out my hand
against the king's son; for in our
hearing the king charged you and
Abishai and Ittai, saying, 'Protect
for me the young man Absalom!'
13 "Otherwise, if I had dealt
treacherously against his life (and
[r]there is nothing hidden from the
king), then you yourself would
have stood aloof." 2 Sam. 14:19
14 Then Joab said, "I will not
[t]waste time here with you." So he
took three spears in his hand and
thrust them through the heart of
Absalom while he was yet alive in
the midst of the oak. *tarry thus*
15 And ten young men who carried Joab's armor gathered
around and struck Absalom and
killed him.
16 Then [r]Joab blew the trumpet,
and the people returned from pursuing Israel, for Joab restrained
the people. 2 Sam. 2:28; 20:22
17 And they took Absalom and
cast him into a deep pit in the forest and erected over him a very
great heap of stones. And all Israel fled, each to his tent.
18 Now Absalom in his lifetime
had taken and [r]set up for himself a
pillar which is in the King's Valley, for he said, "I have no son to
preserve my name." So he named
the pillar after his own name, and
it is called Absalom's monument
to this day. 1 Sam. 15:12
19 Then Ahimaaz the son of Zadok said, "Please let me run and
bring the king news that the LORD
has [t]freed him from the hand of his
enemies." *vindicated*
20 But Joab said to him, "You
are not the man to carry news this
day, but you shall carry news another day; however, you shall carry no news today because the
king's son is dead."
21 Then Joab said to the Cushite, "Go, tell the king what you
have seen." So the Cushite bowed
to Joab and ran.
22 Now Ahimaaz the son of Zadok said once more to Joab, "But
whatever happens, please let me
also run after the Cushite." And
Joab said, "Why would you run,
my son, since [r]you will have no reward for going?" 2 Sam. 18:29
23 "But whatever happens," *he*
said, "I will run." So he said to
him, "Run." Then Ahimaaz ran by
way of the plain and passed up the
Cushite.
24 Now David was sitting between the two gates; and the
watchman went up to the roof of
the gate by the wall, and raised
his eyes and looked, and behold, a
man running by himself.
25 And the watchman called
and told the king. And the king
said, "If he is by himself there is
good news in his mouth." And he
came nearer and nearer.
26 Then the watchman saw another man running; and the

watchman called to the gatekeeper and said, "Behold, *another*
man running by himself." And the
king said, "This one also is bringing good news."
27 And the watchman said, "I
[t]think the running of the first one
is like the running of Ahimaaz the
son of Zadok." And the king said,
"This is a good man and comes
with good news." *see*
28 And Ahimaaz called and said
to the king, "[16]All is well." And he
prostrated himself before the king
with his face to the ground. And
he said, "Blessed is the LORD your
God, who has delivered up the
men who lifted their hands
against my lord the king."
29 And the king said, "Is it well
with the young man Absalom?"
And Ahimaaz answered, "When
Joab sent the king's servant, and
your servant, I saw a great tumult,
but I did not know what *it was.*"
30 Then the king said, "Turn
aside and stand here." So he
turned aside and stood still.
31 And behold, the Cushite arrived, and the Cushite said, "Let
my lord the king receive good
news, for the LORD has freed you
this day from the hand of all those
who rose up against you."
32 Then the king said to the
Cushite, "Is [r]it well with the young
man Absalom?" And the Cushite
answered, "Let the enemies of my
lord the king, and all who rise up
against you for evil, be as that
young man!" 2 Sam. 18:29
33 And the king was deeply
moved and went up to the chamber over the gate and wept. And
thus he said as he walked, "O [r]my
son Absalom, my son, my son Absalom! [r]Would I had died instead
of you, O Absalom, my son, my
son!" 2 Sam. 19:4 • Ex. 32:32

CHAPTER 19

THEN it was told Joab, "Behold,
[r]the king is weeping and mourns
for Absalom." 2 Sam. 18:5, 14
2 And the [t]victory that day was
turned to mourning for all the
people, for the people heard *it*
said that day, "The king is grieved
for his son." *salvation*
3 So the people went by stealth
into the city that day, as people
who are humiliated steal away
when they flee in battle.
4 And the king covered his
face and cried out with a loud
voice, "O my son Absalom, O Absalom, my son, my son!"
5 Then Joab came into the
house to the king and said, "Today you have covered with shame
the faces of all your servants, who
today have saved your life and the
lives of your sons and daughters,
the lives of your wives, and the
lives of your concubines,
6 by loving those who hate
you, and by hating those who love
you. For you have shown today
that [a]princes and servants are
nothing to you; for I know this day
that if Absalom were alive and all
of us were dead today, then you
would be pleased. *commanders*
7 "Now therefore arise, go out
and speak kindly to your servants,
for I swear by the LORD, if you do
not go out, surely not a man will
pass the night with you, and this
will be worse for you than all the

[16]Lit., *Peace.*

evil that has come upon you from your youth until now."

8 So the king arose and sat in the gate. When they told all the people, saying, "Behold, the king is [r]sitting in the gate," then all the people came before the king.

Now [r]Israel had fled, each to his tent. 2 Sam. 15:2 • 2 Sam. 18:17

9 And all the people were quarreling throughout all the tribes of Israel, saying, "The[r] king delivered us from the [t]hand of our enemies and saved us from the [t]hand of the Philistines, but now he has fled out of the land from Absalom. 2 Sam. 8:1-14 • *palm*

10 "However, Absalom, whom we anointed over us, has died in battle. Now then, why are you silent about bringing the king back?"

11 Then King David sent to [r]Zadok and Abiathar the priests, saying, "Speak to the elders of Judah, saying, 'Why are you the last to bring the king back to his house, since the word of all Israel has come to the king, *even* to his house? 2 Sam. 15:29

12 'You are my brothers; [r]you are my bone and my flesh. Why then should you be the last to bring back the king?' 2 Sam. 5:1

13 "And say to [r]Amasa, 'Are you not my bone and my flesh? May God do so to me, and more also, if you will not be commander of the army before me continually in place of Joab.' " 2 Sam. 17:25

14 Thus he turned the hearts of all the men of Judah [r]as one man, so that they sent *word* to the king, *saying*, "Return, you and all your servants." Judg. 20:1

15 The king then returned and came as far as the Jordan. And Judah came to [r]Gilgal in order to go to meet the king, to bring the king across the Jordan. Josh. 5:9

16 Then [r]Shimei the son of Gera, the Benjamite who was from Bahurim, hurried and came down with the men of Judah to meet King David. 2 Sam. 16:5-13

17 And there were a thousand men of Benjamin with him, with [r]Ziba the servant of the house of Saul, and his fifteen sons and his twenty servants with him; and they rushed to the Jordan before the king. 2 Sam. 16:1-4; 19:26, 27

18 Then they kept crossing the ford to bring over the king's household, and to do what was good in his sight. And Shimei the son of Gera fell down before the king as he was about to cross the Jordan.

19 So he said to the king, "Let[r] not my lord consider me guilty, nor remember what your servant did wrong on the day when my lord the king came out from Jerusalem, so that the king should [t]take *it* to heart. 1 Sam. 22:15 • *set*

20 "For your servant knows that I have sinned; therefore behold, I have come today, the first of all the house of Joseph to go down to meet my lord the king."

21 But Abishai the son of Zeruiah answered and said, "Should not Shimei be put to death for this, [r]because he cursed the LORD's anointed?" Ex. 22:28

22 David then said, "What have I to do with you, O sons of Zeruiah, that you should this day be an adversary to me? Should

any man be put to death in Israel
today? For do I not know that I
am king over Israel today?"
23 And the king said to Shimei,
"You[r] shall not die." Thus the king
swore to him. 1 Kin. 2:8
24 Then [r]Mephibosheth the [17]son
of Saul came down to meet the
king; and he had neither [t]cared for
his feet, nor trimmed his mustache, nor washed his clothes,
from the day the king departed
until the day he came *home* in
peace. 2 Sam. 9:6-10 • *done*
25 And it was when he came
from Jerusalem to meet the king,
that the king said to him, "Why[r]
did you not go with me, Mephibosheth?" 2 Sam. 16:17
26 So he answered, "O my lord,
the king, my servant deceived me;
for your servant said, 'I will saddle a donkey for myself that I may
ride on it and go with the king,'
because your servant is lame.
27 "Moreover, [r]he has slandered
your servant to my lord the king;
but my lord the king is like the angel of God, therefore do what is
good in your sight. 2 Sam. 16:3, 4
28 "For all my father's household
was nothing but dead men before
my lord the king; yet you set your
servant among those who ate at
your own table. What right do I
have yet that I should [t]complain
anymore to the king?" *cry out*
29 So the king said to him,
"Why do you still speak of your
affairs? I have decided, 'You and
Ziba shall divide the land.' "
30 And Mephibosheth said to
the king, "Let him even take it all,
since my lord the king has come
safely to his own house."

[17]I.e., grandson

31 Now [r]Barzillai the Gileadite
had come down from Rogelim;
and he went on to the Jordan with
the king to [t]escort him over the
Jordan. 2 Sam. 17:27-29 • *send*
32 Now Barzillai was very old,
being eighty years old; and he had
[a]sustained the king while he stayed
at Mahanaim, for he was a very
great man. *provided food for*
33 And the king said to Barzillai, "You cross over with me and I
will [a]sustain you in Jerusalem with
me." *provide food for*
34 But Barzillai said to the king,
"How[r] long have I yet to live, that I
should go up with the king to Jerusalem? Gen. 47:8
35 "I am now eighty years old.
Can I distinguish between good
and bad? Or can your servant
taste what I eat or what I drink?
Or can I hear anymore the voice
of singing men and women? Why
then should your servant be an
added burden to my lord the king?
36 "Your servant would merely
cross over the Jordan with the
king. Why should the king com-
pensate me *with* this reward?
37 "Please let your servant return, that I may die in my own
city near the grave of my father
and my mother. However, here is
your servant [r]Chimham, let him
cross over with my lord the king,
and do for him what is good in
your sight." 2 Sam. 19:40
38 And the king answered,
"Chimham shall cross over with
me, and I will do for him what is
good in your sight; and whatever
you [t]require of me, I will do for
you." *choose*
39 All the people crossed over

the Jordan and the king crossed
too. The king then[r] kissed Barzillai
and blessed him, and he returned
to his place. Gen. 31:55
40 Now the king went on to Gilgal, and Chimham went on with
him; and all the people of Judah
and also half the people of Israel
accompanied the king.
41 And behold, all the men of Israel came to the king and said to
the king, "Why had our brothers
the men of Judah stolen you
away, and brought the king and
his household and all David's men
with him over the Jordan?"
42 Then all the men of Judah
answered the men of Israel, "Because the king is a close relative
to us. Why then are you angry
about this matter? Have we eaten
at all at the king's *expense*, or has
anything been taken for us?"
43 But the men of Israel answered the men of Judah and said,
"We[r] have ten parts in the king,
therefore we also have more
claim on David than you. Why
then did you treat us with contempt? Was it not our advice first
to bring back our king?" Yet the
words of the men of Judah were
harsher than the words of the men
of Israel. 2 Sam. 5:1

CHAPTER 20

NOW [r]a worthless fellow happened to be there whose name
was Sheba, the son of [r]Bichri, a
Benjamite; and he blew the trumpet and said, 2 Sam. 16:7 • Gen. 46:21
"We[r] have no portion in
David, 2 Sam. 19:43
Nor do we have inheritance
in the son of Jesse;
Every man to his tents, O
Israel!"
2 So all the men of Israel withdrew from following David, *and*
followed Sheba the son of Bichri;
but the men of Judah remained
steadfast to their king, from the
Jordan even to Jerusalem.
3 Then David came to his
house at Jerusalem, and [r]the king
took the ten women, the concubines whom he had left to keep
the house, and placed them under
guard and provided them with
sustenance, but did not go in to
them. So they were shut up until
the day of their death, living as
widows. 2 Sam. 15:16; 16:21, 22
4 Then the king said to [r]Amasa,
"Call out the men of Judah for me
within three days, and be present
here yourself." 2 Sam. 17:25
5 So Amasa went to call out
the men of Judah, but he [r]delayed
longer than the set time which he
had appointed him. 1 Sam. 13:8
6 And David said to [r]Abishai,
"Now Sheba the son of Bichri will
do us more harm than Absalom;
take your lord's servants and pursue him, lest he find for himself
fortified cities and escape from
our sight." 2 Sam. 21:17
7 So Joab's men went out after
him, [r]along with the Cherethites
and the Pelethites and all the
mighty men; and they went out
from Jerusalem to pursue Sheba
the son of Bichri. 2 Sam. 8:18
8 When they were at the large
stone which is in [r]Gibeon, Amasa
came [t]to meet them. Now Joab
was dressed in his military attire,

and over it was a belt with a
sword in its sheath fastened at his
waist; and as he went forward, it
fell out. 2 Sam. 2:13 • *before*
9 And Joab said to Amasa, "Is
it well with you, my brother?"
And [r]Joab took Amasa by the
beard with his right hand to kiss
him. Matt. 26:49
10 But Amasa was not on guard
against the sword which was in
Joab's hand so [r]he struck him in
the belly with it and poured out
his inward parts on the ground,
and did not *strike* him again; and
he died. Then Joab and Abishai
his brother pursued Sheba the son
of Bichri. 2 Sam. 2:23; 3:27
11 Now there stood by him one
of Joab's young men, and said,
"Whoever favors Joab and whoever is for David, [r]*let him* follow
Joab." 2 Sam. 20:13
12 But Amasa lay wallowing in
his blood in the middle of the
highway. And when the man saw
that all the people stood still, he
[t]removed Amasa from the highway into the field and threw a garment over him when he saw that
everyone who came by him stood
still. *caused to turn*
13 As soon as he was removed
from the highway, all the men
passed on after Joab to pursue
Sheba the son of Bichri.
14 Now he went through all the
tribes of Israel to Abel even to
Beth-maacah and all the Berites;
and they were gathered together
and also went after him.
15 And they came and besieged
him in Abel Beth-maacah, and
they cast up a mound against the
city, and it stood by the rampart;
and all the people who were with
Joab were wreaking destruction
in order to topple the wall.
16 Then [r]a wise woman called
from the city, "Hear, hear! Please
tell Joab, 'Come here that I may
speak with you.' " 2 Sam. 14:2
17 So he approached her, and
the woman said, "Are you Joab?"
And he answered, "I am." Then
she said to him, "Listen to the
words of your maidservant." And
he answered, "I am listening."
18 Then she spoke, saying,
"Formerly they used to say, 'They
will surely ask *advice* at Abel,'
and thus they ended *the dispute*.
19 "I am of those who are peaceable *and* faithful in Israel. [r]You are
seeking to destroy a city even a
mother in Israel. Why would you
swallow up the inheritance of the
LORD?" Deut. 20:10
20 And Joab answered and said,
"Far be it, far be it from me that I
should swallow up or destroy!
21 "Such is not the case. But a
man from the hill country of E-
phraim, Sheba the son of Bichri
by name, has lifted up his hand
against King David. Only hand
him over, and I will depart from
the city." And the woman said to
Joab, "Behold, his head will be
thrown to you over the wall."
22 Then the woman wisely
came to all the people. And they
cut off the head of Sheba the son
of Bichri and threw it to Joab. So
he blew the trumpet, and they
were dispersed from the city, each
to his tent. Joab also returned to
the king at Jerusalem.
23 Now Joab was over the
whole army of Israel, and Benaiah

the son of Jehoiada was over the Cherethites and the Pelethites;

24 and Adoram was over the forced labor, and Jehoshaphat the son of Ahilud was the recorder;

25 and Sheva was scribe, and Zadok and Abiathar were priests;

26 and Ira the Jairite was also a priest to David.

CHAPTER 21

NOW there was [r]a famine in the days of David for three years, year after year; and David sought the presence of the LORD. And the LORD said, "It is for Saul and his bloody house, because he put the Gibeonites to death." Gen. 12:10

2 So the king called the Gibeonites and spoke to them (now the Gibeonites were not of the sons of Israel but of the remnant of the Amorites, and the sons of Israel [t]made a covenant with them, but Saul had sought to [t]kill them in his zeal for the sons of Israel and Judah). *had sworn to* • *smite*

3 Thus David said to the Gibeonites, "What should I do for you? And how can I make atonement that you may bless the inheritance of the LORD?"

4 Then the Gibeonites said to him, "We have no *concern* of silver or gold with Saul or his house, nor is it for us to put any man to death in Israel." And he said, "I will do for you whatever you say."

5 So they said to the king, "The [r]man who consumed us, and who planned to exterminate us from remaining within any border of Israel, 2 Sam. 21:1

6 let seven men from his sons be given to us, and we will [t]hang them [r]before the LORD in Gibeah of Saul, the chosen of the LORD." And the king said, "I will give *them*." *expose them* • Num. 25:4

7 But the king spared Mephibosheth, the son of Jonathan the son of Saul, [r]because of the oath of the LORD which was between them, between David and Saul's son Jonathan. 2 Sam. 4:4; 9:10

8 So the king took the two sons of [r]Rizpah the daughter of Aiah, Armoni and Mephibosheth whom she had born to Saul, and the five sons of Merab the daughter of Saul, whom she had born to Adriel the son of Barzillai the Meholathite. 2 Sam. 3:7

9 Then he gave them into the hands of the Gibeonites, and they [t]hanged them in the mountain before the LORD, so that the seven of them fell together; and they were put to death in the first days of harvest at the beginning of barley harvest. *exposed them*

10 And Rizpah the daughter of Aiah took sackcloth and spread it for herself on the rock, from the beginning of harvest until it rained on them from the sky; and she allowed neither the birds of the sky to rest on them by day nor the beasts of the field by night.

11 When it was told David what Rizpah the daughter of Aiah, the concubine of Saul, had done,

12 then David went and took [r]the bones of Saul and the bones of Jonathan his son from the men of Jabesh-gilead, who had stolen them from the open square of Beth-shan, where the Philistines had hanged them on the day the

Philistines struck down Saul in
Gilboa. 1 Sam. 31:11-13
13 And he brought up the bones
of Saul and the bones of Jonathan
his son from there, and they gathered the bones of those who had
been [t]hanged. *exposed*
14 And they buried the bones of
Saul and Jonathan his son in the
country of Benjamin in Zela, in
the grave of Kish his father; thus
they did all that the king commanded, and after that God was
moved by entreaty for the land.
15 Now when [r]the Philistines
were at war again with Israel, David went down and his servants
with him; and as they fought
against the Philistines, David became weary. 2 Sam. 5:17-25
16 Then Ishbi-benob, who was
among the descendants of the
giant, the weight of whose spear
was three hundred *shekels* of
bronze in weight, [t]was girded with
a new *sword,* and he [t]intended to
kill David. *and he was • said*
17 But [r]Abishai the son of
Zeruiah helped him, and struck
the Philistine and killed him. Then
the men of David swore to him,
saying, "You shall not go out
again with us to battle, that you
may not extinguish the lamp of Israel." 2 Sam. 20:6-10
18 Now it came about after this
that there was war again with the
Philistines at Gob; then [r]Sibbecai
the Hushathite struck down Saph,
who was among the descendants
of the giant. 1 Chr. 11:29; 27:11
19 And there was war with the
Philistines again at Gob, and Elhanan the son of Jaare-oregim the
Bethlehemite [t]killed Goliath the
Gittite, the shaft of whose spear
was like a weaver's beam. *smote*
20 And there was war at Gath
again, where there was a man of
great stature who had six fingers
on each hand and six toes on each
foot, twenty-four in number; and
he also had been born to the giant.
21 And when he defied Israel,
Jonathan the son of Shimei, David's brother, struck him down.
22 [r]These four were born to the
giant in Gath, and they fell by the
hand of David and by the hand of
his servants. 1 Chr. 20:8

CHAPTER 22

AND David spoke the words of
this song to the LORD in the day
that the LORD delivered him from
the [t]hand of all his enemies and
from the [t]hand of Saul. *palm*
2 And he said,
"The LORD is my [t]rock and
my fortress and my deliv-
erer; *crag*
3 My God, my rock, in whom
I take refuge;
My shield and the horn of
my salvation, my strong-
hold and my refuge;
My savior, Thou dost save
me from violence.
4 "I call upon the LORD, [r]who is
worthy to be praised;
And I am saved from my
enemies. Ps. 48:1; 96:4
5 "For the waves of death encompassed me;
The torrents of destruction
overwhelmed me;
6 [r]The cords of Sheol surrounded me;

The snares of death confronted me. Ps. 116:3
7 "In[r] my distress I called upon the LORD, Ps. 116:4
Yes, I[a]cried to my God; called
And from His temple He heard my voice,
And my cry for help *came* into His ears.
8 "Then [r]the earth shook and quaked, Judg. 5:4
[r]The foundations of heaven were trembling
And were shaken, because He was angry. Job 26:11
9 "Smoke went up [a]out of His nostrils, *in His wrath*
[r]And fire from His mouth devoured; Ps. 97:3
Coals were kindled by it.
10 "He bowed the heavens also, and came down
With [r]thick darkness under His feet. Ex. 19:16
11 "And[r] He rode on a cherub and flew; 2 Sam. 6:2
And He appeared on the wings of the wind.
12 "And He made darkness canopies around Him,
A mass of waters, thick clouds of the sky.
13 "From the brightness before Him
Coals of fire were kindled.
14 "The[r] LORD thundered from heaven,
And the Most High uttered His voice. Job 37:2-5
15 "And He sent out arrows, and scattered them,
Lightning, and routed them.
16 "Then the channels of the sea appeared,
The foundations of the world were[a]laid bare,
By the rebuke of the LORD,
At the blast of the breath of His nostrils. *uncovered*
17 "He[r] sent from on high, He took me;
[r]He drew me out of many waters. Ps. 144:7 • Ex. 2:10
18 "He delivered me from my strong enemy,
From those who hated me, for they were too strong for me.
19 "They confronted me in the day of my calamity,
[r]But the LORD was my support. Ps. 23:4
20 "He also brought me forth into a broad place;
He rescued me, because He delighted in me.
21 "The[r] LORD has rewarded me according to my righteousness; 1 Sam. 26:23
[r]According to the cleanness of my hands He has recompensed me. Ps. 24:4
22 "For[r]I have kept the ways of the LORD, Gen. 18:19
And have not acted wickedly against my God.
23 "For[r]all His ordinances *were* before me;
And *as for* His statutes, I did not depart from [t]them. Deut. 6:6-9 • *it*
24 "I[r]was also[t]blameless toward Him, Gen. 6:9; 7:1
And I kept myself from my iniquity. *complete*
25 "Therefore the LORD has recompensed me according to my righteousness,

According to my cleanness
before His eyes.
26 "With the kind Thou dost
show Thyself kind,
With the [t]blameless Thou
dost show Thyself [t]blameless; *complete*
27 With the pure Thou dost
show Thyself pure,
And with the perverted
Thou dost show Thyself
[t]astute. *twisted*
28 "And Thou dost save an afflicted people;
[r]But Thine eyes are on the
haughty *whom* Thou dost
abase. Is. 2:11, 12, 17
29 "For[r] Thou art my lamp, O
LORD;
And the LORD illumines my
darkness. 2 Sam. 21:17
30 "For[r] by Thee I can [18]run upon
a troop;
By my God I can leap over a
wall. 2 Sam. 5:6-8
31 "As for God, His way is
[t]blameless; *complete*
The word of the LORD is
tested;
He is a shield to all who
take refuge in Him.
32 "For who is God, besides the
LORD?
[r]And who is a rock, besides
our God? 2 Sam. 22:2
33 "God is my strong fortress;
And He sets the [t]blameless
in His way. *complete*
34 "He makes my feet like
hinds' *feet*,
[r]And sets me on my high
places. Deut. 32:13
35 "He[r] trains my hands for battle,

[18]Or, *crush a troop*

So that my arms can bend a
bow of bronze. Ps. 144:1
36 "Thou hast also given me the
shield of Thy salvation,
And Thy [t]help makes me
great. *answering*
37 "Thou[r] dost enlarge my steps
under me,
And my [t]feet have not
slipped. 2 Sam. 22:20 • *ankles*
38 "I pursued my enemies and
destroyed them,
And I did not turn back until they were consumed.
39 "And I have devoured them
and shattered them, so
that they did not rise;
And they fell under my feet.
40 "For Thou hast girded me
with strength for battle;
Thou hast subdued under
me [r]those who rose up
against me. Ps. 44:5
41 "Thou hast also [r]made my enemies turn *their* backs to
me,
And I [a]destroyed those who
hated me. Ex. 23:27 • *silenced*
42 "They[r] looked, but there was
none to save; Is. 17:7, 8
Even to the LORD, but He
did not answer them.
43 "Then I pulverized them as
the dust of the earth,
[r]I crushed *and* stamped
them as the mire of the
streets. Is. 10:6
44 "Thou[r] hast also delivered me
from the contentions of
my people; 2 Sam. 3:1
Thou hast kept me as head
of the nations;
A people whom I have not
known serve me.

45 "Foreigners[r] pretend obedience to me; Ps. 66:3; 81:15
As soon as they hear, they obey me.
46 "Foreigners lose heart,
And come trembling out of their fortresses.
47 "The LORD lives, and blessed be my rock;
And exalted be God, the rock of my salvation,
48 [r]The God who executes vengeance for me,
[r]And brings down peoples under me, Ps. 94:1 • Ps. 144:2
49 Who also brings me out from my enemies;
Thou dost even lift me above [r]those who rise up against me;
Thou dost rescue me from the violent man. Ps. 44:5
50 "Therefore[r] I will give thanks to Thee, O LORD, among the nations,
And I will sing praises to Thy name. Rom. 15:9
51 "*He* is a tower of [19]deliverance to His king,
And shows lovingkindness to His anointed,
To David and his descendants forever."

CHAPTER 23

NOW these are the last words of David.
David the son of Jesse declares,
And the man who was raised on high declares,
[r]The anointed of the God of Jacob,
And the sweet psalmist of Israel, 1 Sam. 16:12, 13
2 "The[r] Spirit of the LORD spoke by me,
And His word was on my tongue. Matt. 22:43
3 "The God of Israel said,
[r]The Rock of Israel spoke to me, 2 Sam. 22:2, 3, 32
'He[r] who rules over men righteously, Is. 11:1-5
[r]Who rules in the fear of God, 2 Chr. 19:7, 9
4 [r]Is as the light of the morning *when* the sun rises,
A morning without clouds,
When the tender grass *springs* out of the earth,
Through sunshine after rain.' Judg. 5:31; Ps. 72:6
5 "Truly is not my house so with God?
For [r]He has made an everlasting covenant with me,
Ordered in all things, and secured;
For all my salvation and all *my* desire,
Will He not indeed make *it* grow? 2 Sam. 7:12-16
6 "But the worthless, every one of them will be thrust away like thorns,
Because they cannot be taken in hand;
7 But the man who touches them
Must be [t]armed with iron and the shaft of a spear,
And they will be completely burned with fire in *their* [t]place." *filled • sitting*
8 [r]These are the names of the
mighty men whom David had: Jo-
sheb-basshebeth a Tahchemonite,

[19]I.e., victories

chief of the [a]captains, he was
called Adino the Eznite, because
of eight hundred slain *by him* at
one time; 1 Chr. 11:11-47 • *three*
9 and after him was Eleazar
the son of Dodo the Ahohite, one
of the three mighty men with David when they [t]defied the Philistines who were gathered there to
battle and the men of Israel had
[t]withdrawn. *reproached* • *gone up*
10 He arose and struck the Philistines until his hand was weary
and [t]clung to the sword, and the
LORD brought about a great [t]vic-
tory that day; and the people returned after him only to strip *the*
slain. *his hand clung* • *salvation*
11 Now after him was Shammah the son of Agee a [r]Hararite.
And the Philistines were gathered
into a troop, where there was a
plot of ground full of lentils, and
the people fled from the Philistines. 2 Sam. 23:33
12 But he took his stand in the
midst of the plot, defended it and
struck the Philistines; and [r]the
LORD brought about a great [t]vic-
tory. 2 Sam. 23:10 • *salvation*
13 Then three of the thirty chief
men went down and came to David in the harvest time to the [r]cave
of Adullam, while the troop of the
Philistines was camping in the
valley of Rephaim. 1 Sam. 22:1
14 And David was then [r]in the
stronghold, while the garrison of
the Philistines was then in Bethlehem. 1 Sam. 22:4, 5
15 [r]And David had a craving and
said, "Oh that someone would
give me water to drink from the
well of Bethlehem which is by the
gate!" 1 Chr. 11:17
16 So the three mighty men
broke through the camp of the
Philistines, and drew water from
the well of Bethlehem which was
by the gate, and took *it* and
brought *it* to David. Nevertheless
he would not drink it, but [r]poured
it out to the LORD; Gen. 35:14
17 and he said, "Be it far from
me, O LORD, that I should do this.
[r]*Shall I drink* the blood of the men
who went in *jeopardy* of their
lives?" Therefore he would not
drink it. These things the three
mighty men did. Lev. 17:10
18 And Abishai, the brother of
Joab, the son of Zeruiah, was
chief of the thirty. And he swung
his spear against three hundred
[t]and killed *them*, and had a name
as well as the three. *slain ones*
19 He was most honored of the
thirty, therefore he became their
commander; however, he did not
attain to the three.
20 Then Benaiah the son of Jehoiada, the son of a valiant man of
Kabzeel, who had done mighty
deeds,[t] killed the two *sons of* Ariel
of Moab. He also went down and
killed a lion in the middle of a pit
on a snowy day. *smote*
21 And he [t]killed an Egyptian, an
impressive man. Now the Egyptian *had* a spear in his hand, but
he went down to him with a club
and snatched the spear from the
Egyptian's hand, and killed him
with his own spear. *smote*
22 These *things* Benaiah the son
of Jehoiada did, and had a name
as well as the three mighty men.
23 He was honored among the
thirty, but he did not attain to the

three. And David appointed him
over his guard.
24 Asahel the brother of Joab
was among the thirty; Elhanan the
son of Dodo of Bethlehem,
25 Shammah the [r]Harodite, Eli-
ka the Harodite, Judg. 7:1
26 Helez the Paltite, Ira the son
of Ikkesh the Tekoite,
27 Abiezer the Anathothite,
Mebunnai the Hushathite,
28 Zalmon the Ahohite, Maharai the Netophathite,
29 [r]Heleb the son of Baanah the
Netophathite, Ittai the son of Ribai of [r]Gibeah of the sons of Benjamin, 1 Chr. 11:30 • Josh. 18:28
30 Benaiah a Pirathonite, Hid-
dai of the brooks of Gaash,
31 Abi-albon the Arbathite, Azmaveth the Barhumite,
32 Eliahba the Shaalbonite, the
sons of Jashen, Jonathan,
33 [r]Shammah the Hararite,
Ahiam the son of Sharar the Ara-
rite, 2 Sam. 23:11
34 Eliphelet the son of Ahasbai,
the son of the Maacathite, Eliam
the son of Ahithophel the Gilonite,
35 Hezro the [r]Carmelite, Paarai
the Arbite, Josh. 15:55
36 Igal the son of Nathan of [r]Zo-
bah, Bani the Gadite, 2 Sam. 8:3
37 Zelek the Ammonite, Na-
harai the Beerothite, armor bearers of Joab the son of Zeruiah,
38 Ira the [r]Ithrite, Gareb the Ithrite, 1 Chr. 2:53
39 [r]Uriah the Hittite; thirty-
seven in all. 2 Sam. 11:3, 6

CHAPTER 24

NOW again the anger of the
LORD burned against Israel, and it
incited David against them to say,
"Go, number Israel and Judah."
2 And the king said to Joab the
commander of the army who was
with him, "Go about now through
all the tribes of Israel, from Dan to
Beersheba, and [t]register the people, that I may know the number
of the people." *muster*
3 But Joab said to the king,
"Now [r]may the LORD your God
add to the people a hundred times
as many as they are, while the
eyes of my lord the king *still* see;
but why does my lord the king delight in this thing?" Deut. 1:11
4 Nevertheless, the king's
word prevailed against Joab and
against the commanders of the
army. So Joab and the commanders of the army went out from the
presence of the king, to [t]register
the people of Israel. *muster*
5 And they crossed the Jordan
and camped in [r]Aroer, on the right
side of the city that is in the middle of the valley of Gad, and
toward Jazer. Deut. 2:36
6 Then they came to Gilead
and to [20]the land of Tahtim-hodshi,
and they came to Dan-jaan and
around to [r]Sidon, Josh. 19:28
7 and came to the [r]fortress of
Tyre and to all the cities of the Hivites and of the Canaanites, and
they went out to the south of Judah, *to* Beersheba. Josh. 19:29
8 So when they had gone
about through the whole land,
they came to Jerusalem at the end
of nine months and twenty days.
9 And Joab gave the number of
the [t]registration of the people to
the king; and there were in Israel
eight hundred thousand valiant

[20]Or, *Kadesh in the land of the Hittite*

men who drew the sword, and the
men of Judah were five hundred
thousand men. *muster*
10 Now [r]David's heart [t]troubled
him after he had numbered the
people. So David said to the LORD,
"I have sinned greatly in what I
have done. But now, O LORD,
please take away the iniquity of
Thy servant, for I have acted very
foolishly." 1 Sam. 24:5 • *smote*
11 When David arose in the
morning, the word of the LORD
came to [r]the prophet Gad, David's
seer, saying, 1 Sam. 22:5
12 "Go and speak to David, 'Thus
the LORD says, "I am offering you
three things; choose for yourself
one of them, which I may do to
you." ' "
13 So Gad came to David and
told him, and said to him, "Shall
[r]seven years of famine come to
you in your land? Or will you flee
three months before your foes
while they pursue you? Or shall
there be three days' pestilence in
your land? Now consider and see
what answer I shall return to Him
who sent me." 1 Chr. 21:12
14 Then David said to Gad, "I
am in great distress. Let us now
fall into the hand of the LORD for
His mercies are great, but do not
let me fall into the hand of man."
15 So the LORD sent a pestilence
upon Israel from the morning until the appointed time; and seventy thousand men of the people
from Dan to Beersheba died.
16 [r]When the angel stretched
out his hand toward Jerusalem to
destroy it, [r]the LORD relented from
the calamity, and said to the angel
who destroyed the people, "It is
enough! Now relax your hand!"
And the angel of the LORD was by
the threshing floor of Araunah the
Jebusite. Ex. 12:23 • Ex. 32:14
17 Then David spoke to the
LORD when he saw the angel who
was striking down the people, and
said, "Behold, [r]it is I who have
sinned, and it is I who have done
wrong; but these sheep, what
have they done? Please let Thy
hand be against me and against
my father's house." 2 Sam. 24:10
18 So Gad came to David that
day and said to him, "Go up, erect
an altar to the LORD on the threshing floor of [r]Araunah the Jebusite." 1 Chr. 21:18
19 And David went up according to the word of Gad, just as the
LORD had commanded.
20 And Araunah looked down
and saw the king and his servants
crossing over toward him; and A-
raunah went out and bowed his
face to the ground before the king.
21 Then Araunah said, "Why
has my lord the king come to his
servant?" And David said, "To
buy the threshing floor from you,
in order to build an altar to the
LORD, that the plague may be held
back from the people."
22 And Araunah said to David,
"Let my lord the king take and offer up what is good in his sight.
Look, the oxen for the burnt offering, the threshing sledges and the
yokes of the oxen for the wood.
23 "Everything, O king, Araunah
gives to the king." And Araunah
said to the king, "May the LORD
your God accept you."
24 However, the king said to A-
raunah, "No, but I will surely buy

it from you for a price, for[r]I will
not offer burnt offerings to the
LORD my God which cost me
nothing." So David bought the
threshing floor and the oxen for
fifty shekels of silver. Mal. 1:13

25 And David built there an altar to the LORD, and offered burnt
offerings and peace offerings.
Thus the LORD was moved by entreaty for the land, and the plague
was held back from Israel.

THE FIRST BOOK OF THE

KINGS

NOW King David was old, advanced in age; and they covered
him with clothes, but he could not
keep warm.
2 So his servants said to him,
"Let them seek a young virgin for
my lord the king, and let her[t]at-
tend the king and become his
nurse; and let her lie in your bosom, that my lord the king may
keep warm." *stand before*
3 So they searched for a beautiful girl throughout all the territory of Israel, and found Abishag
the[r]Shunammite, and brought her
to the king. Josh. 19:18
4 And the girl was very beautiful; and she became the king's
nurse and served him, but the
king did not cohabit with her.
5 Now Adonijah the son of
Haggith exalted himself, saying,
"I will be king." So he prepared
for himself chariots and horsemen
with fifty men to run before him.
6 And his father had never
[t]crossed him at any time by asking, "Why have you done so?"
And he was also a very handsome
man; and[r]he was born after Absalom. *pained him* • 2 Sam. 3:3, 4

7 And he had conferred with
Joab the son of Zeruiah and with
Abiathar the priest; and following
Adonijah they helped him.
8 But Zadok the priest, Benaiah the son of Jehoiada, Nathan
the prophet, Shimei, Rei, and the
mighty men who belonged to David, were not with Adonijah.
9 And Adonijah sacrificed
sheep and oxen and fatlings by
the [1]stone of Zoheleth, which is
beside[r]En-rogel; and he invited all
his brothers, the king's sons, and
all the men of Judah, the king's
servants. Josh. 15:7; 18:16
10 But he did not invite Nathan
the prophet, Benaiah, the mighty
men, and Solomon his brother.
11 Then Nathan spoke to[r]Bath-
sheba the mother of Solomon,
saying, "Have you not heard that
Adonijah the son of Haggith has
become king, and David our lord
does not know *it*? 2 Sam. 12:24
12 "So now come, please let me
[r]give you counsel and save your
life and the life of your son Solomon. Prov. 15:22
13 "Go[t]at once to King David and
say to him, 'Have you not, my

[1]Or, *Gliding* or *Serpent Stone*

lord, O king, sworn to your maidservant, saying, "Surely[r] Solomon
your son shall be king after me,
and he shall sit on my throne"?
Why then has Adonijah become
king?' *and enter* • 1 Kin. 1:30
14 "Behold, while you are still
there speaking with the king, I
will come in after you and confirm
your words."
15 So Bathsheba went in to the
king in the bedroom. Now [r]the
king was very old, and Abishag
the Shunammite was ministering
to the king. 1 Kin. 1:1
16 Then Bathsheba bowed and
prostrated herself[t] before the king.
And the king said, "What [t]do you
wish?" *to* • *to you*
17 And she said to him, "My
lord, you swore to your maidservant by the LORD your God, *saying,* [r]'Surely your son Solomon
shall be king after me and he shall
sit on my throne.' 1 Kin. 1:13
18 "And now, behold, Adonijah
is king; and now, my lord the king,
you do not know *it.*
19 "And[r] he has sacrificed oxen
and fatlings and sheep in abundance, and has invited all the sons
of the king and Abiathar the priest
and Joab the commander of the
army; but he has not invited Solomon your servant. 1 Kin. 1:9
20 "And as for you now, my lord
the king, the eyes of all Israel are
on you, to tell them who shall sit
on the throne of my lord the king
after him.
21 "Otherwise it will come about,
as soon as my lord the king sleeps
with his fathers, that I and my son
Solomon will be considered [t]of-
fenders." *sinners*
22 And behold, while she was
still speaking with the king, Nathan the prophet came in.
23 And they told the king, saying, "Here is Nathan the prophet."
And when he came in before the
king, he prostrated himself[t] before
the king with his face to the
ground. *to*
24 Then Nathan said, "My lord
the king, have you said, 'Adonijah
shall be king after me, and he
shall sit on my throne'?
25 "For he has gone down today
and has sacrificed oxen and fatlings and sheep in abundance, and
has invited all the king's sons and
the commanders of the army and
Abiathar the priest, and behold,
they are eating and drinking before him; and they say, [r]'*Long* live
King Adonijah!' 1 Sam. 10:24
26 "But[r] me, *even* me your servant, and Zadok the priest and Benaiah the son of Jehoiada and
your servant Solomon, he has not
invited. 1 Kin. 1:8, 10
27 "Has this thing been done by
my lord the king, and you have
not shown to your servants who
should sit on the throne of my lord
the king after him?"
28 Then King David answered
and said, "Call Bathsheba to me."
And she came into the king's presence and stood before the king.
29 And the king vowed and
said, "As[r] the LORD lives, who has
redeemed my life from all distress, 2 Sam. 4:9
30 surely as[r] I vowed to you by
the LORD the God of Israel, saying,
'Your son Solomon shall be king
after me, and he shall sit on my

throne in my place'; I will indeed
do so this day." 1 Kin. 1:13, 17
31 Then Bathsheba bowed with
her face to the ground, and prostrated herself [t]before the king and
said, "May [r]my lord King David
live forever." *to* • Dan. 2:4; 3:9
32 Then King David said, "Call
to me [r]Zadok the priest, Nathan
the prophet, and Benaiah the son
of Jehoiada." And they came into
the king's presence. 1 Kin. 1:8
33 And the king said to them,
"Take with you the servants of
your lord, and have my son Solomon ride on my own mule, and
bring him down to Gihon.
34 "And let Zadok the priest and
Nathan the prophet [r]anoint him
there as king over Israel, and blow
the trumpet and say, '*Long* live
King Solomon!' 1 Sam. 10:1
35 "Then you shall come up after
him, and he shall come and sit on
my throne and be king in my
place; for I have appointed him to
be ruler over Israel and Judah."
36 And Benaiah the son of Jehoiada answered the king and
said, "Amen! Thus may the LORD,
the God of my lord the king, say.
37 "As the LORD has been with
my lord the king, so may He be
with Solomon, and [r]make his
throne greater than the throne of
my lord King David!" 1 Kin. 1:47
38 So Zadok the priest, Nathan
the prophet, Benaiah the son of
Jehoiada, the Cherethites, and the
Pelethites went down and had
Solomon ride on King David's
mule, and brought him to Gihon.
39 Zadok the priest then [r]took
the horn of oil from the tent and
anointed Solomon. Then they
[r]blew the trumpet, and all the people said, "Long live King Solomon!" Ex. 30:23-32 • 1 Kin. 1:34
40 And all the people went up
after him, and the people [t]were
playing on flutes and rejoicing
with great joy, so that the earth
shook at their noise. *fluting*
41 Now Adonijah and all the
guests who were with him heard
it, as they finished eating. When
Joab heard the sound of the trumpet, he said, "Why is the city making such an uproar?"
42 While he was still speaking,
behold, [r]Jonathan the son of Abiathar the priest came. Then Adonijah said, "Come in, for you are a
valiant man and bring good
news." 2 Sam. 15:27, 36; 17:17
43 But Jonathan answered and
said to Adonijah, "No! Our lord
King David has made Solomon
king.
44 "The king has also sent with
him Zadok the priest, Nathan the
prophet, Benaiah the son of Jehoiada, the Cherethites, and the
Pelethites; and they have made
him ride on the king's mule.
45 "And Zadok the priest and
Nathan the prophet have anointed
him king in Gihon, and they have
come up from there rejoicing, so
that the city is in an uproar. This
is the noise which you have heard.
46 "Besides, [r]Solomon has even
taken his seat on the throne of the
kingdom. 1 Chr. 29:23
47 "And moreover, the king's
servants came to bless our lord
King David, saying, 'May [r]your
God make the name of Solomon
better than your name and his
throne greater than your throne!'

And[r] the king bowed himself on
the bed. 1 Kin. 1:37 • Gen. 47:31
48 "The king has also said thus,
'Blessed be the LORD, the God of
Israel, who[r] has granted one to sit
on my throne today while my own
eyes see *it.*' " 2 Sam. 7:12
49 Then all the guests of Adonijah were terrified; and they arose
and each went on his way.
50 And Adonijah was afraid of
Solomon, and he arose, went and
took hold of the horns of the altar.
51 Now it was told Solomon,
saying, "Behold, Adonijah is
afraid of King Solomon, for behold, he has taken hold of the
horns of the altar, saying, 'Let
King Solomon swear to me today
that he will not put his servant to
death with the sword.' "
52 And Solomon said, "If he will
be a worthy man,[r] not one of his
hairs will fall to the ground; but if
wickedness is found in him, he
will die." 1 Sam. • 14:45
53 So King Solomon sent, and
they brought him down from the
altar. And he came and prostrated
himself[t] before King Solomon, and
Solomon said to him, "Go to your
house." *to*

CHAPTER 2

AS David's[t] time to die drew near,
he charged Solomon his son, saying, *days*
2 "I am going the way of all the
earth. Be strong, therefore, and
show yourself a man.
3 "And keep the charge of the
LORD your God, to walk in His
ways, to keep His statutes, His
commandments, His ordinances,
and His testimonies, [r]according to
what is written in the law of
Moses, that you may succeed in
all that you do and wherever you
turn, Deut. 17:18-20
4 so that[r] the LORD may carry
out His promise which He spoke
concerning me, saying, 'If your
sons are careful of their way, to
walk before Me in [2]truth with all
their heart and with all their soul,
you shall not lack a man on the
throne of Israel.' 2 Sam. 7:25
5 "Now you also know what
Joab the son of Zeruiah did to me,
what he did to the two commanders of the armies of Israel, to Abner the son of Ner, and to Amasa
the son of Jether, whom he killed;
he also shed the blood of war in
peace. And he put the blood of
war on his belt about his waist,
and on his sandals on his feet.
6 "So act according to your wisdom, and do not let his gray hair
go down to Sheol in peace.
7 "But show kindness to the
sons of Barzillai the Gileadite, and
let them be among those who eat
at your table; for they[t] assisted me
when I fled from Absalom your
brother. *came near to*
8 "And behold, there is with you
Shimei the son of Gera the Benjamite, of Bahurim; now it was he
who cursed me with a violent
curse on the day I went to Mahanaim. But when he came down to
me at the Jordan, I swore to him
by the LORD, saying, 'I will not put
you to death with the sword.'
9 "Now therefore, do not let
him go unpunished,[r] for you are a
wise man; and you will know
what you ought to do to him, and

[2]Or, *faithfulness*

you will bring his gray hair down
to Sheol with blood." 1 Kin. 2:6
10 Then ʳDavid slept with his fathers and was buried in ʳthe city of
David. Acts 2:29 • 2 Sam. 5:7
11 And ʳthe days that David
reigned over Israel *were* forty
years: seven years he reigned in
Hebron, and thirty-three years he
reigned in Jerusalem. 1 Chr. 3:4
12 And Solomon sat on the
throne of David his father, and his
kingdom was firmly established.
13 Now Adonijah the son of
Haggith came to Bathsheba the
mother of Solomon. And she said,
"Do you come peacefully?" And
he said, "Peacefully."
14 Then he said, "I have something *to say* to you." And she said,
"Speak."
15 So he said, "You know that
the kingdom was mine and that all
Israel expected me to be king;
however, the kingdom has turned
about and become my brother's,
for it was his from the LORD.
16 "And now I am making one
request of you; do not [3]refuse me."
And she said to him, "Speak."
17 Then he said, "Please speak
to Solomon the king, for he will
not refuse you, that he may give
me ʳAbishag the Shunammite as a
wife." 1 Kin. 1:3, 4
18 And Bathsheba said, "Very
well; I will speak to the king for
you."
19 So Bathsheba went to King
Solomon to speak to him for Adonijah. And the king arose to meet
her, bowed before her, and sat on
his throne; then he ʳhad a throne
set for the king's mother, and she
sat on his right. 1 Kin. 15:13
20 Then she said, "I am making
one small request of you; ʳdo not
refuse me." And the king said to
her, "Ask, my mother, for I will
not refuse you." 1 Kin. 2:16
21 So she said, "Let Abishag the
Shunammite be given to Adonijah
your brother as a wife."
22 And King Solomon answered
and said to his mother, "And why
are you asking Abishag the Shunammite for Adonijah? Ask for
him also the kingdom—for he is
my older brother—even for him,
for Abiathar the priest, and for
Joab the son of Zeruiah!"
23 Then King Solomon swore
by the LORD, saying, "May God do
so to me and more also, if Adonijah has not spoken this word
against his own ᵗlife. *soul*
24 "Now therefore, as the LORD
lives, who has established me and
set me on the throne of David my
father, and ʳwho has made me a
house as He promised, surely
Adonijah will be put to death today." 2 Sam. 7:11, 13
25 So King Solomon sent Benaiah the son of Jehoiada; and he fell
upon him so that he died.
26 Then to Abiathar the priest
the king said, "Go to Anathoth to
your own field, for you deserve to
die; but I will not put you to death
at this time, because you carried
the ark of the Lord GOD before my
father David, and because you
were afflicted in everything with
which my father was afflicted."
27 So Solomon dismissed Abiathar from being priest to the
LORD, in order to fulfill ʳthe word
of the LORD, which He had spoken

[3]Lit., *turn away my (your) face,* and so in vv. 17, 20

concerning the house of Eli in Shiloh. 1 Sam. 2:27-36
28 Now the news came to Joab,
[r]for Joab had followed Adonijah,
although he had not followed Absalom. And Joab fled to the tent of
the LORD and took hold of the
horns of the altar. 1 Kin. 1:7
29 And it was told King Solomon that Joab had fled to the tent
of the LORD, and behold, he is beside the altar. Then Solomon sent
Benaiah the son of Jehoiada, saying, "Go, fall upon him."
30 So Benaiah came to the tent
of the LORD, and said to him,
"Thus the king has said, 'Come
out.'" But he said, "No, for I will
die here." And Benaiah brought
the king word again, saying,
"Thus spoke Joab, and thus he answered me."
31 And the king said to him,
"Do as he has spoken and fall
upon him and bury him, that you
may remove from me and from
my father's house the blood which
Joab shed without cause.
32 "And [r]the LORD will return his
blood on his own head, because he
fell upon two men more righteous
and better than he and killed them
with the sword, while my father
David did not know *it:* [r]Abner the
son of Ner, commander of the
army of Israel, and Amasa the son
of Jether, commander of the army
of Judah. Gen. 9:6 • 2 Sam. 3:27
33 "So shall their blood return on
the head of Joab and on the head
of his descendants forever; but to
David and his descendants and his
house and his throne, may there
be peace from the LORD forever."
34 Then [r]Benaiah the son of Jehoiada went up and fell upon him
and put him to death, and he was
buried at his own house in the wilderness. 1 Kin. 2:25
35 And [r]the king appointed Benaiah the son of Jehoiada over the
army in his place, and the king appointed Zadok the priest in the
place of Abiathar. 1 Kin. 4:4
36 Now the king sent and called
for Shimei and said to him, "Build
for yourself a house in Jerusalem
and live there, and do not go out
from there to any place.
37 "For it will happen on the day
you go out and [r]cross over the
[a]brook Kidron, you will know for
certain that you shall surely die;
your blood shall be on your own
head." 2 Sam. 15:23 • *wadi*
38 Shimei then said to the king,
"The word is good. As my lord the
king has said, so your servant will
do." So Shimei lived in Jerusalem
many days.
39 But it came about at the end
of three years, that two of the servants of Shimei ran away [r]to A-
chish son of Maacah, king of
Gath. And they told Shimei, saying, "Behold, your servants are in
Gath." 1 Sam. 27:2
40 Then Shimei arose and saddled his donkey, and went to Gath
to Achish to look for his servants.
And Shimei went and brought his
servants from Gath.
41 And it was told Solomon that
Shimei had gone from Jerusalem
to Gath, and had returned.
42 So the king sent and called
for Shimei and said to him, "Did I
not make you swear by the LORD
and solemnly warn you, saying,
'You will know for certain that on

the day you depart and go anywhere, you shall surely die'? And
you said to me, 'The word which I
have heard is good.'
43 "Why then have you not kept
the oath of the LORD, and the command which I have laid on you?"
44 The king also said to Shimei,
"You know all the evil which you
acknowledge in your heart, which
you did to my father David; therefore [r]the LORD shall return your
evil on your own head. Ps. 7:16
45 "But King Solomon shall be
blessed, and [r]the throne of David
shall be established before the
LORD forever." 2 Sam. 7:13
46 So the king commanded Benaiah the son of Jehoiada, and he
went out and fell upon him so that
he died. [r]Thus the kingdom was established in the hands of Solomon. 1 Kin. 2:12; 2 Chr. 1:1

CHAPTER 3

THEN [r]Solomon formed a marriage alliance with Pharaoh king
of Egypt, and took Pharaoh's
daughter and brought her to the
city of David, until he had finished
building his own house and the
house of the LORD and the wall
around Jerusalem. 1 Kin. 7:8
2 [r]The people were still sacrificing on the high places, because
there was no house built for the
name of the LORD until those
days. Lev. 17:3-5; Deut. 12:2, 13
3 Now [r]Solomon loved the
LORD, [r]walking in the statutes of
his father David, except he sacrificed and burned incense on the
high places. Deut. 6:5 • 1 Kin. 2:3
4 [r]And the king went to [r]Gibeon
to sacrifice there, for that was the
great high place; Solomon offered
a thousand burnt offerings on that
altar. 2 Chr. 1:3 • Josh. 18:21-25
5 In Gibeon the LORD appeared
to Solomon [r]in a dream at night;
and God said, "Ask what *you wish*
me to give you." Matt. 1:20; 2:13
6 Then Solomon said, "Thou
hast shown great lovingkindness
to Thy servant David my father,
according as he walked before
Thee in [4]truth and righteousness
and uprightness of heart toward
Thee; and Thou hast reserved for
him this great lovingkindness,
that Thou hast given him a son to
sit on his throne, as *it is* this day.
7 "And now, O LORD my God,
Thou hast made Thy servant king
in place of my father David, yet I
am but a little child; I do not know
how to go out or come in.
8 "And [r]Thy servant is in the
midst of Thy people which Thou
hast chosen, a great people who
cannot be numbered or counted
for multitude. Ex. 19:6
9 "So give Thy servant an understanding heart to judge Thy
people to discern between good
and evil. For who is able to judge
this great people of Thine?"
10 And [t]it was pleasing in the
sight of the Lord that Solomon
had asked this thing. *the thing*
11 And God said to him, "Because you have asked this thing
and have not asked for yourself
[t]long life, nor have asked riches for
yourself, nor have you asked for
the life of your enemies, but have
asked for yourself discernment to
understand justice, *many days*
12 behold, I have done accord-

[4]Or, *faithfulness*

ing to your words. Behold, I have given you a wise and discerning heart, so that there has been no one like you before you, nor shall one like you arise after you.

13 "And I have also given you what you have not asked, both [r]riches and honor, so that there will not be any among the kings like you all your days. Prov. 3:16

14 "And [r]if you walk in My ways, keeping My statutes and commandments, as your father David walked, then I will [r]prolong your days." 1 Kin. 3:6 • Ps. 91:16

15 Then Solomon awoke, and behold, it was a dream. And he came to Jerusalem and stood before the ark of the covenant of the Lord, and offered burnt offerings and made peace offerings, and made a feast for all his servants.

16 Then two women who were harlots came to the king and stood before him.

17 And the one woman said, "Oh, my lord, [t]this woman and I live in the same house; and I gave birth to a child while she *was* in the house. *I and this woman*

18 "And it happened on the third day after I gave birth, that this woman also gave birth to a child, and we were together. There was no stranger with us in the house, only the two of us in the house.

19 "And this woman's son died in the night, because she lay on it.

20 "So she arose in the middle of the night and took my son from beside me while your maidservant slept, and laid him in her bosom, and laid her dead son in my bosom.

21 "And when I rose in the morning to nurse my son, behold, he was dead; but when I looked at him carefully in the morning, behold, he was not my son, whom I had borne."

22 Then the other woman said, "No! For the living one is my son, and the dead one is your son." But the first woman said, "No! For the dead one is your son, and the living one is my son." Thus they spoke before the king.

23 Then the king said, "The [t]one says, 'This is my son who is living, and your son is the dead one'; and the other says, 'No! For your son is the dead one, and my son is the living one.' " *this one*

24 And the king said, "Get me a sword." So they brought a sword before the king.

25 And the king said, "Divide the living child in two, and give half to the one and half to the other."

26 Then the woman whose child *was* the living one spoke to the king, for she was deeply stirred over her son and said, "Oh, my lord, give her the living child, and by no means kill him." But the other said, "He shall be neither mine nor yours; divide *him!*"

27 Then the king answered and said, "Give the first woman the living child, and by no means kill him. She is his mother."

28 When all Israel heard of the judgment which the king had [t]handed down, they feared the king; for they saw that the wisdom of God was in him to [t]administer justice. *judged • do*

CHAPTER 4

NOW King Solomon was king
over all Israel.
2 And these were his officials:
Azariah the son of Zadok *was*[r] the
priest; 1 Chr. 6:10
3 Elihoreph and Ahijah, the
sons of Shisha *were* secretaries;
[r]Jehoshaphat the son of Ahilud
was the recorder; 2 Sam. 8:16
4 and Benaiah the son of Jehoiada *was* over the army; and
Zadok and Abiathar *were* priests;
5 and Azariah the son of Nathan *was* over[r] the deputies; and
Zabud the son of Nathan, a priest,
was the king's friend; 1 Kin. 4:7
6 and Ahishar was over the
household; and Adoniram the son
of Abda *was* over the men subject
to forced labor.
7 And Solomon had twelve
deputies over all Israel, who[t] provided for the king and his household; each man had to provide for
a month in the year. *nourished*
8 And these are their names:
Ben-hur, in the[r] hill country of E-
phraim; Josh. 24:33
9 Ben-deker in Makaz and
[r]Shaalbim and Beth-shemesh and
Elonbeth-hanan; Judg. 1:35
10 Ben-hesed, in Arubboth (So-
coh[r] *was* his and all the land of[r] Hepher); Josh. 15:35 • Josh. 12:17
11 Ben-abinadab, *in* all the
height of Dor (Taphath the daughter of Solomon was his wife);
12 Baana the son of Ahilud, *in*
Taanach and Megiddo, and all
Beth-shean which is beside Zarethan below Jezreel, from Beth-
shean to Abel-meholah as far as
the other side of Jokmeam;
13 Ben-geber, in Ramoth-gilead
(the towns of Jair, the son of Manasseh, which are in Gilead were
his: the region of Argob, which is
in Bashan, sixty great cities with
walls and bronze bars *were* his);
14 Ahinadab the son of Iddo, *in*
[r]Mahanaim; Josh. 13:26
15 [r]Ahimaaz, in Naphtali (he
also married Basemath the daughter of Solomon); 2 Sam. 15:27
16 Baana the son of Hushai, in
Asher and[a] Bealoth; *in Aloth*
17 Jehoshaphat the son of Paru-
ah, in Issachar;
18 [r]Shimei the son of Ela, in Benjamin; 1 Kin. 1:8
19 Geber the son of Uri, in the
land of Gilead, the country of Sihon king of the Amorites and of
Og king of Bashan; and *he was* the
only deputy who *was* in the land.
20 Judah and Israel *were* as numerous as the sand that is on the
seashore in abundance; *they* were
eating and drinking and rejoicing.
21 Now Solomon ruled over all
the kingdoms[r] from the [5]River *to*
the land of the Philistines and to
the border of Egypt; *they* brought
tribute and served Solomon all the
days of his life. Gen. 15:18
22 And Solomon's provision for
one day was thirty [6]kors of fine
flour and sixty kors of meal,
23 ten fat oxen, twenty[t] pasture-
fed oxen, a hundred sheep besides
deer, gazelles, roebucks, and fattened fowl. *oxen of the pasture*
24 For he had dominion over
everything[t] west of the River, from
Tiphsah even to[r] Gaza, over all the
kings west of the River; and he

[5] I.e., Euphrates, and so through v. 24
[6] I.e., One kor equals approx. 10 bushels

had peace on all sides around about him. *beyond* • Judg. 1:18

25 [r]So Judah and Israel lived in safety, every man under his vine and his fig tree,[r]from Dan even to Beersheba, all the days of Solomon. Jer. 23:6 • 1 Sam. 3:20

26 And Solomon had [7]40,000 stalls of horses for his chariots, and 12,000 horsemen.

27 And those deputies[a]provided for King Solomon and all who came to King Solomon's table, each in his month; they left nothing lacking. *nourished*

28 They also brought barley and straw for the horses and swift steeds to the place where it should be, each according to his charge.

29 Now God gave Solomon wisdom and very great discernment and breadth of[t]mind, like the sand that is on the seashore. *heart*

30 And Solomon's wisdom surpassed the wisdom of all[r]the sons of the east and[r]all the wisdom of Egypt. Gen. 29:1 • Acts 7:22

31 For [r]he was wiser than all men, than Ethan the Ezrahite, Heman, Calcol and Darda, the sons of Mahol; and his [t]fame was *known* in all the surrounding nations. 1 Kin. 3:12 • *name*

32 He also spoke 3,000 proverbs, and his songs were 1,005.

33 And he spoke of trees, from the cedar that is in Lebanon even to the hyssop that grows on the wall; he spoke also of animals and birds and creeping things and fish.

34 And[t]men [r]came from all peoples to hear the wisdom of Solomon, from all the kings of the earth who had heard of his wisdom. *they* • 1 Kin. 10:1

[7]One ms. reads 4,000, cf. 2 Chr. 9:25

CHAPTER 5

NOW Hiram king of Tyre sent his servants to Solomon, when he heard that they had anointed him king in place of his father, for[r]Hiram had [t]always been a friend of David. 2 Sam. 5:11 • *all the day*

2 Then [r]Solomon sent *word* to Hiram, saying, 2 Chr. 2:3

3 "You know that David my father was unable to build a house for the name of the LORD his God because of the wars which surrounded him, until the LORD put them under the soles of his feet.

4 "But now the LORD my God has given me rest on every side; there is neither adversary nor[t]misfortune. *evil occurrence*

5 "And behold,[r]I[t]intend to build a house for the name of the LORD my God, as the LORD spoke to David my father, saying, 'Your son, whom I will set on your throne in your place, he will build the house for My name.' 2 Chr. 2:4 • *say*

6 "Now therefore, command that they cut for me [r]cedars from Lebanon, and my servants will be with your servants; and I will give you wages for your servants according to all that you say, for you know that there is no one among us who knows how to cut timber like the Sidonians." 2 Chr. 2:8

7 And it came about when Hiram heard the words of Solomon, that he rejoiced greatly and said, "Blessed be the LORD today, who has given to David a wise son over this great people."

8 So Hiram sent *word* to Solomon, saying, "I have heard *the message* which you have sent me;

I will do what you desire concerning the cedar and cypress timber.
9 "My servants will bring *them*
down from Lebanon to the sea;
and I will make them into rafts *to*
go by sea to the place where you
[t]direct me, and I will have them
broken up there, and you shall
carry *them* away. Then you shall
accomplish my desire by giving
food to my household." *send*
10 So Hiram [t]gave Solomon as
much as he desired of the cedar
and cypress timber. *was giving*
11 Solomon then gave Hiram
20,000 kors of wheat as food for
his household, and twenty kors of
beaten oil; thus Solomon would
give Hiram year by year.
12 And the LORD gave wisdom
to Solomon, just as He promised
him; and there was peace between
Hiram and Solomon, and the two
of them made a covenant.
13 Now King Solomon [t]levied
forced laborers from all Israel;
and the forced laborers [t]numbered
30,000 men. *raised up • was*
14 And he sent them to Lebanon, 10,000 a month in relays;
they were in Lebanon a month
and two months at home. And
[r]Adoniram *was* over the forced laborers. 1 Kin. 4:6; 12:18
15 Now Solomon had 70,000
transporters, and 80,000 hewers
of stone in the mountains,
16 besides Solomon's 3,300
chief deputies who *were* over the
project *and* who ruled over the
people who were doing the work.
17 Then the king commanded,
and they quarried great stones,
costly stones, to lay the foundation of the house with cut stones.
18 So Solomon's builders and
Hiram's builders and the Gebal-
ites [a]cut them, and prepared the
timbers and the stones to build
the house. *chiseled*

CHAPTER 6

NOW it came about in the four
hundred and eightieth year after
the sons of Israel came out of the
land of Egypt, in the fourth year of
Solomon's reign over Israel, in the
month of Ziv which is the second
month, that he [t]began to build the
house of the LORD. *built*
2 As for the house which King
Solomon built for the LORD, its
length *was* sixty [8]cubits and its
width twenty *cubits* and its height
thirty cubits.
3 And the porch in front of the
nave of the house *was* twenty cubits [t]in length, corresponding to
the width of the house, *and* its
depth along the front of the house
was ten cubits. *in its length*
4 Also for the house he made
windows with *artistic* frames.
5 And [r]against the wall of the
house he built stories encompass-
ing the walls of the house around
both the nave and the inner sanctuary; thus he made side chambers all around. Ezek. 41:6
6 The lowest story *was* five cubits wide, and the middle *was* six
cubits wide, and the third *was*
seven cubits wide; for on the outside he [t]made offsets *in the wall* of
the house all around in order that
the beams should not be inserted
in the walls of the house. *gave*
7 And the house, while it was
being built, was built of stone [t]pre-

[8]I.e., One cubit equals approx. 18 in.

pared at the quarry, and there was
neither hammer nor axe nor any
iron tool heard in the house while
it was being built. *finished*
8 The doorway for the [9]lowest
side chamber *was* on the right
side of the house; and they would
go up by winding stairs to the
middle *story,* and from the middle
to the third.
9 So he built the house and finished it; and he covered the house
with beams and planks of cedar.
10 He also built the stories
against the whole house, each five
cubits high; and they [t]were fastened to the house with timbers of
cedar. *took hold*
11 Now the word of the LORD
came to Solomon saying,
12 "*Concerning* this house which
you are building, [r]if you will walk
in My statutes and execute My ordinances and keep all My commandments by walking in them,
then I will carry out My word with
you which I spoke to David your
father. 2 Sam. 7:5-16; 1 Kin. 9:4
13 "And [r]I will dwell among the
sons of Israel, and will not forsake
My people Israel." Ex. 25:8
14 [r]So Solomon built the house
and finished it. 1 Kin. 6:9, 38
15 Then he built the walls of the
house on the inside with boards of
cedar; from the floor of the house
to the ceiling he overlaid *the walls*
on the inside with wood, and he
overlaid the floor of the house
with boards of cypress.
16 And he built twenty cubits
on the rear part of the house with
boards of cedar from the floor to
the ceiling; he built *them* for it on
the inside as an inner sanctuary,
even as the most holy place.
17 And the house, that is, the
nave in front of *the inner sanctuary,* was forty cubits *long.*
18 And there was cedar on the
house within, carved *in the shape*
of [r]gourds and open flowers; all
was cedar, there was no stone
seen. 1 Kin. 7:24
19 Then he prepared an inner
sanctuary within the house in order to place there the ark of the
covenant of the LORD.
20 And [t]the inner sanctuary *was*
twenty cubits in length, twenty
cubits in width, and twenty cubits
in height, and he overlaid it with
pure gold. He also overlaid the altar with cedar. *before*
21 So Solomon overlaid the inside of the house with pure gold.
And he drew chains of gold across
the front of the inner sanctuary;
and he overlaid it with gold.
22 And he overlaid the whole
house with gold, until all the
house was finished. Also [r]the
whole altar which was by the inner sanctuary he overlaid with
gold. Ex. 30:1, 3, 6
23 Also in the inner sanctuary
he made two cherubim of olive
wood, each ten cubits high.
24 And five cubits *was* the one
wing of the cherub and five cubits
the other wing of the cherub; from
the end of one wing to the end of
the other wing *were* ten cubits.
25 And the other cherub *was*
ten cubits; both the cherubim
were of the same measure and the
same form.
26 The height of the one cherub

[9]So with Gr. and versions; M.T., *middle*

was ten cubits, and so *was* the other cherub.

27 And he placed the cherubim in the midst of the inner house, and [r]the wings of the cherubim were spread out, so that the wing of the one was touching the *one* wall, and the wing of the other cherub was touching the other wall. So their wings were touching each other in the center of the house. Ex. 25:20; 37:9; 1 Kin. 8:7

28 He also overlaid the cherubim with gold.

29 Then he carved all the walls of the house round about with carved engravings of cherubim, palm trees, and open flowers, inner and outer *sanctuaries*.

30 And he overlaid the floor of the house with gold, inner and outer *sanctuaries*.

31 And for the entrance of the inner sanctuary he made doors of olive wood, the lintel *and* five-sided doorposts.

32 So *he made* two doors of olive wood, and he carved on them carvings of cherubim, palm trees, and open flowers, and overlaid them with gold; and he spread the gold on the cherubim and on the palm trees.

33 So also he made for the entrance of the nave four-sided doorposts of olive wood

34 and [r]two doors of cypress wood; the two leaves of the one door turned on pivots, and the two leaves of the other door turned on pivots. Ezek. 41:23-25

35 And he carved *on it* cherubim, palm trees, and open flowers; and he overlaid *them* with gold evenly applied on the engraved work.

36 And [r]he built the inner court with three rows of cut stone and a row of cedar beams. 1 Kin. 7:12

37 In the fourth year the foundation of the house of the LORD was laid, in the month of Ziv.

38 And in the eleventh year, in the month of Bul, which is the eighth month, the house was finished throughout all its parts and according to all its plans. So he was seven years in building it.

CHAPTER 7

NOW [r]Solomon was building his own house thirteen years, and he finished all his house. 1 Kin. 3:1

2 And he built the house of the forest of Lebanon; its length was 100 [10]cubits and its width 50 cubits and its height 30 cubits, on four rows of cedar pillars with cedar beams on the pillars.

3 And it was paneled with cedar above the side chambers which were on the 45 pillars, 15 in each row.

4 And *there were artistic window* frames in three rows, and window was opposite window in three ranks.

5 And all the doorways and doorposts had squared *artistic* frames, and window was opposite window in three ranks.

6 Then he made the hall of pillars; its length was 50 cubits and its width 30 cubits, and a porch *was* in front of them and pillars and a threshold in front of them.

7 And he made the hall of the throne where he was to judge, the

[10]I.e., One cubit equals approx. 18 in.

hall of judgment, and it was paneled with cedar from floor to floor.
8 And his house where he was to live, the other court inward from the hall, was of the same workmanship. ʳHe also made a house like this hall for Pharaoh's daughter, ʳwhom Solomon had married. 1 Kin. 9:24 • 1 Kin. 3:1
9 All these were of costly stones, of stone cut according to measure, sawed with saws, inside and outside; even from the foundation to the coping, and so on the outside to the great court.
10 And the foundation was of costly stones, *even* large stones, stones of ten cubits and stones of eight cubits.
11 And above were costly stones, stone cut according to measure, and cedar.
12 So the great court all around had three rows of cut stone and a row of cedar beams even as the inner court of the house of the LORD, and the porch of the house.
13 Now King Solomon sent and brought Hiram from Tyre.
14 He was a widow's son from the tribe of Naphtali, and his father was a man of Tyre, a worker in bronze; andʳhe was filled with wisdom and understanding and skill for doing any work in bronze. So he came to King Solomon and performed all his work. Ex. 28:3
15 And he fashioned the two pillars of bronze; eighteen cubits was the height of one pillar, and a line of twelve cubits measured the circumference of both.
16 He also made two capitals of molten bronze to set on the tops of the pillars; the height of the one capital was five cubits and the height of the other capital was five cubits.
17 *There were* nets of network and twisted threads of chainwork for the capitals which were on the top of the pillars; seven for the one capital and seven for the other capital.
18 So he made the pillars, and two rows around on the one network to cover the capitals which were on the top of the pomegranates; and so he did for the other capital.
19 And the capitals which *were* on the top of the pillars in the porch were of lily design, four cubits.
20 And *there were* capitals also on the two pillars, close to the rounded projection which was beside the network; and the pomegranates *numbered* two hundred in rows around both capitals.
21 Thus he set up the pillars at the porch of the nave; and he set up the right pillar and named it [11]Jachin, and he set up the left pillar and named it [12]Boaz.
22 And on the top of the pillars was lily design. So the work of the pillars was finished.
23 Now he made the sea of cast *metal* ten cubits from brim to brim, circular in form, and its height was five cubits, and thirty cubits in circumference.
24 And under its brim gourds went around encircling it ten to a cubit, completely surrounding the sea; the gourds were in two rows, castᵗwith the rest. ***in its casting***

[11] I.e., he shall establish [12] I.e., in it is strength

25 It stood on twelve oxen,
three facing north, three facing
west, three facing south, and
three facing east; and the sea *was*
set on top of them, and all their
rear parts *turned* inward.
26 And it was a handbreadth
thick, and its brim was made like
the brim of a cup, *as* a lily blossom; it could hold two thousand
baths.
27 Then he made the ten stands
of bronze; the length of each stand
was four cubits and its width four
cubits and its height three cubits.
28 And this was the design of
the stands: they had borders, even
borders between the [13]frames,
29 and on the borders which
were between the [13]frames *were*
lions, oxen and cherubim; and on
the [13]frames there *was* a pedestal
above, and beneath the lions and
oxen *were* wreaths of hanging
work.
30 Now each stand had four
bronze wheels with bronze axles,
and its four feet had supports; beneath the basin *were* cast supports with wreaths at each side.
31 And its opening inside the
crown at the top *was* a cubit, and
its opening *was* round like the design of a pedestal, a cubit and a
half; and also on its opening *there*
were engravings, and their borders were square, not round.
32 And the four wheels *were* underneath the borders, and the
axles of the wheels *were* on the
stand. And the height of a wheel
was a cubit and a half.
33 And the workmanship of the
wheels *was* like the workmanship
of a chariot wheel. Their axles,
their rims, their spokes, and their
hubs *were* all cast.
34 Now *there were* four supports at the four corners of each
stand; its supports *were* part of
the stand itself.
35 And on the top of the stand
there was a circular form half a
cubit high, and on the top of the
stand its [t]stays and its borders
were part of it. ***hands***
36 And he engraved on the
plates of its stays and on its borders, cherubim, lions and palm
trees, according to the clear space
on each, with wreaths *all* around.
37 He made the ten stands like
this: all of them had one casting,
one measure and one form.
38 [r]And he made ten basins of
bronze, one basin held forty
baths; each basin *was* four cubits,
and on each of the ten stands *was*
one basin. **Ex. 30:18; 2 Chr. 4:6**
39 Then he set the stands, five
on the right side of the house and
five on the left side of the house;
and he set the sea of cast metal on
the right side of the house eastward toward the south.
40 Now Hiram made the basins
and the shovels and the bowls. So
Hiram finished doing all the work
which he performed for King
Solomon *in* the house of the LORD:
41 the two pillars and the two
bowls of the capitals which *were*
on the top of the two pillars, and
the two networks to cover the two
bowls of the capitals which *were*
on the top of the pillars;
42 and the four hundred pomegranates for the two networks,

[13]Or, *crossbars*

two rows of pomegranates for each network to cover the two bowls of the capitals which *were* on the tops of the pillars;

43 and the ten stands with the ten basins on the stands;

44 and the one sea and the twelve oxen under the sea;

45 and the pails and the shovels and the bowls; even all these utensils which Hiram made for King Solomon *in* the house of the LORD *were* of polished bronze.

46 In the plain of the Jordan the king cast them, in the clay ground between Succoth and Zarethan.

47 And Solomon left all the utensils *unweighed*, because *they were* too many; the weight of the bronze could not be ascertained.

48 And Solomon made all the furniture which *was in* the house of the LORD: the golden altar and the golden table on which *was* the [r]bread of the Presence; Ex. 25:30

49 and the lampstands, five on the right side and five on the left, in front of the inner sanctuary, of pure gold; and the flowers and the lamps and the tongs, of gold;

50 and the cups and the snuffers and the bowls and the spoons and the firepans, of pure gold; and the hinges both for the doors of the inner house, the most holy place, *and* for the doors of the house, *that is*, of the nave, of gold.

51 Thus all the work that King Solomon performed *in* the house of the LORD was finished. And Solomon brought in the things dedicated by his father David, the silver and the gold and the utensils, *and* he put them in the treasuries of the house of the LORD.

CHAPTER 8

THEN Solomon assembled the elders of Israel and all the heads of the tribes, the leaders of the fathers' *households* of the sons of Israel, to King Solomon in Jerusalem, to bring up the ark of the covenant of the LORD from the city of David, which is Zion.

2 And all the men of Israel assembled themselves to King Solomon at [r]the feast, in the month Ethanim, which is the seventh month. Lev. 23:34; 1 Kin. 8:65

3 Then all the elders of Israel came, and [r]the priests took up the ark. Num. 7:9; Deut. 31:9

4 And they brought up the ark of the LORD and [r]the tent of meeting and all the holy utensils, which were in the tent, and the priests and the Levites brought them up. 1 Kin. 3:4; 2 Chr. 1:3

5 And King Solomon and all the congregation of Israel, who were assembled to him, were with him before the ark, sacrificing so many sheep and oxen they could not be counted or numbered.

6 Then [r]the priests brought the ark of the covenant of the LORD to its place, into the inner sanctuary of the house, to the most holy place, under the wings of the cherubim. 1 Kin. 8:3

7 For the cherubim spread *their* wings over the place of the ark, and the cherubim made a covering over the ark and its poles from above.

8 But [r]the poles were so long that the ends of the poles could be seen from the holy place before the inner sanctuary, but they

could not be seen outside; they are
there to this day. Ex. 25:13-15
9 There was nothing in the ark
except the two tablets of stone
which Moses put there at Horeb,
where the LORD made a covenant
with the sons of Israel, when they
came out of the land of Egypt.
10 And it came about when the
priests came from the holy place,
that [r]the cloud filled the house of
the LORD, Ex. 40:34, 35
11 so that the priests could not
stand to minister because of the
cloud, for the glory of the LORD
filled the house of the LORD.
12 Then Solomon said,
"The LORD has said that He
would dwell in the thick
cloud.
13 "I [r]have surely built Thee a
lofty house, 2 Sam. 7:13
[r]A place for Thy dwelling
forever." Ex. 15:17; Ps. 132:14
14 Then the king faced about
and [r]blessed all the assembly of Israel, while all the assembly of Israel was standing. 2 Sam. 6:18
15 And he said, "Blessed [r]be the
LORD, the God of Israel, who
spoke with His mouth to my father David and has fulfilled *it* with
His hand, saying, Neh. 9:5
16 'Since the day that I brought
My people Israel from Egypt, I did
not choose a city out of all the
tribes of Israel *in which* to build a
house that [r]My name might be
there, but I chose David to be over
My people Israel.' Deut. 12:5, 11
17 "Now [r]it was [t]in the heart of
my father David to build a house
for the name of the LORD, the God
of Israel. 2 Sam. 7:2, 3 • *with*
18 "But the LORD said to my father David, 'Because it was [t]in
your heart to build a house for My
name, you did well that it was in
your heart. *with*
19 'Nevertheless you shall not
build the house, but your son who
shall be born to you, he shall build
the house for My name.'
20 "Now the LORD has fulfilled
His word which He spoke; for I
have risen in place of my father
David and sit on the throne of Israel, as the LORD promised, and
have built the house for the name
of the LORD, the God of Israel.
21 "And there I have set a place
for the ark, in which is the covenant of the LORD, which He made
with our fathers when He brought
them from the land of Egypt."
22 Then [r]Solomon stood before
the altar of the LORD in the presence of all the assembly of Israel
and [r]spread out his hands toward
heaven. 1 Kin. 8:54 • Ex. 9:33
23 And he said, "O LORD, the
God of Israel, there is no God like
Thee in heaven above or on earth
beneath, who art keeping covenant and showing lovingkindness to Thy servants who walk before Thee with all their heart,
24 who hast kept with Thy servant, my father David, that which
Thou hast [t]promised him; indeed,
Thou hast spoken with Thy mouth
and hast fulfilled it with Thy hand
as it is this day. *spoken to*
25 "Now therefore, O LORD, the
God of Israel, keep with Thy servant David my father that which
Thou hast [t]promised him, saying,
'You [r]shall not lack a man to sit on
the throne of Israel, if only your
sons take heed to their way to

walk before Me as you have
walked.' *spoken to* • 1 Kin. 2:4
26 "Now therefore, O God of Israel, let Thy word, I pray Thee, be
confirmed[r] which Thou hast spoken to Thy servant, my father David. 2 Sam. 7:25
27 "But will God indeed dwell on
the earth? Behold,[r] heaven and the
highest heaven cannot contain
Thee, how much less this house
which I have built! 2 Chr. 2:6
28 "Yet have regard to the[r] prayer
of Thy servant and to his supplication, O LORD my God, to listen to
the cry and to the prayer which
Thy servant prays before Thee today; Phil. 4:6
29 that Thine eyes may be open
toward this house night and day,
toward[r] the place of which Thou
hast said, 'My name shall be
there,' to listen to the prayer
which Thy servant shall pray
toward this place. Deut. 12:11
30 "And listen to the supplication
of Thy servant and of Thy people
Israel, when they pray toward this
place; hear Thou in heaven Thy
dwelling place; hear and forgive.
31 "If[r] a man sins against his
neighbor and is made to take an
oath, and he comes *and* takes an
oath before Thine altar in this
house, Ex. 22:8-11
32 then hear Thou in heaven
and act and judge Thy servants,
[r]condemning the wicked by bringing his way on his own head and
justifying the righteous by giving
him according to his righteousness. Deut. 25:1
33 "When Thy people Israel are
[t]defeated before an enemy, because they have sinned against
Thee, if they turn to Thee again
and confess Thy name and pray
and make supplication to Thee in
this house, *smitten*
34 then hear Thou in heaven,
and forgive the sin of Thy people
Israel, and bring them back to the
land which Thou didst give to
their fathers.
35 "When[r] the heavens are shut
up and there is no rain, because
they have sinned against Thee,
and they pray toward this place
and confess Thy name and turn
from their sin when Thou dost afflict them, Lev. 26:19
36 then hear Thou in heaven
and forgive the sin of Thy servants and of Thy people Israel,[r] indeed, teach them the good way in
which they should walk. And[r] send
rain on Thy land, which Thou hast
given Thy people for an inheritance. 1 Sam. 12:23 • Jer. 14:22
37 "If there is famine in the land,
if there is pestilence, if there is
blight *or* mildew, locust *or* grasshopper, if their enemy besieges
them in the land of their [t]cities,
whatever plague, whatever sickness there is, *gates*
38 whatever prayer or supplication is made by any man *or* by all
Thy people Israel, [t]each knowing
the affliction of his own heart, and
spreading his hands toward this
house; *who shall know each*
39 then hear Thou in heaven
Thy dwelling place, and forgive
and act and render to each according to all his ways,[r] whose
heart Thou knowest, for Thou
alone dost know the hearts of all
the sons of men, 1 Sam. 2:3; 16:7
40 that they may [14]fear Thee all

[14]Or, *revere*

the days that they live[t]in the land
which Thou hast given to our fathers. *on the face of the land*
41 "Also concerning the foreigner who is not of Thy people Israel, when he comes from a far
country for Thy name's sake
42 (for they will hear of Thy
great name[r]and Thy mighty hand,
and of Thine outstretched arm);
when he comes and prays toward
this house, Ex. 13:3; Deut. 3:24
43 hear Thou in heaven Thy
dwelling place, and do according
to all for which the foreigner calls
to Thee, in order that all the peoples of the earth may know Thy
name, to [14]fear Thee, as *do* Thy
people Israel, and that they may
know that this house which I have
built is called by Thy name.
44 "When Thy people go out to
battle against [t]their enemy, by
whatever way Thou shalt send
them, and they pray to the LORD
toward the city which Thou hast
chosen and the house which I
have built for Thy name, *his*
45 then hear in heaven their
prayer and their supplication, and
maintain their cause.
46 "When they sin against Thee
(for[r]there is no man who does not
sin) and Thou art angry with them
and dost deliver them to an enemy, so that they take them away
captive to the land of the enemy,
far off or near; Ps. 130:3, 4
47 if they take thought in the
land where they have been taken
captive, and repent and make supplication to Thee in the land of
those who have taken them captive, saying,[r]'We have sinned and

[14]Or, *revere*

have committed iniquity, we have
acted wickedly'; Ezra 9:6, 7
48 if they return to Thee with all
their heart and with all their soul
in the land of their enemies who
have taken them captive, and[r]pray
to Thee toward their land which
Thou hast given to their fathers,
the city which Thou hast chosen,
and the house which I have built
for Thy name; Dan. 6:10
49 then hear their prayer and
their supplication in heaven Thy
dwelling place, and maintain their
[t]cause, *judgment*
50 and forgive Thy people who
have sinned against Thee and all
their transgressions which they
have transgressed against Thee,
and make them *objects of* compassion before those who have
taken them captive, that they may
have compassion on them
51 [r](for they are Thy people and
Thine inheritance which Thou
hast brought forth from Egypt,
[r]from the midst of the iron furnace), Ex. 32:11, 12 • Deut. 4:20
52 that Thine eyes may be open
to the supplication of Thy servant
and to the supplication of Thy
people Israel, to listen to them
whenever they call to Thee.
53 "For Thou hast separated
them from all the peoples of the
earth as Thine inheritance, [r]as
Thou didst speak through Moses
Thy servant, when Thou didst
bring our fathers forth from
Egypt, O Lord GOD." Ex. 19:5, 6
54 And it came about that when
Solomon had finished praying this
entire prayer and supplication to
the LORD, he arose from before
the altar of the LORD, from kneel-

ing on his knees with his [t]hands
spread toward heaven. *palms*
55 And he stood and [r]blessed all
the assembly of Israel with a loud
voice, saying, Num. 6:23-26
56 "Blessed be the LORD, who
has given rest to His people Israel,
according to all that He promised;
not one word has failed of all His
good promise, which He promised
through Moses His servant.
57 "May the LORD our God be
with us, as He was with our fathers; [r]may He not leave us or forsake us, Deut. 31:6, 17; Josh. 1:5
58 that [r]He may incline our
hearts to Himself, to walk in all
His ways and to keep His commandments and His statutes and
His ordinances, which He commanded our fathers. Ps. 119:36
59 "And may these words of
mine, with which I have made
supplication before the LORD, be
near to the LORD our God day and
night, that He may maintain the
[t]cause of His servant and the cause
of His people Israel, as each day
requires, *judgment*
60 so that all the peoples of the
earth may know that the LORD is
God; there is no one else.
61 "Let your heart therefore be
[t]wholly devoted to the LORD our
God, to walk in His statutes and to
keep His commandments, as at
this day." *complete with*
62 Now the king and all Israel
with him [r]offered sacrifice before
the LORD. 2 Sam. 6:17-19
63 And Solomon offered for the
sacrifice of peace offerings, which
he offered to the LORD, 22,000
oxen and 120,000 sheep. So the
king and all the sons of Israel
dedicated the house of the LORD.
64 On the same day the king
consecrated the middle of the
court that *was* before the house of
the LORD, because there he [t]of-
fered the burnt offering and the
grain offering and the fat of the
peace offerings; for the bronze altar that *was* before the LORD *was*
too small to hold the burnt offering and the grain offering and the
fat of the peace offerings. *made*
65 So Solomon observed the
feast at that time, and all Israel
with him, a great assembly from
the entrance of Hamath to the
brook of Egypt, before the LORD
our God, for seven days and seven
more days, *even* fourteen days.
66 On the eighth day he sent the
people away and they blessed the
king. Then they went to their tents
joyful and glad of heart for all the
goodness that the LORD had
[t]shown to David His servant and to
Israel His people. *done*

CHAPTER 9

NOW it came about when Solomon had finished building the
house of the LORD, and [r]the king's
house, and all that Solomon desired to do, 1 Kin. 7:1, 2
2 that the LORD appeared to
Solomon a second time, as He had
appeared to him at Gibeon.
3 And the LORD said to him, "I
have heard your prayer and your
supplication, which you have
made before Me; I have consecrated this house which you have
built by putting My name there
forever, and My eyes and My
heart will be there perpetually.

4 "And as for you,[r] if you will walk before Me as your father David walked, in integrity of heart and uprightness, doing according to all that I have commanded you *and* will keep My statutes and My ordinances, 1 Kin. 3:6, 14

5 then [r]I will establish the throne of your kingdom over Israel forever, just as I[t] promised to your father David, saying, 'You shall not lack a man on the throne of Israel.' 2 Sam. 7:12, 16 • *spoke*

6 "But[r] if you or your sons shall indeed turn away from following Me, and shall not keep My commandments and My statutes which I have set before you and shall go and serve other gods and worship them, 2 Sam. 7:14-16

7 then I will cut off Israel from the land which I have given them, and[r] the house which I have consecrated for My name, I will[t] cast out of My sight. So Israel will become a proverb and a byword among all peoples. Jer. 7:4-14 • *send*

8 "And this house will become [r]a heap of ruins; everyone who passes by will be astonished and hiss and say,[r] 'Why has the LORD done thus to this land and to this house?' 2 Kin. 25:9 • 2 Chr. 7:21

9 "And they will say,[r] 'Because they forsook the LORD their God, who brought their fathers out of the land of Egypt, and adopted other gods and worshiped them and served them, therefore the LORD has brought all this adversity on them.' " Deut. 29:25-28

10 And it came about[r] at the end of twenty years in which Solomon had built the two houses, the house of the LORD and the king's house 1 Kin. 6:37, 38

11 (Hiram king of Tyre had supplied Solomon with cedar and cypress timber and gold according to all his desire), then King Solomon gave Hiram twenty cities in the land of Galilee.

12 So Hiram came out from Tyre to see the cities which Solomon had given him, and they did not please him.

13 And he said, "What are these cities which you have given me, my brother?" So they were called the land of [15]Cabul to this day.

14 [r]And Hiram sent to the king 120 talents of gold. 1 Kin. 9:11

15 Now this is the account of the forced labor which King Solomon[r] levied to build the house of the LORD, his own house, the [16]Millo, the wall of Jerusalem, Hazor, Megiddo, and Gezer. 1 Kin. 5:13

16 *For* Pharaoh king of Egypt had gone up and captured Gezer, and burned it with fire, and killed the Canaanites who lived in the city, and had given it *as* a dowry to his daughter, Solomon's wife.

17 So Solomon rebuilt Gezer and the lower Beth-horon

18 and [r]Baalath and Tamar in the wilderness, in the land *of Judah,* Josh. 19:44

19 and all the storage cities which Solomon had, even the cities for his chariots and the cities for [t]his horsemen, and all that it pleased Solomon to build in Jerusalem, in Lebanon, and in all the land[t] under his rule. *the* • *of*

20 *As for* all the people who were left of the Amorites, the Hit-

[15] I.e., as good as nothing [16] I.e., citadel

tites, the Perizzites, the Hivites
and the Jebusites, who were not
of the sons of Israel,
21 their descendants who were
left after them in the land [r]whom
the sons of Israel were unable to
destroy utterly, from them Solomon levied forced laborers, even
to this day. Josh. 15:63; 17:12, 13
22 But Solomon [r]did not make
slaves of the sons of Israel; for
they were men of war, his servants, his princes, his captains, his
chariot commanders, and his
horsemen. Lev. 25:39
23 These *were* the chief officers
who were over Solomon's work,
five hundred and fifty, who ruled
over the people doing the work.
24 As soon as [r]Pharaoh's daughter came up from the city of David
to her house which *Solomon* had
built for her, [r]then he built the Millo. 1 Kin. 3:1; 7:8 • 2 Sam. 5:9
25 Now [r]three times in a year
Solomon offered burnt offerings
and peace offerings on the altar
which he built to the LORD, burning incense with them *on the altar*
which *was* before the LORD. So he
finished the house. Ex. 23:14-17
26 King Solomon also built a
fleet of ships in [r]Ezion-geber,
which is near Eloth on the shore
of the [t]Red Sea, in the land of
Edom. Deut. 2:8 • *Sea of Reeds*
27 [r]And Hiram sent his servants
with the fleet, sailors who knew
the sea, along with the servants of
Solomon. 1 Kin. 5:6, 9; 10:11
28 And they went to Ophir, and
took four hundred and twenty talents of gold from there, and
brought *it* to King Solomon.

CHAPTER 10

NOW when the [r]queen of Sheba
heard about the fame of Solomon
concerning the name of the LORD,
she came to test him with difficult
questions. 2 Chr. 9:1
2 So she came to Jerusalem
with a very large retinue, with
camels [r]carrying spices and very
much gold and precious stones.
When she came to Solomon, she
spoke with him about all that was
in her heart. 1 Kin. 10:10
3 And Solomon [t]answered all
her questions; nothing was hidden
from the king which he did not explain to her. *told her all her words*
4 When the queen of Sheba
perceived all the wisdom of Solomon, the house that he had built,
5 the food of his table, the
seating of his servants, the attendance of his waiters and their attire, his cupbearers, and his stairway by which he went up to the
house of the LORD, there was no
more spirit in her.
6 Then she said to the king, "It
was a true report which I heard in
my own land about your words
and your wisdom.
7 "Nevertheless I did not believe the [t]reports, until I came and
my eyes had seen it. And behold,
the half was not told me. You exceed *in* wisdom and prosperity
the report which I heard. *words*
8 "How blessed are your men,
how blessed are these your servants who stand before you continually *and* hear your wisdom.
9 "Blessed be the LORD your
God who delighted in you to set
you on the throne of Israel; be-

cause the LORD loved Israel forever, therefore He made you king,
to do justice and righteousness."
10 And she gave the king a hundred and twenty talents of gold,
and a very great *amount* of spices
and precious stones. Never again
did such abundance of spices
come in as that which the queen
of Sheba gave King Solomon.
11 [r]And also the ships of Hiram,
which brought gold from Ophir,
brought in from Ophir a very
great *number of* almug trees and
precious stones. 1 Kin. 9:27, 28
12 And[r]the king made of the almug trees supports for the house
of the LORD and for the king's
house, also lyres and harps for the
singers; such almug trees have not
come in *again,* nor have they been
seen to this day. 2 Chr. 9:11
13 And King Solomon gave to
the queen of Sheba all her desire
which she requested, besides
what he gave her according to his
royal bounty. Then she turned and
went to her own land[t]together
with her servants. *she and*
14 Now the weight of gold
which came in to Solomon in one
year *was* 666 talents of gold,
15 besides *that* from the traders
and the [17]wares of the merchants
and all the kings of the Arabs and
the governors of the country.
16 And King Solomon made 200
large shields of beaten gold,[t]using
600 *shekels of* gold on each large
shield. *he brought up*
17 And *he made* 300 shields of
beaten gold,[t]using three minas of
gold on each shield, and the king
put them in the house of the forest
of Lebanon. *he brought up*

18 Moreover, the king made a
great throne of[r]ivory and overlaid
it with refined gold. 1 Kin. 10:22
19 There *were* six steps to the
throne and a round top to the
throne at its rear, and arms on
each side of the seat, and two
lions standing beside the arms.
20 And twelve lions were standing there on the six steps on the
one side and on the other; nothing
like *it* was made for any other
kingdom.
21 And all King Solomon's
drinking vessels *were* of gold, and
all the vessels of the house of the
forest of Lebanon *were* of pure
gold. None was of silver; it was
not considered [18]valuable in the
days of Solomon.
22 For[r]the king had at sea the
ships of Tarshish with the ships of
Hiram; once every three years the
ships of Tarshish came bringing
gold and silver, ivory and apes
and peacocks. 1 Kin. 9:26-28
23 So King Solomon became
greater than all the kings of the
earth in riches and in wisdom.
24 And all the earth was seeking the presence of Solomon,[r]to
hear his wisdom which God had
put in his heart. 1 Kin. 3:9, 12, 28
25 And[r]they brought every man
his gift, articles of silver and gold,
garments, weapons, spices,
horses, and mules, so much year
by year. Ps. 68:29
26 Now Solomon gathered
chariots and horsemen; and he
had 1,400 chariots and 12,000
horsemen, and he stationed them
in the [r]chariot cities and with the
king in Jerusalem. 1 Kin. 9:19
27 [r]And the king made silver *as*

[17]Or, *traffic*

[18]Lit., *anything*

common as stones in Jerusalem,
and he made cedars as plentiful as
sycamore trees that are in the
[19]lowland. Deut. 17:17
28 Also Solomon's import of
horses was from Egypt and Kue,
and the king's merchants procured *them* from Kue for a price.
29 And a chariot[t]was imported
from Egypt for 600 *shekels* of silver, and a horse for 150; and by
the same means they exported
them to all the kings of the Hittites and to the kings of the Arameans. *came up and went out from*

CHAPTER 11

NOW[r]King Solomon loved many
foreign women along with the
daughter of Pharaoh: Moabite,
Ammonite, Edomite, Sidonian,
and Hittite women, Deut. 17:17
2 from the nations concerning
which the LORD had said to the
sons of Israel, "You shall not[t]asso-
ciate with them, neither shall they
associate with you, for they will
surely turn your heart away after
their gods." Solomon held fast to
these in love. *go among*
3 And he had seven hundred
wives, princesses, and three hundred concubines, and his wives
turned his heart away.
4 For it came about when Solomon was old, his wives turned his
heart away after other gods; and
his heart was not [20]wholly devoted
to the LORD his God, as the heart
of David his father *had been.*
5 For Solomon went after Ashtoreth the goddess of the Sidonians and after Milcom the detestable idol of the Ammonites.

6 And Solomon did what was
evil in the sight of the LORD, and
did not follow the LORD fully, as
David his father *had done.*
7 Then Solomon built a high
place for Chemosh the detestable
idol of Moab, on the mountain
which is [t]east of Jerusalem, and
for Molech the detestable idol of
the sons of Ammon. *before*
8 Thus also he did for all his
foreign wives, who burned incense and sacrificed to their gods.
9 Now [r]the LORD was angry
with Solomon because his heart
was turned away from the LORD,
the God of Israel, who had appeared to him twice, Ps. 90:7
10 and [r]had commanded him
concerning this thing, that he
should not go after other gods; but
he did not observe what the LORD
had commanded. 1 Kin. 6:12
11 So the LORD said to Solomon,
"Because you have done this, and
you have not kept My covenant
and My statutes, which I have
commanded you, I will surely tear
the kingdom from you, and will
give it to your servant.
12 "Nevertheless I will not do it
in your days for the sake of your
father David, *but* I will tear it out
of the hand of your son.
13 "However, [r]I will not tear
away all the kingdom, but I will
give one tribe to your son for the
sake of My servant David and for
the sake of Jerusalem which I
have chosen." 2 Sam. 7:15
14 Then the LORD raised up an
adversary to Solomon, Hadad the
Edomite; he was of the [t]royal line
in Edom. *king's seed*
15 For it came about, when Da-

[19]Or, *Shephelah* [20]Lit., *complete with*

vid was in Edom, and Joab the
commander of the army had gone
up to bury the slain, and had
struck down every male in Edom
16 (for Joab and all Israel
stayed there six months, until he
had cut off every male in Edom),
17 that Hadad fled to Egypt, he
and certain Edomites of his father's servants with him, while
Hadad *was* a young boy.
18 And they arose from Midian
and came to [r]Paran; and they took
men with them from Paran and
came to Egypt, to Pharaoh king of
Egypt, who gave him a house and
assigned him food and gave him
land. Num. 10:12; Deut. 1:1
19 Now Hadad found great favor [t]before Pharaoh, so that he
gave him in marriage the sister of
his own wife, the sister of Tahpenes the queen. *in the sight of*
20 And the sister of Tahpenes
bore his son Genubath, whom
Tahpenes weaned in Pharaoh's
house; and Genubath was in Pharaoh's house among the sons of
Pharaoh.
21 But [r]when Hadad heard in
Egypt that David slept with his fathers, and that Joab the commander of the army was dead, Hadad said to Pharaoh, "Send me
away, that I may go to my own
country." 1 Kin. 2:10
22 Then Pharaoh said to him,
"But what have you lacked with
me, that behold, you are seeking
to go to your own country?" And
he answered, "Nothing; nevertheless you must surely let me go."
23 God also raised up *another*
adversary to him, Rezon the son
of Eliada, who had fled from his
lord Hadadezer king of Zobah.
24 And he gathered men to himself and became leader of a marauding band, after David slew
them of *Zobah;* and they went to
Damascus and stayed [t]there, and
reigned in Damascus. *in it*
25 So he was an adversary to Israel all the days of Solomon, along
with the evil that Hadad *did;* and
he abhorred Israel and reigned
over Aram.
26 Then Jeroboam the son of
Nebat, an Ephraimite of Zeredah,
Solomon's servant, whose mother's name was Zeruah, a widow,
also rebelled against the king.
27 Now this was the reason why
he [t]rebelled against the king: Solomon built the Millo, *and* closed up
the breach of the city of his father
David. *lifted up a hand*
28 Now the man Jeroboam was
a valiant warrior, and when Solomon saw that the young man was
[t]industrious, he appointed him
over all the forced labor of the
house of Joseph. *a doer of work*
29 And it came about at that
time, when Jeroboam went out of
Jerusalem, that [r]the prophet Ahijah the Shilonite found him on the
road. Now [t]Ahijah had clothed
himself with a new cloak; and
both of them were alone in the
field. 1 Kin. 12:15; 14:2 • *he*
30 Then Ahijah took hold of the
new cloak which was on him, and
tore it into twelve pieces.
31 And he said to Jeroboam,
"Take for yourself ten pieces; for
thus says the LORD, the God of Israel, 'Behold, I will tear the king-

dom out of the hand of Solomon
and give you ten tribes
32 (but he will have one tribe,
for the sake of My servant David
and for the sake of Jerusalem, the
city which I have chosen from all
the tribes of Israel),
33 because they have forsaken
Me, and [r]have worshiped Ashtoreth the goddess of the Sidonians,
Chemosh the god of Moab, and
Milcom the god of the sons of Ammon; and they have not walked in
My ways, doing what is right in
My sight and *observing* My statutes and My ordinances, as his father David *did*. 1 Sam. 7:3
34 'Nevertheless I will not take
the whole kingdom out of his
hand, but I will make him [a]ruler all
the days of his life, for the sake of
My servant David whom I chose,
who observed My command-
ments and My statutes; *prince*
35 but I will take the kingdom
from his son's hand and give it to
you, *even* ten tribes.
36 'But [r]to his son I will give one
tribe, [r]that My servant David may
have a lamp always before Me in
Jerusalem, the city where I have
chosen for Myself to put My
name. 1 Kin. 11:13 • 1 Kin. 15:4
37 'And I will take you, and you
shall reign over whatever [t]you desire, and you shall be king over Israel. *your soul desires*
38 'Then it will be, that if you listen to all that I command you and
walk in My ways, and do what is
right in My sight by observing My
statutes and My commandments,
as My servant David did, then I
will be with you and build you an
enduring house as I built for David, and I will give Israel to you.
39 'Thus I will afflict the [t]de-
scendants of David for this, but
not always.'" *seed*
40 Solomon sought therefore to
put Jeroboam to death; but Jeroboam arose and fled to Egypt to
[r]Shishak king of Egypt, and he was
in Egypt until the death of Solomon. 1 Kin. 14:25; 2 Chr. 12:2-9
41 [r]Now the rest of the acts of
Solomon and whatever he did,
and his wisdom, are they not written in the book of the acts of Solomon? 2 Chr. 9:29
42 Thus [r]the time that Solomon
reigned in Jerusalem over all Israel was forty years. 2 Chr. 9:30
43 And Solomon slept with his
fathers and was buried in the city
of his father David, and his son
Rehoboam reigned in his place.

CHAPTER 12

THEN Rehoboam went to Shechem, for all Israel had come to
Shechem to make him king.
2 Now it came about when
Jeroboam the son of Nebat heard
of it, that [t]he was living in Egypt
(for he was yet in Egypt, where he
had fled from the presence of
King Solomon). *Jeroboam*
3 Then they sent and called
him, and Jeroboam and all the assembly of Israel came and spoke
to Rehoboam, saying,
4 "Your father made our yoke
hard; therefore lighten the hard
service of your father and his
heavy yoke which he put on us,
and we will serve you."
5 Then he said to them, "De-

part for three days, then return to me." So the people departed.

6 And King Rehoboam consulted with the elders who had [t]served his father Solomon while he was still alive, saying, "How do you counsel *me* to answer this people?" *stood before*

7 Then they spoke to him, saying, "If you will be a servant to this people today, will serve them, [t]grant them their petition, and speak good words to them, then they will be your servants forever." *answer them*

8 But he forsook the counsel of the elders which they had given him, and consulted with the young men who grew up with him [t]and served him. *who stood before*

9 So he said to them, "What counsel do you give that we may answer this people who have spoken to me, saying, 'Lighten the yoke which your father put on us' ?"

10 And the young men who grew up with him spoke to him, saying, "Thus you shall say to this people who spoke to you, saying, 'Your father made our yoke heavy, now you make it lighter for us!' But you shall speak to them, 'My little finger is thicker than my father's loins!

11 'Whereas my father loaded you with a heavy yoke, I will add to your yoke; my father disciplined you with whips, but I will discipline you with scorpions.' "

12 Then Jeroboam and all the people came to Rehoboam on the third day as the king had [t]directed, saying, "Return [r]to me on the third day." *spoken* • 1 Kin. 12:5

13 And the king answered the people harshly, for he forsook the advice of the elders which they had [t]given him, *advised*

14 and he spoke to them according to the advice of the young men, saying, "My father made your yoke heavy, but I will add to your yoke; my father disciplined you with whips, but I will discipline you with scorpions."

15 So the king did not listen to the people; [r]for it was a turn *of events* from the LORD, that He might establish His word, which the LORD spoke through Ahijah the Shilonite to Jeroboam the son of Nebat. Deut. 2:30; Judg. 14:4

16 When all Israel *saw* that the king did not listen to them, the people answered the king, saying,

"What portion do we have in
David?
We have no inheritance in
the son of Jesse;
To your tents, O Israel!
Now look after your own
house, David!"

So Israel departed to their tents.

17 But as for the sons of Israel who lived in the cities of Judah, Rehoboam reigned over them.

18 Then King Rehoboam sent [r]Adoram, who was over the forced labor, and all Israel stoned him to death. And King Rehoboam made haste to mount his chariot to flee to Jerusalem. 2 Sam. 20:24

19 So [r] Israel has been in rebellion against the house of David to this day. 2 Kin. 17:21

20 And it came about when all Israel heard that Jeroboam had returned, that they sent and called him to the assembly and made

him king over all Israel.ʳNone but
the tribe of Judah followed the
house of David. 1 Kin. 11:13, 32
21 ʳNow when Rehoboam had
come to Jerusalem, he assembled
all the house of Judah and the
tribe of Benjamin, 180,000 chosen
men who were warriors, to fight
against the house of Israel to restore the kingdom to Rehoboam
the son of Solomon. 2 Chr. 11:1
22 But the word of God came to
Shemaiah the man of God, saying,
23 "Speak to Rehoboam the son
of Solomon, king of Judah, and to
all the house of Judah and Benjamin and to theʳrest of the people,
saying, 1 Kin. 12:17
24 'Thus says the LORD, "You
must not go up and fight against
yourᵗrelatives the sons of Israel;
return every man to his house,ʳfor
this thing has come from Me." ' "
So they listened to the word of the
LORD, and returned and went *their*
way according to the word of the
LORD. *brothers* • 1 Kin. 12:15
25 Then Jeroboam built Shechem in the hill country of Ephraim, and lived there. And he went
out from there and built Penuel.
26 And Jeroboam said in his
heart, "Now the kingdom will return to the house of David.
27 "Ifʳthis people go up to offer
sacrifices in the house of the LORD
at Jerusalem, then the heart of
this people will return to their
lord, *even* to Rehoboam king of
Judah; and they will kill me and
return to Rehoboam king of Judah." Deut. 12:5-7, 14
28 So the king consulted, and
made two golden calves, and he
said to them, "It is too much for
you to go up to Jerusalem; behold
your gods, O Israel, that brought
you up from the land of Egypt."
29 And he set one in Bethel, and
the other he put in Dan.
30 Now this thing became a sin,
for the people went *to worship* before the one as far as Dan.
31 And he made houses on high
places, and made priests from
among all the people who were
not of the sons of Levi.
32 And Jeroboam instituted a
feast in the eighth month on the
fifteenth day of the month, like
the feast which is in Judah, and he
went up to the altar; thus he did in
Bethel, sacrificing to the calves
which he had made. And he stationed in Bethel the priests of the
high places which he had made.
33 Then he went up to the altar
which he had made in Bethel on
the fifteenth day in the eighth
month, even in the month which
he hadᵗdevised in his own heart;
and heᵗinstituted a feast for the
sons of Israel, and went up to the
altar to burn incense. *made*

CHAPTER 13

NOW behold, there cameʳa man
of God from Judah to Bethel by
the word of the LORD, while Jeroboam was standing by the altar to
burn incense. 1 Kin. 12:22
2 Andʳhe cried against the altar by the word of the LORD, and
said, "O altar, altar, thus says the
LORD, 'Behold, a son shall be born
to the house of David, Josiah by
name; and on you he shall sacrifice the priests of the high places
who burn incense on you, and

human bones shall be burned on
you.' " 1 Kin. 13:32
3 Then he gave a[t]sign the same
day, saying, "This is the [t]sign
which the LORD has spoken, 'Behold, the altar shall be split apart
and the ashes which are on it shall
be poured out.' " *wonder*
4 Now it came about when the
king heard the saying of the man
of God, which he cried against the
altar in Bethel, that Jeroboam
stretched out his hand from the altar, saying, "Seize him." But his
hand which he stretched out
against him dried up, so that he
could not draw it back to himself.
5 The altar also was split apart
and the ashes were poured out
from the altar, according to the
sign which the man of God had
given by the word of the LORD.
6 And the king answered and
said to the man of God, "Please
[21]entreat the LORD your God, and
pray for me, that my hand may be
restored to me." So the man of
God [21]entreated the LORD, and the
king's hand was restored to him,
and it became as it was before.
7 Then the king said to the
man of God, "Come home with
me and refresh yourself, and[l]I will
give you a reward." 2 Kin. 5:15
8 But the man of God said to
the king, "If you were to give me
half your house I would not go
with you, nor would I eat bread or
drink water in this place.
9"For so it was commanded me
by the word of the LORD, saying,
'You shall eat no bread, nor drink
water, nor return by the way
which you came.' "
10 So he went another way, and
did not return by the way which
he came to Bethel.
11 Now an old prophet was living in Bethel; and his[t]sons came
and told him all the deeds which
the man of God had done that day
in Bethel; the words which he had
spoken to the king, these also they
related to their father. *son*
12 And their father said to
them, "Which way did he go?"
Now his sons had seen the way
which the man of God who came
from Judah had gone.
13 Then he said to his sons,
"Saddle the donkey for me." So
they saddled the donkey for him
and he rode away on it.
14 So he went after the man of
God and found him sitting under
an oak; and he said to him, "Are
you the man of God who came
from Judah?" And he said, "I am."
15 Then he said to him, "Come
home with me and eat bread."
16 And he said, "I[r]cannot return
with you, nor go with you, nor will
I eat bread or drink water with
you in this place. 1 Kin. 13:8, 9
17"For a command *came* to me
by the word of the LORD, 'You
shall eat no bread, nor drink water
there; do not return by going the
way which you came.' "
18 And he said to him, "I[r] also
am a prophet like you, and an angel spoke to me by the word of the
LORD, saying, 'Bring him back
with you to your house, that he
may eat bread and drink water.' "
But he lied to him. Matt. 7:15
19 So he went back with him,
and ate bread in his house and
drank water.
20 Now it came about, as they

[21] Lit., *soften(ed) the face of*

were sitting down at the table,
that the word of the LORD came to
the prophet who had brought him
back;
21 and he cried to the man of
God who came from Judah, saying, "Thus says the LORD, 'Because you have [t]disobeyed the
command of the LORD, and have
not observed the commandment
which the LORD your God commanded you, *rebelled* against
22 but have returned and eaten
bread and drunk water in the
place of which He said to you,
"Eat no bread and drink no water"; your body shall not come to
the grave of your fathers.'"
23 And it came about after he
had eaten bread and after he had
drunk, that he saddled the donkey
for him, for the prophet whom he
had brought back.
24 Now when he had gone, a
lion met him on the way and killed
him, and his body was thrown on
the road, with the donkey standing beside it; the lion also was
standing beside the body.
25 And behold, men passed by
and saw the body thrown on the
road, and the lion standing beside
the body; so they came and told *it*
in the city where the old prophet
lived.
26 Now when the prophet who
brought him back from the way
heard *it*, he said, "It is the man of
God, who disobeyed the com-
mand of the LORD; therefore the
LORD has given him to the lion,
which has torn him and killed
him, according to the word of the
LORD which He spoke to him."
27 Then he spoke to his sons,
saying, "Saddle the donkey for
me." And they saddled *it*.
28 And he went and found his
body thrown on the road with the
donkey and the lion standing beside the body; the lion had not eat-
en the body nor torn the donkey.
29 So the prophet took up the
body of the man of God and laid it
on the donkey, and brought it
back and he came to the city of
the old prophet to mourn and to
bury him.
30 And he laid his body in his
own grave, and they mourned
over him, *saying*, "Alas,[r] my
brother!" Jer. 22:18
31 And it came about after he
had buried him, that he spoke to
his sons, saying, "When I die,
bury me in the grave in which the
man of God is buried; lay my
bones beside his bones.
32 "For the thing shall surely
come to pass which he cried by
the word of the LORD against the
altar in Bethel and against all the
houses of the high places which
are in the cities of Samaria."
33 After this event Jeroboam
did not return from his evil way,
but again he made priests of the
high places from among [a]all the
people; [r]any who would, he ordained, to be priests of the high
places. *extremities of* • Judg. 17:5
34 And this event became sin to
the house of Jeroboam, even to
blot *it* out and destroy *it* from off
the face of the earth.

CHAPTER 14

AT that time Abijah the son of
Jeroboam became sick.
2 And Jeroboam said to his

wife, "Arise now, and disguise yourself so that they may not know that you are the wife of Jeroboam, and go to Shiloh; behold, Ahijah the prophet is there, who spoke concerning me *that I would be* king over this people.

3 "And take ten loaves with you, *some* cakes and a jar of honey, and go to him. He will tell you what will happen to the boy."

4 And Jeroboam's wife did so, and arose and went to Shiloh, and came to the house of Ahijah. Now Ahijah could not see, for his eyes were dim because of his age.

5 Now the LORD had said to Ahijah, "Behold, the wife of Jeroboam is coming to [t]inquire of you concerning her son, for he is sick. You shall say thus and thus to her, for it will be when she arrives that she will pretend to be another woman." *seek a word from*

6 And it came about when Ahijah heard the sound of her feet coming in the doorway, that he said, "Come in, wife of Jeroboam, why do you pretend to be another woman? For I am sent to you *with* a harsh *message.*

7 "Go, say to Jeroboam, 'Thus says the LORD God of Israel, "Because I exalted you from among the people and made you leader over My people Israel,

8 and [r]tore the kingdom away from the house of David and gave it to you—yet you have not been like My servant David, who kept My commandments and who followed Me with all his heart, [r]to do only that which was right in My sight; 1 Kin. 11:31 • 1 Kin. 15:5

9 you also have done more evil than all who were before you, and have gone and made for yourself other gods and molten images to provoke Me to anger, and have cast Me behind your back—

10 therefore behold, I am bringing calamity on the house of Jeroboam, and will cut off from Jeroboam every male person, both bond and free in Israel, and I will make a clean sweep of the house of Jeroboam, as one sweeps away dung until it is all gone.

11 "Anyone[r] belonging to Jeroboam who dies in the city the dogs will eat. And he who dies in the field the birds of the heavens will eat; for the LORD has spoken *it.*"' 1 Kin. 16:4; 21:24

12 "Now you arise, go to your house. When your feet enter the city the child will die.

13 "And all Israel shall mourn for him and bury him, for [t]he alone of Jeroboam's *family* shall come to the grave, because in him [r]something good was found toward the LORD God of Israel in the house of Jeroboam. *the one* • 2 Chr. 19:3

14 "Moreover, the LORD will raise up for Himself a king over Israel who shall cut off the house of Jeroboam this day [t]and from now on. *and what even now?*

15 "For the LORD will strike Israel, as a reed is shaken in the water; and [r]He will uproot Israel from [r]this good land which He gave to their fathers, and will scatter them beyond the *Euphrates* River, because they have made their [22]Asherim, provoking the LORD to anger. Deut. 29:28 • Josh. 23:15, 16

16 "And He will give up Israel on

[22] I.e., wooden symbols of a female deity. Also v. 23

account of the sins of Jeroboam,
which he committed and with
which he made Israel to sin."
17 Then Jeroboam's wife arose
and departed and came to Tirzah.
As she was entering the threshold
of the house, the child died.
18 [r]And all Israel buried him and
mourned for him, according to the
word of the LORD which He spoke
through His servant Ahijah the
prophet. 1 Kin. 14:13
19 Now the rest of the acts of
Jeroboam, how he made war and
how he reigned, behold, they are
written in the Book of the Chronicles of the Kings of Israel.
20 And the time that Jeroboam
reigned *was* twenty-two years;
and he slept with his fathers, and
Nadab his son reigned in his
place.
21 Now Rehoboam the son of
Solomon reigned in Judah. Rehoboam was forty-one years old
when he became king, and he
reigned seventeen years in Jerusalem,[r] the city which the LORD had
chosen from all the tribes of Israel
to put His name there. And his
mother's name was Naamah the
Ammonitess. 1 Kin. 11:32, 36
22 And Judah did evil in the
sight of the LORD, and they [r]pro-
voked Him to jealousy more than
all that their fathers had done,
with [t]the sins which they [t]commit-
ted. Deut. 32:21 • *their* • *sinned*
23 For they also built for themselves [r]high places and *sacred* [r]pil-
lars and Asherim on every high
hill and beneath every luxuriant
tree. Deut. 12:2 • Deut. 16:22
24 And there were also [r]male
cult prostitutes in the land. They
did according to all the abominations of the nations which the
LORD dispossessed before the
sons of Israel. Gen. 19:5
25 Now it came about in the
fifth year of King Rehoboam, that
Shishak the king of Egypt came
up against Jerusalem.
26 And he took away the treasures of the house of the LORD and
the treasures of the king's house,
and [r]he took everything, even taking all the shields of gold which
Solomon had made. 2 Chr. 12:9
27 So King Rehoboam made
shields of bronze in their place,
and [r]committed them to the [t]care
of the commanders of the [23]guard
who guarded the doorway of the
king's house. 1 Sam. 8:11 • *hand*
28 Then it happened as often as
the king entered the house of the
LORD, that the [23]guards would carry them and would bring them
back into the guards' room.
29 Now the rest of the acts of
Rehoboam and all that he did, are
they not written in the Book of the
Chronicles of the Kings of Judah?
30 [r]And there was war between
Rehoboam and Jeroboam continually. 1 Kin. 12:21; 15:6
31 And Rehoboam slept with
his fathers, and was buried with
his fathers in the city of David;
and [r]his mother's name was Naamah the Ammonitess. And Abijam his son became king in his
place. 1 Kin. 14:21

CHAPTER 15

NOW in the eighteenth year of
King Jeroboam, the son of Nebat,
Abijam became king over Judah.
2 He reigned three years in

[23] Lit., *runner(s)*

Jerusalem; and his mother's name
was [r]Maacah the daughter of A-
bishalom. 2 Chr. 13:2
3 And he walked in all the sins
of his father which he had committed before him; and his heart
was not [t]wholly devoted to the
LORD his God, like the heart of his
father David. *complete with*
4 But for David's sake the
LORD his God gave him a [r]lamp in
Jerusalem, to raise up his son after him and to establish Jerusalem; 2 Sam. 21:17; 1 Kin. 11:36
5 because David did what was
right in the sight of the LORD, and
had not turned aside from anything that He commanded him all
the days of his life, except in the
case of Uriah the Hittite.
6 [r]And there was war between
Rehoboam and Jeroboam all the
days of his life. 1 Kin. 14:30
7 Now the rest of the acts of
Abijam and all that he did, are
they not written in the Book of the
Chronicles of the Kings of Judah?
And there was war between Abijam and Jeroboam.
8 And Abijam slept with his fathers and they buried him in the
city of David; and Asa his son became king in his place.
9 So in the twentieth year of
Jeroboam the king of Israel, Asa
began to reign as king of Judah.
10 And he reigned forty-one
years in Jerusalem; and [r]his mother's name was Maacah the daughter of Abishalom. 1 Kin. 15:2
11 And [r]Asa did what was right
in the sight of the LORD, like David his father. 2 Chr. 14:2
12 He also put away the male
cult prostitutes from the land, and
[r]removed all the idols which his fathers had made. 1 Kin. 11:7, 8
13 And he also removed Maacah his mother from *being* queen
mother, because she had made a
horrid image as an Asherah; and
Asa cut down her horrid image
and burned *it* at the brook Kidron.
14 But the high places were not
taken away; nevertheless the
heart of Asa was wholly devoted
to the LORD all his days.
15 And [r]he brought into the
house of the LORD the dedicated
things of his father and his own
dedicated things: silver and gold
and utensils. 1 Kin. 7:51
16 [r]Now there was war between
Asa and Baasha king of Israel all
their days. 1 Kin. 15:32
17 And Baasha king of Israel
went up against Judah and [t]forti-
fied Ramah in order to prevent
anyone from going out or coming
in to Asa king of Judah. *built*
18 Then Asa took all the silver
and the gold which were left in
the treasuries of the house of the
LORD and the treasuries of the
king's house, and delivered them
into the hand of his servants. And
King Asa sent them to Ben-hadad
the son of Tabrimmon, the son of
Hezion, king of Aram, who lived
in Damascus, saying,
19 "*Let there be* a treaty between
you and me, *as* between my father
and your father. Behold, I have
sent you a present of silver and
gold; go, break your treaty with
Baasha king of Israel so that he
will withdraw from me."
20 So Ben-hadad listened to
King Asa and sent the commanders of his armies against the cities

of Israel, and [t]conquered [r]Ijon,
Dan, Abel-beth-maacah and all
Chinneroth, besides all the land of
Naphtali. *smote* • 2 Kin. 15:29
21 And it came about when Baasha heard *of it* that he ceased
[t]fortifying Ramah, and remained
in Tirzah. *building*
22 Then King Asa made a proclamation to all Judah—none was
exempt—and they carried away
the stones of Ramah and its timber with which Baasha had built.
And King Asa built with them
Geba of Benjamin and Mizpah.
23 [r]Now the rest of all the acts of
Asa and all his might and all that
he did and the cities which he
built, are they not written in the
Book of the Chronicles of the
Kings of Judah? But in the time of
his old age he was diseased in his
feet. 2 Chr. 16:11-14
24 And Asa slept with his fathers and was buried with his fathers in the city of David his father; and [r]Jehoshaphat his son
reigned in his place. Matt. 1:8
25 Now [r]Nadab the son of Jeroboam became king over Israel in
the second year of Asa king of Judah, and he reigned over Israel
two years. 1 Kin. 14:20
26 And he did evil in the sight of
the LORD, and walked in the way
of his father and [r]in his sin which
he made Israel sin. 1 Kin. 14:16
27 Then Baasha the son of Ahijah of the house of Issachar conspired against him, and Baasha
struck him down at Gibbethon,
which belonged to the Philistines,
while Nadab and all Israel were
laying siege to Gibbethon.
28 So Baasha killed him in the
third year of Asa king of Judah,
and reigned in his place.
29 And it came about, as soon
as he was king, he struck down all
the household of Jeroboam. He
did not leave to Jeroboam [t]any
persons alive, until he had destroyed them, according to the
word of the LORD, which He spoke
by His servant Ahijah the Shilonite, *any breath*
30 *and* because of the sins of
Jeroboam which he sinned, and
[r]which he made Israel sin, because
of his provocation with which he
provoked the LORD God of Israel
to anger. 1 Kin. 15:26
31 Now the rest of the acts of
Nadab and all that he did, are they
not written in the Book of the
Chronicles of the Kings of Israel?
32 [r]And there was war between
Asa and Baasha king of Israel all
their days. 1 Kin. 15:16
33 In the third year of Asa king
of Judah, Baasha the son of Ahijah became king over all Israel at
Tirzah, and reigned twenty-four
years.
34 And he did evil in the sight of
the LORD, and [r]walked in the way
of Jeroboam and in his sin which
he made Israel sin. 1 Kin. 15:26

CHAPTER 16

NOW the word of the LORD came
to [r]Jehu the son of Hanani against
Baasha, saying, 1 Kin. 16:7
2 "Inasmuch as I [r]exalted you
from the dust and made you
leader over My people Israel, and
you have walked in the way of
Jeroboam and have made My peo-

ple Israel sin, provoking Me to anger with their sins, 1 Sam. 2:8
3 behold, I will consume Baasha and his house, and I will
make your house like the house of
Jeroboam the son of Nebat.
4 "Anyone of Baasha who dies
in the city the dogs shall eat, and
anyone of his who dies in the field
the birds of the heavens will eat."
5 [r]Now the rest of the acts of
Baasha and what he did and his
might, are they not written in the
Book of the Chronicles of the
Kings of Israel? 1 Kin. 14:19
6 And Baasha slept with his fathers and was buried in [r]Tirzah,
and Elah his son became king in
his place. 1 Kin. 4:17; 15:21
7 Moreover, the word of the
LORD through the prophet Jehu
the son of Hanani also came
against Baasha and his household,
both because of all the evil which
he did in the sight of the LORD,
provoking Him to anger with the
work of his hands, in being like
the house of Jeroboam, and because he struck [a]it. *him*
8 In the twenty-sixth year of
Asa king of Judah, Elah the son of
Baasha became king over Israel at
Tirzah, *and reigned* two years.
9 And his servant Zimri, commander of half his chariots, conspired against him. Now he *was* at
Tirzah drinking himself drunk in
the house of Arza, who *was* over
the household at Tirzah.
10 Then Zimri went in and
struck him and put him to death,
in the twenty-seventh year of Asa
king of Judah, and became king in
his place.
11 And it came about, when he
became king, as soon as he sat on
his throne, that he killed all the
household of Baasha; he did not
leave a single male, neither of his
relatives nor of his friends.
12 Thus Zimri destroyed all the
household of Baasha, [r]according to
the word of the LORD, which He
spoke against Baasha through
Jehu the prophet, 1 Kin. 16:3
13 for all the sins of Baasha and
the sins of Elah his son, which
they sinned and which they made
Israel sin, [r]provoking the LORD
God of Israel to anger with their
[t]idols. Deut. 32:21 • *vanities*
14 Now the rest of the acts of
Elah and all that he did, are they
not written in the Book of the
Chronicles of the Kings of Israel?
15 In the twenty-seventh year
of Asa king of Judah, Zimri
reigned seven days at Tirzah. Now
the people were camped against
[r]Gibbethon, which belonged to the
Philistines. 1 Kin. 15:27
16 And the people who were
camped heard [t]it said, "Zimri has
conspired and has also struck
down the king." Therefore all Israel made Omri, the commander
of the army, king over Israel that
day in the camp. *saying*
17 Then Omri and all Israel with
him went up from Gibbethon, and
they besieged Tirzah.
18 And it came about, when
Zimri saw that the city was taken,
that he went into the citadel of the
king's house and burned the
king's house over him with fire,
and [r]died, 1 Sam. 31:4, 5
19 because of his sins which he
sinned, doing evil in the sight of
the LORD, walking in the way of

Jeroboam, and in his sin which he
did, making Israel sin.
20 Now the rest of the acts of
Zimri and his conspiracy which he
[t]carried out, are they not written in
the Book of the Chronicles of the
Kings of Israel? *conspired*
21 Then the people of Israel
were divided into two parts: half
of the people followed Tibni the
son of Ginath, to make him king;
the *other* half followed Omri.
22 But the people who followed
Omri prevailed over the people
who followed Tibni the son of
Ginath. And Tibni died and Omri
became king.
23 In the thirty-first year of Asa
king of Judah, Omri became king
over Israel, and reigned twelve
years; he reigned six years at [r]Tir-
zah. 1 Kin. 15:21
24 And he bought the hill Samaria from Shemer for two talents of silver; and he built on the
hill, and named the city which he
built Samaria, after the name of
Shemer, the owner of the hill.
25 And [r]Omri did evil in the
sight of the LORD, and [r]acted more
wickedly than all who *were* before
him. Mic. 6:16 • 1 Kin. 14:9
26 For he walked in all the way
of Jeroboam the son of Nebat and
in his sins which he made Israel
sin, provoking the LORD God of Israel with their [t]idols. *vanities*
27 Now the rest of the acts of
Omri which he did and his might
which he [t]showed, are they not
written in the Book of the Chronicles of the Kings of Israel? *did*
28 So Omri slept with his fathers, and was buried in Samaria;
and Ahab his son became king in
his place.
29 Now Ahab the son of Omri
became king over Israel in the
thirty-eighth year of Asa king of
Judah, and Ahab the son of Omri
reigned over Israel in Samaria
twenty-two years.
30 And Ahab the son of Omri
did evil in the sight of the LORD
[r]more than all who were before
him. 1 Kin. 14:9; 16:25
31 And it came about, as though
it had been a trivial thing for him
to walk in the sins of Jeroboam
the son of Nebat, that he married
Jezebel the daughter of Ethbaal
king of the Sidonians, and went to
serve Baal and worshiped him.
32 So he erected an altar for
Baal in [r]the house of Baal, which
he built in Samaria. 2 Kin. 10:21
33 And Ahab also made [r]the [24]A-
sherah. Thus Ahab did more to
provoke the LORD God of Israel
than all the kings of Israel who
were before him. 2 Kin. 13:6
34 In his days Hiel the Bethelite
built Jericho; he laid its foundations with the *loss of* Abiram his
first-born, and set up its gates
with the *loss of* his youngest son
Segub, according to the word of
the LORD, which He spoke by
Joshua the son of Nun.

CHAPTER 17

NOW Elijah the Tishbite, who
was of [a]the settlers of Gilead, said
to Ahab, "As the LORD, the God of
Israel lives, before whom I stand,
surely there shall be neither dew
nor rain these years, except by my
word." *Tishbe in Gilead*

[24] I.e., wooden symbol of a female deity

2 And the word of the LORD came to him, saying,

3 "Go away from here and turn eastward, and hide yourself by the brook Cherith, which is [t]east of the Jordan. *before*

4 "And it shall be that you shall drink of the brook, and [r]I have commanded the ravens to provide for you there." 1 Kin. 17:9

5 So he went and did according to the word of the LORD, for he went and lived by the brook Cherith, which is east of the Jordan.

6 And the ravens brought him bread and meat in the morning and bread and meat in the evening, and he would drink from the brook.

7 And it happened after a while, that the brook dried up, because there was no rain in the land.

8 Then the word of the LORD came to him, saying,

9 "Arise, go to Zarephath, which belongs to Sidon, and stay there; behold, I have commanded a widow there to provide for you."

10 So he arose and went to Zarephath, and when he came to the gate of the city, behold, a widow was there gathering sticks; and he called to her and said, "Please get me a little water in a [a]jar, that I may drink." *vessel*

11 And as she was going to get *it*, he called to her and said, "Please bring me a piece of bread in your hand."

12 But she said, "As the LORD your God lives, I have no [t]bread, only a handful of flour in the [t]bowl and a little oil in the jar; and behold, I am gathering [t]a few sticks that I may go in and prepare for me and my son, that we may eat it and die." *cake · pitcher · two*

13 Then Elijah said to her, "Do not fear; go, do as you have said, but make me a little bread cake from it first, and bring *it* out to me, and afterward you may make *one* for yourself and for your son.

14 "For thus says the LORD God of Israel, 'The [t]bowl of flour shall not be exhausted, nor shall the jar of oil [t]be empty, until the day that the LORD sends rain on the face of the earth.' " *pitcher · lack*

15 So she went and did according to the word of Elijah, and she and he and her household ate for *many* days.

16 The [t]bowl of flour was not exhausted nor did the jar of oil [t]become empty, according to the word of the LORD which He spoke through Elijah. *pitcher · lack*

17 Now it came about after these things, that the son of the woman, the mistress of the house, became sick; and his sickness was so severe, that there was no breath left in him.

18 So she said to Elijah, "What do I have to do with you, O man of God? [a]You have come to me to bring my iniquity to remembrance, and to put my son to death!" *Have you come . . . death?*

19 And he said to her, "Give me your son." Then he took him from her bosom and carried him up to the upper room where he was living, and laid him on his own bed.

20 And he called to the LORD and said, "O LORD my God, hast Thou also brought calamity to the

widow with whom I am staying,
by causing her son to die?"
21 Then he stretched himself
upon the child three times, and
called to the LORD, and said, "O
LORD my God, I pray Thee, let this
child's life return to him."
22 And the LORD heard the
voice of Elijah, and the life of the
child returned [t]to him and he revived. *upon his inward part*
23 And Elijah took the child,
and brought him down from the
upper room into the house and
gave him to his mother; and Elijah
said, "See, your son is alive."
24 Then the woman said to Elijah, "Now I know that you are a
man of God, and that the word of
the LORD in your mouth is truth."

CHAPTER 18

NOW it came about [r]*after* many
days, that the word of the LORD
came to Elijah in the third year,
saying, "Go, show yourself to
Ahab, and I will send rain on the
face of the earth." 1 Kin. 17:1
2 So Elijah went to show himself to Ahab. Now the famine *was*
severe in Samaria.
3 And Ahab called Obadiah
[r]who *was* over the household.
(Now Obadiah [25]feared the LORD
greatly; 1 Kin. 16:9
4 for it came about, when Jezebel [t]destroyed the prophets of the
LORD, that Obadiah took a hundred prophets and hid them by fifties in a cave, and provided them
with bread and water.) *cut off*
5 Then Ahab said to Obadiah,
"Go through the land to all the
springs of water and to all the val-

[25]Or, *revered*

leys; perhaps we will find grass
and keep the horses and mules
alive, and not [t]have to kill some of
the cattle." *cut off*
6 So they divided the land between them to [t]survey it; Ahab
went one way by himself and
Obadiah went another way by
himself. *pass through*
7 Now as Obadiah was on the
way, behold, Elijah [t]met him, and
he recognized him and fell on his
face and said, "Is this you, Elijah
my master?" *to meet*
8 And he said to him, "It is I.
Go, say to your master, 'Behold,
Elijah *is here.*' "
9 And he said, "What sin have
I committed, that you are giving
your servant into the hand of
Ahab, to put me to death?
10 "As the LORD your God lives,
there is no nation or kingdom
where my master has not sent to
search for you; and when they
said, 'He is not *here*,' he made the
kingdom or nation swear that
they could not find you.
11 "And now you are saying, 'Go,
say to your master, "Behold, Elijah *is here.*" '
12 "And it will come about when
I leave you [r]that the Spirit of the
LORD will carry you where I do
not know; so when I come and tell
Ahab and he cannot find you, he
will kill me, although *I* your servant have [a]feared the LORD from
my youth. 2 Kin. 2:16 • *revered*
13 "Has [r]it not been told to my
master what I did when Jezebel
killed the prophets of the LORD,
that I hid a hundred prophets of
the LORD by fifties in a cave, and

provided them with bread and water? 1 Kin. 18:4
14 "And now you are saying, 'Go,
say to your master, "Behold, Elijah *is here*" '; he will then kill me."
15 And Elijah said, "As[r] the
LORD of hosts lives, before whom
I stand, I will surely show myself
to him today." 1 Kin. 17:1
16 So Obadiah went to meet
Ahab, and told him; and Ahab
went to meet Elijah.
17 And it came about, when
Ahab saw Elijah that [r]Ahab said to
him, "Is this you, you troubler of
Israel?" Josh. 7:25; 1 Kin. 21:20
18 And he said, "I have not
troubled Israel, but you and your
father's house *have*, because [r]you
have forsaken the commandments of the LORD, and you have
followed the Baals. 1 Kin. 9:9
19 "Now then send *and* gather to
me all Israel at Mount Carmel, *together* with 450 prophets of Baal
and 400 prophets of the Asherah,
who eat at Jezebel's table."
20 So Ahab sent *a message*
among all the sons of Israel, and
brought the prophets together at
Mount Carmel.
21 And Elijah came near to all
the people and said, "How long
will you [r]hesitate between two
opinions? If the LORD is God, follow Him; but if Baal, follow him."
But the people did not answer him
a word. 2 Kin. 17:41
22 Then Elijah said to the people, "I [r]alone am left a prophet of
the LORD, but Baal's prophets are
450 men. 1 Kin. 19:10, 14
23 "Now let them give us two
oxen; and let them choose one ox
for themselves and cut it up, and
place it on the wood, but put no
fire *under it*; and I will prepare the
other ox, and lay it on the wood,
and I will not put a fire *under it*.
24 "Then you call on the name of
your god, and I will call on the
name of the LORD, and the God
who answers by fire, He is God."
And all the people answered and
said, "[26]That is a good idea."
25 So Elijah said to the prophets of Baal, "Choose one ox for
yourselves and prepare it first for
you are many, and call on the
name of your god, but put no fire
under it."
26 Then they took the ox which
was given them and they prepared
it and called on the name of Baal
from morning until noon saying,
"O Baal, answer us." But there
was no voice and no one answered. And they leaped about
the altar which they made.
27 And it came about at noon,
that Elijah mocked them and said,
"Call out with a loud voice, for he
is a god; either he is occupied or
gone aside, or is on a journey, or
perhaps he is asleep and needs to
be awakened."
28 So they cried with a loud
voice and [r]cut themselves according to their custom with swords
and lances until the blood gushed
out on them. Lev. 19:28
29 And it came about when
midday was past, that they [t]raved
until the time of the offering of the
evening sacrifice; but there was no
voice, no one answered, and no
one paid attention. ***prophesied***
30 Then Elijah said to all the

[26] Lit., *The matter is good*

people, "Come near to me." So all
the people came near to him. And
he repaired the altar of the LORD
which had been torn down.
31 And Elijah took twelve
stones according to the number of
the tribes of the sons of Jacob, to
whom the word of the LORD had
come, saying, "Israel[r]shall be your
name." Gen. 32:28; 35:10
32 So with the stones he built an
altar in[r]the name of the LORD, and
he made a trench around the altar,
large enough to hold two measures of seed. Col. 3:17
33 [r]Then he arranged the wood
and cut the ox in pieces and laid *it*
on the wood. And he said, "Fill
four pitchers with water and pour
it on the burnt offering and on the
wood." Gen. 22:9; Lev. 1:7, 8
34 And he said, "Do it a second
time," and they did it a second
time. And he said, "Do it a third
time," and they did it a third time.
35 And the water flowed around
the altar, and he also filled the
trench with water.
36 Then it came about at the
time of the offering of the *evening*
sacrifice, that Elijah the prophet
came near and said, "O LORD, the
God of Abraham, Isaac and Israel,
today let it be known that Thou
art God in Israel, and that I am
Thy servant, and that I have done
all these things at Thy word.
37 "Answer me, O LORD, answer
me, that this people may know
that Thou, O LORD, art God, and
that Thou hast turned their heart
back again."
38 Then the[r]fire of the LORD fell,
and consumed the burnt offering
and the wood and the stones and
the dust, and licked up the water
that was in the trench. Job 1:16
39 And when all the people saw
it, they fell on their faces; and
they said, "The LORD, He is God;
the LORD, He is God."
40 Then Elijah said to them,
"Seize the prophets of Baal; do
not let one of them escape." So
they seized them; and Elijah
brought them down to the brook
Kishon, and slew them there.
41 Now Elijah said to Ahab,
"Go up, eat and drink; for there is
the sound of the roar of a *heavy*
shower."
42 So Ahab went up to eat and
drink. But Elijah went up to the
top of Carmel; and he crouched
down on the earth, and put his
face between his knees.
43 And he said to his servant,
"Go up now, look toward the
sea." So he went up and looked
and said, "There is nothing." And
he said, "Go back" seven times.
44 And it came about at the seventh *time*, that he said, "Behold, a
cloud as small as a man's hand is
coming up from the sea." And he
said, "Go up, say to Ahab, [t]'Prepare *your chariot* and go down, so
that the *heavy* shower does not
stop you.'" *Tie, harness*
45 So it came about in a little
while, that the sky grew black
with clouds and wind, and there
was a heavy shower. And Ahab
rode and went to Jezreel.
46 Then[r]the hand of the LORD
was on Elijah, and he girded up
his loins and[t]outran Ahab to Jezreel. 2 Kin. 3:15 • *ran before*

CHAPTER 19

NOW Ahab told Jezebel all that
Elijah had done, and[t]how he had
killed all the prophets with the
sword. *all* about *how*
2 Then Jezebel sent a messenger to Elijah, saying, "So[r]may the
gods do to me and even more, if I
do not make your [27]life as the[t]life
of one of them by tomorrow about
this time." Ruth 1:17 • *soul*
3 And he was afraid and arose
and ran for his [27]life and came to
Beersheba, which belongs to Judah, and left his servant there.
4 But he himself went a day's
journey into the wilderness, and
came and sat down under a[a]juni-
per tree; and he requested for
himself that he might die, and
said, "It is enough; now, O LORD,
take my [27]life, for I am not better
than my fathers." *broom-tree*
5 And he lay down and slept
under a juniper tree; and behold,
there was an angel touching him,
and he said to him, "Arise, eat."
6 Then he looked and behold,
there was at his head a bread cake
baked on hot stones, and a jar of
water. So he ate and drank and
lay down again.
7 And the angel of the LORD
came again a second time and
touched him and said, "Arise, eat,
because the journey is too great
for you."
8 So he arose and ate and
drank, and went in the strength of
that food[r]forty days and forty
nights to[r]Horeb, the mountain of
God. Ex. 24:18; 34:28 • Ex. 3:1
9 Then he came there to a
cave, and lodged there; and behold, the word of the LORD *came*
to him, and He said to him, "What
are you doing here, Elijah?"
10 And he said, "I[r] have been
very zealous for the LORD, the
God of hosts; for the sons of Israel
have forsaken Thy covenant, torn
down Thine altars and killed Thy
prophets with the sword. And I
alone am left; and they seek my
life, to take it away." Ex. 20:5
11 So He said, "Go[r] forth, and
stand on the mountain before the
LORD." And behold, the LORD was
passing by! And [r]a great and
strong wind was rending the
mountains and breaking in pieces
the rocks before the LORD; *but* the
LORD *was* not in the wind. And after the wind an earthquake, *but*
the LORD *was* not in the earthquake. Ex. 19:20 • Ezek. 1:4
12 And after the earthquake a
fire, *but* the LORD *was* not in the
fire; and after the fire[r]a sound of a
gentle blowing. Job 4:16
13 And it came about when Elijah heard *it*, that[r]he wrapped his
face in his mantle, and went out
and stood in the entrance of the
cave. And behold, a voice *came* to
him and said, "What are you
doing here, Elijah?" Ex. 3:6
14 Then he said, "I have been
very zealous for the LORD, the
God of hosts; for the sons of Israel
have forsaken Thy covenant, torn
down Thine altars and killed Thy
prophets with the sword. And I
alone am left; and they seek my
life, to take it away."
15 And the LORD said to him,
"Go, return on your way to the
wilderness of Damascus, and

[27]Lit., *soul*

when you have arrived, you shall
anoint Hazael king over Aram;
16 and Jehu the son of Nimshi
you shall anoint king over Israel;
and Elisha the son of Shaphat of
Abel-meholah you shall anoint as
prophet in your place.
17 "And it shall come about, the
[r]one who escapes from the sword
of Hazael, Jehu [r]shall put to death,
and the one who escapes from the
sword of Jehu, Elisha shall put to
death. 2 Kin. 8:12 • 2 Kin. 9:14
18 "Yet I will leave 7,000 in Israel, all the knees that have not
bowed to Baal and every mouth
that has not kissed him."
19 So he departed from there
and found Elisha the son of Shaphat, while he was plowing with
twelve pairs *of oxen* before him,
and he with the twelfth. And Elijah passed over to him and threw
[r]his mantle on him. 1 Sam. 28:14
20 And he left the oxen and ran
after Elijah and said, "Please let
me kiss my father and my mother,
then I will follow you." And he
said to him, "Go back again, for
what have I done to you?"
21 So he returned from following him, and took the pair of oxen
and sacrificed them and [r]boiled
their flesh with the implements of
the oxen, and gave *it* to the people
and they ate. Then he arose and
followed Elijah and ministered to
him. 2 Sam. 24:22

CHAPTER 20

NOW Ben-hadad king of Aram
gathered all his army, and there
were thirty-two kings with him,
and horses and chariots. And he
went up and besieged Samaria,
and fought against it.
2 Then he sent messengers to
the city to Ahab king of Israel,
and said to him, "Thus says Ben-
hadad,
3 'Your silver and your gold are
mine; your most beautiful wives
and children are also mine.' "
4 And the king of Israel answered and said, "It is according
to your word, my lord, O king; I
am yours, and all that I have."
5 Then the messengers re-
turned and said, "Thus says [t]Ben-
hadad, 'Surely, I sent to you saying, "You shall give me your silver
and your gold and your wives and
your children," *Ben-hadad, saying*
6 but about this time tomorrow I will send my servants to
you, and they will search your
house and the houses of your servants; and it shall come about,
whatever is desirable in your eyes,
they will [t]take in their hand and
carry away.' " *put*
7 Then the king of Israel called
all the elders of the land and said,
"Please observe and see how this
man is looking for trouble; for he
sent to me for my wives and my
children and my silver and my
gold, and I did not refuse him."
8 And all the elders and all the
people said to him, "Do not listen
or consent."
9 So he said to the messengers
of Ben-hadad, "Tell my lord the
king, 'All that you sent for to your
servant at the first I will do, but
this thing I cannot do.' " And the
messengers departed and brought
him word again.
10 And Ben-hadad sent to him

and said, "May the gods do so to
me and more also, if the dust of
Samaria shall suffice for handfuls
for all the people who follow me."
11 Then the king of Israel answered and said, "Tell *him,* 'Let
not him who girds on *his armor*
boast like him who takes *it* off.' "
12 And it came about when
Ben-hadad heard this message, as
he was drinking with the kings in
the temporary shelters, that he
said to his servants, "Station
yourselves." So they stationed
themselves against the city.
13 Now behold, a prophet approached Ahab king of Israel and
said, "Thus says the LORD, 'Have
you seen all this great multitude?
Behold, I will deliver them into
your hand today, and you shall
know that I am the LORD.' "
14 And Ahab said, "By whom?"
So he said, "Thus says the LORD,
'By the young men of the rulers of
the provinces.' " Then he said,
"Who shall [t]begin the battle?" And
he answered, "You." *bind*
15 Then he mustered the young
men of the rulers of the provinces,
and there were 232; and after
them he mustered all the people,
even all the sons of Israel, 7,000.
16 And they went out at noon,
while Ben-hadad was drinking
himself drunk in the [a]temporary
shelters with the thirty-two kings
who helped him. *booths*
17 And the young men of the
rulers of the provinces went out
first; and Ben-hadad sent out and
they told him, saying, "Men have
come out from Samaria."
18 Then he said, "If they have
come out for peace, take them
alive; or if they have come out for
war, take them alive."
19 So these went out from the
city, the young men of the rulers
of the provinces, and the army
which followed them.
20 And they [t]killed each his
man; and the Arameans fled, and
Israel pursued them, and Ben-hadad king of Aram escaped on a
horse with horsemen. *smote*
21 And the king of Israel went
out and [t]struck the horses and
chariots, and [t]killed the Arameans
with a great slaughter. *smote*
22 Then [r]the prophet came near
to the king of Israel, and said to
him, "Go, strengthen yourself and
observe and see what you have to
do; for [r]at the turn of the year the
king of Aram will come up against
you." 1 Kin. 20:13 • 2 Sam. 11:1
23 Now the servants of the king
of Aram said to him, "Their gods
are gods of the mountains, therefore they were stronger than we;
but rather let us fight against
them in the plain, *and* surely we
shall be stronger than they.
24 "And do this thing: remove
the kings, each from his place,
and put captains in their place,
25 and muster an army like the
army that you have lost, horse for
horse, and chariot for chariot.
Then we will fight against them in
the plain, and surely we shall be
stronger than they." And he listened to their voice and did so.
26 So it came about at the turn
of the year, that Ben-hadad mustered the Arameans and went up
to Aphek to fight against Israel.
27 And the sons of Israel were
mustered and were provisioned

and went to meet them; and the
sons of Israel camped before them
like two little flocks of goats, but
the Arameans filled the country.
28 Then a man of God came
near and spoke to the king of Israel and said, "Thus says the
LORD, 'Because the Arameans
have said, "The LORD is a god of
the mountains, but He is not a god
of *the* valleys"; therefore I will
give all this great multitude into
your hand, and you shall know
that I am the LORD.' "
29 So they camped one over
against the other seven days. And
it came about that on the seventh
day, the battle was joined, and the
sons of Israel [t]killed *of* the Arameans 100,000 foot soldiers in one
day. *smote*
30 But the rest fled to Aphek
into the city, and the wall fell on
27,000 men who were left. And
Ben-hadad fled and came into the
city into an inner chamber.
31 And his servants said to him,
"Behold now, we have heard that
the kings of the house of Israel are
merciful kings, please let us put
sackcloth on our loins and ropes
on our heads, and go out to the
king of Israel; perhaps he will
save your [t]life." *soul*
32 So [r]they girded sackcloth on
their loins and *put* ropes on their
heads, and came to the king of Israel and said, "Your servant Ben-
hadad says, 'Please let me live.' "
And he said, "Is he still alive? He
is my brother." 1 Kin. 20:31
33 Now the men [t]took this as an
omen, and quickly catching his
word said, "Your brother Ben-hadad." Then he said, "Go, bring
him." Then Ben-hadad came out
to him, and he took him up into
the chariot. *divined*
34 And *Ben-hadad* said to him,
"The cities which my father took
from your father I will restore,
and you shall make streets for
yourself in Damascus, as my father made in Samaria." *Ahab
said*, "And I will let you go with
this covenant." So he made a covenant with him and let him go.
35 Now a certain man of the
sons of the prophets said to another by the word of the LORD,
"Please strike me." But the man
refused to strike him.
36 Then he said to him, "Because you have not listened to the
voice of the LORD, behold, as soon
as you have departed from me, a
lion will kill you." And as soon as
he had departed from him a lion
found him, and killed him.
37 Then he found another man
and said, "Please [t]strike me." And
the man [t]struck him, wounding
him. *smite • smote*
38 So the prophet departed and
waited for the king by the way,
and [r]disguised himself with a bandage over his eyes. 1 Kin. 14:2
39 And as the king passed by,
he cried to the king and said,
"Your servant went out into the
midst of the battle; and behold, a
man turned aside and brought a
man to me and said, 'Guard this
man; if for any reason he is missing, [r]then your life shall be for his
life, or else you shall pay a talent
of silver.' 2 Kin. 10:24
40 "And while your servant was
busy here and there, he was
gone." And the king of Israel said

to him, "So shall your judgment be; you yourself have decided *it*."

41 Then he hastily took the bandage away from his eyes, and the king of Israel recognized him that he was of the prophets.

42 And he said to him, "Thus says the LORD, 'Because you have let go out of *your* hand the man whom I had devoted to destruction, therefore [r]your [t]life shall go for his life, and your people for his people.' " 1 Kin. 20:39 • *soul*

43 So [r]the king of Israel went to his house sullen and vexed, and came to Samaria. 1 Kin. 21:4

CHAPTER 21

NOW it came about after these things, that Naboth the Jezreelite had a vineyard which *was* in [r]Jezreel beside the palace of Ahab king of Samaria. Judg. 6:33

2 And Ahab spoke to Naboth, saying, "Give me your vineyard, that I may have it for a vegetable garden because it is close beside my house, and I will give you a better vineyard than it in its place; if you like, I will give you the price of [t]it in money." *this*

3 But Naboth said to Ahab, "The LORD forbid me [r]that I should give you the inheritance of my fathers." Lev. 25:23; Num. 36:7

4 So Ahab came into his house sullen and vexed because of the word which Naboth the Jezreelite had spoken to him; for he said, "I will not give you the inheritance of my fathers." And he lay down on his bed and turned away his face and ate no [t]food. *bread*

5 But Jezebel his wife came to him and said to him, "How is it that your spirit is so sullen that you are not eating [t]food?" *bread*

6 So he said to her, "Because I spoke to Naboth the Jezreelite, and said to him, 'Give me your vineyard for money; or else, if it pleases you, I will give you a vineyard in its place.' But he said, 'I will not give you my vineyard.' "

7 And Jezebel his wife said to him, "Do you now [t]reign over Israel? Arise, eat bread, and let your heart be joyful; I will give you the vineyard of Naboth the Jezreelite." *exercise kingship*

8 [r]So she wrote letters in Ahab's name and sealed them with his seal, and sent letters to [r]the elders and to the nobles who were living with Naboth in his city. Esth. 3:12 • 1 Kin. 20:7

9 Now she wrote in the letters, saying, "Proclaim a fast, and seat Naboth at the head of the people;

10 and seat two worthless men before him, and let them testify against him, saying, 'You cursed God and the king.' Then take him out and stone him to death."

11 So the men of his city, the elders and the nobles who lived in his city, did as Jezebel had sent *word* to them, just as it was written in the letters which she had sent them.

12 They [r]proclaimed a fast and seated Naboth at the head of the people. Is. 58:4

13 Then the two worthless men came in and sat before him; and the worthless men testified against him, even against Naboth, before the people, saying, "Na-

both cursed God and the king." So
they took him outside the city and
stoned him to death with stones.
14 Then they sent *word* to Jezebel, saying, "Naboth has been
stoned, and is dead."
15 And it came about when Jezebel heard that Naboth had been
stoned and was dead, that Jezebel
said to Ahab, "Arise, take possession of the vineyard of Naboth,
the Jezreelite, which he refused to
give you for money; for Naboth is
not alive, but dead."
16 And it came about when
Ahab heard that Naboth was
dead, that Ahab arose to go down
to the vineyard of Naboth the Jezreelite, to take possession of it.
17 Then the word of the LORD
came to Elijah the Tishbite, saying,
18 "Arise, go down to meet Ahab
king of Israel, who is in Samaria;
behold, he is in the vineyard of
Naboth where he has gone down
to take possession of it.
19 "And you shall speak to him,
saying, 'Thus says the LORD,
"Have[r] you murdered, and also
taken possession?"' And you
shall speak to him, saying, 'Thus
says the LORD, "In the place
where the dogs licked up the
blood of Naboth the dogs shall
lick up your blood, even
yours."'" 2 Sam. 12:9
20 And Ahab said to Elijah,
"Have[r] you found me, O my enemy?" And he [t]answered, "I have
found *you*, because you have sold
yourself to do evil in the sight of
the LORD. 1 Kin. 18:17 • *said*
21 "Behold, I will bring evil upon
you, and [r]will utterly sweep you
away, and will cut off from Ahab
every male, both bond and free in
Israel; 1 Kin. 14:10; 2 Kin. 9:8
22 and I will make your house
like the house of Jeroboam the
son of Nebat, and like the house of
Baasha the son of Ahijah, because
of the provocation with which you
have provoked *Me* to anger, and
because you have made Israel sin.
23 "And of Jezebel also has the
LORD spoken, saying, 'The dogs
shall eat Jezebel in the [t]district of
Jezreel.' *portion*
24 "The[r] one belonging to Ahab,
who dies in the city, the dogs shall
eat, and the one who dies in the
field the birds of heaven shall
eat." 1 Kin. 14:11; 16:4
25 Surely there was no one like
Ahab who sold himself to do evil
in the sight of the LORD, because
Jezebel his wife incited him.
26 And [r]he acted very abominably in following idols, according
to all that the Amorites had done,
whom the LORD cast out before
the sons of Israel. 1 Kin. 15:12
27 And it came about when
Ahab heard these words, that he
tore his clothes and put on [t]sack-
cloth and fasted, and he lay in
sackcloth and went about despon-
dently. *sackcloth on his flesh*
28 Then the word of the LORD
came to Elijah the Tishbite, saying,
29 "Do you see how Ahab has
humbled himself before Me? Because he has humbled himself before Me, I will not bring the evil in
his days, *but* I will bring the evil
upon his house in his son's days."

CHAPTER 22

AND three years passed without
war between Aram and Israel.
2 And it came about in the
third year, that [r]Jehoshaphat the
king of Judah came down to the
king of Israel. 1 Kin. 15:24
3 Now the king of Israel said to
his servants, "Do you know that
Ramoth-gilead belongs to us, and
we [t]are still doing nothing to take
it out of the hand of the king of
Aram?" *are silent so as not*
4 And he said to Jehoshaphat,
"Will you go with me to battle at
Ramoth-gilead?" And Jehoshaphat said to the king of Israel, "I[r]
am as you are, my people as your
people, my horses as your
horses." 2 Kin. 3:7
5 Moreover, Jehoshaphat said
to the king of Israel, "Please inquire [t]first for the word of the
LORD." *as the day*
6 Then [r]the king of Israel gathered the prophets together, about
four hundred men, and said to
them, "Shall I go against Ramoth-
gilead to battle or shall I refrain?"
And they said, "Go up, for the
Lord will give *it* into the hand of
the king." 1 Kin. 18:19
7 But [r]Jehoshaphat said, "Is
there not yet a prophet of the
LORD here, that we may inquire of
him?" 2 Kin. 3:11
8 And the king of Israel said to
Jehoshaphat, "There is yet one
man by whom we may inquire of
the LORD, but I hate him, because
he does not prophesy good concerning me, but evil. *He is* Micaiah
son of Imlah." But Jehoshaphat
said, "Let not the king say so."
9 Then the king of Israel called
an officer and said, "Bring quickly
Micaiah son of Imlah."
10 Now the king of Israel and
Jehoshaphat king of Judah were
sitting each on his throne, arrayed
in *their* robes, at the threshing
floor at the entrance of the gate of
Samaria; and all the prophets
were prophesying before them.
11 Then Zedekiah the son of
Chenaanah made [r]horns of iron for
himself and said, "Thus says the
LORD, 'With these you shall gore
the Arameans until they are consumed.'" Zech. 1:18-21
12 And all the prophets were
prophesying thus, saying, "Go up
to Ramoth-gilead and prosper, for
the LORD will give *it* into the hand
of the king."
13 Then the messenger who
went to summon Micaiah spoke to
him saying, "Behold now, the
words of the prophets are uniformly favorable to the king.
Please let your word be like the
word of one of them, and speak
favorably."
14 But Micaiah said, "As the
LORD lives, what the LORD says to
me, that I will speak."
15 When he came to the king,
the king said to him, "Micaiah,
shall we go to Ramoth-gilead to
battle, or shall we refrain?" And
he [t]answered him, "Go up and succeed, and the LORD will give *it* into
the hand of the king." *said to*
16 Then the king said to him,
"How many times must I adjure
you to speak to me nothing but
the truth in the name of the
LORD?"

17 So he said,
"I saw all Israel
Scattered on the mountains,
[r]Like sheep which have no shepherd. Num. 27:17
And the LORD said, 'These have no master.
Let each of them return to his house in peace.'"
18 Then the king of Israel said
to Jehoshaphat, "Did I not tell you
that he would not prophesy good
concerning me, but evil?"
19 And [t]Micaiah said, "Therefore,
hear the word of the LORD: [r]I
saw the LORD sitting on His
throne, and all the host of heaven
standing by Him on His right and
on His left. *he* • Is. 6:1
20 "And the LORD said, 'Who will
entice Ahab to go up and fall at
Ramoth-gilead?' And one said this
while another said that.
21 "Then a spirit came forward
and stood before the LORD and
said, 'I will entice him.'
22 "And the LORD said to him,
'How?' And he said, 'I will go out
and be a deceiving spirit in the
mouth of all his prophets.' Then
He said, 'You are to entice *him*
and also prevail. Go and do so.'
23 "Now therefore, behold, [r]the
LORD has put a deceiving spirit in
the mouth of all these your prophets;
and the LORD has proclaimed
disaster against you." Ezek. 14:9
24 Then Zedekiah the son of
Chenaanah came near and struck
Micaiah on the cheek and said,
"How did the Spirit of the LORD
pass from me to speak to you?"
25 And Micaiah said, "Behold,
you shall see on that day when
you [r]enter an inner room to hide
yourself." 1 Kin. 20:30
26 Then the king of Israel said,
"Take Micaiah and return him to
Amon the governor of the city and
to Joash the king's son;
27 and say, 'Thus says the king,
"Put this man in prison, and feed
him sparingly with bread and water
until I return safely."'"
28 And Micaiah said, "If you indeed
return safely the LORD has
not spoken by me." And he said,
"Listen, all you people."
29 So the king of Israel and Jehoshaphat
king of Judah went up
against Ramoth-gilead.
30 And the king of Israel said to
Jehoshaphat, "I [r]will disguise myself
and go into the battle, but you
put on your robes." So the king of
Israel disguised himself and went
into the battle. 2 Chr. 35:22
31 Now the king of Aram had
commanded the thirty-two captains
of his chariots, saying, "Do
not fight with small or great, but
with the king of Israel alone."
32 So it came about, when the
captains of the chariots saw Jehoshaphat,
that they said, "Surely
it is the king of Israel," and they
turned aside to fight against him,
and Jehoshaphat cried out.
33 Then it happened, when the
captains of the chariots saw that it
was not the king of Israel, that
they turned back from pursuing
him.
34 Now a certain man drew his
bow at random and struck the
king of Israel in a joint of the armor.
So he said to the driver of his
chariot, "Turn [t]around, and take

me out of the fight; for I am severely wounded." *your hand*
35 And the battle raged that
day, and the king was propped up
in his chariot in front of the Arameans, and died at evening, and
the blood from the wound ran into
the bottom of the chariot.
36 Then a cry passed throughout the army close to sunset, saying, "Every man to his city and every man to his [t]country." *land*
37 So the king died and was
brought to Samaria, and they buried the king in Samaria.
38 And they washed the chariot
by the pool of Samaria, and the
dogs licked up his blood (now the
harlots bathed themselves *there*),
[r]according to the word of the LORD
which He spoke. 1 Kin. 21:19
39 Now the rest of the acts of
Ahab and all that he did and the
ivory house which he built and all
the cities which he built, are they
not written in the Book of the
Chronicles of the Kings of Israel?
40 So Ahab slept with his fathers, and Ahaziah his son became king in his place.
41 [r]Now Jehoshaphat the son of
Asa became king over Judah in
the fourth year of Ahab king of Israel. 2 Chr. 20:31
42 Jehoshaphat was thirty-five
years old when he became king,
and he reigned twenty-five years
in Jerusalem. And his mother's
name was Azubah the daughter of
Shilhi.
43 And he walked in all the way
of Asa his father; he did not turn
aside from it, doing right in the
sight of the LORD. However, the
high places were not taken away;
the people still sacrificed and
burnt incense on the high places.
44 Jehoshaphat also made
peace with the king of Israel.
45 Now the rest of the acts of
Jehoshaphat, and his might which
he showed and how he warred,
are they not written [r]in the Book of
the Chronicles of the Kings of Judah? 2 Chr. 20:34
46 And the remnant of [r]the sod-
omites who remained in the days
of his father Asa, he [t]expelled from
the land. Gen. 19:5 • *consumed*
47 Now there was no king in
Edom; a deputy was king.
48 Jehoshaphat made ships of
Tarshish to go to Ophir for gold,
but they did not go for the ships
were broken at Ezion-geber.
49 Then Ahaziah the son of
Ahab said to Jehoshaphat, "Let
my servants go with your servants
in the ships." But Jehoshaphat
was not willing.
50 And Jehoshaphat slept with
his fathers and was buried with
his fathers in the city of his father
David, and Jehoram his son became king in his place.
51 Ahaziah the son of Ahab became king over Israel in Samaria
in the seventeenth year of Jehoshaphat king of Judah, and he
reigned two years over Israel.
52 And he did evil in the sight of
the LORD and walked in the way
of his father and in the way of his
mother and in the way of Jeroboam the son of Nebat, who
caused Israel to sin.
53 [r]So he served Baal and worshiped him and provoked the
LORD God of Israel to anger according to all that his father had
done. Judg. 2:11; 1 Kin. 16:30-32

THE SECOND BOOK OF THE

KINGS

NOW Moab rebelled against Israel after the death of Ahab.
2 And Ahaziah fell through the
lattice in his upper chamber
which *was* in Samaria, and became ill. So he sent messengers
and said to them, "Go,[r]inquire of
Baal-zebub, the god of Ekron,
whether I shall recover from this
sickness." 2 Kin. 1:3, 6, 16
3 But the angel of the LORD
said to[r]Elijah the Tishbite, "Arise,
go up to meet the messengers of
the king of Samaria and say to
them, 'Is it because there is no
God in Israel *that* you are going to
inquire of[r]Baal-zebub, the god of
Ekron?' 1 Kin. 17:1 • 2 Kin. 1:2
4 "Now therefore thus says the
LORD, 'You shall not come down
from the bed where you have
gone up, but you shall surely
die.'" Then Elijah departed.
5 When the messengers re-
turned to him he said to them,
"Why have you returned?"
6 And they said to him, "A
man came up to meet us and said
to us, 'Go, return to the king who
sent you and say to him, "Thus
says the LORD, 'Is it because there
is no God in Israel *that* you are
sending[r]to inquire of Baal-zebub,
the god of Ekron? Therefore you
shall not come down from the bed
where you have gone up, but shall
surely die.'"'" 2 Kin. 1:2
7 And he said to them, "What
kind of man was he who came up
to meet you and spoke these
words to you?"
8 And they answered him, "*He
was* a hairy man with a leather
girdle bound about his loins." And
he said, "It is Elijah the Tishbite."
9 Then *the king*[r]sent to him a
captain of fifty with his fifty. And
he went up to him, and behold, he
was sitting on the top of the hill.
And he said to him, "O man of
God, the king says, 'Come
down.'" 2 Kin. 6:13, 14
10 And Elijah answered and
said to the captain of fifty, "If I am
a man of God,[r]let fire come down
from heaven and consume you
and your fifty." Then fire came
down from heaven and consumed
him and his fifty. 1 Kin. 18:36-38
11 So he again sent to him another captain of fifty with his fifty.
And he answered and said to him,
"O man of God, thus says the
king, 'Come down quickly.'"
12 And Elijah answered and
said to them, "If I am a man of
God, let fire come down from
heaven and consume you and
your fifty." Then the fire of God
came down from heaven and consumed him and his fifty.
13 So he again sent the captain
of a third fifty with his fifty. When
the third captain of fifty went up,
he came and bowed down on his
knees before Elijah, and begged
him and said to him, "O man of
God, please let my life and the

lives of these fifty servants of
yours be precious in your sight.
14 "Behold fire came down from
heaven, and consumed the first
two captains of fifty with their fifties; but now let my [t]life be precious in your sight." *soul*
15 And [r]the angel of the LORD
said to Elijah, "Go down with him;
[r]do not be afraid of him." So he
arose and went down with him to
the king. 2 Kin. 1:3 • Is. 51:12
16 Then he said to him, "Thus
says the LORD, 'Because you have
sent messengers to inquire of
Baal-zebub, the god of Ekron—is
it because there is no God in Israel
to inquire of His word?—therefore you shall not come down
from the bed where you have
gone up, but shall surely die.' "
17 So Ahaziah died according
to the word of the LORD which Elijah had spoken. And because he
had no son, Jehoram became king
in his place [r]in the second year of
Jehoram the son of Jehoshaphat,
king of Judah. 2 Kin. 3:1; 8:16
18 Now the rest of the acts of
Ahaziah which he did, are they
not written in the Book of the
Chronicles of the Kings of Israel?

CHAPTER 2

AND it came about when the
LORD was about to take up Elijah
by a whirlwind to heaven, that Elijah went with Elisha from Gilgal.
2 And Elijah said to Elisha,
"Stay [r]here please, for the LORD
has sent me as far as Bethel." But
Elisha said, "As [r]the LORD lives
and as you yourself live, I will not
leave you." So they went down to
Bethel. Ruth 1:15 • 1 Sam. 1:26
3 Then the sons of the prophets who *were at* Bethel came out
to Elisha and said to him, "Do you
know that the LORD will take
away your master from over [t]you
today?" And he said, "Yes, I
know; be still." *your head*
4 And Elijah said to him, "Elisha, please stay here, for the LORD
has sent me to Jericho." But he
said, "As the LORD lives, and as
you yourself live, I will not leave
you." So they came to Jericho.
5 And the sons of the prophets
who *were* at Jericho approached
Elisha and said to him, "Do you
know that the LORD will take
away your master from over [t]you
today?" And he [t]answered, "Yes, I
know; be still." *your head • said*
6 Then Elijah said to him,
"Please stay here, for the LORD
has sent me to the Jordan." And
he said, "As the LORD lives, and as
you yourself live, I will not leave
you." So the two of them went on.
7 Now [r]fifty men of the sons of
the prophets went and stood opposite *them* at a distance, while
the two of them stood by the Jordan. 2 Kin. 2:15, 16
8 And Elijah took his mantle
and folded it together and struck
the waters, and they were divided
here and there, so that the two of
them crossed over on dry ground.
9 Now it came about when
they had crossed over, that Elijah
said to Elisha, "Ask what I shall
do for you before I am taken from
you." And Elisha said, "Please, let
a [r]double portion of your spirit be
upon me." Num. 11:17-25

10 And he said, "You have asked a hard thing. *Nevertheless,* if you see me when I am taken from you, it shall be so for you; but if not, it shall not be so."

11 Then it came about as they were going along and talking, that behold, *there appeared* [r]a chariot of fire and horses of fire which separated the two of them. And Elijah went up by a [a]whirlwind to heaven. 2 Kin. 6:17 • *windstorm*

12 And Elisha saw *it* and cried out, "My [r]father, my father, the [t]chariots of Israel and its horsemen!" And he saw him no more. Then he took hold of his own clothes and tore them in two pieces. 2 Kin. 13:14 • *chariot*

13 He also took up the mantle of Elijah that fell from him, and returned and stood by the bank of the Jordan.

14 And he took the mantle of Elijah that fell from him, and [r]struck the waters and said, "Where is the LORD, the God of Elijah?" And when he also had struck the waters, they were divided here and there; and Elisha crossed over. 2 Kin. 2:8

15 Now when [r]the sons of the prophets who *were* at Jericho opposite *him* saw him, they said, "The spirit of Elijah rests on Elisha." And they came to meet him and bowed themselves to the ground before him. 2 Kin. 2:7

16 And they said to him, "Behold now, there are with your servants fifty strong men, please let them go and search for your master; [t]perhaps [r]the Spirit of the LORD has taken him up and cast him on some mountain or into some valley." And he said, "You shall not send." *lest* • 1 Kin. 18:12

17 But when they urged him until he was ashamed, he said, "Send." They sent therefore fifty men; and they searched three days, but did not find him.

18 And they returned to him while he was staying at Jericho; and he said to them, "Did I not say to you, 'Do not go'?"

19 Then the men of the city said to Elisha, "Behold now, the situation of this city is pleasant, as my lord sees; but the water is bad, and the land is unfruitful."

20 And he said, "Bring me a new jar, and put salt [t]in it." So they brought *it* to him. *there*

21 And he went out to the spring of water, and threw salt [t]in it and said, "Thus says the LORD, 'I have [t]purified these waters; there shall not be from there death or unfruitfulness any longer.' " *there* • *healed*

22 So the waters have been purified to this day, according to the word of Elisha which he spoke.

23 Then he went up from there to Bethel; and as he was going up by the way, young lads came out from the city and mocked him and said to him, "Go up, you baldhead; go up, you baldhead!"

24 When he looked behind him and saw them, he cursed them in the name of the LORD. Then two female bears came out of the woods and tore up forty-two lads of [t]their number. *them*

25 And he went from there to [r]Mount Carmel, and from there he returned to Samaria. 2 Kin. 4:25

CHAPTER 3

NOW Jehoram the son of Ahab
became king over Israel at Samaria[r] in the eighteenth year of Jehoshaphat king of Judah, and
reigned twelve years. 2 Kin. 1:17
2 And he did evil in the sight of
the LORD, though not like his father and his mother; for he put
away the *sacred* pillar of Baal
which his father had made.
3 Nevertheless, he clung to the
sins of Jeroboam the son of Nebat, which he made Israel sin; he
did not depart from them.
4 Now Mesha king of Moab
was a sheep breeder, and [r]used to
pay the king of Israel 100,000
lambs and the wool of 100,000
rams. 2 Sam. 8:2; Is. 16:1, 2
5 But it came about, when
Ahab died, the king of Moab rebelled against the king of Israel.
6 And King Jehoram went out
of Samaria [t]at that time and mustered all Israel. *in that day*
7 Then he went and sent *word*
to Jehoshaphat the king of Judah,
saying, "The king of Moab has rebelled against me. Will you go
with me to fight against Moab?"
And he said, "I will go up; I am as
you are, my people as your people, my horses as your horses."
8 And he said, "Which way
shall we go up?" And he [t]an-
swered, "The way of the wilderness of Edom." *said*
9 So [r]the king of Israel went
with [r]the king of Judah and the
king of Edom; and they made a
circuit of seven days' journey, and
there was no water for the army
or for the cattle that followed
them. 2 Kin. 3:1 • 2 Kin. 3:7
10 Then the king of Israel said,
"Alas! For the LORD has called
these three kings to give them into
the hand of Moab."
11 But Jehoshaphat said, "Is
there not a prophet of the LORD
here, that we may inquire of the
LORD by him?" And one of the
king of Israel's servants answered
and said, "Elisha the son of Shaphat is here, who used to pour water on the hands of Elijah."
12 And Jehoshaphat said, "The
word of the LORD is with him." So
the king of Israel and Jehoshaphat
and the king of Edom went down
to him.
13 Now Elisha said to the king
of Israel, "What do I have to do
with you? [r]Go to the prophets of
your father and to the prophets of
your mother." And the king of Israel said to him, "No, for the LORD
has called these three kings *to-*
gether to give them into the hand
of Moab." 1 Kin. 18:19; 22:6-11
14 And Elisha said, "As[r] the
LORD of hosts lives, before whom
I stand, were it not that I regard
the presence of Jehoshaphat the
king of Judah, I would not look at
you nor see you. 1 Kin. 17:1
15 "But now bring me a minstrel." And it came about, when
the minstrel played, that the hand
of the LORD came upon him.
16 And he said, "Thus says the
LORD, 'Make this valley full of
trenches.'
17 "For thus says the LORD, 'You
shall not see wind nor shall you
see rain; yet that valley [r]shall be
filled with water, so that you shall

drink, both you and your cattle
and your beasts. Ps. 107:35
18 'And this is but a [r]slight thing
in the sight of the LORD; He shall
also give the Moabites into your
hand. Jer. 32:17, 27; Mark 10:27
19 'Then[r] you shall strike every
fortified city and every choice
city, and fell every good tree and
stop all springs of water, and mar
every good piece of land with
stones.' " 2 Kin. 3:25
20 And it happened in the morning about the time of offering the
sacrifice, that behold, water came
by the way of Edom, and the
country was filled with water.
21 Now all the Moabites heard
that the kings had come up to
fight against them. And all who
were able to put on armor and
older were summoned, and stood
on the border.
22 And they rose early in the
morning, and the sun shone on the
water, and the Moabites saw the
water opposite *them* as red as
blood.
23 Then they said, "This is
blood; the kings have surely
fought together, and they have
slain one another. Now therefore,
Moab, to the spoil!"
24 But when they came to the
camp of Israel, the Israelites arose
and struck the Moabites, so that
they fled before them; and they
went forward into the land,
slaughtering the Moabites.
25 [r]Thus they destroyed the
cities; and each one threw a stone
on every piece of good land and
filled it. So they stopped all the
springs of water and felled all the
good trees, until in [r]Kir-hareseth
only they left its stones; however,
the slingers went about *it* and
struck it. 2 Kin. 3:19 • Is. 16:7
26 When the king of Moab saw
that the battle was too fierce for
him, he took with him 700 men
who drew swords, to break
through to the king of Edom; but
they could not.
27 Then he took his oldest son
who was to reign in his place, and
[r]offered him as a burnt offering on
the wall. And there came great
wrath against Israel, and they departed from him and returned to
their own land. Amos 2:1

CHAPTER 4

NOW a certain woman of the
wives of the sons of the prophets
cried out to [t]Elisha, "Your servant
my husband is dead, and you
know that your servant feared the
LORD; and the creditor has come
to take my two children to be his
slaves." *Elisha, saying*
2 And Elisha said to her,
"What shall I do for you? Tell me,
what do you have in the house?"
And she said, "Your maidservant
has nothing in the house except [r]a
jar of oil." 1 Kin. 17:12
3 Then he said, "Go, borrow
vessels at large for yourself from
all your neighbors, *even* empty
vessels; do not get a few.
4 "And you shall go in and shut
the door behind you and your
sons, and pour out into all these
vessels; and you shall set aside
what is full."
5 So she went from him and
shut the door behind her and her

sons; they were bringing *the vessels* to her and she poured.

6 And it came about when [r]the vessels were full, that she said to her son, "Bring me another vessel." And he said to her, "There is not one vessel more." And the oil stopped. Matt. 14:20

7 Then she came and told [r]the man of God. And he said, "Go, sell the oil and pay your debt, and you *and* your sons can live on the rest." 1 Kin. 12:22

8 Now there came a day when Elisha passed over to Shunem, where there was a [t]prominent woman, and she persuaded him to eat [t]food. And so it was, as often as he passed by, he turned in there to eat [t]food. *great • bread*

9 And she said to her husband, "Behold now, I perceive that this is a holy [r]man of God passing by us continually. 2 Kin. 4:7

10 "Please, let us make a little walled upper chamber and let us set a bed for him there, and a table and a chair and a lampstand; and it shall be, when he comes to us, *that* he can turn in there."

11 One day he came there and turned in to the upper chamber and [t]rested. *lay there*

12 Then he said to [r]Gehazi his servant, "Call this Shunammite." And when he had called her, she stood before him. 2 Kin. 4:29-31

13 And he said to him, "Say now to her, 'Behold, you have been careful for us with all this care; what can I do for you? Would you be spoken for to the king or to the captain of the army?' " And she answered, "I live among my own people."

14 So he said, "What then is to be done for her?" And Gehazi [t]answered, "Truly she has no son and her husband is old." *said*

15 And he said, "Call her." When he had called her, she stood in the doorway.

16 Then he said, "At [r]this season next year you shall embrace a son." And she said, "No, my lord, O man of God, do not lie to your maidservant." Gen. 18:14

17 And the woman conceived and bore a son at that season [t]the next year, as Elisha had said to her. *when the time revived*

18 When the child was grown, the day came that he went out to his father to the reapers.

19 And he said to his father, "My head, my head." And he said to his servant, "Carry him to his mother."

20 When he had taken him and brought him to his mother, he sat on her [t]lap until noon, and *then* died. *knees*

21 And she went up and [r]laid him on the bed of the man of God, and shut *the door* behind him, and went out. 2 Kin. 4:32

22 Then she called to her husband and said, "Please send me one of the servants and one of the donkeys, that I may run to the man of God and return."

23 And he said, "Why will you go to him today? It is neither [r]new moon nor sabbath." And she said, "*It will be* well." Num. 10:10

24 Then she saddled a donkey and said to her servant, "Drive and go forward; do not slow down the pace for me unless I tell you."

25 So she went and came to the

man of God to Mount Carmel.
And it came about when the man
of God saw her at a distance, that
he said to Gehazi his servant, "Behold, yonder is the Shunammite.
26 "Please run now to meet her
and say to her, 'Is it well with
you? Is it well with your husband?
Is it well with the child?'" And
she [t]answered, "It is well." *said*
27 When she came to the man
of God to the hill, she caught hold
of his feet. And Gehazi came near
to push her away; but the man of
God said, "Let her alone, for her
soul is [t]troubled within her; and
the LORD has hidden it from me
and has not told me." *bitter*
28 Then she said, "Did I ask for
a son from my lord? Did I not say,
'Do not deceive me'?"
29 Then he said to Gehazi,
"Gird up your loins and take my
staff in your hand, and go your
way; if you meet any man, do not
salute him, and if anyone salutes
you, do not answer him; and lay
my staff on the lad's face."
30 And the mother of the lad
said, "As[r] the LORD lives and as
you yourself live, I will not leave
you." And he arose and followed
her. 2 Kin. 2:2, 4
31 Then Gehazi passed on before them and laid the staff on the
lad's face, but there was neither
sound nor response. So he returned to meet him and told him,
"The lad has not awakened."
32 When Elisha came into the
house, behold the lad was dead
and laid on his bed.
33 So he entered and [r]shut the
door behind them both, and
prayed to the LORD. 2 Kin. 4:4
34 And [r]he went up and lay on
the child, and put his mouth on his
mouth and his eyes on his eyes
and his hands on his hands, and
he stretched himself on him; and
the flesh of the child became
warm. 1 Kin. 17:21-23
35 Then he returned and walked
in the house once back and forth,
and went up and [r]stretched himself on him; and the lad sneezed
seven times and the lad opened
his eyes. 1 Kin. 17:21
36 And he called Gehazi and
said, "Call this Shunammite." So
he called her. And when she came
in to him, he said, "Take up your
son."
37 Then she went in and fell at
his feet and bowed herself to the
ground, and [r]she took up her son
and went out. Heb. 11:35
38 When Elisha returned to [r]Gil-
gal, *there was* a famine in the
land. [t]As the sons of the prophets
were sitting before him, he said to
his servant, "Put on the large pot
and boil stew for the sons of the
prophets." 2 Kin. 2:1 • *And*
39 Then one went out into the
field to gather herbs, and found a
wild vine and gathered from it his
lap full of wild gourds, and came
and sliced them into the pot of
stew, for they did not know *what
they were.*
40 So they poured *it* out for the
men to eat. And it came about as
they were eating of the stew, that
they cried out and said, "O man of
God, there is death in the pot."
And they were unable to eat.
41 But he said, "Now bring
meal." [r]And he threw it into the
pot, and he said, "Pour *it* out for

the people that they may eat."
Then there was no harm in the
pot. Ex. 15:25; 2 Kin. 2:21
42 Now a man came from Baal-
shalishah, and brought the man of
God bread of the first fruits,
twenty loaves of barley and fresh
ears of grain in his sack. And he
said, "Give *them* to the people
that they may eat."
43 And his attendant said,
"What, [r]shall I set this before a
hundred men?" But he said, "Give
them to the people that they may
eat, for thus says the LORD, 'They
shall eat and have *some* left
over.'" Luke 9:13; John 6:9
44 So he set *it* before them, and
they ate and [r]had *some* left over,
according to the word of the
LORD. Matt. 14:20; 15:37

CHAPTER 5

NOW Naaman, captain of the
army of the king of Aram, was a
great man with his master, and
highly respected, because by him
the LORD had given victory to
Aram. The man was also a valiant
warrior, *but he was* a leper.
2 Now the Arameans had gone
out in bands, and had taken captive a little girl from the land of
Israel; and she [t]waited on Naaman's wife. *was before*
3 And she said to her mistress,
"I wish that my master were [t]with
the prophet who is in Samaria!
Then he would cure him of his leprosy." *before*
4 And [t]Naaman went in and
told his master, saying, "Thus and
thus spoke the girl who is from
the land of Israel." *he*
5 Then the king of Aram said,
"Go [t]now, and I will send a letter
to the king of Israel." And he departed and [r]took with him ten talents of silver and six thousand
shekels of gold and ten changes of
clothes. *enter* • 1 Sam. 9:7
6 And he brought the letter to
the king of Israel, saying, "And
now as this letter comes to you,
behold, I have sent Naaman my
servant to you, that you may cure
him of his leprosy."
7 And it came about when the
king of Israel read the letter, that
he tore his clothes and said, "Am I
God, to kill and to make alive, that
this man is sending *word* to me to
cure a man of his leprosy? But
consider now, and see how he is
seeking a quarrel against me."
8 And it happened when Elisha
[r]the man of God heard that the
king of Israel had torn his clothes,
that he sent *word* to the king, saying, "Why have you torn your
clothes? Now let him come to me,
and he shall know that there is a
prophet in Israel." 1 Kin. 12:22
9 So Naaman came with his
horses and his chariots, and stood
at the doorway of the house of Elisha.
10 And Elisha sent a messenger
to him, saying, "Go[r] and wash in
the Jordan seven times, and your
flesh shall be restored to you and
you shall be clean." John 9:7
11 But Naaman was furious and
went away and said, "Behold, I
[t]thought, 'He will surely come out
to me, and stand and call on the
name of the LORD his God, and
wave his hand over the place, and
cure the leper.' *said*

12 "Are not Abanah and Pharpar,
the rivers of Damascus, better
than all the waters of Israel?
Could I not wash in them and be
clean?" So he turned and [r]went
away in a rage. Prov. 14:17
13 Then his servants came near
and spoke to him and said, "My[r]
father, had the prophet told you *to*
do some great thing, would you
not have done *it*? How much more
then, when he says to you, 'Wash,
and be clean'?" 2 Kin. 2:12
14 So he went down and dipped
himself seven times in the Jordan,
according to the word of the man
of God; and [r]his flesh was restored
like the flesh of a little child, and
he was clean. 2 Kin. 5:10
15 When he returned to the
man of God with all his company,
and came and stood before him,
he said, "Behold now, I know that
there is no God in all the earth,
but in Israel; so please take a present from your servant now."
16 But he said, "As the LORD
lives, before whom I stand, I will
take nothing." And he urged him
to take *it*, but he refused.
17 And Naaman said, "If not,
please let your servant at least be
given two mules' load of earth; for
your servant will no more offer
burnt offering nor will he sacrifice
to other gods, but to the LORD.
18 "In this matter may the LORD
pardon your servant: when my
master goes into the house of
Rimmon to worship there, and he
leans on my hand and I bow myself in the house of Rimmon,
when I bow myself in the house of
Rimmon, the LORD pardon your
servant in this matter."
19 And he said to him, "Go[r] in
peace." So he departed from him
some distance. Ex. 4:18
20 But Gehazi, the servant of
Elisha the man of God, [t]thought,
"Behold, my master has spared
this Naaman the Aramean, [t]by not
receiving from his hands what he
brought. As the LORD lives, I will
run after him and take something
from him." *said* · *from*
21 So Gehazi pursued Naaman.
When Naaman saw one running
after him, he came down from the
chariot to meet him and said, "Is
all well?"
22 And he said, "All[r] is well. My
master has sent me, saying, 'Behold, just now two young men of
the sons of the prophets have
come to me from the hill country
of Ephraim. Please give them a
talent of silver and two changes of
clothes.'" 2 Kin. 4:26
23 And Naaman said, "Be
pleased to take two talents." And
he urged him, and bound two talents of silver in two bags with two
changes of clothes, and gave them
to two of his servants; and they
carried *them* before him.
24 When he came to the [t]hill, he
took them from their hand and [r]de-
posited them in the house, and he
sent the men away, and they departed. *Ophel* · 1 Kin. 21:16
25 But he went in and stood before his master. And Elisha said to
him, "Where have you been, Gehazi?" And he said, "Your[r] servant
went nowhere." 2 Kin. 5:22
26 Then he said to him, "Did not
my heart go *with you*, when the
man turned from his chariot to
meet you? [r]Is it a time to receive

money and to receive clothes and
olive groves and vineyards and
sheep and oxen and male and female servants? 2 Kin. 5:16
27 "Therefore, the leprosy of
Naaman shall cleave to you and to
your [t]descendants forever." So he
went out from his presence a leper
as white as snow. *seed*

CHAPTER 6

NOW the sons of the prophets
said to Elisha, "Behold now, the
place before you where we are living is too limited for us.
2 "Please let us go to the Jordan, and each of us take from
there a beam, and let us make a
place there for ourselves where
we may live." So he said, "Go."
3 Then one said, "Please be
willing to go with your servants."
And he answered, "I shall go."
4 So he went with them; and
when they came to the Jordan,
they cut down trees.
5 But as one was felling a
beam, [t]the axe head fell into the
water; and he cried out and said,
"Alas, my master! For it was borrowed." *as for the iron, it fell*
6 Then the man of God said,
"Where did it fall?" And when he
showed him the place, [r]he cut off a
stick, and threw *it* in there, and
made the iron float. Ex. 15:25
7 And he said, "Take it up for
yourself." So he put out his hand
and took it.
8 Now the king of Aram was
warring against Israel; and he
[t]counseled with his servants saying, "In such and such a place
shall be my camp." *took counsel*
9 And [r]the man of God sent
word to the king of Israel saying,
"Beware that you do not pass this
place, for the Arameans are coming down there." 2 Kin. 4:1, 7
10 And the king of Israel sent to
the place about which the man of
God had told him; thus he warned
him, so that he guarded himself
there, more than once or twice.
11 Now the heart of the king of
Aram was enraged over this thing;
and he called his servants and
said to them, "Will you tell me
which of us is for the king of Israel?"
12 And one of his servants said,
"No, my lord, O king; but Elisha,
the prophet who is in Israel, tells
the king of Israel the words that
you speak in your bedroom."
13 So he said, "Go and see
where he is, that I may send and
take him." And it was told him,
saying, "Behold, he is in Dothan."
14 And he sent horses and
chariots and a great army there,
and they came by night and surrounded the city.
15 Now when the attendant of
the man of God had risen early
and gone out, behold, an army
with horses and chariots was circling the city. And his servant said
to him, "Alas, my master! [t]What
shall we do?" *How*
16 So he [t]answered, "Do[r] not
fear, for those who are with us are
more than those who are with
them." *said* • Ex. 14:13
17 Then Elisha prayed and said,
"O LORD, I pray, open his eyes
that he may see." And the LORD
opened the servant's eyes, and he
saw; and behold, the mountain

was full of [r]horses and chariots of
fire all around Elisha. Ps. 68:17
18 And when they came down
to him, Elisha prayed to the LORD
and said, "Strike this [t]people with
blindness, I pray." So He struck
them with blindness according to
the word of Elisha. *nation*
19 Then Elisha said to them,
"This is not the way, nor is this
the city; follow me and I will bring
you to the man whom you seek."
And he brought them to Samaria.
20 And it came about when
they had come into Samaria, that
Elisha said, "O LORD, open the
eyes of these *men,* that they may
see." So the LORD opened their
eyes, and they saw; and behold,
they were in the midst of Samaria.
21 Then the king of Israel when
he saw them, said to Elisha, "My[r]
father, shall I [t]kill them? Shall I [t]kill
them?" 2 Kin. 2:12 • *smite*
22 And he [t]answered, "You shall
not [t]kill *them.* Would you [t]kill those
you have taken captive with your
sword and with your bow? Set
bread and water before them, that
they may eat and drink and go to
their master." *said* • *smite*
23 So he prepared a great feast
for them; and when they had eat-
en and drunk he sent them away,
and they went to their master.
And [r]the marauding bands of Arameans did not come again into the
land of Israel. 2 Kin. 5:2; 24:2
24 Now it came about after this,
that Ben-hadad king of Aram
gathered all his army and went up
and besieged Samaria.
25 And there was a great [r]fam-
ine in Samaria; and behold, they
besieged it, until a donkey's head
was sold for eighty *shekels* of silver, and a fourth of a [1]kab of
dove's dung for five *shekels* of silver. Lev. 26:26
26 And as the king of Israel was
passing by on the wall a woman
cried out to him, saying, "Help,
my lord, O king!"
27 And he said, "If the LORD
does not help you, from where
shall I help you? From the threshing floor, or from the wine press?"
28 And the king said to her,
"What [t]is the matter with you?"
And she answered, "This woman
said to me, 'Give your son that we
may eat him today, and we will
eat my son tomorrow.' *to you*
29 "So [r]we boiled my son and ate
him; and I said to her on the next
day, 'Give your son, that we may
eat him'; but she has hidden her
son." Lev. 26:27-29; Lam. 4:10
30 And it came about when the
king heard the words of the
woman, that he tore his clothes—
now he was passing by on the
wall—and the people looked, and
behold, he had sackcloth [t]beneath
on his [t]body. *within* • *flesh*
31 Then he said, "May God do
so to me and more also, if the
head of Elisha the son of Shaphat
[t]remains on him today." *stands*
32 Now Elisha was sitting in his
house, and the elders were sitting
with him. And *the king* sent a man
from his presence; but before the
messenger came to him, he said to
the elders, "Do you see how this
son of a murderer has sent to take
away my head? Look, when the
messenger comes, shut the door
and hold the door shut against

[1]I.e., One kab equals approx. 2 quarts

him. Is not the sound of his master's feet behind him?"
33 And while he was still talking with them, behold, the messenger came down to him, and he
said, "Behold,[r] this evil is from the
LORD; why should I wait for the
LORD any longer?" Is. 8:21

CHAPTER 7

THEN Elisha said, "Listen to the
word of the LORD; thus says the
LORD, 'Tomorrow[r] about this time
a measure of fine flour shall be
sold for a shekel, and two measures of barley for a shekel, in the
gate of Samaria.'" 2 Kin. 7:18
2 And [r]the royal officer on
whose hand the king was leaning
answered the man of God and
said, "Behold, if the LORD should
make windows in heaven, could
this thing be?" Then he said, "Behold you shall see it with your
own eyes, but you shall not eat [t]of
it." 2 Kin. 5:18 • *from there*
3 Now there were four leprous
men at the entrance of the gate;
and they said to one another,
"Why do we sit here until we die?
4 "If we say, 'We will enter the
city,' then the famine is in the city
and we shall die there; and if we
sit here, we die also. Now therefore come, and let us [t]go over to
the camp of the Arameans. If they
spare us, we shall live; and if they
kill us, we shall but die." *fall*
5 And they arose at twilight to
go to the camp of the Arameans;
when they came to the outskirts
of the camp of the Arameans, behold, there was no one there.
6 For the Lord had caused the
army of the Arameans to hear a
sound of chariots and a sound of
horses, *even* the sound of a great
army, so that they said to one another, "Behold, the king of Israel
has hired against us the kings of
the Hittites and the kings of the
Egyptians, to come upon us."
7 Therefore they [r]arose and fled
in the twilight, and left their tents
and their horses and their donkeys, even the camp just as it was,
and fled for their life. Ps. 48:4-6
8 When these lepers came to
the outskirts of the camp, they entered one tent and ate and drank,
and [r]carried from there silver and
gold and clothes, and went and
hid *them*; and they returned and
entered another tent and carried
from there *also*, and went and hid
them. Josh. 7:21
9 Then they said to one another, "We are not doing right.
This day is a day of good news,
but we are keeping silent; if we
wait until morning light, punishment will [t]overtake us. Now therefore come, let us go and tell the
king's household." *find*
10 So they came and called to
the gatekeepers of the city, and
they told them, saying, "We came
to the camp of the Arameans, and
behold, there was no one there,
nor the voice of man, only the
horses tied and the donkeys tied,
and the tents just as they were."
11 And the gatekeepers called,
and told *it* within the king's
household.
12 Then the king arose in the
night and said to his servants, "I
will now tell you what the Arameans have done to us. They know

that we are hungry; therefore they have gone from the camp to hide themselves in the field, saying, 'When they come out of the city, we shall capture them alive and get into the city.' "

13 And one of his servants answered and said, "Please, let some *men* take five of the horses which remain, which are left in the city. Behold, they *will be in any case* like all the multitude of Israel who are left in it; behold, they *will be in any case* like all the multitude of Israel who have already perished, so let us send and see."

14 They took therefore two chariots with horses, and the king sent after the army of the Arameans, saying, "Go and see."

15 And they went after them to the Jordan, and behold, all the way was full of clothes and equipment, which the Arameans had thrown away in their haste. Then the messengers returned and told the king.

16 So the people went out and plundered the camp of the Arameans. Then a measure of fine flour *was sold* for a shekel and two measures of barley for a shekel, [r]according to the word of the LORD. 2 Kin. 7:1

17 Now the king appointed the royal officer on whose hand he leaned to have charge of the gate; but the people trampled on him at the gate, and he died just as the man of God had said, who spoke when the king came down to him.

18 And it came about just as the man of God had spoken to the king, saying, "Two[r] measures of barley for a shekel and a measure of fine flour for a shekel, shall be *sold* tomorrow about this time at the gate of Samaria." 2 Kin. 7:1

19 Then the royal officer answered the man of God and said, "Now behold, [r]if the LORD should make windows in heaven, could such a thing be?" And he said, "Behold, you shall see it with your own eyes, but you shall not eat [t]of it." 2 Kin. 7:2 · *from there*

20 And so it happened to him, for the people trampled on him at the gate, and he died.

CHAPTER 8

NOW Elisha spoke to the woman whose son he had restored to life, saying, "Arise and go [t]with your household, and sojourn wherever you can sojourn; for the LORD has called for a famine, and it shall even come on the land for seven years." *you and your*

2 So the woman arose and did according to the word of the man of God, and she went with her household and sojourned in the land of the Philistines seven years.

3 And it came about at the end of seven years, that the woman returned from the land of the Philistines; and she went out to [t]appeal to the king for her house and for her field. *cry out*

4 Now the king was talking with [r]Gehazi, the servant of the man of God, saying, "Please relate to me all the great things that Elisha has done." 2 Kin. 4:12

5 And it came about, as he was relating to the king how he had restored to life the one who was dead, that behold, the woman

whose son he had restored to life,
[t]appealed to the king for her house
and for her field. And Gehazi said,
"My lord, O king, this is the
woman and this is her son, whom
Elisha restored to life." *cried out*
6 When the king asked the
woman, she related *it* to him. So
the king appointed for her a certain officer, saying, "Restore all
that was hers and all the produce
of the field from the day that she
left the land even until now."
7 Then Elisha came to [r]Damas-
cus. Now [r]Ben-hadad king of Aram
was sick, and it was told him, saying, "The man of God has come
here." 1 Kin. 11:24 • 2 Kin. 6:24
8 And the king said to [r]Hazael,
"Take a gift in your hand and go
to meet the man of God, and inquire of the LORD by him, saying,
'Will I recover from this sickness?' " 1 Kin. 19:15, 17
9 So Hazael went to meet him
and took a gift in his hand, even
every kind of good thing of Damascus, forty camels' loads; and
he came and stood before him and
said, "Your [r]son Ben-hadad king of
Aram has sent me to you, saying,
'Will I recover from this sickness?' " 2 Kin. 5:13
10 Then Elisha said to him, "Go,
say to him, 'You shall surely recover,' but the LORD has shown
me that he will certainly die."
11 And he fixed his gaze steadily *on him* until he was ashamed,
and the man of God wept.
12 And Hazael said, "Why does
my lord weep?" Then he [t]an-
swered, "Because I know the evil
that you will do to the sons of Israel: their strongholds you will set
on fire, and their young men you
will kill with the sword, and their
little ones you [r]will dash in pieces,
and their women with child you
will rip up." *said* • 2 Kin. 15:16
13 Then Hazael said, "But what
is your servant, *who is but* a dog,
that he should do this great
thing?" And Elisha [t]answered,
"The Lord has shown me that you
will be king over Aram." *said*
14 So he departed from Elisha
and returned to his master, who
said to him, "What did Elisha say
to you?" And he [t]answered, "He
told me that [r]you would surely recover." *said* • 2 Kin. 8:10
15 And it came about on the
morrow, that he took the cover
and dipped it in water and spread
it on his face, so that he died. And
Hazael became king in his place.
16 Now in the fifth year of [r]Jo-
ram the son of Ahab king of Israel, Jehoshaphat being then the
king of Judah, Jehoram the son of
Jehoshaphat king of Judah became king. 2 Kin. 1:17; 3:1
17 He was thirty-two years old
when he became king, and he
reigned eight years in Jerusalem.
18 And he walked in the way of
the kings of Israel, just as the
house of Ahab had done, for [r]the
daughter of Ahab became his
wife; and he did evil in the sight of
the LORD. 2 Kin. 8:27
19 However, the LORD was not
willing to destroy Judah, for the
sake of David His servant, [r]since
He had [t]promised him to give a
lamp to him through his sons always. 2 Sam. 7:12-15 • *said*
20 In his days Edom revolted
from under the hand of Judah,

and made a king over themselves.
21 Then Joram crossed over to
Zair, and all his chariots with him.
And it came about that he arose
by night and struck the Edomites
who had surrounded him and the
captains of the chariots; but *his*
army fled to their tents.
22 So Edom revolted against Judah to this day. Then Libnah revolted at the same time.
23 And the rest of the acts of Joram and all that he did, are they
not written in the Book of the
Chronicles of the Kings of Judah?
24 So Joram slept with his fathers, and [r]was buried with his fathers in the city of David; and A-
haziah his son became king in his
place. 2 Chr. 21:20
25 In the twelfth year of Joram
the son of Ahab king of Israel, A-
haziah the son of Jehoram king of
Judah began to reign.
26 [r]Ahaziah *was* twenty-two
years old when he became king,
and he reigned one year in Jerusalem. And his mother's name *was*
Athaliah the granddaughter of
Omri king of Israel. 2 Chr. 22:2
27 And [r]he walked in the way of
the house of Ahab, and did evil in
the sight of the LORD, like the
house of Ahab *had done,* because
he was a son-in-law of the house
of Ahab. 2 Chr. 22:3
28 Then he went with Joram the
son of Ahab to war against [r]Hazael
king of Aram at Ramoth-gilead,
and the Arameans [t]wounded Joram. 2 Kin. 8:15 • *smote*
29 So King Joram returned to
be healed in Jezreel of the wounds
which the Arameans had [t]inflicted
on him at Ramah, when he fought
against Hazael king of Aram.
Then Ahaziah the son of Jehoram
king of Judah went down to see
Joram the son of Ahab in Jezreel
because he was sick. *struck*

CHAPTER 9

NOW Elisha the prophet called
one of [r]the sons of the prophets,
and said to him, "Gird[r] up your
loins, and take this flask of oil in
your hand, and go to Ramoth-gilead. 2 Kin. 2:3 • 2 Kin. 4:29
2 "When you arrive there,
search out Jehu the son of Jehoshaphat the son of Nimshi, and
go in and [t]bid him arise from
among his brothers, and bring him
to an inner room. *cause him to*
3 "Then take the flask of oil and
pour it on his head and say, 'Thus
says the LORD, "I[r] have anointed
you king over Israel." ' Then open
the door and flee and do not
wait." 2 Chr. 22:7
4 So [r]the young man, the servant of the prophet, went to Ramoth-gilead. 2 Kin. 9:1
5 When he came, behold, the
captains of the army were sitting,
and he said, "I have a word for
you, O captain." And Jehu said,
"For which *one* of us?" And he
said, "For you, O captain."
6 And he arose and went into
the house, and he poured the oil
on his head and said to him, "Thus
says the LORD, the God of Israel, 'I[r]
have anointed you king over the
people of the LORD, *even* over Israel. 1 Sam. 2:7, 8; 1 Kin. 19:16
7 'And you shall strike the
house of Ahab your master, [r]that I
may avenge the blood of My ser-

vants the prophets, and the blood
of all the servants of the LORD, at
the hand of Jezebel. 1 Kin. 18:4
8 'For the whole house of Ahab
shall perish, and I will cut off from
Ahab every male person both
bond and free in Israel.
9 'And [r]I will make the house of
Ahab like the house of Jeroboam
the son of Nebat, and like the
house of Baasha the son of Ahijah. 1 Kin. 14:10, 11; 15:29
10 'And the dogs shall eat Jezebel in the territory of Jezreel, and
none shall bury *her.*' " Then he
opened the door and fled.
11 Now Jehu came out to the
servants of his master, and one
said to him, "Is all well? Why did
this mad fellow come to you?"
And he said to them, "You know
very well the man and his talk."
12 And they said, "It is a lie, tell
us now." And he said, "Thus and
thus he said to me, 'Thus says the
LORD, "I have anointed you king
over Israel." ' "
13 Then [r]they hurried and each
man took his garment and placed
it under him on the bare steps,
and blew the trumpet, saying,
"Jehu is king!" Matt. 21:7, 8
14 So Jehu the son of Jehoshaphat the son of Nimshi conspired
against Joram. Now Joram [t]with
all Israel was [t]defending Ramoth-
gilead against Hazael king of
Aram, *he and • keeping*
15 but King [2]Joram had returned to Jezreel to be healed of
the wounds which the Arameans
had inflicted on him when he
fought with Hazael king of Aram.
So Jehu said, "If this is your mind,

[2]Heb., *Jehoram,* and so throughout this
context

then let no one escape *or* leave the
city to go tell *it* in Jezreel."
16 Then Jehu rode in a chariot
and went to Jezreel, for Joram
was lying there. [r]And Ahaziah king
of Judah had come down to see
Joram. 2 Kin. 8:29
17 Now the watchman was
standing on the tower in Jezreel
and he saw the [t]company of Jehu
as he came, and said, "I see a
[t]company." And Joram said,
"Take a horseman and send him
to meet them and let him say, 'Is it
peace?' " *multitude*
18 So a horseman went to meet
him and said, "Thus says the king,
'Is it peace?' " And Jehu said,
"What have you to do with peace?
Turn behind me." And the watchman [t]reported, "The messenger
came to them, but he did not return." *told, saying*
19 Then he sent out a second
horseman, who came to them and
said, "Thus says the king, 'Is it
peace?' " And Jehu [t]answered,
"What have you to do with peace?
Turn behind me." *said*
20 And the watchman reported,
"He came even to them, and he
did not return; and the driving is
like the driving of Jehu the son of
Nimshi, for he drives furiously."
21 Then Joram said, "Get[t]
ready." And they made his chariot
ready. And Joram king of Israel
and Ahaziah king of Judah went
out, each in his chariot, and they
went out to meet Jehu and found
him in the property of Naboth the
Jezreelite. *Yoke the chariot*
22 And it came about, when Joram saw Jehu, that he said, "Is it
peace, Jehu?" And he answered,

"What peace, so long as the harlotries of your mother Jezebel and
her witchcrafts are so many?"
23 So Joram reined about and
fled and said to Ahaziah, "*There is*
treachery, O Ahaziah!"
24 And Jehu drew his bow with
his full strength and [t]shot Joram
between his arms; and the arrow
went through his heart, and he
sank in his chariot. *smote*
25 Then *Jehu* said to Bidkar his
officer, "Take *him* up and cast him
into the [3]property of the field of
Naboth the Jezreelite, for I remember when[t]you and I were riding together after Ahab his father,
that the LORD laid this [r]oracle
against him: *I and you* • Is. 13:1
26 'Surely I have seen yesterday
the blood of Naboth and the blood
of his sons,' says the LORD, 'and I
will repay you in this [3]property,'
says the LORD. Now then, take
and cast him into the property, according to the word of the LORD."
27 When Ahaziah the king of
Judah saw *this,* he fled by the way
of the garden house. And Jehu
pursued him and said, "Shoot[t]him
too, in the chariot." *So they shot
him* at the ascent of Gur, which is
at Ibleam. But he fled to Megiddo
and died there. *smite*
28 Then his servants carried
him in a chariot to Jerusalem, and
buried him in his grave with his
fathers in the city of David.
29 Now in the eleventh year of
Joram, the son of Ahab, Ahaziah
became king over Judah.
30 When Jehu came to Jezreel,
Jezebel heard *of it,* and she
painted her eyes and adorned her
head, and looked out the window.

[3]Lit., *portion,* and so throughout this context

31 And as Jehu entered the
gate, she said, "Is it [t]well, Zimri,
your master's murderer?" *peace*
32 Then he lifted up his face to
the window and said, "Who is on
my side? Who?" And two or three
officials looked down at him.
33 And he said, "Throw her
down." So they threw her down,
and some of her blood was sprinkled on the wall and on the
horses, and he trampled her under
foot.
34 When he came in, he ate and
drank; and he said, "See now to
this cursed woman and bury her,
for she is a king's daughter."
35 And they went to bury her,
but they found no more of her
than the skull and the feet and the
palms of her hands.
36 Therefore they returned and
told him. And he said, "This is the
word of the LORD, which He spoke
by His servant Elijah the Tishbite,
saying, 'In[r]the property of Jezreel
the dogs shall eat the flesh of Jezebel; 1 Kin. 21:23
37 and [r]the corpse of Jezebel
shall be as dung on the face of the
field in the property of Jezreel, so
they cannot say, "This is Jezebel." ' " Jer. 8:1-3

CHAPTER 10

NOW Ahab had seventy sons in
[r]Samaria. And Jehu wrote letters
and sent *them* to Samaria, to the
rulers of Jezreel, the elders, and to
the guardians of *the children of*
Ahab, saying, 1 Kin. 16:24-29
2"And now, when this letter
comes to you, since your master's
sons are with you, as well as the

chariots and horses and a fortified
city and the weapons,
3 select the best and [4]fittest of
your master's sons, and set *him*
on his father's throne, and fight
for your master's house."
4 But they feared greatly and
said, "Behold, [r]the two kings did
not stand before him; how then
can we stand?" 2 Kin. 9:24, 27
5 And the one who *was* over
the household, and he who *was*
over the city, the elders, and the
guardians of *the children,* sent
word to Jehu, saying, "We[r] are
your servants, all that you say to
us we will do, we will not make
any man king; do what is good in
your sight." Josh. 9:8, 11
6 Then he wrote a letter to
them a second time saying, "If
you are on my side, and you will
listen to my voice, take the heads
of the men, your master's sons,
and come to me at Jezreel tomorrow about this time." Now the
king's sons, seventy persons, *were*
with the great men of the city,
who were rearing them.
7 And it came about when the
letter came to them, that they
took the king's sons, and slaughtered *them,* seventy persons, and
put their heads in baskets, and
sent *them* to him at Jezreel.
8 When the messenger came
and told him, saying, "They have
brought the heads of the king's
sons," he said, "Put them in two
heaps at the entrance of the gate
until morning."
9 Now it came about in the
morning, that he went out and
stood, and said to all the people,
"You are [t]innocent; behold, I conspired against my master and
killed him, but who [t]killed all
these? *just* · *smote*
10 "Know then that there shall
fall to the earth nothing of the
word of the LORD, which the LORD
spoke concerning the house of
Ahab, for the LORD has done what
He spoke [t]through His servant Elijah." *by the hand of*
11 So Jehu [t]killed all who remained of the house of Ahab in
[r]Jezreel, and all his great men and
his acquaintances and his priests,
until he left him without a survivor. *smote* · Hos. 1:4
12 Then he arose and departed,
and went to Samaria. On the way
while he was at [5]Beth-eked of the
shepherds,
13 Jehu met the relatives of A-
haziah king of Judah and said,
"Who are you?" And they answered, "We are the relatives of
Ahaziah; and we have come down
to greet the sons of the king and
the sons of the queen mother."
14 And he said, "Take them
alive." So they took them alive,
and killed them at the pit of Beth-
eked, forty-two men; and he left
none of them.
15 Now when he had departed
from there, he [t]met Jehonadab the
son of Rechab *coming* to meet
him; and he [t]greeted him and said
to him, "Is your heart right, as my
heart is with your heart?" And Jehonadab [t]answered, "It is." *Jehu
said,* "If it is, give *me* your hand."
And he gave him his hand, and he
took him up to him into the
chariot. *found* · *blessed* · *said*
16 And he said, "Come with me
and see my zeal for the LORD." So

[4]Lit., *most upright*

[5]I.e., house of binding

he made him ride in his chariot.
17 And when he came to Samaria,[r] he[t] killed all who remained
to Ahab in Samaria, until he had
destroyed him, according to the
word of the LORD, which He spoke
to Elijah. 2 Kin. 9:8 • *smote*
18 Then Jehu gathered all the
people and said to them, "Ahab
served Baal a little; Jehu will
serve him much.
19 "And now, summon all the
prophets of Baal, all his worshipers and all his priests; let no one
be missing, for I have a great sacrifice for Baal; whoever is missing
shall not live." But Jehu did it in
cunning, in order that he might
destroy the worshipers of Baal.
20 And Jehu said, "Sanctify[r] a
solemn assembly for Baal." And
they proclaimed *it*. Joel 1:14
21 Then Jehu sent [t]throughout
Israel and all the worshipers of
Baal came, so that there was not a
man left who did not come. And
when they went into the house of
Baal, the house of Baal was filled
from one end to the other. *in all*
22 And he said to the one who
was in charge of the wardrobe,
"Bring out garments for all the
worshipers of Baal." So he
brought out garments for them.
23 And Jehu went into the
house of Baal with Jehonadab the
son of Rechab; and he said to the
worshipers of Baal, "Search and
see that there may be here with
you none of the servants of the
LORD, but only the worshipers of
Baal."
24 Then they went in to offer
sacrifices and burnt offerings.
Now Jehu had stationed for himself eighty men outside, and he
had said, "The one who permits
any of the men whom I bring into
your hands to escape, shall give
up his life in exchange."
25 Then it came about, as soon
as he had finished offering the
burnt offering, that Jehu said to
the guard and to the royal officers,
"Go in, kill them; let none come
out." And they killed them with
the edge of the sword; and the
guard and the royal officers threw
them out, and went to the inner
room of the house of Baal.
26 And they brought out the *sacred* [r]pillars of the house of Baal,
and burned them. 1 Kin. 14:23
27 They also broke down the *sacred* pillar of Baal and broke down
the house of Baal, and [r]made it a
latrine to this day. Ezra 6:11
28 Thus Jehu eradicated Baal
out of Israel.
29 However, *as for* the sins of
Jeroboam the son of Nebat, which
he made Israel sin, from these
Jehu did not depart, *even* the
golden calves that *were* at Bethel
and that *were* at Dan.
30 And the LORD said to Jehu,
"Because you have done well in
executing what is right in My
eyes, *and* have done to the house
of Ahab according to all that *was*
in My heart, [r]your sons of the
fourth generation shall sit on the
throne of Israel." 2 Kin. 15:12
31 But Jehu [t]was not careful to
walk in the law of the LORD, the
God of Israel, with all his heart; he
did not depart from the sins of
Jeroboam, which he made Israel
sin. *did not watch*
32 In those days the LORD be-

gan to cut off *portions* from Israel;
and Hazael defeated them
throughout the territory of Israel:
33 from the Jordan eastward, all
the land of Gilead, the Gadites
and the Reubenites and the Manassites, from [r]Aroer, which is by
the valley of the Arnon, even Gilead and Bashan. Deut. 2:36
34 Now the rest of the acts of
Jehu and all that he did and all his
might, are they not written in the
Book of the Chronicles of the
Kings of Israel?
35 And Jehu slept with his fathers, and they buried him in Samaria. And Jehoahaz his son became king in his place.
36 Now the [t]time which Jehu
reigned over Israel in Samaria
was twenty-eight years. *days*

CHAPTER 11

WHEN Athaliah the mother of
Ahaziah saw that her son was
dead, she rose and destroyed all
the royal [t]offspring. *seed*
2 But Jehosheba, the daughter
of King Joram, sister of Ahaziah,
[r]took Joash the son of Ahaziah and
stole him from among the king's
sons who were being put to death,
and placed him and his nurse in
the bedroom. So they hid him
from Athaliah, and he was not put
to death. 2 Kin. 11:21; 12:1
3 So he was hidden with her in
the house of the LORD six years,
while Athaliah was reigning over
the land.
4 Now in the seventh year Jehoiada sent and brought the captains of hundreds of the Carites
and of the [6]guard, and brought
them to him in the house of the
LORD. Then he made a covenant
with them and put them under
oath in the house of the LORD, and
showed them the king's son.
5 And he commanded them,
saying, "This is the thing that you
shall do: one third of you, who
come in on the sabbath and keep
watch over the king's house
6 (one third also *shall be* at the
gate Sur, and one third at the gate
behind the [6]guards), shall keep
watch over the house for defense.
7 "And two parts of you, *even*
all who go out on the sabbath,
shall also keep watch over the
house of the LORD for the king.
8 "Then you shall surround the
king, each with his weapons in his
hand; and whoever comes within
the ranks shall be put to death.
And be with the king when he
goes out and when he comes in."
9 So the captains of hundreds
[r]did according to all that Jehoiada
the priest commanded. And each
one of them took his men who
were to come in on the sabbath,
with those who were to go out on
the sabbath, and came to Jehoiada
the priest. 2 Chr. 23:8
10 And [r]the priest gave to the
captains of hundreds the spears
and shields that had been King
David's, which *were* in the house
of the LORD. 2 Sam. 8:7
11 And the [t]guards stood each
with his weapons in his hand,
from the right [t]side of the house to
the left [t]side of the house, by the
altar and by the house, around the
king. *runners* • *shoulder*
12 Then he brought the king's
son out and put the crown on him,

[6]Lit., *runners*

[6]Lit., *runners*

and *gave him* the testimony; and
they made him king and anointed
him, and they clapped their hands
and said, "Long live the king!"
13 ʳWhen Athaliah heard the
noise of the guard *and of* the people, she came to the people in the
house of the LORD. 2 Chr. 23:12
14 And she looked and behold,
the king was standing ʳby the pillar, according to the custom, with
the captains and the ᵗtrumpeters
beside the king; and all the people
of the land rejoiced and blew
trumpets. Then Athaliah tore her
clothes and cried, "Treason! Treason!" 2 Kin. 23:3 • *trumpets*
15 And Jehoiada the priest commanded the captains of hundreds
who were appointed over the
army, and said to them, "Bring
her out between the ranks, and
whoever follows her put to death
with the sword." For the priest
said, "Let her not be put to death
in the house of the LORD."
16 So they ᵗseized her, and when
she arrived at the horses' entrance
of the king's house, she was put to
death there. *placed hands to her*
17 Then Jehoiada made a covenant between the LORD and the
king and the people, that they
should be the LORD's people, also
between the king and the people.
18 And all the people of the land
went to the house of Baal, and
tore it down; his altars and his images they broke in pieces thoroughly, and killed Mattan the
priest of Baal before the altars.
And the priest appointed officers
over the house of the LORD.
19 And he took the captains of
hundreds and the ʳCarites and the
ᵗguards and all the people of the
land; and they brought the king
down from the house of the LORD,
and came by the way of the gate
of the ᵗguards to the king's house.
And he sat on the throne of the
kings. 2 Kin. 11:4 • *runners*
20 So ʳall the people of the land
rejoiced and the city was quiet.
For they had put Athaliah to
death with the sword at the king's
house. Prov. 11:10
21 Jehoash was seven years old
when he became king.

CHAPTER 12

IN the seventh year of Jehu, ʳJeho-
ash became king, and he reigned
forty years in Jerusalem; and his
mother's name was Zibiah of
Beersheba. 2 Chr. 24:1
2 And Jehoash did right in the
sight of the LORD all his days in
which Jehoiada the priest instructed him.
3 Only ʳthe high places were
not taken away; the people still
sacrificed and burned incense on
the high places. 2 Kin. 14:4
4 Then Jehoash said to the
priests, "All the money of the sacred things ʳwhich is brought into
the house of the LORD, in current
money, *both* the money of each
man's assessment *and* all the
money which any man's heart
prompts him to bring into the
house of the LORD, 2 Kin. 22:4
5 let the priests take it for
themselves, each from his ac-
quaintance; and they shall repair
the [7]damages of the house wherever any damage may be found.
6 But it came about that in the

[7]Lit., *breaches*, and so through v. 12

twenty-third year of King Jehoash
the priests had not repaired the
damages of the house.
7 Then King Jehoash called for
Jehoiada the priest, and for the
other priests and said to them,
"Why do you not repair the damages of the house? Now therefore
take no *more* money from your
acquaintances, but pay it for the
damages of the house."
8 So the priests agreed that
they should take no *more* money
from the people, nor repair the
damages of the house.
9 But [r]Jehoiada the priest took
a chest and bored a hole in its lid,
and put it beside the altar, on the
right side as one comes into the
house of the LORD; and the priests
who guarded the threshold put in
it all the money which was
brought into the house of the
LORD. Mark 12:41; Luke 21:1
10 And when they saw that
there was much money in the
chest, [r]the king's scribe and the
high priest came up and tied *it* in
bags and counted the money
which was found in the house of
the LORD. 2 Sam. 8:17
11 And they gave the money
which was weighed out into the
hands of those who did the work,
who had the oversight of the
house of the LORD; and they [t]paid
it out to the carpenters and the
builders, who worked on the
house of the LORD; *brought*
12 and to the masons and the
stonecutters, and for buying timber and hewn stone to repair the
damages to the house of the LORD,
and for all that was [t]laid out for
the house to repair it. *went out*
13 But [r]there were not made for
the house of the LORD silver cups,
snuffers, bowls, trumpets, any
vessels of gold, or vessels of silver
from the money which was
brought into the house of the
LORD; 2 Chr. 24:14
14 for they gave that to those
who did the work, and with it they
repaired the house of the LORD.
15 Moreover, they did not require an accounting from the men
into whose hand they gave the
money to pay to those who did the
work, for they dealt faithfully.
16 The [r]money from the guilt offerings and the money from the
sin offerings, was not brought into
the house of the LORD; it was for
the priests. Lev. 5:15-18
17 Then Hazael king of Aram
went up and fought against Gath
and captured it, and Hazael set his
face to go up to Jerusalem.
18 And Jehoash king of Judah
took all the sacred things that Jehoshaphat and Jehoram and Ahaziah, his fathers, kings of Judah,
had dedicated, and his own sacred
things and all the gold that was
found among the treasuries of the
house of the LORD and of the
king's house, and sent *them* to
Hazael king of Aram. Then he
went away from Jerusalem.
19 Now the rest of the acts of
Joash and all that he did, are they
not written in the Book of the
Chronicles of the Kings of Judah?
20 And his servants arose and
made a conspiracy, and struck
down Joash at the house of Millo
as he was going down to Silla.
21 For Jozacar the son of Shimeath, and Jehozabad the son of

[r]Shomer, his servants, struck *him*,
and he died; and they buried him
with his fathers in the city of David, and Amaziah his son became
king in his place. 2 Chr. 24:26

CHAPTER 13

IN the twenty-third year of Joash
the son of Ahaziah, king of Judah,
Jehoahaz the son of Jehu became
king over Israel at Samaria, *and
he reigned* seventeen years.
2 And he did evil in the sight of
the LORD, and followed the sins of
Jeroboam the son of Nebat, with
which he made Israel sin; he did
not turn from them.
3 So the anger of the LORD was
kindled against Israel, and He
gave them continually into the
hand of [r]Hazael king of Aram, and
into the hand of Ben-hadad the
son of Hazael. 2 Kin. 12:17
4 Then Jehoahaz entreated the
favor of the LORD, and the LORD
listened to him; for He saw the oppression of Israel, how the king of
Aram oppressed them.
5 And the LORD gave Israel a
[8]deliverer, so that they escaped
from under the hand of the Arameans; and the sons of Israel lived
in their tents as formerly.
6 Nevertheless they did not
turn away from the sins of the
house of Jeroboam, with which he
made Israel sin, but walked in
[t]them; and the Asherah also remained standing in Samaria. *it*
7 For he left to Jehoahaz of the
army not more than fifty horsemen and ten chariots and 10,000
footmen, for the king of Aram had
destroyed them and made them
like the dust at threshing.
8 Now the rest of the acts of
Jehoahaz, and all that he did and
his might, are they not written in
the Book of the Chronicles of the
Kings of Israel?
9 And Jehoahaz slept with his
fathers, and they buried him in
Samaria; and Joash his son became king in his place.
10 In the thirty-seventh year of
Joash king of Judah, Jehoash the
son of Jehoahaz, became king
over Israel in Samaria, *and
reigned* sixteen years.
11 And he did evil in the sight of
the LORD; he did not turn away
from all the sins of Jeroboam the
son of Nebat, with which he made
Israel sin, but he walked in them.
12 [r]Now the rest of the acts of
Joash and all that he did and his
might with which he fought
against Amaziah king of Judah,
are they not written in the Book of
the Chronicles of the Kings of Israel? 2 Kin. 13:14-19; 14:8-15
13 So Joash slept with his fathers, and Jeroboam sat on his
throne; and Joash was buried in
Samaria with the kings of Israel.
14 When Elisha became sick
with the illness of which he was to
die, Joash the king of Israel came
down to him and wept over [t]him
and said, "My father, my father,
the chariots of Israel and its
horsemen!" *his face*
15 And Elisha said to him,
"Take a bow and arrows." So he
took a bow and arrows.
16 Then he said to the king of
Israel, "Put your hand on the
bow." And he put his hand *on it*,

[8]Or, *savior*

then Elisha laid his hands on the
king's hands.
17 And he said, "Open the window toward the east," and he
opened *it.* Then Elisha said,
"Shoot!" And he shot. And he
said, "The LORD's arrow of victory, even the arrow of victory
over Aram; for you shall [t]defeat
the Arameans at Aphek until you
have destroyed *them.*" *smite*
18 Then he said, "Take the arrows," and he took them. And he
said to the king of Israel, "Strike
the ground," and he struck *it*
three times and [t]stopped. *stood*
19 So the man of God was angry
with him and said, "You should
have struck five or six times, then
you would have struck Aram until
you would have [t]destroyed *it.* But
now you shall strike Aram *only*
three times." *made an end of*
20 And Elisha died, and they
buried him. Now [r]the bands of the
Moabites would invade the land in
the spring of the year. 2 Kin. 3:7
21 And as they were burying a
man, behold, they saw a marauding band; and they cast the man
into the grave of Elisha. And when
the man touched the bones of Elisha he [r]revived and stood up on his
feet. Matt. 27:52
22 Now [r]Hazael king of Aram
had oppressed Israel all the days
of Jehoahaz. 2 Kin. 8:12, 13
23 But the LORD was gracious to
them and had compassion on
them and turned to them because
of His covenant with Abraham,
Isaac, and Jacob, and would not
destroy them or cast them from
His presence until now.
24 When Hazael king of Aram
died, Ben-hadad his son became
king in his place.
25 Then Jehoash the son of Jehoahaz took again from the hand
of Ben-hadad the son of Hazael
the cities which he had taken in
war from the hand of Jehoahaz
his father. Three times Joash [t]de-
feated him and recovered the
cities of Israel. *smote*

CHAPTER 14

IN the second year of Joash son
of Joahaz king of Israel, [r]Amaziah
the son of Joash king of Judah became king. 2 Kin. 13:10
2 He was twenty-five years old
when he became king, and he
reigned twenty-nine years in Jerusalem. And his mother's name
was Jehoaddin of Jerusalem.
3 And he did right in the sight
of the LORD, yet not like David his
father; he did according to all that
Joash his father had done.
4 Only [r]the high places were
not taken away; the people still
sacrificed and burned incense on
the high places. 2 Kin. 12:3
5 Now it came about, as soon
as the kingdom was firmly in his
hand, that he killed his servants
who had slain the king his father.
6 But the sons of the slayers he
did not put to death, according to
what is written in the book of the
law of Moses, as the LORD commanded, saying, "The fathers
shall not be put to death for the
sons, nor the sons be put to death
for the fathers; but each shall be
put to death for his own sin."
7 He [t]killed *of* Edom in [r]the Valley of Salt 10,000 and took Sela by

war, and named it Joktheel to this
day. *smote* • 2 Sam. 8:13
8 Then Amaziah sent messengers to Jehoash, the son of Jehoahaz son of Jehu, king of Israel,
saying, "Come,[r] let us face each
other." 2 Sam. 2:14-17
9 And Jehoash king of Israel
sent to Amaziah king of Judah,
saying, "The thorn bush which
was in Lebanon sent to the cedar
which was in Lebanon, saying,
'Give your daughter to my son in
marriage.' But there passed by a
wild beast that was in Lebanon,
and trampled the thorn bush.
10 "You have indeed [t]defeated
Edom, and your heart has [t]become
proud. Enjoy your glory and stay
at home; for why should you provoke trouble so that you, even
you, should fall, and Judah with
you?" *smitten* • *lifted you up*
11 But Amaziah would not listen. So Jehoash king of Israel
went up; and he and Amaziah
king of Judah faced each other at
[r]Beth-shemesh, which belongs to
Judah. Josh. 19:38
12 And Judah was defeated [t]by
Israel, and [r]they fled each to his
tent. *before* • 2 Sam. 18:17
13 Then Jehoash king of Israel
captured Amaziah king of Judah,
the son of Jehoash the son of Ahaziah, at Beth-shemesh, and came
to Jerusalem and tore down the
wall of Jerusalem from [r]the Gate
of Ephraim to the Corner Gate,
400 cubits. Neh. 8:16; 12:39
14 And he took all the gold and
silver and all the utensils which
were found in the house of the
LORD, and in the treasuries of the
king's house, the hostages also,
and returned to Samaria.
15 Now the rest of the acts of
Jehoash which he did, and his
might and how he fought with
Amaziah king of Judah, are they
not written in the Book of the
Chronicles of the Kings of Israel?
16 So Jehoash slept with his fathers and was buried in Samaria
with the kings of Israel; and Jeroboam his son became king in his
place.
17 And Amaziah the son of
Joash king of Judah lived fifteen
years after the death of Jehoash
son of Jehoahaz king of Israel.
18 Now the rest of the acts of
Amaziah, are they not written in
the Book of the Chronicles of the
Kings of Judah?
19 And they conspired against
him in Jerusalem, and he fled to
Lachish; but they sent after him to
Lachish and killed him there.
20 Then they brought him on
horses and he was buried at Jerusalem with his fathers in the city
of David.
21 And all the people of Judah
took Azariah, who *was* sixteen
years old, and made him king in
the place of his father Amaziah.
22 [r]He built Elath and restored it
to Judah, after the king slept with
his fathers. 1 Kin. 9:26
23 In the fifteenth year of Amaziah the son of Joash king of Judah, Jeroboam the son of Joash
king of Israel became king in
Samaria, *and reigned* forty-one
years.
24 And he did evil in the sight of
the LORD; he did not depart from
all the sins of Jeroboam the son of

Nebat, which he made Israel sin.
25 He restored the border of Israel from the entrance of Hamath
as far as the Sea of the Arabah,
according to the word of the
LORD, the God of Israel, which He
spoke [t]through His servant Jonah
the son of Amittai, the prophet,
who was of Gath-hepher. *by*
26 For the [r]LORD saw the affliction of Israel, *which was* very bitter; for [r]there was neither bond nor
free, nor was there any helper for
Israel. 2 Kin. 13:4 • Deut. 32:36
27 And the LORD did not say
that He would blot out the name
of Israel from under heaven, but
He saved them by the hand of
Jeroboam the son of Joash.
28 Now the rest of the acts of
Jeroboam and all that he did and
his might, how he fought and how
he recovered for Israel, [r]Damascus
and Hamath, *which had belonged*
to Judah, are they not written in
the Book of the Chronicles of the
Kings of Israel? 1 Kin. 11:24
29 And Jeroboam slept with his
fathers, even with the kings of Israel, and Zechariah his son became king in his place.

CHAPTER 15

[r]IN the twenty-seventh year of
Jeroboam king of Israel, Azariah
son of Amaziah king of Judah became king. 2 Kin. 14:17
2 He was sixteen years old
when he became king, and he
reigned fifty-two years in Jerusalem; and his mother's name was
Jecoliah of Jerusalem.
3 And he did right in the sight
of the LORD, according to all that
his father Amaziah had done.
4 Only [r]the high places were
not taken away; the people still
sacrificed and burned incense on
the high places. 2 Kin. 12:3
5 And the LORD struck the
king, so that he was a leper to the
day of his death. And he [r]lived in a
separate house, [t]while Jotham the
king's son was over the household, judging the people of the
land. Lev. 13:46 • *and*
6 Now the rest of the acts of
Azariah and all that he did, are
they not written in the Book of the
Chronicles of the Kings of Judah?
7 And Azariah slept with his
fathers, and they buried him with
his fathers in the city of David,
and Jotham his son became king
in his place.
8 [r]In the thirty-eighth year of
Azariah king of Judah, Zechariah
the son of Jeroboam became king
over Israel in Samaria *for* six
months. 2 Kin. 15:1
9 And he did evil in the sight of
the LORD, as his fathers had done;
he did not depart from the sins of
Jeroboam the son of Nebat, which
he made Israel sin.
10 Then Shallum the son of Jabesh conspired against him and
[r]struck him before the people and
[t]killed him, and reigned in his
place. Amos 7:9 • *smote*
11 Now the rest of the acts of
Zechariah, behold they are written in the Book of the Chronicles
of the Kings of Israel.
12 This is the word of the LORD
which He spoke to Jehu, saying,
"Your sons to the fourth genera-

tion shall sit on the throne of Israel." And so it was.
13 Shallum son of Jabesh became king in the thirty-ninth year
of Uzziah king of Judah, and he
reigned one month in Samaria.
14 Then Menahem son of Gadi
went up from Tirzah and came to
Samaria, and struck Shallum son
of Jabesh in Samaria, and killed
him and became king in his place.
15 Now the rest of the acts of
Shallum and his conspiracy which
he made, behold they are written
in the Book of the Chronicles of
the Kings of Israel.
16 Then Menahem struck Tiphsah and all who were in it and its
borders from Tirzah, because they
did not open *to him,* therefore he
struck *it;* and he ripped up all its
women who were with child.
17 In the [r]thirty-ninth year of
Azariah king of Judah, Menahem
son of Gadi became king over Israel *and reigned* ten years in Samaria. 2 Kin. 15:1, 8, 13
18 And he did evil in the sight of
the LORD; he did not depart all his
days from the sins of Jeroboam
the son of Nebat, which he made
Israel sin.
19 Pul, king of Assyria, came
against the land, and Menahem
gave Pul a thousand talents of silver so that his hand might be with
him to strengthen the kingdom
[t]under his rule. *in his hand*
20 Then Menahem exacted the
money from Israel, even from all
the mighty men of wealth, from
each man fifty shekels of silver to
pay the king of Assyria. So the
king of Assyria returned and did
not remain there in the land.
21 Now the rest of the acts of
Menahem and all that he did, are
they not written in the Book of the
Chronicles of the Kings of Israel?
22 And Menahem slept with his
fathers, and Pekahiah his son became king in his place.
23 In [r]the fiftieth year of Azariah
king of Judah, Pekahiah son of
Menahem became king over Israel
in Samaria, *and reigned* two
years. 2 Kin. 15:1, 8, 13, 17
24 And he did evil in the sight of
the LORD; he did not depart from
the sins of Jeroboam son of Nebat, which he made Israel sin.
25 Then Pekah son of Remaliah,
his officer, conspired against him
and struck him in Samaria, in [r]the
castle of the king's house with Argob and Arieh; and with him were
fifty men of the Gileadites, and he
killed him and became king in his
place. 1 Kin. 16:18
26 Now the rest of the acts of
Pekahiah and all that he did, behold they are written in the Book
of the Chronicles of the Kings of
Israel.
27 In [r]the fifty-second year of
Azariah king of Judah, Pekah son
of Remaliah became king over Israel in Samaria, *and reigned*
twenty years. 2 Kin. 15:23
28 And he did evil in the sight of
the LORD; he did not depart from
the sins of Jeroboam son of Nebat, which he made Israel sin.
29 In the days of Pekah king of
Israel, Tiglath-pileser king of Assyria came and [t]captured Ijon and
Abel-beth-maacah and Janoah
and Kedesh and Hazor and Gilead
and Galilee, all the land of Naph-

tali; and he carried them captive
to Assyria. *took*
30 And Hoshea the son of Elah
made a conspiracy against Pekah
the son of Remaliah, and struck
him and put him to death and became king in his place, in the
twentieth year of Jotham the son
of Uzziah.
31 Now the rest of the acts of
Pekah and all that he did, behold,
they are written in the Book of the
Chronicles of the Kings of Israel.
32 In the second year of Pekah
the son of Remaliah king of Israel,
Jotham the son of Uzziah king of
Judah became king.
33 He was twenty-five years old
when he became king, and he
reigned sixteen years in Jerusalem; and his mother's name *was*
Jerusha the daughter of Zadok.
34 And[r]he did what was right in
the sight of the LORD; he did according to all that his father Uzziah had done. 2 Kin. 15:3, 4
35 Only the high places were
not taken away; the people still
sacrificed and burned incense on
the high places. He built the upper
gate of the house of the LORD.
36 Now the rest of the acts of
Jotham and all that he did, are
they not written in the Book of the
Chronicles of the Kings of Judah?
37 In those days[r]the LORD began
to send Rezin king of Aram and
Pekah the son of Remaliah against
Judah. 2 Kin. 16:5; Is. 7:1
38 And Jotham slept with his fathers, and he was buried with his
fathers in the city of David his father; and Ahaz his son became
king in his place.

CHAPTER 16

IN the seventeenth year of Pekah
the son of Remaliah, [r]Ahaz the son
of Jotham, king of Judah, became
king. 2 Chr. 28:1
2 Ahaz *was* twenty years old
when he became king, and he
reigned sixteen years in Jerusalem; and he did not do what was
right in the sight of the LORD his
God, as his father David *had done.*
3 But he walked in the way of
the kings of Israel, [r]and even made
his son pass through the fire, according to the abominations of the
nations whom the LORD had
[a]driven out from before the sons of
Israel. Lev. 18:21 • *dispossessed*
4 And he[r]sacrificed and burned
incense on the high places and on
the hills and under every green
tree. Deut. 12:2; 2 Kin. 14:4
5 Then [r]Rezin king of Aram
and Pekah son of Remaliah, king
of Israel, came up to Jerusalem to
wage war; and they besieged
Ahaz, but could not [t]overcome
him. 2 Kin. 15:37; Is. 7:1 • *fight*
6 At that time Rezin king of
Aram recovered Elath for Aram,
and cleared the Judeans out of
[t]Elath entirely; and the Arameans
came to Elath, and have lived
there to this day. *Eloth*
7 So Ahaz sent messengers to
Tiglath-pileser king of Assyria,
saying, "I am your servant and
your son; come up and deliver me
from the [t]hand of the king of
Aram, and from the [t]hand of the
king of Israel, who are rising up
against me." *palm*
8 And Ahaz took the silver and
gold that was found in the house

of the LORD and in the treasuries
of the king's house, and sent a
present to the king of Assyria.
9 So the king of Assyria listened to him; and the king of Assyria went up against Damascus
and captured it, and carried *the
people of* it away into exile to Kir,
and put Rezin to death.
10 Now King Ahaz went to Damascus to meet Tiglath-pileser
king of Assyria, and saw the altar
which *was* at Damascus; and King
Ahaz sent to Urijah the priest the
pattern of the altar and its model,
according to all its workmanship.
11 So Urijah the priest built an
altar; according to all that King
Ahaz had sent from Damascus,
thus Urijah the priest made *it*, [t]be-
fore the coming of King Ahaz
from Damascus. *until*
12 And when the king came
from Damascus, the king saw the
altar; then the king approached
the altar and went up to it,
13 and [t]burned his burnt offering
and his meal offering, and poured
his libation and sprinkled the
blood of his peace offerings on the
altar. *offered in smoke*
14 And the bronze altar, which
was before the LORD, [t]he brought
from the front of the house, from
between *his* altar and the house of
the LORD, and he put it on the
north side of *his* altar. *he also*
15 Then King Ahaz commanded
Urijah the priest, saying, "Upon
the great altar burn the morning
burnt offering and the evening
meal offering and the king's burnt
offering and his meal offering,
with the burnt offering of all the
people of the land and their meal
offering and their libations; and
sprinkle on it all the blood of the
burnt offering and all the blood of
the sacrifice. But the bronze altar
shall be for me to inquire *by*."
16 So Urijah the priest did according to all that King Ahaz
commanded.
17 Then King Ahaz cut off the
borders of the stands, and removed the laver from them; he
also took down the sea from the
bronze oxen which were under it,
and put it on a pavement of stone.
18 And the covered way for the
sabbath which they had built in
the house, and the outer entry of
the king, he removed from the
house of the LORD because of the
king of Assyria.
19 Now the rest of the acts of
Ahaz which he did, are they not
written in the Book of the Chronicles of the Kings of Judah?
20 So Ahaz slept with his fathers, and was buried with his fathers in the city of David; and his
son Hezekiah reigned in his place.

CHAPTER 17

IN the twelfth year of Ahaz king
of Judah, Hoshea the son of Elah
became king over Israel in Samaria, *and reigned* nine years.
2 And he did evil in the sight of
the LORD, only not as the kings of
Israel who were before him.
3 Shalmaneser king of Assyria
came up [r]against him, and Hoshea
became his servant and paid him
tribute. 2 Kin. 18:9-12
4 But the king of Assyria found
conspiracy in Hoshea, who had
sent messengers to So king of
Egypt and had offered no tribute

to the king of Assyria, as *he had*
done year by year; so the king of
Assyria shut him up and bound
him in prison.
5 Then the king of Assyria invaded the whole land and went up
to [r]Samaria and besieged it three
years. Hos. 13:16
6 In the ninth year of Hoshea,
[r]the king of Assyria captured Samaria and [r]carried Israel away into
exile to Assyria, and settled them
in Halah and Habor, *on* the river
of Gozan, and in the cities of the
Medes. Hos. 13:16 • Deut. 28:64
7 Now [r]this came about, because the sons of Israel had
sinned against the LORD their
God, [r]who had brought them up
from the land of Egypt from under
the hand of Pharaoh, king of
Egypt, and they had [9]feared other
gods Josh. 23:16 • Ex. 14:15-30
8 and [r]walked in the [t]customs of
the nations whom the LORD had
driven out before the sons of Israel, and *in the customs* of the
kings of Israel which they had [t]in-
troduced. Lev. 18:3 • *statutes* • *made*
9 And the sons of Israel [a]did
things secretly which were not
right, against the LORD their God.
Moreover, they built for themselves high places in all their
towns, from watchtower to fortified city. *uttered words which*
10 And [r]they set for themselves
sacred pillars and [10]Asherim on every high hill and under every
green tree, Ex. 34:12-14
11 and there they burned incense on all the high places as the
nations *did* which the LORD had
carried away to exile before them;

[9]Lit., *revered,* and so throughout this context
[10]I.e., wooden symbols of a female deity

and they did evil things provoking
the LORD.
12 And they served idols, [r]con-
cerning which the LORD had said
to them, "You shall not do this
thing." Ex. 20:4
13 Yet the LORD warned Israel
and Judah, through all His prophets *and* every seer, saying, "Turn
from your evil ways and keep My
commandments, My statutes according to all the law which I
commanded your fathers, and
which I sent to you through My
servants the prophets."
14 However, they did not listen,
but stiffened their neck [t]like their
fathers, who did not believe in the
LORD their God. *like the neck of*
15 And [r]they rejected His statutes and [r]His covenant which He
made with their fathers, and His
warnings with which He warned
them. And they followed vanity
and became vain, and *went* after
the nations which surrounded
them, concerning which the LORD
had commanded them not to do
like them. Jer. 8:9 • Ex. 24:6-8
16 And they forsook all the
commandments of the LORD their
God and made for themselves
molten images, *even* [r]two calves,
and made an Asherah and worshiped all the host of heaven and
served Baal. 1 Kin. 12:28
17 Then they made their sons
and their daughters pass through
the fire, and practiced divination
and enchantments, and sold themselves to do evil in the sight of the
LORD, provoking Him.
18 So the LORD was very angry
with Israel, and removed them

from His [t]sight; none was left except the tribe of Judah. *face*
19 Also Judah did not keep the
commandments of the LORD their
God, but walked in the customs
which Israel had introduced.
20 And the LORD rejected all the
[t]descendants of Israel and afflicted
them and gave them into the hand
of plunderers, until He had cast
them out of His sight. *seed*
21 When [r]He had torn Israel
from the house of David, they
made Jeroboam the son of Nebat
king. Then Jeroboam drove Israel
away from following the LORD,
and made them [t]commit a great
sin. 1 Kin. 11:11, 31 • *sin*
22 And the sons of Israel
walked in all the sins of Jeroboam
which he did; they did not depart
from them,
23 until the LORD removed Israel from His sight, as He spoke
through all His servants the
prophets. So Israel was carried
away into exile from their own
land to Assyria until this day.
24 And the king of Assyria
brought *men* from Babylon and
from Cuthah and from Avva and
from Hamath and Sephar-vaim,
and settled *them* in the cities of
Samaria in place of the sons of Israel. So they possessed Samaria
and lived in its cities.
25 And it came about at the beginning of their living there, that
they did not fear the LORD; therefore the LORD sent lions among
them which killed some of them.
26 So they spoke to the king of
Assyria, saying, "The nations
whom you have carried away into
exile in the cities of Samaria do
not know the custom of the god of
the land; so he has sent lions
among them, and behold, they kill
them because they do not know
the custom of the god of the
land."
27 Then the king of Assyria
commanded, saying, "Take there
one of the priests whom you carried away into [t]exile, and let him
go and live there; and let him
teach them the custom of the god
of the land." *exile from there*
28 So one of the priests whom
they had carried away into exile
from Samaria came and lived at
Bethel, and taught them how they
should fear the LORD.
29 But every nation still made
gods of its own and put them [r]in
the houses of the high places
which the people of Samaria had
made, every nation in their cities
in which they lived. 1 Kin. 12:31
30 And the men of Babylon
made Succoth-benoth, the men of
Cuth made Nergal, the men of Hamath made Ashima,
31 and the Avvites made Nib-
haz and Tartak; and the Sephar-
vites burned their children in the
fire to Adrammelech and Anam-
melech the gods of Sepharvaim.
32 They also feared the LORD
and [r]appointed from among themselves priests of the high places,
who acted for them in the houses
of the high places. 1 Kin. 12:31
33 They feared the LORD and
served their own gods according
to the custom of the nations from
among whom they had been carried away into exile.
34 To this day they do according to the earlier customs: they do

not fear the LORD, nor do they follow their statutes or their ordinances or the law, or the commandments which the LORD
commanded the sons of Jacob,
whom He named Israel;
35 with whom the LORD made a
covenant and commanded them,
saying, "You shall not fear other
gods, nor bow down yourselves to
them nor serve them nor sacrifice
to them. Judg. 6:10 • Ex. 20:5
36 "But the LORD, who brought
you up from the land of Egypt
with great power and with an outstretched arm, Him you shall fear,
and to Him you shall bow yourselves down, and to Him you shall
sacrifice. Ex. 14:15-30 • Ex. 6:6
37 "And the statutes and the ordinances and the law and the
commandment, which He wrote
for you, you shall observe to do
forever; and you shall not fear
other gods. Deut. 5:32
38 "And the covenant that I have
made with you, you shall not forget, nor shall you fear other gods.
39 "But the LORD your God you
shall fear; and He will deliver you
from the hand of all your enemies."
40 However, they did not listen,
but they did according to their
earlier custom.
41 So while these nations feared
the LORD, they also served their
idols; their children likewise and
their grandchildren, as their fathers did, so they do to this day.

CHAPTER 18

NOW it came about in the third
year of Hoshea, the son of Elah
king of Israel, that Hezekiah the
son of Ahaz king of Judah became
king. 2 Kin. 16:2 • 2 Chr. 28:27
2 He was twenty-five years old
when he became king, and he
reigned twenty-nine years in Jerusalem; and his mother's name was
Abi the daughter of Zechariah.
3 And he did right in the sight
of the LORD, according to all that
his father David had done.
4 He removed the high places
and broke down the *sacred* pillars
and cut down the [11]Asherah. He
also broke in pieces the bronze
serpent that Moses had made, for
until those days the sons of Israel
burned incense to it; and it was
called [12]Nehushtan. Num. 21:8, 9
5 He trusted in the LORD, the
God of Israel; so that after him
there was none like him among all
the kings of Judah, nor *among
those* who were before him.
6 For he clung to the LORD; he
did not depart from following
Him, but kept His commandments, which the LORD had commanded Moses. Deut. 10:20
7 And the LORD was with him;
wherever he went he prospered.
And he rebelled against the king
of Assyria and did not serve him.
8 He defeated the Philistines
as far as Gaza and its territory,
from watchtower to fortified city.
9 Now it came about in the
fourth year of King Hezekiah,
which was the seventh year of Hoshea son of Elah king of Israel,
that Shalmaneser king of Assyria
came up against Samaria and besieged it. 2 Kin. 17:3-7
10 And at the end of three years
they captured it; in the sixth year

[11] I.e., wooden symbol of a female deity
[12] I.e., a piece of bronze

of Hezekiah, which was [r]the ninth
year of Hoshea king of Israel, Samaria was captured. 2 Kin. 17:6
11 Then the king of Assyria carried Israel away into exile to Assyria, and put them in Halah and
on the Habor, the river of Gozan,
and in the cities of the Medes,
12 because they did not obey
the voice of the LORD their God,
but transgressed His covenant,
even all that Moses the servant of
the LORD commanded; they would
neither listen, nor do *it*.
13 [r]Now in the fourteenth year
of King Hezekiah, Sennacherib
king of Assyria came up against
all the fortified cities of Judah and
seized them. 2 Chr. 32:1
14 Then Hezekiah king of Judah
sent to the king of Assyria at Lachish, saying, "I have done wrong.
[t]Withdraw from me; whatever you
[t]impose on me I will bear." So the
king of Assyria [t]required of Hezekiah king of Judah three hundred
talents of silver and thirty talents
of gold. *Return • give • put on*
15 And Hezekiah gave *him* all
the silver which was found in the
house of the LORD, and in the treasuries of the king's house.
16 At that time Hezekiah cut off
the gold from the doors of the
temple of the LORD, and *from* the
doorposts which Hezekiah king of
Judah had overlaid, and gave it to
the king of Assyria.
17 Then the king of Assyria sent
[r]Tartan and Rab-saris and Rabshakeh from Lachish to King Hezekiah with a large army to Jerusalem. So they went up and came to
Jerusalem. And when they went
up, they came and stood by the
[r]conduit of the upper pool, which
is on the highway of the [13]fuller's
field. Is. 20:1 • 2 Kin. 20:20
18 When they called to the king,
[r]Eliakim the son of Hilkiah, who
was over the household, and
[r]Shebnah the scribe and Joah the
son of Asaph the recorder, came
out to them. Is. 22:20 • Is. 22:15
19 Then Rabshakeh said to
them, "Say now to Hezekiah,
'Thus says the great king, the king
of Assyria, "What is this confidence that you [t]have? *trust*
20 "You say (but *they are* only
empty words), '*I have* counsel and
strength for the war.' Now on
whom do you rely, [r]that you have
rebelled against me? 2 Kin. 18:7
21 "Now behold, you [t]rely on the
staff of this crushed reed, *even* on
Egypt; on which if a man leans, it
will go into his hand and pierce it.
So is Pharaoh king of Egypt to all
who rely on him. *rely for yourself*
22 "But if you say to me, 'We
trust in the LORD our God,' is it
not He whose high places and
whose altars Hezekiah has taken
away, and has said to Judah and
to Jerusalem, 'You shall worship
before this altar in Jerusalem'?
23 "Now therefore, come, make
a bargain with my master the king
of Assyria, and I will give you two
thousand horses, if you are able
on your part to set riders on them.
24 "How then can you repulse
one official of the least of my master's servants, and rely on Egypt
for chariots and for horsemen?
25 "Have I now come up without
the LORD's approval against this
place to destroy it? The LORD said
to me, 'Go up against this land
and destroy it.' " ' "

[13] I.e., launderer's

26 Then Eliakim the son of Hilkiah, and Shebnah and Joah, said to Rabshakeh, "Speak now to your servants in Aramaic, for we [t]understand *it;* and do not speak with us in [r]Judean, in the hearing of the people who are on the wall." *hear* • Ezra 4:7; Dan. 2:4

27 But Rabshakeh said to them, "Has my master sent me only to your master and to you to speak these words, *and* not to the men who sit on the wall, *doomed* to eat their own dung and drink their own urine with you?"

28 Then Rabshakeh stood and cried with a loud voice in Judean, saying, "Hear the word of the great king, the king of Assyria.

29 "Thus says the king, 'Do[r] not let Hezekiah deceive you, for he will not be able to deliver you from my hand; 2 Chr. 32:15

30 nor let Hezekiah make you trust in the LORD, saying, "The LORD will surely deliver us, and this city shall not be given into the hand of the king of Assyria."

31 'Do not listen to Hezekiah, for thus says the king of Assyria, "Make your peace with me and come out to me, and eat [r]each of his vine and each of his fig tree and drink each of the waters of his own cistern, 1 Kin. 4:20, 25

32 until I come and take you away[r]to a land like your own land, a land of grain and new wine, a land of bread and vineyards, a land of olive trees and honey, that you may live and not die." But do not listen to Hezekiah, when he misleads you, saying, "The LORD will deliver us." Deut. 8:7-9

33 'Has[r] any one of the gods of the nations delivered his land from the hand of the king of Assyria? 2 Kin. 19:12; Is. 10:10, 11

34 'Where are the gods of Hamath and [r]Arpad? Where are the gods of Sepharvaim, Hena and Ivvah? Have they delivered Samaria from my hand? Is. 10:9

35 'Who among all the gods of the lands[t]have delivered their land from my hand, [r]that the LORD should deliver Jerusalem from my hand?' " *who have* • Ps. 2:1-3

36 But the people were silent and answered him not a word, for the king's commandment was, "Do not answer him."

37 Then Eliakim the son of Hilkiah, who was over the household, and Shebna the scribe and Joah the son of Asaph, the recorder, came to Hezekiah with their clothes torn and told him the words of Rabshakeh.

CHAPTER 19

AND when King Hezekiah heard *it,* he tore his clothes, covered himself with sackcloth and entered the house of the LORD.

2 Then he sent Eliakim who was over the household with Shebna the scribe and the elders of the priests, [r]covered with sackcloth, to Isaiah the prophet the son of Amoz. 2 Sam. 3:31

3 And they said to him, "Thus says Hezekiah, 'This day is a day of distress, rebuke, and rejection; for children have come to birth, and there is no strength to *deliver.*

4 'Perhaps the LORD your God will hear all the words of Rabshakeh, whom his master the king of

Assyria has sent [r]to reproach the
living God, and will rebuke the
words which the LORD your God
has heard. Therefore, offer a
prayer for [r]the remnant that is
left.' " 2 Kin. 18:35 • Is. 1:9
5 So the servants of King Hezekiah came to Isaiah.
6 And Isaiah said to them,
"Thus you shall say to your master, 'Thus says the LORD, "Do not
be afraid because of the words
that you have heard, with which
the servants of the king of Assyria
have blasphemed Me.
7 "Behold, I will put a spirit in
him so that [r]he shall hear a rumor
and return to his own land. And I
will make him fall by the sword in
his own land." ' " 2 Kin. 7:6
8 Then Rabshakeh returned
and found the king of Assyria
fighting against [r]Libnah, for he had
heard that [t]the king had left Lachish. Josh. 10:29 • *he*
9 When he heard *them* say
concerning Tirhakah king of
Cush, "Behold, he has come out to
fight against you," he sent messengers again to Hezekiah saying,
10 "Thus you shall say to Hezekiah king of [t]Judah, 'Do not let
your God in whom you trust deceive you saying, "Jerusalem shall
not be given into the hand of the
king of Assyria." *Judah, saying,*
11 'Behold, you have heard what
the kings of Assyria have done to
all the lands, destroying them
completely. So will you be
[t]spared? *delivered*
12 'Did the gods of [t]those nations
which my fathers destroyed deliver them, *even* Gozan and Haran
and Rezeph and the sons of Eden
who *were* in Telassar? *the*
13 'Where [r]is the king of Hamath,
the king of Arpad, the king of the
city of Sepharvaim, and *of* Hena
and Ivvah?' " 2 Kin. 18:34
14 Then [r]Hezekiah took the letter from the hand of the messengers and read it, and he went up to
the house of the LORD and spread
it out before the LORD. Is. 37:14
15 And Hezekiah prayed before
the LORD and said, "O LORD, the
God of Israel, who art [t]enthroned
above the cherubim, Thou art the
God, Thou alone, of all the kingdoms of the earth. Thou hast
made heaven and earth. *seated*
16 "Incline Thine ear, O LORD,
and hear; [r]open Thine eyes, O
LORD, and see; and listen to the
words of Sennacherib, which he
has sent [r]to reproach the living
God. 1 Kin. 8:29 • 2 Kin. 19:4
17 "Truly, O LORD, the kings of
Assyria have devastated the nations and their lands
18 and have cast their gods into
the fire, [r]for they were not gods
but the work of men's hands,
wood and stone. So they have destroyed them. Is. 44:9-20
19 "And now, O LORD our God, I
pray, deliver us from his hand [r]that
all the kingdoms of the earth may
know that Thou alone, O LORD, art
God." 1 Kin. 8:42, 43
20 Then Isaiah the son of Amoz
sent to Hezekiah saying, "Thus
says the LORD, the God of Israel,
'Because you have prayed to Me
about Sennacherib king of Assyria, I have heard *you.*'
21 "This is the word that the
LORD has spoken against him:

'She has despised you and
mocked you,
ʳThe virgin daughter of Zion;
She has shaken *her* head
behind you, Jer. 14:17
The daughter of Jerusalem!
22 'Whom have you ʳreproached and blasphemed?
And against whom have
you raised *your* voice,
And ᵗhaughtily lifted up
your eyes?
Against the Holy One of Israel! 2 Kin. 19:4 • *on high*
23 'Throughʳ your messengers
you have reproached the
Lord,
And you have said, "With
my many chariots
I came up to the heights of
the mountains,
To the remotest parts of
Lebanon;
And I cut down its tall cedars *and* its choice cypresses.
And I entered its farthest
lodging place, its thickest
forest. 2 Kin. 18:17
24 "I dug *wells* and drank foreign waters,
And with the sole of my
feet I dried up
All the rivers of Egypt."
25 'Haveʳ you not heard?
Long ago I did it;
From ancient times I
planned it.
ʳNow I have brought it to
pass,
That you should turn fortified cities into ruinous
heaps. Is. 45:7 • Is. 10:5

26 'Therefore their inhabitants
were short of strength,
They were dismayed and
put to shame;
They wereʳ as the vegetation
of the field and as the
green herb,
As grass on the housetops
is scorched before it is
grown up. Ps. 129:6
27 'But ʳI know your sitting
down,
And your going out and
your coming in,
And your raging against
Me. Ps. 139:1
28 'Because of your raging
against Me,
And because your arrogance has come up to My
ears,
Therefore I will put My
hook in your nose,
And My bridle in your lips,
And I will turn you back by
the way which you came.

29 'Then this shall be ʳthe sign
for you: ᵗyou shall eat this year
what grows of itself, in the second
year what springs from the same,
and in the third year sow, reap,
plant vineyards, and eat their
fruit. Ex. 3:12; 2 Kin. 20:8, 9 • *eating*
30 'Andʳ the surviving remnant
of the house of Judah shall again
take root downward and bear
fruit upward. 2 Kin. 19:4
31 'For out of Jerusalem shall go
forth a remnant, and ʳout of Mount
Zion survivors. The zeal of [14]the
LORD shall perform this. Is. 10:20
32 'Therefore thus says the LORD
concerning the king of Assyria,
"He shall not come to this city or
shoot an arrow there; neither shall

[14]Some ancient mss. read *the LORD of hosts*

he come before it with a shield,
nor throw up a mound against it.
33 "By[r] the way that he came, by
the same he shall return, and he
shall not come to this city," ' declares the LORD. 2 Kin. 19:28
34 'For I will defend this city to
save it for My own sake and for
My servant David's sake.' "
35 Then it happened that night
that the angel of the LORD went
out, and struck 185,000 in the
camp of the Assyrians; and when
[t]men rose early in the morning, behold, all of them were dead. *they*
36 So Sennacherib king of
Assyria departed and returned
home, and lived at Nineveh.
37 And it came about as he was
worshiping in the house of Nisroch his god, that Adrammelech
and Sharezer killed him with the
sword; and they escaped into the
land of Ararat. And Esarhaddon
his son became king in his place.

CHAPTER 20

IN those days Hezekiah became
[t]mortally ill. And Isaiah the
prophet the son of Amoz came to
him and said to him, "Thus says
the LORD, 'Set your house in order, for you shall die and not
live.' " *sick to the point of death*
2 Then he turned his face to
the wall, and prayed to the LORD,
saying,
3 "Remember now, O LORD, I
beseech Thee, how I have walked
before Thee in truth and with a
whole heart, and have done what
is good in Thy sight." And Hezekiah wept[t] bitterly. *great weeping*
4 And it came about before
Isaiah had gone out of the middle
court, that the word of the LORD
came to him, saying,
5 "Return and say to [r]Hezekiah
the leader of My people, 'Thus
says the LORD, the God of your father David, "I have heard your
prayer, I have seen your tears; behold, I will heal you. On the third
day you shall go up to the house
of the LORD. 1 Sam. 9:16
6 "And I will add fifteen years
to your [t]life, and I will deliver you
and this city from the hand of the
king of Assyria; and I will defend
this city for My own sake and for
My servant David's sake." ' " *days*
7 Then Isaiah said, "Take a
cake of figs." And they took and
laid *it* on the boil, and he recovered.
8 Now Hezekiah said to Isaiah,
"What will be the sign that the
LORD will heal me, and that I shall
go up to the house of the LORD the
third day?"
9 And Isaiah said, "This[r] shall
be the sign to you from the LORD,
that the LORD will do the thing
that He has spoken: shall the
shadow go forward ten steps or go
back ten steps?" Is. 38:7
10 So Hezekiah [t]answered, "It is
easy for the shadow to decline ten
steps; no, but let the shadow turn
backward ten steps." *said*
11 And Isaiah the prophet cried
to the LORD, and He brought the
shadow on the [t]stairway back ten
steps by which it had gone down
on the stairway of Ahaz. *steps*
12 At that time Berodach-bala-
dan a son of Baladan, king of
Babylon, sent letters and a pres-

ent to Hezekiah, for he heard that
Hezekiah had been sick.
13 And Hezekiah listened to
them, and showed them all his
treasure house, the silver and the
gold and the spices and the precious oil and the house of his armor and all that was found in his
treasuries. There was nothing in
his house, nor in all his dominion,
that Hezekiah did not show them.
14 Then Isaiah the prophet
came to King Hezekiah and said
to him, "What did these men say,
and from where have they come
to you?" And Hezekiah said,
"They have come from a far country, from Babylon."
15 And he said, "What have
they seen in your house?" So Hezekiah answered, "They have seen
all that is in my house; there is
nothing among my treasuries that
I have not shown them." *said*
16 Then Isaiah said to Hezekiah, "Hear the word of the
LORD.
17 'Behold, the days are coming
when all that is in your house, and
all that your fathers have laid up
in store to this day shall be carried
to Babylon; nothing shall be left,'
says the LORD. 2 Kin. 24:13; 25:13-15
18 'And some of your sons who
shall issue from you, whom you
shall beget, shall be taken away;
and they shall become officials in
the palace of the king of Babylon.'" 2 Kin. 24:12 • Dan. 1:3-7
19 Then Hezekiah said to Isaiah,
"The word of the LORD which you
have spoken is good." For he
thought, "Is it not so, if there shall
be peace and truth in my days?"
20 Now the rest of the acts of
Hezekiah and all his might, and
how he made the pool and the
conduit, and brought water into
the city, are they not written in
the Book of the Chronicles of the
Kings of Judah? 2 Chr. 32:32
21 So Hezekiah slept with his
fathers, and Manasseh his son became king in his place.

CHAPTER 21

MANASSEH was twelve years
old when he became king, and he
reigned fifty-five years in Jerusalem; and his mother's name was
Hephzibah. 2 Chr. 33:1-9
2 And he did evil in the sight of
the LORD, according to the abominations of the nations whom the
LORD dispossessed before the
sons of Israel. Jer. 15:4 • 2 Kin. 16:3
3 For he rebuilt the high places
which Hezekiah his father had destroyed; and he erected altars for
Baal and made an Asherah, as
Ahab king of Israel had done, and
worshiped all the host of heaven
and served them. 2 Kin. 18:4
4 And he built altars in the
house of the LORD, of which the
LORD had said, "In Jerusalem I
will put My name." 2 Kin. 16:10-16
5 For he built altars for all the
host of heaven in the two courts
of the house of the LORD.
6 And he made his son pass
through the fire, practiced witchcraft and used divination, and
dealt with mediums and spiritists.
He did much evil in the sight of
the LORD provoking *Him to anger.*
7 Then he set the carved image
of Asherah that he had made, in
the house of which the LORD said

to David and to his son Solomon,
"In[r] this house and in Jerusalem,
which I have chosen from all the
tribes of Israel, I will put My name
forever. Deut. 16:21 • 1 Kin. 8:29
8 "And I will not make the feet
of Israel wander anymore from
the land which I gave their fathers, if only they will observe to
do according to all that I have
commanded them, and according
to all the law that My servant
Moses commanded them."
9 But they did not listen, and
Manasseh[r] seduced them to do evil
more than the nations whom the
LORD destroyed before the sons of
Israel. Prov. 29:12
10 Now the LORD spoke through
His servants the prophets, saying,
11 "Because Manasseh king of
Judah has done these abominations, having done wickedly more
than all the Amorites did who
were before him, and has also
made Judah sin with his idols;
12 therefore thus says the LORD,
the God of Israel, 'Behold, I am
bringing *such* calamity on Jerusalem and Judah, that whoever
hears of it, [r] both his ears shall
tingle. 1 Sam. 3:11; Jer. 19:3
13 'And[r] I will stretch over Jerusalem the line of Samaria and the
plummet of the house of Ahab,
and I will wipe Jerusalem as one
wipes a dish, wiping it and turning
it upside down. Is. 34:11
14 'And I will abandon the remnant of My inheritance and deliver
them into the hand of their enemies, and they shall become as
plunder and spoil to all their enemies;
15 because they have done evil
in My sight, and have been provoking Me to anger, since the day
their fathers came from Egypt,
even to this day.' "
16 Moreover, Manasseh shed
very much innocent blood until he
had filled Jerusalem from one end
to another; besides his sin with
which he made Judah sin, in doing
evil in the sight of the LORD.
17 Now the rest of the acts of
Manasseh and all that he did and
his sin which he committed, are
they not written in the Book of the
Chronicles of the Kings of Judah?
18 And Manasseh slept with his
fathers and was buried in the garden of his own house, in the garden of Uzza, and Amon his son
became king in his place.
19 [r]Amon was twenty-two years
old when he became king, and he
reigned two years in Jerusalem;
and his mother's name *was* Me-
shullemeth the daughter of Haruz
of Jotbah. 2 Chr. 33:21-23
20 And he did evil in the sight of
the LORD, [r]as Manasseh his father
had done. 2 Kin. 21:2-6, 11, 16
21 For he walked in all the way
that his father had walked, and
served the idols that his father
had served and worshiped them.
22 So he forsook the LORD, the
God of his fathers, and did not
walk in the way of the LORD.
23 And the servants of Amon
conspired against him and killed
the king in his own house.
24 Then the people of the land
[t]killed all those who had conspired
against King Amon, and the people of the land made Josiah his
son king in his place. *smote*
25 Now the rest of the acts of

Amon which he did, are they not written in the Book of the Chronicles of the Kings of Judah?

26 And he was buried in his grave [r]in the garden of Uzza, and Josiah his son became king in his place. 2 Kin. 21:18

CHAPTER 22

[r]JOSIAH was eight years old when he became king, and he reigned thirty-one years in Jerusalem; and his mother's name *was* Jedidah the daughter of Adaiah of [r]Bozkath. 2 Chr. 34:1 • Josh. 15:39

2 And he did right in the sight of the LORD and walked in all the way of his father David, nor did he [r]turn aside to the right or to the left. Deut. 5:32; Josh. 1:7

3 Now [r]it came about in the eighteenth year of King Josiah that the king sent Shaphan, the son of Azaliah the son of Meshullam the scribe, to the house of the LORD saying, 2 Chr. 34:8

4 "Go up to Hilkiah the high priest that he may [a]count the money brought in to the house of the LORD which the doorkeepers have gathered from the people. *total*

5 "And let them deliver it into the hand of the workmen who have the oversight of the house of the LORD, and let them give it to the workmen who are in the house of the LORD to repair the [t]damages of the house, *breach*

6 to the carpenters and the builders and the masons and for buying timber and hewn stone to repair the house.

7 "Only [r]no accounting shall be made with them for the money delivered into their hands, for they deal faithfully." 2 Kin. 12:15

8 Then Hilkiah the high priest said to Shaphan the scribe, "I [r]have found the book of the law in the house of the LORD." And Hilkiah gave the book to Shaphan who read it. Deut. 31:24-26

9 And Shaphan the scribe came to the king and brought back word to the king and said, "Your servants have emptied out the money that was found in the house, and have delivered it into the hand of the workmen who have the oversight of the house of the LORD."

10 Moreover, Shaphan the scribe told the king saying, "Hilkiah the priest has given me a book." And Shaphan read it in the presence of the king.

11 And it came about when the king heard the words of the book of the law, that he tore his clothes.

12 Then the king commanded Hilkiah the priest, Ahikam the son of Shaphan, Achbor the son of Micaiah, Shaphan the scribe, and Asaiah the king's servant saying,

13 "Go, inquire of the LORD for me and the people and all Judah concerning the words of this book that has been found, for great is the wrath of the LORD that burns against us, because our fathers have not listened to the words of this book, to do according to all that is written concerning us."

14 So Hilkiah the priest, Ahikam, Achbor, Shaphan, and Asaiah went to Huldah the prophetess, the wife of Shallum the son of Tikvah, the son of Harhas, keeper of the wardrobe (now she

lived in Jerusalem in the Second
Quarter); and they spoke to her.
15 And she said to them, "Thus
says the LORD God of Israel, 'Tell
the man who sent you to me,
16 thus says the LORD, "Behold,
I [r]bring evil on this place and on its
inhabitants, *even* all the words of
the book which the king of Judah
has read. Deut. 29:27; Dan. 9:11-14
17 "Because they have forsaken
Me and have burned incense to
other gods that they might provoke Me to anger with all the
work of their hands, therefore My
wrath burns against this place,
and it shall not be quenched." '
18 "But to [r]the king of Judah who
sent you to inquire of the LORD
thus shall you say to him, 'Thus
says the LORD God of Israel, "*Regarding* the words which you have
heard, 2 Chr. 34:26
19 [r]because your heart was tender and [r]you humbled yourself before the LORD when you heard
what I spoke against this place
and against its inhabitants that
they should become a desolation
and a curse, and you have torn
your clothes and wept before Me,
I truly have heard you," declares
the LORD. 1 Sam. 24:5 • Ex. 10:3
20 "Therefore, behold, I will
gather you to your fathers, and
you shall be gathered to your
grave in peace, neither shall your
eyes see all the evil which I will
bring on this place." ' " So they
brought back word to the king.

CHAPTER 23

THEN the king sent, and they
gathered to him all the elders of
Judah and of Jerusalem.
2 And the king went up to the
house of the LORD and all the men
of Judah and all the inhabitants of
Jerusalem with him, and the
priests and the prophets and all
the people, both small and great;
and [r]he read in their hearing all the
words of the book of the covenant, which was found in the
house of the LORD. Deut. 31:10-13
3 And the king stood by the
pillar and made a covenant before
the LORD, to walk after the LORD,
and to keep His commandments
and His testimonies and His statutes with all *his* heart and all *his*
soul, to carry out the words of this
covenant that were written in this
book. And all the people [t]entered
into the covenant. *took a stand in*
4 Then the king commanded
Hilkiah the high priest and the
priests of the second order and
the [t]doorkeepers, to bring out of
the temple of the LORD all the vessels that were made for Baal, for
[15]Asherah, and for all the host of
heaven; and he burned them outside Jerusalem in the fields of the
Kidron, and carried their ashes to
Bethel. *keepers of the threshold*
5 And he did away with the
idolatrous priests whom the kings
of Judah had appointed to burn incense in the high places in the
cities of Judah and in the surrounding area of Jerusalem, also
those who burned incense to Baal,
to the sun and to the moon and to
the constellations and to all the
[r]host of heaven. 2 Kin. 21:3
6 And he brought out the A-
sherah from the house of the LORD
outside Jerusalem to the brook
Kidron, and burned it at the brook

[15]I.e., wooden symbol of a female deity

Kidron, and ground *it* to dust, and threw its dust on the graves of the [t]common people. *sons of the people*

7 He also broke down the houses of the [r]*male* cult prostitutes which *were* in the house of the LORD, where the women were weaving [t]hangings for the Asherah. 1 Kin. 14:24 • *houses*

8 Then he brought all the priests from the cities of Judah, and defiled the high places where the priests had burned incense, from [r]Geba to Beersheba; and he broke down the high places of the gates which *were* at the entrance of the gate of Joshua the governor of the city, which *were* on one's left at the city gate. Josh. 21:17

9 Nevertheless the priests of the high places did not go up to the altar of the LORD in Jerusalem, but they ate unleavened bread among their brothers.

10 He also defiled [16]Topheth, which is in the valley of the son of Hinnom, that no man might make his son or his daughter pass through the fire for Molech.

11 And he did away with the horses which the kings of Judah had given to the [r]sun, at the entrance of the house of the LORD, by the chamber of Nathan-melech the official, which *was* in the precincts; and he burned the chariots of the sun with fire. Deut. 4:19

12 And the altars which *were* on the roof, the upper chamber of Ahaz, which the kings of Judah had made, and the altars which Manasseh had made in the two courts of the house of the LORD, the king broke down; and he [17]smashed them there, and threw their dust into the brook Kidron.

13 And the high places which *were* before Jerusalem, which *were* on the right of the mount of destruction which Solomon the king of Israel had built for Ashtoreth the abomination of the Sidonians, and for Chemosh the abomination of Moab, and for Milcom the abomination of the sons of Ammon, the king defiled.

14 And [r]he broke in pieces the *sacred* pillars and cut down the Asherim and filled their places with human bones. Deut. 7:5, 25

15 Furthermore, the altar that *was* at Bethel *and* the high place which Jeroboam the son of Nebat, who made Israel sin, had made, even that altar and the high place he broke down. Then he demolished its stones, ground them to dust, and burned the Asherah.

16 Now when Josiah turned, he saw the graves that *were* there on the mountain, and he sent and took the bones from the graves and burned *them* on the altar and defiled it [r]according to the word of the LORD which the man of God proclaimed, who proclaimed these things. 1 Kin. 13:2

17 Then he said, "What is this monument that I see?" And the men of the city told him, "It is the grave of the man of God who came from Judah and proclaimed these things which you have done against the altar of Bethel."

18 And he said, "Let him alone; let no one disturb his bones." So they left his bones undisturbed [r]with the bones of the prophet who came from Samaria. 1 Kin. 13:11

[16] I.e., place of burning

[17] Or, *ran from there*

19 And Josiah also removed all
the houses of the high places
which *were* ʳin the cities of Samaria,
which the kings of Israel
had made provoking the LORD;
and he did to them just as he had
done in Bethel. 2 Chr. 34:6, 7
20 And all the priests of the
high places who *were* there he
slaughtered on the altars and
burned human bones on them;
then he returned to Jerusalem.
21 Then the king commanded
all the people saying, "Celebrate
the Passover to the LORD your
God ʳas it is written in this book of
the covenant." 2 Chr. 35:1-17
22 Surely such a Passover had
not been celebrated from the days
of the judges who judged Israel,
nor in all the days of the kings of
Israel and of the kings of Judah.
23 But in the eighteenth year of
King Josiah, this Passover was observed
to the LORD in Jerusalem.
24 Moreover, Josiah ᵗremoved
the mediums and the spiritists and
the teraphim and the idols and all
the abominations that were seen
in the land of Judah and in Jerusalem,
that he might [a] confirm the
words of the law which were written
in the book that Hilkiah the
priest found in the house of the
LORD. *consumed • perform*
25 And before him there was no
king ʳlike him who turned to the
LORD with all his heart and with
all his soul and with all his might,
according to all the law of Moses;
nor did any like him arise after
him. 2 Kin. 18:5
26 However, the LORD did not
turn from the fierceness of His
great wrath with which His anger
burned against Judah, because of
all the provocations with which
Manasseh had provoked Him.
27 And the LORD said, "I will remove
Judah also from My sight,
as I have removed Israel. And I
will cast off Jerusalem, this city
which I have chosen, and the ᵗtemple
of which I said, 'My name
shall be there.' " *house*
28 Now the rest of the acts of
Josiah and all that he did, are they
not written in the Book of the
Chronicles of the Kings of Judah?
29 In his days Pharaoh Neco
king of Egypt went up to the king
of Assyria to the river Euphrates.
And King Josiah went to meet
him, and when *Pharaoh Neco* saw
him he killed him at Megiddo.
30 And ʳhis servants drove ᵗhis
body in a chariot from Megiddo,
and brought him to Jerusalem and
buried him in his own tomb. Then
the people of the land took Jehoahaz
the son of Josiah and anointed
him and made him king in place of
his father. 2 Kin. 9:28 • *him, dead*
31 ʳJehoahaz was twenty-three
years old when he became king,
and he reigned three months in Jerusalem;
and his mother's name
was Hamutal the daughter of Jeremiah
of Libnah. 1 Chr. 3:15
32 And he did evil in the sight of
the LORD, ʳaccording to all that his
fathers had done. 2 Kin. 21:2-7
33 And Pharaoh Neco imprisoned
him at Riblah in the land of
Hamath, that he might not reign
in Jerusalem; and he imposed on
the land a fine of one hundred talents
of silver and a talent of gold.
34 And Pharaoh Neco made
ʳEliakim the son of Josiah king in

the place of Josiah his father, and
[r]changed his name to Jehoiakim.
But he took Jehoahaz away and
brought *him* to Egypt, and he died
there. 1 Chr. 3:15 • 2 Kin. 24:17
35 So Jehoiakim gave the silver
and gold to Pharaoh, but he taxed
the land in order to give the money at the [t]command of Pharaoh.
He exacted the silver and gold
from the people of the land, each
according to his valuation, to give
it to Pharaoh Neco. *mouth*
36 [r]Jehoiakim was twenty-five
years old when he became king,
and he reigned eleven years in Jerusalem; and his mother's name
was Zebidah the daughter of Pedaiah of Rumah. 2 Chr. 36:5
37 And he did evil in the sight of
the LORD, [r]according to all that his
fathers had done. 2 Kin. 23:32

CHAPTER 24

[r]IN his days Nebuchadnezzar king
of Babylon came up, and Jehoiakim became his servant *for* three
years; then he turned and rebelled
against him. 2 Chr. 36:6; Jer. 25:1
2 And the LORD sent against
him [r]bands of Chaldeans, [r]bands of
Arameans, bands of Moabites,
and bands of Ammonites. So He
sent them against Judah to destroy it, according to the word of
the LORD, which He had spoken
through His servants the prophets. Jer. 35:11f. • 2 Kin. 6:23
3 Surely at the command of
the LORD it came upon Judah, to
remove *them* from His sight because of the sins of Manasseh, according to all that he had done,
4 and also for the innocent
blood which he shed, for he filled
Jerusalem with innocent blood;
and the LORD would not forgive.
5 Now the rest of the acts of
Jehoiakim and all that he did, are
they not written in the Book of the
Chronicles of the Kings of Judah?
6 So [r]Jehoiakim slept with his
fathers, and Jehoiachin his son became king in his place. Jer. 22:18
7 And [r]the king of Egypt did
not come out of his land again, for
the king of Babylon had taken all
that belonged to the king of Egypt
from the brook of Egypt to the
river Euphrates. Jer. 37:5-7
8 [r]Jehoiachin was eighteen
years old when he became king,
and he reigned three months in Jerusalem; and his mother's name
was Nehushta the daughter of Elnathan of Jerusalem. 1 Chr. 3:16
9 And he did evil in the sight of
the LORD, [r]according to all that his
father had done. 2 Kin. 21:2-7
10 At that time the servants of
Nebuchadnezzar king of Babylon
went up to Jerusalem, and the city
came under siege.
11 And Nebuchadnezzar the
king of Babylon came to the city,
while his servants were besieging
it.
12 And [r]Jehoiachin the king of
Judah went out to the king of
Babylon, he and his mother and
his servants and his captains and
his officials. So the king of Babylon took him captive in the eighth
year of his reign. Jer. 22:24-30; 24:1
13 And [r]he carried out from
there all the treasures of the house
of the LORD, and the treasures of

the king's house, and cut in pieces
all the vessels of gold which Solomon king of Israel had made in
the temple of the LORD, just as the
LORD had said. 2 Kin. 20:17
14 Then [r]he led away into exile
all Jerusalem and all the captains
and all the mighty men of valor,
ten thousand captives, and all the
craftsmen and the smiths. None
remained except the poorest people of the land. Jer. 24:1
15 So [r]he led Jehoiachin away
into exile to Babylon; also the
king's mother and the king's
wives and his officials and the
leading men of the land, he led
away into exile from Jerusalem to
Babylon. 2 Chr. 36:10; Jer. 22:24-28
16 And all the men of valor,
seven thousand, and the craftsmen and the smiths, one thousand, all strong and fit for war,
and these the king of Babylon
brought into exile to Babylon.
17 [r]Then the king of Babylon
made his uncle Mattaniah, king in
his place, and changed his name
to Zedekiah. 2 Chr. 36:10-13
18 [r]Zedekiah was twenty-one
years old when he became king,
and he reigned eleven years in Jerusalem; and his mother's name
was Hamutal the daughter of Jeremiah of Libnah. Jer. 27:1; 28:1
19 And he did evil in the sight of
the LORD, [r]according to all that Jehoiakim had done. 2 Kin. 23:37
20 For [r]through the anger of the
LORD *this* came about in Jerusalem and Judah until He cast them
out from His presence. And [r]Zede-
kiah rebelled against the king of
Babylon. Deut. 4:24 • 2 Chr. 36:13

CHAPTER 25

NOW it came about in the ninth
year of his reign, on the tenth day
of the tenth month, that Nebuchadnezzar king of Babylon came,
he and all his army, against Jerusalem, camped against it, and
built a siege wall all around it.
2 So the city was under siege
until the eleventh year of King
Zedekiah.
3 On the ninth day of the
fourth month the famine was so
severe in the city that there was
no food for the people of the land.
4 Then the city was broken
into, and all the men of war fled
by night by way of the gate between the two walls beside the
king's garden, though the Chaldeans were all around the city. And
they went by way of the Arabah.
5 But the army of the Chaldeans pursued the king and overtook him in the plains of Jericho
and all his army was scattered
from him.
6 Then [r]they captured the king
and brought him to the king of
Babylon at Riblah, and he passed
sentence on him. Jer. 34:21, 22
7 And they slaughtered the
sons of Zedekiah before his eyes,
then put out the eyes of Zedekiah
and bound him with bronze fetters and brought him to Babylon.
8 Now on the seventh day of
the fifth month, which was the
nineteenth year of King Nebuchadnezzar, king of Babylon,
Nebuzaradan the captain of the
guard, a servant of the king of
Babylon, came to Jerusalem.
9 And [r]he burned the house of

the LORD,[r]the king's house, and all
the houses of Jerusalem; even every great house he burned with
fire. 1 Kin. 9:8 • Amos 2:5
10 So all the army of the Chaldeans who *were with* the captain
of the guard[r]broke down the walls
around Jerusalem. 2 Kin. 14:13
11 Then [r]the rest of the people
who were left in the city and the
deserters who had deserted to the
king of Babylon and the rest of the
multitude, Nebuzaradan the captain of the guard carried away
into exile. 2 Chr. 36:20
12 But the captain of the guard
left some of [r]the poorest of the
land to be vinedressers and plowmen. 2 Kin. 24:14; Jer. 40:7
13 Now the bronze pillars
which were in the house of the
LORD, and the stands and the
bronze sea which were in the
house of the LORD, the Chaldeans
broke in pieces and carried the
[t]bronze to Babylon. *bronze of them*
14 [r]And they took away the pots,
the shovels, the snuffers, the
spoons, and all the bronze vessels
which were used in *temple* service. Ex. 27:3; 1 Kin. 7:47-50
15 The captain of the guard also
took away the firepans and the basins, what was fine gold and what
was fine silver.
16 The two pillars, the one sea,
and the stands which Solomon
had made for the house of the
LORD—the bronze of all these vessels was beyond weight.
17 [r]The height of the one pillar
was eighteen cubits, and a bronze
capital was on it; the height of the
capital was three cubits, with a
network and pomegranates on the
capital all around, all of bronze.
And the second pillar was like
these with network. 1 Kin. 7:15-22
18 Then the captain of the
guard took Seraiah the chief
priest and Zephaniah the second
priest, with the three [t]officers of
the temple. *keepers of the door*
19 And from the city he took
one official who was overseer of
the men of war, and five of the
king's advisers who were found in
the city; and the scribe of the captain of the army, who mustered
the people of the land; and sixty
men of the people of the land who
were found in the city.
20 And Nebuzaradan the captain of the guard took them and
brought them to the king of Babylon at [r]Riblah. 2 Kin. 23:33
21 Then the king of Babylon
struck them down and put them
to death at Riblah in the land of
Hamath. So Judah was led away
into exile from its land.
22 Now *as for* the people who
were left in the land of Judah,
whom Nebuchadnezzar king of
Babylon had left, he appointed
Gedaliah the son of Ahikam, the
son of Shaphan over them.
23 When all the captains of the
forces, they and *their* men, heard
that the king of Babylon had appointed Gedaliah *governor,* they
came to Gedaliah to Mizpah,
namely, Ishmael the son of Nethaniah, and Johanan the son of Kareah, and Seraiah the son of Tanhumeth the Netophathite, and
Jaazaniah the son of the Maacathite, they and their men.
24 And Gedaliah swore to them
and their men and said to them,

"Do not be afraid of the servants of the Chaldeans; live in the land and serve the king of Babylon, and it will be well with you."

25 [r]But it came about in the seventh month, that Ishmael the son of Nethaniah, the son of Elishama, of the royal [t]family, came with ten men and struck Gedaliah down so that he died along with the Jews and the Chaldeans who were with him at Mizpah. Jer. 41:1, 2 • *seed*

26 [r]Then all the people, both small and great, and the captains of the forces arose and went to Egypt; for they were afraid of the Chaldeans. Jer. 43:4-7

27 Now it came about in the thirty-seventh year of the exile of Jehoiachin king of Judah, in the twelfth month, on the twenty-seventh *day* of the month, that Evil-merodach king of Babylon, in the year that he became king, [t]released Jehoiachin king of Judah from prison; *lifted up the head of*

28 and he [r]spoke kindly to him and set his throne above the throne of the kings who *were* with him in Babylon. Dan. 2:37; 5:18, 19

29 And Jehoiachin changed his prison clothes, and had his meals in the king's presence regularly all the days of his life;

30 and for his [r]allowance, a regular allowance was given him by the king, a portion for each day, all the days of his life. Neh. 11:23

THE FIRST BOOK OF THE

CHRONICLES

ADAM, Seth, Enosh,

2 Kenan, Mahalalel, Jared,

3 Enoch, Methuselah, Lamech,

4 Noah, Shem, Ham and Japheth.

5 The sons of Japheth *were* Gomer, Magog, Madai, Javan, Tubal, Meshech, and Tiras.

6 And the sons of Gomer *were* Ashkenaz, Diphath, and Togarmah.

7 And the sons of Javan *were* Elishah, Tarshish, Kittim, and Rodanim.

8 The sons of Ham *were* Cush, Mizraim, Put, and Canaan.

9 And the sons of Cush *were* Seba, Havilah, Sabta, Raama, and Sabteca; and the sons of Raamah *were* Sheba and Dedan.

10 And Cush [t]became the father of Nimrod; he began to be a mighty one in the earth. *begot*

11 [r]And Mizraim became the father of the people of Lud, Anam, Lehab, Naphtuh, Gen. 10:13-18

12 Pathrus, Casluh, from which the Philistines came, and Caphtor.

13 And Canaan became the father of Sidon, his first-born, Heth,

14 and the Jebusites, the Amorites, the Girgashites,

15 the Hivites, the Arkites, the Sinites,

16 the Arvadites, the Zemarites, and the Hamathites.

17 The sons of Shem *were* Elam,
Asshur, Arpachshad, Lud, Aram,
Uz, Hul, Gether, and Meshech.
18 And Arpachshad became the
father of Shelah and Shelah became the father of Eber.
19 And two sons were born to
Eber, the name of the one was Peleg, for in his days the earth was
divided, and his brother's name
was Joktan.
20 And Joktan became the father of Almodad, Sheleph, Hazarmaveth, Jerah,
21 Hadoram, Uzal, Diklah,
22 Ebal, Abimael, Sheba,
23 Ophir, Havilah, and Jobab;
all these *were* the sons of Joktan.
24 Shem, Arpachshad, Shelah,
25 Eber, Peleg, Reu,
26 Serug, Nahor, Terah,
27 Abram, that is Abraham.
28 The sons of Abraham *were*
Isaac and Ishmael.
29 [r]These are their genealogies:
the first-born of Ishmael *was* Nebaioth, then Kedar, Adbeel, Mibsam, Gen. 25:13-16
30 Mishma, Dumah, Massa, Hadad, Tema,
31 Jetur, Naphish and Kedemah; these *were* the sons of Ishmael.
32 [r]And the sons of Keturah,
Abraham's concubine, *whom* she
bore, *were* Zimran, Jokshan, Medan, Midian, Ishbak, and Shuah.
And the sons of Jokshan *were*
Sheba and Dedan. Gen. 25:1-4
33 And the sons of Midian *were*
Ephah, Epher, Hanoch, Abida,
and Eldaah. All these were the
sons of Keturah.
34 And [r]Abraham became the
father of Isaac. The sons of Isaac
were Esau and Israel. 1 Chr. 1:28
35 [r]The sons of Esau *were* Eliphaz, Reuel, Jeush, Jalam, and
Korah. Gen. 36:4-10
36 The sons of Eliphaz *were* Teman, Omar, Zephi, Gatam, Kenaz,
Timna, and Amalek.
37 The sons of Reuel *were* Nahath, Zerah, Shammah, and Mizzah.
38 And the sons of Seir *were* Lotan, Shobal, Zibeon, Anah, Dishon, Ezer, and Dishan.
39 And the sons of Lotan *were*
Hori and Homam; and Lotan's sister *was* Timna.
40 The sons of Shobal *were*
Alian, Manahath, Ebal, Shephi,
and Onam. And the sons of
Zibeon *were* Aiah and Anah.
41 The [t]son of Anah *was* Dishon.
And the sons of Dishon *were*
Hamran, Eshban, Ithran, and Cheran. *sons*
42 The sons of Ezer *were* Bilhan,
Zaavan and [a]Jaakan. The sons of
Dishan *were* Uz and Aran. *Akan*
43 [r]Now these are the kings who
reigned in the land of Edom before any king of the sons of Israel
reigned. Bela *was* the son of Beor,
and the name of his city was Dinhabah. Gen. 36:31-43
44 When Bela died, Jobab the
son of Zerah of [r]Bozrah became
king in his place. Is. 34:6
45 When Jobab died, Husham
of the land of [r]the Temanites became king in his place. Job 2:11
46 When Husham died, Hadad
the son of Bedad, who [t]defeated
Midian in the field of Moab, became king in his place; and the
name of his city *was* Avith. *smote*

47 When Hadad died, Samlah of
Masrekah became king in his
place.
48 When Samlah died, Shaul of
Rehoboth by the River became
king in his place.
49 When Shaul died, Baal-hanan the son of Achbor became
king in his place.
50 When Baal-hanan died, Hadad became king in his place; and
the name of his city was Pai, and
his wife's name was Mehetabel,
the daughter of Matred, the
daughter of Mezahab.
51 Then Hadad died. Now the
chiefs of Edom were: chief Timna,
chief Aliah, chief Jetheth,
52 chief Oholibamah, chief
Elah, chief Pinon,
53 chief Kenaz, chief Teman,
chief Mibzar,
54 chief Magdiel, chief Iram.
These *were* the chiefs of Edom.

CHAPTER 2

[r]THESE are the sons of Israel:
Reuben, Simeon, Levi, Judah, Issachar, Zebulun, Gen. 35:22-26
2 Dan, Joseph, Benjamin,
Naphtali, Gad, and Asher.
3 [r]The sons of Judah *were* Er,
Onan, and Shelah; *these* three
were born to him by Bath-shua
the Canaanitess. And Er, Judah's
first-born, was wicked in the sight
of the LORD, so He put him to
death. Gen. 38:2-10
4 And Tamar his daughter-in-
law bore him Perez and Zerah. Judah had five sons in all.
5 The sons of Perez *were* Hezron and Hamul.
6 And the sons of Zerah *were*
Zimri, Ethan, Heman, Calcol, and
Dara; five of them in all.
7 And the [t]son of Carmi *was* [r]A-
char, the troubler of Israel, who
violated the ban. *sons* • Josh. 7:1
8 And the [t]son of Ethan *was*
Azariah. *sons*
9 Now the sons of Hezron,
who were born to him *were* Jerahmeel, Ram, and Chelubai.
10 And Ram [t]became the father
of Amminadab, and Amminadab
became the father of Nahshon,
leader of the sons of Judah; *begot*
11 Nahshon became the father
of Salma, Salma became the father of Boaz,
12 Boaz became the father of
Obed, and Obed became the father of Jesse;
13 and Jesse became the father
of Eliab his first-born, then Abinadab the second, Shimea the third,
14 Nethanel the fourth, Raddai
the fifth,
15 Ozem the sixth, David the
seventh;
16 and their sisters *were*
Zeruiah and Abigail. And the
three sons of Zeruiah *were* Abshai, Joab, and Asahel.
17 And Abigail bore Amasa,
and the father of Amasa was Jether the Ishmaelite.
18 Now Caleb the son of Hezron had sons by Azubah *his* wife,
and by Jerioth; and these were her
sons: Jesher, Shobab, and Ardon.
19 When Azubah died, Caleb
married Ephrath, who bore him
Hur.
20 And Hur became the father
of Uri, and Uri became the father
of Bezalel.
21 Afterward Hezron went in to

the daughter of Machir the father
of Gilead, whom he married when
he was sixty years old; and she
bore him Segub.
22 And Segub became the father of Jair, who had twenty-three
cities in the land of Gilead.
23 But Geshur and Aram took
the towns of Jair from them, with
Kenath and its villages, *even* sixty
cities. All these were the sons of
Machir, the father of Gilead.
24 And after the death of Hezron in Caleb-ephrathah, Abijah,
Hezron's wife, bore him Ashhur
the father of Tekoa.
25 Now the sons of Jerahmeel
the first-born of Hezron *were* Ram
the first-born, then Bunah, Oren,
Ozem, *and* Ahijah.
26 And Jerahmeel had another
wife, whose name was Atarah;
she was the mother of Onam.
27 And the sons of Ram, the
first-born of Jerahmeel, were
Maaz, Jamin, and Eker.
28 And the sons of Onam were
Shammai and Jada. And the sons
of Shammai *were* Nadab and
Abishur.
29 And the name of Abishur's
wife *was* Abihail, and she bore
him Ahban and Molid.
30 And the sons of Nadab *were*
Seled and Appaim, and Seled died
without sons.
31 And the [t]son of Appaim *was*
Ishi. And the son of Ishi *was* Sheshan. And the son of Sheshan *was*
Ahlai. *sons*
32 And the sons of Jada the
brother of Shammai *were* Jether
and Jonathan, and Jether died
without sons.
33 And the sons of Jonathan
were Peleth and Zaza. These were
the sons of Jerahmeel.
34 Now Sheshan had no sons,
only daughters. And Sheshan had
an Egyptian servant whose name
was Jarha.
35 And Sheshan gave his
daughter to Jarha his servant in
marriage, and she bore him Attai.
36 And Attai became the father
of Nathan, and Nathan became
the father of Zabad,
37 and Zabad became the father
of Ephlal, and Ephlal became the
father of Obed,
38 and Obed became the father
of Jehu, and Jehu became the father of Azariah,
39 and Azariah became the father of Helez, and Helez became
the father of Eleasah,
40 and Eleasah became the father of Sismai, and Sismai became
the father of Shallum,
41 and Shallum became the father of Jekamiah, and Jekamiah
became the father of Elishama.
42 Now the sons of Caleb, the
brother of Jerahmeel, *were* Mesha
his first-born, who was the father
of Ziph; and his son was Mareshah, the father of Hebron.
43 And the sons of Hebron *were*
Korah and Tappuah and Rekem
and Shema.
44 And Shema became the father of Raham, the father of Jor-
keam; and Rekem became the father of Shammai.
45 And the son of Shammai was
Maon, and Maon *was* the father of
Bethzur.
46 And Ephah, Caleb's concubine, bore Haran, Moza, and Ga-

zez; and Haran became the father of Gazez.

47 And the sons of Jahdai *were* Regem, Jotham, Geshan, Pelet, Ephah, and Shaaph.

48 Maacah, Caleb's concubine, bore Sheber and Tirhanah.

49 She also bore Shaaph the father of Madmannah, Sheva the father of Machbena and the father of Gibea; and the daughter of Caleb *was* Achsah.

50 These were the sons of Caleb.

The [t]sons of Hur, the first-born of Ephrathah, *were* Shobal the father of Kiriath-jearim, *son*

51 Salma the father of Bethlehem *and* Hareph the father of Beth-gader.

52 And Shobal the father of Kiriath-jearim had sons: Haroeh, half of the Manahathites,

53 and the families of Kiriath-jearim: the Ithrites, the Puthites, the Shumathites, and the Mishraites; from these came the Zorathites and the Eshtaolites.

54 The sons of Salma *were* Bethlehem and the Netophathites, Atroth-beth-joab and half of the Manahathites, the Zorites.

55 And the families of scribes who lived at Jabez *were* the Tirathites, the Shimeathites, *and* the Sucathites. Those are the Kenites who came from Hammath, the father of the house of Rechab.

CHAPTER 3

[r]NOW these were the sons of David who were born to him in Hebron: the first-born *was* Amnon, by Ahinoam the Jezreelitess; the second *was* Daniel, by Abigail the Carmelitess; 2 Sam. 3:2-5

2 the third *was* Absalom the son of Maacah, the daughter of Talmai king of Geshur; the fourth *was* Adonijah the son of Haggith;

3 the fifth *was* Shephatiah, by Abital; the sixth *was* Ithream, by his wife Eglah.

4 Six were born to him in Hebron, and [r]there he reigned seven years and six months. And in Jerusalem he reigned thirty-three years. 2 Sam. 2:11; 5:4, 5; 1 Kin. 2:11

5 [r]And these were born to him in Jerusalem: Shimea, Shobab, Nathan, and [r]Solomon, four, by Bath-shua the daughter of Ammiel; 2 Sam. 5:14-16 • 2 Sam. 12:24, 25

6 and Ibhar, Elishama, Eliphelet,

7 Nogah, Nepheg, and Japhia,

8 Elishama, Eliada, and Eliphelet, nine.

9 All *these were* the sons of David, besides the sons of the concubines; and [r]Tamar *was* their sister. 2 Sam. 13:1

10 Now Solomon's son *was* Rehoboam, Abijah *was* his son, Asa his son, Jehoshaphat his son,

11 Joram his son, Ahaziah his son, Joash his son,

12 Amaziah his son, Azariah his son, Jotham his son,

13 Ahaz his son, Hezekiah his son, Manasseh his son,

14 Amon his son, Josiah his son.

15 And the sons of Josiah *were* Johanan the first-born, and the second *was* Jehoiakim, the third Zedekiah, the fourth Shallum.

16 And the sons of Jehoiakim *were* Jeconiah his son, Zedekiah his son.

17 And the sons of Jeconiah, the
prisoner, *were* Shealtiel his son,
18 and Malchiram, Pedaiah,
Shenazzar, Jekamiah, Hoshama,
and Nedabiah.
19 And the sons of Pedaiah
were Zerubbabel and Shimei. And
the [t]sons of Zerubbabel *were* Meshullam and Hananiah, and Shelomith *was* their sister; *son*
20 and Hashubah, Ohel, Berechiah, Hasadiah, and Jushab-
hesed, five.
21 And the [t]sons of Hananiah
were Pelatiah and Jeshaiah, the
sons of Rephaiah, the sons of Ar-
nan, the sons of Obadiah, the sons
of Shecaniah. *son*
22 And the [1]son of Shecaniah
was Shemaiah, and the sons of
Shemaiah *were* Hattush, Igal, Ba-
riah, Neariah, and Shaphat, six.
23 And the [t]sons of Neariah
were Elioenai, Hizkiah, and Azrikam, three. *son*
24 And the sons of Elioenai
were Hodaviah, Eliashib, Pelaiah,
Akkub, Johanan, Delaiah, and
Anani, seven.

CHAPTER 4

THE sons of Judah *were* Perez,
Hezron, Carmi, Hur, and Shobal.
2 And Reaiah the son of Shobal became the father of Jahath,
and Jahath became the father of
Ahumai and Lahad. These *were*
the families of the Zorathites.
3 And these *were* the sons of
Etam: Jezreel, Ishma, and Idbash;
and the name of their sister *was*
Hazzelelponi.
4 And Penuel *was* the father of
Gedor, and Ezer the father of Hu-
shah. These *were* the sons of Hur,
the first-born of Ephrathah, the father of Bethlehem.
5 And Ashhur, the father of
Tekoa, had two wives, Helah and
Naarah.
6 And Naarah bore him Ahuz-
zam, Hepher, Temeni, and Haa-
hashtari. These were the sons of
Naarah.
7 And the sons of Helah *were*
Zereth, Izhar and Ethnan.
8 And Koz became the father
of Anub and Zobebah, and the
families of Aharhel the son of Ha-
rum.
9 And Jabez was more honorable than his brothers, and his
mother named him Jabez saying,
"Because I bore *him* with pain."
10 Now Jabez called on the God
of Israel, saying, "Oh that Thou
wouldst bless me indeed, and enlarge my border, and that Thy
hand might be with me, and that
Thou wouldst keep *me* from harm,
that *it* may not pain me!" And
God granted him what he requested.
11 And Chelub the brother of
Shuhah became the father of Me-
hir, who was the father of Eshton.
12 And Eshton became the father of Beth-rapha and Paseah,
and Tehinnah the father of Ir-na-
hash. These are the men of Recah.
13 Now the sons of Kenaz *were*
Othniel and Seraiah. And the [t]son
of Othniel *was* Hathath. *sons*
14 And Meonothai became the
father of Ophrah, and Seraiah became the father of Joab the father
of [a]Ge-harashim, for they were
craftsmen. *valley of craftsmen*
15 And the sons of Caleb the

[1]Lit., *sons*

son of Jephunneh *were* Iru, Elah
and Naam; and the [t]son of Elah
was [t]Kenaz. *sons · and Kenaz*
16 And the sons of Jehallelel
were Ziph and Ziphah, Tiria and
Asarel.
17 And the sons of Ezrah *were*
Jether, Mered, Epher, and Jalon.
(And these are the sons of Bithia
the daughter of Pharaoh, whom
Mered took) and she conceived
and *bore* Miriam, Shammai, and
Ishbah the father of Eshtemoa.
18 And his Jewish wife bore
Jered the father of Gedor, and Heber the father of Soco, and Jeku-
thiel the father of Zanoah.
19 And the sons of the wife of
Hodiah, the sister of Naham, *were*
the fathers of Keilah the Garmite
and Eshtemoa the Maacathite.
20 And the sons of Shimon *were*
Amnon and Rinnah, Benhanan
and Tilon. And the sons of Ishi
were Zoheth and Ben-zoheth.
21 The sons of Shelah the son of
Judah *were* Er the father of Lecah
and Laadah the father of Mareshah, and the families of the
house of the linen workers at
Beth-ashbea;
22 and Jokim, the men of Coze-
ba, Joash, Saraph, who ruled in
Moab, and Jashubi-lehem. And
the [t]records are ancient. *words*
23 These were the potters and
the inhabitants of Netaim and
Gederah; they lived there with the
king for his work.
24 The sons of Simeon *were*
Nemuel and Jamin, Jarib, Zerah,
Shaul;
25 Shallum his son, Mibsam his
son, Mishma his son.
26 And the sons of Mishma
were Hammuel his son, Zaccur his
son, Shimei his son.
27 Now Shimei had sixteen sons
and six daughters; but his brothers did not have many sons, nor
did all their family multiply like
the sons of Judah.
28 And they lived at Beersheba,
Moladah, and Hazar-shual,
29 at Bilhah, Ezem, Tolad,
30 Bethuel, Hormah, Ziklag,
31 Beth-marcaboth, Hazar-su-
sim, Beth-biri, and Shaaraim.
These *were* their cities until the
reign of David.
32 And their villages *were*
Etam, Ain, Rimmon, Tochen, and
Ashan, five cities;
33 and all their villages that
were around the same cities as far
as Baal. These *were* their settlements, and they have their genealogy.
34 And Meshobab and Jamlech
and Joshah the son of Amaziah,
35 and Joel and Jehu the son of
Joshibiah, the son of Seraiah, the
son of Asiel,
36 and Elioenai, Jaakobah,
Jeshohaiah, Asaiah, Adiel, Jesimi-
el, Benaiah,
37 Ziza the son of Shiphi, the
son of Allon, the son of Jedaiah,
the son of Shimri, the son of
Shemaiah;
38 these mentioned by name
were leaders in their families; and
their fathers' houses increased
greatly.
39 And they went to the entrance of Gedor, even to the east
side of the valley, to seek pasture
for their flocks.
40 And they found rich and
good pasture, and [r]the land was

broad and quiet and peaceful; for those who lived there formerly *were* Hamites. Judg. 18:7-10

41 And these, recorded by name, came in the days of Hezekiah king of Judah, and [t]attacked their tents, and the Meunites who were found there, and destroyed them utterly to this day, and lived in their place; because there was pasture for their flocks. *smote*

42 And from them, from the sons of Simeon, five hundred men went to Mount Seir, with Pelatiah, Neariah, Rephaiah, and Uzziel, the sons of Ishi, as their leaders.

43 And [r]they [t]destroyed the remnant of the Amalekites who escaped, and have lived there to this day. 1 Sam. 15:7, 8; 30:17 • *smote*

CHAPTER 5

NOW the sons of Reuben the first-born of Israel (for [r]he was the first-born, but because he defiled his father's bed, his birthright was given to the sons of Joseph the son of Israel; so that he is not enrolled in the genealogy according to the birthright. Gen. 29:32

2 [r]Though Judah prevailed over his brothers, and from him *came* the leader, yet the birthright belonged to Joseph), Gen. 49:8-10

3 [r]the sons of Reuben the first-born of Israel *were* Hanoch and Pallu, Hezron and Carmi. Ex. 6:14

4 The sons of Joel *were* Shemaiah his son, Gog his son, [r]Shimei his son, 1 Chr. 5:8

5 Micah his son, Reaiah his son, Baal his son,

6 Beerah his son, whom Tilgath-pilneser king of Assyria carried away into exile; he was leader of the Reubenites.

7 And his [t]kinsmen by their families, in the genealogy of their generations, *were* Jeiel the chief, then Zechariah *brothers*

8 and Bela the son of Azaz, the son of Shema, the son of Joel, who lived in [r]Aroer, even to Nebo and Baal-meon. Num. 32:34; Josh. 12:2

9 And to the east he settled as far as the entrance of the wilderness from the river Euphrates, [r]because their cattle had increased in the land of Gilead. Josh. 22:8, 9

10 And in the days of Saul they made war with the Hagrites, who fell by their hand, so that they [t]occupied their tents throughout all the land east of Gilead. *dwelt in*

11 Now the sons of Gad lived opposite them in the land of [r]Bashan as far as Salecah. Josh. 13:11

12 Joel *was* the chief, and Shapham the second, then Janai and Shaphat in Bashan.

13 And their [t]kinsmen of their fathers' households *were* Michael, Meshullam, Sheba, Jorai, Jacan, Zia, and Eber, seven. *brother*

14 These *were* the sons of Abihail, the son of Huri, the son of Jaroah, the son of Gilead, the son of Michael, the son of Jeshishai, the son of Jahdo, the son of Buz;

15 Ahi the son of Abdiel, the son of Guni, *was* head of their fathers' households.

16 And they lived in Gilead, in Bashan and in its towns, and in all the pasture lands of Sharon, as far as their [t]borders. *goings out*

17 All of these were enrolled in the genealogies in the days of Jotham king of Judah and in the

days of Jeroboam king of Israel.
18 The sons of Reuben and the
Gadites and the half-tribe of Manasseh, *consisting* of valiant men,
men who bore shield and sword
and shot with bow, and *were* skillful in battle, *were* 44,760, who
[r]went to war. Num. 1:3
19 And they made war against
[r]the Hagrites, [r]Jetur, Naphish, and
Nodab. 1 Chr. 5:10 • Gen. 25:15
20 And they were helped
against them, and the Hagrites
and all who *were* with them were
given into their hand; for they
cried out to God in the battle, and
He was entreated for them, because they trusted in Him.
21 And they took away their
cattle: their 50,000 camels,
250,000 sheep, 2,000 donkeys,
and 100,000 [t]men. *souls of men*
22 For many fell slain, because
the war *was* of God. And they settled in their place until the exile.
23 Now the sons of the half-
tribe of Manasseh lived in the
land; from Bashan to Baal-hermon
and [r]Senir and Mount Hermon
they were numerous. Deut. 3:9
24 And these were the heads of
their fathers' households, even
Epher, Ishi, Eliel, Azriel, Jeremiah, Hodaviah, and Jahdiel, mighty
men of valor, famous men, heads
of their fathers' households.
25 But they [r]acted treacherously
against the God of their fathers,
and [r]played the harlot after the
gods of the peoples of the land,
whom God had destroyed before
them. Deut. 32:15-18 • Ex. 34:15
26 So the God of Israel stirred
up the spirit of [r]Pul, king of Assyria, even the spirit of Tilgath-
pilneser king of Assyria, and he
carried them away into exile,
namely the Reubenites, the Gadites, and the half-tribe of Manasseh, and brought them to Halah,
Habor, Hara, and to the river of
Gozan, to this day. 2 Kin. 15:19, 29

CHAPTER 6

[r]THE sons of Levi *were* Gershon,
Kohath and Merari. Gen. 46:11
2 And the sons of Kohath *were*
Amram, Izhar, Hebron, and Uzziel.
3 And the children of Amram
were Aaron, Moses, and Miriam.
And the sons of Aaron *were* Nadab, Abihu, Eleazar, and Ithamar.
4 Eleazar [t]became the father of
Phinehas, *and* Phinehas became
the father of Abishua, *begot*
5 and Abishua became the father of Bukki, and Bukki became
the father of Uzzi,
6 and Uzzi became the father
of Zerahiah, and Zerahiah became
the father of Meraioth,
7 Meraioth became the father
of Amariah, and Amariah became
the father of Ahitub,
8 and [r]Ahitub became the father of Zadok, and Zadok became
the father of Ahimaaz, 2 Sam. 8:17
9 and Ahimaaz became the father of Azariah, and Azariah became the father of Johanan,
10 and Johanan became the father of Azariah [r](it was he who
served as the priest in the house
[r]which Solomon built in Jerusalem), 2 Chr. 26:17 • 1 Kin. 6:1
11 and Azariah became the father of Amariah, and Amariah became the father of Ahitub,

12 and Ahitub became the father of Zadok, and Zadok became the father of Shallum,

13 and Shallum became the father of Hilkiah, and Hilkiah became the father of Azariah,

14 and Azariah became the father of Seraiah, and Seraiah became the father of Jehozadak;

15 and Jehozadak went *along* when the LORD carried Judah and Jerusalem away into exile [t]by Nebuchadnezzar. *by the hand of*

16 The sons of Levi *were* Gershom, Kohath, and Merari.

17 And these are the names of the sons of Gershom: Libni and Shimei.

18 And the sons of Kohath *were* Amram, Izhar, Hebron, and Uzziel.

19 The sons of Merari *were* Mahli and Mushi. And these are the families of the Levites according to their fathers' *households.*

20 Of Gershom: Libni his son, Jahath his son, Zimmah his son,

21 Joah his son, Iddo his son, Zerah his son, Jeatherai his son.

22 The sons of Kohath *were* Amminadab his son, Korah his son, Assir his son,

23 Elkanah his son, Ebiasaph his son, and Assir his son,

24 Tahath his son, Uriel his son, Uzziah his son, and Shaul his son.

25 And the sons of Elkanah *were* Amasai and Ahimoth.

26 *As for* Elkanah, the sons of Elkanah *were* Zophai his son and Nahath his son,

27 Eliab his son, Jeroham his son, Elkanah his son.

28 And the sons of Samuel *were* [r]Joel, the first-born and Abijah, the second. 1 Sam. 8:2; 1 Chr. 6:33

29 The sons of Merari *were* Mahli, Libni his son, Shimei his son, Uzzah his son,

30 Shimea his son, Haggiah his son, Asaiah his son.

31 Now these are those whom David appointed over the service of song in the house of the LORD, after the ark rested *there.*

32 And they ministered with song before the tabernacle of the tent of meeting, until Solomon had built the house of the LORD in Jerusalem; and they [t]served in their office according to their order. *stood over*

33 And these are those who [t]served with their sons. From the sons of the Kohathites *were* Heman the singer, the son of Joel, the son of Samuel, *stood*

34 the son of Elkanah, the son of Jeroham, the son of Eliel, the son of Toah,

35 the son of Zuph, the son of Elkanah, the son of Mahath, the son of Amasai,

36 the son of Elkanah, the son of Joel, the son of Azariah, the son of Zephaniah,

37 the son of Tahath, the son of Assir, the son of Ebiasaph, the son of Korah,

38 the son of Izhar, the son of Kohath, the son of Levi, the son of Israel.

39 And *Heman's* brother Asaph stood at his right hand, even Asaph the son of Berechiah, the son of Shimea,

40 the son of Michael, the son of Baaseiah, the son of Malchijah,

41 the son of Ethni, the son of
Zerah, the son of Adaiah,
42 the son of Ethan, the son of
Zimmah, the son of Shimei,
43 the son of Jahath, the son of
Gershom, the son of Levi.
44 And on the left hand *were*
their [t]kinsmen the sons of Merari:
Ethan the son of Kishi, the son of
Abdi, the son of Malluch, *brothers*
45 the son of Hashabiah, the son
of Amaziah, the son of Hilkiah,
46 the son of Amzi, the son of
Bani, the son of Shemer,
47 the son of Mahli, the son of
Mushi, the son of Merari, the son
of Levi.
48 And their [t]kinsmen the Levites were [t]appointed for all the
service of the tabernacle of the
house of God. *brothers · given*
49 But Aaron and his sons offered on the altar of burnt offering
and on the altar of incense, for all
the work of the most holy place,
and to make atonement for Israel,
according to all that Moses the
servant of God had commanded.
50 [r]And these are the sons of
Aaron: Eleazar his son, Phinehas
his son, Abishua his son, Ezra 7:5
51 Bukki his son, Uzzi his son,
Zerahiah his son,
52 Meraioth his son, Amariah
his son, Ahitub his son,
53 Zadok his son, Ahimaaz his
son.
54 Now these are their settlements according to their camps
within their borders. To the sons
of Aaron of the families of the Kohathites (for theirs was the [r]*first*
lot), Josh. 21:4, 10
55 to them they gave [r]Hebron in
the land of Judah, and its pasture
lands around it; Josh. 14:13; 21:11f.
56 [r]but the fields of the city and
its villages, they gave to Caleb the
son of Jephunneh. Josh. 15:13
57 And [r]to the sons of Aaron
they gave the *following* cities of
refuge: Hebron, Libnah also with
its pasture lands, Jattir, Eshtemoa
with its pasture lands, Josh. 21:13
58 Hilen with its pasture lands,
Debir with its pasture lands,
59 Ashan with its pasture lands,
and Beth-shemesh with its pasture lands;
60 and from the tribe of Benjamin: Geba with its pasture lands,
Allemeth with its pasture lands,
and Anathoth with its pasture
lands. All their cities throughout
their families were thirteen cities.
61 [r]Then to the rest of the sons
of Kohath *were given* by lot, from
the family of the tribe, from the
half-tribe, the half of Manasseh,
ten cities. Josh. 21:5; 1 Chr. 6:66-70
62 And to the sons of Gershom,
according to their families, *were
given* from the tribe of Issachar
and from the tribe of Asher, the
tribe of Naphtali, and the tribe of
Manasseh, thirteen cities in Bashan.
63 [r]To the sons of Merari *were
given* by lot, according to their
families, from the tribe of Reuben,
the tribe of Gad, and the tribe of
Zebulun, twelve cities. Josh. 21:7
64 [r]So the sons of Israel gave to
the Levites the cities with their
pasture lands. Num. 35:1-8
65 And they gave by lot from
the tribe of the sons of Judah, the
tribe of the sons of Simeon, and
the tribe of the sons of Benjamin,

[r]these cities which are mentioned by name. 1 Chr. 6:57-60

66 [r]Now some of the families of the sons of Kohath had cities of their territory from the tribe of Ephraim. Josh. 21:20-26

67 And they gave to them the *following* cities of refuge: Shechem in the hill country of Ephraim with its pasture lands, Gezer also with its pasture lands,

68 Jokmeam with its pasture lands, Beth-horon with its pasture lands,

69 Aijalon with its pasture lands, and Gath-rimmon with its pasture lands;

70 and from the half-tribe of Manasseh: Aner with its pasture lands and Bileam with its pasture lands, for the rest of the family of the sons of Kohath.

71 To the sons of Gershom *were given,* from the family of the half-tribe of Manasseh: Golan in Bashan with its pasture lands and Ashtaroth with its pasture lands;

72 and from the tribe of Issachar: Kedesh with its pasture lands, Daberath with its pasture lands,

73 and Ramoth with its pasture lands, Anem with its pasture lands;

74 and from the tribe of Asher: Mashal with its pasture lands, Abdon with its pasture lands,

75 Hukok with its pasture lands, and Rehob with its pasture lands;

76 and from the tribe of Naphtali: Kedesh in Galilee with its pasture lands, Hammon with its pasture lands, and Kiriathaim with its pasture lands.

77 To the rest of *the Levites,* the sons of Merari, *were given,* from the tribe of Zebulun: Rimmono with its pasture lands, Tabor with its pasture lands;

78 and beyond the Jordan at Jericho, on the east side of the Jordan, *were given them,* from the tribe of Reuben: Bezer in the wilderness with its pasture lands, Jahzah with its pasture lands,

79 Kedemoth with its pasture lands, and Mephaath with its pasture lands;

80 and from the tribe of Gad: Ramoth in Gilead with its pasture lands, Mahanaim with its pasture lands,

81 Heshbon with its pasture lands, and Jazer with its pasture lands.

CHAPTER 7

NOW the sons of Issachar *were* four: Tola, Puah, Jashub, and Shimron.

2 And the sons of Tola *were* Uzzi, Rephaiah, Jeriel, Jahmai, Ibsam, and Samuel, heads of their fathers' households. *The sons* of Tola *were* mighty men of valor in their generations; their number in the days of David was 22,600.

3 And the [t]son of Uzzi *was* Izrahiah. And the sons of Izrahiah *were* Michael, Obadiah, Joel, Isshiah; all five of them *were* [r]chief men. *sons* • 1 Chr. 5:24

4 And with them by their generations according to their fathers' households were 36,000 troops of the army for war, for they had many wives and sons.

5 And their [t]relatives among all the families of Issachar *were*

mighty men of valor, enrolled by
genealogy, in all 87,000. *brothers*
6 [r]*The sons of* Benjamin *were*
three: Bela and Becher and Jediael. 1 Chr. 8:1-40
7 And the sons of Bela were
five: Ezbon, Uzzi, Uzziel, Jerimoth, and Iri. They *were* heads of
fathers' households, mighty men
of valor, and were 22,034 enrolled
by genealogy.
8 And the sons of Becher *were*
Zemirah, Joash, Eliezer, Elioenai,
Omri, Jeremoth, Abijah, Anathoth, and Alemeth. All these
were the sons of Becher.
9 And they were enrolled by
genealogy, according to their generations, heads of their fathers'
households, 20,200 mighty men of
valor.
10 And the [t]son of Jediael *was*
Bilhan. And the sons of Bilhan
were Jeush, Benjamin, Ehud, Chenaanah, Zethan, Tarshish, and
Ahishahar. *sons*
11 All these *were* sons of Jediael, according to the heads of their
fathers' households, 17,200
mighty men of valor, who were
[t]ready to go out with the army to
war. *going out*
12 And Shuppim and Huppim
were the sons of Ir; Hushim *was*
the [t]son of Aher. *sons*
13 The sons of Naphtali *were*
Jahziel, Guni, Jezer, and Shallum,
the sons of Bilhah.
14 The sons of Manasseh *were*
Asriel, whom his Aramean concubine bore; she bore Machir the father of Gilead.
15 And Machir took a wife for
Huppim and Shuppim, [t]whose sister's name was Maacah. And the
name of the second was Zelophehad, and Zelophehad had daughters. *and his*
16 And Maacah the wife of Machir bore a son, and she named
him Peresh; and the name of his
brother *was* Sheresh, and his sons
were Ulam and Rakem.
17 And the [t]son of Ulam *was* Be-
dan. These *were* the sons of Gilead
the son of Machir, the son of Manasseh. *sons*
18 And his sister Hammole-
cheth bore Ishhod and Abiezer
and Mahlah.
19 And the sons of Shemida
were Ahian and Shechem and Lik-
hi and Aniam.
20 And [r]the sons of Ephraim
were Shuthelah and Bered his son,
Tahath his son, Eleadah his son,
Tahath his son, Num. 26:35, 36
21 Zabad his son, Shuthelah his
son, and Ezer and Elead whom the
men of Gath who were born in the
land killed, because they came
down to take their livestock.
22 And their father Ephraim
mourned many days, and his relatives came to comfort him.
23 Then he went in to his wife,
and she conceived and bore a son,
and he named him Beriah, because misfortune had come upon
his house.
24 And his daughter was Shee-
rah, who built lower and upper
Beth-horon, also Uzzen-sheerah.
25 And Rephah was his son
along with Resheph, Telah his
son, Tahan his son,
26 Ladan his son, Ammihud his
son, Elishama his son,
27 Non his son, and [r]Joshua his
son. Ex. 17:9-14; 24:13

28 And [r]their possessions and
settlements *were* Bethel with its
towns, and to the east Naaran,
and to the west Gezer with its
towns, and Shechem with its
towns as far as Ayyah with its
towns, Josh. 16:2
29 and along the borders of the
sons of Manasseh, Beth-shean
with its towns, Taanach with its
towns, Megiddo with its towns,
Dor with its towns. In these lived
the [r]sons of Joseph the son of Israel. Judg. 1:22-29
30 [r]The sons of Asher *were* Imnah, Ishvah, Ishvi and Beriah, and
Serah their sister. Gen. 46:17
31 And the sons of Beriah *were*
Heber and Malchiel, who was the
father of Birzaith.
32 And Heber [t]became the father of Japhlet, Shomer and Hotham, and Shua their sister. *begot*
33 And the sons of Japhlet *were*
Pasach, Bimhal, and Ashvath.
These were the sons of Japhlet.
34 And the sons of Shemer *were*
Ahi and Rohgah, Jehubbah and
Aram.
35 And the [t]sons of his brother
Helem *were* Zophah, Imna, She-
lesh, and Amal. *son*
36 The sons of Zophah *were*
Suah, Harnepher, Shual, Beri, and
Imrah,
37 Bezer, Hod, Shamma, Shil-
shah, Ithran, and Beera.
38 And the sons of Jether *were*
Jephunneh, Pispa, and Ara.
39 And the sons of Ulla *were*
Arah, Hanniel, and Rizia.
40 All these *were* the sons of
Asher, heads of the fathers'
houses, choice and mighty men of
valor, heads of the princes. And
the number of them enrolled by
genealogy for service in war was
26,000 men.

CHAPTER 8

AND Benjamin became the father of Bela his first-born, Ashbel
the second, Aharah the third,
2 Nohah the fourth, and Rapha
the fifth.
3 And Bela had sons: Addar,
Gera, Abihud,
4 Abishua, Naaman, Ahoah,
5 Gera, Shephuphan, and Huram.
6 And these are the sons of
Ehud: these are the heads of fathers' *households* of the inhabitants of Geba, and they carried
them into exile to Manahath,
7 namely, Naaman, Ahijah,
and Gera—he carried them into
exile; and he became the father of
Uzza and Ahihud.
8 And Shaharaim became the
father of children in the [t]country of
Moab, after he had sent away Hushim and Baara his wives. *field*
9 And by Hodesh his wife he
became the father of Jobab, Zibia,
Mesha, Malcam,
10 Jeuz, Sachia, Mirmah. These
were his sons, heads of fathers'
households.
11 And by Hushim he became
the father of Abitub and Elpaal.
12 And the sons of Elpaal *were*
Eber, Misham, and Shemed, who
built Ono and Lod, with its towns;
13 and Beriah and Shema, who
were heads of fathers' *households*
of the inhabitants of Aijalon, who
put to flight the inhabitants of
Gath;

14 and [a]Ahio, Shashak, and Jeremoth. *his brothers*
15 And Zebadiah, Arad, Eder,
16 Michael, Ishpah, and Joha
were the sons of Beriah.
17 And Zebadiah, Meshullam,
Hizki, Heber,
18 Ishmerai, Izliah, and Jobab
were the sons of Elpaal.
19 And Jakim, Zichri, Zabdi,
20 Elienai, Zillethai, Eliel,
21 Adaiah, Beraiah, and Shim-
rath *were* the sons of Shimei.
22 And Ishpan, Eber, Eliel,
23 Abdon, Zichri, Hanan,
24 Hananiah, Elam, Anthothi-
jah,
25 Iphdeiah, and Penuel *were*
the sons of Shashak.
26 And Shamsherai, Shehariah,
Athaliah,
27 Jaareshiah, Elijah, and Zichri
were the sons of Jeroham.
28 These were heads of the fathers' *households* according to
their generations, chief men, [t]who
lived in Jerusalem. *these*
29 Now in Gibeon, *Jeiel*, the father of Gibeon lived, and his
wife's name was Maacah;
30 and his first-born son *was*
Abdon, then Zur, Kish, Baal, Nadab,
31 Gedor, Ahio, and Zecher.
32 And Mikloth became the father of Shimeah. And they also
lived with their [t]relatives in Jerusalem opposite their *other* [t]rela-
tives. *brothers*
33 And Ner became the father
of Kish, and Kish became the father of Saul, and Saul became the
father of Jonathan, Malchi-shua,
Abinadab, and Eshbaal.
34 And the son of Jonathan *was*
Merib-baal, and Merib-baal became the father of Micah.
35 And the sons of Micah *were*
Pithon, Melech, Tarea, and Ahaz.
36 And Ahaz became the father
of Jehoaddah, and Jehoaddah became the father of Alemeth, Azmaveth, and Zimri; and Zimri became the father of Moza.
37 And Moza became the father
of Binea; Raphah *was* his son, Eleasah his son, Azel his son.
38 And Azel had six sons, and
these *were* their names: Azrikam,
Bocheru, Ishmael, Sheariah, Obadiah and Hanan. All these *were*
the sons of Azel.
39 And the sons of Eshek his
brother *were* Ulam his first-born,
Jeush the second, and Eliphelet
the third.
40 And the sons of Ulam were
mighty men of valor, archers, and
had many sons and grandsons,
150 *of them*. All these *were* of the
sons of Benjamin.

CHAPTER 9

SO all Israel was enrolled by genealogies; and behold, they are
written in the Book of the Kings of
Israel. And [r]Judah was carried
away into exile to Babylon for
their unfaithfulness. 1 Chr. 5:25, 26
2 Now the first who lived in
their possessions 'in their cities
were Israel, the priests, the Levites and the temple servants.
3 And some of the sons of Judah, of the sons of Benjamin, and
of the sons of Ephraim and Manasseh lived in Jerusalem:
4 Uthai the son of Ammihud,
the son of Omri, the son of Imri,

the son of Bani, from the sons of
Perez the [r]son of Judah. Gen. 46:12
5 And from the Shilonites *were*
Asaiah the first-born and his sons.
6 And from the sons of Zerah
were Jeuel and their [t]relatives, 690
of them. *brothers*
7 And from the sons of Benjamin *were* Sallu the son of Meshullam, the son of Hodaviah, the son
of Hassenuah,
8 and Ibneiah the son of Jeroham, and Elah the son of Uzzi, the
son of Michri, and Meshullam the
son of Shephatiah, the son of
Reuel, the son of Ibnijah;
9 and their relatives according
to their generations, 956. All these
were heads of fathers' *households*
according to their fathers' houses.
10 And from the priests *were*
Jedaiah, Jehoiarib, Jachin,
11 and Azariah the son of Hilkiah, the son of Meshullam, the
son of Zadok, the son of Meraioth,
the son of Ahitub, [r]the chief officer
of the house of God; Jer. 20:1
12 and Adaiah the son of Jeroham, the son of Pashhur, the son
of Malchijah, and Maasai the son
of Adiel, the son of Jahzerah, the
son of Meshullam, the son of Me-
shillemith, the son of Immer;
13 and their relatives, heads of
their fathers' households, 1,760
very able men for the work of the
service of the house of God.
14 And of the Levites *were*
Shemaiah the son of Hasshub, the
son of Azrikam, the son of Hashabiah, of the sons of Merari;
15 and Bakbakkar, Heresh and
Galal and Mattaniah the son of
Mica, the son of Zichri, the son of
Asaph,
16 and Obadiah the son of
Shemaiah, the son of Galal, the
son of Jeduthun, and Berechiah
the son of Asa, the son of Elkanah,
who lived in the villages of the
Netophathites.
17 Now the gatekeepers *were*
Shallum and Akkub and Talmon
and Ahiman and their relatives
(Shallum the chief
18 *being stationed* until now at
[r]the king's gate to the east). These
were the gatekeepers for the camp
of the sons of Levi. Ezek. 44:1
19 And Shallum the son of
Kore, the son of Ebiasaph, the son
of Korah, and his relatives, of his
father's house, the Korahites,
were over the work of the service,
keepers of the thresholds of the
tent; and their fathers had been
over the camp of the LORD, keepers of the entrance.
20 And Phinehas the son of Eleazar was ruler over them previously, *and* the LORD was with him.
21 Zechariah the son of Meshelemiah was gatekeeper of the
entrance of the tent of meeting.
22 All these who were chosen to
be gatekeepers in the thresholds
were 212. These were enrolled by
genealogy in their villages, whom
David and Samuel the seer appointed in their office of trust.
23 So they and their sons [t]had
charge of the gates of the house of
the LORD, *even* the house of the
tent, as guards. *were over the gates*
24 The gatekeepers were [t]on the
four sides, to the east, west, north,
and south. *to the four winds*
25 And their relatives in their
villages [r]*were* to come in every

seven days from time to time *to be*
with[t]them; 2 Kin. 11:5, 7 · *these*
26 for the four chief gatekeepers who *were* Levites, were in an
office of trust, and were over the
chambers and over the treasuries
in the house of God.
27 And they spent the night
around the house of God, because
the watch was committed to
them; and they *were* in charge of
opening *it* morning by morning.
28 Now some of them [t]had
charge of the utensils of service,
for they counted them when they
brought them in and when they
took them out. *were over the*
29 Some of them also were appointed over the furniture and
over all the utensils of the sanctuary and [r]over the fine flour and the
wine and the oil and the frankincense and the spices. 1 Chr. 23:29
30 And some of [r]the sons of the
priests prepared the mixing of the
spices. Ex. 30:23-25
31 And Mattithiah, one of the
Levites, who was the first-born of
Shallum the Korahite, had the [t]re-
sponsibility over the things which
were baked in pans. *office of trust*
32 And some of their relatives
of the sons of the Kohathites [r]*were*
over the showbread to prepare it
every sabbath. Lev. 24:5-8
33 Now these are the singers,
heads of fathers' *households* of
the Levites, *who lived* in the
chambers *of the temple* free *from
other service;* for they were engaged in their work day and night.
34 These were heads of fathers'
households of the Levites according to their generations, chief
men, [t]who lived in Jerusalem. *these*
35 And in Gibeon Jeiel the father of Gibeon lived, and his
wife's name was Maacah,
36 and his first-born son *was*
Abdon, then Zur, Kish, Baal, Ner,
Nadab,
37 Gedor, Ahio, Zechariah, and
Mikloth.
38 And Mikloth became the father of Shimeam. And they also
lived with their relatives in Jerusalem opposite their *other* relatives.
39 And Ner became the father
of Kish, and Kish became the father of Saul, and Saul became the
father of Jonathan, Malchi-shua,
Abinadab, and Eshbaal.
40 And the son of Jonathan *was*
Merib-baal; and Merib-baal became the father of Micah.
41 And the sons of Micah *were*
Pithon, Melech, Tahrea, [r]*and
Ahaz.* 1 Chr. 8:35-37
42 And Ahaz became the father
of Jarah, and Jarah became the father of Alemeth, Azmaveth, and
Zimri; and Zimri became the father of Moza,
43 and Moza became the father
of Binea and Rephaiah his son, Eleasah his son, Azel his son.
44 And Azel had six sons whose
names are these: Azrikam, Bocheru and Ishmael and Sheariah and
Obadiah and Hanan. These were
the sons of Azel.

CHAPTER 10

NOW the Philistines fought
against Israel; and the men of Israel fled before the Philistines,
and fell slain on Mount Gilboa.
2 And the Philistines closely

pursued Saul and his sons, and the
Philistines struck down Jonathan,
[r]Abinadab and Malchi-shua, the
sons of Saul. 1 Sam. 31:4
3 And the battle became heavy
against Saul, and the archers
[t]overtook him; and he was
wounded by the archers. *found him*
4 Then Saul said to his armor
bearer, "Draw your sword and
thrust me through with it, lest
these uncircumcised come and
abuse me." But his armor bearer
would not, for he was greatly
afraid. [r]Therefore Saul took his
sword and fell on it. 1 Sam. 31:4
5 And when his armor bearer
saw that Saul was dead, he likewise fell on his sword and died.
6 [r]Thus Saul died with his three
sons, and all *those* of his house
died together. 1 Sam. 31:6
7 When all the men of Israel
who were in the valley saw that
they had fled, and that Saul and
his sons were dead, they forsook
their cities and fled; and the Philistines came and lived in them.
8 And it came about the next
day, when the Philistines came to
strip the slain, that they found
Saul and his sons fallen on Mount
Gilboa.
9 [r]So they stripped him and
took his head and his armor and
sent *messengers* around the land
of the Philistines, to carry the
good news to their idols and to the
people. 1 Sam. 31:9
10 And they put his armor in the
house of their gods and fastened
his head in the house of Dagon.
11 When all Jabesh-gilead
heard all that the Philistines had
done to Saul,
12 all the valiant men arose and
took away the body of Saul and
the bodies of his sons, and
brought them to Jabesh and buried their bones under the oak in
Jabesh, and fasted seven days.
13 So Saul died for his trespass
which he committed against the
LORD, because of the word of the
LORD which he did not keep; and
also because he asked counsel of a
medium, making inquiry *of it*,
14 and did not inquire of the
LORD. Therefore He killed him,
and [r]turned the kingdom to David
the son of Jesse. 1 Sam. 15:28

CHAPTER 11

THEN all Israel gathered to David at Hebron and said, "Behold,
we are your bone and your flesh.
2 "In times past, even when
Saul was king, you *were* the one
who led out and brought in Israel;
and the LORD your God said to
you, 'You [r]shall shepherd My people Israel, and you shall be prince
over My people Israel.' " 2 Sam. 5:2
3 So all the elders of Israel
came to the king at Hebron, and
David made a covenant with them
in Hebron before the LORD; and
[r]they anointed David king over Israel, according to the word of the
LORD through Samuel. 2 Sam. 2:4
4 Then David and all Israel
went to Jerusalem [r](that is, Jebus);
and the Jebusites, the inhabitants
of the land, *were* there. Judg. 1:21
5 And the inhabitants of Jebus
said to David, "You shall not enter
here." Nevertheless David captured the stronghold of Zion (that
is, the city of David).

6 Now David had said, "Whoever strikes down a Jebusite first
shall be chief and commander."
And Joab the son of Zeruiah went
up first, so he became chief.
7 Then David dwelt in the
stronghold; therefore it was called
the city of David.
8 And he built the city all
around, from the [2]Millo even to
the surrounding area; and Joab [r]re-
paired the rest of the city. *revived*
9 And [r]David became greater
and greater, for the LORD of hosts
was with him. 2 Sam. 3:1
10 [r]Now these are the heads of
the mighty men whom David had,
who gave him strong support in
his kingdom, together with all Israel, to make him king, according
to the word of the LORD concerning Israel. 2 Sam. 23:8-39
11 And these *constitute* the list
of the mighty men whom David
had: Jashobeam, the son of a
Hachmonite, the chief of the
thirty; he lifted up his spear
against three hundred [t]whom he
killed at one time. *slain ones*
12 And after him was Eleazar
the son of Dodo, the Ahohite, who
was one of the three mighty men.
13 He was with David at Pas-
dammim when the Philistines
were gathered together there to
battle, and there was a plot of
ground full of barley; and the people fled before the Philistines.
14 And they took their stand in
the midst of the plot, and defended it, and struck down the
Philistines; and the LORD saved
them by a great [a]victory. *salvation*
15 Now three of the thirty chief
men went down to the rock to David, into the cave of Adullam,
while [r]the army of the Philistines
was camping in the valley of
Rephaim. 1 Chr. 14:9
16 And David was then in the
stronghold, while [r]the garrison of
the Philistines *was* then in Bethlehem. 1 Sam. 10:5
17 And David had a craving and
said, "Oh that someone would
give me water to drink from the
well of Bethlehem, which is by the
gate!"
18 So the three broke through
the camp of the Philistines, and
drew water from the well of Bethlehem which *was* by the gate, and
took *it* and brought *it* to David;
nevertheless David would not
drink it, but poured it out to the
LORD;
19 and he said, "Be it far from
me before my God that I should
do this. Shall I drink the blood of
these men *who went* at the risk of
their lives? For at the risk of their
lives they brought it." Therefore
he would not drink it. These
things the three mighty men did.
20 As for Abshai the brother of
Joab, he was chief of the thirty,
and he swung his spear against
three hundred [t]and killed them;
and he had a name as well as the
thirty. *slain ones*
21 Of the three in the second
rank he was the most honored,
and became their commander;
however, he did not attain to the
first three.
22 [r]Benaiah the son of Jehoiada,
the son of a valiant man of Kabzeel, mighty in deeds, struck
down the two *sons of* Ariel of
Moab. He also went down and

[2]I.e., citadel

[t]killed a lion inside a pit on a
snowy day. 2 Sam. 8:18 • *smote*
23 And he[t]killed an Egyptian, a
man of *great* stature five cubits
tall. Now in the Egyptian's hand
was a spear like a weaver's beam,
but he went down to him with a
club and snatched the spear from
the Egyptian's hand, and [t]killed
him with his own spear. *smote*
24 These *things* Benaiah the son
of Jehoiada did, and had a name
as well as the three mighty men.
25 Behold, he was honored
among the thirty, but he did not
attain to the three; and David appointed him over his guard.
26 Now the mighty men of the
armies *were* Asahel the brother of
Joab, Elhanan the son of Dodo of
Bethlehem,
27 Shammoth the Harorite, Helez the Pelonite,
28 Ira the son of Ikkesh the
Tekoite, Abiezer the Anathothite,
29 Sibbecai the Hushathite, Ilai
the Ahohite,
30 Maharai the Netophathite,
Heled the son of Baanah the Netophathite,
31 Ithai the son of Ribai of Gibeah of the sons of Benjamin, Benaiah the Pirathonite,
32 Hurai of the brooks of
Gaash, Abiel the Arbathite,
33 Azmaveth the Baharumite,
Eliahba the Shaalbonite,
34 the sons of Hashem the Gi-
zonite, Jonathan the son of Sha-
gee the Hararite,
35 Ahiam the son of Sacar the
Hararite, Eliphal the son of Ur,
36 Hepher the Mecherathite,
Ahijah the Pelonite,
37 Hezro the Carmelite, Naarai
the son of Ezbai,
38 Joel the brother of Nathan,
Mibhar the son of Hagri,
39 Zelek the Ammonite, Na-
harai the Berothite, the armor
bearer of Joab the son of Zeruiah,
40 Ira the Ithrite, Gareb the Ithrite,
41 Uriah the Hittite, Zabad the
son of Ahlai,
42 Adina the son of Shiza the
Reubenite, a chief of the Reubenites, and thirty with him,
43 Hanan the son of Maacah
and Joshaphat the Mithnite,
44 Uzzia the Ashterathite, Sha-
ma and Jeiel the sons of Hotham
the Aroerite,
45 Jediael the son of Shimri and
Joha his brother, the Tizite,
46 Eliel the Mahavite and Jeri-
bai and Joshaviah, the sons of El-
naam, and Ithmah the Moabite,
47 Eliel and Obed and Jaasiel
the Mezobaite.

CHAPTER 12

[r]NOW these are the ones who
came to David at Ziklag, while he
was still restricted because of
Saul the son of Kish; and they
were among the mighty men who
helped *him* in war. 1 Sam. 27:2-6
2 They were equipped with
bows, [r]using both the right hand
and the left *to sling* stones and *to*
shoot arrows from the bow; [r]*they*
were Saul's kinsmen from Benjamin. Judg. 3:15; 20:16 • 1 Chr. 12:29
3 The chief was Ahiezer, then
Joash, the sons of Shemaah the
Gibeathite; and Jeziel and Pelet,

the sons of Azmaveth, and Bera-
cah and Jehu the Anathothite,
4 and Ishmaiah the Gibeonite,
a mighty man among the thirty,
and over the thirty. Then Jeremiah, Jahaziel, Johanan, Jozabad the
Gederathite,
5 Eluzai, Jerimoth, Bealiah,
Shemariah, Shephatiah the Haru-
phite,
6 Elkanah, Isshiah, Azarel,
Joezer, Jashobeam, the Korahites,
7 and Joelah and Zebadiah, the
sons of Jeroham of Gedor.
8 And from the Gadites there
[t]came over to David in the stronghold in the wilderness, mighty
men of valor, men trained for war,
who could handle shield and
spear, and whose faces were like
the faces of lions, and *they were*
as swift as the gazelles on the
mountains. *separated themselves*
9 Ezer *was* the first, Obadiah
the second, Eliab the third,
10 Mishmannah the fourth, Jeremiah the fifth,
11 Attai the sixth, Eliel the seventh,
12 Johanan the eighth, Elzabad
the ninth,
13 Jeremiah the tenth, Mach-
bannai the eleventh.
14 These of the sons of Gad
were captains of the army; he who
was least was equal to a hundred
and the greatest to a thousand.
15 [r]These are the ones who
crossed the Jordan in the first
month when it was overflowing
all its banks and they put to flight
all those in the valleys, both to the
east and to the west. Josh. 3:15
16 Then some of the sons of
Benjamin and Judah came to the
stronghold to David.
17 And David went out to meet
them, and answered and said to
them, "If you come peacefully to
me to help me, my heart shall be
united with you; but if to betray
me to my adversaries, since there
is no[t]wrong in my hands, may the
God of our fathers look on *it* and
decide." *violence*
18 Then the Spirit came upon
Amasai, who was the chief of the
thirty, *and he said,*

"*We* are yours, O David,
And with you, O son of
Jesse!
Peace, peace to you,
And peace to him who
helps you;
Indeed, your God helps
you!"

Then David received them and
made them captains of the band.
19 [r]From Manasseh also some
defected to David, when he was
about to go to battle with the Philistines against Saul. But they did
not help them, for the lords of the
Philistines after consultation sent
him away, saying, "At *the cost of*
our heads he may defect to his
master Saul." 1 Sam. 29:2-9
20 As he went to Ziklag, there
defected to him from Manasseh:
Adnah, Jozabad, Jediael, Michael,
Jozabad, Elihu, and Zillethai,[a]cap-
tains of thousands who belonged
to Manasseh. *chiefs*
21 And they helped David
against the band of raiders, for
they were all mighty men of valor,
and were captains in the army.
22 For day by day *men* came to
David to help him, until there was

a great army like the army of God.
23 Now these are the numbers
of the [t]divisions equipped for war,
[r]who came to David at Hebron, to
turn the kingdom of Saul to him,
according to the [t]word of the
LORD. *heads* · 2 Sam. 2:3 · *mouth*
24 The sons of Judah who bore
shield and spear *were* 6,800,
equipped for war.
25 Of the sons of Simeon,
mighty men of valor for war,
7,100.
26 Of the sons of Levi 4,600.
27 Now Jehoiada was the leader
of *the house of* Aaron, and with
him were 3,700,
28 also Zadok, a young man
mighty of valor, and of his father's
house twenty-two captains.
29 And of the sons of Benjamin,
[r]Saul's kinsmen, 3,000; for until
now the greatest part of them had
kept their allegiance to the house
of Saul. 1 Chr. 12:2
30 And of the sons of Ephraim
20,800, mighty men of valor, famous men in their fathers' households.
31 And of the half-tribe of Manasseh 18,000, who were designated by name to come and make
David king.
32 And of the sons of Issachar,
[r]men who understood the times,
with knowledge of what Israel
should do, their chiefs were two
hundred; and all their kinsmen
were at their command. Esth. 1:13
33 Of Zebulun, there were
50,000 who went out in the army,
who could draw up in battle formation with all kinds of weapons
of war and helped *David* [t]with an
undivided heart. *not of double heart*
34 And of Naphtali *there were*
1,000 captains, and with them
37,000 with shield and spear.
35 And of the Danites who
could draw up in battle formation,
there were 28,600.
36 And of Asher *there were*
40,000 who went out in the army
to draw up in battle formation.
37 And from the other side of
the Jordan, of the Reubenites and
the Gadites and of the half-tribe of
Manasseh, *there were* 120,000
with all *kinds* of weapons of war
for the battle.
38 All these, being men of war,
who could draw up in battle formation, came to Hebron with [r]a
perfect heart, to make David king
over all Israel; and all the rest also
of Israel were of one mind to
make David king. 2 Sam. 5:1-3
39 And they were there with
David three days, eating and
drinking; for their kinsmen had
prepared for them.
40 Moreover those who were
near to them, *even* as far as Issachar and Zebulun and Naphtali,
[r]brought food on donkeys, camels,
mules, and on oxen, great quantities of flour cakes, fig cakes and
bunches of raisins, wine, oil, oxen
and sheep. There was joy indeed
in Israel. 1 Sam. 25:18

CHAPTER 13

THEN David consulted with the
captains of the thousands and the
hundreds, even with every leader.
2 And David said to all the assembly of Israel, "If it seems good
to you, and if it is from the LORD

our God, let us send everywhere
to our kinsmen who remain in all
the land of Israel, also to the
priests and Levites who are with
them in their cities with pasture
lands, that they may meet with us;
3 and let us bring back the ark
of our God to us, for we did not
seek it in the days of Saul."
4 Then all the assembly said
that they would do so, for the
thing was right in the eyes of all
the people.
5 [r]So David assembled all Israel
together, from the Shihor of Egypt
even to the entrance of Hamath,
to bring the ark of God from Kiriath-jearim. 2 Sam. 6:1; 1 Kin. 8:65
6 And David and all Israel
went up to Baalah, *that is,* to Kiriath-jearim, which belongs to Judah, to bring up from there the
ark of God, the LORD who is enthroned *above* the cherubim,
where His name is called.
7 And they [t]carried the ark of
God on a new cart from the house
of Abinadab, and Uzza and Ahio
drove the cart. *caused to ride*
8 And David and all Israel
were celebrating before God with
all *their* might, [r]even with songs
and with lyres, harps, tambourines, cymbals, and with trumpets. 1 Chr. 15:16
9 When they came to the
threshing floor of Chidon, Uzza
put out his hand to hold the ark,
because the oxen nearly upset *it.*
10 And the anger of the LORD
burned against Uzza, so He struck
him down [r]because he put out his
hand to the ark; and he died there
before God. 1 Chr. 15:13, 15
11 Then David became angry
because of the LORD's outburst
against Uzza; and he called that
place [3]Perez-uzza to this day.
12 And David was afraid of God
that day, saying, "How can I bring
the ark of God *home* to me?"
13 So David did not take the ark
with him to the city of David, but
took it aside [r]to the house of Obed-
edom the Gittite. 2 Chr. 15:25
14 Thus the ark of God remained with the family of Obed-
edom in his house three months;
and the LORD blessed the family of
Obed-edom with all that he had.

CHAPTER 14

[r]NOW Hiram king of Tyre sent
messengers to David with cedar
trees, masons, and carpenters, to
build a house for him. 2 Sam. 5:11
2 And David realized that the
LORD had established him as king
over Israel, *and* that his kingdom
was highly exalted, for the sake of
His people Israel.
3 Then David took more wives
at Jerusalem, and David [t]became
the father of more sons and
daughters. *begot*
4 [r]And these are the names of
the children [t]born *to him* in Jerusalem: Shammua, Shobab, Nathan,
Solomon, 1 Chr. 3:5-8 • *were to*
5 Ibhar, Elishua, Elpelet,
6 Nogah, Nepheg, Japhia,
7 Elishama, Beeliada and E-
liphelet.
8 When the Philistines heard
that David had been anointed king
over all Israel, all the Philistines

[3]I.e., the breakthrough of Uzza

went up in search of David; and David heard of it and went out against them.

9 Now the Philistines had come and [r]made a raid in the valley of Rephaim. 1 Chr. 11:15; 14:13

10 And David inquired of God, saying, "Shall I go up against the Philistines? And wilt Thou give them into my hand?" Then the LORD said to him, "Go up, for I will give them into your hand."

11 So they came up to Baal-perazim, and David [t]defeated them there; and David said, "God has broken through my enemies by my hand, like the breakthrough of waters." Therefore they named that place [4]Baal-perazim. *smote*

12 And they abandoned their gods there; so David gave the order and they were burned with fire.

13 And the Philistines made yet another raid in the valley.

14 And David inquired again of God, and God said to him, "You shall not go up after them; circle around behind them, and come at them in front of the balsam trees.

15 "And it shall be when you hear the sound of marching in the tops of the balsam trees, then you shall go out to battle, for God will have gone out before you to strike the army of the Philistines."

16 And David did just as God had commanded him, and they struck down the army of the Philistines from Gibeon even as far as Gezer.

17 Then the fame of David went out into all the lands; and [r]the LORD brought the fear of him on all the nations. Ex. 15:14-16

CHAPTER 15

NOW *David* built houses for himself in the city of David; and he prepared a place for the ark of God, and pitched a tent for it.

2 Then David said, "No [r]one is to carry the ark of God but the Levites; for the LORD chose them to carry the ark of God, and to minister to Him forever." Num. 4:15

3 And [r]David assembled all Israel at Jerusalem, to bring up the ark of the LORD to its place, which he had prepared for it. 1 Kin. 8:1

4 And David gathered together the sons of Aaron, and [r]the Levites: 1 Chr. 6:16-30; 12:26

5 of the sons of Kohath, Uriel the chief, and 120 of his relatives;

6 of the sons of Merari, Asaiah the chief, and 220 of his relatives;

7 of the sons of Gershom, Joel the chief, and 130 of his relatives;

8 of the sons of Elizaphan, Shemaiah the chief, and 200 of his relatives;

9 of the sons of Hebron, Eliel the chief, and 80 of his relatives;

10 of the sons of Uzziel, Amminadab the chief, and 112 of his relatives.

11 Then David called for Zadok and Abiathar the priests, and for the Levites, for Uriel, Asaiah, Joel, Shemaiah, Eliel, and Amminadab,

12 and said to them, "You are the heads of the fathers' *households* of the Levites; [r]consecrate yourselves both you and your relatives, that you may bring up the ark of the LORD God of Israel,

[4] I.e., the master of breakthrough

to *the place* that I have prepared
for it. Ex. 19:14, 15; 2 Chr. 35:6
13 "Because[r] you did not *carry it*
at the first, the LORD our God
made an outburst on us, for we
did not seek Him according to the
ordinance." 2 Sam. 6:3; 1 Chr. 13:7
14 [r]So the priests and the Levites
consecrated themselves to bring
up the ark of the LORD God of Israel. 1 Chr. 15:12
15 And the sons of the Levites
carried the ark of God on their
shoulders, with the poles thereon
as Moses had commanded according to the word of the LORD.
16 Then David spoke to the
chiefs of the Levites [r]to appoint
their relatives the singers, with instruments of music, harps, lyres,
loud-sounding cymbals, to raise
sounds of joy. 1 Chr. 13:8; 25:1
17 So[r] the Levites appointed Heman the son of Joel, and from his
relatives, Asaph the son of Berechiah; and from the sons of Merari
their relatives, Ethan the son of
Kushaiah, 1 Chr. 25:1
18 and with them their relatives
of the second rank, Zechariah,
Ben, Jaaziel, Shemiramoth, Jehiel,
Unni, Eliab, Benaiah, Maaseiah,
Mattithiah, Eliphelehu, Mikneiah,
Obed-edom, and Jeiel, the gatekeepers.
19 So the singers, Heman,
Asaph, and Ethan *were appointed*
to sound aloud cymbals of bronze;
20 and Zechariah, Aziel, Shemiramoth, Jehiel, Unni, Eliab, Maaseiah, and Benaiah, with harps
tuned to alamoth;
21 and Mattithiah, Eliphelehu,
Mikneiah, Obed-edom, Jeiel, and
Azaziah, to lead with[a] lyres tuned
to the sheminith. *octave harps*
22 And Chenaniah, chief of the
Levites, was *in charge of* the singing; he gave instruction in singing
because he was skillful.
23 And Berechiah and Elkanah
were gatekeepers for the ark.
24 And Shebaniah, Joshaphat,
Nethanel, Amasai, Zechariah, Benaiah, and Eliezer, the priests,
blew the trumpets before the ark
of God. Obed-edom and Jehiah
also *were* gatekeepers for the ark.
25 So *it was* David, with the elders of Israel and the captains
over thousands, who went to
bring up the ark of the covenant
of the LORD from [r]the house of
Obed-edom with joy. 1 Chr. 13:13
26 And it came about because
God was helping the Levites who
were carrying the ark of the covenant of the LORD, that they sacrificed seven bulls and seven rams.
27 Now David was clothed with
a robe of fine linen with all the Levites who were carrying the ark,
and the singers and Chenaniah the
leader of the singing *with* the
singers. [r]David also wore an ephod
of linen. 2 Sam. 6:14
28 Thus all Israel brought up the
ark of the covenant of the LORD
with shouting, and with sound of
the horn, with trumpets, with
loud-sounding cymbals, with
harps and lyres.
29 And it happened when the
ark of the covenant of the LORD
came to the city of David, that Michal the daughter of Saul looked
out of the window, and saw King
David leaping and making merry;
and she despised him in her heart.

CHAPTER 16

AND they brought in the ark of
God and placed it inside the tent
which David had pitched for it,
and they offered burnt offerings
and peace offerings before God.
2 When David had finished offering the burnt offering and the
peace offerings, he blessed the
people in the name of the LORD.
3 And he distributed to everyone of Israel, both man and
woman, to everyone a loaf of
bread and a portion *of meat* and a
raisin cake.
4 And he appointed some of
the Levites *as* ministers before the
ark of the LORD, even to celebrate
and to thank and praise the LORD
God of Israel:
5 Asaph the chief, and second
to him Zechariah, *then* Jeiel, Shemiramoth, Jehiel, Mattithiah,
Eliab, Benaiah, Obed-edom, and
Jeiel, with musical instruments,
harps, lyres; also Asaph *played*
loud-sounding cymbals,
6 and Benaiah and Jahaziel the
priests *blew* trumpets continually
before the ark of the covenant of
God.
7 Then on that day David first
assigned Asaph and his relatives
to give thanks to the LORD.

8 Oh give thanks to the LORD,
call upon His name;
Make known His deeds
among the peoples.
9 Sing to Him, sing praises to
Him;
[5]Speak of all His wonders.
10 Glory in His holy name;
Let the heart of those who
seek the LORD be glad.
11 Seek the LORD and His
strength;
Seek His face continually.
12 Remember His wonderful
deeds which He has
done,
His marvels and the judg-
ments from His mouth,
13 O seed of Israel His servant,
Sons of Jacob, His chosen
ones!
14 He is the LORD our God;
[r]His judgments are in all the
earth. Ps. 48:10
15 Remember His covenant
forever,
The word which He com-
manded to a thousand
generations,
16 *The covenant* which He
made with Abraham,
And His oath to Isaac.
17 [r]He also confirmed it to Jacob for a statute,
To Israel as an everlasting
covenant, Gen. 35:11, 12
18 Saying, "To[r] you I will give
the land of Canaan,
As the portion of your inheritance." Gen. 13:15
19 [r]When they were only a few
in number,
Very few, and strangers in
it, Gen. 34:30; Deut. 7:7
20 And they wandered about
from nation to nation,
And from *one* kingdom to
another people,
21 He permitted no man to oppress them,
And He reproved kings for
their sakes, *saying,*
22 "Do not touch My anointed
ones,

[5]Or, *Meditate on*

And [r]do My prophets no
harm." Gen. 20:7
23 [r]Sing to the LORD, all the
earth;
Proclaim good tidings of
His salvation from day to
day. Ps. 96:1-13
24 Tell of His glory among the
nations,
His wonderful deeds among
all the peoples.
25 For [r]great is the LORD, and
greatly to be praised;
He also is to be feared
above all gods. Ps. 144:3-6
26 For all the gods of the peoples are [a]idols,
But the LORD made the
heavens. *non-existent things*
27 Splendor and majesty are
before Him,
Strength and joy are in His
place.
28 Ascribe to the LORD, O families of the peoples,
Ascribe to the LORD glory
and strength.
29 Ascribe to the LORD the glory due His name;
[a]Bring an offering, and come
before Him;
Worship the LORD in holy
array. *a grain offering*
30 Tremble before Him, all the
earth;
Indeed, the world is firmly
established, it will not be
moved.
31 [r]Let the heavens be glad,
and let the earth rejoice;
And let them say among
the nations, "The LORD
reigns." Is. 44:23; 49:13
32 Let the sea roar, and [t]all it
contains;
Let the field exult, and all
that is in it. *its fulness*
33 Then the trees of the forest
will sing for joy before
the LORD;
For He is coming to judge
the earth.
34 [r]O give thanks to the LORD,
for *He is* good;
For His lovingkindness is
everlasting. 2 Chr. 5:13
35 Then say, "Save us, O God
of our salvation,
And gather us and deliver
us from the nations,
To give thanks to Thy holy
name,
And glory in Thy praise."
36 [r]Blessed be the LORD, the
God of Israel,
From everlasting even to
everlasting. Ps. 72:18
Then all the people said, "Amen,"
and praised the LORD.
37 So he left Asaph and his [t]rela-
tives there before the ark of the
covenant of the LORD, to minister
before the ark continually, as every day's work required; *brothers*
38 and Obed-edom with [t]his 68
relatives; Obed-edom, also the son
of Jeduthun, and Hosah as gatekeepers. *their brothers, 68*
39 And *he left* Zadok the priest
and his relatives the priests before
the tabernacle of the LORD in the
high place which *was* at Gibeon,
40 to offer burnt offerings to the
LORD on the altar of burnt offering
continually morning and evening,
[r]even according to all that is written in the law of the LORD, which
He commanded Israel. Ex. 29:38-42
41 And with them *were* [r]Heman
and Jeduthun, and the rest who

were chosen, who were designated by name, to give thanks to
the LORD, because His lovingkindness is everlasting. 1 Chr. 6:33
42 And with them *were* Heman
and Jeduthun *with* trumpets and
cymbals for those who should
sound aloud, and *with* instruments *for* the songs of God, and
the sons of Jeduthun for the gate.
43 Then all the people departed
each to his house, and David returned to bless his household.

CHAPTER 17

AND it came about, when David
dwelt in his house, that David said
to Nathan the prophet, "Behold, I
am dwelling in a house of cedar,
but the ark of the covenant of the
LORD is under curtains."
2 Then Nathan said to David,
"Do all that is in your heart, for
God is with you."
3 And it came about the same
night, that the word of God came
to Nathan, saying,
4 "Go and tell David My servant, 'Thus says the LORD, "You[r]
shall not build a house for Me to
dwell in; 1 Chr. 28:2, 3
5 for I have not dwelt in a
house since the day that I brought
up Israel to this day, but I have
gone from tent to tent and from
one dwelling place *to another.*
6 "In all places where I have
walked with all Israel, have I spoken a word[r] with any of the judges
of Israel, whom I commanded to
shepherd My people, saying, 'Why
have you not built for Me a house
of cedar?' " ' 2 Sam. 7:7
7 "Now, therefore, thus shall
you say to My servant David,
'Thus says the LORD of hosts, "I
took you from the pasture, from
following the sheep, that you
should be leader over My people
Israel.
8 "And I have been with you
wherever you have gone, and
have cut off all your enemies from
before you; and I will make you a
name like the name of the great
ones who are in the earth.
9 "And I will appoint a place for
My people Israel, and will plant
them, that they may dwell in their
own place and be moved no more;
neither shall the wicked waste
them anymore as formerly,
10 even from the day that I
commanded judges *to be* over My
people Israel. And I will subdue
all your enemies. Moreover, I tell
you that the LORD will build a
house for you.
11 "And it shall come about
when your days are fulfilled that
you must go *to be* with your fathers, that I will set up *one of* your
[t]descendants after you, who shall
be of your sons; and I will establish his kingdom. *seed*
12 "He shall build for Me a
house, and I will establish his
throne forever.
13 "I[r] will be his father, and he
shall be My son; and I will not
take My lovingkindness away
from him, as I took it from him
who was before you. 2 Cor. 6:18
14 "But I will settle him in My
house and in My kingdom forever,
and his throne shall be established
forever." ' "
15 According to all these words

and according to all this vision, so Nathan spoke to David.

16 Then David the king went in and sat before the LORD and said, "Who[r] am I, O LORD God, and what is my house that Thou hast brought me this far? 2 Sam. 7:18

17 "And this was a small thing in Thine eyes, O God; but Thou hast spoken of Thy servant's house for a great while to come, and hast regarded me according to the standard of a man of high degree, O LORD God.

18 "What more can David still *say* to Thee concerning the honor *bestowed* on Thy servant? For Thou knowest Thy servant.

19 "O LORD, [r]for Thy servant's sake, and according to Thine own heart, Thou hast wrought all this greatness, to make known all these great things. 2 Sam. 7:21

20 "O LORD, there is none like Thee, neither is there any God besides Thee, according to all that we have heard with our ears.

21 "And what one nation in the earth is like Thy people Israel, whom God went to redeem for Himself *as* a people, to make Thee a name by great and terrible things, in driving out nations from before Thy people, whom Thou didst redeem out of Egypt?

22 "For[r] Thy people Israel Thou didst make Thine own people forever, and Thou, O LORD, didst become their God. Ex. 19:5, 6

23 "And now, O LORD, let the word that Thou hast spoken concerning Thy servant and concerning his house, be established forever, and do as Thou hast spoken.

24 "And let Thy name be established and magnified forever, saying, 'The LORD of hosts is the God of Israel, *even* a God to Israel; and the house of David Thy servant is established before Thee.'

25 "For Thou, O my God, hast revealed to Thy servant that Thou wilt build for him a house; therefore Thy servant hath found *courage* to pray before Thee.

26 "And now, O LORD, Thou art God, and hast [t]promised this good thing to Thy servant. *said*

27 "And now it hath pleased Thee to bless the house of Thy servant, that it may [t]continue forever before Thee; for Thou, O LORD, hast blessed, and it is blessed forever." *be*

CHAPTER 18

NOW after this [r]it came about that David [t]defeated the Philistines and subdued them and took Gath and its towns from the hand of the Philistines. 2 Sam. 8:1-18 • *smote*

2 And he defeated Moab, and the Moabites became servants to David, bringing tribute.

3 David also defeated Hadadezer king of Zobah *as far as* Hamath, as he went to establish his [t]rule to the Euphrates River. *hand*

4 And David took from him 1,000 chariots and 7,000 horsemen and 20,000 foot soldiers, and David hamstrung all the chariot horses, but reserved *enough* of them for 100 chariots.

5 When the Arameans of Damascus came to help Hadadezer king of Zobah, David [t]killed 22,000 men of the Arameans. *smote*

6 Then David put *garrisons*

among the Arameans of Damascus; and the Arameans became
servants to David, bringing tribute. And the LORD helped David
wherever he went.
7 And David took the shields
of gold which were [t]carried by the
servants of Hadadezer, and
brought them to Jerusalem. *on*
8 Also from Tibhath and from
Cun, cities of Hadadezer, David
took a very large amount of
bronze, with which Solomon
made the bronze sea and the pillars and the bronze utensils.
9 Now when Tou king of Hamath heard that David had [t]de-
feated all the army of Hadadezer
king of Zobah, *smitten*
10 he sent Hadoram his son to
King David, to greet him and to
bless him, because he had fought
against Hadadezer and had defeated him; for Hadadezer had
been at war with Tou. And *Hadoram brought* all kinds of articles
of gold and silver and bronze.
11 King David also dedicated
these to the LORD with the silver
and the gold which he had carried
away from all the nations: from
Edom, Moab, the sons of Ammon,
the Philistines, and from Amalek.
12 Moreover Abishai the son of
Zeruiah [t]defeated 18,000 Edomites
in the Valley of Salt. *smote*
13 Then he put garrisons in
Edom, and all the Edomites became servants to David. And the
LORD helped David wherever he
went.
14 So David reigned over all Israel; and he [t]administered justice
and righteousness for all his people. *was doing*
15 And [r]Joab the son of Zeruiah
was over the army, and Jehoshaphat the son of Ahilud *was* recorder; 1 Chr. 11:6
16 and Zadok the son of Ahitub
and Abimelech the son of Abiathar *were* priests, and Shavsha
was secretary;
17 and Benaiah the son of Jehoiada *was* over the Cherethites
and the Pelethites, and the sons of
David *were* chiefs at the king's
side.

CHAPTER 19

NOW it came about after this,
that Nahash the king of the sons
of Ammon died, and his son became king in his place.
2 Then David said, "I will show
kindness to Hanun the son of Nahash, because his father showed
kindness to me." So David sent
messengers to console him concerning his father. And David's
servants came into the land of the
sons of Ammon to Hanun, to console him.
3 But the princes of the sons of
Ammon said to Hanun, "Do you
think that David is honoring your
father, in that he has sent comforters to you? Have not his servants come to you to search and
to overthrow and to spy out the
land?"
4 So Hanun took David's servants and shaved them, and cut
off their garments in the middle as
far as their hips, and sent them
away.
5 Then *certain persons* went
and told David about the men.
And he sent to meet them, for the

men were greatly humiliated. And
the king said, “Stay[t] at Jericho until your beards grow, and *then* return.” *Return to*
6 When the sons of Ammon
saw that they had made themselves odious to David, Hanun
and the sons of Ammon sent 1,000
talents of silver to hire for themselves chariots and horsemen
from Mesopotamia, from Aram-
maacah, and from Zobah.
7 So they hired for themselves
32,000 chariots, and the king of
Maacah and his people, who came
and camped before [r]Medeba. And
the sons of Ammon gathered together from their cities and came
to battle. Num. 21:30; Josh. 13:9, 16
8 When David heard *of it,* he
sent Joab and all the army, the
mighty men.
9 And the sons of Ammon
came out and drew up in battle array at the entrance of the city, and
the kings who had come were by
themselves in the field.
10 Now when Joab saw that the
[t]battle was set against him in front
and in the rear, he selected from
all the choice men of Israel and
they arrayed themselves against
the Arameans. *the face of the battle*
11 But the remainder of the people he placed in the hand of Abshai his brother; and they arrayed
themselves against the sons of
Ammon.
12 And he said, “If the Arameans are too strong for me, then
you shall help me; but if the sons
of Ammon are too strong for you,
then I will help you.
13 “Be strong, and let us show
ourselves courageous for the sake
of our people and for the cities of
our God; and may the LORD do
what is good in His sight.”
14 So Joab and the people who
were with him drew near to the
battle against the Arameans, and
they fled before him.
15 When the sons of Ammon
saw that the Arameans fled, they
also fled before Abshai his
brother, and entered the city.
Then Joab came to Jerusalem.
16 When the Arameans saw
that they had been defeated by Israel, they sent messengers, and
brought out the Arameans who
were beyond the [6]River, with Shophach the commander of the army
of Hadadezer[t] leading them. *before*
17 When it was told David, he
gathered all Israel together and
crossed the Jordan, and came
upon them and drew up in formation against them. And when David drew up in battle array against
the Arameans, they fought
against him.
18 And the Arameans fled before Israel, and David killed of the
Arameans 7,000 charioteers and
40,000 foot soldiers, and put to
death Shophach the commander
of the army.
19 So when the servants of Hadadezer saw that they were defeated by Israel, they made peace
with David and served him. Thus
the Arameans were not willing to
help the sons of Ammon anymore.

CHAPTER 20

THEN it happened in the spring,
at the time when kings go out *to*
battle, that Joab led out the army

[6] I.e., Euphrates

and ravaged the land of the sons
of Ammon, and came and besieged Rabbah. But David stayed
at Jerusalem. And Joab struck
Rabbah and overthrew it.
2 [r]And David took the crown of
their king from his head, and he
found it to weigh a talent of gold,
and there was a precious stone in
it; and it was placed on David's
head. And he brought out the
spoil of the city, a very great
amount. 2 Sam. 12:30, 31
3 And he brought out the peo-
ple who *were* in it, [r]and cut *them*
with saws and with sharp instruments and with axes. And thus
David did to all the cities of the
sons of Ammon. Then David and
all the people returned *to* Jerusalem. 2 Sam. 12:31
4 Now it came about after this,
that war [t]broke out at Gezer with
the Philistines; then Sibbecai the
Hushathite [t]killed Sippai, one of
the descendants of the giants, and
they were subdued. *stood up • smote*
5 And there was war with the
Philistines again, and Elhanan the
son of Jair [t]killed Lahmi the
brother of Goliath the Gittite, the
[r]shaft of whose spear *was* like a
weaver's beam. *smote* • 1 Chr. 11:23
6 And again there was war at
Gath, where there was a man of
great stature who had twenty-four
fingers and toes, six *fingers on
each hand* and six *toes on each
foot;* and he also was descended
from the giants.
7 And when he taunted Israel,
Jonathan the son of Shimea, David's brother, [t]killed him. *smote*
8 These were descended from
the giants in Gath, and they fell by
the hand of David and by the hand
of his servants.

CHAPTER 21

[r]THEN Satan stood up against Israel and moved David to number
Israel. 2 Sam. 24:1-25
2 So David said to Joab and to
the princes of the people, "Go,
number Israel from Beersheba
even to Dan, and bring me *word*
that I may know their number."
3 And Joab said, "May the
LORD add to His people a hundred
times as many as they are! But,
my lord the king, are they not all
my lord's servants? Why does my
lord seek this thing? Why should
he be a cause of guilt to Israel?"
4 Nevertheless, the king's
word prevailed against Joab.
Therefore, Joab departed and
went throughout all Israel, and
came to Jerusalem.
5 And Joab gave the [t]number of
the [t]census of all the people to David. And all Israel *were* 1,100,000
men who drew the sword; and Judah *was* 470,000 men who drew
the sword. *muster • numbering*
6 But he did not [t]number Levi
and Benjamin among them, for
the king's [t]command was abhorrent to Joab. *muster • word*
7 And [t]God was displeased
with this thing, so He struck Israel. *it was evil in the sight of God*
8 And David said to God, "I
have sinned greatly, in that I have
done this thing. [r]But now, please
take away the iniquity of Thy servant, for I have done very foolishly." 2 Sam. 12:13

9 And the LORD spoke to [r]Gad,
David's seer, saying, 2 Sam. 24:11
10 "Go and speak to David, saying, 'Thus says the LORD, "I [t]offer
you three things; choose for yourself one of them, that I may do *it*
to you." ' " *stretch out to*
11 So Gad came to David and
said to him, "Thus says the LORD,
'Take for yourself
12 [r]either three years of famine,
or three months to be swept away
before your foes, while the sword
of your enemies overtakes *you*, or
else three days of the sword of the
LORD, even pestilence in the land,
and the angel of the LORD destroying throughout all the territory of
Israel.' Now, therefore, consider
what answer I shall return to Him
who sent me." 2 Sam. 24:13
13 And David said to Gad, "I am
in great distress; please let me fall
into the hand of the LORD, for His
mercies are very great. But do not
let me fall into the hand of man."
14 So the LORD sent a pestilence
on Israel; 70,000 men of Israel fell.
15 And God sent an angel to Jerusalem to destroy it; but as he
was about to destroy *it*, the LORD
saw and was sorry over the calamity, and said to the destroying
angel, "It is enough; now relax
your hand." And the angel of the
LORD was standing by the threshing floor of Ornan the Jebusite.
16 Then David lifted up his eyes
and saw the angel of the LORD
standing between earth and
heaven, with his drawn sword in
his hand stretched out over Jerusalem. Then David and the elders,
[r]covered with sackcloth, fell on
their faces. 1 Kin. 21:27

17 And David said to God, "Is it
not I who [t]commanded to count
the people? Indeed, I am the one
who has sinned and done very
wickedly, [r]but these sheep, what
have they done? O LORD my God,
please let Thy hand be against me
and my father's household, but
not against Thy people that they
should be plagued." *said* • Ps. 74:1
18 Then the angel of the LORD
commanded Gad to say to David,
that David should go up and build
an altar to the LORD on the threshing floor of Ornan the Jebusite.
19 So David went up at the
word of Gad, which he spoke in
the name of the LORD.
20 Now Ornan turned back and
saw the angel, and his four sons
who were with him hid themselves. And Ornan was threshing
wheat.
21 And as David came to Ornan,
Ornan looked and saw David, and
went out from the threshing floor,
and prostrated himself [t]before David with his face to the ground. *to*
22 Then David said to Ornan,
"Give me the [t]site of *this* threshing
floor, that I may build on it an altar to the LORD; for the full price
you shall give it to me, that the
plague may be restrained from the
people." *place*
23 And Ornan said to David,
"Take *it* for yourself; and let my
lord the king do what is good in
his sight. See, I will give the oxen
for burnt offerings and the threshing sledges for wood and the
wheat for the grain offering; I will
give *it* all."
24 But King David said to Ornan, "No, but I will surely buy *it*

for the full price; for I will not take
what is yours for the LORD, or offer a burnt offering [t]which costs
me nothing." *gratuitously*
25 So [r]David gave Ornan 600
shekels of gold by weight for the
[t]site. 2 Sam. 24:24 • *place*
26 Then David built an altar to
the LORD there, and offered burnt
offerings and peace offerings. And
he called to the LORD and He answered him with fire from heaven
on the altar of burnt offering.
27 And the LORD commanded
the angel, and he put his sword
back in its sheath.
28 At that time, when David
saw that the LORD had answered
him on the threshing floor of Ornan the Jebusite, he offered sacrifice there.
29 For the tabernacle of the
LORD, which Moses had made in
the wilderness, and the altar of
burnt offering *were* in the high
place at Gibeon at that time.
30 But David could not go before it to inquire of God, for he
was terrified by the sword of the
angel of the LORD.

CHAPTER 22

THEN David said, "This[r] is the
house of the LORD God, and this is
the altar of burnt offering for Israel." 1 Chr. 21:18-28; 2 Chr. 3:1
2 So David [t]gave orders to
gather the foreigners who were in
the land of Israel, and he set
stonecutters to hew out stones to
build the house of God. *said to*
3 And David prepared large
quantities of iron [t]to make the
nails for the doors of the gates and
for the clamps, and more bronze
than could be weighed; *for*
4 and timbers of cedar logs beyond number, for the Sidonians
and Tyrians brought large quantities of cedar timber to David.
5 And David said, "My son
Solomon is young and inexperienced, and the house that is to be
built for the LORD shall be exceedingly magnificent, famous and
glorious throughout all lands.
Therefore I will make preparation
for it." So David made ample
preparations before his death.
6 Then [r]he called for his son
Solomon, and charged him to
build a house for the LORD God of
Israel. 1 Kin. 2:1
7 And David said to Solomon,
"My son, [t]I had intended to build a
house to the name of the LORD my
God. *as for me, it was in my heart*
8 "But the word of the LORD
came to me, saying, 'You[r] have
shed much blood, and have [t]waged
great wars; you shall not build a
house to My name, because you
have shed *so* much blood on the
earth before Me. 1 Chr. 28:3 • *made*
9 'Behold, a son shall be born to
you, who shall be a man of rest;
and [r]I will give him rest from all
his enemies on every side; for his
name shall be [7]Solomon, and I will
give peace and quiet to Israel in
his days. 1 Kin. 4:20, 25
10 'He[r] shall build a house for My
name, and he shall be My son, and
I will be his father; and I will establish the throne of his kingdom
over Israel forever.' 2 Sam. 7:13, 14
11 "Now, my son, [r]the LORD be
with you that you may be successful, and build the house of the

[7]I.e., peaceful

LORD your God just as He has spoken concerning you. 1 Chr. 22:16
12 "Only [r]the LORD give you discretion and understanding, and
give you charge over Israel, so
that you may keep the law of the
LORD your God. 1 Kin. 3:9-12
13 "Then [r]you shall prosper, if
you are careful to observe the
statutes and the ordinances which
the LORD commanded Moses concerning Israel. [r]Be strong and courageous, do not fear nor be dismayed. 1 Chr. 28:7 • Josh. 1:6-9
14 "Now behold, with great pains
I have prepared for the house of
the LORD 100,000 talents of gold
and 1,000,000 talents of silver, and
bronze and iron beyond weight,
for [t]they are in great quantity; also
timber and stone I have prepared,
and you may add to them. *it is*
15 "Moreover, there are many
workmen with you, stonecutters
and masons of stone and carpenters, and all men who are skillful
in every kind of work.
16 "Of the gold, the silver and
the bronze and the iron, there is
no limit. Arise and work, and may
the LORD be with you."
17 [r]David also commanded all
the leaders of Israel to help his
son Solomon, *saying,* 1 Chr. 28:1-6
18 "Is not the LORD your God
with you? And [r]has He not given
you rest on every side? For He has
given the inhabitants of the land
into my hand, and the land is subdued before the LORD and before
His people. 1 Chr. 22:9; 23:25
19 "Now [r]set your heart and your
soul to seek the LORD your God;
arise, therefore, and build the
sanctuary of the LORD God, so
that you may bring the ark of the
covenant of the LORD, and the
holy vessels of God into the house
that is to be built for the name of
the LORD." 1 Chr. 28:9

CHAPTER 23

[r]NOW when David reached old
age, he made his son Solomon
king over Israel. 1 Chr. 29:28
2 And he gathered together all
the leaders of Israel with the
priests and the Levites.
3 And the Levites were numbered from thirty years old and
upward, and their number by [t]cen-
sus of men was 38,000. *their heads*
4 Of these, 24,000 were [r]to
oversee the work of the house of
the LORD; and 6,000 *were* [r]officers
and judges, Ezra 3:8, 9 • 1 Chr. 26:29
5 and 4,000 *were* gatekeepers,
and 4,000 *were* praising the LORD
with the instruments which [t]David
made for giving praise. *I made*
6 And David divided them into
divisions [r]according to the sons of
Levi: Gershon, Kohath, and Merari. 1 Chr. 6:1
7 Of the Gershonites *were* Ladan and Shimei.
8 The sons of Ladan *were* Jehiel the first and Zetham and Joel,
three.
9 The sons of Shimei *were*
Shelomoth and Haziel and Haran,
three. These were the heads of the
fathers' *households* of Ladan.
10 And the sons of Shimei *were*
Jahath, Zina, Jeush, and Beriah.
These four *were* the sons of
Shimei.
11 And Jahath was the first, and
Zizah the second; but Jeush and

Beriah did not have many sons, so they became a father's household, one [t]class. *mustering*

12 The sons of Kohath were four: Amram, Izhar, Hebron and Uzziel.

13 [r]The sons of Amram were Aaron and Moses. And [r]Aaron was set apart to sanctify him as most holy, he and his sons forever, to burn incense before the LORD, to minister to Him and to bless in His name forever. Ex. 6:20 • Ex. 28:1

14 But *as for* [r]Moses the man of God, his sons were named among the tribe of Levi. Deut. 33:1

15 The sons of Moses *were* Gershom and Eliezer.

16 The [t]son of Gershom *was* Shebuel the chief. *sons*

17 And the son of Eliezer was Rehabiah the chief; and Eliezer had no other sons, but the sons of Rehabiah were very many.

18 The [t]son of Izhar was Shelomith the chief. *sons*

19 The sons of Hebron *were* Jeriah the first, Amariah the second, Jahaziel the third and Jekameam the fourth.

20 The sons of Uzziel *were* Micah the first and Isshiah the second.

21 The sons of Merari were Mahli and Mushi. The sons of Mahli *were* Eleazar and Kish.

22 And Eleazar died and had no sons, but daughters only, so their brothers, the sons of Kish, took them *as wives.*

23 The sons of Mushi *were* three: Mahli, Eder, and Jeremoth.

24 These were the sons of Levi according to their fathers' households, *even* the heads of the fathers' *households* of those of them who were [t]counted, in the number of names by their census, doing the work for the service of the house of the LORD, from twenty years old and upward. *mustered*

25 For David said, "The LORD God of Israel [r]has given rest to His people, and He dwells in Jerusalem forever. 1 Chr. 22:18

26 "And also, [r]the Levites will no longer need to carry the tabernacle and all its utensils for its service." Num. 4:5, 15; 7:9; Deut. 10:8

27 For by the last words of David the sons of Levi *were* numbered, from twenty years old and upward.

28 For their office is [t]to assist the sons of Aaron with the service of the house of the LORD, in the courts and in the chambers and in the purifying of all holy things, even the work of the service of the house of God, *at the hand of*

29 [r]and with the showbread, and [r]the fine flour for a grain offering, and unleavened wafers, or what is baked in the pan, or what is well-mixed, and all measures of volume and size. Lev. 24:5-9 • Lev. 6:20

30 And they are to stand every morning to thank and to praise the LORD, and likewise at evening,

31 and to offer all burnt offerings to the LORD, [r]on the sabbaths, the new moons and the fixed festivals in the number *set* by the ordinance concerning them, continually before the LORD. Is. 1:13, 14

32 Thus [r]they are to keep charge of the tent of meeting, and charge of the holy place, and charge of the sons of Aaron their [t]relatives,

for the service of the house of the
LORD. Num. 1:53 · *brothers*

CHAPTER 24

NOW the divisions of the [t]de-
scendants of Aaron *were these:*
the sons of Aaron *were* Nadab,
Abihu, Eleazar, and Ithamar. *sons*
2 But Nadab and Abihu died
before their father and had no
[a]sons. So Eleazar and Ithamar
served as priests. *children*
3 And David, with Zadok of
the sons of Eleazar and Ahimelech of the sons of Ithamar, divided them according to their offices for their ministry.
4 Since more chief men were
found from the [t]descendants of Eleazar than the [t]descendants of
Ithamar, they divided them thus:
there were sixteen heads of fathers' households of the [t]descend-
ants of Eleazar, and eight of the
[t]descendants of Ithamar according
to their fathers' households. *sons*
5 Thus they were divided by
lot, the one as the other; for they
were officers of the sanctuary and
officers of God, both from the [t]de-
scendants of Eleazar and the [t]de-
scendants of Ithamar. *sons*
6 And Shemaiah, the son of
Nethanel the scribe, from the Levites, recorded them in the presence of the king, the princes, Zadok the priest, [r]Ahimelech the son
of Abiathar, and the heads of the
fathers' *households* of the priests
and of the Levites; one father's
household taken for Eleazar and
one taken for Ithamar. 1 Chr. 18:16
7 Now the first lot came out
for Jehoiarib, the second for Jedaiah,
8 the third for Harim, the
fourth for Seorim,
9 the fifth for Malchijah, the
sixth for Mijamin,
10 the seventh for Hakkoz, the
eighth for [r]Abijah, Neh. 12:4
11 the ninth for Jeshua, the
tenth for Shecaniah,
12 the eleventh for Eliashib, the
twelfth for Jakim,
13 the thirteenth for Huppah,
the fourteenth for Jeshebeab,
14 the fifteenth for Bilgah, the
sixteenth for Immer,
15 the seventeenth for Hezir,
the eighteenth for Happizzez,
16 the nineteenth for Pethahiah,
the twentieth for Jehezkel,
17 the twenty-first for Jachin,
the twenty-second for Gamul,
18 the twenty-third for Delaiah,
the twenty-fourth for Maaziah.
19 [r]These were their offices for
their ministry, when *they* came in
to the house of the LORD according to the ordinance *given* to them
through Aaron their father, just as
the LORD God of Israel had commanded him. 1 Chr. 9:25
20 Now for the rest of the sons
of Levi: of the sons of Amram,
Shubael; of the sons of Shubael,
Jehdeiah.
21 Of Rehabiah: of the sons of
Rehabiah, Isshiah the first.
22 Of the Izharites, Shelomoth;
of the sons of Shelomoth, Jahath.
23 And the sons [r]*of Hebron:* Jeriah *the first,* Amariah the second,
Jahaziel the third, Jekameam the
fourth. 1 Chr. 23:19
24 *Of* the sons of Uzziel, Micah;
of the sons of Micah, Shamir.

25 The brother of Micah, Isshiah; of the sons of Isshiah, Zechariah.
26 The sons of Merari, Mahli
and Mushi; the sons of Jaaziah,
Beno.
27 The sons of Merari: by Jaaziah *were* Beno, Shoham, Zaccur,
and Ibri.
28 By Mahli: Eleazar, who had
no sons.
29 By Kish: the sons of Kish, Jerahmeel.
30 And the sons of Mushi:
Mahli, Eder, and Jerimoth. These
were the sons of the Levites according to their fathers' households.
31 [r]These also cast lots just as
their [t]relatives the sons of Aaron in
the presence of David the king,
Zadok, Ahimelech, and the heads
of the fathers' *households* of the
priests and of the Levites—the
head of fathers' *households* as
well as those of his younger
brother. 1 Chr. 24:5, 6 • *brothers*

CHAPTER 25

MOREOVER, David and the
commanders of the army set apart
for the service *some* of the sons of
[r]Asaph and of Heman and of Jeduthun, who *were* to prophesy with
lyres, harps, and cymbals; and the
number of those who performed
their service was: 1 Chr. 6:33, 39
2 Of the sons of Asaph: Zaccur, Joseph, Nethaniah, and Asha-
relah; the sons of Asaph *were* under the [t]direction of Asaph, who
prophesied under the [t]direction of
the king. *hand*(s)
3 Of Jeduthun, the sons of Jeduthun: Gedaliah, Zeri, Jeshaiah,
Shimei, Hashabiah, and Mattithiah, six, under the direction of
their father Jeduthun with the
harp, who prophesied in giving
thanks and praising the LORD.
4 Of Heman, the sons of Heman: Bukkiah, Mattaniah, Uzziel,
Shebuel and Jerimoth, Hananiah,
Hanani, Eliathah, Giddalti and Ro-
mamti-ezer, Joshbekashah, Mallo-
thi, Hothir, Mahazioth.
5 All these *were* the sons of
Heman the king's seer to exalt
him according to the words of
God, for God gave fourteen sons
and three daughters to Heman.
6 All these were under the [t]di-
rection of their father to sing in
the house of the LORD, with cymbals, harps and lyres, for the service of the house of God. Asaph,
Jeduthun and Heman *were* under
the direction of the king. *hands*
7 And their number who were
trained in singing to the LORD,
with their [8]relatives, all who were
skillful, *was* [r]288. 1 Chr. 23:5
8 And [r]they cast lots for their
duties, all alike, the small as well
as the great, the teacher *as well* as
the pupil. 1 Chr. 26:13
9 Now the first lot came out
for Asaph to Joseph, the second
for Gedaliah, he with his relatives
and sons *were* twelve;
10 the third to Zaccur, his sons
and his relatives, twelve;
11 the fourth to Izri, his sons
and his relatives, twelve;
12 the fifth to Nethaniah, his
sons and his relatives, twelve;

[8]Lit., *brothers*, and so throughout this context

13 the sixth to Bukkiah, his sons
and his relatives, twelve;
14 the seventh to Jesharelah, his
sons and his relatives, twelve;
15 the eighth to Jeshaiah, his
sons and his relatives, twelve;
16 the ninth to Mattaniah, his
sons and his relatives, twelve;
17 the tenth to Shimei, his sons
and his relatives, twelve;
18 the eleventh to Azarel, his
sons and his relatives, twelve;
19 the twelfth to Hashabiah, his
sons and his relatives, twelve;
20 for the thirteenth, Shubael,
his sons and his relatives, twelve;
21 for the fourteenth, Mattithiah, his sons and his relatives,
twelve;
22 for the fifteenth to Jeremoth,
his sons and his relatives, twelve;
23 for the sixteenth to Hananiah, his sons and his relatives,
twelve;
24 for the seventeenth to Joshbekashah, his sons and his relatives, twelve;
25 for the eighteenth to Hanani,
his sons and his relatives, twelve;
26 for the nineteenth to Mallo-
thi, his sons and his relatives,
twelve;
27 for the twentieth to Eliathah,
his sons and his relatives, twelve;
28 for the twenty-first to Hothir,
his sons and his relatives, twelve;
29 for the twenty-second to Giddalti, his sons and his relatives,
twelve;
30 for the twenty-third to Mahazioth, his sons and his relatives,
twelve;
31 for the twenty-fourth to Ro-
mamti-ezer, his sons and his relatives, twelve.

CHAPTER 26

FOR the divisions of the gatekeepers *there were* of the Korahites, Meshelemiah the son of
Kore, of the sons of Asaph.
2 And Meshelemiah had sons:
Zechariah the first-born, Jediael
the second, Zebadiah the third,
Jathniel the fourth,
3 Elam the fifth, Johanan the
sixth, Eliehoenai the seventh.
4 And Obed-edom had sons:
Shemaiah the first-born, Jehozabad the second, Joah the third, Sacar the fourth, Nethanel the fifth,
5 Ammiel the sixth, Issachar
the seventh, *and* Peullethai the
eighth; God had indeed blessed
him.
6 Also to his son Shemaiah
sons were born who ruled over
the house of their father, for they
were mighty men of valor.
7 The sons of Shemaiah *were*
Othni, Rephael, Obed, and Elzabad, whose brothers, Elihu and
Semachiah, were valiant men.
8 All these *were* of the sons of
Obed-edom; they and their sons
and their [t]relatives *were* able men
with strength for the service, 62
from Obed-edom. *brothers*
9 And Meshelemiah had sons
and relatives, 18 valiant men.
10 Also [r]Hosah, *one* of the sons
of Merari had sons: Shimri the
first (although he was not the
first-born, his father made him
first), 1 Chr. 16:38
11 Hilkiah the second, Tebaliah
the third, Zechariah the fourth; all
the sons and relatives of Hosah
were 13.
12 To these divisions of the

gatekeepers, the chief men, *were*
given duties like their relatives to
minister in the house of the LORD.
13 [r]And they cast lots, the small
and the great alike, according to
their fathers' households, for every gate. 1 Chr. 24:5, 31; 25:8
14 And the lot to the east fell to
Shelemiah. Then they cast lots *for*
his son Zechariah, a counselor
with insight, and his lot came out
to the north.
15 For Obed-edom *it fell* to the
south, and to his sons went the
storehouse.
16 For Shuppim and Hosah *it*
was to the west, by the gate of
Shallecheth, on the ascending
highway. Guard corresponded to
guard.
17 On the east there were six
Levites, on the north four daily, on
the south four daily, and at the
storehouse two by two.
18 At the [r][9]Parbar on the west
there were four at the highway
and two at the Parbar. 2 Kin. 23:11
19 These were the divisions of
the gatekeepers of the sons of Korah and of the sons of Merari.
20 [10]And the Levites, their relatives, had charge of the treasures
of the house of God, and of the
treasures of the dedicated gifts.
21 The sons of Ladan, the sons
of the Gershonites belonging to
Ladan, *namely,* the Jehielites,
were the heads of the fathers'
households, belonging to Ladan
the Gershonite.
22 The sons of Jehieli, Zetham
and Joel his brother, [t]had charge
of the treasures of the house of
the LORD. *were over*

[9]Possibly *court* or *colonnade*
[10]So Gr.; Heb., *As for the Levites, Ahijah had*

23 As for the Amramites, the Izharites, the Hebronites, and the
Uzzielites,
24 Shebuel the son of Gershom,
the son of Moses, was officer over
the treasures.
25 And his relatives by Eliezer
were Rehabiah his son, Jeshaiah
his son, Joram his son, Zichri his
son, and Shelomoth his son.
26 This Shelomoth and his relatives [t]had charge of all the treasures of the dedicated gifts, which
King David and the heads of the
fathers' *households,* the commanders of thousands and hundreds, and commanders of the
army, had dedicated. *were over*
27 They dedicated part of the
spoil won in battles to repair the
house of the LORD.
28 And all that Samuel the seer
had dedicated and Saul the son of
Kish, Abner the son of Ner and
Joab the son of Zeruiah, everyone
who had dedicated *anything, all*
of this was in the care of Shelomoth and his relatives.
29 As for the Izharites, Chenaniah and his sons [r]were *assigned* to
outside duties for Israel, as officers and judges. Neh. 11:16
30 As for the Hebronites, Hashabiah and his relatives, 1,700 capable men, had charge of the affairs of Israel west of the Jordan,
for all the work of the LORD and
the service of the king.
31 As for the Hebronites, Jeri-
jah the chief (these Hebronites
were investigated according to
their genealogies and fathers'
households, in the fortieth year of
David's reign, and men of outstanding capability were found
among them at Jazer of Gilead)

32 and his relatives, capable men, *were* 2,700 in number, heads of fathers' *households*. And King David made them overseers of the Reubenites, the Gadites and the half-tribe of the Manassites [r]concerning all the affairs of God and of the king. 2 Chr. 19:11

CHAPTER 27

NOW *this is* the enumeration of the sons of Israel, the heads of fathers' *households*, the commanders of thousands and of hundreds, and their officers who served the king in all the affairs of the divisions which came in and went out month by month throughout all the months of the year, each division *numbering* 24,000.

2 Jashobeam the son of Zabdiel [r][1]had charge of the first division for the first month; and in his division *were* 24,000. 2 Sam. 23:8-30

3 *He was* from the sons of Perez, *and was* chief of all the commanders of the army for the first month.

4 Dodai the Ahohite and his division had charge of the division for the second month, Mikloth *being* the chief officer; and in his division *were* 24,000.

5 The third commander of the army for the third month *was* Benaiah, the son of Jehoiada the priest, *as* chief; and in his division *were* 24,000.

6 This Benaiah *was* the mighty man of the thirty, and had charge of thirty; and over his division was Ammizabad his son.

7 The fourth for the fourth month *was* Asahel the brother of Joab, and Zebadiah his son after him; and in his division *were* 24,000.

8 The fifth for the fifth month *was* the commander Shamhuth the Izrahite; and in his division *were* 24,000.

9 The sixth for the sixth month *was* Ira the son of Ikkesh the Tekoite; and in his division *were* 24,000.

10 The seventh for the seventh month *was* Helez the Pelonite of the sons of Ephraim; and in his division *were* 24,000.

11 The eighth for the eighth month *was* Sibbecai the Hushathite of the Zerahites; and in his division *were* 24,000.

12 The ninth for the ninth month *was* Abiezer the Anathothite of the Benjamites; and in his division *were* 24,000.

13 The tenth for the tenth month *was* Maharai the Netophathite of the Zerahites; and in his division *were* 24,000.

14 The eleventh for the eleventh month *was* Benaiah the Pirathonite of the sons of Ephraim; and in his division *were* 24,000.

15 The twelfth for the twelfth month *was* Heldai the Netophathite of Othniel; and in his division *were* 24,000.

16 Now in charge of the tribes of Israel: chief officer for the Reubenites was Eliezer the son of Zichri; for the Simeonites, Shephatiah the son of Maacah;

17 for Levi, Hashabiah the son of Kemuel; for Aaron, Zadok;

18 for Judah, Elihu, *one* of David's brothers; for Issachar, Omri the son of Michael;

[1] Lit., *was over*, and so throughout the ch.

19 for Zebulun, Ishmaiah the
son of Obadiah; for Naphtali, Jeremoth the son of Azriel;
20 for the sons of Ephraim, Hoshea the son of Azaziah; for the
half-tribe of Manasseh, Joel the
son of Pedaiah;
21 for the half-tribe of Manasseh in Gilead, Iddo the son of
Zechariah; for Benjamin, Jaasiel
the son of Abner;
22 for Dan, Azarel the son of
Jeroham. [r]These *were* the princes
of the tribes of Israel. 1 Chr. 28:1
23 But David did not [t]count
those twenty years of age and under, because the LORD had said He
would multiply Israel as the stars
of heaven. *take their number from*
24 Joab the son of Zeruiah had
begun to count *them,* but did not
finish; and because of this, wrath
came upon Israel, and the number
was not included in the account of
the chronicles of King David.
25 Now Azmaveth the son of
Adiel had charge of the king's
storehouses. And Jonathan the
son of Uzziah had charge of the
storehouses in the country, in the
cities, in the villages, and in the
towers.
26 And Ezri the son of Chelub
had charge of the agricultural
workers who tilled the soil.
27 And Shimei the Ramathite
had charge of the vineyards; and
Zabdi the Shiphmite had charge
of the produce of the vineyards
stored in the wine cellars.
28 And Baal-hanan the Gederite
had charge of the olive and [r]syca-
more trees in the [12]Shephelah; and
Joash had charge of the stores of
oil. 1 Kin. 10:27; 2 Chr. 1:15

[12]Or, *lowlands*

29 And Shitrai the Sharonite
had charge of the cattle which
were grazing in Sharon; and Shaphat the son of Adlai had charge
of the cattle in the valleys.
30 And Obil the Ishmaelite had
charge of the camels; and Jehdeiah the Meronothite had charge of
the donkeys.
31 And Jaziz the Hagrite had
charge of the flocks. All these
were overseers of the property
which belonged to King David.
32 Also Jonathan, David's uncle, *was* a counselor, a man of understanding, and a scribe; and Jehiel the son of Hachmoni [t]tutored
the king's sons. *was with*
33 And Ahithophel was counselor to the king; and Hushai the
Archite was the king's friend.
34 And Jehoiada the son of Benaiah, and Abiathar succeeded
Ahithophel; and Joab was the
commander of the king's army.

CHAPTER 28

NOW [r]David assembled at Jerusalem all the officials of Israel, the
princes of the tribes, and the commanders of the divisions that
served the king, and the commanders of thousands, and the
commanders of hundreds, and the
overseers of all the property and
livestock belonging to the king
and his sons, with the officials and
the mighty men, even all the valiant men. 1 Chr. 23:2; 27:1-31
2 Then King David rose to his
feet and said, "Listen to me, my
brethren and my people; I [r]*had* [13]in-
tended to build a [14]permanent
home for the ark of the covenant

[13]Lit., *in my heart* [14]Lit., *house of rest*

of the LORD and for the footstool
of our God. So I had made preparations to build *it*. 1 Chr. 17:1, 2
3 "But God said to me, 'You
shall not build a house for My
name because you are a man of
war and have shed blood.'
4 "Yet, the LORD, the God of Israel, [r]chose me from all the house
of my father to be king over Israel
forever. For He has chosen Judah
to be a leader; and in the house of
Judah, my father's house, and
among the sons of my father He
took pleasure in me to make *me*
king over all Israel. 1 Sam. 16:6-13
5 "And of all my sons (for the
LORD has given me many sons),
He has chosen my son Solomon to
sit on the throne of the kingdom
of the LORD over Israel.
6 "And He said to me, 'Your son
Solomon is the one who shall
build My house and My courts; for
I have chosen him to be a son to
Me, and I will be a father to him.
7 'And I will establish his kingdom forever, if he resolutely performs My commandments and
My ordinances, as is done now.'
8 "So now, in the sight of all Israel, the assembly of the LORD,
and in the hearing of our God, observe and seek after all the commandments of the LORD your God
in order that you may possess the
good land and bequeath *it* to your
sons after you forever.
9 "As for you, my son Solomon,
know the God of your father, and
[r]serve Him with [a]a whole heart and
a willing [t]mind; for the LORD
searches all hearts, and understands every intent of the
thoughts. If you seek Him, He will
let you find Him; but if you forsake Him, He will reject you forever. 1 Kin. 8:61 • *the same* • *soul*
10 "Consider now, for the LORD
has chosen you to build a house
for the sanctuary; [r]be courageous
and act." 1 Chr. 22:13
11 Then David gave to his son
Solomon [r]the plan of [r]the porch *of
the temple,* its buildings, its storehouses, its upper rooms, its inner
rooms, and the room for the mercy seat; Ex. 25:40 • 1 Kin. 6:3
12 and the plan of all that he
had in [t]mind, for the courts of the
house of the LORD, and for all the
surrounding rooms, for the storehouses of the house of God, and
for the storehouses of the dedicated things; *the spirit with him*
13 also for [r]the divisions of the
priests and [r]the Levites and for all
the work of the service of the
house of the LORD and for all the
utensils of service in the house of
the LORD; 1 Chr. 24:1 • 1 Chr. 23:6
14 for the golden *utensils,* the
weight of gold for all utensils for
every kind of service; for the silver utensils, the weight *of silver*
for all utensils for every kind of
service;
15 and the weight *of gold* for
the [r]golden lampstands and their
golden lamps, with the weight of
each lampstand and its lamps; and
the weight of silver for the silver
lampstands, with the weight of
each lampstand and its lamps according to the use of each lampstand; Ex. 25:31-39
16 and the gold by weight for
the tables of showbread, for each
table; and silver for the silver tables;

17 and the forks, the basins, and the pitchers of pure gold; and for the golden bowls with the weight for each bowl; and for the silver bowls with the weight for each bowl;

18 and for the altar of incense refined gold by weight; and gold for the model of the chariot, *even* the cherubim, that spread out *their wings,* and covered the ark of the covenant of the LORD.

19 "All *this,*" *said David,* "the LORD made me understand in writing by His hand upon me, all the [t]details of this pattern." *works*

20 Then David said to his son Solomon, "Be[r] strong and courageous, and act; do not fear nor be dismayed, for the LORD God, my God, is with you. He will not fail you nor forsake you until all the work for the service of the house of the LORD is finished. 1 Chr. 22:13

21 "Now behold,[r] *there are* the divisions of the priests and the Levites for all the service of the house of God, and every willing man of any skill will be with you in all the work for all kinds of service. The officials also and all the people will be entirely at your command." 1 Chr. 28:13

CHAPTER 29

THEN King David said to the entire assembly, "My son Solomon, whom alone God has chosen, is still young and inexperienced and the work is great; for the temple is not for man, but for the LORD God.

2 "Now with all my ability I have provided for the house of my God the gold for the *things of* gold, and the silver for the *things of* silver, and the bronze for the *things of* bronze, the iron for the *things of* iron, and wood for the *things of* wood, onyx stones and inlaid *stones,* stones of antimony, and stones of various colors, and all kinds of precious stones, and alabaster in abundance.

3 "And moreover, in my delight in the house of my God, the treasure I have of gold and silver, I give to the house of my God, over and above all that I have already provided for the holy [15]temple,

4 *namely,* 3,000 talents of gold, of the gold of Ophir, and 7,000 talents of refined silver, to overlay the walls of the [t]buildings; *houses*

5 of gold for the *things of* gold, and of silver for the *things of* silver, that is, for all the work done by the craftsmen. Who then is willing [t]to consecrate himself this day to the LORD?" *to fill his hand*

6 Then the rulers of the fathers' *households,* and the princes of the tribes of Israel, and the commanders of thousands and of hundreds, with the overseers over the king's work, offered willingly;

7 and for the service for the house of God they gave 5,000 talents and 10,000[r] darics of gold, and 10,000 talents of silver, and 18,000 talents of brass, and 100,000 talents of iron. Ezra 2:69; Neh. 7:70

8 And whoever possessed *precious* stones gave them to the treasury of the house of the LORD, in care of Jehiel the Gershonite.

9 Then the people rejoiced because they had offered so willingly, for they made their offering to the LORD [r]with a whole heart,

[15] Lit., *house*

and King David also rejoiced greatly. 1 Kin. 8:61; 2 Cor. 9:7

10 So David blessed the LORD in the sight of all the assembly; and David said, "Blessed art Thou, O LORD God of Israel our father, forever and ever.

11 "Thine, O LORD, is the greatness and the power and the glory and the victory and the majesty, indeed everything that is in the heavens and the earth; Thine is the dominion, O LORD, and Thou dost exalt Thyself as head over all.

12 "Both [r]riches and honor *come* from Thee, and Thou dost rule over all, and [r]in Thy hand is power and might; and it lies in Thy hand to make great, and to strengthen everyone. 2 Chr. 1:12 • 2 Chr. 20:6

13 "Now therefore, our God, we thank Thee, and praise Thy glorious name.

14 "But who am I and who are my people that we should [t]be able to offer as generously as this? For all things come from Thee, and from Thy hand we have given Thee. *retain strength*

15 "For [r]we are sojourners before Thee, and tenants, as all our fathers were; [r]our days on the earth are like a shadow, and there is no hope. Lev. 25:23 • Job 14:2, 10-12

16 "O LORD our God, all this abundance that we have provided to build Thee a house for Thy holy name, it is from Thy hand, and all is Thine.

17 "Since I know, O my God, that [r]Thou triest the heart and delightest in uprightness, I, in the integrity of my heart, have willingly offered all these *things;* so now with joy I have seen Thy people, who are present here, make *their* offerings willingly to Thee. 1 Chr. 28:9

18 "O LORD, the God of Abraham, Isaac, and Israel, our fathers, preserve this forever in the intentions of the heart of Thy people, and direct their heart to Thee;

19 "and give to my son Solomon a perfect heart to keep Thy commandments, Thy testimonies, and Thy statutes, and to do *them* all, and to build the [t]temple, for which I have made provision." *palace*

20 Then David said to all the assembly, "Now bless the LORD your God." And [r]all the assembly blessed the LORD, the God of their fathers, and [r]bowed low and did homage to the LORD and to the king. Josh. 22:33 • Ex. 4:31

21 And on the next day [r]they [t]made sacrifices to the LORD and offered burnt offerings to the LORD, 1,000 bulls, 1,000 rams *and* 1,000 lambs, with their libations and sacrifices in abundance for all Israel. 1 Kin. 8:62, 63 • *sacrificed*

22 So they ate and drank that day before the LORD with great gladness.

And they made Solomon the son of David king a second time, and they anointed *him* as ruler for the LORD and Zadok as priest.

23 Then Solomon sat on the throne of the LORD as king instead of David his father; and he prospered, and all Israel obeyed him.

24 And all the officials, the mighty men, and also all the sons of King David pledged allegiance to King Solomon.

25 And the LORD highly exalted Solomon in the sight of all Israel,

and bestowed on him royal majesty which had not been on any king
before him in Israel.
26 Now David the son of Jesse
reigned over all Israel.
27 And the period which he
reigned over Israel *was* forty
years; he reigned in Hebron seven
years and in Jerusalem thirty-
three *years*.
28 Then he died in a ripe old
age, full of days, riches and honor;
and his son Solomon reigned in
his place.
29 Now the acts of King David,
from first to last, are written in
the chronicles of Samuel the seer,
in the chronicles of Nathan the
prophet, and in the chronicles of
Gad the seer,
30 with all his reign, his power,
and the circumstances which
came on him, on Israel, and on all
the kingdoms of the lands.

THE SECOND BOOK OF THE

CHRONICLES

NOW [r]Solomon the son of David
established himself securely over
his kingdom, and the LORD his
God *was* with him and exalted
him greatly. 1 Kin. 2:12, 46
2 And Solomon spoke [r]to all Israel, to the commanders of thousands and of hundreds and to the
judges and to every leader in all
Israel, the heads of the fathers'
households. 1 Chr. 28:1
3 Then Solomon, and all the
assembly with him, went to [r]the
high place which was at Gibeon;
[r]for God's tent of meeting was
there, which Moses the servant of
the LORD had made in the wilderness. 1 Kin. 3:4 • Ex. 36:8
4 However, David had brought
up [r]the ark of God from Kiriath-jearim to the place he had prepared
for it; for he had pitched a tent for
it in Jerusalem. 1 Chr. 15:25-28
5 Now [r]the bronze altar, which
Bezalel the son of Uri, the son of
Hur, had made, [t]was there before
the tabernacle of the LORD, and
Solomon and the assembly sought
it out. Ex. 31:9; 38:1-7 • *he put*
6 And Solomon went up there
before the LORD to the bronze altar which *was* at the tent of meeting, and [r]offered a thousand burnt
offerings on it. 1 Kin. 3:4
7 In that night God appeared
to Solomon and said to him, "Ask
what I shall give you."
8 And Solomon said to God,
"Thou hast dealt with my father
David with great lovingkindness,
and [r]hast made me king in his
place. 1 Chr. 28:5
9 "Now, O LORD God, Thy
[t]promise to my father David is fulfilled; for Thou hast made me king
over [r]a people as numerous as the
dust of the earth. *word* • Gen. 13:16
10 "Give [r] me now wisdom and
knowledge, [r]that I may go out and
come in before this people; for

who can rule this great people of
Thine?" 1 Kin. 3:9 • Num. 27:17
11 And God said to Solomon,
"Because [t]you had this in mind,
and did not ask for riches, wealth,
or honor, or the life of those who
hate you, nor have you even asked
for long life, but you have asked
for yourself wisdom and knowledge, that you may rule My people, over whom I have made you
king, *this was in your heart*
12 wisdom and knowledge have
been granted to you. And [r]I will
give you riches and wealth and
honor, such as none of the kings
who were before you has possessed, nor those who will [t]come
after you." 1 Chr. 29:25 • *be*
13 So Solomon went from the
high place which was at Gibeon,
from the tent of meeting, to Jerusalem, and he reigned over Israel.
14 [r]And Solomon amassed
chariots and horsemen. He had
1,400 chariots, and 12,000 horsemen, and he stationed them in the
chariot cities and with the king at
Jerusalem. 1 Kin. 10:26-29
15 And [r]the king made silver and
gold as plentiful in Jerusalem as
stones, and he made cedars as
plentiful as sycamores in the lowland. 1 Kin. 10:27
16 And Solomon's horses were
imported from Egypt and from
Kue; the king's traders procured
them from Kue for a price.
17 And they [t]imported chariots
from Egypt for 600 *shekels* of silver apiece, and horses for 150
apiece, and by the same means
they exported them to all the
kings of the Hittites and the kings
of Aram. *brought up and brought out*

CHAPTER 2

NOW Solomon decided to build a
house for the name of the LORD,
and a royal palace for himself.
2 So Solomon assigned 70,000
men to carry loads, and 80,000
men to quarry *stone* in the mountains, and 3,600 to supervise them.
3 Then Solomon sent *word* to
Huram the king of Tyre, saying,
"As you dealt with David my father, and sent him cedars to build
him a house to dwell in, so do for
me.
4 "Behold, I am about to build a
house for the name of the LORD
my God, dedicating it to Him, [r]to
burn fragrant incense before Him,
and *to set out* the [r]showbread continually, and to offer burnt offerings morning and evening, on sabbaths and on new moons and on
the appointed feasts of the LORD
our God, this *being required* forever in Israel. Ex. 30:7 • Ex. 25:30
5 "And the house which I am
about to build *will be* great; for
[r]greater is our God than all the
gods. Ex. 15:11; 1 Chr. 16:25
6 "But who is able to build a
house for Him, for the heavens
and the highest heavens cannot
contain Him? So who am I, that I
should build a house for Him, except to [1]burn *incense* before Him?
7 "And now send me a skilled
man to work in gold, silver, brass
and iron, and in purple, crimson
and violet *fabrics*, and who knows
how to make engravings, to *work*
with the skilled men whom I have
in Judah and Jerusalem, whom
David my father provided.
8 "Send me also cedar, cypress

[1]Lit., *offer up in smoke*

and algum timber from Lebanon,
for I know that your servants
know how to cut timber of Lebanon; and indeed, my servants *will*
work with your servants,
9 to prepare timber in abundance for me, for the house which
I am about to build *will be* great
and wonderful.
10 "Now behold, I will give to
your servants, the woodsmen who
cut the timber, 20,000 [2]kors of
crushed wheat, and 20,000 kors of
barley, and 20,000 baths of wine,
and 20,000 baths of oil."
11 Then Huram, king of Tyre,
[t]answered in a letter sent to Solomon: "Because the LORD loves His
people, He has made you king
over them." *said . . . and he sent*
12 Then Huram [t]continued,
"Blessed be the LORD, the God of
Israel, who has made heaven and
earth, who has given King David a
wise son, endowed with discretion
and understanding, who will build
a house for the LORD and a royal
palace for himself. *said*
13 "And now I am sending a
skilled man, endowed with understanding, Huram-abi,
14 the son of a [t]Danite woman
and a Tyrian father, who knows
how to work in gold, silver,
bronze, iron, stone and wood, *and*
in purple, violet, linen and crimson fabrics, and *who knows how*
to make all kinds of engravings
and to execute any design which
may be assigned to him, *to work*
with your skilled men, and with
those of my lord David your father. *a woman of the daughters of Dan*
15 "Now then, let my lord send
to his servants wheat and barley,
oil and wine, of [r]which he has spoken. 2 Chr. 2:10
16 "And [r]we will cut whatever
timber you need from Lebanon,
and bring it to you on rafts by sea
to Joppa, so that you may carry it
up to Jerusalem." 1 Kin. 5:8, 9
17 And Solomon numbered all
the aliens who *were* in the land of
Israel, following the [t]census which
his father David had taken; and
153,600 were found. *numbering*
18 [r]And he appointed 70,000 of
them to carry loads, and 80,000 to
quarry *stones* in the mountains,
and 3,600 supervisors to make the
people work. 2 Chr. 2:2

CHAPTER 3

[r]THEN Solomon began to build
the house of the LORD in Jerusalem on Mount Moriah, where *the*
LORD had appeared to his father
David, at the place that David had
prepared, on the threshing floor of
Ornan the Jebusite. 1 Kin. 6:1
2 And he began to build on the
second *day* in the second month
[t]of the fourth year of his reign. *in*
3 Now these are the founda-
tions which Solomon laid for
building the house of God. The
length in [3]cubits, according to the
old standard *was* sixty cubits, and
the width twenty cubits.
4 And the porch which was in
front of the house was as long as
the width of the house, twenty cubits, and the height 120; and inside he overlaid it with pure gold.
5 And he overlaid the [t]main
room with cypress wood and
overlaid it with fine gold, and [t]or-

[2]I.e., A kor equals approx. 10 bushels

[3]I.e., One cubit equals approx. 18 in.

namented it with palm trees and
chains. *great house • put on it palm trees*
6 Further, he adorned the
house with precious stones; and
the gold was gold from Parvaim.
7 ʳHe also overlaid the house
with gold—the beams, the thresholds, and its walls, and its doors;
and he ʳcarved cherubim on the
walls. 1 Kin. 6:20-22 • 1 Kin. 6:29-35
8 Now he made ʳthe ᵗroom of
the holy of holies: its length,
across the width of the house, *was*
twenty cubits, and its width *was*
twenty cubits; and he overlaid it
with fine gold, *amounting* to 600
talents. Ex. 26:33; 1 Kin. 6:16 • *house*
9 And the weight of the nails
was fifty shekels of gold. He also
overlaid ʳthe upper rooms with
gold. 1 Chr. 28:11
10 Then he made two ᵗsculp-
tured cherubim in the room of the
holy of holies and overlaid them
with gold. *cherubim of sculptured work*
11 And the wingspan of the
cherubim *was* twenty cubits; the
wing of one, of five cubits,
touched the wall of the house, and
its other wing, of five cubits,
touched the wing of the other
cherub.
12 And the wing of the other
cherub, of five cubits, touched the
wall of the house; and *its* other
wing of five cubits, was attached
to the wing of the first cherub.
13 The wings of these cherubim
extended twenty cubits, and they
stood on their feet ᵗfacing the *main*
room. *and their faces to*
14 And he made the veil of violet, purple, crimson and fine linen,
and he worked cherubim on it.
15 He also made two pillars for
the front of the house, thirty-five
cubits ᵗhigh, and the capital on the
top of each *was* five cubits. *long*
16 And he made chains in the
inner sanctuary, and placed *them*
on the tops of the pillars; and he
made one hundred pomegranates
and placed *them* on the chains.
17 And he erected the pillars in
front of the temple, one on the
right and the other on the left, and
named the one on the right Jachin
and the one on the left Boaz.

CHAPTER 4

THEN he made a bronze altar,
twenty cubits in length and
twenty cubits in width and ten cubits in height.
2 ʳAlso he made the cast *metal*
sea, ten cubits from brim to brim,
circular in form, and its height
was five cubits and its circumference thirty cubits. 1 Kin. 7:23-26
3 Now figures like oxen *were*
under it *and* all around it, ten cubits, entirely encircling the sea.
The oxen *were* in two rows, cast ᵗin
one piece. *in its casting*
4 It stood on twelve oxen,
three facing the north, three facing west, three facing south, and
three facing east; and the sea *was*
set on top of them, and all their
hindquarters turned inwards.
5 And it was a handbreadth
thick, and its brim was made like
the brim of a cup, *like* a lily blossom; it could hold 3,000 baths.
6 He also made ten basins in
which to wash, and he set five on
the right side and five on the left,
ᵗto rinse things for the burnt offer-

ing; but the sea *was* for the priests
to wash in. *in which to*
7 Then [r]he made the ten golden
lampstands in the way prescribed
for them, and he set them in the
temple, five on the right side and
five on the left. Ex. 25:31-40
8 He also made [r]ten tables and
placed them in the temple, five on
the right side and five on the left.
And he made one hundred golden
bowls. 1 Kin. 7:48
9 Then he made [r]the court of
the priests and the great court and
doors for the court, and overlaid
their doors with bronze. 1 Kin. 6:36
10 And [r]he set the sea on the
right [t]side *of the house* toward the
southeast. 1 Kin. 7:39 • *shoulder*
11 Huram also made the pails,
the shovels, and the bowls. So Huram finished doing the work
which he performed for King
Solomon in the house of God:
12 the two pillars, the bowls and
the two capitals on top of the pillars, and the two networks to cover the two bowls of the capitals
which were on top of the pillars,
13 and [r]the four hundred pomegranates for the two networks,
two rows of pomegranates for
each network to cover the two
bowls of the capitals which were
on the pillars. 1 Kin. 7:20
14 He also made the stands and
he made the basins on the stands,
15 *and* the one sea with the
twelve oxen under it.
16 And the pails, the shovels,
the forks, and all its utensils, [r]Hu-
ram-abi made of polished bronze
for King Solomon for the house of
the LORD. 1 Kin. 7:14; 2 Chr. 2:13
17 On the plain of the Jordan
the king cast them, in the clay
ground between Succoth and
Zeredah.
18 [r]Thus Solomon made all these
utensils in great quantities, for the
weight of the bronze could not be
found out. 1 Kin. 7:47
19 Solomon also made all the
things that *were* in the house of
God: even the golden altar, [r]the tables with the bread of the Presence on them, 2 Chr. 4:8
20 the lampstands with their
lamps of pure gold, to burn in
front of the inner sanctuary in the
way prescribed;
21 the flowers, the lamps, and
the tongs of gold, of purest gold;
22 and the snuffers, the bowls,
the spoons, and the firepans of
pure gold; and the entrance of the
house, its inner doors for the holy
of holies, and the doors of the
house, *that is,* of the nave, of gold.

CHAPTER 5

THUS all the work that Solomon
performed for the house of the
LORD was finished. And Solomon
brought in the things that David
his father had dedicated, even the
silver and the gold and all the
utensils, *and* put *them* in the treasuries of the house of God.
2 [r]Then Solomon assembled to
Jerusalem the elders of Israel and
all the heads of the tribes, the
leaders of the fathers' *households*
of the sons of Israel, to bring up
the ark of the covenant of the
LORD out of the city of David,
which is Zion. 1 Kin. 8:1-9
3 And [r]all the men of Israel assembled themselves to the king at

[r]the feast, that is *in* the seventh
month. 1 Kin. 8:2 • 2 Chr. 7:8-10
4 Then all the elders of Israel
came, and [r]the Levites took up the
ark. Josh. 3:6; 2 Chr. 5:7
5 And they brought up the ark
and the tent of meeting and all the
holy utensils which *were* in the
tent; the Levitical priests brought
them up.
6 And King Solomon and all
the congregation of Israel who
were assembled with him before
the ark were sacrificing so many
sheep and oxen, that they could
not be counted or numbered.
7 Then the priests brought the
ark of the covenant of the LORD to
its place, into the inner sanctuary
of the house, to the holy of holies,
under the wings of the cherubim.
8 For the cherubim spread
their wings over the place of the
ark, so that the cherubim made a
covering over the ark and its
[t]poles. *poles above*
9 And the poles were so long
that the ends of the poles of the
ark could be seen in front of the
inner sanctuary, but they could
not be seen outside; and [t]they are
there to this day. *it is*
10 [r]There was nothing in the ark
except the two tablets which
Moses put *there* at Horeb, where
the LORD made a covenant with
the sons of Israel, when they came
out of Egypt. Deut. 10:2-5
11 And when the priests came
forth from the holy place (for all
the priests who were present had
sanctified themselves, without regard [r]to divisions), 1 Chr. 24:1-5
12 and all the Levitical singers,
[r]Asaph, Heman, Jeduthun, and
their sons and kinsmen, clothed in
fine linen, with cymbals, harps,
and lyres, standing east of the altar, and with them one hundred
and twenty priests [r]blowing trumpets 1 Chr. 25:1-4 • 2 Chr. 7:6
13 in unison when the trumpeters and the singers were to make
themselves heard with one voice
to praise and to glorify the LORD,
and when they lifted up their
voice [r]accompanied by trumpets
and cymbals and instruments of
music, and when they praised the
LORD *saying*, "*He* [r]indeed is good
for His lovingkindness is everlasting," then the house, the house
of the LORD, was filled with a
cloud, 1 Chr. 16:42 • 1 Chr. 16:34
14 so that the priests could not
stand to minister because of the
cloud, for [r]the glory of the LORD
filled the house of God. Ex. 40:35

CHAPTER 6

[r]THEN Solomon said,
"The LORD has said that He
would dwell in the thick
cloud. 1 Kin. 8:12-50
2 "I have built Thee a lofty
house,
And a place for Thy dwelling forever."
3 Then the king faced about
and blessed all the assembly of Israel, while all the assembly of Israel was standing.
4 And he said, "Blessed be the
LORD, the God of Israel, who
spoke with His mouth to my father David and has fulfilled *it* with
His hands, saying,
5 'Since the day that I brought
My people from the land of Egypt,

I did not choose a city out of all
the tribes of Israel *in which* to
build a house that My name might
be there, nor did I choose any man
for a leader over My people Israel;
6 but [r]I have chosen Jerusalem
that My name might be there, and
I have chosen David to be over
My people Israel.' 2 Chr. 12:13
7 "Now it was [t]in the heart of
my father David to build a house
for the name of the LORD, the God
of Israel. *with*
8 "But the LORD said to my father David, 'Because it was [t]in
your heart to build a house for My
name, you did well that it was in
your heart. *with*
9 'Nevertheless you shall not
build the house, but your son who
shall be born to you, he shall build
the house for My name.'
10 "Now the LORD has fulfilled
His word which He spoke; for I
have risen in the place of my father David and sit on the throne of
Israel, as the LORD promised, and
have built the house for the name
of the LORD, the God of Israel.
11 "And there I have set the ark,
[r]in which is the covenant of the
LORD, which He made with the
sons of Israel." 2 Chr. 5:7, 10
12 Then he stood before the altar of the LORD in the presence of
all the assembly of Israel and
spread out his hands.
13 Now Solomon had made a
bronze platform, five cubits long,
five cubits wide, and three cubits
high, and had set it in the midst of
the court; and he stood on it, knelt
on his knees in the presence of all
the assembly of Israel, and spread
out his hands toward heaven.
14 And he said, "O LORD, the
God of Israel, [r]there is no god like
Thee in heaven or on earth, keeping covenant and showing lovingkindness to Thy servants who
walk before Thee with all their
heart; Ex. 15:11; Deut. 3:24
15 who has kept with Thy servant David, my father, that which
Thou hast promised him; indeed,
Thou hast spoken with Thy
mouth, and hast fulfilled it with
Thy hand, as it is this day.
16 "Now therefore, O LORD, the
God of Israel, keep with Thy servant David, my father, that which
Thou hast [t]promised him, saying,
'You shall not lack a man to sit on
the throne of Israel, if only your
sons take heed to their way, to
walk in My law as you have
walked before Me.' *spoken to*
17 "Now therefore, O LORD, the
God of Israel, let Thy word be
confirmed which Thou hast spoken to Thy servant David.
18 "But [r]will God indeed dwell
with mankind on the earth? Behold, heaven and the [t]highest
heaven cannot contain Thee; how
much less this house which I have
built. Ps. 113:5, 6 • *heaven of heavens*
19 "Yet have regard to the prayer
of Thy servant and to his supplication, O LORD my God, to listen to
the cry and to the prayer which
Thy servant prays before Thee;
20 that Thine [r]eyes may be open
toward this house day and night,
toward the place of which Thou
hast said that *Thou wouldst* put
Thy name there, to listen to the
prayer which Thy servant shall
pray toward this place. Ps. 33:18
21 "And listen to the supplica-

tions of Thy servant and of Thy
people Israel, when they pray
toward this place; hear Thou from
Thy dwelling place, from heaven;
[r]hear Thou and forgive. Is. 43:25
22 "If a man sins against his
neighbor, and is made to take an
oath, and he comes *and* takes an
oath before Thine altar in this
house,
23 then hear Thou from heaven
and act and judge Thy servants,
punishing the wicked by bringing
his way on his own head and justifying the righteous by giving him
according to his righteousness.
24 "And if Thy people Israel [t]are
defeated before an enemy, because [r]they have sinned against
Thee, and they return *to Thee* and
confess Thy name, and pray and
make supplication before Thee in
this house, *smitten* • Ps. 51:4
25 then hear Thou from heaven
and forgive the sin of Thy people
Israel, and bring them back to the
land which Thou hast given to
them and to their fathers.
26 "When the [r]heavens are shut
up and there is no rain because
they have sinned against Thee,
and they pray toward this place
and confess Thy name, and turn
from their sin when Thou dost afflict them; 1 Kin. 17:1
27 then hear Thou in heaven
and forgive the sin of Thy servants and Thy people Israel, indeed, [r]teach them the good way in
which they should walk. And send
rain on Thy land, which Thou hast
given to Thy people for an inheritance. Ps. 94:12
28 "If there is famine in the land,
if there is pestilence, if there is
blight or mildew, if there is locust
or grasshopper, if their enemies
besiege them in the land of their
[t]cities, whatever plague or whatever sickness *there is,* *gates*
29 whatever prayer or supplication is made by any man or by all
Thy people Israel, each knowing
his own affliction and his own
pain, and spreading his hands
toward this house,
30 then hear Thou from heaven
Thy dwelling place, and forgive,
and render to each according to
all his ways, whose heart Thou
knowest [r]for Thou alone dost
know the hearts of the sons of
men, 1 Sam. 16:7; 1 Chr. 28:9
31 that they may [a][4]fear Thee, to
walk in Thy ways as long as they
live in the land which Thou hast
given to our fathers. *reverence*
32 "Also concerning the foreigner who is not from Thy people
Israel, when he comes from a far
country for Thy great name's sake
and Thy mighty hand and Thine
outstretched arm, when they
come and pray toward this house,
33 then hear Thou from heaven,
from Thy dwelling place, and do
according to all for which the foreigner calls to Thee, in order that
all the peoples of the earth may
know Thy name, and [a][4]fear Thee,
as *do* Thy people Israel, and that
they may know that this house
which I have built is [r]called by Thy
name. *reverence* • 2 Chr. 7:14
34 "When Thy people go out to
battle against their enemies, by
whatever way Thou shalt send
them, and they pray to Thee
toward this city which Thou hast

[4]Or, *reverence*

chosen, and the house which I have built for Thy name,

35 then hear Thou from heaven their prayer and their supplication, and maintain their cause.

36 "When they sin against Thee (for there is no man who does not sin) and Thou art angry with them and dost deliver them to an enemy, so that they take them away captive to a land far off or near,

37 if they take thought in the land where they are taken captive, and repent and make supplication to Thee in the land of their captivity, saying, 'We have sinned, we have committed iniquity, and have acted wickedly';

38 [r]if they return to Thee with all their heart and with all their soul in the land of their captivity, where they have been taken captive, and pray toward their land which Thou hast given to their fathers, and the city which Thou hast chosen, and toward the house which I have built for Thy name, Jer. 29:12, 13

39 then hear from heaven, from Thy dwelling place, their prayer and supplications, and maintain their cause, and forgive Thy people who have sinned against Thee.

40 "Now, O my God, I pray Thee, [r]let Thine eyes be open, and Thine ears attentive to the prayer *offered* in this place. 2 Chr. 7:15

41 "Now therefore arise, O LORD God, to Thy resting place, Thou and the ark of Thy might; let Thy priests, O LORD God, be clothed with salvation, and let Thy godly ones rejoice in what is good.

42 "O LORD God, do not turn away the face of Thine anointed; [r]remember *Thy* lovingkindness to Thy servant David." Ps. 89:24, 28

CHAPTER 7

NOW when Solomon had finished praying, [r]fire came down from heaven and consumed the burnt offering and the sacrifices; and the glory of the LORD filled the house. Lev. 9:23f.

2 And [r]the priests could not enter into the house of the LORD, because the glory of the LORD filled the LORD's house. 2 Chr. 5:14

3 And all the sons of Israel, seeing the fire come down and the glory of the LORD upon the house, bowed down on the pavement with their faces to the ground, and they worshiped and gave praise to the LORD, *saying*, "Truly[r] He is good, truly His lovingkindness is everlasting." 2 Chr. 5:13; 20:21

4 [r]Then the king and all the people offered sacrifice before the LORD. 1 Kin. 8:62, 63

5 And King Solomon offered a sacrifice of 22,000 oxen, and 120,000 sheep. Thus the king and all the people dedicated the house of God.

6 And the priests stood at their posts and [r]the Levites, with the instruments of music to the LORD, which King David had made for giving praise to the LORD—"for His lovingkindness is everlasting"—whenever [t]he gave praise by their [t]means, while the priests on the other side blew trumpets; and all Israel was standing. 1 Chr. 15:16-21 • *David* • *hand*

7 Then Solomon consecrated the middle of the court that *was*

before the house of the LORD, for
there he offered the burnt offerings and the fat of the peace offerings, because the bronze altar
which Solomon had made was not
able to contain the burnt offering,
the grain offering, and the fat.
8 So [r]Solomon observed the
feast at that time for seven days,
and all Israel with him, a very
great assembly, *who came* from
the entrance of Hamath to the
brook of Egypt. 1 Kin. 8:65
9 And on the eighth day they
held [r]a solemn assembly, for the
dedication of the altar they observed seven days, and the feast
seven days. Lev. 23:36
10 Then on the twenty-third day
of the seventh month he sent the
people to their tents, rejoicing and
happy of heart because of the
goodness that the LORD had
shown to David and to Solomon
and to His people Israel.
11 [r]Thus Solomon finished the
house of the LORD and the king's
palace, and successfully completed all that he had planned on
doing in the house of the LORD
and in his palace. 1 Kin. 9:1-9
12 Then the LORD appeared to
Solomon at night and said to him,
"I have heard your prayer, and
have chosen this place for Myself
as a house of sacrifice.
13 "If [r]I shut up the heavens so
that there is no rain, or if I command the locust to devour the
land, or if I send pestilence among
My people, 2 Chr. 6:26-28
14 [r]and My people who are
called by My name humble themselves and pray, and seek My face
and turn from their wicked ways,
then I will hear from heaven, will
forgive their sin, and will heal
their land. 2 Chr. 6:37-39; James 4:10
15 "Now My eyes shall be open
and My ears attentive to the
prayer *offered* in this place.
16 "For [r]now I have chosen and
consecrated this house that My
name may be there forever, and
My eyes and My heart will be
there perpetually. 2 Chr. 7:12
17 "And as for you, if you walk
before Me as your father David
walked even to do according to all
that I have commanded you and
will keep My statutes and My ordinances,
18 then I will establish your
royal throne as I covenanted with
your father David, saying, 'You[r]
shall not lack a man *to be* ruler in
Israel.' 1 Kin. 2:4; 2 Chr. 6:16
19 "But if you turn away and forsake My statutes and My commandments which I have set before you and shall go and serve
other gods and worship them,
20 [r]then I will uproot you from
My land which I have given[a] you,
and this house which I have consecrated for My name I will cast
out of My sight, and I will make it
a proverb and a byword among all
peoples. Deut. 29:28 • *them*
21 "As for this house, which was
exalted, everyone who passes by
it will be astonished and say,
'Why has the LORD done thus to
this land and to this house?'
22 "And they will say, 'Because
[r]they forsook the LORD, the God of
their fathers, who brought them
from the land of Egypt, and they
adopted other gods and worshiped them and served them,

therefore He has brought all this
adversity on them.' " Judg. 2:13

CHAPTER 8

NOW it came about at the end of
the twenty years in which Solomon had built the house of the
LORD and his own house
2 that he built the cities which
Huram had given to him, and settled the sons of Israel there.
3 Then Solomon went to Ha-
math-zobah and captured it.
4 And he built Tadmor in the
wilderness and all the storage
cities which he had built in Hamath.
5 He also built upper Beth-horon and lower Beth-horon, fortified cities *with* walls, gates, and
bars;
6 and Baalath and all the storage cities that Solomon had, and
all the cities for [t]his chariots and
cities for [t]his horsemen, and all
that it pleased Solomon to build in
Jerusalem, in Lebanon, and in all
the land [t]under his rule. *the · of*
7 All of the people who were
left of the Hittites, the Amorites,
the Perizzites, the Hivites, and the
Jebusites, who were not of Israel,
8 namely, from their descendants who were left after them in
the land whom the sons of Israel
had not destroyed, [r]them Solomon
raised as forced laborers to this
day. 1 Kin. 4:6; 9:21
9 But Solomon did not make
slaves for his work from the sons
of Israel; they were men of war,
his chief captains, and commanders of his chariots and his horsemen.
10 And these were the chief [a]offi-
cers of King Solomon, two hundred and fifty who ruled over the
people. *deputies*
11 Then Solomon brought Pharaoh's daughter up from the city
of David to the house which he
had built for her; for he said, "My
wife shall not dwell in the house
of David king of Israel, because
the places are holy where the ark
of the LORD has entered."
12 Then Solomon offered burnt
offerings to the LORD on [r]the altar
of the LORD which he had built before the porch; 2 Chr. 4:1
13 and [r]*did so* according to the
daily rule, offering *them* up according to the commandment of
Moses, for the sabbaths, the new
moons, and the three annual
feasts—the Feast of Unleavened
Bread, the Feast of Weeks, and
the Feast of Booths. Ex. 29:38-42
14 Now according to the ordinance of his father David, he appointed [r]the divisions of the priests
for their service, and the Levites
for their duties of praise and ministering before the priests according to the daily rule, and the gatekeepers by their divisions at every
gate; for David the man of God
had so commanded. 1 Chr. 24:1
15 And they did not depart from
the commandment of the king to
the priests and Levites in any
manner or concerning the storehouses.
16 Thus all the work of Solomon was carried out [a]from the day
of the foundation of the house of
the LORD, and until it was finished. So the house of the LORD
was completed. *as far as*
17 Then Solomon went to

Ezion-geber and to Eloth on the seashore in the land of Edom.

18 And Huram by his servants sent him ships and servants who knew the sea; and they went with Solomon's servants to Ophir, and took from there four hundred and fifty talents of gold, and brought them to King Solomon.

CHAPTER 9

NOW when the queen of Sheba heard of the fame of Solomon, she came to Jerusalem to test Solomon with difficult questions. She had a very large retinue, with camels carrying spices, and a large amount of gold and precious stones; and when she came to Solomon, she spoke with him about all that was on her heart.

2 And Solomon [t]answered all her questions; nothing was hidden from Solomon which he did not explain to her. *told her all her words*

3 And when the queen of Sheba had seen the wisdom of Solomon, the house which he had built,

4 the food at his table, the seating of his servants, the attendance of his ministers and their attire, his cupbearers and their attire, and his stairway by which he went up to the house of the LORD, she was breathless.

5 Then she said to the king, "It was a true report which I heard in my own land about your words and your wisdom.

6 "Nevertheless I did not believe their reports until I came and my eyes had seen it. And behold, the half of the greatness of your wisdom was not told me. You surpass the report that I heard.

7 "How blessed are your men, how blessed are these your servants who stand before you continually and hear your wisdom.

8 "Blessed be the LORD your God who delighted in you, [r]setting you on His throne as king for the LORD your God; [r]because your God loved Israel establishing them forever, therefore He made you king over them, to do justice and righteousness." 1 Chr. 28:5 • Deut. 7:8

9 Then she gave the king one hundred and twenty talents of gold, and a very great *amount of* spices and precious stones; there had never been spice like that which the queen of Sheba gave to King Solomon.

10 And the servants of Huram and the servants of Solomon [r]who brought gold from Ophir, also brought algum trees and precious stones. 1 Kin. 10:11; 2 Chr. 8:18

11 And from the algum the king made steps for the house of the LORD and for the king's palace, and lyres and harps for the singers; and none like that was seen before in the land of Judah.

12 And King Solomon gave to the queen of Sheba all her desire which she requested besides *a return for* what she had brought to the king. Then she turned and went to her own land with her servants.

13 Now the weight of gold which came to Solomon in one year was 666 talents of gold,

14 besides that which the traders and merchants brought; and all the kings of Arabia and the

governors of the country brought
gold and silver to Solomon.
15 And King Solomon made 200
large shields of beaten gold,[t]using
600 *shekels of* beaten gold on each
large shield. *he brought up*
16 And *he made* 300 shields of
beaten gold, using three hundred
shekels of gold on each shield, and
the king put them in the house of
the forest of Lebanon.
17 Moreover, the king made a
great throne of ivory and overlaid
it with pure gold.
18 And *there were* six steps to
the throne and a footstool in gold
attached to the throne, and arms
on each side of the seat, and two
lions standing beside the arms.
19 And twelve lions were standing there on the six steps on the
one side and on the other; nothing
like *it* was made for any *other*
kingdom.
20 And all King Solomon's
drinking vessels *were* of gold, and
all the vessels of the house of the
forest of Lebanon *were* of pure
gold; silver was not considered
valuable in the days of Solomon.
21 [r]For the king had ships which
went to Tarshish with the servants of Huram; once every three
years the ships of Tarshish came
bringing gold and silver, ivory and
apes and peacocks. 2 Chr. 20:36
22 So King Solomon became
greater than all the kings of the
earth in riches and wisdom.
23 And all the kings of the earth
were seeking the presence of
Solomon, to hear his wisdom
which God had put in his heart.
24 And [r]they brought every man
his gift, articles of silver and gold,
garments, weapons, spices,
horses, and mules, so much year
by year. Ps. 72:10
25 Now Solomon had [r]4,000
stalls for horses and chariots and
12,000 horsemen, and he stationed
them in the chariot cities and with
the king in Jerusalem. Deut. 17:16
26 [r]And he was the ruler over all
the kings from the Euphrates
River even to the land of the Philistines, and as far as the border of
Egypt. Gen. 15:18; 1 Kin. 4:21, 24
27 [r]And the king made silver *as
common* as stones in Jerusalem,
and he made cedars as plentiful as
sycamore trees that are in the
lowland. 2 Chr. 1:15-17
28 [r]And they were bringing
horses for Solomon from Egypt
and from all countries. 2 Chr. 1:16
29 [r]Now the rest of the acts of
Solomon, from first to last, are
they not written in the [t]records of
Nathan the prophet, and in the
prophecy of Ahijah the Shilonite,
and in the visions of Iddo the seer
concerning Jeroboam the son of
Nebat? 1 Kin. 11:41-43 • *words*
30 And Solomon reigned forty
years in Jerusalem over all Israel.
31 And Solomon slept with his
fathers and was buried in the city
of his father David; and his son
Rehoboam reigned in his place.

CHAPTER 10

THEN Rehoboam went to Shechem, for all Israel had come to
Shechem to make him king.
2 And it came about when
Jeroboam the son of Nebat heard
of it (for [r]he was in Egypt where he
had fled from the presence of

King Solomon), that Jeroboam returned from Egypt. 1 Kin. 11:40
3 So they sent and summoned
him. When Jeroboam and all Israel came, they spoke to Rehoboam, saying,
4 "Your father made our yoke
hard; now therefore lighten the
hard service of your father and his
heavy yoke which he put on us,
and we will serve you."
5 And he said to them, "Return
to me again in three days." So the
people departed.
6 Then King Rehoboam [r]con-
sulted with the elders who had
[t]served his father Solomon while
he was still alive, saying, "How do
you counsel *me* to answer this
people?" Job 8:8, 9 • *stood before*
7 And they spoke to him, saying, "If you will be kind to this
people and please them and speak
good words to them, then they
will be your servants forever."
8 But he forsook the counsel of
the elders which they had given
him, and consulted with the
young men who grew up with him
[t]and served him. *who stood before*
9 So he said to them, "What
counsel do you give that we may
answer this people, who have spoken to me, saying, 'Lighten the
yoke which your father put on
us'?"
10 And the young men who
grew up with him spoke to him,
saying, "Thus you shall say to the
people who spoke to you, saying,
'Your father made our yoke
heavy, but you make it lighter for
us.' Thus you shall say to them,
'My little finger is thicker than my
father's loins!
11 'Whereas my father loaded
you with a heavy yoke, I will add
to your yoke; my father disciplined you with whips, but I *will
discipline you* with scorpions.'"
12 So Jeroboam and all the people came to Rehoboam on the
third day as the king had [t]directed,
saying, "Return to me on the third
day." *spoken*
13 And the king answered them
harshly, and King Rehoboam forsook the counsel of the elders.
14 And he spoke to them according to the advice of the young
men, saying, "My father made
your yoke heavy, but I will add to
it; my father disciplined you with
whips, but I *will discipline you*
with scorpions."
15 So the king did not listen to
the people, [r]for it was a turn *of
events* from God [r]that the LORD
might establish His word, which
He spoke through Ahijah the Shilonite to Jeroboam the son of Nebat. 2 Chr. 25:16-20 • 1 Kin. 11:29-39
16 And when all Israel *saw* that
the king did not listen to them the
people answered the king, saying,

"What [r]portion do we have in
David?
We have no inheritance in
the son of Jesse.
Every man to your tents, O
Israel;
Now look after your own
house, David."

[r]So all Israel departed to their
tents. 2 Sam. 20:1 • 2 Chr. 10:19
17 But as for the sons of Israel
who lived in the cities of Judah,
Rehoboam reigned over them.
18 Then King Rehoboam sent
Hadoram, who was over the
forced labor, and the sons of Is-

rael stoned him ᵗto death. And
King Rehoboam made haste to
mount his chariot to flee to Jerusalem. *with stones that he died*
19 So ʳIsrael has been in rebellion against the house of David to
this day. 1 Kin. 12:19

CHAPTER 11

ʳNOW when Rehoboam had come
to Jerusalem, he assembled the
house of Judah and Benjamin,
180,000 chosen men who were
warriors, to fight against Israel to
restore the kingdom to Rehoboam. 1 Kin. 12:21-24
2 But the word of the LORD
came to ʳShemaiah the man of
God, saying, 2 Chr. 12:5-7, 15
3 "Speak to Rehoboam the son
of Solomon, king of Judah, and to
all Israel in Judah and Benjamin,
saying,
4 'Thus says the LORD, "You
shall not go up or fight against
your relatives; return every man
to his house, for this thing is from
Me." ' " So they listened to the
words of the LORD and returned
from going against Jeroboam.
5 Rehoboam lived in Jerusalem and ʳbuilt cities for defense in
Judah. 2 Chr. 8:2-6; 11:23
6 Thus he built Bethlehem,
Etam, Tekoa,
7 Beth-zur, Soco, Adullam,
8 Gath, Mareshah, Ziph,
9 Adoraim, Lachish, Azekah,
10 Zorah, Aijalon, and Hebron,
which are fortified cities in Judah
and in Benjamin.
11 He also strengthened the fortresses and put officers in them
and stores of food, oil and wine.
12 And *he put* shields and
spears in every city and
strengthened them greatly. So he
held Judah and Benjamin.
13 Moreover, the priests and
the Levites who were in all Israel
stood with him from all their districts.
14 For ʳthe Levites left their pasture lands and their property and
came to Judah and Jerusalem, for
Jeroboam and his sons had excluded them from serving as
priests to the LORD. Num. 35:2-5
15 And ʳhe set up priests of his
own for the high places, for the
satyrs, and for the calves which
he had made. 1 Kin. 12:31; 13:33
16 And ʳthose from all the tribes
of Israel who set their hearts on
seeking the LORD God of Israel,
ᵗfollowed them to Jerusalem to
sacrifice to the LORD God of their
fathers. 2 Chr. 15:9 • *came after*
17 ʳAnd they strengthened the
kingdom of Judah and supported
Rehoboam the son of Solomon for
three years, for they walked in the
way of David and Solomon for
three years. 2 Chr. 12:1
18 Then Rehoboam took as a
wife Mahalath the daughter of
Jerimoth the son of David *and of*
Abihail the daughter of ʳEliab the
son of Jesse, 1 Sam. 16:6
19 and she bore him sons:
Jeush, Shemariah, and Zaham.
20 And after her he took ʳMaa-
cah the daughter of Absalom, and
she bore him Abijah, Attai, Ziza,
and Shelomith. 1 Kin. 15:2
21 And Rehoboam loved Maacah the daughter of Absalom
more than all his *other* wives and
concubines. For he had taken

eighteen wives and sixty concubines and fathered twenty-eight sons and sixty daughters.

22 And Rehoboam appointed Abijah the son of Maacah as head and leader among his brothers, for he *intended* to make him king.

23 And he acted wisely and distributed [t]some of his sons through all the territories of Judah and Benjamin to all the fortified cities, and he gave them food in abundance. And he sought many wives *for them*. *from all*

CHAPTER 12

IT took place when the kingdom of Rehoboam was established and strong that he and all Israel with him forsook the law of the LORD.

2 And it came about in King Rehoboam's fifth year, because they had been unfaithful to the LORD, that Shishak king of Egypt came up against Jerusalem

3 with 1,200 chariots and 60,000 horsemen. And the people who came with him from Egypt were without number: the Lubim, the Sukkiim, and the Ethiopians.

4 And he captured [r]the fortified cities of Judah and came as far as Jerusalem. 2 Chr. 11:5-12

5 Then Shemaiah the prophet came to Rehoboam and the princes of Judah who had gathered at Jerusalem because of Shishak, and he said to them, "Thus says the LORD, 'You have forsaken Me, so I also have forsaken you [t]to Shishak.'" *in the hand of*

6 So the princes of Israel and the king humbled themselves and said, "The LORD is righteous."

7 And when the LORD saw that they humbled themselves, the word of the LORD came to Shemaiah, saying, "They have humbled themselves so I will not destroy them, but I will grant them some *measure* of deliverance, and My wrath shall not be poured out on Jerusalem by means of Shishak.

8 "But they will become his slaves so [r]that they may learn *the difference between* My service and the service of the kingdoms of the countries." Deut. 28:47, 48

9 So Shishak king of Egypt came up against Jerusalem, and took the treasures of the house of the LORD and the treasures of the king's palace. He took everything; he even took the golden shields which Solomon had made.

10 Then King Rehoboam made shields of bronze in their place, and committed them to the [t]care of the commanders of the [t]guard who guarded the door of the king's house. *hands • runners*

11 And it happened as often as the king entered the house of the LORD, the guards came and carried them and *then* brought them back into the guards' room.

12 And when he humbled himself, the anger of the LORD turned away from him, so as not to destroy *him* completely; and also conditions were good in Judah.

13 [r]So King Rehoboam strengthened himself in Jerusalem, and reigned. Now Rehoboam was forty-one years old when he began to reign, and he reigned seventeen years in Jerusalem, the city which the LORD had chosen from all the tribes of Israel, to put

His name there. And his mother's
name was Naamah the Ammonitess. 1 Kin. 14:21
14 And he did evil [r]because he
did not set his heart to seek the
LORD. 2 Chr. 19:3
15 Now the acts of Rehoboam,
from first to last, are they not
written in the [t]records of Shemaiah the prophet and of Iddo the
seer, according to genealogical
enrollment? And *there were* wars
between Rehoboam and Jeroboam continually. *words*
16 And Rehoboam slept with
his fathers, and was buried in the
city of David; and his son Abijah
became king in his place.

CHAPTER 13

[r]IN the eighteenth year of King
Jeroboam, Abijah became king
over Judah. 1 Kin. 15:1, 2
2 He reigned three years in Jerusalem; and his mother's name
was Micaiah the daughter of Uriel
of Gibeah. And there was war between Abijah and Jeroboam.
3 And Abijah began the battle
with an army of valiant warriors,
400,000 chosen men, while Jeroboam drew up in battle formation
against him with 800,000 chosen
men *who were* valiant warriors.
4 Then Abijah stood on Mount
[r]Zemaraim, which is in the hill
country of Ephraim, and said,
"Listen to me, Jeroboam and all
Israel: Josh. 18:22
5 "Do you not know that the
LORD God of Israel gave the rule
over Israel forever to David and
his sons by a covenant of salt?
6 "Yet Jeroboam the son of Nebat, the servant of Solomon the
son of David, rose up and rebelled
against his [a]master, *lord*
7 and worthless men gathered
about him, scoundrels, who
proved too strong for Rehoboam,
the son of Solomon, when he was
young and timid and could not
hold his own against them.
8 "So now you intend to resist
the kingdom of the LORD through
the sons of David, being a great
multitude and *having* with you the
golden calves which Jeroboam
made for gods for you.
9 "Have you not driven out the
priests of the LORD, the sons of
Aaron and the Levites, and made
for yourselves priests like the peoples of *other* lands? Whoever
comes [r]to consecrate himself with
a young bull and seven rams, even
he may become a priest of *what
are* no gods. Ex. 29:29-33
10 "But as for us, the LORD is our
God, and we have not forsaken
Him; and the sons of Aaron are
ministering to the LORD as priests,
and the Levites [t]attend to their
work. *in the work*
11 "And every morning and evening they burn to the LORD burnt
offerings and fragrant incense,
and the showbread is *set* on the
clean table, and the golden lampstand with its lamps is *ready* to
light every evening; for we keep
the charge of the LORD our God,
but you have forsaken Him.
12 "Now behold, God is with us
at *our* head and [r]His priests with
the signal trumpets to sound the
alarm against you. O sons of Israel, do not fight against the LORD

God of your fathers, for you will not succeed." Num. 10:8, 9

13 But Jeroboam had set an ambush to come from the rear, so that *Israel* was in front of Judah, and the ambush was behind them.

14 When Judah turned around, behold, they were attacked both front and rear; so [r]they cried to the LORD, and the priests blew the trumpets. 2 Chr. 14:11

15 Then the men of Judah raised a war cry, and when the men of Judah raised the war cry, then it was that God [t]routed [r]Jeroboam and all Israel before Abijah and Judah. *smote* • 2 Chr. 14:12

16 And when the sons of Israel fled before Judah, [r]God gave them into their hand. 2 Chr. 16:8

17 And Abijah and his people defeated them with a great slaughter, so that 500,000 chosen men of Israel fell slain.

18 Thus the sons of Israel were subdued at that time, and the sons of Judah [t]conquered because they trusted in the LORD, the God of their fathers. *were strong*

19 And Abijah pursued Jeroboam, and captured from him *several* cities, Bethel with its villages, Jeshanah with its villages, and Ephron with its villages.

20 And Jeroboam did not again recover strength in the days of Abijah; and the [r]LORD struck him and he died. 1 Sam. 25:38

21 But Abijah became powerful, and took fourteen wives to himself; and became the father of twenty-two sons and sixteen daughters.

22 Now the rest of the acts of Abijah, and his ways and his words are written in the treatise of the prophet Iddo.

CHAPTER 14

[r]SO Abijah slept with his fathers, and they buried him in the city of David, and his son Asa became king in his place. The land was undisturbed for ten years during his days. 1 Kin. 15:8

2 And Asa did good and right in the sight of the LORD his God,

3 for he removed [r]the foreign altars and [r]high places, tore down the *sacred* pillars, cut down the [5]Asherim, Deut. 7:5 • 1 Kin. 15:12-14

4 and commanded Judah to seek the LORD God of their fathers and to observe the law and the commandment.

5 He also removed the high places and the [r]incense altars from all the cities of Judah. And the kingdom was undisturbed under him. 2 Chr. 34:4, 7

6 And he built fortified cities in Judah, since the land was undisturbed, and [t]there was no one at war with him during those years, because the LORD had given him rest. *there was not with him war*

7 For he said to Judah, "Let [r]us build these cities and surround *them* with walls and towers, gates and bars. The land is still [t]ours, because we have sought the LORD our God; we have sought Him, and He has given us rest on every side." So they built and prospered. 2 Chr. 8:5 • *before us*

8 Now Asa had an army of [r]300,000 from Judah, bearing large shields and spears, and 280,000

[5]I.e., wooden symbols of a female deity

from Benjamin, bearing shields
and wielding bows; all of them
were valiant warriors. 2 Chr. 13:3
9 Now Zerah the Ethiopian
[r]came out against them with an
army of a million men and 300
chariots, and he came to [r]Mare-
shah. 2 Chr. 12:2, 3; 16:8 • 2 Chr. 11:8
10 So Asa went out [t]to meet
him, and they drew up in battle
formation in the valley of Zepha-
thah at Mareshah. *before him*
11 Then Asa called to the LORD
his God, and said, "LORD, there is
no one besides Thee to help *in the*
battle between the powerful and
those who have no strength; so
help us, O LORD our God, for we
trust in Thee, and in Thy name
have come against this multitude.
O LORD, Thou art our God; let not
man prevail against Thee."
12 So the LORD routed the Ethiopians before Asa and before Judah, and the Ethiopians fled.
13 And Asa and the people who
were with him pursued them as
far as [r]Gerar; and so many Ethiopians fell that they could not recover, for they were shattered before the LORD, and before His
army. And they carried away very
much plunder. Gen. 10:19
14 And they [t]destroyed all the
cities around Gerar,[r]for the dread
of the LORD had fallen on them;
and they despoiled all the cities,
for there was much plunder in
them. *smote* • 2 Chr. 17:10
15 They also struck down those
who owned livestock, and they
carried away large numbers of
sheep and camels. Then they returned to Jerusalem.

CHAPTER 15

NOW the Spirit of God came on
Azariah the son of Oded,
2 and he went out to meet Asa
and said to him, "Listen to me,
Asa, and all Judah and Benjamin:
the LORD is with you when you are
with Him. And if you seek Him,
He will let you find Him; but if you
forsake Him, He will forsake you.
3 "And [r]for many days Israel
was without the true God and
without a teaching priest and
without law. 1 Kin. 12:28-33
4 "But [r]in their distress they
turned to the LORD God of Israel,
and they sought Him, and He let
them find Him. Deut. 4:29
5 "And in those times there was
no peace to him who went out or
to him who came in, for many disturbances [t]afflicted all the inhabitants of the lands. *were on*
6 "And [r]nation was crushed by
nation, and city by city, for God
troubled them with every kind of
distress. Matt. 24:7
7 "But you,[r]be strong and do not
lose courage, for there is reward
for your work." Josh. 1:7, 9
8 Now when Asa heard these
words and the prophecy which
Azariah the son of Oded the
prophet spoke, he took courage
and removed the abominable idols
from all the land of Judah and
Benjamin and from [r]the cities
which he had captured in the hill
country of Ephraim. [r]He then restored the altar of the LORD which
was in front of the porch of the
LORD. 2 Chr. 13:19 • 2 Chr. 4:1
9 And he gathered all Judah
and Benjamin and those from

Ephraim, Manasseh, and Simeon
[r]who resided with them, for many
defected to him from Israel when
they saw that the LORD his God
was with him. 2 Chr. 11:16
10 So they assembled at Jerusalem in the third month of the fifteenth year of Asa's reign.
11 And [r]they sacrificed to the
LORD that day 700 oxen and 7,000
sheep from the spoil they had
brought. 2 Chr. 14:13-15
12 And [r]they entered into the
covenant to seek the LORD God of
their fathers with all their heart
and soul; 2 Chr. 23:16
13 and whoever would not seek
the LORD God of Israel [r]should be
put to death, whether small or
great, man or woman. Ex. 22:20
14 Moreover, they made an oath
to the LORD with a loud voice,
with shouting, with trumpets, and
with horns.
15 And all Judah rejoiced concerning the oath, for they had
sworn with their whole heart and
had sought Him earnestly, and He
let them find Him. So the LORD
gave them rest on every side.
16 And he also removed Maacah, the mother of King Asa, from
the *position of* queen mother, because she had made a horrid
image as an Asherah, and Asa cut
down her horrid image, crushed *it*
and burned *it* at the brook Kidron.
17 But the high places were not
removed from Israel; nevertheless
Asa's heart was blameless all his
days.
18 And he brought into the
house of God the dedicated things
of his father and his own dedicated things: silver and gold and
utensils.
19 And there was no more war
until the thirty-fifth year of Asa's
reign.

CHAPTER 16

IN the thirty-sixth year of Asa's
reign Baasha king of Israel came
up against Judah and [t]fortified Ramah in order to prevent *anyone*
from going out or coming in to
Asa king of Judah. *built*
2 Then Asa brought out silver
and gold from the treasuries of
the house of the LORD and the
king's house, and sent them to
Ben-hadad king of Aram, who
lived in Damascus, saying,
3 "*Let there be* a treaty between
[t]you and me, *as* between my father
and your father. Behold, I have
sent you silver and gold; go, break
your treaty with Baasha king of
Israel so that he will withdraw
from me." *me and you*
4 So Ben-hadad listened to
King Asa and sent the commanders of his armies against the cities
of Israel, and they [t]conquered Ijon,
Dan, Abel-maim, and all the store
cities of Naphtali. *smote*
5 And it came about when Baasha heard *of it* that he ceased
[t]fortifying Ramah and stopped his
work. *building*
6 Then King Asa brought all
Judah, and they carried away the
stones of Ramah and its timber
with which Baasha had been
building, and with them he [t]forti-
fied Geba and Mizpah. *built*
7 At that time [r]Hanani the seer
came to Asa king of Judah and

said to him, "Because you have
relied on the king of Aram and
have not relied on the LORD your
God, therefore the army of the
king of Aram has escaped out of
your hand. 1 Kin. 16:1
8 "Were not [r]the Ethiopians and
the Lubim [r]an immense army with
very many chariots and horsemen? Yet, because you relied on
the LORD, He delivered them into
your hand. 2 Chr. 14:9 • 2 Chr. 12:3
9 "For the eyes of the LORD
move to and fro throughout the
earth that He may strongly support those whose heart is completely His. You have acted foolishly in this. Indeed, from now on
you will surely have wars."
10 Then Asa was angry with the
seer and put him in prison, for he
was enraged at him for this. And
Asa oppressed some of the people
at the same time.
11 [r]And now, the acts of Asa
from first to last, behold, they are
written in the Book of the Kings of
Judah and Israel. 1 Kin. 15:23, 24
12 And in the thirty-ninth year
of his reign Asa became diseased
in his feet. His disease was severe,
yet even in his disease he did not
seek the LORD, but the physicians.
13 So Asa slept with his fathers,
[t]having died in the forty-first year
of his reign. *and*
14 And they buried him in his
own tomb which he had cut out
for himself in the city of David,
and they laid him in the resting
place which he had filled [r]with
spices of various kinds blended by
the perfumers' art; and they made
a very great fire for him. Gen. 50:2

CHAPTER 17

JEHOSHAPHAT his son then became king in his place, and made
his position over Israel firm.
2 He placed troops in all the
fortified cities of Judah, and set
garrisons in the land of Judah, and
in the cities of Ephraim which Asa
his father had captured.
3 And the LORD was with Jehoshaphat because he followed
the example of his father David's
earlier days and did not seek the
Baals,
4 but sought the God of his father, [t]followed His commandments, [r]and did not act as Israel
did. *walked in* • 1 Kin. 12:28
5 So the LORD established the
kingdom in his [t]control, and all Judah brought tribute to Jehoshaphat, and [r]he had great riches and
honor. *hand* • 2 Chr. 18:1
6 And he took great pride in
the ways of the LORD and again
removed the high places and the
Asherim from Judah.
7 Then in the third year of his
reign he sent his officials, Ben-
hail, Obadiah, Zechariah, Nethanel, and Micaiah, [r]to teach in the
cities of Judah; 2 Chr. 15:3· 35:3
8 and with them [r]the Levites,
Shemaiah, Nethaniah, Zebadiah,
Asahel, Shemiramoth, Jehonathan, Adonijah, Tobijah, and
Tobadonijah, the Levites; and
with them Elishama and Jehoram,
the priests. 2 Chr. 19:8
9 And they taught in Judah,
having the book of the law of the
LORD with them; and they went
throughout all the cities of Judah
and taught among the people.

10 Now[r] the dread of the LORD
was on all the kingdoms of the
lands which *were* around Judah,
so that they did not make war
against Jehoshaphat. 2 Chr. 14:14
11 And some of the Philistines
[r]brought gifts and silver as tribute
to Jehoshaphat; the Arabians also
brought him flocks, 7,700 rams
and 7,700 male goats. 2 Chr. 9:14
12 So Jehoshaphat grew greater
and greater, and he built fortresses and store cities in Judah.
13 And he had large supplies in
the cities of Judah, and warriors,
valiant men, in Jerusalem.
14 And this was their muster
according to their fathers' households: of Judah, commanders of
thousands, Adnah *was* the commander, and with him 300,000 valiant warriors;
15 and next to him *was* Johanan
the commander, and with him
280,000;
16 and next to him Amasiah the
son of Zichri, [r]who volunteered for
the LORD, and with him 200,000
valiant warriors; Judg. 5:2, 9
17 and of Benjamin, Eliada a
valiant warrior, and with him
200,000 armed with bow and
shield;
18 and next to him Jehozabad,
and with him 180,000 equipped
for war.
19 These are they who served
the king, apart from [r]those whom
the king put in the fortified cities
through all Judah. 2 Chr. 17:2

CHAPTER 18

NOW Jehoshaphat had great
riches and honor; and he allied
himself by marriage with Ahab.
2 [r]And some years later he
went down to *visit* Ahab at Samaria. And Ahab slaughtered
many sheep and oxen for him and
the people who were with him,
and induced him to go up against
Ramoth-gilead. 1 Kin. 22:2-35
3 And Ahab king of Israel said
to Jehoshaphat king of Judah,
"Will you go with me *against* Ramoth-gilead?" And he said to him,
"I am as you are, and my people
as your people, and *we will be*
with you in the battle."
4 Moreover, Jehoshaphat said
to the king of Israel, "Please inquire [t]first for the word of the
LORD." *as the day*
5 Then the king of Israel assembled the prophets, four hundred men, and said to them,
"Shall we go against Ramoth-gilead to battle, or shall I refrain?"
And they said, "Go up, for God
will give *it* into the hand of the
king."
6 But Jehoshaphat said, "Is
there not yet a prophet of the
LORD here that we may inquire of
him?"
7 And the king of Israel said to
Jehoshaphat, "There is yet one
man by whom we may inquire of
the LORD, but I hate him, for he
never prophesies good concerning
me but always evil. He is Micaiah,
son of Imla." But Jehoshaphat
said, "Let not the king say so."
8 Then the king of Israel called
an officer and said, "Bring[t]quickly
Micaiah, Imla's son." *Hasten*
9 Now the king of Israel and
Jehoshaphat the king of Judah
were sitting each on his throne,
arrayed in *their* robes, and *they*

were sitting at the threshing floor
at the entrance of the gate of Samaria; and all the prophets were
prophesying before them. Ruth 4:1
10 And Zedekiah the son of
Chenaanah made horns of iron for
himself and said, "Thus says the
LORD, 'With these you shall gore
the Arameans, until they are consumed.' "
11 And all the prophets were
prophesying thus, saying, "Go up
to Ramoth-gilead and succeed, for
the LORD will give *it* into the hand
of the king."
12 Then the messenger who
went to summon Micaiah spoke to
him saying, "Behold, the words of
the prophets are uniformly favorable to the king. So please let your
word be like one of them and
speak favorably."
13 But Micaiah said, "As the
LORD lives, what my God says,
that I will speak."
14 And when he came to the
king, the king said to him, "Micaiah, shall we go to Ramoth-gilead
to battle, or shall I refrain?" He
said, "Go up and succeed, for they
will be given into your hand."
15 Then the king said to him,
"How many times must I adjure
you to speak to me nothing but
the truth in the name of the
LORD?"
16 So he said,
"I saw all Israel
Scattered on the moun-
tains,
Like sheep which have no
shepherd; Num. 27:17
And the LORD said,
'These have no master.
Let each of them return to
his house in peace.' "
17 Then the king of Israel said
to Jehoshaphat, "Did I not tell you
that he would not prophesy good
concerning me, but evil?"
18 And Micaiah said, "Therefore, hear the word of the LORD. I
saw the LORD sitting on His
throne, and all the host of heaven
standing on His right and on His
left. Is. 6:1-5; Dan. 7:9, 10
19 "And the LORD said, 'Who will
entice Ahab king of Israel to go up
and fall at Ramoth-gilead?' And
one said this while another said
that.
20 "Then a spirit came forward
and stood before the LORD and
said, 'I will entice him.' And the
LORD said to him, 'How?'
21 "And he said, 'I will go and be
a deceiving spirit in the mouth of
all his prophets.' Then He said,
'You are to entice *him* and prevail
also. Go and do so.' John 8:44
22 "Now therefore, the LORD has
put a deceiving spirit in the mouth
of these your prophets; for the
LORD has proclaimed disaster
against you." Is. 19:14; Ezek. 14:9
23 Then Zedekiah the son of
Chenaanah came near and struck
Micaiah on the cheek and said,
"How did the Spirit of the LORD
pass from me to speak to you?"
24 And Micaiah said, "Behold,
you shall see on that day, when
you enter an inner room to hide
yourself."
25 Then the king of Israel said,
"Take Micaiah and return him to
Amon the governor of the city,
and to Joash the king's son;
26 and say, 'Thus says the king,

"Put this *man* in prison, and feed
him sparingly with bread and water until I return safely."'"
27 And Micaiah said, "If you indeed return safely, the LORD has
not spoken by me." And he said,
"Listen,[r] all you people." Mic. 1:2
28 So the king of Israel and Jehoshaphat king of Judah went up
against Ramoth-gilead.
29 And the king of Israel said to
Jehoshaphat, "I will disguise myself and go into battle, but you put
on your robes." So the king of Israel disguised himself, and they
went into battle.
30 Now the king of Aram had
commanded the captains of his
chariots, saying, "Do not fight
with small or great, but with the
king of Israel alone."
31 So it came about when the
captains of the chariots saw Jehoshaphat, that they said, "It is
the king of Israel," and they
turned aside to fight against him.
But Jehoshaphat [r]cried out, and
the LORD helped him, and God di-
verted them from him. 2 Chr. 13:14
32 Then it happened when the
captains of the chariots saw that it
was not the king of Israel, that
they turned back from pursuing
him.
33 And a certain man drew his
bow at random and struck the
king of Israel in a joint of the armor. So he said to the driver of
the chariot, "Turn [t]around, and
take me out of the fight; for I am
severely wounded." *your hand*
34 And the battle raged that
day, and the king of Israel
propped himself up in his chariot
in front of the Arameans until the
evening; and at sunset he died.

CHAPTER 19

THEN Jehoshaphat the king of
Judah returned in safety to his
house in Jerusalem.
2 And [r]Jehu the son of Hanani
the seer went out to meet him
and said to King Jehoshaphat,
"Should you help the wicked and
love those who hate the LORD and
[t]so *bring* wrath on yourself from
the LORD? 1 Kin. 16:1 • *by this*
3 "But there is *some* good in
you, for you have removed the
Asheroth from the land and you
have set your heart to seek God."
4 So Jehoshaphat lived in Jerusalem and went out again among
the people from Beersheba to the
hill country of Ephraim and
brought them back to the LORD,
the God of their fathers.
5 And he appointed [r]judges in
the land in all the fortified cities of
Judah, city by city. Deut. 16:18-20
6 And he said to the judges,
"Consider what you are doing, for
[r]you do not judge for man but for
the LORD who is with you when
you render judgment. Lev. 19:15
7 "Now then let the fear of the
LORD be upon you; [t]be very careful
what you do, for the LORD our
God will have no part in unrighteousness, or partiality, or the taking of a bribe." *be careful and do*
8 And in Jerusalem also Jehoshaphat appointed some [r]of the
Levites and priests, and some of
the heads of the fathers' *households* of Israel, for the judgment
of the LORD and to judge disputes

among the inhabitants of Jerusalem. 2 Chr. 17:8, 9
9 Then he charged them saying, "Thus you shall do in the fear
of the LORD, faithfully and whole-
heartedly.
10 "And whenever any dispute
comes to you from your brethren
who live in their cities, between
blood and blood, between law and
commandment, statutes and ordinances, you shall warn them that
they may not be guilty before the
LORD, and wrath may *not* come on
you and your brethren. Thus you
shall do and you will not be guilty.
11 "And behold, Amariah the
chief priest will be over you in all
that pertains to the LORD; and
Zebadiah the son of Ishmael, the
ruler of the house of Judah, in all
that pertains to the king. Also the
Levites shall be officers before
you. Act resolutely, and the LORD
be with the upright."

CHAPTER 20

NOW it came about after this
that the sons of Moab and the
sons of Ammon, together with
some of the Meunites, came to
make war against Jehoshaphat.
2 Then some came and re-
ported to Jehoshaphat, saying, "A
great multitude is coming against
you from beyond the sea, out of
Aram and behold, they are in Hazazon-tamar (that is Engedi)."
3 And Jehoshaphat was afraid
and [t]turned his attention to seek
the LORD; and proclaimed a fast
throughout all Judah. *set his face*
4 So Judah gathered together
to [r]seek help from the LORD; they
even came from all the cities of
Judah to seek the LORD. Joel 1:14
5 Then Jehoshaphat stood in
the assembly of Judah and Jerusalem, in the house of the LORD before the new court,
6 and he said, "O LORD, the
God of our fathers, [r]art Thou not
God in the heavens? And art Thou
not ruler over all the kingdoms of
the nations? Power and might are
in Thy hand so that no one can
stand against Thee. Deut. 4:39
7 "Didst Thou not, O our God,
drive out the inhabitants of this
land before Thy people Israel, and
[r]give it to the descendants of Abraham Thy friend forever? Is. 41:8
8 "And they lived in it, and have
built Thee a sanctuary there for
Thy name, saying,
9 'Should[r] evil come upon us,
the sword, *or* judgment, or pestilence, or famine, we will stand before this house and before Thee
(for [r]Thy name is in this house)
and cry to Thee in our distress,
and Thou wilt hear and deliver
us.' 2 Chr. 6:28-30 • 2 Chr. 6:20
10 "And now behold, [r]the sons of
Ammon and Moab and Mount
Seir, whom Thou didst not let Israel invade when they came out of
the land of Egypt (they turned
aside from them and did not destroy them), 2 Chr. 20:1, 22
11 behold *how* they are reward-
ing us, by coming to drive us out
from Thy possession which Thou
hast given us as an inheritance.
12 "O our God, [r]wilt Thou not
judge them? For we are powerless
before this great multitude who
are coming against us; nor do we

know what to do, but [r]our eyes are
on Thee." Judg. 11:27 • Ps. 25:15
13 And all Judah was standing
before the LORD, with their infants, their wives, and their children.
14 Then in the midst of the assembly the Spirit of the LORD
came upon Jahaziel the son of
Zechariah, the son of Benaiah, the
son of Jeiel, the son of Mattaniah,
the Levite of the sons of Asaph;
15 and he said, "Listen, all Judah and the inhabitants of Jerusalem and King Jehoshaphat: thus
says the LORD to you, 'Do[r] not fear
or be dismayed because of this
great multitude, for the battle is
not yours but God's. Ex. 14:13
16 'Tomorrow go down against
them. Behold, they will come up
by the ascent of Ziz, and you will
find them at the end of the valley
in front of the wilderness of Jeru-
el.
17 'You *need* not fight in this
battle; station yourselves, stand
and see the salvation of the LORD
on your behalf, O Judah and Jerusalem.' Do not fear or be dismayed; tomorrow go out to face
them, for the LORD is with you."
18 And Jehoshaphat bowed his
head with *his* face to the ground,
and all Judah and the inhabitants
of Jerusalem fell down before the
LORD, worshiping the LORD.
19 And the Levites, from the
sons of the Kohathites and of the
sons of the Korahites, stood up to
praise the LORD God of Israel,
with a very loud voice.
20 And they rose early in the
morning and went out to the wilderness of Tekoa; and when they
went out, Jehoshaphat stood and
said, "Listen to me, O Judah and
inhabitants of Jerusalem, [r]put your
trust in the LORD your God, and
you will be established. Put your
trust in His prophets and succeed." Is. 7:9
21 And when he had consulted
with the people, he appointed
those who sang to the LORD and
those who [r]praised *Him* in holy attire, as they went out before the
army and said, "Give thanks to
the LORD, for His lovingkindness
is everlasting." 1 Chr. 16:29
22 And when they began singing and praising, the LORD set am-
bushes against the sons of Ammon, Moab, and Mount Seir, who
had come against Judah; so they
were [t]routed. *struck down*
23 For the sons of Ammon and
Moab rose up against the inhabitants of Mount Seir destroying
them completely, and when they
had finished with the inhabitants
of Seir, [r]they helped to destroy one
another. Judg. 7:22; 1 Sam. 14:20
24 When Judah came to the
lookout of the wilderness, they
looked toward the multitude; and
behold, they *were* corpses lying on
the ground, and no one had escaped.
25 And when Jehoshaphat and
his people came to take their
spoil, they found much among
them, *including* goods, garments,
and valuable things which they
took for themselves, more than
they could carry. And they were
three days taking the spoil because there was so much.
26 Then on the fourth day they
assembled in the valley of Bera-

cah, for there they blessed the LORD. Therefore they have named that place "The Valley of [6]Beracah" until today.

27 And every man of Judah and Jerusalem returned with Jehoshaphat at their head, returning to Jerusalem with joy, [r]for the LORD had made them to rejoice over their enemies. Neh. 12:43

28 And they came to Jerusalem with harps, lyres, and trumpets to the house of the LORD.

29 And [r]the dread of God was on all the kingdoms of the lands when they heard that the LORD had fought against the enemies of Israel. 2 Chr. 14:14; 17:10

30 So the kingdom of Jehoshaphat was at peace, for his God gave him rest on all sides.

31 [r]Now Jehoshaphat reigned over Judah. He *was* thirty-five years old when he became king, and he reigned in Jerusalem twenty-five years. And his mother's name *was* Azubah the daughter of Shilhi. 1 Kin. 22:41-43

32 And he walked in the way of his father Asa and did not depart from it, doing right in the sight of the LORD.

33 [r]The high places, however, were not removed; the people had not yet directed their hearts to the God of their fathers. 2 Chr. 17:6

34 Now the rest of the acts of Jehoshaphat, first [t]to last, behold, they are written in the annals of [r]Jehu the son of Hanani, which is [t]recorded in the Book of the Kings of Israel. *and* • 2 Chr. 19:2 • *taken up*

35 And after this Jehoshaphat king of Judah allied himself with Ahaziah king of Israel. He acted wickedly [t]in so doing. *to do*

36 So he allied himself with him to make ships to go [r]to Tarshish, and they made the ships in Ezion-geber. 2 Chr. 9:21

37 Then Eliezer the son of Dodavahu of Mareshah prophesied against Jehoshaphat saying, "Because you have allied yourself with Ahaziah, the LORD has destroyed your works." So the ships were broken and could not go to Tarshish.

CHAPTER 21

[r]THEN Jehoshaphat slept with his fathers and was buried with his fathers in the city of David, and Jehoram his son became king in his place. 1 Kin. 22:50

2 And he had brothers, the sons of Jehoshaphat: Azariah, Jehiel, Zechariah, Azaryahu, Michael, and Shephatiah. All these *were* the sons of Jehoshaphat king [r]of Israel. 2 Chr. 12:6; 23:2

3 And their father gave them many gifts of silver, gold and precious things, [r]with fortified cities in Judah, but he gave the kingdom to Jehoram because he was the first-born. 2 Chr. 11:5

4 Now when Jehoram had [t]taken over the kingdom of his father and made himself [t]secure, he killed all his brothers with the sword, and some of the rulers of Israel also. *risen up* • *strong*

5 [r]Jehoram *was* thirty-two years old when he became king, and he reigned eight years in Jerusalem. 2 Kin. 8:17-22

6 And he walked in the way of

[6]I.e., blessing

the kings of Israel, just as the
house of Ahab did (for Ahab's
daughter was his wife), and he did
evil in the sight of the LORD.
7 Yet the LORD was not willing
to destroy the house of David because of the covenant which he
had made with David, and since
He had promised to give a lamp to
him and his sons forever.
8 In his days Edom revolted
[7]against the rule of Judah, and set
up a king over themselves.
9 Then Jehoram crossed over
with his commanders and all his
chariots with him. And it came
about that he arose by night and
struck down the Edomites who
were surrounding him and the
commanders of the chariots.
10 So Edom revolted [7]against
Judah to this day. Then Libnah revolted at the same time against
his rule, because he had forsaken
the LORD God of his fathers.
11 Moreover, [r]he made high
places in the mountains of Judah,
and caused the inhabitants of Jerusalem [r]to play the harlot and led
Judah astray. 1 Kin. 11:7 • Lev. 20:5
12 Then a letter came to him
from Elijah the prophet saying,
"Thus says the LORD God of your
father David, 'Because you have
not walked in the ways of Jehoshaphat your father and the
ways of [r]Asa king of Judah,
13 but [r]have walked in the way
of the kings of Israel, and have
caused Judah and the inhabitants
of Jerusalem to play the harlot as
the house of Ahab played the harlot, and you have also killed your
brothers, your own family, who
were better than you, 2 Chr. 21:6

[7]Lit., *from under the hand of*

14 behold, the LORD is going to
strike your people, your sons,
your wives, and all your possessions with a great [t]calamity; *blow*
15 and you will suffer [t]severe
sickness, a disease of your bowels, until your bowels come out
because of the sickness, day by
day.' " *in many sicknesses*
16 Then the LORD stirred up
against Jehoram the spirit of the
Philistines and the Arabs who
bordered the Ethiopians;
17 and they came against Judah
and invaded it, and carried away
all the possessions found in the
king's house together with his
sons and his wives, so that no son
was left to him except Jehoahaz,
the youngest of his sons.
18 So after all this the LORD
smote him [r]in his bowels with an
incurable sickness. 2 Chr. 21:15
19 Now it came about in the
course of time, at the end of two
years, that his bowels came out
because of his sickness and he
died in great pain. And his people
made no fire for him like [r]the fire
for his fathers. 2 Chr. 16:14
20 He was thirty-two years old
when he became king, and he
reigned in Jerusalem eight years;
and he departed [t]with no one's regret, and they buried him in the
city of David, but not in the tombs
of the kings. *without desire*

CHAPTER 22

THEN the inhabitants of Jerusalem made Ahaziah, his youngest
son, king in his place, for the band
of men who came with the Arabs
to the camp had slain all the older

sons. So Ahaziah the son of Jehoram king of Judah began to reign.
2 Ahaziah *was* twenty-
two years old when he became
king, and he reigned one year in
Jerusalem. And his mother's
name was Athaliah, the [t]grand-
daughter of Omri. *daughter*
3 He also walked in the ways
of the house of Ahab, for his
mother was his counselor to do
wickedly.
4 And he did evil in the sight of
the LORD like the house of Ahab,
for they were his counselors after
the death of his father, to[r]his destruction. Prov. 13:20
5 He also walked according to
their counsel, and went with Jehoram the son of Ahab king of Israel
to wage war against Hazael king
of Aram at Ramoth-gilead. But
the Arameans wounded Joram.
6 So he returned to be healed
in Jezreel of the wounds [t]which
they had inflicted on him at Ramah, when he fought against Hazael king of Aram. And Ahaziah,
the son of Jehoram king of Judah,
went down to see Jehoram the son
of Ahab in Jezreel, because he
was sick. *with which . . . smitten*
7 Now[r]the destruction of Ahaziah was from God, in that [t]he
went to Joram. For when he came,
he went out with Jehoram against
Jehu the son of Nimshi, whom the
LORD had anointed to cut off the
house of Ahab. 2 Chr. 10:15 • *to go*
8 And it came about when
Jehu was executing judgment on
the house of Ahab, he found the
princes of Judah and the sons of
Ahaziah's brothers, ministering to
Ahaziah, and slew them.
9 [r]He also sought Ahaziah, and
they caught him while he was hiding in Samaria; they brought him
to Jehu, put him to death,[r]and buried him. For they said, "He is the
son of Jehoshaphat, who sought
the LORD with all his heart." So
there was no one of the house of
Ahaziah to retain the power of the
kingdom. 2 Kin. 9:27 • 2 Kin. 9:28
10 Now when Athaliah the
mother of Ahaziah saw that her
son was dead, she rose and destroyed all the royal [t]offspring of
the house of Judah. *seed*
11 But Jehoshabeath the king's
daughter took Joash the son of A-
haziah, and stole him from among
the king's sons who were being
put to death, and placed him and
his nurse in the bedroom. So Jehoshabeath, the daughter of King Jehoram, the wife of Jehoiada the
priest (for she was the sister of A-
haziah), hid him from Athaliah so
that she would not put him to
death.
12 And he was hidden with
them in the house of God six years
while Athaliah reigned over the
land.

CHAPTER 23

[r]NOW in the seventh year Jehoiada strengthened himself, and
took captains of hundreds: Azariah the son of Jeroham, Ishmael
the son of Johanan, Azariah the
son of Obed, Maaseiah the son of
Adaiah, and Elishaphat the son of
Zichri, *and they entered* into a
covenant with him. 2 Kin. 11:4-20
2 And they went throughout
Judah and gathered the Levites

from all the cities of Judah, and
the heads of the fathers' *households* of [r]Israel, and they came to
Jerusalem. 2 Chr. 11:13-17; 21:2
3 Then all the assembly made
a covenant with the king in the
house of God. And Jehoiada said
to them, "Behold, the king's son
shall reign, as the LORD has spoken concerning the sons of David.
4 "This is the thing which you
shall do: one third of you, of the
priests and Levites [r]who come in
on the sabbath, *shall be* gatekeepers, 1 Chr. 9:25
5 and one third *shall be* at the
king's house, and a third at the
Gate of the Foundation; and all
the people *shall be* in the courts of
the house of the LORD.
6 "But let no one enter the
house of the LORD except the
priests and the ministering Levites; they may enter, for they are
holy. And let all the people keep
the charge of the LORD.
7 "And the Levites will surround the king, each man with his
weapons in his hand; and whoever
enters the house, let him be killed.
Thus be with the king when he
comes in and when he goes out."
8 So the Levites and all Judah
did according to all that Jehoiada
the priest commanded. And each
one of them took his men who
were to come in on the sabbath,
with those who were to go out on
the sabbath, for Jehoiada the
priest did not dismiss *any of* [r]the
divisions. 1 Chr. 24:1
9 Then Jehoiada the priest
gave to the captains of hundreds
the spears and the large and small
shields which had been King David's, which *were* in the house of
God.
10 And he stationed all the people, each man with his weapon in
his hand, from the right [t]side of the
house to the left side of the house,
by the altar and by the house,
around the king. *shoulder*
11 Then they brought out the
king's son and put the crown on
him, and *gave him* the testimony,
and made him king. And Jehoiada
and his sons anointed him and
said, "*Long* live the king!"
12 When Athaliah heard the
noise of the people running and
praising the king, she came into
the house of the LORD to the people.
13 And she looked, and behold,
the king was standing by his pillar
at the entrance, and the captains
and the trumpeters *were* beside
the king. And all the people of the
land rejoiced and blew trumpets,
the singers with *their* musical instruments leading the praise.
Then Athaliah tore her clothes
and said, "Treason! Treason!"
14 And Jehoiada the priest
brought out the captains of hundreds who were appointed over
the army, and said to them,
"Bring her out between the ranks;
and whoever follows her, put to
death with the sword." For the
priest said, "Let her not be put to
death in the house of the LORD."
15 So they seized her, and when
she arrived at the entrance of the
Horse Gate of the king's house,
they put her to death there.
16 Then Jehoiada made a covenant between himself and all the

people and the king, that they
should be the LORD's people.
17 And all the people went to
the house of Baal, and tore it
down, and they broke in pieces his
altars and his images, and [r]killed
Mattan the priest of Baal before
the altars. Deut. 13:6-9
18 Moreover, Jehoiada placed
the offices of the house of the
LORD under the [t]authority of [r]the
Levitical priests, whom David had
assigned over the house of the
LORD, to offer the burnt offerings
of the LORD, as it is written in the
law of Moses—with rejoicing and
singing according to the [t]order of
David. *hand* · 2 Chr. 5:5 · *hands of*
19 And he stationed the gatekeepers of the house of the LORD,
so that no one should enter *who*
was in any way unclean.
20 And he took the captains of
hundreds, the nobles, the rulers of
the people, and all the people of
the land, and brought the king
down from the house of the LORD,
and came through the upper gate
to the king's house. And they
placed the king upon the royal
throne. 2 Kin. 11:19
21 So all of the people of the
land rejoiced and the city was
quiet. For they had put Athaliah
to death with the sword.

CHAPTER 24

[r]JOASH *was* seven years old when
he became king, and he reigned
forty years in Jerusalem; his
mother's name *was* Zibiah from
Beersheba. 2 Kin. 11:21; 12:1-15
2 And Joash did what was
right in the sight of the LORD all
the days of Jehoiada the priest.
3 And Jehoiada took two
wives for him, and he became the
father of sons and daughters.
4 Now it came about after this
that Joash decided [r]to restore the
house of the LORD. 2 Chr. 24:7
5 And he gathered the priests
and Levites, and said to them, "Go
out to the cities of Judah, and collect money from all Israel to [t]re-
pair the house of your God annually, and you shall do the matter
quickly." But the Levites did not
act quickly. *to strengthen*
6 So the king summoned Jehoiada the chief *priest* and said to
him, "Why have you not required
the Levites to bring in from Judah
and from Jerusalem the levy *fixed*
by Moses the servant of the LORD
on the congregation of Israel for
the tent of the testimony?"
7 For the sons of the wicked
Athaliah had broken into the
house of God and even [t]used the
holy things of the house of the
LORD for the Baals. *made*
8 So the king commanded, and
[r]they made a chest and set it outside by the gate of the house of
the LORD. 2 Kin. 12:9
9 And [r]they made a proclamation in Judah and Jerusalem to
bring to the LORD the levy *fixed by*
Moses the servant of God on Israel in the wilderness. 2 Chr. 36:22
10 And all the officers and all
the people rejoiced and brought in
their levies and dropped *them* into
the chest until they had finished.
11 And it came about whenever
the chest was brought in to the
king's officer by the Levites, and

when [r]they saw that there was much money, then the king's scribe and the chief priest's officer would come, empty the chest, take it, and return it to its place. Thus they did daily and collected much money. 2 Kin. 12:10

12 And the king and Jehoiada gave it to those who did the work of the service of the house of the LORD; and they hired masons and carpenters to restore the house of the LORD, and also workers in iron and bronze to [t]repair the house of the LORD. *to strengthen*

13 So the workmen labored, and the repair work progressed in their hands, and they [t]restored the house of God [t]according to its specifications, and strengthened it. *set up* · *upon its proportion*

14 And when they had finished, they brought the rest of the money before the king and Jehoiada; and it was made into utensils for the house of the LORD, utensils for the service and the burnt offering, and pans and utensils of gold and silver. And they offered burnt offerings in the house of the LORD continually all the days of Jehoiada.

15 Now when Jehoiada [t]reached a ripe old age he died; he was one hundred and thirty years old at his death. *became old and satisfied with days*

16 And they buried him in the city of David among the kings, because he had done well in Israel and [t]to God and His house. *with*

17 But after the death of Jehoiada the officials of Judah came and bowed down to the king, and the king listened to them.

18 And they abandoned [r]the house of the LORD, the God of their fathers, and served the [8]Asherim and the idols; so wrath came upon Judah and Jerusalem for this their guilt. 2 Chr. 24:4

19 Yet He sent prophets to them to bring them back to the LORD; though they testified against them, they would not listen.

20 Then the Spirit of God [t]came on Zechariah the son of Jehoiada the priest; and he stood above the people and said to them, "Thus God has said, 'Why do you transgress the commandments of the LORD and do not prosper? Because you have forsaken the LORD, He has also forsaken you.' " *clothed*

21 So they conspired against him and at the command of the king they stoned him to death in the court of the house of the LORD.

22 Thus Joash the king did not remember the kindness which his father Jehoiada had shown him, but he murdered his son. And as he died he said, "May [r]the LORD see and [t]avenge!" Gen. 9:5 · *seek*

23 Now it came about at the turn of the year that the army of the Arameans came up against him; and they came to Judah and Jerusalem, destroyed all the officials of the people from among the people, and sent all their spoil to the king of Damascus.

24 Indeed the army of the Arameans came with a small number of men; yet [r]the LORD delivered a very great army into their hands, [r]because they had forsaken the LORD, the God of their fathers. Thus they executed judgment on Joash. 2 Chr. 16:7, 8 · 2 Chr. 24:20

25 [r]And when they had departed

[8]I.e., wooden symbols of a female deity

from him (for they left him very sick), his own servants conspired against him because of the blood of the son of Jehoiada the priest, and murdered him on his bed. So he died, and they buried him in the city of David, but they did not bury him in the tombs of the kings. 2 Kin. 12:20, 21

26 Now these are those who conspired against him: Zabad the son of Shimeath the Ammonitess, and Jehozabad the son of Shimrith the Moabitess.

27 As to his sons and the many [a]oracles against him and the [t]rebuilding of the house of God, behold, they are written in the treatise of the Book of the Kings. Then Amaziah his son became king in his place. *burdens upon • founding*

CHAPTER 25

AMAZIAH was twenty-five years old when he became king, and he reigned twenty-nine years in Jerusalem. And his mother's name was Jehoaddan of Jerusalem.

2 And he did right in the sight of the LORD,[r]yet not with a whole heart. 2 Chr. 25:14

3 Now it came about as soon as the kingdom was firmly in his grasp, that he killed his servants who had slain his father the king.

4 However, he did not put their children to death, but *did* as it is written in the law in the book of Moses, which the LORD commanded, saying, "Fathers[r] shall not be put to death for sons, nor sons be put to death for fathers, but each shall be put to death for his own sin." Deut. 24:16

5 Moreover, Amaziah assembled Judah and appointed them according to *their* fathers' households under commanders of thousands and commanders of hundreds throughout Judah and Benjamin; and he took a census of those from twenty years old and upward, and found them to be 300,000 choice men, *able* to go to war *and* handle spear and shield.

6 He hired also 100,000 valiant warriors out of Israel for one hundred talents of silver.

7 But a man of God came to him saying, "O king, do not let the army of Israel go with you, for the LORD is not with Israel *nor with* any of the sons of Ephraim.

8 "But if you do go, do *it,* be strong for the battle; *yet* God will [t]bring you down before the enemy, for God has power to help and to bring down." *cause to stumble*

9 And Amaziah said to the man of God, "But what *shall we* do for the hundred talents which I have given to the troops of Israel?" And the man of God answered, "The LORD has much more to give you than this."

10 Then Amaziah [t]dismissed them, the troops which came to him from Ephraim, to go home; so their anger burned against Judah and they returned[t]home in fierce anger. *separated • to their own place*

11 Now Amaziah strengthened himself, and led his people forth, and went to[r]the Valley of Salt, and struck down 10,000 of the sons of Seir. 2 Kin. 14:7

12 The sons of Judah also captured 10,000 alive and brought them to the top of the cliff, and

threw them down from the top of
the cliff so that they were all
dashed to pieces.
13 But the troops whom Amaziah sent back from going with him
to battle, raided the cities of Judah, from Samaria to Beth-horon,
and struck down 3,000 of them,
and plundered much spoil.
14 Now it came about after
Amaziah came from slaughtering
the Edomites that [r]he brought the
gods of the sons of Seir, set them
up as his gods, bowed down before them, and burned incense to
them. 2 Chr. 28:23
15 Then the anger of the LORD
burned against Amaziah, and He
sent him a prophet who said to
him, "Why have you sought the
gods of the people [r]who have not
delivered their own people from
your hand?" 2 Chr. 25:11, 12
16 And it came about as he was
talking with him that [t]the king said
to him, "Have we appointed you a
royal counselor? Stop! Why
should you be struck down?"
Then the prophet stopped and
said, "I know that God has
planned to destroy you, because
you have done this, and have not
listened to my counsel." *he*
17 Then Amaziah king of Judah
took counsel and sent to Joash the
son of Jehoahaz the son of Jehu,
the king of Israel, saying, "Come,
let us face each other."
18 And Joash the king of Israel
sent to Amaziah king of Judah,
saying, "The thorn bush which
was in Lebanon sent to the cedar
which was in Lebanon, saying,
'Give your daughter to my son in
marriage.' But there passed by a
wild beast that was in Lebanon,
and trampled the thorn bush.
19 "You said, 'Behold, you have
[t]defeated Edom.' And [r]your heart
has become proud in boasting.
Now stay at home; for why should
you provoke trouble that you,
even you, should fall and Judah
with you?" *smitten* • 2 Chr. 26:16
20 But Amaziah would not listen, for it was from God, that He
might deliver them into the hand
of Joash because they had sought
the gods of Edom.
21 So Joash king of Israel went
up, and he and Amaziah king of
Judah faced each other at Beth-
shemesh, which belonged to Judah.
22 And Judah was defeated [t]by
Israel, and they fled each to his
tent. *before*
23 Then Joash king of Israel
captured Amaziah king of Judah,
the son of Joash the son of Jehoahaz, at Beth-shemesh, and
brought him to Jerusalem, and
tore down the wall of Jerusalem
from the Gate of Ephraim to the
Corner Gate, 400 cubits.
24 And *he took* all the gold and
silver, and all the utensils which
were found in the house of God
with [r]Obed-edom, and the treasures of the king's house, the hostages also, and returned to Samaria. 1 Chr. 26:15
25 And Amaziah, the son of
Joash king of Judah, lived fifteen
years after the death of Joash, son
of Jehoahaz, king of Israel.
26 Now the rest of the acts of
Amaziah, from first to last, behold, are they not written in the

Book of the Kings of Judah and Israel?
27 And from the time that Amaziah turned away from following
the LORD they conspired against
him in Jerusalem, and he fled to
Lachish; but they sent after him to
Lachish and killed him there.
28 Then they brought him on
horses and buried him with his fathers in the city of Judah.

CHAPTER 26

AND all the people of Judah took
Uzziah, who *was* sixteen years
old, and made him king in the
place of his father Amaziah.
2 He built Eloth and restored it
to Judah after the king slept with
his fathers.
3 Uzziah was [r]sixteen years old
when he became king, and he
reigned fifty-two years in Jerusalem; and his mother's name was
Jechiliah of Jerusalem. 2 Kin. 15:2, 3
4 And he did right in the sight
of the LORD according to all that
his father Amaziah had done.
5 And he continued to seek
God in the days of Zechariah, who
had understanding through the vision of God; and [t]as long as he
sought the LORD, God prospered
him. *in the days of his seeking*
6 Now he went out and [r]warred
against the Philistines, and broke
down the wall of Gath and the
wall of Jabneh and the wall of
Ashdod; and he built cities in *the
area of* Ashdod and among the
Philistines. Is. 14:29
7 And [r]God helped him against
the Philistines, and against the
Arabians who lived in Gur-baal,
and the Meunites. 2 Chr. 21:16
8 The Ammonites also gave
tribute to Uzziah, and his fame extended to the border of Egypt, for
he became very strong.
9 Moreover, Uzziah built towers in Jerusalem at [r]the Corner
Gate and at the [r]Valley Gate and at
the corner buttress and fortified
them. 2 Chr. 25:23 • Neh. 2:13, 15
10 And he built towers in the
wilderness and [r]hewed many cisterns, for he had much livestock,
both in the lowland and in the
plain. *He also had* plowmen and
vinedressers in the hill country
and the fertile fields, for he loved
the soil. Gen. 26:18-21
11 Moreover, Uzziah had an
army ready for battle, which [t]en-
tered combat by divisions, according to the number of their muster,
prepared by Jeiel the scribe and
Maaseiah the official, under the
direction of Hananiah, one of the
king's officers. *goes out to*
12 The total number of the
heads of the households, of valiant warriors, was 2,600.
13 And under their direction
was an [t]elite army of [r]307,500, who
could wage war with great power,
to help the king against the enemy. *powerful* • 2 Chr. 25:5
14 Moreover, Uzziah prepared
[t]for all the army shields, spears,
helmets, body armor, bows and
sling stones. *for them, for all*
15 And in Jerusalem he made
engines *of war* invented by skillful
men to be on the towers and on
the corners, for the purpose of
shooting arrows and great stones.
Hence his [t]fame spread afar, for he

was marvelously helped until he
was strong. *name*
16 But [r]when he became strong,
his heart was so [t]proud that he
acted corruptly, and he was unfaithful to the LORD his God, for
he entered the temple of the LORD
to burn incense on the altar of incense. Deut. 32:15 • *lifted up*
17 Then [r]Azariah the priest entered after him and with him
eighty priests of the LORD, valiant
men. 1 Chr. 6:10
18 And [r]they opposed Uzziah the
king and said to him, "It is not for
you, Uzziah, to burn incense to
the LORD, but for the priests, the
sons of Aaron who are consecrated to burn incense. Get out of
the sanctuary, for you have been
unfaithful, and will have no honor
from the LORD God." 2 Chr. 19:2
19 But Uzziah, with a censer in
his hand for burning incense, was
enraged; and while he was enraged with the priests, the leprosy
broke out on his forehead before
the priests in the house of the
LORD, beside the altar of incense.
20 And Azariah the chief priest
and all the priests looked at him,
and behold, he *was* leprous on his
forehead; and they hurried him
out of there, and he himself also
hastened to get out because the
LORD had smitten him.
21 And King Uzziah was a leper
to the day of his death; and he
lived in a separate house, being a
leper, for he was cut off from the
house of the LORD. And Jotham
his son *was* over the king's house
judging the people of the land.
22 Now the rest of the acts of
Uzziah, first to last, the prophet
[r]Isaiah, the son of Amoz, has written. Is. 1:1
23 So Uzziah slept with his fathers, and they buried him with
his fathers [r]in the field of the grave
which belonged to the kings, for
they said, "He is a leper." And Jotham his son became king in his
place. 2 Chr. 21:20; 28:27

CHAPTER 27

JOTHAM was twenty-five years
old when he became king, and he
reigned sixteen years in Jerusalem. And his mother's name was
Jerushah the daughter of Zadok.
2 And he did right in the sight
of the LORD, according to all that
his father Uzziah had done; [r]how-
ever he did not enter the temple of
the LORD. But the people continued acting corruptly. 2 Chr. 26:16
3 He built the upper gate of the
house of the LORD, and he built
extensively the wall of Ophel.
4 Moreover, he built [r]cities in
the hill country of Judah, and he
built fortresses and towers on the
wooded *hills*. 2 Chr. 11:5
5 He fought also with the king
of the Ammonites and prevailed
over them so that the Ammonites
gave him during that year one
hundred talents of silver, ten
thousand [9]kors of wheat and ten
thousand of barley. The Ammonites also paid him this *amount* in
the second and in the third year.
6 [r]So Jotham became mighty
because he ordered his ways before the LORD his God. 2 Chr. 26:5
7 [r]Now the rest of the acts of
Jotham, even all his wars and his
acts, behold, they are written in

[9]I.e., A kor equals approx. 10 bushels

the Book of the Kings of Israel
and Judah. 2 Kin. 15:36
8 He was[r]twenty-five years old
when he became king, and he
reigned sixteen years in Jerusalem. 2 Chr. 27:1
9 And Jotham slept with his fathers, and they buried him in the
city of David; and Ahaz his son
became king in his place.

CHAPTER 28

AHAZ *was* twenty years old
when he became king, and he
reigned sixteen years in Jerusalem; and[r]he did not do right in the
sight of the LORD as David his father *had done.* 2 Chr. 27:2
2 But he walked in the ways of
the kings of Israel; he also made
molten images for the Baals.
3 Moreover,[r]he burned incense
in the valley of Ben-hinnom, and
burned his sons in fire, according
to the abominations of the nations
whom the LORD had driven out
before the sons of Israel. Josh. 15:8
4 And he sacrificed and burned
incense on the high places, on the
hills, and under every green tree.
5 Wherefore, the LORD his God
delivered him into the hand of the
king of Aram; and they defeated
him and carried away from him a
great number of captives, and
brought *them* to Damascus. And
he was also delivered into the
hand of the king of Israel, who inflicted him with heavy casualties.
6 For[r]Pekah the son of Remaliah slew in Judah 120,000 in one
day, all valiant men, because they
had forsaken the LORD God of
their fathers. 2 Kin. 16:5
7 And Zichri, a mighty man of
Ephraim, slew Maaseiah the
king's son, and Azrikam the ruler
of the house and Elkanah the second to the king.
8 And the sons of Israel carried away captive of their brethren 200,000 women, sons, and
daughters; and took also a great
deal of spoil from them, and they
brought the spoil to Samaria.
9 But a prophet of the LORD
was there, whose name *was* Oded;
and he went out to meet the army
which came to Samaria and said
to them, "Behold, because the
LORD, the God of your fathers,
was angry with Judah, He has delivered them into your hand, and
you have slain them in a rage
which has even reached heaven.
10 "And now you are proposing
to [r]subjugate for yourselves the
people of Judah and Jerusalem for
male and female slaves. Surely, *do*
you not *have* transgressions of
your own against the LORD your
God? Lev. 25:39
11 "Now therefore, listen to me
and return the captives[r]whom you
captured from your brothers, for
the burning anger of the LORD is
against you." 2 Chr. 28:8
12 Then some of the heads of
the sons of Ephraim—Azariah the
son of Johanan, Berechiah the son
of Meshillemoth, Jehizkiah the
son of Shallum, and Amasa the
son of Hadlai—arose against
those who were coming from the
battle,
13 and said to them, "You must
not bring the captives in here, for
you are proposing *to bring* upon
us guilt against the LORD adding

to our sins and our guilt; for our
guilt is great so that *His* burning
anger is against Israel."
14 So the armed men left the
captives and the spoil before the
officers and all the assembly.
15 Then [r]the men who were designated by name arose, took the
captives, and they clothed all their
naked ones from the spoil; and
they gave them clothes and sandals, fed them and [r]gave them
drink, anointed them *with oil,* led
all their feeble ones on donkeys,
and brought them to Jericho, the
city of palm trees, to their brothers; then they returned to Samaria. 2 Chr. 28:12 • 2 Kin. 6:22
16 At that time King Ahaz sent
to the [10]kings of Assyria for help.
17 For again the Edomites had
come and attacked Judah, and
carried away captives.
18 [r]The Philistines also had invaded the cities of the lowland
and of the Negev of Judah, and
had taken Beth-shemesh, Aijalon,
Gederoth, and Soco with its villages, Timnah with its villages,
and Gimzo with its villages, and
they settled there. Ezek. 16:57
19 For the LORD humbled Judah
because of Ahaz king of [r]Israel, for
he had brought about a lack of restraint in Judah and was very unfaithful to the LORD. 2 Chr. 21:2
20 So [r]Tilgath-pilneser king of
Assyria came against him and afflicted him instead of strengthening him. 1 Chr. 5:26
21 And Ahaz took a portion out
of the house of the LORD and out
of the palace of the king and of
the princes, and gave *it* to the king
of Assyria; but it did not help him.

[10]Ancient versions read *king*

22 Now in the time of his distress this same King Ahaz became
yet more unfaithful to the LORD.
23 For he sacrificed to the gods
of Damascus which had defeated
him, and said, "Because the gods
of the kings of Aram helped them,
I will sacrifice to them that they
may help me." But they became
the downfall of him and all Israel.
24 Moreover, when Ahaz gathered together the utensils of the
house of God, he [r]cut the utensils
of the house of God in pieces; and
he [r]closed the doors of the house of
the LORD, and made altars for
himself in every corner of Jerusalem. 2 Kin. 16:17 • 2 Chr. 29:7
25 And in every city of Judah he
made high places to burn incense
to other gods, and provoked the
LORD, the God of his fathers, to
anger.
26 Now the rest of his acts and
all his ways, from first to last, behold, they are written in the Book
of the Kings of Judah and Israel.
27 [r]So Ahaz slept with his fathers, and they buried him in the
city, in Jerusalem, for they did not
bring him into the tombs of the
kings of Israel; and Hezekiah his
son reigned in his place. Is. 14:28

CHAPTER 29

[r]HEZEKIAH became king *when*
he was twenty-five years old; and
he reigned twenty-nine years in
Jerusalem. And his mother's
name *was* Abijah, the daughter of
Zechariah. 2 Kin. 18:1-3
2 And he did right in the sight
of the LORD, according to all that
his father David had done.

3 In the first year of his reign,
in the first month, he [r]opened the
doors of the house of the LORD
and repaired them. 2 Chr. 28:24
4 And he brought in the priests
and the Levites, and gathered
them into the square on the east.
5 Then he said to them, "Listen
to me, O Levites. Consecrate
yourselves now, and consecrate
the house of the LORD, the God of
your fathers, and carry the uncleanness out from the holy place.
6 "For our fathers have been
unfaithful and have done evil in
the sight of the LORD our God, and
have forsaken Him and turned
their faces away from the dwelling place of the LORD, and have
[t]turned *their* backs. *given*
7 "They have also shut the
doors of the porch and put out the
lamps, and have not burned incense or offered burnt offerings in
the holy place to the God of Israel.
8 "Therefore [r]the wrath of the
LORD was against Judah and Jerusalem, and He has made them an
object of terror, of horror, and of
[r]hissing, as you see with your own
eyes. 2 Chr. 24:20 • Jer. 25:9, 18
9 "For behold, our fathers have
fallen by the sword, and our sons
and our daughters and our wives
are in captivity for this.
10 "Now it is in my heart to
make a covenant with the LORD
God of Israel, that His burning anger may turn away from us.
11 "My sons, do not be negligent
now, for [r]the LORD has chosen you
to stand before Him, to minister
to Him, and to be His ministers
and burn incense." Num. 3:6; 8:6
12 Then the Levites arose: [r]Ma-
hath, the son of Amasai and Joel
the son of Azariah, from the sons
of the Kohathites; and from the
sons of Merari, Kish the son of
Abdi and Azariah the son of Jehallelel; and from the Gershonites,
Joah the son of Zimmah and Eden
the son of Joah; 2 Chr. 31:13
13 and from the sons of Elizaphan, Shimri and [a]Jeiel; and from
the sons of Asaph, Zechariah and
Mattaniah; *Jeuel*
14 and from the sons of Heman,
[a]Jehiel and Shimei; and from the
sons of Jeduthun, Shemaiah and
Uzziel. *Jehuel,* 1 Chr. 15:18, 20
15 And they assembled their
brothers, [r]consecrated themselves,
and went in to cleanse the house
of the LORD, according to the commandment of the king by the
words of the LORD. 2 Chr. 29:5
16 So the priests went in to the
inner part of the house of the
LORD to cleanse *it,* and every unclean thing which they found in
the temple of the LORD they
brought out to the court of the
house of the LORD. Then the Levites received *it* to carry out to [r]the
Kidron [a]valley. 2 Chr. 15:16 • *wadi*
17 Now they began the consecration on the first *day* of the first
month, and on the eighth day of
the month they entered the porch
of the LORD. Then they consecrated the house of the LORD in
eight days, and finished on the
sixteenth day of the first month.
18 Then they went in to King
Hezekiah and said, "We have
cleansed the whole house of the
LORD, the altar of burnt offering
with all of its utensils, and the ta-

ble of showbread with all of its utensils.

19 "Moreover, all the utensils which King Ahaz had discarded during his reign in his unfaithfulness, we have prepared and consecrated; and behold, they are before the altar of the LORD."

20 Then King Hezekiah arose early and assembled the princes of the city and went up to the house of the LORD.

21 And they brought seven bulls, seven rams, seven lambs, and seven male goats [r]for a sin offering for the kingdom, the sanctuary, and Judah. And he ordered the priests, the sons of Aaron, to offer *them* on the altar of the LORD. Lev. 4:3-14

22 So they slaughtered the bulls, and the priests took the blood and sprinkled it on the altar. They also slaughtered the rams and sprinkled the blood on the altar; they slaughtered the lambs also and [r]sprinkled the blood on the altar. Lev. 4:18

23 Then they brought the male goats of the sin offering before the king and the assembly, and [r]they laid their hands on them. Lev. 4:15

24 And the priests slaughtered them and purged the altar with their blood [r]to atone for all Israel, for the king ordered the burnt offering and the sin offering for all Israel. Lev. 4:26

25 He then stationed the Levites in the house of the LORD with cymbals, with harps, and with lyres, according to the command of David and of Gad the king's seer, and of Nathan the prophet; for the command was from the LORD through His prophets.

26 And the Levites stood with the *musical* instruments of David, and the priests with the trumpets.

27 Then Hezekiah gave the order to offer the burnt offering on the altar. When the burnt offering began, [r]the song to the LORD also began with the trumpets, *accompanied* by the instruments of David, king of Israel. 2 Chr. 23:18

28 While the whole assembly worshiped, the singers also sang and the trumpets sounded; all this *continued* until the burnt offering was finished.

29 Now at the completion of the burnt offerings, the king and all who were present with him bowed down and worshiped.

30 Moreover, King Hezekiah and the officials ordered the Levites to sing praises to the LORD with the words of David and Asaph the seer. [r]So they sang praises with joy, and bowed down and worshiped. Ps. 100:1; 106:12

31 Then Hezekiah answered and said, "Now *that* you have [t]consecrated yourselves to the LORD, come near and bring sacrifices and thank offerings to the house of the LORD." And the assembly brought sacrifices and thank offerings, and all those who were willing *brought* burnt offerings.

filled your hands

32 And the number of the burnt offerings which the assembly brought was 70 bulls, 100 rams, and 200 lambs; all these were for a burnt offering to the LORD.

33 And the consecrated things were 600 bulls and 3,000 sheep.

34 But the priests were too few,
so that they were unable to skin
all the burnt offerings; therefore
their brothers the Levites helped
them until the work was completed, and until the *other* priests
had consecrated themselves. For
the Levites were more [t]conscien-
tious to consecrate themselves
than the priests. *upright of heart*
35 And there *were* also many
burnt offerings with the fat of the
peace offerings and with the libations for the burnt offerings. Thus
the service of the house of the
LORD was established *again.*
36 Then Hezekiah and all the
people rejoiced over what God
had prepared for the people, because the thing came about suddenly.

CHAPTER 30

NOW Hezekiah sent to all Israel
and Judah and wrote letters also
to Ephraim and Manasseh, that
they should come to the house of
the LORD at Jerusalem to [t]cele-
brate the Passover to the LORD
God of Israel. *do,* so in vv. 2, 3, 5, 13
2 For the king and his princes
and all the assembly in Jerusalem
had decided to celebrate the Passover in the second month,
3 since they could not celebrate it [r]at that time, because the
priests had not consecrated themselves in sufficient numbers, nor
had the people been gathered to
Jerusalem. 2 Chr. 29:17, 34
4 Thus the thing was right in
the sight of the king and [t]all the
assembly. *in the sight of all*
5 So they established a decree
to circulate a [t]proclamation
throughout all Israel from Beersheba even to Dan, that they
should come to celebrate the
Passover to the LORD God of Israel at Jerusalem. For they had
not celebrated *it* in great numbers
as it was [t]prescribed. *voice • written*
6 And the [t]couriers went
throughout all Israel and Judah
with the letters from the hand of
the king and his princes, even according to the command of the
king, saying, "O sons of Israel, return to the LORD God of Abraham,
Isaac, and Israel, that He may return to those of you who escaped
and are left from the [t]hand of the
kings of Assyria. *runners • palm*
7 "And do not be like your fathers and your brothers, who were
unfaithful to the LORD God of
their fathers, so that He made
them a horror, as you see.
8 "Now do not stiffen your neck
like your fathers, but [t]yield to the
LORD and enter His sanctuary
which He has consecrated forever, and serve the LORD your
God, that His burning anger may
turn away from you. *give a hand*
9 "For [r]if you return to the LORD,
your brothers and your sons *will
find* compassion before those who
led them captive, and will return
to this land. [r]For the LORD your
God is gracious and compassionate, and will not turn *His* face
away from you if you return to
Him." Deut. 30:2 • Ex. 34:6, 7
10 So the couriers passed from
city to city through the country of
Ephraim and Manasseh, and as
far as Zebulun, but they laughed
them to scorn, and mocked them.

11 Nevertheless [r]some men of
Asher, Manasseh, and Zebulun
humbled themselves and came to
Jerusalem. 2 Chr. 30:18, 21, 25
12 The [r]hand of God was also on
Judah to give them one heart to
do what the king and the princes
commanded by the word of the
LORD. 2 Cor. 3:5; Phil. 2:13
13 Now many people were
gathered at Jerusalem to celebrate the Feast of Unleavened
Bread [r]in the second month, a very
large assembly. 2 Chr. 30:2
14 And they arose and removed
the altars which *were* in Jerusalem; they also [r]removed all the incense altars and cast *them* into
the brook Kidron. 2 Chr. 28:24
15 Then they slaughtered the
Passover *lambs* on the fourteenth
of the second month. And the
priests and Levites were ashamed
of themselves and consecrated
themselves, and brought burnt offerings to the house of the LORD.
16 And they stood at their stations after their custom, according to the law of Moses the man of
God; the priests sprinkled the
blood *which they received* from
the hand of the Levites.
17 For *there were* many in the
assembly who had not consecrated themselves; therefore, the
Levites *were* over the slaughter of
the Passover *lambs* for everyone
who *was* unclean, in order to consecrate *them* to the LORD.
18 For a multitude of the people, *even* many from Ephraim and
Manasseh, Issachar and Zebulun,
had not purified themselves, yet
they ate the Passover otherwise
than [t]prescribed. For Hezekiah
prayed for them, saying, "May the
good LORD pardon *written*
19 [r]everyone who prepares his
heart to seek God, the LORD God
of his fathers, though not according to the purification *rules* of the
sanctuary." 2 Chr. 19:3
20 So the LORD heard Hezekiah
and healed the people.
21 And the sons of Israel present in Jerusalem [r]celebrated the
Feast of Unleavened Bread *for*
seven days with great joy, and the
Levites and the priests praised the
LORD day after day with loud instruments to the LORD. Ex. 12:15
22 Then Hezekiah spoke en-
couragingly to all the Levites who
showed good insight *in the things*
of the LORD. So they ate for the
appointed seven days, sacrificing
peace offerings and giving thanks
to the LORD God of their fathers.
23 Then the whole assembly decided to celebrate *the feast* another seven days, so they celebrated the seven days with joy.
24 For Hezekiah king of Judah
had contributed to the assembly
1,000 bulls and 7,000 sheep, and
the princes had contributed to the
assembly 1,000 bulls and 10,000
sheep; and a large number of
priests consecrated themselves.
25 And all the assembly of Judah rejoiced, with the priests and
the Levites, and all the assembly
that came from Israel, both the sojourners who came from the land
of Israel and those living in Judah.
26 So there was great joy in Jerusalem, because there was nothing like this in Jerusalem [r]since the
days of Solomon the son of David,
king of Israel. 2 Chr. 7:8-10

27 Then [r]the Levitical priests
arose and blessed the people; and
their voice was heard and their
prayer came to His holy dwelling
place, to heaven. 2 Chr. 23:18

CHAPTER 31

NOW when all this was finished,
all Israel who were present went
out to the cities of Judah, [r]broke
the pillars in pieces, cut down the
[11]Asherim, and pulled down the
high places and the altars
throughout all Judah and Benjamin, as well as in Ephraim and
Manasseh, until they had destroyed them all. Then all the sons
of Israel returned to their cities,
each to his possession. 2 Kin. 18:4
2 And Hezekiah appointed [r]the
divisions of the priests and the Levites by their divisions, each according to his service, *both* the
priests and the Levites, for burnt
offerings and for peace offerings,
to minister and to give thanks and
to praise in the gates of the camp
of the LORD. 1 Chr. 24:1
3 *He* also *appointed* the king's
portion of his goods for the burnt
offerings, *namely*, for the morning
and evening burnt offerings, and
the burnt offerings for the sabbaths and for the new moons and
for the fixed festivals, as it is written in the law of the LORD.
4 Also he [t]commanded the people who lived in Jerusalem to give
[r]the portion due to the priests and
the Levites, that they might devote themselves to the law of the
LORD. *said to* • Num. 18:8
5 And as soon as the [t]order
spread, the sons of Israel provided
in abundance the first fruits of
grain, new wine, oil, honey, and of
all the produce of the field; and
they brought in abundantly [r]the
tithe of all. *word* • Neh. 13:12
6 And the sons of Israel and
Judah who lived in the cities of
Judah, also brought in the tithe of
oxen and sheep, and [r]the tithe of
sacred gifts which were consecrated to the LORD their God, and
placed *them* in heaps. Lev. 27:30
7 In the third month they began to make the heaps, and finished *them* by the seventh month.
8 And when Hezekiah and the
rulers came and saw the heaps,
they blessed the LORD and [r]His
people Israel. Deut. 33:29
9 Then Hezekiah questioned
the priests and the Levites concerning the heaps.
10 And Azariah the chief priest
of the house of Zadok said to him,
"Since the contributions began to
be brought into the house of the
LORD, we have had enough to eat
with plenty left over, for the LORD
has blessed His people, and this
great quantity is left over."
11 Then Hezekiah commanded
them to prepare [r]rooms in the
house of the LORD, and they prepared *them*. 1 Kin. 6:5, 8
12 And they faithfully brought
in the contributions and the tithes
and the consecrated things; and
Conaniah the Levite *was* the officer in charge of them and his
brother Shimei *was* second.
13 And Jehiel, Azaziah, Nahath,
Asahel, Jerimoth, Jozabad, Eliel,
Ismachiah, Mahath, and Benaiah
were overseers [t]under the authority of Conaniah and Shimei his

[11]I.e., wooden symbols of a female deity

brother by the appointment of King Hezekiah, and ʳAzariah *was* the *chief* officer of the house of God. *from the hand of* • 2 Chr. 31:10

14 And Kore the son of Imnah the Levite, the keeper of the eastern *gate, was* over the freewill offerings of God, to apportion the contributions for the LORD and the most holy things.

15 And under his authority *were* Eden, Miniamin, Jeshua, Shemaiah, Amariah, and Shecaniah in the cities of the priests, to distribute faithfully *their portions* to their brothers by divisions, whether great or small,

16 without regard to their genealogical enrollment, to the males from ʳthirty years old and upward—everyone who entered the house of the LORD ʳfor his daily obligations—for their work in their duties according to their divisions; 1 Chr. 23:3 • Ezra 3:4

17 as well as the priests who were enrolled genealogically according to their fathers' households, and the Levites from twenty years old and upwards, by their duties *and* their divisions.

18 And the genealogical enrollment *included* all their little children, their wives, their sons, and their daughters, for the whole assembly, for they consecrated themselves faithfully in holiness.

19 Also for the sons of Aaron the priests *who were* in ʳthe pasture lands of their cities, or in each and every city, *there were* men who were designated by name to distribute portions to every male among the priests and to everyone genealogically enrolled among the Levites. Lev. 25:34

20 And thus Hezekiah did throughout all Judah; and ʳhe did what *was* good, right, and true before the LORD his God. 2 Kin. 20:3

21 And every work which he began in the service of the house of God in law and in commandment, seeking his God, he did with all his heart and prospered.

CHAPTER 32

AFTER these acts of faithfulness Sennacherib king of Assyria came and invaded Judah and besieged the fortified cities, and ᵗthought to break into them for himself. *said*

2 Now when Hezekiah saw that Sennacherib had come, and that ᵗhe intended to make war on Jerusalem, *his face for war against*

3 he decided with his officers and his warriors to cut off the *supply of* water from the springs which *were* outside the city, and they helped him.

4 So many people assembled ʳand stopped up all the springs and the stream which flowed through the region, saying, "Why should the kings of Assyria come and find abundant water?" 2 Kin. 20:20

5 And he took courage and rebuilt all the wall that had been broken down, and erected towers on it, and *built* another outside wall, and strengthened the Millo *in* the city of David, and made weapons and shields in great number.

6 And he appointed military officers over the people, and gathered them to him in the square at

the city gate, and spoke encourag-
ingly to them, saying,
7 "Be strong and courageous,
do not fear or be dismayed because of the king of Assyria, nor
because of all the multitude which
is with him; for the one with us is
greater than the one with him.
8 "With him is *only* [r]an arm of
flesh, but [r]with us is the LORD our
God to help us and to fight our
battles." And the people relied on
the words of Hezekiah king of Judah. Jer. 17:5 • 2 Chr. 20:17
9 After this Sennacherib king
of Assyria sent his servants to Jerusalem while he *was* besieging
Lachish with all his forces with
him, against Hezekiah king of Judah and against all Judah who
were at Jerusalem, saying,
10 "Thus says Sennacherib king
of Assyria, 'On what are you
trusting that you are remaining in
Jerusalem under siege?
11 'Is not Hezekiah misleading
you to give yourselves over to die
by hunger and by thirst, saying,
"The LORD our God will deliver us
from the [t]hand of the king of Assyria"? *palm*
12 'Has not the same Hezekiah
taken away His high places and
His altars, and said to Judah and
Jerusalem, "You shall worship before one altar, and on it you shall
[t]burn incense"? *offer up in smoke*
13 'Do you not know what I and
my fathers have done to all the
peoples of the lands? [r]Were the
gods of the nations of the lands
able at all to deliver their land
from my hand? 2 Kin. 18:33-35
14 'Who *was there* among all the
gods of those nations which my
fathers utterly destroyed who
could deliver his people out of my
hand, that your God should be
able to deliver you from my hand?
15 'Now therefore, do not let
Hezekiah deceive you or mislead
you like this, and do not believe
him, for [r]no god of any nation or
kingdom was able to deliver his
people from my hand or from the
hand of my fathers. How much
less shall your God deliver you
from my hand?' " Ex. 5:2
16 And his servants spoke further against the LORD God and
against His servant Hezekiah.
17 He also wrote letters to insult the LORD God of Israel, and to
speak against Him, saying, "As
the gods of the nations of the
lands [t]have not delivered their
people from my hand, so the God
of Hezekiah shall not deliver His
people from my hand." *who have*
18 And [r]they called this out with
a loud voice in the language of Judah to the people of Jerusalem
who were on the wall, to frighten
and terrify them, so that they
might take the city. 2 Kin. 18:28
19 And they spoke [t]of the God of
Jerusalem as of [r]the gods of the
peoples of the earth, the work of
men's hands. *to* • Ps. 115:4-8
20 But King Hezekiah and Isaiah the prophet, the son of Amoz,
prayed about this and cried out to
heaven.
21 And the LORD sent an angel
who destroyed every mighty warrior, commander and officer in the
camp of the king of Assyria. So he
returned [t]in shame to his own
land. And when he had entered
the temple of his god, some of his

own children killed him there with
the sword. *in shame of face*
22 So the LORD [r]saved Hezekiah
and the inhabitants of Jerusalem
from the hand of Sennacherib the
king of Assyria, and from the
hand of all *others*, and guided
them on every side. Is. 31:5
23 And many were bringing
gifts to the LORD at Jerusalem and
choice presents to Hezekiah king
of Judah, so that he was exalted in
the sight of all nations thereafter.
24 In those days Hezekiah became mortally ill; and he prayed
to the LORD, and the LORD spoke
to him and gave him a sign.
25 But Hezekiah gave no return
for the benefit [t]he received, because his heart was proud; therefore wrath came on him and on
Judah and Jerusalem. *to him*
26 However, [r]Hezekiah [t]humbled
the pride of his heart, both he and
the inhabitants of Jerusalem, so
that the wrath of the LORD did not
come on them in the days of Hezekiah. Jer. 26:18 • *humbled himself in*
27 Now Hezekiah had immense
riches and honor; and he made for
himself treasuries for silver, gold,
precious stones, spices, shields
and all kinds of valuable articles,
28 storehouses also for the produce of grain, wine and oil, pens
for all kinds of cattle and sheepfolds for the flocks.
29 And he made cities for himself, and acquired flocks and
herds in abundance; for God had
given him very great wealth.
30 It was Hezekiah who
[r]stopped the upper outlet of the
waters of Gihon and directed
them to the west side of the city of
David. And Hezekiah prospered in
all that he did. 2 Kin. 20:20
31 And even *in the matter of* [r]the
envoys of the rulers of Babylon,
who sent to him to inquire of the
wonder that had happened in the
land, God left him *alone only* to
test him, that He might know all
that was in his heart. Is. 39:1
32 Now the rest of the acts of
Hezekiah and his deeds of devotion, behold, they are written in
the vision of Isaiah the prophet,
the son of Amoz, in the Book of
the Kings of Judah and Israel.
33 So Hezekiah slept with his
fathers, and they buried him in the
[a]upper section of the tombs of the
sons of David; and all Judah and
the inhabitants of Jerusalem [r]hon-
ored him at his death. And his son
Manasseh became king in his
place. *ascent to* • Ps. 112:6

CHAPTER 33

[r]MANASSEH was twelve years
old when he became king, and he
reigned fifty-five years in Jerusalem. 2 Kin. 21:1-9
2 And [r]he did evil in the sight of
the LORD according to the abominations of the nations whom the
LORD dispossessed before the
sons of Israel. 2 Chr. 28:3
3 For he rebuilt the high places
which Hezekiah his father had
broken down; he also erected altars for the Baals and made [12]A-
sherim, and worshiped all the host
of heaven and served them.
4 And [r]he built altars in the
house of the LORD of which the
LORD had said, "My name shall be
in Jerusalem forever." 2 Chr. 28:24

[12] I.e., wooden symbols of a female deity

5 For he built altars for all the
host of heaven in [r]the two courts
of the house of the LORD. 2 Chr. 4:9
6 And [r]he made his sons pass
through the fire in the valley of
Ben-hinnom; and he practiced
witchcraft, used divination, practiced sorcery, and dealt with mediums and spiritists. He did much
evil in the sight of the LORD, provoking Him *to anger*. 2 Chr. 28:3
7 Then he put the carved
image of the idol which he had
made in the house of God, of
which God had said to David and
to Solomon his son, "In this house
and in Jerusalem, which I have
chosen from all the tribes of Israel, I will put My name forever;
8 and I will not again remove
the foot of Israel from the land
[r]which I have appointed for your
fathers, if only they will observe
to do all that I have commanded
them according to all the law, the
statutes, and the ordinances *given*
through Moses." 2 Sam. 7:10
9 Thus Manasseh misled Judah
and the inhabitants of Jerusalem
to do more evil than the nations
whom the LORD destroyed before
the sons of Israel.
10 And the LORD spoke to Manasseh and his people, but [r]they
paid no attention. Neh. 9:29
11 Therefore the LORD brought
the commanders of the army of
the king of Assyria against them,
and they captured Manasseh with
[13]hooks, bound him with bronze
chains, and took him to Babylon.
12 And when [r]he was in distress,
he entreated the LORD his God and
humbled himself greatly before
the God of his fathers. Ps. 118:5

[13]I.e., thong put through the nose

13 When he prayed to Him, He
was moved by his entreaty and
heard his supplication, and
brought him again to Jerusalem to
his kingdom. Then Manasseh
knew that the LORD *was* God.
14 Now after this he built the
outer wall of the city of David on
the west side of [r]Gihon, in the valley, even to the entrance of the
[r]Fish Gate; and he encircled the
Ophel *with it* and made it very
high. Then he put army commanders in all the fortified cities of Judah. 1 Kin. 1:33 • Neh. 3:3
15 He also [r]removed the foreign
gods and the idol from the house
of the LORD, as well as all the altars which he had built on the
mountain of the house of the LORD
and in Jerusalem, and he threw
them outside the city. 2 Chr. 33:3-7
16 And he set up the altar of the
LORD and sacrificed [r]peace offerings and thank offerings on it; and
he ordered Judah to serve the
LORD God of Israel. Lev. 7:11-18
17 Nevertheless [r]the people still
sacrificed in the high places, *al-*
though only to the LORD their
God. 2 Chr. 32:12
18 Now the rest of the acts of
Manasseh even [r]his prayer to his
God, and the words of the seers
who spoke to him in the name of
the LORD God of Israel, behold,
they are among the records of the
kings of Israel. 2 Chr. 33:12, 13
19 His prayer also and *how God*
was entreated by him, and all his
sin, his unfaithfulness, and the
sites on which he built high places
and erected the Asherim and the
carved images, before he humbled

himself, behold, they are written
in the records of the Hozai.
20 So Manasseh slept with his
fathers, and they buried him in his
own house. And Amon his son became king in his place.
21 Amon *was* twenty-two years
old when he became king, and he
reigned two years in Jerusalem.
22 And he did evil in the sight of
the LORD as Manasseh his father
[r]had done, and Amon sacrificed to
all the carved images which his
father Manasseh had made, and
he served them. 2 Chr. 33:2-7
23 Moreover, he did not humble
himself before the LORD as his father Manasseh had done, but
Amon multiplied guilt.
24 Finally his servants conspired against him and put him to
death in his own house.
25 But the people of the land
[t]killed all the conspirators against
King Amon, and the people of the
land made Josiah his son king in
his place. *smote*

CHAPTER 34

JOSIAH *was* eight years old when
he became king, and he reigned
thirty-one years in Jerusalem.
2 And [r]he did right in the sight
of the LORD, and walked in the
ways of his father David and did
not turn aside to the right or to the
left. 2 Chr. 29:2
3 For in the eighth year of his
reign while he was still a youth, he
began to [r]seek the God of his father David; and in the twelfth year
he began to purge Judah and Jerusalem of the high places, the
Asherim, the carved images, and
the molten images. 2 Chr. 15:2
4 And they tore down the altars of the Baals in his presence,
and [r]the incense altars that were
high above them he chopped
down; also the Asherim, the
carved images, and the molten images he broke in pieces and
ground to powder and scattered *it*
on the graves of those who had
sacrificed to them. 2 Kin. 23:4, 5
5 Then he burned the bones of
the priests on their altars, and
purged Judah and Jerusalem.
6 And [r]in the cities of Manasseh, Ephraim, Simeon, even as far
as Naphtali, in their surrounding
ruins, 2 Kin. 23:15, 19
7 he also tore down the altars
and beat the Asherim and the
carved images into powder, and
chopped down all the incense altars throughout the land of Israel.
Then he returned to Jerusalem.
8 Now in the eighteenth year
of his reign, when he had purged
the land and the house, he sent
Shaphan the son of Azaliah, and
Maaseiah [r]an official of the city,
and Joah the son of Joahaz the recorder, to repair the house of the
LORD his God. 2 Chr. 18:25
9 And they came to Hilkiah the
high priest and delivered the money that was brought into the
house of God, which the Levites,
the doorkeepers, had collected
from Manasseh and Ephraim, and
from all the remnant of Israel,
and from all Judah and Benjamin
and the inhabitants of Jerusalem.
10 Then they gave *it* into the
hands of the workmen who had
the oversight of the house of the

LORD, and the workmen who were
working in the house of the LORD
used it to restore and repair the
house. *gave*
11 They in turn gave *it* to the
carpenters and to the builders to
buy quarried stone and timber for
couplings and to make beams for
the houses which the kings of Judah had let go to ruin.
12 And the men did the work
faithfully with foremen over them
to supervise: Jahath and Obadiah,
the Levites of the sons of Merari,
Zechariah and Meshullam of the
sons of the Kohathites, and the
Levites, all who were skillful with
musical instruments. 2 Kin. 12:15
13 *They were* also over the burden bearers, and supervised all
the workmen from job to job; and
some of the Levites *were* scribes
and officials and gatekeepers.
14 When they were bringing out
the money which had been
brought into the house of the
LORD, Hilkiah the priest found the
book of the law of the LORD *given*
by Moses. 2 Chr. 34:9
15 And Hilkiah responded and
said to Shaphan the scribe, "I
have found the book of the law in
the house of the LORD." And Hilkiah gave the book to Shaphan.
16 Then Shaphan brought the
book to the king and reported further word to the king, saying,
"Everything that was entrusted to
your servants they are doing.
17 "They have also emptied out
the money which was found in the
house of the LORD, and have delivered it into the hands of the supervisors and the workmen."
18 Moreover, Shaphan the
scribe told the king saying, "Hilkiah the priest gave me a book."
And Shaphan read from it in the
presence of the king.
19 And it came about when the
king heard the words of the law
that he tore his clothes. Josh. 7:6
20 Then the king commanded
Hilkiah, Ahikam the son of Shaphan, Abdon the son of Micah,
Shaphan the scribe, and Asaiah
the king's servant, saying,
21 "Go, inquire of the LORD for
me and for those who are left in
Israel and in Judah, concerning
the words of the book which has
been found; for great is the wrath
of the LORD which is poured out
on us because our fathers have
not observed the word of the
LORD, to do according to all that is
written in this book." 2 Chr. 29:8
22 So Hilkiah and *those* whom
the king had told went to Huldah
the prophetess, the wife of Shallum the son of Tokhath, the son of
Hasrah, the keeper of the wardrobe (now she lived in Jerusalem
in the Second Quarter); and they
spoke to her regarding this.
23 And she said to them, "Thus
says the LORD, the God of Israel,
'Tell the man who sent you to Me,
24 thus says the LORD, "Behold,
I am bringing evil on this place
and on its inhabitants, *even* all the
curses written in the book which
they have read in the presence of
the king of Judah. 2 Chr. 36:14-20
25 "Because they have forsaken
Me and have burned incense to
other gods, that they might provoke Me to anger with all the
works of their hands, therefore
My wrath will be poured out on

this place, and it shall not be quenched." ' 2 Chr. 33:3

26 "But to the king of Judah who sent you to inquire of the LORD, thus you will say to him, 'Thus says the LORD God of Israel *regarding* the words which you have heard,

27 "Because your heart was tender and you humbled yourself before God, when you heard His words against this place and against its inhabitants, and *because* you humbled yourself before Me, tore your clothes, and wept before Me, I truly have heard you," declares the LORD.

28 "Behold, I will gather you to your fathers and you shall be gathered to your grave in peace, so your eyes shall not see all the evil which I will bring on this place and on its inhabitants." ' " And they brought back word to the king.

29 [r]Then the king sent and gathered all the elders of Judah and Jerusalem. 2 Kin. 23:1-3

30 And the king went up to the house of the LORD and all the men of Judah, the inhabitants of Jerusalem, the priests, the Levites, and all the people, from the greatest to the least; and he read in their hearing all the words of the book of the covenant which was found in the house of the LORD.

31 Then the king stood in his place and made a covenant before the LORD to walk after the LORD, and to keep His commandments and His testimonies and His statutes with all his heart and with all his soul, to perform the words of the covenant written in this book.

32 Moreover, he made all who were present in Jerusalem and Benjamin to stand *with him.* So the inhabitants of Jerusalem did according to the covenant of God, the God of their fathers.

33 And Josiah removed all the abominations from all the lands belonging to the sons of Israel, and made all who were present in Israel to serve the LORD their God. Throughout his [t]lifetime they did not turn from following the LORD God of their fathers. *days*

CHAPTER 35

THEN Josiah celebrated the Passover to the LORD in Jerusalem, and they slaughtered the Passover *animals* on the fourteenth *day* of the first month.

2 And he set the priests in their offices and [r]encouraged them in the service of the house of the LORD. 2 Chr. 29:11

3 He also said to [r]the Levites who taught all Israel *and* who were holy to the LORD, "Put the holy ark in the house which Solomon the son of David king of Israel built; it will be a burden on *your* shoulders no longer. Now serve the LORD your God and His people Israel. 2 Chr. 17:8, 9

4 "And [r]prepare *yourselves* by your fathers' households in your divisions, according to the writing of David king of Israel and [r]according to the writing of his son Solomon. 1 Chr. 9:10-13 • 2 Chr. 8:14

5 "Moreover, [r]stand in the holy place according to the sections of the fathers' households of your brethren the lay people, and ac-

cording to the Levites, by division
of a father's household. Ezra 6:18
6 "Now [r]slaughter the Passover
animals, [r]sanctify yourselves, and
prepare for your brethren to do
according to the word of the LORD
by Moses." 2 Chr. 35:1 • 2 Chr. 29:5
7 And Josiah contributed to
the lay people, to all who were
present, flocks of lambs and kids,
all for the Passover offerings,
numbering 30,000 plus 3,000 bulls;
these were from the king's possessions.
8 His officers also contributed
a freewill offering to the people,
the priests, and the Levites. Hilkiah and Zechariah and Jehiel, [r]the
officials of the house of God, gave
to the priests for the Passover offerings 2,600 *from the flocks* and
300 bulls. 2 Chr. 31:13
9 [r]Conaniah also, and Shemaiah and Nethanel, his brothers,
and Hashabiah and Jeiel and Jozabad, the officers of the Levites,
contributed to the Levites for the
Passover offerings 5,000 *from the
flocks* and 500 bulls. 2 Chr. 31:12
10 So the service was prepared,
and [r]the priests stood at their stations and the Levites by their divisions according to the king's command. 2 Chr. 35:5
11 And [r]they slaughtered the
Passover *animals,* and while the
priests sprinkled the blood *received* from their hand, the Levites skinned them. 2 Chr. 35:1, 6
12 Then they removed the burnt
offerings that *they* might give
them to the sections of the fathers' households of the lay people to present to the LORD, as it is
written in the book of Moses.
They did this also with the bulls.
13 So [r]they roasted the Passover
animals on the fire according to
the ordinance, and they boiled the
holy things in pots, in kettles, in
pans, and carried *them* speedily to
all the lay people. Ex. 12:8, 9
14 And afterwards they prepared for themselves and for the
priests, because the priests, the
sons of Aaron, *were* offering the
burnt offerings and the fat until
night; therefore the Levites prepared for themselves and for the
priests, the sons of Aaron.
15 The singers, the sons of
Asaph, *were* also at their stations
[r]according to the command of David, Asaph, Heman, and Jeduthun
the king's seer; and the gatekeepers at each gate did not have to
depart from their service, because
the Levites their brethren prepared for them. 1 Chr. 25:1
16 So all the service of the LORD
was prepared on that day to celebrate the Passover, and to offer
burnt offerings on the altar of the
LORD according to the command
of King Josiah.
17 Thus the sons of Israel who
were present celebrated the Passover at that time, and the Feast of
Unleavened Bread seven days.
18 And [r]there had not been celebrated a Passover like it in Israel
since the days of Samuel the
prophet; nor had any of the kings
of Israel celebrated such a Passover as Josiah did with the priests,
the Levites, all Judah and Israel
who were present, and the inhabitants of Jerusalem. 2 Kin. 23:21
19 In the eighteenth year of Jo-

siah's reign this Passover was
celebrated.
20 After all this, when Josiah
had set the temple in order, Neco
king of Egypt came up to make
war at Carchemish on the Euphrates, and Josiah went out to engage
him. *house*
21 But Neco sent messengers to
him, saying, "What have we to do
with each other, O King of Judah?
I am not *coming* against you today but against the house with
which I am at war, and God has
ordered me to hurry. Stop for
your own sake from *interfering
with* God who is with me, that He
may not destroy you." *he*
22 However, Josiah would not
turn away from him, but disguised
himself in order to make war with
him; nor did he listen to the words
of Neco from the mouth of God,
but came to make war on the
plain of Megiddo. *his face*
23 And the archers shot King
Josiah, and the king said to his
servants, "Take me away, for I am
badly wounded."
24 So his servants took him out
of the chariot and carried him in
the second chariot which he had,
and brought him to Jerusalem
where he died and was buried in
the tombs of his fathers. And all
Judah and Jerusalem mourned for
Josiah. *and* • Zech. 12:11
25 Then Jeremiah chanted a lament for Josiah. And all the male
and female singers speak about
Josiah in their lamentations to
this day. And they made them an
ordinance in Israel; behold, they
are also written in the Lamentations. Jer. 22:10; Lam. 4:20
26 Now the rest of the acts of
Josiah and his deeds of devotion
as written in the law of the LORD,
27 and his acts, first to last, behold, they are written in the Book
of the Kings of Israel and Judah.

CHAPTER 36

THEN the people of the land took
[14]Joahaz the son of Josiah, and
made him king in place of his father in Jerusalem. 2 Kin. 23:30-34
2 Joahaz was twenty-three
years old when he became king,
and he reigned three months in Jerusalem.
3 Then the king of Egypt deposed him at Jerusalem, and imposed on the land a fine of one
hundred talents of silver and one
talent of gold.
4 And the king of Egypt made
Eliakim his brother king over Judah and Jerusalem, and changed
his name to Jehoiakim. But Neco
took Joahaz his brother and
brought him to Egypt. Jer. 22:10
5 Jehoiakim was twenty-five
years old when he became king,
and he reigned eleven years in Jerusalem; and he did evil in the
sight of the LORD his God.
6 Nebuchadnezzar king of
Babylon came up against him and
bound him with bronze *chains* to
take him to Babylon. 2 Kin. 24:1
7 Nebuchadnezzar also
brought *some* of the articles of the
house of the LORD to Babylon and
put them in his temple at Babylon.
8 Now the rest of the acts of
Jehoiakim and the abominations
which he did, and what was found

[14]I.e., short form of Jehoahaz

against him, behold, they are written in the Book of the Kings of Israel and Judah. And Jehoiachin
his son became king in his place.
9 Jehoiachin was eight years
old when he became king, and he
reigned three months and ten
days in Jerusalem, and he did evil
in the sight of the LORD.
10 And [r]at the turn of the year
King Nebuchadnezzar sent and
brought him to Babylon with the
valuable articles of the house of
the LORD, and he made his kinsman Zedekiah king over Judah
and Jerusalem. 2 Sam. 11:1
11 [r]Zedekiah was twenty-one
years old when he became king,
and he reigned eleven years in Jerusalem. 2 Kin. 24:18-20; Jer. 27:1
12 And he did evil in the sight of
the LORD his God; he did not humble himself before Jeremiah the
prophet who spoke for the LORD.
13 And he also rebelled against
King Nebuchadnezzar who had
made him swear *allegiance* by
God. But he stiffened his neck and
hardened his heart against turning
to the LORD God of Israel.
14 Furthermore, all the officials
of the priests and the people were
very unfaithful *following* all the
abominations of the nations; and
they defiled the house of the LORD
which He had sanctified in Jerusalem.
15 And the LORD, the God of
their fathers, [r]sent *word* to them
again and again by His messengers, because He had compassion
on His people and on His dwelling
place; Jer. 7:13; 25:3
16 but they *continually* mocked
the messengers of God, despised
His words and scoffed at His
prophets, until the wrath of the
LORD arose against His people,
until there was no remedy.
17 [r]Therefore He brought up
against them the king of the Chaldeans who slew their young men
with the sword in the house of
their sanctuary, and had no compassion on young man or virgin,
old man or infirm; He gave *them*
all into his hand. 2 Kin. 25:1-7
18 And all the articles of the
house of God, great and small,
and the treasures of the house of
the LORD, and the treasures of the
king and of his officers, he
brought *them* all to Babylon.
19 Then they burned the house
of God, and broke down the wall
of Jerusalem and burned all its
fortified buildings with fire, and
destroyed all its valuable articles.
20 And those who had escaped
from the sword he carried away to
Babylon; and they were servants
to him and to his sons until the
rule of the kingdom of Persia,
21 to fulfill the word of the LORD
by the mouth of Jeremiah, until
[r]the land had enjoyed its sabbaths.
All the days of its desolation it
kept sabbath until seventy years
were complete. Lev. 26:34
22 Now in the first year of Cyrus king of Persia—in order to fulfill the word of the LORD by the
mouth of Jeremiah—the LORD
stirred up the spirit of Cyrus king
of Persia, so that he sent a proclamation throughout his kingdom,
and also *put it* in writing, saying,
23 "Thus says Cyrus king of Per-

sia, 'The LORD, the God of heaven,
has given me all the kingdoms of
the earth, and He has appointed
me to build Him a house in Jerusalem, which is in Judah. Whoever there is among you of all His
people, may the LORD his God be
with him, and let him go up!' "

THE BOOK OF
EZRA

NOW in the first year of Cyrus
king of Persia, in order to fulfill
the word of the LORD by the
mouth of Jeremiah, the LORD
stirred up the spirit of Cyrus king
of Persia, so that he [r]sent a proclamation throughout all his kingdom, and also *put it* in writing,
saying, Ezra 5:13
2 "Thus says Cyrus king of Persia, 'The LORD, the God of heaven,
has given me all the kingdoms of
the earth, and [r]He has appointed
me to build Him a house in Jerusalem, which is in Judah. Is. 44:28
3 'Whoever there is among you
of all His people, may his God be
with him! Let him go up to Jerusalem which is in Judah, and rebuild
the house of the LORD, the God of
Israel; [r]He is the God who is in Jerusalem. 1 Kin. 8:23; 18:39
4 'And every survivor, at whatever place he may [a]live, let the men
of that place support him with silver and gold, with goods and cattle, together with a freewill offering for the house of God which is
in Jerusalem.' " *reside as an alien*
5 Then the heads of fathers'
households of Judah and Benjamin and the priests and the Levites arose, [r]even everyone whose
spirit God had stirred to go up and
rebuild the house of the LORD
which is in Jerusalem. Ezra 1:1, 2
6 And all those about them [t]en-
couraged them with articles of silver, with gold, with goods, with
cattle, and with valuables, aside
from all that was given as a freewill offering. *strengthened their hands*
7 Also King Cyrus brought out
the articles of the house of the
LORD, which Nebuchadnezzar had
carried away from Jerusalem and
put in the house of his gods;
8 and Cyrus, king of Persia,
had them brought out by the hand
of Mithredath the treasurer, and
he counted them out to [r]Sheshbaz-
zar, the prince of Judah. Ezra 5:14
9 Now this *was* their number:
30 [r]gold dishes, 1,000 silver dishes,
29 duplicates; Ezra 8:27
10 30 gold bowls, 410 silver
bowls of a second *kind, and* 1,000
other articles.
11 All the articles of gold and
silver *numbered* 5,400. Sheshbazzar brought them all up with the
exiles who went up from Babylon
to Jerusalem.

CHAPTER 2

NOW these are the people of the
province who came up out of the

captivity of the exiles whom
Nebuchadnezzar the king of
Babylon had carried away to
Babylon, and returned to Jerusalem and Judah, each to his city.
2 These came with Zerubbabel, Jeshua, Nehemiah, Seraiah,
Reelaiah, Mordecai, Bilshan, Mis-
par, Bigvai, Rehum, and Baanah.
The number of the men of the
people of Israel:
3 the sons of Parosh, 2,172;
4 the sons of Shephatiah, 372;
5 the sons of Arah, 775;
6 the sons of [r]Pahath-moab of
the sons of Jeshua *and* Joab,
2,812; Neh. 7:11
7 the sons of Elam, 1,254;
8 the sons of Zattu, 945;
9 the sons of Zaccai, 760;
10 the sons of Bani, 642;
11 the sons of Bebai, 623;
12 the sons of Azgad, 1,222;
13 the sons of Adonikam, 666;
14 the sons of Bigvai, 2,056;
15 the sons of Adin, 454;
16 the sons of Ater of Hezekiah,
98;
17 the sons of Bezai, 323;
18 the sons of Jorah, 112;
19 the sons of Hashum, 223;
20 the sons of Gibbar, 95;
21 the men of Bethlehem, 123;
22 the men of Netophah, 56;
23 the men of Anathoth, 128;
24 the sons of Azmaveth, 42;
25 the sons of Kiriath-arim,
Chephirah, and Beeroth, 743;
26 the sons of [r]Ramah and Geba,
621; Josh. 18:25
27 the men of Michmas, 122;
28 the men of Bethel and Ai,
223;
29 the sons of Nebo, 52;
30 the sons of Magbish, 156;
31 the sons of the other Elam,
1,254;
32 the sons of Harim, 320;
33 the sons of Lod, Hadid, and
Ono, 725;
34 the men of Jericho, 345;
35 the sons of Senaah, 3,630.
36 The priests: the sons of Jedaiah of the house of Jeshua, 973;
37 the sons of Immer, 1,052;
38 the sons of Pashhur, 1,247;
39 the sons of Harim, 1,017.
40 The Levites: the sons of
Jeshua and Kadmiel, of the sons
of Hodaviah, 74.
41 The singers: the sons of
Asaph, 128.
42 The sons of the gatekeepers:
the sons of Shallum, the sons of
Ater, the sons of Talmon, the sons
of Akkub, the sons of Hatita, the
sons of Shobai, in all 139.
43 The [r]temple servants: the
sons of Ziha, the sons of Hasupha,
the sons of Tabbaoth, 1 Chr. 9:2
44 the sons of Keros, the sons of
Siaha, the sons of Padon,
45 the sons of Lebanah, the sons
of Hagabah, the sons of Akkub,
46 the sons of Hagab, the sons
of Shalmai, the sons of Hanan,
47 the sons of Giddel, the sons
of Gahar, the sons of Reaiah,
48 the sons of Rezin, the sons of
Nekoda, the sons of Gazzam,
49 the sons of Uzza, the sons of
Paseah, the sons of Besai,
50 the sons of Asnah, the sons
of Meunim, the sons of Nephisim,
51 the sons of Bakbuk, the sons
of Hakupha, the sons of Harhur,
52 the sons of Bazluth, the sons
of Mehida, the sons of Harsha,
53 the sons of Barkos, the sons
of Sisera, the sons of Temah,

54 the sons of Neziah, the sons
of Hatipha.
55 The sons of Solomon's servants: the sons of Sotai, the sons
of [r]Hassophereth, the sons of Peru-
da, 1 Kin. 9:21
56 the sons of Jaalah, the sons
of Darkon, the sons of Giddel,
57 the sons of Shephatiah, the
sons of Hattil, the sons of Poche-
reth-hazzebaim, the sons of Ami.
58 All the [r]temple servants, and
the sons of [r]Solomon's servants,
were 392. 1 Chr. 9:2 • 1 Kin. 9:21
59 Now these are those who
came up from Tel-melah, Tel-har-
sha, Cherub, Addan, *and* Immer,
but they were not able to [t]give evidence of their fathers' households,
and their [t]descendants, whether
they were of Israel: *tell • seed*
60 the sons of Delaiah, the sons
of Tobiah, the sons of Nekoda,
652.
61 And of the sons of the
priests: the sons of Habaiah, the
sons of Hakkoz, the sons of Barzillai, who took a wife from the
daughters of [r]Barzillai the Gileadite, and he was called by their
name. 2 Sam. 17:27; 1 Kin. 2:7
62 These searched *among* their
ancestral registration, but they
could not be located; therefore
they were considered unclean *and*
excluded from the priesthood.
63 And the governor said to
them [r]that they should not eat
from the most holy things until a
priest stood up with [r]Urim and
Thummim. Lev. 2:3, 10 • Ex. 28:30
64 The whole assembly [t]num-
bered 42,360, *together was*
65 besides their male and female servants, [t]who numbered
7,337; and they had 200 singing
men and women. *they were*
66 Their horses were 736; their
mules, 245;
67 their camels, 435; *their* donkeys, 6,720.
68 And some of the heads of fathers' *households,* when they arrived at the house of the LORD
which is in Jerusalem, offered
willingly for the house of God to
restore it on its foundation.
69 According to their ability
they gave to the treasury for the
work 61,000 gold drachmas, and
5,000 silver minas, and 100
priestly [a]garments. *tunics*
70 Now the priests and the Levites, some of the people, the singers, the gatekeepers, and the temple servants lived in their cities,
and all Israel in their cities.

CHAPTER 3

NOW when the seventh month
came, and the sons of Israel *were*
in the cities, the people gathered
together as one man to Jerusalem.
2 Then [r]Jeshua the son of Jozadak and his brothers the priests,
and Zerubbabel the son of Shealtiel, and his brothers arose and
built the altar of the God of Israel,
to offer burnt offerings on it, as it
is written in the law of Moses, the
man of God. Neh. 12:1, 8
3 So they set up the altar on its
foundation, for they were terrified
because of the peoples of the
lands; and they offered burnt offerings on it to the LORD, burnt offerings morning and evening.
4 And they celebrated the
Feast of [1]Booths, as it is written,

[1] Or, *Tabernacles*

and *offered* [t]the fixed number of
burnt offerings daily, according to
the ordinance, as each day required; *by number*
5 and afterward *there was* a
[r]continual burnt offering, also for
the new moons and for all the
fixed festivals of the LORD that
were consecrated, and from
everyone who offered a freewill
offering to the LORD. Ex. 29:38
6 From the first day of the seventh month they began to offer
burnt offerings to the LORD, but
the foundation of the temple of
the LORD had not been laid.
7 Then they gave money to the
masons and carpenters, and [r]food,
drink, and oil to the Sidonians and
to the Tyrians, [r]to bring cedar
wood from Lebanon to the sea at
Joppa, according to the permission they had [t]from Cyrus king of
Persia. 2 Chr. 2:10 • 2 Chr. 2:16 • *of*
8 Now in the second year of
their coming to the house of God
at Jerusalem in the second month,
Zerubbabel the son of Shealtiel
and Jeshua the son of Jozadak
and the rest of their brothers the
priests and the Levites, and all
who came from the captivity to
Jerusalem, began *the work* and
appointed the Levites from
twenty years and older to oversee
the work of the house of the LORD.
9 Then [r]Jeshua *with* his sons
and brothers stood united *with*
Kadmiel and his sons, the sons of
Judah *and* the sons of Henadad
with their sons and brothers the
Levites, to oversee the workmen
in the temple of God. Ezra 2:40
10 Now when the builders had
laid the foundation of the temple
of the LORD, [t]the priests stood in
their apparel with trumpets, and
the Levites, the sons of Asaph,
with cymbals, to praise the LORD
according to the directions of
King David of Israel. *hands*
11 And they sang, praising and
giving thanks to the LORD, *saying*,
"For He is good, for His lovingkindness is upon Israel forever."
And all the people shouted with a
great shout when they praised the
LORD because the foundation of
the house of the LORD was laid.
12 Yet many of the priests and
Levites and heads of fathers'
households, [r]the old men who had
seen the first [t]temple, wept with a
loud voice when the foundation of
this house was laid before their
eyes, while many shouted aloud
for joy; Hag. 2:3 • *house*
13 so that the people could not
distinguish the sound of the shout
of joy from the sound of the weeping of the people, for the people
shouted with a loud shout, and the
sound was heard far away.

CHAPTER 4

NOW when the enemies of Judah
and Benjamin heard that the people of the exile were building a
temple to the LORD God of Israel,
2 they approached Zerubbabel
and the heads of fathers' *households*, and said to them, "Let us
build with you, for we, like you,
seek your God; and we have been
sacrificing to Him since the days
of Esarhaddon king of Assyria,
who brought us up here."
3 But Zerubbabel and Jeshua
and the rest of the heads of fa-

thers' *households* of Israel said to
them, "You have nothing in common with us in building a house to
our God; but we ourselves will together build to the LORD God of
Israel, as King Cyrus, the king of
Persia has commanded us."
4 Then the people of the land
discouraged the people of Judah,
and frightened them from building, Ezra 3:3 • *weakened the hands of*
5 and hired counselors against
them to frustrate their counsel all
the days of Cyrus king of Persia,
even until the reign of Darius king
of Persia.
6 Now in the reign of [2]Ahasue-
rus, in the beginning of his reign,
they wrote an accusation against
the inhabitants of Judah and Jerusalem. Esth. 1:1; Dan. 9:1
7 And in the days of Artaxerxes, Bishlam, Mithredath, Tabeel,
and the rest of his colleagues,
wrote to Artaxerxes king of Persia; and the text of the letter was
written in Aramaic and translated
from Aramaic. *writing* • 2 Kin. 18:26
8 Rehum the commander and
Shimshai the scribe wrote a letter
against Jerusalem to King Artaxerxes, as follows—
9 then *wrote* Rehum the commander and Shimshai the scribe
and the rest of their colleagues,
the judges and the lesser governors, the officials, the secretaries,
the men of Erech, the Babylonians, the men of Susa, that is, the
Elamites, 2 Kin. 17:24 • Ezra 5:6
10 and the rest of the nations
which the great and honorable Os-
nappar deported and settled in the
city of Samaria, and in the rest of

[2]Or, *Xerxes*

the region beyond the [3]River. And
now Ezra 4:11, 17; 7:12
11 this is the copy of the letter
which they sent to him: "To King
Artaxerxes: Your servants, the
men in the region beyond the
River, and now
12 let it be known to the king,
that the Jews who came up from
you have come to us at Jerusalem;
they are rebuilding the rebellious
and evil city, and are finishing the
walls and repairing the foundations. 2 Chr. 36:13 • Ezra 5:3, 9
13 "Now let it be known to the
king, that if that city is rebuilt and
the walls are finished, they will
not pay tribute, custom, or toll,
and it will damage the revenue of
the kings. Ezra 4:20; 7:24
14 "Now because we are in the
service of the palace, and it is not
fitting for us to see the king's dishonor, therefore we have sent and
informed the king, *eat the salt*
15 so that a search may be
made in the record books of your
fathers. And you will discover in
the record books, and learn that
that city is a rebellious city and
damaging to kings and provinces,
and that they have incited revolt
within it in past days; therefore
that city was laid waste.
16 "We inform the king that, if
that city is rebuilt and the walls
finished, as a result you will have
no possession in *the province* beyond the River."
17 *Then* the king sent an answer
to Rehum the commander, to
Shimshai the scribe, and to the
rest of their colleagues who live in
Samaria and in the rest of *the*

[3]I.e., Euphrates, and so throughout this
context

provinces beyond the River:
"Peace. And now
18 the document which you sent
to us has been [t]translated and read
before me. *plainly read before*
19 "And a decree has been [t]issued
by me, and a search has been
made and it has been discovered
that that city has risen up against
the kings in past days, that rebellion and revolt have been perpe-
trated in it, *put* forth
20 [r]that mighty kings have [t]ruled
over Jerusalem, governing all *the*
provinces beyond the River, and
that tribute, custom, and toll were
paid to them. 1 Kin. 4:21 • *been*
21 "So, now issue a decree to
make these men stop *work*, that
the city may not be rebuilt until a
decree is issued by me.
22 "And beware of being negligent in carrying out this *matter*;
why should damage increase to
the detriment of the kings?"
23 Then as soon as the copy of
King Artaxerxes' document was
read before Rehum and Shimshai
the scribe and their colleagues,
they went in haste to Jerusalem to
the Jews and stopped them by
force of arms.
24 Then work on the house of
God in Jerusalem ceased, and it
was stopped until the second year
of the reign of Darius king of Persia.

CHAPTER 5

WHEN the prophets, [r]Haggai the
prophet and [r]Zechariah the son of
Iddo, prophesied to the Jews who
were in Judah and Jerusalem, in
the name of the God of Israel, who
was over them, Hag. 1:1 • Zech. 1:1
2 then [r]Zerubbabel the son of
Shealtiel and Jeshua the son of
Jozadak arose and began to rebuild the house of God which is in
Jerusalem; and [r]the prophets of
God were with them supporting
them. Ezra 3:2 • Ezra 6:14
3 At that time [r]Tattenai, the
governor of *the province* beyond
the River, and Shethar-bozenai
and their colleagues came to them
and spoke to them thus, "Who [r]is-
sued you a decree to rebuild this
[4]temple and to finish this structure?" Ezra 6:6, 13 • Ezra 1:3; 5:9
4 [r]Then we told them accordingly what the names of the men
were who were reconstructing
this building. Ezra 5:10
5 But [r]the eye of their God was
on the elders of the Jews, and they
did not stop them until a report
should come to Darius, and then a
written reply be returned concerning it. Ezra 7:6, 28
6 *This is* the copy of the letter
which [r]Tattenai, the governor of
the province beyond the River,
and Shethar-bozenai and his colleagues [r]the officials, who were beyond the River, sent to Darius the
king. Ezra 5:3 • Ezra 4:9
7 They sent a report to him in
which it was written thus: "To Darius the king, all peace.
8 "Let it be known to the king,
that we have gone to the province
of Judah, to the house of the great
God, which is being built with
huge stones, and beams are being
laid in the walls; and this work is
going on with great care and is
succeeding in their hands.
9 "Then we asked those elders
and said to them thus, 'Who is-

[4]Lit., *house*, and so throughout this context

sued you a decree to rebuild this
temple and to finish this structure?'
10 "We also asked them their
names so as to inform you, and
that we might write down the
names of the men who were at
their head.
11 "And thus they [t]answered us,
saying, 'We are the servants of the
God of heaven and earth and are
rebuilding the temple that was
built many years ago, which a
great king of Israel built and finished. *returned us the word*
12 'But [r]because our fathers had
provoked the God of heaven to
wrath, He gave them into the
hand of Nebuchadnezzar king of
Babylon, the Chaldean, *who* destroyed this temple and deported
the people to Babylon. 2 Chr. 36:16
13 'However, [r]in the first year of
Cyrus king of Babylon, King Cyrus [r]issued a decree to rebuild this
house of God. Ezra 1:1 • Ezra 1:1-4
14 'And also [r]the gold and silver
utensils of the house of God which
Nebuchadnezzar had taken from
the temple in Jerusalem, and
brought them to the temple of
Babylon, these King Cyrus took
from the temple of Babylon, and
they were given to one whose
name was Sheshbazzar, whom he
had appointed governor. Ezra 1:7
15 'And he said to him, "Take
these utensils, go *and* deposit
them in the temple [t]in Jerusalem,
and let the house of God be rebuilt
in its place." *that is in*
16 'Then that Sheshbazzar came
and laid the foundations of the
house of God [t]in Jerusalem; and
from then until now it has been
under construction, and it is not
yet completed.' *that is in*
17 "And now, if it pleases the
king [r]let a search be conducted in
the king's treasure house, which is
there in Babylon, if it be that a decree was issued by King Cyrus to
rebuild this house of God at Jerusalem; and let the king send to us
his decision concerning this *matter.*" Ezra 6:1, 2

CHAPTER 6

THEN King Darius issued a decree, and [r]search was made in the
[5]archives, where the treasures
were stored in Babylon. Ezra 5:17
2 And in [6]Ecbatana in the fortress, which is [r]in the province of
Media, a scroll was found and
there was written in it as follows:
"Memorandum— 2 Kin. 17:6
3 "In [r]the first year of King Cyrus, Cyrus the king issued a decree: '*Concerning* the house of
God at Jerusalem, let the temple,
the place where sacrifices are offered, be rebuilt and let its foundations be [t]retained, its height
being 60 cubits and its width 60
cubits; Ezra 1:1 • *fixed, laid*
4 with three layers of huge
stones, and one layer of timbers.
And let the cost be paid from the
[t]royal treasury. *king's house*
5 'And also let [r]the gold and silver utensils of the temple of God,
which Nebuchadnezzar took from
the temple in Jerusalem and
brought to Babylon, be returned
and [t]brought to their places in the
temple in Jerusalem; and you
shall put *them* in the house of
God.' Ezra 1:7; 5:14 • *go*

[5]Lit., *house of the books* [6]Aram., *Achmetha*

6 "Now therefore, Tattenai,
governor of *the province* beyond
the River, Shethar-bozenai, and
your colleagues, the officials of
the provinces beyond the River,
[t]keep away from there. *be distant*
7 "Leave this work on the house
of God alone; let the governor of
the Jews and the elders of the
Jews rebuild this house of God on
its site.
8 "Moreover, I issue a decree
concerning what you are to do for
these elders of Judah in the rebuilding of this house of God: the
full cost is to be paid to these people from the royal treasury out of
the taxes of *the provinces* beyond
the River, and that without delay.
9 "And whatever is needed,
both young bulls, rams, and lambs
for a burnt offering to the God of
heaven, and wheat, salt, wine, and
anointing oil, as the priests in Jerusalem request, *it* is to be given
to them daily without fail,
10 that they may offer [7]accept-
able sacrifices to the God of
heaven and pray for the life of the
king and his sons.
11 "And I issued a decree that
any man who violates this edict, a
timber shall be drawn from his
house and he shall be impaled on
it and his house shall be made a
refuse heap on account of this.
12 "And may the God who [t]has
caused His name to dwell there
overthrow any king or people who
attempts to change *it*, so as to destroy this house of God in Jerusalem. I, Darius, have issued *this* decree, let *it* be carried out with all
diligence!" *sends his hand*
13 Then [r]Tattenai, the governor

[7] Lit., *pleasing* or *sweet-smelling sacrifices*

of *the province* beyond the River,
Shethar-bozenai, and their colleagues carried out *the decree*
with all diligence, just as King Darius had sent. Ezra 6:6
14 And [r]the elders of the Jews
were successful in building
through the prophesying of Haggai the prophet and Zechariah the
son of Iddo. And they finished
building according to the command of the God of Israel and the
decree of Cyrus, Darius, and Artaxerxes king of Persia. Ezra 5:1
15 And this temple was completed on the third day of the
month Adar; it was the sixth year
of the reign of King Darius.
16 And the sons of Israel, the
priests, the Levites, and the rest of
the exiles, celebrated the dedication of this house of God with joy.
17 And they offered for the
dedication of this temple of God
100 bulls, 200 rams, 400 lambs,
and as a sin offering for all Israel
12 male goats, corresponding to
the number of the tribes of Israel.
18 Then they appointed the
priests to their divisions and the
Levites in their orders for the service of God in Jerusalem, as it is
written in the book of Moses.
19 And [r]the exiles observed the
Passover on [r]the fourteenth of the
first month. Ezra 1:11 • Ex. 12:6
20 [r]For the priests and the Levites had purified themselves together; all of them were pure.
Then they slaughtered the Passover *lamb* for all the exiles, both
for their brothers the priests and
for themselves. 2 Chr. 29:34
21 And the sons of Israel who
returned from exile and [r]all those

who had separated themselves
from [r]the impurity of the nations
of the land to *join* them, to seek
the LORD God of Israel, ate *the*
Passover. Neh. 9:2; 10:28 • Ezra 9:11

22 And [r]they observed the Feast
of Unleavened Bread seven days
with joy, for the LORD had caused
them to rejoice, and had turned
the heart of the king of Assyria
toward them to encourage them
in the work of the house of God,
the God of Israel. Ex. 12:15

CHAPTER 7

NOW after these things, in the
reign of Artaxerxes king of Persia,
there went up Ezra son of Seraiah,
son of Azariah, son of Hilkiah,

2 son of Shallum, son of Zadok, son of Ahitub,

3 son of Amariah, son of Azariah, son of Meraioth,

4 son of Zerahiah, son of Uzzi,
son of Bukki,

5 son of Abishua, son of Phinehas, son of Eleazar, son of Aaron
the chief priest.

6 This Ezra went up from
Babylon, and he was a scribe
skilled in the law of Moses, which
the LORD God of Israel had given;
and the king granted him all he requested because the hand of the
LORD his God *was* upon him.

7 And some of the sons of Israel and some of the priests, the
Levites, the singers, the gatekeepers, and the temple servants went
up to Jerusalem in the seventh
year of King Artaxerxes.

8 And he came to Jerusalem in
the fifth month, which was in the
seventh year of the king.

9 For on the first of the first
month [t]he began to go up from
Babylon; and on the first of the
fifth month he came to Jerusalem,
because the good hand of his God
was upon him. *was the foundation*

10 For Ezra had set his heart to
study the law of the LORD, and to
practice *it,* and to teach *His* statutes and ordinances in Israel.

11 Now this is the copy of the
decree which King Artaxerxes
gave to Ezra the priest, the scribe,
[t]learned in the words of the commandments of the LORD and His
statutes to Israel: *the scribe of*

12 "Artaxerxes, [r]king of kings, to
Ezra the priest, the scribe of the
law of the God of heaven, perfect
peace. And now Ezek. 26:7

13 I have issued a decree that
any of the people of Israel and
their priests and the Levites in my
kingdom who are willing to go to
Jerusalem, may go with you.

14 "Forasmuch as you are sent
[t]by the king and his [r]seven counselors to inquire concerning Judah
and Jerusalem according to the
law of your God which is in your
hand, *from before* • Ezra 7:15

15 and to bring the silver and
gold, which the king and his counselors have freely offered to the
God of Israel, [r]whose dwelling is in
Jerusalem, 2 Chr. 6:2; Ezra 6:12

16 with all the silver and gold
which you shall find in the whole
province of Babylon, along with
the freewill offering of the people
and of the priests, who offered
willingly for the house of their
God which is in Jerusalem;

17 with this money, therefore,
you shall diligently buy bulls,

rams, and lambs, [r]with their grain
offerings and their libations and
[r]offer them on the altar of the
house of your God which is in Jerusalem. Num. 15:4-13 • Deut. 12:5-11
18 "And whatever seems good to
you and to your brothers to do
with the rest of the silver and
gold, you may do according to the
will of your God.
19 "Also the utensils which are
given to you for the service of the
house of your God, deliver in full
before the God of Jerusalem.
20 "And the rest of the needs for
the house of your God, for which
you may have occasion to provide, [r]provide *for it* from the royal
treasury. Ezra 6:4
21 "And I, even I King Artaxerxes, issue a decree to all the treasurers who are *in the provinces*
beyond the River, that whatever
Ezra the priest, [r]the scribe of the
law of the God of heaven, may require of you, it shall be done diligently, Ezra 7:6
22 *even* up to 100 talents of silver, 100 kors of wheat, 100 baths
of wine, 100 baths of oil, and salt
[t]as needed. *without prescription*
23 "Whatever is [t]commanded by
the God of heaven, let it be done
with zeal for the house of the God
of heaven, lest there be wrath
against the kingdom of the king
and his sons. *from the decree of*
24 "We also inform you that [r]it is
not allowed to [t]impose tax, tribute
or toll *on* any of the priests, Levites, singers, doorkeepers, Nethinim, or servants of this house of
God. Ezra 4:13, 20 • *throw on them*
25 "And you, Ezra, according to
the wisdom of your God which is
in your hand, [r]appoint magistrates
and judges that they may judge all
the people who are in *the province*
beyond the River, *even* all those
who know the laws of your God;
and you may teach anyone who is
ignorant *of them.* Ex. 18:21
26 "And whoever will not observe the law of your God and the
law of the king, let judgment be
executed upon him strictly,
whether for death or for [t]banish-
ment or for confiscation of goods
or for imprisonment." *rooting out*
27 Blessed be the LORD, the God
of our fathers, [r]who has put *such a*
thing as this in the king's heart, to
adorn the house of the LORD
which is in Jerusalem, Ezra 6:22
28 and has extended lovingkindness to me before the king
and his counselors and before all
the king's mighty princes. Thus I
was strengthened according to the
hand of the LORD my God upon
me, and I gathered leading men
from Israel to go up with me.

CHAPTER 8

NOW these are the heads of their
fathers' *households* and the genealogical enrollment of those
who went up with me from Babylon in the reign of King Artaxerxes:
2 of the sons of Phinehas, Gershom; of the sons of Ithamar,
Daniel; of the sons of David, [r]Hat-
tush; 1 Chr. 3:22
3 of the sons of Shecaniah *who*
was of the sons of Parosh, Zechariah and with him 150 males *who*
were in the genealogical list;
4 of the sons of Pahath-moab,

Eliehoenai the son of Zerahiah
and 200 males with him;
5 of the sons of Shecaniah, the
son of Jahaziel and 300 males
with him;
6 and of the sons of [r]Adin, Ebed
the son of Jonathan and 50 males
with him; Ezra 2:15; Neh. 7:20
7 and of the sons of Elam, Jeshaiah the son of Athaliah and 70
males with him;
8 and of the sons of Shephatiah, Zebadiah the son of Michael
and 80 males with him;
9 of the sons of Joab, Obadiah
the son of Jehiel and 218 males
with him;
10 and of the sons of Shelomith,
the son of Josiphiah and 160
males with him;
11 and of the sons of Bebai,
Zechariah the son of Bebai and 28
males with him;
12 and of the sons of Azgad, Johanan the son of Hakkatan and
110 males with him;
13 and of the sons of Adonikam,
the last ones, these being their
names, Eliphelet, Jeuel, and
Shemaiah and 60 males with
them;
14 and of the sons of Bigvai, U-
thai and [a]Zabbud and 70 males
with [a]them. *Zakkur* • *him*
15 Now I assembled them at [r]the
river that runs to Ahava, where
we camped for three days; and
when I observed the people and
the priests, I [r]did not find any Levites there. Ezra 8:21 • Ezra 7:7
16 So I sent for Eliezer, Ariel,
Shemaiah, Elnathan, Jarib, Elnathan, Nathan, Zechariah, and Meshullam, leading men, and for Joiarib and Elnathan, teachers.
17 And I sent them to Iddo the
[t]leading man at the place Casiphia;
and I told them what to say to
Iddo *and* his brothers, the temple
servants at the place Casiphia,
that is, to bring ministers to us for
the house of our God. *head*
18 And according to the good
hand of our God upon us they
brought us a man of insight of the
sons of Mahli, the son of Levi, the
son of Israel, namely Sherebiah,
and his sons and brothers, 18 men;
19 and Hashabiah and Jeshaiah
of the sons of Merari, with his
brothers and their sons, 20 men;
20 and 220 of [r]the temple servants, whom David and the
princes had given for the service
of the Levites, all of them designated by name. Ezra 2:43; 7:7
21 Then I proclaimed a fast
there at the river of Ahava, that
we might humble ourselves before
our God to seek from Him a [t]safe
journey for us, our little ones, and
all our possessions. *straight way*
22 For I was ashamed to request from the king troops and
horsemen to [t]protect us from the
enemy on the way, because we
had said to the king, "The hand of
our God is favorably disposed to
all those who seek Him, but His
power and His anger are against
all those who forsake Him." *help*
23 So we fasted and sought our
God concerning this *matter,* and
He listened to our entreaty.
24 Then I set apart twelve of the
leading priests, [r]Sherebiah, Hashabiah, and with them ten of their
brothers; Ezra 8:18, 19
25 and I weighed out to them
the silver, the gold, and the uten-

sils, the offering for the house of
our God which the king and his
counselors and his princes, and all
Israel present *there,* had offered.
26 [r]Thus I weighed into their
hands 650 talents of silver, and
silver utensils *worth* 100 talents,
and gold talents, Ezra 1:9-11
27 and 20 gold bowls, *worth*
1,000 darics; and two utensils of
fine shiny bronze, precious as
gold.
28 Then I said to them, "You are
holy to the LORD, and the utensils
are holy; and the silver and the
gold are a freewill offering to the
LORD God of your fathers.
29 "Watch and keep *them* [r]until
you weigh *them* before the leading priests, the Levites, and the
heads of the fathers' *households*
of Israel at Jerusalem, *in* the
chambers of the house of the
LORD." Ezra 8:33, 34
30 So the priests and the Levites
[r]accepted the weighed out silver
and gold and the utensils, to bring
them to Jerusalem to the house of
our God. Ezra 1:9
31 Then we journeyed from [r]the
river Ahava on the twelfth of the
first month to go to Jerusalem;
and the hand of our God was over
us, and He delivered us from the
hand of the enemy and the am-
bushes by the way. Ezra 8:15, 21
32 Thus we came to Jerusalem
and remained there three days.
33 And on the fourth day the silver and the gold and the utensils
[r]were weighed out in the house of
our God into the hand of [r]Mer-
emoth the son of Uriah the priest,
and with him *was* Eleazar the son
of Phinehas; and with them *were*
the Levites, Jozabad the son of
Jeshua and Noadiah the son of
Binnui. Ezra 8:30 • Neh. 3:4, 21
34 Everything *was* numbered
and weighed, and all the weight
was recorded at that time.
35 [r]The exiles who had come
from the captivity offered burnt
offerings to the God of Israel: [r]12
bulls for all Israel, 96 rams, 77
lambs, 12 male goats for a sin offering, all as a burnt offering to
the LORD. Ezra 2:1 • Ezra 6:17
36 Then [r]they delivered the
king's edicts to the king's satraps,
and to the governors *in the provinces* beyond the River, and they
supported the people and the
house of God. Ezra 7:21-24

CHAPTER 9

NOW when these things had
been completed, the princes approached me, saying, "The people
of Israel and the priests and the
Levites have not [r]separated themselves from the peoples of the
lands, [r]according to their abominations, *those* of the Canaanites, the
Hittites, the Perizzites, the Jebusites, the Ammonites, the Moabites, the Egyptians, and the Amorites. Ezra 6:21 • Lev. 18:24-30
2 "For they have taken some of
their daughters *as wives* for themselves and for their sons, so that
the holy [t]race has intermingled
with the peoples of the lands; indeed, the hands of the princes and
the rulers have been foremost in
this unfaithfulness." *seed*
3 And when I heard about this
matter, I [r]tore my garment and my
robe, and pulled some of the hair

from my head and my beard, and
sat down appalled. 2 Kin. 18:37
4 Then [r]everyone who trembled
at the words of the God of Israel
on account of the unfaithfulness
of the exiles gathered to me, and I
sat appalled until [r]the evening offering. Ezra 10:3 • Ex. 29:39
5 But at the evening offering I
arose from my [t]humiliation, even
with my garment and my robe
torn, and I fell on my knees and
stretched out my [t]hands to the
LORD my God; *fasting • palms*
6 and I said, "O my God, I am
ashamed and embarrassed to lift
up my face to Thee, my God, for
our iniquities have risen above
our heads, and our guilt has
grown even to the heavens.
7 "Since [r]the days of our fathers
to this day we *have been* in great
guilt, and on account of our iniquities we, our kings *and* our priests
have been given into the hand of
the kings of the lands, to the
sword, to captivity, and to plunder
and to [t]open shame, as *it is* this
day. 2 Chr. 29:6 • *shame of faces*
8 "But now for a brief moment
grace has been *shown* from the
LORD our God, [r]to leave us an escaped remnant and to give us a
[r]peg in His holy place, that our
God may enlighten our eyes and
grant us a little reviving in our
bondage. Ezra 9:13-15 • Is. 22:23
9 "For we are slaves; yet in our
bondage, our God has not forsaken us, but has extended lovingkindness to us in the sight of the
kings of Persia, to give us reviving
to raise up the house of our God,
to restore its ruins, and to give us
a wall in Judah and Jerusalem.
10 "And now, our God, what
shall we say after this? For we
have forsaken Thy commandments,
11 which Thou hast com-
manded by Thy servants the
prophets, saying, 'The land which
you are entering to possess is an
unclean land with the uncleanness
of the peoples of the lands, with
their abominations which have
filled it from end to end and [r]with
their impurity. Ezra 6:21
12 'So now do not give your
daughters to their sons nor take
their daughters to your sons, and
never seek their peace or their
prosperity, that you may be
strong and eat the good *things* of
the land and leave *it* as an inheritance to your sons forever.'
13 "And after all that has come
upon us for our evil deeds and our
great guilt, since Thou our God
hast requited *us* less than our iniquities *deserve,* and hast given us
an escaped remnant as this,
14 shall we again break Thy
commandments and intermarry
with the peoples who commit
these abominations? Wouldst
Thou not be angry with us to the
point of destruction, until there is
no remnant nor any who escape?
15 "O LORD God of Israel, [r]Thou
art righteous, for we have been
left an escaped remnant, as *it is*
this day; behold, we are before
Thee in [r]our guilt, for no one can
stand before Thee because of
this." Neh. 9:33 • Ezra 9:6

CHAPTER 10

NOW while Ezra was praying
and making confession, weeping

and prostrating himself before the
house of God, a very large assembly, men, women, and children,
gathered to him from Israel; for
the people wept bitterly.
2 And Shecaniah the son of Jehiel, one of the sons of Elam, answered and said to Ezra, "We
have been unfaithful to our God,
and have [t]married foreign women
from the peoples of the land; yet
now there is hope for Israel in
spite of this. *given dwelling to*
3 "So now let us make a covenant with our God to put away
all the wives and [t]their children,
according to the counsel of [8]my
lord and of those who tremble at
the commandment of our God;
and let it be done according to the
law. *that which is born of them*
4 "Arise! For *this* matter is your
responsibility, but we will be with
you; be courageous and act."
5 Then Ezra rose and made the
leading priests, the Levites, and
all Israel, take oath that they
would do according to this proposal; so they took the oath.
6 Then Ezra [r]rose from before
the house of God and went into
the chamber of Jehohanan the son
of Eliashib. Although he went
there, [r]he did not eat bread, nor
drink water, for he was mourning
over the unfaithfulness of the exiles. Ezra 10:1 • Deut. 9:18
7 And they made a proclamation throughout Judah and Jerusalem to all the exiles, that they
should assemble at Jerusalem,
8 and that whoever would not
come within three days, according
to the counsel of the leaders and
the elders, all his possessions
should be forfeited and he himself
excluded from the assembly of the
exiles.
9 So all the men of Judah and
Benjamin assembled at Jerusalem
within the three days. It was the
ninth month on the twentieth of
the month, and all the people sat
in the open square *before* the
house of God, trembling because
of this matter and the heavy rain.
10 Then Ezra the priest stood up
and said to them, "You have been
unfaithful and have married foreign wives adding to the guilt of
Israel.
11 "Now, therefore, [r]make confession to the LORD God of your
fathers, and [r]do His will; and separate yourselves from the peoples
of the land and from the foreign
wives." Lev. 26:40 • Rom. 12:2
12 Then all the assembly answered and said with a loud voice,
"That's right! As you have said, so
it is [t]our duty to *do*. *upon us*
13 "But there are many people, it
is the rainy season, and we are not
able to stand in the open. Nor can
the task be done in one or two
days, for we have transgressed
greatly in this matter.
14 "Let our leaders [t]represent the
whole assembly and let all those
in our cities who have married
foreign wives come at appointed
times, together with the elders
and judges of each city, until the
fierce anger of our God on account of this matter is turned
away from us." *stand for*
15 Only Jonathan the son of

[8]Or, *the Lord*

Asahel and Jahzeiah the son of
Tikvah [t]opposed this, with Meshullam and Shabbethai the Levite
supporting them. *stood against*
16 But the exiles did so. And
Ezra the priest selected men *who
were* heads of fathers' *households*
for each of their father's *households,* all of them by name. So
they [t]convened on the first day of
the tenth month to investigate the
matter. *sat*
17 And they finished *investigating* all the men who had married
foreign wives by the first of the
first month.
18 And among the sons of the
priests who had married foreign
wives were found of the sons of
[r]Jeshua the son of Jozadak, and his
brothers: Maaseiah, Eliezer, Jarib,
and Gedaliah. Ezra 5:2; Hag. 1:1
19 And they pledged to put
away their wives, and being
guilty, [r]*they offered* a ram of the
flock for their offense. Lev. 5:15
20 And of the sons of Immer
there were Hanani and Zebadiah;
21 and of the sons of Harim:
Maaseiah, Elijah, Shemaiah, Jehiel, and Uzziah;
22 and of the sons of Pashhur:
Elioenai, Maaseiah, Ishmael, Nethanel, Jozabad, and Elasah.
23 And of Levites *there were*
Jozabad, Shimei, Kelaiah (that is,
Kelita), Pethahiah, Judah, and Eliezer.
24 And of the singers *there was*
Eliashib; and of the gatekeepers:
Shallum, Telem, and Uri.
25 And of Israel, of the sons of
[r]Parosh *there were* Ramiah, Izziah,
Malchijah, Mijamin, Eleazar, Malchijah, and Benaiah; Ezra 2:3
26 and of the sons of Elam: Mattaniah, Zechariah, Jehiel, Abdi,
Jeremoth, and Elijah;
27 and of the sons of [r]Zattu: Elioenai, Eliashib, Mattaniah, Jeremoth, Zabad, and Aziza; Ezra 2:8
28 and of the sons of Bebai:
Jehohanan, Hananiah, Zabbai,
and Athlai;
29 and of the sons of Bani: Meshullam, Malluch, and Adaiah, Jashub, Sheal, *and* Jeremoth;
30 and of the sons of Pahath-
moab: Adna, Chelal, Benaiah, Maaseiah, Mattaniah, Bezalel, Binnui, and Manasseh;
31 and *of* the sons of Harim: Eliezer, Isshijah, [r]Malchijah, Shemaiah, Shimeon, Neh. 3:11
32 Benjamin, Malluch, *and*
Shemariah;
33 of the sons of Hashum: Mattenai, Mattattah, Zabad, Eliphelet,
Jeremai, Manasseh, *and* Shimei;
34 of the sons of Bani: Maadai,
Amram, Uel,
35 Benaiah, Bedeiah, Cheluhi,
36 Vaniah, Meremoth, Eliashib,
37 Mattaniah, Mattenai, Jaasu,
38 Bani, Binnui, Shimei,
39 Shelemiah, Nathan, Adaiah,
40 Machnadebai, Shashai, Sha-
rai,
41 Azarel, Shelemiah, Shemariah,
42 Shallum, Amariah, *and*
Joseph.
43 Of the sons of Nebo *there
were* Jeiel, Mattithiah, Zabad, Ze-
bina, Jaddai, Joel, *and* Benaiah.
44 All these had married foreign
wives, and some of them had
wives *by whom* they had children.

THE BOOK OF
NEHEMIAH

THE words of [r]Nehemiah the son
of Hacaliah. Neh. 10:1
Now it happened in the month
Chislev, *in* the twentieth year,
while I was in Susa the [1]capitol,
2 that Hanani, one of my
brothers, and some men from Judah came; and I asked them concerning the Jews who had escaped *and* had survived the
captivity, and about Jerusalem.
3 And they said to me, "The
remnant there in the [r]province
who survived the captivity are in
great distress and [r]reproach, and
the wall of Jerusalem is broken
down and its gates are burned
with fire." Neh. 7:6 • Neh. 2:17
4 Now it came about when I
heard these words, [r]I sat down and
wept and mourned for days; and I
was fasting and praying before
the God of heaven. Ezra 9:3; 10:1
5 And I said, "I beseech Thee,
O LORD God of heaven, [r]the great
and awesome God, who preserves
the covenant and lovingkindness
for those who love Him and keep
His commandments, Neh. 4:14
6 let Thine ear now be attentive and Thine eyes open to hear
the prayer of Thy servant which I
am praying before Thee now, day
and night, on behalf of the sons of
Israel Thy servants, [r]confessing
the sins of the sons of Israel which
we have sinned against Thee; [r]I
and my father's house have
sinned. Ezra 10:1 • 2 Chr. 29:6
7 "We[r] have acted very corruptly against Thee and have not
kept the commandments, nor the
statutes, nor the ordinances [r]which
Thou didst command Thy servant
Moses. Dan. 9:5 • Deut. 28:14
8 "Remember the word which
Thou didst command Thy servant
Moses, saying, 'If [r]you are unfaithful I will scatter you among the
peoples; Lev. 26:33
9 but if you return to Me and
keep My commandments and do
them, though those of you who
have been scattered were in the
most remote part of the heavens, I
[r]will gather them from there and
will bring them [r]to the place where
I have chosen to cause My name
to dwell.' Deut. 30:4 • Deut. 12:5
10 "And [r]they are Thy servants
and Thy people whom Thou didst
redeem by Thy great power and
by Thy strong hand. Ex. 32:11
11 "O Lord, I beseech Thee, [r]may
Thine ear be attentive to the
prayer of Thy servant and the
prayer of Thy servants who delight to [a]revere Thy name, and
make Thy servant successful today, and grant him compassion
before this man."
Now I was the [r]cupbearer to the
king. Neh. 1:6 • *fear* • Gen. 40:21; Neh. 2:1

CHAPTER 2

AND it came about in the month
Nisan, in the twentieth year of
King Artaxerxes, that wine *was*
before him, and I took up the wine

[1]Or, *palace or citadel*

and gave it to the king. Now I had
not been sad in his presence.
2 So the king said to me, "Why
is your face sad though you are
not sick? [r]This is nothing but sad-
ness of heart." Then I was very
much afraid. Prov. 15:13
3 And I said to the king, "Let[r]
the king live forever. Why should
my face not be sad when the city,
the place of my fathers' tombs,
lies desolate and its gates have
been consumed by fire?" Dan. 2:4
4 Then the king said to me,
"What would you request?" So I
prayed to the God of heaven.
5 And I said to the king, "If it
please the king, and if your servant has found favor before you,
send me to Judah, to the city of
my fathers' tombs, that I may rebuild it."
6 Then the king said to me, the
queen sitting beside him, "How
long will your journey be, and
when will you return?" So it
pleased the king to send me, and [r]I
gave him a definite time. Neh. 13:6
7 And I said to the king, "If it
please the king, let letters be giv-
en me for the governors *of the
provinces* beyond the River, that
they may allow me to pass
through until I come to Judah,
8 and a letter to Asaph the
keeper of the king's forest, that he
may give me timber to make
beams for the gates of the fortress
which is by the [2]temple, for the
wall of the city, and for the house
to which I will go." And the king
granted *them* to me because the
good hand of my God *was* on me.
9 Then I came to the governors
of the provinces beyond the River

[2]Lit., *house*

and gave them the king's letters.
Now the king had sent with me officers of the army and horsemen.
10 And when Sanballat the
Horonite and Tobiah the Ammonite official heard *about it*, it was
very displeasing to them that
someone had come to seek the
welfare of the sons of Israel.
11 So I [r]came to Jerusalem and
was there three days. Ezra 8:32
12 And I arose in the night, I
and a few men with me. I did not
tell anyone what my God was putting into my [t]mind to do for Jerusalem and there was no animal
with me except the animal on
which I was riding. *heart*
13 So I went out at night by the
Valley Gate in the direction of the
Dragon's Well and *on* to the [t]Ref-
use Gate, inspecting the walls of
Jerusalem which were broken
down and its gates which were
consumed by fire. *Gate of Ash-heaps*
14 Then I passed on to [r]the
Fountain Gate and the King's
Pool, but there was no place for
my mount to pass. Neh. 3:15
15 So I went up at night by the
[r]ravine and inspected the wall.
Then I entered the Valley Gate
again and returned. John 18:1
16 And the officials did not
know where I had gone or what I
had done; nor had I as yet told the
Jews, the priests, the nobles, the
officials, or the rest who did the
work.
17 Then I said to them, "You
see the bad situation we are in,
that Jerusalem is desolate and its
gates burned by fire. Come, let us
rebuild the wall of Jerusalem that
we may no longer be a reproach."

18 And I told them how the
hand of my God had been favorable to me, and also about the
king's words which he had spoken
to me. Then they said, "Let us
arise and build." So they put their
hands to the good *work*.
19 But when Sanballat the
Horonite, and Tobiah the Ammonite [t]official, and Geshem the Arab
heard *it*, they mocked us and despised us and said, "What is this
thing you are doing? Are you re-
belling against the king?" *servant*
20 So I answered them and said
to them, "The God[r] of heaven will
give us success; therefore we His
servants will arise and build, but
you have no portion, right, or memorial in Jerusalem." Ezra 4:3

CHAPTER 3

THEN [r]Eliashib the high priest
arose with his brothers the priests
and built the Sheep Gate; they
consecrated it and hung its doors.
They consecrated [t]the wall to the
Tower of the Hundred *and* the
Tower of Hananel. Neh. 3:20 • *it*
2 And next to him the men of
Jericho built, and next to [t]them
Zaccur the son of Imri built. *him*
3 Now the sons of Hassenaah
built [r]the Fish Gate; they laid its
beams and hung its doors with its
bolts and bars. Neh. 12:39
4 And next to them Meremoth
the son of Uriah the son of Hakkoz made repairs. And next to
him Meshullam the son of Berechiah the son of Meshezabel made
repairs. And next to [t]him Zadok
the son of Baana also made repairs. *them*
5 Moreover, next to [t]him the
Tekoites made repairs, but their
nobles did not support the work of
their masters. *them*
6 And Joiada the son of Paseah
and Meshullam the son of Besode-
iah repaired the Old Gate; they
laid its beams and hung its doors,
with its bolts and its bars.
7 Next to them Melatiah the
Gibeonite and Jadon the Meronothite, the men of Gibeon and of
Mizpah, also made repairs for the
official seat of the governor *of the*
province beyond the River.
8 Next to him Uzziel the son of
Harhaiah of the goldsmiths made
repairs. And next to him Hananiah, one of the perfumers, made
repairs, and they restored Jerusalem as far as the Broad Wall.
9 And next to them Rephaiah
the son of Hur, [r]the official of half
the district of Jerusalem, made repairs. Neh. 3:12, 17
10 Next to them Jedaiah the son
of Harumaph made repairs opposite his house. And next to him
Hattush the son of Hashabneiah
made repairs.
11 Malchijah the son of Harim
and Hasshub the son of Pahath-
moab repaired another section
and the Tower of Furnaces.
12 And next to him Shallum the
son of Hallohesh, [r]the official of
half the district of Jerusalem,
made repairs, he and his daughters. Neh. 3:9
13 Hanun and the inhabitants of
Zanoah repaired the Valley Gate.
They built it and hung its doors
with its bolts and its bars, and a
thousand cubits of the wall to the
[t]Refuse Gate. *Gate of Ash-heaps*

14 And Malchijah the son of Rechab, the official of the district of Beth-haccherem repaired the Refuse Gate. He built it and hung its doors with its bolts and its bars.

15 Shallum the son of Col-hozeh, the official of the district of Mizpah, [r]repaired the Fountain Gate. He built it, covered it, and hung its doors with its bolts and its bars, and the wall of the Pool of Shelah at the king's garden as far as the steps that descend from the city of David. Neh. 2:17

16 After him Nehemiah the son of Azbuk, [r]official of half the district of Beth-zur, made repairs as far as *a point* opposite the tombs of David, and as far as [r]the artificial pool and the house of the mighty men. Neh. 3:9 • Is. 7:3

17 After him the Levites carried out repairs *under* Rehum the son of Bani. Next to him Hashabiah, the official of half the district of Keilah, carried out repairs for his district.

18 After him their brothers carried out repairs *under* Bavvai the son of Henadad, official of *the other* half of the district of Keilah.

19 And next to him Ezer the son of Jeshua,[r] the official of Mizpah, repaired [t]another section, in front of the ascent of the armory at the Angle. Neh. 3:15 • *a second measure*

20 After him Baruch the son of Zabbai zealously repaired another section, from the Angle to the doorway of the house of [r]Eliashib the high priest. Neh. 3:1

21 After him Meremoth the son of Uriah the son of Hakkoz repaired another section, from the doorway of Eliashib's house even as far as the end of his house.

22 And after him the priests, [r]the men of the [3]valley, carried out repairs. Neh. 12:28

23 After [t]them Benjamin and Hasshub carried out repairs in front of their house. After [t]them Azariah the son of Maaseiah, son of Ananiah carried out repairs beside his house. *him*

24 After him Binnui the son of Henadad repaired another section, from the house of Azariah as far as [r]the Angle and as far as the corner. Neh. 3:19

25 Palal the son of Uzai *made repairs* in front of the Angle and the tower projecting from the upper house of the king, which is by [r]the court of the guard. After him Pedaiah the son of Parosh *made repairs.* Jer. 32:2

26 And [r]the temple servants living in [r]Ophel *made repairs* as far as the front of the Water Gate toward the east and the projecting tower. Neh. 7:46 • Neh. 11:21

27 After him [r]the Tekoites repaired another section in front of the great projecting tower and as far as the wall of Ophel. Neh. 3:5

28 Above [r]the Horse Gate the priests carried out repairs, each in front of his house. 2 Kin. 11:16

29 After [t]them Zadok the son of Immer carried out repairs in front of his house. And after him Shemaiah the son of Shecaniah, the keeper of the East Gate, carried out repairs. *him*

30 After him Hananiah the son of Shelemiah, and Hanun the sixth son of Zalaph, repaired another section. After him Meshul-

[3]Lit., *circle;* i.e., lower Jordan valley

lam the son of Berechiah carried
out repairs in front of his own
[a]quarters. *cell*
31 After him Malchijah [t]one of
the goldsmiths, carried out repairs
as far as the house of the temple
servants and of the merchants, in
front of the [a]Inspection Gate and
as far as the upper room of the
corner. *son of* • *Mustering*
32 And between the upper room
of the corner and [r]the Sheep Gate
the goldsmiths and the merchants
carried out repairs. Neh. 3:1

CHAPTER 4

NOW it came about that when
[r]Sanballat heard that we were rebuilding the wall, he became furious and very angry and mocked
the Jews. Neh. 2:10
2 And he spoke in the presence
of his brothers and the wealthy
men of Samaria and said, "What
are these feeble Jews doing? Are
they going to restore *it* for themselves? Can they offer sacrifices?
Can they finish in a day? Can they
revive the stones from the dusty
rubble even the burned ones?"
3 Now Tobiah the Ammonite
was near him and he said, "Even
what they are building—if a fox
should [t]jump on *it,* he would break
their stone wall down!" *go up*
4 [r]Hear, O our God, how we are
despised! [r]Return their reproach
on their own heads and give them
up for plunder in a land of captivity. Ps. 123:3, 4 • Ps. 79:12
5 Do not [t]forgive their iniquity
and let not their sin be blotted out
before Thee, for they have demoralized the builders. *cover*
6 So we built the wall and the
whole wall was joined together to
half its *height,* for the people had
a [t]mind to work. *heart*
7 Now it came about when
Sanballat, Tobiah, the Arabs, the
Ammonites, and the Ashdodites
heard that the [t]repair of the walls
of Jerusalem went on, *and* that
the breaches began to be closed,
they were very angry. *healing*
8 And all of them [r]conspired together to come *and* fight against
Jerusalem and to cause a disturbance in it. Ps. 83:3
9 But we prayed to our God,
and because of them we set up a
guard against them day and night.
10 Thus in Judah it was said,
"The strength of the burden
bearers is failing,
Yet there is much [t]rubbish;
And we ourselves are un-
able
To rebuild the wall." *dust*
11 And our enemies said, "They
will not know or see until we
come among them, kill them, and
put a stop to the work."
12 And it came about when the
Jews who lived near them came
and told us ten times, "They will
come up against us from every
place where you may turn,"
13 then I stationed *men* in the
lowest parts of the space behind
the wall, the [t]exposed places, and I
[r]stationed the people in families
with their swords, spears, and
bows. *bare* • Neh. 4:17, 18
14 When I saw *their fear,* I rose
and spoke to the nobles, the officials, and the rest of the people:
"Do[r] not be afraid of them; remember the Lord who is great and

awesome, and [r]fight for your brothers, your sons, your daughters, your wives, and your houses." Num. 14:9 • 2 Sam. 10:12

15 And it happened when our enemies heard that it was known to us, and that God had frustrated their plan, then all of us returned to the wall, each one to his work.

16 And it came about from that day on, that half of my servants carried on the work while half of them held the spears, the shields, the bows, and the breastplates; and the captains *were* behind the whole house of Judah.

17 Those who were rebuilding the wall and those who carried burdens took *their* load with one hand doing the work and the other holding a weapon.

18 As for the builders, each *wore* his sword girded at his side as he built, while the trumpeter *stood* near me.

19 And I said to the nobles, the officials, and the rest of the people, "The work is great and extensive, and we are separated on the wall far from one another.

20 "At whatever place you hear the sound of the trumpet, [t]rally to us there. [r]Our God will fight for us." *assemble yourselves* • Ex. 14:14

21 So we carried on the work with half of them holding spears from [t]dawn until the stars [t]appeared. *rising of the dawn* • *came out*

22 At that time I also said to the people, "Let each man with his servant spend the night within Jerusalem so that they may be a guard for us by night and a laborer by day."

23 So neither I, my brothers, my servants, nor the men of the guard who followed me, none of us removed our clothes, each *took* his weapon *even to* the water.

CHAPTER 5

NOW there was a great outcry of the people and of their wives against their Jewish brothers.

2 For there were those who said, "We, our sons and our daughters, are many; therefore let us [r]get grain that we may eat and live." Hag. 1:6

3 And there were others who said, "We are mortgaging our fields, our vineyards, and our houses that we might get grain because of the famine."

4 Also there were those who said, "We have borrowed money [r]for the king's tax *on* our fields and our vineyards. Ezra 4:13; 7:24

5 "And now [r]our flesh is like the flesh of our brothers, our children like their children. Yet behold, we are forcing our sons and our daughters to be slaves, and some of our daughters are forced into bondage *already*, and we are helpless because our fields and vineyards belong to others." Gen. 37:27

6 Then I was very [r]angry when I had heard their outcry and these words. Ex. 11:8

7 And I consulted with myself, and contended with the nobles and the rulers and said to them, "You[r] are exacting usury, each from his brother!" Therefore, I held a great assembly against them. Ex. 22:25; Lev. 25:36

8 And I said to them, "We according to our ability have

[t]redeemed our Jewish brothers
who were sold to the nations; now
would you even sell your brothers
that they may be sold to us?"
Then they were silent and could
not find a word *to say.* *bought*

9 Again I said, "The thing
which you are doing is not good;
should you not walk in the fear of
our God because of the reproach
of the nations, our enemies?

10 "And likewise I, my brothers
and my servants, are lending them
money and grain. Please, let us
leave off this usury.

11 "Please, give back to them
this very day their fields, their
vineyards, their olive groves, and
their houses, also the hundredth
part of the money and of the
grain, the new wine, and the oil
that you are exacting from them."

12 Then they said, "We [r]will give
it back and will require nothing
from them; we will do exactly as
you say." So I called the priests
and took an oath from them that
they would do according to this
[t]promise. 2 Chr. 28:15 • *word*

13 I also shook out the front of
my garment and said, "Thus may
God shake out every man from his
house and from his possessions
who does not fulfill this promise;
even thus may he be shaken out
and emptied." And all the assembly said, "Amen!" And they
praised the LORD. Then the people
did according to this promise.

14 Moreover, from the day that
I was appointed to be their governor in the land of Judah, from the
twentieth year to the thirty-sec-
ond year of King Artaxerxes, *for*
twelve years, neither I nor my
[t]kinsmen have eaten the governor's food *allowance.* *brothers*

15 But the former governors
who were before me [t]laid burdens
on the people and took from them
bread and wine besides forty
shekels of silver; even their servants domineered the people. But
I did not do so [r]because of the fear
of God. *made heavy* • Neh. 5:9

16 And I also [t]applied myself to
the work on this wall; we did not
buy any land, and all my servants
were gathered there for the work.

17 Moreover, [r]*there were* at my
table one hundred and fifty Jews
and officials, besides those who
came to us from the nations that
were around us. 1 Kin. 18:19

18 Now [r]that which was prepared for each day was one ox
and six choice sheep, also birds
were prepared for me; and once in
ten days all sorts of wine *were furnished* in abundance. Yet for all
this [r]I did not demand the governor's food *allowance,* because the
servitude was heavy on this people. 1 Kin. 4:22, 23 • 2 Thess. 3:8

19 Remember me, O my God,
for good, *according to* all that I
have done for this people.

CHAPTER 6

NOW it came about when it was
reported to Sanballat, Tobiah, to
Geshem the Arab, and to the rest
of our enemies that I had rebuilt
the wall, and *that* no breach remained in it, [r]although at that time
I had not set up the doors in the
gates, Neh. 3:1, 3

2 that Sanballat and Geshem
sent *a message* to me, saying,

[t]Or, *held fast*

"Come, let us meet together at [5]Chephirim in the plain of [r]Ono." But they were planning to [t]harm me. 1 Chr. 8:12 • *do evil to me*

3 So I sent messengers to them, saying, "I am doing a great work and I cannot come down. Why should the work stop while I leave it and come down to you?"

4 And they sent *messages* to me four times in this manner, and I answered them in the same way.

5 Then Sanballat sent his servant to me in the same manner a fifth time with an open letter in his hand.

6 In it was written, "It is reported among the nations, and Gashmu says, that [r]you and the Jews are planning to rebel; therefore you are rebuilding the wall. And you are to be their king, according to these reports. Neh. 2:19

7 "And you have also appointed prophets to proclaim in Jerusalem concerning [t]you, 'A king is in Judah!' And now it will be reported to the king according to these reports. So come now, let us take counsel together." *you, saying*

8 Then I sent *a message* to him saying, "Such things as you are saying have not been done, but you are inventing them [t]in your own mind." *from your heart*

9 For all of them were *trying* to frighten us, [t]thinking, "They will become discouraged with the work and it will not be done." But now, [r]*O God*, strengthen my hands. *saying* • Ps. 138:3

10 And when I entered the house of Shemaiah the son of Delaiah, son of Mehetabel, who was confined at home, he said, "Let us meet together in the house of God, within the temple, and let us close the doors of the temple, for they are coming to kill you, and they are coming to kill you at night."

11 But I said, "Should a man like me flee? And could one such as I go into the temple [t]to save his life? I will not go in." *and live*

12 Then I perceived [t]that surely God had not sent him, but he uttered *his* prophecy against me because Tobiah and Sanballat had hired him. *and behold God*

13 He was hired for this reason, [r]that I might become frightened and act accordingly and sin, so that they might have an evil report in order that they could reproach me. Neh. 6:6

14 Remember, O my God, Tobiah and Sanballat according to these works of theirs, and also Noadiah [r]the prophetess and the rest of the prophets who were *trying* to frighten me. Ezek. 13:17

15 So [r]the wall was completed on the twenty-fifth of *the month* Elul, in fifty-two days. Neh. 4:1

16 And it came about when all our enemies heard *of it*, and all the nations surrounding us saw *it*, they lost their confidence; for they recognized that this work had been accomplished [t]with the help of our God. *from our God*

17 Also in those days many letters went from the nobles of Judah to Tobiah, and Tobiah's *letters* came to them.

18 For many in Judah were bound by oath to him because he was the son-in-law of Shecaniah the son of Arah, and his son Jehohanan had married the daughter

[5]Another reading is, one of *the villages*

of Meshullam the son of Berechiah.
19 Moreover, they were speaking about his good deeds in my
presence and reported my words
to him. Then Tobiah sent letters to
frighten me.

CHAPTER 7

NOW it came about when [r]the
wall was rebuilt and I had set up
the doors, and the gatekeepers
and the singers and the Levites
were appointed, Neh. 6:1, 15
2 that I put Hanani my brother,
and Hananiah the commander of
the fortress, in charge of Jerusalem, for he was a faithful man and
feared God more than many.
3 Then I said to them, "Do not
let the gates of Jerusalem be
opened until the sun is hot, and
while they are standing *guard*, let
them shut and bolt the doors. Also
appoint guards from the inhabitants of Jerusalem, each at his
post, and each in front of his own
house."
4 Now the city was large and
spacious, but the people in it were
few and the houses were not built.
5 [r]Then my God put it into my
heart to assemble the nobles, the
officials, and the people to be enrolled by genealogies. Then I
found the book of the genealogy
of those who came up first [t]in
which I found the following rec-
ord: Prov. 2:6 • *and I found written in it*
6 These are the [t]people of the
province who came up from the
captivity of the exiles whom
Nebuchadnezzar the king of
Babylon had carried away, and
who returned to Jerusalem and
Judah, each to his city, *sons*
7 who came with Zerubbabel,
Jeshua, Nehemiah, Azariah, Ra-
amiah, Nahamani, Mordecai, Bilshan, Mispereth, Bigvai, Nehum,
Baanah.
The number of men of the people of Israel:
8 the sons of Parosh, 2,172;
9 the sons of Shephatiah, 372;
10 the sons of Arah, 652;
11 the sons of Pahath-moab of
the sons of Jeshua and Joab,
2,818;
12 the sons of Elam, 1,254;
13 the sons of Zattu, 845;
14 the sons of Zaccai, 760;
15 the sons of Binnui, 648;
16 the sons of Bebai, 628;
17 the sons of Azgad, 2,322;
18 the sons of Adonikam, 667;
19 the sons of Bigvai, 2,067;
20 the sons of Adin, 655;
21 the sons of Ater, of Hezekiah, 98;
22 the sons of Hashum, 328;
23 the sons of Bezai, 324;
24 the sons of Hariph, 112;
25 the sons of Gibeon, 95;
26 the men of Bethlehem and
Netophah, 188;
27 the men of Anathoth, 128;
28 the men of Beth-azmaveth,
42;
29 the men of Kiriath-jearim,
Chephirah, and Beeroth, 743;
30 the men of Ramah and Geba,
621;
31 the men of Michmas, 122;
32 the men of Bethel and Ai,
123;
33 the men of the other Nebo,
52;

34 the sons of the other Elam,
1,254;
35 the sons of Harim, 320;
36 the [t]men of Jericho, 345; *sons*
37 the sons of Lod, Hadid, and
Ono, 721;
38 the sons of Senaah, 3,930.
39 The priests: the sons of Jedaiah of the house of Jeshua, 973;
40 the sons of Immer, 1,052;
41 the sons of Pashhur, 1,247;
42 the sons of Harim, 1,017.
43 The Levites: the sons of
Jeshua, of Kadmiel, of the sons of
Hodevah, 74.
44 The singers: the sons of
Asaph, 148.
45 The gatekeepers: the sons of
Shallum, the sons of Ater, the
sons of Talmon, the sons of Akkub, the sons of Hatita, the sons
of Shobai, 138.
46 The temple servants: the
sons of Ziha, the sons of Hasupha,
the sons of Tabbaoth,
47 the sons of Keros, the sons of
Sia, the sons of Padon,
48 the sons of Lebana, the sons
of Hagaba, the sons of Shalmai,
49 the sons of Hanan, the sons
of Giddel, the sons of Gahar,
50 the sons of Reaiah, the sons
of Rezin, the sons of Nekoda,
51 the sons of Gazzam, the sons
of Uzza, the sons of Paseah,
52 the sons of Besai, the sons of
Meunim, the sons of Nephushe-
sim,
53 the sons of Bakbuk, the sons
of Hakupha, the sons of Harhur,
54 the sons of Bazlith, the sons
of Mehida, the sons of Harsha,
55 the sons of Barkos, the sons
of Sisera, the sons of Temah,
56 the sons of Neziah, the sons
of Hatipha.
57 The sons of Solomon's servants: the sons of Sotai, the sons
of Sophereth, the sons of Perida,
58 the sons of Jaala, the sons of
Darkon, the sons of Giddel,
59 the sons of Shephatiah, the
sons of Hattil, the sons of Poche-
reth-hazzebaim, the sons of
Amon.
60 All the temple servants and
the sons of Solomon's servants
were 392.
61 And these *were* they who
came up from Tel-melah, Tel-har-
sha, Cherub, Addon, and Immer;
but they could not show their fathers' houses or their descendants, whether they were of Israel:
62 the sons of Delaiah, the sons
of Tobiah, the sons of Nekoda,
642.
63 And of the priests: the sons
of Hobaiah, the sons of Hakkoz,
the sons of Barzillai, who took a
wife of the daughters of Barzillai,
the Gileadite, and was named after them.
64 These searched *among* their
ancestral registration, but it could
not be located; therefore they
were considered unclean *and excluded* from the priesthood.
65 And [r]the governor said to
them that they should not eat
from the most holy things until a
priest arose with [r]Urim and Thummim. Neh. 8:9 • Ex. 28:30
66 The whole assembly together
was 42,360,
67 besides their male and their
female servants, [t]of whom *there
were* 7,337; and they had 245 male
and female singers. *these*

68 [r]Their horses were 736; their
mules, 245; Ezra 2:66
69 *their* camels, 435; *their* donkeys, 6,720.
70 And some from among the
heads of fathers' *households* gave
to the work. The governor gave to
the treasury 1,000 gold drachmas,
50 basins, 530 priests' garments.
71 And some of the heads of fathers' *households* gave into the
treasury of the work 20,000 gold
drachmas, and 2,200 silver minas.
72 And that which the rest of
the people gave was 20,000 gold
drachmas and 2,000 silver minas,
and 67 priests' garments.
73 Now [r]the priests, the Levites,
the gatekeepers, the singers, some
of the people, the temple servants,
and all Israel, lived in their cities.
[r]And when the seventh month
came, the sons of Israel *were* in
their cities. 1 Chr. 9:2 • Ezra 3:1

CHAPTER 8

AND all the people gathered as
one man at the square which was
in front of the Water Gate, and
they [t]asked Ezra the scribe to
bring the book of the law of
Moses which the LORD had [t]given
to Israel. *said to* • *commanded*
2 Then Ezra the priest brought
the law before the assembly of
men, women, and all who *could*
listen with understanding, on the
first day of the seventh month.
3 And he read from it before
the square which was in front of
[r]the Water Gate from [t]early morning until midday, in the presence
of men and women, those who
could understand; and all the people were attentive to the book of
the law. Neh. 8:1 • *the light*
4 And Ezra the scribe stood at
a wooden podium which they had
made for the purpose. And beside
him stood Mattithiah, Shema,
Anaiah, Uriah, Hilkiah, and Maaseiah on his right hand; and Pedaiah, Mishael, Malchijah, Hashum,
Hashbaddanah, Zechariah, *and*
Meshullam on his left hand.
5 And Ezra opened [r]the book in
the sight of all the people for he
was standing above all the people;
and when he opened it, all the
people stood up. Neh. 8:3
6 Then Ezra blessed the LORD
the great God. And all the people
answered, "Amen,[r] Amen!" while
lifting up their hands; then [r]they
bowed low and worshiped the
LORD with *their* faces to the
ground. Neh. 5:13 • Ex. 4:31
7 Also Jeshua, Bani, Sherebiah, Jamin, Akkub, Shabbethai,
Hodiah, Maaseiah, Kelita, Azariah, Jozabad, Hanan, Pelaiah, and
the Levites, explained the law to
the people while the people *re-*
mained in their place.
8 And they read from the
book, from the law of God, translating to give the sense so that
they understood the reading.
9 Then Nehemiah, who was
the [r]governor, and Ezra the priest
and scribe, and the Levites who
taught the people said to all the
people, "This day is holy to the
LORD your God; do not mourn or
weep." For all the people were
weeping when they heard the
words of the law. Neh. 7:65
10 Then he said to them, "Go,
eat of the fat, drink of the sweet,

and [r]send portions to him who has
nothing prepared; for this day is
holy to our Lord. Do not be
grieved, for the joy of the LORD is
your strength." Deut. 26:11-13
11 So the Levites calmed all the
people, saying, "Be still, for the
day is holy; do not be grieved."
12 And all the people went
away to eat, to drink, [r]to send portions and to celebrate a great festival, because they understood the
words which had been made
known to them. Neh. 8:10
13 Then on the second day the
heads of fathers' *households* of all
the people, the priests, and the Levites were gathered to Ezra the
scribe that they might gain insight
into the words of the law.
14 And they found written in
the law how the LORD had commanded through Moses that the
sons of Israel [r]should live in booths
during the feast of the seventh
month. Lev. 23:34, 40, 42
15 So they proclaimed and circulated a proclamation in all their
cities and [r]in Jerusalem, saying,
"Go [r]out to the hills, and bring olive branches, and wild olive
branches, myrtle branches, palm
branches, and branches of *other*
leafy trees, to make booths, as it is
written." Deut. 16:16 • Lev. 23:40
16 So the people went out and
brought *them* and made booths
for themselves, each [r]on his roof,
and in their courts, and in the
courts of the house of God, and in
the square at [r]the Water Gate, and
in the square at [r]the Gate of Ephraim. Jer. 32:29 • Neh. 8:1 • 2 Kin. 14:13
17 And the entire assembly of
those who had returned from the
captivity made booths and lived in
them. The sons of Israel had indeed not done so from the days of
Joshua the son of Nun to that day.
And there was great rejoicing.
18 And [r]he read from the book of
the law of God daily, from the first
day to the last day. And they [r]cele-
brated the feast seven days, and
on the eighth day *there was* a solemn assembly according to the ordinance. Deut. 31:11 • Lev. 23:36

CHAPTER 9

NOW on the twenty-fourth day
of this month the sons of Israel assembled with fasting, in sackcloth, and with dirt upon them.
2 And the [t]descendants of Israel separated themselves from all
foreigners, and stood and [r]con-
fessed their sins and the iniquities
of their fathers. *seed* • Prov. 28:13
3 While they stood in their
place, they read from the book of
the law of the LORD their God for
a fourth of the day; and for *another* fourth they confessed and
worshiped the LORD their God.
4 [r]Now on the Levites' platform
stood Jeshua, Bani, Kadmiel,
Shebaniah, Bunni, Sherebiah,
Bani, *and* Chenani, and they cried
with a loud voice to the LORD their
God. Neh. 8:7
5 Then the Levites, Jeshua,
Kadmiel, Bani, Hashabnei-
ah, Sherebiah, Hodiah, Shebaniah, *and* Pethahiah, said, "Arise,
bless the LORD your God forever
and ever!

O may Thy glorious name be
blessed
And exalted above all blessing and praise!

6"Thou alone art the LORD.
Thou hast made the heavens,
The heaven of heavens with all their host,
The earth and all that is on it,
The seas and all that is in them.
[r]Thou dost give life to all of them Col. 1:16f.
And the heavenly host bows down before Thee.
7"Thou art the LORD God,
[r]Who chose Abram Gen. 12:1
And brought him out from Ur of the Chaldees,
And [r]gave him the name Abraham. Gen. 17:5
8"And Thou didst find his heart faithful before Thee,
And didst make a covenant with him
To give *him* the land of the Canaanite,
Of the Hittite and the Amorite,
Of the Perizzite, the Jebusite, and the Girgashite—
To give *it* to his descendants.
And Thou hast fulfilled Thy promise,
For Thou art righteous.

9"Thou didst see the affliction of our fathers in Egypt,
And didst hear their cry by the [t]Red Sea. *Sea of Reeds*
10"Then Thou didst perform [r]signs and wonders against Pharaoh, Ex. 5:2
Against all his servants and all the people of his land;
For Thou didst know that they acted arrogantly toward them,
And didst make a name for Thyself as *it is* this day.
11"And Thou didst divide the sea before them,
So they passed through the midst of the sea on dry ground;
And their pursuers Thou didst hurl into the depths,
Like a stone into [t]raging waters. *strong, mighty*
12"And with a pillar of cloud [r]Thou didst lead them by day, Ex. 13:21, 22
And with a pillar of fire by night
To light for them the way
In which they were to go.
13"Then [r]Thou didst come down on Mount Sinai, Ex. 19:11
And didst [r]speak with them from heaven; Ex. 20:1
Thou didst give to them just ordinances and true laws,
Good statutes and commandments.
14"So Thou didst make known to them [r]Thy holy sabbath, Ex. 16:23; 20:8
And didst lay down for them commandments, statutes, and law,
Through Thy servant Moses.
15"Thou didst [r]provide bread from heaven for them for their hunger, Ex. 16:4
Thou didst [r]bring forth water from a rock for them for their thirst, Ex. 17:6
And Thou didst tell them to enter in order to possess
The land which Thou didst swear to give them.

16"But they, our fathers, [r]acted arrogantly; Neh. 9:10

They [6]became stubborn and
would not listen to Thy
commandments.
17 "And they refused to listen,
And [r]did not remember Thy
wondrous deeds which
Thou hadst performed
among them; Ps. 78:11
So they [6]became stubborn
and [r]appointed a leader to
return to their slavery in
Egypt. Num. 14:4
But Thou art a God [r]of forgiveness, Ex. 34:6, 7
Gracious and compassionate,
Slow to anger, and abounding in lovingkindness;
And Thou didst not forsake
them.
18 "Even when they [r]made for
themselves Ex. 32:4-8
A calf of molten metal
And said, 'This is your God
Who brought you up from
Egypt,'
And committed great [7]blasphemies,
19 [r]Thou, in Thy great compassion, Deut. 8:2-4
Didst not forsake them in the
wilderness;
The pillar of cloud did not
leave them by day,
To guide them on their way,
Nor the pillar of fire by night,
to light for them the way
in which they were to go.
20 "And [r]Thou didst give Thy
good Spirit to instruct
them, Num. 11:17
Thy manna Thou didst not
withhold from their
mouth,

[6]Lit., *stiffened their neck*
[7]Lit., *acts of contempt*

And Thou didst give them
water for their thirst.
21 "Indeed, [r]forty years Thou
didst provide for them in
the wilderness *and* they
were not in want; Deut. 2:7
Their clothes did not wear
out, nor did their feet
swell.
22 "Thou didst also give them
kingdoms and peoples,
And Thou didst allot *them* to
them as a boundary.
[r]And they took possession of
the land of Sihon the king
of Heshbon, Num. 21:21-35
And the land of Og the king
of Bashan.
23 "And Thou didst make their
sons numerous as [r]the
stars of heaven,
And Thou didst bring them
into the land
Which Thou hadst told their
fathers to enter and possess. Gen. 15:5; 22:17
24 "So their sons entered and
possessed the land.
And [r]Thou didst subdue before them the inhabitants
of the land, the Canaanites, Josh. 18:1
And Thou didst give them
into their hand, with their
kings, and the peoples of
the land,
To do with them as they desired.
25 "And they captured fortified
cities and a fertile land.
They took possession of
[r]houses full of every good
thing, Deut. 6:11
Hewn cisterns, vineyards, olive groves,
Fruit trees in abundance.

So they ate, were filled, and [r]grew fat, Deut. 32:15
And [r]reveled in Thy great goodness. 1 Kin. 8:66

26 "But [r]they became disobedient and rebelled against Thee, Judg. 2:11
And cast Thy law behind their backs
And killed Thy prophets who had admonished them
So that they might return to Thee,
And [r]they committed great [7]blasphemies. Neh. 9:18
27 "Therefore Thou didst [r]deliver them into the hand of their oppressors who oppressed them, Judg. 2:14
But when they cried to Thee [r]in the time of their distress, Deut. 4:29
Thou didst hear from heaven, and according to Thy great compassion
Thou didst [r]give them deliverers who delivered them from the hand of their oppressors. Judg. 2:16
28 "But [r]as soon as they had rest, they did evil again before Thee; Judg. 3:11
Therefore Thou didst abandon them to the hand of their enemies, so that they ruled over them.
When they cried again to Thee, Thou didst hear from heaven,
And many times Thou didst rescue them according to Thy compassion,
29 And [r]admonished them in order to turn them back to Thy law. Neh. 9:26, 30
Yet [r]they acted arrogantly and did not listen to Thy commandments but sinned against Thine ordinances, Neh. 9:10, 16
By which if a man observes them he shall live.
And they [t]turned a stubborn shoulder and stiffened their neck, and would not listen. *gave*
30 "However, [r] Thou didst bear with them for many years, Ps. 95:10
And admonished them by Thy Spirit through Thy prophets,
Yet they would not give ear.
Therefore Thou didst give them into the hand of the peoples of the lands.
31 "Nevertheless, in Thy great compassion Thou didst not make an end of them or forsake them,
For Thou art a gracious and compassionate God.

32 "Now therefore, our God, [r]the great, the mighty, and the awesome God, who dost keep covenant and lovingkindness, Neh. 1:5
Do not let all the hardship seem insignificant before Thee,
Which has come upon us, our kings, our princes, our priests, our prophets, our fathers, and on all Thy people,
From the days of the kings of Assyria to this day.
33 "However, [r]Thou art just in all that has come upon us;

[7]Lit., *acts of contempt*

For Thou hast dealt faithfully, but we have acted wickedly. Gen. 18:25
34 "For our kings, our leaders, our priests, and our fathers have not kept Thy law
Or paid attention to Thy commandments and Thine [t]admonitions with which Thou hast admonished them. *testimonies*
35 "But [r]they, in their own kingdom, Deut. 28:47
[r]With Thy great goodness which Thou didst give them, Neh. 9:25
With the broad and rich land which Thou didst set before them,
Did not serve Thee or turn from their evil deeds.
36 "Behold, we are slaves today,
And as to the land which Thou didst give to our fathers to eat of its fruit and its bounty,
Behold, we are slaves on it.
37 "And its abundant produce is for the kings
Whom Thou hast set over us because of our sins;
They also rule over our bodies
And over our cattle as they please,
So we are in great distress.
38 "Now because of all this
We are making an agreement in writing;
And on the [r]sealed document *are the names of* our leaders, our Levites *and* our priests." Neh. 10:1

CHAPTER 10

NOW on the [r]sealed document
were the names of: Nehemiah the
governor, the son of Hacaliah, and
Zedekiah, Neh. 9:38
2 Seraiah, Azariah, Jeremiah,
3 Pashhur, Amariah, Malchijah,
4 Hattush, Shebaniah, Malluch,
5 Harim, Meremoth, Obadiah,
6 Daniel, Ginnethon, Baruch,
7 Meshullam, Abijah, Mijamin,
8 Maaziah, Bilgai, Shemaiah.
These *were* the priests.
9 And the Levites: Jeshua the
son of Azaniah, Binnui of the sons
of Henadad, Kadmiel;
10 also their brothers Shebaniah, Hodiah, Kelita, Pelaiah, Hanan,
11 Mica, Rehob, Hashabiah,
12 Zaccur, Sherebiah, Shebaniah,
13 Hodiah, Bani, Beninu.
14 The leaders of the people:
Parosh, Pahath-moab, Elam, Zattu, Bani,
15 Bunni, Azgad, Bebai,
16 Adonijah, Bigvai, Adin,
17 Ater, Hezekiah, Azzur,
18 Hodiah, Hashum, Bezai,
19 Hariph, Anathoth, Nebai,
20 Magpiash, Meshullam, Hezir,
21 Meshezabel, Zadok, Jaddua,
22 Pelatiah, Hanan, Anaiah,
23 Hoshea, Hananiah, Hasshub,
24 Hallohesh, Pilha, Shobek,
25 Rehum, Hashabnah, Maaseiah,
26 Ahiah, Hanan, Anan,
27 Malluch, Harim, Baanah.
28 Now the rest of the people,
the priests, the Levites, the gate-

keepers, the singers, the temple servants, and all those who had separated themselves from the peoples of the lands to the law of God, their wives, their sons and their daughters, all those who had knowledge and understanding,

29 are joining with their [t]kinsmen, their nobles, and are [t]taking on themselves a curse and an oath to walk in God's law, which was given through Moses, God's servant, and to keep and to observe all the commandments of GOD our Lord, and His ordinances and His statutes; *brothers • entering into a*

30 and [r]that we will not give our daughters to the peoples of the land or take their daughters for our sons. Ex. 34:16; Deut. 7:3

31 As for the peoples of the land who bring wares or any grain on the sabbath day to sell, we will not buy from them on the sabbath or a holy day; and we will forego *the crops* the [r]seventh year and the exaction of every debt. Ex. 23:10

32 We also placed ourselves under obligation to contribute yearly one third of a shekel for the service of the house of our God:

33 for the showbread, for the continual grain offering, for the continual burnt offering, the sabbaths, the new moon, for the appointed times, for the holy things and for the sin offerings to make atonement for Israel, and all the work of the house of our God.

34 Likewise [r]we cast lots for the supply of wood *among* the priests, the Levites, and the people in order that they might bring it to the house of our God, according to our fathers' households, at fixed times annually, to burn on the altar of the LORD our God as it is written in the law; Neh. 11:1

35 and in order that they might bring the first fruits of our ground and [r]the first fruits of all the fruit of every tree to the house of the LORD annually, Ex. 23:19

36 and [r]bring to the house of our God the first-born of our sons and of our cattle, and the first-born of our herds and our flocks as it is written in the law, for the priests who are ministering in the house of our God. Ex. 13:2

37 We will also bring the first of our [a]dough, our contributions, the fruit of every tree, the new wine and the oil to the priests at the chambers of the house of our God, and the tithe of our ground to the Levites, for the Levites are they who receive the tithes in all the rural towns. *coarse meal*

38 And [r]the priest, the son of Aaron, shall be with the Levites when the Levites receive tithes, and the Levites shall bring up the tenth of the tithes to the house of our God, to the chambers of the storehouse. Num. 18:26

39 For the sons of Israel and the sons of Levi shall bring the [r]contribution of the grain, the new wine and the oil, to the chambers; there are the utensils of the sanctuary, the priests who are ministering, the gatekeepers, and the singers. Thus we will not [t]neglect the house of our God. Deut. 12:6 • *forsake*

CHAPTER 11

NOW the leaders of the people lived in Jerusalem, but the rest of

the people cast lots to bring one
out of ten to live in Jerusalem, the
holy city, while nine-tenths *remained* in the *other* cities.
2 And the people blessed all
the men who [r]volunteered to live
in Jerusalem. Judg. 5:9
3 Now these are the heads of
the provinces who lived in Jerusalem, but in the cities of Judah
each lived on his own property in
their cities—the [t]Israelites, the
priests, the Levites, the temple
servants and the descendants of
Solomon's servants. *Israel*
4 And some of the sons of Judah and some of the sons of Benjamin lived in Jerusalem. From
the sons of Judah: Athaiah the son
of Uzziah, the son of Zechariah,
the son of Amariah, the son of
Shephatiah, the son of Mahalalel,
of the sons of Perez;
5 and Maaseiah the son of Baruch, the son of Col-hozeh, the son
of Hazaiah, the son of Adaiah, the
son of Joiarib, the son of Zechariah, the son of the Shilonite.
6 All the sons of Perez who
lived in Jerusalem were 468 able
men.
7 Now these are the sons of
Benjamin: Sallu the son of Meshullam, the son of Joed, the son
of Pedaiah, the son of Kolaiah, the
son of Maaseiah, the son of Ithiel,
the son of Jeshaiah;
8 and after him Gabbai *and*
Sallai, 928.
9 And Joel the son of Zichri
was their overseer, and Judah the
son of Hassenuah was second [t]in
command of the city. *over*
10 From the priests: Jedaiah the
son of Joiarib, Jachin,

11 Seraiah the son of Hilkiah,
the son of Meshullam, the son of
Zadok, the son of Meraioth, the
son of Ahitub, the leader of the
house of God,
12 and their [8]kinsmen who performed the work of the [t]temple,
822; and Adaiah the son of Jeroham, the son of Pelaliah, the son
of Amzi, the son of Zechariah, the
son of Pashhur, the son of Malchijah, *house*
13 and his kinsmen, heads of fathers' *households*, 242; and
Amashsai the son of Azarel, the
son of Ahzai, the son of Meshillemoth, the son of Immer,
14 and their brothers, valiant
warriors, 128. And their overseer
was Zabdiel, the son of [a]Haggedo-
lim. *the great ones*
15 Now from the Levites:
Shemaiah the son of Hasshub, the
son of Azrikam, the son of Hashabiah, the son of Bunni;
16 and Shabbethai and Jozabad,
from the [t]leaders of the Levites,
who were in charge of the outside
work of the house of God; *heads*
17 and Mattaniah the son of
Mica, the son of Zabdi, the son of
Asaph, who was the leader in beginning the thanksgiving at
prayer, and Bakbukiah, the second among his brethren; and
Abda the son of Shammua, the
son of Galal, the son of Jeduthun.
18 All the Levites in [r]the holy
city *were* 284. Neh. 11:1
19 Also the gatekeepers, Akkub, Talmon, and their brethren,
who kept watch at the gates, *were*
172.
20 And the rest of Israel, of the
priests, *and* of the Levites, *were* in

[8]Lit., *brothers*, and so throughout this context

all the cities of Judah, each [r]on his
own inheritance. Neh. 11:3
21 But [r]the temple servants were
living in Ophel, and Ziha and
Gishpa were [t]in charge of the temple servants. Neh. 3:26 • *over*
22 Now the overseer of the Levites in Jerusalem was Uzzi the
son of Bani, the son of Hashabiah,
the son of Mattaniah, the son of
Mica, from the sons of Asaph,
who were the singers for the [a]ser-
vice of the house of God. *work*
23 [r]For *there was* a commandment from the king concerning
them and a firm regulation for the
song leaders day by day. Ezra 6:8
24 And Pethahiah the son of
Meshezabel, of the sons of Zerah
the son of Judah, was the king's
[t]representative in all matters concerning the people. *hand*
25 Now as for the villages with
their fields, some of the sons of
Judah lived in Kiriath-arba and its
[9]towns, in Dibon and its towns,
and in Jekabzeel and its villages,
26 and in Jeshua, in Moladah
and Beth-pelet,
27 and in Hazar-shual, in Beersheba and its towns,
28 and in Ziklag, in Meconah
and in its towns,
29 and in En-rimmon, in Zorah
and in Jarmuth,
30 Zanoah, Adullam, and their
villages, Lachish and its fields,
Azekah and its towns. So they encamped from Beersheba as far as
the valley of Hinnom.
31 The sons of Benjamin also
lived from Geba *onward,* at Michmash and Aija, at Bethel and its
towns,

[9]Lit., *daughters,* and so through this ch.

32 at Anathoth, Nob, Ananiah,
33 Hazor, Ramah, Gittaim,
34 Hadid, Zeboim, Neballat,
35 Lod and Ono, the valley of
craftsmen.
36 And from the Levites, *some*
divisions in Judah belonged to
Benjamin.

CHAPTER 12

NOW these are the priests and
the Levites who came up with Zerubbabel the son of Shealtiel, and
Jeshua: Seraiah, Jeremiah, Ezra,
2 Amariah, Malluch, Hattush,
3 Shecaniah, Rehum, Mer-
emoth,
4 Iddo, Ginnethoi, Abijah,
5 Mijamin, Maadiah, Bilgah,
6 Shemaiah and Joiarib, Jedaiah,
7 Sallu, Amok, Hilkiah, and
Jedaiah. These were the heads of
the priests and their [t]kinsmen in
the days of Jeshua. *brothers*
8 And the Levites *were* Jeshua,
Binnui, Kadmiel, Sherebiah, Judah, *and* Mattaniah *who was* [t]in
charge of the songs of thanksgiving, he and his brothers. *over*
9 Also Bakbukiah and Unni,
their brothers, stood opposite
them in *their* service divisions.
10 And Jeshua [t]became the father of Joiakim, and Joiakim became the father of Eliashib, and
Eliashib became the father of Joiada, *begot,* and so in vv. 11, 12
11 and Joiada became the father
of Jonathan, and Jonathan became the father of Jaddua.
12 Now in the days of Joiakim
the priests, the heads of fathers'

households were: of Seraiah, Me-
raiah; of Jeremiah, Hananiah;
13 of Ezra, Meshullam; of Amariah, Jehohanan;
14 of Malluchi, Jonathan; of
Shebaniah, Joseph;
15 of Harim, Adna; of Meraioth,
Helkai;
16 of Iddo, Zechariah; of Ginnethon, Meshullam;
17 of Abijah, Zichri; of Miniamin, of Moadiah, Piltai;
18 of Bilgah, Shammua; of
Shemaiah, Jehonathan;
19 of Joiarib, Mattenai; of Jedaiah, Uzzi;
20 of Sallai, Kallai; of Amok,
Eber;
21 of Hilkiah, Hashabiah; of
Jedaiah, Nethanel.
22 As for the Levites, the heads
of fathers' *households* were registered in the days of Eliashib, Joiada, and Johanan, and Jaddua; so
were the priests in the reign of Darius the Persian.
23 The sons of Levi, the heads
of fathers' *households*, were registered in the Book of the Chronicles up to the days of Johanan the
son of Eliashib.
24 And the heads of the Levites
were Hashabiah, Sherebiah, and
Jeshua the son of Kadmiel, with
their brothers opposite them, to
praise *and* give thanks, [t]as prescribed by David the man of God,
division corresponding to division. *in the commandment of*
25 Mattaniah, and Bakbukiah,
Obadiah, Meshullam, Talmon,
and Akkub were gatekeepers
keeping watch at [r]the storehouses
of the gates. 1 Chr. 26:15
26 These *served* in the days of
Joiakim the son of Jeshua, the son
of Jozadak, and in the days of [r]Ne-
hemiah the governor and of Ezra
the priest *and* scribe. Neh. 8:9
27 Now at the dedication of the
wall of Jerusalem they sought out
the Levites from all their places,
to bring them to Jerusalem so that
they might celebrate the dedication with gladness, with hymns of
thanksgiving and with songs [r]*to*
the accompaniment of cymbals,
harps, and lyres. 1 Chr. 15:16, 28
28 So the sons of the singers
were assembled from the district
around Jerusalem, and from the
villages of the Netophathites,
29 from Beth-gilgal, and from
their fields in Geba and Azmaveth, for the singers had built
themselves villages around Jerusalem.
30 And the priests and the Levites [r]purified themselves; they
also purified the people, the gates,
and the wall. Neh. 13:22, 30
31 Then I had the leaders of Judah come up on top of the wall,
and I appointed two great [t]choirs,
the first proceeding to the right on
top of the wall toward the Refuse
Gate. *thanksgiving choirs*
32 Hoshaiah and half of the
leaders of Judah followed them,
33 with Azariah, Ezra, Meshullam,
34 Judah, Benjamin, Shemaiah,
Jeremiah,
35 and some of the sons of the
priests with trumpets; *and* Zechariah the son of Jonathan, the son
of Shemaiah, the son of Mattaniah, the son of Micaiah, the son
of Zaccur, the son of Asaph,

36 and his [t]kinsmen, Shemaiah,
Azarel, Milalai, Gilalai, Maai, Nethanel, Judah *and* Hanani, with
the musical instruments of David
the man of God. And Ezra the
scribe went before them. ***brothers***
37 And at the Fountain Gate
they went directly up the steps of
the city of David by the stairway
of the wall above the house of David to the Water Gate on the east.
38 The second choir proceeded
to the [t]left, while I followed them
with half of the people on the
wall, above the Tower of Furnaces, to the Broad Wall, ***front***
39 and above the Gate of Ephraim, by the Old Gate, by the Fish
Gate, the Tower of Hananel, and
the Tower of the Hundred, as far
as the Sheep Gate, and they
stopped at the Gate of the Guard.
40 Then the two choirs took
their stand in the house of God. So
did I and half of the officials with
me;
41 and the priests, Eliakim, Maaseiah, Miniamin, Micaiah, Elioenai, Zechariah, and Hananiah,
with the trumpets;
42 and Maaseiah, Shemaiah, Eleazar, Uzzi, Jehohanan, Malchijah, Elam, and Ezer. And the singers [t]sang, with Jezrahiah *their*
leader, ***caused their voices to be heard***
43 and on that day they offered
great sacrifices and rejoiced because [r]God had given them great
joy, even the women and children
rejoiced, so that the joy of Jerusalem was heard from afar. Ps. 9:2
44 On that day men were also
appointed over the chambers for
the stores, the contributions, the
first fruits, and the tithes, to
gather into them from the fields of
the cities the portions required by
the law for the priests and Levites;
for Judah rejoiced over the priests
and Levites who [t]served. ***stood***
45 For they performed the worship of their God and the service
of purification, together with the
singers and the gatekeepers in accordance with the command of
David *and* of his son Solomon.
46 For in the days of David and
[r]Asaph, in ancient times, *there*
were [r]leaders of the singers, songs
of praise and hymns of thanksgiving to God. 2 Chr. 29:30 • 1 Chr. 9:33
47 And so all Israel in the days
of Zerubbabel and Nehemiah gave
the portions due the singers and
the gatekeepers [r]as each day required, and [r]set apart the consecrated *portion* for the Levites, and
the Levites set apart the consecrated *portion* for the sons of Aaron. Neh. 11:23 • Num. 18:21

CHAPTER 13

ON that day they read aloud
from the book of Moses in the
hearing of the people; and there
was found written in it that no
Ammonite or Moabite should ever
enter the assembly of God,
2 because they did not meet
the sons of Israel with bread and
water, but [r]hired Balaam against
them to curse them. However, [r]our
God turned the curse into a blessing. Num. 22:3-11 • Deut. 23:5
3 So it came about, that when
they heard the law, they excluded
all foreigners from Israel.
4 Now prior to this, Eliashib
the priest, who was appointed

over the chambers of the house of
our God, being related to Tobiah,
5 had prepared a large room
for him, where formerly they put
the grain offerings, the frankincense, the utensils, and the tithes
of grain, wine and oil prescribed
for the Levites, the singers and the
gatekeepers, and the [t]contribu-
tions for the priests. *heave offerings*
6 But during all this *time* I was
not in Jerusalem, for in [r]the thirty-
second year of Artaxerxes king of
Babylon I had gone to the king.
After some time, however, I asked
leave from the king, Neh. 5:14
7 and I came to Jerusalem and
learned about the evil that Eliashib had done for Tobiah, by preparing a room for him in the
courts of the house of God.
8 And it was very displeasing
to me, so I threw all of Tobiah's
household goods out of the room.
9 Then I gave an order and
they cleansed the rooms; and I returned there the utensils of the
house of God with the grain offerings and the frankincense.
10 I also discovered that the
portions of the Levites had not
been given *them,* so that the Levites and the singers who performed the service had gone
away, each to his own field.
11 So I [a]reprimanded the officials
and said, "Why is the house of
God forsaken?" Then I gathered
them together and restored them
to their posts. *contended with*
12 All Judah then brought [r]the
tithe of the grain, wine, and oil
into the storehouses. Neh. 10:37
13 And in charge of the storehouses I appointed Shelemiah the
priest, Zadok the scribe, and Pedaiah of the Levites, and in addition to them was Hanan the son of
Zaccur, the son of Mattaniah; for
they were considered reliable, and
it was [t]their task to distribute to
their [t]kinsmen. *on them to • brothers*
14 [r]Remember me for this, O my
God, and do not blot out my loyal
deeds which I have performed for
the house of my God and its services. Neh. 5:19; 13:22, 31
15 In those days I saw in Judah
some who were treading wine
presses [r]on the sabbath, and bringing in sacks of grain and loading
them on donkeys, as well as wine,
grapes, figs, and all kinds of loads,
[r]and they brought *them* into Jerusalem on the sabbath day. So I admonished *them* on the day they
sold food. Ex. 20:8 • Neh. 10:31
16 Also men of Tyre were living
[t]there *who* imported fish and all
kinds of merchandise, and sold
them to the sons of Judah on the
sabbath, even in Jerusalem. *in it*
17 Then I [a]reprimanded the
nobles of Judah and said to them,
"What is this evil thing you are
doing, [t]by profaning the sabbath
day? *contended with • and*
18 "Did [r]not your fathers do the
same so that our God brought on
us, and on this city, all this trouble? Yet you are adding to the
wrath on Israel by profaning the
sabbath." Ezra 9:13
19 And it came about that just
as it grew dark at the gates of Jerusalem before the sabbath, I
commanded that the doors should
be shut and that they should not
open them until after the sabbath.
Then I stationed some of my ser-

vants at the gates *that* no load
should enter on the sabbath day.
20 Once or twice the traders
and merchants of every kind of
merchandise spent the night outside Jerusalem.
21 Then I warned them and said
to them, "Why do you spend the
night in front of the wall? If you
do so again, I will use force
against you." From that time on
they did not come on the sabbath.
22 And I commanded the Levites that they should purify
themselves and come as gatekeepers to sanctify the sabbath
day. *For* this also remember me, O
my God, and have compassion on
me according to the greatness of
Thy lovingkindness. Neh. 12:30
23 In those days I also saw that
the Jews had married women
from Ashdod, Ammon, *and* Moab.
24 As for their children, half
spoke in the language of Ashdod,
and none of them was able to
speak the language of Judah, but
the language of his own people.
25 So I contended with them
and cursed them and struck some
of them and pulled out their hair,
and made them swear by God,
"You shall not give your daughters to their sons, nor take of their
daughters for your sons or for
yourselves. Neh. 13:11 • Deut. 25:2
26 "Did not Solomon king of Israel sin regarding these things?
Yet among the many nations
there was no king like him, and he
was loved by his God, and God
made him king over all Israel;
nevertheless the foreign women
caused even him to sin.
27 "Do we then hear about you
that you have committed all this
great evil by acting unfaithfully
against our God by marrying foreign women?" *giving dwelling to*
28 Even one of the sons of Joiada, the son of Eliashib the high
priest, was a son-in-law of Sanballat the Horonite, so I drove him
away from me. Neh. 2:10, 19; 4:1
29 Remember them, O my God,
because they have defiled the
priesthood and the covenant of
the priesthood and the Levites.
30 Thus I purified them from
everything foreign and appointed
duties for the priests and the Levites, each in his task, Neh. 10:30
31 and *I arranged* for the supply
of wood at appointed times and
for the first fruits. Remember me,
O my God, for good. Neh. 10:34

THE BOOK OF

ESTHER

NOW it took place in the days of
[r]Ahasuerus, the Ahasuerus who
reigned from India to [t]Ethiopia
over 127 provinces, Ezra 4:6 · *Cush*
2 in those days as King Ahasuerus [r]sat on his royal throne which
was in Susa the capital, 1 Kin. 1:46
3 in the third year of his reign,
he gave a banquet for all his
princes and attendants, the army
officers of Persia and Media, the
nobles, and the princes of his
provinces being in his presence.
4 [t]And he displayed the riches
of his royal glory and the splendor
of his great majesty for many
days, 180 days. *When*
5 And when these days were
completed, the king gave a banquet lasting seven days for all the
people who were present in Susa
the capital, from the greatest to
the least, in the court of the garden of the king's palace.
6 *There were hangings of* fine
white and violet linen held by
cords of fine purple linen on silver
rings and marble columns, *and*
[r]couches of gold and silver on a
mosaic pavement of porphyry,
marble, mother-of-pearl, and precious stones. Ezek. 23:41
7 Drinks were served in golden
vessels of various kinds, and the
royal wine was plentiful according to the king's [t]bounty. *hand*
8 And the drinking was *done*
according to the law, there was no
compulsion, for so the king had
given orders to each official of his
household that he should do according to the desires of each person.
9 Queen Vashti also gave a
banquet for the women in the [t]pal-
ace which belonged to King Ahasuerus. *royal house*
10 On the seventh day, when
the heart of the king was merry
with wine, he commanded Mehu-
man, Biztha, Harbona, Bigtha,
Abagtha, Zethar, and Carkas, the
seven eunuchs who served in the
presence of King Ahasuerus,
11 to bring Queen Vashti before
the king with *her* royal [r]crown in
order to display her beauty to the
people and the princes, for she
was beautiful. Esth. 2:17; 6:8
12 But Queen Vashti refused to
come at the king's command delivered by the eunuchs. Then the
king became very angry and his
wrath burned within him.
13 Then the king said to the
wise men who understood the
times—for it was the custom of
the king so *to speak* before all
who knew law and justice,
14 and were close to him: Car-
shena, Shethar, Admatha, Tarshish, Meres, Marsena, and Memucan, the seven princes of
Persia and Media who had access
to the king's presence and sat in
the first place in the kingdom—
15 "According to law, what is to
be done with Queen Vashti, because she did not [t]obey the command of King Ahasuerus *delivered* by the eunuchs?" *do*
16 And in the presence of the

king and the princes, Memucan said, "Queen Vashti has wronged not only the king but *also* all the princes, and all the peoples who are in all the provinces of King Ahasuerus.

17 "For the queen's conduct will [t]become known to all the women causing them to look with contempt on their husbands by saying, 'King Ahasuerus commanded Queen Vashti to be brought in to his presence, but she did not come.' *go forth*

18 "And this day the ladies of Persia and Media who have heard of the queen's conduct will speak in *the same way* to all the king's princes, and there will be plenty of contempt and anger.

19 "If it pleases the king, let a royal edict be issued by him and let it be written in the laws of Persia and Media so that it cannot [t]be repealed, that Vashti should come no more into the presence of King Ahasuerus, and let the king give her royal position to another who is more worthy than she. *pass away*

20 "And when the king's edict which he shall make is heard throughout all his kingdom, [t]great as it is, then [r]all women will give honor to their husbands, great and small." *for great is it* • Eph. 5:22

21 And *this* word pleased the king and the princes, and the king did as Memucan proposed.

22 So he sent letters to all the king's provinces, to each province according to its script and to every people according to their language, that every man should be the master in his own house and the one who speaks in the language of his own people.

CHAPTER 2

AFTER these things when the anger of King Ahasuerus had subsided, he remembered Vashti and what she had done and what had been decreed against her.

2 Then the king's attendants, who served him, said, "Let [r]beautiful young virgins be sought for the king. 1 Kin. 1:2

3 "And let the king appoint overseers in [r]all the provinces of his kingdom that they may gather every beautiful young virgin to Susa the capital, to the harem, into the custody of Hegai, the king's eunuch, who was in charge of the women; and let their cosmetics be given *them*. Esth. 1:1, 2

4 "Then let the young lady who pleases the king be queen in place of Vashti." And the matter pleased the king, and he did accordingly.

5 *Now* there was a Jew in Susa the capital whose name was [r]Mordecai, the son of Jair, the son of Shimei, the son of Kish, a Benjamite, Esth. 3:2

6 [r]who had been taken into exile from Jerusalem with the captives who had been exiled with Jeconiah king of Judah, whom Nebuchadnezzar the king of Babylon had exiled. 2 Kin. 24:14

7 And he was bringing up Hadassah, that is Esther, his uncle's daughter, for she had neither father nor mother. Now the young lady was beautiful of form and [t]face, and when her father and her mother died, Mordecai took her as his own daughter. *good of appearance*

8 So it came about when the command and decree of the king were heard and [r]many young ladies were gathered to Susa the capital into the custody of [r]Hegai, that Esther was taken to the king's [t]palace into the custody of Hegai, who was in charge of the women. Esth. 2:3 · Esth. 2:3 · *house*

9 Now the young lady pleased him and found favor with him. So he quickly provided her with her [r]cosmetics and [t]food, gave her seven choice maids from the king's palace, and transferred her and her maids to the best place in the harem. Esth. 2:3 · *portions*

10 Esther did not make known her people or her kindred, for Mordecai had instructed her that she should not make *them* known.

11 And every day Mordecai walked back and forth in front of the court of the harem to learn how Esther was and how she fared.

12 Now when the turn of each young lady came to go in to King Ahasuerus, after the end of her twelve months under the regulations for the women—for the days of their beautification were completed as follows: six months with oil of myrrh and six months with spices and the cosmetics for women—

13 the young lady would go in to the king in this way: anything that she [t]desired was given her to take with her from the harem to the king's palace. *said*

14 In the evening she would go in and in the morning she would return to the second harem, to the [t]custody of Shaashgaz, the king's eunuch who was in charge of the concubines. She would not again go in to the king unless the king delighted in her and she was summoned by name. *hand*

15 Now when the turn of Esther, [r]the daughter of Abihail the uncle of Mordecai who had taken her as his daughter, came to go in to the king, she did not request anything except what Hegai, the king's eunuch who was in charge of the women, [t]advised. And Esther found favor in the eyes of all who saw her. Esth. 2:7 · *said*

16 So Esther was taken to King Ahasuerus to his royal palace in the tenth month which is the month Tebeth, in the seventh year of his reign.

17 And the king loved Esther more than all the women, and she found favor and kindness with him more than all the virgins, so that [r]he set the royal crown on her head and made her queen instead of Vashti. Esth. 1:11

18 Then [r]the king gave a great banquet, Esther's banquet, for all his princes and his servants; he also made a holiday for the provinces and gave gifts according to the king's bounty. Esth 1:3

19 And [r]when the virgins were gathered together the second time, then Mordecai was sitting at the king's gate. Esth. 2:3, 4

20 Esther had not yet made known her kindred or her people, even as Mordecai had commanded her, for Esther did what Mordecai told her as she had done [r]when under his care. Esth. 2:7

21 In those days, while Mordecai was sitting at the king's gate, Bigthan and Teresh, two of the king's officials from those who guarded the door, became angry

and sought to [t]lay hands on King
Ahasuerus. *send a hand against*
22 But the plot became known
to Mordecai, and he told Queen
Esther, and Esther [t]informed the
king in Mordecai's name. *told*
23 Now when the plot was investigated and found *to be so,*
they were both hanged on a [1]gal-
lows; and it was written in [r]the
Book of the Chronicles in the
king's presence. Esth. 10:2

CHAPTER 3

AFTER these events King Ahasuerus promoted Haman, the son of
Hammedatha the Agagite, and advanced him and [t]established his
authority over all the princes who
were with him. *set his seat*
2 And all the king's servants
who were at the king's gate
bowed down and paid homage to
Haman; for so the king had commanded concerning him. But [r]Mor-
decai neither bowed down nor
paid homage. Esth. 2:19; 5:9
3 Then the king's servants who
were at the king's gate said to
Mordecai, "Why are you transgressing the king's command?"
4 Now it was when they had
spoken daily to him and he would
not listen to them, that they told
Haman to see whether Mordecai's
reason would stand; for he had
told them that he was a Jew.
5 When Haman saw that [r]Mor-
decai neither bowed down nor
paid homage to him, Haman was
filled with rage. Esth. 5:9
6 But he [t]disdained to lay hands
on Mordecai alone, for they had
told him *who* the people of Mordecai *were;* therefore Haman [r]sought
to destroy all the Jews, the people
of Mordecai, who *were* throughout the whole kingdom of Ahasuerus. *despised in his eyes* • Ps. 83:4
7 In the first month, which is
the month Nisan, in the twelfth
year of King Ahasuerus, Pur, that
is the lot, was cast before Haman
from day to day and from month
to month, until the twelfth month,
that is [r]the month Adar. Ezra 6:15
8 Then Haman said to King
Ahasuerus, "There is a certain
people scattered and dispersed
among the peoples in all the provinces of your kingdom; their laws
are different from *those* of all *oth-*
er people, and they do not observe
the king's laws, so it is not in the
king's interest to let them remain.
9 "If it is pleasing to the king,
let it be [t]decreed that they be destroyed, and I will pay ten thousand talents of silver into the
hands of those who carry on the
king's business, to put into the
king's treasuries." *written*
10 Then [r]the king took his signet
ring from his hand and gave it to
Haman, the son of Hammedatha
[r]the Agagite, the enemy of the
Jews. Gen. 41:42 • Esth. 3:1
11 And the king said to Haman,
"The silver is [t]yours, and the people *also,* to do with them as you
please." *given to you*
12 Then the king's scribes were
summoned on the thirteenth day
of the first month, and it was written just as Haman commanded to
[r]the king's satraps, to the governors who were over each province, and to the princes of each
people, each province according
to its script, each people accord-

[1]Lit., *tree*

ing to its language, being written [r]in the name of King Ahasuerus and sealed with the king's signet ring. Ezra 8:36 • 1 Kin. 21:8

13 And letters were sent by [r]couriers to all the king's provinces [r]to destroy, to kill, and to annihilate all the Jews, both young and old, women and children, in one day, the thirteenth *day* of the twelfth month, which is the month Adar, and to seize their possessions as plunder. 2 Chr. 30:6 • Esth. 7:4

14 [r]A copy of the edict to be [t]issued as law in every province was published to all the peoples so that they should be ready for this day. Esth. 8:13, 14 • *given*

15 The couriers went out impelled by the king's command while the decree was [t]issued in Susa the capital; and while the king and Haman sat down to drink, [r]the city of Susa was in confusion. *given* • Esth. 8:15

CHAPTER 4

WHEN Mordecai learned all that had been done, he tore his clothes, put on sackcloth and ashes, and went out into the midst of the city and wailed loudly and bitterly.

2 And he went as far as the king's gate, for no one was to enter the king's gate clothed in sackcloth.

3 And in each and every province where the command and decree of the king came, there was great mourning among the Jews, with [r]fasting, weeping, and wailing; and many lay on sackcloth and ashes. Esth. 4:16

4 Then Esther's maidens and her eunuchs came and told her, and the queen writhed in great anguish. And she sent garments to clothe Mordecai that he might remove his sackcloth from him, but he did not accept *them.*

5 Then Esther summoned Hathach from the king's eunuchs, whom [t]the king had appointed to attend her, and ordered him *to go* to Mordecai to learn what this *was* and why it *was.* *he*

6 So Hathach went out to Mordecai to the city square in front of the king's gate.

7 And Mordecai told him all that had happened to him, and [r]the exact amount of money that Haman had promised to pay to the king's treasuries for the destruction of the Jews. Esth. 3:9

8 He also gave him [r]a copy of the text of the edict which had been issued in Susa for their destruction, that he might show Esther and inform her, and to order her to go in to the king to implore his favor and to plead with him for her people. Esth. 3:14

9 And Hathach came back and related Mordecai's words to Esther.

10 Then Esther spoke to Hathach and ordered him *to reply* to Mordecai:

11 "All the king's servants and the people of the king's provinces know that for any man or woman who [r]comes to the king to the inner court who is not summoned, he has but one law, that he be put to death, unless the king holds out to him the golden scepter so that he may live. And I have not been summoned to come to the king for these thirty days." Esth. 5:1; 6:4

12 And they related Esther's
words to Mordecai.
13 Then Mordecai told *them* to
reply to Esther, "Do not imagine
that you in the king's palace can
escape any more than all the
Jews.
14 "For if you remain silent at
this time, relief and [r]deliverance
will arise for the Jews from another place and you and your father's house will perish. And who
knows whether you have not attained royalty for such a time as
this?" Lev. 26:42; 2 Kin. 13:5
15 Then Esther told *them* to reply to Mordecai,
16 "Go, assemble all the Jews
who are found in Susa, and fast
for me; do not eat or drink for
three days, night or day. I and my
maidens also will fast in the same
way. And thus I will go in to the
king, which is not according to the
law; and if I perish, I perish."
17 So Mordecai went away and
did just as Esther had commanded him.

CHAPTER 5

NOW it came about on the third
day that Esther put on her royal
robes and stood in the inner court
of the king's palace in front of the
king's [t]rooms, and the king was
sitting on his royal throne in the
throne room, opposite the entrance to the palace. *house*
2 And it happened when the
king saw Esther the queen standing in the court, [r]she obtained favor in his sight; and the king extended to Esther the golden
scepter which was in his hand. So
Esther came near and touched the
top of the scepter. Esth. 2:9
3 Then the king said to her,
"What is *troubling* you, Queen Esther? And what is your request?
[r]Even to half of the kingdom it will
be given to you." Esth. 7:2
4 And Esther said, "If it please
the king, may the king and Haman
come this day to the banquet that
I have prepared for him."
5 Then the king said, "Bring
Haman quickly that we may do as
Esther desires." So the king and
Haman came to the banquet
which Esther had prepared.
6 And, as they drank their
wine at the banquet, the king said
to Esther, "What is your petition,
for it shall be granted to you. And
what is your request? Even to half
of the kingdom it shall be done."
7 So Esther answered and said,
"My petition and my request is:
8 if I have found favor in the
sight of the king, and if it please
the king to grant my petition and
do [t]what I request, may the king
and Haman come to [r]the banquet
which I shall prepare for them,
and tomorrow I will do as the king
says." *my request* • Esth. 6:14
9 Then Haman went out that
day glad and pleased of heart; but
when Haman saw Mordecai in the
king's gate, and that he did not
stand up or [a]tremble before him,
Haman was filled with anger
against Mordecai. *move for*
10 Haman controlled himself,
however, went to his house, and
[t]sent for his friends and his wife
[r]Zeresh. *sent and brought* • Esth. 6:13
11 Then Haman recounted to
them the glory of his riches, and
the [t]number of his sons, and every

instance where the king had magnified him, and how he had promoted him above the princes and servants of the king. *multitude*

12 Haman also said, "Even Esther the queen let no one but me come with the king to the banquet which she had prepared; and tomorrow also I am [t]invited by her with the king. *summoned to her*

13 "Yet all of this does not satisfy me every time I see Mordecai the Jew sitting at the king's gate."

14 Then Zeresh his wife and all his friends said to him, "Have[r] a [t]gallows fifty cubits high made and in the morning ask the king to have Mordecai hanged on it, then go joyfully with the king to the banquet." And the [t]advice pleased Haman, so he had the gallows made. Esth. 6:4 · *tree* · *thing*

CHAPTER 6

DURING that night [t]the king could not sleep so he gave an order to bring the book of records, the chronicles, and they were read before the king. *the king's sleep fled*

2 And it was found written what Mordecai had reported concerning Bigthana and Teresh, two of the king's eunuchs who were doorkeepers, that they had sought to lay hands on King Ahasuerus.

3 And the king said, "What honor or dignity has been bestowed on Mordecai for this?" Then the king's servants who attended him said, "Nothing has been done for him."

4 So the king said, "Who is in the court?" Now Haman had just [r]entered the outer court of the king's palace in order to speak to the king about hanging Mordecai on the gallows which he had prepared for him. Esth. 4:11

5 And the king's servants said to him, "Behold, Haman is standing in the court." And the king said, "Let him come in."

6 So Haman came in and the king said to him, "What is to be done for the man [r]whom the king desires to honor?" And Haman said [t]to himself, "Whom would the king desire to honor more than me?" Esth. 6:7, 9, 11 · *in his heart*

7 Then Haman said to the king, "For the man whom the king desires to honor,

8 let them bring a royal robe which the king has worn, and the horse on which the king has ridden, and on whose head [r]a royal crown has been placed; Esth. 1:11

9 and let the robe and the horse be handed over to one of the king's most noble princes and let them array the man whom the king desires to honor and lead him on horseback through the city square, and proclaim before him, 'Thus it shall be done to the man whom the king desires to honor.' "

10 Then the king said to Haman, "Take quickly the robes and the horse as you have said, and do so for Mordecai the Jew, who is sitting at the king's gate; do not fall short in anything of all that you have said."

11 So Haman took the robe and the horse, and arrayed Mordecai, and led him *on horseback* through the city square, and proclaimed before him, "Thus it shall be done to the man whom the king desires to honor."

12 Then Mordecai returned to

the king's gate. But Haman hurried home, mourning, ʳwith *his* head covered. 2 Sam. 15:30

13 And Haman recounted ʳto Zeresh his wife and all his friends everything that had happened to him. Then his wise men and Zeresh his wife said to him, "If Mordecai, before whom you have begun to fall, is of Jewish origin, you will not overcome him, but will surely fall before him." Esth. 5:10

14 While they were still talking with him, the king's eunuchs arrived and hastily ʳbrought Haman to the banquet which Esther had prepared. Esth. 5:8

CHAPTER 7

NOW the king and Haman came to drink *wine* with Esther the queen.

2 And the king said to Esther on the second day also as they drank their wine at the banquet, "What is your petition, Queen Esther? It shall be granted you. And what is your request? Even to half of the kingdom it shall be done."

3 Then Queen Esther answered and said, "If ʳI have found favor in your sight, O king, and if it please the king, let my life be given me as my petition, and my people as my request; Esth. 5:8; 8:5

4 for we have been sold, I and my people, to be destroyed, to be killed and to be annihilated. Now if we had only been sold as slaves, men and women, I would have remained silent, for the trouble would not be commensurate with the annoyance to the king."

5 Then King Ahasuerus ᵗasked Queen Esther, "Who is he, and where is he, who would presume to do thus?" *said and said to*

6 And Esther said, "A foe and an enemy, is this wicked Haman!" Then Haman became terrified before the king and queen.

7 And the king arose in his anger from drinking wine *and went* into the palace garden; but Haman stayed to beg for his life from Queen Esther, for he saw that harm had been determined against him by the king.

8 Now when the king returned from the palace garden into the ᵗplace where they were drinking wine, Haman was falling on the couch where Esther was. Then the king said, "Will he even assault the queen with me in the house?" As the word went out of the king's mouth, they covered Haman's face. *house of the banquet of wine*

9 Then Harbonah, one of the eunuchs who *were* before the king said, "Behold indeed, ʳthe gallows standing at Haman's house fifty cubits high, which Haman made for Mordecai who spoke good on behalf of the king!" And the king said, "Hang him on it." Esth. 5:14

10 So they hanged Haman on the ᵗgallows which he had prepared for Mordecai, ʳand the king's anger subsided. *tree* • Esth. 7:7, 8

CHAPTER 8

ON that day King Ahasuerus gave the house of Haman, ʳthe enemy of the Jews, to Queen Esther; and Mordecai came before the king, for Esther had disclosed what he was to her. Esth. 7:6

2 And the king took off his signet ring which he had taken away
from Haman, and gave it to Mordecai. And Esther set Mordecai
over the house of Haman.
3 Then Esther spoke again to
the king, fell at his feet, wept, and
implored him to avert the evil
scheme of Haman the Agagite and
his plot which he had devised
against the Jews.
4 [r]And the king extended the
golden scepter to Esther. So Esther arose and stood before the
king. Esth. 4:11; 5:2
5 Then she said, "If [r]it pleases
the king and if I have found favor
before him and the matter *seems*
proper to the king and I am pleasing in his sight, let it be written to
revoke the letters devised by Haman, the son of Hammedatha the
Agagite, which he wrote to destroy the Jews who are in all the
king's provinces. Esth. 5:8; 7:3
6 "For [r]how can I endure to see
the calamity which shall befall my
people, and how can I endure to
see the destruction of my kindred?" Esth. 7:4; 9:1
7 So King Ahasuerus said to
Queen Esther and to Mordecai the
Jew, "Behold, I have given the
house of Haman to Esther, and
him they have hanged on the gallows because he had stretched out
his hands against the Jews.
8 "Now you write to the Jews as
you see fit, in the king's name, and
[r]seal *it* with the king's signet ring;
for a decree which is written in
the name of the king and sealed
with the king's signet ring may
not be revoked." Esth. 3:12; 8:10

9 So the king's scribes were
called at that time in the third
month (that is, the month Sivan),
on the twenty-third [t]day; and it
was written according to all that
Mordecai commanded to the
Jews, the satraps, the governors,
and the princes of the provinces
which *extended* from India to
[t]Ethiopia, 127 provinces, to every
province according to its script,
and to every people according to
their language, as well as to the
Jews according to their script and
their language. *in it* • *Cush*
10 And he wrote in the name of
King Ahasuerus, and sealed it
with the king's signet ring, and
sent letters by couriers on [r]horses,
riding on steeds sired by the royal
stud. 1 Kin. 4:28
11 [t]In them the king granted the
Jews who were in each and every
city *the right* to assemble and to
defend their lives, to destroy, to
kill, and to annihilate the entire
army of any people or province
which might attack them, including children and women, and to
plunder their spoil, *Which*
12 on one day in all the provinces of King Ahasuerus, the thirteenth *day* of the twelfth month
(that is, the month Adar).
13 A copy of the edict to be issued as law in each and every
province, was published to all the
peoples, so that the Jews should
be ready for this day to avenge
themselves on their enemies.
14 The couriers, hastened and
impelled by the king's command,
went out, riding on the royal
steeds; and the decree was given
out in Susa the capital.

15 Then Mordecai went out
from the presence of the king [r]in
royal robes of [a]blue and white,
with a large crown of gold and a
garment of fine linen and purple;
and the city of Susa shouted and
rejoiced. Esth. 5:11 • *violet*
16 For the Jews there was light
and gladness and joy and honor.
17 And in each and every province, and in each and every city,
wherever the king's commandment and his decree arrived, there
was gladness and joy for the
Jews, a feast and a holiday. And
many among the peoples of the
land became Jews, for the dread
of the Jews had fallen on them.

CHAPTER 9

NOW in the twelfth month (that
is, the month Adar), on the thirteenth day when the king's command and edict were about to be
executed, on the day when the enemies of the Jews hoped to gain
the mastery over them, it was
turned to the contrary so that the
Jews themselves gained the mastery over those who hated them.
2 The Jews assembled in their
cities throughout all the provinces
of King Ahasuerus to lay hands on
those who sought their harm; and
no one could stand before them,
[r]for the dread of them had fallen
on all the peoples. Esth. 8:17
3 Even all the princes of the
provinces, the satraps, the governors, and those who were doing
the king's business [t]assisted the
Jews, because the dread of Mordecai had fallen on them. *lifted up*
4 Indeed, Mordecai was great
in the king's house, and his fame
spread throughout all the provinces; for the man Mordecai became greater and greater.
5 Thus [r]the Jews struck all their
enemies with [t]the sword, killing
and destroying; and they did what
they pleased to those who hated
them. Esth. 3:13 • *the stroke of*
6 And in Susa the capital the
Jews killed and destroyed five
hundred men,
7 and Parshandatha, Dalphon,
Aspatha,
8 Poratha, Adalia, Aridatha,
9 Parmashta, Arisai, Aridai,
and Vaizatha,
10 the ten sons of Haman the
son of Hammedatha, the Jews'
enemy; but [r]they did not lay their
hands on the plunder. Esth. 8:11
11 On that day the number of
those who were killed in Susa the
capital was reported to the king.
12 And the king said to Queen
Esther, "The Jews have killed and
destroyed five hundred men and
the ten sons of Haman in Susa the
capital. What then have they done
in the rest of the king's provinces!
[r]Now what is your petition? It shall
even be granted you. And what is
your further request? It shall also
be done." Esth. 5:6; 7:2
13 Then said Esther, "If it
pleases the king, [r]let tomorrow
also be granted to the Jews who
are in Susa to do according to the
edict of today; and let Haman's
ten sons be hanged on the gallows." Esth. 8:11; 9:15
14 So the king commanded that
it should be done so; and an edict

was issued in Susa, and Haman's
ten sons were hanged.
15 And the Jews who were in
Susa assembled also on the fourteenth day of the month Adar and
killed [r]three hundred men in Susa,
but [r]they did not lay their hands on
the plunder. Esth. 9:12 · Esth. 9:10
16 Now the rest of the Jews
who *were* in the king's provinces
assembled, to defend their lives
and rid themselves of their enemies, and kill 75,000 of those
who hated them; but they did not
lay their hands on the plunder.
17 *This was done* on [r]the thirteenth day of the month Adar, and
on the fourteenth [t]day they rested
and made it a day of feasting and
rejoicing. Esth. 9:1 · *in it*
18 But the Jews who were in
Susa assembled on the thirteenth
and the fourteenth [t]of the same
month, and they rested on the fifteenth day and made it a day of
feasting and rejoicing. *in it*
19 Therefore the Jews of the rural areas, who live in the rural
towns, make the fourteenth day of
the month Adar *a* holiday for rejoicing and feasting and sending
portions *of food* to one another.
20 Then Mordecai recorded
these events, and he sent letters to
all the Jews who were in all the
provinces of King Ahasuerus,
both near and far,
21 obliging them to celebrate
the fourteenth day of the month
Adar, and the fifteenth day [t]of the
same month, annually, *in it*
22 because on those days the
Jews [t]rid themselves of their enemies, and *it was a* month which
was turned for them from sorrow
into gladness and from mourning
into a [t]holiday; that they should
make them days of feasting and
rejoicing and sending portions *of
food* to one another and gifts to
the poor. *had rest from · good day*
23 Thus the Jews undertook
what they had started to do, and
what Mordecai had written to
them.
24 For Haman the son of Hammedatha, the Agagite, the adversary of all the Jews, had schemed
against the Jews to destroy them,
and had cast Pur, that is the lot, to
disturb them and destroy them.
25 But when it came to the
king's attention, he commanded
by letter that his wicked scheme
which he had devised against the
Jews, should return on his own
head, and that he and his sons
should be hanged on the gallows.
26 Therefore they called these
days Purim after the name of Pur.
And [r]because of the instructions in
this letter, both what they had
seen in this regard and what had
happened to them, Esth. 9:20
27 the Jews established and
[t]made a custom for themselves,
and for their [t]descendants, and for
all those who allied themselves
with them, so that they should not
fail to celebrate these two days
according to their [t]regulation, and
according to their appointed time
annually. *received · seed · writing*
28 So these days were to be
remembered and celebrated
throughout every generation, every family, every province, and
every city; and these days of Pu-

rim were not to fail from among
the Jews, or their memory [t]fade
from their descendants. *end*
29 Then Queen Esther, [r]daughter
of Abihail, with Mordecai the Jew,
wrote with full authority to confirm [r]this second letter about Purim. Esth. 2:15 • Esth. 9:20, 21
30 And he sent letters to all the
Jews, to the 127 provinces of the
kingdom of Ahasuerus, namely,
words of peace and truth,
31 to establish these days of Purim at their appointed times, just
as Mordecai the Jew and Queen
Esther had established for them,
and just as they had established
for themselves and for their [t]de-
scendants with [t]instructions for
their times of fasting and their lamentations. *seed* • *words*
32 And the command of Esther
established these [t]customs for [r]Pu-
rim, and it was written in the
book. *words* • Esth. 9:26

CHAPTER 10

NOW King Ahasuerus laid a tribute on the land and on the [r]coast-
lands of the sea. Is. 11:11; 24:15
2 And all the accomplishments
of his authority and strength, and
the full account of the greatness
of Mordecai, to which the king advanced him, are they not written
in the Book of the Chronicles of
the Kings of Media and Persia?
3 For Mordecai the Jew was
[r]second *only* to King Ahasuerus
and great among the Jews, and in
favor with the multitude of his
kinsmen, [r]one who sought the
good of his people and one who
spoke for the welfare of his whole
nation. Gen. 41:43, 44 • Neh. 2:10

THE BOOK OF JOB

THERE was a man in the [r]land of
Uz, whose name was [r]Job, and that
man was [r]blameless, upright, fearing God, and turning away from
evil. Jer. 25:20 • Ezek. 14:14 • Gen. 6:9
2 And seven sons and three
daughters were born to him.
3 His possessions also were
7,000 sheep, 3,000 camels, 500
yoke of oxen, 500 female donkeys,
and very many servants; and that
man was [r]the greatest of all the
[t]men of the east. Job 29:25 • *sons*
4 And his sons used to go and
hold a feast in the house of each
one on his day, and they would
send and invite their three sisters
to eat and drink with them.
5 And it came about, when the
days of feasting had completed
their cycle, that Job would send
and consecrate them, rising up
early in the morning and offering
burnt offerings *according to* the
number of them all; for Job said,
"Perhaps[r] my sons have sinned
and cursed God in their hearts."
Thus Job did continually. Job 8:4

6 Now there was a day when the sons of God came to present themselves before the LORD, and [1]Satan also came among them.

7 And the LORD said to Satan, "From where do you come?" Then Satan answered the LORD and said, "From roaming about on the earth and walking around on it."

8 And the LORD said to Satan, "Have you considered My servant Job? For there is no one like him on the earth, a blameless and upright man, [a]fearing God and turning away from evil." *revering*

9 Then Satan answered the [t]LORD, "Does Job fear God for nothing? *LORD and said*

10 "Hast Thou not made a hedge about him and his house and all that he has, on every side? [r]Thou hast blessed the work of his hands, and his possessions have increased in the land. Job 31:25

11 "But put forth Thy hand now and touch all that he has; he will surely curse Thee to Thy face."

12 Then the LORD said to Satan, "Behold, all that he has is in your power, only do not put forth your hand on him." So Satan departed from the presence of the LORD.

13 Now it happened on the day when his sons and his daughters were eating and drinking wine in their oldest brother's house,

14 that a messenger came to Job and said, "The oxen were plowing and the [t]donkeys feeding beside them, *female donkeys*

15 and [t]the Sabeans [t]attacked and took them. They also slew the servants with the edge of the sword, and I alone have escaped to tell you." *Sheba • fell upon*

[1]I.e., the adversary; so through chs. 1 and 2

16 While he was still speaking, another also came and said, "The fire of God fell from heaven and burned up the sheep and the servants and consumed them, and I alone have escaped to tell you."

17 While he was still speaking, another also came and said, "The [r]Chaldeans formed three bands and made a raid on the camels and took them and [t]slew the servants with the edge of the sword; and I alone have escaped to tell you." Gen. 11:28, 31 • *smote*

18 While he was still speaking, another also came and said, "Your sons and your daughters were eating and drinking wine in their oldest brother's house,

19 and behold, a great wind came from across the wilderness and struck the four corners of the house, and it fell on the young people and they died; and I alone have escaped to tell you."

20 Then Job arose and tore his robe and shaved his head, and he fell to the ground and worshiped.

21 And he said,

"Naked[r] I came from my
mother's womb, Eccl. 5:15
And naked I shall return
there.
The [r]LORD gave and the
LORD has taken away.
Blessed be the name of the
LORD." 1 Sam. 2:7, 8

22 Through all this Job did not sin nor did he blame God.

CHAPTER 2

AGAIN there was a day when the sons of God came to present themselves before the LORD, and

Satan also came among them to
present himself before the LORD.
2 And the LORD said to Satan,
"Where have you come from?"
Then Satan answered the LORD
and said, "From roaming about on
the earth, and walking around on
it."
3 And the LORD said to Satan,
"Have you [t]considered My servant
Job? For there is no one like him
on the earth, a blameless and upright man fearing God and turning
away from evil. And he still holds
fast his integrity, although you incited Me against him, to ruin him
without cause." *set your heart to*
4 And Satan answered the
LORD and said, "Skin for skin!
Yes, all that a man has he will give
for his life.
5 "However,[r] put forth Thy
hand, now, and [r]touch his bone
and his flesh; he will curse Thee to
Thy face." Job 1:11 • Job 19:20
6 So the LORD said to Satan,
"Behold, he is in your [t]power, only
spare his life." *hand*
7 Then Satan went out from
the presence of the LORD, and
smote Job with [r]sore boils from
the sole of his foot to the crown of
his head. Job 7:5; 13:28
8 And he took a potsherd to
scrape himself while [r]he was sitting among the ashes. Job 42:6
9 Then his wife said to him,
"Do you still hold fast your integrity? Curse God and die!"
10 But he said to her, "You
speak as one of the foolish women
speaks. [r]Shall we indeed accept
good from God and not accept adversity?" [r]In all this Job did not sin
with his lips. Job 1:21 • Job 1:22

11 Now when Job's three
friends heard of all this adversity
that had come upon him, they
came each one from his own
place, Eliphaz the [r]Temanite, Bildad the [r]Shuhite, and Zophar the
Naamathite; and they made an appointment together to come to
[r]sympathize with him and comfort
him. Gen. 36:11 • Gen. 25:2 • Job 42:11
12 And when they lifted up their
eyes at a distance, and did not recognize him, they raised their
voices and wept. And each of
them [r]tore his robe, and they [r]threw
dust over their heads toward the
sky. Job 1:20 • Josh. 7:6; Neh. 9:1
13 Then they sat down on the
ground with him for seven days
and seven nights with no one
speaking a word to him, for they
saw that *his* pain was very great.

CHAPTER 3

AFTERWARD Job opened his
mouth and cursed [t]the day of his
birth. *his day*
2 And Job said,
3 "Let the day perish on which I
was to be born,
And the night *which* said, 'A
boy is conceived.'
4 "May that day be darkness;
Let not God above care for it,
Nor light shine on it.
5 "Let [r]darkness and black
gloom claim it; Jer. 13:16
Let a cloud settle on it;
Let the blackness of the day
terrify it.
6 "*As for* that night, let darkness seize it;
Let it not rejoice among the
days of the year;

Let it not come into the number of the months.
7 "Behold, let that night be barren;
Let no joyful shout enter it.
8 "Let those curse it who curse the day,
Who are [a]prepared to rouse Leviathan. *skillful*
9 "Let the stars of its twilight be darkened;
Let it wait for light but have none,
Neither let it see the [t]breaking dawn; *eyelids*
10 Because it did not shut the opening of my *mother's* womb,
Or hide trouble from my eyes.

11 "Why did I not die [t]at birth,
Come forth from the womb and expire? *from the womb*
12 "Why did the knees receive me,
And why the breasts, that I should suck?
13 "For now I would have lain down and been quiet;
I would have slept then, I would have been at rest,
14 With kings and *with* counselors of the earth,
Who rebuilt [r]ruins for themselves; Job 15:28
15 Or with [r]princes who had gold, Job 12:21
Who were filling their houses *with* silver.
16 "Or like a miscarriage which is [t]discarded, I would not be, *hidden*
As infants that never saw light.
17 "There the wicked cease from raging,
And there the [t]weary are at rest. *weary of strength*
18 "The prisoners are at ease together;
They do not hear the voice of the taskmaster.
19 "The small and the great are there,
And the slave is free from his master.

20 "Why is [r]light given to him who suffers, Jer. 20:18
And life to the bitter of soul;
21 Who [t]long for death, but there is none, *wait*
And dig for it more than for hidden treasures;
22 Who rejoice greatly,
They exult when they find the grave?
23 "*Why is light given* to a man whose way is hidden,
And whom [r]God has hedged in? Job 19:8; Ps. 88:8
24 "For my groaning comes at the sight of my food,
And [r]my cries pour out like water. Job 30:16; Ps. 42:4
25 "For [t]what I fear comes upon me, *the fear I fear and*
And what I dread befalls me.
26 "I [r]am not at ease, nor am I quiet, Job 7:13, 14
And I am not at rest, but turmoil comes."

CHAPTER 4

THEN Eliphaz the Temanite [t]answered, *answered and said*
2 "If one ventures a word with you, will you become impatient?

But who can refrain [t]from
speaking? *in words*
3 "Behold [r]you have admonished
many, Job 4:3, 4; 29:15
And you have strengthened
weak hands.
4 "Your words have helped the
tottering to stand,
And you have strengthened
[t]feeble knees. *bowing*
5 "But now it has come to you,
and you are impatient;
It [r]touches you, and you are
dismayed. Job 19:21
6 "Is not your [2]fear *of God* [r]your
confidence, Prov. 3:26
And the integrity of your
ways your hope?

7 "Remember now, [r]who *ever*
perished being innocent?
Or where were the upright
destroyed? Job 8:20
8 "According to what I have
seen, [r]those who plow iniquity Job 15:31
And those who sow trouble
harvest it.
9 "By [r]the breath of God they
perish, Job 15:30
And by the blast of His anger
they come to an end.
10 "The [r]roaring of the lion and
the voice of the *fierce*
lion, Job 5:15; Ps. 58:6
And the teeth of the young
lions are broken.
11 "The [r]lion perishes for lack of
prey, Job 29:17
And the [r]whelps of the lioness
are scattered. Job 5:4

12 "Now a word was brought to
me stealthily,
And my ear received a [r]whis-
per of it. Job 26:14

13 "Amid disquieting [r]thoughts
from the visions of the
night, Job 33:15
When deep sleep falls on
men,
14 Dread came upon me, and
trembling,
And made [t]all my bones
shake. *the multitude of*
15 "Then a [3]spirit passed by my
face;
The hair of my flesh bristled
up.
16 "It stood still, but I could not
discern its appearance;
A form *was* before my eyes;
There was silence, then I
heard a voice:
17 'Can [r]mankind be just before
God? Job 9:2
Can a man be pure [t]before his
Maker? *from*
18 'He puts no trust even in His
servants;
And against His angels He
charges error.
19 'How much more those who
dwell in houses of clay,
Whose [r]foundation is in the
dust, Gen. 2:7; 3:19
Who are crushed before the
moth!
20 'Between morning and evening they are broken in
pieces;
Unobserved, they [r]perish forever. Job 14:20; 20:7
21 'Is not their tent-cord plucked
up within them?
They die, yet [r]without wisdom.' Job 18:21; 36:12

CHAPTER 5

"CALL now, is there anyone
who will answer you?

[2]Or, *reverence*

[3]Or, *breath passed over*

And to which of the holy ones will you turn?
2 "For [r]vexation slays the foolish man, Prov. 12:16; 27:3
And anger kills the simple.
3 "I have seen the [r]foolish taking root, Jer. 12:2
And I [r]cursed his abode immediately. Job 24:18
4 "His sons are far from safety,
They are even [4]oppressed in the gate,
Neither is there a deliverer.
5 "His[t] harvest the hungry devour, *Whose*
And take it to a *place of* thorns;
And the [r]schemer is eager for their wealth. Job 18:8-10
6 "For [r]affliction does not come from the dust, Job 15:35
Neither does trouble sprout from the ground,
7 For man is born for trouble,
As sparks fly upward.

8 "But as for me, I would [r]seek God, Job 13:2, 3; Ps. 50:15
And I would place my cause before God;
9 Who does great and unsearchable things,
Wonders without number.
10 "He [r]gives rain on the earth,
And sends water on the fields, Job 36:27-29
11 So that [r]He sets on high those who are lowly, Job 22:29
And those who mourn are lifted to safety.
12 "He [r]frustrates the plotting of the shrewd, Ps. 33:10
So that their hands cannot attain success.

[4]Lit., *crushed*

13 "He captures the wise by their own shrewdness
And the advice of the cunning is quickly thwarted.
14 "By day they [r]meet with darkness, Job 12:25
And grope at noon as in the night.
15 "But He saves from [r]the sword of their mouth, Job 4:10
And [r]the poor from the hand of the mighty. Job 29:17
16 "So the helpless has hope,
And unrighteousness must shut its mouth.

17 "Behold, how [r]happy is the man whom God reproves, Ps. 94:12
So do not despise the discipline of the Almighty.
18 "For He inflicts pain, and [t]gives relief; *binds*
He wounds, and His hands *also* heal.
19 "From[t] six troubles [r]He will deliver you, *In* • Ps. 34:19
Even in seven [r]evil will not touch you. Ps. 91:10
20 "In famine He will redeem you from death,
And [r]in war from the power of the sword. Ps. 144:10
21 "You will be hidden from the scourge of the tongue,
Neither will you be afraid of violence when it comes.
22 "You will [r]laugh at violence and famine, Job 8:21
[r]Neither will you be afraid of wild beasts. Ps. 91:13
23 "For you will be in league with the stones of the field;
And the beasts of the field will be at peace with you.

24"And you will know that your
[r]tent is secure, Job 8:6
For you will visit your abode
and fear no loss.
25"You will know also that your
[r]descendants will be
many, Ps. 112:2
And your offspring as the
grass of the earth.
26"You will [r]come to the grave in
full vigor, Job 42:17
Like the stacking of grain in
its season.
27"Behold this, we have investigated it, thus it is;
Hear it, and know for yourself."

CHAPTER 6

THEN Job answered,
2"Oh that my vexation were
actually weighed,
And laid in the balances together with my iniquity!
3"For then it would be [r]heavier
than the sand of the seas,
Therefore my words have
been rash. Job 23:2
4"For the arrows of the Almighty are within me;
[r]Their [r]poison my spirit
drinks; *Whose* · Job 20:16
The terrors of God are arrayed against me.
5"Does the [r]wild donkey bray
over *his* grass, Job 39:5-8
Or does the ox low over his
fodder?
6"Can something tasteless be
eaten without salt,
Or is there any taste in the
white of an egg?
7"My soul [r]refuses to touch
them; Job 3:24; 33:20
They are like loathsome food
to me.

8"Oh that my request might
come to pass,
And that God would grant
my longing!
9"Would that God were [r]willing
to crush me; Num. 11:15
That He would loose His
hand and cut me off!
10"But it is still my consolation,
And I rejoice in unsparing
pain,
That I have not denied the
words of the Holy One.
11"What is my strength, that I
should wait?
And what is my end, that I
should [r]endure? Job 21:4
12"Is my strength the strength
of stones,
Or is my flesh bronze?
13"Is it that my [r]help is not
within me, Job 26:2
And that deliverance is
driven from me?

14"For the [r]despairing man *there should be* kindness from
his friend; Job 4:5
Lest he forsake the [a]fear of
the Almighty. *reverence*
15"My brothers have acted deceitfully like a wadi,
Like the torrents of [a]wadis
which vanish, *brooks*
16 Which are turbid because of
ice,
And into which the snow
melts.
17"When they become waterless, they [a]are silent, *cease*
When it is hot, they vanish
from their place.

18 "The paths of their course wind along,
They go up into nothing and perish.
19 "The caravans of [r]Tema looked, Gen. 25:15
The travelers of [r]Sheba hoped for them. Job 1:15
20 "They were [t]disappointed for they had trusted, *ashamed*
They came there and were confounded.
21 "Indeed, you have now become such,
[r]You see a terror and are afraid. Ps. 38:11
22 "Have I said, 'Give me *something,*'
Or, 'Offer a bribe for me from your wealth,'
23 Or, 'Deliver me from the hand of the adversary,'
Or, 'Redeem me from the hand of the tyrants'?

24 "Teach me, and [r]I will be silent; Ps. 39:1
And show me how I have erred.
25 "How painful are honest words!
But what does your argument prove?
26 "Do you intend to reprove *my* words,
When the words of one in despair belong to the wind?
27 "You would even [r]cast *lots* for the orphans, Joel 3:3
And barter over your friend.
28 "And now please look at me,
And *see* if I lie to your face.
29 "Desist now, let there be no injustice;
Even desist, my righteousness is yet in it.
30 "Is there injustice on my tongue?
Cannot my palate discern [a]calamities? *words*

CHAPTER 7

"IS not man [r]forced to labor on earth, Job 5:7; 10:17
And *are not* his days like the days of a hired man?
2 "As a slave who pants for the shade,
And as a hired man who eagerly waits for his wages,
3 So am I allotted months of vanity,
And [r]nights of trouble are appointed me. Job 16:7
4 "When I lie down I say, 'When shall I arise?'
But the night continues,
And I am [t]continually tossing until dawn. *sated with*
5 "My [r]flesh is clothed with worms and a crust of dirt; Job 2:7; 17:14
My skin hardens and runs.
6 "My days are swifter than a weaver's shuttle,
And come to an end [r]without hope. Job 13:15; 14:19

7 "Remember that my life [r]is *but* breath, Job 7:16
My eye will [r]not again see good. Job 9:25
8 "The eye of him who sees me will behold me no more;
Thine eyes *will be* on me, but [r]I will not be. Job 7:21
9 "When a [r]cloud vanishes, it is gone, Job 30:15

So he who goes down to
Sheol does not come up.
10 "He will not return again to
his house,
Nor will [r]his place know him
anymore. Job 8:18

11 "Therefore, [r]I will not restrain
my mouth; Job 10:1
I will speak in the anguish of
my spirit,
I will complain in the bitterness of my soul.
12 "Am I the sea, or [r]the sea monster, Ezek. 32:2, 3
That Thou dost set a guard
over me?
13 "If I say, 'My [r]bed will comfort
me, Job 7:4
My couch will [t]ease my complaint,' *bear*
14 Then Thou dost frighten me
with dreams
And terrify me by visions;
15 So that my soul would
choose suffocation,
Death rather than my pains.
16 "I [a]waste away; I will not live
forever. *loathe*
Leave me alone, for my days
are *but* a breath.
17 "What is man that Thou dost
magnify him,
And that Thou art concerned
about him,
18 That [r]Thou dost examine him
every morning, Job 14:3
And try him every moment?
19 "Wilt Thou never turn Thy
gaze away from me,
Nor let me alone until I swallow my spittle?
20 "Have I sinned? What have I
done to Thee,
O [r]watcher of men? Ps. 36:6
Why hast Thou set me as
Thy target,
So that I am a burden to myself?
21 "Why then dost Thou not pardon my transgression
And take away my iniquity?
For now I will [r]lie down in the
dust; Job 10:9
And Thou wilt seek me, [r]but I
will not be." Job 7:8

CHAPTER 8

THEN Bildad the Shuhite [t]answered, *answered and said*
2 "How long will you say these
things,
And the words of your
mouth be a mighty wind?
3 "Does God pervert justice
Or does the Almighty pervert
what is right?
4 "If [r]your sons sinned against
Him, Job 1:5
Then He delivered them into
the [t]power of their transgression. *hand*
5 "If you would seek God
And implore the compassion
of the Almighty,
6 If you are pure and upright,
Surely now He would rouse
Himself for you
And restore your righteous
[t]estate. *place*
7 "Though your beginning was
insignificant,
Yet your [r]end will increase
greatly. Job 42:12

8 "Please [r]inquire of past generations, Deut. 4:32
And consider the things
searched out by their fathers.

9 "For we are *only* of yesterday
and know nothing,
Because our days on earth
are as a shadow.
10 "Will they not teach you *and*
tell you,
And bring forth words from
their minds?

11 "Can the papyrus grow up
without marsh?
Can the rushes grow without
water?
12 "While it is still green *and* not
cut down,
Yet it withers before any *oth-*
er[t]plant. *reed*
13 "So are the paths of [r]all who
forget God, Ps. 9:17
And the [r]hope of the godless
will perish, Job 11:20
14 Whose confidence is fragile,
And whose trust a [r]spider's
[t]web. Is. 59:5, 6 • *house*
15 "He [t]trusts in his house, but it
does not stand; *leans on*
He holds fast to it, but it does
not endure.
16 "He thrives before the sun,
And his shoots spread out
over his garden.
17 "His roots wrap around a rock
pile,
He grasps a house of stones.
18 "If he is [t]removed from his
place, *swallowed up*
Then it will deny him, *saying,*
'I never saw you.'
19 "Behold, [r]this is the joy of His
way; Job 20:5
And out of the dust others
will spring.
20 "Lo, [r]God will not reject *a man*
of integrity, Job 4:7
Nor [r]will He support the evildoers. Job 21:30
21 "He will yet fill [r]your mouth
with laughter, Job 5:22
And your lips with shouting.
22 "Those who hate you will be
clothed with shame;
And the tent of the wicked
will be no more."

CHAPTER 9

THEN Job answered,
2 "In truth I know that this is
so,
But how can a man be in the
right before God?
3 "If one wished to [r]dispute with
Him, Job 10:2; 13:19
He could not answer Him
once in a thousand *times.*
4 "Wise in heart and [r]mighty in
strength, Job 9:19; 23:6
Who has defied Him [t]without
harm? *and remained safe*
5 "*It is God* who removes the
mountains, they know
not *how,*
When He overturns them in
His anger;
6 Who [r]shakes the earth out of
its place, Is. 2:19, 21
And its pillars tremble;
7 Who commands the [r]sun [t]not
to shine, Is. 13:10
And sets a seal upon the
stars; *and it does not shine*
8 Who alone [r]stretches out the
heavens, Gen. 1:1
And tramples down the
waves of the sea;
9 Who makes the Bear, Orion,
and the Pleiades,
And the [r]chambers of the
south; Job 37:9

10 Who [r]does great things, unfathomable, Job 5:9
And wondrous works without number.
11 "Were He to pass by me, I would not see Him;
Were He to move past *me,* I would not perceive Him.
12 "Were He to snatch away, who could restrain Him?
Who could say to Him, 'What art Thou doing?'

13 "God will not turn back His anger;
Beneath Him crouch the helpers of Rahab.
14 "How then can I answer Him,
And choose my words [t]before Him? *with*
15 "For though I were right, I could not answer;
I would have to implore the mercy of my judge.
16 "If I called and He answered me,
I could not believe that He was listening to my voice.
17 "For He [r]bruises me with a tempest, Job 16:12, 14
And multiplies my wounds without cause.
18 "He will [r]not allow me to get my breath, Job 7:19
But saturates me with [r]bitterness. Job 13:26
19 "If *it is a matter* of power, [r]behold, *He is* the strong one! Job 9:4
And if *it is a matter* of justice, who can summon Him?
20 "Though I am righteous, my mouth will condemn me;
Though I am guiltless, He will declare me guilty.
21 "I am [r]guiltless; Job 1:1
I do not take notice of myself;
I [r]despise my life. Job 7:16
22 "It is *all* one; therefore I say,
'He [r]destroys the guiltless and the wicked.' Job 10:7
23 "If the scourge kills suddenly,
He [r]mocks the despair of the innocent. Job 24:12
24 "The earth is given into the hand of the wicked;
He [r]covers the faces of its judges. Job 12:17
If *it is* not *He,* then who is it?

25 "Now [r]my days are swifter than a runner; Job 7:6
They flee away, [r]they see no good. Job 7:7
26 "They slip by like reed boats, *reed*
Like an eagle that swoops on [t]its prey. *food*
27 "Though I say, 'I will forget my complaint,
I will leave off my *sad* countenance and be cheerful,'
28 I am afraid of all my pains,
I know that [r]Thou wilt not acquit me. Job 7:21
29 "I am accounted [r]wicked,
Why then should I toil in vain? Job 10:2
30 "If I should [r]wash myself with snow Jer. 2:22
And cleanse [r]my hands with lye, Job 31:7
31 Yet Thou wouldst plunge me into the pit,
And my own clothes would abhor me.
32 "For *He is* not a man as I am that I may answer Him,

That we may go to [t]court together. *judgment*
33 "There is no [r]umpire between us, 1 Sam. 2:25
Who may lay his hand upon us both.
34 "Let Him [r]remove His rod from me, Job 13:21
And let not dread of Him terrify me.
35 "*Then* I [r]would speak and not fear Him; Job 13:22
But I am not like that in myself.

CHAPTER 10

"I LOATHE my own life;
I will give full vent to [r]my complaint; Job 7:11
I will speak in the bitterness of my soul.
2 "I will say to God, 'Do[r] not condemn me; Job 9:29
Let me know why Thou dost contend with me.
3 'Is it [t]right for Thee indeed to oppress, *good*
To reject [r]the labor of Thy hands, Job 10:8; 14:15
And to look favorably on the schemes of the wicked?
4 'Hast Thou eyes of flesh?
Or dost Thou [r]see as a man sees? 1 Sam. 16:7
5 'Are Thy days as the days of a mortal,
Or Thy years as man's years,
6 That [r]Thou shouldst seek for my guilt, Job 14:16
And search after my sin?
7 'According to Thy knowledge I am indeed not guilty;
Yet there is [r]no deliverance from Thy hand. Job 9:12
8 'Thy hands fashioned and made me altogether,
[r]And wouldst Thou destroy me? Job 9:22
9 'Remember now, that Thou hast made me as clay;
And wouldst Thou turn me into dust again?
10 'Didst Thou not pour me out like milk,
And curdle me like cheese;
11 Clothe me with skin and flesh,
And knit me together with bones and sinews?
12 'Thou hast [r]granted me life and lovingkindness;
And Thy care has preserved my spirit. Job 33:4
13 'Yet [r]these things Thou hast concealed in Thy heart;
I know that this is within Thee: Job 23:13
14 If I sin, then Thou wouldst take note of me,
And [r]wouldst not acquit me of my guilt. Job 7:21
15 'If I am wicked, woe to me!
And if I am righteous, I dare not lift up my head.
I am sated with disgrace and conscious of my misery.
16 'And should *my head* be lifted up, [r]Thou wouldst hunt me like a lion; Is. 38:13
And again Thou wouldst show Thy [r]power against me. Job 5:9
17 'Thou dost renew Thy witnesses against me,
And increase Thine anger toward me,
[r]Hardship after hardship is with me. Job 7:1

18 'Why then hast Thou brought me out of the womb?
Would that I had died and no eye had seen me!
19 'I should have been as though I had not been,
Carried from womb to tomb.'
20 "Would He not let ʳmy few days alone? Job 14:1
Withdraw from me that I may have a little cheer
21 Before I go—ʳand I shall not return— 2 Sam. 12:23
To the land of darkness and deep shadow;
22 The land of utter gloom as darkness *itself*,
Of deep shadow without order,
And which shines as the darkness."

CHAPTER 11

THEN Zophar the Naamathite answered,ᵗ *answered and said*
2 "Shall a multitude of words go unanswered,
And a ʳtalkative man be acquitted? Job 8:2; 15:2
3 "Shall your boasts silence men?
And shall you ʳscoff and none rebuke? Job 17:2; 21:3
4 "For you have said, 'My teaching is pure,
And ʳI am innocent in your eyes.' Job 10:7
5 "But would that God might speak,
And open His lips against you,
6 And show you the secrets of wisdom!
For sound wisdom ᵗhas two sides. *is double*
Know then that God forgets a part of your iniquity.

7 "Canʳ you discover the depths of God? Job 33:12, 13
Can you discover the limits of the Almighty?
8 "*They are* high as the heavens, what can you do?
Deeper than ʳSheol, what can you know? Job 26:6
9 "Its measure is longer than the earth,
And broader than the sea.
10 "If He passes by or shuts up,
Or calls an assembly, who can restrain Him?
11 "For He knows false men,
And He sees iniquity without investigating.
12 "And ᵗan idiot will become intelligent *a hollow man*
When the foal of a wild donkey is born a man.

13 "If you would ʳdirect your heart right, 1 Sam. 7:3
And ʳspread out your hand to Him; Job 22:27
14 If iniquity is in your hand, put it far away,
And do not let wickedness dwell in your tents.
15 "Then, indeed, you could ʳlift up your face without *moral* defect, Job 22:26
And you would be steadfast and ʳnot fear. Ps. 27:3
16 "For you would ʳforget *your* trouble, Is. 65:16
As ʳwaters that have passed by, you would remember *it*. Job 22:11

17"And your [t]life would be brighter than noonday;
Darkness would be like the morning. *duration of life*
18"Then you would trust, because there is hope;
And you would look around and rest securely.
19"You would lie down and none would disturb *you,*
And many would entreat your [t]favor. *face*
20"But the [r]eyes of the wicked will fail, Deut. 28:65
And there will [r]be no escape for them; Job 27:22
And their hope is [r]to breathe their last." Job 6:9

CHAPTER 12

THEN Job responded,
2"Truly then [r]you are the people, Job 17:10
And with you wisdom will die!
3"But [r]I have intelligence as well as you; Job 13:2
I am not inferior to you.
And who does not know such things as these?
4"I am a joke to [t]my friends.
The one who called on God, and He answered him;
The just *and* blameless *man* is a joke. *his*
5"He who is at ease holds calamity in contempt,
As prepared for those whose feet slip.
6"The [r]tents of the destroyers prosper, Job 9:24; 21:7-9
And those who provoke God [r]are secure, Job 24:23
Whom God brings into [5]their power.

[5]Lit., *his*

7"But now ask the beasts, and let them teach you;
And the birds of the heavens, and let them tell you.
8"Or speak to the earth, and let it teach you;
And let the fish of the sea declare to you.
9"Who among all these does not know
That [r]the hand of the LORD has done this, Is. 41:20
10 In whose hand is the life of every living thing,
And [r]the breath of all mankind? Job 27:3; 33:4
11"Does not the ear test words,
As the palate tastes its food?
12"Wisdom is with aged men,
With [t]long life is understanding. *length of days*

13"With Him are [r]wisdom and [r]might; Job 9:4 • Job 9:4
To Him belong counsel and [r]understanding. Job 11:6
14"Behold, He tears down, and it cannot be rebuilt;
He imprisons a man, and there can be no release.
15"Behold, He restrains the waters, and they dry up;
And He sends them out, and they inundate the earth.
16"With Him are strength and sound wisdom,
The misled and the misleader belong to Him.
17"He makes counselors walk [a]barefoot, *stripped*
And makes fools of judges.
18"He loosens the [a]bond of kings,
And binds their loins with a girdle. *discipline*

19"He makes priests walk[a]barefoot, *stripped*
And overthrows [r]the secure ones. Job 24:22
20"He deprives the trusted ones of speech,
And takes away the discernment of the elders.
21"He [r]pours contempt on nobles, Job 34:19
And [r]loosens the belt of the strong. Job 12:18
22"He [r]reveals mysteries from the darkness, Dan. 2:22
And brings the deep darkness into light.
23"He [r]makes the nations great, then destroys them; Is. 9:3
He enlarges the nations, then leads them away.
24"He [r]deprives of intelligence the chiefs of the earth's people, Job 12:20
And makes them wander in a pathless waste.
25"They [r]grope in darkness with no light, Job 5:14
And He makes them stagger like a drunken man.

CHAPTER 13

"BEHOLD, my eye has seen all *this,*
My ear has heard and understood it.
2"What you know I also know.
I am not inferior to you.

3"But [r]I would speak to the Almighty, Job 13:22
And I desire to [r]argue with God. Job 13:15
4"But you smear with lies;
You are all [r]worthless physicians. Jer. 23:32
5"O that you would [r]be completely silent, Job 13:13
And that it would become your wisdom!
6"Please hear my argument,
And listen to the contentions of my lips.
7"Will you [r]speak what is unjust for God, Job 27:4
And speak what is deceitful for Him?
8"Will you [r]show partiality for Him? Lev. 19:15
Will you contend for God?
9"Will it be well when He examines you?
Or will you deceive Him as one deceives a man?
10"He will surely reprove you,
If you secretly [r]show partiality. Job 13:8; 32:21
11"Will not [r]His [t]majesty terrify you, Job 31:23 • *exaltation*
And the dread of Him fall on you?
12"Your memorable sayings are proverbs of ashes,
Your defenses are defenses of clay.

13"Be[r] silent before me so that I may speak; Job 13:5
Then let come on me what may.
14"Why should I take my flesh in my teeth,
And put my life in my hands?
15"Though[r] He slay me, Job 7:6
I will hope in Him.
Nevertheless I will argue my ways before Him.
16"This also will be my [r]salvation, Job 23:7
For [r]a godless man may not come before His presence. Job 34:21-23

17 "Listen carefully to my speech,
And let my declaration *fill* your ears.
18 "Behold now, I have ʳprepared my case; Job 23:4
I know that ʳI will be vindicated. Job 9:21; 10:7
19 "Who will contend with me?
For then I would be silent and ʳdie. Job 7:21

20 "Only two things do not do to me,
Then I will not hide from Thy face:
21 Remove Thy ᵗhand from me,
And let not the dread of Thee terrify me. *palm*
22 "Then call, and ʳI will answer;
Or let me speak, then reply to me. Job 9:16; 14:15
23 "How many are my iniquities and sins?
Make known to me my rebellion and my sin.
24 "Why dost Thou ʳhide Thy face, Ps. 13:1; 44:24
And consider me ʳThine enemy? Job 19:11
25 "Wilt Thou cause a ʳdriven leaf to tremble? Lev. 26:36
Or wilt Thou pursue the dry ʳchaff? Job 21:18
26 "For Thou dost write bitter things against me,
And dost ʳmake me to inherit the iniquities of my youth. Ps. 25:7
27 "Thou ʳdost put my feet in the stocks, Job 33:11
And dost watch all my paths;
Thou dost set a limit for the soles of my feet,
28 While ᵗI am decaying like a rotten thing, *he is*
Like a garment that is moth-eaten.

CHAPTER 14

"MAN, who is born of woman,
Is ᵗshort-lived and full of turmoil. *short of days*
2 "Like a flower he comes forth and withers.
He also flees like a shadow and does not remain.
3 "Thou also dost ʳopen Thine eyes on him, Ps. 8:4
And ʳbring him into judgment with Thyself. Ps. 143:2
4 "Who can make the clean out of the unclean?
No one!
5 "Since his days are determined,
The ʳnumber of his months is with Thee, Job 21:21
And his limits Thou hast set so that he cannot pass.
6 "Turn Thy gaze from him that he may ᵗrest, *cease*
Until he fulfills his day like a hired man.

7 "For there is hope for a tree,
When it is cut down, that it will sprout again,
And its shoots will not fail.
8 "Though its roots grow old in the ground,
And its stump dies in the dry soil,
9 At the scent of water it will flourish
And put forth sprigs like a plant.

10 "But ʳman dies and lies prostrate. Job 3:13; 14:10-15
Man ʳexpires, and where is he? Job 13:9
11 "*As* water ᵗevaporates from the sea, *disappears*
And a river becomes parched and dried up,
12 So ʳman lies down and does not rise. Job 3:13
Until the heavens be no more,
He will not awake nor be aroused out of his sleep.

13 "Oh that Thou wouldst hide me in Sheol,
That Thou wouldst conceal me ʳuntil Thy wrath returns *to Thee,* Is. 26:20
That Thou wouldst set a limit for me and remember me!
14 "If a man dies, will he live *again?*
All the days of my struggle I will wait,
Until my change comes.
15 "Thou wilt call, and I will answer Thee;
Thou wilt long for ʳthe work of Thy hands. Job 10:3
16 "For now Thou dost ʳnumber my steps, Job 31:4
Thou dost not ʳobserve my sin. Job 10:6
17 "My transgression is sealed up in a bag,
And Thou dost ᵗwrap up my iniquity. *plaster*

18 "But the falling mountain ᵗcrumbles away, *withers*
And the rock moves from its place;
19 Water wears away stones,
Its torrents wash away the dust of the earth;
So Thou dost ʳdestroy man's hope. Job 7:6
20 "Thou dost forever overpower him and he departs;
Thou dost change his appearance and send him away.
21 "His sons achieve honor, but ʳhe does not know *it;*
Or they become insignificant, but he does not perceive it. Eccl. 9:5
22 "But his ᵗbody pains him,
And he mourns only for himself." *flesh*

CHAPTER 15

THEN Eliphaz the Temanite ᵗresponded, *answered and said*
2 "Should a wise man answer with windy knowledge,
And fill ᵗhimself with the east wind? *his belly*
3 "Should he argue with useless talk,
Or with words which are not profitable?
4 "Indeed, you do away with ᵗreverence, *fear*
And hinder meditation before God.
5 "For ʳyour guilt teaches your mouth, Job 22:5
And you choose the language of ʳthe crafty. Job 5:12
6 "Your ʳown mouth condemns you, and not I; Job 18:7
And your own lips testify against you.

7 "Were you the first man to be born,

Or were you brought forth before the hills?

8 "Do you hear the [r]secret counsel of God, Job 29:4
And limit wisdom to yourself?

9 "What do you know that we do not know?
What do you understand that we do not?

10 "Both the gray-haired and the aged are among us,
Older than your father.

11 "Are the consolations of God too small for you,
Even the [r]word *spoken* gently with you? Job 6:10; 23:12

12 "Why does your [r]heart carry you away? Job 11:13
And why do your eyes flash,

13 That you should turn your spirit against God,
And allow *such* words to go out of your mouth?

14 "What is man, that [r]he should be pure, Job 14:4
Or [r]he who is born of a woman, that he should be righteous? Job 25:4

15 "Behold, He puts no trust in His [r]holy ones, Job 5:1
And the [r]heavens are not pure in His sight; Job 25:5

16 How much less one who is detestable and corrupt,
Man, who [r]drinks iniquity like water! Job 34:7

17 "I will tell you, listen to me;
And what I have seen I will also declare;

18 What wise men have told,
And have not concealed from their fathers,

19 To whom alone the land was given,
And no alien passed among them.

20 "The wicked man writhes in pain all *his* days,
And numbered are the years stored up for the ruthless.

21 "Sounds[t] of terror are in his ears, *A sound of terrors is*
While at peace the destroyer comes upon him.

22 "He does not believe that he will [r]return from darkness, Job 15:30
And he is destined for [r]the sword. Job 19:29

23 "He wanders about for food, saying, 'Where is it?'
He knows that a day of darkness is at hand.

24 "Distress and anguish terrify him,
They overpower him like a king ready for the attack,

25 Because he has stretched out his hand against God,
And conducts himself [r]arrogantly against the Almighty. Job 36:9

26 "He rushes headlong at Him
With his massive shield.

27 "For he has [r]covered his face with his fat, Ps. 73:7
And made his thighs heavy with flesh.

28 "And he has [r]lived in desolate cities, Job 3:14; Is. 5:8, 9
In houses no one would inhabit,
Which are destined to become [a]ruins. *heaps*

29 "He will not become rich, nor will his wealth endure;

And his grain will not bend down to the ground.
30"He will not [t]escape from darkness; *turn aside*
The [r]flame will wither his shoots, Job 15:34
And by the breath of His mouth he will go away.
31"Let him not trust in emptiness, deceiving himself;
For emptiness will be his [t]reward. *exchange*
32"It will be accomplished [r]before his time, Job 22:16
And his palm [r]branch will not be green. Job 18:16
33"He will drop off his unripe grape like the vine,
And will cast off his flower like the olive tree.
34"For the company of [r]the godless is barren, Job 8:13
And fire consumes the tents of [t]the corrupt. ***a bribe***
35"They [r]conceive mischief and bring forth iniquity,
And their [t]mind prepares deception." Ps. 7:14 • ***belly***

CHAPTER 16

THEN Job answered,
2"I have heard many such things;
Sorry comforters are you all.
3"Is there *no* limit to [r]windy words? Job 6:26
Or what plagues you that you answer?
4"I too could speak like you,
If I were in your place.
I could compose words against you,
And shake my head at you.
5"I could strengthen you with my mouth,
And the solace of my lips could lessen *your pain.*

6"If I speak, [r]my pain is not lessened, Job 9:27, 28
And if I hold back, what has left me?
7"But now He has [r]exhausted me; Job 7:3
Thou hast laid [r]waste all my company. Job 16:20
8"And Thou hast shriveled me up,
It has become a witness;
And my [r]leanness rises up against me, Job 19:20
It testifies to my face.
9"His anger has torn me and hunted me down,
He has [r]gnashed at me with His teeth; Ps. 35:16
My adversary glares at me.
10"They have [r]gaped at me with their mouth, Ps. 22:13
They have slapped me on the cheek with contempt;
They have massed themselves against me.
11"God hands me over to ruffians,
And tosses me into the hands of the wicked.
12"I was at ease, but [r]He shattered me, Job 9:17
And He has grasped me by the neck and shaken me to pieces;
He has also set me up as His [r]target. Job 7:20
13"His arrows surround me.
Without mercy He splits my kidneys open;

He pours out [r]my gall on the ground. Job 20:25
14 "He breaks through me with breach after breach;
He runs at me like a warrior.
15 "I have sewed [r]sackcloth over my skin, Gen. 37:34
And [r]thrust my horn in the dust. Ps. 7:5
16 "My face is flushed from [r]weeping, Job 16:20
[r]And deep darkness is on my eyelids, Job 24:17
17 Although there is no violence in my hands,
And my prayer is pure.

18 "O earth, do not cover my blood,
And let there be no *resting* place for my cry.
19 "Even now, behold, my witness is in heaven,
And my advocate is on high.
20 "My friends are my scoffers;
My eye weeps to God.
21 "O that a man might plead with God
As a man with his neighbor!
22 "For when a few years are past,
I shall go the way [r]of no return. Job 3:13

CHAPTER 17

"MY spirit is broken, my days are extinguished,
The grave is *ready* for me.
2 "Surely mockers are with me,
And my eye [t]gazes on their provocation. *lodges*

3 "Lay down, now, a pledge for me with Thyself;
Who is there that will be my guarantor?
4 "For Thou hast [t]kept their heart from understanding; *hidden*
Therefore Thou wilt not exalt *them*.
5 "He who [r]informs against friends for a share *of the spoil*, Lev. 19:13
The [r]eyes of his children also shall languish. Job 11:20

6 "But He has made me a byword of the people,
And I am [t]one at whom men spit. *a spitting to the faces*
7 "My eye has also grown dim because of grief,
And all my [r]members are as a shadow. Job 16:8
8 "The upright shall be appalled at this,
And the [r]innocent shall stir up himself against the godless. Job 22:19
9 "Nevertheless the righteous shall hold to his way,
And [r]he who has clean hands shall grow stronger and stronger. Job 22:30
10 "But come again all of you now,
For I [r]do not find a wise man among you. Job 12:2
11 "My days are past, my plans are torn apart,
Even the wishes of my heart.
12 "They make night into day, *saying*,
'The light is near,' in the presence of darkness.
13 "If I look for [r]Sheol as my home, Job 3:13

I [t]make my bed in the darkness; *spread out*
14 If I call to the [r]pit, 'You are my father'; Job 7:5
To the worm, 'my mother and my sister';
15 Where now is my hope?
And who regards my hope?
16"Will it go down with me to Sheol?
Shall we together [r]go down into the dust?" Job 3:17

CHAPTER 18

THEN Bildad the Shuhite [t]responded, *answered and said*
2"How long will you hunt for words?
Show understanding and then we can talk.
3"Why are we [r]regarded as beasts, Ps. 73:22
As stupid in your eyes?
4"O you who tear yourself in your anger—
For your sake is the earth to be abandoned,
Or the rock to be moved from its place?
5"Indeed, the light of the wicked goes out,
And the [t]flame of his fire gives no light. *spark*
6"The light in his tent is [r]darkened, Job 12:25
And his lamp goes out above him.
7"His [t]vigorous stride is shortened, *steps of his strength*
And his own scheme brings him down.
8"For he is thrown into the net by his own feet,
And he steps on the webbing.
9"A snare seizes *him* by the heel,
And a trap snaps shut on him.
10"A noose for him is hidden in the ground,
And a trap for him on the path.
11"All around [r]terrors frighten him, Job 15:21
And harry him at every step.
12"His strength is famished,
And calamity is ready at his side.
13"His skin is devoured by disease,
The first-born of death devours his [a]limbs. *parts*
14"He is [r]torn from the security of his tent, Job 8:22
And they march him before the king of terrors.
15"There dwells in his tent nothing of his;
[r]Brimstone is scattered on his habitation. Ps. 11:6
16"His roots are dried below,
And his [r]branch is cut off above. Job 15:30, 32
17"Memory of him perishes from the earth,
And he has no name abroad.
18"He is driven from light [r]into darkness, Job 5:14
And [r]chased from the inhabited world. Job 20:8
19"He has no [r]offspring or posterity among his people,
Nor any survivor where he sojourned. Job 27:14
20"Those in the west are appalled at his fate,
And those in the east are seized with horror.

21 "Surely such are the ʳdwellings
of the wicked, Job 21:28
And this is the place of him
who does not know
God."

CHAPTER 19

THEN Job responded,
2 "How long will you torment
ᵗme, *my soul*
And crush me with words?
3 "These ten times you have insulted me,
You are not ashamed to
wrong me.
4 "Even if I have truly erred,
My error lodges with me.
5 "If indeed you ʳvaunt yourselves against me,
And prove my disgrace to
me, Ps. 35:26; 38:16
6 Know then that ʳGod has
wronged me, Job 16:11
And has closed ʳHis net
around me. Job 18:8-10

7 "Behold, I cry, 'Violence!' but
I get no answer;
I shout for help, but there is
no justice.
8 "He has walled up my way so
that I cannot pass;
And He has put ʳdarkness on
my paths. Job 30:26
9 "He has ʳstripped my honor
from me, Job 12:17, 19
And removed the ʳcrown
from my head. Job 16:15
10 "He breaks me down on every
side, and I am gone;
And He has uprooted my
hope like a tree.
11 "He has also ʳkindled His anger against me, Job 16:9
And ʳconsidered me as His
enemy. Job 13:24; 33:10
12 "His troops come together,
And ʳbuild up their way
against me, Job 30:12
And camp around my tent.

13 "He has ʳremoved my brothers
far from me, Job 16:7
And my ʳacquaintances are
completely estranged
from me. Job 16:20
14 "My relatives have failed,
And my intimate friends
have forgotten me.
15 "Those who live in my house
and my maids consider
me a stranger.
I am a foreigner in their
sight.
16 "I call to my servant, but he
does not answer,
I have to implore him with
my mouth.
17 "My breath is ᵗoffensive to my
wife, *strange*
And I am loathsome to my
own brothers.
18 "Even young children despise
me;
I rise up and they speak
against me.
19 "All my ʳassociates abhor me,
And those I love have turned
against me. Ps. 38:11
20 "My bone clings to my skin
and my flesh,
And I have escaped *only* by
the skin of my teeth.
21 "Pity me, pity me, O you my
friends,
For the ʳhand of God has
struck me. Job 1:11
22 "Why do you ʳpersecute me as
God *does*, Job 13:24, 25

And are not satisfied with my flesh?
23 "Oh that my words were written!
Oh that they were ʳinscribed in a book! Is. 30:8
24 "That with an iron stylus and lead
They were engraved in the rock forever!
25 "And as for me, I know that my Redeemer lives,
And at the last He will take His stand on the earth.
26 "Even after my skin is destroyed,
Yet from my flesh I shall ʳsee God; Ps. 17:15
27 Whom I myself shall behold,
And whom my eyes shall see and not another.
My heart faints within me.
28 "If you say, 'How shall we persecute him?'
And 'What pretext for a case against him can we find?'
29 *Then* be afraid of ʳthe sword for yourselves, Job 15:22
For wrath *brings* the punishment of the sword,
So that you may know ʳthere is judgment." Job 22:4

CHAPTER 20

THEN Zophar the Naamathite answered,ᵗ *answered and said*
2 "Therefore my disquieting thoughts make me ᵗrespond, *return*
Even because of my ᵗinward agitation. *haste within me*
3 "I listened to ʳthe reproof which insults me, Job 19:3
And the spirit of my understanding makes me answer.
4 "Do you know this from ʳof old, Job 8:8
From the establishment of man on earth,
5 That the triumphing of the wicked is short,
And ʳthe joy of the godless momentary? Job 8:13
6 "Though his loftiness ᵗreaches the heavens, *goes up to*
And his head touches the clouds,
7 He ʳperishes forever like his refuse; Job 4:20
Those who have seen him will say, 'Where is he?'
8 "He flies away like a dream, and they cannot find him;
Even like a vision of the night he is chased away.
9 "The ʳeye which saw him sees him no more, Job 7:8
And ʳhis place no longer beholds him. Job 7:10
10 "His sons[a] favor the poor,
And his hands give back his wealth. *seek the favor of*
11 "His ʳbones are full of his youthful vigor, Job 21:23
But it lies down with him ᵗin the dust. *on*

12 "Though ʳevil is sweet in his mouth, Job 15:16
And he hides it under his tongue,
13 *Though* he desires it and will not let it go,
But holds it in his mouth,
14 *Yet* his food in his stomach is changed

To the [t]venom of cobras
within him. *gall*
15 "He swallows riches,
But will [r]vomit them up;
God will expel them from his
belly. Job 20:10, 20
16 "He sucks [r]the poison of cobras;
Deut. 32:24, 33
The viper's tongue slays him.
17 "He does not look at [r]the
streams, Deut. 32:13, 14
The rivers flowing with honey and curds.
18 "He [r]returns what he has attained
Job 20:10, 15
And cannot swallow *it;*
As to the riches of his trading,
He cannot even enjoy *them.*
19 "For he has oppressed *and*
forsaken the poor;
He has seized a house which
he has not built.

20 "Because he knew no quiet
[t]within him *in his belly*
He does [r]not retain anything
he desires. Eccl. 5:13-15
21 "Nothing remains [a]for him to
devour, *of what he devours*
Therefore [r]his prosperity does
not endure. Job 15:29
22 "In the fulness of his plenty he
will be cramped;
The [r]hand of everyone who
suffers will come *against*
him. Job 5:5
23 "When he fills his belly,
God will send His fierce anger on him
And will rain *it* on him [a]while
he is eating. *as his food*
24 "He may [r]flee from the iron
weapon, Is. 24:18
But the bronze bow will
pierce him.
25 "It is drawn forth and comes
out of his back,
Even the glittering point
from [r]his gall. Job 16:13
Terrors come upon him,
26 Complete darkness is held in
reserve for his treasures,
And unfanned [r]fire will devour him; Job 15:30
It will consume the survivor
in his tent.
27 "The [r]heavens will reveal his
iniquity, Deut. 31:28
And the earth will rise up
against him.
28 "The [r]increase of his house will
depart; Deut. 28:31
His possessions will flow
away [r]in the day of His
anger. Job 20:15
29 "This is the wicked man's portion from God,
Even the heritage decreed to
him by God."

CHAPTER 21

THEN Job answered,
2 "Listen carefully to my
speech,
And let this be your *way of*
consolation.
3 "Bear with me that I may
speak;
Then after I have spoken,
you may [r]mock. Job 11:3
4 "As for me, is my complaint
[a]to man? *against*
And why should [t]I not be impatient? *my spirit*
5 "Look at me, and be astonished,

And [r]put *your* hand over *your*
mouth. Judg. 18:19
6 "Even when I remember, I am
disturbed,
And [r]horror takes hold of my
flesh. Ps. 55:5
7 "Why [r]do the wicked *still* live,
Continue on, also become
very powerful? Job 9:24
8 "Their [t]descendants are established with them in their
sight, *seed*
And their offspring before
their eyes,
9 Their houses [r]are safe from
fear, Job 12:6
Neither is the rod of God on
them.
10 "His ox mates [t]without fail;
His cow calves and does not
abort. *and does not fail*
11 "They send forth their little
ones like the flock,
And their children skip
about.
12 "They [t]sing to the timbrel and
harp *lifted up the voice*
And rejoice at the sound of
the flute.
13 "They [r]spend their days in
prosperity, Job 21:23
And suddenly they go down
to Sheol.
14 "And they say to God, [r]'Depart
from us! Job 22:17
We do not even desire the
knowledge of Thy ways.
15 'Who is the Almighty, that we
should serve Him,
And what would we gain if
we entreat Him?'
16 "Behold, their prosperity is
not in their hand;
The [r]counsel of the wicked is
far from me. Job 22:18

17 "How often is [r]the lamp of the
wicked put out, Job 18:5
Or *does* their [r]calamity fall on
them? Job 31:2, 3
Does [t]God apportion destruction in His anger? *He*
18 "Are they as [r]straw before the
wind, Job 13:25
And like chaff which the
storm carries away?
19 "*You say,* 'God stores away [t]a
man's iniquity for his
sons.' *his*
Let [t]God repay him so that he
may know *it.* *Him*
20 "Let his [r]own eyes see his decay, Num. 14:28-32
And let him drink of the
wrath of the Almighty.
21 "For what does he care for his
household [6]after him,
When the number of his
months is cut off?
22 "Can anyone [r]teach God
knowledge, Job 35:11
In that He [r]judges those on
high? Job 4:18
23 "One dies in his full strength,
Being wholly at ease and [a]sat-
isfied; *quiet*
24 His sides are filled out with
fat,
And the [r]marrow of his bones
is moist, Prov. 3:8
25 While another dies with a
bitter soul,
Never even [t]tasting *anything*
good. *eating*
26 "Together they [r]lie down in the
dust, Job 3:13; 20:11
And worms cover them.

27 "Behold, I know your
thoughts,

[6]I.e., after he dies

And the plans by which you would wrong me.
28 "For you say, 'Where is the house of the nobleman,
And where is the [r]tent, the dwelling places of the wicked?' Job 8:22
29 "Have you not asked wayfaring men,
And do you not recognize their [t]witness? *signs*
30 "For the wicked is reserved for the day of calamity;
They will be led forth at [r]the day of fury. Job 21:17
31 "Who will confront him with his actions,
And who will repay him for what he has done?
32 "While he is carried to the grave,
Men will keep watch over *his* tomb.
33 "The clods of the valley will gently cover him;
Moreover, all men will [t]follow after him, *draw*
While countless ones *go* before him.
34 "How then will you vainly [r]comfort me, Job 16:2
For your answers remain *full of* [a]falsehood?" *faithlessness*

CHAPTER 22

THEN Eliphaz the Temanite [t]responded, *answered and said*
2 "Can a vigorous [r]man be of use to God, Job 35:7
Or a wise man be useful to himself?
3 "Is there any pleasure to the Almighty if you are righteous,
Or profit if you make your ways perfect?
4 "Is it because of your [a]reverence that He reproves you, *fear*
That He enters into judgment against you?
5 "Is not [r]your wickedness great,
And your iniquities without end? Job 11:6; 15:5
6 "For you have [r]taken pledges of your brothers without cause, Ex. 22:26
And stripped men naked.
7 "To the weary you have given no water to drink,
And from the hungry you have withheld bread.
8 "But the earth [r]belongs to the mighty man, Job 9:24
And [r]the honorable man dwells in it. Is. 3:3; 9:15
9 "You have sent [r]widows away empty, Job 24:3, 21
And the strength of the orphans has been crushed.
10 "Therefore [r]snares surround you, Job 18:8
And sudden [r]dread terrifies you, Job 15:21
11 Or [r]darkness, so that you cannot see, Job 5:14
And an [r]abundance of water covers you. Job 38:34

12 "Is not God [r]*in* the height of heaven? Job 11:7-9
Look also at the distant stars, how high they are!
13 "And you say, [r]'What does God know? Ps. 10:11
Can He judge through the thick darkness?
14 'Clouds are a hiding place for

Him, so that He cannot see;
And He walks on the [t]vault of heaven.' *circle*
15 "Will you keep to the ancient path
Which [r]wicked men have trod, Job 34:36
16 Who were snatched away before their time,
Whose foundations were washed away by a river?
17 "They [r]said to God, 'Depart from us!' Job 21:14, 15
And 'What can the Almighty do to them?'
18 "Yet He filled their houses with good *things;*
But the counsel of the wicked is far from me.
19 "The [r]righteous see and are glad, Ps. 52:6; 58:10
And the innocent mock them,
20 *Saying,* 'Truly our adversaries are cut off,
And their [a]abundance the fire has consumed.' *excess*

21 "Yield [a]now and be at peace with Him; *Know intimately*
Thereby good will come to you.
22 "Please receive [a]instruction from His mouth, *law*
And establish His words in your heart.
23 "If you return to the Almighty, you will be [t]restored; *built up*
If you remove unrighteousness far from your tent,
24 And [r]place *your* [t]gold in the dust, Job 31:24, 25 • *ore*
And *the gold of* Ophir among the stones of the brooks,
25 Then the Almighty will be your [t]gold *ore*
And choice silver to you.
26 "For then you will [r]delight in the Almighty, Job 27:10
And lift up your face to God.
27 "You will pray to Him, and He will hear you;
And you will pay your vows.
28 "You will also decree a thing, and it will be established for you;
And [r]light will shine on your ways. Job 11:17
29 "When [t]you are cast down, you will speak with confidence *they cast* you *down*
And the [t]humble person He will save. *lowly of eyes*
30 "He will deliver one who is not innocent,
And he will be [r]delivered through the cleanness of your hands." Job 42:7, 8

CHAPTER 23

THEN Job replied,
2 "Even today my [r]complaint is rebellion; Job 7:11
His hand is [r]heavy despite my groaning. Job 6:2, 3
3 "Oh that I knew where I might find Him,
That I might come to His seat!
4 "I would [r]present *my* case before Him Job 13:18
And fill my mouth with arguments.
5 "I would learn the words *which* He would [t]answer,

And perceive what He would
say to me. *answer me*
6 "Would He contend with me
by [r]the greatness of *His*
power? Job 9:4
No, surely He would pay attention to me.
7 "There the upright would [r]reason with Him; Job 13:3
And I would be delivered forever from my Judge.

8 "Behold, I go forward but He
is not *there,*
And backward, but I [r]cannot
perceive Him; Job 9:11
9 When He acts on the left, I
cannot behold *Him;*
He turns on the right, I cannot see Him.
10 "But He knows the way I take;
When He has tried me, I
shall come forth as gold.
11 "My foot has [r]held fast to His
path; Job 31:7
I have kept His way and not
turned aside.
12 "I have not departed from the
command of His lips;
I have treasured the [r]words of
His mouth more than my
necessary food. Job 6:10
13 "But He is unique and who
can turn Him?
And *what* His soul desires,
that He does.
14 "For He performs what is appointed for me,
And many such *decrees* are
with Him.
15 "Therefore, I would be dismayed at His presence;
When I consider, I am terrified of Him.
16 "*It is* God *who* has made my
[r]heart faint, Deut. 20:3
And the Almighty *who* has
dismayed me,
17 But I [r]am not silenced by the
darkness, Job 10:18, 19
Nor [r]deep gloom *which* covers *me.* Job 19:8

CHAPTER 24

"WHY are times not stored up
by the Almighty,
And why do those who know
Him not see His days?
2 "Some remove the landmarks;
They seize and devour flocks.
3 "They drive away the donkeys
of the [r]orphans; Job 6:27
They take the [r]widow's ox for
a pledge. Deut. 24:17
4 "They push [r]the needy aside
from the road; Job 24:14
The [r]poor of the land are
made to hide themselves
altogether. Job 29:12
5 "Behold, as wild donkeys in
the wilderness
They [r]go forth seeking food in
their activity, Ps. 104:23
As [t]bread for *their* children in
the desert. *his bread*
6 "They harvest their fodder in
the field,
And they glean the vineyard
of the wicked.
7 "They spend the night naked,
without clothing,
And have no covering
against the cold.
8 "They are wet with the mountain rains,
And they hug the rock for
want of a shelter.

9 "Others[t] snatch the orphan from the breast, *They*
And against the poor they take a pledge.
10 "They cause *the poor* to go about naked without clothing,
And they take away the sheaves from the hungry.
11 "Within the walls they produce oil;
They tread wine presses but thirst.
12 "From the city men groan,
And the souls of the wounded cry out;
Yet God [r]does not pay attention to folly. Job 9:23

13 "Others[t] have been with those who rebel against the light; *They*
They do not want to know its ways,
Nor abide in its paths.
14 "The murderer arises at dawn;
He [r]kills the poor and the needy, Ps. 10:8
And at night he is as a thief.
15 "And the eye of the adulterer waits for the twilight,
Saying, 'No eye will see me.'
And he disguises his face.
16 "In the dark they [r]dig into houses, Ex. 22:2
They [r]shut themselves up by day; John 3:20
They do not know the light.
17 "For the morning is the same to him as thick darkness,
For he is familiar with the terrors of thick darkness.

18 "They are insignificant on the surface of the water;
Their portion is [r]cursed on the earth. Job 5:3
They do not turn [t]toward the vineyards. *to the path of*
19 "Drought and heat [t]consume the snow waters, *seize*
So does [r]Sheol *those who* have sinned. Job 21:13
20 "A mother will forget him;
The [r]worm feeds sweetly till he is remembered no more. Job 21:26
And wickedness will be broken [r]like a tree. Job 19:10
21 "He wrongs the barren woman,
And does no good for [r]the widow. Job 22:9
22 "But He drags off the valiant by [r]His power; Job 9:4
He rises, but [r]no one has assurance of life. Job 18:20
23 "He provides them [r]with security, and they are supported; Job 12:6
And His [r]eyes are on their ways. Job 10:4; 11:11
24 "They are exalted a little while, then they are gone;
Moreover, they are [r]brought low and like everything gathered up; Job 14:21
Even like the heads of grain they are cut off.
25 "Now if it is not so, [r]who can prove me a liar,
And make my speech worthless?" Job 6:28; 27:4

CHAPTER 25

THEN Bildad the Shuhite [t]answered, *answered and said*
2 "Dominion and awe [t]belong to Him *are with Him*

Who establishes peace in [r]His
heights. Job 16:19; 31:2
3 "Is there any number to [r]His
troops? Job 16:13
And upon whom does His
light not rise?
4 "How then can a man be [r]just
with God? Job 4:17; 9:2
Or how can he be clean who
is born of woman?
5 "If even [r]the moon has no
brightness Job 31:26
And the [r]stars are not pure in
His sight, Job 15:15
6 How much less man, *that*
[r]maggot, Job 17:14
And the son of man, *that*
worm!"

CHAPTER 26

THEN Job responded,
2 "What a help you are to [t]the
weak! *no power*
How you have saved the arm
[r]without strength! Ps. 71:9
3 "What counsel you have given
to *one* without wisdom!
What helpful insight you
have abundantly [t]provided! *made known*
4 "To whom have you uttered
words?
And whose spirit was expressed through you?

5 "The [a]departed spirits tremble
Under the waters and their
inhabitants. *shades*
6 "Naked is Sheol before Him
And [7]Abaddon has no covering.
7 "He [r]stretches out the north
over empty space, Job 9:8
And hangs the earth on nothing.
8 "He [r]wraps up the waters in
His clouds; Job 37:11
And the cloud does not burst
under them.
9 "He [t]obscures the face of the
full moon, *covers*
And spreads His cloud over
it.
10 "He has inscribed a circle on
the surface of the waters,
At the [r]boundary of light and
darkness. Job 38:19
11 "The pillars of heaven tremble,
And are amazed at His rebuke.
12 "He [r]quieted the sea with His
power, Is. 51:15
And by His understanding
He shattered Rahab.
13 "By His breath the [r]heavens
are cleared; Job 9:8
His hand has pierced [r]the
fleeing serpent. Is. 27:1
14 "Behold, these are the fringes
of His ways;
And how faint [r]a word we
hear of Him! Job 4:12
But His mighty thunder, who
can understand?"

CHAPTER 27

THEN Job [a]continued his discourse and said, *again took up*
2 "As God lives, [r]who has taken
away my right, Job 16:11
And the Almighty, who has
embittered my soul,
3 For as long as [t]life is in me,
And the breath of God is in
my nostrils, *breath*

[7]I.e., place of destruction

4 My lips certainly will not speak unjustly,
Nor will [r]my tongue mutter deceit. Job 6:28; 33:3
5 "Far be it from me that I should declare you right;
Till I die I will not put away my integrity from me.
6 "I [r]hold fast my righteousness and will not let it go.
My heart does not reproach any of my days. Job 2:3

7 "May my enemy be as the wicked,
And my opponent as the unjust.
8 "For what is the hope of the godless [a]when he is cut off, *though he gains*
When God requires his life?
9 "Will God hear his cry,
When [r]distress comes upon him? Prov. 1:27
10 "Will he take [r]delight in the Almighty, Job 22:26, 27
Will he call on God at all times?
11 "I will instruct you in the [t]power of God; *hand*
What is with the Almighty I will not conceal.
12 "Behold, all of you have seen *it;*
Why then do you [a]act foolishly? *speak vanity*

13 "This is the portion of a wicked man from God,
And the inheritance *which* [r]tyrants receive from the Almighty. Job 15:20
14 "Though his sons are many, they are destined [r]for the sword; Job 15:22; 18:19
And his descendants will not be satisfied with bread.
15 "His survivors will be buried because of the plague,
And their [r]widows will not be able to weep. Ps. 78:64
16 "Though he piles up silver like dust,
And prepares garments as *plentiful as* the clay;
17 He may prepare *it,* [r]but the just will wear *it,*
And the innocent will divide the silver. Job 20:18-21
18 "He has built his [r]house like the spider's web, Job 8:15
Or as a hut *which* the watchman has made.
19 "He lies down rich, but never again;
He opens his eyes, and it is no more.
20 "Terrors overtake him like a flood;
A tempest steals him away [r]in the night. Job 20:8
21 "The east wind carries him away, and he is gone,
For it whirls him [r]away from his place. Job 7:10
22 "For it will hurl at him [r]without sparing; Jer. 13:14
He will surely try to flee from its [t]power. *hand*
23 "*Men* will clap their hands at him,
And will [r]hiss him from his place. Job 18:18; 20:8

CHAPTER 28

"SURELY there is a [8]mine for silver,
And a place [t]where they refine gold. *for gold they refine*

[8]Or, *source*

2 "Iron is taken from the dust,
And from rock copper is smelted.
3 "*Man* puts an end to darkness,
And ʳto the farthest limit he searches out Eccl. 1:13
The rock in gloom and deep shadow.
4 "He ᵗsinks a shaft far from habitation, *breaks open*
Forgotten by the foot;
They hang and swing to and fro far from men.
5 "The earth, from it comes food,
And underneath it is turned up as fire.
6 "Its rocks are the [a]source of sapphires, *place*
And its dust *contains* gold.
7 "The path no bird of prey knows,
Nor has the falcon's eye caught sight of it.
8 "The ᵗproud beasts have not trodden it, *sons of pride*
Nor has the *fierce* lion passed over it.
9 "He puts his hand on the flint;
He overturns the mountains at the ᵗbase. *roots*
10 "He hews out channels through the rocks;
And his eye sees anything precious.
11 "He dams up the streams from ᵗflowing; *weeping*
And what is hidden he brings out to the light.

12 "But ʳwhere can wisdom be found? Job 28:23, 28
And where is the place of understanding?
13 "Manʳ does not know its value,
Nor is it found in the land of the living. Matt. 13:44-46
14 "The deep says, 'It is not in me';
And the sea says, 'It is not with me.'
15 "Pureʳ gold cannot be given in exchange for it,
Nor can silver be weighed as its price. Prov. 3:13, 14
16 "It cannot be valued in the gold of Ophir,
In precious onyx, or sapphire.
17 "Gold or glass cannot equal it,
Nor can it be exchanged for articles of fine gold.
18 "Coral and crystal are not to be mentioned;
And the acquisition of ʳwisdom is above *that of* pearls. Prov. 8:11
19 "The topaz of Ethiopia cannot equal it,
Nor can it be valued in ʳpure gold. Prov. 8:19
20 "Whereʳ then does wisdom come from? Job 28:23
And where is the place of understanding?
21 "Thus it is hidden from the eyes of all living,
And concealed from the birds of the sky.
22 "[9]Abaddon and Death say,
'With our ears we have heard a report of it.'

23 "God understands its way;
And He knows its place.
24 "For He ʳlooks to the ends of the earth, Ps. 11:4; 33:13
And sees everything under the heavens.

[9]I.e., Destruction

25 "When He imparted ʳweight to the wind, Ps. 135:7
And ʳmeted out the waters by measure, Job 12:15
26 When He set a ʳlimit for the rain, Job 37:6, 11, 12
And a course for the ʳthunderbolt, Job 37:3
27 Then He saw it and declared it;
He established it and also searched it out.
28 "And to man He said, 'Behold, the ʳfear of the Lord, that is wisdom; Ps. 111:10
And to depart from evil is understanding.' "

CHAPTER 29

AND Job again took up his ʳdiscourse and said, Num. 23:7
2 "Oh that I were as in months gone by,
As in the days when God watched over me;
3 When ʳHis lamp shone over my head, Job 18:6
And by His light I walked through darkness;
4 As I was in [10]the prime of my days,
When the friendship of God *was* over my tent;
5 When the Almighty was yet with me,
And my children were around me;
6 When my steps were bathed in ʳbutter, Deut. 32:14
And the rock poured out for me streams of oil!
7 "When I went out to ʳthe gate of the city, Job 31:21
When I ᵗtook my seat in the square; *sat up*
8 The young men saw me and hid themselves,
And the old men arose *and* stood.
9 "The princes stopped talking,
And ʳput *their* hands on their mouths; Job 21:5
10 The voice of the nobles was ᵗhushed, *hidden*
And their ʳtongue stuck to their palate. Ps. 137:6
11 "For when the ear heard, it called me blessed;
And when the eye saw, it gave witness of me,
12 Because I delivered the poor who cried for help,
And the ʳorphan who had no helper. Job 31:17, 21
13 "The blessing of the one ready to perish came upon me,
And I made the widow's heart sing for joy.
14 "I ʳput on righteousness, and it clothed me; Job 27:5, 6
My justice was like a robe and a turban.
15 "I was eyes to the blind,
And feet to the lame.
16 "I was a father to the needy,
And I investigated the case which I did not know.
17 "And I ʳbroke the jaws of the wicked, Ps. 3:7
And snatched the prey from his teeth.
18 "Then I ᵗthought, 'I shall die ᵗin my nest, *said* • *with*
And I shall multiply *my* days as the sand.
19 'My ʳroot is spread out to the waters, Jer. 17:8

[10]Lit., *the days of my autumn*

And ʳdew lies all night on my
branch. Hos. 14:5
20 'My glory is *ever* new with
me,
And my ʳbow is renewed in
my hand.' Gen. 49:24

21 "To me ʳthey listened and
waited, Job 4:3; 29:9
And kept silent for my counsel.
22 "After my words they did not
ʳspeak again, Job 29:10
And ʳmy speech dropped on
them. Deut. 32:2
23 "And they waited for me as
for the rain,
And opened their mouth as
for the spring rain.
24 "I smiled on them when they
did not believe,
And the light of my face they
did not cast down.
25 "I chose a way for them and
sat as ʳchief, Job 1:3
And dwelt as a king among
the troops,
As one who ʳcomforted the
mourners. Job 4:4

CHAPTER 30

"BUT now those younger than I
ʳmock me, Job 12:4
Whose fathers I disdained to
put with the dogs of my
flock.
2 "Indeed, what *good was* the
strength of their hands to
me?
Vigor had perished from
them.
3 "From want and famine they
are gaunt
Who gnaw the dry ground by
night in waste and desolation,
4 Who pluck [1]mallow by the
bushes,
And whose food is the root of
the broom shrub.
5 "They are driven from the
community;
They shout against them as
against a thief,
6 So that they dwell in dreadful ᵃvalleys, *wadis*
In holes of the earth and of
the rocks.
7 "Among the bushes they ᵃcry
out; *bray*
Under the nettles they are
gathered together.
8 "Fools, even ᵗthose without a
name, *sons*
They were scourged from the
land.

9 "And now I have become
their ᵗtaunt, *song*
I have even become a ʳbyword to them. Job 17:6
10 "They abhor me *and* stand
aloof from me,
And they do not refrain from
spitting at my face.
11 "Because ᵃHe has loosed His
bowstring and ʳafflicted
me, *they* • Ruth 1:21
They have cast off ʳthe bridle
before me. Ps. 32:9
12 "On the right hand their brood
arises;
They thrust aside my feet
and build up against me
their ways of destruction.
13 "They break up my path,
They profit ᵗfrom my destruction, *for*
No one restrains them.

[1] I.e., plant of the salt marshes

14"As *through* a wide breach they come,
[t]Amid the tempest they roll on. *Under*
15"Terrors[r] are turned against me,
They pursue my[a]honor as the wind, Job 3:25 · *nobility*
And my prosperity has passed away like a cloud.

16"And now my soul is poured out [t]within me; *upon*
Days of affliction have seized me.
17"At night it pierces my bones [t]within me, *from upon*
And my gnawing *pains* take no rest.
18"By a great force my garment is [r]distorted; Job 2:7
It binds me about as the collar of my coat.
19"He has cast me into the [r]mire,
And I have become like dust and ashes. Ps. 69:2, 14
20"I [r]cry out to Thee for help, but Thou dost not answer me; Job 19:7
I stand up, and Thou dost turn Thy attention against me.
21"Thou hast [t]become cruel to me; *turned to be*
With the might of Thy hand Thou dost persecute me.
22"Thou dost [r]lift me up to the wind *and* cause me to ride; Job 9:17; 27:21
And Thou dost dissolve me in a storm.
23"For I know that Thou wilt bring me to death
And to the [r]house of meeting for all living. Job 3:19

24"Yet does not one in a heap of ruins stretch out *his* hand,
Or in his disaster therefore [r]cry out for help? Job 19:7
25"Have I not wept for the one whose life is hard?
Was not my soul grieved for [r]the needy? Job 24:4
26"When I [r]expected good, then evil came; Job 3:25, 26
When I waited for light, then darkness came.
27"I am seething [r]within, and cannot relax; Lam. 2:11
Days of affliction confront me.
28"I go about [r]mourning without comfort; Job 30:31
I stand up in the assembly *and* cry out for help.
29"I have become a brother to [r]jackals, Ps. 44:19; Mic. 1:8
And a companion of ostriches.
30"My skin turns black [t]on me,
And my bones burn with [t]fever. *from upon · heat*
31"Therefore my harp [t]is turned to mourning, *becomes*
And my flute to the sound of those who weep.

CHAPTER 31

"I HAVE made a covenant with my [r]eyes; Matt. 5:28
How then could I gaze at a virgin?
2"And what is the portion of God from above
Or the heritage of the Almighty from on high?
3"Is it not calamity to the unjust,

And disaster to [r]those who work iniquity? Job 34:22
4 "Does He not see my ways,
And number all my steps?

5 "If I have [r]walked with falsehood, Job 15:31; Mic. 2:11
And my foot has hastened after deceit,
6 Let Him weigh me with [t]accurate scales,
And let God know [r]my integrity. *just* • Job 23:10; 27:5, 6
7 "If my step has [r]turned from the way, Job 23:11
Or my heart [t]followed my eyes, *walked after*
Or if any [r]spot has stuck to my hands, Job 9:30
8 Let me sow and another eat,
And let my [a]crops be uprooted. *offspring*

9 "If my heart has been enticed by a woman,
Or I have lurked at my neighbor's doorway,
10 May my wife [r]grind for another, Is. 47:2
And let [r]others kneel down over her. Deut. 28:30
11 "For that would be a [r]lustful crime; Lev. 20:10
Moreover, it would be an iniquity *punishable* by judges.
12 "For it would be fire that consumes to Abaddon,
And would uproot all my [a]increase. *yield*

13 "If I have despised the claim of my male or female slaves
When they filed a complaint against me,
14 What then could I do when God arises,
And when He calls me to account, what will I answer Him?
15 "Did not He who made me in the womb make him,
And the same one fashion us in the womb?

16 "If I have kept [r]the poor from *their* desire, Job 5:16
Or have caused the eyes of the widow to fail,
17 Or have [r]eaten my morsel alone, Job 22:7
And the orphan has not [t]shared it *eaten from it*
18 (But from my youth he grew up with me as with a father,
And from [t]infancy I guided her), *my mother's womb*
19 If I have seen anyone perish for lack of clothing,
Or that [r]the needy had no covering, Job 24:4
20 If his loins have not [t]thanked me, *blessed*
And if he has not been warmed with the fleece of my sheep,
21 If I have lifted up my hand against the orphan,
Because I saw [t]I had support in the gate, *my help*
22 Let my shoulder fall from the socket,
And my [r]arm be broken off at the elbow. Job 38:15
23 "For calamity from God is a terror to me,
And because of [r]His majesty I can do nothing. Job 13:11

24 "If I have put my confidence
in [r]gold, Job 22:24
And called fine gold my
trust,
25 If I have gloated because my
wealth was great,
And because my hand had
secured *so* much;
26 If I have looked at the [t]sun
when it shone, *light*
Or the moon going in splendor,
27 And my heart became secretly enticed,
And my hand threw a kiss
from my mouth,
28 That too would have been an
iniquity *calling for* [t]judgment, *judges*
For I would have [r]denied God
above. Josh. 24:27

29 "Have I rejoiced at the extinction of my enemy,
Or [t]exulted when evil befell
him? *lifted myself up*
30 "No, [r]I have not allowed my
mouth to sin Ps. 7:4
By asking for his life in [r]a
curse. Job 5:3
31 "Have the men of my tent not
said,
'Who can [t]find one who has
not been [r]satisfied with
his meat'? *give* · Job 22:7
32 "The alien has not lodged outside,
For I have opened my doors
to the traveler.
33 "Have I covered my transgressions like Adam,
By hiding my iniquity in my
bosom,
34 Because I [r]feared the great
multitude, Ex. 23:2
And the contempt of families
terrified me,
And kept silent and did not
go out of doors?
35 "Oh that I had one to hear me!
Behold, here is my [t]signature;
Let the Almighty answer me!
And the indictment which
my [r]adversary has written, *mark* · Job 27:7
36 Surely I would carry it on my
shoulder;
I would bind it to myself like
a crown.
37 "I would declare to Him the
number of my steps;
Like [r]a prince I would approach Him. Job 1:3

38 "If my [r]land cries out against
me, Job 24:2
And its furrows weep together;
39 If I have eaten its [t]fruit without money, *strength*
Or have caused its owners to
lose their lives,
40 Let briars [t]grow instead of
wheat, *come forth*
And stinkweed instead of
barley."
The words of Job are ended.

CHAPTER 32

THEN these three men ceased
answering Job, because he was
righteous in his own eyes.
2 But the anger of Elihu the
son of Barachel the Buzite, of the
family of Ram burned; against Job
his anger burned, because he justified himself before God.
3 And his anger burned against
his three friends because they had

found no answer, and yet had condemned Job.
4 Now Elihu had waited to speak to Job because they were years older than he.
5 And when Elihu saw that there was no answer in the mouth of the three men his anger burned.
6 So Elihu the son of Barachel the Buzite spoke out and said,
"I am young in years and you are [r]old; Job 15:10
Therefore I was shy and afraid to tell you [t]what I think. *my knowledge*
7 "I [t]thought age should speak,
And [t]increased years should teach wisdom. *said • many*
8 "But it is a spirit in man,
And the [r]breath of the Almighty gives them understanding. Job 33:4
9 "The [a]abundant *in years* may not be wise, *nobles*
Nor may elders understand justice.
10 "So I say, 'Listen to me,
I too will tell what I think.'

11 "Behold, I waited for your words,
I listened to your reasonings,
While you [t]pondered what to say. *searched out words*
12 "I even paid close attention to you,
[t]Indeed, there was no one who refuted Job, *Behold*
Not one of you who answered his words.
13 "Do [t]not say, *Lest you say*
'We have found wisdom;
God will rout him, not man.'
14 "For he has not arranged *his* words against me;
Nor will I reply to him with your [t]arguments. *words*

15 "They are dismayed, they answer no more;
Words have failed them.
16 "And shall I wait, because they do not speak,
Because they [t]stop *and* answer no more? *stand*
17 "I too will answer my share,
I also will tell my opinion.
18 "For I am full of words;
The spirit within me constrains me.
19 "Behold, my belly is like unvented wine,
Like new wineskins it is about to burst.
20 "Let me speak that I may get relief;
Let me open my lips and answer.
21 "Let me now [r]be partial to no one; Lev. 19:15; Job 13:8
Nor flatter *any* man.
22 "For I do not know how to flatter,
Else my Maker would soon take me away.

CHAPTER 33

"HOWEVER now, Job, please [r]hear my speech, Job 13:6
And listen to all my words.
2 "Behold now, I open my mouth,
My tongue in my [t]mouth speaks. *palate*
3 "My words are *from* the uprightness of my heart;
And my lips speak [r]knowledge sincerely. Job 6:28
4 "The [r]Spirit of God has made me, Gen. 2:7; Job 10:3

And the breath of the Almighty gives me life.
5 "Refute me if you can;
Array yourselves before me, take your stand.
6 "Behold, I belong to God like you;
I too have been [t]formed out of the clay. *cut out of*
7 "Behold, [r]no fear of me should terrify you, Job 13:21
Nor should my pressure weigh heavily on you.

8 "Surely you have spoken in my hearing,
And I have heard the sound of *your* words:
9 'I am [r]pure, without transgression; Job 9:21
I am innocent and there [r]is no guilt in me. Job 10:14
10 'Behold, He [t]invents pretexts against me; *finds*
He counts me as His enemy.
11 'He [r]puts my feet in the stocks; Job 13:27
He watches all my paths.'
12 "Behold, let me tell you, you are not right in this,
For God is greater than man.

13 "Why do you [r]complain against Him, Job 40:2
That He does not give an account of all His doings?
14 "Indeed [r]God speaks once,
Or twice, *yet* no one notices it. Job 33:29; 40:5
15 "In a [r]dream, a vision of the night, Job 4:12-17
When sound sleep falls on men,
While they slumber in their beds,
16 Then [r]He opens the ears of men, Job 36:10, 15
And seals their instruction,
17 That He may turn man aside *from his* conduct,
And keep man from pride;
18 He [r]keeps back his soul from the pit, Job 33:22, 24
And his life from passing over [r]into Sheol. Job 15:22

19 "Man [t]is also chastened with pain on his bed, *He*
And with unceasing complaint in his bones;
20 So that his life loathes bread,
And his soul favorite food.
21 "His [r]flesh wastes away from sight, Job 16:8
And his bones which were not seen stick out.
22 "Then [r]his soul draws near to the pit, Job 33:18, 28
And his life to those who bring death.

23 "If there is an angel *as* mediator for him,
One out of a thousand,
To remind a man what is [t]right for him, *his uprightness*
24 Then let him be gracious to him, and say,
'Deliver him from [r]going down to the pit, Job 33:18
I have found a ransom';
25 Let his flesh become fresher than in youth,
Let him return to the days of his youthful vigor;
26 Then he will pray to God, and He will accept him,
That [r]he may see His face with joy, Job 22:26
And He may restore His righteousness to man.

27"He will sing to men and say,
'I[r]have sinned and perverted
what is right, 2 Sam. 12:13
And it is not proper for me.
28 'He has redeemed my soul
from going to the pit,
And my life shall [r]see the
light.' Job 22:28

29"Behold, God does all these
oftentimes with men,
30 To[r]bring back his soul from
the pit, Job 33:18
That he may be enlightened
with the light of life.
31"Pay attention, O Job, listen
to me;
Keep silent and let me speak.
32"*Then* if[t]you have anything to
say, answer me;
Speak, for I desire to justify
you. *there are words*
33"If not,[r]listen to me; Ps. 34:11
Keep silent, and I will teach
you wisdom."

CHAPTER 34

THEN Elihu continued and said,
2"Hear my words, you wise
men,
And listen to me, you who
know.
3"For the ear tests words,
As the palate tastes food.
4"Let us choose for ourselves
what is right;
Let us know among ourselves
what is good.
5"For Job has said, 'I[r]am righteous,
Job 13:18
But[r]God has taken away my
right; Job 27:2
6 Should I lie concerning my
right?
My [t]wound is incurable,
though I am without
transgression.' *arrow*
7"What man is like Job,
Who[r]drinks up derision like
water, Job 15:16
8 Who goes in company with
the workers of iniquity,
And walks with wicked men?
9"For he has said, 'It profits a
man nothing
When he [a]is pleased with
God.' *takes delight in God*

10"Therefore, listen to me, you
men of understanding.
Far be it from God to [r]do
wickedness, Gen. 18:25
And from the Almighty to do
wrong.
11"For He pays a man according
to[r]his work, Job 34:25
And makes him find it according
to his way.
12"Surely, [r]God will not act
wickedly, Job 34:10
And the Almighty will not
pervert justice.
13"Who [r]gave Him authority
over the earth? Job 38:4
And who[r]has laid *on Him* the
whole world? Job 38:5
14"If He should[t]determine to do
so, *set His mind on Himself*
If He should[r]gather to Himself
His spirit and His
breath, Job 12:10
15 All [r]flesh would perish together,
Gen. 7:21
And man would [r]return to
dust. Gen. 3:19; Job 10:9

16"But if *you have* understanding,
hear this;
Listen to the sound of my
words.

17 "Shall [r]one who hates justice rule? 2 Sam. 23:3
And will you condemn a righteous mighty one,
18 Who says to a king, 'Worthless one,'
To nobles, 'Wicked ones';
19 Who shows no [r]partiality to princes, Lev. 19:15
Nor regards the rich above the poor,
For they all are the [r]work of His hands? Job 10:3
20 "In a moment they die, and [r]at midnight Ex. 12:29
People are shaken and pass away,
And the mighty are taken away without a hand.

21 "For His eyes are upon the ways of a man,
And He sees all his steps.
22 "There is [r]no darkness or deep shadow Ps. 139:11, 12
Where the workers of iniquity may hide themselves.
23 "For He does not *need to* consider a man further,
That he should go before God in judgment.
24 "He breaks in pieces [r]mighty men without inquiry,
And sets others in their place. Job 12:19
25 "Therefore He [r]knows their works, Job 34:11
And [r]He overthrows *them* in the night, Job 34:20
And they are crushed.
26 "He [r]strikes them like the wicked Ps. 9:5; 11:5
In a public place,
27 Because they turned aside from following Him,
And [r]had no regard for any of His ways; Job 21:14
28 So that they caused [r]the cry of the poor to come to Him, Job 35:9; James 5:4
And that He might hear the cry of the afflicted—
29 When He keeps quiet, who then can condemn?
And when He hides His face, who then can behold Him,
That is, in regard to both nation and man?—
30 So that [r]godless men should not rule, Job 5:15; 20:5
Nor be snares of the people.

31 "For has anyone said to God,
'I have borne *chastisement;*
I will not offend *anymore;*
32 Teach Thou me what I do not see;
If I have done iniquity,
I will do it no more'?
33 "Shall He [r]recompense on your terms, because you have rejected *it?* Job 41:11
For you must choose, and not I;
Therefore declare what you know.
34 "Men of understanding will say to me,
And a wise man who hears me,
35 'Job [r]speaks without knowledge, Job 35:16; 38:2
And his words are without wisdom.
36 'Job ought to be tried[a] to the limit, *to the end*

Because he answers [r]like wicked men. Job 22:15
37 'For he adds [r]rebellion to his sin; Job 23:2
He claps his hands among us,
And multiplies his words against God.' "

CHAPTER 35

THEN Elihu continued and said,
2 "Do you think this is according to [r]justice? Job 27:2
Do you say, 'My righteousness is more than God's'?
3 "For you say, 'What advantage will it be to You?
[r]What profit shall I have, more than if I had sinned?' Job 9:30, 31
4 "I will answer you,
And your friends with you.
5 "Look at the heavens and see;
And behold the clouds—they are higher than you.
6 "If you have sinned, [r]what do you accomplish against Him? Job 7:20
And if your transgressions are many, what do you do to Him?
7 "If you are righteous, what do you give to Him?
Or what does He receive from your hand?
8 "Your wickedness is for a man like yourself,
And your righteousness is for a son of man.

9 "Because of the multitude of oppressions they cry out;
They cry for help because of the arm of the mighty.
10 "But [r]no one says, 'Where is God my Maker, Is. 51:13
Who gives songs in the night,
11 Who teaches us more than the beasts of the earth,
And makes us wiser than the birds of the heavens?'
12 "There they cry out, but He does not answer
Because of the pride of evil men.
13 "Surely God will not listen to [a]an empty *cry*, *falsehood*
Nor will the Almighty regard it.
14 "How much less when [r]you say you do not behold Him, Job 9:11; 23:8, 9
The case is before Him, and you must wait for Him!
15 "And now, because He has not visited *in* His anger,
Nor has He acknowledged transgression well,
16 So Job opens his mouth [t]emptily; *vainly*
He multiplies words [r]without knowledge." Job 34:35

CHAPTER 36

THEN Elihu continued and said,
2 "Wait for me a little, and I will show you
That there is yet more to be said in God's behalf.
3 "I will fetch my knowledge from afar,
And I will ascribe righteousness to my Maker.
4 "For truly [r]my words are not false; Job 33:3
One who is perfect in knowledge is with you.
5 "Behold, God is mighty but does not despise *any*;

He is [r]mighty in strength of
understanding. Job 12:13
6 "He does not [r]keep the wicked
alive, Job 8:22; 34:26
But gives justice to [r]the afflicted. Job 5:15
7 "He does not withdraw His
eyes from the righteous;
But with kings on the throne
He has seated them forever,
and they are exalted.
8 "And if they are bound in fetters,
And are caught in the cords
of [r]affliction, Job 36:15
9 Then he declares to them
their work
And their transgressions, that they have
magnified themselves.
10 "And [r]He opens their ear to instruction, Job 33:16; 36:15
And commands that they return from evil.
11 "If they hear and serve *Him,*
They shall [r]end their days in
prosperity, 1 Tim. 4:8
And their years in pleasures.
12 "But if they do not hear, they
shall [t]perish by the sword,
And they shall die without
knowledge. *pass away*
13 "But the godless in heart lay
up anger;
They do not cry for help
when He binds them.
14 "They die in youth,
And their life *perishes* among
the cult prostitutes.
15 "He delivers the afflicted in
[t]their affliction, *his*
And [r]opens their ear in *time*
of oppression. Job 36:10
16 "Then indeed, He [r]enticed you
from the mouth of distress, Hos. 2:14
Instead of it, a broad place
with no constraint;
And that which was set on
your table was full of fatness.[a] *rich food*

17 "But you were full of [r]judgment on the wicked;
Judgment and justice take
hold *of you.* Job 22:5, 10
18 "*Beware* lest [r]wrath entice you
to scoffing; Jon. 4:4, 9
And do not let the greatness
of the [r]ransom turn you
aside. Job 33:24
19 "Will your [a]riches keep *you*
from distress, *cry*
Or all the forces of *your*
strength?
20 "Do not long for the night,
When people [t]vanish in their
place. *go up*
21 "Be careful, do [r]not turn to
evil; Job 36:10
For you have preferred this
to [r]affliction. Job 36:8
22 "Behold, God is exalted in His
power;
Who is a teacher like Him?
23 "Who has appointed Him His
way,
And who has said, 'Thou [r]hast
done wrong'? Deut. 32:4

24 "Remember that you should
exalt His work,
Of which men have sung.
25 "All men have seen it;
Man beholds from afar.
26 "Behold, God is exalted, and
we do not know *Him;*
The [r]number of His years is
unsearchable. Job 10:5

27"For [r]He draws up the drops of water, Job 5:10; 36:26-29
They distill rain from [t]the [a]mist, its · flood
28 Which the clouds pour down,
They drip upon man abundantly.
29"Can anyone understand the spreading of the clouds,
The thundering of His [t]pavilion? booth
30"Behold, He spreads His [t]lightning about Him, light
And He covers the depths of the sea.
31"For by these He [r]judges peoples; Job 37:13
He gives food in abundance.
32"He covers *His* hands with the [t]lightning, light
And commands it to strike the mark.
33"Its noise declares [t]His presence; concerning Him
The cattle also, concerning what is coming up.

CHAPTER 37

"AT this also my heart trembles,
And leaps from its place.
2"Listen closely to the [r]thunder of His voice, Job 36:33
And the rumbling that goes out from His mouth.
3"Under the whole heaven He lets it loose,
And His [t]lightning to the ends of the earth. light
4"After it, a voice roars;
He thunders with His majestic voice;
And He does not restrain [t]the lightnings when His voice is heard. them
5"God [r]thunders with His voice wondrously, Job. 26:14
Doing great things which we cannot comprehend.
6"For to the snow He says, 'Fall on the earth,'
And to the downpour and the rain, 'Be strong.'
7"He [r]seals the hand of every man, Job 12:14
That [r]all men may know His work. Ps. 111:2
8"Then the beast goes into its [r]lair, Job 38:40
And remains in its den.
9"Out of the [t]south comes the storm, chamber
And out of the [t]north the cold. scattering winds
10"From the breath of God [r]ice is made, Job 38:29
And the expanse of the waters is frozen.
11"Also with moisture He loads the thick cloud;
He disperses the cloud of His [t]lightning. light
12"And it changes direction, turning around by His guidance,
That it may do whatever He commands [t]it them
On the face of the inhabited earth.
13"Whether for correction, or for His world,
Or for lovingkindness, He causes it to happen.

14"Listen to this, O Job,
Stand and consider the wonders of God.
15"Do you know how God establishes them,

And makes the ^t^lightning of
His cloud to shine? *light*
16 "Do you know about the layers of the thick clouds,
The wonders of one perfect
in knowledge,
17 You whose garments are hot,
When the land is still because of the south wind?
18 "Can you, with Him, ^r^spread
out the skies, Job 9:8
Strong as a molten mirror?
19 "Teach us what we shall say
to Him;
We cannot arrange *our case*
because of darkness.
20 "Shall it be told Him that I
would speak?
Or should a man say that he
would be swallowed up?
21 "And now ^t^men do not see the
light which is bright in
the skies; *they*
But the wind has passed and
cleared them.
22 "Out of the north comes
golden *splendor;*
Around God is awesome
majesty.
23 "The Almighty—^r^we cannot
find Him; Job 11:7, 8
He is exalted in power;
And ^r^He will not do violence
to justice and abundant
righteousness. Is. 63:9
24 "Therefore men fear Him;
He does not regard any who
are wise of heart."

CHAPTER 38

THEN the LORD answered Job
out of the whirlwind and said,
2 "Who is this that ^r^darkens
counsel Job 35:16; 42:3
By words without knowledge?
3 "Now ^r^gird up your loins like a
man, Job 40:7
And ^r^I will ask you, and you
instruct Me! Job 42:4
4 "Where were you ^r^when I laid
the foundation of the
earth! Job 15:7
Tell *Me,* if you have understanding,
5 Who set its measurements,
since you know?
Or who stretched the line on
it?
6 "On what ^r^were its bases
sunk? Job 26:7
Or who laid its cornerstone,
7 When the morning stars sang
together,
And all the ^r^sons of God
shouted for joy? Job 1:6
8 "Or *who* ^r^enclosed the sea with
doors, Gen. 1:9
When, bursting forth, it went
out from the womb;
9 When I made a cloud its garment,
And thick darkness its swaddling band,
10 And I ^t^placed boundaries on
it, *broke My decree on it*
And I set a bolt and doors,
11 And I said, 'Thus far you
shall come, but no farther;
And here shall your proud
waves stop'?
12 "Have you ever in your life
commanded the morning,
And caused the dawn to
know its place;
13 That it might take hold of the
ends of the earth,

And [r]the wicked be shaken
out of it? Job 34:25
14 "It is changed like clay *under*
the seal;
And they stand forth like a
garment.
15 "And from the wicked their
light is withheld,
And the [r]uplifted arm is broken. Num. 15:30; Ps. 10:15

16 "Have you entered into the
springs of the sea?
Or have you walked in the
recesses of the deep?
17 "Have the gates of death been
revealed to you?
Or have you seen the gates of
deep darkness?
18 "Have you understood the expanse of the earth?
Tell *Me,* if you know all this.

19 "Where is the way to the
dwelling of light?
And darkness, where is its
place,
20 That you may take it to [r]its
territory, Job 26:10
And that you may discern
the paths to its home?
21 "You know, for [r]you were born
then, Job 15:7
And the number of your days
is great!
22 "Have you entered the storehouses of the snow,
Or have you seen the storehouses of the hail,
23 Which I have reserved for
the time of distress,
For the day of war and battle?
24 "Where is the way that the
light is divided,
Or the east wind scattered on
the earth?

25 "Who has cleft a channel for
the flood,
Or a way for the thunderbolt;
26 To bring [r]rain on a land without [t]people, Job 36:27 • *man*
On a desert without a man in
it,
27 To [r]satisfy the waste and
desolate land, Ps. 104:13
And to make the [a]seeds of
grass to sprout? *growth*
28 "Has the rain a father?
Or who has begotten the
drops of dew?
29 "From whose womb has come
the [r]ice? Job 37:10
And the frost of heaven, who
has given it birth?
30 "Water [t]becomes hard like
stone, *hides itself*
And the surface of the deep
is imprisoned.

31 "Can you bind the chains of
the [r]Pleiades, Job 9:9
Or loose the cords of Orion?
32 "Can you lead forth a constel-
lation in its season,
And guide the Bear with her
[t]satellites? *sons*
33 "Do you know the [r]ordinances
of the heavens, Ps. 148:6
Or fix their rule over the
earth?

34 "Can you lift up your voice to
the clouds,
So that an abundance of water may cover you?
35 "Can you [r]send forth lightnings that they may go
And say to you, 'Here we
are'? Job 36:32; 37:3

36 "Who has [r]put wisdom in the
innermost being, Job 9:4
Or has given understanding
to the [a]mind? *cock*
37 "Who can count the clouds by
wisdom,
Or [r]tip the water jars of the
heavens, Job 38:34
38 When the dust hardens into a
mass,
And the clods stick together?

39 "Can you hunt the [r]prey for
the lion, Ps. 104:21
Or satisfy the appetite of the
young lions,
40 When they [r]crouch in *their*
dens, Job 37:8
And lie in wait in *their* lair?
41 "Who prepares for the raven
its nourishment,
When its young cry to God,
And wander about without
food?

CHAPTER 39

"DO you know the time the
[t]mountain goats give
birth? *goats of the rock*
Do you observe the calving
of the [r]deer? Ps. 29:9
2 "Can you count the months
they fulfill,
Or do you know the time
they give birth?
3 "They kneel down, they bring
forth their young,
They get rid of their labor
pains.
4 "Their offspring become
strong, they grow up in
the open field;
They leave and do not return
to them.

5 "Who sent out the [r]wild donkey
free? Job 6:5; 11:12
And who loosed the bonds of
the swift donkey,
6 To whom I gave [r]the wilderness
for a home, Job 24:5
And the salt land for his
dwelling place?
7 "He scorns the tumult of the
city,
The shoutings of the driver
he does not hear.
8 "He explores the mountains
for his pasture,
And he searches after every
green thing.
9 "Will the [r]wild ox consent to
serve you? Num. 23:22
Or will he spend the night at
your manger?
10 "Can you bind the wild ox in a
furrow with [t]ropes? *his rope*
Or will he harrow the valleys
after you?
11 "Will you trust him because
his strength is great
And leave your labor to him?
12 "Will you have faith in him
that he will return your
[t]grain, *seed*
And gather *it from* your
threshing floor?

13 "The ostriches' wings flap joyously
With the pinion and plumage
of [12]love,
14 For she abandons her eggs to
the earth,
And warms them in the dust,
15 And she forgets that a foot
may crush [t]them,
Or that a wild beast may
trample [t]them. *it*

[12] Or, *a stork*

16 "She treats her young cruelly,
as if *they* were not hers;
Though her labor be in vain,
she is unconcerned;
17 Because God has made her
forget wisdom,
And has not given her a
share of understanding.
18 "When she lifts herself [a]on
high, *to flee*
She laughs at the horse and
his rider.

19 "Do you give the horse *his*
might?
Do you clothe his neck with a
mane?
20 "Do you make him [r]leap like
the locust? Joel 2:5
His majestic [r]snorting is terrible. Jer. 8:16
21 "He paws in the valley, and
rejoices in *his* strength;
He [r]goes out to meet the
weapons. Jer. 8:6
22 "He laughs at fear and is not
dismayed;
And he does not turn back
from the sword.
23 "The quiver rattles against
him,
The flashing spear and javelin.
24 "With shaking and rage he
races over the ground;
And he does not stand still at
the voice of the trumpet.
25 "As often as the trumpet
sounds he says, 'Aha!'
And he scents the battle
from afar,
And thunder of the captains,
and the war cry.

26 "Is it by your understanding
that the hawk soars,
Stretching his wings toward
the south?
27 "Is it at your command that
the eagle mounts up,
And makes his nest on high?
28 "On the cliff he dwells and
lodges,
Upon the rocky crag, an in-
accessible place.
29 "From there he spies out food;
His eyes see *it* from afar.
30 "His young ones also suck up
blood;
And [r]where the slain are,
there is he." Matt. 24:28

CHAPTER 40

THEN the LORD said to Job,
2 "Will the faultfinder contend
with the Almighty?
Let him who [r]reproves God
answer it." Job 13:3; 23:4

3 Then Job answered the LORD
and said,
4 "Behold, I am insignificant;
what can I reply to Thee?
I lay my hand on my mouth.
5 "Once I have spoken, and [r]I
will not answer; Job 9:3
Even twice, and I will add no
more."

6 Then the [r]LORD answered Job
out of the storm, and said, Job 38:1
7 "Now [r]gird up your loins like a
man; Job 38:3
I will [r]ask you, and you instruct Me. Job 38:3; 42:4
8 "Will you really [r]annul My
judgment? Rom. 3:4
Will you condemn Me that
you may be justified?
9 "Or do you have an arm like
God,

And can you [r]thunder with a voice like His? Job 37:5

10"Adorn yourself with eminence and dignity;
And clothe yourself with honor and majesty.
11"Pour out [r]the overflowings of your anger; Is. 42:25
And look on everyone who is [r]proud, and make him low. Is. 2:12; Dan. 4:37
12"Look on everyone who is proud, *and* humble him;
And tread down the wicked where they stand.
13"Hide[r] them in the dust together; Is. 2:10-12
Bind [a]them in the hidden *place.* *their faces*
14"Then I will also [a]confess to you, *praise you*
That your own right hand can save you.

15"Behold now, [13]Behemoth, which I made [t]as well as you; *with*
He eats grass like an ox.
16"Behold now, his strength in his loins,
And his power in the muscles of his belly.
17"He bends his tail like a cedar;
The sinews of his thighs are knit together.
18"His bones are tubes of bronze;
His [t]limbs are like bars of iron. *bones*
19"He is the first of the ways of God;
Let his [r]maker bring near his sword. Job 40:15
20"Surely the mountains [r]bring him food, Ps. 104:14
And all the beasts of the field [r]play there. Ps. 104:26
21"Under the lotus plants he lies down,
In the covert of the reeds and the marsh.
22"The lotus plants cover him with [t]shade; *his shade*
The willows of the brook surround him.
23"If a river [a]rages, he is not alarmed; *oppresses*
He is confident, though the [r]Jordan rushes to his mouth. Gen. 13:10
24"Can anyone capture him when he is on watch,
With [t]barbs can anyone pierce *his* nose? *snares*

CHAPTER 41

"CAN you draw out [14]Leviathan with a fishhook?
Or press down his tongue with a cord?
2"Can you put a [t]rope in his nose? *rope of rushes*
Or pierce his jaw with a [a]hook? *thorn* or *ring*
3"Will he make many supplications to you?
Or will he speak to you soft words?
4"Will he make a covenant with you?
Will you take him for a servant forever?
5"Will you play with him as with a bird?
Or will you bind him for your maidens?
6"Will the [t]traders bargain over him? *partners*
Will they divide him among the merchants?

[13]Or, *the hippopotamus*

[14]Or, *the crocodile*

7 "Can you fill his skin with harpoons,
Or his head with fishing spears?
8 "Lay your hand on him;
Remember the battle; you will not do it again!
9 "Behold, [t]your expectation is false; *his*
Will [t]you be laid low even at the sight of him? *he*
10 "No one is so fierce that he dares to arouse him;
Who then is he that can stand before Me?
11 "Who has given to Me that I should repay *him?*
Whatever is [r]under the whole heaven is Mine. Ex. 19:5

12 "I will not keep silence concerning his limbs,
Or his mighty strength, or his [a]orderly frame. *graceful*
13 "Who can strip off his outer armor?
Who can come within his double mail?
14 "Who can open the doors of his face?
Around his teeth there is terror.
15 "*His* [t]strong scales are *his* pride, *rows of shields*
Shut up *as with* a tight seal.
16 "One is so near to another,
That no air can come between them.
17 "They are joined one to another;
They clasp each other and cannot be separated.
18 "His sneezes flash forth light,
And his eyes are like the eyelids of the morning.
19 "Out of his mouth go burning torches;
Sparks of fire leap forth.
20 "Out of his nostrils smoke goes forth,
As *from* a boiling pot and *burning* rushes.
21 "His breath kindles coals,
And a flame goes forth from his mouth.
22 "In his neck lodges strength,
And dismay leaps before him.
23 "The folds of his flesh are joined together,
Firm on him and immovable.
24 "His heart is as hard as a stone;
Even as hard as a lower millstone.
25 "When he raises himself up, the [a]mighty fear; *gods*
Because of the crashing they are bewildered.
26 "The sword that reaches him cannot avail;
Nor the spear, the dart, or the javelin.
27 "He regards iron as straw,
Bronze as rotten wood.
28 "The [t]arrow cannot make him flee; *son of the bow*
Slingstones are turned into stubble for him.
29 "Clubs are regarded as stubble;
He laughs at the rattling of the javelin.
30 "His underparts are *like* sharp potsherds;
He spreads out *like* a threshing sledge on the mire.
31 "He makes the depths boil like a pot;
He makes the sea like a jar of ointment.

32 "Behind him he makes a wake
to shine;
One would think the deep to
be gray-haired.
33 "Nothing on earth is like him,
One made without fear.
34 "He looks on everything that
is high;
He is king over all the [r]sons of
pride." Job 28:8

CHAPTER 42

THEN Job answered the LORD, and said,

2 "I know that [r]Thou canst do all
things, Gen. 18:14
And that no purpose of Thine
can be thwarted.
3 'Who is this that hides counsel
without knowledge?'
"Therefore I have declared
that which I did not understand,
Things too wonderful for me,
which I did not know."
4 'Hear, now, and I will speak;
I will [r]ask Thee, and do Thou
instruct me.' Job 38:3
5 "I have heard of Thee by the
hearing of the ear;
But now my eye sees Thee;
6 Therefore I retract,
And I repent in dust and
ashes."

7 And it came about after the LORD had spoken these words to Job, that the LORD said to Eliphaz the Temanite, "My wrath is kindled against you and against your two friends, because you have not spoken of Me what is right [r]as My servant Job has. Job 40:3-5; 42:1-6

8 "Now therefore, take for yourselves seven bulls and seven rams, and go to My servant Job, and offer up a burnt offering for yourselves, and My servant Job will pray for you. For I will accept him so that I may not do with you *according to your* folly, because you have not spoken of Me what is right, as My servant Job has."

9 So Eliphaz the Temanite and Bildad the Shuhite *and* Zophar the Naamathite went and did as the LORD told them; and the LORD [t]accepted Job. *lifted up the face of*

10 And the LORD restored the fortunes of Job when he prayed for his friends, and the LORD increased all that Job had twofold.

11 Then all his brothers, and all his sisters, and all who had known him before, came to him, and they ate bread with him in his house; and they consoled him and comforted him for all the evil that the LORD had brought on him. And each one gave him one piece of money, and each a ring of gold.

12 [r]And the LORD blessed the latter *days* of Job more than his beginning, [r]and he had 14,000 sheep, and 6,000 camels, and 1,000 yoke of oxen, and 1,000 female donkeys. Job 1:10 • Job 1:3

13 And [r]he had seven sons and three daughters. Job 1:2

14 And he named the first Jemimah, and the second Keziah, and the third Keren-happuch.

15 And in all the land no women were found so fair as Job's daughters; and their father gave them inheritance among their brothers.

16 And after this Job lived 140 years, and saw his sons, and his grandsons, four generations.

17 [r]And Job died, an old man and full of days. Job 5:26

THE PSALMS

The following expressions occur often in the Psalms:

Selah	May mean *Pause, Crescendo* or *Musical Interlude*
Maskil	Possibly, *Contemplative,* or *Didactic,* or *Skillful Psalm*
Mikhtam	Possibly, *Epigrammatic Poem,* or *Atonement Psalm*
Sheol	The nether world

BOOK 1

PSALM 1

HOW blessed is the man who [r]does not walk in the counsel of the wicked,
Nor stand in the [a]path [r]of sinners, Prov. 4:14 • *way* • Ps. 17:4
Nor sit in the seat of scoffers!
2 But his [r]delight is in the law of the LORD, Ps. 119:14, 16
And in His law he meditates [r]day and night. Ps. 25:5
3 And he will be like a tree *firmly* planted by [a]streams of water, *canals*
Which yields its fruit in its season,
And its leaf does not wither;
And in whatever he does, he [r]prospers. Gen. 39:2, 3, 23

4 The wicked are not so,
But they are like chaff which the wind drives away.
5 Therefore the wicked will not stand in the judgment,
Nor sinners in the assembly of the righteous.
6 For the LORD knows the way of the righteous,
But the way of [r]the wicked will perish. Ps. 9:5, 6

PSALM 2

WHY are the [a]nations in an uproar, *Gentiles*
And the peoples [r]devising a vain thing? Ps. 21:11
2 The [r]kings of the earth take their stand, Ps. 48:4-6
And the rulers take counsel together
[r]Against the LORD and against His [1]Anointed: Ps. 74:18
3 "Let us [r]tear their fetters apart,
And cast away their cords from us!" Jer. 5:5

4 He who [2]sits in the heavens [r]laughs, Ps. 37:13
The Lord scoffs at them.
5 Then He will speak to them in His [r]anger Ps. 21:8, 9
And terrify them in His fury:
6 "But as for Me, I have installed My King
Upon Zion, [r]My holy mountain." Ps. 48:1, 2

7 "I will surely tell of the decree of the LORD:
He said to Me, 'Thou art [r]My Son, Acts 13:33
Today I have begotten Thee.

[1]Or, *Messiah* [2]Or, *is enthroned*

8 'Ask of Me, and I will surely give the [a]nations as Thine inheritance, *Gentiles*
And the *very* ends of the earth as Thy possession.
9 'Thou shalt [3]break them with a rod of iron,
Thou shalt shatter them like earthenware.' "

10 Now therefore, O kings, show discernment;
Take warning, O [4]judges of the earth.
11 Worship the LORD with [a]reverence, *fear*
And rejoice with trembling.
12 Do homage to the Son, lest He become angry, and you perish *in* the way,
For [r]His wrath may [5]soon be kindled. Rev. 6:16, 17
How blessed are all who [r]take refuge in Him! Ps. 5:11

PSALM 3

A Psalm of David, when he fled from Absalom his son.

O LORD, how [r]my adversaries have increased!
Many are rising up against me. Ps. 69:4
2 Many are saying of my soul,
"There is no deliverance for him in God." [[6]Selah.

3 But Thou, O LORD, art a shield about me,
My [r]glory, and the One who lifts my head. Ps. 62:7
4 I was crying to the LORD with my voice,
And He answered me from His holy mountain. [Selah.
5 I lay down and slept;
I awoke, for the LORD sustains me.
6 I will not be afraid of ten thousands of people
Who have set themselves against me round about.

7 Arise, O LORD; [r]save me, O my God! Ps. 6:4; 22:21
For Thou hast smitten all my enemies on the cheek;
Thou hast [r]shattered the teeth of the wicked. Ps. 57:4
8 Salvation belongs to the LORD;
Thy blessing *be* upon Thy people! [Selah.

PSALM 4

For the choir director; on stringed instruments.
A Psalm of David.

ANSWER me when I call, O God of my righteousness!
Thou hast [t]relieved me in my distress; *made room for*
Be [r]gracious to me and hear my prayer. Ps. 25:16

2 O sons of men, how long will my [a]honor become [r]a reproach? *glory* • Ps. 69:7-10
How long will you love what is worthless and aim at deception? [Selah.
3 But know that the LORD has set apart the [r]godly man for Himself; Ps. 31:23
The LORD [r]hears when I call to Him. Ps. 6:8, 9; 17:6

[3]Another reading is *rule* [4]Or, *leaders*
[5]Or, *quickly, suddenly, easily*
[6]*Selah* may mean: *Pause, Crescendo* or *Musical Interlude*

4 Tremble, and do not sin;
Meditate in your heart upon your bed, and be still. [Selah.
5 Offer the [r]sacrifices of righteousness, Deut. 33:19
And trust in the LORD.

6 Many are saying, "Who will show us *any* good?"
Lift up the light of Thy countenance upon us, O LORD!
7 Thou hast put [r]gladness in my heart, Ps. 97:11, 12
More than when their grain and new wine abound.
8 In peace I will both [r]lie down and sleep, Job 11:19
For Thou alone, O LORD, dost make me to [r]dwell in safety. Lev. 25:18

PSALM 5

For the choir director; for flute accompaniment.
A Psalm of David.

GIVE ear to my words, O LORD,
Consider my [1]groaning.
2 Heed [r]the sound of my cry for help, my King and my God, Ps. 140:6
For to Thee do I pray.
3 In the morning, O LORD, Thou wilt hear my voice;
In the morning I will order *my prayer* to Thee and *eagerly* watch.

4 For Thou art not a God [r]who takes pleasure in wickedness; Ps. 11:5; 34:16
No evil dwells with Thee.
5 The boastful shall not stand before Thine eyes;
Thou [r]dost hate all who do iniquity. Ps. 11:5; 45:7
6 Thou dost destroy those who speak falsehood;
The LORD abhors the man of bloodshed and deceit.
7 But as for me, by Thine abundant lovingkindness I will enter Thy house,
[a]At [r]Thy holy temple I will bow in reverence for Thee. *Toward* • Ps. 138:2

8 O LORD, [r]lead me [r]in Thy righteousness because of my foes; Ps. 31:3 • Ps. 31:1
Make Thy way [a]straight before me. *smooth*
9 There is nothing [a]reliable in what they say;
Their [r]inward part is destruction *itself*;
Their throat is an open grave;
They flatter with their tongue. *true* • Ps. 7:14
10 Hold them guilty, O God;
[r]By their own devices let them fall! Ps. 9:16
In the multitude of their transgressions [r]thrust them out, Ps. 36:12
For they are [r]rebellious against Thee. Ps. 107:10

11 But let all who [r]take refuge in Thee be glad, Ps. 2:12
Let them ever sing for joy;
And [a]mayest Thou shelter them, *Thou dost shelter*
That those who love Thy name may exult in Thee.
12 For it is Thou who dost [r]bless the righteous man, O LORD, Ps. 29:11
Thou dost surround him with favor as with a shield.

[1]Or, *meditation*

PSALM 6

For the choir director; with stringed instruments, upon an eight-stringed lyre.
A Psalm of David.

O LORD, [r]do not rebuke me in Thine anger,
Nor chasten me in Thy wrath. Ps. 38:1
2 Be gracious to me, O LORD, for I *am* pining away;
Heal me, O LORD, for my bones are dismayed.
3 And my [r]soul is greatly dismayed;
But Thou, O LORD—[r]how long? Ps. 88:3 • Ps. 90:13

4 Return, O LORD, [r]rescue my [8]soul;
Save me because of Thy lovingkindness. Ps. 17:13
5 For there is no [9]mention of Thee in death;
In Sheol who will give Thee thanks?

6 I am [r]weary with my sighing;
Every night I make my bed swim,
I dissolve my couch with [r]my tears. Ps. 69:3 • Ps. 42:3
7 My [r]eye has wasted away with grief; Job 17:7
It has become old because of all my adversaries.

8 Depart from me, all you who do iniquity,
For the LORD has heard the voice of my weeping.
9 The LORD [r]has heard my supplication, Ps. 116:1
The LORD [r]receives my prayer. Ps. 66:19, 20
10 All my enemies shall [r]be ashamed and greatly dismayed; Ps. 71:13, 24
They shall turn back, they shall [r]suddenly be ashamed. Ps. 73:19

PSALM 7

A [10]Shiggaion of David, which he sang to the Lord concerning Cush, a Benjamite.

O LORD my God, in Thee I have taken refuge;
Save me from all those who pursue me, and [r]deliver me, Ps. 31:15
2 Lest he tear [a]my soul [r]like a lion, *me* • Ps. 57:4; Is. 38:13
Dragging me away, while there is none to deliver.

3 O LORD my God, if I have done this,
If there is [r]injustice in my hands, 1 Sam. 24:11
4 If I have [r]rewarded evil to my friend, Ps. 109:4, 5
Or have [r]plundered him who without cause was my adversary, 1 Sam. 24:7
5 Let the enemy pursue my soul and overtake *it*;
And let him trample my life down to the ground,
And lay my glory in the dust. [Selah.

6 [r]Arise, O LORD, in Thine anger; Ps. 3:7
Lift up Thyself against the rage of my adversaries,

[8]Or, *life* [9]Or, *remembrance*

[10]I.e., Dithyrambic rhythm, or, wild, passionate song

And [r]arouse Thyself for me;
Thou hast appointed judgment. Ps. 35:23; 44:23
7 And let the assembly of the [r]peoples encompass Thee;
And over [t]them return Thou on high. Ps. 22:27 • *it*
8 The LORD judges the peoples;
[t]Vindicate me, O LORD, according to my righteousness and my integrity that is in me. *Judge*
9 O let the evil of the wicked come to an end, but establish the righteous;
For the righteous God tries the hearts and [11]minds.
10 My shield is [t]with God, *upon*
Who [r]saves the upright in heart. Ps. 97:10, 11
11 God is a righteous judge,
And a God who has indignation every day.

12 If a man does not repent, He will sharpen His sword;
He has bent His bow and [t]made it ready. *fixed it*
13 He has also prepared for Himself deadly weapons;
He makes His [r]arrows fiery shafts. Ps. 18:14; 45:5
14 Behold, he travails with wickedness,
And he [r]conceives mischief, and brings forth falsehood. Job 15:35
15 He has dug a pit and hollowed it out,
And has fallen into the hole which he made.
16 His [r]mischief will return upon his own head, Esth. 9:25
And his [r]violence will descend upon [12]his own pate. Ps. 140:11
17 I will give thanks to the LORD [r]according to His righteousness, Ps. 71:15, 16
And will [r]sing praise to the name of the LORD Most High. Ps. 9:2; 66:1, 2, 4

PSALM 8

For the choir director; on the Gittith. A Psalm of David.

O LORD, our Lord,
How majestic is Thy name in all the earth,
Who hast [a]displayed Thy splendor above the heavens! *set*
2 From the mouth of infants and nursing babes Thou hast established strength,
Because of Thine adversaries,
To make the enemy and the revengeful cease.

3 When I [a]consider [r]Thy heavens, the work of Thy fingers, *see* • Ps. 89:11
The moon and the stars, which Thou hast [a]ordained; *appointed, fixed*
4 What is man, that Thou dost take thought of him?
And the son of man, that Thou dost care for him?
5 Yet Thou hast made him a little lower than God,
And dost crown him with glory and majesty!
6 Thou dost make him to [r]rule over the works of Thy hands; Gen. 1:26, 28

[11] Lit., *kidneys*, figurative for inner man

[12] I.e., the crown of his own head

Thou hast [r]put all things under his feet, 1 Cor. 15:27
7 All sheep and oxen,
And also the [a]beasts of the field, *animals*
8 The birds of the heavens, and the fish of the sea,
Whatever passes through the paths of the seas.

9 [r]O LORD, our Lord,
How majestic is Thy name in all the earth! Ps. 8:1

PSALM 9

For the choir director; on [13]Muthlabben.
A Psalm of David.

I WILL give thanks to the LORD with all my heart;
I will tell of all Thy wonders.
2 I will be glad and [r]exult in Thee; Ps. 5:11; 104:34
I will sing praise to Thy name, O Most High.

3 When my enemies turn back,
They stumble and [r]perish before Thee. Ps. 27:2
4 For Thou hast [r]maintained my just cause; Ps. 140:12
Thou dost sit on the throne judging righteously.
5 Thou hast rebuked the nations; Thou hast destroyed the wicked;
Thou hast blotted out their name forever and ever.
6 The enemy has come to an end in perpetual ruins,
And Thou hast uprooted the cities;
The very [r]memory of them has perished. Ps. 34:16

7 But the [r]LORD [14]abides forever; Ps. 10:16
He has established His throne for judgment,
8 And He will judge the world in righteousness;
He will execute judgment for the peoples with equity.
9 The LORD also will be a [r]stronghold for the oppressed,
A stronghold in times of trouble, Ps. 32:7; 59:9, 16
10 And those who [r]know Thy name will put their trust in Thee; Ps. 91:14
For Thou, O LORD, hast not [r]forsaken those who seek Thee. Ps. 37:28; 94:14

11 Sing praises to the LORD, who dwells in Zion;
[r]Declare among the peoples His deeds. Ps. 105:1
12 For He who [15]requires blood remembers them;
He does not forget [r]the cry of the afflicted. Ps. 9:18
13 Be gracious to me, O LORD;
Behold my affliction from those who hate me,
Thou who dost lift me up from the gates of death;
14 That I may tell of [r]all Thy praises, Ps. 106:2
That in the gates of the daughter of Zion
I may rejoice in Thy [a]salvation. *deliverance*
15 The nations have sunk down [r]in the pit which they have made; Ps. 7:15, 16
In the [r]net which they hid, their own foot has been caught. Ps. 57:6

[13]I.e., "Death to the Son"

[14]Or, *sits* as king [15]I.e., avenges bloodshed

16 The LORD has [r]made Himself known; Ex. 7:5
He has executed judgment.
In the work of his own hands the wicked is snared. [Higgaion Selah.
17 The wicked will [a]return to Sheol,
Even all the nations who [r]forget God. *turn* · Job 8:13
18 For the [r]needy will not always be forgotten, Ps. 9:12
Nor the [r]hope of the afflicted perish forever. Ps. 62:5
19 Arise, O LORD, do not let man prevail;
Let the nations be [r]judged before Thee. Ps. 9:5
20 Put them in fear, O LORD;
Let the nations know that they are but men. [Selah.

PSALM 10

WHY [r]dost Thou stand afar off, O LORD? Ps. 22:1
Why dost Thou hide *Thyself* in times of trouble?
2 In pride the wicked hotly pursue the afflicted;
[a]Let them be caught in the plots which they have devised. *They will be caught*
3 For the wicked [r]boasts of his heart's desire, Ps. 49:6
And [16]the greedy man curses *and* spurns the LORD.
4 The wicked, in the haughtiness of his countenance, does not seek *Him*.
All his [a]thoughts are, "There is no God." *plots*
5 His ways [t]prosper at all times; *are strong*
Thy judgments are on high, out of his sight;
As for all his adversaries, he snorts at them.
6 He says to himself, "I shall not be moved;
Throughout all generations I shall not be in adversity."
7 His [r]mouth is full of curses and deceit and [r]oppression; Rom. 3:14 · Ps. 73:8
[r]Under his tongue is mischief and wickedness. Job 20:12
8 He sits in the [r]lurking places of the villages; Ps. 11:2
In the hiding places he [r]kills the innocent; Ps. 94:6
His eyes stealthily watch for the [a]unfortunate. *poor*
9 He lurks in a hiding place as a lion in his lair;
He lurks to catch [r]the afflicted; Ps. 10:2
He catches the afflicted when he draws him into his net.
10 He crouches, he bows down,
And the unfortunate fall [17]by his mighty ones.
11 He says to himself, "God has forgotten;
He has hidden His face; He will never see it."
12 Arise, O LORD; O God, [r]lift up Thy hand. Ps. 17:7
Do not forget the afflicted.
13 Why has the wicked [r]spurned God?
He has said to himself, "Thou wilt not require *it*." Ps. 10:3
14 Thou hast seen *it*, for Thou hast beheld mischief and

[16] Or, *blesses the greedy man*

[17] Or, *into his claws*

vexation to [t]take it into
Thy hand. *put, give*
The [a]unfortunate commits
himself to Thee; *poor*
Thou hast been the [r]helper of
the orphan. Ps. 68:5
15 Break the arm of the wicked
and the evildoer,
Seek out his wickedness until
Thou dost find none.

16 The LORD is [r]King forever and
ever; Ps. 29:10
[r]Nations have perished from
His land. Deut. 8:20
17 O LORD, Thou hast heard the
desire of the [18]humble;
Thou wilt [r]strengthen their
heart, Thou wilt incline
Thine ear 1 Chr. 29:18
18 To [19]vindicate the orphan and
the oppressed,
That man who is of the earth
may cause [r]terror no
more. Is. 29:20

PSALM 11

For the choir director. *A Psalm* of David.

IN the LORD I take refuge;
How can you say to my soul,
"Flee *as* a bird to your
[r]mountain; Ps. 121:1
2 For, behold, the wicked bend
the bow,
They [a]make ready their arrow
upon the string,
To shoot in darkness at the
upright in heart. *fixed*
3 If the [r]foundations are destroyed,
Ps. 82:5; 87:1
What can the righteous do?"

4 The LORD is in His [r]holy temple;
the LORD's throne is
in heaven; Ps. 18:6; Mic. 1:2
His eyes behold, His eyelids
test the sons of men.
5 The LORD tests the righteous
and the wicked,
And the one who loves violence
His soul hates.
6 Upon the wicked He will rain
[20]snares;
Fire and brimstone and burning
wind will be the portion
of their cup.
7 For the LORD is righteous; He
loves righteousness;
The upright will [r]behold His
face. Ps. 16:11; 17:15

PSALM 12

For the choir director; upon an eight-stringed lyre.
A Psalm of David.

HELP, LORD, for [r]the godly man
ceases to be,
For the faithful disappear
from among the sons of
men. Is. 57:1
2 They speak [a]falsehood to one
another; *emptiness*
With [r]flattering [t]lips and with
a double heart they
speak. Ps. 28:3 • *lip*
3 May the LORD cut off all flattering
lips,
The tongue that [r]speaks great
things; Dan. 7:8; Rev. 13:5
4 Who have said, "With our
tongue we will prevail;
Our lips are [t]our own; who is
lord over us?" *with us*
5 "Because of the [r]devastation of
the afflicted, because of

[18]Or, *afflicted* [19]Lit., *judge*

[20]Or, *coals of fire*

the groaning of the
needy, Ps. 9:9; 10:18
Now [r]"I will arise," says the
LORD; "I will set him in
the safety for which he
longs." Is. 33:10

6 The [r]words of the LORD are
pure words; 2 Sam. 22:31
As silver [r]tried in a furnace on
the earth, refined seven
times. Prov. 30:5
7 Thou, O LORD, wilt keep
them;
Thou wilt preserve him from
this generation forever.
8 The [r]wicked strut about on
every side, Ps. 55:10, 11
When [21]vileness is exalted
among the sons of men.

PSALM 13

For the choir director. A Psalm of David.

HOW long, O LORD? Wilt Thou
forget me forever?
How long wilt Thou hide Thy
face from me?
2 How long shall I [r]take counsel
in my soul, Ps. 42:4
Having [r]sorrow in my heart
all the day? Ps. 42:9
How long will my enemy be
exalted over me?

3 Consider *and* answer me, O
LORD, my God;
Enlighten my eyes, lest I
sleep the *sleep of* death,
4 Lest my enemy [r]say, "I have
overcome him," Ps. 12:4
Lest my adversaries rejoice
when I am shaken.

5 But I have [r]trusted in Thy
lovingkindness; Ps. 52:8
My heart shall [r]rejoice in Thy
salvation. Ps. 9:14
6 I will sing to the LORD,
Because He has dealt bountifully with me.

PSALM 14

For the choir director. *A Psalm* of David.

THE fool has said in his heart,
"There is no God."
They are corrupt, they have
committed abominable
[t]deeds;
There is [r]no one who does
good. *doings* • Ps. 14:1-3
2 The LORD has [r]looked down
from heaven upon the
sons of men, Ps. 33:13, 14
To see if there are any who
[a]understand, *act wisely*
Who seek after God.
3 They have all [r]turned aside;
together they have be-
come corrupt; Ps. 58:3
There is no one who does
good, not even one.

4 Do all the workers of wickedness not know,
Who eat up my people *as*
they eat bread,
And [r]do not call upon the
Lord? Ps. 79:6; Is. 64:7
5 There they are in great
dread,
For God is with the [r]righteous
generation. Ps. 73:15
6 You would put to shame the
counsel of the afflicted,
But the LORD is his refuge.

[21]Or, *worthlessness*

7 Oh, that the salvation of Israel would come out of Zion!
When the LORD [22]restores His captive people,
Jacob will rejoice, Israel will be glad.

PSALM 15

A Psalm of David.

O LORD, who may [t]abide in Thy tent?
Who may dwell on Thy [r]holy hill? *sojourn* · Ps. 24:3
2 He who walks with integrity, and works righteousness,
And [r]speaks truth in his heart. Zech. 8:16
3 He does not slander [t]with his tongue, *according to*
Nor does evil to his neighbor,
Nor takes up a reproach against his friend;
4 In [t]whose eyes a reprobate is despised,
But [t]who honors those who fear the LORD; *his* · *he*
He swears to his own hurt, and does not change;
5 He does not put out his money [23]at interest,
Nor does he take a bribe against the innocent.
He who does these things will never be shaken.

PSALM 16

A [24]Mikhtam of David.

PRESERVE me, O God, for [r]I take refuge in Thee. Ps. 7:1
2 I said to the LORD, "Thou art [a]my Lord; *the Lord*
I [r]have no good besides Thee." Ps. 73:25
3 As for the [t]saints who are in the earth, *holy ones*
They are the majestic ones in whom is all my delight.
4 The sorrows of those who have bartered for another *god* will be multiplied;
I shall not pour out their libations of [r]blood, Ps. 106:37, 38
Nor shall I [r]take their names upon my lips. Ex. 23:13

5 The LORD is the [r]portion of my inheritance and my cup; Ps. 73:26; 119:57
Thou dost support my lot.
6 The lines have fallen to me in pleasant places;
Indeed, my heritage is [r]beautiful to me. Jer. 3:19

7 I will bless the LORD who has [r]counseled me; Ps. 73:24
Indeed, my [r]mind instructs me in the night. Ps. 77:6
8 I have set the LORD continually before me;
Because He is [r]at my right hand, I will not be shaken. Ps. 73:23
9 Therefore my heart is glad, and my glory rejoices;
My flesh also will [r]dwell securely. Ps. 4:8
10 For Thou wilt not abandon my soul to Sheol;
Neither wilt Thou allow Thy Holy One to [25]undergo decay.

[22] Or, *restores the fortunes of His people*
[23] I.e., to a fellow Israelite
[24] Possibly Epigrammatic Poem, or, Atonement Psalm
[25] Or, *see corruption* or *the pit*

11 Thou wilt make known to me the path of life;
In [r]Thy presence is fulness of joy; Ps. 21:6; 43:4
In Thy right hand there are pleasures forever.

PSALM 17

A Prayer of David.

HEAR a just cause, O LORD, give heed to my cry;
Give ear to my prayer, which is not from deceitful lips.
2 Let my judgment come forth from Thy presence;
Let Thine eyes look with [r]equity. Ps. 98:9; 99:4
3 Thou hast tried my heart;
Thou hast visited *me* by night;
Thou hast tested me and dost find [26]nothing;
I have [r]purposed that my mouth will not transgress. Ps. 39:1
4 As for the deeds of men, by the word of Thy lips
I have kept from the [r]paths of the violent. Ps. 10:5-11
5 My steps have held fast to Thy [t]paths. *tracks*
My feet have not slipped.

6 I have [r]called upon Thee, for Thou wilt answer me, O God; Ps. 86:7; 116:2
[r]Incline Thine ear to me, hear my speech. Ps. 88:2
7 Wondrously show Thy lovingkindness,
O Savior of those who take refuge at Thy right hand
From those who rise up *against them.*
8 Keep me as [27]the apple of the eye;
Hide me [r]in the shadow of Thy wings, Ruth 2:12
9 From the [r]wicked who despoil me, Ps. 31:20
My [r]deadly enemies, who surround me. Ps. 27:12
10 They have closed their [t]unfeeling *heart;*
With their mouth they [r]speak proudly. *fat* • 1 Sam. 2:3
11 They have now surrounded us in our steps;
They set their eyes to cast *us* down to the ground.
12 He is [r]like a lion that is eager to tear,
And as a young lion lurking in hiding places. Ps. 7:2

13 Arise, O LORD, confront him, bring him low;
Deliver my soul from the wicked with Thy sword,
14 From men with [r]Thy hand, O LORD,
From men of the world, [r]whose portion is in *this* life; Ps. 17:7 • Ps. 73:3-7
And whose belly Thou dost fill with Thy treasure;
They are satisfied with children,
And leave their abundance to their babes.
15 As for me, I shall behold Thy face in righteousness;
I will be satisfied with Thy likeness when I awake.

[26]Or, *no evil device in me*

[27]Lit., *the pupil, the daughter of the eye*

PSALM 18

For the choir director. *A Psalm* of David the servant of the LORD, who spoke to the LORD the words of this song in the day that the LORD delivered him from the hand of all his enemies and from the hand of Saul. And he said,

"I LOVE Thee, O LORD, [r]my strength." Ps. 59:17
2 The LORD is [r]my rock and my fortress and my deliverer, Deut. 32:18
My God, my rock, in whom I take refuge;
My shield and the horn of my salvation, my stronghold.
3 I call upon the LORD, who is worthy to be praised,
And I am [r]saved from my enemies. Ps. 34:6

4 The [r]cords of death encompassed me, Ps. 116:3
And the torrents of [28]ungodliness terrified me.
5 The cords of Sheol surrounded me;
The snares of death confronted me.
6 In my [r]distress I called upon the LORD, Ps. 50:15
And cried to my God for help;
He heard my voice [r]out of His temple, Ps. 3:4
And my cry for help before Him came into His ears.

7 Then the [r]earth shook and quaked; Judg. 5:4; Ps. 68:7
And the [r]foundations of the mountains were trembling Ps. 114:4, 6
And were shaken, because He was angry.
8 Smoke went up [a]out of His nostrils, *in His wrath*
And [r]fire from His mouth devoured; Ps. 50:3
Coals were kindled by it.
9 He bowed the heavens also, and came down
With thick [r]darkness under His feet. Ps. 97:2
10 And He rode upon a [r]cherub and flew; Ps. 80:1; 99:1
And He sped upon the [r]wings of the wind. Ps. 104:3
11 He made darkness His hiding place, His [a]canopy around Him, *pavilion*
Darkness of waters, thick clouds of the skies.
12 From the [r]brightness before Him passed His thick clouds, Ps. 104:2
Hailstones and coals of fire.
13 The LORD also [r]thundered in the heavens, Ps. 29:3
And the Most High uttered His voice,
Hailstones and coals of fire.
14 And He sent out His arrows, and scattered them,
And lightning flashes in abundance, and [r]routed them. *confused*
15 Then the channels of water appeared,
And the foundations of the world were laid bare
At Thy rebuke, O LORD,
At the blast of the [r]breath of Thy nostrils. Ps. 18:8

16 He [r]sent from on high, He took me;
He drew me out of [r]many waters. Ps. 144:7 • Ps. 32:6

[28]Or, *destruction*

17 He [r]delivered me from my strong enemy, Ps. 59:1
And from those who hated me, for they were [r]too mighty for me. Ps. 35:10
18 They confronted me in the day of my calamity,
But the LORD was my stay.
19 He brought me forth also into a broad place;
He rescued me, because He delighted in me.

20 The LORD has [r]rewarded me according to my righteousness; 1 Sam. 24:19
According to the cleanness of my hands He has recompensed me.
21 For I have [r]kept the ways of the LORD, Ps. 37:34
And have not wickedly departed from my God.
22 For all [r]His ordinances were before me, Ps. 119:30
And I did not put away His statutes from me.
23 I was also [29]blameless with Him,
And I [r]kept myself from my iniquity. Ps. 19:12, 13
24 Therefore the LORD has recompensed me according to my righteousness,
According to the cleanness of my hands in His eyes.

25 With the kind Thou dost show Thyself kind;
With the blameless [r]Thou dost show Thyself blameless; Ps. 18:30
26 With the pure Thou dost show Thyself pure;
And with the crooked Thou dost show Thyself [30]astute.
27 For Thou dost [r]save an afflicted people; Ps. 72:12
But [r]haughty eyes Thou dost abase. Ps. 101:5
28 For Thou dost light my lamp;
The LORD my God [r]illumines my darkness. Ps. 27:1
29 For by Thee I can [31]run upon a troop;
And by my God I can [r]leap over a wall. Ps. 18:33

30 As for God, His way is [r]blameless; Deut. 32:4
The [r]word of the LORD is tried; Ps. 12:6
He is a shield to all who take refuge in Him.
31 For [r]who is God, but the LORD? Deut. 32:39
And who is a [r]rock, except our God, Deut. 32:31
32 The God who [r]girds me with strength,
And makes my way [r]blameless? Ps. 18:39 • Ps. 18:23
33 He makes my feet like hinds' *feet*,
And [r]sets me upon my high places. Deut. 32:13
34 He [r]trains my hands for battle, Ps. 144:1
So that my arms can bend a bow of bronze.
35 Thou hast also given me the shield of Thy salvation,
And Thy [r]right hand upholds me; Ps. 63:8; 119:117
And Thy gentleness makes me great.
36 Thou dost enlarge my steps under me,

[29] Lit., *complete;* or, *having integrity*
[30] Lit., *twisted* [31] Or, *crush a troop*

And my [t]feet have not slipped. *ankles*

37 I pursued my enemies and overtook them,
And I did not turn back until they were consumed.
38 I shattered them, so that they were not able to rise;
They fell under my feet.
39 For Thou hast girded me with strength for battle;
Thou hast [r]subdued under me those who rose up against me. Ps. 18:47
40 Thou hast also made my enemies [r]turn their backs to me,
And I [32]destroyed those who hated me. Ps. 21:12
41 They cried for help, but there was none to save,
Even to the LORD, but He did not answer them.
42 Then I beat them fine as the dust before the wind;
I emptied them out as the mire of the streets.

43 Thou hast delivered me from the [r]contentions of the people; 2 Sam. 3:1; 19:9
Thou hast placed me as head of the nations;
A people whom I have not known serve me.
44 As soon as they hear, they obey me;
Foreigners [33]submit to me.
45 Foreigners fade away,
And come trembling out of their fortresses.

46 The LORD [r]lives, and blessed be [r]my rock; Job 19:25
And exalted be the God of my salvation, Ps. 18:2
47 The God who executes vengeance for me,
And [r]subdues peoples under me. Ps. 18:43; 47:3
48 He [r]delivers me from my enemies;
Surely Thou dost lift me above those who rise up against me;
Thou dost rescue me from the violent man. Ps. 3:7
49 Therefore I will give thanks to Thee among the nations, O LORD,
And I will [r]sing praises to Thy name. Ps. 108:1
50 He gives great [34]deliverance to His king,
And shows lovingkindness to [r]His anointed, Ps. 28:8
To David and his [t]descendants forever. *seed*

PSALM 19

For the choir director. A Psalm of David.

THE heavens are telling of the glory of God;
And their [r]expanse is declaring the work of His hands. Gen. 1:6, 7
2 Day to [r]day pours forth speech, Ps. 74:16
And [r]night to night reveals knowledge. Ps. 139:12
3 There is no speech, nor are there words;
Their voice is not heard.
4 Their [35]line has gone out through all the earth,

[32] Or, *silenced* [33] I.e., give feigned obedience

[34] I.e., victories [35] Another reading is *sound*

And their utterances to the end of the world.
In them He has [r]placed a tent for the sun, Ps. 104:2
5 Which is as a bridegroom coming out of his chamber;
It rejoices as a strong man to run his course.
6 Its rising is from [t]one end of the heavens, *the*
And its circuit to the [t]other end of them; *the ends*
And there is nothing hidden from its heat.

7 The law of the LORD is [36]perfect, restoring the soul;
The testimony of the LORD is sure, making [r]wise the simple. Ps. 119:98-100
8 The precepts of the LORD are right, rejoicing the heart;
The commandment of the LORD is pure, enlightening the eyes.
9 The fear of the LORD is clean, enduring forever;
The judgments of the LORD are true; they are righteous altogether.
10 They are more desirable than [r]gold, yes, than much fine gold; Ps. 119:72, 127
[r]Sweeter also than honey and the drippings of the honeycomb. Ps. 119:103
11 Moreover, by them Thy servant is warned;
In keeping them there is great reward.
12 Who can discern *his* errors? Acquit me of [r]hidden *faults.* Ps. 90:8
13 Also keep back Thy servant from presumptuous *sins;*
Let them not rule over me;
Then I shall be [37]blameless,
And I shall be acquitted of great transgression.
14 Let the words of my mouth and [r]the meditation of my heart
Be acceptable in Thy sight,
O LORD, my rock and my Redeemer. Ps. 104:34

PSALM 20

For the choir director. A Psalm of David.

MAY the LORD answer you in the day of trouble!
May the [r]name of the God of Jacob set you *securely* on high! Ps. 91:14
2 May He send you help [r]from the sanctuary, Ps. 3:4
And support you from Zion!
3 May He remember all your meal offerings,
And find your burnt offering acceptable! [Selah.
4 May He grant you your heart's desire,
And fulfill all your [38]counsel!
5 We will sing for joy over your [a]victory, *salvation*
And in the name of our God we will [r]set up our banners. Ps. 60:4
May the LORD [r]fulfill all your petitions. 1 Sam. 1:17

6 Now I know that the LORD saves His anointed;
He will [r]answer him from His holy heaven, Is. 58:9
With the [r]saving strength of His right hand. Ps. 28:8

[36] I.e., blameless

[37] Lit., *complete* [38] Or, *purpose*

7 Some *boast* in chariots, and
some in horses;
But [r]we will boast in the
name of the LORD, our
God. 2 Chr. 32:8
8 They have [r]bowed down and
fallen; Is. 2:11, 17
But we have [r]risen and stood
upright. Ps. 37:24
9 Save, O LORD;
May the King answer us in
the day we call.

PSALM 21

For the choir director. A Psalm of David.

O LORD, in Thy strength the
king will be glad,
And in Thy [39]salvation how
greatly he will rejoice!
2 Thou hast given him his
heart's desire,
And Thou hast not withheld
the request of his lips.
[Selah.
3 For Thou [r]dost meet him with
the blessings of good
things; Ps. 59:10
Thou dost set a crown of fine
gold on his head.
4 He asked life of Thee,
[r]Thou didst give it to him,
[r]Length of days forever and
ever. Ps. 91:16
5 His glory is great through
Thy [39]salvation,
Splendor and majesty Thou
dost place upon him.
6 For Thou dost make him
most blessed forever;
Thou dost make him joyful
[r]with gladness in Thy
presence. Ps. 43:4
7 For the king [r]trusts in the
LORD, Ps. 125:1
And through the lovingkindness of the Most High he
will not be shaken.
8 Your hand will find out all
your enemies;
Your right hand will find out
those who hate you.
9 You will make them [r]as a fiery oven in the time of
your anger; Mal. 4:1
The LORD will swallow them
up in His wrath,
And fire will devour them.
10 Their [40]offspring Thou wilt
destroy from the earth,
And their [41]descendants from
among the sons of men.
11 Though they [t]intended evil
against Thee, *stretched out*
And [r]devised a plot, Ps. 10:2
They will not succeed.
12 For Thou wilt make them
turn their back;
Thou wilt aim with Thy bow-
strings at their faces.
13 Be Thou exalted, O LORD, in
Thy strength;
We will [r]sing and praise Thy
power. Ps. 59:16; 81:1

PSALM 22

For the choir director; upon [42]Aijeleth Hashshahar. A Psalm of David.

MY God, my God, why hast
Thou forsaken me?
Far from my deliverance are
the words of my [t]groan-
ing. *roaring*

[39]Or, *victory*

[40]Lit., *fruit* [41]Lit., *seed*
[42]Lit., *the hind of the morning*

2 O my God, I cry by day, but Thou dost not answer;
And by night, but I have no rest.
3 Yet Thou art holy,
O Thou who art enthroned upon the praises of Israel.
4 In Thee our fathers trusted;
They trusted, and Thou didst [r]deliver them. Ps. 107:6
5 To Thee they cried out, and were delivered;
In Thee they trusted, and were not disappointed.

6 But I am a [r]worm, and not a man, Job 25:6; Is. 41:14
A reproach of men, and despised by the people.
7 All who see me sneer at me;
They [43]separate with the lip, they [r]wag the head, *saying,* Matt. 27:39
8 "[44]Commit *yourself* to the LORD; [r]let Him deliver him; Ps. 91:14; Matt. 27:43
Let Him rescue him, because He delights in him."

9 Yet Thou art He who [r]didst bring me forth from the womb;
Thou didst make me trust *when* upon my mother's breasts. Ps. 71:5, 6
10 Upon Thee I was cast [r]from [t]birth; Is. 46:3 • *a womb*
Thou hast been my God from my mother's womb.

11 Be not far from me, for [a]trouble is near; *distress*
For there is none to help.
12 Many [r]bulls have surrounded me; Ps. 22:21
Strong *bulls* of [r]Bashan have encircled me. Deut. 32:14
13 They [r]open wide their mouth at me, Ps. 35:21
As a ravening and a roaring [r]lion. Ps. 10:9; 17:12
14 I am poured out like water,
And all my [r]bones are out of joint; Ps. 31:10; Dan. 5:6
My heart is like wax;
It is melted within me.
15 My strength is dried up like a potsherd,
And my tongue cleaves to my jaws;
And Thou dost lay me [t]in the dust of death. *to*
16 For [r]dogs have surrounded me; Ps. 59:6, 7
A band of evildoers has encompassed me;
They [r]pierced my hands and my feet. Matt. 27:35
17 I can count all my bones.
They look, they stare at me;
18 They divide my garments among them,
And for my clothing they cast lots.

19 But Thou, O LORD, [r]be not far off; Ps. 22:11
O Thou my help, [r]hasten to my assistance. Ps. 70:5
20 Deliver my [a]soul from the sword,
My only *life* from the [t]power of the dog. *life* • *paw*
21 Save me from the lion's mouth;
And from the horns of the wild oxen Thou dost answer me.

22 I will tell of Thy name to my brethren;

[43] I.e., make mouths at me
[44] Another reading is *He committed* himself

In the midst of the assembly
I will praise Thee.
23 You who fear the LORD,
praise Him;
All you [t]descendants of Jacob, glorify Him,
And [r]stand in awe of Him, all
you descendants of Israel. *seed* • Ps. 33:8
24 For He has not despised nor
abhorred the affliction of
the afflicted;
Neither has He hidden His
face from him;
But when he cried to Him for
help, He heard.

25 From Thee *comes* my praise
in the great assembly;
I shall pay my vows before
those who fear Him.
26 The [45]afflicted shall eat and [r]be
satisfied; Ps. 107:9
Those who seek Him will
praise the LORD.
Let your heart live forever!
27 All the [r]ends of the earth will
remember and turn to the
LORD, Ps. 2:8; 82:8
And all the [r]families of the
nations will worship before Thee. Ps. 86:9
28 For the kingdom is the
LORD'S,
And He rules over the nations.
29 All the [t]prosperous of the
earth will eat and worship, *fat ones*
All those who go down to the
dust will bow before
Him,
Even he who [a]cannot keep his
soul alive. *did not*
30 Posterity will serve Him;
It will be told of the Lord to
the *coming* generation.
31 They will come and will declare His righteousness
To a people who will be born,
that He has performed *it*.

PSALM 23

A Psalm of David.

THE LORD is my shepherd,
I [a]shall not want. *do*
2 He makes me lie down in
green pastures;
He leads me beside [t]quiet waters. *waters of rest*
3 He restores my soul;
He guides me in the [t]paths of
righteousness
For His name's sake. *tracks*
4 Even though I walk through
the [46]valley of the shadow
of death,
I [r]fear no [47]evil; for Thou art
with me; Ps. 3:6; 27:1
Thy [r]rod and Thy staff, they
comfort me. Mic. 7:14
5 Thou dost prepare a table before me in the presence
of my enemies;
Thou [a]hast anointed my head
with oil; *dost anoint*
My [r]cup overflows. Ps. 16:5
6 Surely goodness and lovingkindness will follow me
all the days of my life,
And I will [48]dwell in the house
of the LORD forever.

PSALM 24

A Psalm of David.

THE earth is the LORD'S, and [49]all
it contains,

45 Or, *poor*

46 Or, *valley of deep darkness* 47 Or, *harm*
48 Another reading is *return to*
49 Lit., *its fulness*

The [r]world, and those who
dwell in it. Ps. 89:11
2 For He has [r]founded it upon
the seas,
And established it upon the
rivers. Ps. 104:3, 5
3 Who may [r]ascend into the hill
of the LORD? Ps. 15:1
And who may stand in His
holy [r]place? Ps. 65:4
4 He who has clean hands and
a pure heart,
Who has not lifted up his
soul to falsehood,
And has not [r]sworn deceitfully. Ps. 15:4
5 He shall receive a [r]blessing
from the LORD Ps. 115:13
And righteousness from the
God of his salvation.
6 This is the generation of
those who seek Him,
Who seek Thy face—*even*
Jacob. [Selah.

7 Lift up your heads, O gates,
And be lifted up, O [50]ancient
doors,
That the King of [r]glory may
come in! Ps. 29:2, 9
8 Who is the King of glory?
The LORD strong and mighty,
The LORD mighty in battle.
9 Lift up your heads, O gates,
And lift *them* up, O [50]ancient
doors,
That the King of [r]glory may
come in! Ps. 26:8; 57:11
10 Who is this King of glory?
The LORD of hosts,
He is the King of glory.
[Selah.

[50]Lit., *everlasting*

PSALM 25

A Psalm of David.

TO Thee, O LORD, I [r]lift up my
soul. Ps. 86:4; 143:8
2 O my God, in Thee I trust,
Do not let me be ashamed;
Do not let my [r]enemies exult
over me. Ps. 13:4; 41:11
3 Indeed, [r]none of those who
wait for Thee will be
ashamed; Ps. 37:9; 40:1
Those who [r]deal treacherously without cause will
be ashamed. Ps. 119:158

4 Make me know Thy ways, O
LORD;
Teach me Thy paths.
5 Lead me in [r]Thy truth and
teach me, Ps. 25:10
For Thou art the [r]God of my
salvation; Ps. 79:9
For Thee I wait all the day.
6 Remember, O LORD, Thy
compassion and Thy lov-
ingkindnesses,
For they have been [50]from of
old.
7 Do not remember the [r]sins of
my youth or my trans-
gressions; Job 13:26
According to Thy lovingkindness remember Thou me,
For Thy [r]goodness' sake, O
LORD. Ps. 31:19

8 Good and [r]upright is the
LORD; Ps. 92:15
Therefore He instructs sin-
ners in the way.
9 He [r]leads the [a]humble in jus-
tice, Ps. 23:3 • *afflicted*
And He [r]teaches the humble
His way. Ps. 27:11

[50]Lit., *everlasting*

10 All the paths of the LORD are lovingkindness and truth
To [r]those who keep His covenant and His testimonies. Ps. 103:18
11 For [r]Thy name's sake, O LORD,
Pardon my iniquity, for it is great. Ps. 31:3; 79:9

12 Who is the man who [r]fears the LORD? Ps. 31:19
He will instruct him in the way he should choose.
13 His soul will abide in [t]prosperity, *good*
And his [51]descendants will inherit the [a]land. *earth*
14 The secret of the LORD is for those who fear Him,
And He will make them know His covenant.
15 My eyes are continually toward the LORD,
For He will [t]pluck my feet out of the net. *bring out*

16 [r]Turn to me and be gracious to me, Ps. 69:16
For I am lonely and afflicted.
17 The [r]troubles of my heart are enlarged; Ps. 40:12
Bring me [r]out of my distresses. Ps. 107:6
18 Look upon my affliction and my [52]trouble,
And forgive all my sins.
19 Look upon my enemies, for they are many;
And they [r]hate me with violent hatred. Ps. 9:13
20 Guard my soul and deliver me;
Do not let me be ashamed, for I take refuge in Thee.
21 Let [r]integrity and uprightness preserve me, Ps. 41:12
For [r]I wait for Thee. Ps. 25:3
22 Redeem Israel, O God,
Out of all his troubles.

PSALM 26

A Psalm of David.

[53] VINDICATE me, O LORD, for I have [r]walked in my integrity; 2 Kin. 20:3
And I have trusted in the LORD without wavering.
2 Examine me, O LORD, and try me;
Test my [54]mind and my heart.
3 For Thy lovingkindness is before my eyes,
And I have walked in Thy [a]truth. *faithfulness*
4 I do not [r]sit with [55]deceitful men, Ps. 1:1
Nor will I go with pretenders.
5 I [r]hate the assembly of evildoers,
And I will not sit with the wicked. Ps. 31:6; 139:21
6 I shall [r]wash my hands in innocence, Ps. 73:13
And I will go about [r]Thine altar, O LORD, Ps. 43:3, 4
7 That I may proclaim with the voice of thanksgiving,
And declare all Thy wonders.
8 O LORD, I [r]love the habitation of Thy house, Ps. 27:4
And the place where Thy [r]glory dwells. Ps. 24:7
9 Do not take my soul away *along* with sinners,
Nor my life with men of bloodshed,

[51] Lit., *seed* [52] Lit., *toil*

[53] Lit., *Judge*
[54] Lit., *kidneys*, figurative for inner man
[55] Or, *worthless*

10 In whose hands is a [r]wicked scheme, Ps. 37:7
And whose right hand is full of [r]bribes. Ps. 15:5
11 But as for me, I shall [r]walk in my integrity;
Redeem me, and be gracious to me. Ps. 26:1
12 My foot stands on a [r]level place;
In the congregations I shall bless the LORD. Ps. 27:11

PSALM 27

A Psalm of David.

THE LORD is my [r]light and my [r]salvation; Ps. 18:28 • Ex. 15:2
Whom shall I fear?
The LORD is the [a]defense of my life;
Whom shall I dread? *refuge*
2 When evildoers came upon me to devour my flesh,
My adversaries and my enemies, they [r]stumbled and fell. Ps. 9:3
3 Though a host encamp against me,
My heart will not fear;
Though war arise against me,
In *spite of* this I [t]shall be confident. *am confident*
4 One thing I have asked from the LORD, that I shall seek:
That I may dwell in the house of the LORD all the days of my life,
To behold the [56]beauty of the LORD,
And to [57]meditate in His temple.

[56]Lit., *delightfulness* [57]Lit., *inquire*

5 For in the day of trouble He will conceal me in His [a]tabernacle; *shelter*
In the secret place of His tent He will hide me;
He will lift me up on a rock.
6 And now my head will be lifted up above my enemies around me;
And I will offer in His tent sacrifices [t]with shouts of joy; *of shouts*
I will sing, yes, I will sing praises to the LORD.

7 Hear, O LORD, when I cry with my voice,
And be gracious to me and [r]answer me. Ps. 13:3
8 *When Thou didst say,* "Seek[r] My face," my heart said to Thee,
"Thy face, O LORD, [r]I shall seek." Ps. 105:4 • Ps. 34:4
9 Do not hide Thy face from me,
Do not turn Thy servant away in [r]anger; Ps. 6:1
Thou hast been my help;
Do not abandon me nor [r]forsake me, Ps. 37:28
O God of my salvation!
10 For my father and [r]my mother have forsaken me,
But [r]the LORD will take me up. Is. 49:15 • Is. 40:11

11 Teach me Thy way, O LORD,
And lead me in a level path,
Because of my foes.
12 Do not deliver me over to the desire of my adversaries;
For [r]false witnesses have risen against me, Ps. 35:11

And such as[r] breathe out violence. Acts 9:1
13 *I would have despaired* unless I had believed that I would see the [r]goodness of the LORD Ps. 31:19
In the land of the living.
14 Wait for the LORD;
Be [r]strong, and let your heart take courage; Ps. 31:24
Yes, wait for the LORD.

PSALM 28

A Psalm of David.

TO Thee, O LORD, I call;
My [r]rock, do not be deaf to me, Ps. 18:2
Lest, if Thou be silent to me,
I become like those who go down to the pit.
2 Hear the [r]voice of my supplications when I cry to Thee for help,
When I lift up my hands toward [58]Thy holy sanctuary. Ps. 140:6
3 Do not drag me away with the wicked
And with those who work iniquity;
Who [r]speak peace with their neighbors, Ps. 12:2
While evil is in their hearts.
4 Requite them [r]according to their work and according to the evil of their practices;
Requite them according to the deeds of their hands;
Repay them their [59]recompense. Ps. 62:12

[58] Lit., *the innermost place of Thy sanctuary*
[59] Or, *dealings*

5 Because they do not regard the works of the LORD
Nor the deeds of His hands,
He will tear them down and not build them up.

6 Blessed be the LORD,
Because He has heard the voice of my supplication.
7 The LORD is my [r]strength and my shield; Ps. 18:2
My heart [r]trusts in Him, and I am helped; Ps. 13:5
Therefore my heart exults,
And with [r]my song I shall thank Him. Ps. 40:3
8 The LORD is their strength,
And He is a [r]saving defense to His anointed. Ps. 27:1
9 Save Thy people, and bless Thine inheritance;
Be their shepherd also, and carry them forever.

PSALM 29

A Psalm of David.

ASCRIBE to the LORD, O [a]sons of the mighty, *sons of gods*
Ascribe to the LORD glory and strength.
2 Ascribe to the LORD the glory due to His name;
Worship the LORD in [a]holy array. *the majesty of holiness*

3 The voice of the LORD is upon the waters;
The God of glory thunders,
The LORD is over [a]many waters. *great*
4 The voice of the LORD is [r]powerful,
The voice of the LORD is majestic. Ps. 68:33

5 The voice of the LORD breaks the cedars;
Yes, the LORD breaks in pieces [r]the cedars of Lebanon. Judg. 9:15
6 And He makes Lebanon [r]skip like a calf,
And [r]Sirion like a young wild ox. Ps. 114:4, 6 • Deut. 3:9
7 The voice of the LORD hews out flames of fire.
8 The voice of the LORD shakes the wilderness;
The LORD shakes the wilderness of Kadesh.
9 The voice of the LORD makes the deer to calve,
And strips the forests bare,
And [r]in His temple everything says, "Glory!" Ps. 26:8

10 The LORD sat *as King* at the [r]flood; Gen. 6:17
Yes, the LORD sits as [r]King forever. Ps. 10:16
11 The LORD will give [r]strength to His people;
The LORD will bless His people with peace. Ps. 28:8

PSALM 30

A Psalm; a Song at the Dedication of the House.
A Psalm of David.

I WILL extol Thee, O LORD, for Thou hast lifted me up,
And hast not let my enemies rejoice over me.
2 O LORD my God,
I cried to Thee for help, and Thou didst heal me.
3 O LORD, Thou hast brought up my soul from Sheol;
Thou hast kept me alive, that I should not [r]go down to the pit. Ps. 28:1
4 Sing praise to the LORD, you His godly ones,
And give thanks to His holy [t]name. *memorial*
5 For [r]His anger is but for a moment, Ps. 103:9; Is. 26:20
His favor is for a lifetime;
Weeping may [r]last for the night, Ps. 126:5
But a shout of joy *comes* in the morning.

6 Now as for me, I said in my prosperity,
"I will never be moved."
7 O LORD, by Thy favor Thou hast made my mountain to stand strong;
Thou didst hide Thy face, I was dismayed.
8 To Thee, O LORD, I called,
And to the LORD I made supplication:
9 "What profit is there in my blood, if I [r]go down to the pit?
Will the [r]dust praise Thee? Will it declare Thy faithfulness? Ps. 28:1 • Ps. 6:5

10 "Hear, O LORD, and be gracious to me;
O LORD, be Thou my helper."
11 Thou hast turned for me my mourning into dancing;
Thou hast [r]loosed my sackcloth and girded me with gladness; Is. 20:2
12 That *my* soul may sing praise to Thee, and not be silent.
O LORD my God, I will give thanks to Thee forever.

PSALM 31

For the choir director. A Psalm of David.

IN Thee, O LORD, I have taken refuge;
Let me never be ashamed;
[r]In Thy righteousness deliver me. Ps. 143:1
2 Incline Thine ear to me, rescue me quickly;
Be Thou to me a rock of [a]strength, *refuge*
A stronghold to save me.
3 For Thou art my rock and [r]my fortress; Ps. 18:2
For [r]Thy name's sake Thou wilt lead me and guide me. Ps. 23:3; 25:11
4 Thou wilt pull me out of the net which they have secretly laid for me;
For Thou art my strength.
5 Into Thy hand I commit my spirit;
Thou hast ransomed me, O LORD, God of truth.

6 I hate those who regard [t]vain idols; *empty vanities*
But I trust in the LORD.
7 I will rejoice and be glad in Thy lovingkindness,
Because Thou hast [r]seen my affliction;
Thou hast known the troubles of my soul, Ps. 10:14
8 And Thou hast not [r]given me over into the hand of the enemy;
Thou hast set my feet in a large place. Deut. 32:30

9 Be gracious to me, O LORD, for I am in distress;
My [r]eye is wasted away from grief, my soul and my body *also*. Ps. 6:7
10 For my life is spent with [r]sorrow, Ps. 13:2
And my years with sighing;
My strength has failed because of my iniquity,
And my [a]body has wasted away. *bones, substance*
11 Because of all my adversaries, I have become a [r]reproach, Ps. 69:19
Especially to my neighbors,
And an object of dread to my acquaintances;
Those who see me in the street flee from me.
12 I am forgotten as a dead man, out of mind,
I am like a broken vessel.
13 For I have heard the [t]slander of many, *whispering*
Terror is on every side;
While they took counsel together against me,
They [r]schemed to take away my life. Ps. 41:7

14 But as for me, I trust in Thee, O LORD,
I say, "Thou art my God."
15 My times are in Thy hand;
Deliver me from the hand of my enemies, and from those who persecute me.
16 Make Thy face to shine upon Thy servant;
[r]Save me in Thy lovingkindness. Ps. 6:4
17 Let me not be [r]put to shame, O LORD, for I call upon Thee; Ps. 25:2, 20
Let the wicked be put to

shame, let them [r]be silent in Sheol. 1 Sam. 2:9
18 Let the lying lips be dumb,
Which speak arrogantly against the righteous
With pride and contempt.

19 How great is Thy goodness,
Which Thou hast stored up for those who fear Thee,
Which Thou hast wrought for those who take refuge in Thee,
Before the sons of men!
20 Thou dost hide them in the secret place of Thy presence from the [r]conspiracies of man; Ps. 37:12
Thou dost keep them secretly in a shelter from the strife of tongues.
21 Blessed be the LORD,
For He has made marvelous His lovingkindness to me in a besieged city.
22 As for me, [r]I said in my alarm, Ps. 116:11
"I am [r]cut off from before Thine eyes"; Ps. 88:5
Nevertheless Thou didst [r]hear the voice of my supplications Ps. 18:6
When I cried to Thee.

23 O love the LORD, all you [r]His godly ones! Ps. 30:4
The LORD [r]preserves the faithful, Ps. 145:20
And fully [r]recompenses the proud doer. Deut. 32:41
24 Be strong, and let your heart take courage,
All you who [a]hope in the LORD. *wait for*

PSALM 32

A Psalm of David. A [60]Maskil.

HOW blessed is he whose transgression is forgiven,
Whose sin is covered!
2 How blessed is the man to whom the LORD does not impute iniquity,
And in whose spirit there is [r]no deceit! John 1:47

3 When I kept silent *about my sin*, [r]my body wasted away
Through my [t]groaning all day long. Ps. 31:10 • *roaring*
4 For day and night Thy hand was heavy upon me;
My vitality was drained away *as* with the fever heat of summer. [Selah.
5 I [r]acknowledged my sin to Thee, Lev. 26:40
And my iniquity I [r]did not hide; Job 31:33
I said, "I [r]will confess my transgressions to the LORD"; Ps. 38:18
And Thou didst forgive the guilt of my sin. [Selah.
6 Therefore, let everyone who is godly pray to Thee [r]in a time when Thou mayest be found;
Surely [r]in a flood of great waters they shall not reach him. Ps. 69:13 • Ps. 46:1-3
7 Thou art my hiding place;
Thou dost preserve me from trouble;
Thou dost surround me with songs of deliverance. [Selah.

[60]Possibly, *Contemplative* or *Didactic*, or *Skillful Psalm*

8 I will [r]instruct you and teach you in the way which you should go; Ps. 25:8
I will counsel you [r]with My eye upon you. Ps. 33:18
9 Do not be as the horse or as the mule which have no understanding,
Whose trappings include bit and bridle to hold them in check,
Otherwise they will not come near to you.
10 Many are the [r]sorrows of the wicked; Ps. 16:4
But he who trusts in the LORD, lovingkindness shall surround him.
11 Be glad in the LORD and rejoice you righteous ones,
And shout for joy all you who are upright in heart.

PSALM 33

SING for joy in the LORD, O you righteous ones;
Praise is [r]becoming to the upright. Ps. 92:1; 147:1
2 Give thanks to the LORD with the [r]lyre; Ps. 71:22
Sing praises to Him with a harp of ten strings.
3 Sing to Him a new song;
Play skillfully with [r]a shout of joy. Ps. 98:4
4 For the word of the LORD [r]is upright; Ps. 19:8
And all His work is *done* [r]in faithfulness. Ps. 119:90
5 He [r]loves righteousness and justice; Ps. 11:7; 37:28
The earth is full of the lovingkindness of the LORD.
6 By the word of the LORD the heavens were made,
And by the breath of His mouth all their host.
7 He gathers the waters of the sea together as a heap;
He lays up the deeps in storehouses.
8 Let [r]all the earth fear the LORD;
Let all the inhabitants of the world [r]stand in awe of Him. Ps. 67:7 • Ps. 96:9
9 For [r]He spoke, and it was done; Gen. 1:3; Ps. 148:5
He commanded, and it [a]stood fast. *stood forth*
10 The LORD nullifies the counsel of the nations;
He frustrates the plans of the peoples.
11 The counsel of the LORD stands forever,
The plans of His heart from generation to generation.
12 Blessed is the nation whose God is the LORD,
The people whom He has [r]chosen for His own inheritance. Ex. 19:5
13 The LORD looks from heaven;
He sees all the sons of men;
14 From [r]His dwelling place He looks out
On all the inhabitants of the earth, 1 Kin. 8:39, 43
15 He who [r]fashions the hearts of them all, Job 10:8
He who [r]understands all their works. 2 Chr. 16:9
16 The king is not saved by a mighty army;
A warrior is not delivered by great strength.

17 A [r]horse is a false hope for
victory; Ps. 20:7; 147:10
Nor does it deliver anyone by
its great strength.

18 Behold, the eye of the LORD
is on those who fear Him,
On those who hope for His
lovingkindness,
19 To [r]deliver their soul from
death, Ps. 56:13
And to keep them alive [r]in
famine. Job 5:20
20 Our soul waits for the LORD;
He is our help and our shield.
21 For our [r]heart rejoices in
Him,
Because we trust in His holy
name. Ps. 13:5; 28:7
22 Let Thy lovingkindness, O
LORD, be upon us,
According as we have [a]hoped
in Thee. *waited for*

PSALM 34

A Psalm of David when he feigned madness before Abimelech, who drove him away and he departed.

I WILL [r]bless the LORD at all
times; Eph. 5:20
His praise shall continually
be in my mouth.
2 My soul shall [r]make its boast
in the LORD; Ps. 44:8
The [r]humble shall hear it and
rejoice. Ps. 69:32
3 O magnify the LORD with me,
And let us [r]exalt His name together.
Ps. 18:46

4 I sought the LORD, and He
answered me,
And [r]delivered me from all
my fears. Ps. 34:6, 17, 19
5 They [r]looked to Him and
were radiant, Ps. 36:9
And their faces shall [r]never
be ashamed. Ps. 25:3
6 This poor man cried and the
LORD heard him,
And saved him out of all his
troubles.
7 The [r]angel of the LORD encamps
around those who
fear Him,
And rescues them. Ps. 91:11

8 O [r]taste and see that the LORD
is good; Ps. 119:103
How blessed is the man who
takes refuge in Him!
9 O fear the LORD, you [r]His
saints; Ps. 31:23
For to those who fear Him,
there is no want.
10 The young lions do lack and
suffer hunger;
But they who seek the LORD
shall not be in want of
any good thing.
11 [r]Come, you children, listen to
me; Ps. 66:16
I will teach you [r]the fear of
the LORD. Ps. 111:10
12 Who is the man who desires
life,
And loves *length of* days that
he may see good?
13 Keep your tongue from evil,
And your lips from speaking
[r]deceit. 1 Pet. 2:22
14 Depart from evil, and do
good;
Seek peace, and pursue it.

15 The eyes of the LORD are
toward the righteous,
And His ears are *open* to
their cry.
16 The face of the LORD is
against evildoers,
To cut off the memory of
them from the earth.

17 *The righteous* [r]cry and the LORD hears,
And delivers them out of all their troubles. Ps. 34:6
18 The LORD [r]is near to the brokenhearted, Ps. 145:18
And saves those who are [61]crushed in spirit.

19 Many are the afflictions of the righteous;
But the LORD delivers him out of them all.
20 He keeps all his bones;
Not one of them is broken.
21 Evil shall slay the wicked;
And those who hate the righteous will be [a]condemned. *held guilty*
22 The LORD redeems the soul of His servants;
And none of those who take refuge in Him will be condemned.

PSALM 35

A Psalm of David.

CONTEND, O LORD, with those who contend with me;
Fight against those who [r]fight against me. Ps. 56:2
2 Take hold of [62]buckler and shield,
And rise up for my help.
3 Draw also the spear and the battle-axe to meet those who pursue me;
Say to my soul, "I am [r]your salvation." Ps. 62:2
4 Let those be [r]ashamed and dishonored who seek my [a]life; Ps. 70:2 • *soul*
Let those be turned back and humiliated who devise evil against me.

[61]Or, *contrite* [62]I.e., small shield

5 Let them be [r]like chaff before the wind, Job 21:18
With the angel of the LORD driving *them* on.
6 Let their way be dark and [r]slippery, Ps. 73:18
With the angel of the LORD pursuing them.
7 For without cause they hid their net for me;
Without cause they dug a pit for my soul.
8 Let destruction come upon him unawares;
And [r]let the net which he hid catch himself; Ps. 9:15
Into that very [r]destruction let him fall. Ps. 73:18

9 And my soul shall [r]rejoice in the LORD; Is. 61:10
It shall exult in His salvation.
10 All my bones will say, "LORD, who is like Thee,
Who delivers the afflicted from him who is too strong for him,
And [r]the afflicted and the needy from him who robs him?" Ps. 37:14; 109:16
11 Malicious witnesses rise up;
They ask me of things that I do not know.
12 They repay me evil for good,
To the bereavement of my soul.
13 But as for me, when they were sick, my clothing was sackcloth;
I [r]humbled my soul with fasting; Ps. 69:10
And my prayer kept returning to my bosom.
14 I went about as though it were my friend or brother;

I bowed down[a]mourning, as one who sorrows for a mother. *dressed in black*
15 But at my [63]stumbling they rejoiced, and gathered themselves together;
The [a]smiters whom I did not know gathered together against me, *smitten ones*
They [t]slandered me without ceasing. *tore*
16 Like godless jesters at a feast,
They [r]gnashed at me with their teeth. Job 16:9

17 Lord, [r]how long wilt Thou look on? Ps. 13:1
Rescue my soul [r]from their ravages, Ps. 35:7
My only *life* from the lions.
18 I will give Thee thanks in the great congregation;
I will [r]praise Thee among a mighty throng. Ps. 22:25
19 Do not let those who are wrongfully my enemies rejoice over me;
Neither let those who hate me without cause [a]wink maliciously. *wink the eye*
20 For they do not speak peace,
But they devise deceitful words against those who are quiet in the land.
21 And they opened their mouth wide against me;
They said, "Aha, aha, our eyes have seen it!"

22 Thou hast seen it, O LORD, do not keep silent;
O Lord, [r]do not be far from me. Ps. 10:1; 22:11
23 Stir up Thyself, and awake to my right,
And to my cause, my God and my Lord.
24 Judge me, O LORD my God, according to Thy righteousness;
And [r]do not let them rejoice over me. Ps. 35:19
25 Do not let them say in their heart, "Aha, our desire!"
Do not let them say, "We have swallowed him up!"
26 Let [r]those be ashamed and humiliated altogether who rejoice at my distress; Ps. 40:14
Let those be [r]clothed with shame and dishonor who [r]magnify themselves over me. Ps. 109:29 • Job 19:5

27 Let them [r]shout for joy and rejoice, who favor my vindication; Ps. 32:11
And let them say continually, "The LORD be magnified,
Who delights in the prosperity of His servant."
28 And my tongue shall declare Thy righteousness
And Thy praise all day long.

PSALM 36

For the choir director. *A Psalm* of David the servant of the LORD.

TRANSGRESSION speaks to the ungodly within his heart;
There is [r]no fear of God before his eyes. Rom. 3:18
2 For[a]it flatters him in his *own* eyes, *he flatters himself*
Concerning the discovery of his iniquity *and* the hatred *of it*.

[63]Or, *limping*

3 The words of his mouth are wickedness and deceit;
He has ʳceased to be wise *and* to do good. Ps. 94:8
4 He ʳplans wickedness upon his bed; Prov. 4:16
He sets himself on a ʳpath that is not good; Is. 65:2
He does not despise evil.

5 Thy lovingkindness, O LORD, extends to the heavens,
Thy faithfulness *reaches* to the skies.
6 Thy righteousness is like the mountains of God;
Thy ʳjudgments are *like* a great deep.
O LORD, Thou preservest man and beast. Job 11:8
7 How precious is Thy lovingkindness, O God!
And the children of men ʳtake refuge in the shadow of Thy wings. Ruth 2:12
8 They drink their fill of the abundance of Thy house;
And Thou dost give them to drink of the ʳriver of Thy delights. Job 20:17
9 For with Thee is the ʳfountain of life; Jer. 2:13
In Thy light we see light.

10 O continue Thy lovingkindness to ʳthose who know Thee, Jer. 22:16
And Thy ʳrighteousness to the upright in heart. Ps. 24:5
11 Let not the foot of pride come upon me,
And let not the hand of the wicked drive me away.
12 There the doers of iniquity have fallen;
They have been thrust down and cannot rise.

PSALM 37

A Psalm of David.

DO not fret because of evildoers,
Be not ʳenvious toward wrongdoers. Ps. 73:3
2 For they will ʳwither quickly like the grass, Job 14:2
And fade like the green herb.
3 ʳTrust in the LORD, and do good; Ps. 62:8
Dwell in the land and [64]cultivate faithfulness.
4 Delight yourself in the LORD;
And He will give you the desires of your heart.
5 Commit your way to the LORD,
Trust also in Him, and He will do it.
6 And He will bring forth ʳyour righteousness as the light, Ps. 97:11; Is. 58:8, 10
And your judgment ʳas the noonday. Job 11:17

7 [65]Rest in the LORD and wait [66]patiently for Him;
Do not fret because of him who prospers in his way,
Because of the man who carries out wicked schemes.
8 Cease from anger, and ʳforsake wrath;
Do not fret, *it leads* only to evildoing. Eph. 4:31
9 For evildoers will be cut off,
But those who wait for the LORD, they will ʳinherit the land. Ps. 25:13
10 Yet ʳa little while and the wicked man will be no more; Job 24:24

[64]Or, *feed securely*, or, *feed on His faithfulness* [65]Or, *Be still* [66]Or, *longingly*

And you will look carefully
for [r]his place, and he will
not be *there*. Job 7:10
11 But [r]the humble will inherit
the land, Matt. 5:5
And will delight themselves
in abundant prosperity.

12 The wicked [r]plots against the
righteous, Ps. 31:13, 20
And [r]gnashes at him with his
teeth. Ps. 35:16
13 The Lord laughs at him;
For He sees [r]his day is coming. 1 Sam. 26:10
14 The wicked have drawn the
sword and [r]bent their
bow, Ps. 11:2; Lam 2:4
To cast down the [r]afflicted
and the needy, Ps. 35:10
To [r]slay those who are upright in conduct. Ps. 11:2
15 Their sword will enter their
own heart,
And their [r]bows will be broken. 1 Sam. 2:4

16 Better is the little of the
righteous
Than the abundance of many
wicked.
17 For the arms of the wicked
will be broken;
But the LORD [r]sustains the
righteous. Ps. 71:6
18 The LORD knows the days of
the [t]blameless;
And their inheritance will be
forever. *complete*
19 They will not be ashamed in
the time of evil;
And [r]in the days of famine
they will have abun-
dance. Job 5:20; Ps. 33:19
20 But the wicked will perish;
And the enemies of the LORD
will be like the [67]glory of
the pastures,
They vanish—like smoke
they vanish away.
21 The wicked borrows and
does not pay back,
But the righteous [r]is gracious
and gives. Ps. 112:5, 9
22 For those blessed by Him
will inherit the land;
But those [r]cursed by Him will
be cut off. Job 5:3

23 The steps of a man are established by the LORD;
And He delights in his way.
24 When he falls, he shall not be
hurled headlong;
Because the LORD is the One
who holds his hand.
25 I have been young, and now I
am old;
Yet [r]I have not seen the righteous forsaken,
Or his [t]descendants begging
bread. Ps. 37:28 • *seed*
26 All day long [r]he is gracious
and lends;
And his [t]descendants are a
blessing. Deut. 15:8 • *seed*

27 Depart from evil, and do
good,
So you will abide forever.
28 For the LORD loves justice,
And [r]does not forsake His
godly ones; Ps. 37:25
They are preserved forever;
But the descendants of the
wicked will be cut off.
29 The righteous will [r]inherit the
land, Ps. 37:9; Prov. 2:21
And dwell in it forever.
30 The mouth of the righteous
utters wisdom,

[67]I.e., flowers

And his tongue [r]speaks justice. Ps. 101:1; 119:13
31 The [r]law of his God is in his
heart; Deut. 6:6; Ps. 40:8
His steps do not slip.
32 The [r]wicked spies upon the
righteous, Ps. 10:8
And seeks to kill him.
33 The LORD will [r]not leave him
in his hand, Ps. 31:8
Or let him be condemned
when he is judged.
34 Wait for the LORD, and keep
His way,
And He will exalt you to inherit the land;
When the [r]wicked are cut off,
you will see it. Ps. 52:5, 6
35 I have [r]seen a violent, wicked
man
Spreading himself like a luxuriant [t]tree in its native
soil. Job 5:3 • *native*
36 Then he passed away, and lo,
he was no more;
I sought for him, but he
could not be found.
37 Mark the blameless man, and
behold the upright;
For the man of peace will
have a posterity.
38 But transgressors will be altogether destroyed;
The [t]posterity of the wicked
will be cut off. *end*
39 But the salvation of the righteous is from the LORD;
He is their strength [r]in time of
trouble. Ps. 9:9; 37:19
40 And the LORD helps them,
and delivers them;
He delivers them from the
wicked, and saves them,
Because they take refuge in
Him.

PSALM 38

A Psalm of David, for a memorial.

O LORD, [r]rebuke me not in Thy
wrath;
And chasten me not in Thy
burning anger. Ps. 6:1
2 For Thine arrows have sunk
deep into me,
And Thy hand has pressed
down on me.
3 There is [r]no soundness in my
flesh because of Thine indignation; Is. 1:6
There is no health in my
bones because of my sin.
4 For my iniquities are gone
over my head;
As a heavy burden they
weigh too much for me.
5 My [a]wounds grow foul *and*
fester.
Because of my folly, *stripes*
6 I am bent over and greatly
bowed down;
I go mourning all day long.
7 For my loins are filled with
[r]burning; Ps. 102:3
And there is [r]no soundness in
my flesh. Ps. 38:3
8 I am benumbed and [a]badly
crushed; *greatly*
I groan because of the [t]agita-
tion of my heart. *growling*
9 Lord, all my desire is [a]before
Thee; known *to Thee*
And my [r]sighing is not hidden
from Thee. Ps. 6:6; 102:5
10 My heart throbs, my strength
fails me;
And the light of my eyes,
even [t]that has gone from
me. *they have*
11 My [a]loved ones and my
friends stand aloof from
my plague; *lovers*

And my kinsmen [r]stand afar
off. Luke 23:49
12 Those who seek my life lay
snares *for me;*
And those who seek to injure
me have [t]threatened destruction,
And they devise treachery all
day long. *spoken*
13 But I, like a deaf man, do not
hear;
And I am like a [r]dumb man
who does not open his
mouth. Ps. 39:2, 9
14 Yes, I am like a man who
does not hear,
And in whose mouth are no
arguments.
15 For I hope in Thee, O LORD;
Thou [r]wilt answer, O Lord my
God. Ps. 17:6
16 For I said, "May they not rejoice over me,
Who, when my foot slips,
would magnify themselves against me."
17 For I am ready to fall,
And my [68]sorrow is continually before me.
18 For I confess my iniquity;
I am full of [r]anxiety because
of my sin. 2 Cor. 7:9, 10
19 But my enemies are vigorous
and [69]strong;
And many are those who
hate me wrongfully.
20 And those who [r]repay evil for
good, Ps. 35:12
They oppose me, because I
follow what is good.
21 Do not forsake me, O LORD;
O my God, [r]do not be far from
me! Ps. 22:19; 35:22

[68]Lit., *pain* [69]Or, *numerous*

22 Make haste to help me,
O Lord, my salvation!

PSALM 39

For the choir director, for Jeduthun.
A Psalm of David.

I SAID, "I will guard my ways,
That I [r]may not sin with my
tongue; Job 2:10
I will guard [r]my mouth as
with a muzzle,
While the wicked are in my
presence." Ps. 141:3
2 I was dumb and silent,
I [70]refrained *even* from good;
And my [68]sorrow grew worse.
3 My heart was hot within me;
While I was musing the fire
burned;
Then I spoke with my
tongue:
4 "LORD, make me to know [r]my
end, Job 6:11; Ps. 90:12
And what is the extent of my
days,
Let me know how [r]transient I
am. Ps. 78:39; 103:14
5 "Behold, Thou hast made my
days *as* handbreadths,
And my lifetime as nothing
in Thy sight,
Surely every man at his best
is a mere breath. [Selah.
6 "Surely every man walks
about as [71]a phantom;
Surely they make an [r]uproar
for nothing; Ps. 127:2
He [r]amasses *riches,* and does
not know who will gather
them. Ps. 49:10

7 "And now, Lord, for what do I
wait?

[68]Lit., *pain* [70]Lit., *kept silence*
[71]Lit., *an image*

My [r]hope is in Thee. Ps. 38:15
8 "Deliver me from all my transgressions;
Make me not the [r]reproach of the foolish. Ps. 44:13
9 "I have become dumb, I do not open my mouth,
Because it is [r]Thou who hast done *it*. 2 Sam. 16:10
10 "Remove Thy plague from me;
Because of the opposition of Thy hand, I am perishing.
11 "With [r]reproofs Thou dost chasten a man for iniquity; Ezek. 5:15
Thou dost [r]consume as a moth what is precious to him; Job 13:28; Ps. 90:7
Surely every man is a mere breath. [Selah.

12 "Hear my prayer, O LORD, and give ear to my cry;
Do not be silent at my tears;
For I am [r]a stranger with Thee, Lev. 25:23
A [r]sojourner like all my fathers. Gen. 47:9
13 "Turn Thy gaze away from me, that I may [72]smile *again*,
Before I depart and am no more."

PSALM 40

For the choir director. A Psalm of David.

I WAITED [73]patiently for the LORD;
And He inclined to me, and heard my cry.
2 He brought me up out of the [r]pit of destruction, out of the miry clay; Ps. 69:2, 14
And [r]He set my feet upon a rock making my footsteps firm. Ps. 27:5
3 And He put a [r]new song in my mouth, a song of praise to our God; Ps. 32:7
Many will see and fear,
And will trust in the LORD.

4 How [r]blessed is the man who has made the LORD his trust, Ps. 34:8; 84:12
And has not turned to the proud, nor to those who lapse into falsehood.
5 Many, O LORD my God, are [r]the wonders which Thou hast done, Job 5:9
And Thy thoughts toward us;
There is none to compare with Thee;
If I would declare and speak of them,
They [r]would be too numerous to count. Ps. 71:15

6 Sacrifice and meal offering Thou hast not desired;
My ears Thou hast [74]opened;
Burnt offering and sin offering Thou hast not required.
7 Then I said, "Behold, I come;
In the scroll of the book it is written of me;
8 [r]I delight to do Thy will, O my God; John 4:34
Thy Law is within my heart."

9 I have proclaimed glad tidings of righteousness in the great congregation;
Behold, I will [r]not restrain my lips, Ps. 119:13
O LORD, Thou knowest.

[72]Or, *become cheerful* [73]Or, *intently* [74]Lit., *dug*, or possibly, *pierced*

10 I have [r]not hidden Thy righteousness within my heart; Acts 20:20, 27
I have [r]spoken of Thy faithfulness and Thy salvation; Ps. 89:1
I have not concealed Thy lovingkindness and Thy truth from the great congregation.

11 Thou, O LORD, wilt not withhold Thy compassion from me;
Thy [r]lovingkindness and Thy truth will continually preserve me. Ps. 43:3; 57:3
12 For evils beyond number have surrounded me;
My [r]iniquities have overtaken me, so that I am not able to see; Ps. 38:4; 65:3
They are [r]more numerous than the hairs of my head; Ps. 69:4
And my heart has failed me.

13 [r]Be pleased, O LORD, to deliver me; Ps. 70:1
Make [r]haste, O LORD, to help me. Ps. 22:19; 71:12
14 Let those be ashamed and humiliated together
Who seek my [75]life to destroy it;
Let those be turned back and dishonored
Who delight [76]in my hurt.
15 Let those be appalled because of their shame
Who say to me, "Aha, aha!"
16 Let all who seek Thee rejoice and be glad in Thee;
Let those who love Thy salvation say continually,
"The LORD be magnified!"
17 Since [r]I am afflicted and needy, Ps. 70:5; 86:1
[a]Let the Lord be mindful of me; *The Lord is mindful*
Thou art my help and my deliverer;
Do not delay, O my God.

PSALM 41

For the choir director. A Psalm of David.

HOW blessed is he who considers the helpless;
The LORD will deliver him in a day of trouble.
2 The LORD will protect him, and keep him alive,
And he shall be called blessed upon the earth;
And do not give him over to the desire of his enemies.
3 The LORD will sustain him upon his sickbed;
In his illness, Thou dost [77]restore him to health.

4 As for me, I said, "O LORD, be gracious to me;
Heal my soul, for I have sinned against Thee."
5 My enemies [r]speak evil against me,
"When will he die, and his name perish?" Ps. 38:12
6 And when he comes to see *me*, he speaks falsehood;
His heart gathers wickedness to itself;
When he goes outside, he tells it.
7 All who hate me whisper together against me;
Against me they [r]devise my hurt, *saying*, Ps. 56:5

[75]Or, *soul* [76]Or, *to injure me* [77]Lit., *turn all his bed*

8 "A wicked thing is poured out [a]upon him, *within*
That when he lies down, he will not rise up again."
9 Even my close friend, in whom I trusted,
Who ate my bread,
Has lifted up his heel against me.

10 But Thou, O LORD, be gracious to me, and [r]raise me up, Ps. 3:3
That I may repay them.
11 By this I know that Thou art pleased with me,
Because [r]my enemy does not shout in triumph over me. Ps. 25:2
12 As for me, Thou dost uphold me in my integrity,
And Thou dost set me in Thy presence forever.

13 Blessed be the LORD, the God of Israel,
From everlasting to everlasting.
Amen, and Amen.

BOOK 2

PSALM 42

For the choir director.
A Maskil of the sons of Korah.

As the deer [78]pants for the water brooks,
So my soul pants for Thee, O God.
2 My soul [r]thirsts for God, for the living God; Ps. 63:1
When shall I come and appear before God?
3 My [r]tears have been my food day and night, Ps. 80:5
While *they* [r]say to me all day long, "Where is your God?" Ps. 79:10
4 These things I remember, and I [r]pour out my soul within me. 1 Sam. 1:15
For I [r]used to go along with the throng *and* lead them in procession to the house of God, Ps. 55:14
With the voice of [r]joy and thanksgiving, a multitude keeping festival. Ps. 100:4

5 Why are you [a]in despair, O my soul? *sunk down*
And *why* have you become disturbed within me?
[a]Hope in God, for I shall again praise Him *Wait for*
For the help of His presence.
6 O my God, my soul is in despair within me;
Therefore I [r]remember Thee from the land of the Jordan, Ps. 61:2
And the peaks of Hermon, from Mount Mizar.
7 Deep calls to deep at the sound of Thy waterfalls;
All Thy [r]breakers and Thy waves have rolled over me. Ps. 69:1, 2; 88:7
8 The LORD will [r]command His lovingkindness in the daytime; Ps. 57:3; 133:3
And His song will be with me [r]in the night, Job 35:10
A prayer to [r]the God of my life. Eccl. 5:18; 8:15

9 I will say to God [r]my rock, "Why hast Thou forgotten me? Ps. 18:2
Why do I go [r]mourning because of the oppression of the enemy?" Ps. 38:6

[78] Lit., *longs for*

10 As a shattering of my bones,
my adversaries revile me,
While they [r]say to me all day
long, "Where is your
God?" Ps. 42:3; Joel 2:17
11 Why are you [a]in despair, O
my soul? *sunk down*
And why have you become
disturbed within me?
[a]Hope in God, for I shall yet
praise Him, *wait for*
The help of my countenance,
and my God.

PSALM 43

VINDICATE me, O God, and
plead my case against an
ungodly nation;
O deliver me from the deceitful and unjust man!
2 For Thou art the [r]God of my
strength; why hast Thou
rejected me? Ps. 18:1
Why do I go [r]mourning because of the oppression
of the enemy? Ps. 42:9

3 O send out Thy light and Thy
truth, let them lead me;
Let them bring me to Thy
[r]holy hill, Ps. 2:6; 3:4
And to Thy dwelling places.
4 Then I will go to [r]the altar of
God, Ps. 26:6
To God my exceeding joy;
And upon the [r]lyre I shall
praise Thee, O God, my
God. Ps. 33:2; 49:4

5 Why are you [a]in despair, O
my soul? *sunk down*
And why are you disturbed
within me?
Hope in God, for I shall [a]again
praise Him, *still*
The help of my countenance,
and my God.

PSALM 44

For the choir director.
A Maskil of the sons of Korah.

O GOD, we have heard with our
ears,
Our fathers have told us,
The [r]work that Thou didst in
their days, Ps. 78:12
In the days of old.
2 Thou with Thine own hand
didst [r]drive out the nations; Josh. 3:10
Then Thou didst plant them;
Thou didst afflict the peoples,
Then Thou didst [r]spread them
abroad. Ps. 80:9-11
3 For by their own sword they
did not possess the land;
And their own arm did not
save them;
But Thy right hand, and
Thine arm, and the light
of Thy presence,
For Thou didst favor them.

4 Thou art my King, O God;
Command [t]victories for Jacob. *salvation*
5 Through Thee we will push
back our adversaries;
Through Thy name we will
trample down those who
rise up against us.
6 For I will [r]not trust in my
bow, 1 Sam. 17:47
Nor will my sword save me.
7 But Thou hast saved us from
our adversaries,
And Thou hast put to shame
those who hate us.
8 In God we have [r]boasted all
day long, Ps. 34:2

And we will give thanks to
Thy name forever.
[Selah.

9 Yet Thou [r]hast rejected *us*
and brought us to dishonor, Ps. 43:2; 60:1, 10
And [r]dost not go out with our
armies. Ps. 60:10; 108:11
10 Thou dost cause us to turn
back from the adversary;
And those who hate us [r]have
taken spoil for themselves. Ps. 89:41
11 Thou dost give us as sheep [t]to
be eaten, *for food*
And hast [r]scattered us among
the nations. Lev. 26:33
12 Thou dost sell Thy people
[t]cheaply,
And hast not [79]profited by
their sale. *for no wealth*
13 Thou dost make us a reproach to our neighbors,
A scoffing and a derision to
those around us.
14 Thou dost make us a byword
among the nations,
A [r]laughingstock among the
peoples. 2 Kin. 19:21
15 All day long my dishonor is
before me,
And my humiliation has
overwhelmed me,
16 Because of the voice of him
who [r]reproaches and reviles, Ps. 74:10
Because of the presence of
the [r]enemy and the
avenger. Ps. 8:2

17 All this has come upon us,
but we have [r]not forgotten Thee, Ps. 78:7; 119:61
And we have not [r]dealt
falsely with Thy covenant. Ps. 78:57
18 Our heart has not [r]turned
back, Ps. 78:57
And our steps have not deviated from Thy way,
19 Yet Thou hast crushed us in
a place of jackals,
And covered us with the
shadow of death.

20 If we had [r]forgotten the name
of our God, Ps. 78:11
Or extended our [t]hands to a
strange god; *palms*
21 Would not God find this out?
For He knows the secrets of
the heart.
22 But for Thy sake we are
killed all day long;
We are considered as sheep
to be slaughtered.
23 Arouse Thyself, why dost
Thou sleep, O Lord?
Awake, [r]do not reject us forever. Ps. 77:7
24 Why dost Thou [r]hide Thy
face, Job 13:24
And forget our affliction and
our oppression?
25 For our soul has sunk down
into the dust;
Our body cleaves to the
earth.
26 Rise up, be our help,
And redeem us for the sake
of Thy lovingkindness.

PSALM 45

For the choir director; according to the [80]Shoshannim. A Maskil of the sons of Korah. A Song of Love.

MY heart [81]overflows with a good
theme;

[79] Or, *set a high price on them*

[80] Possibly, *Lilies* [81] Lit., *is astir*

I [t]address my verses to the King; *am saying*
My tongue is the pen of [r]a ready writer. Ezra 7:6
2 Thou art fairer than the sons of men;
[r]Grace is poured upon Thy lips; Luke 4:22
Therefore God has [r]blessed Thee forever. Ps. 21:6

3 Gird Thy sword on *Thy* thigh, O Mighty One,
In Thy splendor and Thy majesty!
4 And in Thy majesty ride on victoriously,
For the cause of truth and [r]meekness *and* righteousness; Zeph. 2:3
Let Thy right hand teach Thee awesome things.
5 Thine arrows are sharp;
The peoples fall under Thee;
Thine arrows are in the heart of the King's enemies.

6 Thy throne, O God, is forever and ever;
A scepter of [r]uprightness is the scepter of Thy kingdom. Ps. 98:9
7 Thou hast [r]loved righteousness, and hated wickedness; Ps. 11:7; 33:5
Therefore God, Thy God, has [r]anointed Thee
With the oil of joy above Thy fellows. Ps. 2:2
8 All Thy garments are fragrant with myrrh and aloes *and* cassia;
Out of ivory palaces [r]stringed instruments have made Thee glad. Ps. 150:4
9 Kings' daughters are among Thy noble ladies;
At Thy right hand stands the queen in gold from Ophir.

10 Listen, O daughter, give attention and incline your ear;
Forget your people and your father's house;
11 Then the King will desire your beauty;
Because He is your Lord, bow down to Him.
12 And the daughter of Tyre *will come* with a gift;
The rich among the people will entreat your favor.

13 The King's daughter is all glorious within;
Her clothing is [r]interwoven with gold. Ex. 39:2, 3
14 She will be led to the King in embroidered work;
The [r]virgins, her companions who follow her, Ps. 45:9
Will be brought to Thee.
15 They will be led forth with gladness and rejoicing;
They will enter into the King's palace.

16 In place of your fathers will be your sons;
You shall make them princes in all the earth.
17 I will cause [r]Thy name to be remembered in all generations; Mal. 1:11
Therefore the peoples [r]will give Thee thanks forever and ever. Ps. 138:4

PSALM 46

For the choir director. A *Psalm* of the sons of Korah, [82]set to Alamoth. A Song.

GOD is our refuge and strength,
[83]A very present help in trouble.
2 Therefore we will [r]not fear, though the earth should change, Ps. 23:4; 27:1
And though [r]the mountains slip into the heart of the [t]sea; Ps. 18:7 · *seas*
3 Though its [r]waters roar *and* foam, Ps. 93:3, 4
Though the mountains quake at its swelling pride. [Selah.

4 There is a [r]river whose streams make glad the city of God,
The holy dwelling places of the Most High. Ps. 36:8
5 God is in the midst of her, she will not be moved;
God will help her when morning dawns.
6 The nations made an uproar, the kingdoms tottered;
He [t]raised His voice, the earth melted. *gave forth*
7 The LORD of hosts is with us;
The God of Jacob is our stronghold. [Selah.

8 Come, [r]behold the works of the LORD, Ps. 66:5
Who has wrought desolations in the earth.
9 He makes wars to cease to the end of the earth;
He breaks the bow and cuts the spear in two;
He [r]burns the chariots with fire. Is. 9:5; Ezek. 39:9
10 "Cease *striving* and [r]know that I am God; Ps. 100:3
I will be [r]exalted among the nations, I will be exalted in the earth." Is. 2:11, 17
11 The LORD of hosts is with us;
The God of Jacob is our stronghold. [Selah.

[82] Possibly, *for soprano voices*
[83] Or, *Abundantly available for help*

PSALM 47

For the choir director.
A Psalm of the sons of Korah.

O CLAP your hands, all peoples;
Shout to God with the voice of [a]joy. *a ringing cry*
2 For the LORD Most High is to be [r]feared, Deut. 7:21
A [r]great King over all the earth. Mal. 1:14
3 He [r]subdues peoples under us, Ps. 18:47
And nations under our feet.
4 He chooses our [r]inheritance for us, 1 Pet. 1:4
The glory of Jacob whom He loves. [Selah.

5 God has [r]ascended with a shout, Ps. 68:18
The LORD, with the [r]sound of a trumpet. Ps. 98:6
6 Sing praises to God, sing praises;
Sing praises to [r]our King, sing praises. Ps. 89:18
7 For God is the [r]King of all the earth; Zech. 14:9
Sing praises [r]with a skillful psalm. 1 Cor. 14:15
8 God reigns over the nations,
God sits on His holy throne.

9 The princes of the people
have assembled themselves
as the people of
the God of Abraham;
For the [r]shields of the earth
belong to God; Ps. 89:18
He is [r]highly exalted. Ps. 97:9

PSALM 48

A Song; a Psalm of the sons of Korah.

GREAT is the LORD, and greatly
to be praised,
In the city of our God, His
holy mountain.
2 Beautiful in elevation, the joy
of the whole earth,
Is Mount Zion *in* the far
north,
The city of the great King.
3 God, in her palaces,
Has made Himself known as
a [r]stronghold. Ps. 46:7

4 For, lo, the [r]kings assembled
themselves, 2 Sam. 10:6-19
They passed by together.
5 They saw *it*, then they were
amazed;
They were [r]terrified, they fled
in alarm. Ex. 15:15
6 Panic seized them there,
Anguish, as of [r]a woman in
childbirth. Is. 13:8
7 With the east wind
Thou [r]dost break the ships of
Tarshish. 1 Kin. 22:48
8 As we have heard, so have
we seen
In the city of the LORD of
hosts, in the city of our
God;
God will establish her forever.
[Selah.

9 We have thought on Thy
lovingkindness, O God,
In the midst of Thy temple.
10 As is Thy name, O God,
So is Thy [r]praise to the ends
of the earth; Ps. 65:1, 2
Thy [r]right hand is full of
righteousness. Is. 41:10
11 Let Mount Zion be glad,
Let the [r]daughters of Judah
rejoice, Ps. 97:8
Because of Thy judgments.
12 Walk about Zion, and go
around her;
Count her [r]towers; Neh. 3:1
13 Consider her ramparts;
Go through her palaces;
That you may tell *it* to the
next generation.
14 For such is God,
Our God forever and ever;
He will guide us [84]until death.

PSALM 49

For the choir director.
A Psalm of the sons of Korah.

HEAR this, all peoples;
Give ear, all [r]inhabitants of
the world, Ps. 33:8
2 Both [r]low and high, Ps. 62:9
Rich and poor together.
3 My mouth will [r]speak wisdom;
Ps. 37:30
And the meditation of my
heart *will be* [r]understanding.
Ps. 119:130
4 I will incline my ear to [r]a
proverb; Ps. 78:2
I will [t]express my riddle on
the harp. *open up*

5 Why should I [r]fear in days of
adversity, Ps. 23:4; 27:1

[84] Some mss. and the Gr. read *forever*

When the iniquity of my [t]foes
surrounds me, *supplanters*
6 Even those who [r]trust in their
wealth, Job 31:24
And boast in the abundance
of their riches?
7 No man can by any means
redeem *his* brother,
Or give to God a [r]ransom for
him— Job 36:18, 19
8 For the redemption of [t]his
soul is costly,
And he should cease *trying*
forever— *their*
9 That he should [r]live on eter-
nally;
That he should not [85]undergo
decay. Ps. 22:29

10 For he sees *that even* [r]wise
men die; Eccl. 2:16
The [r]stupid and the senseless
alike perish, Ps. 92:6; 94:8
And [r]leave their wealth to
others. Ps. 39:6; Eccl. 2:18
11 Their [86]inner thought is, *that*
their houses are forever,
And their dwelling places to
all generations;
They have called their lands
after their own names.
12 But man in *his* [t]pomp will not
endure;
He is like the beasts that [t]per-
ish. *honor • are destroyed*

13 This is the [r]way of those who
are foolish, Jer. 17:11
And of those after them who
approve their words.
[Selah.
14 As sheep they are appointed
[r]for Sheol; Ps. 9:17
Death shall be their shepherd;
And the [r]upright shall rule
over them in the morn-
ing; Dan. 7:18
And their form shall be for
Sheol to consume,
So that they have no habitation.
15 But God will redeem my soul
from the power of Sheol;
For He will receive me.
[Selah.

16 Do not be afraid [r]when a man
becomes rich,
When the [87]glory of his house
is increased; Ps. 37:7
17 For when he dies he will carry nothing away;
His [87]glory will not descend
after him.
18 Though while he lives he
congratulates himself—
And though *men* praise you
when you do well for
yourself—
19 He shall [r]go to the generation
of his fathers; Gen. 15:15
They shall never see [r]the
light. Job 33:30; Ps. 56:13
20 Man in *his* pomp, yet without
understanding,
Is like the beasts that perish.

PSALM 50

A Psalm of Asaph.

THE Mighty One, God, the LORD,
has spoken,
And summoned the earth
[r]from the rising of the sun
to its setting. Ps. 113:3
2 Out of Zion, [r]the perfection of
beauty, Ps. 48:2
God has shone forth.

[85]Or, *see corruption* or *the pit*
[86]Some versions read *graves are their houses*
[87]Or, *wealth*

3 May our God ^r^come and not keep silence; Ps. 96:13
Fire devours before Him,
And it is very ^r^tempestuous around Him. Ps. 18:12, 13
4 He ^r^summons the heavens above,
And the earth, to judge His people: Deut. 4:26; 31:28
5 "Gather My godly ones to Me,
Those who have made a ^r^covenant with Me by sacrifice." Ex. 24:7; 2 Chr. 6:11
6 And the heavens declare His righteousness,
For God Himself is judge. [Selah.

7 "Hear, O My people, and I will speak;
O Israel, I will testify[a] against you;
I am God, your God. *to*
8 "I do ^r^not reprove you for your sacrifices, Ps. 40:6; 51:16
And your burnt offerings are continually before Me.
9 "I shall take no ^r^young bull out of your house,
Nor male goats out of your folds. Ps. 69:31
10 "For ^r^every beast of the forest is Mine,
The cattle on a thousand hills. Ps. 104:24
11 "I know every ^r^bird of the mountains, Matt. 6:26
And everything that moves in the field is [88]Mine.
12 "If I were hungry, I would not tell you;
For the world is Mine, and ^t^all it contains. *its fulness*
13 "Shall I eat the flesh of bulls,
Or drink the blood of male goats?
14 "Offer to God ^r^a sacrifice of thanksgiving, Ps. 27:6
And ^r^pay your vows to the Most High; Num. 30:2
15 And ^r^call upon Me in the day of trouble; Ps. 91:15
I shall rescue you, and you will honor Me."

16 But to the wicked God says,
"What right have you to tell of My statutes,
And to take ^r^My covenant in your mouth? Is. 29:13
17 "For you hate discipline,
And you ^r^cast My words behind you. 1 Kin. 14:9
18 "When you see a thief, you are pleased with him,
And ^t^you associate with adulterers. *your part is with*
19 "You ^t^let your mouth loose in evil, *send*
And your ^r^tongue frames deceit. Ps. 36:3; 52:2
20 "You sit and ^r^speak against your brother;
You slander your own mother's son. Job 19:18
21 "These things you have done, and I kept silence;
You thought that I was just like you;
I will ^r^reprove you, and state *the case* in order before your eyes. Ps. 90:8

22 "Now consider this, you who ^r^forget God, Job 8:13
Lest I tear *you* in pieces, and there be none to deliver.
23 "He who offers a sacrifice of thanksgiving honors Me;

[88]Or, *in My mind*

And to him who [t]orders *his* way *aright*
I shall [r]show the salvation of God." *sets* • Ps. 91:16

PSALM 51

For the choir director. A Psalm of David, when Nathan the prophet came to him, after he had gone in to Bathsheba.

BE gracious to me, O God, according to Thy lovingkindness;
According to the greatness of Thy compassion blot out my transgressions.
2 Wash me thoroughly from my iniquity,
And cleanse me from my sin.
3 For [a]I know my transgressions,
And my sin is ever before me. *I myself know*
4 Against Thee, Thee only, I have sinned,
And done what is [r]evil in Thy sight, Luke 15:21
So that Thou [89]art justified when Thou dost speak,
And [t]blameless when Thou dost judge. *pure*
5 Behold, I was [r]brought forth in iniquity,
And in sin my mother conceived me. Job 14:4
6 Behold, Thou dost desire truth in the [a]innermost being, *inward parts*
And in the hidden part Thou wilt [r]make me know wisdom. Prov. 2:6; Eccl. 2:26
7 Purify me with hyssop, and I shall be clean;
Wash me, and I shall be whiter than snow.
8 Make me to hear [r]joy and gladness, Is. 35:10
Let the bones which Thou hast broken rejoice.
9 Hide Thy face from my sins,
And blot out all my iniquities.
10 Create [t]in me a clean heart, O God,
And renew [a]a steadfast spirit within me. *for* • *an upright*
11 Do not cast me away from Thy presence,
And do not take Thy [r]Holy Spirit from me. Is. 63:10
12 Restore to me the [r]joy of Thy salvation, Ps. 13:5
And sustain me with a [r]willing spirit. Ps. 110:3
13 *Then* I will teach transgressors Thy ways,
And sinners will [90]be converted to Thee.
14 Deliver me from bloodguiltiness, O God, Thou [r]God of my salvation; Ps. 25:5
Then my [r]tongue will joyfully sing of Thy righteousness. Ps. 35:28; 71:15
15 O LORD, open my lips,
That my mouth may [r]declare Thy praise. Ps. 9:14
16 For Thou [r]dost not delight in sacrifice, otherwise I would give it;
Thou art not pleased with burnt offering. Ps. 40:6
17 The sacrifices of God are a [r]broken spirit;
A broken and a contrite heart, O God, Thou wilt not despise. Ps. 34:18

[89]Or, *mayest be in the right*

[90]Or, *turn back*

18 [r]By Thy favor do good to Zion; Ps. 69:35; Is. 51:3
Build the walls of Jerusalem.
19 Then Thou wilt delight in righteous sacrifices,
In burnt offering and whole burnt offering;
Then young bulls will be offered on Thine altar.

PSALM 52

For the choir director. A Maskil of David, when Doeg the Edomite came and told Saul, and said to him, "David has come to the house of Ahimelech."

WHY do you [r]boast in evil, O mighty man? Ps. 94:4
The lovingkindness of God *endures* all day long.
2 Your tongue devises [r]destruction, Ps. 5:9
Like a [r]sharp razor, O worker of deceit. Ps. 57:4; 59:7
3 You [r]love evil more than good, Ps. 36:4
Falsehood more than speaking what is right. [Selah.
4 You love all words that devour,
O [r]deceitful tongue. Ps. 120:3

5 But God will break you down forever;
He will snatch you up, and [r]tear you away from *your* tent, Is. 22:18, 19
And uproot you from the land of the living. [Selah.
6 And the righteous will [r]see and fear, Ps. 37:34; 40:3
And will [r]laugh at him, *saying,* Job 22:19
7 "Behold, the man who would not make God his refuge,
But trusted in the abundance of his riches,
And was strong in [a]his *evil* desire." *his destruction*
8 But as for me, I am like a [r]green olive tree in the house of God; Ps. 92:12
I trust in the lovingkindness of God forever and ever.
9 I will [r]give Thee thanks forever, because Thou hast done *it,* Ps. 30:12
And I will wait on Thy name, for *it is* good, in the presence of Thy godly ones.

PSALM 53

For the choir director; according to [91]Mahalath.
A Maskil of David.

THE fool has said in his heart, "There is no God,"
They are corrupt, and have committed abominable injustice;
[r]There is no one who does good. Rom. 3:10
2 God has looked down from heaven upon the sons of men,
To see if there is anyone who [a]understands, *acts wisely*
Who seeks after God.
3 [r]Every one of them has turned aside; together they have become corrupt; Rom. 3:12
There is no one who does good, not even one.

4 Have the workers of wickedness no knowledge,

[91] I.e., sickness, a sad tone

Who eat up My people *as*
though they ate bread,
And have not called upon
God?
5 There they were in great fear
where no fear had been;
For God [r]scattered the bones
of him who encamped
against you; Ps. 141:7
You [r]put *them* to shame, because
God had rejected
them. Ps. 44:7
6 Oh, that the salvation of Israel
would come out of
Zion!
When God restores His captive
people,
Let Jacob rejoice, let Israel
be glad.

PSALM 54

For the choir director; on stringed instruments. A Maskil of David, when the Ziphites came and said to Saul, "Is not David hiding himself among us?"

SAVE me, O God, by Thy name,
And [92]vindicate me by [r]Thy
power. 2 Chr. 20:6
2 Hear my prayer, O God;
[r]Give ear to the words of my
mouth. Ps. 5:1
3 For strangers have [r]risen
against me, Ps. 86:14
And [r]violent men have sought
my life; Ps. 18:48; 86:14
They have not set God before
them. [Selah.
4 Behold, God is my helper;
The Lord is the [r]sustainer of
my soul. Ps. 37:17, 24
5 [93]He will recompense the evil
to my foes;
[a]Destroy them in Thy faithfulness.
Put to silence
6 Willingly I will sacrifice to
Thee;
I will give [r]thanks to Thy
name, O LORD, for it is
good. Ps. 50:14
7 For He has delivered me
from all trouble;
And my eye has [r]looked *with*
satisfaction upon my enemies.
Ps. 59:10; 92:11

PSALM 55

For the choir director; on stringed instruments.
A Maskil of David.

GIVE ear to my prayer, O God;
And [r]do not hide Thyself from
my supplication. Ps. 27:9
2 Give [r]heed to me, and answer
me;
I am restless in my complaint
and [94]am surely distracted,
Ps. 66:19; 86:6, 7
3 Because of the voice of the
enemy,
Because of the [r]pressure of
the wicked; Ps. 17:9
For they bring down [a]trouble
upon me, *wickedness*
And in anger they bear a
grudge against me.
4 My [r]heart is in anguish within
me,
And the terrors of death have
fallen upon me. Ps. 38:8
5 Fear and [r]trembling come
upon me; Ps. 119:120
And [t]horror has overwhelmed
me. *shuddering*
6 And I said, "Oh, that I had
wings like a dove!

[92] Lit., *judge* [93] Lit., *The evil will return*

[94] Or, *I must moan*

I would fly away and [95]be at
rest.
7 "Behold, I would wander far
away,
I would lodge in the wilderness.
[Selah.
8 "I would hasten to my place of
refuge
From the [r]stormy wind *and*
tempest." Is. 4:6; 25:4

9 Confuse, O Lord, [r]divide their
tongues, Gen. 11:9
For I have seen [r]violence and
strife in the city. Ps. 11:5
10 Day and night they go
around her upon her
walls;
And iniquity and mischief
are in her midst.
11 Destruction is in her midst;
Oppression and deceit do not
depart from her streets.

12 For it is [r]not an enemy who
reproaches me, Ps. 41:9
Then I could bear *it*;
Nor is it one who hates me
who [r]has exalted himself
against me, Ps. 35:26
Then I could hide myself
from him.
13 But it is you, a man my
equal,
My companion and my familiar friend.
14 We who had sweet [96]fellowship together,
[r]Walked in the house of God
in the throng. Ps. 42:4
15 Let death come [r]deceitfully
upon them; Ps. 64:7
Let them [r]go down alive to
Sheol, Num. 16:30, 33
For evil is in their dwelling,
in their midst.

16 As for me, I shall [r]call upon
God, Ps. 57:2, 3
And the LORD will save me.
17 Evening and [r]morning and at
noon, I will complain and
murmur, Ps. 5:3; 88:13
And He will hear my voice.
18 He will redeem my soul in
peace from the battle
which is against me,
For they are [r]many *who strive*
with me. Ps. 56:2
19 God will [r]hear and answer
them— Ps. 78:59
Even the one who sits enthroned from of old—
[Selah.
With whom there [t]is no
change, *are no changes*
And who do not fear God.
20 He has put forth his hands
against those who were
at peace with him;
He has [97]violated his covenant.
21 His [t]speech was smoother
than butter, *mouth*
But his heart was war;
His words were [r]softer than
oil, Ps. 12:2; 28:3
Yet they were drawn swords.

22 Cast your burden upon the
LORD, and He will sustain
you;
He will never allow the righteous to be shaken.
23 But Thou, O God, wilt bring
them down to the [a]pit of
destruction; *lowest pit*
Men of bloodshed and deceit
will [r]not live out half their
days. Job 15:32
But I will trust in Thee.

[95] Lit., *settle down* [96] Lit., *counsel*

[97] Lit., *profaned*

PSALM 56

For the choir director; according to Jonath elem rehokim.
A Mikhtam of David, when the Philistines seized him in Gath.

BE gracious, O God, for man has trampled upon me;
Fighting all day long he ʳoppresses me. Ps. 17:9
2 My foes have trampled upon me all day long,
For they are many who fight proudly against me.
3 When I am afraid,
I will put my trust in Thee.
4 In God, whose word I praise,
In God I have put my trust;
I shall not be afraid.
ʳWhat can *mere* ᵗman do to me? Ps. 118:6 • *flesh*
5 All day long they [98]distort my words;
All their thoughts are against me for evil.
6 They [99]attack, they lurk,
They watch my steps,
As they have ʳwaited *to take* my ᵗlife. Ps. 71:10 • *soul*
7 Because of wickedness, ʳcast them forth, Ps. 36:12
In anger ʳput down the peoples, O God! Ps. 55:23

8 Thou hast taken account of my wanderings;
Put my tears in Thy bottle;
Are *they* not in Thy book?
9 Then my enemies will ʳturn back ʳin the day when I call;
This I know, [100]that God is for me. Ps. 9:3 • Ps. 102:2
10 In God, *whose* word I praise,
In the LORD, *whose* word I praise,
11 In God I have put my [101]trust,
I shall not be afraid.
What can man do to me?
12 Thy ʳvows are *binding* upon me, O God;
I will render thank offerings to Thee. Ps. 50:14
13 For Thou hast delivered my soul from death,
Indeed ʳmy feet from stumbling, Ps. 116:8
So that I may ʳwalk before God Ps. 116:9
In the light of the living.

PSALM 57

For the choir director; *set to* [102]Al-tashheth.
A Mikhtam of David, when he fled from Saul, in the cave.

BE gracious to me, O God, be gracious to me,
For my soul ʳtakes refuge in Thee; Ps. 2:12; 34:22
And in the shadow of Thy wings I will take refuge,
Until destruction passes by.
2 I will cry to God Most High,
To God who accomplishes *all things* for me.
3 He will ʳsend from heaven and save me;
He reproaches him who tramples upon me. [Selah.
God will send forth His lovingkindness and His truth. Ps. 18:16

4 My soul is among lions;
I must lie among those who breathe forth fire,

[98]Or, *trouble my affairs* [99]Or, *stir up strife*
[100]Or, *because*
[101]Or, *trust without fear*
[102]Lit., *Do Not Destroy*

Even the sons of men, whose [r]teeth are spears and arrows, Prov. 30:14
And their [r]tongue a sharp sword. Ps. 55:21; 59:7
5 Be exalted above the heavens, O God;
Let Thy glory *be* above all the earth.
6 They have [103]prepared a net for my steps;
My soul is bowed down;
They dug a pit before me;
They *themselves* have fallen into the midst of it. [Selah.

7 My heart is steadfast, O God, my heart is steadfast;
I will sing, yes, I will sing praises!
8 Awake, [r]my glory; Ps. 16:9
Awake, harp and lyre,
I will awaken the dawn!
9 I will give thanks to Thee, O Lord, among the peoples;
I will sing praises to Thee among the nations.
10 For Thy lovingkindness is great to the heavens,
And Thy truth to the clouds.
11 [r]Be exalted above the heavens, O God;
Let Thy glory *be* above all the earth. Ps. 57:5

PSALM 58

For the choir director; *set to* Al-tashheth. A Mikhtam of David.

DO you indeed speak righteousness, O [104]gods?
Do you judge [105]uprightly, O sons of men?

[103] Or, *spread* [104] Or, *judges*
[105] Or, *uprightly the sons of men?*

2 No, in heart you work unrighteousness;
On earth you weigh out the violence of your hands.
3 The wicked are estranged [r]from the womb; Ps. 51:5
These who speak lies go astray from birth.
4 They have venom like the venom of a serpent;
Like a deaf cobra that stops up its ear,
5 So that it does not hear the voice of charmers,
Or a skillful caster of spells.

6 O God, [r]shatter their teeth in their mouth; Job 4:10
Break out the fangs of the young lions, O LORD.
7 Let them flow away like water that runs off;
When he [t]aims his arrows, let them be as headless shafts. *bends*
8 *Let them be* as a snail which melts away as it goes along,
Like the [r]miscarriages of a woman which never see the sun. Job 3:16
9 Before your pots can feel *the fire of* thorns,
He will [r]sweep them away with a whirlwind, the [t]green and the burning alike. Job 27:21 • *living*

10 The [r]righteous will rejoice when he sees the vengeance; Job 22:19
He will wash his feet in the blood of the wicked.
11 And men will say, "Surely there is a [t]reward for the righteous; *fruit*

Surely there is a God who judges on earth!"

PSALM 59

For the choir director; *set to* Al-tashheth. A Mikhtam of David, when Saul sent *men*, and they watched the house in order to kill him.

DELIVER me from my enemies, O my God;
Set me *securely* on high away from those who rise up against me.
2 Deliver me from ʳthose who do iniquity, Ps. 28:3
And save me from ʳmen of bloodshed. Ps. 26:9
3 For behold, they have set an ambush for my life;
Fierce men [106]launch an attack against me,
Not for my transgression nor for my sin, O LORD,
4 ᵗFor no guilt of *mine*, they run and set themselves against me. *Without guilt*
ʳArouse Thyself to ᵗhelp me, and see! Ps. 7:6 • *meet*
5 And Thou, O LORD God of hosts, the God of Israel,
Awake to ᵗpunish all the nations; *visit*
Do not be gracious to any *who are* treacherous in iniquity. [Selah.
6 They ʳreturn at evening, they howl like a dog, Ps. 59:14
And go around the city.
7 Behold, they ʳbelch forth with their mouth; Ps. 94:4
Swords are in their lips,
For, *they say,* "Who hears?"
8 But Thou, O LORD, dost ʳlaugh at them; Ps. 37:13
Thou dost ʳscoff at all the nations. Ps. 2:4

9 *Because of* [107]his strength I will watch for Thee,
For God is my stronghold.
10 My God in His lovingkindness will meet me;
God will let me look *triumphantly* upon my foes.
11 Do not slay them, ʳlest my people forget; Deut. 4:9
Scatter them by Thy power, and bring them down,
O Lord, ʳour shield. Ps. 84:9
12 *On account of* the ʳsin of their mouth *and* the words of their lips, Prov. 12:13
Let them even be ʳcaught in their pride, Zeph. 3:11
And on account of curses and lies which they utter.
13 [108]Destroy *them* in wrath, [108]destroy *them*, that they may be no more;
That *men* may know that God rules in Jacob,
To the ends of the earth. [Selah.
14 And they return at evening, they howl like a dog,
And go around the city.
15 They ʳwander about [109]for food,
And growl if they are not satisfied. Job 15:23

16 But as for me, I shall ʳsing of Thy strength; Ps. 21:13
Yes, I shall ʳjoyfully sing of Thy lovingkindness in the morning, Ps. 101:1

[106] Or, *stir up strife*

[107] Many mss. and some ancient versions read *My strength*

[108] Lit., *Bring to an end* [109] Or, *to devour*

For Thou hast been my [r]stronghold, Ps. 59:9
And a [r]refuge in the day of my distress. 2 Sam. 22:3
17 O my strength, I will sing praises to Thee;
For God is my stronghold, the God who shows me lovingkindness.

PSALM 60

For the choir director; according to [110]Shushan Eduth. A Mikhtam of David, to teach; when he struggled with Aram-naharaim and with Aram-zobah, and Joab returned, and smote twelve thousand of Edom in the Valley of Salt.

O GOD, Thou hast rejected us. Thou hast broken us;
Thou hast been [r]angry; O, [r]restore us. Ps. 79:5 • Ps. 80:3
2 Thou hast made the [a]land quake, Thou hast split it open;
[r]Heal its breaches, for it totters. *earth* • 2 Chr. 7:14
3 Thou hast made Thy people experience hardship;
Thou hast given us [t]wine to drink that makes us stagger. *wine of staggering*
4 Thou hast given a banner to those who fear Thee,
That it may be displayed because of the truth. [Selah.
5 That Thy [r]beloved may be delivered, Deut. 33:12
[r]Save with Thy right hand, and answer us! Ps. 17:7

6 God has spoken in His [111]holiness:
"I will exult, I will portion out Shechem and measure out the valley of Succoth.
7 "Gilead[r] is Mine, and Manasseh is Mine; Josh. 13:31
Ephraim also is the [t]helmet of My head; *protection*
Judah is My [112]scepter.
8 "Moab is My washbowl;
Over [r]Edom I shall throw My shoe; 2 Sam. 8:14
Shout loud, O [r]Philistia, because of Me!" 2 Sam. 8:1

9 Who will bring me into the besieged city?
Who will lead me to Edom?
10 Hast not Thou Thyself, O God, rejected us?
And wilt Thou not go forth with our armies, O God?
11 O give us help against the adversary,
For [r]deliverance [t]by man is in vain. Ps. 146:3 • *of*
12 Through God we shall [r]do valiantly, Num. 24:18
And it is He who will tread down our adversaries.

PSALM 61

For the choir director; on a stringed instrument.
A Psalm of David.

HEAR my cry, O God;
Give heed to my prayer.
2 From the end of the earth I call to Thee, when my heart is [r]faint; Ps. 77:3
Lead me to [r]the rock that is higher than I. Ps. 18:2
3 For Thou hast been a [r]refuge for me, Ps. 62:7

[110] Lit., *The lily of testimony* [111] Or, *sanctuary* [112] Or, *lawgiver*

A tower of strength [t]against
the enemy. *from*
4 Let me [a]dwell in Thy tent forever; *sojourn*
Let me take refuge in the shelter of Thy wings. [Selah.

5 For Thou hast heard my [r]vows, O God; Ps. 56:12
Thou hast given *me* the inheritance of those who [r]fear Thy name. Ps. 86:11
6 Thou wilt [t]prolong the king's [t]life; *add days to*
His years will be as many generations. *days*
7 He will [a]abide before God forever; *sit enthroned*
Appoint [r]lovingkindness and truth, that they may preserve him. Ps. 40:11
8 So I will sing praise to Thy name forever,
That I may [r]pay my vows day by day. Ps. 65:1; Is. 19:21

PSALM 62

For the choir director; according to Jeduthun.
A Psalm of David.

MY soul *waits* in silence for God only;
From Him is my salvation.
2 He only is my [r]rock and my salvation,
My stronghold; I shall not be greatly shaken. Ps. 89:26
3 How long will you assail a man,
That you may murder *him*, all of you,
Like a [r]leaning wall, like a tottering fence? Is. 30:13
4 They have counseled only to thrust him down from his high position;
They delight in falsehood;
They bless with their mouth,
But inwardly they curse. [Selah.

5 My soul, [r]wait in silence for God only, Ps. 62:1
For my hope is from Him.
6 He only is [r]my rock and my salvation,
My stronghold; I shall not be shaken. Ps. 62:2
7 On God my [r]salvation and my glory *rest*; Ps. 85:9
The rock of my strength, my [r]refuge is in God. Ps. 46:1
8 Trust in Him at all times, O people;
Pour out your heart before Him;
God is a refuge for us. [Selah.

9 Men of [r]low degree are only vanity, and men of rank are a lie; Ps. 49:2
In the balances they go up;
They are together lighter than breath.
10 Do not trust in oppression,
And do not vainly hope in [r]robbery; Is. 61:8
If riches increase, do not set *your* heart *upon them.*

11 [113]Once God has spoken;
[114]Twice I have heard this:
That power belongs to God;
12 And lovingkindness [r]is Thine, O Lord, Ps. 86:5; 103:8
For Thou [r]dost recompense a man according to his work. Job 34:11

[113]Or, *One thing*
[114]Or, *These two things I have heard*

PSALM 63

A Psalm of David, when he was in the wilderness of Judah.

O GOD, Thou art my God; I shall seek Thee [115]earnestly;
My soul thirsts for Thee, my flesh yearns for Thee,
In a dry and weary land where there is no water.
2 Thus I have ʳbeheld Thee in the sanctuary,
To see Thy power and Thy glory. Ps. 27:4
3 Because Thy lovingkindness is better than life,
My lips will praise Thee.
4 So I will bless Thee ʳas long as I live; Ps. 104:33
I will ʳlift up my hands in Thy name. Ps. 28:2; 143:6
5 My soul is satisfied as with [116]marrow and fatness,
And my mouth offers praises with joyful lips.

6 When I remember Thee ʳon my bed, Ps. 4:4
I meditate on Thee in the ʳnight watches, Ps. 16:7
7 For Thou hast been my help,
And in the shadow of Thy wings I sing for joy.
8 My soul clings to Thee;
Thy right hand upholds me.

9 But those who seek my ᵗlife, to destroy it,
Will go into the ᵗdepths of the earth. *soul • lowest places*
10 They will be ᵗdelivered over to the power of the sword; *poured out by*
They will be a prey for foxes.
11 But the ʳking will rejoice in God; Ps. 21:1
Everyone who swears by Him will glory,
For the ʳmouths of those who speak lies will be stopped. Job 5:16

[115] Lit., *early* [116] Lit., *fat*

PSALM 64

For the choir director. A Psalm of David.

HEAR my voice, O God, in my [117]complaint;
Preserve my life from dread of the enemy.
2 Hide me from the secret counsel of evildoers,
From the tumult of those who do iniquity,
3 Who have sharpened their tongue like a sword.
They ʳaimed bitter speech *as* their arrow, Ps. 58:7
4 To shoot from concealment at the blameless;
Suddenly they shoot at him, and do not fear.
5 They hold fast to themselves an evil purpose;
They ᵗtalk of ʳlaying snares secretly; *tell of* • Ps. 140:5
They say, "Whoʳ can see them?" Job 22:13
6 They [118]devise injustices, *saying,*
"We are ready with a well-conceived plot";
For the inward thought and the heart of a man are [119]deep.

7 But God [a] will shoot at them with an arrow;
Suddenly they will be wounded. *shot*

[117] Or, *concern* [118] Or, *search out*
[119] Or, *unsearchable*

8 So they[a] will [r]make him stumble; *made* • Ps. 9:3
[r]Their own tongue is against them; Prov. 12:13; 18:7
All who see them will [r]shake the head. Ps. 22:7; 44:14
9 Then all men will fear,
And[a] will declare the work of God, *declared*
And will consider [t]what He has done. *His work*
10 The righteous man will be glad in the LORD, and will take refuge in Him;
And all the upright in heart will glory.

PSALM 65

For the choir director. A Psalm of David. A Song.

THERE will be silence [t]before Thee, *and* praise in Zion, O God; *to*
And to Thee the [r]vow will be performed. Ps. 116:18
2 O Thou who dost hear prayer,
To Thee all men come.
3 Iniquities prevail against me;
As for our transgressions, Thou dost forgive them.
4 How blessed is the one whom Thou dost choose, and bring near *to Thee,*
To dwell in Thy courts.
We will be satisfied with the goodness of Thy house,
Thy holy temple.

5 By [r]awesome *deeds* Thou dost answer us in righteousness, O God of our salvation, Ps. 45:4; 66:3
Thou who art the trust of all the ends of the earth and of the farthest sea;
6 Who dost [r]establish the mountains by His strength, Ps. 95:4
Being girded with might;
7 Who dost [r]still the roaring of the seas, Ps. 89:9; 93:3, 4
The roaring of their waves,
And the [r]tumult of the peoples. Ps. 2:1; 74:23
8 And they who dwell in the ends *of the earth* stand in awe of Thy signs;
Thou dost make the dawn and the sunset shout for joy.

9 Thou dost visit the earth, and cause it to overflow;
Thou dost greatly enrich it;
The [t]stream of God is full of water;
Thou dost prepare their grain, for thus Thou dost prepare the earth. *it*
10 Thou dost water its furrows abundantly;
Thou dost settle its ridges;
Thou dost soften it [r]with showers; Deut. 32:2
Thou dost bless its growth.
11 Thou hast crowned the year with Thy bounty,
And Thy paths [r]drip *with* fatness. Job 36:28
12 [r]The pastures of the wilderness drip, Job 38:26, 27
And the [r]hills gird themselves with rejoicing. Ps. 98:8
13 The meadows are clothed with flocks,
And the valleys are [r]covered with grain; Ps. 72:16
They [r]shout for joy, yes, they sing. Ps. 98:8; Is. 44:23

PSALM 66

For the choir director. A Song. A Psalm.

SHOUT joyfully to God, all the earth;
2 Sing the glory of His name;
Make His praise glorious.
3 Say to God, "How [r]awesome are Thy works! Ps. 47:2
Because of the greatness of Thy power Thine enemies will [t]give feigned obedience to Thee. *deceive*
4 "All[r] the earth will worship Thee, Ps. 22:27; 67:7
And will sing praises to Thee;
They will sing praises to Thy name." [Selah.

5 [r]Come and see the works of God, Ps. 46:8
Who is [r]awesome in *His* deeds toward the sons of men. Ps. 106:22
6 He [r]turned the sea into dry land; Ex. 14:21
They passed through [r]the river on foot; Josh. 3:16
There let us rejoice in Him!
7 He [r]rules by His might forever; Ps. 145:13
His [r]eyes keep watch on the nations; Ps. 11:4
Let not the rebellious exalt themselves. [Selah.

8 Bless our God, O peoples,
And [r]sound His praise abroad, Ps. 98:4
9 Who keeps us in life,
And [r]does not allow our feet to slip. Ps. 121:3
10 For Thou hast [r]tried us, O God; Job 23:10; Ps. 7:9
Thou hast refined us as silver is refined.
11 Thou [r]didst bring us into the net; Lam. 1:13; Ezek. 12:13
Thou didst lay an oppressive burden upon our loins.
12 Thou didst make men ride over our heads;
We went through [r]fire and through water; Ps. 78:21
Yet Thou [r]didst bring us out into *a place of* abundance. Ps. 18:19
13 I shall come into Thy house with burnt offerings;
I shall pay Thee my vows,
14 Which my lips uttered
And my mouth spoke when I was in distress.
15 I shall offer to Thee burnt offerings of fat beasts,
With the smoke of rams;
I shall make *an offering of* bulls with male goats. [Selah.

16 Come *and* hear, all who [120]fear God,
And I will tell of what He has done for my soul.
17 I cried to Him with my mouth,
And He was extolled with my tongue.
18 If I [121]regard wickedness in my heart,
The Lord will not hear;
19 But certainly God has heard;
He has given heed to the voice of my prayer.
20 Blessed be God,
Who [r]has not turned away my prayer,
Nor His lovingkindness from me. Ps. 22:24

[120] Or, *revere*
[121] Or, *had regarded . . . would not have heard*

PSALM 67

For the choir director; with stringed instruments.
A Psalm. A Song.

GOD be gracious to us and bless us,
And cause His face to shine upon us— [Selah.
2 That Thy way may be known on the earth,
Thy salvation among all nations. Ps. 98:2 • Is. 52:10
3 Let the peoples praise Thee, O God;
Let all the peoples praise Thee. Ps. 66:4
4 Let the nations be glad and sing for joy; Ps. 100:1, 2
For Thou wilt judge the peoples with uprightness,
And guide the nations on the earth. [Selah.
5 Let the peoples praise Thee, O God;
Let all the peoples praise Thee. Ps. 67:3
6 The earth has yielded its produce; Lev. 26:4; Ps. 85:12
God, our God, blesses us.
7 God blesses us,
[122]That all the ends of the earth may fear Him.

PSALM 68

For the choir director. A Psalm of David. A Song.

LET God arise, let His enemies be scattered; Num. 10:35
And let those who hate Him flee before Him.
2 As smoke is driven away, *so* drive *them* away;
As wax melts before the fire,
So let the wicked perish before God. Ps. 9:3; 37:20
3 But let the righteous be glad; let them exult before God;
Yes, let them rejoice with gladness. Ps. 32:11; 64:10
4 Sing to God, sing praises to His name; Ps. 66:2
Cast up a highway for Him who rides through the deserts, Deut. 33:26
Whose name is the LORD, and exult before Him.

5 A father of the fatherless and a judge [123]for the widows,
Is God in His holy habitation.
6 God makes a home for the lonely; Ps. 107:4-7; 113:9
He leads out the prisoners into prosperity, Ps. 69:33
Only the rebellious dwell in a parched land. Ps. 78:17

7 O God, when Thou didst go forth before Thy people,
When Thou didst march through the wilderness, [Selah.
8 The earth quaked;
The heavens also dropped *rain* at the presence of God; Judg. 5:4; Ps. 18:9
Sinai itself *quaked* at the presence of God, the God of Israel. Ex. 19:18
9 Thou didst shed abroad a plentiful rain, O God;
Thou didst confirm Thine inheritance, when it was parched. *weary*
10 Thy creatures settled in it;
Thou didst provide in Thy goodness for the poor, O God. Ps. 65:9; 74:19

[122] Or, *And let all . . . earth fear Him*

[123] Lit., *of*

11 The Lord gives the [t]command; *word*
The [r]women who proclaim the *good* tidings are a great host: Ex. 15:20
12 "Kings[r] of armies flee, they flee, Josh. 10:16
And she who remains at home will [r]divide the spoil!" Judg. 5:30
13 [124]When you lie down among the [125]sheepfolds,
You are like the wings of a dove covered with silver,
And its pinions with glistening gold.
14 When the Almighty scattered the kings there,
It was snowing in Zalmon.

15 A mountain of God is the mountain of Bashan;
A mountain *of many* peaks is the mountain of Bashan.
16 Why do you look with envy, O mountains with *many* peaks,
At the mountain which God has [r]desired for His abode? Deut. 12:5
Surely, [r]the LORD will dwell *there* forever. Ps. 132:14
17 The chariots of God are [126]myriads, thousands upon thousands;
The Lord is among them *as at* Sinai, in holiness.
18 Thou hast [r]ascended on high, Thou hast led captive *Thy* captives;
Thou hast received gifts among men, Ps. 7:7; 47:5
Even *among* the rebellious also, that the LORD God may dwell *there.*

19 Blessed be the Lord, who daily bears our burden,
The God *who* is our salvation. [Selah.
20 God is to us a [r]God of deliverances; Ps. 106:43
And to GOD the Lord belong escapes from death.
21 Surely God will shatter the head of His enemies,
The hairy crown of him who goes on in his guilty deeds.
22 The Lord said, "I will bring *them* back from Bashan.
I will bring *them* back from the depths of the sea;
23 That [r]your foot may shatter *them* in blood, Ps. 58:10
The tongue of your [r]dogs *may have* its portion from *your* enemies." Jer. 15:3

24 They have seen Thy [t]procession, O God, *goings*
The procession of my God, my King, [t]into the sanctuary. *in the sanctuary*
25 The singers went on, the musicians after *them*,
In the midst of the maidens beating tambourines.
26 Bless God in the congregations,
Even the LORD, *you who are* of the fountain of Israel.
27 There is Benjamin, the youngest, ruling them,
The princes of Judah *in* their throng,

[124] Lit., *If*
[125] Or, *cooking stones*, or, *saddle bags*
[126] Lit., *twice ten thousand*

The princes of Zebulun, the
princes of Naphtali.

28 Your God has [r]commanded
your strength;
Show Thyself strong, O God,
who hast acted [t]on our behalf. Ps. 29:11 • *for us*
29 Because of Thy temple at Jerusalem
[r]Kings will bring gifts to
Thee. 1 Kin. 10:10, 25
30 Rebuke the [r]beasts [t]in the
reeds, Job 40:21 • *of*
The herd of bulls with the
calves of the peoples,
Trampling under foot the
pieces of silver;
He has scattered the peoples
who delight in war.
31 Envoys will come out of
[r]Egypt; Is. 19:19, 21
Ethiopia will quickly stretch
out her hands to God.

32 Sing to God, O [r]kingdoms of
the earth; Ps. 102:22
Sing praises to the Lord,
[Selah.
33 To Him who rides upon the
highest heavens, which
are from ancient times;
Behold, He speaks forth with
His voice, a mighty voice.
34 Ascribe strength to God;
His majesty is over Israel,
And [r]His strength is in the
[t]skies. Ps. 150:1 • *clouds*
35 O God, *Thou art* awesome
from Thy sanctuary.
The God of Israel Himself
gives [r]strength and power
to the people.
Blessed be God! Ps. 29:11

PSALM 69

For the choir director; according to [127]Shoshannim. *A Psalm* of David.

SAVE me, O God,
For the [r]waters have threatened my life. Job 22:11
2 I have sunk in deep mire, and
there is no foothold;
I have come into deep waters, and a flood overflows me.
3 I am weary with my crying;
my throat is parched;
My [r]eyes fail while I wait for
my God. Deut. 28:32
4 Those who hate me without a
cause are more than the
hairs of my head;
Those who would [a]destroy me
are powerful,
What I did not steal, I then
have to restore. *silence*

5 O God, it is Thou who dost
know [r]my folly, Ps. 38:5
And [r]my wrongs are not hidden from Thee. Ps. 44:21
6 May those who wait for Thee
not be ashamed through
me, O Lord GOD of hosts;
May those who seek Thee
not be dishonored
through me, O God of Israel,
7 Because for Thy sake I have
borne reproach;
[r]Dishonor has covered my
face. Ps. 44:15; Is. 50:6
8 I have become estranged
[t]from my brothers,
And an alien to my mother's
sons. *to*
9 For zeal for Thy house has
consumed me,

[127]Or possibly, *Lilies*

And the reproaches of those who reproach Thee have fallen on me.
10 When I wept[r] in my soul with fasting, Ps. 35:13
It became my reproach.
11 When I made [r]sackcloth my clothing, 1 Kin. 20:31
I became a byword to them.
12 Those who [r]sit in the gate talk about me, Gen. 19:1
And I *am* the [t]song of the drunkards. *songs*

13 But as for me, my prayer is to Thee, O LORD, [r]at an acceptable time;
O God, in the greatness of Thy lovingkindness,
Answer me with Thy saving truth. Ps. 32:6
14 Deliver me from the mire, and do not let me sink;
May I be [r]delivered from my foes, and from the deep waters. Ps. 144:7
15 May the [t]flood of water not overflow me, *stream*
And may the deep not swallow me up,
And may the [r]pit not shut its mouth on me. Num. 16:33

16 Answer me, O LORD, for Thy lovingkindness is good;
According to the greatness of Thy compassion, [r]turn to me, Ps. 25:16; 86:16
17 And do not hide Thy face from Thy servant,
For I am [r]in distress; answer me quickly. Ps. 31:9; 66:14
18 Oh draw near to my soul *and* [r]redeem it; 2 Sam. 4:9
[r]Ransom me because of my enemies! Ps. 119:134
19 Thou dost know my [r]reproach and my shame and my dishonor;
All my adversaries are [128]before Thee. Ps. 22:6; 31:11

20 Reproach has broken my heart, and I am so sick.
And I looked for sympathy, but there was none,
And for [r]comforters, but I found none. Job 16:2
21 They also gave me [129]gall for my food,
And for my thirst they gave me vinegar to drink.

22 May their table before them become a snare;
And when they are in peace, *may it become* a trap.
23 May their eyes grow dim so that they cannot see,
And make their [r]loins shake continually. Dan. 5:6
24 Pour out Thine indignation on them,
And may Thy burning anger overtake them.
25 May their [t]camp be desolate;
May none dwell in their tents. *encampment*
26 For they have [r]persecuted him whom Thou Thyself hast smitten, 2 Chr. 28:9
And they tell of the pain of those whom Thou hast [t]wounded. *pierced*
27 Do Thou add [r]iniquity to their iniquity, Neh. 4:5
And may they not come into Thy righteousness.
28 May they be [r]blotted out of the book of life, Ex. 32:32

[128]Or, known *to Thee* [129]Or, *poison*

And may they not be [t]recorded with the righteous. *written*

29 But I am [r]afflicted and in pain; Ps. 70:5
May Thy salvation, O God, set me *securely* on high.
30 I will [r]praise the name of God with song, Ps. 28:7
And shall [r]magnify Him with thanksgiving. Ps. 34:3
31 And it will please the LORD better than an ox
Or a young bull with horns and hoofs.
32 The [r]humble have seen *it and* are glad; Ps. 34:2
You who seek God, let your heart [a]revive. *live*
33 For [r]the LORD hears the needy, Ps. 12:5
And does not despise His *who are* prisoners.

34 Let [r]heaven and earth praise Him, Ps. 96:11; 98:7
The seas and [r]everything that moves in them. Is. 55:12
35 For God will save Zion and build the cities of Judah,
That they may dwell there and possess it.
36 And the descendants of His servants will inherit it,
And those who love His name will dwell in it.

PSALM 70

For the choir director. *A Psalm* of David; for a memorial.

O GOD, *hasten* to deliver me;
O LORD, hasten to my help!
2 Let those be ashamed and humiliated
Who seek my [a]life; *soul*
Let those be turned back and dishonored
Who delight in my hurt.
3 Let those be turned back because of their shame
Who say, "Aha, aha!"

4 Let all who seek Thee rejoice and be glad in Thee;
And let those who love Thy salvation say continually,
"Let God be magnified."
5 But I am afflicted and needy;
Hasten to me, O God!
Thou art my help and my deliverer;
O LORD, do not delay.

PSALM 71

IN Thee, O LORD, I have taken refuge;
Let me never be ashamed.
2 In Thy righteousness deliver me, and rescue me;
[r]Incline Thine ear to me, and save me. Ps. 17:6
3 Be Thou to me a rock of habitation, to which I may continually come;
Thou hast given commandment to save me,
For Thou art [r]my rock and my fortress. Ps. 18:2
4 Rescue me, O my God, out of the hand of the wicked,
Out of the [t]grasp of the wrongdoer and ruthless man, *palm*
5 For Thou art my hope;
O Lord GOD, *Thou art* my [r]confidence from my youth. Ps. 22:9
6 By Thee I have been sustained from *my* birth;

Thou art He who took me from my mother's womb;
My [r]praise is continually [t]of Thee. Ps. 34:1 • *in*
7 I have become a [r]marvel to many; Is. 8:18; 1 Cor. 4:9
For Thou art [r]my strong refuge. Ps. 61:3
8 My mouth is filled with Thy praise,
And with [r]Thy glory all day long. Ps. 96:6; 104:1
9 Do not cast me off in the time of old age;
Do not forsake me when my strength fails.
10 For my enemies have spoken against me;
And those who watch for my [t]life have consulted together, *soul*
11 Saying, "God[r] has forsaken him;
Pursue and seize him, for there is [r]no one to deliver." Ps. 3:2 • Ps. 7:2

12 O God, [r]do not be far from me; Ps. 10:1; 22:11
O my God, [r]hasten to my help! Ps. 38:22; 40:13
13 Let those who are adversaries of my soul be ashamed *and* consumed;
Let them be covered with reproach and dishonor, who seek to injure me.
14 But as for me, I will [r]hope continually, Ps. 130:7
And will [r]praise Thee yet more and more. Ps. 71:8
15 My mouth shall tell of Thy righteousness,
And of [r]Thy salvation all day long;
For I do not know the [t]sum *of them.* Ps. 96:2 • *numbers*
16 I will come with the mighty deeds of the Lord GOD;
I will [r]make mention of Thy righteousness, Thine alone. Ps. 51:14

17 O God, Thou hast taught me from my youth;
And I still [r]declare Thy wondrous deeds. Ps. 26:7
18 And even when *I am* [r]old and gray, O God, do not forsake me,
Until I declare Thy [t]strength to *this* generation,
Thy power to all who are to come. Ps. 71:9 • *arm*
19 For Thy righteousness, O God, *reaches* to the [t]heavens, *height*
Thou who hast [r]done great things; Ps. 126:2
O God, who is like Thee?
20 Thou, who hast shown [130]me many troubles and distresses,
Wilt revive [130]me again,
And wilt bring [130]me up again from the depths of the earth.
21 Mayest Thou increase my greatness,
And turn *to* comfort me.

22 I will also praise Thee with [r]a harp, Ps. 33:2; 81:2
Even Thy truth, O my God;
To Thee I will sing praises with the lyre,
O Thou Holy One of Israel.
23 My lips will shout for joy when I sing praises to Thee;

[130] Another reading is *us*

And my soul, which Thou hast redeemed.
24 My [r]tongue also will utter Thy righteousness all day long; Ps. 35:28
For they are [r]ashamed, for they are humiliated who seek my hurt. Ps. 71:13

PSALM 72

A Psalm of Solomon.

GIVE the king [r]Thy judgments, O God, 1 Kin. 3:9
And [r]Thy righteousness to the king's son. Ps. 24:5
2 May he judge Thy people with righteousness,
And [131]Thine afflicted with justice.
3 Let the mountains bring peace to the people,
And the hills in righteousness.
4 May he vindicate the afflicted of the people,
Save the children of the needy,
And crush the oppressor.

5 Let them fear Thee [r]while the sun endures, Ps. 72:17
And [t]as long as the moon, throughout all generations. *before the moon*
6 May he come down like rain upon the mown grass,
Like [r]showers that water the earth. Ps. 65:10
7 In his days may the [r]righteous flourish, Ps. 92:12
And abundance of peace till the moon is no more.

8 May he also rule [r]from sea to sea, Ex. 23:31; Zech. 9:10
And from the River to the ends of the earth.
9 Let the nomads of the desert bow before him,
And his enemies [r]lick the dust. Is. 49:23; Mic. 7:17
10 Let the kings of Tarshish and of the [a]islands bring presents; *coastlands*
The kings of Sheba and Seba offer [a]gifts. *tribute*
11 And let all kings bow down before him,
All nations serve him.

12 For he will deliver the needy when he cries for help,
The afflicted also, and him who has no helper.
13 He will have compassion on the poor and needy,
And the [t]lives of the needy he will save. *souls*
14 He will rescue their life from oppression and violence;
And their blood will be precious in his sight;
15 So may he live; and may the [r]gold of Sheba be given to him;
And let [t]them pray for him continually;
Let them bless him all day long. Is. 60:6 • *him*

16 May there be abundance of grain in the earth on top of the mountains;
Its fruit will wave like *the cedars of* Lebanon;
And may those from the city flourish like [r]vegetation of the earth. Job 5:25
17 May his [r]name endure forever; Ex. 3:15; Ps. 135:13
May his name increase as long as the sun *shines*;

[131]Or, *Thy humble*

And let *men* [r]bless themselves by him;
Let all nations call him blessed. Gen. 12:3
18 Blessed be the LORD God, the God of Israel,
Who alone works wonders.
19 And blessed be His [r]glorious name forever;
And may the whole earth be filled with His glory.
Amen, and Amen. Neh. 9:5
20 The prayers of David the son of Jesse are ended.

BOOK 3

PSALM 73

A Psalm of Asaph.

SURELY God is good to Israel,
To those who are [r]pure in heart! Ps. 24:4; 51:10
2 But as for me, my feet came close to stumbling;
My steps had almost slipped.
3 For I was envious of the [a]arrogant, *boasters*
As I saw the [r]prosperity of the wicked. Job 21:7
4 For there are no pains in their death;
And their [a]body is fat. *belly*
5 They are not in trouble *as other* men;
Nor are they plagued [t]like mankind. *with*
6 Therefore pride is [r]their necklace; Gen. 41:42
The [r]garment of violence covers them. Ps. 109:18
7 Their eye [t]bulges from fatness; *goes forth*
The imaginations of *their* heart [t]run riot. *overflow*
8 They mock, and wickedly speak of oppression;
They speak from on high.
9 They have set their mouth against the heavens,
And their tongue parades through the earth.

10 Therefore his people return to this place;
And waters of abundance are drunk by them.
11 And they say, "How[r] does God know? Job 22:13
And is there knowledge [t]with the Most High?" *in*
12 Behold, these are the wicked;
And always at ease, they have increased *in* wealth.
13 Surely in vain I have [a]kept my heart pure, *cleansed my heart*
And [r]washed my hands in innocence; Ps. 26:6
14 For I have been stricken all day long,
And [t]chastened every morning. *my chastening*

15 If I had said, "I will speak thus,"
Behold, I should have betrayed the generation of Thy children.
16 When I pondered to understand this,
It was [t]troublesome in my sight *labor, trouble*
17 Until I came into the [t]sanctuary of God; *sanctuaries*
Then I perceived their end.
18 Surely Thou dost set them in slippery places;
Thou dost cast them down to destruction.

19 How they are destroyed in a moment!
They are utterly swept away by sudden terrors!
20 Like a [r]dream when one awakes, Job 20:8
O Lord, when aroused, Thou wilt despise their form.

21 When my [r]heart was embittered, Judg. 10:16
And I was pierced within,
22 Then I was senseless and ignorant;
I was *like* a beast [t]before Thee. *with Thee*
23 Nevertheless [r]I am continually with Thee;
Thou hast taken hold of my right hand. Ps. 16:8
24 With Thy counsel Thou wilt [r]guide me, Ps. 32:8; 48:14
And afterward receive me [a]to glory. *with honor*

25 Whom have I in heaven *but Thee*?
And besides Thee, I desire nothing on earth.
26 My [r]flesh and my heart may fail, Ps. 38:10; 40:12
But God is the [t]strength of my heart and my portion forever. *rock*
27 For, behold, those who are far from Thee will perish;
Thou hast destroyed all those who [t]are unfaithful to Thee. *go to a whoring from*
28 But as for me, the nearness of God is my good;
I have made the Lord GOD my [r]refuge,
That I may tell of all Thy works. Ps. 14:6; 71:7

PSALM 74

A Maskil of Asaph.

O GOD, why hast Thou [r]rejected *us* forever? Ps. 44:9; 77:7
Why does Thine anger smoke against the sheep of Thy pasture?
2 Remember Thy congregation, which Thou hast purchased of old,
Which Thou hast [r]redeemed to be the tribe of Thine inheritance; Ex. 15:13
And Mount Zion, where Thou hast dwelt.
3 Turn Thy footsteps toward the perpetual ruins;
The enemy [r]has damaged everything within the sanctuary. Ps. 79:1
4 Thine adversaries have roared in the midst of Thy meeting place;
They have set up their own standards for signs.
5 It seems as if one had lifted up
His axe in a forest of trees.
6 And now all its carved work
They smash with hatchet and [a]hammers. *axes*
7 They have burned Thy sanctuary to the ground;
They have defiled the dwelling place of Thy name.
8 They said in their heart, "Let us [t]completely subdue them." *altogether*
They have burned all the meeting places of God in the land.
9 We do not see our signs;
There is [r]no longer any prophet, 1 Sam. 3:1

Nor is there any among us
who knows how long.
10 How long, O God, will the
adversary revile,
And the enemy [r]spurn Thy
name forever? Lev. 24:16
11 Why [r]dost Thou withdraw
Thy hand, even Thy right
hand? Lam. 2:3
From within Thy bosom, [r]destroy *them*! Ps. 59:13

12 Yet God is [r]my king from of
old,
Who works deeds of deliverance in the midst of the
earth. Ps. 44:4
13 [132]Thou didst divide the sea by
Thy strength;
Thou didst break the heads
of the sea monsters [t]in the
waters. *on*
14 Thou didst crush the heads
of Leviathan;
Thou didst give him as food
for the [t]creatures of the
wilderness. *people*
15 Thou didst break open
springs and torrents;
Thou didst [r]dry up ever-flowing streams. Ex. 14:21, 22
16 Thine is the day, Thine is the
night;
Thou hast prepared the [a]light
and the sun. *luminary*
17 Thou hast established all the
boundaries of the earth;
Thou hast [a]made summer and
winter. *formed*

18 Remember this, O LORD, that
the enemy has reviled;
And a foolish people has
spurned Thy name.
19 Do not deliver the soul of
Thy [r]turtledove to the
wild beast; Song 2:14
Do not forget the life of
Thine afflicted forever.
20 Consider the covenant;
For the dark places of the
land are full of the habitations of violence.
21 Let not the [r]oppressed return
dishonored; Ps. 103:6
Let the afflicted and needy
praise Thy name.

22 Do arise, O God, *and* plead
Thine own cause;
Remember how the [r]foolish
man reproaches Thee all
day long. Ps. 14:1; 53:1
23 Do not forget the voice of
Thine adversaries,
The uproar of those who rise
against Thee which ascends continually.

PSALM 75

For the choir director; *set to*
Al-tashheth.
A Psalm of Asaph, a Song.

WE give thanks to Thee, O God,
we give thanks,
For Thy name is near;
Men declare [r]Thy wondrous
works. Ps. 26:7; 44:1
2 "When I select an [r]appointed
time, Ps. 102:13
It is I who judge with equity.
3 "The earth and all who dwell
in it [133]melt;
It is I who have firmly set its
pillars. [Selah.
4 "I said to the boastful, 'Do not
boast,'

[132] Or, *Thou Thyself,* and so through v. 17

[133] Or, *totter*

And to the wicked, 'Do not lift up the horn;
5 Do not lift up your horn on high,
[r]Do not speak with insolent [t]pride.' " Ps. 94:4 • *neck*

6 For not from the east, nor from the west,
Nor from the [r]desert *comes* exaltation; Ps. 3:3
7 But God is the Judge;
He [r]puts down one, and exalts another. 1 Sam. 2:7
8 For a [r]cup is in the hand of the LORD, and the wine foams; Job 21:20; Ps. 11:6
It is well mixed, and He pours out of this;
Surely all the wicked of the earth must drain *and* drink down its dregs.

9 But as for me, I will [r]declare *it* forever;
I will sing praises to the God of Jacob. Ps. 22:22; 40:10
10 And all the horns of the wicked He will cut off,
But the horns of the righteous will be lifted up.

PSALM 76

For the choir director; on stringed instruments.
A Psalm of Asaph, a Song.

GOD is known in Judah;
His name is great in Israel.
2 And His [t]tabernacle is in Salem; *shelter*
His [r]dwelling place also is in Zion. Ps. 9:11; 132:13
3 There He [r]broke the flaming arrows, Ps. 46:9
The shield, and the sword, and the weapons of war. [Selah.

4 Thou art resplendent,
More majestic than the mountains of prey.
5 The [r]stouthearted were plundered; Is. 10:12; 46:12
They sank into sleep;
And none of the warriors could use his hands.
6 At Thy [r]rebuke, O God of Jacob, Ps. 80:16
Both rider and horse were cast into a dead sleep.
7 Thou, even Thou, art [r]to be feared; 1 Chr. 16:25
And who may stand in Thy presence when once Thou art angry?

8 Thou didst cause judgment to be heard from heaven;
The earth [r]feared, and was still, 1 Chr. 16:30
9 When God [r]arose to judgment, Ps. 9:7, 8; 74:22
To save all the humble of the earth. [Selah.
10 For the [t]wrath of man shall praise Thee; *wraths*
With a remnant of wrath Thou shalt gird Thyself.

11 Make vows to the LORD your God and fulfill *them*;
Let all who are around Him [r]bring gifts to Him who is to be feared. 2 Chr. 32:23
12 He will cut off the spirit of princes;
He is [t]feared by the kings of the earth. *awesome*

PSALM 77

For the choir director; according to Jeduthun.
A Psalm of Asaph.

MY voice *rises* to God, and I will
ʳcry aloud; Ps. 3:4; 142:1
My voice *rises* to God, and
He will hear me.
2 In the day of my trouble I
sought the Lord;
In the night my ʳhand was
stretched out [134]without
weariness; Job 11:13
My soul ʳrefused to be comforted. Gen. 37:35
3 *When* I remember God, then
I am disturbed;
When I sigh, then my spirit
grows faint. [Selah.
4 Thou hast held my eyelids
open;
I am so troubled that I ʳcan-
not speak. Ps. 39:9
5 I have considered the ʳdays of
old, Deut. 32:7; Ps. 44:1
The years of long ago.
6 I will remember my ʳsong in
the night; Ps. 42:8
I ʳwill meditate with my
heart; Ps. 4:4
And my spirit ponders.

7 Will the Lord reject forever?
And will He ʳnever be favorable again? Ps. 85:1, 5
8 Has His lovingkindness
ceased forever?
Has *His* ᵗpromise come to an
end forever? *word*
9 Has God ʳforgotten to be gracious? Is. 49:15
Or has He in anger with-
drawn His compassion?
[Selah.

[134]Lit., *and did not grow numb*

10 Then I said, "It is my grief,
That the right hand of the
Most High has changed."

11 I shall remember the ʳdeeds
of the LORD; Ps. 105:5
Surely I will remember Thy
wonders of old.
12 I will ʳmeditate on all Thy
work, Ps. 145:5
And muse on Thy deeds.
13 Thy way, O God, is holy;
What god is great like our
God?
14 Thou art the ʳGod who work-
est wonders;
Thou hast ʳmade known Thy
strength among the peo-
ples. Ps. 72:18 • Ps. 106:8
15 Thou hast by Thy power redeemed Thy people,
The sons of Jacob and
Joseph. [Selah.

16 The waters saw Thee, O God;
The waters saw Thee, they
were in anguish;
The deeps also trembled.
17 The clouds poured out water;
The skies gave forth a sound;
Thy arrows ᵗflashed here and
there. *went*
18 The sound of Thy thunder
was in the whirlwind;
The ʳlightnings lit up the
world; Ps. 97:4
The ʳearth trembled and
shook. Judg. 5:4; Ps. 18:7
19 Thy way was in the sea,
And Thy paths in the mighty
waters,
And Thy footprints may not
be known.
20 Thou ʳdidst lead Thy people
like a flock, Ex. 13:21
By the hand of ʳMoses and
Aaron. Ex. 6:26; Ps. 105:26

PSALM 78

A Maskil of Asaph.

LISTEN, O my people, to my instruction;
Incline your ears to the words of my mouth.
2 I will [r]open my mouth in a parable;
I will utter [r]dark sayings of old, Ps. 49:4 • Prov. 1:6
3 Which we have heard and known,
And our fathers have told us.
4 We will not conceal them from their children,
But [r]tell to the generation to come the praises of the LORD, Ex. 13:8, 14
And His strength and His [r]wondrous works that He has done. Job 37:16

5 For He established a [r]testimony in Jacob, Ps. 19:7
And appointed a [r]law in Israel, Ps. 147:19
Which He [r]commanded our fathers, Deut. 6:4-9
That they should teach them to their children,
6 That the generation to come might know, *even* the children *yet* to be born,
That they may arise and tell *them* to their children,
7 That they should put their confidence in God,
And [r]not forget the works of God, Deut. 4:9; 6:12
But [r]keep His commandments, Deut. 4:2; 5:1
8 And not be like their fathers,
A stubborn and rebellious generation,
A generation that did not [135]prepare its heart,
And whose spirit was not [r]faithful to God. Ps. 51:10

9 The sons of Ephraim [a]were archers equipped with bows, *being*
Yet [r]they turned back in the day of battle. Judg. 20:39
10 They did not keep the covenant of God,
And refused to [r]walk in His law; Ps. 119:1; Jer. 32:23
11 And they forgot His deeds,
And His miracles that He had shown them.
12 He wrought wonders before their fathers,
In the land of Egypt, in the [r]field of Zoan. Num. 13:22
13 He [r]divided the sea, and caused them to pass through; Ex. 14:21
And He made the waters stand up like a heap.
14 Then He led them with the cloud by [r]day, Ex. 13:21
And all the night with a [r]light of fire. Ex. 14:24
15 He [r]split the rocks in the wilderness,
And gave *them* abundant drink like the ocean depths. Ex. 17:6
16 He brought forth streams also from the rock,
And caused waters to run down like rivers.

17 Yet they still continued to sin against Him,
To rebel against the Most High in the desert.
18 And in their heart they [r]put God to the test Ex. 17:6

[135] Or, *put right*

By asking ʳfood according to their desire. Num. 11:4
19 Then they spoke against God;
They said, "Can God prepare a table in the wilderness?
20 "Behold, He ʳstruck the rock, so that waters gushed out, Num. 20:11; Ps. 78:15, 16
And streams were overflowing;
Can He give bread also?
Will He provide ᵗmeat for His people?" *flesh*

21 Therefore the LORD heard and was full of wrath,
And a fire was kindled against Jacob,
And anger also mounted against Israel;
22 Because they ʳdid not believe in God,
And did not trust in His salvation. Deut. 1:32; 9:23
23 Yet He commanded the clouds above,
And ʳopened the doors of heaven; Gen. 7:11
24 And He rained down manna upon them to eat,
And gave them ᵗfood from heaven. *grain*
25 Man did eat the bread of ᵗangels; *mighty ones*
He sent them food ᵗin abundance. *to satiation*
26 He caused the east wind to blow in the heavens;
And by His power He directed the south wind.
27 When He rained meat upon them like the dust,
Even winged fowl like the sand of the seas,
28 Then He let *them* fall in the midst of their camp,
Round about their dwellings.
29 So they ʳate and were well filled;
And their desire He gave to them. Num. 11:19, 20
30 Before they had satisfied their desire,
ʳWhile their food was in their mouths, Num. 11:33
31 The ʳanger of God rose against them, Num. 11:33
And killed some of their ʳstoutest ones, Is. 10:16
And subdued the choice men of Israel.
32 In spite of all this they still sinned,
And did not believe in His wonderful works.
33 So He brought their days to an end in futility,
And their years in sudden terror.

34 When He killed them, then they sought Him,
And returned and searched diligently for God;
35 And they remembered that God was their rock,
And the Most High God their ʳRedeemer. Ex. 15:13
36 But they ʳdeceived Him with their mouth, Ex. 24:7, 8
And ʳlied to Him with their tongue. Ex. 32:7, 8
37 For their heart was not steadfast toward Him,
Nor were they faithful in His covenant.
38 But He, being compassionate, ᵗforgave *their* iniquity, and did not destroy *them*; *covered over*

And often He [t]restrained His
anger, *turned away*
And did not arouse all His
wrath.
39 Thus He remembered that
they were but flesh,
A [a]wind that passes and does
not return. *breath*
40 How often they [r]rebelled
against Him in the wil-
derness, Ps. 95:8, 9; 106:43
And [r]grieved Him in the desert! Ps. 95:10; Is. 63:10
41 And again and again they
[136]tempted [r]God, Num. 14:22
And pained the [r]Holy One of
Israel. 2 Kin. 19:22
42 They did not remember His
[t]power, *hand*
The day when He redeemed
them from the adversary,
43 When He performed His
signs in Egypt,
And His [r]marvels in the field
of Zoan, Ex. 4:21; 7:3
44 And [r]turned their rivers to
blood, Ex. 7:20; Ps. 105:29
And their streams, they
could not drink.
45 He sent among them swarms
of [r]flies, which devoured
them, Ex. 8:24; Ps. 105:31
And [r]frogs which destroyed
them. Ex. 8:6; Ps. 105:30
46 He gave also their crops to
the grasshopper,
And the product of their labor to the locust.
47 He destroyed their vines
with hailstones,
And their sycamore trees
with frost.
48 He gave over their cattle also
to the hailstones,
And their herds to bolts of
lightning.
49 He [r]sent upon them His burning anger, Ex. 15:7
Fury, and indignation, and
trouble,
A band of destroying angels.
50 He leveled a path for His anger;
He did not spare their soul
from death,
But [r]gave over their life to the
plague, Ex. 12:29, 30
51 And [r]smote all the first-born
in Egypt, Ex. 12:29
The first *issue* of their virility
in the tents of Ham.
52 But He led forth His own
people like sheep,
And guided them in the wilderness like a flock;
53 And He led them safely, so
that they did not fear;
But [r]the sea engulfed their enemies. Ex. 14:27, 28
54 So He brought them to His
holy [t]land, *border, territory*
To this [a]hill country which
His right hand had
gained. *mountain*
55 He also drove out the nations
before them,
And He apportioned them
for an inheritance by
measurement,
And made the tribes of Israel
dwell in their tents.
56 Yet they [136]tempted and [r]re-
belled against the Most
High God,
And did not keep His testimonies, Judg. 2:11-13
57 But turned back and [r]acted

[136] Or, *put to the test*

treacherously like their fathers; Ezek. 20:27, 28
They turned aside like a treacherous bow.
58 For they provoked Him with their high places,
And aroused His jealousy with their graven images.
59 When God heard, He was filled with wrath,
And greatly abhorred Israel;
60 So that He abandoned the dwelling place at Shiloh,
The tent which He had pitched among men,
61 And gave up His [r]strength to captivity, Ps. 63:2; 132:8
And His glory into the hand of the adversary.
62 He also [r]delivered His people to the sword, Judg. 20:21
And was filled with wrath at His inheritance.
63 Fire devoured [a]His young men; *their*
And His [r]virgins had no wedding songs. Jer. 7:34
64 His priests fell by the sword;
And His [r]widows could not weep. Job 27:15

65 Then the Lord [r]awoke as *if from* sleep, Ps. 44:23
Like a warrior [a]overcome by wine. *sobered up from*
66 And He [t]drove His adversaries backward;
He put on them an everlasting reproach. *smote*
67 He also [r]rejected the tent of Joseph,
And did not choose the tribe of Ephraim, Ps. 78:60
68 But chose the tribe of Judah,
Mount Zion which He loved.
69 And He built His sanctuary like the heights,
Like the earth which He has founded forever.
70 He also [r]chose David His servant, 1 Sam. 16:11, 12
And took him from the sheepfolds;
71 From [t]the care of the ewes with suckling lambs He brought him, *following*
To [r]shepherd Jacob His people, 2 Sam. 5:2
And Israel His inheritance.
72 So he shepherded them according to the [r]integrity of his heart, 1 Kin. 9:4
And guided them with his skillful hands.

PSALM 79

A Psalm of Asaph.

O GOD, the nations have invaded Thine inheritance;
They have defiled Thy [r]holy temple; Ps. 74:3, 7
They have [r]laid Jerusalem in ruins. 2 Kin. 25:9, 10
2 They have given the [r]dead bodies of Thy servants for food to the birds of the heavens, Deut. 28:26
The flesh of Thy godly ones to the beasts of the earth.
3 They have poured out their blood like water round about Jerusalem;
And there was [r]no one to bury them. Jer. 14:16
4 We have become a reproach to our neighbors,
A scoffing and derision to those around us.
5 How long, O LORD? Wilt Thou be angry forever?

Will Thy jealousy [r]burn like
fire? Ps. 89:46; Zeph. 3:8
6 Pour out Thy wrath upon the
nations which [r]do not
know Thee, 1 Thess. 4:5
And upon the kingdoms
which [r]do not call upon
Thy name. Ps. 14:4; 53:4
7 For they have [r]devoured Jacob,
And laid waste his [t]habitation. Ps. 53:4 • *pasture*
8 Do not remember the iniquities of *our* forefathers
against us;
Let Thy compassion come
quickly to meet us;
For we are brought very low.
9 Help us, O God of our salvation, for the glory of [r]Thy
name; Ps. 31:3
And deliver us, and [a]forgive
our sins, for Thy name's
sake. *cover over, atone for*
10 Why should the nations say,
"Where is their God?"
Let there be known among
the nations in our sight,
Vengeance for the blood of
Thy servants, which has
been shed.
11 Let the groaning of the prisoner come before Thee;
According to the greatness
of Thy [t]power preserve
those who are [r]doomed to
die. *arm* • Ps. 102:20
12 And return to our neighbors
[r]sevenfold into their bosom Gen. 4:15
[t]The reproach with which
they have reproached
Thee, O Lord. *Their*
13 So we Thy people and the
sheep of Thy pasture
Will [r]give thanks to Thee forever;
To all generations we will tell
of Thy praise. Ps. 44:8

PSALM 80

For the choir director; *set to*
El Shoshannim; Eduth.
A Psalm of Asaph.

OH, give ear, Shepherd of Israel,
Thou who dost lead [r]Joseph
like a flock; Ps. 77:15
Thou who [r]art enthroned
above the cherubim,
shine forth! Ex. 25:22
2 Before Ephraim and Benjamin and Manasseh, [r]stir
up Thy power, Ps. 35:23
And come to save us!
3 O God, restore us,
And [r]cause Thy face to shine
upon us, and we will be
saved. Num. 6:25; Ps. 4:6
4 O LORD God *of* hosts,
How long wilt Thou [t]be angry
with the prayer of Thy
people? *smoke against*
5 Thou hast fed them with the
bread of tears,
And Thou hast made them to
drink tears in [t]large measure. *a third part of a*
6 Thou dost make us [137]an object of contention to our
neighbors;
And our enemies laugh
among themselves.
7 O God *of* hosts, restore us,
And cause Thy face to shine
upon us, [138]and we will be
saved.
8 Thou didst remove a [r]vine
from Egypt; Ps. 80:15

[137] Lit., *a strife to* [138] Or, *that we may*

Thou didst drive out the nations, and didst plant it.
9 Thou didst [r]clear *the ground* before it, Ex. 23:28
And it [r]took deep root and filled the land. Hos. 14:5
10 The mountains were covered with its shadow;
And the cedars of God with its [r]boughs. Gen. 49:22
11 It was sending out its branches to the sea,
And its shoots to the River.
12 Why hast Thou broken down its [a]hedges, *walls, fences*
So that all who pass *that* way pick its *fruit*?
13 A boar from the forest [r]eats it away,
And whatever moves in the field feeds on it. Jer. 5:6

14 O God *of* hosts, turn again now, we beseech Thee;
[r]Look down from heaven and see, and take care of this vine, Ps. 102:19
15 Even the shoot which Thy right hand has planted,
And on the son whom Thou hast [a]strengthened for Thyself. *secured*
16 It is [r]burned with fire, it is cut down; 2 Chr. 36:19
They perish at the rebuke of Thy countenance.
17 Let Thy hand be upon the man of Thy right hand,
Upon the son of man whom Thou [r]didst make strong for Thyself. Ps. 80:15
18 Then we shall not [r]turn back from Thee;
Revive us, and we will call upon Thy name. Is. 50:5
19 O LORD God of hosts, [r]restore us; Ps. 80:3
Cause Thy face to shine *upon us*, and we will be saved.

PSALM 81

For the choir director; on the Gittith.
A Psalm of Asaph.

SING for joy to God our strength;
Shout [r]joyfully to the God of Jacob. Ps. 66:1; 95:2
2 Raise a song, strike [r]the timbrel, Ex. 15:20; Ps. 149:3
The sweet sounding [r]lyre with the harp. Ps. 92:3
3 Blow the trumpet at the [r]new moon, Num. 10:10
At the full moon, on our [r]feast day. Lev. 23:24
4 For it is a statute for Israel,
An ordinance of the God of Jacob.
5 He established it for a testimony in Joseph,
When he went throughout the land of Egypt.
I heard a [r]language that I did not know: Deut. 28:49

6 "I [r]relieved his shoulder of the burden, Is. 9:4; 10:27
His hands were freed from the basket.
7 "You [r]called in trouble, and I rescued you; Ex. 2:23
I answered you in the hiding place of thunder;
I proved you at the waters of Meribah. [Selah.
8 "Hear, O My people, and I will admonish you;
O Israel, if you [r]would listen to Me! Ps. 95:7
9 "Let there be no strange god among you;

Nor shall you worship any
foreign god.
10 "I, the LORD, am your God,
Who brought you up from
the land of Egypt;
Open your mouth wide and I
will [r]fill it. Ps. 37:4; 78:25

11 "But My people [r]did not listen
to My voice; Deut. 32:15
And Israel did not obey Me.
12 "So I gave [t]them over to the
stubbornness of their
heart, *him*
To walk in their own devices.
13 "Oh that My people [r]would listen to Me, Deut. 5:29
That Israel would [r]walk in My
ways! Ps. 128:1
14 "I would quickly [r]subdue their
enemies, Ps. 18:47
And turn My hand against
their adversaries.
15 "Those who hate the LORD
would [r]pretend obedience
to Him; Ps. 18:44; 66:3
And their time *of punishment* would be forever.
16 "But I would feed you with
the finest of the wheat;
And with [r]honey from the
rock I would satisfy
you." Deut. 32:13

PSALM 82

A Psalm of Asaph.

GOD takes His stand in His own
congregation;
He judges in the midst of the
[t]rulers. *gods*
2 How long will you judge unjustly,
And show partiality to the
wicked? [Selah.
3 Vindicate the weak and fatherless;
Do justice to the afflicted and
destitute.
4 Rescue the weak and needy;
Deliver *them* out of the hand
of the wicked.

5 They do not know nor do
they understand;
They walk about in darkness;
All the foundations of the
earth are shaken.
6 I said, "You are gods,
And all of you are [r]sons of the
Most High. Ps. 89:26
7 "Nevertheless [r]you will die like
men, Job 21:32
And fall like *any* [r]one of the
princes." Ps. 83:11
8 Arise, O God, [r]judge the
earth! Ps. 58:11; 96:13
For it is Thou who dost possess all the nations.

PSALM 83

A Song, a Psalm of Asaph.

O GOD, do not remain quiet;
Do not be silent and, O God,
do not be still.
2 For, behold, Thine enemies
make an uproar;
And those who hate Thee
have exalted themselves.
3 They make shrewd plans
against Thy people,
And [a]conspire together
against [r]Thy treasured
ones. *consult* • Ps. 27:5
4 They have said, "Come, and
let us wipe them out [t]as a
nation, *from*
That the name of Israel be remembered no more."

5 For they have conspired together with one mind;
Against Thee do they make a covenant:
6 The tents of Edom and the Ishmaelites;
Moab, and the Hagrites;
7 Gebal, and [r]Ammon, and Amalek; 2 Chr. 20:10
Philistia with the inhabitants of [r]Tyre; Ezek. 27:3
8 Assyria also has joined with them;
They have become a help to the children of Lot. [Selah.
9 Deal with them [r]as with Midian, Judg. 7:1-24
As with Sisera *and* Jabin, at the torrent of Kishon,
10 Who were destroyed at En-dor,
Who [r]became as dung for the ground. Zeph. 1:17
11 Make their nobles like [r]Oreb and Zeeb, Judg. 7:25
And all their princes like Zebah and Zalmunna,
12 Who said, "Let us possess for ourselves
The pastures of God."
13 O my God, make them like the [139]whirling dust;
Like chaff before the wind.
14 Like [r]fire that burns the forest, Is. 9:18
And like a flame that sets the mountains on fire,
15 So pursue them [r]with Thy tempest,
And terrify them with Thy storm. Job 9:17
16 Fill their faces with dishonor,
That they may seek Thy name, O LORD.
17 Let them be ashamed and dismayed forever;
And let them be humiliated and perish,
18 That they may [r]know that Thou alone, whose name is the LORD, Ps. 59:13
Art the [r]Most High over all the earth. Ps. 9:2; 18:13

PSALM 84

For the choir director; on the Gittith. A Psalm of the sons of Korah.

HOW lovely are Thy [r]dwelling places, Ps. 43:3; 132:5
O LORD of hosts!
2 My [r]soul longed and even yearned for the courts of the LORD; Ps. 42:1, 2
My heart and my flesh sing for joy to the living God.
3 The bird also has found a house,
And the swallow a nest for herself, where she may lay her young,
Even Thine [r]altars, O LORD of hosts, Ps. 43:4
My King and my God.
4 How blessed are those who dwell in Thy house!
They are ever praising Thee. [Selah.
5 How blessed is the man whose [r]strength is in Thee; Ps. 81:1
In [t]whose heart are the highways *to Zion*! *their*
6 Passing through the valley of [140]Baca, they make it a [a]spring, *place of springs*

[139] Or, *tumbleweed*

[140] Probably, *Weeping* or *Balsam trees*

The early rain also covers it
with blessings.
7 They [r]go from strength to
strength, Prov. 4:18
Every one of them appears
before God in Zion.
8 O [r]LORD God of hosts, hear
my prayer; Ps. 59:5; 80:4
Give ear, O God of Jacob!
[Selah.
9 Behold our shield, O God,
And look upon the face of
Thine anointed.
10 For [r]a day in Thy courts is
better than a thousand
outside.
I would rather stand at the
threshold of the house of
my God,
Than dwell in the tents of
wickedness. Ps. 27:4
11 For the LORD God is a sun
and [r]shield; Gen. 15:1
The LORD gives grace and
[r]glory; Ps. 85:9
No good thing does He withhold from those who
walk uprightly.
12 O LORD of hosts,
How blessed is the man who
trusts in Thee!

PSALM 85

For the choir director.
A Psalm of the sons of Korah.

O LORD, Thou didst show [r]favor
to Thy land;
Thou didst [141]restore the captivity of Jacob. Ps. 77:7
2 Thou didst forgive the iniquity of Thy people;
Thou didst cover all their sin.
[Selah.
3 Thou didst [r]withdraw all Thy
fury; Ps. 78:38; 106:23
Thou didst turn away from
Thy burning anger.
4 [r]Restore us, O God of our salvation, Ps. 80:3, 7
And cause Thine indignation
toward us to cease.
5 Wilt [r]Thou be angry with us
forever? Ps. 74:1; 79:5
Wilt Thou prolong Thine anger to all generations?
6 Wilt Thou not Thyself [a]revive
us again, *bring to life*
That Thy people may [r]rejoice
in Thee? Ps. 33:1; 90:14
7 Show us Thy lovingkindness,
O LORD,
And grant us Thy salvation.
8 I will hear what God the
LORD will say;
For He will [r]speak peace to
His people, [t]to His godly
ones; Ps. 29:11 · *even to*
But let them not turn back to
[a]folly. *stupidity*
9 Surely His salvation is near
to those who [142]fear Him,
That [r]glory may dwell in our
land. Ps. 84:11; Hag. 2:7
10 Lovingkindness and truth
have met together;
Righteousness and peace
have kissed each other.
11 Truth springs from the earth;
And righteousness looks
down from heaven.
12 Indeed, [r]the LORD will give
what is good; Ps. 84:11
And our [r]land will yield its
produce. Lev. 26:4
13 Righteousness will go before
Him,

[141] Or, *restore the fortunes*

[142] Or, *reverence*

And will make His footsteps into a way.

PSALM 86

A Prayer of David.

INCLINE Thine ear, O LORD, *and* answer me;
For I am afflicted and needy.
2 Do preserve my[a] soul, for I am a godly man;
O Thou my God, save Thy servant who [r] trusts in Thee. *life* • Ps. 25:2; 31:14
3 Be gracious to me, O Lord,
For to Thee I cry all day long.
4 Make glad the soul of Thy servant,
For to Thee, O Lord,[r] I lift up my soul. Ps. 25:1; 143:8
5 For Thou, Lord, art good, and ready to forgive,
And[r] abundant in lovingkindness to all who call upon Thee. Ex. 34:6
6 Give ear, O LORD, to my prayer;
And give heed to the voice of my supplications!
7 In the day of my trouble I shall call upon Thee,
For Thou wilt answer me.
8 There is no one like Thee among the gods, O Lord;
Nor are there any works[r] like Thine. Deut. 3:24
9 All nations whom Thou hast made shall come and worship before Thee, O Lord;
And they shall glorify Thy name.
10 For Thou art[r] great and doest wondrous deeds;
Thou alone art God. Ps. 77:13
11 Teach me Thy way, O LORD;
I will walk in Thy truth;
[r]Unite my heart to fear Thy name. Jer. 32:39
12 I will[r] give thanks to Thee, O Lord my God, with all my heart,
And will glorify Thy name forever. Ps. 111:1
13 For Thy lovingkindness toward me is great,
And Thou hast[r] delivered my soul from the depths of Sheol. Ps. 30:3

14 O God, arrogant men have risen up against me,
And a band of violent men have sought my life,
And they have not set Thee before them.
15 But Thou, O Lord, art a God merciful and gracious,
Slow to anger and abundant in lovingkindness and [a]truth. *faithfulness*
16 [r]Turn to me, and be gracious to me; Ps. 25:16
Oh[r] grant Thy strength to Thy servant, Ps. 68:35
And save the [r] son of Thy handmaid. Ps. 116:16
17 Show me a sign for good,
That those who hate me may see *it*, and be ashamed,
Because Thou, O LORD,[r] hast helped me and comforted me. Ps. 118:13

PSALM 87

A Psalm of the sons of Korah.
A Song.

HIS [r]foundation is in the holy mountains. Ps. 78:69
2 The LORD[r] loves the gates of Zion Ps. 78:67, 68

More than all the *other*
dwelling places of Jacob.
3 [r]Glorious things are spoken of
you, Is. 60:1
O city of God. [Selah.
4 "I shall mention [143]Rahab and
Babylon among those
who know Me;
Behold, Philistia and Tyre
with Ethiopia:
'This one was born there.' "
5 But of Zion it shall be said,
"This one and that one
were born in her";
And the Most High Himself
will establish her.
6 The LORD shall count when
He registers the peoples,
"This one was born there."
[Selah.
7 Then those who sing as well
as those who [a]play the
flutes *shall say*,
"All my [r]springs *of joy* are in
you." *dance* • Ps. 36:9

PSALM 88

A Song. A Psalm of the sons of
Korah. For the choir director;
according to Mahalath Leannoth.
A Maskil of Heman the Ezrahite.

O LORD, the [r]God of my salvation, Ps. 24:5; 27:9
I have cried out by day and
in the night before Thee.
2 Let my prayer [r]come before
Thee; Ps. 18:6
Incline Thine ear to my cry!
3 For my [r]soul has had enough
troubles, Ps. 107:26
And [r]my life has drawn near
to Sheol. Ps. 107:18
4 I am reckoned among those
who go down to the pit;
I have become like a man
without strength,
5 Forsaken among the dead,
Like the slain who lie in the
grave,
Whom Thou dost remember
no more,
And they are [r]cut off from
Thy hand. Ps. 31:22
6 Thou hast put me in [r]the lowest pit, Ps. 86:13
In dark places, in the depths.
7 Thy wrath [r]has rested upon
me, Ps. 32:4; 39:10
And Thou hast afflicted me
with all Thy waves.
[Selah.
8 Thou hast removed my acquaintances far from me;
Thou hast made me an [144]ob-
ject of loathing to them;
I am [r]shut up and cannot go
out. Ps. 142:7; Jer. 32:2
9 My eye has wasted away because of affliction;
I have called upon Thee every day, O LORD;
I have spread out my [t]hands
to Thee. *palms*
10 Wilt Thou perform wonders
for the dead?
Will the departed spirits rise
and praise Thee? [Selah.
11 Will Thy lovingkindness be
declared in the grave,
Thy faithfulness in Abaddon?
12 Will Thy wonders be made
known in the darkness?
And Thy righteousness in the
land of forgetfulness?

13 But I, O LORD, have cried out
to Thee for help,

[143] I.e., Egypt

[144] Lit., *abomination to them*

And [r]in the morning my prayer comes before Thee. Ps. 5:3; 119:147
14 O LORD, why [r]dost Thou reject my soul? Ps. 43:2
Why dost Thou [r]hide Thy face from me? Job 13:24
15 I was afflicted and about to die from my youth on;
I suffer Thy terrors; I am [a]overcome. *embarrassed*
16 Thy burning anger has passed over me;
Thy terrors have [a]destroyed me. *silenced*
17 They have surrounded me like water all day long;
They have [r]encompassed me altogether. Ps. 17:11; 22:12
18 Thou hast removed lover and friend far from me;
My acquaintances are *in* darkness.

PSALM 89

A Maskil of Ethan the Ezrahite.

I WILL sing of the lovingkindness of the LORD forever;
To all generations I will make known Thy faithfulness with my mouth.
2 For I have said, [r]"Lovingkindness will be built up forever; Ps. 103:17
In the heavens Thou wilt establish Thy faithfulness."
3 "I have made a covenant with [r]My chosen; 1 Kin. 8:16
I have [r]sworn to David My servant, Ps. 132:11
4 I will establish your [r]seed forever, 2 Sam. 7:16
And build up your throne to all generations." [Selah.
5 And the heavens will praise Thy wonders, O LORD;
Thy faithfulness also [r]in the assembly of the holy ones. Ps. 149:1
6 For who in the skies is comparable to the LORD?
Who among the sons of the mighty is like the LORD,
7 A God greatly feared in the council of the holy ones,
And [r]awesome above all those who are around Him? Ps. 96:4
8 O LORD God of hosts, [r]who is like Thee, O mighty LORD? Ps. 35:10; 71:19
Thy faithfulness also surrounds Thee.
9 Thou dost rule the swelling of the sea;
When its waves rise, Thou [r]dost still them. Ps. 65:7
10 Thou Thyself didst crush Rahab like one who is slain;
Thou didst [r]scatter Thine enemies with Thy mighty arm. Ps. 18:14; 68:1

11 The heavens are Thine, the earth also is Thine;
The [r]world and [145]all it contains, Thou hast founded them. Ps. 24:1
12 The north and the south, Thou hast created them;
Tabor and Hermon shout for joy at Thy name.
13 Thou hast a strong arm;
Thy hand is mighty, Thy right hand is exalted.
14 [r]Righteousness and justice are the foundation of Thy throne; Ps. 97:2

[145] Lit., *its fulness*

[r] Lovingkindness and truth go
before Thee. Ps. 85:13
15 How blessed are the people
who know the [146]joyful
sound!
O LORD, they walk in the
light of Thy countenance.
16 In [r]Thy name they rejoice all
the day, Ps. 105:3
And by Thy righteousness
they are exalted.
17 For Thou art the glory of
[r]their strength, Ps. 28:8
And by Thy favor our [r]horn is
exalted. Ps. 75:10; 92:10
18 For our [r]shield belongs to the
LORD,
[147]And our king to the Holy
One of Israel. Ps. 47:9

19 Once Thou didst speak in vision to Thy godly ones,
And didst say, "I have [t]given
help to one who is
mighty; *placed help upon*
I have exalted one chosen
from the people.
20 "I have [r]found David My servant; 1 Sam. 13:14
With My holy oil I have
anointed him,
21 With whom [r]My hand will be
established;
My arm also will [r]strengthen
him. Ps. 18:35 • Ps. 18:32
22 "The enemy will not [148]deceive
him,
Nor the [a]son of wickedness
afflict him. *wicked man*
23 "But I shall crush his adversaries before him,
And strike those who hate
him.

24 "And My [r]faithfulness and My
lovingkindness will be
with him,
And in My name his horn
will be exalted. Ps. 89:1
25 "I shall also set his hand [r]on
the sea,
And his right hand on the rivers. Ps. 72:8
26 "He will cry to Me, 'Thou art
[r]my Father, 2 Sam. 7:14
My God, and the [r]rock of my
salvation.' 2 Sam. 22:47
27 "I also shall make him *My*
[r]first-born,
The highest of the kings of
the earth. Ex. 4:22
28 "My lovingkindness I will
keep for him forever,
And My covenant shall be
confirmed to him.
29 "So I will establish his descendants forever,
And his throne [r]as the days of
heaven. Deut. 11:21

30 "If his sons forsake My law,
And do not walk in My judgments,
31 If they [149]violate My statutes,
And do not keep My com-
mandments,
32 Then I will visit their transgression with the rod,
And their iniquity with
stripes.
33 "But I will not break off My
lovingkindness from him,
Nor deal falsely in My faithfulness.
34 "My covenant I will not [t]vio-
late, *profane*
Nor will I [r]alter the utterance
of My lips. Num. 23:19

[146] Or, *blast of the trumpet, shout of joy*
[147] Or, *Even to the Holy One of Israel our King*
[148] Or, *exact usury from him*
[149] Lit., *profane*

35 "[150]Once I have [r]sworn by My holiness; Ps. 60:6; Amos 4:2
I will not lie to David.
36 "His [t]descendants shall endure forever,
And his [r]throne as the sun before Me. *seed* • Ps. 72:5
37 "It shall be established forever like the moon,
And the witness in the sky is faithful." [Selah.

38 But Thou hast [r]cast off and rejected, Ps. 44:9
Thou hast been full of wrath against Thine anointed.
39 Thou hast spurned the covenant of Thy servant;
Thou hast profaned his crown in the dust.
40 Thou hast [r]broken down all his walls; Ps. 80:12
Thou hast brought his strongholds to ruin.
41 All who pass along the way plunder him;
He has become a [r]reproach to his neighbors. Ps. 44:13
42 Thou hast exalted the right hand of his adversaries;
Thou hast made all his enemies rejoice.
43 Thou dost also turn back the edge of his sword,
And hast [r]not made him stand in battle. Ps. 44:10
44 Thou hast made his [t]splendor to cease, *clearness, luster*
And cast his throne to the ground.
45 Thou hast shortened the days of his youth;
Thou hast covered him with shame. [Selah.

46 How long, O LORD?
Wilt Thou hide Thyself forever?
Will Thy [r]wrath burn like fire? Ps. 79:5; 80:4
47 [r]Remember what my span of life is; Job 7:7; 10:9
For what [r]vanity Thou hast created all the sons of men! Ps. 39:5; 62:9
48 What man can live and not [r]see death? Ps. 22:29; 49:9
Can he deliver his soul from the power of Sheol? [Selah.

49 Where are Thy former lovingkindnesses, O Lord,
Which Thou didst [r]swear to David in Thy faithfulness? 2 Sam. 7:15
50 Remember, O Lord, the reproach of Thy servants;
How I do bear in my bosom *the reproach of* all the many peoples,
51 With which [r]Thine enemies have reproached, O LORD, Ps. 74:10, 18, 22
With which they have reproached the footsteps of Thine anointed.

52 Blessed be the LORD forever!
Amen and Amen.

BOOK 4

PSALM 90

A Prayer of Moses the man of God.

LORD, Thou hast been our [151]dwelling place in all generations.

[150] Or, *One thing*

[151] Or, *hiding place;* some ancient mss. read *place of refuge*

2 Before [r]the mountains were born, Job 15:7; Prov. 8:25
Or Thou didst give birth to the earth and the world,
Even [r]from everlasting to everlasting, Thou art God. Ps. 93:2; 102:24, 27

3 Thou dost [r]turn man back into dust, Gen. 3:19
And dost say, "Return, O children of men."
4 For [r]a thousand years in Thy sight 2 Pet. 3:8
Are like [r]yesterday when it passes by, Ps. 39:5
Or *as* a watch in the night.
5 Thou hast swept them away like a flood, they [t]fall asleep; *become asleep*
In the morning they are like grass which [a]sprouts anew. *passes away*
6 In the morning it flourishes, and sprouts anew;
Toward evening it [r]fades, and withers away. Ps. 92:7

7 For we have been consumed by Thine anger,
And by Thy wrath we have been dismayed.
8 Thou hast placed our iniquities before Thee,
Our [r]secret *sins* in the light of Thy presence. Ps. 19:12
9 For all our days have declined in Thy fury;
We have finished our years like a [a]sigh. *whisper*
10 As for the days of our [t]life, [t]they contain seventy years,
Or if due to strength, eighty years, *years • in them are*
Yet their pride is *but* labor and sorrow;
For soon it is gone and we [r]fly away. Job 20:8; Ps. 78:39
11 Who understands the power of Thine anger,
And Thy fury, according to the fear that is due Thee?
12 So [r]teach us to number our days, Deut. 32:29
That we may present to Thee a heart of wisdom.

13 Do return, O LORD; how [r]long *will it be*? Ps. 6:3; 74:10
And be [r]sorry for Thy servants. Ex. 32:12
14 O satisfy us in the morning with Thy lovingkindness,
That we may sing for joy and be glad all our days.
15 Make us glad according to the days Thou hast afflicted us,
And the years we have seen [152]evil.
16 Let Thy [r]work appear to Thy servants, Deut. 32:4
And Thy majesty [a]to their children. *upon*
17 And let the favor of the Lord our God be upon us;
And do [153]confirm for us the work of our hands;
Yes, [153]confirm the work of our hands.

PSALM 91

HE who dwells in the shelter of the Most High
Will abide in the [r]shadow of the Almighty. Ps. 17:8
2 I will say to the LORD, "My refuge and my fortress,
My God, in whom I trust!"

[152] Or, *trouble* [153] Or, *give permanence to*

3 For it is He who delivers you
from the [r]snare of the
trapper, Ps. 124:7
And from the deadly [r]pestilence. 1 Kin. 8:37
4 He will [r]cover you with His
pinions,
And under His wings you
may seek refuge;
His faithfulness is a shield
and bulwark. Is. 51:16

5 You will not be afraid of the
terror by night,
Or of the [r]arrow that flies by
day; Ps. 64:4
6 Of the pestilence that [a]stalks
in darkness,
Or of the destruction that
lays waste at noon. *walks*
7 A thousand may fall at your
side,
And ten thousand at your
right hand;
But it shall not approach you.
8 You will only look on with
your eyes,
And [r]see the recompense of
the wicked. Ps. 37:34
9 For you have made the LORD,
[r]my refuge, Ps. 91:2
Even the Most High, [r]your
dwelling place. Ps. 90:1
10 No evil will befall you,
Nor will any plague come
near your [a]tent. *dwelling*

11 For He will give His angels
charge concerning you,
To guard you in all your
ways.
12 They will [r]bear you up in their
hands,
Lest you strike your foot
against a stone. Matt. 4:6
13 You will tread upon the lion
and cobra,
The young lion and the [a]serpent
you will trample
down. *dragon*

14 "Because [r]he has loved Me,
therefore I will deliver
him; Ps. 145:20
I will set him *securely* on
high, because he has
known My name.
15 "He will call upon Me, and I
will answer him;
I will be with him in trouble;
I will rescue him, and [r]honor
him. 1 Sam. 2:30
16 "With a [r]long life I will satisfy
him, Deut. 6:2; Ps. 21:4
And [r]let him behold My salvation."
Ps. 50:23

PSALM 92

A Psalm, a Song for the Sabbath day.

IT is [r]good to give thanks to the
LORD, Ps. 147:1
And to sing praises to Thy
name, O Most High;
2 To declare Thy lovingkindness
in the morning,
And Thy faithfulness [t]by
night, *nights*
3 With the ten-stringed lute,
and with the harp;
With resounding music [t]upon
the lyre. *by means of*
4 For Thou, O LORD, hast made
me glad by [t]what Thou
hast done, *Thy working*
I will sing for joy at the
works of Thy hands.

5 How [r]great are Thy works, O
LORD! Ps. 40:5; 111:2
Thy thoughts are very deep.
6 A senseless man has no
knowledge;

Nor does a stupid man understand this:
7 That when the wicked sprouted up like grass,
And all [r] who did iniquity flourished,
It *was only* that they might be [r] destroyed forevermore. Ps. 94:4 • Ps. 37:38
8 But Thou, O LORD, art [r] on high forever. Ps. 83:18
9 For, behold, Thine enemies, O LORD,
For, behold, [r] Thine enemies will perish; Ps. 37:20
All who do iniquity will be [r] scattered. Ps. 68:1

10 But Thou hast exalted my [r] horn like *that of* the wild ox; Ps. 75:10; 89:17
I have [a] been anointed with fresh oil. *become moist*
11 And my eye has looked *exultantly* upon my foes,
My ears hear of the evildoers who rise up against me.
12 The righteous man will flourish like the palm tree,
He will grow like a [r] cedar in Lebanon. Ps. 104:16
13 Planted in the house of the LORD,
They will flourish in the courts of our God.
14 They will still [a] yield fruit in old age;
They shall be [154] full of sap and very green, *thrive in*
15 To [a] declare that the LORD is upright; *show forth*
He is my [r] rock, and there is no unrighteousness in Him. Deut. 32:4

[154] Lit., *fat and*

PSALM 93

THE LORD reigns, He is [r] clothed with majesty; Ps. 104:1
The LORD has [r] clothed and girded Himself with strength; Ps. 65:6
Indeed, the [r] world is firmly established, it will not be moved. Ps. 96:10
2 Thy [r] throne is established from of old; Ps. 45:6
Thou art from everlasting.

3 The [r] floods have lifted up, O LORD, Ps. 96:11; 98:7, 8
The floods have lifted up their voice;
The floods lift up their pounding waves.
4 More than the sounds of many waters,
Than the mighty breakers of the sea,
The LORD on high is mighty.
5 Thy [r] testimonies are fully confirmed; Ps. 19:7
Holiness befits Thy house,
O LORD, forevermore.

PSALM 94

O LORD, God of vengeance;
God of vengeance, [a] shine forth! *has shone forth*
2 Rise up, O Judge of the earth;
Render recompense [r] to the proud. Ps. 31:23
3 How long shall the wicked, O LORD,
How long shall the [r] wicked exult? Job 20:5
4 They pour forth *words*, they speak arrogantly;
All who do wickedness [r] vaunt themselves. Ps. 10:3

5 They [r]crush Thy people, O LORD, Is. 3:15
And afflict Thy heritage.
6 They [r]slay the widow and the stranger, Is. 10:2
And murder the orphans.
7 And they have said, "The LORD does not see,
Nor does the God of Jacob pay heed."

8 Pay heed, you senseless among the people;
And when will you understand, stupid ones?
9 He who [r]planted the ear, does He not hear? Ex. 4:11
He who formed the eye, does He not see?
10 He who chastens the nations, will He not rebuke,
Even He who teaches man knowledge?
11 The LORD knows the thoughts of man,
That they are a *mere* breath.

12 Blessed is the man whom [r]Thou dost chasten, O LORD, Deut. 8:5
And [r]dost teach out of Thy law; Ps. 119:171
13 That Thou mayest grant him relief from the days of adversity,
Until [r]a pit is dug for the wicked. Ps. 9:15; 55:23
14 For the LORD will not abandon His people,
Nor will He [r]forsake His inheritance. Ps. 37:28
15 For [r]judgment will again be righteous;
And all the upright in heart will follow it. Ps. 97:2
16 Who will stand up for me against evildoers?
Who will take his stand for me against those who do wickedness?

17 If [r]the LORD had not been my help,
My soul would soon have dwelt in *the abode of* silence. Ps. 124:1, 2
18 If I should say, [r]"My foot has slipped," Ps. 38:16; 73:2
Thy lovingkindness, O LORD, will hold me up.
19 When my anxious thoughts multiply within me,
Thy [r]consolations delight my soul. Is. 57:18; 66:13
20 Can a throne of destruction be allied with Thee,
One which devises [a]mischief by decree? *trouble*
21 They band themselves together against the life of the righteous,
And condemn [t]the innocent to death. *innocent blood*
22 But the LORD has been my [r]stronghold, Ps. 9:9
And my God the [r]rock of my refuge. Ps. 18:2; 71:7
23 And He has [r]brought back their wickedness upon them, Ps. 7:16
And will [a]destroy them in their evil; *silence*
The LORD our God will destroy them.

PSALM 95

O COME, let us sing for joy to the LORD;
Let us shout joyfully to the rock of our salvation.

2 Let us come before His presence with thanksgiving;
Let us shout joyfully to Him [r]with psalms. Ps. 81:2
3 For the LORD is a great God,
And a great King[r]above all gods, Ps. 96:4; 97:9
4 In whose hand are the[r]depths of the earth;
The peaks of the mountains are His also. Ps. 135:6
5 The sea is His, for it was He [r]who made it;
And His hands formed the dry land. Gen. 1:9, 10

6 Come, let us [r]worship and bow down; Ps. 96:9
Let us[r]kneel before the LORD our Maker. 2 Chr. 6:13
7 For He is our God,
And[r]we are the people of His pasture, and the sheep of His hand. Ps. 79:13
[r]Today, if you would hear His voice, Heb. 3:7-11, 15
8 Do not harden your hearts, as at [155]Meribah,
As in the day of [156]Massah in the wilderness;
9 "When your fathers [r] tested Me, Num. 14:22
They tried Me, though they had seen My work.
10 "For[r]forty years I loathed *that* generation,
And said they are a people who err in their heart,
And they do not know My ways. Acts 7:36
11 "Therefore I[r]swore in My anger, Num. 14:23, 28-30
Truly they shall not enter into My rest."

[155]Or, *place of strife* [156]Or, *temptation*

PSALM 96

SING to the LORD a new song;
Sing to the LORD, all the earth.
2 Sing to the LORD, bless His name;
[r]Proclaim good tidings of His salvation from day to day. Ps. 71:15
3 Tell of[r]His glory among the nations,
His wonderful deeds among all the peoples. Ps. 145:12
4 For great is the LORD, and greatly to be praised;
He is to be[r]feared above all gods. Ps. 89:7
5 For[r]all the gods of the peoples are idols, 1 Chr. 16:26
But[r]the LORD made the heavens. Ps. 115:15; Is. 42:5
6 Splendor and majesty are before Him,
Strength and beauty are in His sanctuary.

7 [157]Ascribe to the LORD, O families of the peoples,
[157]Ascribe to the LORD glory and strength.
8 [157]Ascribe to the LORD the glory of His name;
Bring an offering, and come into His courts.
9 Worship the LORD in [158]holy attire;
[r]Tremble before Him, all the earth. Ps. 33:8; 114:7
10 Say among the nations,[r]"The LORD reigns;
Indeed, the world is firmly established, it will not be moved; Ps. 93:1; 97:1

[157]Lit., *Give* [158]Or, *the splendor of holiness*

He will judge the peoples with [159]equity."

11 Let the heavens be glad, and let the earth rejoice;
Let the sea roar, and [t]all it contains; *its fulness*
12 Let the [r]field exult, and all that is in it. Ps. 65:13
Then all the trees of the forest will sing for joy
13 Before the LORD,[r] for He is coming;
For He is coming to judge the earth.
He will judge the world in righteousness,
And the peoples in His faithfulness. Ps. 98:9

PSALM 97

THE LORD reigns; let the [r]earth rejoice; Ps. 96:11
Let the many [160]islands be glad.
2 [r]Clouds and thick darkness surround Him; Ex. 19:9
[r]Righteousness and justice are the foundation of His throne. Ps. 89:14
3 Fire goes before Him,
And [r]burns up His adversaries round about. Mal. 4:1
4 His [r] lightnings lit up the world; Ex. 19:16
The earth saw and trembled.
5 The mountains [r]melted like wax at the presence of the LORD, Ps. 46:6
At the presence of the Lord of the whole earth.
6 The [r] heavens declare His righteousness, Ps. 19:1
And [r] all the peoples have seen His glory. Ps. 98:2

[159] Or, *uprightness* [160] Or, *coastlands*

7 Let all those be ashamed who serve [r] graven images, Ps. 78:58; Is. 42:17
Who boast themselves of [r]idols; Ps. 106:36
Worship Him, all you gods.
8 Zion heard *this* and was glad,
And the daughters of Judah have rejoiced
Because of Thy judgments, O LORD.
9 For Thou art the LORD Most High over all the earth;
Thou art exalted far above all [a]gods. *supernatural powers*

10 [r]Hate evil, you who love the LORD, Ps. 34:14
Who preserves the souls of His godly ones;
He delivers them from the hand of the wicked.
11 Light is sown *like seed* for the righteous,
And [r]gladness for the upright in heart. Ps. 64:10
12 Be glad in the LORD, you righteous ones;
And [r]give thanks to His holy name. Ps. 30:4

PSALM 98

A Psalm.

O SING to the LORD a new song,
For He has done [r]wonderful things, Ps. 40:5; 96:3
His right hand and His holy arm have [161]gained the victory for Him.
2 [r]The LORD has made known His salvation; Is. 52:10
He has [r]revealed His righteousness in the sight of the nations. Is. 62:2

[161] Or, *accomplished salvation*

3 He has [r]remembered His
lovingkindness and His
faithfulness to the house
of Israel; Luke 1:54, 72
[r]All the ends of the earth have
seen the salvation of our
God. Ps. 22:27

4 [r]Shout joyfully to the LORD,
all the earth; Ps. 100:1
Break forth and sing for joy
and sing praises.
5 Sing praises to the LORD with
the [r]lyre; Ps. 92:3
With the lyre and the [a]sound
of melody. *voice of song*
6 With [r]trumpets and the sound
of the horn Num. 10:10
Shout joyfully before [r] the
King, the LORD. Ps. 47:7

7 Let the sea roar and [t]all it
contains, *its fulness*
The [r]world and those who
dwell in it. Ps. 24:1
8 Let the rivers clap their
hands;
Let the mountains sing together
for joy
9 Before the LORD; for He is
coming to [r] judge the
earth; Ps. 96:13
He will judge the world with
righteousness,
And the peoples with equity.

PSALM 99

THE LORD reigns, let the peoples
tremble;
He is [t]enthroned *above* the
cherubim, let the earth
shake! *sits*
2 The LORD is great in Zion,
And He is [r]exalted above all
the peoples. Ps. 97:9

3 Let them praise Thy great
and awesome name;
Holy is He.
4 And the strength of the King
loves [162]justice;
Thou hast established equity;
Thou hast [r]executed [162]justice
and righteousness in Jacob.
Ps. 103:6; 146:7
5 Exalt the LORD our God,
And worship at His footstool;
Holy is He.

6 Moses and Aaron were
among His priests,
And [r] Samuel was among
those who called on His
name; Jer. 15:1
They called upon the LORD,
and He answered them.
7 He [r]spoke to them in the pillar
of cloud;
They kept His testimonies,
And the statute that He gave
them. Ex. 33:9
8 O LORD our God, Thou didst
[r]answer them; Ps. 106:44
Thou wast a [r]forgiving God to
them, Num. 14:20
And *yet* an [r]avenger of their
evil deeds. Ex. 32:28
9 Exalt the LORD our God,
And worship at His holy hill;
For holy is the LORD our God.

PSALM 100

A Psalm for Thanksgiving.

SHOUT joyfully to the LORD, all
the earth.
2 [r]Serve the LORD with gladness;
Deut. 12:11, 12
[r]Come before Him with joyful
singing. Ps. 95:2

[162] Or, *judgment*

3 Know that the LORD[a] Himself
is God;
It is He who has made us,
and [163]not we ourselves;
We are His people and the
sheep of His pasture. *He*
4 Enter His gates with[a] thanksgiving, *a thank offering*
And His courts with praise.
Give thanks to Him; [r] bless
His name. Ps. 96:2
5 For the LORD is good;
[r] His lovingkindness is everlasting, Ps. 136:1
And His [r] faithfulness to all
generations. Ps. 119:90

PSALM 101

A Psalm of David.

I WILL sing of lovingkindness
and[a] justice,
To Thee, O LORD, I will sing
praises. *judgment*
2 I will give heed to the
[164]blameless way.
When wilt Thou come to me?
I will walk within my house
in the [a] integrity of my
heart. *blamelessness*
3 I will set no worthless thing
before my eyes;
I hate the work of those who
[r] fall away;
It shall not fasten its grip on
me. Josh. 23:6
4 A [r] perverse heart shall depart
from me; Prov. 11:20
I will know no evil.
5 Whoever secretly slanders
his neighbor, him I will
[a] destroy; *silence*
No one who has a haughty
look and an arrogant
heart will I endure.
6 My eyes shall be upon the
faithful of the land, that
they may dwell with me;
He who walks in a [164]blame-
less way is the one who
will minister to me.
7 He who [r] practices deceit shall
not dwell within my
house; Ps. 43:1; 52:2
He who speaks falsehood
shall not maintain his position before me.
8 Every morning I will [165]de-
stroy all the wicked of
the land,
So as to [r] cut off from the city
of the LORD all those who
do iniquity. Ps. 118:10-12

PSALM 102

A Prayer of the Afflicted, when he is faint, and pours out his complaint before the LORD.

HEAR my prayer, O LORD!
And let my cry for help [r] come
to Thee. Ex. 2:23
2 [r] Do not hide Thy face from
me in the day of my dis-
tress; Ps. 69:17
Incline Thine ear to me;
In the day when I call [r] answer
me quickly. Ps. 69:17
3 For my days have been consumed in smoke,
And my bones have been
scorched like a hearth.
4 My heart has been smitten
like [t] grass and has withered away, *herbage*
Indeed, I [r] forget to eat my
bread. 1 Sam. 1:7

[163] Some mss. read *His we are*
[164] Or, *way of integrity*
[164] Or, *way of integrity* [165] Or, *silence*

5 Because of the [t]loudness of
my groaning *voice*
My bones cling to my flesh.
6 I resemble a [r]pelican of the
wilderness; Is. 34:11
I have become like an owl of
the waste places.
7 I [r]lie awake, Ps. 77:4
I have become like a lonely
bird on a housetop.

8 My enemies have reproached
me all day long;
Those who deride me have
used my *name* as a curse.
9 For I have eaten ashes like
bread,
And [r]mingled my drink with
weeping, Ps. 42:3; 80:5
10 [r]Because of Thine indignation
and Thy wrath; Ps. 38:3
For Thou hast lifted me up
and cast me away.
11 My days are like a [r]length-
ened shadow; Job 14:2
And I wither away like grass.

12 But Thou, O LORD, dost [a]abide
forever; *sit enthroned*
And Thy [t]name to all generations. *memorial*
13 Thou wilt arise *and* have
compassion on Zion;
For [r]it is time to be gracious
to her, Ps. 119:126
For the [r]appointed time has
come. Ps. 75:2
14 Surely Thy servants find
pleasure in her stones,
And feel pity for her dust.
15 So the nations will fear the
name of the LORD,
And [r]all the kings of the earth
Thy glory. Ps. 138:4
16 For the LORD has [r]built up
Zion; Ps. 147:2
He has appeared in His glory.
17 He has regarded the prayer
of the [a]destitute,
And has not despised their
prayer. *naked*

18 This will be written for the
generation to come;
That [r]a people yet to be created may praise the
LORD. Ps. 22:31; 78:6f.
19 For He looked down from
His holy height;
From heaven the LORD gazed
[t]upon the earth, *toward*
20 To hear the [r]groaning of the
prisoner; Ps. 79:11
To set free those who were
doomed to death;
21 That *men* may [r]tell of the
name of the LORD in
Zion, Ps. 22:22
And His praise in Jerusalem;
22 When [r]the peoples are gathered together,
And the kingdoms, to serve
the LORD. Ps. 22:27

23 He has weakened my
strength in the way;
He has shortened my days.
24 I say, "O my God, do not
take me away in the
midst of my days,
Thy [r]years are throughout all
generations. Job 36:26
25 "Of old Thou didst [r]found the
earth; Gen. 1:1; Neh. 9:6
And the heavens are the
work of Thy hands.
26 "Even they will perish, but
Thou dost endure;
And all of them will wear out
like a garment;
Like clothing Thou wilt
change them, and they
will be changed.

27 "But Thou art[t] the same,
And Thy years will not come to an end. *He*
28 "The children of Thy servants will continue,
And their [t] descendants will be established before Thee." *seed*

PSALM 103

A Psalm of David.

BLESS the LORD, O my soul;
And all that is within me, *bless* His holy name.
2 Bless the LORD, O my soul,
And[r] forget none of His benefits; Deut. 6:12; 8:11
3 Who[r] pardons all your iniquities; Ex. 34:7
Who heals all your diseases;
4 Who[r] redeems your life from the pit; Ps. 49:15
Who [r] crowns you with lovingkindness and compassion; Ps. 5:12
5 Who satisfies your [166] years with good things,
So *that* your youth is renewed like the eagle.

6 The LORD[r] performs righteous deeds, Ps. 99:4; 146:7
And judgments for all who are[r] oppressed. Ps. 12:5
7 He[r] made known His ways to Moses, Ex. 33:13; Ps. 99:7
His acts to the sons of Israel.
8 The LORD is compassionate and gracious,
Slow to anger and abounding in lovingkindness.
9 He [r] will not always strive *with us*; Ps. 30:5
Nor will He[r] keep *His anger* forever. Jer. 3:5, 12
10 He has not dealt with us according to our sins,
Nor rewarded us according to our iniquities.
11 For as high as the heavens are above the earth,
So great is His lovingkindness toward those who [167] fear Him.
12 As far as the east is from the west,
So far has He removed our transgressions from us.
13 Just as a father has compassion on *his* children,
So the LORD has compassion on those who fear Him.
14 For[r] He Himself knows [168] our frame; Is. 29:16
He[r] is mindful that we are *but* dust. Ps. 78:39

15 As for man, his days are[r] like grass; Ps. 90:5
As a[r] flower of the field, so he flourishes. Job 14:2
16 When the wind has passed over it, it is no more;
And its[r] place acknowledges it no longer. Job 7:10
17 But the lovingkindness of the LORD is from everlasting to everlasting on those who [167] fear Him,
And His righteousness to children's children,
18 To[r] those who keep His covenant, Deut. 7:9; Ps. 25:10
And who remember His precepts to do them.

19 The LORD has established His[r] throne in the heavens; Ps. 11:4

[166] Or, *desire*

[167] Or, *revere* [168] I.e., what we are made of

And His [169]sovereignty rules over all.
20 Bless the LORD, you [r]His angels, Ps. 148:2
Mighty in strength, who perform His word,
[r]Obeying the voice of His word! Ps. 91:11
21 Bless the LORD, all you [r]His hosts, 1 Kin. 22:19
You [r]who serve Him, doing His will. Ps. 104:4
22 Bless the LORD, [r]all you works of His, Ps. 145:10
In all places of His dominion;
Bless the LORD, O my soul!

PSALM 104

BLESS the LORD, O my soul!
O LORD my God, Thou art very great;
Thou art clothed with splendor and majesty,
2 Covering Thyself with light as with a cloak,
[r]Stretching out heaven like a *tent* curtain. Is. 40:22
3 [170]He lays the beams of His upper chambers in the waters;
He makes the [r]clouds His chariot; Is. 19:1
He walks upon the [r]wings of the wind; Ps. 18:10
4 He makes [171]the winds His messengers,
[172]Flaming fire His ministers.
5 He established the earth upon its foundations,
So that it will not [173]totter forever and ever.

[169] Or, *kingdom*
[170] Lit., *Who, so through v. 4, and vv. 13, 14*
[171] Or, *His angels, spirits*
[172] Or, *His ministers flames of fire*
[173] Or, *move out of place*

6 Thou didst cover it with the deep as with a garment;
The waters were standing above the mountains.
7 At Thy rebuke they fled;
At the sound of Thy thunder they hurried away.
8 The mountains rose; the valleys sank down
To the place which Thou didst establish for them.
9 Thou didst set a [r]boundary that they may not pass over; Job 38:10, 11
That they may not return to cover the earth.

10 He sends forth [r]springs in the valleys;
They flow between the mountains; Ps. 107:35
11 They give drink to every beast of the field;
The [r]wild donkeys quench their thirst. Job 39:5
12 Beside them the birds of the heavens dwell;
They lift up *their* voices among the branches.
13 He waters the mountains from His upper chambers;
The earth is satisfied with the fruit of His works.

14 He causes the [r]grass to grow for the cattle, Job 38:27
And [r]vegetation for the labor of man, Gen. 1:29
So that he may bring forth food from the earth,
15 And wine which makes man's heart glad,
So that he may make *his* face glisten with oil,
And [t]food which sustains man's heart. *bread*

16 The trees of the LORD[t] drink
their fill, *are satisfied*
The cedars of Lebanon which
He planted,
17 Where the[r] birds build their
nests, Ps. 104:12
And the[r] stork, *whose home* is
the fir trees. Lev. 11:19

18 The high mountains are for
the[r] wild goats;
The cliffs are a refuge for the
rock badgers. Job 39:1
19 He made the moon[r] for the
seasons; Gen. 1:14
The[r] sun knows the place of
its setting. Ps. 19:6
20 Thou dost appoint darkness
and it becomes night,
In which all the beasts of the
forest prowl about.
21 The[r] young lions roar after
their prey, Job 38:39
And[r] seek their food from
God. Ps. 145:15
22 *When* the sun rises they
withdraw,
And lie down in their dens.
23 Man goes forth to his work
And to his labor until evening.

24 O LORD, how[r] many are Thy
works! Ps. 40:5
In[r] wisdom Thou hast made
them all; Ps. 136:5
The earth is full of Thy [174]pos-
sessions.
25 There is the[r] sea, great and
broad,
In which are swarms without
number,
Animals both small and
great. Ps. 8:8; 69:34

[174] Or, *creatures*

26 There the ships move along,
And [175]Leviathan, which Thou
hast formed to sport in it.

27 They all wait for Thee,
To give them their food in
[176]due season.
28 Thou dost give to them, they
gather *it* up;
Thou[r] dost open Thy hand,
they are satisfied with
good. Ps. 145:16
29 Thou dost hide Thy face,
they are dismayed;
Thou dost take away their
[177]spirit, they expire,
And return to their dust.
30 Thou dost send forth Thy
[177]Spirit, they are created;
And Thou dost renew the
face of the ground.

31 Let the[r] glory of the LORD endure forever; Ps. 86:12
Let the LORD[r] be glad in His
works; Gen. 1:31
32 He[r] looks at the earth, and it
trembles; Judg. 5:5
He touches the mountains,
and they smoke.
33 I will sing to the LORD[t] as long
as I live; *in my lifetime*
I will sing praise to my God
while I have my being.
34 Let my[r] meditation be pleasing to Him; Ps. 19:14
As for me, I shall[r] be glad in
the LORD. Ps. 9:2
35 Let sinners be consumed
from the earth,
And let the[r] wicked be no
more.
Bless the LORD, O my soul.
Praise the LORD! Ps. 37:10

[175] Or, *a sea monster*
[176] Lit., *its appointed time* [177] Or, *breath*

PSALM 105

OH give thanks to the LORD, call
upon His name;
Make known His deeds
among the peoples.
2 Sing to Him,[r] sing praises to
Him; Ps. 96:1; 98:5
[178]Speak of all His wonders.
3 Glory in His holy name;
Let the heart of those who
seek the LORD be glad.
4 Seek the LORD and [r] His
strength; Ps. 63:2
Seek His face continually.
5 Remember His wonders
which He has done,
His marvels, and the judgments [t] uttered by His
mouth, *of His mouth*
6 O seed of [r]Abraham, His servant, Ps. 105:42
O sons of Jacob, His[r]chosen
ones! 1 Chr. 16:13
7 He is the LORD our God;
His[r]judgments are in all the
earth. Is. 26:9
8 He has remembered His covenant forever,
The word which He com-
manded to a [r] thousand
generations, Deut. 7:9
9 *The covenant* which He
made with Abraham,
And His oath to Isaac.
10 Then He confirmed it to Jacob for a statute,
To Israel as an everlasting
covenant,
11 Saying, "To you I will give
the land of Canaan
As the[t]portion of your inheritance," *measuring line*
12 When they were only a few
men in number,
Very few, and strangers in it.
13 And they wandered about
from nation to nation,
From *one* kingdom to an-
other people.
14 He[r]permitted no man to oppress them, Gen. 20:7
And He[r]reproved kings for
their sakes: Gen. 12:17
15 "Do[r] not touch My anointed
ones,
And do My prophets no
harm." Gen. 26:11
16 And He called for a famine
upon the land;
He[r]broke the whole staff of
bread. Lev. 26:26; Is. 3:1
17 He sent a man before them,
Joseph, *who* was[r]sold as a
slave. Gen. 37:28, 36
18 They afflicted his[r]feet with
fetters, Gen. 39:20; 40:15
He himself was laid in irons;
19 Until the time that his word
came to pass,
The word of the LORD[a]tested
him. *refined*
20 The[r]king sent and released
him,
The ruler of peoples, and set
him free. Gen. 41:14
21 He[r]made him lord of his
house,
And ruler over all his possessions, Gen. 41:40-44
22 To[t]imprison his princes[t]at
will, *bind • at his*
That he might teach his elders wisdom.
23 Israel also came into Egypt;
Thus Jacob sojourned in the
land of Ham.
24 And He caused His people to
be very fruitful,

[178]Or, *Meditate on*

And made them stronger
than their adversaries.
25 He [r]turned their heart to hate
His people, Ex. 1:8; 4:21
To [r]deal craftily with His servants. Ex. 1:10
26 He sent Moses His servant,
And [r]Aaron whom He had
chosen. Ex. 4:14
27 They performed His wondrous acts among them,
And miracles in the land of
Ham.
28 He [r]sent darkness and made
it dark; Ex. 10:21, 22
And they did not rebel
against His words.
29 He [r]turned their waters into
blood, Ex. 7:20, 21
And caused their fish to die.
30 Their land swarmed with
[r]frogs Ex. 8:6
Even in the [r]chambers of their
kings. Ex. 8:3
31 He spoke, and there came a
[r]swarm of flies Ex. 8:21
And [r]gnats in all their territory. Ex. 8:16, 17
32 He gave them hail for rain,
And flaming fire in their
land.
33 He struck down their vines
also and their fig trees,
And shattered the trees of
their territory.
34 He spoke, and locusts came,
And young locusts, even
without number,
35 And ate up all vegetation in
their land,
And ate up the fruit of their
ground.
36 He also struck down all the
first-born in their land,
The [r]first fruits of all their
vigor. Gen. 49:3
37 Then He brought them out
with silver and gold;
And among His tribes there
was not one who stumbled.
38 Egypt was [r]glad when they
departed; Ex. 12:33
For the dread of them had
fallen upon them.
39 He spread a cloud for a [179]covering,
And fire to illumine by night.
40 They asked, and He brought
[r]quail, Ex. 16:13
And satisfied them with the
[a]bread of heaven. *food*
41 He opened the rock, and water flowed out;
[t]It ran in the dry places *like* a
river. *They went*
42 For He [r]remembered His holy
word Gen. 15:13, 14
With Abraham His servant;
43 And He brought forth His
people with joy,
His chosen ones with a joyful
[r]shout. Ex. 15:1
44 He gave them also the lands
of the nations,
That they might take possession of *the fruit of* the
peoples' labor,
45 So that they might [r]keep His
statutes, Deut. 4:1, 40
And observe His laws,
Praise the LORD!

PSALM 106

PRAISE the LORD!
Oh give thanks to the LORD,
for He is good;
For [r]His lovingkindness is
everlasting. 1 Chr. 16:34

[179]Or, *curtain*

2 Who can speak of the mighty
deeds of the LORD,
Or can show forth all His
praise?
3 How blessed are those who
keep[a] justice, *judgment*
Who [r] practice righteousness
at all times! Ps. 15:2

4 Remember me, O LORD, in
Thy [r] favor[a] toward Thy
people; Ps. 44:3 • *of*
Visit me with Thy salvation,
5 That I may see the prosperity
of Thy chosen ones,
That I may rejoice in the
gladness of Thy nation,
That I may glory with Thine
[180]inheritance.

6 [r] We have sinned [t] like our fathers, 1 Kin. 8:47
We have committed iniquity,
we have behaved wick-
edly. *with*
7 Our fathers in Egypt did not
understand Thy wonders;
They [r] did not remember
Thine abundant kind-
nesses,
But rebelled by the sea, at
the [181]Red Sea. Judg. 3:7
8 Nevertheless He saved them
for the sake of His name,
That He might [r] make His
power known. Ex. 9:16
9 Thus He rebuked the [181]Red
Sea and it dried up;
And He [r] led them through the
deeps, as through the wilderness. Is. 63:11-13
10 So He [r] saved them from the
hand of the one who
hated *them*, Ex. 14:30
And redeemed them from
the hand of the enemy.

[180]I.e., people [181]Lit., *Sea of Reeds*

11 And [r] the waters covered their
adversaries; Ex. 14:27, 28
Not one of them was left.
12 Then they [r] believed His
words; Ex. 14:31
They sang His praise.

13 They quickly [r] forgot His
works; Ex. 15:24; 16:2
They [r] did not wait for His
counsel, Ps. 107:11
14 But craved intensely in the
wilderness,
And[a] tempted God in the desert. *put God to the test*
15 So He [r] gave them their request,
But sent a wasting disease
among them. Num. 11:31

16 When they became envious
of Moses in the camp,
And of Aaron, the holy one
of the LORD,
17 The earth opened and swallowed up Dathan,
And engulfed the company
of Abiram.
18 And a [r] fire blazed up in their
company;
The flame consumed the
wicked. Num. 16:35

19 They made a calf in Horeb,
And worshiped a molten
image.
20 Thus they [r] exchanged their
glory
For the image of an ox that
eats grass. Jer. 2:11
21 They forgot God their Savior,
Who had done [r] great things
in Egypt, Deut. 10:21
22 Wonders in the land of Ham,
And awesome things by the
[181]Red Sea.

[181]Lit., *Sea of Reeds*

23 Therefore He said that He
would destroy them,
Had not [r]Moses His chosen
one stood in the breach
before Him, Ex. 32:11-14
To turn away His wrath from
destroying *them.*
24 Then they despised the
pleasant land;
They [r]did not believe in His
word, Deut. 1:32
25 But grumbled in their tents;
They did not listen to the
voice of the LORD.
26 Therefore He swore to them,
That He would cast them
down in the wilderness,
27 And that He would cast their
seed among the nations,
And [r]scatter them in the
lands. Lev. 26:33; Ps. 44:11

28 They [r]joined themselves also
to Baal-peor, Num. 25:3
And ate [r]sacrifices offered to
the dead. Num. 25:2
29 Thus they provoked *Him* to
anger with their deeds;
And the plague broke out
among them.
30 Then Phinehas [r]stood up and
interposed; Num. 25:7
And so the [r]plague was
stayed. Num. 25:8
31 And it was reckoned to him
for righteousness,
To all generations forever.

32 They also provoked *Him* to
wrath at the waters of
[182]Meribah,
So that it went hard with
Moses on their account;
33 Because they were rebellious
against His Spirit,
He spoke rashly with his lips.

34 They [r]did not destroy the peoples, Judg. 1:21
As [r]the LORD commanded
them, Deut. 7:2, 16
35 But [r]they mingled with the
nations, Judg. 3:5, 6
And learned their practices,
36 And served their idols,
[r]Which became a snare to
them. Deut. 7:16
37 They even sacrificed their
sons and their daughters
to the demons,
38 And shed innocent blood,
The blood of their sons and
their daughters,
Whom they sacrificed to the
idols of Canaan;
And the land was polluted
with the blood.
39 Thus they became unclean in
their [t]practices, *works*
And [r]played the harlot in
their deeds. Lev. 17:7

40 Therefore the [r]anger of the
LORD was kindled against
His people, Judg. 2:14
And He abhorred His [r]inheri-
tance. Deut. 9:29
41 Then He gave them into the
hand of the nations;
And those who hated them
ruled over them.
42 Their enemies also [r]oppressed
them, Judg. 4:3; 10:12
And they were subdued un-
der their [t]power. *hand*
43 Many times He would [r]deliver
them; Judg. 2:16-18
They, however, were rebellious in their counsel,
And so [r]sank down in their iniquity. Judg. 6:6

[182] Lit., *strife*

44 Nevertheless He looked upon their distress,
When He heard their cry;
45 And He remembered His covenant for their sake,
And relented according to the greatness of His lovingkindness.
46 He also made them [r]*objects* of compassion
In the presence of all their captors. 1 Kin. 8:50

47 Save us, O LORD our God,
And [r]gather us from among the nations, Ps. 147:2
To give thanks to Thy holy name,
And glory in Thy praise.
48 [r]Blessed be the LORD, the God of Israel, Ps. 41:13; 72:18
From everlasting even to everlasting.
And let all the people say, "Amen."
Praise the LORD!

BOOK 5

PSALM 107

OH give thanks to the LORD, for [r]He is good;
For His lovingkindness is everlasting. 2 Chr. 5:13
2 Let [r]the redeemed of the LORD say so, Is. 35:9, 10
Whom He has [r]redeemed from the hand of the adversary, Ps. 78:42
3 And gathered from the lands,
From the east and from the west,
From the north and from the [t]south. *sea*
4 They wandered in the wilderness in a desert region;
They did not find a way to an inhabited [r]city. Ps. 107:7
5 *They were* hungry [t]and thirsty;
Their [r]soul fainted within them. *also* • Ps. 77:3
6 Then they cried out to the LORD in their trouble;
He delivered them out of their distresses.
7 He led them also by a straight way,
To go to an inhabited city.
8 Let them give thanks to the LORD for His lovingkindness,
And for His wonders to the sons of men!
9 For He has [r]satisfied the thirsty soul, Ps. 22:26
And the hungry soul He has filled with what is good.

10 There were those who dwelt in darkness and in the shadow of death,
Prisoners in [t]misery and [t]chains, *affliction* • *irons*
11 Because they had rebelled against the words of God,
And spurned the counsel of the Most High.
12 Therefore He humbled their heart with labor;
They stumbled and there was none to help.
13 Then they cried out to the LORD in their trouble;
He saved them out of their distresses.
14 He [r]brought them out of darkness and the shadow of death, Ps. 86:13; 107:10
And broke their bands apart.

15 [r]Let them give thanks to the
LORD for His lovingkind-
ness, Ps. 107:8, 21, 31
And for His wonders to the
sons of men!
16 For He has [r]shattered gates of
bronze, Is. 45:1,2
And cut bars of iron asunder.

17 Fools, because of their rebellious way,
And because of their iniquities, were afflicted.
18 Their [r]soul abhorred all kinds
of food; Job 33:20
And they [r]drew near to the
gates of death. Job 33:22
19 Then they cried out to the
LORD in their trouble;
He saved them out of their
distresses.
20 He [r]sent His word and healed
them, Ps. 147:15,18
And delivered *them* from
their [183]destructions.
21 [r]Let them give thanks to the
LORD for His lovingkind-
ness,
And for His wonders to the
sons of men! Ps. 107:8
22 Let them also offer sacrifices
of thanksgiving,
And tell of His works with
joyful singing.

23 Those who [r]go down to the
sea in ships,
Who do business on great
waters; Is. 42:10
24 They have seen the works of
the LORD,
And His wonders in the deep.
25 For He [r]spoke and raised up a
stormy wind,
Which lifted up the waves [t]of
the sea. Ps. 105:31 • *of it*

[183]Or, *pits*

26 They rose up to the heavens,
they went down to the
depths;
Their soul [r]melted away in
their misery. Ps. 22:14
27 They reeled and staggered
like a drunken man,
And [184]were at their wits' end.
28 Then they cried to the LORD
in their trouble,
And He brought them out of
their distresses.
29 He [r]caused the storm to be
still, Ps. 65:7; 89:9
So that the waves [t]of the sea
were hushed. *of it*
30 Then they were glad because
they were quiet;
So He guided them to their
desired haven.
31 [r]Let them give thanks to the
LORD for His lovingkind-
ness, Ps. 107:8, 15, 21
And for His [r]wonders to the
sons of men! Ps. 78:4
32 Let them [r]extol Him also in
the congregation of the
people, Ps. 34:3; 99:5
And [r]praise Him at the seat of
the elders. Ps. 35:18

33 He [185]changes rivers into a
wilderness,
And springs of water into a
thirsty ground;
34 A fruitful land into a [r]salt
waste, Job 39:6
Because of the wickedness of
those who dwell in it.
35 He changes a wilderness into
a pool of water,
And a dry land into springs
of water;

[184]Lit., *all their wisdom was swallowed up*
[185]Or, *turns rivers into a desert*

36 And there He makes the hungry to dwell,
So that they may establish an inhabited city,
37 And sow fields, and [r]plant vineyards, 2 Kin. 19:29
And gather a fruitful harvest.
38 Also He blesses them and they multiply greatly;
And He does not let their cattle decrease.

39 When they are diminished and bowed down
Through oppression, misery, and sorrow,
40 He [r]pours contempt upon princes, Job 12:21
And [r]makes them wander in a pathless waste. Job 12:24
41 But He [r]sets the needy securely on high away from affliction, 1 Sam. 2:8
And [r]makes *his* families like a flock. Job 21:11
42 The [r]upright see it, and are glad; Job 22:19
But all [r]unrighteousness shuts its mouth. Job 5:16
43 Who is wise? Let him give heed to these things;
And consider the lovingkindnesses of the LORD.

PSALM 108

A Song, a Psalm of David.

MY heart is steadfast, O God;
I will sing, I will sing praises, even with my soul.
2 Awake, harp and lyre;
I will awaken the dawn!
3 I will give thanks to Thee, O LORD, among the peoples;
And I will sing praises to Thee among the nations.
4 For Thy lovingkindness is great above the heavens;
And Thy truth *reaches* to the skies.
5 [r]Be exalted, O God, above the heavens,
And Thy glory above all the earth. Ps. 57:5
6 [r]That Thy beloved may be delivered, Ps. 60:5-12
Save with Thy right hand, and answer me!

7 God has spoken in His [186]holiness:
"I will exult, I will portion out Shechem,
And measure out the valley of Succoth.
8 "Gilead is Mine, Manasseh is Mine;
Ephraim also is the [t]helmet of My head; *protection*
Judah is My [187]scepter.
9 "Moab is My washbowl;
Over Edom I shall throw My shoe;
Over Philistia I will shout aloud."

10 Who will bring me into the besieged city?
Who will lead me to Edom?
11 Hast not Thou Thyself, O God, rejected us?
And wilt Thou not go forth with our armies, O God?
12 Oh give us help against the adversary,
For [r]deliverance [t]by man is in vain. Is. 30:3 · *of*
13 Through God we shall do valiantly;
And it is He who will tread down our adversaries.

[186] Or, *sanctuary* [187] Or, *lawgiver*

PSALM 109

For the choir director. A Psalm of David.

O GOD of my praise,
[r]Do not be silent! Ps. 28:1
2 For they have opened the wicked and deceitful mouth against me;
They have spoken against me with a lying tongue.
3 They have also surrounded me with words of hatred,
And fought against me[r]without cause. Ps. 35:7; 69:4
4 In return[r]for my love they act as my accusers; Ps. 38:20
But[r]I am *in* prayer. Ps. 69:13
5 Thus they have[t]repaid me evil for good, *laid upon me*
And hatred for my love.

6 Appoint a wicked man over him;
And let an accuser stand at his right hand.
7 When he is judged, let him come forth guilty;
And let his[r]prayer become sin. Prov. 28:9
8 Let his days be few;
Let another take his office.
9 Let his children be fatherless,
And his wife a widow.
10 Let his[r]children wander about and beg; Gen. 4:12
And let them[r]seek *sustenance* far from their ruined homes. Ps. 37:25
11 Let[r]the creditor seize all that he has; Neh. 5:7; Job 5:5
And let strangers plunder the product of his labor.
12 Let there be none to extend lovingkindness to him,
Nor any to be gracious to his fatherless children.
13 Let his posterity be cut off;
In a following generation let their[r]name be blotted out. Ps. 9:5; Prov. 10:7

14 Let[r]the iniquity of his fathers be remembered[t]before the LORD, Ex. 20:5 • *to*
And do not let the sin of his mother be blotted out.
15 Let[r]them be before the LORD continually, Ps. 90:8
That He may cut off their memory from the earth;
16 Because he did not remember to show lovingkindness,
But persecuted the[r]afflicted and needy man, Ps. 37:14
And the despondent in heart, to put *them* to death.
17 He also loved cursing, so[r]it came to him;
And he did not delight in blessing, so it was far from him. Prov. 14:14
18 But he[r]clothed himself with cursing as with his garment, Ps. 73:6; 109:29
And it entered into[t]his body like water, *his inward parts*
And like oil into his bones.
19 Let it be to him as[r]a garment with which he covers himself, Ps. 73:6; 109:29
And for a belt with which he constantly girds himself.
20 Let this be the reward of my accusers from the LORD,
And of those who speak evil against my soul.

21 But Thou, O GOD, the Lord, deal *kindly* with me for Thy name's sake;

Because Thy lovingkindness
is good, deliver me;
22 For I am afflicted and needy,
And my heart is [r]wounded
within me. Job 24:12
23 I am passing like a shadow
when it lengthens;
I am shaken off [r]like the locust. Ex. 10:19
24 My [r]knees are weak from
fasting; Heb. 12:12
And my flesh has grown
lean, without fatness.
25 I also have become a reproach to them;
When they see me, they [r]wag
their head. Ps. 22:7

26 Help me, O LORD my God;
Save me according to Thy
lovingkindness.
27 And let them [r]know that this
is Thy hand; Job 37:7
Thou, LORD, hast done it.
28 [r]Let them curse, but do Thou
bless; 2 Sam. 16:11, 12
When they arise, they shall
be ashamed,
But Thy [r]servant shall be
glad. Is. 65:14
29 Let my accusers be clothed
with dishonor,
And let them cover themselves with their own
shame as with a robe.

30 With my mouth I will give
thanks abundantly to the
LORD;
And in the midst of many I
will praise Him.
31 For He stands at the right
hand of the needy,
To save him from those who
judge his soul.

PSALM 110

A Psalm of David.

THE LORD says to my Lord:
"Sit at My right hand,
Until I make Thine enemies a
footstool for Thy feet."
2 The LORD will stretch forth
Thy strong [r]scepter from
Zion, *saying*, Ps. 45:6
[r]"Rule in the midst of Thine
enemies." Ps. 2:9; 72:8
3 Thy [r]people will volunteer
freely in the day of Thy
[a]power; Judg. 5:2 • *army*
[r]In holy array, from the womb
of the dawn, 1 Chr. 16:29
Thy youth are to Thee *as* the
[r]dew. 2 Sam. 17:12

4 The LORD has sworn and will
not change His mind,
"Thou art a priest forever
According to the order of
Melchizedek."
5 The Lord is [r]at Thy right
hand; Ps. 16:8; 109:31
He will shatter kings in the
day of His wrath.
6 He will [r]judge among the nations, Is. 2:4; Joel 3:12
He [a]will fill *them* with
corpses, *has filled*
He will shatter the chief men
over a broad country.
7 He will drink from the brook
by the wayside;
Therefore He will [r]lift up *His*
head. Ps. 27:6

PSALM 111

PRAISE the LORD!
I will give thanks to the LORD
with all *my* heart,

In the [r]company of the upright and in the assembly. Ps. 89:7
2 [r]Great are the works of the LORD; Ps. 92:5
They are [r]studied by all who delight in them. Ps. 143:5
3 [t]Splendid and majestic is His work; *Splendor and majesty*
And [r]His righteousness endures forever. Ps. 112:3, 9
4 He has made His wonders to be remembered;
The LORD is gracious and compassionate.
5 He has given food to those who [188]fear Him;
He will [r]remember His covenant forever. Ps. 105:8
6 He has made known to His people the power of His works,
In giving them the heritage of the nations.

7 The works of His hands are truth and justice;
All His precepts are sure.
8 They are [r]upheld forever and ever; Ps. 119:160; Is. 40:8
They are performed in [r]truth and uprightness. Ps. 19:9
9 He has sent [r]redemption to His people; Luke 1:68
He has ordained His covenant forever;
[r]Holy and awesome is His name. Ps. 99:3
10 The [189]fear of the LORD is the beginning of wisdom;
A good understanding have all those who [t]do *His commandments*; *do them*
His praise endures forever.

[188]Or, *revere* [189]Or, *reverence for*

PSALM 112

PRAISE the LORD!
How [r]blessed is the man who fears the LORD, Ps. 128:1
Who greatly delights in His commandments.
2 His [190]descendants will be mighty on earth;
The generation of the upright will be blessed.
3 [r]Wealth and riches are in his house, Prov. 3:16; 8:18
And his righteousness endures forever.
4 Light arises in the darkness for the upright;
He is gracious and compassionate and righteous.
5 It is well with the man who is gracious and lends;
He will maintain his cause in judgment.
6 For he will never be shaken;
The righteous will be remembered forever.

7 He will not fear evil tidings;
His heart is steadfast, trusting in the LORD.
8 His [r]heart is upheld, he will not fear, Heb. 13:9
Until he looks *with satisfaction* on his adversaries.
9 He [r]has given freely to the poor; 2 Cor. 9:9
His righteousness endures forever;
His [r]horn will be exalted in honor. Ps. 75:10; 89:17

10 The wicked will see it and be [a]vexed; *angry*
He will gnash his teeth and [r]melt away; Ps. 58:7

[190]Lit., *seed*

The desire of the wicked will
perish.

PSALM 113

PRAISE the LORD!
Praise, O [r]servants of the
LORD. Ps. 34:22; 69:36
Praise the name of the LORD.
2 [r]Blessed be the name of the
LORD
From this time forth and forever. Ps. 145:21
3 [r]From the rising of the sun to
its setting Is. 59:19
The [r]name of the LORD is to
be praised. Ps. 18:3
4 The LORD is [r]high above all
nations; Ps. 97:9; 99:2
His [r]glory is above the heavens. Ps. 8:1; 57:11
5 [r]Who is like the LORD our
God, Ps. 35:10; 89:6
Who is enthroned on high,
6 Who [r]humbles Himself to behold Ps. 11:4; 138:6
The things that are in heaven
and in the earth?
7 He [r]raises the poor from the
dust,
And lifts the needy from the
ash heap, 1 Sam. 2:8
8 To make *them* sit with
[a]princes,
With the [a]princes of His people. *nobles*
9 He makes the barren woman
abide in the house
As a joyful mother of children.
[a]Praise the LORD! *Hallelujah!*

PSALM 114

WHEN Israel went forth [r]from
Egypt, Ex. 12:51; 13:3
The house of Jacob from a
people of [r]strange lan-
guage, Ps. 81:5
2 Judah became His sanctuary,
Israel, His dominion.
3 The sea looked and fled;
The Jordan turned back.
4 The mountains [r]skipped like
rams, Ex. 19:18; Judg. 5:5
The hills, like lambs.
5 What [r]ails you, O sea, that
you flee?
O Jordan, that you turn
back? Hab. 3:8
6 O mountains, that you skip
like rams?
O hills, like lambs?
7 [r]Tremble, O earth, before the
Lord, Ps. 96:9
Before the God of Jacob,
8 Who [r]turned the rock into a
pool of water,
The flint into a fountain of
water. Ex. 17:6

PSALM 115

NOT to us, O LORD, not to us,
But to Thy name give glory
Because of Thy lovingkindness, because of Thy
[a]truth. *faithfulness*
2 Why should the nations say,
"Where, now, is their God?"
3 But our [r]God is in the heavens; Ps. 103:19
He [r]does whatever He
pleases. Ps. 135:6
4 Their idols are silver and
gold,
The work of man's hands.
5 They have mouths, but they
[r]cannot speak; Jer. 10:5
They have eyes, but they
cannot see;

6 They have ears, but they cannot hear;
They have noses, but they cannot smell;
7 [t]They have hands, but they cannot feel; *Their hands*
[t]They have feet, but they cannot walk; *Their feet*
They cannot make a sound with their throat.
8 Those who make them will become like them,
Everyone who trusts in them.

9 O Israel, trust in the LORD;
He is their [r]help and their shield. Ps. 33:20
10 O house of [r]Aaron, trust in the LORD;
He is their help and their shield. Ps. 118:2
11 You who [191]fear the LORD, trust in the LORD;
He is their help and their shield.
12 The LORD has been mindful of us; He will bless *us*;
He will bless the house of Israel;
He will bless the house of Aaron.
13 He will bless those who [191]fear the LORD,
[r]The small together with the great. Rev. 11:18; 19:5
14 May the LORD [r]give you increase, Deut. 1:11
You and your children.
15 May you be blessed of the LORD,
Maker of heaven and earth.

16 The heavens are [r]the heavens of the LORD; Ps. 89:11
But the earth He has given to the sons of men.
17 The [r]dead do not praise the LORD, Ps. 6:5; 88:10-12
Nor *do* any who go down into [r]silence; Ps. 31:17
18 But as for us, we will [r]bless the LORD Dan. 2:20
From this time forth and forever.
[a]Praise the LORD! *Hallelujah!*

PSALM 116

I LOVE the LORD, because He [r]hears
My voice *and* my supplications. Ps. 6:8; 66:19
2 Because He has [r]inclined His ear to me, Ps. 17:6
Therefore I shall call *upon Him* as long as I live.
3 The [r]cords of death encompassed me, Ps. 18:4, 5
And the [t]terrors of Sheol came upon me; *straits*
I found distress and sorrow.
4 Then [r]I called upon the name of the LORD: Ps. 18:6
"O LORD, I beseech Thee, [a]save my life!" *deliver my soul*

5 Gracious is the LORD, and [r]righteous;
Yes, our God is compassionate. Ezra 9:15
6 The LORD preserves [r]the simple; Ps. 19:7; Prov. 1:4
I was brought low, and He saved me.
7 Return to your [r]rest, O my soul, Jer. 6:16; Matt. 11:29
For the LORD has dealt bountifully with you.
8 For Thou hast [r]rescued my soul from death,
My eyes from tears, Ps. 49:15

[191]Or, *revere*

My feet from stumbling.
9 I shall walk before the LORD
In the land of the living.
10 I believed when I said,
"I am greatly afflicted."
11 I ʳsaid in my alarm,
"All men are liars." Ps. 31:22

12 What shall I ʳrender to the LORD 1 Thess. 3:9
For all His ʳbenefits ᵗ toward me? Ps. 103:2 • *upon*
13 I shall lift up the ʳcup of salvation,
And call upon the name of the LORD. Ps. 16:5
14 I shall ʳpay my vows to the LORD, Ps. 50:14
Oh *may it be* in the presence of all His people.
15 ʳPrecious in the sight of the LORD
Is the death of His godly ones. Ps. 72:14
16 O LORD, ᵃ surely I am Thy servant, *because*
I am Thy servant, the ʳson of Thy handmaid, Ps. 86:16
Thou hast loosed my bonds.
17 To Thee I shall offer a sacrifice of thanksgiving,
And ʳcall upon the name of the LORD. Ps. 116:13
18 I shall ʳpay my vows to the LORD, Ps. 116:14
Oh *may it be* in the presence of all His people,
19 In the courts of the LORD's house,
In the midst of you, O Jerusalem.
ᵃ Praise the LORD! *Hallelujah!*

PSALM 117

PRAISE the LORD, all nations;
Laud Him, all peoples!
2 For His lovingkindness [192]is great toward us,
And the truth of the LORD is everlasting.
ᵃ Praise the LORD! *Hallelujah!*

PSALM 118

GIVE thanks to the LORD, for ʳHe is good; 2 Chr. 5:13; 7:3
For His lovingkindness is everlasting.
2 Oh let ʳIsrael say,
"His lovingkindness is everlasting." Ps. 115:9
3 Oh let the ʳhouse of Aaron say,
"His lovingkindness is everlasting." Ps. 115:10
4 Oh let those who [193]fear the LORD say,
"His lovingkindness is everlasting."

5 From *my* ʳdistress I called upon the LORD; Ps. 18:6
The LORD answered me *and set me* in a large place.
6 The LORD is ʳfor me; I will not fear; Job 19:27; Ps. 56:9
What can man do to me?
7 The LORD is for me among those who help me;
Therefore I shall ʳlook *with satisfaction* on those who hate me. Ps. 54:7
8 It is ʳbetter to take refuge in the LORD Ps. 40:4
Than to trust in man.
9 It is ʳbetter to take refuge in the LORD Ps. 146:3
Than to trust in princes.

10 All nations surrounded me;
In the name of the LORD I will surely cut them off.

[192] Lit., *prevails over us* [193] Or, *revere*

11 They surrounded me, yes, they surrounded me;
In the name of the LORD I will surely cut them off.
12 They surrounded me [r] like bees; Deut. 1:44
They were extinguished as a [r] fire of thorns; Ps. 58:9
In the name of the LORD I will surely cut them off.
13 You pushed me violently so that I[a] was falling, *fell*
But the LORD helped me.
14 [r] The LORD is my strength and song, Ex. 15:2; Is. 12:2
And He has become [r] my salvation. Ps. 27:1

15 The sound of joyful shouting and salvation is in the tents of the righteous;
The [r] right hand of the LORD does valiantly. Luke 1:51
16 The [r] right hand of the LORD is exalted;
The right hand of the LORD does valiantly. Ps. 89:13
17 I shall not die, but live,
And [r] tell of the works of the LORD. Ps. 73:28; 107:22
18 The LORD has [r] disciplined me severely, 1 Cor. 11:32
But He has [r] not given me over to death. Ps. 86:13

19 [r] Open to me the gates of righteousness;
I shall enter through them, I shall give thanks to the LORD. Is. 26:2
20 This is the gate of the LORD;
The [r] righteous will enter through it. Ps. 15:1, 2
21 I shall give thanks to Thee, for Thou hast [r] answered me; Ps. 116:1
And Thou hast [r] become my salvation. Ps. 118:14

22 The [r] stone which the builders rejected
Has become the chief corner *stone*. Acts 4:11
23 This is [194] the LORD's doing;
It is marvelous in our eyes.
24 This is the day which the LORD has made;
Let us [r] rejoice and be glad in it. Ps. 31:7
25 O LORD, [r] do save, we beseech Thee; Ps. 106:47
O LORD, we beseech Thee, do send prosperity!
26 [r] Blessed is the one who comes in the name of the LORD; Matt. 21:9; 23:39
We have blessed you from the house of the LORD.
27 The LORD is God, and He has given us light;
Bind the festival sacrifice with cords [r] to the horns of the altar. *unto*
28 Thou art my God, and I give thanks to Thee;
Thou art my God, [r] I extol Thee. Ex. 15:2; Is. 25:1
29 Give thanks to the LORD, for He is good;
For His lovingkindness is everlasting.

PSALM 119

Aleph.

HOW blessed are those whose way is [195] blameless,
Who [r] walk in the law of the LORD. Ps. 128:1
2 How blessed are those who observe His testimonies,

[194] Lit., *from the LORD*
[195] Lit., *complete*, or, *having integrity*

Who ʳseek Him with all *their*
heart. Deut. 4:29
3 They also ʳdo no unrighteousness; 1 John 3:9
They walk in His ways.
4 Thou hast ᵗordained Thy precepts, *commanded*
ᵗThat we should keep *them*
diligently. *To keep*
5 Oh that my ʳways may be established Ps. 40:2
To keep Thy statutes!
6 Then I shall not be ashamed
When I look ᵗupon all Thy
commandments. *to*
7 I shall ʳgive thanks to Thee
with uprightness of
heart,
When I learn Thy righteous
judgments. Ps. 119:62
8 I shall keep Thy statutes;
Do not forsake me utterly!

Beth.

9 How can a young man keep
his way pure?
By ʳkeeping *it* according to
Thy word. 1 Kin. 2:4
10 With ᵗall my heart I have
sought Thee; 2 Chr. 15:15
Do not let me wander from
Thy commandments.
11 Thy word I have ʳtreasured in
my heart,
That I may not sin against
Thee. Luke 2:19, 51
12 Blessed art Thou, O LORD;
Teach me Thy statutes.
13 With my lips I have told of
All the ʳordinances of Thy
mouth. Ps. 119:72
14 I have rejoiced in the way of
Thy testimonies,
As much as in all riches.
15 I will meditate on Thy precepts,
And regard Thy ways.
16 I shall ᵗdelight in Thy statutes; *delight myself*
I shall not forget Thy word.

Gimel.

17 ʳDeal bountifully with Thy
servant,
That I may live and keep Thy
word. Ps. 13:6; 116:7
18 Open my eyes, that I may behold
Wonderful things from Thy
law.
19 I am a stranger in the earth;
Do not hide Thy commandments from me.
20 My soul is crushed ᵗwith longing
After Thine ordinances at all
times. *for*
21 Thou dost ʳrebuke the arrogant, the cursed,
Who wander from Thy commandments. Ps. 68:30
22 ʳTake away reproach and
contempt from me,
For I ʳobserve Thy testimonies. Ps. 39:8; 119:39 • Ps. 119:2
23 Even though princes sit and
talk against me,
Thy servant ʳmeditates on
Thy statutes. Ps. 119:15
24 Thy testimonies also are my
ʳdelight; Ps. 119:16
They are my counselors.

Daleth.

25 My ʳsoul cleaves to the dust;
Revive me according to Thy
word. Ps. 44:25
26 I have told of my ways, and
Thou hast answered me;
Teach me Thy statutes.
27 Make me understand the
way of Thy precepts,

So I will [r]meditate on Thy
wonders. Ps. 105:2
28 My soul [t]weeps because of
grief; *drops*
[r]Strengthen me according to
Thy word. Ps. 20:2
29 Remove the false way from
me,
And graciously grant me Thy
law.
30 I have chosen the faithful
way;
I have placed Thine ordi-
nances *before me.*
31 I [r]cleave to Thy testimonies;
O LORD, do not put me to
shame! Deut. 11:22
32 I shall run the way of Thy
commandments,
For Thou wilt [r]enlarge my
heart. 1 Kin. 4:29

He.

33 [r]Teach me, O LORD, the way
of Thy statutes,
And I shall observe it to the
end. Ps. 119:5, 12
34 Give me understanding, that
I may [r]observe Thy law,
And keep it with all *my*
heart. 1 Chr. 22:12
35 Make me walk in the [r]path of
Thy commandments,
For I delight in it. Ps. 25:4
36 Incline my heart to Thy testimonies,
And not to *dishonest* gain.
37 Turn away my eyes from
looking at vanity,
And revive me in Thy ways.
38 Establish Thy [a]word to Thy
servant, *promise*
As that which produces reverence for Thee.
39 [r]Turn away my reproach
which I dread,
For Thine ordinances are
good. Ps. 119:22
40 Behold, I [r]long for Thy precepts; Ps. 119:20
Revive me through Thy
righteousness.

Vav.

41 May Thy lovingkindnesses
also come to me, O LORD,
Thy salvation according to
Thy [a]word; *promise*
42 So I shall have an answer for
him who reproaches me,
For I trust in Thy word.
43 And do not take the word of
truth utterly out of my
mouth,
For I [a]wait for Thine ordinances. *hope in*
44 So I will [r]keep Thy law continually, Ps. 119:33
Forever and ever.
45 And I will walk at liberty,
For I seek Thy precepts.
46 I will also speak of Thy testimonies before kings,
And shall not be ashamed.
47 And I shall delight in Thy
commandments,
Which I love.
48 And I shall lift up my hands
to Thy commandments,
Which I love;
And I will [r]meditate on Thy
statutes. Ps. 119:15

Zayin.

49 Remember the word to Thy
servant,
[t]In which Thou hast made me
hope. *On*
50 This is my comfort in my affliction,
That Thy word has [a]revived
me. *preserved me alive*

51 The arrogant [r]utterly deride
me, Job 30:1
Yet I do not [r]turn aside from
Thy law. Job 23:11
52 I have [r]remembered Thine ordinances from [196]of old, O
LORD, Ps. 103:18
And comfort myself.
53 Burning [r]indignation has
seized me because of the
wicked, Ex. 32:19
Who forsake Thy law.
54 Thy statutes are my songs
In the house of my [r]pilgrimage. Gen. 47:9
55 O LORD, I [r]remember Thy
name in the night,
And keep Thy law. Ps. 63:6
56 This has become mine,
That I observe Thy precepts.

Heth.

57 The LORD is my portion;
I have promised to [r]keep Thy
words. Deut. 33:9
58 I entreated Thy favor [r]with all
my heart; Ps. 119:2
Be gracious to me according
to Thy [a]word. *promise*
59 I considered my ways,
And turned my feet to Thy
testimonies.
60 I hastened and did not delay
To keep Thy commandments.
61 The [r]cords of the wicked have
encircled me,
But I have not forgotten Thy
law. Job 36:8
62 At midnight I shall rise to
give thanks to Thee
Because of Thy [r]righteous ordinances. Ps. 119:7
63 I am a companion of all those
who [a]fear Thee,
And of those who keep Thy
precepts. *revere*
64 The earth is full of Thy
lovingkindness, O LORD;
Teach me Thy statutes.

Teth.

65 Thou hast dealt well with
Thy servant,
O LORD, according to Thy
word.
66 Teach me good [a]discernment
and knowledge,
For I believe in Thy commandments. *judgment*
67 [r]Before I was afflicted I went
astray, Heb. 12:5-11
But now I keep Thy word.
68 Thou art [r]good and doest
good; Ps. 86:5
Teach me Thy statutes.
69 The arrogant [197]have forged a
lie against me;
With all *my* heart I will observe Thy precepts.
70 Their heart is [t]covered with
fat, *gross like fat*
But I delight in Thy law.
71 It is [r]good for me that I was
afflicted,
That I may learn Thy statutes. Ps. 119:67, 75
72 The [r]law of Thy mouth is better to me
Than thousands of gold and
silver *pieces*. Ps. 19:10

Yodh.

73 Thy hands made me and
[198]fashioned me;
[r]Give me understanding, that
I may learn Thy commandments. Ps. 119:34

[196] Or, *everlasting*

[197] Lit., *besmear me with lies*

[198] Lit., *established*

74 May those who fear Thee see me and be glad,
Because I wait for Thy word.
75 I know, O LORD, that Thy judgments are righteous,
And that in faithfulness Thou hast afflicted me.
76 O may Thy lovingkindness comfort me,
According to Thy [a]word to Thy servant. *promise*
77 May Thy compassion come to me that I may live,
For Thy law is my delight.
78 May the arrogant be ashamed, for they subvert me with a lie;
But I shall [r]meditate on Thy precepts. Ps. 119:15
79 May those who [a]fear Thee turn to me,
Even those who know Thy testimonies. *revere*
80 May my heart be blameless in Thy statutes,
That I may not be ashamed.

Kaph.

81 My [r]soul languishes for Thy salvation; Ps. 84:2
I [a]wait for Thy word. *hope in*
82 My eyes fail *with longing* for Thy [a]word, *promise*
While I say, "When wilt Thou comfort me?"
83 Though I have become like a wineskin in the smoke,
I do not forget Thy statutes.
84 How many are the [r]days of Thy servant? Ps. 39:4
When wilt Thou [r]execute judgment on those who persecute me? Rev. 6:10
85 The arrogant have [r]dug pits for me, Jer. 18:22
Men who are not in accord with Thy law.
86 All Thy commandments are [r]faithful; Ps. 119:138
They have persecuted me with a lie; help me!
87 They almost destroyed me [t]on earth, *in the earth*
But as for me, I did not forsake Thy precepts.
88 Revive me according to Thy lovingkindness,
So that I may keep the testimony of Thy mouth.

Lamedh.

89 [r]Forever, O LORD,
Thy word [199]is settled in heaven. Ps. 89:2
90 Thy [r]faithfulness *continues* [t]throughout all generations; Ps. 36:5 · *to*
Thou didst establish the earth, and it stands.
91 They stand this day according to Thine ordinances,
For [r]all things are Thy servants. Ps. 104:2-4
92 If Thy law had not been my [r]delight, Ps. 119:16
Then I would have perished in my affliction.
93 I will never forget Thy precepts,
For by them Thou hast [a]revived me. *kept me alive*
94 I am Thine, [r]save me;
For I have sought Thy precepts. Ps. 119:146
95 The wicked [r]wait for me to destroy me;
I shall diligently consider Thy testimonies. Is. 32:7
96 I have seen [t]a limit to all perfection; *an end of*

[199] Lit., *stands firm*

Thy commandment is exceedingly broad.

Mem.

97 O how I love Thy law!
It is my [r]meditation all the day. Ps. 1:2; 119:15
98 Thy [r]commandments make me wiser than my enemies, Ps. 119:130
For they are ever mine.
99 I have more insight than all my teachers,
For Thy testimonies are my [r]meditation. Ps. 119:15
100 I understand [r]more than the aged, Job 32:7-9
Because I have observed Thy precepts.
101 I have restrained my feet from every evil way,
That I may keep Thy word.
102 I have not turned aside from Thine ordinances,
For Thou Thyself hast taught me.
103 How sweet are Thy words to my [t]taste!
Yes, sweeter than honey to my mouth! *palate*
104 From Thy precepts I [r]get understanding; Ps. 119:130
Therefore I [r]hate every false way. Ps. 119:128

Nun.

105 Thy word is a [r]lamp to my feet, Prov. 6:23
And a light to my path.
106 I have [r]sworn, and I will confirm it, Neh. 10:29
That I will keep Thy righteous ordinances.
107 I am exceedingly afflicted;
Revive me, O LORD, according to Thy word.
108 O accept the [r]freewill offerings of my mouth, O LORD, Heb. 13:15
And [r]teach me Thine ordinances. Ps. 119:12
109 My life is continually [200]in my hand,
Yet I do not forget Thy law.
110 The wicked have [r]laid a snare for me, Ps. 91:3
Yet I have not gone astray from Thy precepts.
111 I have [r]inherited Thy testimonies forever, Deut. 33:4
For they are the [r]joy of my heart. Ps. 119:14, 162
112 I have inclined my heart to perform Thy statutes
Forever, *even* to the end.

Samekh.

113 I hate those who are [r]double-minded, James 1:8
But I love Thy law.
114 Thou art my hiding place and my shield;
I wait for Thy word.
115 Depart from me, evildoers,
That I may observe the commandments of my God.
116 Sustain me according to Thy word, that I may live;
And do not let me be ashamed of my hope.
117 Uphold me that I may be [r]safe, Ps. 12:5
That I may have regard for Thy statutes continually.
118 Thou hast [t]rejected all those who wander from Thy statutes, *made light of*
For their deceitfulness is [t]useless. *falsehood*
119 Thou hast [t]removed all the

[200] I.e., in danger

wicked of the earth *like*
dross; *caused to cease*
Therefore I [r]love Thy testimonies. Ps. 119:47
120 My flesh [t]trembles for fear of
Thee, *bristles up from*
And I am [r]afraid of Thy judgments. Ps. 119:161

Ayin.

121 I have [r]done justice and
righteousness;
Do not leave me to my op-
pressors. Job 29:14
122 Be [r]surety for Thy servant for
good; Heb. 7:22
Do not let the arrogant [r]op-
press me. Ps. 119:134
123 My eyes fail *with longing* for
Thy salvation,
And for Thy righteous word.
124 Deal with Thy servant according to Thy loving-
kindness,
And teach me Thy statutes.
125 I am Thy servant; give me
understanding,
That I may know Thy testimonies.
126 It is time for the LORD to [r]act,
For they have broken Thy
law. Jer. 18:23
127 Therefore I [r]love Thy commandments
Above gold, yes, above fine
gold. Ps. 19:10
128 Therefore I esteem right all
Thy [r]precepts concerning
everything, Ps. 19:8
I hate every false way.

Pe.

129 Thy testimonies are [r]wonder-
ful; Ps. 119:18
Therefore my soul [r]observes
them. Ps. 119:22
130 The [r]unfolding of Thy words
gives light;
It gives understanding to the
simple. Prov. 6:23
131 I [r]opened my mouth wide and
panted,
For I longed for Thy com-
mandments. Ps. 81:10
132 [r]Turn to me and be gracious
to me, Ps. 25:16; 106:4
After Thy manner with those
who love Thy name.
133 Establish my footsteps in
Thy [a]word, *promise*
And do not let any iniquity
have dominion over me.
134 [r]Redeem me from the oppression of man,
That I may keep Thy pre-
cepts. Ps. 119:84
135 Make Thy face shine upon
Thy servant,
And teach me Thy statutes.
136 My eyes [t]shed streams of water,
Because they do not keep
Thy law. *run down*

Tsadhe.

137 Righteous art Thou, O LORD,
And upright are Thy judg-
ments.
138 Thou hast commanded Thy
testimonies in [r]righteous-
ness Ps. 19:7-9
And exceeding faithfulness.
139 My zeal has consumed me,
Because my adversaries have
forgotten Thy words.
140 Thy word is very pure,
Therefore Thy servant [r]loves
it. Ps. 119:47
141 I am small and despised,
Yet I do not forget Thy precepts.

142 Thy righteousness is an everlasting righteousness,
And Thy law is truth.
143 Trouble and anguish have [t]come upon me; *found me*
Yet Thy commandments are my [r]delight. Ps. 119:24
144 Thy testimonies are righteous forever;
[r]Give me understanding that I may live. Ps. 119:27

Qoph.

145 I cried with all my heart; answer me, O LORD!
I will observe Thy statutes.
146 I cried to Thee; save me,
And I shall keep Thy testimonies.
147 I rise before dawn and cry for help;
I wait for Thy words.
148 My eyes anticipate the [r]night watches,
That I may meditate on Thy [a]word. Ps. 63:6 · *promise*
149 Hear my voice according to Thy lovingkindness;
Revive me, O LORD, according to Thine ordinances.
150 Those who follow after wickedness draw near;
They are far from Thy law.
151 Thou art near, O LORD,
And all Thy commandments are [r]truth. Ps. 119:142
152 Of old I have known from Thy testimonies,
That Thou hast founded them [r]forever. Luke 21:33

Resh.

153 Look upon my [r]affliction and rescue me, Ps. 119:50
For I do not forget Thy law.
154 Plead my cause and [r]redeem me; Ps. 119:134
Revive me according to Thy [a]word. *promise*
155 Salvation is [r]far from the wicked,
For they do not seek Thy statutes. Job 5:4
156 [a]Great are Thy mercies, O LORD;
Revive me according to Thine ordinances. *Many*
157 Many are my persecutors and my adversaries,
Yet I do not turn aside from Thy testimonies.
158 I behold the [r]treacherous and loathe *them*, Is. 21:2
Because they do not keep Thy [a]word. *promise*
159 Consider how I [r]love Thy precepts; Ps. 119:47
[r]Revive me, O LORD, according to Thy lovingkindness. Ps. 119:25
160 The [r]sum of Thy word is truth,
And every one of Thy righteous ordinances is everlasting. Ps. 139:17

Shin.

161 Princes persecute me without cause,
But my heart stands in awe of Thy words.
162 I rejoice at Thy word,
As one who finds great spoil.
163 I [r]hate and despise falsehood,
But I love Thy law. Ps. 31:6
164 Seven times a day I praise Thee,
Because of Thy [r]righteous ordinances. Ps. 119:7, 160
165 Those who love Thy law have great peace,

And [r]nothing causes them to
stumble. Prov. 3:23
166 I [r]hope for Thy salvation, O
LORD, Gen. 49:18
And do Thy commandments.
167 My [r]soul keeps Thy testimonies, Ps. 119:129
And I love them exceedingly.
168 I [r]keep Thy precepts and Thy
testimonies, Ps. 119:22
For all my [r]ways are before
Thee. Prov. 5:21

Tav.

169 Let my cry come before
Thee, O LORD;
Give me understanding according to Thy word.
170 Let my supplication come
before Thee;
Deliver me according to Thy
[a]word. *promise*
171 Let my lips utter praise,
For Thou [r]dost teach me Thy
statutes. Ps. 94:12
172 Let my tongue sing of Thy
[a]word, *promise*
For all Thy commandments
are righteousness.
173 Let Thy hand be [t]ready to
help me, *to help me*
For I have [r]chosen Thy precepts. Josh. 24:22
174 I [r]long for Thy salvation, O
LORD, Ps. 119:166
And Thy law is my delight.
175 Let my [r]soul live that it may
praise Thee,
And let Thine ordinances
help me. Is. 55:3
176 I have gone astray like a lost
sheep; seek Thy servant,
For I do not forget Thy commandments.

PSALM 120

A Song of Ascents.

IN my trouble I cried to the LORD,
And He answered me.
2 Deliver my soul, O LORD,
from lying lips,
From a deceitful tongue.
3 What shall be given to you,
and what more shall be
done to you,
You deceitful tongue?
4 Sharp arrows of the warrior,
With the *burning* coals of the
broom tree.

5 Woe is me, for I sojourn in
[r]Meshech, Gen. 10:2
For I dwell among the [r]tents
of Kedar! Song 1:5
6 Too long has my soul had its
dwelling
With those who hate peace.
7 I [r]am *for* peace, but when I
speak, Ps. 109:4
They are [r]for war. Ps. 55:21

PSALM 121

A Song of Ascents.

I WILL lift up my eyes to [r]the
mountains;
From whence shall my help
come? Ps. 87:1
2 My [r]help *comes* from the
LORD, Ps. 124:8
Who made heaven and earth.
3 He will not [r]allow your foot to
slip; 1 Sam. 2:9
He who [r]keeps you will not
slumber. Ps. 41:2
4 Behold, He who keeps Israel
Will neither slumber nor
sleep.

5 The LORD is your keeper;
The LORD is your shade on your right hand.
6 The [r]sun will not smite you by day, Jon. 4:8; Rev. 7:16
Nor the moon by night.
7 The LORD will [201]protect you from all evil;
He will keep your soul.
8 The LORD will [201]guard your going out and your coming in
[r]From this time forth and forever. Ps. 113:2

PSALM 122

A Song of Ascents, of David.

I WAS glad when they said to me,
"Let us [r]go to the house of the LORD." Ps. 42:4
2 Our feet are standing
Within your [r]gates, O Jerusalem, Jer. 7:2
3 Jerusalem, that is built
As a city that is [r]compact together; 2 Sam. 5:9
4 To which the tribes [r]go up, even the tribes of the LORD—
An ordinance for Israel—
To give thanks to the name of the LORD. Ex. 23:17
5 For there thrones were set for judgment,
The thrones of the house of David.
6 Pray for the [r]peace of Jerusalem:
"May they prosper who [r]love you. Ps. 29:11 • Ps. 102:14
7 "May peace be within your [r]walls, Ps. 51:18
And prosperity within your [r]palaces." Jer. 17:27
8 For the sake of my brothers and my friends,
I will now say, "May peace be within you."
9 For the sake of the house of the LORD our God
I will seek your good.

PSALM 123

A Song of Ascents.

TO Thee I lift up my eyes,
O Thou who [r]art enthroned in the heavens! Ps. 121:1
2 Behold, as the eyes of [r]servants *look* to the hand of their master, Mal. 1:6
As the eyes of a maid to the hand of her mistress;
So our [r]eyes *look* to the LORD our God, Ps. 25:15
Until He shall be gracious to us.
3 Be gracious to us, O LORD, be gracious to us;
For we are greatly filled [r]with contempt. Neh. 4:4
4 Our soul is greatly filled
With the scoffing of those who are at ease,
And with the [r]contempt of the proud. Ps. 119:22

PSALM 124

A Song of Ascents, of David.

"HAD it not been the LORD who was on our side,"
Let Israel now say,
2 "Had it not been the LORD who was on our side,
When men rose up against us;

[201] Or, *keep*

3 Then they would have swallowed us alive,
When their anger was kindled against us;
4 Then the ʳwaters would have engulfed us, Job 22:11
The stream would have swept over our soul;
5 Then the raging waters would have ᵃswept over our soul." *passed over*

6 Blessed be the LORD,
Who has not given us to be torn by their teeth.
7 Our soul has ʳescaped as a bird out of the snare of the trapper; 2 Cor. 11:33
The snare is broken and we have escaped.
8 Ourʳ help is in the name of the LORD, Ps. 121:2
Who made heaven and earth.

PSALM 125

A Song of Ascents.

THOSE who trust in the LORD
Are as Mount Zion, which cannot be moved, but ʳabides forever. Ps. 61:7
2 As the mountains surround Jerusalem,
So ʳthe LORD surrounds His people Zech. 2:5
ʳFrom this time forth and forever. Ps. 121:8
3 For the scepter of wickedness shall not rest upon the land of the righteous;
That the righteous ʳmay not put forth their hands to do wrong. Acts 12:1

4 Do good, O LORD, to those who are good,
And to those who are ʳupright in their hearts. Ps. 7:10
5 But as for those who ʳturn aside to their crooked ways,
The LORD will lead them away with the ʳdoers of iniquity. Ps. 40:4 • Ps. 92:7
Peace be upon Israel.

PSALM 126

A Song of Ascents.

WHEN the LORD brought back the captive ones of Zion,
We were ʳlike those who dream. Acts 12:9
2 Then our ʳmouth was filled with laughter, Job 8:21
And our ʳtongue with joyful shouting; Ps. 51:14
Then they said among the nations,
"The LORD has done great things for them."
3 The LORD has done great things for us;
We are ʳglad. Zeph. 3:14

4 Restore our captivity, O LORD,
As the streams in the South.
5 Those who sow in ʳtears shall reap with joyful shouting. Jer. 31:9, 16
6 He who goes to and fro weeping, carrying *his* bag of seed,
Shall indeed come again with a shout of joy, bringing his sheaves *with him.*

PSALM 127

A Song of Ascents, of Solomon.

UNLESS the LORD ʳbuilds the house, Ps. 78:69

They labor in vain who build it;
Unless the LORD [r]guards the city, Ps. 121:4
The watchman keeps awake in vain.
2 It is vain for you to rise up early,
To [t]retire late,
To eat the bread of [t]painful labors; *delay sitting* • *toils*
For He gives to His beloved *even in his* sleep.

3 Behold, children are a [a]gift of the LORD;
The [r]fruit of the womb is a reward. *heritage* • Is. 13:18
4 Like arrows in the hand of a [r]warrior,
So are the children of one's youth. Ps. 112:2
5 How [r]blessed is the man whose quiver is full of them; Ps. 128:2, 3
They shall not be ashamed,
When they speak with their enemies in the gate.

PSALM 128

A Song of Ascents.

HOW blessed is everyone who fears the LORD,
Who walks in His ways.
2 When you shall eat of the [202]fruit of your hands,
You will be happy and it will be well with you.
3 Your wife shall be like a [r]fruitful vine, Ezek. 19:10
Within your house,
Your children like [r]olive plants Ps. 52:8
Around your table.
4 Behold, for thus shall the man be blessed
Who fears the LORD.

5 The LORD bless you [r]from Zion, Ps. 20:2
And may you see the prosperity of Jerusalem all the days of your life.
6 Indeed, may you see your children's children.
Peace be upon Israel!

PSALM 129

A Song of Ascents.

"MANY times they have [r]persecuted me from my [r]youth up," Ex. 1:11 • Is. 47:12
Let Israel now say,
2 "Many times they have [t]persecuted me from my youth up; *showed hostility toward*
Yet they have [r]not prevailed against me. Jer. 1:19
3 "The plowers plowed upon my back;
They lengthened their furrows."
4 The LORD is righteous;
He has cut in two the cords of the wicked.

5 May all who hate Zion,
Be [r]put to shame and turned backward, Ps. 70:3
6 Let them be like grass upon the housetops,
Which withers before it [t]grows up; *draws out*
7 With which the reaper does not fill his [t]hand,
Or the binder of sheaves his [r]bosom; *palm* • Ps. 79:12
8 Nor do those who pass by say,

[202] Lit., *labor*

"The [r]blessing of the LORD be upon you;
We bless you in the name of the LORD." Ruth 2:4

PSALM 130

A Song of Ascents.

OUT of the [r]depths I have cried to Thee, O LORD. Ps. 42:7
2 Lord, hear my voice!
Let Thine ears be attentive
To the [r]voice of my supplications. Ps. 28:2
3 If Thou, LORD, shouldst mark iniquities,
O Lord, who could stand?
4 But there is [r]forgiveness with Thee, Neh. 9:17
That Thou mayest be feared.

5 I wait for the LORD, my [r]soul does wait, Ps. 27:14
And in His word do I hope.
6 My soul *waits* for the Lord
More than the watchmen [r]for the morning; Ps. 63:6
Indeed, more than the watchmen for the morning.
7 O Israel, hope in the LORD;
For with the LORD there is lovingkindness,
And with Him is [r]abundant redemption. Eph. 1:7
8 And He will redeem Israel
From all his iniquities.

PSALM 131

A Song of Ascents, of David.

O LORD, my heart is not proud, nor my eyes haughty;
Nor do I involve myself in [r]great matters,
Or in things too [a]difficult for me. Jer. 45:5 • *marvelous*
2 Surely I have composed and quieted my soul;
Like a weaned child *rests* against his mother,
My soul is like a weaned child [a]within me. *upon*
3 O Israel, hope in the LORD
[r]From this time forth and forever. Ps. 113:2

PSALM 132

A Song of Ascents.

REMEMBER, O LORD, on David's behalf,
All his affliction;
2 How he swore to the LORD,
And vowed to the Mighty One of Jacob,
3 "Surely I will not enter [r]my house,
Nor lie on my bed; Job 21:28
4 I will not [r]give sleep to my eyes, Prov. 6:4
Or slumber to my eyelids;
5 Until I find a [r]place for the LORD, 1 Kin. 8:17
A dwelling place for the Mighty One of Jacob."

6 Behold, we heard of it in [r]Ephrathah; Gen. 35:19
We found it in the field of [a]Jaar. *the wood*
7 Let us go into His [t]dwelling place; *dwelling places*
Let us [r]worship at His footstool. Ps. 5:7
8 Arise, O LORD, to Thy [r]resting place; Ps. 132:14
Thou and the ark of Thy [r]strength. Ps. 78:61
9 Let Thy priests be clothed with righteousness;
And let Thy [r]godly ones sing for joy. Ps. 30:4

10 For the sake of David Thy servant,
Do not turn away the face of Thine anointed.
11 The LORD has ʳsworn to David, Ps. 89:3, 35
A truth from which He will not turn back;
"Of the fruit of your body I will set upon your throne.
12 "If your sons will keep My covenant,
And My testimony which I will teach them,
Their sons also shall sit upon your throne forever."

13 For the LORD has ʳchosen Zion; Ps. 48:1, 2
He has ʳdesired it for His habitation. Ps. 68:16
14 "This is My ʳresting place forever; Ps. 132:8
Here I will ʳdwell, for I have desired it. Ps. 68:16
15 "I will abundantly ʳbless her provision; Ps. 147:14
I will ʳsatisfy her needy with bread. Ps. 107:9
16 "Her priests also I will clothe with salvation;
And her ʳgodly ones will sing aloud for joy. Ps. 132:9
17 "There I will cause the horn of David to spring forth;
I have prepared a ʳlamp for Mine anointed. Ps. 18:28
18 "His enemies I will ʳclothe with shame; Job 8:22
But upon himself his ʳcrown shall shine." Ps. 21:3

PSALM 133

A Song of Ascents, of David.

BEHOLD, how good and how pleasant it is
For brothers to dwell together in unity!
2 It is like the precious ʳoil upon the head,
Coming down upon the beard,
Even Aaron's beard,
Coming down upon the edge of his robes. Ex. 29:7
3 It is like the dew of Hermon,
Coming down upon the mountains of Zion;
For there the LORD commanded the blessing—
ʳlife forever. Ps. 21:4

PSALM 134

A Song of Ascents.

BEHOLD, bless the LORD, all servants of the LORD,
Who serve by night in the house of the LORD!
2 Lift up your hands to the ʳsanctuary,
And bless the LORD. Ps. 63:2
3 May the LORD ʳbless you from Zion, Ps. 128:5
He who ʳmade heaven and earth. Ps. 124:8

PSALM 135

PRAISE the LORD!
Praise the name of the LORD;
Praise *Him*, O ʳservants of the LORD, Ps. 134:1
2 You who stand in the house of the LORD,
In the ʳcourts of the house of our God! Ps. 92:13
3 Praise the LORD, for ʳthe LORD is good; Ps. 100:5
ʳSing praises to His name, for it is lovely. Ps. 68:4

4 For the LORD has chosen Jacob for Himself,
Israel for His [a]own possession. *special treasure*

5 For I know that [r]the LORD is great, Ps. 48:1
And that our Lord is [r]above all gods. Ps. 97:9
6 [r]Whatever the LORD pleases, He does, Ps. 115:3
In heaven and in earth, in the seas and in all deeps.
7 He [r]causes the vapors to ascend from the ends of the earth; Jer. 10:13
Who [r]makes lightnings for the rain; Zech. 10:1
Who brings forth the wind from His treasuries.

8 [t]He smote the first-born of Egypt, *The one who*
Both of man and beast.
9 He sent signs and wonders into your midst, O Egypt,
Upon [r]Pharaoh and all his servants. Ps. 136:15
10 He smote many nations,
And slew mighty kings,
11 Sihon, king of the Amorites,
And Og, king of Bashan,
And [r]all the kingdoms of Canaan; Josh. 12:7-24
12 And He [r]gave their land as a heritage,
A heritage to Israel His people. Deut. 29:8
13 Thy [r]name, O LORD, is everlasting, Ex. 3:15
Thy [a]remembrance, O LORD, [t]throughout all generations. *memorial • to*
14 For the LORD will [r]judge His people, Ps. 50:4
And [r]will have compassion on His servants. Ps. 90:13
15 The idols of the nations are *but* silver and gold,
The work of man's hands.
16 They have mouths, but they do not speak;
They have eyes, but they do not see;
17 They have ears, but they do not hear;
Nor is there any breath at all in their mouths.
18 Those who make them will be like them,
Yes, everyone who trusts in them.

19 O house of [r]Israel, bless the LORD;
O house of Aaron, bless the LORD; Ps. 115:9
20 O house of Levi, bless the LORD;
You who [203]revere the LORD, bless the LORD.
21 Blessed be the LORD [r]from Zion, Ps. 128:5; 134:3
Who dwells in Jerusalem.
Praise the LORD!

PSALM 136

GIVE thanks to the LORD, for [r]He is good; Ezra 3:11
For [r]His lovingkindness is everlasting. Ps. 118:1-4
2 Give thanks to the [r]God of gods,
For His lovingkindness is everlasting. Deut. 10:17
3 Give thanks to the [r]Lord of lords,
For His lovingkindness is everlasting. Deut. 10:17
4 To Him who [r]alone does great wonders,
For His lovingkindness is everlasting; Job 9:10

[203] Or, *fear*

5 To Him who [r]made the heavens with skill,
For His lovingkindness is everlasting; Gen. 1:1
6 To Him who spread out the earth above the waters,
For His lovingkindness is everlasting;
7 To Him who [r]made *the* great lights,
For His lovingkindness is everlasting: Ps. 74:16
8 The sun to rule by day,
For His lovingkindness is everlasting,
9 The moon and stars to rule [a]by night,
For His lovingkindness is everlasting. *over the*

10 To Him who smote the Egyptians in their first-born,
For His lovingkindness is everlasting,
11 And [r]brought Israel out from their midst,
For His lovingkindness is everlasting, Ex. 12:51
12 With a strong hand and an outstretched arm,
For His lovingkindness is everlasting;
13 To Him who divided the Red Sea [t]asunder,
For His lovingkindness is everlasting, *in parts*
14 And made Israel pass through the midst of it,
For His lovingkindness is everlasting;
15 But He [t]overthrew Pharaoh and his army in the Red Sea,
For His lovingkindness is everlasting. *shook off*
16 To Him who led His people through the wilderness,
For His lovingkindness is everlasting;
17 To Him who [r]smote great kings,
For His lovingkindness is everlasting, Ps. 135:10-12
18 And slew mighty kings,
For His lovingkindness is everlasting:
19 Sihon, king of the Amorites,
For His lovingkindness is everlasting,
20 And Og, king of Bashan,
For His lovingkindness is everlasting,
21 And [r]gave their land as a heritage,
For His lovingkindness is everlasting, Josh. 12:1
22 Even a heritage to Israel His [r]servant,
For His lovingkindness is everlasting. Ps. 105:6

23 Who [r]remembered us in our low estate,
For His lovingkindness is everlasting, Ps. 9:12
24 And has [r]rescued us from our adversaries,
For His lovingkindness is everlasting; Judg. 6:9
25 Who gives food to all flesh,
For His lovingkindness is everlasting.
26 Give thanks to the [r]God of heaven, Ezra 1:2; 5:11
For His lovingkindness is everlasting.

PSALM 137

BY the rivers of Babylon,
There we sat down and wept,

When we remembered Zion.
2 Upon the [a]willows in the midst of it *poplars*
We hung our [t]harps. *lyres*
3 For there our captors demanded of us songs,
And [r]our tormentors mirth, *saying*,
"Sing us one of the songs of Zion." Is. 49:17

4 How can we sing [r]the LORD's song 2 Chr. 29:27
In a foreign land?
5 If I forget you, O Jerusalem,
May my right hand forget *her skill*.
6 May my tongue cleave to the roof of my mouth,
If I do not remember you,
If I do not exalt Jerusalem
Above my chief joy.

7 Remember, O LORD, against the sons of Edom
The day of Jerusalem,
Who said, "Raze it, raze it,
To its very foundation."
8 O daughter of Babylon, you devastated one,
How blessed will be the one who repays you
With [t]the recompense with which you have repaid us. *your recompense*
9 How blessed will be the one who seizes and dashes your little ones
Against the rock.

PSALM 138

A Psalm of David.

I WILL give Thee thanks with all my heart;
I will sing praises to Thee before the gods.
2 I will bow down [r]toward Thy holy temple,
And give thanks to Thy name for Thy lovingkindness and Thy truth;
For Thou hast magnified Thy [a]word according to all Thy name. Ps. 5:7 • *promise*
3 On the day I called Thou didst answer me;
Thou didst make me bold with strength in my soul.

4 [r]All the kings of the earth will give thanks to Thee, O LORD, Ps. 72:11
When they have heard the words of Thy mouth.
5 And they will sing of the ways of the LORD.
For [r]great is the glory of the LORD. Ps. 21:5
6 For [r]though the LORD is exalted,
Yet He regards the lowly;
But the haughty He knows from afar. Ps. 113:4-7

7 Though I walk in the midst of trouble, Thou wilt [a]revive me; *keep me alive*
Thou wilt [r]stretch forth Thy hand against the wrath of my enemies, Ex. 7:5
And Thy right hand will [r]save me. Ps. 20:6; 60:5
8 The LORD will accomplish what concerns me;
Thy [r]lovingkindness, O LORD, is everlasting; Ps. 136:1
Do not forsake the [r]works of Thy hands. Job 10:3

PSALM 139

For the choir director. A Psalm of David.

O LORD, Thou hast [r]searched me
and known *me.* Ps. 17:3
2 Thou dost know when I sit
down and when I rise up;
Thou dost understand my
thought from afar.
3 Thou dost scrutinize my path
and my lying down,
And art intimately ac-
quainted with all my
ways.
4 Even before there is a word
on my tongue,
Behold, O LORD, Thou [r]dost
know it all. Heb. 4:13
5 Thou hast [r]enclosed me behind and before, Ps. 34:7
And laid Thy hand upon me.
6 *Such* [r]knowledge is too wonderful for me;
It is *too* high, I cannot attain
to it. Rom. 11:33

7 [r]Where can I go from Thy
Spirit?
Or where can I flee from Thy
presence? Jer. 23:24
8 [r]If I ascend to heaven, Thou
art there; Amos 9:2-4
If I make my bed in Sheol,
behold, Thou art there.
9 If I take the wings of the
dawn,
If I dwell in the remotest part
of the sea,
10 Even there Thy hand will
[r]lead me,
And Thy right hand will lay
hold of me. Ps. 23:2, 3
11 If I say, "Surely the darkness
will overwhelm me,
And the light around me will
be night,"
12 Even the darkness is not
dark [t]to Thee,
And the night is as bright as
the day.
Darkness and light are alike
to Thee. *from*

13 For Thou didst form my [t]in-
ward parts;
Thou didst weave me in my
mother's womb. *kidneys*
14 I will give thanks to Thee, for
[204]I am fearfully and won-
derfully made;
Wonderful are Thy works,
And my soul knows it very
well.
15 My [t]frame was not hidden
from Thee, *bones were*
When I was made in secret,
And skillfully wrought in the
depths of the earth.
16 Thine eyes have seen my un-
formed substance;
And in [r]Thy book they were
all written, Ps. 56:8
The [r]days that were ordained
for me, Job 14:5
When as yet there was not
one of them.

17 How precious also are Thy
thoughts to me, O God!
How vast is the sum of them!
18 If I should count them, they
would [r]outnumber the
sand.
When [r]I awake, I am still with
Thee. Ps. 40:5 • Ps. 3:5

19 O that Thou wouldst slay the
wicked, O God;
Depart from me, therefore,
men of bloodshed.

[204] Some ancient versions read *Thou art fearfully wonderful*

20 For they [r]speak [a]against Thee
wickedly, Jude 15 • *of*
And Thine enemies [r]take *Thy*
name in vain. Ex. 20:7
21 Do I not hate those who hate
Thee, O LORD?
And do I not [r]loathe those
who rise up against
Thee? Ps. 119:158
22 I hate them with the utmost
hatred;
They have become my en-
emies.

23 [r]Search me, O God, and know
my heart; Job 31:6
[r]Try me and know my anxious thoughts; Ps. 7:9
24 And see if there be any hurt-
ful way in me,
And lead me in the [r]ever-
lasting way. Ps. 16:11

PSALM 140

For the choir director. A Psalm of David.

RESCUE me, O LORD, from evil
men;
Preserve me from [r]violent
men, Ps. 18:48
2 Who [r]devise evil things in
their hearts;
They [r]continually stir up
wars. Ps. 7:14 • Ps. 56:6
3 They [r]sharpen their tongues
as a serpent; Ps. 57:4
Poison of a viper is under
their lips. [Selah.

4 Keep me, O LORD, from the
hands of the wicked;
[r]Preserve me from violent
men, Ps. 140:1
Who have [a]purposed to [205]trip
up my feet. *devised*
5 The proud have hidden a trap
for me, and cords;
They have spread a net by
the [t]wayside; *track*
They have set snares for me.
[Selah.

6 I [r]said to the LORD, "Thou art
my God;
[r]Give ear, O LORD, to the
voice of my supplica-
tions. Ps. 16:2 • Ps. 143:1
7 "O GOD the Lord, the strength
of my salvation,
Thou hast covered my head
in the day of battle.
8 "Do not grant, O LORD, the desires of the wicked;
Do not promote his *evil* device, *lest* they be exalted.
[Selah.

9 "As for the head of those who
surround me,
May the [r]mischief of their lips
cover them. Ps. 7:16
10 "May [r]burning coals fall upon
them; Ps. 11:6
May they be [r]cast into the
fire, Matt. 3:10
Into deep pits from which
they cannot rise.
11 "May a slanderer not be established in the earth;
May evil hunt the violent
man [206]speedily."

12 I know that the LORD will
[r]maintain the cause of the
afflicted, Ps. 9:4
And justice for the poor.
13 Surely the righteous will give
thanks to Thy name;
The [r]upright will dwell in Thy
presence. Ps. 11:7

[205] Lit., *push violently*

[206] Lit., *thrust upon thrust*

PSALM 141

A Psalm of David.

O LORD, I call upon Thee; [r]hasten
to me! Ps. 22:19
[r]Give ear to my voice when I
call to Thee! Ps. 5:1
2 May my prayer be counted
as incense before Thee;
The lifting up of my hands as
the evening offering.
3 Set a [r]guard, O LORD, [t]over my
mouth;
Keep watch over the door of
my lips. Ps. 34:13 • to
4 Do not incline my heart to
any evil thing,
To practice deeds [t]of wickedness in
With men who do iniquity;
And [r]do not let me eat of their
delicacies. Prov. 23:6
5 Let the righteous smite me in
kindness and reprove me;
It is oil upon the head;
Do not let my head refuse it,
For still my prayer is against
their wicked deeds.
6 Their judges are [r]thrown
down by the sides of the
rock, 2 Chr. 25:12
And they hear my words, for
they are pleasant.
7 As when one plows and
breaks open the earth,
Our [r]bones have been scattered at the mouth of
Sheol. Ps. 53:5
8 For my eyes are toward
Thee, O GOD, the Lord;
In Thee I take refuge; do not
leave me defenseless.
9 Keep me from the [r]jaws of
the trap which they have
set for me, Ps. 38:12
And from the [r]snares of those
who do iniquity. Ps. 140:5
10 Let the wicked [r]fall into their
own nets, Ps. 7:15; 35:8
While I pass by safely.

PSALM 142

Maskil of David, when he was in the cave. A Prayer.

I [r]CRY aloud with my voice to the
LORD; Ps. 77:1
I make supplication with my
voice to the LORD.
2 I [r]pour out my complaint be-
fore Him; Ps. 102:title
I declare my [r]trouble before
Him. Ps. 77:2
3 When my spirit was over-
whelmed within me,
Thou didst know my path.
In the way where I walk
They have [r]hidden a trap for
me. Ps. 140:5
4 Look to the right and see;
For there is [r]no one who re-
gards me; Ps. 31:11
There is no escape for me;
No one cares for my soul.
5 I cried out to Thee, O LORD;
I said, "Thou art my refuge,
My [r]portion in the land of the
living. Ps. 16:5; 73:26
6 "Give heed to my cry,
For I am brought very low;
Deliver me from my persecu-
tors,
For they are too [r]strong for
me. Ps. 18:17
7 "Bring my soul out of prison,
So that I may give thanks to
Thy name;
The righteous will surround
me,
For Thou wilt deal bounti-
fully with me."

PSALM 143

A Psalm of David.

HEAR my prayer, O LORD,
Give ear to my supplications!
Answer me in Thy faithfulness, in Thy righteousness! Ps. 89:1, 2
2 And do not enter into judgment with Thy servant,
For in Thy sight no man living is righteous.
3 For the enemy has persecuted my soul;
He has crushed my life to the ground;
He has made me dwell in dark places, like those who have long been dead. Ps. 44:25 • Ps. 88:6
4 Therefore my spirit is overwhelmed within me;
My heart is [207]appalled within me.

5 I remember the days of old;
I meditate on all Thy doings;
I muse on the work of Thy hands. Ps. 105:2
6 I stretch out my hands to Thee; Job 11:13
My soul *longs* for Thee, as a parched land. [Selah.

7 Answer me quickly, O LORD, my spirit fails;
Do not hide Thy face from me, Jer. 8:18 • Ps. 27:9
Lest I become like those who go down to the pit.
8 Let me hear Thy lovingkindness in the morning;
For I trust in Thee; Ps. 25:2
Teach me the way in which I should walk; Ps. 27:11
For to Thee I lift up my soul.

[207]Or, *desolate*

9 Deliver me, O LORD, from my enemies; Ps. 31:15
I take refuge in Thee.

10 Teach me to do Thy will,
For Thou art my God;
Let Thy good Spirit lead me on level ground. *land*
11 For the sake of Thy name, O LORD, revive me.
In Thy righteousness bring my soul out of trouble.
12 And in Thy lovingkindness cut off my enemies,
And destroy all those who afflict my soul; Ps. 52:5
For I am Thy servant.

PSALM 144

A Psalm of David.

BLESSED be the LORD, my rock,
Who trains my hands for war, 2 Sam. 22:35
And my fingers for battle;
2 My lovingkindness and my fortress,
My stronghold and my deliverer; Ps. 18:2 • Ps. 59:9
My shield and He in whom I take refuge; Ps. 3:3
Who subdues my people under me. Ps. 18:39
3 O LORD, what is man, that Thou dost take knowledge of him? Heb. 2:6
Or the son of man, that Thou dost think of him?
4 Man is like a mere breath;
His days are like a passing shadow. Job 8:9; 14:2

5 Bow Thy heavens, O LORD, and come down;
Touch the mountains, that they may smoke.

6 Flash forth [r]lightning and
scatter them; Ps. 18:14
Send out Thine [r]arrows and
confuse them. Ps. 7:13
7 Stretch forth Thy hand [r]from
on high; Ps. 18:16
Rescue me and deliver me
out of great waters,
Out of the hand of aliens
8 Whose mouths speak deceit,
And whose right hand is a
right hand of falsehood.

9 I will sing a [r]new song to
Thee, O God; Ps. 33:3
Upon a harp of ten strings I
will sing praises to Thee,
10 Who dost [r]give salvation to
kings; Ps. 18:50
Who [r]dost rescue David His
servant from the evil
sword. 2 Sam. 18:7
11 Rescue me, and deliver me
out of the hand of aliens,
Whose mouth speaks deceit,
And whose right hand is a
right hand of falsehood.

12 Let our sons in their youth be
as grown-up plants,
And our daughters as [r]corner
pillars fashioned as for a
palace; Song 4:4
13 *Let* our [r]garners be full, furnishing every kind of pro-
duce, Prov. 3:9, 10
And our flocks bring forth
thousands and ten thou-
sands in our fields;
14 *Let* our cattle bear,
Without [l]mishap and without
loss, *bursting forth*
Let there be no [r]outcry in our
streets! Is. 24:11
15 How blessed are the people
who are so situated;
How blessed are the people
whose God is the LORD!

PSALM 145

A Psalm of Praise, of David.

I WILL [r]extol Thee, my God, O
King; Ps. 30:1; 66:17
And I will bless Thy name
forever and ever.
2 Every day I will bless Thee,
And I will praise Thy name
forever and ever.
3 [r]Great is the LORD, and highly
to be praised; Ps. 48:1
And His [r]greatness is unsearchable. Rom. 11:33
4 One generation shall praise
Thy works to another,
And shall declare Thy
mighty acts.
5 On the [r]glorious splendor of
Thy majesty, Ps. 145:12
And on Thy wonderful
works, I will meditate.
6 And men shall speak of the
[a]power of Thine awesome
acts; *strength*
And I will [r]tell of Thy greatness. Deut. 32:3
7 They shall eagerly utter the
memory of Thine [r]abun-
dant goodness, Is. 63:7
And shall shout joyfully of
Thy righteousness.

8 The LORD is [r]gracious and
merciful; Num. 14:18
Slow to anger and great in
lovingkindness.
9 The LORD is good to all,
And His [r]mercies are over all
His works. Ps. 145:15
10 All Thy works shall give
thanks to Thee, O LORD,

And Thy [r]godly ones shall
bless Thee. Ps. 68:26
11 They shall speak of the [r]glory
of Thy kingdom, Jer. 14:21
And talk of Thy power;
12 To make known to the sons
of men Thy mighty acts,
And the glory of the majesty
of Thy kingdom.
13 Thy kingdom is an everlasting kingdom,
And Thy dominion *endures*
throughout all genera-
tions.

14 The LORD [r]sustains all who
fall, Ps. 37:24
And [r]raises up all who are
bowed down. Ps. 146:8
15 The eyes of all look to Thee,
And Thou dost give them
their food in due time.
16 Thou dost open Thy hand,
And dost satisfy the desire of
every living thing.

17 The LORD is [r]righteous in all
His ways, Ps. 116:5
And kind in all His deeds.
18 The LORD is [r]near to all who
call upon Him, Deut. 4:7
To all who call upon Him [r]in
truth. John 4:24
19 He will fulfill the desire of
those who fear Him;
He will also hear their cry
and will save them.
20 The LORD [r]keeps all who love
Him; Ps. 31:23; 91:14
But all the [r]wicked, He will
destroy. Ps. 9:5
21 My mouth will speak the
praise of the LORD;
And [r]all flesh will bless His
holy name forever and
ever. Ps. 65:2; 150:6

PSALM 146

PRAISE the LORD!
Praise the LORD, O my soul!
2 I will praise the LORD [r]while I
live; Ps. 63:4
I will sing praises to my God
while I have my being.
3 Do not trust in princes,
In mortal man, in whom
there is no salvation.
4 His spirit departs, he returns
to [t]the earth; *his earth*
In that very day his [r]thoughts
perish. 1 Cor. 2:6
5 How blessed is he whose
help is the God of Jacob,
Whose [r]hope is in the LORD
his God; Ps. 71:5
6 Who made heaven and earth,
The [r]sea and all that is in
them; Acts 14:15
Who keeps faith forever;
7 Who [r]executes justice for the
oppressed; Ps. 103:6
Who [r]gives food to the hungry. Ps. 107:9; 145:15
The LORD [r]sets the prisoners
free. Ps. 68:6; Is. 61:1

8 The LORD [r]opens *the eyes of*
the blind; Matt. 9:30
The LORD raises up those
who are bowed down;
The LORD [r]loves the righteous; Ps. 11:7
9 The LORD protects the
[a]strangers; *sojourners*
He [a]supports the fatherless
and the widow; *relieves*
But He thwarts the way of
the wicked.
10 The LORD will reign forever,
Thy God, O Zion, to all generations.
[a]Praise the LORD! *Hallelujah*

PSALM 147

PRAISE the LORD!
For [r]it is good to sing praises
to our God;
For [208]it is pleasant *and* praise
is becoming. Ps. 92:1
2 The LORD [r]builds up Jerusalem; Ps. 51:18; 102:16
He [r]gathers the outcasts of Israel. Is. 11:12; 56:8
3 He heals the brokenhearted,
And binds up their [209]wounds.
4 He [r]counts the number of the
stars; Gen. 15:5
He [r]gives names to all of
them. Is. 40:26
5 Great is our Lord, and abundant in strength;
His understanding is infinite.
6 The LORD [210]supports the afflicted;
He brings down the wicked
to the ground.

7 [r]Sing to the LORD with
thanksgiving;
Sing praises to our God on
the lyre, Ps. 33:2
8 Who [r]covers the heavens
with clouds, Job 26:8
Who [r]provides rain for the
earth, Job 5:10; 38:26
Who makes grass to grow on
the mountains.
9 He gives to the beast its food,
And to the [r]young ravens
which cry. Job 38:41
10 He does not delight in the
strength of the horse;
He does not take pleasure in
the legs of a man.
11 The LORD [r]favors those who
fear Him, Ps. 149:4
Those who wait for His
lovingkindness.

12 Praise the LORD, O Jerusalem!
Praise your God, O Zion!
13 For He has strengthened the
bars of your gates;
He has [r]blessed your sons
within you. Ps. 37:26
14 He makes [t]peace in your borders; *your borders peace*
He satisfies you with the [t]finest of the wheat. *fat*
15 He sends forth His [r]command
to the earth; Ps. 148:5
His word runs very swiftly.
16 He gives snow like wool;
He scatters the [r]frost like
ashes. Job 38:29
17 He casts forth His [r]ice as
fragments; Job 37:10
Who can stand before His
[r]cold? Job 37:9
18 He [r]sends forth His word and
melts them; Ps. 33:9
He causes His wind to blow
and the waters to flow.
19 He [r]declares His words to Jacob, Deut. 33:3, 4
His statutes and His ordinances to Israel.
20 He [r]has not dealt thus with
any nation; Rom. 3:1, 2
And as for His ordinances,
they have [r]not known
them. Ps. 79:6; Jer. 10:25
Praise the LORD!

PSALM 148

PRAISE the LORD!
Praise the LORD [r]from the
heavens; Ps. 69:34
Praise Him in the heights!
2 Praise Him, all His angels;
Praise Him, all His hosts!

[208]Or, *He is gracious* [209]Lit., *sorrows*
[210]Or, *relieves*

3 Praise Him, sun and moon;
Praise Him, all stars of light!
4 Praise Him, highest heavens,
And the waters that are above the heavens!
5 Let them praise the name of the LORD,
For [r]He commanded and they were created. Gen. 1:1
6 He has also established them forever and ever;
He has made a decree which will not pass away.

7 Praise the LORD from the earth,
Sea monsters and all deeps;
8 Fire and hail, [r]snow and clouds; Ps. 147:16
[r]Stormy wind, fulfilling His word; Ps. 107:25
9 Mountains and all hills;
Fruit trees and all cedars;
10 Beasts and all cattle;
[r]Creeping things and winged fowl; Hos. 2:18
11 [r]Kings of the earth and all peoples;
Princes and all judges of the earth; Ps. 102:15
12 Both young men and virgins;
Old men and children.

13 Let them praise the name of the LORD,
For His [r]name alone is exalted; Is. 12:4
His [r]glory is above earth and heaven. Ps. 8:1; 113:4
14 And He has [r]lifted up a horn for His people,
Praise for all His godly ones;
Even for the sons of Israel, a people near to Him.
Praise the LORD! 1 Sam. 2:1

PSALM 149

PRAISE the LORD!
Sing to the LORD a new song,
And His praise in the congregation of the godly ones.
2 Let Israel be glad in [r]his Maker; Ps. 95:6
Let the sons of Zion rejoice in their [r]King. Ps. 47:6
3 Let them praise His name with [r]dancing; Ps. 150:4
Let them sing praises to Him with timbrel and lyre.
4 For the LORD [r]takes pleasure in His people; Job 36:11
He will beautify the afflicted ones with salvation.

5 Let the [r]godly ones exult in glory; Ps. 132:16
Let them [r]sing for joy on their beds. Job 35:10; Ps. 42:8
6 *Let* the high praises of God *be* in their mouth,
And a [r]two-edged sword in their hand, Heb. 4:12
7 To [r]execute vengeance on the nations,
And punishment on the peoples; Ezek. 25:17
8 To bind their kings [r]with chains, Job 36:8
And their [r]nobles with fetters of iron; Nah. 3:10
9 To execute on them the judgment written;
This is an [r]honor for all His godly ones.
Praise the LORD! Ps. 112:9

PSALM 150

PRAISE the LORD!
Praise God in His sanctuary;

Praise Him in His mighty expanse.
2 Praise Him for His mighty deeds;
Praise Him according to His excellent greatness.

3 Praise Him with trumpet sound;
Praise Him with harp and lyre.
4 Praise Him with timbrel and dancing;
Praise Him with stringed instruments and pipe.
5 Praise Him with loud cymbals;
Praise Him with resounding cymbals.
6 Let everything that has breath praise the LORD.
Praise the LORD!

THE PROVERBS

THE proverbs of Solomon the son of David, king of Israel:
2 To know [r]wisdom and instruction, Prov. 15:33
To discern the sayings of [r]understanding, Prov. 4:1
3 To [r]receive instruction in wise behavior, Prov. 2:1
[r]Righteousness, justice and equity; Prov. 2:9
4 To give prudence to the [t]naive, *simple ones*
To the youth [r]knowledge and discretion, Prov. 2:10, 11
5 A wise man will hear and increase in learning,
And a man of understanding will acquire wise counsel,
6 To understand a proverb and a figure,
The words of the wise and their [r]riddles. Num. 12:8

7 [r]The fear of the LORD is the beginning of knowledge;
Fools despise wisdom and instruction. Job 28:28

8 [r]Hear, my son, your father's instruction, Prov. 4:1
And do not forsake your mother's teaching;
9 Indeed, they are a graceful wreath to your head,
And [t]ornaments about your neck. *necklaces*
10 My son, if sinners [r]entice you,
Do not consent. Prov. 16:29
11 If they say, "Come with us,
Let us [r]lie in wait for blood,
Let us ambush the innocent without cause; Prov. 12:6
12 Let us [r]swallow them alive like Sheol, Ps. 124:3
Even whole, as those who [r]go down to the pit; Ps. 28:1
13 We shall find all *kinds* of precious wealth,
We shall fill our houses with spoil;
14 Throw in your lot with us,
We shall all have one purse,"
15 My son, [r]do not walk in the way with them. Ps. 1:1

ʳKeep your feet from their
path, Ps. 119:101
16 Forʳtheir feet run to evil,
And they hasten to shed
blood. Prov. 6:17, 18; Is. 59:7
17 Indeed, it isᵗuseless to spread
the net *in vain*
In the eyes of any bird;
18 But theyʳlie in wait for their
own blood; Prov. 11:19
They ambush their own lives.
19 So are the ways of everyone
who ʳgains by violence;
It takes away the life of its
possessors. Prov. 15:27

20 ʳWisdom shouts in the street,
She ᵗlifts her voice in the
square; Prov. 8:1-3 • *gives*
21 At the head of the noisy
streets she cries out;
At the entrance of the gates
in the city, she utters her
sayings:
22 "How long, O naive ones, will
you love simplicity?
And scoffers delight themselves in scoffing,
And fools hate knowledge?
23 "Turn to my reproof,
Behold, I will ʳpour out my
spirit on you; Is. 32:15
I will make my words known
to you.
24 Becauseʳ I called, and you refused; Is. 65:12; 66:4
I stretched out my hand, and
no one paid attention;
25 And you ʳneglected all my
counsel, Ps. 107:11
And did not ʳwant my re-
proof; Prov. 15:10
26 I will evenʳlaugh at your calamity; Ps. 2:4
I will mock when your ʳdread
comes, Prov. 10:24
27 When your dread comes like
a storm,
And your calamity comes on
like aʳwhirlwind,
When distress *and* anguish
come on you. Prov. 10:25
28 "Then they will call on me,
but I will not answer;
They will ʳseek me diligently,
but they shall not find
me, Prov. 8:17
29 Because they ʳhated knowledge, Job 21:14; Prov. 1:22
And did not choose the fear
of the LORD.
30 "They ʳwould not accept my
counsel, Ps. 81:11
They spurned all my reproof.
31 "So they shall eat of the fruit
of their own way,
And be ʳsatiated with their
own devices. Prov. 14:14
32 "For the waywardness of the
naive shall kill them,
And the complacency of
fools shall destroy them.
33 "But he who listens to me
shallᵗlive securely, *dwell*
And shall be at ease from the
dread of evil."

CHAPTER 2

MY son, if you will ʳreceive my
sayings, Prov. 4:10
And treasure my command-
ments within you,
2 ʳMake your ear attentive to
wisdom, Prov. 22:17
Incline your heart to understanding;
3 For if you cry for discernment,
ᵗLift your voice for understanding; *Give*
4 If you seek her as silver,

And search for her as for hidden treasures;
5 Then you will discern the [r]fear of the LORD, Prov. 1:7
And discover the knowledge of God.
6 For [r]the LORD gives wisdom;
From His mouth *come* knowledge and understanding. 1 Kin. 3:12
7 He stores up sound wisdom for the upright;
He is a [r]shield to those who walk in integrity, Ps. 84:11
8 Guarding the paths of justice,
And He [r]preserves the way of His godly ones. Ps. 66:9
9 Then you will discern righteousness and justice
And equity *and* every [r]good course. Prov. 4:18
10 For [r]wisdom will enter your heart, Prov. 14:33
And knowledge will be pleasant to your soul;
11 Discretion will [r]guard you,
Understanding will watch over you, Prov. 4:6; 6:22
12 To [r]deliver you from the way of evil, Prov. 28:26
From the man who speaks perverse things;
13 From those who leave the paths of uprightness,
To walk in the [r]ways of darkness; Ps. 82:5; Prov. 4:19
14 Who delight in doing evil,
And rejoice in the perversity of evil;
15 Whose paths are [r]crooked,
And who are devious in their ways; Ps. 125:5; Prov. 21:8
16 To [r]deliver you from the strange woman, Prov. 6:24
From the adulteress who flatters with her words;
17 That leaves the [r]companion of her youth, Mal. 2:14, 15
And forgets the [r]covenant of her God; Gen. 2:24
18 For her house [t]sinks down to death, *bows down*
And her tracks *lead* to the [t]dead; *departed spirits*
19 None [r]who go to her return again, Eccl. 7:26
Nor do they reach the paths of life.
20 So you will walk in the way of good men,
And keep to the paths of the righteous.
21 For the upright will [a]live in the land, *dwell*
And the blameless will remain in it;
22 But the wicked will be cut off from the land,
And the treacherous will be uprooted from it.

CHAPTER 3

MY son, do not forget my [a]teaching, *law*
But let your heart keep my commandments;
2 For [r]length of days and years of life, Ps. 91:16
And peace they will add to you.
3 Do not let [r]kindness and truth leave you; 2 Sam. 15:20
Bind them around your neck,
Write them on the tablet of your heart.
4 So you will find favor and good repute
In the sight of God and man.
5 Trust in the LORD with all your heart,

And do not lean on your own
understanding.
6 In all your ways [r]acknowledge Him, 1 Chr. 28:9
And He will [r]make your paths
straight. Is. 45:13
7 [r]Do not be wise in your own
eyes; Rom. 12:16
[r]Fear the LORD and turn away
from evil. Job 1:1
8 It will be healing to your
[t]body, *navel*
And [r]refreshment to your
bones. Job 21:24
9 [r]Honor the LORD from your
wealth, Is. 43:23
And from the first of all your
produce;
10 So your [r]barns will be filled
with plenty, Deut. 28:8
And your vats will overflow
with new wine.
11 My son, do not reject the discipline of the LORD,
Or loathe His reproof,
12 For [r]whom the LORD loves He
reproves, Rev. 3:19
Even as a father, the son in
whom he delights.

13 [r]How blessed is the man who
finds wisdom, Prov. 8:32, 34
And the man who gains understanding.
14 For its profit is better than
the profit of silver,
And its gain than fine gold.
15 She is more precious than
[t]jewels; *corals*
And nothing you desire compares with her.
16 [t]Long life is in her right hand;
In her left hand are riches
and honor. *Length of days*
17 Her ways are pleasant ways,
And all her paths are peace.
18 She is a [r]tree of life to those
who take hold of her,
And happy are all who hold
her fast. Gen. 2:9
19 The LORD by wisdom
founded the earth;
By understanding He established the heavens.
20 By His knowledge the deeps
were broken up,
And the skies drip with dew.
21 My son, [r]let them not depart
from your sight; Prov. 4:21
Keep sound wisdom and discretion,
22 So they will be [r]life to your
soul, Deut. 32:47; Prov. 4:22
And adornment to your neck.
23 Then you will walk in your
way securely,
And your foot will not [r]stumble. Ps. 91:12
24 When you [r]lie down, you will
not be afraid; Job 11:19
When you lie down, your
sleep will be sweet.
25 [r]Do not be afraid of sudden
fear, Ps. 91:5
Nor of the onslaught of the
wicked when it comes;
26 For the LORD will be [a]your
confidence, *at your side*
And will keep your foot from
being caught.

27 Do not withhold good from
[t]those to whom it is due,
When it is in your power to
do *it*. *its owners*
28 Do not say to your neighbor,
"Go, and come back,
And tomorrow I will give *it*,"
When you have it with you.
29 Do not devise harm against
your neighbor,

While he lives in security beside you.
30 Do not contend with a man without cause,
If he has done you no harm.
31 ʳDo not envy a man of violence, Ps. 37:1
And do not choose any of his ways.
32 For the crooked *man* is an abomination to the LORD;
But He is ʳintimate with the upright. Job 29:4
33 The ʳcurse of the LORD is on the house of the wicked,
But He blesses the dwelling of the righteous. Ps. 1:3
34 Though ʳHe scoffs at the scoffers, James 4:6
Yet He gives grace to the afflicted.
35 The wise will inherit honor,
But fools display dishonor.

CHAPTER 4

HEAR, O sons, the ʳinstruction of a father, Ps. 34:11
And give attention that you may gain understanding,
2 For I give you ᵗsound teaching; *good*
Do not abandon my [a]instruction. *law*
3 When I was a son to my father,
Tender and the only son in the sight of my mother,
4 Then he ʳtaught me and said to me, Eph. 6:4
"Let your heart ʳhold fast my words; Ps. 119:168
ʳKeep my commandments and live; Prov. 7:2
5 Acquire wisdom! Acquire understanding!
Do not forget, nor turn away from the words of my mouth.
6 "Do not forsake her, and she will guard you;
ʳLove her, and she will watch over you. 2 Thess. 2:10
7 "The beginning of wisdom *is:*
Acquire wisdom;
And with all your acquiring, get understanding.
8 "Prizeʳ her, and she will exalt you; 1 Sam. 2:30
She will honor you if you embrace her.
9 "She will place on your head a garland of grace;
She will present you with a crown of beauty."

10 Hear, my son, and ʳaccept my sayings, Prov. 2:1
And the ʳyears of your life will be many. Prov. 3:2
11 I have ʳdirected you in the way of wisdom;
I have led you in upright paths. 1 Sam. 12:23
12 When you walk, your steps will not be impeded;
And if you run, you ʳwill not stumble. Prov. 3:23
13 ʳTake hold of instruction; do not let go. Prov. 3:18
Guard her, for she is your ʳlife. Prov. 3:22
14 ʳDo not enter the path of the wicked, Ps. 1:1; Prov. 1:15
And do not proceed in the way of evil men.
15 Avoid it, do not pass by it;
Turn away from it and pass on.
16 For they cannot sleep unless they do evil;
And they are robbed of sleep

unless they make *someone* stumble.
17 For they [r]eat the bread of wickedness, Prov. 13:2
And drink the wine of violence.
18 But the path of the righteous is like the light of dawn,
That shines brighter and brighter until the full day.
19 The [r]way of the wicked is like darkness; Job 18:5
They do not know over what they [a]stumble. *may stumble*

20 My son, [r]give attention to my words; Prov. 5:1
[r]Incline your ear to my sayings. Prov. 2:2
21 [r]Do not let them depart from your sight; Prov. 3:21
[r]Keep them in the midst of your heart. Prov. 7:1, 2
22 For they are life to those who find them,
And health to all [t]their whole body. *his*
23 Watch over your heart with all diligence,
For [r]from it *flow* the springs of life. Matt. 12:34
24 Put away from you a [r]deceitful mouth, Prov. 6:12
And [r]put devious lips far from you. Prov. 19:1
25 Let your eyes look directly ahead,
And let your gaze be fixed straight in front of you.
26 Watch the path of your feet,
And all your [r]ways will be established. Ps. 119:5
27 Do not turn to the right nor to the left;
Turn your foot from evil.

CHAPTER 5

MY son, [r]give attention to my wisdom, Prov. 4:20
[r]Incline your ear to my understanding; Prov. 22:17
2 That you may [r]observe discretion, Prov. 3:21
And your [r]lips may reserve knowledge. Mal. 2:7
3 For the lips of an [r]adulteress drip honey, Prov. 2:16
And smoother than oil is her [t]speech; *palate*
4 But in the end she is bitter as wormwood,
Sharp as a two-edged sword.
5 Her feet go down to death,
Her steps lay hold of Sheol.
6 She does not ponder the [r]path of life; Prov. 4:26
Her ways are unstable, she does not know *it.*

7 [r]Now then, *my* sons, listen to me, Prov. 7:24
And do not depart from the words of my mouth.
8 Keep your way far from her,
And do not go near the [r]door of her house, Prov. 9:14
9 Lest you give your vigor to others,
And your years to the cruel one;
10 Lest strangers be filled with your strength,
And your hard-earned goods go to the house of an alien;
11 And you groan at your latter end,
When your flesh and your body are consumed;
12 And you say, "How I have hated instruction!

And my heart spurned re-
proof!
13 "And I have not listened to the
voice of my [r]teachers,
Nor inclined my ear to my instructors! Prov. 1:8
14 "I was almost in utter ruin
In the midst of the assembly
and congregation."

15 Drink water from your own
cistern,
And [t]fresh water from your
own well. *flowing*
16 Should your [r]springs be dispersed abroad, Prov. 5:18
Streams of water in the
streets?
17 Let them be yours alone,
And not for strangers with
you.
18 Let your [r]fountain be blessed,
And rejoice in the wife of
your youth. Prov. 9:17
19 *As* a loving [r]hind and a graceful doe, Song 2:9, 17
Let her breasts satisfy you at
all times;
Be [t]exhilarated always with
her love. *intoxicated*
20 For why should you, my son,
be exhilarated with an
[t]adulteress, *strange woman*
And embrace the bosom of a
foreigner?
21 For the [r]ways of a man are
before the eyes of the
LORD, Job 14:16; 31:4
And He [r]watches all his
paths. Prov. 4:26
22 His own iniquities will capture the wicked,
And he will be held with the
cords of his sin.
23 He will [r]die for lack of instruction, Job 4:21
And in the greatness of his
folly he will go astray.

CHAPTER 6

MY son, if you have become
surety for your neighbor,
Have given a pledge for a
stranger,
2 *If* you have been snared with
the words of your mouth,
Have been caught with the
words of your mouth,
3 Do this then, my son, and deliver yourself;
Since you have come into the
hand of your neighbor,
Go, humble yourself, and im-
portune your neighbor.
4 Do not give [r]sleep to your
eyes, Ps. 132:4
Nor slumber to your eyelids;
5 Deliver yourself like a gazelle from *the hunter's*
hand,
And like a bird from the
hand of the fowler.

6 Go to the [r]ant, O sluggard,
Observe her ways and be
wise, Prov. 30:24, 25
7 Which, having [r]no chief,
Officer or ruler, Prov. 30:27
8 Prepares her food [r]in the
summer, Prov. 10:5
And gathers her provision in
the harvest.
9 How long will you lie down,
O sluggard?
When will you arise from
your sleep?
10 "A little sleep, a little slumber,
A little folding of the hands
to [t]rest"— *lie down*
11 And your poverty will come
in like a vagabond,

And your need like [t]an armed
man. *a man with a shield*

12 A [r]worthless person, a
wicked man, Prov. 16:27
Is the one who walks with a
[r]false mouth, Prov. 4:24
13 Who winks with his eyes,
who signals with his feet,
Who points with his fingers;
14 Who *with* [r]perversity in his
heart devises evil continually,
Prov. 17:20
Who spreads strife.
15 Therefore his calamity will
come suddenly;
Instantly he will be broken,
and there will be [r]no healing.
2 Chr. 36:16

16 There are six things which
the LORD hates,
Yes, seven which are an
abomination to Him:
17 [r]Haughty eyes, a [r]lying
tongue, Ps. 18:27
And hands that shed innocent
blood, Ps. 31:18
18 A heart that devises [r]wicked
plans, Gen. 6:5; Prov. 24:2
Feet that run rapidly to evil,
19 A [r]false witness *who* utters
lies, Ps. 27:12; Prov. 12:17
And one who spreads strife
among brothers.

20 My son, observe the commandment
of your father,
And do not forsake the
teaching of your mother;
21 [r]Bind them continually on
your heart; Prov. 3:3
Tie them around your neck.
22 When you walk about, they
will guide you;
When you sleep, they will
watch over you;
And when you awake, they
will talk to you.
23 For the commandment is a
lamp, and the [a]teaching is
light; *law*
And reproofs for discipline
are the way of life,
24 To [r]keep you from the evil
woman, Prov. 5:3; 7:5, 21
From the smooth tongue of
the adulteress.
25 [r]Do not desire her beauty in
your heart, Matt. 5:28
Nor let her catch you with
her [r]eyelids. Jer. 4:30
26 For [r]on account of a harlot
one is reduced to a loaf of
bread, Prov. 5:9, 10
And an adulteress hunts for
the precious life.
27 Can a man [t]take fire in his
bosom, *snatch up*
And his clothes not be
burned?
28 Or can a man walk on hot
coals,
And his feet not be scorched?
29 So is the one who goes in to
his neighbor's wife;
Whoever touches her will
not go unpunished.
30 Men do not despise a thief if
he steals
To satisfy himself when he is
hungry;
31 But when he is found, he
must repay sevenfold;
He must give all the substance
of his house.
32 The one who commits adultery
with a woman is
lacking [t]sense; *heart*
He who would destroy [t]himself
does it. *his soul*
33 Wounds and disgrace he will
find,

And his reproach will not be
blotted out.
34 For jealousy enrages a man,
And he will not spare in the
day of vengeance.
35 He will not accept any ransom,
Nor will he be [t]content
though you give many
[t]gifts. *willing • bribes*

CHAPTER 7

MY son, keep my words,
And treasure my command-
ments within you.
2 [r]Keep my commandments
and live, Prov. 4:4
And my [t]teaching as the apple of your eye. *law*
3 Bind them on your fingers;
[r]Write them on the tablet of
your heart. Prov. 3:3
4 Say to wisdom, "You are my
sister,"
And call understanding *your*
intimate friend;
5 That they may keep you
from an adulteress,
From the foreigner who flatters with her words.

6 For [r]at the window of my
house Judg. 5:28
I looked out [r]through my lattice, Song 2:9
7 And I saw among the naive,
I discerned among the
[t]youths, *sons*
A young man lacking sense,
8 Passing through the street
near her corner;
And he [t]takes the way to her
house, *steps*
9 In the twilight, in the [t]eve-
ning, *evening of the day*
In the middle of the night
and *in* the darkness.
10 And behold, a woman *comes*
to meet him,
[r]Dressed as a harlot and cunning of heart. 1 Tim. 2:9
11 She is [r]boisterous and rebellious; Prov. 9:13
Her [r]feet do not remain at
home; 1 Tim. 5:13
12 *She is* now in the streets,
now in the squares,
And lurks by every corner.
13 So she seizes him and kisses
him,
And with a [r]brazen face she
says to him: Prov. 21:29
14 "I was due to offer [r]peace offerings; Lev. 7:11
Today I have paid my vows.
15 "Therefore I have come out to
meet you,
To seek your presence earnestly, and I have found
you.
16 "I have spread my couch with
[r]coverings, Prov. 31:22
With colored linens of Egypt.
17 "I have sprinkled my bed
With [r]myrrh, aloes and [r]cinna-
mon. Ps. 45:8 • Ex. 30:23
18 "Come, let us drink our fill of
love until morning;
Let us delight ourselves with
caresses.
19 "For the man is not at home,
He has gone on a long journey;
20 He has taken a bag of money
[t]with him, ***in his hand***
At full moon he will come
home."
21 With her many persuasions
she entices him;
With her [t]flattering lips she
seduces him. ***smooth***

22 Suddenly he follows her,
As an ox goes to the slaughter,
Or as *one in* fetters to the discipline of a fool,
23 Until an arrow pierces through his liver;
As a [r]bird hastens to the snare, Eccl. 9:12
So he does not know that it *will cost him* his life.

24 Now therefore, *my* sons, [r]listen to me, Prov. 5:7
And pay attention to the words of my mouth.
25 Do not let your heart turn aside to her ways,
Do not stray into her paths.
26 For many are the victims she has cast down,
And [r]numerous are all her slain. Prov. 9:18
27 Her [r]house is the way to Sheol, Prov. 2:18; 5:5; 9:18
Descending to the chambers of death.

CHAPTER 8

DOES not wisdom call,
And understanding [t]lift up her voice? *give*
2 On top of [r]the heights beside the way, Prov. 9:3,14
Where the paths meet, she takes her stand;
3 Beside the [r]gates, at the opening to the city, Job 29:7
At the entrance of the doors, she cries out:
4 "To you, O men, I call,
And my voice is to the sons of men.
5 "O [t]naive ones, discern prudence; *simple*
And, O fools, discern [t]wisdom. *heart*
6 "Listen, for I shall speak [r]noble things; Prov. 22:20
And the opening of my lips *will produce* right things.
7 "For my [r]mouth will utter truth; Ps. 37:30
And wickedness is an abomination to my lips.
8 "All the utterances of my mouth are in righteousness;
There is nothing crooked or perverted in them.
9 "They are all [r]straightforward to him who understands,
And right to those who find knowledge. Prov. 14:6
10 "Take my [r]instruction, and not silver, Prov. 3:14, 15
And knowledge rather than choicest gold.
11 "For wisdom is better than [t]jewels; *corals*
And all desirable things can not compare with her.

12 "I, wisdom, [r]dwell with prudence, Prov. 8:5
And I find [r]knowledge *and* discretion. Prov. 1:4
13 "The [r]fear of the LORD is to hate evil; Prov. 3:7; 16:6
Pride and arrogance and [r]the evil way, Prov. 15:9
And the [r]perverted mouth, I hate. Prov. 6:12
14 "Counsel is mine and [r]sound wisdom; Prov. 2:7; 3:21
I am understanding, [r]power is mine. Eccl. 7:19; 9:16
15 "By me kings reign,
And rulers decree justice.
16 "By me princes rule, and nobles,

All who judge rightly.
17 "I love those who love me;
And those who diligently seek me will find me.
18 "Riches[r] and honor are with me, Prov. 3:16
Enduring [r]wealth and righteousness. Ps. 112:3
19 "My fruit is better than gold, even pure gold,
And my yield than [r]choicest silver. Prov. 10:20
20 "I walk in the way of righteousness,
In the midst of the paths of justice,
21 To endow those who love me with wealth,
That I may [r]fill their treasuries. Prov. 24:4

22 "The LORD possessed me at the beginning of His way,
Before His works of old.
23 "From everlasting I was [a]established, *consecrated*
From the beginning, [r]from the earliest times of the earth. John 17:5
24 "When there were no depths I was brought forth,
When there were no springs abounding with water.
25 "Before the mountains were settled,
Before the hills I was [a]brought forth; *born*
26 While He had not yet made the earth and the [t]fields,
Nor the first dust of the world. *outside places*
27 "When He established the heavens, I was there,
When He inscribed a circle on the face of the deep,
28 When He made firm the skies above,
When the springs of the deep became [t]fixed, *strong*
29 When [r]He set for the sea its boundary, Job 38:10
So that the water should not transgress His command,
When He marked out the foundations of the earth;
30 Then I was beside Him, *as* a master workman;
And I was daily *His* delight,
[a]Rejoicing always before Him, *Playing*
31 [a]Rejoicing in the world, His earth, *Playing*
And *having* [r]my delight in the sons of men. Ps. 16:3

32 "Now therefore, *O* sons, [r]listen to me, Prov. 5:7; 7:24
For blessed are they who keep my ways.
33 "Heed[r] instruction and be wise, Prov. 4:1
And do not neglect *it*.
34 "Blessed[r] is the man who listens to me, Prov. 3:13, 18
Watching daily at my gates,
Waiting at my doorposts.
35 "For [r]he who finds me finds life, Prov. 4:22; John 17:3
And [r]obtains favor from the LORD. Prov. 3:4
36 "But he who sins against me injures himself;
All those who hate me [r]love death." Prov. 21:6

CHAPTER 9

WISDOM has [r]built her house,
She has hewn out her seven pillars; 1 Cor. 3:9, 10
2 She has prepared her food, she has mixed her wine;

She has also set her table;
3 She has [r]sent out her maidens, she calls Ps. 68:11
From the [r]tops of the heights of the city: Prov. 9:14
4 "Whoever is [t]naive, let him turn in here!" *simple*
To him who lacks understanding she says,
5 "Come, [r]eat of my food,
And drink of the wine I have mixed. Song 5:1; Is. 55:1
6 "Forsake *your* folly and live,
And proceed in the way of understanding."

7 He who corrects a scoffer gets dishonor for himself,
And he who reproves a wicked man *gets* [t]insults for himself. *a blemish*
8 [r]Do not reprove a scoffer, lest he hate you, Prov. 15:12
[r]Reprove a wise man, and he will love you. Prov. 10:8
9 Give *instruction* to a wise man, and he will be still wiser,
Teach a righteous man, and he will [r]increase *his* learning. Prov. 1:5
10 The [r]fear of the LORD is the beginning of wisdom,
And the knowledge of the Holy One is understanding. Job 28:28
11 For [r]by me your days will be multiplied, Prov. 3:16
And years of life will be added to you.
12 If you are wise, you are wise [r]for yourself, Job 22:2
And if you [r]scoff, you alone will bear it. Prov. 19:29

13 The [a]woman of folly is boisterous, *foolish woman*
She is [t]naive, and knows nothing. *simple*
14 And she sits at the doorway of her house,
On a seat by [r]the high places of the city, Prov. 9:3
15 Calling to those who pass by,
Who are making their paths straight:
16 "Whoever is [t]naive, let him turn in here," *simple*
And to him who lacks understanding she says,
17 "Stolen water is sweet;
And [r]bread *eaten* in secret is pleasant." Prov. 20:17
18 But he does not know that the dead are there,
That her guests are in the depths of Sheol.

CHAPTER 10

THE proverbs of Solomon.
[r]A wise son makes a father glad, Prov. 15:20; 29:3
But a foolish son is a grief to his mother.
2 [r]Ill-gotten gains do not profit,
But righteousness delivers from death. Ps. 49:7
3 The LORD will not allow the righteous to hunger,
But He will thrust *aside* the craving of the wicked.
4 Poor is he who works with a negligent hand,
But the [r]hand of the diligent makes rich. Prov. 13:4
5 He who gathers in summer is a son who acts wisely,
But he who sleeps in harvest is a son who acts shamefully.
6 [r]Blessings are on the head of the righteous, Prov. 28:20

But the mouth of the wicked
conceals violence.
7 The [r]memory of the righteous
is blessed, Ps. 112:6
But [r]the name of the wicked
will rot. Ps. 9:5, 6
8 The [r]wise of heart will receive
commands, Prov. 9:8
But a babbling fool will be
thrown down.
9 He [r]who walks in integrity
walks securely, Ps. 23:4
But he who perverts his ways
will be found out.
10 He [r]who winks the eye causes
trouble, Ps. 35:19; Prov. 6:13
And a [r]babbling fool will be
thrown down. Prov. 10:8
11 The mouth of the righteous is
a fountain of life,
But the mouth of the wicked
conceals violence.
12 Hatred stirs up strife,
But [r]love covers all transgressions. James 5:20; 1 Pet. 4:8
13 On the lips of the discerning,
wisdom is found,
But [r]a rod is for the back of
him who lacks under-
standing. Prov. 19:29
14 Wise men [r]store up knowledge, Prov. 9:9
But with the mouth of the
foolish, ruin is at hand.
15 The rich man's wealth is his
[t]fortress, *strong city*
The [r]ruin of the poor is their
poverty. Prov. 19:7
16 The [a]wages of the righteous is
life, *work*
The income of the wicked,
punishment.
17 He [r]is *on* the path of life who
heeds instruction,
But he who forsakes reproof
goes astray. Prov. 6:23
18 He [r]who conceals hatred *has*
lying lips, Prov. 26:24
And he who spreads slander
is a fool.
19 When there are [r]many words,
transgression is unavoid-
able, Job 11:2; Prov. 18:21
But he [r]who restrains his lips
is wise. James 1:19
20 The tongue of the righteous
is *as* [r]choice silver,
The heart of the wicked is
worth little. Prov. 8:19
21 The lips of the righteous feed
many,
But fools die for lack of [t]un-
derstanding. *heart*
22 It is the blessing of the LORD
that makes rich,
And He adds no sorrow to it.
23 Doing wickedness is like
[r]sport to a fool; Prov. 2:14
And *so is* wisdom to a man of
understanding.
24 What the wicked fears will
come upon him,
And the desire of the righteous will be granted.
25 When the whirlwind passes,
the wicked is no more,
But the righteous *has* an
everlasting foundation.
26 Like vinegar to the teeth and
smoke to the eyes,
So is the [r]lazy one to those
who send him. Prov. 26:6
27 The fear of the LORD prolongs [t]life, *days*
But the years of the wicked
will be shortened.
28 The [r]hope of the righteous is
gladness, Prov. 11:23
But the expectation of the
wicked perishes.
29 The way of the LORD is a
stronghold to the upright,

But [r]ruin to the workers of iniquity. Prov. 21:15
30 The [r]righteous will never be shaken, Ps. 37:29; 125:1
But [r]the wicked will not dwell in the land. Prov. 2:22
31 The mouth of the righteous flows with wisdom,
But the [r]perverted tongue will be cut out. Prov. 17:20
32 The lips of the righteous bring forth [r]what is acceptable, Eccl. 12:10
But the mouth of the wicked, what is perverted.

CHAPTER 11

A [r]FALSE balance is an abomination to the LORD,
But a just weight is His delight. Lev. 19:35, 36
2 When [r]pride comes, then comes dishonor,
But with the humble is wisdom. Prov. 16:18; 18:12
3 The integrity of the upright will guide them,
But the [r]falseness of the treacherous will destroy them. Prov. 19:3; 22:12
4 [r]Riches do not profit in the day of wrath, Zeph. 1:18
But [r]righteousness delivers from death. Gen. 7:1
5 The [r]righteousness of the blameless will smooth his way, Prov. 3:6
But the wicked will fall by his own wickedness.
6 The righteousness of the upright will deliver them,
But the treacherous will [r]be caught by *their* own greed. Ps. 7:15, 16; 9:15
7 When a wicked man dies, *his* expectation will perish,
And the [r]hope of strong men perishes. Job 8:13, 14
8 The righteous is delivered from trouble,
But the wicked [t]takes his place. *enters*
9 With *his* [r]mouth the godless man destroys his neighbor, Prov. 16:29
But through knowledge the [r]righteous will be delivered. Prov. 11:6
10 When it [r]goes well with the righteous, the city rejoices, Prov. 28:12
And when the wicked perish, there is glad shouting.
11 By the blessing of the upright a city is exalted,
But by the mouth of the wicked it is torn down.
12 He who despises his neighbor lacks [t]sense, *heart*
But a man of understanding keeps silent.
13 He who goes about as a talebearer reveals secrets,
But he who is trustworthy conceals a matter.
14 Where there is no [r]guidance, the people fall, Prov. 15:22
But in abundance of counselors there is victory.
15 He who is [r]surety for a stranger will surely suffer for it, Prov. 6:1; 27:13
But he who hates going surety is safe.
16 A [r]gracious woman attains honor, Prov. 31:28, 30
And violent men attain riches.
17 The [r]merciful man does himself good, Matt. 5:7

But the cruel man does himself harm.
18 The wicked earns deceptive
wages,
But he who sows righteousness *gets* a true reward.
19 He who is steadfast in [r]right-
eousness *will attain* to
life, Prov. 10:16; 12:28
And [r]he who pursues evil *will*
bring about his own
death. Prov. 21:16; Rom. 6:23
20 The perverse in heart are an
abomination to the LORD,
But the blameless in *their*
walk are His delight.
21 Assuredly, the evil man will
not go unpunished,
But the [t]descendants of the
righteous will be deliv-
ered. *seed*
22 *As* a [r]ring of gold in a swine's
snout, Gen. 24:47
So is a beautiful woman who
lacks [1]discretion.
23 The desire of the righteous is
only good,
But the expectation of the
wicked is wrath.
24 There is one who scatters,
yet increases all the
more,
And there is one who withholds what is justly due,
but *it results* only in
want.
25 The generous man will be
[t]prosperous, *made fat*
And he who waters will himself be watered.
26 He who withholds grain, the
people will curse him,
But blessing will be on the
head of him who sells *it*.

[1] Lit., *taste*

27 He who diligently seeks good
seeks favor,
But he who searches after
evil, it will come to him.
28 He who [r]trusts in his riches
will fall, Ps. 49:6
But the righteous will flourish like the *green* leaf.
29 He who troubles his own
house will inherit wind,
And the foolish will be servant to the wisehearted.
30 The fruit of the righteous is [r]a
tree of life, Prov. 3:18
And he who is wise [t]wins
souls. *takes*
31 If the righteous will be rewarded in the earth,
How much more the wicked
and the sinner!

CHAPTER 12

WHOEVER loves [a]discipline
loves knowledge,
But he who hates reproof is
stupid. *instruction*
2 A [r]good man will obtain favor
from the LORD, Prov. 3:4
But He will condemn a man
who devises evil.
3 A man will not be established by wickedness,
But the root of the righteous
will not be moved.
4 An excellent wife is the
crown of her husband,
But she who shames *him* is
as [r]rottenness in his
bones. Prov. 14:30; Hab. 3:16
5 The thoughts of the righteous are just,
But the counsels of the
wicked are deceitful.
6 The words of the wicked lie
in wait for blood,

But the mouth of the upright
will deliver them.
7 The wicked are overthrown
and are no more,
But the house of the righteous will stand.
8 A man will be praised according to his insight,
But one of perverse [t]mind will
be despised. *heart*
9 Better is he who is lightly esteemed and has a servant,
Than he who honors himself
and lacks bread.
10 A [r]righteous man has regard
for the life of his beast,
But the compassion of the
wicked is cruel. Deut. 25:4
11 He who tills his land will
have plenty of bread,
But he who pursues vain
things lacks sense.
12 The wicked desires the [t]booty
of evil men, *net*
But the root of the righteous
yields *fruit.*
13 An evil man is ensnared by
the transgression of his
lips,
But the [r]righteous will escape
from trouble. Prov. 11:8
14 A man will be [r]satisfied with
good by the fruit of his
[t]words, Prov. 13:2 • *mouth*
And the deeds of a man's
hands will return to him.
15 The [r]way of a fool is right in
his own eyes, Prov. 14:12
But a wise man is he who listens to counsel.
16 A [r]fool's vexation is known at
once, Prov. 14:33; 27:3
But a prudent man conceals
dishonor.
17 He who [t]speaks truth tells
what is right, *breathes*
But a false witness, deceit.
18 There is one who [r]speaks
rashly like the thrusts of
a sword, Ps. 57:4
But the [r]tongue of the wise
brings healing. Prov. 4:22
19 Truthful lips will be established forever,
But a [r]lying tongue is only for
a moment. Ps. 52:4, 5
20 Deceit is in the heart of those
who devise evil,
But counselors of peace have
joy.
21 [r]No harm befalls the righteous, Ps. 91:10; 121:7
But the wicked are filled with
trouble.
22 Lying lips are an abomination to the LORD,
But those who deal faithfully
are His delight.
23 A [r]prudent man conceals
knowledge, Prov. 10:14
But the heart of fools proclaims folly.
24 The hand of the diligent will
rule,
But the slack *hand* will be
put to forced labor.
25 Anxiety in the heart of a man
weighs it down,
But a [r]good word makes it
glad. Is. 50:4
26 The righteous is a guide to
his neighbor,
But the way of the wicked
leads them astray.
27 A slothful man does not
roast his prey,
But the precious possession
of a man *is* diligence.
28 [r]In the way of righteousness
is life, Deut. 30:15f.

And in *its* pathway there is
no death.

CHAPTER 13

A [r]WISE son *accepts his* father's
discipline, Prov. 10:1
But a [r]scoffer does not listen
to rebuke. Prov. 9:7, 8
2 From the fruit of a man's
mouth he enjoys good,
But the desire of the treacherous is violence.
3 The one who guards his
mouth preserves his life;
The one who opens wide his
lips comes to ruin.
4 The soul of the sluggard
craves and *gets* nothing,
But the soul of the diligent is
made fat.
5 A righteous man [r]hates falsehood, Col. 3:9
But a wicked man [r]acts dis-
gustingly and shame-
fully. Prov. 3:35
6 Righteousness [r]guards the
one whose way is blame-
less, Prov. 11:3
But wickedness subverts the
[t]sinner. *sin*
7 There is one who pretends to
be rich, but has nothing;
Another pretends to be poor,
but has great wealth.
8 The ransom of a man's life is
his riches,
But the poor hears no re-
buke.
9 The [r]light of the righteous [2]re-
joices, Job 29:3
But the [r]lamp of the wicked
goes out. Job 18:5
10 Through presumption comes
nothing but strife,
But with those who receive
counsel is wisdom.
11 Wealth *obtained* by [t]fraud
dwindles, *vanity*
But the one who gathers by
labor increases *it.*
12 Hope deferred makes the
heart sick,
But desire [t]fulfilled is a tree of
life. *coming*
13 The one who [r]despises the
word will be in debt to it,
But the one who fears the
commandment will be re-
warded. Num. 15:31
14 The [a]teaching of the wise is a
fountain of life, *law*
To turn aside from the [r]snares
of death. Ps. 18:5
15 [r]Good understanding produces favor, Prov. 3:4
But the way of the treacherous is hard.
16 Every [r]prudent man acts with
knowledge, Prov. 12:23
But a fool displays folly.
17 A wicked messenger falls
into adversity,
But [r]a faithful envoy *brings*
healing. Prov. 25:13
18 Poverty and shame *will
come* to him who ne-
glects discipline,
But he who regards reproof
will be honored.
19 Desire realized is sweet to
the soul,
But it is an abomination to
fools to depart from evil.
20 [r]He who walks with wise men
will be wise, Prov. 2:20
But the companion of fools
will suffer harm.
21 Adversity pursues sinners,
But the righteous will be rewarded with prosperity.

[2]I.e., shines brightly

22 A good man leaves an inheritance to his [t]children's children, *sons' sons*
And the [r]wealth of the sinner is stored up for the righteous. Job 27:16, 17
23 [r]Abundant food *is in* the fallow ground of the poor,
But it is swept away by injustice. Prov. 12:11
24 He who [r]spares his rod hates his son, Prov. 19:18; 22:15
But he who loves him disciplines him diligently.
25 The righteous has enough to satisfy his appetite,
But the stomach of the wicked is in want.

CHAPTER 14

THE [r]wise woman builds her house, Ruth 4:11
But the foolish tears it down with her own hands.
2 He who walks in his uprightness fears the LORD,
But he who is crooked in his ways despises Him.
3 In the mouth of the foolish is a rod for *his* back,
But [r]the lips of the wise will preserve them. Prov. 12:6
4 Where no oxen are, the manger is clean,
But much increase comes by the strength of the ox.
5 A faithful witness will not lie,
But a false witness [t]speaks lies. *breathes out*
6 A scoffer seeks wisdom, and *finds* none,
But knowledge is easy to him who has understanding.
7 Leave the presence of a fool,
Or you will not discern words of knowledge.
8 The wisdom of the prudent is to understand his way,
But [r]the folly of fools is deceit. 1 Cor. 3:19
9 Fools mock at [t]sin,
But among the upright there is good will. *guilt*
10 The heart knows its own [r]bitterness, 1 Sam. 1:10
And a stranger does not share its joy.
11 The [r]house of the wicked will be destroyed, Job 8:15
But the tent of the upright will flourish.
12 There is a way *which seems* right to a man,
But its [r]end is the way of death. Rom. 6:21
13 Even in laughter the heart may be in pain,
And the [r]end of joy may be grief. Eccl. 2:1, 2
14 The backslider in heart will have his [r]fill of his own ways, Prov. 1:31; 12:21
But a good man will *be satisfied* with his.
15 The [t]naive believes everything, *simple*
But the prudent man considers his steps.
16 A wise man [t]is cautious and turns away from evil,
But a fool is arrogant and careless. *fears*
17 A quick-tempered man acts foolishly,
And a man of evil devices is hated.
18 The [t]naive inherit folly,
But the prudent are crowned with knowledge. *simple*

19 The [r]evil will bow down before the good, 1 Sam. 2:36
And the wicked at the gates of the righteous.
20 The [r]poor is hated even by his neighbor, Prov. 19:7
But those who love the rich are many.
21 He who [r]despises his neighbor sins, Prov. 11:12
But happy is he who is gracious to the [a]poor. *afflicted*
22 Will they not go astray who [r]devise evil? Ps. 36:4
But kindness and truth *will be to* those who devise good.
23 In all labor there is profit,
But [t]mere talk *leads* only to poverty. *word of lips*
24 The [r]crown of the wise is their riches,
But the folly of fools is foolishness. Prov. 10:22; 13:8
25 A truthful witness saves lives,
But he who [t]speaks lies is treacherous. *breathes out*
26 In the [3]fear of the LORD there is strong confidence,
And [a]his children will have refuge. *His*
27 The [3]fear of the LORD is a fountain of life,
That one may avoid the snares of death.
28 In a multitude of people is a king's glory,
But in the dearth of people is a prince's ruin.
29 He who is slow to anger has great understanding,
But he who is quick-tempered exalts folly.

[3]Or, *reverence*

30 A [r]tranquil heart is life to the body, Prov. 15:13
But passion is [r]rottenness to the bones. Hab. 3:16
31 He who oppresses the poor reproaches his Maker,
But he who is gracious to the needy honors Him.
32 The wicked is thrust down by his wrongdoing,
But the righteous has a refuge when he dies.
33 Wisdom rests in the heart of one who has understanding,
But in the [t]bosom of fools it is made known. *midst*
34 Righteousness exalts a nation,
But sin is a disgrace to *any* people.
35 The king's favor is toward a servant who acts wisely,
But his anger is toward him who acts shamefully.

CHAPTER 15

A [r]GENTLE answer turns away wrath, Judg. 8:1-3
But a [t]harsh word stirs up anger. *painful*
2 The tongue of the wise makes knowledge [t]acceptable, *good*
But the [r]mouth of fools spouts folly. Prov. 12:23
3 The [r]eyes of the LORD are in every place, 2 Chr. 16:9
Watching the evil and the good.
4 A [t]soothing tongue is a tree of life, *healing*
But perversion in it crushes the spirit.

5 A fool[a]rejects his father's discipline, *despises*
But he who regards reproof is prudent.
6 Much wealth is *in* the house of the[r]righteous, Prov. 8:21
But trouble is in the income of the wicked.
7 The lips of the wise spread knowledge,
But the hearts of fools are not so.
8 The[r]sacrifice of the wicked is an abomination to the LORD, Prov. 21:27
But[r]the prayer of the upright is His delight. Prov. 15:29
9 The way of the wicked is an abomination to the LORD,
But He loves him who pursues righteousness.
10 Stern discipline is for him who forsakes the way;
He who hates reproof will die.
11 Sheol and Abaddon *lie open* before the LORD,
How much more the hearts of[t]men! *sons of Adam*
12 A scoffer does not love one who reproves him,
He will not go to the wise.
13 A joyful heart makes a [t]cheerful face, *good*
But when the heart is sad, the spirit is broken.
14 The[r]mind of the intelligent seeks knowledge,
But the mouth of fools feeds on folly. Prov. 18:15
15 All the days of the afflicted are bad,
But a[t]cheerful heart *has* a continual feast. *good*
16 Better is a little with the[a]fear of the LORD, *reverence*
Than great treasure and turmoil with it.
17 Better is a[a]dish of[a]vegetables where love is, *portion • herbs*
Than a fattened ox and hatred with it.
18 A[r]hot-tempered man stirs up strife, Prov. 16:28; 26:21
But the[r]slow to anger pacifies contention. Prov. 14:29
19 The way of the sluggard is as a hedge of thorns,
But the path of the upright is a highway.
20 A[r]wise son makes a father glad, Prov. 10:1; 29:3
But a foolish man[r]despises his mother. Prov. 30:17
21 Folly is joy to him who lacks [t]sense, *heart*
But a man of understanding [r]walks straight. Eph. 5:15
22 Without consultation, plans are frustrated,
But with many counselors they[a]succeed. *are established*
23 A man has joy in an[t]apt answer, *answer of his mouth*
And how delightful is a timely[r]word! Prov. 25:11
24 The[r]path of life *leads* upward for the wise, Prov. 4:18
That he may keep away from Sheol below.
25 The LORD will tear down the house of the proud,
But He will establish the boundary of the widow.
26 Evil plans are an abomination to the LORD,
But pleasant words are pure.
27 He who profits illicitly troubles his own house,
But he who[r]hates bribes will live. Ex. 23:8; Deut. 16:19

28 The heart of the righteous ponders how to answer,
But the mouth of the wicked pours out evil things.
29 The LORD is [r]far from the wicked, Ps. 18:41
But He hears the prayer of the righteous.
30 Bright eyes gladden the heart;
Good news puts fat on the bones.
31 He whose ear listens to the life-giving reproof
Will dwell among the wise.
32 He who neglects discipline despises himself,
But he who listens to reproof acquires understanding.
33 The [a]fear of the LORD is the instruction for wisdom,
And before honor *comes* humility. *reverence*

CHAPTER 16

THE [r]plans of the heart belong to man, Prov. 16:9; 19:21
But the answer of the tongue is from the LORD.
2 All the ways of a man are clean in his own sight,
But the LORD weighs the [t]motives. *spirits*
3 [t]Commit your works to the LORD, *Roll*
And your plans will be established.
4 The LORD has made everything for [a]its own purpose, *His*
Even the wicked for the day of evil.
5 Everyone who is proud in heart is an abomination to the LORD;
Assuredly, he will not be unpunished.
6 By lovingkindness and truth iniquity is atoned for,
And by the [a]fear of the LORD one keeps away from evil. *reverence*
7 When a man's ways are pleasing to the LORD,
He makes even his enemies to be at peace with him.
8 Better is a little with righteousness
Than great income with injustice.
9 The mind of [r]man plans his way, Prov. 16:1; 19:21
But [r]the LORD directs his steps. Jer. 10:23
10 A divine decision is in the lips of the king;
His mouth should not [t]err in judgment. *be unfaithful*
11 A just balance and scales belong to the LORD;
All the [t]weights of the bag are His concern. *stones*
12 It is an abomination for kings to commit wickedness,
For a [r]throne is established on righteousness. Prov. 25:5
13 Righteous lips are the delight of kings,
And he who speaks right is loved.
14 The wrath of a king is *as* messengers of death,
But a wise man will appease it.
15 In the light of a king's face is life,
And his favor is like a cloud with the spring rain.
16 How much better it is to get wisdom than gold!

And to get understanding is
to be chosen above silver.
17 The highway of the upright is
to depart from evil;
He who watches his way preserves
his [t]life. *soul*
18 [r]Pride *goes* before destruction,
Prov. 11:2; 18:12
And a haughty spirit before
stumbling.
19 It is better to be of a humble
spirit with the lowly,
Than to [r]divide the spoil with
the proud. Ex. 15:9
20 He who gives attention to the
word shall find good,
And [r]blessed is he who trusts
in the LORD. Ps. 2:12
21 The wise in heart will be
called discerning,
And sweetness of speech increases
persuasiveness.
22 Understanding is a fountain
of life to him who has it,
But the discipline of fools is
folly.
23 The [r]heart of the wise teaches
his mouth, Ps. 37:30
And adds [a]persuasiveness to
his lips. *learning*
24 [r]Pleasant words are a honeycomb,
Ps. 19:10
Sweet to the soul and [r]healing
to the bones. Prov. 4:22
25 [r]There is a way *which seems*
right to a man,
But its end is the way of
death. Prov. 12:15
26 A worker's appetite works
for him,
For his hunger urges him *on.*
27 A [r]worthless man digs up
evil, Prov. 6:12, 14, 18
While [t]his words are as a
scorching fire. *on his lips*
28 A perverse man spreads
strife,
And a slanderer separates intimate
friends.
29 A man of violence [r]entices his
neighbor, Prov. 1:10; 12:26
And leads him in a way that
is not good.
30 He who winks his eyes *does
so* to devise perverse
things;
He who compresses his lips
brings evil to pass.
31 A [r]gray head is a crown of
glory; Prov. 20:29
It [r]is found in the way of
righteousness. Prov. 3:1, 2
32 He who is slow to anger is
better than the mighty,
And he who rules his spirit,
than he who captures a
city.
33 The lot is cast into the lap,
But its every [r]decision is from
the LORD. Prov. 29:26

CHAPTER 17

BETTER is a dry morsel and quietness
with it
Than a house full of feasting
with strife.
2 A servant who acts wisely
will rule over a son who
acts shamefully,
And will share in the inheritance
among brothers.
3 The refining pot is for silver
and the furnace for gold,
But the LORD tests hearts.
4 An [r]evildoer listens to wicked
lips, Prov. 14:15
A liar pays attention to a destructive
tongue.
5 He who mocks the poor reproaches
his Maker;

He who rejoices at calamity
will not go unpunished.
6 [r]Grandchildren are the crown
of old men, Gen. 48:11
And the [r]glory of sons is their
fathers. Mal. 1:6
7 [t]Excellent speech is not fitting for a fool;
Much less are lying lips to a
prince. *A lip of abundance*
8 A bribe is a [t]charm in the
sight of its owner;
Wherever he turns, he prospers. *stone of favor*
9 He who [r]covers a transgression seeks love,
But he who repeats a matter
separates intimate
friends. Prov. 10:12
10 A rebuke goes deeper into
one who has understanding
Than a hundred blows into a
fool.
11 A rebellious man seeks only
evil,
So a cruel messenger will be
sent against him.
12 Let a man meet a [r]bear
robbed of her cubs,
Rather than a fool in his folly. 2 Sam. 17:8; Hos. 13:8
13 He who [r]returns evil for good,
Evil will not depart from his
house. Ps. 35:12; 109:5
14 The beginning of strife is *like*
letting out water,
So abandon the quarrel before it breaks out.
15 He who [r]justifies the wicked,
and he who condemns
the righteous, Ex. 23:7
Both of them alike are an
abomination to the LORD.
16 Why is there a price in the
hand of a fool to [r]buy wisdom, Prov. 23:23
When he has no sense?
17 A [r]friend loves at all times,
And a brother is born for adversity. Ruth 1:16
18 A man lacking in sense
[t]pledges, *shakes hands*
And becomes surety in the
presence of his neighbor.
19 He who [r]loves transgression
loves strife; Prov. 29:22
He who [r]raises his door seeks
destruction. Prov. 16:18
20 He who has a crooked [t]mind
finds no good, *heart*
And he who is [r]perverted in
his language falls into
evil. James 3:8
21 He who [r]begets a fool *does* so
to his sorrow,
And the father of a fool has
no joy. Prov. 10:1
22 A joyful heart [t]is good medicine, *causes good healing*
But a broken spirit [r]dries up
the bones. Ps. 22:15
23 A wicked man receives a
bribe from the bosom
To [r]pervert the ways of justice. Mic. 3:11; 7:3
24 Wisdom is in the presence of
the one who has understanding,
But the eyes of a fool are on
the ends of the earth.
25 A [r]foolish son is a grief to his
father, Prov. 19:13
And [r] bitterness to her who
bore him. Prov. 10:1
26 It is also not good to [r]fine the
righteous, Prov. 17:15
Nor to strike the noble for
their uprightness.
27 He who restrains his words
has knowledge,

And he who has a [r]cool spirit
is a man of understand-
ing. Prov. 14:29
28 Even a fool, when he keeps
silent, is considered wise;
When he closes his lips, he is
counted prudent.

CHAPTER 18

HE who separates himself seeks
his own desire,
He [t]quarrels against all sound
wisdom. *breaks out*
2 A fool does not delight in understanding,
But only [r]in revealing his own
[t]mind. Prov. 12:23 • *heart*
3 When a wicked man comes,
contempt also comes,
And with dishonor *comes* reproach.
4 The words of a man's mouth
are [r]deep waters;
The fountain of wisdom is a
bubbling brook. Prov. 20:5
5 To show partiality to the
wicked is not good,
Nor to thrust aside the righteous in judgment.
6 A fool's lips [t]bring strife,
And his mouth calls for
blows. *come with*
7 A [r]fool's mouth is his ruin,
And his lips are the snare of
his soul. Ps. 64:8; 140:9
8 The words of a whisperer are
like dainty morsels,
And they go down into the
[t]innermost parts of the
body. *chambers of the belly*
9 He also who is [r]slack in his
work Prov. 10:4
[r]Is brother to him who destroys. Prov. 28:24
10 The [r]name of the LORD is a
strong tower; Ex. 3:15
The righteous runs into it
and is [t]safe. *set on high*
11 A [r]rich man's wealth is his
strong city, Prov. 10:15
And like a high wall in his
own imagination.
12 Before destruction the heart
of man is haughty,
But [r]humility *goes* before
honor. Prov. 15:33
13 He who gives an answer before he hears,
It is folly and shame to him.
14 The spirit of a man can endure his sickness,
But a [r]broken spirit who can
bear? Prov. 15:13
15 The [t]mind of the prudent acquires knowledge, *heart*
And the ear of the wise seeks
knowledge.
16 A man's [r]gift makes room for
him, Gen. 32:20
And brings him before great
men.
17 The first [t]to plead his case
seems just, *in his plea*
Until [t]another comes and examines him. *his neighbor*
18 The [r]lot puts an end to contentions, Prov. 16:33
And [t]decides between the
mighty. *makes a division*
19 A brother offended *is harder*
to be won than a strong
city,
And contentions are like the
bars of a castle.
20 With the fruit of a man's
mouth his stomach will
be satisfied;
He will be satisfied *with* the
product of his lips.

21 Death and life are in the
[t]power of the tongue,
And those who love it will
eat its fruit. *hand*
22 He who finds a [r]wife finds a
good thing, Gen. 2:18
And [r]obtains favor from the
LORD. Prov. 8:35
23 The [r]poor man utters supplications, Prov. 19:7
But the [r]rich man answers
roughly. James 2:3, 6
24 A man of *many* friends
comes to ruin,
But there is a [a]friend who
sticks closer than a
brother. *lover*

CHAPTER 19

BETTER is a poor man who
walks in his integrity
Than he who is perverse in
speech and is a fool.
2 Also it is not good for a person to be without knowl-
edge,
And he who makes haste
with his feet [t]errs. *sins*
3 The [r]foolishness of man subverts his way, Prov. 11:3
And his heart [r]rages against
the LORD. Is. 8:21
4 Wealth adds many friends,
But a poor man is separated
from his friend.
5 A [r]false witness will not go
unpunished, Ex. 23:1
And he who [t]tells lies will not
escape. *breathes*
6 Many will entreat the favor
of a [a]generous man, *noble*
And every man is a friend to
him who gives gifts.
7 All the brothers of a poor
man hate him;
How much more do his
friends go far from him!
He pursues *them with* words,
but they are [t]gone. *not*
8 He who gets [t]wisdom loves
his own soul; *heart*
He who keeps understanding
will [r]find good. Prov. 16:20
9 A [r]false witness will not go
unpunished, Prov. 19:5
And he who [t]tells lies will
perish. *breathes*
10 Luxury is [r]not fitting for a
fool; Prov. 17:7; 26:1
Much less for a [r]slave to rule
over princes. Prov. 30:22
11 A man's discretion makes
him slow to anger,
And it is his glory to overlook a transgression.
12 The king's wrath is like the
roaring of a lion,
But his favor is like [r]dew on
the grass. Gen. 27:28
13 A [r]foolish son is destruction
to his father, Prov. 17:25
And the contentions of a wife
are a constant dripping.
14 House and wealth are an [r]in-
heritance from fathers,
But a prudent wife is from
the LORD. 2 Cor. 12:14
15 [r]Laziness casts into a deep
sleep, Prov. 6:9, 10
And an idle [t]man will suffer
hunger. *soul*
16 He who keeps the commandment keeps his soul,
But he who is careless of his
ways will die.
17 He who is gracious to a poor
man lends to the LORD,
And He will repay him for
his [a]good deed. *benefits*
18 Discipline your son while
there is hope,

And do not desire his death.
19 *A man of* great anger shall bear the penalty,
For if you rescue *him,* you will only have to do it again.
20 [r]Listen to counsel and accept discipline, Prov. 4:1; 8:33
That you may be wise the rest of your days.
21 Many are the [r]plans in a man's heart, Prov. 16:1, 9
But the [r]counsel of the LORD, it will stand. Is. 14:26, 27
22 What is desirable in a man is his [4]kindness,
And *it is* better to be a poor man than a liar.
23 The [a]fear of the LORD *leads* to life, *reverence*
So that one may sleep satisfied, untouched by evil.
24 The [r]sluggard buries his hand in the dish, Prov. 26:15
And will not even bring it back to his mouth.
25 Strike a scoffer and the naive may become shrewd,
But reprove one who has understanding and he will gain knowledge.
26 He [r]who assaults *his* father *and* drives *his* mother away Prov. 28:24
Is a shameful and disgraceful son.
27 Cease listening, my son, to discipline,
And you will stray from the words of knowledge.
28 A rascally witness makes a mockery of justice,
And the mouth of the wicked [a]spreads iniquity. *swallows*

[4]Or, *loyalty*

29 Judgments are prepared for scoffers,
And blows for the back of fools.

CHAPTER 20

WINE is a mocker, strong drink a brawler,
And whoever [t]is intoxicated by it is not wise. *errs*
2 The terror of a king is like the growling of a lion;
He who provokes him to anger forfeits his own life.
3 Keeping away from strife is an honor for a man,
But any fool will quarrel.
4 The sluggard does not plow after the autumn,
So he begs during the harvest and has nothing.
5 A plan in the heart of a man is *like* deep water,
But a man of understanding draws it out.
6 Many a man [r]proclaims his own loyalty, Prov. 25:14
But who can find a [r]trustworthy man? Ps. 12:1
7 A righteous man who walks in his integrity—
[r]How blessed are his sons after him. Ps. 37:26; 112:2
8 [r]A king who sits on the throne of justice Prov. 20:26; 25:5
[a]Disperses all evil with his eyes. *Sifts*
9 Who can say, "I have cleansed my heart,
I am pure from my sin"?
10 [r]Differing weights and differing measures, Prov. 11:1
Both of them are abominable to the LORD.

11 It is by his deeds that a lad
[a]distinguishes himself
If his conduct is pure and
right. *makes himself known*
12 The hearing [r]ear and the seeing eye, Ex. 4:11; Ps. 94:9
The LORD has made both of
them.
13 [r]Do not love sleep, lest you
become poor; Prov. 6:9, 10
Open your eyes, *and* you will
be satisfied with food.
14 "Bad, bad," says the buyer;
But when he goes his way,
then he boasts.
15 There is gold, and an abundance of [a]jewels; *corals*
But the lips of knowledge are
a more precious thing.
16 Take his garment when he
becomes surety for a
stranger;
And for foreigners, hold him
in pledge.
17 Bread obtained by falsehood
is sweet to a man,
But afterward his mouth will
be filled with gravel.
18 Prepare [r]plans by consultation, Prov. 11:14; 15:22
And [r]make war by wise guidance. Luke 14:31
19 He who [r]goes about as a slanderer reveals secrets,
Therefore do not associate
with a gossip. Prov. 11:13
20 He who [r]curses his father or
his mother, Ex. 21:17
His [r]lamp will go out in time
of darkness. Job 18:5
21 An inheritance gained hurriedly at the beginning,
Will not be blessed in the
end.
22 [r]Do not say, "I will repay
evil"; Prov. 24:29
Wait for the LORD, and He
will save you.
23 Differing weights are an
abomination to the LORD,
And a false scale is not good.
24 [r]Man's steps are *ordained* by
the LORD, Prov. 16:9
How then can man under-
stand his way?
25 It is a snare for a man to say
rashly, "It is holy!"
And [r]after the vows to make
inquiry. Eccl. 5:4, 5
26 A [r]wise king winnows the
wicked, Prov. 20:8
And [t]drives the *threshing*
wheel over them. *turns*
27 The [t]spirit of man is the lamp
of the LORD, *breath*
Searching all the innermost
parts of his being.
28 [t]Loyalty and truth preserve
the king, *Covenant loyalty*
And he upholds his throne by
righteousness.
29 The glory of young men is
their strength,
And the [a]honor of old men is
their gray hair. *splendor*
30 [r]Stripes that wound scour
away evil, Ps. 89:32
And strokes *reach* the innermost parts.

CHAPTER 21

THE king's heart is *like* channels
of water in the hand of
the LORD;
He [r]turns it wherever He
wishes. Ezra 6:22
2 Every man's way is right in
his own eyes,
But the LORD [r]weighs the
hearts. Prov. 16:2

3 To do [r]righteousness and justice Prov. 15:8 ; Is. 1:11, 16, 17
Is desired by the LORD rather than sacrifice.
4 Haughty eyes and a proud heart,
The [r]lamp of the wicked, is sin. Prov. 24:20; Luke 11:34
5 The plans of the diligent *lead* surely to advantage,
But everyone who is hasty *comes* surely to poverty.
6 The [r]getting of treasures by a lying tongue Prov. 13:11
Is a fleeting vapor, the [t]pursuit of death. *seekers*
7 The violence of the wicked will drag them away,
Because they [r]refuse to act with justice. Mic. 3:9
8 The way of a guilty man is [r]crooked, Prov. 2:15
But as for the pure, his conduct is upright.
9 It is better to live in a corner of a roof,
Than in a house shared with a contentious woman.
10 The soul of the wicked desires evil;
His [r]neighbor finds no favor in his eyes. Ps. 52:3
11 When the [r]scoffer is punished, the [t]naive becomes wise; Prov. 19:25
But when the wise is instructed, he receives knowledge. *simple*
12 The righteous one considers the house of the wicked,
Turning the wicked to ruin.
13 He who shuts his ear to the cry of the poor
Will also cry himself and not be [r]answered. James 2:13
14 A [r]gift in secret subdues anger, Prov. 18:16; 19:6
And a bribe in the bosom, strong wrath.
15 The execution of justice is joy for the righteous,
But is [r]terror to the workers of iniquity. Prov. 10:29
16 A man who wanders from the way of understanding
Will rest in the assembly of the [t]dead. *departed spirits*
17 He who loves pleasure *will become* a poor man;
He who loves wine and oil will not become rich.
18 The wicked is a [r]ransom for the righteous, Is. 43:3
And the treacherous is in the place of the upright.
19 [r]It is better to live in a desert land, Prov. 21:9
Than with a contentious and vexing woman.
20 There is precious [r]treasure and oil in the dwelling of the wise, Ps. 112:3
But a foolish man [r]swallows it up. Job 20:15, 18
21 He who [r]pursues righteousness and loyalty Prov. 15:9
Finds life, righteousness and honor.
22 A [r]wise man scales the city of the mighty, 2 Sam. 5:6-9
And brings down the stronghold in which they trust.
23 He who [r]guards his mouth and his tongue, Prov. 12:13
Guards his soul from troubles.
24 "Proud," "Haughty," "Scoffer," are his names,
Who acts with insolent pride.
25 The desire of the sluggard puts him to death,

For his hands refuse to work;
26 All day long he is craving,
While the righteous gives and does not hold back.
27 The sacrifice of the wicked is an abomination,
How much more when he brings it with evil intent!
28 A [r]false witness will perish,
But the man who listens *to the truth* will speak forever. Prov. 19:5, 9
29 A wicked man [t]shows a bold face, *makes firm with his face*
But as for the upright, he makes his way sure.
30 There is [r]no wisdom and no understanding Jer. 9:23
And no counsel against the LORD.
31 The [r]horse is prepared for the day of battle, Ps. 20:7
But [r]victory belongs to the LORD. Ps. 3:8

CHAPTER 22

A [r]*GOOD* name is to be more desired than great riches,
Favor is better than silver and gold. Eccl. 7:1
2 The rich and the poor [t]have a common bond,
The LORD is the maker of them all. *meet together*
3 The [r]prudent sees the evil and hides himself, Prov. 14:16
But the [t]naive go on, and are punished for it. *simple*
4 The reward of humility *and* the fear of the LORD
Are riches, honor and life.
5 Thorns *and* snares are in the way of the perverse;
He who guards himself will be far from them.
6 [r]Train up a child in the way he should go, Eph. 6:4
Even when he is old he will not depart from it.
7 The rich rules over the poor,
And the borrower *becomes* the lender's slave.
8 He who [r]sows iniquity will reap vanity, Job 4:8
And the [r]rod of his fury will perish. Ps. 125:3
9 He who [t]is generous will be blessed, *has a good eye*
For he [r]gives some of his food to the poor. Luke 14:13
10 [r]Drive out the scoffer, and contention will go out,
Even strife and dishonor will cease. Gen. 21:9, 10
11 He who loves purity of heart
And [t]whose speech is gracious, the king is his friend. *has grace on his lips*
12 The eyes of the LORD preserve knowledge,
But He overthrows the words of the treacherous man.
13 The [r]sluggard says, "There is a lion outside;
I shall be slain in the streets!" Prov. 26:13
14 The mouth of [t]an adulteress is a deep pit; *strange woman*
He who is cursed of the LORD will fall [t]into it. *there*
15 Foolishness is bound up in the heart of a child;
The rod of discipline will remove it far from him.
16 He who oppresses the poor to make much for himself
Or who gives to the rich, *will* only *come to* poverty.

17 [r]Incline your ear and hear the words of the wise,
And apply your mind to my knowledge; Prov. 5:1
18 For it will be pleasant if you keep them within you,
[t]That they may be ready on your lips. *They together*
19 So that your [r]trust may be in the LORD, Prov. 3:5
I have [t]taught you today, even you. *made you know*
20 Have I not written to you [a]excellent things *previous*
Of counsels and knowledge,
21 To make you know the [t]certainty of the words of truth *truth*
That you may [t]correctly answer to him who sent you? *return words of truth*

22 [r]Do not rob the poor because he is poor, Ex. 23:6
Or [r]crush the afflicted at the gate; Zech. 7:10; Mal. 3:5
23 For the LORD will [r]plead their case, 1 Sam. 25:39
And take the life of those who rob them.

24 Do not associate with a man *given* to anger;
Or go with a [r]hot-tempered man, Prov. 29:22
25 Lest you learn his ways,
And find a snare for yourself.

26 Do not be among those who give [t]pledges, *strike hands*
Among those who become sureties for debts.
27 If you have nothing with which to pay,
Why should he take your bed from under you?

28 [r]Do not move the ancient boundary Deut. 19:14
Which your fathers have set.

29 Do you see a man skilled in his work?
He will stand before kings;
He will not stand before obscure men.

CHAPTER 23

WHEN you sit down to dine with a ruler,
Consider carefully [a]what is before you; *who*
2 And put a knife to your throat,
If you are a [r]man of *great* appetite. Prov. 23:20
3 Do not desire his delicacies,
For it is deceptive food.

4 [r]Do not weary yourself to gain wealth, Prov. 15:27
Cease from your [a]consideration *of it*. *understanding*
5 When you set your eyes on it, it is gone.
For [r]*wealth* certainly makes itself wings, Prov. 27:24
Like an eagle that flies *toward* the heavens.

6 Do not eat the bread of [t]a selfish man, *an evil eye*
Or desire his delicacies;
7 For as he thinks within himself, so he is.
He says to you, "Eat and drink!"
But his heart is not with you.
8 You will vomit up [t]the morsel you have eaten, *your*
And waste your [t]compliments. *pleasant words*

9 Do not speak in the [t]hearing of a fool, *ears*
For he will despise the wisdom of your words.

10 Do not move the ancient boundary,
Or [r]go into the fields of the fatherless; Jer. 22:3
11 For their Redeemer is strong;
[r]He will plead their case against you. Prov. 22:23
12 Apply your heart to discipline,
And your ears to words of knowledge.

13 Do not hold back discipline from the child,
Although you beat him with the rod, he will not die.
14 You shall [t]beat him with the rod, *smite*
And [r]deliver his soul from Sheol. 1 Cor. 5:5

15 My son, if your heart is [r]wise,
My own heart also will be glad; Prov. 23:24f.
16 And my [t]inmost being will rejoice, *kidneys*
When your lips speak [r]what is right. Prov. 8:6

17 [r]Do not let your heart envy sinners, Ps. 37:1
But *live* in the [a]fear of the LORD always. *reverence*
18 Surely there is a [t]future,
And your hope will not be cut off. *latter end*
19 Listen, my son, and be wise,
And [r]direct your heart in the way. Prov. 4:23; 9:6
20 Do not be with [r]heavy drinkers of wine, Prov. 20:1
Or with [r]gluttonous eaters of meat; Deut. 21:20
21 For the [r]heavy drinker and the glutton will come to poverty, Prov. 21:17
And drowsiness will clothe *a man* with rags.

22 [r]Listen to your father who begot you, Prov. 1:8
And do not despise your mother when she is old.
23 Buy truth, and do not sell *it*,
Get wisdom and instruction and understanding.

24 The father of the righteous will greatly rejoice,
And he who begets a wise son will be glad in him.
25 Let your [r]father and your mother be glad,
And let her rejoice who gave birth to you. Prov. 27:11

26 Give me your heart, my son,
And let your eyes [r]delight in my ways. Ps. 1:2; 119:24
27 For a harlot is a deep pit,
And an [t]adulterous woman is a narrow well. *strange*
28 Surely she lurks as a robber,
And increases the [t]faithless among men. *treacherous*

29 Who has [r]woe? Who has sorrow? Is. 5:11, 22
Who has contentions? Who has complaining?
Who has wounds without cause?
Who has redness of eyes?
30 Those who [r]linger long over wine, 1 Sam. 25:36
Those who go to [a]taste mixed wine. *search out*
31 Do not look on the wine when it is red,

When it sparkles in the cup,
When it goes down smoothly;
32 At the last it [r]bites like a serpent, Job 20:16
And stings like a viper.
33 Your eyes will see strange things,
And your [t]mind will utter perverse things. *heart*
34 And you will be like one who lies down in the [t]middle of the sea, *heart*
Or like one who lies down on the top of a [5]mast.
35 "They [r]struck me, *but* I did not become ill; Prov. 27:22
They beat me, *but* I did not know *it*.
When shall I awake?
I will seek another drink."

CHAPTER 24

Do not be envious of evil men,
Nor desire to be with them;
2 For their [t]minds devise violence, *hearts*
And their lips talk of trouble.

3 [r]By wisdom a house is built,
And by understanding it is established; Prov. 9:1
4 And by knowledge the rooms are [r]filled Prov. 8:21
With all precious and pleasant riches.

5 A wise man is strong,
And a man of knowledge increases power.
6 For by wise guidance you will wage war,
And in abundance of counselors there is victory.

[5]Or, *lookout*

7 Wisdom is [r]too high for a fool, Ps. 10:5
He does not open his mouth [r]in the gate. Job 5:4

8 He who plans to do evil,
Men will call him a schemer.
9 The devising of folly is sin,
And the scoffer is an abomination to men.

10 If you [r]are slack in the day of distress, Job 4:5
Your strength is limited.

11 [r]Deliver those who are being taken away to death,
And those who are staggering to slaughter, O hold *them* back. Ps. 82:4
12 If you say, "See, we did not know this,"
Does He not consider *it* who weighs the hearts?
And does He not know *it* who keeps your soul?
And will He not [t]render to man according to his work? *bring back*

13 My son, eat [r]honey, for it is good, Ps. 19:10
Yes, the [r]honey from the comb is sweet to your taste; Prov. 16:24
14 Know *that* [r]wisdom is thus for your soul; Prov. 2:10
If you find *it*, then there will be a [t]future, *latter end*
And your hope will not be cut off.

15 [r]Do not lie in wait, O wicked man, against the dwelling of the righteous;
Do not destroy his resting place; Ps. 10:9, 10

16 For a righteous man falls
seven times, and rises
again, Job 5:19; Ps. 37:24
But the wicked stumble in
time of calamity.

17 Do not rejoice when your
enemy falls, Job 31:29
And do not let your heart be
glad when he stumbles;
18 Lest the LORD see *it* and be
displeased,
And He turn away His anger
from him.

19 Do not fret because of evildoers, Ps. 37:1
Or be envious of the wicked;
20 For there will be no future
for the evil man;
The lamp of the wicked will
be put out. Job 18:5, 6

21 My son, [a]fear the LORD and
the king; *reverence*
Do not associate with those
who are given to change;
22 For their calamity will rise
suddenly, Prov. 24:16
And who knows the ruin *that
comes* from both of
them?

23 These also are sayings of the
wise. Prov. 1:6; 22:17
To show partiality in judgment is not good.
24 He who says to the wicked,
"You are righteous,"
Peoples will curse him, nations will abhor him;
25 But to those who rebuke the
wicked will be delight,
And a good blessing will
come upon them.
26 He kisses the lips
Who gives a right answer.

27 Prepare your work outside,
And make it ready for yourself in the field;
Afterwards, then, build your
house. Prov. 27:23-27

28 Do not be a witness against
your neighbor without
cause, Prov. 25:18
And do not deceive with
your lips. Lev. 6:2, 3
29 Do not say, "Thus I shall do
to him as he has done to
me; Prov. 20:22
I will render to the man according to his work."

30 I passed by the field of the
sluggard,
And by the vineyard of the
man lacking [t]sense; *heart*
31 And behold, it was completely overgrown with
thistles, Gen. 3:18
Its surface was covered with
nettles,
And its stone wall was broken down.
32 When I saw, I [t]reflected upon
it; *set my heart*
I looked, *and* received instruction.
33 "A little sleep, a little slumber,
A little folding of the hands
to rest," Prov. 6:10
34 Then your poverty will come
as[a] a robber, *a vagabond*
And your want like [t]an armed
man. *a man with a shield*

CHAPTER 25

THESE also are proverbs of Solomon which the men of Hezekiah,
king of Judah, transcribed.
2 It is the glory of God to conceal a matter,

But the glory of kings is to
search out a matter.
3 *As* the heavens for height
and the earth for depth,
So the heart of kings is unsearchable.
4 Take away the [r]dross from
the silver, Prov. 26:23
And there comes out a vessel
for the [r]smith; Mal. 3:2, 3
5 Take away the wicked *from*
before the king,
And his throne will be established in righteousness.
6 Do not claim honor in the
presence of the king,
And do not stand in the place
of great men;
7 For [r]it is better that it be said
to you, "Come up here,"
Than that you should be put
lower in the presence of
the prince, Luke 14:7-11
Whom your eyes have seen.

8 Do not go out hastily to [t]ar-
gue *your case;* *contend*
[t]Otherwise, what will you do
in [t]the end, *Lest • its*
When your neighbor puts
you to shame?
9 [t]Argue your case with your
neighbor, *Contend*
And [r]do not reveal the secret
of another, Prov. 11:13
10 Lest he who hears *it* reproach you,
And the evil report about you
not [t]pass away. *return*

11 *Like* apples of gold in settings of silver
Is a word spoken in [t]right circumstances. *its*
12 *Like* an earring of gold and
an ornament of fine gold
Is a wise reprover to a [r]listen-
ing ear. Prov. 15:31
13 Like the cold of snow in the
[t]time of harvest *day*
Is a faithful messenger to
those who send him,
For he refreshes the soul of
his masters.
14 *Like* [r]clouds and wind without rain Jude 12
Is a man who boasts of his
gifts falsely.
15 By [r]forbearance a ruler may
be persuaded, Gen. 32:4
And a soft tongue breaks the
bone.
16 Have you found honey? Eat
only [t]what you need,
Lest you have it in excess
and vomit it. *your sufficiency*
17 Let your foot rarely be in
your neighbor's house,
Lest he become weary of you
and hate you.
18 *Like* a club and a [r]sword and
a sharp arrow Ps. 57:4
Is a man who bears false witness against his neighbor.
19 *Like* a bad tooth and [t]an un-
steady foot *a slipping foot*
Is confidence in a faithless
man in time of trouble.
20 *Like* one who takes off a garment on a cold day, *or*
like vinegar on soda,
Is he who sings songs to [t]a
troubled heart. *an evil*
21 If your enemy is hungry, give
him food to eat;
And if he is thirsty, give him
water to drink;
22 For you will [t]heap burning
coals on his head,
And the LORD will reward
you. *snatch up*

23 The north wind brings forth rain,
And a backbiting tongue, an angry countenance.
24 It is[r] better to live in a corner of the roof Prov. 21:9
Than in a house shared with a contentious woman.
25 *Like* cold water to a weary soul,
So is[r] good news from a distant land. Prov. 15:30
26 *Like* a trampled spring and a [t]polluted well *ruined*
Is a righteous man who gives way before the wicked.
27 It is not good to eat much honey,
Nor is it glory to search out [t]one's own glory. *their*
28 *Like* a city that is broken into *and* without walls
Is a man[r] who has no control over his spirit. Neh. 1:3

CHAPTER 26

LIKE snow in summer and like rain in harvest,
So honor is not [r]fitting for a fool. Prov. 17:7
2 Like a sparrow in *its* [t]flitting, like a swallow in *its* flying, *wandering*
So a curse without cause does not [t]alight. *come*
3 A whip is for the horse, a bridle for the donkey,
And a [r]rod for the back of fools. Prov. 10:13; 19:29
4 Do not answer a fool according to his folly,
Lest you also be like him.
5 [r]Answer a fool as his folly *deserves,* Matt. 16:1-4
Lest he be [r]wise in his own eyes. Prov. 3:7; 28:11
6 He cuts off *his own* feet, *and* drinks violence
Who sends a message by the hand of a fool.
7 *Like* the legs *which* hang down from the lame,
So is a proverb in the mouth of fools.
8 Like [t]one who binds a stone in a sling, *the binding of*
So is he who gives honor to a fool.
9 *Like* a thorn *which* [t]falls into the hand of a drunkard,
So is a proverb in the mouth of fools. *goes up*
10 *Like* an archer who wounds everyone,
So is he who hires a fool or who hires those who pass by.
11 Like [r]a dog that returns to its vomit 2 Pet. 2:22
Is a fool who [r]repeats his folly. Ex. 8:15
12 Do you see a man [r]wise in his own eyes? Prov. 3:7
[r]There is more hope for a fool than for him. Prov. 29:20
13 The sluggard says, "There is a lion in the road!
A lion is in the open square!"
14 *As* the door turns on its hinges,
So *does* the [r]sluggard on his bed. Prov. 6:9
15 The [r]sluggard buries his hand in the dish; Prov. 19:24
He is weary of bringing it to his mouth again.
16 The sluggard is [r]wiser in his own eyes Prov. 27:11
Than seven men who can give a discreet answer.

17 *Like* one who takes a dog by the ears
Is he who passes by *and* meddles with strife not belonging to him.
18 Like a madman who throws [r]Firebrands, arrows and death, Is. 50:11
19 So is the man who [r]deceives his neighbor, Prov. 24:28
And says, "Was[r] I not joking?" Eph. 5:4
20 For lack of wood the fire goes out,
And where there is no [r]whisperer, contention quiets down. Prov. 16:28
21 *Like* charcoal to hot embers and wood to fire,
So is a [r]contentious man to kindle strife. Prov. 15:18
22 The words of a whisperer are like dainty morsels,
And they go down into the [t]innermost parts of the body. *chambers of the belly*
23 *Like* an earthen [r]vessel overlaid with silver dross
Are burning lips and a wicked heart. Matt. 23:27
24 He who [r]hates disguises *it* with his lips, Ps. 41:6
But he lays up deceit in his [t]heart. *inward part*
25 When he speaks graciously, do not believe him,
For there are seven abominations in his heart.
26 *Though his* hatred covers itself with guile,
His wickedness will be [r]revealed before the assembly. Luke 8:17
27 He who [r]digs a pit will fall into it, Esth. 7:10
And he who rolls a stone, it will come back on him.
28 A lying tongue hates [t]those it crushes, *its crushed ones*
And a [r]flattering mouth works ruin. Prov. 29:5

CHAPTER 27

Do not boast about tomorrow,
For you do not know what a day may bring forth.
2 Let [r]another praise you, and not your own mouth;
A stranger, and not your own lips. Prov. 25:27
3 A stone is heavy and the sand weighty,
But the provocation of a fool is heavier than both of them.
4 Wrath is fierce and anger is a flood,
But [r]who can stand before jealousy? Prov. 6:34
5 Better is open rebuke
Than love that is concealed.
6 Faithful are the [r]wounds of a friend, Ps. 141:5
But [a]deceitful are the kisses of an enemy. *excessive*
7 A sated man loathes honey,
But to a famished man any bitter thing is sweet.
8 Like a [r]bird that wanders from her nest, Is. 16:2
So is a man who wanders from his [t]home. *place*
9 [r]Oil and perfume make the heart glad, Ps. 23:5
So a [t]man's counsel is sweet to his friend. *soul's*
10 Do not forsake your own friend or [r]your father's friend, 1 Kin. 12:6-8

And do not go to your brother's house in the day of your calamity;
Better is a neighbor who is near than a brother far away.
11 [r]Be wise, my son, and make my heart glad, Prov. 10:1
That I may reply to him who reproaches me.
12 A prudent man sees evil *and* hides himself,
The [t]naive proceed *and* pay the penalty. *simple*
13 [r]Take his garment when he becomes surety for a stranger; Prov. 20:16
And for an [t]adulterous woman hold him in pledge. *strange*
14 [r]He who blesses his friend with a loud voice early in the morning, Ps. 12:2
It will be reckoned a curse to him.
15 A [r]constant dripping on a day of steady rain Prov. 19:13
And a contentious woman are alike;
16 He who would [t]restrain her [t]restrains the wind,
And [t]grasps oil with his right hand. *hide(s) • encounters*
17 Iron sharpens iron,
So one man sharpens another.
18 He who tends the [r]fig tree will eat its fruit; Is. 36:16
And he who cares for his master will be honored.
19 As in water face *reflects* face,
So the heart of man *reflects* man.
20 [r]Sheol and Abaddon are never satisfied, Job 26:6
Nor are the [r]eyes of man ever satisfied. Eccl. 1:8; 4:8
21 The crucible is for silver and the furnace for gold,
And a man *is tested* by the praise accorded him.
22 Though you [r]pound a fool in a mortar with a pestle along with crushed grain,
Yet his folly will not depart from him. Prov. 23:35

23 Know well the [t]condition of your flocks, *face*
And pay attention to your herds;
24 For riches are not forever,
Nor does a crown *endure* to all generations.
25 *When* the grass disappears, the new growth is seen,
And the herbs of the mountains are gathered in,
26 The lambs *will be* for your clothing,
And the goats *will bring* the price of a field,
27 And *there will be* goats' milk enough for your food,
For the food of your household,
And sustenance for your maidens.

CHAPTER 28

THE wicked [r]flee when no one is pursuing, Ps. 53:5
But the righteous are [t]bold as a lion. *confident*
2 By the transgression of a land many are its princes,
But [r]by a man of understanding *and* knowledge, so it endures. Prov. 11:11
3 A [r]poor man who oppresses the lowly Matt. 18:28

Is *like* a driving rain which
leaves no food.
4 Those who forsake the law
praise the wicked,
But those who keep the law
strive with them.
5 Evil men [r]do not understand
justice, Ps. 92:6; Is. 6:9
But those who seek the LORD
understand all things.
6 Better is the poor who walks
in his integrity,
Than he who is crooked
though he be rich.
7 He who keeps the law is a
discerning son,
But he who is a companion
of [r]gluttons humiliates his
father. Prov. 23:20
8 He who increases his wealth
by interest and usury,
Gathers it for him who is gracious
to the poor.
9 He who turns away his ear
from listening to the law,
Even his [r]prayer is an abomination.
Ps. 66:18; 109:7
10 He who leads the upright
astray in an evil way
Will [r]himself fall into his own
pit, Ps. 7:15; Prov. 26:27
But the [r]blameless will inherit
good. Heb. 6:12; 1 Pet. 3:9
11 The rich man is [r]wise in his
own eyes, Prov. 3:7; 26:5, 12
But the poor who has understanding
[t]sees through
him. *examines him*
12 When the righteous triumph,
there is great glory,
But when the wicked rise,
men hide themselves.
13 He who [r]conceals his transgressions
will not prosper,
Job 31:33; Ps. 32:3
But he who confesses and
forsakes *them* will find
compassion.
14 How blessed is the man who
[r]fears always, Prov. 23:17
But he who hardens his heart
will fall into calamity.
15 *Like* a [r]roaring lion and a
rushing bear 1 Pet. 5:8
Is a [r]wicked ruler over a poor
people. Ex. 1:14; Prov. 29:2
16 A [r]leader who is a great oppressor
lacks understanding,
Is. 3:12
But he who hates unjust gain
will prolong *his* days.
17 A man who is laden with the
guilt of human blood
Will be a fugitive until death;
let no one support him.
18 He who walks blamelessly
will be delivered,
But he who is [r]crooked will
fall all at once. Prov. 10:27
19 He who tills his land will
have plenty of food,
But he who follows empty
pursuits will have poverty
in plenty.
20 A faithful man will abound
with blessings,
But he who [r]makes haste to
be rich will not go unpunished.
Prov. 20:21; 28:22
21 To [t]show partiality is not
good, *regard the face*
Because for a piece of bread
a man will transgress.
22 A man with an evil eye hastens
after wealth,
And does not know that
want will come upon
him.
23 He who [r]rebukes a man will
afterward find *more* favor
Prov. 27:5, 6

Than he who [r]flatters with the
tongue. Prov. 29:5
24 He who [r]robs his father or his
mother,
And says, "It is not a transgression,'' Prov. 19:26
Is the [r]companion of a man
who destroys. Prov. 18:9
25 An [t]arrogant man stirs up
strife, *broad soul*
But he who trusts in the
LORD will prosper.
26 He who [r]trusts in his own
heart is a fool, Prov. 3:5
But he who walks wisely will
be delivered.
27 He who [r]gives to the poor will
never want, Prov. 11:24
But he who shuts his eyes
will have many curses.
28 When the wicked rise, men
hide themselves;
But when they perish, the
righteous increase.

CHAPTER 29

A MAN who hardens *his* neck after much reproof
Will [r]suddenly be broken beyond remedy. Prov. 6:15
2 When the righteous increase,
the people rejoice,
But when a wicked man
rules, people groan.
3 A man who loves wisdom
makes his father glad,
But he who [r]keeps company
with harlots wastes *his*
wealth. Prov. 5:10; 6:26
4 The king gives stability to
the land by justice,
But a man who takes bribes
overthrows it.
5 A man who [r]flatters his neighbor Ps. 5:9
Is spreading a net for his
steps.
6 By transgression an evil man
is [r]ensnared, Prov. 22:5
But the righteous [r]sings and
rejoices. Ex. 15:1
7 The righteous is concerned
for the rights of the poor,
The wicked does not understand *such* concern.
8 Scorners set a city aflame,
But [r]wise men turn away anger. Prov. 16:14
9 When a wise man has a controversy with a foolish
man,
[t]The foolish man either rages
or laughs, and there is no
rest. *He*
10 Men of [r]bloodshed hate the
blameless, Gen. 4:5-8
But the upright are con-
cerned for his life.
11 A fool [t]always loses his tem-
per, *sends forth all his spirit*
But a wise man holds it back.
12 If a [r]ruler pays attention to
falsehood, 1 Kin. 12:14
All his ministers *become*
wicked.
13 The poor man and the oppressor [t]have this in common: *meet together*
The LORD gives [r]light to the
eyes of both. Ps. 13:3
14 If a [r]king judges the poor with
truth, Ps. 72:4; Is. 11:4
His [r]throne will be established forever. Prov. 16:12
15 The [r]rod and reproof give wisdom, Prov. 13:24; 22:15
But a child [t]who gets his own
way brings shame to his
mother. *left to himself*
16 When the wicked increase,
transgression increases;

But the [r]righteous will see
their fall. Ps. 37:34, 36
17 Correct your son, and he will
give you comfort;
He will also [t]delight your
soul. *give delight to*
18 Where there is no [a]vision, the
people are unrestrained,
But happy is he who keeps
the law. *revelation*
19 A slave will not be instructed
by words *alone;*
For though he understands,
there will be no response.
20 Do you see a man who is hasty in his words?
There is [r]more hope for a fool
than for him. Prov. 26:12
21 He who pampers his slave
from childhood
Will in the end find him to be
a son.
22 An angry man stirs up strife,
And a hot-tempered man
abounds in transgression.
23 A man's [r]pride will bring him
low, Prov. 11:2; 16:18
But a [r]humble spirit will obtain honor. Prov. 15:33
24 He who is a partner with a
thief hates his own life;
He [r]hears the oath but tells
nothing. Lev. 5:1
25 The fear of man [t]brings a
snare, *gives*
But he who trusts in the
LORD will be exalted.
26 Many seek the ruler's favor,
But justice for man *comes*
from the LORD.
27 An unjust man is abominable
to the righteous,
And he who is [r]upright in the
way is abominable to the
wicked. Ps. 69:4

CHAPTER 30

THE words of Agur the son of Jakeh, the [a]oracle. *burden*
The man declares to Ithiel, to
Ithiel and Ucal:
2 Surely I am more [r]stupid than
any man, Prov. 12:1
And I do not have the understanding of a man.
3 Neither have I learned wisdom,
Nor do I have the knowledge
of the Holy One.
4 Who has ascended into
heaven and descended?
Who has gathered the [r]wind
in His fists? Ex. 15:10
Who has wrapped the waters
in [t]His garment? *the*
Who has established all the
ends of the earth?
What is His [r]name or His
son's name? Rev. 19:12
Surely you know!

5 Every word of God is tested;
He is a shield to those who
take refuge in Him.
6 Do not add to His words
Lest He reprove you, and you
be proved a liar.

7 Two things I asked of Thee,
Do not refuse me before I
die:
8 Keep deception and [t]lies far
from me, *words of falsehood*
Give me neither poverty nor
riches;
Feed me with the [r]food that is
my portion, Job 23:12
9 Lest I be [r]full and deny *Thee*
and say, "Who is the
LORD?" Deut. 8:12; 31:20
Or lest I be in want and steal,

And ʳprofane the name of my
God. Ex. 20:7

10 Do not slander a slave to his
master,
Lest he ʳcurse you and you be
found guilty. Eccl. 7:21

11 There is a [6]kind of *man* who
ʳcurses his father,
And does not bless his
mother. Ex. 21:17
12 There is a kind who is ʳpure in
his own eyes, Is. 65:5
Yet is not washed from his
filthiness.
13 There is a kind—oh how
lofty are his eyes!
And his eyelids are raised *in
arrogance.*
14 There is a kind of *man* whose
teeth are *like* swords,
And his ʳjaw teeth *like*
knives, Job 29:17
To ʳdevour the afflicted from
the earth, Ps. 14:4
And the needy from among
men.

15 The leech has two daughters,
"Give," "Give."
There are three things that
will not be satisfied,
Four that will not say,
"Enough":
16 ʳSheol, and the barren womb,
Earth that is never satisfied
with water, Prov. 27:20
And fire that never says,
"Enough."
17 The eye that mocks a father,
And scorns a mother,
The ʳravens of the valley will
pick it out, Deut. 28:26
And the young eagles will eat
it.

18 There are three things which
are too wonderful for me,
Four which I do not understand:
19 The way of an ʳeagle in the
sky, Deut. 28:49; Jer. 48:40
The way of a serpent on a
rock,
The way of a ship in the middle of the sea,
And the way of a man with a
maid.
20 This is the way of an ʳadulter-
ous woman: Prov. 5:6
She eats and wipes her
mouth,
And says, "I have done no
wrong."

21 Under three things the earth
quakes,
And under four, it cannot
bear up:
22 Under a ʳslave when he becomes king, Prov. 19:10
And a fool when he is satisfied with food,
23 Under an unloved woman
when she gets a husband,
And a maidservant when she
supplants her mistress.

24 Four things are small on the
earth,
But they are exceedingly
wise:
25 The ʳants are not a strong
folk, Prov. 6:6
But they prepare their food
in the summer;
26 The ʳbadgers are not mighty
folk, Lev. 11:5; Ps. 104:18
Yet they make their houses
in the rocks;
27 The locusts have no king,

[6]Or, *generation;* so through v. 14

Yet all of them go out in
ʳranks; Joel 2:7
28 The lizard you may grasp
with the hands,
Yet it is in kings' palaces.

29 There are three things which
are stately in *their* march,
Even four which are stately
when they walk:
30 The lion *which* is ʳmighty
among beasts Judg. 14:18
And does not ᵗretreat before
any, *turn back*
31 The strutting cock, the male
goat also,
And a king *when his* army is
with him.

32 If you have been foolish in
exalting yourself
Or if you have plotted *evil,*
ʳ*put your* hand on your
mouth. Job 21:5; 40:4
33 For the ᵗchurning of milk produces butter, *pressing*
And pressing the nose brings
forth blood;
So the churning of ʳanger produces strife. Prov. 10:12

CHAPTER 31

THE words of King Lemuel, the
ᵃoracle which his mother taught
him. *burden*
2 What, O my son?
And what, O ʳson of my
womb? Is. 49:15
And what, O son of my
ʳvows? 1 Sam. 1:11
3 ʳDo not give your strength to
women, Prov. 5:9
Or your ways to that which
ʳdestroys kings. 1 Kin. 11:1
4 It is not for kings, O Lemuel,
It is not for kings to ʳdrink
wine, Prov. 20:1
Or for rulers to desire strong
drink,
5 Lest they drink and forget
what is decreed,
And pervert the ᵗrights of all
the afflicted. *judgment*
6 Give strong drink to him who
is ʳperishing, Job 29:13
And wine to him ᵗwhose life
is bitter. *bitter of soul*
7 Let him drink and forget his
poverty,
And remember his trouble no
more.
8 ʳOpen your mouth for the
dumb, Job 29:12-17
For the ᵗrights of all the unfortunate. *judgment*
9 Open your mouth, ʳjudge
righteously, Lev. 19:15
And defend the rights of the
afflicted and needy.

10 An ʳexcellent wife, who can
find? Ruth 3:11; Prov. 12:4
For her worth is far ʳabove
jewels. Job 28:18
11 The heart of her husband
trusts in her,
And he will have no lack of
gain.
12 She does him good and not
evil
All the days of her life.
13 She looks for wool and flax,
And works with her ᵗhands ᵃin
delight. *palms • willingly*
14 She is like ʳmerchant ships;
She brings her food from
afar. Ezek. 27:25
15 She ʳrises also while it is still
night, Prov. 20:13

And [r]gives food to her household, Luke 12:42
And portions to her maidens.
16 She considers a field and buys it;
From her earnings she plants a vineyard.
17 She girds [t]herself with strength, *her loins*
And makes her arms strong.
18 She senses that her gain is good;
Her lamp does not go out at night.
19 She stretches out her hands to the distaff,
And her [t]hands grasp the spindle. *palms*
20 She [t]extends her hand to the poor; *spreads out her palm*
And she stretches out her hands to the needy.
21 She is not afraid of the snow for her household,
For all her household are clothed with scarlet.
22 She makes [r]coverings for herself; Prov. 7:16
Her clothing is [r]fine linen and purple. Gen. 41:42
23 Her husband is known [r]in the gates, Deut. 16:18
When he sits among the elders of the land.
24 She makes [r]linen garments and sells *them,* Judg. 14:12
And [t]supplies belts to the tradesmen. *gives*
25 Strength and [r]dignity are her clothing, 1 Tim. 2:9, 10
And she smiles at the future.
26 She [r]opens her mouth in wisdom, Prov. 10:31
And the [a]teaching of kindness is on her tongue. *law*
27 She looks well to the ways of her household,
And does not eat the [r]bread of idleness. Prov. 19:15
28 Her children rise up and bless her;
Her husband *also,* and he praises her, *saying:*
29 "Many daughters have done nobly,
But you excel them all."
30 Charm is deceitful and beauty is vain,
But a woman who [a]fears the LORD, she shall be praised. *reverences*
31 Give her the [t]product of her hands, *fruit*
And let her works praise her in the gates.

THE BOOK OF

ECCLESIASTES

THE words of the Preacher, the son of David, king in Jerusalem.

2 "[1]Vanity of vanities," says the Preacher,
"[1]Vanity of vanities! All is [a]vanity." *futile*

3 What advantage does man have in all his work
Which he does under the sun?
4 A generation goes and a generation comes,
But the earth [t]remains forever. *stands*
5 Also, [r]the sun rises and the sun sets; Ps. 19:6
And hastening to its place it rises there *again*.
6 Blowing toward the south,
Then turning toward the north,
The wind continues [t]swirling along; *turning*
And on its circular courses the wind returns.
7 All the rivers [t]flow into the sea,
Yet the sea is not full.
To the place where the rivers [t]flow,
There they [t]flow again. *go*
8 All things are wearisome;
Man is not able to tell *it*.
[r]The eye is not satisfied with seeing, Eccl. 4:8
Nor is the ear filled with hearing.
9 [r]That which has been is that which will be, Eccl. 1:10
And that which has been done is that which will be done.
So, there is nothing new under the sun.
10 Is there anything of which one might say,
"See this, it is new"?
Already it has existed for ages
Which were before us.
11 There is no remembrance of earlier things;
And also of the later things which will occur,
There will be for them no remembrance
Among those who will come [t]later *still*. *latter* or *after*

12 I, the Preacher, have been
king over Israel in Jerusalem.
13 And I set my [t]mind to seek
and explore by wisdom concerning all that has been done under
heaven. *It* is a grievous task *which*
God has given to the sons of men
to be afflicted with. *heart*
14 I have seen all the works
which have been done under the
sun, and behold, all is [a]vanity and
striving after wind. *futility*
15 What is [r]crooked cannot be
straightened, and what is lacking
cannot be counted. Eccl. 7:13
16 I said to myself, "Behold, I
have magnified and increased wisdom more than all who were over
Jerusalem before me; and my
mind has observed a wealth of
wisdom and knowledge."

[1]Or, *Futility of futilities*

17 And I set my[t] mind to know wisdom and to know madness and folly; I realized that this also is striving after wind. *heart*

18 Because [r]in much wisdom there is much grief, and increasing knowledge *results in* increasing pain. Eccl. 2:23; 12:12

CHAPTER 2

I SAID[t] to myself, "Come now, I will test you with pleasure. So enjoy yourself." And behold, it too was futility. *in my heart*

2 [r]I said of laughter, "It is madness," and of pleasure, "What does it accomplish?" Prov. 14:13

3 I explored with my[t] mind *how* to stimulate my body with wine while my [t]mind was guiding *me* wisely, and how to take hold of folly, until I could see what good there is for the sons of men to do under heaven the [t]few years of their lives. *heart • days*

4 I enlarged my works: I[r] built houses for myself, I planted vineyards for myself; 1 Kin. 7:1-12

5 I made[r] gardens and parks for myself, and I planted in them all kinds of fruit trees; Song 4:16; 5:1

6 I made ponds of water for myself from which to irrigate a forest of growing trees.

7 I bought male and female slaves, and I had homeborn slaves. Also I possessed flocks and herds larger than all who preceded me in Jerusalem.

8 Also, I collected for myself silver and [r]gold, and the treasure of kings and provinces. I provided for myself male and female singers and the pleasures of men—many concubines. 1 Kin. 9:28

9 Then I became great and increased more than all who preceded me in Jerusalem. My wisdom also stood by me.

10 And all that my eyes desired I did not refuse them. I did not withhold my heart from any pleasure, for my heart was pleased because of all my labor and this was my reward for all my labor.

11 Thus I considered all my activities which my hands had done and the labor which I had exerted, and behold all was [2]vanity and striving after wind and there was no profit under the sun.

12 So I turned to [r]consider wisdom, madness and folly, for what *will* the man *do* who will come after the king *except* what has already been done? Eccl. 1:17

13 And I saw that wisdom excels folly as light excels darkness.

14 The wise man's eyes are in his head, but the [r]fool walks in darkness. And yet I know that one fate befalls them both. 1 John 2:11

15 Then I said to myself, "As is the fate of the fool, it will also befall me. Why then have I been extremely wise?" So I said to myself, "This too is vanity."

16 For there is no [t]lasting remembrance of the wise man *as* with the fool, inasmuch as *in* the coming days all will be forgotten. And how the wise man and the fool alike die! *forever*

17 So I hated life, for the work which had been done under the sun was [t]grievous to me; because

[2]Or, *futility*, and so throughout this context

everything is futility and striving
after wind. *evil*
18 Thus I hated [r]all the fruit of
my labor for which I had labored
under the sun, for I must [r]leave it
to the man who will come after
me. Eccl. 1:3; 2:11 • Ps. 39:6
19 And who knows whether he
will be a wise man or a fool? Yet
he will have control over all the
fruit of my labor for which I have
labored by acting wisely under the
sun. This too is vanity.
20 Therefore I [t]completely despaired of all the fruit of my labor
for which I had labored under the
sun. *turned aside my heart to despair*
21 When there is a man who has
labored with wisdom, knowledge
and [r]skill, then he gives his [t]legacy
to one who has not labored with
them. This too is vanity and a
great evil. Eccl. 4:4 • *share*
22 For what does a man get in
all his labor and in [t]his striving
with which he labors under the
sun? *the striving of his heart*
23 Because all his days his task
is painful and grievous; even at
night his [t]mind does not rest. This
too is vanity. *heart*
24 There is [r]nothing better for a
man *than* to eat and drink and tell
himself that his labor is good. This
also I have seen, that it is from the
hand of God. Eccl. 2:3; 3:12, 13
25 For who can eat and who can
have enjoyment without Him?
26 For to a person who is good
in His sight [r]He has given wisdom
and knowledge and joy, while to
the sinner He has given the task of
gathering and collecting so that he
may give to one who is good in
God's sight. This too is vanity and
striving after wind. Job 32:8

CHAPTER 3

THERE is an appointed time for
everything. And there is a time for
every event under heaven—
2 A time to give birth, and a
[r]time to die; Job 14:5
A time to plant, and a time
to uproot what is planted.
3 A [r]time to kill, and a time to
heal; Gen. 9:6; 1 Sam. 2:6
A time to tear down, and a
time to build up.
4 A time to [r]weep, and a time
to laugh; Rom. 12:15
A time to mourn, and a time
to [r]dance. Ex. 15:20
5 A time to throw stones, and
a time to gather stones;
A time to embrace, and a
time to shun embracing.
6 A time to search, and a time
to give up as lost;
A time to keep, and a time
to throw away.
7 A time to tear apart, and a
time to sew together;
A time to [r]be silent, and a
time to speak. Amos 5:13
8 A time to love, and a time
to [r]hate; Ps. 101:3
A time for war, and a time
for peace.
9 [r]What profit is there to the
worker from that in which he
toils? Eccl. 1:3; 2:11; 5:16
10 I have seen the task which
God has given the sons of men
with which to occupy themselves.
11 He has made everything [3]ap-
propriate in its time. He has also
set eternity in their heart, yet so
that man will not find out the
work which God has done from
the beginning even to the end.

[3]Lit., *beautiful*

12 I know that there is nothing better for them than to rejoice and to do good in one's lifetime;

13 moreover, that every man who eats and drinks sees good in all his labor—it is the gift of God.

14 I know that everything God does will remain forever; there is nothing to add to it and there is nothing to take from it, for God has *so* worked that men should [a]fear Him. *be in awe before Him*

15 That [r]which is has been already, and that which will be has already been, for God seeks what has passed by. Eccl. 1:9; 6:10

16 Furthermore, I have seen under the sun *that* in the place of justice there is [r]wickedness, and in the place of righteousness there is wickedness. Eccl. 4:1; 5:8; 8:9

17 I said [t]to myself, "God will judge both the righteous man and the wicked man," for a time for every [a]matter and for every deed is there. *in my heart* • *delight*

18 I said to myself concerning the sons of men, "God has surely tested them in order for them to see that they are but beasts."

19 For the fate of the sons of men and the fate of beasts [t]is the same. As one dies so dies the other; indeed, they all have the same breath and there is no advantage for man over beast, for all is vanity. *and they have one fate*

20 All go to the same place. All came from the [r]dust and all return to the dust. Gen. 3:19; Ps. 103:14

21 Who knows that the [r]breath of man ascends upward and the breath of the beast descends downward to the earth?

22 And I have seen that nothing is better than that man should be happy in his activities, for that is his lot. For who will bring him to see what will occur after him?

CHAPTER 4

THEN I looked again at all the acts of [r]oppression which were being done under the sun. And behold *I saw* the tears of the oppressed and *that* they had no one to comfort *them;* and on the side of their oppressors was power, but they had no one to comfort *them.* Job 35:9; Ps. 12:5; Eccl. 3:16

2 So I congratulated the dead who are already dead more than the living who are still living.

3 But [r]better *off* than both of them is the one who has never existed, who has never seen the evil activity that is done under the sun. Job 3:11-22; Eccl. 6:3; Luke 23:29

4 And I have seen that every labor and every [r]skill which is done is *the result of* rivalry between a man and his neighbor. This too is [r]vanity and striving after wind. Eccl. 2:21 • Eccl. 1:14

5 The fool folds his hands and [r]consumes his own flesh. Is. 9:20

6 One hand full of rest is [r]better than two fists full of labor and striving after wind. Prov. 15:16, 17

7 Then I looked again at vanity under the sun.

8 There was a certain man without a [t]dependent, having neither a son nor a brother, yet there was no end to all his labor. Indeed, his eyes were not satisfied with riches *and he never asked,* "And [r]for whom am I laboring and depriving myself of pleasure?" This too is vanity and it is a grievous task. *second* • Eccl. 2:21

9 Two are better than one because they have a good return for
their labor.
10 For if either of them falls, the
one will lift up his companion. But
woe to the one who falls when
there is not another to lift him up.
11 Furthermore, if two lie down
together they keep warm, but how
can one be warm *alone?*
12 And if [t]one can overpower
him who is alone, two can resist
him. A cord of three *strands* is not
quickly torn apart. *he*
13 A [r]poor, yet wise lad is better
than an old and foolish king who
no longer knows *how* to receive
[a]instruction. Eccl. 7:19; 9:15 • *warning*
14 For he has come [r]out of
prison to become king, even
though he was born poor in his
kingdom. Gen. 41:14, 41-43
15 I have seen all the living under the sun throng to the side of
the second lad who replaces him.
16 There is no end to all the people, to all who were before them,
and even the ones who will come
later will not be happy with him,
for this too is [r]vanity and striving
after wind. Eccl. 1:14

CHAPTER 5

GUARD your steps as you go to
the house of God, and draw near
to listen rather than to offer the
sacrifice of fools; for they do not
know they are doing evil.
2 Do not be hasty [t]in word or
[t]impulsive in thought to bring up a
matter in the presence of God. For
God is in heaven and you are on
the earth; therefore let your words
be few. *with your mouth* • *hurry your heart*
3 For the dream comes
through much [t]effort, and the
voice of a [r]fool through many
words. *task* • Job 11:2; Prov. 15:2
4 When you [r]make a vow to
God, do not be late in paying it,
for He takes no delight in fools.
Pay what you vow! Num. 30:2
5 It is [r]better that you should
not vow than that you should vow
and not pay. Prov. 20:25; Acts 5:4
6 Do not let your [t]speech cause
[t]you to sin and do not say in the
presence of the messenger *of God*
that it was a mistake. Why should
God be angry on account of your
voice and destroy the work of
your hands? *mouth* • *your body*
7 For in many dreams and in
many words there is [t]emptiness.
Rather, fear God. *vanity*
8 If you see oppression of the
poor and denial of justice and
righteousness in the province, do
not be shocked at the [t]sight, for
one [t]official watches over another
official, and there are higher officials over them. *delight* • *high one*
9 After all, a king who culti-
vates the field is an advantage to
the land.
10 He who loves money will not
be satisfied with money, nor he
who loves abundance *with its* income. This too is [a]vanity. *futility*
11 When good things increase,
those who consume them increase. So what is the advantage
to their owners except to look on?
12 The sleep of the working
man is pleasant, whether he eats
little or much. But the [t]full stomach of the rich man does not allow
him to sleep. *satiety*
13 There is a grievous evil
which I have seen under the sun:

riches being [t]hoarded by their owner to his hurt. *guarded*

14 When those riches were lost through a bad investment and he had fathered a son, then there was nothing [t]to support him. *in his hand*

15 As he had come naked from his mother's womb, so will he return as he came. He will take nothing from the fruit of his labor that he can carry in his hand.

16 And this also is a grievous evil—exactly as a man [t]is born, thus will he [t]die. So, what is the advantage to him who [r]toils for the wind? *comes* • *go* • Eccl. 1:3

17 Throughout his life *he* also eats in darkness with great vexation, sickness and anger.

18 Here is what I have seen to be good and [t]fitting: to eat, to drink and [t]enjoy oneself in all one's labor in which he toils under the sun *during* the few years of his life which God has given him; for this is his reward. *beautiful* • *see good*

19 Furthermore, as for every man to whom [r]God has given riches and wealth, He has also empowered him to eat from them and to receive his [a]reward and rejoice in his labor; this is the gift of God. 2 Chr. 1:12; Eccl. 6:2 • *share*

20 For he will not often [t]consider the [a]years of his life, because God keeps him occupied with the gladness of his heart. *remember* • *days*

CHAPTER 6

THERE is an [r]evil which I have seen under the sun and it is prevalent [t]among men— Eccl. 5:13 • *upon*

2 a man to whom God has given riches and wealth and honor so that his soul lacks nothing of all that he desires, but God has not empowered him to eat from them, for a foreigner enjoys them. This is vanity and a severe affliction.

3 If a man fathers a hundred *children* and lives many years, however many they be, but his soul is not satisfied with good things, and he does not even have a *proper* burial, *then* I say, "Better the miscarriage than he,

4 for it comes in futility and goes into obscurity; and its name is covered in obscurity.

5 "It never sees the sun and it never knows *anything;* it is better off than he.

6 "Even if the *other* man lives a thousand years twice and does not [t]enjoy good things—[r]do not all go to one place?" *see* • Eccl. 2:14

7 [r]All a man's labor is for his mouth and yet the [t]appetite is not [t]satisfied. Prov. 16:26 • *soul* • *filled*

8 For [r]what advantage does the wise man have over the fool? What *advantage* does the poor man have, knowing *how* to walk before the living? Eccl. 2:15

9 What the eyes see is better than what the soul [t]desires. This too is [r]futility and a striving after wind. *goes after* • Eccl. 1:14

10 Whatever exists has already been named, and it is known what man is; for he cannot dispute with him who is stronger than he is.

11 For there are many words which increase futility. What *then* is the advantage to a man?

12 For who knows what is good for a man during *his* lifetime, *during* the few years of his futile life? He will spend them like a shadow. For who can tell a man what will be after him under the sun?

CHAPTER 7

A [r]GOOD name is better than a
good ointment, Prov. 22:1
And the [r]day of *one's* death
is better than the day of
one's birth. Eccl. 4:2; 7:8
2 It is better to go to a house
of mourning
Than to go to a house of
feasting,
Because that is the end of
every man,
And the living [t]takes *it* to
[t]heart. *gives* • *his heart*
3 [r]Sorrow is better than laughter, Eccl. 2:2
For when a face is sad a
heart may be happy.
4 The mind of the wise is in
the house of mourning,
While the mind of fools is in
the house of pleasure.
5 It is better to [r]listen to the
rebuke of a wise man
Than for one to listen to the
song of fools. Ps. 141:5
6 For as the [t]crackling of
thorn bushes under a pot,
So is the [r]laughter of the
fool, *voice* • Eccl. 2:2
And this too is futility.
7 For [r]oppression makes a
wise man mad, Eccl. 4:1
And a bribe [t]corrupts the
heart. *destroys*
8 The end of a matter is better than its beginning;
[r]Patience of spirit is better
than haughtiness of
spirit. Prov. 14:29; 16:32
9 Do not be [r]eager in your
heart to be angry,
For anger resides in the
bosom of fools. Prov. 14:17
10 Do not say, "Why is it that
the former days were
better than these?"
For it is not from wisdom
that you ask about this.
11 Wisdom along with an inheritance is good
And an advantage to those
who see the sun.
12 For [r]wisdom is [t]protection
just as money is protection. Eccl. 7:19 • *in a shadow*
But the advantage of
knowledge is that wis-
dom preserves the lives
of its possessors.
13 Consider the [r]work of God,
For who is able to
straighten what He has
bent? Eccl. 3:11; 8:17
14 [r]In the day of prosperity be
happy, Deut. 26:11
But [r]in the day of adversity
consider— Deut. 8:5
God has made the one as
well as the other
So that man may not dis-
cover anything *that will*
be after him.
15 I have seen everything during my [t]lifetime of futility; there is
a righteous man who perishes in
his righteousness, and there is a
wicked man who prolongs *his life*
in his wickedness. *days*
16 Do not be excessively righteous, and do not be overly wise.
Why should you ruin yourself?
17 Do not be excessively
wicked, and do not be a fool. Why
should you die before your time?
18 It is good that you grasp one
thing, and also not let go of the
other; for the one who fears God
comes forth with both of them.

19 [r]Wisdom strengthens a wise
man more than ten rulers who are
in a city. Eccl. 7:12; 9:13-18
20 Indeed, [r]there is not a righteous man on earth who *continually* does good and who never
sins. 1 Kin. 8:46; 2 Chr. 6:36
21 Also, do not [t]take seriously
all words which are spoken, lest
you hear your servant [r]cursing
you. *give your heart to* • Prov. 30:10
22 For you also have realized
that you likewise have many
times cursed others.
23 I tested all this with wisdom,
and I said, "I will be wise," [r]but it
was far from me. Eccl. 3:11; 8:17
24 What has been is remote and
[r]exceedingly [t]mysterious. Who can
discover it? Rom. 11:33 • *deep*
25 I [t]directed my mind to know,
to investigate, and to seek wisdom
and an explanation, and to know
the evil of folly and the foolishness of madness. *turned about*
26 And I discovered more [r]bitter
than death the woman whose
heart is snares and nets, whose
hands are chains. One who is
pleasing to God will escape from
her, but [r]the sinner will be captured by her. Prov. 5:4 • Prov. 22:14
27 "Behold, I have discovered
this," says the Preacher, "*adding*
one thing to another to find an explanation,
28 which [t]I am still seeking but
have not found. I have found one
man among a thousand, but I have
not found a woman among all
these. *my soul still seeks*
29 "Behold, I have found only
this, that [r]God made men upright,
but they have sought out many
devices." Gen. 1:27

CHAPTER 8

WHO is like the wise man and
who knows the interpretation of a
matter? A man's wisdom illumines [t]him and causes his stern
face to [a]beam. *his face* • *change*
2 I say, "Keep the [t]command of
the king because of the [r]oath [t]be-
fore God. *mouth* • Ex. 22:11 • *of*
3 "Do not be in a hurry [t]to leave
him. Do not join in an evil matter,
for he will do whatever he
pleases." *to go out from his presence*
4 Since the word of the king is
authoritative, [r]who will say to him,
"What are you doing?" Job 9:12
5 He who keeps a *royal* command experiences no [t]trouble, for
a wise heart knows the proper
time and procedure. *evil thing*
6 For [r]there is a proper time
and procedure for every delight,
when a man's trouble is heavy
upon him. Eccl. 3:1, 17
7 If no one [r]knows what will
happen, who can tell him when it
will happen? Eccl. 3:22; 6:12
8 No man has authority to restrain the wind with the wind, or
authority over the day of death;
and there is no discharge in the
time of war, and evil will not deliver those who practice it.
9 All this I have seen and applied my [t]mind to every deed that
has been done under the sun
wherein a man has exercised [r]au-
thority over *another* man to his
hurt. *heart* • Eccl. 4:1; 5:8; 7:7
10 So then, I have seen the
wicked buried, those who used to
go in and out from the holy place,
and they are [r]*soon* forgotten in the
city where they did thus. This too
is futility. Eccl. 1:11; 2:16; 9:5, 15

11 Because the [r]sentence against
an evil deed is not executed
quickly, therefore the hearts of
the sons of men among them are
given fully to do evil. Ex. 34:6
12 Although a sinner does evil a
hundred *times* and may lengthen
his *life*, still I know that it will be
well for those who fear God, who
fear [t]Him openly. *before Him*
13 But it will [r]not be well for the
evil man and he will not lengthen
his days like a shadow, because he
does not fear God. Eccl. 8:8; Is. 3:11
14 There is futility which is
done on the earth, that is, there
are [r]righteous men to whom it happens according to the deeds of the
wicked. On the other hand, there
are evil men to whom it [t]happens
according to the deeds of the
righteous. I say that this too is futility. Ps. 73:14; Eccl. 7:15 • *strikes*
15 So I commended pleasure,
for there is nothing good for [r]a
man under the sun except to eat
and to drink and to be merry, and
this will stand by him in his [t]toils
throughout the days of his life
which God has given him under
the sun. Eccl. 2:24; 3:12, 13 • *labor*
16 When I [r]gave my heart to
know wisdom and to see the task
which has been done on the earth
(even though one should never
sleep day or night), Eccl. 1:13, 14
17 and I saw every work of God,
I concluded that [r]man cannot discover the work which has been
done under the sun. Even though
man should seek laboriously, he
will not discover; and though the
wise man should say, "I know,"
he cannot discover. Eccl. 3:11

CHAPTER 9

FOR I have taken all this to my
heart and explain it that righteous
men, wise men, and their deeds
are in the hand of God. Man does
not know whether *it will be* love
or hatred; anything awaits him.
2 It is the same for all. There is
one fate for the righteous and for
the wicked; for the good, for the
clean, and for the unclean; for the
man who offers a sacrifice and for
the one who does not sacrifice. As
the good man is, so is the sinner;
as the swearer is, so is the one
who is afraid to swear.
3 This is an evil in all that is
done under the sun, that there is
one fate for all men. Furthermore,
the hearts of the sons of men are
full of evil, and insanity is in their
hearts throughout their lives. Afterwards they go to the dead.
4 For whoever is joined with
the living, there is hope; surely a
live dog is better than a dead lion.
5 For the living know they will
die; but the dead [r]do not know
anything, nor have they any
longer a reward, for their [r]memory
is forgotten. Job 14:21 • Ps. 88:12
6 Indeed their love, their hate,
and their zeal have already perished, and they will no longer
have a [r]share in all that is done under the sun. Eccl. 2:10; 3:22
7 Go *then*, eat your bread in
happiness, and drink your wine
with a cheerful heart; for God has
already approved your works.
8 Let your [r]clothes be white all
the time, and let not [r]oil be lacking
on your head. Rev. 3:4 • Ps. 23:5
9 Enjoy life with the woman
whom you love all the days of

your [r]fleeting life which He has
given to you under the sun; for
this is your reward in life, and in
your toil in which you have labored under the sun. Eccl. 6:12
10 Whatever your hand finds to
do, verily, [r]do *it* with all your
might; for there is no activity or
planning or wisdom in Sheol
where you are going. Eccl. 11:6
11 I again saw under the sun
that the [r]race is not to the swift,
and the battle is not to the warriors, and neither is bread to the
wise, nor wealth to the discerning,
nor favor to men of ability; for
time and [r]chance overtake them
all. Amos 2:14, 15 • 1 Sam. 6:9
12 Moreover, man does not
know his time: like fish caught in
a treacherous net, and birds
trapped in a snare, so the sons of
men are ensnared at an evil time
when it suddenly falls on them.
13 Also this I came to see as
wisdom under the sun, and [t]it im-
pressed me. *great it was to me*
14 There [r]was a small city with
few men in it and a great king
came to it, surrounded it, and con-
structed large siegeworks against
it. 2 Sam. 20:16-22
15 But there was found in it a
poor wise man and he delivered
the city by his wisdom. Yet no one
remembered that poor man.
16 So I said, "Wisdom [r]is better
than strength." But the wisdom of
the poor man is despised and his
words are not heeded. Prov. 21:22
17 The words of the wise heard
in quietness are *better* than the
shouting of a ruler among fools.
18 [r]Wisdom is better than weapons of war, but one sinner destroys much good. Eccl. 9:16

CHAPTER 10

DEAD flies make a perfumer's
oil stink, so a little foolishness is
weightier than wisdom *and* honor.
2 A wise man's heart *directs*
him toward the right, but the
foolish [r]man's heart *directs him*
toward the left. Matt. 6:33
3 Even when the fool walks
along the road his [t]sense is lacking, and he demonstrates to
everyone *that* he is a fool. *heart*
4 If the ruler's [t]temper rises
against you, do not abandon your
position, because composure al-
lays great offenses. *spirit*
5 There is an evil I have seen
under the sun, like an error which
goes forth from the ruler—
6 [r]folly is set in many exalted
places while rich men sit in humble places. Esth. 3:1, 5f.
7 I have seen [r]slaves *riding* on
horses and princes walking like
slaves on the land. Prov. 19:10
8 He who digs a pit may fall
into it, and a serpent may bite him
who breaks through a wall.
9 He who quarries stones may
be hurt by them, and he who splits
logs may be endangered by them.
10 If the axe is dull and he does
not sharpen *its* edge, then he must
exert more strength. Wisdom has
the advantage of giving success.
11 If the serpent bites [t]before
being charmed, there is no profit
for the charmer. *without enchantment*
12 Words from the mouth of a
wise man are gracious, while the
lips of a fool consume him;
13 the beginning of [t]his talking is
folly, and the end of it is wicked
madness. *the words of his mouth*
14 Yet the fool multiplies

words. No man knows what will happen, and who can tell him what will come after him?

15 The toil of [t]a fool *so* wearies him that he does not *even* know how to go to a city. *fools*

16 Woe to you, O land, whose king is a lad and whose princes [t]feast in the morning. *eat*

17 Blessed *are* you, O land, whose king is of nobility and whose princes eat at the appropriate time—for strength, and not for [r]drunkenness. Prov. 31:4; Is. 5:11

18 Through [r]indolence the rafters sag, and through slackness the house leaks. Prov. 24:30-34

19 *Men* prepare a meal for enjoyment, and wine makes life merry, and money [t]is the answer to everything. *answers all*

20 Furthermore, [r]in your bedchamber do not curse a king, and in your sleeping rooms do not curse a rich man, for a bird of the heavens will carry the sound, and the winged creature will make the matter known. 2 Kin. 6:12

CHAPTER 11

CAST your bread on the surface of the waters, for you [r]will find it after many days. Deut. 15:10

2 [r]Divide your portion to seven, or even to eight, for you do not know what misfortune may occur on the earth. Ps. 112:9; Matt. 5:42

3 If the clouds are full, they pour out rain upon the earth; and whether a tree falls toward the south or toward the north, wherever the tree falls, there it lies.

4 He who watches the wind will not sow and he who looks at the clouds will not reap.

5 Just as you do not know the path of the wind and how bones *are formed* in the womb of the [t]pregnant woman, so you do not know the activity of God who makes all things. *full*

6 Sow your seed in the morning, and do not be idle in the evening, for you do not know whether morning or evening sowing will succeed, or whether both of them alike will be good.

7 The light is pleasant, and *it is* good for the eyes to see the sun.

8 Indeed, if a man should live many years, let him [r]rejoice in them all, and let him remember the days of darkness, for they shall be many. Everything that is to come *will be* futility. Eccl. 9:7

9 Rejoice, young man, during your childhood, and let your heart be pleasant during the days of young manhood. And follow the [t]impulses of your heart and the [t]desires of your eyes. Yet know that God will bring you to judgment for all these things. *ways • sights*

10 So, remove vexation from your heart and put away [t]pain from your body, because childhood and the prime of life are fleeting. *evil*

CHAPTER 12

REMEMBER also your Creator in the days of your youth, before the [r]evil days come and the years draw near when you will say, "I have no delight in them"; Eccl. 11:8

2 before the sun, the light, the moon, and the stars are darkened, and clouds return after the rain;

3 in the day that the watchmen of the house tremble, and mighty

men stoop, the grinding ones stand idle because they are few, and those who look through[a] windows grow dim; *holes*

4 and the doors on the street are shut as the [r]sound of the grinding mill is low, and one will arise at the sound of the bird, and all the daughters of song will [t]sing softly. Jer. 25:10 • *be brought low*

5 Furthermore, [t]men are afraid of a high place and of terrors on the road; the almond tree blossoms, the grasshopper drags himself along, and the caperberry is ineffective. For man goes to his eternal home while mourners go about in the street. *they*

6 *Remember Him* before the silver cord is broken and the [r]golden bowl is crushed, the pitcher by the well is shattered and the wheel at the cistern is crushed; Zech. 4:2, 3

7 then the dust will return to the earth as it was, and the spirit will return to God who gave it.

8 "Vanity[r] of vanities," says the Preacher, "all is vanity!" Eccl. 1:2

9 In addition to being a wise man, the Preacher also taught the people knowledge; and he pondered, searched out and arranged [r]many proverbs. 1 Kin. 4:32

10 The Preacher sought to find [r]delightful words and to write words of truth correctly. Prov. 10:32

11 The [r]words of wise men are like goads, and masters of *these* collections are like [t]well-driven nails; they are given by one Shepherd. Prov. 1:6; 22:17 • *planted*

12 But beyond this, my son, be warned: the [t]writing of many books is endless, and excessive [r]devotion *to books* is wearying to the body. *making* • Eccl. 1:18

13 The conclusion, when all has been heard, *is:* [r]fear God and keep His commandments, because this *applies to* every person. Eccl. 3:14

14 For God will bring every act to judgment, everything which is hidden, whether it is good or evil.

THE SONG OF SOLOMON

THE [1]Song of [r]Songs, which is Solomon's. 1 Kin. 4:32

2 "[2]May he kiss me with the
kisses of his mouth!
For your [r]love is better than
wine. Song 1:4; 4:10
3 "Your [r]oils have a pleasing fragrance, Song 4:10
Your name is *like* [t]purified
oil; *oil which is emptied*
Therefore the [a]maidens love
you. *virgins*
4 "Draw me after you *and* let us
run *together!*
The [r]king has brought me into
his chambers." Ps. 45:14, 15

"[3]We will rejoice in you and
be glad;
We will extol your [r]love more
than wine. Song 1:4; 4:10

[1] Or, *Best of the Songs* [2] BRIDE [3] CHORUS

Rightly do they love you."

5 "[4]I am black but lovely,
O [r]daughters of Jerusalem,
Like the tents of Kedar,
Like the curtains of Solomon. Song 2:14; 4:3; 6:4
6 "Do not stare at me because I am [a]swarthy, *black*
For the sun has burned me.
My [r]mother's sons were angry with me; Ps. 69:8
They made me [r]caretaker of the vineyards, Song 8:11
But I have not taken care of my own vineyard.
7 "Tell me, O you [r]whom my soul loves, Song 3:1-4
Where do you [r]pasture *your flock,* Song 2:16; 6:3
Where do you make *it* [r]lie down at noon? Is. 13:20
For why should I be like one who veils herself
Beside the flocks of your [r]companions?" Song 8:13

8 "[5]If you yourself do not know,
[r]Most beautiful among women, Song 5:9; 6:1
Go forth on the trail of the flock,
And pasture your young goats
By the tents of the shepherds.

9 "To[t] me, [r]my darling, you are like *I have compared you to*
My mare among the chariots of Pharaoh. Song 1:15; 2:2
10 "Your [r]cheeks are lovely with ornaments, Song 5:13
Your neck with strings of [r]beads." Gen. 24:53

[4]BRIDE [5]BRIDEGROOM

11 "[6]We will make for you ornaments of gold
With beads of silver."

12 "[4]While the king was at his [a]table, *couch*
My [t]perfume gave forth its fragrance. *nard*
13 "My beloved is to me a pouch of [r]myrrh Ps. 45:8
Which lies all night between my breasts.
14 "My beloved is to me a cluster of henna blossoms
In the vineyards of Engedi."

15 "[5]How beautiful [t]you are, my darling, *Behold*
How beautiful you are!
Your eyes are *like* doves."

16 "[4]How[t] handsome you are, my beloved, *Behold*
And so pleasant!
Indeed, our couch is luxuriant!
17 "The beams of our houses are [r]cedars, 1 Kin. 6:9, 10
Our rafters, cypresses.

CHAPTER 2

"[4]I AM the [t]rose of Sharon,
The lily of the valleys." *crocus*

2 "[5]Like a lily among the thorns,
So is my darling among the [t]maidens." *daughters*

3 "[7]Like an apple tree among the trees of the forest,
So is my beloved among the [t]young men. *sons*
In his shade I took great delight and sat down,

[4]BRIDE [5]BRIDEGROOM
[6]CHORUS [7]BRIDE

And his [r]fruit was sweet to
my taste. Song 4:13, 16
4 "He has brought me to *his* [t]banquet hall, *house of wine*
And his [r]banner over me is
love. Ps. 20:5
5 "Sustain me with raisin cakes,
Refresh me with apples,
Because I am lovesick.
6 "*Let* [r]his left hand be under my
head Song 8:3
And his right hand [r]embrace
me." Prov. 4:8

7 "[8]I [r]adjure you, O daughters of
Jerusalem, Song 3:5; 5:8, 9
By the gazelles or by the
[r]hinds of the field,
That you will not arouse or
awaken *my* love, Hab. 3:19
Until she pleases."

8 "[7]Listen! My beloved!
Behold, he is coming,
Climbing on the mountains,
Leaping on the hills!
9 "My beloved is like a gazelle
or a young [t]stag.
Behold, he is standing behind
our wall, *of the stags*
He is looking through the
windows,
He is peering [r]through the lat-
tice. Judg. 5:28

10 "My beloved responded and
said to me,
'Arise[r], my darling, my beautiful one, Song 2:13
And come along.
11 'For behold, the winter is
past,
The rain is over *and* gone.
12 'The flowers have *already* appeared in the land;
The time has arrived for
[a]pruning *the vines*, *singing*
And the voice of the turtledove has been heard in
our land.
13 'The [r]fig tree has ripened its
figs, Matt. 24:32
And the [r]vines in blossom
have given forth *their* fragrance. Song 7:12
Arise, my darling, my beautiful one,
And come along!' "
14 "O [r]my dove, in the clefts of
the rock, Song 5:2; 6:9
In the secret place of the
steep pathway,
Let me see your form,
Let me hear your voice;
For your voice is sweet,
And your form is lovely."

15 "Catch the foxes for us,
The [a]little foxes that are ruin-
ing the vineyards, *young*
While our [r]vineyards are in
blossom." Song 2:13
16 "My [r]beloved is mine, and I am
his; Song 6:3; 7:10
He [r]pastures *his flock* among
the lilies. Song 4:5; 6:2, 3
17 "Until [t]the cool of the day
when the shadows flee
away, *the day blows*
Turn, my beloved, and be
like a [r]gazelle Song 2:9
Or a young stag on the
mountains of Bether."

CHAPTER 3

"[9]ON my bed night after night I
sought him
[r]Whom my soul loves; Song 1:7
I [r]sought him but did not find
him. Song 5:6

[7]BRIDE [8]BRIDEGROOM [9]BRIDE

2 'I[a] must arise now and go
about the city; *Let me arise*
In the [r]streets and in the
squares Jer. 5:1
[a]I must seek him whom my
soul loves.' *Let me seek*
I sought him but did not find
him.
3 "The[r] watchmen who make
the rounds in the city
found me, Song 5:7
And I said, 'Have you seen
him whom my soul
loves?'
4 "Scarcely had I[t]left them
When I found him whom my
soul loves; *passed*
I [r]held on to him and would
not let him go, Prov. 4:13
Until I had brought him to
my mother's house,
And into the room of her
who conceived me."

5 "[10]I adjure[r]you, O daughters of
Jerusalem, Song 2:7; 5:8
By the gazelles or by the
hinds of the field,
That you will not arouse or
awaken *my* love,
Until[a]she pleases." *it*

6 "[11]What is this coming up
from the wilderness
Like columns of smoke,
Perfumed with [r]myrrh and
frankincense, Song 1:13; 4:6
With all scented powders of
the merchant?
7 "Behold, it is the *traveling*
couch of Solomon;
Sixty mighty men around it,
Of the mighty men of Israel.
8 "All of them are wielders of
the sword,
[r]Expert in war; Jer. 50:9
Each man has his [r]sword at
his side, Ps. 45:3
Guarding against the [r]terrors
of the night. Ps. 91:5
9 "King Solomon has made for
himself a sedan chair
From the timber of Lebanon.
10 "He made its posts of silver,
Its[a]back of gold *support*
And its seat of purple fabric,
With its interior lovingly
fitted out
By the[r]daughters of Jerusalem. Song 1:5
11 "Go forth, O [r]daughters of
Zion, Is. 3:16, 17; 4:4
And gaze on King Solomon
with the[a]crown *wreath*
With which his mother has
crowned him
On the [r]day of his wedding,
And on the day of his gladness of heart." Is. 62:5

CHAPTER 4

"[10]HOW[t] beautiful you are, my
darling, *Behold*
How beautiful you are!
Your [r]eyes are *like* doves be-
hind your veil; Song 1:15
Your [r]hair is like a flock of
goats Song 6:5
That have descended from
Mount [r]Gilead. Mic. 7:14
2 "Your [r]teeth are like a flock of
newly shorn ewes
Which have come up from
their washing, Song 6:6
All of which bear twins,
And not one among them has
[a]lost her young. *miscarried*

[10]BRIDEGROOM [11]CHORUS

[10]BRIDEGROOM

3 "Your lips are like a [r]scarlet
thread, Josh. 2:18
And your mouth is lovely.
Your [r]temples are like a slice
of a pomegranate
Behind your veil. Song 6:7
4 "Your [r]neck is like the tower of
David Song 7:4
Built [a]with rows of stones,
On which are hung a thousand shields, *for an arsenal*
All the round [r]shields of the
mighty men. 2 Sam. 1:21
5 "Your [r]two breasts are like
two fawns, Song 7:3
Twins of a gazelle,
Which feed among the lilies.
6 "Until [t]the cool of the day
When the shadows flee
away, *the day blows*
I will go my way to the
mountain of myrrh
And to the hill of [r]frankincense. Song 4:14

7 "You [r]are altogether beautiful,
my darling, Song 1:15
And there is no blemish in
you.
8 "*Come* with me from [r]Lebanon, *my* bride, 1 Kin. 4:33
May you come with me from
Lebanon.
[a]Journey down from the summit of Amana, *Look*
From the summit of [r]Senir
and Hermon, Deut. 3:9
From the dens of lions,
From the mountains of leopards.
9 "You have made my heart
beat faster, [r]my sister, *my*
bride; Song 4:10, 12
You have made my heart
beat faster with a single
glance of your eyes,
With a single strand of your
[r]necklace. Gen. 41:42
10 "How beautiful is your love,
my sister, *my* bride!
How much [r]better is your
love than wine, Song 1:2, 4
And the [r]fragrance of your
oils Song 1:3
Than all *kinds* of spices!
11 "Your lips, *my* bride, [r]drip honey; Prov. 5:3
Honey and milk are under
your tongue,
And the fragrance of your
garments is like the fragrance of Lebanon.
12 "A garden locked is my sister,
my bride,
A [t]rock garden locked, a
spring sealed up. *stone heap*
13 "Your shoots are an orchard
of pomegranates
With choice fruits, henna
with nard plants,
14 Nard and saffron, calamus
and [r]cinnamon, Ex. 30:23
With all the trees of [r]frankincense, Song 4:6
Myrrh and aloes, along with
all the finest spices.
15 "*You are* a garden spring,
A well of [t]fresh water, *living*
And streams *flowing* from
Lebanon."

16 "[12]Awake, O north *wind,*
And come, *wind of* the south;
Make my [r]garden breathe out
fragrance, Song 5:1; 6:2
Let its [a]spices be wafted
abroad. *balsam odors*
May [r]my beloved come into
his garden Song 1:13
And eat its choice fruits!"

[12]BRIDE

CHAPTER 5

"[13]I HAVE come into my garden,
my sister, *my* bride;
I have gathered my myrrh
along with my balsam.
I have eaten my honeycomb
[t]and my honey; *with*
I have drunk my wine [a]and
my milk. *become drunk*
Eat, [r]friends; Judg. 14:11, 20
Drink and imbibe deeply, O
lovers."

2 "[14]I was asleep, but my heart
was awake.
A voice! My beloved was
knocking:
'Open to me, [r]my sister, my
darling, Song 4:9
My dove, my perfect one!
For my head is [t]drenched
with dew, *filled*
My locks with the [t]damp of
the night.' *drops*
3 "I have taken off my dress,
How can I put it on *again?*
I have washed my feet,
How can I dirty them *again?*
4 "My beloved extended his
hand through the open-
ing,
And my [t]feelings were
aroused for him. *bowels*
5 "I arose to open to my beloved;
And my hands [r]dripped with
myrrh, Song 5:13
And my fingers with [t]liquid
myrrh, *passing*
On the handles of the bolt.
6 "I opened to my beloved,
But my beloved had turned
away *and* had gone!
My [t]heart went out *to him* as
he spoke. *soul*
I [r]searched for him, but I did
not find him; Song 3:1
I [r]called him, but he did not
answer me. Prov. 1:28
7 "The [r]watchmen who make
the rounds in the city
found me, Song 3:3
They struck me *and*
wounded me;
The guardsmen of the walls
took away my shawl
from me.
8 "I [r]adjure you, O daughters of
Jerusalem, Song 2:7; 3:5
If you find my beloved,
As to what you will tell him:
For [r]I am lovesick." Song 2:5

9 "[15]What kind of beloved is
your beloved,
O [r]most beautiful among
women? Song 1:8; 6:1
What kind of beloved is your
beloved,
That thus you adjure us?"

10 "[14]My beloved is dazzling and
[r]ruddy, 1 Sam. 16:12
[r]Outstanding among ten thousand. Ps. 45:2
11 "His head is *like* gold, pure
gold;
His [r]locks are *like* clusters of
dates, Song 5:2
And black as a raven.
12 "His [r]eyes are like doves,
Beside streams of water,
Bathed in milk, Song 1:15
And reposed in *their* setting.
13 "His cheeks are like a [r]bed of
balsam, Song 6:2
Banks of sweet-scented
herbs;

[13]BRIDEGROOM [14]BRIDE

[14]BRIDE [15]CHORUS

His lips are [r]lilies, Song 2:1
Dripping with liquid myrrh.
14 "His hands are rods of gold
Set with [r]beryl; Ex. 28:20
His abdomen is carved ivory
Inlaid with sapphires.
15 "His legs are pillars of alabaster
Set on pedestals of pure gold;
His appearance is like [r]Lebanon, Song 7:4
Choice as the cedars.
16 "His [t]mouth is *full of* sweetness. *palate*
And he is wholly [r]desirable.
This is my beloved and this is my friend, 2 Sam. 1:23
O daughters of Jerusalem."

CHAPTER 6

"[16]WHERE[r] has your beloved gone, Song 5:6
O [r]most beautiful among women? Song 1:8
Where has your beloved turned,
That we may seek him with you?"

2 "[17]My beloved has gone down
to his [r]garden, Song 4:16; 5:1
To the beds of balsam,
To [r]pasture *his flock* in the gardens Song 1:7
And gather lilies.
3 "I[r] am my beloved's and my beloved is mine, Song 2:16
He who pastures *his flock* among the lilies."

4 "[18]You are as beautiful as [r]Tirzah, my darling, 1 Kin. 14:17
As lovely as Jerusalem,
As awesome as [t]an army with banners. *bannered ones*

5 "Turn your eyes away from me,
For they have confused me;
[r]Your hair is like a flock of goats Song 4:1
That have descended from Gilead.
6 "Your[r] teeth are like a flock of ewes Song 4:2
Which have come up from *their* washing,
All of which bear twins,
And not one among them has [a]lost her young. *miscarried*
7 "Your[r] temples are like a slice of a pomegranate
Behind your veil. Song 4:3
8 "There are sixty queens and eighty concubines,
And [a]maidens without number; *virgins*
9 *But* [r]my dove, my perfect one, is unique: Song 2:14; 5:2
She is her mother's [t]only *daughter*; *one*
She is the pure *child* of the one who bore her.
The maidens saw her and called her blessed,
The queens and the concubines *also*, and they praised her, *saying*,

10 'Who is this that [t]grows like the dawn, *looks down*
As beautiful as the full moon,
As pure [r]as the sun, Matt. 17:2
As awesome as [t]an army with banners?' *bannered ones*
11 "I went down to the orchard of nut trees
To see the blossoms of the valley,
To see whether [r]the vine had budded Song 7:12

[16]CHORUS [17]BRIDE [18]BRIDEGROOM

Or the [r]pomegranates had
bloomed. Song 4:13
12 "Before I was aware, my soul
set me
Over the chariots of my
noble people."

13 "[19]Come back, come back, O
Shulammite;
Come back, come back, that
we may gaze at you!"

"[20]**Why** should you gaze at the
Shulammite,
As at the [r]dance of the two
companies? Judg. 21:21

CHAPTER 7

"HOW beautiful are your feet in
sandals,
O [a]prince's daughter! *nobleman's*
The curves of your hips are
like [a]jewels, *ornaments*
The work of the hands of an
artist.
2 "Your navel is *like* a round
goblet
Which never lacks mixed
wine;
Your belly is like a heap of
wheat
Fenced about with lilies.
3 "Your [r]two breasts are like
two fawns, Song 4:5
Twins of a gazelle.
4 "Your [r]neck is like a tower of
ivory, Song 4:4
Your eyes *like* the pools in
[r]Heshbon Num. 21:26
By the gate of Bath-rabbim;
Your nose is like the tower of
Lebanon,
Which faces toward Damas-
cus.
5 "Your head [t]crowns you like
Carmel, *is upon*
And the flowing locks of
your head are like purple
threads;
The king is captivated by
your tresses.
6 "How [r]beautiful and how delightful you are,
My love, with *all* your
charms! Song 1:15, 16
7 "Your [t] stature is like a palm
tree, *This stature of yours*
And your breasts are *like its*
clusters.
8 "I said, 'I will climb the palm
tree,
I will take hold of its fruit
stalks.'
Oh, may your breasts be like
clusters of the vine,
And the fragrance of your
breath like apples,
9 And your [t]mouth like the best
wine!" *palate*

"[21]**It** [r]goes *down* smoothly for
my beloved, Prov. 23:31
Flowing gently *through* the
lips of those who fall
asleep.

10 "I am my beloved's,
And his desire is for me.
11 "Come, my beloved, let us go
out into the country,
Let us spend the night in the
villages.
12 "Let us rise early *and go* to
the vineyards;
Let us [r]see whether the vine
has budded Song 6:11
And its blossoms have
opened,
And whether the pomegranates have bloomed.

[19]CHORUS [20]BRIDEGROOM [21]BRIDE

There I will give you my love.
13 "The [r]mandrakes have given forth fragrance; Gen. 30:14
And over our doors are all [r]choice *fruits*, Song 2:3
Both new and old,
Which I have saved up for you, my beloved.

CHAPTER 8

"OH that you were like a brother to me
Who nursed at my mother's breasts.
If I found you outdoors, I would kiss you;
No one would despise me, either.
2 "I would lead you *and* [r]bring you Song 3:4
Into the house of my mother, who used to instruct me;
I would give you spiced wine to drink from the juice of my pomegranates.
3 "Let [r]his left hand be under my head, Song 2:6
And his right hand embrace me."

4 "[22]I want you to swear, O daughters of Jerusalem,
[a]Do not arouse or awaken *my* love, *Why should you arouse*
Until she pleases."

5 "[23]Who [r]is this coming up from the wilderness, Song 3:6
Leaning on her beloved?"

"[22]**B**eneath the [a]apple tree I awakened you; *apricot*
There your mother was in labor with you,
There she was in labor *and* gave you birth.
6 "Put me like a [24]seal over your heart,
Like a [r]seal on your arm.
For love is as strong as death, Is. 49:16
[a]Jealousy is as severe as Sheol; *Its ardor is inflexible*
Its flashes are flashes of fire,
The *very* flame of the LORD.
7 "Many waters cannot quench love,
Nor will rivers overflow it;
[r]If a man were to give all the riches of his house for love, Prov. 6:35
It would be utterly despised."

8 "[25]We have a little sister,
And she [r]has no breasts;
What shall we do for our sister Ezek. 16:7
On the day when she is spoken for?
9 "If she is a wall,
We shall build on her a battlement of silver;
But if she is a door,
We shall barricade her with [r]planks of cedar." 1 Kin. 6:15

10 "[26]I was a wall, and my breasts were like towers;
Then I became in his eyes as one who finds peace.
11 "Solomon had a [r]vineyard at Baal-hamon; Eccl. 2:4
He [r]entrusted the vineyard to caretakers; Matt. 21:33
Each one was to bring a [r]thousand *shekels* of silver for its fruit. Is. 7:23
12 "My very own vineyard is [t]at my disposal; *before me*

[22]BRIDEGROOM [23]CHORUS [24]Or, *signet* [25]CHORUS [26]BRIDE

The thousand *shekels* are for you, Solomon,
And two hundred are for those who take care of its fruit."
13 "[27]O you who sit in the gardens,

[27]BRIDEGROOM

My [r]companions are listening for your voice— Song 1:7
Let me hear it!"
14 "[26]Hurry, my beloved,
And be [r]like a gazelle or a young stag Song 2:7, 9, 17
On the mountains of spices."

[26]BRIDE

THE BOOK OF

ISAIAH

THE vision of Isaiah the son of
Amoz, concerning Judah and Jerusalem which he saw during the
reigns of Uzziah, Jotham, Ahaz,
and Hezekiah, kings of Judah.

2 Listen, O heavens, and hear, O [r]earth; Deut. 32:1
For the LORD speaks,
"Sons[r] I have reared and brought up, Jer. 3:22
But they have [r]revolted against Me. Is. 30:1, 9
3 "An ox knows its owner,
And a donkey its master's manger,
But Israel [r]does not know,
My people do not understand." Jer. 9:3, 6

4 Alas, sinful nation,
People weighed down with iniquity,
Offspring of evildoers,
Sons who act corruptly!
They have [r]abandoned the LORD, Is. 1:28
They have [r]despised the Holy One of Israel, Is. 5:24
They have turned away [t]from Him. *backward*

5 Where will you be stricken again,
As you [r]continue in *your* rebellion? Is. 31:6
The whole head is sick,
And the whole heart is faint.
6 From the sole of the foot even to the head
There is [r]nothing sound in it,
Only bruises, welts, and raw wounds, Ps. 38:3
Not pressed out or bandaged,
Nor softened with oil.

7 Your [r]land is desolate,
Your cities are burned with fire, Jer. 44:6
Your fields—strangers are devouring them in your presence;
It is desolation, as overthrown by strangers.
8 And the daughter of Zion is left like a shelter in a vineyard,
Like a watchman's hut in a cucumber field, like a besieged city.
9 Unless the LORD of hosts
Had left us a few survivors,

We would be like Sodom,
We would be like Gomorrah.

10 Hear the word of the LORD,
You rulers of Sodom;
Give ear to the instruction of our God,
You people of Gomorrah.
11 "What[r] are your multiplied sacrifices to Me?" Ps. 50:8
Says the LORD.
"I have had enough of burnt offerings of rams,
And the fat of fed cattle.
And I take no pleasure in the blood of bulls, lambs, or goats.
12 "When you come [r]to appear before Me, Ex. 23:17
Who requires of you this trampling of My courts?
13 "Bring your worthless offerings no longer,
[r]Incense is an abomination to Me. Is. 66:3
New moon and sabbath, the calling of assemblies—
I cannot endure iniquity and the solemn assembly.
14 "I hate your new moon *festivals* and your [r]appointed feasts, Is. 29:1, 2
They have become a burden to Me.
I am weary of bearing *them.*
15 "So when you spread out your hands *in prayer,*
I will hide My eyes from you,
Yes, even though you [r]multiply prayers, Mic. 3:4
I will not listen.
[r]Your hands are covered with blood. Is. 59:3

16 "Wash yourselves, make yourselves clean;
Remove the evil of your deeds from My sight.
[r]Cease to do evil, Jer. 25:5
17 Learn to do good;
Seek justice,
Reprove the ruthless;
Defend the orphan,
Plead for the widow.

18 "Come now, and [r]let us reason together," Is. 41:1, 21
Says the LORD,
"Though[r] your sins are as scarlet, Ps. 51:7
They will be as white as snow;
Though they are red like crimson,
They will be like wool.
19 "If you consent and obey,
You will [r]eat the best of the land; Is. 55:2
20 "But if you refuse and rebel,
You will be [r]devoured by the sword." Is. 3:25; 65:12
Truly, [r]the mouth of the LORD has spoken. Is. 40:5

21 How the faithful city has become [r]a harlot,
She *who* was full of justice!
Righteousness once lodged in her, Is. 57:3-9; Jer. 2:20
But now murderers.
22 Your silver has become dross,
Your drink diluted with water.
23 Your rulers are rebels,
And companions of thieves;
Everyone loves a bribe,
And chases after rewards.
They do not [a]defend the [a]orphan, *vindicate • fatherless*
Nor does the widow's plea come before them.

24 Therefore the Lord GOD of hosts,
The [r]Mighty One of Israel declares, Is. 49:26; 60:16
"Ah, I will be relieved of My adversaries,
And [r]avenge Myself on My foes. Is. 35:4; 59:18
25 "I will also turn My hand against you,
And will smelt away your dross as with lye,
And will remove all your alloy.
26 "Then I will restore your judges as at the first,
And your counselors as at the beginning;
After that you will be called the [r]city of righteousness,
A faithful city." Is. 33:5; 60:14

27 Zion will be [r]redeemed with justice, Is. 39:9f.; 62:12; 63:4
And her [a]repentant ones with righteousness. *returnees*
28 But transgressors and sinners will be [r]crushed together, Ps. 9:5; Is. 66:24
And those who forsake the LORD shall come to an end.
29 Surely, you will be ashamed of the [a]oaks which you have desired, *terebinths*
And you will be embarrassed at the [r]gardens which you have chosen. Is. 65:3; 66:17
30 For you will be like an oak whose leaf fades away,
Or as a garden that has no water.
31 And the strong man will become tinder,
His work also a spark.
Thus they shall both [r]burn together, Is. 5:24; 9:19
And there will be [r]none to quench *them.* Is. 66:24

CHAPTER 2

THE word which [r]Isaiah the son
of Amoz saw concerning Judah
and Jerusalem. Is. 1:1
2 Now it will come about that
[r]In the last days, Mic. 4:1-3
The [r]mountain of the house of the LORD Is. 27:13; 66:20
Will be established as the chief of the mountains,
And will be raised above the hills;
And [r]all the nations will stream to it. Is. 56:7
3 And many peoples will come and say,
"Come, let us go up to the mountain of the LORD,
To the house of the God of Jacob;
That He may teach us [a]concerning His ways,
And that we may walk in His paths." *some of*
For the [a]law will go forth from Zion, *instruction*
And the word of the LORD from Jerusalem.
4 And He will judge between the nations,
And will [a]render decisions for many peoples; *reprove many*
And they will hammer their swords into plowshares, and their spears into pruning hooks.
[r]Nation will not lift up sword against nation,
And never again will they learn war. Is. 9:5, 7; 11:6-9

5 Come, [r]house of Jacob, and
let us walk in the light of
the LORD. Is. 58:1
6 For Thou hast [r]abandoned
Thy people, the house of
Jacob, Deut. 31:17
Because they are filled with
influences from the east,
And *they are* soothsayers
like the Philistines,
And they [r]strike *bargains*
with the children of for-
eigners. 2 Kin. 16:7, 8
7 Their land has also been
filled with silver and
gold,
And there is no end to their
treasures;
Their land has also been
filled with [r]horses, Is. 30:16
And there is no end to their
chariots.
8 Their land has also been
[r]filled with idols; Is. 10:11
They worship the [r]work of
their hands, Ps. 115:4-8
That which their fingers have
made.
9 So [r]the *common* man has
been humbled, Ps. 49:2
And the man *of importance*
has been abased,
But do not forgive them.
10 [r]Enter the rock and hide in
the dust Is. 2:19, 21
[r]From the terror of the LORD
and from the splendor of
His majesty. 2 Thess. 1:9
11 The [r]proud look of man will
be abased, Is. 5:15; 37:23
And the [r]loftiness of man will
be humbled, Ps. 18:27
And the LORD alone will be
exalted in that day.

12 For the LORD of hosts will
have a day of reckoning
Against [r]everyone who is
proud and lofty, Is. 24:4, 21
And against everyone who is
lifted up,
That he may be abased.
13 And *it will be* against all the
cedars of Lebanon that
are lofty and lifted up,
Against all the [r]oaks of Bashan, Zech. 11:2
14 Against all the [r]lofty mountains, Is. 40:4
Against all the hills that are
lifted up,
15 Against every high tower,
Against every fortified wall,
16 Against all the [r]ships of Tarshish, Is. 23:1, 14
And against all the beautiful
craft.
17 And the pride of man will be
humbled,
And the loftiness of men will
be abased,
And the LORD alone will be
exalted in that day.
18 But the [r]idols will completely
vanish. Is. 21:9; Mic. 1:7
19 And *men* will [r]go into caves
of the rocks, Is. 2:10
And into holes of the ground
Before the terror of the LORD,
And before the splendor of
His majesty,
When He arises [r]to make the
earth tremble. Is. 2:21
20 In that day men will [r]cast
away to the moles and
the bats Is. 30:22; 31:7
Their idols of silver and their
idols of gold,
Which they made for them-
selves to worship,

21 In order to [r]go into the caverns of the rocks and the clefts of the cliffs, Is. 2:19
Before the terror of the LORD and the splendor of His majesty,
When He arises to make the earth tremble.
22 [t]Stop regarding man, whose breath *of life* is in his nostrils; *Cease from man*
For [t]why should he be esteemed? *in what*

CHAPTER 3

FOR behold, the Lord GOD of hosts [r]is going to remove from Jerusalem and Judah Is. 5:13; 9:20
Both [t]supply and support, the whole supply of bread,
And the whole [t]supply of water; *staff*
2 [r]The mighty man and the warrior, 2 Kin. 24:14
The judge and the prophet,
The diviner and the elder,
3 The captain of fifty and the honorable man,
The counselor and the expert artisan,
And the skillful enchanter.
4 And I will make mere [r]lads their princes Eccl. 10:16
And capricious children will rule over them,
5 And the people will be [r]oppressed, Mic. 7:3-6
Each one by another, and each one by his neighbor;
The youth will storm against the elder,
And the inferior against the honorable.
6 When a man [r]lays hold of his brother in his father's house, *saying,* Is. 4:1
"You have a cloak, you shall be our ruler,
And these ruins will be under your [t]charge," *hand*
7 On that day will he [t]protest, saying, *lift up his voice*
"I will not be *your* healer,
For in my house there is neither bread nor cloak;
You should not appoint me ruler of the people."
8 For Jerusalem has stumbled, and Judah has fallen,
Because their [t]speech and their actions are against the LORD, *tongue*
To [r]rebel against His glorious presence. Is. 65:3
9 [a]The expression of their faces bears witness against them. *Their partiality bears*
And they display their sin like [r]Sodom; Gen. 13:13
They do not *even* conceal *it.*
Woe to [t]them! *their soul*
For they have [r]brought evil on themselves. Rom. 6:23
10 Say to the righteous that *it will go* well *with them,*
For they will eat the fruit of their actions.
11 Woe to the wicked! *It will go* badly *with him,*
For [r]what he deserves will be done to him. Is. 65:6, 7
12 O My people! Their oppressors are children,
And women rule over them.
O My people! [r]Those who guide you lead *you* astray, Is. 9:16; 28:14, 15
And confuse the direction of your paths.

13 The LORD arises to contend,
And stands to judge the people.
14 The LORD enters into judgment with the elders and princes of His people,
"It is you who have [r]devoured the vineyard; Ps. 14:4
The [r]plunder of the poor is in your houses. Ps. 10:9
15 "What do you mean by [r]crushing My people, Ps. 94:5
And grinding the face of the poor?"
Declares the Lord GOD of hosts.

16 Moreover, the LORD said, "Because the daughters of Zion are proud,
And walk with heads held high and seductive eyes,
And go along with mincing steps,
And tinkle the bangles on their feet,
17 Therefore the Lord will afflict the scalp of the daughters of Zion with scabs,
And the LORD will make their foreheads bare."
18 In that day the Lord will take
away the beauty of *their* anklets,
headbands, crescent ornaments,
19 dangling earrings, bracelets,
veils,
20 headdresses, ankle chains,
sashes, perfume boxes, amulets,
21 finger rings, nose rings,
22 festal robes, outer tunics,
cloaks, money purses,
23 hand mirrors, undergarments, turbans, and veils.
24 Now it will come about that instead of [a]sweet perfume there will be putrefaction; *balsam oil*
Instead of a belt, a rope;
Instead of well-set hair, a plucked-out scalp;
Instead of fine clothes, a donning of sackcloth;
And branding instead of beauty.
25 Your men will [r]fall by the sword, Is. 1:20; 65:12
And your mighty ones in battle.
26 And her [t]gates will lament and mourn; *entrances*
And deserted she will [r]sit on the ground. Lam. 2:10

CHAPTER 4

FOR seven women will take hold
of [r]one man in that day, saying,
"We will eat our own bread and
wear our own clothes, only let us
be called by your name; take
away our reproach!" Is. 13:12
2 In that day the [r]Branch of the
LORD will be beautiful and glorious, and the fruit of the earth *will*
be the pride and the adornment of
the survivors of Israel. Is. 11:1
3 And it will come about that
he who is [r]left in Zion and remains
in Jerusalem will be called holy—
everyone who is recorded for life
in Jerusalem. Is. 28:5; 46:3
4 When the LORD has washed
away the filth of the daughters of
Zion, and [t]purged the bloodshed of
Jerusalem from her midst, by the
spirit of judgment and the spirit of
burning, *rinsed away*
5 then the LORD will create
over the whole area of Mount
Zion and over her assemblies a
cloud by day, even smoke, and the

brightness of a flaming fire by
night; for over all the [r]glory will be
a canopy. Is. 60:1, 2
6 And there will be a shelter to
give shade from the heat by day,
and refuge and [r]protection from
the storm and the rain. *a hiding place*

CHAPTER 5

LET me sing now for my well-beloved
A song of my beloved concerning His vineyard.
My well-beloved had a vineyard on a fertile hill.
2 And He dug it all around, removed its stones,
And planted it with the choicest vine.
And He built a tower in the middle of it,
And hewed out a [a]wine vat in it; *wine press*
Then He expected *it* to produce *good* grapes,
But it produced *only* [a]worthless ones. *wild grapes*
3 "And now, O inhabitants of Jerusalem and men of Judah,
[r]Judge between Me and My vineyard. Matt. 21:40
4 "What more was there to do for My vineyard that I have not done in it?
Why, when I expected *it* to produce *good* grapes did it produce [a]worthless ones? *wild grapes*
5 "So now let Me tell you what I am going to do to My vineyard:
I will remove its hedge and it will be consumed;
I will [r]break down its wall and it will become trampled ground. Ps. 80:12
6 "And I will [r]lay it waste;
It will not be pruned or hoed,
But briars and thorns will come up. 2 Chr. 36:19-21
I will also charge the clouds to rain no rain on it."

7 For the [r]vineyard of the LORD of hosts is the house of Israel, Ps. 80:8-11
And the men of Judah His delightful plant.
Thus He looked for justice, but behold, bloodshed;
For righteousness, but behold, a cry of distress.

8 Woe to those who [r]add house to house *and* join field to field, Jer. 22:13-17; Mic. 2:2
Until there is no more room,
So that you have to live alone in the midst of the land!
9 In my ears the LORD of hosts *has sworn,* "Surely, [r]many houses shall become desolate, Is. 6:11, 12
Even great and fine ones, without occupants.
10 "For [r]ten acres of vineyard will yield *only* one [1]bath *of wine,* Lev. 26:26; Is. 7:23
And a [r]homer of seed will yield *but* an [2]ephah of grain." Ezek. 45:11
11 Woe to those who rise early in the morning that they may pursue [r]strong drink;
Who stay up late in the evening that wine may inflame them! Prov. 23:29, 30
12 And their banquets are *accompanied* by lyre and

[1]I.e., Approx. 10½ gal. [2]I.e., Approx. one bu.

harp, by tambourine and flute, and by wine;
But they do not pay attention to the deeds of the LORD,
Nor do they consider the work of His hands.

13 Therefore My people go into exile for their [r]lack of knowledge; Is. 1:3; 27:11
And their [r]honorable men are famished, Is. 3:3
And their multitude is parched with thirst.
14 Therefore Sheol has enlarged its throat and opened its mouth without measure;
And Jerusalem's splendor, her multitude, her din *of revelry,* and the jubilant within her, descend *into it.*
15 So the *common* man will be humbled, and the man of *importance* abased,
The [r]eyes of the proud also will be abased. Is. 2:11
16 But the LORD of hosts will be exalted in judgment,
And the holy God will show Himself [r]holy in righteousness. Is. 8:13; 29:23
17 [r]Then the lambs will graze as in their pasture, Is. 7:25
And strangers will eat in the waste places of the [t]wealthy. *the fat*

18 Woe to those who drag [r]iniquity with the cords of falsehood, Is. 59:4-8
And sin as if with cart ropes;
19 [r]Who say, "Let Him make speed, let Him hasten His work, that we may see *it;*
And let the purpose of the Holy One of Israel draw near Ezek. 12:22; 2 Pet. 3:4
And come to pass, that we may know *it!*"
20 Woe to those who call evil good, and good evil;
Who [t]substitute darkness for light and light for darkness; *set*
Who substitute bitter for sweet, and sweet for bitter!
21 Woe to those who are [r]wise in their own eyes, Prov. 3:7
And clever in their own sight!
22 [r]Woe to those who are heroes in drinking wine,
And valiant men in mixing strong drink; Hab. 2:15
23 [r]Who justify the wicked for a bribe, Ex. 23:8; Is. 1:23
And [r]take away the [t]rights of the ones who are in the right! Ps. 94:21 • *righteousness*

24 Therefore, [r]as a tongue of fire consumes stubble,
And dry grass collapses into the flame, Is. 9:18, 19
So their root will become like rot and their blossom blow away as dust;
For they have rejected the law of the LORD of hosts,
And despised the word of the Holy One of Israel.
25 On this account the anger of the LORD has burned against His people,
And He has stretched out His hand against them and struck them down,
And the mountains quaked; and their corpses [t]lay like

refuse in the middle of the streets. *were*
For all this His anger ᵗis not spent, *has not turned away*
But His ʳhand is still stretched out. Ex. 7:19; Is. 23:11
26 He will also lift up a standard to the distant nation,
And will whistle for it from the ends of the earth;
And behold, it will ʳcome with speed swiftly. Is. 13:4, 5
27 ʳNo one in it is weary or stumbles, Joel 2:7, 8
None slumbers or sleeps;
Nor is the ʳbelt at its waist undone, Job 12:18
Nor its sandal strap broken.
28 Its arrows are sharp, and all its bows are bent;
The hoofs of its horses seem like flint, and its *chariot* wheels like a whirlwind.
29 Its ʳroaring is like a lioness, and it roars like young lions; Jer. 51:38; Zeph. 3:3
It growls as it ʳseizes the prey, Is. 10:6; 49:24, 25
And carries *it* off with ʳno one to deliver *it*. Is. 42:22
30 And it shall ʳgrowl over it in that day like the roaring of the sea. Is. 17:12; Jer. 6:23
If one ʳlooks to the land, behold, there is darkness *and* distress; Is. 8:22
Even the light is darkened by its clouds.

CHAPTER 6

IN the year of King Uzziah's
death, I saw the Lord sitting on a
throne, lofty and exalted, with the
train of His robe filling the temple.
2 Seraphim stood above Him,
ʳeach having six wings; with two
he covered his face, and with two
he covered his feet, and with
two he flew. Rev. 4:8
3 And one called out to another and said,
"Holy, Holy, Holy, is the LORD of hosts,
The whole earth is full of His glory."
4 And the foundations of the
thresholds trembled at the voice
of him who called out, while the
temple was filling with smoke.
5 Then I said,
"Woe is me, for I am ruined!
Because I am a man of ʳunclean lips, Ex. 6:12, 30
And I live among a ʳpeople of unclean lips; Is. 59:3
For my eyes have seen the King, the LORD of hosts."
6 Then one of the seraphim
flew to me, with a burning coal in
his hand which he had taken from
the ʳaltar with tongs. Rev. 8:3
7 And he ʳtouched my mouth
with it and said, "Behold, this has
touched your lips; and your iniquity is taken away, and your sin is
ᵗforgiven." Jer. 1:9 • *atoned for*
8 Then I heard the voice of the
Lord, saying, "Whom shall I send,
and who will go for Us?" Then I
said, "Here am I. Send me!"
9 And He said, "Go, and tell this people:
'Keep on ʳlistening, but do not perceive; Is. 43:8; Matt. 13:14
Keep on looking, but do not understand.'
10 "Render the hearts of this people insensitive,
Their ears dull,
And their eyes dim,
Lest they see with their eyes,
Hear with their ears,

Understand with their hearts,
And return and be healed."
11 Then I said, "Lord, how long?" And He answered,
"Until cities are devastated *and* without inhabitant,
Houses are without people,
And the land is utterly desolate,
12 "The LORD has [r]removed men far away, Deut. 28:64
And the [a]forsaken places are many in the midst of the land. *forsakenness will be great*
13 "Yet there will be a tenth portion in it,
And it will again be *subject* to burning,
Like a terebinth or an oak
Whose stump remains when it is felled.
The holy seed is its stump."

CHAPTER 7

NOW it came about in the days of [r]Ahaz, the son of Jotham, the son of Uzziah, king of Judah, that Rezin the king of Aram and Pekah the son of Remaliah, king of Israel, went up to Jerusalem to *wage* war against it, but could not conquer it. 2 Kin. 16:1; Is. 1:1
2 When it was reported to the house of David, saying, "The Arameans have camped in Ephraim," his heart and the hearts of his people shook as the trees of the forest shake [t]with the wind. *from before*
3 Then the LORD said to Isaiah, "Go out now to meet Ahaz, you and your son Shear-jashub, at the end of the conduit of the upper pool, on the highway to the fuller's field,
4 and say to him, 'Take care, and be calm, have no fear and do not be fainthearted because of these two stubs of smoldering firebrands, on account of the fierce anger of Rezin and Aram, and the son of Remaliah.
5 'Because Aram, *with* Ephraim and the son of Remaliah, has planned evil against you, saying,
6 "Let us go up against Judah and terrorize it, and make for ourselves a breach in its walls, and set up the son of Tabeel as king in the midst of it,"
7 thus says the Lord GOD, "It shall not stand nor shall it come to pass.
8 "For the head of Aram is Damascus and the head of Damascus is Rezin (now within another 65 years Ephraim will be shattered, *so that it is* no longer a people),
9 and the head of Ephraim is Samaria and the head of Samaria is the son of Remaliah. [r]If you will not believe, you surely shall not [a]last." 2 Chr. 20:20 • *be established*
10 Then the LORD spoke again to Ahaz, saying,
11 "Ask a sign for yourself from the LORD your God; make *it* deep as Sheol or high as heaven."
12 But Ahaz said, "I will not ask, nor will I test the LORD!"
13 Then he said, "Listen now, O [r]house of David! Is it too slight a thing for you to try the patience of men, that you will try the patience of my God as well? Is. 7:2
14 "Therefore the Lord Himself will give you a sign: Behold, [r]a [a]virgin will be with child and bear a son, and she will call His name [3]Immanuel. Matt. 1:23 • *maiden*

[3] I.e., God is with us

15 "He will eat curds and honey
at the time He knows *enough* to
refuse evil and choose good.
16 "For before the boy will know
enough to refuse evil and choose
good, the land whose two kings
you dread will be forsaken.
17 "The LORD will bring on you,
on your people, and on your father's house such days as have
never come since the day that [r]E-
phraim separated from Judah, the
king of Assyria." 1 Kin. 12:16
18 And it will come about in
that day, that the LORD will [r]whis-
tle for the fly that is in the [r]remot-
est part of the rivers of Egypt, and
for the bee that is in the land of
Assyria. Is. 5:26 • Is. 13:5
19 And they will all come and
settle on the steep [a]ravines, on the
[r]ledges of the cliffs, on all the thorn
bushes, and on all the [a]watering
places. *wadis* • Is. 2:19 • *pastures*
20 In that day the Lord will
shave with a razor, hired from regions beyond the Euphrates (*that
is,* with the king of Assyria), the
head and the hair of the legs; and
it will also remove the beard.
21 Now it will come about in
that day that a man may keep
alive a heifer and a pair of sheep;
22 and it will happen that because of the abundance of the
milk produced he will eat curds,
for everyone that is left within the
land will eat curds and honey.
23 And it will come about in
that day, [r]that every place where
there used to be a thousand vines,
valued at a thousand *shekels* of
silver, will become [r]briars and
thorns. Is. 5:10; 32:13, 14 • Is. 5:6
24 *People* will come there with
bows and arrows because all the
land will be briars and thorns.
25 And as for all the hills which
used to be cultivated with the hoe,
you will not go there for fear of
briars and thorns; but they will
become a place for [t]pasturing oxen
and for sheep to trample. *sending*

CHAPTER 8

THEN the LORD said to me,
"Take for yourself a large tablet
and write on it [t]in ordinary letters:
Swift is the booty, speedy is the
prey. *with the stylus of man*
2 "And I will take to Myself
faithful witnesses for testimony,
[r]Uriah the priest and Zechariah the
son of Jeberechiah." 2 Kin. 16:10, 11
3 So I approached the prophetess, and she conceived and gave
birth to a son. Then the LORD said
to me, "Name him [r][4]Maher-shalal-
hash-baz; Is. 8:1
4 for [r]before the boy knows
how to cry out 'My father' or 'My
mother,' the wealth of [r]Damascus
and the spoil of Samaria will be
carried away before the king of
Assyria." Is. 7:16 • Is. 7:8, 9
5 And again the LORD spoke to
me further, saying,
6 "Inasmuch as these people
have [r]rejected the gently
flowing waters of Shilo-
ah, Is. 1:20; 5:24; 7:9
And rejoice in Rezin and
the son of Remaliah;
7 "Now therefore, behold, the
Lord is about to bring on
them the strong and
abundant waters of the
[t]Euphrates, *River*

[4] I.e., swift is the booty, speedy is the prey

Even the king of Assyria
and all his glory;
And it will [r]rise up over all
its channels and go over
all its banks. Amos 8:8; 9:5
8 "Then it will sweep on into
Judah, it will overflow
and pass through,
It will [r]reach even to the
neck; Is. 30:28
And the spread of its wings
will fill the breadth of
your land, O Immanuel.

9 "Be broken, O peoples, and
be [a]shattered; *dismayed*
And give ear all remote
places of the earth.
Gird yourselves, yet be
shattered;
Gird yourselves, yet be
shattered.
10 "Devise [r]a plan but it will be
thwarted; Job 5:12; Is. 28:18
State a [t]proposal, but it will
not stand, *word*
For God is with us."
11 For thus the LORD spoke to
me with mighty power and instructed me not to walk in the
way of this people, saying,
12 "You are not to say, '*It is* a
conspiracy!'
In regard to all that this
people call a conspiracy,
And you are not to fear
[t]what they fear or be in
dread of *it*. *their fear*
13 "It is the [r]LORD of hosts
whom you should regard
as holy. Is. 5:16; 29:23
And He shall be your fear,
And He shall be your dread.
14 "Then He shall become a
[r]sanctuary; Is. 4:6; 25:4
But to both the houses of Israel, a stone to strike and
a rock to stumble over,
And a snare and a [r]trap for
the inhabitants of Jerusalem. Is. 24:17, 18
15 "And many [r]will stumble
over them, Is. 28:13; 59:10
Then they will fall and be
broken;
They will even be snared
and caught."
16 Bind up the testimony, seal
the law among my disciples.
17 And I will [r]wait for the LORD
who is hiding His face from the
house of Jacob; I will even look
eagerly for Him. Is. 25:9; 30:18
18 [r]Behold, I and the children
whom the LORD has given me are
for signs and wonders in Israel
from the LORD of hosts, who
dwells on Mount Zion. Heb. 2:13
19 And when they say to you,
"Consult the mediums and the
spiritists who whisper and mutter," should not a people consult
their God? *Should they consult*
the dead on behalf of the living?
20 To the [a]law and to the testimony! If they do not speak according to this word, it is because
they have no dawn. *teaching*
21 And they will pass through
[t]the land [r]hard-pressed and famished, and it will turn out that
when they are hungry, they will
be enraged and curse [a]their king
and their God as they face up-
ward. *it* • Is. 9:20, 21 • *by their king*
22 Then they will [r]look to the
earth, and behold, distress and
darkness, the gloom of anguish;
and *they will be* driven away into
darkness. Is. 5:30; 59:9

CHAPTER 9

BUT there will be no *more* gloom for her who was in anguish; in earlier times He treated the land of Zebulun and the land of Naphtali with contempt, but later on He shall make *it* glorious, by the way of the sea, on the other side of Jordan, Galilee of the Gentiles.

2 [r]The people who walk in darkness Matt. 4:16
Will see a great light;
Those who live in a dark land,
The light will shine on them.
3 [r]Thou shalt multiply the nation, Is. 26:15
Thou shalt increase [t]their gladness; *the*
They will be glad in Thy presence
As with the gladness [t]of harvest, *in*
As [t]men rejoice when they divide the spoil. *they*
4 For [r]Thou shalt break the yoke of their burden and the staff on their shoulders, Is. 10:27; 14:25
The rod of their oppressor, as at the battle of Midian.
5 For every boot of the booted warrior in the *battle* tumult,
And cloak rolled in blood, will be for burning, fuel for the fire.
6 For a child will be born to us, a son will be given to us;
And the government will [t]rest on His shoulders; *be*
And His name will be called [r]Wonderful Counselor, Mighty God, Is. 28:29
Eternal [r]Father, Prince of Peace. Is. 63:16; 64:8
7 There will be no end to the increase of *His* government or of peace,
On the throne of David and over his kingdom,
To establish it and to uphold it with [r]justice and righteousness Is. 11:4, 5
From then on and forevermore.
The zeal of the LORD of hosts will accomplish this.

8 The Lord sends a [t]message against Jacob, *word*
And it falls on Israel.
9 And all the people know *it,*
That is, Ephraim and the inhabitants of Samaria,
Asserting in pride and in arrogance of heart:
10 "The bricks have fallen down,
But we will [r]rebuild with smooth stones; Mal. 1:4
The sycamores have been cut down,
But we will replace *them* with cedars."
11 Therefore the LORD raises against them adversaries from [r]Rezin, Is. 7:1, 8
And spurs their enemies on,
12 The Arameans on the east and the [r]Philistines on the west; 2 Chr. 28:18
And they devour Israel with gaping jaws.
In *spite of* all this His anger does not turn away,
And His hand is still stretched out.

13 Yet the people [r]do not turn back to Him who struck them, Jer. 5:3; Hos. 7:10

Nor do they [r]seek the LORD of hosts. Is. 31:1; Hos. 3:5
14 So the LORD cuts off head and tail from Israel,
Both palm branch and bulrush in a single day.
15 The head is [r]the elder and honorable man, Is. 3:2, 3
And the prophet who teaches falsehood is the tail.
16 [r]For those who guide this people are leading *them* astray; Is. 3:12; Matt. 15:14
And those who are guided by them are [a]brought to confusion. *swallowed up*
17 Therefore the Lord does [r]not take pleasure in their young men, Amos 4:10; 8:13
[r]Nor does He have pity on their [a]orphans or their widows; Is. 27:11 • *fatherless*
For every one of them is godless and an evildoer,
And every [r]mouth is speaking foolishness. Matt. 12:34
In *spite of* all this His anger does not turn away,
And His hand is still stretched out.

18 [r]For wickedness burns like a fire; Ps. 83:14; Is. 1:7
It consumes briars and thorns;
It even sets the thickets of the forest aflame,
And they roll upward in a column of smoke.
19 By the [r]fury of the LORD of hosts the land is burned up, Is. 10:6; 13:9, 13; 42:25
And the [r]people are like fuel for the fire; Is. 1:31; 24:6
No man spares his brother.
20 And [t]they slice off *what is* on the right hand but *still* are hungry, *he slices*
And [t]they eat *what is* on the left hand but they are not satisfied; *he eats*
Each of them eats the [r]flesh of his own arm. Is. 49:26
21 Manasseh *devours* Ephraim, and Ephraim Manasseh,
[r]*And* together they are against Judah. Is. 11:13
In *spite of* all this His anger does not turn away,
And His hand is still stretched out.

CHAPTER 10

WOE to those who [r]enact evil statutes, Is. 29:21; 59:4, 13
And to those who constantly record unjust decisions,
2 So as to [t]deprive the needy of justice, *turn aside from*
And rob the poor of My people of *their* rights,
In order [r]that widows may be their spoil, Is. 1:23; 3:14
And that they may plunder the [a]orphans. *fatherless*
3 Now what will you do in the day of punishment,
And in the devastation which will come from afar?
[r]To whom will you flee for help? Is. 20:6; 30:5, 7
And where will you leave your wealth?
4 Nothing *remains* but to crouch [t]among the [r]captives *under* • Is. 24:22
Or fall among the slain.
In *spite of* all this His anger does not turn away,

And His hand is still stretched out.

5 Woe to [r]Assyria, the rod of My anger Is. 7:17; 8:7
And the staff in whose hands is My indignation,
6 I send it against a [r]godless nation Is. 9:17
And commission it against the people of My fury
To capture booty and [r]to seize plunder, Is. 5:29
And to trample them down like mud in the streets.
7 Yet it does not so intend
Nor does [t]it plan so in its heart, *its heart so plan*
But rather it is [t]its purpose to destroy, *in its heart*
And to cut off many nations.
8 For it says, "Are not my princes all kings?
9 "Is not [r]Calno like Carchemish, Gen. 10:10; Amos 6:2
Or Hamath like Arpad,
Or Samaria like Damascus?
10 "As my hand has reached to the [r]kingdoms of the idols, 2 Kin. 19:17, 18
Whose graven images *were* greater than those of Jerusalem and Samaria,
11 Shall I not [t]do to Jerusalem and her images *do thus*
Just as I have done to Samaria and her idols?"
12 So it will be that when the
Lord has completed all His work
on Mount Zion and on Jerusalem,
He will say, "I will [t]punish the fruit
of the arrogant heart of the king
of Assyria and the pomp of his
haughtiness." *visit*
13 For he has said,
"By the power of my hand and by my wisdom I did *this,*
For I have understanding;
And I removed the boundaries of the peoples,
And plundered their treasures,
And like a mighty man I brought down *their* inhabitants,
14 And my hand reached to the riches of the peoples like a nest,
And as one gathers abandoned eggs, I gathered all the earth;
And there was not one that flapped its wing or opened *its* beak or chirped."

15 Is the [r]axe to boast itself over the one who chops with it? Jer. 51:20
Is the saw to exalt itself over the one who wields it?
That would be like a club wielding those who lift it,
Or like [r]a rod lifting *him who* is not wood. Is. 10:5
16 Therefore the Lord, the GOD of hosts, will send a [r]wasting disease among his stout warriors; Ps. 106:15
And under his [r]glory a fire will be kindled like a burning flame. Is. 8:7
17 And the light of Israel will become a fire and his Holy One a flame,
And it will burn and devour his thorns and his briars in a single day.
18 And He will [r]destroy the glory of his forest and of his

fruitful garden, both soul
and body; Is. 10:33, 34
And it will be as when a sick
man wastes away.
19 And the [r]rest of the trees of
his forest will be so small
in number Is. 21:17
That a child could write them
down.

20 Now it will come about in that day that the remnant of Israel, and those of the house of Jacob who have escaped, will never again rely on the one who struck them, but will truly rely on the LORD, the Holy One of Israel.

21 A [r]remnant will return, the
remnant of Jacob, to the
mighty God. Is. 7:3
22 For [r]though your people, O Israel,
may be like the sand
of the sea, Rom. 9:27, 28
Only a remnant within them
will return;
A [r]destruction is determined,
overflowing with righteousness.
Is. 28:22
23 For a complete destruction,
one that is decreed, [r]the Lord GOD
of hosts will execute in the midst
of the whole land. Is. 28:22; Dan. 9:27

24 Therefore thus says the Lord GOD of hosts, "O My people who dwell in Zion, do not fear the Assyrian who strikes you with the rod and lifts up his staff against you, the way Egypt *did.*

25 "For in a very little while My indignation *against you* will be spent, and My anger *will be directed* to their destruction."

26 And the LORD of hosts will arouse a scourge against him like the slaughter of Midian at the rock of Oreb; and His staff will be over the sea, and He will lift it up the way *He did* in Egypt.

27 So it will be in that day, that his burden will be removed from your shoulders and his yoke from your neck, and the yoke will be broken because of fatness.

28 He has come against Aiath,
He has passed through [r]Migron;
1 Sam. 14:2
At [r]Michmash he deposited
his baggage. 1 Sam. 13:2, 5
29 They have gone through [r]the
pass, saying, 1 Sam. 13:23
[r]"Geba will be our lodging
place." Josh. 21:17
[r]Ramah is terrified, and Gibeah
of Saul has fled
away. Josh. 18:25; 1 Sam. 7:17
30 Cry aloud with your voice, O
daughter of Gallim!
Pay attention, Laishah and
wretched Anathoth!
31 Madmenah has fled.
The inhabitants of Gebim
have sought refuge.
32 Yet today he will halt at Nob;
He shakes his fist at the
mountain of the daughter
of Zion, the hill of Jerusalem.

33 Behold, the Lord, the GOD of
hosts, will lop off the
boughs with a terrible
crash;
Those also who are [r]tall in
stature will be cut down,
And those who are lofty will
be abased. Ezek. 31:3
34 And He will cut down the
thickets of the forest with
an iron *axe,*
And Lebanon will fall[a] by the
Mighty One. ***as a mighty one***

CHAPTER 11

THEN a shoot will spring from the stem of Jesse,
And a branch from [r]his roots will bear fruit. Rev. 5:5
2 And the Spirit of the LORD will rest on Him,
The spirit of [r]wisdom and understanding, John 16:13
The spirit of counsel and [r]strength, 2 Tim. 1:7
The spirit of knowledge and the fear of the LORD.
3 And He will delight in the fear of the LORD,
And He will not judge by what His eyes see,
Nor make a decision by what His ears hear;
4 But with righteousness He will judge the poor,
And decide with fairness for the afflicted of the earth;
And He will strike the earth with the [r]rod of His mouth, Ps. 2:9; Is. 49:2
And with the [r]breath of His lips He will slay the wicked. Is. 30:28, 33
5 Also righteousness will be the belt about His loins,
And [r]faithfulness the belt about His waist. Is. 25:1

6 And the [r]wolf will dwell with the lamb, Is. 65:25
And the leopard will lie down with the kid,
And the calf and the young lion [5]and the fatling together;
And a little boy will lead them.
7 Also the cow and the bear will graze;
Their young will lie down together;
And the [r]lion will eat straw like the ox. Is. 65:25
8 And the nursing child will play by the hole of the cobra,
And the weaned child will put his hand on the viper's den.
9 They will not hurt or destroy in all My holy mountain,
For the [r]earth will be full of the knowledge of the LORD Ps. 98:2, 3
As the waters cover the sea.

10 Then it will come about in that day
That the nations will resort to the root of Jesse,
Who will stand as a signal for the peoples;
And His [r]resting place will be [t]glorious. Is. 14:3; 28:12 • *glory*

11 Then it will happen on that day that the Lord
Will again recover the second time with His hand
The remnant of His people, who will remain,
From [r]Assyria, Egypt, Pathros, Cush, Elam, Shinar, Hamath, Is. 19:23-25
And from the [a]islands of the sea. *coastlands*
12 And He will lift up a standard for the nations,
And will assemble the banished ones of Israel,
And will gather the dispersed of Judah
From the four corners of the earth.

[5]Some versions read *will feed together*

13 Then the [r]jealousy of Ephraim will depart, Is. 9:21
And those who harass Judah will be cut off;
Ephraim will not be jealous of Judah,
And Judah will not harass Ephraim.
14 And they will swoop down on the slopes of the Philistines on the west;
Together they will plunder the sons of the east;
They will possess [r]Edom and Moab; Is. 63:1; Dan. 11:41
And the sons of Ammon will be subject to them.
15 And the LORD will [r]utterly destroy Is. 43:16; 44:27
The tongue of the Sea of Egypt;
And He will wave His hand over the [r]River Is. 7:20
With His scorching wind;
And He will strike it into seven streams,
And make *men* walk over [t]dry-shod. *in sandals*
16 And there will be a [r]highway from Assyria Is. 19:23
For the remnant of His people who will be left,
Just as there was for Israel
In the day that they came up out of the land of Egypt.

CHAPTER 12

THEN you will say on that day,
"I [r]will give thanks to Thee, O LORD; Ps. 9:1; Is. 25:1
For [r]although Thou wast angry with me, Ps. 30:5
Thine anger is turned away,
And Thou dost comfort me.
2 "Behold, God is my salvation,
I will trust and not be afraid;
For the LORD GOD is my strength and song,
And He has become my salvation."
3 Therefore you will joyously [r]draw water John 4:10
From the [r]springs of salvation. Is. 41:18; Jer. 2:13
4 And in that day you will say,
"Give [r]thanks to the LORD, call on His name. Ps. 105:1
Make known His deeds among the peoples;
Make *them* remember that His name is exalted."
5 Praise the LORD in song, for He has done [a]excellent things; *gloriously*
Let this be known throughout the earth.
6 Cry aloud and shout for joy, O inhabitant of Zion,
For great in your midst is the Holy One of Israel.

CHAPTER 13

THE [a]oracle [r] concerning Babylon which Isaiah the son of Amoz saw. *burden of* • Is. 14:28; 15:1
2 [r]Lift up a standard on the [6]bare hill, Is. 5:26; Jer. 50:2
Raise your voice to them,
Wave the hand that they may [r]enter the doors of the nobles. Is. 45:1-3
3 I have commanded My consecrated ones,
I have even called My [r]mighty warriors, Joel 3:11
My proudly exulting ones,
To *execute* My anger.
4 A [r]sound of tumult on the mountains, Joel 3:14

[6]Or, *wind-swept mountain*

Like that of many people!
A sound of the uproar of kingdoms,
Of nations gathered together!
The LORD of hosts is mustering the army for battle.
5 They are coming from a far country
From the farthest horizons,
The LORD and His instruments of indignation,
To destroy the whole land.
6 Wail, for the [r]day of the LORD is near! Is. 2:12; 10:3
It will come as destruction from the Almighty.
7 Therefore [r]all hands will fall limp, Ezek. 7:17
And every man's [r]heart will melt. Is. 19:1; Ezek. 21:7
8 And they will be [r]terrified,
Pains and anguish will take hold of *them*; Is. 21:3
They will [r]writhe like a woman in labor, Is. 26:17
They will look at one another in astonishment,
Their faces aflame.
9 Behold, [r]the day of the LORD is coming, Is. 13:6
Cruel, with fury and burning anger,
To make the land a desolation;
And He will exterminate its sinners from it.
10 For the stars of heaven and their constellations
Will not flash forth their light;
The [r]sun will be dark when it rises, Is. 24:23; 50:3
And the moon will not shed its light.
11 Thus I will [r]punish the world for its evil, Is. 26:21
And the [r]wicked for their iniquity; Is. 3:11; 11:4; 14:5
I will also put an end to the arrogance of the proud,
And abase the haughtiness of the [a]ruthless. *tyrants, despots*
12 I will make mortal man scarcer than pure gold,
And mankind than the [r]gold of Ophir. 1 Kin. 9:28
13 Therefore I shall make the [r]heavens tremble, Is. 34:4
And [r]the earth will be shaken from its place Ps. 18:7
At the fury of the LORD of hosts
In [r]the day of His burning anger. Lam. 1:12
14 And it will be that like a hunted gazelle,
Or like [r]sheep with none to gather *them*, 1 Kin. 22:17
They will each turn to his own people,
And each one flee to his own land.
15 Anyone who is found will be [r]thrust through, Is. 14:19
And anyone who is captured will fall by the sword.
16 Their [r]little ones also will be dashed to pieces
Before their eyes; Ps. 137:8, 9
Their houses will be plundered
And their wives ravished.

17 Behold, I am going to stir up the Medes against them,
Who will not value silver or take pleasure in gold,
18 And *their* bows will mow down the young men,

They will not even have compassion on the fruit of the womb,
Nor will their [r]eye pity [t]children. Ezek. 9:5, 10 • *sons*
19 And Babylon, the beauty of kingdoms, the glory of the Chaldeans' pride,
Will be as when God [r]overthrew Sodom and Gomorrah. Gen. 19:24
20 It will [r]never be inhabited or lived in from generation to generation; Is. 14:23
Nor will the [r]Arab pitch *his* tent there, 2 Chr. 17:11
Nor will shepherds make *their flocks* lie down there.
21 But [r]desert creatures will lie down there, Is. 34:11-15
And their houses will be full of [a]owls, *howling creatures*
Ostriches also will live there, and [a]shaggy goats will frolic there. *goat demons*
22 And hyenas will howl in their fortified towers
And jackals in their luxurious [r]palaces. Is. 25:2; 32:14
Her *fateful* time also [t]will soon come *is near to come*
And her days will not be prolonged.

CHAPTER 14

WHEN the LORD will [r]have compassion on Jacob, and again choose Israel, and settle them in their own land, then strangers will join them and attach themselves to the house of Jacob. Ps. 102:13
2 And the peoples will take them along and bring them to their place, and the [r]house of Israel will possess them as an inheritance in the land of the LORD as male servants and female servants; and they will take their captors captive, and will rule over their oppressors. Is. 45:14; 49:23
3 And it will be in the day when the LORD gives you [r]rest from your pain and turmoil and harsh service in which you have been enslaved, Ezra 9:8, 9
4 that you will [r]take up this [a]taunt against the king of Babylon, and say, Hab. 2:6 • *proverb*
"How [r]the oppressor has ceased, Is. 9:4; 16:4; 49:26
And how fury has ceased!
5 "The LORD has broken the staff of the wicked,
The scepter of rulers
6 [r]Which used to strike the peoples in fury with unceasing strokes, Is. 10:14; 47:6
Which subdued the nations in anger with unrestrained persecution.
7 "The whole earth is at rest *and* is quiet;
They [r]break forth into shouts of joy. Ps. 47:1-3; 98:1-9
8 "Even the [r]cypress trees rejoice over you, *and* the cedars of Lebanon, *saying*, Is. 55:12; Ezek. 31:16
'Since you were laid low, no *tree* cutter comes up against us.'
9 "Sheol from beneath is excited over you to meet you when you come;
It arouses for you the [a]spirits of the dead, all the leaders of the earth; *shades*
It raises all the kings of the nations from their thrones.

10 "They[r] will all respond and say
to you, Ezek. 32:21
'Even you have been made
weak as we,
You have become like *us.*
11 'Your[r] pomp *and* the music of
your harps Is. 5:14
Have been brought down to
Sheol;
Maggots are spread out *as
your bed* beneath you,
And worms are your cover-
ing.'
12 "How you have [r]fallen from
heaven, Is. 34:4; Luke 10:18
O [r]star of the morning, son of
the dawn! 2 Pet. 1:19
You have been cut down to
the earth,
You who have weakened the
nations!
13 "But you said in your heart,
'I will ascend to heaven;
I will raise my throne above
the stars of God,
And I will sit on the mount of
assembly
In the recesses of the north.
14 'I will ascend above the
heights of the clouds;
[r]I will make myself like the
Most High.' Is. 47:8
15 "Nevertheless you will be
thrust down to Sheol,
To the recesses of the pit.
16 "Those who see you will gaze
at you,
They will ponder over you,
saying,
'Is this the man who made the
earth tremble,
Who shook kingdoms,
17 Who made the world like a
wilderness
And overthrew its cities,
Who did not allow his prisoners to go home?'
18 "All the kings of the nations
lie in glory,
Each in his own [t]tomb. *house*
19 "But you have been [r]cast out
of your tomb Is. 22:16-18
Like a rejected branch,
Clothed with the slain who
are pierced with a sword,
Who go down to the stones
of the [r]pit, Jer. 41:7, 9
Like a trampled corpse.
20 "You will not be united with
them in burial,
Because you have ruined
your country,
You have slain your people.
May the [r]offspring of evildoers not be mentioned
forever. Job 18:16, 19
21 "Prepare for his sons a place
of slaughter
Because of the [r]iniquity of
their fathers. Ex. 20:5
They must not arise and take
possession of the earth
And fill the face of the world
with cities."
22 "And I will rise up against
them," declares the LORD of hosts,
"and will cut off from Babylon
name and survivors, offspring and
posterity," declares the LORD.
23 "I will also make it a possession for the hedgehog, and
swamps of water, and I will sweep
it with the broom of destruction,"
declares the LORD of hosts.
24 The LORD of hosts has sworn
saying, "Surely, [r]just as I have intended so it has happened, and
just as I have planned so it will
stand, Job 23:13; Is. 46:11; 55:8, 9
25 to break Assyria in My land,

and I will trample him on My mountains. Then his yoke will be removed from them, and his burden removed from their shoulder.
26 "This is the plan devised against the whole earth; and this is the hand that is stretched out against all the nations.
27 "For the LORD of hosts has planned, and who can frustrate *it*? And as for His stretched-out hand, who can turn it back?"
28 In the year that King Ahaz died this [a]oracle came: *burden*
29 "Do not rejoice, O Philistia, all of you, Is. 2:6; 11:14
Because the rod that [r]struck you is broken; 2 Chr. 26:6
For from the serpent's root a viper will come out,
And its fruit will be a [r]flying serpent. Is. 30:6
30 "And those who are most [r]helpless will eat,
And the needy will lie down in security; Is. 3:14, 15
I will [t]destroy your root with famine, *put to death*
And it will kill off your survivors.
31 "Wail, O gate; cry, O city;
[a]Melt away, O Philistia, all of you; *Become demoralized*
For smoke comes from the [r]north, Jer. 1:14
And [r]there is no straggler in his ranks. Is. 34:16
32 "How then will one answer the [r]messengers of the nation? Is. 37:9
That [r]the LORD has founded Zion, Ps. 87:1, 5; 102:16
And the afflicted of His people will seek refuge in it."

CHAPTER 15

THE oracle concerning Moab.
Surely in a night Ar of Moab is devastated *and* ruined;
Surely in a night Kir of Moab is devastated *and* ruined.
2 They have gone up to the [t]temple and *to* [r]Dibon, *even* to the high places to weep. *house* • Jer. 48:18, 22
Moab wails over Nebo and Medeba;
Everyone's head is bald and every beard is cut off.
3 In their streets they have girded themselves with [r]sackcloth; Jon. 3:6-8
[r]On their housetops and in their squares Jer. 48:38
Everyone is wailing, [r]dissolved in tears. Is. 22:4
4 [r]Heshbon and Elealeh also cry out, Num. 21:28; 32:3
Their voice is heard all the way to Jahaz;
Therefore the armed men of Moab cry aloud;
His soul trembles within him.
5 My heart cries out for Moab;
His fugitives are as far as [r]Zoar *and* Eglath-shelishiyah, Jer. 48:34
For they go up the [r]ascent of Luhith weeping; Jer. 48:5
Surely on the road to Horonaim they raise a cry of distress over *their* ruin.
6 For the waters of Nimrim are [t]desolate. *desolations*
Surely the grass is withered, the tender grass died out,
There is no green thing.
7 Therefore the [r]abundance *which* they have acquired and stored up Is. 30:6

They carry off over the brook of [a]Arabim. *the poplars*
8 For the cry of distress has gone around the territory of Moab,
Its wail *goes* as far as Eglaim and its wailing even to Beer-elim.
9 For the waters of Dimon are full of blood;
Surely I will bring added *woes* upon Dimon,
A lion upon the fugitives of Moab and upon the remnant of the land.

CHAPTER 16

[r]SEND the *tribute* lamb to the ruler of the land, 2 Kin. 3:4
From Sela by way of the wilderness to the mountain of the daughter of Zion.
2 Then, like fleeing birds *or* scattered nestlings,
The daughters of [r]Moab will be at the fords of the Arnon. Jer. 48:20, 46
3 "Give[t] *us* advice, make a decision; *Bring*
[t]Cast your shadow like night at high noon; *Set*
[r]Hide the outcasts, do not betray the fugitive. 1 Kin. 18:4
4 "Let the outcasts of Moab stay with you;
Be a hiding place to them from the destroyer."
For the extortioner has come to an end, destruction has ceased,
[r]Oppressors have completely *disappeared* from the land. Is. 9:4; 14:4; 49:26
5 A throne will even be established in lovingkindness,
And a judge will sit on it in faithfulness in the tent of [r]David; Is. 9:6, 7
Moreover, he will seek justice
And be prompt in righteousness.
6 [r]We have heard of the pride of Moab, an excessive pride; Jer. 48:29; Amos 2:1
Even of his arrogance, pride, and fury;
His idle boasts are false.
7 Therefore Moab shall wail; everyone of Moab shall wail.
You shall moan for the raisin cakes of Kir-hareseth
As those who are utterly stricken.
8 For the fields of Heshbon have withered, the vines of Sibmah *as well*;
The lords of the nations have trampled down its choice clusters
Which reached as far as Jazer *and* wandered to the deserts;
[r]Its tendrils spread themselves out *and* passed over the sea. Jer. 48:32
9 Therefore I will [r]weep bitterly for Jazer, for the vine of Sibmah; Jer. 48:32
I will drench you with my tears, O [r]Heshbon and Elealeh; Is. 15:4
For the shouting over your summer fruits and your harvest has fallen away.
10 And [r]gladness and joy are taken away from the fruitful field; Is. 24:8
In the vineyards also there

will be no cries of joy or
jubilant shouting,
No [r]treader treads out wine in
the presses, Job 24:11
For I have made the shouting
to cease.
11 Therefore my heart intones
like a harp for Moab,
And my [t]inward feelings for
Kir-hareseth. *inward part*
12 So it will come about when
Moab presents himself,
When he wearies himself
upon *his* [r]high place,
And comes to his sanctuary
to pray, Is. 15:2
That he will not prevail.

13 This is the word which the LORD spoke earlier concerning Moab.

14 But now the LORD speaks, saying, "Within three years, as [r]a hired man would count them, the glory of Moab will be degraded along with all *his* great population, and *his* remnant will be very small *and* impotent." Job 7:1; 14:6

CHAPTER 17

THE [a]oracle[r] concerning Damascus. *burden of* • Is. 13:1

"Behold, Damascus is about
to be [r]removed from
being a city, Is. 7:16; 8:4
And it will become a [r]fallen
ruin. Is. 25:2; Jer. 49:2
2 "The cities of [r]Aroer are forsaken; Num. 32:34
They will be for [r]flocks to lie
down in, Is. 7:21, 22
And there will be [r]no one to
frighten *them*. Mic. 4:4
3 "The fortified city will disappear from Ephraim,
And [a]sovereignty from Damascus *royal power, kingdom*
And the remnant of Aram;
They will be like the [r]glory of
the sons of Israel," Is. 17:4
Declares the LORD of hosts.

4 Now it will come about in
that day that the glory of
Jacob will [t]fade, *become thin*
And the fatness of his flesh
will become lean.
5 It will be [r]even like the reaper
gathering the standing
grain, Is. 17:11; Jer. 51:33
As his arm harvests the ears,
Or it will be like one gleaning
ears of grain
In the valley of Rephaim.
6 Yet [r]gleanings will be left in it
like the [t]shaking of an olive tree, Deut. 4:27 • *striking*
Two *or* three olives on the
topmost bough,
Four *or* five on the branches
of a fruitful tree,
Declares the LORD, the God
of Israel.
7 In that day man will have regard for his Maker,
And his eyes will look to the
Holy One of Israel.
8 And he will not have regard
for the [r]altars, the work of
his hands, 2 Chr. 34:7
Nor will he look to that
which his [r]fingers have
made, Is. 2:8, 20; 30:22; 31:7
Even the [7]Asherim and [a]incense stands. *sun pillars*
9 In that day their strong cities
will be like forsaken
places in the forest,
Or like [a]branches which they
abandoned before the
sons of Israel; *the treetop*

[7]I.e., wooden symbols of a female deity

And [t]the land will be a desolation. *it*
10 For you have forgotten the God of your salvation
And have not remembered the [r]rock of your refuge.
Therefore you plant delightful plants Deut. 32:4, 18, 31
And set them with vine slips of a strange *god*.
11 In the day that you plant *it* you carefully fence *it* in,
And in the [r]morning you bring your seed to blossom; Ps. 90:6
But the harvest will [r]be a heap Job 4:8; Hos. 8:7
In a day of sickliness and incurable pain.

12 Alas, the uproar of many peoples
[r]Who roar like the roaring of the seas, Is. 5:30; Jer. 6:23
And the rumbling of nations
Who rush on like the rumbling of mighty waters!
13 The [r]nations rumble on like the rumbling of many waters, Is. 33:3
But He will rebuke them and they will flee far away,
And be chased [r]like chaff in the mountains before the wind, Ps. 1:4; 83:13
Or like whirling dust before a gale.
14 At evening time, behold, *there is* terror!
Before morning [r]they are no more. 2 Kin. 19:35; Is. 41:12
Such *will be* the portion of those who plunder us,
And the lot of those who pillage us.

CHAPTER 18

ALAS, oh land of whirring wings
Which lies beyond the rivers of [8]Cush[r] Zeph. 2:12; 3:10
2 Which sends envoys by the sea,
Even in papyrus vessels on the surface of the waters.
Go, swift messengers, to a nation tall and smooth,
To a people feared [t]far and wide, *from it and beyond*
A powerful and oppressive nation
Whose land the rivers divide.
3 [r]All you inhabitants of the world and dwellers on earth, Ps. 49:1; Mic. 1:2
As soon as a standard is raised on the mountains,
[r]you will see *it*, Is. 26:11
And as soon as the trumpet is blown, you will hear *it*.
4 For thus the LORD has told me,
"I will look [t]from My [r]dwelling place quietly *in* • Is. 26:21
Like dazzling heat in the [t]sunshine[r], *light* • 2 Sam. 23:4
Like a cloud of [r]dew in the heat of harvest." Is. 26:19
5 For before the harvest, as soon as the bud blossoms
And the flower becomes a ripening grape,
Then He will cut off the sprigs with pruning knives
And remove *and* cut away the spreading branches.
6 They will be left together for mountain birds [r]of prey,
And for the beasts of the earth; Is. 46:11; 56:9

[8]Or, *Ethiopia*

And the birds of prey will spend the summer *feeding* on them,
And all the beasts of the earth will spend harvest time on them.
7 At that time a gift of homage will be brought to the LORD of hosts
From a people [t]tall and smooth, *drawn out*
Even from a people feared far and wide,
A powerful and oppressive nation,
Whose land the rivers divide—
To the [r]place of the name of the LORD of hosts, *even* Mount Zion. Zech. 14:16, 17

CHAPTER 19

THE oracle concerning Egypt.
Behold, the LORD is riding on a swift cloud, and is about to come to Egypt;
The idols of Egypt will tremble at His presence,
And the [r]heart of the Egyptians will melt within them. Josh. 2:11; Is. 13:7
2 "So I will incite Egyptians against Egyptians;
And they will [r]each fight against his brother, and each against his neighbor, Judg. 7:22; 1 Sam. 14:20
City against city, *and* kingdom against kingdom.
3 "Then the spirit of the Egyptians will be demoralized within them;
And I will confound their strategy,
So that [r]they will resort to idols and ghosts of the dead, Is. 8:19; Dan. 2:2
And to [a]mediums and spiritists. *ghosts and spirits*
4 "Moreover, I will deliver the Egyptians into the hand of a cruel master,
And a mighty king will rule over them," declares the Lord GOD of hosts.

5 [r]And the waters from the sea will dry up,
And the river will be parched and dry. Is. 50:2; Jer. 51:36
6 And the [t]canals[r] will emit a stench, *rivers* • Ex. 7:18
The streams of Egypt will thin out and dry up;
[r]The reeds and rushes will rot away. Ex. 2:3; Job 8:11
7 The bulrushes by the Nile, by the edge of the Nile
And all the sown fields by the Nile
Will become dry, be driven away, and be no more.
8 And the [r]fishermen will lament, Ezek. 47:10; Hab. 1:15
And all those who cast a line into the Nile will mourn,
And those who spread nets on the waters will [a]pine away. *languish*
9 Moreover, the manufacturers of linen made from combed flax
And the weavers of white [r]cloth will be utterly dejected. Prov. 7:16; Ezek. 27:7
10 And the [r]pillars *of Egypt* will be crushed; Ps. 11:3
All the hired laborers will be grieved in soul.

11 The princes of [a]Zoan are mere
fools; *Tanis*
The advice of Pharaoh's wisest advisers has become
[a]stupid. *brutish*
How can you *men* say to
Pharaoh,
"I am a son of the wise, a son
of ancient kings"?
12 Well then, where are your
wise men?
Please let them tell you,
And let them understand
what the LORD of hosts
Has purposed against Egypt.
13 The princes of [a]Zoan have
acted foolishly, *Tanis*
The princes of [r]Memphis are
deluded; Jer. 2:16; 46:14, 19
Those who are the cornerstone of her tribes
Have led Egypt astray.
14 The LORD has mixed within
her a spirit of distortion;
They have led Egypt astray
in all that it does,
As a [r]drunken man staggers
in his vomit. Is. 28:7
15 And there will be no work for
Egypt
[r]Which *its* head or tail, *its*
palm branch or bulrush,
may do. Is. 9:14, 15

16 In that day the Egyptians will become like women, and they will tremble and be in dread because of the waving of the hand of the LORD of hosts, which He is going to wave over them.

17 And the land of Judah will become a [a]terror to Egypt; everyone to whom it is mentioned will be in dread of it, because of the [r]purpose of the LORD of hosts which He is purposing against them. *cause of shame* • Is. 14:24

18 In that day five cities in the land of Egypt will be speaking the language of Canaan and [r]swearing *allegiance* to the LORD of hosts; one will be called the City of [9]Destruction. Is. 45:23; 65:16

19 In that day there will be an [r]altar to the LORD in the midst of the land of Egypt, and a pillar to the LORD near its border. Is. 56:7

20 And it will become a sign and a witness to the LORD of hosts in the land of Egypt; for they will cry to the LORD because of oppressors, and He will send them a Savior and a [t]Champion, and He will deliver them. *Mighty One*

21 Thus the LORD will make Himself known to Egypt, and the Egyptians will know the LORD in that day. They will even worship with [r]sacrifice and offering, and will make a vow to the LORD and perform it. Is. 56:7; 60:7

22 And the LORD will strike Egypt, striking but [r]healing; so they will return to the LORD, and He will respond to them and will heal them. Deut. 32:39; Is. 30:26; 57:18

23 In that day there will be a [r]highway from Egypt to Assyria, and the Assyrians will come into Egypt and the Egyptians into Assyria, and the Egyptians will worship with the Assyrians. Is. 11:16

24 In that day Israel will be the third *party* with Egypt and Assyria, a blessing in the midst of the earth,

25 whom the LORD of hosts has blessed, saying, "Blessed is [r]Egypt My people, and Assyria [r]the work of My hands, and Israel My inheritance." Is. 45:14 • Ps. 100:3

[9]Some ancient mss. and versions read *the Sun*

CHAPTER 20

IN the year that the commander
came to [r]Ashdod, when Sargon the
king of Assyria sent him and he
fought against Ashdod and captured it, 1 Sam. 5:1
2 at that time the LORD spoke
through Isaiah the son of Amoz,
saying, "Go and loosen the sackcloth from your hips, and take
your shoes off your feet." And he
did so, going naked and barefoot.
3 And the LORD said, "Even as
My servant Isaiah has gone naked
and barefoot three years as a [r]sign
and token against Egypt and
[r]Cush, Is. 8:18 • Is. 37:9; 43:3
4 so the [r]king of Assyria will
lead away the captives of Egypt
and the exiles of Cush, young and
old, naked and barefoot with but-
tocks uncovered, to the [t]shame of
Egypt. Is. 19:4 • *nakedness*
5 "Then they shall be dismayed
and ashamed because of Cush
their hope and Egypt their boast.
6 "So the inhabitants of this
coastland will say in that day, 'Behold, such is our hope, where we
fled [r]for help to be delivered from
the king of Assyria; and we, how
shall we escape?' " Is. 10:3; 30:7

CHAPTER 21

THE [a]oracle concerning the [10]wil-
derness of the sea. *burden of*
As [r]windstorms in the Negev
sweep on, Zech. 9:14
It comes from the wilder-
ness, from a terrifying
land.
2 A [r]harsh vision has been
shown to me; Ps. 60:3
The [r]treacherous one still
deals treacherously, *and*
the destroyer still de-
stroys. Is. 24:16; 33:1
Go up, [r]Elam, lay siege, Media; Is. 22:6; Jer. 49:34
I have made an end of all the
groaning she has caused.
3 For this reason my [r]loins are
full of anguish; Is. 13:8
Pains have seized me like the
pains of a [r]woman in labor. Ps. 48:6; Is. 13:8
I am so bewildered I cannot
hear, so terrified I cannot
see.
4 My mind reels, [t]horror over-
whelms me; *shuddering*
The twilight I longed for has
been [r]turned for me into
trembling. Deut. 28:67
5 They set the table, they
[11]spread out the cloth,
they eat, they drink;
"Rise up, captains, oil the
shields,"
6 For thus the Lord says to me,
"Go, station the lookout, let
him report what he sees.
7 "When he sees [r]riders, horsemen in pairs, Is. 21:9
A train of donkeys, a train of
camels,
Let him pay close attention,
very close attention."
8 Then the lookout called,
"O [r] Lord, I stand continually
by day on the watch-
tower, Hab. 2:1
And I am stationed every
night at my guard post.
9 "Now behold, here comes a
troop of riders, horsemen
in pairs."

[10]Or, *sandy wastes, sea country*

[11]Or, *spread out the rugs;* or possibly, *arranged the seating*

And one answered and said,
"Fallen, fallen is Babylon;
And all the [r]images of her
gods are shattered on the
ground." Is. 46:1
10 O my [r]threshed *people,* and
my [t]afflicted of the threshing floor! Mic. 4:13 • *son*
What I have heard from the
LORD of hosts,
The God of Israel, I make
known to you.

11 The [a]oracle concerning [r]Edom.
One keeps calling to me from
Seir, *burden* • Gen. 25:14
"Watchman, [12]how far gone is
the night?
Watchman, [12]how far gone is
the night?"
12 The watchman says,
"Morning comes but also
night.
If you would inquire, inquire;
Come back again."

13 The oracle about Arabia.
In the thickets of Arabia you
must spend the night,
O caravans of Dedanites.
14 Bring water [t]for the thirsty,
O inhabitants of the land of
Tema, *to meet*
Meet the fugitive with bread.
15 For they have [r]fled from the
swords, Is. 13:14, 15; 17:13
From the drawn sword, and
from the bent bow,
And from the press of battle.
16 For thus the Lord said to me,
"In a year, as [t]a hired man would
count it, all the splendor of Kedar
will terminate; *the years of a hireling*
17 and the [r]remainder of the
number of bowmen, the mighty
men of the sons of Kedar, will be
few; for the LORD God of Israel
has [r]spoken." Is. 10:19 • Zech. 1:6

[12] Lit., *what* is the time *of the night?*

CHAPTER 22

THE [a]oracle concerning the [r]valley
of vision. *burden of* • Ps. 125:2
What is the matter with you
now, that you have all
gone up to the [r]house-
tops? Is. 15:3
2 You who were full of noise,
You boisterous town, you [r]ex-
ultant city; Is. 23:7
Your slain were [r]not slain
with the sword, Lam. 2:20
Nor did they die in battle.
3 [r]All your rulers have fled together, Is. 21:15
And have been captured
without the bow;
All of you who were found
were taken captive to-
gether,
Though they had fled far
away.
4 Therefore I say, "Turn your
eyes away from me,
Let me weep bitterly,
Do not try to comfort me
concerning the destruc-
tion of the daughter of
my people."
5 For the Lord GOD of hosts
has a day of panic, subju-
gation, and confusion
In the valley of vision,
A breaking down of walls
And a crying [a]to the mountain. *against*
6 And Elam took up the quiver
With the chariots, infantry,
and horsemen;
And [r]Kir uncovered the
shield. 2 Kin. 16:9

7 Then your choicest valleys
were full of chariots,
And the horsemen took up
fixed positions at the
gate.
8 And He removed the [t]defense
of Judah. *screen, covering*
In that day you depended on
the weapons of the house
of the forest,
9 And you saw that the
breaches
In the *wall* of the city of David were many;
And you collected the waters
of the lower pool.
10 Then you counted the houses
of Jerusalem,
And you tore down houses to
fortify the wall.
11 And you made a reservoir
between the two walls
For the waters of the [r]old
pool. 2 Kin. 20:20; 2 Chr. 32:3
But you did not depend on
Him who made it,
Nor did you [t]take into consideration Him who planned
it long ago. *see . . . Him*

12 Therefore in that day the
Lord GOD of hosts, called
you to [r]weeping, to wailing, Is. 32:11; Joel 1:13
To shaving the head, and to
wearing sackcloth.
13 Instead, there is [r]gaiety and
gladness, Is. 5:11, 22; 28:7, 8
Killing of cattle and slaughtering of sheep,
Eating of meat and drinking
of wine:
"Let us eat and drink, for tomorrow we may die."
14 But the LORD of hosts revealed Himself to me,
"Surely this iniquity shall not
be forgiven you
[r]Until you die," says the Lord
GOD of hosts. Is. 65:20

15 Thus says the Lord GOD of
hosts,
"Come, go to this steward,
To Shebna, who is in charge
of the *royal* household,
16 'What right do you have here,
And whom do you have here,
That you have [r]hewn a tomb
for yourself here,
You who hew a tomb on the
height, 2 Sam. 18:18
You who carve a resting
place for [t]yourself in the
rock? *himself*
17 'Behold, the LORD is about to
hurl you headlong, O
man.
And He is about to grasp you
firmly,
18 *And* roll you tightly like a
ball,
To be [r]*cast* into a vast country; Job 18:18; Is. 17:13
There you will die,
And there your splendid
chariots will be,
You shame of your master's
house.'
19 "And I will [r]depose you from
your office, Job 40:11, 12
And I will pull you down
from your station.
20 "Then it will come about in
that day,
That I will summon My servant [r]Eliakim the son of
Hilkiah 2 Kin. 18:18
21 And I will clothe him with
your tunic,
And tie your sash securely
about him,

I will entrust him with your
[t]authority, *rule*
And he will become a [r]father
to the inhabitants of Jerusalem and to the house
of Judah. Job 29:16
22 "Then I will set [r]the key of the
[r]house of David on his
shoulder, Rev. 3:7
When he opens no one will
shut, Is. 7:2, 13
When he shuts no one will
[r]open. Job 12:14
23 "And I will drive him *like* a
peg in a firm place,
And he will become a [r]throne
of glory to his father's
house. 1 Sam. 2:8; Job 36:7
24 "So they will hang on him all
the glory of his father's house, offspring and issue, all the least of
vessels, from bowls to all the jars.
25 "In that day," declares the
LORD of hosts, "the peg driven in a
firm place will give way; it will
even break off and fall, and the
load hanging on it will be cut off,
for the LORD has spoken."

CHAPTER 23

THE oracle concerning Tyre.
Wail, O ships of Tarshish,
For *Tyre* is destroyed, without house *or* harbor;
It is reported to them from
the land of Cyprus.
2 [r]Be silent, you inhabitants of
the coastland, Is. 47:5
You merchants of Sidon;
Your messengers crossed the
sea
3 And *were* on many waters.
[r]The grain of the Nile, the harvest of the River was her
revenue; Is. 19:7-9
And she was the [r]market of
nations. Ezek. 27:3-23
4 Be ashamed, O [r]Sidon;
For the sea speaks, the
stronghold of the sea,
saying, Gen. 10:15, 19
"I have neither travailed nor
given birth,
I have neither brought up
young men *nor* reared
virgins."
5 When the report *reaches*
Egypt,
They will be in [r]anguish at the
report of Tyre. Josh. 2:9-11
6 Pass over to [r]Tarshish;
Wail, O inhabitants of the
coastland. Is. 23:1
7 Is this your [r]jubilant *city*,
Whose origin is from antiquity, Is. 22:2; 32:13
Whose feet used to carry
her to [t]colonize distant
places? *sojourn afar off*

8 Who has planned this
against Tyre, [r]the bestower of crowns, Ezek. 28:2
Whose merchants were
princes, whose traders
were the honored of the
earth?
9 The LORD of hosts has
planned it to defile the
pride of all beauty,
To despise all the [r]honored of
the earth. Is. 5:13; 9:15
10 [t]Overflow your land like the
Nile, O daughter of Tarshish, *Pass over*
There is no more restraint.
11 He has stretched His hand
out over the sea,
He has [r]made the kingdoms
tremble; Is. 13:13

The LORD has given a command concerning Canaan
to [r]demolish its strongholds. Is. 25:2
12 And He has said, "You shall exult no more, O crushed
virgin daughter of Sidon.
Arise, pass over to [r]Cyprus;
even there you will find no rest." Is. 23:1
13 Behold, the land of the Chaldeans—this is the people *which*
was not; Assyria appointed it for
desert creatures—they erected
their siege towers, they stripped
its palaces, they made it a ruin.
14 Wail, O [r]ships of Tarshish,
For your stronghold is destroyed. Is. 2:16
15 Now it will come about in
that day that Tyre will be forgotten for seventy years like the days
of one king. At the end of seventy
years it will happen to Tyre as *in*
the song of the harlot:
16 Take *your* harp, walk about the city,
O forgotten harlot;
Pluck the strings skillfully, sing many songs,
That you may be remembered.
17 And it will come about at the
end of seventy years that the
LORD will visit Tyre. Then she will
go back to her harlot's wages, and
will play the harlot with all the
kingdoms on the face of the earth.
18 And her [r]gain and her harlot's
wages will be set apart to the
LORD; it will not be stored up or
hoarded, but her gain will become
sufficient food and choice attire
for those who dwell in the presence of the LORD. Ps. 72:10, 11

CHAPTER 24

BEHOLD, the LORD [r]lays the
earth waste, devastates it, distorts
its surface, and scatters its inhabitants. Is. 2:19; 13:13; 24:19, 20
2 And the people will be like
the priest, the servant like his
master, the maid like her mistress,
the buyer like the seller, the
lender like the borrower, the
creditor like the debtor.
3 The earth will be completely
laid waste and completely despoiled, for the LORD has spoken
this word.
4 The [r]earth mourns *and* withers, the world fades *and* withers,
the exalted of the people of the
earth fade away. Is. 33:9
5 The earth is also polluted by
its inhabitants, for they transgressed laws, violated statutes,
broke the everlasting covenant.
6 Therefore, a curse devours
the earth, and those who live in it
are held guilty. Therefore, the inhabitants of the earth are burned,
and few men are left.
7 The new wine mourns,
The vine decays,
All the merry-hearted sigh.
8 The [r]gaiety of tambourines ceases, Is. 5:12, 14
The noise of revelers stops,
The gaiety of the harp ceases.
9 They do not drink wine with song;
Strong drink is bitter to those who drink it.
10 The [r]city of chaos is broken down; Is. 34:11
Every house is shut up so that none may enter.

11 There is an ʳoutcry in the streets concerning the wine; Jer. 14:2; 46:12
All joyᵗturns to gloom.
The gaiety of the earth is banished. *is darkened*
12 Desolation is left in the city,
And the ʳgate is battered to ruins. Is. 14:31; 45:2
13 For ʳthus it will be in the midst of the earth among the peoples, Is. 17:6; 27:12
As the ᵗshaking of an olive tree, *striking*
As the gleanings when the grape harvest is over.
14 ʳThey raise their voices, they shout for joy. Is. 12:6; 48:20
They cry out from the ᵗwest concerning the majesty of the LORD. *sea*
15 Therefore glorify the LORD in the ᵗeast, *region of light*
The ʳname of the LORD, the God of Israel Mal. 1:11
In the coastlands of the sea.
16 From the ends of the earth we hear songs, "Glory to the Righteous One,"
But I say, "Woe to me! Woe to me! Alas for me!
The ʳtreacherous deal treacherously, Is. 21:2; 33:1
And the treacherous deal very treacherously."
17 Terror and pit and snare
ᵗConfront you, O inhabitant of the earth. *Are upon you*
18 Then it will be that he who flees the report of disaster will fall into the pit,
And he who ᵗclimbs out of the pit will be caught in the snare; *from the height*
For the windows above are opened, and the foundations of the earth shake.
19 The earth is broken asunder,
The earth is split through,
The earth is shaken violently.
20 The earth ʳreels to and fro like a drunkard, Is. 19:14; 24:1
And it totters like a shack,
For its ʳtransgression is heavy upon it, Is. 1:28
And it will fall, ʳnever to rise again. Dan. 11:19
21 So it will happen in that day,
That the LORD will punish the host of heaven, on high,
And the ʳkings of the earth, on earth. Ps. 76:12
22 And they will be gathered together
Like ʳprisoners in the dungeon, Is. 10:4; 42:22
And will be confined in prison;
And after many days they will be punished.
23 Then the ʳmoon will be abashed and the sun ashamed, Is. 13:10
For the ʳLORD of hosts will reign on Mount Zion and in Jerusalem, Is. 60:19, 20
And *His* glory will be before His elders.

CHAPTER 25

O LORD, Thou art my God;
I will exalt Thee, I will give thanks to Thy name;
For Thou hast ʳworked wonders, Ps. 40:5; 98:1
Plans formed long ago, with perfect faithfulness.
2 For Thou hast made a city into a ʳheap, Is. 17:1; 26:5
A fortified city into a ruin;

A [r]palace of strangers is a city no more, Is. 13:22; 32:14
It will never be rebuilt.
3 Therefore a strong people will [r]glorify Thee; Is. 24:15
[r]Cities of ruthless nations will revere Thee. Is. 13:11
4 For Thou hast been a [r]defense for the helpless, Is. 14:32
A defense for the needy in his distress,
A refuge from the storm, a shade from the heat;
For the breath of the [r]ruthless
Is like a *rain* storm *against* a wall. Is. 29:5, 20
5 Like heat in drought, Thou dost subdue the [r]uproar of aliens; Jer. 51:54-56
Like heat by the shadow of a cloud, the song of the ruthless is silenced.

6 And [r]the LORD of hosts will prepare a lavish banquet for all peoples on this mountain; Is. 1:19
A banquet of [t]aged wine, choice pieces with marrow, *wine on the lees*
And refined, aged wine.
7 And on this mountain He will swallow up the covering which is over all peoples,
Even the veil which is [t]stretched over all nations. *woven*
8 He will [r]swallow up death for all time, Hos. 13:14
And the Lord GOD will wipe tears away from all faces,
And He will remove the reproach of His people from all the earth;
For the LORD has spoken.
9 And it will be said in that day,
"Behold, this is our God for whom we have waited that He might save us.
This is the LORD for whom we have waited;
[r]Let us rejoice and be glad in His salvation." Ps. 20:5
10 For the hand of the LORD will rest on this mountain,
And Moab will be trodden down in his place
As straw is trodden down in the water of a manure pile.
11 And he will spread out his hands in the middle of it
As a swimmer spreads out *his hands* to swim,
But *the Lord* will lay low his pride together with the trickery of his hands.
12 And the [r]unassailable fortifications of your walls He will bring down, Is. 15:1
Lay low, *and* cast to the ground, even to the dust.

CHAPTER 26

[r]IN that day this song will be sung in the land of Judah: Is. 4:2; 12:1
"We have a strong city;
He sets up walls and ramparts for security.
2 "Open the [r]gates, that the righteous nation may enter, Is. 60:11, 18
The one that [t]remains faithful. *keeps faithfulness*
3 "The steadfast of mind Thou wilt keep in perfect [r]peace, Is. 26:12; 27:5
Because he trusts in Thee.

4 "Trust in the LORD forever,
For in GOD the LORD, *we have* an everlasting Rock.
5 "For He has brought low those who dwell on high, the unassailable city;
[r]He lays it low, He lays it low to the ground, He casts it to the dust. Job 40:11-13
6 "The foot will trample it,
The feet of the afflicted, the steps of the helpless."

7 The [r]way of the righteous is smooth; Is. 57:2
O Upright One, [r]make the path of the righteous level. Ps. 25:4, 5; 27:11
8 Indeed, *while following* the way of [r]Thy judgments, O LORD, Is. 51:4; 56:1
We have waited for Thee eagerly;
[r]Thy name, even Thy [r]memory, is the desire of *our* souls. Is. 12:4 • Ex. 3:15
9 At night [t]my soul longs for Thee, *with my soul I long*
Indeed, my spirit within me seeks Thee diligently;
For when the earth experiences Thy judgments
The inhabitants of the world learn righteousness.
10 *Though* the wicked is shown favor,
He does not [r]learn righteousness; Is. 22:12, 13; 32:6, 7
He [r]deals unjustly in the land of uprightness, Hos. 11:7
And does not perceive the majesty of the LORD.

11 O LORD, Thy hand is lifted up *yet* they do not see it.
They see [r]*Thy* zeal for the people and are put to shame; Is. 9:7; 37:32
Indeed, [r]fire will devour Thine enemies. Is. 5:24; 9:18, 19
12 LORD, Thou wilt establish [r]peace for us, Is. 26:3
Since Thou hast also performed for us all our works.
13 O LORD our God, [r]other masters besides Thee have ruled us; Is. 2:8; 10:11
But through Thee alone we confess Thy name.
14 [r]The dead will not live, the [a]departed spirits will not rise; Deut. 4:28 • *shades*
Therefore Thou hast [r]punished and destroyed them, Is. 10:3
And Thou hast wiped out all remembrance of them.
15 [r]Thou hast increased the nation, O LORD, Is. 9:3
Thou hast increased the nation, Thou art glorified;
Thou hast extended all the borders of the land.
16 O LORD, they sought Thee [r]in distress; Is. 37:3; Hos. 5:15
They [t]could only whisper a prayer, *sound forth a whisper*
Your chastening was upon them.
17 [r]As the pregnant woman approaches *the time* to give birth, Is. 13:8; 21:3
She writhes *and* cries out in her labor pains,
Thus were we before Thee, O LORD.
18 We were pregnant, we writhed *in labor*,
We [r]gave birth, as it were, *only* to wind. Is. 33:11

We could not accomplish deliverance for the earth
Nor were inhabitants of the world [t]born. *fallen*
19 Your dead will live;
Their corpses will rise.
You who lie in the dust, awake and shout for joy,
For your dew is as the dew of the [t]dawn, *lights*
And the earth will give birth to the departed spirits.

20 Come, my people, [r]enter into your rooms, Ex. 12:22, 23
And close your doors behind you;
Hide for a little while,
Until indignation [t]runs *its* course. *passes over*
21 For behold, the LORD is about to [r]come out from His place Mic. 1:3; Jude 14
To [r]punish the inhabitants of the earth for their iniquity; Is. 13:11; 30:12-14
And the earth will [r]reveal her bloodshed, Job 16:18
And will no longer cover her slain.

CHAPTER 27

In that day the LORD will punish [a]Leviathan the fleeing serpent, *sea monster*
With His fierce and great and mighty sword,
Even Leviathan the twisted serpent;
And He will kill the dragon who *lives* in the sea.

2 In that day,
"A vineyard of wine, sing of it!
3 "I, the LORD, am its keeper;
I water it every moment.
Lest anyone damage it,
I guard it night and day.
4 "I have no wrath.
Should [t]someone give Me [r]briars *and* thorns in battle, *who* • 2 Sam. 23:6
Then I would step on them, [r]I would burn them completely. Is. 33:12
5 "Or let him [t]rely on My protection, *take hold of*
Let him make peace with Me,
Let him [r]make peace with Me." Job 22:21
6 [t]In the days to come Jacob will take root, *Those coming*
Israel will [r]blossom and sprout; Is. 35:1, 2; Hos. 14:5, 6
And they will fill the whole world with [r]fruit. Is. 4:2

7 Like the striking of Him who has struck them, has [r]He struck them? Is. 10:12, 17
Or like the slaughter of His slain, [t]have they been slain? *he was slain*
8 Thou didst contend with them by banishing them, by driving them away.
With His fierce wind He has expelled *them* on the day of the [r]east wind. Jer. 4:11
9 Therefore through this Jacob's iniquity will be [r]forgiven; Is. 1:25; 48:10
And this will be [t]the full price of the [t]pardoning of his sin: *all the fruit* • *removing*
When he makes all the altar stones like pulverized chalk stones;
When Asherim and incense altars will not stand.

10 For the fortified city is [r]isolated, Is. 32:13, 14
A homestead forlorn and forsaken like the desert;
There the calf will graze,
And there it will lie down and feed on its branches.
11 When its [r]limbs are dry, they are broken off; Is. 18:5
Women come *and* make a fire with them.
For they are not a people of [r]discernment, Deut. 32:28
Therefore [r]their Maker will not have compassion on them. Deut. 32:18
And their Creator will not be gracious to them.

12 And it will come about in
that day, that the LORD [r]will start
His threshing from the flowing
stream of the Euphrates to the
brook of Egypt; and you will be
gathered up one by one, O sons of
Israel. Is. 11:11; 17:6; 24:13; 56:8
13 It will come about also in
that day that a great [r]trumpet will
be blown; and those who were
perishing in the land of Assyria
and who were scattered in the
land of Egypt will come and worship the LORD in the holy mountain at Jerusalem. Lev. 25:9

CHAPTER 28

WOE to the proud crown of the drunkards of Ephraim,
And to the fading flower of its glorious beauty,
Which is at the head of the [t]fertile valley *valley of fatness*
Of those who are [t]overcome with wine! *smitten*
2 Behold, the Lord has a strong and mighty *agent;*
As a storm of [r]hail, a tempest of destruction, Is. 28:17
Like a storm of [r]mighty overflowing waters, Is. 8:6, 7
He has cast *it* down to the earth with *His* hand.
3 The proud crown of the drunkards of Ephraim is trodden under foot.
4 And the fading flower of its glorious beauty,
Which is at the head of the fertile valley,
Will be like the [r]first-ripe fig prior to summer; Hos. 9:10
Which one sees,
And [t]as soon as it is in his [t]hand, *while it is yet* • *palm*
He swallows it.
5 In that day the [r]LORD of hosts will become a beautiful crown Is. 41:16; 45:25
And a glorious diadem to the remnant of His people;
6 A spirit of justice for him who sits in judgment,
A [r]strength to those who repel the onslaught at the gate. 2 Chr. 32:6-8
7 And these also [r]reel with wine and stagger from strong drink: Is. 5:11, 22; 22:13
The priest and the prophet reel with strong drink,
They are confused by wine, they stagger from [r]strong drink; Hab. 2:15, 16
They reel while [t]having [r]visions, *seeing* • Is. 29:11
They totter *when rendering* judgment.
8 For all the tables are full of filthy vomit, without a *single clean* place.

9 "To [r]whom would He teach knowledge? Is. 2:3; 28:26
And to whom would He interpret the message?
Those *just* [r]weaned from milk? Ps. 131:2
Those *just* taken from the breast?
10 "For *He says,*
'Order [r]on order, order on order, 2 Chr. 36:15; Neh. 9:30
Line on line, line on line,
A little here, a little there.' "
11 Indeed, He will speak to this people
Through stammering lips and a foreign tongue,
12 He who said to them, "Here is [r]rest, give rest to the weary," Is. 11:10; 30:15
And, "Here is repose," but they would not listen.
13 So the word of the LORD to them will be,
"Order on order, order on order,
Line on line, line on line,
A little here, a little there,"
That they may go and [r]stumble backward, be broken, snared, and taken captive. Is. 8:15; Matt. 21:44
14 Therefore, hear the word of the LORD, O scoffers,
Who rule this people who are in Jerusalem,
15 Because you have said, "We have made a [r]covenant with death, Is. 28:18
And with Sheol we have made a pact.
The overwhelming [a]scourge will not reach us when it passes by, *flood*
For we have made [r]falsehood our refuge and we have concealed ourselves with deception." Ezek. 13:22
16 Therefore thus says the Lord GOD,
"Behold, I am laying in Zion a stone, a tested stone,
A costly cornerstone *for* the foundation, [t]firmly placed. *well-laid*
He who believes *in it* will not be [t]disturbed. *in a hurry*
17 "And I will make [r]justice the measuring line, 2 Kin. 21:13
And righteousness the level;
Then hail shall sweep away the refuge of lies,
And the waters shall overflow the secret place.
18 "And your [r]covenant with death shall be canceled,
And your pact with Sheol shall not stand; Is. 28:15
When the overwhelming scourge passes through,
Then you become its [r]trampling *place.* Is. 28:3
19 "As often as it passes through, it will [t]seize you. *take*
For [r]morning after morning it will pass through, *anytime* during the day or night. Is. 50:4
And it will be [t]sheer terror to understand what it means." *only*
20 The bed is too short on which to stretch out,
And the blanket is too small to wrap oneself in.
21 For the LORD will rise up as *at* Mount Perazim,
He will be stirred up as in the valley of Gibeon;

To do His task, His [t]unusual task, *task is strange*
And to work His work, His extraordinary work.
22 And now do not carry on as [r]scoffers, Is. 28:14
Lest your fetters be made stronger;
For I have heard from the Lord GOD of hosts,
Of decisive [r]destruction on all the earth. Is. 10:22, 23

23 Give ear and hear my voice,
Listen and hear my words.
24 Does the farmer plow continually to plant seed?
Does he *continually* turn and harrow the ground?
25 Does he not level its surface,
And sow dill and scatter [r]cummin, Matt. 23:23
And plant wheat in rows,
Barley in its place, and rye within its [t]area? *region*
26 For his God instructs and teaches him properly.
27 For dill is not threshed with a [r]threshing sledge, Amos 1:3
Nor is the cartwheel [t]driven over cummin; *rolled*
But dill is beaten out with a rod, and cummin with a club.
28 *Grain for* bread is crushed,
Indeed, he does not continue to thresh it forever.
Because the wheel of *his* cart and his horses *eventually* [t]damage *it*, *discomfit*
He does not thresh it longer.
29 This also comes from the LORD of hosts,
Who has made *His* counsel [r]wonderful and *His* wisdom great. Is. 9:6

CHAPTER 29

WOE, O Ariel, Ariel the city *where* David *once* [r]camped! 2 Sam. 5:9
Add year to year, observe *your* feasts on schedule.
2 And I will bring distress to Ariel,
And she shall be *a city of* lamenting and mourning;
And she shall be like an Ariel to me.
3 And I will [r]camp against you encircling *you,*
And I will set siegeworks against you, Luke 19:43, 44
And I will raise up battle towers against you.
4 Then you shall [r]be brought low; Is. 8:19
From the earth you shall speak,
And from the dust *where* you are prostrate,
Your words *shall come.*
Your voice shall also be like that of a [a]spirit from the ground, *ghost*
And your speech shall whisper from the dust.

5 But the multitude of your [t]enemies shall become like fine dust, *strangers*
And the multitude of the ruthless ones like the chaff which blows away;
And it shall happen [r]instantly, suddenly. 1 Thess. 5:3
6 From the LORD of hosts you will be [r]punished with thunder and earthquake and loud noise, Is. 10:3
With whirlwind and tempest

and the flame of a consuming fire.
7 And the [r]multitude of all the nations who wage war against Ariel, Mic. 4:11, 12
Even all who wage war against her and her stronghold, and who distress her,
Shall be like a dream, a vision of the night.
8 And it will be as when a hungry man dreams—
And behold, he is eating;
But when he awakens, his hunger is not satisfied,
Or as when a thirsty man dreams—
And behold, he is drinking,
But when he awakens, behold, he is faint,
And his [t]thirst is not quenched. *soul*
[r]Thus the multitude of all the nations shall be, Is. 54:17
Who wage war against Mount Zion.

9 [r]Be delayed and wait. Is. 29:1
Blind yourselves and be blind.
They [r]become drunk, but not with wine; Is. 51:17, 21, 22
They stagger, but not with strong drink.
10 For the LORD has poured over you a spirit of deep [r]sleep, Ps. 69:23; Is. 6:9, 10
He has [r]shut your eyes, the prophets; Is. 44:18
And He has covered your heads, the seers.
11 And the entire vision shall be
to you like the words of a sealed
book, which when they give it to
the one who is literate, saying,
"Please read this," he will say, "I
cannot, for it is sealed."
12 Then the [a]book will be given
to the one who is illiterate, saying,
"Please read this." And he will
say, "I cannot read." *scroll*
13 Then the Lord said,
"Because this people draw near with their words
And honor Me with their [t]lip service, *lips*
But they remove their hearts far from Me,
And their reverence for Me consists of tradition learned *by rote,*
14 Therefore behold, I will once again deal marvelously with this people, wondrously marvelous;
And the wisdom of their wise men shall perish,
And the discernment of their discerning men shall be concealed.

15 Woe to those who deeply [r]hide their [t]plans from the LORD, Ps. 10:11, 13 • *counsel*
And whose [r]deeds are *done* in a dark place, Job 22:13
And they say, "Who sees us?" or "Who knows us?"
16 You turn *things* around!
Shall the potter be considered [t]as equal with the clay, *like*
That [r]what is made should say to its maker, "He did not make me"; Is. 45:9
Or what is formed say to him who formed it, "He has no understanding"?

17 Is it not yet just a little while

Before Lebanon will be turned into a fertile field,
And the fertile field will be considered as a forest?
18 And on that day the [r]deaf shall hear words of a book, Is. 35:5; 42:18, 19
And out of *their* gloom and darkness the [r]eyes of the blind shall see. Ps. 119:18
19 The [r]afflicted also shall increase their gladness in the LORD, Ps. 25:9; 37:11
And the [r]needy of mankind shall rejoice in the Holy One of Israel. Matt. 11:5
20 For the ruthless will come to an end, and the [r]scorner will be finished, Is. 28:14
Indeed all who are intent on doing evil will be cut off;
21 Who cause a person to be indicted by a word,
And ensnare him who adjudicates at the gate,
And [t]defraud the one in the right with meaningless arguments. *turn aside*

22 Therefore thus says the
LORD, who redeemed Abraham,
concerning the house of Jacob,

"Jacob shall not now be ashamed, nor shall his face now turn pale;
23 But when he sees his children, the work of My hands, in his midst,
They will sanctify My name;
Indeed, they will sanctify the Holy One of Jacob,
And will stand in awe of the God of Israel.
24 "And those who err in mind will know the truth,
And those who criticize will accept instruction.

CHAPTER 30

"WOE to the rebellious children," declares the LORD,
"Who [r]execute a plan, but not Mine, Is. 29:15
And make an alliance, but not of My Spirit,
In order to add sin to sin;
2 Who proceed down to Egypt,
Without consulting Me,
[r]To take refuge in the safety of Pharaoh, Is. 36:9
And to seek shelter in the shadow of Egypt!
3 "Therefore the safety of Pharaoh will be [r]your shame,
And the shelter in the shadow of Egypt, your humiliation. Jer. 42:18, 22
4 "For [r]their princes are at Zoan,
And their ambassadors arrive at Hanes. Is. 19:11
5 "Everyone will be ashamed because of a people who cannot profit them,
Who are [r]not for help or profit, but for shame and also for reproach." Is. 10:3

6 The [a]oracle concerning the
beasts of the Negev. *burden of*

Through a land of [r]distress and anguish, Ex. 5:10, 21
From [t]where *come* lioness and lion, viper and [r]flying serpent, *them* • Deut. 8:15
They carry their riches on the [t]backs of young donkeys *shoulders*
And their treasures on [r]camels' humps, 1 Kin. 10:2
To a people who cannot profit *them;*
7 Even Egypt, whose [r]help is vain and empty. Is. 30:5

Therefore, I have called her
"Rahab[r] who has been exterminated." Job 9:13
8 Now go,[r] write it on a tablet
before them Is. 8:1
And inscribe it on a scroll,
That it may[t] serve in the time
to come *be*
As a witness forever.
9 For this is a [r]rebellious people, false sons, Is. 30:1
Sons who refuse to listen
To the [a]instruction of the
LORD; *law*
10 Who say to the seers, "You
must not see *visions*";
And to the prophets, "You
must not [r]prophesy to us
what is right, Jer. 11:21
Speak to us pleasant words,
Prophesy illusions.
11 "Get out of the way, turn
aside from the path,
Let us hear no more about
the Holy One of Israel."
12 Therefore thus says the Holy
One of Israel,
"Since[r] you have rejected this
word, Is. 5:24; 7:9
And have put your trust in
oppression and guile, and
have relied on them,
13 Therefore this [r]iniquity will
be to you Is. 26:21
Like a breach about to fall,
A bulge in a high wall,
Whose collapse comes sud-
denly in an instant.
14 "And whose collapse is like
the smashing of a [r]pot-
ter's jar; Jer. 19:10, 11
So ruthlessly shattered
That a sherd will not be
found among its pieces
To take fire from a hearth,
Or to scoop water from a cistern."
15 For thus the Lord GOD, the
Holy One of Israel, has
said,
"In [t]repentance and rest you
shall be saved, *returning*
In [r]quietness and trust is your
strength." Is. 7:4; 32:17
But you were not willing,
16 And you said, "No, for we
will flee on horses,"
Therefore you shall flee!
"And we will ride on swift
horses,"
Therefore those who pursue
you shall be swift.
17 One thousand *shall flee* at
the threat of one *man*,
You shall flee at the threat of
five;
Until you are left as a [t]flag on
a mountain top, *pole*
And as a signal on a hill.

18 Therefore the LORD longs to
be gracious to you,
And therefore He [t]waits on
high to have compassion
on you. *is on high*
For the LORD is a [r]God of justice; Is. 5:16; 28:17
How blessed are all those
who long for Him.
19 O people in Zion, [r]inhabitant
in Jerusalem, you will weep no
longer. He will surely be gracious
to you at the sound of your cry;
when He hears it, He will answer
you. Is. 65:9; Ezek. 37:25, 28
20 Although the Lord has given
you [r]bread of privation and water
of oppression, *He*, your Teacher
will no longer hide Himself, but
your eyes will behold your
Teacher. 1 Kin. 22:27; Ps. 80:5

21 And your ears will hear a word behind you, "This is the way, walk in it," whenever you turn to the right or to the left.

22 And you will defile your graven [r]images, overlaid with silver, and your molten images plated with gold. You will scatter them as an impure thing; *and* say to them, "Be gone!" Ex. 32:2, 4

23 Then He will give *you* rain for [t]the seed which you will sow in the ground, and bread *from* the yield of the ground, and it will be [t]rich and plenteous; on that day your livestock will graze in a roomy pasture. *your · fatness*

24 Also the oxen and the donkeys which work the ground will eat salted fodder, which has been winnowed with shovel and fork.

25 And on every lofty mountain and on [r]every high hill there will be streams running with water on the day of the great slaughter, when the towers fall. Is. 35:6, 7

26 And the light of the moon will be as the light of the sun, and the light of the sun will be seven times *brighter*, like the light of seven days, on the day the LORD binds up the fracture of His people and heals the bruise [t]He has inflicted. *of His blow*

27 Behold, the name of the LORD comes from a [t]remote place; *distance*
Burning is His anger, and dense is *His* smoke;
His lips are filled with [r]indignation, Is. 10:5; 13:5; 66:14
And His tongue is like a [r]consuming fire; Is. 66:15
28 And His breath is like an overflowing torrent,
Which reaches to the neck,
To shake the nations back and forth in a sieve,
And to *put* in the jaws of the peoples the bridle which [t]leads to ruin. *misleads*
29 You will have [t]songs as in the night when you keep the festival; *the song*
And gladness of heart as when one marches to *the sound of* the flute,
To go to the mountain of the LORD, to the Rock of Israel.
30 And the LORD will cause [t]His voice of authority to be heard. *the majesty of His voice*
And the [t]descending of His arm to be seen in fierce anger, *descent*
And *in* the flame of a consuming fire,
In cloudburst, downpour, and hailstones.
31 For at the voice of the LORD Assyria will be terrified,
When He strikes with the [r]rod. Is. 10:26; 11:4
32 And every [t]blow of the rod of punishment, *passing*
Which the LORD will lay on him,
Will be with *the music of* tambourines and lyres;
And in battles, [r]brandishing weapons, He will fight them. Ezek. 32:10
33 For [13]Topheth [r]has long been ready, 2 Kin. 23:10
Indeed, it has been prepared for the king.
He has made it deep and large,

[13] I.e., the place of human sacrifice to Molech

A[t] pyre of fire with plenty of
wood; *Its pile*
The [r]breath of the LORD, like a
torrent of brimstone, sets
it afire. Is. 11:4; 30:28

CHAPTER 31

WOE to those who go down to
[r]Egypt for help, Is. 30:2, 7
And rely on horses,
And trust in chariots because
they are many,
And in horsemen because
they are very strong,
But they do not [r]look to the
Holy One of Israel, nor
seek the LORD! Dan. 9:13
2 Yet He also is [r]wise and will
bring disaster, Rom. 16:27
And does [r]not retract His
words, Num. 23:19; Jer. 44:29
But will arise against the
house of evildoers,
And against the help of the
workers of iniquity.
3 Now the Egyptians are [r]men,
and not God, 2 Thess. 2:4
And their [r]horses are flesh
and not spirit; Is. 36:9
So the LORD will [r]stretch out
His hand, Jer. 15:6
And [r]he who helps will stumble Is. 30:5, 7; Matt. 15:14
And he who is helped will
fall,
And all of them will come to
an end together.

4 For thus says the LORD to
me,
"As the lion or the young lion
growls over his prey,
Against which a band of
shepherds is called out,
Will not be terrified at their
voice, nor disturbed at
their noise,
So will the LORD of hosts
come down to wage [r]war
on Mount Zion and on its
hill." Is. 42:13; Zech. 12:8
5 Like [a]flying [r]birds so the LORD
of hosts will protect Jerusalem. *hovering* • Ps. 91:4
He will [r]protect and deliver *it;*
He will pass over and rescue
it. Is. 37:35; 38:6
6 [r]Return to Him from whom
you have [r]deeply defected, O sons
of Israel. Is. 44:22; 55:7 • Is. 1:2, 5
7 For in that day every man
will [r]cast away his silver idols and
his gold idols, which your hands
have made as a sin. Is. 2:20
8 And the Assyrian will fall by
a sword not of man,
And a [r]sword not of man will
devour him. Is. 66:16
So he will [t]not escape the
sword, *flee*
And his young men will become forced laborers.
9 "And his rock will pass away
because of panic,
And his princes will be terrified at the standard,"
Declares the LORD, whose
fire is in Zion and whose
furnace is in Jerusalem.

CHAPTER 32

BEHOLD, a [r]king will reign righteously, Ps. 72:1-4
And princes will rule justly.
2 And each will be like a refuge from the wind,
And a shelter from the
storm,

Like [t]streams of water in a dry country, *canals*
Like the shade of a huge rock in a parched land.
3 Then the eyes of those who see will not be blinded,
And the ears of those who hear will listen.
4 And the mind of the hasty will discern the truth,
And the tongue of the stammerers will hasten to speak clearly.
5 No longer will the [r]fool be called noble, 1 Sam. 25:25
Or the rogue be spoken of *as* generous.
6 For a fool speaks nonsense,
And his heart inclines toward wickedness,
To practice [r]ungodliness and to speak error against the LORD, Is. 9:17; 10:6
To [r]keep the hungry person unsatisfied Is. 3:15; 10:2
And to withhold drink from the thirsty.
7 As for a rogue, his weapons are evil;
He devises wicked schemes
To [r]destroy *the* afflicted with slander, Is. 11:4; 61:1
Even though *the* needy one speaks what is right.
8 But [r]the noble man devises noble plans; Prov. 11:25
And by noble plans he stands.

9 Rise up you [r]women who are at ease, Amos 6:1; Zeph. 2:15
And hear my voice;
Give ear to my word,
You complacent daughters.
10 Within a year and *a few* days,
You will be troubled, O complacent *daughters*;
For the vintage is ended,
And the *fruit* gathering will not come.
11 Tremble, you *women* who are at ease;
[r]Be troubled, you complacent *daughters*; Is. 22:12
Strip, undress, and put *sackcloth* on *your* waist,
12 [r]Beat your breasts for the pleasant fields, for the fruitful vine, Nah. 2:7
13 [r]For the land of my people *in which* thorns *and* briars shall come up; Is. 5:6, 10, 17
Yea, for all the joyful houses, *and for* the jubilant city.
14 Because the palace has been abandoned, the populated city forsaken.
Hill and watch-tower have become caves forever,
A delight for wild donkeys, a pasture for flocks;
15 Until the Spirit is poured out upon us from on high,
And the wilderness becomes a [r]fertile field Ps. 107:35
And the fertile field is considered as a forest.
16 Then [r]justice will dwell in the wilderness, Zech. 8:3
And righteousness will abide in the fertile field.
17 And the work of righteousness will be peace,
And the service of righteousness, quietness and [a]confidence forever. *security*
18 Then my people will live in a peaceful habitation,
And in secure dwellings and in undisturbed [r]resting places; Hos. 2:18-23

19 And it will [r]hail when the forest comes down, Is. 28:2, 17
And [r]the city will be utterly laid low. Is. 24:10, 12
20 How [r]blessed will you be, you who sow beside all waters, Eccl. 11:1
Who let out freely the ox and the donkey.

CHAPTER 33

WOE [r]to you, O destroyer,
While you were not destroyed; Is. 10:6; 21:2
And he who is treacherous, while *others* did not deal treacherously with him.
As soon as you shall finish destroying, [r]you shall be destroyed; Hab. 2:8
As soon as you shall cease to deal treacherously, *others* shall [r]deal treacherously with you. Matt. 7:2
2 O LORD, be gracious to us; we have waited for Thee.
Be Thou their [t]strength every morning, *arm*
Our salvation also in the [r]time of distress. Is. 37:3
3 At the sound of the tumult [r]peoples flee; Is. 17:13
At the lifting up of Thyself nations disperse.
4 And your spoil is gathered *as* the caterpillar gathers;
As locusts rushing about, men rush about on it.
5 The LORD is [r]exalted, for He dwells on high; Ps. 97:9
He has filled Zion with justice and righteousness.
6 And He shall be the [a]stability of your times, *faithfulness*
A wealth of salvation, wisdom, and knowledge;
The [r]fear of the LORD is his treasure. 2 Kin. 18:7
7 Behold, their brave men cry [t]in the streets,
The ambassadors of peace weep bitterly. *the outside*
8 The highways are desolate, the traveler has ceased,
He has [r]broken the covenant, he has despised the cities, Is. 24:5
He has no regard for man.
9 [r]The land mourns and pines away, Is. 3:26; 24:4
[r]Lebanon is shamed and withers; Is. 2:13; 10:34
[r]Sharon is like a desert plain,
And Bashan and Carmel lose *their foliage.* Is. 35:2
10 "Now [r]I will arise," says the LORD, Ps. 12:5; Is. 2:19, 21
"Now I will be exalted, now I will be lifted up.
11 "You have [r]conceived [t]chaff, you will give birth to stubble; Ps. 7:14 • *dry grass*
My [r]breath will consume you like a fire. Is. 1:31
12 "And the peoples will be burned to lime,
Like cut thorns which are burned in the fire.

13 "You who are far away, hear what I have done;
And you who are near, acknowledge My might."
14 Sinners in Zion are terrified;
[r]Trembling has seized the godless. Is. 32:11
"Who among us can live with the consuming fire?
Who among us can live with continual burning?"

15 He who ʳwalks righteously,
and speaks with sincerity, Ps. 15:2; 24:4
He who rejects unjust gain,
And shakes his hands so that
they hold no bribe;
He who stops his ears from
hearing about bloodshed,
And shuts his eyes from
looking upon evil;
16 He will dwell on the heights;
ʳHis refuge will be the impregnable rock; Is. 25:4
His bread will be given *him;*
His water will be sure.

17 Your eyes will see ʳthe King
in His beauty; Is. 6:5; 24:23
They will behold ʳa far-distant
land. Is. 26:15
18 Your heart will meditate on
ʳterror: Is. 17:14
"Where is he who counts?
Where is he who weighs?
Where is he who counts the
towers?"
19 You will no longer see a
fierce people,
A people of ʳunintelligible
speech which no one
comprehends, Deut. 28:49
Of a stammering tongue
which no one understands.
20 Look upon Zion, the city of
our appointed feasts;
Your eyes shall see Jerusalem an ʳundisturbed habitation, Ps. 46:5; 125:1, 2
ʳA tent which shall not be
folded, Is. 54:2
Its stakes shall never be
pulled up
Nor any of its cords be torn
apart.
21 But there the majestic *One,*
the LORD, shall be for us
A place of ʳrivers and wide
canals, Is. 41:18
On which no boat with oars
shall go,
And on which no mighty ship
shall pass—
22 For the LORD is our judge,
The LORD is our lawgiver,
The LORD is our king;
He will save us—
23 Your tackle hangs slack;
It cannot hold the base of its
mast firmly,
Nor spread out the sail.
Then the prey of an abundant
spoil will be divided;
ʳThe lame will take the plunder. 2 Kin. 7:8; Is. 35:6
24 And no resident will say, "I
am ʳsick"; Jer. 30:17
The people who dwell ᵗthere
will be forgiven *their* iniquity. *in it*

CHAPTER 34

DRAW near, O nations, to hear;
and listen, O peoples!
ʳLet the earth and ᵗall it contains hear, and the world
and all that springs from
it. Deut. 32:1 • *its fulness*
2 For the LORD's ʳindignation is
against all the nations,
And *His* wrath against all
their armies; Is. 26:20
He has ᵗutterly destroyed
them, *put under the ban*
He has given them over to
ʳslaughter. Is. 30:25; 63:6
3 So their slain will be ʳthrown
out, Is. 14:19
And their corpses will give
off their ʳstench, Amos 4:10

And the mountains will [t]be drenched with their blood. *dissolve*
4 And all the host of heaven will [t]wear away, *rot*
And the [r]sky will be rolled up like a scroll; Rev. 6:12-14
All their hosts will also wither away
As a leaf withers from the vine,
Or as *one* withers from the fig tree.
5 For [r]My sword is satiated in heaven, Deut. 32:41, 42
Behold it shall descend for judgment upon Edom,
And upon the people whom I have [r]devoted to destruction. Is. 24:6; 43:28
6 The sword of the LORD is filled with blood,
It is sated with fat, with the blood of lambs and goats,
With the fat of the kidneys of rams.
For the LORD has a sacrifice in [r]Bozrah, Is. 63:1; Jer. 49:13
And a great slaughter in the land of [r]Edom. Is. 63:1
7 Wild oxen shall also [t]fall with them, *go down*
And [r]young bulls with strong ones; Ps. 68:30
Thus their land shall be soaked with blood,
And their dust [t]become greasy with fat. *made fat*
8 For the LORD has a day of [r]vengeance, Is. 13:6; 35:4
A year of recompense for the [a]cause of Zion. *controversy*
9 And its streams shall be turned into pitch,
And its loose earth into [r]brimstone, Deut. 29:23
And its land shall become burning pitch.
10 It shall [r]not be quenched night or day; Is. 1:31
Its [r]smoke shall go up forever; Rev. 14:11; 19:3
From generation to generation it shall be desolate;
None shall pass through it forever and ever.
11 But [r]pelican and hedgehog shall possess it, Zeph. 2:14
And [a]owl and raven shall dwell in it; *great horned owl*
And He shall stretch over it the line of desolation
And the [t]plumb line of emptiness. *stones of void*
12 Its nobles—there is [r]no one there Jer. 27:20; 39:6
Whom they may proclaim king—
And all its princes shall be [r]nothing. Is. 41:11, 12
13 And thorns shall come up in its fortified towers,
Nettles and thistles in its fortified cities;
It shall also be a haunt of [r]jackals Ps. 44:19
And an abode of ostriches.
14 And the desert creatures shall meet with the [a]wolves, *howling creatures*
The [a]hairy goat also shall cry to its kind; *demon*
Yes, the night monster shall settle there
And shall find herself a resting place.
15 The tree snake shall make its nest and lay *eggs* there,
And it will hatch and gather *them* under its [t]protection. *shade*

Yes, the [a]hawks shall be gathered there, *kites*
Every one with its kind.

16 Seek from the book of the
LORD, and read:
Not one of these will be miss-
ing;
None will lack its mate.
For [r]His mouth has com-
manded, Is. 1:20; 40:5
And His Spirit has gathered
them.
17 And He has cast the [r]lot for
them, Jer. 13:25
And His hand has divided it
to them by line.
They shall possess it forever;
From generation to genera-
tion they shall dwell in it.

CHAPTER 35

THE [r]wilderness and the desert
will be glad, Is. 6:11
And the [a]Arabah will rejoice
and blossom; *desert*
Like the crocus
2 It will blossom profusely
And rejoice with rejoicing
and shout of joy.
The [r]glory of Lebanon will be
given to it, Is. 60:13
The majesty of [r]Carmel and
Sharon. Song 7:5
They will see the [r]glory of the
LORD, Is. 25:9
The majesty of our God.
3 Encourage the [t]exhausted,
and strengthen the [t]fee-
ble. *slack hands • tottering knees*
4 Say to those with [r]anxious
heart, Is. 32:4
"Take courage, fear not.
Behold, your God will come
with vengeance;
The [r]recompense of God will
come, Is. 34:8; 59:18
But He will save you."
5 Then the [r]eyes of the blind
will be opened, Is. 29:18
And the ears of the deaf will
be unstopped.
6 Then the [r]lame will leap like a
deer, Matt. 15:30; John 5:8, 9
And the tongue of the dumb
will shout for joy.
For waters will break forth in
the [r]wilderness John 7:38
And streams in the Arabah.
7 And the [a]scorched land will
become a pool, *mirage*
And the thirsty ground
springs of water;
In the [r]haunt of jackals, its
resting place, Is. 13:22
Grass *becomes* reeds and
rushes.
8 And [r]a highway will be there,
a roadway, Is. 11:16
And it will be called the
Highway of Holiness.
The unclean will not travel
on it,
But it *will* be for him who
walks *that* way,
And [r]fools will not wander *on*
it. Is. 33:8
9 No lion will be there,
Nor will any vicious beast go
up on it;
[t]These will not be found
there. *It*
But [r] the redeemed will walk
there, Is. 51:10; 62:12
10 And [r]the ransomed of the
LORD will return, Is. 1:27
And come with joyful shouting to Zion,
With everlasting joy upon
their heads.

They will [t]find gladness and
joy, *overtake*
And [r]sorrow and sighing will
flee away. Rev. 7:17; 21:4

CHAPTER 36

[r]NOW it came about in the fourteenth year of King Hezekiah, Sennacherib king of Assyria came up against all the fortified cities of Judah and seized them. 2 Kin. 18:13

2 And the king of Assyria sent Rabshakeh from Lachish to Jerusalem to King Hezekiah with a large army. And he stood by the conduit of the upper pool on the highway of the fuller's field.

3 Then [r]Eliakim the son of Hilkiah, who was over the household, and [r]Shebna the scribe, and Joah the son of Asaph, the recorder, came out to him. Is. 22:20 • Is. 22:15

4 Then Rabshakeh said to them, "Say now to Hezekiah, 'Thus says the great king, the king of Assyria, "What is this confidence that you [t]have? *trust*

5 "I say, 'Your counsel and strength for the war are only [t]empty words.' Now on whom do you rely, that [r]you have rebelled against me? *words of lips* • 2 Kin. 18:7

6 "Behold, you rely on the staff of this crushed reed, *even* on Egypt; on which if a man leans, it will go into his [t]hand and pierce it. So is Pharaoh king of Egypt to all who rely on him. *palm*

7 "But if you say to me, 'We trust in the LORD our God,' is it not He [r]whose high places and whose altars Hezekiah has taken away, and has said to Judah and to Jerusalem, 'You shall worship before this altar'? 2 Kin. 18:4, 5

8 "Now therefore, come make a bargain with my master the king of Assyria, and I will give you two thousand horses, if you are able on your part to set riders on them.

9 "How then can you repulse one official of the least of my master's servants, and rely on Egypt for chariots and for horsemen?

10 "And have I now come up without the LORD's approval against this land to destroy it? The LORD said to me, 'Go up against this land, and destroy it.' " ' "

11 Then Eliakim and Shebna and Joah said to Rabshakeh, "Speak now to your servants in Aramaic, for we [t]understand *it;* and do not speak with us in Judean, in the hearing of the people who are on the wall." *hear*

12 But Rabshakeh said, "Has my master sent me only to your master and to you to speak these words, *and* not to the men who sit on the wall, *doomed* to eat their own dung and drink their own urine with you?"

13 Then Rabshakeh stood and cried with a loud voice in Judean, and said, "Hear the words of the great king, the king of Assyria.

14 "Thus says the king, 'Do not let Hezekiah deceive you, for he will not be able to deliver you;

15 nor let Hezekiah make you trust in the LORD, saying, "The LORD will surely deliver us, this city shall not be given into the hand of the king of Assyria."

16 'Do not listen to Hezekiah,' for thus says the king of Assyria, 'Make your peace with me and come out to me, and eat each of his vine and each of his fig tree

and drink each of the [r]waters of his
own cistern, Prov. 5:15
17 until I come and take you
away to a land like your own land,
a land of grain and new wine, a
land of bread and vineyards.
18 '*Beware* lest Hezekiah misleads you, saying, "The [r]LORD will
deliver us." Has any one of the
gods of the nations delivered his
land from the hand of the king of
Assyria? Is. 36:15
19 'Where are the gods of [r]Ha-
math and Arpad? Where are the
gods of Sepharvaim? And when
have they delivered Samaria from
my hand? Is. 10:9-11; 37:11-13
20 'Who among all the [r]gods of
these lands have delivered their
land from my hand, that the [r]LORD
should deliver Jerusalem from my
hand?' " 1 Kin. 20:23, 28 • Is. 36:15
21 But they were silent and [r]an-
swered him not a word; for the
king's commandment was, "Do
not answer him." Prov. 9:7, 8
22 Then Eliakim the son of Hilkiah, who was over the household,
and [r]Shebna the scribe and Joah
the son of Asaph, the recorder,
came to Hezekiah with their
clothes torn and told him the
words of Rabshakeh. Is. 22:15

CHAPTER 37

AND when King Hezekiah heard
it, he tore his clothes, covered
himself with sackcloth and entered the house of the LORD.
2 Then he sent [r]Eliakim who
was over the household with
[r]Shebna the scribe and the elders
of the priests, covered with sackcloth, to Isaiah the prophet, the
son of Amoz. Is. 22:20 • Is. 22:15
3 And they said to him, "Thus
says Hezekiah, 'This day is a day
of distress, rebuke, and rejection;
for children have come to birth,
and there is no strength to deliver.
4 'Perhaps the LORD your God
will hear the words of Rabshakeh,
whom his master the king of Assyria has sent to [r]reproach the living God, and will rebuke the
words which the LORD your God
has heard. Therefore, offer a
prayer for the remnant that is
left.' " Is. 36:13-15, 18, 20
5 So the servants of King Hezekiah came to Isaiah.
6 And Isaiah said to them,
"Thus you shall say to your master, 'Thus says the LORD, "Do [r]not
be afraid because of the words
that you have heard, with which
the servants of the king of Assyria
have blasphemed Me. Is. 7:4
7 "Behold, I will put a spirit in
him so that he shall hear a rumor
and [r]return to his own land. And I
will make him fall by the sword in
his own land." ' " Is. 37:37, 38
8 Then Rabshakeh returned
and found the king of Assyria
fighting against [r]Libnah, for he had
heard that [t]the king had left Lachish. Num. 33:20; Josh. 10:29 • *he*
9 When he heard *them* say
concerning Tirhakah king of
[a]Cush, "He has come out to fight
against you," and when he heard
it he sent messengers to Hezekiah, saying, ***Ethiopia***
10 "Thus you shall say to Hezekiah king of [t]Judah, 'Do not let
your God in whom you trust deceive you, saying, "Jerusalem
shall not be given into the hand of
the king of Assyria." ***Judah, saying***

11 'Behold,[r] you have heard what
the kings of Assyria have done to
all the lands, destroying them
completely. So will you be
[t]spared? Is. 10:9-11 • *delivered*
12 'Did the gods of those nations
which my fathers have destroyed
deliver them, *even* Gozan and Haran and Rezeph and the sons of
Eden who *were* in Telassar?
13 'Where is the king of Hamath,
the king of Arpad, the king of the
city of Sepharvaim, *and of* Hena
and Ivvah?' "
14 Then Hezekiah took the [t]let-
ter from the hand of the messengers and read it, and he went up to
the house of the LORD and spread
it out before the LORD. *letters*
15 And Hezekiah prayed to the
LORD saying,
16 "O LORD of hosts, the God of
Israel, [r]who art enthroned *above*
the cherubim, Thou art the God,
Thou alone, of all the kingdoms of
the earth. Thou hast made heaven
and earth. 1 Sam. 4:4; Ps. 80:1; 99:1
17 "Incline Thine ear, O LORD,
and hear; open Thine eyes, O
LORD, and see; and listen to all the
words of Sennacherib, who sent
them to reproach the living God.
18 "Truly, O LORD, the kings of
Assyria have devastated all the
countries and their lands,
19 and have cast their gods into
the fire, for they were not gods
but the [r]work of men's hands,
wood and stone. So they have destroyed them. Is. 2:8; 17:8; 41:24, 29
20 "And now, O LORD our God,
[r]deliver us from his hand that all
the kingdoms of the earth may
know that Thou alone, LORD, art
God." Is. 25:9; 33:22; 35:4

21 Then [r]Isaiah the son of Amoz
sent word to Hezekiah, saying,
"Thus says the LORD, the God of
Israel, 'Because you have prayed
to Me about Sennacherib king of
Assyria, Is. 37:2
22 this is the word that the
LORD has spoken against him:
"She has despised you and
mocked you,
The virgin daughter of Zion;
She has [r]shaken *her* head behind you, Job 16:4
The daughter of Jerusalem!
23 "Whom have you reproached
and blasphemed?
And against whom have you
raised *your* voice,
And [t]haughtily lifted up your
eyes? *on high*
Against the [r]Holy One of Is-
rael! Ezek. 39:7; Hab. 1:12
24 "Through your servants you
have reproached the
Lord,
And you have said, 'With my
many chariots I came up
to the heights of the
mountains,
To the remotest parts of
[r]Lebanon; Is. 10:33, 34
And I cut down its tall cedars
and its choice cypresses.
And I will go to its highest
peak, its thickest forest.
25 'I dug *wells* and drank waters,
And [r]with the sole of my feet
I dried up Deut. 11:10
All the rivers of Egypt.'
26 "Have you not heard?
Long ago I did it,
From ancient times I [r]planned
it. Acts 2:23; 4:27, 28
Now [r]I have brought it to
pass, Is. 46:11

That you should turn fortified cities into ruinous heaps. Is. 10:6

27 "Therefore their inhabitants were short of strength,
They were dismayed and put to shame;
They were *as* the vegetation of the field and *as* the green herb, Is. 40:7
As grass on the housetops is scorched before it is grown up. Ps. 129:6

28 "But I know your sitting down, Ps. 139:1
And your going out and your coming in,
And your raging against Me.

29 "Because of your raging against Me,
And because your arrogance has come up to My ears,
Therefore I will put My hook in your nose, Ezek. 29:4
And My bridle in your lips,
And I will turn you back by the way which you came.

30 "Then this shall be the sign
for you: you shall eat this year
what grows of itself, in the second
year what springs from the same,
and in the third year sow, reap,
plant vineyards, and eat their
fruit. *eating* • Lev. 25:5, 11
31 "And the surviving remnant
of the house of Judah shall again
take root downward and bear
fruit upward. Is. 4:2; 10:20
32 "For out of Jerusalem shall go
forth a remnant, and out of Mount
Zion survivors. The zeal of the
LORD of hosts shall perform
this." ' Is. 37:4 • 2 Kin. 19:31
33 "Therefore, thus says the
LORD concerning the king of Assyria,
'He shall not come to this
city, or shoot an arrow there; neither
shall he come before it with a
shield, nor throw up a mound
against it. Jer. 6:6; 32:24
34 'By the way that he came, by
the same he shall return, and he
shall not come to this city,' declares
the LORD. Is. 37:29
35 'For I will defend this city to
save it for My own sake and for
My servant David's sake.' "
36 Then the angel of the LORD
went out, and struck 185,000 in
the camp of the Assyrians; and
when men arose early in the
morning, behold, all of these were
dead. *they* • *dead bodies*
37 So Sennacherib, king of Assyria,
departed and returned
home, and lived at Nineveh.
38 And it came about as he was
worshiping in the house of Nisroch
his god, that Adrammelech
and Sharezer his sons killed him
with the sword; and they escaped
into the land of Ararat. And Esarhaddon
his son became king in his
place. Gen. 8:4; Jer. 51:27 • Ezra 4:2

CHAPTER 38

IN those days Hezekiah became
mortally ill. And Isaiah the
prophet the son of Amoz came to
him and said to him, "Thus says
the LORD, 'Set your house in order,
for you shall die and not
live.' " *sick to the point of death*
2 Then Hezekiah turned his
face to the wall, and prayed to the
LORD,
3 and said, "Remember now, O
LORD, I beseech Thee, how I have
walked before Thee in truth and
with a whole heart, and have done

what is good in Thy sight." And
Hezekiah [r]wept bitterly. Ps. 6:6-8
4 Then the word of the LORD
came to Isaiah, saying,
5 "Go and say to Hezekiah,
'Thus says the LORD, the God of
your father David, "I have heard
your prayer, I have seen your
tears; behold, I will add [r]fifteen
years to your [t]life. 2 Kin. 18:2, 13 • *days*
6 "And I will [r]deliver you and
this city from the hand of the king
of Assyria; and I will defend this
city." ' Is. 31:5; 37:35
7 "And this shall be the [r]sign to
you from the LORD, that the LORD
will do this thing that He has spoken: Judg. 6:17, 21, 36-40
8 "Behold, I will cause the
shadow on the stairway, which
has gone down with the sun on
the stairway of Ahaz, to go back
ten steps." So the sun's *shadow*
went back ten steps on the stairway on which it had gone down.
9 A writing of Hezekiah king
of Judah, after his illness and [t]re-
covery: *he lived after his illness*

10 I said, "In [r]the middle of my [t]life Ps. 102:24 • *days*
I am to enter the [r]gates of Sheol; Ps. 107:18
I am to be deprived of the rest of my years."
11 I said, "I shall not see the LORD,
The LORD [r]in the land of the living; Ps. 27:13; 116:9
I shall look on man no more among the inhabitants of the world.
12 "Like a shepherd's tent my dwelling is pulled up and removed from me;
As a [r]weaver I [r]rolled up my life. Job 7:6 • Heb. 1:12
He [r]cuts me off from the loom; Job 6:9
From day until night Thou dost make an end of me.
13 "I composed *my soul* until morning.
[r]Like a lion—so He breaks all my bones, Job 10:16
From day until night Thou dost make an end of me.
14 "Like [r]a swallow, *like* a crane, so I twitter; Job 30:29
I moan like a dove;
My [r]eyes look wistfully to the heights; Ps. 119:123
O Lord, I am oppressed, be my [r]security. Job 17:3
15 "What [r]shall I say? Ps. 39:9
For He has spoken to me, and He Himself has done it;
I shall wander about all my years because of the bitterness of my soul.
16 "O Lord, [r]by *these* things *men* live; Ps. 119:71, 75
And in all these is the life of my spirit;
[t]O restore me to health, and let me live! *Thou wilt*
17 "Lo, for *my own* welfare I had great bitterness;
It is Thou who hast kept my soul from the pit of [a]nothingness, *destruction*
For Thou hast cast all my sins behind Thy back.
18 "For Sheol cannot thank Thee,
Death cannot praise Thee;
Those who go down [r]to the pit cannot hope for Thy faithfulness. Ps. 28:1
19 "It is the [r]living who give thanks to Thee, as I do today; Ps. 118:17; 119:175

A father tells his sons about
Thy faithfulness.
20 "The LORD will surely save
me;
So we will play my songs on
stringed instruments
All *the* days of our life at the
house of the LORD."
21 Now [r]Isaiah had said, "Let
them take a cake of figs, and apply it to the boil, that he may recover." 2 Kin. 20:7, 8
22 Then Hezekiah had said,
"What is the sign that I shall go
up to the house of the LORD?"

CHAPTER 39

AT that time Merodach-baladan
son of Baladan, king of Babylon,
sent letters and a present to Hezekiah, for he heard that he had
been sick and had recovered.
2 And Hezekiah [t]was pleased,
and showed them all his treasure
house, the silver and the gold and
the spices and the precious oil and
his whole armory and all that was
found in his treasuries. There was
nothing in his house, nor in all his
dominion, that Hezekiah did not
show them. *rejoiced over them*
3 Then Isaiah the prophet
came to King Hezekiah and said
to him, "What did these men say,
and from where have they come
to you?" And Hezekiah said,
"They have come to me from a far
[r]country, from Babylon." Jer. 5:15
4 And he said, "What have
they seen in your house?" So Hezekiah [t]answered, "They have seen
all that is in my house; there is
nothing among my treasuries that
I have not shown them." *said*
5 Then Isaiah said to Hezekiah,
"Hear the [r]word of the LORD of
hosts, 1 Sam. 13:13, 14; 15:16
6 'Behold, the days are coming
when [r]all that is in your house, and
all that your fathers have laid up
in store to this day shall be carried
to Babylon; nothing shall be left,'
says the LORD. 2 Kin. 24:13; 25:13-15
7 'And *some* of your sons who
shall issue from you, whom you
shall beget, [r]shall be taken away;
and they shall become officials in
the palace of the king of Babylon.' " 2 Kin. 24:10-16; 2 Chr. 36:10
8 Then Hezekiah said to Isaiah,
"The word of the LORD which you
have spoken is good." For he
[t]thought, "For there will be peace
and truth in my days." *said*

CHAPTER 40

"COMFORT, O comfort My peo-
ple," says your God.
2 "Speak kindly to Jerusalem;
And call out to her, that her
warfare has ended,
That her [r]iniquity has been re-
moved, Is. 33:24; 53:5, 6, 11
That she has received of the
LORD's hand
Double for all her sins."

3 A voice is calling,
"Clear the way for the LORD in
the wilderness;
Make smooth in the desert a
highway for our God.
4 "Let every valley be lifted up,
And every mountain and hill
be made low;
And let the rough ground become a plain,
And the rugged terrain a
broad valley;

5 Then the [r]glory of the LORD
will be revealed, Is. 6:3
And [r]all flesh will see *it* together; Is. 52:10; Joel 2:28
For the mouth of the LORD
has spoken."
6 A voice says, "Call out."
Then he answered, "What
shall I call out?"
[r]All flesh is grass, and all its
loveliness is like the
flower of the field. Job 14:2
7 The [r]grass withers, the flower
fades, James 1:10, 11
[a]When the breath of the LORD
blows upon it; *Because*
Surely the people are grass.
8 The grass withers, the flower
fades,
But [r]the word of our God
stands forever. Matt. 5:18

9 Get yourself up on a [r]high
mountain, Is. 52:7
O Zion, bearer of good news,
Lift up your voice mightily,
O Jerusalem, bearer of good
news;
Lift *it* up, do not fear.
Say to the cities of Judah,
"Here [r]is your God!" Is. 25:9
10 Behold, the Lord GOD will
come with might,
With His arm ruling for Him.
Behold, His [r]reward is with
Him, Is. 62:11; Rev. 22:12
And His recompense before
Him.
11 Like a shepherd He will [r]tend
His flock, Ezek. 34:12-14, 23
In His arm He will gather the
lambs,
And carry *them* in His bosom;
He will gently lead the nursing *ewes*.

12 Who has [r]measured the waters in the hollow of His
hand, Ps. 102:25, 26; Is. 48:13
And marked off the heavens
by the span,
And calculated the dust of
the earth by the measure,
And weighed the mountains
in a balance,
And the hills in a pair of
scales?
13 [r]Who has directed the Spirit
of the LORD, Rom. 11:34
Or as His [r]counselor has informed Him? Is. 41:28
14 With whom did He consult
and *who* [r]gave Him understanding? Job 21:22
And *who* taught Him in the
path of justice and taught
Him knowledge,
And informed Him of the
way of understanding?
15 Behold, the nations are like a
drop from a bucket,
And are regarded as a speck
of dust on the scales;
Behold, He lifts up the islands like fine dust.
16 Even Lebanon is not enough
to burn,
Nor its [r]beasts enough for a
burnt offering. Mic. 6:6, 7
17 [r]All the nations are as nothing
before Him, Is. 29:7
They are regarded by Him as
less than nothing and
[a]meaningless. *void*

18 [r]To whom then will you liken
God? Ex. 8:10; 15:11
Or what likeness will you
compare with Him?
19 *As for* the [a]idol, a craftsman
casts it, *graven image*

A goldsmith [r]plates it with
gold, Is. 2:20; 30:22
And a silversmith *fashions*
chains of silver.
20 He who is too impoverished
for *such* an offering
Selects a [r]tree that does not
rot; Is. 44:14
He seeks out for himself a
skillful craftsman
To [a]prepare an idol that will
not totter. *set up*

21 [r]Do you not know? Have you
not heard? Ps. 19:1; 50:6
Has it not been declared to
you from the beginning?
Have you not understood
[r]from the foundations of
the earth? Is. 48:13; 51:13
22 It is He who [14]sits above the
[15]vault of the earth,
And its inhabitants are like
[r]grasshoppers, Num. 13:33
Who stretches out the heavens like a curtain
And spreads them out like a
[r]tent to dwell in. Job 36:29
23 He *it is* who reduces [r]rulers to
nothing, Job 12:21
Who makes the judges of the
earth [a]meaningless. *void*
24 [16]Scarcely have they been
planted,
[16]Scarcely have they been
sown,
[16]Scarcely has their stock
taken root in the earth,
But He merely blows on
them, and they wither,
And the storm carries them
away like stubble.
25 "To [r]whom then will you liken
Me Is. 40:18
That I should be *his* equal?"
says the Holy One.
26 Lift up your eyes on high
And see [r]who has created
these *stars*, Is. 42:5; 48:12
The One who leads forth
their host by number,
He calls them all by name;
Because of the greatness of
His might and the
strength of *His* power
Not one *of them* is missing.

27 Why do you say, O Jacob,
and assert, O Israel,
"My way is [r]hidden from the
LORD, Is. 54:8
And the justice due me [t]es-
capes the notice of my
God"? *passes by my God*
28 [r]Do you not know? Have you
not heard? Is. 40:21
The Everlasting God, the
LORD, the Creator of the
ends of the earth
Does not become weary or
tired.
His understanding is [r]inscru-
table. Ps. 147:5; Rom. 11:33
29 He gives strength to the
[r]weary, Is. 50:4; Jer. 31:25
And to *him who* lacks might
He increases power.
30 Though [r]youths grow weary
and tired, Jer. 6:11; 9:21
And vigorous [r]young men
stumble badly, Is. 9:17
31 Yet those who [a]wait for the
LORD *hope in*
Will gain new strength;
They will [a]mount up *with*
wings like eagles,
They will run and not get
tired, *sprout wings*
They will walk and not become weary.

[14]Or, *is enthroned* [15]Or, *circle*
[16]Or, *Not even*

CHAPTER 41

"COASTLANDS, listen to Me in silence, Is. 11:11 • Hab. 2:20
And let the peoples gain new strength; Is. 40:31
Let them come forward, then let them speak; Is. 34:1
Let us come together for judgment. Is. 1:18; 43:26
2 "Who has aroused one from the east Is. 41:25; 45:1-3
Whom He calls in righteousness to His feet? Is. 42:6
He delivers up nations before him, 2 Chr. 36:23; Ezra 1:2
And subdues kings.
He makes them like dust with his sword, 2 Sam. 22:43
As the wind-driven chaff with his bow. Is. 40:24
3 "He pursues them, passing on in safety,
By a way he had not been traversing with his feet.
4 "Who has performed and accomplished *it*, Is. 41:26
Calling forth the generations from the beginning?
'I, the LORD, am the first, and with the last. I am He.' "
5 The coastlands have seen and are afraid; Is. 41:1
The ends of the earth tremble; Josh. 5:1; Ps. 67:7
They have drawn near and have come.
6 Each one helps his neighbor,
And says to his brother, "Be strong!"
7 So the craftsman encourages the smelter, Is. 44:12, 13
And he who smooths *metal* with the hammer *encourages* him who beats the anvil,
Saying of the soldering, "It is good";
And he fastens it with nails,
That it should not totter.
8 "But you, Israel, My servant,
Jacob whom I have chosen,
Descendant of Abraham My friend, Is. 29:22; 51:2
9 "You whom I have taken from the ends of the earth,
And called from its remotest parts, Is. 43:5-7
And said to you, 'You are My servant, Is. 42:1; 44:1
I have chosen you and not rejected you. Ps. 135:4
10 'Do not fear, for I am with you; Deut. 20:1; 31:6
Do not anxiously look about you, for I am your God.
I will strengthen you, surely I will help you, Is. 41:14; 44:2
Surely I will uphold you with My righteous right hand.'
11 "Behold, all those who are angered at you will be shamed and dishonored;
Those who contend with you will be as nothing, and will perish. Is. 17:13
12 "You will seek those who quarrel with you, but will not find them, Job 20:7-9
Those who war with you will be as nothing, and nonexistent.
13 "For I am the LORD your God, who upholds your right hand, Is. 42:6; 45:1
Who says to you, 'Do not fear, I will help you.'
14 "Do not fear, you worm Jacob, you men of Israel;
I will help you," declares the LORD, "and your Re-

deemer is the Holy One of Israel. Is. 35:10
15 "Behold, I have made you a new, sharp threshing sledge with double edges;
[r]You will thresh the mountains, and pulverize *them,* Mic. 4:13; Hab. 3:12
And will make the hills like chaff.
16 "You will [r]winnow them, and the wind will carry them away, Jer. 51:2
And the storm will scatter them;
But you will [r]rejoice in the LORD, Is. 25:9; 35:10
You will glory in the Holy One of Israel.

17 "The [a]afflicted and needy are seeking water, but there is none, *poor*
And their tongue is parched with thirst;
I, the LORD, [r]will answer them Myself, Is. 30:19; 65:24
As the God of Israel I will not forsake them.
18 "I will open [r]rivers on the bare heights, Is. 30:25; 43:19
And springs in the midst of the valleys;
I will make [r]the wilderness a pool of water, Is. 35:6, 7
And the dry land fountains of water.
19 "I will put the cedar in the wilderness,
The acacia, and the myrtle, and the [a]olive tree; *oleaster*
I will place the [r]juniper in the desert, Is. 35:1; 55:13; 60:13
Together with the box tree and the cypress,
20 That [r]they may see and recognize, Is. 40:5; 43:10
And consider and gain insight as well,
That the [r]hand of the LORD has done this, Job 12:9
And the Holy One of Israel has created it.

21 "Present [t]your case," the LORD says. *Bring near*
"Bring forward your strong *arguments,*"
The King of Jacob says.
22 [r]Let them bring forth and declare to us what is going to take place; Is. 44:7
As for the former *events,* declare what they *were,*
That we may consider them, and know their outcome;
Or announce to us what is coming.
23 Declare the things that are going to come afterward,
That we may know that you are gods;
Indeed, [r]do good or evil, that we may anxiously look about us and fear together. Jer. 10:5
24 Behold, [r]you are of [t]no account, Ps. 115:8 • *nothing*
And [r]your work amounts to nothing; Is. 37:19; 41:29
He who chooses you is an [r]abomination. Prov. 3:32

25 "I have aroused one from the north, and he has come;
From the rising of the sun he will call on My name;
And he will come upon rulers as *upon* mortar,
Even as the potter treads clay."

26 Who has ʳdeclared *this* from
the beginning, that we
might know? Is. 41:22
Or from former times, that
we may say, "*He is*
right!"?
Surely there was ʳno one who
declared, Hab. 2:18, 19
Surely there was no one who
proclaimed,
Surely there was no one who
heard your words.
27 "Formerly *I said* to Zion, 'Behold,
here they are.'
And to Jerusalem, 'I will give
a ʳmessenger of good
news.' Is. 40:9; 44:28
28 "But ʳwhen I look, there is no
one, Is. 50:2; 59:16; 63:5
And there is no counselor
ᵗamong them *out of those*
Who, if I ask, can ʳgive an answer.
Is. 46:7
29 "Behold, all of them are [17]false;
Their works are worthless,
Their molten images are
wind and emptiness.

CHAPTER 42

"BEHOLD, My ʳServant, whom I
ᵃuphold; Is. 41:8 • *hold fast*
My ʳchosen one *in whom* My
soul delights. Luke 9:35
I have put My ʳSpirit upon
Him; Is. 11:2; 59:21
He will bring forth ʳjustice to
the nations. Is. 2:4
2 "He will not cry out or raise
His voice,
Nor make His voice heard in
the street.
3 "A bruised reed He will not
break,
And a dimly burning wick He
will not extinguish;
He will faithfully bring forth
ʳjustice. Ps. 72:2, 4; 96:13
4 "He will not be ʳdisheartened
or crushed, Is. 40:28
Until He has established justice
in the earth;
And the coastlands will wait
expectantly for His law."

5 Thus says God the LORD,
Who created the heavens
and stretched them out,
Who spread out the ʳearth
and its offspring, Ps. 24:1, 2
Who ʳgives breath to the people
on it, Job 12:10; 33:4
And spirit to those who walk
in it,
6 "I am the LORD, I have called
you in righteousness,
I will also ʳhold you by the
hand and watch over
you, Is. 41:13; 45:1
And I will appoint you as a
covenant to the people,
As a light to the nations,
7 To open blind eyes,
To ʳbring out prisoners from
the dungeon, Is. 49:9; 61:1
And those who dwell in darkness
from the prison.
8 "I am the LORD, that is ʳMy
name; Ex. 3:15; Ps. 83:18
I will not give My ʳglory to
another, Ex. 20:3-5
Nor My praise to ᵃgraven images.
idols
9 "Behold, the former things
have come to pass,
Now I declare new things;
Before they spring forth I
proclaim *them* to you."

10 Sing to the LORD a new song,

[17] Another reading is *nothing*

Sing His praise from the ʳend
of the earth! Is. 49:6; 62:11
You who go down to the sea,
and all that is in it.
You ʳislands and those who
dwell on them. Is. 42:4
11 Let the wilderness and its
cities lift up *their voices*,
The settlements where ʳKedar
inhabits. Is. 21:16; 60:7
Let the inhabitants of ʳSela
sing aloud, Is. 16:1
Let them shout for joy from
the tops of the ʳmoun-
tains. Is. 52:7; Nah. 1:15
12 Let them ʳgive glory to the
LORD, Is. 24:15
And declare His praise in the
ʳcoastlands. Is. 42:4
13 ʳThe LORD will go forth like a
warrior, Ex. 15:3
He will arouse *His* ʳzeal like a
man of war. Is. 9:7; 26:11
He will utter a shout, yes, He
will raise a war cry.
He will ʳprevail against His
enemies. Is. 66:14-16

14 "I ʳhave kept silent for a long
time, Ps. 50:21; Is. 57:11
I have kept still and re-
strained Myself.
Now like a woman in labor I
will groan,
I will both gasp and pant.
15 "I will ʳlay waste the mountains and hills, Is. 2:12-16
And wither all their vegetation;
I will ʳmake the rivers into
coastlands, Is. 44:27
And dry up the ponds.
16 "And I will lead the blind by a
way they do not know,
In paths they do not know I
will guide them.
I will ʳmake darkness into
light before them Eph. 5:8
And ʳrugged places into
plains. Is. 40:4; Luke 3:5
These are the things I will do,
And I will ʳnot leave them undone." Josh. 1:5
17 They shall be turned back
and be ʳutterly put to
shame, Ps. 97:7
Who trust in idols,
Who say to molten images,
"You are our gods."

18 Hear, you deaf!
And look, you blind, that you
may see.
19 Who is blind but My servant,
Or so deaf as My ʳmessenger
whom I send? Is. 44:26
Who is so blind as he that is
at peace *with Me*,
Or so blind as the servant of
the LORD?
20 ʳYou have seen many things,
but you do not observe
them; Rom. 2:21
Your ears are open, but none
hears.
21 The LORD was pleased for
His righteousness' sake
To make the law ʳgreat and
glorious. Is. 42:4; 51:4
22 But this is a people plundered and despoiled;
All of them are ʳtrapped in
caves, Is. 24:18
Or are ʳhidden away in prisons; Is. 24:22
They have become a prey
with none to deliver
them,
And a spoil, with none to say,
"Give *them* back!"

23 Who among you will give ear
to this?

Who will give heed and listen hereafter?
24 Who gave Jacob up for spoil, and Israel to plunderers?
Was it not the LORD, against whom we have sinned,
And in whose ways they were not willing to walk,
And whose law they did not obey? Is. 48:18; 57:17
25 So He poured out on him the heat of His anger
And the fierceness of battle;
And it set him aflame all around,
Yet he did not recognize *it;*
And it burned him, but he paid no attention.

CHAPTER 43

BUT now, thus says the LORD, your Creator, O Jacob,
And He who formed you, O Israel, Is. 43:7, 21
"Do not fear, for I have redeemed you; Is. 43:5
I have called you by name; you are Mine! Gen. 32:28
2 "When you pass through the waters, I will be with you; Ps. 66:12; Is. 8:7, 8
And through the rivers, they will not overflow you.
When you walk through the fire, you will not be scorched, Is. 29:6; 30:27-29
Nor will the flame burn you.
3 "For I am the LORD your God,
The Holy One of Israel, your Savior; Is. 19:20; 43:11
I have given Egypt as your ransom,
Cush and Seba in your place.
4 "Since you are precious in My sight, Ex. 19:5, 6
Since you are honored and I love you, Is. 49:5 • Is. 63:9
I will give *other* men in your place and *other* peoples in exchange for your life.
5 "Do not fear, for I am with you; Is. 8:10; 43:2
I will bring your offspring from the east, Is. 41:8
And gather you from the west. Is. 49:12
6 "I will say to the north, 'Give *them* up!' Ps. 107:3
And to the south, 'Do not hold *them* back.'
Bring My sons from afar,
And My daughters from the ends of the earth,
7 Everyone who is called by My name, Is. 56:5; 62:2
And whom I have created for My glory, Ps. 100:3
Whom I have formed, even whom I have made."

8 Bring out the people who are blind, even though they have eyes, Is. 6:9; 42:19
And the deaf, even though they have ears.
9 All the nations have gathered together Is. 34:1; 41:1
In order that the peoples may be assembled.
Who among them can declare this Is. 41:22, 23, 26
And proclaim to us the former things?
Let them present their witnesses that they may be justified, Is. 44:9
Or let them hear and say, "It is true."
10 "You are My witnesses," declares the LORD,

"And [r]My servant whom I have chosen, Is. 41:8
In order that you may know and believe Me,
And understand that [r]I am He. Is. 41:4
[r]Before Me there was no God formed, Is. 45:5, 6
And there will be none after Me.
11 "I, even I, am the LORD;
And there is no [r]savior besides Me. Is. 43:3; 45:21
12 "It is I who have declared and saved and proclaimed,
And there was no strange *god* among you;
So you are My witnesses," declares the LORD,
"And I am God.
13 "Even from eternity I am He;
And there is none who can deliver out of My hand;
[r]I act and who can reverse it?" Job 9:12; Is. 14:27

14 Thus says the LORD your [r]Redeemer, the Holy One of Israel, Is. 41:14
"For your sake I have sent to Babylon,
And will bring them all down as fugitives,
[18]Even the [r]Chaldeans, into the [r]ships in which they rejoice. Is. 23:13 • Jer. 51:13
15 "I am the LORD, your Holy One,
[r]The Creator of Israel, your [r]King." Is. 43:1 • Is. 41:20; 44:6
16 Thus says the LORD,
Who [r]makes a way through the sea Ex. 14:21, 22
And a path through the mighty waters,
17 Who brings forth the [r]chariot and the horse, Ex. 15:19
The army and the mighty man
(They will lie down together *and* not rise again;
They have been [r]quenched *and* extinguished like a wick): Ps. 118:12; Is. 1:31
18 "Do [r]not call to mind the former things, Is. 65:17
Or ponder things of the past.
19 "Behold, I will do something [r]new, Is. 42:9; 48:6
Now it will spring forth;
Will you not be aware of it?
I will even make a roadway in the wilderness,
Rivers in the desert.
20 "The beasts of the field will glorify Me;
The [r]jackals and the ostriches; Is. 13:22; 35:7
Because I have given waters in the wilderness
And rivers in the desert,
To give drink to My chosen people.
21 "The people whom [r]I formed for Myself, Is. 43:1
Will declare My praise.

22 "Yet you have not called on Me, O Jacob;
But you have become weary of Me, O Israel.
23 "You have [r]not brought to Me the sheep of your burnt offerings; Amos 5:25
Nor have you honored Me with your sacrifices.
I have not [r]burdened you with offerings, Jer. 7:21-26
Nor wearied you with [r]incense. Lev. 2:1; 24:7

[18]Another reading is *As for the Chaldeans, their rejoicing is turned into lamentations*

24 "You have bought Me no
sweet cane with money,
Neither have you [a]filled Me
with the fat of your sacrifices; *saturated*
Rather you have burdened
Me with your sins,
You have [r]wearied Me with
your iniquities. Is. 1:14

25 "I, even I, am the one who
wipes out your transgres-
sions for My own sake;
And I will [r]not remember
your sins. Jer. 31:34
26 "Put[a] Me in remembrance; let
us argue our case to-
gether, *Report to Me*
State your *cause*, that you
may be proved right.
27 "Your first forefather sinned,
And your spokesmen have
transgressed against Me.
28 "So I will pollute the princes
of the sanctuary;
And I will consign Jacob to
the [r]ban, and Israel to re-
vilement. Is. 24:6

CHAPTER 44

"BUT now listen, O Jacob, My
[r]servant; Is. 41:8
And Israel, whom I have chosen:
2 Thus says the LORD who
made you
And formed you from the
womb, who will help you,
'Do not fear, O Jacob My servant;
And you [r]Jeshurun whom I
have chosen. Deut. 32:15
3 'For I will pour out water on
the thirsty *land*
And streams on the dry
ground;
I will [r]pour out My Spirit on
your offspring, Is. 32:15
And My blessing on your descendants;
4 And they will spring up
among the grass
Like [r]poplars by streams of
water.' Lev. 23:40; Job 40:22
5 "This one will say, 'I am the
LORD'S';
And that one will call on the
name of Jacob;
And another will [r]write[a] *on* his
hand, 'Belonging to the
LORD,' Ex. 13:9 • *with*
And will name Israel's name
with honor.

6 "Thus says the LORD, the [r]King
of Israel Is. 41:21; 43:15
And his [r]Redeemer, the LORD
of hosts: Is. 41:14
'I am the [r]first and I am the
last, Rev. 1:8, 17
And there is no God [r]besides
Me. Is. 43:11; 44:8
7 'And who is like Me? Let him
proclaim and declare it;
Yes, let him recount it to Me
in order,
From the time that I established the ancient nation.
And let them declare to them
the things that are com-
ing
And the events that are
going to take place.
8 'Do not tremble and do not be
afraid;
[r]Have I not long since announced it to you and de-
clared it? Is. 42:9; 48:5
And you are My witnesses.
Is there any God besides Me,
Or is there any *other* Rock?
I know of none.' "

9 Those who fashion[a] a graven
image are all of them futile, and
their precious things are of no
profit; even their own witnesses
fail to see or know, so that they
will be put to shame. *an idol*
10 Who has fashioned a god or
cast an idol to no profit?
11 Behold, all his companions
will be [r]put to shame, for the
craftsmen themselves are mere
men. Let them all assemble themselves, let them stand up, let them
tremble, let them together be put
to shame. Ps. 97:7; Is. 42:17
12 The man shapes iron into a
cutting tool, and does his work
over the coals, fashioning it with
hammers, and working it with his
strong arm. He also gets hungry
and his strength fails; he drinks no
water and becomes weary.
13 *Another* shapes wood, he extends a measuring line; he outlines it with red chalk. He works it
with planes, and outlines it with a
compass, and makes it like the
form of a man, like the beauty of
man, so that it may sit in a house.
14 Surely he cuts cedars for
himself, and takes a[a] cypress or an
oak, and [t]raises *it* for himself
among the trees of the forest. He
plants a fir, and the rain makes it
grow. *holm-oak • makes strong*
15 Then it becomes *something*
for a man to burn, so he takes one
of them and warms himself; he
also makes a fire to bake bread.
He also makes a god and worships
it; he makes it a graven image,
and falls down before it.
16 Half of it he burns in the fire;
over *this* half he eats meat as he
roasts a roast, and is satisfied. He
also warms himself and says,
"Aha! I am warm, I have seen the
fire."
17 But the rest of it he makes
into a god, his graven image. He
falls down before it and worships;
he also prays to it and says, "Deliver me, for thou art my god."
18 They do not know, nor do
they understand, for He has
smeared over their eyes so that
they cannot see and their hearts
so that they cannot comprehend.
19 And no one recalls, nor is
there knowledge or understanding
to say, "I have burned half of it in
the fire, and also have baked
bread over its coals. I roast meat
and eat *it*. Then I make the rest of
it into an abomination, I fall down
before a block of wood!"
20 He [a]feeds on ashes; a deceived heart has turned him aside.
And he cannot deliver himself,
nor say, "Is there not a lie in my
right hand?" *is a companion of ashes*

21 "Remember[r] these things, O
Jacob, Is. 46:8; Zech. 10:9
And Israel, for you are [r]My
servant; Is. 44:1, 2
I have formed you, you are
My servant,
O Israel, you will [r]not be forgotten by Me. Is. 49:15
22 "I have [r]wiped out your transgressions like a thick
cloud, Ps. 51:1,9; Is. 43:25
And your sins like a [a]heavy
mist. *cloud*
[r]Return to Me, for I have redeemed you." Is. 31:6; 55:7
23 Shout for joy, O heavens, for
the LORD has done *it!*
Shout joyfully, you lower
parts of the earth;
Break forth into a shout of
joy, you mountains,

O forest, and every tree in it;
For ʳthe LORD has redeemed
Jacob *Is. 43:1*
And in Israel He ʳshows forth
His glory. *Is. 49:3; 61:3*
24 Thus says the LORD, your ʳRedeemer, and the one who
formed you from the
womb, *Is. 41:14; 43:14*
"I, the LORD, am the maker of
all things,
ʳStretching out the heavens
by Myself, *Is. 40:22; 42:5*
And spreading out the earth
all alone,
25 Causing the ᵗomens of boasters to fail, *signs*
Making fools out of diviners,
ʳCausing wise men to draw
back, *2 Sam. 15:31*
And ᵗturning their knowledge
into foolishness, *He turns*
26 ʳConfirming the word of His
servant, *Zech. 1:6*
And performing the purpose
of His messengers.
It is I who says of Jerusalem,
'She shall be inhabited!'
And of the cities of Judah,
'They shall be built.'
And I will raise up her ruins
again.
27 "*It is I* who says to the depth
of the sea, 'Be dried up!'
And I will make your rivers
ʳdry. *Is. 42:15; 50:2*
28 "*It is I* who says of Cyrus, '*He
is* My shepherd!
And he will perform all My
desire.'
And he declares of Jerusalem, 'She will be built,'
And of the temple, 'Your
foundation will be laid.' "

CHAPTER 45

THUS says the LORD to ʳCyrus
His anointed, *Is. 44:28*
Whom I have taken by the
right ʳhand, *Ps. 72:23*
To ʳsubdue nations before
him, *Jer. 50:3, 35*
And ᵗto loose the loins of
kings; *I will loose*
To open doors before him so
that gates will not be
shut:
2 "I will go before you and
ʳmake the rough places
smooth; *Is. 40:4*
I will shatter the doors of
bronze, and cut through
their iron bars.
3 "And I will give you the treasures of darkness,
And hidden wealth of secret
places,
In order that you may know
that it is I,
The LORD, the God of Israel,
who ʳcalls you by your
name. *Ex. 33:12, 17*
4 "For the sake of ʳJacob My servant, *Is. 41:8, 9; 44:1*
And Israel My chosen *one,*
I have also ʳcalled you by
your name; *Is. 43:1*
I have given you a title of
honor
Though you have ʳnot known
Me. *Acts 17:23*
5 "I am the LORD, and ʳthere is
no other; *Is. 45:6, 14, 18, 21*
Besides Me there is no God.
I will gird you, though you
have not known Me;
6 That ᵗmen may know from
the rising to the setting of
the sun *they*

That there is [r]no one besides
Me. Is. 45:5
I am the LORD, and there is
no other,
7 The One forming light and
creating darkness,
Causing [a]well-being and creating calamity; *peace*
I am the LORD who does all
these.

8 "Drip [r]down, O heavens, from
above, Ps. 72:6; Hos. 10:12
And let the clouds pour
down righteousness;
Let the earth open up and
salvation bear fruit,
[r]And righteousness spring up
with it. Is. 60:21; 61:11
I, the LORD, have created it.

9 "Woe to *the one* who quarrels
with his Maker—
An earthenware vessel
[t]among the vessels of
earth! *with*
Will the [r]clay say to the potter, 'What are you
doing?' Jer. 18:6
Or the thing you are making
say, 'He has no hands'?
10 "Woe to him who says to a father, 'What are you be-
getting?'
Or to a woman, 'To what are
you giving birth?' "

11 Thus says the LORD, the Holy
One of Israel, and his
[t]Maker: *Fashioner*
"Ask [a]Me about the things to
come concerning My
sons, *Will you ask*
And you shall commit to Me
the work of My hands.
12 "It is I who made the earth,
and created man upon it.
I stretched out the heavens
with My hands,
And I ordained all their host.
13 "I have aroused him in [r]right-
eousness, Is. 41:2
And I will [r]make all his ways
smooth; Is. 45:2
He will build My city, and
will let My exiles go free,
Without any payment or reward," says the LORD of
hosts.

14 Thus says the LORD,
"The products of Egypt and
the merchandise of Cush
And the Sabeans, men of
stature,
Will [r]come over to you and
will be yours; Is. 14:1, 2
They will walk behind you,
they will come over in
[r]chains Ps. 149:8
And will bow down to you;
They will make supplication
to you:
'Surely, God is [a]with you, and
there is none else, *in*
No other God.' "
15 Truly, Thou art a God who
[r]hides Himself, Ps. 44:24
O God of Israel, Savior!
16 They will be [r]put to shame
and even humiliated, all
of them; Is. 42:17; 44:9
The [r]manufacturers of idols
will go away together in
humiliation. Is. 44:11
17 Israel has been saved by the
LORD
With an [r]everlasting salvation; Rom. 11:26
You will not be put to shame
or humiliated
To all eternity.

18 For thus says the LORD, who
created the heavens
(He is the God who formed
the earth and made it,
He established it and did not
create it a waste place,
But formed it to be ʳinhab-
ited), Gen. 1:26; Ps. 115:16
"I am the LORD, and ʳthere is
none else. Is. 45:5
19 "I ʳhave not spoken in secret,
In some dark land; Is. 48:16
I did not say to the ᵗoffspring
of Jacob, *seed*
'Seek Me in a waste place';
I, the LORD, ʳspeak righteousness Ps. 19:8; Is. 45:23
ʳDeclaring things that are upright. Is. 43:12; 44:8

20 "Gather yourselves and come;
Draw near together, you fugitives of the nations;
They have no knowledge,
Who ʳcarry about their
wooden idol, Jer. 10:5
And ʳpray to a god who cannot save. Is. 44:17; 46:6, 7
21 "Declare ʳ and set forth *your*
case; Is. 41:23; 43:9
Indeed, let them consult together.
ʳWho has announced this
from of old? Is. 41:26
Who has long since declared
it?
Is it not I, the LORD?
And there is ʳno other God
besides Me, Is. 45:5
A righteous God and a ʳSav-
ior; Is. 43:3, 11
There is none except Me.
22 "Turn to Me, and be saved, all
the ends of the earth;
For I am God, and there is no
other.
23 "I have sworn by Myself,
The ʳword has gone forth
from My mouth in right-
eousness Gen. 22:16
And will not turn back,
That to Me every knee will
bow, every tongue will
swear *allegiance.*
24 "They will say of Me, 'Only
in the LORD are right-
eousness and strength.'
Men will come to Him,
And ʳall who were angry at
Him shall be put to
shame. Is. 41:11
25 "In the LORD all the offspring
of Israel
Will be ʳjustified, and will glory." 1 Kin. 8:32; Is. 53:11

CHAPTER 46

ʳBEL has bowed down, Nebo
stoops over; Is. 2:18
Their images are *consigned*
to the beasts and the cattle.
The things that you carry are
burdensome,
A load for the weary *beast.*
2 They stooped over, they have
bowed down together;
They could not rescue the
burden,
But have themselves ʳgone
into captivity. Hos. 10:5, 6

3 "Listen ʳ to Me, O house of Jacob, Is. 46:12
And all ʳthe remnant of the
house of Israel, Is. 10:21, 22
You who have been ʳborne by
Me from birth, Is. 49:1
And have been carried from
the womb;
4 Even to your old age, I ᵗshall
be the same, *I am He*

And even to your graying
years I shall bear *you!*
I have [a]done *it,* and I shall
carry *you;* *made you*
And I shall bear *you,* and I
shall deliver *you.*

5 "To[r] whom would you liken
Me, Is. 40:18, 25
And make Me equal and
compare Me,
That we should be alike?
6 "Those who [r]lavish gold from
the purse Jer. 10:4
And weigh silver on the scale
Hire a goldsmith, and he
makes it *into* a god;
They [r]bow down, indeed they
worship it. Is. 44:15, 17
7 "They [r]lift it upon the shoulder
and carry it; Jer. 10:5
They set it in its place and it
stands *there.*
[r]It does not move from its
place. Is. 40:20; 41:7
Though one may cry to it, it
[r]cannot answer; Is. 41:28
It [r]cannot deliver him from
his distress. Is. 45:20

8 "Remember this, and be [t]assured;
Recall it to [t]mind, you transgressors. *firm • heart*
9 "Remember the [r]former things
long past, Deut. 32:7
For I am God, and there is [r]no
other; Is. 45:5, 21
I am God, and there is [r]no one
like Me, Is. 41:26, 27
10 Declaring the end from the
beginning
And from ancient times
things which have not
been done,
Saying, 'My [r]purpose will be
established, Ps. 33:11
And I will accomplish all My
good pleasure';
11 Calling a [r]bird of prey from
the [r]east, Is. 18:6 • Is. 41:2
The man of [t]My purpose from
a far country. *His*
Truly I have spoken; truly I
will bring it to pass.
I have planned *it, surely* I
will do it.

12 "Listen to Me, you [r]stubborn-minded, Ps. 76:5; Is. 48:4
Who are [r]far from righteousness. Ps. 119:150
13 "I bring near My righteousness, it is not far off;
And My salvation will not
delay.
And I will grant [r]salvation in
Zion, Joel 3:17; 1 Pet. 2:6
And My glory for Israel.

CHAPTER 47

"COME[r] down and sit in the
dust, Is. 3:26; Jer. 48:18
O [r]virgin [r]daughter of Babylon; Jer. 46:11 • Jer. 50:42
Sit on the ground without a
throne,
O daughter of the Chaldeans.
For you shall no longer be
called [r]tender and delicate. Deut. 28:56
2 "Take the [r]millstones and
grind meal. Ex. 11:5
Remove your [r]veil, strip off
the skirt, Gen. 24:65
Uncover the leg, cross the
rivers.
3 "Your [r]nakedness will be uncovered, Ezek. 16:37
Your shame also will be exposed;
I will take vengeance and
will not spare a man."

4 Our Redeemer, the LORD of
hosts is His name,
The Holy One of Israel.
5 "Sit[r] silently, and go into darkness, Jer. 8:14; Lam. 2:10
O daughter of the Chaldeans;
For you will no more be
called
The queen of kingdoms.
6 "I was angry with My people,
I profaned My heritage,
And gave them into your
hand.
You did not show mercy to
them,
On the aged you made your
yoke very heavy.
7 "Yet you said, 'I shall be a
[r]queen forever.' Is. 47:5
These things you did not [r]con-
sider, Is. 42:25; 57:11
Nor remember the [r]outcome
of them. Deut. 32:29

8 "Now, then, hear this, you
sensual one,
Who dwells securely,
Who says in your heart,
'I[r] am, and there is no one besides me. Zeph. 2:15
I shall [r]not sit as a widow,
Nor shall I know loss of children.' Rev. 18:7
9 "But these [r]two things shall
come on you suddenly in
one day: Is. 13:16, 18
Loss of children and widowhood.
They shall come on you in
full measure
In spite of your many [r]sorcer-
ies, Nah. 3:4; Rev. 18:23
In spite of the great power of
your spells.
10 "And you felt secure in your
wickedness and said,
'No[r] one sees me,' Ezek. 8:12
Your wisdom and your
knowledge, [t]they have deluded you; *it has*
For you have said in your
heart,
'I[r] am, and there is no one besides me.' Is. 47:8
11 "But evil will come on you
Which you will not know
how to charm away;
And disaster will fall on you
For which you cannot atone,
And destruction about which
you do not know
Will come on you suddenly.

12 "Stand *fast* now in your spells
And in your many sorceries
With which you have labored
from your youth;
Perhaps you will be able to
profit,
Perhaps you may cause
trembling.
13 "You are [r]wearied with your
many counsels; Jer. 51:58
Let now the astrologers,
Those who prophesy by the
stars,
Those who predict by the
new moons,
Stand up and save you from
what will come upon you.
14 "Behold, they have become
[r]like stubble, Nah. 1:10
[r]Fire burns them; Jer. 51:30
They cannot deliver them-
selves from the power of
the flame;
There will be [r]no coal to
warm by, Is. 44:16
Nor a fire to sit before!
15 "So have those become to you
with whom you have la-
bored,

Who have trafficked with you from your youth;
Each has wandered in his own [t]way. *side, region*
There is none to save you.

CHAPTER 48

"HEAR this, O house of Jacob, who are named Israel
And who came forth from the [t]loins of Judah, *waters*
Who [r]swear by the name of the LORD Deut. 6:13
And invoke the God of Israel,
But not in truth nor in [r]righteousness. Is. 58:2; Jer. 4:2
2 "For they call themselves after the holy city,
And [r]lean on the God of Israel; Jer. 7:4; 21:2
The LORD of hosts is His name.
3 "I [r]declared the former things long ago Is. 41:22; 42:9; 43:9
And they went forth from My mouth, and I proclaimed them.
[r]Suddenly I acted, and they came to pass. Is. 29:5
4 "Because I know that you are [a]obstinate, *harsh*
And your [r]neck is an iron sinew, 2 Chr. 36:13
And your forehead bronze,
5 Therefore I declared *them* to you long ago,
Before they took place I proclaimed *them* to you,
Lest you should say, 'My [r]idol has done them, Jer. 44:15-18
And my graven image and my molten image have commanded them.'
6 "You have heard; look at all this.
And you, will you not declare it?
I proclaim to you [r]new things from this time, Is. 42:9
Even hidden things which you have not known.
7 "They are created now and not long ago;
And before today you have not heard them,
Lest you should say, 'Behold, I knew them.'
8 "You have not heard, you have not known.
Even from long ago your ear has not been open,
Because I knew that you would deal very treacherously;
And you have been called a rebel from birth.
9 "For the sake of My name I [r]delay My wrath, Is. 30:18
And *for* My praise I restrain *it* for you,
In order not to cut you off.
10 "Behold, I have refined you, but not as silver;
I have tested you in the furnace of affliction.
11 "For My own sake, for My own sake, I will act;
For how can *My name* be profaned?
And My [r]glory I will not give to another. Deut. 32:26, 27

12 "Listen to Me, O Jacob, even Israel whom I called;
[r]I am He, I am the first, I am also the last. Is. 41:4
13 "Surely My hand [r]founded the earth, Ex. 20:11; Ps. 102:25
And My right hand spread out the heavens;

When I [r]call to them, they
stand together. Is. 40:26
14 "Assemble[r], all of you, and listen!
Is. 43:9; 45:20
Who among them has declared these things?
The LORD loves him; he shall carry out His good pleasure on [r]Babylon,
And His arm *shall be against* the Chaldeans. Is. 13:4, 5
15 "I, even I, have spoken; indeed I have called him,
I have brought him, and He will make his ways successful.
16 "Come[r] near to Me, listen to this: Is. 34:1; 41:1; 57:3
From the first I have [r]not spoken in secret, Is. 45:19
[r]From the time it took place, I was there. Is. 43:13
And now the Lord GOD has sent Me, and His Spirit."

17 Thus says the LORD, your [r]Redeemer, the Holy One of Israel; Is. 41:14; 43:14
"I am the LORD your God, who teaches you to profit,
Who [r]leads you in the way you should go. Ps. 32:8
18 "If only you had [r]paid attention to My commandments! Deut. 5:29; 32:29
Then your well-being would have been like a river,
And your righteousness like the waves of the sea.
19 "Your [r]descendants would have been like the sand,
And your offspring like its grains; Gen. 22:17; Is. 10:22
[r]Their name would never be cut off or destroyed from My presence." Is. 56:5; 66:22

20 Go forth from Babylon! Flee from the Chaldeans!
Declare with the sound of [r]joyful shouting, proclaim this, Is. 42:10; 49:13
[r]Send it out to the end of the earth; Jer. 31:10; 50:2
Say, "The[r] LORD has redeemed His servant Jacob." Is. 43:1; 52:9; 63:9
21 And they did not [r]thirst when He led them through the deserts. Is. 30:25; 35:6, 7
He made the water flow out of the rock for them;
He split the rock, and [r]the water gushed forth. Ps. 78:20
22 "There is no peace for the wicked," says the LORD.

CHAPTER 49

LISTEN to Me, O islands,
And pay attention, you peoples from afar.
[r]The LORD called Me from the womb; Is. 44:2, 24
From the [t]body of My mother He named Me. *inward parts*
2 And He has made My mouth like a sharp sword;
In the shadow of His hand He has concealed Me,
And He has also made Me a [a]select arrow; *sharpened*
He has hidden Me in His quiver.
3 And He said to Me, "You are My Servant, Israel,
In Whom I will [a]show My glory." *glorify Myself*
4 But I said, "I have [r]toiled in vain, Is. 65:23
I have spent My strength for nothing and vanity;

Yet surely the justice *due* to
Me is with the LORD,
And My [r]reward with My
God." Is. 35:4; 59:18

5 And now says the LORD, who
formed Me from the
womb to be His Servant,
To bring Jacob back to Him,
in order that Israel might
be gathered to Him
(For I am [r]honored in the
sight of the LORD, Is. 43:4
And My God is My strength),
6 He says, "It is too [t]small a
thing that You should be
My Servant *light*
To raise up the tribes of Jacob,
and to restore the
preserved ones of Israel;
I will also make You a light
[a]of the nations *to*
So that My salvation may
[t]reach to the [r]end of the
earth." *be* • Is. 48:20
7 Thus says the LORD, the [r]Redeemer
of Israel, *and* its
Holy One, Is. 48:17
To the [r]despised One,
To the One abhorred by the
nation, Ps. 22:6-8
To the Servant of rulers,
"Kings shall see and arise,
Princes shall also bow down;
Because of the LORD who is
faithful, the Holy One of
Israel who has chosen
You."

8 Thus says the LORD, "In a [r]favorable
time I have answered
You, 2 Cor. 6:2
And in a day of salvation I
have helped You;
And I will [r]keep You and give
You for a covenant of the
people, Is. 26:3; 27:3
To [t]restore the land, to make
them inherit the desolate
heritages; *establish*
9 Saying to those who are
bound, 'Go forth,'
To those who are in darkness,
'Show yourselves.'
Along the roads they will
feed,
And their pasture will be on
all [r]bare heights. Is. 41:18
10 "They will [r]not hunger or
thirst, Is. 33:16; 48:21
Neither will the scorching
[r]heat or sun strike them
down; Ps. 121:6
For He who has compassion
on them will lead them,
And will guide them to
[r]springs of water. Is. 35:7
11 "And I will make all My
mountains a road,
And My [r]highways will be
raised up. Is. 11:16; 19:23
12 "Behold, these shall come
[r]from afar; Is. 49:1; 60:4
And lo, these *will come* from
the [r]north and from the
west, Is. 43:5, 6
And these from the land of
Sinim."
13 Shout for joy, O heavens!
And rejoice, O earth!
Break forth into joyful shouting,
O mountains!
For the LORD has comforted
His people, Is. 40:1; 51:3, 12
And will [r]have compassion on
His afflicted. Is. 54:7, 8, 10

14 But Zion said, "The LORD has
forsaken me,
And the Lord has forgotten
me."
15 "Can a woman forget her
nursing child,

And have no compassion on
the son of her womb?
Even these may forget, but I
will not forget you.
16 "Behold, I have [r]inscribed you
on the palms *of My*
hands; Song 8:6; Hag. 2:23
Your [r]walls are continually
before Me. Ps. 48:12, 13
17 "Your builders hurry;
Your [r]destroyers and
devastators Is. 10:6; 37:18
Will depart from you.
18 "Lift[r] up your eyes and look
around; Is. 60:4; John 4:35
All of them gather together,
they come to you.
As I live," declares the LORD,
"You shall surely put on all of
them as jewels, and bind
them on as a bride.
19 "For [r]your waste and desolate
places, and your de-
stroyed land— Is. 1:7; 3:8
Surely now you will be [r]too
cramped for the inhabi-
tants, Zech. 10:10
And those who swallowed
you will be far away.
20 "The [r]children of whom you
were bereaved will yet
say in your ears, Is. 54:1-3
'The place is too cramped for
me;
Make room for me that I may
live *here.*'
21 "Then you will [r]say in your
heart, Is. 29:23; 54:6, 7
'Who has begotten these for
me,
Since I have been bereaved
of my children,
And am [r]barren, an exile and
a wanderer? Lam. 1:1
And who has reared these?
Behold, I was left alone;
[r]From where did these
come?' " Is. 60:8

22 Thus says the Lord GOD,
"Behold, I will lift up My hand
to the nations,
And set up My [r]standard to
the peoples; Is. 11:10, 12
And they will bring your
sons in *their* bosom,
And your daughters will be
carried on *their* shoul-
ders.
23 "And [r]kings will be your
guardians, Is. 14:1, 2
And their princesses your
nurses.
They will [r]bow down to you
with their faces to the
earth, Is. 45:14; 60:14
And [r]lick the dust of your
feet; Ps. 72:9; Mic. 7:17
And *you* will [r]know that I am
the LORD; Is. 41:20; 43:10
Those who hopefully [r]wait for
Me will not be put to
shame. Ps. 37:9; Is. 25:9

24 "Can[r] the prey be taken from
the mighty man,
Or the captives of a tyrant be
rescued?" Matt. 12:29
25 Surely, thus says the LORD,
"Even the [r]captives of the
mighty man will be taken
away, Jer. 50:33, 34
And the prey of the tyrant
will be rescued;
For I will contend with the
one who contends with
you,
And I will save your sons.
26 "And I will feed your oppressors with their own flesh,
And they will become drunk

with their own blood as with sweet wine;
And ʳall flesh will know that I, the LORD, am your Savior, Is. 45:6; Ezek. 39:7
And your Redeemer, the Mighty One of Jacob."

CHAPTER 50

THUS says the LORD,
"Where is the ʳcertificate of divorce, Deut. 24:1, 3
By which I have ʳsent your mother away? Is. 54:6, 7
Or to whom of My creditors did I ʳsell you? Deut. 32:30
Behold, you were sold for your ʳiniquities, Is. 52:3
And for your ʳtransgressions your mother ʳwas sent away. Is. 1:28 • Jer. 3:8
2 "Why was there ʳno man when I came? Is. 41:28; 59:16
When I called, *why* was there none to answer?
Is My ʳhand so short that it cannot ransom?
Or have I no power to deliver? Gen. 18:14
Behold, I dry up the sea with My rebuke,
I ʳmake the rivers a wilderness; Josh. 3:16; Is. 42:15
Their fish stink for lack of water,
And die of thirst.
3 "I ʳclothe the heavens with blackness, Rev. 6:12
And I make sackcloth their covering."

4 The Lord GOD has given Me the tongue of disciples,
That I may know how to ʳsustain the weary one with a word. Is. 57:19; Jer. 31:25
He awakens *Me* ʳmorning by morning, Ps. 5:3; 88:13
He awakens My ear to listen as a disciple.
5 The Lord GOD has ʳopened My ear; Ps. 40:6
And I was not disobedient,
Nor did I turn back.
6 I ʳgave My back to those who strike *Me,* Matt. 26:67
And My cheeks to those who pluck out the beard;
I did not cover My face from humiliation and spitting.
7 For the Lord GOD ʳhelps Me,
Therefore, I am not disgraced; Is. 42:1; 49:8
Therefore, I have set My face like ʳflint, Ezek. 3:8, 9
And I know that I shall not be ashamed.
8 He who ʳvindicates Me is near; Is. 45:25; Rom. 8:33, 34
Who will contend with Me?
Let us ʳstand up to each other; Is. 1:18; 41:1
Who has a case against Me?
Let him draw near to Me.
9 Behold, ʳthe Lord GOD helps Me; Is. 41:10
ʳWho is he who condemns Me? Is. 54:17
Behold, ʳthey will all wear out like a garment; Job 13:28
The moth will eat them.
10 Who is among you that fears the LORD,
That obeys the voice of His ʳservant, Is. 49:2, 3; 50:4
That ʳwalks in darkness and has no light? Eph. 5:8
Let him ʳtrust in the name of the LORD and rely on his God. Is. 12:2; 26:4
11 Behold, all you who ʳkindle a fire, Prov. 26:18

Who [t]encircle yourselves with firebrands, *gird*
Walk in the light of your fire
And among the brands you have set ablaze.
This you will have from My hand;
And you will [r]lie down in torment. Amos 4:9, 10

CHAPTER 51

"LISTEN to me, you who [r]pursue righteousness, Ps. 94:15
Who seek the LORD:
Look to the rock from which you were hewn,
And to the quarry from which you were dug.
2 "Look to [r]Abraham your father, Is. 29:22; 41:8; 63:16
And to Sarah who gave birth to you in pain;
When *he* [r]*was* one I called him, Deut. 1:10; Ezek. 33:24
Then I blessed him and multiplied him."
3 Indeed, [r]the LORD will comfort Zion; Is. 40:1; 49:13
He will comfort all her [r]waste places. Is. 52:9
And her wilderness He will make like Eden,
And her desert like the garden of the LORD;
[r]Joy and gladness will be found in her, Is. 25:9
Thanksgiving and sound of a melody.

4 "Pay[r] attention to Me, O My people; Ps. 50:7; 78:1
And give ear to Me, O My [a]nation; *people*
For a [r]law will go forth from Me, Deut. 18:18; Is. 2:3
And I will set My justice for a light of the peoples.
5 "My righteousness is near, My salvation has gone forth,
And My [r]arms will judge the peoples; Is. 40:10
The [r]coastlands will wait for Me, Is. 42:4; 60:9
And for My arm they will wait expectantly.
6 "Lift up your eyes to the sky,
Then look to the earth beneath;
For the [r]sky will vanish like smoke, Is. 40:26
And the [r]earth will wear out like a garment, Ps. 102:25
And its inhabitants will die[a] in like manner, *like gnats*
But My [r]salvation shall be forever, Is. 45:17
And My righteousness shall not [t]wane. *be broken*
7 "Listen[r] to Me, you who know righteousness, Is. 51:1
A people in whose [r]heart is My law; Ps. 37:31
Do not fear the [r]reproach of man, Matt. 5:11; Acts 5:41
Neither be dismayed at their revilings.
8 "For the [r]moth will eat them like a garment, Is. 50:9
And the [r]grub will eat them like wool. Is. 14:11
But My [r]righteousness shall be forever, Is. 51:6
And My salvation to all generations."

9 [r]Awake, awake, put on strength, O arm of the LORD; Is. 51:17; 52:1
Awake as in the [r]days of old, the generations of long ago. Ex. 6:6; Deut. 4:34

Was it not Thou who cut Rahab in pieces, Job 26:12
Who pierced the dragon?
10 Was it not Thou who dried
up the sea, Is. 11:15; 16
The waters of the great deep;
Who made the depths of the
sea a pathway
For the redeemed to cross
over? Ex. 15:13
11 So the ransomed of the LORD
will return, Jer. 31:11, 12
And come with joyful shouting to Zion;
And everlasting joy *will be*
on their heads. Is. 60:19
They will obtain gladness
and joy,
And sorrow and sighing will
flee away. Rev. 7:17

12 "I, even I, am He who comforts you. Is. 51:3
Who are you that you are
afraid of man who dies,
And of the son of man who is
made like grass;
13 That you have forgotten the
LORD your Maker,
Who stretched out the heavens, Job 9:8; Ps. 104:2
And laid the foundations of
the earth;
That you fear continually all
day long because of the
fury of the oppressor,
As he makes ready to de-
stroy?
But where is the fury of the
oppressor? Is. 49:26
14 "The exile will soon be set
free, and will not die in the dungeon, nor will his bread be lacking. *one in chains*
15 "For I am the LORD your God,
who stirs up the sea and its waves
roar (the LORD of hosts is His
name). Ps. 107:25; Jer. 31:35
16 "And I have put My words in
your mouth, and have covered
you with the shadow of My hand,
to establish the heavens, to found
the earth, and to say to Zion, 'You
are My people.' " *plant*
17 Rouse yourself! Rouse yourself! Arise, O Jerusalem,
You who have drunk from
the LORD's hand the cup
of His anger; Job 21:20
The chalice of reeling you
have drained to the
dregs. *drunk*
18 There is none to guide her
among all the sons she
has borne; Ps. 88:18
Nor is there one to take her
by the hand among all
the sons she has reared.
19 These two things have befall-
en you;
Who will mourn for you?
The devastation and destruction, famine and sword;
How shall I comfort you?
20 Your sons have fainted,
They lie *helpless* at the head
of every street,
Like an antelope in a net,
Full of the wrath of the LORD,
The rebuke of your God.

21 Therefore, please hear this,
you afflicted, Is. 54:11
Who are drunk, but not with
wine: Is. 29:9; 51:17
22 Thus says your Lord, the
LORD, even your God
Who contends for His peo-
ple, Jer. 50:34
"Behold, I have taken out of
your hand the cup of reeling; Is. 51:17

The chalice of My anger,
You will never drink it again.
23 "And I will put it into the hand
of your tormentors,
Who have said to [t]you, 'Lie
down that we may walk
over you.' *your soul*
You have even made your
back like the ground,
And like the street for those
who walk over *it*."

CHAPTER 52

[r]AWAKE, awake, Is. 51:9, 17
Clothe yourself in your
strength, O Zion;
Clothe yourself in your [r]beau-
tiful garments, Ex. 28:2, 40
O Jerusalem, the holy city.
For the uncircumcised and
the [r]unclean Is. 35:8
Will no more come into you.
2 Shake yourself [r]from the
dust, rise up, Is. 29:4
O captive Jerusalem;
Loose yourself from the
chains around your neck,
O captive daughter of Zion.
3 For thus says the LORD, "You
were sold for nothing and you will
be redeemed without money."
4 For thus says the Lord GOD,
"My people [r]went down at the first
into Egypt to reside there, then
the Assyrian oppressed them
without cause. Gen. 46:6
5 "Now therefore, what do I
have here," declares the LORD,
"seeing that My people have been
taken away without cause?"
Again the LORD declares, "Those
who rule over them howl, and My
[r]name is continually blasphemed
all day long. Ezek. 36:20, 23
6 "Therefore My people shall
[r]know My name; therefore in that
day I am the one who is speaking,
'Here I am.' " Is. 49:23
7 How lovely on the mountains
Are the feet of him who
brings good news,
Who announces peace
And brings good news of
[t]happiness, *good*
Who announces salvation,
And says to Zion, "Your God
[a]reigns!" *is King*
8 Listen! Your watchmen lift
up *their* [r]voices, Is. 62:6
They shout joyfully together;
For they will see [t]with their
own eyes *eye to eye*
When the LORD restores
Zion.
9 [r]Break forth, shout joyfully
together, Ps. 98:4; Is. 44:23
You [r]waste places of Jerusa-
lem; Is. 44:26; 51:3; 61:4
For the LORD has comforted
His people,
He has redeemed Jerusalem.
10 The LORD has bared His holy
[r]arm Ps. 98:1-3; Is. 51:9
In the sight of all the nations,
That [t]all the ends of the earth
may see *And . . . earth will see*
The salvation of our God.

11 [r]Depart, depart, go out from
there, Is. 48:20; Jer. 50:8
[r]Touch nothing unclean;
Go out of the midst of her,
purify yourselves,
You who carry the vessels of
the LORD. Num. 19:11, 16
12 But you will not go out in
[r]haste, Ex. 12:11, 33
Nor will you go as fugitives;
For the [r]LORD will go before
you, Is. 26:7; 42:16

And the God of Israel *will be* your rear guard.

13 Behold, My [r]servant will prosper, Is. 42:1; 49:1-7
He will be high and lifted up, and greatly exalted.
14 Just as many were astonished at you, *My people,*
So His [r]appearance was marred more than any man, Is. 53:2, 3
And His form more than the sons of men.
15 Thus He will [r]sprinkle many nations, Num. 19:18-21
Kings will shut their mouths on account of Him;
For what had not been told them they will see,
And what they had not heard they will understand.

CHAPTER 53

WHO has believed our message?
And to whom has the arm of the LORD been revealed?
2 For He grew up before Him like a tender shoot,
And like a root out of parched ground;
He has [r]no *stately* form or majesty Is. 52:14
That we should look upon Him,
Nor appearance that we should [19]be attracted to Him.
3 He was [r]despised and forsaken of men, Ps. 22:6
A man of sorrows, and acquainted with grief;
And like one from whom men hide their face,
He was despised, and we did not esteem Him.

4 Surely our [20]griefs He Himself [r]bore, Matt. 8:17
And our sorrows He carried;
Yet we ourselves esteemed Him stricken,
Smitten of God, and afflicted.
5 But He was [21]pierced through for our transgressions,
He was crushed for [r]our iniquities; Is. 53:10; Rom. 4:25
The chastening for our well-being *fell* upon Him,
And by [r]His scourging we are healed. 1 Pet. 2:24, 25
6 All of us like sheep have gone astray,
Each of us has turned to his own way;
But the LORD has caused the iniquity of us all
To [t]fall on Him. *encounter Him*

7 He was oppressed and He was afflicted,
Yet He did not [r]open His mouth; Mark 14:61; 15:5
[r]Like a lamb that is led to slaughter, Acts 8:32, 33
And like a sheep that is silent before its shearers,
So He did not open His mouth.
8 By oppression and judgment He was taken away;
And as for His generation, who considered
That He was cut off out of the land of the living,
For the transgression of my people to whom the stroke *was due?*

[19] Lit., *desire*

[20] Or, *sickness* [21] Or, *wounded*

9 His grave was assigned with wicked men,
Yet He was with a [r]rich man in His death, Matt. 27:57-60
[r]Because He had [r]done no violence, Is. 42:1-3 • 1 Pet. 2:22
Nor was there any deceit in His mouth.

10 But the LORD was pleased
To [r]crush Him, putting *Him* to grief; Is. 53:5
If He would render Himself *as* a guilt offering,
He will see *His* offspring,
He will prolong *His* days,
And the good pleasure of the LORD will prosper in His hand.
11 As a result of the [a]anguish of His soul, *toilsome labor*
He will [r]see *it* and be satisfied; John 10:14-18
By His [r]knowledge the Righteous One, Rom. 5:18, 19
My Servant, will justify the many,
As He will [r]bear their iniquities. Is. 53:5, 6
12 Therefore, I will allot Him a portion with the great,
And He will divide the booty with the strong;
Because He poured out [t]Himself to death, *His soul*
And was [r]numbered with the transgressors; Mark 15:28
Yet He Himself [r]bore the sin of many, 2 Cor. 5:21
And interceded for the transgressors.

CHAPTER 54

"SHOUT[r] for joy, O barren one, you who have borne no *child;* Gal. 4:27
Break forth into joyful shouting and cry aloud, you who have not travailed;
For the sons of the [r]desolate one *will be* more numerous Is. 62:4
Than the sons of the married woman," says the LORD.
2 "Enlarge[r] the place of your tent; Is. 33:20; 49:19, 20
[t]Stretch out the curtains of your dwellings, spare not; *Let them stretch out*
Lengthen your cords,
And strengthen your pegs.
3 "For you will spread abroad to the right and to the left.
And your [t]descendants will possess nations, *seed*
And they will [r]resettle the desolate cities. Is. 49:19

4 "Fear not, for you will [r]not be put to shame; Is. 45:17
Neither feel humiliated, for you will not be disgraced;
But you will forget the shame of your youth,
And the reproach of your widowhood you will remember no more.
5 "For your [r]husband is your Maker, Jer. 3:14; Hos. 2:19
Whose name is the LORD of hosts;
And your Redeemer is the Holy One of Israel,
Who is called the [r]God of all the earth. Is. 6:3; 11:9
6 "For the LORD has called you,
Like a wife forsaken and grieved in spirit,
Even like a wife of *one's* youth when she is rejected,"
Says your God.

7"For ᵀa ʳbrief moment I forsook you, *in* • Is. 26:20
But with great compassion I will ʳgather you. Is. 11:12
8"In an outburst of anger
I hid My face from you for a moment;
But with everlasting lovingkindness I will have compassion on you,"
Says the LORD your ʳRedeemer. Is. 54:5
9"For this is like the days of Noah to Me;
When I swore that the waters of Noah
Should ʳnot ᵀflood the earth again, Gen. 9:11 • *cross over*
So I have sworn that I will not be angry with you,
Nor will I rebuke you.
10"For the ʳmountains may be removed and the hills may shake, Ps. 102:26
But My lovingkindness will not be removed from you,
And My covenant of peace will not be shaken,"
Says ʳthe LORD who has compassion on you. Is. 54:8
11"O afflicted one, storm-tossed, and not comforted,
Behold, I will set your stones in antimony,
And your foundations I will ʳlay in sapphires. Is. 14:32
12"Moreover, I will make your battlements of rubies,
And your gates of crystal,
And your entire wall of precious stones.
13"And all your sons will be taught of the LORD;
And the well-being of your sons will be great.
14"In ʳrighteousness you will be established; Is. 1:26, 27
You will be far from oppression, for you will not fear;
And from terror, for it will not come near you.
15"If anyone fiercely assails *you* it will not be from Me.
ʳWhoever assails you will fall because of you. Is. 41:11-16
16"Behold, I Myself have created the smith who blows the fire of coals,
And brings out a weapon for its work;
And I have created the destroyer to ruin.
17"No weapon that is formed against you shall prosper;
And every tongue that accuses you in judgment you will condemn.
This is the heritage of the servants of the LORD,
And their vindication is from Me," declares the LORD.

CHAPTER 55

"HO! Every one who thirsts, come to the waters;
And you who have no money come, buy and eat.
Come, buy wine and milk
ʳWithout money and without cost. Hos. 14:4; Matt. 10:8
2"Why do you spend money for what is not bread,
And your wages for what does not satisfy?
Listen carefully to Me, and eat what is good,
And ʳdelight yourself in abundance. Is. 25:6; Jer. 31:14

3"Incline[r] your ear and come to Me. Is. 51:4
Listen, that you may live;
And I will make [r]an everlasting covenant with you, Is. 61:8
According to the faithful mercies shown to David.
4"Behold, I have made him a witness to the peoples,
A [r]leader and commander for the peoples. Dan. 9:25
5"Behold, you will call a [r]nation you do not know, Is. 45:14
And a nation which knows you not will [r]run to you,
Because of the LORD your God, even the Holy One of Israel; Zech. 8:22
For He has glorified you."

6 Seek the LORD while He may be found;
Call upon Him while He is near.
7 [r]Let the wicked forsake his way, Is. 1:16, 19; 58:6
And the unrighteous man his [r]thoughts; Is. 32:7; 59:7
And let him [r]return to the LORD, Is. 31:6; 44:22
And He will have [r]compassion on him; Is. 14:1; 54:8, 10
And to our God,
For He will [r]abundantly pardon. Is. 1:18; 40:2; 43:25
8"For My thoughts are not [r]your thoughts, Is. 65:2
Neither are [r]your ways My ways," declares the LORD. Is. 53:6
9"For [r]as the heavens are higher than the earth, Ps. 103:11
So are My ways higher than your ways,
And My thoughts than your thoughts.
10"For as the rain and the snow come down from heaven,
And do not return there without watering the earth,
And making it bear and sprout,
And furnishing [r]seed to the sower and bread to the eater; 2 Cor. 9:10
11 So shall My [r]word be which goes forth from My mouth; Matt. 24:35
It shall [r]not return to Me empty, Is. 44:26; 59:21
Without [r]accomplishing what I desire, Is. 46:10; 53:10
And without succeeding *in the matter* for which I sent it.
12"For you will go out with joy,
And be led forth with peace;
The mountains and the hills will break forth into shouts of joy before you,
And all the trees of the field will clap *their* hands.
13"Instead of the thorn bush the cypress will come up;
And instead of the nettle the myrtle will come up;
And it will be a [t]memorial to the LORD, name
For an everlasting [r]sign which [r]will not be cut off." Is. 19:20 • Is. 56:5

CHAPTER 56

THUS says the LORD,
"Preserve[r] justice, and do righteousness, Is. 1:17
For My [r]salvation is about to come Ps. 85:9

And My righteousness to be revealed.
2 "How ʳblessed is the man who does this, Ps. 112:1
And the son of man who ʳtakes hold of it; Is. 56:4, 6
Who ʳkeeps from profaning the sabbath, Ex. 20:8-11
And keeps his hand from doing any evil."
3 Let not the ʳforeigner who has joined himself to the LORD say, Is. 14:1; 56:6
"The LORD will surely separate me from His people."
Neither let the eunuch say, "Behold, I am a dry tree."
4 For thus says the LORD,
"To the eunuchs who ʳkeep My sabbaths, Is. 56:2, 6
And choose what pleases Me,
And hold fast My covenant,
5 To them I will give in My house and within My walls a memorial,
And a name better than that of sons and daughters;
I will give them an everlasting ʳname which will not be cut off. Is. 62:2

6 "Also the foreigners who join themselves to the LORD,
To minister to Him, and to love the name of the LORD,
To be His servants, every one who ʳkeeps from profaning the sabbath, Is. 56:2, 4
And holds fast My covenant;
7 Even ʳthose I will bring to My holy mountain, Is. 2:2, 3
And ʳmake them joyful in My house of prayer. Is. 61:10
Their burnt offerings and their sacrifices will be acceptable on My altar;
For ʳMy house will be called a house of prayer for all the peoples." Matt. 21:13
8 The Lord GOD, who ʳgathers the dispersed of Israel, declares, Is. 11:12
"Yet ʳ*others* I will gather to them, to those *already* gathered." Is. 60:3-11

9 All you beasts of the field,
All you beasts in the forest,
Come to eat.
10 His watchmen are blind,
All of them know nothing.
All of them are dumb dogs unable to bark,
Dreamers lying down, who love to slumber;
11 And the dogs are greedy, they are not satisfied.
And they are shepherds who have no understanding;
They have all ʳturned to their own way, Jer. 22:17
Each one to his unjust gain, to the last one.
12 "Come," *they say,* "let us get wine, and let us drink heavily of strong drink;
And tomorrow will be like today, only more so."

CHAPTER 57

THE righteous man perishes, and no man ʳtakes it to heart;
And devout men are taken away, while no one understands. Is. 42:25
For the righteous man is taken away from evil,
2 He enters into peace;
They rest in their beds,

Each one who [r]walked in his
upright way. Is. 26:7
3 "But come here, you sons of a
[r]sorceress, Mal. 3:5
[r]Offspring of an adulterer and
a prostitute. Matt. 16:4
4 "Against whom do you jest?
Against whom do you open
wide your mouth
And stick out your tongue?
Are you not children of
[r]rebellion, Is. 48:8
Offspring of deceit,
5 *Who* inflame yourselves
among the [r]oaks, Is. 1:29
Under every luxuriant tree,
Who [r]slaughter the children
in the ravines, Jer. 7:31
Under the clefts of the crags?
6 "Among the [r]smooth *stones* of
the ravine Jer. 3:9; Hab. 2:19
Is your portion, [t]they are your
lot; *they, they*
Even to them you have
poured out a libation,
You have made a grain offering.
Shall I [a]relent concerning
these things? *repent*
7 "Upon a [r]high and lofty mountain Jer. 3:6; Ezek. 16:16
You have made your bed.
You also went up there to offer sacrifice.
8 "And behind the door and the
doorpost
You have set up your sign;
Indeed, far removed from
Me, you have [r]uncovered
yourself; Ezek. 23:18
And have gone up and made
your bed wide.
And you have made an
agreement for yourselves
with them,
You have loved their bed,
You have looked on *their*
[t]manhood. *hand*
9 "And you have journeyed to
the king with oil
And increased your per-
fumes;
You have [r]sent your envoys a
great distance,
And made *them* go down to
Sheol. Ezek. 23:16, 40
10 "You were tired out by the
length of your road,
Yet you did not say, 'It[r] is
hopeless.' Jer. 2:25; 18:12
You found renewed strength,
Therefore you did not faint.

11 "Of [r]whom were you worried
and fearful, Prov. 29:25
When you lied, and did [r]not
remember Me, Jer. 2:32
Nor give *Me* a thought?
Was I not silent even for a
long time
So you do not fear Me?
12 "I will declare your righteousness and your deeds,
But they will not profit you.
13 "When you cry out, [r]let your
collection *of idols* deliver
you. Jer. 22:20; 30:14
But the wind will carry all of
them up,
And a breath will take *them*
away.
But he who takes refuge in
Me shall inherit the land,
And shall [r]possess My holy
mountain." Is. 65:9

14 And it shall be said,
"Build[r] up, build up, prepare
the way, Is. 62:10; Jer. 18:15
Remove *every* obstacle out of
the way of My people."
15 For thus says the high and
exalted One

Who ʳlives forever, whose
name is Holy, Deut. 33:27
"I ʳdwell *on* a high and holy
place, Is. 33:5; 66:1
And *also* with the contrite
and lowly of spirit
In order to ʳrevive the spirit of
the lowly Ps. 147:3
And to revive the heart of the
contrite.
16 "For I will ʳnot contend forever, Gen. 6:3
ʳNeither will I always be angry; Ps. 85:5; 103:9
For the spirit would grow
faint before Me,
And the breath *of those
whom* I have made.
17 "Because of the iniquity of his
ʳunjust gain I was angry
and struck him; Is. 2:7
I hid *My face* and was angry,
And he went on ʳturning
away, in the way of his
heart. Is. 1:4; Jer. 3:14, 22
18 "I have seen his ways, but I
will ʳheal him; Is. 19:22
I will ʳlead him and restore
comfort to him and to his
mourners, Is. 52:12
19 Creating the ᵗpraise of the
lips. *fruit of the lips*
ʳPeace, peace to him who is
far and to him who is
near," Is. 26:12; 32:17
Says the LORD, "and I will
heal him."
20 But the ʳwicked are like the
tossing sea, Job 18:5-14
For it cannot be quiet,
And its waters toss up refuse
and mud.
21 "There is no peace," says my
God, "for the wicked."

CHAPTER 58

"CRY ʳloudly, do not hold back;
Raise your voice like a trumpet, Is. 40:6
And declare to My people
their transgression,
And to the house of Jacob
their sins.
2 "Yet they ʳseek Me day by day,
and delight to know My
ways, Is. 1:11; Titus 1:16
As a nation that has done
ʳrighteousness, Jer. 7:9
And has not forsaken the ordinance of their God.
They ask Me *for* just decisions,
They delight ʳin the nearness
of God. Ps. 119:150
3 'Why have we fasted and
Thou dost not see?
Why have we humbled ourselves and Thou dost not
ᵗnotice?' *know*
Behold, on the day of your
fast you find *your* desire,
And drive hard all your
workers.
4 "Behold, you fast for contention and strife and to
strike with a wicked fist.
You do not fast like *you do*
today to ʳmake your voice
heard on high. Joel 2:12-14
5 "Is it a fast like this which I
choose, a day for a man
to humble himself?
Is it for bowing ᵗone's head
like a reed, *his*
And for spreading out sackcloth and ashes as a bed?
Will you call this a fast, even
an ʳacceptable day to the
LORD? Is. 49:8; 61:2

6"Is this not the fast which I
choose,
To [r]loosen the bonds of wickedness, Neh. 5:10-12
To undo the bands of the
yoke,
And to [r]let the oppressed go
free, Is. 1:17
And break every yoke?
7"Is it not to divide your bread
with the hungry,
And [r]bring the homeless poor
into the house; Heb. 13:2
When you see the [r]naked, to
cover him; Luke 3:11
And not to hide yourself
from your own flesh?
8"Then your light will break
out like the dawn,
And your recovery will
speedily spring forth;
And your [r]righteousness will
go before you; Ps. 85:13
The glory of the LORD will be
your rear guard.
9"Then you will call, and the
LORD will answer;
You will cry, and He will say,
'Here I am.'
If you [r]remove the yoke from
your midst, Is. 58:6
The [t]pointing of the finger,
and speaking wicked-
ness, *sending out*
10 And if you [t]give yourself to
the hungry, *furnish*
And satisfy the [a]desire of the
afflicted, *soul*
Then your [r]light will rise in
darkness, Job 11:17
And your gloom *will become*
like midday.
11"And the [r]LORD will continually guide you, Is. 49:10
And satisfy your [a]desire in
scorched places, *soul*
And [r]give strength to your
bones; Is. 66:14
And you will be like a [r]wa-
tered garden, Song 4:15
And like a spring of water
whose waters do not fail.
12"And those from among you
will [r]rebuild the ancient
ruins; Is. 49:8; 61:4
You will [r]raise up the age-old
foundations; Is. 44:28
And you will be called the re-
pairer of the breach,
The restorer of the [t]streets in
which to dwell. *paths*

13"If because of the sabbath,
you turn your foot
From doing your *own* pleasure on My holy day,
And call the sabbath a delight, the holy *day* of the
LORD honorable,
And shall honor it, desisting
from your *own* ways,
From seeking your *own* pleasure,
And [r]speaking *your own*
word, Is. 59:13
14 Then you will take [r]delight in
the LORD, Job 22:26
And I will make you ride on
the heights of the earth;
And I will feed you *with* the
heritage of Jacob your father,
For the [r]mouth of the LORD
has spoken." Is. 1:20; 40:5

CHAPTER 59

BEHOLD, [r]the LORD's hand is not
so short Num. 11:23
That it cannot save;
Neither is His ear so dull
That it cannot hear.

2 But your iniquities have made a separation between you and your God,
And your sins have hidden *His* face from you, so that
He does [r]not hear. Is. 58:4
3 For your [r]hands are defiled with blood, Jer. 2:30, 34
And your fingers with iniquity;
Your lips have spoken [r]falsehood, Is. 28:15; 30:9
Your tongue mutters wickedness.
4 No one sues righteously and no one pleads honestly.
They [r]trust in confusion, and speak lies; Jer. 7:4, 8
They conceive mischief, and bring forth iniquity.
5 They hatch adders' eggs and weave the spider's web;
He who eats of their eggs dies,
And *from* that which is crushed a snake breaks forth.
6 Their webs will not become clothing,
Nor will they cover themselves with their works;
Their [r]works are works of iniquity, Is. 57:12; Jer. 6:7
And an [r]act of violence is in their hands. Ezek. 7:11
7 Their feet run to evil,
And they hasten to shed innocent blood;
[r]Their thoughts are thoughts of iniquity; Mark 7:21, 22
Devastation and destruction are in their highways.
8 They do not know the [r]way of peace, Luke 1:79
And there is [r]no justice in their tracks; Hos. 4:1
They have made their paths crooked;
Whoever treads on them does not know peace.

9 Therefore, [r]justice is far from us, Is. 59:14
And righteousness does not overtake us;
We [r]hope for light, but behold, darkness; Is. 5:30
For brightness, but we walk in gloom.
10 We [r]grope along the wall like blind men, Job 5:14
We grope like those who have no eyes;
We [r]stumble at midday as in the twilight, Is. 8:14, 15
Among those who are vigorous we are like dead men.
11 All of us growl like bears,
And moan sadly like doves;
We hope for [r]justice, but there is none, Is. 59:9, 14
For salvation, *but* it is far from us.
12 For our transgressions are multiplied before Thee,
And our [r]sins [t]testify against us; Is. 3:9 • *answer*
For our transgressions are with us,
And we know our iniquities:
13 Transgressing and [r]denying the LORD, Josh. 24:27
And turning away from our God,
Speaking [r]oppression and revolt, Jer. 9:3, 4
Conceiving *in* and [r]uttering from the heart lying words. Mark 7:21, 22
14 And justice is turned back,
And [r]righteousness stands far away; Is. 46:12; Hab. 1:4

For truth has stumbled in the
street,
And uprightness cannot enter.
15 Yes, truth is lacking;
And he who turns aside from
evil [r]makes himself a
prey. Is. 5:23; 10:2; 29:21

Now the LORD saw,
And it was[a]displeasing in His
sight [r]that there was no
justice. *evil* • Is. 1:21-23
16 And He saw that there was
[r]no man, Ezek. 22:30
And was astonished that
there was no one to intercede;
Then His own arm brought
salvation to Him;
And His righteousness upheld Him.
17 And He put on righteousness
like a breastplate,
And a [r]helmet of salvation on
His head; Eph. 6:17
And He put on garments of
vengeance for clothing,
And wrapped Himself with
zeal as a mantle.
18 According to *their* [t]deeds, so
He will repay, *recompense*
Wrath to His adversaries,
recompense to His enemies;
To the coastlands He will
make recompense.
19 So they will fear the name of
the LORD from the west
And His glory from the [r]rising
of the sun, Ps. 113:3
For He will come like a [t]rushing stream, *narrow*
Which the wind of the LORD
drives.

20 "And a [r]Redeemer will come
to Zion, Rom. 11:26
And to those who turn from
transgression in Jacob,"
declares the LORD.
21 "And as for Me, this is My
covenant with them," says the
LORD: "My Spirit which is upon
you, and My words which I have
put in your mouth, shall not depart from your mouth, nor from
the mouth of your offspring, nor
from the mouth of your offspring's offspring," says the LORD,
"from now and forever."

CHAPTER 60

"ARISE, shine; for your [r]light has
come, Is. 52:2
And the glory of the LORD
has risen upon you.
2 "For behold, [r]darkness will
cover the earth, Col. 1:13
And deep darkness the peoples;
But the LORD will rise upon
you,
And His [r]glory will appear
upon you. Is. 4:5
3 "And [r]nations will come to
your light, Is. 2:3; 45:14
And kings to the brightness
of your rising.

4 "Lift up your eyes round
about, and see;
They all gather together,
they come to you.
Your sons will come from
afar,
And your daughters will be
carried in the arms.
5 "Then you will see and be [r]radiant, Ps. 34:5
And your heart will thrill and
rejoice;

Because the [r]abundance of the sea will be turned to you, Is. 23:18; 24:14
The wealth of the nations will come to you.
6"A multitude of camels will cover you,
The young camels of Midian and [r]Ephah; Gen. 25:4
All those from [r]Sheba will come; Gen. 25:3; Ps. 72:10
They will bring [r]gold and frankincense, Matt. 2:11
And will bear good news of the praises of the LORD.
7"All the flocks of [r]Kedar will be gathered together to you, Gen. 25:13
The rams of Nebaioth will minister to you;
They will go up with acceptance on My altar,
And I shall [a]glorify My glorious house. *beautify*
8"Who[r] are these who fly like a cloud, Is. 49:21
And like the doves to their [a]lattices? *dovecotes, windows*
9"Surely the [r]coastlands will wait for Me; Is. 11:11
And the [r]ships of Tarshish *will come* first, Ps. 48:7
To bring your sons from afar,
Their silver and their gold with them,
For the name of the LORD your God,
And for the Holy One of Israel because He has [t]glorified you. *beautified*

10"And [r]foreigners will build up your walls, Is. 14:1, 2
And their [r]kings will minister to you; Rev. 21:24
For in My wrath I struck you,
And in My favor I have had compassion on you.
11"And your [r]gates will be open continually; Is. 26:2
They will not be closed day or night,
So that *men* may [r]bring to you the wealth of the nations, Is. 60:5
With [r]their kings led in procession. Ps. 149:8; Is. 24:21
12"For the [r]nation and the kingdom which will not serve you will perish,
And the nations will be utterly ruined. Zech. 14:17
13"The [r]glory of Lebanon will come to you, Is. 35:2
The juniper, the box tree, and the cypress together,
To beautify the place of My sanctuary;
And I shall make the place of My feet glorious.
14"And the sons of those who afflicted you will come bowing to you,
And all those who despised you will bow themselves at the soles of your feet;
And they will call you the city of the LORD,
The [r]Zion of the Holy One of Israel. Heb. 12:22

15"Whereas you have been forsaken and hated
With no one passing through,
I will make you an everlasting [r]pride, Is. 4:2
A joy from generation to generation.
16"You will also [r]suck the milk of nations, Is. 66:11

And will suck the breast of
kings;
Then you will know that I,
the LORD, am your [r]Savior, Is. 19:20; 43:3, 11
And your Redeemer, the
Mighty One of Jacob.
17 "Instead of bronze I will bring
gold,
And instead of iron I will
bring silver,
And instead of wood, bronze,
And instead of stones, iron.
And I will make peace your
administrators,
And righteousness your
overseers.
18 "Violence will not be heard
again in your land,
Nor devastation or destruction within your borders;
But you will call your [r]walls
salvation, and your [r]gates
praise. Is. 26:1 • Is. 60:11
19 "No longer will you have the
sun for light by day,
Nor for brightness will the
moon give you light;
But you will have the LORD
for an everlasting light,
And your God for your glory.
20 "Your [r]sun will set no more,
Neither will your moon
wane; Is. 30:26
For you will have the LORD
for an everlasting light,
And the days of your mourning will be finished.
21 "Then all your [r]people *will be*
righteous; Is. 45:24, 25
They will [r]possess the land
forever, Ps. 37:11, 22
The branch of My planting,
The work of My hands,
That I may be glorified.
22 "The smallest one will become
a [a]clan, *thousand*
And the least one a mighty
nation.
I, the LORD, will hasten it in
its time."

CHAPTER 61

THE [r]Spirit of the Lord GOD is
upon me, Luke 4:18
Because the LORD has
anointed me
To bring good news to the [a]afflicted; *humble*
He has sent me to bind up
the brokenhearted,
To [r]proclaim liberty to captives, Is. 42:7; 49:9
And freedom to prisoners;
2 To proclaim the favorable
year of the LORD,
And the [r]day of vengeance of
our God; Is. 2:12; 13:6
To comfort all who mourn,
3 To [r]grant those who mourn *in*
Zion, Is. 60:20
Giving them a garland instead of ashes,
The [r]oil of gladness instead of
mourning, Ps. 23:5; 45:7
The mantle of praise instead
of a spirit of fainting.
So they will be called [a]oaks of
righteousness, *terebinths*
The planting of the LORD,
that He may be glorified.

4 Then they will [r]rebuild the
ancient ruins, Is. 49:8
They will raise up the former
devastations,
And they will repair the
ruined cities,
The desolations of many generations.

5 And strangers will stand and pasture your flocks,
And foreigners will be your farmers and your vinedressers.
6 But you will be called the priests of the LORD;
You will be spoken of *as* ministers of our God.
You will eat the [r]wealth of nations, Is. 60:5, 11
And in their [a]riches you will boast. *glory*
7 Instead of your [r]shame *you will have a* [r]double *portion,* Is. 54:4 • Is. 40:2
And *instead of* humiliation they will shout for joy over their portion.
Therefore they will possess a double *portion* in their land,
Everlasting joy will be theirs.
8 For I, the LORD, love justice,
I hate robbery [a]in the burnt offering; *with iniquity*
And I will faithfully give them their recompense,
And I will make an [r]everlasting covenant with them. Ps. 105:10; Is. 55:3
9 Then their offspring will be known among the nations,
And their descendants in the midst of the peoples.
All who see them will recognize them
Because they are the [r]offspring *whom* the LORD has blessed. Is. 44:3

10 I will [r]rejoice greatly in the LORD, Is. 12:1, 2
My soul will exult in my God;
For He has clothed me with garments of salvation,
He has wrapped me with a robe of righteousness,
As a bridegroom decks himself with a garland,
And as a bride adorns herself with her jewels.
11 For as the [r]earth brings forth its sprouts, Is. 4:2; 55:10
And as a garden causes the things sown in it to spring up,
So the Lord GOD will cause righteousness and praise
To spring up before all the nations.

CHAPTER 62

FOR Zion's sake I will not keep silent,
And for Jerusalem's sake I will not keep quiet,
Until her righteousness goes forth like brightness,
And her salvation like a torch that is burning.
2 And the [r]nations will see your righteousness, Is. 60:3
And all kings your glory;
And you will be called by a new [r]name, Is. 56:5
Which the mouth of the LORD will designate.
3 You will also be a [r]crown of beauty in the hand of the LORD, Is. 28:5; Zech. 9:16
And a royal diadem in the hand of your God.
4 It will no longer be said to you, "Forsaken,"
Nor to your land will it any longer be said, "Desolate";

But you will be called, "My
delight is in her,"
And your land, "Married";
For the LORD delights in you,
And *to Him* your land will be
married.
5 For *as* a young man marries
a virgin,
So your sons will marry you;
And *as* the bridegroom rejoices over the bride,
So your [r]God will rejoice over
you. Is. 65:19

6 On your walls, O Jerusalem,
I have appointed [r]watch-
men; Is. 52:8; Jer. 6:17
All day and all night they will
never keep silent.
You who [r]remind the LORD,
take no rest for your-
selves; Jer. 14:21
7 And [r]give Him no rest until
He establishes Luke 18:1-8
And makes Jerusalem a
praise in the earth.
8 [r]The LORD has sworn by His
right hand and by His
strong arm, Is. 45:23; 54:9
"I will [r]never again give your
grain *as* food for your enemies; Deut. 28:31, 33
Nor will foreigners drink
your new wine, for which
you have labored."
9 But those who [r]garner it will
eat it, and praise the
LORD; Is. 65:13, 21-23
And those who gather it will
drink it in the courts of
My sanctuary.

10 Go through, [r]go through the
gates; Is. 26:1; 60:11, 18
Clear the way for the people;
[r]Build up, build up the highway; Is. 57:14
Remove the stones, lift up a
[r]standard over the peo-
ples. Is. 11:10, 12
11 Behold, the LORD has proclaimed to the [r]end of the
earth, Is. 42:10; 49:6
[r]Say to the daughter of Zion,
"Lo, your salvation
comes; Matt. 21:5; Zech. 9:9
Behold His reward is with
Him, and His recom-
pense before Him."
12 And they will call them, "The [r]
holy people, Deut. 7:6
The redeemed of the LORD";
And you will be called,
"Sought out, a city [r]not
forsaken." Is. 41:17; 42:16

CHAPTER 63

WHO is this who comes from
[r]Edom, Ps. 137:7; Is. 34:5, 6
With garments of glowing
colors from Bozrah,
This One who is majestic in
His apparel,
[t]Marching in the greatness of
His strength? *Inclining*
"It is I who speak in righteousness, [r]mighty to
save." Zeph. 3:17
2 Why is Your apparel red,
And Your garments like the
one who [r]treads in the
wine press? Rev. 19:13, 15
3 "I [r] have trodden the wine
trough alone, Rev. 14:20
And from the peoples there
was no man with Me.
I also trod them in My anger,
And [r]trampled them in My
wrath; Mic. 7:10
And their lifeblood is sprinkled on My garments,
And I stained all My raiment.

4 "For the day of vengeance was in My heart,
And My year of redemption has come.
5 "And I looked, and there was no one to help,
And I was astonished and there was [r]no one to uphold; Is. 59:16
So My [r]own arm brought salvation to Me; Ps. 44:3
And My wrath upheld Me.
6 "And I [r]trod down the peoples in My anger, Is. 22:5; 34:2
And made them [r]drunk in My wrath, Is. 29:9; 51:17, 21
And I poured out their lifeblood on the earth."

7 I shall make mention of the [r]lovingkindnesses of the LORD, the praises of the LORD, Ps. 25:6; 92:2
According to all that the LORD has granted us,
And the great [r]goodness toward the house of Israel, 1 Kin. 8:66; Neh. 9:25
Which He has granted them according to His [r]compassion, Ps. 51:1; 86:5
And according to the multitude of His lovingkindnesses.
8 For He said, "Surely, they are [r]My people, Ex. 6:7
Sons who will not deal falsely."
So He became their Savior.
9 In all their affliction [r]He was afflicted, Judg. 10:16
And the angel of His presence saved them;
In His love and in His mercy He redeemed them;
And He [r]lifted them and carried them all the days of old. Deut. 1:31; 32:10-12
10 But they rebelled
And grieved His Holy Spirit;
Therefore, He turned Himself to become their enemy,
He fought against them.
11 Then [r]His people remembered the days of old, of Moses. Ps. 106:44, 45
Where is [r]He who brought them up out of the sea with the shepherds of His flock? Is. 51:10
Where is He who [r]put His Holy Spirit in the midst of them, Hag. 2:5
12 Who caused His [r]glorious arm to go at the right hand of Moses, Ex. 6:6
Who [r]divided the waters before them to make for Himself an everlasting name, Ex. 14:21, 22
13 Who led them through the depths?
Like the horse in the wilderness, they did not [r]stumble; Jer. 31:9
14 As the cattle which go down into the valley,
The Spirit of the [r]LORD gave them rest. Josh. 21:44; 23:1
So didst Thou [r]lead Thy people, Deut. 32:12
To make for Thyself a glorious name.

15 Look down from heaven, and see from Thy holy and glorious habitation;
Where are Thy [r]zeal and Thy mighty deeds? Is. 9:7
The stirrings of Thy heart

and Thy compassion are restrained toward me.
16 For Thou art our [r]Father, though Abraham does not know us, Is. 1:2; 64:8
And Israel does not recognize us.
Thou, O LORD, art our Father,
Our [r]Redeemer from of old is Thy name. Is. 41:14; 44:6
17 Why, O LORD, dost Thou [r]cause us to stray from Thy ways, Ezek. 14:7-9
And [r]harden our heart from fearing Thee? Is. 29:13, 14
[r]Return for the sake of Thy servants, the tribes of Thy heritage. Num. 10:36
18 Thy holy people possessed Thy sanctuary for a little while,
Our adversaries have [r]trodden *it* down. Ps. 74:3-7
19 We have become *like* those over whom Thou hast never ruled,
Like those who were not called by Thy name.

CHAPTER 64

OH, that Thou wouldst rend the heavens *and* come down,
That the mountains might quake at Thy presence—
2 As fire kindles the brushwood, *as* fire causes water to boil—
To make Thy name known to Thine adversaries,
That the nations may tremble at Thy presence!
3 When Thou didst [r]awesome things which we did not expect, Ps. 65:5; 66:3, 5
Thou didst come down, the mountains quaked at Thy presence.
4 For from of old [r]they have not heard nor perceived by ear, 1 Cor. 2:9
Neither has the eye seen a God besides Thee,
Who acts in behalf of the one who waits for Him.
5 Thou dost [r]meet him who rejoices in [r]doing righteousness, Ex. 20:24 • Is. 56:1
Who [r]remembers Thee in Thy ways. Is. 26:13; 63:7
Behold, [r]Thou wast angry, for we sinned, Is. 12:1
We continued in them a long time;
And shall we be saved?
6 For all of us have become like one who is unclean,
And all our righteous deeds are like a filthy garment;
And all of us [r]wither like a leaf, Ps. 90:5, 6
And our iniquities, like the wind, take us away.
7 And there is [r]no one who calls on Thy name, Ezek. 22:30
Who arouses himself to take hold of Thee;
For Thou hast [r]hidden Thy face from us, Deut. 31:18
And hast delivered us into the power of our iniquities.

8 But now, O LORD, [r]Thou art our Father, Is. 63:16
We are the [r]clay, and Thou our potter; Is. 29:16; 45:9
And all of us are the [r]work of Thy hand. Ps. 100:3
9 Do not be angry beyond measure, O LORD,

[r]Neither remember iniquity
forever; Is. 43:25; Mic. 7:18
Behold, look now, all of us
are[r]Thy people. Ps. 79:13
10 Thy[r]holy cities have become
a wilderness, Is. 48:2
Zion has become a wilderness,
Jerusalem a desolation.
11 Our holy and beautiful
[r]house, 2 Kin. 25:9
Where our fathers praised
Thee,
Has been burned *by* fire;
And all our precious things
have become a ruin.
12 Wilt Thou restrain Thyself at
these things, O LORD?
Wilt Thou keep silent and afflict
us beyond measure?

CHAPTER 65

"I PERMITTED Myself to be
sought by[r]those who did
not ask *for Me;*
I permitted Myself to be
found by those who did
not seek Me. Rom. 9:24-26
I said, 'Here am I, here am I,'
To a nation which did not
call on My name.
2 "I[r]have spread out My hands
all day long to a rebellious
people, Rom. 10:21
Who walk *in* the way which
is not good, following
their own thoughts,
3 A people who continually
provoke Me to My face,
Offering sacrifices in[r]gardens
and burning incense on
bricks; Is. 1:29; 66:17
4 Who sit among graves, and
spend the night in secret
places;
Who eat swine's flesh,
And the broth of unclean
meat is *in* their pots.
5 "Who say, 'Keep to yourself,
do not come near me,
For I am holier than you!'
These are smoke in My[t]nostrils,
nose
A fire that burns all the day.
6 "Behold, it is written before
Me,
I will[r]not keep silent, but I
will repay; Ps. 50:3, 21
I will even repay into their
bosom,
7 Both[t]their own[r]iniquities and
the iniquities of their fathers
together," says the
LORD. *your* • Is. 13:11
"Because they have burned incense
on the mountains,
And scorned Me on the hills,
Therefore I will[r]measure
their former work into
their bosom." Jer. 5:29

8 Thus says the LORD,
"As the new wine is found in
the cluster,
And one says, 'Do not destroy
it, for there is[t]benefit
in it,' *blessing*
So I will act on behalf of My
servants
In order[r]not to destroy[t]all of
them. Is. 1:9 • *the whole*
9 "And I will bring forth offspring
from Jacob,
And an[r]heir of My mountains
from Judah; Is. 49:8
Even[r]My chosen ones shall
inherit it, Is. 57:13
And[r]My servants shall dwell
there. Is. 32:18
10 "And Sharon shall be a pasture
land for flocks,

And the valley of Achor a resting place for herds,
For My people who seek Me.
11 "But you who [r]forsake the LORD, Deut. 29:24, 25
Who forget My [r]holy mountain, Is. 2:2, 3; 66:20
Who set a table for Fortune,
And who fill *cups* with mixed wine for Destiny,
12 I will destine you for the [r]sword, Is. 27:1; 34:5, 6
And all of you shall bow down to the slaughter.
Because I called, but you [r]did not answer; 2 Chr. 36:15, 16
I spoke, but you did not hear.
And you did evil in My sight,
And chose that in which I did not delight."

13 Therefore, thus says the Lord GOD,
"Behold, My servants shall [r]eat, but you shall be [r]hungry. Is. 1:19 • Is. 8:21
Behold, My servants shall [r]drink, but you shall be [r]thirsty. Is. 41:17, 18 • Is. 5:13
Behold, My servants shall [r]rejoice, but you shall be [r]put to shame. Is. 61:7 • Is. 42:17
14 "Behold, My servants shall [r]shout joyfully with a glad heart, Ps. 66:4
But you shall cry out with a [t]heavy heart, *pain of*
And you shall wail with a broken spirit.
15 "And you will leave your name for a [r]curse to My chosen ones, Jer. 24:9
And the Lord GOD will slay you.
But My servants will be called by another name.
16 "Because he who [a]is blessed in the earth *bless(es) himself*
Shall be blessed by the [r]God of truth; Ex. 34:6; Ps. 31:5
And he who swears in the earth
Shall [r]swear by the God of truth; Is. 19:18; 45:23
Because the former troubles are forgotten,
And because they are hidden from My sight!

17 "For behold, I create new heavens and a new earth;
And the [r]former things shall not be remembered or come to mind. Is. 43:18
18 "But be glad and rejoice forever in what I create;
For behold, I create Jerusalem *for* rejoicing,
And her people *for* gladness.
19 "I will also [r]rejoice in Jerusalem, and be glad in My people; Jer. 32:41
And there will no longer be heard in her
The voice of weeping and the sound of crying.
20 "No longer will there be *in it* an infant *who lives but a few* days,
Or an old man who does not live out his days;
For the youth will die at the age of one hundred
And the [t]one who does not reach the age of one hundred *one who misses the mark*
Shall be *thought* accursed.
21 "And they shall build houses and inhabit *them;*
They shall also plant vineyards and eat their fruit.

22 "They shall not build, and [r]another inhabit, Is. 62:8, 9
They shall not plant, and another eat;
For [r]as the [t]lifetime of a tree, *so shall be* the days of My people, Ps. 92:12-14 • *days*
And My chosen ones shall [r]wear out the work of their hands. Ps. 21:4; 91:16
23 "They shall not labor in vain,
Or bear *children* for calamity;
For they are the [r]offspring of those blessed by the LORD, Jer. 32:38, 39
And their descendants with them.
24 "It will also come to pass that
before they call, I will [r]answer; and
while they are still speaking, I will
hear. Ps. 91:15; Is. 55:6; 58:9
25 "The wolf and the lamb shall
graze together, and the lion shall
eat straw like the ox; and dust
shall be the serpent's food. They
shall do no evil or harm in all My
holy mountain," says the LORD.

CHAPTER 66

THUS says the LORD,
"Heaven is My throne, and the earth is My footstool.
Where then is a house you could build for Me?
And where is a place that [t]I may rest? *is My resting place?*
2 "For [r]My hand made all these things, Is. 40:26
Thus all these things came into being," declares the LORD.
"But to this one I will look,
To him who is humble and contrite of spirit, and who [r]trembles at My word. Ps. 119:120; Is. 66:5
3 "*But* he who kills an ox is *like* one who slays a man;
He who sacrifices a lamb is *like* the one who breaks a dog's neck;
He who offers a grain offering *is like one who offers* [r]swine's blood; Is. 65:4
He who [r]burns incense is *like* the one who blesses an idol. Lev. 2:2; Is. 1:13
As they have chosen their [r]own ways, Is. 57:17; 65:2
And their soul delights in their abominations,
4 So I will choose their [t]punishments, *ill treatments*
And I will bring on them what they dread.
Because I called, but [r]no one answered; Prov. 1:24
I spoke, but they did not listen.
And they did evil in My sight,
And chose that in which I did not delight."
5 Hear the word of the LORD, you who [r]tremble at His word: Is. 66:2
"Your brothers who [r]hate you, who exclude you for My name's sake, Ps. 38:20
Have said, 'Let the LORD be glorified, that we may see your joy.'
But [r]they will be put to shame. Luke 13:17
6 "A voice of uproar from the city, a voice from the temple,
The voice of the LORD who is [r]rendering recompense to His enemies. Joel 3:7

7 "Before she travailed, she brought forth;
Before her pain came, she gave birth to a boy.
8 "Who[r] has heard such a thing?
Who has seen such things? Is. 64:4
Can a land be [t]born in one day? *travailed with*
Can a nation be brought forth all at once?
As soon as Zion travailed, she also brought forth her sons.
9 "Shall I bring to the point of birth, and not give delivery?" says the LORD.
"Or shall I who gives delivery shut *the womb?*" says your God.
10 "Be[r] joyful with Jerusalem and rejoice for her, all you who love her; Deut. 32:43
Be exceedingly [r]glad with her, all you who mourn over her, Ps. 137:6
11 That you may nurse and [r]be satisfied with her comforting breasts, Is. 49:23
That you may suck and be delighted with her [r]bountiful bosom." Is. 60:1, 2
12 For thus says the LORD, "Behold, I extend [r]peace to her like a river, Ps. 72:3, 7
And the [r]glory of the nations like an overflowing stream; Is. 60:5; 61:6
And you shall [t]be nursed, you shall be carried on the [t]hip and fondled on the knees. *nurse • side*
13 "As one whom his mother comforts, so I will [r]comfort you; Is. 12:1
And you shall be comforted in Jerusalem."
14 Then you shall see *this,* and your heart shall be glad,
And your bones shall flourish like the new grass;
And the [r]hand of the LORD shall be made known to His servants, Ezra 7:9; 8:31
But He shall be indignant toward His enemies.
15 For behold, the LORD will come in [r]fire Is. 10:17
And His [r]chariots like the whirlwind, Ps. 68:17
To render His anger with fury,
And His rebuke with flames of fire.
16 For the LORD will execute judgment by fire
And by His [r]sword on all flesh, Is. 65:12; Ezek. 38:21
And those slain by the LORD will be many.
17 "Those who sanctify and purify themselves *to* go to the [r]gardens, Is. 1:29
Following one in the center,
Who eat swine's flesh, detestable things, and mice,
Shall [r]come to an end altogether," declares the LORD. Is. 1:28, 31
18 "For I know their works and
their thoughts; [t]the time is coming
to gather all nations and tongues.
And they shall come and see My
glory. *it is coming*
19 "And I will set a [r]sign among
them and will send survivors from
them to the nations: Tarshish, Put,
Lud, Meshech, Rosh, Tubal, and
Javan, to the distant coastlands
that have neither heard My fame
nor seen My glory. And they will

declare My glory among the nations. Is. 11:10, 12; 49:22; 62:10

20 "Then they shall [r]bring all your brethren from all the nations as a grain offering to the LORD, on horses, in chariots, in litters, on mules, and on camels, to My holy mountain Jerusalem," says the LORD, "just as the sons of Israel bring their grain offering in a clean vessel to the house of the LORD. Is. 43:6; 49:22; 60:4

21 "I will also take some of them for [r]priests *and* for Levites," says the LORD. Ex. 19:6; Is. 61:6

22 "For just as the new heavens
and the new earth
Which I make will endure
before Me," declares the
LORD,
"So your offspring and your
name will endure.
23 "And it shall be from new
moon to new moon
And from sabbath to sabbath,
All [t]mankind will come to
bow down before Me,"
says the LORD. *flesh*
24 "Then they shall go forth and
look
On the corpses of the men
Who have [a]transgressed
against Me. *rebelled*
For their worm shall not die,
[r]And their fire shall not be
quenched; Matt. 3:12
And they shall be an abhorrence to all mankind."

THE BOOK OF

JEREMIAH

THE words of [r]Jeremiah, the son of Hilkiah, of the priests who were in [r]Anathoth in the land of Benjamin, 2 Chr. 35:25 • Josh. 21:18

2 to whom the word of the LORD came in the days of Josiah, the son of Amon, king of Judah, in the thirteenth year of his reign.

3 It came also in the days of [r]Jehoiakim, the son of Josiah, king of Judah, until the end of the eleventh year of [r]Zedekiah, the son of Josiah, king of Judah, until the exile of Jerusalem in the fifth month. 2 Kin. 23:34 • Jer. 39:2

4 Now the word of the LORD came to me saying,

5 "Before I formed you in the
womb I knew you,
And before you were born I
consecrated you;
I have appointed you a
prophet to the nations."
6 Then I said, "Alas, Lord GOD!
Behold, I do not know how to
speak,
Because I am a youth."
7 But the LORD said to me,
"Do not say, 'I am a youth,'
Because everywhere I send
you, you shall go,
And all that I command you,
you shall speak.
8 "Do not be afraid of them,

For I am with you to deliver
you," declares the LORD.
9 Then the LORD stretched out
His hand and [r]touched my mouth,
and the LORD said to me, Is. 6:7
"Behold, I have put My words
in your mouth.
10 "See, I have appointed you
this day over the nations
and over the kingdoms,
To pluck up and to break
down,
To destroy and to overthrow,
To build and to plant."
11 And the word of the LORD
came to me saying, "What do you
see, Jeremiah?" And I said, "I see
a rod of an almond tree."
12 Then the LORD said to me,
"You have seen well, for [r]I am
watching over My word to perform it." Jer. 31:28
13 And the word of the LORD
came to me a second time saying,
"What [r]do you see?" And I said, "I
see a boiling pot, facing away
from the north." Zech. 4:2
14 Then the LORD said to me,
"Out of the north the evil [t]will
break forth on all the inhabitants
of the land. *will be opened*
15 "For, behold, I am calling [r]all
the families of the kingdoms of
the north," declares the LORD;
"and they will come, and they will
set each one his throne at the entrance of the gates of Jerusalem,
and against all its walls round
about, and against all the [r]cities of
Judah. Jer. 25:9 • Jer. 4:16; 9:11
16 "And I will [t]pronounce My
judgments on them concerning all
their wickedness, whereby they
have forsaken Me and have [a]of-
fered sacrifices to other gods, and
worshiped the works of their own
hands. *speak • burned incense*
17 "Now, [r]gird up your loins, and
arise, and speak to them all which
I command you. Do not be dismayed before them, lest I dismay
you before them. 1 Kin. 18:46
18 "Now behold, I have made
you today as a fortified city, and
as a pillar of iron and as walls of
bronze against the whole land, to
the kings of Judah, to its princes,
to its priests and to the people of
the land.
19 "And they will fight against
you, but they will not overcome
you, for I am with you to deliver
you," declares the LORD.

CHAPTER 2

NOW the word of the LORD came
to me saying,
2 "Go and [r]proclaim in the ears
of Jerusalem, saying, 'Thus says
the LORD, Is. 58:1
"I remember concerning you
the [a]devotion of your
youth, *lovingkindness*
The love of your betrothals,
Your following after Me in
the wilderness,
Through a land not sown.
3 "Israel was holy to the LORD,
The first of His harvest;
[r]All who ate of it became
guilty; Jer. 30:16
Evil came upon them," de-
clares the LORD.' "
4 Hear the word of the LORD, O
house of Jacob, and all the families of the house of Israel.
5 Thus says the LORD,
"What [r]injustice did your fathers find in Me, Is. 5:4
That they went far from Me

And walked after emptiness
and became empty?
6 "And they did not say, 'Where
is the LORD
Who [r]brought us up out of the
land of Egypt, Ex. 20:2
Who [r]led us through the wilderness, Deut. 8:15
Through a land of deserts
and of pits,
Through a land of drought
and of [a]deep darkness,
Through a land that no one
crossed *the shadow of death*
And where no man dwelt?'
7 "And I brought you into the
[r]fruitful land, Deut. 8:7-9
To eat its fruit and its good
things.
But you came and [r]defiled My
land, Ps. 106:38
And My inheritance you
made an abomination.
8 "The priests did not say,
'Where is the LORD?'
And those who handle the
law did not know Me;
The [t]rulers also transgressed
against Me, *shepherds*
And the prophets prophesied
by Baal
And walked after [r]things that
did not profit. Hab. 2:18

9 "Therefore I will yet [r]contend
with you," declares the
LORD, Jer. 2:35
"And with your sons' sons I
will contend.
10 "For [r]cross to the coastlands of
Kittim and see, Is. 23:12
And send to [r]Kedar and observe closely, Is. 21:16
And see if there has been
such *a thing* as this!
11 "Has a nation changed gods,
When [r]they were not gods?
But My people have [r]changed
their glory
For that which does not
profit. Is. 37:19 • Rom. 1:23
12 "Be appalled, [r]O heavens, at
this, Is. 1:2; Jer. 4:23
And shudder, be very desolate," declares the LORD.
13 "For My people have committed two evils:
They have forsaken Me,
The fountain of living waters,
To hew for themselves [r]cisterns, Jer. 14:3
Broken cisterns,
That can hold no water.

14 "Is Israel a slave? Or is he a
homeborn servant?
Why has he become a prey?
15 "The young lions have roared
at him,
They have [t]roared loudly.
And they have [r]made his land
a waste; *given their voice*
His cities have been destroyed, without inhabitant. Jer. 4:7
16 "Also the [a]men of Memphis
and Tahpanhes
Have [t]shaved the crown of
your head. *sons • grazed*
17 "Have you not [r]done this to
yourself, Jer. 4:18
By your forsaking the LORD
your God,
When He led you in the way?
18 "But now what are you doing
on the road to Egypt,
To drink the waters of the
Nile?
Or what are you doing on the
road to Assyria,
To drink the waters of the
[t]Euphrates? *River*

19 "Your[r] own wickedness will
correct you, Is. 3:9
And your [r]apostasies will reprove you; Hos. 11:7
Know therefore and see that
it is evil and bitter
For you to forsake the LORD
your God,
And [r]the dread of Me is not in
you," declares the Lord
GOD of hosts. Ps. 36:1

20 "For long ago [a]I broke your
yoke *you*
And tore off your bonds;
But you said, 'I will not
serve!'
For on every [r]high hill
And under every green tree
You have lain down as a harlot. Deut. 12:2
21 "Yet I planted you a choice
vine,
A completely faithful seed.
How then have you turned
yourself before Me
Into the [r]degenerate shoots of
a foreign vine? Is. 5:4
22 "Although you [r]wash yourself
with lye Jer. 4:14
And use much soap,
The stain of your iniquity is
before Me," declares the
Lord GOD.
23 "How [r]can you say, 'I am not
defiled, Prov. 30:12
I have not gone after the
[r]Baals'? Jer. 9:14
Look at your way in the valley!
Know what you have done!
You are a swift young camel
entangling her ways,
24 A [r]wild donkey accustomed
to the wilderness,
That sniffs the wind in her
passion.
In *the time of* her [t]heat who
can turn her away?
All who seek her will not become weary;
In her month they will find
her. Jer. 14:6 • *occasion*
25 "Keep your feet from being
unshod
And your throat from thirst;
But you said, 'It is [a]hopeless!
No! For I have loved strangers, *desperate*
And after them I will walk.'

26 "As the [r]thief is shamed when
he is discovered,
So the house of Israel is
shamed; Jer. 48:27
They, their kings, their
princes,
And their priests, and their
prophets,
27 Who say to a tree, 'You are
my father,'
And to a stone, 'You gave me
birth.'
For they have turned *their*
[r]back to Me, Jer. 18:17
And not *their* face;
But in the time of their [a]trouble they will say,
'Arise and save us.' *evil*
28 "But where are your [r]gods
Which you made for yourself? Deut. 32:37
Let them arise, if they can
save you
In the time of your [a]trouble;
For *according to* the number
of your cities *evil*
Are your gods, O Judah.

29 "Why do you contend with
Me?

You have [r]all transgressed
against Me," declares the
LORD. Jer. 5:1; 6:13
30 "In[r] vain I have struck your
sons; Is. 1:5
They accepted no chastening.
Your [r]sword has devoured
your prophets Acts 7:52
Like a destroying lion.
31 "O generation, heed the word
of the LORD.
Have I been a wilderness to
Israel,
Or a [r]land of thick darkness?
Why do My people say, 'We
are free to roam; Is. 45:19
We will come no more to
Thee'?
32 "Can a virgin forget her ornaments,
Or a bride her attire?
Yet My people have [r]forgotten Me Ps. 106:21
Days without number.
33 "How well you prepare your
way
To seek love!
Therefore even [a]the wicked
women *in wickedness*
You have taught your ways.
34 "Also on your skirts is found
The [r]lifeblood of the innocent
poor; 2 Kin. 21:16
You did not find them [r]breaking in. Ex. 22:2
But in spite of all these
things,
35 Yet you said, 'I am innocent;
Surely His anger is turned
away from me.'
Behold, I will [r]enter into judgment with you Jer. 25:31
Because you say, 'I have not
sinned.'
36 "Why do you [r]go around so
much Hos. 12:1
Changing your way?
Also, [r]you shall be put to
shame by Egypt Is. 30:3
As you were put to shame by
[r]Assyria. 2 Chr. 28:16
37 "From this *place* also you
shall go out
With [r]your hands on your
head; Jer. 14:3, 4
For the LORD has rejected
[r]those in whom you trust,
And you shall not prosper
with them." Jer. 37:7-10

CHAPTER 3

GOD says, "If a husband divorces his wife,
And she goes from him,
And belongs to another man,
Will he still return to her?
Will not that land be completely [a]polluted? *alienated*
But you are a harlot *with*
many [t]lovers; *companions*
Yet you [r]turn to Me," declares the LORD. Jer. 4:1
2 "Lift up your eyes to the [r]bare
heights and see; Deut. 12:2
Where have you not been
violated?
By the roads you have [r]sat for
them Gen. 38:14
Like an Arab in the desert,
And you have [r]polluted a land
With your harlotry and with
your wickedness. Jer. 2:7
3 "Therefore the [r]showers have
been withheld, Lev. 26:19
And there has been no spring
rain.
Yet you had a harlot's forehead;
You refused to be ashamed.

4 "Have you not just now called
to Me,
'My Father, Thou art the
[t]friend of my youth? *leader*
5 'Will He be angry forever?
Will He [t]be indignant to the
end?' *keep it*
Behold, you have spoken
And have done evil things,
And you have [t]had your
way." *been able*
6 Then the LORD said to me in
the days of Josiah the king, "Have
you seen what faithless Israel did?
She[r]went up on every high hill and
under every green tree, and she
was a harlot there. Jer. 17:2
7 "And I[t]thought, 'After she has
done all these things, she will return to Me'; but she did not return,
and her [r]treacherous sister Judah
saw it. *said* • Jer. 3:11
8 "And I saw that for all the
adulteries of faithless Israel, I had
sent her away and given her a writ
of divorce, yet her treacherous
sister Judah did not fear; but she
went and was a harlot also.
9 "And it came about because
of the lightness of her harlotry,
that she [r]polluted the land and
committed adultery with stones
and trees. Jer. 2:7; 3:2
10 "And yet in spite of all this her
treacherous sister Judah did not
return to Me with all her heart,
but rather in [r]deception," declares
the LORD. Jer. 12:2
11 And the LORD said to me,
"Faithless[r] Israel has proved herself more righteous than treacherous Judah. Ezek. 16:51, 52
12 "Go, and proclaim these
words toward the north and say,
'Return[r], faithless Israel,' declares the LORD; Jer. 3:14
'I[r] will not look upon you in
anger. Jer. 3:5
For I am gracious,' declares
the LORD;
'I will not be angry forever.
13 'Only [t]acknowledge your iniquity, *know*
That you have transgressed
against the LORD your
God
And have scattered your favors to the strangers un-
der every green tree,
And you have not obeyed My
voice,' declares the LORD.
14 'Return, O faithless sons,' declares the LORD;
'For I am a master to you,
And I will take you one from
a city and two from a
family,
And I will bring you to Zion.'
15 "Then I will give you [r]shep-
herds after My own heart, who
will feed you on knowledge and
understanding. Jer. 23:4; 31:10
16 "And it shall be in those days
when you are multiplied and increased in the land," declares the
LORD, "they shall [r]say no more,
'The ark of the covenant of the
LORD.' And it shall not come to
mind, nor shall they remember it,
nor shall they miss *it*, nor shall it
be made again. Is. 65:17
17 "At that time they shall call
Jerusalem 'The Throne of the
LORD,' and all the nations will be
gathered to it, to Jerusalem, for
the name of the LORD; nor shall
they walk anymore after the stubbornness of their evil heart.
18 "In those days the house of
Judah will walk with the house of
Israel, and they will come together from the land of the north

to the land that I gave your fathers as an inheritance.

19 "Then I said,
'How I would set you among [t]My sons, *the*
And give you a pleasant land,
The most beautiful inheritance of the nations!'
And I said, 'You shall call Me, [r]My Father, Jer. 3:4
And not turn away from following Me.'
20 "Surely, as a woman treacherously departs from her [a]lover, *companion*
So you have [r]dealt treacherously with Me, Is. 48:8
O house of Israel," declares the LORD.

21 A voice is heard on the [r]bare heights, Is. 15:2
The weeping *and* the supplications of the sons of Israel;
Because they have perverted their way,
They have [r]forgotten the LORD their God. Jer. 2:32
22 "Return, O faithless sons,
[r]I will heal your faithlessness." Jer. 30:17; 33:6
"Behold, we come to Thee;
For Thou art the LORD our God.
23 "Surely, the hills are a deception,
A tumult *on* the mountains.
Surely, in the LORD our God
Is the salvation of Israel.

24 "But [r]the shameful thing has
consumed the labor of our fathers
since our youth, their flocks and
their herds, their sons and their
daughters. Hos. 9:10
25 "Let us lie down in our shame,
and let our humiliation cover us;
for we have sinned against the
LORD our God, we and our fathers,
since our youth even to this day.
And we have not obeyed the voice
of the LORD our God."

CHAPTER 4

"IF you will [r]return, O Israel," declares the LORD,
"*Then* you should return to Me. Jer. 3:22
And [r]if you will put away your detested things from My presence,
And will not waver, Jer. 7:3
2 And you will [r]swear, 'As the LORD lives,' Deut. 10:20
In truth, in justice, and in righteousness;
Then the nations will bless themselves in Him,
And in Him they will glory."

3 For thus says the LORD to the men of Judah and to Jerusalem,
"Break [r]up your fallow ground,
And do not sow among thorns. Hos. 10:12
4 "Circumcise [r]yourselves to the LORD Deut. 10:16
And remove the foreskins of your heart,
Men of Judah and inhabitants of Jerusalem,
Lest My [r]wrath go forth like fire Is. 30:27, 33
And burn with [r]none to quench it, Amos 5:6
Because of the evil of your deeds."

5 Declare in Judah and proclaim in Jerusalem, and say,

"Blow[r] the trumpet in the land;
Cry aloud and say, Jer. 6:1
'Assemble yourselves, and let
us go
Into the fortified cities.'
6 "Lift up a [r]standard toward
Zion! Is. 62:10
Seek refuge, do not stand
still,
For I am bringing [r]evil from
the north, Jer. 1:14
And great destruction.
7 "A [r]lion has gone up from his
thicket, Jer. 5:6
And a [r]destroyer of nations
has set out; Jer. 25:9
He has gone out from his
place
To make your land a waste.
Your cities will be ruins
Without inhabitant.
8 "For this, [r]put on sackcloth,
Lament and wail; Is. 22:12
For the [r]fierce anger of the
LORD Is. 5:25
Has not turned back from
us."
9 "And it shall come about in
that day," declares the LORD,
"that the heart of the king and the
heart of the princes will fail; and
the priests will be appalled, and
the prophets will be astounded."
10 Then I said, "Ah, Lord GOD!
Surely Thou hast utterly deceived
this people and Jerusalem, saying,
'You will have peace'; whereas a
sword touches the throat."
11 In that time it will be said to
this people and to Jerusalem, "A
[r]scorching wind from the bare
heights in the wilderness in the direction of the daughter of My people—not to winnow, and not to
cleanse, Jer. 13:24 • Hos. 13:15
12 a wind too strong for [t]this—
will come [t]at My command; now I
will also pronounce judgments
against them. *these • for Me*
13 "Behold, he [r]goes up like
clouds, Is. 19:1
And his [r]chariots like the
whirlwind; Is. 5:28
His horses are [r]swifter than
eagles. Lam. 4:19
Woe to us, for [r]we are
ruined!" Is. 3:8

14 Wash your heart from evil, O
Jerusalem,
That you may be saved.
How long will your [r]wicked
thoughts Prov. 1:22
Lodge within you?
15 For a voice declares from
[r]Dan, Jer. 8:16
And proclaims wickedness
from Mount Ephraim.
16 "Report *it* to the nations, now!
Proclaim over Jerusalem,
'Besiegers come from a [r]far
country, Is. 39:3
And lift their voices against
the cities of Judah.
17 'Like watchmen of a field
they are [r]against her
round about, 2 Kin. 25:1, 4
Because she has rebelled
against Me,' declares the
LORD.
18 "Your [r]ways and your deeds
Have [t]brought these things to
you. Is. 50:1 • *done*
This is your evil. How bitter!
How it has touched your
heart!"
19 My [t]soul, my soul! I am in anguish! Oh, my heart!
My heart is pounding in me;
I cannot be silent, *inward parts*

Because you have heard, O my soul,
The sound of the trumpet,
The alarm of war.
20 [r]Disaster on disaster is proclaimed, Ps. 42:7
For the [r]whole land is devastated; Jer. 4:27
Suddenly my [r]tents are devastated, Jer. 10:20
My curtains in an instant.
21 How long must I see the standard,
And hear the sound of the trumpet?
22 "For [r]My people are foolish,
They know Me not;
They are stupid children,
And they have no understanding. Jer. 5:4, 21
They are shrewd to [r]do evil,
But to do good they do not know." Jer. 9:3; 13:23

23 I looked on the earth, and behold, *it was* [r]formless and void; Gen. 1:2; Is. 24:19
And to the heavens, and they had no light.
24 I looked on the mountains, and behold, they were [r]quaking, Is. 5:25
And all the hills [t]moved to and fro. *moved lightly*
25 I looked, and behold, there was no man,
And all the [r]birds of the heavens had fled. Jer. 9:10
26 I looked, and behold, [a]the [r]fruitful land was a wilderness, *Carmel* • Jer. 9:10
And all its cities were pulled down
Before the LORD, before His fierce anger.

27 For thus says the LORD,
"The [r]whole land shall be a desolation, Jer. 12:11
Yet I will not execute a complete destruction.
28 "For this the [r]earth shall mourn, Jer. 12:4
And the [r]heavens above be dark, Is. 5:30
Because I have spoken, I have purposed,
And I will not [t]change My mind, nor will I turn from it." *be sorry*
29 At the sound of the horseman and bowman [r]every city flees; 2 Kin. 25:4
They go into the thickets and climb among the rocks;
Every city is forsaken,
And no man dwells in them.
30 And you, O desolate one, [r]what will you do?
Although you dress in scarlet, Is. 10:3; 20:6; Jer. 13:21
Although you decorate *yourself with* ornaments of gold,
Although you [r]enlarge your eyes with paint, 2 Kin. 9:30
In vain you make yourself beautiful;
Your [r]lovers despise you;
They seek your life. Jer. 22:20
31 For I heard a [t]cry as of a woman in labor, *sound*
The anguish as of one giving birth to her first child,
The cry of the daughter of Zion gasping for breath,
Stretching out her [t]hands, *saying,* *palms*
"Ah, woe is me, for I faint before murderers."

CHAPTER 5

"ROAM[r] to and fro through the
streets of Jerusalem,
And look now, and take note.
And seek in her open
squares, Dan. 12:4
If you can find a man,
If there is one who does justice, who seeks truth,
Then I will pardon her.
2 "And [r]although they say, 'As
the LORD lives,' Is. 48:1
Surely they swear falsely."
3 O LORD, do not [r]Thine eyes
look for truth? 2 Chr. 16:9
Thou hast smitten them,
But they did not weaken;
Thou hast consumed them,
But they [r]refused to take correction. Jer. 7:28; 8:5
They have made their faces
harder than rock;
They have refused to repent.

4 Then I said, "They are only
the poor,
They are foolish;
For they [r]do not know the
way of the LORD
Or the ordinance of their
God. Is. 27:11
5 "I will go to the great
And will speak to them,
For [r]they know the way of the
LORD, Mic. 3:1
And the ordinance of their
God."
But they too, with one accord, have [r]broken the
yoke Ex. 32:25
And burst the bonds.
6 Therefore a lion from the forest shall slay them,
A wolf of the deserts shall
destroy them,
A [r]leopard is watching their
cities. Hos. 13:7
Everyone who goes out of
them shall be torn in
pieces,
Because their [r]transgressions
are many, Jer. 30:14, 15
Their apostasies are numerous.

7 "Why should I pardon you?
Your sons have forsaken Me
And [r]sworn by those who are
[r]not gods. Josh. 23:7
When I had fed them to the
full, Deut. 32:21
They [r]committed adultery
And trooped to the harlot's
house. Jer. 7:9
8 "They were well-fed lusty
horses,
Each one neighing after his
neighbor's wife.
9 "Shall I not punish these *people*," declares the LORD,
"And on a nation such as this
Shall I not avenge Myself?

10 "Go up through her vine rows
and destroy,
But do not execute a complete destruction;
Strip away her branches,
For they are not the LORD's.
11 "For the [r]house of Israel and
the house of Judah
Have dealt very treacherously with Me," declares
the LORD. Jer. 3:6, 7, 20
12 They have [r]lied about the
LORD 2 Chr. 36:16
And said, "[1]Not[r] He; Jer. 14:22
Misfortune will [r]not come on
us; Jer. 23:17
And we [r]will not see sword or
famine. Jer. 14:13

[1] Lit., *He is not*

13 "And the [r]prophets are *as* wind,
And the word is not in them.
Thus it will be done to them!" Job 8:2; Jer. 14:13

14 Therefore, thus says the LORD, the God of hosts,
"Because you have spoken this word,
Behold, I am making My words in your mouth fire
And this people wood, and it will consume them.
15 "Behold, I am [r]bringing a nation against you from afar, O house of Israel," declares the LORD.
"It is an enduring nation,
It is an ancient nation,
A nation whose language you do not know,
Nor can you understand what they say. Is. 5:26
16 "Their [r]quiver is like an open grave, Is. 5:28; 13:18
All of them are mighty men.
17 "And they will devour your harvest and your food;
They will devour your sons and your daughters;
They will devour your flocks and your herds;
They will devour your vines and your fig trees;
They will demolish with the sword your fortified cities in which you trust.

18 "Yet even in those days," declares the LORD, "I will not make
you a complete destruction.
19 "And it shall come about
when [a]they say, 'Why has the LORD
our God done all these things to
us?' then you shall say to them,
'As you have forsaken Me and
served foreign gods in your land,
so you shall serve strangers in a
land that is not yours.' *you*

20 "Declare this in the house of Jacob
And proclaim it in Judah, saying,
21 'Hear this, O foolish and senseless people,
Who have eyes, but see not;
Who have ears, but hear not.
22 'Do you not [r]fear Me?' declares the LORD.
'Do you not tremble in My presence? Deut. 28:58
For I have placed the sand as a boundary for the sea,
An eternal decree, so it cannot cross over it.
Though the waves toss, yet they cannot prevail;
Though they roar, yet they cannot cross over it.
23 'But this people has a [r]stubborn and rebellious heart;
They have turned aside and departed. Deut. 21:18
24 'They do not say in their heart,
"Let us now fear the LORD our God,
Who [r]gives rain in its season,
Both the autumn rain and the spring rain, Ps. 147:8
Who keeps for us
The [r]appointed weeks of the harvest." Gen. 8:22
25 'Your [r]iniquities have turned these away, Jer. 2:17
And your sins have withheld good from you.
26 'For wicked men are found among My people,
They [r]watch like fowlers lying in wait; Ps. 10:9

They set a trap,
They catch men.
27 'Like a cage full of birds,
So their houses are full of [r]deceit; Jer. 9:6
Therefore they have become great and rich.
28 'They are [r]fat, they are sleek,
They also [2]excel in deeds of wickedness; Deut. 32:15
They do not plead the cause,
The cause of the orphan, that they may prosper;
And they do not defend the rights of the poor.
29 'Shall I not punish these *people?*' declares the LORD,
'On a nation such as this
Shall I not avenge Myself?'

30 "An appalling and [r]horrible thing Jer. 23:14
Has happened in the land:
31 The [r]prophets prophesy falsely, Ezek. 13:6
And the priests rule on their *own* authority;
And My people [r]love it so!
But what will you do at the end of it? Mic. 2:11

CHAPTER 6

"FLEE for safety, O sons of Benjamin,
From the midst of Jerusalem!
Now blow a trumpet in Tekoa,
And raise a signal over [r][3]Beth-haccerem; Neh. 3:14
For evil looks down from the north,
And a great destruction.
2 "The comely and dainty one,
[r]the daughter of Zion, I will cut off. Is. 1:8; Jer. 4:31
3 "Shepherds and their flocks will come to her,
They will [r]pitch *their* tents around her, Jer. 4:17
They will pasture each in his [t]place. *hand*
4 "Prepare [t]war against her; *Sanctify*
Arise, and let us [t]attack at [r]noon. *go up*
Woe to us, for the day declines, Jer. 15:8
For the shadows of the evening lengthen!
5 "Arise, and let us [t]attack by night *go up*
And destroy her palaces!"
6 For thus says the LORD of hosts,
"Cut down her trees,
And cast up a [r]siege against Jerusalem. Jer. 32:24
This is the city to be punished,
In whose midst there is only [r]oppression. Jer. 22:17
7 "As a well [t]keeps its waters fresh, *keeps cold*
So she keeps fresh her wickedness.
[r]Violence and destruction are heard in her; Jer. 20:8
[r]Sickness and wounds are ever before Me. Jer. 30:12
8 "Be warned, O Jerusalem,
Lest I be alienated from you;
Lest I make you a desolation,
A land not inhabited."

9 Thus says the LORD of hosts,
"They will [r]thoroughly glean as the vine the remnant of Israel; Jer. 16:16
Pass your hand again like a grape gatherer

[2]Or, *overlook deeds*
[3]I.e., house of the vineyard

Over the branches."
10 To whom shall I speak and
give warning,
That they may hear?
Behold, their ears are [t]closed,
And they cannot listen.
Behold, the word of the LORD
has become a reproach to
them; *uncircumcised*
They have no delight in it.
11 But I am full of the wrath of
the LORD:
I am weary with holding *it* in.
"Pour *it* out on the children in
the street,
And on the gathering of
young men together;
For both husband and wife
shall be taken,
The aged and the very old.
12 "And their [r]houses shall be
turned over to others,
Their fields and their wives
together; Deut. 28:30
For I will [r]stretch out My
hand Jer. 15:6
Against the inhabitants of
the land," declares the
LORD.
13 "For [r]from the least of them
even to the greatest of
them, Jer. 8:10
Everyone is [r]greedy for gain,
And from the prophet even
to the priest Is. 56:11
Everyone deals falsely.
14 "And they have [r]healed the
brokenness of My people
superficially, Jer. 8:11
Saying, 'Peace, peace,'
But there is no peace.
15 "Were they [r]ashamed because
of the abomination they
have done? Jer. 3:3
They were not even ashamed
at all;
They did not even know how
to blush.
Therefore they shall fall
among those who fall;
At the time that I punish
them,
They shall be cast down,"
says the LORD.

16 Thus says the LORD,
"Stand by the ways and see
and ask for the [r]ancient
paths, Is. 8:20; Jer. 12:16
Where the good way is, and
walk in it;
And you shall find rest for
your souls.
But they said, 'We will not
walk *in it.*'
17 "And I set [r]watchmen over
you, *saying,* Is. 21:11
'Listen to the sound of the
trumpet!' Jer. 25:4
But they said, 'We will not
listen.' Hab. 2:1
18 "Therefore hear, O nations,
And know, O congregation,
what is among them.
19 "Hear,[r] O earth: behold, I am
bringing disaster on this
people, Is. 1:2
The fruit of their [a]plans,
Because they have not listened to My words,
And as for My law, they have
rejected it also. *devices*
20 "For[r] what purpose does
frankincense come to Me
from Sheba, Ps. 50:7-9
And the [t]sweet cane from a
distant land? *good*
[r]Your burnt offerings are not
acceptable, Ps. 40:6
And your sacrifices are not
pleasing to Me."

21 Therefore, thus says the
LORD,
"Behold, [r]I am [t]laying stumbling blocks before this
people. Is. 8:14 · *giving*
And they will stumble
against them,
Fathers and sons together;
Neighbor and [t]friend will perish." *his friend*

22 Thus says the LORD,
"Behold, a people is coming
from the north land,
And a great nation will be
aroused from the remote
parts of the earth.
23 "They seize [r]bow and spear;
They are cruel and have no
mercy; Is. 13:18
Their voice roars like the sea,
And they ride on horses,
Arrayed as a man for the battle
Against you, O daughter of
Zion!"
24 We have [r]heard the report of
it; Is. 28:19; Jer. 4:19-21
Our hands are limp.
[r]Anguish has seized us,
Pain as of a woman in childbirth. Jer. 4:31
25 Do not go out into the field,
And do not walk on the road,
For the enemy has a sword,
Terror is on every side.
26 O daughter of my people, [r]put
on sackcloth Jer. 4:8
And [r]roll in ashes; Jer. 25:34
[r]Mourn as for an only son,
A lamentation most bitter.
For suddenly the destroyer
Will come upon us. Amos 8:10

27 "I have [r]made you an assayer
and a tester among My
people, Jer. 1:18
That you may know and assay their way."
28 All of them are stubbornly
rebellious,
Going about as a talebearer.
They are [r]bronze and iron;
They, all of them, are corrupt. Ezek. 22:18
29 The bellows blow fiercely,
The lead is consumed by the
fire;
In vain the refining goes on,
But the wicked are not [a]separated. *drawn off*
30 [r]They call them rejected silver, Ps. 119:119
Because the [r]LORD has rejected them. Jer. 7:29

CHAPTER 7

THE word that came to Jeremiah
from the LORD, saying,
2 "Stand[r] in the gate of the
LORD's house and proclaim there
this word, and say, 'Hear the word
of the LORD, all you of Judah, who
enter by these gates to worship
the LORD!' " Jer. 17:19; 26:2
3 Thus says the LORD of hosts,
the God of Israel, "Amend your
ways and your deeds, and I will let
you dwell in this place.
4 "Do not trust in deceptive
words, saying, 'This is the temple
of the LORD, the temple of the
LORD, the temple of the LORD.'
5 "For [r]if you truly amend your
ways and your deeds, if you truly
practice justice between a man
and his neighbor, Is. 1:19
6 *if* you do not oppress the
alien, the [r]orphan, or the widow,
and do not shed innocent blood in
this place, nor walk after other
gods to your own ruin, Ex. 22:21

7 then I will let you dwell in this place, in the land that I gave to your fathers forever and ever.

8"Behold, you are trusting in deceptive words to no avail.

9"Will you steal, murder, and commit adultery, and swear falsely, and offer sacrifices to Baal, and walk after other gods that you have not known,

10 then come and stand before Me in [r]this house, which is called by My name, and say, 'We are delivered!'—that you may do all these abominations? Jer. 7:11

11"Has [r]this house, which is called by My name, become a [r]den of robbers in your sight? Behold, I, even I, have seen *it*," declares the LORD. Is. 56:7 • Luke 19:46

12"But go now to My place which was in [r]Shiloh, where I made My name dwell at the first, and [r]see what I did to it because of the wickedness of My people Israel. Judg. 18:31 • Ps. 78:60-64

13"And now, because you have done all these things," declares the LORD, "and I spoke to you, [r]rising up early and speaking, but you did not hear, and I called you but you did not answer, Jer. 7:25

14 therefore, I will do to the house which is called by My name, in which you trust, and to the place which I gave you and your fathers, as I did to Shiloh.

15"And I will [r]cast you out of My sight, as I have cast out all your brothers, all the [t]offspring of Ephraim. Jer. 15:1; 52:3 • *seed*

16"As for you, [r]do not pray for this people, and do not lift up cry or prayer for them, and do not intercede with Me; for I do not hear you. Ex. 32:10; Deut. 9:14

17"Do you not see what they are doing in the cities of Judah and in the streets of Jerusalem?

18"The children gather wood, and the fathers kindle the fire, and the women knead dough to make cakes for the queen of heaven; and *they* pour out libations to other gods in order to spite Me.

19"Do they spite Me?" declares the LORD. "Is it not themselves *they spite*, to their own shame?"

20 Therefore thus says the Lord GOD, "Behold, My anger and My wrath will be poured out on this place, on man and on beast and on the trees of the field and on the fruit of the ground; and it will burn and not be quenched."

21 Thus says the LORD of hosts, the God of Israel, "Add your [r]burnt offerings to your sacrifices and [r]eat flesh. Is. 1:11 • Hos. 8:13

22"For I did not [r]speak to your fathers, or command them in the day that I brought them out of the land of Egypt, concerning burnt offerings and sacrifices. Hos. 6:6

23"But this is [t]what I commanded them, saying, 'Obey My voice, and I will be your God, and you will be My people; and you will walk in all the way which I command you, that it may be well with you.' *the word which*

24"Yet they did not obey or incline their ear, but walked in *their own* counsels *and* in the stubbornness of their evil heart, and went backward and not forward.

25"Since the day that your fathers came out of the land of Egypt until this day, I have [r]sent you all My servants the prophets, daily rising early and sending *them*. 2 Chr. 36:15; Luke 11:49

26 "Yet they did not listen to Me
or incline their ear, but [r]stiffened
their neck; they did evil more than
their fathers. Neh. 9:16; Jer. 17:23
27 "And you shall [r]speak all these
words to them, but they will not
listen to you; and you shall call to
them, but they will [r]not answer
you. Jer. 1:7; 26:2 • Zech. 7:13
28 "And you shall say to them,
'This is the nation that did not
obey the voice of the LORD their
God or accept correction; [t]truth
has perished and has been cut off
from their mouth. *faithfulness*
29 'Cut off your hair and cast *it*
away,
And take up a lamentation
on the bare heights;
For the LORD has [r]rejected
and forsaken Jer. 6:30
The generation of His wrath.'
30 "For the sons of Judah have
done that which is evil in My
sight," declares the LORD, "they
have [r]set their detestable things in
the house which is called by My
name, to defile it. 2 Kin. 21:3f.
31 "And they have built the high
places of Topheth, which is in the
valley of the son of Hinnom, to
[r]burn their sons and their daughters in the fire, which I did not
command, and it did not come
into My [t]mind. Ps. 106:38 • *heart*
32 "Therefore, behold, days are
coming," declares the LORD,
"when it will no more be called
Topheth, or the valley of the son
of Hinnom, but the valley of the
Slaughter; for they will bury in
Topheth[a] because there is no *other*
place. *until there is no place left*
33 "And the [r]dead bodies of this
people will be food for the birds of
the sky, and for the beasts of the
earth; and no one will frighten
them away. Deut. 28:26; Ps. 79:2
34 "Then I will make to [r]cease
from the cities of Judah and from
the streets of Jerusalem the voice
of joy and the voice of gladness,
the voice of the bridegroom and
the voice of the bride; for the land
will become a ruin. Is. 24:7, 8

CHAPTER 8

"AT that time," declares the
LORD, "they will [r]bring out the
bones of the kings of Judah, and
the bones of its princes, and the
bones of the priests, and the bones
of the prophets, and the bones of
the inhabitants of Jerusalem from
their graves. Ezek. 6:5
2 "And they will spread them
out to the sun, the moon, and to
all the host of heaven, which they
have loved, and which they have
served, and which they have gone
after, and which they have sought,
and which they have worshiped.
They will not be gathered [r]or buried; they will be as dung on the
face of the ground. Jer. 22:19
3 "And death will be chosen
rather than life by all the remnant
that remains of this evil family,
that remains in all the places to
which I have driven them," declares the LORD of hosts.
4 "And you shall say to them,
'Thus says the LORD,
"Do *men* [r]fall and not get up
again? Prov. 24:16
Does one turn away and not
[t]repent? *turn back*
5 "Why then has this people, Jerusalem,
[r]Turned away in continual
apostasy? Jer. 5:6; 7:24

They hold fast to deceit,
They refuse to return.
6 "I [r]have listened and heard,
They have spoken what is
not right; Ps. 14:2
[r]No man repented of his
wickedness, Mic. 7:2
Saying, 'What have I done?'
Everyone turned to his
course,
Like a [r]horse charging into
the battle. Job 39:21
7 "Even the stork in the sky
Knows her seasons;
And the turtledove and the
swift and the thrush
Observe the time of their [t]mi-
gration; *coming*
But My people do not know
The ordinance of the LORD.

8 "How [r]can you say, 'We are
wise, Job 5:12, 13
And the law of the LORD is
with us'? Jer. 4:22
But behold, the lying pen of
the scribes Rom. 1:22
Has made *it* into a lie.
9 "The wise men are [r]put to
shame, Is. 19:11
They are dismayed and
caught; Jer. 6:15
Behold, they have [r]rejected
the word of the LORD,
And what kind of wisdom do
they have? Jer. 6:19
10 "Therefore I will give their
wives to others,
Their fields to [t]new owners;
Because from the least even
to the greatest
Everyone is greedy for gain;
From the prophet even to the
priest *possessing ones*
Everyone practices deceit.
11 "And they heal the brokenness of the daughter of
My people superficially,
Saying, 'Peace, peace,'
But there is no peace.
12 "Were they [r]ashamed because
of the abomination they
had done? Ps. 52:1, 7
They certainly were not
ashamed, Is. 3:9
And they did not know how
to blush; Jer. 3:3
Therefore they shall [r]fall
among those who fall;
At the time of their punishment they shall be
brought down," Is. 9:14
Declares the LORD.

13 "I will [r]surely snatch them
away," declares the
LORD; Jer. 14:12
"There will be [r]no grapes on
the vine, Jer. 5:17
And no figs on the fig tree,
And the leaf shall wither;
And what I have given them
shall pass away." ' "
14 Why are we sitting still?
Assemble yourselves, and let
us [r]go into the fortified
cities, 2 Sam. 20:6
And let us perish there,
Because the LORD our God
has doomed us
And given us [r]poisoned water
to drink, Deut. 29:18
For [r]we have sinned against
the LORD. Jer. 3:25
15 *We* [r]waited for peace, but no
good *came;* Jer. 8:11
For a time of healing, but behold, terror! Jer. 14:19
16 From Dan is heard the snort-
ing of his horses;
At the sound of the neighing
of his [r]stallions Judg. 5:22

The whole land quakes;
For they come and devour
the land and its fulness,
The city and its inhabitants.
17 "For behold, I am sending serpents against you,
Adders, for which there is [r]no
charm, Ps. 58:4, 5
And they will bite you," declares the LORD.

18 My [r]sorrow is beyond healing, Is. 22:4
My heart is faint *within me!*
19 Behold, listen! The cry of the
daughter of my people
from a distant land:
"Is the LORD not in Zion? Is
her King not within her?"
"Why have they provoked Me
with their graven images,
with foreign idols?"
20 "Harvest is past, summer is
ended,
And we are not saved."
21 For the [r]brokenness of the
daughter of my people I
am broken; Jer. 4:19
I [r]mourn, dismay has taken
hold of me. Nah. 2:10
22 Is there no balm in Gilead?
Is there no physician there?
Why then has not the health
of the daughter of my
people been restored?

CHAPTER 9

[r]OH, that my head were waters,
And my eyes a fountain of
tears, Is. 22:4
That I might weep day and
night Jer. 8:18
For the slain of the [r]daughter
of my people! Jer. 6:26
2 [r]O that I had in the desert
A wayfarers' lodging place;
That I might leave my people, Ps. 55:6, 7; 120:5, 6
And go from them!
For all of them are [r]adulterers, Jer. 5:7, 8
An assembly of treacherous
men.
3 "And they [r]bend their tongue
like their bow; Ps. 64:3
Lies and not truth prevail in
the land;
For they [r]proceed from evil to
evil, Jer. 4:22
And they do not know Me,"
declares the LORD.
4 "Let everyone be on guard
against his neighbor,
And do not trust any brother;
Because every [r]brother deals
craftily, Gen. 27:35
And every neighbor goes
about as a slanderer.
5 "And everyone [r]deceives his
neighbor, Mic. 6:12
And does not speak the
truth,
They have taught their
tongue to speak lies;
They weary themselves committing iniquity.
6 "Your [r]dwelling is in the midst
of deceit; Ps. 120:5, 6
Through deceit they [r]refuse to
know Me," declares the
LORD. Job 21:14, 15

7 Therefore thus says the LORD
of hosts,
"Behold, I will refine them and
[r]assay them; Is. 1:25
For what *else* can I do, because of the daughter of
My people?
8 "Their [r]tongue is a deadly arrow; Jer. 9:3
It speaks deceit;

With his mouth one speaks
peace to his neighbor,
But inwardly he [r]sets an ambush for him. Jer. 5:26
9 "Shall [r]I not punish them for
these things?" declares
the LORD. Is. 1:24
"On a nation such as this
Shall I not avenge Myself?

10 "For the [r]mountains I will take
up a weeping and wail-
ing, Jer. 4:24; 7:29
And for the pastures of the
wilderness a dirge,
Because they are [r]laid waste,
so that no one passes
through, Jer. 12:4
And the lowing of the cattle
is not heard;
Both the [r]birds of the sky and
the beasts have fled; they
are gone. Jer. 4:25
11 "And I will make Jerusalem a
[r]heap of ruins, Is. 25:2
A haunt of jackals;
And I will make the cities of
Judah a desolation, with-
out inhabitant."
12 Who is the [r]wise man that
may understand this? And *who is*
he to whom the mouth of the
LORD has spoken, that he may declare it? Why is the land ruined,
laid waste like a desert, so that no
one passes through? Ps. 107:43
13 And the LORD said, "Because
they have [r]forsaken My law which
I set before them, and have not
obeyed My voice nor walked according to it, 2 Chr. 7:19
14 but have [r]walked after the
stubbornness of their heart and
after the Baals, as their fathers
taught them," Jer. 7:24; 11:8
15 therefore thus says the LORD
of hosts, the God of Israel, "behold, I will feed them, this people,
with wormwood and give them
poisoned water to drink.
16 "And I will [r]scatter them
among the nations, whom neither
they nor their fathers have
known; and I will send the [r]sword
after them until I have annihilated
them." Lev. 26:33 • Jer. 44:27
17 Thus says the LORD of hosts,
"Consider and call for the
[r]mourning women, that
they may come;
And send for the wailing
women, that they may
come! 2 Chr. 35:25
18 "And let them make haste,
and take up a wailing for
us,
That our [r]eyes may shed
tears,
And our eyelids flow with
water. Is. 22:4; Jer. 9:1; 14:17
19 "For a voice of wailing is
heard from Zion,
'How are we ruined!
We are put to great shame,
For we have left the land,
Because they have cast down
our dwellings.'"
20 Now hear the word of the
LORD, O you [r]women,
And let your ear receive the
word of His mouth;
Teach your daughters wailing, Is. 32:9
And everyone her neighbor a
dirge.
21 For [r]death has come up
through our windows;
It has entered our palaces
To cut off the children from
the streets, Jer. 15:7

The young men from the
town squares.

22 Speak, "Thus declares the
LORD,
'The corpses of men will fall
[r]like dung on the open
field, Ps. 83:10
And like the sheaf after the
reaper, Is. 5:25
But no one will gather
them.' " Jer. 8:2

23 Thus says the LORD, "Let[r]not a wise man boast of his wisdom, and let not the mighty man boast of his might, let not a rich man boast of his riches; Eccl. 9:11

24 but let him who boasts boast of this, that he understands and knows Me, that I am the LORD who exercises lovingkindness, justice, and righteousness on earth; for I delight in these things," declares the LORD.

25 "Behold, the days are coming," declares the LORD, "that I will punish all who are circumcised and yet uncircumcised—

26 Egypt, and Judah, and Edom, and the sons of Ammon, and Moab, and [r]all those inhabiting the desert who clip the hair on their temples; for all the nations are uncircumcised, and all the house of Israel are [r]uncircumcised of heart." Jer. 25:23 • Ezek. 44:7

CHAPTER 10

HEAR the word which the LORD speaks to you, O house of Israel.

2 Thus says the LORD,
"Do[r] not learn the way of the
nations, Lev. 18:3
And do not be terrified by the
signs of the heavens
Although the nations are terrified by them;

3 For the customs of the peoples are [t]delusion; *vanity*
Because [r]it is wood cut from
the forest, Is. 44:9-20
The work of the hands of a
craftsman with a cutting
tool.

4 "They [r]decorate *it* with silver
and with gold; Is. 40:19
They [r]fasten it with nails and
with hammers Is. 40:20
So that it will not totter.

5 "Like a scarecrow in a cucum-
ber field are they,
And they cannot speak;
They must be [r]carried,
Because they cannot walk!
Do not fear them, Ps. 115:7
For they can do no harm,
Nor can they do any good."

6 [r]There is none like Thee, O
LORD; Ex. 15:11
Thou art great, and great is
Thy name in might.

7 [r]Who would not fear Thee, O
King of the nations?
Indeed it is Thy due!
For among all the wise men
of the nations, Rev. 15:4
And in all their kingdoms,
There is none like Thee.

8 But they are altogether stupid and foolish
In their discipline of delu-
sion—their idol is wood!

9 Beaten [r]silver is brought from
Tarshish, Is. 40:19
And gold from Uphaz,
The work of a craftsman and
of the hands of a gold-
smith;
Violet and purple are their
clothing;

They are all the [r]work of
skilled men. Ps. 115:4
10 But the LORD is the true God;
He is the living God and the
everlasting King.
At His wrath the earth
quakes,
And the nations cannot endure His indignation.
11 Thus you shall say to them,
"The [r]gods that did not make the
heavens and the earth shall perish
from the earth and from under the
[a]heavens." Ps. 96:5 • *these heavens*
12 *It is* [r]He who made the earth
by His power, Gen. 1:1, 6
Who established the world
by His wisdom;
And by His understanding
He has [r]stretched out the
heavens. Job 9:8
13 When He utters His voice,
there is a tumult of waters in the heavens,
And He causes the [r]clouds to
ascend from the end of
the earth; Job 36:27
He makes lightning for the
rain,
And brings out the wind
from His storehouses.
14 Every man is [r]stupid, devoid
of knowledge; Jer. 10:8
Every goldsmith is put to
shame by his [a]idols;
For his molten images are
deceitful, *graven image*
And there is no breath in
them.
15 They are [r]worthless, a work
of mockery; Is. 41:24
In the time of their punishment they will perish.
16 The [r]portion of Jacob is not
like these; Ps. 16:5
For the [t]Maker of all is He,
And Israel is the tribe of His
inheritance;
The LORD of hosts is His
name. *Fashioner*

17 [r]Pick up your bundle from the
ground, Ezek. 12:3-12
You who dwell under siege!
18 For thus says the LORD,
"Behold, I am [r]slinging out the
inhabitants of the land
At this time, 1 Sam. 25:29
And will cause them distress,
That they may be found."

19 Woe is me, because of my [t]in-
jury! *breaking*
My [r]wound is incurable.
But I said, "Truly this is a
sickness, Jer. 14:17
And I must bear it."
20 My tent is destroyed,
And all my ropes are broken;
My sons have gone from me
and are no more.
There is [r]no one to stretch out
my tent again Is. 51:18
Or to set up my curtains.
21 For the shepherds have be-
come stupid
And [r]have not sought the
LORD; Jer. 2:8
Therefore they have not
prospered,
And [r]all their flock is scat-
tered. Jer. 23:2
22 The sound of a [r]report! Be-
hold, it comes— Jer. 4:15
A great commotion out of
the land of the north—
To make the cities of Judah
A desolation, a haunt of jack-
als.

23 I know, O LORD, that a man's
way is not in himself;

Nor is it in a man who walks
to direct his steps.
24 [r]Correct me, O LORD, but with
justice; Ps. 6:1
Not with Thine anger, lest
Thou [t]bring me to noth-
ing. *diminish me*
25 [r]Pour out Thy wrath on the
nations that do not know
Thee, Ps. 79:6, 7
And on the families that do
not call Thy name;
For they have devoured Jacob;
They have [r]devoured him and
consumed him, Jer. 8:16
And have laid waste his [a]habi-
tation. *pasture*

CHAPTER 11

THE word which came to Jeremiah from the LORD, saying,
2 "Hear[r] the words of this [r]cov-
enant, and speak to the men of Judah and to the inhabitants of Jerusalem; Jer. 11:6 • Ex. 19:5
3 and say to them, 'Thus says
the LORD, the God of Israel,
"Cursed is the man who does not
heed the words of this covenant
4 which I commanded your
forefathers in the day that I
brought them out of the land of
Egypt, from the iron furnace, saying, 'Listen to My voice, and do
according to all which I command
you; so you shall be My people,
and I will be your God,'
5 in order to confirm the oath
which I swore to your forefathers,
to give them a land flowing with
milk and honey, as *it is* this
day." ' " Then I answered and
said, "Amen, O LORD."
6 And the LORD said to me,
"Proclaim[r] all these words in the
cities of Judah and in the streets
of Jerusalem, saying, 'Hear[r] the
words of this covenant and do
them. Jer. 3:12; 7:2 • Jer. 11:2
7 'For I solemnly warned your
fathers in the day that I brought
them up from the land of Egypt,
even to this day, [t]warning persis-
tently, saying, "Listen to My
voice." *rising early and warning*
8 'Yet they did not obey or incline their ear, but walked, each
one, in the stubbornness of his
evil heart; therefore I brought on
them all the words of this covenant, which I commanded *them*
to do, but they did not.' "
9 Then the LORD said to me,
"A [r]conspiracy has been found
among the men of Judah and
among the inhabitants of Jerusalem. Ezek. 22:25; Hos. 6:9
10 "They have turned back to the
iniquities of their ancestors who
refused[r] to hear My words, and
they have gone after other gods to
serve them; the house of Israel
and the house of Judah have broken My covenant which I made
with their fathers." Ps. 78:8-10
11 Therefore thus says the
LORD, "Behold I am [r]bringing disaster on them which they will [r]not
be able to escape; though they will
cry to Me, yet I will not listen to
them. 2 Kin. 22:16 • Is. 24:17
12 "Then the cities of Judah and
the inhabitants of Jerusalem will
go[r] and cry to the gods to whom
they burn incense, but they surely
will not save them in the time of
their disaster. Deut. 32:37
13 "For your gods are [t]as many as
your cities, O Judah; and as many

as the streets of Jerusalem are the
altars you have set up to the
shameful thing, altars to burn incense to Baal. *the number of*
14 "Therefore [r]do not pray for
this people, nor lift up a cry or
prayer for them; for I will not listen when they call to Me because
of their disaster. Ex. 32:10
15 "What right has My [r]beloved
in My house Jer. 13:27
When [r]she has done many
vile deeds? Ezek. 16:25
Can the sacrificial flesh take
away from you your di-
saster,
So *that* you can rejoice?"
16 The LORD called your name,
"A green olive tree, beautiful
in fruit and form";
With the [r]noise of a great tumult Ps. 83:2
He has [r]kindled fire on it,
And its branches are worthless. Ps. 80:16
17 And the LORD of hosts, who
[r]planted you, has pronounced evil
against you because of the evil of
the house of Israel and of the
house of Judah, which they have
done to provoke Me by offering up
sacrifices to Baal. Is. 5:2
18 Moreover, the LORD [r]made it
known to me and I knew
it; 1 Sam. 23:11
Then Thou didst show me
their deeds. Ezek. 8:6
19 But I was like a gentle lamb
led to the slaughter;
And I did not know that they
had [r]devised plots against
me, *saying*, Jer. 18:18
"Let us destroy the tree with
its [t]fruit, *bread*
And let us cut him off from
the land of the living,
That his name be remem-
bered no more."
20 But, O LORD of hosts, who
judges righteously,
Who tries the [t]feelings and
the heart, *kidneys*
Let me see Thy vengeance on
them,
For to Thee have I [t]commit-
ted my cause. *revealed*
21 Therefore thus says the LORD
concerning the men of [r]Anathoth,
who seek your life, saying, "Do
not prophesy in the name of the
LORD, that you might not [r]die at
our hand"; Jer. 1:1 · Jer. 26:8
22 therefore, thus says the LORD
of hosts, "Behold, I am about to
punish them! The young men will
die by the sword, their sons and
daughters will die by famine;
23 and a remnant [r]will not be left
to them, for I will bring disaster
on the men of Anathoth—the year
of their punishment." Jer. 6:9

CHAPTER 12

RIGHTEOUS art Thou, O LORD,
that I would plead *my*
case with Thee;
Indeed I would discuss matters of justice with Thee:
Why has the way of the
wicked prospered?
Why are all those who deal
in treachery at ease?
2 Thou hast [r]planted them, they
have also taken root;
They grow, they have even
produced fruit. Jer. 11:17
Thou art near to their lips
But far from their mind.
3 But Thou [r]knowest me, O
LORD; Ps. 139:1-4
Thou seest me;
And Thou dost [r]examine my

heart's *attitude* toward
Thee. Ps. 7:9
Drag them off like sheep for
the slaughter
And set them apart for a [r]day
of carnage! Jer. 17:18
4 How long is the [r]land to
mourn Jer. 4:28
And the vegetation of the
countryside to wither?
For the wickedness of those
who dwell in it,
[r]Animals and birds have been
snatched away,
Because *men* have said, "He
will not see our latter
ending." Jer. 4:25

5 "If you have run with footmen
and they have tired you
out,
Then how can you compete
with horses?
If you fall down in a land of
peace,
How will you do in the
thicket of the Jordan?
6 "For even your [r]brothers and
the household of your fa-
ther, Gen. 37:4-11
Even they have dealt treacherously with you,
Even they have cried aloud
after you. Job 6:15
Do not believe them, al-
though they may say [r]nice
things to you." Ps. 12:2

7 "I have [r]forsaken My house,
I have abandoned My inher-
itance; Is. 2:6
I have given the [r]beloved of
My soul Jer. 11:15
Into the hand of her enemies.
8 "My inheritance has become
to Me
Like a lion in the forest;
She has [t]roared against Me;
Therefore I have come to
hate her. *raised her voice*
9 "Is My inheritance like a
speckled bird of prey to
Me?
Are the birds of prey against
her on every side?
Go, gather all the [r]beasts of
the field, Is. 56:9
Bring them to devour!
10 "Many shepherds have ruined
My [r]vineyard, Is. 5:1-7
They have [r]trampled down
My field; Is. 63:18
They have made My [r]pleasant
field Jer. 3:19
A desolate wilderness.
11 "It[t] has been made a desola-
tion, *One has made it*
Desolate, it mourns [a]before
Me; *Upon*
The [r]whole land has been
made desolate, Jer. 4:20
Because no man [r]lays it to
heart. Is. 42:25
12 "On all the [r]bare heights in the
wilderness Jer. 3:2
Destroyers have come,
For a [r]sword of the LORD is
devouring Is. 34:6
From one end of the land
even to the other;
There is no peace for anyone.
13 "They have sown wheat and
have reaped thorns,
They have strained them-
selves to no profit.
But be ashamed of your [r]har-
vest
Because of the fierce anger
of the LORD." Jer. 17:10

14 Thus says the LORD concerning all My [r]wicked neighbors who
strike at the inheritance with
which I have endowed My people

Israel, "Behold I am about to uproot them from their land and will
uproot the house of Judah from
among them. Jer. 49:1, 7
15 "And it will come about that
after I have uprooted them, I will
[r]again have compassion on them;
and I will bring them back, each
one to his inheritance and each
one to his land. Jer. 48:47; 49:6
16 "Then it will come about that
if they will really learn the ways
of My people, to swear by My
name, 'As the LORD lives,' even as
they taught My people to swear
by Baal, then they will be built up
in the midst of My people.
17 "But if they will not listen,
then I will [r]uproot that nation, uproot and destroy it," declares the
LORD. Ps. 2:8-12; Is. 60:12

CHAPTER 13

THUS the LORD said to me, "Go
and buy yourself a linen waistband, and put it around your
waist, but do not put it in water."
2 So I bought the waistband in
accordance with the word of the
LORD and put it around my waist.
3 Then the word of the LORD
came to me a second time, saying,
4 "Take the waistband that you
have bought, which is around
your waist, and arise, go to [a]the
Euphrates and hide it there in a
crevice of the rock." *Parah*
5 So I went and hid it by the
Euphrates, [r]as the LORD had commanded me. Ex. 39:42, 43
6 And it came about after
many days that the LORD said to
me, "Arise, go to the Euphrates
and take from there the waistband
which I commanded you to hide
there."
7 Then I went to the Euphrates
and dug, and I took the waistband
from the place where I had hidden
it; and lo, the waistband was
ruined, it was totally worthless.
8 Then the word of the LORD
came to me, saying,
9 "Thus says the LORD, 'Just so
will I destroy the pride of Judah
and the great pride of Jerusalem.
10 'This wicked people, who [r]re-
fuse to listen to My words, who
walk in the stubbornness of their
hearts and have gone after other
gods to serve them and to bow
down to them, let them be just
like this waistband, which is totally worthless. Num. 14:11
11 'For as the waistband clings
to the waist of a man, so I made
the whole household of Israel and
the whole household of Judah
cling to Me,' declares the LORD,
'that they might be for Me a people, for renown, for praise, and for
glory; but they did not listen.'
12 "Therefore you are to speak
this word to them, 'Thus says the
LORD, the God of Israel, "Every
jug is to be filled with wine."'
And when they say to you, 'Do we
not very well know that every jug
is to be filled with wine?'
13 then say to them, 'Thus says
the LORD, "Behold I am about to
fill all the inhabitants of this
land—the kings that sit for David
on his throne, the priests, the
prophets and all the inhabitants of
Jerusalem—with drunkenness!
14 "And I will dash them against
each other, both the fathers and
the sons together," declares the
LORD. "I will not show pity nor be
sorry nor have compassion that I
should not destroy them."'"

15 Listen and give heed, do not
be [r]haughty, Prov. 16:5
For the LORD has spoken.
16 [r]Give glory to the LORD your
God, Josh. 7:19
Before He brings darkness
And before your [r]feet stumble
On the dusky mountains,
And while you are hoping for
light Prov. 4:19
He makes it into [r]deep dark-
ness, Ps. 44:19
And turns *it* into gloom.
17 But if you will not listen to it,
My soul will [r]sob in secret for
such pride;
And my eyes will bitterly
weep Jer. 9:1; Luke 19:41
And flow down with tears,
Because the [r]flock of the
LORD has been taken cap-
tive. Ps. 80:1
18 Say to the king and the
queen mother,
"Take a lowly seat,
For your beautiful [r]crown
Has come down from your
head." Ex. 39:28
19 The [r]cities of the Negev have
been locked up,
And there is no one to open
them; Jer. 32:44
All [r]Judah has been carried
into exile, Jer. 20:4
Wholly carried into exile.

20 "Lift up your eyes and see
Those coming [r]from the
north. Jer. 1:15; 6:22
Where is the [r]flock that was
given you, Jer. 13:17; 23:2
Your beautiful sheep?
21 "What will you say when He
appoints over you—
And you yourself had taught
them—
Former [a]companions to be
head over you?
Will not pangs take hold of
you, *chieftains*
Like a woman in childbirth?
22 "And if you say in your heart,
'Why have these things happened to me?'
Because of the [r]magnitude of
your iniquity Jer. 2:17-19
[r]Your skirts have been removed, Is. 47:2
And your heels have [a]been exposed. *suffered violence*
23 "Can the Ethiopian change his
skin
Or the leopard his spots?
Then you also can [r]do good
Who are accustomed to do
evil. Jer. 4:22; 9:5
24 "Therefore I will scatter them
like drifting straw
To the desert [r]wind. Jer. 4:11
25 "This is your [r]lot, the portion
measured to you
From Me," declares the
LORD, Job 20:29
"Because you have [r]forgotten
Me Ps. 9:17
And trusted in falsehood.
26 "So I Myself have also
[r]stripped your skirts off
over your face, Lam. 1:8
That your shame may be
seen. Ezek. 23:29
27 "As for your adulteries and
your *lustful* neighings,
The [r]lewdness of your prosti-
tution Jer. 11:15
On the [r]hills in the field,
I have seen your abomina-
tions. Jer. 2:20
Woe to you, O Jerusalem!
How [r]long will you remain
unclean?" Prov. 1:22

CHAPTER 14

THAT which came as the word of
the LORD to Jeremiah in regard to
the [r]drought: Jer. 17:8
2 "Judah mourns,
And [r]her gates languish
They sit on the ground in
mourning, Is. 3:26
And the [r]cry of Jerusalem has
ascended. Jer. 11:11
3 "And their nobles have sent
their servants for water;
They have come to the cisterns
and found no water.
They have returned with
their vessels empty;
They have been put to shame
and humiliated,
And they cover their heads.
4 "Because the ground is
[t]cracked, *shattered*
For there has been [r]no rain on
the land; Jer. 3:3
The [r]farmers have been put to
shame, Joel 1:11
They have covered their
heads.
5 "For even the doe in the field
has given birth only to
abandon *her young,*
Because there is no grass.
6 "And the [r]wild donkeys stand
on the bare heights;
They pant for air like jackals,
Their eyes fail Job 39:5, 6
For there is no vegetation.
7 "Although our iniquities testify
against us,
O LORD, act [r]for Thy name's
sake! Jer. 14:21
Truly our apostasies have
been many,
We have sinned against
Thee.
8 "Thou [r]Hope of Israel,
Its [r]Savior in time of distress,
Why art Thou like a stranger
in the land Jer. 17:13
Or like a traveler who has
pitched his *tent* for the
night? Is. 43:3
9 "Why art Thou like a man dismayed,
Like a mighty man who [r]cannot
save? Num. 11:23
Yet [r]Thou art in our midst, O
LORD, Ex. 29:45
And we are [r]called by Thy
name; Is. 63:19
Do not forsake us!"

10 Thus says the LORD to this
people, "Even so they have loved
to wander; they have not kept
their feet in check. Therefore the
LORD does not accept them; now
He will remember their iniquity
and call their sins to account."
11 So the LORD said to me, "Do [r]
not pray for the welfare of this
people. Ex. 32:10; Jer. 7:16
12 "When they fast, I am not
going to listen to their cry; and
when they offer burnt offering and
grain offering, I am not going to
accept them. Rather I am going to
make an end of them by the
sword, famine and pestilence."
13 But, "Ah, Lord GOD!" I said,
"Look, the prophets are telling
them, 'You will not see the sword
nor will you have famine, but I
will give you [t]lasting peace in this
place.'" *peace of truth*
14 Then the LORD said to me,
"The prophets are prophesying
falsehood in My name. I have neither
sent them nor commanded
them nor spoken to them; they are
prophesying to you a false vision,
divination, futility and the deception
of their own [t]minds. *hearts*

15 "Therefore thus says the LORD
concerning the prophets who are
prophesying in My name, although it was not I who sent
them—yet they keep saying,
'There shall be no sword or famine in this land'—by sword and
famine those prophets shall [t]meet
their end! *be finished*
16 "The people also to whom
they are prophesying will be
[r]thrown out into the streets of Jerusalem because of the famine
and the sword; and there will be
no one to bury them—*neither*
them, *nor* their wives, nor their
sons, nor their daughters—for I
shall pour out their *own* wickedness on them. Ps. 79:2, 3
17 "And you will say this word to them,
[r]'Let my eyes flow down with tears night and day,
And let them not cease;
For the virgin daughter of my people has been crushed with a mighty blow, Jer. 9:1; 13:17
With a sorely [r]infected wound. Jer. 10:19
18 'If I go out to the country,
Behold, those [t]slain with the sword! *pierced*
Or if I enter the city,
Behold, diseases of famine!
For [r]both prophet and priest
Have gone roving about in the land that they do not know.'" Jer. 6:13

19 Hast Thou completely rejected Judah?
Or hast [t]Thou loathed Zion?
Why hast Thou stricken us so that we are beyond healing? *Thy soul*
We [r]waited for peace, but nothing good *came;*
And for a time of healing, but behold, terror! Job 30:26
20 We [r]know our wickedness, O LORD, Ps. 32:5
The iniquity of our fathers, for [r]we have sinned against Thee. Jer. 8:14
21 Do not despise *us,* for Thine own name's sake;
Do not disgrace the [r]throne of Thy glory; Jer. 3:17
Remember *and* do not annul Thy covenant with us.
22 Are there any among the [t]idols of the nations who [r]give rain? *vanities*
Or can the heavens grant showers? 1 Kin. 17:1
Is it not Thou, O LORD our God?
Therefore we [a]hope in Thee,
For Thou art the one who hast done all these things. *wait for*

CHAPTER 15

THEN the LORD said to me,
"Even though Moses and Samuel
were to stand before Me, My [t]heart
would not be with this people;
send them away from My presence and let them go! *soul*
2 "And it shall be that when
they say to you, 'Where should we
go?' then you are to tell them,
'Thus says the LORD:
"Those *destined* [r]for death, to death; Jer. 14:12
And those *destined* for the sword, to the sword;
And those *destined* for famine, to famine;

And those *destined* for captivity, to captivity." '
3 "And I shall appoint over them four kinds *of doom*," declares the LORD: "the sword to slay, the dogs to drag off, and the birds of the sky and the beasts of the earth to devour and destroy.
4 "And I shall [r]make them an object of horror among all the kingdoms of the earth because of Manasseh, the son of Hezekiah, the king of Judah, for what he did in Jerusalem. Lev. 26:33
5 "Indeed, who will have pity on you, O Jerusalem,
Or who will mourn for you,
Or who will turn aside to ask about your welfare?
6 "You who have forsaken Me," declares the LORD,
"You keep going backward.
So I will [r]stretch out My hand against you and destroy you; Jer. 6:12
I am tired of relenting!
7 "And I will winnow them with a winnowing fork
At the gates of the land;
I will [r]bereave *them* of children, I will destroy My people; Jer. 18:21
They did not [t]repent of their ways. *turn back from*
8 "Their widows will be more numerous before Me
Than the sand of the seas;
I will bring against them, against the mother of a young man,
A [r]destroyer at noonday;
I will suddenly bring down on her Jer. 22:7
Anguish and dismay.
9 "She who [r]bore seven *sons* pines away; 1 Sam. 2:5
Her breathing is labored.
Her sun has set while it was yet day;
She has been [r]shamed and humiliated. Jer. 6:4
So I shall give over their survivors to the sword
Before their enemies," declares the LORD.

10 Woe to me, my mother, that you have borne me
As a [r]man of strife and a man of contention to all the land! Jer. 1:18, 19; 15:20
I have neither lent, nor have men lent money to me,
Yet everyone curses me.
11 The LORD said, "Surely I will [r]set you free for *purposes of* good; Ps. 138:3
Surely I will cause the [r]enemy to make supplication to you Jer. 21:2; 37:3
In a time of disaster and a time of distress.

12 "Can anyone smash iron,
[r]Iron from the north, or bronze? Jer. 28:14
13 "Your [r]wealth and your treasures Jer. 17:3
I will give for booty [r]without cost, Ps. 44:12
Even for all your sins
And within all your borders.
14 "Then I will cause your enemies to bring *it*
Into a land you do not know;
For a [r]fire has been kindled in My anger, Deut. 32:22
It will burn upon you."

15 [r]Thou who knowest, O LORD,
Remember me, take notice of me, Jer. 12:3
And take vengeance for me on my persecutors.

Do *not,* in view of Thy patience, take me away;
Know that for Thy sake I endure reproach.
16 Thy words were found and I [r]ate them, Ezek. 3:3
And Thy [r]words became for me a joy and the delight of my heart; Job 23:12
For I have been [r]called by Thy name, Jer. 14:9
O LORD God of hosts.
17 I [r]did not sit in the circle of merrymakers, Ps. 1:1
Nor did I exult.
Because of Thy hand *upon me* I sat [r]alone, Ps. 102:7
For Thou didst [r]fill me with indignation. Jer. 6:11
18 Why has my pain been perpetual
And my [r]wound incurable, refusing to be healed?
Wilt Thou indeed be to me like a deceptive *stream*
With water that is unreliable? Job 34:6
19 Therefore, thus says the LORD,
"[r]If you return, then I will restore you— Jer. 4:1
Before Me you will stand;
And [r]if you extract the precious from the worthless,
You will become My spokesman. Jer. 6:29; Ezek. 22:26
They for their part may turn to you,
But as for you, you must not turn to them.
20 "Then I will [r]make you to this people Jer. 1:18, 19
A fortified wall of bronze;
And though they fight against you,
They will not prevail over you;
For [r]I am with you to save you Ps. 46:7; Is. 41:10
And deliver you," declares the LORD.
21 "So I will deliver you from the hand of the wicked,
And I will redeem you from the grasp of the violent."

CHAPTER 16

THE word of the LORD also came to me saying,
2 "You shall not take a wife for yourself nor have sons or daughters in this place."
3 For thus says the LORD concerning the sons and daughters born in this place, and concerning their [r]mothers who bear them, and their [r]fathers who beget them in this land: Jer. 15:8 • Jer. 6:21
4 "They will die of deadly diseases, they will not be lamented or buried; they will be as dung on the surface of the ground and come to an end by sword and famine, and their carcasses will become food for the birds of the sky and for the beasts of the earth."
5 For thus says the LORD, "Do not enter a house of [a]mourning, or go to lament or to console them; for I have withdrawn My peace from this people," declares the LORD, "*My* lovingkindness and compassion. banqueting
6 "Both [r]great men and small will die in this land; they will not be buried, they will not be lamented, nor will anyone [r]gash himself or shave his head for them. 2 Chr. 36:17 • Deut. 14:1
7 "Neither will men break *bread* in mourning for them, to comfort

anyone for the dead, nor give them a cup of consolation to drink for anyone's father or mother.

8 "Moreover you shall not go into a house of feasting to sit with them to eat and drink."

9 For thus says the LORD of hosts, the God of Israel: "Behold, I am going to [t]eliminate from this place, before your eyes and in your time, the voice of rejoicing and the voice of gladness, the voice of the groom and the voice of the bride. *cause to cease*

10 "Now it will come about when you tell this people all these words that they will say to you, [r]'For what reason has the LORD declared all this great calamity against us? And what is our iniquity, or what is our sin which we have committed against the LORD our God?' Deut. 29:24

11 "Then you are to say to them, '*It is* [r]because your forefathers have forsaken Me,' declares the LORD, 'and have followed [r]other gods and served them and bowed down to them; but Me they have forsaken and have not kept My law. Deut. 29:25 • 1 Kin. 9:9

12 'You too have done evil, *even* [r]more than your forefathers; for behold, you are each one walking according to the [r]stubbornness of his own evil heart, without listening to Me. Jer. 7:26 • Jer. 7:24

13 'So I will hurl you out of this land into the land which you have not known, neither you nor your fathers; and there you will serve other gods day and night, for I shall grant you no favor.'

14 "Therefore behold, days are coming," declares the LORD, "when it will no longer be said, 'As the LORD lives, who [r]brought up the sons of Israel out of the land of Egypt,' Ex. 20:2

15 but, 'As the LORD lives, who brought up the sons of Israel from the [r]land of the north and from all the countries where He had banished them.' For I will restore them to their own land which I gave to their fathers. Jer. 3:18

16 "Behold, I am going to send for many [r]fishermen," declares the LORD, "and they will fish for them; and afterwards I shall send for many hunters, and they will hunt them from every mountain and every hill, and from the clefts of the rocks. Hab. 1:14, 15

17 "For My eyes are on all their ways; they are not hidden from My face, [r]nor is their iniquity concealed from My eyes. Jer. 2:22

18 "And I will first [r]doubly repay their iniquity and their sin, because they have [r]polluted My land; they have filled My inheritance with the carcasses of their detestable idols and with their abominations." Jer. 17:18 • Jer. 2:7; 3:9

19 O LORD, my [r]strength and my stronghold, Ps. 18:1, 2
And my [r]refuge in the day of distress, Nah. 1:7
To Thee the [r]nations will come Is. 2:2; Jer. 3:17
From the ends of the earth and say,
"Our fathers have inherited nothing but falsehood,
Futility and [r]things of no profit." Is. 44:10

20 Can man make gods for himself?
Yet they are not gods!

21 "Therefore behold, I am going
to make them know—
This time I will [r]make them
know Ps. 9:16
My power and My might;
And they shall know that My
name is the LORD."

CHAPTER 17

THE sin of Judah is written down
with an iron stylus;
With a diamond point it is
[r]engraved upon the tablet
of their heart, Prov. 3:3
And on the horns of their altars, Is. 49:16
2 As they remember their [r]chil-
dren, Jer. 7:18
So they *remember* their altars and their Asherim
By [r]green trees on the high
hills. Jer. 3:6
3 O [r]mountain of Mine in the
countryside, Jer. 26:18
I will [r]give over your wealth
and all your treasures for
booty, 2 Kin. 24:13
Your high places for sin
throughout your borders.
4 And you will, even of yourself, [r]let go of your inheritance Jer. 12:7
That I gave you;
And I will make you serve
your [r]enemies Is. 14:3
In the [r]land which you do not
know; Jer. 16:13
For you have [r]kindled a fire in
My anger Is. 5:25
Which will burn forever.

5 Thus says the LORD,
[r]"Cursed is the man who trusts
in mankind Ps. 146:3
And makes [r]flesh his
[t]strength, 2 Chr. 32:8
And whose heart turns away
from the LORD. *arm*
6 "For he will be like a [r]bush in
the desert Jer. 48:6
And will not see when prosperity comes,
But will live in stony wastes
in the wilderness,
A land of salt [t]without inhabitant. *and is not inhabited*
7 "Blessed is the man who
trusts in the LORD
And whose trust is the LORD.
8 "For he will be like a tree
planted by the water,
That extends its roots by a
stream
And will not fear when the
heat comes;
But its leaves will be green,
And it will not be anxious in
a year of drought
Nor cease to yield fruit.

9 "The [r]heart is more deceitful
than all else Eccl. 9:3
And is desperately sick;
Who can understand it?
10 "I, the LORD, search the heart,
I test the [t]mind, *kidneys*
Even to give to each man according to his ways,
According to the [t]results of
his deeds. *fruit*
11 "As a partridge that hatches
eggs which it has not
laid,
So is he who [r]makes a fortune, but unjustly;
In the midst of his days it
will forsake him,
And in [t]the end he will be a
fool." Jer. 6:13 • *his*

12 A glorious throne on high
from the beginning
Is the place of our sanctuary.

13 O LORD, the hope of Israel,
All who [r]forsake Thee will be put to shame. Is. 1:28
Those who turn away on earth will be [r]written down, Luke 10:20
Because they have forsaken the fountain of living water, even the LORD.
14 Heal me, O LORD, and I will be healed;
Save me and I will be saved,
For Thou art my praise.
15 Look, they keep [r]saying to me, Is. 5:19; 2 Pet. 3:4
"Where is the word of the LORD?
Let it come now!"
16 But as for me, I have not hurried away from *being* a shepherd after Thee,
Nor have I longed for the woeful day;
Thou Thyself knowest the utterance of my lips
Was in Thy presence.
17 Do not be a terror to me;
Thou art my refuge in the day of disaster.
18 Let those who persecute me be [r]put to shame, but as for me, let me not be put to shame; Ps. 35:4
Let them be dismayed, but let me not be dismayed.
[r]Bring on them a day of disaster, Ps. 35:8
And crush them with twofold destruction!

19 Thus the LORD said to me,
"Go and stand in the public gate,
through which the kings of Judah
come in and go out, as well as in
all the gates of Jerusalem;
20 and say to them, 'Listen[r] to
the word of the LORD, kings of Judah, and all Judah, and all inhabitants of Jerusalem, who come in
through these gates: Ezek. 2:7
21 'Thus says the LORD, "Take[r]
heed for yourselves, and do not
carry any load on the sabbath day
or bring anything in through the
gates of Jerusalem. Deut. 4:9
22 "And you shall not bring a
load out of your houses on the
sabbath day nor do any work, but
keep the sabbath day holy, as I
commanded your forefathers.
23 "Yet they [r]did not listen or incline their ears, but stiffened their
necks in order not to listen or take
correction. Jer. 7:24, 28; 11:10
24 "But it will come about, if you
[r]listen attentively to Me," declares
the LORD, "to bring no load in
through the gates of this city on
the sabbath day, but to keep the
sabbath day holy by doing no
work on it, Ex. 15:26; Is. 21:7
25 then there will come in
through the gates of this city
kings and princes sitting on the
throne of David, riding in chariots
and on horses, they and their
princes, the men of Judah, and the
inhabitants of Jerusalem; and this
city will be inhabited forever.
26 "They will come in from the
[r]cities of Judah and from the environs of Jerusalem, from the land
of Benjamin, from the lowland,
from the hill country, and from
the Negev, bringing burnt offerings, sacrifices, grain offerings
and incense, and bringing sacrifices of thanksgiving to the house
of the LORD. Jer. 32:44; 33:13
27 "But if you do not listen to Me
to keep the sabbath day holy by
not carrying a load and coming in
through the gates of Jerusalem on

the sabbath day, then I shall kindle a fire in its gates, and it will devour the palaces of Jerusalem and not be quenched." ' "

CHAPTER 18

THE word which came to Jeremiah from the LORD saying,

2 "Arise and go down to the potter's house, and there I shall announce My words to you."

3 Then I went down to the potter's house, and there he was, making something on the wheel.

4 But the vessel that he was making of clay was spoiled in the hand of the potter; so he remade it into another vessel, as it pleased the potter to make.

5 Then the word of the LORD came to me saying,

6 "Can I not, O house of Israel, deal with you as this potter *does*?" declares the LORD. "Behold, like the [r]clay in the potter's hand, so are you in My hand, O house of Israel. Is. 45:9; 64:8; Rom. 9:21

7 "At one moment I might speak concerning a nation or concerning a kingdom to uproot, to pull down, or to destroy *it;*

8 if that nation against which I have spoken turns from its evil, I will [4]relent concerning the calamity I planned to bring on it.

9 "Or at another moment I might speak concerning a nation or concerning a kingdom to [r]build up or to plant *it;* Jer. 1:10

10 if it does evil in My sight by not obeying My voice, then I will [4]think better of the good with which I had promised to bless it.

11 "So now then, speak to the men of Judah and against the inhabitants of Jerusalem saying, 'Thus says the LORD, "Behold, I am fashioning calamity against you and devising a plan against you. Oh turn back, each of you from his evil way, and reform your ways and your deeds." '

12 "But [r]they will say, 'It's hopeless! For we are going to follow our own plans, and each of us will act according to the stubbornness of his evil heart.' Is. 57:10

13 "Therefore thus says the LORD,
'Ask now among the nations,
Who ever heard the like of
[t]this? *these*
The [r]virgin of Israel Jer. 14:17
Has done a most [r]appalling
thing. Jer. 5:30
14 'Does the snow of Lebanon
forsake the rock of the
open country?
Or is the cold flowing water
from a foreign *land* ever
snatched away?
15 'For [r]My people have forgotten Me, Jer. 2:32
[r]They burn incense to worthless gods Is. 65:7
And they have stumbled
from their ways,
[a]From the [r]ancient paths, *in*
To walk in bypaths, Jer. 6:16
Not on a [r]highway, Is. 57:14
16 To make their land a [r]desolation, Jer. 25:9; 49:13
An object of perpetual [r]hissing; 1 Kin. 9:8
Everyone who passes by it
will be astonished
And shake his head.
17 'Like an [r]east wind I will [r]scatter them Ps. 48:7
Before the enemy; Job 27:21

[4]Lit., *repent (of)*

I will show them My back
and not *My* face
[r]In the day of their calamity.' " Jer. 46:21
18 Then they said, "Come and
let us [r]devise plans against Jeremiah. Surely the law is not going to
be lost to the priest, nor counsel to
the sage, nor the *divine* word to
the prophet! Come on and let us
[r]strike at him with *our* tongue, and
let us give no heed to any of his
words." Jer. 11:19 • Ps. 52:2
19 Do give heed to me, O LORD,
And listen to what my opponents are saying!
20 [r]Should good be repaid with evil? Ps. 109:4
For they have dug a pit for [t]me. *my soul*
Remember how I [r]stood before Thee Ps. 106:23
To speak good on their behalf,
So as to turn away Thy wrath from them.
21 Therefore, give their children over to famine,
And deliver them up to the [t]power of the sword;
And let their wives become [r]childless and widowed.
Let their men also be smitten to death,
Their young men struck down by the sword in battle. *hands of* • Is. 13:18
22 May an [r]outcry be heard from their houses, Jer. 6:26
When Thou suddenly bringest raiders upon them;
[r]For they have dug a pit to capture me Jer. 18:20
And [r]hidden snares for my feet. Ps. 140:5
23 Yet Thou, O LORD, knowest
All their [t]deadly designs against me; *unto death*
[r]Do not forgive their iniquity
Or blot out their sin from Thy sight. Neh. 4:5
But may they be [r]overthrown before Thee; Jer. 6:15
Deal with them in the [r]time of Thine anger! Jer. 7:20

CHAPTER 19

THUS says the LORD, "Go and
buy a potter's earthenware jar,
and *take* some of the [r]elders of the
people and some of the [a]senior
priests. Num. 11:16 • *elders of*
2 "Then go out to the [r]valley of
Ben-hinnom, which is by the entrance of the potsherd gate; and
proclaim there the words that I
shall tell you, 2 Kin. 23:10
3 and say, 'Hear the word of
the LORD, O kings of Judah and inhabitants of Jerusalem: thus says
the LORD of hosts, the God of Israel, "Behold I am about to bring
a [r]calamity upon this place, at
which the ears of everyone that
hears of it will tingle. Jer. 6:19
4 "Because they have forsaken
Me and have made this an alien
place and have burned [a]sacrifices
in it to [r]other gods that neither
they nor their forefathers nor the
kings of Judah had *ever* known,
and *because* they have filled this
place with the blood of the innocent *incense* • Jer. 7:9; 11:13
5 and have built the high
places of Baal to burn their [r]sons in
the fire as burnt offerings to Baal,
a thing which I never commanded
or spoke of, nor did it *ever* enter
My [t]mind; 2 Kin. 17:17 • *heart*
6 therefore, behold, [r]days are

coming," declares the LORD, "when this place will no longer be called Topheth or the valley of Ben-hinnom, but rather the valley of Slaughter. Jer. 7:32

7 "And I shall [r]make void the counsel of Judah and Jerusalem in this place, and I shall cause them to fall by the sword before their enemies and by the hand of those who seek their life; and I shall give over their carcasses as food for the birds of the sky and the beasts of the earth. Jer. 8:8, 9

8 "I shall also make this city a desolation and an *object of* hissing; everyone who passes by it will be astonished and hiss because of all its [t]disasters. *blows*

9 "And I shall make them [r]eat the flesh of their sons and the flesh of their daughters, and they will eat one another's flesh in the siege and in the distress with which their enemies and those who seek their life will distress them."' Lev. 26:29 ; Is. 9:20

10 "Then you are to break the [r]jar in the sight of the men who accompany you Jer. 19:1

11 and say to them, 'Thus says the LORD of hosts, "Just so shall I [r]break this people and this city, even as one breaks a potter's vessel, which cannot again be repaired; and they will bury in Topheth because there is no *other* place for burial. Ps. 2:9

12 "This is how I shall treat this place and its inhabitants," declares the LORD, "so as to make this city like Topheth.

13 "And the houses of Jerusalem and the houses of the kings of Judah will be [r]defiled like the place Topheth, because of all the houses on whose rooftops they burned [a]sacrifices to all the heavenly host and poured out libations to other gods."' " 2 Kin. 23:10 • *incense*

14 Then Jeremiah came from Topheth, where the LORD had sent him to prophesy; and he stood in the [r]court of the LORD's house and said to all the people: Jer. 26:2

15 "Thus says the LORD of hosts, the God of Israel, 'Behold, I am about to bring on this city and all its towns the entire calamity that I have declared against it, because they have stiffened their necks so as not to heed My words.' "

CHAPTER 20

WHEN Pashhur the priest, the son of [r]Immer, who was chief officer in the house of the LORD, heard Jeremiah prophesying these things, 1 Chr. 24:14

2 Pashhur had Jeremiah the prophet beaten, and put him in the stocks that were at the upper [r]Benjamin Gate, which was by the house of the LORD. Jer. 37:13

3 Then it came about on the next day, when Pashhur released Jeremiah from the stocks, that Jeremiah said to him, "Pashhur is not the name the LORD has called you, but rather [5]Magor-missabib.

4 "For thus says the LORD, 'Behold, I am going to make you a terror to yourself and to all your friends; and while your eyes look on, they will fall by the sword of their enemies. So I shall give over all Judah to the hand of the king of Babylon, and he will carry them away as exiles to Babylon and will slay them with the sword.

[5]I.e., terror on every side

5 'I shall also give over all the wealth of this city, all its produce, and all its costly things; even all the treasures of the kings of Judah I shall give over to the hand of their enemies, and they will plunder them, take them away, and bring them to Babylon.

6 'And you, [r]Pashhur, and all who live in your house will go into captivity; and you will enter Babylon, and there you will die, and there you will be buried, you and all your friends to whom you have falsely prophesied.' " Jer. 20:1

7 O LORD, Thou hast deceived
me and I was deceived;
Thou hast [r]overcome me and
prevailed. Ezek. 3:14
I have become a laughing-
stock all day long;
Everyone mocks me.
8 For each time I speak, I cry
aloud;
I [r]proclaim violence and destruction, Jer. 6:7
Because for me the word of
the LORD has [t]resulted
In reproach and derision all
day long. *become*
9 But if I say, "I will not [r]re-
member Him 1 Kin. 19:3
Or speak anymore in His
name,"
Then in my heart it becomes
like a burning fire
Shut up in my bones;
And I am weary of holding *it*
in,
And I cannot endure *it*.
10 For I have heard the whispering of many,
"Terror on every side!
[r]Denounce *him;* yes, let us denounce him!" Neh. 6:6-13
All my trusted friends,
Watching for my fall, say:
"Perhaps he will be [a]deceived,
so that we may [r]prevail
against him *persuaded*
And take our revenge on
him." 1 Kin. 19:2
11 But the LORD is with me like
a dread champion;
Therefore my [r]persecutors
will stumble and not pre-
vail. Deut. 32:35, 36
They will be utterly
ashamed, because they
have failed,
With an everlasting disgrace
that will not be forgotten.
12 Yet, O LORD of hosts, Thou
who dost test the right-
eous,
Who seest the [t]mind and the
heart; *kidneys*
Let me [r]see Thy vengeance on
them; Ps. 54:7; 59:10
For [r]to Thee I have set forth
my cause. Ps. 62:8
13 [r]Sing to the LORD, praise the
LORD! Jer. 31:7
For He has delivered the soul
of the needy one
From the hand of evildoers.

14 Cursed be the [r]day when I
was born;
Let the day not be blessed
when my mother bore
me! Job 3:3-6
15 Cursed be the man who
brought the news
To my father, saying,
"A [t]baby boy has been born to
you!" *male child*
And made him very happy.
16 But let that man be like the
cities

Which the LORD overthrew
without [6]relenting,
And let him hear an [r]outcry in
the morning Jer. 18:22
And a [a]shout of alarm at
noon; *trumpet blast*
17 Because he did not kill me
[t]before birth,
So that my mother would
have been my grave,
And her womb ever preg-
nant. *from the womb*
18 Why did I ever come forth
from the womb
To [r]look on trouble and sorrow, Job 3:20; 5:7; 14:1
So that my days have been
spent in shame?

CHAPTER 21

THE word which came to Jeremiah from the LORD when [r]King
Zedekiah sent to him Pashhur the
son of Malchijah, and Zephaniah
the priest, the son of Maaseiah,
saying, 2 Kin. 24:17, 18
2 "Please inquire of the LORD on
our behalf, for Nebuchadnezzar
king of Babylon is warring against
us; perhaps the LORD will deal
with us according to all His [a]won-
derful acts, that *the enemy* may
withdraw from us." *miracles*
3 Then Jeremiah said to them,
"You shall say to Zedekiah as follows:
4 'Thus says the LORD God of
Israel, "Behold, I am about to [r]turn
back the weapons of war which
are in your hands, with which you
are warring against the king of
Babylon and the Chaldeans who
are besieging you outside the wall;
and I shall gather them into the
center of this city. Jer. 32:5
5 "And I [r]Myself shall war
against you with an [r]outstretched
hand and a mighty arm, even in
anger and wrath and great indignation. Is. 63:10 • Jer. 6:12
6 "I shall also strike down the
inhabitants of this city, both man
and beast; they will die of a great
[r]pestilence. Jer. 14:12; 32:24
7 "Then afterwards," declares
the LORD, "I shall give over Zedekiah king of Judah and his servants and the people, even those
who survive in this city from the
pestilence, the sword, and the
famine, into the hand of Nebuchadnezzar king of Babylon, and
into the hand of their foes, and
into the hand of those who seek
their lives; and he will strike them
down with the edge of the sword.
He will not spare them nor have
pity nor compassion." '
8 "You shall also say to this
people, 'Thus says the LORD, "Behold, I set before you the way of
life and the way of death.
9 "He who [r]dwells in this city
will die by the sword and by famine and by pestilence; but he who
goes out and falls away to the
Chaldeans who are besieging you
will live, and he will have his own
life as booty. Jer. 38:2, 17-23
10 "For I have [r]set My face
against this city for [t]harm and not
for good," declares the LORD. "It
will be given into the hand of the
king of Babylon, and he will burn
it with fire." ' Lev. 17:10 • *evil*
11 "Then *say* to the household of
the [r]king of Judah, 'Hear the word
of the LORD, Jer. 17:20
12 O house of David, thus says
the LORD:

[6]Lit., *being sorry*

"Administer justice [a]every morning; *in the*
And deliver the *person* who has been robbed from the [t]power of his oppressor,
That My wrath may not go forth like fire *hand*
And [r]burn with none to extinguish *it,* Is. 1:31
Because of the evil of their deeds.

13"Behold, [r]I am against you, O valley dweller, Ezek. 13:8
O rocky plain," declares the LORD,
"You men who say, 'Who[r] will come down against us?
Or who will enter into our habitations?' 2 Sam. 5:6, 7
14"But I shall punish you according to the [t]results of your deeds," declares the LORD, *fruit*
"And I shall [r]kindle a fire in its forest 2 Chr. 36:19
That it may devour all its environs." ' "

CHAPTER 22

THUS says the LORD, "Go down
to the house of the king of Judah,
and there speak this word,
2 and say, 'Hear the word of
the LORD, O king of Judah, who
[r]sits on David's throne, you and
your servants and your people
who enter these gates. Is. 9:7
3 'Thus says the LORD, "Do justice and righteousness, and deliver the one who has been robbed
from the power of *his* oppressor.
Also do not mistreat *or* do violence to the stranger, the orphan,
or the widow; and do not shed innocent blood in this place.
4"For if you men will indeed
perform this thing, then kings will
enter the gates of this house, sitting in David's place on his
throne, riding in chariots and on
horses, *even the king* himself and
his servants and his people.
5"But if you will not obey these
words, I swear by Myself," declares the LORD, "that this house
will become a desolation." ' "
6 For thus says the LORD concerning the house of the king of
Judah:

"You are *like* Gilead to Me,
Like the summit of Lebanon;
Yet most assuredly I shall make you like a [r]wilderness, Ps. 107:34
Like cities which are not inhabited.
7"For I shall set apart destroyers against you,
Each with his weapons;
And they will [r]cut down your choicest cedars Is. 10:33
And throw *them* on the fire.

8"And many nations will pass
by this city; and they will say to
one another, 'Why has the LORD
done thus to this great city?'
9"Then they will [t]answer, 'Because they [r]forsook the covenant
of the LORD their God and bowed
down to other gods and served
them.' " *say* • 2 Kin. 22:17

10 [r]Do not weep for the dead or mourn for him, Is. 57:1
But weep continually for the one who goes away;
For he will never return
Or see his native land.

11 For thus says the LORD in regard to Shallum the son of Josiah,
king of Judah, who became king
in the place of Josiah his father,

who went forth from this place,
"He will never return there;
12 but in the place where they
led him captive, there he will die
and not see this land again.

13 "Woe to him who builds his house [r]without righteousness Jer. 17:11
And his [a]upper rooms without justice, *roof chambers*
Who uses his neighbor's services without pay
And [r]does not give him his wages, Lev. 19:13
14 Who says, 'I will build myself a roomy house
With spacious upper rooms,
And cut out its windows,
Paneling *it* with cedar and painting *it* bright red.'
15 "Do you become a king because you are competing in cedar?
Did not your father eat and drink,
And [r]do justice and righteousness? 2 Kin. 23:25
Then it was well with him.
16 "He pled the cause of the [r]afflicted and needy;
Then it was well. Ps. 72:1-4
[r]Is not that what it means to know Me?" 1 Chr. 28:9
Declares the LORD.
17 "But your eyes and your heart
Are *intent* only upon your own dishonest gain,
And on [r]shedding innocent blood 2 Kin. 24:4
And on practicing oppression and extortion."

18 Therefore thus says the LORD
in regard to Jehoiakim the son of
Josiah, king of Judah,

"They will not lament for him:
'Alas,[r] my brother!' or, 'Alas, sister!' 1 Kin. 13:30
They will not lament for him:
'Alas for the master!' or, 'Alas for his splendor!'
19 "He will be [r]buried with a donkey's burial, 1 Kin. 21:23, 24
Dragged off and thrown out beyond the gates of Jerusalem.
20 "Go up to Lebanon and cry out,
And lift up your voice in Bashan;
Cry out also from [r]Abarim,
For all your lovers have been crushed. Num. 27:12
21 "I spoke to you in your prosperity;
But [r]you said, 'I will not listen!' Jer. 13:10
[r]This has been your practice from your youth,
That you have not obeyed My voice. Jer. 3:25
22 "The wind will sweep away all your [r]shepherds,
And your lovers will go into captivity; Jer. 23:1
Then you will surely be [r]ashamed and humiliated
Because of all your wickedness. Is. 65:13
23 "You who dwell in Lebanon,
Nested in the cedars,
How you will groan when pangs come upon you,
[r]Pain like a woman in childbirth! Jer. 4:31; 6:24

24 "As I live," declares the LORD,
"even though [7]Coniah the son of
Jehoiakim king of Judah were a
[r]signet *ring* on My right hand, yet I
would pull you off; Song 8:6
25 and I shall [r]give you over into

[7]I.e., Jehoiachin

the hand of those who are seeking your life, yes, into the hand of those whom you dread, even into the hand of Nebuchadnezzar king of Babylon, and into the hand of the Chaldeans. 2 Kin. 24:15, 16

26 "I shall hurl you and your mother who bore you into another country where you were not born, and there you will die.

27 "But as for the land to which they desire to return, they will not return to it.

28 "Is this man Coniah a despised, shattered jar?
Or is he an [r]undesirable vessel? Ps. 31:12
Why have he and his descendants been [r]hurled out Jer. 15:1
And cast into a land that they had not known?
29 "O land, land, land,
Hear the word of the LORD!
30 "Thus says the LORD,
'Write this man down [r]childless, 1 Chr. 3:17
A man who will [r]not prosper in his days; Jer. 2:37
For no man of his [r]descendants will prosper
Sitting on the throne of David Ps. 94:20
Or ruling again in Judah.' "

CHAPTER 23

"WOE[r] to the [r]destroying and scattering the sheep of My pasture!" declares the LORD. Ezek. 13:3 • Jer. 10:21

2 Therefore thus says the LORD God of Israel concerning the shepherds who are tending My people: "You have scattered My flock and driven them away, and have not attended to them; behold, I am about to attend to you for the evil of your deeds," declares the LORD.

3 "Then I Myself shall [r]gather the remnant of My flock out of all the countries where I have driven them and shall bring them back to their pasture; and they will be fruitful and multiply.

4 "I shall also raise up shepherds over them and they will [a]tend them; and they will not be afraid any longer, nor be terrified, [r]nor will any be missing," declares the LORD. *shepherd* • 1 Pet. 1:5

5 "Behold, *the* days are coming," declares the LORD,
"When I shall raise up for David a righteous Branch;
And He will reign as king and act wisely
And do justice and righteousness in the land.
6 "In His days Judah will be saved,
And [r]Israel will dwell securely; Deut. 33:28
And this is His name by which He will be called,
'The LORD our righteousness.'

7 "Therefore[r] behold, *the* days are coming," declares the LORD, "when they will no longer say, 'As the LORD lives, who brought up the sons of Israel from the land of Egypt,' Is. 43:18, 19

8 but, 'As the LORD lives, who [r]brought up and led back the descendants of the household of Israel from *the* north land and from all the countries where I had driven them.' Then they will live on their own soil." Is. 43:5, 6

9 As for the prophets:
My [r]heart is broken within me, Jer. 8:18; Hab. 3:16

All my bones tremble;
I have become like a drunken man,
Even like a man overcome with wine,
Because of the LORD
And because of His holy words.
10 For the land is full of ʳadulterers; Jer. 9:2
For the land ʳmourns because of the curse. Jer. 12:4
The pastures of the wilderness have dried up.
Their course also is evil,
And their might is not right.
11 "For ʳboth prophet and priest are polluted; Jer. 6:13
Even in My house I have found their wickedness,"
declares the LORD.
12 "Therefore their way will be like ʳslippery paths to them, Ps. 35:6
They will be driven away into the ʳgloom and fall down in it; Is. 8:22
For I shall bring ʳcalamity upon them, Jer. 11:23
The year of their punishment," declares the LORD.

13 "Moreover, among the prophets of Samaria I saw an ʳoffensive thing:
They prophesied by Baal and led My people Israel astray. Hos. 9:7, 8
14 "Also among the prophets of Jerusalem I have seen a ʳhorrible thing: Jer. 5:30
The committing of ʳadultery and walking in falsehood;
And they strengthen the hands of ʳevildoers,
So that no one has turned back from his wickedness. Jer. 29:23 • Jer. 23:22
All of them have become to Me like Sodom,
And her inhabitants like Gomorrah.
15 "Therefore thus says the LORD of hosts concerning the prophets,
'Behold, I am going to feed them wormwood
And make them drink poisonous water,
For from the prophets of Jerusalem
Pollution has gone forth into all the land.' "

16 Thus says the LORD of hosts,
"Do not listen to the words of the prophets who are prophesying to you.
They are ʳleading you into futility; Gal. 1:8
They speak a vision of their own ᵗimagination, *heart*
Not ʳfrom the mouth of the LORD. Jer. 9:12, 20
17 "They keep saying to those who despise Me,
'The LORD has said, "You will have peace" ';
And as for everyone who walks in the stubbornness of his own heart,
They say, 'Calamity will not come upon you.'
18 "But ʳwho has stood in the council of the LORD,
That he should see and hear His word? Job 15:8
Who has given heed to His word and listened?
19 "Behold, the ʳstorm of the

LORD has gone forth in
wrath, Jer. 25:32
Even a whirling tempest;
It will swirl down on the
head of the wicked.
20 "The ʳanger of the LORD will
not turn back Jer. 30:24
Until He has ʳperformed and
carried out the purposes
of His heart; Is. 55:11
In the last days you will
clearly understand it.
21 "I ʳdid not send *these* prophets,
But they ran. Jer. 14:14
I did not speak to them,
But they prophesied.
22 "But if they had ʳstood in My
council, Jer. 9:12
Then they would have ʳannounced My words to My
people, Jer. 35:15
And would have turned them
back from their evil way
And from the evil of their
deeds.

23 "Am I a God who is near," declares the LORD,
"And not a God far off?
24 "Can a man ʳhide himself in
hiding places, Job 22:13
So I do not see him?" declares the LORD.
"Do ʳI not fill the heavens and
the earth?" declares the
LORD. 1 Kin. 8:27
25 "I have heard what the prophets have said who prophesy
falsely in My name, saying, 'I had
a dream, I had a dream!'
26 "How long? Is there *anything*
in the hearts of the prophets who
prophesy falsehood, even *these*
prophets of the ʳdeception of their
own heart, 1 Tim. 4:1, 2
27 who intend to make My people forget My name by their
dreams which they relate to one
another, just as their fathers forgot My name because of Baal?
28 "The prophet who has a
dream may relate *his* dream, but
let him who has My word speak
My word in truth. What does
straw have *in common* with
grain?" declares the LORD.
29 "Is not My word like fire?" declares the LORD, "and like a hammer which shatters a rock?
30 "Therefore behold, ʳI am
against the prophets," declares
the LORD, "who steal My words
from each other. Deut. 18:20
**31 "Behold, I am against the
prophets," declares the LORD,
"who use their tongues and declare, '*The Lord* declares.'**
32 "Behold, I am against those
who have prophesied ʳfalse
dreams," declares the LORD, "and
related them, and led My people
astray by their falsehoods and
reckless boasting; yet I did not
send them or command them, nor
do they ʳfurnish this people the
slightest benefit," declares the
LORD. Deut. 13:1, 2 • Jer. 7:8
33 "Now when this people or the
prophet or a priest asks you saying, 'What is the [8]oracle of the
LORD?' then you shall say to them,
'What oracle?' The LORD declares,
'I shall ʳabandon you.' Jer. 12:7
34 "Then as for the prophet or
the priest or the people who say,
'The ʳoracle of the LORD,' I shall
bring punishment upon that man
and his household. Lam. 2:14
35 "Thus shall each of you say to
his neighbor and to his brother,

[8]Or, *burden*, and so throughout the ch.

'What has the LORD answered?'
or, 'What has the LORD spoken?'
36"For you will no longer remember the oracle of the LORD,
because every man's own word
will become the oracle, and you
have [r]perverted the words of the
[r]living God, the LORD of hosts, our
God. Gal. 1:7, 8 • 2 Kin. 19:4
37"Thus you will say to *that*
prophet, 'What has the LORD answered you?' and, 'What has the
LORD spoken?'
38"For if you say, 'The oracle of
the LORD!' surely thus says the
LORD, 'Because you said this
word, "The oracle of the LORD!" I
have also sent to you, saying,
"You shall not say, 'The oracle of
the LORD!' " '
39"Therefore behold, [r]I shall
surely forget you and cast you
away from My presence, along
with the city which I gave you and
your fathers. Jer. 7:14, 15
40"And I will put an everlasting
[r]reproach on you and an everlasting humiliation which will not
be forgotten." Jer. 20:11; 42:18

CHAPTER 24

AFTER Nebuchadnezzar king of
Babylon had carried away captive
Jeconiah the son of Jehoiakim,
king of Judah, and the officials of
Judah with the craftsmen and
smiths from Jerusalem and had
brought them to Babylon, the
LORD showed me: behold, two
[r]baskets of figs set before the temple of the LORD! Amos 8:1
2 One basket had very good
figs, like [r]first-ripe figs; and the
other basket had [r]very bad figs,
which could not be eaten due to
rottenness. Mic. 7:1 • Jer. 29:17
3 Then the LORD said to me,
"What[r] do you see, Jeremiah?"
And I said, "Figs, the good figs,
very good; and the bad *figs,* very
bad, which cannot be eaten due to
rottenness." Jer. 1:11, 13
4 Then the word of the LORD
came to me, saying,
5"Thus says the LORD God of
Israel, 'Like these good figs, so I
will regard [r]as good the captives of
Judah, whom I have sent out of
this place *into* the land of the
Chaldeans. Nah. 1:7
6 'For I will set My eyes on
them for good, and I will [r]bring
them again to this land; and I will
build them up and not overthrow
them, and I will plant them and
not pluck *them* up. Jer. 12:15
7 'And I will give them a heart
to know Me, for I am the LORD;
and they will be My people, and I
will be their God, for they will return to Me with their whole heart.
8 'But like the [r]bad figs which
cannot be eaten due to rottenness—indeed, thus says the
LORD—so I will [t]abandon Zedekiah king of Judah and his officials, and the remnant of Jerusalem who remain in this land, and
the ones who dwell in the land of
Egypt. Jer. 29:17 • *give up*
9 'And I will [r]make them a terror *and an* evil for all the kingdoms of the earth, as a reproach
and a proverb, a taunt and a curse
in all places where I shall scatter
them. Jer. 15:4; 29:18; 34:17
10 'And I will send the [r]sword,
the famine, and the pestilence
upon them until they are de-

stroyed from the land which I
gave to them and their forefathers.' " Is. 51:19; Jer. 21:9

CHAPTER 25

THE word that came to Jeremiah
concerning all the people of Judah, in the fourth year of Jehoiakim the son of Josiah, king of Judah (that was the first year of
Nebuchadnezzar king of Babylon), Jer. 36:1; 46:2
2 which Jeremiah the prophet
spoke to all the people of Judah
and to all the inhabitants of Jerusalem, saying, Jer. 18:11
3 "From the thirteenth year of
Josiah the son of Amon, king of
Judah, even to this day, these
twenty-three years the word of
the LORD has come to me, and I
have spoken to you again and
again, but you have not listened.
4 "And the LORD has sent to you
all His servants the prophets
again and again, but you have not
listened nor inclined your ear to
hear, *rising early and sending*
5 saying, 'Turn now everyone
from his evil way and from the
evil of your deeds, and dwell on
the land which the LORD has given
to you and your forefathers forever and ever; 2 Kin. 17:13
6 and do not go after other
gods to serve them and to worship
them, and do not provoke Me to
anger with the work of your
hands, and I will do you no harm.'
7 "Yet you have not listened to
Me," declares the LORD, "in order
that you might provoke Me to anger with the work of your hands
to your own harm. Jer. 7:19
8 "Therefore thus says the LORD
of hosts, 'Because you have not
obeyed My words,
9 behold, I will send and take
all the families of the north,' declares the LORD, 'and *I will send* to
Nebuchadnezzar king of Babylon,
My servant, and will bring them
against this land, and against its
inhabitants, and against all these
nations round about; and I will utterly destroy them, and make
them a horror, and a hissing, and
an everlasting desolation.
10 'Moreover, I will take from
them the voice of joy and the
voice of gladness, the voice of
the bridegroom and the voice of
the bride, the sound of the millstones and the light of the lamp.
11 'And this whole land shall be
a desolation and a horror, and
these nations shall serve the king
of Babylon seventy years.
12 'Then it will be when seventy
years are completed I will punish
the king of Babylon and that nation,' declares the LORD, 'for their
iniquity, and the land of the Chaldeans; and I will make it an everlasting desolation. Ezra 1:1
13 'And I will bring upon that
land all My words which I have
pronounced against it, all that is
written in this book, which Jeremiah has prophesied against all
the nations. Jer. 36:4, 29, 32
14 '(For many nations and great
kings shall make slaves of them,
even them; and I will recompense
them according to their deeds,
and according to the work of their
hands.)' " Jer. 27:7; 50:9, 41
15 For thus the LORD, the God
of Israel, says to me, "Take this
cup of the wine of wrath from My

hand, and cause all the nations, to
whom I send you, to drink it.
16 "And they shall [r]drink and
stagger and go mad because of
the sword that I will send among
them." Nah. 3:11
17 Then I took the cup from the
LORD's hand, and [r]made all the nations drink, to whom the LORD
sent me: Jer. 1:10; 25:28
18 [r]Jerusalem and the cities of
Judah, and its kings *and* its
princes, to make them a ruin, a
horror, a hissing, and a curse, as it
is this day; Ps. 60:3; Is. 51:17
19 [r]Pharaoh king of Egypt, his
servants, his princes, and all his
people; Jer. 46:2-28
20 and all the foreign people, all
the kings of the land of Uz, all the
kings of the land of the Philistines
(even Ashkelon, Gaza, Ekron, and
the remnant of Ashdod);
21 [r]Edom, Moab, and the sons of
[r]Ammon; Ps. 137:7 • Jer. 49:1-6
22 and all the kings of [r]Tyre, all
the kings of Sidon, and the kings
of the coastlands which are beyond the sea; Jer. 47:4
23 and [r]Dedan, Tema, Buz, and
all who [r]cut the corners *of their*
hair; Is. 21:13 • Jer. 9:26; 49:32
24 and all the kings of Arabia
and all the kings of the foreign
people who dwell in the desert;
25 and all the kings of Zimri, all
the kings of [r]Elam, and all the
kings of Media; Gen. 10:22
26 and all the kings of the north,
near and far, one with another;
and all the kingdoms of the earth
which are upon the face of the
ground, and the king of Sheshach
shall drink after them.
27 "And you shall say to them,
'Thus says the LORD of hosts, the
God of Israel, "Drink,[r] be drunk,
vomit, fall, and rise no more because of the sword which I will
send among you." ' Jer. 25:16
28 "And it will be, if they refuse
to take the cup from your hand to
drink, then you will say to them,
'Thus says the LORD of hosts:
"You shall surely drink!
29 "For behold, I am [r]beginning
to work calamity in *this* city
which is called by My name, and
shall you be completely free from
punishment? You will not be free
from punishment; for I am summoning a sword against all the inhabitants of the earth," declares
the LORD of hosts.' Prov. 11:31
30 "Therefore you shall prophesy
against them all these words, and
you shall say to them,

'The [r]LORD will roar from on
high, Is. 42:13
And utter His voice from His
holy habitation;
He will roar mightily against
His [a]fold. *pasture*
He will shout like those who
tread *the grapes*,
Against all the inhabitants of
the earth.
31 'A clamor has come to the
end of the earth,
Because the LORD has a controversy with the nations.
He is entering into [r]judgment
with all flesh; Joel 3:2
As for the wicked, He has
given them to the sword,'
declares the LORD."

32 Thus says the LORD of hosts,
"Behold, evil is going forth
From [r]nation to nation,
And a great [r]storm is being
stirred up 2 Chr. 15:6

From the remotest parts of
the earth. Jer. 23:19
33 "And those slain by the LORD
on that day shall be from one end
of the earth to the other. They
shall not be lamented, gathered,
or buried; they shall be like dung
on the face of the ground.
34 "Wail, you shepherds, and
cry;
And [r]wallow *in ashes,* you
masters of the flock;
For the days of your slaughter and your dispersions
[t]have come, Jer. 6:26
And you shall fall like a
choice vessel. *are full*
35 "Flight[r] shall perish from the
shepherds,
And escape from the masters
of the flock. Job 11:20
36 "*Hear* the sound of the cry of
the shepherds,
And the wailing of the masters of the flock!
For the LORD is destroying
their pasture,
37 "And the peaceful [a]folds are
made silent *pastures*
Because of the fierce anger
of the LORD.
38 "He has left His hiding place
[r]like the lion; Hos. 5:14
For their land has become a
horror
Because of the fierceness of
the [a]oppressing *sword,*
And because of His fierce anger." *oppressor*

CHAPTER 26

IN the beginning of the reign of
[r]Jehoiakim the son of Josiah, king
of Judah, this word came from the
LORD, saying, 2 Kin. 23:36
2 "Thus says the LORD, 'Stand[r]
in the court of the LORD's house,
and speak to all the cities of Judah, who have come to worship *in*
the LORD's house, [r]all the words
that I have commanded you to
speak to them. Do not omit a
word! 2 Chr. 24:20, 21 • Jer. 1:17
3 'Perhaps they will listen and
everyone will turn from his evil
way, that[r] I may repent of the calamity which I am planning to do
to them because of the evil of
their deeds.' Jer. 18:8
4 "And you will say to them,
'Thus says the LORD, "If you will
not listen to Me, to walk in My
law, which I have set before you,
5 to listen to the words of My
servants the prophets, whom I
have been sending to you [t]again
and again, but you have not listened; *rising early and sending*
6 then I will make this house
like [r]Shiloh, and this city I will
make a curse to all the nations of
the earth." ' " Josh. 18:1
7 And the priests and the
prophets and all the people heard
Jeremiah speaking these words in
the house of the LORD.
8 And when Jeremiah finished
speaking all that the LORD had
commanded *him* to speak to all
the people, the priests and the
prophets and all the people seized
him, saying, "You must die!
9 "Why have you prophesied in
the name of the LORD saying, 'This
house will be like Shiloh, and this
city will be [r]desolate, without inhabitant'?" And all the people
gathered about Jeremiah in the
house of the LORD. Jer. 9:11
10 And when the [r]princes of Judah heard these things, they came

up from the king's house to the
house of the LORD and sat in
the entrance of the New Gate of
the LORD's *house.* Jer. 26:21
11 Then the priests and the
prophets spoke to the officials and
to all the people, saying, "A death
sentence for this man! For he has
prophesied against this city as you
have heard in your hearing."
12 Then Jeremiah spoke to all
the officials and to all the people,
saying, [r]"The LORD sent me to
prophesy against this house and
against this city all the words that
you have heard. Jer. 1:17, 18
13 "Now therefore amend your
ways and your deeds, and obey
the voice of the LORD your God;
and the LORD will change His
mind about the misfortune which
He has pronounced against you.
14 "But as for me, behold, I am in
your hands; do with me as is good
and right in your sight.
15 "Only know for certain that if
you put me to death, you will
bring innocent blood on yourselves, and on this city, and on its
inhabitants; for truly the LORD has
sent me to you to speak all these
words in your hearing."
16 Then the officials and all the
people [r]said to the priests and to
the prophets, "No death sentence
for this man! For he has spoken to
us in the name of the LORD our
God." Jer. 26:11; 36:19, 25
17 Then [r]some of the elders of
the land rose up and spoke to all
the assembly of the people, saying, Acts 5:34
18 "Micah[r] of Moresheth prophesied in the days of Hezekiah king
of Judah; and he spoke to all the
people of Judah, saying, 'Thus the
LORD of hosts has said, Mic. 1:1
"Zion[r] will be plowed *as* a
field, Neh. 4:2
And Jerusalem will become
ruins,
And the [r]mountain of the
house as the high places
of a forest." ' Is. 2:2, 3
19 "Did Hezekiah king of Judah
and all Judah put him to death?
Did he not fear the LORD and entreat the favor of the LORD, and
the LORD [t]changed His mind about
the misfortune which He had pronounced against them? But we are
committing a great evil against
ourselves." *was sorry for*
20 Indeed, there was also a man
who prophesied in the name of the
LORD, Uriah the son of Shemaiah
from Kiriath-jearim; and he
prophesied against this city and
against this land words similar to
all those of Jeremiah.
21 When King Jehoiakim and
all his mighty men and all the officials heard his words, then the
king sought to put him to death;
but Uriah heard *it,* and he was
afraid and fled, and went to Egypt.
22 Then King Jehoiakim sent
men to Egypt: [r]Elnathan the son of
Achbor and *certain* men with him
went into Egypt. Jer. 36:12
23 And they brought Uriah from
Egypt and led him to King Jehoiakim, who slew him with a sword,
and cast his dead body into the
[t]burial place of the [t]common people. *graves • sons of the people*
24 But the hand of [r]Ahikam the
son of Shaphan was with Jeremiah, so that he was not given into
the hands of the people to put him
to death. 2 Kin. 22:12-14

CHAPTER 27

IN the beginning of the reign of
Zedekiah the son of Josiah, king
of Judah, this word came to Jeremiah from the LORD, saying—
2 thus says the LORD to me—
"Make for yourself bonds and
yokes and put them on your neck,
3 and send[t] word to the king of
Edom, to the king of Moab, to the
king of the sons of Ammon, to the
king of Tyre, and to the king of Sidon[t] by the messengers who come
to Jerusalem to Zedekiah king of
Judah. *them • by the hand of*
4 "And command them *to* go to
their masters, saying, 'Thus says
the LORD of hosts, the God of Israel, thus you shall say to your
masters,
5 "I have made the earth, the
men and the beasts which are on
the face of the earth by My great
power and by My outstretched
arm, and I will give it to the one
who is pleasing in My sight.
6 "And now I [r]have given all
these lands into the hand of Nebuchadnezzar king of Babylon, My
servant, and I have given him also
the wild animals of the field to
serve him. Jer. 21:7; 22:25
7 "And all the nations shall
serve him, and his son, and his
grandson, until the time of his
own land comes; then many nations and great kings will [a]make
him their servant. *enslave him*
8 "And it will be, *that* the nation
or the kingdom which will not
serve him, Nebuchadnezzar king
of Babylon, and which will not put
its neck under the yoke of the king
of Babylon, I will punish that nation with the [r]sword, with famine,
and with pestilence," declares the
LORD, "until I have destroyed[t] it by
his hand. Ezek. 14:21 • *them*
9 "But as for you, do not listen
to your prophets, your diviners,
your [t]dreamers, your soothsayers,
or your sorcerers, who speak to
you, saying, 'You shall not serve
the king of Babylon.' *dreams*
10 "For they prophesy a lie to
you, in order to remove you far
from your land; and I will drive
you out, and you will perish.
11 "But the nation which will
bring its neck under the yoke of
the king of Babylon and serve
him, I will let remain on its land,"
declares the LORD, "and they will
till it and dwell in it." ' "
12 And I spoke words like all
these to [r]Zedekiah king of Judah,
saying, "Bring your necks under
the yoke of the king of Babylon,
and serve him and his people, and
live! Jer. 27:3; 28:1; 38:17
13 "Why will you die, you and
your people, by the sword, famine, and pestilence, as the LORD
has spoken to that nation which
will not serve the king of Babylon?
14 "So [r]do not listen to the words
of the prophets who speak to you,
saying, 'You shall not serve the
king of Babylon,' for they prophesy a lie to you; Jer. 27:9
15 for I have not sent them," declares the LORD, "but they prophesy falsely in My name, in order
that I may drive you out, and that
you may perish, you and the
prophets who prophesy to you."
16 *Then* I spoke to the priests
and to all this people, saying,
"Thus says the LORD: Do not listen to the words of your prophets
who prophesy to you, saying, 'Be-

hold, the vessels of the LORD's
house will now shortly be brought
again from Babylon'; for they are
prophesying a lie to you.
17 "Do not listen to them; serve
the king of Babylon, and live!
Why should this city become a
ruin? Jer. 7:34
18 "But if they are prophets, and
if the word of the LORD is with
them, let them now entreat the
LORD of hosts, that the vessels
which are left in the house of the
LORD, in the house of the king of
Judah, and in Jerusalem, may not
go to Babylon. 1 Kin. 18:24
19 "For thus says the LORD of
hosts concerning the pillars, concerning the sea, concerning the
stands, and concerning the rest of
the vessels that are left in this
city, 1 Kin. 7:15; 2 Kin. 25:13, 17
20 which Nebuchadnezzar king
of Babylon did not take when he
carried into exile Jeconiah the son
of Jehoiakim, king of Judah, from
Jerusalem to Babylon, and all the
nobles of Judah and Jerusalem.
21 "Yes, thus says the LORD of
hosts, the God of Israel, concerning the vessels that are left in the
house of the LORD, and in the
house of the king of Judah, and in
Jerusalem,
22 'They shall be carried to
Babylon, and they shall be there
until the day I visit them,' declares
the LORD. 'Then I will bring them
back and restore them to this
place.' " Jer. 25:11, 12 • *up*

CHAPTER 28

NOW it came about in the same
year, in the beginning of the reign
of Zedekiah king of Judah, in the
fourth year, in the fifth month,
that Hananiah the son of Azzur,
the prophet, who was from Gibeon, spoke to me in the house of
the LORD in the presence of the
priests and all the people, saying,
2 "Thus says the LORD of hosts,
the God of Israel, 'I have broken
the yoke of the king of Babylon.
3 'Within two years I am going
to bring back to this place all the
vessels of the LORD's house,
which Nebuchadnezzar king of
Babylon took away from this
place and carried to Babylon.
4 'I am also going to bring back
to this place Jeconiah the son of
Jehoiakim, king of Judah, and all
the exiles of Judah who went to
Babylon,' declares the LORD, 'for I
will break the yoke of the king of
Babylon.' " Jer. 22:26, 27
5 Then the prophet Jeremiah
spoke to the prophet Hananiah in
the presence of the priests and in
the presence of all the people who
were standing in the house of the
LORD, Jer. 28:1
6 and the prophet Jeremiah
said, "Amen! May the LORD do so;
may the LORD confirm your words
which you have prophesied to
bring back the vessels of the
LORD's house and all the exiles,
from Babylon to this place.
7 "Yet hear now this word
which I am about to speak in your
hearing and in the hearing of all
the people! 1 Kin. 22:28
8 "The prophets who were before me and before you from ancient times prophesied against
many lands and against great
kingdoms, of war and of calamity
and of pestilence. Is. 5:5-7
9 "The prophet who prophesies

of peace, when the word of the prophet shall come to pass, then that prophet will be known *as* one whom the LORD has truly sent."

10 Then Hananiah the prophet took the [r]yoke from the neck of Jeremiah the prophet and broke it. Jer. 27:2

11 And Hananiah spoke in the presence of all the people, saying, "Thus[r] says the LORD, 'Even so will I break within two full years, the yoke of Nebuchadnezzar king of Babylon from the neck of all the nations.' " Then the prophet Jeremiah went his way. Jer. 14:14

12 And the [r]word of the LORD came to Jeremiah, after Hananiah the prophet had broken the yoke from off the neck of the prophet Jeremiah, saying, Jer. 1:2

13 "Go and speak to Hananiah, saying, 'Thus says the LORD, "You have broken the yokes of wood, but you have made instead of them [r]yokes of iron." Is. 45:2

14 'For thus says the LORD of hosts, the God of Israel, "I have put a yoke of iron on the neck of all these nations, that they may serve Nebuchadnezzar king of Babylon; and they shall serve him. And I have also given him the beasts of the field." ' "

15 Then Jeremiah the prophet said to Hananiah the prophet, "Listen now, Hananiah, the LORD has not sent you, and you have made this people trust in a lie.

16 "Therefore thus says the LORD, 'Behold, I am about to remove you from the face of the earth. This year you are going to die, because you have counseled rebellion against the LORD.' "

17 So Hananiah the prophet died in the same year in the seventh month.

CHAPTER 29

NOW these are the words of the [r]letter which Jeremiah the prophet sent from Jerusalem to the rest of the elders of the exile, the priests, the prophets, and all the people whom Nebuchadnezzar had taken into exile from Jerusalem to Babylon. 2 Chr. 30:1, 6; Esth. 9:20

2 (This was after King [r]Jeconiah and the queen mother, the court officials, the princes of Judah and Jerusalem, the craftsmen and the smiths had departed from Jerusalem.) 2 Kin. 24:12-16

3 *The letter was sent* by the hand of Elasah the son of Shaphan, and Gemariah the son of [r]Hilkiah, whom Zedekiah king of Judah sent to Babylon to Nebuchadnezzar king of Babylon, saying, 1 Chr. 6:13

4 "Thus says the LORD of hosts, the God of Israel, to all the exiles whom I have sent into exile from Jerusalem to Babylon,

5 'Build[r] houses and live *in them;* and plant gardens, and eat their [t]produce. Jer. 29:28 • *fruit*

6 'Take [r]wives and [t]become the fathers of sons and daughters, and take wives for your sons and give your daughters to husbands, that they may bear sons and daughters; and multiply there and do not decrease. Jer. 16:2-4 • *beget*

7 'And seek the [a]welfare of the city where I have sent you into exile, and [r]pray to the LORD on its behalf; for in its welfare you will have welfare.' *peace* • Dan. 4:19

8 "For thus says the LORD of
hosts, the God of Israel, 'Do not
let your prophets who are in your
midst and your diviners deceive
you, and do not listen to the
dreams which they dream.
9 'For they prophesy falsely to
you in My name; I have not sent
them,' declares the LORD.
10 "For thus says the LORD,
'When [r]seventy years have been
completed for Babylon, I will visit
you and fulfill My good word to
you, to bring you back to this
place. 2 Chr. 36:21-23; Dan. 9:2
11 'For I know the plans that I
[t]have for you,' declares the LORD,
'plans for welfare and not for calamity to give you a future and a
[r]hope. *am planning* • Hos. 2:15
12 'Then you will [r]call upon Me
and come and pray to Me, and I
will listen to you. Ps. 50:15
13 'And you will [r]seek Me and
find *Me,* when you search for Me
with all your heart. Deut. 4:29
14 'And I will be found by you,'
declares the LORD, 'and I will [r]re-
store your [a]fortunes and will
gather you from all the nations
and from all the places where I
have driven you,' declares the
LORD, 'and I will bring you back to
the place from where I sent you
into exile.' Jer. 30:3 • *captivity*
15 "Because you have said, 'The
LORD has raised up [r]prophets for
us in Babylon'— Jer. 29:21, 24
16 for thus says the LORD concerning the king who sits on the
throne of David, and concerning
all the people who dwell in this
city, your brothers who did not go
with you into exile—
17 thus says the LORD of hosts,
'Behold, I am sending upon them
the [r]sword, famine, and pestilence,
and I will make them like split-
open figs that cannot be eaten due
to rottenness. Jer. 27:8; 29:18
18 'And I will pursue them with
the sword, with famine and with
pestilence; and I will [r]make them a
terror to all the kingdoms of the
earth, to be a curse, and a horror,
and a hissing, and a reproach
among all the nations where I
have driven them, Deut. 28:25
19 because they have [r]not listened to My words,' declares the
LORD, 'which I sent to them again
and again by My servants the
prophets; but you did not listen,'
declares the LORD. Jer. 6:19
20 "You, therefore, hear the
word of the LORD, all you exiles,
whom I have [r]sent away from Jerusalem to Babylon. Jer. 24:5
21 "Thus says the LORD of hosts,
the God of Israel, concerning
Ahab the son of Kolaiah and concerning Zedekiah the son of Maaseiah, who are [r]prophesying to you
falsely in My name, 'Behold, I will
deliver them into the hand of
Nebuchadnezzar king of Babylon,
and he shall slay them before your
eyes. Jer. 14:14, 15; 29:8, 9
22 'And because of them a curse
shall be [t]used by all the exiles from
Judah who are in Babylon, saying,
"May the LORD make you like
Zedekiah and like Ahab, whom
the king of Babylon [r]roasted in the
fire, *taken* • Dan. 3:6, 21
23 because they have acted
foolishly in Israel, and have committed adultery with their neighbors' wives, and have spoken
words in My name falsely, which I
did not command them; and I am

He who knows, and am a witness," declares the LORD.' "
24 And to Shemaiah the Nehelamite you shall speak, saying,
25"Thus says the LORD of hosts,
the God of Israel, 'Because you
have sent letters in your own
name to all the people who are in
Jerusalem, and to Zephaniah the
son of Maaseiah, the priest, and to
all the priests, saying,
26"The LORD has made you
priest instead of Jehoiada the
priest, to be the [t]overseer in the
house of the LORD over every
[r]madman who prophesies, to put
him in the stocks and in the iron
collar, *overseers* • 2 Kin. 9:11
27 now then, why have you not
rebuked Jeremiah of Anathoth
who prophesies to you?
28"For he has [r]sent to us in Babylon, saying, '*The exile* will be long;
build houses and live *in them* and
plant gardens and eat their [t]pro-
duce.' " ' " Jer. 29:1 • *fruit*
29 And Zephaniah the priest
read this letter [t]to Jeremiah the
prophet. *in the ears of*
30 Then came the word of the
LORD to Jeremiah, saying,
31"Send to [r]all the exiles, saying,
'Thus says the LORD concerning
Shemaiah the Nehelamite, "Because Shemaiah has prophesied to
you, although I did not send him,
and he has [r]made you trust in a
lie," Jer. 29:20 • Jer. 28:15
32 therefore thus says the LORD,
"Behold, I am about to punish
Shemaiah the Nehelamite and his
[t]descendants; he shall not have
anyone living among this people,
and he shall not see the good that
I am about to do to My people,"
declares the LORD, "because he
has [t]preached rebellion against the
LORD." ' " *seed* • *spoken*

CHAPTER 30

THE word which came to Jeremiah from the LORD, saying,
2"Thus says the LORD, the God
of Israel, [r]"Write all the words
which I have spoken to you in a
book. Is. 30:8; Jer. 25:13
3 'For, behold, days are coming,' declares the LORD, 'when I
will [r]restore the [a]fortunes of My
people Israel and Judah.' The
LORD says, 'I will also bring them
back to the land that I gave to
their forefathers, and they shall
possess it.' " Jer. 29:14 • *captivity*
4 Now these are the words
which the LORD spoke concerning
Israel and concerning Judah,
5"For thus says the LORD,
'I[t] have heard a sound of [r]ter-
ror, *We*
Of dread, and there is no
peace. Is. 5:30; Jer. 6:25
6 'Ask now, and see,
If a male can give birth.
Why do I see every man
With his hands on his loins,
[r]as a woman in childbirth?
And *why* have all faces
turned pale? Jer. 4:31
7 'Alas! for that [r]day is great,
There is none like it;
And it is the time of Jacob's
distress, Is. 2:12
But he will be saved from it.
8 'And it shall come about on
that day,' declares the LORD of
hosts, 'that I will [r]break his yoke
from off their neck, and will tear
off their bonds; and strangers

shall no longer make [t]them their slaves. Is. 9:4 • *him their slave*
9 'But they shall serve the LORD their God, and David their king, whom I will raise up for them.
10 'And[r] fear not, O Jacob My
servant,' declares the
LORD, Is. 41:13; 43:5; 44:2
'And do not be dismayed, O
Israel;
For behold, I will save you
[r]from afar, Is. 60:4
And your [t]offspring from the
land of their captivity.
And Jacob shall return, and
shall be quiet and at ease,
And no one shall make him
afraid. *seed*
11 'For I am with you,' declares
the LORD, 'to save you;
For I will destroy completely
all the nations where I
have scattered you,
Only I will [r]not destroy you
completely. Jer. 4:27
But I will chasten you justly,
And will by no means leave
you unpunished.'

12 "For thus says the LORD,
'Your wound is incurable,
And your injury is serious.
13 'There is no one to plead your
cause;
No healing for *your* sore,
No recovery for you.
14 'All your [r]lovers have forgotten you, Jer. 22:20, 22
They do not seek you;
For I have wounded you with
the wound of an enemy,
With the punishment of a
[r]cruel one, Jer. 6:23
Because your [r]iniquity is
great Jer. 32:30-35
And your sins are numerous.
15 'Why do you cry out over
your injury?
Your pain is incurable.
Because your iniquity is
great
And your sins are numerous,
I have done these things to
you.
16 'Therefore all who [r]devour
you shall be devoured;
And all your adversaries, every one of them, shall go
into captivity; Jer. 2:3
And those who plunder you
shall be for plunder,
And all who prey upon you I
will give for prey.
17 'For I will [t]restore you to
[r]health *cause to go up*
And I will heal you of your
wounds,' declares the
LORD, Ex. 15:26
'Because they have called you
an outcast, saying:
"It is Zion; no one [t]cares for
her." ' *is seeking*

18 "Thus says the LORD,
'Behold, I will [r]restore the [a]for-
tunes of the tents of Ja-
cob Jer. 30:3 • *captivity*
And have compassion on his
dwelling places;
And the [r]city shall be rebuilt
on its ruin, Jer. 31:4
And the palace shall stand on
its rightful place.
19 'And from them shall proceed
[r]thanksgiving Is. 12:1
And the voice of those who
[a]make merry; *dance*
And I will [r]multiply them, and
they shall not be dimin-
ished; Jer. 33:22
I will also [r]honor them, and

they shall not be insignificant. Is. 55:5; 60:9
20 'Their[t] children also shall be as formerly, *His*
And [t]their congregation shall be [r]established before Me;
And I will punish all their oppressors. *his* • Is. 54:14
21 'And [t]their [r]leader shall be one of them, *his* • Jer. 30:9
And their ruler shall come forth from their midst;
And I will bring him near, and he shall approach Me;
For who would dare to risk his life to [r]approach Me?'
declares the LORD. Ex. 3:5
22 'And you shall be My people,
And I will be your God.' "

23 Behold, the [r]tempest of the LORD! Jer. 23:19
Wrath has gone forth,
A [a]sweeping tempest;
It will burst on the head of the wicked. *raging*
24 The [r]fierce anger of the LORD will not turn back, Jer. 4:8
Until He has performed, and until He has accomplished
The intent of His heart;
In the latter days you will understand this.

CHAPTER 31

"AT that time," declares the
LORD, "I will be the [r]God of all the
[r]families of Israel, and they shall
be My people." Jer. 30:22 • Gen. 17:7
2 Thus says the LORD,
"The people who survived the sword
[r]Found grace in the wilderness— Num. 14:20
Israel, when it went to [r]find its rest." Ex. 33:14
3 The LORD appeared to [t]him from afar, *saying*, *me*
"I have loved you with an everlasting love;
Therefore I have drawn you with lovingkindness.
4 "Again [r]I will build you, and you shall be rebuilt,
O virgin of Israel! Jer. 24:6
Again you shall take up your [r]tambourines, Is. 30:32
And go forth to the dances of the merrymakers.
5 "Again you shall [r]plant vineyards Ps. 107:37
On the hills of Samaria;
The planters shall plant
And shall enjoy *them*.
6 "For there shall be a day when watchmen
On the hills of Ephraim shall call out,
'Arise, and [r]let us go up *to* Zion, Is. 2:3; Jer. 31:12
To the LORD our God.' "

7 For thus says the LORD,
"Sing [r]aloud with gladness for Jacob, Ps. 14:7
And shout among the [t]chiefs of the nations; *heads*
Proclaim, give praise, and say,
'O LORD, save Thy people,
The remnant of Israel.'
8 "Behold, I am bringing them from the north country,
And I will [r]gather them from the remote parts of the earth, Deut. 30:4
Among them the blind and the lame,
The woman with child and

she who is in labor with
child, together;
A great[a] company, they shall
return here. *assembly*
9 "With[r] weeping they shall
come, Ps. 126:5
And by supplication I will
lead them;
I will make them walk by
streams of waters,
On a straight path in which
they shall [r]not stumble;
For I am a father to Israel,
And Ephraim is My first-
born." Is. 63:13

10 Hear the word of the LORD, O
nations,
And declare in the [r]coast-
lands afar off, Is. 66:19
And say, "He who scattered
Israel will gather him,
And keep him as a [r]shepherd
keeps his flock." Is. 40:11
11 For the LORD has [r]ransomed
Jacob, Is. 44:23
And redeemed him from the
hand of him who was
stronger than he.
12 "And they shall [r]come and
shout for joy on the
height of Zion, Jer. 31:6
And they shall be radiant
over the [t]bounty of the
LORD— *goodness*
Over the grain, and the new
wine, and the oil,
And over the young of the
flock and the herd;
And their life shall be like a
watered garden,
And they shall [r]never languish again. Is. 35:10
13 "Then the virgin shall rejoice
in the [r]dance, Judg. 21:21
And the young men and the
old, together,
For I will [r]turn their mourning into joy, Is. 61:3
And will comfort them, and
give them [r]joy for their
sorrow. Is. 51:11
14 "And I will fill the soul of the
priests with abundance,
And My people shall be satisfied with My goodness,"
declares the LORD.

15 Thus says the LORD,
"A[r] voice is heard in [r]Ramah,
Lamentation *and* bitter
weeping. Matt. 2:18
Rachel is weeping for her
children; Josh. 18:25
She refuses to be comforted
for her children,
Because they are no more."
16 Thus says the LORD,
"Restrain[r] your voice from
weeping, Is. 25:8
And your eyes from tears;
For your [r]work shall be re-
warded," declares the
LORD, Ruth 2:12
"And they shall return from
the land of the enemy.
17 "And there is [r]hope for your
future," declares the
LORD, Jer. 29:11
"And *your* children shall re-
turn to their own terri-
tory.
18 "I have surely heard Ephraim
[r]grieving, Jer. 3:21
'Thou hast [r]chastised me, and
I was chastised, Job 5:17
Like an untrained calf;
[r]Bring me back that I may be
restored, Ps. 80:3
For Thou art the LORD my
God.

19 'For after I turned back, I [r]repented; Ezek. 36:31
And after I was instructed, I smote on *my* thigh;
I was [r]ashamed, and also humiliated, Jer. 3:25
Because I bore the reproach of my youth.'
20 "Is [r]Ephraim My dear son?
Is he a delightful child?
Indeed, as often as I have spoken against him,
I certainly *still* remember him; Hos. 11:8
Therefore My [t]heart yearns for him; *inward parts*
I will surely have mercy on him," declares the LORD.

21 "Set up for yourself roadmarks,
Place for yourself guideposts;
[r]Direct your [t]mind to the highway, Jer. 50:5 • *heart*
The way by which you went.
Return, O virgin of Israel,
Return to these your cities.
22 "How long will you go here and there,
O [r]faithless daughter?
For the LORD has created a new thing in the earth—
A woman will encompass a man." Jer. 3:6; 49:4

23 Thus says the LORD of hosts,
the God of Israel, "Once again
they will speak this word in the
land of Judah and in its cities,
when I restore their [a]fortunes,
'The LORD bless you, O abode of righteousness,
O holy hill!' *captivity*
24 "And Judah and all its cities
will [r]dwell together in it, the
farmer and they who go about
with flocks. Jer. 31:12
25 "For [r]I satisfy the weary ones
and [t]refresh everyone who languishes." Ps. 107:9 • *fill*
26 At this I awoke and looked,
and my sleep was pleasant to me.
27 "Behold, days are coming,"
declares the LORD, "when I will
sow the house of Israel and the
house of Judah with the seed of
man and with the seed of beast.
28 "And it will come about that
as I have [r]watched over them to
pluck up, to break down, to overthrow,
to destroy, and to bring disaster,
so I will watch over them
to [r]build and to plant," declares
the LORD. Jer. 44:27 • Jer. 24:6
29 "In those days they will not say again,
'The [r]fathers have eaten sour grapes, Lam. 5:7
And the children's teeth are [a]set on edge.' *dull*
30 "But [r]everyone will die for his
own iniquity; each man who eats
the sour grapes, his teeth will be
[a]set on edge. Deut. 24:16 • *dull*
31 "Behold, days are coming,"
declares the LORD, "when I will
make a [r]new covenant with the
house of Israel and with the house
of Judah, Jer. 32:40; 33:14
32 not like the covenant which I
made with their fathers in the day
I [r]took them by the hand to bring
them out of the land of Egypt, My
covenant which they broke, although
I was a husband to them,"
declares the LORD. Is. 63:12
33 "But [r]this is the covenant
which I will make with the house
of Israel after those days," declares
the LORD, "I will put My
law within them, and on their

heart I will write it; and [r]I will be
their God, and they shall be My
people. Jer. 32:40 • Jer. 24:7
34 "And they shall not teach
again, each man his neighbor and
each man his brother, saying,
'Know the LORD,' for they shall all
[r]know Me, from the least of them
to the greatest of them," declares
the LORD, "for I will forgive their
iniquity, and their sin I will remember no more." Is. 11:9
35 Thus says the LORD,
Who [r]gives the sun for light
by day, Gen. 1:14-18
And the [t]fixed order of the
moon and the stars for
light by night, *statutes*
Who [r]stirs up the sea so that
its waves roar; Is. 51:15
[r]The LORD of hosts is His
name: Jer. 10:16; 32:18
36 "If [r]this fixed order departs
From before Me," declares
the LORD, Ps. 89:36, 37
"Then the offspring of Israel
also shall [r]cease
From being a nation before
Me forever." Amos 9:8, 9
37 Thus says the LORD,
"If [r]the heavens above can be
measured, Is. 40:12
And the foundations of the
earth searched out be-
low,
Then I will also cast off all
the offspring of Israel
For all that they have done,"
declares the LORD.
38 "Behold, days are coming,"
declares the LORD, "when the [r]city
shall be rebuilt for the LORD from
the Tower of Hananel to the Corner Gate. Jer. 30:18; 31:4
39 "And the [r]measuring line shall
go out farther straight ahead to
the hill Gareb; then it will turn to
Goah. Zech. 2:1
40 "And the whole valley of the
dead bodies and of the ashes, and
all the fields as far as the brook
Kidron, to the corner of the Horse
Gate toward the east, shall be
[r]holy to the LORD; it shall not be
plucked up, or overthrown anymore forever." Joel 3:17

CHAPTER 32

THE word that came to Jeremiah
from the LORD in the [r]tenth year of
Zedekiah king of Judah, which
was the eighteenth year of Nebuchadnezzar. 2 Kin. 25:1, 2
2 Now at that time the army of
the king of Babylon was besieging
Jerusalem, and Jeremiah the
prophet was shut up in the court
of the guard, which was *in* the
house of the king of Judah,
3 because Zedekiah king of Judah had [r]shut him up, saying,
"Why do you prophesy, saying,
'Thus says the LORD, "Behold, I
am about to give this city into the
hand of the king of Babylon, and
he will take it; 2 Kin. 6:32
4 and Zedekiah king of Judah
shall not escape out of the hand of
the Chaldeans, but he shall surely
be given into the hand of the king
of Babylon, and he shall speak
with him [t]face to face, and see him
eye to eye; *mouth to mouth*
5 and he shall take Zedekiah to
Babylon, and he shall be there until I visit him," declares the LORD.
"If you fight against the Chaldeans, you shall not succeed" ' ? "
6 And Jeremiah said, "The
word of the LORD came to me,
saying,

7 'Behold, Hanamel the son of Shallum your uncle is coming to you, saying, "Buy for yourself my field which is at [r]Anathoth, for you have the right of redemption to buy *it*."' Jer. 1:1; 11:21

8 "Then Hanamel my uncle's son came to me in the [r]court of the guard according to the word of the LORD, and said to me, 'Buy my field, please, that is at Anathoth, which is in the land of Benjamin; for you have the right of possession and the redemption is yours; buy *it* for yourself.' Then I knew that this was the [r]word of the LORD. Jer. 32:2; 33:1 • Jer. 32:25

9 "And I bought the field which was at Anathoth from Hanamel my uncle's son, and I [r]weighed out the silver for him, seventeen shekels of silver. Gen. 23:16

10 "And I [a]signed and sealed the deed, and called in witnesses, and weighed out the silver on the scales. *wrote . . . on the document*

11 "Then I took the deeds of purchase, both the sealed *copy containing* the [r]terms and conditions, and the open *copy*; Luke 2:27

12 and I gave the deed of purchase to Baruch the son of Neriah, the son of Mahseiah, in the sight of Hanamel my uncle's *son*, and in the sight of the witnesses who signed the deed of purchase, before all the Jews who were sitting in the court of the guard.

13 "And I commanded Baruch in their presence, saying,

14 'Thus says the LORD of hosts, the God of Israel, "Take these deeds, this sealed deed of purchase, and this open deed, and put them in an earthenware jar, that they may last a long time."

15 'For thus says the LORD of hosts, the God of Israel, "Houses and fields and vineyards shall again be bought in this land."'

16 "After I had given the deed of purchase to Baruch the son of Neriah, then I [r]prayed to the LORD, saying, Gen. 32:9-12

17 'Ah Lord GOD! Behold, Thou hast made the heavens and the earth by Thy great power and by Thine outstretched arm! Nothing is too difficult for Thee,

18 who showest lovingkindness to thousands, but repayest the iniquity of fathers into the bosom of their children after them, O [r]great and mighty God. The LORD of hosts is His name; Ps. 145:3

19 great in counsel and mighty in deed, whose [r]eyes are open to all the ways of the sons of men, [r]giving to everyone according to his ways and according to the fruit of his deeds; Job 34:21 • Ps. 62:12

20 who hast [r]set signs and wonders in the land of Egypt, *and* even to this day both in Israel and among mankind; and Thou hast [r]made a name for Thyself, as at this day. Ps. 78:43 • Ex. 9:16

21 'And Thou didst [r]bring Thy people Israel out of the land of Egypt with signs and with wonders, and with a strong hand and with an outstretched arm, and with great terror; Ex. 6:6

22 and gavest them this land, which Thou didst swear to their forefathers to give them, a land flowing with milk and honey.

23 'And they came in and took possession of it, but they did not obey Thy voice or walk in Thy law; they have done nothing of all that Thou commandedst them to

do; therefore Thou hast made all this calamity come upon them.

24 'Behold, the [r]siege mounds have reached the city to take it; and the city is given into the hand of the Chaldeans who fight against it, because of the [r]sword, the famine, and the pestilence; and what Thou hast spoken has come to pass; and, behold, Thou seest *it*. Jer. 33:4 • Jer. 14:12

25 'And Thou hast said to me, O Lord GOD, "Buy for yourself the field with money, and call in witnesses"—although the city is given into the hand of the Chaldeans.'"

26 Then the word of the LORD came to Jeremiah, saying,

27 "Behold, I am the LORD, the [r]God of all flesh; is anything too difficult for Me?" Num. 16:22

28 Therefore thus says the LORD, "Behold, I am about to [r]give this city into the hand of the Chaldeans and into the hand of Nebuchadnezzar king of Babylon, and he shall take it. 2 Kin. 25:11

29 "And the Chaldeans who are fighting against this city shall enter and [r]set this city on fire and burn it, with the houses where *people* have offered incense to Baal on their roofs and poured out libations to other gods to provoke Me to anger. 2 Chr. 36:19

30 "Indeed the sons of Israel and the sons of Judah have been doing only [r]evil in My sight from their youth; for the sons of Israel have been only provoking Me to anger by the work of their hands," declares the LORD. Deut. 9:7-12

31 "Indeed this city has been to Me *a [r]provocation of* My anger and My wrath from the day that they built it, even to this day, that it should be removed from before My face, 1 Kin. 11:7, 8

32 because of all the evil of the sons of Israel and the sons of Judah, which they have done to provoke Me to anger—they, their kings, their leaders, their priests, their prophets, the men of Judah, and the inhabitants of Jerusalem.

33 "And they have turned *their* back to Me, and not *their* face; though *I* taught them, teaching again and again, they would not listen and receive instruction.

34 "But they put their detestable things in the house which is called by My name, to defile it.

35 "And they built the [r]high places of Baal that are in the valley of Ben-hinnom to cause their sons and their daughters to pass through *the fire* to Molech, which I had not commanded them nor had it entered My mind that they should do this abomination, to cause Judah to sin. 2 Chr. 28:2, 3

36 "Now therefore thus says the LORD God of Israel concerning this city of which you say, 'It is [r]given into the hand of the king of Babylon by sword, by famine, and by pestilence.' Jer. 32:24

37 "Behold, I will [r]gather them out of all the lands to which I have driven them in My anger, in My wrath, and in great indignation; and I will bring them back to this place and [r]make them dwell in safety. Deut. 30:3 • Jer. 23:6

38 "And they shall be [r]My people, and I will be their God; Jer. 24:7

39 and I will [r]give them one heart and one way, that they may fear Me always, for their own

good, and for *the good of* their
children after them. Jer. 31:33
40 "And I will make an everlasting covenant with them that I
will not turn away from them, to
do them good; and I will put the
fear of Me in their hearts so that
they will not turn away from Me.
41 "And I will rejoice over them
to do them good, and I will faithfully plant them in this land with
all My heart and with all My soul.
42 "For thus says the LORD, 'Just[r]
as I brought all this great disaster
on this people, so I am going to
bring on them all the good that I
am promising them. Jer. 31:28
43 'And [r]fields shall be bought in
this land of which you say, "It is a
desolation, without man or beast;
it is given into the hand of the
Chaldeans." Jer. 32:15, 25
44 'Men shall buy fields for money, sign and seal deeds, and call in
witnesses in the land of Benjamin,
in the environs of Jerusalem, in
the cities of Judah, in the cities of
the hill country, in the cities of the
lowland, and in the cities of the
[9]Negev; for I will restore their fortunes,' declares the LORD."

CHAPTER 33

THEN the word of the LORD
came to Jeremiah the second
time, while he was still confined in
the court of the guard, saying,
2 "Thus says [r]the LORD who
made [t]*the earth,* the LORD who
formed it to establish it, the LORD
is His name, Jer. 51:19 • *it*
3 'Call [r]to Me, and I will answer
you, and I will tell you great and
mighty things, [r]which you do not
know.' Ps. 50:15 • Is. 48:6
4 "For thus says the LORD God
of Israel concerning the houses of
this city, and concerning the
houses of the kings of Judah,
which are broken down to *make a
defense* against the siege mounds
and against the sword,
5 'While *they* are coming to
fight with the Chaldeans, and to
fill them with the corpses of men
whom I have slain in My anger
and in My wrath, and I have hidden My face from this city because of all their wickedness:
6 'Behold, I will bring to it
health and healing, and I will heal
them; and I will reveal to them an
abundance of peace and truth.
7 'And I will restore the [a]for-
tunes of Judah and the fortunes of
Israel, and I will rebuild them as
they were at first. *captivity*
8 'And I will [r]cleanse them from
all their iniquity by which they
have sinned against Me, and I will
pardon all their iniquities by
which they have sinned against
Me, and by which they have transgressed against Me. Ps. 51:2
9 'And [10]it shall be to Me a [r]name
of joy, praise, and glory before [r]all
the nations of the earth, which
shall hear of all the good that I do
for them, and they shall fear and
tremble because of all the good
and all the peace that I make for
it.' Is. 62:2, 4, 7 • Jer. 3:17, 19
10 "Thus says the LORD, 'Yet
again there shall be heard in this
place, of which you say, "It is a
[r]waste, without man and without
beast," *that is,* in the cities of Ju-

[9]I.e., South country

[10]I.e., this city

dah and in the streets of Jerusalem that are desolate, without
man and without inhabitant and
without beast, Jer. 32:43
11 the voice of [r]joy and the voice
of gladness, the voice of the bridegroom and the voice of the bride,
the voice of those who say,

"Give[r] thanks to the LORD of
hosts, Is. 35:10
For the LORD is good,
For His lovingkindness is
everlasting"; 1 Chr. 16:8

and of those who bring a [r]thank offering into the house of the LORD.
For I will restore the [a]fortunes of
the land as they were at first,' says
the LORD. Lev. 7:12 • *captivity*
12 "Thus says the LORD of hosts,
'There shall again be in this place
which is waste, [r]without man or
beast, and in all its cities, a [a]habita-
tion of shepherds who rest their
flocks. Jer. 32:43; 36:29 • *pasture*
13 'In the cities of the hill country, in the cities of the lowland, in
the cities of the Negev, in the land
of Benjamin, in the environs of Jerusalem, and in the cities of Judah, the flocks shall again pass
under the hands of the one who
numbers them,' says the LORD.
14 'Behold, days are coming,'
declares the LORD, 'when I will
fulfill the good word which I have
spoken concerning the house of
Israel and the house of Judah.
15 'In those days and at that
time I will cause a righteous
Branch of David to spring forth;
and He shall execute justice and
righteousness on the earth.
16 'In those days Judah shall be
saved, and Jerusalem shall dwell
in safety; and this is *the name* by
which she shall be called: the
LORD is our righteousness.'
17 "For thus says the LORD, 'David shall [r]never lack a man to sit
on the throne of the house of Israel; 2 Sam. 7:16; 1 Kin. 2:4; 8:25
18 and the [r]Levitical priests shall
never lack a man before Me to offer burnt offerings, to burn grain
offerings, and to prepare sacrifices continually.' " Deut. 18:1
19 And the word of the LORD
came to Jeremiah, saying,
20 "Thus says the LORD, 'If you
can break My covenant for the
day, and My covenant for the
night, so that day and night will
not be at their appointed time,
21 then My covenant may also
be broken with David My servant
that he shall not have a son to
reign on his throne, and with the
Levitical priests, My ministers.
22 'As the host of heaven cannot
be counted, and the sand of the
sea cannot be measured, so I will
multiply the [t]descendants of David
My servant and the Levites who
minister to Me.' " *seed*
23 And the word of the LORD
came to Jeremiah, saying,
24 "Have you not observed what
this people have spoken, saying,
'The [r]two families which the LORD
chose, He has rejected them'?
Thus they despise My people, no
longer are they as a nation [t]in their
sight. Is. 7:17 • *to their faces*
25 "Thus says the LORD, 'If My
[r]covenant *for* day and night *stand*
not, *and* the [t]fixed patterns of
heaven and earth I have not established, Gen. 8:22 • *statutes*
26 then I would reject the [t]de-
scendants of Jacob and David My
servant, [t]not taking from his de-

scendants rulers over the descendants of Abraham, Isaac, and
Jacob. But I will restore their fortunes and will have mercy on
them.' " *seed* • *from taking*

CHAPTER 34

THE word which came to Jeremiah from the LORD, when Nebuchadnezzar king of Babylon and
all his army, with all the kingdoms
of the earth that were under his
dominion and all the peoples,
were fighting against Jerusalem
and against all its cities, saying,
2 "Thus says the LORD God of
Israel, 'Go[r] and speak to Zedekiah
king of Judah and say to him:
"Thus says the LORD, 'Behold, I
am giving this city into the hand
of the king of Babylon, and he will
burn it with fire. 2 Chr. 36:11
3 'And you will not escape from
his hand, for you will surely be
captured and delivered into his
hand; and you will see the king of
Babylon eye to eye, and he will
speak with you face to face, and
you will go to Babylon.' " '
4 "Yet hear the word of the
LORD, O Zedekiah king of Judah!
Thus says the LORD concerning
you, 'You will not die by the
sword.
5 'You will die in peace; and as
spices were burned for your fathers, the former kings who were
before you, so they will [r]burn
spices for you; and they will lament for you, "Alas, lord!" ' For I
have spoken the word," declares
the LORD. 2 Chr. 16:14; 21:19
6 Then Jeremiah the prophet
spoke all these words to Zedekiah
king of Judah in Jerusalem
7 when the army of the king of
Babylon was fighting against Jerusalem and against all the remaining cities of Judah, *that is,*
Lachish and Azekah, for they
alone remained as fortified cities
among the cities of Judah.
8 The word which came to Jeremiah from the LORD, after King
Zedekiah had [r]made a covenant
with all the people who were in
Jerusalem to proclaim [a]release to
them: 2 Kin. 11:17; 23:2, 3 • *liberty*
9 that each man should set free
his male servant and each man his
female servant, a [r]Hebrew man or
a Hebrew woman; so that no one
should keep them, a Jew his
brother, in bondage. Ex. 2:6
10 And all the officials and all
the people obeyed, who had entered into the covenant that each
man should set free his male servant and each man his female servant, so that no one should keep
them any longer in bondage; they
obeyed, and set *them free.*
11 But afterward they turned
around and took back the male
servants and the female servants,
whom they had set free, and
brought them into subjection for
male servants and for female servants.
12 Then the word of the LORD
came to Jeremiah from the LORD,
saying,
13 "Thus says the LORD God of
Israel, 'I [r]made a covenant with
your forefathers in the day that I
brought them out of the land of
Egypt, from the house of bondage,
saying, Ex. 24:3, 7, 8
14 "At[r] the end of seven years
each of you shall set free his He-

brew brother, who[a]has been sold
to you and has served you six
years, you shall send him out free
from you; but your forefathers did
not obey Me, or incline their ear to
Me. Ex. 21:2 • *has sold himself*
15 "Although recently you *had*
turned and [r]done what is right in
My sight, each man proclaiming
[a]release to his neighbor, and you
had made a covenant before Me in
the house which is called by My
name. Jer. 34:8 • *liberty*
16 "Yet you turned and profaned
My name, and each man took
back his male servant and each
man his female servant, whom
you had set free according to their
desire, and you brought them into
subjection to be your male servants and female servants." '
17 "Therefore thus says the
LORD, 'You have not obeyed Me in
proclaiming[a]release each man to
his brother, and each man to his
neighbor. Behold, I am proclaiming a release to you,' declares the
LORD, 'to the sword, to the pestilence, and to the famine; and I will
make you a terror to all the kingdoms of the earth. *liberty*
18 'And I will give the men who
have [r]transgressed My covenant,
who have not fulfilled the words
of the covenant which they made
before Me, *when* they [r]cut the calf
in two and passed between its
parts— Deut. 17:2 • Gen. 15:10
19 the officials of Judah, and the
officials of Jerusalem, the court
officers, and the priests, and all
the people of the land, who passed
between the parts of the calf—
20 and I will give them into the
hand of their enemies and into the
hand of those who seek their life.
And their dead bodies shall be
food for the birds of the sky and
the beasts of the earth.
21 'And Zedekiah king of Judah
and his officials I will give into the
hand of their enemies, and into
the hand of those who seek their
life, and into the hand of the army
of the king of Babylon which has
gone away from you.
22 'Behold, I am going to command,' declares the LORD, 'and I
will bring them back to this city;
and they shall fight against it and
take it and burn it with fire; and I
will make the cities of Judah a
desolation without inhabitant.' "

CHAPTER 35

THE word which came to Jeremiah from the LORD in the days of
[r]Jehoiakim the son of Josiah, king
of Judah, saying, 2 Chr. 36:5-7
2 "Go to the house of the Rechabites, and speak to them, and
bring them into the house of the
LORD, into one of the chambers,
and give them wine to drink."
3 Then I took Jaazaniah the
son of Jeremiah, son of Habazzini-
ah, and his brothers, and all his
sons, and the whole house of the
Rechabites,
4 and I brought them into the
house of the LORD, into the chamber of the sons of Hanan the son
of Igdaliah, the man of God,
which was near the chamber of
the officials, which was above the
chamber of Maaseiah the son of
Shallum, the doorkeeper.
5 Then I set before the men of
the house of the Rechabites pitch-

ers full of wine, and cups; and I
said to them, "Drink wine!"
6 But they said, "We will not
drink wine, for Jonadab the son of
Rechab, our father, commanded
us, saying, 'You shall not drink
wine, you or your sons, forever.
7 'And you shall not build a
house, and you shall not sow seed,
and you shall not plant a vineyard
or own one; but in [r]tents you shall
dwell all your days, that you may
live many days in the land where
you sojourn.' Gen. 25:27
8 "And we have obeyed the
voice of Jonadab the son of Rechab, our father, in all that he
commanded us, not to drink wine
all our days, we, our wives, our
sons, or our daughters,
9 nor to build ourselves houses
to dwell in; and we do not have
vineyard or field or seed.
10 "We have only dwelt in tents,
and have obeyed, and have done
according to all that Jonadab our
father commanded us.
11 "But it came about, when
[r]Nebuchadnezzar king of Babylon
came up against the land, that we
said, 'Come and let us go to Jerusalem before the army of the
Chaldeans and before the army of
the Arameans.' So we have dwelt
in Jerusalem." 2 Kin. 24:1, 2
12 Then the word of the LORD
came to Jeremiah, saying,
13 "Thus says the LORD of hosts,
the God of Israel, 'Go and say to
the men of Judah and the inhabitants of Jerusalem, "Will you not
receive instruction by listening to
My words?" declares the LORD.
14 "The words of Jonadab the
son of Rechab, which he commanded his sons not to drink
wine, are observed. So they do not
drink *wine* to this day, for they
have obeyed their father's command. But I have spoken to you
[r]again and again; yet you have not
listened to Me. 2 Chr. 36:15
15 "Also I have sent to you all
My [r]servants the prophets, sending
them again and again, saying:
'Turn now every man from his evil
way, and amend your deeds, and
do not go after other gods to worship them, then you shall dwell in
the land which I have given to you
and to your forefathers; but you
have not inclined your ear or listened to Me. Jer. 7:25; 25:4
16 'Indeed, the sons of Jonadab
the son of Rechab have [r]observed
the command of their father
which he commanded them, but
this people has not listened to
Me.' " ' Jer. 35:14; Mal. 1:6
17 "Therefore thus says the
LORD, the God of hosts, the God of
Israel, 'Behold, I am bringing on
Judah and on all the inhabitants of
Jerusalem all the disaster that I
have pronounced against them;
because I spoke to them but they
did not listen, and I have called
them but they did not answer.' "
18 Then Jeremiah said to the
house of the Rechabites, "Thus
says the LORD of hosts, the God of
Israel, 'Because you have [r]obeyed
the command of Jonadab your father, kept all his commands, and
done according to all that he commanded you; Ex. 20:12
19 therefore thus says the LORD
of hosts, the God of Israel, "Jonadab the son of Rechab shall not
lack a man to stand before Me [t]al-
ways." ' " *all the days*

CHAPTER 36

AND it came about in the [r]fourth year of Jehoiakim the son of Josiah, king of Judah, that this word came to Jeremiah from the LORD, saying, 2 Kin. 24:1; Dan. 1:1

2 "Take a [r]scroll and write on it all the words which I have spoken to you concerning Israel, and concerning Judah, and concerning all the nations, from the day I *first* spoke to you, from the days of Josiah, even to this day. Is. 8:1

3 "Perhaps the house of Judah will hear all the calamity which I plan to bring on them, in order that every man will turn from his evil way; then I will forgive their iniquity and their sin."

4 Then Jeremiah called Baruch the son of Neriah, and Baruch wrote at the dictation of Jeremiah all the words of the LORD, which He had spoken to him, on a scroll.

5 And Jeremiah commanded Baruch, saying, "I am [t]restricted; I cannot go into the house of the LORD. *shut up*

6 "So you go and read from the scroll which you have written at my dictation the words of the LORD to the people in the LORD's house on a fast day. And also you shall read them to all *the people of* Judah who come from their cities.

7 "Perhaps their supplication will come before the LORD, and everyone will turn from his evil way, for great is the anger and the wrath that the LORD has pronounced against this people."

8 And Baruch the son of Neriah did according to all that Jeremiah the prophet commanded him, [r]reading from the book the words of the LORD in the LORD's house. Jer. 1:17; 36:6

9 Now it came about in the [r]fifth year of Jehoiakim the son of Josiah, king of Judah, in the ninth month, that all the people in Jerusalem and all the people who came from the cities of Judah to Jerusalem proclaimed a fast before the LORD. Jer. 36:1

10 Then Baruch read from the book the words of Jeremiah in the house of the LORD in the chamber of Gemariah the son of Shaphan the scribe, in the upper court, at the entry of the New Gate of the LORD's house, to all the people.

11 Now when Micaiah the son of Gemariah, the son of Shaphan, had heard all the words of the LORD from the book,

12 he went down to the king's house, into the scribe's chamber. And, behold, all the officials were sitting there—[r]Elishama the scribe, and [r]Delaiah the son of Shemaiah, and Elnathan the son of Achbor, and Gemariah the son of Shaphan, and Zedekiah the son of Hananiah, and all the *other* officials. Jer. 36:20 • Jer. 36:25

13 And Micaiah declared to them all the words that he had heard, when Baruch read from the book to the people.

14 Then all the officials sent [r]Jehudi the son of Nethaniah, the son of Shelemiah, the son of Cushi, to Baruch, saying, "Take in your hand the scroll from which you have read to the people and come." So Baruch the son of Neriah took the scroll in his hand and went to them. Jer. 36:21

15 And they said to him, "Sit

down please, and read it to us."
So Baruch read it to them.
16 Now it came about when
they had heard all the words, they
turned in fear one to another and
said to Baruch, "We will surely report all these words to the king."
17 And they asked Baruch, saying, "Tell us please, how did you
write all these words? *Was it* [t]at
his dictation?" *from his mouth*
18 Then Baruch said to them,
"He [r]dictated all these words to
me, and I wrote them with ink on
the book." Jer. 36:4
19 Then the officials said to Baruch, "Go, hide yourself, you and
Jeremiah, and do not let anyone
know where you are."
20 So they went to the king in
the court, but they had deposited
the scroll in the chamber of Elishama the scribe, and they reported
all the words to the king.
21 Then the king sent Jehudi to
get the scroll, and he took it out of
the chamber of Elishama the
scribe. And Jehudi read it to the
king as well as to all the officials
who stood beside the king.
22 Now the king was sitting in
the [r]winter house in the ninth
month, with *a fire* burning in the
brazier before him. Judg. 3:20
23 And it came about, when Jehudi had read three or four columns, *the king* cut it with a
scribe's knife and threw *it* into the
fire that was in the brazier, until
all the scroll was consumed in the
fire that was in the brazier.
24 Yet the king and all his servants who heard all these words
were not afraid, nor did they [r]rend
their garments. Gen. 37:29
25 Even though Elnathan and
Delaiah and Gemariah entreated
the king not to burn the scroll, he
would not listen to them.
26 And the king commanded Jerahmeel the king's son, Seraiah
the son of Azriel, and Shelemiah
the son of Abdeel to seize Baruch
the scribe and Jeremiah the
prophet, but the LORD hid them.
27 Then the word of the LORD
came to Jeremiah after the king
had [r]burned the scroll and the
words which [r]Baruch had written
at the dictation of Jeremiah, saying, Jer. 36:23 • Jer. 36:4, 18
28 "Take again another scroll
and write on it all the former
words that were [r]on the first scroll
which Jehoiakim the king of Judah burned. Jer. 36:4, 23
29 "And concerning Jehoiakim
king of Judah you shall say, 'Thus
says the LORD, "You have burned
this scroll, saying, 'Why have you
written on it that the king of
Babylon shall certainly come and
destroy this land, and shall make
man and beast to cease from it?' "
30 'Therefore thus says the LORD
concerning Jehoiakim king of Judah, "He shall have [r]no one to sit
on the throne of David, and his
dead body shall be cast out to the
heat of the day and the frost of the
night. 2 Kin. 24:12-15
31 "I shall also [r]punish him and
his [t]descendants and his servants
for their iniquity, and I shall bring
on them and the inhabitants of Jerusalem and the men of Judah all
the calamity that I have declared
to them—but they did not listen." ' " Jer. 23:34 • *seed*
32 Then Jeremiah took another
scroll and gave it to Baruch the
son of Neraiah, the scribe, and he

[r]wrote on it at the dictation of Jeremiah all the words of the book
which Jehoiakim king of Judah
had burned in the fire; and many
[t]similar words were added to
them. Ex. 4:15, 16 • *like those*

CHAPTER 37

NOW [r]Zedekiah the son of Josiah
whom Nebuchadnezzar king of
Babylon had made king in the
land of Judah, reigned as king in
place of [r]Coniah the son of Jehoiakim. 2 Kin. 24:17 • 1 Chr. 3:16
2 But [r]neither he nor his servants nor the people of the land
listened to the words of the LORD
which He spoke through Jeremiah
the prophet. 2 Kin. 24:19, 20
3 Yet King Zedekiah sent Je-
hucal the son of Shelemiah, and
Zephaniah the son of Maaseiah,
the priest, to Jeremiah the
prophet, saying, "Please pray to
the LORD our God on our behalf."
4 Now Jeremiah was *still* coming in and going out among the
people, for they had not *yet* [r]put
him in the prison. Jer. 32:2, 3
5 Meanwhile, [r]Pharaoh's army
had set out from Egypt; and when
the Chaldeans who had been besieging Jerusalem heard the report about them, they lifted the
siege from Jerusalem. 2 Kin. 24:7
6 Then the word of the LORD
came to Jeremiah the prophet,
saying,
7 "Thus says the LORD God of
Israel, 'Thus you are to say to the
king of Judah, who sent you to Me
to inquire of Me: "Behold, Pharaoh's army which has come out
for your assistance is going to return to its own land of Egypt.
8 "The Chaldeans will also [r]re-
turn and fight against this city,
and they will capture it and burn
it with fire." ' Jer. 34:22; 38:23
9 "Thus says the LORD, 'Do not
deceive yourselves, saying, "The
Chaldeans will surely go away
from us," for they will not go.
10 'For [r]even if you had defeated
the entire army of Chaldeans who
were fighting against you, and
there were *only* wounded men left
among them, each man in his tent,
they would rise up and burn this
city with fire.' " Lev. 26:36-38
11 Now it happened, when the
army of the Chaldeans had lifted
the siege from Jerusalem because
of Pharaoh's army,
12 that Jeremiah went out from
Jerusalem to go to the land of
Benjamin in order to [r]take possession of *some* property there
among the people. Jer. 32:8
13 While he was at the Gate of
Benjamin, a captain of the guard
whose name was Irijah, the son of
Shelemiah the son of Hananiah
was there; and he arrested Jeremiah the prophet, saying, "You are
going over to the Chaldeans!"
14 But Jeremiah said, "A lie! I
am not going over to the Chaldeans"; yet he would not listen to
him. So Irijah arrested Jeremiah
and brought him to the officials.
15 Then the officials were angry
at Jeremiah and beat him, and
they put him in jail in the house of
Jonathan the scribe, which they
had made into the prison.
16 For Jeremiah had come into
the [t]dungeon, that is, the vaulted
cell; and Jeremiah stayed there
many days. *house of the cistern-pit*

17 Now King Zedekiah sent and
took him *out;* and in his palace the
king [r]secretly asked him and said,
"Is there a [r]word from the LORD?"
And Jeremiah said, "There is!"
Then he said, "You will be given
into the hand of the king of Babylon!" 1 Kin. 14:1-4 • Jer. 15:11
18 Moreover Jeremiah said to
King Zedekiah, "*In*[r] what *way*
have I sinned against you, or
against your servants, or against
this people, that you have put me
in prison? 1 Sam. 24:9; 26:18
19 "Where[r] then are your prophets who prophesied to you, saying,
'The king of Babylon will not
come against you or against this
land'? Deut. 32:37, 38; Jer. 2:28
20 "But now, please listen, O my
lord the king; please let my [r]peti-
tion [t]come before you, and do not
make me return to the house of
Jonathan the scribe, that I may
not die there." Jer. 36:7; 38:26 • *fall*
21 Then King Zedekiah gave
commandment, and they committed Jeremiah to the [r]court of the
guardhouse and gave him a loaf of
[r]bread daily from the bakers'
street, until all the bread in the
city was gone. So Jeremiah remained in the court of the guardhouse. Jer. 32:2 • Ps. 33:18, 19

CHAPTER 38

NOW Shephatiah the son of Mattan, and Gedaliah the son of Pashhur, and Jucal the [r]son of Shelemiah, and Pashhur the son of
Malchijah heard the words that
Jeremiah was speaking to all the
people, saying, Jer. 37:3
2 "Thus says the LORD, 'He who
stays in this city will die by the
sword and by famine and by pestilence, but he who goes out to the
Chaldeans will live and have his
own life as booty and stay alive.'
3 "Thus says the LORD, 'This
city will certainly be [r]given into
the hand of the army of the king
of Babylon, and he will capture
it.' " Jer. 21:10; 32:3-5
4 Then the officials said to the
king, "Now let this man be put to
death, inasmuch as he is discour-
aging the men of war who are left
in this city and [t]all the people, by
speaking such words to them; for
this man is not seeking the well-
being of this people, but rather
their harm." *the hands of all*
5 So King Zedekiah said, "Behold, he is in your hands; for the
king can *do* nothing against you."
6 Then they took Jeremiah and
cast him into the cistern *of* Malchijah the king's son, which was
in the court of the guardhouse;
and they let Jeremiah down with
ropes. Now in the cistern there
was no water but only mud, and
Jeremiah sank into the mud.
7 But Ebed-melech the Ethiopian, [a]a eunuch, while he was in
the king's palace, heard that they
had put Jeremiah into the cistern.
Now the king was sitting in the
Gate of Benjamin; *an official*
8 and Ebed-melech went out
from the king's palace and spoke
to the king, saying,
9 "My lord the king, these men
have acted wickedly in all that
they have done to Jeremiah the
prophet whom they have cast into
the cistern; and he will die right
where he is because of the famine,
for there is [r]no more bread in the
city." Jer. 37:21; 52:6

10 Then the king commanded Ebed-melech the Ethiopian, saying, "Take thirty men from here [t]under your authority, and bring up Jeremiah the prophet from the cistern before he dies." *in your hand*

11 So Ebed-melech took the men under his [t]authority and went into the king's palace to *a place* beneath the storeroom and took from there worn-out clothes and worn-out rags and let them down by ropes into the cistern to Jeremiah. *hand*

12 Then Ebed-melech the Ethiopian said to Jeremiah, "Now put these worn-out clothes and rags under your armpits under the ropes"; and Jeremiah did so.

13 So they pulled Jeremiah up with the ropes and lifted him out of the cistern, and Jeremiah stayed in the [r]court of the guardhouse. Neh. 3:25; Acts 23:35; 24:27

14 Then King Zedekiah [r]sent and had Jeremiah the prophet brought to him at the third entrance that is in the house of the LORD; and the king said to Jeremiah, "I am going to ask you something; do not hide anything from me." Jer. 21:1, 2

15 Then Jeremiah said to Zedekiah, "If [r]I tell you, will you not certainly put me to death? Besides, if I give you advice, you will not listen to me." Luke 22:67, 68

16 But King Zedekiah swore to Jeremiah in [r]secret saying, "As the LORD lives, who made this [t]life for us, surely I will not put you to death nor will I give you over to the hand of these men who are seeking your life." John 3:2 • *soul*

17 Then Jeremiah said to Zedekiah, "Thus says the LORD God of hosts, the God of Israel, 'If you will indeed go out to the officers of the king of Babylon, then [t]you will live, this city will not be burned with fire, and you and your household will [t]survive. *your soul* • *live*

18 'But if you will [r]not go out to the officers of the king of Babylon, then this city [r]will be given over to the hand of the Chaldeans; and they will burn it with fire, and you yourself will not escape from their hand.' " Jer. 27:8 • 2 Kin. 25:4-10

19 Then King Zedekiah said to Jeremiah, "I dread the Jews who have gone over to the Chaldeans, lest they give me over into their hand and they abuse me."

20 But Jeremiah said, "They will not give you over. Please obey the LORD in what I am saying to you, that it may go well with you and [t]you may live. *your soul*

21 "But if you keep refusing to go out, this is the word which the LORD has shown me:

22 'Then behold, all of the women who have been left in the palace of the king of Judah are going to be brought out to the [a]officers of the king of Babylon; and those women will say, *princes*

"Your close friends
Have misled and overpowered you;
While your feet were sunk in the mire,
They turned back."

23 'They will also bring out all your wives and your [r]sons to the Chaldeans, and you yourself will not escape from their hand, but will be seized by the hand of the king of Babylon, and this city will be burned with fire.' " Jer. 39:6

24 Then Zedekiah said to Jeremiah, "Let no man know about

these words and you will not die.
25 "But if the [r]officials hear that I
have talked with you and come to
you and say to you, 'Tell us now
what you said to the king, and
what the king said to you; do not
hide *it* from us, and we will not
put you to death,' Jer. 38:4-6, 27
26 then you are to say to them,
'I was [r]presenting my petition before the king, not to make me return to the house of Jonathan to
die there.' " Jer. 37:20
27 Then all the officials came to
Jeremiah and questioned him. So
he reported to them in accordance
with all these words which the
king had commanded; and they
ceased speaking with him, since
the [t]conversation had not been
overheard. *word*
28 So Jeremiah stayed in the
court of the guardhouse until the
day that Jerusalem was captured.

CHAPTER 39

NOW it came about when Jerusalem was captured [r]in the ninth
year of Zedekiah king of Judah, in
the tenth month, Nebuchadnezzar
king of Babylon and all his army
came to Jerusalem and laid siege
to it; 2 Kin. 25:1-12; Jer. 52:4
2 in the eleventh year of Zedekiah, in the fourth month, in the
ninth *day* of the month, the city
wall was [r]breached. Jer. 52:7
3 Then all the officials of the
king of Babylon came in and sat
down at the Middle Gate: Nergal-
sar-ezer, Samgar-nebu, Sar-sekim
the Rab-saris, Nergal-sar-ezer *the*
Rab-mag, and all the rest of the
officials of the king of Babylon.
4 And it came about, when
Zedekiah the king of Judah and all
the men of war saw them, that
they [r]fled and went out of the city
at night by way of the king's garden through the gate between the
two walls; and he went out toward
the [11]Arabah. 2 Kin. 25:4; Is. 30:16
5 But the army of the [r]Chalde-
ans pursued them and overtook
Zedekiah in the plains of Jericho;
and they seized him and brought
him up to Nebuchadnezzar king
of Babylon at Riblah in the land of
Hamath, and he passed sentence
on him. Jer. 32:4, 5; 38:18, 23
6 Then the [r]king of Babylon
slew the sons of Zedekiah before
his eyes at Riblah; the king of
Babylon also slew all the nobles of
Judah. 2 Kin. 25:7; Jer. 52:10
7 He then blinded Zedekiah's
eyes and bound him in fetters of
bronze to bring him to Babylon.
8 The Chaldeans also [r]burned
with fire the king's palace and the
houses of the people, and they
broke down the walls of Jerusalem. 2 Kin. 25:9; Jer. 21:10
9 And as for the rest of the
people who were left in the city,
the deserters who had gone over
to him and the rest of the people
who remained, Nebuzaradan the
captain of the bodyguard carried
them into exile in Babylon.
10 But some of the [r]poorest people who had nothing, Nebuzaradan the captain of the bodyguard
left behind in the land of Judah,
and gave them vineyards and
fields at that time. 2 Kin. 25:12
11 Now Nebuchadnezzar king
of Babylon gave orders about Jeremiah through Nebuzaradan the
captain of the bodyguard, saying,

[11] I.e., Jordan valley

12 "Take him and [t]look after him,
and do nothing harmful to him;
but rather deal with him just as he
tells you." *set your eyes on*
13 So Nebuzaradan the captain
of the bodyguard sent *word,* along
with Nebushazban the Rab-saris,
and Nergal-sar-ezer the Rab-mag,
and all the leading officers of the
king of Babylon;
14 they even sent and took Jeremiah out of the court of the guardhouse and entrusted him to Gedaliah, the son of Ahikam, the son of
Shaphan, to take him home. So he
stayed among the people.
15 Now the word of the LORD
had come to Jeremiah while he
was [r]confined in the court of the
guardhouse, saying, Jer. 38:28
16 "Go and speak to Ebed-melech the Ethiopian, saying, 'Thus
says the LORD of hosts, the God of
Israel, "Behold, I am about to
bring My words on this city for disaster and not for [t]prosperity; and
they will [r]take place before you on
that day. *good* • Ps. 91:8
17 "But I will deliver you on that
day," declares the LORD, "and you
shall not be given into the hand of
the men whom you dread.
18 "For I will certainly rescue
you, and you will not fall by the
sword; but you will have your
own [r]life as booty, because you
have trusted in Me," declares the
LORD.' " Jer. 21:9; 38:2; 45:5

CHAPTER 40

THE word which came to Jeremiah from the LORD after [r]Nebuzara-
dan captain of the bodyguard had
released him from Ramah, when
he had taken him bound in [r]chains,
among all the exiles of Jerusalem
and Judah, who were being exiled
to Babylon. Jer. 39:9, 11 • Eph. 6:20
2 Now the captain of the bodyguard had taken Jeremiah and
said to him, "The [r]LORD your God
promised this calamity against
this place; Lev. 26:14-38
3 and the LORD has brought *it*
on and done just as He promised.
Because you *people* sinned
against the LORD and did not listen to His voice, therefore this
thing has happened to you.
4 "But now, behold, I am [r]free-
ing you today from the chains
which are on your hands. If you
would prefer to come with me to
Babylon, come *along,* and I will
look after you; but if you would
prefer not to come with me to
Babylon, [t]never mind. Look, the
whole land is before you; go wherever it seems good and right for
you to go." Jer. 39:11, 12 • *refrain!*
5 As Jeremiah was still not
going back, *he said,* "Go on back
then to Gedaliah the son of Ahikam, the son of Shaphan, whom
the king of Babylon has appointed
over the cities of Judah, and stay
with him among the people; or
else go anywhere it seems right
for you to go." So the captain of
the bodyguard gave him a ration
and a gift and let him go.
6 Then Jeremiah went to [r]Miz-
pah to [r]Gedaliah the son of Ahikam and stayed with him among
the people who were left in the
land. Judg. 20:1; 21:1 • Jer. 39:14
7 Now all the [a]commanders of
the forces that were in the field,
they and their men, heard that the
king of Babylon had appointed
Gedaliah the son of Ahikam over

the land and that he had put him
in charge of the men, women and
ᵗchildren, those of the poorest of
the land who had not been exiled
to Babylon. *princes • infants*
8 So they came to Gedaliah at
Mizpah, along with ʳIshmael the
son of Nethaniah, and Johanan
and Jonathan the sons of Kareah,
and Seraiah the son of Tanhumeth, and the sons of Ephai the
Netophathite, and Jezaniah the
son of the Maacathite, *both* they
and their men. Jer. 40:14; 41:2
9 Then Gedaliah the son of
Ahikam, the son of Shaphan,
swore to them and to their men,
saying, "Do not be afraid of serving the Chaldeans; stay in the land
and serve the king of Babylon,
that it may go well with you.
10 "Now as for me, behold, I am
going to stay at Mizpah to ʳstand
for you before the Chaldeans who
come to us; but as for you, gather
in wine and summer fruit and oil,
and put *them* in your *storage* vessels, and live in your cities that
you have taken over." Deut. 1:38
11 Likewise also all the Jews
who were in Moab and among the
sons of Ammon and in ʳEdom, and
who were in all the *other* countries, heard that the king of Babylon had left a remnant for Judah
and that he had appointed over
them Gedaliah the son of Ahikam,
the son of Shaphan. Is. 11:14
12 Then all the Jews ʳreturned
from all the places to which they
had been driven away and came
to the land of Judah, to Gedaliah
at Mizpah, and gathered in wine
and summer fruit in great abundance. Jer. 43:5
13 Now Johanan the son of Kareah and all the commanders of
the forces that were in the field
came to Gedaliah at Mizpah,
14 and said to him, "Are you
well aware that Baalis the king of
the sons of Ammon has sent Ishmael the son of Nethaniah to take
your life?" But Gedaliah the son of
Ahikam did not believe them.
15 Then Johanan the son of Kareah spoke secretly to Gedaliah in
Mizpah, saying, "Let me go and
kill Ishmael the son of Nethaniah,
and not a man will know! Why
should he take your life, so that all
the Jews who are gathered to you
should be scattered and the ʳremnant of Judah perish?" Jer. 42:2
16 But Gedaliah the son of Ahikam said to Johanan the son of
Kareah, "Do ʳnot do this thing, for
you are telling a lie about Ishmael." Matt. 10:16; 1 Cor. 13:5

CHAPTER 41

NOW it came about in the seventh month that Ishmael the son
of Nethaniah, the son of Elishama,
of the royal ᵗfamily and *one* of the
chief officers of the king, along
with ten men, came to Mizpah to
Gedaliah the son of Ahikam.
While they were eating bread together there in Mizpah, *seed*
2 Ishmael the son of Nethaniah
and the ten men who were with
him arose and ʳstruck down Gedaliah the son of Ahikam, the son of
Shaphan, with the sword and put
to death the one whom the king of
Babylon had appointed over the
land. 2 Sam. 3:27; 20:9, 10
3 Ishmael also struck down all
the Jews who were with him, *that*

is with Gedaliah at Mizpah, and the Chaldeans who were found there, the men of war.

4 Now it happened on the next day after the killing of Gedaliah, when no one knew about *it,*

5 that eighty men came from Shechem, from Shiloh, and from Samaria with their beards shaved off and their clothes torn and their bodies gashed, having grain offerings and incense in their hands to bring to the house of the LORD.

6 Then Ishmael the son of Nethaniah went out from Mizpah to meet them, weeping as he went; and it came about as he met them that he said to them, "Come to Gedaliah the son of Ahikam!"

7 Yet it turned out that as soon as they came inside the city, Ishmael the son of Nethaniah and the men that were with him ⸢slaughtered them, *and cast them* into the cistern. Ps. 55:23; Is. 59:7

8 But ten men who were found among them said to Ishmael, "Do not put us to death; for we have ⸢stores of wheat, barley, oil and honey hidden in the field." So he refrained and did not put them to death along with their companions. Is. 45:3

9 Now as for the cistern where Ishmael had cast all the corpses of the men whom he had struck down because of Gedaliah, it was the one that King Asa had made on ⸢account of Baasha, king of Israel; Ishmael the son of Nethaniah filled it with the slain. Judg. 6:2

10 Then Ishmael took captive all the remnant of the people who were in Mizpah, the king's daughters and all the people who were left in Mizpah, whom Nebuzaradan the captain of the bodyguard had put under the charge of Gedaliah the son of Ahikam; thus Ishmael the son of Nethaniah took them captive and proceeded to cross over to the sons of Ammon.

11 But Johanan the son of Kareah and all the commanders of the forces that were with him heard of all the evil that Ishmael the son of Nethaniah had done.

12 So they took all the men and went to fight with Ishmael the son of Nethaniah and they found him by the great pool that is in Gibeon.

13 Now it came about, as soon as all the people who were with Ishmael saw Johanan the son of Kareah and the commanders of the forces that were with him, they were glad.

14 So all the people whom Ishmael had taken captive from Mizpah turned around and came back, and went to Johanan the son of Kareah.

15 But Ishmael the son of Nethaniah ⸢escaped from Johanan with eight men and went to the sons of Ammon. Job 21:30

16 Then Johanan the son of Kareah and all the commanders of the forces that were with him took from Mizpah all the remnant of the people whom he had recovered from Ishmael the son of Nethaniah, after he had struck down Gedaliah the son of Ahikam, *that is,* the men who were soldiers, *the* women, *the* children, and *the* eunuchs, whom he had brought back from Gibeon.

17 And they went and stayed in ⸢Geruth Chimham, which is beside Bethlehem, in order to proceed into Egypt 2 Sam. 19:37, 38, 40

18 because of the Chaldeans;
for they were afraid of them, since
Ishmael the son of Nethaniah had
struck down Gedaliah the son of
Ahikam, whom the king of Babylon had appointed over the land.

CHAPTER 42

THEN all the[a]commanders of the
forces, Johanan the son of Kareah, Jezaniah the son of Hoshaiah, and all the people both small
and great approached *princes*
2 and said to Jeremiah the
prophet, "Please let our petition
[t]come before you, and pray for us
to the LORD your God, *that is* for
all this remnant; because we are
left *but* a few out of many, as your
own eyes *now* see us, *fall*
3 that the LORD your God may
tell us the[r]way in which we should
walk and the thing that we should
do." Ps. 86:11; Prov. 3:6
4 Then Jeremiah the prophet
said to them, "I have heard *you*.
Behold, I am going to pray to the
LORD your God in accordance
with your words; and it will come
about that the whole [t]message
which the LORD will answer you I
will tell you. I will[r]not keep back a
word from you." *word* • Ps. 40:10
5 Then they said to Jeremiah,
"May the [r]LORD be a true and
faithful witness against us, if we
do not act in accordance with the
whole [t]message with which the
LORD your God will send you to
us. Mic. 1:2; Mal. 2:14; 3:5 • *word*
6 "Whether *it* is[t]pleasant or[t]un-
pleasant, we will listen to the
voice of the LORD our God to
whom we are sending you, in order that it may go well with us
when we listen to the voice of the
LORD our God." *good* • *evil*
7 Now it came about at the
end of ten days that the word of
the LORD came to Jeremiah.
8 Then he called for Johanan
the son of Kareah, and all the
[a]commanders of the forces that
were with him, and for all the people both small and great, *princes*
9 and said to them, "Thus says
the LORD the God of Israel, to
whom you sent me to present
your petition before Him:
10 'If you will indeed stay in this
land, then I will build you up and
not tear you down, and I will plant
you and not uproot you; for I shall
relent concerning the calamity
that I have inflicted on you.
11 'Do[r] not be afraid of the king
of Babylon, whom you are *now*
fearing; do not be afraid of him,'
declares the LORD, 'for I am with
you to save you and deliver you
from his hand. Jer. 27:12, 17
12 'I will also show you compassion, so that[r]he will have compassion on you and restore you to
your own soil. Ps. 106:46
13 'But if you are going to say,
"We will[r]not stay in this land," so
as not to listen to the voice of the
LORD your God, Ex. 5:2
14 saying, "No, but we will go
to the land of Egypt, where we
shall not see war or hear the
sound of a trumpet or hunger for
bread, and we will stay there";
15 then in that case listen to the
word of the LORD, O remnant of
Judah. Thus says the LORD of
hosts, the God of Israel, "If you
really set your mind to enter

Egypt, and go in to reside there,
16 then it will come about that
the sword, which you are afraid of
will overtake you there in the land
of Egypt; and the famine, about
which you are anxious, will follow
closely after you there *in* Egypt;
and you will die there. Ezek. 11:8
17 "So all the men who set their
mind to go to Egypt to reside
there will die by the sword, by
famine, and by pestilence; and
they will have no survivors or
refugees from the calamity that I
am going to bring on them." ' "
18 For thus says the LORD of
hosts, the God of Israel, "As My
anger and wrath have been
poured out on the inhabitants of
Jerusalem, so My wrath will be
poured out on you when you enter
Egypt. And you will become a
curse, an object of horror, an imprecation, and a reproach; and
you will see this place no more."
19 The LORD has spoken to you,
O remnant of Judah, "Do not go
into Egypt!" You should clearly
understand that today I have testified against you. Deut. 17:16
20 For you have *only* deceived
yourselves; for it is you who sent
me to the LORD your God, saying,
"Pray for us to the LORD our God;
and whatever the LORD our God
says, tell us so, and we will do it."
21 So, I have told you today, but
you have not obeyed the LORD
your God, even in whatever He
has sent me to *tell* you. Jer. 43:4
22 Therefore you should now
clearly understand that you will
die by the sword, by famine, and
by pestilence, in the place where
you wish to go to reside. Hos. 9:6

CHAPTER 43

BUT it came about, as soon as
Jeremiah whom the LORD their
God had sent, had finished telling
all the people all the words of the
LORD their God—that is, all these
words— Jer. 26:8; 51:63
2 that Azariah the son of
Hoshaiah, and Johanan the son of
Kareah, and all the arrogant men
said to Jeremiah, "You are telling
a lie! The LORD our God has not
sent you to say, 'You are not to
enter Egypt to reside there';
3 but Baruch the son of Neriah
is inciting you against us to give
us over into the hand of the Chaldeans, so they may put us to death
or exile us to Babylon."
4 So Johanan the son of Kareah and all the commanders of
the forces, and all the people, did
not obey the voice of the LORD, so
as to stay in the land of Judah.
5 But Johanan the son of Kareah and all the commanders of
the forces took the entire remnant
of Judah who had returned from
all the nations to which they had
been driven away, in order to reside in the land of Judah—
6 the men, the women, the
children, the king's daughters and
every person that Nebuzaradan
the captain of the bodyguard had
left with Gedaliah the son of Ahikam and grandson of Shaphan, together with Jeremiah the prophet
and Baruch the son of Neriah—
7 and they entered the land of
Egypt (for they did not obey the
voice of the LORD) and went in as
far as Tahpanhes. Jer. 2:16; 44:1
8 Then the word of the LORD

came to Jeremiah in [r]Tahpanhes, saying, Jer. 2:16; 44:1

9 "Take *some* large stones in your hands and hide them in the mortar in the [a]brick *terrace* which is at the entrance of Pharaoh's palace in Tahpanhes, in the sight of some *of the* Jews; *brickwork*

10 and say to them, 'Thus says the LORD of hosts, the God of Israel, "Behold, I am going to send and get [r]Nebuchadnezzar the king of Babylon, [r]My servant, and I am going to set his throne *right* over these stones that I have hidden; and he will spread his canopy over them. Jer. 25:9, 11 • Is. 44:28

11 "He will also come and [r]strike the land of Egypt; those who are *meant* for death *will be given over* to death, and those for captivity to captivity, and those for the sword to the sword. Ezek. 29:19, 20

12 "And I shall set fire to the temples of the [r]gods of Egypt, and he will burn them and take them captive. So he will wrap himself with the land of Egypt as a shepherd wraps himself with his garment, and he will depart from there safely. Ex. 12:12; Is. 19:1

13 "He will also shatter the [a]obelisks of Heliopolis, which is in the land of Egypt; and the temples of the gods of Egypt he will burn with fire." ' " *stone pillars*

CHAPTER 44

THE word that came to Jeremiah for all the Jews living in the land of Egypt, those who were living in Migdol, Tahpanhes, Memphis, and the land of Pathros, saying,

2 "Thus says the LORD of hosts, the God of Israel, 'You yourselves have seen all the calamity that I have brought on Jerusalem and all the cities of Judah; and behold, this day they are in [r]ruins and no one lives in them, Is. 6:11

3 [r]because of their wickedness which they committed so as to provoke Me to anger by continuing to burn [a]sacrifices *and* to serve other gods whom they had not known, *neither* they, you, nor your fathers. Neh. 9:33 • *incense*

4 'Yet I sent you all My servants the prophets, again and again, saying, "Oh, do not do this abominable thing which I hate."

5 'But they did not listen or incline their ears to turn from their wickedness, so as not to burn [a]sacrifices to other gods. *incense*

6 'Therefore My wrath and My anger were poured out and burned in the cities of Judah and in the streets of Jerusalem, so they have become a ruin and a desolation as it is this day.

7 'Now then thus says the LORD God of hosts, the God of Israel, "Why are you doing great harm to yourselves, so as to cut off from you man and woman, child and infant, from among Judah, leaving yourselves without remnant,

8 [r]provoking Me to anger with the works of your hands, burning sacrifices to other gods in the land of Egypt, where you are entering to reside, so that you might be cut off and become a curse and a reproach among all the nations of the earth? 2 Kin. 17:15-17

9 "Have you forgotten the [r]wickedness of your fathers, the wickedness of the kings of Judah, and the wickedness of their wives, your own wickedness, and the

wickedness of your wives, which
they committed in the land of Judah and in the streets of Jerusalem? Jer. 7:9, 10, 17, 18
10 "But they [r]have not become
[t]contrite even to this day, nor have
they feared nor walked in My law
or My statutes, which I have set
before you and before your fathers." ' Jer. 6:15; 8:12 • *crushed*
11 "Therefore thus says the LORD
of hosts, the God of Israel, 'Behold, I am going to [r]set My face
against you for [t]woe, even to cut
off all Judah. Amos 9:4 • *evil*
12 'And I will take away the
remnant of Judah who have set
their [t]mind on entering the land of
Egypt to reside there, and they
will all meet their end in the land
of Egypt; they will fall by the
sword *and* [t]meet their end by famine. Both small and great will die
by the sword and famine; and
they will become a curse, an object of horror, an imprecation and
a reproach. *face • be finished*
13 'And I will [r]punish those who
live in the land of Egypt, as I have
punished Jerusalem, with the
sword, with famine, and with pestilence. Jer. 11:22; 44:27, 28
14 'So there will be [r]no refugees
or survivors for the remnant of Judah who have entered the land of
Egypt to reside there and then to
return to the land of Judah, to
which they are longing to return
and live; for none will return except *a few* refugees.' " Jer. 22:10
15 Then [r]all the men who were
aware that their wives were burning [t]sacrifices to other gods, along
with all the women who were
standing by, *as* a large assembly,
[t]including all the people who were
living in Pathros in the land of
Egypt, responded to Jeremiah,
saying, Is. 1:5 • *incense • and*
16 "As for the [t]message [r]that you
have spoken to us in the name of
the LORD, we are not going to listen to you! *word* • Jer. 43:2
17 "But rather we will certainly
carry out every word that has proceeded from our mouths, [a]by burning sacrifices to the queen of
heaven and pouring out libations
to her, just as we ourselves, our
forefathers, our kings and our
princes did in the cities of Judah
and in the streets of Jerusalem;
for *then* we had plenty of food,
and were well off, and saw no misfortune. *so as to burn*
18 "But since we stopped burning [a]sacrifices to the queen of
heaven and pouring out libations
to her, we have lacked everything
and have met our end by the
sword and by famine." *incense*
19 "And," *said the women,*
"when we were burning sacrifices
to the queen of heaven, and [t]were
pouring out libations to her, was it
without our husbands that we
made for her *sacrificial* cakes in
her image and poured out libations to her?" *to pour*
20 Then Jeremiah said to all the
people, to the men and women—
even to all the people who were
giving him *such* an answer—saying,
21 "As for the smoking sacrifices
that you burned in the cities of Judah and in the streets of Jerusalem, you and your forefathers,
your kings and your princes, and
the people of the land, did not the

LORD remember them, and did not
all this come into His mind?
22 "So the LORD was [r]no longer
able to endure *it,* because of the
evil of your deeds, because of the
abominations which you have
committed; thus your land has become a ruin, an object of horror
and a curse, without an inhabitant, as *it is* this day. Is. 7:13
23 "Because you have burned
sacrifices and have sinned against
the LORD and not obeyed the voice
of the LORD or walked in His law,
His statutes or His testimonies,
therefore this calamity has befall-
en you, as *it has* this day."
24 Then Jeremiah said to all the
people, including all the women,
"Hear[r] the word of the LORD, all
Judah who are in the land of
Egypt, Jer. 42:15; 44:16
25 thus says the LORD of hosts,
the God of Israel, as follows: 'As
for you and your wives, you have
spoken with your mouths and fulfilled *it* with your hands, saying,
"We will certainly perform our
vows that we have vowed, to burn
sacrifices to the queen of heaven
and pour out libations to her." Go
ahead and confirm your vows, and
certainly perform your vows!'
26 "Nevertheless[t] hear the word
of the LORD, all Judah who are living in the land of Egypt, 'Behold, I
have sworn by My great name,'
says the LORD, 'never shall My
name be invoked again by the
mouth of any man of Judah in all
the land of Egypt, saying, "As the
Lord GOD lives." *Therefore*
27 'Behold, I am watching over
them for harm and not for good,
and all the men of Judah who are
in the land of Egypt will [t]meet
their end by the sword and by
famine until they [t]are completely
gone. ***be finished • come to an end***
28 'And those who escape the
sword will return out of the land
of Egypt to the land of Judah[t]few
in number. Then all the remnant
of Judah who have gone to the
land of Egypt to reside there will
know whose word will stand,
Mine or theirs. ***men of number***
29 'And this will be the[r]sign to
you,' declares the LORD, 'that I am
going to punish you in this place,
so that you may know that My
words will surely stand against
you for harm.' Is. 7:11, 14; 8:18
30 "Thus says the LORD, 'Behold,
I am going to give over Pharaoh
Hophra king of Egypt to the hand
of his enemies, to the hand of
those who seek his life, just as I
gave over Zedekiah king of Judah
to the hand of Nebuchadnezzar
king of Babylon, *who was* his enemy and was seeking his life.' "

CHAPTER 45

THIS is the message which Jeremiah the prophet spoke to Baruch
the son of Neriah, when he had
written down these words in a
book [t]at Jeremiah's dictation, in
the fourth year of Jehoiakim the
son of Josiah, king of Judah, saying: *from the mouth of Jeremiah*
2 "Thus says the LORD the God
of Israel to you, O Baruch:
3 'You said, "Ah, woe is me!
For the LORD has added sorrow to
my pain; I am [r]weary with my
groaning and have found no
rest." ' Ps. 6:6; 69:3
4 "Thus you are to say to him,
'Thus says the LORD, "Behold,

[r]what I have built I am about to tear down, and what I have planted I am about to uproot, that is, the whole land." Is. 5:5

5 'But you, are you seeking great things for yourself? Do not seek *them;* for behold, I am going to bring disaster on all flesh,' declares the LORD, 'but I will give your life to you as booty in all the places where you may go.' "

CHAPTER 46

THAT which came as the word of the LORD to Jeremiah the prophet [r]concerning the nations. Jer. 1:10

2 To [r]Egypt, concerning the army of Pharaoh Neco king of Egypt, which was by the Euphrates River at [r]Carchemish, which Nebuchadnezzar king of Babylon defeated in the fourth year of Jehoiakim the son of Josiah, king of Judah: Jer. 46:14 • Is. 10:9

3 "Line up the shield and buckler,
And draw near for the battle!
4 "Harness the horses,
And mount the steeds,
And take your stand with helmets *on!*
Polish the spears,
Put on the scale-armor!
5 "Why have I seen *it?*
They are terrified,
They are drawing back,
And their [r]mighty men are defeated Is. 5:25; Ezek. 39:18
And have taken refuge in flight,
Without facing back;
Terror is on every side!"
Declares the LORD.
6 Let not the swift man flee,
Nor the mighty man escape;
In the north beside the river Euphrates
They have [r]stumbled and fallen. Jer. 46:12, 16
7 Who is this that [r]rises like the Nile, Jer. 47:2
Like the rivers whose waters surge about?
8 Egypt rises like the Nile,
Even like the rivers whose waters surge about;
And He has said, "I will rise and cover *that* land;
I will surely destroy the city and its inhabitants."
9 Go up, you horses, and drive madly, you chariots,
That the mighty men may [t]march forward: *go forth*
Ethiopia and [r]Put, that handle the shield, Nah. 3:9
And the Lydians, that handle *and* bend the bow.
10 For that day belongs to the Lord GOD of hosts,
A day of [r]vengeance, so as to avenge Himself on His foes; Jer. 50:15, 18
And the [r]sword will devour and be satiated Is. 31:8
And [t]drink its fill of their blood; *be saturated with*
For there will be a [r]slaughter for the Lord GOD of hosts, Is. 34:6; Zeph. 1:7
In the land of the north by the river Euphrates.
11 Go [r]up to Gilead and obtain balm, Jer. 8:22
O virgin daughter of Egypt!
In vain have you multiplied [t]remedies; *healings*
There is no healing for you.
12 The nations have heard of your [r]shame, Jer. 2:36

And the earth is full of your
cry *of distress;*
For one warrior has stumbled over another,
And both of them have fallen
down together.

13 *This is* the message which
the LORD spoke to Jeremiah the
prophet about the coming of
Nebuchadnezzar king of Babylon
to smite the land of Egypt:

14 "Declare in Egypt and proclaim in [r]Migdol, Jer. 44:1
Proclaim also in Memphis
and [r]Tahpanhes; Jer. 43:8
Say, 'Take your stand and
get yourself ready,
For the [r]sword has devoured
those around you.' Is. 1:20
15 "Why have your mighty ones
become prostrate?
They do not stand because
the LORD has [r]thrust them
down. Ps. 18:14, 39
16 "They have repeatedly [r]stumbled; Lev. 26:36, 37
Indeed, they have fallen one
against another.
Then they said, 'Get up! And
[r]let us go back Jer. 51:9
To our own people and our
native land
Away from the [r]sword of the
oppressor.' Jer. 50:16
17 "They cried there, 'Pharaoh
king of Egypt *is but* [r]a big
noise; Ex. 15:9, 10
He has let the appointed time
pass by!'
18 "As I live," declares the King
Whose name is the LORD of
hosts,
"Surely one shall come *who
looms up* like Tabor
among the mountains,
Or like Carmel by the sea.
19 "Make your baggage ready for
[r]exile, Is. 20:4
O [r]daughter dwelling in
Egypt, Jer. 48:18
For [r]Memphis will become a
desolation; Ezek. 30:13
It will even be burned down
and bereft of inhabitants.
20 "Egypt is a pretty heifer,
But a [a]horsefly is coming
from the north—it is
coming! *mosquito*
21 "Also her [r]mercenaries in her
midst 2 Sam. 10:6
Are like fattened calves,
For even they too have
turned back *and* have
fled away together;
They did not stand *their
ground.*
For the day of their calamity
has come upon them,
The time of their [r]punishment. Hos. 9:7; Obad. 13
22 "Its sound moves along like a
serpent;
For they move on [a]like an
army *in force*
And come to her as woodcutters with axes.
23 "They have cut down her forest," declares the LORD;
"Surely it will no *more* be
found,
Even though they are *now*
more numerous than [r]locusts Judg. 6:5; 7:12
And are without number.
24 "The daughter of Egypt has
been put to shame,
Given over to the power of
the people of the north."

25 The LORD of hosts, the God
of Israel, says, "Behold, I am
going to punish Amon of [r]Thebes,

and Pharaoh, and Egypt along
with her gods and her kings, even
Pharaoh and those who trust in
him. Ezek. 30:14-16; Nah. 3:8
26 "And I shall give them over to
the ᵗpower of those who are seeking their lives, even into the hand
of Nebuchadnezzar king of Babylon and into the hand of his ᵗoffi-
cers. Afterwards, however, it will
be inhabited as in the days of old,"
declares the LORD. *hand • servants*

27 "But as for you, O Jacob My
servant, do not fear,
Nor be dismayed, O Israel!
For, see, I am going to ʳsave
you from afar, Is. 11:11
And your descendants from
the land of their captivity;
And Jacob shall return and
be ʳundisturbed Jer. 23:6
And secure, with no one
making *him* tremble.
28 "O Jacob My servant, do not
fear," declares the LORD,
"For ʳI am with you. Is. 8:10
For I shall make a full end of
all the nations
Where I have driven you,
Yet I shall ʳnot make a full
end of you; Amos 9:8, 9
But I shall ʳcorrect you properly Jer. 10:24; Hab. 3:2
And by no means leave you
unpunished."

CHAPTER 47

THAT which came as the word of the LORD to Jeremiah the prophet concerning the Philistines, before Pharaoh conquered Gaza.

2 Thus says the LORD:
"Behold, waters are going to
rise from the north
And become an overflowing
torrent,
And ʳoverflow the land and
all its fulness, Is. 8:7, 8
The city and those who live
in it;
And the men will cry out,
And every inhabitant of the
land will wail.
3 "Because of the noise of the
ᵗgalloping hoofs of his
stallions, *stamping of the*
The tumult of his chariots,
and the rumbling of his
wheels,
The fathers have not turned
back for *their* children,
Because of the limpness of
their hands,
4 On account of the day that is
coming
To destroy all the Philistines,
To cut off from ʳTyre and Sidon Is. 23:5
Every ally that is left;
For the LORD is going to destroy the Philistines,
The remnant of the coastland
of ʳCaphtor. Gen. 10:14
5 "Baldnessʳ has come upon
Gaza; Jer. 48:37; Mic. 1:16
Ashkelon has been ruined.
O remnant of their valley,
How long will you ʳgash yourself? Jer. 16:6; 41:5
6 "Ah, ʳsword of the LORD,
How long will you not be
quiet? Judg. 7:20
Withdraw into your sheath;
Be at rest and stay still.
7 "How can it be quiet,
When the LORD has ʳgiven it
an order? Ezek. 14:17
Against Ashkelon and
against the seacoast—
There He has assigned it."

CHAPTER 48

CONCERNING Moab.
Thus says the LORD of hosts, the God of Israel,
"Woe to ʳNebo, for it has been destroyed; Num. 32:3, 38
ʳKiriathaim has been put to shame, it has been captured; Num. 32:37
The lofty stronghold has been put to shame and ᵃshattered. *dismayed*
2 "There is praise for Moab no longer;
In ʳHeshbon they have devised calamity against her: Num. 21:25
'Come and let us cut her off from *being* a nation!'
You too, [12]Madmen, will be silenced;
The sword will follow after you.
3 "The sound of an outcry from ʳHoronaim, Is. 15:5; Jer. 48:5
'Devastation and great destruction!'
4 "Moab is broken,
Her little ones have sounded out a cry *of distress.*
5 "For by the ascent of Luhith
They will ascend with continual weeping;
For at the descent of Horonaim
They have heard the ᵗanguished cry of destruction. *distresses of outcry*
6 "Flee, save your lives,
That you may be like a juniper in the wilderness.
7 "For because of your ʳtrust in your own achievements and treasures, Is. 59:4
Even you yourself will be captured;
And ʳChemosh will go off into exile Num. 21:29
Together with his priests and his princes.
8 "And a destroyer will come to every city,
So that no city will escape;
The valley also will be ruined,
And the ʳplateau will be destroyed, Josh. 13:9, 17, 21
As the LORD has said.
9 "Give ᵃwings to Moab, *salt*
For she will flee away;
And her cities will become a ʳdesolation, Jer. 44:22
Without inhabitants in them.
10 "Cursed ʳbe the one who does the LORD'S work negligently, Jer. 11:3
And cursed be the one who restrains his ʳsword from blood. Jer. 47:6, 7

11 "Moab has been ʳat ease since his youth; Ezek. 16:49
He has also been ʳundisturbed on his lees, Zeph. 1:12
Neither has he been emptied from vessel to vessel,
Nor has he gone into exile.
Therefore he retains his flavor,
And his aroma has not changed.

12 "Therefore behold, the days
are coming," declares the LORD,
"when I shall send to him those
who tip *vessels,* and they will tip
him over, and they will empty his
vessels and shatter his jars.
13 "And Moab will be ʳashamed
of Chemosh, as the house of Israel

[12] I.e., a city of Moab

was ashamed of Bethel, their confidence. Is. 45:16; Jer. 48:39
14"How can you say, 'We are
mighty warriors,
And men valiant for battle'?
15"Moab has been destroyed,
and[t]men have gone up to
[t]his cities; *one has • her*
His choicest young men have
also gone down to the
slaughter,"
Declares the [r]King, whose
name is the LORD of
hosts. Jer. 46:18; 51:57
16"The disaster of Moab will
[r]soon come, Is. 13:22
And his calamity has swiftly
hastened.
17"Mourn for him, all you who
live around him,
Even all of you who know his
name;
Say, 'How has the mighty
scepter been broken,
A staff of splendor!'
18"Come down from your glory
And sit [t]on the parched
ground, *in thirst*
O daughter dwelling in [r]Di-
bon, Num. 21:30; Josh. 13:9
For the destroyer of Moab
has come up against you,
He has ruined your strongholds.
19"Stand by the road and keep
watch,
O inhabitant of Aroer;
[r]Ask him who flees and her
who escapes
And say, 'What has hap-
pened?' 1 Sam. 4:13, 14, 16
20"Moab has been put to shame,
for it has been shattered.
Wail and cry out;
Declare by the Arnon
That Moab has been de-
stroyed.
21"Judgment has also come
upon the plain, upon Holon, Jahzah, and against Mephaath,
22 against Dibon, Nebo, and
Beth-diblathaim,
23 against Kiriathaim, Beth-ga-
mul, and[r]Beth-meon, Josh. 13:17
24 against[r]Kerioth, Bozrah, and
all the cities of the land of Moab,
far and near. Jer. 48:41; Amos 2:2
25"The[r]horn of Moab has been
cut off, and his arm broken," declares the LORD. Ps. 75:10
26"Make[r] him drunk, for he has
become arrogant toward the
LORD; so Moab will wallow in his
vomit, and he also will become a
laughingstock. Jer. 25:15
27"Now was not Israel a[r]laugh-
ingstock to you? Or was he caught
among thieves? For each time you
speak about him you shake *your*
head in scorn. Lam. 2:15-17
28"Leave the cities and dwell
among the[r]crags,
O inhabitants of Moab,
And be like a dove that nests
Beyond the mouth of the
chasm. Judg. 6:2; Is. 2:19
29"We[r] have heard of the pride
of Moab—he *is* very
proud— Is. 16:6; Zeph. 2:8
Of his haughtiness, his[r]pride,
his arrogance and his
self-exaltation. Job 40:11, 12
30"I know his [r]fury," declares
the LORD, Is. 37:28
"But it is futile;
His idle boasts have accomplished nothing.
31"Therefore I shall [r]wail for
Moab, Is. 15:5; 16:7, 11
Even for all Moab shall I cry
out;

I will moan for the men of
[r]Kir-heres. 2 Kin. 3:25
32 "More than the [r]weeping for
[r]Jazer Is. 16:8, 9
I shall weep for you, O vine
of Sibmah! Num. 21:32
Your tendrils stretched
across the sea,
They reached to the sea of
Jazer;
Upon your summer fruits
and your grape harvest
The destroyer has fallen.
33 "So [r]gladness and joy are
taken away Is. 16:10
From the fruitful field, even
from the land of Moab.
And I have made the wine to
[r]cease from the wine
presses; Is. 5:10; Hag. 2:16
No one will tread *them* with
shouting,
The shouting will not be
shouts *of joy.*
34 "From [r]the outcry at Heshbon
even to Elealeh, even to Jahaz
they have [t]raised their voice, from
[r]Zoar even to Horonaim *and to* Eglath-shelishiyah; for even the waters of Nimrim will become deso-
late. Is. 15:4-6 • *given forth* • Is. 15:5, 6
35 "And I shall make an end of
Moab," declares the LORD, "the
one who offers *sacrifice* on the
[r]high place and the one who burns
incense to his gods. Is. 15:2; 16:12
36 "Therefore My heart wails for
Moab like flutes; My heart also
wails like flutes for the men of
Kir-heres. Therefore they have
lost the abundance it produced.
37 "For [r]every head is bald and
every beard cut short; there are
gashes on all the hands and sackcloth on the loins. Is. 15:2
38 "On all the housetops of Moab
and in its streets there is lamentation everywhere; for I have broken Moab like an undesirable vessel," declares the LORD.
39 "How [a]shattered it is! *How*
they have wailed! How Moab has
turned his back—he is ashamed!
So Moab will become a laughingstock and an [r]object of terror to all
around him." *dismayed* • Ezek. 26:16
40 For thus says the LORD,
"Behold, one will [r]fly swiftly
like an eagle, Hos. 8:1
And [r]spread out his wings
against Moab. Is. 8:8
41 "Kerioth has been captured
And the strongholds have
been seized,
So the hearts of the mighty
men of Moab in that day
Will be like the heart of a
[r]woman in labor. Is. 13:8
42 "And Moab will be destroyed
from *being* a people
Because he has become arrogant toward the LORD.
43 "Terror, pit, and snare are
coming upon you,
O inhabitant of Moab," declares the LORD.
44 "The one who [r]flees from the
terror 1 Kin. 19:17; Is. 24:18
Will fall into the pit,
And the one who climbs up
out of the pit
Will be caught in the snare;
For I shall bring upon her,
even upon Moab,
The year of their [r]punish-
ment," declares the
LORD. Jer. 46:21

45 "In the shadow of Heshbon
The fugitives stand without
strength;

For a fire has gone forth from
Heshbon,
And a [r]flame from the midst
of Sihon, Num. 21:28, 29
And it has devoured the [r]fore-
head of Moab Num. 24:17
And the scalps of the [t]riotous
revelers. *sons of tumult*
46 "Woe to you, Moab!
The people of [r]Chemosh have
perished; Judg. 11:24
For your sons have been
taken away captive,
And your daughters into captivity.
47 "Yet I will restore the [a]fortunes
of Moab *captivity*
In the [t]latter days," declares
the LORD.
Thus far the judgment on
Moab. *end of the days*

CHAPTER 49

CONCERNING the sons of [r]Am-
mon. Deut. 23:3, 4; 2 Chr. 20:1
Thus says the LORD:
"Does Israel have no sons?
Or has he no heirs?
Why then has Malcam taken
possession of Gad
And his people settled in its
cities?
2 "Therefore behold, the days
are coming," declares the
LORD,
"That I shall cause a trumpet
blast of war to be heard
Against [r]Rabbah of the sons
of Ammon; Deut. 3:11
And it will become a desolate
heap,
And her [r]towns will be set on
fire. Josh. 17:11, 16
Then Israel will take posses-
sion of his possessors,"
Says the LORD.
3 "Wail, O [r]Heshbon, for Ai has
been destroyed! Jer. 48:2
Cry out, O daughters of Rabbah,
Gird yourselves with sackcloth and lament,
And rush back and forth inside the walls;
For Malcam will go into exile
Together with his priests and
his princes.
4 "How [r]boastful you are about
the valleys! Jer. 9:23
Your valley is flowing *away,*
O backsliding daughter
Who trusts in her [r]treasures,
saying, Ps. 62:10
'Who will come against me?'
5 "Behold, I am going to bring
terror upon you,"
Declares the Lord GOD of
hosts,
"From all *directions* around
you;
And each of you will be
driven out headlong,
With no one to gather the [r]fu-
gitives together. Lam. 4:15
6 "But afterward I will restore
The [a]fortunes of the sons of
Ammon,"
Declares the LORD. *captivity*

7 Concerning Edom.
Thus says the LORD of hosts,
"Is there no longer any [r]wis-
dom in Teman?
Has good counsel been lost
to the prudent? Job 2:11
Has their wisdom decayed?
8 "Flee away, turn back, dwell
in the depths,
O inhabitants of Dedan,
For I will bring the disaster
of Esau upon him

At the time I punish him.
9 "If ʳgrape gatherers came to you, Obad. 5
Would they not leave gleanings?
If thieves *came* by night,
They would destroy *only* until they had enough.
10 "But I have ʳstripped Esau bare, Jer. 13:26
I have uncovered his hiding places
So that he will not be able to conceal himself;
His ᵗoffspring has been destroyed along with his ᵗrelatives *seed • brothers*
And his neighbors, and ʳhe is no more. Is. 17:14
11 "Leave your orphans behind, I will keep *them* alive;
And let your ʳwidows trust in Me." Ps. 68:5; Zech. 7:10
12 For thus says the LORD, "Be-
hold, those who were not sen-
tenced to drink the ʳcup will certainly drink *it,* and are you the one
who will be completely acquitted?
You will not be acquitted, but you
will certainly drink *it.* Jer. 25:15
13 "For I have ʳsworn by Myself,"
declares the LORD, "that Bozrah
will become an object of horror, a
reproach, a ruin and a curse; and
all its cities will become perpetual
ruins." Gen. 22:16; Is. 45:23
14 I have ʳheard a message from the LORD, Obad. 1-4
And an envoy is sent among the nations, *saying,*
"Gather yourselves together and come against her,
And rise up for battle!"
15 "For behold, I have made you small among the nations,
Despised among men.
16 "As for the terror of you,
The arrogance of your heart has deceived you,
O you who live in the clefts of the ʳrock, 2 Kin. 14:7
Who occupy the height of the hill.
Though you make your nest as high as an eagle's,
I will ʳbring you down from there," declares the LORD. Amos 9:2
17 "And Edom will become an
object of horror; everyone who
passes by it will be horrified and
will hiss at all its wounds.
18 "Like the ʳoverthrow of Sodom
and Gomorrah with its neighbors," says the LORD, "no one will
live there, nor will a son of man
reside in it. Gen. 19:24, 25
19 "Behold, one will come up like
a lion from the thickets of the Jordan against a perennially watered
pasture; for in an instant I shall
make him run away from it, and
whoever is chosen I shall appoint
over it. For who is like Me, and
who will summon Me *into court?*
And who then is the shepherd
who can stand against Me?"
20 Therefore hear the ʳplan of
the LORD which He has planned
against Edom, and His purposes
which He has purposed against
the inhabitants of Teman: surely
they will drag them off, *even* the
little ones of the flock; surely He
will make their pasture desolate
because of them. Is. 14:24, 27
21 The ʳearth has quaked at the
noise of their downfall. There is
an outcry! The noise of it has been
heard at the Red Sea. Jer. 50:46
22 Behold, He will mount up
and swoop like an eagle, and

spread out His wings against Bozrah; and the hearts of the mighty
men of Edom in that day will be
like the heart of a woman in labor.
23 Concerning Damascus.
"Hamath [r]and Arpad are put to
shame, Is. 10:9; Jer. 39:5
For they have heard bad
news;
They are disheartened.
There is anxiety by the sea,
It cannot be calmed.
24 "Damascus has become helpless;
She has turned away to flee,
And panic has gripped her;
Distress and pangs have
taken hold of her
Like a woman in childbirth.
25 "How the city of praise has
not been deserted,
The town of My joy!
26 "Therefore, her young men
will fall in her streets,
And all the men of war will
be [a]silenced in that day,"
declares the LORD of
hosts. *destroyed*
27 "And I shall [r]set fire to the wall
of Damascus, Amos 1:3-5
And it will devour the [a]forti-
fied towers of [r]Ben-ha-
dad." *palaces* • 2 Kin. 13:3
28 Concerning Kedar and the
kingdoms of Hazor, which Nebuchadnezzar king of Babylon defeated. Thus says the LORD,
"Arise, go up to Kedar
And devastate the [r]men of the
east. Job 1:3; Is. 11:14
29 "They will take away their
tents and their flocks;
They will carry off for themselves
Their tent curtains, all their
goods, and their camels,
And they will call out to one
another, 'Terror [r]on every
side!' Jer. 46:5
30 "Run away, flee! Dwell in the
depths,
O inhabitants of Hazor," declares the LORD;
"For [r]Nebuchadnezzar king of
Babylon has formed a
plan against you
And devised a scheme
against you. Jer. 25:9; 27:6
31 "Arise, go up against a nation
which is at ease,
Which lives securely," declares the LORD.
"It has no gates or bars;
They [r]dwell alone. Mic. 7:14
32 "And their camels will become plunder,
And the multitude of their
cattle for booty,
And I shall scatter to all the
winds those who cut the
corners *of their hair;*
And I shall bring their disaster from every side," de-
clares the LORD.
33 "And Hazor will become a
[r]haunt of jackals,
A desolation forever;
No one will live there,
Nor will a son of man reside
in it." Jer. 9:11
34 That which came as the
word of the LORD to Jeremiah
the prophet concerning Elam, at
the beginning of the reign of Zedekiah king of Judah, saying,
35 "Thus says the LORD of hosts,
'Behold, I am going to break
the bow of Elam,
The finest of their might.
36 'And I shall bring upon Elam
the [r]four winds Rev. 7:1

From the four ends of heaven,
And shall [r]scatter them to all these winds; Amos 9:9
And there will be no nation
To which the outcasts of Elam will not go.
37 'So I shall [a]shatter Elam before their enemies *dismay*
And before those who seek their lives;
And I shall [r]bring calamity upon them, Jer. 6:19
Even My [r]fierce anger,' declares the LORD, Jer. 30:24
'And I shall [r]send out the sword after them Jer. 9:16
Until I have consumed them.
38 'Then I shall set My throne in Elam,
And I shall destroy [a]out of it king and princes,'
Declares the LORD. *from there*
39 'But it will come about in the last days
That I shall restore the [a]fortunes of Elam,'"
Declares the LORD. *captivity*

CHAPTER 50

THE word which the LORD spoke concerning [r]Babylon, the land of the Chaldeans, through Jeremiah the prophet: Gen. 10:10; 11:9
2 "Declare [r]and proclaim among the nations. Jer. 4:16
Proclaim it and [r]lift up a standard. Jer. 51:27
Do not conceal *it but* say,
'Babylon has been captured,
[r]Bel has been put to shame,
Marduk has been [a]shattered; Is. 46:1 • *dismayed*
Her images have been put to shame, her idols have been shattered.'
3 "For a nation has come up
against her out of the north; it will
make her land an object of horror,
and there will be no inhabitant in
it. Both man and beast have wandered off, they have gone away!
4 "In those days and at that
time," declares the LORD, "the
sons of Israel will come, *both* they
and the sons of Judah [r]as well;
they will go along weeping as they
go, and it will be the LORD their
God they will seek. Is. 11:12, 13
5 "They will [r]ask for the way to
Zion, *turning* their faces in its direction; they will come that they
may join themselves to the LORD
in an everlasting covenant that
will not be forgotten. Is. 35:8
6 "My people have become [r]lost sheep; Ezek. 34:15, 16
[r]Their shepherds have led them astray. Jer. 23:11-14
They have made them turn aside *on* the mountains;
They have gone along from mountain to hill
And have forgotten their [r]resting place. Jer. 33:12
7 "All who came upon them have devoured them;
And their adversaries have said, 'We are not guilty,
Inasmuch as they have sinned against the LORD
who is the [r]habitation of righteousness, Jer. 31:23
Even the LORD, the [r]hope of their fathers.' Ps. 22:4
8 "Wander away from the [r]midst of Babylon, Rev. 18:4
And go forth from the land of the Chaldeans;

Be also like male goats at the
head of the flock.
9 "For behold, I am going to
[r]arouse and bring up
against Babylon Jer. 51:1
A horde of great nations
from the land of the
north,
And they will draw up *their*
battle lines against her;
From there she will be taken
captive.
Their arrows will be like an
expert warrior
Who does not return empty-
handed.
10 "And [r]Chaldea will become
plunder; Jer. 51:24, 35
All who plunder her will
have enough," declares
the LORD.

11 "Because you are glad, because you are jubilant,
O you who [r]pillage My heritage, Jer. 12:14
Because you skip about like
a threshing heifer
And neigh like stallions,
12 Your [r]mother will be greatly
ashamed, Jer. 15:9
She who gave you birth[a] will
be humiliated. *has become*
Behold, *she will be* the least
of the nations,
A wilderness, a parched
land, and a desert.
13 "Because of the indignation of
the LORD she will [r]not be
inhabited, Jer. 34:22
But she will be [r]completely
desolate; Jer. 51:26
Everyone who passes by
Babylon will be horrified
And will hiss because of all
her wounds.
14 "Draw up your battle lines
against Babylon on every
side,
All you who bend the bow;
Shoot at her, do not be sparing with *your* arrows,
For she has [r]sinned against
the LORD. Hab. 2:8, 17
15 "Raise your battle cry against
her on every side!
She has [r]given herself up, her
pillars have fallen,
Her walls have been torn
down. 1 Chr. 29:24
For this is the [r]vengeance of
the LORD: Jer. 46:10
Take vengeance on her;
[r]As she has done *to others,* so
do to her. Ps. 137:8
16 "Cut off the [r]sower from Babylon, Joel 1:11
And the one who wields the
sickle at the time of harvest;
From before the [r]sword of the
oppressor Jer. 25:38
They will each turn back to
his own people,
And they will each flee to his
own land.

17 "Israel is a scattered flock, the
lions have driven *them* away. The
first one *who* devoured him was
the king of Assyria, and this last
one *who* has broken his bones is
Nebuchadnezzar king of Babylon.
18 "Therefore thus says the LORD
of hosts, the God of Israel: 'Behold, I am going to punish the
king of Babylon and his land, just
as I punished the king of Assyria.
19 'And I shall bring Israel back
to his pasture, and he will graze
on Carmel and Bashan, and his
desire will be satisfied in the hill
country of Ephraim and Gilead.

20 'In those days and at that
time,' declares the LORD, 'search
will be made for the iniquity of Israel, but there will be none; and
for the sins of Judah, but they will
not be found; for I shall pardon
those whom I leave as a remnant.'

21 "Against the land of [13]Merathaim, go up against it,
And against the inhabitants of [14]Pekod.ʳ Ezek. 23:23
Slay and utterly destroy them," declares the LORD,
"And do according to all that I have commanded you.

22 "The ʳnoise of battle is in the land, Jer. 4:19-21
And great destruction.

23 "How the ʳhammer of the whole earth
Has been cut off and broken!
How Babylon has become
An object of horror among the nations! Jer. 51:20-24

24 "I ʳset a snare for you, and you were also caught, O Babylon, Jer. 48:43, 44
While you yourself were not aware;
You have been found and also seized
Because you have engaged in conflict with the LORD."

25 The LORD has opened His armory
And has brought forth the ʳweapons of His indignation, Is. 13:5
For it is a ʳwork of the Lord GOD of hosts Jer. 50:15
In the land of the Chaldeans.

26 Come to her from the ᵗfarthest border; *end*
Open up her barns,
Pile her up like heaps
And utterly destroy her,
Let nothing be left to her.

27 ʳPut all her young bulls to the sword; Is. 34:7
Let them ʳgo down to the slaughter! Jer. 48:10
Woe be upon them, for their ʳday has come, Ps. 37:13
The time of their punishment.

28 There is a ʳsound of fugitives and refugees from the land of Babylon, Is. 48:20
To declare in Zion the ʳvengeance of the LORD our God, Ps. 149:6-9
Vengeance for His temple.

29 "Summon [15]many against Babylon,
All those who bend the bow:
Encamp against her on every side,
Let there be no escape.
Repay her according to her work;
According to all that she has done, *so* do to her;
For she has become arrogant against the LORD,
Against the Holy One of Israel.

30 "Therefore her young men will fall in her streets,
And all her men of war will be silenced in that day,"
declares the LORD.

31 "Behold, ʳI am against you, O arrogant one," Nah. 2:13
Declares the Lord GOD of hosts,
"For your day has come,

[13]Or, *Double Rebellion* [14]Or, *Punishment*

[15]Another reading is *archers*

The time when I shall punish
you.
32 "And the [r]arrogant one will
stumble and fall Is. 10:12-15
With no one to raise him up;
And I shall [r]set fire to his
cities, Jer. 21:14; 49:27
And it will devour all his environs."

33 Thus says the LORD of hosts,
"The sons of Israel are oppressed,
And the sons of Judah as
well;
And [r]all who took them captive have held them fast,
They have refused to let
them go. Is. 14:17; 58:6
34 "Their [r]Redeemer is strong,
the LORD of hosts is His
name; Prov. 23:11
He will vigorously [r]plead
their case, Mic. 7:9
So that He may [r]bring rest to
the earth, Is. 14:3-7
But turmoil to the inhabitants of Babylon.
35 "A sword against the Chaldeans," declares the LORD,
"And against the inhabitants
of Babylon,
And against her [r]officials and
her wise men! Dan. 5:1, 2
36 "A sword against the [r]oracle
priests, and they will become fools! Is. 44:25
A sword against her mighty
men, and they will be
[a]shattered! *dismayed*
37 "A sword against their [r]horses
and against their chariots, Ps. 20:7, 8
And against all the [t]foreigners who are in the midst
of her, *mixed multitude*
And they will become
[r]women! Jer. 48:41; 51:30
A sword against her treasures, and they will be
plundered!
38 "A drought on her waters, and
they will be dried up!
For it is a land of idols,
And they are mad over fearsome idols.
39 "Therefore the [r]desert creatures will live *there* along
with the jackals; Is. 13:21
The ostriches also will live in
it,
And it will [r]never again be inhabited Is. 13:20; Jer. 25:12
Or dwelt in from generation
to generation.
40 "As when God overthrew
[r]Sodom Gen. 19:24, 25
And Gomorrah with its
neighbors," declares the
LORD,
"No man will live there,
Nor will *any* son of man reside in it.

41 "Behold, a people is coming
[r]from the north, Is. 13:2-5
And a great nation and many
kings
Will be aroused from the remote parts of the earth.
42 "They [r]seize *their* bow and
javelin; Jer. 6:23
They are [r]cruel and have no
mercy. Is. 13:17, 18; 47:6
Their voice roars like the sea,
And they ride on horses,
[r]Marshalled like a man for the
battle Jer. 50:9, 14; Joel 2:5
Against you, O daughter of
Babylon.
43 "The [r]king of Babylon has

heard the report about
them, Jer. 51:31
And his hands hang limp;
[r]Distress has gripped him,
Agony like a woman in childbirth. Jer. 30:6; 49:24

44 "Behold, one will come up like
a lion from the [t]thicket of the Jordan
to a perennially watered pasture;
for in an instant I shall make them run away from it,
and whoever is chosen I shall appoint over it.
For who is like Me, and who will summon Me *into court*?
And who then is the shepherd who can stand before Me?" *pride*

45 Therefore hear the plan of the LORD which He has planned against Babylon, and His purposes which He has purposed against the land of the Chaldeans: surely they will drag them off, *even* the little ones of the flock; surely He will make their pasture desolate because of them.

46 At the [t]shout, "Babylon has been seized!" the [r]earth is shaken, and an outcry is heard among the nations. *voice* • Ezek. 26:18; 31:16

CHAPTER 51

THUS says the LORD:
"Behold, I am going to arouse
against Babylon
And against the inhabitants
of [16]Leb-kamai
The spirit of a destroyer.
2 "And I shall dispatch foreigners
to Babylon that they
may winnow her
And may devastate her land;
For on every side they will be
opposed to her
In the day of *her* calamity.
3 "Let not him who [r]bends his
bow bend *it*, Jer. 50:14, 29
Nor let him rise up in his
[r]scale-armor; Jer. 46:4
So do not spare her young
men;
Devote all her army to destruction.
4 "And they will fall down [a]slain
in the land of the Chaldeans, *wounded*
And [r]pierced through in their
streets." Is. 13:15; 14:19

5 For neither Israel nor Judah
has been forsaken
By his God, the LORD of
hosts,
Although their land is [r]full of
guilt Hos. 4:1, 2
[t]Before the Holy One of Israel. *From*
6 [r]Flee from the midst of Babylon, Jer. 50:8, 28; Rev. 18:4
And each of you save his life!
Do not be [r]destroyed in her
punishment, Num. 16:26
For this is the [r]LORD's time of
vengeance; Jer. 50:15
He is going to [r]render recompense
to her. Jer. 25:14
7 Babylon has been a golden
[r]cup in the hand of the
LORD, Hab. 2:16; Rev. 17:4
Intoxicating all the earth.
The [r]nations have drunk of
her wine; Rev. 14:8; 18:3
Therefore the nations are
[r]going mad. Jer. 25:16
8 Suddenly Babylon has fallen
and been broken;
[r]Wail over her! Is. 13:6
Bring balm for her pain;
Perhaps she may be healed.
9 We applied healing to

[16]Cryptic name for Chaldea

Babylon, but she was not healed;
Forsake her and let us each go to his own country,
For her judgment has [r]reached to heaven Ezra 9:6
And [t]towers up to the very skies. *is lifted*
10 The LORD has brought [t]about our vindication; *forth*
Come and let us [r]recount in Zion Is. 40:2; Jer. 50:28
The work of the LORD our God!

11 [r]Sharpen the arrows, fill the quivers! Joel 3:9, 10
The LORD has aroused the spirit of the kings of the Medes,
Because His purpose is against Babylon to destroy it;
For it is the [r]vengeance of the LORD, vengeance for His temple. Jer. 50:28
12 Lift up a signal against the walls of Babylon;
Post a strong guard,
Station [a]sentries, *watchmen*
Place men in ambush!
For the LORD has both purposed and performed
What He spoke concerning the inhabitants of Babylon.
13 O you who [r]dwell by many waters, Rev. 17:1
Abundant in treasures,
Your end has come,
The measure of your end.
14 The [r]LORD of hosts has sworn by Himself: Jer. 49:13
"Surely I will fill you with a population like locusts,
And they will cry out with shouts of victory over you."

15 *It is* [r]He who made the earth by His power, Gen. 1:1
Who established the world by His wisdom,
And by His understanding He [r]stretched out the heavens. Ps. 146:5, 6
16 When He utters His voice, *there is* a tumult of waters in the heavens,
And He causes the [r]clouds to ascend from the end of the earth; Ps. 135:7
He makes lightning for the rain,
And brings forth the wind from His storehouses.
17 [r]All mankind is stupid, devoid of knowledge; Jer. 10:14
Every goldsmith is put to shame by his idols,
For his molten images are [r]deceitful, Hab. 2:18, 19
And there is no breath in them.
18 They are [r]worthless, a work of mockery; Jer. 18:15
In the time of their punishment they will perish.
19 The [r]portion of Jacob is not like these; Ps. 73:26
For the Maker of all is He,
And of the tribe of His inheritance;
The [r]LORD of hosts is His name. Jer. 50:34
20 *He says,* "You are My [t]war-club, *My* weapon of war;
And with you I shatter nations, *shatterer*
And with you I destroy kingdoms.

21 "And with you I shatter the horse and his rider,
22 And with you I shatter the chariot and its rider,
And with you I shatter [r]man and woman, 2 Chr. 36:17
And with you I shatter old man and [r]youth, Is. 13:18
And with you I shatter young man and virgin,
23 And with you I shatter the shepherd and his flock,
And with you I shatter the farmer and his team,
And with you I shatter governors and prefects.

24 "But I will repay Babylon and
all the inhabitants of [r]Chaldea for
all their evil that they have done
in Zion before your eyes," declares the LORD. Jer. 50:10

25 "Behold, I am against you, O destroying mountain,
Who destroy the whole earth," declares the LORD,
"And I will stretch out My hand against you,
And roll you down from the crags
And I will make you a [r]burnt out mountain. Rev. 8:8
26 "And they will not take from you *even* a stone for a corner
Nor a stone for foundations,
But you will be desolate forever," declares the LORD.

27 Lift up a signal in the land,
Blow a trumpet among the nations!
Consecrate the nations against her,
Summon against her the kingdoms of Ararat, Minni and Ashkenaz;
Appoint a marshal against her,
Bring up the [r]horses like bristly locusts. Jer. 50:42
28 Consecrate the nations against her,
The kings of the Medes,
[t]Their governors and all their prefects,
And every land of [t]their dominion. *Her • his*
29 So the [r]land quakes and writhes, Jer. 8:16; 10:10
For the purposes of the LORD against Babylon stand,
To make the land of Babylon
[a]A desolation without inhabitants. *An object of horror*
30 The mighty men of Babylon have ceased fighting,
They stay in the strongholds;
Their strength is exhausted,
They are becoming [r]*like* women; Is. 13:7, 8
Their dwelling places are set on fire,
The [r]bars of her *gates* are broken. Is. 45:1, 2; Lam. 2:9
31 One [t]courier runs to meet [t]another, *runner*
And one [t]messenger to meet another, *announcer*
To tell the king of Babylon
That his city has been captured from end *to end;*
32 The fords also have been seized,
And they have burned the marshes with fire,
And the men of war are terrified.

33 For thus says the LORD of hosts, the God of Israel:

"The daughter of Babylon is like a threshing floor
At the time [t]it is stamped firm; *of treading it*
Yet in a little while the time of [r]harvest will come for her." Is. 17:5; Hos. 6:11

34 "Nebuchadnezzar king of Babylon has devoured me *and* crushed me,
He has set me down *like* an [r]empty vessel; Is. 24:1-3
He has [r]swallowed me like a monster, Job 20:15
He has filled his stomach with my delicacies;
He has washed me away.
35 "May the [r]violence *done* to me and to my flesh be upon Babylon," Ps. 137:8
The [t]inhabitant of Zion will say; *inhabitress*
And, "May my blood be upon the inhabitants of Chaldea,"
Jerusalem will say.
36 Therefore thus says the LORD,
"Behold, I am going to [r]plead your case Ps. 140:12
And [r]exact full vengeance for you; Jer. 51:6, 11
And I shall dry up her sea
And make her fountain dry.
37 "And [r]Babylon will become a heap *of ruins,* a haunt of jackals, Rev. 18:2
An object of horror and hissing, without inhabitants.
38 "They will roar together like [r]young lions, Jer. 2:15
They will growl like lions' cubs.
39 "When they become heated up, I shall serve *them* their banquet
And [r]make them drunk, that they may become jubilant Jer. 25:27; 48:26
And may [r]sleep a perpetual sleep Ps. 76:5
And not wake up," declares the LORD.
40 "I shall bring them down like lambs to the slaughter,
Like rams together with male goats.

41 "How [17]Sheshak [r]has been captured, Jer. 25:26
And the praise of the whole earth been seized!
How Babylon has become an object of horror among the nations!
42 "The [a]sea has come up over Babylon; *broad river*
She has been engulfed with its tumultuous waves.
43 "Her cities have become an object of horror,
A parched land and a desert,
A land in which no man lives,
And through which no son of man passes.
44 "And [r]I shall punish Bel in Babylon, Is. 46:1; Jer. 50:2
And I shall make what he has swallowed [r]come out of his mouth; Ezra 1:7, 8
And the nations will no longer stream to him.
Even the [r]wall of Babylon has fallen down! Jer. 50:15

45 "Come forth from her midst, My people,
And each of you [r]save yourselves Gen. 19:12-16

[17]Cryptic name for Babylon

From the fierce anger of the LORD.
46 "Now [r]lest your heart grow faint, Jer. 46:27, 28
And you be afraid at the [r]report that *will be* heard in the land— 2 Kin. 19:7
For the report will come [t]one year, in the
And after that [t]another report in [t]another year, the
And violence *will be* in the land
With ruler against ruler—
47 Therefore behold, days are coming
When I shall punish the [r]idols of Babylon; Is. 21:9; 46:1, 2
And her whole land will be [r]put to shame,
And all her slain will fall in her midst. Jer. 50:12, 35-37
48 "Then heaven and earth and all that is in them
Will shout for joy over Babylon,
For the destroyers will come to her from the north,"
Declares the LORD.

49 Indeed Babylon is to fall *for* the slain of Israel,
As also for Babylon [r]the slain of all the earth have fallen. Rev. 18:24
50 You [r]who have escaped the sword, Jer. 44:28
Depart! Do not stay!
[r]Remember the LORD from afar, Deut. 4:29-31
And let Jerusalem come to your mind.
51 We are ashamed because we have heard reproach;
Disgrace has covered our faces,
For aliens have entered
The holy places of the LORD's house.

52 "Therefore behold, the days are coming," declares the LORD,
"When I shall punish her [r]idols, Jer. 50:38
And the mortally wounded will groan throughout her land.
53 "Though Babylon should ascend to the heavens,
And though she should fortify her lofty stronghold,
From [r]Me destroyers will come to her," declares the LORD. Is. 13:3

54 The [r]sound of an outcry from Babylon, Jer. 48:3-5
And of great destruction from the land of the Chaldeans!
55 For the LORD is going to destroy Babylon,
And He will make *her* loud noise vanish from her.
And their waves will roar like many waters;
The tumult of their voices [t]sounds forth. is given
56 For the [r]destroyer is coming against her, against Babylon, Jer. 51:48, 53
And her mighty men will be captured,
Their bows are shattered;
For the LORD is a God of recompense,
He will fully repay.
57 "And I shall make her princes and her wise men drunk,
Her governors, her prefects, and her mighty men,

That they may sleep a ʳperpetual sleep and not wake up," Ps. 76:5, 6
ʳDeclares the King, whose name is the LORD of hosts. Jer. 46:18; 48:15
58 Thus says the LORD of hosts,
"The broad wall of Babylon will be completely razed,
And her high ʳgates will be set on fire; Is. 45:1, 2
So the peoples will ʳtoil for nothing, Hab. 2:13
And the nations become exhausted *only* for fire."
59 The ᵗmessage which Jeremiah the prophet commanded Seraiah the son of ʳNeriah, the grandson of Mahseiah, when he went with Zedekiah the king of Judah to Babylon in the fourth year of his reign. (Now Seraiah was quartermaster.) *word* • Jer. 32:12; 36:4
60 So Jeremiah wrote in a single scroll all the calamity which would come upon Babylon, *that is,* all these words which have been written concerning Babylon.
61 Then Jeremiah said to Seraiah, "As soon as you come to Babylon, then see that you read all these words aloud,
62 and say, 'Thou, O LORD, hast ᵗpromised concerning this place to cut it off, so that there will be nothing dwelling in it, whether man or beast, but it will be a perpetual desolation.' *spoken*
63 "And it will come about as soon as you finish reading this ᵃscroll, you will tie a stone to it and ʳthrow it into the middle of the Euphrates, *book* • Rev. 18:21
64 and say, 'Just so shall Babylon sink down and not rise again, because of the calamity that I am going to bring upon her; and they will become exhausted.'" Thus far are the words of Jeremiah.

CHAPTER 52

ZEDEKIAH was twenty-one years old when he became king, and he reigned eleven years in Jerusalem; and his mother's name was ʳHamutal the daughter of Jeremiah of Libnah. 2 Kin. 22:31
2 And he did ʳevil in the sight of the LORD like all that Jehoiakim had done. 1 Kin. 14:22; 2 Kin. 24:19
3 For through the ʳanger of the LORD *this* came about in Jerusalem and Judah until He cast them out from His presence. And Zedekiah rebelled against the king of Babylon. 2 Kin. 24:20; Is. 3:1, 4, 5
4 Now it came about in the ninth year of his reign, on the tenth day of the tenth month, that Nebuchadnezzar king of Babylon came, he and all his army, against Jerusalem, camped against it, and built a siege wall all around it.
5 ʳSo the city was under siege until the eleventh year of King Zedekiah. 2 Kin. 25:2
6 On the ninth day of the fourth month the famine was so severe in the city that there was no food for the people of the land.
7 Then the city was broken into, and all the men of war fled and went forth from the city at night by way of the gate between the two walls which *was* by the king's garden, though the Chaldeans were all around the city. And they went by way of the Arabah.
8 But the army of the Chaldeans pursued the king and ʳovertook Zedekiah in the ᵗplains of

Jericho, and all his army was scattered from him. Jer. 21:7 • *Arabah*
9 Then they captured the king
and brought him up to the king of
Babylon at Riblah in the land of
Hamath; and he [t]passed sentence
on him. *spoke judgments with*
10 And the king of Babylon
[r]slaughtered the sons of Zedekiah
before his eyes, and he also
slaughtered all the princes of Judah in Riblah. 2 Kin. 25:7
11 Then he [r]blinded the eyes of
Zedekiah; and the king of Babylon
bound him with bronze fetters
and brought him to Babylon, and
put him in prison until the day of
his death. Jer. 39:7; Ezek. 12:13
12 Now on the tenth day of the
fifth month, which was the nineteenth year of King Nebuchadnezzar, king of Babylon, Nebuzaradan the captain of the bodyguard,
who was in the service of the king
of Babylon, came to Jerusalem.
13 And he [r]burned the house of
the LORD, the king's house, and all
the houses of Jerusalem; even every large house he burned with
fire. 1 Kin. 9:8; 2 Kin. 25:9
14 So all the army of the Chaldeans who *were* with the captain
of the guard [r]broke down all the
walls around Jerusalem. Neh. 1:3
15 Then Nebuzaradan the captain of the guard [r]carried away
into exile some of the poorest of
the people, the rest of the people
who were left in the city, the deserters who had [r]deserted to the
king of Babylon, and the rest of
the artisans. 2 Kin. 25:11 • Jer. 39:9
16 But Nebuzaradan the captain
of the guard left some of the poorest of the land to be vinedressers
and [a]plowmen. *unpaid laborers*
17 Now the bronze pillars
which belonged to the house of
the LORD and the stands and the
bronze sea, which were in the
house of the LORD, the Chaldeans
broke in pieces and carried all
their bronze to Babylon.
18 And they also took away the
pots, the shovels, the snuffers, the
basins, the [a]pans, and all the
bronze vessels which were used in
temple service. *spoons* for *incense*
19 The captain of the guard also
took away the [r]bowls, the firepans,
the basins, the pots, the lampstands, the pans and the libation
bowls, what was fine gold and
what was fine silver. 1 Kin. 7:49, 50
20 The two pillars, the one sea,
and the twelve bronze bulls that
were under the sea, *and* the
stands, which King Solomon had
made for the house of the LORD—
the bronze of all these vessels was
[r]beyond weight. 2 Kin. 25:16
21 As for the pillars, the height
of each pillar was eighteen cubits,
and it was twelve cubits in circumference and four fingers in
thickness, *and* hollow.
22 Now a capital of bronze was
on it; and the height of each capital was five cubits, with network
and pomegranates upon the capital all around, all of bronze. And
the second pillar was like these,
including pomegranates.
23 And there were ninety-six
exposed pomegranates; all the
pomegranates *numbered* a hundred on the network all around.
24 Then the captain of the
guard took Seraiah the chief
priest and Zephaniah the second
priest, with the three [t]officers of
the temple. *keepers of the door*

25 He also took from the city one official who was overseer of the men of war, and seven of the [r]king's advisers who were found in the city, and the scribe of the commander of the army who mustered the people of the land, and sixty men of the people of the land who were found in the midst of the city. 2 Kin. 25:19; Esth. 1:14

26 And Nebuzaradan the captain of the guard took them and [r]brought them to the king of Babylon at Riblah. 2 Kin. 25:20

27 Then the king of Babylon struck them down and put them to death at Riblah in the land of Hamath. So Judah was [r]led away into exile from its land. Is. 6:11, 12

28 These are the people whom Nebuchadnezzar carried away into exile: in the [a]seventh year 3,023 Jews; *seventeenth*

29 in the eighteenth year of Nebuchadnezzar 832 persons from Jerusalem;

30 in the twenty-third year of Nebuchadnezzar, Nebuzaradan the captain of the guard carried into exile 745 Jewish people; there were 4,600 persons in all.

31 Now it came about in the thirty-seventh year of the exile of Jehoiachin king of Judah, in the twelfth month, on the twenty-fifth of the month, that Evil-merodach king of Babylon, in the *first* year of his reign, showed favor to Jehoiachin king of Judah and brought him out of prison.

32 [r]Then he spoke kindly to him and set his throne above the thrones of the kings who *were* with him in Babylon. 2 Kin. 25:28

33 So [t]Jehoiachin changed his prison clothes, and [t]had his meals in the king's presence regularly all the days of his life. ***he • ate***

34 And for his allowance, a [r]regular allowance was given him by the king of Babylon, a daily portion all the days of his life until the day of his death. 2 Sam. 9:10

THE LAMENTATIONS
OF JEREMIAH

HOW lonely sits the city
That was full of people!
She has become like a widow
Who was once [r]great among
the nations! Ezra 4:20
She who was a princess
among the provinces
Has become a forced laborer!
2 She [r]weeps bitterly in the
night, Ps. 6:6; 77:2-6
And her tears are on her
cheeks;
She has none to comfort her
Among all her lovers.
All her friends have dealt
treacherously with her;
They have become her enemies.
3 [r]Judah has gone into exile under affliction, Jer. 13:19

And under harsh servitude;
She dwells [r]among the na-
tions, Deut. 28:64-67
But she has found no rest;
All [r]her pursuers have over-
taken her 2 Kin. 25:4, 5
In the midst of distress.
4 The roads [a]of Zion are in
mourning *to*
Because no one comes to the
appointed feasts.
All her gates are desolate;
Her priests are groaning,
Her virgins are afflicted,
And she herself is bitter.
5 Her adversaries have be-
come her masters,
Her enemies prosper;
For the LORD has [r]caused her
grief Ezek. 8:17, 18; 9:9, 10
Because of the multitude of
her transgressions;
Her little ones have gone
away
As captives before the adversary.
6 And all her [r]majesty Jer. 13:18
Has departed from the
daughter of Zion;
Her princes have become
like bucks
That have found no pasture;
And they have [t]fled without
strength *gone*
Before the pursuer.
7 In the days of her affliction
and homelessness
[r]Jerusalem remembers all her
precious things Ps. 42:4
That were from the days of
old
When her people fell into the
hand of the adversary,
And no one helped her.
The adversaries saw her,
They mocked at her ruin.
8 Jerusalem sinned [r]greatly,
Therefore she has become an
unclean thing. Is. 59:2-13
All who honored her despise
her
Because they have seen her
nakedness;
Even [r]she herself groans and
turns away. Lam. 1:11
9 Her [r]uncleanness was in her
skirts; Jer. 2:34; Ezek. 24:13
She did not consider her [r]fu-
ture; Deut. 32:29; Is. 47:7
Therefore she has [t]fallen as-
tonishingly; *come down*
She has no comforter.
"See, O LORD, my affliction,
For the enemy has [r]magnified
himself!" Ps. 74:23
10 The adversary has stretched
out his hand
Over all her precious things,
For she has seen the nations
enter her sanctuary,
The ones whom Thou didst
command
That they should not enter
into Thy congregation.
11 All her people groan [r]seeking
bread; Jer. 38:9; 52:6
They have given their precious things for food
To [r]restore their lives themselves. 1 Sam. 30:12
"See, O LORD, and look,
For I am [r]despised." Jer. 15:19
12 "Is [r]it nothing to all you who
pass this way? Jer. 18:16
Look and see if there is any
pain like my pain
Which was severely dealt out
to me,
Which the [r]LORD inflicted on
the day of His fierce an-
ger. Jer. 30:23, 24

13 "From on high He sent fire
into my ʳbones, Ps. 22:14
And it prevailed *over them;*
He has spread a ʳnet for my
feet; Job 19:6; Ps. 66:11
He has turned me back;
He has made me desolate,
ᵃFaint all day long. *Sick*
14 "The ʳyoke of my transgressions is bound; Is. 47:6
By His hand they are knit together;
They have ʳcome upon my
neck; Jer. 28:13, 14
He has made my strength
ᵗfail; *stumble*
The Lord ʳhas given me into
the hands Ezek. 25:4, 7
Of *those against whom* I am
not able to stand.
15 "The ʳLord has rejected all my
strong men Jer. 13:24; 37:10
In my midst;
He has called an appointed
ᵃtime against me *feast*
To crush my young men;
The Lord has ʳtrodden *as in* a
wine press Mal. 4:3
The virgin daughter of Judah.
16 "For these things I weep;
ᵗMy eyes run down with water; *My eye, my eye*
Because far from me is a
ʳcomforter,
One who restores my soul;
My children are desolate
Because the enemy has prevailed." Eccl. 4:1; Lam. 1:2
17 Zion stretches out her hands;
There is no one to comfort
her;
The LORD has commanded
concerning Jacob
That the ones round about
him should be his adversaries;
Jerusalem has become an unclean thing among them.
18 "The LORD is righteous;
For I have ʳrebelled against
His command; Jer. 4:17
Hear now, all peoples,
And behold my pain;
ʳMy virgins and my young
men Deut. 28:32, 41
Have gone into captivity.
19 "I called to my lovers, *but*
they deceived me;
My priests and my elders
perished in the city,
While they sought food to ʳrestore ᵗtheir strength themselves. Lam. 1:11 • *their soul*
20 "See, O LORD, for I am in distress;
My spirit is greatly troubled;
My heart is overturned
within me,
For I have been very ʳrebellious. Jer. 14:20
In the street the sword slays;
In the house it is like death.
21 "They have heard that I groan;
There is no one to comfort
me;
All my enemies have heard
of my ᵗcalamity; *evil*
They are ʳglad that Thou hast
done *it.* Ps. 35:15
Oh, that Thou wouldst bring
the day which Thou hast
proclaimed,
That they may become ʳlike
me. Is. 14:5, 6; 47:6, 11
22 "Let all their wickedness
come before Thee;
And deal with them as Thou
hast dealt with me
For all my transgressions;

For my groans are many, and
my heart is faint."

CHAPTER 2

HOW the Lord has covered the
daughter of Zion
With a cloud in His anger!
He has [r]cast from heaven to
earth Is. 14:12-15
The [r]glory of Israel, Is. 64:11
And has not remembered His
[r]footstool Ps. 99:5; 132:7
In the day of His anger.
2 The Lord has swallowed up;
He has not spared
All the habitations of Jacob.
In His wrath He has [r]thrown
down Lam. 2:5; Mic. 5:11, 14
The strongholds of the
daughter of Judah;
He has [r]brought *them* down
to the ground; Is. 25:12
He has profaned the king-
dom and its princes.
3 In fierce anger He has cut off
All the strength of Israel;
He has [r]drawn back His right
hand Ps. 74:11; Jer. 21:4, 5
From before the enemy.
And He has burned in Jacob
like a flaming fire
Consuming round about.
4 He has bent His [r]bow like an
enemy, Job 6:4; 16:13
He has set His right hand like
an adversary
And slain all that were [r]pleas-
ant to the eye; Ezek. 24:25
In the tent of the daughter of
Zion
He has [r]poured out His wrath
like fire. Is. 42:25
5 The Lord has become like an
[r]enemy. Jer. 30:14
He has swallowed up Israel;
He has swallowed up all its
[r]palaces; Jer. 52:13
He has destroyed its strongholds
And [r]multiplied in the daughter of Judah Jer. 9:17-20
Mourning and moaning.
6 And He has violently treated
His [t]tabernacle like a garden *booth;* *booth*
He has destroyed His ap-
pointed meeting place;
The LORD has [r]caused to be
forgotten Jer. 17:27
The appointed feast and sabbath in Zion,
And He has [r]despised king
and priest Lam. 4:16
In the indignation of His anger.
7 The Lord has [r]rejected His altar, Ps. 78:59-61; Is. 64:11
He has abandoned His sanctuary;
He has delivered into the
hand of the enemy
The walls of her palaces.
They have made a noise in
the house of the LORD
As in the day of an appointed
feast.
8 The LORD [t]determined to destroy *thought*
The wall of the daughter of
Zion.
He has stretched out a line,
He has not restrained His
hand from destroying;
And He has caused rampart
and wall to lament;
They have languished to-
gether.
9 Her [r]gates have sunk into the
ground, Neh. 1:3
He has destroyed and broken
her bars.

Her king and her princes are among the nations;
The [r]law is no more; Hos. 3:4
Also, her prophets find
No vision from the LORD.
10 The elders of the daughter of Zion
[r]Sit on the ground, they are silent. Job 2:13; Is. 3:26; 47:1
They have thrown [r]dust on their heads; Job 2:12
They have girded themselves with [r]sackcloth. Is. 15:3
The virgins of Jerusalem
Have bowed their heads to the ground.
11 My eyes fail because of tears,
My spirit is greatly troubled;
My [t]heart is poured out on the earth, *liver*
[r]Because of the [t]destruction of the daughter of my people, Is. 22:4 • *breaking*
When [r]little ones and infants faint Jer. 44:7; Lam. 2:19
In the streets of the city.
12 They say to their mothers,
"Where is grain and wine?"
As they faint like a wounded man
In the streets of the city,
As their life is poured out
On their mothers' bosom.
13 How shall I admonish you?
To what shall I compare you,
O daughter of Jerusalem?
To what shall I liken you as I comfort you,
O virgin daughter of Zion?
For your [t]ruin is as vast as the sea; *breaking*
Who can heal you?
14 Your [r]prophets have seen for you Jer. 23:25-29; 29:8, 9
False and foolish visions;
And they have not [r]exposed your iniquity Ezek. 23:36
So as to restore you from captivity,
But they have [r]seen for you false and misleading oracles. Ezek. 22:25, 28
15 All who pass along the way
[r]Clap their hands *in derision* at you; Job 27:23
They [r]hiss and shake their heads Jer. 18:16; 19:8
At the daughter of Jerusalem,
"Is this the city of which they said,
'The perfection of beauty,
A joy to all the earth'?"
16 All [r]your enemies Ps. 22:13
Have opened their mouths wide against you;
They hiss and [r]gnash *their* teeth. Ps. 35:16; 37:12
They say, "We have [r]swallowed *her* up! Ps. 56:2
Surely this is the day for which we waited;
We have reached *it*, we have seen *it*."
17 The LORD has [r]done what He purposed; Jer. 4:28
He has accomplished His word
Which He commanded from days of old.
He has thrown down [r]without sparing, Ezek. 5:11; 7:8, 9
And He has caused the enemy to rejoice over you;
He has exalted the might of your adversaries.
18 Their [r]heart cried out to the Lord, Ps. 119:145; Hos. 7:14
"O [r]wall of the daughter of Zion, Lam. 2:8; Hab. 2:11

Let *your* tears run down like
a river day and night;
Give yourself no relief;
Let your eyes have no rest.
19 "Arise, cry aloud in the night
At the beginning of the night
watches;
ʳPour out your heart like water Ps. 42:4; 62:8
Before the presence of the
Lord;
Lift up your hands to Him
For the life of your little ones
Who are ʳfaint because of
hunger Is. 51:20
At the head of every street."
20 See, O LORD, and look!
With ʳwhom hast Thou dealt
thus? Ex. 32:11; Deut. 9:26
Should women ʳeat their offspring, Jer. 19:9; Lam. 4:10
The little ones who were
born healthy?
Should ʳpriest and prophet be
slain Jer. 14:15; 23:11, 12
In the sanctuary of the Lord?
21 On the ground in the streets
Lie ʳyoung and old, Jer. 6:11
My ʳvirgins and my young
men Ps. 78:62, 63
Have fallen by the sword.
Thou hast slain *them* in the
day of Thine anger,
Thou hast slaughtered, ʳnot
sparing. Zech. 11:6
22 Thou didst call as in the day
of an appointed feast
My terrors on every side;
And there was no one who
escaped or survived
In the day of the LORD's anger.
Those ʳwhom I bore and
reared, Jer. 16:2-4; 44:7
My enemy annihilated them.

CHAPTER 3

I AM the man who has ʳseen affliction Ps. 88:7, 15, 16
Because of the rod of His
wrath.
2 He has driven me and made
me walk
In darkness and not in light.
3 Surely against me He has
turned His hand
Repeatedly all the day.
4 He has caused my flesh and
my skin to waste away,
He has broken my bones.
5 He has besieged and encompassed me with bitterness and hardship.
6 In ʳdark places He has made
me dwell, Ps. 88:5, 6; 143:3
Like those who have long
been dead.
7 He has ʳwalled *me* in so that I
cannot go out; Job 3:23
He has made my ᵗchain
heavy. *bronze piece*
8 Even when I cry out and call
for help,
He shuts out my prayer.
9 He has blocked my ways
with hewn stone;
He has made my paths
crooked.
10 He is to me like a bear lying
in wait,
Like a lion in secret places.
11 He has turned aside my ways
and torn me to pieces;
He has made me desolate.
12 He ʳbent His bow Ps. 7:12
And ʳset me as a target for
the arrow. Job 6:4; 7:20
13 He made the ᵗarrows of His
ʳquiver *sons* • Jer. 5:16
To enter into my ᵗinward
parts. *kidneys*

14 I have become a laughingstock to all my people,
Their *mocking* [r]song all the day. Job 30:9; Lam. 3:63
15 He has [r]filled me with bitterness, Jer. 9:15
He has made me drunk with wormwood.
16 And He has [r]broken my teeth with gravel; Ps. 3:7; 58:6
He has made me cower in the [r]dust. Jer. 6:26
17 And my soul has been rejected from peace;
I have forgotten happiness.
18 So I say, "My strength has perished,
And *so has* my [r]hope from the LORD." Job 17:15; Ezek. 37:11

19 Remember my affliction and my wandering, the [r]wormwood and bitterness. Jer. 9:15
20 Surely my soul remembers
And is [r]bowed down within me. Ps. 42:5, 6, 11; 43:5
21 This I recall to my mind,
Therefore I have hope.
22 The LORD's lovingkindnesses indeed never cease,
[r]For His compassions never fail. Mal. 3:6
23 *They* are new every morning;
Great is Thy faithfulness.
24 "The LORD is my [r]portion," says my soul, Ps. 16:5
"Therefore I [r]have hope in Him." Ps. 33:18
25 The LORD is good to those who [r]wait for Him, Is. 25:9
To the [t]person who [r]seeks Him. *soul* • Is. 26:9
26 *It is* good that he [r]waits silently Ps. 37:7
For the salvation of the LORD.
27 *It is* good for a man that he should bear
The yoke in his youth.
28 Let him [r]sit alone and be silent Jer. 15:17
Since He has laid *it* on him.
29 Let him [t]put his mouth in the [r]dust, *give* • Job 16:15
Perhaps there is hope.
30 Let him give his [r]cheek to the smiter; Job 16:10; Is. 50:6
Let him be filled with reproach.
31 For the Lord will [r]not reject forever, Ps. 77:7; 94:14
32 For if He causes grief,
Then He will have [r]compassion Ps. 78:38; 106:43-45
According to His abundant lovingkindness.
33 For He does not afflict [t]willingly, *from His heart*
Or grieve the sons of men.
34 To crush under His feet
All the prisoners of the land,
35 To deprive a man of justice
In the presence of the Most High,
36 To [t]defraud a man in his lawsuit— *make crooked*
Of these things the Lord does not [t]approve. *see*
37 Who is [t]there who speaks and it comes to pass, *this*
Unless the Lord has commanded *it*?
38 *Is it* not from the mouth of the Most High
That [r]both good and ill go forth? Job 2:10; Is. 45:7

39 Why should *any* living mortal, or *any* man,

Offer complaint [a]in view of
his sins? *on the basis of*
40 Let us [r]examine and probe
our ways, Ps. 119:59
And let us return to the
LORD.
41 We [r]lift up our heart and
hands Ps. 25:1; 28:2
Toward God in heaven;
42 We have [r]transgressed and
rebelled, Neh. 9:26
Thou hast not pardoned.
43 Thou hast covered *Thyself*
with [r]anger Lam. 2:21
And [r]pursued us; Ps. 83:15
Thou hast slain *and* [r]hast not
spared. Lam. 2:2, 17, 21
44 Thou hast [r]covered Thyself
with a cloud Ps. 97:2
So that [r]no prayer can pass
through. Lam. 3:8; Zech. 7:13
45 *Mere* offscouring and refuse
Thou hast made us
In the midst of the peoples.
46 All our enemies have opened
their mouths against us.
47 [r]Panic and pitfall have befall-
en us, Is. 24:17, 18
Devastation and destruction;
48 My eyes run down with
streams of water
Because of the destruction of
the daughter of my peo-
ple.
49 My eyes pour down [r]unceas-
ingly, Ps. 77:2; Jer. 14:17
Without stopping,
50 Until the LORD looks down
And sees from heaven.
51 My eyes bring pain to my
soul
Because of all the daughters
of my city.
52 My enemies without cause
Hunted me down like a bird;
53 They have silenced [t]me [r]in the
pit *my life* • Jer. 37:16
And have [a]placed a stone on
me. *cast stones*
54 Waters flowed over my head;
I said, "I am cut off!"
55 I [r]called on Thy name, O
LORD, Ps. 130:1; Jon. 2:2
Out of the lowest pit.
56 Thou hast heard my voice,
"Do not hide Thine ear from
my *prayer for* relief,
From my cry for help."
57 Thou didst [r]draw near when I
called on Thee; Ps. 145:18
Thou didst say, "Do not
fear!"
58 O Lord, Thou didst plead my
soul's cause;
Thou hast redeemed my life.
59 O LORD, Thou hast [r]seen my
oppression; Jer. 18:19, 20
[r]Judge my case. Ps. 26:1
60 Thou hast seen all their vengeance,
All their schemes against me.
61 Thou hast heard their reproach, O LORD,
All their schemes against me.
62 The lips of my assailants and
their whispering
Are against me all day long.
63 Look on their [r]sitting and
their rising; Ps. 139:2
I am their mocking song.
64 Thou wilt [r]recompense them,
O LORD, Jer. 51:6, 24, 56
According to the work of
their hands.
65 Thou wilt give them [a]hard-
ness of heart, *insolence*
Thy curse will be on them.
66 Thou wilt pursue them in anger and destroy them
From under the [r]heavens of
the LORD! Ps. 8:3

CHAPTER 4

HOW dark the gold has become,
How the pure gold has changed!
The sacred stones are poured out
At the corner of every street.
2 The precious sons of Zion,
Weighed against fine gold,
How they are regarded as [r]earthen jars, Is. 30:14
The work of a potter's hands!
3 Even jackals offer the breast,
They nurse their young;
But the daughter of my people has become cruel
Like [r]ostriches in the wilderness. Job 39:14-17
4 The [r]tongue of the infant cleaves Ps. 22:15
To the roof of its mouth because of thirst;
The little ones [r]ask for bread,
But no one breaks *it* for them. Lam. 2:12
5 Those who ate delicacies
Are desolate in the streets;
Those reared in purple
Embrace ash pits.
6 For the iniquity of the daughter of my people
Is greater than the [a]sin of Sodom, *punishment for sin*
Which was [r]overthrown as in a moment, Gen. 19:25
And no hands were [a]turned toward her. *wrung over her*
7 Her consecrated ones were purer than snow,
They were whiter than milk;
They were more ruddy *in* body than corals,
Their polishing *was* like lapis lazuli.
8 Their appearance is [r]blacker than soot, Job 30:30
They are not recognized in the streets;
Their [r]skin is shriveled on their bones, Job 19:20
It is withered, it has become like wood.
9 Better are those [r]slain with the sword Jer. 16:4
Than those [t]slain with hunger; *pierced*
For they [t]pine away, being stricken *flow away*
For lack of the fruits of [t]the field. *my fields*
10 The hands of compassionate women
Boiled their own children;
They became food for them
Because of the destruction of the daughter of my people.
11 The LORD has [r]accomplished His wrath, Jer. 7:20
He has poured out His fierce anger;
And He has [r]kindled a fire in Zion Deut. 32:22; Jer. 17:27
Which has consumed its foundations.
12 The kings of the earth did not believe,
Nor *did* any of the inhabitants of the world,
That the adversary and the enemy
Could [r]enter the gates of Jerusalem. Jer. 21:13
13 Because of the sins of her [r]prophets Jer. 5:31; 6:13
And the iniquities of her priests,
Who have shed in her midst
The blood of the righteous,

14 They wandered, [r]blind, in the
streets; Deut. 28:28, 29
They were defiled with blood
So that no one could touch
their [r]garments. Jer. 2:34
15 "Depart! [r]Unclean!" they cried
of themselves.
"Depart, depart, do not
touch!" Lev. 13:45, 46
So they fled and wandered;
Men among the nations said,
"They shall not continue to
dwell *with us.*"
16 The presence of the LORD has
scattered them;
He will not continue to regard
them.
They did not [r]honor the
priests, Jer. 52:24-27
They did not favor the elders.
17 Yet our eyes failed;
Looking for help was useless.
In our watching we have
watched
For a [r]nation that could not
save. Ezek. 29:6, 7, 16
18 They hunted our steps
So that we could not walk in
our streets;
Our end drew near,
Our days were finished
For our end had come.
19 Our pursuers were swifter
Than the eagles of the sky.
They chased us on the mountains;
They waited in ambush for
us in the wilderness.
20 The breath of our nostrils,
the LORD's anointed,
Was captured in their pits,
Of whom we had said, "Under
his [r]shadow Dan. 4:12
We shall live among the nations."
21 Rejoice and be glad, O
daughter of Edom,
Who dwells in the land of Uz;
But the [r]cup will come around
to you as well, Obad. 16
You will become drunk and
make yourself naked.
22 *The punishment* of your iniquity
has been completed,
O daughter of Zion;
He will exile you no longer.
But He [r]will punish your iniquity,
O daughter of
Edom; Jer. 49:10; Mal. 1:3, 4
He will expose your sins!

CHAPTER 5

REMEMBER, O LORD, what has
befallen us;
Look, and see our reproach!
2 Our inheritance has been
turned over to strangers,
Our houses to aliens.
3 We have become orphans
without a father,
Our mothers are like widows.
4 We have to pay for our
drinking [r]water, Is. 3:1
Our wood comes *to us* at a
price.
5 Our pursuers are at our
necks;
We are worn out, there is [r]no
rest for us. Neh. 9:36, 37
6 We have submitted to [r]Egypt
and Assyria to get
enough bread. Hos. 9:3
7 Our [r]fathers sinned, *and* are
no more; Jer. 14:20; 16:12
It is we who have borne their
iniquities.
8 Slaves rule over us;
There is no one to deliver us
from their hand.

9 We get our bread [t]at the risk
of our lives *with our soul*
[a]Because of the sword in the
wilderness. *In the face of*
10 Our skin has become as [r]hot
as an oven, Job 30:30
Because of the burning heat
of famine.
11 They ravished the [r]women in
Zion, Is. 13:16; Zech. 14:2
The virgins in the cities of Judah.
12 Princes were hung by their
hands;
Elders were not respected.
13 Young men [t]worked at the
grinding mill; *carry*
And youths [r]stumbled under
loads of wood. Jer. 7:18
14 Elders [t]are gone from the
gate, *have ceased*
Young men from their music.
15 The joy of our hearts has
[r]ceased; Jer. 25:10; Amos 8:10
Our dancing has been turned
into mourning.
16 The [r]crown has fallen from
our head; Ps. 89:39
[r]Woe to us, for we have
sinned! Is. 3:9-11
17 Because of this our [r]heart is
faint; Is. 1:5
Because of these things our
[r]eyes are dim; Job 17:7
18 Because of Mount Zion
which lies desolate,
[r]Foxes prowl in it. Neh. 4:3

19 Thou, O LORD, dost [t]rule forever; *sit*
Thy throne is from generation to generation.
20 Why dost Thou [r]forget us forever; Ps. 13:1; 44:24
Why dost Thou forsake us so
long?
21 Restore us to Thee, O LORD,
that we may be restored;
Renew our days as of old,
22 Unless [r]Thou hast utterly rejected us, Ps. 60:1, 2
And art exceedingly [r]angry
with us. Is. 64:9

THE BOOK OF

EZEKIEL

NOW it came about in the thirtieth year, on the fifth *day* of the
fourth month, while I was by the
[r]river Chebar among the exiles, the
heavens were opened and I saw
visions of God. Ezek. 3:23
2 (On the fifth of the month in
the [r]fifth year of King Jehoiachin's
exile, 2 Kin. 24:12-15
3 the [r]word of the LORD came
expressly to Ezekiel the priest,
son of Buzi, in the land of the
Chaldeans by the river Chebar;
and there the hand of the LORD
came upon him.) 2 Pet. 1:21
4 And as I looked, behold, a
storm wind was coming from the
north, a great cloud with fire
flashing forth continually and a
bright light around it, and in its
midst something like glowing
metal in the midst of the fire.
5 And within it there were figures resembling four living be-

ings. And this was their appearance: they had human form.
6 Each of them had [r]four faces
and four wings. Ezek. 1:10; 10:14, 21
7 And their legs were straight
and [t]their feet were like a calf's
hoof, and they gleamed like burnished bronze. *the soles of their feet*
8 Under their wings on their
[r]four sides *were* human hands. As
for the faces and wings of the four
of them, Ezek. 1:17; 10:11
9 their wings touched one another; their *faces* did [r]not turn
when they moved, each went
straight forward. Ezek. 1:17
10 As for the form of their
faces, *each* had the face of a man,
[t]all four had the face of a lion on
the right and the face of a bull on
the left, and all four had the face
of an eagle. *the four of them*
11 Such were their faces. Their
wings were spread out above;
each had two touching another
being, and [r]two covering their bodies. Is. 6:2; Ezek. 1:23
12 And [r]each went straight forward; wherever the spirit was
about to go, they would go, without turning as they went. Ezek. 1:9
13 In the midst of the living beings there was something that
looked like burning coals of [r]fire,
like torches darting back and
forth among the living beings. The
fire was bright, and lightning was
flashing from the fire. Ps. 104:4
14 And the living beings ran to
and fro like bolts of lightning.
15 Now as I looked at the living
beings, behold, there was one
[r]wheel on the earth beside the living beings, for *each of* the four of
them. Ezek. 1:19-21; 10:9
16 The [r]appearance of the
wheels and their workmanship
was like sparkling beryl, and all
four of them had the same form,
their appearance and workmanship *being* as if one wheel were
within another. Ezek. 10:9-11
17 Whenever they [t]moved, they
moved in any of their four [t]direc-
tions, without turning as they
moved. *went • sides*
18 As for their rims they were
lofty and awesome, and the rims
of all four of them were [r]full of
eyes round about. Rev. 4:6, 8
19 And [r]whenever the living beings moved, the wheels moved
with them. And whenever the living beings rose from the earth, the
wheels rose *also.* Ezek. 10:16
20 [r]Wherever the spirit was
about to go, they would go in that
direction. And the wheels rose
close beside them; for the spirit of
the living beings *was* in the
wheels. Ezek. 1:12
21 [r]Whenever those went, these
went; and whenever those stood
still, these stood still. And whenever those rose from the earth, the
wheels rose close beside them; for
the spirit of the living beings *was*
in the wheels. Ezek. 10:17
22 Now [r]over the heads of the
living beings *there was* something
like an expanse, like the awesome
gleam of [a]crystal, extended over
their heads. Ezek. 10:1 • *ice*
23 And under the expanse their
wings *were stretched out* straight,
one toward the other; each one
also had [r]two wings covering their
bodies on the one side and on the
other. Ezek. 1:6, 11
24 I also heard the sound of
their wings like the [r]sound of
abundant waters as they went,

like the voice of the Almighty, a sound of tumult like the sound of an army camp; whenever they stood still, they dropped their wings. Rev. 1:15; 19:6

25 And there came a voice from above the expanse that was over their heads; whenever they stood still, they dropped their wings.

26 Now above the expanse that was over their heads there was something resembling a throne, like lapis lazuli in appearance; and on that which resembled a throne, high up, *was* a figure with the appearance of a man. Ezek. 1:22; 10:1

27 Then I noticed from the appearance of His loins and upward something like glowing metal that looked like fire all around within it, and from the appearance of His loins and downward I saw something like fire; and *there was* a radiance around Him. *saw*

28 As the appearance of the rainbow in the clouds on a rainy day, so *was* the appearance of the surrounding radiance. Such *was* the appearance of the likeness of the glory of the LORD. And when I saw *it,* I fell on my face and heard a voice speaking. *which occurs in*

CHAPTER 2

THEN He said to me, "Son of man, stand on your feet that I may speak with you!" Dan. 10:11

2 And as He spoke to me the Spirit entered me and set me on my feet; and I heard *Him* speaking to me. Ezek. 3:24; Dan. 8:18

3 Then He said to me, "Son of man, I am sending you to the sons of Israel, to a rebellious people who have rebelled against Me; they and their fathers have transgressed against Me to this very day. 1 Sam. 8:7, 8; Jer. 3:25

4 "And I am sending you to them who are stubborn and obstinate children; and you shall say to them, 'Thus says the Lord GOD.'

5 "As for them, whether they listen or not—for they are a rebellious house—they will know that a prophet has been among them.

6 "And you, son of man, neither fear them nor fear their words, though thistles and thorns are with you and you sit on scorpions; neither fear their words nor be dismayed at their presence, for they are a rebellious house.

7 "But you shall speak My words to them whether they listen or not, for they are rebellious.

8 "Now you, son of man, listen to what I am speaking to you; do not be rebellious like that rebellious house. Open your mouth and eat what I am giving you."

9 Then I looked, behold, a hand was extended to me; and lo, a scroll *was* in it. *scroll of a book*

10 When He spread it out before me, it was written on the front and back; and written on it were lamentations, mourning and woe. Is. 3:11; Rev. 8:13

CHAPTER 3

THEN He said to me, "Son of man, eat what you find; eat this scroll, and go, speak to the house of Israel." Ezek. 2:9

2 So I opened my mouth, and He fed me this scroll. Jer. 25:17

3 And He said to me, "Son of man, feed your stomach, and fill your body with this scroll which I

am giving you." Then I ate it, and
it was sweet as honey in my
mouth. Jer. 6:11; 20:9
4 Then He said to me, "Son of
man, go to the house of Israel and
speak with My words to them.
5 "For [r]you are not being sent to
a people of unintelligible speech
or difficult language, *but* to the
house of Israel, Acts 14:11; 26:17
6 nor to many peoples of unintelligible speech or difficult language, whose words you cannot
understand. But I have sent you to
them who should listen to you;
7 yet the house of Israel will
not be willing to listen to you,
since they are not willing to listen
to Me. Surely the whole house of
Israel is stubborn and obstinate.
8 "Behold, I have made your
face as hard as their faces, and
your forehead as hard as their
foreheads.
9 "Like [t]emery harder than flint I
have made your forehead. Do not
be afraid of them or be dismayed
before them, though they are a rebellious house." *corundum*
10 Moreover, He said to me,
"Son of man, take into your heart
all My [r]words which I shall speak
to you, and listen closely. Job 22:22
11 "And [t]go to the exiles, to the
sons of your people, and speak to
them and tell them, whether they
listen or [t]not, 'Thus says the Lord
GOD.'" *go, come* • *forbear*
12 Then the Spirit lifted me up,
and I heard a great rumbling
sound behind me, "Blessed be the
glory of the LORD in His place."
13 And I *heard* the sound of the
wings of the living beings touching one another, and the sound of
the [r]wheels beside them, even a
great rumbling sound. Ezek. 1:15
14 So the Spirit lifted me up and
took me away; and I went embittered in the rage of my spirit, and
[r]the hand of the LORD was strong
on me. 2 Kin. 3:15
15 Then I came to the exiles
who lived beside the river Chebar
at Tel-abib, and I sat there seven
days where they were living, causing consternation among them.
16 Now it came about at the
end of seven days that the word of
the LORD came to me, saying,
17 "Son of man, I have appointed
you a [r]watchman to the house of
Israel; whenever you hear a word
from My mouth, warn them from
Me. Is. 52:8; 56:10; 62:6
18 "When I say to the wicked,
'You shall surely die'; and you do
not warn him or speak out to
warn the wicked from his wicked
way that he may live, that wicked
man shall die in his iniquity, but
his [r]blood I will require at your
hand. Ezek. 3:20; 33:6, 8
19 "Yet if you have warned the
wicked, and he does not turn from
his wickedness or from his wicked
way, he shall die in his iniquity;
but you have delivered yourself.
20 "Again, [r]when a righteous man
turns away from his righteousness
and commits iniquity, and I place
an [r]obstacle before him, he shall
die; since you have not warned
him, he shall die in his sin, and his
righteous deeds which he has
done shall not be remembered;
but his blood I will require at your
hand. Ps. 125:5; Zeph. 1:6 • Is. 8:14
21 "However, if you have warned
the righteous man that the righteous should not sin, and he does

not sin, he shall surely live because he took warning; and you
have delivered yourself."
22 And the hand of the LORD
was on me there, and He said to
me, "Get up, go out to the plain,
and there I will speak to you."
23 So I got up and went out to
the plain; and behold, the glory of
the LORD was standing there, like
the glory which I saw by the river
Chebar, and I fell on my face.
24 The [r]Spirit then entered me
and made me stand on my feet,
and He spoke with me and said to
me, "Go, shut yourself up in your
house. Ezek. 2:2
25 "As for you, son of man, they
will [r]put ropes on you and bind you
with them, so that you cannot go
out among them. Ezek. 4:8
26 "Moreover, [r]I will make your
tongue stick to [t]the roof of your
mouth so that you will be dumb,
and cannot be a man who rebukes
them, for they are a rebellious
house. Luke 1:20, 22 • *your palate*
27 "But [r]when I speak to you, I
will open your mouth, and you
will say to them, 'Thus says the
Lord GOD.' He who hears, let him
hear; and he who refuses, let him
refuse; for they are a rebellious
house. Ezek. 24:27; 33:22

CHAPTER 4

"NOW you son of man, [r]get yourself a brick, place it before you,
and inscribe a city on it, Jerusalem. Is. 20:2; Jer. 13:1
2 "Then lay siege against it,
build a siege wall, raise up a ramp,
pitch camps, and place battering
rams against it all around.
3 "Then get yourself an iron
plate and set it up as an iron wall
between you and the city, and set
your face toward it so that it is under siege, and besiege it. This is a
sign to the house of Israel.
4 "As for you, lie down on your
left side, and lay the iniquity of
the house of Israel on it; you shall
bear their iniquity for the number
of days that you lie on it.
5 "For I have assigned you a
number of days corresponding to
the years of their iniquity, three
hundred and ninety days; thus [r]you
shall bear the iniquity of the house
of Israel. Num. 14:34
6 "When you have completed
these, you shall lie down a second
time, *but* on your right side, and
bear the iniquity of the house of
Judah; I have assigned it to you
for forty days, a day for each year.
7 "Then you shall set your face
toward the siege of Jerusalem
with your arm bared, and [r]proph-
esy against it. Ezek. 21:2
8 "Now behold, I will [r]put ropes
on you so that you cannot turn
from one side to the other, until
you have completed the days of
your siege. Ezek. 3:25
9 "But as for you, take wheat,
barley, beans, lentils, millet and
[r]spelt, put them in one vessel and
make them into bread for yourself; you shall eat it according to
the number of the days that you
lie on your side, three hundred
and ninety days. Ex. 9:32; Is. 28:25
10 "And your food which you eat
shall be [r]twenty shekels a day by
weight; you shall eat it from time
to time. Ezek. 45:12
11 "And the water you drink will
be the sixth part of a hin by mea-

sure; you shall drink it from time
to time.
12 "And you shall eat it as a barley cake, having baked *it* in their
sight over human [r]dung." Is. 36:12
13 Then the LORD said, "Thus
shall the sons of Israel eat their
bread unclean among the nations
where I shall banish them."
14 But I said, "Ah,[r] Lord GOD!
Behold, I have [r]never been defiled;
for from my youth until now I
have never eaten what died of itself or was torn by beasts, nor has
any unclean meat ever entered my
mouth." Jer. 1:6 • Acts 10:14
15 Then He said to me, "See, I
shall give you cow's dung in place
of human dung over which you
will prepare your bread."
16 Moreover, He said to me,
"Son of man, behold, I am going
to [r]break the staff of bread in Jerusalem, and they will eat bread by
weight and with anxiety, and
drink water by measure and in
horror, Lev. 26:26; Is. 3:1
17 because bread and water will
be scarce; and they will be appalled with one another and [r]waste
away in their iniquity. Lev. 26:39

CHAPTER 5

"AS for you, son of man, take a
[r]sharp sword; take and use it *as* a
barber's razor on your head and
beard. Then take scales for weighing and divide the hair. Is. 7:20
2 "One third you shall burn in
the fire at the center of the city,
when the [r]days of the siege are
completed. Then you shall take
one third and strike *it* with the
sword all around [t]the city, and one
third you shall scatter to the wind;
and I will unsheathe a sword behind them. Jer. 39:1, 2 • *it*
3 "Take also a few in number
from [t]them and bind them in the
edges of your *robes*. *there*
4 "And take again some of them
and throw them into the fire, and
burn them in the fire; from it a fire
will [t]spread to all the house of Israel. *go out*
5 "Thus says the Lord GOD,
'This is Jerusalem; I have set her
at the center of the nations, with
lands around her.
6 'But she has rebelled against
My ordinances more wickedly
than the nations and against My
statutes more than the lands
which surround her; for they have
rejected My ordinances and have
not walked in My statutes.'
7 "Therefore, thus says the Lord
GOD, 'Because you have [r]more turmoil than the nations which surround you, and have not walked in
My statutes, nor observed My ordinances, nor observed the ordinances of the nations which surround you,' 2 Kin. 21:9-11
8 therefore, thus says the Lord
GOD, 'Behold, I, even I, am [r]against
you, and I will [r]execute judgments
among you in the sight of the nations. Jer. 21:5 • Jer. 24:9
9 'And because of all your
abominations, I will do among
you what I have not done, and the
like of which I will never do again.
10 'Therefore, [r]fathers will eat
their sons among you, and sons
will eat their fathers; for I will execute judgments on you, and [r]scat-
ter all your remnant to every
wind. Lev. 26:29 • Zech. 2:6; 7:14
11 'So as I live,' declares the
Lord GOD, 'surely, because you

have [r]defiled My sanctuary with all your [r]detestable idols and with all your abominations, therefore I will also withdraw, and My eye shall have no pity and I will not spare. Jer. 7:9-11 • Jer. 16:18

12 'One third of you will die by [r]plague or be consumed by famine among you, one third will fall by the sword around you, and one third I will scatter to every wind, and I will unsheathe a sword behind them. Jer. 15:2; 21:9

13 'Thus My anger will be spent, and I will [t]satisfy My wrath on them, and I shall be [t]appeased; then they will know that I, the LORD, have spoken in My zeal when I have spent My wrath upon them. *cause to rest* • *comforted*

14 'Moreover, I will make you a desolation and a reproach among the nations which surround you, in the sight of all who pass by.

15 'So it will be a reproach, a reviling, a [r]warning and an object of horror to the nations who surround you, when I execute judgments against you in anger, wrath, and raging rebukes. I, the LORD, have spoken. Is. 26:9

16 'When I send against them the [t]deadly arrows of famine which were for the destruction of those whom I shall send to destroy you, then I shall also intensify the famine upon you, and break the staff of bread. *evil*

17 'Moreover, [r]I will send on you famine and wild beasts, and they will bereave you of children; plague and bloodshed also will pass through you, and I will bring the sword on you. I, the LORD, have spoken.' " Rev. 6:8

CHAPTER 6

AND the word of the LORD came to me saying,

2 "Son of man, set your face toward the mountains of Israel, and prophesy against them,

3 and say, 'Mountains of Israel, listen to the word of the Lord GOD! Thus says the Lord GOD to the mountains, the hills, the ravines and the valleys: "Behold, I Myself am going to bring a sword on you, and [r]I will destroy your high places. Lev. 26:30

4 "So your [r]altars will become desolate, and your incense altars will be smashed; and I shall make your slain fall in front of your idols. Lev. 26:30; 2 Chr. 14:5; Is. 27:9

5 "I shall also lay the dead bodies of the sons of Israel in front of their idols; and I shall scatter your bones around your altars.

6 "In all your dwellings, [r]cities will become waste and the high places will be desolate, that your altars may become waste and desolate, your [r]idols may be broken and brought to an end, your incense altars may be cut down, and your works may be blotted out. Lev. 26:31; Is. 6:11 • Mic. 1:7

7 "And the slain will fall among you, and you will know that I am the LORD.

8 "However, I shall leave a [r]remnant, for you will have those who escaped the sword among the nations when you are scattered among the countries. Is. 6:13

9 "Then those of you who escape will [r]remember Me among the nations to which they will be carried captive, how I have been hurt by their adulterous hearts

which turned away from Me, and
by their eyes, which played the
harlot after their idols; and they
will loathe themselves in their
own sight for the evils which they
have committed, for all their
abominations. Deut. 4:29; 30:2
10 "Then they will know that I
am the LORD; I have not said in
vain [t]that I would inflict this disaster on them." ' *to do this evil to*
11 "Thus says the Lord GOD,
'Clap your hand, [r]stamp your foot,
and say, "Alas, because of all the
evil abominations of the house of
Israel, which will fall by sword,
famine, and plague! Ezek. 25:6
12 "He who is [r]far off will die by
the plague, and he who is near will
fall by the sword, and he who remains and is besieged will die by
the famine. Thus shall I [r]spend My
wrath on them. Dan. 9:7 • Lam. 4:11, 22
13 "Then you will know that I am
the LORD, when their [r]slain are
among their idols around their altars, on [r]every high hill, on all the
tops of the mountains, under every green tree, and under every
leafy oak—the places where they
offered soothing aroma to all their
idols. Ezek. 6:4-7 • 1 Kin. 14:23
14 "So throughout all their habitations I shall [r]stretch out My hand
against them and make the land
more desolate and waste than the
wilderness toward Diblah; thus
they will know that I am the
LORD." ' " Is. 5:25; 9:12; Ezek. 14:13

CHAPTER 7

MOREOVER, the word of the
LORD came to me saying,
2 "And you, son of man, thus
says the Lord GOD to the land of
Israel, 'An end! The end is coming
on the four corners of the land.
3 'Now the end is upon you,
and I shall send My anger against
you; I shall judge you according to
your ways, and I shall bring all
your abominations upon you.
4 'For My eye will have no pity
on you, nor shall I spare *you,* but I
shall [r]bring your ways upon you,
and your abominations will be
among you; then you will know
that I am the LORD!' Hos. 9:7
5 "Thus says the Lord GOD, 'A
[r]disaster, unique disaster, behold it
is coming! 2 Kin. 21:12, 13
6 'An end is coming; the end
has come! It has awakened
against you; behold, it has come!
7 'Your doom has come to you,
O inhabitant of the land. The [r]time
has come, the [r]day is near—tumult
rather than joyful shouting on the
mountains. Ezek. 7:12 • Is. 22:5
8 'Now I will shortly pour out
My wrath on you, and spend My
anger against you, judge you according to your ways, and bring
on you all your abominations.
9 'And My eye will show no
pity, nor will I spare. I will [t]repay
you according to your ways, while
your abominations are in your
midst; then you will know that I,
the LORD, do the smiting. *give*
10 'Behold, the day! Behold, it is
coming! *Your* doom has gone
forth; the [r]rod has budded, arrogance has blossomed. Ps. 89:32
11 'Violence has grown into a
rod of wickedness. None of them
shall remain, none of their multitude, none of their wealth, nor
anything eminent among them.
12 'The [r]time has come, the day
has arrived. Let not the buyer re-

joice nor the seller mourn; for
wrath is against all their multitude. Ezek. 7:5-7, 10; 1 Cor. 7:29-31
13 'Indeed, the seller will not regain what he sold as long as they
both live; for the vision regarding
all their multitude will not be
averted, nor will any of them
maintain his life by his iniquity.
14 'They have [r]blown the trumpet and made everything ready,
but no one is going to the battle;
for My wrath is against all [t]their
multitude. Num. 10:9; Jer. 4:5 • *her*
15 'The [r]sword is outside, and the
plague and the famine are within.
He who is in the field will die by
the sword; famine and the plague
will also consume those in the
city. Ezek. 5:12; 6:11, 12; 12:16
16 'Even when their survivors
[r]escape, they will be on the mountains like doves of the valleys, all
of them [t]mourning, each over his
own iniquity. Ezra 9:15 • *moaning*
17 'All hands will hang limp, and
all knees will become like water.
18 'And they will gird themselves with sackcloth, and shuddering will overwhelm them; and
shame *will be* on all faces, and
baldness on all their heads.
19 'They shall [r]fling their silver
into the streets, and their gold
shall become an abhorrent thing;
their silver and their gold shall not
be able to deliver them in the day
of the wrath of the LORD. They
cannot satisfy their appetite, nor
can they fill their stomachs, for
their iniquity has become an occasion of stumbling. Is. 2:20; 30:22
20 'And they transformed the
beauty of His ornaments into
pride, and [r]they made the images
of their abominations *and* their
detestable things with it; therefore
I will make it an abhorrent thing
to them. Jer. 7:30
21 'And I shall give it into the
hands of the foreigners as plunder
and to the wicked of the earth as
spoil, and they will profane it.
22 'I shall also turn My [r]face from
them, and they will profane My
secret place; then robbers will enter and profane it. Jer. 18:17
23 'Make[r] the chain, for the land
is full of bloody crimes, and the
city is full of violence. Jer. 27:2
24 'Therefore, I shall bring the
worst of the nations, and they will
possess their houses. I shall also
make the pride of the strong ones
cease, and their [r]holy places will
be profaned. 2 Chr. 7:20
25 'When anguish comes, they
will seek [r]peace, but there will be
none. Ezek. 13:10, 16
26 'Disaster[r] will come upon disaster, and rumor will be *added* to
rumor; then they will seek a vision
from a prophet, but the [r]law will
be lost from the priest and counsel
from the elders. Is. 47:11 • Mic. 3:6
27 'The king will mourn, the
prince will be clothed with horror,
and the hands of the people of the
land will tremble. According to
their conduct I shall deal with
them, and by their judgments I
shall judge them. And they will
know that I am the LORD.' "

CHAPTER 8

AND it came about in the sixth
year, on the fifth *day* of the sixth
month, as I was sitting in my
house with the elders of Judah sitting before me, that the hand of
the Lord GOD fell on me there.

2 Then I looked, and behold, a likeness as the appearance of a man; from His loins and downward *there was* the appearance of fire, and from His loins and upward the appearance of brightness, like the appearance of[a]glowing metal. *electrum*

3 And He stretched out the form of a hand and caught me by a lock of my head; and the Spirit lifted me up between earth and heaven and brought me in the visions of God to Jerusalem, to the entrance of the north gate of the inner *court,* where the seat of the idol of jealousy, which provokes to jealousy, was *located.*

4 And behold, the [r]glory of the God of Israel *was* there, like the appearance which I saw in the plain. Ezek. 1:28; 3:22, 23

5 Then He said to me, "Son of man, raise your eyes, now, toward the north." So I raised my eyes toward the north, and behold, to the north of the altar gate *was* this idol of jealousy at the entrance.

6 And He said to me, "Son of man, do you see what they are doing, the great [r]abominations which the house of Israel are committing here, that I should be far from My sanctuary? But yet you will see still greater abominations." 2 Kin. 23:4, 5; Ezek. 5:11

7 Then He brought me to the entrance of the court, and when I looked, behold, a hole in the wall.

8 And He said to me, "Son of man, now [r]dig through the wall." So I dug through the wall, and behold, an entrance. Is. 29:15

9 And He said to me, "Go in and see the wicked abominations that they are committing here."

10 So I entered and looked, and behold, every form of creeping things and beasts *and* detestable things, with all the idols of the house of Israel, were carved on the wall all around.

11 And standing in front of them were [r]seventy elders of the house of Israel, with Jaazaniah the son of Shaphan standing among them, each man with his censer in his hand, and the fragrance of the cloud of incense rising. Num. 11:16, 25; Luke 10:1

12 Then He said to me, "Son of man, do you see what the elders of the house of Israel are committing in the dark, each man in the room of his carved images? For they say, 'The[r] LORD does not see us; the LORD has [r]forsaken the land.' " Ps. 14:1; Is. 29:15 • Ps. 10:11

13 And He said to me, "Yet you will see still greater abominations which they are committing."

14 Then He brought me to the entrance of the [r]gate of the LORD's house which *was* toward the north; and behold, women were sitting there weeping for Tammuz. Ezek. 44:4; 46:9

15 And He said to me, "Do you see *this,* son of man? Yet you will see still greater abominations than these."

16 Then He brought me into the inner court of the LORD's house. And behold, at the entrance to the temple of the LORD, between the porch and the altar, *were* about twenty-five men with their backs to the temple of the LORD and their faces toward the east; and they were prostrating themselves eastward toward the sun.

17 And He said to me, "Do you
see *this,* son of man? Is it too light
a thing for the house of Judah to
commit the abominations which
they have committed here, that
they have [r]filled the land with violence and provoked Me repeatedly? For behold, they are putting
the twig to their nose. Mic. 2:2
18 "Therefore, I indeed shall deal
in wrath. My eye will have no pity
nor shall I spare; and though they
cry in My ears with a loud voice,
yet I shall not listen to them."

CHAPTER 9

THEN He cried out in my hearing
with a loud [r]voice saying, "Draw
near, [t]O executioners of the city,
each with his destroying weapon
in his hand." Is. 6:8 • *you who punish*
2 And behold, six men came
from the direction of the upper
gate which faces north, each with
his shattering weapon in his hand;
and among them was [r]a certain
man clothed in linen with a [a]writ-
ing case at his loins. And they
went in and stood beside the
bronze altar. Lev. 16:4 • *scribal inkhorn*
3 Then the glory of the God of
Israel went up from the cherub on
which it had been, to the threshold of the temple. And He called
to the man clothed in linen at
whose loins was the writing case.
4 And the LORD said to him,
"Go through the midst of the city,
even through the midst of Jerusalem, and put a [r]mark on the foreheads of the men who sigh and
groan over all the abominations
which are being committed in its
midst." Ex. 12:7, 13; Rev. 7:2, 3; 9:4
5 But to the others He said in
my hearing, "Go through the city
after him and strike; do not let
your eye have pity, and do not
spare.
6 "Utterly slay old men, young
men, maidens, little children, and
women, but do not touch any man
on whom is the mark; and you
shall start from My sanctuary."
So they started with the elders
who *were* before the temple.
7 And He said to them, "Defile[r]
the [t]temple and fill the courts with
the slain. Go out!" Thus they went
out and struck down *the people* in
the city. 2 Chr. 36:17 • *house*
8 Then it came about as they
were striking and I *alone* was left,
that I fell on my face and cried out
saying, "Alas, Lord GOD! Art Thou
destroying the whole remnant of
Israel [t]by pouring out Thy wrath
on Jerusalem?" *by Thy pouring*
9 Then He said to me, "The iniquity of the house of Israel and
Judah is very, very great, and the
land is filled with blood, and the
city is full of perversion; for they
say, 'The LORD has forsaken the
land, and the LORD does not see!'
10 "But as for Me, [r]My eye will
have no pity nor shall I spare, but
[r]I shall bring their conduct upon
their heads." Is. 65:6 • Hos. 9:7
11 Then behold, the man
clothed in linen at whose loins
was the writing case reported,
saying, "I have done just as Thou
hast commanded me."

CHAPTER 10

THEN I looked, and behold, in
the [a]expanse that was over the
heads of the cherubim something

like a sapphire stone, in appearance resembling a throne, appeared above them. *firmament*
2 And He spoke to the man
clothed in linen and said, "Enter
between the [r]whirling wheels under the cherubim, and fill your
hands with coals of fire from between the cherubim, and scatter
them over the city." And he entered in my sight. Ezek. 1:15-21
3 Now the cherubim were
standing on the right side of the
temple when the man entered,
and the cloud filled the [r]inner
court. Ezek. 8:3, 16
4 Then the [r]glory of the LORD
went up from the cherub to the
threshold of the temple, and the
temple was filled with the cloud,
and the court was filled with the
brightness of the glory of the
LORD. Ezek. 9:3; 11:22, 23
5 Moreover, the sound of the
wings of the cherubim was heard
as far as the outer court, like the
[r]voice of God Almighty when He
speaks. Job 40:9; Rev. 10:3
6 And it came about when He
commanded the man clothed in
linen, saying, "Take fire from between the whirling wheels, from
between the cherubim," he entered and stood beside a wheel.
7 Then the cherub stretched
out his hand from between the
cherubim to the fire which *was*
between the cherubim, took some
and put it into the hands of the
one clothed in linen, who took *it*
and went out.
8 And the cherubim appeared
to have the form of a man's hand
under their wings.
9 Then I looked, and behold,
four wheels beside the cherubim,
one wheel beside each cherub;
and the appearance of the wheels
was like the gleam of a [r]Tarshish
stone. Dan. 10:6; Rev. 21:20
10 And as for their appearance,
all four of them had the same likeness, as if one wheel were within
another wheel.
11 When they moved, they went
in *any of* their four [t]directions
without turning as they went; but
they followed in the direction
which [t]they faced, without turning
as they went. *sides • the head*
12 And their [r]whole body, their
backs, their hands, their wings,
and the wheels were full of eyes
all around, the wheels belonging
to all four of them. Rev. 4:6, 8
13 The wheels were called in my
hearing, the whirling wheels.
14 And [r]each one had four faces.
The first face *was* the face of a
cherub, the second face *was* the
face of a man, the third the face of
a lion, and the fourth the face of
an eagle. 1 Kin. 7:29, 36
15 Then the cherubim rose up.
They are the living beings that I
saw by the river Chebar.
16 Now when the cherubim
moved, the wheels would go beside them; also when the cherubim lifted up their wings to rise
from the ground, the wheels
would not turn from beside them.
17 When [t]the cherubim [r]stood
still, [t]the wheels would stand still;
and when they rose up, [t]the wheels
would rise with them; for the
spirit of the living beings *was* in
them. *they* • Ezek. 1:21
18 Then the glory of the LORD
departed from the threshold of the
temple and stood [r]over the cherubim. Ps. 18:10

19 When [r]the cherubim departed, they lifted their wings and rose up from the earth in my sight with the wheels beside them; and they stood still at the entrance of the east gate of the LORD's house. And the glory of the God of Israel hovered over them. Ezek. 11:22

20 These are the living beings that I saw beneath the God of Israel by [r]the river Chebar; so I knew that they *were* cherubim. Ezek. 1:1

21 [r]Each one had four faces and each one four wings, and beneath their wings *was* the form of human hands. Ezek. 1:6, 8; 10:14

22 As for the likeness of their faces, they were the same faces whose appearance I had seen by the river Chebar. Each one went straight ahead.

CHAPTER 11

MOREOVER, the Spirit lifted me up and brought me to the east gate of the LORD's house which faced eastward. And behold, *there were* twenty-five men at the entrance of the gate, and among them I saw Jaazaniah son of Azzur and [r]Pelatiah son of Benaiah, leaders of the people. Ezek. 11:13

2 And He said to me, "Son of man, these are the men who devise iniquity and [r]give evil advice in this city, Ps. 2:1, 2; 52:2

3 who say, 'Is not *the time* near to build houses? This *city* is the pot and we are the flesh.'

4 "Therefore, prophesy against them, son of man, prophesy!"

5 Then the Spirit of the LORD fell upon me, and He said to me, "Say, 'Thus says the LORD, "So you think, house of Israel, for [r]I know your thoughts. Jer. 11:20

6 "You have [r]multiplied your slain in this city, filling its streets with [t]them." Is. 1:15 • *the slain*

7 'Therefore, thus says the Lord GOD, "Your slain whom you have laid in the midst of the city are the flesh, and this *city* is the pot; but I shall bring you out of it.

8 "You have [r]feared a sword; so I will bring a sword upon you," the Lord GOD declares. Is. 66:4

9 "And I shall bring you out of the midst of [t]the city, and I shall deliver you into the hands of [r]strangers and execute judgments against you. *it* • Ps. 106:41

10 "You will [r]fall by the sword. I shall judge you to the border of Israel; so you shall know that I am the LORD. Jer. 52:9, 10

11 "This *city* will [r]not be a pot for you, nor will you be flesh in the midst of it, *but* I shall judge you to the border of Israel. Ezek. 11:3, 7

12 "Thus you will know that I am the LORD; for you have not walked in My statutes nor have you executed My ordinances, but have acted according to the ordinances of the nations around you." ' "

13 Now it came about as I prophesied, that [r]Pelatiah son of Benaiah died. Then I fell on my face and cried out with a loud voice and said, "Alas, Lord GOD! Wilt Thou bring the remnant of Israel to a complete end?" Ezek. 11:1

14 Then the word of the LORD came to me, saying,

15 "Son of man, your brothers, your [t]relatives, your fellow exiles, and the whole house of Israel, all of them, *are those* to whom the inhabitants of Jerusalem have said,

'Go far from the LORD; this land
has been given [r]us as a possession.' *brothers* • Ezek. 33:24
16"Therefore say, 'Thus says the
Lord GOD, "Though I had removed them far away among the
nations, and though I had scattered them among the countries,
yet I was a [r]sanctuary for them a
little while in the countries where
they had gone."' Ps. 31:20; 90:1
17"Therefore say, 'Thus says the
Lord GOD, "I shall [r]gather you
from the peoples and assemble
you out of the countries among
which you have been scattered,
and I shall give you the land of Israel."' Is. 11:11-16; Jer. 3:12, 18
18"When they come there, they
will [r]remove all its [r]detestable
things and all its abominations
from it. Ezek. 37:23 • Ezek. 5:11
19"And I shall give them one
heart, and shall put a new spirit
within them. And I shall take the
heart of stone out of their flesh
and give them a heart of flesh,
20 that they may [r]walk in My
statutes and keep My ordinances,
and do them. Then they will be
My people, and I shall be their
God. Ps. 105:45; Ezek. 36:27
21"But as for those whose
hearts go after their detestable
things and abominations, I shall
bring their conduct down on their
heads," declares the Lord GOD.
22 Then the cherubim lifted up
their wings with the wheels beside
them, and the glory of the God of
Israel hovered over them.
23 And the [r]glory of the LORD
went up from the midst of the
city, and stood over the mountain
which is east of the city. Ezek. 8:4
24 And the Spirit lifted me up
and brought me in a vision by the
Spirit of God to the exiles in Chaldea. So the vision that I had seen
[t]left me. *went up from*
25 Then I [r]told the exiles all the
things that the LORD had shown
me. Ezek. 2:7; 3:4, 17, 27

CHAPTER 12

THEN the word of the LORD
came to me saying,
2"Son of man, you live in the
midst of the rebellious house, who
have eyes to see but do not see,
ears to hear but do not hear; for
they are a rebellious house.
3"Therefore, son of man, prepare for yourself baggage for exile
and go into exile by day in their
sight; even go into exile from your
place to another place in their
sight. Perhaps they will [a]under-
stand though they are a rebellious
house. *see that they are*
4"And bring your baggage out
by day in their sight, as baggage
for exile. Then you will go out [r]at
evening in their sight, as those
going into exile. 2 Kin. 25:4; Jer. 39:4
5"Dig a hole through the wall
in their sight and [t]go out through
it. *bring it out*
6"Load *the baggage* on *your*
shoulder in their sight, *and* carry
it out in the dark. You shall cover
your face so that you can not see
the land, for I have set you as a
sign to the house of Israel."
7 And I [r]did so, as I had been
commanded. By day I brought out
my baggage like the baggage of
an exile. Then in the evening I dug
through the wall with my hands; I

went out in the dark *and* carried
the baggage on *my* shoulder in
their sight. Ezek. 24:18; 37:7, 10
8 And in the morning the word
of the LORD came to me, saying,
9"Son of man, has not the
house of Israel, the [r]rebellious
house, said to you, 'What are you
doing?' Ezek. 2:5-8; 12:1-3
10"Say to them, 'Thus says the
Lord GOD, "This[a]burden *concerns*
the prince in Jerusalem, as well as
all the house of Israel who are [t]in
it." ' *oracle* • *in their midst*
11"Say, 'I am [t]a sign to you. As I
have done, so it will be done to
them; they will [r]go into exile, into
captivity.' *your sign* • Jer. 15:2; 52:15
12"And the [r]prince who is among
them will load *his baggage* on *his*
shoulder in the dark and go out.
They will dig a hole through the
wall to bring *it* out. He will cover
his face so that he can not see the
land with *his* eyes. 2 Kin. 25:4
13"I shall also spread My [r]net
over him, and he will be caught in
My snare. And I shall bring him to
Babylon in the land of the Chaldeans; yet he will not see it, though
he will die there. Is. 24:17, 18
14"And I shall scatter to every
wind all who are around him, his
helpers and all his troops; and I
shall draw out a sword after them.
15"So they will know that I am
the LORD when I scatter them
among the nations, and spread
them among the countries.
16"But I shall spare a few of
them from the sword, the famine,
and the pestilence that they may
tell all their abominations among
the nations where they go, and
may know that I am the LORD."
17 Moreover, the word of the
LORD came to me saying,
18"Son of man, eat your bread
with trembling, and drink your
water with quivering and anxiety.
19"Then say to the people of the
land, 'Thus says the Lord GOD
concerning the inhabitants of Jerusalem in the land of Israel,
"They will eat their bread with
anxiety and drink their water with
horror, because their land will be
stripped of its fulness on account
of the violence of all who live in it.
20"And the inhabited [r]cities will
be laid waste, and the land will be
a desolation. So you will know
that I am the LORD." ' " Is. 3:26
21 Then the word of the LORD
came to me saying,
22"Son of man, what is this
proverb you *people* have concerning the land of Israel, saying, 'The
[r]days are long and every vision
fails'? Amos 6:3; 2 Pet. 3:4
23"Therefore say to them, 'Thus
says the Lord GOD, "I will make
this proverb cease so that they
will no longer use it as a proverb
in Israel." But tell them, "The
days draw near as well as the [t]ful-
fillment of every vision. *word*
24"For there will no longer be
any false vision or flattering divination within the house of Israel.
25"For I the LORD shall speak,
and whatever [r]word I speak will be
performed. It will no longer be delayed, for in your days, O rebellious house, I shall speak the word
and perform it," declares the Lord
GOD.' " Num. 14:28-34; Is. 14:24
26 Furthermore, the word of the
LORD came to me saying,
27"Son of man, behold, the
house of Israel is saying, 'The vi-

sion that he sees is for many years *from now,* and he prophesies of times far off.' Dan. 10:14 · *days*

28 "Therefore say to them, 'Thus says the Lord GOD, "None of My words will be delayed any longer. Whatever word I speak will be performed," ' " declares the Lord GOD.

CHAPTER 13

THEN the word of the LORD came to me saying,

2 "Son of man, prophesy against the prophets of Israel who prophesy, and say to those who prophesy from their own inspiration, 'Listen to the word of the LORD! Is. 9:15; Jer. 37:19

3 'Thus says the Lord GOD, "Woe to the foolish prophets who are following their own spirit and have seen nothing. Lam. 2:14

4 "O Israel, your prophets have been like foxes among ruins.

5 "You have not gone up into the breaches, nor did you build the wall around the house of Israel to stand in the battle on the day of the LORD. Ps. 106:23

6 "They see falsehood and lying divination who are saying, 'The LORD declares,' when the LORD has not sent them; yet they hope for the fulfillment of *their* word.

7 "Did you not see a false vision and speak a lying divination when you said, **'The LORD declares,'** but it is not I who have spoken?" ' "

8 Therefore, thus says the Lord GOD, "Because you have spoken falsehood and seen a lie, therefore behold, I am against you," declares the Lord GOD. *vanity*

9 "So My hand will be against the prophets who see false visions and utter lying divinations. They will have no place in the council of My people, nor will they be written down in the register of the house of Israel, nor will they enter the land of Israel, that you may know that I am the Lord GOD.

10 "It is definitely because they have misled My people by saying, 'Peace!' when there is no peace. And when anyone builds a wall, behold, they plaster it over with whitewash; Jer. 23:32; 50:6

11 *so* tell those who plaster it over with whitewash, that it will fall. A flooding rain will come, and you, O hailstones, will fall; and a violent wind will break out.

12 "Behold, when the wall has fallen, will you not be asked, 'Where is the plaster with which you plastered *it*?' "

13 Therefore, thus says the Lord GOD, "I will make a violent wind break out in My wrath. There will also be in My anger a flooding rain and hailstones to consume *it* in wrath. Ex. 9:24, 25; Ps. 18:12, 13

14 "So I shall tear down the wall which you plastered over with whitewash and bring it down to the ground, so that its foundation is laid bare; and when it falls, you will be consumed in its midst. And you will know that I am the LORD.

15 "Thus I shall spend My wrath on the wall and on those who have plastered it over with whitewash; and I shall say to you, 'The wall is gone and its plasterers are gone,

16 *along with* the prophets of Israel who prophesy to Jerusalem, and who see visions of peace for

her when there is no peace,' declares the Lord GOD. Jer. 6:14
17 "Now you, son of man, set
your face against the daughters of
your people who are [r]prophesying
from their own [t]inspiration. Prophesy against them, Judg. 4:4 • *heart*
18 and say, 'Thus says the Lord
GOD, "Woe to the women who
sew *magic* bands on [t]all wrists,
and make veils for the heads of
persons of every stature to hunt
down lives! Will you hunt down
the lives of My people, but preserve the lives *of others* for yourselves? *all joints of the hand*
19 "And for handfuls of barley
and fragments of bread, you have
profaned Me to My people to put
to death some who should not die
and to keep others alive who
should not live, by your lying to
My people who listen to lies."' "
20 Therefore, thus says the Lord
GOD, "Behold, I am against your
magic bands by which you hunt
[t]lives there as [a]birds, and I will tear
them off your arms; and I will let
them go, even those lives whom
you hunt as birds. *souls • flying ones*
21 "I will also tear off your veils
and deliver My people from your
hands, and they will no longer be
in your hands to be hunted; and
you will know that I am the LORD.
22 "Because you [r]disheartened
the righteous with falsehood
when I did not cause him grief,
but have encouraged the wicked
not to turn from his wicked way
and preserve his life, Amos 5:12
23 therefore, you women will no
longer see false visions or practice
divination, and I will deliver My
people out of your hand. Thus you
will know that I am the LORD."

CHAPTER 14

THEN some elders of Israel came
to me and sat down before me.
2 And the word of the LORD
came to me saying,
3 "Son of man, these men have
[r]set up their idols in their hearts,
and have [r]put right before their
faces the stumbling block of their
iniquity. Should I be consulted by
them at all? Ezek. 20:16 • Zeph. 1:3
4 "Therefore speak to them and
tell them, 'Thus says the Lord
GOD, "Any man of the house of Israel who sets up his idols in his
heart, puts right before his face
the stumbling block of his iniquity, and *then* comes to the
prophet, I the LORD will be
brought to give him an answer in
the matter in view of the [r]multi-
tude of his idols, 1 Kin. 21:20-24
5 in order to lay hold of [t]the
hearts of the house of Israel who
are [r]estranged from Me through all
their idols."' *their* • Is. 1:4; Jer. 2:11
6 "Therefore say to the house of
Israel, 'Thus says the Lord GOD,
"Repent and turn away from your
idols, and turn your faces away
from all your abominations.
7 "For anyone of the house of
Israel or of the immigrants who
stay in Israel who separates himself from Me, sets up his idols in
his heart, puts right before his
face the stumbling block of his iniquity, and *then* comes to the
prophet to inquire of Me for himself, I the LORD will be brought to
answer him in My own person.
8 "And I shall set My face
against that man and make him a
[r]sign and [t]a proverb, and I shall cut

him off from among My people.
So you will know that I am the
LORD. Is. 65:15 • *proverbs*
9 "But if the prophet is [a]pre-
vailed upon to speak a word, it is
I, the LORD, who have prevailed
upon that prophet, and I will
stretch out My hand against him
and [t]destroy him from among My
people Israel. *enticed* • Jer. 6:14, 15
10 "And they will bear *the punishment of* their iniquity; as the iniquity of the inquirer is, so the iniquity of the prophet will be,
11 in order that the house of Israel may no longer [r]stray from Me
and no longer defile themselves
with all their transgressions. Thus
they will be My people, and I shall
be their God," ' declares the Lord
GOD." Ezek. 44:10, 15; 48:11
12 Then the word of the LORD
came to me saying,
13 "Son of man, if a country sins
against Me by committing unfaithfulness, and I stretch out My
hand against it, [t]destroy its [r]supply
of bread, send famine against it,
and cut off from it both man and
beast, *break the staff* • Lev. 26:26
14 even *though* these three men,
Noah, Daniel, and Job were in its
midst, by their *own* righteousness
they could *only* deliver themselves," declares the Lord GOD.
15 "If I were to cause wild beasts
to pass through the land, and they
[t]depopulated it, and it became
desolate so that no one would
pass through it because of the
beasts, *bereave of children*
16 *though* these three men were
in its midst, as I live," declares the
Lord GOD, "they could not deliver
either *their* sons or *their* daughters. [r]They alone would be delivered, but the country would be
desolate. Gen. 19:29; Ezek. 18:20
17 "Or *if* I should bring a sword
on that country and say, 'Let the
sword pass through the country
and cut off man and beast from it,'
18 even *though* these three men
were in its midst, as I live," declares the Lord GOD, "they could
not deliver either *their* sons or
their daughters, but they alone
would be delivered.
19 "Or *if* I should send a [r]plague
against that country and pour out
My wrath in blood on it, to cut off
man and beast from it, Jer. 14:12
20 even *though* Noah, Daniel,
and Job were in its midst, as I
live," declares the Lord GOD,
"they could not deliver either
their son or *their* daughter. They
would deliver only themselves by
their righteousness."
21 For thus says the Lord GOD,
"How much more when I send My
four [t]severe judgments against Jerusalem: sword, famine, wild
beasts, and plague to cut off man
and beast from it! *evil*
22 "Yet, behold, [t]survivors will be
left in it who will be brought out,
both sons and daughters. Behold,
they are going to come forth to
you and you will see their conduct
and actions; then you will be comforted for the calamity which I
have brought against Jerusalem
for everything which I have
brought upon it. *escaped ones*
23 "Then they will comfort you
when you see their conduct and
actions, for you will know that I
have not done in vain whatever I
did to it," declares the Lord GOD.

CHAPTER 15

THEN the word of the LORD came to me saying,

2 "Son of man, how is the wood of the [r]vine *better* than any wood of a branch which is among the trees of the forest? Ps. 80:8-16

3 "Can wood be taken from it to make [t]anything, or can *men* take a peg from it on which to hang any vessel? *a work*

4 "If it has been put into the fire for fuel, *and* the fire has consumed both of its ends, and its middle part has been charred, is it *then* useful for [t]anything? *a work*

5 "Behold, while it is intact, it is not made into anything. How much less, when the fire has consumed it and it is charred, can it still be made into anything!

6 "Therefore, thus says the Lord GOD, 'As the wood of the vine among the trees of the forest, which I have given to the fire for fuel, so have I given up the inhabitants of Jerusalem;

7 and I [r]set My face against them. *Though* they have come out of the fire, yet the fire will consume them. Then you will know that I am the LORD, when I set My face against them. Lev. 26:17

8 'Thus I will make the land desolate, because they have [r]acted unfaithfully,' " declares the Lord GOD. Ezek. 14:13; 17:20

CHAPTER 16

THEN the word of the LORD came to me saying,

2 "Son of man, make known to Jerusalem her abominations,

3 and say, 'Thus says the Lord GOD to Jerusalem, "Your origin and your birth are from the land of the Canaanite, your father was an Amorite and your mother a Hittite.

4 "As for your birth, [r]on the day you were born your navel cord was not cut, nor were you washed with water for cleansing; you were not rubbed with salt or even wrapped in cloths. Hos. 2:3

5 "No eye looked with pity on you to do any of these things for you, to have compassion on you. Rather you were thrown out into the open field, for you were abhorred on the day you were born.

6 "When I passed by you and saw you squirming in your blood, I said to you *while you were* in your blood, 'Live!' I said to you while you were in your blood, 'Live!'

7 "I [r]made you [t]numerous like plants of the field. Then you grew up, became tall, and reached the age for fine ornaments; *your* breasts were formed and your hair had grown. Yet you were naked and bare. Ex. 1:7 • *a myriad*

8 "Then I passed by you and saw you, and behold, you were at the time for love; so I [r]spread My skirt over you and covered your nakedness. I also swore to you and entered into a covenant with you so that you became Mine," declares the Lord GOD. Ruth 3:9

9 "Then I bathed you with water, washed off your blood from you, and anointed you with oil.

10 "I also clothed you with [r]embroidered cloth, and put sandals of porpoise skin on your feet; and I wrapped you with fine linen and covered you with silk. Ex. 26:36

11 "And I adorned you with ornaments, put [r]bracelets on your
hands, and a necklace around
your neck. Gen. 24:22, 47
12 "I also put a ring in your nostril, earrings in your ears, and a
beautiful crown on your head.
13 "Thus you were adorned with
[r]gold and silver, and your dress
was of fine linen, silk, and embroidered cloth. You ate fine flour,
honey, and oil; so you were exceedingly beautiful and advanced
to royalty. Ps. 45:13, 14
14 "Then your [r]fame went forth
among the nations on account of
your beauty, for it was [r]perfect because of My splendor which I bestowed on you," declares the Lord
GOD. 1 Kin. 10:1, 24 • Ps. 50:2
15 "But you trusted in your
beauty and played the harlot because of your fame, and you
poured out your harlotries on every passer-by [t]who might be *will-*
ing. *to whom it might be*
16 "And you took some of your
clothes, made for yourself high
places of various colors, and
played the harlot on them, which
should never come about nor happen.
17 "You also took your beautiful
[t]jewels *made* of My gold and of My
silver, which I had given you, and
made for yourself male images
that you might play the harlot
with them. *articles of beauty*
18 "Then you took your embroidered cloth and covered them,
and offered My oil and My incense
before them.
19 "Also [r]My bread which I gave
you, fine flour, oil, and honey with
which I fed you, [t]you would offer
before them for a soothing aroma;
so it happened," declares the Lord
GOD. Hos. 2:8 • *and you . . . offer it*
20 "Moreover, you took your
sons and daughters whom you
had borne to [r]Me, and you sacrificed them to idols to be devoured.
Were your harlotries so small a
matter? Ex. 13:2, 12; Deut. 29:11, 12
21 "You slaughtered [r]My children, and offered them up to idols
by [r]causing them to pass through
the fire. Ex. 13:2 • Jer. 19:5
22 "And besides all your abominations and harlotries you did not
remember the days of your youth,
when you were naked and bare
and squirming in your blood.
23 "Then it came about after all
your wickedness ('Woe, woe to
you!' declares the Lord GOD),
24 that you built yourself a
[r]shrine and made yourself a high
place in every square. Jer. 11:13
25 "You built yourself a high
place at the top of [r]every street,
and made your beauty abominable; and you spread your legs to
every passer-by to multiply your
harlotry. Prov. 9:14
26 "You also played the harlot
with the Egyptians, your lustful
neighbors, and multiplied your
harlotry to make Me angry.
27 "Behold now, I have stretched
out My hand against you and diminished your rations. And I delivered you up to the desire of
those who hate you, the daughters
of the Philistines, who are
ashamed of your lewd conduct.
28 "Moreover, you played the
harlot with the [r]Assyrians because
you were not satisfied; you even
played the harlot with them and
still were not satisfied. Hos. 10:6

29 "You also multiplied your harlotry with the land of merchants,
Chaldea, yet even with this you
were not satisfied." ' "
30 "How languishing is your
heart," declares the Lord GOD,
"while you do all these things, the
actions of a bold-faced harlot.
31 "When you built your shrine
at the beginning of every street
and made your high place in every
square, in [r]disdaining money, you
were not like a harlot. Is. 52:3
32 "You adulteress wife, who
takes strangers instead of her husband!
33 "Men give gifts to all harlots,
but you [r]give your gifts to all your
lovers to bribe them to come to
you from every direction for your
harlotries. Hos. 8:9, 10
34 "Thus you are different from
those women in your harlotries, in
that no one plays the harlot [t]as you
do, because you give money and
no money is given you; thus you
are different." *after you*
35 Therefore, O harlot, hear the
word of the LORD.
36 Thus says the Lord GOD, "Because your lewdness was poured
out and your nakedness uncovered through your harlotries with
your lovers and with all your detestable [r]idols, and because of the
blood of your sons which you
gave to idols, Jer. 19:5; Ezek. 20:31
37 therefore, behold, I shall
[r]gather all your lovers with whom
you took pleasure, even all those
whom you loved *and* all those
whom you hated. So I shall gather
them against you from every direction and expose your nakedness to them that they may see all
your nakedness. Jer. 13:22, 26
38 "Thus I shall judge you, like
women who commit adultery or
shed blood are judged; and I shall
bring on you the blood of [r]wrath
and jealousy. Ps. 79:3, 5; Jer. 18:21
39 "I shall also give you into the
hands of your lovers, and they will
tear down your shrines, demolish
your high places, strip you of your
clothing, take away your [t]jewels,
and will leave you naked and
bare. *articles of beauty*
40 "They will [t]incite a crowd
against you, and they will stone
you and cut you to pieces with
their swords. *bring up an assembly*
41 "And they will [r]burn your
houses with fire and execute judgments on you in the sight of many
women. Then I shall stop you
from playing the harlot, and you
will also no longer pay [t]your lovers. 2 Kin. 25:9 • *a harlot's hire*
42 "So I shall calm My fury
against you, and My jealousy will
depart from you, and I shall be
pacified and angry no more.
43 "Because you have [r]not remembered the days of your youth
but have enraged Me by all these
things, behold, I in turn will bring
your conduct down on your own
head," declares the Lord GOD, "so
that you will not commit this
lewdness on top of all your *other*
abominations. Ps. 78:42; 106:13
44 "Behold, everyone who
quotes proverbs will quote *this*
proverb concerning you, saying,
'Like [t]mother, [t]like daughter.' *Her*
45 "You are the daughter of your
mother, who loathed her husband
and children. You are also the sister of your sisters, who [r]loathed
their husbands and children. Your

mother was a Hittite and your father an Amorite. Is. 1:4; Zech. 11:8

46 "Now your older sister is Samaria, who lives north of you with her daughters; and your younger sister, who lives south of you, is Sodom with her daughters.

47 "Yet you have not merely walked in their ways or done according to their abominations; but, as if that were [r]too little, you acted more corruptly in all your conduct than they. 1 Kin. 16:31

48 "As I live," declares the Lord GOD, "Sodom, your sister, and her daughters, have not done as you and your daughters have done.

49 "Behold, this was the guilt of your sister Sodom: she and her daughters had [r]arrogance, abundant food, and careless ease, but she did not help the poor and needy. Gen. 19:9; Ps. 138:6; Is. 3:9

50 "Thus they were haughty and committed [r]abominations before Me. Therefore I removed them when I saw *it*. Gen. 13:13; 18:20

51 "Furthermore, Samaria did not commit half of your sins, for you have multiplied your abominations more than they. Thus you have made your sisters appear righteous by all your abominations which you have committed.

52 "Also bear your disgrace in that you have made judgment favorable for your sisters. Because of your sins in which you acted more abominably than they, they are more in the right than you. Yes, be also ashamed and bear your disgrace, in that you made your sisters appear righteous.

53 "Nevertheless, I will restore their captivity, the captivity of Sodom and her daughters, the captivity of Samaria and her daughters, and [t]along with them your own captivity, *in their midst*

54 in order that you may bear your humiliation, and feel [r]ashamed for all that you have done when you become [r]a consolation to them. Jer. 2:26 • Ezek. 14:22, 23

55 "And your sisters, Sodom with her daughters and Samaria with her daughters, will return to their former state, and you with your daughters will *also* return to your former state.

56 "As *the name of* your sister Sodom was not heard from your lips in your day of pride,

57 before your wickedness was uncovered, so now you have become the reproach of the daughters of Edom, and of all who are around her, of the daughters of the Philistines—those surrounding *you* who despise you.

58 "You have borne *the penalty of* your lewdness and abominations," the LORD declares.

59 For thus says the Lord GOD, "I will also do with you as you have done, you who have [r]despised the oath by breaking the covenant. Is. 24:5; Ezek. 17:19

60 "Nevertheless, I will remember My covenant with you in the days of your youth, and I will establish an [r]everlasting covenant with you. Is. 55:3; Jer. 32:38-41

61 "Then you will remember your ways and be ashamed when you receive your sisters, *both* your older and your younger; and I will give them to you as daughters, but not because of your covenant.

62 "Thus I will establish My covenant with you, and you shall know that I am the LORD,

63 in order that you may [r]remember and be ashamed, and [r]never open your mouth anymore because of your humiliation, when I have forgiven you for all that you have done," the Lord GOD declares. Dan. 9:7, 8 • Ps. 39:9

CHAPTER 17

NOW the word of the LORD came to me saying,

2 "Son of man, propound a riddle, and speak a [r]parable to the house of Israel, Ezek. 20:49; 24:3

3 [t]saying, 'Thus says the Lord GOD, "A great eagle with great wings, long pinions and a full plumage of many colors, came to Lebanon and took away the top of the cedar. *and you shall say*

4 "He plucked off the topmost of its young twigs and brought it to a land of merchants; he set it in a city of traders.

5 "He also took some of the seed of the land and planted it in [t]fertile soil. He [t]placed *it* beside abundant waters; he set it *like* a willow. *a field of seed • took*

6 "Then it sprouted and became a low, spreading vine with its branches turned toward him, but its roots remained under it. So it became a vine, and yielded shoots and sent out branches.

7 "But there was another great eagle with great wings and much plumage; and behold, this vine bent its roots toward him and sent out its branches toward him from the beds where it was [r]planted, that he might water it. Ezek. 31:4

8 "It was planted in good [t]soil beside abundant waters, that it might yield branches and bear fruit, *and* become a splendid vine." ' *field*

9 "Say, 'Thus says the Lord GOD, "Will it thrive? Will he not pull up its roots and cut off its fruit, so that it withers—so that all its sprouting leaves wither? And neither by great [t]strength nor by many people can it be raised from its roots *again*. *arm*

10 "Behold, though it is planted, will it thrive? Will it not [r]completely wither as soon as the east wind strikes it—wither on the beds where it grew?" ' " Hos. 13:15

11 Moreover, the word of the LORD came to me saying,

12 "Say now to the rebellious house, 'Do you not know what these things *mean?*' Say, 'Behold, the [r]king of Babylon came to Jerusalem, took its king and princes, and brought them to him in Babylon. 2 Kin. 24:11, 12, 15

13 'And he took one of the royal [t]family and made a covenant with him, putting him under [r]oath. He also took away the mighty of the land, *seed* • 2 Chr. 36:13

14 that the kingdom might [r]be [t]in subjection, not exalting itself, *but* keeping his covenant, that it might continue. Ezek. 29:14 • *low*

15 'But he rebelled against him by sending his envoys to Egypt that they might give him horses and many troops. Will he succeed? Will he who does such things escape? Can he indeed break the covenant and escape?

16 'As I live,' declares the Lord GOD, 'Surely in the [t]country of the king who put him on the throne, whose oath he despised, and whose covenant he broke, in Babylon he shall die. *place*

17 'And Pharaoh with *his* mighty
army and great company will not
help him in the war, when they
cast up mounds and build siege
walls to cut off many lives.
18 'Now he despised the oath by
breaking the covenant, and behold, he [t]pledged his allegiance,
yet did all these things; he shall
not escape.' " *gave his hand*
19 Therefore, thus says the Lord
GOD, "As I live, surely My oath
which he despised and My covenant which he broke, I will [t]inflict
on his head. *give it*
20 "And I will spread My [r]net
over him, and he will be caught in
My snare. Then I will bring him to
Babylon and enter into judgment
with him there *regarding* the unfaithful act which he has committed against Me. Ezek. 12:13
21 "And all the choice men in all
his troops will fall by the sword,
and the survivors will be scattered
to every wind; and you will know
that I, the LORD, have spoken."
22 Thus says the Lord GOD, "I
shall also take *a sprig* from the
lofty top of the cedar and set *it*
out; I shall pluck from the topmost of its young twigs a tender
one, and I shall plant *it* on a [r]high
and lofty mountain. Ps. 72:16
23 "On the high mountain of Israel I shall plant it, that it may
bring forth boughs and bear fruit,
and become a stately [r]cedar. And
birds of every [t]kind will nest under
it; they will nest in the shade of its
branches. Ps. 92:12 • *wing*
24 "And all the [r]trees of the field
will know that I am the LORD; I
bring down the high tree, exalt the
low tree, dry up the green tree,
and make the dry tree flourish. I
am the LORD; I have spoken, and I
will perform *it*." Ps. 96:12; Is. 55:12

CHAPTER 18

THEN the word of the LORD
came to me saying,
2 "What [r]do you mean by using
this proverb concerning the land
of Israel saying, Is. 3:15

> 'The [r]fathers eat the sour
> grapes, Jer. 31:29
> But the children's teeth [t]are
> set on edge'? *become dull*

3 "As I live," declares the Lord
GOD, "you are surely not going to
use this proverb in Israel anymore.
4 "Behold, all [a]souls are Mine;
the soul of the father as well as
the soul of the son is Mine. The
soul who sins will die. *lives*
5 "But if a man is righteous, and
practices justice and righteousness,
6 and does not [r]eat at the
mountain *shrines* or lift up his
eyes to the idols of the house of
Israel, or defile his neighbor's
wife, or approach a woman during
her menstrual period— Ezek. 6:13
7 if a man does not oppress
anyone, but [r]restores to the debtor
his pledge, does not commit robbery, *but* gives his bread to the
hungry, and covers the naked
with clothing, Deut. 24:13
8 if he does not lend *money* on
[r]interest or take increase, *if* he
keeps his hand from iniquity, *and*
executes true justice between
man and man, Deut. 23:19, 20
9 *if* he walks in [r]My statutes
and My ordinances so as to deal
faithfully—[r]he is righteous *and*

will surely live," declares the Lord
GOD. Lev. 18:5 • Rom. 8:1
10 "Then he may[t] have a violent
son who sheds blood, and who
does any of these things to a
brother *beget*
11 (though he himself did not do
any of these things), that is, he
even eats at the mountain *shrines,*
and defiles his neighbor's wife,
12 oppresses the [r]poor and
needy, commits robbery, does not
restore a pledge, but lifts up his
eyes to the idols, *and* commits
abomination, Amos 4:1; Zech. 7:10
13 he [r]lends *money* on interest
and takes increase; will he live?
He will not live! He has committed all these abominations, he will
surely be put to death; his blood
will be on his own head. Ex. 22:25
14 "Now behold, he has a son
who has observed all his father's
sins which he committed, and observing does not do likewise.
15 "He does not eat at the mountain *shrines* or lift up his eyes to
the idols of the house of Israel, or
defile his neighbor's wife,
16 or oppress anyone, or retain
a pledge, or commit robbery, *but*
he [r]gives his bread to the hungry,
and covers the naked with clothing, Job 31:16, 20; Ps. 41:1
17 he keeps his hand from the
poor, does not take interest or increase, *but* executes My ordinances, and walks in My statutes;
[r]he will not die for his father's iniquity, he will surely live. Rom. 2:7
18 "As for his father, because he
practiced extortion, robbed *his*
brother, and did what was not
good among his people, behold, he
will die for his iniquity.

19 "Yet you say, 'Why[r] should the
son not bear the punishment for
the father's iniquity?' When the
son has practiced justice and
righteousness, and has observed
all My statutes and done them, he
shall surely live. Ex. 20:5; Jer. 15:4
20 "The person who [r]sins will die.
The son will not bear the punishment for the father's iniquity, nor
will the father bear the punishment for the son's iniquity; the
righteousness of the righteous will
be upon himself, and the wickedness of the wicked will be upon
himself. 2 Kin. 14:6; 22:18-20
21 "But if the [r]wicked man turns
from all his sins which he has
committed and observes all My
statutes and practices justice and
righteousness, he shall surely live;
he shall not die. Ezek. 18:27, 28
22 "All[r] his transgressions which
he has committed will not be remembered against him; because
of his righteousness which he has
practiced, he will live. Is. 43:25
23 "Do[r] I have any pleasure in the
death of the wicked," declares the
Lord GOD, "rather[t] than that he
should turn from his ways and
live? Ezek. 18:32 • *is it not*
24 "But when a righteous man
[r]turns away from his righteousness, commits iniquity, and does
according to all the abominations
that a wicked man does, will he
live? All his righteous deeds
which he has done will not be remembered for his treachery which
he has committed and his sin
which he has committed; for them
he will die. 2 Chr. 24:2, 17-22
25 "Yet you say, 'The[r] way of the
Lord is not right.' Hear now, O

house of Israel! Is My way not right? Is it not your ways that are not right? Mal. 2:17; 3:13-15

26 “When a righteous man turns away from his righteousness, commits iniquity, and dies because of it, for his iniquity which he has committed he will die.

27 “Again, when a wicked man turns away [r]from his wickedness which he has committed and practices justice and righteousness, he will save his life. Is. 1:18; 55:7

28 “Because he considered and turned away from all his transgressions which he had committed, he shall surely live; he shall not die.

29 “But the house of Israel says, ‘The way of the Lord is not right.’ Are My ways not right, O house of Israel? Is it not your ways that are not right?

30 “Therefore I will judge you, O house of Israel, each according to his conduct,” declares the Lord GOD. “Repent[r] and turn away from all your transgressions, so that iniquity may not become a stumbling block to you. Hos. 12:6

31 “Cast[r] away from you all your transgressions which you have committed, and make yourselves a new heart and a new spirit! For why will you die, O house of Israel? Is. 1:16, 17; 55:7

32 “For I have[r] no pleasure in the death of anyone who dies,” declares the Lord GOD. “Therefore, repent and live.” Ezek. 18:23

CHAPTER 19

“AS for you, take up a lamentation for the princes of Israel,

2 and say,
‘What was your mother?
A lioness among lions!
She lay down among young lions,
She reared her cubs.
3 ‘When she brought up one of her cubs,
He became a lion,
And he learned to tear *his* prey;
He devoured men.
4 ‘Then nations heard about him;
He was captured in their pit,
And they[r] brought him with hooks 2 Kin. 23:34
To the land of Egypt.
5 ‘When she saw, as she waited,
That her hope was lost,
She took [t]another of her cubs *one*
And made him a young lion.
6 ‘And he walked about among the lions;
He became a young lion,
He learned to tear *his* prey;
He devoured men.
7 ‘And he destroyed their [a]fortified towers *widows*
And laid waste their cities;
And the land and its fulness were appalled
Because of the sound of his roaring.
8 ‘Then [r]nations set against him 2 Kin. 24:11
On every side from *their* provinces,
And they spread their net over him;
He was captured in their pit.

9 ‘And[r]they put him in a cage
with hooks 2 Chr. 36:6
And [r]brought him to the
king of Babylon;
They brought him in hunt-
ing nets 2 Kin. 24:15
So that his voice should be
heard no more
On the mountains of Israel.
10 ‘Your mother was[r]like a vine
in your vineyard,
Planted by the waters;
It was fruitful and full of
branches
Because of abundant wa-
ters. Ps. 80:8-11
11 ‘And it had strong branches
fit for scepters of rulers,
And its [r]height was raised
above the clouds
So that it was seen in its
height with the mass of
its branches. Ezek. 31:3
12 ‘But it was [r]plucked up in
fury; Jer. 31:28
It was [r]cast down to the
ground; Lam. 2:1; Ezek. 28:17
And the[r]east wind dried up
its fruit. Hos. 13:15
Its [r]strong branch was torn
off Is. 27:11; Ezek. 19:11
So that it withered;
The fire consumed it.
13 ‘And now it is planted in the
[r]wilderness, 2 Kin. 24:12-16
In a dry and thirsty land.
14 ‘And[r]fire has gone out from
its branch; Ezek. 15:4
It has consumed its shoots
and fruit,
So that there is not in it a
strong branch,
A scepter to rule.’ ”
This is a lamentation, and has become a lamentation.

CHAPTER 20

NOW it came about in the seventh year, in the fifth *month*, on
the tenth of the month, that [t]cer-
tain of the[r]elders of Israel came to
inquire of the LORD, and sat before me. *men* • Ezek. 8:1, 11, 12
2 And the word of the LORD
came to me saying,
3 “Son of man, speak to the elders of Israel, and say to them,
‘Thus says the Lord GOD, “Do you
come to inquire of Me? As I live,”
declares the Lord GOD, “I[r]will not
be inquired of by you.” ’ Ezek. 14:3
4 “Will you judge them, will
you judge them, son of man?
[r]Make them know the abominations of their fathers; Matt. 23:32
5 and say to them, ‘Thus says
the Lord GOD, “On the day when I
[r]chose Israel and swore to the [t]de-
scendants of the house of Jacob
and made Myself known to them
in the land of Egypt, when I swore
to them, saying, I am the LORD
your God, Ex. 6:6-8 • *seed*
6 on that day I swore to them,
[r]to bring them out from the land of
Egypt into a land that I had [t]se-
lected for them, flowing with milk
and honey, which is the glory of
all lands. Jer. 32:22 • *spied out*
7 “And I said to them, ‘Cast
away, each of you, the detestable
things of his eyes, and do not defile yourselves with the idols of
Egypt; I am the LORD your God.’
8 “But they [r]rebelled against Me
and were not willing to listen to
Me;[t]they did not cast away the detestable things of their eyes, nor
did they forsake the idols of
Egypt. Deut. 9:7 • *each one*
Then I[t]resolved to pour out My

wrath on them, to accomplish My anger against them in the midst of the land of Egypt. *said*

9 "But I acted [r]for the sake of My name, that it should not be profaned in the sight of the nations among whom they *lived*, in whose sight I made Myself known to them by bringing them out of the land of Egypt. Ex. 32:11-14

10 "So I took them out of the land of Egypt and brought them into the [r]wilderness. Ex. 19:1

11 "And I gave them My statutes and informed them of My ordinances, by which, if a man [t]observes them, he will live. *does*

12 "And also I gave them My sabbaths to be a [r]sign between Me and them, that they might know that I am the LORD who sanctifies them. Ex. 31:13, 17; Ezek. 20:20

13 "But the house of Israel rebelled against Me in the wilderness. They did not walk in My statutes, and they rejected My ordinances, by which, if a man [t]observes them, he will live; and My sabbaths they greatly profaned. Then I [t]resolved to pour out My wrath on them in the wilderness, to annihilate them. *does • said*

14 "But I acted for the sake of My name, that it should not be profaned in the sight of the nations, before whose sight I had brought them out.

15 "And also [r]I swore to them in the wilderness that I would not bring them into the land which I had given them, flowing with milk and honey, which is the glory of all lands, Num. 14:30; Ps. 95:11

16 because they rejected My ordinances, and as for My statutes, they did not walk in them; they even profaned My sabbaths, for their [r]heart continually went after their idols. Ezek. 11:21; 14:3-7

17 "Yet My eye spared them rather than destroying them, and I did not cause their [r]annihilation in the wilderness. Jer. 4:27; 5:18

18 "And I said to their [t]children in the wilderness, 'Do not walk in the statutes of your fathers, or keep their ordinances, or defile yourselves with their idols. *sons*

19 'I am the LORD your God; walk in My statutes, and keep My ordinances, and observe them.

20 'And sanctify My sabbaths; and they shall be a sign between Me and you, that you may know that I am the LORD your God.'

21 "But the [r]children rebelled against Me; they did not walk in My statutes, nor were they careful to observe My ordinances, by which, *if* a man observes them, he will live; they profaned My sabbaths. So I [t]resolved to pour out My wrath on them, to accomplish My anger against them in the wilderness. Num. 21:5; 25:1-3 • *said*

22 "But I withdrew My hand and acted for the sake of My name, that it should not be profaned in the sight of the nations in whose sight I had brought them out.

23 "Also I swore to them in the wilderness that I would scatter them among the nations and disperse them among the lands,

24 because they had not observed My ordinances, but had rejected My statutes, and had profaned My sabbaths, and their eyes were on the idols of their fathers.

25 "And I also gave them statutes that were [r]not good and ordi-

nances by which they could not
live; Ps. 81:12; Is. 66:4
26 and I pronounced them [r]un-
clean because of their gifts, in that
they caused all their first-born to
pass through *the fire* so that I
might make them desolate, in order that they might know that I
am the LORD."' Lev. 18:21; 20:2-5
27 "Therefore, son of man, [r]speak
to the house of Israel, and say to
them, 'Thus says the Lord GOD,
"Yet in this your fathers have
blasphemed Me by acting treacherously against Me. Ezek. 2:7
28 "When I had [r]brought them
into the land which I swore to give
to them, then they saw every high
hill and every leafy tree, and they
offered there their sacrifices, and
there they presented the provocation of their offering. There also
they made their soothing aroma,
and there they poured out their libations. Josh. 23:3, 14; Neh. 9:22-26
29 "Then I said to them, 'What is
the high place to which you go?'
So its name is called [1]Bamah to
this day."'
30 "Therefore, say to the house
of Israel, 'Thus says the Lord GOD,
"Will you defile yourselves [t]after
the manner of your fathers and
play the harlot after their detestable things? *in the way of*
31 "And [t]when you offer your
gifts, when you cause your sons to
pass through the fire, you are defiling yourselves with all your
idols to this day. And shall I be inquired of by you, O house of Israel? As I live," declares the Lord
GOD, "I will not be inquired of by
you. *in your lifting up*

[1]Or, *High Place*

32 "And what [r]comes into your
mind will not come about, when
you say: 'We will be like the nations, like the tribes of the lands,
serving wood and stone.' Ezek. 11:5
33 "As I live," declares the Lord
GOD, "surely with a mighty hand
and with an [r]outstretched arm and
with wrath poured out, I shall be
[r]king over you. Jer. 21:5 • Jer. 51:57
34 "And I shall bring you out
from the peoples and gather you
from the lands where you are
scattered, with a mighty hand and
with an outstretched arm and
with [r]wrath poured out; Lam. 2:4
35 and I shall bring you into the
[r]wilderness of the peoples, and
there I shall enter into judgment
with you face to face. Hos. 2:14
36 "As I entered into judgment
with your fathers in the wilderness of the land of Egypt, so I will
enter into judgment with you,"
declares the Lord GOD.
37 "And I shall make you pass
under the rod, and I shall bring
you into the bond of the covenant;
38 and I shall purge from you
the rebels and those who transgress against Me; I shall bring
them out of the land where they
sojourn, but they will not enter
the land of Israel. Thus you will
know that I am the LORD.
39 "As for you, O house of Israel," thus says the Lord GOD,
"Go[r], serve everyone his idols; but
later, you will surely listen to Me,
and My holy name you will profane no longer with your gifts and
with your idols. Jer. 44:25, 26
40 "For on My holy mountain, on
the high mountain of Israel," declares the Lord GOD, "there the
whole house of Israel, all of them,

will serve Me in the land; there I shall accept them, and there I shall [a]seek your contributions and the choicest of your gifts, with all your holy things. *require*

41 "As[t] a soothing aroma I shall accept you, when I [r]bring you out from the peoples and gather you from the lands where you are scattered; and I shall prove Myself holy among you in the sight of the nations. *With* • Is. 27:12, 13

42 "And [r]you will know that I am the LORD, when I bring you into the land of Israel, into the land which I swore to give to your forefathers. Ezek. 36:23; 38:23

43 "And there you will remember your ways and all your deeds, with which you have defiled yourselves; and you will loathe yourselves in your own sight for all the evil things that you have done.

44 "Then [r]you will know that I am the LORD when I have dealt with you [r]for My name's sake, not according to your evil ways or according to your corrupt deeds, O house of Israel," declares the Lord GOD.' " Ezek. 24:24 • Ezek. 36:22

45 Now the word of the LORD came to me saying,

46 "Son of man, set your face toward [a]Teman, and speak out against the south, and prophesy against the forest [t]land of the Negev, *the South* • *of the field*

47 and say to the forest of the Negev, 'Hear the word of the LORD: thus says the Lord GOD, "Behold, I am about to kindle a fire in you, and it shall consume every [t]green tree in you, as well as every dry tree; the blazing flame will not be quenched, and the whole surface from south to north will be burned by it. *moist*

48 "And all flesh will see that I, the LORD, have kindled it; it shall [r]not be quenched." ' " Jer. 7:20; 17:27

49 Then I said, "Ah Lord GOD! They are saying of me, 'Is he not *just* speaking parables?' "

CHAPTER 21

AND the word of the LORD came to me saying,

2 "Son of man, set your face toward Jerusalem, and [t]speak against the sanctuaries, and prophesy against the land of Israel; *flow*

3 and say to the land of Israel, 'Thus says the LORD, "Behold, [r]I am against you; and I shall draw My sword out of its sheath and cut off from you the righteous and the wicked. Jer. 21:13; Nah. 2:13; 3:5

4 "Because I shall cut off from you the righteous and the wicked, therefore My sword shall go forth from its sheath against [r]all flesh from south *to* north. Jer. 12:12

5 "Thus all flesh will know that I, the LORD, have drawn My sword out of its sheath. It will [r]not return *to its sheath* again." ' Nah. 1:9

6 "As for you, son of man, groan with breaking heart and bitter grief, groan in their sight.

7 "And it will come about when they say to you, 'Why do you groan?' that you will say, 'Because of the news that is coming; and [r]every heart will melt, all hands will be feeble, every spirit will [t]faint, and all knees will [t]be weak as water. Behold, it comes and it will happen,' declares the Lord GOD." Is. 13:7 • *be dim* • *flow*

8 Again the word of the LORD
came to me saying,
9 "Son of man, prophesy and
say, 'Thus says the LORD.' Say,
"A sword, a sword sharp-
ened Deut. 32:41
And also polished!
10 'Sharpened to make a
[r]slaughter,
Polished to flash like lightning!' Is. 34:5, 6
Or shall we rejoice, the rod of My
son despising every tree?
11 "And it is given to be polished, that it may be handled; the
sword is sharpened and polished,
to give it into the hand of the
slayer.
12 "Cry[r] out and wail, son of man;
for it is against My people, it is
against all the officials of Israel.
They are delivered over to the
sword with My people, therefore
strike *your* thigh. Joel 1:13
13 "For *there is* a testing; and
what if even the[a] rod which despises will be no more?" declares the
Lord GOD. *scepter*
14 "You therefore, son of man,
prophesy, and clap *your* hands together; and let the sword be[r] dou-
bled the third time, the sword for
the slain. It is the sword for the
great one slain, which surrounds
them, Lev. 26:21, 24
15 that *their*[r] hearts may melt,
and many fall at all their gates. I
have given the glittering sword.
Ah! It is made *for striking* like
lightning, it is wrapped up *in*
readiness for slaughter. Josh. 2:11
16 "Show[a] yourself sharp, go to
the right; set yourself; go to the
left, wherever your [t]edge is appointed. *Unite yourself • face*

17 "I shall also clap My hands together, and I shall appease My
wrath; I, the LORD, have spoken."
18 And the word of the LORD
came to me saying,
19 "As for you, son of man, make
two ways for the sword of the
king of Babylon to come; both of
them will go out of one land. And
make a signpost; make it at the
head of the way to the city.
20 "You shall[t] mark a way for the
sword to come to Rabbah of the
sons of Ammon, and to Judah into
fortified Jerusalem. *set*
21 "For the king of Babylon
stands at the parting of the way,
at the head of the two ways, to
use divination; he shakes the arrows, he consults the household
idols, he looks at the liver.
22 "Into his right hand came the
divination, 'Jerusalem,' to set battering rams, to open the mouth for
slaughter, to lift up the voice with
a battle cry, to set battering rams
against the gates, to cast up
mounds, to build a siege wall.
23 "And it will be to them like a
false divination in their eyes; they
have *sworn* solemn oaths. But he
brings iniquity to remembrance,
that they may be seized.
24 "Therefore, thus says the Lord
GOD, 'Because you have made
your iniquity to be remembered,
in that your transgressions are uncovered, so that in all your deeds
your sins appear—because you
have come to remembrance, you
will be seized with the hand.
25 'And you, O slain, wicked
one, the prince of Israel, whose
day has come, in the time of the
[a]punishment of the end,' *iniquity*

26 thus says the Lord GOD, 'Remove the turban, and take off the
crown; this will *be* no more the
same.[r]Exalt that which is low, and
abase that which is high. Ps. 75:7
27 'A ruin, a ruin, a ruin, I shall
make it. This also will be no more,
until[r]He comes whose right it is;
and I shall give it *to Him.*' Ps. 2:6
28 "And you, son of man, prophesy and say, 'Thus says the Lord
GOD concerning the sons of Ammon and concerning their reproach,' and say: 'A sword, a
sword is drawn, polished for the
slaughter, to cause it to consume,
that it may be like lightning—
29 while they see for you false
visions, while they divine lies for
you—to place you on the necks of
the wicked who are slain, whose
day has come, in the time of the
[a]punishment of the end. *iniquity*
30 'Return[r]*it* to its sheath. In the
[r]place where you were created, in
the land of your origin, I shall
judge you. Jer. 47:6, 7 • Ezek. 25:5
31 'And I shall pour out My indignation on you; I shall blow on
you with the fire of My wrath, and
I shall give you into the hand of
brutal men, skilled in destruction.
32 'You will be[t]fuel for the fire;
your blood will be in the midst of
the land. You will[r]not be remembered, for I, the LORD, have spoken.' " *food* • Ezek. 25:10

CHAPTER 22

THEN the word of the LORD
came to me saying,
2 "And you, son of man, will
you judge, will you judge the
bloody city? Then cause her to
know all her abominations.
3 "And you shall say, 'Thus says
the Lord GOD, "A city[r]shedding
blood in her midst, so that her
time will come, and that makes
idols, contrary to her *interest,* for
defilement! Ezek. 22:6, 27
4 "You have become guilty by
[t]the blood which you have shed,
and defiled by your idols which
you have made. Thus you have
brought your[t]day near and have
come to your years; therefore I
have made you a[r]reproach to the
nations, and a mocking to all the
lands. *your* • *days* • Ps. 44:13, 14
5 "Those who are near and
those who are far from you will
mock you, you of ill repute, full of
[r]turmoil. Is. 22:2
6 "Behold, the[r]rulers of Israel,
each according to his[t]power, have
been in you for the purpose of
shedding blood. Is. 1:23 • *arm*
7 "They have treated father and
mother lightly within you. The
alien they have oppressed in your
midst; the fatherless and the
widow they have wronged in you.
8 "You have despised My holy
things and profaned My sabbaths.
9 "Slanderous men have been in
you for the purpose of shedding
blood, and in you they have eaten
at the mountain *shrines.* In your
midst they have[r]committed acts
of lewdness. Hos. 4:2, 10, 14
10 "In you[t]they have[r]uncovered
their fathers' nakedness; in you
they have humbled her who was
[r]unclean in her menstrual impurity. *he has* • Lev. 18:8 • Lev. 18:19
11 "And one has committed
abomination with his neighbor's
wife, and another has lewdly defiled his daughter-in-law. And an-

other in you has humbled his sister, his father's daughter.
12"In you they have [r]taken
bribes to shed blood; you have
taken interest and profits, and you
have injured your neighbors for
gain by oppression, and you have
forgotten Me," declares the Lord
GOD. Ex. 23:8; Deut. 16:19; 27:25
13"Behold, then, I smite My
hand at your dishonest gain which
you have acquired and at the
bloodshed which is among you.
14"Can [r]your heart endure, or
can your hands be strong, in the
days that I shall deal with you?[r]I,
the LORD, have spoken and shall
act. Ezek. 21:7 • Ezek. 17:24
15"And I shall [r]scatter you
among the nations, and I shall disperse you through the lands, and I
shall consume your uncleanness
from you. Deut. 4:27; Neh. 1:8
16"And you will profane yourself in the sight of the nations, and
you will [r]know that I am the
LORD." ' " Ps. 83:18; Ezek. 6:7
17 And the word of the LORD
came to me saying,
18"Son of man, the house of Israel has become [r]dross to Me; all
of them are bronze and tin and
iron and lead in the furnace; they
are the dross of silver. Is. 1:22
19"Therefore, thus says the Lord
GOD, 'Because all of you have become dross, therefore, behold, I
am going to gather you into the
midst of Jerusalem.
20 'As they gather silver and
bronze and iron and lead and tin
into the [r]furnace to blow fire on it
in order to melt *it*, so I shall gather
you in My anger and in My wrath,
and I shall lay you *there* and melt
you. Is. 1:25
21 'And I shall gather you and
blow on you with the fire of My
wrath, and you will be melted in
the midst of it.
22 'As silver is melted in the furnace, so you will be melted in the
midst of it; and you will know that
I, the LORD, have [r]poured out My
wrath on you.' " Hos. 5:10
23 And the word of the LORD
came to me saying,
24"Son of man, say to her, 'You
are a land that is [r]not cleansed or
rained on in the day of indignation.' Is. 9:13; Jer. 2:30
25"There is a [r]conspiracy of her
prophets in her midst, like a roaring lion tearing the prey. They
have devoured lives; they have
taken treasure and precious
things; they have made many widows in the midst of her. Hos. 6:9
26"Her [r]priests have done violence to My law and have profaned My holy things; they have
made no distinction between the
holy and the profane, and they
have not taught the difference between the unclean and the clean;
and they hide their eyes from My
sabbaths, and I am profaned
among them. Jer. 2:8, 26; Ezek. 7:26
27"Her princes within her are
like wolves tearing the prey, by
shedding blood *and* [r]destroying
lives in order to get [r]dishonest
gain. Ezek. 22:25 • Ezek. 22:13
28"And her prophets have
smeared whitewash for them, seeing [r]false visions and divining lies
for them, saying, 'Thus says the
Lord GOD,' when the LORD has not
spoken. Jer. 23:25-32; Ezek. 13:6
29"The people of the land have
practiced [r]oppression and committed robbery, and they have

wronged the poor and needy and
have oppressed the sojourner
without justice. Is. 5:7
30 "And I searched for a man
among them who should build up
the wall and stand in the gap before Me for the land, that I should
not destroy it; but I found no one.
31 "Thus I have poured out My
[r]indignation on them; I have consumed them with the fire of My
wrath; their way I have brought
upon their heads," declares the
Lord GOD. Is. 10:5; 13:5; 30:27

CHAPTER 23

THE word of the LORD came to
me again saying,
2 "Son of man, there were [r]two
women, the daughters of one
mother; Ezek. 16:46
3 and they played the harlot in
Egypt. They [r]played the harlot in
their youth; there their breasts
were pressed, and there their virgin bosom was handled. Jer. 3:9
4 "And their names were Oholah the elder and Oholibah her sister. And they became Mine, and
they bore sons and daughters.
And *as for* their names, Samaria
is Oholah, and Jerusalem is Oholibah.
5 "And Oholah played the harlot while she was Mine; and she
lusted after her lovers, after the
Assyrians, *her* neighbors,
6 who were clothed in purple,
[r]governors and officials, all of them
desirable young men, horsemen
riding on horses. Ezek. 23:12, 13
7 "And she bestowed her harlotries on them, all of whom *were*
the choicest men of Assyria; and
with all whom she lusted after,
with all their idols she [r]defiled herself. Ezek. 20:7; 22:3, 4; Hos. 5:3
8 "And she did not forsake her
harlotries [r]from the time in Egypt;
for in her youth [t]men had lain with
her, and they handled her virgin
bosom and poured out their [t]lust
on her. Ex. 32:4 • *they* • *harlotry*
9 "Therefore, I gave her into the
hand of her lovers, into the hand
of the [t]Assyrians, after whom she
lusted. *sons of Asshur*
10 "They uncovered her nakedness; they took her sons and her
daughters, but they slew her with
the sword. Thus she became a byword among women, and they executed judgments on her.
11 "Now her sister Oholibah saw
this, yet she was [r]more corrupt in
her lust than she, and her harlotries were more than the harlotries
of her sister. Jer. 3:8-11; Ezek. 16:51
12 "She lusted after the Assyrians, governors and officials, the
ones near, magnificently dressed,
horsemen riding on horses, all of
them desirable young men.
13 "And I saw that she had defiled herself; they both took [t]the
same way. *one*
14 "So she increased her harlotries. And she saw men portrayed
on the wall, images of the Chaldeans portrayed with vermilion,
15 girded with belts on their
loins, with flowing turbans on
their heads, all of them looking
like officers, like the Babylonians
in Chaldea, the land of their birth.
16 "And when she saw them she
lusted after them and sent messengers to them in Chaldea.
17 "And the [t]Babylonians came to
her to the bed of love, and they
defiled her with their harlotry.

And when she had been defiled by them, [t]she became disgusted with them. *sons of Babel • her soul*

18 "And she uncovered her harlotries and uncovered her nakedness; then [t]I became disgusted with her, as I had become disgusted with her sister. *My soul*

19 "Yet she multiplied her harlotries, remembering the days of her youth, when she played the harlot in the land of Egypt.

20 "And she lusted after their paramours, whose flesh is *like* the flesh of donkeys and whose issue is *like* the issue of horses.

21 "Thus you longed for the [r]lewdness of your youth, when the Egyptians handled your bosom because of the breasts of your youth. Jer. 3:9; Ezek. 23:3

22 "Therefore, O Oholibah, thus says the Lord GOD, 'Behold I will arouse your lovers against you, from whom you were alienated, and I will bring them against you from every side:

23 the Babylonians and all the [r]Chaldeans, Pekod and Shoa and Koa, *and* all the Assyrians with them; desirable young men, governors and officials all of them, officers and men of renown, all of them riding on horses. Job 1:17

24 'And they will come against you with weapons, chariots, and wagons, and with a company of peoples. They will set themselves against you on every side with buckler and shield and helmet; and I shall commit the judgment to them, and they will judge you according to their customs.

25 'And I will set My [r]jealousy against you, that they may deal with you in wrath. They will remove your nose and your ears; and your survivors will fall by the sword. They will take your sons and your daughters; and your [t]survivors will be consumed by the fire. Ex. 34:14; Zeph. 1:18 • *remainder*

26 'They will also [r]strip you of your clothes and take away your beautiful jewels. Jer. 13:22

27 'Thus [r]I shall make your lewdness and your harlotry *brought* from the land of Egypt to cease from you, so that you will not lift up your eyes to them or remember Egypt anymore.' Ezek. 16:41

28 "For thus says the Lord GOD, 'Behold, I will give you into the hand of those whom you [r]hate, into the hand of those from whom you were alienated. Jer. 21:7-10

29 'And they will deal with you in hatred, take all your property, and leave you naked and bare. And the nakedness of your harlotries shall be uncovered, both your lewdness and your harlotries.

30 'These things will be done to you because you have [r]played the harlot with the nations, because you have defiled yourself with their idols. Ezek. 6:9

31 'You have walked in the way of your sister; therefore I will give her cup into your hand.'

32 "Thus says the Lord GOD,

'You will [r]drink your sister's
cup, Ps. 60:3; Is. 51:17
Which is deep and wide.
You will be [r]laughed at and
held in derision;
It contains much. Ezek. 5:14

33 'You will be filled with
drunkenness and sorrow,
The cup of horror and desolation,

The cup of your sister Samaria.
34 'And you will ʳdrink it and drain it.
Then you will gnaw its fragments
And tear your breasts;
for I have spoken,' declares the Lord GOD. Ps. 75:8; Is. 51:17
35"Therefore, thus says the Lord GOD, 'Because you have forgotten Me and cast Me behind your back, bear now the *punishment* of your lewdness and your harlotries.' "
36 Moreover, the LORD said to me, "Son of man, will you judge Oholah and Oholibah? Then declare to them their abominations.
37"For they have committed adultery, and blood is on their hands. Thus they have committed adultery with their idols and even caused their sons, whom they bore to Me, to pass through *the fire* to them as food.
38"Again, they have done this to Me: they have ʳdefiled My sanctuary on the same day and have profaned My sabbaths. 2 Kin. 21:4, 7
39"For when they had slaughtered their children for their idols, they entered My sanctuary on the same day to profane it; and lo, thus they did within My house.
40"Furthermore, they have even sent for men who come from afar, to whom a messenger was sent; and lo, they came—for whom you bathed, ʳpainted your eyes, and decorated yourselves with ornaments; 2 Kin. 9:30; Jer. 4:30
41 and you sat on a splendid ʳcouch with a table arranged before it, on which you had set My incense and My oil. Esth. 1:6
42"And the sound of a carefree multitude was with her; and drunkards were brought from the wilderness with men of the common sort. And they put bracelets on the hands of the women and beautiful crowns on their heads.
43"Then I said concerning her who was worn out by adulteries, 'Will they now commit adultery with her when she is *thus*?'
44"But they went in to her as they would go in to a harlot. Thus they went in to Oholah and to Oholibah, the lewd women.
45"But they, righteous men, will ʳjudge them with the judgment of adulteresses, and with the judgment of women who shed blood, because they are adulteresses and blood is on their hands. Ezek. 16:38
46"For thus says the Lord GOD, 'Bring up a company against them, and give them over to ʳterror and plunder. Jer. 15:4; 24:9; 29:18
47 'And the company will stone them with stones and cut them down with their swords; they will slay their sons and their daughters and burn their houses with fire.
48 'Thus I shall make lewdness cease from the land, that all women may be admonished and not commit ˡlewdness as you have done. *according to your lewdness*
49 'And your lewdness will be requited upon you, and you will bear the penalty of *worshiping* your idols; thus you will know that I am the Lord GOD.' "

CHAPTER 24

AND the word of the LORD came to me in the ninth year, in the

tenth month, on the tenth of the
month, saying,
2 "Son of man, write the name
of the day, this very day. The king
of Babylon [t]has laid siege to Jerusalem this very day. *leaned on*
3 "And speak a parable to the
rebellious house, and say to them,
'Thus says the Lord GOD,
"Put on the pot, put *it* on,
and also pour water in it;
4 Put in it the pieces,
Every good piece, the thigh,
and the shoulder;
Fill *it* with choice bones.
5 "Take the [r]choicest of the
flock, Jer. 39:6; 52:10
And also pile [t]wood under
[t]the pot. *bones • it*
Make it boil vigorously.
Also seethe its bones in it."

6 'Therefore, thus says the
Lord GOD,
"Woe to the [r]bloody city,
To the pot in which there is
rust 2 Kin. 24:3, 4
And whose rust has not
gone out of it!
Take out of it piece after
piece,
Without making a choice.
7 "For her blood is in her
midst;
She placed it on the bare
rock;
She did not [r]pour it on the
ground Lev. 17:13
To cover it with dust.
8 "That it may [r]cause wrath to
come up to take ven-
geance, Is. 26:21
I have put her blood on the
bare rock,
That it may not be cov-
ered."

9 'Therefore, thus says the
Lord GOD,
[r]"Woe to the bloody city!
I also shall make the pile
great. Hab. 2:12
10 "Heap on the wood, kindle
the fire,
Boil the flesh well,
And mix in the spices,
And let the bones be
burned.
11 "Then [r]set it empty on its
coals, Jer. 21:10; Mal. 4:1
So that it may be hot,
And its bronze may glow,
And its [r]filthiness may be
melted in it, Ezek. 22:15
Its rust consumed.
12 "She has [r]wearied *Me* with
toil, Jer. 9:5
Yet her great rust has not
gone from her;
Let her rust *be* in the fire!
13 "In your filthiness is lewdness.
Because I *would* have
cleansed you,
Yet you are not clean,
You will not be cleansed
from your filthiness
again,
Until I have [t]spent My wrath
on you. *caused to rest*
14 "I, the LORD, have spoken; it is
[r]coming and I shall act. I shall not
relent, and I shall not pity, and I
shall not be sorry; according to
your ways and according to your
deeds I shall judge you," declares
the Lord GOD.' " Ps. 33:9; Is. 55:11
15 And the word of the LORD
came to me saying,
16 "Son of man, behold, I am
about to take from you the [r]desire
of your eyes with a blow; but you
shall not mourn, and you shall not

weep, and your tears shall not
come. Song 7:10; Ezek. 24:18
17 "Groan silently; make [r]no
mourning for the dead. Bind on
your turban, and put your shoes
on your feet, and do not cover
your mustache, and do not eat the
bread of men." Lev. 21:10-12
18 So I spoke to the people in
the morning, and in the evening
my wife died. And in the morning
I did as I was commanded.
19 And the people said to me,
"Will you not tell us what these
things that you are doing mean for
us?"
20 Then I said to them, "The
word of the LORD came to me saying,
21 'Speak to the house of Israel,
"Thus says the Lord GOD, 'Behold,
I am about to profane My sanctuary, the pride of your power, the
[r]desire of your eyes, and the delight of your soul; and your sons
and your daughters whom you
have left behind will fall by the
sword. Ps. 27:4; 84:1; Ezek. 24:16
22 'And you will do as I have
done; you will not cover *your*
mustache, and you will not eat the
bread of men.
23 'And your turbans will be on
your heads and your shoes on
your feet. You will not mourn, and
you will not weep; but you will rot
away in your iniquities, and you
will groan to one another.
24 'Thus Ezekiel will be a [r]sign to
you; according to all that he has
done you will do; when it comes,
then you will know that I am the
Lord GOD.'" Luke 11:29, 30
25 'As for you, son of man, will
it not be on the day when I take
from them their stronghold, the
joy of their [a]pride, the desire of
their eyes, and [t]their heart's delight, their sons and their daughters, *beauty • the lifting up of their soul*
26 that on that day he who [r]es-
capes will come to you with information for *your* ears? 1 Sam. 4:12
27 'On that day your [r]mouth will
be opened to him who escaped,
and you will speak and be dumb
no longer. Thus you will be a sign
to them, and they will know that I
am the LORD.'" Ezek. 3:26

CHAPTER 25

AND the word of the LORD came
to me saying,
2 "Son of man, set your face
toward the [r]sons of Ammon, and
prophesy against them, Zeph. 2:9
3 and say to the sons of Ammon, 'Hear the word of the Lord
GOD! Thus says the Lord GOD,
"Because you said, 'Aha!' against
My sanctuary when it was profaned, and against the land of Israel when it was made desolate,
and against the house of Judah
when they went into exile,
4 therefore, behold, I am going
to give you to the [r]sons of the east
for a possession, and they will set
their encampments among you
and make their dwellings among
you; they will eat your fruit and
drink your milk. Judg. 6:3, 33
5 "And I shall make [r]Rabbah a
pasture for camels and the sons of
Ammon a resting place for flocks.
Thus you will know that I am the
LORD." Deut. 3:11; 2 Sam. 12:26
6 'For thus says the Lord GOD,
"Because you have clapped your
hands and stamped your feet and

rejoiced with all the scorn of your
soul against the land of Israel,
7 therefore, behold, I have
[r]stretched out My hand against
you, and I shall give you for spoil
to the nations. And I shall cut you
off from the peoples and make
you perish from the lands; I shall
destroy you. Thus you will know
that I am the LORD." Zeph. 1:4
8 'Thus says the Lord GOD,
"Because [r]Moab and Seir say, 'Behold, the house of Judah is like all
the nations,' Is. 15:1; Jer. 48:1
9 therefore, behold, I am going
to [t]deprive the flank of Moab of *its*
cities, of its cities which are on its
[t]frontiers, the glory of the land,
Beth-jeshimoth, Baal-meon, and
Kiriathaim, *open • end*
10 and I will give it for a possession, along with the sons of Ammon, to the sons of the east, that
the sons of Ammon may not be remembered among the nations.
11 "Thus I will execute judgments on Moab, and they will
know that I am the LORD."
12 'Thus says the Lord GOD,
"Because [r]Edom has acted against
the house of Judah by taking vengeance, and has incurred grievous
guilt, and avenged themselves
upon them," 2 Chr. 28:17; Ps. 137:7
13 therefore, thus says the Lord
GOD, "I will also stretch out My
hand against Edom and cut off
man and beast from it. And I will
lay it waste; from Teman even to
Dedan they will fall by the sword.
14 "And I will lay My vengeance
on Edom by the hand of My people Israel. Therefore, they will act
in Edom according to My anger
and according to My wrath; thus
they will know My vengeance,"
declares the Lord GOD.
15 'Thus says the Lord GOD,
"Because the Philistines have
acted in revenge and have taken
vengeance with scorn of soul to
destroy with everlasting enmity,"
16 therefore, thus says the Lord
GOD, "Behold, I will [r]stretch out
My hand against the Philistines,
even cut off the [r]Cherethites and
destroy the remnant of the seacoast. Jer. 25:20; 47:1-7 • Zeph. 2:5
17 "And I will execute great vengeance on them with wrathful rebukes; and they will [r]know that I
am the LORD when I lay My vengeance on them."'" Ps. 9:16

CHAPTER 26

NOW it came about in the eleventh year, on the first of the
month, that the word of the LORD
came to me saying,
2 "Son of man, because [r]Tyre
has said concerning Jerusalem,
'Aha, the gateway of the peoples
is broken; it has [t]opened to me. I
shall be filled, *now that* she is laid
waste,' 2 Sam. 5:11; Is. 23:1 • *turned*
3 therefore, thus says the Lord
GOD, 'Behold, I am against you, O
Tyre, and I will bring up [r]many nations against you, as the sea
brings up its waves. Mic. 4:11
4 'And they will [r]destroy the
walls of Tyre and break down her
towers; and I will scrape her debris from her and make her a bare
rock. Is. 23:11; Ezek. 26:9; Amos 1:10
5 'She will be a place for the
spreading of nets in the midst of
the sea, for I have spoken,' declares the Lord GOD, 'and she will
become spoil for the nations.

6 'Also her daughters who are
[t]on the mainland will be slain by
the sword, and they will know
that I am the LORD.'" *in the field*
7 For thus says the Lord GOD,
"Behold, I will bring upon Tyre
from the north Nebuchadnezzar
king of Babylon, [r]king of kings,
with horses, chariots, cavalry, and
a great army. Ezra 7:12; Is. 10:8
8 "He will slay your daughters
[t]on the mainland with the sword;
and he will make siege walls
against you, cast up a mound
against you, and raise up a large
shield against you. *in the field*
9 "And the blow of his battering
rams he will direct against your
walls, and with his [t]axes he will
break down your towers. *swords*
10 "Because of the multitude of
his horses, the dust *raised by*
them will cover you; your walls
will shake at the noise of cavalry
and [t]wagons and chariots, when he
enters your gates as men enter a
city that is breached. *wheels*
11 "With the hoofs of his horses
he will trample all your streets. He
will slay your people with the
sword; and your strong pillars will
come down to the ground.
12 "Also they will make a spoil of
your riches and a prey of your
[r]merchandise, break down your
walls and destroy your pleasant
houses, and throw your stones
and your timbers and your debris
into the water. Is. 23:8, 18; Zech. 9:3
13 "So I will silence the sound of
your songs, and the sound of your
harps will be heard no more.
14 "And I will make you a bare
rock; you will be a place for the
spreading of nets. You will be
built no more, for I the LORD have
spoken," declares the Lord GOD.
15 Thus says the Lord GOD to
Tyre, "Shall not the coastlands
[r]shake at the sound of your fall
when the wounded groan, when
the slaughter occurs in your
midst? Jer. 49:21; Ezek. 31:16
16 "Then all the princes of the
sea will go down from their
thrones, remove their robes, and
strip off their embroidered garments. They will clothe themselves with trembling; they will sit
on the ground, tremble every moment, and be appalled at you.
17 "And they will take up a lamentation over you and say to you,

> [r]'How you have perished, O
> inhabited one, Is. 14:12
> From the seas, O renowned
> city,
> Which was [r]mighty on the
> sea, Ezek. 27:3, 10,11
> She and her inhabitants,
> Who imposed her terror
> On all her inhabitants!
> 18 'Now the [r]coastlands will
> tremble Is. 41:5
> On the day of your fall;
> Yes, the coastlands which
> are by the sea
> Will be terrified at your
> [r]passing.'" Is. 23:5-7, 10, 11

19 For thus says the Lord GOD,
"When I shall make you a desolate city, like the cities which are
not inhabited, when I shall bring
up the deep over you, and the
great waters will cover you,
20 then I shall bring you down
with those who go down to the
pit, to the people of old, and I shall
make you dwell in the lower parts
of the earth, like the ancient waste
places, with those who go down to

the pit, so that you will not[a] be inhabited; but I shall set glory in the land of the living. *return*

21 "I shall bring [r]terrors on you, and you will be no more; though you will be sought,[r] you will never be found again," declares the Lord GOD. Ezek. 26:15, 16 • Rev. 18:21

CHAPTER 27

MOREOVER, the word of the LORD came to me saying,

2 "And you, son of man, take up a lamentation over Tyre;

3 and say to Tyre, who dwells at the entrance to the sea, merchant of the peoples to many coastlands, 'Thus says the Lord GOD,

"O Tyre, you have said, 'I am
perfect in beauty.'

4 "Your borders are in the
heart of the seas;
Your builders have perfected your beauty.

5 "They have [t]made all *your*
planks of fir trees from
[r]Senir; *built* • Duet. 3:9
They have taken a cedar
from Lebanon to make a
mast for you.

6 "Of oaks from Bashan they
have made your oars;
With ivory they have [t]inlaid
your deck of boxwood
from the coastlands of
Cyprus. *made*

7 "Your sail was of fine embroidered linen from
Egypt
So that it became your[a] distinguishing mark; *standard*
Your [t]awning was blue and
purple from the coastlands of Elishah. *covering*

8 "The inhabitants of Sidon
and [r]Arvad were your
rowers; Gen. 10:18
Your wise men, O Tyre,
were [t]aboard; they were
your pilots. *in you*

9 "The elders of Gebal and her
wise men were with you
repairing your seams;
All the ships of the sea and
their sailors were with
you in order to deal in
your merchandise.

10 "Persia and Lud and Put were in your army, your men of war. They hung shield and helmet in you; they set forth your splendor.

11 "The sons of Arvad and your army were on your walls, *all* around, and the Gammadim were in your towers. They hung their shields on your walls, *all* around; they perfected your beauty.

12 "Tarshish was your customer because of the abundance of all *kinds* of wealth; with silver, iron, tin, and lead, they paid for your wares.

13 "Javan, Tubal, and Meshech, they were your traders; with the lives of men and vessels of bronze they paid for your merchandise.

14 "Those from Beth-togarmah gave horses and war horses and mules for your wares.

15 "The sons of Dedan were your traders. Many coastlands were your market; ivory tusks and ebony they brought as your payment.

16 "[r]Aram was your customer because of the abundance of your [t]goods; they paid for your wares with emeralds, purple, embroidered work, fine linen, coral, and rubies. Is. 7:1-8 • *works*

17"Judah and the land of Israel,
they were your traders; with the
wheat of [r]Minnith, [t]cakes, honey,
oil, and balm they paid for your
merchandise. Judg. 11:33 • *pannag*
18"Damascus[r] was your customer because of the abundance
of your [t]goods, because of the
abundance of all *kinds* of wealth,
because of the wine of Helbon and
white wool. Gen. 14:15 • *works*
19"Vedan and Javan paid for
your wares from Uzal; wrought
iron, cassia, and [a]sweet cane were
among your merchandise. *calamus*
20"Dedan[r] traded with you in
saddlecloths for riding. Gen. 25:3
21"Arabia and all the princes of
Kedar, they were your customers
for lambs, rams, and goats; for
these they were your customers.
22"The traders of [r]Sheba and
Raamah, they traded with you;
they paid for your wares with the
best of all *kinds* of [r]spices, and
with all *kinds* of precious stones,
and gold. Gen. 10:7 • 1 Kin. 10:2
23"Haran, Canneh, Eden, the
traders of Sheba, Asshur, *and*
Chilmad traded with you.
24"They traded with you in
choice garments, in clothes of
[a]blue and embroidered work, and
in carpets of many colors, *and*
tightly wound cords, *which were*
among your merchandise. *violet*
25"The ships of Tarshish were
[t]the carriers for your merchandise.
And you were filled and were
very glorious *your travelers*
In the heart of the seas.

26"Your rowers have brought
you
Into [r]great waters; Ezek. 26:19
The east wind has broken
you
In the heart of the seas.
27"Your wealth, your wares,
your merchandise,
Your sailors, and your pilots,
Your repairers of seams,
your dealers in merchan-
dise,
And all your men of war who
are in you,
With all your company that
is in your midst,
Will fall into the heart of the
seas
On the day of your over-
throw.
28"At the sound of the cry of
your pilots
The pasture lands will shake.
29"And all who handle the oar,
The [r]sailors, *and* all the pilots
of the sea Rev. 18:17-19
Will come down from their
ships;
They will stand on the land,
30 And they will [r]make their
voice heard over you
And will cry bitterly. Is. 23:1-6
They will [r]cast dust on their
heads, Rev. 18:19
They will wallow in ashes.
31"Also they will make themselves [r]bald for you
And gird themselves with
sackcloth; Is. 15:2
And they will [r]weep for you
in bitterness of soul
With bitter mourning. Is. 16:9
32"Moreover, in their wailing
they will take up a [r]lam-
entation for you
And lament over you:
'Who is like Tyre, Ezek. 26:17
Like her who is silent in the
midst of the sea?

33 'When your wares went out from the seas,
You satisfied many peoples;
With the [r]abundance of your wealth and your merchandise Ezek. 27:12
You enriched the kings of earth.
34 'Now[t] that you are broken by the seas *The time*
In the depths of the waters,
Your [r]merchandise and all your company
Have fallen in the midst of you. Zech. 9:3, 4
35 'All the [r]inhabitants of the coastlands
Are appalled at you,
And their kings are horribly afraid;
They are troubled in countenance. Is. 23:6; Ezek. 26:16
36 'The merchants among the peoples hiss at you;
You have become[t] terrified,
And you will be no more.' " ' " *terrors*

CHAPTER 28

THE word of the LORD came
again to me saying,
2 "Son of man, say to the[a] leader
of Tyre, 'Thus says the Lord GOD,
"Because your heart is lifted up *ruler, prince*
And you have said, 'I am a god,
I sit in the seat of[a] gods, *God*
In the heart of the seas';
Yet you are a [r]man and not God, Ps. 9:20
Although you make your heart like the heart of God—
3 Behold, you are wiser than [r]Daniel; Dan. 1:20
There is no secret that is a match for you.
4 "By your wisdom and understanding
You have acquired [r]riches for yourself, Ezek. 27:33
And have acquired gold and silver for your treasuries.
5 "By your great wisdom, by your [r]trade Ezek. 27:12
You have increased your riches,
And your heart is lifted up because of your riches—
6 Therefore, thus says the Lord GOD,
'Because you have [r]made your heart Ex. 9:17
Like the heart of God,
7 Therefore, behold, I will bring [r]strangers upon you,
The [r]most ruthless of the nations. Ezek. 26:7 • Hab. 1:6-8
And they will draw their swords
Against the beauty of your wisdom
And defile your splendor.
8 'They will bring you down to the pit,
And you will die the death of those who are slain
In the heart of the seas.
9 'Will you still say, "I am a god,"
In the presence of your slayer,
Although you are a man and not God,
In the hands of those who wound you?
10 'You will die the death of the [r]uncircumcised 1 Sam. 17:26
By the hand of strangers,

For I have spoken!' declares
the Lord GOD!"'"

11 Again the word of the LORD
came to me saying,
12"Son of man,[r]take up a lamentation over the king of Tyre, and
say to him, 'Thus says the Lord
GOD, Ezek. 19:1; 26:17; 27:2

"You had the seal of perfection,
Full of wisdom and perfect in
beauty.
13"You were in[r]Eden, the garden of God; Gen. 2:8
[r]Every precious stone was
your covering: Ezek. 27:16
The[r]ruby, the topaz, and the
diamond; Ex. 28:17-20
The beryl, the onyx, and the
jasper;
The lapis lazuli, the turquoise, and the emerald;
And the gold, the workmanship of your[a]settings and
[a]sockets, *tambourines • flutes*
Was in you.
On the day that you were
created
They were prepared.
14"You were the anointed
cherub who covers,
And I placed you *there.*
You were on the holy[r]moun-
tain of God; Ezek. 20:40
You walked in the midst of
the stones of fire.
15"You were[r]blameless in your
ways Ezek. 27:3, 4
From the day you were created,
Until [r]unrighteousness was
found in you. Ezek. 28:17, 18
16"By the [r]abundance of your
trade Ezek. 27:12
You were internally filled
with violence,
And you sinned;
Therefore I have cast you as
profane
From the mountain of God.
And I have destroyed you, O
[a]covering cherub,
From the midst of the stones
of fire. *guardian*
17"Your heart was lifted up because of your beauty;
You[r]corrupted your wisdom
by reason of your splen-
dor. Is. 19:11
I cast you to the ground;
I put you before kings,
That they may see you.
18"By the multitude of your iniquities,
In the unrighteousness of
your trade,
You profaned your sanctuar-
ies.
Therefore I have brought fire
from the midst of you;
It has consumed you,
And I have turned you to
ashes on the earth
In the eyes of all who see
you.
19"All who know you among the
peoples
Are appalled at you;
You have become terrified,
And you will be no more."'"

20 And the word of the LORD
came to me saying,
21"Son of man, [r]set your face
toward [r]Sidon, prophesy against
her, Ezek. 6:2; 25:2 • Gen. 10:15, 19
22 and say, 'Thus says the Lord
GOD,

"Behold, I am against you, O
Sidon,
And I shall[a]be glorified in
your midst. *glorify Myself*

Then they will know that I
am the LORD, when I ex-
ecute judgments in her,
And I shall manifest My holiness in her.
23"For[r]I shall send pestilence to
her Ezek. 38:22
And blood to her streets,
And the[r]wounded will fall in
her midst Jer. 51:52
By the sword upon her on every side;
Then they will know that I
am the LORD.
24"And there will be no more for
the house of Israel a[r]prickling
brier or a painful thorn from any
round about them who scorned
them; then they will know that I
am the Lord GOD." Num. 33:55
25 'Thus says the Lord GOD,
"When I[r]gather the house of Israel
from the peoples among whom
they are scattered, and shall manifest My holiness in them in the
sight of the nations, then they will
live in their land which I gave to
My servant Jacob. Ps. 106:47
26"And they will live in it securely; and they will build houses,
plant vineyards, and live securely,
when I execute judgments upon
all who scorn them round about
them. Then they will know that I
am the LORD their God." ' "

CHAPTER 29

IN the[r]tenth year, in the tenth
month, on the twelfth of the
month, the word of the LORD
came to me saying, Ezek. 26:1; 29:17
2"Son of man, set your face
against[r]Pharaoh, king of Egypt,
and prophesy against him and
against all Egypt. Jer. 44:30
3"Speak and say, 'Thus says
the Lord GOD,
"Behold, I am against you,
Pharaoh, king of Egypt,
The great monster that lies in
the midst of his rivers,
That[r]has said, 'My Nile is
mine, and I myself have
made it.' Ezek. 29:9; 30:12
4"And I shall put[r]hooks in your
jaws, 2 Kin. 19:28
And I shall make the fish of
your rivers cling to your
scales.
And I shall bring you up out
of the midst of your[a]riv-
ers, *Nile*
And all the fish of your rivers
will cling to your scales.
5"And I shall abandon you to
the wilderness, you and
all the fish of your rivers;
You will fall on the open
field; you will not be
brought together or[r]gath-
ered. Jer. 8:2; 25:33
I have given you for[r]food to
the beasts of the earth
and to the birds of the
sky. Jer. 7:33; 34:20
6"Then all the inhabitants of
Egypt will know that I
am the LORD,
Because they have been *only*
a staff *made* of reed to
the house of Israel.
7"When they took hold of you
with the hand,
You[r]broke and tore all their
hands; 2 Kin. 18:21; Is. 36:6
And when they leaned on
you,
You broke and made all their
loins[t]quake." *stand*
8 'Therefore, thus says the Lord

GOD, "Behold, I shall [r]bring upon
you a sword, and I shall cut off
from you man and beast. Jer. 46:13
9"And the [r]land of Egypt will
become a desolation and waste.
Then they will know that I am the
LORD. Ezek. 29:10-12; 30:7, 8, 13-19
Because you said, 'The Nile is
mine, and I have made *it,*'
10 therefore, behold, I am
against you and against your rivers, and I will make the land of
Egypt an utter waste and desolation, from Migdol *to* Syene and
even to the border of Ethiopia.
11"A man's foot will not pass
through it, and the foot of a beast
will not pass through it, and it will
not be inhabited for forty years.
12"So I shall make the land of
Egypt a desolation in the midst of
desolated lands. And her cities, in
the midst of cities that are laid
waste, will be desolate forty
years; and I shall scatter the Egyptians among the nations and disperse them among the lands."
13 'For thus says the Lord GOD,
"At the end of forty years I shall
[r]gather the Egyptians from the
peoples among whom they were
scattered. Is. 19:22; Jer. 46:26
14"And I shall turn the fortunes
of Egypt and shall make them return to the land of Pathros, to the
land of their origin; and there they
will be a lowly kingdom.
15"It will be the [r]lowest of the
kingdoms; and it will never again
lift itself up above the nations.
And I shall make them so small
that they will not rule over the nations. Ezek. 17:6, 14; 30:13
16"And it will never again be the
confidence of the house of Israel,
[t]bringing to mind the iniquity of
their having turned to Egypt. Then
they will know that I am the Lord
GOD."'" *causing to remember*
17 Now in the twenty-seventh
year, in the first *month,* on the
first of the month, the word of the
LORD came to me saying,
18"Son of man, Nebuchadnezzar king of Babylon made his
army labor hard against Tyre; every head was made bald, and every shoulder was rubbed bare. But
he and his army had no wages
from Tyre for the labor that he
had performed against it."
19 Therefore, thus says the Lord
GOD, "Behold, I shall give the land
of Egypt to Nebuchadnezzar king
of Babylon. And he will carry off
her [a]wealth, and capture her spoil
and seize her plunder; and it will
be wages for his army. *multitude*
20"I have given him the land of
Egypt *for* his labor which he performed, because they acted for
Me," declares the Lord GOD.
21"On that day I shall make a
horn sprout for the house of Israel, and I shall open your mouth
in their midst. Then they will
know that I am the LORD."

CHAPTER 30

THE word of the LORD came
again to me saying,
2"Son of man, prophesy and
say, 'Thus says the Lord GOD,
"Wail, 'Alas for the day!'
3 "For the day is near,
Even [r]the day of the LORD is
near;
It will be a day of clouds,
A time *of doom* for the nations. Ezek. 7:19; 13:5

4 "And a sword will come
upon Egypt,
And anguish will be in [t]Ethi-
opia, *Cush*
When the slain fall in
Egypt,
They take away her wealth,
And her foundations are
torn down.
5 "Ethiopia, Put, Lud, all [a]Ara-
bia, Libya, and the people of the
land that is in league will fall with
them by the sword." *the mixed people*
6 'Thus says the LORD,
"Indeed, those who support
[r]Egypt will fall, Is. 20:3-6
And the pride of her power
will come down;
From Migdol *to* Syene
They will fall within her by
the sword,"
Declares the Lord GOD.
7 "And they will be desolate
In the [r]midst of the desolated lands; Jer. 25:18-26
And her cities will be
In the midst of the devastated cities.
8 "And they will [r]know that I
am the LORD, Ps. 58:11
When I set a fire in Egypt
And all her helpers are broken.
9 "On that day [r]messengers will
go forth from Me in ships to
frighten [r]secure Ethiopia; and [r]an-
guish will be on them as on the
day of Egypt; for, behold, it
comes!" Is. 18:1, 2 • Is. 47:8 • Is. 19:17
10 'Thus says the Lord GOD,
"I will also make the multitude of Egypt cease
By the hand of Nebuchad-
nezzar king of Babylon.
11 "He and his people with him,
[r]The most ruthless of the nations, Ezek. 28:7
Will be brought in to de-
stroy the land;
And they will draw their
swords against Egypt
And fill the land with the
slain.
12 "Moreover, I will make the
[r]Nile canals dry Ezek. 29:3
And [r]sell the land into the
hands of evil men.
And I will make the land
desolate, Is. 19:4
And all that is in it,
By the hand of strangers; I,
the LORD, have spoken."
13 'Thus says the Lord GOD,
"I will also destroy the idols
And make the [a]images cease
from Memphis. *futile ones*
And there will no longer be
a prince in the land of
Egypt;
And I will put fear in the
land of Egypt.
14 "And I will make [r]Pathros
desolate, Is. 11:11
Set a fire in [r]Zoan,
And execute judgments on
[2]Thebes. Ps. 78:12, 43
15 "And I will pour out My
wrath on [3]Sin,
The stronghold of Egypt;
I will also cut off the multitude of Thebes.
16 "And I will set a fire in
Egypt;
Sin will writhe in anguish,
Thebes will be breached,
And [4]Memphis *will have*
distresses daily.
17 "The young men of [5]On and
of Pi-beseth

[2]Or, *No* [3]Or, *Pelusium* [4]Or, *Noph*
[5]Or, *Aven*

Will fall by the sword,
And[t] the women will go into
captivity. *they*
18 "And in Tehaphnehes the
day will be dark
When I break there the
yoke bars of Egypt.
Then the pride of her power
will cease in her;
A cloud will cover her,
And her daughters will go
into captivity.
19 "Thus I will [r]execute judgments on Egypt, Ps. 9:16
And they will know that I
am the LORD."'"

20 And it came about in the
[r]eleventh year, in the first *month,*
on the seventh of the month, that
the word of the LORD came to me
saying, Ezek. 26:1; 29:1, 17; 31:1
21 "Son of man, I have broken
the arm of Pharaoh king of Egypt;
and, behold, it has not been bound
up[t] for healing or wrapped with a
bandage, that it may be strong to
hold the sword. *to give healing*
22 "Therefore, thus says the Lord
GOD, 'Behold, I am [r]against Pharaoh king of Egypt and will break
his arms, both the strong and the
broken; and I will make the sword
fall from his hand. Jer. 46:25
23 'And I will scatter the Egyptians among the nations and disperse them among the lands.
24 'For I will strengthen the
arms of the king of Babylon and
put My sword in his hand; and I
will break the arms of Pharaoh, so
that he will groan before him with
the groanings of a wounded man.
25 'Thus I will strengthen the
arms of the king of Babylon, but
the arms of Pharaoh will fall. Then
they will know that I am the LORD,
when I put My sword into the
hand of the king of Babylon and
he [r]stretches it out against the land
of Egypt. Josh. 8:18; 1 Chr. 21:16
26 'When I scatter the Egyptians
among the nations and disperse
them among the lands, then they
will know that I am the LORD.'"

CHAPTER 31

AND it came about in the [r]elev-
enth year, in the third *month,* on
the first of the month, that the
word of the LORD came to me saying, Jer. 52:5, 6; Ezek. 30:20; 32:1
2 "Son of man, say to Pharaoh
king of Egypt, and to his [r]multi-
tude, Ezek. 29:19; 30:10; Nah. 3:9
'Whom are you like in your
greatness?
3 'Behold, Assyria *was* a [r]ce-
dar in Lebanon Is. 10:33, 34
With beautiful branches
and forest shade,
And [r]very high; Is. 10:33
And its top was among the
clouds.
4 'The waters made it grow,
the deep made it high.
With its rivers it continually extended all around
its planting place,
And it sent out its channels
to all the trees of the
field.
5 'Therefore [r]its height was
loftier than all the trees
of the field Dan. 4:11
And its boughs became
many and its branches
long
Because of many waters as
it spread them out.

6 'All the birds of the heavens nested in its boughs,
And under its branches all the beasts of the field gave birth,
And all great nations lived under its shade.
7 'So it was beautiful in its greatness, in the length of its branches;
For its [t]roots extended to many waters. *root was*
8 'The cedars in God's garden could not match it;
The cypresses could not compare with its boughs,
And the plane trees could not match its branches.
No tree in [r]God's garden could compare with it in its beauty. Gen. 2:8, 9; 13:10
9 'I made it beautiful with the multitude of its branches,
And all the trees of Eden, which were in the garden of God, were jealous of it.

10 'Therefore, thus says the Lord GOD, "Because it is high in stature, and it has set its top among the clouds, and its [r]heart is haughty in its loftiness, Is. 10:12
11 therefore, I will give it into the hand of a [a]despot of the nations; he will thoroughly deal with it. According to its wickedness I have driven it away. *mighty one*
12 "And [r]alien tyrants of the nations have cut it down and left it; on the mountains and in all the valleys its branches have fallen, and its boughs have been broken in all the ravines of the land. And all the peoples of the earth have gone down from its shade and left it. Ezek. 7:21; 28:7; 30:12; Hab. 1:6
13 "On its ruin all the [r]birds of the heavens will dwell. And all the beasts of the field will be on its *fallen* branches Is. 18:6
14 in order that all the trees by the waters may not be exalted in their stature, nor set their top among the [a]clouds, nor their [t]well-watered mighty ones stand *erect* in their height. For they have all been given over to death, to the earth beneath, among the sons of men, with those who go down to the pit." *thick boughs* · *drinkers of water*
15 'Thus says the Lord GOD, "On the day when it went down to Sheol I caused lamentations; I closed the deep over it and held back its rivers. And *its* many waters were stopped up, and I made Lebanon [t]mourn for it, and all the trees of the field wilted away on account of it. *be darkened*
16 "I made the nations [r]quake at the sound of its fall when I made it go down to Sheol with those who go down to the pit; and all the well-watered trees of Eden, the choicest and best of Lebanon, were comforted in the earth beneath. Ezek. 26:15; 27:28; Hag. 2:7
17 "They also went down with it to Sheol to those who were slain by the sword; and those who were its [t]strength lived under its shade among the nations. *arm*
18 "To which among the trees of Eden are you thus [t]equal in glory and greatness? Yet you will be brought down with the trees of Eden to the earth beneath; you will lie in the midst of the uncircumcised, with those who were slain by the sword. [r]So is Pharaoh and all his multitude!"' declares the Lord GOD." *like* · Ps. 52:7

CHAPTER 32

AND it came about in the twelfth
year, in the twelfth *month,* on the
first of the month, that the word
of the LORD came to me saying,
2 "Son of man, take up a [r]lamen-
tation over Pharaoh king of Egypt,
and say to him, Ezek. 19:1; 27:2

'You compared yourself to a
young lion of the nations,
Yet you are like the [r]mon-
ster in the seas; Is. 27:1
And you [r]burst forth in your
rivers, Jer. 46:7, 8
And muddied the waters
with your feet,
And fouled their rivers.' "

3 Thus says the Lord GOD,
"Now I will [r]spread My net
over you Ezek. 12:13
With a company of many
peoples,
And they shall lift you up in
My net.
4 "And I will leave you on the
land;
I will cast you on the [t]open
field. *surface of the field*
And I will cause all the
[r]birds of the heavens to
dwell on you, Is. 18:6
And I will satisfy the beasts
of the whole earth [t]with
you. *from*
5 "And I will lay your flesh [r]on
the mountains, Ezek. 31:12
And fill the valleys with
your refuse.
6 "I will also make the land
drink the discharge of
your [r]blood, Is. 34:3, 7
As far as the mountains,
And the ravines shall be full
of you.
7 "And when *I* extinguish you,
I will cover the heavens,
and darken their stars;
I will cover the [r]sun with a
cloud, Joel 2:2, 31; 3:15
And the moon shall not give
its light.
8 "All the shining [r]lights in the
heavens Gen. 1:14
I will darken over you
And will set darkness on
your land,"
Declares the Lord GOD.

9 "I will also [r]trouble the hearts
of many peoples, when I bring
your destruction among the nations, into lands which you have
not known. Rev. 18:10-15
10 "And I will make many peoples [r]appalled at you, and their
kings shall be horribly afraid of
you when I brandish My sword
before them; and [r]they shall tremble every moment, every man for
his own life, on the day of your
fall." Ezek. 27:35 • Ezek. 26:16
11 For [r]thus says the Lord GOD,
"The sword of the king of Babylon
shall come upon you. Jer. 46:26
12 "By the swords of the mighty
ones I will cause your multitude to
fall; all of them are [r]tyrants of the
nations, Ezek. 28:7

And they shall [r]devastate
the pride of Egypt,
And all its multitude shall
be destroyed. Ezek. 28:19
13 "I will also destroy all its cattle from beside many wa-
ters;
And [r]the foot of man shall
not muddy them any-
more, Ezek. 29:11
And the hoofs of beasts
shall not muddy them.

14 "Then I will make their waters settle,
And will cause their rivers to run like oil,"
Declares the Lord GOD.
15 "When I make the land of Egypt a desolation,
And the land is destitute of that which filled it,
When I smite all those who live in it,
Then they shall [r]know that I am the LORD. Ps. 9:16
16 "This is a [r]lamentation and
they shall chant it. The daughters
of the nations shall chant it. Over
Egypt and over all her multitude
they shall chant it," declares the
Lord GOD. 2 Sam. 1:17; 3:33, 34
17 And it came about in the
twelfth year, on the fifteenth of
the month, that the word of the
LORD came to me saying,
18 "Son of man, [r]wail for the multitude of Egypt, and bring it down,
her and the daughters of the powerful nations, to the nether world,
with those who go down to the
pit; Is. 16:9; Ezek. 21:6; 32:2, 16; Mic. 1:8
19 'Whom do you surpass in beauty?
Go down and make your bed with the uncircumcised.'
20 "They shall fall in the midst of
those who are slain by the sword.
She is given over to the sword;
they have [r]drawn her and all her
multitudes away. Ps. 28:3
21 "The [r]strong among the
mighty ones shall speak of him
and his helpers from the midst of
Sheol, 'They have gone down,
they lie still, the uncircumcised,
slain by the sword.' Is. 14:9-12
22 "Assyria is there and all her
company; [t]her graves are round
about her. All of them are slain,
fallen by the sword, *his*
23 whose [r]graves are set in the
remotest parts of the pit, and her
company is round about her
grave. All of them are slain, fallen
by the sword, who spread terror
in the land of the living. Is. 14:15
24 "Elam[r] is there and all her
multitude around her grave; all of
them slain, fallen by the sword,
who went down uncircumcised to
the lower parts of the earth, who
instilled their terror in the land of
the living, and bore their disgrace
with those who went down to the
pit. Gen. 10:22; 14:1; Is. 11:11
25 "They have made a [r]bed for
her among the slain with all her
multitude. Her graves are around
it, they are all uncircumcised,
slain by the sword (although their
terror was [t]instilled in the land of
the living), and they bore their disgrace with those who go down to
the pit; they were put in the midst
of the slain. Ps. 139:8 • *given*
26 "Meshech, Tubal and all their
multitude are there; their graves
surround them. All of them were
slain by the sword uncircumcised,
though they instilled their terror
in the land of the living.
27 "Nor do they lie beside the
fallen [a]heroes of the uncircumcised, who went down to Sheol
with their weapons of war, and
whose swords were laid under
their heads; but the punishment
for their iniquity rested on their
bones, though the terror of *these*
heroes *was* once in the land of the
living. *mighty ones*
28 "But in the midst of the uncircumcised you will be broken and
lie with those slain by the sword.

29 "There also is Edom, its kings,
and all its princes, who for *all*
their might are laid with those
slain by the sword; they will lie
with the uncircumcised, and with
those who go down to the pit.
30 "There also are the [a]chiefs of
the north, all of them, and all the
Sidonians, who in spite of the terror resulting from their might, in
shame went down with the slain.
So they lay down uncircumcised
with those slain by the sword, and
bore their disgrace with those
who go down to the pit. *princes*
31 "These Pharaoh will see, and
he will be [r]comforted for all his
multitude slain by the sword, *even*
Pharaoh and all his army," declares the Lord GOD. Ezek. 14:22
32 "Though I instilled a terror of
him in the land of the living, yet
he will be made to lie down
among *the* uncircumcised *along*
with those slain by the sword,
even Pharaoh and all his multitude," declares the Lord GOD.

CHAPTER 33

AND the word of the LORD came
to me saying,
2 "Son of man, speak to the
sons of your people, and say to
them, 'If I bring a sword upon a
land, and the people of the land
take one man from among them
and make him their watchman;
3 and he sees the sword coming upon the land, and he [r]blows
on the trumpet and warns the people, Neh. 4:18-20; Is. 58:1; Hos. 8:1
4 then he who hears the sound
of the trumpet and [r]does not take
warning, and a sword comes and
takes him away, his blood will be
on his *own* head. 2 Chr. 25:16
5 'He heard the sound of the
trumpet, but did not take warning;
his blood will be on himself. But
had he taken warning, he would
have [r]delivered his life. Heb. 11:7
6 'But if the watchman sees the
sword coming and does not blow
the trumpet, and the people are
not warned, and a sword comes
and takes a person from them, he
is [r]taken away in his iniquity; but
his blood I will require from the
watchman's hand.' Ezek. 18:20, 24
7 "Now as for you, son of man, I
have appointed you a watchman
for the house of Israel; so you will
hear a message from My mouth,
and give them warning from Me.
8 "When I say to the wicked, 'O
wicked man, you shall [r]surely die,'
and you do not speak to warn the
wicked from his way, that wicked
man shall die in his iniquity, but
his blood I will require from your
hand. Is. 3:11; Ezek. 18:4, 13, 18, 20
9 "But if you on your part warn
a wicked man to turn from his
way, and he does not turn from
his way, he will die in his iniquity;
but you have delivered your life.
10 "Now as for you, son of man,
say to the house of Israel, 'Thus
you have spoken, saying, "Surely
our transgressions and our sins
are upon us, and we are [r]rotting
away in them; [r]how then can we
[t]survive?"' Lev. 26:39 • Is. 49:14 • *live*
11 "Say to them, [r]'As I live!' declares the Lord GOD, 'I take no
pleasure in the death of the
wicked, but rather that the wicked
turn from his way and live. Turn
back, turn back from your evil

ways! Why then will you die, O
house of Israel?' Is. 49:18; Ezek. 5:11
12"And you, son of man, say to
your fellow citizens, 'The [r]right-
eousness of a righteous man will
not deliver him in the day of his
transgression, and as for the wickedness of the wicked, he will not
stumble because of it in the day
when he turns from his wickedness; whereas a righteous man
will not be able to live [t]by his
righteousness on the day when he
commits sin.' Ezek. 3:18; 18:24 • *by it*
13"When I say to the righteous
he will surely live, and he *so* trusts
in his righteousness that he [r]com-
mits iniquity, none of his righteous deeds will be remembered;
but in that same iniquity of his
which he has committed he will
die. Heb. 10:38; 2 Pet. 2:20, 21
14"But when I say to the
wicked, 'You will surely die,' and
he [r]turns from his sin and practices
justice and righteousness, Is. 55:7
15 *if a* wicked man restores a
pledge, [r]pays back what he has
taken by robbery, walks by the
statutes which ensure life without
committing iniquity, he will surely
live; he shall not die. Ex. 22:1-4
16"None [r]of his sins that he has
committed will be remembered
against him. He has practiced justice and righteousness; he will
surely live. Is. 1:18; 43:25
17"Yet [t]your fellow citizens say,
'The way of the Lord is not right',
when it is their own way that is
not right. *the sons of your people*
18"When the righteous turns
from his righteousness and [r]com-
mits iniquity, then he shall die in
[t]it. Ezek. 3:20; 18:24; 33:12, 13 • *them*
19"But when the wicked turns
from his wickedness and practices
justice and righteousness, he will
live by them.
20"Yet you say, [r]'The way of the
Lord is not right.' O house of Israel, I will judge each of you according to his ways." Ezek. 18:25
21 Now it came about in the
twelfth year of our exile, on the
fifth of the tenth month, that the
[a]refugees from Jerusalem came to
me, saying, [r]"The city has been
[t]taken." *refugee* • Jer. 39:8 • *smitten*
22 Now the hand of the LORD
had been upon me in the evening,
before the refugees came. And He
opened my mouth at the time *they*
came to me in the morning; so my
mouth was opened, and I was no
longer [a]speechless. *dumb*
23 Then the word of the LORD
came to me saying,
24"Son of man, they who [r]live in
these waste places in the land of
Israel are saying, [r]'Abraham was
only one, yet he possessed the
land; so to us who are many the
land has been given as a possession.' Jer. 39:10; 40:7 • Is. 51:2
25"Therefore, say to them, 'Thus
says the Lord GOD, "You eat *meat*
with the [r]blood *in it,* lift up your
eyes to your idols as you shed
blood. Should you then possess
the land? Lev. 17:10, 12, 14
26"You [t]rely [r]on your sword, you
commit abominations, and each
of you defiles his neighbor's wife.
Should you then possess the
land?" ' *stand* • Mic. 2:1, 2; Zeph. 3:3
27"Thus you shall say to them,
'Thus says the Lord GOD, "As I
live, surely those who are in the
waste places will fall by the
sword, and whoever is in the open

field I will give to the beasts to be
devoured, and those who are in
the strongholds and in the [r]caves
will die of pestilence. Is. 2:19
28 "And I shall [r]make the land a
desolation and a waste, and the
pride of her power will cease; and
the mountains of Israel will be
desolate, so that no one will pass
through. Ezek. 5:14; 6:14; Mic. 7:13
29 "Then they will know that I
am the LORD, when I make the
land a desolation and a waste because of all their abominations
which they have committed." '
30 "But as for you, son of man,
[t]your fellow citizens who talk
about you by the walls and in the
doorways of the houses, speak to
one another, each to his brother,
saying, 'Come now, and hear what
the message is which comes forth
from the LORD.' *the sons of your people*
31 "And they come to you as
people come, and sit before you *as*
My people, and hear your words,
but they do not do them, for they
do the lustful desires *expressed* by
their [r]mouth, *and* their heart goes
after their gain. Ps. 78:36, 37
32 "And behold, you are to them
like a sensual song by one who
has a [r]beautiful voice and plays
well on an instrument; for they
hear your words, but they do not
practice them. Mark 6:20
33 "So when it comes to pass—
[t]as surely it will—then they will
know that a prophet has been in
their midst." *behold, it is coming*

CHAPTER 34

THEN the word of the LORD
came to me saying,
2 "Son of man, prophesy
against the [r]shepherds of Israel.
Prophesy and say to those shepherds, 'Thus says the Lord GOD,
"Woe, shepherds of Israel who
have been feeding themselves!
Should not the shepherds feed the
flock? Jer. 2:8; 3:15; 10:21; 12:10
3 "You eat the fat and clothe
yourselves with the wool, you
slaughter the fat *sheep* without
[t]feeding the flock. *pasturing*
4 "Those who are sickly you
have not strengthened, the [t]dis-
eased you have not healed, [r]the
broken you have not bound up,
the scattered you have not
brought back, nor have you
sought for the lost; but with force
and with severity you have domi-
nated them. *sick* • Zech. 11:16
5 "And they were scattered for
lack of a shepherd, and they became food for every beast of the
field and were scattered.
6 "My flock wandered through
all the mountains and on every
high hill, and My flock was scattered over all the surface of the
earth; and there was no one to
search or seek *for them.*" ' "
7 Therefore, you shepherds,
hear the word of the LORD:
8 "As I live," declares the Lord
GOD, "surely because My flock
has become a [r]prey, My flock has
even become food for all the
beasts of the field for lack of a
shepherd, and My shepherds did
not search for My flock, but *rather*
the shepherds fed themselves and
did not feed My flock; Acts 20:29
9 therefore, you shepherds,
hear the word of the LORD:
10 'Thus says the Lord GOD, "Behold, I am against the shepherds,

and I shall demand My sheep
from them and make them cease
from feeding sheep. So the shepherds will not feed themselves
anymore, but I shall deliver My
flock from their mouth, that they
may not be food for them."'"
11 For thus says the Lord GOD,
"Behold, I Myself will search for
My sheep and seek them out.
12"As a shepherd [a]cares for his
herd in the day when he is among
his scattered [a]sheep, so I will care
for My sheep and will deliver
them from all the places to which
they were scattered on a cloudy
and gloomy day. *seek(s) out • flock*
13"And I will bring them out
from the peoples and gather them
from the countries and bring them
to their own land; and I will feed
them on the mountains of Israel,
by the streams, and in all the inhabited places of the land.
14"I will feed them in a [r]good
pasture, and their grazing ground
will be on the mountain heights of
Israel. There they will lie down in
good grazing ground, and they
will feed in [t]rich pasture on the
mountains of Israel. Ps. 23:2 • *fat*
15"I will feed My flock and I will
[t]lead them to rest," declares the
Lord GOD. *cause them to lie down*
16"I will seek the lost, bring
back the scattered, bind up the
broken, and strengthen the sick;
but the [r]fat and the strong I will
destroy. I will [r]feed them with
judgment. Is. 10:16 • Is. 49:26
17"And as for you, My flock,
thus says the Lord GOD, 'Behold, I
will [r]judge between one [a]sheep and
another, between the rams and
the male goats. Mal. 4:1 • *lamb*
18 'Is it too slight a thing for you
that you should feed in the good
pasture, that you must tread down
with your feet the rest of your
pastures? Or that you should
drink of the clear waters, that you
must foul the rest with your feet?
19 'And as for My flock, they
must eat what you tread down
with your feet, and they must
drink what you [t]foul with your
feet!'" *foul by trampling*
20 Therefore, thus says the Lord
GOD to them, "Behold, I, even I,
will judge between the fat sheep
and the lean sheep.
21"Because you push with side
and with shoulder, and thrust at
all the weak with your horns, until
you have scattered them abroad,
22 therefore, I will [r]deliver My
flock, and they will no longer be a
prey; and I will judge between one
sheep and another. Ps. 72:12-14
23"Then I will [r]set over them one
[r]shepherd, My servant David, and
he will feed them; he will feed
them himself and be their shepherd. Rev. 7:17 • Is. 40:11
24"And I, the LORD, will be their
God, and My servant [r]David will
be prince among them; I, the
LORD, have spoken. Is. 55:3
25"And I will make a [r]covenant
of peace with them and eliminate
harmful beasts from the land, so
that they may live securely in the
wilderness and sleep in the
woods. Ezek. 16:60; 20:37; 37:26
26"And I will make them and
the places around My hill a blessing. And I will cause showers to
come down in their season; they
will be showers of blessing.
27"Also the tree of the field will
yield its fruit, and the earth will

yield its increase, and they will be
[r]secure on their land. Then they
will know that I am the LORD,
when I have broken the bars of
their yoke and have delivered
them from the hand of those who
enslaved them. Ezek. 38:8, 11

28 "And they will no longer be a
prey to the nations, and the beasts
of the earth will not devour them;
but they will live securely, and no
one will make *them* afraid.

29 "And I will establish for them
a [r]renowned planting place, and
they will not again be victims of
famine in the land, and they will
not endure the insults of the nations anymore. Is. 4:2; 60:21; 61:3

30 "Then they will know that [r]I,
the LORD their God, am with
them, and that they, the house of
Israel, are My people," declares
the Lord GOD. Ps. 46:7, 11

31 "As for you, My [r]sheep, the
sheep of My pasture, you are men,
and I am your God," declares the
Lord GOD. Ps. 78:52; 80:1

CHAPTER 35

MOREOVER, the word of the
LORD came to me saying,

2 "Son of man, set your face
against [r]Mount Seir, and prophesy
against it, Gen. 36:8; Ezek. 25:12

3 and say to it, 'Thus says the
Lord GOD,

"Behold, I am against you,
Mount Seir,
And I will [r]stretch out My
hand against you, Jer. 6:12
And I will make you a deso-
lation and a waste.

4 "I will [r]lay waste your cities,
And you will become a
desolation. Mal. 1:3, 4
Then you will know that I
am the LORD.

5 "Because you have had everlasting enmity and have [t]delivered
the sons of Israel to the power of
the sword at the time of their calamity, at the time of the [a]punish-
ment of the end, *poured* • *iniquity*

6 therefore, as I live," declares
the Lord GOD, "I will give you
over to bloodshed, and bloodshed
will pursue you; since you have
not hated bloodshed, therefore
bloodshed will pursue you.

7 "And I will make Mount Seir a
waste and a desolation, and I will
cut off from it the one who passes
through and returns.

8 "And I will [r]fill its mountains
with its slain; on your hills and in
your valleys and in all your ravines those slain by the sword will
[t]fall. Is. 34:5, 6 • *fall in them*

9 "I will make you an everlasting desolation, and your cities
will not be inhabited. Then you
will know that I am the LORD.

10 "Because you have [r]said,
'These two nations and these two
lands will be mine, and we will
possess [t]them,' although the LORD
was there, Ps. 83: 4-12 • *it*

11 therefore, as I live," declares
the Lord GOD, "I will deal *with
you* [r]according to your anger and
according to your envy which you
showed because of your hatred
against them; so I will [r]make Myself known among them when I
judge you. Ps. 137:7 • Ps. 9:16

12 "Then you will know that I,
the LORD, have heard all your revilings which you have spoken
against the mountains of Israel
saying, 'They are laid desolate;
they are given to us for food.'

13 "And you have [r]spoken arrogantly against Me and have multiplied your words against Me; I have heard." Is. 10:13, 14; 36:20

14 'Thus says the Lord GOD, "As all the [r]earth rejoices, I will make you a desolation. Is. 44:23; 49:13

15 "As you [r]rejoiced over the inheritance of the house of Israel because it was desolate, so I will do to you. You will be a desolation, O Mount Seir, and all Edom, all of it. Then they will know that I am the LORD." ' Jer. 50:11

CHAPTER 36

"AND you, son of man, prophesy to the mountains of Israel and say, 'O mountains of Israel, hear the word of the LORD.

2 'Thus says the Lord GOD, "Because the enemy has spoken against you, 'Aha!' and, 'The everlasting [r]heights have become our possession,' Ps. 78:69; Is. 58:14

3 therefore, prophesy and say, 'Thus says the Lord GOD, "For good cause they have made you desolate and crushed you from every side, that you should become a possession of the rest of the nations, and you have been taken up in the [t]talk and the whispering of the people." ' " *lip of the tongue*

4 'Therefore, O [r]mountains of Israel, hear the word of the Lord GOD. Thus says the Lord GOD to the mountains and to the hills, to the ravines and to the valleys, to the desolate wastes and to the forsaken cities, which have become a prey and a derision to the rest of the nations which are round about, Deut. 11:11; Ezek. 36:1, 6

5 therefore, thus says the Lord GOD, "Surely in the fire of My [r]jealousy I have spoken against the rest of the nations, and against all Edom, who [t]appropriated My land for themselves as a possession with wholehearted joy *and* with scorn of soul, to drive it out for a prey." Ezek. 5:13; 36:6 • *gave*

6 'Therefore, prophesy concerning the land of Israel, and say to the mountains and to the hills, to the ravines and to the valleys, "Thus says the Lord GOD, 'Behold, I have spoken in My jealousy and in My wrath because you have endured the insults of the nations.'

7 "Therefore, thus says the Lord GOD, 'I have sworn that surely the nations which are around you will themselves endure their insults.

8 'But you, O mountains of Israel, you will [r]put forth your branches and bear your fruit for My people Israel; for they will soon come. Is. 4:2; 27:6

9 'For, behold, I am for you, and I will turn to you, and you shall be cultivated and sown.

10 'And I will multiply men on you, [r]all the house of Israel, all of it; and the cities will be inhabited, and the waste places will be rebuilt. Is. 27:6; 49:17-23

11 'And I will multiply on you man and beast; and they will increase and be fruitful; and I will cause you to be inhabited as you were formerly and will treat you better than at the first. Thus you will know that I am the LORD.

12 'Yes, I will cause men—My people Israel—to walk on you and possess you, so that you will become their inheritance and never again bereave them of children.'

13 "Thus says the Lord GOD, 'Because they say to you, "You are a
devourer of men and have bereaved your nation of children,"
14 therefore, you will no longer
devour men, and no longer bereave your nation of children,' declares the Lord GOD.
15 "And I will not let you hear [r]in-
sults from the nations anymore,
nor will you bear [r]disgrace from
the peoples any longer, nor will
you cause your nation to stumble
any longer," declares the Lord
GOD.' " Is. 60:14 • Ps. 89:50; Is. 54:4
16 Then the word of the LORD
came to me saying,
17 "Son of man, when the house
of Israel was living in their own
land, they [r]defiled it by their ways
and their deeds; their way before
Me was like the uncleanness of a
woman in her impurity. Jer. 2:7
18 "Therefore, I [r]poured out My
wrath on them for the blood
which they had shed on the land,
because they had defiled it with
their idols. 2 Chr. 34:21, 25; Lam. 2:4
19 "Also I [r]scattered them among
the nations, and they were dispersed throughout the lands. According to their ways and their
deeds I judged them. Amos 9:9
20 "When they came to the nations where they went, they [r]pro-
faned My holy name, because it
was said of them, 'These are the
people of the LORD; yet they have
come out of His land.' Is. 52:5
21 "But I had [t]concern for My
holy name, which the house of Israel had profaned among the nations where they went. *compassion*
22 "Therefore, say to the house
of Israel, 'Thus says the Lord GOD,
"It is [r]not for your sake, O house of
Israel, that I am about to act, but
for My holy name, which you
have profaned among the nations
where you went. Deut. 7:7, 8
23 "And I will vindicate the holiness of My great name which has
been profaned among the nations,
which you have profaned in their
midst. Then the nations will know
that I am the LORD," declares the
Lord GOD, "when I prove Myself
holy among you in their sight.
24 "For I will [r]take you from the
nations, gather you from all the
lands, and bring you into your
own land. Is. 43:5, 6; Ezek. 34:13
25 "Then I will sprinkle clean water on you, and you will be clean; I
will cleanse you from all your
filthiness and from all your idols.
26 "Moreover, I will give you a
new heart and put a new spirit
within you; and I will remove the
heart of stone from your flesh and
give you a heart of flesh.
27 "And I will put My Spirit
within you and cause you to walk
in My statutes, and you will be
careful to observe My ordinances.
28 "And you will live in the land
that I gave to your forefathers; so
you will be [r]My people, and I will
be your God. Ezek. 14:11; 37:23, 27
29 "Moreover, I will save you
from all your uncleanness; and I
will call for the grain and multiply
it, and I [r]will not bring a famine on
you. Ezek. 34:27, 29; Hos. 2:21-23
30 "And I will [r]multiply the fruit
of the tree and the produce of the
field, that you may not receive
again the disgrace of famine
among the nations. Lev. 26:4
31 "Then you will [r]remember
your evil ways and your deeds
that were not good, and you will

loathe yourselves in your own sight for your iniquities and your abominations. Ezek. 16:61-63

32 "I am not doing *this*[r] for your sake," declares the Lord GOD, "let it be known to you. Be ashamed and confounded for your ways, O house of Israel!" Deut. 9:5

33 'Thus says the Lord GOD, "On the day that I cleanse you from all your iniquities, I will cause the cities to be inhabited, and the waste places will be rebuilt.

34 "And the desolate land will be cultivated instead of being a desolation in the sight of everyone who passed by.

35 "And they will say, 'This desolate land has become like the[r] garden of Eden; and the waste, desolate, and ruined cities are fortified *and* inhabited.' Is. 51:3; Joel 2:3

36 "Then the nations that are left round about you will know that I, the LORD, have rebuilt the ruined places *and* planted that which was desolate; I, the LORD, have spoken and[r] will do it." Hos. 14:4-9

37 'Thus says the Lord GOD, "This also I will let the house of Israel ask Me to do for them: I will increase their men like a flock.

38 "Like the flock[t] for sacrifices, like the flock at Jerusalem during her appointed feasts, so will the waste cities be filled with flocks of men. Then they will know that I am the LORD."' " *of holy things*

CHAPTER 37

THE hand of the LORD was upon me, and He brought me out[a] by the Spirit of the LORD and set me down in the middle of the valley; and it was full of bones. *in*

2 And He caused me to pass among them round about, and behold, *there were* very many on the surface of the valley; and lo, *they were* very dry.

3 And He said to me, "Son of man,[r] can these bones live?" And I answered, "O Lord GOD,[r] Thou knowest." Ezek. 26:19 • Deut. 32:39

4 Again He said to me, "Prophesy over these bones, and say to them, 'O dry bones,[r] hear the word of the LORD.' Jer. 22:29; Ezek. 36:1

5 "Thus says the Lord GOD to these bones, 'Behold, I will cause [6]breath[r] to enter you that you may come to life. Ps. 104:29, 30

6 'And I will put sinews on you, make flesh grow back on you, cover you with skin, and put breath in you that you may come alive; and you will[r] know that I am the LORD.' " Is. 49:23; Ezek. 35:9

7 So I prophesied as I was commanded; and as I prophesied, there was a noise, and behold, a rattling; and the bones came together, bone to its bone.

8 And I looked, and behold, sinews were on them, and flesh grew, and skin covered them; but there was no breath in them.

9 Then He said to me, "Prophesy to the breath, prophesy, son of man, and say to the breath, 'Thus says the Lord GOD, "Come from the four winds, O breath, and [r] breathe on these slain, that they come to life." ' " Ps. 104:30

10 So I prophesied as He commanded me, and the[r] breath came into them, and they came to life, and stood on their feet, an exceedingly great army. Rev. 11:11

[6] Or, *spirit*, and so throughout this context

11 Then He said to me, "Son of
man, these bones are the [r]whole
house of Israel; behold, they say,
'Our[r]bones are dried up, and our
hope has perished. We are completely cut off.' Jer. 33:24 • Ps. 141:7
12"Therefore prophesy, and say
to them, 'Thus says the Lord GOD,
"Behold, I will open your graves
and cause you to come up out of
your graves, My people; and I will
bring you into the land of Israel.
13"Then you will know that I am
the LORD, when I have opened
your graves and caused you to
come up out of your graves, My
people.
14"And I will put My [7]Spirit
within you, and you will come to
life, and I will place you on your
own land. Then you will know
that I, the LORD, have spoken and
done it," declares the LORD.' "
15 The word of the LORD came
again to me saying,
16"And you, son of man, take
for yourself [r]one stick and write on
it, 'For[r]Judah and for the sons of
Israel, his companions'; then take
another stick and write on it, 'For
Joseph, the stick of Ephraim and
all the house of Israel, his companions.' Num. 17:2, 3 • 2 Chr. 10:17
17"Then[r]join them for yourself
one to another into one stick, that
they may become one in your
hand. Is. 11:13; Jer. 50:4
18"And when the sons of your
people speak to you saying, 'Will
you not declare to us [r]what you
mean by these?' Ezek. 12:9; 17:12
19 say to them, 'Thus says the
Lord GOD, "Behold, I will take
the stick of Joseph, which is in the
hand of Ephraim, and the tribes of
Israel, his companions; and I will
put them with it, with the stick of
Judah, and make them one stick,
and they will be one in My
hand." '
20"And the sticks on which you
write will be in your hand before
their eyes.
21"And say to them, 'Thus says
the Lord GOD, "Behold, I will[r]take
the sons of Israel from among the
nations where they have gone,
and I will gather them from every
side and bring them into their own
land; Is. 43:5, 6; Jer. 29:14; Ezek. 36:24
22 and I will make them [r]one nation in the land, on the mountains
of Israel; and one king will be king
for all of them; and they will no
longer be two nations, and they
will no longer be divided into two
kingdoms. Jer. 3:18; 50:4, 5
23"And they will no longer defile
themselves with their idols, or
with their detestable things, or
with any of their transgressions;
but I will deliver them from all
their [8]dwelling places in which
they have sinned, and will cleanse
them. And they will be My people,
and I will be their God.
24"And My servant [r]David will
be king over them, and they will
all have one shepherd; and they
will walk in My ordinances, and
keep My statutes, and observe
them. Jer. 30:9; Ezek. 34:24
25"And they shall live on the
land that I gave to Jacob My servant, in which your fathers lived;
and they will live on it, they, and
their sons, and their sons' sons,
forever; and David My servant
shall be their prince forever.
26"And I will make a covenant

[7]Or, *breath*

[8]Another reading is *backslidings*

of peace with them; it will be an
everlasting covenant with them.
And I will place them and multiply them, and will set My sanctuary in their midst forever.
27 "My dwelling place also will
be with them; and I will be their
God, and they will be My people.
28 "And the nations will know
that I am the LORD [r]who sanctifies
Israel, when My sanctuary is in
their midst forever." ' " Ex. 31:13

CHAPTER 38

AND the word of the LORD came
to me saying,
2 "Son of man, set your face
toward Gog of the land of Magog,
the prince of Rosh, Meshech, and
Tubal, and prophesy against him,
3 and say, 'Thus says the Lord
GOD, "Behold, I am against you, O
Gog, [a]prince of Rosh, Meshech,
and Tubal. *chief prince of Meshech*
4 "And I will turn you about,
and put hooks into your jaws, and
I will bring you out, and all your
army, horses and horsemen, all of
them splendidly attired, a great
company *with* buckler and shield,
all of them wielding swords;
5 [r]Persia, [t]Ethiopia, and Put
with them, all of them *with* shield
and helmet; 2 Chr. 36:20 • *Cush*
6 Gomer with all its troops;
Beth-togarmah *from* the remote
parts of the north with all its
troops—many peoples with you.
7 "Be prepared, and prepare
yourself, you and all your companies that are assembled about
you, and be a guard for them.
8 "[r]After many days you will be
summoned; in the latter years you
will come into the land that is restored from the sword, *whose inhabitants* have been gathered
from many [t]nations to the mountains of Israel which had been a
continual waste; but [t]its people
were brought out from the nations, and they are living securely,
all of them. Is. 24:22 • *peoples* • *it was*
9 "And you will go up, you will
come [r]like a storm; you will be like
a cloud covering the land, you and
all your troops, and many peoples
with you." Is. 5:28; 21:1; 25:4; 28:2
10 'Thus says the Lord GOD, "It
will come about on that day, that
[t]thoughts will come into your
mind, and you will [r]devise an evil
plan, *words* • Ps. 36:4; Mic. 2:1
11 and you will say, 'I will go up
against the land of [9]unwalled villages. I will go against those who
are at rest, that live securely, all of
them living without walls, and
having no bars or gates,
12 to [r]capture spoil and to seize
plunder, to turn your hand against
the waste places which are *now*
inhabited, and against the people
who are gathered from the nations, who have acquired cattle
and goods, who live at the [t]center
of the world.' Is. 10:6 • *navel*
13 "Sheba, and Dedan, and the
merchants of Tarshish, with all its
villages, will say to you, 'Have you
come to capture spoil? Have you
assembled your company to seize
plunder, to carry away silver and
gold, to take away cattle and
goods, to capture great spoil?' " '
14 "Therefore, prophesy, son of
man, and say to Gog, 'Thus says
the Lord GOD, "On that day when

[9]Or, *open country*

My people Israel are living securely, will you not know *it*?
15 "And [r]you will come from your
place out of the remote parts of
the north, you and many peoples
with you, all of them riding on
horses, a great assembly and a
mighty army; Ezek. 39:2
16 and you will come up against
My people Israel like a cloud to
cover the land. It will come about
in the last days that I shall bring
you against My land, in order that
the nations may [r]know Me when I
shall be sanctified through you before their eyes, O Gog." Ps. 83:18
17 'Thus says the Lord GOD,
"Are you the one of whom I spoke
in former days through My servants the prophets of Israel, who
[r]prophesied in those days for *many*
years that I would bring you
against them? Is. 5:26-29; 34:1-6
18 "And it will come about on
that day, when Gog comes against
the land of Israel," declares the
Lord GOD, "that My fury will
mount up in My [r]anger. Ps. 18:8, 15
19 "And in My [r]zeal and in My
blazing wrath I declare *that* on
that day there will surely be a
great [a]earthquake in the land of Israel. Deut. 32:22; Ps. 18:7, 8 • *shaking*
20 "[r]And the fish of the sea, the
birds of the heavens, the beasts of
the field, all the creeping things
that creep on the earth, and all the
men who are on the face of the
earth will shake at My presence;
the mountains also will be thrown
down, the steep pathways will
[t]collapse, and every wall will fall
to the ground. Jer. 4:24, 25 • *fall*
21 "And I shall call for a sword
against him on all My mountains,"
declares the Lord GOD. "Every [r]
man's sword will be against his
brother. Judg. 7:22; 1 Sam. 14:20
22 "And with pestilence and with
blood I shall enter into judgment
with him; and I shall rain on him,
and on his troops, and on the
many peoples who are with him, [t]a
torrential rain, with hailstones,
fire, and brimstone. *an overflowing*
23 "And I shall magnify Myself,
sanctify Myself, and [r]make Myself
known in the sight of many nations; and they will know that I
am the LORD."' Ps. 9:16

CHAPTER 39

"AND you, son of man, prophesy
against Gog, and say, 'Thus says
the Lord GOD, "Behold, I am
against you, O Gog, prince of
Rosh, Meshech, and Tubal;
2 and I shall turn you around,
drive you on, take you up from the
remotest parts of the north, and
bring you against the mountains
of Israel.
3 "And I shall [r]strike your bow
from your left hand, and dash
down your arrows from your right
hand. Ps. 76:3; Jer. 21:4, 5
4 "You shall fall on the mountains of Israel, you and all your
troops, and the peoples who are
with you; I shall give you as food
to every [t]kind of predatory bird
and beast of the field. *wing*
5 "You will fall on the [t]open
field; for it is I who have spoken,"
declares the Lord GOD. *face of the*
6 "And I shall send fire upon
Magog and those who inhabit the
coastlands in safety; and they will
know that I am the LORD.
7 "And My holy name I shall

make known in the midst of My
people Israel; and I shall not let
My holy name be [r]profaned anymore. And the nations will know
that I am the Lord, the [r]Holy One
in Israel. Ex. 20:7 • Is. 12:6; 43:3, 14
8 "Behold, it is coming and it
shall be done," declares the Lord
GOD. "That is the day of which I
have spoken.
9 "Then those who inhabit the
cities of Israel will go out, and
make fires with the weapons and
burn *them*, both shields and buck-
lers, bows and arrows, war clubs
and spears and for seven years
they will make fires of them.
10 "And they will not take wood
from the field or gather firewood
from the forests, for they will
make fires with the weapons; and
they will take the spoil of those
who despoiled them, and seize the
plunder of those who plundered
them," declares the Lord GOD.
11 "And it will come about on
that day that I shall give Gog a
burial ground there in Israel, the
valley of those who pass by east
of the sea, and it will block off the
passers-by. So they will bury Gog
there with all his multitude, and
they will call *it* the valley of [a]Ha-
mon-gog. *the multitude of Gog*
12 "For seven months the house
of Israel will be burying them in
order to cleanse the land.
13 "Even all the people of the
land will bury *them*; and it will be
[a]to their renown *on* the day that I
glorify Myself," declares the Lord
GOD. *a memorial for them*
14 "And they will set apart men
who will constantly pass through
the land, [r]burying those who were
passing through, even those left
on the surface of the ground, in
order to cleanse it. At the end of
seven months they will make a
search. Jer. 14:16
15 "And as those who pass
through the land pass through and
anyone sees a man's bone, then he
will [t]set up a marker by it until the
buriers have buried it in the valley
of Hamon-gog. *build*
16 "And even *the* name of *the*
city will be Hamonah. So they will
cleanse the land." '
17 "And as for you, son of man,
thus says the Lord GOD, 'Speak to
every [t]kind of [r]bird and to every
beast of the field, "Assemble and
come, gather from every side to
My sacrifice which I am going to
sacrifice for you, as a great sacrifice on the mountains of Israel,
that you may eat flesh and drink
blood. *wing* • Is. 56:9; Jer. 12:9
18 "You shall [r]eat the flesh of
mighty men, and drink the blood
of the princes of the earth, as
though they were rams, lambs,
goats, and bulls, all of them fatlings of Bashan. Rev. 19:18
19 "So you will eat fat until you
are glutted, and drink blood until
you are drunk, from My sacrifice
which I have sacrificed for you.
20 "And you will be glutted at
My table with [r]horses and charioteers, with mighty men and all
the men of war," declares the
Lord GOD. Ps. 76:5, 6; Ezek. 38:4
21 "And I shall set My glory
among the nations; and all the nations will see My judgment which
I have executed, and My hand
which I have laid on them.
22 "And the house of Israel will

know that I am the LORD their God from that day onward.

23 "And the nations will know that the house of Israel went into exile for their [r]iniquity because they acted treacherously against Me, and I hid My face from them; so I gave them into the hand of their adversaries, and all of them fell by the sword. Jer. 22:8, 9; 44:22

24 "According to their uncleanness and according to their transgressions I dealt with them, and I hid My face from them." ' "

25 Therefore thus says the Lord GOD, "Now I shall restore the fortunes of Jacob, and have mercy on the whole house of Israel; and I shall be jealous for My holy name.

26 "And they shall [r][10]forget their disgrace and all their treachery which they [11]perpetrated against Me, when they live securely on their *own* land with no one to make them afraid. Ezek. 16:63

27 "When I [r]bring them back from the peoples and gather them from the lands of their enemies, then I shall be sanctified [t]through them in the sight of the many nations. Ezek. 36:24; 37:21 • *in*

28 "Then they will know that I am the LORD their God because I made them go into exile among the nations, and then gathered them *again* to their own land; and I will leave none of them there any longer.

29 "And I will not hide My face from them any longer, for I shall have [r]poured out My Spirit on the house of Israel," declares the Lord GOD. Is. 32:15; Ezek. 36:27; Joel 2:28

[10] Another reading is *bear*
[11] Lit., *did treacherously*

CHAPTER 40

IN the twenty-fifth year of our exile, at the beginning of the year, on the tenth of the month, in the fourteenth year after the city was [t]taken, on that same day the hand of the LORD was upon me and He brought me there. *struck*

2 In the visions of God He brought me into the land of Israel, and set me on a very high mountain; and on it to the south *there was* a structure like a city.

3 So He brought me there; and behold, there was a man whose appearance was like the appearance of [r]bronze, with a line of flax and a measuring rod in his hand; and he was standing in the gateway. Ezek. 1:7; Dan. 10:6; Rev. 1:15

4 And the man said to me, "Son of man, see with your eyes, hear with your ears, and give attention to all that I am going to show you; for you have been brought here in order to show *it* to you. [r]Declare to the house of Israel all that you see." Is. 21:10

5 And behold, there was a wall on the outside of the [t]temple all around, and in the man's hand was a measuring rod of six cubits, *each of which was* a cubit and a handbreadth. So he measured the thickness of the wall, one rod; and the height, one rod. *house*

6 Then he went to the gate which faced [r]east, went up its steps, and measured the threshold of the gate, one rod [a]in width; and the other threshold *was* one rod in width. Ezek. 8:16; 11:1 • *in depth*

7 And the guardroom *was* one rod long and one rod wide; and *there were* five cubits between the

guardrooms. And the threshold of
the gate by the porch of the gate
facing inward *was* one rod.
8 Then he measured the porch
of the gate facing inward, one rod.
9 And he measured the porch
of the gate, eight cubits; and its
side pillars, two cubits. And the
porch of the gate was [t]faced inward. *from the house*
10 And the guardrooms of the
gate toward the east *numbered*
three on each side; the three of
them had the same measurement.
The side pillars also had the same
measurement on each side.
11 And he measured the width
of the gateway, ten cubits, and the
length of the gate, thirteen cubits.
12 And *there was* a [t]barrier *wall*
one cubit *wide* in front of the
guardrooms on each side; and the
guardrooms *were* six cubits
square on each side. *border*
13 And he measured the gate
from the roof of the one guardroom to the roof of the other, a
width of twenty-five cubits from
one door to *the* door opposite.
14 And he made the side pillars
sixty cubits *high;* the gate *extended* round about to the side pillar of the [r]courtyard. Ex. 27:9
15 And *from* the front of the entrance gate to the front of the inner porch of the gate *was* fifty cubits.
16 And *there were* shuttered
windows *looking* toward the
guardrooms, and toward their
side pillars within the gate all
around, and likewise for the
porches. And *there were* windows
all around inside; and on *each* side
pillar *were* palm tree ornaments.

17 Then he brought me into the
[r]outer court, and behold, *there
were* [r]chambers and a pavement,
made for the court all around;
thirty chambers [t]faced the pavement. Rev. 11:2 • 2 Kin. 23:11 • *to*
18 And the pavement (*that is,*
the lower pavement) *was* by the
[t]side of the gates, corresponding to
the length of the gates. *shoulder*
19 Then he measured the width
from the front of the lower gate to
the front of the exterior of the inner court, a hundred cubits on the
east and on the north.
20 And *as for* the [r]gate of the
outer court which faced the north,
he measured its length and its
width. Ezek. 40:6
21 And it had three guardrooms
on each side; and its side pillars
and its porches had the same measurement as the first gate. Its
length *was* fifty cubits, and the
width twenty-five cubits.
22 And its windows, and its
porches, and its palm tree ornaments *had* the same measurements as the gate which faced
toward the east; and it was
reached by seven steps, and its
porch *was* in front of them.
23 And the inner court had a
gate opposite the gate on the
north as well as *the gate* on the
east; and he measured a hundred
cubits from gate to gate.
24 Then he led me toward the
south, and behold, there was a
[r]gate toward the south; and he
measured its side pillars and its
porches according to those same
measurements. Ezek. 40:6, 20, 35
25 And [t]the gate and its porches
had windows all around like [t]those
other windows; the length *was* fif-

ty cubits and the width twenty-
five cubits. *it • these windows*
26 And *there were* seven steps
going up to it, and its porches
were in front of them; and it had
palm tree ornaments on its side
pillars, one on each side.
27 And the inner court had a
gate toward the [r]south; and he
measured from gate to gate
toward the south, a[r] hundred cubits. Ezek. 40:23, 32 • Ezek. 40:19
28 Then he brought me to the
inner court by the south gate; and
he measured the south gate [r]ac-
cording to those same measurements. Ezek. 40:32, 35
29 Its guardrooms also, its side
pillars, and its porches *were* according to those same measurements. And [t]the gate and its
porches had windows all around;
it *was* fifty cubits long and
twenty-five cubits wide. *it*
30 And *there were* [r]porches all
around, twenty-five cubits long
and five cubits wide. Ezek. 40:16, 21
31 And its porches *were* toward
the outer court; and palm tree ornaments *were* on its side pillars,
and its stairway had eight steps.
32 And he brought me into the
inner court toward the east. And
he measured the gate according to
those same measurements.
33 Its guardrooms also, its side
pillars, and its porches *were* according to those same measurements. And [t]the gate and its
porches had windows all around;
it *was* fifty cubits long and
twenty-five cubits wide. *it*
34 And its[r]porches *were* toward
the outer court; and palm tree ornaments *were* on its side pillars,
on each side, and its stairway had
eight steps. Ezek. 40:16
35 Then he brought me to the
[r]north gate; and he measured *it* according to those same measurements, Ezek. 40:27, 32; 44:4
36 *with* its guardrooms, its side
pillars, and its porches. And [t]the
gate had windows all around;
the length *was* fifty cubits and the
width twenty-five cubits. *it*
37 And its side pillars *were*
toward the outer court; and[r]palm
tree ornaments *were* on its side
pillars on each side, and its stairway had eight steps. Ezek. 40:16
38 And a[r]chamber with its doorway was by the side pillars at the
gates; there they rinse the burnt
offering. 1 Chr. 28:12; Neh. 13:5, 9
39 And in the porch of the gate
were two tables on each side, on
which to slaughter the[r]burnt offering, the sin offering, and the guilt
offering. Lev. 1:3-17
40 And on the outer[t]side, as one
went up to the gateway toward
the north, were two tables; and on
the other side of the porch of the
gate *were* two tables. *shoulder*
41 Four tables *were* on each
side[t]next to the gate; *or*, eight tables on which they slaughter *sacrifices*. *by the shoulder of*
42 And for the burnt offering
there were four tables of [r]hewn
stone, a cubit and a half long, a
cubit and a half wide, and one cubit high, on which they lay the instruments with which they
slaughter the burnt offering and
the sacrifice. Ex. 20:25
43 And the double[a]hooks, one
handbreadth in length, were installed[a]in the house all around;

and on the tables *was* the flesh of
the offering. *ledges • inside*
44 And from the outside to the
inner gate were chambers for the
singers in the inner court, *one of*
which was at the side of the north
gate, with its front toward the
south, and one at the side of the
east gate facing toward the north.
45 And he said to me, "This is
the chamber which faces toward
the south, *intended* for the priests
who keep charge of the temple;
46 but the chamber which faces
toward the north is for the priests
who keep charge of the altar.
These are the sons of Zadok, who
from the sons of Levi come near
to the LORD to minister to Him."
47 And he measured the court, a
perfect square, a [r]hundred cubits
long and a hundred cubits wide;
and the altar was in front of the
[t]temple. Ezek. 40:19, 23, 27 • *house*
48 Then he brought me to the
[r]porch of the temple and measured
each side pillar of the porch, five
cubits on each side; and the width
of the gate was three cubits on
each side. 1 Kin. 6:3; 2 Chr. 3:4
49 The length of the porch was
twenty cubits, and the width
eleven cubits; and at the stairway
by which it was ascended *were*
[r]columns belonging to the side pillars, one on each side. Rev. 3:12

CHAPTER 41

THEN he brought me to the nave
and measured the side pillars; six
cubits wide on each side *was* the
width of the side pillar.
2 And the width of the entrance *was* ten cubits, and the
[t]sides of the entrance were five cubits on each side. And he measured [t]the length of the nave, forty
cubits, and the width, twenty cubits. *shoulders • its length*
3 Then he went inside and
measured each side pillar of the
doorway, two cubits, and the
doorway, six cubits *high;* and
the width of the doorway, seven
cubits.
4 And he measured its length,
[r]twenty cubits, and the width,
twenty cubits, before the nave;
and he said to me, "This is the
most holy *place.*" 1 Kin. 6:20
5 Then he measured the wall
of the temple, six cubits; and the
width of the [r]side chambers, four
cubits, all around about the house
on every side. 1 Kin. 6:5
6 And the side chambers were
in three stories, [t]one above another, and thirty in each story;
and the side chambers extended
to the wall which *stood* on their
inward side all around, that they
might be fastened, and not be fastened into the wall of the temple
itself. *chamber upon chamber*
7 And the side chambers surrounding the temple were wider
at each successive story. Because
the [r]structure surrounding the
temple went upward by stages on
all sides of the temple, therefore
the width of the temple increased
as it went higher; and thus one
went up from the lowest *story* to
the highest by way of the [t]second
story. 1 Kin. 6:8 • *middle*
8 I saw also that the house had
a raised [t]platform all around; the
foundations of the side chambers
were a full rod of six [a]long cubits
in height. *height • to the joint*
9 The [t]thickness of the outer

wall of the side chambers was five cubits. But the [r]free space between the side chambers belonging to the temple *width* • Ezek. 41:11

10 and the *outer* chambers *was* twenty cubits in width all around the temple on every side.

11 And the [t]doorways of the [t]side chambers toward the free space *consisted of* one doorway toward the north and another doorway toward the south; and the width of the free space was five cubits all around. *doorway* • *side chamber*

12 And the [r]building that *was* in front of the separate area at the side toward the west *was* seventy cubits wide; and the wall of the building was five cubits thick all around, and its length *was* ninety cubits. Ezek. 41:13, 15; 42:1

13 Then he measured the temple, a [r]hundred cubits long; the separate area with the building and its walls *were* also a hundred cubits long. Ezek. 40:47

14 Also the width of the front of the temple and *that of* the separate [t]areas along the east *side totaled* a hundred cubits. *area*

15 And he measured the length of the building along the front of the separate area behind it, with a gallery on each side, a hundred cubits; *he* also *measured* the inner nave and the porches of the court.

16 The thresholds, the [a]latticed windows, and the galleries round about their three stories, opposite the threshold, were paneled with wood all around, and *from* the ground to the windows (but the windows were covered), *framed*

17 over the entrance, and to the inner house, and on the outside, and on all the wall all around inside and outside, by measurement.

18 And it was [t]carved with [r]cherubim and palm trees; and a palm tree was between cherub and cherub, and every cherub had two faces, *made* • 1 Kin. 6:29, 32, 35

19 a man's face toward the palm tree on one side, and a young lion's face toward the palm tree on the other side; they were carved on all the house all around.

20 From the ground to above the entrance cherubim and palm trees were [t]carved, as well as *on* the wall of the nave. *made*

21 The [r]doorposts of the nave were square; as for the front of the sanctuary, the appearance of one doorpost was like that of the other. 1 Kin. 6:33; Ezek. 40:9, 14, 16

22 The altar *was* of wood, three cubits high, and its length two cubits; its corners, its [t]base, and its [t]sides *were* of wood. And he said to me, "This is the table that is before the LORD." *length* • *walls*

23 And the nave and the sanctuary each had a double door.

24 And each of the doors had two leaves, two [a]swinging leaves; two *leaves* for one door and two leaves for the other. *turning*

25 Also there were carved on them, on the doors of the nave, cherubim and palm trees like those carved on the walls; and *there was* a threshold of wood on the front of the porch outside.

26 And *there were* [a]latticed windows and palm trees on one side and on the other, on the sides of the porch; thus *were* the side chambers of the house and the [a]thresholds. *framed* • *canopies*

CHAPTER 42

THEN he brought me out into the
outer court, the way toward the
north; and he brought me to
the chamber which *was* opposite
the separate area and opposite the
building toward the north.
2 Along the length, *which was*
a hundred cubits, *was* the north
door; the width *was* fifty cubits.
3 Opposite the [r]twenty *cubits*
which belonged to the inner court,
and opposite the pavement which
belonged to the outer court, *was*
gallery corresponding to [a]gallery in
three stories. Ezek. 41:10 • *passageway*
4 And before the chambers
was an inner walk ten cubits wide,
a way of one *hundred* cubits; and
their openings *were* on the north.
5 Now the upper chambers
were [t]smaller because the galleries
took more *space* away from them
than from the lower and middle
ones in the building. *shorter*
6 For they *were* in three stories
and had no pillars like the pillars
of the courts; therefore *the upper
chambers* were [a]set back from the
ground upward, more than the
lower and middle ones. *reduced*
7 As for the outer wall by the
side of the chambers, toward the
outer court facing the chambers,
its length *was* fifty cubits.
8 For the length of the chambers which *were* in the outer court
was fifty cubits; and behold, *the
length of those* facing the temple
was a hundred cubits.
9 And below these chambers
was the [r]entrance on the east side,
as one enters them from the outer
court. Ezek. 44:5; 46:19
10 In the thickness of the wall
of the court toward the east, facing the separate area and facing
the building, *there were* chambers.
11 And the way in front of them
was like the appearance of the
chambers which *were* on the
north, according to their length so
was their width; and all their exits
were both according to their arrangements and openings.
12 And corresponding to the
openings of the chambers which
were toward the south was an
opening at the head of the way,
the way in front of the [r]wall
toward the east, as one enters
them. Ezek. 42:7
13 Then he said to me, "The
north chambers *and* the south
chambers, which are opposite the
separate area, they are the holy
chambers where the priests who
are near to the LORD shall eat the
most holy things. There they shall
lay the most holy things, the grain
offering, the sin offering, and the
guilt offering; for the place is holy.
14 "When the priests enter, then
they shall not go out into the outer
court from the sanctuary without
laying there their garments in
which they minister, for they are
holy. They shall put on other garments; then they shall approach
that which is for the people."
15 Now when he had finished
measuring the inner house, he
brought me out by the way of the
gate which faced toward the east,
and measured it all around.
16 He measured on the east side
with the measuring reed five hundred reeds, by the [r]measuring
reed. Ezek. 40:3
17 He measured on the north

side five hundred reeds by the
measuring reed.
18 On the south side he measured five hundred reeds with the
measuring reed.
19 He turned to the west side,
and measured five hundred reeds
with the measuring reed.
20 He measured it on the four
sides; it had a [r]wall all around, the
length five hundred and the width
five hundred, to divide between
the holy and the profane. Is. 60:18

CHAPTER 43

THEN he led me to the gate, the
gate facing toward the east;
2 and behold, the [r]glory of the
God of Israel was coming from
the way of the east. And His [r]voice
was like the sound of many waters; and the earth [r]shone with His
glory. Is. 6:3 • Rev. 1:15; 14:2 • Rev. 18:1
3 And *it was* like the appear-
ance of the vision which I saw,
like the vision which I saw when
He came to [r]destroy the city. And
the visions *were* like the vision
which I saw by the river Chebar;
and I fell on my face. Jer. 1:10
4 And the glory of the LORD
came into the house by the way of
the gate facing toward the east.
5 And the [r]Spirit lifted me up
and brought me into the inner
court; and behold, the glory of the
LORD filled the house. 2 Cor. 12:2-4
6 Then I heard one speaking to
me from the house, while a [r]man
was standing beside me. Ezek. 1:26
7 And He said to me, "Son of
man, *this is* the place of My
throne and the place of the soles
of My feet, where I will dwell
among the sons of Israel forever.
And the house of Israel will not
again defile My holy name, neither they nor their kings, by their
harlotry and by the [12]corpses of
their kings [13]when they die,
8 by setting their threshold by
My threshold, and their door post
beside My door post, with *only*
the wall between Me and them.
And they have defiled My holy
name by their abominations
which they have committed. So I
have consumed them in My anger.
9 "Now let them [r]put away their
harlotry and the [12]corpses of their
kings far from Me; and I will dwell
among them forever. Ezek. 18:30, 31
10 "As for you, son of man, [t]de-
scribe the temple to the house of
Israel, that they may be ashamed
of their iniquities; and let them
measure the plan. *declare*
11 "And if they are ashamed of
all that they have done, make
known to them the design of the
house, its structure, its exits, its
entrances, all its designs, all its
statutes, and all its laws. And
write *it* in their sight, so that they
may observe its whole design and
all its statutes, and do them.
12 "This is the [a]law of the house:
its entire [t]area on the top of the
[r]mountain all around *shall be* most
holy. Behold, this is the law of the
house. *instruction for* • *border* • Ezek. 40:2
13 "And these are the measure-
ments of the altar by cubits (the
cubit being a cubit and a handbreadth): the [t]base *shall be* a cubit,
and the width a cubit, and its border on its edge round about one
span; and this *shall be* the *height
of the* base of the altar. *lap*

[12] Or, *monuments* [13] Or, *in their high places*

14 "And from the base on the ground to the lower ledge *shall be* two cubits, and the width one cubit; and from the smaller ledge to the larger ledge *shall be* four cubits, and the width one cubit.

15 "And the altar hearth *shall be* four cubits; and from the altar hearth shall extend upwards four [r]horns. Ex. 27:2; Lev. 9:9; Ps. 118:27

16 "Now the altar hearth *shall be* twelve *cubits* long by twelve wide, [r]square in its four sides. Ex. 27:1

17 "And the ledge *shall be* fourteen *cubits* long by fourteen wide in its four sides, the border around it *shall be* half a cubit, and its base *shall be* a cubit round about; and its steps shall face the east."

18 And He said to me, "Son of man, thus says the Lord GOD, 'These are the statutes for the altar on the day it is built, to offer [r]burnt offerings on it and to [r]sprinkle blood on it. Ex. 40:29 • Lev. 1:5, 11

19 'And you shall give to the Levitical priests who are from the offspring of [r]Zadok, who draw near to Me to minister to Me,' declares the Lord GOD, 'a young bull for a sin offering. 1 Kin. 2:35

20 'And you shall take some of its blood, and put it on its four horns, and on the four corners of the ledge, and on the border round about; thus you shall cleanse it and make atonement for it.

21 'You shall also take the bull for the sin offering; and it *shall be* burned in the appointed place of the house, outside the sanctuary.

22 'And on the second day you shall offer a male goat without blemish for a sin offering; and they shall cleanse the altar, as they cleansed *it* with the bull.

23 'When you have finished cleansing *it,* you shall present a [r]young bull without blemish and a [r]ram without blemish from the flock. Ex. 29:1, 10 • Ex. 29:1

24 'And you shall present them before the LORD, and the priests shall throw [r]salt on them, and they shall offer them up as a burnt offering to the LORD. Lev. 2:13

25 [r]'For seven days you shall prepare daily a goat for a sin offering; also a young bull and a ram from the flock, without blemish, shall be prepared. Ex. 29:35-37

26 'For seven days they shall make atonement for the altar and purify it; so shall they [t]consecrate it. *fill its hands*

27 'And when they have completed the days, it shall be that on the eighth day and onward, the priests shall offer your burnt offerings on the altar, and your peace offerings; and I will accept you,' declares the Lord GOD."

CHAPTER 44

THEN He brought me back by the way of the [r]outer gate of the sanctuary, which faces the east; and it was shut. Ezek. 40:6, 17

2 And the LORD said to me, "This gate shall be shut; it shall not be opened, and no one shall enter by it, for the [r]LORD God of Israel has entered by it; therefore it shall be shut. Ezek. 43:2-4

3 "As for the prince, he shall sit in it as prince to eat bread before the LORD; he shall enter by way of the porch of the gate, and shall go out [t]by the same way." *by his way*

4 Then He brought me by way of the north gate to the front of the house; and I looked, and behold, the [r]glory of the LORD filled the house of the LORD, and I fell on my face. Is. 6:3, 4; Hag. 2:7

5 And the LORD said to me, "Son of man, [t]mark well, see with your eyes, and hear with your ears all that I say to you concerning all the statutes of the house of the LORD and concerning all its laws; and mark well the entrance of the house, with all exits of the sanctuary. *set your heart on*

6 "And you shall say to the [t]rebellious ones, to the house of Israel, 'Thus says the Lord GOD, "Enough of all your abominations, O house of Israel, *rebellion*

7 when you brought in [r]foreigners, [r]uncircumcised in heart and uncircumcised in flesh, to be in My sanctuary to profane it, *even* My house, when you offered My food, the fat and the blood; for they made My covenant void—*this* in addition to all your abominations. Ex. 12:43-49 • Lev. 26:41

8 "And you have not kept charge of My holy things yourselves, but you have set *foreigners* to keep charge of My sanctuary."

9 'Thus says the Lord GOD, [r]"No foreigner, uncircumcised in heart and uncircumcised in flesh, of all the foreigners who are among the sons of Israel, shall enter My sanctuary. Joel 3:17; Zech. 14:21

10 "But the Levites who went far from Me, when Israel went astray, who went astray from Me after their idols, shall [r]bear the punishment for their iniquity. Num. 18:23

11 "Yet they shall be [r]ministers in My sanctuary, having oversight at the gates of the house and ministering in the house; they shall slaughter the burnt offering and the sacrifice for the people, and they shall stand before them to minister to them. Num. 3:5-37

12 "Because they ministered to them before their idols and became a stumbling block of iniquity to the house of Israel, therefore I have [t]sworn against them," declares the Lord GOD, "that they shall bear the punishment for their iniquity. *lifted up My hand*

13 "And they shall not come near to Me to serve as a priest to Me, nor come near to any of My holy things, to the things that are most holy; but they shall bear their shame and their abominations which they have committed.

14 "Yet I will [t]appoint them [t]to keep charge of the house, of all its service, and of all that shall be done in it. *give • keepers of the charge*

15 "But the Levitical priests, the sons of Zadok, who kept charge of My sanctuary when the sons of Israel went astray from Me, shall come near to Me to minister to Me; and they shall stand before Me to offer Me the fat and the blood," declares the Lord GOD.

16 "They shall [r]enter My sanctuary; they shall come near to My table to minister to Me and keep My charge. Num. 18:5, 7, 8

17 "And it shall be that when they enter at the gates of the inner court, they shall be clothed with linen garments; and wool shall not [t]be on them while they are ministering in the gates of the inner court and in the house. *come upon*

18 "Linen [r]turbans shall be on their heads, and [r]linen undergarments shall be on their loins; they shall not gird themselves with

anything which makes them sweat. Ex. 28:40; Is. 3:20 • Lev. 16:4

19 "And when they go out into the outer court, into the outer court to the people, they shall[r] put off their garments in which they have been ministering and lay them in the holy chambers; then they shall put on other garments that they may not transmit holiness to the people with their garments. Lev. 6:10; 16:4, 23, 24

20 "Also they shall not shave their heads, yet they shall not let their locks grow long; they shall only[r] trim *the hair of* their heads.

21 [n]"Nor shall any of the priests drink wine when they enter the inner court. Lev. 10:9

22 "And they shall not[t] marry a widow or a divorced woman but shall take virgins from the offspring of the house of Israel, or a widow who is the widow of a priest. *take as wives for themselves*

23 "Moreover, they shall teach My people *the difference* between the holy and the profane, and cause them to discern between the unclean and the clean.

24 "And in a dispute[r] they shall take their stand to judge; they shall judge it according to My ordinances. They shall also keep My laws and My statutes in all My appointed feasts, and sanctify My sabbaths. Deut. 17:8, 9; 19:17; 21:5

25 "And[t] they[r] shall not go to a dead person to defile *themselves;* however, for father, for mother, for son, for daughter, for brother, or for a sister who has not had a husband, they may defile themselves. *he* • Lev. 21:1-4

26 "And after he is cleansed, seven days shall [14]elapse for him.

27 "And on the day that he goes into the sanctuary, into the[r] inner court to minister in the sanctuary, he shall offer his sin offering," declares the Lord GOD. Ezek. 44:17

28 "And it shall be with regard to an inheritance for them, *that* I am their inheritance; and you shall give them no possession in Israel—I am their possession.

29 "They shall eat the grain offering, the sin offering, and the guilt offering; and every[a] devoted thing in Israel shall be theirs. *dedicated*

30 "And the first of all the first fruits of every kind and every[a] contribution of every kind, from all your contributions, shall be for the priests; you shall also give to the priest the first of your[a] dough to cause a blessing to rest on your house. *heave offering(s)* • *coarse meal*

31 "The priests shall not eat any bird or beast that has[r] died a natural death or has been torn to pieces. Lev. 22:8; Deut. 14:21

CHAPTER 45

"AND when you shall divide by lot the land for inheritance, you shall offer an allotment to the LORD, a holy portion of the land; the length shall be the length of 25,000 *cubits,* and the width shall be 10,000. It shall be holy within all its boundary round about.

2 "Out of this there shall be for the holy place a square round about five hundred by five hundred *cubits,* and fifty cubits for its open space round about.

3 "And from this[t] area you shall measure a length of 25,000 *cubits,*

[14] Lit., *be counted*

and a width of 10,000 *cubits;* and in it shall be the sanctuary, the most holy place. *measure*

4 "It shall be the holy portion of the land; it shall be for the priests, the ministers of the sanctuary, who [r]come near to minister to the LORD, and it shall be a place for their houses and a holy place for the sanctuary. Num. 16:5

5 "And *an area* [r]25,000 *cubits* in length and 10,000 in width shall be for the Levites, the ministers of the house, *and* for their possession cities to dwell in. Ezek. 48:13

6 "And you shall give the city possession of *an area* 5,000 *cubits* wide and 25,000 *cubits* long, alongside the [15]allotment of the holy portion; it shall be for the whole house of Israel.

7 "And the prince shall have *land* on either side of the holy [15]allotment and the property of the city, adjacent to the holy [15]allotment and the property of the city, on the west side toward the west and on the east side toward the east, and in length comparable to one of the portions, from the west border to the east border.

8 "This shall be his land for a possession in Israel; so My princes shall no longer oppress My people, but they shall give *the rest of* the land to the house of Israel according to their tribes."

9 'Thus says the Lord GOD, "Enough, you princes of Israel; put away violence and destruction, and [r]practice justice and righteousness. Stop your expropriations from My people," declares the Lord GOD. Jer. 22:3

[15]Or, *contribution*

10 "You shall have just balances, a just ephah, and a just bath.

11 "The ephah and the bath shall be the same quantity, so that the bath may contain a tenth of a [r]homer, and the ephah a tenth of a homer; their standard shall be according to the homer. Is. 5:10

12 "And the shekel shall be twenty gerahs; twenty shekels, twenty-five shekels, *and* fifteen shekels shall be your maneh.

13 "This is the offering that you shall offer: a sixth of an ephah from a homer of wheat; a sixth of an ephah from a homer of barley;

14 and the prescribed portion of oil (*namely,* the bath of oil), a tenth of a bath from *each* kor (*which is* ten baths *or* a homer, for ten baths are a homer);

15 and one sheep from *each* flock of two hundred from the watering places of Israel—for a [r]grain offering, for a burnt offering, and for peace offerings, to [r]make atonement for them," declares the Lord GOD. Ezek. 45:17 • Lev. 1:4

16 "All the people of the land shall give to this offering for the [r]prince in Israel. Is. 16:1

17 "And it shall be the prince's part *to provide* the burnt offerings, the grain offerings, and the libations, at the feasts, on the [r]new moons, and on the sabbaths, at all the appointed feasts of the house of Israel; he shall provide the sin offering, the grain offering, the burnt offering, and the peace offerings, to make atonement for the house of Israel." Is. 66:23

18 'Thus says the Lord GOD, "In the [r]first *month,* on the first of the month, you shall take a young bull

[r]without blemish and cleanse the sanctuary. Ex. 12:2 • Lev. 22:20

19 "And the priest shall take some of the blood from the sin offering and put *it* on the door posts of the house, on the [r]four corners of the ledge of the altar, and on the posts of the gate of the inner court. Lev. 16:18-20; Ezek. 43:20

20 "And thus you shall do on the seventh *day* of the month for everyone who goes astray or is [t]naive; so you shall make atonement for the house. *simple*

21 "In the first *month,* on the fourteenth day of the month, you shall have the [r]Passover, a feast of seven days; unleavened bread shall be eaten. Ex. 12:1-24

22 "And on that day the prince shall provide for himself and all the people of the land a [r]bull for a sin offering. Lev. 4:14

23 "And *during* the [r]seven days of the feast he shall provide as a [r]burnt offering to the LORD seven bulls and seven rams without blemish on every day of the seven days, and a male goat daily for a sin offering. Lev. 23:8 • Num. 28:16-25

24 "And he shall provide as a grain offering an ephah [t]with a bull, an ephah with a ram, and a hin of oil with an ephah. *for*

25 "In the seventh *month,* on the fifteenth day of the month, at the feast, he shall provide like this, seven days [t]for the sin offering, the burnt offering, the grain offering, and the oil." *according to*

CHAPTER 46

'THUS says the Lord GOD, "The [r]gate of the inner court facing east shall be shut the six working days; but it shall be opened on the sabbath day, and opened on the day of the new moon. Ezek. 45:19

2 "And the prince shall enter by way of the porch of the gate from outside and stand by the post of the gate. Then the priests shall provide his burnt offering and his peace offerings, and he shall worship at the threshold of the gate and then go out; but the gate shall not be shut until the evening.

3 "The people of the land shall also worship at the doorway of that gate before the LORD on the sabbaths and on the new moons.

4 "And the [r]burnt offering which the prince shall offer to the LORD on the sabbath day shall be six lambs without blemish and a ram without blemish; Ezek. 45:17

5 and the grain offering shall be an ephah with the ram, and the grain offering [t]with the lambs as much as he is able to give, and a hin of oil with an ephah. *for*

6 "And on the day of the [r]new moon *he shall offer* a young bull without blemish, also six lambs and a ram, *which* shall be without blemish. Ezek. 46:1

7 "And he shall provide a grain offering, an ephah [t]with the bull, and an ephah with the ram, and with the lambs as [t]much as he is able, and a hin of oil with an ephah. *for • his hand can reach*

8 "And when the [r]prince enters, he shall go in by way of the porch of the gate and go out [t]by the same way. Ezek. 44:3; 46:2 • *by its way*

9 "But when the people of the land come [r]before the LORD at the appointed feasts, he who enters by way of the north gate to worship shall go out by way of the

south gate. And he who enters by way of the south gate shall go out by way of the north gate. [t]No one shall return by way of the gate by which he entered but shall go straight out. Ex. 34:23 • *He shall not*

10 "And when they go in, the prince shall go in [r]among them; and when they go out, he shall go out. 2 Sam. 6:14, 15; 1 Chr. 29:20, 22

11 "And at the festivals and the appointed feasts the grain offering shall be an ephah with a bull and an ephah [t]with a ram, and with the lambs as [t]much as one is able to give, and a hin of oil with an ephah. *for • a gift of his hand*

12 "And when the prince provides a [r]freewill offering, a burnt offering, or peace offerings *as* a freewill offering to the LORD, the gate facing east shall be opened for him. And he shall provide his burnt offering and his peace offerings as he does on the sabbath day. Then he shall go out, and the gate shall be shut after he goes out. Lev. 23:38; 2 Chr. 29:31

13 "And you shall provide a [r]lamb a year old without blemish for a burnt offering to the LORD daily; [r]morning by morning you shall provide it. Num. 28:3-5 • Is. 50:4

14 "Also you shall provide a grain offering with it morning by morning, a [r]sixth of an ephah, and a third of a hin of oil to moisten the fine flour, a grain offering to the LORD continually by a perpetual [t]ordinance. Num. 28:5 • *statute*

15 "Thus they shall provide the lamb, the grain offering, and the oil, morning by morning, for a continual burnt offering."

16 'Thus says the Lord GOD, "If the prince gives a gift *out of* his inheritance to any of his sons, it shall belong to his sons; it is their possession by inheritance.

17 "But if he gives a gift from his inheritance to one of his servants, it shall be his until the [r]year of liberty; then it shall return to the prince. His inheritance *shall be* only his sons'; it shall belong to them. Lev. 25:10

18 "And the prince shall [r]not take from the people's inheritance, [t]thrusting them out of their possession; he shall give his sons inheritance from his own possession so that My people shall not be scattered, anyone from his possession." ' " Ezek. 45:8 • *oppressing*

19 Then he brought me through the [r]entrance, which *was* at the side of the gate, into the holy chambers for the priests, which faced north; and behold, there *was* a place at the extreme rear toward the west. Ezek. 42:9; 44:5

20 And he said to me, "This is the place where the priests shall boil the guilt offering and the sin offering, *and* where they shall [r]bake the grain offering, in order that they may not bring *them* out into the outer court to transmit holiness to the people." Lev. 2:4-7

21 Then he brought me out into the outer court and led me across to the four corners of the court; and behold, in every corner of the court *there was* a *small* court.

22 In the four corners of the court *there were* enclosed courts, forty *cubits* long and thirty wide; these four in the corners *were* [t]the same size. *one measure*

23 And *there was* a row *of masonry* round about in them, around the four of them, and boil-

ing places were made under the
rows round about.
24 Then he said to me, "These
are the boiling places where the
ministers of the house shall boil
the sacrifices of the people."

CHAPTER 47

THEN he brought me back to the
door of the house; and behold, water was flowing from under the
threshold of the house toward the
east, for the house faced east. And
the water was flowing down from
under, from the right side of the
house, from south of the altar.
2 And he brought me out by
way of the north gate and led me
around [t]on the outside to the outer
gate by way of *the gate* that faces
east. And behold, water was trick-
ling from the south side. *by way of*
3 When the man went out
toward the east with a line in his
hand, he measured a thousand cubits, and he led me through the
water, water *reaching* the ankles.
4 Again he measured a thousand and led me through the water, water *reaching* the knees.
Again he measured a thousand
and led me through *the water*, water *reaching* the loins.
5 Again he measured a thousand; *and it was* a river that I
could not ford, for the water had
risen, *enough* water to swim in, a
river that could not be forded.
6 And he said to me, "Son of
man, have you [r]seen *this*?" Then
he brought me back to the bank of
the river. Ezek. 8:6; 40:4; 44:5
7 Now when I had returned,
behold, on the bank of the river
there *were* very many trees on the
one side and on the other.
8 Then he said to me, "These
waters go out toward the eastern
region and go down into the [r]Ara-
bah; then they go toward the sea,
being made to flow into the sea,
and the waters *of the sea* become
[t]fresh. Deut. 3:17; Is. 35:6 • *healed*
9 "And it will come about that
every living creature which
swarms in every place where the
[t]river goes, will live. And there will
be very many fish, for these waters go there, and *the others* become fresh; so everything will live
where the river goes. *two rivers*
10 "And it will come about that
fishermen will stand beside it;
from [r]Engedi to Eneglaim there
will be a place for the spreading of
nets. Their fish will be according
to their kinds, like the fish of the
Great Sea, very many. Gen. 14:7
11 "But its swamps and marshes
will not become [t]fresh; they will be
[t]left for [r]salt. *healed* • *given* • Deut. 29:23
12 "And by the river on its bank,
on one side and on the other, will
grow all *kinds of* trees for food.
Their leaves will not wither, and
their fruit will not fail. They will
bear every month because their
water flows from the sanctuary,
and their fruit will be for food and
their leaves for healing."
13 Thus says the Lord GOD,
"This *shall be* the [r]boundary by
which you shall divide the land for
an inheritance among the twelve
tribes of Israel; Joseph *shall have*
two portions. Num. 34:2-12
14 "And you shall divide it for an
inheritance, each one equally with
the other; for I swore to give it to

your forefathers, and this land shall fall to you as an inheritance.

15"And this *shall be* the boundary of the land: on the north side, from the Great Sea *by* the way of Hethlon, to the entrance of Zedad;

16[a]Hamath, Berothah, Sibraim, which is between the border of Damascus and the border of Hamath; Hazer-hatticon, which is by the border of Hauran. *Zedad*

17"And the boundary shall[t]extend from the sea *to*[r]Hazar-enan *at* the border of Damascus, and on the north toward the north is the border of Hamath. This is the north side. *be* • Num. 34:9

18"And the east side, from between Hauran, Damascus,[r]Gilead, and the land of Israel, *shall be* the Jordan; from the *north* border to the eastern sea you shall measure. This is the east side. Gen. 37:25

19"And the south side toward the south *shall extend* from Tamar as far as the waters of Meribath-kadesh, to the brook *of Egypt, and* to the Great Sea. This is the south side toward the south.

20"And the west side *shall be* the Great Sea, from the *south* border to a point opposite Lebo-hamath. This is the west side.

21"So you shall divide this land among yourselves according to the tribes of Israel.

22"And it will come about that you shall divide it by lot for an inheritance among yourselves and among the aliens who stay in your midst, who bring forth sons in your midst. And they shall be to you as the native-born among the sons of Israel; they shall be allotted an inheritance with you among the tribes of Israel.

23"And it will come about that in the tribe with which the alien stays, there you shall give *him* his inheritance," declares the Lord GOD.

CHAPTER 48

"NOW[r]these are the names of the tribes: from the northern extremity, beside the way of Hethlon to Lebo-hamath, *as far as* Hazar-enan *at* the border of Damascus, toward the north beside Hamath, running from east to west, Dan, one *portion.* Ex. 1:1

2"And beside the border of Dan, from the east side to the west side, Asher, one *portion.*

3"And beside the border of Asher, from the east side to the west side, Naphtali, one *portion.*

4"And beside the border of Naphtali, from the east side to the west side, Manasseh, one *portion.*

5"And beside the border of Manasseh, from the east side to the west side, Ephraim, one *portion.*

6"And beside the border of Ephraim, from the east side to the west side, Reuben, one *portion.*

7"And beside the border of Reuben, from the east side to the west side, Judah, one *portion.*

8"And beside the border of Judah, from the east side to the west side, shall be the [16]allotment which you shall[t]set apart, 25,000 *cubits* in width, and in length like one of the portions, from the east side to the west side; and the sanctuary shall be in the middle of it. *offer*

9"The allotment that you shall set apart to the LORD *shall be*

[16]Or, *contribution*, and so throughout this context

25,000 *cubits* in length, and 10,000 in width.

10 "And the holy allotment shall be for these, *namely* for the [r]priests, toward the north 25,000 *cubits in length,* toward the west 10,000 in width, toward the east 10,000 in width, and toward the south 25,000 in length; and the sanctuary of the LORD shall be in its midst. Ezek. 44:28; 45:4

11 "*It shall be* for the priests who are sanctified of the [r]sons of Zadok, who have kept My charge, who did not go astray when the sons of Israel went astray, as the Levites went astray. Ezek. 40:46

12 "And it shall be an allotment to them from the allotment of the land, a most holy place, by the border of the Levites.

13 "And alongside the border of the priests the Levites *shall have* 25,000 *cubits* in length and 10,000 in width. The whole length *shall be* 25,000 *cubits* and the width 10,000.

14 "Moreover, they shall not sell or exchange any of it, or alienate this [t]choice *portion* of land; for it is holy to the LORD. *first* or *first fruits*

15 "And the remainder, 5,000 *cubits* in width and 25,000 [t]in length, shall be for common use for the city, for dwellings and for [a]open spaces; and the city shall be in its midst. *in front • pasture land*

16 "And these *shall be* its measurements: the north side 4,500 *cubits,* the south side [r]4,500 *cubits,* the east side 4,500 *cubits,* and the west side 4,500 *cubits.* Rev. 21:16

17 "And the city shall have [a]open spaces: on the north 250 *cubits,* on the south 250 *cubits,* on the east 250 *cubits,* and on the west 250 *cubits.* *pasture land*

18 "And the remainder of the length alongside the holy allotment shall be 10,000 *cubits* toward the east, and 10,000 toward the west; and it shall be [a]alongside the holy allotment. And its produce shall be food for the workers of the city. *exactly as*

19 "And the workers of the city, out of all the tribes of Israel, shall cultivate it.

20 "The whole allotment *shall be* 25,000 by 25,000 *cubits;* you shall [t]set apart the holy allotment, a [t]square, with the [a]property of the city. *offer • fourth • possession*

21 "And the remainder *shall be* for the prince, on the one side and on the other of the holy allotment and of the property of the city; in front of the 25,000 *cubits* of the allotment toward the east border and westward in front of the 25,000 toward the west border, alongside the portions, *it shall be* for the prince. And the holy allotment and the sanctuary of the house shall be in the middle of it.

22 "And exclusive of the [a]property of the Levites and the property of the city, *which* are in the middle of that which belongs to the prince, *everything* between the border of Judah and the border of Benjamin shall be for the prince. *possession*

23 "As for the rest of the tribes: from the east side to the west side, Benjamin, one *portion.*

24 "And beside the border of Benjamin, from the east side to the west side, [r]Simeon, one *portion.* Josh. 19:1-9

25"And beside the border of
Simeon, from the east side to the
west side, Issachar, one *portion.*
26"And beside the border of Issachar, from the east side to the
west side, Zebulun, one *portion.*
27"And beside the border of
Zebulun, from the east side to the
west side, Gad, one *portion.*
28"And beside the border of
Gad, at the south side toward the
south, the border shall be from
[r]Tamar to the waters of Meribath-
kadesh, to the brook *of Egypt,* to
the Great Sea. Gen. 14:7; 2 Chr. 20:2
29"This is the land which you
shall divide by lot to the tribes of
Israel for an inheritance, and
these are their *several* portions,"
declares the Lord GOD.
30"And these are the exits of the
city: on the north side, 4,500 *cubits* by measurement,
31 shall be the gates of the city,
named for the tribes of Israel,
three gates toward the north: the
gate of Reuben, one; the gate of
Judah, one; the gate of Levi, one.
32"And on the east side, 4,500
cubits,[t] shall be three gates: the
gate of Joseph, one; the gate of
Benjamin, one; the gate of Dan,
one. *and*
33"And on the south side, 4,500
cubits by measurement,[t]shall be
three gates: the gate of Simeon,
one; the gate of Issachar, one; the
gate of Zebulun, one. *and*
34"On the west side, 4,500 *cubits, shall be* three gates: the gate
of Gad, one; the gate of Asher,
one; the gate of Naphtali, one.
35"*The city shall be* 18,000 *cubits* round about; and the[r]name of
the city from *that* day *shall be,*
'The LORD is there.'" Jer. 23:6

THE BOOK OF
DANIEL

IN the third year of the reign of
Jehoiakim king of Judah, Nebuchadnezzar king of Babylon came
to Jerusalem and besieged it.
2 And the[r]Lord gave Jehoiakim king of Judah into his hand,
along with some of the[r]vessels of
the house of God; and he brought
them to the land of Shinar, to the
house of his [1]god, and he brought
the vessels into the treasury of his
[1]god. Is. 42:24 • 2 Chr. 36:7
3 Then the king ordered Ash-
penaz, the chief of his [2]officials, to
bring in some of the sons of Israel,
including some of the[t]royal family
and of the nobles, *seed of the*
4 youths in whom was no defect, who were good-looking,
showing intelligence in every
branch of wisdom, endowed with
understanding, and discerning
knowledge, and who had ability
for[t]serving in the king's[t]court; and
he ordered him to teach them the
[3]literature and language of the
Chaldeans. *standing • palace*
5 And the king appointed for

[1]Or, *gods*
[2]Or, *eunuchs,* and so throughout the ch.
[3]Or, *writing*

them a daily ration from the
king's choice food and from the
wine which he drank, and *ap-*
pointed that they should be[a] educated three years, at the end of
which they were to enter the
king's personal service. *reared*
6 Now among them from the
sons of Judah were Daniel, Hananiah, Mishael and Azariah.
7 Then the commander of the
officials assigned *new* names to
them; and to Daniel he assigned
the name Belteshazzar, to Hananiah Shadrach, to Mishael Meshach, and to Azariah Abed-nego.
8 But Daniel made up his mind
that he would not defile himself
with the king's choice food or
with the wine which he drank; so
he sought *permission* from the
commander of the officials that he
might not defile himself.
9 Now God granted Daniel favor and compassion in the sight of
the commander of the officials,
10 and the commander of the
officials said to Daniel, "I am
afraid of my lord the king, who
has appointed your food and your
drink; for why should he see your
faces looking more haggard than
the youths who are your own age?
Then you would make me forfeit
my head to the king."
11 But Daniel said to the overseer whom the commander of the
officials had appointed over Daniel, Hananiah, Mishael and Azariah,
12 "Please test your servants for
ten days, and let us be[r] given some
vegetables to eat and water to
drink. Dan. 1:16
13 "Then let our appearance be
[t] observed in your presence, and
the appearance of the youths who
are eating the king's choice food;
and deal with your servants according to what you see." *seen*
14 So he listened to them in this
matter and tested them for ten
days.
15 And at the end of ten days
their appearance seemed better
and[t] they were fatter than all the
youths who had been eating the
king's choice food. *fat of flesh*
16 So the overseer continued to
withhold their choice food and the
wine they were to drink, and kept
giving them vegetables.
17 And as for these four youths,
God gave them knowledge and intelligence in every *branch of*[a] literature and wisdom; Daniel even
understood all *kinds of* visions
and dreams. *writing*
18 Then at the end of the days
which the king had[t] specified for
presenting them, the commander
of the officials presented them before Nebuchadnezzar. *said*
19 And the king talked with
them, and out of them all not one
was found like Daniel, Hananiah,
Mishael and Azariah; so they entered the king's personal service.
20 And as for every matter of
wisdom[t] and understanding about
which the king consulted them, he
found them ten times better than
all the magicians *and* conjurers
who *were* in all his realm. *of*
21 And Daniel continued until
the first year of Cyrus the king.

CHAPTER 2

NOW in the second year of the
reign of Nebuchadnezzar, Nebuchadnezzar[t] had dreams; and his

spirit was troubled and his sleep
left him. *dreamed dreams*
2 Then the king [t]gave orders to
call in the [4]magicians, the conjurers, the sorcerers and the [5]Chalde-
ans, to tell the king his dreams. So
they came in and stood before the
king. *said to call*
3 And the king said to them, "I
had a dream, and my spirit is anxious to understand the dream."
4 Then the Chaldeans spoke to
the king in [r]Aramaic: "O king, live
forever! Tell the dream to your
servants, and we will declare the
interpretation." Ezra 4:7
5 The king answered and said
to the Chaldeans, "The command
from me is firm: if you do not
make known to me the dream and
its interpretation, you will be torn
limb from limb, and your houses
will be made a rubbish heap.
6 "But if you declare the dream
and its interpretation, you will receive from me [r]gifts and a reward
and great honor; therefore declare
to me the dream and its interpretation." Dan. 2:48; 5:7, 16, 29
7 They answered a second
time and said, "Let the king tell
the dream to his servants, and we
will declare the interpretation."
8 The king answered and said,
"I know for certain that you are
[t]bargaining for time, inasmuch as
you have seen that the command
from me is firm, *buying*
9 that if you do not make the
dream known to me, there is only
one [a]decree for you. For you have
agreed together to speak lying
and corrupt [t]words before me until
the situation is changed; therefore
tell me the dream, that I may
know that you can declare to me
its interpretation." *law • word*
10 The Chaldeans answered the
king and said, "There is not a man
on earth who could declare the
matter for the king, inasmuch as
no great king or ruler has *ever*
asked anything like this of any
magician, conjurer or Chaldean.
11 "Moreover, the thing which
the king demands is [a]difficult, and
there is no one else who could declare it [t]to the king except gods,
whose dwelling place is not with
mortal flesh." *rare • before*
12 Because of this the king became [r]indignant and very furious,
and gave orders to destroy all the
wise men of Babylon. Ps. 76:10
13 So the decree went forth that
the wise men should be slain; and
they looked for Daniel and his
friends to [t]kill *them*. *be killed*
14 Then Daniel replied with discretion and discernment to Arioch, the captain of the king's
bodyguard, who had gone forth to
slay the wise men of Babylon;
15 he answered and said to Arioch, the king's commander, "For
what reason is the decree from
the king *so* urgent?" Then Arioch
informed Daniel about the matter.
16 So Daniel went in and requested of the king that he would
[a]give him time, in order that he
might declare the interpretation
to the king. *appoint a time for him*
17 Then Daniel went to his
house and informed his friends,
[r]Hananiah, Mishael and Azariah,
about the matter, Dan. 1:6
18 in order that they might request compassion from the God of

[4]Or, *soothsayer priests*
[5]Or, *master astrologers*, and so throughout this context

heaven concerning this mystery,
so that Daniel and his friends
might not be destroyed with the
rest of the wise men of Babylon.
19 Then the mystery was revealed to Daniel in a night [r]vision.
Then Daniel blessed the God of
heaven; Num. 12:6; Job 33:15, 16
20 Daniel answered and said,
"Let the name of God be
[r]blessed forever and ever,
For wisdom and power be-
long to Him. Ps. 103:1, 2
21 "And it is He who changes
the times and the epochs;
He removes kings and [a]es-
tablishes kings; *sets up*
He gives [r]wisdom to wise
men, 1 Kin. 3:9, 10
And knowledge to [t]men of
understanding. *knowers*
22 "It is He who [r]reveals the
profound and hidden
things; Job 12:22
[r]He knows what is in the
darkness, Job 26:6
And the [r]light dwells with
Him. Ps. 36:9
23 "To Thee, O [r]God of my fathers, I give thanks and
praise, Gen. 31:42
For Thou hast given me
wisdom and power;
Even now Thou hast made
known to me what we re-
quested of Thee,
For Thou hast made known
to us the king's matter."
24 Therefore, Daniel went in to
Arioch, whom the king had appointed to destroy the wise men
of Babylon; he went and spoke to
him as follows: "Do not destroy
the wise men of Babylon! Take me
[t]into the king's presence, and I will
declare the interpretation to the
king." *in before the king*
25 Then Arioch hurriedly
brought Daniel [t] into the king's
presence and spoke to him as follows: "I have found a man among
the exiles from Judah who can
make the interpretation known to
the king!" *in before the king*
26 The king answered and said
to Daniel, whose name was Belteshazzar, "Are you able to make
known to me the dream which I
have seen and its interpretation?"
27 Daniel answered before the
king and said, "As for the mystery
about which the king has inquired, neither wise men, conjurers, magicians, *nor* diviners are
able to declare *it* to the king.
28 "However, there is a God in
heaven who reveals mysteries,
and He has made known to King
Nebuchadnezzar what will take
place in the latter days. This was
your dream and the visions in
your mind *while* on your bed.
29 "As for you, O king, *while* on
your bed your thoughts [t]turned to
what would take place in the future; and He who reveals mysteries has made known to you what
will take place. *came up*
30 "But as for me, this mystery
has not been revealed to me for
any wisdom [t]residing in me more
than *in* any *other* living man, but
for the purpose of making the interpretation known to the king,
and that you may understand the
thoughts of your mind. *which is*
31 "You, O king, were looking
and behold, there was a single
great statue; that statue, which
was large and [t]of extraordinary

splendor, was standing in front of
you, and its appearance was awesome. *its splendor was surpassing*
32 "The[r] head of that statue *was*
made of fine gold, its breast and
its arms of silver, its belly and its
thighs of bronze, Dan. 2:38
33 its legs of iron, its feet partly
of iron and partly of clay.
34 "You [t]continued looking until
a [r] stone was cut out without
hands, and it struck the statue on
its feet of iron and clay, and
crushed them. *were* • Dan. 2:45
35 "Then the iron, the clay, the
bronze, the silver and the gold
were crushed [t]all at the same time,
and became like chaff from the
summer threshing floors; and the
wind carried them away so that
not a trace of them was found. But
the stone that struck the statue
became a great mountain and
filled the whole earth. *like one*
36 "This *was* the dream; now we
shall tell [r]its interpretation before
the king. Dan. 2:24
37 "You, O king, are the king of
kings, to whom the God of heaven
has given the kingdom, the power,
the strength, and the glory;
38 and wherever the sons of
men dwell, *or* the beasts of the
field, or the birds of the sky, He
has given *them* into your hand
and has caused you to rule over
them all. You are the head of gold.
39 "And after you there will arise
another kingdom inferior to you,
then another third kingdom of
bronze, which will rule over all
the earth.
40 "Then there will be a [r]fourth
kingdom as strong as iron; inasmuch as iron crushes and shatters
all things, so, like iron that breaks
in pieces, it will crush and break
all these in pieces. Dan. 7:23
41 "And in that you saw the feet
and toes, partly of potter's clay
and partly of iron, it will be a divided kingdom; but it will have in
it the toughness of iron, inasmuch
as you saw the iron mixed with
[t]common clay. *clay of mud*
42 "And *as* the toes of the feet
were partly of iron and partly of
pottery, *so* some of the kingdom
will be strong and part of it will be
brittle.
43 "And in that you saw the iron
mixed with [t]common clay, they
will combine with one another [a]in
the seed of men; but they will not
adhere to one another, even as
iron does not combine with pottery. *clay of mud* • *with*
44 "And in the days of those
kings the God of heaven will set
up a kingdom which will never be
destroyed, and *that* kingdom will
not be [a]left for another people; it
will crush and put an end to all
these kingdoms, but it will itself
endure forever. *passed on to*
45 "Inasmuch as you saw that a
stone was cut out of the mountain
without hands and that it crushed
the iron, the bronze, the clay, the
silver, and the gold, the great God
has made known to the king what
will take place [t]in the future; so the
dream is true, and its interpretation is trustworthy." *after this*
46 Then King Nebuchadnezzar
fell on his face and did [r]homage to
Daniel, and gave orders to present
to him an offering and [t]fragrant incense. Dan. 3:5, 7 • *sweet odors*
47 The king answered Daniel
and said, "Surely [r]your God is a
God of gods and a Lord of kings

and a[r]revealer of mysteries, since you have been able to reveal this mystery." Dan. 3:15 • Amos 3:7

48 Then the king[t] promoted Daniel and gave him many great gifts, and he made him ruler over the whole province of Babylon and chief prefect over all the wise men of Babylon. *made great*

49 And Daniel made request of the king, and he appointed Shadrach, Meshach and Abed-nego over the administration of the province of Babylon, while Daniel *was* at the king's[t]court. *gate*

CHAPTER 3

NEBUCHADNEZZAR the king made an[r]image of gold, the height of which *was* sixty cubits *and* its width six cubits; he set it up on the plain of Dura in the province of Babylon. 1 Kin. 12:28; Is. 46:6

2 Then Nebuchadnezzar the king sent *word* to assemble the[r]satraps, the prefects and the governors, the counselors, the treasurers, the judges, the magistrates and all the rulers of the provinces to come to the dedication of the image that Nebuchadnezzar the king had set up. Dan. 3:3, 27

3 Then the satraps, the prefects and the governors, the counselors, the treasurers, the judges, the magistrates and all the rulers of the provinces were assembled for the dedication of the image that Nebuchadnezzar the king had set up; and they stood before the image that Nebuchadnezzar had set up.

4 Then the herald loudly proclaimed: "To you[t]the command is given, O peoples, nations and *men of every* language, *they command*

5 that at the moment you hear the sound of the horn, flute,[a]lyre, trigon, psaltery, bagpipe, and all kinds of music, you are to fall down and worship the golden image that Nebuchadnezzar the king has set up. *zither*

6 "But whoever does not fall down and worship shall immediately be cast into the midst of a furnace of blazing fire."

7 Therefore at that time, when all the peoples heard the sound of the horn, flute, lyre, trigon, psaltery, bagpipe, and all kinds of music, all the peoples, nations and *men of every*[t]language fell down *and* worshiped the golden image that Nebuchadnezzar the king had set up. *tongue*

8 For this reason at that time certain Chaldeans came forward and[t]brought charges against the Jews. *ate the pieces of*

9 They responded and said to Nebuchadnezzar the king: [r]"O king, live forever! Dan. 2:4

10 "You yourself, O king, have [r]made a decree that every man who hears the sound of the horn, flute, lyre, trigon, psaltery, and bagpipe, and all kinds of music, is to fall down and worship the golden image. Esth. 3:12-14

11 "But whoever does not fall down and worship shall be cast into the midst of a furnace of blazing fire.

12 "There are certain Jews whom you have[r]appointed over the administration of the province of Babylon, *namely* Shadrach, Meshach and Abed-nego. These men, O king, have disregarded you;

they do not serve your gods or worship the golden image which you have set up." Dan. 2:49

13 Then Nebuchadnezzar in rage and anger gave orders to bring Shadrach, Meshach and Abed-nego; then these men were brought before the king.

14 Nebuchadnezzar responded and said to them, "Is it true, Shadrach, Meshach and Abed-nego, that you do not serve[r] my gods or worship the golden image that I have set up? Is. 46:1; Jer. 50:2

15 "Now if you are ready, at the moment you hear the sound of the horn, flute, lyre, trigon, psaltery, and bagpipe, and all kinds of music, to fall down and worship the image that I have made, *very well.* But if you will not worship, you will immediately be cast into the midst of a furnace of blazing fire; and what god is there who can deliver you out of my hands?"

16 [r]Shadrach, Meshach and Abed-nego answered and said to the king, "O Nebuchadnezzar, we do not need to give you an answer concerning this. Dan. 1:7; 3:12

17 [a]"If it be *so,* our God whom we serve is able to deliver us from the furnace of blazing fire;[a] and He will deliver us out of your hand, O king. *If our God . . . is able • then*

18 "But *even* if *He does* not,[r] let it be known to you, O king, that we are not going to serve your gods or worship the golden image that you have set up." Heb. 11:25

19 Then Nebuchadnezzar was filled with wrath, and his facial expression was altered toward Shadrach, Meshach and Abed-nego. He answered[t] by giving orders to heat the furnace seven times more than it was usually heated. *and ordered to*

20 And he commanded certain valiant warriors who *were* in his army to tie up Shadrach, Meshach and Abed-nego, in order to cast *them* into the furnace of blazing fire.

21 Then these men were tied up in their[a] trousers, their coats, their caps and their *other* clothes, and were cast into the midst of the furnace of blazing fire. *cloaks*

22 For this reason, because the king's[t] command *was*[a] urgent and the furnace had been made extremely hot, the flame of the fire slew those men who carried up Shadrach, Meshach and Abed-nego. *word • harsh*

23 But these three men, Shadrach, Meshach and Abed-nego, fell into the midst of the furnace of blazing fire *still* tied up.

24 Then Nebuchadnezzar the king was astounded and stood up in haste; he responded and said to his high officials, "Was it not three men we cast bound into the midst of the fire?" They answered and said to the king, "Certainly, O king."

25 He answered and said, "Look! I see four men loosed *and* [r]walking *about* in the midst of the fire without harm, and the appearance of the fourth is like a son of *the*[r] gods!" Ps. 91:3-9 • Jer. 15:21

26 Then Nebuchadnezzar came near to the door of the furnace of blazing fire; he responded and said, "Shadrach, Meshach and Abed-nego, come out, you servants of the[r] Most High God, and come here!" Then Shadrach, Me-

shach and Abed-nego came out of
the midst of the fire. Dan. 3:17
27 And the satraps, the prefects,
the governors and the king's high
officials gathered around *and* saw
in regard to these men that the
fire had no[t] effect on[t] the bodies of
these men nor was the hair of
their head singed, nor were their
[a] trousers damaged, nor had the
smell of fire *even* come upon
them. *power over* • *their* • *cloaks*
28 Nebuchadnezzar responded
and said, "Blessed be the God of
Shadrach, Meshach and Abed-
nego, who has sent His angel and
delivered His servants who put
their trust in Him, [t] violating the
king's command, and yielded up
their bodies so as not to serve or
worship any god except their own
God. *and changed the king's word*
29 "Therefore, I make a decree
that any people, nation or tongue
that speaks anything offensive
against the God of Shadrach, Meshach and Abed-nego shall be
torn limb from limb and their
houses reduced to a rubbish heap,
inasmuch as there is no other god
who is able to deliver in this way."
30 Then the king [r] caused Shadrach, Meshach and Abed-nego to
prosper in the province of Babylon. Dan. 2:49; 3:12

CHAPTER 4

NEBUCHADNEZZAR the king
to all the peoples, nations, and
men of every[t] language that live in
all the earth: "May your [a] peace
abound! *tongue* • *welfare* or *prosperity*
2 "It has seemed good to me to
declare the signs and wonders
which the [r] Most High God has
done for me. Dan. 3:26
3 "How great are His [r] signs,
And how mighty are His
wonders! Ps. 77:19
His kingdom is an ever-
lasting kingdom,
And His dominion is from
generation to generation.
4 "I, Nebuchadnezzar, was at
ease in my house and [r] flourishing
in my palace. Ps. 30:6; Is. 47:7, 8
5 "I saw a dream and it made
me fearful; and *these* fantasies *as I
lay* on my bed and the visions in
my mind kept alarming me.
6 "So I gave orders to [r] bring into
my presence all the wise men of
Babylon, that they might make
known to me the interpretation of
the dream. Gen. 41:8; Dan. 2:2
7 "Then the [a] magicians, the conjurers, the Chaldeans, and the diviners came in, and I related the
dream [t] to them; but they could not
make its interpretation known to
me. *soothsayer priests* • *before*
8 "But finally Daniel came in
before me, whose name is Belteshazzar according to the name of
my god, and in whom is [6] a spirit of
the holy gods; and I related the
dream [t] to him, *saying,* *before*
9 'O Belteshazzar, [r] chief of the
magicians, since I know that [r] a
spirit of the holy gods is in you
and no mystery baffles you, tell
me the visions of my dream which
I have seen, along with its interpretation. Dan. 1:20 • Dan. 4:8
10 'Now *these were* the visions
in my mind *as I lay* on my bed: I
was looking, and behold, *there*

[6] Or possibly, *the Spirit of the holy God,* and so throughout this context

was a tree in the midst of the
earth, and its height *was* great.
11 'The tree grew large and became strong,
And its height [r]reached to the sky, **Deut. 9:1**
And it *was* visible to the end of the whole earth.
12 'Its foliage *was* beautiful and its fruit abundant,
And in it *was* food for all.
The beasts of the field found shade under it,
And the birds of the sky dwelt in its branches,
And all living creatures fed themselves from it.
13 'I was looking in the visions
in my mind *as I lay* on my bed,
and behold, an *angelic* watcher, a
holy one, descended from heaven.
14 'He shouted out and spoke as follows:
[r]"Chop down the tree and cut off its branches,
Strip off its foliage and scatter its fruit;
Let the[r]beasts flee from under it, **Ezek. 31:10-14**
And the birds from its branches. **Dan. 4:12**
15 "Yet[r]leave the stump[t]with its roots in the ground,
But with a band of iron and bronze *around it*
In the new grass of the field; **Job 14:7-9** · *of*
And let him be drenched with the dew of heaven,
And let[t]him share with the beasts in the grass of the earth. ***his portion be with***
16 "Let his[t] mind be changed from *that of* a man,
And let a beast's mind be given to him, ***heart***
And let seven periods of time pass over him.
17 "This sentence is by the decree of the *angelic* watchers,
And the decision is a command of the holy ones,
In order that the living may [r]know **Ps. 9:16; 83:18**
That the Most High is ruler over the realm of mankind,
And[r]bestows it on whom He wishes, **Jer. 27:5-7**
And sets over it the[r]lowliest of men." **1 Sam. 2:8**
18 'This is the dream *which* I,
King Nebuchadnezzar, have seen.
Now you, Belteshazzar, tell *me* its
interpretation, inasmuch as none
of the wise men of my kingdom is
able to make known to me the interpretation;
but you are able, for
a spirit of the holy gods is in you.'
19"Then Daniel, whose name is
Belteshazzar, was appalled for a
while as his [r]thoughts alarmed
him. The king responded and said,
'Belteshazzar, do not let the
dream or its interpretation alarm
you.' Belteshazzar answered and
said,[r]"My lord, *if only* the dream
applied to those who hate you,
and its interpretation to your adversaries!
Jer. 4:19 · Dan. 4:24
20 'The tree that you saw, which
became large and grew strong,
whose height reached to the sky
and was visible to all the earth,
21 and whose foliage *was* beautiful
and its fruit abundant, and in
which *was* food for all, under
which the beasts of the field dwelt
and in whose branches the birds
of the sky lodged—

22 it is[r]you, O king; for you have become great and grown strong, and your [t]majesty has become great and reached to the sky and your dominion to the end of the earth. 2 Sam. 12:7 • *greatness*

23 'And in that the king saw an *angelic* watcher, a holy one, descending from heaven and saying, "Chop down the tree and destroy it; yet leave the stump with its roots in the ground, but with a band of iron and bronze *around it* in the new grass of the field, and let him be drenched with the dew of heaven, and let him share with the beasts of the field until seven periods of time pass over him";

24 this is the interpretation, O king, and this is the decree of the Most High, which has[r]come upon my lord the king: Job 40:11, 12

25 that you be [r] driven away from mankind, and your dwelling place be with the beasts of the field, and you be given grass to eat like cattle and be drenched with the dew of heaven; and seven periods of time will pass over you, until you recognize that the Most High is ruler over the realm of mankind, and bestows it on whomever He wishes. Dan. 4:33

26 'And in that it was commanded to leave the stump[t]with the roots of the tree, your kingdom will be[t]assured to you after you recognize that *it is* Heaven *that* rules. *of* • *enduring*

27 'Therefore, O king, may my advice be pleasing to you: break away now from your sins by *doing* righteousness, and from your iniquities by showing mercy to *the* poor, in case there may be a prolonging of your prosperity.'

28 "All *this*[r]happened to Nebuchadnezzar the king. Zech. 1:6

29 "Twelve[r]months later he was walking on the *roof of* the royal palace of Babylon. 2 Pet. 3:9

30 "The king[t]reflected and said, 'Is this not Babylon the great, which I myself have built as a royal[t]residence by the might of my power and for the glory of my majesty?' *answered* • *house*

31 "While the word *was* in the king's mouth, a voice[t]came from heaven, *saying,* 'King Nebuchadnezzar, to you it is declared:[a]sovereignty has been removed from you, *fell* • *kingdom*

32 and[r]you will be driven away from mankind, and your dwelling place *will be* with the beasts of the field. You will be given grass to eat like cattle, and seven periods of time will pass over you, until you recognize that the Most High is ruler over the realm of mankind, and bestows it on whomever He wishes.' Dan. 4:25

33 "Immediately the word concerning Nebuchadnezzar was fulfilled; and he was [r]driven away from mankind and began eating grass like cattle, and his body was drenched with the dew of heaven, until his hair had grown like eagles' *feathers* and his nails like birds' *claws.* Dan. 4:25; 5:21

34 "But at the end of[t]that period I, Nebuchadnezzar, raised my eyes toward heaven, and my reason returned to me, and I blessed the Most High and praised and honored Him who lives forever;

For His dominion is an
everlasting dominion,
And His kingdom *endures*

from generation to generation. *the days*

35 "And [r]all the inhabitants of the earth are accounted as nothing, Ps. 39:5
But [r]He does according to His will in the host of heaven Dan. 6:27
And *among* the inhabitants of earth;
And no one can [t]ward off His hand *strike against*
Or say to Him, [r]'What hast Thou done?' Job 9:12

36 "At that time my [t]reason returned to me. And my majesty and splendor were [t]restored to me for the glory of my kingdom, and my counselors and my nobles began seeking me out; so I was reestablished in my sovereignty, and surpassing greatness was added to me. *knowledge • returning*

37 "Now I Nebuchadnezzar praise, exalt, and honor the King of heaven, for all His works are [t]true and His ways [t]just, and He is able to humble those who walk in pride." *truth • justice*

CHAPTER 5

BELSHAZZAR the king held a great feast for a thousand of his nobles, and he was drinking wine in the presence of the thousand.

2 When Belshazzar tasted the wine, he gave orders to bring the gold and silver [r]vessels which Nebuchadnezzar his [a]father had taken out of the temple which *was* in Jerusalem, in order that the king and his nobles, his wives, and his concubines might drink from them. 2 Kin. 24:13 • *forefather*

3 Then they brought the gold vessels that had been taken out of the temple, the house of God which *was* in Jerusalem; and the king and his nobles, his wives, and his concubines drank from them.

4 They [r]drank the wine and praised the gods of [r]gold and silver, of bronze, iron, wood, and stone. Is. 42:8 • Ps. 115:4

5 Suddenly the fingers of a man's hand emerged and began writing opposite the lampstand on the plaster of the wall of the king's palace, and the king saw the [a]back of the hand that did the writing. *palm*

6 Then the king's [t]face grew pale, and his thoughts alarmed him; and his hip joints went slack, and his knees began knocking together. *brightness changed for him*

7 The king called aloud to bring in the conjurers, the [a]Chaldeans and the diviners. The king spoke and said to the wise men of Babylon, "Any man who can read this inscription and explain its interpretation to me will be clothed with purple, and *have* a necklace of gold around his neck, and have authority as third *ruler* in the kingdom." *master astrologers*

8 Then all the king's wise men came in, but they could not read the inscription or make known its interpretation to the king.

9 Then King Belshazzar was greatly [r]alarmed, his [r]face grew *even* paler, and his nobles were perplexed. Job 18:11 • Is. 13:6-8

10 The queen entered the banquet hall because of the words of the king and his nobles; the queen spoke and said, "O king, live for-

ever! Do not let your thoughts
alarm you or your face be pale.
11 "There is a man in your kingdom in whom is a spirit of the
holy gods; and in the days of your
father, illumination, insight, and
wisdom like the wisdom of the
gods were found in him. And King
Nebuchadnezzar, your father,
your father the king, appointed
him chief of the magicians, conjurers, Chaldeans, *and* diviners.
12 "*This was* because an extraordinary spirit, knowledge and insight, interpretation of dreams,
explanation of enigmas, and solv-
ing of difficult problems were
found in this Daniel, whom the
king named Belteshazzar. Let
Daniel now be summoned, and he
will declare the interpretation."
13 Then Daniel was brought in
before the king. The king spoke
and said to Daniel, "Are you that
Daniel who is one of the exiles
from Judah, whom my father the
king brought from Judah?
14 "Now I have heard about you
that [a] a spirit of the gods is in you,
and that illumination, insight, and
extraordinary wisdom have been
found in you. ***the Spirit of God***
15 "Just now the wise men *and*
the conjurers were brought in before me that they might read this
inscription and make its interpretation known to me, but they
could not declare the interpretation of the [t] message. ***word***
16 "But I personally have heard
about you, that you are able to
give interpretations and solve difficult problems. Now if you are
able to read the inscription and
make its interpretation known to
me, you will be clothed with purple and *wear* a necklace of gold
around your neck, and you will
have authority as the [a] third *ruler* in
the kingdom." ***triumvir***
17 Then Daniel answered and
said before the king, [t] "Keep your
gifts for yourself, or give your rewards to someone else; however, I
will read the inscription to the
king and make the interpretation
known to him. ***Let . . . be for***
18 "O [t] king, the Most High God
granted sovereignty, grandeur,
glory, and majesty to Nebuchadnezzar your father. ***You, O king***
19 "And because of the grandeur
which He bestowed on him, all the
peoples, nations, and *men of every*
language feared and trembled before him; whomever he wished he
killed, and whomever he wished
he spared alive; and whomever he
wished he elevated, and whomever he wished he humbled.
20 "But when his heart was lifted
up and his spirit became so [t] proud
that he behaved arrogantly, he
was deposed from his royal
throne, and *his* glory was taken
away from him. ***strong***
21 "He was also driven away
from mankind, and his heart was
made like *that of* beasts, and his
dwelling place *was* with the wild
donkeys. He was given grass to
eat like cattle, and his body was
drenched with the dew of heaven,
until he recognized that the Most
High God is ruler over the realm
of mankind, and *that* He sets over
it whomever He wishes.
22 "Yet you, his son, Belshazzar,
have not humbled your heart,
even though you knew all this,
23 but you have exalted yourself against the Lord of heaven;

and they have brought the vessels of His house before you, and you and your nobles, your wives and your concubines have been drinking wine from them; and you have praised the gods of silver and gold, of bronze, iron, wood and stone, which do not see, hear or understand. But the God in whose hand are your life-breath and your ways, you have not glorified.

24 "Then the[t] hand was sent from Him, and this inscription was written out. *palm of the hand*

25 "Now this is the inscription that was written out: 'MENĒ, MENĒ, TEKĒL, UPHARSIN.'

26 "This is the interpretation of the[t] message: 'MENĒ'—God has numbered your kingdom and[r] put an end to it. *word* • Jer. 50:41-43

27 " 'TEKĒL'—you have been [r]weighed on the scales and found deficient. Job 31:6; Ps. 62:9

28 " 'PERĒS'—your kingdom has been divided and given over to the [r]Medes and Persians." Is. 13:17

29 Then Belshazzar gave orders, and they clothed Daniel with purple and *put* a necklace of gold around his neck, and issued a proclamation concerning him that he *now* had authority as the[a] third *ruler* in the kingdom. *triumvir*

30 That same night Belshazzar the Chaldean king was slain.

31 So[r] Darius the Mede received the kingdom at about the age of sixty-two. Dan. 6:1; 9:1

CHAPTER 6

IT seemed good to Darius to appoint 120 satraps over the kingdom, that they should be in charge of the whole kingdom,

2 and over them three commissioners (of whom Daniel was one), that these satraps might be accountable to them, and that the king might not suffer loss.

3 Then this Daniel began distinguishing himself [t] among the commissioners and satraps because[t] he possessed an extraordinary spirit, and the king planned to appoint him over the entire kingdom. *above* • *there was in him*

4 Then the commissioners and satraps began trying to find a ground of accusation against Daniel in regard to government affairs; but they could find no ground of accusation or *evidence of* corruption, inasmuch as he was faithful, and no negligence or corruption was *to be* found in him.

5 Then these men said, "We shall not find any ground of accusation against this Daniel unless we find *it* against him with regard to the law of his God."

6 Then these commissioners and satraps came by agreement to the king and spoke to him as follows: "King Darius, live forever!

7 "All the commissioners of the kingdom, the prefects and the satraps, the high officials and the governors have consulted together that the king should establish a statute and enforce an injunction that anyone who makes a petition to any god or man besides you, O king, for thirty days, shall be cast into the lions'[a] den. *pit*

8 "Now, O king, establish the injunction and sign the document so that it may not be changed, according to the law of the Medes and Persians, which[t] may not be revoked." *does not pass away*

9 Therefore King Darius
[r]signed the document, that is, the
injunction. Ps. 118:9; 146:3
10 Now when Daniel knew that
the document was signed, he entered his house (now in his roof
chamber he had windows open
toward Jerusalem); and he continued kneeling on his knees three
times a day, praying and giving
thanks before his God,[a] as he had
been doing previously. *because*
11 Then these men came[a] by
agreement and found Daniel making petition and supplication before his God. *thronging*
12 Then they approached and
spoke before the king about the
king's injunction, "Did you not
sign an injunction that any man
who makes a petition to any god
or man besides you, O king, for
thirty days, is to be cast into the
lions' den?" The king answered
and said, "The statement is true,
according to the law of the Medes
and Persians, which[t] may not be
revoked." *does not pass away*
13 Then they answered and
spoke before the king, "Daniel,
who is one of the exiles from Judah, pays no attention to you, O
king, or to the injunction which
you signed, but keeps making his
petition three times a day."
14 Then, as soon as the king
heard this statement, he was
deeply[r] distressed and set *his* mind
on delivering Daniel; and even until sunset he kept exerting himself
to rescue him. Mark 6:26
15 Then these men came[a] by
agreement to the king and said to
the king, "Recognize, O king, that
it is a[r] law of the Medes and Persians that no injunction or statute
which the king establishes may be
changed." *thronging* • Esth. 8:8
16 Then the king gave orders,
and Daniel was brought in and
cast into the lions' den. The king
spoke and said to Daniel, "Your
God whom you constantly serve
will Himself deliver you."
17 And a[r] stone was brought and
laid over the mouth of the den;
and the king sealed it with his
own signet ring and with the signet rings of his nobles, so that
nothing might be changed in regard to Daniel. Lam. 3:53
18 Then the king went off to his
palace and spent the night[r] fasting,
and no entertainment was
brought before him; and his sleep
fled from him. 2 Sam. 12:16, 17
19 Then the king arose with the
dawn, at the break of day, and
went in haste to the lions' den.
20 And when he had come near
the den to Daniel, he cried out
with a troubled voice. The king
spoke and said to Daniel, "Daniel,
servant of the living God, has[r] your
God, whom you constantly serve,
been[r] able to deliver you from the
lions?" Dan. 6:16, 27 • Dan. 3:17
21 Then Daniel spoke[t] to the
king, "O king, live forever! *with*
22 "My God sent His angel and
shut the lions' mouths, and they
have not harmed me, inasmuch as
I was found innocent before Him;
and also toward you, O king, I
have committed no crime."
23 Then the king was very
pleased and gave orders for Daniel to be taken up out of the den.
So Daniel was taken up out of the
den, and[r] no injury whatever was

found on him, because he had
trusted in his God. Dan. 3:25, 27
24 The king then gave orders,
and they brought those men who
had maliciously accused Daniel,
and they [r]cast them, their children,
and their wives into the lions'
den; and they had not reached the
bottom of the den before the lions
overpowered them and crushed
all their bones. Deut. 19:18, 19
25 Then Darius the king wrote
to all the peoples, nations, and
men of every [t]language who were
living in all the land: "May your
peace abound! *tongue*
26 "I [r]make a decree that in all
the dominion of my kingdom men
are to fear and tremble before the
God of Daniel; Ezra 6:8-12

> For He is the living God and
> [r]enduring forever,
> And His kingdom is one
> which will not be destroyed, Ps. 93:1, 2
> And His dominion *will be*
> [t]forever. *to the end*
> 27 "He delivers and rescues and
> performs [r]signs and wonders Dan. 4:2, 3
> In heaven and on earth,
> Who has *also* delivered
> Daniel from the [t]power of
> the lions." *hand*

28 So this Daniel enjoyed success in the reign of Darius and in
the reign of Cyrus the Persian.

CHAPTER 7

IN the first year of Belshazzar
king of Babylon Daniel saw a
dream and visions in his mind *as
he lay* on his bed; then he wrote
the dream down *and* related the
following summary of [t]it. *words*
2 Daniel said, "I was looking in
my vision by night, and behold,
the four winds of heaven were
stirring up the great sea.
3 "And four great [r]beasts were
coming up from the sea, different
from one another. Dan. 7:17
4 "The first *was* like a lion and
had *the* wings of an eagle. I kept
looking until its wings were
plucked, and it was lifted up from
the ground and made to stand on
two feet like a man; a human
[t]mind also was given to it. *heart*
5 "And behold, another beast, a
second one, resembling a bear.
And it was raised up on one side,
and three ribs *were* in its mouth
between its teeth; and thus they
said to it, 'Arise, devour much
meat!'
6 "After this I kept looking, and
behold, another one, [r]like a leopard, which had on its [a]back four
wings of a bird; the beast also had
four heads, and dominion was given to it. Rev. 13:2 • *sides*
7 "After this I kept looking in
the night visions, and behold, a
[r]fourth beast, dreadful and terrifying and extremely strong; and it
had large iron teeth. It devoured
and crushed, and trampled down
the remainder with its feet; and it
was different from all the beasts
that were before it, and it had ten
horns. Dan. 7:19, 20, 23
8 "While I was contemplating
the horns, behold, another horn, a
little one, came up among them,
and three of the first horns were
pulled out by the roots before it;
and behold, this horn possessed
eyes like the eyes of a man, and a
mouth uttering great *boasts*.

9 "I kept looking
Until[r]thrones were set up,
And the Ancient of Days took *His* seat; Rev. 20:4
His[r]vesture *was* like white snow, Mark 9:3
And the hair of His head like pure wool.
His throne *was*[t]ablaze with flames, *flames of fire*
Its[r]wheels *were* a burning fire. Ezek. 10:2, 6
10 "A river of[r]fire was flowing
And coming out from before Him; Ps. 18:8
[r]Thousands upon thousands were attending Him,
And myriads upon myriads were standing before Him; Deut. 33:2
The[r]court sat, Ps. 96:11-13
And [r]the books were opened. Dan. 12:1
11 "Then I kept looking because
of the sound of the boastful words
which the horn was speaking; I
kept looking until the beast was
slain, and its body was destroyed
and given to the burning fire.
12 "As for the rest of the beasts,
their dominion was taken away,
but an extension of life was
granted to them for an appointed
period of time.
13 "I kept looking in the night visions,
And behold, with the clouds of heaven
One like a[r]Son of Man was coming, Matt. 24:30; 26:64
And He came up to the Ancient of Days
And was presented before Him.
14 "And to Him was given[r]dominion, Dan. 7:27
Glory and a kingdom,
That all the peoples, nations, and *men of every* [t]language *tongue*
Might serve Him.
His dominion is an everlasting dominion
Which will not pass away;
[r]And His kingdom is one
Which will not be destroyed. Heb. 12:28
15 "As for me, Daniel, my spirit
was distressed[t]within me, and the
visions in my mind kept alarming
me. *in the midst of its sheath*
16 "I approached one of those
who were standing by and began
asking him the[t]exact meaning of
all this. So he told me and made
known to me the interpretation of
these things: *truth concerning*
17 'These great beasts, which
are four *in number,* are four kings
who will arise from the earth.
18 'But the[t]saints of the Highest
One will receive the kingdom and
possess the kingdom forever, for
all ages to come.' *holy ones*
19 "Then I desired to know the
exact meaning of the fourth beast,
which was different from all[t]the
others, exceedingly dreadful, with
its teeth of iron and its claws of
bronze, *and which* devoured,
crushed, and trampled down the
remainder with its feet, *of them*
20 and *the meaning* of the ten
horns that *were* on its head, and
the other *horn* which came up,
and before which three *of them*
fell, namely, that horn which had
eyes and a mouth uttering great
boasts, and which was larger in
appearance than its associates.
21 "I kept looking, and that horn

was waging war with the saints and overpowering them

22 until the Ancient of Days came, and judgment was [t]passed in favor of the saints of the Highest One, and the time arrived when the saints took possession of the kingdom. *given for*

23 "Thus he said: 'The fourth beast will be a fourth kingdom on the earth, which will be different from all the *other* kingdoms, and it will devour the whole earth and tread it down and crush it.

24 'As for the [r]ten horns, out of this kingdom ten kings will arise; and another will arise after them, and he will be different from the previous ones and will subdue three kings. Dan. 7:7; Rev. 17:12

25 'And he will speak [t] out against the Most High and wear down the [t]saints of the Highest One, and he will intend to make alterations in times and in law; and they will be given into his hand for a time, times, and half a time. *words* • *holy ones*

26 'But the court will sit *for judgment,* and his dominion will be taken away, annihilated and destroyed [t]forever. *to the end*

27 'Then the sovereignty, the dominion, and the greatness of *all* the kingdoms under the whole heaven will be given to the people of the saints of the Highest One; His kingdom *will be* an everlasting kingdom, and all the dominions will serve and obey Him.'

28 "At this point the revelation ended. As for me, Daniel, my thoughts were greatly alarming me and my face grew pale, but I kept the matter to myself."

CHAPTER 8

IN the third year of the reign of Belshazzar the king a vision appeared to me, [t]Daniel, subsequent to the one which appeared to me previously. *I, Daniel*

2 And I [r]looked in the vision, and it came about while I was looking, that I was in the citadel of Susa, which is in the province of Elam; and I looked in the vision, and I myself was beside the Ulai [a]Canal. Num. 12:6 • *river*

3 Then I lifted my gaze and looked, and behold, a ram which had two horns was standing in front of the [a]canal. Now the two horns *were* long, but one *was* longer than the other, with the longer one coming up last. *river*

4 I saw the ram [r]butting westward, northward, and southward, and no *other* beasts could stand before him, nor was there anyone to rescue from his [t]power; but he did as he pleased and magnified *himself.* Deut. 33:17 • *hand*

5 While I was observing, behold, a male goat was coming from the west over the surface of the whole earth without touching the ground; and the [t]goat *had* a [r]conspicuous horn between his eyes. *buck* • Dan. 8:8, 21; 11:3

6 And he came up to the ram that had the two horns, which I had seen standing in front of the [a]canal, and rushed at him in his mighty wrath. *river*

7 And I saw him come beside the ram, and he was enraged at him; and he struck the ram and shattered his two horns, and the ram had no strength to withstand him. So he hurled him to the

ground and trampled on him, and
there was none to rescue the ram
from his[t]power. *hand*
8 Then the male goat magnified *himself* exceedingly. But as
soon as[r]he was mighty, the[r]large
horn was broken; and in its place
there came up four conspicuous
horns toward the four winds of
heaven. 2 Chr. 26:16 • Dan. 8:22
9 And out of one of them came
forth a rather small horn which
grew exceedingly great toward
the south, toward the east, and
toward the [7]Beautiful *Land.*
10 And it grew up to the host of
heaven and caused some of the
host and some of the[r]stars to fall
to the earth, and it[r]trampled them
down. Is. 14:13 • Dan. 7:7
11 It even magnified *itself*[t]to be
equal with the[a]Commander of the
host; and it removed the regular
sacrifice from Him, and the place
of His sanctuary was thrown
down. *up to the • Prince*
12 And on account of transgression the host will be given over *to*
the horn along with the regular
sacrifice; and it will[r]fling truth to
the ground and perform *its will*
and prosper. Is. 59:14
13 Then I heard a holy one
speaking, and another holy one
said to that particular one who
was speaking, "How long will the
vision *about* the regular sacrifice
apply, while the transgression
causes horror, so as to allow both
the holy place and the host[t]to be
trampled?" *as a trampling*
14 And he said to me, "For
2,300 evenings *and* mornings;
then the holy place will be[t]prop-
erly restored." *vindicated*

[7]I.e., Palestine

15 And it came about when[r]I,
Daniel, had seen the vision, that I
sought to understand it; and behold, standing before me was one
who looked like a man. Dan. 8:1
16 And I heard the voice of a
man between *the banks of* Ulai,
and he called out and said, "Gabriel, give this *man* an understanding of the vision."
17 So he came near to where I
was standing, and when he came I
was frightened and fell on my
face; but he said to me, "Son of
man, understand that the vision
pertains to the time of the end."
18 Now while he was talking
with me, I sank into a deep sleep
with my face to the ground; but he
touched me and made me stand
[t]upright. *on my standing*
19 And he said, "Behold, I am
going to let you know what will
occur at the final period of the indignation, for *it* pertains to the appointed time of the end.
20 "The ram which you saw with
the two horns represents the
kings of Media and Persia.
21 "And the shaggy [t]goat *repre-*
sents the kingdom of Greece, and
the large horn that is between his
eyes is the first king. *buck*
22 "And the broken *horn* and the
four *horns that* arose in its place
represent four kingdoms *which*
will arise from *his* nation, although not with his power.
23 "And in the latter period of
their[a]rule, *kingdom*
When the transgressors
have[t]run *their course,*
A king will arise *finished*
[t]Insolent and skilled in intrigue. *Strong of face*

24 “And his power will be
mighty, but not by his
own power,
And he will[a]destroy to an
extraordinary degree
And prosper and perform
his will; *corrupt*
He will destroy mighty men
and the holy people.
25 “And through his shrewdness
He will cause deceit to succeed by his[t]influence;
And he will magnify *him-
self* in his heart, *hand*
And he will destroy many
while *they are* at ease.
He will even oppose the
Prince of princes,
But he will be broken without human agency.
26 “And the vision of the evenings and mornings
Which has been told is true;
But keep the vision secret,
For *it* pertains to many
days *in the future.*”

27 Then I, Daniel, was [a]exhausted and sick for days. Then I got up *again* and carried on the king’s business; but I was astounded at the vision, and there was none to explain *it.* *done in*

CHAPTER 9

IN the first year of Darius the son of Ahasuerus, of Median descent, who was made king over the kingdom of the Chaldeans—

2 in the first year of his reign I, Daniel, observed in the books the number of the years which was *revealed as* the word of the LORD to Jeremiah the prophet for the completion of the desolations of Jerusalem, *namely,* seventy years.

3 So I[t]gave my attention to the Lord God to seek *Him by* prayer and supplications, with fasting, sackcloth, and ashes. *set my face*

4 And I prayed to the LORD my God and confessed and said, “Alas, O Lord, the[r]great and awesome God, who keeps His covenant and lovingkindness for those who love Him and keep His commandments, Deut. 7:21

5 we have sinned, committed iniquity, acted wickedly, and[r]rebelled, even[r]turning aside from Thy commandments and ordinances. Lam. 1:18,20 • Is. 53:6

6 “Moreover, we have not listened to Thy servants the prophets, who spoke in Thy name to our kings, our princes, our fathers, and all the people of the land.

7 “Righteousness belongs to Thee, O Lord, but to us[t]open shame, as it is this day—to the men of Judah, the inhabitants of Jerusalem, and all Israel, those who are nearby and those who are far away in all the countries to which Thou hast driven them, because of their unfaithful deeds which they have committed against Thee. *the shame of face*

8 “Open shame belongs to us, O Lord, to our kings, our princes, and our fathers, because we have sinned against Thee.

9 “To the Lord our God belong compassion and forgiveness, for we have rebelled against Him;

10 nor have we obeyed the voice of the LORD our God, to walk in His[a]teachings which He set before us through His servants the prophets. *laws*

11 "Indeed [r]all Israel has transgressed Thy law and turned aside, not obeying Thy voice; so the curse has been poured out on us, along with the oath which is written in the law of Moses the servant of God, for we have sinned against Him. Is. 1:3, 4

12 "Thus He has confirmed His words which He had spoken against us and against our [t]rulers who ruled us, to bring on us great calamity; for under the whole heaven there has not been done *anything* like what was done to Jerusalem. *judges who judged us*

13 "As it is written in the law of Moses, all this calamity has come on us; yet we have not sought the favor of the LORD our God by turning from our iniquity and giving attention to Thy truth.

14 "Therefore, the LORD has kept the calamity in store and brought it on us; for the LORD our God is righteous with respect to all His deeds which He has done, but we have not obeyed His voice.

15 "And now, O Lord our God, who hast brought Thy people out of the land of Egypt with a mighty hand and hast made a name for Thyself, as it is this day—we have sinned, we have been wicked.

16 "O Lord, in accordance with all Thy [t]righteous acts, let now Thine anger and Thy wrath turn away from Thy city Jerusalem, Thy holy mountain; for because of our sins and the iniquities of our fathers, Jerusalem and Thy people *have become* a reproach to all those around us. *righteousnesses*

17 "So now, our God, listen to the prayer of Thy servant and to his supplications, and for Thy sake, O Lord, let Thy face shine on Thy desolate sanctuary.

18 "O my God, incline Thine ear and hear! Open Thine eyes and see our desolations and the city which is called by Thy name; for we are not presenting our supplications before Thee on account of any merits of our own, but on account of Thy great compassion.

19 "O Lord, hear! O Lord, forgive! O Lord, listen and take action! For Thine own sake, O my God, [r]do not delay, because Thy city and Thy people are called by Thy name." Ps. 44:23; 74:10, 11

20 Now while I was [r]speaking and praying, and confessing my sin and the sin of my people Israel, and [t]presenting my supplication before the LORD my God in behalf of the holy mountain of my God, Ps. 145:18 • *causing to fall*

21 while I was still speaking in prayer, then the man [r]Gabriel, whom I had seen in the vision previously, came to me in *my* extreme weariness about the time of the evening offering. Dan. 8:16

22 And he gave *me* instruction and talked with me, and said, "O Daniel, I have now come forth to give you insight with [r]understanding. Dan. 8:16; 10:21; Zech. 1:9

23 "At the beginning of your supplications the command was issued, and I have come to tell *you*, for you are highly esteemed; so give heed to the message and gain understanding of the vision.

24 "Seventy weeks have been decreed for your people and your holy city, to finish the transgression, to make an end of sin, to make atonement for iniquity, to bring in everlasting righteousness,

to seal up vision and prophecy,
and to anoint the most holy *place.*
25 "So you are to know and discern *that* from the issuing of a [t]de-
cree to restore and rebuild Jerusalem until [a]Messiah the Prince *there*
will be seven weeks and sixty-two
weeks; it will be built again, with
plaza and moat, even in times of
distress. *word • an anointed one*
26 "Then after the sixty-two
weeks the Messiah will be cut off
and have nothing, and the people
of the prince who is to come will
destroy the city and the sanctuary. And its end *will come* with a
flood; even to the end there will be
war; desolations are determined.
27 "And he will make a firm covenant with the many for one
week, but in the middle of the
week he will put a stop to sacrifice
and grain offering; and on the
wing of abominations *will come*
one who makes desolate, even until a complete destruction, one
that is decreed, is poured out on
the one who makes desolate."

CHAPTER 10

IN the third year of [r]Cyrus king of
Persia a [t]message was revealed to
Daniel, who was named Belteshazzar; and the [t]message was
true and *one of* great [a]conflict, but
he understood the [t]message and
had an understanding of the vision. Dan. 1:21 • *word • warfare*
2 In those days I, Daniel, had
been [r]mourning for three entire
weeks. Ezra 9:4, 5; Neh. 1:4
3 I [r]did not eat any tasty food,
nor did meat or wine enter my
mouth, nor did I use any ointment
at all, until the entire three weeks
were completed. Dan. 6:18
4 And on the twenty-fourth
day of the first month, while I was
by the bank of the great [r]river, that
is, the Tigris, Ezek. 1:3; Dan. 8:2
5 I lifted my eyes and looked,
and behold, there was a certain
man [r]dressed in linen, whose waist
was girded with *a belt of* pure
gold of Uphaz. Ezek. 9:2
6 His body also was like beryl,
his face [t]had the appearance of
lightning, his eyes were like flaming torches, his arms and feet like
the gleam of polished bronze, and
the sound of his words like the
sound of a [a]tumult. *like • roaring*
7 Now I, Daniel, [r]alone saw the
vision, while the men who were
with me did not see the vision;
nevertheless, a great dread fell on
them, and they ran away to hide
themselves. 2 Kin. 6:17-20
8 So I was left alone and saw
this great vision; yet no strength
was left in me, for my [t]natural col-
or turned to a deathly pallor, and I
retained no strength. *splendor*
9 But I heard the sound of his
words; and as soon as I heard the
sound of his words, I [r]fell into a
deep sleep on my face, with my
face to the ground. Gen. 15:12
10 Then behold, a hand [r]touched
me and set me trembling on my
hands and knees. Dan. 8:18
11 And he said to me, "O Daniel, man of high esteem, understand the words that I am about to
tell you and stand upright, for I
have now been sent to you." And
when he had spoken this word to
me, I stood up trembling.
12 Then he said to me, "Do not
be afraid, Daniel, for from the first

day that you set your heart on understanding *this* and on humbling
yourself before your God, your
words were heard, and I have
come in response to your words.
13 "But the prince of the kingdom of Persia was [t]withstanding
me for twenty-one days; then behold, Michael, one of the chief
princes, came to help me, for I had
been left there with the kings of
Persia. *standing opposite*
14 "Now I have come to give you
an understanding of what will
happen to your people in the [t]latter
days, for the vision pertains to the
days yet *future*." *end of the days*
15 And when he had spoken to
me according to these words, I
[t]turned my face toward the ground
and became speechless. *set*
16 And behold, one who resembled a human being was touching
my lips; then I opened my mouth
and spoke, and said to him who
was standing before me, "O my
lord, as a result of the vision anguish has come upon me, and I
have retained no strength.
17 "For how can such a servant
of my lord talk with such as my
lord? As for me, there remains
just now no strength in me, nor
has any breath been left in me."
18 Then *this* one with human
appearance touched me again and
[r]strengthened me. Is. 35:3, 4
19 And he said, "O man of high
esteem, do not be afraid. Peace be
with you; take courage and be
courageous!" Now as soon as he
spoke to me, I received strength
and said, "May my lord speak, for
you have strengthened me."
20 Then he said, "Do you [t]under-
stand why I came to you? But I
shall now return to fight against
the prince of Persia; so I am going
forth, and behold, the prince of
Greece is about to come. *know*
21 "However, I will tell you what
is inscribed in the writing of truth.
Yet there is no one who [t]stands
firmly with me against these
forces except Michael your
prince. *shows himself strong*

CHAPTER 11

"AND in the first year of Darius
the Mede, I arose to be an encouragement and a protection for him.
2 "And now I will tell you the
truth. Behold, three more kings
are going to arise [t]in Persia. Then a
fourth will gain far more riches
than all *of them;* as soon as he becomes strong through his riches,
he will arouse the whole *empire*
against the realm of Greece. *for*
3 "And a mighty king will arise,
and he will rule with great authority and do as he pleases.
4 "But as soon as he has arisen,
his kingdom will be broken up and
parceled out toward the four
[t]points of the compass, though not
to his *own* descendants, nor according to his authority which he
wielded; for his sovereignty will
be uprooted and *given* to others
besides them. *winds of the heaven*
5 "Then the king of the South
will grow strong, [t]along with *one*
of his princes [t]who will gain ascen-
dancy over him and obtain dominion; his domain *will be* a great dominion *indeed.* *and • and he*
6 "And after some years they
will form an alliance, and the
daughter of the king of the South
will come to the king of the North

to carry out a peaceful arrangement. But she will not retain her position of power, nor will he remain with his[t]power, but she will be given up, along with those who brought her in, and the one who sired her, as well as he who supported her in *those* times. *arm*

7"But one of the[t]descendants of her line will arise in his place, and he will come against *their* army and enter the fortress of the king of the North, and he will deal with them and display *great* strength. *branch of her roots*

8"And also their[r]gods with their metal images *and* their precious vessels of silver and gold he will take into captivity to Egypt, and he on his part will refrain from *attacking* the king of the North for *some* years. Is. 37:19

9"Then the latter will enter the realm of the king of the South, but will return to his *own* land.

10"And his sons will mobilize and assemble a multitude of great forces; and one of them will keep on coming and overflow and pass through, that he may again wage war up to his *very* fortress.

11"And the king of the South will be enraged and go forth and fight[t]with the king of the North. Then the latter will raise a great multitude, but *that* multitude will be given into[t]the hand of the *former*. *with him, with • his hand*

12"When the multitude is carried away, his heart will be lifted up, and he will cause tens of thousands to fall; yet he will not prevail.

13"For the king of the North will again raise a greater multitude than the former, and after an interval of some years he will[a]press on with a great army and much equipment. *keep on coming*

14"Now in those times many will rise up against the king of the South; the violent ones among your people will also lift themselves up in order to fulfill the vision, but they will fall down.

15"Then the king of the North will come, cast up a siege mound, and capture a well-fortified city; and the forces of the South will not stand *their ground*, not even [t]their choicest troops, for there will be no strength to make a stand. *the people of its choice ones*

16"But he who comes against him will[r]do as he pleases, and no one will *be able to* withstand him; he will also stay *for a time* in the Beautiful Land, with destruction in his hand. Dan. 5:19; 11:3, 36

17"And he will set his face to come with the power of his whole kingdom,[t]bringing with him a proposal of peace which he will put into effect; he will also give him the daughter of women to ruin it. But she will not take a stand *for him* or be on his side. *and*

18"Then he will turn his face to the[r]coastlands and capture many. But a commander will put a stop to his scorn against him; moreover, he will[r]repay him for his scorn. Gen. 10:5 • Hos. 12:14

19"So he will turn his face toward the fortresses of his own land, but he will[r]stumble and fall and be found no more. Ps. 27:2

20"Then in his place one will arise who will send an[a]oppressor through the [8]Jewel of *his* kingdom;

[8]Lit., *adornment;* i.e., probably Jerusalem and its temple

yet within a few days he will be
shattered, though neither in anger
nor in battle. *exactor* of tribute
21“And in his place a despicable
person will arise, on whom the
honor of kingship has not been
conferred, but he will come in a
time of tranquility and seize the
kingdom by intrigue.
22“And the overflowing [r]forces
will be flooded away before him
and shattered, and also the prince
of the covenant. Dan. 9:26
23“And after an alliance is made
with him he will practice deception, and he will go up and gain
power with a small *force of* people.
24“In a time of tranquility he
will enter the richest *parts* of the
[a]realm, and he will accomplish
what his fathers never did, nor his
ancestors; he will distribute plunder, booty, and possessions
among them, and he will devise
his schemes against strongholds,
but *only* for a time. *province*
25“And he will stir up his
strength and [t]courage against the
king of the South with a large
army; so the king of the South will
mobilize an extremely large and
mighty army for war; but he will
not stand, for schemes will be devised against him. *heart*
26“And those who eat his choice
food will [t]destroy him, and his
army will overflow, but many will
fall down slain. *break*
27“As for both kings, their
hearts will be *intent* on evil, and
they will speak lies *to each other*
at the same table; but it will not
succeed, for the end is still *to
come* at the appointed time.

28“Then he will return to his
land with much plunder; but his
heart will be *set* against the holy
covenant, and he will take action
and *then* return to his *own* land.
29“At the appointed time he will
return and come into the South,
but this last time it will not turn
out the way it did before.
30“For ships of [r]Kittim will come
against him; therefore he will be
disheartened, and will return and
become enraged at the holy covenant and take action; so he will
come back and show regard for
those who forsake the holy covenant. Gen. 10:4; Num. 24:24
31“And forces from him will
arise, desecrate the sanctuary fortress, and do away with the regular sacrifice. And they will set up
the abomination of desolation.
32“And by smooth *words* he will
[a]turn to godlessness those who act
wickedly toward the covenant,
but the people who know their
God will display [r]strength and take
action. *pollute those* • Mic. 5:7-9
33“And [r]those who have insight
among the people will give understanding to the many; yet they
will fall by sword and by flame, by
captivity and by plunder, for
many days. Mal. 2:7
34“Now when they fall they will
be granted a little help, and many
will join with them in hypocrisy.
35“And some of those who have
insight will fall, in order to refine,
purge, and make them pure, until
the end time; because *it is* still *to
come* at the appointed time.
36“Then the king will do as he
pleases, and he will exalt and
magnify himself above every god,
and will speak [t]monstrous things

against the God of gods; and he
will prosper until the indignation
is finished, for that which is decreed will be done. *extraordinary*
37 "And he will show no regard
for the [a]gods of his fathers or for
the desire of women, nor will he
show regard for any *other* god; for
he will magnify himself above
them all. *God*
38 "But instead he will honor a
god of fortresses, a god whom his
fathers did not know; he will hon-
or *him* with gold, silver, costly
stones, and treasures.
39 "And he will take action
against the strongest of fortresses
with *the help of* a foreign god; he
will give great honor to [t]those who
acknowledge *him,* and he will
cause them to rule over the many,
and will parcel out land for a
price. *the one who acknowledges*
40 "And at the end time the king
of the South will collide with him,
and the king of the North will
storm against him with chariots,
with horsemen, and with many
ships; and he will enter countries,
overflow *them,* and pass through.
41 "He will also enter the Beautiful Land, and many *countries* will
fall; but these will be rescued out
of his hand: Edom, Moab and the
foremost of the sons of Ammon.
42 "Then he will stretch out his
hand against *other* countries, and
the land of Egypt will not escape.
43 "But he will gain control over
the hidden treasures of gold and
silver, and over all the precious
things of Egypt; and Libyans and
Ethiopians *will follow* at his heels.
44 "But rumors from the East
and from the North will disturb
him, and he will go forth with
great wrath to destroy and [t]annihi-
late many. *devote to destruction*
45 "And he will pitch the tents of
his royal pavilion between the
seas and the beautiful Holy Mountain; yet he will come to his end,
and no one will help him.

CHAPTER 12

"NOW at that time Michael, the
great prince who stands *guard*
over the sons of your people, will
arise. And there will be a time of
distress such as never occurred
since there was a nation until that
time; and at that time your people,
everyone who is found written in
the book, will be rescued.
2 "And many of those who
sleep in the dust of the ground will
awake, these to everlasting life,
but the others to disgrace *and*
everlasting [t]contempt. *abhorrence*
3 "And [a]those who have insight
will shine brightly like the brightness of the expanse of heaven,
and those who lead the many to
righteousness, like the stars forever and ever. *the instructors will*
4 "But as for you, Daniel, [r]con-
ceal these words and seal up the
book until the end of time; many
will go back and forth, and knowledge will increase." Dan. 8:26
5 Then I, Daniel, looked and
behold, two others were standing,
one on this bank of the river, and
the other on that bank of the river.
6 And [r]one said to the man
dressed in linen, who was above
the waters of the river, "How long
will it be until the end of *these*
wonders?" Dan. 8:16
7 And I heard the man dressed
in linen, who was above the wa-

ters of the river, as he raised his
right hand and his left toward
heaven, and swore by Him who
lives forever that it would be for a
time, times, and half *a time;* and
as soon as they finish shattering
the power of the holy people, all
these *events* will be completed.
8 As for me, I heard but could
not understand; so I said, "My
lord, what *will be* the[a]outcome of
these *events?"* *final end*
9 And he said, "Go *your way,*
Daniel, for *these* words are concealed and[r]sealed up until the end
time. Dan. 12:4
10 "Many will be purged, purified and refined; but the wicked
will act wickedly, and none of the
wicked will understand, but those
who have insight will understand.
11 "And from the time that the
regular sacrifice is abolished, and
the abomination of desolation is
set up, *there will be* 1,290 days.
12 "How[r]blessed is he who keeps
waiting and attains to the[r]1,335
days! Is. 30:18 • Dan. 8:14
13 "But as for you, go *your way*
to the end; then you will enter into
rest and rise *again* for your allotted portion at the end of the age."

THE BOOK OF

HOSEA

THE word of the LORD which
came to[r]Hosea the son of Beeri,
during the days of[r]Uzziah, Jotham, Ahaz, *and* Hezekiah, kings
of Judah, and during the days of
Jeroboam the son of Joash, king
of Israel. Rom. 9:25 • Is. 1:1
2 When the LORD first spoke
through Hosea, the LORD said to
Hosea, [r]"Go, take to yourself a
wife of harlotry, and *have* children of harlotry; for[r]the land commits flagrant harlotry, forsaking
the LORD." Hos. 3:1 • Jer. 3:1
3 So he went and took Gomer
the daughter of Diblaim, and she
conceived and bore him a son.
4 And the LORD said to him,
"Name him Jezreel; for yet a little
while, and I will punish the house
of Jehu for the bloodshed of Jezreel, and I will put an end to the
kingdom of the house of Israel.
5 "And it will come about on
that day, that I will break the bow
of Israel in the valley of Jezreel."
6 Then she conceived again
and gave birth to a daughter. And
[t]the LORD said to him, "Name her
[1]Lo-ruhamah, for I will no longer
[r]have compassion on the house of
Israel, that I should ever forgive
them. *He* • Hos. 2:4
7 "But I will have[r]compassion
on the house of Judah and deliver
them by the LORD their God, and
will not deliver them by[r]bow,
sword, battle, horses, or horsemen." 2 Kin. 19:29-35 • Zech. 4:6
8 When she had weaned Lo-ru-
hamah, she conceived and gave
birth to a son.
9 And the LORD said, "Name
him [2]Lo-ammi, for you are not My

[1]I.e., she has not obtained compassion
[2]I.e., not my people

people and I am not your God."
10 Yet the number of the sons
of Israel
Will be like the [r]sand of the
sea, Gen. 22:17; 32:12
Which cannot be measured
or numbered;
And [r]it will come about that,
in the place Rom. 9:26
Where it is said to them,
"You are [r]not My people,"
It will be said to them,
"*You are* the sons of the living
God." Is. 65:1; Hos. 1:9
11 And the [r]sons of Judah and
the sons of Israel will be
[r]gathered together,
And they will appoint for
themselves one leader,
And they will go up from the
land, Is. 11:12 • Jer. 23:5, 6
For great will be the day of
Jezreel.

CHAPTER 2

SAY to your brothers, "[3]Ammi,"
and to your sisters, "[4]Ruhamah."
2 "Contend with your mother,
[r]contend, Ezek. 23:45
For she is not my wife, and I
am not her husband;
And let her put away her harlotry from her face,
And her adultery from be-
tween her breasts,
3 Lest I strip her [r]naked
And expose her as on the day
when she was born.
I will also make her like a
wilderness, Jer. 13:22
Make her like desert land,
And slay her with thirst.
4 "Also, I will have no compassion on her children,

[3]I.e., my people
[4]I.e., she has obtained compassion

Because they are [r]children of
harlotry. Jer. 13:14
5 "For their mother has [r]played
the harlot;
She who conceived them has
acted shamefully.
For she said, [r]'I will go after
my lovers, Is. 1:21
Who [r]give *me* my bread and
my water, Jer. 44:17, 18
My wool and my flax, my [r]oil
and my drink.' Hos. 2:8
6 "Therefore, behold, I will
[r]hedge up her way with
thorns, Job 19:8
And I will build a wall
against her so that she
cannot find her paths.
7 "And she will [r]pursue her lovers, but she will not overtake them; Hos. 5:13
And she will seek them, but
will not find *them*.
Then she will say, 'I will go
back to my first husband,
For it was [r]better for me then
than now!' Jer. 14:22
8 "For she does [r]not know that it
was [r]I who gave her the
grain, the new wine, and
the oil, Is. 1:3 • Ezek. 16:19
And lavished on her silver
and gold,
Which they used for Baal.
9 "Therefore, I will [r]take back
My grain at [t]harvest time
And My new wine in its season. Hos. 8:7; 9:2
I will also take away My
wool and My flax
Given to cover her nakedness. *its time*
10 "And then I will [r]uncover her
lewdness Ezek. 16:37
In the sight of her lovers,

And no one will rescue her out of My hand.
11 "I will also [r]put an end to all her gaiety, Jer. 7:34
Her [r]feasts, her new moons, her sabbaths, Hos. 3:4
And all her festal assemblies.
12 "And I will [r]destroy her vines and fig trees,
Of which she said, 'These are my wages
Which my lovers have given me.' Jer. 5:17; 8:13
And I will [r]make them a forest, Is. 5:5; 7:23
And the beasts of the field will devour them.
13 "And I will punish her for the days of the Baals
When she used to [r]offer sacrifices to them Jer. 7:9
And adorn herself with her earrings and jewelry,
And follow her lovers, so that she forgot Me," declares the LORD.

14 "Therefore, behold, I will allure her,
[r]Bring her into the wilderness, Ezek. 20:33-38
And speak kindly to her.
15 "Then I will give her her vineyards from there,
And the valley of Achor as a door of hope.
And she will [a]sing there as in the days of her youth,
As in the day when she came up from the land of Egypt. *give answer*
16 "And it will come about in that day," declares the LORD,
"That you will call Me [5]Ishi
And will no longer call Me [6]Baali.
17 "For [r]I will remove the names of the Baals from her mouth, Ex. 23:13
So that they will be [a]mentioned by their names no more. *remembered*
18 "In that day I will also make a covenant for them
With the [r]beasts of the field,
The birds of the sky,
And the creeping things of the ground. Job 5:23
And I will [t]abolish the bow, the sword, and war from the land, *break*
And will make them [r]lie down in safety. Lev. 26:5
19 "And I will [r]betroth you to Me forever; Is. 62:4, 5
Yes, I will betroth you to Me in [r]righteousness and in justice, Is. 1:27
In lovingkindness and in compassion,
20 And I will betroth you to Me in faithfulness.
Then you will [r]know the LORD. Jer. 31:33, 34

21 "And it will come about in that day that [r]I will respond," declares the LORD. Is. 55:10
"I will respond to the heavens, and they will respond to the earth,
22 And the [r]earth will respond to the grain, to the new wine, and to the oil,
And they will respond to [7]Jezreel. Jer. 31:12
23 "And I will [r]sow her for Myself in the land. Jer. 31:27

[5]I.e., my Husband
[6]I.e., my Master, or, my Baal [7]I.e., God sows

I will also have compassion on her who had not obtained compassion,
And I will say to those who were not My people,
'You are My people!'
And[t] they will say, '*Thou art* my God!' " *he*

CHAPTER 3

THEN the LORD said to me, "Go again, love a woman *who* is loved by *her* husband, yet an adulteress, even as the LORD loves the sons of Israel, though they turn to other gods and love raisin cakes."
2 So I bought her for myself for fifteen *shekels* of silver and a homer and a half of barley.
3 Then I said to her, "You shall stay with me for many days. You shall not play the harlot, nor shall you have a[a] man; so I will also be toward you." *husband*
4 For the sons of Israel will remain for many days[r] without king or prince, without sacrifice or *sacred* pillar, and without ephod or household idols. Hos. 10:3
5 Afterward the sons of Israel will [r]return and seek the LORD their God and David their king; and they will come trembling to the LORD and to His goodness in the last days. Jer. 50:4, 5

CHAPTER 4

[r]LISTEN to the word of the LORD, O sons of Israel, Hos. 5:1
For the LORD has a [r]case against the inhabitants of the land, Hos. 12:2
Because there is no[a] faithfulness or[a] kindness
Or knowledge of God in the land. *truth · loyalty*
2 *There is*[r] swearing, deception, murder, stealing, and adultery. Deut. 5:11
They employ violence, so that bloodshed [t]follows bloodshed. *touches*
3 Therefore the land[r] mourns,
And everyone who lives in it languishes Is. 24:4; 33:9
Along with the beasts of the field and the birds of the sky;
And also the fish of the sea disappear.

4 Yet let no one[t] find fault, and let none offer reproof;
For your people are like those who contend with the priest. *contend*
5 So you will[r] stumble by day,
And the prophet also will stumble with you by night; Ezek. 14:3, 7
And I will destroy your [r]mother. Jer. 15:8
6 My people are destroyed for lack of knowledge.
Because you have [r]rejected knowledge, Hos. 4:14
I also will reject you from being My priest.
Since you have forgotten the [r]law of your God,
I also will forget your children. Hos. 8:1, 12

7 The more they [r]multiplied, the more they sinned against Me; Hos. 10:1
I will[r] change their glory into shame. Hab. 2:16
8 They feed on the[a] sin of My people, *sin offering*

And direct their desire
toward their iniquity.
9 And it will be, like people,
[r]like priest; Is. 24:2
So I will [r]punish them for
their ways, Hos. 8:13; 9:9
And repay them for their
deeds.
10 And [r]they will eat, but not
have enough; Is. 65:13
They will [r]play the harlot, but
not increase, Hos. 7:4
Because they have stopped
giving heed to the LORD.

11 Harlotry, wine, and new
wine take away the [t]un-
derstanding. *heart*
12 My people [r] consult their
wooden idol, and their *di-*
viner's wand informs
them; Is. 44:19; Jer. 2:27
For a spirit of harlotry has
led *them* astray,
And they have played the
harlot, *departing* [t] from
their God. *from under*
13 They offer sacrifices on the
tops of the mountains
And [a]burn incense on the
hills, *offer sacrifices*
[r]Under oak, poplar, and terebinth, Is. 1:29; Jer. 2:20
Because their shade is pleasant.
Therefore your daughters
play the harlot,
And your brides commit
adultery.
14 I will not punish your daughters when they play the
harlot
Or your brides when they
commit adultery,
For *the men* themselves go
apart with harlots
And offer sacrifices with
temple prostitutes;
So the people without understanding are ruined.

15 Though you, Israel, play the
harlot,
Do not let Judah become
guilty;
Also do not go to Gilgal,
Or go up to Beth-aven,
And take the oath:
"As the LORD lives!"
16 Since Israel is stubborn
Like a stubborn heifer,
Can the LORD now [r]pasture
them Is. 5:17; 7:25
Like a lamb in a large field?
17 Ephraim is joined to [r]idols;
Let him alone. Hos. 13:2
18 Their liquor gone,
They play the harlot continually;
Their [t] rulers dearly love
shame. *shields*
19 [r]The wind wraps them in its
wings,
And they will be ashamed
because of their sacri-
fices. Hos. 12:1; 13:15

CHAPTER 5

HEAR this, O priests!
Give heed, O house of Israel!
Listen, O house of the king!
For the judgment applies to
you,
For you have been a [r]snare at
Mizpah, Hos. 9:8
And a net spread out on Ta-
bor.
2 And the [r]revolters have gone
deep in depravity,
But I will chastise all of
them. Hos. 9:15

3 I know Ephraim, and Israel is not hidden from Me;
For now, O Ephraim, you have played the harlot,
Israel has defiled itself.
4 Their deeds will not allow them
To return to their God.
For a [r]spirit of harlotry is within them, Hos. 4:12
And they [r]do not know the LORD. Hos. 4:6, 14
5 Moreover, the [r]pride of Israel testifies against him,
And Israel and Ephraim stumble in their iniquity;
Judah also has stumbled with them. Hos. 7:10
6 They will [r]go with their flocks and herds Hos. 8:13
To seek the LORD, but they will not find *Him*;
He has [r] withdrawn from them. Ezek. 8:6
7 They have dealt treacherously against the LORD,
For they have borne [t]illegitimate children. *strange*
Now the new moon will devour them with their [t]land. *portions*

8 Blow the horn in [r]Gibeah,
The trumpet in Ramah.
Sound an alarm at Beth-aven: Hos. 9:9; 10:9
"Behind you, Benjamin!"
9 Ephraim will become a [r]desolation in the day of rebuke; Is. 28:1-4
Among the tribes of Israel I declare what is sure.
10 The princes of Judah have become like those who move a boundary;
On them I will pour out My wrath like water.
11 Ephraim is [r] oppressed, crushed in judgment,
Because he was determined to follow *man's* command. Deut. 28:33
12 Therefore I am like a [r]moth to Ephraim, Ps. 39:11
And like rottenness to the house of Judah.
13 When Ephraim saw his sickness,
And Judah his wound,
Then Ephraim went to [r]Assyria Hos. 7:11
And sent to King Jareb.
But he is unable to heal you,
Or to cure you of your [a]wound. *ulcer*
14 For I *will be* [r]like a lion to Ephraim, Ps. 7:2
And like a young lion to the house of Judah.
[r]I, even I, will tear to pieces and go away, Ps. 50:22
I will carry away, and there will be none to deliver.
15 I will go away *and* return to My place
Until they acknowledge their guilt and seek My face;
In their affliction they will earnestly seek Me.

CHAPTER 6

"COME,[r] let us return to the LORD. Jer. 50:4, 5
For He has torn *us*, but [r]He will heal us; Jer. 30:17
He has [t]wounded *us*, but He will bandage us. *struck*
2 "He will [r]revive us after two days; Ps. 30:5

He will [r]raise us up on the third day 1 Cor. 15:4
That we may live before Him.
3 "So let us know, let us press on to know the LORD.
His [r]going forth is as certain as the dawn; Ps. 19:6
And He will come to us like the [r]rain, Job 29:23
Like the spring rain watering the earth."

4 What shall I do with you, O [r]Ephraim? Hos. 7:1
What shall I do with you, O Judah?
For your loyalty is like a [r]morning cloud,
And like the dew which goes away early. Ps. 78:34-37
5 Therefore I have hewn *them* in pieces by the prophets;
I have slain them by the [r]words of My mouth;
And the judgments on you are *like* the light that goes forth. Jer. 23:29
6 For [r]I delight in loyalty rather than sacrifice,
And in the knowledge of God rather than burnt offerings. Matt. 9:13; 12:7
7 But like [a]Adam they have transgressed the covenant; *men*
There they have dealt treacherously against Me.
8 Gilead is a city of wrongdoers,
Tracked with [r]bloody *footprints.* Hos. 4:2
9 And as [r]raiders wait for a man, Hos. 7:1
So a band of priests murder on the way to Shechem;
Surely they have committed [a]crime. *lewdness*
10 In the house of Israel I have seen a horrible thing;
Ephraim's harlotry is there,
Israel has defiled itself.
11 Also, O Judah, there is a [r]harvest appointed for you,
When I restore the fortunes of My people. Joel 3:13

CHAPTER 7

WHEN I [r]would heal Israel,
The iniquity of Ephraim is uncovered, Ezek. 24:13
And the evil deeds of Samaria,
For they deal falsely;
The thief enters in,
Bandits raid outside,
2 And they do not consider in their hearts
That I [r]remember all their wickedness. Ps. 25:7
Now their [r]deeds are all around them; Jer. 2:19
They are before My face.
3 With their wickedness they make the [r]king glad,
And the princes with their lies. Jer. 28:1-4
4 They are [r]all adulterers
Like an oven heated by the baker, Jer. 9:2; 23:10
Who ceases to stir up *the fire*
From the kneading of the dough until it is leavened.
5 On the day of our king, the princes became sick with the heat of wine;
He stretched out his hand with [r]scoffers, Is. 28:14
6 For their hearts are like an [r]oven Ps. 21:9

As they approach their[t]plot-
ting; *ambush*
Their anger [t] smolders all
night, *sleeps*
In the morning it burns like a
flaming fire.
7 All of them are hot like an
oven,
And they consume their[r]rul-
ers; Hos. 13:10
All their kings have fallen.
None of them calls on Me.

8 Ephraim[r]mixes himself with
the[t]nations; Ps. 106:35
Ephraim has become a cake
not turned. *peoples*
9 [r]Strangers devour his
strength, Is. 1:7
Yet he[r]does not know *it*;
Gray hairs also are sprinkled
on him, Hos. 4:6
Yet he does not know *it*.
10 Though the[r]pride of Israel
testifies against him,
Yet [r]they have neither returned to the LORD their
God, Hos. 5:5 • Is. 9:13
Nor have they sought Him,
for all this.
11 So Ephraim has become like
a silly dove, without
[t]sense; *heart*
They call to[r]Egypt, they go to
Assyria. Hos. 8:13
12 When they go, I will spread
My net over them;
I will bring them down like
the birds of the sky.
I will chastise them in accordance with the proclama-
tion to their assembly.
13 Woe to them, for they have
[r]strayed from Me! Jer. 14:10
Destruction is theirs, for they
have rebelled against Me!
I would redeem them, but
they speak lies against
Me.
14 And[r]they do not cry to Me
from their heart
When they wail on their
beds; Job 35:9-11
For the sake of grain and
new wine they[r]assemble
themselves, Judg. 9:27
They turn away from Me.
15 Although I trained *and*
strengthened their arms,
Yet they[r]devise evil against
Me. Nah. 1:9
16 They turn, *but* not[a]upward,
They are like a deceitful bow;
Their princes will fall by the
sword *to the Most High*
Because of the[r]insolence of
their tongue. Ps. 12:3, 4
This *will be* their derision in
the land of Egypt.

CHAPTER 8

PUT the trumpet to your[t]lips!
Like an eagle *the enemy*
comes against the house
of the LORD, *palate*
Because they have trans-
gressed My covenant,
And rebelled against My law.
2 They cry out to Me,
"My God,[r]we of Israel know
Thee!" Titus 1:16
3 Israel has rejected the good;
The enemy will pursue him.
4 They have set up kings, but
not by Me;
They have appointed princes,
but I did not know *it*.
With their [r]silver and gold
they have made idols for
themselves, Hos. 2:8
That they might be cut off.

5 He has rejected your [r]calf, O
Samaria, saying,
"My anger burns against
them!" Hos. 10:5; 13:2
How long will they be in-
capable of innocence?
6 For from Israel is even this!
A [r]craftsman made it, so it is
not God; Hos. 13:2
Surely the calf of Samaria
will be broken to pieces.
7 For they sow the wind,
And they reap the whirlwind.
The standing grain has no
[t]heads; *growth*
It yields no [a]grain. *meal*
Should it yield, strangers
would swallow it up.

8 Israel is [r]swallowed up;
They are now among the nations 2 Kin. 17:6
Like a [r]vessel in which no one
delights. Jer. 22:28
9 For they have gone up to [r]As-
syria, Hos. 7:11
Like a wild donkey all alone;
Ephraim has hired lovers.
10 Even though they hire *allies*
among the nations,
Now I will gather them up;
And they will begin to [a]dimin-
ish *suffer for awhile*
Because of the burden of the
[r]king of princes. Is. 10:8

11 Since Ephraim has multiplied altars for sin,
They have become altars of
sinning for him.
12 Though I wrote for him ten
thousand *precepts* of My
[r]law, Hos. 4:6
They are regarded as a
strange thing.
13 As for My sacrificial gifts,
They [r]sacrifice the flesh and
eat *it,* Jer. 6:20; 7:21
But the LORD has taken no
delight in them.
Now He will [r]remember their
iniquity, Jer. 14:10
And [r]punish *them* for their
sins; Hos. 4:9; 9:7
They will return to Egypt.
14 For Israel has [r]forgotten his
Maker and built palaces;
And Judah has multiplied
fortified cities, Deut. 32:18
But I will send a fire on its
cities that it may con-
sume its palatial dwell-
ings.

CHAPTER 9

Do not rejoice, O Israel, [t]with exultation like the [t]nations!
For you have played the harlot, forsaking your God.
You have loved *harlots'*
earnings on every thresh-
ing floor. *to • peoples*
2 Threshing floor and wine
press will [r]not feed them,
And the new wine will fail
[t]them. Hos. 2:9 • *her*
3 They will not remain in [r]the
LORD's land, Jer. 2:7
But Ephraim will return to
Egypt,
And in Assyria they will eat
unclean *food.*
4 They will not pour out libations of wine to the LORD,
Their sacrifices will not
please Him.
Their bread will [t]*be* like
mourners' bread;
All who eat of it will be defiled, *be to them*

For their bread will be for
[t]themselves *alone*;
It will not enter the house of
the LORD. *their appetite*
5 What will you do on the day
of the appointed festival
And on the day of the [r]feast
of the LORD? Hos. 2:11
6 For behold, they will go because of destruction;
Egypt will gather them up,
Memphis will bury them.
Weeds will take over their
treasures of silver;
Thorns *will be* in their tents.

7 The days of [r]punishment have
come, Is. 10:3; Jer. 10:15
The days of [r]retribution have
come; Is. 34:8; Jer. 16:18
Let Israel know *this*!
The prophet is a fool,
The [t]inspired man is demented, *man of the spirit*
Because of the grossness of
your [r]iniquity,
And *because* your hostility is
so great. Ezek. 14:9, 10
8 Ephraim *was* a watchman
with my God, a prophet;
Yet the snare of a bird
catcher is in all his ways,
And there is *only* hostility in
the house of his God.
9 They have gone [r]deep [t]in depravity Is. 31:6
As in the days of Gibeah;
He will remember their iniquity, *they have corrupted*
He will punish their sins.

10 I found Israel like [r]grapes in
the wilderness; Mic. 7:1
I saw your forefathers as the
earliest fruit on the fig
tree in its first *season*.
But they came to [r]Baal-peor
and devoted themselves
to [8]shame, Num. 25:1-5
And they became as [r]detestable as that which they
loved. Ps. 115:8
11 As for Ephraim, their [r]glory
will fly away like a bird—
No birth, no pregnancy, and
no conception! Hos. 4:7
12 Though they bring up their
children,
Yet I will bereave them until
not a man is left.
Yes, woe to them indeed
when I depart from them!
13 Ephraim, as I have seen,
Is planted in a pleasant
meadow like Tyre;
But Ephraim will bring out
his children for slaughter.
14 Give them, O LORD—what
wilt Thou give?
Give them a miscarrying
womb and dry breasts.

15 All their evil is at [r]Gilgal;
Indeed, I came to hate them
there! Hos. 4:15; 12:11
Because of the [r]wickedness of
their deeds Hos. 4:9
I will drive them out of My
house!
I will love them no more;
All their princes are rebels.
16 Ephraim is stricken, their
root is dried up,
They will bear [r]no fruit.
Even though they bear children, Hos. 8:7
I will slay the precious ones
of their womb.
17 My God will cast them away
Because they have not listened to Him;

[8]I.e., Baal

And they will be wanderers
among the nations.

CHAPTER 10

ISRAEL is a[a]luxuriant vine;
He produces fruit for himself. *degenerate*
The more his fruit,
The more altars he made;
The[a]richer his land, *better*
The better[t]he made the *sacred* pillars. *they*
2 Their heart is[t]faithless;
Now they must bear their guilt. *smooth*
[t]The LORD will[r]break down their altars
And destroy their *sacred* pillars. *He* • Hos. 10:8
3 Surely now they will say,
"We have[r]no king, Ps. 12:4
For we do not revere the LORD.
As for the king, what can he do for us?"
4 They speak *mere* words,
With worthless oaths they make covenants;
And judgment sprouts like poisonous weeds in the furrows of the field.
5 The inhabitants of Samaria will fear
For the[r]calf of Beth-aven.
Indeed, its people will mourn for it, Hos. 8:5, 6
And its idolatrous priests will cry out over it,
Over its glory, since it has departed from it.
6 The thing itself will be carried to Assyria
As tribute to King Jareb;
Ephraim will be[r]seized with shame, Hos. 4:7
And Israel will be ashamed of its own counsel.
7 Samaria will be[r]cut off *with* her king, Hos. 13:11
Like a stick on the surface of the water.
8 Also the[r]high places of Aven, the sin of Israel, will be destroyed; Hos. 4:13
[r]Thorn and thistle will grow on their altars, Hos. 9:6
Then they will[r]say to the mountains, Is. 2:19
"Cover us!" And to the hills, "Fall on us!"
9 From the days of Gibeah you have sinned, O Israel;
There they stand!
Will not the battle against the sons of iniquity overtake them in Gibeah?
10 When it is My desire, I will [a]chastise them; *bind*
And the peoples will be gathered against them
When they are bound for their double guilt.

11 And Ephraim is a trained [r]heifer that loves to thresh, Jer. 50:11
But I will come over her fair neck *with a yoke*;
I will harness Ephraim,
Judah will plow, Jacob will harrow for himself.
12 [r]Sow with a view to righteousness, Prov. 11:18
Reap in accordance with [a]kindness; *loyalty*
Break up your fallow ground,
For it is time to[r]seek the LORD Hos. 12:6
Until He comes to[a]rain righteousness on you. *teach*
13 You have[r]plowed wicked-

ness, you have reaped injustice, Job 4:8
You have eaten the fruit of [r]lies. Hos. 4:2; 7:3
Because you have trusted in your way, in your[r]numerous warriors, Ps. 33:16
14 Therefore, a tumult will arise among your people,
And all your[r]fortresses will be destroyed, Is. 17:3
As Shalman destroyed Beth-arbel on the day of battle,
When[r]mothers were dashed in pieces with *their* children. Hos. 13:16
15 Thus it will be done to you at Bethel because of your great wickedness.
At dawn the king of Israel will be completely cut off.

CHAPTER 11

WHEN Israel *was* a youth I loved him,
And[r]out of Egypt I called My son. Hos. 2:15; 12:9, 13
2 The more they called them,
The more they went from them;
They kept [r]sacrificing to the Baals Hos. 2:13; 4:13
And burning incense to idols.
3 Yet it is I who taught Ephraim to walk,
I took them in My arms;
But they did not know that I [r]healed them. Jer. 30:17
4 I led them with cords of a man, with bonds of love,
And[r]I became to them as one who lifts the yoke from their jaws; Lev. 26:13
And I bent down *and* [r]fed them. Ex. 16:32; Ps. 78:25
5 [t]They will not return to the land of Egypt;
But Assyria—he will be[t]their king,
Because they refused to return *to Me*. *He • his*
6 And the sword will whirl against[t]their cities,
And will demolish[t]their gate bars *his*
And consume *them* because of their counsels.
7 So My people are bent on turning from Me.
Though they call[t]them to *the One* on high, *him*
None at all exalts *Him*.
8 How can I give you up, O Ephraim?
How can I surrender you, O Israel?
How can I[t]make you like Admah?
How can I treat you like Zeboiim?
My heart is turned over within Me,
[t]All my compassions are kindled. *give • Together*
9 I will[r]not execute My fierce anger; Deut. 13:17
I will not destroy Ephraim [r]again. Jer. 26:3
For I am God and not man,
the [r]Holy One in your midst, Is. 5:24; 12:6
And I will not come in wrath.
10 They will [r] walk after the LORD, Hos. 3:5; 6:1-3
He will roar like a lion;
Indeed He will roar,
And His sons will come trembling from the west.

11 They will come trembling like birds from Egypt,
And like [r]doves from the land of Assyria; Is. 60:8
And I will [r]settle them in their houses, declares the LORD. Ezek. 28:25, 26

12 Ephraim surrounds Me with [r]lies, Hos. 4:2; 7:3
And the house of Israel with deceit;
Judah is also unruly against God,
Even against the Holy One who is faithful.

CHAPTER 12

EPHRAIM feeds on [r]wind,
And pursues the [r]east wind continually; Jer. 22:22
He multiplies lies and violence. Gen. 41:6
Moreover, he makes a covenant with Assyria,
And oil is carried to Egypt.
2 The LORD also has a [r]dispute with Judah, Hos. 4:1
And will punish Jacob [r]according to his ways;
He will repay him according to his deeds. Hos. 4:9
3 In the womb he took his brother by the heel,
And in his maturity he contended with God.
4 Yes, he wrestled with the angel and prevailed;
He wept and [r]sought His favor. Gen. 32:26
He found Him at Bethel,
And there He spoke with us,
5 Even the LORD, the God of hosts;
The LORD is His name.
6 Therefore, [r]return to your God, Hos. 6:1-3
Observe [a]kindness and justice, *loyalty*
And [r]wait for your God continually. Mic. 7:7
7 A merchant, in whose hands are false balances,
He loves to oppress.
8 And Ephraim said, "Surely I have become [r]rich,
I have found wealth for myself; Ps. 62:10
In all my labors they will find in me
[r]No iniquity, which *would be* sin." Hos. 4:8; 14:1
9 But I *have been* the LORD your God since the land of Egypt;
I will make you [r]live in tents again, Lev. 23:42
As in the days of the appointed festival.
10 I have also spoken to the [r]prophets,
And I gave numerous visions; 2 Kin. 17:13
And through the prophets I gave parables.
11 Is there iniquity *in* Gilead?
Surely they are worthless.
In Gilgal they sacrifice bulls,
Yes, [r]their altars are like the stone heaps
Beside the furrows of the field. Hos. 8:11; 10:1, 2

12 Now Jacob fled to the [t]land of Aram, *field*
And Israel worked for a wife,
And for a wife he kept *sheep*.
13 But by a [r]prophet the LORD brought Israel from Egypt, Ex. 14:19-22

And by a prophet he was kept.
14 Ephraim has provoked to bitter anger;
So his Lord will leave his bloodguilt on him,
And bring back his[r]reproach to him. Dan. 11:18

CHAPTER 13

WHEN Ephraim spoke, *there was* trembling.
He exalted himself in Israel,
But through Baal he did wrong and died.
2 And now they sin more and more,
And make for themselves molten images,
Idols [r]skillfully made from their silver, Is. 44:17-20
All of them the [r]work of craftsmen. Hos. 8:6
They say of them, "Let the men who sacrifice kiss the[r]calves!" Hos. 8:5, 6
3 Therefore, they will be like the morning cloud,
And like dew which[t]soon disappears, *goes away early*
Like [r]chaff which is blown away from the threshing floor, Ps. 1:4; Is. 17:13
And like smoke from a[t]chimney. *window*

4 Yet I *have been* the [r]LORD your God Hos. 12:9
Since the land of Egypt;
And you were not to know any god except Me,
For there is no savior[r]besides Me. Is. 43:11; 45:21, 22
5 I[a]cared for you in the wilderness, *knew*
In the land of drought.
6 As *they had* their pasture, they became satisfied,
And being satisfied, their heart became proud;
Therefore, they forgot Me.
7 So I will be[r]like a lion to them; Lam. 3:10
Like a leopard I will lie in wait by the wayside.
8 I will encounter them[r]like a bear robbed of her cubs,
And I will tear open their chests; 2 Sam. 17:8
There I will also[r]devour them like a lioness,
As a wild beast would tear them. Ps. 50:22

9 *It is* your destruction, O Israel,
That *you are* against Me, against your help.
10 Where now is your[r]king
That he may save you in all your cities, 2 Kin. 17:4
And your judges of whom you[t]requested, *said*
"Give me a king and princes"?
11 I[r]gave you a king in My anger, 1 Sam. 8:7
And[r]took him away in My wrath. 1 Sam. 15:26

12 The iniquity of Ephraim is bound up;
His sin is stored up.
13 The pains of[r]childbirth come upon him; Is. 13:8
He is not a wise son,
For it is not the time that he should delay at the opening of the womb.
14 I will ransom them from the [t]power of Sheol; *hand*
I will redeem them from death.

[r]O Death, where are your
thorns? 1 Cor. 15:55
O Sheol, where is your sting?
Compassion will be hidden
from My sight.

15 Though he flourishes among
the[a]reeds, *brothers*
An east wind will come,
The wind of the LORD coming
up from the wilderness;
And his fountain will[r]become
dry, Jer. 51:36
And his spring will be dried
up;
It will plunder *his* treasury of
every precious article.
16 Samaria will be held [r]guilty,
For she has rebelled against
her God. Hos. 10:2
They will fall by the sword,
Their little ones will be
dashed in pieces,
And their pregnant women
will be ripped open.

CHAPTER 14

[r]RETURN, O Israel, to the LORD
your God, Hos. 6:1
For you have stumbled be-
cause of your iniquity.
2 Take words with you and return to the LORD.
Say to Him,[r]"Take away all
iniquity, Mic. 7:18, 19
And receive *us* graciously,
That we may present the
fruit of our lips.
3 "Assyria will not save us,
We will[r]not ride on horses;
Nor will we say again, 'Our
god,' Ps. 33:17
To the work of our hands;
For in Thee the[a]orphan finds
mercy." *fatherless*

4 I will heal their apostasy,
I will love them freely,
For My anger has turned
away from them.
5 I will be like the[r]dew to Israel; Prov. 19:12
He will blossom like the lily,
And he will take root like *the*
cedars of Lebanon.
6 His shoots will[t]sprout, *go*
And his[a]beauty will be like
the olive tree, *splendor*
And his fragrance like *the ce-*
dars of Lebanon.
7 Those who[r]live in his shadow
Will again raise grain,
And they will blossom like
the vine. Ezek. 17:23
His renown *will be* like the
wine of Lebanon.

8 O Ephraim, what more have
I to do with idols?
It is I who answer and look
after[t]you. *him*
I am like a luxuriant cypress;
From Me comes your fruit.

9 Whoever is wise, let him understand these things;
Whoever is discerning, let
him know them.
For the[r]ways of the LORD are
right, Ps. 111:7, 8
And the[r]righteous will walk
in them, Is. 26:7
But[r]transgressors will stumble in them. Is. 1:28

THE BOOK OF

JOEL

THE word of the LORD that came to Joel, the son of Pethuel.

2 Hear this, O [r]elders, Job 8:8
And listen, all inhabitants of the land.
Has *anything like* this happened in your days
Or in your fathers' days?
3 [r]Tell your sons about it,
And *let* your sons *tell* their sons, Ex. 10:2; Ps. 78:4
And their sons the next generation.

4 What the [r]gnawing locust has left, the swarming locust has eaten; Deut. 28:38
And what the swarming locust has left, the creeping locust has eaten;
And what the creeping locust has left, the [r]stripping locust has eaten. Is. 33:4
5 Awake, [r]drunkards, and weep; Joel 3:3
And wail, all you wine drinkers,
On account of the sweet wine
That is [r]cut off from your mouth. Is. 32:10
6 For a nation has [t]invaded my land, *come up against*
Mighty and without number;
[r]Its teeth are the teeth of a lion, Rev. 9:8
And it has the fangs of a lioness.
7 It has made my vine a waste,
And my fig tree [a]splinters.
It has stripped them bare and cast *them* away; *a stump*
Their branches have become white.

8 [r]Wail like a virgin [r]girded with sackcloth
For the bridegroom of her youth. Is. 22:12 • Joel 1:13
9 The grain offering and the libation are cut off
From the house of the LORD.
The priests mourn,
The ministers of the LORD.
10 The field is ruined,
The land mourns,
For the grain is ruined,
The new wine dries up,
Fresh oil fails.
11 Be ashamed, O farmers,
Wail, O vinedressers,
For the wheat and the barley;
Because the harvest of the field is destroyed.
12 The vine dries up,
And the fig tree [t]fails;
The pomegranate, the palm also, and the apple tree,
All the trees of the field dry up. *wastes away*
Indeed, rejoicing dries up
From the sons of men.

13 [r]Gird yourselves *with sackcloth,* Jer. 4:8
And lament, O priests;
[r]Wail, O ministers of the altar! Jer. 9:10
Come, [r]spend the night in sackcloth, 1 Kin. 21:27
O ministers of my God,
For the grain offering and the libation

Are withheld from the house
of your God.
14 Consecrate a fast,
Proclaim a [r]solemn assembly;
Gather the elders Lev. 23:36
And all the inhabitants of the
land
To the house of the LORD
your God,
And cry out to the LORD.
15 Alas for the day!
For the [r]day of the LORD is
near, Joel 2:1, 11, 31
And it will come as destruction
from the Almighty.
16 Has not [r]food been cut off before
our eyes, Is. 3:7
Gladness and joy from the
house of our God?
17 The [a]seeds shrivel under their
[a]clods;
The storehouses are desolate,
dried figs • shovels
The barns are torn down,
For the grain is dried up.
18 How [r]the beasts groan!
The herds of cattle wander
aimlessly 1 Kin. 8:5
Because there is no pasture
for them;
Even the flocks of sheep [t]suffer.
bear punishment
19 To Thee, O LORD, I cry;
For [r]fire has devoured the
pastures of the wilderness,
Jer. 9:10
And the flame has burned up
all the trees of the field.
20 Even the beasts of the field
[t]pant for Thee; *long for*
For the [r]water brooks are
dried up, 1 Kin. 17:7
And fire has devoured the
pastures of the wilderness.

CHAPTER 2

BLOW a trumpet in Zion,
And sound an alarm on My
holy mountain!
Let all the inhabitants of the
land tremble,
For the [r]day of the LORD is
coming; Joel 1:15
Surely it is near,
2 A day of [r]darkness and
gloom, Joel 2:10, 31
A day of clouds and thick
darkness.
As the dawn is spread over
the mountains,
So there is a [r]great and
mighty people; Joel 1:6
There has [r]never been *anything*
like it, Lam. 1:12
Nor will there be again after
it
To the years of many generations.
3 A [r]fire consumes before them,
And behind them a flame
burns. Ps. 97:3
The land is [r]like the garden of
Eden before them,
But a [r]desolate wilderness behind
them,
And nothing at all escapes
them. Is. 51:3 • Ex. 10:5, 15
4 Their [r]appearance is like the
appearance of horses;
And like war horses, so they
run. Rev. 9:7
5 With a [r]noise as of chariots
They leap on the tops of the
mountains, Rev. 9:9
Like the [t]crackling of a flame
of fire consuming the
stubble, *noise*
Like a mighty people arranged
for battle.

6 Before them the people are in
[r]anguish; Is. 13:8
All faces turn pale.
7 They run like mighty men;
They climb the wall like soldiers;
And they each march[t] in line,
Nor do they deviate from
their paths. *in his ways*
8 They do not crowd each other;
They march everyone in his
path.
When they[t] burst through the
defenses, *fall*
They do not break ranks.
9 They rush on the city,
They run on the wall;
They climb into the houses,
They enter through the windows like a thief.
10 Before them the earth
[r]quakes, Ps. 18:7
The heavens tremble,
The[r] sun and the moon grow
dark, Is. 13:10; 34:4
And the stars lose their
brightness.
11 And the LORD [r]utters His
voice before His army;
Surely His camp is very
great, Ps. 46:6
For[r] strong is He who carries
out His word. Rev. 18:8
The[r] day of the LORD is indeed great and very awesome, Jer. 30:7
And who can endure it?
12 "Yet even now," declares the
LORD,
[r]"Return to Me with all your
heart, Deut. 4:29
And with[r] fasting, weeping,
and mourning; Dan. 9:3
13 And rend your heart and not
your[r] garments."
Now return to the LORD your
God, Gen. 37:34
For He is[r] gracious and compassionate, Ex. 34:6
Slow to anger, abounding in
lovingkindness,
And relenting of evil.
14 Who knows whether He will
not turn and relent,
And leave a[r] blessing behind
Him, Hag. 2:19
Even[r] a grain offering and a
libation Joel 1:9, 13
For the LORD your God?
15 Blow a trumpet in Zion,
Consecrate a fast, proclaim a
solemn assembly,
16 Gather the people, sanctify
the congregation,
Assemble the elders,
Gather the children and the
nursing infants.
Let the[r] bridegroom come out
of his room Ps. 19:5
And the bride out of her *bridal* chamber.
17 Let the priests, the LORD's
ministers,
Weep[r] between the porch and
the altar, 2 Chr. 8:12
And let them say, "Spare
Thy people, O LORD,
And do not make Thine inheritance a[r] reproach,
A byword among the nations. Ps. 44:13
Why should they among the
peoples say,
'Where is their God?' "

18 Then the LORD[a] will be zealous for His land,
And will have pity on His
people. *was zealous*
19 And the LORD[a] will answer
and say to His people,

"Behold, I am going to send
you grain, new wine, and
oil, *answered and said*
And you will be satisfied *in*
full with[t]them; *it*
And I will never again make
you a reproach among
the nations.
20 "But I will remove the[r]northern *army* far from you,
And I will drive it into a
parched and desolate
land, Jer. 1:14, 15
And its vanguard into the
[r]eastern sea, Zech. 14:8
And its rear guard into the
western sea.
And its[r]stench will arise and
its foul smell will come
up, Is. 34:3; Amos 4:10
For it has done great things."

21 [r]Do not fear, O land, rejoice
and be glad, Is. 54:4
For the LORD has done[r]great
things. Ps. 126:3
22 Do not fear, beasts of the
field,
For the[r]pastures of the wilderness have turned
green, Ps. 65:12, 13
For the tree has borne its
fruit,
The fig tree and the vine have
yielded in full.
23 So rejoice, O sons of Zion,
And[r]be glad in the LORD your
God; Is. 12:2-6
For He has[r]given you the
[1]early rain for *your* vindication. Deut. 11:14
And He has poured down for
you the rain,
The [1]early and [2]latter[r]rain as
before. Lev. 26:4

[1] I.e., autumn [2] I.e., spring

24 And the threshing floors will
be full of grain,
And the vats will[r]overflow
with the new wine and
oil. Lev. 26:10
25 "Then I will make up to you
for the years
That the swarming[r]locust
has eaten, Joel 1:4-7
The creeping locust, the
stripping locust, and the
gnawing locust,
My great army which I sent
among you.
26 "And you shall have plenty to
eat and be satisfied,
And praise the name of the
LORD your God,
Who has[r]dealt wondrously
with you; Is. 25:1
Then My people will[r]never be
put to shame. Is. 45:17
27 "Thus you will[r]know that I am
in the midst of Israel,
And that I am the LORD your
God Lev. 26:11, 12
And there is no other;
And My people will never be
[r]put to shame. Is. 49:23

28 "And it will come about after
this
That I will[r]pour out My Spirit
on all[t]mankind;
And your sons and daughters
will prophesy,
Your old men will dream
dreams,
Your young men will see visions. Is. 32:15 • *flesh*
29 "And even on the[r]male and female servants 1 Cor. 12:13
I will pour out My Spirit in
those days.
30 "And I will[r]display wonders in
the sky and on the earth,

Blood, fire, and columns of
smoke. Matt. 24:29
31 "The [r]sun will be turned into
darkness, Is. 13:10
And the moon into blood,
Before the [r]great and awesome
day of the LORD
comes. Is. 13:9
32 "And it will come about that
[r]whoever calls on the
name of the LORD
Will be delivered; Jer. 33:3
For [r]on Mount Zion and in Jerusalem
Is. 46:13
There will be those who [r]escape,
Is. 4:2
As the LORD has said,
Even among the survivors
whom the LORD calls.

CHAPTER 3

"FOR behold, [r]in those days and
at that time, Jer. 30:3
When I restore the fortunes
of Judah and Jerusalem,
2 I will gather all the nations,
And bring them down to the
valley of Jehoshaphat.
Then I will [r]enter into judgment
with them there
On behalf of My people and
My inheritance, Israel,
Whom they have scattered
among the nations;
And they have divided up My
land. Is. 66:16
3 "They have also [r]cast lots for
My people, Obad. 11
[t]Traded a boy for a harlot,
And sold a girl for wine that
they may drink. *Given*
4 "Moreover, what are you to
Me, O [r]Tyre, Sidon, and all the regions of Philistia? Are you rendering Me a recompense? But if you
do recompense Me, swiftly and
speedily I will return your recompense on your head. Is. 23:1-18
5 "Since you have taken My silver and My gold, brought My precious treasures to your temples,
6 and sold the sons of Judah
and Jerusalem to the [t]Greeks in order to remove them far from their
territory, *sons of Javan*
7 behold, I am going to arouse
them from the place where you
have sold them, and return your
recompense on your head.
8 "Also I will [r]sell your sons and
your daughters into the hand of
the sons of Judah, and they will
sell them to the [r]Sabeans, to a distant nation," for the LORD has spoken. Is. 14:2; 60:14 • Job 1:15
9 [r]Proclaim this among the nations:
Jer. 51:27
[r]Prepare a war; rouse the
mighty men! Jer. 6:4
Let all the soldiers draw
near, let them come up!
10 [r]Beat your plowshares into
swords, Is. 2:4
And your pruning hooks into
spears;
Let the weak say, "I am a
mighty man."
11 [a]Hasten and come, all you
surrounding nations,
And gather yourselves there.
Bring down, O LORD, Thy
mighty ones. *Lend aid*
12 Let the nations be aroused
And come up to the [r]valley of
Jehoshaphat, Joel 3:2, 14
For there I will sit to judge
All the surrounding nations.
13 Put in the sickle, for the [r]harvest
is ripe. Jer. 51:33
Come, tread, for the [r]wine
press is full; Is. 63:3

The vats overflow, for their
wickedness is great.
14 Multitudes, multitudes in the
[r]valley of decision!
For the day of the LORD is
near in the valley of decision. Joel 3:2, 12
15 The [r]sun and moon grow
dark, Joel 2:10, 31
And the stars lose their
brightness.
16 And the LORD [r]roars from
Zion Hos. 11:10
And [r]utters His voice from Jerusalem, Joel 2:11
And the [r]heavens and the
earth tremble. Hag. 2:6
But the LORD is a [r]refuge for
His people Ps. 61:3
And a [r]stronghold to the sons
of Israel. Jer. 16:19
17 Then you will know that I am
the LORD your God,
Dwelling in Zion My [r]holy
mountain. Is. 11:9; 56:7
So Jerusalem will be holy,
And strangers will pass
through it no more.

18 And it will come about in
that day
That the [r]mountains will drip
with sweet wine,
And the hills will flow with
milk, Amos 9:13
And all the brooks of Judah
will flow with water;
And a spring will go out from
the house of the LORD,
To water the valley of [a]Shit-
tim. *acacias*
19 Egypt will become a waste,
And Edom will become a
desolate wilderness,
Because of the [r]violence done
to the sons of Judah,
In whose land they have shed
innocent blood. Obad. 10
20 But Judah will be [r]inhabited
forever, Ezek. 37:25
And Jerusalem for all generations.
21 And I will [r]avenge their blood
which I have not
avenged, Is. 4:4
For the LORD dwells in Zion.

THE BOOK OF
AMOS

THE words of Amos, who was
among the sheepherders from Tekoa, which he envisioned in visions concerning Israel in the days
of Uzziah king of Judah, and in
the days of Jeroboam son of
Joash, king of Israel, two years
before the earthquake.
2 And he said,
"The LORD roars from Zion,
And from Jerusalem He ut-
ters His voice;
And the shepherds' pasture
grounds mourn,
And the [t]summit of Carmel
dries up." *head*

3 Thus says the LORD,
"For [r]three transgressions of
[r]Damascus and for four

I will not revoke its *punish-*
ment, Amos 2:1, 4, 6
Because they threshed Gilead with *implements* of
sharp iron. Is. 8:4
4 "So I will send fire upon the
house of Hazael,
And it will consume the citadels of Ben-hadad.
5 "I will also [r]break the *gate* bar
of Damascus, Jer. 51:30
And cut off the inhabitant
from the valley of Aven,
And him who holds the scepter, from Beth-eden;
So the people of Aram will
go exiled to [r]Kir,"
Says the LORD. 2 Kin. 16:9

6 Thus says the LORD,
"For three transgressions of
[r]Gaza and for four
I will not revoke its *punish-*
ment, 1 Sam. 6:17
Because they deported an entire population
To deliver *it* up to Edom.
7 "So I will send fire upon the
wall of Gaza,
And it will consume her citadels.
8 "I will also cut off the inhabitant from Ashdod,
And him who holds the scepter, from Ashkelon;
I will even unleash My [t]power
upon Ekron, *hand*
And the remnant of the Philistines will perish,"
Says the Lord GOD.

9 Thus says the LORD,
"For three transgressions of
[r]Tyre and for four
I will not revoke its *punish-*
ment, Is. 23:1-18
Because they delivered up an
entire population to
Edom
And did not remember *the*
covenant of brotherhood.
10 "So I will [r]send fire upon the
wall of Tyre, Zech. 9:4
And it will consume her citadels."

11 Thus says the LORD,
"For three transgressions of
[r]Edom and for four
I will not revoke its *punish-*
ment, Is. 34:5, 6; 63:1-6
Because he pursued his
brother with the sword,
While he [t]stifled his compassion; *corrupted*
His anger also [r]tore continually, Is. 57:16
And he maintained his fury
forever.
12 "So I will send fire upon [r]Te-
man, Jer. 49:7, 20
And it will consume the citadels of Bozrah."

13 Thus says the LORD,
"For three transgressions of
the sons of [r]Ammon and
for four Jer. 49:1-6
I will not revoke its *punish-*
ment,
Because they [r]ripped open the
pregnant women of Gil-
ead 2 Kin. 15:16
In order to [r]enlarge their borders. Is. 5:8; Ezek. 35:10
14 "So I will kindle a fire on the
wall of [r]Rabbah,
And it will consume her citadels Deut. 3:11
Amid [a]war cries on the day of
battle *shouts*
And a [r]storm on the day of
tempest. Is. 29:6; 30:30
15 "Their [r]king will go into exile,

He and his princes together,"
says the LORD. Jer. 49:3

CHAPTER 2

THUS says the LORD,
"For three transgressions of
[r]Moab and for four
I will not revoke its *punishment*, Is. 15:1–16:14
Because he[r]burned the bones
of the king of Edom to
lime. 2 Kin. 3:26, 27
2"So I will send fire upon
Moab,
And it will consume the citadels of Kerioth;
And Moab will die amid[r]tumult, Jer. 48:45
With[a]war cries and the sound
of a trumpet. *shouts*
3"I will also cut off the[r]judge
from her midst, Ps. 2:10
And slay all her princes with
him," says the LORD.

4 Thus says the LORD,
"For three transgressions of
[r]Judah and for four
I will not revoke its *punishment*, 2 Kin. 17:19
Because they[r]rejected the
law of the LORD
And have not kept His statutes; Judg. 2:17-20
Their[a]lies also have led them
astray, *false gods*
Those after which their[r]fathers walked. Jer. 9:14
5"So I will[r]send fire upon Judah, Jer. 17:27; 21:10
And it will consume the citadels of Jerusalem."

6 Thus says the LORD,
"For three transgressions of
[r]Israel and for four
I will not revoke its *punishment*, 2 Kin. 18:11, 12
Because they[r]sell the righteous for money
And the needy for a pair of
sandals. Joel 3:3
7"These who pant after the
very dust of the earth on
the head of the[r]helpless
Also turn aside the way of
the humble; Amos 8:4
And a[r]man and his father[t]resort to the same girl
In order to profane My holy
name. Hos. 4:14 • *go*
8"And on garments[r]taken as
pledges they stretch out
beside every altar,
And in the house of their God
they drink the wine of
those who have been
fined. Ex. 22:26

9"Yet it was I who destroyed
the Amorite before them,
[t]Though his height *was* like
the height of cedars
And he *was* strong as the
oaks; *Whose height*
I even destroyed his fruit
above and his root below.
10"And it was I who[r]brought
you up from the land of
Egypt, Ex. 12:51; 20:2
And I led you in the wilderness forty years
[t]That you might take possession of the land of the
Amorite. *To possess*
11"Then I raised up some of
your sons to be prophets
And some of your young
men to be Nazirites.
Is this not so, O sons of Israel?" declares the LORD.

12 "But you made the Nazirites drink wine,
And you commanded the prophets saying, 'You shall not prophesy!'
13 "Behold, I am[a] weighted down beneath you *tottering*
As a wagon[a] is weighted down when filled with sheaves. *totters*
14 "Flight[a] will perish from the swift, *A place of refuge*
And the stalwart will not strengthen his power,
Nor the mighty man save his [t]life. *soul*
15 "He who [r]grasps the bow will not stand *his ground*,
The swift of foot will not escape, Jer. 51:56
Nor will he who rides the horse save his [t]life. *soul*
16 "Even the [t]bravest among the warriors will flee naked in that day," declares the LORD. *stout of heart*

CHAPTER 3

HEAR this word which the LORD
has spoken against you, sons of
Israel, against the entire [r]family
which [t]He brought up from the
land of Egypt, Jer. 8:3 • *I*
2 "You only have I [t]chosen among all the families of the earth; *known*
Therefore, I will punish you for all your iniquities."
3 Do two men walk together unless they have made an appointment?
4 Does a lion roar in the forest when he has no prey?
Does a young lion growl from his den unless he has captured *something*?
5 Does a bird fall into a trap on the ground when there is no bait in it?
Does a trap spring up from the earth when it captures nothing at all?
6 If a [r]trumpet is blown in a city will not the people tremble? Jer. 4:5, 19, 21
If a calamity occurs in a city has not the LORD done it?
7 [a]Surely the LORD God does nothing *For*
Unless He [r]reveals His secret counsel Gen. 6:13
To His servants the prophets.
8 A [r]lion has roared! Who will not fear? Amos 1:2
The Lord GOD has spoken! Who can but prophesy?

9 Proclaim on the citadels in
[r]Ashdod and on the citadels in the
land of Egypt and say, "Assemble
yourselves on the [r]mountains of
Samaria and see *the* great tumults
within her and *the* oppressions in
her midst. 1 Sam. 5:1 • Amos 4:1
10 "But they [r]do not know how to
do what is right," declares the
LORD, "these who [r]hoard up violence and devastation in their citadels." Ps. 14:4 • Hab. 2:8-10
11 Therefore, thus says the Lord
GOD,
"An enemy, even one surrounding the land,
Will pull down your [a]strength from you *stronghold*
And your [r]citadels will be looted." Amos 2:5
12 Thus says the LORD,
"Just as the shepherd snatches from the lion's mouth a couple of legs or a piece of an ear,

So will the sons of Israel dwelling in Samaria be snatched away—
With *the* corner of a bed and *the* cover of a couch!
13 "Hear and [r]testify against the house of Jacob," Ezek. 2:7
Declares the Lord GOD, the God of hosts.
14 "For on the day that I punish Israel's transgressions,
I will also punish the altars of [r]Bethel; 2 Kin. 23:15
The horns of the altar will be cut off,
And they will fall to the ground.
15 "I will also smite the [a]winter house together with the summer house; *autumn*
The houses of [r]ivory will also perish 1 Kin. 22:39
And the great houses will come to an end,"
Declares the LORD.

CHAPTER 4

HEAR this word, you cows of Bashan who are on the mountain of Samaria,
Who oppress the poor, who crush the needy,
Who say to [t]your husbands, "Bring now, that we may drink!" *their lords*
2 The Lord GOD has [r]sworn by His [r]holiness, Amos 6:8
"Behold, the days are coming upon you Ps. 89:35
When [t]they will take you away with meat hooks,
And the last of you with [r]fish hooks. *he* • Jer. 16:16
3 "You will go out *through* breaches *in the walls*,
Each one straight before her,
And you will be cast to Harmon," declares the LORD.

4 "Enter Bethel and transgress;
In Gilgal multiply transgression!
[r]Bring your sacrifices every morning, Num. 28:3
Your tithes every three days.
5 "Offer [t]a thank offering also from that which is leavened, *Offer up in smoke*
And proclaim freewill offerings, make them known.
For so you love *to do*, you sons of Israel,"
Declares the Lord GOD.

6 "But I gave you also [r]cleanness of teeth in all your cities
And lack of bread in all your places, Is. 3:1
Yet you have not returned to Me," declares the LORD.
7 "And furthermore, I [r]withheld the rain from you
While there *were* still three months until harvest.
Then I would send rain on one city Deut. 11:17
And on another city I would not send rain;
One part would be rained on,
While the part not rained on would dry up.
8 "So two or three cities would stagger to another city to drink [r]water, Jer. 14:4
But would not be satisfied;
Yet you have not returned to Me," declares the LORD.
9 "I smote you with scorching *wind* and mildew;
And the [r]caterpillar was devouring Joel 1:4, 7

Your many gardens and
vineyards, fig trees and
olive trees;
Yet you have not returned to
Me," declares the LORD.
10 "I sent a [r]plague among you after the manner of Egypt;
I slew your young men by
the sword along with
your captured horses,
And I made the stench of
your camp rise up in your
nostrils; Ex. 9:3
Yet you have not returned to
Me," declares the LORD.
11 "I overthrew you as [r]God overthrew Sodom and Go-
morrah, Gen. 19:24, 25
And you were like a [r]fire-
brand snatched from a
blaze; Zech. 3:2
Yet you have not returned to
Me," declares the LORD.
12 "Therefore, thus I will do to
you, O Israel;
Because I shall do this to
you,
Prepare to [r]meet your God, O
Israel." Is. 32:11; 64:2
13 For behold, He who [r]forms
mountains and creates
the wind Job 38:4-7
And declares to man what
are His thoughts,
He who [r]makes dawn into
darkness Jer. 13:16
And [r]treads on the high
places of the earth,
The LORD God of hosts is His
name. Mic. 1:3

CHAPTER 5

HEAR this word which I take up
for you as a [r]dirge, O house of Israel. Jer. 7:29; 9:10, 17
2 She has fallen, she will [r]not
rise again— Amos 8:14
The [r]virgin Israel. Jer. 14:17
She *lies* neglected on her
land;
There is none to raise her up.
3 For thus says the Lord GOD,
"The city which goes forth a
thousand *strong*
Will have a [r]hundred left,
And the *one* which goes forth
a hundred *strong* Is. 6:13
Will have ten left to the
house of Israel."

4 For thus says the LORD to the
house of Israel,
"Seek Me that you may live.
5 "But do not [t]resort to Bethel,
And do not come to Gilgal,
Nor cross over to Beersheba;
For Gilgal will certainly go
into captivity, *seek*
And Bethel will [a]come to
trouble. *become iniquity*
6 "Seek [r]the LORD that you may
live, Is. 55:3, 6, 7
Lest He break forth like a
fire, O house of Joseph,
And it consume with none to
quench *it* for Bethel,
7 *For* those who turn [r]justice
into wormwood Amos 2:3
And cast righteousness down
to the earth."

8 He who made the [r]Pleiades
and Orion Job 9:9
And [r]changes deep darkness
into morning, Is. 42:16
[t]Who also darkens day *into*
night, *And He darkened*
Who [r]calls for the waters of
the sea Ps. 104:6-9
And pours them out on the
surface of the earth,

The LORD is His name.
9 It is He who [r]flashes forth
with destruction upon
the strong, Is. 29:5
So that destruction comes
upon the fortress.

10 They hate him who [r]reproves
in the gate, Is. 29:21
And they abhor him who
speaks *with* integrity.
11 Therefore, because you impose heavy rent on the
poor
And exact a tribute of grain
from them,
Though you have built
[r]houses of well-hewn
stone, Amos 3:15; 6:11
Yet you will not live in them;
You have planted pleasant
vineyards, yet you will
not drink their wine.
12 For I know your transgressions are many and your
sins are great,
You who distress the righteous *and* accept bribes,
And [t]turn aside the poor in
the gate. *they turn*
13 Therefore, at such a time the
prudent person keeps si-
lent, for it is an evil time.

14 Seek good and not evil, that
you may live;
And thus may the LORD God
of hosts be with you,
Just as you have said!
15 [r]Hate evil, love good,
And establish justice in the
gate! Ps. 97:10
Perhaps the LORD God of
hosts
May be gracious to the remnant of Joseph.

16 Therefore, thus says the
LORD God of hosts, the
Lord,
"There is [r]wailing in all the pla-
zas, Jer. 9:10, 18-20
And in all the streets they
say, 'Alas! Alas!'
They also call the [r]farmer to
mourning Joel 1:11
And professional mourners
to lamentation.
17 "And in all the [r]vineyards *there*
is wailing, Is. 16:10
Because I shall pass through
the midst of you," says
the LORD.

18 Alas, you who are longing
for the [r]day of the LORD,
For what purpose *will* the
day of the LORD *be* to
you? Is. 5:19; Jer. 30:7
It *will be* [r]darkness and not
light; Is. 5:30
19 As when a man [r]flees from a
lion, Job 20:24
And a bear meets him,
[a]Or goes home, leans his hand
against the wall, *Then*
And a snake bites him.
20 *Will* not the day of the LORD
be [r]darkness instead of
light, Is. 13:10
Even gloom with no brightness in it?

21 "I hate, I reject your festivals,
Nor do I delight in your sol-
emn assemblies.
22 "Even though you [r]offer up to
Me burnt offerings and
your grain offerings,
I will not accept *them*;
And I will not *even* look at
the peace offerings of
your fatlings. Is. 66:3

23 "Take away from Me the noise of your songs;
I will not even listen to the sound of your harps.
24 "But let[r]justice roll down like waters Jer. 22:3
And righteousness like an ever-flowing stream.

25 "Did[r]you present Me with sacrifices and grain offerings in the wilderness for forty years, O house of Israel? Deut. 32:17

26 "You also carried along Sikkuth your king and Kiyyun, your images, the star of your gods which you made for yourselves.

27 "Therefore, I will make you go into exile beyond Damascus," says the LORD, whose name is the God of hosts.

CHAPTER 6

[r]WOE to those who are at ease in Zion,
And to those who *feel* secure in the mountain of Samaria, Is. 32:9-11
The[r]distinguished men of the foremost of nations,
To whom the house of Israel comes. Ex. 19:5
2 Go over to[r]Calneh and look,
And go from there to Hamath the great, Is. 10:9
Then go down to[r]Gath of the Philistines. 1 Sam. 5:8
Are[a] they better than these kingdoms, *you*
Or is their territory greater than yours?
3 Do you[r]put off the day of calamity, Is. 56:12
And would you bring near the seat of violence?
4 Those who recline on beds of ivory
And sprawl on their[r]couches,
And eat lambs from the flock
And calves from the midst of the stall, Amos 3:12
5 Who improvise to the sound of the harp,
And like David have composed[r] songs for themselves, 1 Chr. 15:16
6 Who[r]drink wine from[t]sacrificial bowls Amos 2:8
While they anoint themselves with the finest of oils, *sprinkling basins*
Yet they have not grieved over the ruin of Joseph.
7 Therefore, they will now[r]go into exile at the head of the exiles, Amos 7:11
And the sprawlers' banqueting will pass away.

8 The Lord GOD has[r]sworn by Himself, the LORD God of hosts has declared:
"I loathe the arrogance of Jacob, Gen. 22:16
And I[t]detest his citadels;
Therefore, I will deliver up *the* city and[t]all it contains." *hate • its fulness*
9 And it will be, if ten men are left in one house, they will die.

10 Then one's uncle, or his[t]undertaker, will lift him up to carry out *his* bones from the house, and he will say to the one who is in the innermost part of the house, "Is anyone else with you?" And that one will say, "No one." Then he will answer, "Keep quiet. For the name of the LORD is not to be mentioned." *one who burns him*

11 For behold, the LORD is going

to command that the great house
be smashed to pieces and the
small house to fragments.

12 Do horses run on rocks?
Or does one plow them with
oxen?
Yet you have turned[r] justice
into poison, Hos. 10:4
And the fruit of righteousness into [1]wormwood,
13 You who rejoice in [2]Lo-de-
bar,
And say, "Have we not by
our *own* strength taken
[3]Karnaim for ourselves?"
14 "For behold, [r]I am going to
raise up a nation against
you, Jer. 5:15
O house of Israel," declares
the LORD God of hosts,
"And they will afflict you from
the entrance of Hamath
To the brook of the Arabah.

CHAPTER 7

THUS the Lord GOD showed me,
and behold, He was forming a[r] lo-
cust-swarm when the spring crop
began to sprout. And behold, the
spring crop *was* after the king's
[a]mowing. Joel 1:4 • *shearings*
2 And it came about,[t] when it
had finished eating the vegetation
of the land, that I said,
"Lord GOD, please pardon!
[t]How can Jacob stand,
For he is small?" *if* • *As who*
3 The LORD[a] changed His mind
about this. *relented*
"It shall not be," said the
LORD.

4 Thus the Lord GOD showed
me, and behold, the Lord GOD was

[1]I.e., bitterness [2]Lit., *a thing of nothing*
[3]Lit., *a pair of horns*

calling to contend *with them* by
fire, and it consumed the great
deep and began to consume the
[t]farm land. *portion*
5 Then I said,
[r]"Lord GOD, please stop!
How can Jacob stand, for he
is small?" Ps. 85:4
6 The LORD[a] changed His mind
about this. *relented*
"This too shall not be," said
the Lord GOD.

7 Thus He showed me, and behold, the Lord was standing by a
[t]vertical wall, with a plumb line in
His hand. *wall of a plumb line*
8 And the LORD said to me,
[r]"What do you see, Amos?" And I
said, "A plumb line." Then the
Lord said, Jer. 1:11; Amos 8:2
"Behold I am about to put a
[r]plumb line
In the midst of My people Israel. 2 Kin. 21:13
I will spare them no longer.
9 "The[r] high places of Isaac will
be desolated Gen. 46:1
And the[r] sanctuaries of Israel
laid waste. Lev. 26:31
Then shall I rise up against
the house of Jeroboam
with the sword."

10 Then Amaziah, the priest of
Bethel, sent *word* to Jeroboam,
king of Israel, saying, "Amos has
conspired against you in the midst
of the house of Israel; the land is
unable to endure all his words.
11 "For thus Amos says, 'Jeroboam will die by the sword and Israel will certainly go from its land
into exile.' "
12 Then Amaziah said to Amos,
"Go, you seer, flee away to the
land of Judah, and there eat bread
and there do your prophesying!

13"But no longer prophesy at
Bethel, for it is a sanctuary of the
king and a royal residence."
14 Then Amos answered and
said to Amaziah, "I am not a
prophet, nor am I the son of a
prophet; for I am a herdsman and
a grower of sycamore figs.
15"But the LORD took me from
[t]following the flock and the LORD
said to me, 'Go prophesy to My
people Israel.' *behind*
16"And now hear the word of
the LORD: you are saying, 'You
shall not prophesy against Israel
nor shall you [t]speak against the
house of Isaac.' *flow*
17"Therefore, thus says the
LORD, 'Your wife will become a
harlot in the city, your sons and
your daughters will fall by the
sword, your land will be parceled
up by a *measuring* line, and you
yourself will die [a]upon unclean
soil. Moreover, Israel will certainly go from its land into
exile.' " *in an unclean land*

CHAPTER 8

THUS the Lord GOD showed me,
and behold, *there was* a basket of
summer fruit.
2 And He said, "What do you
see, Amos?" And I said, "A basket
of summer fruit." Then the LORD
said to me, "The end has come for
My people Israel. I will [t]spare
them no longer. *pass him by*
3"The songs of the palace will
turn to wailing in that day," declares the Lord GOD. "Many *will*
be the corpses; in every place they
will cast them forth in silence."
4 Hear this, you who [a]trample
the needy, to do away with the
humble of the land, *snap at*
5 saying,
"When will the new moon [t]be
over, *pass by*
So that we may buy grain,
And the [r]sabbath, that we
may open the wheat *mar-*
ket, Ex. 31:13-17
To make the [t]bushel smaller
and the shekel bigger,
And to cheat with dishonest
scales, *ephah*
6 So as to [r]buy the helpless for
[t]money Amos 2:6 • *silver*
And the needy for a pair of
sandals,
And *that* we may sell the refuse of the wheat?"

7 The LORD has sworn by the
pride of Jacob,
"Indeed, I will never forget
any of their deeds.
8"Because of this will not the
land [r]quake Ps. 18:7
And everyone who dwells in
it [r]mourn? Hos. 4:3
Indeed, all of it will [r]rise up
like the Nile, Jer. 46:7, 8
And it will be tossed about,
And subside like the Nile of
Egypt.
9"And it will come about in
that day," declares the
Lord GOD,
"That I shall make the [r]sun go
down at noon Job 5:14
And [r]make the earth dark in
broad daylight. Is. 59:9
10"Then I shall turn your festivals into mourning
And all your songs into [a]lam-
entation; *a dirge*
And I will bring [r]sackcloth on
everyone's loins Is. 15:2, 3

And baldness on every head.
And I will make it[r] like *a time of* mourning for an only son, Jer. 6:26
And the end of it will be like a bitter day.

11 "Behold, days are coming," declares the Lord GOD,
"When I will send a famine on the land,
Not a famine for bread or a thirst for water,
But rather for hearing the words of the LORD.
12 "And people will stagger from sea to sea,
And from the north even to the east;
They will go to and fro to [r]seek the word of the LORD, Ezek. 20:3, 31
But they will not find *it.*
13 "In that day the beautiful [r]virgins Lam. 1:18; 2:21
And the young men will [r]faint from thirst. Is. 41:17
14 "*As for* those who swear by the [a]guilt of Samaria, Ashimah
Who say, 'As your god lives, O Dan,'
And, 'As the way of [r]Beersheba lives,' Amos 5:5
They will fall and [r]not rise again." Amos 5:2

CHAPTER 9

I SAW the Lord standing beside the [r]altar, and He said,
"Smite the capitals so that the thresholds will shake,
And break them on the heads of them all! Amos 3:14
Then I will slay the rest of them with the sword;
They will [r]not have a fugitive who will flee, Jer. 11:11
Or a refugee who will escape.
2 "Though they dig into [r]Sheol,
From there shall My hand take them; Ps. 139:8
And though they [r]ascend to heaven, Jer. 51:53
From there will I bring them down.
3 "And though they hide on the summit of Carmel,
I will [r]search them out and take them from there;
And though they conceal themselves from My sight on the floor of the sea, Jer. 16:16
From there I will command the [r]serpent and it will bite them. Is. 27:1
4 "And though they go into [r]captivity before their enemies, Lev. 26:33
From there I will command the sword that it slay them,
And I will set My eyes against them for evil and not for good."

5 And the Lord GOD of hosts,
The One who [r]touches the land so that it melts,
And [r]all those who dwell in it mourn,
And all of it rises up like the Nile Ps. 104:32 • Amos 8:8
And subsides like the Nile of Egypt;
6 The One who builds His [a]upper chambers in the heavens, stairs
And has founded His vaulted dome over the earth,

He who[r]calls for the waters
of the sea Amos 5:8
And pours them out on the
face of the earth,
The LORD is His name.

7"Are you not as the sons of
[r]Ethiopia to Me,
O sons of Israel?" declares
the LORD. Is. 20:4; 43:3
"Have I not brought up Israel
from the land of Egypt,
And the [r]Philistines from
Caphtor and the Arame-
ans from Kir? Jer. 47:4
8"Behold, the[r]eyes of the Lord
GOD are on the sinful
kingdom, Jer. 44:27
And I will[r]destroy it from the
face of the earth;
Nevertheless, I will not totally destroy the house of
Jacob," Amos 7:17
Declares the LORD.
9"For behold, I am commanding,
And I will shake the house of
Israel among all nations
As *grain* is shaken in a sieve,
But not a[a]kernel will fall to
the ground. *pebble*
10"All the[r]sinners of My people
will die by the sword,
Those who say, 'The calamity will not overtake or
confront us.' Is. 33:14
11"In that day I will raise up the
fallen[r]booth of David,
And wall up its breaches;
I will also raise up its ruins,
And rebuild it as in the days
of old; Is. 16:5
12 That they may possess the
remnant of Edom
And all the[a]nations who are
called by My name,"
Declares the LORD who does
this. *Gentiles*

13"Behold, days are coming,"
declares the LORD,
"When the [r]plowman will
overtake the reaper
And the treader of grapes
him who sows seed;
When the mountains will
drip sweet wine,
And all the hills will be dissolved. Lev. 26:5
14"Also I will[r]restore the[a]captiv-
ity of My people Israel,
And they will [r]rebuild the
ruined cities and live *in*
them, Ps. 53:6; Is. 60:4
They will also plant vineyards and drink their
wine, *fortunes*
And make gardens and eat
their fruit. Is. 61:4
15"I will also plant them on their
land,
And[r]they will not again be
rooted out from their
land Is. 60:21
Which I have given them,"
Says the LORD your God.

THE BOOK OF

OBADIAH

THE vision of Obadiah.
Thus says the Lord GOD concerning[r] Edom—
[r]We have heard a report from the LORD, Ps. 137:7
And an envoy has been sent among the nations saying, Jer. 49:14-16
"Arise and let us go against her for battle"—
2 "Behold, I will make you small among the nations;
You are greatly despised.
3 "The arrogance of your heart has deceived you,
You who live in the clefts of [a]the[r] rock, *Sela*
In the loftiness of your dwelling place, 2 Kin. 14:7
Who say in your heart,
[r]'Who will bring me down to earth?' Is. 14:13-15
4 "Though you[r] build high like the eagle, Job 20:6, 7
Though you set your nest among the[r] stars,
From there I will bring you down," declares the LORD. Is. 14:12-15
5 "If thieves came to you,
If robbers by night—
O how you will be ruined!—
Would they not steal *only*
[t]until they had enough?
If grape gatherers came to you, *their sufficiency*
[r]Would they not leave *some* gleanings? Deut. 24:21
6 "O how Esau will be[r] ransacked, Jer. 49:10
And his hidden treasures searched out!
7 "All the[r] men[t] allied with you
Will send you forth to the border, Jer. 30:14
And the men at peace with you *of your covenant*
Will deceive you and overpower you.
They who eat your[r] bread
Will set an ambush for you.
(There is no understanding in him.) Ps. 41:9
8 "Will I not on that day," declares the LORD,
"Destroy[r] wise men from Edom Job 5:12-14
And understanding from the mountain of Esau?
9 "Then your mighty men will be dismayed, O Teman,
In order that everyone may be cut off from the mountain of Esau by slaughter.
10 "Because of[r] violence to your brother Jacob,
You will be covered *with* shame, Gen. 27:41
[r]And you will be cut off forever. Ezek. 35:9
11 "On the day that you[r] stood aloof, Ps. 83:5, 6; 137:7
On the day that strangers carried off his wealth,
And foreigners entered his gate
And[r] cast lots for Jerusalem— Joel 3:3
You too were as one of them.

12 "Do not[t] gloat over your brother's day, *look on*
The day of his misfortune.
And[r] do not rejoice over the sons of Judah
In the day of their destruction; Prov. 17:5
Yes, do not boast
In the day of *their* distress.
13 "Do not enter the gate of My people
In the day of their disaster.
Yes, you, do not[t] gloat over their calamity *look on*
In the day of their disaster.
And do not loot their wealth
In the day of their disaster.
14 "And do not[r] stand at the fork of the road Is. 16:3, 4
To cut down their fugitives;
And do not imprison their survivors
In the day of their distress.

15 "For the[r] day of the LORD draws near on all the nations. Ezek. 30:3
[r]As you have done, it will be done to you. Jer. 50:29
Your dealings will return on your own head.
16 "Because just as you[r] drank on My holy mountain,
All the nations will drink continually. Jer. 49:12
They will drink and[a] swallow,
And become as if they had never existed. *stagger*
17 "But on Mount Zion there will be those who escape,
And it will be holy.
And the house of Jacob will [r]possess their possessions. Is. 14:1, 2
18 "Then the house of Jacob will be a[r] fire Is. 5:24
And the house of Joseph a flame;
But the house of Esau *will be* as stubble.
And they will set them on fire and consume them,
So that there will be[r] no survivor of the house of Esau," Jer. 11:23
For the LORD has spoken.
19 Then *those of* the [1]Negev will [r]possess the mountain of Esau, Is. 11:14
And *those of* the [2]Shephelah the Philistine *plain*;
Also, they will [r]possess the territory of Ephraim and the territory of Samaria,
And Benjamin *will possess* Gilead. Jer. 31:5; 32:44
20 And the exiles of this host of the sons of Israel,
Who are *among* the Canaanites as far as[r] Zarephath,
And the exiles of Jerusalem who are in Sepharad
Will possess the cities of the Negev. 1 Kin. 17:9
21 The [r]deliverers will ascend Mount Zion Neh. 9:27
To judge the mountain of Esau,
And the[r] kingdom will be the LORD'S. Ps. 22:28

[1] I.e., South country [2] I.e., the foothills

THE BOOK OF

JONAH

THE word of the LORD came to
Jonah the son of Amittai saying,
2 "Arise, go to [r]Nineveh the
great city, and [r]cry against it, for
their wickedness has come up before Me." Gen. 10:11 • Is. 58:1
3 But Jonah rose up to flee to
[r]Tarshish [r]from the presence of the
LORD. So he went down to Joppa,
found a ship which was going to
Tarshish, paid the fare, and went
down into it to go with them to
Tarshish from the presence of the
LORD. Is. 23:1, 6, 10 • Gen. 4:16
4 And the LORD hurled a great
wind on the sea and there was a
great storm on the sea so that the
ship was about to break up.
5 Then the sailors became
afraid, and every man cried to his
god, and they threw the [t]cargo
which was in the ship into the sea
to lighten *it* for them. But Jonah
had gone below into the hold of
the ship, lain down, and fallen
sound asleep. *vessels*
6 So the captain approached
him and said, "How is it that you
are sleeping? Get up, [r]call on your
god. Perhaps *your* god will be concerned about us so that we will
not perish." Ps. 107:28
7 And each man said to his
mate, "Come, let us [r]cast lots so
we may [t]learn on whose account
this calamity *has struck* us." So
they cast lots and the lot fell on
Jonah. Josh. 7:14-18 • *know*
8 Then they said to him, [r]"Tell
us, now! On whose account *has*
this calamity *struck* us? What is
your [r]occupation? And where do
you come from? What is your
country? From what people are
you?" Josh. 7:19 • Gen. 47:3
9 And he said to them, "I am a
[r]Hebrew, and I fear the LORD God
of heaven who made the sea and
the dry land." Gen. 14:13
10 Then the men became extremely frightened and they said
to him, "How could you do this?"
For the men knew that he was
fleeing from the presence of the
LORD, because he had told them.
11 So they said to him, "What
should we do to you that the sea
may become calm [t]for us?"—for
the sea was becoming increas-
ingly stormy. *from upon us*
12 And he said to them, "Pick
me up and throw me into the sea.
Then the sea will become calm [t]for
you, for I know that on account of
me this great storm *has come*
upon you." *from upon you*
13 However, the men [t]rowed
desperately to return to land but
they could not, for the sea was becoming *even* stormier against
them. *dug their oars into the water*
14 Then they called on the [r]LORD
and said, "We earnestly pray, O
LORD, do not let us perish on account of this man's life and do not
put innocent blood on us; for
Thou, O LORD, hast done as Thou
hast pleased." Ps. 107:28
15 So they picked up Jonah,
threw him into the sea, and the
sea [r]stopped its raging. Ps. 65:7
16 Then the men feared the

LORD greatly, and they offered a
sacrifice to the LORD and made
[r]vows. Ps. 50:14; 66:13, 14
17 And the LORD appointed a
great fish to swallow Jonah, and
Jonah was in the stomach of the
fish three days and three nights.

CHAPTER 2

THEN Jonah prayed to the LORD
his God [r]from the stomach of the
fish, Job 13:15; Ps. 130:1, 2
2 and he said,
"I [r]called out of my distress to
the LORD, 1 Sam. 30:6
And He answered me.
I cried for help from the
[t]depth of Sheol; *belly*
Thou didst hear my voice.
3 "For Thou hadst [r]cast me into
the deep, Lam. 3:54
Into the heart of the seas,
And the current engulfed me.
All Thy breakers and billows
passed over me.
4 "So I said, 'I have been [r]ex-
pelled from Thy sight.
Nevertheless I will look
again toward Thy holy
temple.' Ps. 31:22
5 "Water encompassed me to
the [t]point of death. *soul*
The great deep [t]engulfed me,
Weeds were wrapped around
my head. *surrounded*
6 "I [r]descended to the roots of
the mountains. Ps. 18:5
The earth with its bars *was*
around me forever,
But Thou hast brought up my
life from [a]the pit, O LORD
my God. *corruption*
7 "While I was [r]fainting away,
I remembered the LORD;
And my prayer came to
Thee, Ps. 142:3
Into Thy holy temple.
8 "Those who regard vain idols
Forsake their faithfulness,
9 But I will [r]sacrifice to Thee
With the voice of thanksgiving. Ps. 50:14, 23
That which I have vowed I
will [r]pay. Job 22:27
Salvation is from the LORD."
10 Then the LORD commanded
the [r]fish, and it vomited Jonah up
onto the dry land. Jon. 1:17

CHAPTER 3

NOW the word of the LORD came
to Jonah the second time, saying,
2 "Arise, go to [r]Nineveh the
great city and [r]proclaim to it the
proclamation which I am going to
tell you." Zeph. 2:13 • Jer. 1:17
3 So Jonah arose and went to
Nineveh according to the word of
the LORD. Now Nineveh was [1]an
[r]exceedingly great city, a three
days' walk. Jon. 1:2; 4:11
4 Then Jonah began to go
through the city one day's walk;
and he [r]cried out and said, "Yet
forty days and Nineveh will be
overthrown." Matt. 12:41
5 Then the people of Nineveh
believed in God; and they called a
fast and put on sackcloth from the
greatest to the least of them.
6 When the word reached the
king of Nineveh, he arose from his
throne, laid aside his robe from
him, covered *himself* with sackcloth, and sat on the [a]ashes. *dust*
7 And he issued a proclamation
and it said, "In Nineveh by
the decree of the king and his

[1]Lit., *a great city to God*

nobles: Do not let man, beast,
herd, or flock taste a thing. Do not
let them eat or drink water.
8 "But both man and beast must
be covered with sackcloth; and let
[t]men call on God earnestly that
each may turn from his wicked
way and from the violence which
is in[t]his hands. *them • their*
9 "Who[r] knows, God may turn
and relent, and withdraw His
burning anger so that we shall not
perish?" 2 Sam. 12:22; Joel 2:14
10 When God saw their deeds,
that they turned from their
wicked way, then God relented
concerning the calamity which He
had declared He would[t]bring upon
them. And He did not do *it*. *do*

CHAPTER 4

BUT it greatly displeased Jonah,
and he became angry.
2 And he prayed to the LORD
and said, "Please LORD, was not
this what I said while I was still in
my *own* country? Therefore, in order to forestall this I fled to Tarshish, for I knew that Thou art a
gracious and compassionate God,
slow to anger and abundant in
lovingkindness, and one who re-
lents concerning calamity.
3 "Therefore now, O LORD,
please take my life from me, for
death is better to me than life."
4 And the LORD said, "Do you
have good reason to be angry?"
5 Then Jonah went out from
the city and sat east of[t]it. There he
made a shelter for himself and[r]sat
under it in the shade until he
could see what would happen in
the city. *the city* • 1 Kin. 19:9, 13
6 So the LORD God appointed a
plant and it grew up over Jonah to
be a shade over his head to deliver
him from his discomfort. And Jonah was[t]extremely happy about
the plant. *greatly*
7 But God appointed a worm
when dawn came the next day,
and it attacked the plant and it
[r]withered. Joel 1:12
8 And it came about when the
sun came up that God appointed a
scorching east wind, and the sun
beat down on Jonah's head so that
he became faint and begged with
all his soul to die, saying, "Death
is better to me than life."
9 Then God said to Jonah, "Do
you have good reason to be angry
about the plant?" And he said, "I
have good reason to be angry,
even to death."
10 Then the LORD said, "You
had compassion on the plant for
which you did not work, and
which you did not cause to grow,
which *came up*[t]overnight and perished[t]overnight. *a son of a night*
11 "And should I not[r]have compassion on Nineveh, the great city
in which there are more than
120,000 persons who do not[r]know
the difference between their right
and left hand, as well as many animals?" Jon. 3:10 • Deut. 1:39

THE BOOK OF

MICAH

THE [r]word of the LORD which came *to* Micah of Moresheth in the days of [r]Jotham, Ahaz, *and* Hezekiah, kings of Judah, which he saw concerning Samaria and Jerusalem. 2 Pet. 1:21 • Hos. 1:1

2 Hear, O peoples, all of [t]you;
[r]Listen, O earth and [t]all it contains, *them* • Jer. 6:19
And let the Lord GOD be a witness against you,
The Lord from His holy temple. *its fulness*
3 For behold, the LORD is [r]coming forth from His place.
He will come down and tread on the high places of the [a]earth. Is. 26:21 • *land*
4 [r]The mountains will melt under Him, Ps. 97:5
And the valleys will be split,
Like wax before the fire,
Like water poured down a steep place.
5 All this is for the rebellion of Jacob
And for the sins of the house of Israel.
What is the [r]rebellion of Jacob? Jer. 2:19
Is it not [r]Samaria? Is. 7:9
What is the high [t]place of Judah? *places*
Is it not Jerusalem?
6 For I will make Samaria a [r]heap of ruins [t]in the open country, 2 Kin. 19:25
Planting places for a vineyard. *of the field*
I will pour her stones down into the valley,
And will [r]lay bare her foundations. Ezek. 13:14
7 All of her [r]idols will be smashed, Deut. 9:21
All of her earnings will be burned with fire,
And all of her images I will make desolate,
For she collected *them* from a harlot's earnings,
And to the earnings of a harlot they will return.

8 Because of this I must lament and wail,
I must go [r]barefoot and naked; Is. 32:11
I must make a lament like the [r]jackals Is. 13:21, 22
And a mourning like the ostriches.
9 For her [t]wound is incurable,
For it has come to Judah;
It has reached the gate of my people,
Even to Jerusalem. *wounds*
10 Tell it not in Gath,
Weep not at all.
At [1]Beth-le-aphrah roll yourself in the dust.
11 Go on your way, inhabitant of [2]Shaphir, in [r]shameful nakedness. Ezek. 23:29
The inhabitant of [3]Zaanan does not [t]escape. *go out*
The lamentation of [4]Beth-ezel: "He will take from you its support."
12 For the inhabitant of [5]Maroth

[1]I.e., house of dust [2]I.e., pleasantness
[3]I.e., going out [4]I.e., house of removal
[5]I.e., bitterness

Becomes weak [r]waiting for
good, Is. 59:9-11
Because a calamity has come
down from the LORD
To the gate of Jerusalem.
13 Harness the chariot to the
team of horses,
O inhabitant of Lachish—
She was the beginning of sin
To the daughter of Zion—
Because in you were found
The rebellious acts of Israel.
14 Therefore, you will give parting [r]gifts 2 Kin. 16:8
On behalf of Moresheth-
gath;
The houses of Achzib *will*
become a deception
To the kings of Israel.
15 Moreover, I will bring on you
The one who takes posses-
sion,
O inhabitant of [6]Mareshah.
The glory of Israel will enter
[r]Adullam. Josh. 12:15
16 Make yourself [r]bald and cut
off your hair, Is. 22:12
Because of the children of
your delight;
Extend your baldness like
the eagle,
For they will [r]go from you
into exile. 2 Kin. 17:6

CHAPTER 2

WOE to those who [r]scheme iniquity, Ps. 36:4; Is. 32:7
Who work out evil on their
beds!
[r]When morning comes, they
do it, Hos. 7:6, 7
For it is in the [r]power of their
hands. Gen. 31:29

[6]I.e., possession

2 They [r]covet fields and then
[r]seize *them*, Jer. 22:17
And houses, and take *them*
away. Is. 5:8
They [t]rob a man and his
house, *oppress*
A man and his inheritance.
3 Therefore, thus says the
LORD,
"Behold, I am [r]planning
against this family a ca-
lamity Deut. 28:48
From which you cannot re-
move your necks;
And you will not walk
[r]haughtily, Is. 2:11, 12
For it will be an evil time.
4 "On that day they will take up
against you a [a]taunt
And [t]utter a bitter lamentation *and* say,
'We are completely de-
stroyed! *proverb • lament*
He exchanges the portion of
my people;
How He removes it from me!
To the apostate He appor-
tions our fields.'
5 "Therefore, you will have no
one [t]stretching a measuring line *casting*
For you by lot in the assembly of the LORD.
6 'Do not [t]speak out,' *so* they
[t]speak out.
But if they do not [t]speak out
concerning these things,
Reproaches will not be
turned back. *flow*
7 "Is it being said, O house of
Jacob:
'Is the Spirit of the LORD [r]im-
patient? Is. 50:2; 59:1
Are these His doings?'
Do not My words do good

To the one [r]walking uprightly? Ps. 15:2; 84:11
8 "Recently[t] My people have arisen as an enemy—
You strip the [a]robe off the garment,
From unsuspecting passersby,
From those returned from war.

And yesterday *ornaments*

9 "The women of My people you[r]evict, Jer. 10:20
Each *one* from her pleasant house.
From her children you take My splendor forever.
10 "Arise and go,
For this is no place [r]of rest
Because of the uncleanness that brings on destruction, Deut. 12:9
A painful destruction.
11 "If a man walking after wind and[r]falsehood Jer. 5:31
Had told lies *and said,*
'I will[t]speak out to you concerning wine and liquor,'
He would be spokesman to this people.

flow

12 "I will surely[r]assemble all of you, Jacob, Mic. 4:6, 7
I will surely gather the[r]remnant of Israel. Mic. 5:7, 8
I will put them together like sheep in the fold;
Like a flock in the midst of its pasture
They will be noisy with men.
13 "The breaker goes up before them;
They break out, pass through the gate, and go out by it.
So their king goes on before them,
And the LORD at their head."

CHAPTER 3

AND I said,
[r]"Hear now, heads of Jacob
And rulers of the house of Israel. Is. 1:10; Mic. 3:9
Is it not for you to[r]know justice? Ps. 82:1-5; Jer. 5:5
2 "You who hate good and love evil,
Who[r]tear off their skin from them Ps. 53:4
And their flesh from their bones,
3 And who[r]eat the flesh of my people, Ps. 14:4; 27:2
Strip off their skin from them,
Break their bones,
And[r]chop *them* up as for the pot Ezek. 11:3, 6, 7
And as meat in a kettle."
4 Then they will[r]cry out to the LORD, Ps. 18:41
But He will not answer them.
Instead, He will[r]hide His face from them at that time,
Because they have practiced evil deeds. Deut. 31:17

5 Thus says the LORD concerning the prophets
Who lead my people astray;
When they have *something* to bite with their teeth,
They[r]cry, "Peace," Jer. 6:14
But against him who puts nothing in their mouths,
They declare holy war.
6 Therefore *it will be*[r]night for you—without vision,
And darkness for you—without divination.
The sun will go down on the prophets, Is. 8:20-22

And the day will become
dark over them.
7 The seers will be [r]ashamed
And the diviners will be embarrassed. Zech. 13:4
Indeed, they will all cover
their [t]mouths *mustache*
Because there is no answer
from God.
8 On the other hand [r]I am filled
with power— Jer. 1:18
With the Spirit of the LORD—
And with justice and courage
To [r]make known to Jacob his
rebellious act, Is. 58:1
Even to Israel his sin.
9 Now hear this, heads of the
house of Jacob
And rulers of the house of Israel,
Who [r]abhor justice Ps. 58:1, 2
And twist everything that is
straight,
10 Who [r]build Zion with
bloodshed Jer. 22:13, 17
And Jerusalem with violent
injustice.
11 Her leaders pronounce [r]judg-
ment for a bribe, Is. 1:23
Her [r]priests instruct for a
price, Jer. 6:13
And her prophets divine for
money.
Yet they lean on the LORD
saying,
"Is [r]not the LORD in our midst?
Calamity will not come upon
us." Is. 48:2
12 Therefore, on account of you,
[r]Zion will be plowed as a
field, Jer. 26:18
[r]Jerusalem will become a
heap of ruins, Ps. 79:1
And the mountain of the
[t]temple *will become* high
places of a forest. *house*

CHAPTER 4

AND it will come about in the
[r]last days Is. 2:2-4
That the [r]mountain of the
house of the LORD
Will be established [t]as the
chief of the mountains.
It will be raised above the
hills, Ezek. 43:12 • *on*
And the [r]peoples will stream
to it. Ps. 22:27; 86:9
2 And many nations will come
and say,
"Come and let us go up to the
mountain of the LORD
And to the house of the God
of Jacob,
That [r]He may teach us about
His ways Ps. 25:8, 9, 12
And that we may walk in His
paths."
For from Zion will go forth
the law,
Even the word of the LORD
from Jerusalem.
3 And He will judge between
many peoples
And render decisions for
mighty, [t]distant nations.
Then they will hammer their
swords into plowshares
And their spears into pruning
hooks; *at a distance*
Nation will not lift up sword
against nation,
And never again will they
[t]train for war. *learn*
4 And each of them will sit under his vine
And under his fig tree,
With [r]no one to make *them*
afraid, Lev. 26:6
For the mouth of the LORD of
hosts has spoken.

5 Though all the peoples walk
Each in the name of his god,
As for us, we will walk
In the name of the LORD our
God forever and ever.

6 "In that day," declares the
LORD,
"I will assemble the [r]lame,
And gather the outcasts,
Even those whom I have af-
flicted. Zeph. 3:19
7 "I will make the lame a [r]rem-
nant, Mic. 5:7, 8; 7:18
And the outcasts a strong na-
tion,
And the LORD will reign over
them in Mount Zion
From now on and forever.
8 "And as for you, [r]tower of the
flock, Ps. 48:3, 12; 61:3
Hill of the daughter of Zion,
To you it will come—
Even the [r]former dominion
will come, Is. 1:26
The kingdom of the daughter
of Jerusalem.

9 "Now, why do you [r]cry out
loudly? Jer. 8:19
Is there no king among you,
Or has your [r]counselor perished, Is. 3:1-3
That agony has gripped you
like a woman in child-
birth?
10 "Writhe[r] and labor to give
birth, Mic. 5:3
Daughter of Zion,
Like a woman in childbirth,
For now you will [r]go out of
the city, 2 Kin. 20:18
Dwell in the field,
And go to Babylon.
There you will be rescued;
[r]There the LORD will redeem
you Is. 48:20; 52:9-12
From the hand of your en-
emies.
11 "And now [r]many nations have
been assembled against
you Is. 5:25-30; 17:12-14
Who say, 'Let her be pol-
luted,
And let our eyes [t]gloat over
Zion.' *look on*
12 "But they do not [r]know the
thoughts of the LORD,
And they do not understand
His purpose;
For He has gathered them
like sheaves to the
threshing floor. Ps. 147:19
13 "Arise and [r]thresh, daughter of
Zion, Is. 41:15
For your horn I will make
iron
And your hoofs I will make
bronze,
That you may pulverize
many peoples,
That you may [r]devote to the
LORD their unjust gain
And their wealth to the Lord
of all the earth. Is. 60:9

CHAPTER 5

"NOW [t] muster yourselves in
troops, daughter of
troops; *He has*
They have laid siege against
us;
With a rod they will [r]smite
the judge of Israel on the
cheek. 1 Kin. 22:24
2 "But as for you, Bethlehem
Ephrathah,
Too little to be among the
clans of Judah,
From [r]you One will go forth
for Me to be ruler in Is-
rael. Is. 11:1

His goings forth are [r]from
long ago, Ps. 102:25
From the days of eternity."
3 Therefore, He will [r]give them
up until the time Hos. 11:8
When she [r]who is in labor has
borne a child. Mic. 4:9, 10
Then the [r]remainder of His
brethren Is. 10:20-22
Will return to the sons of Israel.
4 And He will arise and [r]shep-
herd *His flock* Is. 40:11
In the strength of the LORD,
In the majesty of the name of
the LORD His God.
And they will remain,
Because [t]at that time He will
be great *now*
To the ends of the earth.
5 And this One [r]will be *our*
peace. Is. 9:6; Luke 2:14

When the [r]Assyrian invades
our land, Is. 8:7, 8
When he tramples on our
[a]citadels, *palaces*
Then we will raise against
him
Seven shepherds and eight
leaders of men.
6 And they will [r]shepherd the
land of Assyria with the
sword, Nah. 2:11-13
The land of [r]Nimrod at its entrances; Gen. 10:8-11
And He will [r]deliver *us* from
the Assyrian Is. 14:25
When he attacks our land
And when he tramples our
territory.

7 Then the remnant of Jacob
Will be among many peoples
Like dew from the LORD,
Like showers on vegetation
Which do not wait for man
Or delay for the sons of men.
8 And the remnant of Jacob
Will be among the nations,
Among many peoples
[r]Like a lion among the beasts
of the forest, Gen. 49:9
Like a young lion among
flocks of sheep,
Which, if he passes through,
Tramples down and tears,
And there is none to rescue.
9 Your hand will be [r]lifted up
against your adversaries,
And all your enemies will be
cut off. Ps. 10:12; 21:8

10 "And it will be in that day,"
declares the LORD,
"That I will cut off your [r]horses
from among you Is. 2:7
And destroy your chariots.
11 "I will also cut off the [r]cities of
your land Is. 1:7; 6:11
And tear down all your [r]forti-
fications. Is. 2:12-17
12 "I will cut off [r]sorceries from
your hand, Is. 2:6
And you will have fortune-
tellers no more.
13 "I [r]will cut off your carved images Is. 2:18; 17:8
And your *sacred* pillars from
among you,
So that you will no longer
bow down
To the work of your hands.
14 "I will root out your Asherim
from among you
And destroy your cities.
15 "And I will [r]execute vengeance
in anger and wrath
On the nations which have
not obeyed." Is. 1:24

CHAPTER 6

HEAR now what the LORD is saying,
"Arise, plead your case[t] before the mountains, *with*
And let the hills hear your voice.
2 "Listen, you mountains, to the indictment of the LORD,
And you enduring foundations of the earth,
Because the[r] LORD has a case against His people;
Even with Israel He will dispute. Hos. 4:1; 12:2
3 "My people,[r] what have I done to you, Jer. 2:5
And how have I wearied you? Answer Me.
4 "Indeed, I brought you up from the land of Egypt
And ransomed you from the house of slavery,
And I sent before you Moses, Aaron, and Miriam.
5 "My people, remember now
What [r] Balak king of Moab counseled Num. 22:5, 6
And what Balaam son of Beor answered him,
And from Shittim to Gilgal,
In order[t] that you might know the righteous acts of the LORD." *to know*

6 With[r] what shall I come to the LORD Ps. 40:6-8
And bow myself before the God on high?
Shall I come to Him with burnt offerings,
With yearling calves?
7 Does the LORD take delight in [r] thousands of rams, Is. 1:1
In ten thousand rivers of oil?
Shall I present my first-born *for* my rebellious acts,
The fruit of my body for the sin of my soul?
8 He has told you, O man, what is good;
And[r] what does the LORD require of you Deut. 10:12
But to do justice, to love [a] kindness, *loyalty*
And to walk[a] humbly with your God? *circumspectly*

9 The voice of the LORD will call to the city—
And it is sound wisdom to fear Thy name:
"Hear, O tribe. Who has appointed its[t] time? *it*
10 "Is there yet a man in the wicked house,
Along with treasures of [r] wickedness, Amos 3:10
And a [t] short measure *that is* cursed? *shrunken ephah*
11 "Can I justify wicked[r] scales
And a bag of deceptive weights? Lev. 19:36
12 "For the rich men of *the*[t] city are full of[r] violence, *her*
Her residents speak lies,
And their tongue is deceitful in their mouth. Is. 1:23
13 "So also I will make *you* sick, striking you down,
[r] Desolating *you* because of your sins. Is. 1:7; 6:11
14 "You will eat, but you will[r] not be satisfied, Is. 9:20
And your [7] vileness will be in your midst.
You will *try to* remove *for safekeeping,*
But you will [r] not preserve *anything,* Is. 30:6

[7] Or possibly, *garbage* or *excreta*

And what you do preserve I
will give to the sword.
15 "You will sow but you will [r]not
reap. Deut. 28:38-40
You will tread the olive but
will not anoint yourself
with oil;
And the grapes, but you will
not drink wine.
16 "The statutes of Omri
And all the works of the
house of [r]Ahab are observed; 1 Kin. 16:29-33
And in their devices you
[r]walk. Jer. 7:24
Therefore, I will give you up
for destruction
And [t]your inhabitants for derision, *her*
And you will bear the reproach of My people."

CHAPTER 7

WOE is me! For I am
Like the fruit pickers and the
[r]grape gatherers.
There is not a cluster of
grapes to eat,
Or a first-ripe fig *which* [t]I
crave. Is. 24:13 • *my soul*
2 The [a]godly person has perished from the land,
And there is no upright *person* among men. *loyal*
All of them lie in wait for
[r]bloodshed; Is. 59:7
Each of them hunts the other
with a net.
3 Concerning evil, both hands
do it [r]well. Prov. 4:16, 17
The prince asks, also the
judge, for a bribe,
And a great man speaks the
desire of his soul;
So they weave it together.
4 The best of them is like a
[r]briar, Ezek. 2:6; 28:24
The most upright like a [r]thorn
hedge. Nah. 1:10
The day when you post a
watchman,
Your punishment will come.
Then their [r]confusion will occur. Is. 22:5
5 Do not [r]trust in a neighbor;
Do not have confidence in a
friend. Jer. 9:4
From her who lies in your
bosom
Guard your lips.
6 For [r]son treats father contemptuously,
Daughter rises up against her
mother, Matt. 10:21, 35
Daughter-in-law against her
mother-in-law;
A man's enemies are the men
of his own household.

7 But as for me, I will [r]watch
expectantly for the LORD;
I will wait for the God of my
salvation. Hab. 2:1
My God will hear me.
8 Do not rejoice over me, O [r]my
enemy. Mic. 7:10
Though I fall I will rise;
Though I dwell in darkness,
the LORD is a light for me.

9 I will bear the indignation of
the LORD
Because I have sinned
against Him,
Until He [r]pleads my case and
executes justice for me.
He will bring me out to the
[r]light,
And I will see His righteousness. Jer. 50:34 • Ps. 37:6
10 Then my enemy will see,

And shame will cover her who[r] said to me,
"Where is the LORD your God?" Joel 2:17
My eyes will look on her;
[t]At that time she will be trampled down, *Now*
Like mire of the streets.
11 *It will be* a day for[r] building your walls. Is. 54:11
On that day will your boundary be extended.
12 It *will be* a day when[t] they will[r] come to you *he*
From Assyria and the cities of Egypt, Is. 19:23-25
From Egypt even to the[t] Euphrates, *River*
Even from sea to sea and mountain to mountain.
13 And the earth will become [r]desolate because of her inhabitants, Jer. 25:11
On account of the[r] fruit of their deeds. Mic. 3:4

14 Shepherd Thy people with Thy[r] scepter, Lev. 27:32
The flock of Thy[a] possession
Which dwells by itself in the woodland, *inheritance*
In the midst of[a] a fruitful field.
Let them feed in Bashan and Gilead *Carmel*
As in the days of old.
15 "As in the days when you came out from the land of Egypt,
I will show you miracles."
16 Nations [r]will see and be ashamed Is. 26:11
Of all their might.
They will[r] put *their* hand on *their* mouth, Mic. 3:7
Their ears will be deaf.
17 They will[r] lick the dust like a serpent, Ps. 72:9
Like reptiles of the earth.
They will come trembling out of their[t] fortresses;
To the LORD our God they will come in dread,
And they will be afraid before Thee. *fastnesses*
18 Who is a God like Thee, who pardons iniquity
And passes over the rebellious act of the remnant of His[a] possession?
He does not retain His anger forever, *inheritance*
Because He[r] delights in unchanging love. Jer. 32:41
19 He will again have compassion on us;
[r]He will tread our iniquities under foot. Jer. 50:20
Yes, Thou wilt[r] cast all their sins Is. 38:17; 43:25
Into the depths of the sea.
20 Thou wilt give[a] truth to Jacob
And unchanging love to Abraham, *faithfulness*
Which Thou didst swear to our forefathers
From the days of old.

THE BOOK OF

NAHUM

THE [1]oracle of [r]Nineveh. The book of the vision of Nahum the Elkoshite. 2 Kin. 19:36; Jon. 1:2

2 A [r]jealous and avenging God
is the LORD; Ex. 20:5
The LORD is avenging and
wrathful.
The LORD takes [r]vengeance
on His adversaries,
And He reserves wrath for
His enemies. Ps. 94:1
3 The LORD is [r]slow to anger
and great in power,
And the LORD will by no
means leave *the guilty*
unpunished. Ex. 34:6, 7
In [r]whirlwind and storm is
His way, Ex. 19:16
And [r]clouds are the dust beneath His feet. Ps. 104:3
4 He [r]rebukes the sea and
makes it dry; Ps. 106:9
He dries up all the rivers.
[r]Bashan and Carmel wither;
The blossoms of Lebanon
wither. Is. 33:9
5 Mountains [r]quake because of
Him, Ex. 19:18
And the hills dissolve;
Indeed the earth is upheaved
by His presence,
The [r]world and all the inhabitants in it. Ps. 98:7
6 Who can stand before His indignation?
Who can endure the [r]burning
of His anger? Is. 13:13
His [r]wrath is poured out like
fire, Is. 66:15
And the [r]rocks are broken up
by Him. 1 Kin. 19:11
7 The LORD is [r]good, Ps. 25:8
A stronghold in the day of
trouble,
And He knows those who
take refuge in Him.
8 But with an [r]overflowing
flood Is. 28:2, 17f.
He will make a complete end
of its site,
And will pursue His enemies
into darkness.

9 Whatever you [r]devise against
the LORD,
He will make a [r]complete end
of it.
Distress will not rise up
twice. Ps. 2:1 • Is. 28:22
10 Like tangled thorns,
And like those who are
drunken with their drink,
They are [r]consumed
As stubble completely withered. Is. 5:24; 10:17
11 From you has gone forth
One who [r]plotted evil against
the LORD, Is. 10:7-11
A wicked counselor.
12 Thus says the LORD,
"Though they are at full
strength and likewise
many,
Even so, they will be cut off
and pass away.
Though I have afflicted you,
I will afflict you no longer.
13 "So now, I will [r]break his yoke
bar from upon you, Is. 9:4

[1]Or, *burden*

And I will tear off your
shackles."

14 The LORD has issued a command concerning you:
"Your name will [r]no longer be
perpetuated. Job 18:17
I will cut off idol and image
From the house of your gods.
I will prepare your grave,
For you are contemptible."

15 Behold, [r]on the mountains the
feet of him who brings
good news, Is. 40:9
Who announces peace!
[r]Celebrate your feasts, O Judah; Lev. 23:2, 4
Pay your vows.
For never again will the
[a]wicked one pass through
you; *worthless one*
He is cut off completely.

CHAPTER 2

THE one who scatters has come
up against [t]you. *your face*
Man the fortress, watch the
road;
Strengthen your back, summon all *your* strength.
2 For the LORD will restore the
[r]splendor of Jacob
Like the splendor of Israel,
Even though devastators
have devastated them
And destroyed their vine
branches. Is. 60:15

3 The shields of his mighty
men are *colored* red,
The warriors are dressed in
[r]scarlet, Ezek. 23:14, 15
The chariots are *enveloped* in
[t]flashing steel
When he is prepared *to
march*, *fire of steel*
And the cypress [r]*spears* are
brandished. Job 39:23
4 The [r]chariots race madly in
the streets, Is. 66:15
They rush wildly in the
[t]squares, *broad places*
Their appearance is like
torches,
They dash to and fro like
lightning flashes.
5 He remembers his nobles;
They stumble in their march,
They hurry to her wall,
And the mantelet is set up.
6 The gates of the rivers are
opened,
And the palace is dissolved.
7 And it is fixed:
She is stripped, she is carried
away,
And her handmaids are
[r]moaning like the sound
of doves, Is. 38:14
Beating on their breasts.

8 Though Nineveh *was* like a
pool of water throughout
her days,
Now they are fleeing;
"Stop, stop,"
But no one turns back.
9 Plunder the silver!
Plunder the gold!
For there is no limit to the
treasure—
Wealth from every kind of
desirable object.
10 She is emptied! Yes, she is
desolate and waste!
[r]Hearts are melting and knees
knocking! Is. 13:7, 8
Also anguish is in [t]the whole
body, *all the loin*
And all their [r]faces are grown
pale! Joel 2:6
11 Where is the den of the lions

And the feeding place of the
[r]young lions, Is. 5:29
Where the lion, lioness, and
lion's cub prowled,
With nothing to disturb
them?
12 The lion tore enough for his
cubs,
[t]Killed *enough* for his lioness-
es, *Strangled*
And filled his lairs with prey
And his dens with torn flesh.
13 "Behold, [r]I am against you,"
declares the LORD of hosts. "I will
[r]burn up her chariots in smoke, a
sword will devour your young
lions, I will cut off your prey from
the land, and no longer will the
voice of your messengers be
heard." Jer. 21:13 • Josh. 11:6, 9

CHAPTER 3

WOE[r] to the bloody city, completely full of lies *and* pillage; Ezek. 24:6, 9
Her prey never departs.
2 The [r]noise of the whip,
The noise of the rattling of
the wheel, Job 39:22-25
Galloping horses,
And bounding chariots!
3 Horsemen charging,
Swords flashing, [r]spears
gleaming, Hab. 3:11
[r]Many slain, a mass of
corpses, Is. 34:3; 66:16
And [t]countless dead bodies—
They stumble over the dead
bodies! *there is no end to*
4 *All* because of the many harlotries of the harlot,
The charming one, the mistress of sorceries,
Who [r]sells nations by her harlotries Rev. 18:3
And families by her sorceries.
5 "Behold, [r]I am against you,"
declares the LORD of
hosts; Jer. 50:31
"And I will [t]lift up your skirts
over your face,
And show to the nations
your nakedness
And to the kingdoms your
disgrace. *uncover your*
6 "I will throw [t]filth on you
And make you vile,
And set you up as a spectacle. *detestable things*
7 "And it will come about that
all who see you
Will [t]shrink from you and
say, *flee*
'Nineveh is devastated!
[r]Who will grieve for her?'
Where will I seek comforters
for you?" Is. 51:19

8 Are you better than [2]No-
amon,
Which was situated by the
[r]waters of the Nile,
With water surrounding her,
Whose rampart *was* the sea,
Whose wall *consisted* of the
sea? Is. 19:6-8
9 Ethiopia [r]was *her* might,
And Egypt too, without lim-
its. Is. 20:5
Put and Lubim were among
[t]her helpers. *your*
10 Yet she became an exile,
She went into captivity;
Also her small children were
dashed to pieces
At the head of every street;
They [r]cast lots for her honor-
able men, Joel 3:3

[2]I.e., the city of Amon: Thebes

And all her great men were
bound with fetters.
11 You too will become drunk,
You will be[r]hidden. Is. 2:10
You too will search for a refuge from the enemy.
12 All your fortifications are fig
trees with ripe fruit—
When shaken, they fall into
the eater's mouth.
13 Behold, your people are
[r]women in your midst!
The gates of your land are
[r]opened wide to your enemies;
Fire consumes your gate
bars. Is. 19:16 • Is. 45:1, 2
14 [r]Draw for yourself water for
the siege! 2 Chr. 32:3, 4
[r]Strengthen your fortifications! Nah. 2:1
Go into the clay and tread
the mortar!
Take hold of the brick mold!
15 There[r]fire will consume you,
The sword will cut you
down; Is. 66:15, 16
It will[r]consume you as the locust *does*. Joel 1:4

Multiply yourself like the
creeping locust,
Multiply yourself like the
swarming locust.
16 You have increased your
[r]traders more than the
stars of heaven—
The creeping locust strips
and flies away. Is. 23:8
17 Your[a]guardsmen are like the
swarming locust.
Your [r]marshals are like
hordes of grasshoppers
Settling in the stone walls on
a cold day. *officials*
The sun rises and they flee,
And the place where they are
is not known. Jer. 51:27
18 Your shepherds are sleeping,
O king of Assyria;
Your[r]nobles are lying down.
Your people are[r]scattered on
the mountains, Nah. 2:5
And there is no one to re-
gather *them*. Is. 13:14
19 There is[r]no relief for your
breakdown, Jer. 46:11
Your wound is incurable.
All who hear[t]about you
Will clap *their* hands over
you, *your report*
For on whom has not your
evil passed continually?

THE BOOK OF

HABAKKUK

THE [1]oracle which Habakkuk the prophet saw.

2 [r]How long, O LORD, will I call
for help, Ps. 13:1, 2
And Thou wilt not hear?
I cry out to Thee, "Violence!"
Yet Thou dost not save.
3 Why dost Thou make me [r]see
iniquity, Ps. 55:9-11
And cause *me* to look on
wickedness?
Yes, [r]destruction and violence are before me;
Strife exists and contention
arises. Jer. 20:8
4 Therefore, the law is [t]ignored
And justice is never upheld.
For the wicked [r]surround the
righteous; *numbed*
Therefore, justice comes out
perverted. Ps. 22:12

5 "Look [r]among the nations! Observe! Acts 13:41
Be astonished! Wonder!
Because *I* am doing something in your days—
You would not believe if [t]you
were told. *it*
6 "For behold, I am raising up
the Chaldeans,
That [t]fierce and impetuous
people *bitter*
Who march [t]throughout the
earth *the breadth of*
To seize dwelling places
which are not theirs.
7 "They are dreaded and feared.
Their justice and [t]authority
originate with themselves. *eminence*

[1]Or, *burden*

8 "Their [r]horses are swifter than
leopards Jer. 4:13
And keener than [r]wolves in
the evening. Zeph. 3:3
Their horsemen come galloping,
Their horsemen come from
afar;
They fly like an eagle swooping *down* to devour.
9 "All of them come for violence.
Their horde of [r]faces *moves*
forward. 2 Kin. 12:17
They collect captives like
sand.
10 "They [r]mock at kings,
And rulers are a laughing
matter to them.
They laugh at every fortress,
And heap up rubble to capture it. 2 Chr. 36:6, 10
11 "Then they will sweep
through *like* the [r]wind and
pass on. Jer. 4:11, 12
But they will be held [r]guilty,
They whose strength is their
god." Jer. 2:3

12 Art Thou not from [r]everlasting, Deut. 33:27
O LORD, my God, my Holy
One?
We will not die.
Thou, O LORD, hast appointed them to judge;
And Thou, O Rock, hast established them to correct.
13 *Thine* eyes are too pure to
[t]approve evil, *look at*
And Thou canst not look on
wickedness *with favor.*

Why dost Thou [r]look with favor Jer. 12:1, 2
On those who deal [r]treacherously? Is. 24:16
Why art Thou [r]silent when the wicked swallow up
Those more righteous than they? Ps. 50:21
14 *Why* hast Thou made men like the fish of the sea,
Like creeping things without a ruler over them?
15 *The Chaldeans* [r]bring all of them up with a hook,
[r]Drag them away with their net, Jer. 16:16 • Ps. 10:9
And gather them together in their fishing net.
Therefore, they rejoice and are glad.
16 Therefore, they offer a sacrifice to their net.
And [a]burn incense to their fishing net; *sacrifice*
Because through these things their catch is large,
And their food is plentiful.
17 Will they therefore empty their [r]net Is. 19:8
And continually slay nations without sparing?

CHAPTER 2

I WILL stand on my guard post
And station myself on the rampart;
And I will [r]keep watch to see [r]what He will speak to me, Ps. 5:3 • Ps. 85:8
And how I may reply when I am reproved.
2 Then the LORD answered me and said,
[r]"Record the vision Deut. 27:8
And inscribe *it* on tablets,
That the one who reads it may run.
3 "For the vision is yet for the appointed time;
It [t]hastens toward the goal, and it will not fail.
Though it tarries, wait for it;
For it will certainly come, it will not delay. *pants*

4 "Behold, as for the [r]proud one,
His soul is not right within him; Ps. 49:18; Is. 13:11
But the righteous will live by his [a]faith. *faithfulness*
5 "Furthermore, [r]wine betrays the [r]haughty man,
So that he does not [r]stay at home. Prov. 20:1
He [r]enlarges his appetite like Sheol, Prov. 21:24
And he is like death, never satisfied. 2 Kin. 14:10
He also gathers to himself all nations Prov. 27:20
And collects to himself all peoples.

6 "Will not all of these [r]take up a taunt-song against him,
Even mockery *and* insinuations against him,
And say, 'Woe to him who increases what is not his— Is. 14:4-10
For how long—
And makes himself [t]rich with loans?' *heavy*
7 "Will not your creditors [r]rise up suddenly, Prov. 29:1
And those who collect from you awaken?
Indeed, you will become plunder for them.

8 "Because you have [r]looted many nations,
All the remainder of the peoples will loot you—
Because of human bloodshed and violence done to the land,
To the town and all its inhabitants. Is. 33:1; Jer. 27:7

9 "Woe to him who gets evil gain for his house
To put his nest on high
To be delivered from the hand of calamity!
10 "You have devised a shameful thing for your house
By cutting off many peoples;
So you are [r]sinning against yourself. Jer. 26:19
11 "Surely the stone will cry out from the wall,
And the rafter will answer it from the framework.

12 "Woe to him who builds a city with bloodshed
And founds a town with [a]violence! *injustice*
13 "Is it not indeed from the LORD of hosts
That peoples [r]toil for fire,
And nations grow weary for nothing? Is. 50:11
14 "For the earth will be filled
With the knowledge of the glory of the LORD,
As the waters cover the sea.

15 "Woe to you who make [t]your neighbors drink,
Who mix in your venom even to make *them* drunk
So as to look on their nakedness! *his neighbor*
16 "You will be filled with disgrace rather than honor.
Now you yourself [r]drink and expose your *own* nakedness. Lam. 4:21
The [r]cup in the LORD's right hand will come around to you, Jer. 25:15, 17
And [r]utter disgrace *will come* upon your glory. Nah. 3:6
17 "For the [r]violence done to Lebanon will [t]overwhelm you, Joel 3:19 • *cover*
And the devastation of *its* beasts [t]by which you terrified them,
[r]Because of human bloodshed and violence *done* to the land, which *terrified them*
To the town and all its inhabitants. Hab. 2:8

18 "What [r]profit is the idol when its maker has carved it,
Or [t]an image, a teacher of falsehood? Is. 42:17
For *its* maker trusts in his *own* handiwork
When he fashions speechless idols. a *cast* metal *image*
19 "Woe to him who says to a *piece of* wood, 'Awake!'
To a dumb stone, 'Arise!'
And that is *your* teacher?
Behold, it is overlaid with gold and silver,
And there is [r]no breath at all inside it. Ps. 135:17
20 "But the [r]LORD is in His holy temple. Mic. 1:2
Let all the earth be [r]silent before Him." Zeph. 1:7

CHAPTER 3

A PRAYER of Habakkuk the prophet, according to [2]Shigionoth.

[2]I.e., A highly emotional poetic form

2 Lord, I have heard the report
about Thee *and* I fear.
O Lord, revive Thy work in
the midst of the years,
In the midst of the years
make it known;
In wrath remember mercy.

3 God comes from Teman,
And the Holy One from
Mount Paran. [Selah.
His [r]splendor covers the
heavens, Ps. 113:4
And the [r]earth is full of His
praise. Ps. 48:10
4 *His* [r]radiance is like the sun-
light; Ps. 18:12
He has rays *flashing* from
His hand,
And there is the hiding of His
[r]power. Job 26:14
5 Before Him goes pestilence,
And plague comes after Him.
6 He stood and surveyed the
earth;
He looked and [r]startled the
nations. Job 21:18
Yes, the perpetual mountains
were shattered,
The ancient hills collapsed.
His ways are everlasting.
7 I saw the tents of Cushan under distress,
The tent curtains of the land
of [r]Midian were trem-
bling. Num. 31:7, 8

8 Did the Lord rage against
the [r]rivers, Ex. 7:19, 20
Or *was* Thine anger against
the rivers,
Or *was* Thy wrath against
the [r]sea, Ex. 14:16, 21
That Thou didst [r]ride on Thy
horses, Deut. 33:26
On Thy chariots of salvation?
9 Thy bow was made bare,
The rods of [t]chastisement
were sworn. [Selah.
Thou didst cleave the earth
with rivers. *word*
10 The mountains saw Thee *and*
quaked;
The downpour of waters
swept by.
The deep [r]uttered forth its
voice, Ps. 93:3; 98:7, 8
It lifted high its hands.
11 [r]Sun *and* moon stood in their
places; Josh. 10:12-14
They went away at the light
of Thine arrows,
At the radiance of Thy
gleaming spear.
12 In indignation Thou didst
march through the earth;
In anger Thou didst [a]trample
the nations. *thresh*
13 Thou didst go forth for the
[r]salvation of Thy people,
For the salvation of Thine
anointed. Ex. 15:2
Thou didst strike the head of
the house of the evil
To lay him open from thigh
to neck. [Selah.
14 Thou didst pierce with his
own [t]spears *shafts*
The head of his [a]throngs.
They stormed in to scatter
[t]us; *warriors* or *villagers* • *me*
Their exultation *was* like
those
Who [r]devour the oppressed in
secret. Ps. 10:8; 64:2-5
15 Thou didst tread on the sea
with Thy horses,
On the surge of many waters.

16 I heard and my [t]inward parts
[r]trembled, *belly*
At the sound my lips quiv-
ered. Dan. 10:8

Decay enters my bones,
And in my place I tremble.
Because I must wait quietly
for the day of distress,
For the [r]people to arise *who*
will invade us. Jer. 5:15
17 Though the [r]fig tree should
not blossom, Amos 4:9
And there be no [t]fruit on the
vines, *produce*
Though the yield of the [r]olive
should fail, Mic. 6:15
And the fields produce no
food,
Though the flock should be
cut off from the fold,
And there be [r]no cattle in the
stalls, Jer. 5:17
18 Yet I will exult in the LORD,
I will rejoice in the [r]God of
my salvation. Ps. 25:5
19 The Lord GOD is my [r]strength,
And He has made my feet
like hinds' *feet*,
And makes me walk on my
high places. Ps. 18:32, 33

For the choir director, on my stringed instruments.

THE BOOK OF

ZEPHANIAH

THE word of the LORD which
came to Zephaniah son of Cushi,
son of Gedaliah, son of Amariah,
son of Hezekiah, in the days of Josiah son of Amon, king of Judah,
2 "I will completely [r]remove all
things Gen. 6:7
From the face of the earth,"
declares the LORD.
3 "I will remove [r]man and beast;
I will remove the birds of the
sky Is. 6:11, 12
And the fish of the sea,
And the [a]ruins along with the
wicked; *stumbling blocks*
And I will cut off man from
the face of the [t]earth," declares the LORD. *ground*
4 "So I will [r]stretch out My hand
against Judah Jer. 6:12
And against all the inhabitants of Jerusalem.
And I will [r]cut off the remnant of Baal from this
place, Mic. 5:13
And the names of the [r]idola-
trous priests along with
the priests. 2 Kin. 23:5
5 "And those who bow down on
the [r]housetops to the host
of heaven, 2 Kin. 23:12
And those who bow down
and swear to the LORD
and *yet* swear by Milcom,
6 And those who have [r]turned
back from following the
LORD, Is. 1:4; Hos. 7:10
And those who have [r]not
sought the LORD or in-
quired of Him." Is. 9:13

7 Be [t]silent before the Lord
GOD! *Hush*
For the [r]day of the LORD is
near, Zeph. 1:14

For the LORD has prepared a
ʳsacrifice, Is. 34:6
He has ʳconsecrated His
guests. Is. 13:3
8 "Then it will come about on
the day of the LORD's sacrifice,
That I will ʳpunish the
princes, the king's sons,
And all who clothe themselves
with foreign garments. Is. 24:21
9 "And I will punish on that day
all who leap on the *temple*
threshold,
Who fill the house of their
lord with violence and
deceit.
10 "And on that day," declares
the LORD,
"There will be the sound of a
cry from the ʳFish Gate,
A wail from the [1]Second
Quarter, 2 Chr. 33:14
And a loud crash from the
ʳhills. Ezek. 6:13
11 "Wail, O inhabitants of the
[1]Mortar,
For all the people of Canaan
will be silenced;
All who weigh out ʳsilver will
be cut off. Hos. 9:6
12 "And it will come about at
that time
That I will ʳsearch Jerusalem
with lamps, Amos 9:1-3
And I will punish the men
Who are stagnant in spirit,
Who say in their hearts,
'The LORD will ʳnot do good or
evil!' Ezek. 8:12; 9:9
13 "Moreover, their wealth will
become plunder,
And their houses desolate;
Yes, they will build houses
but not inhabit *them*,
And plant vineyards but not
drink their wine."

14 Near is the ʳgreat ʳday of the
LORD, Jer. 30:7
Near and coming very
quickly; Ezek. 7:7, 12
Listen, the day of the LORD!
ᵗIn it the warrior cries out bitterly.
There
15 A day of wrath is that day,
A day of ʳtrouble and distress,
A day of destruction and
desolation, Is. 22:5
A day of ʳdarkness and
gloom, Joel 2:2, 31
A day of clouds and thick
darkness,
16 A day of ʳtrumpet and battle
cry, Is. 27:13; Jer. 4:19
Against the fortified cities
And the high corner towers.
17 And I will bring ʳdistress on
men, Jer. 10:18
So that they will walk ʳlike
the blind, Deut. 28:29
Because they have sinned
against the LORD;
And their blood will be
poured out like dust,
And their flesh like dung.
18 Neither their ʳsilver nor their
gold Ezek. 7:19
Will be able to deliver them
On the day of the LORD's
wrath;
And ʳall the earth will be devoured
Zeph. 3:8
In the fire of His jealousy,
For He will ʳmake a complete
end, Gen. 6:7
Indeed a terrifying one,
Of all the inhabitants of the
earth.

[1]I.e., a district of Jerusalem

CHAPTER 2

GATHER yourselves together,
yes,[r]gather, Joel 1:14
O nation without shame,
2 Before the decree[t] takes effect— *is born*
The day passes [r] like the chaff— Is. 17:13
Before the[r] burning anger of the LORD comes upon you, Lam. 4:11
Before the day of the LORD's anger comes upon you.
3 Seek the LORD,
All you humble of the[a]earth
Who have carried out His[a]ordinances; *land • justice*
Seek righteousness, seek humility.
Perhaps you will be[r]hidden
In the day of the LORD's anger. Ps. 57:1; Is. 26:20

4 For[r]Gaza will be abandoned,
And Ashkelon a desolation;
[r]Ashdod will be driven out at noon, Amos 1:7, 8
And Ekron will be uprooted.
5 Woe to the inhabitants of the seacoast,
The nation of the [2]Cherethites!
The word of the LORD is [r]against you, Amos 3:1
O Canaan, land of the Philistines;
And I will[r]destroy you,
So that there will be no inhabitant. Is. 14:29, 30
6 So the seacoast will be[r]pastures, Is. 5:17; 7:25
With caves for shepherds and folds for flocks.
7 And the coast will be
For the[r]remnant of the house of Judah, Is. 11:16
They will[r]pasture on it.
In the houses of Ashkelon they will lie down at evening; Is. 32:14
For the LORD their God will care for them
And restore their fortune.

8 "I have heard the[t]taunting of Moab *reproach*
And the[r]revilings of the sons of Ammon, Ezek. 25:3
With which they have taunted My people
And become arrogant against their territory.
9 "Therefore, as I live," declares the LORD of hosts,
The God of Israel,
"Surely[r]Moab will be like Sodom, Is. 15:1-9
And the sons of Ammon like Gomorrah—
A place possessed by nettles and salt pits,
And a perpetual desolation.
The remnant of My people will plunder them,
And the remainder of My nation will inherit them."
10 This they will have in return
for their[r]pride, because they have
[t]taunted and become arrogant
against the people of the LORD of
hosts. Is. 16:6 • *reproached*
11 The LORD will be terrifying to
them, for He will [t]starve all the
gods of the earth; and all the
coastlands of the nations will bow
down to Him, everyone from his
own place. *make lean*
12 "You also, O Ethiopians, will be slain by My sword."

[2]I.e., a segment of the Philistines with roots in Crete

13 And He will[r] stretch out His hand against the north
And destroy Assyria,
And He will make Nineveh a desolation, Is. 14:26
Parched like the wilderness.
14 And flocks will lie down in her midst,
All beasts which range in herds;
Both the[a] pelican and the hedgehog *owl* or *jackdaw*
Will lodge in[t] the tops of her pillars; *her capitals*
[t]Birds will sing in the window, *A voice*
Desolation *will be* on the threshold;
For He has laid bare the cedar work.
15 This is the[r] exultant city
Which dwells securely,
Who says in her heart,
"I am, and there is no one besides me." Is. 22:2
How she has become a[r] desolation, Is. 32:14
A resting place for beasts!
[r]Everyone who passes by her will hiss Jer. 18:16; 19:8
And wave his hand *in contempt.*

CHAPTER 3

WOE to her who is[r] rebellious and defiled, Jer. 5:23
The tyrannical city!
2 She heeded no voice;
She accepted no instruction.
She did not trust in the LORD;
She did not[r] draw near to her God. Ps. 73:28
3 Her[r] princes within her are roaring lions, Ezek. 22:27
Her judges are[r] wolves at evening; Jer. 5:6
They leave nothing for the morning.
4 Her prophets are[r] reckless, treacherous men;
Her priests have profaned the sanctuary. Judg. 9:4
They have done violence to the law.
5 The LORD is[r] righteous within her; Deut. 32:4
He will do no injustice.
[r]Every morning He brings His justice to light; Job 7:18
He does not fail.
But the unjust[r] knows no shame. Zeph. 2:1
6 "I have cut off nations;
Their corner towers are in ruins.
I have made their streets [r]desolate, Jer. 9:12
With no one passing by;
Their[r] cities are laid waste,
Without a man, without an inhabitant. Lev. 26:31
7 "I said, 'Surely you will revere Me,
[r]Accept instruction.' Job 36:10
So her dwelling will[r] not be cut off Jer. 7:7
According to all that I have appointed concerning her.
But they were eager to corrupt all their deeds.

8 "Therefore,[r] wait for Me," declares the LORD,
"For the day when I rise up to the prey. Ps. 27:14
Indeed, My decision is to gather nations,
To assemble kingdoms,

To pour out on them My indignation,
All My burning anger;
For [r]all the earth will be devoured Zeph. 1:18
By the fire of My zeal.
9 "For then I will [t]give to the peoples purified lips,
That all of them may call on the name of the LORD,
To serve Him shoulder to shoulder. *change*
10 "From beyond the rivers of [r]Ethiopia Ps. 68:31
My [a] worshipers, My dispersed ones, *suppliants*
Will bring My offerings.
11 "In that day you will [r]feel no shame Is. 45:17; 54:4
Because of all your deeds
By which you have rebelled against Me;
For then I will remove from your midst
Your [r]proud, exulting ones,
And you will never again be haughty Is. 2:12; 5:15
On My holy mountain.
12 "But I will leave among you
A humble and lowly people,
And they will take refuge in the name of the LORD.
13 "The [r]remnant of Israel will do no wrong Is. 10:20-22
And tell no lies,
Nor will a deceitful tongue
Be found in their mouths;
For they shall [r]feed and lie down Ezek. 34:13-15
With no one to make them tremble."

14 Shout for joy, O daughter of Zion!
[r]Shout *in triumph,* O Israel!
Rejoice and exult with all *your* heart, Zech. 9:9
O daughter of Jerusalem!
15 The LORD has taken away [r]*His* judgments against you, Ps. 19:9; John 5:30
He has cleared away your enemies.
The King of Israel, the LORD, is in your midst;
You will [r] fear disaster no more. Is. 54:14
16 [r]In that day it will be said to Jerusalem:
"Do [r]not be afraid, O Zion;
Do not let your hands fall limp. Is. 25:9 • Is. 35:3, 4
17 "The LORD your God is [r]in your midst, Zeph. 3:5, 15
A [t]victorious warrior.
He will [r]exult over you with joy, *A warrior who saves*
He will be quiet in His love,
He will rejoice over you with shouts of joy. Is. 62:5
18 "I will gather those who grieve about the appointed feasts—
They [t]came from you, O *Zion;*
The reproach *of exile* is a burden on them. *were*
19 "Behold, I am going to deal at that time
With all your [r]oppressors,
I will save the lame
And gather the outcast,
And I will turn their shame into praise and renown
In all the earth. Is. 60:14
20 "At that time I will [r]bring you in, Ezek. 37:12, 21
Even at the time when I gather you together;

Indeed, I will give you[r] renown and praise
Among all the peoples of the
earth, Deut. 26:18, 19
When I[r] restore your fortunes
before your eyes,"
Says the LORD. Jer. 29:14

THE BOOK OF

HAGGAI

IN the second year of Darius the
king, on the first day of the sixth
month, the word of the LORD
came by the prophet Haggai to
Zerubbabel the son of Shealtiel,
governor of Judah, and to Joshua
the son of Jehozadak, the high
priest saying,
2 "Thus says the LORD of[t] hosts,
'This people says, "The time has
not come, *even* the time for the
house of the LORD to be rebuilt." ' " *hosts, saying*
3 Then the word of the LORD
came by Haggai the prophet saying,
4 "Is it time for you yourselves
to dwell in your paneled houses
while this house *lies* desolate?"
5 Now therefore, thus says the
LORD of hosts, [t]"Consider your
ways! *Set your heart on*
6 "You have sown much, but
harvest little; *you* eat, but *there is*
not *enough* to be satisfied; *you*
drink, but *there is* not *enough* to
become drunk; *you* put on clothing, but no one is warm *enough*;
and he who earns, earns wages *to
put* into a purse with holes."
7 Thus says the LORD of hosts,
"Consider your ways!
8 "Go up to the mountains,
bring wood and rebuild the temple, that I may be pleased with it
and be glorified," says the LORD.
9 "*You* look for much, but behold, *it comes* to little; when you
bring *it* home, I[r] blow it *away*.
Why?" declares the LORD of hosts,
"Because of My house which *lies*
desolate, while each of you runs
to his own house. Is. 40:7
10 "Therefore, because of you
the[r] sky has withheld[t] its dew, and
the earth has withheld its produce. Deut. 28:23, 24 • *from dew*
11 "And I called for a drought on
the land, on the mountains, on the
grain, on the new wine, on the oil,
on what the ground produces, on
men, on cattle, and on all the labor
of[t] your hands." *the palms*
12 Then Zerubbabel the son of
Shealtiel, and Joshua the son of
Jehozadak, the high priest, with
all the remnant of the people,
obeyed the voice of the LORD their
God and the words of Haggai the
prophet, as the LORD their God
had sent him. And the people
showed reverence for the LORD.
13 Then Haggai, the messenger
of the LORD, spoke[a] by the commission of the LORD to the people
saying, " 'I am with you,' declares
the LORD." *the message*
14 So the LORD stirred up the

spirit of [r]Zerubbabel the son of
Shealtiel,[r]governor of Judah, and
the spirit of Joshua the son of Jehozadak, the high priest, and the
spirit of all the remnant of the
people; and they came and
worked on the house of the LORD
of hosts, their God, Hag. 1:1
15 on the twenty-fourth day of
the sixth month in the second year
of Darius the king.

CHAPTER 2

ON the twenty-first of the seventh month, the word of the LORD
came by[r]Haggai the prophet saying, Hag. 1:1
2 "Speak now to Zerubbabel the
son of Shealtiel, governor of Judah, and to Joshua the son of Jehozadak, the high priest, and to
the remnant of the people saying,
3 'Who is left among you who
saw this[t]temple in its former glory? And how do you see it now?
Does it not seem to you like nothing in comparison? *house*
4 'But now [t]take courage, Zerubbabel,' declares the LORD,
'take courage also, Joshua son of
Jehozadak, the high priest, and all
you people of the land take courage,' declares the LORD, 'and
work; for I am with you,' says the
LORD of hosts. *be strong*
5 'As for the[t]promise which I
made you when you came out of
Egypt, My Spirit is abiding in your
midst; do not fear!' *word*
6 "For thus says the LORD of
hosts, 'Once more[t]in a[r]little while,
I am going to shake the heavens
and the earth, the sea also and the
dry land. *it is a little* • Is. 10:25
7 'And I will shake[r]all the nations; and they will come with the
wealth of all nations; and I will fill
this house with glory,' says the
LORD of hosts. Dan. 2:44
8 'The[r]silver is Mine, and the
gold is Mine,' declares the LORD of
hosts. 1 Chr. 29:14, 16; Is. 60:17
9 'The latter[r]glory of this house
will be greater than the former,'
says the LORD of hosts, 'and in this
place I shall give peace,' declares
the LORD of hosts." Zech. 2:5
10 On the[r]twenty-fourth of the
ninth *month*, in the second year of
Darius, the word of the LORD
came to Haggai the prophet saying, Hag. 2:20
11 "Thus says the LORD of hosts,
'Ask now the priests *for* a ruling:
12 'If a man carries holy meat in
the [t]fold of his garment, and
touches bread with[t]this fold, or
cooked food, wine, oil, or any *other* food, will it become holy?' "
And the priests answered and
said, "No." *wing* • *his wing*
13 Then Haggai said, "If one
who is unclean from a [t]corpse
touches any of these, will *the latter* become unclean?" And the
priests answered and said, "It will
become unclean." *soul*
14 Then Haggai answered and
said,[r]" 'So is this people. And so is
this nation before Me,' declares
the LORD, 'and so is every work of
their hands; and what they offer
there is unclean. Prov. 15:8
15 'But now, do [t]consider from
this day onward: before one stone
was placed on another in the temple of the LORD, *set your heart*
16 from that time *when* one
came to a *grain* heap of twenty

measures, there would be only
ten; and *when* one came to the
wine vat to draw fifty measures,
there would be *only* twenty.
17 'I smote you *and* every work
of your hands with[r]blasting wind,
mildew, and hail; yet you did not
come *back* to Me,' declares the
LORD. Deut. 28:22; 1 Kin. 8:37
18 'Do consider from this day
onward, from the twenty-fourth
day of the ninth *month;* from the
day when the temple of the LORD
was founded, consider:
19 'Is the seed still in the barn?
Even including the vine, the fig
tree, the pomegranate, and the olive tree, it has not borne fruit. Yet
from this day on I will[r] bless
you.' " Ps. 128:1-6; Jer. 31:12, 14
20 Then the word of the LORD
came a second time to Haggai on
the [r]twenty-fourth *day* of the
month saying, Hag. 2:10
21 "Speak to Zerubbabel governor of Judah saying, 'I am going to
shake the heavens and the earth.
22 'And I will [r]overthrow the
thrones of kingdoms and destroy
the power of the kingdoms of the
[a]nations; and I will overthrow
the chariots and their riders, and
the horses and their riders will go
down, everyone by the sword of
another.' Ezek. 26:16 • *Gentiles*
23 'On that day,' declares the
LORD of hosts, 'I will take you, Zerubbabel, son of Shealtiel, my servant,' declares the LORD, 'and I
will make you like a[a]signet *ring,*
for I have chosen you,' " declares
the LORD of hosts. *seal*

THE BOOK OF
ZECHARIAH

IN the eighth month of the second year of[r]Darius, the word of
the LORD came to Zechariah the
prophet, the son of Berechiah, the
son of Iddo saying, Ezra 4:24
2 "The LORD was very [r]angry
with your fathers. 2 Chr. 36:16
3 "Therefore say to them, 'Thus
says the LORD of hosts,[r] "Return to
Me," declares the LORD of hosts,
"that I may return to you," says
the LORD of hosts. Is. 31:6
4 "Do not be[r]like your fathers,
to whom the[r]former prophets proclaimed, saying, 'Thus says the
LORD of hosts, "Return now from
your evil ways and from your evil
deeds." ' But they did not listen or
give heed to Me," declares the
LORD. Ps. 78:8 • 2 Chr. 24:19
5 "Your [r] fathers, where are
they? And the prophets, do they
live forever? Lam. 5:7
6 "But did not My words and
My statutes, which I commanded
My servants the prophets, [r]over-
take your fathers? Then they repented and said, 'As the LORD of
hosts purposed to do to us in accordance with our ways and our
deeds, so He has dealt with
us.' " ' " Jer. 12:16, 17; 44:28, 29
7 On the twenty-fourth day of
the eleventh month, which is the

month Shebat, in the second year
of Darius, the word of the LORD
came to Zechariah the prophet,
the son of Berechiah, the son of
Iddo, as follows:
8 I saw at night, and behold, a
man was riding on a [r]red horse,
and he was standing among the
myrtle trees which were in the ravine, with red, sorrel, and white
horses behind him. Zech. 6:2
9 Then I said, "My lord, what
are these?" And the angel who
was speaking with me said to me,
"I will show you what these are."
10 And the man who was standing among the myrtle trees answered and said, "These are those
whom the LORD has sent to [t]patrol
the earth." *walk about through*
11 So they answered the angel
of the LORD who was standing
among the myrtle trees, and said,
"We have [t]patrolled the earth, and
behold, all the earth is peaceful
and quiet." *walked about through*
12 Then the angel of the LORD
answered and said, "O LORD of
hosts, [r]how long wilt Thou [r]have no
compassion for Jerusalem and the
cities of Judah, with which Thou
hast been indignant these seventy
years?" Ps. 74:10 • Ps. 102:13
13 And the LORD answered the
[r]angel who was speaking with me
with [t]gracious words, comforting
words. Zech. 1:9; 4:1 • *good*
14 So the angel who was speaking with me said to me, "Proclaim, saying, 'Thus says the LORD
of hosts, "I am exceedingly jealous for Jerusalem and Zion.
15 "But I am very [r]angry with the
nations who are at ease; for while
I was only a little angry, they fur-
thered the disaster." Zech. 1:2
16 'Therefore, thus says the
LORD, "I will [r]return to Jerusalem
with compassion; My [r]house will
be built in it," declares the LORD
of hosts, "and a measuring line
will be stretched over Jerusalem." ' Is. 54:8-10 • Zech. 4:9
17 "Again, proclaim, saying,
'Thus says the LORD of hosts, "My
[r]cities will again overflow with
prosperity, and the LORD will
again comfort Zion and again
choose Jerusalem." ' " Is. 44:26
18 Then I lifted up my eyes and
looked, and behold, *there were*
four horns.
19 So I said to the angel who
was speaking with me, "What are
these?" And he answered me,
"These are the [r]horns which have
scattered Judah, Israel, and Jerusalem." 1 Kin. 22:11; Ps. 75:4, 5
20 Then the LORD showed me
four [r]craftsmen. Is. 44:12; 54:16
21 And I said, "What are these
coming to do?" And he said,
"These are the [r]horns which have
scattered Judah, so that no man
lifts up his head; but these *craftsmen* have come to terrify them, to
throw down the horns of the nations who have lifted up *their*
horns against the land of Judah in
order to scatter it." Zech. 1:19

CHAPTER 2

THEN I lifted up my eyes and
looked, and behold, *there was* a
man with a [r]measuring line in his
hand. Jer. 31:39; Ezek. 40:3; 47:3
2 So I said, "Where are you
going?" And he said to me, "To

measure Jerusalem, to see how
wide it is and how long it is."
3 And behold, the [r]angel who
was speaking with me was going
out, and another angel was coming out to meet him, Zech. 1:9
4 and said to him, "Run, speak
to that young man, saying, 'Jerusalem will be inhabited without
walls, because of the multitude of
men and cattle within it.
5 'For I,' declares the LORD,
'will be a [r]wall of fire [t]around her,
and I will be the glory in her
midst.' " Is. 4:5; 26:1 • *to her*
6 "Ho[t] there! Flee from the land
of the north," declares the LORD,
"for I have dispersed you as the
four winds of the heavens," declares the LORD. *Ho! ho!*
7 "Ho, Zion! [r]Escape, you who
are living with the daughter of
Babylon." Is. 48:20; Jer. 51:6
8 For thus says the LORD of
hosts, "After glory He has sent me
against the nations which plunder
you, for he who touches you,
touches the apple of His eye.
9 "For behold, I will [r]wave My
hand over them, so that they will
be plunder for their slaves. Then
you will know that the LORD of
hosts has sent Me. Is. 19:16
10 "Sing for joy and be glad, O
daughter of Zion; for behold I am
coming and I will dwell in your
midst," declares the LORD.
11 "And many nations will join
themselves to the LORD in that
day and will become My people.
Then I will dwell in your midst,
and you will know that the LORD
of hosts has sent Me to you.
12 "And the LORD will [a]possess
Judah as His portion in the holy
land, and will again [r]choose Jerusalem. *inherit* • 2 Chr. 6:6
13 "Be[t] silent, all flesh, before the
LORD; for He is aroused from His
holy habitation." *Hush*

CHAPTER 3

THEN he showed me Joshua the
high priest standing before the angel of the LORD, and [a]Satan standing at his right hand to accuse
him. the *Adversary* or *Accuser*
2 And the LORD said to Satan,
"The LORD rebuke you, Satan! Indeed, the LORD who has chosen
Jerusalem rebuke you! Is this not
a brand plucked from the fire?"
3 Now Joshua was clothed
with [r]filthy garments and standing
before the angel. Ezra 9:15
4 And he spoke and said to
those who were standing before
him saying, "Remove the filthy
garments from him." Again he
said to him, "See, I have taken
your iniquity away from you and
will clothe you with festal robes."
5 Then I said, "Let them put a
clean [r]turban on his head." So they
put a clean turban on his head and
clothed him with garments, while
the angel of the LORD was standing by. Job 29:14; Is. 3:23
6 And the angel of the LORD
admonished Joshua saying,
7 "Thus says the LORD of hosts,
'If you will walk in My ways, and
if you will perform My service,
then you will also govern My
house and also have charge of My
courts, and I will grant you [t]free
access among these who are
standing *here*. *goings*
8 'Now listen, Joshua the high
priest, you and your friends who

are sitting in front of you—indeed
they are men who are a symbol,
for behold, I am going to bring in
My servant the[t]Branch. *Sprout*
9 'For behold, the stone that I
have set before Joshua; on one
stone are[r] seven eyes. Behold, I
will engrave an inscription on it,'
declares the LORD of hosts, 'and I
will remove the iniquity of that
land in one day. Zech. 4:10
10 'In that day,' declares the
LORD of hosts, 'every one of you
will invite his neighbor to *sit* under *his*[r] vine and under *his* fig
tree.' " 1 Kin. 4:25; Is. 36:16

CHAPTER 4

THEN[r]the angel who was speaking with me returned, and roused
me as a man who is awakened
from his sleep. Zech. 1:9
2 And he said to me, "What do
you see?" And I said, "I see, and
behold, a lampstand all of gold
with its bowl on the top of it, and
its seven lamps on it with seven
spouts belonging to each of the
lamps which are on the top of it;
3 also two olive trees by it, one
on the right side of the bowl and
the other on its left side."
4 Then I answered and said to
the angel who was speaking with
me saying, "What are these,[r] my
lord?" Zech. 1:9; 4:5, 13; 6:4
5 So the angel who was speaking with me answered and said to
me, "Do you not know what these
are?" And I said, "No, my lord."
6 Then he answered and said
to me, "This is the word of the
LORD to Zerubbabel saying, 'Not
by might nor by power, but by My
Spirit,' says the LORD of hosts.
7 'What are you, O great[r]moun-
tain? Before Zerubbabel *you will
become* a plain; and he will bring
forth the top stone with shouts of
"Grace, grace to it!" ' " Is. 40:4
8 Also the word of the LORD
came to me saying,
9"The hands of Zerubbabel
have laid the foundation of this
house, and his hands will finish *it*.
Then you will know that the LORD
of hosts has sent me to you.
10"For who has despised the
day of small things? But these
[r]seven will be glad when they see
the plumb line in the hand of Zerubbabel—*these are* the eyes of
the LORD which range to and fro
throughout the earth." Rev. 8:2
11 Then I answered and said to
him, "What are these[r]two olive
trees on the right of the lampstand
and on its left?" Zech. 4:3
12 And I answered the second
time and said to him, "What are
the two olive[a]branches which are
beside the two golden pipes,
which empty the golden *oil* from
themselves?" *clusters*
13 So he answered me saying,
"Do you not know what these
are?" And I said, "No, my lord."
14 Then he said, "These are the
two[t]anointed ones, who are standing by the Lord of the whole
earth." *sons of fresh oil*

CHAPTER 5

THEN I lifted up my eyes again
and looked, and behold, *there was*
a flying[r]scroll. Jer. 36:2
2 And he said to me, "What do
you see?" And I answered, "I see
a flying scroll; its length is twenty
cubits and its width ten cubits."

3 Then he said to me, "This is
the[r]curse that is going forth over
the face of the whole[a]land; surely
everyone who steals will be
purged away according to[t] the
writing on one side, and everyone
who swears will be purged away
according to the writing on the
other side. Is. 24:6 • *earth* • *it*
4"I will[r]make it go forth," declares the LORD of hosts, "and it
will enter the house of the thief
and the house of the one who
swears falsely by My name; and it
will spend the night within that
house and consume it with its timber and stones." Mal. 3:5
5 Then[r] the angel who was
speaking with me went out, and
said to me, "Lift up now your
eyes, and see what this is, going
forth." Zech. 1:9
6 And I said, "What is it?" And
he said, "This is the ephah going
forth." Again he said, "This is
their appearance in all the land
7 (and behold, a lead cover
was lifted up); and this is a
woman sitting inside the ephah."
8 Then he said, "This is[r]Wick-
edness!" And he threw her down
into the middle of the ephah and
cast the lead weight on its[t]open-
ing. Hos. 12:7 • *mouth*
9 Then I lifted up my eyes and
looked, and there two women
were coming out with the wind in
their wings; and they had wings
like the wings of a[r]stork, and they
lifted up the ephah between the
earth and the heavens. Jer. 8:7
10 And I said to the angel who
was speaking with me, "Where
are they taking the ephah?"
11 Then he said to me, "To build
a[t]temple for her in the land of[r]Shi-
nar; and when it is prepared, she
will be set there on her own pedestal." *house* • Gen. 10:10

CHAPTER 6

NOW I lifted up my eyes again
and looked, and behold, [r]four
chariots were coming forth from
between the two mountains; and
the mountains *were* bronze mountains. Dan. 7:3; 8:22; Zech. 1:18
2 With the first chariot *were*
[r]red horses, with the second
chariot black horses, Zech. 1:8
3 with the third chariot white
horses, and with the fourth
chariot strong dappled horses.
4 Then I spoke and said to the
angel who was speaking with me,
"What are these, my lord?"
5 And the angel answered and
said to me, "These are the[r]four
spirits of heaven, going forth after
standing before the Lord of all the
earth, Jer. 49:36; Ezek. 37:9
6 with one of which the black
horses are going forth to the[r]north
country; and the white ones go
forth after them, while the
dappled ones go forth to the south
country. Jer. 1:14, 15; 4:6; 6:1
7"When the strong ones went
out, they[t]were eager to go to patrol the earth." And He said, "Go,
patrol the earth." So they pa-
trolled the earth. *sought to go*
8 Then He cried out to me and
spoke to me saying, "See, those
who are going to the land of the
north have appeased My wrath in
the land of the north."
9 The[r]word of the LORD also
came to me saying, Zech. 1:1
10"Take *an offering* from the exiles, from Heldai, Tobijah, and

Jedaiah; and you go the same day and enter the house of Josiah the son of Zephaniah, where they have arrived from Babylon.

11 "And take silver and gold, make an *ornate* crown, and set *it* on the head of Joshua the son of Jehozadak, the high priest.

12 "Then say to him, 'Thus says the LORD of hosts, "Behold, a man whose name is [t]Branch, for He will [t]branch out from where He is; and He will build the temple of the LORD. *Sprout* · *sprout up*

13 "Yes, it is He who will build the temple of the LORD, and He who will bear the honor and sit and rule on His throne. Thus, He will be a priest on His throne, and the counsel of peace will be between the two [t]offices." ' *of them*

14 "Now the crown will become a reminder in the temple of the LORD to Helem, Tobijah, Jedaiah, and Hen the son of Zephaniah.

15 "And [r]those who are far off will come and [t]build the temple of the LORD." Then you will know that the LORD of hosts has sent me to you. And it will take place, if you completely obey the LORD your God. Is. 56:6-8 · *build in*

CHAPTER 7

THEN it came about in the fourth year of King Darius, that the word of the LORD came to Zechariah on the fourth *day* of the ninth month, *which is* [r]Chislev. Neh. 1:1

2 Now *the town of* Bethel had sent Sharezer and Regemmelech and [t]their men to [t]seek the favor of the LORD, *his* · *soften the face of*

3 speaking to the priests who belong to the house of the LORD of hosts, and to the prophets saying, "Shall I weep in the fifth month [t]and abstain, as I have done these many years?" *abstaining*

4 Then the word of the LORD of hosts came to me saying,

5 "Say to all the people of the land and to the priests, 'When you fasted and mourned in the fifth and seventh months [t]these seventy years, was it actually for Me that you fasted? *and these*

6 'And when you eat and drink, do you not eat for yourselves and do you not drink for yourselves?

7 'Are not *these* the words which the LORD [r]proclaimed by the former prophets, when Jerusalem was inhabited and [a]prosperous with its cities around it, and the Negev and the foothills were inhabited?' " Is. 1:16-20 · *at ease*

8 Then the word of the LORD came to Zechariah saying,

9 "Thus has the LORD of hosts said, [r]'Dispense true justice, and practice kindness and compassion each to his brother; Ezek. 18:8

10 and do not oppress the widow or the [a]orphan, the [a]stranger or the poor; and do not devise evil in your hearts against one another.' *fatherless* · *resident alien*

11 "But they refused to pay attention, and [t]turned a stubborn shoulder and [t]stopped their ears from hearing. *gave* · *made heavy*

12 "And they made their hearts like flint so that they could not hear the law and the words which the LORD of hosts had sent by His Spirit through the former prophets; therefore great wrath came from the LORD of hosts.

13 "And it came about that just as [r]He called and they would not

listen, so[r]they called and I would
not listen," says the LORD of
hosts; Jer. 11:10, 14 • Is. 1:15
14 "but I[r]scattered them with a
storm wind among all the nations
whom they have not known. Thus
the land is desolated behind them,
so that no one went back and
forth, for they made the pleasant
land desolate." Deut. 4:27; 28:64

CHAPTER 8

THEN the word of the LORD of
hosts came saying,
2 "Thus says the LORD of hosts,
'I am[r] exceedingly jealous for
Zion, yes, with great wrath I am
jealous for her.' Zech. 1:14
3 "Thus says the LORD, 'I will
return to Zion and will[r]dwell in
the midst of Jerusalem. Then Jerusalem will be called the City of
Truth, and the mountain of the
LORD of hosts *will be called* the
Holy Mountain.' Zech. 2:10, 11
4 "Thus says the LORD of hosts,
'Old[r] men and old women will
again sit in the [1]streets of Jerusalem, each man with his staff in his
hand because of age. Is. 65:20
5 'And the [1]streets of the city
will be filled with boys and girls
playing in its [1]streets.'
6 "Thus says the LORD of hosts,
'If it is[a]too difficult in the sight of
the remnant of this people in
those days, will it also be[a]too difficult in My sight?' declares the
LORD of hosts. *wonderful*
7 "Thus says the LORD of hosts,
'Behold, I am going to save My
people from the land of the east
and from the land of the west;
8 and I will bring them *back,*

[1]Or, *squares*

and they will live in the midst of
Jerusalem, and they will be My
people and I will be their God in
truth and righteousness.'
9 "Thus says the LORD of hosts,
'Let your hands be[r]strong, you
who are listening in these days to
these words from the mouth of
the prophets, *those* who *spoke* in
the day that the foundation of the
house of the LORD of hosts was
laid, to the end that the temple
might be built. 1 Chr. 22:13
10 'For before those days there
was no wage for man or any wage
for animal; and for him who went
out or came in there was no peace
because of his enemies, and I set
all men one against another.
11 'But now I will[r]not[t]treat the
remnant of this people as in the
former days,' declares the LORD of
hosts. Ps. 103:9 • *be to the*
12 'For *there will be*[r]peace for
the seed: the vine will yield its
fruit, the land will yield its produce, and the heavens will give
their dew; and I will cause the
remnant of this people to inherit
all these *things.* Lev. 26:3-6
13 'And it will come about that
just as you were a[r]curse among
the nations, O house of Judah and
house of Israel, so I will save you
that you may become a[r]blessing.
Do not fear; let your hands be
strong.' Jer. 29:18 • Ps. 72:17
14 "For thus says the LORD of
hosts, 'Just as I[r]purposed to do
harm to you when your fathers
provoked Me to wrath,' says the
LORD of hosts, 'and I have not[r]re-
lented, Jer. 31:28 • Jer. 4:28
15 so I have again purposed in
these days to[r]do good to Jerusa-

lem and to the house of Judah.[r] Do not fear! Jer. 29:11 • Zech. 8:13

16 'These are the things which you should do: speak the truth to one another; judge with truth and judgment for peace in your [2]gates.

17 'Also let none of you devise evil in your heart against another, and do not love[t] perjury; for all these are what I hate,' declares the LORD." *false oath*

18 Then the word of the LORD of hosts came to me saying,

19 "Thus says the LORD of hosts, 'The fast of the fourth, the fast of the fifth, the fast of the seventh, and the fast of the tenth *months* will become joy, gladness, and cheerful feasts for the house of Judah; so love truth and peace.'

20 "Thus says the LORD of hosts, '*It will* yet *be* that[r] peoples will come, even the inhabitants of many cities. Ps. 117:1; Jer. 16:19

21 And the inhabitants of one will go to another saying, "Let us go at once to[r] entreat the favor of the LORD, and to seek the LORD of hosts; I will also go." Zech. 7:2

22 'So many peoples and mighty nations will come to seek the LORD of hosts in Jerusalem and to entreat the favor of the LORD.'

23 "Thus says the LORD of hosts, 'In those days ten men from all the nations will[r] grasp the garment of a Jew saying, "Let us go with you, for we have heard that God is with you."'" Is. 45:14, 24; 60:14

CHAPTER 9

THE[a] burden of the word of the LORD is against the land of Hadrach, with Damascus as its resting place (for the eyes of men, especially of all the tribes of Israel, are toward the LORD), *oracle*

2 And[r] Hamath also, which
borders on it; Jer. 49:23
Tyre and Sidon, though
they are very wise.
3 For Tyre built herself a[r] fortress Josh. 19:29
And[r] piled up silver like
dust, Job 27:16
And gold like the mire of
the streets.
4 Behold, the Lord will[r] dispossess her Ezek. 26:3-5
And cast her wealth into
the sea;
And she will be[r] consumed
with fire. Ezek. 28:18
5 Ashkelon will see *it* and be
afraid.
Gaza too will writhe in
great pain;
Also Ekron, for her expectation has been confounded.
Moreover, the king will perish from Gaza,
And Ashkelon will not be
inhabited.
6 And a mongrel race will
dwell in Ashdod,
And I will cut off the pride
of the Philistines.
7 And I will remove their
blood from their mouth,
And their detestable things
from between their teeth.
Then they also will be a
remnant for our God,
And be like a clan in Judah,
And Ekron like a Jebusite.
8 But I will camp around My
house because of an
army,

[2]I.e., the place where court was held

Because of[r]him who passes by and returns; Is. 52:1
And[r]no oppressor will pass over them anymore,
For now I have seen with My eyes. Is. 54:14
9 Rejoice greatly, O daughter of Zion!
Shout *in triumph,* O daughter of Jerusalem!
Behold, your king is coming to you;
He is just and [r]endowed with salvation, Is. 43:3, 11
[r]Humble, and mounted on a donkey, Is. 57:15
Even on a[r]colt, the foal of a donkey. Is. 30:6
10 And I will cut off the chariot from Ephraim,
And the horse from Jerusalem;
And the[r]bow of war will be cut off. Hos. 2:18
And He will speak[r]peace to the nations; Is. 57:19
And His dominion will be from sea to sea,
And from the [3]River to the ends of the earth.

11 As for you also, because of the[r]blood of *My* covenant with you,
I have set your [r]prisoners free from the waterless pit. Ex. 24:8 • Is. 24:22
12 Return to the[a]stronghold, O prisoners [t]who have the hope; *Stronghold*
This very day I am declaring that I will restore double to you. *of the hope*
13 For I will[r]bend Judah[t]as My bow, Jer. 51:20 • *for Me*
I will fill the bow with Ephraim.
And I will stir up your sons, O Zion, against your sons, O Greece;
And I will make you like a warrior's sword.
14 Then the LORD will appear [r]over them, Is. 31:5
And His arrow will go forth like lightning;
And the Lord GOD will blow the[r]trumpet, Is. 27:13
And will march in the storm winds of the south.
15 The LORD of hosts will defend them.
And they will[r]devour, and trample on the sling stones; Zech. 12:6
And they will drink, *and* be boisterous as with wine;
And they will be filled like a *sacrificial* basin,
Drenched like the [r]corners of the altar. Ex. 27:2
16 And the LORD their God will save them in that day
As the flock of His people;
For *they are as* the stones of a[r]crown, Is. 62:3
Sparkling in His land.
17 For what comeliness and beauty *will be*[t]theirs! *his*
Grain will make the young men flourish, and new wine the virgins.

CHAPTER 10

ASK rain from the LORD at the time of the spring rain—
The LORD who makes the [a]storm clouds; *thunderbolts*
And He will give them showers of rain, vegeta-

[3]I.e., Euphrates

tion in the field to *each*
man.
2 For the teraphim speak[a]in-
iquity, *futility*
And the diviners see[t]lying
visions, a *lie*
And tell false dreams;
They comfort in vain.
Therefore *the people*[t]wan-
der like sheep, *journey*
They are afflicted, because
there is no shepherd.
3 "My[r]anger is kindled against
the shepherds,
And I will punish the male
goats; Jer. 25:34-36
For the LORD of hosts has
[r]visited His flock, the
house of Judah,
And will make them like
His majestic horse in battle. Ezek. 34:12
4 "From[t]them will come the
cornerstone,
From[t]them the tent peg,
From[t]them the bow of battle,
From[t]them every ruler, *all*
of them together. *him*
5 "And they will be as mighty
men,
[r]Treading down *the enemy*
in the mire of the streets
in battle; 2 Sam. 22:43
And they will fight, for the
LORD *will be* with them;
And the riders on horses
will be put to shame.
6 "And I shall strengthen the
house of Judah,
And I shall[r]save the house
of Joseph, Zech. 8:7
And I shall[a]bring them
back, *make them dwell*
Because I have had com-
passion on them;
And they will be as though I
had not rejected them,
For I am the LORD their
God, and I will answer
them.
7 "And Ephraim will be like a
mighty man,
And their heart will be glad
as if *from* wine;
Indeed, their[r]children will
see *it* and be glad,
Their heart will rejoice in
the LORD. Is. 54:13
8 "I will whistle for them to
gather them together,
For I have redeemed them;
And they will be as numerous as they were before.
9 "When I[t]scatter them among
the peoples, *sow*
They will[r]remember Me in
far countries,
And they with their chil-
dren will live and come
back. 1 Kin. 8:47, 48
10 "I will[r]bring them back from
the land of Egypt,
And gather them from As-
syria;
And I will bring them into
the land of Gilead and
Lebanon,
[t]Until no *room* can be found
for them. Is. 11:11 • *And*
11 "And He will pass through
the[r]sea *of* distress,
And strike the waves in the
sea, Is. 51:9, 10
So that all the depths of the
Nile will dry up;
And the pride of Assyria
will be brought down,
And the scepter of[r]Egypt
will depart. Ezek. 30:13
12 "And I shall[r]strengthen them
in the LORD, Zech. 10:6

And in His name they will
walk," declares the LORD.

CHAPTER 11

OPEN your doors, O Lebanon,
That a[r] fire may feed on
your cedars. Jer. 22:6, 7
2 Wail, O[a] cypress, for the cedar has fallen, *juniper*
Because the glorious *trees*
have been destroyed;
Wail, O oaks of Bashan,
For the impenetrable forest
has come down.
3 There is a sound of the
shepherds' wail,
For their glory is ruined;
There is a sound of the
young lions' roar,
For the[a] pride of the Jordan
is ruined. *jungle*
4 Thus says the LORD my God,
"Pasture the flock *doomed* to
slaughter[r]. Ps. 44:22; Zech. 11:7
5 "Those who buy them slay
them and go unpunished, and
each of those who sell them says,
'Blessed be the LORD, for I have
become rich!' And their own shepherds have no pity on them.
6 "For I shall[r] no longer have
pity on the inhabitants of the
land," declares the LORD; "but behold, I shall cause the men to[t] fall,
each into another's[t] power and
into the[t] power of his king; and
they will strike the land, and I
shall not deliver *them* from their
[t]power." Jer. 13:14 • *find* • *hand*
7 So I pastured the flock
doomed to slaughter, hence the
afflicted of the flock. And I took
for myself two staffs: the one I
called[a] Favor, and the other I
called[a] Union; so I pastured the
flock. *Pleasantness* • *Cords*
8 Then I annihilated the three
shepherds in one month, for my
soul was impatient with them, and
their soul also was weary of me.
9 Then I said, "I will not pasture you. What is to die, let it die,
and what is to be annihilated, let it
be annihilated; and let those who
are left eat one another's flesh."
10 And I took my staff,[a] Favor,
and cut it in pieces, to break my
covenant which I had made with
all the peoples. *Pleasantness*
11 So it was broken on that day,
and [4]thus the afflicted of the flock
who were watching me realized
that it was the word of the LORD.
12 And I said to them, "If it is
good in your sight, give *me* my
wages; but if not,[t] never mind!" So
they weighed out thirty *shekels* of
silver as my wages. *cease*
13 Then the LORD said to me,
"Throw it to the[r] potter, *that* magnificent price at which I was valued by them." So I took the thirty
shekels of silver and threw them
to the potter in the house of the
LORD. Matt. 27:3-10; Acts 1:18, 19
14 Then I cut my second staff,
[a]Union, in pieces, to[r] break the
brotherhood between Judah and
Israel. *Cords* • Is. 9:21
15 And the LORD said to me,
"Take again for yourself the
equipment of a foolish shepherd.
16 "For behold, I am going to
raise up a shepherd in the land
who will[r] not care for the perishing, seek the scattered, heal the
broken, or sustain the one standing, but will[r] devour the flesh of

[4]Another reading is *the sheep dealers who*

the fat *sheep* and tear off their hoofs. Jer. 23:2 • Ezek. 34:2-6

17 [r]"Woe to the worthless shepherd Jer. 23:1
Who leaves the flock!
A sword will be on his arm
And on his right eye!
His [r]arm will be totally withered, Ezek. 30:21, 22
And his right eye will be blind."

CHAPTER 12

THE [5]burden of the word of the LORD concerning Israel.

Thus declares the LORD who stretches out the heavens, lays the foundation of the earth, and forms the spirit of man within him,

2 "Behold, I am going to make Jerusalem a cup that causes reeling to all the peoples around; and when the siege is against Jerusalem, it will also be against Judah.

3 "And it will come about in that day that I will make Jerusalem a heavy stone for all the peoples; all who lift it will be severely injured. And all the nations of the earth will be gathered against it.

4 "In that day," declares the LORD, "I will strike every horse with bewilderment, and his rider with madness. But I will [t]watch over the house of Judah, while I strike every horse of the peoples with blindness. *open My eyes*

5 "Then the clans of Judah will say in their hearts, [t]'A strong support for us are the inhabitants of Jerusalem through the LORD of hosts, their God.' *My strength is*

6 "In that day I will make the clans of Judah like a firepot among pieces of wood and a flaming torch among sheaves, so they will consume on the right hand and on the left all the surrounding peoples, while the inhabitants of Jerusalem again dwell on their own sites in Jerusalem.

7 "The LORD also will [r]save the tents of Judah first in order that the glory of the house of David and the glory of the inhabitants of Jerusalem may not be magnified above Judah. Jer. 30:18

8 "In that day the LORD will defend the inhabitants of Jerusalem, and the one who [a]is feeble among them in that day will be like David, and the house of David *will be* like God, like the angel of the LORD before them. *stumbles*

9 "And it will come about in that day that I will [t]set about to destroy all the nations that come against Jerusalem. *seek to*

10 "And I will pour out on the house of David and on the inhabitants of Jerusalem, the Spirit of grace and of supplication, so that they will look on Me whom they have pierced; and they will mourn for Him, as one mourns for an only son, and they will weep bitterly over Him, like the bitter weeping over a first-born.

11 "In that day there will be great [r]mourning in Jerusalem, like the mourning of Hadadrimmon in the plain of Megiddo. Rev. 1:7

12 "And the land will mourn, every family by itself; the family of the house of David by itself, and their wives by themselves; the family of the house of Nathan by itself, and their wives by themselves;

[5]Or, *oracle*

13 the family of the house of
Levi by itself, and their wives by
themselves; the family of the
Shimeites by itself, and their
wives by themselves;
14 all the families that remain,
every family by itself, and their
wives by themselves.

CHAPTER 13

"IN that day a fountain will be
opened for the house of David and
for the inhabitants of Jerusalem,
for sin and for [r]impurity. Is. 4:4
2 "And it will come about in
that day," declares the LORD of
hosts, "that I will [r]cut off the
names of the idols from the land,
and they will no longer be remembered; and I will also remove the
prophets and the unclean spirit
from the land. Ex. 23:13
3 "And it will come about that if
anyone still prophesies, then his
father and mother who gave birth
to him will say to him, 'You shall
not live, for you have spoken
falsely in the name of the LORD';
and his father and mother who
gave birth to him will pierce him
through when he prophesies.
4 "Also it will come about in
that day that the prophets will
each be [r]ashamed of his vision
when he prophesies, and they will
not put on a [r]hairy robe in order to
deceive; Jer. 6:15 • 2 Kin. 1:8
5 but he will say, 'I am [r]not a
prophet; I am a tiller of the
ground, for a man sold me as a
slave in my youth.' Amos 7:14
6 "And one will say to him,
'What are these wounds between
your arms?' Then he will say,
'*Those* with which I was wounded
in the house of my friends.'
7 "Awake, O [r]sword, against
My Shepherd, Jer. 47:6
And against the man, My
[r]Associate," Ps. 2:2
Declares the LORD of hosts.
[r]"Strike the Shepherd that
the sheep may be scat-
tered; Is. 53:4, 5, 10
And I will turn My hand
against the little ones.
8 "And it will come about in
all the land,"
Declares the LORD,
"That [r]two parts in it will be
cut off *and* perish;
But the third will be left in
it. Is. 6:13
9 "And I will bring the third
part through the [r]fire,
Refine them as silver is refined, Is. 48:10; Mal. 3:3
And test them as gold is
tested.
They will call on My name,
And I will answer them;
I will say, 'They are [r]My
people,' Hos. 2:23
And they will say, 'The
LORD is my God.'"

CHAPTER 14

BEHOLD, a day is coming for the
LORD when the spoil taken from
you will be divided among you.
2 For I will gather all the nations against Jerusalem to battle,
and the city will be captured, the
houses plundered, the women ravished, and half of the city exiled,
but the rest of the people will not
be cut off from the city.
3 Then the LORD will go forth

and fight against those nations, as
when He fights on a day of battle.
4 And in that day His feet will
stand on the Mount of Olives,
which is in front of Jerusalem on
the east; and the Mount of Olives
will be split in its middle from east
to west by a very large valley, so
that half of the mountain will
move toward the north and the
other half toward the south.
5 And you will flee by the valley of My mountains, for the valley of the mountains will reach to
Azel; yes, you will flee just as you
fled before the [r]earthquake in the
days of Uzziah king of Judah.
[r]Then the LORD, my God, will
come, *and* all the holy ones with
Him! Is. 29:6 • Ps. 96:13
6 And it will come about in
that day that there will be no light;
the luminaries will dwindle.
7 For it will be [r]a unique day
which is known to the LORD, neither day nor night, but it will
come about that at evening time
there will be light. Jer. 30:7
8 And it will come about in
that day that [r]living waters will
flow out of Jerusalem, half of
them toward the eastern sea and
the other half toward the western
sea; it will be in summer as well as
in winter. Ezek. 47:1-12
9 And the LORD will be [r]king
over all the earth; in that day the
LORD will be *the only* one, and His
name *the only* one. Is. 2:2-4
10 All the land will be changed
into a plain from [r]Geba to Rimmon
south of Jerusalem; but [t]Jerusalem
will rise and remain on its site
from Benjamin's Gate as far as
the place of the First Gate to the
Corner Gate, and from the Tower
of Hananel to the king's wine
presses. 1 Kin. 15:22 • *it*
11 And people will live in it, and
there will be no more curse, for
Jerusalem will dwell in security.
12 Now this will be the plague
with which the LORD will strike all
the peoples who have gone to war
against Jerusalem; their flesh will
[r]rot while they stand on their feet,
and their eyes will rot in their
sockets, and their tongue will rot
in their mouth. Lev. 26:16
13 And it will come about in
that day that a great panic from
the LORD will fall on them; and
they will seize one another's hand,
and the hand of one will be lifted
against the hand of another.
14 And Judah also will fight at
Jerusalem; and the wealth of all
the surrounding nations will be
gathered, gold and silver and garments in great abundance.
15 So also like this [r]plague, will
be the plague on the horse, the
mule, the camel, the donkey, and
all the cattle that will be in those
camps. Zech. 14:12
16 Then it will come about that
any who are left of all the nations
that went against Jerusalem will
[r]go up from year to year to worship the King, the LORD of hosts,
and to celebrate the Feast of
Booths. Is. 60:6-9; 66:18-21, 23
17 And it will be that whichever
of the families of the earth does
not go up to Jerusalem to worship
the King, the LORD of hosts, there
will be no rain on them.
18 And if the family of Egypt
does not go up or enter, then no
rain will fall on them; it will be
the [r]plague with which the LORD
smites the nations who do not go

up to celebrate the Feast of
Booths. Zech. 14:12, 15
19 This will be the punishment
of Egypt, and the punishment of
all the nations who do not go up to
celebrate the Feast of Booths.
20 In that day there will *be in-*
scribed on the bells of the horses,
[r]"HOLY TO THE LORD." And the
[r]cooking pots in the LORD's house
will be like the bowls before the
altar. Ex. 28:36-38 • Ezek. 46:20
21 And every cooking pot in Jerusalem and in Judah will be[r]holy
to the LORD of hosts; and all who
sacrifice will come and take of
them and boil in them. And there
will no longer be a[a]Canaanite in
the house of the LORD of hosts in
that day. Neh. 8:10 • *merchant*

THE BOOK OF

MALACHI

THE oracle of the word of the
LORD to Israel through Malachi.
2 "I have loved you," says the
LORD. But you say, "How hast
Thou loved us?" "*Was* not Esau
Jacob's brother?" declares the
LORD. "Yet I have loved Jacob;
3 but I have hated Esau, and I
have[r]made his mountains a desolation, and *appointed* his inheritance for the jackals of the wilderness." Jer. 49:10, 16-18
4 Though Edom says, "We
have been beaten down, but we
will return and build up the ruins"; thus says the LORD of hosts,
"They may build, but I will tear
down; and *men* will call them the
[t]wicked territory, and the people
toward whom the LORD is indignant forever." *border of wickedness*
5 And your eyes will see this
and you will say, "The LORD[a] be
magnified beyond the[a]border of
Israel!" *will be great • territory*
6 "'A son honors *his* father, and
a servant his master. Then if I am
a father, where is My honor? And
if I am a master, where is My[t]re-
spect?' says the LORD of hosts to
you, O priests who despise My
name. But you say, 'How have we
despised Thy name?' *fear*
7 "*You* are presenting defiled
[t]food upon My altar. But you say,
'How have we defiled Thee?' In
that you say, 'The table of the
LORD is to be despised.' *bread*
8 "But when you present the
blind for sacrifice, is it not evil?
And when you present the lame
and sick, is it not evil?[t] Why not
offer it to your governor? Would
he be pleased with you? Or would
he receive you kindly?" says the
LORD of hosts. *Offer it, please*
9 "But now[t]will you not[r]entreat

God's favor, that He may be gracious to us? With such an offering on your part, will He receive any of you kindly?" says the LORD of hosts. *entreat, please* · Jer. 27:18

10 "Oh that there were one among you who would shut the gates, that you might not uselessly kindle *fire on* My altar! I am not pleased with you," says the LORD of hosts, "nor will I accept an offering from[t] you. *your hand*

11 "For from the [r]rising of the sun, even to its setting,[r] My name *will be* great among the nations, and in every place incense is going to be offered to My name, and a grain offering *that is* pure; for My name *will be* great among the nations," says the LORD of hosts. Is. 45:6 · Ps. 111:9

12 "But you are profaning it, in that you say, 'The table of the Lord is defiled, and as for its fruit, its food is to be despised.'

13 "You also say, 'My, how [r]tiresome it is!' And you disdainfully sniff at it," says the LORD of hosts, "and you bring what was taken by robbery, and *what is* lame or sick; so you bring the offering! Should I receive that from your hand?" says the LORD. Is. 43:22

14 "But cursed be the swindler who has a male in his flock, and vows it, but sacrifices a blemished animal to the Lord, for I am a great King," says the LORD of hosts, "and My name is [a]feared among the nations." *revered*

CHAPTER 2

"AND now, this commandment is for you, O priests.

2 "If you do [r]not listen, and if you do not take it to heart to give honor to My name," says the LORD of hosts, "then I will send the curse upon you, and I will curse your blessings; and indeed, I have [r]cursed them *already*, because you are not taking *it* to heart. Lev. 26:14, 15 · Mal. 3:9

3 "Behold, I am going to rebuke your [t]offspring, and I will spread [a]refuse on your faces, the [a]refuse of your feasts; and you will be taken away[t] with it. *seed · vomit · to*

4 "Then you will know that I have sent this commandment to you,[a] that My covenant may [t]continue with Levi," says the LORD of hosts. *to be My covenant with · be*

5 "My covenant with him was *one of* life and peace, and I gave them to him *as an object of* [a]reverence; so he revered Me, and stood in awe of My name. *fear*

6 "True[a] instruction was in his mouth, and unrighteousness was not found on his lips; he walked [r]with Me in peace and uprightness, and he turned many back from iniquity. *Law of truth* · Ps. 37:37

7 "For the lips of a priest should preserve knowledge, and [t]men should seek [a]instruction from his mouth; for he is the messenger of the LORD of hosts. *they · law*

8 "But as for you, you have turned aside from the way; you have caused many to stumble[a] by the instruction; you have corrupted the covenant of Levi," says the LORD of hosts. *in the law*

9 "So I also have made you despised and abased[t] before all the people, just as you are not keep-

ing My ways, but are showing partiality in the instruction. *to*

10 "Do we not all have[r] one father? Has not one God created us? Why do we deal[r] treacherously each against his brother so as to profane the covenant of our fathers? Is. 63:16 • Jer. 9:4, 5

11 "Judah has dealt treacherously, and an abomination has been committed in Israel and in Jerusalem; for Judah has profaned the sanctuary of the LORD which He loves, and has married the daughter of a foreign god.

12 "*As* for the man who does this, may the LORD cut off from the tents of Jacob *everyone* who awakes and answers, or who presents[a] an offering to the LORD of hosts. *a grain offering*

13 "And this is[t] another thing you do: you cover the altar of the LORD with tears, with weeping and with groaning, because He no longer regards the[a] offering or accepts *it with* favor from your hand. *second • grain offering*

14 "Yet you say, 'For what reason?' Because the LORD has been a witness between you and the[r] wife of your youth, against whom you have dealt treacherously, though she is your companion and your wife by covenant. Is. 54:6

15 "But not one has done *so* who has a remnant of the Spirit. And what did *that* one *do* while he was seeking a godly[t] offspring? Take heed then, to your spirit, and let no one deal treacherously against the wife of your youth. *seed*

16 "For I hate divorce," says the LORD, the God of Israel, "and him who covers his garment with wrong," says the LORD of hosts. "So take heed to your spirit, that you do not deal treacherously."

17 You have wearied the LORD with your words. Yet you say, "How have we wearied *Him*?" In that you say, "Everyone who does evil is good in the sight of the LORD, and He delights in them," or, "Where is the God of justice?"

CHAPTER 3

"BEHOLD, I am going to send My messenger, and he will clear the way before Me. And the Lord, whom you seek, will suddenly come to His temple; and the messenger of the covenant, in whom you delight, behold, He is coming," says the LORD of hosts.

2 "But who can[r] endure the day of His coming? And who can stand when He appears? For He is like a refiner's fire and like[t] fullers' soap. Is. 33:14 • *laundrymen's*

3 "And He will sit as a smelter and purifier of silver, and He will purify the sons of Levi and refine them like gold and silver, so that they may[r] present to the LORD offerings in righteousness. Ps. 4:5

4 "Then the[a] offering of Judah and Jerusalem will be pleasing to the LORD, as in the days of old and as in former years. *grain offering*

5 "Then I will draw near to you for judgment; and I will be a swift witness against the sorcerers and against the adulterers and against those who swear falsely, and against those who oppress the wage earner in his wages, the widow and the[a] orphan, and those

who turn aside the [a]alien, and do not fear Me," says the LORD of hosts. *fatherless • sojourner*

6 "For I, the LORD, do not change; therefore you, O sons of Jacob, are not consumed.

7 "From the [r]days of your fathers you have turned aside from My statutes, and have not kept *them.* Return to Me, and I will return to you," says the LORD of hosts. "But you say, 'How shall we return?' Jer. 7:25, 26

8 "Will a man [1]rob God? Yet you are robbing Me! But you say, 'How have we robbed Thee?' In tithes and offerings.

9 "You are [r]cursed with a curse, for you are [1]robbing Me, the whole nation *of you*! Mal. 2:2

10 "Bring the whole tithe into the storehouse, so that there may be [t]food in My house, and test Me now in this," says the LORD of hosts, "if I will not [r]open for you the windows of heaven, and pour out for you a blessing until [2]it overflows. *prey* • Ps. 78:23-29

11 "Then I will rebuke the [r]devourer for you, so that it may not [t]destroy the fruits of the ground; nor will your vine in the field cast *its grapes*," says the LORD of hosts. Joel 1:4; 2:25 • *ruin*

12 "And [r]all the nations will call you blessed, for you shall be a [r]delightful land," says the LORD of hosts. Is. 61:9 • Is. 62:4

13 "Your words have been [t]arrogant against Me," says the LORD. "Yet you say, 'What have we spoken against Thee?' *strong*

14 "You have said, 'It is vain to serve God; and what profit is it that we have kept His charge, and that we have walked in mourning before the LORD of hosts?

15 'So now we [r]call the arrogant blessed; not only are the doers of wickedness built up, but they also test God and escape.' " Is. 2:22

16 Then those who [3]feared the LORD spoke to one another, and the LORD [r]gave attention and heard *it,* and a book of remembrance was written before Him for those who [3]fear the LORD and who esteem His name. Ps. 34:15

17 "And they will be Mine," says the LORD of hosts, "on the day that I [t]prepare *My* [a]own possession, and I will spare them as a man spares his own son who serves him." *make • special treasure*

18 So you will again [r]distinguish between the righteous and the wicked, between one who serves God and one who does not serve Him. Gen. 18:25; Amos 5:15

CHAPTER 4

"FOR behold, the day is coming, [r]burning like a furnace; and all the arrogant and every evildoer will be [r]chaff; and the day that is coming will set them ablaze," says the LORD of hosts, "so that it will leave them neither root nor branch." Ps. 21:9 • Is. 5:24

2 "But for you who [3]fear My name the sun of righteousness will rise with healing in its wings; and you will go forth and skip about like calves from the stall.

3 "And you will tread down the wicked, for they shall be ashes un-

[1]Or, *defraud(ing)*
[2]Or, *there is not room enough*

[3]Or, *revere(d)*

der the soles of your feet on the
day[a] which I am preparing," says
the LORD of hosts. *when I act*
4 "Remember the law of Moses
My servant, *even the* statutes and
ordinances which I commanded
him in Horeb for all Israel.
5 "Behold, I am going to send
you[r] Elijah the prophet before the
coming of the great and terrible
day of the LORD. **Matt. 11:14**
6 "And he will restore the
hearts of the fathers to *their* children, and the hearts of the children to their fathers, lest I come
and smite the land with a curse."

THE

NEW TESTAMENT

THE GOSPEL ACCORDING TO

MATTHEW

THE book of the genealogy of
Jesus Christ,[r]the son of David, the
son of Abraham. 2 Sam. 7:12-16
2 To Abraham was born Isaac;
and to Isaac, Jacob; and to Jacob,
[1]Judah and his brothers;
3 and to Judah were born Perez and Zerah by Tamar; and to
[r]Perez was born Hezron; and to
Hezron, Ram; Ruth 4:18-22
4 and to Ram was born Am-
minadab; and to Amminadab,
Nahshon; and to Nahshon, Salmon;
5 and to Salmon was born
Boaz by Rahab; and to Boaz was
born Obed by Ruth; and to Obed,
Jesse;
6 and to Jesse was born David
the king.
And to David [r]was born Solomon by her *who had been the wife*
of Uriah; 2 Sam. 11:27; 12:24
7 and to Solomon was born
Rehoboam; and to Rehoboam,
Abijah; and to Abijah, Asa;
8 and to Asa was born Je-
hoshaphat; and to Jehoshaphat,
Joram; and to Joram, Uzziah;
9 and to Uzziah was born Jotham; and to Jotham, Ahaz; and to
Ahaz, Hezekiah;
10 and to Hezekiah was born
Manasseh; and to Manasseh,
Amon; and to Amon, Josiah;
11 and to Josiah were born Jeconiah and his brothers, at the time
of the deportation to Babylon.

[1]Gr., *Judas*. Names of Old Testament characters will be given in their Old Testament form.

12 And after the [r]deportation to
Babylon, to Jeconiah was born
Shealtiel; and to Shealtiel, Zerubbabel; 2 Kin. 24:14f.; Jer. 27:20
13 and to Zerubbabel was born
Abiud; and to Abiud, Eliakim; and
to Eliakim, Azor;
14 and to Azor was born Zadok;
and to Zadok, Achim; and to A-
chim, Eliud;
15 and to Eliud was born Eleazar; and to Eleazar, Matthan; and
to Matthan, Jacob;
16 and to Jacob was born
Joseph the husband of Mary, by
whom was born Jesus, who is
called Christ.
17 Therefore all the generations
from Abraham to David are fourteen generations; and from David
to the [r]deportation to Babylon
fourteen generations; and from
the deportation to Babylon to *the*
time of Christ fourteen generations. 2 Kin. 24:14f.; Jer. 27:20
18 Now the birth of Jesus Christ
was as follows. When His [r]mother
Mary had been betrothed to
Joseph, before they came together
she was found to be with child by
the Holy Spirit. Matt. 12:46
19 And Joseph her husband,
being a righteous man, and not
wanting to disgrace her, desired
[2]to put her away secretly.
20 But when he had considered
this, behold, an angel of the Lord
appeared to him in a dream, saying, "Joseph, son of David, do not
be afraid to take Mary as your

[2]Or, *to divorce her*

wife; for that which has been [3]con-
ceived in her is of the Holy Spirit.
21 "And she will bear a Son; and
[r]you shall call His name Jesus, for
it is He who will save His people
from their sins." Luke 1:31; 2:21
22 Now all this [a]took place that
what was spoken by the Lord
through the prophet might be fulfilled, saying, *has taken place*
23 "BEHOLD, THE VIRGIN SHALL BE
WITH CHILD, AND SHALL BEAR A
SON, AND THEY SHALL CALL HIS
NAME IMMANUEL," which translated means, "GOD WITH US."
24 And Joseph arose from his
sleep, and did as the angel of the
Lord commanded him, and took
her as his wife,
25 and [4]kept her a virgin until
she gave birth to a Son; and he
called His name Jesus.

CHAPTER 2

NOW after Jesus was [r]born in
Bethlehem of Judea in the days of
Herod the king, behold, [5]magi
from the east arrived in Jerusalem, saying, Mic. 5:2
2 "Where is He who has been
born King of the Jews? For we
saw His star in the east, and have
come to worship Him."
3 And when Herod the king
heard it, he was troubled, and all
Jerusalem with him.
4 And gathering together all
the chief priests and scribes of the
people, he *began* to inquire of
them where the Christ was to be
born.

[3] Lit., *begotten* [4] Lit., *was not knowing her*
[5] Pronounced may-ji, a caste of wise men specializing in astrology, medicine and natural science

5 And they said to him, "In
Bethlehem of Judea, for so it has
been written by the prophet,
6 'AND [r]YOU, BETHLEHEM, LAND
OF JUDAH, Mic. 5:2
ARE BY NO MEANS LEAST
AMONG THE LEADERS OF
JUDAH;
FOR OUT OF YOU SHALL
COME FORTH A RULER,
WHO WILL SHEPHERD MY
PEOPLE ISRAEL.'"
7 Then Herod secretly called
the magi, and ascertained from
them the time the star appeared.
8 And he sent them to Bethlehem, and said, "Go and make
careful search for the Child; and
when you have found *Him,* report
to me, that I too may come and
worship Him."
9 And having heard the king,
they went their way; and lo, the
star, which they had seen in the
east, went on before them, until it
came and stood over where the
Child was.
10 And when they saw the star,
they rejoiced exceedingly with
great joy.
11 And they came into the
house and saw the Child with
Mary His mother; and they fell
down and worshiped Him; and
opening their treasures they presented to Him gifts of gold and
frankincense and myrrh.
12 And having been warned *by
God* in a dream not to return to
Herod, they departed for their
own country by another way.
13 Now when they had departed, behold, an [r]angel of the
Lord *appeared to Joseph in a
dream, saying, "Arise and take

the Child and His mother, and flee
to Egypt, and remain there until I
tell you; for Herod is going to
search for the Child to destroy
Him." Acts 5:19; 10:7; 12:7-11
14 And he arose and took the
Child and His mother by night,
and departed for Egypt;
15 and was there until the death
of Herod, that what was spoken
by the Lord through the prophet
might be fulfilled, saying, "OUT OF
EGYPT DID I CALL MY SON."
16 Then when Herod saw that
he had been tricked by [r]the magi,
he became very enraged, and sent
and slew all the male children
who were in Bethlehem and in all
its environs, from two years old
and under, according to the time
which he had ascertained from
the magi. Matt. 2:1
17 Then that which was spoken
through Jeremiah the prophet was
fulfilled, saying,
18 "A[r] VOICE WAS HEARD IN RA-
MAH, Jer. 31:15
WEEPING AND GREAT
MOURNING,
RACHEL WEEPING FOR HER
CHILDREN;
AND SHE REFUSED TO BE
COMFORTED,
BECAUSE THEY WERE NO
MORE."
19 But when Herod was dead,
behold, an angel of the Lord [r]*appeared in a dream to Joseph in
Egypt, saying, Matt. 1:20; 2:12
20 "Arise and take the Child and
His mother, and go into the land
of Israel; for those who sought the
Child's life are dead."
21 And he arose and took the
Child and His mother, and came
into the land of Israel.
22 But when he heard that Ar-
chelaus was reigning over Judea
in place of his father Herod, he
was afraid to go there. And being
warned *by God* in a dream, he departed for the regions of Galilee,
23 and came and resided in a
city called [r]Nazareth, that what
was spoken through the prophets
might be fulfilled, "He shall be
called a Nazarene." Luke 1:26

CHAPTER 3

NOW in those days John the
Baptist *came, preaching in the
wilderness of Judea, saying,
2 "Repent, for the kingdom of
heaven [t]is at hand." *has come near*
3 For this is the one referred to
[t]by Isaiah the prophet, saying,
"THE[r] VOICE OF ONE CRYING IN
THE WILDERNESS, *through*
'MAKE READY THE WAY OF
THE LORD,
MAKE HIS PATHS
STRAIGHT!'" Is. 40:3
4 Now John himself had a garment of camel's hair, and a leather
belt about his waist; and his food
was locusts and wild honey.
5 Then Jerusalem was going
out to him, and all Judea, and all
the district around the Jordan;
6 and they were being baptized
by him in the Jordan River, as
they confessed their sins.
7 But when he saw many of
the [r]Pharisees and Sadducees coming for baptism, he said to them,
"You brood of vipers, who
warned you to flee from the wrath
to come? Matt. 16:1ff.; 23:13, 15
8 "Therefore bring forth fruit in
keeping with repentance;
9 and do not suppose that you

can say to yourselves, 'We have
Abraham for our father'; for I say
to you, that God is able from these
stones to raise up children to
Abraham. Luke 3:8; 16:24
10 "And the axe is already laid at
the root of the trees; every tree
therefore that does not bear good
fruit is cut down and thrown into
the fire. Luke 3:9 • Ps. 92:12-14
11 "As for me, I baptize you [6]with
water for repentance, but He who
is coming after me is mightier
than I, and I am not fit to remove
His sandals; He will baptize you
with the Holy Spirit and fire.
12 "And His winnowing fork is in
His hand, and He will thoroughly
clear His threshing floor; and He
will gather His wheat into the
barn, but He will burn up the chaff
with unquenchable fire." Ps. 1:4
13 Then Jesus *arrived from
Galilee at the Jordan *coming* to
John, to be baptized by him.
14 But John tried to prevent
Him, saying, "I have need to be
baptized by You, and do You
come to me?"
15 But Jesus answering said to
him, "Permit *it* at this time; for in
this way it is fitting for us to fulfill
all righteousness." Then he *permitted Him. Ps. 40:7, 8
16 And after being baptized,
Jesus went up immediately from
the water; and behold, the heavens were opened, and he saw the
Spirit of God descending as a
dove, *and* coming upon Him,
17 and behold, a voice out of the
heavens, saying, "This is [7]My beloved Son, in whom I am well-pleased." Ps. 2:7; Is. 42:1

[6] The Gr. here can be translated *in, with* or *by*
[7] Lit., *My Son, the Beloved*

CHAPTER 4

THEN Jesus was led up by the
Spirit into the wilderness to be
tempted by the devil. Heb. 4:15
2 And after He had fasted forty
days and forty nights, He [8]then became hungry. Ex. 34:28
3 And the tempter came and
said to Him, "If You are the Son
of God, command that these
stones become bread." *loaves*
4 But He answered and said,
"It is written, 'MAN SHALL NOT
LIVE ON BREAD ALONE, BUT ON EVERY WORD THAT PROCEEDS OUT OF
THE MOUTH OF GOD.'" Deut. 8:3
5 Then the devil *took Him
into the holy city; and he had Him
stand on the pinnacle of the temple, Neh. 11:1, 18; Dan. 9:24
6 and *said to Him, "If You are
the Son of God throw Yourself
down; for it is written,

'HE WILL GIVE HIS ANGELS CHARGE CONCERNING YOU'; Ps. 91:11, 12

and

'ON *their* HANDS THEY WILL BEAR YOU UP,
LEST YOU STRIKE YOUR FOOT AGAINST A STONE.'"

7 Jesus said to him, "On the
other hand, it is written, 'YOU
SHALL NOT [9]PUT THE LORD YOUR
GOD TO THE TEST.'" *Again*
8 Again, the devil *took Him to
a very high mountain, and
*showed Him all the kingdoms of
the world, and their glory;
9 and he said to Him, "All
these things will I give You, if You
fall down and worship me."
10 Then Jesus *said to him,
"Begone, Satan! For it is written,

[8] Lit., *later, afterward* [9] Or, *tempt . . . God*

'YOU SHALL WORSHIP THE LORD
YOUR GOD, AND [a]SERVE HIM
ONLY.' " *fulfill religious duty to Him*
11 Then the devil *left Him; and
behold, [r]angels came and *began* to
minister to Him. Matt. 26:53
12 Now when He heard that
John had been taken into custody,
He withdrew into Galilee;
13 and leaving Nazareth, He
came and settled in Capernaum,
which is by the sea, in the region
of Zebulun and Naphtali.
14 *This was* to fulfill what was
spoken through Isaiah the
prophet, saying,
15 "THE LAND OF ZEBULUN AND
THE LAND OF NAPHTALI,
BY THE WAY OF THE SEA, BE-
YOND THE JORDAN, GALI-
LEE OF THE [10]GENTILES—
16 "THE [r]PEOPLE WHO WERE SIT-
TING IN DARKNESS SAW A
GREAT LIGHT, Is. 9:2
AND TO THOSE WHO WERE
SITTING IN THE LAND AND
SHADOW OF DEATH,
UPON THEM A LIGHT
DAWNED."
17 From that time Jesus began
to [a]preach and say, "Repent, for
the kingdom of heaven is at
hand." *proclaim*
18 And walking by [r]the Sea of
Galilee, He saw two brothers, Simon who was called Peter, and
Andrew his brother, casting a net
into the sea; for they were fishermen. Matt. 15:29; Mark 7:31
19 And He *said to them, "Follow [t]Me, and I will make you fishers of men." *Come here after Me*
20 And they immediately left
the nets, and followed Him.

[10]Or, *nations*

21 And going on from there He
saw two other brothers, [a]James the
son of Zebedee, and John his
brother, in the boat with Zebedee
their father, mending their nets;
and He called them. *Jacob*
22 And they immediately left
the boat and their father, and followed Him.
23 And *Jesus* was going about
in all Galilee, [r]teaching in their
synagogues, and proclaiming the
[a]gospel of the kingdom, and healing every kind of disease and every kind of sickness among the
people. Matt. 9:35 • *good news*
24 And the news about Him
went out into all Syria; and they
brought to Him all who were ill,
taken with various diseases and
pains, demoniacs, epileptics, para-
lytics; and He healed them.
25 And great multitudes followed Him from Galilee and Decapolis and Jerusalem and Judea
and *from* beyond the Jordan.

CHAPTER 5

AND when He saw the multitudes, He went up on the [a]moun-
tain; and after He sat down, His
disciples came to Him. *hill*
2 And opening His mouth He
began to teach them, saying,
3 "Blessed are the poor in spirit,
for [r]theirs is the kingdom of
heaven. Matt. 5:10; 19:14; 25:34
4 "Blessed are [r]those who
mourn, for they shall be comforted. Is. 61:2; John 16:20; Rev. 7:17
5 "Blessed are the [11]gentle, for
they shall inherit the earth.
6 "Blessed are those who hunger and thirst for righteousness,
for they shall be satisfied.

[11]Or, *humble, meek*

7 "Blessed are the merciful, for
they shall receive mercy.
8 "Blessed are [r]the pure in heart,
for they shall see God. Ps. 24:4
9 "Blessed are the peacemak-
ers, for [r]they shall be called sons of
God. Matt. 5:45; Luke 6:35
10 "Blessed are those who have
been [r]persecuted for the sake of
righteousness, for theirs is the
kingdom of heaven. 1 Pet. 3:14
11 "Blessed are you when *men*
[r]cast insults at you, and persecute
you, and say all kinds of evil
against you falsely, on account of
Me. 1 Pet. 4:14
12 "Rejoice, and be glad, for your
reward in heaven is great, for [r]so
they persecuted the prophets who
were before you. 2 Chr. 36:16
13 "You are the salt of the earth;
but if the salt has become tasteless, how will it be made salty
again? It is good for nothing anymore, except to be thrown out and
trampled under foot by men.
14 "You are the light of the
world. A city set on a [a]hill cannot
be hidden. *mountain*
15 "Nor do *men* light a lamp, and
put it under the peck-measure,
but on the lampstand; and it gives
light to all who are in the house.
16 "Let your light shine before
men in such a way that they may
see your good works, and glorify
your Father who is in heaven.
17 "Do not think that I came to
abolish the [r]Law or the Prophets; I
did not come to abolish, but to fulfill. Matt. 7:12
18 "For truly I say to you, [r]until
heaven and earth pass away, not
the smallest letter or stroke shall
pass away from the Law, until all
is accomplished. Matt. 24:35
19 "Whoever then annuls one of
the least of these commandments,
and so teaches others, shall be
called least in the kingdom of
heaven; but whoever keeps and
teaches *them*, he shall be called
great in the kingdom of heaven.
20 "For I say to you, that unless
your [r]righteousness surpasses *that*
of the scribes and Pharisees, you
shall not enter the kingdom of
heaven. Luke 18:11, 12
21 "You have heard that [t]the ancients were told, 'YOU SHALL NOT
COMMIT MURDER' and 'Whoever
commits murder shall be [12]liable to
the court.' *it was said to the ancients*
22 "But I say to you that everyone who is angry with his
brother[13] shall be [a]guilty before the
court; and whoever shall say to
his brother, '[14]Raca,' shall be guilty
before [15]the supreme court; and
whoever shall say, 'You fool,'
shall be guilty *enough to* go into
the [16]fiery hell. *liable to*
23 "If therefore you are presenting your offering at the altar, and
there remember that your brother
has something against you,
24 leave your [a]offering there before the altar, and go your way;
first be [r]reconciled to your brother,
and then come and present your
offering. *gift* • Rom. 12:17, 18
25 "Make [r] friends quickly with
your opponent at law while you
are with him on the way, in order
that your opponent may not deliver you to the judge, and the

[12] Or, *guilty before*
[13] Some mss. insert here: *without cause*
[14] Aramaic for *empty-head* or, *good for nothing*
[15] Lit., *the Sanhedrin* [16] Lit., *Gehenna of fire*

judge to the officer, and you be
thrown into prison. Prov. 25:8f.
26 "Truly I say to you, you shall
not come out of there, until you
have paid up the last [17]cent.
27 "You have heard that it was
said, 'You[r] SHALL NOT COMMIT
ADULTERY'; Ex. 20:14; Deut. 5:18
28 but I say to you, that everyone who looks on a woman to lust
for her has committed adultery
with her already in his heart.
29 "And if your right eye makes
you stumble, tear it out, and
throw it from you; for it is better
for you that one of the parts of
your body perish, than for your
whole body to be thrown into hell.
30 "And if your right hand makes
you stumble, cut it off, and throw
it from you; for it is better for you
that one of the parts of your body
perish, [t]than for your whole body
to go into hell. *not your whole body*
31 "And it was said, 'WHOEVER
DIVORCES HIS WIFE, LET HIM GIVE
HER A CERTIFICATE OF DISMISSAL';
32 [r]but I say to you that everyone who divorces his wife, except
for *the* cause of unchastity, makes
her commit adultery; and whoever marries a divorced woman
commits adultery. Matt. 19:9
33 "Again, you have heard that
[t]the ancients were told, 'YOU
SHALL NOT MAKE FALSE VOWS, BUT
SHALL FULFILL YOUR VOWS TO THE
LORD.' *it was said to the ancients*
34 "But I say to you, [r]make no
oath at all, either by heaven, for it
is the throne of God, James 5:12
35 or by the earth, for it is the
[r]footstool of His feet, or [a]by Jerusalem, for it is THE CITY OF THE
GREAT KING. Is. 66:1 • *toward*
36 "Nor shall you make an oath
by your head, for you cannot
make one hair white or black.
37 "But let your statement be,
'Yes, yes' *or* 'No, no'; and anything beyond these is of evil.
38 "You have heard that it was
said, 'AN[r] EYE FOR AN EYE, AND A
TOOTH FOR A TOOTH.' Ex. 21:24
39 "But I say to you, do not resist
him who is evil; but [r]whoever slaps
you on your right cheek, turn to
him the other also. Matt. 5:39-42
40 "And if anyone wants to sue
you, and take your [18]shirt, let him
have your [19]coat also.
41 "And whoever shall force you
to go one mile, go with him two.
42 "Give to him who asks of you,
and do not turn away from him
who wants to borrow from you.
43 "You have heard that it was
said, 'YOU SHALL LOVE YOUR
NEIGHBOR, and hate your enemy.'
44 "But I say to you, [r]love your
enemies, and pray for those who
persecute you Luke 6:27f.; 23:34
45 in order that you may be
[r]sons of your Father who is in
heaven; for He causes His sun to
rise on *the* evil and *the* good, and
sends rain on *the* righteous and
the unrighteous. Matt. 5:9
46 "For [r]if you love those who
love you, what reward have you?
Do not even the tax-gatherers do
the same? Luke 6:32
47 "And if you greet your brothers only, what do you do more
than others? Do not even the Gentiles do the same?

[17]Lit., *quadrans* (equaling two lepta or mites); i.e., 1/64 of a denarius

[18]Or, *tunic;* i.e., garment worn next to the body [19]Or, *cloak;* i.e., outer garment

48 "Therefore [r]you are to be perfect, as your heavenly Father is perfect. Lev. 19:2; Deut. 18:13

CHAPTER 6

"BEWARE of practicing your righteousness before men [r]to be noticed by them; otherwise you have no reward with your Father who is in heaven. Matt. 6:5

2 "When therefore you [a]give alms, do not sound a trumpet before you, as the hypocrites do in the synagogues and in the streets, that they may be honored by men. Truly I say to you, they have their reward in full. *do an act of charity*

3 "But when you give alms, do not let your left hand know what your right hand is doing

4 that your alms may be in secret; and your Father who sees in secret will repay you.

5 "And when you pray, you are not to be as the hypocrites; for they love to [r]stand and pray in the synagogues and on the street corners, in order to be seen by men. Truly I say to you, they have their reward in full. Luke 18:11, 13

6 "But you, when you pray, [r]go into your inner room, and when you have shut your door, pray to your Father who is in secret, and your Father who sees in secret will repay you. Matt. 26:36-39

7 "And when you are praying, do not use meaningless repetition, as the Gentiles do, for they suppose that they will be heard for their [r]many words. 1 Kin. 18:26f.

8 "Therefore do not be like them; for your Father knows what you need, before you ask Him.

9 "Pray, then, in this way:
'Our Father who art in [t]heaven, *the heavens*
Hallowed be Thy name.
10 'Thy kingdom come.
Thy will be done,
On earth as it is in heaven.
11 'Give[r] us this day our daily bread. Prov. 30:8
12 'And [r]forgive us our debts, as we also have forgiven our debtors. Ex. 34:7
13 'And do not lead us into temptation, but deliver us from evil. [For Thine is the kingdom, and the power, and the glory, forever. Amen.]'

14 "For if you forgive men for their transgressions, your heavenly Father will also forgive you.

15 "But if you do not forgive men, then your Father will not forgive your transgressions.

16 "And whenever you fast, do not put on a gloomy face as the hypocrites *do,* for they neglect their appearance in order to be seen fasting by men. Truly I say to you, they have their reward in full.

17 "But you, when you fast, [r]anoint your head, and wash your face Ruth 3:3; 2 Sam. 12:20

18 so that you may not be seen fasting by men, but by your Father who is in secret; and your [r]Father who sees in secret will repay you. Matt. 6:4, 6

19 "Do not lay up for yourselves treasures upon earth, where moth and rust destroy, and where thieves break in and steal.

20 "But lay up for yourselves treasures in heaven, where neither moth nor rust destroys, and where thieves do not break in or steal;

21 for where your treasure is, there will your heart be also.

22 "The[r] lamp of the body is the eye; if therefore your eye is[a] clear, your whole body will be full of light. Matt. 6:22, 23 • *healthy*

23 "But if[r] your eye is bad, your whole body will be full of darkness. If therefore the light that is in you is darkness, how great is the darkness! Matt. 20:15

24 "No one can serve two masters; for either he will hate the one and love the other, or he will hold to one and despise the other. You cannot serve God and [20]mammon.

25 "For this reason I say to you, [a]do not be anxious for your life, *as to* what you shall eat, or what you shall drink; nor for your body, *as to* what you shall put on. Is not life more than food, and the body than clothing? *stop being anxious*

26 "Look at the birds of the [t]air, that they do not sow, neither do they reap, nor gather into barns, and *yet* your heavenly Father feeds them. Are you not worth much more than they? *heaven*

27 "And which of you by being anxious can [r]add a *single* cubit to his[a] life's span? Ps. 39:5 • *height*

28 "And why are you [r]anxious about clothing? Observe how the lilies of the field grow; they do not toil nor do they spin, Matt. 6:25

29 yet I say to you that even Solomon in all his glory did not clothe himself like one of these.

30 "But if God so arrays the [r]grass of the field, which is *alive* today and tomorrow is thrown into the furnace, *will He* not much more *do so for* you, O men of little faith? James 1:10, 11; 1 Pet. 1:24

31 "Do not be anxious then, saying, 'What shall we eat?' or 'What shall we drink?' or 'With what shall we clothe ourselves?'

32 "For all these things the Gentiles eagerly seek; for [r]your heavenly Father knows that you need all these things. Matt. 6:8

33 "But seek first His kingdom and His righteousness; and all these things shall be added to you.

34 "Therefore do not be anxious for tomorrow; for tomorrow will care for itself. *Each* day has enough trouble of its own.

CHAPTER 7

"DO[r] not judge lest you be judged. Matt. 7:1-5: *Luke 6:37f., 41f.*

2 "For in the way you judge, you will be judged; and [r]by your standard of measure, it will be measured to you. Mark 4:24

3 "And why do you [r]look at the speck that is in your brother's eye, but do not notice the log that is in your own eye? Rom. 2:1

4 "Or how [t]can you say to your brother, 'Let me take the speck out of your eye,' and behold, the log is in your own eye? *will*

5 "You hypocrite, first take the log out of your own eye, and then you will see clearly to take the speck out of your brother's eye.

6 "Do not give what is holy to dogs, and do not throw your pearls before swine, lest they trample them under their feet, and turn and tear you to pieces.

7 "Ask, and it shall be given to you; [a]seek, and you shall find; knock, and it shall be opened to you. *keep seeking*

[20]Or, *riches*

8 "For everyone who asks receives, and he who seeks finds, and to him who knocks it shall be opened.

9 "Or what man is there among you, when his son shall ask him for a loaf, will give him a stone?

10 "Or [t]if he shall ask for a fish, he will not give him a snake, will he? *also*

11 "If you then, being evil, know how to give good gifts to your children, [r]how much more shall your Father who is in heaven give what is good to those who ask Him! Ps. 84:11; Is. 63:7; Rom. 8:32

12 "Therefore, however you want people to treat you, [a]so treat them, for this is the Law and the Prophets. *you, too, do so for*

13 "Enter[r] by the narrow gate; for the gate is wide, and the way is broad that leads to destruction, and many are those who enter by it. Luke 13:24

14 "For the gate is small, and the way is narrow that leads to life, and few are those who find it.

15 "Beware of the [r]false prophets, who come to you in sheep's clothing, but inwardly are ravenous wolves. Matt. 24:11, 24; Mark 13:22

16 "You will [a]know them by their fruits. Grapes are not gathered from thorn *bushes,* nor figs from thistles, are they? *recognize*

17 "Even so, [r]every good tree bears good fruit; but the bad tree bears bad fruit. Matt. 12:33, 35

18 "A good tree cannot produce bad fruit, nor can a bad tree produce good fruit.

19 "Every[r] tree that does not bear good fruit is cut down and thrown into the fire. Matt. 3:10; Luke 3:9

20 "So then, you will [a]know them by their fruits. *recognize*

21 "Not[r] everyone who says to Me, 'Lord, Lord,' will enter the kingdom of heaven; but he who does the will of My Father who is in heaven. Luke 6:46

22 "Many will say to Me on [r]that day, 'Lord, Lord, did we not prophesy in Your name, and in Your name cast out demons, and in Your name perform many [a]miracles?' Matt. 10:15 • *works of power*

23 "And then I will declare to them, 'I never knew you; [r]DEPART FROM ME, YOU WHO PRACTICE LAWLESSNESS.' Ps. 6:8; Luke 13:27

24 "Therefore everyone who hears these words of Mine, and [t]acts upon them, may be compared to a wise man, who built his house upon the rock. *does*

25 "And the rain descended, and the floods came, and the winds blew, and burst against that house; and *yet* it did not fall, for it had been founded upon the rock.

26 "And everyone who hears these words of Mine, and does not [t]act upon them, will be like a foolish man, who built his house upon the sand. *do*

27 "And the rain descended, and the [t]floods came, and the winds blew, and burst against that house; and it fell, and great was its fall." *rivers*

28 [t]The result was that when Jesus had finished these words, the multitudes were amazed at His teaching; *And it came to pass*

29 for He was teaching them as *one* having authority, and not as their scribes.

CHAPTER 8

AND when He had come down
from the mountain, great multitudes followed Him.
2 And behold, a leper came to
Him, and bowed down to Him,
saying, "Lord, if You are willing,
You can make me clean."
3 And He stretched out His
hand and touched him, saying, "I
am willing; be cleansed." And immediately his [r]leprosy was
cleansed. Matt. 11:5; Luke 4:27
4 And Jesus *said to him, "See
that you tell no one; but go, show
yourself to the priest, and present
the offering that Moses commanded, for a testimony to them."
5 And when He had entered
Capernaum, a centurion came to
Him, entreating Him,
6 and saying, "Lord,[a] my [t]ser-
vant is lying paralyzed at home,
suffering great pain." *Sir • boy*
7 And He *said to him, "I will
come and heal him."
8 But the centurion answered
and said, "Lord,[a] I am not worthy
for You to come under my roof,
but just say the word, and my [t]ser-
vant will be healed. *Sir • boy*
9 "For I, too, am a man under
[r]authority, with soldiers under me;
and I say to this one, 'Go!' and he
goes, and to another, 'Come!' and
he comes, and to my slave, 'Do
this!' and he does *it*." Luke 9:1
10 Now when Jesus heard *this*,
He marveled, and said to those
who were following, "Truly I say
to you, I have not found such
great faith with anyone in Israel.
11 "And I say to you, that many
shall come from east and west,
and [21]recline *at the table* with
Abraham, and Isaac, and Jacob, in
the kingdom of heaven;
12 but [r]the sons of the kingdom
shall be cast out into the outer
darkness; in that place [r]there shall
be weeping and gnashing of
teeth." Matt. 13:38 • Matt. 13:42
13 And Jesus said to the centurion, "Go your way; let it be done
to you [r]as you have believed." And
the [t]servant was healed that *very*
hour. Matt. 9:22, 29 • *boy*
14 [r]And when Jesus had come to
Peter's [a]home, He saw his mother-
in-law lying sick in bed with a fever. Matt. 8:14-16 • *house*
15 And He touched her hand,
and the fever left her; and she
arose, and waited on Him.
16 And when evening had
come, they brought to Him many
who were demon-possessed; and
He cast out the spirits with a
word, and healed all who were ill
17 in order that what was spoken through Isaiah the prophet
might be fulfilled, saying, "[r]HE
HIMSELF TOOK OUR INFIRMITIES,
AND [a]CARRIED AWAY OUR DIS-
EASES." Is. 53:4 • *removed*
18 Now when Jesus saw a
crowd around Him, He gave orders to depart to the other side.
19 And a certain scribe came
and said to Him, "Teacher, I will
follow You wherever You go."
20 And Jesus *said to him, "The
foxes have holes, and the birds of
the [a]air *have* [a]nests; but the Son of
Man has nowhere to lay His
head." *sky • roosting places*
21 And another of the disciples
said to Him, "Lord, permit me
first to go and bury my father."

[21] Or, *dine*

22 But Jesus *said to him, "Follow[r] Me; and allow the dead to
bury their own dead." Matt. 9:9
23 And when He got into the
boat, His disciples followed Him.
24 And behold, there arose a
great storm in the sea, so that the
boat was covered with the waves;
but He Himself was asleep.
25 And they came to *Him,* and
awoke Him, saying, "Save *us,*
Lord; we are perishing!"
26 And He *said to them, "Why
are you timid, you men of little
faith?" Then He arose, and rebuked the winds and the sea; and
it became perfectly calm.
27 And the men marveled, saying, "What kind of a man is this,
that even the winds and the sea
obey Him?"
28 And when He had come to
the other side into the country of
the Gadarenes, two men who
were [r]demon-possessed met Him
as they were coming out of the
tombs; *they were* so exceedingly
violent that no one could pass by
that road. Matt. 4:24
29 And behold, they cried out,
saying, "What[r] do we have to do
with You, Son of God? Have You
come here to torment us before
the time?" Judg. 11:12
30 Now there was at a distance
from them a herd of many swine
feeding.
31 And the demons *began* to entreat Him, saying, "If You are
going to cast us out, send us into
the herd of swine."
32 And He said to them, "Begone!" And they came out, and
went into the swine, and behold,
the whole herd rushed down the
steep bank into the sea and perished in the waters.
33 And the herdsmen ran away,
and went to the city, and reported
everything, [t]including the *incident*
of the [r]demoniacs. *and* • Matt. 4:24
34 And behold, the whole city
came out to meet Jesus; and when
they saw Him, they entreated *Him*
to depart from their region.

CHAPTER 9

AND getting into a boat, He
crossed over, and came to [r]His
own city. Matt. 4:13; Mark 5:21
2 And behold, they were bringing to Him a paralytic, lying on a
bed; and Jesus seeing their faith
said to the paralytic, "Take courage, My [t]son, your sins [t]are forgiven." *child* • *are being forgiven*
3 And behold, some of the
scribes said [t]to themselves, "This
fellow blasphemes." *among*
4 And Jesus knowing their
thoughts said, "Why are you
thinking evil in your hearts?
5 "For which is easier, to say,
'Your sins are forgiven,' or to say,
'Rise, and walk'?
6 "But in order that you may
know that the [r]Son of Man has authority on earth to forgive sins"—
then He *said to the paralytic—
"Rise, take up your bed, and go
home." Matt. 8:20; John 5:27
7 And he rose, and went home.
8 But when the multitudes saw
this, they were [a]filled with awe,
and glorified God, who had given
such authority to men. *afraid*
9 And as Jesus passed on from
there, He saw a man, called Matthew, sitting in the tax office; and

He *said to him, "Follow Me!" And he rose, and followed Him.

10 And it happened that as He was reclining *at the table* in the house, behold many tax-gatherers and sinners came and were dining with Jesus and His disciples.

11 And when the Pharisees saw *this,* they said to His disciples, "Why is your Teacher eating with the tax-gatherers and sinners?"

12 But when He heard this, He said, "*It is* not [r]those who are healthy who need a physician, but those who are sick. Mark 2:17

13 "But go and learn [r]what *this* means, 'I DESIRE [a]COMPASSION, [22]AND NOT SACRIFICE,' for I did not come to call the righteous, but sinners." Matt. 12:7 · *mercy*

14 Then the disciples of John *came to Him, saying, "Why do we and the Pharisees fast, but Your disciples do not fast?"

15 And Jesus said to them, "The attendants of the bridegroom cannot mourn as long as the bridegroom is with them, can they? But the days will come when the bridegroom is taken away from them, and then they will fast.

16 "But no one puts a patch of unshrunk cloth on an old garment; for the patch pulls away from the garment, and a worse tear results.

17 "Nor do *men* put new wine into old wineskins; otherwise the wineskins burst, and the wine pours out, and the wineskins are ruined; but they put new wine into fresh wineskins, and both are preserved."

18 While He was saying these things to them, behold, there came [a]a *synagogue* [t]official, and bowed down before Him, saying, "My daughter has just died; but come and lay Your hand on her, and she will live." *one · ruler*

19 And Jesus rose and *began* to follow him, and *so did* His disciples.

20 And behold, a woman who had been suffering from a hemorrhage for twelve years, came up behind Him and touched the fringe of His [a]cloak; *outer garment*

21 for she was saying [t]to herself, "If I only touch His garment, I shall get well." *in herself*

22 But Jesus turning and seeing her said, "Daughter, take courage; your faith has [t]made you well." And [t]at once the woman was made well. *saved you · from that hour*

23 And when Jesus came into the [t]official's house, and saw [r]the flute-players, and the crowd in noisy disorder, *ruler's* · Jer. 9:17

24 He *began* to say, "Depart; for the girl [r]has not died, but is asleep." And they *began* laughing at Him. John 11:13; Acts 20:10

25 But [r]when the crowd had been put out, He entered and took her by the hand; and the girl [a]arose. Acts 9:40 · *was raised up*

26 And [r]this news went out into all that land. Matt. 4:24; 9:31

27 And as Jesus passed on from there, two blind men followed Him, crying out, and saying, "Have mercy on us, [r]Son of David!" Matt. 1:1; 12:23; 15:22

28 And after He had come into the house, the blind men came up to Him, and Jesus *said to them, "Do you believe that I am able to do this?" They *said to Him, "Yes, Lord."

[22]I.e., more than

29 Then He touched their eyes, saying, "Be it done to you according to your faith."

30 And their eyes were opened. And Jesus [r]sternly warned them, saying, "See *here,* let no one know *about this!*" Matt. 8:4

31 But they went out, and [r]spread the news about Him in all that land. Matt. 4:24; 9:26; 14:1

32 And as they were going out, behold, a dumb man, demon-possessed, was brought to Him.

33 And after the demon was cast out, the dumb man spoke; and the multitudes marveled, saying, "Nothing like this [t]was ever seen in Israel." *ever appeared*

34 But the Pharisees were saying, "He casts out the demons by the ruler of the demons."

35 And Jesus was going about all the cities and the villages, [r]teaching in their synagogues, and proclaiming the gospel of the kingdom, and healing every kind of disease and every kind of sickness. Matt. 4:23; Mark 1:14

36 And seeing the multitudes, He felt compassion for them, because they were distressed and [t]downcast like sheep [t]without a shepherd. *thrown down* • *not having*

37 Then He *said to His disciples, "The[r] harvest is plentiful, but the workers are few. Luke 10:2

38 "Therefore beseech the Lord of the harvest to send out workers into His harvest."

CHAPTER 10

AND [r]having summoned His twelve disciples, He gave them authority over unclean spirits, to cast them out, and to heal every kind of disease and every kind of sickness. Mark 3:13-15; 6:7

2 Now the names of the twelve apostles are these: The first, Simon, who is called Peter, and [r]Andrew his brother; and [a]James the *son* of Zebedee, and John his brother; Matt. 4:18 • *Jacob*

3 Philip and Bartholomew; Thomas and Matthew the tax-gatherer; James the *son* of Alphaeus, and Thaddaeus;

4 Simon the[a]Zealot, and [r]Judas Iscariot, the one who betrayed Him. *Cananaean* • Matt. 26:14

5 These twelve Jesus sent out after instructing them, saying, "Do not[a]go in *the* way of *the* Gentiles, and do not enter *any* city of the[r]Samaritans; *go off to* • Luke 9:52

6 but rather go to the lost sheep of the house of Israel.

7 "And as you go,[a]preach, saying, 'The kingdom of heaven[t]is at hand.' *proclaim* • *has come near*

8 "Heal *the* sick, raise *the* dead, cleanse *the* lepers, cast out demons; freely you received, freely give.

9 "Do[r] not acquire gold, or silver, or copper [t]for your money belts, Matt. 10:9-15 • *into*

10 or a bag for *your* journey, or even two tunics, or sandals, or a staff; for the worker is worthy of his[t]support. *nourishment*

11 "And into whatever city or village you enter, inquire who is worthy in it; and abide there until you go away.

12 "And as you enter the[a]house, give it your greeting. *household*

13 "And if the house is worthy, let your *greeting of* peace come upon it; but if it is not worthy, let

your *greeting of* peace return to
you.
14 "And whoever does not receive you, nor heed your words,
as you go out of that house or that
city, [r]shake off the dust of your
feet. Acts 13:51
15 "Truly I say to you, it will be
more tolerable for *the* land of Sodom and Gomorrah in the day of
judgment, than for that city.
16 "Behold, I send you out as
sheep in the midst of wolves;
therefore be shrewd as serpents,
and innocent as doves.
17 "But beware of men; for they
will deliver you up to *the* [r]courts,
and scourge you [r]in their synagogues; Matt. 5:22 • Matt. 23:34
18 and you shall even be
brought before governors and
kings for My sake, as a testimony
to them and to the Gentiles.
19 "But when they deliver you
up, do not become anxious about
how or what you will speak; for it
shall be given you in that hour
what you are to speak.
20 "For [r]it is not you who speak,
but *it is* the Spirit of your Father
who speaks in you. Luke 12:12
21 "And brother will deliver up
brother to death, and a father *his*
child; and [r]children will rise up
against parents, and cause them
to be put to death. Mic. 7:6
22 "And you will be hated by all
on account of My name, but it is
the one who has endured to the
end who will be saved.
23 "But whenever they [r]persecute
you in this city, flee to [t]the next;
for truly I say to you, you shall not
finish *going through* the cities of
Israel, until the Son of Man
comes. Matt. 23:34 • *the other*

24 "A [r][a]disciple is not above his
teacher, nor a slave above his
master. John 13:16; 15:20 • *pupil*
25 "It is enough for the disciple
that he become as his teacher, and
the slave as his master. If they
have called the head of the house
Beelzebul, how much more the
members of his household!
26 "Therefore do not fear them,
for there is nothing covered that
will not be revealed, and hidden
that will not be known.
27 "What I tell you in the darkness, speak in the light; and what
you hear *whispered* in *your* ear,
proclaim upon the housetops.
28 "And do not fear those who
kill the body, but are unable to kill
the soul; but rather fear Him who
is able to destroy both soul and
body in [r]hell. Matt. 5:22; Luke 12:5
29 "Are [r] not two sparrows sold
for a [23]cent? And *yet* not one of
them will fall to the ground apart
from your Father. Luke 12:6
30 "But the very hairs of your
head are all numbered.
31 "Therefore do not fear; [r]you
are of more value than many sparrows. Matt. 12:12
32 "Everyone therefore who shall
confess [t]Me before men, I will also
confess [t]him before My Father
who is in heaven. *in Me* • *in him*
33 "But [r]whoever shall deny Me
before men, I will also deny him
before My Father who is in
heaven. Mark 8:38; Luke 9:26
34 "Do not think that I came to
bring peace on the earth; I did not
come to bring peace, but a sword.
35 "For I came to [r]SET A MAN
AGAINST HIS FATHER, AND A
DAUGHTER AGAINST HER MOTHER,

[23] Gr., *assarion*, the smallest copper coin

AND A DAUGHTER-IN-LAW AGAINST
HER MOTHER-IN-LAW; Mic. 7:6
36 and A MAN'S ENEMIES WILL BE
THE MEMBERS OF HIS HOUSEHOLD.
37 "He[r] who loves father or
mother more than Me is not worthy of Me; and he who loves son
or daughter more than Me is not
worthy of Me. Deut. 33:9
38 "And[r] he who does not take his
cross and follow after Me is not
worthy of Me. Matt. 16:24
39 "He who has found his life
shall lose it, and he who has lost
his life for My sake shall find it.
40 "He who receives you receives Me, and he who receives
Me receives Him who sent Me.
41 "He who receives a prophet in
the name of a prophet shall receive a prophet's reward; and he
who receives a righteous man in
the name of a righteous man shall
receive a righteous man's reward.
42 "And[r] whoever in the name of
a disciple gives to one of these little ones even a cup of cold water
to drink, truly I say to you he shall
not lose his reward." Mark 9:41

CHAPTER 11

AND it came about that when
Jesus had finished giving instructions to His twelve disciples, He
departed from there to teach and
[a]preach in their cities. *proclaim*
2 Now when John in prison
heard of the works of Christ, he
sent *word* by his disciples,
3 and said to Him, "Are You
the Expected One, or shall we
look for someone else?"
4 And Jesus answered and said
to them, "Go and report to John
what you hear and see:
5 *the* BLIND RECEIVE SIGHT and
the lame walk, *the* lepers are
cleansed and *the* deaf hear, and
the dead are raised up, and *the*
[r]POOR HAVE THE [a]GOSPEL PREACHED
TO THEM. Luke 4:18 • *good news*
6 "And blessed is he who keeps
from stumbling over Me."
7 And as these were going
away, Jesus began to speak to the
multitudes about John, "What did
you go out into[r] the wilderness to
look at? A reed shaken by the
wind? Matt. 3:1
8 "But what did you go out to
see? A man dressed in soft *clothing*? Behold, those who wear soft
clothing are in kings' palaces.
9 "But[a] why did you go out? To
see[r] a prophet? Yes, I say to you,
and one who is more than a
prophet. *Well then,* • Luke 1:76
10 "This is the one about whom it
[t]is written, *has been written*

'BEHOLD, I SEND MY MESSEN-
GER BEFORE YOUR FACE,
WHO WILL PREPARE YOUR
WAY BEFORE YOU.'

11 "Truly, I say to you, among
those born of women there has
not arisen *anyone* greater than
John the Baptist; yet he who is
[t]least in the kingdom of heaven is
greater than he. *less*
12 "And from the days of John
the Baptist until now the kingdom
of heaven suffers violence, and
violent men take it by force.
13 "For all the prophets and the
Law prophesied until John.
14 "And if you care to accept *it*,
he himself is [r]Elijah, who [a]was to
come. Matt. 17:10-13 • *is to come*
15 "He[r] who has ears to hear, let
him hear. Matt. 13:9, 43; Mark 4:9

16 "But to what shall I compare
this generation? It is like children
sitting in the market places, who
call out to the other *children*,
17 and say, 'We played the flute
for you, and you did not dance; we
sang a dirge, and you did not
[t]mourn.' *beat the breast*
18 "For John came neither [r]eating
nor drinking, and they say, 'He
has a demon!' Matt. 3:4
19 "The Son of Man came eating
and drinking, and they say, 'Behold,
a gluttonous man and a
drunkard, a friend of tax-gatherers
and sinners!' [t]Yet wisdom is
vindicated by her deeds." *And*
20 Then He began to reproach
the cities in which most of His
[a]miracles were done, because they
did not repent. *works of power*
21 "Woe to you, Chorazin! Woe
to you, [r]Bethsaida! For if the miracles
had occurred in Tyre and Sidon
which occurred in you, they
would have repented long ago in
sackcloth and ashes. Mark 6:45
22 "Nevertheless I say to you, [r]it
shall be more tolerable for Tyre
and Sidon in *the* day of judgment,
than for you. Matt. 10:15; 11:24
23 "And you, Capernaum, will
not be exalted to heaven, will you?
You shall descend to Hades; for if
the miracles had occurred in Sodom
which occurred in you, it
would have remained to this day.
24 "Nevertheless I say to you
that it shall be more tolerable for
the land of Sodom in *the* day of
judgment, than for you."
25 At that [a]time Jesus answered
and said, "I praise Thee, O Father,
Lord of heaven and earth, that
Thou didst hide these things from
the wise and intelligent and didst
reveal them to babes. *occasion*
26 "Yes, Father, for thus it was
well-pleasing in Thy sight.
27 "All things [t]have been handed
over to Me by My Father; and no
one knows the Son, except the Father;
nor does anyone know the
Father, [r]except the Son, and anyone
to whom the Son wills to reveal
Him. *were given over* • John 7:29
28 "Come[r] to Me, all who are
weary and heavy-laden, and I will
give you rest. Jer. 31:25
29 "Take My yoke upon you, and
learn from Me, for I am gentle and
humble in heart; and YOU SHALL
FIND REST FOR YOUR SOULS.
30 "For My yoke is [a]easy, and My
load is light." *kindly* or *pleasant*

CHAPTER 12

AT that [a]time Jesus went on the
Sabbath through the grainfields,
and His disciples became hungry
and began to pick the heads *of*
grain and eat. *occasion*
2 But when the Pharisees saw
it, they said to Him, "Behold,
Your disciples do what is not lawful
to do on a Sabbath."
3 But He said to them, "Have
you not read what David did,
when he became hungry, he and
his companions;
4 how he entered the house of
God, and they ate the consecrated
bread, which was not lawful for
him to eat, nor for those with him,
but for the priests alone?
5 "Or have you not read in the
Law, that on the Sabbath the
priests in the temple break the
Sabbath, and are innocent?

6 "But I say to you, that something [r]greater than the temple is here. 2 Chr. 6:18; Is. 66:1, 2
7 "But if you had known what this means, 'I DESIRE COMPASSION, AND NOT A SACRIFICE,' you would not have condemned the innocent.
8 "For [r]the Son of Man is Lord of the Sabbath." Matt. 8:20; 12:32
9 And departing from there, He went into their synagogue.
10 And behold, *there was* a man with a withered hand. And they questioned Him, saying, "Is[r] it lawful to heal on the Sabbath?"—in order that they might accuse Him. Matt. 12:2; Luke 13:14
11 And He said to them, "What[r] man shall there be [t]among you, who shall have one sheep, and if it falls into a pit on the Sabbath, will he not take hold of it, and lift it out? Luke 14:5 • *of*
12 "Of [r]how much more value then is a man than a sheep! So then, it is lawful to do [t]good on the Sabbath." Matt. 10:31 • *well*
13 Then He *said to the man, "Stretch out your hand!" And he stretched it out, and it was restored to normal, like the other.
14 But the Pharisees went out, and [r]counseled together against Him, *as to* how they might destroy Him. John 7:30, 44; 8:59
15 But Jesus, [t]aware of *this,* withdrew from there. And many followed Him, and [r]He healed them all, *knowing* • Matt. 4:23
16 and [r]warned them not to make Him known, Matt. 8:4; 9:30
17 in order that what was spoken through Isaiah the prophet, might be fulfilled, saying,
18 "BEHOLD, MY SERVANT WHOM I HAVE CHOSEN;
MY BELOVED IN WHOM MY SOUL IS WELL-PLEASED;
[r]I WILL PUT MY SPIRIT UPON HIM, John 3:34
AND HE SHALL PROCLAIM JUSTICE TO THE GENTILES.
19 "HE[r] WILL NOT QUARREL, NOR CRY OUT; Is. 42:2
NOR WILL ANYONE HEAR HIS VOICE IN THE STREETS.
20 "A BATTERED REED HE WILL NOT BREAK OFF,
AND A SMOLDERING WICK HE WILL NOT PUT OUT,
UNTIL HE [a]LEADS JUSTICE TO VICTORY. *puts forth*
21 "AND IN HIS NAME THE GENTILES WILL HOPE."
22 Then there was brought to Him a [r]demon-possessed man *who was* blind and dumb, and He healed him, so that the dumb man spoke and saw. 2 Thess. 2:9
23 And all the multitudes were amazed, and *began* to say, "This *man* cannot be the [r]Son of David, can he?" Matt. 9:27
24 But when the Pharisees heard it, they said, "This man casts out demons only by Beelzebul the ruler of the demons."
25 And knowing their thoughts He said to them, "Any kingdom divided against itself is laid waste; and any city or house divided against itself shall not stand.
26 "And if Satan casts out Satan, he is divided against himself; how then shall his kingdom stand?
27 "And if I [r]by Beelzebul cast out demons, by whom do your sons cast them out? Consequently they shall be your judges. Matt. 9:34
28 "But if I cast out demons by the Spirit of God, then the kingdom of God has come upon you.

29 "Or how can anyone enter the
strong man's house and carry off
his property, unless he first binds
the strong *man*? And then he will
plunder his house.
30 "He who is not with Me is
against Me; and he who does not
gather with Me scatters.
31 "Therefore I say to you, any
sin and blasphemy shall be forgiven men, but blasphemy against
the Spirit shall not be forgiven.
32 "And[r] whoever shall speak a
word against the Son of Man, it
shall be forgiven him; but whoever shall speak against the Holy
Spirit, it shall not be forgiven him,
either in[r] this age, or in the *age* to
come. Luke 12:10 • Matt. 13:22
33 "Either make the tree good,
and its fruit good; or make the
tree bad, and its fruit bad; for the
tree is known by its fruit.
34 "You brood of vipers, how can
you, being evil, speak what is
good? For the mouth speaks out
of that which fills the heart.
35 "The good man out of *his*
good treasure brings forth[t] what is
good; and the evil man out of *his*
evil treasure brings forth[t] what is
evil. *good things • evil things*
36 "And I say to you, that every
careless word that men shall
speak, they shall render account
for it in the day of judgment.
37 "For by your words you shall
be justified, and by your words
you shall be condemned."
38 Then some of the scribes and
Pharisees answered Him, saying,
"Teacher, we want to see a[a] sign
from You." *attesting miracle*
39 But He answered and said to
them, "An evil and adulterous
generation craves for a sign; and
yet no sign shall be given to it but
the sign of Jonah the prophet;
40 for just as[r] JONAH WAS THREE
DAYS AND THREE NIGHTS IN THE
BELLY OF THE SEA MONSTER, so
shall[r] the Son of Man be three days
and three nights in the heart of the
earth. Jon. 1:17 • Matt. 8:20
41 "The men of Nineveh shall
stand up with this generation at
the judgment, and shall condemn
it because[r] they repented at the
preaching of Jonah; and behold,
[r]something greater than Jonah is
here. Jon. 3:5 • Matt. 12:6, 42
42 "*The* Queen of *the* South shall
rise up with this generation at the
judgment and shall condemn it,
because she came from the ends
of the earth to hear the wisdom of
Solomon; and behold, something
greater than Solomon is here.
43 "Now when the unclean spirit
goes out of a man, it passes
through waterless places, seeking
rest, and does not find *it*.
44 "Then it says, 'I will return to
my house from which I came'; and
when it comes, it finds it unoccu-
pied, swept, and put in order.
45 "Then it goes, and takes along
with it seven other spirits more
wicked than itself, and they go in
and live there; and the last state of
that man becomes worse than the
first. That is the way it will also be
with this evil generation."
46 While He was still speaking
to the multitudes, behold, His
[r]mother and[r] brothers were standing outside, seeking to speak to
Him. John 2:1, 5, 12 • Gal. 1:19
47 And someone said to Him,
"Behold, Your mother and Your
brothers are standing outside
seeking to speak to You."

48 But He answered the one
who was telling Him and said,
"Who is My mother and who are
My brothers?"
49 And stretching out His hand
toward His disciples, He said,
"Behold, My mother and My
brothers!
50 "For whoever does the will of
My Father who is in heaven, he is
My brother and sister and
mother."

CHAPTER 13

ON that day Jesus went out of
[r]the house, and was sitting by the
sea. Matt. 9:28; 13:36
2 And great multitudes gathered to Him, so that [r]He got into a
boat and sat down, and the whole
multitude was standing on the
beach. Luke 5:3
3 And He spoke many things
to them in parables, saying, "Behold, the sower went out to sow;
4 and as he sowed, some *seeds*
fell beside the road, and the birds
came and ate them up.
5 "And others fell upon the
rocky places, where they [t]did not
have much soil; and immediately
they sprang up, because they had
no depth of soil. *were not having*
6 "But when the sun had risen,
they were scorched; and because
they had no root, they withered
away.
7 "And others fell [t]among the
thorns, and the thorns came up
and choked them out. *upon*
8 "And others fell on the good
soil, and *yielded a crop, some a
[r]hundredfold, some sixty, and
some thirty. Gen. 26:12
9 "He[r] who has ears, let him
hear." Matt. 11:15; Rev. 2:7

10 And the disciples came and
said to Him, "Why do You speak
to them in parables?"
11 And He answered and said to
them, "To[r] you it has been granted
to know the mysteries of the kingdom of heaven, but to them it has
not been granted. Matt. 19:11
12 "For whoever has, to him
shall *more* be given, and he shall
have an abundance; but whoever
does not have, even what he has
shall be taken away from him.
13 "Therefore I speak to them in
parables; because while [r]seeing
they do not see, and while hearing
they do not hear, nor do they understand. Deut. 29:4; Is. 42:19, 20
14 "And [t]in their case the prophecy of Isaiah is being fulfilled,
which says, *for them*

'YOU WILL KEEP ON HEARING,
[t]BUT WILL NOT UNDER-
STAND; *and*
AND [t]YOU WILL KEEP ON SEE-
ING, BUT WILL NOT PER-
CEIVE; *seeing you will see*
15 FOR THE HEART OF THIS PEO-
PLE HAS BECOME DULL,
AND WITH THEIR EARS THEY
SCARCELY HEAR,
AND THEY HAVE CLOSED
THEIR EYES
LEST THEY SHOULD SEE
WITH THEIR EYES,
AND HEAR WITH THEIR EARS,
AND UNDERSTAND WITH
THEIR HEART AND RE-
TURN,
AND I SHOULD HEAL THEM.'

16 "But[r] blessed are your eyes,
because they see; and your ears,
because they hear. Matt. 16:17
17 "For truly I say to you, that
many prophets and righteous men
desired to see what you see, and

ıot see *it;* and to hear what
ıear, and did not hear *it.*
Hear[r] then the parable of the
Matt. 13:18-23
When anyone hears[r] the word
kingdom, and does not un-
nd it, the evil *one* comes
atches away what has been
n his heart. This is the one
om seed was sown beside
ıd. Matt. 4:23
nd the one on whom seed
own on the rocky places,
the man who hears the
word, and immediately receives it
with joy;
21 yet he has no *firm* root in
himself, but is *only* temporary,
and when affliction or persecution
arises because of the word, immediately he[r] falls away. Matt. 11:6
22 "And the one on whom seed
was sown among the thorns, this
is the man who hears the word,
and the worry of the[a] world, and
the [r]deceitfulness of riches choke
the word, and it becomes unfruitful. *age* • Matt. 19:23
23 "And the one on whom seed
was sown on the good soil, this is
the man who hears the word and
understands it; who indeed bears
fruit, and brings forth, some [r]a
hundredfold, some sixty, and
some thirty." Matt. 13:8
24 He presented another parable to them, saying, "The kingdom of heaven [t]may be compared
to a man who sowed good seed in
his field. *was compared to*
25 "But while men were sleeping,
his enemy came and sowed [24]tares
also among the wheat, and went
away.

[24]Or, *darnel,* a weed resembling wheat

26 "But when the [t]wheat sprang
up and bore grain, then the tares
became evident also. *grass*
27 "And the slaves of the landowner came and said to him, 'Sir,
did you not sow good seed in your
field? [t]How then does it have
tares?' *From where*
28 "And he said to them, 'An
[t]enemy has done this!' And the
slaves *said to him, 'Do you want
us, then, to go and gather them
up?' *enemy man*
29 "But he *said, 'No; lest while
you are gathering up the tares,
you may root up the wheat with
them.
30 'Allow both to grow together
until the harvest; and in the time
of the harvest I will say to the
reapers, "First gather up the tares
and bind them in bundles to burn
them up; but [r]gather the wheat
into my barn." ' " Matt. 3:12
31 He presented another parable to them, saying, "The[r] kingdom of heaven is like a mustard
seed, which a man took and
sowed in his field; Matt. 13:31, 32
32 and this is smaller than all
other seeds; but when it is full
grown, it is larger than the garden
plants, and becomes a tree, so that
THE BIRDS OF THE [a]AIR come and
NEST IN ITS BRANCHES." *sky*
33 He spoke another parable to
them, "The kingdom of heaven is
like leaven, which a woman took,
and hid in three pecks of meal, until it was all leavened."
34 All these things Jesus spoke
to the multitudes in parables, and
He did not speak to them [r]without
a parable, Mark 4:34; John 10:6
35 so that what was spoken

through the prophet might be fulfilled, saying,

"I[r] WILL OPEN MY MOUTH IN PARABLES; Ps. 78:2
I WILL UTTER THINGS HIDDEN SINCE THE FOUNDATION OF THE WORLD."

36 Then He left the multitudes, and went into [r]the house. And His disciples came to Him, saying, "Explain to us the parable of the tares of the field." Matt. 13:1

37 And He answered and said, "The one who sows the good seed is [r]the Son of Man, Matt. 8:20

38 and the field is the world; and *as for* the good seed, these are the sons of the kingdom; and the tares are the sons of the evil *one;*

39 and the enemy who sowed them is the devil, and the harvest is the [a]end of the age; and the reapers are angels. *consummation*

40 "Therefore just as the tares are gathered up and burned with fire, so shall it be at [r]the [a]end of the age. Matt. 12:32 • *consummation*

41 "The Son of Man will send forth His angels, and they will gather out of His kingdom all [r]stumbling blocks, and those who commit lawlessness, Zeph. 1:3

42 and [r]will cast them into the furnace of fire; in that place [r]there shall be weeping and gnashing of teeth. Matt. 13:50 • Matt. 8:12

43 "Then [r] THE RIGHTEOUS WILL SHINE FORTH AS THE SUN in the kingdom of their Father. He who has ears, let him hear. Dan. 12:3

44 "The kingdom of heaven is like a treasure hidden in the field, which a man found and hid; and from joy over it he goes and sells all that he has, and buys that field.

45 "Again, [r]the kingdom of heaven is like a merchant seeking fine pearls, Matt. 13:24

46 and upon finding one pearl of great value, he went and sold all that he had, and bought it.

47 "Again, [r]the kingdom of heaven is like a dragnet cast into the sea, and gathering *fish* of every kind; Matt. 13:44

48 and when it was filled, they drew it up on the beach; and they sat down, and gathered the good *fish* into containers, but the bad they threw away.

49 "So it will be at the end of the age; the angels shall come forth, and [a]take out the wicked from among the righteous, *separate*

50 and will cast them into the furnace of fire; there shall be weeping and gnashing of teeth.

51 "Have you understood all these things?" They *said to Him, "Yes."

52 And He said to them, "Therefore every scribe who has become a disciple of the kingdom of heaven is like a head of a household, who brings forth out of his treasure things new and old."

53 And it came about that when Jesus had finished these parables, He departed from there.

54 And coming to [a]His home town He *began* teaching them in their synagogue, so that they became astonished, and said, "Where *did* this man *get* this wisdom, and *these* miraculous powers? *His own part of the country*

55 "Is not this the carpenter's son? Is not His mother called Mary, and His brothers, James and Joseph and Simon and Judas?

56 "And His sisters, are they not
all with us? Where then *did* this
man *get* all these things?"
57 And they took [r]offense at
Him. But Jesus said to them, "A
prophet is not without honor except in his home town, and in his
own household." Matt. 11:6
58 And He did not do many [a]mir-
acles there because of their unbelief. *works of power*

CHAPTER 14

At that time Herod the tetrarch
heard the news about Jesus,
2 and said to his servants,
"This is John the Baptist; [a]he has
risen from the dead; and that is
why miraculous powers are at
work in him." *he, himself*
3 For when Herod had John arrested, he bound him, and put him
in prison on account of Herodias,
the wife of his brother Philip.
4 For John had been saying to
him, "It [r]is not lawful for you to
have her." Lev. 18:16; 20:21
5 And although he wanted to
put him to death, he feared the
multitude, because they regarded
him as [r]a prophet. Matt. 11:9
6 But when Herod's birthday
came, the daughter of [r]Herodias
danced [t]before *them* and pleased
Herod. Matt. 14:3 • *in the midst*
7 Thereupon he promised with
an oath to give her whatever she
asked.
8 And having been prompted
by her mother, she *said, "Give
me here on a platter the head of
John the Baptist."
9 And although he was
grieved, the king commanded *it* to
be given because of his oaths, and
because of his dinner guests.
10 And he sent and had John
beheaded in the prison.
11 And his head was brought on
a platter and given to the girl; and
she brought *it* to her mother.
12 And his disciples came and
took away the body and buried [t]it;
and they went and reported to
Jesus. *him*
13 [r]Now when Jesus heard *it*, He
withdrew from there in a boat, to
a lonely place by Himself; and
when the multitudes heard *of this*,
they followed Him on foot from
the cities. Matt. 14:13-21
14 And when He went [t]ashore,
He [r]saw a great multitude, and felt
compassion for them, and healed
their sick. *out* • Matt. 9:36
15 And when it was evening,
the disciples came to Him, saying,
"The place is desolate, and the
time is already past; so send the
multitudes away, that they may
go into the villages and buy food
for themselves."
16 But Jesus said to them,
"They do not need to go away;
you give them *something* to eat!"
17 And they *said to Him, "We
have here only [r]five loaves and two
fish." Matt. 16:9
18 And He said, "Bring them
here to Me."
19 And ordering the multitudes
to recline on the grass, He took
the five loaves and the two fish,
and looking up toward heaven, He
[r]blessed *the food*, and breaking the
loaves He gave them to the disciples, and the disciples *gave* to the
multitudes, 1 Sam. 9:13
20 and they all ate, and were
satisfied. And they picked up

what was left over of the broken
pieces, twelve full baskets.
21 And there were about five
thousand men who ate, aside from
women and children.
22 [r]And immediately He [t]made
the disciples get into the boat, and
go ahead of Him to the other side,
while He sent the multitudes
away. Matt. 14:22-33 • *compelled*
23 And after He had sent the
multitudes away, [r]He went up to
the mountain by Himself to pray;
and when it was evening, He was
there alone. Mark 6:46; Luke 6:12
24 But the boat was already
many [25]stadia away from the land,
[t]battered by the waves; for the
wind was contrary. *tormented*
25 And in [r]the [26]fourth watch of
the night He came to them, walking on the sea. Matt. 24:43
26 And when the disciples saw
Him walking on the sea, they
were [a]frightened, saying, "It is [r]a
ghost!" And they cried out for
fear. *troubled* • Luke 24:37
27 But immediately Jesus spoke
to them, saying, "Take courage, it
is I; do not be afraid."
28 And Peter answered Him
and said, "Lord, if it is You, command me to come to You on the
water."
29 And He said, "Come!" And
Peter got out of the boat, and
walked on the water and came
toward Jesus.
30 But seeing the wind, he became afraid, and beginning to
sink, he cried out, saying, "Lord,
save me!"
31 And immediately Jesus
stretched out His hand and took
hold of him, and *said to him, "O[r]
you of little faith, why did you
doubt?" Matt. 6:30; 8:26; 16:8
32 And when they got into the
boat, the wind stopped.
33 And those who were in the
boat worshiped Him, saying,
"You are certainly God's Son!"
34 And when they had crossed
over, they came to [t]land at [r]Gen-
nesaret. *the land* • Mark 6:53
35 And when the men of that
place [a]recognized Him, they sent
into all that surrounding district
and brought to Him all who were
sick; *knew*
36 and they *began* to entreat
Him that they might just touch
the fringe of His cloak; and as
many as touched *it* were cured.

CHAPTER 15

THEN some Pharisees and
scribes *came to Jesus [r]from Jerusalem, saying, Mark 3:22; 7:1
2 "Why do Your disciples transgress the tradition of the elders?
For they do not wash their hands
when they eat bread."
3 And He answered and said to
them, "And why do [a]you yourselves transgress the commandment of God for the sake of your
tradition? *you also*
4 "For God said, 'HONOR[r] YOUR
FATHER AND MOTHER,' and, 'HE
WHO SPEAKS EVIL OF FATHER OR
MOTHER, LET HIM [t]BE PUT TO
DEATH.' Ex. 20:12 • *die the death*
5 "But you say, 'Whoever shall
say to *his* father or mother, "Anything of mine you might have
been helped by has been [a]given *to
God*," *a gift, an offering*

[25] A stadion was about 600 feet
[26] I.e., 3-6 a.m.

6 he is not to honor his father
[27]or his mother[28].' And *thus* you in-
validated the word of God for the
sake of your tradition.
7 "You hypocrites, rightly did
Isaiah prophesy of you, saying,
8 'THIS PEOPLE HONORS ME
WITH THEIR LIPS,
BUT THEIR HEART IS FAR
AWAY FROM ME.
9 'BUT IN VAIN DO THEY WOR-
SHIP ME,
TEACHING AS DOCTRINES
THE PRECEPTS OF MEN.' "
10 And after He called the multitude to Him, He said to them,
"Hear, and understand.
11 "Not what enters into the
mouth defiles the man, but what
proceeds out of the mouth, this
defiles the man." Matt. 15:18
12 Then the disciples *came and
*said to Him, "Do You know that
the Pharisees were offended when
they heard this statement?"
13 But He answered and said,
"Every plant which My heavenly
Father did not plant shall be
rooted up. Is. 60:21; 61:3
14 "Let them alone; they are
blind guides [29]of the blind. And if a
blind man guides a blind man,
both will fall into a pit."
15 And Peter answered and said
to Him, "Explain the parable to
us." Matt. 13:36
16 And He said, "Are you still
lacking in understanding also?
17 "Do you not understand that
everything that goes into the
mouth passes into the stomach,
and is eliminated? *belly*
18 "But the things that proceed

[27]Many mss. do not contain *or his mother*
[28]I.e., by supporting them with it
[29]Some mss. do not contain *of the blind*

out of the mouth come from the
heart, and those defile the man.
19 "For out of the heart come
evil thoughts, murders, adulteries,
fornications, thefts, false witness,
slanders.
20 "These are the things which
defile the man; but to eat with unwashed hands does not defile the
man."
21 And Jesus went away from
there, and withdrew into the district of Tyre and Sidon.
22 And behold, a Canaanite
woman came out from that region, and *began* to cry out, saying,
"Have mercy on me, O Lord, Son
of David; my daughter is cruelly
demon-possessed." Matt. 9:27
23 But He did not answer her a
word. And His disciples came to
Him and kept asking Him, saying,
"Send her away, for she is shouting out after us."
24 But He answered and said, "I
was sent only to the lost sheep of
the house of Israel." Matt. 10:6
25 But she came and *began* to
bow down before Him, saying,
"Lord, help me!" Matt. 8:2 · *to worship*
26 And He answered and said,
"It is not good to take the children's bread and throw it to the
dogs." *proper*
27 But she said, "Yes, Lord; but
even the dogs feed on the crumbs
which fall from their masters' table." *for*
28 Then Jesus answered and
said to her, "O woman, your faith
is great; be it done for you as you
wish." And her daughter was
healed at once. *from that hour*
29 And departing from there,
Jesus went along by the Sea of

Galilee, and having gone up to the
mountain, He was sitting there.
30 And great multitudes came
to Him, bringing with them *those
who were* lame, crippled, blind,
dumb, and many others, and they
laid them down at His feet; and
[r]He healed them, Matt. 4:23
31 so that the multitude marveled as they saw the dumb
speaking, the crippled [a]restored,
and the lame walking, and the
blind seeing; and they [r]glorified the
God of Israel. *healthy* • Matt. 9:8
32 And Jesus called His disciples to Him, and said, "I feel compassion for the multitude, because
they [t]have remained with Me now
three days and have nothing to
eat; and I do not wish to send
them away hungry, lest they faint
on the way." *are remaining*
33 And the disciples *said to
Him, "Where would we get so
many loaves in a desolate place to
satisfy such a great multitude?"
34 And Jesus *said to them,
"How many loaves do you have?"
And they said, "Seven, and a few
small fish."
35 And He directed the multitude to sit down on the ground;
36 and He took the seven loaves
and the fish; and giving thanks,
He broke them and started giving
them to the disciples, and the disciples *in turn,* to the multitudes.
37 And they all ate, and were
satisfied, and they picked up what
was left over of the broken pieces,
seven large baskets full.
38 And those who ate were four
thousand men, besides women
and children.
39 And sending away the multitudes, He got into the boat, and
came to the region of Magadan.

CHAPTER 16

AND the Pharisees and Sadducees came up, and testing Him
asked Him to show them a [a]sign
from heaven. *attesting miracle*
2 But He answered and said to
them, "When[r] it is evening, you
say, '*It will be* fair weather, for the
sky is red.' Luke 12:54f.
3 "And in the morning, '*There
will be* a storm today, for the sky
is red and threatening.' Do you
know how to discern the appearance of the sky, but cannot *discern* the signs of the times?
4 "An evil and adulterous generation seeks after a sign; and a
sign will not be given it, except
the sign of Jonah." And He left
them, and went away.
5 And the disciples came to
the other side and had forgotten
to take bread.
6 And Jesus said to them,
"Watch out and [r]beware of the
[a]leaven of the Pharisees and Sadducees." Matt. 16:11 • *yeast*
7 And they began to discuss
among themselves, saying, "*It is*
because we took no bread."
8 But Jesus, aware of this,
said, "You men of little faith, why
do you discuss among yourselves
that you have no bread?
9 "Do you not yet understand or
remember [r]the five loaves of the
five thousand, and how many baskets you took up? Matt. 14:17-21
10 "Or the seven loaves of the
four thousand, and how many
large baskets you took up?

11 "How is it that you do not understand that I did not speak to
you concerning bread? But beware of the [a]leaven of the Pharisees and Sadducees." *yeast*
12 Then they understood that
He did not say to beware of the
leaven of bread, but of the teaching of the [r]Pharisees and Sadducees. Matt. 3:7; 5:20; 16:6, 11
13 Now when Jesus came into
the district of [r]Caesarea Philippi,
He *began* asking His disciples,
saying, "Who do people say that
the Son of Man is?" Mark 8:27
14 And they said, "Some *say*
[r]John the Baptist; and others, Elijah; but still others, Jeremiah, or
one of the prophets." Matt. 14:2
15 He *said to them, "But who
do you say that I am?"
16 And Simon Peter answered
and said, "Thou art the Christ, the
Son of the living God."
17 And Jesus answered and said
to him, "Blessed are you, Simon
Barjona, because flesh and blood
did not reveal *this* to you, but My
Father who is in heaven.
18 "And I also say to you that
you are [r]Peter, and upon this rock I
will build My church; and the
gates of Hades shall not overpower it. Matt. 4:18
19 "I will give you [r]the keys of the
kingdom of heaven; and whatever
you shall bind on earth shall be
bound in heaven, and whatever
you shall loose on earth shall be
loosed in heaven." Is. 22:22
20 Then He warned the disciples that they should tell no one
that He was the Christ.
21 From that time Jesus Christ
began to show His disciples that
He must go to Jerusalem, and [r]suf-
fer many things from the elders
and chief priests and scribes, and
be killed, and be raised up on the
third day. Matt. 12:40; 17:9, 12, 22f.
22 And Peter took Him aside
and began to rebuke Him, saying,
"God forbid *it*, Lord! This shall
never [t]happen to You." *be*
23 But He turned and said to Peter, "Get behind Me, Satan! You
are a stumbling block to Me; for
you are not setting your mind on
God's interests, but man's."
24 Then Jesus said to His disciples, "If anyone wishes to come
after Me, let him deny himself,
and [r]take up his cross, and follow
Me. Matt. 10:38; Luke 14:27
25 "For [r]whoever wishes to save
his [a]life shall lose it; but whoever
loses his life for My sake shall find
it. Matt. 10:39 • *soul*
26 "For what will a man be profited, if he gains the whole world,
and forfeits his soul? Or what will
a man give in exchange for his
soul?
27 "For the Son of Man is going
to come in the glory of His Father
with His angels; and WILL THEN
RECOMPENSE EVERY MAN ACCORD-
ING TO HIS [t]DEEDS. *doing*
28 "Truly I say to you, there are
some of those who are standing
here who shall not taste death until they see the [r]Son of Man coming in His kingdom." Matt. 8:20

CHAPTER 17

AND six days later Jesus *took
with Him [r]Peter and [a]James and
John his brother, and *brought
them up to a high mountain by
themselves. Matt. 26:37 • *Jacob*

2 And He was transfigured before them; and His face shone like the sun, and His garments became as white as light.

3 And behold, Moses and Elijah appeared to them, talking with Him.

4 And Peter answered and said to Jesus, "Lord, it is good for us to be here; if You wish, I will make three [a]tabernacles here, one for You, and one for Moses, and one for Elijah." *sacred tents*

5 While he was still speaking, behold, a bright cloud overshadowed them; and behold, a voice out of the cloud, saying, "This is My beloved Son, with whom I am well-pleased; listen to Him!"

6 And when the disciples heard *this,* they fell on their faces and were much afraid.

7 And Jesus came to *them* and touched them and said, "Arise, and do not be afraid."

8 And lifting up their eyes, they saw no one, except Jesus Himself alone.

9 And as they were coming down from the mountain, Jesus commanded them, saying, "Tell the vision to no one until the Son of Man has risen from the dead."

10 And His disciples asked Him, saying, "Why then do the scribes say that Elijah must come first?"

11 And He answered and said, "Elijah is coming and will restore all things;

12 but I say to you, that Elijah already came, and they did not recognize him, but did [t]to him whatever they wished. So also the Son of Man is going to suffer at their hands." *in him;* or, *in his case*

13 Then the disciples understood that He had spoken to them about John the Baptist.

14 [r]And when they came to the multitude, a man came up to Him, falling on his knees before Him, and saying, Matt. 17:14-19

15 "Lord, have mercy on my son, for he is a lunatic, and is very ill; for he often falls into the fire, and often into the water.

16 "And I brought him to Your disciples, and they could not cure him."

17 And Jesus answered and said, "O unbelieving and perverted generation, how long shall I be with you? How long shall I put up with you? Bring him here to Me."

18 And Jesus rebuked him, and the demon came out of him, and the boy was cured at once.

19 Then the disciples came to Jesus privately and said, "Why could we not cast it out?"

20 And He *said to them, "Because of the littleness of your faith; for truly I say to you, [r]if you have faith as a mustard seed, you shall say to this mountain, 'Move from here to there,' and it shall move; and nothing shall be impossible to you. Matt. 21:21f.

21 ["[30]But this kind does not go out except by prayer and fasting."]

22 [r]And while they were gathering together in Galilee, Jesus said to them, "The Son of Man is going to be [a]delivered into the hands of men; Luke 9:44, 45 • *betrayed*

23 and [r]they will kill Him, and He will be raised on the third day." And they were deeply grieved. Matt. 16:21; 17:9

[30] Many mss. do not contain this verse

24 And when they had come to
Capernaum, those who collected
the [31]two-drachma *tax* came to Peter, and said, "Does your teacher
not pay the [31]two-drachma *tax*?"
25 He *said, "Yes." And when
he came into the house, Jesus
spoke to him first, saying, "What
do you think, Simon? From whom
do the kings of the earth collect
customs or poll-tax, from their
sons or from strangers?"
26 And upon his saying, "From
strangers," Jesus said to him,
"Consequently the sons are
[a]exempt. *free*
27 "But, lest we [r]give them offense, go to the sea, and throw in
a hook, and take the first fish that
comes up; and when you open its
mouth, you will find a [32]stater.
Take that and give it to them for
you and Me." Matt. 5:29, 30; 18:6

CHAPTER 18

AT that [t]time the disciples came
to Jesus, saying, "Who then is
[t]greatest in the kingdom of
heaven?" *hour • greater*
2 And He called a child to
Himself and set him before them,
3 and said, "Truly I say to you,
unless you are converted and become like children, you shall not
enter the kingdom of heaven.
4 "Whoever then humbles himself as this child, he is the greatest
in the kingdom of heaven.
5 "And whoever receives one
such child in My name receives
Me;
6 but whoever causes one of
these little ones who believe in Me
to stumble, it is better for him that
a heavy millstone be hung around
his neck, and that he be drowned
in the depth of the sea.
7 "Woe to the world because of
its stumbling blocks! For [r]it is inevitable that stumbling blocks
come; but woe to that man
through whom the stumbling
block comes! Luke 17:1; 1 Cor. 11:19
8 "And [r]if your hand or your foot
causes you to stumble, cut it off
and throw it from you; it is better
for you to enter life crippled or
lame, than having two hands or
two feet, to be cast into the eternal fire. Matt. 5:30; Mark 9:43
9 "And if your eye causes you to
stumble, pluck it out, and throw it
from you. It is better for you to
enter life with one eye, than having two eyes, to be cast into the
[t]fiery hell. *Gehenna of fire*
10 "See that you do not despise
one of these little ones, for I say to
you, that their angels in heaven
continually behold the face of My
Father who is in heaven.
11 ["[33]For the Son of Man has
come to save that which was lost.]
12 "What do you think? If any
man has a hundred sheep, and one
of them has gone astray, does he
not leave the ninety-nine on the
mountains and go and search for
the one that is straying?
13 "And if it turns out that he
finds it, truly I say to you, he rejoices over it more than over the
ninety-nine which have not gone
astray.
14 "Thus it is not *the* will of your
Father who is in heaven that one
of these little ones perish.

[31] Equivalent to two denarii or two days' wages paid as a temple tax
[32] Or, *shekel*, worth four drachmas
[33] Most ancient mss. do not contain this verse

15 "And if your brother sins[34], go and reprove him [t]in private; if he listens to you, you have won your brother. *between you and him alone*

16 "But if he does not listen *to you,* take one or two more with you, so that BY THE MOUTH OF TWO OR THREE WITNESSES EVERY [t]FACT MAY BE CONFIRMED. *word*

17 "And if he refuses to listen to them, tell it to the church; and if he refuses to listen even to the church, let him be to you as [t]a Gentile and a tax-gatherer. *the*

18 "Truly I say to you, whatever you shall [a]bind on earth shall be bound in heaven; and whatever you [a]loose on earth shall be loosed in heaven. *forbid · permit*

19 "Again I say to you, that if two of you agree on earth about anything that they may ask, it shall be done for them [t]by My Father who is in heaven. *from*

20 "For where two or three have gathered together in My name, there I am in their midst."

21 Then Peter came and said to Him, "Lord, how often shall my brother sin against me and I forgive him? Up to seven times?"

22 Jesus *said to him, "I do not say to you, up to seven times, but up to seventy times seven.

23 "For this reason the kingdom of heaven may be compared to a certain king who wished to settle accounts with his slaves.

24 "And when he had begun to settle *them,* there was brought to him one who owed him [35]ten thousand talents.

[34] Many mss. add here: *against you*
[35] About $10,000,000 in silver content but worth much more in buying power

25 "But since he [a]did not have *the means* to repay, his lord commanded him [r]to be sold, along with his wife and children and all that he had, and repayment to be made. *was unable to* · Ex. 21:2

26 "The slave therefore falling down, [r]prostrated himself before him, saying, 'Have patience with me, and I will repay you everything.' Matt. 8:2

27 "And the lord of that slave felt compassion and released him and forgave him the [a]debt. *loan*

28 "But that slave went out and found one of his fellow slaves who owed him a hundred [36]denarii; and he seized him and *began* to choke *him,* saying, 'Pay back what you owe.'

29 "So his fellow slave fell down and *began* to entreat him, saying, 'Have patience with me and I will repay you.'

30 "He was unwilling however, but went and threw him in prison until he should pay back what was owed.

31 "So when his fellow slaves saw what had happened, they were deeply grieved and came and reported to their lord all that had happened.

32 "Then summoning him, his lord *said to him, 'You wicked slave, I forgave you all that debt because you entreated me.

33 'Should you not also have had mercy on your fellow slave, even as I had mercy on you?'

34 "And his lord, moved with anger, handed him over to the torturers until he should repay all that was owed him.

[36] The denarius was equivalent to one day's wage

35"So[r] shall My heavenly Father
also do to you, if each of you does
not forgive his brother from [t]your
heart." Matt. 6:14 • *your hearts*

CHAPTER 19

AND it came about that when
Jesus had finished these words,
He departed from Galilee, and
[r]came into the region of Judea beyond the Jordan; Matt. 19:1-9
2 and great multitudes followed Him, and [r]He healed them
there. Matt. 4:23
3 And *some* Pharisees came to
Him, testing Him, and saying, "Is
it lawful *for a man* to divorce his
wife for any cause at all?"
4 And He answered and said,
"Have you not read, that He who
created *them* from the beginning
MADE THEM MALE AND FEMALE,
5 and said, 'FOR[r] THIS CAUSE A
MAN SHALL LEAVE HIS FATHER AND
MOTHER, AND SHALL CLEAVE TO HIS
WIFE; AND THE TWO SHALL BECOME
ONE FLESH'? Gen. 2:24; Eph. 5:31
6"Consequently they are no
longer two, but one flesh. What
therefore God has joined together,
let no man separate."
7 They *said to Him, "Why[r]
then did Moses command to GIVE
HER A CERTIFICATE AND DIVORCE
HER?" Deut. 24:1-4; Matt. 5:31
*8 He *said to them*, "Because
of your hardness of heart, Moses
permitted you to divorce your
wives; but from the beginning it
has not been this way.
9"And I say to you, whoever divorces his wife, except for immorality, and marries another
woman commits adultery."
10 The disciples *said to Him,
"If the relationship of the man
with his wife is like this, it is better not to marry."
11 But He said to them, "Not[r] all
men *can* accept this statement,
but *only* those to whom it has
been given. 1 Cor. 7:7ff.
12"For there are eunuchs who
were born that way from their
mother's womb; and there are eunuchs who were made eunuchs by
men; and there are *also* eunuchs
who made themselves eunuchs
for the sake of the kingdom of
heaven. He who is able to accept
this, let him accept *it*."
13 Then *some* children were
brought to Him so that He might
lay His hands on them and pray;
and the disciples rebuked them.
14 But Jesus said, "Let[a] the children alone, and do not hinder
them from coming to Me; for the
kingdom of heaven belongs to
such as these." *Permit the children*
15 And after laying His hands
on them, He departed from there.
16 And behold, one came to
Him and said, "Teacher, what
good thing shall I do that I may
obtain [r]eternal life?" Matt. 25:46
17 And He said to him, "Why
are you asking Me about what is
good? There is *only* One who is
good; but if you wish to enter into
life, keep the commandments."
18 He *said to Him, "Which
ones?" And Jesus said, "YOU
SHALL NOT COMMIT MURDER; YOU
SHALL NOT COMMIT ADULTERY;
YOU SHALL NOT STEAL; YOU SHALL
NOT BEAR FALSE WITNESS;
19 HONOR YOUR FATHER AND
MOTHER; and YOU SHALL LOVE
YOUR NEIGHBOR AS YOURSELF."

20 The young man *said to Him, "All these things I have kept; what am I still lacking?"

21 Jesus said to him, "If you wish to be complete, go *and* sell your possessions and give to *the* poor, and you shall have treasure in heaven; and come, follow Me."

22 But when the young man heard this statement, he went away grieved; for he was one who owned much property.

23 And Jesus said to His disciples, "Truly I say to you, [r]it is hard for a rich man to enter the kingdom of heaven. Matt. 13:22

24 "And again I say to you, [r]it is easier for a camel to go through the eye of a needle, than for a rich man to enter the kingdom of God." Mark 10:25; Luke 18:25

25 And when the disciples heard *this*, they were very astonished and said, "Then who can be saved?"

26 And looking upon *them* Jesus said to them, "With[r] men this is impossible, but with God all things are possible." Gen. 18:14

27 Then Peter answered and said to Him, "Behold, we have left everything and followed You; what then will there be for us?"

28 And Jesus said to them, "Truly I say to you, that you who have followed Me, in the regeneration when the Son of Man will sit on His glorious throne, you also shall sit upon twelve thrones, judging the twelve tribes of Israel.

29 "And everyone who has left houses or brothers or sisters or father or mother[37] or children or farms for My name's sake, shall receive many times as much, and shall inherit eternal life.

30 "But many *who are* first will be last; and *the* last, first.

CHAPTER 20

"FOR the kingdom of heaven is like a landowner who went out early in the morning to hire laborers [t]for his vineyard. *into*

2 "And when he had agreed with the laborers for a [38]denarius for the day, he sent them into his vineyard.

3 "And he went out about the [39]third hour and saw others standing idle in the market place;

4 and to those he said, 'You too go into the vineyard, and whatever is right I will give you.' And *so* they went.

5 "Again he went out about the [40]sixth and the ninth hour, and did the same thing.

6 "And about the [41]eleventh *hour* he went out, and found others standing; and he *said to them, 'Why have you been standing here idle all day long?'

7 "They *said to him, 'Because no one hired us.' He *said to them, 'You too go into the vineyard.'

8 "And when [r]evening had come, the [a]owner of the vineyard *said to his foreman, 'Call the laborers and pay them their wages, beginning with the last *group* to the first.' Lev. 19:13 • *lord*

9 "And when those *hired* about the eleventh hour came, each one received a [38]denarius.

10 "And when those *hired* first

[37]Many mss. add here, *or wife*

[38]The denarius was equivalent to one day's wage [39]I.e., 9 a.m. [40]I.e., Noon and 3 p.m. [41]I.e., 5 p.m.

came, they thought that they
would receive more; and they also
received each one a [38]denarius.
11 "And when they received it,
they grumbled at the landowner,
12 saying, 'These last men have
worked *only* one hour, and you
have made them equal to us who
have borne the burden and the
scorching heat of the day.'
13 "But he answered and said to
one of them, 'Friend, I am doing
you no wrong; did you not agree
with me for a [38]denarius?
14 'Take what is yours and go
your way, but I wish to give to
this last man the same as to you.
15 'Is it not lawful for me to do
what I wish with what is my own?
Or is your eye [t]envious because I
am [t]generous?' *evil* • *good*
16 "Thus [r]the last shall be first,
and the first last." Matt. 19:30
17 [r]And as Jesus was about to go
up to Jerusalem, He took the
twelve *disciples* aside by themselves, and on the way He said to
them, Matt. 20:17-19: *Mark 10:32-34*
18 "Behold, we are going up to
Jerusalem; and the Son of Man
will be [a]delivered to the chief
priests and scribes, and they will
condemn Him to death, *betrayed*
19 and [r]will deliver Him to the
Gentiles to mock and scourge and
crucify *Him*, and on the third day
He will be raised up." Matt. 27:2
20 Then the mother of [r]the sons
of Zebedee came to Him with her
sons, bowing down, and making a
request of Him. Matt. 4:21; 10:2
21 And He said to her, "What
do you wish?" She *said to Him,
"Command that in Your kingdom
these two sons of mine [r]may sit,
one on Your right and one on
Your left." Matt. 19:28
22 But Jesus answered and said,
"You do not know what you are
asking for. Are you able to drink
the cup that I am about to drink?"
They *said to Him, "We are able."
23 He *said to them, "My [r]cup
you shall drink; but to sit on My
right and on *My* left, this is not
Mine to give, but it is for those for
whom it has been prepared by My
Father." Acts 12:2; Rev. 1:9
24 And hearing *this*, the ten became indignant with the two
brothers.
25 But Jesus called them to
Himself, and said, "You know
that the rulers of the Gentiles lord
it over them, and *their* great men
exercise authority over them.
26 "It is not so among you, but
whoever wishes to become great
among you shall be your servant,
27 and whoever wishes to be
first among you shall be your
slave;
28 just as [r]the Son of Man did
not come to be served, but to
serve, and to give His [a]life a ransom for many." Matt. 8:20 • *soul*
29 [r]And as they were going out
from Jericho, a great multitude
followed Him. Matt. 20:29-34
30 And behold, two blind men
sitting by the road, hearing that
Jesus was passing by, cried out,
saying, "Lord, [r]have mercy on us,
Son of David!" Matt. 20:31
31 And the multitude sternly
told them to be quiet; but they
cried out all the more, saying,
"Lord, have mercy on us, [r]Son of
David!" Matt. 9:27

[38]The denarius was equivalent to one day's wage

32 And Jesus stopped and called them, and said, "What do you want Me to do for you?"

33 They *said to Him, "Lord, *we want* our eyes to be opened."

34 And moved with compassion, Jesus touched their eyes; and immediately they regained their sight and followed Him.

CHAPTER 21

AND when they had approached Jerusalem and had come to Bethphage, to the Mount of Olives, then Jesus sent two disciples,

2 saying to them, "Go into the village opposite you, and immediately you will find a donkey tied *there* and a colt with her; untie *them,* and bring *them* to Me.

3 "And if anyone says something to you, you shall say, 'The Lord has need of them,' and immediately he will send them."

4 Now this took place that what was spoken through the prophet might be fulfilled, saying,

5 "SAY[r] TO THE DAUGHTER OF
ZION, Is. 62:11
'BEHOLD YOUR KING IS COMING TO YOU,
GENTLE, AND MOUNTED ON A DONKEY,
EVEN ON A COLT, THE FOAL OF A BEAST OF BURDEN.' "

6 And the disciples went and did just as Jesus had directed them,

7 and brought the donkey and the colt, and laid on them their garments, on which He sat.

8 And most of the multitude [r]spread their garments in the road, and others were cutting branches from the trees, and spreading them in the road. 2 Kin. 9:13

9 And the multitudes going before Him, and those who followed after were crying out, saying,
"Hosanna to the [r]Son of David; Matt. 9:27
[r]BLESSED IS HE WHO COMES IN THE NAME OF THE LORD; Ps. 118:26
Hosanna in the highest!"

10 And when He had entered Jerusalem, all the city was stirred, saying, "Who is this?"

11 And the multitudes were saying, "This is the prophet Jesus, from Nazareth in Galilee."

12 And Jesus entered the temple and cast out all those who were buying and selling in the temple, and overturned the tables of the [r]moneychangers and the seats of those who were selling [t]doves. Ex. 30:13 · *the doves*

13 And He *said to them, "It is written, 'MY[r] HOUSE SHALL BE CALLED A HOUSE OF PRAYER'; but you are making it a [r]ROBBERS' [t]DEN." Is. 56:7 · Jer. 7:11 · *cave*

14 And *the* blind and *the* lame came to Him in the temple, and [r]He healed them. Matt. 4:23

15 But when the chief priests and the scribes saw the wonderful things that He had done, and the children who were crying out in the temple and saying, "Hosanna to the [r]Son of David," they became indignant, Matt. 9:27

16 and said to Him, "Do You hear what these are saying?" And Jesus *said to them, "Yes; have you never read, 'OUT OF THE MOUTH OF INFANTS AND NURSING BABES THOU HAST PREPARED PRAISE FOR THYSELF'?"

17 And He left them and went
out of the city to [r]Bethany, and
lodged there. Matt. 26:6
18 [r]Now in the morning, when
He returned to the city, He became hungry. Matt. 21:18-22
19 And seeing a lone [r]fig tree by
the road, He came to it, and found
nothing on it except leaves only;
and He *said to it, "No longer
shall there ever be *any* fruit from
you." And at once the fig tree
withered. Luke 13:6-9
20 And seeing *this,* the disciples
marveled, saying, "How did the
fig tree wither at once?"
21 And Jesus answered and said
to them, "Truly I say to you, if you
have faith, and do not doubt, you
shall not only do what was done
to the fig tree, but even if you say
to this mountain, 'Be taken up and
cast into the sea,' it shall happen.
22 "And [r]all things you ask in
prayer, believing, you shall receive." Matt. 7:7
23 And when He had come into
the temple, the chief priests and
the elders of the people came to
Him [r]as He was teaching, and said,
"By what authority are You doing
these things, and who gave You
this authority?" Matt. 26:55
24 And Jesus answered and said
to them, "I will ask you one [t]thing
too, which if you tell Me, I will
also tell you by what authority I
do these things. *word*
25 "The baptism of John was
from what *source,* from heaven or
from men?" And they *began* reasoning among themselves, saying,
"If we say, 'From heaven,' He will
say to us, 'Then why did you not
believe him?'
26 "But if we say, 'From men,'
we fear the multitude; for they all
hold John to be a prophet."
27 And answering Jesus, they
said, "We do not know." He also
said to them, "Neither will I tell
you by what authority I do these
things.
28 "But what do you think? A
man had two [t]sons, and he came to
the first and said, 'Son, go work
today in the vineyard.' *children*
29 "And he answered and said, 'I
will, sir'; and he did not go.
30 "And he came to the second
and said [t]the same thing. But he
answered and said, 'I will not'; *yet*
he afterward regretted *it* and
went. *likewise*
31 "Which of the two did the will
of his father?" They *said, "The
latter." Jesus *said to them,
"Truly I say to you that the tax-
gatherers and harlots will get into
the kingdom of God before you.
32 "For John came to you in the
way of righteousness and you did
not believe him; but [r]the tax-gatherers and harlots did believe him;
and you, seeing this, did not even
feel remorse afterward so as to
believe him. Luke 3:12; 7:29f.
33 "Listen to another parable.
There was a landowner who
PLANTED A VINEYARD AND PUT A
WALL AROUND IT AND DUG A WINE
PRESS IN IT, AND BUILT A TOWER,
and rented it out to vine-growers,
and went on a journey.
34 "And when the [t]harvest time
approached, he sent his slaves to
the vine-growers to receive his
produce. *the season of the fruits*
35 "And the vine-growers took
his slaves and beat one, and killed
another, and stoned a third.

36 "Again he sent another group
of slaves larger than the first; and
they did the same thing to them.
37 "But afterward he sent his son
to them, saying, 'They will respect
my son.'
38 "But when the vine-growers
saw the son, they said among
themselves, 'This is the heir;
come, let us kill him, and seize his
inheritance.'
39 "And they took him, and
threw him out of the vineyard,
and killed him.
40 "Therefore when the [t]owner of
the vineyard comes, what will he
do to those vine-growers?" *lord*
41 They *said to Him, "He will
bring those wretches to a
wretched end, and will rent out
the vineyard to other vine-growers, who will pay him the proceeds at the *proper* seasons."
42 Jesus *said to them, "Did
you never read in the Scriptures,

'THE[r] STONE WHICH THE BUILDERS REJECTED,
THIS BECAME THE CHIEF CORNER *stone*;
THIS CAME ABOUT FROM THE LORD,
AND IT IS MARVELOUS IN OUR EYES'? 1 Pet. 2:7

43 "Therefore I say to you, the
kingdom of God will be taken
away from you, and be given to a
nation producing the fruit of it.
44 "And [r]he who falls on this
stone will be broken to pieces; but
on whomever it falls, it will scatter him like dust." Is. 8:14, 15
45 And when the chief priests
and the Pharisees heard His parables, they understood that He
was speaking about them.
46 And when they sought to
seize Him, they [r]feared the multitudes, because they held Him to
be a prophet. Matt. 21:26

CHAPTER 22

AND Jesus answered and spoke
to them again in parables, saying,
2 "The kingdom of heaven may
be compared to a king, who gave
a wedding feast for his son.
3 "And he [r]sent out his slaves to
call those who had been invited to
the wedding feast, and they were
unwilling to come. Matt. 21:34
4 "Again he [r]sent out other
slaves saying, 'Tell those who
have been invited, "Behold, I have
prepared my dinner; my oxen and
my fattened livestock are *all*
butchered and everything is
ready; come to the wedding
feast."' Matt. 21:36
5 "But they paid no attention
and went their way, one to his
own farm, another to his business,
6 and the rest seized his slaves
and mistreated them and killed
them.
7 "But the king was enraged
and sent his armies, and destroyed those murderers, and set
their city on fire.
8 "Then he *said to his slaves,
'The wedding is ready, but those
who were invited were not worthy.
9 'Go therefore to [r]the main
highways, and as many as you
find *there*, invite to the wedding
feast.' Ezek. 21:21; Obad. 14
10 "And those slaves went out
into the streets, and gathered together all they found, both evil

and good; and the wedding hall
was filled with dinner guests.
11 "But when the king came in to
look over the dinner guests, he
saw there [r]a man not dressed in
wedding clothes, 2 Kin. 10:22
12 and he *said to him, 'Friend,[r]
how did you come in here [t]without
wedding clothes?' And he was
speechless. Matt. 20:13 • *not having*
13 "Then the king said to the servants,
'Bind him hand and foot,
and cast him into the outer darkness;
in that place there shall be
weeping and gnashing of teeth.'
14 "For many are [a]called, but few
are [r]chosen." *invited* • Matt. 24:22
15 Then the Pharisees went and
counseled together how they
might trap Him in what He said.
16 And they *sent their disciples
to Him, along with the [r]Herodians,
saying, "Teacher, we know
that You are truthful and teach
the way of God in truth, and defer
to no one; for You are not partial
to any. Mark 3:6; 8:15; 12:13
17 "Tell us therefore, what do
You think? Is it lawful to give a
poll-tax to Caesar, or not?"
18 But Jesus perceived their
malice, and said, "Why are you
testing Me, you hypocrites?
19 "Show Me the [r]coin *used* for
the poll-tax." And they brought
Him a denarius. Matt. 17:25
20 And He *said to them,
"Whose likeness and inscription
is this?"
21 They *said to Him, "Caesar's."
Then He *said to them,
"Then render to Caesar the things
that are Caesar's; and to God the
things that are God's."
22 And hearing *this,* they marveled,
and [r]leaving Him, they went
away. Mark 12:12
23 On that day *some* Sadducees
(who say there is no resurrection)
came to Him and questioned Him,
24 saying, "Teacher, Moses
said, 'IF[r] A MAN DIES, HAVING NO
CHILDREN, HIS BROTHER AS NEXT
OF KIN SHALL MARRY HIS WIFE,
AND RAISE UP AN OFFSPRING TO HIS
BROTHER.' Deut. 25:5
25 "Now there were seven brothers
with us; and the first married
and died, and having no offspring
left his wife to his brother;
26 so also the second, and the
third, down to the seventh.
27 "And last of all, the woman
died.
28 "In the resurrection therefore
whose wife of the seven shall she
be? For they all had her."
29 But Jesus answered and said
to them, "You are mistaken, not
[a]understanding the Scriptures, or
the power of God. *knowing*
30 "For in the resurrection they
neither [r]marry, nor are given in
marriage, but are like angels in
heaven. Matt. 24:38; Luke 17:27
31 "But regarding the resurrection
of the dead, have you not
read that which was spoken to
you by God, saying,
32 'I AM THE GOD OF ABRAHAM,
AND THE GOD OF ISAAC, AND THE
GOD OF JACOB'? He is not the God
of the dead but of the living."
33 And when the multitudes
heard *this,* [r]they were astonished
at His teaching. Matt. 7:28
34 But when the Pharisees
heard that He had put [r]the Sadducees
to silence, they gathered
themselves together. Matt. 3:7

35 And one of them, [42]a lawyer, asked Him *a question,* testing Him, Luke 7:30; 10:25; 11:45, 46
36 "Teacher, which is the great commandment in the Law?"
37 And He said to him, " 'YOU SHALL LOVE THE LORD YOUR GOD WITH ALL YOUR HEART, AND WITH ALL YOUR SOUL, AND WITH ALL YOUR MIND.'
38 "This is the great and foremost commandment. *first*
39 "The second is like it, 'YOU SHALL LOVE YOUR NEIGHBOR AS YOURSELF.' Lev. 19:18; Matt. 19:19
40 "On these two commandments depend the whole Law and the Prophets." Matt. 7:12
41 Now while the Pharisees were gathered together, Jesus asked them a question,
42 saying, "What do you think about the Christ, whose son is He?" They *said to Him, "*The son* of David." Matt. 9:27
43 He *said to them, "Then how does David in the Spirit call Him 'Lord,' saying, *by inspiration*
44 'THE LORD SAID TO MY LORD,
"SIT AT MY RIGHT HAND,
UNTIL I PUT THINE ENEMIES
BENEATH THY FEET" '?
45 "If David then calls Him 'Lord,' how is He his son?"
46 And no one was able to answer Him a word, nor did anyone dare from that day on to ask Him another question. Mark 12:34

CHAPTER 23

THEN Jesus spoke to the multitudes and to His disciples,
2 saying, "The scribes and the Pharisees have seated themselves in the chair of Moses; Neh. 8:4
3 therefore all that they tell you, do and observe, but do not do according to their deeds; for they say *things,* and do not do *them.*
4 "And they tie up heavy loads, and lay them on men's shoulders; but they themselves are unwilling to move them with *so much as* a finger. Luke 11:46; Acts 15:10
5 "But they do all their deeds to be noticed by men; for they broaden their [43]phylacteries, and lengthen the tassels *of their garments.* Matt. 6:1, 5, 16 • Ex. 13:9
6 "And they love the place of honor at banquets, and the chief seats in the synagogues,
7 and respectful greetings in the market places, and being called by men, Rabbi. Matt. 23:8
8 "But do not be called Rabbi; for One is your Teacher, and you are all brothers. James 3:1
9 "And do not call *anyone* on earth your father; for One is your Father, He who is in heaven.
10 "And do not be called leaders; for One is your Leader, *that is,* Christ. *teachers*
11 "But the greatest among you shall be your servant. Matt. 20:26
12 "And whoever exalts himself shall be humbled; and whoever humbles himself shall be exalted.
13 "But woe to you, scribes and Pharisees, hypocrites, because you shut off the kingdom of heaven from men; for you do not enter in yourselves, nor do you allow those who are entering to go in. Matt. 23:15, 16 • *in front of*

[42]I.e., an expert in the Mosaic law

[43]I.e., small boxes containing Scripture texts worn for religious purposes

14 ["[44]Woe to you, scribes and
Pharisees, hypocrites, because
you devour widows' houses, even
while for a pretense you make
long prayers; therefore you shall
receive greater condemnation.]
15 "Woe to you, scribes and
Pharisees, hypocrites, because
you travel about on sea and land
to make one [a]proselyte; and when
he becomes one, you make him
twice as much a son of [r]hell as
yourselves. *convert* • Matt. 5:22
16 "Woe to you, blind guides,
who say, 'Whoever swears by the
[a]temple, that is nothing; but whoever swears by the gold of the
temple, he is obligated.' *sanctuary*
17 "You fools and blind men;
which is [t]more important, the gold,
or the [a]temple that sanctified the
gold? *greater* • *sanctuary*
18 "And, 'Whoever swears by
the altar, *that* is nothing, but whoever swears by the [a]offering upon
it, he is obligated.' *gift*
19 "You blind men, which is
[t]more important, the [a]offering or
the altar that sanctifies the offering? *greater* • *gift*
20 "Therefore he who swears,
swears *both* by the altar and by
everything on it.
21 "And he who swears by the
temple, swears *both* by the temple
and by Him who dwells within it.
22 "And he who swears by
heaven, [r]swears *both* by the throne
of God and by Him who sits upon
it. Is. 66:1; Matt. 5:34
23 "Woe[r] to you, scribes and
Pharisees, hypocrites! For you
tithe mint and dill and cummin,
and have neglected the weightier
provisions of the law: justice and
mercy and faithfulness; but these
are the things you should have
done without neglecting the others. Matt. 23:13; Luke 11:42
24 "You blind guides, who strain
out a gnat and swallow a camel!
25 "Woe to you, scribes and
Pharisees, hypocrites! For you
clean the outside of the cup and of
the dish, but inside they are full of
robbery and self-indulgence.
26 "You blind Pharisee, first
clean the inside of the cup and of
the dish, so that the outside of it
may become clean also.
27 "Woe to you, scribes and
Pharisees, hypocrites! For you are
like whitewashed tombs which on
the outside appear beautiful, but
inside they are full of dead men's
bones and all uncleanness.
28 "Even so you too outwardly
appear righteous to men, but inwardly you are full of hypocrisy
and lawlessness.
29 "Woe[r] to you, scribes and
Pharisees, hypocrites! For you
build the tombs of the prophets
and adorn the monuments of the
righteous, Luke 11:47f.
30 and say, 'If we had been *living* in the days of our fathers, we
would not have been partners
with them in *shedding* the blood
of the prophets.'
31 "Consequently you bear witness against yourselves, that you
are [a]sons of those who murdered
the prophets. *descendants*
32 "Fill up then the measure *of
the guilt* of your fathers.
33 "You serpents, you brood of
vipers, how shall you escape the
[a]sentence of hell? *judgment*
34 "Therefore[r] behold, I am sending you prophets and wise men

[44]This verse not found in the earliest mss.

and scribes; some of them you
will kill and crucify, and some of
them you will scourge in your
synagogues, and persecute from
city to city, Matt. 23:34-36
35 that upon you may fall *the*
guilt of all the righteous blood
shed on earth, from the blood of
righteous Abel to the blood of
Zechariah, the son of Berechiah,
whom you murdered between the
[a]temple and the altar. *sanctuary*
36 "Truly I say to you, all these
things shall come upon [r]this generation. Matt. 10:23; 24:34
37 "O Jerusalem, Jerusalem, who
kills the prophets and stones
those who are sent to her! How often I wanted to gather your children together, the way a hen gathers her chicks under her wings,
and you were unwilling.
38 "Behold, your house is being
left to you desolate!
39 "For I say to you, from now
on you shall not see Me until you
say, 'BLESSED IS HE WHO COMES IN
THE NAME OF THE LORD!' "

CHAPTER 24

AND Jesus came out from the
temple and was going away when
His disciples came up to point out
the temple buildings to Him.
2 And He answered and said to
them, "Do you not see all these
things? Truly I say to you, [r]not one
stone here shall be left upon another, which will not be torn
down." Luke 19:44
3 And as He was sitting on [r]the
Mount of Olives, the disciples
came to Him privately, saying,
"Tell us, when will these things
be, and what *will be* the sign of
Your coming, and of the [a]end of
the age?" Matt. 21:1 • *consummation*
4 And Jesus answered and said
to them, "See[r] to it that no one
misleads you. Jer. 29:8
5 "For many will come in My
name, saying, 'I am the Christ,'
and will mislead many.
6 "And you will be hearing of
[r]wars and rumors of wars; see that
you are not frightened, for *those*
things must take place, but *that* is
not yet the end. Rev. 6:4
7 "For nation will rise against
nation, and kingdom against kingdom, and in various places there
will be famines and earthquakes.
8 "But[r] all these things are
merely the beginning of birth
pangs. Matt. 24:8-20; Luke 21:12-24
9 "Then they will deliver you to
tribulation, and will kill you, and
you will be hated by all nations on
account of My name.
10 "And at that time many will
fall away and will deliver up one
another and hate one another.
11 "And many false prophets will
arise, and will mislead many.
12 "And because lawlessness is
increased, [t]most people's love will
grow cold. *the love of many*
13 "But the one who endures to
the end, he shall be saved.
14 "And this [r]gospel of the kingdom shall be preached in the
whole [t]world for a witness to all
the nations, and then the end shall
come. Matt. 4:23 • *inhabited earth*
15 "Therefore when you see the
[r]ABOMINATION OF DESOLATION
which was spoken of through
Daniel the prophet, standing in
the holy place (let the reader understand), Dan. 9:27; 11:31; 12:11

16 then let those who are in Judea flee to the mountains;
17 let him who is on the housetop not go down to get the things
out that are in his house;
18 and let him who is in the field
not turn back to get his cloak.
19 "But [r]woe to those who are
with child and to those who nurse
babes in those days! Luke 23:29
20 "But pray that your flight may
not be in the winter, or on a Sabbath;
21 for then there will be a great
tribulation, such as has not occurred since the beginning of the
world until now, nor ever shall.
22 "And unless those days had
been cut short, no life would have
been saved; but for the sake of the
elect those days shall be cut short.
23 "Then if anyone says to you,
'Behold, here is the Christ,' or
'There *He is,*' do not believe *him.*
24 "For false Christs and false
prophets will arise and will show
great [a]signs and wonders, so as to
mislead, if possible, even the
[a]elect. *attesting miracles • chosen ones*
25 "Behold, I have told you in advance.
26 "If therefore they say to you,
'Behold, He is in the wilderness,'
do not go forth, *or,* 'Behold, He is
in the inner rooms,' do not believe
them.
27 "For just as the lightning
comes from the east, and flashes
even to the west, so shall the coming of the Son of Man be.
28 "Wherever the corpse is, there
the [a]vultures will gather. *eagles*
29 "But immediately after the
tribulation of those days THE SUN
WILL BE DARKENED, AND THE MOON
WILL NOT GIVE ITS LIGHT, AND [r]THE
STARS WILL FALL from [a]the sky,
and the powers of the heavens
will be shaken, Is. 34:4 • *heaven*
30 and then [r]the sign of the Son
of Man will appear in the sky, and
then all the tribes of the earth will
mourn, and they will see [r]the SON
OF MAN COMING ON THE CLOUDS OF
THE SKY with power and great glory. Matt. 24:3; Rev. 1:7 • Dan. 7:13
31 "And He will send forth His
angels with A GREAT TRUMPET and
THEY WILL GATHER TOGETHER His
elect from the four winds, from
one end of the sky to the other.
32 "Now learn the parable from
the fig tree: when its branch has
already become tender, and puts
forth its leaves, you know that
summer is near;
33 even so you too, when you
see all these things, recognize that
He is near, *right* at the door.
34 "Truly I say to you, this [a]gen-
eration will not pass away until all
these things take place. *race*
35 "Heaven[r] and earth will pass
away, but My words shall not
pass away. Matt. 5:18
36 "But [r]of that day and hour no
one knows, not even the angels of
heaven, nor the Son, but the Father alone. Mark 13:32; Acts 1:7
37 "For [t]the coming of the Son of
Man will be just like the days of
Noah. *just as . . . were the days*
38 "For as in those days which
were before the flood they were
eating and drinking, they were
[r]marrying and giving in marriage,
until the day that [r]Noah entered
the ark, Matt. 22:30 • Gen. 7:7
39 and they did not [t]understand
until the flood came and took
them all away; so shall the coming
of the Son of Man be. *know*

40 "Then there shall be two men
in the field; one [t]will be taken, and
one will be left. *is*
41 "Two women *will be* grinding
at the [r]mill; one [t]will be taken, and
one will be left. Ex. 11:5 • *is*
42 "Therefore [r]be on the alert, for
you do not know which day your
Lord is coming. Matt. 24:43
43 "But [t]be sure of this, that if the
head of the house had known at
what time of the night the thief
was coming, he would have been
on the alert and would not have
allowed his house to be [t]broken
into. *know this* • *dug through*
44 "For this reason [r]you be ready
too; for the Son of Man is coming
at an hour when you do not think
He will. Matt. 24:42, 43; 25:10, 13
45 "Who then is the [r]faithful and
sensible slave whom his [a]master
put in charge of his household to
give them their food at the proper
time? Matt. 25:21, 23 • *lord*
46 "Blessed is that slave whom
his [a]master finds so doing when he
comes. *lord*
47 "Truly I say to you, that [r]he
will put him in charge of all his
possessions. Matt. 25:21, 23
48 "But if that evil slave says in
his heart, 'My master [t]is not coming for a long time,' *lingers*
49 and shall begin to beat his
fellow slaves and eat and drink
with drunkards;
50 the [a]master of that slave will
come on a day when he does not
expect *him* and at an hour which
he does not know, *lord*
51 and shall cut him in pieces
and assign him a place with the
hypocrites; weeping shall be there
and the gnashing of teeth.

CHAPTER 25

"THEN the kingdom of heaven
will be comparable to ten virgins,
who took their lamps, and went
out to meet the bridegroom.
2 "And five of them were foolish, and five were prudent.
3 "For when the foolish took
their lamps, they took no oil with
them,
4 but the prudent took oil in
flasks along with their lamps.
5 "Now while the bridegroom
was delaying, they all got drowsy
and *began* to sleep.
6 "But at midnight there was a
shout, 'Behold, the bridegroom!
Come out to meet *him.*'
7 "Then all those virgins rose,
and trimmed their lamps.
8 "And the foolish said to the
prudent, 'Give us some of your oil,
for our lamps are going out.'
9 "But the [r]prudent answered,
saying, 'No, there will not be
enough for us and you *too;* go instead to the dealers and buy *some*
for yourselves.' Matt. 7:24
10 "And while they were going
away to make the purchase, the
bridegroom came, and those who
were [r]ready went in with him to
the wedding feast; and the door
was shut. Matt. 24:42ff.
11 "And later the other virgins
also came, saying, 'Lord,[r] lord,
open up for us.' Matt. 7:21ff.
12 "But he answered and said,
'Truly I say to you, I do not know
you.'
13 "Be on the alert then, for you
do not know the day nor the hour.
14 "For *it is* just like a man [r]*about*
to go on a journey, who called his

own slaves, and entrusted his possessions to them. Matt. 21:33
15 "And to one he gave five [r]tal-
ents, to another, two, and to another, one, each according to his
own ability; and he went on his
journey. Matt. 18:24; Luke 19:13
16 "Immediately the one who
had received the five [r]talents went
and traded with them, and gained
five more talents. Matt. 18:24
17 "In the same manner the one
who had *received* the two *talents*
gained two more.
18 "But he who received the one
talent went away and dug in the
ground, and hid his [a]master's money. *lord's*
19 "Now after a long time the
master of those slaves *came and
*settled accounts with them.
20 "And the one who had received the five [r]talents came up
and brought five more talents,
saying, 'Master, you entrusted five
talents to me; see, I have gained
five more talents.' Matt. 18:24
21 "His master said to him, 'Well
done, good and [r]faithful slave; you
were faithful with a few things, I
will put you in charge of many
things, enter into the joy of your
[a]master.' Matt. 24:45, 47 • *lord*
22 "The one also who had *received* the two talents came up
and said, 'Master, you entrusted
to me two talents; see, I have
gained two more talents.'
23 "His master said to him, 'Well
done, good and [r]faithful slave; you
were faithful with a few things, I
will put you in charge of many
things; enter into the joy of your
master.' Matt. 24:45, 47; 25:21
24 "And the one also who had received the one [r]talent came up and
said, 'Master, I knew you to be a
hard man, reaping where you did
not sow, and gathering where you
scattered no *seed*. Matt. 18:24
25 'And I was afraid, and went
away and hid your talent in the
ground; see, you have what is
yours.'
26 "But his master answered and
said to him, 'You wicked, lazy
slave, you knew that I reap where
I did not sow, and gather where I
scattered no *seed*.
27 'Then you ought to have put
my money in the bank, and on my
arrival I would have received my
money back with interest.
28 'Therefore take away the talent from him, and give it to the
one who has the ten talents.'
29 "For to everyone who has
shall *more* be given, and he shall
have an abundance; but from the
one who does not have, even what
he does have shall be taken away.
30 "And cast out the worthless
slave into the outer darkness; in
that place there shall be weeping
and gnashing of teeth.
31 "But when [r]the Son of Man
comes in His glory, and all the angels with Him, then He will sit on
His glorious throne. Heb. 9:28
32 "And all the nations will be
gathered before Him; and He will
separate them from one another,
as the shepherd separates the
sheep from the goats;
33 and He will put the sheep [r]on
His right, and the goats on the
left. 1 Kin. 2:19; Ps. 45:9
34 "Then the King will say to
those on His right, 'Come, you
who are blessed of My Father, [r]in-
herit the kingdom prepared for

you from the foundation of the
world. Matt. 5:3; 19:29; Luke 12:32
35 'For [r]I was hungry, and you
gave Me *something* to eat; I was
thirsty, and you gave Me drink; I
was a stranger, and you invited
Me in; Is. 58:7; Ezek. 18:7, 16
36 naked, and you clothed Me; I
was sick, and you [r]visited Me; [r]I
was in prison, and you came to
Me.' James 1:27 • 2 Tim. 1:16f.
37 "Then the righteous will answer Him, saying, 'Lord, when did
we see You hungry, and feed You,
or thirsty, and give You drink?
38 'And when did we see You a
stranger, and invite You in, or
naked, and clothe You?
39 'And when did we see You
sick, or in prison, and come to
You?'
40 "And [r]the King will answer
and say to them, 'Truly I say to
you, to the extent that you did it
to one of these brothers of Mine,
even the least *of them*, you did it
to Me.' Matt. 25:34; Luke 19:38
41 "Then He will also say to
those on His left, 'Depart from
Me, accursed ones, into the eternal fire which has been prepared
for the devil and his angels;
42 for I was hungry, and you
gave Me *nothing* to eat; I was
thirsty, and you gave Me nothing
to drink;
43 I was a stranger, and you did
not invite Me in; naked, and you
did not clothe Me; sick, and in
prison, and you did not visit Me.'
44 "Then they themselves also
will answer, saying, 'Lord, when
did we see You hungry, or thirsty,
or a stranger, or naked, or sick, or
in prison, and did not [a]take care of
You?' *serve*
45 "Then He will answer them,
saying, 'Truly I say to you, to the
extent that you did not do it to one
of the least of these, you did not
do it to Me.'
46 "And these will go away into
eternal punishment, but the righteous into eternal life."

CHAPTER 26

AND it came about that when
Jesus had finished all these words,
He said to His disciples,
2 "You know that after two
days [r]the Passover is coming, and
the Son of Man is *to be* delivered
up for crucifixion." John 11:55
3 Then the chief priests and
the elders of the people were gathered together in the court of the
high priest, named Caiaphas;
4 and they [r]plotted together to
seize Jesus by stealth, and kill
Him. Matt. 12:14
5 But they were saying, "Not
during the festival, [r]lest a riot occur among the people." Matt. 27:24
6 Now when Jesus was in
[r]Bethany, at the home of Simon
the leper, Matt. 21:17
7 [r]a woman came to Him with
an alabaster vial of very costly
perfume, and she poured it upon
His head as He reclined *at the table*. Luke 7:37f.
8 But the disciples were indignant when they saw *this*, and said,
"Why this waste?
9 "For this *perfume* might have
been sold for a high price and *the
money* given to the poor."
10 But Jesus, aware of this, said
to them, "Why do you bother the
woman? For she has done a good
deed to Me.

11 "For [r]the poor you have with
you always; but you do not always
have Me. Deut. 15:11
12 "For when she poured this
perfume upon My body, she did it
to prepare Me for burial.
13 "Truly I say to you, [r]wherever
this gospel is preached in the
whole world, what this woman
has done shall also be spoken of in
memory of her." Mark 14:9
14 Then one of the twelve,
named [r]Judas Iscariot, went to the
chief priests, Matt. 10:4; 26:25, 47
15 and said, "What are you willing to give me to deliver Him up
to you?" And they weighed out to
him thirty pieces of silver.
16 And from then on he *began*
looking for a good opportunity to
[a]betray Him. *deliver Him up*
17 Now on the first *day* of [r]Un-
leavened Bread the disciples came
to Jesus, saying, "Where do You
want us to prepare for You to eat
the Passover?" Ex. 12:18-20
18 And He said, "Go into the
city to [r]a certain man, and say to
him, 'The Teacher says, "My time
is at hand; I *am to* keep the Passover at your house with My disciples." ' " Mark 14:13; Luke 22:10
19 And the disciples did as
Jesus had directed them; and they
prepared the Passover.
20 Now when evening had
come, He was reclining *at the table* with the twelve disciples.
21 And as they were eating, He
said, "Truly I say to you that one
of you will betray Me."
22 And being deeply grieved,
they each one began to say to
Him, "Surely not I, Lord?"
23 And He answered and said,
"He [r]who dipped his hand with Me
in the bowl is th
tray Me. P
24 "The Son of
as it is written o , but woe to
that man by whom the Son of
Man is betrayed! It would have
been good for that man if he had
not been born." Matt. 26:31, 54
25 And [r]Judas, who was betraying Him, answered and said,
"Surely it is not I, Rabbi?" He
*said to him, "You have said *it*
yourself." Matt. 26:14
26 And while they were eating,
Jesus took *some* bread, and after a
blessing, He broke *it* and gave *it*
to the disciples, and said, "Take,
eat; this is My body."
27 And when He had taken a
cup and given thanks, He gave *it*
to them, saying, "Drink from it, all
of you;
28 for this is My blood of the
covenant, which is poured out for
many for forgiveness of sins.
29 "But I say to you, I will not
drink of this fruit of the vine from
now on until that day when I
drink it new with you in My Father's kingdom."
30 And after singing a hymn,
they went out to [r]the Mount of Olives. Matt. 21:1
31 Then Jesus *said to them,
"You will all [a]fall away because of
Me this night, for it is written, 'I
WILL STRIKE DOWN THE SHEPHERD,
AND THE SHEEP OF THE FLOCK
SHALL BE SCATTERED.' *stumble*
32 "But after I have been raised, I
will go before you to Galilee."
33 But Peter answered and said
to Him, "*Even* though all may [a]fall
away because of You, I will never
fall away." *stumble*

34 Jesus said to him, "Truly[r] I
say to you that this *very* night, before a cock crows, you shall deny
Me three times." Matt. 26:75
35 Peter *said to Him, "Even[r] if I
have to die with You, I will not
deny You." All the disciples said
the same thing too. John 13:37
36 Then Jesus *came with them
to a place called Gethsemane, and
*said to His disciples, "Sit here
while I go over there and pray."
37 And He took with Him[r] Peter
and the two sons of Zebedee, and
began to be grieved and distressed. Matt. 4:21; 17:1
38 Then He *said to them, "My[r]
soul is deeply grieved, to the point
of death; remain here and keep
watch with Me." John 12:27
39 And He went a little beyond
them, and fell on His face and
prayed, saying, "My Father, if it is
possible, let this cup pass from
Me;[r] yet not as I will, but as Thou
wilt." Matt. 26:42; Mark 14:36
40 And He *came to the disciples and *found them sleeping,
and *said to Peter, "So, you *men*
could not[r] keep watch with Me for
one hour? Matt. 26:38
41 "Keep watching and praying,
that you may not enter into temptation;[r] the spirit is willing, but the
flesh is weak." Mark 14:38
42 He went away again a second time and prayed, saying, "My
Father, if this[r] cannot pass away
unless I drink it, Thy will be
done." Matt. 20:22
43 And again He came and
found them sleeping, for their
eyes were heavy.
44 And He left them again, and
went away and prayed a third
time, saying the same thing once
more.
45 Then He *came to the disciples, and *said to them, "Are you
still sleeping and taking your rest?
Behold, the hour is at hand and
the Son of Man is being betrayed
into the hands of sinners.
46 "Arise, let us be going; behold,
the one who betrays Me is at
hand!"
47 And while He was still
speaking, behold, Judas, one of
the twelve, came up, accompanied
by a great multitude with swords
and clubs, from the chief priests
and elders of the people.
48 Now he who was betraying
Him gave them a sign, saying,
"Whomever I shall kiss, He is the
one; seize Him."
49 And immediately he went to
Jesus and said, "Hail,[r] Rabbi!" and
kissed Him. Matt. 23:7; 26:25
50 And Jesus said to him,
"Friend, *do* what you have come
for." Then they came and laid
hands on Jesus and seized Him.
51 And behold, one of those
who were with Jesus[t] reached and
drew out his sword, and struck
the slave of the high priest, and
cut off his ear. *extended the hand*
52 Then Jesus *said to him,
"Put your sword back into its
place; for[r] all those who take up
the sword shall perish by the
sword. Gen. 9:6; Rev. 13:10
53 "Or do you think that I cannot
appeal to My Father, and He will
at once put at My disposal more
than twelve[45] legions of angels?
54 "How then shall[r] the Scriptures be fulfilled, that it must happen this way?" Matt. 26:24

[45] A legion equaled 6,000 troops

55 At that time Jesus said to the
multitudes, "Have you come out
with swords and clubs to arrest
Me as against a robber? Every day
I used to sit in the temple teaching
and you did not seize Me.
56 "But all this has taken place
that the Scriptures of the prophets
may be fulfilled." Then all the disciples left Him and fled.
57 And those who had seized
Jesus led Him away to [r]Caiaphas,
the high priest, where the scribes
and the elders were gathered together. Matt. 26:3
58 But Peter also was following
Him at a distance as far as the
courtyard of the high priest, and
entered in, and sat down with the
officers to see the outcome.
59 Now the chief priests and the
whole [a]Council kept trying to obtain false testimony against Jesus,
in order that they might put Him
to death; *Sanhedrin*
60 and they did not find *any,*
even though many false witnesses
came forward. But later on [r]two
came forward, Deut. 19:15
61 and said, "This man stated, 'I
am able to destroy the [a]temple of
God and to rebuild it [a]in three
days.'" *sanctuary • after*
62 And the high priest stood up
and said to Him, "Do You make
no answer? What is it that these
men are testifying against You?"
63 But Jesus kept silent. And
the high priest said to Him, "I adjure You by the living God, that
You tell us whether You are the
Christ, the Son of God."
64 Jesus *said to him, "You
have said it *yourself*; nevertheless
I tell you, hereafter you shall see
THE SON OF MAN SITTING AT THE
RIGHT HAND OF POWER, and COM-
ING ON THE CLOUDS OF HEAVEN."
65 Then the high priest tore his
robes, saying, "He has blasphemed! What further need do we
have of witnesses? Behold, you
have now heard the blasphemy;
66 what do you think?" They
answered and said, "He [r]is deserving of death!" Lev. 24:16
67 Then they [r]spat in His face
and beat Him with their fists; and
others slapped Him, Mark 10:34
68 and said, "Prophesy [r] to us,
You Christ; who is the one who hit
You?" Mark 14:65; Luke 22:64
69 Now Peter was sitting outside in the [r]courtyard, and a certain servant-girl came to him and
said, "You too were with Jesus
the Galilean." Matt. 26:3
70 But he denied *it* before them
all, saying, "I do not know what
you are talking about."
71 And when he had gone out to
the gateway, another *servant-girl*
saw him and *said to those who
were there, "This man was with
Jesus of Nazareth."
72 And again he denied *it* with
an oath, "I do not know the man."
73 And a little later the bystanders came up and said to Peter,
"Surely you too are *one* of them;
for the way you talk gives you
away."
74 Then he began to curse and
swear, "I do not know the man!"
And immediately a cock crowed.
75 And Peter remembered the
word which Jesus had said, "Before [r] a cock crows, you will deny
Me three times." And he went out
and wept bitterly. Matt. 26:34

CHAPTER 27

NOW when morning had come,
all the chief priests and the elders
of the people took counsel against
Jesus to put Him to death;
2 and they bound Him, and led
Him away, and delivered Him up
to Pilate the governor.
3 Then when [r]Judas, who had
betrayed Him, saw that He had
been condemned, he felt remorse
and returned the thirty [a]pieces of
silver to the chief priests and elders, Matt. 26:14 • *silver shekels*
4 saying, "I have sinned by betraying innocent blood." But they
said, "What is that to us? [r]See *to*
that yourself!" Matt. 27:24
5 And he threw the pieces of
silver into [r]the sanctuary and departed; and he went away and
hanged himself. Matt. 26:61
6 And the chief priests took
the pieces of silver and said, "It is
not lawful to put them into the
temple treasury, since it is the
price of blood."
7 And they counseled together
and with [t]the money bought the
Potter's Field as a burial place for
strangers. *them*
8 [r]For this reason that field has
been called the Field of Blood to
this day. Acts 1:19
9 Then that which was spoken
through Jeremiah the prophet was
fulfilled, saying, "AND [r]THEY TOOK
THE THIRTY PIECES OF SILVER, THE
PRICE OF THE ONE WHOSE PRICE
HAD BEEN SET by the sons of Israel; Zech. 11:12
10 [r]AND THEY GAVE THEM FOR
THE POTTER'S FIELD, AS THE LORD
DIRECTED ME." Zech. 11:13

11 Now Jesus stood before the
governor, and the governor questioned Him, saying, "Are You the
King of the Jews?" And Jesus said
to him, "*It is as* you say."
12 And while He was being accused by the chief priests and elders, He made no answer.
13 Then Pilate *said to Him,
"Do You not hear how many
things they testify against You?"
14 And [r]He did not answer him
with regard to even a *single*
[t]charge, so that the governor was
quite amazed. John 19:9 • *word*
15 [r]Now at *the* feast the governor was accustomed to release for
the multitude *any* one prisoner
whom they wanted. John 18:39
16 And they were holding at
that time a notorious prisoner,
called Barabbas.
17 When therefore they were
gathered together, Pilate said to
them, "Whom do you want me to
release for you? Barabbas, or
Jesus who is called Christ?"
18 For he knew that because of
envy they had delivered Him up.
19 And while he was sitting on
the judgment seat, his wife sent to
him, saying, "Have nothing to do
with that righteous Man; for [t]last
night I suffered greatly in a dream
because of Him." *today*
20 But the chief priests and the
elders persuaded the multitudes
to [r]ask for Barabbas, and to put
Jesus to death. Acts 3:14
21 But the governor answered
and said to them, "Which of the
two do you want me to release for
you?" And they said, "Barabbas."
22 Pilate *said to them, "Then
what shall I do with Jesus who is

called Christ?" They all *said,
"Let Him be crucified!"
23 And he said, "Why, what evil
has He done?" But they kept
shouting all the more, saying, "Let
Him be crucified!"
24 And when Pilate saw that he
was accomplishing nothing, but
rather that a riot was starting, he
took water and washed his hands
in front of the multitude, saying,
"I am innocent of this Man's
blood; see *to that* yourselves."
25 And all the people answered
and said, "His[r] blood *be* on us and
on our children!" Josh. 2:19
26 Then he released Barabbas
[a]for them; but after having Jesus
[r]scourged, he delivered Him to be
crucified. *to them* • Mark 15:15
27 Then the soldiers of the governor took Jesus into the Praetorium and gathered the whole *Roman* cohort around Him.
28 And they stripped Him, and
put a scarlet robe on Him.
29 And after weaving a crown
of thorns, they put it on His head,
and a[a]reed in His right hand; and
they kneeled down before Him
and mocked Him, saying, "Hail,
King of the Jews!" *staff*
30 And[r]they spat on Him, and
took the reed and *began* to beat
Him on the head. Matt. 26:67
31 And after they had mocked
Him, they took His robe off and
put His garments on Him, and led
Him away to crucify *Him*.
32 And as they were coming
out, they found a man of Cyrene
named Simon, whom they pressed
into service to bear His cross.
33 And when they had come to
a place called Golgotha, which
means Place of a Skull,
34 they gave Him wine to drink
mingled with gall; and after tast-
ing *it*, He was unwilling to drink.
35 And when they had crucified
Him, [r]they divided up His garments among themselves, casting
[t]lots; Ps. 22:18 • *a lot*
36 and sitting down, they *began*
to keep watch over Him there.
37 And they put up above His
head the charge against Him
[t]which read, "THIS IS JESUS THE
KING OF THE JEWS." *written*
38 At that time two robbers
*were crucified with Him, one on
the right and one on the left.
39 And those passing by were
[a]hurling abuse at Him, [r]wagging
their heads, *blaspheming* • Job 16:4
40 and saying, "You who *are
going to* destroy the temple and
rebuild it in three days, save Yourself! If You are the Son of God,
come down from the cross."
41 In the same way the chief
priests also, along with the scribes
and elders, were mocking *Him*,
and saying,
42 "He saved others; He cannot
save Himself.[r]He is the King of Israel; let Him now come down
from the cross, and we shall believe in Him. Matt. 27:37; Luke 23:37
43 "HE[r] TRUSTS IN GOD; LET HIM
DELIVER *Him* now, IF HE TAKES
PLEASURE IN HIM; for He said, 'I
am the Son of God.' " Ps. 22:8
44 And the robbers also who
had been crucified with Him were
casting the same insult at Him.
45 Now from the [46]sixth hour
darkness[a]fell upon all the land until the [47]ninth hour. *occurred*
46 And about the ninth hour

[46]I.e., noon [47]I.e., 3 p.m.

Jesus cried out with a loud voice, saying, "ELI,[r] ELI, LAMA SABACHTHANI?" that is, "MY GOD, MY GOD, WHY HAST THOU FORSAKEN ME?" Ps. 22:1

47 And some of those who were standing there, when they heard it, *began* saying, "This man is calling for Elijah."

48 And immediately one of them ran, and taking a sponge, he filled it with sour wine, and put it on a reed, and gave Him a drink.

49 But the rest *of them* said, "Let us see whether Elijah will come to save Him."[48]

50 And Jesus [r]cried out again with a loud voice, and yielded up *His* spirit. Mark 15:37; Luke 23:46

51 And behold, the veil of the temple was torn in two from top to bottom, and the earth shook; and the rocks were split,

52 and the tombs were opened; and many bodies of the saints who had fallen asleep were raised;

53 and coming out of the tombs after His resurrection they entered [r]the holy city and appeared to many. Matt. 4:5

54 Now the centurion, and those who were with him keeping guard over Jesus, when they saw the earthquake and the things that were happening, became very frightened and said, "Truly this was [r]the Son of God!" Matt. 4:3

55 And many women were there looking on from a distance, who had followed Jesus from Galilee, ministering to Him,

56 among whom was [r]Mary Magdalene, *along with* Mary the mother of James and Joseph, and the mother of the sons of Zebedee. Matt. 28:1; Mark 15:40, 47

57 [r]And when it was evening, there came a rich man from Arimathea, named Joseph, who himself had also become a disciple of Jesus. Matt. 27:57-61: *Mark 15:42-47*

58 This man went to Pilate and asked for the body of Jesus. Then Pilate ordered *it* to be given over *to him.*

59 And Joseph took the body and wrapped it in a clean linen cloth,

60 and laid it in his own new tomb, which he had hewn out in the rock; and he rolled a large stone against the entrance of the tomb and went away.

61 And [r]Mary Magdalene was there, and the other Mary, sitting opposite the grave. Matt. 27:56

62 Now on the next day, which is *the one* after the preparation, the chief priests and the Pharisees gathered together with Pilate,

63 and said, "Sir, we remember that when He was still alive that deceiver said, 'After [r]three days I *am to* rise again.' Matt. 16:21

64 "Therefore, give orders for the grave to be made secure until the third day, lest the disciples come and steal Him away and say to the people, 'He has risen from the dead,' and the last deception will be worse than the first."

65 Pilate said to them, "You have a guard; go, make it *as* secure as you know how."

66 And they went and made the grave secure, and along with the guard they set a seal on the stone.

[48] Some early mss. add: *And another took a spear and pierced His side, and there came out water and blood.* (cf. John 19:34)

CHAPTER 28

NOW after the Sabbath, as it began to dawn toward the first *day*
of the week,[r] Mary Magdalene and
the other Mary came to look at
the grave. Matt. 27:56, 61
2 And behold, a severe earthquake had occurred, for an angel
of the Lord descended from
heaven and came and rolled away
the stone and sat upon it.
3 And[r] his appearance was like
lightning, and his garment as
white as snow; Dan. 7:9; 10:6
4 and the guards shook for fear
of him, and became like dead
men.
5 And the angel answered and
said to the women, "Do[a] not be
afraid; for I know that you are
looking for Jesus who has been
crucified. *Stop being afraid*
6 "He is not here, for He has ris-
en, just as He said. Come, see the
place where He was lying.
7 "And go quickly and tell His
disciples that He has risen from
the dead; and behold, He is going
before you[r] into Galilee, there you
will see Him; behold, I have told
you." Matt. 26:32; 28:10, 16
8 And they departed quickly
from the tomb with fear and great
joy and ran to report it to His disciples.
9 And behold, Jesus met them
[t]and greeted them. And they came
up and took hold of His feet and
worshiped Him. *saying hello*
10 Then Jesus *said to them,
"Do[a] not be afraid; go and take
word to[r] My brethren to leave for
Galilee, and there they shall see
Me." *Stop being afraid* • Rom. 8:29
11 Now while they were on
their way, behold, some of[r] the
guard came into the city and reported to the chief priests all that
had happened. Matt. 27:65, 66
12 And when they had assembled with the elders and counseled together, they gave a large
sum of money to the soldiers,
13 and said, "You are to say,
'His disciples came by night and
stole Him away while we were
asleep.'
14 "And if this should come to
the governor's ears, we will win
him over and[t] keep you out of
trouble." *make you free from care*
15 And they took the money
and did as they had been instructed; and this story was
widely[r] spread among the Jews,
and is to this day. Matt. 9:31
16 But the eleven disciples proceeded to Galilee, to the mountain
which Jesus had designated.
17 And when they saw Him,
they worshiped *Him*; but[r] some
were doubtful. Mark 16:11
18 And Jesus came up and
spoke to them, saying, "All[r] authority has been given to Me in
heaven and on earth. Dan. 7:13f.
19 "Go therefore and make disciples of all the nations, baptizing
them in the name of the Father
and the Son and the Holy Spirit,
20 teaching them to observe all
that I commanded you; and lo, I
am with you[t] always, even to the
end of the age." *all the days*

THE GOSPEL ACCORDING TO

MARK

THE beginning of the gospel of
Jesus Christ, [1]the Son of God.
2 [r]As it is written in Isaiah the
prophet, Mark 1:2-8
"BEHOLD, I SEND MY MESSEN-
GER BEFORE YOUR FACE,
WHO WILL PREPARE YOUR
WAY; Mal. 3:1
3 "THE VOICE OF ONE CRYING IN
THE WILDERNESS,
'MAKE READY THE WAY OF
THE LORD,
MAKE HIS PATHS
STRAIGHT.' "
4 John the Baptist appeared in
the wilderness [r2]preaching a baptism of repentance for the forgiveness of sins. Acts 13:24
5 And all the country of Judea
was going out to him, and all the
people of Jerusalem; and they
were being baptized by him in the
Jordan River, confessing their
sins.
6 And John was clothed with
camel's hair and *wore* a leather
belt around his waist, and his diet
was locusts and wild honey.
7 And he was [a]preaching, and
saying, "After me One is coming
who is mightier than I, and I am
not fit to stoop down and untie the
thong of His sandals. *proclaiming*
8 "I baptized you [3]with water;
but He will baptize you [3]with the
Holy Spirit."
9 And it came about in those
days that Jesus came from Nazareth in Galilee, and was baptized
by John in the Jordan.
10 And immediately coming up
out of the water, He saw the heavens opening, and the Spirit like a
dove descending upon Him;
11 and a voice came out of the
heavens: "Thou art My beloved
Son, in Thee I am well-pleased."
12 [r]And immediately the Spirit
*impelled Him *to go* out into the
wilderness. Mark 1:12, 13
13 And He was in the wilderness forty days being tempted by
[r]Satan; and He was with the wild
beasts, and the angels were ministering to Him. Matt. 4:10
14 And after John had been
[t]taken into custody, Jesus came
into Galilee, [a]preaching the gospel
of God, *delivered up • proclaiming*
15 and saying, "The time is fulfilled, and the kingdom of God is
at hand; repent and [a]believe in the
gospel." *put your trust in*
16 [r]And as He was going along
by the Sea of Galilee, He saw Simon and Andrew, the brother of
Simon, casting a net in the sea; for
they were fishermen. Matt. 4:18
17 And Jesus said to them, "Follow Me, and I will make you become fishers of men."
18 And they immediately left
the nets and followed Him.
19 And going on a little farther,
He saw James the *son* of Zebedee,
and John his brother, who were
also in the boat mending the nets.
20 And immediately He called
them; and they left their father

[1]Many mss. do not contain *the Son of God*
[2]Or, *proclaiming*
[3]The Gr. here can be translated *in, with* or *by*

Zebedee in the boat with the hired
servants, and went away[t]to follow
Him. *after Him*
21 And they *went into Capernaum; and immediately on the
Sabbath He entered the synagogue and *began* to teach.
22 And [r]they were amazed at
His teaching; for He was teaching
them as *one* having authority, and
not as the scribes. Matt. 7:28
23 And just then there was in
their synagogue a man with an
unclean spirit; and he cried out,
24 saying, "What[r] do we have to
do with You, Jesus [4]of Nazareth?
Have You come to destroy us? I
know who You are—[r]the Holy One
of God!" Matt. 8:29 • Luke 1:35
25 And Jesus rebuked him, saying, "Be quiet, and come out of
him!"
26 And throwing him into con-
vulsions, the unclean spirit cried
out with a loud voice, and came
out of him.
27 And they were all amazed, so
that they debated among themselves, saying, "What is this? A
new teaching with authority! He
commands even the unclean spirits, and they obey Him."
28 And immediately the news
about Him went out everywhere
into all the surrounding district of
Galilee.
29 And immediately after they
had come out of the synagogue,
they came into the house of Simon and Andrew, with[a]James and
John. *Jacob*
30 Now Simon's mother-in-law
was lying sick with a fever; and
immediately they *spoke to Him
about her.
31 And He came to her and
raised her up, taking her by the
hand, and the fever left her, and
she [5]waited on them.
32 And when evening had
come, [r]after the sun had set, they
began bringing to Him all who
were ill and those who were demon-possessed. Matt. 8:16
33 And the whole [r]city had gathered at the door. Mark 1:21
34 And He [r]healed many who
were ill with various diseases, and
cast out many demons; and He
was not permitting the demons to
speak, because they [6]knew who
He was. Matt. 4:23
35 And in the early morning,
while it was still dark, He arose
and went out and departed to a
lonely place, and [r]was praying
there. Matt. 14:23; Luke 5:16
36 And Simon and his companions hunted for Him;
37 and they found Him, and
*said to Him, "Everyone is look-
ing for You."
38 And He *said to them, "Let
us go somewhere else to the
towns nearby, in order that I may
[a]preach there also; for that is what
I came out for." *proclaim*
39 And He went into their synagogues throughout all Galilee,
[a]preaching and casting out the demons. *proclaiming*
40 And a leper *came to Him,
beseeching Him and [r]falling on his
knees before Him, and saying to
Him, "If You are willing, You can
make me clean." Matt. 8:2-4

[4]Lit., *the Nazarene*

[5]Or, *served*
[6]Some mss. read: *knew Him to be Christ*

41 And moved with compas-
sion, He stretched out His hand,
and touched him, and *said to
him, "I am willing; be cleansed."
42 And immediately the leprosy
left him and he was cleansed.
43 And He sternly warned him
and immediately sent him away,
44 and He *said to him, "See[r]
that you say nothing to anyone;
but go, show yourself to the priest
and offer for your cleansing what
Moses commanded, for a testimony to them." Matt. 8:4
45 But he went out and began to
proclaim it freely and to spread
the news about, to such an extent
that Jesus could no longer publicly enter a city, but [7]stayed out in
unpopulated areas; and they were
coming to Him from everywhere.

CHAPTER 2

AND when He had come back to
Capernaum several days afterward, it was heard that He was at
home.
2 And [r]many were gathered together, so that there was no
longer room, even near the door;
and He was speaking the word to
them. Mark 1:45; 2:13
3 And they *came, bringing to
Him a [r]paralytic, carried by four
men. Matt. 4:24
4 And being unable to [t]get to
Him because of the crowd, they
removed the roof above Him; and
when they had dug an opening,
they let down the pallet on which
the paralytic was lying. *bring to*
5 And Jesus seeing their faith
*said to the paralytic, "My [8]son,
your sins are forgiven."

[7]Lit., *was* [8]Lit., *child*

6 But there were some of the
scribes sitting there and reasoning
in their hearts,
7 "Why does this man speak
that way? He is blaspheming; who
can forgive sins but God alone?"
8 And immediately Jesus,
aware [t]in His spirit that they were
reasoning that way within themselves, *said to them, "Why are
you reasoning about these things
in your hearts? *by*
9 "Which is easier, to say to the
[r]paralytic, 'Your sins are forgiven';
or to say, 'Arise, and take up your
pallet and walk'? Matt. 4:24
10 "But in order that you may
know that the Son of Man has authority on earth to forgive sins"—
He *said to the paralytic—
11 "I say to you, rise, take up
your pallet and go home."
12 And he rose and immediately
took up the pallet and went out in
the sight of all; so that they were
all amazed and [r]were glorifying
God, saying, "We have never seen
anything like this." Matt. 9:8
13 And He went out again by
the seashore; and [r]all the multitude
were coming to Him, and He was
teaching them. Mark 1:45
14 And as He passed by, He saw
[r]Levi the *son* of Alphaeus sitting in
the tax office, and He *said to
him, "Follow Me!" And he rose
and followed Him. Matt. 9:9
15 And it [t]came about that He
was reclining *at the table* in his
house, and many tax-gatherers
and sinners were dining with
Jesus and His disciples; for there
were many of them, and they
were following Him. *comes*
16 And when [r]the scribes of the
Pharisees saw that He was eating

with the sinners and tax-gatherers, they *began* saying to His disciples, "Why is He eating and
drinking with tax-gatherers and
sinners?" Luke 5:30; Acts 23:9
17 And hearing this, Jesus *said
to them, "*It is* not those who are
healthy who need a physician, but
those who are sick; I did not come
to call the righteous, but sinners."
18 [r]And John's disciples and the
Pharisees were fasting; and they
*came and *said to Him, "Why do
John's disciples and the disciples
of the Pharisees fast, but Your disciples do not fast?" Luke 5:33-38
19 And Jesus said to them,
"While the bridegroom is with
them, the attendants of the bridegroom do not fast, do they? So
long as they have the bridegroom
with them, they cannot fast.
20 "But the [r]days will come when
the bridegroom is taken away
from them, and then they will fast
in that day. Matt. 9:15; Luke 17:22
21 "No one sews a patch of unshrunk cloth on an old garment;
otherwise the patch pulls away
from it, the new from the old, and
a worse tear results.
22 "And no one puts new wine
into old wineskins; otherwise the
wine will burst the skins, and the
wine is lost, and the skins *as well;*
but *one puts* new wine into fresh
wineskins."
23 [r]And it came about that He
was passing through the grainfields on the Sabbath, and His disciples began to make their way
along while picking the heads *of*
grain. Mark 2:23-28
24 And the Pharisees were saying to Him, "See here, [r]why are
they doing what is not lawful on
the Sabbath?" Matt. 12:2
25 And He *said to them, "Have
you never read what David did
when he was in need and became
hungry, he and his companions:
26 how he entered the house of
God in the time of Abiathar *the*
high priest, and ate the consecrated bread, which is not lawful
for *anyone* to eat except the
priests, and he gave *it* also to
those who were with him?"
27 And He was saying to them,
"The Sabbath was made for man,
and not man for the Sabbath.
28 "Consequently, the Son of
Man is Lord even of the Sabbath."

CHAPTER 3

AND He entered again into a
synagogue; and a man was there
with a withered hand.
2 And [r]they were watching Him
to see if He would heal him on the
Sabbath, in order that they might
accuse Him. Luke 6:7; 14:1; 20:20
3 And He *said to the man
with the withered hand, "Rise and
come forward!"
4 And He *said to them, "Is it
lawful on the Sabbath to do good
or to do harm, to save a life or to
kill?" But they kept silent.
5 And after [r]looking around at
them with anger, grieved at their
hardness of heart, He *said to the
man, "Stretch out your hand."
And he stretched it out, and his
hand was restored. Luke 6:10
6 And the Pharisees went out
and immediately *began* [t]taking
counsel with the Herodians
against Him, *as to* how they might
destroy Him. *giving*

7 And Jesus withdrew to the
sea with His disciples; and a great
multitude from Galilee followed;
and *also* from Judea,
8 and from Jerusalem, and
from [r]Idumea, and beyond the Jordan, and the vicinity of Tyre and
Sidon, a great multitude heard of
all that He was doing and came to
Him. Josh. 15:1, 21; Ezek. 35:15
9 [r]And He told His disciples
that a boat should stand ready for
Him because of the multitude, in
order that they might not crowd
Him; Mark 4:1; Luke 5:1-3
10 for He had healed many,
with the result that all those who
had afflictions pressed about Him
in order to touch Him.
11 And whenever the unclean
spirits beheld Him, they would fall
down before Him and cry out,
saying, "You are the Son of God!"
12 And He earnestly warned
them not to make Him known.
13 And He *went up to [r]the
mountain and *summoned those
whom He Himself wanted, and
they came to Him. Matt. 5:1
14 And He appointed twelve[9],
that they might be with Him, and
that He might send them out to
preach,
15 and to have authority to cast
out the demons.
16 And He appointed the
twelve: [r]Simon (to whom He gave
the name Peter), Mark 3:16-19
17 and James, the *son* of Zebedee, and John the brother of
[a]James (to them He gave the name
Boanerges, which means, "Sons
of Thunder"); *Jacob*
18 and Andrew, and Philip, and
Bartholomew, and Matthew, and
Thomas, and [a]James the *son* of Alphaeus, and Thaddaeus, and Simon the Zealot; *Jacob*
19 and Judas Iscariot, who also
betrayed Him.
20 And He *came [10]home, and
the multitude *gathered again, to
such an extent that they could not
even eat a meal.
21 And when His own [11]people
heard *of this,* they went out to
take custody of Him; for they
were saying, "He has lost His
senses."
22 And the scribes who came
down from Jerusalem were saying, "He is possessed by Beelzebul," and "He casts out the demons by the ruler of the demons."
23 And He called them to Himself and began speaking to them
in parables, "How can Satan cast
out Satan?
24 "And if a kingdom is divided
against itself, that kingdom cannot stand.
25 "And if a house is divided
against itself, that house will not
be able to stand.
26 "And if Satan has risen up
against himself and is divided, he
cannot stand, but he is finished!
27 "But [r] no one can enter the
strong man's house and plunder
his property unless he first binds
the strong man, and then he will
plunder his house. Is. 49:24, 25
28 "Truly [r] I say to you, all sins
shall be forgiven the sons of men,
and whatever blasphemies they
utter; Matt. 12:31, 32
29 but [r]whoever blasphemes
against the Holy Spirit never has

[9] Some early mss. add: *whom He named apostles*

[10] Lit., *into a house* [11] Or, *kinsmen*

forgiveness, but is guilty of an
eternal sin" Luke 12:10
30 because they were saying,
"He has an unclean spirit."
31 ʳAnd His mother and His
brothers *arrived, and standing
outside they sent *word* to Him,
and called Him. Mark 3:31-35
32 And a multitude was sitting
around Him, and they *said to
Him, "Behold, Your mother and
Your brothers[12] are outside looking for You."
33 And answering them, He
*said, "Who are My mother and
My brothers?"
34 And looking about on those
who were sitting around Him, He
*said, "Beholdʳ, My mother and
My brothers! Matt. 12:49
35"For whoever does the will of
God, he is My brother and sister
and mother."

CHAPTER 4

AND He began to teach again by
the sea. And such a very great
multitude gathered to Him that
He got into a boat in the sea and
sat down; and the whole multitude was by the sea on the land.
2 And He was teaching them
many things in parables, and was
saying to them in His teaching,
3"Listen *to this*! Behold, the
sower went out to sow;
4 and it came about that as he
was sowing, some *seed* fell beside
the road, and the birds came and
ate it up.
5"And other *seed* fell on the
rocky *ground* where it did not
have much soil; and immediately
it sprang up because it had no
depth of soil.
6"And after the sun had risen,
it was scorched; and because it
had no root, it withered away.
7"And other *seed* fell among
the thorns, and the thorns came
up and choked it, and it yielded no
crop.
8"And other *seeds* fell into the
good soil and as they grew up and
increased, they yielded a crop and
produced thirty, sixty, and a hundredfold."
9 And He was saying, "He who
has ears to hear, let him hear."
10 And as soon as He was
alone, His followers, along with
the twelve, *began* asking Him
about the parables.
11 And He was saying to them,
"To you has been given the mystery of the kingdom of God; but
ʳthose who are outside get everything in parables, 1 Cor. 5:12f.
12 in order that WHILE SEEING,
THEY MAY SEE AND NOT PERCEIVE;
AND WHILE HEARING, THEY MAY
HEAR AND NOT UNDERSTAND LEST
THEY RETURN AND BE FORGIVEN."
13 ʳAnd He *said to them, "Do
you not understand this parable?
And how will you understand all
the parables? Mark 4:13-20
14"The sower sows the word.
15"And these are the ones who
are beside the road where the
word is sown; and when they
hear, immediately Satan comes
and takes away the word which
has been sown in them.
16"And in a similar way these
are the ones on whom seed was
sown on the rocky *places*, who,
when they hear the word, immediately receive it with joy;

[12]Later mss. add: *and Your sisters*

17 and they have no *firm* root in
themselves, but are *only* temporary; then, when affliction or persecution arises because of the
word, immediately they fall away.
18 "And others are the ones on
whom seed was sown among the
thorns; these are the ones who
have heard the word,
19 and the worries of the
[13]world, and the deceitfulness of
riches, and the desires for other
things enter in and choke the
word, and it becomes unfruitful.
20 "And those are the ones on
whom seed was sown on the good
soil; and they hear the word and
accept it, and bear fruit, thirty,
sixty, and a hundredfold."
21 And He was saying to them,
"A lamp is not brought to be put
under a peck-measure, is it, or under a bed? Is it not *brought* to be
put on the lampstand?
22 "For nothing is hidden, except
to be revealed; nor has *anything*
been secret, but that it should
come to light. Luke 8:17; 12:2
23 "If any man has ears to hear,
let him hear." Matt. 11:15; 13:9
24 And He was saying to them,
"Take care what you listen to. By
your standard of measure it shall
be measured to you; and more
shall be given you besides.
25 "For whoever has, to him
shall *more* be given; and whoever
does not have, even what he has
shall be taken away from him."
26 And He was saying, "The
kingdom of God is like a man who
casts seed upon the soil;
27 and goes to bed at night and
gets up by day, and the seed
sprouts up and grows—how, he
himself does not know.
28 "The soil produces crops by itself; first the blade, then the head,
then the mature grain in the head.
29 "But when the crop permits,
he immediately puts in the sickle,
because the harvest has come."
30 And He said, "How shall we
[14]picture the kingdom of God, or
by what parable shall we present
it?
31 "*It is* like a mustard seed,
which, when sown upon the soil,
though it is smaller than all the
seeds that are upon the soil,
32 yet when it is sown, grows
up and becomes larger than all the
garden plants and forms large
branches; so that THE BIRDS OF
THE [15]AIR can NEST UNDER ITS
SHADE."
33 And with many such parables He was speaking the word
to them as they were able to hear
it;
34 and He did not speak to them
without a parable; but He was explaining everything privately to
His own disciples. Matt. 13:34
35 And on that day, when evening had come, He *said to them,
"Let us go over to the other side."
36 And leaving the multitude,
they *took Him along with them,
just as He was, in the boat; and
other boats were with Him.
37 And there *arose a fierce
gale of wind, and the waves were
breaking over the boat so much
that the boat was already filling
up.
38 And He Himself was in the
stern, asleep on the cushion; and

[13]Or, *age*

[14]Lit., *compare* [15]Or, *sky*

they *awoke Him and *said to Him, "Teacher, do You not care that we are perishing?"

39 And being aroused, He rebuked the wind and said to the sea, "Hush, be still." And the wind died down and [t]it became perfectly calm. *a great calm occurred*

40 And He said to them, "Why are you so timid? How is it that you have no faith?"

41 And they became very much afraid and said to one another, "Who then is this, that even the wind and the sea obey Him?"

CHAPTER 5

[r]AND they came to the other side of the sea, into the country of the Gerasenes. Mark 5:1-17

2 And when He had come out of [r]the boat, immediately a man from the tombs with an unclean spirit met Him, Mark 3:9; 4:1, 36

3 and he had his dwelling among the tombs. And no one was able to bind him anymore, even with a chain;

4 because he had often been bound with shackles and chains, and the chains had been torn apart by him, and the shackles broken in pieces, and no one was strong enough to subdue him.

5 And constantly night and day, among the tombs and in the mountains, he was crying out and gashing himself with stones.

6 And seeing Jesus from a distance, he ran up and bowed down before Him;

7 and crying out with a loud voice, he *said, "What do I have to do with You, Jesus, Son of the Most High God? I implore You by God, do not torment me!"

8 For He had been saying to him, "Come out of the man, you unclean spirit!"

9 And He was asking him, "What is your name?" And he *said to Him, "My name is Legion; for we are many."

10 And he *began* to entreat Him earnestly not to send them out of the country.

11 Now there was a big herd of swine feeding there on the mountain.

12 And *the demons* entreated Him, saying, "Send us into the swine so that we may enter them."

13 And He gave them permission. And coming out, the unclean spirits entered the swine; and the herd rushed down the steep bank into the sea, about two thousand *of them;* and they [t]were drowned in the sea. *were drowning*

14 And their herdsmen ran away and reported it in the city and *out* in the country. And *the people* came to see what it was that had happened.

15 And they *came to Jesus and *observed the man who had been [r]demon-possessed sitting down, clothed and in his right mind, the very man who had had the "legion"; and they became frightened. Matt. 4:24; Mark 5:16, 18

16 And those who had seen it described to them how it had happened to the demon-possessed man, and *all* about the swine.

17 And they began to entreat Him to depart from their region.

18 And as He was getting into the boat, the man who had been

[r]demon-possessed was entreating
Him that he might [t]accompany
Him. Matt. 4:24 • *be with Him*
19 And He did not let him, but
He *said to him, "Go home to
your people and report to them
[16]what great things the Lord has
done for you, and *how* He had
mercy on you." Luke 8:39
20 And he went away and began to proclaim in Decapolis what
great things Jesus had done for
him; and everyone marveled.
21 And when Jesus had crossed
over again in [r]the boat to the other
side, a great multitude gathered
about Him; and He [t]stayed by the
seashore. Mark 4:36 • *was*
22 And one of [r]the synagogue [a]of-
ficials named Jairus *came up,
and upon seeing Him, *fell at His
feet, Matt. 9:18 • *rulers*
23 and *entreated Him earnestly, saying, "My little daughter
is at the point of death; *please*
come and lay Your hands on her,
that she may get well and live."
24 And He went off with him;
and a great multitude was following Him and pressing in on Him.
25 And a woman who had had a
hemorrhage for twelve years,
26 and had endured much at the
hands of many physicians, and
had spent all that she had and was
not helped at all, but rather had
grown worse,
27 after hearing about Jesus,
came up in the crowd behind *Him,*
and touched His cloak.
28 For she [t]thought, "If I just
touch His garments, I shall [t]get
well." *was saying* • *be saved*
29 And immediately the flow of
her blood was dried up; and she
felt in her body that she was
healed of her affliction.
30 And immediately Jesus, perceiving in Himself that [r]the power
proceeding from Him had gone
forth, turned around in the crowd
and said, "Who touched My garments?" Luke 5:17
31 And His disciples said to
Him, "You see the multitude
pressing in on You, and You say,
'Who touched Me?' "
32 And He looked around to see
the woman who had done this.
33 But the woman fearing and
trembling, aware of what had
happened to her, came and fell
down before Him, and told Him
the whole truth.
34 And He said to her, "Daughter, your faith has [t]made you well;
go in peace, and be healed of your
affliction." *saved you*
35 While He was still speaking,
they *came from the *house of* the
synagogue official, saying, "Your
daughter has died; why trouble
the Teacher anymore?"
36 But Jesus, overhearing what
was being spoken, *said to the
synagogue official, "Do not be
afraid *any longer,* only believe."
37 And He allowed no one to
follow with Him, except [r]Peter and
[a]James and John the brother of
James. Matt. 17:1; 26:37 • *Jacob*
38 And they *came to the house
of the synagogue official; and He
*beheld a commotion, and *people*
loudly weeping and wailing.
39 And entering in, He *said to
them, "Why make a commotion
and weep? The child has not died,
but is asleep."
40 And they *began* laughing at
Him. But putting them all out, He

[16]Or, *everything that*

*took along the child's father and
mother and His own companions,
and *entered *the room* where the
child was.
41 And taking the child by the
hand, He *said to her, "Talitha
kum!" (which translated means,
"Little girl, I say to you, arise!")
42 And immediately the girl
rose and *began* to walk; for she
was twelve years old. And immediately they were completely astounded.
43 And He gave them strict orders that no one should know
about this; and He said that *something* should be given her to eat.

CHAPTER 6

AND He went out from there,
and He *came into [a]His home
town; and His disciples *followed
Him. *His own part of the country*
2 And when the Sabbath had
come, He began to teach in the
synagogue; and the many listen-
ers were astonished, saying,
"Where did this man *get* these
things, and what is *this* wisdom
given to Him, and such miracles
as these performed by His hands?
3 "Is not this the carpenter, the
son of Mary, and brother of
James, and Joses, and Judas, and
Simon? Are not His sisters here
with us?" And they [t]took offense
at Him. *were being made to stumble*
4 And Jesus said to them, "A[r]
prophet is not without honor except in his home town and among
his *own* relatives and in his *own*
household." Matt. 13:57
5 And He could do no[a]miracle
there except that He laid His
hands upon a few sick people and
healed them. *work of power*
6 And He wondered at their
unbelief.
[r]And He was going around the
villages teaching. Mark 1:39
7 And [r]He *summoned the
twelve and began to send them
out in pairs; and He was giving
them authority over the unclean
spirits; Matt. 10:1, 5; Mark 3:13
8 and He instructed them that
they should take nothing for *their*
journey, except a mere staff; no
bread, no[a]bag, no money in their
belt; *knapsack* or *beggar's bag*
9 but [t]*to* wear sandals; and *He
added,* "Do not put on two [17]tu-
nics." *being shod with*
10 And He said to them, "Wherever you enter a house, stay there
until you leave town.
11 "And any place that does not
receive you or listen to you, as
you go out from there, shake off
the dust [t]from the soles of your
feet for a testimony against
them." *under your feet*
12 And they went out and
preached that *men* should repent.
13 And they were casting out
many demons and [r]were anointing
with oil many sick people and
healing them. James 5:14
14 And King Herod heard *of it,*
for His name had become well
known; and *people* were saying,
"John[r] the Baptist has risen from
the dead, and that is why these
miraculous powers are at work in
Him." Matt. 14:2; Luke 9:19
15 But others were saying, "*He
is* Elijah." And others were saying, "*He is* a prophet, like one of
the prophets *of old.*"

[17]Or, *inner garments*

16 But when Herod heard *of it,*
he kept saying, "John, whom I beheaded, has risen!"
17 For Herod himself had sent
and had John arrested and bound
in prison on account of Herodias,
the wife of his brother Philip, because he had married her.
18 For John had been saying to
Herod, "It is not lawful for you to
have your brother's wife."
19 And Herodias had a grudge
against him and wanted to put
him to death and could not *do so;*
20 for Herod was afraid of John,
knowing that he was a righteous
and holy man, and kept him safe.
And when he heard him, he was
very perplexed;[t]but he used to enjoy listening to him. *and*
21 And a strategic day came
when Herod on his birthday [r]gave
a banquet for his lords and military commanders and the leading
men of Galilee; Esth. 1:3; 2:18
22 and when the daughter of
Herodias herself came in and
danced, she pleased Herod and his
dinner guests; and the king said to
the girl, "Ask me for whatever
you want and I will give it to you."
23 And he swore to her, "Whatever you ask of me, I will give it to
you; up to half of my kingdom."
24 And she went out and said to
her mother, "What shall I ask
for?" And she said, "The head of
John the Baptist."
25 And immediately she came
in haste before the king and
asked, saying, "I want you to give
me right away the head of John
the Baptist on a platter."
26 And although the king was
very sorry, *yet* because of his
oaths and because of [t]his dinner
guests, he was unwilling to refuse
her. *those reclining at the table*
27 And immediately the king
sent an executioner and commanded *him* to bring *back* his
head. And he went and had him
beheaded in the prison,
28 and brought his head on a
platter, and gave it to the girl; and
the girl gave it to her mother.
29 And when his disciples heard
about this, they came and took
away his body and laid it in a
tomb.
30 And the [r]apostles *gathered
together with Jesus; and they reported to Him all that they had
done and taught. Matt. 10:2
31 And He *said to them,
"Come away by yourselves to a
lonely place and rest a while."
(For there were many *people* coming and going, and they did not
even have time to eat.)
32 [r]And they went away in the
boat to a lonely place by themselves. Luke 9:10-17; John 6:5-13
33 And *the people* saw them
going, and many recognized *them,*
and they ran there together on
foot from all the cities, and got
there ahead of them.
34 And when He went [t]ashore,
He saw a great multitude, and He
felt compassion for them because
they were like sheep without a
shepherd; and He began to teach
them many things. *out*
35 And when it was already
quite late, His disciples came up
to Him and *began* saying, "The
place is desolate and it is already
quite late;
36 send them away so that they
may go into the surrounding

countryside and villages and buy
themselves something to eat."
37 But He answered and said to
them, "You give them *something*
to eat!" And they *said to Him,
"Shall we go and spend two hundred [18]denarii on bread and give
them *something* to eat?"
38 And He *said to them, "How
many loaves do you have? Go
look!" And when they found out,
they *said, "Five and two fish."
39 And He commanded them all
to recline by groups on the green
grass.
40 And they reclined in companies of hundreds and of fifties.
41 And He took the five loaves
and the two fish, and looking up
toward heaven, He blessed *the
food* and broke the loaves and He
kept giving *them* to the disciples
to set before them; and He divided
up the two fish among them all.
42 And they all ate and were
satisfied.
43 And they picked up twelve
full baskets of the broken pieces,
and also of the fish. Matt. 14:20
44 And there were five thousand men who ate the loaves.
45 And immediately He made
His disciples get into the boat and
go ahead of *Him* to the other side
to Bethsaida, while He Himself
was sending the multitude away.
46 And after bidding them farewell, He departed to the mountain
to pray. Acts 18:18, 21; 2 Cor. 2:13
47 And when it was evening,
the boat was in the midst of the
sea, and He *was* alone on the land.
48 And seeing them straining at
the oars, for the wind was against
them, at about the fourth watch of
the night, He *came to them,
walking on the sea; and He intended to pass by them.
49 But when they saw Him
walking on the sea, they supposed
that it was a ghost, and cried out;
50 for they all saw Him and
were frightened. But immediately
He spoke with them and *said to
them, "Take courage; it is I, do not
be afraid." *troubled* • Matt. 9:2
51 And He got into the boat
with them, and the wind stopped;
and they were greatly astonished,
52 for they had not gained any
insight from the *incident of* the
loaves, but their heart was hardened. Mark 8:17ff. • Rom. 11:7
53 And when they had crossed
over they came to land at Gennesaret, and moored to the shore.
54 And when they had come out
of the boat, immediately *the people* recognized Him,
55 and ran about that whole
country and began to carry about
on their pallets those who were
sick, to the place they heard He
was.
56 And wherever He entered
villages, or cities, or countryside,
they were laying the sick in the
market places, and entreating
Him that they might just touch
the fringe of His cloak; and as
many as touched it were being
cured. Mark 3:10 • Matt. 9:20

CHAPTER 7

AND the Pharisees and some of
the scribes gathered together
around Him when they had come
from Jerusalem, Matt. 15:1-20
2 and had seen that some of

[18]The denarius was equivalent to one day's wage

His disciples were eating their
bread with [r]impure hands, that is,
unwashed. Matt. 15:2; Mark 7:5
3 (For the Pharisees and all the
Jews do not eat unless they [t]care-
fully wash their hands, *thus* observing the [r]traditions of the elders; *with the fist* • Mark 7:5, 8, 9
4 and *when they come* from
the market place, they do not eat
unless they [a]cleanse themselves;
and there are many other things
which they have received in order
to observe, such as the [t]washing of
cups and pitchers and copper
pots.) *sprinkle* • *baptizing*
5 And the Pharisees and the
scribes *asked Him, "Why do
Your disciples not walk according
to the [r]tradition of the elders, but
eat their bread with impure
hands?" Mark 7:3, 8, 9, 13
6 And He said to them,
"Rightly did Isaiah prophesy of
you hypocrites, as it is written,
'THIS PEOPLE HONORS ME
WITH THEIR LIPS,
BUT THEIR HEART IS FAR
AWAY FROM ME.
7 'BUT [r]IN VAIN DO THEY WOR-
SHIP ME, Is. 29:13
TEACHING AS DOCTRINES
THE PRECEPTS OF MEN.'
8 "Neglecting the commandment of God, you hold to the [r]tra-
dition of men." Mark 7:3, 5, 9
9 He was also saying to them,
"You nicely set aside the commandment of God in order to keep
your [r]tradition. Mark 7:3, 5, 8
10 "For Moses said, 'HONOR[r]
YOUR FATHER AND YOUR MOTHER';
and, 'HE WHO SPEAKS EVIL OF FA-
THER OR MOTHER, LET HIM [t]BE PUT
TO DEATH'; Ex. 20:12 • *die the death*

11 but you say, 'If a man says to
his father or *his* mother, anything
of mine you might have been
helped by is [r]Corban (that is to
say, [19]given *to God*),' Lev. 1:2
12 you no longer permit him to
do anything for *his* father or *his*
mother;
13 *thus* invalidating the word of
God by your tradition which you
have handed down; and you do
many things such as that."
14 And after He called the multitude to Him again, He *began*
saying to them, "Listen to Me, all
of you, and understand:
15 there is nothing outside the
man which going into him can defile him; but the things which proceed out of the man are what defile the man.
16 ["[20]If any man has ears to
hear, let him hear."]
17 And when leaving the multitude, He had entered [r]the house,
His disciples questioned Him
about the parable. Mark 2:1; 3:20
18 And He *said to them, "Are
you so lacking in understanding
also? Do you not understand that
whatever goes into the man from
outside cannot defile him;
19 because it does not go into
his heart, but into his stomach,
and is eliminated?" (*Thus He* declared all foods clean.)
20 And He was saying, "That
which proceeds out of the man,
that is what defiles the man.
21 "For from within, out of the
heart of men, proceed the evil
thoughts, fornications, thefts,
murders, adulteries,

[19] Or, *a gift, an offering*
[20] Many mss. do not contain this verse

22 deeds of coveting *and* wickedness, *as well as* deceit, sensuality, [t]envy, slander,[a]pride *and* foolishness. *an evil eye* · *arrogance*

23 "All these evil things proceed from within and defile the man."

24 [r]And from there He arose and went away to the region of Tyre[21]. And when He had entered a house, He wanted no one to know *of it;* [t]yet He could not escape notice. Mark 7:24-30 · *and*

25 But after hearing of Him, a woman whose little daughter had an unclean spirit, immediately came and fell at His feet.

26 Now the woman was a [22]Gentile, of the Syrophoenician race. And she kept asking Him to cast the demon out of her daughter.

27 And He was saying to her, "Let the children be satisfied first, for it is not [a]good to take the children's bread and throw it to the dogs." *proper*

28 But she answered and *said to Him, "Yes, Lord, *but* even the dogs under the table feed on the children's crumbs."

29 And He said to her, "Because of this [t]answer go your way; the demon has gone out of your daughter." *word*

30 And going back to her home, she found the child lying on the bed, the demon having departed.

31 And again He went out from the region of [r]Tyre, and came through Sidon to the Sea of Galilee, within the region of Decapolis. Matt. 11:21; Mark 7:24

32 And they *brought to Him one who was deaf and spoke with difficulty, and they *entreated Him to lay His hand upon him.

33 And [r]He took him aside from the multitude by himself, and put His fingers into his ears, and after spitting, He touched his tongue *with the saliva;* Mark 8:23

34 and looking up to heaven with a deep [r]sigh, He *said to him, "Ephphatha!" that is, "Be opened!" Mark 8:12

35 And his ears were opened, and the impediment of his tongue [t]was removed, and he *began* speaking plainly. *was loosed*

36 And He gave them orders not to tell anyone; but the more He ordered them, the more widely they continued to proclaim it.

37 And they were utterly astonished, saying, "He has done all things well; He makes even the deaf to hear, and the dumb to speak."

CHAPTER 8

IN those days again, when there was a great multitude and they had nothing to eat, He called His disciples and *said to them,

2 "I feel compassion for the multitude because they have remained with Me now three days, and have nothing to eat;

3 and if I send them away hungry to their home, they will faint on the way; and some of them have come from a distance."

4 And His disciples answered Him, "Where will anyone be able to *find enough to* satisfy these men with [t]bread here in a desolate place?" *loaves*

5 And He was asking them,

[21] Some early mss. add: *and Sidon*
[22] Lit., *Greek*

"How many loaves do you have?" And they said, "Seven."

6 And He *directed the multitude to sit down on the ground; and taking the seven loaves, He gave thanks and broke them, and started giving them to His disciples to serve to them, and they served them to the multitude.

7 They also had a few small fish; and after He had blessed them, He ordered these to be [t]served as well. *set before them*

8 And they ate and were satisfied; and they picked up seven large baskets full of what was left over of the broken pieces.

9 And about four thousand were *there;* and He sent them away.

10 And immediately He entered the boat with His disciples, and came to the district of [r]Dalmanutha. Matt. 15:39

11 And the Pharisees came out and began to argue with Him, seeking from Him a sign from heaven, to test Him.

12 And sighing deeply [a]in His spirit, He *said, "Why does this generation seek for a sign? Truly I say to you, no sign shall be given to this generation." *to Himself*

13 And leaving them, He again embarked and went away to the other side.

14 And they had forgotten to take bread; and [t]did not have more than one loaf in the boat with them. *were not having*

15 And He was giving orders to them, saying, "Watch[r] out! Beware of the leaven of the Pharisees and the leaven of Herod." Luke 12:1

16 And they *began* to discuss with one another *the fact* that they had no bread.

17 And Jesus, aware of this, *said to them, "Why do you discuss *the fact* that you have no bread? Do[r] you not yet see or understand? Do you have a[a] hardened heart? Mark 6:52 • *dull, insensible*

18 "HAVING[r] EYES, DO YOU NOT SEE? AND HAVING EARS, DO YOU NOT HEAR? And do you not remember, Jer. 5:21; Ezek. 12:2

19 when I broke[r] the five loaves for the five thousand, how many baskets full of broken pieces you picked up?" They *said to Him, "Twelve." Mark 6:41-44

20 "And when *I broke*[r] the seven for the four thousand, how many large baskets full of broken pieces did you pick up?" And they *said to Him, "Seven." Mark 8:6-9

21 And He was saying to them, "Do you not yet understand?"

22 And they *came to [r]Bethsaida. And they *brought a blind man to Him, and *entreated Him to touch him. Matt. 11:21

23 And taking the blind man by the hand, He brought him out of the village; and after [r]spitting on his eyes, and laying His hands upon him, He asked him, "Do you see anything?" Mark 7:33

24 And he looked up and said, "I see men, for I am seeing *them* like trees, walking about."

25 Then again He laid His hands upon his eyes; and he looked intently and was restored, and *began* to see everything clearly.

26 And He sent him to his home, saying, "Do not even enter [r]the village." Mark 8:23

27 And Jesus went out, along with His disciples, to the villages

of Caesarea Philippi; and on the
way He questioned His disciples,
saying to them, "Who do people
say that I am?" Matt. 16:13
28 [r]And they told Him, saying,
"John the Baptist; and others *say*
Elijah; but others, one of the
prophets." Mark 6:14
29 And He *continued* by questioning them, "But who do you
say that I am?" [r]Peter *answered
and *said to Him, "Thou art the
Christ." John 6:68, 69
30 And [r]He warned them to tell
no one about Him. Matt. 8:4
31 And He began to teach them
that the Son of Man must suffer
many things and be rejected by
the elders and the chief priests
and the scribes, and be killed, and
after three days rise again.
32 And He was stating the matter plainly. And Peter took Him
aside and began to rebuke Him.
33 But turning around and seeing His disciples, He rebuked Peter, and *said, "Get behind Me,
[r]Satan; for you are not setting your
mind on [23]God's interests, but
man's." Matt. 4:10
34 And He summoned the multitude with His disciples, and said
to them, "If anyone wishes to
come after Me, let him deny himself, and [r]take up his cross, and follow Me. Matt. 10:38; Luke 14:27
35 "For whoever wishes to save
his life shall lose it; but whoever
loses his life for My sake and the
gospel's shall save it.
36 "For what does it profit a man
to gain the whole world, and forfeit his soul?
37 "For what shall a man give in
exchange for his soul?
38 "For whoever is ashamed of
Me and My words in this adulterous and sinful generation, the Son
of Man will also be ashamed of
him when He [r]comes in the glory
of His Father with the holy angels." Mark 13:26; Luke 9:26

CHAPTER 9

AND He was saying to them,
"Truly I say to you, there are
some of those who are standing
here who shall not taste death until they see the kingdom of God after it has come with power."
2 And six days later, Jesus
*took with Him [r]Peter and [a]James
and John, and *brought them up
to a high mountain by themselves.
And He was transfigured before
them; Mark 5:37 • *Jacob*
3 and [r]His garments became radiant and exceedingly white, as no
launderer on earth can whiten
them. Matt. 28:3
4 And Elijah appeared to them
along with Moses; and they were
talking with Jesus.
5 And Peter answered and
*said to Jesus, "Rabbi,[r] it is good
for us to be here; and let us make
three [a]tabernacles, one for You,
and one for Moses, and one for
Elijah." Matt. 23:7 • *sacred tents*
6 For he did not know what to
answer; for they became terrified.
7 Then a cloud formed, overshadowing them, and a voice
came out of the cloud, "This is My
beloved Son, listen to Him!"
8 And all at once they looked
around and saw no one with them
anymore, except Jesus alone.
9 And as they were coming
down from the mountain, He [r]gave

[23]Lit., *the things of God*

them orders not to relate to anyone what they had seen, [t]until the
Son of Man should rise from the
dead. Matt. 8:4 • *except when*
10 And they seized upon [t]that
statement, discussing with one
another what rising from the dead
might mean. *the statement*
11 And they asked Him, saying,
"*Why is it* that the scribes say
that Elijah must come first?"
12 And He said to them, "Elijah
does first come and restore all
things. And *yet* how is it written
of [r]the Son of Man that He should
suffer many things and be treated
with contempt? Mark 9:31
13 "But I say to you, that Elijah
has [t]indeed come, and they did to
him whatever they wished, just as
it is written of him." *also*
14 And when they came *back* to
the disciples, they saw a large
crowd around them, and *some*
scribes arguing with them.
15 And immediately, when the
entire crowd saw Him, they were
[r]amazed, and *began* running up to
greet Him. Mark 14:33; 16:5, 6
16 And He asked them, "What
are you discussing with them?"
17 And one of the crowd answered Him, "Teacher, I brought
You my son, possessed with a
spirit which makes him mute;
18 and whenever it seizes him,
it dashes him *to the ground* and he
foams *at the mouth,* and grinds
his teeth, and stiffens out. And I
told Your disciples to cast it out,
and they could not *do it.*"
19 And He *answered them and
*said, "O unbelieving generation,
how long shall I be with you? How
long shall I put up with you? Bring
him to Me!"
20 And they brought the boy to
Him. And when he saw Him, immediately the spirit threw him
into a convulsion, and falling to
the ground, he *began* rolling about
and foaming *at the mouth.*
21 And He asked his father,
"How long has this been happening to him?" And he said, "From
childhood.
22 "And it has often thrown him
both into the fire and into the water to destroy him. But if You can
do anything, take pity on us and
help us!"
23 And Jesus said to him, " 'If
You can!' All things are possible
to him who believes."
24 Immediately the boy's father
cried out and *began* saying, "I do
believe; help my unbelief."
25 And when Jesus saw that a
crowd was rapidly gathering, He
rebuked the unclean spirit, saying
to it, "You deaf and dumb spirit, I
command you, come out of him
and do not enter him again."
26 And after crying out and
throwing him into terrible convul-
sions, it came out; and *the boy* became so much like a corpse that
most *of them* said, "He is dead!"
27 But Jesus took him by the
hand and raised him; and he got
up.
28 And when He had come into
the house, His disciples *began*
questioning Him privately, "Why
could we not cast it out?"
29 And He said to them, "This
kind cannot come out by anything
but prayer[24]."
30 And from there they went
out and *began* to go through Gali-

[24] Many mss. add: *and fasting*

lee, and He was unwilling for anyone to know *about it.*

31 For He was teaching His disciples and telling them, "The[r] Son of Man is to be [25]delivered into the hands of men, and they will kill Him; and when He has been killed, He will rise three days later." Matt. 16:21; Mark 8:31; 9:12

32 But they did not understand *this* statement, and they were afraid to ask Him.

33 And they came to Capernaum; and when He [t]was in [r]the house, He *began* to question them, "What were you discussing on the way?" *had come* • Mark 3:19

34 But they kept silent, for on the way [r]they had discussed with one another which *of them was* the greatest. Matt. 18:4

35 And sitting down, He called the twelve and *said to them, "If anyone wants to be first, he shall be last of all, and servant of all."

36 And taking a child, He set him before them, and taking him in His arms, He said to them,

37 "Whoever receives [t]one child like this in My name receives Me; and whoever receives Me does not receive Me, but Him who sent Me." *one of such children*

38 John said to Him, "Teacher, we saw someone casting out demons in Your name, and [r]we tried to hinder him because he was not following us." Num. 11:27-29

39 But Jesus said, "Do not hinder him, for there is no one who shall perform a miracle in My name, and be able soon afterward to speak evil of Me.

40 "For[r] he who is not against us is [26]for us. Matt. 12:30; Luke 11:23

41 "For [r]whoever gives you a cup of water to drink because of your name as *followers* of Christ, truly I say to you, he shall not lose his reward. Matt. 10:42

42 "And whoever causes one of these little ones who believe to stumble, it would be better for him if, with a heavy millstone hung around his neck, he had been cast into the sea.

43 "And if your hand causes you to stumble, cut it off; it is better for you to enter life crippled, than having your two hands, to go into hell, into the unquenchable fire,

44 [[27]where THEIR WORM DOES NOT DIE, AND THE FIRE IS NOT QUENCHED.]

45 "And if your foot causes you to stumble, cut it off; it is better for you to enter life lame, than having your two feet, to be cast into [r]hell, Matt. 5:22

46 [[27]where THEIR WORM DOES NOT DIE, AND THE FIRE IS NOT QUENCHED.]

47 "And if your eye causes you to stumble, cast it out; it is better for you to enter the kingdom of God with one eye, than having two eyes, to be cast into hell,

48 where THEIR WORM DOES NOT DIE, AND [r]THE FIRE IS NOT QUENCHED. Matt. 3:12; 25:41

49 "For everyone will be salted with fire.

50 "Salt is good; but if the salt becomes unsalty, with what will you [t]make it salty *again*? Have salt in yourselves, and be at peace with one another." *season it*

[25]Or, *betrayed* [26]Or, *on our side*

[27]Vv. 44 and 46, which are identical with v. 48, are not found in the best ancient mss.

CHAPTER 10

AND rising up, He *went from
there to the region of Judea, and
beyond the Jordan; and crowds
*gathered around Him again, and,
according to His custom, He once
more *began* to teach them.
2 And *some* Pharisees came up
to Him, testing Him, and *began* to
question Him whether it was lawful for a man to divorce a wife.
3 And He answered and said to
them, "What did Moses command
you?"
4 And they said, "Moses[r] permitted *a man* TO WRITE A CERTIFI-
CATE OF DIVORCE AND [a]SEND *her*
AWAY." Matt. 5:31 • *divorce her*
5 But Jesus said to them, "Because of your hardness of heart he
wrote you this commandment.
6 "But [r]from the beginning of
creation, *God* MADE THEM MALE
AND FEMALE. Mark 13:19
7 "FOR THIS CAUSE A MAN SHALL
LEAVE HIS FATHER AND MOTHER,[28]
8 AND THE TWO SHALL BECOME
ONE FLESH; consequently they are
no longer two, but one flesh.
9 "What therefore God has
joined together, let no man separate."
10 And in the house the disciples *began* questioning Him about
this again.
11 And He *said to them,
"Whoever[r] divorces his wife and
marries another woman commits
adultery against her; Matt. 5:32
12 and if she herself divorces
her husband and marries another
man, she is committing adultery."
13 [r]And they were bringing children to Him so that He might
touch them; and the disciples rebuked them. Mark 10:13-16
14 But when Jesus saw this, He
was indignant and said to them,
"Permit the children to come to
Me; do not hinder them; [r]for the
kingdom of God belongs to such
as these. Matt. 5:3
15 "Truly I say to you, [r]whoever
does not receive the kingdom of
God like a child shall not enter it
at all." Matt. 18:3; 19:14
16 And He took them in His
arms and *began* blessing them,
laying His hands upon them.
17 And as He was setting out on
a journey, a man ran up to Him
and knelt before Him, and *began*
asking Him, "Good Teacher, what
shall I do to inherit eternal life?"
18 And Jesus said to him, "Why
do you call Me good? No one is
good except God alone.
19 "You know the command-
ments, 'Do[r] NOT MURDER, DO NOT
COMMIT ADULTERY, DO NOT STEAL,
DO NOT BEAR FALSE WITNESS, Do
not defraud, HONOR YOUR FATHER
AND MOTHER.'" Ex. 20:12-16
20 And he said to Him,
"Teacher, I have kept all these
things from my youth up."
21 And looking at him, Jesus
felt a love for him, and said to
him, "One thing you lack: go and
sell all you possess, and give to
the poor, and you shall have [r]trea-
sure in heaven; and come, follow
Me." Matt. 6:20
22 But at these words [a]his face
fell, and he went away grieved, for
he was one who owned much
property. *he became gloomy*
23 And Jesus, looking around,
*said to His disciples, "How[r] hard
it will be for those who are

[28] Some mss. add: *and shall cleave to his wife*

wealthy to enter the kingdom of God!" Matt. 19:23

24 And the disciples were amazed at His words. But Jesus *answered again and *said to them, "Children, how hard it is [29]to enter the kingdom of God!

25 "It[r] is easier for a camel to go through the eye of [t]a needle than for a rich man to enter the kingdom of God." Matt. 19:24 • *the*

26 And they were even more astonished and said to Him, "Then[t] who can be saved?" *And*

27 Looking upon them, Jesus *said, "With[r] men it is impossible, but not with God; for all things are possible with God." Matt. 19:26

28 Peter began to say to Him, "Behold, we have left everything and followed You."

29 Jesus said, "Truly I say to you, [r]there is no one who has left house or brothers or sisters or mother or father or children or farms, for My sake and for the gospel's sake, Matt. 6:33; 19:29

30 but that he shall receive a hundred times as much now in [t]the present age, houses and brothers and sisters and mothers and children and farms, along with persecutions; and in [r]the age to come, eternal life. *this time* • Matt. 12:32

31 "But many *who are* first, will be last; and the last, first."

32 And they were on the road, going up to Jerusalem, and Jesus was walking on ahead of them; and they were amazed, and those who followed were fearful. And again He took the twelve aside and began to tell them what was going to happen to Him,

33 *saying,* "Behold, we are going up to Jerusalem, and [r]the Son of Man will be [30]delivered to the chief priests and the scribes; and they will condemn Him to death, and will [a]deliver Him to the Gentiles. Mark 8:31 • *betray*

34 "And they will mock Him and [r]spit upon Him, and scourge Him, and kill *Him,* and three days later He will rise again." Matt. 16:21

35 And [a]James and John, the two sons of Zebedee, *came up to Him, saying to Him, "Teacher, we want You to do for us whatever we ask of You." *Jacob*

36 And He said to them, "What do you want Me to do for you?"

37 And they said to Him, "Grant[t] that we [r]may sit in Your glory, one on Your right, and one on *Your* left." *Give to us* • Matt. 19:28

38 But Jesus said to them, "You do not know what you are asking for. Are you able [r]to drink the cup that I drink, or to be baptized with the baptism with which I am baptized?" Matt. 20:22

39 And they said to Him, "We are able." And Jesus said to them, "The cup that I drink [r]you shall drink; and you shall be baptized with the baptism with which I am baptized. Acts 12:2; Rev. 1:9

40 "But to sit on My right or on *My* left, this is not Mine to give; [r]but it is for those for whom it has been prepared." Matt. 13:11

41 [r]And hearing this, the ten began to feel indignant with [a]James and John. Mark 10:42-45 • *Jacob*

42 And calling them to Himself, Jesus *said to them, "You know that those who are recognized as rulers of the Gentiles lord it over

[29]Later mss. insert: *for those who trust in wealth*

[30]Or, *betrayed*

them; and their great men exercise authority over them.
43 "But it is not so among you,
but whoever wishes to become
great among you shall be your
servant; Matt. 20:26; 23:11
44 and whoever wishes to be
first among you shall be slave of
all.
45 "For even the Son of Man did
not come to be served, but to
serve, and to give His life a ransom for many." *soul*
46 And they *came to Jericho.
And as He was going out from
Jericho with His disciples and a
great multitude, a blind beggar
named Bartimaeus, the son of Ti-
maeus, was sitting by the road.
47 And when he heard that it
was Jesus the Nazarene, he began
to cry out and say, "Jesus, Son of
David, have mercy on me!"
48 And many were sternly telling him to be quiet, but he kept
crying out all the more, "Son of
David, have mercy on me!"
49 And Jesus stopped and said,
"Call him *here.*" And they *called
the blind man, saying to him,
"Take courage, arise! He is calling
for you." Matt. 9:2
50 And casting aside his cloak,
he jumped up, and came to Jesus.
51 And answering him, Jesus
said, "What do you want Me to do
for you?" And the blind man said
to Him, "[31]Rabboni, *I want* to regain my sight!" Matt. 23:7
52 And Jesus said to him, "Go
your way; your faith has made
you well." And immediately he regained his sight and *began* following Him on the road. *saved you*

[31] I.e., My Master

CHAPTER 11

AND as they *approached Jerusalem, at Bethphage and Bethany,
near the Mount of Olives, He
*sent two of His disciples,
2 and *said to them, "Go into
the village opposite you, and immediately as you enter it, you will
find a colt tied *there,* on which no
one yet has ever sat; untie it and
bring it *here.*
3 "And if anyone says to you,
'Why are you doing this?' you say,
'The Lord has need of it'; and immediately he will send it back
here." *sends*
4 And they went away and
found a colt tied at the door outside in the street; and they *untied
it.
5 And some of the bystanders
were saying to them, "What are
you doing, untying the colt?"
6 And they spoke to them just
as Jesus had told *them,* and they
gave them permission.
7 And they *brought the colt
to Jesus and put their garments on
it; and He sat upon it.
8 And many spread their garments in the road, and others
spread leafy branches which they
had cut from the fields.
9 And those who went before,
and those who followed after,
were crying out,
"Hosanna!
BLESSED IS HE WHO COMES
IN THE NAME OF THE
LORD; Ps. 118:26
10 Blessed *is* the coming kingdom of our father David;
Hosanna in the highest!"
11 And He entered Jerusalem
and came into the temple; and af-

ter looking all around, He departed for Bethany with the
twelve, since it was already late.
12 And on the next day, when
they had departed from Bethany,
He became hungry.
13 And seeing at a distance a fig
tree in leaf, He went *to see* if perhaps He would find anything on it;
and when He came to it, He found
nothing but leaves, for it was not
the season for figs.
14 And He answered and said to
it, "May no one ever eat fruit from
you again!" And His disciples
were listening.
15 [r]And they *came to Jerusalem. And He entered the temple
and began to cast out those who
were buying and selling in the
temple, and overturned the tables
of the moneychangers and the
seats of those who were selling
[t]doves; Mark 11:15-18 • *the doves*
16 and He would not permit
anyone to carry [t]goods through the
temple. *a vessel*
17 And He *began* to teach and
say to them, "Is it not written,
'MY[r] HOUSE SHALL BE CALLED A
HOUSE OF PRAYER FOR ALL THE NA-
TIONS'? But you have made it a
ROBBERS' [t]DEN." Is. 56:7 • *cave*
18 And the chief priests and the
scribes heard *this,* and [r]*began*
seeking how to destroy Him; for
they were afraid of Him, for all
the multitude was astonished at
His teaching. Matt. 21:46
19 And [r]whenever evening
came, they would go out of the
city. Matt. 21:17; Mark 11:11
20 And as they were passing by
in the morning, they saw the fig
tree withered from the roots *up.*
21 And being reminded, Peter
*said to Him, "Rabbi,[r] behold, the
fig tree which You cursed has
withered." Matt. 23:7
22 And Jesus *answered saying
to them, "Have faith in God.
23 "Truly I say to you, whoever
says to this mountain, 'Be taken
up and cast into the sea,' and does
not doubt in his heart, but believes that what he says is going
to happen, it shall be *granted* him.
24 "Therefore I say to you, [r]all
things for which you pray and
ask, believe that you have received them, and they shall be
granted you. Matt. 7:7f.
25 "And whenever you stand
praying, forgive, if you have anything against anyone; so that your
Father also who is in heaven may
forgive you your transgressions.
26 ["[32]But if you do not forgive,
neither will your Father who is in
heaven forgive your transgressions."]
27 And they *came again to Jerusalem. [r]And as He was walking
in the temple, the chief priests,
and scribes, and elders *came to
Him, Mark 11:27-33: *Matt. 21:23-27*
28 and *began* saying to Him,
"By what authority are You doing
these things, or who gave You this
authority to do these things?"
29 And Jesus said to them, "I
will ask you one question, and you
answer Me, and *then* I will tell you
by what authority I do these
things.
30 "Was the baptism of John
from heaven, or from men? Answer Me."
31 And they *began* reasoning
among themselves, saying, "If we
say, 'From heaven,' He will say,

[32] Many mss. do not contain this verse

'Then why did you not believe
him?'
32 "But shall we say, 'From
men'?"—they were afraid of the
multitude, for all considered John
to have been a prophet indeed.
33 And answering Jesus, they
*said, "We do not know." And
Jesus *said to them, "Neither[r] will
I tell you by what authority I do
these things." *do I tell*

CHAPTER 12

AND He began to speak to them
in parables: "A man PLANTED A
VINEYARD, AND PUT A WALL
AROUND IT, AND DUG A VAT UNDER
THE WINE PRESS, AND BUILT A
TOWER, and rented it out to [33]vine-
growers and went on a journey.
2 "And at the *harvest* time he
sent a slave to the vine-growers,
in order to receive *some* of the
produce of the vineyard from the
vine-growers.
3 "And they took him, and beat
him, and sent him away empty-
handed.
4 "And again he sent them another slave, and they wounded
him in the head, and treated him
shamefully.
5 "And he sent another, and
that one they killed; and *so with*
many others, beating some, and
killing others.
6 "He had one more *to send,* a
beloved son; he sent him last *of
all* to them, saying, 'They will respect my son.'
7 "But those vine-growers said
to one another, 'This is the heir;
come, let us kill him, and the inheritance will be ours!'

[33] Or, *tenant farmers,* also vv. 2, 7, 9

8 "And they took him, and
killed him, and threw him out of
the vineyard.
9 "What will the owner of the
vineyard do? He will come and destroy the vine-growers, and will
give the vineyard to others.
10 "Have you not even read this
Scripture:
'THE[r] STONE WHICH THE
BUILDERS REJECTED,
THIS BECAME THE CHIEF COR-
NER *stone;* Ps. 118:22
11 [r]THIS CAME ABOUT FROM THE
LORD, Ps. 118:23
AND IT IS MARVELOUS IN
OUR EYES'?"
12 And they were seeking to
seize Him; and *yet* they feared the
multitude; for they understood
that He spoke the parable against
them. And *so* [r]they left Him, and
went away. Matt. 22:22
13 [r]And they *sent some of the
Pharisees and Herodians to Him,
in order to trap Him in a statement. Mark 12:13-17: *Matt. 22:15-22*
14 And they *came and *said to
Him, "Teacher, we know that You
are truthful, and defer to no one;
for You are not partial to any, but
teach the way of God in truth. Is it
[a]lawful to pay a poll-tax to Caesar,
or not? *permissible*
15 "Shall we pay, or shall we not
pay?" But He, knowing their hypocrisy, said to them, "Why are
you testing Me? Bring Me a [34]de-
narius to look at."
16 And they brought *one.* And
He *said to them, "Whose likeness and inscription is this?" And
they said to Him, "Caesar's."

[34] The denarius was equivalent to one day's
wage

17 And Jesus said to them,
"Render to Caesar the things that
are Caesar's, and to God the
things that are God's." And they
were amazed at Him.
18 And *some* Sadducees (who
say that there is no resurrection)
*came to Him, and *began* questioning Him, saying,
19 "Teacher, Moses wrote for us
that IF A MAN'S BROTHER DIES, and
leaves behind a wife, AND LEAVES
NO CHILD, HIS BROTHER SHOULD
TAKE THE WIFE, AND RAISE UP OFF-
SPRING TO HIS BROTHER.
20 "There were seven brothers;
and the first took a wife, and died,
leaving no offspring.
21 "And the second one took her,
and died, leaving behind no offspring; and the third likewise;
22 and *so* [t]all seven left no offspring. Last of all the woman died
also. *the seven*
23 "In the resurrection, [35]when
they rise again, which one's wife
will she be? For [t]all seven had her
as wife." *the seven*
24 Jesus said to them, "Is this
not the reason you are mistaken,
that you do not understand the
Scriptures, or the power of God?
25 "For when they rise from the
dead, they neither marry, nor are
given in marriage, but are like angels in heaven.
26 "But regarding the fact that
the dead rise again, have you not
read in the book of Moses, [r]in the
passage about the burning bush,
how God spoke to him, saying, 'I
AM THE GOD OF ABRAHAM, AND
THE GOD OF ISAAC, AND THE GOD
OF JACOB'? Luke 20:37

[35]Most ancient mss. do not contain *when they rise again*

27 "He is not the God of the
dead, but of the living; you are
greatly mistaken."
28 And one of the scribes came
and heard them arguing, and [r]rec-
ognizing that He had answered
them well, asked Him, "What
commandment is the [a]foremost of
all?" Luke 20:39 • *first*
29 Jesus answered, "The foremost is, 'HEAR, O ISRAEL! THE
LORD OUR GOD IS ONE LORD;
30 AND YOU SHALL LOVE THE
LORD YOUR GOD WITH ALL YOUR
HEART, AND WITH ALL YOUR SOUL,
AND WITH ALL YOUR MIND, AND
WITH ALL YOUR STRENGTH.'
31 "The second is this, 'YOU
SHALL LOVE YOUR NEIGHBOR AS
YOURSELF.' There is no other commandment greater than these."
32 And the scribe said to Him,
"Right, Teacher, You have truly
stated that HE IS ONE; AND THERE
IS NO ONE ELSE BESIDES HIM;
33 AND TO LOVE HIM WITH ALL
THE HEART AND WITH ALL THE UN-
DERSTANDING AND WITH ALL THE
STRENGTH, AND TO LOVE ONE'S
NEIGHBOR AS HIMSELF, [r]is much
more than all burnt offerings and
sacrifices." 1 Sam. 15:22; Hos. 6:6
34 And when Jesus saw that he
had answered intelligently, He
said to him, "You are not far from
the kingdom of God." And after
that, no one would venture to ask
Him any more questions.
35 And Jesus answering *began*
to say, as He [r]taught in the temple,
"How *is it that* the scribes say
that the Christ is the son of David? Matt. 26:55; Mark 10:1
36 "David himself said [a]in the
Holy Spirit, *by*

'THE LORD SAID TO MY LORD,
"SIT AT MY RIGHT HAND,
UNTIL I PUT THINE ENEMIES
BENEATH THY FEET." '
37 "David himself calls Him
'Lord'; and so in what sense is He
his son?" And the great crowd enjoyed listening to Him.
38 And in His teaching He was
saying: "Beware of the scribes
who like to walk around in long
robes, and *like* respectful greetings in the market places,
39 and chief seats in the synagogues, and places of honor at
banquets,
40 who devour widows' houses,
and for appearance's sake offer
long prayers; these will receive
greater condemnation."
41 And He sat down opposite
the treasury, and *began* observing
how the multitude were putting
money into the treasury; and
many rich people were putting in
large sums. John 8:20
42 And a poor widow came and
put in two small copper coins,
which amount to a cent.
43 And calling His disciples to
Him, He said to them, "Truly I say
to you, this poor widow put in
more than all the contributors to
the treasury;
44 for they all put in out of their
surplus, but she, out of her poverty, put in all she owned, all she
had to live on." *her whole livelihood*

CHAPTER 13

AND as He was going out of the
temple, one of His disciples *said
to Him, "Teacher, behold [36]what
wonderful stones and what wonderful buildings!" Matt. 24
2 And Jesus said to him, "Do
you see these great buildings? Not
one stone shall be left upon another which will not be torn
down." Luke 19:44
3 And as He was sitting on the
Mount of Olives opposite the temple, Peter and James and John and
Andrew were questioning Him
privately, Matt. 21:1 · *Jacob*
4 "Tell us, when will these
things be, and what *will be* the
sign when all these things are
going to be fulfilled?"
5 And Jesus began to say to
them, "See to it that no one misleads you.
6 "Many will come in My name,
saying, 'I am *He!*' and will mislead
many. John 8:24
7 "And when you hear of wars
and rumors of wars, do not be
frightened; *those things* must take
place; but *that is* not yet the end.
8 "For nation will arise against
nation, and kingdom against kingdom; there will be earthquakes in
various places; there will *also* be
famines. These things are *merely*
the beginning of birth pangs.
9 "But be on your guard; for
they will deliver you to *the* courts,
and you will be flogged in *the*
synagogues, and you will stand
before governors and kings for
My sake, as a testimony to them.
10 "And the gospel must first be
preached to all the nations.
11 "And when they arrest you
and deliver you up, do not be anxious beforehand about what you
are to say, but say whatever is
given you in that hour; for it is not

[36]Lit., *how great*

you who speak, but *it is* the Holy
Spirit. Mark 13:11-13 • *lead*
12 "And brother will deliver
brother to death, and a father *his*
child; and children will rise up
against parents and [t]have them
put to death. *put them to death*
13 "And [r]you will be hated by all
on account of My name, but the
one who endures to the end, he
shall be saved. Matt. 10:22
14 "But when you see the [r]ABOMI-
NATION OF DESOLATION standing
where it should not be (let the
reader understand), then let those
who are in Judea flee to the mountains. Dan. 9:27; 11:31; 12:11
15 "And let him who is on the
housetop not go down, or enter in,
to get anything out of his house;
16 and let him who is in the field
not turn back to get his cloak.
17 "But woe to those who are
with child and to those who nurse
babes in those days!
18 "But pray that it may not happen in the winter.
19 "For those days will be a *time
of* tribulation such as has not occurred [r]since the beginning of the
creation which God created, until
now, and never shall. Dan. 12:1
20 "And unless the Lord had
shortened *those* days, no life
would have been saved; but for
the sake of the elect whom He
chose, He shortened the days.
21 "And then if anyone says to
you, 'Behold, here is the Christ';
or, 'Behold, *He is* there'; do not believe *him;*
22 for false Christs and false
prophets will arise, and will show
signs and wonders, in order, if
possible, to lead the elect astray.
23 "But take heed; behold, I have
told you everything in advance.
24 "But in those days, after that
tribulation, [r]THE SUN WILL BE
DARKENED, AND THE MOON WILL
NOT GIVE ITS LIGHT, Is. 13:10
25 [r]AND THE STARS WILL BE FALL-
ING from heaven, and the powers
that are in [a]the heavens will be
shaken. Is. 34:4 • *heaven*
26 "And then they will see THE
SON OF MAN COMING IN CLOUDS
with great power and glory.
27 "And then He will send forth
the angels, and [r]will gather together His [a]elect from the four
winds, from the farthest end of
the earth, to the farthest end of
heaven. Deut. 30:4 • *chosen ones*
28 "Now learn the parable from
the fig tree: when its branch has
already become tender, and puts
forth its leaves, you know that
summer is near.
29 "Even so, you too, when you
see these things happening, [t]recog-
nize that [a]He is near, *right* at the
[t]door. *know* • *it* • *doors*
30 "Truly I say to you, this [37]gen-
eration will not pass away until all
these things take place.
31 "Heaven and earth will pass
away, but My words will not pass
away.
32 "But [r] of that day or hour no
one knows, not even the angels in
heaven, nor the Son, but the Father *alone.* Matt. 24:36; Acts 1:7
33 "Take heed, [r]keep on the alert;
for you do not know when the *appointed* time is. Eph. 6:18
34 "*It is* like a man, away on a
journey, *who* upon leaving his
house and putting his slaves in
charge, *assigning* to each one his

[37]Or, *race*

task, also commanded the doorkeeper to stay on the alert.
35 "Therefore, [r]be on the alert—
for you do not know when the
[t]master of the house is coming,
whether in the evening, at midnight, at cockcrowing, or in the
morning— Matt. 24:42 · *lord*
36 lest he come suddenly and
find you [r]asleep. Rom. 13:11
37 "And what I say to you I say
to all, 'Be on the alert!' "

CHAPTER 14

NOW the Passover and Unleavened Bread was two days off; and
the chief priests and the scribes
were seeking how to seize Him by
stealth, and kill *Him;*
2 for they were saying, "Not
during the festival, lest there be a
riot of the people."
3 And while He was in Bethany at the home of Simon the leper, and reclining *at the table,* there
came a woman with an alabaster
vial of very costly perfume of pure
nard; *and* she broke the vial and
poured it over His head.
4 But some were indignantly
remarking to one another, "Why
has this perfume been wasted?
5 "For this perfume might have
been sold for over three hundred
[38]denarii, and *the money* given to
the poor." And they were scolding
her.
6 But Jesus said, "Let her
alone; why do you bother her? She
has done a good deed to Me.
7 "For the poor you always
have with you, and whenever you
wish, you can do them good; but
you do not always have Me.
8 "She has done what she could;
[r]she has anointed My body beforehand for the burial. John 19:40
9 "And truly I say to you, wherever the gospel is preached in the
whole world, that also which this
woman has done shall be spoken
of in memory of her."
10 And Judas Iscariot, who was
one of the twelve, went off to the
chief priests, in order to [a]betray
Him to them. *deliver Him up*
11 And they were glad when
they heard *this,* and promised to
give him money. And he *began*
seeking how to betray Him at an
opportune time.
12 And on the first day of Unleavened Bread, when [t]the Passover *lamb* was being sacrificed,
His disciples *said to Him,
"Where do You want us to go and
prepare for You to eat the Passover?" *they were sacrificing*
13 And He *sent two of His disciples, and *said to them, "Go into
the city, and a man will meet you
carrying a pitcher of water; follow
him;
14 and wherever he enters, say
to the owner of the house, 'The
Teacher says, "Where is My guest
room in which I may eat the Passover with My disciples?" '
15 "And he himself will show
you a large upper room furnished
and ready; and prepare for us
there."
16 And the disciples went out,
and came to the city, and found *it*
just as He had told them; and they
prepared the Passover.
17 And when it was evening He
*came with the twelve.

[38] The denarius was equivalent to one day's wage

18 And as they were reclining *at
the table and eating, Jesus said,
"Truly I say to you that one of you
will[a] betray Me—[a] one who is eating
with Me." *deliver Me up* • *the one*
19 They began to be grieved and
to say to Him one by one, "Surely
not I?"
20 And He said to them, *"It is*
one of the twelve, [a] one who dips
with Me in the bowl. *the one*
21 "For the Son of Man *is to* go,
just as it is written of Him; but
woe to that man[a] by whom the Son
of Man is betrayed! *It would have*
been good for that man if he had
not been born." *through*
22 And while they were eating,
He took *some* bread, and [t] after a
blessing He broke *it;* and gave *it*
to them, and said, "Take *it;* this is
My body." *having blessed*
23 And when He had taken a
cup, *and* given thanks, He gave *it*
to them; and they all drank from
it.
24 And He said to them, "This is
My blood of the covenant, which
is poured out for many.
25 "Truly I say to you, I shall
never again drink of the fruit of
the vine until that day when I
drink it new in the kingdom of
God."
26 [r] And after singing a hymn,
they went out to [r] the Mount of Olives. Matt. 26:30 • Matt. 21:1
27 And Jesus *said to them,
"You will all[a] fall away, because it
is written, 'I WILL STRIKE DOWN
THE SHEPHERD, AND THE SHEEP
SHALL BE SCATTERED.' *stumble*
28 "But after I have been raised, I
will go before you to Galilee."[r]
29 But Peter said to Him, *"Even*
though all may[a] fall away, yet I will
not." *stumble*
30 And Jesus *said to him,
"Truly I say to you, that you yourself [t] this very night, before a cock
crows twice, shall three times
deny Me." *today, on this night*
31 But *Peter* kept saying insis-
tently, *"Even* if I have to die with
You, I will not deny You!" And
they all were saying the same
thing, too.
32 [r] And they *came to a place
named Gethsemane; and He *said
to His disciples, "Sit here until I
have prayed." Mark 14:32-42
33 And He *took with Him Peter and [a] James and John, and began to be very [r] distressed and
troubled. *Jacob* • Mark 9:15
34 And He *said to them, "My[r]
soul is deeply grieved to the point
of death; remain here and keep
watch." Matt. 26:38; John 12:27
35 And He went a little beyond
them, and fell to the ground, and
began to pray that if it were possible, the hour might pass Him by.
36 And He was saying, "Abba![r]
Father! All things are possible for
Thee; remove this cup from Me;
yet not what I will, but what Thou
wilt." Rom. 8:15; Gal. 4:6
37 And He *came and *found
them sleeping, and *said to Peter,
"Simon, are you asleep? Could
you not keep watch for one hour?
38 "Keep[r] watching and praying,
that you may not come into temptation; the spirit is willing, but the
flesh is weak." Matt. 26:41
39 And again He went away and
prayed, saying the same words.
40 And again He came and
found them sleeping, for their
eyes were very heavy; and they

did not know what to answer
Him.
41 And He *came the third
time, and *said to them, "Are you
still sleeping and taking your rest?
It is enough; the hour has come;
behold, the Son of Man is being
betrayed into the hands of sinners. *Keep on sleeping therefore*
42 "Arise, let us be going; behold,
the one who betrays Me is at
hand!"
43 And immediately while He
was still speaking, Judas, one of
the twelve, *came up, accompanied by a multitude with swords
and clubs, from the chief priests
and the scribes and the elders.
44 Now he who was betraying
Him had given them a signal, saying, "Whomever I shall kiss, He is
the one; seize Him, and lead Him
away under guard." *safely*
45 And after coming, he immediately went to Him, saying,
"Rabbi!" and kissed Him.
46 And they laid hands on Him,
and seized Him.
47 But a certain one of those
who stood by drew his sword, and
struck the slave of the high priest,
and cut off his ear. *took off*
48 And Jesus answered and said
to them, "Have you come out with
swords and clubs to arrest Me, as
against a robber?
49 "Every day I was with you in
the temple teaching, and you did
not seize Me; but *this has happened* that the Scriptures might
be fulfilled." Luke 19:47; 21:37
50 And they all left Him and
fled.
51 And a certain young man
was following Him, wearing *nothing but* a linen sheet over *his*
naked *body;* and they *seized him.
52 But he left the linen sheet behind, and escaped naked.
53 And they led Jesus away to
the high priest; and all the chief
priests and the elders and the
scribes *gathered together.
54 And Peter had followed Him
at a distance, right into the courtyard of the high priest; and he was
sitting with the officers, and
warming himself at the fire.
55 Now the chief priests and the
whole [39]Council kept trying to obtain testimony against Jesus to
put Him to death; and they were
not finding any. Matt. 5:22
56 For many were giving false
testimony against Him, and *yet*
their testimony was not consistent.
57 And some stood up and *began* to give false testimony
against Him, saying,
58 "We heard Him say, 'I will destroy this temple made with
hands, and in three days I will
build another made without
hands.'" Matt. 26:61 • *sanctuary*
59 And not even in this respect
was their testimony consistent.
60 And the high priest stood up
and came forward and questioned
Jesus, saying, "Do You make no
answer? What is it that these men
are testifying against You?"
61 But He kept silent, and made
no answer. Again the high priest
was questioning Him, and saying
to Him, "Are You the Christ, the
Son of the Blessed *One?*"
62 And Jesus said, "I am; and
you shall see THE SON OF MAN SIT-
TING AT THE RIGHT HAND OF

[39]Or, *Sanhedrin*

POWER, and [r]COMING WITH THE
CLOUDS OF HEAVEN." Dan. 7:13
63 And tearing his clothes, the
high priest *said, "What further
need do we have of witnesses?
64 "You have heard the [r]blas-
phemy; how does it seem to you?"
And they all condemned Him to
be deserving of death. Lev. 24:16
65 And some began to spit at
Him, and [a]to blindfold Him, and to
beat Him with their fists, and to
say to Him, "Prophesy!" And the
officers received Him with slaps
in the face. *cover over His face*
66 And as Peter was below in
the courtyard, one of the servant-
girls of the high priest *came,
67 and seeing Peter [r]warming
himself, she looked at him, and
*said, "You, too, were with Jesus
the Nazarene." Mark 14:54
68 But he denied *it,* saying, "I
neither know nor understand
what you are talking about." And
he went out onto the porch.[40]
69 And the maid saw him, and
began once more to say to the bystanders, "This is *one* of them!"
70 But again he was denying it.
And after a little while the bystanders were again saying to Peter, "Surely you are *one* of them,
for you are a Galilean too."
71 But he began to curse and
swear, "I do not know this man
you are talking about!"
72 And immediately a cock
crowed a second time. And Peter
remembered how Jesus had made
the remark to him, "Before [r]a cock
crows twice, you will deny Me
three times." And he began to
weep. Mark 14:30, 68

[40] Later mss. add: *and a cock crowed*

CHAPTER 15

[r]AND early in the morning the
chief priests with the elders and
scribes, and the whole [r][41]Council,
immediately held a consultation;
and binding Jesus, they led Him
away, and delivered Him up to Pilate. Matt. 27:1 • Matt. 5:22
2 And Pilate questioned Him,
"Are You the King of the Jews?"
And answering He *said to him,
"*It is as* you say."
3 And the chief priests *began*
to accuse Him harshly.
4 And Pilate was questioning
Him again, saying, "Do You make
no answer? See how many
charges they bring against You!"
5 But Jesus [r]made no further
answer; so that Pilate was
amazed. Matt. 27:12
6 Now at *the* feast he used to
release for them *any* one prisoner
whom they requested.
7 And the man named Barabbas had been imprisoned with the
insurrectionists who had committed murder in the insurrection.
8 And the multitude went up
and began asking him *to do* as he
had been accustomed to do for
them.
9 And Pilate answered them,
saying, "Do you want me to release for you the King of the
Jews?"
10 For he was aware that the
chief priests had delivered Him up
because of envy.
11 But the chief priests stirred
up the multitude *to ask* him to release Barabbas for them instead.
12 And answering again, Pilate
was saying to them, "Then what

[41] Or, *Sanhedrin*

shall I do with Him whom you call the King of the Jews?"

13 And they shouted [a]back, "Crucify Him!" *again*

14 But Pilate was saying to them, "Why, what evil has He done?" But they shouted all the more, "Crucify Him!"

15 And wishing to satisfy the multitude, Pilate released Barabbas for them, and after having Jesus [r]scourged, he delivered *Him* to be crucified. Matt. 27:26

16 And the soldiers took Him away into the palace (that is, the Praetorium), and they *called together the whole *Roman* [42]cohort.

17 And they *dressed Him up in purple, and after weaving a crown of thorns, they put it on Him;

18 and they began to acclaim Him, "Hail, King of the Jews!"

19 And they kept beating His head with a [43]reed, and spitting at Him, and kneeling and bowing before Him.

20 And after they had mocked Him, they took the purple off Him, and put His garments on Him. And they *led Him out to crucify Him.

21 And they *pressed into service a passer-by coming from the country, Simon of Cyrene (the father of Alexander and [r]Rufus), to bear His cross. Rom. 16:13

22 And they *brought Him to the place Golgotha, which is translated, Place of a Skull.

23 And they tried to give Him [r]wine mixed with myrrh; but He did not take it. Matt. 27:34

24 And they *crucified Him, and *divided up His garments among themselves, casting lots for them, *to decide* what each should take.

25 And it was the [44]third hour when they crucified Him.

26 And the inscription of the charge against Him read, "THE KING OF THE JEWS."

27 And they *crucified two robbers with Him, one on His right and one on His left.

28 [[45]And the Scripture was fulfilled which says, "And He was numbered with transgressors."]

29 And those passing by were hurling abuse at Him, wagging their heads, and saying, "Ha! You who *are going to* destroy the temple and rebuild it in three days,

30 save Yourself, and come down from the cross!"

31 In the same way the chief priests also, along with the scribes, were mocking *Him* among themselves and saying, "He saved others;[a]He cannot save Himself. *can He not save Himself?*

32 "Let *this* Christ, [r]the King of Israel, now come down from the cross, so that we may see and believe!" And those who were crucified with Him were casting the same insult at Him. Matt. 27:42

33 And when the [46]sixth hour had come, darkness fell over the whole land until the [47]ninth hour.

34 And at the ninth hour Jesus cried out with a loud voice, "ELOI, ELOI, LAMA SABACHTHANI?" which is translated, "MY GOD, MY GOD, WHY HAST THOU FORSAKEN ME?"

35 And when some of the bystanders heard it, they *began* say-

[42]Or, *battalion* [43]Or, *staff* (made of a reed)

[44]I.e., 9 a.m.
[45]Many mss. do not contain this verse
[46]I.e., noon [47]I.e., 3 p.m.

ing, "Behold, He is calling for Elijah."
36 And someone ran and filled a
sponge with sour wine, put it on a
reed, and gave Him a drink, saying, "Let us see whether Elijah
will come to take Him down."
37 [r]And Jesus uttered a loud cry,
and breathed His last. John 19:30
38 [r]And the veil of the temple
was torn in two from top to bottom. Ex. 26:31-33; Matt. 27:51
39 And when the centurion,
who was standing right in front of
Him, saw the way He breathed
His last, he said, "Truly this man
was the Son of God!"
40 And there were also *some*
women looking on from a distance, among whom *were* Mary
Magdalene, and Mary the mother
of [a]James the [t]Less and Joses, and
Salome. *Jacob • little*
41 And when He was in Galilee,
they used to follow Him and [a]min-
ister to Him; and *there were* many
other women who had come up
with Him to Jerusalem. *wait on*
42 And when evening had already come, because it was [r]the
preparation day, that is, the day
before the Sabbath, Matt. 27:62
43 Joseph of Arimathea came, a
[r]prominent member of the Council, who himself was waiting for
the kingdom of God; and he gathered up courage and went in before Pilate, and asked for the body
of Jesus. Matt. 27:57; Luke 23:50
44 And Pilate wondered if He
was dead by this time, and summoning the centurion, he questioned him as to whether He was
already dead.
45 And ascertaining this from
[r]the centurion, he granted the body
to Joseph. Mark 15:39
46 And *Joseph* bought a linen
cloth, took Him down, wrapped
Him in the linen cloth, and laid
Him in a tomb which had been
hewn out in the rock; and he
rolled a stone against the entrance
of the tomb.
47 And [r]Mary Magdalene and
Mary the *mother* of Joses were
looking on *to see* where He was
laid. Matt. 27:56; Mark 15:40; 16:1

CHAPTER 16

AND when the Sabbath was
over, Mary Magdalene, and Mary
the *mother* of James, and Salome,
bought spices, that they might
come and anoint Him.
2 And very early on the first
day of the week, they *came to
the tomb when the sun had risen.
3 And they were saying to one
another, "Who will roll away [r]the
stone for us from the entrance of
the tomb?" Mark 15:46; 16:4
4 And looking up, they *saw
that the stone had been rolled
away, [t]although it was extremely
large. *for*
5 And entering the tomb, they
saw a young man sitting at the
right, wearing a white robe; and
they [r]were amazed. Mark 9:15
6 And he *said to them, "Do
not be amazed; you are looking
for Jesus the Nazarene, who has
been crucified. He has risen; He is
not here; behold, *here is* the place
where they laid Him.
7 "But go, tell His disciples and
Peter, 'He is going before you into
Galilee; there you will see Him,
just as He said to you.' "

8 And they went out and fled from the tomb, for trembling and astonishment had gripped them; and they said nothing to anyone, for they were afraid.

9 [[48]Now after He had risen early on the first day of the week, He first appeared to Mary Magdalene, from whom He had cast out seven demons.

10 [r]She went and reported to those who had been with Him, while they were mourning and weeping. John 20:18

11 And when they heard that He was alive, and had been seen by her, they refused to believe it.

12 And after that, He appeared in a different form to two of them, while they were walking along on their way to the country.

13 And they went away and reported it to the others, but they did not believe them either.

14 And afterward He appeared to the eleven themselves as they were reclining *at the table;* and He reproached them for their unbelief and hardness of heart, because they had not believed those who had seen Him after He had risen.

15 And He said to them, "Go[r] into all the world and preach the gospel to all creation. Acts 1:8

16 "He[r] who has believed and has been baptized shall be saved; but he who has disbelieved shall be condemned. John 3:18, 36

17 "And these [a]signs will accompany those who have believed: in My name they will cast out demons, they will speak with new tongues; *attesting miracles*

18 they will [r]pick up serpents, and if they drink any deadly *poison,* it shall not hurt them; they will lay hands on the sick, and they will recover." Acts 28:3-5

19 So then, when the Lord Jesus had spoken to them, He was received up into heaven, and sat down at the right hand of God.

20 And they went out and preached everywhere, while the Lord worked with them, and confirmed the word by the [a]signs that followed.] *attesting miracles*

[[49]*And they promptly reported all these instructions to Peter and his companions. And after that, Jesus Himself sent out through them from east to west the sacred and imperishable proclamation of eternal salvation.*]

[48] Some of the oldest mss. do not contain vv. 9-20

[49] A few later mss. and versions contain this paragraph, usually after verse 8; a few have it at the end of chapter.

THE GOSPEL ACCORDING TO

LUKE

INASMUCH as many have undertaken to compile an account of the things [r]accomplished among us, Rom. 4:21; 14:5; Col. 2:2

2 just as those who from the beginning [t]were eyewitnesses and servants of the [1]word have handed them down to us, *became*

3 it seemed fitting for me as well, [r]having [a]investigated everything carefully from the beginning, to write *it* out for you in consecutive order, most excellent Theophilus; 1 Tim. 4:6 • *followed*

4 so that you might know the exact truth about the things you have been [r]taught. Acts 18:25

5 In the days of Herod, king of Judea, there was a certain priest named Zacharias, of the [r]division of [2]Abijah; and he had a wife [3]from the daughters of Aaron, and her name was Elizabeth. Matt. 2:1

6 And they were both [r]righteous in the sight of God, walking blamelessly in all the commandments and requirements of the Lord. Gen. 7:1

7 And they had no child, because Elizabeth was barren, and they were both advanced in years.

8 Now it came about, while he was performing his priestly service before God in the *appointed* order of his division,

9 according to the custom of the priestly office, he was chosen by lot [r]to enter the temple of the Lord and burn incense. Ex. 30:7f.

10 And the whole multitude of the people were in prayer outside at the hour of the incense offering.

11 And an angel of the Lord appeared to him, standing to the right of the altar of incense.

12 And Zacharias was troubled when he saw *him*, and [r]fear [a]gripped him. Luke 2:9 • *fell upon*

13 But the angel said to him, "Do not be afraid, Zacharias, for your petition has been heard, and your wife Elizabeth will bear you a son, and you will [t]give him the name John. *call his name*

14 "And you will have joy and gladness, and many will rejoice at his birth.

15 "For he will be great in the sight of the Lord, and he will drink no wine or liquor; and he will be filled with the Holy Spirit, while yet in his mother's womb.

16 "And he will [r]turn back many of the sons of Israel to the Lord their God. Matt. 3:2, 6; Luke 3:3

17 "And it is he who will go *as a forerunner* before Him in the spirit and power of Elijah, TO TURN THE HEARTS OF THE FATHERS BACK TO THE CHILDREN, and the disobedient to the attitude of the righteous; so as to make ready a people prepared for the Lord."

18 And Zacharias said to the angel, "How shall I know this *for certain*? For I am an old man, and my wife is advanced in years."

19 And the angel answered and said to him, "I am Gabriel, who stands in the presence of God; and

[1]I.e., gospel [2]Gr., *Abia*
[3]I.e., of priestly descent

I have been sent to speak to you,
and to bring you this good news.
20 "And behold, you shall be silent and unable to speak until the
day when these things take place,
because you did not believe my
words, which shall be fulfilled in
their proper time."
21 And the people were waiting
for Zacharias, and were wondering at his delay in the temple.
22 But when he came out, he
was unable to speak to them; and
they realized that he had seen a
vision in the temple; and he [r]kept
making signs to them, and remained mute. Luke 1:62
23 And it came about, when the
days of his priestly service were
ended, that he went back home.
24 And after these days Elizabeth his wife became pregnant;
and she kept herself in seclusion
for five months, saying,
25 "This is the way the Lord has
dealt with me in the days when He
looked *with favor* upon *me,* to
[r]take away my disgrace among
men." Gen. 30:23; Is. 4:1; 25:8
26 Now in the sixth month the
angel [r]Gabriel was sent from God
to a city in Galilee, called [r]Naza-
reth, Luke 1:19 • Matt. 2:23
27 to a virgin engaged to a man
whose name was Joseph, of the
[t]descendants of David; and the virgin's name was Mary. *house*
28 And coming in, he said to
her, "Hail, favored one! The Lord
[a]*is* with you."[4] be
29 But she [r]was greatly troubled
at *this statement,* and kept pondering what kind of salutation this
might be. Luke 1:12

30 And the angel said to her,
"Do not be afraid, Mary; for you
have found favor with God.
31 "And behold, you will conceive in your womb, and bear a
son, and you [r]shall name Him
Jesus. Is. 7:14; Matt. 1:21, 25
32 "He will be great, and will be
called the Son of the Most High;
and the Lord God will give Him
the throne of His father David;
33 and He will reign over the
house of Jacob forever; and His
kingdom will have no end."
34 And Mary said to the angel,
"How [t]can this be, since I [t]am a virgin?" *shall • know no man*
35 And the angel answered and
said to her, "The Holy Spirit will
come upon you, and the power of
the Most High will overshadow
you; and for that reason the [t]holy
offspring shall be called the Son of
God. *the holy thing begotten*
36 "And behold, even your relative Elizabeth has also conceived
a son in her old age; and she who
was called barren is now in her
sixth month.
37 "For [t]nothing will be impossible with God." *not any word*
38 And Mary said, "Behold, the
[5]bondslave of the Lord; be it done
to me according to your word."
And the angel departed from her.
39 Now at this time Mary arose
and went with haste to the hill
country, to a city of Judah,
40 and entered the house of
Zacharias and greeted Elizabeth.
41 And it came about that when
Elizabeth heard Mary's greeting,
the baby leaped in her womb; and
Elizabeth was [r]filled with the Holy
Spirit. Luke 1:67; Acts 2:4; 4:8; 9:17

[4] Later mss. add: *you are blessed among women*

[5] I.e., female slave

42 And she cried out with a loud
voice, and said, "Blessed among
women *are* you, and blessed *is* the
fruit of your womb!
43 "And how has it *happened* to
me, that the mother of [r]my Lord
should come to me? Luke 2:11
44 "For behold, when the sound
of your greeting reached my ears,
the baby leaped in my womb for
joy.
45 "And blessed *is* she who believed[t]that there would be a fulfillment of what had been spoken to
her by the Lord." *from*
46 And Mary said:
"My soul exalts the Lord,
47 "And my spirit has rejoiced
in God my Savior.
48 "For [r]He has had regard for
the humble state of His
bondslave;
For behold, from this time
on all generations will
count me blessed. Ps. 138:6
49 "For the Mighty One has
done great things for me;
And holy is His name.
50 "AND[r] HIS MERCY IS UPON
GENERATION AFTER GEN-
ERATION
TOWARD THOSE WHO FEAR
HIM. Ps. 103:17
51 "He has done [t]mighty deeds
with His arm; *might*
He has scattered *those who*
were proud in the
thoughts of their heart.
52 "He has brought down rulers
from *their* thrones,
And has [r]exalted those who
were humble. Job 5:11
53 "HE[r] HAS FILLED THE HUNGRY
WITH GOOD THINGS;
And sent away the rich
empty-handed. Ps. 107:9
54 "He has given help to Israel
His servant,
In remembrance of His
mercy,
55 As He spoke to our fathers,
To Abraham and his off-
spring forever."
56 And Mary stayed with her
about three months, and *then* returned to her home.
57 Now the time [t]had come for
Elizabeth to give birth, and she
brought forth a son. *was fulfilled*
58 And her neighbors and her
relatives heard that the Lord had
[t]displayed[r]His great mercy toward
her; and they were rejoicing with
her. *magnified* • Gen. 19:19
59 And it came about that on
the eighth day they came to circumcise the child, and they were
going to call him Zacharias, [t]after
his father. *after the name of*
60 And his mother answered
and said, "No indeed; but[r]he shall
be called John." Luke 1:13, 63
61 And they said to her, "There
is no one among your relatives
who is called by that name."
62 And they [r]made signs to his
father, as to what he wanted him
called. Luke 1:22
63 And he asked for a tablet,
and wrote as follows, "His[r] name
is John." And they were all astonished. Luke 1:13, 60
64 [r]And at once his mouth was
opened and his tongue *loosed*, and
he *began* to speak in praise of
God. Luke 1:20
65 And fear came on all those
living around them; and all these
matters were being talked about
in all the hill country of Judea.
66 And all who heard them kept
them in mind, saying, "What then

will this child *turn out to* be?" For
the[r]hand of the Lord was certainly
with him. Acts 11:21
67 And his father Zacharias[r]was
filled with the Holy Spirit, and
prophesied, saying: Luke 1:41
68 "Blessed[r]*be* the Lord God of
Israel, 1 Kin. 1:48
For He has visited us and
accomplished redemption for His people,
69 And has raised up a horn of
salvation for us
In the house of David[r]His
servant— Matt. 1:1
70 As He spoke by the mouth
of His holy prophets[r]from
of old— Acts 3:21
71 [a]Salvation FROM OUR ENEMIES, *Deliverance*
And FROM THE HAND OF ALL
WHO HATE US;
72 [r]To show mercy toward our
fathers, Mic. 7:20
[r]And to remember His holy
covenant, Ps. 105:8f.
73 The oath which He swore to
Abraham our father,
74 To grant us that we, being
delivered from the hand
of our enemies,
Might serve Him without
fear,
75 [r]In holiness and righteousness before Him all our
days. Eph. 4:24
76 "And you, child, will be
called the[r]prophet of the
Most High;
For you will go on[r]BEFORE
THE LORD TO PREPARE HIS
WAYS; Matt. 11:9 • Mal. 3:1
77 To give to His people *the*
knowledge of salvation
[a]By the forgiveness of their
sins, *Consisting in*
78 Because of the tender mercy of our God,
With which[r]the Sunrise
from on high shall visit
us, Mal. 4:2; Eph. 5:14
79 TO SHINE UPON THOSE WHO
SIT IN DARKNESS AND THE
SHADOW OF DEATH,
To guide our feet into the
[r]way of peace." Is. 59:8
80 [r]And the child continued to
grow, and to become strong in
spirit, and he lived in the deserts
until the day of his public appearance to Israel. Luke 2:40

CHAPTER 2

NOW it came about in those
days that a decree went out from
Caesar Augustus, that a census be
taken of all [6]the inhabited earth.
2 This was the first census
taken while [7]Quirinius was governor of[r]Syria. Matt. 4:24
3 And all were proceeding to
register for the census, everyone
to his own city.
4 And Joseph also went up
from Galilee, from the city of
Nazareth, to Judea, to the city of
David, which is called Bethlehem,
because[r]he was of the house and
family of David, Luke 1:27
5 in order to register, along
with Mary, who was engaged to
him, and was with child.
6 And it came about that while
they were there, the days were
completed for her to give birth.
7 And she gave birth to her
first-born son; and she wrapped
Him in cloths, and laid Him in a
manger, because there was no
room for them in the inn.

[6]I.e., the Roman empire [7]Gr., *Kyrenios*

8 And in the same region there
were *some* shepherds staying out
in the fields, and keeping watch
over their flock by night.
9 And [r]an angel of the Lord
suddenly stood before them, and
the glory of the Lord shone
around them; and they were terri-
bly frightened. Luke 1:11
10 And the angel said to them,
"Do[r] not be afraid; for behold, I
bring you good news of a great
joy which shall be for all the people; Matt. 14:27
11 for today in the city of David
there has been born for you a Savior, who is [8]Christ the Lord.
12 "And this *will be* a sign for
you: you will find a baby wrapped
in cloths, and lying in a manger."
13 And suddenly there ap-
peared with the angel a multitude
of the heavenly host praising God,
and saying,
14 "Glory to God in the highest,
And on earth peace among
men [9]with whom He is
pleased."
15 And it came about when the
angels had gone away from them
into heaven, that the shepherds
began saying to one another, "Let
us go straight to Bethlehem then,
and see this thing that has happened which the Lord has made
known to us."
16 And they came in haste and
found their way to Mary and
Joseph, and the baby as He lay in
the[a]manger. *feeding trough*
17 And when they had seen this,
they made known the statement
which had been told them about
this Child.
18 And all who heard it wondered at the things which were
told them by the shepherds.
19 But Mary [r]treasured up all
these things, pondering them in
her heart. Luke 2:51
20 And the shepherds went
back, glorifying and praising God
for all that they had heard and
seen, just as had been told them.
21 And when eight days were
completed [t]before His circumcision, His name was *then* called
Jesus, the name given by the angel before He was conceived in
the womb. *so as to circumcise Him*
22 And when the days for their
purification according to the law
of Moses were completed, they
brought Him up to Jerusalem to
present Him to the Lord
23 (as it is written in the Law of
the Lord, "EVERY *first-born* MALE
THAT OPENS THE WOMB SHALL BE
CALLED HOLY TO THE LORD"),
24 and to offer a sacrifice according to what was said in the
Law of the Lord, "A [r]PAIR OF TUR-
TLEDOVES, OR TWO YOUNG PI-
GEONS." Lev. 5:11; 12:8
25 And behold, there was a man
in Jerusalem whose name was
Simeon; and this man was [r]right-
eous and devout, looking for the
consolation of Israel; and the Holy
Spirit was upon him. Luke 1:6
26 And it had been revealed to
him by the Holy Spirit that he
would not see death before he had
seen the Lord's Christ.
27 And he came in the Spirit
into the temple; and when the parents brought in the child Jesus,[t]to

[8]I.e., Messiah
[9]Lit., *of good pleasure;* or possibly, *of good will*

carry out for Him the custom of
the Law, *to do for Him according to*
28 then he took Him into his
arms, and blessed God, and said,
29 "Now Lord, Thou dost let
Thy bond-servant depart
In peace, [r]according to Thy
word; Luke 2:26
30 For my eyes have [r]seen Thy
salvation, [r] Ps. 119:166
31 Which Thou hast prepared
in the presence of all peoples,
32 [r]A LIGHT [a]OF REVELATION TO
THE GENTILES,
And the glory of Thy people
Israel." Is. 9:2; 42:6 · *for*
33 And His father and mother
were amazed at the things which
were being said about Him.
34 And Simeon blessed them,
and said to Mary His mother, "Behold,
this *Child* is appointed for
the fall and rise of many in Israel,
and for a sign to be opposed—
35 and a sword will pierce even
your own soul—to the end that
thoughts from many hearts may
be revealed."
36 And there was a prophetess,
[a]Anna the daughter of Phanuel, of
the tribe of Asher. She was advanced
in years, [t]having lived with
a husband seven years after her
[t]marriage, *Hannah · days · virginity*
37 and then as a widow to the
age of eighty-four. And she never
left the temple, serving night and
day with fastings and prayers.
38 And at that very moment she
came up and *began* giving thanks
to God, and continued to speak of
Him to all those who were looking
for the redemption of Jerusalem.
39 And when they had performed
everything according to
the Law of the Lord, they returned
to Galilee, to [r]their own city of
Nazareth. Matt. 2:23; Luke 1:26
40 And the Child continued to
grow and become strong, increasing
in wisdom; and the grace of
God was upon Him.
41 And His parents used to go
to Jerusalem every year at the
Feast of the Passover.
42 And when He became
twelve, they went up *there* according
to the custom of the
Feast;
43 and as they were returning,
after spending the [r]full number of
days, the boy Jesus stayed behind
in Jerusalem. And His parents
were unaware of it, Ex. 12:15
44 but supposed Him to be in
the caravan, and went a day's
journey; and they *began* looking
for Him among their relatives and
acquaintances.
45 And when they did not find
Him, they returned to Jerusalem,
looking for Him.
46 And it came about that after
three days they found Him in the
temple, sitting in the midst of the
teachers, both listening to them,
and asking them questions.
47 And all who heard Him [r]were
amazed at His understanding and
His answers. Matt. 7:28; 13:54
48 And when they saw Him,
they were astonished; and His
mother said to Him, "Son, why
have You treated us this way? Behold,
Your father and I have been
anxiously looking for You."
49 And He said to them, **"Why
is it that you were looking for Me?
Did you not know that I had to be
in My Father's *house*?"**
50 And [r]they did not understand

the statement which He[t]had made
to them. Mark 9:32 • *had spoken*
51 And He went down with
them, and came to Nazareth; and
He continued in subjection to
them; and His mother treasured
all *these* things in her heart.
52 And Jesus kept increasing in
wisdom and[a]stature, and in favor
with God and men. *age*

CHAPTER 3

NOW in the fifteenth year of the
reign of Tiberius Caesar, when
[r]Pontius Pilate was governor of Judea,
and Herod was tetrarch of
Galilee, and his brother Philip was
tetrarch of the region of Ituraea
and Trachonitis, and Lysanias was
tetrarch of Abilene, Matt. 27:2
2 in the high priesthood of Annas
and Caiaphas, the word of
God came to John, the son of
Zacharias, in the wilderness.
3 And he came into all[r]the district
around the Jordan, preaching
a baptism of repentance for the
forgiveness of sins; Matt. 3:5
4 as it is written in the book of
the words of Isaiah the prophet,

"THE[r]VOICE OF ONE CRYING IN THE WILDERNESS, Is. 40:3
'MAKE READY THE WAY OF THE LORD,
MAKE HIS PATHS STRAIGHT.
5 'EVERY[r] RAVINE SHALL BE FILLED UP, Is. 40:4
AND EVERY MOUNTAIN AND HILL SHALL BE [a]BROUGHT LOW; *leveled*
AND THE CROOKED SHALL BECOME STRAIGHT,
AND THE ROUGH ROADS SMOOTH;
6 AND ALL FLESH SHALL SEE THE SALVATION OF GOD.' "

7 He therefore *began* saying to
the multitudes who were going
out to be baptized by him, "You
brood of vipers, who warned you
to flee from the wrath to come?
8 "Therefore bring forth fruits
in keeping with repentance, and
do not begin to say[a]to yourselves,
'We have Abraham for our father,'
for I say to you that God is
able from these stones to raise up
children to Abraham. *in*
9 "And also the axe is already
laid at the root of the trees; [r]every
tree therefore that does not bear
good fruit is cut down and thrown
into the fire." Matt. 7:19
10 And the multitudes were
questioning him, saying, "Then[r]
what shall we do?" Luke 3:12, 14
11 And he would answer and
say to them, "Let the man who
has two tunics share with him
who has none; and let him who
has food do likewise."
12 And *some* [r][10]tax-gatherers
also came to be baptized, and they
said to him, "Teacher, what shall
we do?" Luke 7:29
13 And he said to them, "Collect[a]no
more than what you have
been ordered to." *Exact*
14 And *some* [11]soldiers were
questioning him, saying, "And
what about us, what shall we do?"
And he said to them, "Do not take
money from anyone by force, or
accuse *anyone* falsely, and be
content with your wages."
15 Now while the people were
in a state of expectation and all
were wondering in their hearts

[10] I.e., Collectors of Roman taxes for profit
[11] I.e., men in active military service

about John, as to whether he
might be the Christ,
16 John answered and said to
them all, "As for me, I baptize you
with water; but One is coming
who is mightier than I, and I am
not fit to untie the thong of His
sandals; He will baptize you with
the Holy Spirit and fire.
17 "And His [r]winnowing fork is in
His hand to thoroughly clear His
threshing floor, and to gather the
wheat into His barn; but He will
burn up the chaff with unquenchable fire." Is. 30:24
18 So with many other exhorta-
tions also he preached the gospel
to the people.
19 But when Herod the tetrarch
was reproved by him on account
of Herodias, his brother's wife,
and on account of all the wicked
things which Herod had done,
20 he added this also to them
all, that [r]he locked John up in
prison. John 3:24
21 Now it came about when all
the people were baptized, that
Jesus also was baptized, and
while He was [r]praying, heaven was
opened, Matt. 14:23; Luke 5:16
22 and the Holy Spirit descended upon Him in bodily form
like a dove, and a voice came out
of heaven, "Thou art My beloved
Son, in Thee I am well-pleased."
23 And when He began His
ministry, Jesus Himself was about
thirty years of age, [t]being suppos-
edly *the* son of Joseph, the *son* of
Eli, *as it was being thought*
24 the *son* of Matthat, the *son* of
Levi, the *son* of Melchi, the *son* of
Jannai, the *son* of Joseph,
25 the *son* of Mattathias, the
son of Amos, the *son* of Nahum,
the *son* of Hesli, the *son* of Nag-
gai,
26 the *son* of Maath, the *son* of
Mattathias, the *son* of Semein, the
son of Josech, the *son* of Joda,
27 the *son* of Joanan, the *son* of
Rhesa, the *son* of Zerubbabel, the
son of Shealtiel, the *son* of Neri,
28 the *son* of Melchi, the *son* of
Addi, the *son* of Cosam, the *son* of
Elmadam, the *son* of Er,
29 the *son* of Joshua, the *son* of
Eliezer, the *son* of Jorim, the *son*
of Matthat, the *son* of Levi,
30 the *son* of Simeon, the *son* of
Judah, the *son* of Joseph, the *son*
of Jonam, the *son* of Eliakim,
31 the *son* of Melea, the *son* of
Menna, the *son* of Mattatha, the
son of Nathan, the *son* of David,
32 the *son* of Jesse, the *son* of
Obed, the *son* of Boaz, the *son* of
Salmon, the *son* of Nahshon,
33 the *son* of Amminadab, the
son of Admin, the *son* of Ram, the
son of Hezron, the *son* of Perez,
the *son* of Judah,
34 the *son* of Jacob, the *son* of
Isaac, the *son* of Abraham, the
son of Terah, the *son* of Nahor,
35 the *son* of Serug, the *son* of
Reu, the *son* of Peleg, the *son* of
Heber, the *son* of Shelah,
36 the *son* of Cainan, the *son* of
Arphaxad, the *son* of Shem, the
son of Noah, the *son* of Lamech,
37 the *son* of Methuselah, the
son of Enoch, the *son* of Jared, the
son of Mahalaleel, the *son* of Cainan,
38 the *son* of Enosh, the *son* of
Seth, the *son* of Adam, the *son* of
God.

CHAPTER 4

AND Jesus, full of the Holy
Spirit, [r]returned from the Jordan
and was led about [t]by the Spirit in
the wilderness Luke 3:3 • *in*
2 for forty days, being tempted
by the devil. And He ate nothing
during those days; and when they
had ended, He became hungry.
3 And the devil said to Him, "If
You are the Son of God, tell this
stone to become bread."
4 And Jesus answered him, "It
is written, 'MAN [r]SHALL NOT LIVE
ON BREAD ALONE.' " Deut. 8:3
5 And he led Him up and
showed Him all the kingdoms of
the world in a moment of time.
6 And the devil said to Him, "I
will give You all this domain and
[t]its glory; [r]for it has been handed
over to me, and I give it to whomever I wish. *their* • 1 John 5:19
7 "Therefore if You worship before me, it shall all be Yours."
8 And Jesus answered and said
to him, "It is written, 'YOU [r]SHALL
WORSHIP THE LORD YOUR GOD AND
SERVE HIM ONLY.' " Deut. 6:13
9 And he led Him to Jerusalem
and had Him stand on the pinnacle of the temple, and said to Him,
"If You are the Son of God, throw
Yourself down from here;
10 for it is written,
'HE WILL GIVE HIS ANGELS
CHARGE CONCERNING YOU
TO GUARD YOU,'
11 and,
'ON [r]*their* HANDS THEY WILL
BEAR YOU UP, Ps. 91:12
LEST YOU STRIKE YOUR
FOOT AGAINST A STONE.' "
12 And Jesus answered and said
to him, "It is said, 'YOU [r]SHALL NOT
[12]PUT THE LORD YOUR GOD TO THE
TEST.' " Deut. 6:16
13 And when the devil had finished every temptation, he departed from Him until an opportune time.
14 And Jesus returned to Galilee in the power of the Spirit; and
news about Him spread through
all the surrounding district.
15 And He *began* [r]teaching in
their synagogues and was praised
by all. Matt. 4:23
16 And He came to Nazareth,
where He had been brought up;
and as was His custom, He entered the synagogue on the Sabbath, and stood up to read.
17 And the book of the prophet
Isaiah was handed to Him. And
He opened the book, and found
the place where it was written,
18 "THE [r]SPIRIT OF THE LORD IS
UPON ME, Is. 61:1
BECAUSE HE ANOINTED ME
TO PREACH THE GOSPEL TO
THE POOR. Matt. 11:5
HE HAS SENT ME TO PRO-
CLAIM RELEASE TO THE
CAPTIVES, Matt. 12:18
AND RECOVERY OF SIGHT TO
THE BLIND, John 3:34
TO SET FREE THOSE WHO ARE
DOWNTRODDEN,
19 TO PROCLAIM THE FAVOR-
ABLE YEAR OF THE LORD."
20 And He closed the book, and
gave it back to the attendant, and
sat down; and the eyes of all in the
synagogue were fixed upon Him.
21 And He began to say to
them, "Today this Scripture has
been fulfilled in your hearing."
22 And all were speaking well
of Him, and wondering at the gra-

[12]Or, *tempt . . . God*

cious words which were falling
from His lips; and they were saying, "Is this not Joseph's son?"
23 And He said to them, "No
doubt you will quote this proverb
to Me, 'Physician, heal yourself!
Whatever we heard was done [r]at
Capernaum, do here in your home
town as well.'" Matt. 4:13
24 And He said, "Truly I say to
you, [r]no prophet is welcome in his
home town. Matt. 13:57
25 "But I say to you in truth,
there were many widows in Israel
in the days of Elijah, when the sky
was shut up for three years and
six months, when a great famine
came over all the land;
26 and yet Elijah was sent to
none of them, but only to Zarephath, in the land of Sidon, to a
woman who was a widow.
27 "And there were many lepers
in Israel in the time of Elisha the
prophet; and none of them was
cleansed, but [r]only Naaman the
Syrian." 2 Kin. 5:1-14
28 And all in the synagogue
were filled with rage as they heard
these things;
29 and they rose up and cast
Him out of the city, and led Him
to the brow of the hill on which
their city had been built, in order
to throw Him down the cliff.
30 But passing through their
midst, He went His way.
31 And [r]He came down to Capernaum, a city of Galilee. And He
was teaching them on the Sabbath; Luke 4:31-37: *Mark 1:21-28*
32 and they were amazed at His
teaching, for His [t]message was
with authority. *word*
33 And there was a man in the
synagogue possessed by the spirit
of an unclean demon, and he cried
out with a loud voice,
34 "Ha! [r]What do we have to do
with You, Jesus [t]of Nazareth?
Have You come to destroy us? I
know who You are—the Holy One
of God!" Matt. 8:29 • *the Nazarene*
35 And Jesus [r]rebuked him, saying, "Be quiet and come out of
him!" And when the demon had
thrown him down in *their* midst,
he came out of him without doing
him any harm. Matt. 8:26
36 And amazement came upon
them all, and they *began* discussing with one another saying,
"What is this message? For [r]with
authority and power He commands the unclean spirits, and
they come out." Luke 4:32
37 And the report about Him
was getting out into every locality
in the surrounding district.
38 And He arose and *left* the
synagogue, and entered Simon's
home. Now Simon's mother-in-
law was [r]suffering from a high fever; and they made request of
Him on her behalf. Matt. 4:24
39 And standing over her, He
rebuked the fever, and it left her;
and she immediately arose and
[a]waited on them. *served*
40 And while [r]the sun was setting, all who had any sick with
various diseases brought them to
Him; and [r]laying His hands on every one of them, He was healing
them. Mark 1:32 • Mark 5:23
41 And demons also were coming out of many, crying out and
saying, "You are the Son of God!"
And rebuking them, He would not
allow them to speak, because they
knew Him to be the Christ.

42 [r]And when day came, He departed and went to a lonely place;
and the multitudes were searching for Him, and came to Him,
and tried to keep Him from going
away from them. Luke 4:42, 43
43 But He said to them, "I must
preach the kingdom of God to the
other cities also,[r]for I was sent for
this purpose." Mark 1:38
44 And He kept on preaching in
the synagogues of [13]Judea.

CHAPTER 5

NOW it came about that while
the multitude were pressing
around Him and listening to the
word of God, He was standing by
the lake of Gennesaret;
2 and He saw two boats lying
at the edge of the lake; but the
fishermen had gotten out of them,
and were washing their nets.
3 And [r]He got into one of the
boats, which was Simon's, and
asked him to put out a little way
from the land. And He sat down
and *began* teaching the multitudes
from the boat. Matt. 13:2
4 And when He had finished
speaking, He said to Simon, "Put
out into the deep water and let
down your nets for a catch."
5 And Simon answered and
said, "Master,[r] we worked hard all
night and caught nothing, but at
Your[a]*bidding I will let* down the
nets." Luke 8:24; 9:33 • *word*
6 And when they had done
this,[r]they enclosed a great quantity of fish; and their nets *began* to
break; John 21:6
7 and they signaled to their
partners in the other boat, for
them to come and help them. And
they came, and filled both of the
boats, so that they began to sink.
8 But when Simon Peter saw
that, he fell down at Jesus' [t]feet,
saying, "Depart from me, for I am
a sinful man, O Lord!" *knees*
9 For amazement had seized
him and all his companions because of the catch of fish which
they had taken;
10 and so also James and John,
sons of Zebedee, who were partners with Simon. And Jesus said
to Simon, "Do not fear, from now
on you will be catching men."
11 And when they had brought
their boats to land, they left everything and followed Him.
12 And it came about that while
He was in one of the cities, behold, *there was* a man full of leprosy; and when he saw Jesus, he
fell on his face and implored Him,
saying, "Lord, if You are willing,
You can make me clean."
13 And He stretched out His
hand, and touched him, saying, "I
am willing; be cleansed." And immediately the leprosy left him.
14 And He ordered him to tell
no one, "But go and [r]show yourself
to the priest, and make an offering
for your cleansing, just as Moses
commanded, for a testimony to
them." Lev. 13:49; 14:2ff.
15 But [r]the news about Him was
spreading even farther, and great
multitudes were gathering to hear
Him and to be healed of their sicknesses. Matt. 9:26
16 But He Himself would *often*
slip away [t]to the [a]wilderness and
pray. *in* • *lonely places*

[13]I.e., the country of the Jews (including Galilee); some mss. read *Galilee*

17 And it came about [t]one day that He was teaching; and there were *some* Pharisees and teachers of the law sitting *there,* who had come from every village of Galilee and Judea and *from* Jerusalem; and the power of the Lord was *present* for Him to perform healing. *on one of the days*

18 And behold, *some* men *were* carrying on a [a]bed a man who was paralyzed; and they were trying to bring him in, and to set him down in front of Him. *stretcher*

19 And not finding any *way* to bring him in because of the crowd, they went up on the roof and let him down [r]through the tiles with his stretcher, right in the center, in front of Jesus. Mark 2:4

20 And seeing their faith, He said, [t]"Friend, [r]your sins are forgiven you." *Man* • Matt. 9:2

21 And the scribes and the Pharisees began to reason, saying, "Who is this *man* who speaks blasphemies? Who can forgive sins, but God alone?"

22 But Jesus, [a]aware of their reasonings, answered and said to them, "Why are you reasoning in your hearts? *perceiving*

23 "Which is easier, to say, 'Your sins have been forgiven you,' or to say, 'Rise and walk'?

24 "But in order that you may know that the Son of Man has authority on earth to forgive sins,"—He said to the paralytic—"I say to you, rise, and take up your stretcher and go home."

25 And at once he rose up before them, and took up what he had been lying on, and went home, [r]glorifying God. Matt. 9:8

26 And they were all seized with astonishment and *began* glorifying God; and they were filled with fear, saying, "We have seen remarkable things today."

27 [r]And after that He went out, and noticed a [14]tax-gatherer named Levi, sitting in the tax office, and He said to him, "Follow Me." Luke 5:27-39: *Matt. 9:9-17*

28 And he [r]left everything behind, and rose and *began* to follow Him. Luke 5:11

29 And [r]Levi gave a big [a]reception for Him in his house; and there was a great crowd of tax-gatherers and other *people* who were reclining *at the table* with them. Matt. 9:9 • *banquet*

30 And [r]the Pharisees and their scribes *began* grumbling at His disciples, saying, "Why do you eat and drink with the tax-gatherers and sinners?" Mark 2:16

31 And Jesus answered and said to them, "It [r]*is* not those who are well who need a physician, but those who are sick. Matt. 9:12

32 "I have not come to call the righteous but sinners to repentance."

33 And they said to Him, "The disciples of John often fast and offer prayers; the *disciples* of the Pharisees also do the same; but Yours eat and drink."

34 And Jesus said to them, "You cannot make the [t]attendants of the bridegroom fast while the bridegroom is with them, can you? *sons of the bridal-chamber*

35 "But [r]*the* days will come; and when the bridegroom is taken away from them, then they will fast in those days." Matt. 9:15

[14] I.e., Collector of Roman taxes for profit

36 And He was also telling them a parable: "No one tears a piece from a new [a]garment and puts it on an old garment; otherwise he will both tear the new, and the piece from the new will not match the old. ***cloak***

37 "And no one puts new wine into old wineskins; otherwise the new wine will burst the skins, and it will be spilled out, and the skins will be ruined.

38 "But new wine must be put into fresh wineskins.

39 "And no one, after drinking old *wine* wishes for new; for he says, 'The old is good *enough.*' "

CHAPTER 6

NOW it came about that on a *certain* Sabbath He was passing through *some* grainfields; and His disciples [r]were picking and eating the heads *of grain,* rubbing them in their hands. **Deut. 23:25**

2 But some of the Pharisees said, "Why do you do what is not lawful on the Sabbath?"

3 And Jesus answering them said, "Have you not even read what David did when he was hungry, he and those who were with him,

4 how he entered the house of God, and took and ate the [15]consecrated bread which is not lawful for any to eat except the priests alone, and gave it to his companions?"

5 And He was saying to them, "The Son of Man is Lord of the Sabbath."

6 And it came about [r]on another Sabbath, that He entered the synagogue and was teaching; and there was a man there whose right hand was withered. **Luke 6:1**

7 And the scribes and the Pharisees were watching Him closely, *to see* if He healed on the Sabbath, in order that they might find *reason* to accuse Him.

8 But He knew [t]what they were thinking, and He said to the man with the withered hand, "Rise and come forward!" And he rose and [t]came forward. ***their thoughts • stood***

9 And Jesus said to them, "I ask you, is it lawful on the Sabbath to do good, or to do harm, to save a life, or to destroy it?"

10 And after looking around at them all, He said to him, "Stretch out your hand!" And he did *so;* and his hand was restored.

11 But they themselves were filled with [t]rage, and discussed together what they might do to Jesus. ***folly***

12 And it was at this time that He went off to the mountain to pray, and He spent the whole night in prayer to God.

13 And when day came, He called His disciples to Him; and chose twelve of them, whom He also named as apostles:

14 Simon, whom He also named Peter, and Andrew his brother; and [a]James and John; and Philip and Bartholomew; ***Jacob***

15 and Matthew and Thomas; James *the son* of Alphaeus, and Simon who was called the Zealot;

16 Judas *the son* of James, and Judas Iscariot, who became a traitor.

17 And He [r]descended with them, and stood on a level place; and *there was* a great multitude of

[15]Or, *showbread,* lit., *loaves of presentation*

His disciples, and a great throng
of people from all Judea and Jerusalem and the coastal region of
Tyre and Sidon, Luke 6:12
18 who had come to hear Him,
and to be healed of their diseases;
and those who were troubled with
unclean spirits were being cured.
19 And all the multitude were
trying to [r]touch Him, for power
was coming from Him and healing
them all. Matt. 9:21; 14:36
20 And turning His gaze on His
disciples, He *began* to say,
"Blessed *are* you *who are* poor,
for yours is the kingdom of God.
21 "Blessed *are* you who hunger
now, for you shall be satisfied.
Blessed *are* you who weep now,
for you shall laugh.
22 "Blessed are you when men
hate you, and [r]ostracize you, and
cast insults at you, and spurn your
name as evil, for the sake of the
Son of Man. John 9:22; 16:2
23 "Be glad in that day, and leap
for joy, for behold, your reward is
great in heaven; for in the same
way their fathers used to [t]treat the
prophets. *do to*
24 "But woe to [r]you who are rich,
for you are receiving your comfort
in full. Luke 16:25; James 5:1
25 "Woe to you who are well-fed
now, for you shall be hungry. Woe
to you who laugh now, for you
shall mourn and weep.
26 "Woe *to you* when all men
speak well of you, for in the same
way their fathers used to [t]treat the
[r]false prophets. *do to* • Matt. 7:15
27 "But I say to you who hear,
love your enemies, do good to
those who hate you,
28 bless those who curse you,
pray for those who mistreat you.
29 "Whoever hits you on the
cheek, offer him the other also;
and whoever takes away your
[a]coat, do not withhold your [a]shirt
from him either. *cloak* • *tunic*
30 "Give to everyone who asks of
you, and whoever takes away
what is yours, do not demand it
back.
31 "And [r]just as you want people
to treat you, [t]treat them in the
same way. Matt. 7:12 • *do to*
32 "And [r]if you love those who
love you, what credit is *that* to
you? For even sinners love those
who love them. Matt. 5:46
33 "And if you do good to those
who do good to you, what credit is
that to you? For even sinners do
the same.
34 "And if you lend to those from
whom you expect to receive, what
credit is *that* to you? Even sinners
lend to sinners, in order to receive
back the same *amount.*
35 "But love your enemies, and
do good, and lend, expecting nothing in return; and your reward will
be great, and you will be sons of
the Most High; for He Himself is
kind to ungrateful and evil *men.*
36 "Be [a]merciful, just as your Father is merciful. *Become*
37 "And do not judge and you
will not be judged; and do not
condemn, and you will not be condemned; [t]pardon, and you will be
pardoned. *release*
38 "Give, and it will be given to
you; [r]good measure, pressed down,
shaken together, running over,
they will pour [r]into your lap. For
by your standard of measure it
will be measured to you in return." Mark 4:24 • Ps. 79:12

39 And He also spoke a parable to them: "A blind man cannot guide a blind man, can he? Will they not both fall into a pit?

40"A[r] [a]pupil is not above his teacher; but everyone, after he has been fully trained, will be like his teacher. **Matt. 10:24 • *disciple***

41"And why do you look at the speck that is in your brother's eye, but do not notice the log that is in your own eye?

42"Or how can you say to your brother, 'Brother, let me take out the speck that is in your eye,' when you yourself do not see the log that is in your own eye? You hypocrite, first take the log out of your own eye, and then you will see clearly to take out the speck that is in your brother's eye.

43"For there is no good tree which produces bad fruit; nor, [t]on the other hand, a bad tree which produces good fruit. ***again***

44"For each tree is known by its own fruit. For men do not gather figs from thorns, nor do they pick grapes from a briar bush.

45"The good man out of the good treasure of his heart brings forth what is good; and the evil *man* out of the evil *treasure* brings forth what is evil; for his mouth speaks from [t]that which fills his heart. ***the abundance of***

46"And [r]why do you call Me, 'Lord, Lord,' and do not do what I say? **Mal. 1:6; Matt. 7:21**

47"Everyone[r] who comes to Me, and hears My words, and [t]acts upon them, I will show you whom he is like: **Luke 6:47-49 • *does***

48 he is like a man building a house, who [t]dug deep and laid a foundation upon the rock; and when a flood rose, the [t]torrent burst against that house and could not shake it, because it had been well built. ***dug and went deep • river***

49"But the one who has heard, and has not acted *accordingly,* is like a man who built a house upon the ground without any foundation; and the [t]torrent burst against it and immediately it collapsed, and the ruin of that house was great." ***river***

CHAPTER 7

WHEN He had completed all His discourse in the hearing of the people, He went to Capernaum.

2 And a certain centurion's slave, who was highly regarded by him, was sick and about to die.

3 And when he heard about Jesus,[r] he sent some Jewish elders asking Him to come and save the life of his slave. **Matt. 8:5**

4 And when they had come to Jesus, they earnestly entreated Him, saying, "He is worthy for You to grant this to him;

5 for he loves our nation, and it was he who built us our synagogue."

6 Now Jesus *started* on His way with them; and when He was already not far from the house, the centurion sent friends, saying to Him, "Lord,[a] do not trouble Yourself further, for I am not worthy for You to come under my roof; ***Sir***

7 for this reason I did not even consider myself worthy to come to You, but just say the word, and my[a]servant will be healed. ***boy***

8"For I, too, am a man under authority, with soldiers under me;

and I say to this one, 'Go!' and he goes; and to another, 'Come!' and he comes; and to my slave, 'Do this!' and he does it."

9 Now when Jesus heard this, He marveled at him, and turned and said to the multitude that was following Him, "I say to you, [r]not even in Israel have I found such great faith." **Matt. 8:10**

10 And when those who had been sent returned to the house, they found the slave in good health.

11 And it came about soon afterwards, that He went to a city called Nain; and His disciples were going along with Him, accompanied by a large multitude.

12 Now as He approached the gate of the city, behold, a dead man was being carried out, the only son of his mother, and she was a widow; and a sizeable crowd from the city was with her.

13 And when the Lord saw her, He felt compassion for her, and said to her, "Do not weep."

14 And He came up and touched the coffin; and the bearers came to a halt. And He said, "Young man, I say to you, arise!"

15 And the dead man sat up, and began to speak. And *Jesus* gave him back to his mother.

16 And fear gripped them all, and they *began* glorifying God, saying, "A great prophet has arisen among us!" and, "God has [a]visited His people!" ***cared for***

17 And this report concerning Him went out all over Judea, and in all the surrounding district.

18 [r]And the disciples of John reported to him about all these things. **Luke 7:18-35:** ***Matt. 11:2-19***

19 And summoning [t]two of his disciples, John sent them to the Lord, saying, "Are You the Expected One, or do we look for someone else?" ***a certain two***

20 And when the men had come to Him, they said, "John the Baptist has sent us to You, saying, 'Are You the Expected One, or do we look for someone else?' "

21 At that [t]very time He [r]cured many *people* of diseases and afflictions and evil spirits; and He granted sight to many *who were* blind. ***hour*** • **Matt. 4:23**

22 And He answered and said to them, "Go and report to John what you have seen and heard: *the* [r]BLIND RECEIVE SIGHT, *the* lame walk, *the* lepers are cleansed, and *the* deaf hear, *the* dead are raised up, *the* POOR HAVE THE GOSPEL PREACHED TO THEM. **Is. 35:5**

23 "And blessed is he who keeps from stumbling over Me."

24 And when the messengers of John had left, He began to speak to the multitudes about John, "What did you go out into the wilderness to look at? A reed shaken by the wind?

25 "But what did you go out to see? A man dressed in soft clothing? Behold, those who are splendidly clothed and live in luxury are *found* in royal palaces.

26 "But what did you go out to see? A prophet? Yes, I say to you, and one who is more than a prophet.

27 "This is the one about whom it [t]is written, ***has been written***

> 'BEHOLD, I SEND MY MESSENGER BEFORE YOUR FACE,
> WHO WILL PREPARE YOUR WAY BEFORE YOU.'

28"I say to you, among those born of women, there is no one greater than John; yet he who is [t]least in the kingdom of God is greater than he." *less*

29 And when all the people and the [16]tax-gatherers heard *this*, they [a]acknowledged God's justice, having been baptized with the baptism of John. *justified God*

30 But the Pharisees and the [17]lawyers rejected God's purpose for themselves, not having been baptized by [t]John. *him*

31"To what then shall I compare the men of this generation, and what are they like?

32"They are like children who sit in the market place and call to one another; and they say, 'We played the flute for you, and you did not dance; we sang a dirge, and you did not weep.'

33"For John the Baptist has come [r]eating no bread and drinking no wine; and you say, 'He has a demon!' Luke 1:15

34"The Son of Man has come eating and drinking; and you say, 'Behold, a gluttonous man, and a [a]drunkard, a friend of tax-gatherers and sinners!' *wine-drinker*

35"Yet[t] wisdom is vindicated by all her children." *And*

36 Now one of the Pharisees was requesting Him to dine with him. And He entered the Pharisee's house, and reclined *at the table.*

37 And behold, there was a woman in the city who was a sinner; and when she learned that He was reclining *at the table* in the Pharisee's house, she brought an alabaster vial of perfume,

38 and standing behind *Him* at His feet, weeping, she began to wet His feet with her tears, and kept wiping them with the hair of her head, and kissing His feet, and anointing them with the perfume.

39 Now when the Pharisee who had invited Him saw this, he said [t]to himself, "If this man were a prophet He would know who and what sort of person this woman is who is touching Him, that she is a sinner." *to himself, saying*

40 And Jesus answered and said to him, "Simon, I have something to say to you." And he [t]replied, "Say it, Teacher." *says*

41"A certain moneylender had two debtors: one owed five hundred [18]denarii, and the other fifty.

42"When they [r]were unable to repay, he graciously forgave them both. Which of them therefore will love him more?" Matt. 18:25

43 Simon answered and said, "I suppose the one whom he forgave more." And He said to him, "You have judged correctly."

44 And turning toward the woman, He said to Simon, "Do you see this woman? I entered your house; you[r] gave Me no water for My feet, but she has wet My feet with her tears, and wiped them with her hair. Gen. 18:4

45"You gave Me no kiss; but she, since the time I came in, has not ceased to kiss My feet.

46"You[r] did not anoint My head with oil, but she anointed My feet with perfume. 2 Sam. 12:20

47"For this reason I say to you,

[16]I.e., Collectors of Roman taxes for profit
[17]I.e., experts in the Mosaic law
[18]The denarius was equivalent to one day's wage

her sins, which are many, have
been forgiven, for she loved much;
but he who is forgiven little, loves
little."
48 And He said to her, "Your
sins have been forgiven."
49 And those who were reclining *at the table* with Him began to
say to themselves, "Who is this
man who even forgives sins?"
50 And He said to the woman,
"Your[r] faith has saved you; go in
peace." Matt. 9:22; Luke 17:19

CHAPTER 8

AND it came about soon afterwards, that He *began* going about
from one city and village to another, proclaiming and preaching
the kingdom of God; and the
twelve were with Him,
2 and *also* [r]some women who
had been healed of evil spirits and
sicknesses: Mary who was called
Magdalene, from whom seven demons had gone out, Matt. 27:55
3 and Joanna the wife of Chu-
za,[r] Herod's steward, and Susanna,
and many others who were contributing to their support out of
their private means. Matt. 14:1
4 [r]And when a great multitude
were coming together, and those
from the various cities were journeying to Him, He spoke by way
of a parable: Luke 8:4-8
5 "The sower went out to sow
his seed; and as he sowed, some
fell beside the road; and it was
trampled under foot, and the birds
of the [t]air ate it up. ***heaven***
6 "And other *seed* fell on rocky
soil, and as soon as it grew up, it
withered away, because it had no
moisture.
7 "And other *seed* fell among
the thorns; and the thorns grew up
with it, and choked it out.
8 "And other *seed* fell into the
good soil, and grew up, and produced a crop a hundred times as
great." As He said these things,
He would call out, "He who has
ears to hear, let him hear."
9 [r]And His disciples *began*
questioning Him as to what this
parable might be. Luke 8:9-15
10 And He said, "To[r] you it has
been granted to know the mysteries of the kingdom of God, but to
the rest *it is* in parables, in order
that [r]SEEING THEY MAY NOT SEE,
AND HEARING THEY MAY NOT UN-
DERSTAND. Matt. 13:11 • Is. 6:9
11 "Now the parable is this: the
seed is the word of God.
12 "And those beside the road
are those who have heard; then
the devil comes and takes away
the word from their heart, so that
they may not believe and be
saved.
13 "And those on the rocky *soil*
are those who, when they hear, receive the word with joy; and these
have no *firm* root;[t] they believe for
a while, and in time of temptation
fall away. ***who believe***
14 "And the *seed* which fell
among the thorns, these are the
ones who have heard, and as they
go on their way they are choked
with worries and riches and pleasures of *this* life, and bring no
fruit to maturity.
15 "And the *seed* in the good soil,
these are the ones who have heard
the word in an honest and good
heart, and hold it fast, and bear
fruit with perseverance.

16"Now [r]no one after lighting a
lamp covers it over with a container, or puts it under a bed; but
he puts it on a lampstand, in order
that those who come in may see
the light. Matt. 5:15; Mark 4:21
17"For nothing is hidden that
shall not become evident, nor *anything* secret that shall not be
known and come to light.
18"Therefore take care how you
listen; for whoever has, to him
shall *more* be given; and whoever
does not have, even what he
[a]thinks he has shall be taken away
from him." *seems to have*
19 [r]And His mother and brothers
came to Him, and they were unable to get to Him because of the
crowd. Luke 8:19-21
20 And it was reported to Him,
"Your mother and Your brothers
are standing outside, wishing to
see You."
21 But He answered and said to
them, "My mother and My brothers are these [r]who hear the word of
God and do it." Luke 11:28
22 Now it came about on one of
those days, that He and His disciples got into a boat, and He said to
them, "Let us go over to the other
side of [r]the lake." And they
launched out. Luke 5:1f.; 8:23
23 But as they were sailing
along He fell asleep; and a fierce
gale of wind descended upon the
lake, and they *began* to be
swamped and to be in danger.
24 And they came to Him and
woke Him up, saying, "Master,
Master, we are perishing!" And
being aroused, He rebuked the
wind and the surging waves, and
they stopped, and it became calm.
25 And He said to them,
"Where is your faith?" And they
were fearful and amazed, saying
to one another, "Who then is this,
that He commands even the
winds and the water, and they
obey Him?"
26 [r]And they sailed to the country of the Gerasenes, which is opposite Galilee. Luke 8:26-37
27 And when He had come out
onto the land, He was met by a
certain man from the city who
was possessed with demons; and
who had not put on any clothing
for a long time, and was not living
in a house, but in the tombs.
28 And seeing Jesus, he cried
out and fell before Him, and said
in a loud voice, "What [r]do I have
to do with You, Jesus, Son of the
Most High God? I beg You, do not
torment me." Matt. 8:29
29 For He had been commanding the unclean spirit to come out
of the man. For it had seized him
many times; and he was bound
with chains and shackles and kept
under guard; and *yet* he would
burst his fetters and be driven by
the demon into the desert.
30 And Jesus asked him, "What
is your name?" And he said, [r]"Legion"; for many demons had entered him. Matt. 26:53
31 And they were entreating
Him not to command them to depart into the abyss.
32 Now there was a herd of
many swine feeding there on the
mountain; and *the demons* entreated Him to permit them to enter [t]the swine. And He gave them
permission. *them*
33 And the demons came out
from the man and entered the
swine; and the herd rushed down

the steep bank into[r]the lake, and
were drowned. Luke 5:1f.
34 And when the herdsmen saw
what had happened, they ran
away and reported it in the city
and *out* in the country.
35 And *the people* went out to
see what had happened; and they
came to Jesus, and found the man
from whom the demons had gone
out, sitting down [r]at the feet of
Jesus, clothed and in his right
mind; and they became frightened. Luke 10:39
36 And those who had seen it
reported to them how the man
who was demon-possessed had
been[a]made well. *saved*
37 And all the people of the
country of the Gerasenes and the
surrounding district asked Him to
depart from them; for they were
gripped with great fear; and He
got into a boat, and returned.
38 [r]But the man from whom the
demons had gone out was begging
Him that he might [t]accompany
Him; but He sent him away, saying, Luke 8:38, 39 • *be with*
39 "Return to your house and describe what great things God has
done for you." And he went away,
proclaiming throughout the whole
city what great things Jesus had
done for him.
40 And as Jesus returned, the
multitude welcomed Him, for they
had all been waiting for Him.
41 And behold, there came a
man named Jairus, and he was an
official of the synagogue; and he
fell at Jesus' feet, and *began* to entreat Him to come to his house;
42 for he had an[a]only daughter,
about twelve years old, and she
was dying. But as He went, the
multitudes were pressing against
Him. *only begotten*
43 And a woman who had a
hemorrhage for twelve years,
[19]and could not be healed by anyone,
44 came up behind Him, and
touched the fringe of His [a]cloak;
and immediately her hemorrhage
stopped. *outer garment*
45 And Jesus said, "Who is the
one who touched Me?" And while
they were all denying it, Peter
said, "Master,[r] the multitudes are
crowding and pressing upon
You." Luke 5:5
46 But Jesus said, "Someone
did touch Me, for I was aware that
power had gone out of Me."
47 And when the woman saw
that she had not escaped notice,
she came trembling and fell down
before Him, and declared in the
presence of all the people the reason why she had touched Him,
and how she had been immediately healed.
48 And He said to her, "Daughter,[r]your faith has[a]made you well;
go in peace." Matt. 9:22 • *saved you*
49 While He was still speaking,
someone *came from *the house of*
the synagogue official, saying,
"Your daughter has died; do not
trouble the Teacher anymore."
50 But when Jesus heard *this,*
He answered him, "Do not be
afraid *any longer;* only believe,
and she shall be made well."
51 And when He had come to
the house, He did not allow anyone to enter with Him, except Peter and John and James, and the
girl's father and mother.

[19] Some mss. add *who had spent all her living upon physicians*

52 Now they were all weeping
and lamenting for her; but He
said, "Stop weeping, for she has
not died, but is asleep."
53 And they *began* laughing at
Him, knowing that she had died.
54 He, however, took her by the
hand and called, saying, "Child,
arise!"
55 And her spirit returned, and
she rose immediately; and He
gave orders for *something* to be
given her to eat.
56 And her parents were
amazed; but He instructed them
to tell no one what had happened.

CHAPTER 9

[r]AND He called the twelve together, and gave them power and
authority over all the demons, and
to heal diseases. Matt. 10:5
2 And He sent them out to [r]pro-
claim the kingdom of God, and to
perform healing. Matt. 10:7
3 And He said to them, "Take
nothing for *your* journey, neither
a staff, nor a [a]bag, nor bread, nor
money; and do not *even* have two
tunics apiece. ***knapsack*** **or** ***beggar's bag***
4 "And whatever house you en-
ter, stay there, and take your
leave from there.
5 "And as for those who do not
receive you, as you go out from
that city, [r]shake off the dust from
your feet as a testimony against
them." Luke 10:11; Acts 13:51
6 And departing, they *began*
going about [a]among the villages,
preaching the gospel, and healing
everywhere. ***from village to village***
7 Now Herod the tetrarch
heard of all that was happening;
and he was greatly perplexed, because it was said by some that
John had risen from the dead,
8 and by some that [r]Elijah had
appeared, and by others, that one
of the prophets of old had risen
again. Matt. 16:14
9 And Herod said, "I myself
had John beheaded; but who is
this man about whom I hear such
things?" And [r]he kept trying to see
Him. Luke 23:8
10 And when the apostles returned, they gave an account to
Him of all that they had done. [r]And
taking them with Him, He withdrew by Himself to a city called
Bethsaida. Luke 9:10-17
11 But the multitudes were
aware of this and followed Him;
and welcoming them, He *began*
speaking to them about the kingdom of God and curing those who
had need of healing.
12 And the day began to decline, and the twelve came and
said to Him, "Send the multitude
away, that they may go into the
surrounding villages and countryside and find lodging and get
something to eat; for here we are
in a desolate place."
13 But He said to them, "You
give them *something* to eat!" And
they said, "We have no more than
five loaves and two fish, unless
perhaps we go and buy food for
all these people."
14 (For there were about five
thousand men.) And He said to
His disciples, "Have them recline
to eat [r]in groups of about fifty
each." Mark 6:39
15 And they did so, and had
them all recline.
16 And He took the five loaves
and the two fish, and looking up to

heaven, He blessed them, and
broke *them,* and kept giving *them*
to the disciples to set before the
multitude.
17 And they all ate and were
satisfied; and the broken pieces
which they had left over were
picked up, twelve baskets *full.*
18 And it came about that while
He was praying alone, the disciples were with Him, and He questioned them, saying, "Who do the
multitudes say that I am?"
19 And they answered and said,
"John the Baptist, and others *say*
Elijah; but others, that one of the
prophets of old has risen again."
20 And He said to them, "But
who do you say that I am?" And
Peter answered and said, "The[r]
Christ of God." John 6:68f.
21 But He[a] warned them, and instructed *them* not to tell this to
anyone, *strictly admonished*
22 saying, "The[r] Son of Man
must suffer many things, and be
rejected by the elders and chief
priests and scribes, and be killed,
and be raised up on the third
day." Matt. 16:21; Luke 9:44
23 And He was saying to *them*
all, "If[r] anyone wishes to come after Me, let him deny himself, and
take up his cross daily, and follow
Me. Matt. 10:38; Luke 14:27
24 "For whoever wishes to save
his[a] life shall lose it, but whoever
loses his life for My sake, he is the
one who will save it. *soul*
25 "For what is a man profited if
he gains the whole world, and
loses or forfeits himself?
26 "For[r] whoever is ashamed of
Me and My words, of him will the
Son of Man be ashamed when He
comes in His glory, and *the glory*
of the Father and of the holy angels. Matt. 10:33; Luke 12:9
27 "But I say to you truthfully,
there are some of those standing
here who shall not taste death until they see the kingdom of God."
28 And some eight days after
these sayings, it came about that
He took along[r] Peter and John and
James, and went up to the mountain to pray. Matt. 17:1
29 And while He was praying,
the appearance of His face became different, and His clothing
became white *and* gleaming.
30 And behold, two men were
talking with Him; and they were
Moses and Elijah,
31 who, appearing in [a]glory,
were speaking of His departure
which He was about to accomplish at Jerusalem. *splendor*
32 Now Peter and his companions had been overcome with
sleep; but when they were fully
awake, they saw His glory and the
two men standing with Him.
33 And it came about, as these
were parting from Him, Peter said
to Jesus, "Master, it is good for us
to be here; and let us make three
tabernacles: one for You, and one
for Moses, and one for Elijah"—
not realizing what he was saying.
34 And while he was saying
this, a cloud formed and *began* to
overshadow them; and they were
afraid as they entered the cloud.
35 And a voice came out of the
cloud, saying, "This is My Son,
My Chosen One; listen to Him!"
36 And when the voice had spoken, Jesus was found alone. And
they kept silent, and reported to
no one in those days any of the
things which they had seen.

37 And it came about on the
next day, that when they had
come down from the mountain, a
great multitude met Him.
38 And behold, a man from the
multitude shouted out, saying,
"Teacher, I beg You to look at my
son, for he is my only *boy*,
39 and behold, a spirit seizes
him, and he suddenly screams,
and it throws him into a convulsion with foaming *at the mouth*,
and as it mauls him, it scarcely
leaves him.
40 "And I begged Your disciples
to cast it out, and they could not."
41 And Jesus answered and
said, "O unbelieving and perverted generation, how long shall
I be with you, and put up with
you? Bring your son here."
42 And while he was still approaching, the demon dashed him
to the ground, and threw him into
a convulsion. But Jesus rebuked
the unclean spirit, and healed the
boy, and gave him back to his father. *tore him*
43 And they were all amazed at
the greatness of God. *majesty*
But while everyone was marveling at all that He was doing, He
said to His disciples,
44 "Let these words sink into
your ears; for the Son of Man is
going to be delivered into the
hands of men." *betrayed*
45 But they did not understand
this statement, and it was concealed from them so that they
might not perceive it; and they
were afraid to ask Him about this
statement. *were not knowing*
46 And an argument arose
among them as to which of them
might be the greatest. *entered in*

47 But Jesus, knowing what
they were thinking in their heart,
took a child and stood him by His
side, *the reasoning;* or, *argument*
48 and said to them, "Whoever
receives this child in My name receives Me; and whoever receives
Me receives Him who sent Me; for
he who is least among you, this is
the one who is great." *lowliest*
49 And John answered and said,
"Master, we saw someone casting
out demons in Your name; and we
tried to hinder him because he
does not follow along with us."
50 But Jesus said to him, "Do
not hinder *him;* for he who is not
against you is for you."
51 And it came about, when the
days were approaching for His as-
cension, that He resolutely set His
face to go to Jerusalem;
52 and He sent messengers on
ahead of Him. And they went, and
entered a village of the Samaritans, to make arrangements for
Him. Matt. 10:5; Luke 10:33 • *prepare*
53 And they did not receive
Him, because He was journeying
with His face toward Jerusalem.
54 And when His disciples
James and John saw *this*, they
said, "Lord, do You want us to
command fire to come down from
heaven and consume them?"
55 But He turned and rebuked
them, [and said, "You do not
know what kind of spirit you are
of;
56 for the Son of Man did not
come to destroy men's lives, but
to save them."] And they went on
to another village.
57 And as they were going
along the road, someone said to

Him, "I will follow You wherever
You go." Luke 9:51
58 And Jesus said to him, "The
foxes have holes, and the birds of
the[a]air *have*[a]nests, but the Son of
Man has nowhere to lay His
head." *sky • roosting-places*
59 And He said to another, "Follow[r] Me." But he said, "[20]Permit
me first to go and bury my father." Matt. 8:22
60 But He said to him, "Allow
the dead to bury their own dead;
but as for you, go and proclaim
everywhere the kingdom of God."
61 And another also said, "I will
follow You, Lord; but[r]first permit
me to say good-bye to those at
home." 1 Kin. 19:20
62 But Jesus said to him, "No[r]
one, after putting his hand to the
plow and looking back, is fit for
the kingdom of God." Phil. 3:13

CHAPTER 10

NOW after this the Lord appointed seventy others, and sent
them two and two ahead of Him
to every city and place where He
Himself was going to come.
2 And He was saying to them,
"The harvest is plentiful, but the
laborers are few; therefore beseech the Lord of the harvest to
send out laborers into His harvest.
3 "Go your ways;[r]behold, I send
you out as lambs in the midst of
wolves. Matt. 10:16
4 "Carry no purse, no[a]bag, no
shoes; and greet no one on the
way. *knapsack* or *beggar's bag*
5 "And whatever house you enter, first say, 'Peace *be* to this
house.'

[20]Some mss. add *Lord*

6 "And if a [t]man of peace is
there, your peace will rest upon
him; but if not, it will return to
you. *son*
7 "And stay in that house, eating and drinking what they give
you; for[r]the laborer is worthy of
his wages. Do not keep moving
from house to house. Matt. 10:10
8 "And whatever city you enter,
and they receive you,[r]eat what is
set before you; 1 Cor. 10:27
9 and heal those in it who are
sick, and say to them, 'The[r] kingdom of God has come near to
you.' Matt. 3:2; 10:7; Luke 10:11
10 "But whatever city you enter
and they do not receive you, go
out into its streets and say,
11 'Even the dust of your city
which clings to our feet, we wipe
off *in protest* against you; yet[t]be
sure of this, that the kingdom of
God has come near.' *know*
12 "I say to you,[r]it will be more
tolerable in that day for Sodom,
than for that city. Gen. 19:24-28
13 "Woe to you, Chorazin! Woe
to you, Bethsaida! For if the[a]mir-
acles had been performed in Tyre
and Sidon which occurred in you,
they would have repented long
ago, sitting in sackcloth and
ashes. *works of power*
14 "But it will be more tolerable
for[r]Tyre and Sidon in the judgment, than for you. Matt. 11:21
15 "And you,[r]Capernaum, will
not be exalted to heaven, will you?
You will be brought down to
Hades! Is. 14:13-15; Matt. 4:13
16 "The one who listens to you
listens to Me, and[r]the one who rejects you rejects Me; and he who
rejects Me rejects the One who
sent Me." John 12:48; 1 Thess. 4:8

17 And the seventy returned with joy, saying, "Lord, even [r]the demons are subject to us in Your name." Mark 16:17

18 And He said to them, "I was watching [r]Satan fall from heaven like lightning. Matt. 4:10

19 "Behold, I have given you authority to [r]tread upon serpents and scorpions, and over all the power of the enemy, and nothing shall injure you. Ps. 91:13; Mark 16:18

20 "Nevertheless do not rejoice in this, that the spirits are subject to you, but rejoice that your names are recorded in heaven."

21 [r]At that very [t]time He rejoiced greatly in the Holy Spirit, and said, "I praise Thee, O Father, Lord of heaven and earth, that Thou didst hide these things from *the* wise and intelligent and didst reveal them to babes. Yes, Father, for thus it was well-pleasing in Thy sight. Luke 10:21, 22 • *hour*

22 "All [r]things have been handed over to Me by My Father, and [r]no one knows who the Son is except the Father, and who the Father is except the Son, and anyone to whom the Son wills to reveal *Him*." John 3:35 • John 10:15

23 And turning to the disciples, He said privately, "Blessed *are* the eyes which see the things you see,

24 for I say to you, that many prophets and kings wished to see the things which you see, and did not see *them*, and to hear the things which you hear, and did not hear *them*."

25 And behold, a certain lawyer stood up and put Him to the test, saying, "Teacher, what shall I do to inherit eternal life?"

26 And He said to him, "What is written in the Law? How [t]does it read to you?" *do you read?*

27 And he answered and said, "YOU [r]SHALL LOVE THE LORD YOUR GOD WITH ALL YOUR HEART, AND WITH ALL YOUR SOUL, AND WITH ALL YOUR STRENGTH, AND WITH ALL YOUR MIND; AND YOUR NEIGHBOR AS YOURSELF." Deut. 6:5

28 And He said to him, "You have answered correctly; [r]DO THIS, AND YOU WILL LIVE." Lev. 18:5

29 But wishing [r]to justify himself, he said to Jesus, "And who is my neighbor?" Luke 16:15

30 Jesus replied and said, "A certain man was going down from Jerusalem to Jericho; and he fell among robbers, and they stripped him and beat him, and went off leaving him half dead.

31 "And by chance a certain priest was going down on that road, and when he saw him, he passed by on the other side.

32 "And likewise a Levite also, when he came to the place and saw him, passed by on the other side.

33 "But a certain [r]Samaritan, who was on a journey, came upon him; and when he saw him, he felt compassion, Matt. 10:5

34 and came to him, and bandaged up his wounds, pouring oil and wine on *them;* and he put him on his own beast, and brought him to an inn, and took care of him.

35 "And on the next day he took out two [21]denarii and gave them to the innkeeper and said, 'Take care of him; and whatever more you

[21] The denarius was equivalent to one day's wage

spend, when I return, I will repay you.'

36 "Which of these three do you think proved to be a neighbor to the man who fell into the robbers' *hands?*"

37 And he said, "The one who showed mercy toward him." And Jesus said to him, "Go and do[a] the same." ***likewise***

38 Now as they were traveling along, He entered a certain village; and a woman named Martha welcomed Him into her home.

39 And she had a sister called [r]Mary, who moreover was listening to the Lord's word, seated at His feet. Luke 10:42; John 11:1f.

40 But Martha was distracted with all her preparations; and she came up *to Him*, and said, "Lord, do You not care that my sister has left me to do all the serving alone? Then tell her to help me."

41 But the Lord answered and said to her, "Martha,[r] Martha, you are worried and bothered about so many things; Luke 10:38, 40

42 but *only* a few things are necessary, [t]really *only* one, for [r]Mary has chosen the good part, which shall not be taken away from her." ***or*** • Luke 10:39

CHAPTER 11

AND it came about that while He was praying in a certain place, after He had finished, one of His disciples said to Him, "Lord, teach us to pray just as John also taught his disciples."

2 And He said to them, "When[r] you pray, say: Luke 11:2-4

'[22]Father, hallowed be Thy name.
Thy kingdom come.

3 'Give us [r]each day our daily bread. Acts 17:11

4 'And forgive us our sins,
For we ourselves also forgive everyone who is indebted to us.
And lead us not into temptation.' "

5 And He said to them, "Suppose one of you shall have a friend, and shall go to him at midnight, and say to him, 'Friend, lend me three loaves;

6 for a friend of mine has come to me from a journey, and I have nothing to set before him';

7 and from inside he shall answer and say, 'Do not bother me; the door has already been shut and my children [t]and I are in bed; I cannot get up and give you *anything.*' ***with me***

8 "I tell you, even though he will not get up and give him *anything* because he is his friend, yet [r]because of his[a] persistence he will get up and give him as much as he needs. Luke 18:1-5 • ***shamelessness***

9 "And I say to you,[a] ask, and it shall be given to you; seek, and you shall find; knock, and it shall be opened to you. ***keep asking***

10 "For everyone who asks, receives; and he who seeks, finds; and to him who knocks, it shall be opened.

11 "Now suppose one of you fathers is asked by his son for a fish; he will not give him a snake instead of a fish, will he?

[22] Some mss. insert phrases from Matt. 6:9–13 to make the two passages closely similar

12 "Or *if* he is asked for an egg,
he will not give him a scorpion,
will he?
13 "If you then, being evil, know
how to give good gifts to your
children, how much more shall
your [t]heavenly Father give the
Holy Spirit to those who ask
Him?" ***Father from heaven***
14 [r]And He was casting out a demon, *and it was* dumb; and it
came about that when the demon
had gone out, the dumb man
spoke; and the multitudes marveled. Luke 11:14, 15
15 But some of them said, "He
casts out demons by Beelzebul,
the ruler of the demons."
16 And others, [t]to test *Him,*
were demanding of Him a sign
from heaven. ***were testing***
17 But He knew their thoughts,
and said to them, "Any[t] kingdom
divided against itself is laid waste;
and a house *divided* against[t] itself
falls. ***every • a house***
18 "And if Satan also is divided
against himself, how shall his
kingdom stand? For you say that I
cast out demons by Beelzebul.
19 "And if I by Beelzebul cast out
demons, by whom do your sons
cast them out? Consequently they
shall be your judges.
20 "But if I cast out demons by
the finger of God, then the kingdom of God has come upon you.
21 "When [t]a strong *man,* fully
armed, guards his own homestead, his possessions are [t]undis-
turbed; ***the • in peace***
22 but when someone stronger
than he attacks him and overpow-
ers him, he takes away from him
all his armor on which he had relied, and distributes his plunder.
23 "He who is not with Me is
against Me; and he who does not
gather with Me, scatters.
24 "When[r] the unclean spirit goes
out of [t]a man, it passes through
waterless places seeking rest, and
not finding any, it says, 'I will return to my house from which I
came.' Luke 11:24-26 • ***the***
25 "And when it comes, it finds it
swept and put in order.
26 "Then it goes and takes *along*
seven other spirits more evil than
itself, and they go in and live
there; and the last state of that
man becomes worse than the
first."
27 And it came about while He
said these things, one of the
women in the crowd raised her
voice, and said to Him, "Blessed is
the womb that bore You, and the
breasts at which You nursed."
28 But He said, "On the contrary, blessed are those who hear
the word of God, and observe it."
29 And as the crowds were increasing, He began to say, "This
generation is a wicked generation;
it [r]seeks for a[a] sign, and *yet* no sign
shall be given to it but the sign of
Jonah. Matt. 12:38 • ***attesting miracle***
30 "For just as Jonah became a
sign to the Ninevites, so shall the
Son of Man be to this generation.
31 "The Queen of the South shall
rise up with the men of this generation at the judgment and condemn them, because she came
from the ends of the earth to hear
the wisdom of Solomon; and behold, something greater than
Solomon is here.
32 "The men of Nineveh shall
stand up with this generation at
the judgment and condemn it, be-

cause they repented at the preaching of Jonah; and behold, something greater than Jonah is here.

33 "No one, after lighting a lamp, puts it away in a cellar, nor under a peck-measure, but on the lampstand, in order that those who enter may see the light.

34 "The lamp of your body is your eye; when your eye is clear, your whole body also is full of light; but when it is bad, your body also is full of darkness.

35 "Then watch out that the light in you may not be darkness.

36 "If therefore your whole body is full of light, with no dark part in it, it shall be wholly illumined, as when the lamp illumines you with its rays."

37 Now when He had spoken, a Pharisee *asked Him to have lunch with him; and He went in, and reclined *at the table.*

38 And when the Pharisee saw it, he was surprised that He had not first [t]ceremonially washed before the [a]meal. *baptized • lunch*

39 But the Lord said to him, "Now you Pharisees clean the outside of the cup and of the platter; but inside of you, you are full of robbery and wickedness.

40 "You [r]foolish ones, did not He who made the outside make the inside also? Luke 12:20

41 "But give that which is within as charity, and [t]then all things are clean for you. *behold*

42 "But woe to you Pharisees! For you pay tithe of mint and rue and every *kind of* garden herb, and *yet* disregard justice and the love of God; but these are the things you should have done without neglecting the others.

43 "Woe to you Pharisees! For you love the front seats in the synagogues, and the respectful greetings in the market places.

44 "Woe to you! For you are like [a]concealed tombs, and the people who walk over *them* are unaware *of it.*" *indistinct, unseen*

45 And one of the [r][23]lawyers *said to Him in reply, "Teacher, when You say this, You insult us too." Matt. 22:35; Luke 11:46, 52

46 But He said, "Woe to you lawyers as well! For you weigh men down with burdens hard to bear, [t]while you yourselves will not even touch the burdens with one of your fingers. *and*

47 "Woe to you! For you build the tombs of the prophets, and *it was* your fathers *who* killed them.

48 "Consequently, you are witnesses and approve the deeds of your fathers; because it was they who killed them, and you build *their tombs.*

49 "For this reason also the wisdom of God said, 'I will send to them prophets and apostles, and *some* of them they will kill and *some* they will persecute,

50 in order that the blood of all the prophets, shed since the foundation of the world, may be charged against this generation,

51 from the blood of Abel to the blood of Zechariah, who perished between the altar and the house *of God;* yes, I tell you, it shall be charged against this generation.'

52 "Woe to you lawyers! For you have taken away the key of knowledge; you did not enter in yourselves, and those who were entering in you hindered."

[23] I.e., experts in the Mosaic law

53 And when He left there, the
scribes and the Pharisees began to
be very hostile and to question
Him closely on many subjects,
54 plotting against Him, to
catch[t] *Him* in something He might
say. *something out of His mouth*

CHAPTER 12

UNDER these circumstances, after[t] so many thousands of the multitude had gathered together that
they were stepping on one another, He began saying to His disciples first *of all*, "Beware[r] of the
leaven of the Pharisees, which is
hypocrisy. *myriads* • Matt. 16:6
2 "But there is nothing covered
up that will not be revealed, and
hidden that will not be known.
3 "Accordingly, whatever you
have said in the dark shall be
heard in the light, and what you
have [t]whispered in the inner
rooms shall be proclaimed upon
the housetops. *spoken in the ear*
4 "And I say to you, My friends,
do not be afraid of those who kill
the body, and after that have no
more that they can do.
5 "But I will warn you whom to
fear: fear the One who after He
has killed has authority to cast
into hell; yes, I tell you, fear Him!
6 "Are not five sparrows sold
for two cents? And *yet* not one of
them is forgotten before God.
7 "Indeed,[r] the very hairs of your
head are all numbered. Do not
fear; you are of more value than
many sparrows. Matt. 10:30
8 "And I say to you, everyone
who confesses Me before men, the
Son of Man shall confess him also
before the angels of God;
9 but[r] he who denies Me before
men shall be denied before the angels of God. Matt. 10:33
10 "And[r] everyone who will
speak a word against the Son of
Man, it shall be forgiven him; but
he who blasphemes against the
Holy Spirit, it shall not be forgiven him. Matt. 12:31, 32
11 "And when they bring you before the synagogues and the rulers
and the authorities, do not become anxious about how or what
you should speak in your defense,
or what you should say;
12 for[r] the Holy Spirit will teach
you in that very hour what you
ought to say." Matt. 10:20
13 And someone [t]in the crowd
said to Him, "Teacher, tell my
brother to divide the *family* inheritance with me." *out of*
14 But He said to him, "Man,[r]
who appointed Me a judge or arbi-
ter over you?" Mic. 6:8; Rom. 2:1
15 And He said to them, "Beware,[r] and be on your guard
against every form of greed; for
not *even* when one has an abundance does his life consist of his
possessions." 1 Tim. 6:6-10
16 And He told them a parable,
saying, "The land of a certain rich
man was very productive.
17 "And he began reasoning to
himself, saying, 'What shall I do,
since I have no place to store my
crops?'
18 "And he said, 'This is what I
will do: I will tear down my barns
and build larger ones, and there I
will store all my grain and my
goods.
19 'And I will say to my soul,
"Soul,[r] you have many goods laid
up for many years *to come*; take

your ease, eat, drink *and* be merry." ' Eccl. 11:9
20 "But God said to him, 'You
fool! This *very* night your soul is
required of you; and *now* who will
own what you have prepared?'
21 "So is the man who lays up
treasure for himself, and is not
rich toward God." Luke 12:33
22 And He said to His disciples,
"For this reason I say to you, do
not be anxious for *your* life, *as to*
what you shall eat; nor for your
body, *as to* what you shall put on.
23 "For life is more than food,
and the body than clothing.
24 "Consider the ravens, for they
neither sow nor reap; and they
have no storeroom nor barn; and
yet God feeds them; how much
more valuable you are than the
birds! Job 38:41
25 "And which of you by being
anxious can add a *single* [24]cubit to
his [25]life's span? Ps. 39:5
26 "If then you cannot do even a
very little thing, why are you anxious about other matters?
27 "Consider the lilies, how they
grow; they neither toil nor spin;
but I tell you, even Solomon in all
his glory did not clothe himself
like one of these. 1 Kin. 10:4-7
28 "But if God so arrays the
grass in the field, which is *alive*
today and tomorrow is thrown
into the furnace, how much more
will He clothe you, O men of little
faith! Matt. 6:30
29 "And do not seek what you
shall eat, and what you shall
drink, and do not keep worrying.
30 "For all these things the nations of the world eagerly seek;
but your Father knows that you
need these things.
31 "But seek for His kingdom,
and these things shall be added to
you. Matt. 6:33
32 "Do not be afraid, little flock,
for your Father has chosen gladly
to give you the kingdom.
33 "Sell your possessions and
give to charity; make yourselves
purses which do not wear out, an
unfailing treasure in heaven,
where no thief comes near, nor
moth destroys. Matt. 6:20
34 "For where your treasure is,
there will your heart be also.
35 "Be dressed in readiness, and
keep your lamps alight.
36 "And be like men who are
waiting for their master when he
returns from the wedding feast, so
that they may immediately open
the door to him when he comes
and knocks.
37 "Blessed are those slaves
whom the master shall find on the
alert when he comes; truly I say to
you, that he will gird himself *to
serve,* and have them recline *at
the table,* and will come up and
wait on them. Luke 17:8
38 "Whether he comes in the
[26]second watch, or even in the
[27]third, and finds *them* so, blessed
are those *slaves.* Matt. 24:43
39 "And be sure of this, that if
the head of the house had known
at what hour the thief was coming, he would not have allowed his
house to be broken into.
40 "You too, be ready; for the
Son of Man is coming at an hour
that you do not expect."

[24] I.e., One cubit equals approx. 18 in.
[25] Or, *height*
[26] I.e., 9 p.m. to midnight
[27] I.e., midnight to 3 a.m.

41 And Peter said, "Lord, are
You addressing this parable to us,
or to everyone *else* as well?"
42 And [r]the Lord said, "Who
then is the faithful and sensible
steward, whom his master will
put in charge of his [t]servants, to
give them their rations at the
proper time? Luke 7:13 • *service*
43 "Blessed is that [r]slave whom
his [a]master finds so doing when he
comes. Luke 12:42 • *lord*
44 "Truly I say to you, that he
will put him in charge of all his
possessions.
45 "But if that slave says in his
heart, 'My master [t]will be a long
time in coming,' and begins to
beat the slaves, *both* men and
women, and to eat and drink and
get drunk; *is delaying to come*
46 the master of that slave will
come on a day when he does not
expect *him,* and at an hour he
does not know, and will cut him in
pieces, and assign him a place
with the unbelievers.
47 "And that slave who knew his
master's will and did not get
ready or act in accord with his
will, shall receive many lashes,
48 but the one who did not
[r]know *it,* and committed deeds
worthy of [t]a flogging, will receive
but few. And from everyone who
has been given much shall much
be required; and to whom they entrusted much, of him they will ask
all the more. Lev. 5:17 • *blows*
49 "I have come to cast fire upon
the earth; and [t]how I wish it were
already kindled! *what do I wish if . . . ?*
50 "But I have a baptism to un-
dergo, and how distressed I am
until it is accomplished!
51 "Do you suppose that I came
to grant peace on earth? I tell you,
no, but rather division;
52 for from now on five *mem-*
bers in one household will be divided, three against two, and two
against three.
53 "They will be divided, father
against son, and son against father; mother against daughter,
and daughter against mother;
mother-in-law against daughter-
in-law, and daughter-in-law
against mother-in-law."
54 And He was also saying to
the multitudes, "When you see a
cloud rising in the west, immediately you say, 'A shower is coming,' and so it turns out.
55 "And when *you see* a south
wind blowing, you say, 'It will be
a [r]hot day,' and it turns out *that*
way. Matt. 20:12
56 "You hypocrites! You know
how to analyze the appearance of
the earth and the sky, but why do
you not analyze this present time?
57 "And [r]why do you not even on
your own initiative judge what is
right? Luke 21:30
58 "For while you are going with
your opponent to appear before
the magistrate, on *your* way *there*
make an effort to [t]settle with him,
in order that he may not drag you
before the judge, and the judge
turn you over to the constable,
and the constable throw you into
prison. *be released from him*
59 "I say to you, you shall not get
out of there until you have paid
the very last [r]cent." Mark 12:42

CHAPTER 13

NOW on the same occasion there
were some present who reported

to Him about the Galileans, whose blood Pilate had [a]mingled with their sacrifices. *shed along with*

2 And He answered and said to them, "Do you suppose that these Galileans were *greater* sinners than all *other* Galileans, because they suffered this *fate?*

3 "I tell you, no, but, unless you [a]repent, you will all likewise perish. *are repentant*

4 "Or do you suppose that those eighteen on whom the tower in Siloam fell and killed them, were *worse* [t]culprits than all the men who live in Jerusalem? *debtors*

5 "I tell you, no, but unless you repent, you will all likewise perish."

6 And He *began* telling this parable: "A certain man had a fig tree which had been planted in his vineyard; and he came looking for fruit on it, and did not find any.

7 "And he said to the vineyard-keeper, 'Behold, for three years I have come looking for fruit on this fig tree [t]without finding any. Cut it down! Why does it even use up the ground?' *and I do not find*

8 "And he answered and said to him, 'Let it alone, sir, for this year too, until I dig around it and put in fertilizer;

9 and if it bears fruit next year, *fine;* but if not, cut it down.' "

10 And He was teaching in one of the synagogues on the Sabbath.

11 And behold, there was a woman who for eighteen years had had a sickness caused by a spirit; and she was bent double, and could not straighten up at all.

12 And when Jesus saw her, He called her over and said to her, "Woman, you are freed from your sickness."

13 And He [r]laid His hands upon her; and immediately she was made erect again, and *began* glorifying God. Mark 5:23

14 And the synagogue official, indignant because Jesus had healed on the Sabbath, *began* saying to the multitude in response, "There are six days in which work should be done; therefore come during them and get healed, and not on the Sabbath day."

15 But [r]the Lord answered him and said, "You hypocrites, does not each of you on the Sabbath untie his ox or his donkey from the stall, and lead him away to water *him?* Luke 7:13

16 "And this woman, [r]a daughter of Abraham as she is, whom Satan has bound for eighteen long years, should she not have been released from this bond on the Sabbath day?" Luke 19:9

17 And as He said this, all His opponents were being humiliated; and [r]the entire multitude was rejoicing over all the glorious things being done by Him. Luke 18:43

18 Therefore He was saying, "What is the kingdom of God like, and to what shall I compare it?

19 "It is like a mustard seed, which a man took and threw into his own garden; and it grew and became a tree; and THE BIRDS OF THE AIR NESTED IN ITS BRANCHES."

20 And again He said, "To [r]what shall I compare the kingdom of God? Matt. 13:24; Luke 13:18

21 "It is like leaven, which a woman took and hid in three pecks of meal, until it was all leavened."

22 And He was passing through from one city and village to another, teaching, and proceeding on His way to Jerusalem.

23 And someone said to Him, "Lord, are there *just* a few who are being saved?" And He said to them,

24 "Strive to enter by the narrow door; for many, I tell you, will seek to enter and will not be able.

25 "Once the head of the house gets up and shuts the door, and you begin to stand outside and knock on the door, saying, 'Lord, open up to us!' [t]then He will answer and say to you, 'I do not know where you are from.' *and*

26 "Then you will [r]begin to say, 'We ate and drank in Your presence, and You taught in our streets'; Luke 3:8

27 and He will say, 'I tell you, [r]I do not know where you are from; [r]DEPART FROM ME, ALL YOU EVILDOERS.' Luke 13:25 • Ps. 6:8

28 "There[r] will be weeping and gnashing of teeth there when you see Abraham and Isaac and Jacob and all the prophets in the kingdom of God, but yourselves being cast out. Matt. 8:12; 22:13; 25:30

29 "And they will come from east and west, and from north and south, and will recline *at the table* in the kingdom of God.

30 "And behold, [r]*some* are last *who will be first and some* are first who will be last." Matt. 19:30

31 Just at that time some Pharisees came up, saying to Him, "Go away and depart from here, for Herod wants to kill You."

32 And He said to them, "Go and tell that fox, 'Behold, I cast out demons and perform cures today and tomorrow, and the third *day* I reach My goal.'

33 "Nevertheless [r]I must journey on today and tomorrow and the next *day;* for it cannot be that a prophet should perish outside of Jerusalem. John 11:9

34 "O Jerusalem, Jerusalem, *the city* that kills the prophets and stones those sent to her! How often I wanted to gather your children together, just as a hen *gathers* her brood under her wings, and you would not *have it!*

35 "Behold, your house is left to you *desolate;* and I say to you, you shall not see Me until *the time* comes when you say, 'BLESSED[r] IS HE WHO COMES IN THE NAME OF THE LORD!'" Ps. 118:26

CHAPTER 14

AND it came about when He went into the house of one of the leaders of the Pharisees on *the* Sabbath to eat bread, that they were watching Him closely.

2 And [t]there, in front of Him was a certain man suffering from dropsy. *behold*

3 And Jesus answered and spoke to the lawyers and Pharisees, saying, "Is it lawful to heal on the Sabbath, or not?"

4 But they kept silent. And He took hold of him, and healed him, and sent him away.

5 And He said to them, "Which one of you shall have a son or an ox fall into a well, and will not immediately pull him out on a Sabbath day?"

6 [r]And they could make no reply to this. Matt. 22:46

7 And He *began* speaking a
parable to the invited guests when
He noticed how they had been
picking out the places of honor *at*
the table; saying to them,
8 "When you are invited by
someone to a wedding feast, [r]do
not [t]take the place of honor, lest
someone more distinguished than
you may have been invited by
him, Prov. 25:6,7 • *recline at*
9 and he who invited you both
shall come and say to you, 'Give
place to this man,' and then [r]in disgrace you [t]proceed to occupy the
last place. Luke 3:8 • *begin*
10 "But when you are invited, go
and recline at the last place, so
that when the one who has invited
you comes, he may say to you,
'Friend, move up higher'; then you
will have honor in the sight of all
who are at the table with you.
11 "For everyone who exalts
himself shall be humbled, and he
who humbles himself shall be exalted."
12 And He also went on to say
to the one who had invited Him,
"When you give a luncheon or a
dinner, do not invite your friends
or your brothers or your relatives
or rich neighbors, lest they also invite you in return, and repayment
come to you.
13 "But when you give a [a]recep-
tion, invite *the* poor, *the* crippled,
the lame, *the* blind, *banquet*
14 and you will be blessed, since
they do not have *the means* to repay you; for you will be repaid at
the resurrection of the righteous."
15 And when one of those who
were reclining *at the table* with
Him heard this, he said to Him,
"Blessed is everyone who shall eat
bread in the kingdom of God!"
16 But He said to him, "A certain man was giving a big dinner,
and he invited many;
17 and at the dinner hour he
sent his slave to say to those who
had been invited, 'Come; for
everything is ready now.'
18 "But they all alike began to
make excuses. The first one said
to him, 'I have bought a piece of
land and I need to go out and look
at it; please consider me excused.'
19 "And another one said, 'I have
bought five yoke of oxen, and I am
going to try them out; [t]please consider me excused.' *I request you*
20 "And another one said, [r]'I have
married a wife, and for that reason I cannot come.' Deut. 24:5
21 "And the slave came *back* and
reported this to his master. Then
the head of the household became
angry and said to his slave, 'Go
out at once into the streets and
lanes of the city and bring in here
the poor and crippled and blind
and lame.'
22 "And the slave said, 'Master,
what you commanded has been
done, and still there is room.'
23 "And the master said to the
slave, 'Go out into the highways
and along the hedges, and compel
them to come in, that my house
may be filled.
24 'For I tell you, none of those
men who were invited shall taste
of my dinner.' "
25 Now great multitudes were
going along with Him; and He
turned and said to them,
26 "If [r]anyone comes to Me, and
does not [28]hate his own father and

[28] I.e., by comparison of his love for Me

mother and wife and children and
brothers and sisters, yes, and even
his own life, he cannot be My disciple. Matt. 10:37
27 "Whoever does not [r]carry his
own cross and come after Me cannot be My disciple. Matt. 10:38
28 "For which one of you, when
he wants to build a tower, does
not first sit down and calculate
the cost, to see if he has enough to
complete it?
29 "Otherwise, when he has laid
a foundation, and is not able to
finish, all who observe it begin to
ridicule him,
30 saying, 'This man began to
build and was not able to finish.'
31 "Or what king, when he sets
out to meet another king in battle,
will not first sit down and take
counsel whether he is strong
enough with ten thousand *men* to
encounter the one coming against
him with twenty thousand?
32 "Or else, while the other is
still far away, he sends a delegation and asks terms of peace.
33 "So therefore, no one of you
can be My disciple who does not
give up all his own possessions.
34 "Therefore, salt is good; but if
even salt has become tasteless,
with what will it be seasoned?
35 "It is useless either for the soil
or for the manure pile; [t]it is thrown
out. He who has ears to hear, let
him hear." *they throw it out*

CHAPTER 15

NOW all the [r]tax-gatherers and
the sinners were coming near Him
to listen to Him. Luke 5:29
2 And both the Pharisees and
the scribes *began* to grumble, saying, "This man receives sinners
and eats with them."
3 And He told them this parable, saying,
4 "What man among you, if he
has a hundred sheep and has lost
one of them, does not leave the
ninety-nine in the [t]open pasture,
and go after the one which is lost,
until he finds it? *wilderness*
5 "And when he has found it, he
lays it on his shoulders, rejoicing.
6 "And when he comes home,
he calls together his friends and
his neighbors, saying to them, 'Rejoice with me, for I have found my
sheep which was lost!'
7 "I tell you that in the same
way, there will be *more* joy in
heaven over one sinner who repents, than over ninety-nine righteous persons who need no repentance.
8 "Or what woman, if she has
ten silver coins and loses one coin,
does not light a lamp and sweep
the house and search carefully until she finds it?
9 "And when she has found it,
she calls together her friends and
neighbors, saying, 'Rejoice with
me, for I have found the coin
which I had lost!'
10 "In the same way, I tell you,
there is joy [r]in the presence of the
angels of God over one sinner who
repents." Matt. 10:32; Luke 15:7
11 And He said, "A certain man
had two sons;
12 and the younger of them said
to his father, 'Father, give me [r]the
share of the estate that falls to
me.' And he divided his [t]wealth between them. Deut. 21:17 • *living*
13 "And not many days later, the
younger son gathered everything

together and went on a journey
into a distant country, and there
he squandered his estate with
loose living.
14"Now when he had spent
everything, a severe famine occurred in that country, and he began to be in need.
15"And he went and attached
himself to one of the citizens of
that country, and he sent him into
his fields to feed swine.
16"And he was longing to fill his
stomach with the pods that the
swine were eating, and no one
was giving *anything* to him.
17"But when he came to [t]his
senses, he said, 'How many of my
father's hired men have more than
enough bread, but I am dying here
with hunger! *himself*
18 'I will get up and go to my father, and will say to him, "Father,
I have sinned against heaven, and
[t]in your sight; *before you*
19"I am no longer worthy to be
called your son; make me as one
of your hired men."'
20"And he got up and came to
[t]his father. But while he was still a
long way off, his father saw him,
and felt compassion *for him,* and
ran and [t]embraced him, and kissed
him. *his own • fell on his neck*
21"And the son said to him, 'Father, I have sinned against heaven
and in your sight; I am no longer
worthy to be called your son.'
22"But the father said to his
slaves, 'Quickly bring out [r]the best
robe and put it on him, and put a
ring on his hand and sandals on
his feet; Zech. 3:4; Rev. 6:11
23 and bring the fattened calf,
kill it, and let us eat and be merry;
24 for this son of mine was
dead, and has come to life again;
he was lost, and has been found.'
And they began to be merry.
25"Now his older son was in the
field, and when he came and approached the house, he heard music and dancing.
26"And he summoned one of the
servants and *began* inquiring
what these things might be.
27"And he said to him, 'Your
brother has come, and your father
has killed the fattened calf, because he has received him back
safe and sound.'
28"But he became angry, and
was not willing to go in; and his
father came out and *began* entreating him.
29"But he answered and said to
his father, 'Look! For so many
years I have been serving you, and
I have never neglected a command of yours; and *yet* you have
never given me a kid, that I might
be merry with my friends;
30 but when this son of yours
came, who has devoured your
[t]wealth with harlots, you killed the
fattened calf for him.' *living*
31"And he said to him, '*My*
child, you have always been with
me, and all that is mine is yours.
32 'But [t]we had to be merry and
rejoice, for this brother of yours
was dead and *has begun* to live,
and *was* lost and has been
found.'" *it was necessary*

CHAPTER 16

NOW He was also saying to the
disciples, "There was a certain
rich man who had a steward, and

this *steward* was reported to him
as squandering his possessions.
2 "And he called him and said
to him, 'What is this I hear about
you? Give an account of your
stewardship, for you can no
longer be steward.'
3 "And the steward said to himself, 'What shall I do, since my
[a]master is taking the stewardship
away from me? I am not strong
enough to dig; I am ashamed to
beg. ***lord***
4 'I know what I shall do, so
that when I am removed from the
stewardship, they will receive me
into their homes.'
5 "And he summoned each one
of his [a]master's debtors, and he *be-*
gan saying to the first, 'How much
do you owe my master?' ***lord's***
6 "And he said, 'A hundred
measures of oil.' And he said to
him, 'Take your bill, and sit down
quickly and write fifty.'
7 "Then he said to another, 'And
how much do you owe?' And he
said, 'A hundred measures of
wheat.' He *said to him, 'Take
your bill, and write eighty.'
8 "And his [a]master praised the
unrighteous steward because he
had acted shrewdly; for the sons
of this age are more shrewd in relation to their own [t]kind than the
sons of light. ***lord • generation***
9 "And I say to you, [r]make
friends for yourselves by means of
the [29]mammon of unrighteousness;
that when it fails, they may receive you into the eternal dwellings. **Matt. 19:21; Luke 11:41**
10 "He[r] who is faithful in a very
little thing is faithful also in much;
and he who is unrighteous in a
very little thing is unrighteous
also in much. **Matt. 25:21, 23**
11 "If therefore you have not
been faithful in the *use of* unrighteous [a]mammon, who will entrust
the true *riches* to you? ***riches***
12 "And if you have not been
faithful in *the use of* that which is
another's, who will give you that
which is your own?
13 "No [a]servant can serve two
masters; for either he will hate the
one, and love the other, or else he
will hold to one, and despise the
other. You cannot serve God and
[a]mammon." ***house-servant • riches***
14 Now the Pharisees, who
were lovers of money, were listening to all these things, and they
were scoffing at Him.
15 And He said to them, "You
are those who justify yourselves
in the sight of men, but God
knows your hearts; for that which
is highly esteemed among men is
detestable in the sight of God.
16 "The Law and the Prophets
were proclaimed until John; since
then the gospel of the kingdom of
God is preached, and everyone is
forcing his way into it.
17 "But[r] it is easier for heaven
and earth to pass away than for
one stroke of a letter of the Law to
fail. **Matt. 5:18**
18 "Everyone[r] who divorces his
wife and marries another commits
adultery; and he who marries one
who is divorced from a husband
commits adultery. **Matt. 5:32**
19 "Now there was a certain rich
man, and he habitually dressed in
purple and fine linen, gaily living
in splendor every day.
20 "And a certain poor man

[29]Or, *riches*

named Lazarus was laid at his
gate, covered with sores,
21 and longing to be fed with
the *crumbs* which were falling
from the rich man's table; besides,
even the dogs were coming and
licking his sores.
22 "Now it came about that the
poor man died and he was carried
away by the angels to [r]Abraham's
bosom; and the rich man also died
and was buried. John 1:18
23 "And in Hades [t]he lifted up his
eyes, being in torment, and *saw
Abraham far away, and Lazarus
in his bosom. *having lifted up*
24 "And he cried out and said,
'Father Abraham, have mercy on
me, and send Lazarus, that he
may dip the tip of his finger in water and cool off my tongue; for I
am in agony in this flame.'
25 "But Abraham said, 'Child, remember that [r]during your life you
received your good things, and
likewise Lazarus bad things; but
now he is being comforted here,
and you are in agony. Luke 6:24
26 'And [t]besides all this, between
us and you there is a great chasm
fixed, in order that those who
wish to come over from here to
you may not be able, and *that*
none may cross over from there to
us.' *in all these things*
27 "And he said, 'Then I beg you,
Father, that you send him to my
father's house—
28 for I have five brothers—that
he may warn them, lest they also
come to this place of torment.'
29 "But Abraham *said, 'They
have [r]Moses and the Prophets; let
them hear them.' Luke 4:17
30 "But he said, 'No, [r]Father
Abraham, but if someone goes to
them from the dead, they will repent!' Luke 3:8; 16:24; 19:9
31 "But he said to him, 'If they do
not listen to Moses and the Prophets, neither will they be persuaded
if someone rises from the dead.' "

CHAPTER 17

AND He said to His disciples, "It
is inevitable that stumbling blocks
should come, but woe to him
through whom they come!
2 "It would be better for him if a
millstone were hung around his
neck and he were thrown into the
sea, than that he should cause one
of these little ones to stumble.
3 "Be on your guard! [r]If your
brother sins, rebuke him; and if he
repents, forgive him. Matt. 18:15
4 "And if he sins against you
seven times a day, and returns to
you seven times, saying, 'I repent,'
[t]forgive him." *you shall forgive*
5 And the apostles said to the
Lord, "Increase our faith!"
6 And the Lord said, "If you
had faith like a mustard seed, you
would say to this mulberry tree,
'Be uprooted and be planted in the
sea'; and it would obey you.
7 "But which of you, having a
slave plowing or tending sheep,
will say to him when he has come
in from the field, 'Come immediately and sit down to eat'?
8 "But will he not say to him,
'Prepare something for me to eat,
and *properly* [t]clothe yourself and
serve me until I have eaten and
drunk; and [t]afterward you will eat
and drink'? *gird • after these things*
9 "He does not thank the slave
because he did the things which
were commanded, does he?

10 "So you too, when you do all
the things which are commanded
you, say, 'We are unworthy
slaves; we have done *only* that
which we ought to have done.'"
11 And it came about while He
was [r]on the way to Jerusalem, that
He was passing between Samaria
and Galilee. Luke 9:51
12 And as He entered a certain
village, ten leprous men who
stood at a distance met Him;
13 and they raised their voices,
saying, "Jesus, [r]Master, have mercy on us!" Luke 5:5
14 And when He saw them, He
said to them, "Go and show yourselves to the priests." And it came
about that as they were going,
they were cleansed.
15 Now one of them, when he
saw that he had been healed,
turned back, [r]glorifying God with a
loud voice, Matt. 9:8
16 and he fell on his face at His
feet, giving thanks to Him. And he
was a [r]Samaritan. Matt. 10:5
17 And Jesus answered and
said, "Were there not ten
cleansed? But the nine—where
are they?
18 "Was no one found who
turned back to give glory to God,
except this foreigner?"
19 And He said to him, "Rise,
and go your way; [r]your faith [30]has
made you well." Matt. 9:22
20 Now having been questioned
by the Pharisees as to when the
kingdom of God was coming, He
answered them and said, "The
kingdom of God is not coming
with signs to be observed;
21 nor will they say, 'Look, here
it is!' or, 'There *it is!*' For behold,
the kingdom of God is [a]in your
midst." *within you*
22 And He said to the disciples,
"The [r]days shall come when you
will long to see one of the days of
the Son of Man, and you will not
see it. Matt. 9:15; Mark 2:20
23 "And they will say to you,
'Look there! Look here!' Do not go
away, and do not run after *them.*
24 "For just as the lightning,
when it flashes out of one part [t]of
the sky, shines to the other part of
the sky, so will the Son of Man be
in His day. *under heaven*
25 "But [r] first He must suffer
many things and be rejected by
this generation. Matt. 16:21
26 "And just as it happened in
the days of Noah, so it shall be
also in the days of the Son of Man:
27 they were eating, they were
drinking, they were marrying,
they were being given in marriage, until the day that Noah entered the ark, and the flood came
and destroyed them all.
28 "It was the same as happened
in the days of Lot: they were eating, they were drinking, they were
buying, they were selling, they
were planting, they were building;
29 but on the day that Lot went
out from Sodom it rained fire and
[a]brimstone from heaven and destroyed them all. *sulphur*
30 "It will be [t]just the same on the
day that the Son of Man is revealed. *according to the same things*
31 "On that day, let not the one
who is [r]on the housetop and whose
goods are in the house go down to
take them away; and likewise let
not the one who is in the field turn
back. Matt. 24:17, 18
32 "Remember Lot's wife.

[30]Or, *has saved you*

33 "Whoever seeks to keep his life shall lose it, and whoever loses *his life* shall preserve it.

34 "I tell you, on that night there will be two men in one bed; one will be taken, and the other will be left.

35 "There[r] will be two women grinding at the same place; one will be taken, and the other will be left. Matt. 24:41

36 ["[31]Two men will be in the field; one will be taken and the other will be left."]

37 And answering they *said to Him, "Where, Lord?" And He said to them, "Where[r] the body *is,* there also will the [a]vultures be gathered." Matt. 24:28 • *eagles*

CHAPTER 18

NOW He was telling them a parable to show that at all times they [r]ought to pray and not to [r]lose heart, Luke 11:5-10 • 2 Cor. 4:1

2 saying, "There was in a certain city a judge who did not fear God, and did not respect man.

3 "And there was a widow in that city, and she kept coming to him, saying, 'Give me legal protection from my opponent.'

4 "And for a while he was unwilling; but afterward he said to himself, 'Even though I do not fear God nor respect man,

5 yet[r] because this widow bothers me, I will give her legal protection, lest by continually coming she wear me out.'" Luke 11:8

6 And the Lord said, "Hear what the unrighteous judge *said;

7 now shall not God bring about justice for His elect, who cry to Him day and night, and will He delay long over them?

8 "I tell you that He will bring about justice for them speedily. However, when the Son of Man comes, [r]will He find [t]faith on the earth?" Luke 17:26ff. • *the faith*

9 And He also told this parable to certain ones who [r]trusted in themselves that they were righteous, and viewed others with contempt: Luke 16:15

10 "Two men went up into the temple to pray, one a Pharisee, and the other a tax-gatherer.

11 "The Pharisee [r]stood and was praying thus to himself, 'God, I thank Thee that I am not like other people: swindlers, unjust, adulterers, or even like this tax-gatherer. Matt. 6:5; Mark 11:25

12 'I fast twice a week; I pay tithes of all that I get.'

13 "But the tax-gatherer, standing some distance away, was even unwilling to lift up his eyes to heaven, but was beating his breast, saying, 'God, be [a]merciful to me, the sinner!' *propitious*

14 "I tell you, this man went down to his house justified rather than the other; [r]for everyone who exalts himself shall be humbled, but he who humbles himself shall be exalted." Matt. 23:12

15 [r]And they were bringing even their babies to Him so that He might touch them, but when the disciples saw it, they *began* rebuking them. Luke 18:15-17

16 But Jesus called for them, saying, "Permit the children to come to Me, and do not hinder them, for the kingdom of God belongs to such as these.

[31] Many mss. do not contain this verse

17 "Truly I say to you,[r] whoever
does not receive the kingdom of
God like a child shall not enter it
at all." Matt. 18:3; 19:14
18 [r]And a certain ruler questioned Him, saying, "Good
Teacher, what shall I do to inherit
eternal life?" Luke 18:18-30
19 And Jesus said to him, "Why
do you call Me good? No one is
good except God alone.
20 "You know the command-
ments, 'Do[r] NOT COMMIT ADUL-
TERY, DO NOT MURDER, DO NOT
STEAL, DO NOT BEAR FALSE WIT-
NESS, HONOR YOUR FATHER AND
MOTHER.' " Ex. 20:12-16
21 And he said, "All these
things I have kept from *my*
youth."
22 And when Jesus heard *this,*
He said to him, "One thing you
still lack; sell all that you possess,
and distribute it to the poor, and
you shall have treasure in heaven;
and come, follow Me."
23 But when he had heard these
things, he became very sad; for he
was extremely rich.
24 And Jesus looked at him and
said, "How[r] hard it is for those
who are wealthy to enter the kingdom of God! Matt. 19:23
25 "For it is easier for a camel to
[t]go through the eye of a needle,
than for a rich man to enter the
kingdom of God." *enter*
26 And they who heard it said,
"Then[t] who can be saved?" *And*
27 But He said, "The[r] things impossible with men are possible
with God." Matt. 19:26
28 And Peter said, "Behold, we
have left[t] our own *homes,* and followed You." *our own things*
29 And He said to them, "Truly
I say to you, there is no one who
has left house or wife or brothers
or parents or children, for the
sake of the kingdom of God,
30 who shall not receive many
times as much at this time and in
the age to come, eternal life."
31 And He took the twelve
aside and said to them, "Behold,
we are going up to Jerusalem, and
all things which are written
through the prophets about the
Son of Man will be accomplished.
32 "For He will be delivered to
the Gentiles, and will be mocked
and mistreated and spit upon,
33 and after they have scourged
Him, they will kill Him; and the
third day He will rise again."
34 And[r] they understood none of
these things, and this saying was
hidden from them, and they did
not comprehend the things that
were said. Mark 9:32
35 And it came about that[r] as He
was approaching Jericho, a certain blind man was sitting by the
road, begging. Matt. 20:29
36 Now hearing a multitude
going by, he *began* to inquire what
this might be.
37 And they told him that Jesus
of Nazareth was passing by.
38 And he called out, saying,
"Jesus,[r] Son of David, have mercy
on me!" Matt. 9:27
39 And those who led the way
were sternly telling him to be
quiet; but he kept crying out all
the more, "Son of David, have
mercy on me!"
40 And Jesus[t] stopped and commanded that he be brought to
Him; and when he had come near,
He questioned him, *stood*

41 "What do you want Me to do for you?" And he said, "Lord, *I want* to regain my sight!"

42 And Jesus said to him, "Receive[a] your sight; your faith has made you well." ***Regain***

43 And immediately he regained his sight, and *began* following Him, [r]glorifying God; and when all the people saw it, they gave praise to God. **Matt. 9:8**

CHAPTER 19

AND He [r]entered and was passing through Jericho. **Luke 18:35**

2 And behold, there was a man called by the name of Zaccheus; and he was a chief tax-gatherer, and he was rich.

3 And he was trying to see who Jesus was, and he was unable because of the crowd, for he was small in stature.

4 And he ran on ahead and climbed up into a sycamore tree in order to see Him, for He was about to pass through that way.

5 And when Jesus came to the place, He looked up and said to him, "Zaccheus, hurry and come down, for today I must stay at your house."

6 And he hurried and came down, and received Him gladly.

7 And when they saw it, they all *began* to grumble, saying, "He has gone[a] to be the guest of a man who is a sinner." ***to find lodging***

8 And Zaccheus stopped and said to the Lord, "Behold, Lord, half of my possessions I will give to the poor, and if I have defrauded anyone of anything, I will give back four times as much."

9 And Jesus said to him, "Today salvation has come to this house, because he, too, is [r]a son of Abraham. **Luke 3:8**

10 "For [r]the Son of Man has come to seek and to save that which was lost." **Matt. 18:11**

11 And while they were listening to these things, He went on to tell a parable, because He was near Jerusalem, and they supposed that the kingdom of God was going to appear immediately.

12 He said therefore, "A certain nobleman went to a distant country to receive a kingdom for himself, and *then* return.

13 "And he called ten of his slaves, and gave them ten [32]minas, and said to them, 'Do business *with this* until I come *back*.'

14 "But his citizens hated him, and sent [a]a delegation after him, saying, 'We do not want this man to reign over us.' ***an embassy***

15 "And it came about that when he returned, after receiving the kingdom, he ordered that these slaves, to whom he had given the money, be called to him in order that he might know what business they had done.

16 "And the first appeared, saying, 'Master[t], your mina has made ten minas more.' ***Lord***

17 "And he said to him, 'Well done, good slave, because you have been [r]faithful in a very little thing, be in authority over ten cities.' **Luke 16:10**

18 "And the second came, saying, 'Your mina, [t]master, has made five minas.' ***lord***

[32] A mina is equal to about 100 days' wages or nearly $20

19 "And he said to him also, 'And
you are to be over five cities.'
20 "And another came, saying,
'Master, behold your mina, which
I kept put away in a handkerchief;
21 for I was afraid of you, because you are an exacting man;
you take up what you did not lay
down, and reap what you did not
sow.'
22 "He *said to him, 'By your
own words I will judge you, you
worthless slave. Did you know
that I am an exacting man, taking
up what I did not lay down, and
reaping what I did not sow?
23 'Then[t] why did you not put the
money in the bank, and having
come, I would have collected it
with interest?' *And*
24 "And he said to the bystanders, 'Take the mina away from
him, and give it to the one who
has the ten minas.'
25 "And they said to him, 'Master, he has ten minas *already*.'
26 "I[r] tell you, that to everyone
who has shall *more* be given, but
from the one who does not have,
even what he does have shall be
taken away. **Matt. 13:12**
27 "But these enemies of mine,
who did not want me to reign over
them, bring them here and slay
them in my presence."
28 And after He had said these
things, He was going on ahead, ascending to Jerusalem.
29 And it came about that when
He approached Bethphage and
Bethany, near the[a] mount that is
called[a] Olivet, He sent two of the
disciples, *hill • Olive Grove*
30 saying, "Go into the village
opposite *you*, in which as you enter you will find a colt tied, on
which no one yet has ever sat; untie it, and bring it *here*.
31 "And if anyone asks you,
'Why are you untying it?' thus
shall you speak, 'The Lord has
need of it.' "
32 And those who were sent
went away and found it just as He
had told them.
33 And as they were untying the
colt, its owners said to them,
"Why are you untying the colt?"
34 And they said, "The Lord has
need of it."
35 And they brought it to Jesus,
and they threw their garments on
the colt, and put Jesus *on it*.
36 And as He was going, they
were spreading their garments in
the road.
37 And as He was now ap-
proaching, near the descent of the
Mount of Olives, the whole multitude of the disciples began to
praise God joyfully with a loud
voice for all the[a] miracles which
they had seen, *works of power*
38 saying,
"BLESSED[r] IS THE King WHO
COMES IN THE NAME OF
THE LORD; **Ps. 118:26**
Peace in heaven and glory
in the highest!"
39 And some of the Pharisees in
the multitude said to Him,
"Teacher, rebuke Your disciples."
40 And He answered and said,
"I tell you, if these become silent,
the stones will cry out!"
41 And when He approached,
He saw the city and wept over it,
42 saying, "If you had known in
this day, even you, the things
which make for peace! But now
they have been hidden from your
eyes.

43 "For the days shall come upon you[t] when your enemies will[r] throw up a bank before you, and surround you, and hem you in on every side, *and* • Eccl. 9:14

44 and will level you to the ground and your children within you, and[r] they will not leave in you one stone upon another, because you did not recognize the time of your visitation." Matt. 24:2

45 [r]And He entered the temple and began to cast out those who were selling, Luke 19:45

46 saying to them, "It is written, 'AND MY HOUSE SHALL BE A HOUSE OF PRAYER,' but you have made it a ROBBERS' [t]DEN." *cave*

47 And[r] He was teaching daily in the temple; but the chief priests and the scribes and the leading men among the people were trying to destroy Him, Matt. 26:55

48 and they could not find anything that they might do, for all the people were hanging upon [t]His words. *Him, listening*

CHAPTER 20

AND it came about on one of the days while He was teaching the people in the temple and preaching the gospel, that the chief priests and the scribes with the elders confronted *Him*,

2 and they spoke, saying to Him, "Tell us by what authority You are doing these things, or who is the one who gave You this authority?"

3 And He answered and said to them, "I shall also ask you a [t]question, and you tell Me: *word*

4 "Was the baptism of John from heaven or from men?"

5 And they reasoned among themselves, saying, "If we say, 'From heaven,' He will say, 'Why did you not believe him?'

6 "But if we say, 'From men,' all the people will stone us to death, for they are convinced that John was a [r]prophet." Matt. 11:9

7 And they answered that they did not know where *it came* from.

8 And Jesus said to them, "Neither will I tell you by what authority I do these things."

9 And He began to tell the people this parable: "A man planted a vineyard and rented it out to [a]vine-growers, and went on a journey for a long time. *tenant farmers*

10 "And at the *harvest* time he sent a slave to the vine-growers, in order that they might give him *some* of the produce of the vineyard; but the vine-growers beat him and sent him away empty-handed.

11 "And he proceeded to send another slave; and they beat him also and treated him shamefully, and sent him away empty-handed.

12 "And he proceeded to send a third; and this one also they wounded and cast out.

13 "And the [t]owner of the vineyard said, 'What shall I do? I will send my beloved son; perhaps they will respect him.' *lord*

14 "But when the vine-growers saw him, they reasoned with one another, saying, 'This is the heir; let us kill him that the inheritance may be ours.'

15 "And they threw him out of the vineyard and killed him. What, therefore, will the owner of the vineyard do to them?

16 "He will come and [r]destroy
these vine-growers and will give
the vineyard to others." And
when they heard it, they said,
"May it never be!" Matt. 21:41
17 But He looked at them and
said, "What then is this that is
written,

'THE STONE WHICH THE
BUILDERS REJECTED,
THIS BECAME [r]THE CHIEF COR-
NER *stone*'? Eph. 2:20

18 "Everyone[r] who falls on that
stone will be broken to pieces; but
on whomever it falls, it will scatter him like dust." Matt. 21:44
19 And the scribes and the chief
priests [r]tried to lay hands on Him
that very hour, and they feared
the people; for they understood
that He spoke this parable against
them. Luke 19:47
20 And they watched Him, and
sent spies who pretended to be
righteous, in order that they might
catch Him in some statement, so
as to deliver Him up to the rule
and the authority of the governor.
21 And they questioned Him,
saying, "Teacher, we know that
You speak and teach correctly,
and You are not partial to any, but
teach the way of God in truth.
22 "Is it lawful for us to pay
taxes to Caesar, or not?"
23 But He detected their trickery and said to them,
24 "Show Me a [33]denarius. Whose
likeness and inscription does it
have?" And they said, "Caesar's."
25 And He said to them, "Then
render to Caesar the things that
are Caesar's, and to God the
things that are God's."

[33]The denarius was equivalent to one day's wage

26 And they were unable to
catch Him in a saying in the presence of the people; and marveling
at His answer, they became silent.
27 Now there came to Him
some of the Sadducees (who say
that there is no resurrection),
28 and they questioned Him,
saying, "Teacher, Moses wrote for
us that [r]IF A MAN'S BROTHER DIES,
having a wife, AND HE IS CHILD-
LESS, HIS BROTHER SHOULD TAKE
THE WIFE AND RAISE UP OFFSPRING
TO HIS BROTHER. Deut. 25:5
29 "Now there were seven brothers; and the first took a wife, and
died childless;
30 and the second
31 and the third took her; and in
the same way all seven died, leaving no children.
32 "Finally the woman died also.
33 "In the resurrection therefore,
which one's wife will she be? For
all seven had her as wife."
34 And Jesus said to them, "The
sons of [r]this age marry and are giv-
en in marriage, Matt. 12:32
35 but those who are considered
worthy to attain to [r]that age and
the resurrection from the dead,
neither marry, nor are given in
marriage; Matt. 12:32
36 for neither can they die anymore, for they are like angels, and
are [r]sons of God, being sons of the
resurrection. Rom. 8:16f.
37 "But that the dead are raised,
even Moses showed, in the *passage about the burning* bush,
where he calls the Lord THE GOD
OF ABRAHAM, AND THE GOD OF
ISAAC, AND THE GOD OF JACOB.
38 "Now[r] He is not the God of the
dead, but of the living; for all live
to Him." Matt. 22:32; Mark 12:27

39 And some of the scribes answered and said, "Teacher, You
have spoken well."
40 For they did not have courage to question Him any longer
about anything. Matt. 22:46
41 And He said to them, "How
is it that they say [34]the Christ is
David's son? Luke 20:41-44
42"For David himself says in the
book of Psalms,
'THE LORD SAID TO MY LORD,
"SIT AT MY RIGHT HAND,
43 UNTIL I MAKE THINE EN-
EMIES A FOOTSTOOL FOR
THY FEET."' Ps. 110:1
44"David therefore calls Him
'Lord,' and how is He his son?"
**45 And while all the people
were listening, He said to the disciples,** Luke 20:45-47
46"Beware of the scribes, who
like to walk around in long robes,
and love respectful greetings in
the market places, and chief seats
in the synagogues, and places of
honor at banquets, Luke 11:43
47 who devour widows' houses,
and for appearance's sake offer
long prayers; these will receive
greater condemnation."

CHAPTER 21

**AND He looked up and saw the
rich putting their gifts into the
treasury.**
2 **And He saw a certain poor
widow putting in two small copper coins.** *therein*
3 **And He said,** "Truly I say to
you, this poor widow put in more
than all *of them;*
4 for they all out of their surplus put into the offering; but she
out of her poverty put in all that
she had to live on." *gifts*
**5 And while some were talking
about the temple, that it was
adorned with beautiful stones and
votive gifts, He said,**
6"*As for* these things which
you are looking at, the days will
come in which there will not be
left one stone upon another which
will not be torn down."
7 And they questioned Him,
saying, "Teacher, when therefore
will these things be? And what
will be the sign when these things
are about to take place?"
8 And He said, "See to it that
you be not misled; for many will
come in My name, saying, 'I am
He,' and, 'The time is at hand'; do
not go after them. John 8:24
9"And when you hear of wars
and disturbances, do not be terrified; for these things must take
place first, but the end *does* not
follow immediately."
**10 Then He continued by saying
to them,** "Nation will rise against
nation, and kingdom against kingdom,
11 and there will be great earthquakes, and in various places
plagues and famines; and there
will be terrors and great signs
from heaven. *attesting miracles*
12"But before all these things,
they will lay their hands on you
and will persecute you, delivering
you to the synagogues and prisons, bringing you before kings
and governors for My name's
sake. Luke 21:12-17 · *being brought*
13"It will lead to an opportunity
for your testimony. Phil. 1:12
14"So make up your minds not

[34]I.e., the Messiah

to prepare beforehand to defend
yourselves; Luke 12:11
15 for [r]I will give you [t]utterance
and wisdom which none of your
opponents will be able to resist or
refute. Luke 12:12 • *a mouth*
16 "But you will be delivered up
even by parents and brothers and
relatives and friends, and they will
put *some* of you to death,
17 and you will be hated by all
on account of My name.
18 "Yet [r]not a hair of your head
will perish. Matt. 10:30
19 "By [r]your endurance you will
gain your [a]lives. Matt. 10:22 • *soul*
20 "But when you see Jerusalem
surrounded by armies, then recognize that her desolation is at hand.
21 "Then let those who are in Judea flee to the mountains, and let
those who are in the midst of the
city depart, and let not those who
are in the country enter the city;
22 because these are days of
vengeance, in order that all things
which are written may be fulfilled.
23 "Woe to those who are with
child and to those who nurse
babes in those days; for there will
be great distress upon the land,
and wrath to this people,
24 and they will fall by the edge
of the sword, and will be led captive into all the nations; and Jerusalem will be trampled under foot
by the Gentiles until the times of
the Gentiles be fulfilled.
25 "And there will be signs in
sun and moon and stars, and upon
the earth dismay among nations,
in perplexity at the roaring of the
sea and the waves,
26 men fainting from fear and
the expectation of the things
which are coming upon the [t]world;
for the powers of [a]the heavens will
be shaken. *inhabited earth* • *heaven*
27 "And then they will see THE
SON OF MAN COMING IN A CLOUD
with power and great glory.
28 "But when these things begin
to take place, straighten up and
lift up your heads, because your
redemption is drawing near."
29 And He told them a parable:
"Behold the fig tree and all the
trees;
30 as soon as they put forth
leaves, you see it and [r]know for
yourselves that summer is now
near. Luke 12:57
31 "Even so you, too, when you
see these things happening, [t]recog-
nize that [r]the kingdom of God is
near. *know* • Matt. 3:2
32 "Truly I say to you, this [a]gen-
eration will not pass away until all
things take place. *race*
33 "Heaven [r] and earth will pass
away, but My words will not pass
away. Matt. 5:18; Luke 16:17
34 "Be on guard, that your hearts
may not be weighted down with
dissipation and drunkenness and
the worries of life, and that day
come on you suddenly like a trap;
35 for it will come upon all
those who dwell on the face of all
the earth.
36 "But [r] keep on the alert at all
times, praying in order that you
may have strength to escape all
these things that are about to take
place, and to stand before the Son
of Man." Mark 13:33; Luke 12:40
37 Now [t]during the day He was
teaching in the temple, but [t]at evening He would go out and spend
the night on the mount that is
called Olivet. *days* • *nights*

38 And all the people would get
up early in the morning *to come* to
Him in the temple to listen to
Him. John 8:2

CHAPTER 22

NOW the Feast of Unleavened
Bread, which is called the Passover, was approaching.
2 And the chief priests and the
scribes were seeking how they
might put Him to death; for they
were afraid of the people.
3 And Satan entered into Judas who was called Iscariot, belonging to the number of the
twelve. Luke 22:3-6 • *being of*
4 And he went away and discussed with the chief priests and
officers how he might betray Him
to them. 1 Chr. 9:11; Neh. 11:11
5 And they were glad, and
agreed to give him money.
6 And he consented, and *began*
seeking a good opportunity to betray Him to them apart from the
multitude. *without a disturbance*
7 Then came the *first* day of
Unleavened Bread on which the
Passover *lamb* had to be sacrificed. Mark 14:12
8 And He sent Peter and John,
saying, "Go and prepare the Passover for us, that we may eat it."
9 And they said to Him,
"Where do You want us to prepare it?"
10 And He said to them, "Behold, when you have entered the
city, a man will meet you carrying
a pitcher of water; follow him into
the house that he enters.
11 "And you shall say to the
owner of the house, 'The Teacher
says to you, "Where is the guest
room in which I may eat the Passover with My disciples?" '
12 "And he will show you a large,
furnished, upper room; prepare it
there."
13 And they departed and found
everything just as He had told
them; and they prepared the Passover.
14 And when the hour had
come He reclined *at the table,* and
the apostles with Him.
15 And He said to them, "I have
earnestly desired to eat this Passover with you before I suffer;
16 for I say to you, I shall never
again eat it until it is fulfilled in
the kingdom of God."
17 And when He had taken a
cup *and* given thanks, He said,
"Take this and share it among
yourselves; Matt. 14:19
18 for I say to you, I will not
drink of the fruit of the vine from
now on until the kingdom of God
comes." Matt. 26:29; Mark 14:25
19 And when He had taken
some bread *and* given thanks, He
broke *it,* and gave *it* to them, saying, "This is My body [35]which is
given for you; do this in remembrance of Me." Matt. 14:19
20 And in the same way *He took*
the cup after they had eaten, saying, "This cup which is poured out
for you is the new covenant in My
blood. Matt. 26:28; Mark 14:24
21 "But behold, the hand of the
one betraying Me is with Me on
the table. Luke 22:21-23
22 "For indeed, the Son of Man is
going as it has been determined;
but woe to that man by whom He
is betrayed!" Acts 2:23; 4:28

[35] Some ancient mss. do not contain the remainder of v. 19 nor any of v. 20

23 And they began to discuss
among themselves which one of
them it might be who was going
to do this thing.
24 And there arose also [r]a dispute among them *as to* which one
of them was regarded to be greatest. Mark 9:34; Luke 9:46
25 [r]And He said to them, "The
kings of the Gentiles lord it over
them; and those who have authority over them are called 'Benefac-
tors.' Luke 22:25-27
26 "But not so with you, but let
him who is the greatest among
you become as the youngest, and
the leader as the servant.
27 "For [r]who is greater, the one
who reclines *at the table,* or the
one who serves? Is it not the one
who reclines *at the table*? But I
am among you as the one who
serves. Luke 12:37
28 "And you are those who have
stood by Me in My trials;
29 and just as My Father has
granted Me a [r]kingdom, I grant
you
30 that you may eat and drink
at My table in My kingdom, and
you will sit on thrones judging the
twelve tribes of Israel.
31 "Simon, Simon, behold, Satan
has demanded *permission* to [r]sift
you like wheat; Amos 9:9
32 but I have prayed for you,
that your faith may not fail; and
you, when once you have turned
again, strengthen your brothers."
33 And he said to Him, "Lord,
with You I am ready to go both to
prison and to death!"
34 And He said, "I say to you,
Peter, the cock will not crow today until you have denied three
times that you know Me."
35 And He said to them, "When
I sent you out without purse and
bag and sandals, you did not lack
anything, did you?" And they
said, "*No,* nothing."
36 And He said to them, "But
now, let him who has a purse take
it along, likewise also a bag, and
let him who has no sword sell his
robe and buy one.
37 "For I tell you, that this which
is written must be fulfilled in Me,
'AND HE WAS NUMBERED WITH
TRANSGRESSORS'; for that which
refers to Me has *its* fulfillment."
38 And they said, "Lord, look,
here are two swords." And He
said to them, "It is enough."
39 And He came out and proceeded as was His custom to the
Mount of Olives; and the disciples
also followed Him.
40 [r]And when He arrived at the
place, He said to them, "Pray that
you may not enter into temptation." Luke 22:40-46
41 And He withdrew from them
about a stone's throw, and He
knelt down and *began* to pray,
42 saying, "Father, if Thou art
willing, remove this [r]cup from Me;
yet not My will, but Thine be
done." Matt. 20:22
43 Now an [r]angel from heaven
appeared to Him, strengthening
Him. Matt. 4:11
44 And being in agony He was
praying very fervently; and His
sweat became like drops of blood,
falling down upon the ground.
45 And when He rose from
prayer, He came to the disciples
and found them sleeping from sorrow,
46 and said to them, "Why are
you sleeping? Rise and pray that

you may not enter into temptation."
47 While He was still speaking,
behold, a multitude *came,* and the
one called Judas, one of the
twelve, was preceding them; and
he approached Jesus to kiss Him.
48 But Jesus said to him, "Judas, are you betraying the Son of
Man with a kiss?"
49 And when those who were
around Him saw what was going
to happen, they said, "Lord, shall
we strike with the sword?"
50 And a certain one of them
struck the slave of the high priest
and cut off his right ear.
51 But Jesus answered and said,
"Stop! No more of this." And He
touched his ear and healed him.
52 And Jesus said to the chief
priests and officers of the temple
and elders who had come against
Him, "Have you come out with
swords and clubs as against a robber? Luke 22:4 • Luke 22:37
53 "While I was with you daily in
the temple, you did not lay hands
on Me; but this hour and the
power of darkness are yours."
54 And having arrested Him,
they led Him *away,* and brought
Him to the house of the high
priest; but Peter was following at
a distance. Matt. 26:57
55 And after they had kindled a
fire in the middle of the courtyard
and had sat down together, Peter
was sitting among them.
56 And a certain servant-girl,
seeing him as he sat in the fire-
light, and looking intently at him,
said, "This man was with Him
too."
57 But he denied *it,* saying,
"Woman, I do not know Him."
58 And a little later, another
saw him and said, "You are *one* of
them too!" But Peter said, "Man, I
am not!" John 18:26
59 And after about an hour had
passed, another man *began* to in-
sist, saying, "Certainly this man
also was with Him, for he is a
Galilean too." Matt. 26:73
60 But Peter said, "Man, I do
not know what you are talking
about." And immediately, while
he was still speaking, a cock
crowed.
61 And the Lord turned and
looked at Peter. And Peter remembered the word of the Lord,
how He had told him, "Before a
cock crows today, you will deny
Me three times." Luke 7:13
62 And he went out and wept
bitterly.
63 And the men who were holding Jesus in custody were mocking Him, and beating Him,
64 and they blindfolded Him
and were asking Him, saying,
"Prophesy, who is the one who hit
You?" Matt. 26:68; Mark 14:65
65 And they were saying many
other things against Him, blaspheming. Matt. 27:39
66 And when it was day, the
[36]Council of elders of the people
assembled, both chief priests and
scribes, and they led Him away to
their council *chamber,* saying,
67 "If You are the Christ, tell us."
But He said to them, "If I tell you,
you will not believe;
68 and if I ask a question, you
will not answer.
69 "But from now on THE SON OF
MAN WILL BE SEATED AT THE

[36]Or, *Sanhedrin*

RIGHT HAND of the power OF GOD."

70 And they all said, "Are You the Son of God, then?" And He said to them, "Yes, I am."

71 And they said, "What further need do we have of testimony? For we have heard it ourselves from His own mouth."

CHAPTER 23

THEN the whole body of them arose and [r]brought Him before Pilate. Matt. 27:2; Mark 15:1

2 And they began to accuse Him, saying, "We found this man [r]misleading our nation and [r]forbidding to pay taxes to Caesar, and saying that He Himself is Christ, a King." Luke 23:14 • Luke 20:22

3 And Pilate asked Him, saying, "Are You the King of the Jews?" And He answered him and said, "*It is as* you say."

4 And Pilate said to the chief priests and the multitudes, "I [r]find no guilt in this man." Matt. 27:23

5 But they kept on insisting, saying, "He stirs up the people, teaching all over Judea, [r]starting from Galilee, even as far as this place." Matt. 4:12

6 But when Pilate heard it, he asked whether the man was a Galilean.

7 And when he learned that He belonged to Herod's jurisdiction, he sent Him to [r]Herod, who himself also was in Jerusalem [t]at that time. Matt. 14:1 • *in these days*

8 Now Herod was very glad when he saw Jesus; for he had wanted to see Him for a long time, because he had been hearing about Him and was hoping to see some sign performed by Him.

9 And he questioned Him [t]at some length; but He answered him nothing. *in many words*

10 And the chief priests and the scribes were standing there, accusing Him vehemently.

11 And Herod with his soldiers, after treating Him with contempt and mocking Him, [r]dressed Him in a gorgeous robe and sent Him back to Pilate. Matt. 27:28

12 Now Herod and Pilate became friends with one another that very day; for before they had been at enmity with each other.

13 And Pilate summoned the chief priests and the [r]rulers and the people, Luke 23:35

14 and said to them, "You brought this man to me as one who [r]incites the people to rebellion, and behold, having examined Him before you, I [r]have found no guilt in this man regarding the charges which you make against Him. Luke 23:2 • Luke 23:4

15 "No, nor has [r]Herod, for he sent Him back to us; and behold, nothing deserving death has been done by Him. Luke 9:9

16 "I will therefore [r]punish Him and release Him." Matt. 27:26

17 [[37]Now he was obliged to release to them at the feast one prisoner.]

18 But they cried out all together, saying, "Away[r] with this man, and release for us Barabbas!" Luke 23:18-25

19 (He was one who had been thrown into prison for a certain insurrection made in the city, and for murder.)

20 And Pilate, wanting to re-

[37] Many mss. do not contain this verse

lease Jesus, addressed them again,

21 but they kept on calling out, saying, "Crucify, crucify Him!"

22 And he said to them the third time, "Why, what evil has this man done? I have found in Him no guilt *demanding* death; I will therefore [r]punish Him and release Him." Luke 23:16

23 But they were insistent, with loud voices asking that He be crucified. And their voices *began* to prevail.

24 And Pilate pronounced sentence that their demand should be granted.

25 And he released the man they were asking for who had been thrown into prison for insurrection and murder, but he delivered Jesus to their will.

26 And when they led Him away, they laid hold of one Simon of Cyrene, coming in from the country, and placed on him the cross to carry behind Jesus.

27 And there were following Him a great multitude of the people, and of women who were mourning and lamenting Him.

28 But Jesus turning to them said, "Daughters of Jerusalem, stop weeping for Me, but weep for yourselves and for your children.

29 "For behold, the days are coming when they will say, 'Blessed are the barren, and the wombs that never bore, and the breasts that never nursed.'

30 "Then they will begin TO SAY TO THE MOUNTAINS, 'FALL ON US,' AND TO THE HILLS, 'COVER US.'

31 "For if they do these things in the green tree, what will happen in the dry?"

32 And two others also, who were criminals, were being led away to be put to death with Him.

33 And when they came to the place called The Skull, there they crucified Him and the criminals, one on the right and the other on the left.

34 But Jesus was saying, "Father, forgive them; for they do not know what they are doing." And they cast lots, dividing up His garments among themselves.

35 And the people stood by, looking on. And even the [r]rulers were sneering at Him, saying, "He saved others; let Him save Himself if this is the Christ of God, His Chosen One." Luke 23:13

36 And the soldiers also mocked Him, coming up to Him, [r]offering Him sour wine, Matt. 27:48

37 and saying, "If You are the King of the Jews, save Yourself!"

38 Now there was also an inscription above Him, "THIS IS THE KING OF THE JEWS."

39 And one of the criminals who were hanged *there* was[a]hurling abuse at Him, saying, "Are You not the Christ? Save Yourself and us!" *blaspheming*

40 But the other answered, and rebuking him said, "Do you not even fear God, since you are under the same sentence of condemnation?

41 "And we indeed justly, for we are receiving what we deserve for our deeds; but this man has done nothing wrong."

42 And he was saying, "Jesus, remember me when You come[a]in Your kingdom!" *into*

43 And He said to him, "Truly I

say to you, today you shall be
with Me in Paradise."
44 And it was now about [38]the
sixth hour, and darkness fell over
the whole land until [39]the ninth
hour, John 19:14 • *occurred*
45 the sun being obscured; and
the veil of the temple was torn in
two. *failing* • *in the middle*
46 And Jesus, crying out with a
loud voice, said, "Father, INTO
THY HANDS I COMMIT MY SPIRIT."
And having said this, He breathed
His last. Matt. 27:50; Mark 15:37
47 Now when the centurion saw
what had happened, he *began*
praising God, saying, "Certainly
this man was innocent."
48 And all the multitudes who
came together for this spectacle,
when they observed what had
happened, *began* to return, beating their breasts. Luke 8:52
49 And all His acquaintances
and the women who accompanied
Him from Galilee, were standing
at a distance, seeing these things.
50 And behold, a man named
Joseph, who was a member of the
Council, a good and righteous
man Luke 23:50-56: *Matt. 27:57*
51 (he had not consented to
their plan and action), *a man* from
Arimathea, a city of the Jews,
who was waiting for the kingdom
of God; Mark 15:43; Luke 2:25
52 this man went to Pilate and
asked for the body of Jesus.
53 And he took it down and
wrapped it in a linen cloth, and
laid Him in a tomb cut into the
rock, where no one had ever lain.
54 And it was the preparation
day, and the Sabbath was about to
begin. Matt. 27:62 • *dawn*

[38]I.e., 12 noon [39]I.e., 3 p.m.

55 Now the women who had
come with Him out of Galilee followed after, and saw the tomb
and how His body was laid.
56 And they returned and prepared spices and perfumes.
And on the Sabbath they rested
according to the commandment.

CHAPTER 24

BUT on the first day of the week,
at early dawn, they came to the
tomb, bringing the spices which
they had prepared.
2 And they found the stone
rolled away from the tomb,
3 but when they entered, they
did not find the body of the Lord
Jesus. Luke 7:13; Acts 1:21
4 And it happened that while
they were perplexed about this,
behold, two men suddenly stood
near them in dazzling apparel;
5 and as *the women* were terrified and bowed their faces to the
ground, *the men* said to them,
"Why do you seek the living One
among the dead?
6 "He is not here, but He has
risen. Remember how He spoke to
you while He was still in Galilee,
7 saying that the Son of Man
must be delivered into the hands
of sinful men, and be crucified,
and the third day rise again."
8 And they remembered His
words, John 2:22
9 and returned from the tomb
and reported all these things to
the eleven and to all the rest.
10 Now they were Mary Magdalene and Joanna and Mary the
mother of James; also the other
women with them were telling
these things to the apostles.

11 And these words appeared to
them as nonsense, and they would
not believe them. *in their sight*
12 [[40]But Peter arose and ran to
the tomb; stooping and looking in,
he *saw the linen wrappings only;
and he went away to his home,
marveling at that which had happened.] *by themselves*
13 And behold, two of them
were going that very day to a village named Emmaus, which was
[41]about seven miles from Jerusalem. Mark 16:12
14 And they were conversing
with each other about all these
things which had taken place.
15 And it came about that while
they were conversing and discussing, Jesus Himself approached,
and *began* traveling with them.
16 But their eyes were prevented from recognizing Him.
17 And He said to them, "What
are these words that you are ex-
changing with one another as you
are walking?" And they stood
still, looking sad.
18 And one of them, named
Cleopas, answered and said to
Him, "Are You the only one visiting Jerusalem and unaware of the
things which have happened here
in these days?"
19 And He said to them, "What
things?" And they said to Him,
"The things about Jesus the Nazarene, who was a prophet mighty
in deed and word in the sight of
God and all the people,
20 and how the chief priests and
our rulers delivered Him up to the
sentence of death, and crucified
Him. Luke 23:13

[40]Some ancient mss. do not contain v. 12
[41]I.e., 60 stadia, one stadion was about 600 feet

21 "But we were hoping that it
was He who was going to redeem
Israel. Indeed, besides all this, it is
the third day since these things
happened. Luke 1:68
22 "But also some women among
us amazed us. When they were at
the tomb early in the morning,
23 and did not find His body,
they came, saying that they had
also seen a vision of angels, who
said that He was alive.
24 "And some of those who were
with us went to the tomb and
found it just exactly as the women
also had said; but Him they did
not see."
25 And He said to them, "O
foolish men and slow of heart to
believe in all that the prophets
have spoken! Matt. 26:24
26 "Was it not necessary for the
Christ to suffer these things and
to enter into His glory?"
27 And beginning with Moses
and with all the prophets, He explained to them the things concerning Himself in all the Scriptures. *from* • Gen. 3:15
28 And they approached the village where they were going, and
He acted as though He would go
farther. Mark 6:48
29 And they urged Him, saying,
"Stay with us, for it is *getting*
toward evening, and the day is
now nearly over." And He went in
to stay with them.
30 And it came about that when
He had reclined *at the table* with
them, He took the bread and
blessed *it*, and breaking *it*, He *be-*
gan giving *it* to them.
31 And their eyes were opened
and they recognized Him; and He
vanished from their sight.

32 And they said to one another,
"Were not our hearts burning
within us while He was speaking
to us on the road, while He was
explaining the Scriptures to us?"
33 And they arose that very
hour and returned to Jerusalem,
and [r]found gathered together the
eleven and [r]those who were with
them, Mark 16:13 • Acts 1:14
34 saying, "The[r] Lord has really
risen, and [r]has appeared to Simon." Luke 24:6 • 1 Cor. 15:5
35 And they *began* to relate
their experiences on the road and
how He was recognized by them
in the breaking of the bread.
36 And while they were telling
these things, He Himself stood in
their midst.[42]
37 But they were startled and
frightened and thought that they
were seeing a spirit.
38 And He said to them, "Why
are you troubled, and why do
doubts arise in your hearts?
39 "See My hands and My feet,
that it is I Myself; touch Me and
see, for a spirit does not have flesh
and bones as you see that I have."
40 [[43]And when He had said this,
He showed them His hands and
His feet.]
41 And while they still could not
believe *it* for joy and were marveling, He said to them, "Have you
anything here to eat?"

[42]Some ancient mss. insert *And He says to them, "Peace be to you."*
[43]Many mss. do not contain this verse

42 And they gave Him a piece of
a broiled fish;
43 and He took it and [r]ate *it* before them. Acts 10:41
44 Now He said to them, "These[r]
are My words which I spoke to
you while I was still with you, that
all things which are written about
Me in the Law of Moses and the
Prophets and the Psalms must be
fulfilled." Luke 9:22, 44f.; 18:31-34
45 Then He opened their minds
to understand the Scriptures,
46 and He said to them, "Thus it
is written, that the Christ should
suffer and rise again from the
dead the third day;
47 and that repentance for forgiveness of sins should be proclaimed in His name to all the nations, beginning from Jerusalem.
48 "You are [r]witnesses of these
things. Acts 1:8, 22; 2:32; 3:15
49 "And behold, I am sending
forth the promise of My Father
upon you; but [r]you are to stay in
the city until you are clothed with
power from on high." Acts 1:4
50 And He led them out as far
as Bethany, and He lifted up His
hands and blessed them.
51 And it came about that while
He was blessing them, He parted
from them.[44]
52 And they[45] returned to Jerusalem with great joy,
53 and were continually in the
temple, [t]praising God. *blessing*

[44]Some mss. add *and was carried up into heaven*
[45]Some mss. insert *worshiped Him, and*

THE GOSPEL ACCORDING TO

JOHN

IN the beginning was [r]the Word,
and the Word was with God, and
the Word was God. John 1:14
2 [t]He was in the beginning with
God. *This one*
3 [r]All things came into being[a] by
Him, and apart from Him nothing
came into being that has come
into being. John 1:10 • *through*
4 In Him was life, and the life
was [r]the light of men. John 8:12
5 And [r]the light shines in the
darkness, and the darkness did
not [1]comprehend it. John 3:19
6 There [2]came a man, sent
from God, whose name was John.
7 [t]He came [r]for a witness, that
he might bear witness of the light,
that all might believe through
him. *This one* • John 1:15, 19, 32
8 [t]He was not the light, but
came that he might bear witness
of the light. *That one*
9 There was [r]the true light
[3]which, coming into the world, enlightens every man. 1 John 2:8
10 He was in the world, and the
world was made through Him,
and the world did not know Him.
11 He came to His [4]own, and
those who were His own did not
receive Him.
12 But as many as received
Him, to them He gave the right to
become children of God, *even* to
those who believe in His name,
13 who were born not of blood,
nor of the will of the flesh, nor of
the will of man, but of God.
14 And the Word became flesh,
and [a]dwelt among us, and we beheld His glory, glory as of the only
begotten from the Father, full of
grace and truth. *tabernacled*
15 John *bore witness of Him,
and cried out, saying, "This was
He of whom I said, 'He who
comes after me [t]has a higher rank
than I, for He existed before
me.'" *is become before me*
16 For of His fulness we have all
received, and grace upon grace.
17 For [r]the Law was given
through Moses; [r]grace and truth
were realized through Jesus
Christ. John 7:19 • John 1:14
18 No man has seen God at any
time; the only begotten [5]God, who
is in the bosom of the Father, [r]He
has explained *Him*. John 3:11
19 And this is the witness of
John, when the Jews sent to him
priests and Levites from Jerusalem to ask him, "Who are you?"
20 And he confessed, and did
not deny, and he confessed, "I [r]am
not the Christ." Luke 3:15f.
21 And they asked him, "What
then? Are you [r]Elijah?" And he
*said, "I am not." "Are you the
Prophet?" And he answered,
"No." Matt. 11:14
22 They said then to him, "Who
are you, so that we may give an
answer to those who sent us?
What do you say about yourself?"

[1] Or, *overpower* [2] Or, *came into being*
[3] Or, *which enlightens every man coming into the world*
[4] Or, *own things, possessions, domain*
[5] Some later mss. read *Son*

23 He said, "I am A VOICE OF
ONE CRYING IN THE WILDERNESS,
'MAKE STRAIGHT THE WAY OF THE
LORD,' as Isaiah the prophet said."
24 Now they had been sent
from the Pharisees.
25 And they asked him, and
said to him, "Why then are you
baptizing, if you are not the
Christ, nor Elijah, nor the
Prophet?" Deut. 18:15, 18
26 John answered them saying,
"I baptize [6]in water, *but* among
you stands One whom you do not
know. Matt. 3:11; Mark 1:8
27 "*It is* He who comes after me,
the thong of whose sandal I am
not worthy to untie." Matt. 3:11
28 These things took place in
Bethany beyond the Jordan,
where John was baptizing.
29 The next day he *saw Jesus
coming to him, and *said, "Behold, the Lamb of God who takes
away the sin of the world!
30 "This is He on behalf of whom
I said, 'After me comes a Man
who has a higher rank than I, for
He existed before me.'
31 "And I did not recognize Him,
but in order that He might be
manifested to Israel, I came baptizing [6]in water."
32 And John bore witness saying, "I have beheld the Spirit descending as a dove out of heaven,
and He remained upon Him.
33 "And I did not recognize Him,
but He who sent me to baptize [6]in
water said to me, 'He upon whom
you see the Spirit descending and
remaining upon Him, this is the
one who baptizes in the Holy
Spirit.' Matt. 3:11; Mark 1:8
34 "And I have seen, and have
borne witness that this is the Son
of God." Matt. 4:3
35 Again the next day John was
standing with two of his disciples,
36 and he looked upon Jesus as
He walked, and *said, "Behold,
the Lamb of God!" John 1:29
37 And the two disciples heard
him speak, and they followed
Jesus.
38 And Jesus turned, and beheld them following, and *said to
them, "What do you seek?" And
they said to Him, "Rabbi (which
translated means Teacher), where
are You staying?"
39 He *said to them, "Come,
and you will see." They came
therefore and saw where He was
staying; and they stayed with Him
that day, for it was about the
[7]tenth hour.
40 One of the two who heard
John *speak,* and followed Him,
was Andrew, Simon Peter's
brother. Matt. 4:18-22
41 He *found first his own
brother Simon, and *said to him,
"We have found the Messiah"
(which translated means Christ).
42 He brought him to Jesus.
Jesus looked at him, and said,
"You are Simon the son of John;
you shall be called Cephas"
(which translated means Peter).
43 The next day He purposed to
go forth into Galilee, and He
*found Philip. And Jesus *said to
him, "Follow Me." Matt. 10:3
44 Now Philip was from Bethsaida, of the city of Andrew and Peter. Matt. 10:3; John 1:44-48
45 Philip *found Nathanael and
*said to him, "We have found
Him of whom Moses in the Law

[6]The Gr. here can be translated *in, with* or *by*

[7]Perhaps 10 a.m. (Roman time)

and *also* the Prophets wrote,
Jesus of [r]Nazareth, [r]the son of
Joseph." Matt. 2:23 • Luke 2:48
46 And Nathanael *said to him,
"Can[r] any good thing come out of
Nazareth?" Philip *said to him,
"Come and see." John 7:41
47 Jesus saw Nathanael coming
to Him, and *said of him, "Behold,
an[r] Israelite indeed, in whom is no
guile!" Rom. 9:4
48 Nathanael *said to Him,
"How do You know me?" Jesus
answered and said to him, "Before
Philip called you, when you were
under the fig tree, I saw you."
49 Nathanael answered Him,
"Rabbi, You are the Son of God;
You are the King of Israel."
50 Jesus answered and said to
him, "Because I said to you that I
saw you under the fig tree, do you
believe? You shall see greater
things than these."
51 And He *said to him, "Truly,
truly, I say to you, you shall see
the heavens opened, and the angels of God ascending and descending on the Son of Man."

CHAPTER 2

AND on the third day there was a
wedding in Cana of Galilee, and
the mother of Jesus was there;
2 and Jesus also was invited,
and His disciples, to the wedding.
3 And when the wine gave out,
the mother of Jesus *said to Him,
"They have no wine."
4 And Jesus *said to her,
"Woman, [r]what do I have to do
with you? My hour has not yet
come." Matt. 8:29
5 His [r]mother *said to the servants, "Whatever He says to you,
do it." Matt. 12:46
6 Now there were six stone
waterpots set there for the Jewish
custom of purification, containing
twenty or thirty gallons each.
7 Jesus *said to them, "Fill the
waterpots with water." And they
filled them up to the brim.
8 And He *said to them,
"Draw *some* out now, and take it
to the [8]headwaiter." And they
took it *to him.*
9 And when the headwaiter
tasted the water [r]which had become wine, and did not know
where it came from (but the servants who had drawn the water
knew), the headwaiter *called the
bridegroom, John 4:46
10 and *said to him, "Every
man serves the good wine first,
and when *men* have[a] drunk freely,
then that which is poorer; you
have kept the good wine until
now." *have become drunk*
11 This beginning of *His* signs
Jesus did in Cana of Galilee, and
manifested His glory, and His disciples believed in Him.
12 After this He went down to
[r]Capernaum, He and His [r]mother,
and *His* [r]brothers, and His disciples; and there they stayed a few
days. Matt. 4:13 • Matt. 12:46
13 And the Passover of the
Jews was at hand, and Jesus [r]went
up to Jerusalem. Luke 2:41
14 [r]And He found in the temple
those who were selling oxen and
sheep and doves, and the moneychangers seated. John 2:14-16
15 And He made a scourge of
cords, and drove *them* all out of
the temple, with the sheep and the

[8] Or, *steward*

oxen; and He poured out the coins of the moneychangers, and overturned their tables;

16 and to those who were selling[r] the doves He said, "Take these things away; stop making[r] My Father's house a house of merchandise." Matt. 21:12 • Luke 2:49

17 His disciples remembered that it was written, "ZEAL FOR THY HOUSE WILL CONSUME ME."

18 The Jews therefore answered and said to Him, "What[r] sign do You show to us, seeing that You do these things?" Matt. 12:38

19 Jesus answered and said to them, "Destroy this temple, and in three days I will raise it up."

20 The Jews therefore said, "It took forty-six years to build this [a]temple, and will You raise it up in three days?" *sanctuary*

21 But He was speaking of the temple of His body.

22 When therefore He was raised from the dead, His disciples remembered that He said this; and they believed the Scripture, and the word which Jesus had spoken.

23 Now when He was in Jerusalem at [r]the Passover, during the feast, many believed in His name, [r]beholding His signs which He was doing. John 2:13 • John 2:11

24 But Jesus, on His part, was not entrusting Himself to them, for He knew all men,

25 and because He did not need anyone to bear witness concerning man [r]for He Himself knew what was in man. Matt. 9:4

CHAPTER 3

NOW there was a man of the Pharisees, named [r]Nicodemus, a ruler of the Jews; John 7:50

2 this man came to Him by night, and said to Him, "Rabbi,[r] we know that You have come from God *as* a teacher; for no one can do these signs that You do unless God is with him." Matt. 23:7

3 Jesus answered and said to him, "Truly, truly, I say to you, unless one is born again, he cannot see the kingdom of God."

4 Nicodemus *said to Him, "How can a man be born when he is old? He cannot enter a second time into his mother's womb and be born, can he?"

5 Jesus answered, "Truly, truly, I say to you, unless one is born of [r]water and the Spirit, he cannot enter into the kingdom of God. Ezek. 36:25-27; Eph. 5:26

6 "That which is born of the flesh is flesh, and that which is born of the Spirit is spirit.

7 "Do not marvel that I said to you, 'You must be born again.'

8 "The[r] wind blows where it wishes and you hear the sound of it, but do not know where it comes from and where it is going; so is everyone who is born of the Spirit." Ps. 135:7; Eccl. 11:5

9 Nicodemus answered and said to Him, "How can these things be?"

10 Jesus answered and said to him, "Are you [r]the teacher of Israel, and do not understand these things? Luke 2:46; 5:17

11 "Truly, truly, I say to you,[r] we speak that which we know, and bear witness of that which we have seen; and you do not receive our witness. John 1:18; 7:16f.

12 "If I told you earthly things and you do not believe, how shall

you believe if I tell you heavenly things?

13 "And [r]no one has ascended into heaven, but He who descended from heaven, *even* the Son of Man. Deut. 30:12

14 "And as Moses lifted up the serpent in the wilderness, even so must the Son of Man be lifted up;

15 that whoever [9]believes may in Him have eternal life.

16 "For God so[r]loved the world, that He gave His [a]only begotten Son, that whoever believes in Him should not perish, but have eternal life. Rom. 5:8 • *unique*

17 "For God did not send the Son into the world to judge the world, but that the world should be saved through Him.

18 "He who believes in Him is not judged; he who does not believe has been judged already, because he has not believed in the name of the[a]only begotten Son of God. *unique*

19 "And this is the judgment, that [r]the light is come into the world, and men loved the darkness rather than the light; for their deeds were evil. John 1:4

20 "For[r] everyone who does evil hates the light, and does not come to the light, lest his deeds should be exposed. John 3:20, 21

21 "But he who practices the truth comes to the light, that his deeds may be manifested as having been wrought in God."

22 After these things Jesus and His disciples came into the land of Judea, and there He was spending time with them and baptizing.

23 And John also was baptizing in Aenon near Salim, because there was [t]much water there; and they were coming and were being baptized. *many waters*

24 For [r]John had not yet been thrown into prison. Matt. 4:12

25 There arose therefore a discussion on the part of John's disciples with a Jew about purification.

26 And they came to John and said to him, "Rabbi,[r] He who was with you beyond the Jordan, to whom you have borne witness, behold, He is baptizing, and all are coming to Him." Matt. 23:7

27 John answered and said, "A man can receive nothing, unless it has been given him from heaven.

28 "You yourselves bear me witness, that I said, 'I[r] am not the Christ,' but, 'I have been sent before Him.' John 1:20, 23

29 "He who has the bride is [r]the bridegroom; but the friend of the bridegroom, who stands and hears him, rejoices greatly because of the bridegroom's voice. And so this joy of mine has been made full. Matt. 9:15; 25:1

30 "He must increase, but I must decrease.

31 "He who comes from above is above all,[r]he who is of the earth is from the earth and speaks of the earth. He who comes from heaven is above all. 1 Cor. 15:47

32 "What He has seen and heard, of that He bears witness; and no man receives His witness.

33 "He who has received His witness[r]has set his seal to *this*, that God is true. John 6:27; Rom. 4:11

34 "For He whom God has sent speaks the words of God; for He gives the Spirit without measure.

[9]Some mss. read *believes in Him may have eternal life*

35 "The Father loves the Son,
and [r]has given all things into His
hand. Matt. 11:27; Luke 10:22
36 "He who believes in the Son
has eternal life; but he who [r]does
not [a]obey the Son shall not see life,
but the wrath of God abides on
him." Acts 14:2 • *believe*

CHAPTER 4

WHEN therefore the Lord knew
that the Pharisees had heard that
Jesus was making and baptizing
more disciples than John
2 (although [r]Jesus Himself was
not baptizing, but His disciples
were), John 3:22, 26
3 He left [r]Judea, and departed
again into Galilee. John 3:22
4 And He had to pass through
[r]Samaria. Luke 9:52
5 So He *came to a city of [r]Sa-
maria, called Sychar, near the parcel of ground that Jacob gave to
his son Joseph; Luke 9:52
6 and Jacob's well was there.
Jesus therefore, being wearied
from His journey, was sitting thus
by the well. It was about [10]the
sixth hour.
7 There *came a woman of Samaria to draw water. Jesus *said
to her, "Give Me a drink."
8 For His disciples had gone
away into the city to buy food.
9 The Samaritan woman therefore *said to Him, "How is it that
You, being a Jew, ask me for a
drink since I am a Samaritan
woman?" (For Jews have no dealings with Samaritans.)
10 Jesus answered and said to
her, "If you knew the gift of God,
and who it is who says to you,
'Give Me a drink,' you would have
asked Him, and He would have
given you living water."
11 She *said to Him, "Sir,[a] You
have nothing to draw with and the
well is deep; where then do You
get that living water? *Lord*
12 "You are not greater than our
father Jacob, are You, who gave
us the well, and drank of it himself, and his sons, and his cattle?"
13 Jesus answered and said to
her, "Everyone who drinks of this
water shall thirst again;
14 but whoever drinks of the
water that I shall give him [r]shall
never thirst; but the water that I
shall give him shall become in him
a well of water springing up to
eternal life." John 6:35; 7:38
15 The woman *said to Him,
"Sir,[a] give me this water, so I will
not be thirsty, nor come all the
way here to draw." *Lord*
16 He *said to her, "Go, call
your husband, and come here."
17 The woman answered and
said, "I have no husband." Jesus
*said to her, "You have well said,
'I have no husband';
18 for you have had five husbands, and the one whom you
now have is not your husband;
this you have said truly."
19 The woman *said to Him,
"Sir,[a] I perceive that You are [r]a
prophet. *Lord* • Matt. 21:11
20 "Our fathers worshiped in this
mountain, and you *people* say that
in Jerusalem is the place where
men ought to worship."
21 Jesus *said to her, "Woman,
believe Me, [r]an hour is coming
when neither in this mountain,

[10]Perhaps 6 p.m. (Roman time)

nor in Jerusalem, shall you worship the Father. John 4:23
22 "You worship that which you
do not know; we worship that
which we know, for [r]salvation is
from the Jews. Rom. 3:1f.; 9:4f.
23 "But an hour is coming, and
now is, when the true worshipers
shall worship the Father in spirit
and truth; for such people the Father seeks to be His worshipers.
24 "God is [a]spirit, and those who
worship Him must worship in
spirit and truth." *a Spirit*
25 The woman *said to Him, "I
know that [r]Messiah is coming (He
who is called Christ); when that
One comes, He will declare all
things to us." Dan. 9:25
26 Jesus *said to her, "I[r] who
speak to you am *He.*" John 8:24
27 And at this point His [r]disci-
ples came, and they marveled that
He had been speaking with a
woman; yet no one said, "What do
You seek?" or, "Why do You
speak with her?" John 4:8
28 So the woman left her water-
pot, and went into the city, and
*said to the men,
29 "Come, see a man who told
me all the things that I *have* done;
this is not the Christ, is it?"
30 They went out of the city,
and were coming to Him.
31 In the meanwhile the disciples were requesting Him, saying,
"Rabbi,[r] eat." Matt. 23:7; 26:25, 49
32 But He said to them, "I have
food to eat that you do not know
about."
33 The [r]disciples therefore were
saying to one another, "No one
brought Him *anything* to eat, did
he?" Luke 6:13-16; John 1:40-49; 2:2
34 Jesus *said to them, "My
food is to [r]do the will of Him who
sent Me, and to accomplish His
work. John 5:30; 6:38
35 "Do you not say, 'There are
yet four months, and *then* comes
the harvest'? Behold, I say to you,
lift up your eyes, and look on the
fields, that they are white [r]for harvest. Matt. 9:37, 38; Luke 10:2
36 "Already he who reaps is receiving [r]wages, and is gathering
fruit for life eternal; that he who
sows and he who reaps may rejoice together. Prov. 11:18
37 "For in this *case* the saying is
true, 'One[r] sows, and another
reaps.' Job 31:8; Mic. 6:15
38 "I sent you to reap that for
which you have not labored; others have labored, and you have
entered into their labor."
39 And from that city many of
the Samaritans believed in Him
because of the word of the woman
who testified, "He told me all the
things that I *have* done."
40 So when the Samaritans
came to Him, they were asking
Him to stay with them; and He
stayed there two days.
41 And many more believed because of His word;
42 and they were saying to the
woman, "It is no longer because
of what you said that we believe,
for we have heard for ourselves
and know that this One is indeed
the Savior of the world."
43 And after the two days He
went forth from there into Galilee.
44 For Jesus Himself testified
that [r]a prophet has no honor in his
own country. Matt. 13:57
45 So when He came to Galilee,

the Galileans received Him, having seen all the things that He did
in Jerusalem at the feast; for they
themselves also went to the feast.
46 He came therefore again to
Cana of Galilee where He had
made the water wine. And there
was a certain royal official, whose
son was sick at Capernaum.
47 When he heard that Jesus
had come [r]out of Judea into Galilee, he went to Him, and was requesting *Him* to come down and
heal his son; for he was at the
point of death. John 4:3, 54
48 Jesus therefore said to him,
"Unless you *people* see [a]signs and
wonders, you *simply* will not believe." *attesting miracles*
49 The royal official *said to
Him, "Sir,[a] come down before my
child dies." *Lord*
50 Jesus *said to him, "Go your
way; your son lives." The man believed the word that Jesus spoke
to him, and he started off.
51 And as he was now going
down, *his* slaves met him, saying
that his son was living.
52 So he inquired of them the
hour when he began to get better.
They said therefore to him, "Yesterday at the [11]seventh hour the fever left him."
53 So the father knew that *it
was* at that hour in which Jesus
said to him, "Your son lives"; and
he himself believed, and [r]his whole
household. Acts 11:14
54 This is again a second [a]sign
that Jesus performed, when He
had come out of Judea into Galilee. *attesting miracle*

[11]Perhaps 7 p.m. (Roman time)

CHAPTER 5

AFTER these things there was [r][12]a
feast of the Jews, and Jesus went
up to Jerusalem. Deut. 16:1
2 Now there is in Jerusalem by
[r]the sheep *gate* a pool, which is
called in Hebrew Bethesda, having five porticoes. Neh. 3:1
3 In these lay a multitude of
those who were sick, blind, lame,
and withered, [[13]waiting for the
moving of the waters;
4 for an angel of the Lord went
down at certain seasons into the
pool, and stirred up the water;
whoever then first, after the stirring up of the water, stepped in
was made well from whatever disease with which he was afflicted.]
5 And a certain man was there,
who had been thirty-eight years in
his sickness.
6 When Jesus saw him lying
there, and knew that he had already been a long time *in that
condition*, He *said to him, "Do
you wish to get well?"
7 The sick man answered Him,
"Sir, I have no man to put me into
the pool when the water is stirred
up, but while I am coming, another steps down before me."
8 Jesus *said to him, "Arise,
take up your pallet, and walk."
9 And immediately the man
became well, and took up his pallet and *began* to walk.
[r]Now it was the Sabbath on that
day. John 9:14
10 Therefore the Jews were saying to him who was cured, "It is
the Sabbath, and it is not permis-

[12]Many mss. read *the feast*, i.e., the Passover
[13]Many mss. do not contain the remainder of
v. 3 nor v. 4

sible for you to carry your pallet."

11 But he answered them, "He who made me well was the one who said to me, 'Take up your pallet and walk.' "

12 They asked him, "Who is the man who said to you, 'Take up *your* pallet, and walk'?"

13 But he who was healed did not know who it was; for Jesus had slipped away while there was a crowd in *that* place.

14 Afterward Jesus *found him in the temple, and said to him, "Behold, you have become well; do not sin anymore, so that nothing worse may befall you."

15 The man went away, and told the Jews that it was Jesus who had made him well.

16 And for this reason [r]the Jews were persecuting Jesus, because He was doing these things on the Sabbath. John 1:19; 5:10, 15, 18

17 But He answered them, "My Father is working until now, and I Myself am working."

18 For this cause therefore the Jews were seeking all the more to kill Him, because He not only was breaking the Sabbath, but also was calling God His own Father, making Himself equal with God.

19 Jesus therefore answered and was saying to them, "Truly, truly, I say to you, the Son can do nothing of Himself, unless *it is* something He sees the Father doing; for whatever *the Father* does, these things the Son also does in like manner.

20 "For the Father loves the Son, and shows Him all things that He Himself is doing; and greater works than these will He show Him, that you may marvel.

21 "For just as the Father raises the dead and [r]gives them life, even so the Son also gives life to whom He wishes. Rom. 4:17; 8:11

22 "For not even the Father judges anyone, but He has given all judgment to the Son,

23 in order that all may honor the Son, even as they honor the Father. [r]He who does not honor the Son does not honor the Father who sent Him. Luke 10:16

24 "Truly, truly, I say to you, he who hears My word, and [r]believes Him who sent Me, has eternal life, and does not come into judgment, but has passed out of death into life. John 3:18; 12:44; 20:31

25 "Truly, truly, I say to you, [r]an hour is coming and now is, when the dead shall hear the voice of the Son of God; and those who hear shall live. John 4:21, 23

26 "For just as the Father has life in Himself, even so He gave to the Son also to have life in Himself;

27 and He gave Him authority to execute judgment, because He is *the* Son of Man.

28 "Do not marvel at this; for [r]an hour is coming, in which [r]all who are in the tombs shall hear His voice, John 4:21

29 and shall come forth; [r]those who did the good *deeds* to a resurrection of life, those who committed the evil *deeds* to a resurrection of judgment. Dan. 12:2

30 "I can do nothing on My own initiative. As I hear, I judge; and My judgment is just, because I do not seek My own will, but the will of Him who sent Me.

31 "If I *alone* bear witness of Myself, My testimony is not true.

32 "There is [r]another who bears
witness of Me, and I know that
the testimony which He bears of
Me is true. John 5:37
33 "You have sent to John, and
he has borne witness to the truth.
34 "But [r]the witness which I receive is not from man, but I say
these things that you may be
saved. John 5:32; 1 John 5:9
35 "He was [r]the lamp that was
burning and was shining and you
were willing to rejoice for a while
in his light. 2 Sam. 21:17
36 "But the witness which I have
is greater than *that of* John; for
the works which the Father has
given Me to accomplish, the very
works that I do, bear witness of
Me, that the Father has sent Me.
37 "And the Father who sent Me,
He has borne witness of Me. You
have neither heard His voice at
any time, nor seen His form.
38 "And you do not have His
word abiding in you, for you do
not believe Him whom He sent.
39 "[14]You search the Scriptures,
because you think that in them
you have eternal life; and it is
these that bear witness of Me;
40 and you are unwilling to
come to Me, that you may have
life.
41 "I [r]do not receive glory from
men; John 5:44; 7:18
42 but I know you, that you do
not have the love of God in yourselves.
43 "I have come in My Father's
name, and you do not receive Me;
if another shall come in his own
name, you will receive him.
44 "How can you believe, when
you receive [a]glory from one an-

[14] Or, (a command) *Search the Scriptures!*

other, and you do not seek the glory that is from the *one and* only
God? *honor or fame*
45 "Do not think that I will accuse you before the Father; the
one who accuses you is Moses, in
whom you have set your hope.
46 "For if you believed Moses,
you would believe Me; for [r]he
wrote of Me. Luke 24:27
47 "But [r]if you do not believe his
writings, how will you believe My
words?" Luke 16:29, 31

CHAPTER 6

AFTER these things Jesus went
away to the other side of the Sea
of Galilee (or Tiberias).
2 And a great multitude was
following Him, because they were
seeing the [a]signs which He was
performing on those who were
sick. *attesting miracles*
3 And [r]Jesus went up on the
mountain, and there He sat with
His disciples. Matt. 5:1
4 Now the Passover, the feast
of the Jews, was at hand.
5 Jesus therefore lifting up His
eyes, and seeing that a great multitude was coming to Him, *said
to Philip, "Where are we to buy
bread, that these may eat?"
6 And this He was saying to
test him; for He Himself knew
what He was intending to do.
7 Philip answered Him, "Two
hundred [15]denarii worth of bread
is not sufficient for them, for
everyone to receive a little."
8 One of His [r]disciples, Andrew, Simon Peter's brother,
*said to Him, John 2:2

[15] The denarius was equivalent to one day's
wage

9 "There is a lad here who has
five barley loaves and two [r]fish,
but what are these for so many
people?" John 6:11; 21:9, 10, 13
10 Jesus said, "Have the people
[t]sit down." Now there was [r]much
grass in the place. So the men [t]sat
down, in number about five thousand. *recline(d)* · Mark 6:39
11 Jesus therefore took the
loaves; and having given thanks,
He distributed to those who were
seated; likewise also of the fish as
much as they wanted.
12 And when they were filled,
He *said to His [r]disciples, "Gather
up the leftover fragments that
nothing may be lost." John 2:2
13 And so they gathered them
up, and filled twelve baskets with
fragments from the five barley
loaves, which were left over by
those who had eaten.
14 When therefore the people
saw the [a]sign which He had performed, they said, "This is of a
truth the Prophet who is to come
into the world." *attesting miracle*
15 Jesus therefore perceiving
that they were intending to come
and take Him by force, to make
Him king, withdrew again to the
mountain by Himself alone.
16 Now when evening came,
His [r]disciples went down to the
sea, John 2:2
17 and after getting into a boat,
they *started to* cross the sea [r]to
Capernaum. And it had already
become dark, and Jesus had not
yet come to them. Mark 6:45
18 And the sea *began* to be
stirred up because a strong wind
was blowing.
19 When therefore they had
rowed about three or four miles,
they *beheld Jesus walking on the
sea and drawing near to the boat;
and they were frightened.
20 But He *said to them, "It is I;
[a]do not be afraid." *stop fearing*
21 They were willing therefore
to receive Him into the boat; and
immediately the boat was at the
land to which they were going.
22 The next day [r]the multitude
that stood on the other side of the
sea saw that there was no other
small boat there, except one, and
that Jesus [r]had not entered with
His disciples into the boat, but
that His disciples had gone away
alone. John 6:2 · John 6:15ff.
23 There came other small
boats from Tiberias near to the
place where they ate the bread after the Lord had given thanks.
24 When the multitude therefore saw that Jesus was not there,
nor His disciples, they themselves
got into the small boats, and came
to Capernaum, seeking Jesus.
25 And when they found Him
on the other side of the sea, they
said to Him, "Rabbi,[r] when did
You get here?" Matt. 23:7
26 Jesus answered them and
said, "Truly, truly, I say to you,
you seek Me, not because you saw
signs, but because you ate of the
loaves, and were filled.
27 "Do not work for the food
which perishes, but for the food
which endures to eternal life,
which the Son of Man shall give to
you, for on Him the Father, *even*
God, has set His seal."
28 They said therefore to Him,
"What shall we do, that we may
work the works of God?"
29 Jesus answered and said to
them, "This is the work of God,

that you believe in Him whom He
has sent."
30 They said therefore to Him,
"What then do You do for a sign,
that we may see, and believe You?
What work do You perform?
31 "Our fathers ate the manna in
the wilderness; as it is written, 'HE[r]
GAVE THEM BREAD OUT OF HEAVEN
TO EAT.'" Ps. 78:24; Ex. 16:4, 15
32 Jesus therefore said to them,
"Truly, truly, I say to you, it is not
Moses who has given you the
bread out of heaven, but it is My
Father who gives you the true
bread out of heaven.
33 "For the bread of God is [16]that
which comes down out of heaven,
and gives life to the world."
34 They said therefore to Him,
"Lord, evermore [r]give us this
bread." John 4:15
35 Jesus said to them, "I am the
bread of life; he who comes to Me
shall not hunger, and he who believes in Me shall never thirst.
36 "But [r]I said to you, that you
have seen Me, and yet do not believe. John 6:26
37 "All[r] that the Father gives Me
shall come to Me, and the one
who comes to Me I will certainly
not cast out. John 6:39
38 "For I have come down from
heaven, not to do My own will,
but the will of Him who sent Me.
39 "And this is the will of Him
who sent Me, that of all that He
has given Me I lose nothing, but
raise it up on the last day.
40 "For this is the will of My Father, that everyone who beholds
the Son and believes in Him, may
have eternal life; and I Myself will
raise him up on the last day."

[16]Or, *He who comes*

41 The Jews therefore were
grumbling about Him, because He
said, "I am the bread that came
down out of heaven."
42 And they were saying, "Is
not this Jesus, the son of Joseph,
whose father and mother we
know? How does He now say, 'I
have come down out of heaven'?"
43 Jesus answered and said to
them, "Do not grumble among
yourselves.
44 "No one can come to Me, unless the Father who sent Me
[r]draws him; and I will raise him up
on the last day. Jer. 31:3
45 "It is written [r]in the prophets,
'AND THEY SHALL ALL BE TAUGHT
OF GOD.' Everyone who has heard
and learned from the Father,
comes to Me. Acts 7:42
46 "Not that any man has seen
the Father, except the One who is
from God; He has seen the Father.
47 "Truly, truly, I say to you, he
who believes has eternal life.
48 "I am the bread of life.
49 "Your fathers ate the manna
in the wilderness, and they died.
50 "This is the bread which
comes down out of heaven, so
that one may eat of it and not die.
51 "I am the living bread that
[r]came down out of heaven; if anyone eats of this bread, he shall live
forever; and the bread also which
I shall give for the life of the world
is My flesh." John 6:41
52 The Jews therefore [r]*began* to
argue with one another, saying,
"How can this man give us *His*
flesh to eat?" John 9:16; 10:19
53 Jesus therefore said to them,
"Truly, truly, I say to you, unless
you eat the flesh of the Son of

Man and drink His blood, you
have no life in yourselves.
54 "He who eats My flesh and
drinks My blood has eternal life,
and I will raise him up on the last
day. John 6:39
55 "For My flesh is true food, and
My blood is true drink.
56 "He who eats My flesh and
drinks My blood abides in Me, and
I in him. John 15:4f.; 17:23
57 "As the living Father sent Me,
and I live because of the Father,
so he who eats Me, he also shall
live because of Me.
58 "This is the bread which came
down out of heaven; not as the fathers ate, and died, he who eats
this bread shall live forever."
59 These things He said in the
synagogue, as He taught in Capernaum. Matt. 4:23 • John 6:24
60 Many therefore of His disciples, when they heard *this* said,
"This is a difficult statement; who
can listen to it?" John 2:2; 6:66; 7:3
61 But Jesus, conscious that His
disciples grumbled at this, said to
them, "Does this cause you to
stumble? John 6:64
62 "*What* then if you should behold the Son of Man ascending
where He was before?
63 "It is the Spirit who gives life;
the flesh profits nothing; the
words that I have spoken to you
are spirit and are life.
64 "But there are some of you
who do not believe." For Jesus
knew from the beginning who
they were who did not believe,
and who it was that would betray
Him. *deliver Him up*
65 And He was saying, "For this
reason I have said to you, that no
one can come to Me, unless it has
been granted him from the Father." John 6:37, 44
66 As a result of this many of
His disciples withdrew, and were
not walking with Him anymore.
67 Jesus said therefore to the
twelve, "You do not want to go
away also, do you?"
68 Simon Peter answered Him,
"Lord, to whom shall we go? You
have words of eternal life.
69 "And we have believed and
have come to know that You are
the Holy One of God."
70 Jesus answered them, "Did I
Myself not choose you, the
twelve, and *yet* one of you is a
devil?" John 15:16, 19 • Matt. 10:2
71 Now He meant Judas *the son*
of Simon Iscariot, for he, one of
the twelve, was going to betray
Him. *was intending to*

CHAPTER 7

AND after these things Jesus was
walking in Galilee; for He was unwilling to walk in Judea, because
the Jews were seeking to kill Him.
2 Now the feast of the Jews,
the Feast of Booths, was at hand.
3 His brothers therefore said to
Him, "Depart from here, and go
into Judea, that Your disciples
also may behold Your works
which You are doing.
4 "For no one does anything in
secret, when he himself seeks to
be *known* publicly. If You do
these things, show Yourself to the
world." *and*
5 For not even His brothers
were believing in Him.
6 Jesus therefore *said to
them, "My time is not yet at hand,

but your time is always opportune.

7 "The world cannot hate you; but it hates Me because I testify of it, that its deeds are evil.

8 "Go up to the feast yourselves; I do not go up to this feast because [r]My time has not yet fully come." John 7:6

9 And having said these things to them, He stayed in Galilee.

10 But when His brothers had gone up to the feast, then He Himself also went up, not publicly, but as it were, in secret.

11 The Jews therefore were seeking Him at the feast, and were saying, "Where is He?"

12 And there was much grumbling among the multitudes concerning Him; some were saying, "He is a good man"; others were saying, "No, on the contrary, He leads the multitude astray."

13 Yet no one was speaking openly of Him for [r]fear of the Jews. John 9:22; 12:42; 19:38

14 But when it was now the midst of the feast Jesus went up into the temple, and *began to* [r]teach. Matt. 26:55; John 7:28

15 [r]The Jews therefore were marveling, saying, "How has this man become learned, having never been educated?" John 1:19

16 Jesus therefore answered them, and said, "My teaching is not Mine, but His who sent Me.

17 "If any man is willing to do His will, he shall know of the teaching, whether it is of God, or *whether* I speak from Myself.

18 "He who speaks from himself seeks his own glory; but He who is seeking the glory of the one who sent Him, He is true, and there is no unrighteousness in Him.

19 "Did [r]not Moses give you the law, and *yet* none of you carries out the law? Why do you seek to kill Me?" John 1:17

20 The multitude answered, "You [a]have a demon! Who seeks to kill You?" *are demented*

21 Jesus answered and said to them, "I did [r]one [a]deed, and you all marvel. John 5:2-9 • *work*

22 "On this account Moses has given you circumcision (not because it is from Moses, but from the fathers), and on *the* Sabbath you circumcise a man.

23 "If [r] a man receives circumcision on *the* Sabbath that the Law of Moses may not be broken, are you angry with Me because I made an entire man well on *the* Sabbath? Matt. 12:2; John 5:9, 10

24 "Do not [r]judge according to appearance, but judge with righteous judgment." Lev. 19:15

25 Therefore some of the people of Jerusalem were saying, "Is this not the man whom they are seeking to kill?

26 "And look, He is speaking publicly, and they are saying nothing to Him. [r]The rulers do not really know that this is the Christ, do they? Luke 23:13; John 3:1

27 "However, we know where this man is from; but whenever the Christ may come, no one knows where He is from."

28 Jesus therefore cried out in the temple, [r]teaching and saying, "You [r] both know Me and know where I am from; and I have not come of Myself, but He who sent Me is true, whom you do not know. John 7:14 • John 6:42

29 "I know Him; because I am
from Him, and He sent Me."
30 They [r]were seeking therefore
to seize Him; and no man laid his
hand on Him, because His hour
had not yet come. Matt. 21:46
31 But many of the multitude
believed in Him; and they were
saying, "When the Christ shall
come, He will not perform more
[a]signs than those which this man
has, will He?" *attesting miracles*
32 The Pharisees heard the multitude muttering these things
about Him; and the chief priests
and the Pharisees sent [r]officers to
seize Him. Matt. 26:58; John 7:45f.
33 Jesus therefore said, "For a
little while longer I am with you,
then I go to Him who sent Me.
34 "You [r]shall seek Me, and shall
not find Me; and where I am, you
cannot come." John 7:36; 8:21
35 [r]The Jews therefore said to
one another, "Where [r] does this
man intend to go that we shall not
find Him? He is not intending to
go to the Dispersion among the
Greeks, and teach the Greeks, is
He? John 7:1 • John 8:22
36 "What is this statement that
He said, 'You [r] will seek Me, and
will not find Me; and where I am,
you cannot come'?" John 7:34
37 Now on [r]the last day, the
great *day* of the feast, Jesus stood
and cried out, saying, "If any man
is thirsty, let him come to Me and
drink. Lev. 23:36; Num. 29:35
38 "He who believes in Me, as
the Scripture said, 'From [t]his innermost being shall flow rivers of
living water.'" *out of his belly*
39 But this He spoke of the
Spirit, whom those who believed
in Him were to receive; for the
Spirit was not yet *given,* because
Jesus was not yet glorified.
40 *Some* of the multitude therefore, when they heard these
words, were saying, "This certainly is the Prophet."
41 Others were saying, "This is
the Christ." Still others were saying, "Surely the Christ is not
going to come from Galilee, is He?
42 "Has not the Scripture said
that the Christ comes from [r]the
offspring of David, and from Bethlehem, the village where David
was?" Ps. 89:4; Mic. 5:2
43 So there arose a division in
the multitude because of Him.
44 And [r]some of them wanted to
seize Him, but no one laid hands
on Him. John 7:30
45 The [r]officers therefore came
to the chief priests and Pharisees,
and they said to them, "Why did
you not bring Him?" John 7:32
46 The [r]officers answered, "Never did a man speak the way this
man speaks." John 7:32
47 The Pharisees therefore answered them, "You have not also
been led astray, have you?
48 "No one of the rulers or Pharisees has believed in Him, has he?
49 "But this multitude which
does not know the Law is accursed."
50 [r]Nicodemus *said to them (he
who came to Him before, being
one of them), John 3:1
51 "Our [r] Law does not judge a
man, unless it first hears from him
and knows what he is doing, does
it?" Ex. 23:1; Deut. 17:6; 19:15
52 They answered and said to
him, "You are not also from Galilee, are you? Search, and see that

no prophet arises out of Galilee."
53 [[17]And everyone went to his
home.

CHAPTER 8

BUT Jesus went to[r]the Mount of
Olives. Matt. 21:1
2 And early in the morning He
came again into the temple, and
all the people were coming to
Him; and[r]He sat down and *began*
to teach them. Matt. 26:55
3 And the scribes and the
Pharisees *brought a woman
caught in adultery, and having set
her in the midst,
4 they *said to Him, "Teacher,
this woman has been caught in
adultery, in the very act.
5 "Now in the Law Moses commanded us to stone such women;
what then do You say?"
6 And they were saying this,
[r]testing Him, in order that they
might have grounds for accusing
Him. But Jesus stooped down, and
with His finger wrote on the
ground. Matt. 16:1; 19:3; 22:18, 35
7 But when they persisted in
asking Him, He straightened up,
and said to them, "He who is
without sin among you, let him *be
the* first to throw a stone at her."
8 And again He stooped down,
and wrote on the ground.
9 And when they heard it, they
began to go out one by one, beginning with the older ones, and He
was left alone, and the woman,
where she had been, in the midst.
10 And straightening up, Jesus
said to her, "Woman, where are
they? Did no one condemn you?"
11 And she said, "No one,
Lord." And Jesus said, "Neither
do I condemn you; go your way.
From now on sin no more."]
12 Again therefore Jesus spoke
to them, saying, "I am the light of
the world; he who follows Me
shall not walk in the darkness, but
shall have the light of life."
13 The Pharisees therefore said
to Him, "You[r]are bearing witness
of Yourself; Your witness is not
[a]true." John 5:31 • *valid*
14 Jesus answered and said to
them, "Even if I bear witness of
Myself, My witness is true; for I
know[r]where I came from, and
where I am going; but you do not
know where I come from, or
where I am going. John 8:42
15 "You[r] people judge according
to the flesh; I am not judging anyone. 1 Sam. 16:7; John 7:24
16 "But even if I do judge, My
judgment is true; for I am not
alone *in it,* but I and [18]He who sent
Me.
17 "Even in[r]your law it has been
written, that the testimony of two
men is true. Deut. 17:6; 19:15
18 "I am He who bears witness
of Myself, and the Father who
sent Me bears witness of Me."
19 And so they were saying to
Him, "Where is Your Father?"
Jesus answered, "You know neither Me, nor My Father; [r]if you
knew Me, you would know My
Father also." John 7:28
20 These words He spoke in the
treasury, as He taught in the temple; and no one seized Him, be-

[17]John 7:53–8:11 is not found in most of the old mss.

[18]Many ancient mss. read *the Father who sent Me*

cause His hour had not yet come.
21 He said therefore again to
them, "I go away, and [r]you shall
seek Me, and [r]shall die in your sin;
where I am going, you cannot
come." John 7:34 • John 8:24
22 Therefore [r]the Jews were saying, "Surely He will not kill Himself, will He, since He says,
'Where I am going, you cannot
come'?" John 1:19; 8:48, 52, 57
23 And He was saying to them,
"You [r]are from below, I am from
above; you are of this world, I am
not of this world. John 3:31
24 "I said therefore to you, that
you shall die in your sins; for unless you believe that I am *He,* you
shall die in your sins."
25 And so they were saying to
Him, "Who are You?" Jesus said
to them, "What have I been saying to you *from* the beginning?
26 "I have many things to speak
and to judge concerning you, but
He who sent Me is true; and the
things which I heard from Him,
these I speak to the world."
27 They did not realize that He
had been speaking to them about
the Father.
28 Jesus therefore said, "When
you lift up the Son of Man, then
you will know that [t]I am *He,* and I
do nothing on My own initiative,
but I speak these things as the Father taught Me. *I AM*
29 "And He who sent Me is with
Me; He [a]has not left Me alone, for I
always do the things that are
pleasing to Him." *did not leave*
30 As He spoke these things,
many came to believe in Him.
31 Jesus therefore was saying
to those Jews who had believed
Him, "If [r]you abide in My word,
then you are truly disciples of
Mine; John 15:7; 2 John 9
32 and [r]you shall know the truth,
and [r]the truth shall make you
free." John 1:14, 17 • John 8:36
33 They answered Him, "We
are Abraham's offspring, and
have never yet been enslaved to
anyone; how is it that You say,
'You shall become free'?"
34 Jesus answered them,
"Truly, truly, I say to you, [r]every-
one who commits sin is the slave
of sin. Rom. 6:16; 2 Pet. 2:19
35 "And the slave does not remain in the house forever; the son
does remain forever.
36 "If therefore the Son [r]shall
make you free, you shall be free
indeed. John 8:32
37 "I know that you are Abraham's offspring; yet you seek to
kill Me, because My word [a]has no
place in you. *makes no progress*
38 "I speak the things which I
have seen with *My* Father; therefore you also do the things which
you heard from *your* father."
39 They answered and said to
Him, "Abraham is [r]our father."
Jesus *said to them, "If you are
Abraham's children, do the deeds
of Abraham. Matt. 3:9
40 "But as it is, you are seeking
to kill Me, a man who has told you
the truth, which I heard from God;
this Abraham did not do.
41 "You are doing the deeds of
your father." They said to Him,
"We were not born of fornication;
we have one Father, *even* God."
42 Jesus said to them, "If God
were your Father, you would love
Me; for I proceeded forth and
have come from God, for I have

not even come on My own initiative, but He sent Me.
43 "Why do you not understand
what I am saying? *It is* because
you cannot hear My word.
44 "You are of *your* father the
devil, and you want to do the desires of your father. He was a
murderer from the beginning, and
does not stand in the truth, because there is no truth in him.
Whenever he speaks a lie, he
speaks from his own *nature;* for
he is a liar, and the father of lies.
45 "But because I speak the
truth, you do not believe Me.
46 "Which one of you convicts
Me of sin? If I speak truth, why do
you not believe Me?
47 "He[r] who is of God hears the
words of God; for this reason you
do not hear *them,* because you are
not of God." 1 John 4:6
48 The Jews answered and said
to Him, "Do we not say rightly
that You are a [r]Samaritan and
have a demon?" Matt. 10:5
49 Jesus answered, "I do not
have a demon; but I honor My Father, and you dishonor Me.
50 "But [r]I do not seek My glory;
there is One who seeks and
judges. John 5:41; 8:54
51 "Truly, truly, I say to you, if
anyone [r]keeps My word he shall
never see death." John 8:55
52 The Jews said to Him, "Now
we know that You[r]have a demon.
Abraham died, and the prophets
also; and You say, 'If anyone
keeps My word, he shall never
taste of death.' John 7:20
53 "Surely You [r]are not greater
than our father Abraham, who
died? The prophets died too;
whom do You make Yourself out
to be?" John 4:12
54 Jesus answered, "If I glorify
Myself, My glory is nothing; it is
My Father who glorifies Me, of
whom you say, 'He is our God';
55 and you have not come to
know Him, but I know Him; and if
I say that I do not know Him, I
shall be a liar like you, but I do
know Him, and keep His word.
56 "Your[r] father Abraham rejoiced to see My day, and he saw
it and was glad." John 8:37, 39
57 [r]The Jews therefore said to
Him, "You are not yet fifty years
old, and have You seen Abraham?" John 1:19
58 Jesus said to them, "Truly,
truly, I say to you, before Abraham was born, I am."
59 Therefore they picked up
stones to throw at Him; but Jesus
[t]hid Himself, and went out of the
temple. *was hidden*

CHAPTER 9

AND as He passed by, He saw a
man blind from birth.
2 And His disciples asked Him,
saying, "Rabbi,[r] who sinned, this
man or his parents, that he should
be born blind?" Matt. 23:7
3 Jesus answered, "*It was* neither *that* this man sinned, nor his
parents; but *it was* in order [r]that
the works of God might be displayed in him. John 11:4
4 "We must work the works of
Him who sent Me, [r]as long as it is
day; night is coming, when no
man can work. John 7:33
5 "While I am in the world, I am
the light of the world."

6 When He had said this, He
[r]spat on the ground, and made clay
of the spittle, and applied the clay
to his eyes, Mark 7:33
7 and said to him, "Go, wash in
[r]the pool of Siloam" (which is
translated, Sent). And so he went
away and washed, and came *back*
seeing. Neh. 3:15; Is. 8:6
8 The neighbors therefore, and
those who previously saw him as
a beggar, were saying, "Is not this
the one who used to sit and beg?"
9 Others were saying, "This is
he," *still* others were saying, "No,
but he is like him." He kept saying, "I am the one."
10 Therefore they were saying
to him, "How then were your eyes
opened?"
11 He answered, "The man who
is called Jesus made clay, and
anointed my eyes, and said to me,
'Go to Siloam, and wash'; so I
went away and washed, and I received sight."
12 And they said to him,
"Where is He?" He *said, "I do
not know."
13 They *brought to the Pharisees him who was formerly blind.
14 Now it was a Sabbath on the
day when Jesus made the clay,
and opened his eyes.
15 Again, therefore, the Pharisees also were asking him how he
received his sight. And he said to
them, "He applied clay to my
eyes, and I washed, and I see."
16 Therefore some of the Pharisees were saying, "This man is not
from God, because He does not
keep the Sabbath." But others
were saying, "How can a man
who is a sinner perform such
signs?" And there was a division
among them.
17 They *said therefore to the
blind man [r]again, "What do you
say about Him, since He opened
your eyes?" And he said, "He is a
prophet." John 9:15
18 The Jews therefore did not
believe *it* of him, that he had been
blind, and had received sight, until
they called the parents of the very
one who had received his sight,
19 and questioned them, saying,
"Is this your son, who you say
was born blind? Then how does he
now see?"
20 His parents answered them
and said, "We know that this is
our son, and that he was born
blind;
21 but how he now sees, we do
not know; or who opened his eyes,
we do not know. Ask him; he is of
age, he shall speak for himself."
22 His parents said this because
they [r]were afraid of the Jews; for
the Jews had already agreed, that
if anyone should confess Him to
be Christ, he should be put out of
the synagogue. John 7:13
23 For this reason his parents
said, "He is of age; ask him."
24 So a second time they called
the man who had been blind, and
said to him, "Give[r] glory to God;
we know that this man is a sinner." Josh. 7:19; Ezra 10:11
25 He therefore answered,
"Whether He is a sinner, I do not
know; one thing I do know, that,
whereas I was blind, now I see."
26 They said therefore to him,
"What did He do to you? How did
He open your eyes?"
27 He answered them, "I told
you already, and you did not lis-

ten; why do you want to hear *it* again? You do not want to become His disciples too, do you?"

28 And they reviled him, and said, "You are His disciple, but we are disciples of Moses.

29 "We know that God has spoken to Moses; but as for this man, [r]we do not know where He is from." John 8:14

30 The man answered and said to them, "Well, here is an amazing thing, that you do not know where He is from, and *yet* He opened my eyes.

31 "We know that [r]God does not hear sinners; but if anyone is God-fearing, and does His will, He hears him. Job 27:8f.; 35:13

32 "Since[t] the beginning of time it has never been heard that anyone opened the eyes of a person born blind. *From antiquity it was not heard*

33 "If this man were not from God, He could do nothing."

34 They answered and said to him, "You were born entirely in sins, and are you teaching us?" And they put him out.

35 Jesus heard that they had [r]put him out; and finding him, He said, "Do you believe in the Son of Man?" John 9:22, 34

36 He answered and said, "And [r]who is He, [a]Lord, that I may believe in Him?" Rom. 10:14 • *Sir*

37 Jesus said to him, "You have both seen Him, and He is the one who is talking with you."

38 And he said, "Lord, I believe." And he worshiped Him.

39 And Jesus said, "For[r] judgment I came into this world, that those who do not see may see; and that those who see may become blind." John 3:19; 5:22, 27

40 Those of the Pharisees who were with Him heard these things, and said to Him, "We[r] are not blind too, are we?" Rom. 2:19

41 Jesus said to them, "If[r] you were blind, you would have no sin; but since you say, 'We see,' your sin remains. John 15:22, 24

CHAPTER 10

"TRULY, truly, I say to you, he who does not enter by the door into the fold of the sheep, but climbs up some other way, he is [r]a thief and a robber. John 10:8

2 "But he who enters by the door is a shepherd of the sheep.

3 "To him the doorkeeper opens, and the sheep hear his voice, and he calls his own sheep by name, and leads them out.

4 "When he puts forth all his own, he goes before them, and the sheep follow him because they know [r]his voice. John 10:5, 16, 27

5 "And a stranger they simply will not follow, but will flee from him, because they do not know the voice of strangers."

6 This [r]figure of speech Jesus spoke to them, but they did not understand what those things were which He had been saying to them. John 16:25, 29; 2 Pet. 2:22

7 Jesus therefore said to them again, "Truly, truly, I say to you, I am the door of the sheep.

8 "All who came before Me are [r]thieves and robbers, but the sheep did not hear them. Jer. 23:1f.

9 "I[r] am the door; if anyone enters through Me, he shall be saved, and shall go in and out, and find pasture. John 10:1f., 9

10 "The thief comes only to steal, and kill, and destroy; I came that they might have life, and might have *it* abundantly.

11 "I am the good shepherd; the good shepherd lays down His life for the sheep. John 10:15, 17, 18

12 "He who is a hireling, and not a shepherd, who is not the owner of the sheep, beholds the wolf coming, and leaves the sheep, and flees, and the wolf snatches them, and scatters *them*. John 10:2

13 "*He flees* because he is a hireling, and is not concerned about the sheep.

14 "I am the good shepherd; and I know My own, and My own know Me, John 10:27

15 even as the Father knows Me and I know the Father; and I lay down My life for the sheep.

16 "And I have other sheep, which are not of this fold; I must bring them also, and they shall hear My voice; and they shall become one flock *with* one shepherd. Is. 56:8 • John 11:52; 17:20f.

17 "For this reason the Father loves Me, because I lay down My life that I may take it again.

18 "No one [19]has taken it away from Me, but I lay it down on My own initiative. I have authority to lay it down, and I have authority to take it up again. This commandment I received from My Father." John 10:11, 15, 17

19 There arose a division again among the Jews because of these words. John 7:43; 9:16

20 And many of them were saying, "He has a demon and is insane. Why do you listen to Him?"

21 Others were saying, "These are not the sayings of one demon-possessed. A demon cannot open the eyes of the blind, can he?"

22 At that time the Feast of the Dedication took place at Jerusalem;

23 it was winter, and Jesus was walking in the temple in the portico of Solomon. Acts 3:11; 5:12

24 The Jews therefore gathered around Him, and were saying to Him, "How long will You keep us in suspense? If You are the Christ, tell us plainly." John 1:19

25 Jesus answered them, "I told you, and you do not believe; the works that I do in My Father's name, these bear witness of Me.

26 "But you do not believe, because you are not of My sheep.

27 "My sheep hear My voice, and I know them, and they follow Me;

28 and I give eternal life to them, and they shall never perish; and no one shall snatch them out of My hand. John 17:2f.

29 "[20]My Father, who has given *them* to Me, is greater than all; and no one is able to snatch *them* out of the Father's hand.

30 "I and the Father are one."

31 The Jews took up stones again to stone Him.

32 Jesus answered them, "I showed you many good works from the Father; for which of them are you stoning Me?"

33 The Jews answered Him, "For a good work we do not stone You, but for blasphemy; and because You, being a man, make Yourself out *to be* God."

[19] Many Gr. mss. read *takes*

[20] Some early mss. read *What My Father has given Me is greater than all*

34 Jesus answered them, "Has
it not been written in your Law, 'I
SAID, YOU ARE GODS'?
35 "If he called them gods, to
whom the word of God came (and
the Scripture cannot be broken),
36 do you say of Him, whom the
Father [r]sanctified and sent into the
world, 'You are blaspheming,' because I said, 'I am the Son of
God'? Jer. 1:5; John 6:69
37 "If I do not do the works of
My Father, do not believe Me;
38 but if I do them, though you
do not believe Me, believe the
works, that you may know and
understand that the Father is in
Me, and I in the Father."
39 Therefore [r]they were seeking
again to seize Him, and He eluded
their grasp. John 7:30
40 And He went away again beyond the Jordan to the place
where John was first baptizing,
and He was staying there.
41 And many came to Him and
were saying, "While John performed no [r]sign, yet [r]everything
John said about this man was
true." John 2:11 • John 1:27
42 And [r]many believed in Him
there. John 7:31

CHAPTER 11

NOW a certain man was sick,
Lazarus of Bethany, the village of
Mary and her sister Martha.
2 And it was the Mary who
anointed the Lord with ointment,
and wiped His feet with her hair,
whose brother Lazarus was sick.
3 The sisters therefore sent to
Him, saying, "Lord, behold, he
whom You love is sick."
4 But when Jesus heard it, He
said, "This sickness is not unto
death, but for [r]the glory of God,
that the Son of God may be glorified by it." John 9:3; 10:38; 11:40
5 Now Jesus loved Martha,
and her sister, and Lazarus.
6 When therefore He heard
that he was sick, He stayed then
two days *longer* in the place
where He was.
7 Then after this He *said to
the disciples, "Let us go to Judea
again."
8 The disciples *said to Him,
"Rabbi, the Jews were just now
seeking to stone You, and are You
going there again?"
9 Jesus answered, "Are there
not twelve hours in the day? If
anyone walks in the day, he does
not stumble, because he sees the
light of this world.
10 "But if anyone walks in the
night, he stumbles, because the
light is not in him."
11 This He said, and after that
He *said to them, "Our [r]friend
Lazarus [r]has fallen asleep; but I go,
that I may awaken him out of
sleep." John 11:3 • Matt. 27:52
12 The disciples therefore said
to Him, "Lord, if he has fallen
asleep, he will recover."
13 Now Jesus had spoken of his
death, but they thought that He
was speaking of literal sleep.
14 Then Jesus therefore said to
them plainly, "Lazarus is dead,
15 and I am glad for your sakes
that I was not there, so that you
may believe; but let us go to him."
16 Thomas therefore, who is
called Didymus, said to *his* fellow
disciples, "Let us also go, that we
may die with Him."

17 So when Jesus came, He
found that he had already been in
the tomb four days. John 11:39
18 Now Bethany was near Jerusalem, about two miles off;
19 and many of the Jews had
come to Martha and Mary, to console them concerning *their*
brother. John 1:19; 11:8
20 Martha therefore, when she
heard that Jesus was coming,
went to meet Him; but Mary still
sat in the house. Luke 10:38-42
21 Martha therefore said to
Jesus, "Lord, if You had been
here, my brother would not have
died. John 11:2 • John 11:32, 37
22 "Even now I know that whatever You ask of God, God will
give You." John 9:31; 11:41f.
23 Jesus *said to her, "Your
brother shall rise again."
24 Martha *said to Him, "I
know that he will rise again in the
resurrection on the last day."
25 Jesus said to her, "I am the
resurrection and the life; he who
believes in Me shall live even if he
dies, John 1:4; 5:26; 6:39f.
26 and everyone who lives and
believes in Me shall never die. Do
you believe this?" John 6:47, 50, 51
27 She *said to Him, "Yes,
Lord; I have believed that You are
the Christ, the Son of God, *even*
He who comes into the world."
28 And when she had said this,
she went away, and called Mary
her sister, saying secretly, "The
Teacher is here, and is calling for
you." John 11:30 • Matt. 26:18
29 And when she heard it, she
*arose quickly, and was coming to
Him.
30 Now Jesus had not yet come
into the village, but was still in the
place where Martha met Him.
31 The Jews then who were
with her in the house, and consoling her, when they saw that Mary
rose up quickly and went out, followed her, supposing that she was
going to the tomb to weep there.
32 Therefore, when Mary came
where Jesus was, she saw Him,
and fell at His feet, saying to Him,
"Lord, if You had been here, my
brother would not have died."
33 When Jesus therefore saw
her weeping, and the Jews who
came with her, *also* weeping, He
was deeply moved in spirit, and
was troubled, *wailing*
34 and said, "Where have you
laid him?" They *said to Him,
"Lord, come and see."
35 Jesus wept. Luke 19:41
36 And so the Jews were saying,
"Behold how He loved him!"
37 But some of them said,
"Could not this man, who opened
the eyes of him who was blind,
have kept this man also from
dying?" John 9:7
38 Jesus therefore again being
deeply moved within, *came to
the tomb. Now it was a cave, and
a stone was lying against it.
39 Jesus *said, "Remove the
stone." Martha, the sister of the
deceased, *said to Him, "Lord, by
this time there will be a stench,
for he has been *dead* four days."
40 Jesus *said to her, "Did I not
say to you, if you believe, you will
see the glory of God?"
41 And so they removed the
stone. And Jesus raised His eyes,
and said, "Father, I thank Thee
that Thou heardest Me.

42 "And I knew that Thou hearest Me always; but [r]because of the people standing around I said it, that they may believe that Thou didst send Me." John 12:30

43 And when He had said these things, He cried out with a loud voice, "Lazarus, come forth."

44 He who had died came forth, [r]bound hand and foot with wrappings; and [r]his face was wrapped around with a cloth. Jesus *said to them, "Unbind him, and let him go." John 19:40 • John 20:7

45 [r]Many therefore of the Jews, [r]who had come to Mary and beheld what He had done, believed in Him. John 7:31 • John 11:19

46 But some of them went away to the Pharisees, and told them the things which Jesus had done.

47 Therefore the chief priests and the Pharisees convened a council, and were saying, "What are we doing? For this man is performing many signs.

48 "If we let Him *go on* like this, all men will believe in Him, and the Romans will come and take away both our [r]place and our nation." Matt. 24:15

49 But a certain one of them, Caiaphas, who was high priest that year, said to them, "You know nothing at all,

50 nor do you take into account that [r]it is expedient for you that one man should die for the people, and that the whole nation should not perish." John 18:14

51 Now this he did not say [t]on his own initiative; but being high priest that year, he prophesied that Jesus was going to die for the nation, *from himself*

52 and not for the nation only, but that He might also gather together into one the children of God who are scattered abroad.

53 So from that day on they planned together to kill Him.

54 Jesus therefore [r]no longer continued to walk publicly among the Jews, but went away from there to the country near the wilderness, into a city called Ephraim; and there He stayed with the disciples. John 7:1

55 Now [r]the Passover of the Jews was at hand, and many went up to Jerusalem out of the country before the Passover, to purify themselves. Matt. 26:1f.

56 Therefore they were seeking for Jesus, and were saying to one another, as they stood in the temple, "What do you think; that He will not come to the feast at all?"

57 Now the chief priests and the Pharisees had given orders that if anyone knew where He was, he should report it, that they might seize Him.

CHAPTER 12

JESUS, therefore, six days before the Passover, came to Bethany where Lazarus was, whom Jesus had raised from the dead.

2 So they made Him a supper there, and Martha was serving; but Lazarus was one of those reclining *at the table* with Him.

3 Mary therefore took a pound of very costly perfume of pure nard, and anointed the feet of Jesus, and wiped His feet with her hair; and the house was filled with the fragrance of the perfume.

4 But [r]Judas Iscariot, one of His
disciples, who was intending to
betray Him, *said, John 6:71
5 "Why was this perfume not
sold for [21]three hundred denarii,
and given to poor *people*?"
6 Now he said this, not because he was concerned about the
poor, but because he was a thief,
and as he had the money box, he
used to pilfer what was put into it.
7 Jesus therefore said, "Let her
alone, in order that she may keep
[22]it for the day of My burial.
8 "For[r] the poor you always
have with you, but you do not always have Me." Deut. 15:11
9 The great multitude therefore of the Jews learned that He
was there; and they came, not for
Jesus' sake only, but that they
might also see Lazarus, whom He
raised from the dead.
10 But the chief priests took
counsel that they might put Lazarus to death also;
11 because on account of him
many of the Jews were going
away, and were believing in Jesus.
12 On the next day the great
multitude who had come to the
feast, when they heard that Jesus
was coming to Jerusalem,
13 took the branches of the
palm trees, and went out to meet
Him, and *began* to cry out, [r]"Hosanna! BLESSED IS HE WHO COMES
IN THE NAME OF THE LORD, even
the King of Israel." Ps. 118:26
14 And Jesus, finding a young
donkey, sat on it; as it is written,
15 "FEAR NOT, DAUGHTER OF
ZION; BEHOLD, YOUR KING IS COM-
ING, SEATED ON A DONKEY'S COLT."

[21] Equivalent to 11 months' wages
[22] I.e., The custom of anointing for burial

16 These things His disciples
did not understand at the first; but
when Jesus [r]was glorified, then
they remembered that these
things were written of Him, and
that they had done these things to
Him. John 7:39; 12:23
17 And so the multitude who
were with Him when He called
Lazarus out of the tomb, and
raised him from the dead, were
bearing Him witness.
18 For this cause also the multitude went and met Him, because
they heard that He had performed
this [a]sign. *attesting miracle*
19 The Pharisees therefore said
to one another, "You see that you
are not doing any good; look, the
world has gone after Him."
20 Now there were certain
Greeks among those who were
going up to worship at the feast;
21 these therefore came to
[r]Philip, who was from [r]Bethsaida of
Galilee, and *began to* ask him,
saying, "Sir, we wish to see
Jesus." John 1:44 • Matt. 11:21
22 Philip *came and *told Andrew; Andrew and Philip *came,
and they *told Jesus.
23 And Jesus *answered them,
saying, "The hour has come for
the Son of Man to be glorified.
24 "Truly, truly, I say to you, [r]un-
less a grain of wheat falls into the
earth and dies, it remains by itself
alone; but if it dies, it bears much
fruit. Rom. 14:9; 1 Cor. 15:36
25 "He who loves his life loses it;
and he who hates his life in this
world shall keep it to life eternal.
26 "If anyone serves Me, let him
follow Me; and [r]where I am, there
shall My servant also be; if anyone

serves Me, the Father will honor
him. John 14:3; 17:24
27 "Now My soul has become
troubled; and what shall I say, 'Father'^r, save Me from ^r this hour'? But
for this purpose I came to this
hour. Matt. 11:25 • John 12:23
28 "Father, glorify Thy name."
There came therefore a voice out
of heaven: "I have both glorified
it, and will glorify it again."
29 The multitude therefore, who
stood by and heard it, were saying
that it had thundered; others were
saying, "An^r angel has spoken to
Him." Acts 23:9
30 Jesus answered and said,
"This voice has not come for My
sake, but for your sakes.
31 "Now judgment is upon this
world; now ^r the ruler of this world
shall be cast out. John 14:30
32 'And I, if I ^r be lifted up from
the earth, will draw all men to
Myself." John 3:14; 8:28
33 But He was saying this ^r to indicate the kind of death by which
He was to die. John 18:32; 21:19
34 The multitude therefore answered Him, "We have heard out
of ^r the Law that ^r the Christ is to remain forever; and how can You
say, 'The Son of Man must be
lifted up'? Who is this Son of
Man?" John 10:34 • Ps. 110:4
35 Jesus therefore said to them,
"For ^r a little while longer the light
is among you. Walk while you
have the light, that darkness may
not overtake you; he who walks in
the darkness does not know
where he goes. John 7:33
36 "While you have the light, ^r believe in the light, in order that you
may become sons of light."

These things Jesus spoke, and
He departed and ^t hid Himself from
them. John 12:46 • *was hidden*
37 But though He had performed so many ^a signs before
them, *yet* they were not believing
in Him; *attesting miracles*
38 that the word of Isaiah the
prophet might be fulfilled, which
he spoke, "LORD^r, WHO HAS BELIEVED OUR REPORT? AND TO
WHOM HAS THE ARM OF THE LORD
BEEN REVEALED?" Is. 53:1
39 For this cause they could not
believe, for Isaiah said again,
40 "HE HAS BLINDED THEIR EYES,
AND HE HARDENED THEIR HEART;
LEST THEY SEE WITH THEIR EYES,
AND PERCEIVE WITH THEIR HEART,
AND ^t BE CONVERTED, AND I HEAL
THEM." *should be turned*
41 These things Isaiah said, because ^r he saw His glory, and he
spoke of Him. Is. 6:1ff.
42 Nevertheless ^r many even of
the rulers believed in Him, but because of the Pharisees they were
not confessing *Him*, lest they
should be put out of the synagogue; John 7:48; 12:11
43 ^r for they loved the approval
of men rather than the approval of
God. John 5:41, 44
44 And Jesus cried out and said,
"He^r who believes in Me does not
believe in Me, but in Him who
sent Me. Matt. 10:40; John 5:24
45 "And he who beholds Me beholds the One who sent Me.
46 "I^r have come *as* light into the
world, that everyone who believes
in Me may not remain in darkness. John 1:4; 3:19; 8:12; 9:5; 12:35f.
47 "And if anyone hears My sayings, and does not keep them, I do
not judge him; for ^r I did not come

to judge the world, but to save the
world. John 3:17; 8:15f.
48 "He who rejects Me, and does
not receive My sayings, has one
who judges him;[r]the word I spoke
is what will judge him at the last
day. Deut. 18:18f.; John 5:45ff.; 8:47
49 "For I did not speak on My
own initiative, but the Father
Himself who sent Me has given
Me commandment, what to say,
and what to speak.
50 "And I know that His commandment is eternal life; therefore the things I speak, I speak
just as the Father has told Me."

CHAPTER 13

NOW before the Feast of the
Passover, Jesus knowing that His
hour had come that He should depart out of this world to the Father, having loved His own who
were in the world, He loved them
[t]to the end. *to the uttermost*
2 And during supper, the devil
having already put into the heart
of Judas Iscariot, *the son* of Simon, to betray Him,
3 *Jesus,*[r]knowing that the Father had given all things into His
hands, and that He had come
forth from God, and was going
back to God, John 3:35
4 *rose from supper, and *laid
aside His garments; and taking a
towel, He girded Himself about.
5 Then He *poured water into
the basin, and began to[r]wash the
disciples' feet, and to wipe them
with the towel with which He was
girded. Gen. 18:4; 19:2; 43:24
6 And so He *came to Simon
Peter. He *said to Him, "Lord, do
You wash my feet?"
7 Jesus answered and said to
him, "What I do you do not realize
now, but you shall understand
[r]hereafter." John 13:12ff.
8 Peter *said to Him, "Never
shall You wash my feet!" Jesus
answered him, "If I do not wash
you, you have no part with Me."
9 Simon Peter *said to Him,
"Lord, not my feet only, but also
my hands and my head."
10 Jesus *said to him, "He who
has bathed needs only to wash his
feet, but is completely clean; and
you are clean, but not all *of you.*"
11 For [r]He knew the one who
was betraying Him; for this reason He said, "Not all of you are
clean." John 6:64; 13:2
12 And so when He had washed
their feet, and taken His garments, and reclined *at the table*
again, He said to them, "Do you
know what I have done to you?
13 "You call Me [r]Teacher and
Lord; and [t]you are right, for so I
am. John 11:28 • *you say well*
14 "If I then, [r]the Lord and the
Teacher, washed your feet, you
also ought to wash one another's
feet. John 11:2; 1 Cor. 12:3
15 "For I gave you [r]an example
that you also should do as I did to
you. 1 Pet. 5:3
16 "Truly, truly, I say to you, [r]a
slave is not greater than his master; neither *is* one who is sent
greater than the one who sent
him. Matt. 10:24; Luke 6:40
17 "If you know these things, you
are blessed if you do them.
18 "I do not speak of all of you. I
know the ones I have chosen; but
it is[r]that the Scripture may be fulfilled, 'HE WHO EATS MY BREAD

HAS LIFTED UP HIS HEEL AGAINST
ME.' John 15:25; 17:12; 18:32; 19:24
19 "From now on I am telling
you before *it* comes to pass, so
that when it does occur, you may
believe that I am *He.*
20 "Truly, truly, I say to you, he
who receives whomever I send receives Me; and he who receives
Me receives Him who sent Me."
21 When Jesus had said this, He
became troubled in spirit, and testified, and said, "Truly, truly, I say
to you, that one of you will[a] betray
Me." *deliver Me up*
22 The disciples *began* looking
at one another, at a loss *to know*
of which one He was speaking.
23 There was reclining on[r] Jesus'
breast one of His disciples, whom
Jesus loved. John 1:18
24 Simon Peter therefore *ges-
tured to him, and *said to him,
"Tell *us* who it is of whom He is
speaking."
25 He, [r]leaning back thus on
Jesus' breast, *said to Him, "Lord,
who is it?" John 21:20
26 Jesus therefore *answered,
"That is the one for whom I shall
dip the morsel and give it to him."
So when He had dipped the morsel, He *took and *gave it to Judas, *the son* of Simon Iscariot.
27 And after the morsel, [r]Satan
then entered into him. Jesus
therefore *said to him, "What you
do, do quickly." Matt. 4:10
28 Now no one of those reclining *at the table* knew for what
purpose He had said this to him.
29 For some were supposing,
because Judas [r]had the money
box, that Jesus was saying to him,
"Buy the things we have need of
[r]for the feast"; or else, that he
should give something to the
poor. John 12:6 • John 13:1
30 And so after receiving the
morsel he went out immediately;
and [r]it was night. Luke 22:53
31 When therefore he had gone
out, Jesus *said, "Now[a] is [r]the Son
of Man glorified, and God is glorified in Him; *was* • Matt. 8:20
32 if God is glorified in Him,
[r]God will also glorify Him in Himself, and will glorify Him immediately. John 17:1
33 "Little children, I am with you
a little while longer. You shall
seek Me; and as I said to the Jews,
I now say to you also, 'Where I am
going, you cannot come.'
34 "A new commandment I give
to you, that you love one another,
even as I have loved you, that you
also love one another.
35 "By this all men will know
that you are My disciples, if you
have love for one another."
36 Simon Peter *said to Him,
"Lord, where are You going?"
Jesus answered, "Where I go, you
cannot follow Me now; but you
shall follow later."
37 Peter *said to Him, "Lord,
why can I not follow You right
now? [r]I will lay down my life for
You." John 13:37, 38
38 Jesus *answered, "Will you
lay down your life for Me? Truly,
truly, I say to you, [r]a cock shall not
crow, until you deny Me three
times. Mark 14:30; John 18:27

CHAPTER 14

"LET[r] not your heart be troubled;
[23]believe in God, believe also in
Me. John 14:27; 16:22, 24

[23] Or, *you believe in God*

2 "In My Father's house are
many dwelling places; if it were
not so, I would have told you; for I
go to prepare a place for you.
3 "And if I go and prepare a
place for you, I will come again,
and receive you to Myself; that
where I am, *there* you may be
also. John 14:18, 28 • John 12:26
4 "[24]And you know the way
where I am going."
5 Thomas *said to Him, "Lord,
we do not know where You are
going, how do we know the way?"
6 Jesus *said to him, "I am the
way, and the truth, and the life; no
one comes to the Father, but
through Me. John 10:9; Rom. 5:2
7 "If you had known Me, you
would have known My Father
also; from now on you know Him,
and have seen Him."
8 Philip *said to Him, "Lord,
show us the Father, and it is
enough for us." John 1:43
9 Jesus *said to him, "Have I
been so long with you, and *yet* you
have not come to know Me,
Philip? He who has seen Me has
seen the Father; how do you say,
'Show us the Father'?
10 "Do you not believe that I am
in the Father, and the Father is in
Me? The words that I say to you I
do not speak on My own initiative,
but the Father abiding in Me does
His works. John 10:38
11 "Believe Me that I am in the
Father, and the Father in Me; otherwise believe on account of the
works themselves. John 10:38
12 "Truly, truly, I say to you, he
who believes in Me, the works
that I do shall he do also; and
greater *works* than these shall he
do; because I go to the Father.
13 "And whatever you ask in My
name, that will I do, that the Father may be glorified in the Son.
14 "If you ask Me anything in My
name, I will do *it*. John 15:16
15 "If you love Me, you will keep
My commandments. 1 John 5:3
16 "And I will ask the Father,
and He will give you another
Helper, that He may be with you
forever; John 7:39
17 *that is* the Spirit of truth,
whom the world cannot receive,
because it does not behold Him or
know Him, *but* you know Him because He abides with you, and
will be in you. John 15:26
18 "I will not leave you as orphans; I will come to you.
19 "After a little while the world
will behold Me no more; but you
will behold Me; because I live, you
shall live also. John 16:16, 22
20 "In that day you shall know
that I am in My Father, and you in
Me, and I in you. John 10:38; 14:11
21 "He who has My commandments and keeps them, he it is
who loves Me; and he who loves
Me shall be loved by My Father,
and I will love him, and will disclose Myself to him."
22 Judas (not Iscariot) *said to
Him, "Lord, what then has happened that You are going to disclose Yourself to us, and not to
the world?" Acts 10:40, 41
23 Jesus answered and said to
him, "If anyone loves Me, he will
keep My word; and My Father will
love him, and We will come to
him, and make Our abode with
him. John 14:15, 21; 15:10
24 "He who does not love Me

[24]Many ancient authorities read *And where I go you know, and the way you know*

does not keep My words; and the
word which you hear is not Mine,
but the Father's who sent Me.
25"These things I have spoken
to you, while abiding with you.
26"But the Helper, the Holy
Spirit, whom the Father will send
in My name, He will teach you all
things, and bring to your remembrance all that I said to you.
27"Peace I leave with you; My
peace I give to you; not as the
world gives, do I give to you. Let
not your heart be troubled, nor let
it be fearful. John 14:1
28"You heard that I said to you,
'I go away, and I will come to
you.' If you loved Me, you would
have rejoiced, because I go to the
Father; for the Father is greater
than I. John 14:3, 18 • John 14:12
29"And now I have told you before it comes to pass, that when it
comes to pass, you may believe.
30"I will not speak much more
with you, for the ruler of the
world is coming, and he has nothing in Me; John 12:31
31 but that the world may know
that I love the Father, and as the
Father gave Me commandment,
even so I do. Arise, let us go from
here. John 10:18; 12:49

CHAPTER 15

"I AM the true vine, and My Father is the vinedresser.
2"Every branch in Me that does
not bear fruit, He takes away; and
every *branch* that bears fruit, He
[25]prunes it, that it may bear more
fruit.
3"You are already clean because of the word which I have
spoken to you. Eph. 5:26
4"Abide in Me, and I in you. As
the branch cannot bear fruit of itself, unless it abides in the vine, so
neither *can* you, unless you abide
in Me. John 6:56; 15:4-7
5"I am the vine, you are the
branches; he who abides in Me,
and I in him, he bears much fruit;
for apart from Me you can do
nothing. John 15:16
6"If anyone does not abide in
Me, he is thrown away as a
branch, and dries up; and they
gather them, and cast them into
the fire, and they are burned.
7"If you abide in Me, and My
words abide in you, ask whatever
you wish, and it shall be done for
you. Matt. 7:7; John 15:16
8"By this is My Father glorified, that you bear much fruit, and
so prove to be My disciples.
9"Just as the Father has loved
Me, I have also loved you; abide in
My love. John 3:35; 17:23, 24, 26
10"If you keep My commandments, you will abide in My love;
just as I have kept My Father's
commandments, and abide in His
love. John 14:15 • John 8:29
11"These things I have spoken
to you, that My joy may be in you,
and *that* your joy may be made
full. John 17:13 • John 3:29
12"This is My commandment,
that you love one another, just as I
have loved you.
13"Greater love has no one than
this, that one lay down his life for
his friends. John 10:11
14"You are My friends, if you do
what I command you.
15"No longer do I call you
slaves, for the slave does not

[25]Lit., *cleanses*

know what his master is doing;
but I have called you friends, for
[r]all things that I have heard from
My Father I have made known to
you. John 8:26; 16:12
16 "You did not choose Me, but I
chose you, and appointed you,
that you should go and [r]bear fruit,
and *that* your fruit should remain,
that [r]whatever you ask of the Father in My name, He may give to
you. John 15:5 • John 14:13
17 "This [r]I command you, that
you love one another. John 15:12
18 "If the world hates you, [a]you
know that it has hated Me before
it hated you. *know that*
19 "If you were of the world, the
world would love its own; but because you are not of the world,
but I chose you out of the world,
therefore the world hates you.
20 "Remember the word that I
said to you, 'A [r]slave is not greater
than his master.' If they persecuted Me, they will also persecute
you; if they kept My word, they
will keep yours also. Matt. 10:24
21 "But all these things they will
do to you [r]for My name's sake, because they do not know the One
who sent Me. Matt. 10:22; 24:9
22 "If [r]I had not come and spoken
to them, they would not have sin,
but now they have no excuse for
their sin. John 9:41; 15:24
23 "He who hates Me hates My
Father also.
24 "If I had not done among
them the works which no one else
did, they would not have sin; but
now they have both seen and
hated Me and My Father as well.
25 "But *they have done this* in order that the word may be fulfilled
that is written in their Law, 'THEY
HATED ME WITHOUT A CAUSE.'
26 "When the Helper comes,
whom I will send to you from the
Father, *that is* the Spirit of truth,
who proceeds from the Father, He
will bear witness of Me,
27 and you *will* bear witness
also, because you have been with
Me from the beginning.

CHAPTER 16

"THESE things I have spoken to
you, that you may be kept from
[r]stumbling. Matt. 11:6
2 "They will [r]make you outcasts
from the synagogue, but an hour
is coming for everyone who kills
you to think that he is offering service to God. John 9:22
3 "And these things they will
do, [r]because they have not known
the Father, or Me. John 8:19, 52
4 "But these things I have spoken to you, that when their hour
comes, you may remember that I
told you of them. And these things
I did not say to you at the beginning, because I was with you.
5 "But now I am going to Him
who sent Me; and none of you
asks Me, 'Where are You going?'
6 "But because I have said these
things to you, [r]sorrow has filled
your heart. John 14:1
7 "But I tell you the truth, it is
to your advantage that I go away;
for if I do not go away, the [r]Helper
shall not come to you; but if I go, I
will send Him to you. John 14:16
8 "And He, when He comes,
will convict the world concerning
sin, and righteousness, and judgment;

9 concerning sin, [r]because they do not believe in Me; John 15:22

10 and concerning righteousness, because I go to the Father, and you no longer behold Me;

11 [r]and concerning judgment, because the ruler of this world has been judged. John 12:31

12 "I have many more things to say to you, but you cannot bear *them* now.

13 "But when He, [r]the Spirit of truth, comes, He will guide you into all the truth; for He will not speak on His own initiative, but whatever He hears, He will speak; and He will disclose to you what is to come. John 14:17

14 "He shall [r]glorify Me; for He shall take of Mine, and shall disclose *it* to you. John 7:39

15 "All [r]things that the Father has are Mine; therefore I said, that He takes of Mine, and will disclose *it* to you. John 17:10

16 "A little while, and you will no longer behold Me; and again a little while, and you will see Me."

17 *Some* of His disciples therefore said to one another, "What is this thing He is telling us, 'A [r]little while, and you will not behold Me; and again a little while, and you will see Me'; and, 'because I go to the Father'?" John 16:16

18 And so they were saying, "What is this that He says, 'A little while'? We do not know what He is talking about."

19 [r]Jesus knew that they wished to question Him, and He said to them, "Are you deliberating together about this, that I said, 'A little while, and you will not behold Me, and again a little while, and you will see Me'? Mark 9:32

20 "Truly, truly, I say to you, that [r]you will weep and lament, but the world will rejoice; you will be sorrowful, but your sorrow will be turned to joy. Mark 16:10

21 "Whenever a woman is in travail she has sorrow, because her hour has come; but when she gives birth to the child, she remembers the anguish no more, for joy that a [t]child has been born into the world. *human being*

22 "Therefore [r]you too now have sorrow; but [r]I will see you again, and your heart will rejoice, and no one takes your joy away from you. John 16:6 • John 16:16

23 "And in that day you will [t]ask Me no question. Truly, truly, I say to you, if you shall ask the Father for anything, He will give it to you in My name. *question Me nothing*

24 "Until now you have asked for nothing in My name; ask, and you will receive, that your [r]joy may be made full. John 3:29; 15:11

25 "These things I have spoken to you in [t]figurative language; an hour is coming when I will speak no more to you in [t]figurative language, but will tell you plainly of the Father. *proverbs*

26 "In [r]that day you will ask in My name, and I do not say to you that I will request the Father on your behalf; John 14:20; 16:23

27 for [r]the Father Himself loves you, because you have loved Me, and have believed that I came forth from the Father. John 14:21

28 "I came forth from the Father, and have come into the world; I am leaving the world again, and [r]going to the Father." John 13:1, 3

29 His disciples *said, "Lo, now
You are speaking plainly, and are
not using a figure of speech.
30 "Now we know that You
know all things, and have no need
for anyone to question You; by
this we [r]believe that You came
from God." John 2:11; 16:27
31 Jesus answered them, "Do
you now believe?
32 "Behold, an hour is coming,
and has *already* come, for you to
be scattered, each to his own
home, and to leave Me alone; and
yet I am not alone, because the
Father is with Me.
33 "These things I have spoken
to you, that in Me you may have
peace. In the world you have
tribulation, but take courage; I
have overcome the world."

CHAPTER 17

THESE things Jesus spoke; and
[r]lifting up His eyes to heaven, He
said, "Father, the hour has come;
glorify Thy Son, that the Son may
glorify Thee, John 11:41
2 even as Thou gavest Him authority over all mankind, that to
all whom Thou hast given Him,
He may give eternal life.
3 "And this is eternal life, that
they may know Thee, [r]the only
true God, and Jesus Christ whom
Thou hast sent. John 5:44
4 "I glorified Thee on the earth,
having accomplished the work
which Thou hast given Me to do.
5 "And now, glorify Thou Me
together with Thyself, Father,
with the glory which I had with
Thee before the world was.
6 "I manifested Thy name to the
men whom [r]Thou gavest Me out of
the world; Thine they were, and
Thou gavest them to Me, and they
have kept Thy word. John 6:37
7 "Now they have come to
know that everything Thou hast
given Me is from Thee;
8 for [r]the words which Thou
gavest Me I have given to them;
and they received *them*, and truly
understood that I came forth from
Thee, and they believed that Thou
didst send Me. John 6:68; 12:49
9 "I ask on their behalf; [r]I do not
ask on behalf of the world, but of
those whom Thou hast given Me;
for they are Thine; Luke 23:34
10 and all things that are Mine
are Thine, and Thine are Mine;
and I have been glorified in them.
11 "And I am no more in the
world; and *yet* [r]they themselves
are in the world, and I come to
Thee. Holy Father, keep them in
Thy name, *the name* which Thou
hast given Me, that they may be
one, even as We *are*. John 13:1
12 "While I was with them, I was
keeping them in Thy name [r]which
Thou hast given Me; and I
guarded them, and not one of
them perished but the son of per-
dition, that the Scripture might be
fulfilled. John 17:6; Phil. 2:9
13 "But now [r]I come to Thee; and
these things I speak in the world,
that they may have My joy made
full in themselves. John 7:33
14 "I have given them Thy word;
and the world has hated them, because they are not of the world,
even as I am not of the world.
15 "I do not ask Thee to take
them out of the world, but to keep
them from the evil *one*.

16 "They are not of the world,
even as I am not of the world.
17 "Sanctify[r] them in the truth;
Thy word is truth. John 15:3
18 "As[r] Thou didst send Me into
the world, I also have sent them
into the world. John 3:17; 17:3, 8
19 "And for their sakes I sanctify
Myself, that they themselves also
may be sanctified in truth.
20 "I do not ask in behalf of these
alone, but for those also who believe in Me through their word;
21 that they may all be one;
even as Thou, Father, *art* in Me,
and I in Thee, that they also may
be in Us; that the world may believe that Thou didst send Me.
22 "And the [r]glory which Thou
hast given Me I have given to
them; that they may be one, just
as We are one; John 1:14
23 I in them, and Thou in Me,
that they may be perfected [t]in
unity, that the world may know
that Thou didst send Me, and
didst love them, even as Thou
didst love Me. ***into a unit***
24 "Father, I desire that they
also, whom Thou hast given Me,
be with Me where I am, in order
that they may behold My glory,
which Thou hast given Me; for
Thou didst love Me before the
foundation of the world.
25 "O righteous Father, [t]although
[r]the world has not known Thee, yet
I have known Thee; and these
have known that Thou didst send
Me; ***and*** • John 17:11
26 and [r]I have made Thy name
known to them, and will make it
known; that the love wherewith
Thou didst love Me may be in
them, and I in them." John 17:6

CHAPTER 18

WHEN Jesus had spoken these
words, He went forth with His disciples over the [t]ravine of the Kidron, where there was a garden,
into which He Himself entered,
and His disciples. ***winter-torrent***
2 Now Judas also, who was[a] betraying Him, knew the place; for
Jesus had often met there with
His disciples. ***delivering Him up***
3 Judas then, having received
the *Roman* cohort, and officers
from the chief priests and the
Pharisees, *came there with lan-
terns and torches and weapons.
4 Jesus therefore, knowing all
the things that were coming upon
Him, went forth, and *said to
them, "Whom do you seek?"
5 They answered Him, "Jesus
the Nazarene." He *said to them,
"I am *He.*" And Judas also who
was betraying Him, was standing
with them.
6 When therefore He said to
them, "I am *He,*" they drew back,
and fell to the ground.
7 Again therefore He asked
them, "Whom do you seek?" And
they said, "Jesus the Nazarene."
8 Jesus answered, "I told you
that I am *He*; if therefore you seek
Me, let these go their way,"
9 that the word might be fulfilled which He spoke, "Of[r] those
whom Thou hast given Me I lost
not one." John 17:12
10 Simon Peter therefore [r]hav-
ing a sword, drew it, and struck
the high priest's slave, and cut off
his right ear; and the slave's name
was Malchus. Matt. 26:51
11 Jesus therefore said to Peter,
"Put the sword into the sheath;

the cup which the Father has given Me, shall I not drink it?"

12 [r]So the *Roman*[a]cohort and the commander, and the officers of the Jews, arrested Jesus and bound Him, John 18:12f. • *battalion*

13 and led Him to [r]Annas first; for he was father-in-law of Caiaphas, who was high priest that year. Luke 3:2; John 18:24

14 Now Caiaphas was the one who had advised the Jews that it was expedient for one man to die on behalf of the people.

15 And [r]Simon Peter was following Jesus, and *so was* another disciple. Now that disciple was known to the high priest, and entered with Jesus into the court of the high priest, Matt. 26:58

16 but Peter was standing at the door outside. So the other disciple, who was known to the high priest, went out and spoke to the doorkeeper, and brought in Peter.

17 [r]The slave-girl therefore who kept the door *said to Peter, "You[r] are not also *one* of this man's disciples, are you?" He *said, "I am not." Acts 12:13 • John 18:25

18 Now the slaves and the [r]officers were standing *there*, having made [r]a charcoal fire, for it was cold and they were warming themselves; and Peter also was with them, standing and warming himself. John 18:3 • John 21:9

19 The high priest therefore questioned Jesus about His disciples, and about His teaching.

20 Jesus answered him, "I have spoken openly to the world; I always taught in [t]synagogues, and in the temple, where all the Jews come together; and I spoke nothing in secret. *the synagogue*

21 "Why do you question Me? Question those who have heard what I spoke to them; behold, these know what I said."

22 And when He had said this, one of the [r]officers standing by [r]gave Jesus a blow, saying, "Is that the way You answer the high priest?" John 18:3 • John 19:3

23 Jesus answered him, "If I have spoken wrongly, bear witness of the wrong; but if rightly, why do you strike Me?"

24 Annas therefore sent Him bound to Caiaphas the high priest.

25 Now [r]Simon Peter was standing and warming himself. They said therefore to him, "You[r] are not also *one* of His disciples, are you?" He denied *it*, and said, "I am not." John 18:18 • John 18:17

26 One of the slaves of the high priest, being a relative of the one [r]whose ear Peter cut off, *said, "Did I not see you in the garden with Him?" John 18:10

27 Peter therefore denied *it* again; and immediately [r]a cock crowed. John 13:38

28 They *led Jesus therefore from [r]Caiaphas into the [26]Praetorium, and it was early; and they themselves did not enter into the Praetorium in order that they might not be defiled, but might eat the Passover. John 18:13

29 [r]Pilate therefore went out to them, and *said, "What accusation do you bring against this Man?" John 18:29-38

30 They answered and said to him, "If this Man were not an evildoer, we would not have delivered Him up to you."

[26]I.e., governor's official residence

31 Pilate therefore said to them, "Take Him yourselves, and judge Him according to your law." The Jews said to him, "We are not permitted to put anyone to death,"

32 that[r]the word of Jesus might be fulfilled, which He spoke, signifying by what kind of death He was about to die. Matt. 20:19

33 Pilate therefore entered again into the [26]Praetorium, and summoned Jesus, and said to Him, "Are[r] You the King of the Jews?" Luke 23:3; John 19:12

34 Jesus answered, "Are you saying this on your own initiative, or did others tell you about Me?"

35 Pilate answered, "I am not a Jew, am I? Your own nation and the chief priests delivered You up to me; what have You done?"

36 Jesus answered, "My[r] kingdom is not of this world. If My kingdom were of this world, then My servants would be fighting, that I might not be delivered up to the Jews; but as it is, My kingdom is not [27]of this realm." John 6:15

37 Pilate therefore said to Him, "So You are a king?" Jesus answered, "You say *correctly* that I am a king. For this I have been born, and for this I have come into the world, to bear witness to the truth. Everyone who is of the truth hears My voice."

38 Pilate *said to Him, "What is truth?"

And when he had said this, he [r]went out again to the Jews, and *said to them, "I find no guilt in Him. John 18:33; 19:4

39 "But you have a custom, that I should release someone[a]for you at the Passover; do you wish then that I release[a]for you the King of the Jews?" *to you*

40 Therefore they cried out again, saying, "Not[r] this Man, but Barabbas." Now Barabbas was a robber. Acts 3:14

CHAPTER 19

THEN Pilate therefore took Jesus, and scourged Him.

2 [r]And the soldiers wove a crown of thorns and put it on His head, and arrayed Him in a purple robe; Matt. 27:27-30: *Mark 15:16-19*

3 and they *began* to come up to Him, and say, "Hail,[r] King of the Jews!" and to give Him blows in the face. Matt. 27:29

4 And Pilate [r]came out again, and *said to them, "Behold, I am bringing Him out to you, that you may know that [r]I find no guilt in Him." John 18:33, 38 • Luke 23:4

5 Jesus therefore came out, wearing the crown of thorns and the purple robe. And *Pilate* *said to them, "Behold, the Man!"

6 When therefore the chief priests and the [r]officers saw Him, they cried out, saying, "Crucify, crucify!" Pilate *said to them, "Take Him yourselves, and crucify Him, for I find no guilt in Him." Matt. 26:58; John 18:3

7 The Jews answered him, "We have a law, and by that law He ought to die because He made Himself out *to be* the Son of God."

8 When Pilate therefore heard this statement, he was the more afraid;

9 and he entered into the [28]Praetorium again, and *said to

[26] I.e., governor's official residence
[27] Lit., *from here*
[28] I.e., governor's official residence

Jesus, "Where are You from?"
But Jesus gave him no answer.
10 Pilate therefore *said to Him,
"You do not speak to me? Do You
not know that I have authority to
release You, and I have authority
to crucify You?"
11 Jesus answered, "You would
have no authority over Me, unless
it had been given you from above;
for this reason he who delivered
Me up to you has *the* greater sin."
12 As a result of this Pilate
[t]made efforts to release Him, but
the Jews cried out, saying, "If you
release this Man, you are no
friend of Caesar; everyone who
makes himself out *to be* a king opposes Caesar." *was seeking to*
13 When Pilate therefore heard
these words, he brought Jesus
out, and [r]sat down on the judgment seat at a place called The
Pavement, but [r]in Hebrew, Gabbatha. Matt. 27:19 • John 5:2; 19:17, 20
14 Now it was [r]the day of preparation for the Passover; it was
about the [29]sixth hour. And he
*said to the Jews, "Behold, your
King!" Matt. 27:62; John 19:31, 42
15 They therefore cried out,
"Away with *Him*, away with *Him*,
crucify Him!" Pilate *said to
them, "Shall I crucify your King?"
The chief priests answered, "We
have no king but Caesar."
16 So he then [r]delivered Him to
them to be crucified. Luke 23:25
17 They took Jesus therefore,
and He went out, [r]bearing His own
cross, to the place called the Place
of a Skull, which is called in Hebrew, Golgotha. Matt. 27:32
18 There they crucified Him,
and with Him [r]two other men, one
on either side, and Jesus in between. Luke 23:32
19 And Pilate wrote an inscription also, and put it on the cross.
And it was written, "JESUS [r]THE
NAZARENE, THE KING OF THE
JEWS." Matt. 27:37
20 Therefore this inscription
many of the Jews read, for the
place where Jesus was crucified
was near the city; and it was written [r]in Hebrew, Latin, *and* in
Greek. John 19:13
21 And so the chief priests of
the Jews were saying to Pilate,
"Do not write, 'The [r]King of the
Jews'; but that He said, 'I am King
of the Jews.'" John 19:14, 19
22 Pilate answered, "What I
have written I have written."
23 The soldiers therefore, when
they had crucified Jesus, took His
outer garments and made four
parts, a part to every soldier and
also the [30]tunic; now the tunic was
seamless, woven in one piece.
24 They said therefore to one
another, "Let [r]us not tear it, but
cast [t]lots for it, *to decide* whose it
shall be"; that the Scripture might
be fulfilled, "THEY DIVIDED MY
OUTER GARMENTS AMONG THEM,
AND FOR MY CLOTHING THEY CAST
LOTS." Ex. 28:32 • *a lot*
25 Therefore the soldiers did
these things. But there were
standing by the cross of Jesus [r]His
mother, and His mother's sister,
Mary the *wife* of Clopas, and
Mary Magdalene. Matt. 12:46
26 When Jesus therefore saw
His mother, and the disciple
whom He loved standing nearby,

[29] Perhaps 6 a.m. (Roman time)

[30] Gr., *khiton*, the garment worn next to the skin

He *said to His mother, "Woman[r],
behold, your son!" John 2:4
27 Then He *said to the disciple,
"Behold, your mother!" And from
that hour the disciple took her
into his own *household*.
28 After this, Jesus, [r]knowing
that all things had already been
accomplished, in order that the
Scripture might be fulfilled, *said,
"I am thirsty." John 13:1; 17:4
29 A jar full of sour wine was
standing there; so [r]they put a
sponge full of the sour wine upon
a branch of hyssop, and brought it
up to His mouth. John 19:29, 30
30 When Jesus therefore had received the sour wine, He said, "It
is finished!" And He bowed His
head, and gave up His spirit.
31 The Jews therefore, because
it was [r]the day of preparation, so
that the bodies should not remain
on the cross on the Sabbath (for
that Sabbath was a high *day*),
asked Pilate that their legs might
be broken, and *that* they might be
taken away. John 19:14, 42
32 The soldiers therefore came,
and broke the legs of the first
man, and of the other man who
was crucified with Him;
33 but coming to Jesus, when
they saw that He was already
dead, they did not break His legs;
34 but one of the soldiers
pierced His side with a spear, and
immediately there came out [r]blood
and water. 1 John 5:6, 8
35 And he who has seen has
[r]borne witness, and his witness is
true; and he knows that he is telling the truth, so that you also may
believe. John 15:27; 21:24
36 For these things came to
pass, that the Scripture might be
fulfilled, "NOT A BONE OF HIM
SHALL BE [a]BROKEN." *crushed*
37 And again another Scripture
says, "THEY [r]SHALL LOOK ON HIM
WHOM THEY PIERCED." Rev. 1:7
38 And after these things
Joseph of Arimathea, being a disciple of Jesus, but a [r]secret *one*, for
fear of the Jews, asked Pilate that
he might take away the body of
Jesus; and Pilate granted permission. He came therefore, and took
away His body. Mark 15:43
39 And [r]Nicodemus came also,
who had first come to Him by
night; bringing a mixture of [r]myrrh
and aloes, about a hundred
pounds *weight*. John 3:1 • Ps. 45:8
40 And so they took the body of
Jesus, and bound it in linen wrappings with the spices, as is the
burial custom of the Jews.
41 Now in the place where He
was crucified there was a garden;
and in the garden a new tomb, in
which no one had yet been laid.
42 Therefore on account of the
Jewish day of [r]preparation, because the tomb was nearby, they
laid Jesus there. John 19:14, 31

CHAPTER 20

NOW on the first *day* of the week
[r]Mary Magdalene *came early to
the tomb, while it *was still dark,
and *saw the stone *already* taken
away from the tomb. John 19:25
2 And so she *ran and *came
to Simon Peter, and to the other
disciple whom Jesus [t]loved, and
*said to them, "They have taken
away the Lord out of the tomb,
and we do not know where they
have laid Him." *was loving*
3 Peter therefore went forth,

and the other disciple, and they
were going to the tomb.
4 And the two were running
together; and the other disciple
ran ahead faster than Peter, and
came to the tomb first;
5 and stooping and looking in,
he *saw the linen wrappings lying
there; but he did not go in.
6 Simon Peter therefore also
*came, following him, and en-
tered the tomb; and he *beheld
the linen wrappings lying *there,*
7 and the face-cloth, which
had been on His head, not lying
with the linen wrappings, but
rolled up in a place by itself.
8 So the other disciple who
[r]had first come to the tomb entered
then also, and he saw and believed. John 20:4
9 For as yet they did not understand the Scripture, that He
must rise again from the dead.
10 So the disciples went away
again to their own homes.
11 But Mary was standing outside the tomb weeping; and so, as
she wept, she [r]stooped and looked
into the tomb; John 20:5
12 and she *beheld two angels
in white sitting, one at the head,
and one at the feet, where the
body of Jesus had been lying.
13 And they *said to her,
"Woman,[r] why are you weeping?"
She *said to them, "Because [r]they
have taken away my Lord, and I
do not know where they have laid
Him." John 20:15 • John 20:2
14 When she had said this, she
turned around, and *beheld[r] Jesus
standing *there,* and did not know
that it was Jesus. Matt. 28:9
15 Jesus *said to her, "Woman,
why are you weeping? Whom are
you seeking?" Supposing Him to
be the gardener, she *said to Him,
"Sir, if you have carried Him
away, tell me where you have laid
Him, and I will take Him away."
16 Jesus *said to her, "Mary!"
She *turned and *said to Him [r]in
Hebrew, "Rabboni!" (which
means, Teacher). John 5:2
17 Jesus *said to her, "Stop
clinging to Me, for I have not yet
ascended to the Father; but go to
[r]My brethren, and say to them, 'I
[r]ascend to My Father and your Father, and My God and your
God.' " Matt. 28:10 • John 7:33
18 Mary Magdalene *came, an-
nouncing to the disciples, "I have
seen the Lord," and *that* He had
said these things to her.
19 When therefore it was evening, on that day, the first *day* of
the week, and when the doors
were shut where the disciples
were, for fear of the Jews, Jesus
came and stood in their midst, and
*said to them, "Peace[t] *be* with
you." *Peace to you*
20 And when He had said this,
[r]He showed them both His hands
and His side. The disciples therefore rejoiced when they saw the
Lord. Luke 24:39, 40
21 Jesus therefore said to them
again, "Peace[r] *be* with you; [r]as the
Father has sent Me, I also send
you." Luke 24:36 • John 17:18
22 And when He had said this,
He breathed on them, and *said to
them, "Receive the Holy Spirit.
23 "If you forgive the sins of any,
their sins have been forgiven
them; if you retain the *sins* of any,
they have been retained."
24 But Thomas, one of the

twelve, called Didymus, was not
with them when Jesus came.
25 The other disciples therefore
were saying to him, "We have
seen the Lord!" But he said to
them, "Unless I shall see in His
hands the imprint of the nails, and
put my finger into the place of the
nails, and put my hand into His
side, I will not believe."
26 And after eight days again
His disciples were inside, and
Thomas with them. Jesus *came,
the doors having been shut, and
stood in their midst, and said,
"Peace[r] *be* with you." John 14:27
27 Then He *said to Thomas,
"Reach here your finger, and see
My hands; and reach here your
hand, and put it into My side; and
be not unbelieving, but believing."
28 Thomas answered and said
to Him, "My Lord and my God!"
29 Jesus *said to him, "Because
you have seen Me, have you believed? Blessed *are* they who did
not see, and *yet* believed."
30 Many other signs therefore
Jesus also performed in the presence of the disciples, which are
not written in this book;
31 but these have been written
[r]that you may believe that Jesus is
the Christ, [r]the Son of God; and
that believing you may have life in
His name. John 19:35 • Matt. 4:3

CHAPTER 21

AFTER these things Jesus manifested Himself again to the disciples at the Sea of Tiberias, and He
manifested *Himself* in this way.
2 There were together Simon
Peter, and Thomas called Didymus, and Nathanael of Cana in
Galilee, and the *sons* of Zebedee,
and two others of His disciples.
3 Simon Peter *said to them,
"I am going fishing." They *said
to him, "We will also come with
you." They went out, and got into
the boat; and [r]that night they
caught nothing. Luke 5:5
4 But when the day was now
breaking, Jesus stood on the
beach; yet the disciples did not
know that it was Jesus.
5 Jesus therefore *said to
them, "Children, [r]you do not have
any fish, do you?" They answered
Him, "No." Luke 24:41
6 And He said to them, "Cast[r]
the net on the right-hand side of
the boat, and you will find *a
catch.*" They cast therefore, and
then they were not able to haul it
in because of the great number of
fish. Luke 5:4ff.
7 That disciple therefore
whom Jesus loved *said to Peter,
"It is the Lord." And so when Simon Peter heard that it was the
Lord, he put his outer garment on
(for he was stripped *for work*),
and threw himself into the sea.
8 But the other disciples came
in the little boat, for they were not
far from the land, but about [t]one
hundred yards away, dragging the
net *full* of fish. *200 cubits*
9 And so when they got out
upon the land, they *saw a charcoal fire *already* laid, and fish
placed on it, and bread.
10 Jesus *said to them, "Bring
some of the [r]fish which you have
now caught." John 6:9, 11; 21:9, 13
11 Simon Peter went up, and
drew the net to land, full of large
fish, a hundred and fifty-three;

and although there were so many,
the net was not torn.
12 Jesus *said to them, "Come
and have[r] breakfast." None of the
disciples ventured to question
Him, "Who are You?" knowing
that it was the Lord. John 21:15
13 Jesus *came and *took [r]the
bread, and *gave them, and the
fish likewise. John 21:9
14 This is now the third time
that Jesus[a] was manifested to the
disciples, after He was raised
from the dead. *made Himself visible*
15 So when they had finished
breakfast, Jesus *said to Simon
Peter, "Simon, *son* of John, do
you love Me more than these?" He
*said to Him, "Yes, Lord; You
know that I love You." He *said to
him, "Tend My lambs."
16 He *said to him again a second time, "Simon, *son* of John, do
you love Me?" He *said to Him,
"Yes, Lord; You know that I love
You." He *said to him, "Shepherd[r]
My sheep." Matt. 2:6
17 He *said to him the third
time, "Simon, *son* of John, do you
love Me?" Peter was grieved because He said to him [r]the third
time, "Do you love Me?" And he
said to Him, "Lord, You know all
things; You know that I love
You." Jesus *said to him, "Tend
My sheep. John 13:38
18 "Truly, truly, I say to you,
when you were younger, you used
to gird yourself, and walk wherever you wished; but when you
grow old, you will stretch out your
hands, and someone else will gird
you, and bring you where you do
not wish to *go*."
19 Now this He said, [r]signifying
by what kind of death he would
glorify God. And when He had
spoken this, He *said to him, "Follow Me!" John 12:33; 18:32
20 Peter, turning around, *saw
the disciple whom Jesus loved following *them;* the one who also
had leaned back on His breast at
the supper, and said, "Lord, who
is the one who betrays You?"
21 Peter therefore seeing him
*said to Jesus, "Lord, and what
about this man?"
22 Jesus *said to him, "If I want
him to remain until I come, what
is that to you? You follow Me!"
23 This saying therefore went
out among [r]the brethren that that
disciple would not die; yet Jesus
did not say to him that he would
not die, but *only*, "If I want him to
remain [r]until I come, what *is that*
to you?" Acts 1:15 • 1 Cor. 4:5
24 This is the disciple who [r]bears
witness of these things, and wrote
these things; and we know that
his witness is true. John 15:27
25 And there are also [r]many other things which Jesus did, which if
they *were written in detail, I suppose that even the world itself
*would not contain the books
which *were written. John 20:30

THE

ACTS OF THE APOSTLES

THE first account I composed, Theophilus, about all that Jesus began to do and teach,

2 until the day when He was taken up, after He had by the Holy Spirit given orders to the apostles whom He had chosen.

3 To [t]these He also presented Himself alive, after His suffering, by many convincing proofs, appearing to them over *a period of* forty days, and speaking of [r]the things concerning the kingdom of God. *whom* • Acts 8:12

4 And gathering them together, He commanded them not to leave Jerusalem, but to wait for [t]what the Father had promised, "Which," *He said,* "you heard of from Me; *the promise of the Father*

5 for John baptized with water, but you shall be baptized [a]with the Holy Spirit [t]not many days from now." *in* • *after these many days*

6 And so when they had come together, they were asking Him, saying, "Lord, [r]is it at this time You are restoring the kingdom to Israel?" Matt. 17:11; Mark 9:12

7 He said to them, "It is not for you to know times or epochs which [r]the Father has fixed by His own authority; Matt. 24:36

8 but you shall receive power [r]when the Holy Spirit has come upon you; and you shall be [r]My witnesses both in Jerusalem, and in all Judea and Samaria, and even to the remotest part of the earth." Acts 2:1-4 • Luke 24:48

9 And after He had said these things, He was lifted up while they were looking on, and a cloud received Him out of their sight.

10 And as they were gazing intently into the sky while He was departing, behold, two men in white clothing stood beside them;

11 and they also said, "Men[r] of Galilee, why do you stand looking into [a]the sky? This Jesus, who has been taken up from you into heaven, will come in just the same way as you have watched Him go into heaven." Acts 2:7 • *heaven*

12 Then they returned to Jerusalem from the mount called Olivet, which is near Jerusalem, a Sabbath day's journey away.

13 And when they had entered, they went up to the upper room, where they were staying; that is, Peter and John and [a]James and Andrew, Philip and Thomas, Bartholomew and Matthew, James *the son* of Alphaeus, and Simon the Zealot, and Judas *the* [a]*son* of James. *Jacob* • possibly, *brother*

14 These all with one mind were continually devoting themselves to prayer, along with *the* women, and Mary the mother of Jesus, and with His brothers.

15 And [t]at this time Peter stood up in the midst of the brethren (a gathering of about one hundred and twenty persons was there together), and said, *in these days*

16 "Brethren, [r]the Scripture had to be fulfilled, which the Holy Spirit foretold by the mouth of

David concerning Judas, who became a guide to those who arrested Jesus. John 13:18; 17:12

17 "For he was [r]counted among us, and received his portion in [r]this ministry." John 6:70f. • Acts 1:25

18 (Now this man acquired a field with the price of his wickedness; and falling headlong, he burst open in the middle and all his bowels gushed out.

19 And it became known to all who were living in Jerusalem; so that in their own language that field was called Hakeldama, that is, Field of Blood.)

20 "For it is written in the book of Psalms,

'LET[r] HIS HOMESTEAD BE MADE DESOLATE,
AND LET NO MAN DWELL IN IT'; Ps. 69:25

and,

'HIS[r] OFFICE LET ANOTHER MAN TAKE.' Ps. 109:8

21 "It is therefore necessary that of the men who have accompanied us all the time that the Lord Jesus went in and out among us—

22 beginning [t]with the baptism of John, until the day that He was taken up from us—one of these should become a witness with us of His resurrection." *from*

23 And they put forward two men, Joseph called Barsabbas (who was also called Justus), and [r]Matthias. Acts 1:26

24 And they prayed, and said, "Thou, Lord, who knowest the hearts of all men, show which one of these two Thou hast chosen

25 to [t]occupy [r]this ministry and apostleship from which Judas turned aside to go to his own place." *take the place of* • Acts 1:17

26 And they [t]drew lots for them, and the lot fell [a]to Matthias; and he was [t]numbered with the eleven apostles. *gave* • *upon* • *chosen*

CHAPTER 2

AND when the day of Pentecost [t]had come, they were all together in one place. *was being fulfilled*

2 And suddenly there came from heaven a noise like a violent, rushing wind, and it filled [r]the whole house where they were sitting. Acts 4:31

3 And there appeared to them tongues as of fire distributing themselves, and [t]they [a]rested on each one of them. *it* • *sat*

4 And they were all filled with the Holy Spirit and began to speak with other tongues, as the Spirit was giving them utterance.

5 Now there were Jews living in Jerusalem, devout men, from every nation under heaven.

6 And when this sound occurred, the multitude came together, and were bewildered, because they were each one hearing them speak in his own language.

7 And [r]they were amazed and marveled, saying, "Why[t], are not all these who are speaking Galileans? Acts 2:12 • *Behold*

8 "And how is it that we each hear *them* in our own [a]language [t]to which we were born? *dialect* • *in*

9 "Parthians and Medes and Elamites, and residents of Mesopotamia, Judea and [r]Cappadocia, Pontus and Asia, 1 Pet. 1:1

10 Phrygia and Pamphylia, Egypt and the districts of Libya around Cyrene, and visitors from

Rome, both Jews and [1]proselytes,
11 Cretans and Arabs—we hear
them in our *own* tongues speaking
of the mighty deeds of God."
12 And [r]they continued in
amazement and great perplexity,
saying to one another, "What
does this mean?" Acts 2:7
13 But others were mocking and
saying, "They[r] are full of [a]sweet
wine." 1 Cor. 14:23 • *new wine*
14 But Peter, taking his stand
with the eleven, raised his voice
and declared to them: "Men of Judea,
and all you who live in Jerusalem,
let this be known to you,
and give heed to my words.
15 "For these men are not drunk,
as you suppose, for it is *only* the
[2]third hour of the day;
16 but this is what was spoken
of through the prophet Joel:
17 'AND IT SHALL BE IN THE LAST DAYS,' God says,
'THAT I WILL POUR FORTH OF MY SPIRIT UPON ALL [t]MANKIND; *flesh*
AND YOUR SONS AND YOUR DAUGHTERS SHALL PROPHESY,
AND YOUR YOUNG MEN SHALL SEE VISIONS,
AND YOUR OLD MEN SHALL DREAM DREAMS;
18 EVEN UPON MY BONDSLAVES, BOTH MEN AND WOMEN,
I WILL IN THOSE DAYS POUR FORTH OF MY SPIRIT
And they shall prophesy.
19 'AND I WILL GRANT WONDERS IN THE SKY ABOVE,
AND SIGNS ON THE EARTH BENEATH,
BLOOD, AND FIRE, AND VAPOR OF SMOKE.
20 'THE SUN SHALL BE TURNED INTO DARKNESS,
AND THE MOON INTO BLOOD,
BEFORE THE GREAT AND GLORIOUS DAY OF THE LORD SHALL COME.
21 'AND IT SHALL BE, THAT EVERYONE WHO CALLS ON THE NAME OF THE LORD SHALL BE SAVED.'
22 "Men of Israel, listen to these
words: Jesus the Nazarene, a man
attested to you by God with miracles
and wonders and signs
which God performed through
Him in your midst, just as you
yourselves know—
23 this *Man*, delivered up by the
[r]predetermined plan and foreknowledge
of God, you nailed to a
cross by the hands of godless men
and put *Him* to death. Acts 3:18
24 "And God raised Him up
again, putting an end to the agony
of death, since it was impossible
for Him to be held in its power.
25 "For David says of Him,
'I[r] WAS ALWAYS BEHOLDING THE LORD IN MY PRESENCE;
FOR HE IS AT MY RIGHT HAND, THAT I MAY NOT BE SHAKEN. Ps. 16:8-11
26 'THEREFORE MY HEART WAS GLAD AND MY TONGUE EXULTED;
MOREOVER MY FLESH ALSO WILL ABIDE IN HOPE;
27 BECAUSE THOU WILT NOT ABANDON MY SOUL TO [r]HADES, Matt. 11:23
NOR ALLOW THY HOLY ONE TO UNDERGO DECAY.

[1] I.e., Gentile converts to Judaism
[2] I.e., 9 a.m.

28 'THOU HAST MADE KNOWN TO
ME THE WAYS OF LIFE;
THOU WILT MAKE ME FULL
OF GLADNESS WITH THY
PRESENCE.'

29 "Brethren,[t] I may confidently say to you regarding the patriarch David that he both died and was buried, and his tomb is [t]with us to this day. *Men brothers* · *among*

30 "And so, because he was [r]a prophet, and knew that GOD HAD SWORN TO HIM WITH AN OATH TO SEAT *one* OF HIS DESCENDANTS UPON HIS THRONE, Matt. 22:43

31 he looked ahead and spoke of the resurrection of [3]the Christ, that [r]HE WAS NEITHER ABANDONED TO HADES, NOR DID His flesh SUFFER DECAY. Matt. 11:23; Acts 2:27

32 "This Jesus [r]God raised up again, to which we are all witnesses. Acts 2:24; 3:15, 26; 4:10

33 "Therefore having been exalted[a] to[r] the right hand of God, and having received from the Father the promise of the Holy Spirit, He has poured forth this which you both see and hear. *by* · Mark 16:19

34 "For it was not David who ascended into [t]heaven, but he himself says: *the heavens*

'THE LORD SAID TO MY LORD,
"SIT AT MY RIGHT HAND,

35 UNTIL I MAKE THINE ENEMIES A FOOTSTOOL FOR
THY FEET." '

36 "Therefore let all the [r]house of Israel know for certain that God has made Him both Lord and [t]Christ—this Jesus whom you crucified." Ezek. 36:22, 32 · *Messiah*

37 Now when they heard *this*, they were pierced to the heart, and said to Peter and the rest of the apostles, "Brethren,[t] what shall we do?" *Men brothers*

38 And Peter *said* to them, "Repent,[r] and let each of you be baptized in the name of Jesus Christ for the forgiveness of your sins; and you shall receive the gift of the Holy Spirit. Mark 1:15

39 "For the promise is for you and your children, and for all who are far off, as many as the Lord our God shall call to Himself."

40 And with many other words he solemnly testified and kept on exhorting them, saying, "Be saved from this perverse generation!"

41 So then, those who had received his word were baptized; and there were added that day about three thousand [4]souls.

42 And they were continually devoting themselves to the apostles' teaching and to fellowship, to the breaking of bread and [t]to[r] prayer. *the prayers* · Acts 1:14

43 And everyone kept feeling a sense of awe; and many [r]wonders and signs were taking place through the apostles[5]. Acts 2:22

44 And all those who had believed [6]were together, and [r]had all things in common; Acts 4:32, 37

45 and they *began* selling their property and possessions, and were sharing them with all, as anyone might have need.

46 And day by day continuing with one mind in the temple, and breaking bread from house to house, they were taking their [t]meals together with gladness and sincerity of heart, *food*

[3] I.e., the Messiah

[4] I.e., persons

[5] Some ancient mss. add *in Jerusalem; and great fear was upon all*

[6] Some ancient mss. do not contain *were*

47 praising God, and [r]having favor with all the people. And the Lord was adding [t]to their number day by day those who were being saved. Acts 5:13 • *together*

CHAPTER 3

NOW Peter and John were going up to the temple at the [7]ninth *hour*, the hour of prayer.

2 And [r]a certain man who had been lame from his mother's womb was being carried along, whom they used to set down every day at the gate of the temple which is called Beautiful, in order to beg [8]alms of those who were entering the temple. Acts 14:8

3 And when he saw Peter and John about to go into the temple, he *began* asking to receive alms.

4 And Peter, along with John, [r]fixed his gaze upon him and said, "Look at us!" Acts 10:4

5 And he *began* to give them his attention, expecting to receive something from them.

6 But Peter said, "I do not possess silver and gold, but what I do have I give to you: [r]In the name of Jesus Christ the Nazarene—walk!" Acts 2:22; 3:16; 4:10

7 And seizing him by the right hand, he raised him up; and immediately his feet and his ankles were strengthened.

8 [r]And [t]with a leap, he stood upright and *began* to walk; and he entered the temple with them, walking and leaping and praising God. Acts 14:10 • *leaping up*

9 And all the people saw him walking and praising God;

10 and they were taking note of him as being the one who used to [r]sit at the Beautiful Gate of the temple to *beg* alms, and they were filled with wonder and amazement at what had happened to him. John 9:8; Acts 3:2

11 And while he was clinging to Peter and John, all the people ran together to them at the so-called [a]portico of Solomon, full of amazement. *colonnade*

12 But when Peter saw *this*, he replied to the people, "Men of Israel, why do you marvel at this, or why do you gaze at us, as if by our own power or piety we had made him walk?

13 "The [r]God of Abraham, Isaac, and Jacob, the God of our fathers, has glorified His [a]servant Jesus, *the one* whom you delivered up, and disowned in the presence of Pilate, when he had decided to release Him. Matt. 22:32 • *Child*

14 "But you disowned the Holy and Righteous One, and asked for a murderer to be granted to you,

15 but put to death the [a]Prince[r] of life, *the one* whom God raised from the dead, *a fact* to which we are witnesses. *Author* • Acts 5:31

16 "And on the basis of faith in His name, *it is* the name of [t]Jesus which has strengthened this man whom you see and know; and the faith which *comes* through Him has given him this perfect health in the presence of you all. *His*

17 "And now, brethren, I know that you acted [r]in ignorance, just as your rulers did also. Eph. 4:18

18 "But the things which [r]God announced beforehand by the mouth of all the prophets, that His [a]Christ should suffer, He has thus fulfilled. Acts 2:23 • *Anointed One*

[7]I.e., 3 p.m. [8]Or, *a gift of charity*

19 "Repent therefore and return, that your sins may be wiped away, in order that [r]times of refreshing may come from the presence of the Lord; 2 Thess. 1:7

20 and that He may send Jesus, the Christ appointed for you,

21 whom heaven must receive until *the* [t]period of restoration of all things about which God spoke by the mouth of His holy prophets from ancient time. *periods, times*

22 "Moses said, 'THE[r] LORD GOD SHALL RAISE UP FOR YOU A PROPHET [a]LIKE ME FROM YOUR BRETHREN; TO HIM YOU SHALL GIVE HEED in everything He says to you. Acts 7:37 • *as* He raised up *me*

23 'And it shall be that every soul that does not heed that prophet shall be utterly destroyed from among the people.'

24 "And likewise, all the prophets who have spoken, from Samuel and *his* successors onward, also announced these days.

25 "It is you who are the sons of the prophets, and of the covenant which God made with your fathers, saying to Abraham, 'AND IN YOUR SEED ALL THE FAMILIES OF THE EARTH SHALL BE BLESSED.'

26 "For you first, God raised up His [a]Servant, and sent Him to bless you by turning every one *of you* from your wicked ways." *Child*

CHAPTER 4

AND as they were speaking to the people, the priests and the *captain of the temple guard*, and the Sadducees, came upon them,

2 being greatly disturbed because they were teaching the people and proclaiming in Jesus the resurrection from the dead.

3 And they laid hands on them, and put them in jail until the next day, for it was already evening.

4 But many of those who had heard the [a]message believed; and the number of the men came to be about five thousand. *word*

5 And it came about on the next day, that their [r]rulers and elders and scribes were gathered together in Jerusalem; Acts 4:8

6 and Annas the high priest *was there*, and Caiaphas and John and Alexander, and all who were of high-priestly descent.

7 And when they had placed them in the center, they *began to* inquire, "By what power, or in what name, have you done this?"

8 Then Peter, filled with the Holy Spirit, said to them, "Rulers and elders of the people,

9 if we are on trial today for a benefit done to a sick man, as to how this man has been made well,

10 let it be known to all of you, and to all the people of Israel, that [r]by the name of Jesus Christ the Nazarene, whom you crucified, whom God raised from the dead—[a]by [a]this *name* this man stands here before you in good health. Acts 2:22 • *in* • *him*

11 "He[t] is the [r]STONE WHICH WAS REJECTED by you, THE BUILDERS, *but* WHICH BECAME THE VERY CORNER *stone*. *This One* • Ps. 118:22

12 "And there is salvation in [r]no one else; for there is no other name under heaven that has been given among men, by which we must be saved." Matt. 1:21

13 Now as they observed the [r]confidence of Peter and John, and

understood that they were unedu-
cated and untrained men, they
were marveling, and *began* to recognize them [t]as having been with
Jesus. Acts 4:31 • *that they had been*
14 And seeing the man who had
been healed standing with them,
they had nothing to say in reply.
15 But when they had ordered
them to go aside out of the[a]Coun-
cil,[r] they *began* to confer with one
another, *Sanhedrin* • Matt. 5:22
16 saying, "What[r] shall we do
with these men? For the fact that
a noteworthy [a]miracle has taken
place through them is apparent to
all who live in Jerusalem, and we
cannot deny it. John 11:47 • *sign*
17 "But in order that it may not
spread any further among the
people, let us warn them to speak
no more to any man in this name."
18 And when they had sum-
moned them, they [r]commanded
them not to speak or teach at all
in the name of Jesus. Acts 5:28f.
19 But [r]Peter and John answered
and said to them, "Whether it is
right in the sight of God to give
heed to you rather than to God,
you be the judge; Acts 4:13
20 for we cannot stop speaking
what we have seen and heard."
21 And when they had threatened them further, they let them
go (finding no basis on which they
might punish them) [r]on account of
the people, because they were all
[r]glorifying God for what had happened; Acts 5:26 • Matt. 9:8
22 for the man was more than
forty years old on whom this[a]mir-
acle of healing had been performed. *sign*
23 And when they had been released, they went to their own
companions, and reported all that
the chief priests and the elders
had said to them.
24 And when they heard *this*,
they lifted their voices to God
with one accord and said, "O
Lord, it is Thou who DIDST MAKE
THE HEAVEN AND THE EARTH AND
THE SEA, AND ALL THAT IS IN THEM,
25 who by the Holy Spirit,
through the mouth of our father
David Thy servant, didst say,

'WHY DID THE [9]GENTILES RAGE,
AND THE PEOPLES DEVISE FUTILE THINGS?
26 'THE KINGS OF THE EARTH TOOK THEIR STAND,
AND THE RULERS WERE GATHERED TOGETHER
AGAINST THE LORD, AND AGAINST HIS CHRIST.'

27 "For truly in this city there
were gathered together against
Thy holy servant Jesus, whom
Thou didst anoint, both Herod and
Pontius Pilate, along with the
Gentiles and the peoples of Israel,
28 to do whatever Thy hand and
Thy purpose predestined to occur.
29 "And now, Lord, take note of
their threats, and grant that Thy
bond-servants may speak Thy
word with all confidence,
30 while Thou dost extend Thy
hand to heal, and signs and wonders take place through the name
of Thy holy servant Jesus."
31 And when they had prayed,
the [r]place where they had gathered
together was shaken, and they
were all filled with the Holy Spirit,
and *began* to speak the word of
God with boldness. Acts 2:1

[9]Or, *nations*

32 And the [a]congregation of
those who believed were of one
heart and soul; and not one *of*
them [t]claimed that anything belonging to him was his own; but
all things were common property
to them. *multitude* · *was saying*
33 And [r]with great power the
apostles were giving witness to
the resurrection of the Lord Jesus,
and abundant grace was upon
them all. Acts 1:8
34 For there was not a needy
person among them, for all who
were owners of land or houses
[r]would sell them and bring the proceeds of the sales, Acts 2:45
35 and lay them at the apostles'
feet; and they would be distributed to each, as any had need.
36 And Joseph, a Levite of Cyp-
rian birth, who was also called
Barnabas by the apostles (which
translated means, Son of [a]Encour-
agement), *Exhortation*
37 and who owned a tract of
land, sold it and brought the money and laid it at the apostles' feet.

CHAPTER 5

BUT a certain man named Ananias, with his wife Sapphira, sold
a piece of property,
2 and [r]kept back *some* of the
price for himself, with his wife's
[a]full knowledge, and bringing a
portion of it, he laid it at the apostles' feet. Acts 5:3 · *collusion*
3 But Peter said, "Ananias,
why has [r]Satan filled your heart to
lie to the Holy Spirit, and to keep
back some of the price of the
land? Matt. 4:10; Luke 22:3
4 "While it remained *unsold*,
did it not remain your own? And
after it was sold, was it not under
your control? Why is it that you
have [a]conceived this deed in your
heart? You have not lied to men,
but to God." *placed*
5 And as he heard these words,
Ananias [r]fell down and breathed
his last; and great fear came upon
all who heard of it. Acts 5:10
6 And the young men arose
and covered him up, and after carrying him out, they buried him.
7 Now there elapsed an interval of about three hours, and his
wife came in, not knowing what
had happened.
8 And Peter responded to her,
"Tell me whether you sold the
land [t]for [r] such and such a price?"
And she said, "Yes, that was the
price." *for so much* · Acts 5:2
9 Then Peter *said* to her, "Why
is it that you have agreed together
to [r]put the Spirit of the Lord to the
test? Behold, the feet of those who
have buried your husband are at
the door, and they shall carry you
out *as well*." Acts 15:10
10 And she [r]fell immediately at
his feet, and breathed her last; and
the young men came in and found
her dead, and they carried her out
and buried her beside her husband. Ezek. 11:13; Acts 5:5
11 And great fear came upon
the whole church, and upon all
who heard of these things.
12 And [t]at the hands of the apostles many signs and wonders were
taking place among the people;
and they were all with one accord
in Solomon's portico. *through*
13 But none of the rest dared to
associate with them; however, the
people held them in high esteem.
14 And all the more believers in

the Lord, multitudes of men and women, were constantly [r]added to *their number*; Acts 2:47; 11:24

15 to such an extent that they even carried the sick out into the streets, and laid them on cots and pallets, so that when Peter came by, [r]at least his shadow might fall on any one of them. Acts 19:12

16 And also the [t]people from the cities in the vicinity of Jerusalem were coming together, bringing people who were sick [10]or afflicted with unclean spirits; and they were all being healed. *multitude*

17 But the high priest rose up, along with all his associates (that is the sect of the Sadducees), and they were filled with jealousy;

18 and they laid hands on the apostles, and [r]put them in a public jail. Acts 4:3

19 But [r]an angel of the Lord during the night opened the gates of the prison, and taking them out he said, Matt. 1:20, 24; 2:13, 19

20 "Go your way, stand and speak to the people in the temple the whole message of this Life."

21 And upon hearing *this*, they entered into the temple about daybreak, and *began* to teach. Now when the high priest and his associates had come, they called the [a]Council together, even all the Senate of the sons of Israel, and sent *orders* to the prison house for them to be brought. *Sanhedrin*

22 But [r]the officers who came did not find them in the prison; and they returned, and reported back, Matt. 26:58; Acts 5:26

23 saying, "We found the prison house locked quite securely and the guards standing at the doors; but when we had opened up, we found no one inside."

24 Now when the captain of the temple *guard* and the chief priests heard these words, they were greatly perplexed about them as to what would come of this.

25 But someone came and reported to them, "Behold, the men whom you put in prison are standing in the temple and teaching the people!"

26 Then the captain went along with the officers and *proceeded* to bring them *back* without violence (for they were afraid of the people, lest they should be stoned).

27 And when they had brought them, they stood them [t]before [r]the Council. And the high priest questioned them, *in* • Matt. 5:22

28 saying, "We gave you [r]strict orders not to continue teaching in this name, and behold, you have filled Jerusalem with your teaching, and intend to bring this man's blood upon us." Acts 4:18

29 But Peter and the apostles answered and said, "We must obey God rather than men.

30 "The God of our fathers raised up Jesus, whom you had put to death by hanging Him on a cross.

31 "He is the one whom God exalted to His right hand as a Prince and a Savior, to grant repentance to Israel, and forgiveness of sins.

32 "And we are witnesses[11] of these things; and [r]*so is* the Holy Spirit, whom God has given to those who obey Him." Heb. 2:4

33 But when they heard this, they were cut to the quick and were intending to slay them.

[10] Lit., *and*

[11] Some mss. add *in Him*, or, *of Him*

34 But a certain Pharisee named [r]Gamaliel, a [r]teacher of the Law, respected by all the people, stood up in the Council and gave orders to put the men outside for a short time. Acts 22:3 • Luke 2:46

35 And he said to them, "Men of Israel, take care what you propose to do with these men.

36 "For some time ago Theudas rose up, claiming to be somebody; and a group of about four hundred men joined up with him. [t]And he was slain; and all who [t]followed him were dispersed and came to nothing. *Who was slain • were obeying*

37 "After this man Judas of Galilee rose up in the days of [r]the census, and drew away *some* people after him, he too perished, and all those who [t]followed him were scattered. Luke 2:2 • *were obeying*

38 "And so in the present case, I say to you, stay away from these men and let them alone, for if this plan or [a]action should be of men, it will be overthrown; *work*

39 but if it is of God, you will not be able to overthrow them; or else you may even be found [r]fighting against God." Acts 11:17

40 And they [t]took his advice; and after calling the apostles in, they flogged them and ordered them to speak no more in the name of Jesus, and *then* released them. *were persuaded by him*

41 So they went on their way from the presence of the [a]Council, rejoicing that they had been considered worthy to suffer shame for *His* name. *Sanhedrin*

42 And every day, in the temple and from house to house, they kept right on teaching and preaching Jesus *as* the Christ.

CHAPTER 6

NOW at this time while the [r]disciples were increasing *in number*, a complaint arose on the part of the [12]Hellenistic *Jews* against the *native* Hebrews, because their widows were being overlooked in the daily serving *of food*. Acts 11:26

2 And the twelve summoned the [a]congregation of the disciples and said, "It is not desirable for us to neglect the word of God in order to serve tables. *multitude*

3 "But select from among you, [r]brethren, seven men of good reputation, full of the Spirit and of wisdom, whom we may put in charge of this task. John 21:23; Acts 1:15

4 "But we will [r]devote ourselves to prayer, and to the [a]ministry of the word." Acts 1:14 • *service*

5 And the statement found approval with the whole congregation; and they chose Stephen, a man full of faith and of the Holy Spirit, and Philip, Prochorus, Nicanor, Timon, Parmenas and Nicolas, a [13]proselyte from Antioch.

6 And these they brought before the apostles; and after praying, they laid their hands on them.

7 And the word of God kept on spreading; and the number of the disciples continued to increase greatly in Jerusalem, and a great many of the priests were becoming obedient to the faith.

8 And Stephen, full of grace and power, was performing great wonders and [a]signs among the people. *attesting miracles*

9 But some men from what was called the Synagogue of the

[12] I.e., non-Palestinian Jews who normally spoke Greek

[13] I.e., a Gentile convert to Judaism

Freedmen, *including* both Cyreni-
ans and Alexandrians, and some
from [r]Cilicia and Asia, rose up and
argued with Stephen. Gal. 1:21
10 And *yet* they were unable to
cope with the wisdom and the
Spirit with which he was speaking.
11 Then they secretly induced
men to say, "We have heard him
speak blasphemous words against
Moses and *against* God."
12 And they stirred up the people, the elders and the scribes, and
they came upon him and dragged
him away, and brought him [t]be-
fore the Council. *into*
13 And they put forward [r]false
witnesses who said, "This man in-
cessantly speaks against this holy
place, and the Law; Acts 7:58
14 for we have heard him say
that [r]this Nazarene, Jesus, will destroy this place and alter the customs which Moses handed down
to us." Matt. 26:61
15 And fixing their gaze on him,
all who were sitting in the [a]Council[r]
saw his face like the face of an angel. *Sanhedrin* • Matt. 5:22

CHAPTER 7

AND the high priest said, "Are
these things so?"
2 And he said, "Hear me,
brethren and fathers! The God of
glory appeared to our father Abraham when he was in Mesopotamia, before he lived in Haran,
3 and said to him, 'DEPART
FROM YOUR COUNTRY AND YOUR
RELATIVES, AND COME INTO THE
LAND THAT I WILL SHOW YOU.'
4 "Then he departed from the
land of the Chaldeans, and settled
in Haran. And [r]from there, after
his father died, *God* removed him
into this country in which you are
now living. Gen. 12:4, 5
5 "And He gave him no inheritance in it, not even a foot of
ground; and *yet,* even when he
had no child, [r]He promised that HE
WOULD GIVE IT TO HIM AS A POS-
SESSION, AND TO HIS OFFSPRING AF-
TER HIM. Gen. 12:7; 13:15
6 "But [r]God spoke to this effect,
that his OFFSPRING WOULD BE
ALIENS IN A FOREIGN LAND, AND
THAT THEY WOULD BE ENSLAVED
AND MISTREATED FOR FOUR HUN-
DRED YEARS. Gen. 15:13f.
7 " 'AND WHATEVER NATION TO
WHICH THEY SHALL BE IN BONDAGE
I MYSELF WILL JUDGE,' said God,
'AND [r]AFTER THAT THEY WILL COME
OUT AND [14]SERVE ME IN THIS
PLACE.' Ex. 3:12
8 "And He gave him [a]the covenant of circumcision; and so
Abraham became the father of
Isaac, and circumcised him on the
eighth day; and Isaac *became the
father of* Jacob, and Jacob *of* the
twelve [r]patriarchs. *a* • Acts 2:29
9 "And the patriarchs [r]became
jealous of Joseph and sold him
into Egypt. And *yet* God was with
him, Gen. 37:11, 28; 39:2, 21f.
10 and rescued him from all his
afflictions, and [r]granted him favor
and wisdom in the sight of Pharaoh, king of Egypt; and he made
him governor over Egypt and all
his household. Gen. 39:21
11 "Now a famine came over all
Egypt and Canaan, and great affliction *with it;* and our fathers
could find no [a]food. *fodder*

[14]Or, *worship*

12"But when Jacob heard that there was grain in Egypt, he sent our fathers *there* the first time.

13"And on the second *visit* Joseph made himself known to his brothers, and [r]Joseph's family was disclosed to Pharaoh. Gen. 45:16

14"And [r]Joseph sent *word* and invited Jacob his father and all his relatives to come to him, seventy-five persons *in all.* Gen. 45:9, 10, 17

15"And [r]Jacob went down to Egypt and *there* passed away, he and our fathers. Gen. 46:1-7

16"And *from there* they were removed to Shechem, and laid in the tomb which Abraham had purchased for a sum of money from the sons of Hamor in Shechem.

17"But as the [r]time of the promise was approaching which God had assured to Abraham, [r]the people increased and multiplied in Egypt, Gen. 15:13 • Ex. 1:7f.

18 until [r]THERE AROSE ANOTHER KING OVER EGYPT WHO KNEW NOTHING ABOUT JOSEPH. Ex. 1:8

19"It was he who took shrewd advantage of our race, and mistreated our fathers so that they would expose their infants and they would not survive.

20"And it was at this time that [r]Moses was born; and he was lovely [t]in the sight of God; and he was nurtured three months in his father's home. Ex. 2:2 • *to God*

21"And after he had been [a]exposed, Pharaoh's daughter took him away, and nurtured him as her own son. *put out to die*

22"And Moses was educated in *all* [r]*the learning* of the Egyptians, and he was a man of power in words and deeds. Is. 19:11

23"But when he was approaching the age of forty, it entered his [t]mind to visit his brethren, the sons of Israel. *heart*

24"And when he saw one *of them* being treated unjustly, he defended him and took vengeance for the oppressed by striking down the Egyptian.

25"And he supposed that his brethren understood that God was granting them deliverance through him; but they did not understand.

26"And on the following day he appeared to them as they were fighting together, and he tried to reconcile them in peace, saying, 'Men, you are brethren, why do you injure one another?'

27"But the one who was injuring his neighbor pushed him away, saying, 'WHO MADE YOU A RULER AND JUDGE OVER US?

28 'YOU [r]DO NOT MEAN TO KILL ME AS YOU KILLED THE EGYPTIAN YESTERDAY, DO YOU?' Ex. 2:14

29"And at this remark MOSES FLED, AND BECAME AN ALIEN IN THE LAND OF MIDIAN, where he became the father of two sons.

30"And after forty years had passed, [r]AN ANGEL APPEARED TO HIM IN THE WILDERNESS OF MOUNT Sinai, IN THE FLAME OF A BURNING THORN BUSH. Ex. 3:1f.; Is. 63:9

31"And when Moses saw it, he *began* to marvel at the sight; and as he approached to look *more* closely, there came the voice of the Lord:

32 'I [r]AM THE GOD OF YOUR FATHERS, THE GOD OF ABRAHAM AND ISAAC AND JACOB.' And Moses shook with fear and would not venture to look. Ex. 3:6

33 "BUT[r] THE LORD SAID TO HIM, 'TAKE[r] OFF THE SANDALS FROM YOUR FEET, FOR THE PLACE ON WHICH YOU ARE STANDING IS HOLY GROUND. Ex. 3:5 • Josh. 5:15

34 'I HAVE CERTAINLY SEEN THE OPPRESSION OF MY PEOPLE IN EGYPT, AND HAVE HEARD THEIR GROANS, AND I HAVE COME DOWN TO DELIVER THEM; COME NOW, AND I WILL SEND YOU TO EGYPT.'

35 "This Moses whom they disowned, saying, 'WHO MADE YOU A RULER AND A JUDGE?' is the one whom God [t]sent *to be* both a ruler and a deliverer with the [t]help of the angel who appeared to him in the thorn bush. *has sent* • *hand*

36 "This man led them out, performing [r]wonders and [a]signs in the land of Egypt and in the Red Sea and in the wilderness for forty years. Ex. 7:3 • *attesting miracles*

37 "This is the Moses who said to the sons of Israel, 'GOD SHALL RAISE UP FOR YOU A PROPHET LIKE ME FROM YOUR BRETHREN.'

38 "This is the one who was in [r]the [a]congregation in the wilderness together with the angel who was speaking to him on Mount Sinai, and *who was* with our fathers; and he received living oracles to pass on to you. Ex. 19:17 • *church*

39 "And our fathers were unwilling to be obedient to him, but repudiated him and in their hearts turned back to Egypt,

40 [r]SAYING TO AARON, 'MAKE FOR US GODS WHO WILL GO BEFORE US; FOR THIS MOSES WHO LED US OUT OF THE LAND OF EGYPT—WE DO NOT KNOW WHAT HAPPENED TO HIM.' Ex. 32:1, 23

41 "And at that time they made a calf and brought a sacrifice to the idol, and were rejoicing in the works of their hands.

42 "But God turned away and delivered them up to serve the host of heaven; as it is written in the book of the prophets, 'IT WAS NOT TO ME THAT YOU OFFERED VICTIMS AND SACRIFICES [r]FORTY YEARS IN THE WILDERNESS, WAS IT, O HOUSE OF ISRAEL? Acts 7:36

43 'YOU ALSO TOOK ALONG THE TABERNACLE OF MOLOCH AND THE STAR OF THE GOD ROMPHA, THE IMAGES WHICH YOU MADE TO WORSHIP THEM. I ALSO WILL REMOVE YOU BEYOND BABYLON.'

44 "Our fathers had the tabernacle of testimony in the wilderness, just as He who spoke to Moses directed *him* to make it according to the pattern which he had seen.

45 "And having received it in their turn, our fathers [r]brought it in with Joshua upon dispossessing the [a]nations whom God drove out before our fathers, until the time of David. Deut. 32:49 • *Gentiles*

46 "And [r]*David* found favor in God's sight, and asked that he might find a dwelling place for the [15]God of Jacob. 2 Sam. 7:8ff.

47 "But it was Solomon who built a house for Him.

48 "However, [r]the Most High does not dwell in *houses* made by *human* hands; as the prophet says: Luke 1:32

49 'HEAVEN[r] IS MY THRONE,
AND EARTH IS THE FOOTSTOOL OF MY FEET;
WHAT KIND OF HOUSE WILL YOU BUILD FOR ME?' says the Lord; Is. 66:1

[15] The earliest mss. read *house* instead of *God;* the Septuagint reads *God*

'OR WHAT PLACE IS THERE
FOR MY REPOSE?
50 'WAS[r] IT NOT MY HAND
WHICH MADE ALL THESE
THINGS?' Is. 66:2

51 "You men who are stiff-necked and uncircumcised in heart and ears are always resisting the Holy Spirit; you are doing just as your fathers did.

52 "Which one of the prophets did your fathers not persecute? And they killed those who had previously announced the coming of [r]the Righteous One, whose betrayers and murderers you have now become; Acts 3:14; 22:14

53 you who received the law as [r]ordained by angels, and *yet* did not keep it." Deut. 33:2; Acts 7:38

54 Now when they heard this, they were [r]cut [t]to the quick, and they *began* gnashing their teeth at him. Acts 5:33 • *in their hearts*

55 But being [r]full of the Holy Spirit, he [r]gazed intently into heaven and saw the glory of God, and Jesus standing at the right hand of God; Acts 2:4 • John 11:41

56 and he said, "Behold, I see the [r]heavens opened up and the Son of Man standing at the right hand of God." John 1:51

57 But they cried out with a loud voice, and covered their ears, and they rushed upon him with one impulse.

58 And when they had driven him out of the city, they *began* stoning *him,* and the witnesses laid aside their robes at the feet of a young man named Saul.

59 And they went on stoning Stephen as he [r]called upon *the Lord* and said, "Lord Jesus, receive my spirit!" Acts 9:14, 21

60 And [r]falling on his knees, he cried out with a loud voice, "Lord, do not hold this sin against them!" And having said this, he [a]fell asleep. Luke 22:41 • *expired*

CHAPTER 8

AND Saul was in hearty agreement with putting him to death.

And on that day a great persecution arose against the church in Jerusalem; and they were all scattered throughout the regions of Judea and Samaria, except the apostles.

2 And *some* devout men buried Stephen, and made loud lamentation over him.

3 But [r]Saul *began* ravaging the church, entering house after house; and dragging off men and women, he would put them in prison. Acts 9:1, 13, 21; 22:4, 19

4 Therefore, those [r]who had been scattered went about preaching the word. Acts 8:1

5 And Philip went down to the city of Samaria and *began* proclaiming Christ to them.

6 And the multitudes with one accord were giving attention to what was said by Philip, as they heard and saw the [a]signs which he was performing. *attesting miracles*

7 For *in the case of* many who had [r]unclean spirits, they were coming out *of them* shouting with a loud voice; and many who had been [r]paralyzed and lame were healed. Mark 16:17 • Matt. 4:24

8 And there was [r]much rejoicing in that city. John 4:40-42

9 Now there was a certain man named Simon, who formerly was practicing [r]magic in the city, and astonishing the people of Samaria, claiming to be someone great; Acts 8:11; 13:6

10 and they all, from smallest to greatest, were giving attention to him, saying, "This man is what is called the Great Power of God."

11 And they were giving him attention because he had for a long time astonished them with his [r]magic arts. Acts 8:9; 13:6

12 But when they believed Philip [r]preaching the good news about the kingdom of God and the name of Jesus Christ, they were being [r]baptized, men and women alike. Acts 1:3; 8:4 • Acts 2:38

13 And even Simon himself believed; and after being baptized, he continued on with Philip; and as he observed [r]signs and great miracles taking place, he was constantly amazed. Acts 8:6

14 Now when the apostles in Jerusalem heard that Samaria had received the word of God, they sent them Peter and John,

15 who came down and prayed for them, [r]that they might receive the Holy Spirit. Acts 2:38; 19:2

16 For He had not yet fallen upon any of them; they had simply been [r]baptized [t]in the name of the Lord Jesus. Acts 2:38 • *into*

17 Then they *began* laying their hands on them, and they were receiving the Holy Spirit.

18 Now when Simon saw that the Spirit was bestowed through the laying on of the apostles' hands, he offered them money,

19 saying, "Give this authority to me as well, so that everyone on whom I lay my hands may receive the Holy Spirit."

20 But Peter said to him, "May your silver perish with you, because you thought you could obtain the gift of God with money!

21 "You have no part or portion in this [t]matter, for your heart is not right before God. *word*

22 "Therefore repent of this wickedness of yours, and pray the Lord that [r]if possible, the intention of your heart may be forgiven you. Is. 55:7

23 "For I see that you are in the gall of bitterness and in [r]the [a]bondage of iniquity." Is. 58:6 • *fetter*

24 But Simon answered and said, "Pray[r] to the Lord for me yourselves, so that nothing of what you have said may come upon me." Gen. 20:7

25 And so, when they had solemnly testified and spoken the word of the Lord, they started back to Jerusalem, and were preaching the gospel to many villages of the Samaritans.

26 But [r]an angel of the Lord spoke to Philip saying, "Arise and go south to the road that descends from Jerusalem to Gaza." (This is a desert *road.*) Acts 5:19; 8:29

27 And he arose and went; and behold, [r]there was an Ethiopian eunuch, a court official of Candace, queen of the Ethiopians, who was in charge of all her treasure; and he had come to Jerusalem to worship. Ps. 68:31; 87:4

28 And he was returning and sitting in his chariot, and was reading the prophet Isaiah.

29 And the Spirit said to Philip, "Go up and join this chariot."

30 And when Philip had run up, he heard him reading Isaiah the

prophet, and said, "Do you understand what you are reading?"
31 And he said, "Well, how
could I, unless someone guides
me?" And he invited Philip to
come up and sit with him.
32 Now the passage of Scripture which he was reading was
this:

"HE[r] WAS LED AS A SHEEP TO
SLAUGHTER; Is. 53:7
AND AS A LAMB BEFORE ITS
SHEARER IS SILENT,
SO HE DOES NOT OPEN HIS
MOUTH.
33 "IN HUMILIATION HIS JUDG-
MENT WAS TAKEN AWAY;
WHO SHALL [a]RELATE HIS
GENERATION? *describe*
FOR HIS LIFE IS REMOVED
FROM THE EARTH."

34 And the eunuch answered
Philip and said, "Please *tell me*, of
whom does the prophet say this?
Of himself, or of someone else?"
35 And Philip [r]opened his
mouth, and beginning from this
Scripture he [r]preached Jesus to
him. Matt. 5:2 • Acts 5:42
36 And as they went along the
road they came to some water;
and the eunuch *said, "Look! Water! [r]What prevents me from being
baptized?" Acts 10:47
37 [[16]And Philip said, "If you believe with all your heart, you
may." And he answered and said,
"I believe that Jesus Christ is the
Son of God."]
38 And he ordered the chariot
to stop; and they both went down
into the water, Philip as well as
the eunuch; and he baptized him.
39 And when they came up out
of the water, [r]the Spirit of the Lord
snatched Philip away; and the eunuch saw him no more, but went
on his way rejoicing. Ezek. 3:12, 14
40 But Philip [a]found himself at
[r]Azotus; and as he passed through
he kept preaching the gospel to all
the cities, until he came to Caesarea. *was found* • Josh. 11:22

CHAPTER 9

NOW Saul, still [r]breathing [t]threats
and murder against the disciples
of the Lord, went to the high
priest, Acts 8:3; 9:13-21 • *threat*
2 and asked for [r]letters from
him to the synagogues at Damascus, so that if he found any belonging to the Way, both men and
women, he might bring them
bound to Jerusalem. Acts 9:14, 21
3 And it came about that as he
journeyed, he was approaching
Damascus, and suddenly a light
from heaven flashed around him;
4 and [r]he fell to the ground, and
heard a voice saying to him,
"Saul, Saul, why are you persecuting Me?" Acts 22:7; 26:14
5 And he said, "Who art Thou,
Lord?" And He *said*, "I am Jesus
whom you are persecuting,
6 but rise, and enter the city,
and [r]it shall be told you what you
must do." Acts 9:16
7 And the men who traveled
with him stood speechless, hearing the voice, but seeing no one.
8 And Saul got up from the
ground, and though his eyes were
open, he could see nothing; and
leading him by the hand, they
brought him into Damascus.
9 And he was three days with-

[16]Many mss. do not contain this verse

out sight, and neither ate nor
drank.
10 Now there was a certain disciple at Damascus, named Ananias; and the Lord said to him in a
vision, "Ananias." And he said,
"Behold, *here am* I, Lord."
11 And the Lord *said* to him,
"Arise and go to the street called
Straight, and inquire at the house
of Judas for a man from [r]Tarsus
named Saul, for behold, he is
praying, Acts 9:30; 11:25; 21:39
12 and he has seen [17]in a vision a
man named Ananias come in and
lay his hands on him, so that he
might regain his sight."
13 But Ananias answered,
"Lord, I have heard from many
about this man, how much harm
he did to Thy saints at Jerusalem;
14 and here he has authority
from the chief priests to bind all
who call upon Thy name."
15 But the Lord said to him,
"Go, for [r]he is a chosen [18]instru-
ment of Mine, to bear My name
before the Gentiles and kings and
the sons of Israel; Acts 13:2
16 for [r]I will show him how
much he must suffer for My
name's sake." Acts 20:23; 21:4, 11
17 And Ananias departed and
entered the house, and after [r]lay-
ing his hands on him said,
"Brother Saul, the Lord Jesus,
who appeared to you on the road
by which you were coming, has
sent me so that you may regain
your sight, and be filled with the
Holy Spirit." Mark 5:23; Acts 6:6
18 And immediately there fell
from his eyes something like
scales, and he regained his sight,
and he arose and was baptized;
19 and he took food and was
strengthened.
Now [r]for several days he was
with [r]the disciples who were at Damascus, Acts 26:20 • Acts 9:26, 38
20 and immediately he *began* to
proclaim Jesus in the synagogues,
saying, "He is the Son of God."
21 And all those hearing him
continued to be amazed, and were
saying, "Is this not he who in Jerusalem [r]destroyed those who
called on this name, and *who* had
come here for the purpose of
bringing them bound before the
chief priests?" Acts 8:3; 9:13
22 But Saul kept increasing in
strength and confounding the
Jews who lived at Damascus by
proving that this *Jesus* is the
Christ.
23 And when [r]many days had
elapsed, the Jews plotted together
to do away with him, Gal. 1:17
24 but [r]their plot became known
to Saul. And they were also
watching the gates day and night
so that they might put him to
death; Acts 20:3, 19; 23:12, 30; 25:3
25 but his disciples took him by
night, and let him down through
an opening in the wall, lowering
him in a large basket.
26 And when he had come to
Jerusalem, he was trying to associate with the disciples; and they
were all afraid of him, not believing that he was a disciple.
27 But [r]Barnabas took hold of
him and brought him to the apostles and described to them how he
had [r]seen the Lord on the road,
and that He had talked to him,
and how at Damascus he had spo-

[17] Some mss. do not contain *in a vision*
[18] Or, *vessel*

ken out boldly in the name of
Jesus. Acts 4:36 • Acts 9:3-6
28 And he was with them [t]mov-
ing about freely in Jerusalem,
speaking out boldly in the name of
the Lord. *going in and going out*
29 And he was talking and arguing with the [r]Hellenistic *Jews;* but
they were attempting to put him
to death. Acts 6:1
30 But when [r]the brethren
learned *of it,* they brought him
down to Caesarea and sent him
away to Tarsus. Acts 1:15
31 So [r]the church throughout all
Judea and Galilee and Samaria
[t]enjoyed peace, being built up;
and, going on in the fear of the
Lord and in the comfort of the
Holy Spirit, it continued to increase. Acts 5:11 • *was having*
32 Now it came about that as
Peter was traveling through all
those parts, he came down also to
the saints who lived at Lydda.
33 And there he found a certain
man named Aeneas, who had
been bedridden eight years, for he
was paralyzed.
34 And Peter said to him, "Aeneas, Jesus Christ heals you; arise,
and make your bed." And immediately he arose.
35 And all who lived at [r]Lydda
and Sharon saw him, and they
turned to the Lord. 1 Chr. 8:12
36 Now in [r]Joppa there was a
certain disciple named Tabitha
(which translated *in Greek* is
called Dorcas); this woman was
abounding with deeds of kindness
and charity, which she continually
did. Josh. 19:46; 2 Chr. 2:16
37 And it came about [t]at that
time that she fell sick and died;
and when they had washed her
body, they laid it in an [r]upper
room. *in those days* • Acts 1:13
38 And since Lydda was near
Joppa, the disciples, having heard
that Peter was there, sent two
men to him, entreating him, "Do
not delay to come to us."
39 And Peter arose and went
with them. And when he had
come, they brought him into the
upper room; and all the widows
stood beside him weeping, and
showing all the [19]tunics and garments that Dorcas used to make
while she was with them.
40 But Peter [r]sent them all out
and [r]knelt down and prayed, and
turning to the body, he said, "Tabitha, arise." And she opened her
eyes, and when she saw Peter, she
sat up. Matt. 9:25 • Luke 22:41
41 And he gave her his hand
and raised her up; and calling [r]the
[a]saints and widows, he presented
her alive. Acts 9:13, 32 • *holy ones*
42 And it became known all
over [r]Joppa, and many believed in
the Lord. Josh. 19:46; 2 Chr. 2:16
43 And it came about that he
stayed many days in Joppa with a
certain tanner, Simon.

CHAPTER 10

NOW *there was* a certain man at
[r]Caesarea named Cornelius, a centurion of what was called the Ital-
ian [20]cohort, Acts 8:40; 10:24
2 a devout man, and [r]one who
feared God with all his household,
and gave many [21]alms to the *Jew-*
ish people, and prayed to God
continually. Acts 10:22, 35; 13:16
3 About [r]the [22]ninth hour of the

[19] Or, *inner garments* [20] Or, *battalion*
[21] Or, *gifts of charity* [22] I.e., 3 p.m.

day he clearly saw [r]in a vision an
angel of God who had *just* come in
to him, and said to him, "Cornelius!" Acts 3:1 • Acts 9:10
4 And fixing his gaze upon him
and being much alarmed, he said,
"What is it, Lord?" And he said to
him, "Your prayers and [a][23]alms
have ascended as a memorial before God. *deeds of charity*
5 "And now dispatch *some* men
to [r]Joppa, and send for a man
named Simon, who is also called
Peter; Acts 9:36
6 he [a]is staying with a certain
tanner *named* Simon, whose
house is by the sea." *is lodging*
7 And when the angel who was
speaking to him had departed, he
summoned two of his [a]servants
and a devout soldier of those who
were in constant attendance upon
him, *household slaves*
8 and after he had explained
everything to them, he sent them
to [r]Joppa. Acts 9:36
9 And on the next day, as they
were on their way, and approaching the city, [r]Peter went up on the
housetop about the [24]sixth hour to
pray. Acts 10:9-32; 11:5-14
10 And he became hungry, and
was desiring to eat; but while they
were making preparations, he [r]fell
into a trance; Acts 11:5; 22:17
11 and he *beheld [r]the [a]sky
opened up, and a certain [25]object
like a great sheet coming down,
lowered by four corners to the
ground, John 1:51 • *heaven*
12 and there were in it all *kinds*
of four-footed animals and
[26]crawling creatures of the earth
and birds of the [a]air. *heaven*
13 And a voice came to him,
"Arise, Peter, kill and eat!"
14 But Peter said, "By no
means, Lord, for I have never eat-
en anything unholy and unclean."
15 And again a voice *came* to
him a second time, "What [r]God
has cleansed, no *longer* consider
[t]unholy." Matt. 15:11 • *common*
16 And this happened three
times; and immediately the object
was taken up into the sky.
17 Now while Peter was greatly
perplexed [t]in mind as to what the
vision which he had seen might
be, behold, the men who had been
sent by Cornelius, having asked
directions for Simon's house, appeared at the gate; *himself*
18 and calling out, they were
asking whether Simon, who was
also called Peter, was [a]staying
there. *lodging*
19 And while Peter was reflect-
ing on [r]the vision, [r]the Spirit said to
him, "Behold, three men are looking for you. Acts 10:3 • Acts 8:29
20 "But arise, go downstairs, and
accompany them without misgivings; for I have sent them Myself."
21 And Peter went down to the
men and said, "Behold, I am the
one you are looking for; what is
the reason for which you have
come?"
22 And they said, "Cornelius, a
centurion, a righteous and God-
fearing man well spoken of by the
entire nation of the Jews, was *di-*
vinely directed by a holy angel to
send for you *to come* to his house
and hear a message from you."
23 And so he invited them in
and gave them lodging.
And on the next day he arose
and went away with them, and

[23]Or, *deeds of charity* [24]I.e., noon
[25]Or, *vessel* [26]Or possibly, *reptiles*

[r]some of the brethren from Joppa
accompanied him. Acts 10:45
24 And on the following day he
entered [r]Caesarea. Now Cornelius
was waiting for them, and had
called together his relatives and
close friends. Acts 8:40; 10:1
25 And when it came about that
Peter entered, Cornelius met him,
and fell at his feet and [a]worshiped
him. *prostrated himself in reverence*
26 But Peter raised him up, saying, "Stand[r] up; I too am *just* a
man." Acts 14:15
27 And as he talked with him,
he entered, and [t]found many people assembled. *finds*
28 And he said to them, "You
yourselves know how unlawful it
is for a man who is a Jew to associate with a foreigner or to visit
him; and *yet* God has shown me
that I should not call any man [a]un-
holy or unclean. *profane*
29 "That is why I came without
even raising any objection when I
was sent for. And so I ask for
what reason you have sent for
me."
30 And Cornelius said, "Four
days ago to this hour, I was praying in my house during the [27]ninth
hour; and behold, a man stood before me in shining garments,
31 and he *said, 'Cornelius,
your prayer has been heard and
your [a]alms have been remembered
before God. *deeds of charity*
32 'Send therefore to Joppa and
invite Simon, who is also called
Peter, to come to you; he is [a]stay-
ing at the house of Simon *the* tanner by the sea.' *lodging*
33 "And so I sent to you immediately, and you have been kind
enough to come. Now then, we
are all here present before God to
hear all that you have been commanded by the Lord."
34 And [r]opening his mouth, Peter said: Matt. 5:2
"I most certainly understand
now that God is not one to show
partiality,
35 but in every nation the man
who fears Him and does what is
right, is welcome to Him.
36 "The word which He sent to
the sons of Israel, preaching [a]peace
through Jesus Christ (He is Lord
of all)— *the gospel of peace*
37 you yourselves know the
thing which took place throughout all Judea, starting from Galilee, after the baptism which John
proclaimed.
38 "*You know of* Jesus of Nazareth, how God anointed Him with
the Holy Spirit and with power,
[t]and *how* He went about doing
good, and healing all who were
oppressed by the devil; for God
was with Him. *who went*
39 "And we are witnesses of all
the things He did both in the land
of the Jews and in Jerusalem. And
they also put Him to death by
hanging Him on a cross.
40 "God raised Him up on the
third day, and granted that He
should become visible,
41 not to all the people, but to
witnesses who were chosen beforehand by God, *that is,* to us,
who ate and drank with Him after
He arose from the dead.
42 "And He ordered us to preach
to the people, and solemnly to testify that this is the One who has
been appointed by God as Judge
of the living and the dead.

[27] I.e., 3 to 4 p.m.

43 "Of Him all the prophets bear witness that through His name everyone who believes in Him receives forgiveness of sins."

44 While Peter was still speaking these words, the Holy Spirit fell upon all those who were listening to the [t]message. *word*

45 And all the circumcised believers who had come with Peter were amazed, because the gift of the Holy Spirit had been poured out upon the Gentiles also.

46 For they were hearing them speaking with tongues and exalting God. Then Peter answered,

47 "Surely no one can refuse the water for these to be baptized who have received the Holy Spirit just as we *did*, can he?"

48 And he ordered them to be baptized in the name of Jesus Christ. Then they asked him to stay on for a few days.

CHAPTER 11

NOW the apostles and the brethren who were throughout Judea heard that the Gentiles also had received the word of God.

2 And when Peter came up to Jerusalem, those who were circumcised took issue with him,

3 saying, "You [a]went to uncircumcised men and ate with them." *entered the house of*

4 But Peter began *speaking* and *proceeded* to explain to them in orderly sequence, saying,

5 "I was in the city of Joppa praying; and in a trance I saw a vision, a certain object coming down like a great sheet lowered by four corners from the sky; and it came right down to me,

6 and when I had fixed my gaze upon it and was observing it [t]I saw the four-footed animals of the earth and the wild beasts and the [28]crawling creatures and the birds of the air. *and I saw*

7 "And I also heard a voice saying to me, 'Arise, Peter; [a]kill and eat.' *sacrifice*

8 "But I said, 'By no means, Lord, for nothing unholy or unclean has ever entered my mouth.'

9 "But a voice from heaven answered a second time, 'What God has cleansed, no longer [t]consider unholy.' *make common*

10 "And this happened three times, and everything was drawn back up into [a]the sky. *heaven*

11 "And behold, at that moment three men appeared before the house in which we were *staying*, having been sent to me from [r]Caesarea. Acts 8:40

12 "And [r]the Spirit told me to go with them without misgivings. And these six brethren also went with me, and we entered the man's house. Acts 8:29

13 "And he reported to us how he had seen the angel standing in his house, and saying, 'Send to Joppa, and have Simon, who is also called Peter, brought here;

14 and he shall speak words to you by which you will be saved, you and all your household.'

15 "And as I began to speak, the Holy Spirit fell upon them, just as *He did* upon us at the beginning.

16 "And I remembered the word of the Lord, how He used to say, 'John[r] baptized with water, but you shall be baptized [a]with the Holy Spirit.' Acts 1:5 • *in*

[28] Or possibly, *reptiles*

17 "If God therefore gave to them the same gift as *He gave* to us also after believing in the Lord Jesus Christ, who was I that I could stand in God's way?"

18 And when they heard this, they quieted down, and glorified God, saying, "Well then, God has granted to the Gentiles also the repentance *that leads* to life."

19 So then those who were scattered because of the [a]persecution that arose in connection with Stephen made their way [t]to Phoenicia and Cyprus and Antioch, speaking the word to no one except to Jews alone. *tribulation • as far as*

20 But there were some of them, men of Cyprus and Cyrene, who came to Antioch and *began* speaking to the [29]Greeks also, preaching the Lord Jesus.

21 And [r]the hand of the Lord was with them, and [r]a large number who believed turned to the Lord. Luke 1:66 • Acts 2:47

22 And the [t]news about them reached the ears of the church at Jerusalem, and they sent Barnabas off to Antioch. *word*

23 Then when he had come and [t]witnessed the grace of God, he rejoiced and *began* to encourage them all with resolute heart to remain *true* to the Lord; *seen*

24 for he was a good man, and full of the Holy Spirit and of faith. And considerable [t]numbers were brought to the Lord. *multitudes*

25 And he left for [r]Tarsus to look for Saul; Acts 9:11

26 and when he had found him, he brought *him* to Antioch. And it came about that for an entire year they met with the church, and taught considerable numbers; and the disciples were first called Christians in Antioch.

27 Now [t]at this time some prophets came down from Jerusalem to Antioch. *in these days*

28 And one of them named Agabus stood up and *began* to indicate by the Spirit that there would certainly be a great famine all over the world. And this took place in the *reign* of Claudius.

29 And in the proportion that any of the disciples had means, each of them determined to send *a contribution* for the relief of the brethren living in Judea.

30 And this they did, sending it [t]in charge of Barnabas and Saul to the elders. *through the hand of*

CHAPTER 12

NOW about that time Herod the king laid hands on some who belonged to the church, in order to mistreat them.

2 And he [r]had James the brother of John put to death with a sword. Matt. 4:21; 20:23

3 And when he saw that it pleased the Jews, he proceeded to arrest Peter also. Now it was during the days of Unleavened Bread.

4 And when he had seized him, he put him in prison, delivering him to four [t]squads of soldiers to guard him, intending after the Passover to bring him out before the people. *quaternions*

5 So Peter was kept in the prison, but prayer for him was being made fervently by the church to God.

6 And on the very night when Herod was about to bring him for-

[29]Some mss. read *Greek-speaking Jews*

ward, Peter was sleeping between two soldiers, [r]bound with two chains; and guards in front of the door were watching over the prison. Acts 21:33

7 And behold, an angel of the Lord suddenly appeared, and a light shone in the cell; and he struck Peter's side and roused him, saying, "Get up quickly." And his chains fell off his hands.

8 And the angel said to him, "Gird yourself and put on your sandals." And he did so. And he *said to him, "Wrap your cloak around you and follow me."

9 And he went out and continued to follow, and he did not know that what was being done by the angel was real, but thought he was seeing [r]a vision. Acts 9:10

10 And when they had passed the first and second guard, they came to the iron gate that leads into the city, which [r]opened for them by itself; and they went out and went along one street; and immediately the angel departed from him. Acts 5:19; 16:26

11 And when Peter [r]came to himself, he said, "Now I know for sure that the Lord has sent forth His angel and rescued me from the hand of Herod and from all that the Jewish people were expecting." Luke 15:17

12 And when he realized *this*, he went to the house of Mary, the mother of [r]John who was also called Mark, where many were gathered together and were praying. Acts 12:25; 13:5,13; 15:37

13 And when he knocked at the door of the gate, a servant-girl named Rhoda came to answer.

14 And when she recognized Peter's voice, because of her joy she did not open the gate, but ran in and announced that Peter was standing in front of the gate.

15 And they said to her, "You are out of your mind!" But she kept insisting that it was so. And they kept saying, "It is his angel."

16 But Peter continued knocking; and when they had opened *the door*, they saw him and were amazed.

17 But motioning to them with his hand to be silent, he described to them how the Lord had led him out of the prison. And he said, "Report these things to James and the brethren." And he departed and went to another place.

18 Now when day came, there was no small disturbance among the soldiers *as to* what could have become of Peter.

19 And when Herod had searched for him and had not found him, he examined the guards and ordered that they be led away *to execution*. And he went down from Judea to Caesarea and was spending time there.

20 Now he was very angry with the people of [r]Tyre and Sidon; and with one accord they came to him, and having won over Blastus the king's chamberlain, they were asking for peace, because [r]their country was fed by the king's country. Matt. 11:21 • 1 Kin. 5:11

21 And on an appointed day Herod, having put on his royal apparel, took his seat on the [a]rostrum and *began* delivering an address to them. *judgment seat*

22 And the people kept crying

out, "The voice of a god and not of
a man!"
23 And immediately an angel of
the Lord struck him because he
did not give God the glory, and he
was eaten by worms and died.
24 But [r]the word of the Lord
continued to grow and to be multiplied. Acts 6:7; 19:20
25 And Barnabas and Saul returned from Jerusalem when they
had fulfilled their [t]mission, taking
along with *them* John, who was
also called Mark. *ministry*

CHAPTER 13

NOW there were at Antioch, in
the church that was *there*, prophets and teachers: Barnabas, and
Simeon who was called Niger, and
Lucius of Cyrene, and Manaen
who had been brought up with
Herod the tetrarch, and Saul.
2 And while they were ministering to the Lord and fasting, the
Holy Spirit said, "Set apart for Me
Barnabas and Saul for the work to
which I have called them."
3 Then, when they had fasted
and prayed and laid their hands
on them, they sent them away.
4 So, being [r]sent out by the
Holy Spirit, they went down to
Seleucia and from there they
sailed to Cyprus. Acts 13:2f.
5 And when they reached Sala-
mis, they *began* to proclaim the
word of God in [r]the synagogues of
the Jews; and they also had John
as their helper. Acts 9:20; 13:14
6 And when they had gone
through the whole island as far as
Paphos, they found a certain magician, a Jewish false prophet
whose name was Bar-Jesus,
7 who was with the [r]proconsul,
Sergius Paulus, a man of intelligence. This man summoned Barnabas and Saul and sought to hear
the word of God. Acts 13:8, 12
8 But Elymas the [r]magician (for
thus his name is translated) was
opposing them, seeking to turn
the [r]proconsul away from the
faith. Acts 8:9 • Acts 13:7, 12
9 But Saul, who was also
known as Paul, [a]filled with the
Holy Spirit, fixed his gaze upon
him, *having* just *been filled*
10 and said, "You who are full
of all deceit and fraud, you [r]son of
the devil, you enemy of all righteousness, will you not cease to
make crooked the straight ways
of the Lord? Matt. 13:38
11 "And now, behold, the hand of
the Lord is upon you, and you will
be blind and not see the sun for a
time." And immediately a mist
and a darkness fell upon him, and
he went about seeking those who
would lead him by the hand.
12 Then the [r]proconsul believed
when he saw what had happened,
being amazed at the teaching of
the Lord. Acts 13:7, 8; 18:12
13 Now Paul and his companions put out to sea from [r]Paphos
and came to Perga in Pamphylia;
and John left them and returned
to Jerusalem. Acts 13:6
14 But going on from Perga,
they arrived at Pisidian Antioch,
and on the Sabbath day they went
into the synagogue and sat down.
15 And after [r]the reading of the
Law and the Prophets the synagogue officials sent to them, saying, "Brethren, if you have any
word of exhortation for the people, say it." Acts 15:21

16 And Paul stood up, and [r]mo-
tioning with his hand, he said,
"**M**en of Israel, and you who fear
God, listen: Acts 12:17
17 "The God of this people Israel
chose our fathers, and made the
people great during their stay in
the land of Egypt, and with an up-
lifted arm He led them out from it.
18 "And for [r]a period of about
forty years He put up with them in
the wilderness. Num. 14:34
19 "And [r]when He had destroyed
[r]seven nations in the land of Canaan, He distributed their land as
an inheritance—*all of which took*
about four hundred and fifty
years. Acts 7:45 • Deut. 7:1
20 "And after these things He
[r]gave *them* judges until [r]Samuel
the prophet. Judg. 2:16 • 1 Sam. 3:20
21 "And then they asked for a
king, and God gave them Saul the
son of Kish, a man of the tribe of
Benjamin, for forty years.
22 "And after He had [r]removed
him, He raised up David to be
their king, concerning whom He
also testified and said, 'I HAVE
FOUND DAVID the son of Jesse, A
MAN AFTER MY HEART, who will do
all My [t]will.' 1 Sam. 15:23 • *wills*
23 "From [r] the offspring of this
man, [r]according to promise, God
has brought to Israel a Savior,
Jesus, Matt. 1:1 • Acts 13:32f.
24 after John had proclaimed
before [t]His coming a baptism of
repentance to all the people of Israel. *the face of His entering*
25 "And while John [r]was com-
pleting his course, [r]he kept saying,
'What do you suppose that I am? I
am not *He*. But behold, one is
coming after me the sandals of
whose feet I am not worthy to untie.' Acts 20:24 • Matt. 3:11
26 "Brethren, sons of Abraham's
family, and those among you who
fear God, to us the word of [r]this
salvation is sent out. John 6:68
27 "For those who live in Jerusalem, and their rulers, recognizing
neither Him nor the [t]utterances of
the prophets which are read every
Sabbath, fulfilled *these* by condemning *Him*. *voices*
28 "And though they found no
ground for *putting Him to* death,
they [r]asked Pilate that He be [t]ex-
ecuted. Acts 3:14 • *destroyed*
29 "And when they had [r]carried
out all that was written concerning Him, they took Him down
from the [t]cross and laid Him in a
tomb. Acts 26:22 • *wood*
30 "But God [r]raised Him from the
dead; Acts 2:24; 13:33, 34, 37
31 and for many days He appeared to those who came up with
Him from Galilee to Jerusalem,
the very ones who are now His
witnesses to the people.
32 "And we [r]preach to you the
good news of the promise made to
the fathers, Acts 5:42; 14:15
33 that God has fulfilled this
promise to our children in that He
raised up Jesus, as it is also written in the second Psalm, 'THOU
ART MY SON; TODAY I HAVE BEGOT-
TEN THEE.'
34 "*And as for the fact* that He
[r]raised Him up from the dead, no
more to return to decay, He has
spoken in this way: 'I WILL GIVE
YOU THE HOLY *and* SURE *blessings*
OF DAVID.' Acts 2:24; 13:30, 33, 37
35 "Therefore He also says in another *Psalm*, 'THOU WILT NOT [t]AL-

LOW THY[a]HOLY ONE TO UNDERGO
DECAY.' *give · Devout*
36"For David, after he had
served the purpose of God in his
own generation, fell asleep, and
was laid among his fathers, and
underwent decay;
37 but He whom God raised did
not [t]undergo decay. *see corruption*
38"Therefore let it be known to
you, brethren, that [r]through [t]Him
forgiveness of sins is proclaimed
to you, Luke 24:47 · *this One*
39 and through Him [r]everyone
who believes is [t]freed from all
things, from which you could not
be freed through the Law of
Moses. Acts 10:43 · *justified*
40"Take heed therefore, so that
the thing spoken of in the Prophets may not come upon *you*:
41 'BEHOLD, YOU SCOFFERS, AND
MARVEL, AND PERISH;
FOR I AM ACCOMPLISHING A
WORK IN YOUR DAYS,
A WORK WHICH YOU WILL
NEVER BELIEVE, THOUGH
SOMEONE SHOULD DE-
SCRIBE IT TO YOU.'"
42 And as [t]Paul and Barnabas
were going out, [t]the people kept
begging that these [t]things might
be spoken to them the next Sabbath. *they were · they · words*
43 Now when *the meeting of* the
synagogue had broken up, many
of the Jews and of the [r]God-fearing
proselytes followed Paul and Barnabas, who, speaking to them,
were urging them to continue in
the grace of God. Acts 13:50
44 And the next Sabbath nearly
the whole city assembled to hear
the word of God.
45 But when the Jews saw the
crowds, they were filled with jealousy, and *began* contradicting the
things spoken by Paul, and were
[a]blaspheming. *reviling*
46 And Paul and Barnabas
spoke out boldly and said, "It was
necessary that the word of God
should be spoken to you [r]first;
since you repudiate it, and judge
yourselves unworthy of eternal
life, behold, we are turning to the
Gentiles. Acts 3:26; 9:20; 13:5, 14
47"For thus the Lord has commanded us,
'I[r] HAVE PLACED YOU AS A
LIGHT FOR THE GENTILES,
THAT YOU SHOULD BRING
SALVATION TO THE END OF
THE EARTH.'" Is. 42:6
48 And when the Gentiles heard
this, they *began* rejoicing and glorifying the word of the Lord; and
as many as had been appointed to
eternal life believed.
49 And [r]the word of the Lord
was being spread through the
whole region. Acts 13:12
50 But the Jews aroused the devout women of prominence and
the leading men of the city, and
instigated a persecution against
Paul and Barnabas, and drove
them out of their district.
51 But they shook off the dust
of their feet *in protest* against
them and went to Iconium.
52 And the disciples were continually [r]filled with joy and with
the Holy Spirit. Acts 2:4

CHAPTER 14

AND it came about that in [r]Ico-
nium they entered the synagogue
of the Jews together, and spoke in
such a manner that a great multi-

tude believed, both of Jews and of
Greeks. Acts 13:51; 14:19, 21
2 But the Jews who disbe-
lieved stirred up the [t]minds of the
Gentiles, and embittered them
against the brethren. *souls*
3 Therefore they spent a long
time *there* speaking boldly *with*
reliance upon the Lord, who was
bearing witness to the word of His
grace, granting that signs and
wonders be done by their hands.
4 But the multitude of the city
was divided; and some [t]sided with
[r]the Jews, and some with the apostles. *were* • Acts 13:45, 50; 14:2
5 And when an attempt was
made by both the Gentiles and [r]the
Jews with their rulers, to mistreat
and to stone them, Acts 13:45, 50
6 they became aware of it and
fled to the cities of [r]Lycaonia, [r]Lys-
tra and Derbe, and the surrounding region; Acts 14:11 • Acts 14:8, 21
7 and there they continued to
[r]preach the gospel. Acts 14:15, 21
8 And at [r]Lystra there was sitting a certain man, without
strength in his feet, lame from his
mother's womb, who had never
walked. Acts 14:6, 21; 16:1f.
9 This man was listening to
Paul as he spoke, who, [r]when he
had fixed his gaze upon him, and
had seen that he had faith to be
[t]made well, Acts 3:4 • *saved*
10 said with a loud voice,
"Stand upright on your feet." And
he leaped up and *began* to walk.
11 And when the multitudes
saw what Paul had done, they
raised their voice, saying in the
[r]Lycaonian language, "The gods
have become like men and have
come down to us." Acts 14:6
12 And they *began* calling Barnabas, Zeus, and Paul, Hermes,
because he was the chief speaker.
13 And the priest of Zeus,
whose *temple* was [t]just outside the
city, brought oxen and garlands to
the gates, and wanted to offer sacrifice with the crowds. *in front of*
14 But when the apostles, Barnabas and Paul, heard of it, they
tore their robes and rushed out
into the crowd, crying out
15 and saying, "Men, why are
you doing these things? We are
also [r]men of the same nature as
you, and preach the gospel to you
in order that you should turn from
these [30]vain things to a living God,
WHO MADE THE HEAVEN AND THE
EARTH AND THE SEA, AND ALL THAT
IS IN THEM. Acts 10:26; James 5:17
16 "And in the generations gone
by He permitted all the [a]nations to
go their own ways; *Gentiles*
17 and yet [r]He did not leave
Himself without witness, in that
He did good and gave you rains
from heaven and fruitful seasons,
[t]satisfying your hearts with food
and gladness." Acts 17:26f. • *filling*
18 And *even* saying these
things, they with difficulty restrained the crowds from offering
sacrifice to them.
19 But Jews came from Antioch
and Iconium, and having won
over the multitudes, they stoned
Paul and dragged him out of the
city, supposing him to be dead.
20 But while the disciples stood
around him, he arose and entered
the city. And the next day he went
away with Barnabas to Derbe.
21 And after they had [r]preached
the gospel to that city and had

[30]I.e., idols

made many disciples, they returned to Lystra and to Iconium
and to Antioch, Acts 14:7
22 strengthening the souls of
the disciples, encouraging them to
continue in the faith, and *saying,*
"Through many tribulations we
must enter the kingdom of God."
23 And when they had ap-
pointed elders for them in every
church, having prayed with fasting, they commended them to the
Lord in whom they had believed.
24 And they passed through Pisidia and came into Pamphylia.
25 And when they had spoken
the word in [r]Perga, they went
down to Attalia; Acts 13:13
26 and from there they sailed to
[r]Antioch, from which they had
been commended to the grace of
God for the work that they had [t]ac-
complished. Acts 11:19 • *fulfilled*
27 And when they had arrived
and gathered the church together,
they *began* to [r]report all things
that God had done with them and
[t]how He had opened a door of faith
to the Gentiles. Acts 15:3, 4, 12 • *that*
28 And they spent [t]a long time
with the disciples. *not a little*

CHAPTER 15

AND some men came down from
Judea and *began* teaching the
brethren, "Unless you are circumcised according to the custom of
Moses, you cannot be saved."
2 And when Paul and Barnabas had great dissension and de-
bate with them, *the brethren determined that* Paul and Barnabas
and certain others of them should
go up to Jerusalem to the apostles
and elders concerning this issue.
3 Therefore, being [r]sent on
their way by the church, they
were passing through both Phoenicia and Samaria, describing in
detail the conversion of the Gentiles, and were bringing great joy
to all the brethren. Acts 20:38
4 And when they arrived at Jerusalem, they were received by
the church and the apostles and
the elders, and they reported all
that God had done with them.
5 But certain ones of [r]the sect
of the Pharisees who had believed, stood up, saying, "It is necessary to circumcise them, and to
direct them to observe the Law of
Moses." Acts 5:17; 24:5, 14; 26:5
6 And the apostles and the elders came together to [t]look into
this [t]matter. *see about • word*
7 And after there had been
much [r]debate, Peter stood up and
said to them, "Brethren, you know
that [t]in the early days God made a
choice among you, that by my
mouth the Gentiles should hear
the word of the gospel and believe. Acts 15:2 • *from days of old*
8 "And God, [r]who knows the
heart, bore witness to them, giving them the Holy Spirit, just as
He also did to us; Acts 1:24
9 and [r]He made no distinction
between us and them, cleansing
their hearts by faith. Acts 10:28
10 "Now therefore why do you
put God to the test by placing
upon the neck of the disciples a
yoke which neither our fathers
nor we have been able to bear?
11 "But we believe that we are
saved through [r]the grace of the
Lord Jesus, in the same way as
they also are." Rom. 3:24; 5:15

12 And all the multitude kept silent, and they were listening to
Barnabas and Paul as they were
[r]relating what signs and wonders
God had done through them
among the Gentiles. Acts 14:27
13 And after they had stopped
speaking, James answered, saying, "Brethren, listen to me.
14 "Simeon[r] has related how God
first concerned Himself about taking from among the Gentiles a
people for His name. Acts 15:7
15 "And with this the words of
[r]the Prophets agree, just as it is
written, Acts 13:40
16 'AFTER[r] THESE THINGS I WILL
RETURN,
AND I WILL REBUILD THE
[a]TABERNACLE OF DAVID
WHICH HAS FALLEN,
AND I WILL REBUILD ITS RU-
INS, Amos 9:11 • *tent*
AND I WILL RESTORE IT,
17 IN ORDER THAT THE REST OF
[t]MANKIND MAY SEEK THE
LORD, *men*
AND ALL THE GENTILES WHO
ARE CALLED BY MY NAME,'
18 SAYS[r] THE LORD, WHO MAKES
THESE THINGS KNOWN
FROM OF OLD. Amos 9:12
19 "Therefore it is [r]my judgment
that we do not trouble those who
are turning to God from among
the Gentiles, Acts 15:28; 21:25
20 but that we write to them
that they abstain from [t]things con-
taminated by idols and from fornication and from what is strangled
and from blood. *the pollutions of*
21 "For [r]Moses from ancient generations has in every city those
who preach him, since he is read
in the synagogues every Sabbath." Acts 13:15; 2 Cor. 3:14f.

22 Then it seemed good to the
apostles and the elders, with the
whole church, to choose men
from among them to send to Antioch with Paul and Barnabas—Judas called Barsabbas, and Silas,
leading men among the brethren,
23 and they [t]sent this letter by
them, *wrote by their hand*
"The apostles and the
brethren who are elders,
to the brethren in Anti-
och and Syria and Cili-
cia who are from the
Gentiles, greetings.
24 "Since we have heard
that some of our number
to whom we gave no in-
struction have disturbed
you with *their* words,
unsettling your souls,
25 it seemed good to us,
having [a]become of one
mind, to select men to
send to you with our be-
loved Barnabas and
Paul, *met together*
26 men who have risked
their lives for the name
of our Lord Jesus Christ.
27 "Therefore we have sent
Judas and Silas, who
themselves will also re-
port the same things by
word *of mouth*.
28 "For it seemed good to
the Holy Spirit and to us
to lay upon you no
greater burden than
these essentials:
29 that you abstain from
things sacrificed to idols
and from [r]blood and
from things strangled
and from fornication; if

you keep yourselves free from such things, you will do well. Farewell." Acts 15:20

30 So, when they were sent away,[r] they went down to Antioch; and having gathered the [a]congregation together, they delivered the letter. Acts 15:22f. • *multitude*

31 And when they had read it, they rejoiced because of its [a]encouragement. *exhortation*

32 And Judas and Silas, also being prophets themselves, encouraged and strengthened the brethren with a lengthy message.

33 And after they had spent time *there*, they were sent away from the brethren in peace to those who had sent them out.

34 [[31]But it seemed good to Silas to remain there.]

35 But [r]Paul and Barnabas stayed in Antioch, teaching and preaching, with many others also, the word of the Lord. Acts 12:25

36 And after some days Paul said to Barnabas, "Let us return and visit the brethren in [r]every city in which we proclaimed the word of the Lord, *and see* how they are." Acts 13:4, 13, 14, 51; 14:6

37 And Barnabas was desirous of taking [r]John, called Mark, along with them also. Acts 12:12

38 But Paul kept insisting that they should not take him along who had deserted them [t]in Pamphylia and had not gone with them to the work. *from*

39 And there arose such a sharp disagreement that they separated *from one another*, and Barnabas took [r]Mark with him and sailed away to Cyprus. Acts 12:12

40 But Paul chose Silas and departed, being committed by the brethren to the grace of the Lord.

41 And he was traveling through Syria and Cilicia, strengthening the churches.

CHAPTER 16

AND he came also to [r]Derbe and to Lystra. And behold, a certain disciple was there, named Timothy, the son of a Jewish woman who was a believer, but his father was a Greek, Acts 14:6

2 and he was well spoken of by [r]the brethren who were in Lystra and Iconium. Acts 16:40

3 Paul wanted this man to [t]go with him; and he [r]took him and circumcised him because of the Jews who were in those parts, for they all knew that his father was a Greek. *go out* • Gal. 2:3

4 Now while they were passing through the cities, they were delivering the decrees, which had been decided upon by the apostles and [r]elders who were in Jerusalem, for them to observe. Acts 11:30

5 So the churches were being strengthened in the faith, and were increasing in number daily.

6 And they passed through the [a]Phrygian and Galatian region, having been forbidden by the Holy Spirit to speak the word in Asia; *Phrygia and the Galatian region*

7 and when they had come to Mysia, they were trying to go into Bithynia, and the Spirit of Jesus did not permit them;

8 and passing [a]by Mysia, they came down to Troas. *through*

9 And a vision appeared to Paul in the night: a certain man of

[31] Many mss. do not contain this verse

Macedonia was standing and appealing to him, and saying, "Come over to Macedonia and help us."

10 And when he had seen the vision, immediately we sought to [t]go into Macedonia, concluding that God had called us to preach the gospel to them. *go out*

11 Therefore putting out to sea from Troas, we ran a straight course to Samothrace, and on the day following to Neapolis;

12 and from there to [r]Philippi, which is a leading city of the district of Macedonia, a *Roman* colony; and we were staying in this city for some days. Acts 20:6

13 And on [r]the Sabbath day we went outside the gate to a riverside, where we were supposing that there would be a place of prayer; and we sat down and began speaking to the women who had assembled. Acts 13:14

14 And a certain woman named Lydia, from the city of Thyatira, a seller of purple fabrics, a worshiper of God, was listening; [t]and the Lord opened her heart to respond to the things spoken by Paul. *whose heart the Lord opened*

15 And when she and her household had been baptized, she urged us, saying, "If you have judged me to be faithful to the Lord, come into my house and stay." And she prevailed upon us.

16 And it happened that as we were going to [r]the place of prayer, a certain slave-girl having a spirit of divination met us, who was bringing her masters much profit by fortunetelling. Acts 16:13

17 Following after Paul and us, she kept crying out, saying, "These men are bond-servants of [r]the Most High God, who are proclaiming to you [t]the way of salvation." Mark 5:7 • *a way*

18 And she continued doing this for many days. But Paul was greatly annoyed, and turned and said to the spirit, "I command you in the name of Jesus Christ to come out of her!" And it came out at that very [t]moment. *hour*

19 But when her masters saw that their hope of profit was gone, they seized Paul and Silas and dragged them into the market place before the authorities,

20 and when they had brought them to the chief magistrates, they said, "These men are throwing our city into confusion, being Jews,

21 and [r]are proclaiming customs which it is not lawful for us to accept or to observe, being [r]Romans." Esth. 3:8 • Acts 16:12

22 And the crowd rose up together against them, and the chief magistrates tore their robes off them, and proceeded to order *them* to be beaten with rods.

23 And when they had inflicted many blows upon them, they threw them into prison, commanding [r]the jailer to guard them securely; Acts 16:27, 36

24 and he, having received such a command, threw them into the inner prison, and fastened their feet in [r]the stocks. Job 13:27

25 But about midnight Paul and Silas were praying and singing hymns of praise to God, and the prisoners were listening to them;

26 and suddenly there came a great earthquake, so that the foundations of the prison house

were shaken; and immediately all the doors were opened, and everyone's chains were unfastened.

27 And when [r]the jailer had been roused out of sleep and had seen the prison doors opened, he drew his sword and was about to kill himself, supposing that the prisoners had escaped. Acts 16:23

28 But Paul cried out with a loud voice, saying, "Do yourself no harm, for we are all here!"

29 And he called for lights and rushed in and, trembling with fear, he fell down before [r]Paul and Silas, Acts 16:19

30 and after he brought them out, he said, "Sirs, [r]what must I do to be saved?" Acts 2:37; 22:10

31 And they said, "Believe in the Lord Jesus, and you shall be saved, you and your household."

32 And they spoke the word of the Lord to him together with all who were in his house.

33 And he took them that *very* hour of the night and washed their wounds, and immediately he was baptized, he and all his *household*.

34 And he brought them into his house and set [t]food before them, and rejoiced greatly, having believed in God with [r]his whole household. *a table* • Acts 11:14

35 Now when day came, the chief magistrates sent their policemen, saying, "Release those men."

36 And [r]the jailer reported these words to Paul, *saying*, "The chief magistrates have sent to release you. Now therefore, come out and go in peace." Acts 16:27

37 But Paul said to them, "They have beaten us in public without trial, [r]men who are Romans, and have thrown us into prison; and now are they sending us away secretly? No indeed! But let them come themselves and bring us out." Acts 22:25-29

38 And the policemen reported these words to the chief magistrates. And [r]they were afraid when they heard that they were Romans, Acts 22:29

39 and they came and appealed to them, and when they had brought them out, they kept begging them to leave the city.

40 And they went out of the prison and entered *the house of* [r]Lydia, and when they saw the brethren, they [a]encouraged them and departed. Acts 16:14 • *exhorted*

CHAPTER 17

NOW when they had traveled through Amphipolis and Apollonia, they came to [r]Thessalonica, where there was a synagogue of the Jews. Acts 17:11, 13; 20:4

2 And according to Paul's custom, he went to them, and for three Sabbaths reasoned with them from the Scriptures,

3 explaining and giving evidence that the Christ had to suffer and rise again from the dead, and *saying*, "This Jesus whom I am proclaiming to you is the Christ."

4 And some of them were persuaded and joined Paul and Silas, along with a great multitude of the God-fearing Greeks and a number of the leading women.

5 But the Jews, becoming jealous and taking along some wicked men from the market place, formed a mob and set the city in an uproar; and coming upon the

house of Jason, they were seeking
to bring them out to the people.
6 And when they did not find
them, they *began* dragging Jason
and some brethren before the city
authorities, shouting, "These men
who have upset [r32]the world have
come here also; Matt. 24:14
7 and Jason has welcomed
them, and they all act contrary to
the decrees of Caesar, saying that
there is another king, Jesus."
8 And they stirred up the
crowd and the city authorities
who heard these things.
9 And when they had received
a [a]pledge from Jason and the others, they released them. *bond*
10 And [r]the brethren immediately sent Paul and Silas away by
night to Berea; and when they arrived, they went into the synagogue of the Jews. Acts 1:15
11 Now these were more noble-
minded than those in Thessalonica, for they received the word
with great eagerness, examining
the Scriptures daily, *to see*
whether these things were so.
12 Many of them therefore believed, [t]along with a number of
prominent Greek women and
men. *and not a few*
13 But when the Jews of [r]Thes-
salonica found out that the word
of God had been proclaimed by
Paul in Berea also, they came
there likewise, agitating and stirring up the crowds. Acts 17:1
14 And then immediately [r]the
brethren sent Paul out to go as far
as the sea; and Silas and Timothy
remained there. Acts 1:15; 17:6
15 Now those who conducted
Paul brought him as far as Athens; and receiving a command for
Silas and Timothy to come to him
as soon as possible, they departed.
16 Now while Paul was waiting
for them at [r]Athens, his spirit was
being provoked within him as he
was beholding the city full of
idols. Acts 17:15, 21f.; 18:1
17 So he was reasoning in the
synagogue with the Jews and the
God-fearing *Gentiles,* and in the
market place every day with those
who happened to be present.
18 And also some of the Epicu-
rean and Stoic philosophers were
[a]conversing with him. And some
were saying, "What would this
idle babbler wish to say?" Others,
"He seems to be a proclaimer of
strange [t]deities,"—because he was
preaching Jesus and the resurrection. *disputing • demons*
19 And they took him and
brought him [a]to the [a]Areopagus,
saying, "May we know what this
new teaching is which you are
proclaiming? *before • Hill of Ares*
20 "For you are bringing some
strange things to our ears; we
want to know therefore what
these things mean."
21 (Now all the Athenians and
the strangers [r]visiting there used
to spend their time in nothing other than telling or hearing something new.) Acts 2:10
22 And Paul stood in the midst
of the Areopagus and said, "Men
of Athens, I observe that you are
very religious in all respects.
23 "For while I was passing
through and examining the objects of your worship, I also found
an altar with this inscription, 'TO
AN UNKNOWN GOD.' What

32 Lit., *the inhabited earth*

therefore you worship in ignorance, this I proclaim to you.
24 "The God who made the
world and all things in it, since He
is Lord of heaven and earth, does
not dwell in temples made with
hands; 1 Kin. 8:27; Acts 7:48
25 neither is He served by human hands, as though He needed
anything, since He Himself gives
to all life and breath and all
things; Job 22:2; Ps. 50:10-12
26 and He made from [33]one, every nation of mankind to live on
all the face of the earth, having
determined *their* appointed times,
and the boundaries of their habitation, Deut. 32:8; Job 12:23
27 that they should seek God, if
perhaps they might grope for Him
and find Him, though He is not far
from each one of us; Deut. 4:7
28 for in Him we live and move
and exist, as even some of your
own poets have said, 'For we also
are His offspring.' *are*
29 "Being then the offspring of
God, we ought not to think that
the Divine Nature is like gold or
silver or stone, an image formed
by the art and thought of man.
30 "Therefore having overlooked
the times of ignorance, God is
now declaring to men that all
everywhere should repent,
31 because He has fixed a day in
which He will judge the world in
righteousness through a Man
whom He has appointed, having
furnished proof to all men by raising Him from the dead."
32 Now when they heard of the
resurrection of the dead, some *began* to sneer, but others said, "We
shall hear you again concerning
this." Acts 17:18, 31 • *also again*
33 So Paul went out of their
midst.
34 But some men joined him
and believed, among whom also
was Dionysius the Areopagite and
a woman named Damaris and others with them. Acts 17:19, 22

CHAPTER 18

AFTER these things he left Athens and went to Corinth.
2 And he found a certain Jew
named Aquila, a native of Pontus,
having recently come from Italy
with his wife Priscilla, because
Claudius had commanded all the
Jews to leave Rome. He came to
them, Acts 18:18, 26; Rom. 16:3
3 and because he was of the
same trade, he stayed with them
and they were working; for by
trade they were tent-makers.
4 And he was reasoning in the
synagogue every Sabbath and trying to persuade Jews and Greeks.
5 But when Silas and Timothy
came down from Macedonia, Paul
began devoting himself completely to the word, solemnly testifying to the Jews that Jesus was
the Christ. Acts 15:22; 16:1
6 And when they resisted and
blasphemed, he shook out his garments and said to them, "Your
blood *be* upon your own heads! I
am clean. From now on I shall go
to the Gentiles." Neh. 5:13
7 And he departed from there
and went to the house of a certain
man named Titius Justus, a worshiper of God, whose house was
next to the synagogue. Acts 13:43
8 And Crispus, the leader of

[33] Some later mss. read *one blood*

the synagogue, believed in the
Lord with all his household, and
many of the Corinthians when
they heard were believing and
being baptized. 1 Cor. 1:14
9 And the Lord said to Paul in
the night by a vision, "Do not be
afraid *any longer*, but go on
speaking and do not be silent;
10 for I am with you, and no
man will attack you in order to
harm you, for I have many people
in this city."
11 And he settled *there* a year
and six months, teaching the word
of God among them.
12 But while Gallio was [r]procon-
sul of [r]Achaia, the Jews with one
accord rose up against Paul and
brought him before the judgment
seat, Acts 13:7 • Acts 18:27
13 saying, "This man persuades
men to worship God contrary to
[r]the law." John 19:7; Acts 18:15
14 But when Paul was about to
open his mouth, Gallio said to the
Jews, "If it were a matter of
wrong or of vicious crime, O
Jews, it would be reasonable for
me to put up with you;
15 but if there are [r]questions
about words and names and your
own law, look after it yourselves; I
am unwilling to be a judge of
these matters." Acts 23:29; 25:19
16 And he drove them away
from the judgment seat.
17 And they all took hold of
[r]Sosthenes, the leader of the synagogue, and *began* beating him in
front of the judgment seat. And
Gallio was not concerned about
any of these things. 1 Cor. 1:1
18 And Paul, having remained
many days longer, took leave of
the brethren and put out to sea for
Syria, and with him were Priscilla
and Aquila. In Cenchrea [t]he had
his hair cut, for he was keeping a
vow. *having his hair cut*
19 And they came to Ephesus,
and he left them there. Now he
himself entered the synagogue
and reasoned with the Jews.
20 And when they asked him to
stay for a longer time, he did not
consent,
21 but [r]taking leave of them and
saying, "I will return to you again
[r]if God wills," he set sail from Ephesus. Mark 6:46 • Rom. 1:10
22 And when he had landed at
[r]Caesarea, he went up and greeted
the church, and went down to [r]An-
tioch. Acts 8:40 • Acts 11:19
23 And having spent some time
there, he departed and passed suc-
cessively through the [r]Galatian region and Phrygia, strengthening
all the disciples. Acts 16:6
24 Now a certain Jew named
Apollos, an Alexandrian by birth,
[a]an eloquent man, came to Ephesus; and he was mighty in the
Scriptures. *a learned man*
25 This man had been in-
structed in [r]the way of the Lord;
and being fervent in spirit, he was
speaking and teaching accurately
the things concerning Jesus, being
acquainted only with the baptism
of John; Acts 9:2; 18:26
26 and he began to speak out
boldly in the synagogue. But when
[r]Priscilla and Aquila heard him,
they took him aside and explained
to him [r]the way of God more accurately. Acts 18:2, 18 • Acts 18:25
27 And when he wanted to go
across to [r]Achaia, the brethren encouraged him and wrote to the
disciples to welcome him; and

when he had arrived, he helped greatly those who had believed through grace; Acts 18:12

28 for he powerfully refuted the Jews in public, demonstrating by the Scriptures that Jesus was the Christ. Acts 8:35 • Acts 18:5

CHAPTER 19

AND it came about that while Apollos was at Corinth, Paul having passed through the upper country came to Ephesus, and found some disciples, Acts 18:24

2 and he said to them, "Did you receive the Holy Spirit when you believed?" And they *said* to him, "No, we have not even heard whether there is a Holy Spirit."

3 And he said, "Into what then were you baptized?" And they said, "Into John's baptism."

4 And Paul said, "John baptized with the baptism of repentance, telling the people to believe in Him who was coming after him, that is, in Jesus." Matt. 3:11

5 And when they heard this, they were baptized in the name of the Lord Jesus. Acts 8:12 • *into*

6 And when Paul had laid his hands upon them, the Holy Spirit came on them, and they *began* speaking with tongues and prophesying. Acts 6:6; 8:17

7 And there were in all about twelve men.

8 And he entered the synagogue and continued speaking out boldly for three months, reasoning and persuading *them* about the kingdom of God. Acts 9:20

9 But when some were becoming hardened and disobedient, speaking evil of the Way before the multitude, he withdrew from them and took away the disciples, reasoning daily in the school of Tyrannus. Acts 14:4 • Acts 9:2

10 And this took place for two years, so that all who lived in Asia heard the word of the Lord, both Jews and Greeks. Acts 19:8

11 And God was performing extraordinary [a]miracles by the hands of Paul, *works of power*

12 so that handkerchiefs or aprons were even carried from his body to the sick, and the diseases left them and the evil spirits went out. Mark 16:17

13 But also some of the Jewish exorcists, who went from place to place, attempted to name over those who had the evil spirits the name of the Lord Jesus, saying, "I adjure you by Jesus whom Paul preaches." Matt. 12:27

14 And seven sons of one Sceva, a Jewish chief priest, were doing this.

15 And the evil spirit answered and said to them, "I recognize Jesus, and I know about Paul, but who are you?"

16 And the man, in whom was the evil spirit, leaped on them and subdued all of them and overpowered them, so that they fled out of that house naked and wounded.

17 And this became known to all, both Jews and Greeks, who lived in Ephesus; and fear fell upon them all and the name of the Lord Jesus was being magnified.

18 Many also of those who had believed kept coming, confessing and disclosing their practices.

19 And many of those who practiced magic brought their books together and *began* burning

them in the sight of all; and they
counted up the price of them and
found it [r]fifty thousand pieces of
silver. Luke 15:8
20 So the word of the Lord was
growing mightily and prevailing.
21 Now after these things were
finished, Paul purposed in the
[a]spirit to [r]go to Jerusalem after he
had passed through Macedonia
and Achaia, saying, "After I have
been there, I must also see
Rome." *Spirit* • Acts 20:16
22 And having sent into [r]Mace-
donia two of those who ministered to him, Timothy and Erastus, he himself stayed in Asia for a
while. Acts 16:9; 19:21
23 And about that time there
arose no small disturbance concerning [r]the Way. Acts 19:9
24 For a certain man named Demetrius, a silversmith, who made
silver shrines of Artemis, [r]was
bringing no little [a]business to the
craftsmen; Acts 16:16, 19f. • *profit*
25 these he gathered together
with the workmen of similar
trades, and said, "Men, you know
that our prosperity [t]depends upon
this business. *is from*
26 "And you see and hear that
not only in [r]Ephesus, but in almost
all of [r]Asia, this Paul has persuaded and turned away a considerable number of people, saying
that gods made with hands are no
gods *at all.* Acts 18:19 • Acts 19:10
27 "And not only is there danger
that this trade of ours fall into dis-
repute, but also that the temple of
the great goddess Artemis be regarded as worthless and that she
whom all of Asia and the world
worship should even be dethroned
from her magnificence."

28 And when they heard *this*
and were filled with rage, they *began* crying out, saying, "Great is
Artemis of the Ephesians!"
29 And the city was filled with
the confusion, and they rushed
with one accord into the theater,
[t]dragging along Gaius and Aristarchus, Paul's traveling companions
from Macedonia. *having dragged*
30 And when Paul wanted to go
into the [t]assembly, the disciples
would not let him. *people*
31 And also some of the
[34]Asiarchs who were friends of his
sent to him and repeatedly urged
him not to [t] venture into the theater. *give himself*
32 So then, some were shouting
one thing and some another, for
the assembly was in confusion,
and the majority did not know [a]for
what cause they had come together. *on whose account*
33 And some of the crowd concluded *it was* Alexander, since the
Jews had put him forward; and
having motioned with his hand,
Alexander was intending to make
a defense to the assembly.
34 But when they recognized
that he was a Jew, a *single* outcry
arose from them all as they
shouted for about two hours,
"Great is Artemis of the Ephesians!"
35 And after quieting the multitude, the town clerk *said, "Men
of Ephesus, what man is there after all who does not know that the
city of the Ephesians is guardian
of the temple of the great Artemis,
and of the *image* which fell down
from [t]heaven? *Zeus*

[34] I.e., political or religious officials of the province of Asia

36 "Since then these are undeni-
able facts, you ought to keep calm
and to do nothing rash.
37 "For you have brought these
men *here* who are neither [r]robbers
of temples nor blasphemers of our
goddess. Rom. 2:22
38 "So then, if Demetrius and the
craftsmen who are with him have
a complaint against any man, the
courts are in session and procon-
suls are *available*; let them bring
charges against one another.
39 "But if you want anything beyond this, it shall be settled in the
[a]lawful assembly. *regular*
40 "For indeed we are in danger
of being accused of a riot in connection with today's affair, since
there is no *real* cause *for it*; and in
this connection we shall be unable
to account for this disorderly
gathering."
41 And after saying this he dismissed the assembly.

CHAPTER 20

AND after the uproar had ceased,
Paul sent for the disciples and
when he had exhorted them and
taken his leave of them, he departed to go to Macedonia.
2 And when he had gone
through those districts and had
given them much exhortation, he
came to Greece.
3 And *there* he spent three
months, and when [r]a plot was
formed against him by the Jews
as he was about to set sail for Syria, he determined to return
through Macedonia. Acts 9:23f.
4 And he was accompanied by
Sopater of Berea, *the son* of Pyr-
rhus; and by Aristarchus and Se-
cundus of the Thessalonians; and
Gaius of Derbe, and Timothy; and
Tychicus and Trophimus of Asia.
5 But these had gone on ahead
and were waiting for us at Troas.
6 And [r]we sailed from Philippi
after the days of Unleavened
Bread, and came to them at Troas
within five days; and there we
stayed seven days. Acts 16:10
7 And on [r]the first day of the
week, when we were gathered together to break bread, Paul *began*
talking to them, intending to depart the next day, and he prolonged his [t]message until midnight. 1 Cor. 16:2 • *word, speech*
8 And there were many [r]lamps
in the upper room where we were
gathered together. Matt. 25:1
9 And there was a certain
young man named Eutychus sitting on the window sill, sinking
into a deep sleep; and as Paul kept
on talking, he was overcome by
sleep and fell down from the third
floor, and was picked up dead.
10 But Paul went down and fell
upon him and after embracing
him, he said, "Do not be troubled,
for his life is in him."
11 And when he had gone *back*
up, and had [r]broken the bread and
[t]eaten, he talked with them a long
while, until daybreak, and so departed. Acts 2:42; 20:7 • *tasted*
12 And they took away the boy
alive, and were greatly comforted.
13 But we, going ahead to the
ship, set sail for Assos, intending
from there to take Paul on board;
for thus he had arranged it, intending himself to go by land.
14 And when he met us at Assos, we took him on board and
came to Mitylene.

15 And sailing from there, we arrived the following day opposite Chios; and the next day we crossed over to Samos; and the day following we came to Miletus.

16 For Paul had decided to sail past [r]Ephesus in order that he might not have to spend time in Asia; for he was hurrying to be in Jerusalem, if possible, on the day of Pentecost. Acts 18:19

17 And from Miletus he sent to [r]Ephesus and called to him the elders of the church. Acts 18:19

18 And when they had come to him, he said to them,

"**Y**ou yourselves know, [r]from the first day that I set foot in Asia, how I was with you the whole time, Acts 18:19; 19:1, 10; 20:4

19 serving the Lord with all humility and with tears and with trials which came upon me through [r]the plots of the Jews; Acts 20:3

20 how I did not shrink from declaring to you anything that was profitable, and teaching you publicly and from house to house,

21 solemnly [r]testifying to both Jews and Greeks of repentance toward God and faith in our Lord Jesus Christ. Luke 16:28

22 "And now, behold, bound in [a]spirit, I am on my way to Jerusalem, not knowing what will happen to me there, *the Spirit*

23 except that [r]the Holy Spirit solemnly testifies to me in every city, saying that bonds and afflictions await me. Acts 8:29

24 "But [r]I do not consider my life of any account as dear to myself, in order that I may finish my course, and the ministry which I received from the Lord Jesus, to testify solemnly of the gospel of the grace of God. Acts 21:13

25 "And now, behold, I know that all of you, among whom I went about preaching the kingdom, will see my face no more.

26 "Therefore I testify to you this day, that I am [t]innocent of the blood of all men. *pure from*

27 "For I [r]did not shrink from declaring to you the whole purpose of God. Acts 20:20

28 "Be on guard for yourselves and for all the flock, among which the Holy Spirit has made you overseers, to shepherd the church of God which He [t]purchased with His own blood. *acquired*

29 "I know that after my departure savage wolves will come in among you, not sparing the flock;

30 and from among your own selves men will arise, speaking perverse things, to draw away [r]the disciples after them. Acts 11:26

31 "Therefore be on the alert, remembering that night and day for a period of [r]three years I did not cease to admonish each one with tears. Acts 19:8, 10; 24:17

32 "And now I commend you to God and to the word of His grace, which is able to build *you* up and to give *you* the inheritance among all those who are sanctified.

33 "I [r]have coveted no one's silver or gold or clothes. 1 Cor. 9:4-18

34 "You yourselves know that [r]these hands ministered to my *own* needs and to the men who were with me. Acts 18:3

35 "In everything I showed you that by working hard in this manner you must help the weak and remember the words of the Lord Jesus, that He Himself said, 'It is

more blessed to give than to receive.' "

36 And when he had said these
things, he knelt down and prayed
with them all.

37 And they *began* to weep
aloud and [r]embraced Paul, and repeatedly kissed him, Luke 15:20

38 [t]grieving especially over the
word which he had spoken, that
they should see his face no more.
And they were accompanying him
to the ship. *suffering pain*

CHAPTER 21

AND when it came about that we
had parted from them and had set
sail, we ran a straight course to
Cos and the next day to Rhodes
and from there to Patara;

2 and having found a ship
crossing over to Phoenicia, we
went aboard and set sail.

3 And when we had come in
sight of Cyprus, leaving it on the
left, we kept sailing to Syria and
landed at Tyre; for there the ship
was to unload its cargo.

4 And after looking up [r]the disciples, we stayed there seven
days; and they kept telling Paul
through the Spirit not to set foot
in Jerusalem. Acts 11:26; 21:16

5 And when it came about that
[t]our days there were ended, we departed and started on our journey,
while they all, with wives and
children, escorted us until *we
were* out of the city. And after
kneeling down on the beach and
praying, we said farewell to one
another. *we had completed the days*

6 Then we went on board the
ship, and they returned [r]home
again. John 19:27

7 And when we had finished
the voyage from [r]Tyre, we arrived
at Ptolemais; and after greeting
the brethren, we stayed with them
for a day. Acts 12:20; 21:3

8 And on the next day we departed and came to Caesarea; and
entering the house of Philip the
evangelist, who was one of the
seven, we stayed with him.

9 Now this man had four virgin
daughters who were [r]prophetess-
es. Luke 2:36; Acts 13:1

10 And as we were staying
there for some days, a certain
prophet named [r]Agabus came
down from Judea. Acts 11:28

11 And coming to us, he [r]took
Paul's belt and bound his own feet
and hands, and said, "This is what
the Holy Spirit says: 'In this way
the Jews at Jerusalem will bind
the man who owns this belt and
deliver him into the hands of the
Gentiles.' " 1 Kin. 22:11; Is. 20:2

12 And when we had heard this,
we as well as the local residents
began begging him [r]not to go up to
Jerusalem. Acts 21:15

13 Then Paul answered, "What
are you doing, weeping and breaking my heart? For [r]I am ready not
only to be bound, but even to die
at Jerusalem for the name of the
Lord Jesus." Acts 20:24

14 And since he would not be
persuaded, we fell silent, remarking, "The[r] will of the Lord be
done!" Luke 22:42

15 And after these days we got
ready and [r]started on our way up
to Jerusalem. Acts 21:12

16 And *some* of the disciples
from Caesarea also came with us,
taking us to Mnason of Cyprus, a

disciple of long standing with whom we were to lodge.

17 And when we had come to Jerusalem, [r]the brethren received us gladly. Acts 1:15; 21:7

18 And now the following day Paul went in with us to James, and all the elders were present.

19 And after he had greeted them, he [r]*began* to relate one by one the things which God had done among the Gentiles through his ministry. Acts 14:27

20 And when they heard it they *began* [r]glorifying God; and they said to him, "You see, brother, how many thousands there are among the Jews of those who have believed, and they are all zealous for the Law; Matt. 9:8

21 and they have been told about you, that you are [r]teaching all the Jews who are among the Gentiles to forsake Moses, telling them not to circumcise their children nor to walk according to the customs. Acts 21:28

22 "What, then, is *to be done*? They will certainly hear that you have come.

23 "Therefore do this that we tell you. We have four men who [r]are under a vow; Num. 6:13-21

24 take them and purify yourself along with them, and [t]pay their expenses in order that they may shave their [t]heads; and all will know that there is nothing to the things which they have been told about you, but that you yourself also walk orderly, keeping the Law. *spend on them* • *head*

25 "But concerning the Gentiles who have believed, we wrote, having decided that they should abstain from [t]meat sacrificed to idols and from blood and from what is strangled and from fornication." *the thing*

26 Then Paul took the men, and the next day, [r]purifying himself along with them, went into the temple, giving notice of the completion of the days of purification, until the sacrifice was offered for each one of them. John 11:55

27 And when the seven days were almost over, the Jews from Asia, upon seeing him in the temple, *began* to stir up all the multitude and laid hands on him,

28 crying out, "Men of Israel, come to our aid! [r]This is the man who preaches to all men everywhere against our people, and the Law, and this place; and besides he has even brought Greeks into the temple and has defiled this holy place." Acts 6:13f.

29 For they had previously seen [r]Trophimus the Ephesian in the city with him, and they supposed that Paul had brought him into the temple. Acts 20:4

30 And all the city was aroused, and the people rushed together; and taking hold of Paul, they [r]dragged him out of the temple; and immediately the doors were shut. 2 Kin. 11:15; Acts 16:19

31 And while they were seeking to kill him, a report came up to the [35]commander of the [r]*Roman* [a]cohort that all Jerusalem was in confusion. Acts 10:1 • *battalion*

32 And at once he took along *some* soldiers and centurions, and ran down to them; and when they saw the commander and the soldiers, they stopped beating Paul.

[35] I.e., chiliarch, in command of one thousand troops

33 Then the commander came
up and took hold of him, and ordered him to be bound with two
chains; and he *began* asking who
he was and what he had done.
34 But among the crowd some
were shouting one thing *and* some
another, and when he could not
find out the facts on account of
the uproar, he ordered him to be
brought into the barracks.
35 And when he got to the
stairs, it so happened that he was
carried by the soldiers because of
the violence of the mob;
36 for the multitude of the people kept following behind, crying
out, "Away with him!"
37 And as Paul was about to be
brought into the barracks, he said
to the commander, "May I say
something to you?" And he *said,
"Do you know Greek?
38 "Then you are not [r]the Egyptian who some time ago stirred up
a revolt and led the four thousand
men of the Assassins out into the
wilderness?" Acts 5:36
39 But Paul said, "I am a Jew of
Tarsus in Cilicia, a citizen of no insignificant city; and I beg you, allow me to speak to the people."
40 And when he had given him
permission, Paul, standing on [r]the
stairs, motioned to the people
with his hand; and when there
[t]was a great hush, he spoke to
them in the Hebrew dialect, saying, Acts 21:35 • *occurred*

CHAPTER 22

"BRETHREN[r] and fathers, hear
my defense which I now *offer* to
you." Acts 7:2
2 And when they heard that he
was addressing them in the Hebrew dialect, they became even
more quiet; and he *said,
3 "I am a Jew, born in Tarsus of
[r]Cilicia, but brought up in this city,
educated under Gamaliel, strictly
according to the law of our fathers, being zealous for God, just
as you all are today. Acts 6:9
4 "And [r]I persecuted this Way to
the death, binding and putting
both men and women into prisons, Acts 8:3; 22:19f.
5 as also the high priest and all
the Council of the elders [t]can testify. From them I also received
letters to the brethren, and started
off for Damascus in order to bring
even those who were there to Jerusalem as prisoners to be punished. *testifies for me*
6 "And it came about that as I
was on my way, approaching Damascus about noontime, a very
bright light suddenly flashed from
heaven all around me,
7 and I fell to the ground and
heard a voice saying to me, 'Saul,
Saul, why are you persecuting
Me?'
8 "And I answered, 'Who art
Thou, Lord?' And He said to me, 'I
am [r]Jesus the Nazarene, whom
you are persecuting.' Acts 26:9
9 "And those who were with me
beheld the light, to be sure, but
did not understand the voice of
the One who was speaking to me.
10 "And I said, 'What[r] shall I do,
Lord?' And the Lord said to me,
'Arise and go on into Damascus;
and there you will be told of all
that has been appointed for you to
do.' Acts 16:30
11 "But since I could not see because of the [a]brightness of that

light, I was led by the hand by
those who were with me, and
came into Damascus. *glory*
12 "And a certain Ananias, a
man who was devout by the standard of the Law, *and* well spoken
of by all the Jews who lived there,
13 came to me, and standing
near said to me, 'Brother Saul, receive your sight!' And at that very
time I looked up at him.
14 "And he said, 'The God of our
fathers has appointed you to
know His will, and to see the
Righteous One, and to hear an utterance from His mouth.
15 'For you will be [r]a witness for
Him to all men of what you have
seen and heard. Acts 23:11
16 'And now why do you delay?
[r]Arise, and be baptized, and [r]wash
away your sins, calling on His
name.' Acts 9:18 • Acts 2:38
17 "And it came about when I [r]re-
turned to Jerusalem and was
praying in the temple, that I fell
into a trance, Acts 9:26
18 and I saw Him saying to me,
'Make[r] haste, and get out of Jerusalem quickly, because they will
not accept your testimony about
Me.' Acts 9:29
19 "And I said, 'Lord, they themselves understand that in one
synagogue after another [r]I used to
imprison and beat those who believed in Thee. Acts 8:3; 22:4
20 'And when the blood of Thy
witness Stephen was being shed, I
also was standing by approving,
and watching out for the cloaks of
those who were slaying him.'
21 "And He said to me, 'Go! For I
will send you far away [r]to the Gentiles.' " Acts 9:15

22 And they listened to him up
to this statement, and *then* they
raised their voices and said,
"Away[r] with such a fellow from
the earth, for he should not be allowed to live!" Acts 21:36
23 And as they were crying out
and throwing off their cloaks and
tossing dust into the air,
24 the [36]commander ordered
him to be brought into [r]the barracks, stating that he should be
examined by scourging so that he
might find out the reason why
they were shouting against him
that way. Acts 21:34
25 And when they stretched
him out [t]with thongs, Paul said to
the centurion who was standing
by, "Is it lawful for you to scourge
a man who is a Roman and uncon-
demned?" *for the thongs*
26 And when the centurion
heard *this*, he went to the commander and told him, saying,
"What are you about to do? For
this man is a Roman."
27 And the commander came
and said to him, "Tell me, are you
a Roman?" And he said, "Yes."
28 And the commander an-
swered, "I acquired this citizen-
ship with a large sum of money."
And Paul said, "But I was actually
born *a citizen*."
29 Therefore those who were
about to examine him immediately let go of him; and the commander also was afraid when he
found out that he was a Roman,
and because he had [t]put him in
chains. *bound him*
30 But on the next day, wishing
to know for certain why he had

[36] I.e., chiliarch, in command of one thousand troops

been accused by the Jews, he released him and ordered the chief priests and all the Council to assemble, and brought Paul down and set him before them.

CHAPTER 23

AND Paul, looking intently at [r]the [a]Council, said, "Brethren, I have lived my life with a perfectly good conscience before God up to this day." Acts 22:30 • *Sanhedrin*

2 And the high priest [r]Ananias commanded those standing beside him to strike him on the mouth. Acts 24:1

3 Then Paul said to him, "God is going to strike you, [r]you whitewashed wall! And do you sit to try me according to the Law, and in violation of the Law order me to be struck?" Matt. 23:27

4 But the bystanders said, "Do you revile God's high priest?"

5 And Paul said, "I was not aware, brethren, that he was high priest; for it is written, 'YOU [r]SHALL NOT SPEAK EVIL OF A RULER OF YOUR PEOPLE.' " Ex. 22:28

6 But perceiving that one part were Sadducees and the other Pharisees, Paul *began* crying out in the [a]Council, "Brethren, I am a Pharisee, a son of Pharisees; I am on trial for the hope and resurrection of the dead!" *Sanhedrin*

7 And as he said this, there arose a dissension between the Pharisees and Sadducees; and the assembly was divided.

8 For the Sadducees say that there is no resurrection, nor an angel, nor a spirit; but the Pharisees acknowledge them all.

9 And there arose a great uproar; and some of [r]the scribes of the Pharisaic party stood up and *began* to argue heatedly, saying, "We find nothing wrong with this man; suppose a spirit or an angel has spoken to him?" Mark 2:16

10 And as a great dissension was developing, the [37]commander was afraid Paul would be torn to pieces by them and ordered the troops to go down and take him away from them by force, and bring him into the barracks.

11 But on the night *immediately* following, the Lord stood at his side and said, "Take courage; for as you have solemnly witnessed to My cause at Jerusalem, so you must witness at Rome also."

12 And when it was day, [r]the Jews formed a [a]conspiracy and bound themselves under an oath, saying that they would neither eat nor drink until they had killed Paul. Acts 9:23; 23:30 • *mob*

13 And there were more than forty who formed this plot.

14 And they came to the chief priests and the elders, and said, "We have bound ourselves under a solemn oath to taste nothing until we have killed Paul.

15 "Now, therefore, you [t]and the [a]Council notify the commander to bring him down to you, as though you were going to determine his case by a more thorough investigation; and we for our part are ready to slay him before he comes near *the place*." *with* • *Sanhedrin*

16 But the son of Paul's sister heard of their ambush, and he came and entered [r]the barracks and told Paul. Acts 21:34

[37]I.e., chiliarch, in command of one thousand troops

17 And Paul called one of the centurions to him and said, "Lead this young man to the commander, for he has something to report to him."

18 So he took him and led him to the commander and *said, "Paul [r]the prisoner called me to him and asked me to lead this young man to you since he has something to tell you." Eph. 3:1

19 And the commander took him by the hand and stepping aside, *began* to inquire of him privately, "What is it that you have to report to me?"

20 And he said, "The Jews have agreed to ask you to bring Paul down tomorrow to the [a]Council, as though they were going to inquire somewhat more thoroughly about him. *Sanhedrin*

21 "So do not listen to them, for more than forty of them are lying in wait for him who have bound themselves under a curse not to eat or drink until they slay him; and now they are ready and waiting for the promise from you."

22 Therefore the commander let the young man go, instructing him, "Tell no one that you have notified me of these things."

23 And he called to him two of the centurions, and said, "Get two hundred soldiers ready by [38]the third hour of the night to proceed to Caesarea, with seventy horsemen and two hundred spearmen."

24 *They were* also to provide mounts to put Paul on and bring him safely to Felix the governor.

25 And he wrote a letter having this form:

[38]I.e., 9 p.m.

26 "Claudius Lysias, to the most excellent governor Felix, greetings.

27 "When this man was arrested by the Jews and was about to be slain by them, [r]I came upon them with the troops and rescued him, having learned that he was a Roman. Acts 21:32f.

28 "And wanting to ascertain the charge for which they were accusing him, I brought him down to their Council;

29 and I found him to be accused over questions about their Law, but [t]under no accusation deserving death or imprisonment. *having*

30 "And when I was [r]informed that there would be a plot against the man, I sent him to you at once, also instructing his accusers to bring charges against him before you." Acts 23:20f.

31 So the soldiers, in accordance with their orders, took Paul and brought him by night to Antipatris.

32 But the next day, leaving the horsemen to go on with him, they returned to the barracks.

33 And when these had come to [r]Caesarea and delivered the letter to the governor, they also presented Paul to him. Acts 8:40

34 And when he had read it, he asked from what province he was; and when he learned that [r]he was from Cilicia, Acts 6:9; 21:39

35 he said, "I will give you a
hearing after your accusers arrive
also," giving orders for him to be
kept in Herod's [39]Praetorium.

CHAPTER 24

AND after five days the high
priest Ananias came down with
some elders, [t]with a certain [t]attor-
ney *named* Tertullus; and they
brought charges to the governor
against Paul. *and • orator*
2 And after *Paul* had been
summoned, Tertullus began to accuse him, saying *to the governor,*
"Since we have through you attained much peace, and since by
your providence reforms are
being carried out for this nation,
3 we acknowledge *this* in every way and everywhere, [r]most excellent Felix, with all thankfulness. Acts 23:26; 26:25
4 "But, that I may not weary
you any further, I beg you [t]to grant
us, by your kindness, a brief hearing. *to hear . . . briefly*
5 "For we have found this man
a real pest and a fellow who stirs
up dissension among all the Jews
throughout [40]the world, and a ring-
leader of the [r]sect of the Naza-
renes. Acts 15:5; 24:14
6 "And he even tried to desecrate the temple; and then we arrested him. [[41]And we wanted to
judge him according to our own
Law.
7 "But Lysias the commander
came along, and with much violence took him out of our hands,
8 ordering his accusers to
come before you.] And by examining him yourself concerning all
these matters, you will be able to
ascertain the things of which we
accuse him."
9 And [r]the Jews also joined in
the attack, asserting that these
things were so. 1 Thess. 2:16
10 And when [r]the governor had
nodded for him to speak, Paul responded: Acts 23:24
"Knowing that for many years
you have been a judge to this nation, I cheerfully make my defense,
11 since you can take note of
the fact that no more than [r]twelve
days ago I went up to Jerusalem
to worship. Acts 21:18
12 "And neither in the temple,
nor in the synagogues, nor in the
city *itself* did they find me carrying on a discussion with anyone or
causing [t]a riot. *an attack of a mob*
13 "Nor [r]can they prove to you
the charges of which they now accuse me. Acts 25:7
14 "But this I admit to you, that
according to the Way which they
call a sect I do serve [t]the God of
our fathers, believing everything
that is in accordance with the
Law, and that is written in the
Prophets; *the ancestral god*
15 having a hope in God, which
[r]these men cherish themselves,
that there shall certainly be a resurrection of both the righteous
and the wicked. Dan. 12:2
16 "In view of this, I also [t]do my
best to maintain always a blameless conscience *both* before God
and before men. *practice myself*
17 "Now after several years I

[39] I.e., governor's official residence
[40] Lit., *the inhabited earth*
[41] Many mss. do not contain the remainder of v. 6, v. 7, nor the first part of v. 8

came to bring [42]alms to my nation
and to present offerings;
18 in which they found me *oc-*
cupied in the temple, having been
[r]purified, without *any* crowd or uproar. But *there were* certain Jews
from Asia— Acts 21:26
19 who ought to have been present before you, and to [r]make accusation, if they should have anything against me. Acts 23:30
20 "Or else let these men themselves tell what misdeed they
found when I stood before [r]the
[a]Council, Matt. 5:22 • *Sanhedrin*
21 other than for this one statement which I shouted out while
standing among them, 'For the
resurrection of the dead I am on
trial before you today.' "
22 But Felix, having a more
exact knowledge about the Way,
put them off, saying, "When Lysias the [43]commander comes down,
I will decide your case."
23 And he gave orders to the
centurion for him to be kept in
custody and *yet* have *some* freedom, and not to prevent any of his
friends from ministering to him.
24 But some days later, Felix arrived with Drusilla, his [t]wife who
was a Jewess, and sent for Paul,
and heard him *speak* about faith
in Christ Jesus. *own wife*
25 And as he was discussing
[r]righteousness, self-control and the
judgment to come, Felix became
frightened and said, "Go away for
the present, and when I find time,
I will summon you." Titus 2:12
26 At the same time too, he was
hoping that money would be giv-
en him by Paul; therefore he also
used to send for him quite often
and converse with him.
27 But after two years had
passed, [r]Felix was succeeded by
Porcius [r]Festus; and wishing to do
the Jews a favor, Felix left Paul
imprisoned. Acts 25:1, 4, 9, 12

CHAPTER 25

FESTUS therefore, having arrived in [r]the province, three days
later went up to Jerusalem from
Caesarea. Acts 23:34
2 And the chief priests and the
leading men of the Jews [r]brought
charges against Paul; and they
were urging him, Acts 24:1
3 requesting a concession
against [t]Paul, that he might have
him brought to Jerusalem (*at the*
same time, setting an ambush to
kill him on the way). *him*
4 Festus then answered that
Paul was being kept in custody at
[r]Caesarea and that he himself was
about to leave shortly. Acts 8:40
5 "Therefore," he *said, "let the
influential men among you [t]go
there with me, and if there is anything wrong about the man, let
them prosecute him." *go down*
6 And after he had spent not
more than eight or ten days
among them, he went down to
Caesarea; and on the next day he
took his seat on the tribunal and
ordered Paul to be brought.
7 And after he had arrived, the
Jews who had come down from
Jerusalem stood around him,
bringing [r]many and serious
charges against him which they
could not prove; Acts 24:5f.
8 while Paul said in his own

[42]Or, *gifts to charity*
[43]I.e., chiliarch, in command of one thousand troops

defense, "I have committed no offense either against the Law of the Jews or against the temple or against Caesar." Acts 6:13

9 But Festus, wishing to do the Jews a favor, answered Paul and said, "Are you willing to go up to Jerusalem and stand trial before me on these charges?" *be judged*

10 But Paul said, "I am standing before Caesar's tribunal, where I ought to be tried. I have done no wrong to *the* Jews, as you also very well know. Matt. 27:19

11 "If then I am a wrongdoer, and have committed anything worthy of death, I do not refuse to die; but if none of those things is *true* of which these men accuse me, no one can hand me over to them. I appeal to Caesar."

12 Then when Festus had conferred with his council, he answered, "You have appealed to Caesar, to Caesar you shall go."

13 Now when several days had elapsed, King Agrippa and Bernice arrived at Caesarea, and paid their respects to Festus.

14 And while they were spending many days there, Festus laid Paul's case before the king, saying, "There is a certain man left a prisoner by Felix; Acts 24:27

15 and when I was at Jerusalem, the chief priests and the elders of the Jews brought charges against him, asking for a sentence of condemnation upon him.

16 "And I answered them that it is not the custom of the Romans to hand over any man before the accused meets his accusers face to face, and has an opportunity to make his defense against the charges. Acts 25:4f.

17 "And so after they had assembled here, I made no delay, but on the next day took my seat on the tribunal, and ordered the man to be brought. Matt. 27:19

18 "And when the accusers stood up, they *began* bringing charges against him not of such crimes as I was expecting;

19 but they *simply* had some points of disagreement with him about their own religion and about a certain dead man, Jesus, whom Paul asserted to be alive.

20 "And being at a loss how to investigate such matters, I asked whether he was willing to go to Jerusalem and there stand trial on these matters. Acts 25:9 • *these*

21 "But when Paul appealed to be held in custody for [44]the Emperor's decision, I ordered him to be kept in custody until I send him to Caesar." Acts 25:11f.

22 And Agrippa *said* to Festus, "I also would like to hear the man myself." "Tomorrow," he *said, "you shall hear him." Acts 9:15

23 And so, on the next day when Agrippa had come together with Bernice, amid great pomp, and had entered the auditorium [45]accompanied by the commanders and the prominent men of the city, at the command of Festus, Paul was brought in. Acts 25:13

24 And Festus *said, "King Agrippa, and all you gentlemen here present with us, you behold this man about whom all the people of the Jews appealed to me, both at Jerusalem and here, loudly declaring that he ought not to live any longer. Acts 25:2, 7

[44] Lit., *the Augustus'* (in this case Nero)
[45] Lit., *and with*

25"But I found that he had committed [r]nothing worthy of death;
and since he himself appealed to
the Emperor, I decided to send
him. Luke 23:4
26"Yet I have nothing definite
about him to write to my lord.
Therefore I have brought him before you *all* and especially before
you, King Agrippa, so that after
the investigation has taken place,
I may have something to write.
27"For it seems absurd to me in
sending a prisoner, not to indicate
also the charges against him."

CHAPTER 26

AND [r]Agrippa said to Paul, "You
are permitted to speak for yourself." Then Paul stretched out his
hand and *proceeded* to make his
defense: Acts 9:15
2"In regard to all the things of
which I am accused by the Jews, I
consider myself fortunate, King
Agrippa, that I am about to make
my defense before you today;
3 especially because you are
an expert in all customs and questions among *the* Jews; therefore I
beg you to listen to me patiently.
4"So then, all Jews know [r]my
manner of life from my youth up,
which from the beginning was
spent among my *own* nation and
at Jerusalem; Gal. 1:13f.
5 since they have known about
me for a long time previously, if
they are willing to testify, that I
lived *as* a Pharisee according to
the strictest sect of our religion.
6"And now I am [t]standing trial
for the hope of the promise made
by God to our fathers; *being tried*
7 *the promise* to which our
twelve tribes hope to attain, as
they earnestly serve *God* night
and day. And for this hope, O
King, I am being accused by Jews.
8"Why is it considered incredi-
ble among you *people* [r]if God does
raise the dead? Acts 23:6
9"So then, [r]I thought to myself
that I had to do many things hostile to the name of Jesus of Nazareth. John 16:2; 1 Tim. 1:13
10"And this is [t]just what I did in
Jerusalem; not only did I lock up
many of the saints in prisons, having received authority from the
chief priests, but also when they
were being put to death I cast my
vote against them. *also*
11"And as I punished them often
in all the synagogues, I tried to
force them to blaspheme; and
being furiously enraged at them, I
kept pursuing them [r]even to [a]for-
eign cities. Acts 22:5 • *outlying*
12"While[t] thus engaged as I was
journeying to Damascus with the
authority and commission of the
chief priests, *In which things*
13 at midday, O King, I saw on
the way a light from heaven,
brighter than the sun, shining all
around me and those who were
journeying with me.
14"And when we had [r]all fallen
to the ground, I heard a voice saying to me in the Hebrew dialect,
'Saul, Saul, why are you persecuting Me? It is hard for you to kick
against the goads.' Acts 9:7
15"And I said, 'Who art Thou,
Lord?' And the Lord said, 'I am
Jesus whom you are persecuting.
16 'But arise, and stand on your
feet; for this purpose I have appeared to you, to appoint you a
minister and a witness not only to

the things which you have seen,
but also to the things in which I
will appear to you;
17 delivering you from the *Jewish* people and from the Gentiles,
to whom I am sending you,
18 to [r]open their eyes so that
they may turn from darkness to
light and from the dominion of Satan to God, in order that they may
receive forgiveness of sins and an
inheritance among those who
have been sanctified by faith in
Me.' Is. 35:5; 42:7, 16; Eph. 5:8
19 "Consequently, King Agrippa,
I did not prove disobedient to the
heavenly vision,
20 but *kept* declaring both [r]to
those of Damascus first, and *also*
at Jerusalem and *then* throughout
all the region of Judea, and *even*
to the Gentiles, that they should
repent and turn to God, performing deeds appropriate to repentance. Acts 9:19ff.
21 "For this reason *some* Jews
[r]seized me in the temple and tried
to put me to death. Acts 21:27
22 "And so, having obtained help
from God, I stand to this day [r]testi-
fying both to small and great, stating nothing but what the Prophets
and Moses said was going to take
place; Luke 16:28
23 [t]that the Christ was [t]to suffer,
and that by reason of *His* resurrection from the dead He should
be the first to proclaim light both
to the *Jewish* people and to the
Gentiles." *whether • subject to suffering*
24 And while *Paul* was saying
this in his defense, Festus *said in
a loud voice, "Paul, you are out of
your mind! *Your* great [r]learning is
driving you mad." John 7:15
25 But Paul *said, "I am not out
of my mind, most excellent Festus, but I utter words [t]of sober
truth. *of truth and rationality*
26 "For the king knows about
these matters, and I speak to him
also with confidence, since I am
persuaded that none of these
things escape his notice; for this
has not been done in a corner.
27 "King Agrippa, do you believe
the Prophets? I know that you
do."
28 And Agrippa *replied* to Paul,
"In a short time you will persuade
me to become a Christian."
29 And Paul *said*, "I[t] would to
God, that whether in a short or
long time, not only you, but also
all who hear me this day, might
become such as I am, except for
these chains." *I would pray to*
30 And the king arose and the
governor and Bernice, and those
who were sitting with them,
31 and when they had drawn
aside, they *began* talking to one
another, saying, "This man is not
doing anything worthy of death or
[t]imprisonment." *bonds*
32 And Agrippa said to Festus,
"This man might have been [r]set
free if he had not appealed to Caesar." Acts 28:18

CHAPTER 27

AND when it was decided that
we should sail for [r]Italy, they proceeded to deliver Paul and some
other prisoners to a centurion of
the Augustan [46]cohort named Julius. Acts 18:2; 27:6
2 And embarking in an Adra-
myttian ship, which was about to

[46]Or, *battalion*

sail to the regions along the coast
of ʳAsia, we put out to sea, accompanied by Aristarchus, a Macedo-
nian of Thessalonica. Acts 2:9
3 And the next day we put in
at ʳSidon; and Julius treated Paul
with consideration and allowed
him to go to his friends and receive care. Matt. 11:21
4 And from there we put out to
sea and sailed under the shelter of
ʳCyprus because ʳthe winds were
contrary. Acts 4:36 • Acts 27:7
5 And when we had sailed
through the sea along the coast of
ʳCilicia and Pamphylia, we landed
at Myra in Lycia. Acts 6:9
6 And there the centurion
found an Alexandrian ship sailing
for Italy, and he put us aboard it.
7 And when we had sailed
slowly for a good many days, and
with difficulty had arrived off Cni-
dus, since the wind did not permit
us *to go* farther, we sailed under
the shelter of Crete, off Salmone;
8 and with difficulty ʳsailing
past it we came to a certain place
called Fair Havens, near which
was the city of Lasea. Acts 27:13
9 And when considerable time
had passed and the voyage was
now dangerous, since even ʳthe
[47]fast was already over, Paul *began*
to admonish them, Lev. 16:29-31
10 and said to them, "Men, I
perceive that the voyage will certainly be *attended* with ʳdamage
and great loss, not only of the cargo and the ship, but also of our
lives." Acts 27:21
11 But the centurion was more
persuaded by the pilot and the
captain of the ship, than by what
was being said by Paul.
12 And because the harbor was
not suitable for wintering, the majority reached a decision to put
out to sea from there, if somehow
they could reach Phoenix, a harbor of Crete, facing[a]southwest and
northwest, and spend the winter
there. *northeast and southeast*
13 And when a moderate south
wind came up, supposing that
they had gained their purpose,
they weighed anchor and *began*
sailing along Crete, close *inshore.*
14 But before very long there
rushed down from the land a violent wind, called [48]Euraquilo;
15 and when the ship was
caught *in it,* and could not face
the wind, we gave way *to it,* and
let ourselves be driven along.
16 And running under the shelter of a small island called Clauda,
we were scarcely able to get the
ship's boat under control.
17 And after they had hoisted it
up, they used supporting cables in
undergirding the ship; and fearing
that they might run aground on
the shallows of Syrtis, they let
down the sea anchor, and so let
themselves be driven along.
18 The next day as we were
being violently storm-tossed, they
began to jettison the cargo;
19 and on the third day they
threw the ship's tackle overboard
with their own hands.
20 And since neither sun nor
stars appeared for many days, and
no small storm was assailing *us,*
from then on all hope of our being
saved was gradually abandoned.
21 And when they had gone a

[47]I.e., Day of Atonement in September or October

[48]I.e., a northeaster

long time without food, then Paul
stood up in their midst and said,
"Men, you ought to have [t]followed
my advice and not to have set sail
from Crete, and incurred this
damage and loss. *obeyed me*
22 "And *yet* now I urge you to
[r]keep up your courage, for there
shall be no loss of life among you,
but *only* of the ship. Acts 27:25
23 "For this very night an angel
of the God to whom I belong and
whom I serve stood before me,
24 saying, 'Do not be afraid,
Paul; you must stand before Caesar;
and behold, God has granted
you [r]all those who are sailing with
you.' Acts 27:31, 42, 44
25 "Therefore, keep up your
courage, men, for I believe God,
that [t]it will turn out exactly as I
have been told. *it will be*
26 "But we must run aground on
a certain [r]island." Acts 28:1
27 But when the fourteenth
night had come, as we were being
driven about in the Adriatic Sea,
about midnight the sailors *began*
to surmise that they were approaching
some land.
28 And they took soundings,
and found *it to be* twenty fathoms;
and a little farther on they took
another sounding and found *it to
be* fifteen fathoms.
29 And fearing that we might
[r]run aground somewhere on the
rocks, they cast four anchors from
the stern and wished for daybreak.
Acts 27:17, 26
30 And as the sailors were trying
to escape from the ship, and
had let down [r]the *ship's* boat into
the sea, on the pretense of intending
to lay out anchors from the
bow, Acts 27:16
31 Paul said to the centurion
and to the soldiers, "Unless these
men remain in the ship, you yourselves
cannot be saved."
32 Then the soldiers cut away
the [r]ropes of the *ship's* boat, and
let it fall away. John 2:15
33 And until the day was about
to dawn, Paul was encouraging
them all to take some food, saying,
"Today is the fourteenth day
that you have been constantly
watching and going without eating,
having taken nothing.
34 "Therefore I encourage you to
take some food, for this is for your
preservation; for [r]not a hair from
the head of any of you shall perish."
Matt. 10:30
35 And having said this, he took
bread and [r]gave thanks to God in
the presence of all; and he broke it
and began to eat. Matt. 14:19
36 And all of them [t]were encouraged,
and they themselves also
took food. *became cheerful*
37 And all of us in the ship were
two hundred and seventy-six [t]persons.[r]
souls • Acts 2:41
38 And when they had eaten
enough, they *began* to lighten the
ship by [r]throwing out the wheat
into the sea. Jon. 1:5
39 And when day came, they
[a]could not recognize the land; but
they did observe a certain bay
with a beach, and they resolved to
[49]drive the ship onto it if they
could. *were not recognizing*
40 And casting off the anchors,
they left them in the sea while at
the same time they were loosening
the ropes of the rudders, and

[49] Some ancient mss. read *bring the ship safely ashore*

hoisting the foresail to the wind, they were heading for the beach.

41 But striking a [t]reef where two seas met, they ran the vessel aground; and the prow stuck fast and remained immovable, but the stern *began* to be broken up by the force *of the waves.* *place*

42 And the soldiers' plan was to [r]kill the prisoners, that none *of them* should swim away and escape; Acts 12:19

43 but the centurion, wanting to bring Paul safely through, kept them from their intention, and commanded that those who could swim should [t]jump overboard first and get to land, *cast themselves*

44 and the rest *should follow,* some on planks, and others on various things from the ship. And thus it happened that they all were brought safely to land.

CHAPTER 28

AND when they had been brought safely through, then we found out that [r]the island was called Malta. Acts 27:26

2 And the natives showed us extraordinary kindness; for because of the rain that had set in and because of the cold, they kindled a fire and received us all.

3 But when Paul had gathered a bundle of sticks and laid them on the fire, a viper came out [a]because of the heat, and fastened on his hand. *from the heat*

4 And when the natives saw the creature hanging from his hand, they *began* saying to one another, "Undoubtedly this man is a murderer, and though he has been saved from the sea, justice has not allowed him to live."

5 However [r]he shook the creature off into the fire and suffered no harm. Mark 16:18

6 But they were expecting that he was about to swell up or suddenly fall down dead. But after they had waited a long time and had seen nothing unusual happen to him, they changed their minds and [r]*began* to say that he was a god. Acts 14:11

7 Now in the neighborhood of that place were lands belonging to the leading man of the island, named Publius, who welcomed us and entertained us courteously three days.

8 And it came about that the father of Publius was lying *in bed* afflicted with *recurrent* fever and dysentery; and Paul went in *to see* him and after he had [r]prayed, he laid his hands on him and healed him. Acts 9:40; James 5:14f.

9 And after this had happened, the rest of the people on the island who had diseases were coming to him and getting cured.

10 And they also honored us with many marks of respect; and when we were setting sail, they supplied *us* with all we needed.

11 And at the end of three months we set sail on an Alexandrian ship which had wintered at the island, and which had the Twin Brothers for its figurehead.

12 And after we put in at Syracuse, we stayed there for three days.

13 And from there we sailed around and arrived at Rhegium, and a day later a south wind

sprang up, and on the second day
we came to Puteoli.
14 [t]There we found *some* brethren, and were invited to stay with
them for seven days; and thus we
came to Rome. *where*
15 And the [r]brethren, when they
heard about us, came from there
as far as the Market of Appius and
Three Inns to meet us; and when
Paul saw them, he thanked God
and took courage. Acts 1:15
16 And when we entered Rome,
Paul was [r]allowed to stay by himself, with the soldier who was
guarding him. Acts 24:23
17 And it happened that after
three days he called together
those who were [r]the leading men
of the Jews, and when they had
come together, he *began* saying to
them, "Brethren, though I had
done nothing against our people,
or the customs of our [a]fathers, yet I
was delivered prisoner from Jerusalem into the hands of the Romans. Acts 13:50 • *forefathers*
18 "And when they had examined me, they were willing to release me because there was no
ground for putting me to death.
19 "But when the Jews [t]objected,
I was forced to appeal to Caesar;
not that I had any accusation
against my nation. *spoke against it*
20 "For this reason therefore, I
requested to see you and to speak
with you, for I am wearing [r]this
chain for the sake of the hope of
Israel." Acts 21:33
21 And they said to him, "We
have neither received letters from
Judea concerning you, nor have
any of [r]the brethren come here and
reported or spoken anything bad
about you. Acts 3:17; 22:5
22 "But we desire to hear from
you what [t]your views are; for concerning this [r]sect, it is known to us
that it is spoken against everywhere." *you think* • Acts 24:14
23 And when they had set a day
for him, they came to him at [r]his
lodging in large numbers; and he
was explaining to them by solemnly testifying about the kingdom of God, and trying to persuade them concerning Jesus,
from both the Law of Moses and
from the Prophets, from morning
until evening. Philem. 22
24 And some were being persuaded by the things spoken, but
others would not believe.
25 And when they did not agree
with one another, they *began* leaving after Paul had spoken one
parting word, "The Holy Spirit
rightly spoke through Isaiah the
prophet to your fathers,
26 saying,

'GO TO THIS PEOPLE AND SAY,
"YOU [t]WILL KEEP ON HEARING,
BUT WILL NOT UNDER-
STAND; *with a hearing*
AND [t]YOU WILL KEEP ON SEE-
ING, BUT WILL NOT PER-
CEIVE; *seeing you will see*
27 [r]FOR THE HEART OF THIS PEO-
PLE HAS BECOME DULL,
AND WITH THEIR EARS THEY
SCARCELY HEAR,
AND THEY HAVE CLOSED
THEIR EYES;
LEST THEY SHOULD SEE
WITH THEIR EYES,
AND HEAR WITH THEIR EARS,
AND UNDERSTAND WITH
THEIR HEART AND RE-
TURN, Is. 6:10

AND I SHOULD HEAL
THEM." '
28 "Let it be known to you therefore, that this salvation of God has
been sent [r]to the Gentiles; they will
also listen." Acts 9:15; 13:46
29 [[50]And when he had spoken
these words, the Jews departed,

[50]Many mss. do not contain this verse

having a great dispute among
themselves.]
30 And he stayed two full years
[a]in his own rented quarters, and
was welcoming all who came to
him, *at his own expense*
31 [r]preaching the kingdom of
God, and teaching concerning the
Lord Jesus Christ with all open-
ness, unhindered. *proclaiming*

THE EPISTLE OF PAUL TO THE
ROMANS

PAUL, a bond-servant of Christ
Jesus, called *as* an apostle, set
apart for the gospel of God,
2 which He [r]promised beforehand through His prophets in the
holy Scriptures, Titus 1:2
3 concerning His Son, who
was born of a [t]descendant of David according to the flesh, *seed*
4 who was declared [r]the Son of
God with power [1]by the resurrection from the dead, according to
the [a]spirit of holiness, Jesus Christ
our Lord, Matt. 4:3 • *spirit*
5 through whom we have received grace and apostleship [t]to
bring about *the* obedience of faith
among all the Gentiles, for His
name's sake, *for obedience*
6 among whom you also are
the called of Jesus Christ;
7 to all who are beloved of God
in Rome, called *as* saints: Grace to
you and peace from God our Father and the Lord Jesus Christ.
8 First, [r]I thank my God

[1]Or, *as a result of*

through Jesus Christ for you all,
because [r]your faith is being proclaimed throughout the whole
world. 1 Cor. 1:4 • Acts 28:22
9 For [r]God, whom I [r]serve in my
spirit in the *preaching of the* gospel of His Son, is my witness *as to*
how unceasingly I make mention
of you, Rom. 9:1 • Acts 24:14
10 always in my prayers making
request, if perhaps now at last by
[r]the will of God I may succeed in
coming to you. Acts 18:21
11 For [r]I long to see you in order
that I may impart some spiritual
gift to you, that you may be established; Acts 19:21; Rom. 15:23
12 that is, that I may be encouraged together with you *while*
among you, each of us by the other's faith, both yours and mine.
13 And I do not want you to be
unaware, brethren, that often I
have planned to come to you (and
have been prevented thus far) in
order that I might obtain some
fruit among you also, even as
among the rest of the Gentiles.

14 I am [2]under obligation both
to Greeks and to barbarians, both
to the wise and to the foolish.
15 Thus, for my part, I am eager
to [r]preach the gospel to you also
who are in Rome. Rom. 15:20
16 For I am not [r]ashamed of the
gospel, for it is the power of God
for salvation to everyone who believes, to the Jew first and also to
the Greek. Mark 8:38
17 For in it *the* righteousness of
God is revealed from faith to faith;
as it is written, "BUT THE RIGHT-
EOUS *man* SHALL LIVE BY FAITH."
18 For [r]the wrath of God is revealed from heaven against all ungodliness and unrighteousness of
men, who suppress the truth [a]in
unrighteousness, Eph. 5:6 • *by*
19 because that which is known
about God is evident within them;
for God made it evident to them.
20 For [r]since the creation of the
world His invisible attributes, His
eternal power and divine nature,
have been clearly seen, [r]being understood through what has been
made, so that they are without excuse. Mark 10:6 • Job 12:7-9
21 For even though they knew
God, they did not [3]honor Him as
God, or give thanks; but they became [r]futile in their speculations,
and their foolish heart was darkened. 2 Kin. 17:15; Jer. 2:5
22 [r]Professing to be wise, they
became fools, Jer. 10:14
23 and exchanged the glory of
the incorruptible God for an
image in the form of corruptible
man and of birds and four-footed
animals and [4]crawling creatures.

[2] Lit., *debtor* [3] Lit., *glorify*
[4] Or possibly, *reptiles*

24 Therefore God gave them
over in the lusts of their hearts to
impurity, that their bodies might
be dishonored among them.
25 For they exchanged the truth
of God for [t]a lie, and worshiped
and served the creature rather
than the Creator, who is blessed
forever. Amen. *the lie*
26 For this reason God gave
them over to degrading passions;
for their women exchanged the
natural function for that which is
[t]unnatural, *against nature*
27 and in the same way also the
men abandoned the natural function of the woman and burned in
their desire toward one another,
men with men committing [t]in-
decent acts and receiving in their
own persons the due penalty of
their error. *the shameless deed*
28 And just as they did not see
fit to acknowledge God any
longer, God gave them over to a
depraved mind, to do those things
which are not proper,
29 being filled with all unrighteousness, wickedness, greed, evil;
full of envy, murder, strife, deceit,
malice; *they are* gossips,
30 slanderers, [a]haters of God, insolent, arrogant, boastful, inven-
tors of evil, [r]disobedient to parents, *hateful to God* • 2 Tim. 3:2
31 without understanding, untrustworthy, [r]unloving, unmerci-
ful; 2 Tim. 3:3
32 and, although they know the
ordinance of God, that those who
practice such things are worthy of
death, they not only do the same,
but also give hearty approval to
those who practice them.

CHAPTER 2

THEREFORE you are [r]without excuse, every man *of you* who passes judgment, for in that you judge another, you condemn yourself; for you who judge practice the same things. Rom. 1:20

2 And we know that the judgment of God rightly falls upon those who practice such things.

3 And do you suppose this, O man, [t]when you pass judgment upon those who practice such things and do the same *yourself,* that you will escape the judgment of God? *who pass judgment*

4 Or do you think lightly of [r]the riches of His kindness and forbearance and patience, not knowing that the kindness of God leads you to repentance? Rom. 9:23

5 But [a]because of your stubbornness and unrepentant heart you are storing up wrath for yourself in the day of wrath and revelation of the righteous judgment of God, *in accordance with*

6 who WILL RENDER TO EVERY MAN ACCORDING TO HIS DEEDS:

7 to those who by [r]perseverance in doing good seek for [r]glory and honor and immortality, eternal life; Luke 8:15 • Rom. 2:10

8 but to those who are selfishly ambitious and do not obey the truth, but obey unrighteousness, wrath and indignation.

9 *There will be* [r]tribulation and distress [t]for every soul of man who does evil, of the Jew first and also of the Greek, Rom. 8:35 • *upon*

10 but [r]glory and honor and peace to every man who does good, to the Jew [r]first and also to the Greek. Rom. 2:7 • Rom. 2:9

11 For [r]there is no partiality with God. Deut. 10:17; Acts 10:34

12 For all who have sinned [a]without the Law will also perish [a]without the Law; and all who have sinned under the Law will be judged by the Law; *without law*

13 for not the hearers of the Law are just before God, but the doers of the Law will be justified.

14 For when Gentiles who do not have [a]the Law do [t]instinctively the things of the Law, these, not having [a]the Law, are a law to themselves, *law • by nature*

15 in that they show the work of the Law written in their hearts, their conscience bearing witness, and their thoughts alternately accusing or else defending them,

16 on the day when, [r]according to my gospel, [r]God will judge the secrets of men through Christ Jesus. Rom. 16:25 • Acts 10:42

17 But if you bear the name "Jew," and rely [a]upon the Law, and boast in God, *upon law*

18 and know *His* will, and approve the things that are essential, being instructed out of the Law,

19 and are confident that you yourself are a guide to the blind, a light to those who are in darkness,

20 a corrector of the foolish, a teacher of the immature, having in the Law the embodiment of knowledge and of the truth,

21 you, therefore, who teach another, do you not teach yourself? You who [a]preach that one should not steal, do you steal? *proclaim*

22 You who say that one should not commit adultery, do you commit adultery? You who abhor idols, do you rob temples?

23 You who boast[a] in the Law,
through your breaking the Law,
do you dishonor God? *in law*
24 For "THE[r] NAME OF GOD IS
BLASPHEMED AMONG THE GENTILES
[r]BECAUSE OF YOU," just as it is written. Is. 52:5 • 2 Pet. 2:2
25 For indeed circumcision is of
value, if you practice[a] the Law; but
if you are a transgressor of the
Law, your circumcision has become uncircumcision. *law*
26 If therefore [r]the [t]uncircum-
cised man keeps the requirements
of the Law, will not his uncircumcision be regarded as circumcision? Rom. 3:30 • *uncircumcision*
27 And will not he who is physi-
cally uncircumcised, if he keeps
the Law, will he not judge you
who though having the letter *of
the Law* and circumcision are a
transgressor[a] of the Law? *of law*
28 For[r] he is not a Jew who is
one outwardly; neither is circumcision that which is outward in the
flesh. John 8:39; Rom. 2:17; 9:6
29 But he is a Jew who is one
inwardly; and circumcision is that
which is of the heart, by the Spirit,
not by the letter; and his praise is
not from men, but from God.

CHAPTER 3

THEN what advantage has the
Jew? Or what is the benefit of circumcision?
2 Great in every respect. First
of all, that they were entrusted
with the oracles of God.
3 What then? If some did not
believe, their unbelief will not nullify the faithfulness of God, will it?
4 May it never be! Rather, let
God be found true, though every
man *be found* [r]a liar, as it is written, Ps. 116:11
"THAT THOU MIGHTEST BE
JUSTIFIED IN THY WORDS,
AND MIGHTEST PREVAIL
WHEN THOU ART
JUDGED."
5 But if our unrighteousness
[a]demonstrates the righteousness of
God, what shall we say? The God
who inflicts wrath is not unrighteous, is He? (I am speaking in human terms.) *commends*
6 [r]May it never be! For otherwise how will [r]God judge the
world? Luke 20:16 • Rom. 2:16
7 But if through my lie [r]the
truth of God abounded to His glory, why am I also still being
judged as a sinner? Rom. 3:4
8 And why not *say* (as we are
slanderously reported and as
some affirm that we say), "Let us
do evil that good may come"?
Their condemnation is just.
9 What then? Are we better
than they? Not at all; for we have
already charged that both Jews
and Greeks are all under sin;
10 as it is written,
"THERE IS NONE RIGHTEOUS,
NOT EVEN ONE;
11 THERE IS NONE WHO UNDER-
STANDS,
THERE IS NONE WHO SEEKS
FOR GOD;
12 ALL HAVE TURNED ASIDE,
TOGETHER THEY HAVE BE-
COME USELESS;
THERE IS NONE WHO DOES
GOOD,
THERE IS NOT EVEN ONE."
13 "THEIR THROAT IS AN OPEN
GRAVE,
WITH THEIR TONGUES THEY
KEEP DECEIVING,"

"THE POISON OF ASPS IS UN-
DER THEIR LIPS";
14 "WHOSE[r] MOUTH IS FULL OF
CURSING AND BITTER-
NESS"; Ps. 10:7
15 "THEIR[r] FEET ARE SWIFT TO
SHED BLOOD, Is. 59:7f.
16 DESTRUCTION AND MISERY
ARE IN THEIR PATHS,
17 AND THE PATH OF PEACE
HAVE THEY NOT KNOWN."
18 "THERE IS NO FEAR OF GOD
BEFORE THEIR EYES."
19 Now we know that whatever
the [r]Law says, it speaks to those
who are [t]under the Law, that every
mouth may be closed, and all the
world may become accountable to
God; John 10:34 • *in*
20 because by the works of the
Law no flesh will be justified in
His sight; for through the Law
comes the knowledge of sin.
21 But now apart from the Law
the righteousness of God has been
manifested, being witnessed by
the Law and the Prophets,
22 even *the* [r]righteousness of
God through faith in Jesus Christ
for all those who believe; for there
is no distinction; Rom. 1:17
23 for all have sinned and fall
short of the glory of God,
24 being justified as a gift by
His grace through the redemption
which is in Christ Jesus;
25 whom God displayed pub-
licly as a [a]propitiation in His blood
through faith. *This was* to demonstrate His righteousness, because
in the forbearance of God He
passed over the sins previously
committed; *a propitiatory sacrifice*
26 for the demonstration, *I say,*
of His righteousness at the present time, that He might be just
and the justifier of the one who
has faith in Jesus.
27 Where then is boasting? It is
excluded. By what kind of law? Of
works? No, but by a law of faith.
28 For we maintain that a man
is justified by faith apart from
works [a]of the Law. *of law*
29 Or is God *the God* of Jews
only? Is He not *the God* of Gentiles also? Yes, of Gentiles also,
30 since indeed God who will
justify the [t]circumcised [t]by faith
and the uncircumcised through
faith is one. *circumcision • out of*
31 Do we then nullify [a]the Law
through faith? [r]May it never be! On
the contrary, we establish the
Law. *law* • Luke 20:16

CHAPTER 4

WHAT then shall we say that
Abraham, our forefather according to the flesh, has found?
2 For if Abraham was justified
by works, he has something to
boast about; but not before God.
3 For what does the Scripture
say? "AND ABRAHAM BELIEVED
GOD, AND IT WAS RECKONED TO
HIM AS RIGHTEOUSNESS."
4 Now to the one who works,
his wage is not reckoned as a favor, but as what is due.
5 But to the one who does not
work, but believes in Him who
justifies the ungodly, his faith is
reckoned as righteousness,
6 just as David also speaks of
the blessing upon the man to
whom God reckons righteousness
apart from works:
7 "BLESSED[r] ARE THOSE WHOSE
LAWLESS DEEDS HAVE
BEEN FORGIVEN, Ps. 32:1

AND WHOSE SINS HAVE BEEN
COVERED.
8 "BLESSED IS THE MAN WHOSE
SIN THE LORD WILL NOT
TAKE INTO ACCOUNT."
9 Is this blessing then upon the
circumcised, or upon the uncircumcised also? For we say,
"FAITH WAS RECKONED TO ABRA-
HAM AS RIGHTEOUSNESS."
10 How then was it reckoned?
While he was circumcised, or uncircumcised? Not while circumcised, but while uncircumcised;
11 and he [r]received the sign of
circumcision, a seal of the righteousness of the faith which he had
while uncircumcised, that he
might be the father of all who believe without being circumcised,
that righteousness might be reckoned to them, Gen. 17:10f.
12 and the father of circumcision to those who not only are of
the circumcision, but who also follow in the steps of the faith of our
father Abraham which he had
while uncircumcised.
13 For the promise to Abraham
or to his [t]descendants that he
would be heir of the world was
not through the Law, but through
the righteousness of faith. *seed*
14 For if those who are of the
Law are heirs, faith is made void
and the promise is nullified;
15 for the Law brings about
wrath, but where there is no law,
neither is there violation.
16 For this reason *it is* by faith,
that *it might be* in accordance
with grace, in order that the
promise may be certain to all the
descendants, not only to those
who are of the Law, but also to
those who are of the faith of Abraham, who is the father of us all,
17 (as it is written, "A FATHER
OF MANY NATIONS HAVE I MADE
YOU") in the sight of Him whom
he believed, *even* God, who gives
life to the dead and calls into
being that which does not exist.
18 In hope against hope he believed, in order that he might become [r]a father of many nations,
according to that which had been
spoken, "SO SHALL YOUR [t]DESCEND-
ANTS BE." Rom. 4:17 • *seed*
19 And without becoming weak
in faith he contemplated his own
body, now [r]as good as dead since
[r]he was about a hundred years old,
and the deadness of Sarah's
womb; Heb. 11:12 • Gen. 17:17
20 yet, with respect to the
promise of God, he did not waver
in unbelief, but grew strong in
faith, giving glory to God,
21 and [r]being fully assured that
what He had promised, He was
able also to perform. Rom. 14:5
22 Therefore also IT WAS RECK-
ONED TO HIM AS RIGHTEOUSNESS.
23 Now [r]not for his sake only
was it written, that it was reckoned to him, Rom. 15:4
24 but for our sake also, to
whom it will be reckoned, as
those [r]who believe in Him who
[r]raised Jesus our Lord from the
dead, 1 Pet. 1:21 • Acts 2:24
25 *He* who was [r]delivered up because of our transgressions, and
was [r]raised because of our justification. Gal. 2:20 • 2 Cor. 5:15

CHAPTER 5

[r]THEREFORE having been justified by faith, [r]we have peace with

God through our Lord Jesus
Christ, Rom. 3:28 • Rom. 5:11
2 through whom also we have
[r]obtained our introduction by faith
into this grace in which we stand;
and[a]we exult in hope of the glory
of God. Eph. 2:18 • *let us exult*
3 And not only this, but we
also [r]exult in our tribulations,
knowing that tribulation brings
about perseverance; Matt. 5:12
4 and [r]perseverance, [r]proven
character; and proven character,
hope; Luke 21:19 • Phil. 2:22
5 and hope [r]does not disap-
point, because the love of God has
been poured out within our hearts
through the Holy Spirit who was
given to us. Ps. 119:116
6 For while we were still[r]help-
less, at the right time Christ died
for the ungodly. Rom. 5:8, 10
7 For one will hardly die for a
righteous man; though perhaps
for the good man someone would
dare even to die.
8 But God [r]demonstrates His
own love toward us, in that while
we were yet sinners, [r]Christ died
for us. Rom. 3:5 • Rom. 4:25
9 Much more then, having now
been justified[a]by His blood, we
shall be saved from the wrath *of*
God through Him. *in*
10 For if while we were [r]en-
emies, we were reconciled to God
through the death of His Son,
much more, having been reconciled, we shall be saved[a]by His
life. Rom. 11:28 • *in*
11 And not only this, [t]but we
also exult in God through our
Lord Jesus Christ, through whom
we have now received the reconciliation. *but also exulting*

12 Therefore, just as through
[r]one man sin entered into the
world, and death through sin, and
so death spread to all men, because all sinned— Gen. 2:17
13 for[a]until the Law sin was in
the world; but sin is not imputed
when there is no law. *until law*
14 Nevertheless death reigned
from Adam until Moses, even
over those who had not sinned[r]in
the likeness of the offense of
Adam, who is a [5]type of Him who
was to come. Hos. 6:7
15 But the free gift is not like
the transgression. For if by the
transgression of[r]the one the many
died, much more did the grace of
God and the gift by the grace of
the one Man, Jesus Christ, abound
to the many. Rom. 5:12, 18, 19
16 And the gift is not like *that*
which came through the one who
sinned; for on the one hand the
judgment *arose* from one *trans-*
gression resulting in condemnation, but on the other hand the
free gift *arose* from many transgressions resulting in justification.
17 For if by the transgression of
the one, death reigned[r]through the
one, much more those who receive the abundance of grace and
of the gift of righteousness will
reign in life through the One,
Jesus Christ. Gen. 2:17; 3:6, 19
18 So then as through one transgression [t]there resulted condemnation to all men, even so through
one act of righteousness there resulted justification of life to all
men. *to condemnation*
19 For as through the one man's
disobedience the many were
made sinners, even so through[r]the

[5]Or, *foreshadowing*

obedience of the One the many
will be made righteous. Phil. 2:8
20 And [a]the Law came in that
the transgression might increase;
but where sin increased, grace
abounded all the more, *law*
21 that, as sin reigned in death,
even so grace might reign through
righteousness to eternal life
through Jesus Christ our Lord.

CHAPTER 6

WHAT shall we say then? Are
we to [r]continue in sin that grace
might increase? Rom. 3:8; 6:15
2 May it never be! How shall
we who died to sin still live in it?
3 Or do you not know that all
of us who have been [r]baptized into
Christ Jesus have been baptized
into His death? Matt. 28:19
4 Therefore we have been buried with Him through baptism
into death, in order that as Christ
was raised from the dead through
the glory of the Father, so we too
might walk in newness of life.
5 For if we have become
[a]united with *Him* in the likeness of
His death, certainly we shall be
also *in the likeness* of His resurrection, *united with the likeness*
6 knowing this, that our [r]old
self was crucified with *Him,* that
our body of sin might be done
away with, that we should no
longer be slaves to sin; Col. 3:9
7 for [r]he who has died is [a]freed
from sin. 1 Pet. 4:1 • *acquitted*
8 Now [r]if we have died with
Christ, we believe that we shall
also live with Him, Rom. 6:4
9 knowing that Christ, having
been [r]raised from the dead, is never to die again; death no longer is
master over Him. Acts 2:24
10 For the death that He died,
He died to sin, once for all; but the
life that He lives, He lives to God.
11 Even so consider yourselves
to be [r]dead to sin, but alive to God
in Christ Jesus. Rom. 6:2; 7:4, 6
12 Therefore do not let sin [r]reign
in your mortal body that you
should obey its lusts, Rom. 6:14
13 and do not go on presenting
the members of your body to sin
as instruments of unrighteousness; but present yourselves to
God as those alive from the dead,
and your members *as* instruments
of righteousness to God.
14 For sin shall not be master
over you, for [r]you are not under
law, but under grace. Gal. 4:21
15 What then? Shall we sin because we are not under law but
under grace? May it never be!
16 Do you not know that when
you present yourselves to someone *as* slaves for obedience, you
are slaves of the one whom you
obey, either of sin [t]resulting in
death, or of obedience resulting in
righteousness? *to death*
17 But [r]thanks be to God that
though you were slaves of sin, you
became obedient from the heart
to that form of teaching to which
you were committed, Rom. 1:8
18 and having been [r]freed from
sin, you became slaves of righteousness. John 8:32; Rom. 6:22
19 I am speaking in human
terms because of the weakness of
your flesh. For just as you presented your members *as* slaves to
impurity and to lawlessness, [t]re-
sulting in *further* lawlessness, so
now present your members *as*

slaves to righteousness, resulting in sanctification. *to lawlessness*

20 For [r]when you were slaves of sin, you were free in regard to righteousness. Rom. 6:16

21 Therefore what [t]benefit were you then [t]deriving [t]from the things of which you are now ashamed? For the outcome of those things is death. *fruit • having • in*

22 But now having been freed from sin and enslaved to God, you [t]derive your [t]benefit, resulting in sanctification, and the outcome, eternal life. *have • fruit*

23 For the wages of sin is death, but the free gift of God is eternal life in Christ Jesus our Lord.

CHAPTER 7

OR do you not know, [r]brethren (for I am speaking to those who know the law), that the law has jurisdiction over a person as long as he lives? Rom. 1:13

2 For the married woman is bound by law to her husband while he is living; but if her husband dies, she is released from the law concerning the husband.

3 So then if, while her husband is living, she is joined to another man, she shall be called an adulteress; but if her husband dies, she is free from the law, so that she is not an adulteress, though she is joined to another man.

4 Therefore, my brethren, you also were [r]made to die [r]to the Law through the body of Christ, that you might be joined to another, to Him who was raised from the dead, that we might bear fruit for God. Rom. 6:2; 7:6 • Rom. 8:2

5 For while we were in the flesh, the sinful passions, which were *aroused* by the Law, were at work in the members of our body to bear fruit for death.

6 But now we have been [r]released from the Law, having [r]died to that by which we were bound, so that we serve in newness of the [6]Spirit and not in oldness of the letter. Rom. 7:2 • Rom. 6:2

7 What shall we say then? Is the Law sin? May it never be! On the contrary, I would not have come to know sin except [a]through the Law; for I would not have known about [a]coveting if the Law had not said, "YOU SHALL NOT COVET." *through law • lust*

8 But sin, taking opportunity through the commandment, produced in me [a]coveting of every kind; for apart [a]from the Law sin *is* dead. *lust • from law*

9 And I was once alive apart [a]from the Law; but when the commandment came, sin became alive, and I died; *from law*

10 and this commandment, which was [t]to result in life, proved to result in death for me; *to life*

11 for sin, [r]taking opportunity [r]through the commandment, deceived me, and through it killed me. Rom. 7:8 • Rom. 3:20; 7:8

12 [r]So then, the Law is holy, and the commandment is holy and righteous and good. Rom. 7:16

13 Therefore did that which is good become *a cause of* death for me? May it never be! Rather it was sin, in order that it might be shown to be sin by effecting my death through that which is good, that through the commandment sin might become utterly sinful.

[6]Or, *spirit*

14 For we know that the Law is spiritual; but I am of flesh, sold [t]into bondage to sin. *under sin*

15 For that which I am doing,[r] I do not understand; for I am not practicing [r]what I *would* like to *do,* but I am doing the very thing I hate. John 15:15 • Rom. 7:19

16 But if I do the very thing I do not wish *to do,* I agree with the Law, *confessing* that it is good.

17 So now, [r]no longer am I the one doing it, but sin which indwells me. Rom. 7:20

18 For I know that nothing good dwells in me, that is, in my flesh; for the wishing is present in me, but the doing of the good *is* not.

19 For [r]the good that I wish, I do not do; but I practice the very evil that I do not wish. Rom. 7:15

20 But if I am doing the very thing I do not wish,[r] I am no longer the one doing it, but sin which dwells in me. Rom. 7:17

21 I find then the [t]principle that evil is present in me, the one who wishes to do good. *law*

22 For I joyfully concur with the law of God in the inner man,

23 but I see a different law in [t]the members of my body, waging war against the law of my mind, and making me a prisoner [t]of the law of sin which is in my members. *my members • in*

24 Wretched man that I am! Who will set me free from [r]the body of this death? Rom. 6:6

25 Thanks be to God through Jesus Christ our Lord! So then, on the one hand I myself with my mind am serving the law of God, but on the other, with my flesh [r]the law of sin. Rom. 7:21, 23; 8:2

CHAPTER 8

THERE is therefore now no [r]condemnation for those who are in Christ Jesus. Rom. 5:16; 8:34

2 For [r]the law of the Spirit of life in Christ Jesus [r]has set [7]you free from the law of sin and of death. 1 Cor. 15:45 • Rom. 7:4

3 For what the Law could not do, weak as it was through the flesh, God *did:* sending His own Son in the likeness of sinful flesh and *as an offering* for sin, He condemned sin in the flesh,

4 in order that the requirement of the Law might be fulfilled in us, who do not walk according to the flesh, but according to the Spirit.

5 For those who are according to the flesh set their minds on [r]the things of the flesh, but those who are according to the Spirit, the things of the Spirit. Gal. 5:19-21

6 [r]For the mind set on the flesh is death, but the mind set on the Spirit is life and peace, Gal. 6:8

7 because the mind set on the flesh is [r]hostile toward God; for it does not subject itself to the law of God, for it is not even able *to do so;* James 4:4

8 and those who are in the flesh cannot please God.

9 However, you are not in the flesh but in the Spirit, if indeed the Spirit of God dwells in you. But if anyone does not have the Spirit of Christ, he does not belong to Him.

10 And if Christ is in you, though the body is dead because of sin, yet the spirit is [t]alive because of righteousness. *life*

11 But if the Spirit of Him who raised Jesus from the dead dwells

[7]Some ancient mss. read *me*

in you, He who raised Christ Jesus
from the dead will also give life to
your mortal bodies [8]through His
Spirit who indwells you.
12 So then, brethren, we are under obligation, not to the flesh, to
live according to the flesh—
13 for if you are living according to the flesh, you [a]must die; but
if by the Spirit you are putting to
death the deeds of the body, you
will live. *are about to*
14 For all who are [r]being led by
the Spirit of God, these are [r]sons of
God. Gal. 5:18 • Hos. 1:10
15 For you have not received a
spirit of slavery [t]leading to fear
again, but you have received [a]a
spirit of adoption as sons by
which we cry out, "Abba! Father!" *for fear again • the Spirit*
16 The Spirit Himself [r]bears witness with our spirit that we are
children of God, Acts 5:32
17 and if children, [r]heirs also,
heirs of God and fellow heirs with
Christ, if indeed we suffer with
Him in order that we may also be
glorified with *Him*. Acts 20:32
18 For I consider that the sufferings of this present time are not
worthy to be compared with the
glory that is to be revealed to us.
19 For the anxious longing of
the creation waits eagerly for the
revealing of the sons of God.
20 For the creation [r]was subjected to futility, not of its own
will, but because of Him who subjected it, [9]in hope Gen. 3:17-19
21 that the creation itself also
will be set free from its slavery to

[8]Some ancient mss. read *because of*
[9]Some ancient mss. read *in hope; because the creation*

corruption into the freedom of the
glory of the children of God.
22 For we know that the whole
creation [r]groans and suffers the
pains of childbirth together until
now. Jer. 12:4, 11
23 And not only this, but also
we ourselves, having [r]the first
fruits of the Spirit, even we ourselves [r]groan within ourselves,
waiting eagerly for *our* adoption
as sons, the redemption of our
body. Rom. 8:16 • 2 Cor. 5:2, 4
24 For [r]in hope we have been
saved, but hope that is seen is not
hope; for [10]why does one also hope
for what he sees? Rom. 8:20
25 But [r]if we hope for what we
do not see, with perseverance we
wait eagerly for it. 1 Thess. 1:3
26 And in the same way the
Spirit also helps our weakness; for
[r]we do not know how to pray as
we should, but the Spirit Himself
intercedes for *us* with groanings
too deep for words; Matt. 20:22
27 and He who searches the
hearts knows what the mind of
the Spirit is, because He intercedes for the [a]saints according to
the will of God. *holy ones*
28 And we know that [11]God
causes [r]all things to work together
for good to those who love God, to
those who are called according to
His purpose. Rom. 8:32
29 For whom He foreknew, He
also predestined *to become* conformed to the image of His Son,
that He might be the first-born
among many brethren;
30 and whom He [r]predestined,
these He also called; and whom

[10]Some ancient mss. read *who hopes for what he sees?*
[11]Some ancient mss. read *all things work together for good*

He called, these He also justified;
and whom He justified, these He
also glorified. Rom. 9:23; 11:29
31 What then shall we say to
these things? If God *is* for us, who
is against us? Ps. 118:6
32 He who did not spare His
own Son, but delivered Him up for
us all, how will He not also with
Him freely give us all things?
33 Who will bring a charge
against God's elect? God is the
one who justifies; Luke 18:7
34 who is the one who condemns? Christ Jesus is He who
died, yes, rather who was [12]raised,
who is at the right hand of God,
who also intercedes for us.
35 Who shall separate us from
the love of [13]Christ? Shall tribulation, or distress, or persecution, or
famine, or nakedness, or peril, or
sword? Rom. 8:37f. • Rom. 2:9
36 Just as it is written,
"FOR THY SAKE WE ARE
BEING PUT TO DEATH ALL
DAY LONG;
WE WERE CONSIDERED AS
SHEEP TO BE SLAUGH-
TERED." Ps. 44:22
37 But in all these things we
overwhelmingly conquer through
Him who loved us. John 16:33
38 For I am convinced that neither death, nor life, nor angels,
nor principalities, nor things present, nor things to come, nor powers, 1 Cor. 3:22 • 1 Cor. 15:24
39 nor height, nor depth, nor
any other created thing, shall be
able to separate us from the love
of God, which is in Christ Jesus
our Lord. Rom. 5:8 • Rom. 8:1

[12] Some ancient mss. read *raised from the dead*

[13] Some ancient mss. read *God*

CHAPTER 9

I AM telling the truth in Christ, I
am not lying, my conscience bearing me witness in the Holy Spirit,
2 that I have great sorrow and
unceasing grief in my heart.
3 For I could wish that I myself
were accursed, *separated* from
Christ for the sake of my brethren, my kinsmen according to the
flesh, Ex. 32:32 • *pray* • 1 Cor. 12:3
4 who are Israelites, to whom
belongs the adoption as sons and
the glory and the covenants and
the giving of the Law and the *temple* service and the promises,
5 whose are the fathers, and
from whom is the Christ according to the flesh, who is over all,
God blessed forever. Amen.
6 But *it is* not as though the
word of God has failed. For they
are not all Israel who are *descended* from Israel; John 1:47
7 neither are they all children
because they are Abraham's descendants, but: "THROUGH ISAAC
YOUR DESCENDANTS WILL BE
NAMED." John 8:33, 39 • *seed*
8 That is, it is not the children
of the flesh who are children of
God, but the children of the promise are regarded as descendants.
9 For this is a word of promise:
"AT THIS TIME I WILL COME, AND
SARAH SHALL HAVE A SON."
10 And not only this, but there
was Rebekah also, when she had
conceived *twins* by one man, our
father Isaac; Gen. 25:21
11 for though *the twins* were
not yet born, and had not done
anything good or bad, in order
that God's purpose according to
His choice might stand, not be-

cause of works, but because of
Him who calls, Rom. 4:17; 8:28
12 it was said to her, "THE
OLDER WILL SERVE THE YOUNGER."
13 Just as it is written, "JACOB I
LOVED, BUT ESAU I HATED."
14 What shall we say then?
There is no injustice with God, is
there? May it never be!
15 For He says to Moses, "I[r]
WILL HAVE MERCY ON WHOM I
HAVE MERCY, AND I WILL HAVE
COMPASSION ON WHOM I HAVE
COMPASSION." Ex. 33:19
16 So then it *does* not *depend* on
the man who wills or the man who
runs, but on God who has mercy.
17 For the Scripture says to
Pharaoh, "FOR THIS VERY PURPOSE
I RAISED YOU UP, TO DEMONSTRATE
MY POWER IN YOU, AND THAT MY
NAME MIGHT BE PROCLAIMED
THROUGHOUT THE WHOLE EARTH."
18 So then He has mercy on
whom He desires, and He [r]hardens
whom He desires. Ex. 4:21; 7:3
19 You will say to me then,
"Why [r]does He still find fault? For
who resists His will?" Rom. 3:7
20 On the contrary, who are
you, O man, who answers back to
God? The thing molded will not
say to the molder, "Why did you
make me like this," will it?
21 Or does not the potter have a
right over the clay, to make from
the same lump one vessel [t]for honorable use, and another for common use? *for honor*
22 What if God, although willing to demonstrate His wrath and
to make His power known, endured with much patience vessels
of wrath prepared for destruction?
23 And *He did so* in order that
He might make known [r]the riches
of His glory upon vessels of mercy, which He prepared beforehand for glory, Rom. 2:4
24 *even* us, whom He also
called, not from among Jews only,
but also from among Gentiles.
25 As He says also in Hosea,
"I WILL CALL THOSE WHO
WERE NOT MY PEOPLE,
'MY PEOPLE,'
AND HER WHO WAS NOT BE-
LOVED, 'BELOVED.'"
26 "AND IT SHALL BE THAT IN
THE PLACE WHERE IT WAS
SAID TO THEM, 'YOU ARE
NOT MY PEOPLE,'
THERE THEY SHALL BE
CALLED SONS OF [r]THE LIV-
ING GOD." Matt. 16:16
27 And Isaiah cries out concern-
ing Israel, "THOUGH THE NUMBER
OF THE SONS OF ISRAEL BE AS THE
SAND OF THE SEA, IT IS THE REM-
NANT THAT WILL BE SAVED;
28 [r]FOR THE LORD WILL EXECUTE
HIS WORD UPON THE EARTH, THOR-
OUGHLY AND QUICKLY." Is. 10:23
29 And just as Isaiah foretold,
"EXCEPT THE LORD OF SABA-
OTH HAD LEFT TO US A
[t]POSTERITY, *seed*
WE WOULD HAVE BECOME AS
SODOM, AND WOULD HAVE
RESEMBLED GOMORRAH."
30 What shall we say then?
That Gentiles, who did not pursue
righteousness, attained righteousness, even the righteousness
which is [t]by faith; *out of*
31 but Israel, [r]pursuing a law of
righteousness, did not [r]arrive at
that law. Is. 51:1 • Gal. 5:4
32 Why? Because *they did* not
pursue it [t]by faith, but as though *it*
were [t]by works. They stumbled
over the stumbling stone, *out of*

33 just as it is written,
"BEHOLD, I LAY IN ZION A
STONE OF STUMBLING AND
A ROCK OF OFFENSE,
AND HE WHO BELIEVES IN
HIM WILL NOT BE [t]DISAP-
POINTED." *put to shame*

CHAPTER 10

BRETHREN, my heart's desire
and my prayer to God for them is
for *their* salvation.
2 For I bear them witness that
they have a zeal for God, but not
in accordance with knowledge.
3 For not knowing about [r]God's
righteousness, and seeking to establish their own, they did not
subject themselves to the righteousness of God. Rom. 1:17
4 For Christ is the [a]end of the
law for righteousness to [r]everyone
who believes. *goal* • Rom. 3:22
5 For Moses writes that the
man who practices the righteousness which is based on law shall
live [t]by that righteousness. *by it*
6 But the righteousness [t]based
on faith speaks thus, "DO NOT SAY
IN YOUR HEART, 'WHO WILL AS-
CEND INTO HEAVEN?' (that is, to
bring Christ down), *out of, from*
7 or 'WHO WILL DESCEND INTO
THE ABYSS?' (that is, to bring
Christ up from the dead)."
8 But what does it say? "THE[r]
WORD IS NEAR YOU, IN YOUR
MOUTH AND IN YOUR HEART"—that
is, the word of faith which we are
preaching, Deut. 30:14
9 that if you confess with your
mouth Jesus *as* Lord, and believe
in your heart that God raised Him
from the dead, you shall be saved;
10 for with the heart man believes, resulting in righteousness,
and with the mouth he confesses,
resulting in salvation.
11 For the Scripture says,
"WHOEVER BELIEVES IN HIM WILL
NOT BE DISAPPOINTED."
12 For [r]there is no distinction between Jew and Greek; for the
same *Lord* is Lord of all, abounding in riches for all who call upon
Him; Rom. 3:22, 29
13 for "WHOEVER[r] WILL CALL
UPON THE NAME OF THE LORD WILL
BE SAVED." Joel 2:32; Acts 2:21
14 How then shall they call
upon Him in whom they have not
believed? And how shall they believe in Him [r]whom they have not
heard? And how shall they hear
without a preacher? Eph. 2:17
15 And how shall they preach
unless they are sent? Just as it is
written, "HOW BEAUTIFUL ARE THE
FEET OF THOSE WHO BRING GLAD
TIDINGS OF GOOD THINGS!"
16 However, they did not all
heed the [t]glad tidings; for Isaiah
says, "LORD, WHO HAS BELIEVED
OUR REPORT?" *gospel*
17 So faith *comes* from hearing,
and hearing by the word of Christ.
18 But I say, surely they have
never heard, have they? Indeed
they have;
"THEIR VOICE HAS GONE OUT
INTO ALL THE EARTH,
AND THEIR WORDS TO THE
ENDS OF THE WORLD."
19 But I say, surely Israel did
not know, did they? At the first
Moses says,
"I[r] WILL MAKE YOU JEALOUS
BY THAT WHICH IS NOT A
NATION, Deut. 32:21

BY A NATION WITHOUT UN-
DERSTANDING WILL I AN-
GER YOU."
20 And Isaiah is very bold and
says,
"I[r] WAS FOUND BY THOSE WHO
SOUGHT ME NOT,
I BECAME MANIFEST TO
THOSE WHO DID NOT ASK
FOR ME." Is. 65:1
21 But as for Israel He says,
"ALL[r] THE DAY LONG I HAVE
STRETCHED OUT MY HANDS TO A
DISOBEDIENT AND OBSTINATE PEO-
PLE." Is. 65:2

CHAPTER 11

I SAY then, God has not [r]rejected
His people, has He? May it never
be! For I too am an Israelite, a descendant of Abraham, of the tribe
of Benjamin. 1 Sam. 12:22
2 God [r]has not rejected His
people whom He [r]foreknew. Or do
you not know what the Scripture
says in *the passage about* Elijah,
how he pleads with God against
Israel? Ps. 94:14 • Rom. 8:29
3 "Lord, [r]THEY HAVE KILLED THY
PROPHETS, THEY HAVE TORN DOWN
THINE ALTARS, AND I ALONE AM
LEFT, AND THEY ARE SEEKING MY
LIFE." 1 Kin. 19:10, 14
4 But what [t]is the divine response to him? "I[r] HAVE KEPT for
Myself SEVEN THOUSAND MEN WHO
HAVE NOT BOWED THE KNEE TO
BAAL." *says* • 1 Kin. 19:18
5 In the same way then, there
has also come to be at the present
time a remnant according to
God's gracious choice.
6 But if it is by grace, it is no
longer on the basis of works, oth-
erwise grace is no longer grace.
7 What then? That which Is-
rael is seeking for, it has not ob-
tained, but [t]those who were chosen obtained it, and the rest were
hardened; *the election*
8 just as it is written,
"GOD[r] GAVE THEM A SPIRIT OF
STUPOR, Is. 29:10
EYES TO SEE NOT AND EARS
TO HEAR NOT,
DOWN TO THIS VERY DAY."
9 And David says,
"LET[r] THEIR TABLE BECOME A
SNARE AND A TRAP,
AND A STUMBLING BLOCK
AND A RETRIBUTION TO
THEM. Ps. 69:22
10 "LET[r] THEIR EYES BE DARK-
ENED TO SEE NOT,
AND BEND THEIR BACKS FOR-
EVER." Ps. 69:23
11 I say then, they did not stumble so as to fall, did they? May it
never be! But by their transgression salvation *has come* to the
Gentiles, to make them jealous.
12 Now if their transgression be
riches for the world and their failure be riches for the Gentiles, how
much more will their [a]fulfillment
be! *fulness*
13 But I am speaking to you
who are Gentiles. Inasmuch then
as [r]I am an apostle of Gentiles, I
magnify my ministry, Acts 9:15
14 if somehow I might move to
jealousy my [t]fellow countrymen
and save some of them. *flesh*
15 For if their rejection be the
[r]reconciliation of the world, what
will *their* acceptance be but life
from the dead? Rom. 5:11
16 And if the [r]first piece *of
dough* be holy, the lump is also;

and if the root be holy, the branches are too. Num. 15:18ff.

17 But if some of the branches were broken off, and you, being a wild olive, were grafted in among them and became partaker with them of the [t]rich root of the olive tree, *root of the fatness*

18 do not be arrogant toward the branches; but if you are arrogant, *remember that* [r]it is not you who supports the root, but the root *supports* you. John 4:22

19 [r]You will say then, "Branches were broken off so that I might be grafted in." Rom. 9:19

20 Quite right, they were broken off for their unbelief, but you [r]stand by your faith. Do not be conceited, but fear; Rom. 5:2

21 for if God did not spare the natural branches, neither will He spare you.

22 Behold then the kindness and severity of God; to those who fell, severity, but to you, God's [r]kindness, [r]if you continue in His kindness; otherwise you also will be cut off. Rom. 2:4 • 1 Cor. 15:2

23 And they also, [r]if they do not continue in their unbelief, will be grafted in; for God is able to graft them in again. 2 Cor. 3:16

24 For if you were cut off from what is by nature a wild olive tree, and were grafted contrary to nature into a cultivated olive tree, how much more shall these who are the natural *branches* be grafted into their own olive tree?

25 For [r]I do not want you, brethren, to be uninformed of this mystery, lest you be wise in your own estimation, that a partial [r]hardening has happened to Israel until the fulness of the Gentiles has come in; Rom. 1:13 • Rom. 11:7

26 and thus all Israel will be saved; just as it is written,

"THE[r] DELIVERER WILL COME
FROM ZION, Is. 59:20
HE WILL REMOVE UNGODLINESS FROM JACOB."

27 "AND[r] THIS IS MY COVENANT
WITH THEM,
[r]WHEN I TAKE AWAY THEIR
SINS." Is. 59:21 • Is. 27:9

28 From the standpoint of the gospel they are enemies for your sake, but from the standpoint of *God's* choice they are beloved for the sake of the fathers;

29 for the gifts and the [r]calling of God are irrevocable. Rom. 8:28

30 For just as you once were disobedient to God, but now have been shown mercy because of their disobedience,

31 so these also now have been disobedient, in order that because of the mercy shown to you they also may now be shown mercy.

32 For [r]God has shut up all in disobedience that He might show mercy to all. Rom. 3:9

33 Oh, the depth of the riches [a]both of the wisdom and knowledge of God! How unsearchable are His judgments and unfathomable His ways! *and the wisdom*

34 For WHO HAS KNOWN THE MIND OF THE LORD, OR WHO BECAME HIS COUNSELOR?

35 Or [r]WHO HAS FIRST GIVEN TO HIM THAT IT MIGHT BE PAID BACK TO HIM AGAIN? Job 35:7; 41:11

36 For from Him and through Him and to Him are all things. To Him *be* the glory forever. Amen.

CHAPTER 12

I URGE you therefore, brethren, by the mercies of God, to present your bodies a living and holy sacrifice, acceptable to God, *which is* your spiritual service of worship.

2 And do not be conformed to this[a] world, but be transformed by the renewing of your mind, that you may prove what the will of God is, that which is good and acceptable and perfect. *age*

3 For through the grace given to me I say to every man among you not to think more highly of himself than he ought to think; but to think so as to have sound judgment, as God has allotted to each a measure of faith.

4 For [r]just as we have many members in one body and all the members do not have the same function, 1 Cor. 12:12-14

5 so we, who are many, are one body in Christ, and individually members one of another.

6 And since we have gifts that differ according to the grace given to us, *let each exercise them accordingly:* if prophecy, according to the proportion of his faith;

7 if service, in his serving; or he who teaches, in his teaching;

8 or he who exhorts, in his exhortation; he who gives, with [14]liberality; he who [a]leads, with diligence; he who shows mercy, with cheerfulness. *gives aid*

9 Let [r]love be without hypocrisy. Abhor what is evil; cling to what is good. 2 Cor. 6:6

10 Be devoted to one another in brotherly love; give preference to one another [r]in honor; Phil. 2:3

11 not lagging behind in diligence, [r]fervent in spirit, serving the Lord; Acts 18:25

12 [r]rejoicing in hope, persevering in tribulation, [r]devoted to prayer, Rom. 5:2 • Acts 1:14

13 contributing to the needs of the saints, practicing hospitality.

14 Bless those who persecute [15]you; bless and curse not.

15 [r]Rejoice with those who rejoice, and weep with those who weep. Job 30:25; Heb. 13:3

16 Be of the same mind toward one another; [r]do not be haughty in mind, but associate with the lowly. [r]Do not be wise in your own estimation. Rom. 11:20 • Prov. 3:7

17 Never pay back evil for evil to anyone. Respect what is right in the sight of all men.

18 If possible, [r]so far as it depends on you, [r]be at peace with all men. Rom. 1:15 • Mark 9:50

19 Never take your own revenge, beloved, but leave room for the wrath *of God*, for it is written, "VENGEANCE[r] IS MINE, I WILL REPAY," says the Lord. Ps. 94:1

20 "BUT IF YOUR ENEMY IS HUNGRY, FEED HIM, AND IF HE IS THIRSTY, GIVE HIM A DRINK; FOR IN SO DOING YOU WILL HEAP BURNING COALS UPON HIS HEAD."

21 Do not be overcome by evil, but overcome evil with good.

CHAPTER 13

LET every person be in subjection to the governing authorities. For there is no authority except [t]from God, and those which exist are established by God. *by*

[14]Or, *simplicity*

[15]Some ancient mss. do not contain *you*

2 Therefore he who resists authority has opposed the ordinance
of God; and they who have opposed will receive condemnation
upon themselves.
3 For [r]rulers are not a cause of
fear for [t]good behavior, but for
evil. Do you want to have no fear
of authority? Do what is good, and
you will have praise from the
same; 1 Pet. 2:14 • *good work*
4 for it is a minister of God to
you for good. But if you do what is
evil, be afraid; for it does not bear
the sword for nothing; for it is a
minister of God, an [r]avenger who
brings wrath upon the one who
practices evil. 1 Thess. 4:6
5 Wherefore it is necessary to
be in subjection, not only because
of wrath, but also [r]for conscience'
sake. Eccl. 8; 1 Pet. 2:13, 19
6 For because of this you also
pay taxes, for *rulers* are servants
of God, devoting themselves to
this very thing.
7 Render to all what is due
them: tax to whom tax *is due;* custom to whom custom; fear to
whom fear; honor to whom honor.
8 Owe nothing to anyone except to love one another; for he
who loves [t]his neighbor has fulfilled *the* law. *the other*
9 For this, "YOU SHALL NOT
COMMIT ADULTERY, YOU SHALL
NOT MURDER, YOU SHALL NOT
STEAL, YOU SHALL NOT COVET,"
and if there is any other commandment, it is summed up in
this saying, "YOU SHALL LOVE
YOUR NEIGHBOR AS YOURSELF."
10 Love [t]does no wrong to a
neighbor; love therefore is the fulfillment of *the* law. *works no evil*
11 And this *do,* knowing the
time, that it is already the hour for
you to awaken from sleep; for
now [16]salvation is nearer to us
than when we believed.
12 The night is almost gone, and
the day is at hand. Let us therefore lay aside the deeds of darkness and put on the armor of light.
13 Let us [t]behave properly as in
the day, not in carousing and
drunkenness, not in sexual pro-
miscuity and sensuality, not in
strife and jealousy. *walk*
14 But put on the Lord Jesus
Christ, and make no provision for
the flesh in regard to *its* lusts.

CHAPTER 14

NOW [r]accept the one who is
[r]weak in faith, *but* not for *the purpose of* passing judgment on his
opinions. Acts 28:2 • Rom. 14:2
2 One man has faith that he
may eat all things, but he who is
weak eats vegetables *only.*
3 Let not him who eats [r]regard
with contempt him who does not
eat, and let not him who does not
eat judge him who eats, for God
has accepted him. Luke 18:9
4 Who are you to judge the
servant of another? To his own
[t]master he stands or falls; and
stand he will, for the Lord is able
to make him stand. *lord*
5 One man regards one day
above another, another regards
every day *alike.* Let each man be
fully convinced in his own mind.
6 He who observes the day, observes it for the Lord, and he who
eats, does so for the Lord, for he
gives thanks to God; and he who

[16]Or, *our salvation is nearer than when*

eats not, for the Lord he does not
eat, and gives thanks to God.
7 For not one of us [r]lives for
himself, and not one dies for himself; Rom. 8:38f.; 2 Cor. 5:15
8 for if we live, we live for the
Lord, or if we die, we die for the
Lord; therefore whether we live or
die, we are the Lord's.
9 For to this end [r]Christ died
and lived *again,* that He might be
[r]Lord both of the dead and of the
living. Rev. 1:18 • Matt. 28:18
10 But you, why do you judge
your brother? Or you again, why
do you regard your brother with
contempt? For we shall all stand
before the judgment seat of God.
11 For it is written,

"AS[r] I LIVE, SAYS THE LORD,
EVERY KNEE SHALL BOW
TO ME, Is. 45:23
AND EVERY TONGUE SHALL
GIVE PRAISE TO GOD."

12 So then each one of us shall
give account of himself to God.
13 Therefore let us not [r]judge
one another anymore, but rather
determine this—not to put an obstacle or a stumbling block in a
brother's way. Matt. 7:1
14 I know and am convinced in
the Lord Jesus that [r]nothing is unclean in itself; but to him who
thinks anything to be unclean, to
him it is unclean. Acts 10:15
15 For if because of food your
brother is hurt, you are no longer
[r]walking according to love. Do not
destroy with your food him for
whom Christ died. Eph. 5:2
16 Therefore [r]do not let what is
for you a good thing be [t]spoken of
as evil; Titus 2:5 • *blasphemed*
17 for the kingdom of God [r]is not
eating and drinking, but righteousness and peace and joy in the
Holy Spirit. 1 Cor. 8:8
18 For he who in this *way*
serves Christ is [r]acceptable to God
and approved by men. Phil. 4:8
19 So then [17]let us pursue the
things which make for peace and
the building up of one another.
20 Do not tear down the work of
God for the sake of food. All
things indeed are clean, but they
are evil for the man who eats [t]and
gives offense. *with offense*
21 It is good not to eat meat or
to drink wine, or *to do anything*
by which your brother stumbles.
22 The faith which you have,
have [t]as your own conviction before God. Happy is he who does
not condemn himself in what he
approves. *according to yourself*
23 But he who doubts is condemned if he eats, because *his
eating is* not from faith; and whatever is not from faith is sin.

CHAPTER 15

NOW we who are strong ought
to bear the weaknesses of [r]those
without strength and not *just*
please ourselves. Rom. 14:1
2 Let each of us [r]please his
neighbor for his good, to his [r]edifi-
cation. 1 Cor. 9:22 • Rom. 14:19
3 For even [r]Christ did not
please Himself; but as it is written, "THE[r] REPROACHES OF THOSE
WHO REPROACHED THEE FELL UPON
ME." 2 Cor. 8:9 • Ps. 69:9
4 For [r]whatever was written in
earlier times was written for our
instruction, that through perseverance and the encouragement

[17]Many ancient mss. read *we pursue*

of the Scriptures we might have
hope. Rom. 4:23f.; 2 Tim. 3:16
5 Now may the God[t]who gives
perseverance and encouragement
grant you to be of the same mind
with one another according to
Christ Jesus; *of perseverance*
6 that with one accord you
may with one [t]voice glorify [r]the
God and Father of our Lord Jesus
Christ. *mouth* • Rev. 1:6
7 Wherefore, accept one another, just as Christ also accepted
us to the glory of God.
8 For I say that Christ has become a servant to [r]the circumcision on behalf of the truth of God
to confirm the promises *given* to
the fathers, Matt. 15:24
9 and for [r]the Gentiles to [r]glo-
rify God for His mercy; as it is
written, Rom. 3:29 • Matt. 9:8

"THEREFORE I WILL [a]GIVE
PRAISE TO THEE AMONG
THE GENTILES, *confess*
AND I WILL SING TO THY
NAME."

10 And again he says,

"REJOICE, O GENTILES, WITH
HIS PEOPLE."

11 And again,

"PRAISE[r] THE LORD ALL YOU
GENTILES, Ps. 117:1
AND LET ALL THE PEOPLES
PRAISE HIM."

12 And again Isaiah says,

"THERE SHALL COME THE
ROOT OF JESSE,
AND HE WHO ARISES TO
RULE OVER THE GENTILES,
[r]IN HIM SHALL THE GENTILES
HOPE." Matt. 12:21

13 Now may the God of hope fill
you with all [r]joy and peace in believing, that you may abound in
hope [r]by the power of the Holy
Spirit. Rom. 14:17 • Rom. 15:19
14 And concerning you, my
brethren, I myself also am convinced that you yourselves are full
of [r]goodness, filled with all knowledge, and able also to admonish
one another. Eph. 5:9
15 But I have written very
boldly to you on some points, so
as to remind you again, because of
[r]the grace that was given me from
God, Rom. 12:3
16 to be [r]a minister of Christ
Jesus to the Gentiles, ministering
as a priest the gospel of God, that
my offering of the Gentiles might
become acceptable, sanctified by
the Holy Spirit. Acts 9:15
17 Therefore in Christ Jesus I
have found reason for boasting in
things pertaining to God.
18 For I will not presume to
speak of anything except what
Christ has accomplished through
me, resulting in the obedience of
the Gentiles by word and deed,
19 in the power of signs and
wonders, [r]in the power of the
Spirit; so that from Jerusalem and
round about as far as Illyricum I
have [t]fully preached the gospel of
Christ. Rom. 15:13 • *fulfilled*
20 And thus I aspired to [r]preach
the gospel, not where Christ was
already named, [r]that I might not
build upon another man's foundation; Rom. 1:15 • 1 Cor. 3:10
21 but as it is written,

"THEY[r] WHO HAD NO NEWS OF
HIM SHALL SEE,
AND THEY WHO HAVE NOT
HEARD SHALL UNDER-
STAND." Is. 52:15

22 For this reason [r]I have often

been hindered from coming to
you; Rom. 1:13; 1 Thess. 2:18
23 but now, with no further
place for me in these regions, and
since I have had for many years a
longing to come to you
24 whenever I go to Spain—for
I hope to see you in passing, and
to be helped on my way there by
you, when I have first enjoyed
your company for a while—
25 but now, I am going to Jerusalem serving the saints.
26 For [r]Macedonia and Achaia
have been pleased to make a contribution for the poor among the
saints in Jerusalem. Acts 16:9
27 Yes, they were pleased *to do
so,* and they are indebted to them.
For [r]if the Gentiles have shared in
their spiritual things, they are indebted to minister to them also in
material things. 1 Cor. 9:11
28 Therefore, when I have finished this, and have put my seal
on this fruit of theirs, I will go on
by way of you to Spain.
29 And I know that when I
come to you, I will come in the
fulness of the blessing of Christ.
30 Now I urge you, brethren, by
our Lord Jesus Christ and by [r]the
love of the Spirit, to strive together with me in your prayers to
God for me, Gal. 5:22; Col. 1:8
31 that I may be [r]delivered from
those who are disobedient in Judea, and *that* my service for Jerusalem may prove acceptable to
the saints; 2 Cor. 1:10
32 so that I may come to you in
joy by the will of God and find *refreshing* rest in your company.
33 Now [r]the God of peace be
with you all. Amen. Rom. 16:20

CHAPTER 16

I COMMEND to you our sister
Phoebe, who is a servant of the
church which is at Cenchrea;
2 that you receive her in the
Lord in a manner worthy of the
saints, and that you help her in
whatever matter she may have
need of you; for she herself has
also been a helper of many, [t]and of
myself as well. *and of me, myself*
3 Greet Prisca and Aquila, my
fellow workers in Christ Jesus,
4 who for my life risked their
own necks, to whom not only do I
give thanks, but also all the
churches of the Gentiles;
5 also *greet* the church that is
in their house. Greet Epaenetus,
my beloved, who is the first convert to Christ from Asia.
6 Greet Mary, who has worked
hard for you.
7 Greet Andronicus and Juni-
as, my kinsmen, and my fellow
prisoners, who are outstanding
among the apostles, who also
were in Christ before me.
8 Greet Ampliatus, my beloved
in the Lord.
9 Greet Urbanus, our fellow
worker [r]in Christ, and Stachys my
beloved. Rom. 8:11ff.; 16:3, 7, 10
10 Greet Apelles, the approved
in Christ. Greet those who are of
the *household* of Aristobulus.
11 Greet Herodion, my kinsman. Greet those of the *household*
of Narcissus, who are in the Lord.
12 Greet Tryphaena and Try-
phosa, workers in the Lord. Greet
Persis the beloved, who has
worked hard in the Lord.
13 Greet [r]Rufus, a choice man in

the Lord, also his mother and
mine. Mark 15:21
14 Greet Asyncritus, Phlegon,
Hermes, Patrobas, Hermas and
the brethren with them.
15 Greet Philologus and Julia,
Nereus and his sister, and Olym-
pas, and all [r]the saints who are
with them. Rom. 16:2, 14
16 [r]Greet one another with a
holy kiss. All the churches of
Christ greet you. 1 Cor. 16:20
17 Now I urge you, brethren,
keep your eye on those who cause
dissensions and [t]hindrances contrary to the teaching which you
learned, and turn away from
them. *occasions of stumbling*
18 For such men are [r]slaves, not
of our Lord Christ but of their
own [t]appetites; and by their
smooth and flattering speech they
deceive the hearts of the unsuspecting. Rom. 14:18 • *belly*
19 For the report of your obedience has reached to all; therefore I
am rejoicing over you, but I want
you to be wise in what is good,
and innocent in what is evil.
20 And [r]the God of peace will
soon crush Satan under your feet.
The grace of our Lord Jesus be
with you. Rom. 15:33
21 Timothy my fellow worker
greets you, and *so do* Lucius and
Jason and Sosipater, my kinsmen.
22 I, Tertius, who write this letter, greet you in the Lord.
23 [r]Gaius, host to me and to the
whole church, greets you. Erastus,
the city treasurer greets you, and
Quartus, the brother. Acts 19:29
24 [[18]The grace of our Lord Jesus
Christ be with you all. Amen.]
25 Now to Him who is able to
establish you according to my
gospel and the preaching of Jesus
Christ, according to the revelation
of the mystery which has been
kept secret for long ages past,
26 but now is manifested, and
by [r]the Scriptures of the prophets,
according to the commandment of
the eternal God, has been made
known to all the nations, *leading*
to obedience of faith; Rom. 1:2
27 to the only wise God,
through Jesus Christ, [r]be the glory
forever. Amen. Rom. 11:36

[18] Many mss. do not contain this verse

THE FIRST EPISTLE OF PAUL TO THE

CORINTHIANS

PAUL, called *as* an apostle of
Jesus Christ by the will of God,
and Sosthenes our brother,
2 to the church of God which is
at Corinth, to those who have
been sanctified in Christ Jesus,
saints by calling, with all who in
every place call upon the name of
our Lord Jesus Christ, their *Lord*
and ours:
3 [r]Grace to you and peace from
God our Father and the Lord
Jesus Christ. Rom. 1:7
4 [r]I thank [1]my God always concerning you, for the grace of God

[1] Some ancient mss. do not contain *my*

which was given you in Christ Jesus, Rom. 1:8

5 that in everything you were [r]enriched in Him, in all speech and all knowledge, 2 Cor. 9:11

6 even as [r]the testimony concerning Christ was confirmed [a]in you, 2 Thess. 1:10 • *among*

7 so that you are not lacking in any gift, awaiting eagerly the revelation of our Lord Jesus Christ,

8 [r]who shall also confirm you to the end, blameless in the day of our Lord Jesus Christ. Phil. 1:6

9 [r]God is faithful, through whom you were [r]called into fellowship with His Son, Jesus Christ our Lord. Deut. 7:9 • Rom. 8:28

10 Now I exhort you, brethren, by the name of our Lord Jesus Christ, that you all [t]agree, and there be no divisions among you, but you be made complete in the same mind and in the same judgment. *speak the same thing*

11 For I have been informed concerning you, my brethren, by Chloe's *people*, that there are quarrels among you.

12 Now I mean this, that each one of you is saying, "I am of Paul," and "I of Apollos," and "I of Cephas," and "I of Christ."

13 Has Christ been divided? Paul was not crucified for you, was he? Or were you baptized [t]in the name of Paul? *into*

14 [2]I thank God that I [r]baptized none of you except Crispus and [r]Gaius, Acts 18:8 • Rom. 16:23

15 that no man should say you were baptized [t]in my name. *into*

16 Now I did baptize also the [r]household of Stephanas; beyond that, I do not know whether I baptized any other. 1 Cor. 16:15, 17

17 [r]For Christ did not send me to baptize, but to preach the gospel, not in [t]cleverness of speech, that the cross of Christ should not be made void. John 4:2 • *wisdom*

18 For the word of the cross is to those who are perishing foolishness, but to us who are being saved it is the power of God.

19 For it is written,

"I[r] WILL DESTROY THE WISDOM OF THE WISE,
AND THE CLEVERNESS OF THE CLEVER I WILL SET ASIDE." Is. 29:14

20 Where is the wise man? Where is the scribe? Where is the debater of [r]this age? Has not God made foolish the wisdom of [r]the world? Matt. 13:22 • John 12:31

21 For since in the wisdom of God the world through its wisdom did not *come to* know God, God was well-pleased through the foolishness of the message preached to save those who believe.

22 For indeed Jews ask for [a]signs, and Greeks search for wisdom; *attesting miracles*

23 but we preach [3]Christ crucified, to Jews a stumbling block, and to Gentiles foolishness,

24 but to those who are [r]the called, both Jews and Greeks, Christ the power of God and the wisdom of God. Rom. 8:28

25 Because the [r]foolishness of God is wiser than men, and the weakness of God is stronger than men. 1 Cor. 1:18, 21, 23; 2:14

26 For consider your calling, brethren, that there were not

[2]Some ancient mss. read *I give thanks that*

[3]I.e., Messiah

many wise according to the flesh,
not many mighty, not many noble;
27 but God has chosen the foolish things of the world to shame
the wise, and God has chosen the
weak things of the world to shame
the things which are strong,
28 and the base things of [r]the
world and the despised, God has
chosen, the things that are not,
that He might nullify the things
that are, 1 Cor. 1:20
29 that [r]no [t]man should boast before God. Eph. 2:9 · *flesh*
30 But [t]by His doing you are in
Christ Jesus, who became to us
wisdom from God, [a]and righteousness and sanctification, and
redemption, *of Him* · *both*
31 that, just as it is written,
"LET[r] HIM WHO BOASTS, BOAST IN
THE LORD." Jer. 9:23f.

CHAPTER 2

AND when I came to you, brethren, I [r]did not come with superior-
ity of speech or of wisdom, proclaiming to you the [4]testimony of
God. 1 Cor. 1:17; 2:4, 13
2 For I determined to know
nothing among you except Jesus
Christ, and Him crucified.
3 And I was with you in [r]weak-
ness and in [r]fear and in much
trembling. 1 Cor. 4:10 · Is. 19:16
4 And my [t]message and my
preaching were [r]not in persuasive
words of wisdom, but in demonstration of the Spirit and of
power, *word* · 1 Cor. 1:17
5 that your faith should not
[t]rest on the wisdom of men, but on
the power of God. *be*
6 Yet we do speak wisdom
among those who are [r]mature; a
wisdom, however, not of this age,
nor of the rulers of this age, who
are passing away; Eph. 4:13
7 but we speak God's wisdom
in a [r]mystery, the hidden *wisdom*,
which God predestined before the
ages to our glory; Rom. 11:25
8 *the wisdom* [r]which none of
the rulers of this age has understood; for if they had understood
it, they would not have crucified
the Lord of glory; 1 Cor. 1:26
9 but just as it is written,

"THINGS[r] WHICH EYE HAS NOT
SEEN AND EAR HAS NOT
HEARD,
AND *which* HAVE NOT EN-
TERED THE HEART OF MAN,
ALL THAT GOD HAS PRE-
PARED FOR THOSE WHO
LOVE HIM." Is. 64:4; 65:17

10 [5]For to us God revealed *them*
[r]through the Spirit; for the Spirit
searches all things, even the
depths of God. John 14:26
11 For who among men knows
the *thoughts* of a man except the
[r]spirit of the man, which is in him?
Even so the *thoughts* of God no
one knows except the Spirit of
God. Prov. 20:27
12 Now we [r]have received, not
the spirit of the world, but the
Spirit who is from God, that we
might know the things freely giv-
en to us by God, Rom. 8:15
13 which things we also speak,
not in words taught by human
wisdom, but in those taught by
the Spirit, combining spiritual
thoughts with spiritual *words*.
14 But [a]a natural man does not
accept the things of the Spirit of

[4] Some ancient mss. read *mystery*

[5] Some ancient mss. use *But*

God; for they are foolishness to
him, and he cannot understand
them, because they are spiritually
appraised. *an unspiritual*
15 But he who is spiritual ap-
praises all things, yet he himself is
appraised by no man.
16 For WHO HAS KNOWN THE
MIND OF THE LORD, THAT HE
SHOULD INSTRUCT HIM? But we
have the mind of Christ.

CHAPTER 3

AND I, brethren, could not speak
to you as to [r]spiritual men, but as
to [r]men of flesh, as to babes in
Christ. 1 Cor. 2:15 • Rom. 7:14
2 I gave you milk to drink, not
solid food; for you were not yet
able *to receive it.* Indeed, even
now you are not yet able,
3 for you are still fleshly. For
since there is jealousy and strife
among you, are you not fleshly,
and are you not walking[t]like mere
men? *according to man*
4 For when one says, "I am of
Paul," and another, "I am of Apollos," are you not *mere* men?
5 What then is Apollos? And
what is Paul? [r]Servants through
whom you believed, even [r]as the
Lord gave *opportunity* to each
one. Rom. 15:16 • Rom. 12:6
6 I planted, Apollos watered,
but God was causing the growth.
7 So then neither the one who
plants nor the one who waters is
anything, but God who causes the
growth.
8 Now he who plants and he
who waters are one; but each will
receive his own [a]reward according
to his own labor. *wages*
9 For we are God's fellow
workers; you are God's [a]field,
God's building. *cultivated land*
10 According to the grace of
God which was given to me, as a
wise master builder I laid a foundation, and another is building
upon it. But let each man be careful how he builds upon it.
11 For no man can lay a foundation other than the one which is
laid, which is Jesus Christ.
12 Now if any man builds upon
the foundation with gold, silver,
precious stones, wood, hay, straw,
13 [r]each man's work will become evident; for [r]the day will
show it, because it is *to be* revealed with fire; and the fire itself
will test the quality of each man's
work. 1 Cor. 4:5 • Matt. 10:15
14 If any man's work which he
has built upon it remains, he shall
[r]receive a reward. 1 Cor. 3:8
15 If any man's work is burned
up, he shall suffer loss; but he
himself shall be saved, yet [r]so as
through fire. Job 23:10; Jude 23
16 Do you not know that you
are a temple of God, and *that* the
Spirit of God dwells in you?
17 If any man destroys the [a]tem-
ple of God, God will destroy him,
for the [a]temple of God is holy, and
that is what you are. *sanctuary*
18 Let no man deceive himself.
[r]If any man among you thinks that
he is wise in [r]this age, let him become foolish that he may become
wise. 1 Cor. 8:2 • 1 Cor. 1:20
19 For [r]the wisdom of this world
is foolishness before God. For it is
written, "*He is* THE ONE WHO
CATCHES THE WISE IN THEIR
CRAFTINESS"; 1 Cor. 1:20
20 and again, "THE [r]LORD KNOWS

THE REASONINGS of the wise, THAT
THEY ARE USELESS." Ps. 94:11
21 So then let no one boast in
men. For all things belong to you,
22 whether Paul or Apollos or
Cephas or the world or life or
death or things present or things
to come; all things belong to you,
23 and [r]you belong to Christ; and
Christ belongs to God. Gal. 3:29

CHAPTER 4

LET a man regard us in this manner,
as servants of Christ, and
stewards of the mysteries of God.
2 In this case, moreover, it is
required [t]of stewards that one be
found trustworthy. *in*
3 But to me it is a very small
thing that I should be examined
by you, or by *any* human [t]court; in
fact, I do not even examine myself.
day
4 I am conscious of nothing
against myself, yet I am not by
this acquitted; but the one who
examines me is the Lord.
5 Therefore do not go on passing
judgment before [6]the time, *but
wait* until the Lord comes who
will both bring to light the things
hidden in the darkness and disclose
the motives of *men's* hearts;
and then each man's praise will
come to him from God.
6 Now these things, brethren, I
have figuratively applied to myself
and Apollos for your sakes,
that in us you might learn not to
exceed what is written, in order
that no one of you might become
[t]arrogant in behalf of one against
the other. *puffed up*
7 For who regards you as superior?
And what do you have that
you did not receive? But if you did
receive it, why do you boast as if
you had not received it?
8 You are already filled, you
have already become rich, you
have become kings without us;
and *I* would indeed that you had
become kings so that we also
might reign with you.
9 For, I think, God has exhibited
us apostles last of all, as men
condemned to death; because we
have become a spectacle to the
world, both to angels and to men.
10 We are fools for Christ's
sake, but you are prudent in
Christ; we are weak, but you are
strong; you are distinguished, but
we are without honor.
11 To this present hour we are
both hungry and thirsty, and are
poorly clothed, and are roughly
treated, and are homeless;
12 and we toil, [r]working with
our own hands; when we are reviled,
we bless; when we are persecuted,
we endure; Acts 18:3
13 when we are slandered, we
try to conciliate; we have become
as the scum of the world, the
dregs of all things, *even* until now.
14 I do not write these things to
shame you, but to admonish you
as my beloved children.
15 For if you were to have
countless tutors in Christ, yet *you
would* not *have* many fathers; for
in Christ Jesus I became your father
through the gospel.
16 I exhort you therefore, be
[r]imitators of me. 1 Cor. 11:1
17 For this reason I have sent to
you Timothy, who is my beloved
and faithful child in the Lord, and
he will remind you of my ways

[6]I.e., the appointed time of judgment

which are in Christ, just as I teach
everywhere in every church.
18 Now some have become [t]ar-
rogant, as though I were not coming to you. *puffed up*
19 But I will come to you soon,
if the Lord wills, and I shall find
out, not the words of those who
are arrogant, but their power.
20 For the kingdom of God does
not consist in words, but in power.
21 What do you desire? Shall I
come to you with a rod or with
love and a spirit of gentleness?

CHAPTER 5

IT is actually reported that there
is immorality among you, and immorality of such a kind as does
not exist even among the Gentiles,
that someone has [r]his father's
wife. Lev. 18:8; Deut. 22:30
2 And you have become arrogant, and have not mourned instead, in order that the one who
had done this deed might be removed from your midst.
3 For I, on my part, though [r]ab-
sent in body but present in spirit,
have already judged him who has
so committed this, as though I
were present. Col. 2:5
4 In the name of our Lord
Jesus, when you are assembled,
and I with you in spirit, with the
power of our Lord Jesus,
5 *I have decided* to [r]deliver
such a one to Satan for the destruction of his flesh, that his
spirit may be saved in the day of
the Lord [7]Jesus. Prov. 23:14
6 Your boasting is not good.
[r]Do you not know that [r]a little
leaven leavens the whole lump *of*
dough? Rom. 6:16 • Hos. 7:4
7 Clean out the old leaven, that
you may be a new lump, just as
you are *in fact* unleavened. For
Christ our [r]Passover also has been
sacrificed. Mark 14:12
8 Let us therefore celebrate the
feast, not with old leaven, nor
with the leaven of malice and
wickedness, but with the unleavened bread of sincerity and truth.
9 I wrote you in my letter not
to associate with immoral people;
10 I *did* not at all *mean* with the
immoral people of this world, or
with the covetous and swindlers,
or with idolaters; for then you
would have to go out of the world.
11 But [a]actually, I wrote to you
not to associate with any so-called
brother if he should be an immoral person, or covetous, or an
idolater, or a reviler, or a drunkard, or a swindler—not even to
eat with such a one. *now I write*
12 For what have I to do with
judging [r]outsiders? Do you not
judge those who are within *the*
church? Mark 4:11
13 But those who are outside,
God judges. REMOVE THE WICKED
MAN FROM AMONG YOURSELVES.

CHAPTER 6

DOES any one of you, when he
has a [t]case against his neighbor,
dare to go to law before the unrighteous, and not before the
[a]saints? *matter* • *holy ones*
2 Or do you not know that the
saints will judge the world? And if
the world is judged by you, are
you not competent *to constitute*
the smallest law courts?

[7]Some ancient mss. do not contain *Jesus*

3 Do you not know that we
shall judge angels? How much
more, matters of this life?
4 If then you have law courts
dealing with matters of this life,
[a]do you appoint them as judges
who are of no account in the
church? *appoint them . . . church*
5 I say *this* to your shame. *Is it*
so, *that* there is not among you
one wise man who will be able to
decide between his brethren,
6 but brother goes to law with
brother, and that before [r]unbeliev-
ers? 2 Cor. 6:14f.; 1 Tim. 5:8
7 Actually, then, it is already a
defeat for you, that you have law-
suits with one another. Why not
rather be wronged? Why not
rather be defrauded?
8 On the contrary, you yourselves wrong and defraud, and
that *your* [r]brethren. 1 Thess. 4:6
9 Or do you not know that the
unrighteous shall not inherit the
kingdom of God? Do not be deceived; neither fornicators, nor
idolaters, nor adulterers, nor [8]ef-
feminate, nor homosexuals,
10 nor thieves, nor *the* covetous,
nor drunkards, nor revilers, nor
swindlers, shall [r]inherit the kingdom of God. Acts 20:32
11 And [r]such were some of you;
but you were washed, but you
were sanctified, but you were justified in the name of the Lord
Jesus Christ, and in the Spirit of
our God. 1 Cor. 12:2; Eph. 2:2f.
12 All things are lawful for me,
but not all things are profitable.
All things are lawful for me, but I
will not be mastered by anything.
13 Food is for the [t]stomach, and
the [t]stomach is for food; but God
will do away with both of them.
Yet the body is not for immorality, but for the Lord; and the Lord
is for the body. *belly*
14 Now God has not only [r]raised
the Lord, but will also raise us up
through His power. Acts 2:24
15 Do you not know that [r]your
bodies are members of Christ?
Shall I then take away the members of Christ and make them
members of a harlot? [r]May it never
be! Rom. 12:5 • Luke 20:16
16 Or [r]do you not know that the
one who joins himself to a harlot
is one body *with her*? For He says,
"THE [r] TWO WILL BECOME ONE
FLESH." 1 Cor. 6:3 • Gen. 2:24
17 But the one who joins himself to the Lord is [r]one spirit *with*
Him. John 17:21-23; Rom. 8:9-11
18 Flee immorality. Every *other*
sin that a man commits is outside
the body, but the immoral man
sins against his own body.
19 Or do you not know that
your body is a [a]temple of the Holy
Spirit who is in you, whom you
have from God, and that you are
not your own? *sanctuary*
20 For [r]you have been bought
with a price: therefore glorify God
in your body. Acts 20:28

CHAPTER 7

NOW concerning the things
about which you wrote, it is good
for a man not to touch a woman.
2 But because of immoralities,
let each man have his own wife,
and let each woman have her own
husband.
3 Let the husband [t]fulfill his

[8]I.e., effeminate by perversion

duty to his wife, and likewise also the wife to her husband. *render*

4 The wife does not have authority over her own body, but the husband *does*; and likewise also the husband does not have authority over his own body, but the wife *does*.

5 Stop depriving one another, except by agreement for a time that you may devote yourselves to prayer, and [t]come together again lest Satan tempt you because of your lack of self-control. *be*

6 But this I say by way of concession, not of command.

7 [9]Yet I wish that all men were [r]even as I myself am. However, each man has his own gift from God, one in this manner, and another in that. 1 Cor. 7:8; 9:5

8 But I say to the unmarried and to widows that it is good for them if they remain even as I.

9 But if they do not have self-control, let them marry; for it is better to marry than to burn.

10 But to the married I give instructions,[r]not I, but the Lord, that the wife should not[t]leave her husband Mal. 2:16 • *depart from*

11 (but if she does leave, let her remain unmarried, or else be reconciled to her husband), and that the husband should not[a]send his wife away. *leave his wife*

12 But to the rest I say, not the Lord, that if any brother has a wife who is an unbeliever, and she consents to live with him, let him not[a]send her away. *leave her*

13 And a woman who has an unbelieving husband, and he consents to live with her, let her not send her husband away.

14 For the unbelieving husband is sanctified through his wife, and the unbelieving wife is sanctified through her believing husband; for otherwise your children are unclean, but now they are holy.

15 Yet if the unbelieving one leaves, let him leave; the brother or the sister is not under bondage in such *cases*, but God has called [10]us[t]to peace. *in*

16 For how do you know, O wife, whether you will [r]save your husband? Or how do you know, O husband, whether you will save your wife? Rom. 11:14; 1 Pet. 3:1

17 Only, [r]as the Lord has assigned to each one, as God has called each, in this manner let him walk. And thus I direct in all the churches. Rom. 12:3

18 Was any man called *already* circumcised? Let him not become uncircumcised. Has anyone been called in uncircumcision?[r]Let him not be circumcised. Acts 15:1ff.

19 Circumcision is nothing, and uncircumcision is nothing, but *what matters is* the keeping of the commandments of God.

20 Let each man remain in that condition in which he was called.

21 Were you called while a slave? Do not worry about it; but if you are able also to become free, rather [t]do that. *use*

22 For he who was called in the Lord while a slave, is the Lord's freedman; likewise he who was called while free, is Christ's slave.

23 [r]You were bought with a

[9]Some ancient mss. read *For*

[10]Some ancient mss. read *you*

price; do not become slaves of
men. 1 Cor. 6:20
24 Brethren, let each man remain with God in that *condition*
in which he was called.
25 Now concerning virgins I
have [r]no command of the Lord, but
I give an opinion as one who [r]by
the mercy of the Lord is trustworthy. 1 Cor. 7:6 • 2 Cor. 4:1
26 I think then that this is good
in view of the [a]present distress,
that it is good for a man [t]to remain
as he is. *impending • so to be*
27 Are you bound to a wife? Do
not seek to be released. Are you
released from a wife? Do not seek
a wife.
28 But if you should marry, you
have not sinned; and if a virgin
should marry, she has not sinned.
Yet such will have trouble in this
life, and I am trying to spare you.
29 But this I say, brethren, [r]the
time has been shortened, so that
from now on those who have
wives should be as though they
had none; Rom. 13:11f.
30 and those who weep, as
though they did not weep; and
those who rejoice, as though they
did not rejoice; and those who
buy, as though they did not possess;
31 and those who use the world,
as though they did not [r]make full
use of it; for the form of this world
is passing away. 1 Cor. 9:18
32 But I want you to be free
from concern. One who is [r]unmar-
ried is concerned about the things
of the Lord, how he may please
the Lord; 1 Tim. 5:5
33 but one who is married is
concerned about the things of the
world, how he may please his
[11]wife,
34 and *his interests* are divided.
And the woman who is unmarried, and the virgin, is concerned
about the things of the Lord, that
she may be holy both in body and
spirit; but one who is married is
concerned about the things of the
world, how she may please her
husband.
35 And this I say for your own
benefit; not to put a restraint upon
you, but to promote what is
seemly, and *to secure* undistract-
ed devotion to the Lord.
36 But if any man thinks that he
is acting unbecomingly toward his
virgin *daughter*, if she should be
of full age, and if it must be so, let
him do what he wishes, he does
not sin; let [t]her marry. *them*
37 But he who stands firm in his
heart, being under no constraint,
but has authority over his own
will, and has decided this in his
own heart, to keep his own virgin
daughter, he will do well.
38 So then both he who gives
his own virgin *daughter* in marriage does well, and he who does
not give her in marriage will do
better.
39 A wife is bound as long as
her husband lives; but if her husband [t]is dead, she is free to be
married to whom she wishes, only
in the Lord. *has fallen asleep*
40 But [r]in my opinion she is hap-
pier if she remains as she is; and I
think that I also have the Spirit of
God. 1 Cor. 7:6, 25

[11] Some mss. read *wife. And there is a difference also between the wife and the virgin. One who is unmarried is concerned . . .*

CHAPTER 8

NOW concerning things sacrificed to idols, we know that we all
have knowledge. Knowledge
makes arrogant, but love edifies.
2 If anyone supposes that he
knows anything, he has not yet
known as he ought to know;
3 but if anyone loves God, he[r]is
known by Him. Ps. 1:6; Jer. 1:5
4 Therefore concerning the
eating of things sacrificed to idols,
we know that [12]there is no such
thing as an idol in the world, and
that there is no God but one.
5 For even if there are so-
called gods whether in heaven or
on earth, as indeed there are many
gods and many lords,
6 yet for us [r]there is *but* one
God, the Father, from whom are
all things, and we *exist* for Him;
and one Lord, Jesus Christ, by
whom are all things, and we *exist*
through Him. Deut. 4:35, 39
7 However not all men have
this knowledge; but [r]some, being
accustomed to the idol until now,
eat food as if it were sacrificed to
an idol; and their conscience being
weak is defiled. 1 Cor. 8:4ff.
8 But food will not commend
us to God; we are neither [t]the
worse if we do not eat, nor the
better if we do eat. *lacking*
9 But take care lest this liberty
of yours somehow become a
stumbling block to the weak.
10 For if someone sees you, who
have [r]knowledge, dining in an
idol's temple, will not his conscience, if he is weak, be
strengthened to eat things sacrificed to idols? 1 Cor. 8:4ff.

[12]I.e., has no real existence

11 For through [r]your knowledge
he who is weak [r]is ruined, the
brother for whose sake Christ
died. 1 Cor. 8:4ff. • Rom. 14:15
12 And thus, by sinning against
the brethren and wounding their
conscience when it is weak, you
sin [r]against Christ. Matt. 25:45
13 Therefore, if food causes my
brother to stumble, I will never
eat meat again, that I might not
cause my brother to stumble.

CHAPTER 9

AM I not [r]free? Am I not an [r]apos-
tle? Have I not seen Jesus our
Lord? Are you not my work in the
Lord? 1 Cor. 9:19 • Acts 14:14
2 If to others I am not an apostle, at least I am to you; for you
are the [r]seal of my [r]apostleship in
the Lord. John 3:33 • Acts 1:25
3 My defense to those who examine me is this:
4 [r]Do we not have a right to eat
and drink? 1 Cor. 9:14
5 Do we not have a right to
take along a believing wife, even
as the rest of the apostles, and the
brothers of the Lord, and Cephas?
6 Or do only [t]Barnabas and I
not have a right to refrain from
working? *I and Barnabas*
7 Who at any time serves [r]as a
soldier at his own expense? Who
plants a vineyard, and does not
eat the fruit of it? Or who tends a
flock and does not [t]use the milk of
the flock? 2 Cor. 10:4 • *eat of*
8 I am not speaking these
things according to [t]human judgment, am I? Or does not the Law
also say these things? *man*
9 For it is written in the Law of
Moses, "YOU[r] SHALL NOT MUZZLE

THE OX WHILE HE IS THRESHING."
God is not concerned about [r]oxen,
is He? Deut. 25:4 • Prov. 12:10
10 Or is He speaking altogether
for our sake? Yes, [r]for our sake it
was written, because the plow-
man ought to plow in hope, and
the thresher *to thresh* in hope of
sharing *the crops.* Rom. 4:23f.
11 If we sowed spiritual things
in you, is it too much if we should
reap material things from you?
12 If others share the right over
you, do we not more? Nevertheless, we [r]did not use this right, but
we endure all things, [r]that we may
cause no hindrance to the gospel
of Christ. Acts 18:3 • 2 Cor. 6:3
13 Do you not know that those
who perform sacred services eat
the *food* of the temple, *and* those
who attend regularly to the altar
have their share with the altar?
14 So also the Lord directed
those who proclaim the gospel to
get their living from the gospel.
15 But I have used none of these
things. And I am not writing these
things that it may be done so in
my case; for it would be better for
me to die than have any man
make my boast an empty one.
16 For if I preach the gospel, I
have nothing to boast of, for I am
under compulsion; for woe is me
if I do not preach the gospel.
17 For if I do this voluntarily, I
have a [r]reward; but if against my
will, I have a stewardship entrusted to me. John 4:36
18 What then is my reward?
That, when I preach the gospel, I
may offer the gospel without
charge, so as not to make full use
of my right in the gospel.
19 For though I am free from all
men, I have made myself a slave
to all, that I might win the more.
20 And [r]to the Jews I became as
a Jew, that I might win Jews; to
those who are under [a]the Law, as
under [a]the Law, though not being
myself under [a]the Law, that I
might win those who are under
[a]the Law; Acts 16:3 • *law*
21 to those who are [r]without
law, [r]as without law, though not
being without the law of God but
under the law of Christ, that I
might win those who are without
law. Rom. 2:12, 14 • Gal. 2:3
22 To the weak I became weak,
that I might win the weak; I have
become all things to all men, that I
may by all means save some.
23 And I do all things for the
sake of the gospel, that I may become a fellow partaker of it.
24 Do you not know that those
who run in a race all run, but *only*
one receives the prize? Run in
such a way that you may win.
25 And everyone who [r]competes
in the games exercises self-control in all things. They then *do it* to
receive a perishable wreath, but
we an imperishable. Eph. 6:12
26 Therefore I run in such a
way, as not without aim; I box in
such a way, as not beating the air;
27 but I buffet my body and
make it my slave, lest possibly, after I have preached to others, I
myself should be disqualified.

CHAPTER 10

FOR I do not want you to be unaware, brethren, that our fathers
were all under the cloud, and all
[r]passed through the sea; Ps. 66:6

2 and all [13]were baptized into
Moses in the cloud and in the sea;
3 and all [r]ate the same spiritual
food; Ex. 16:4, 35; Deut. 8:3
4 and all [r]drank the same spiritual drink, for they were drinking
from a spiritual rock which followed them; and the rock was
Christ. Ex. 17:6; Num. 20:11
5 Nevertheless, with most of
them God was not well-pleased;
for [r]they were laid low in the wilderness. Num. 14:29ff., 37; 26:65
6 Now these things happened
as [r]examples for us, that we should
not crave evil things, as [r]they also
craved. 1 Cor. 10:11 • Num. 11:4
7 And do not be [r]idolaters, as
some of them were; as it is written, "THE[r] PEOPLE SAT DOWN TO
EAT AND DRINK, AND STOOD UP TO
PLAY." Ex. 32:4 • Ex. 32:6
8 Nor let us act immorally, as
some of them did, and twenty-
three thousand fell in one day.
9 Nor let us try the Lord, as
some of them did, and were destroyed by the serpents.
10 Nor grumble, as some of
them [t]did, and were destroyed by
the destroyer. *grumbled*
11 Now these things happened
to them as an [r]example, and they
were written for our instruction,
upon whom the ends of the ages
have come. 1 Cor. 10:6
12 Therefore let him who thinks
he stands take heed lest he fall.
13 No temptation has overtaken
you but such as is common to
man; and [r]God is faithful, who will
not allow you to be tempted beyond what you are able, but with
the temptation will provide the
way of escape also, that you may
be able to endure it. 1 Cor. 1:9
14 Therefore, my [r]beloved, flee
from idolatry. Heb. 6:9
15 I speak as to wise men; you
judge what I say.
16 Is not the cup of blessing
which we bless a sharing in the
blood of Christ? Is not the [t]bread
which we break a sharing in the
body of Christ? *loaf*
17 Since there is one bread, we
who are many are one body; for
we all partake of the one bread.
18 Look at the nation [r]Israel; are
not those who eat the sacrifices
sharers in the altar? Rom. 1:3
19 What do I mean then? That a
thing sacrificed to idols is anything, or that an idol is anything?
20 No, but *I say* that the things
which the Gentiles sacrifice, they
sacrifice to demons, and not to
God; and I do not want you to become sharers in demons.
21 You cannot drink the cup of
the Lord and the cup of demons;
you cannot partake of the table of
the Lord and the table of demons.
22 Or do we [r]provoke the Lord
to jealousy? We are not stronger
than He, are we? Deut. 32:21
23 All things are lawful, but not
all things are profitable. All things
are lawful, but not all things edify.
24 Let no one seek his own
good, but that of his neighbor.
25 Eat anything that is sold in
the meat market, without asking
questions for conscience' sake;
26 FOR THE EARTH IS THE
LORD'S, AND ALL IT CONTAINS.
27 If [r]one of the unbelievers in-
vites you, and you wish to go, eat
anything that is set before you,

[13]Some ancient mss. read *received baptism*

without asking questions for conscience' sake. 1 Cor. 5:10
28 But [r]if anyone should say to
you, "This is meat sacrificed to
idols," do not eat *it*, for the sake of
the one who informed *you*, and for
conscience' sake; 1 Cor. 8:7
29 I mean not your own conscience, but the other *man's*; for
why is my freedom judged by another's conscience?
30 If I partake with thankfulness, why am I slandered concerning that for which I give thanks?
31 Whether, then, you eat or
drink or [r]whatever you do, do all to
the glory of God. Col. 3:17
32 [r]Give no offense either to
Jews or to Greeks or to [r]the church
of God; Acts 24:16 • Phil. 3:6
33 just as I also please all men
in all things, not seeking my own
profit, but the *profit* of the many,
that they may be saved.

CHAPTER 11

[r]BE imitators of me, just as I also
am of Christ. 1 Cor. 4:16
2 Now I praise you because
you remember me in everything,
and hold firmly to the traditions,
just as I delivered them to you.
3 But I want you to understand
that Christ is the [r]head of every
man, and [r]the man is the head of a
woman, and God is the head of
Christ. Eph. 1:22 • Gen. 3:16
4 Every man who has *something* on his head while praying or
prophesying, disgraces his head.
5 But every woman who has
her head uncovered while praying
or prophesying, disgraces her
head; for she is one and the same
with her whose head is shaved.
6 For if a woman does not cover [t]her head, let her also have her
hair cut off; but if it is disgraceful
for a woman to have her hair cut
off or [t]her head shaved, let her
cover [t]her head. *herself*
7 For a man ought not to have
his head covered, since he is the
image and glory of God; but the
woman is the glory of man.
8 For [r]man [t]does not originate
from woman, but woman from
man; Gen. 2:21-23 • *it not from*
9 for indeed man was not created for the woman's sake, but
woman for the man's sake.
10 Therefore the woman ought
to have *a symbol of* authority on
her head, because of the angels.
11 However, in the Lord, neither is woman [t]independent of
man, nor is man [t]independent of
woman. *without*
12 For as the woman [t]originates
from the man, so also the man has
his birth through the woman; and
all things originate from God. *is*
13 Judge [t]for yourselves: is it
proper for a woman to pray to
God *with head* uncovered? *in*
14 Does not even nature itself
teach you that if a man has long
hair, it is a dishonor to him,
15 but if a woman has long hair,
it is a glory to her? For her hair is
given to her for a covering.
16 But if one is inclined to be
contentious, [r]we have no [t]other
practice, nor have the churches of
God. 1 Cor. 4:5 • *such*
17 But in giving this instruction,
[r]I do not praise you, because you
come together not for the better
but for the worse. 1 Cor. 11:2, 22
18 For, in the first place, when
you come together as a church, I

hear that divisions exist among you; and in part, I believe it.

19 For there must also be factions among you, in order that those who are approved may have become evident among you.

20 Therefore when you meet together, it is not to eat the Lord's Supper,

21 for in your eating each one takes his own supper first; and one is hungry and [r]another is drunk. Jude 12

22 What! Do you not have houses in which to eat and drink? Or do you despise the [r]church of God, and shame those who have nothing? What shall I say to you? Shall I praise you? In this I will not praise you. 1 Cor. 10:32

23 For [r]I received from the Lord that which I also delivered to you, that [r]the Lord Jesus in the night in which He was betrayed took bread; 1 Cor. 15:3 • 1 Cor. 10:16

24 and when He had given thanks, He broke it, and said, "This is My body, which [14]is for you; do this in remembrance of Me."

25 In the same way *He took* the cup also, after supper, saying, "This cup is the new covenant in My blood; do this, as often as you drink *it*, in remembrance of Me."

26 For as often as you eat this bread and drink the cup, you proclaim the Lord's death [r]until He comes. John 21:22; 1 Cor. 4:5

27 Therefore whoever eats the bread or drinks the cup of the Lord in an unworthy manner, shall be [r]guilty of the body and the blood of the Lord. Heb. 10:29

28 But let a man examine himself, and so let him eat of the bread and drink of the cup.

29 For he who eats and drinks, eats and drinks judgment to himself, if he does not judge the body rightly.

30 For this reason many among you are weak and sick, and a number [r]sleep. Acts 7:60

31 But if we judged ourselves rightly, we should not be judged.

32 But when we are judged, we are disciplined by the Lord in order that we may not be condemned along with the world.

33 So then, my brethren, when you come together to eat, wait for one another.

34 If anyone is [r]hungry, let him eat at home, so that you may not come together for judgment. And the remaining matters I shall arrange when I come. 1 Cor. 11:21

CHAPTER 12

NOW concerning [r]spiritual *gifts*, brethren, [r]I do not want you to be unaware. 1 Cor. 12:4 • Rom. 1:13

2 You know that when you were pagans, *you were* [r]led astray to the [r]dumb idols, however you were led. 1 Thess. 1:9 • Is. 46:7

3 Therefore I make known to you, that no one speaking [a]by the Spirit of God says, "Jesus is [r]accursed"; and no one can say, "Jesus is Lord," except by the Holy Spirit. *in* • Rom. 9:3

4 Now there are varieties of gifts, but the same Spirit.

5 And there are varieties of ministries, and the same Lord.

6 And there are varieties of ef-

[14]Some ancient mss. read *is broken*

fects, but the same God who
works all things in all *persons.*
7 But to each one is given the
manifestation of the Spirit[r] for the
common good. 1 Cor. 12:12-30
8 For to one is given the word
of wisdom through the Spirit, and
to another the word of knowledge
according to the same Spirit;
9 to another faith by the same
Spirit, and to another gifts of[t] healing by the one Spirit, *healings*
10 and to another the[t] effecting
of miracles, and to another prophecy, and to another the[t] distinguishing of spirits, to another *various* kinds of tongues, and to
another the interpretation of
tongues. *effects* • *distinguishings*
11 But one and the same Spirit
works all these things,[r] distributing to each one individually just
as He wills. 1 Cor. 12:4
12 For even as the body is one
and *yet* has many members, and
all the members of the body,
though they are many, are one
body, so also is Christ.
13 For[a] by one Spirit we were all
baptized into one body, whether
Jews or Greeks, whether slaves or
free, and we were all made to
drink of one Spirit. *in*
14 For[r] the body is not one member, but many. 1 Cor. 12:20
15 If the foot should say, "Because I am not a hand, I am not *a
part* of the body," it is not for this
reason[t] any the less *a part* of the
body. *not* a part
16 And if the ear should say,
"Because I am not an eye, I am
not *a part* of the body," it is not
for this reason[t] any the less *a part*
of the body. *not* a part
17 If the whole body were an
eye, where would the hearing be?
If the whole were hearing, where
would the sense of smell be?
18 But now God has placed the
members, each one of them, in the
body, just as He desired.
19 And if they were all one
member, where would the body
be?
20 But now there are many
members, but one body.
21 And the eye cannot say to
the hand, "I have no need of you";
or again the head to the feet, "I
have no need of you."
22 On the contrary, it is much
truer that the members of the
body which seem to be weaker
are necessary;
23 and those *members* of the
body, which we deem less honorable, on these we bestow more
abundant honor, and our un-
seemly *members come to* have
more abundant seemliness,
24 whereas our seemly *members* have no need *of it.* But God
has *so* composed the body, giving
more abundant honor to that
member which lacked,
25 that there should be no[t] division in the body, but *that* the
members should have the same
care for one another. *schism*
26 And if one member suffers,
all the members suffer with it; if
one member is honored, all the
members rejoice with it.
27 Now you are Christ's body,
and individually members of it.
28 And God has[t] appointed in
the church, first apostles, second
prophets, third teachers, then miracles, then gifts of healings, helps,

administrations, *various* kinds of
tongues. *set some in*
29 All are not apostles, are
they? All are not prophets, are
they? All are not teachers, are
they? All are not *workers of* [a]mir-
acles, are they? *works of power*
30 All do not have gifts of healings, do they? All do not speak
with tongues, do they? All do not
[r]interpret, do they? 1 Cor. 12:10
31 But [r]earnestly desire the
greater gifts. 1 Cor. 14:1, 39
And I show you a still more excellent way.

CHAPTER 13

IF I speak with the tongues of
men and of angels, but do not
have love, I have become a noisy
gong or a clanging cymbal.
2 And if I have *the gift of*
[r]prophecy, and know all [r]mysteries
and all knowledge; and if I have
all faith, so as to remove mountains, but do not have love, I am
nothing. Acts 13:1 • 1 Cor. 14:2
3 And if I [r]give all my possessions to feed *the poor,* and if I [r]de-
liver my body [15]to be burned, but
do not have love, it profits me
nothing. Matt. 6:2 • Dan. 3:28
4 Love is patient, love is kind,
and is not jealous; love does not
brag *and* is not arrogant,
5 does not act unbecomingly; it
[r]does not seek its own, is not provoked, does not take into account
a wrong *suffered,* 1 Cor. 10:24
6 [r]does not rejoice in unrighteousness, but [r]rejoices with the
truth; 2 Thess. 2:12 • 2 John 4
7 [a]bears all things, believes all
things, hopes all things, endures
all things. *covers*
8 Love never fails; but if *there*
are gifts of prophecy, they will be
done away; if *there are* tongues,
they will cease; if *there is* knowledge, it will be done away.
9 For we [r]know in part, and we
prophesy in part; 1 Cor. 8:2
10 but when the perfect comes,
the partial will be done away.
11 When I was a child, I used to
speak as a child, think as a child,
reason as a child; when I became
a man, I did away with childish
things.
12 For now we see in a mirror
[t]dimly, but then face to face; now I
know in part, but then I shall
know fully just as I also have been
fully known. *in a riddle*
13 But now abide faith, hope,
love, these three; but the [t]greatest
of these is love. *greater*

CHAPTER 14

PURSUE love, yet desire earnestly spiritual *gifts,* but especially that you may prophesy.
2 For one who speaks in a
tongue does not speak to men, but
to God; for no one [t]understands,
but [a]in *his* spirit he speaks mysteries. *hears • by the Spirit*
3 But one who prophesies
speaks to men for edification and
exhortation and consolation.
4 One who speaks in a tongue
edifies himself; but one who
prophesies edifies the church.
5 Now I wish that you all
spoke in tongues, but *even* more
that you would prophesy; and
greater is one who prophesies
than one who speaks in tongues,

[15] Some ancient mss. read *that I may boast*

unless he interprets, so that the
church may receive edifying.
6 But now, brethren, if I come
to you speaking in tongues, what
shall I profit you, unless I speak to
you either by way of [r]revelation or
of knowledge or of prophecy or of
teaching? 1 Cor. 14:26
7 Yet *even* lifeless things, either flute or harp, in producing a
sound, if they do not produce a
distinction in the tones, how will it
be known what is played on the
flute or on the harp?
8 For if the [t]bugle produces an
indistinct sound, who will prepare
himself for battle? *trumpet*
9 So also you, unless you utter
by the tongue speech that is clear,
how will it be known what is spoken? For you will be [r]speaking into
the air. 1 Cor. 9:26
10 There are, perhaps, a great
many kinds of [t]languages in the
world, and no *kind* is without
meaning. *voices*
11 If then I do not know the
meaning of the language, I shall
be to the one who speaks a barbarian, and the one who speaks
will be a barbarian to me.
12 So also you, since you are
zealous of [t]spiritual *gifts,* seek to
abound for the [r]edification of the
church. *spirits* • Rom. 14:19
13 Therefore let one who speaks
in a tongue pray that he may interpret.
14 For if I pray in a tongue, my
spirit prays, but my mind is unfruitful.
15 What is *the outcome* then? I
shall pray with the spirit and I
shall pray with the mind also; I
shall sing with the spirit and I
shall sing with the mind also.
16 Otherwise if you bless [a]in the
spirit *only,* how will the one who
fills the place of the ungifted say
the "Amen" at your giving of
thanks, since he does not know
what you are saying? *with the*
17 For you are giving thanks
well enough, but the other man is
not [r]edified. Rom. 14:19
18 I thank God, I speak in
tongues more than you all;
19 however, in the church I desire to speak five words with my
mind, that I may instruct others
also, rather than ten thousand
words in a tongue.
20 Brethren, [r]do not be children
in your thinking; yet in evil [r]be
babes, but in your thinking be mature. Eph. 4:14 • Ps. 131:2
21 In [r]the Law it is written, "BY
MEN OF STRANGE TONGUES AND BY
THE LIPS OF STRANGERS I WILL
SPEAK TO THIS PEOPLE, AND EVEN
SO THEY WILL NOT LISTEN TO ME,"
says the Lord. John 10:34
22 So then tongues are for a
sign, not to those who believe, but
to unbelievers; but [r]prophecy *is for*
a sign, not to unbelievers, but to
those who believe. 1 Cor. 14:1
23 If therefore the whole church
should assemble together and all
speak in tongues, and ungifted
men or unbelievers enter, will
they not say that you are mad?
24 But if all prophesy, and an
unbeliever or an ungifted man enters, he is convicted by all, he is
called to account by all;
25 the secrets of his heart are
disclosed; and so he will fall on his
face and worship God, declaring
that God is certainly among you.

26 What is *the outcome* then,
brethren? When you assemble,
each one has a psalm, has a teaching, has a revelation, has a tongue,
has an interpretation. Let all
things be done for edification.
27 If anyone speaks in a[r]tongue,
it should be by two or at the most
three, and *each* in turn, and let
one interpret; 1 Cor. 14:2
28 but if there is no interpreter,
let him keep silent in the church;
and let him speak to himself and
to God.
29 And let two or three [r]proph-
ets speak, and let the others pass
judgment. 1 Cor. 13:2; 14:32, 37
30 But if a revelation is made to
another who is seated, let the first
keep silent.
31 For you can all prophesy one
by one, so that all may learn and
all may be exhorted;
32 and the spirits of prophets
are subject to prophets;
33 for God is not *a God* of confusion but of peace, as in all the
churches of the [r]saints. Acts 9:13
34 Let the women[r]keep silent in
the churches; for they are not permitted to speak, but let them subject themselves, just as the Law
also says. 1 Cor. 11:5, 13
35 And if they desire to learn
anything, let them ask their own
husbands at home; for it is [a]im-
proper for a woman to speak in
church. *disgraceful*
36 Was it from you that the
word of God *first* went forth? Or
has it come to you only?
37 If anyone thinks he is a
prophet or[r]spiritual, let him recognize that the things which I write
to you [r]are the Lord's commandment. 1 Cor. 2:15 • 1 John 4:6
38 But if anyone [16]does not recognize *this*, he is not recognized.
39 Therefore, my brethren, desire earnestly to prophesy, and do
not forbid to speak in tongues.
40 But [r]let all things be done
properly and in an orderly manner. 1 Cor. 14:33

CHAPTER 15

NOW I make known to you,
brethren, the gospel which I
preached to you, which also you
received, in which also you stand,
2 by which also you are saved,
if you hold fast [t]the word which I
preached to you, unless you believed in vain. *to what word I*
3 For I delivered to you as of
first importance what I also received, that Christ died for our
sins according to the Scriptures,
4 and that He was buried, and
that He was raised on the third
day according to the Scriptures,
5 and that He appeared to Cephas, then to the twelve.
6 After that He appeared to
more than five hundred brethren
at one time, most of whom remain
until now, but some [r]have fallen
asleep; Acts 7:60
7 then He appeared to [t]James,
then to all the apostles; *Jacob*
8 and last of all, as it were [t]to
one untimely born, He appeared
to me also. *to an untimely birth*
9 For I am the least of the
apostles, who am not fit to be
called an apostle, because I persecuted the church of God.
10 But by [r]the grace of God I am
what I am, and His grace toward

[16]Some ancient mss. read *is ignorant, let him be ignorant*

me did not prove vain; but I [r]la-
bored even more than all of them,
yet not I, but the grace of God
with me. Rom. 12:3 • Col. 1:29
11 Whether then *it was* I or
they, so we preach and so you believed.
12 Now if Christ is preached,
that He has been raised from the
dead, how do some among you
say that there [r]is no resurrection of
the dead? Acts 17:32; 23:8
13 But if there is no resurrection
of the dead, not even Christ has
been raised;
14 and if Christ has not been
raised, then our preaching is vain,
your faith also is vain.
15 Moreover we are even found
to be false witnesses of God, because we witnessed [a]against God
that He raised [17]Christ, whom He
did not raise, if in fact the dead
are not raised. *concerning*
16 For if the dead are not raised,
not even Christ has been raised;
17 and if Christ has not been
raised, your faith is worthless; [r]you
are still in your sins. Rom. 4:25
18 Then those also who [r]have
fallen asleep in Christ have perished. 1 Cor. 15:6; 1 Thess. 4:16
19 If we have hoped in Christ in
this life only, we are [r]of all men
most to be pitied. 1 Cor. 4:9
20 But now Christ has been
raised from the dead, the first
fruits of those who are asleep.
21 For since [r]by a man *came*
death, by a man also *came* the resurrection of the dead. Rom. 5:12
22 For [r]as in Adam all die, so
also in Christ all shall be made
alive. Rom. 5:14-18

[17] I.e., the Messiah

23 But each in his own order:
Christ [r]the first fruits, after that
[r]those who are Christ's at His coming, Acts 26:23 • 1 Cor. 6:14
24 then *comes* the end, when He
delivers up [r]the kingdom to the
God and Father, when He has
abolished all rule and all authority
and power. Dan. 2:44; 7:14, 27
25 For He must reign [r]until He
has put all His enemies under His
feet. Ps. 110:1; Matt. 22:44
26 The last enemy that will be
[r]abolished is death. 2 Tim. 1:10
27 For HE HAS PUT ALL THINGS
IN SUBJECTION UNDER HIS FEET.
But when He says, "All things are
put in subjection," it is evident
that He is excepted who put all
things in subjection to Him.
28 And when all things are subjected to Him, then the Son Himself also will be subjected to the
One who subjected all things to
Him, that God may be all in all.
29 Otherwise, what will those
do who are baptized for the dead?
If the dead are not raised at all,
why then are they baptized for
them?
30 Why are we also [r]in danger
every hour? 2 Cor. 11:26
31 I protest, brethren, by the
boasting in you, which I have in
Christ Jesus our Lord, I die daily.
32 If [t]from human motives I
fought with wild beasts at Ephesus, what does it profit me? If the
dead are not raised, LET US EAT
AND DRINK, FOR TOMORROW WE
DIE. *according to man*
33 Do not be deceived: "Bad
company corrupts good morals."
34 Become sober-minded as you
ought, and stop sinning; for some

have no knowledge of God. I
speak *this* to your shame.
35 But someone will say, "How
are the dead raised? And with
what kind of body do they come?"
36 ʳYou fool! That which you
ʳsow does not come to life unless it
dies; Luke 11:40 • John 12:24
37 and that which you sow, you
do not sow the body which is to
be, but a bare grain, perhaps of
wheat or of something else.
38 But God gives it a body just
as He wished, and to each of the
seeds a body of its own.
39 All flesh is not the same
flesh, but there is *one flesh* of
men, and another flesh of beasts,
and another flesh of birds, and another of fish.
40 There are also heavenly bodies and earthly bodies, but the glory of the heavenly is one, and the
glory of the earthly is another.
41 There is one glory of the sun,
and another glory of the moon,
and another glory of the stars; for
star differs from star in glory.
42 ʳSo also is the resurrection of
the dead. It is sown ᵗa perishable
body, it is raised an imperishable
body; Dan. 12:3 • *in corruption*
43 it is sown in dishonor, it is
raised in glory; it is sown in weakness, it is raised in power;
44 it is sown a ʳnatural body, it is
raised a spiritual body. If there is
a natural body, there is also a
spiritual *body*. 1 Cor. 2:14
45 So also it is written, "The
first ʳMAN, Adam, BECAME A LIVING
SOUL." The last Adam *became* a
life-giving spirit. Gen. 2:7
46 However, the spiritual is not
first, but the natural; then the
spiritual.
47 The first man is from the
earth, ᵗearthy; the second man is
from heaven. *made of dust*
48 As is the earthy, so also are
those who are earthy; and as is the
heavenly, ʳso also are those who
are heavenly. Phil. 3:20f.
49 And just as we have ʳborne
the image of the earthy, [18]we ʳshall
also bear the image of the heavenly. Gen. 5:3 • Rom. 8:29
50 Now I say this, brethren, that
flesh and blood cannot inherit the
kingdom of God; nor does the perishable inherit the imperishable.
51 Behold, I tell you a ʳmystery;
we shall not all sleep, but we shall
all be changed, 1 Cor. 13:2
52 in a moment, in the twinkling
of an eye, at the last trumpet; for
the trumpet will sound, and the
dead will be raised imperishable,
and we shall be changed.
53 For this perishable must put
on the imperishable, and this mortal must put on immortality.
54 But when this perishable will
have put on the imperishable, and
this mortal will have put on immortality, then will come about
the saying that is written, "DEATH
IS SWALLOWED UP in victory.
55 "O ʳDEATH, WHERE IS YOUR VICTORY? O DEATH, WHERE IS YOUR
STING?" Hos. 13:14
56 The sting of death is sin, and
the power of sin is the law;
57 but ʳthanks be to God, who
gives us the victory through our
Lord Jesus Christ. Rom. 7:25
58 Therefore, my beloved brethren, be steadfast, immovable, always abounding in the work of
the Lord, knowing that your toil is
not *in* vain in the Lord.

[18] Some ancient mss. read *let us also*

CHAPTER 16

NOW concerning [r]the collection
for [r]the saints, as I directed the
churches of Galatia, so do you
also. Acts 24:17 • Acts 9:13
2 On [r]the first day of every
week let each one of you [t]put aside
and save, as he may prosper, that
no collections be made when I
come. Acts 20:7 • *put by himself*
3 And when I arrive, whomever you may approve, I shall
send them with letters to carry
your gift to Jerusalem;
4 and if it is fitting for me to go
also, they will go with me.
5 But I shall come to you after
I go through Macedonia, for I am
going through Macedonia;
6 and perhaps I shall stay with
you, or even spend the winter,
that you may [r]send me on my way
wherever I may go. Acts 15:3
7 For I do not wish to see you
now [r]*just* in passing; for I hope to
remain with you for some time, if
the Lord permits. 2 Cor. 1:15f.
8 But I shall remain in [r]Ephesus
until Pentecost; Acts 18:19
9 for a wide door [t]for effective
service has opened to me, and
there are many adversaries. *and*
10 Now if Timothy comes, see
that he is with you without cause
to be afraid; for he is doing the
Lord's work, as I also am.
11 Let no one therefore despise
him. But send him on his way in
peace, so that he may come to me;
for I expect him with the brethren.
12 But concerning [r]Apollos our
brother, I encouraged him greatly
to come to you with the brethren;
and it was not at all *his* desire to
come now, but he will come when
he has opportunity. Acts 18:24
13 Be on the alert, stand firm in
the faith, act like men, be strong.
14 Let all that you do be done [r]in
love. 1 Cor. 14:1
15 Now I urge you, brethren
(you know the household of
Stephanas, that [t]they were the first
fruits of Achaia, and that they
have devoted themselves for ministry to the saints), *it was*
16 that you also be in subjection
to such men and to everyone who
helps in the work and labors.
17 And I rejoice over the [a]com-
ing of Stephanas and Fortunatus
and Achaicus; because they have
supplied what was lacking on
your part. *presence*
18 For they have refreshed my
spirit and yours. Therefore [r]ac-
knowledge such men. Phil. 2:29
19 The churches of Asia greet
you. Aquila and Prisca greet you
heartily in the Lord, with the
church that is in their house.
20 All the brethren greet you.
[r]Greet one another with a holy
kiss. Rom. 16:16
21 The greeting is in my own
hand—[t]Paul. *Paul's*
22 If anyone does not love the
Lord, let him be [r]accursed. [r]Mara-
natha. Rom. 9:3 • Phil. 4:5
23 [r]The grace of the Lord Jesus
be with you. Rom. 16:20
24 My love be with you all in
Christ Jesus. Amen.

THE SECOND EPISTLE OF PAUL TO THE

CORINTHIANS

PAUL, [r]an apostle of Christ Jesus
by the will of God, and Timothy
our brother, to the church of God
which is at Corinth with all the
[a]saints who are throughout Achaia: Rom. 1:1 • *holy ones*
2 [r]Grace to you and peace from
God our Father and the Lord
Jesus Christ. Rom. 1:7
3 [r]Blessed *be* the God and Father of our Lord Jesus Christ, the
Father of mercies and [r]God of all
comfort; Eph. 1:3 • Rom. 15:5
4 who [r]comforts us in all our affliction so that we may be able to
comfort those who are in any affliction with the comfort with
which we ourselves are comforted
by God. Is. 51:12; 66:13
5 For just as the sufferings of
Christ are [t]ours in abundance, so
also our comfort is abundant
through Christ. *to us*
6 But if we are afflicted, it is
for your comfort and salvation; or
if we are comforted, it is for your
comfort, which is effective in the
patient enduring of the same sufferings which we also suffer;
7 and our hope for you is
firmly grounded, knowing that [r]as
you are sharers of our sufferings,
so also you are *sharers* of our
comfort. Rom. 8:17
8 For we do not want you to be
unaware, brethren, of our affliction which came *to us* in Asia,
that we were burdened excessively, beyond our strength, so
that we despaired even of life;
9 [t]indeed, we had the sentence
of death within ourselves in order
that we should not trust in ourselves, but in God who raises the
dead; *but we ourselves*
10 who [r]delivered us from so
great a *peril of* death, and will deliver *us*, He [r]on whom we have set
our hope. And He will yet deliver
us, Rom. 15:31 • 1 Tim. 4:10
11 you also joining in [r]helping us
through your prayers, that thanks
may be given by [r]many persons on
our behalf for the favor bestowed
upon us through *the prayers of*
many. Rom. 15:30 • 2 Cor. 4:15
12 For our proud confidence is
this, the testimony of our conscience, that in holiness and godly
sincerity, not in fleshly wisdom
but in the grace of God, we have
conducted ourselves in the world,
and especially toward you.
13 For we write nothing else to
you than what you read and understand, and I hope you will understand until the end;
14 just as you also partially did
understand us, that we are your
reason to be proud as you also are
ours, in the day of our Lord Jesus.
15 And in this confidence I intended at first to come to you, that
you might [t]twice receive a blessing; *have a second grace*
16 [t]that is, to pass [t]your way into
Macedonia, and again from Macedonia to come to you, and by you
to be helped on my journey to Judea. *and • through you into*
17 Therefore, I was not vacillat-

ing when I intended to do this,
was I? Or that which I purpose, do
I purpose according to the flesh,
that with me there should be yes,
yes and no, no *at the same time*?
18 But as God is faithful, our
word to you is not yes and no.
19 For [r]the Son of God, Christ
Jesus, who was preached among
you by us—by me and Silvanus
and Timothy—was not yes and
no, but is yes in Him. Matt. 4:3
20 For [r]as many as may be the
promises of God, [r]in Him they are
yes; wherefore also by Him is our
Amen to the glory of God through
us. Rom. 15:8 • Heb. 13:8
21 Now He who [r]establishes us
with you in Christ and [r]anointed us
is God, 1 Cor. 1:8 • 1 John 2:20
22 who also sealed us and gave
us the Spirit in our hearts as a
[a]pledge. *down payment*
23 But I call God as witness [t]to
my soul, that to spare you I came
no more to Corinth. *upon*
24 Not that we [r]lord it over your
faith, but are workers with you for
your joy; for in your faith you are
standing firm. 2 Cor. 4:5

CHAPTER 2

BUT I determined this for my
own sake, that I would not come
to you in sorrow again.
2 For if I cause you sorrow,
who then makes me glad but the
one whom I made sorrowful?
3 And this is the very thing I
wrote you, lest, when I came, I
should have sorrow from those
who ought to make me rejoice;
having confidence in you all, that
my joy would be *the joy* of you all.
4 For out of much affliction
and anguish of heart I wrote to
you with many tears; not that you
should be made sorrowful, but
that you might know the love
which I have especially for you.
5 But if any has caused sorrow, he has caused sorrow not to
me, but in some degree—[t]in order
not to say too much—to all of
you. *that I be not burdensome*
6 Sufficient for such a one is
this punishment which was *inflicted by* the majority,
7 so that on the contrary you
should rather [r]forgive and comfort
him, lest somehow such a one be
overwhelmed by excessive sorrow. Gal. 6:1; Eph. 4:32
8 Wherefore I urge you to reaf-
firm *your* love for him.
9 For to this end also I wrote
that I might [t]put you to the test,
whether you are obedient in all
things. *know the proof of you*
10 But whom you forgive anything, I *forgive* also; for indeed
what I have forgiven, if I have forgiven anything, *I did it* for your
sakes in the presence of Christ,
11 in order that no advantage be
taken of us by Satan; for we are
not ignorant of his schemes.
12 Now when I came to [r]Troas
for the [r]gospel of Christ and when
a door was opened for me in the
Lord, Acts 16:8 • Rom. 1:1
13 I [r]had no rest for my spirit,
not finding Titus my brother; but
taking my leave of them, I went
on to Macedonia. 2 Cor. 7:5
14 But thanks be to God, who
always leads us in His triumph in
Christ, and manifests through us
the [r]sweet aroma of the knowledge
of Him in every place. Eph. 5:2
15 For we are a [r]fragrance of

Christ to God among those who are being saved and among those who are perishing; Ezek. 20:41

16 to the one an aroma from death to death, to the other an aroma from life to life. And who is adequate for these things?

17 For we are not like many, [1]peddling the word of God, but [r]as from sincerity, but as from God, we speak in Christ [r]in the sight of God. 1 Cor. 5:8 • 2 Cor. 12:19

CHAPTER 3

ARE we beginning to [r]commend ourselves again? Or do we need, as some, letters of commendation to you or from you? 2 Cor. 5:12

2 [r]You are our letter, written in our hearts, known and read by all men; 1 Cor. 9:2

3 being manifested that you are a letter of Christ, [t]cared for by us, written not with ink, but with the Spirit of the living God, not on tablets of stone, but on tablets of human hearts. *served*

4 And such confidence we have through Christ toward God.

5 Not that we are adequate in ourselves to consider anything as *coming* from ourselves, but our adequacy is from God,

6 who also made us adequate *as* [r]servants of a [r]new covenant, not of the letter, but of the Spirit; for the letter kills, but the Spirit gives life. 1 Cor. 3:5 • Jer. 31:31

7 But if the ministry of death, in letters engraved on stones, came with glory, so that the sons of Israel could not look intently at the face of Moses because of the glory of his face, fading *as* it was,

8 how shall the ministry of the Spirit fail to be even more with glory?

9 For if [r]the ministry of condemnation has glory, much more does the ministry of righteousness abound in glory. Deut. 27:26

10 For indeed what had glory, in this case has no glory on account of the glory that surpasses *it*.

11 For if that which fades away *was* with glory, much more that which remains *is* in glory.

12 [r]Having therefore such a hope, [r]we use great boldness in *our* speech, 2 Cor. 7:4 • Eph. 6:19

13 and *are* not as Moses, [r]*who* used to put a veil over his face that the sons of Israel might not look intently at the end of what was fading away. Ex. 34:33-35

14 But their minds were hardened; for until this very day at the reading of the old covenant the same veil remains unlifted, because it is removed in Christ.

15 But to this day whenever Moses is read, a veil lies over their heart;

16 but whenever a man turns to the Lord, the veil is taken away.

17 Now the Lord is the Spirit; and where [r]the Spirit of the Lord is, *there* is liberty. Is. 61:1f.

18 But we all, with unveiled face [r]beholding as in a mirror the glory of the Lord, are being transformed into the same image from glory to glory, just as from the Lord, the Spirit. 1 Cor. 13:12

CHAPTER 4

THEREFORE, since we have this [r]ministry, as we received mercy, we do not lose heart, 1 Cor. 3:5

[1]Or, *corrupting*

2 but we have renounced the
things hidden because of shame,
not walking in craftiness or adul-
terating the word of God, but by
the manifestation of truth commending ourselves to every man's
conscience in the sight of God.
3 And even if our [r]gospel is
veiled, it is veiled [t]to those who are
perishing, 2 Cor. 2:12 • *in*
4 in whose case [r]the god of this
[t]world has blinded the minds of
the unbelieving, that they might
not see the light of the gospel of
the glory of Christ, who is the
image of God. John 12:31 • *age*
5 For we do not preach ourselves but Christ Jesus as Lord,
and ourselves as your bond-servants for Jesus' sake.
6 For God, who said, "Light[r]
shall shine out of darkness," is the
One who has [r]shone in our hearts
to give the light of the knowledge
of the glory of God in the face of
Christ. Gen. 1:3 • 2 Pet. 1:19
7 But we have this treasure in
earthen vessels, that the surpassing greatness of the power may be
of God and not from ourselves;
8 *we are* [r]afflicted in every way,
but not crushed; perplexed, but
not despairing; 2 Cor. 1:8; 7:5
9 persecuted, but not forsaken;
struck down, but not destroyed;
10 always carrying about in the
body the dying of Jesus, that [r]the
life of Jesus also may be manifested in our body. Rom. 6:8
11 For we who live are constantly being delivered over to
death for Jesus' sake, that the life
of Jesus also may be manifested
in our mortal flesh.
12 So death works in us, but life
in you.
13 But having the same [r]spirit of
faith, according to what is written, "I BELIEVED, THEREFORE I
SPOKE," we also believe, therefore
also we speak; 1 Cor. 12:9
14 knowing that He who [r]raised
the Lord Jesus will raise us also
with Jesus and will [r]present us
with you. Acts 2:24 • Eph. 5:27
15 For all things *are* [r]for your
sakes, that the grace which is
[r]spreading to more and more people may cause the giving of
thanks to abound to the glory of
God. Rom. 8:28 • 1 Cor. 9:19
16 Therefore we do not lose
heart, but though our outer man is
decaying, yet our inner man is
being renewed day by day.
17 For momentary, [r]light affliction is producing for us an eternal
weight of glory far beyond all
comparison, Rom. 8:18
18 while we [r]look not at the
things which are seen, but at the
things which are not seen; for the
things which are seen are tempo-
ral, but the things which are not
seen are eternal. Rom. 8:24

CHAPTER 5

FOR we know that if the earthly
tent which is our house is torn
down, we have a building from
God, a house not made with
hands, eternal in the heavens.
2 For indeed in this *house* we
groan, longing to be clothed with
our dwelling from heaven;
3 inasmuch as we, having put
it on, shall not be found naked.
4 For indeed while we are in
this tent, we [r]groan, being burdened, because we do not want to
be unclothed, but to be clothed, in

order that what is [r]mortal may be
swallowed up by life. 2 Cor. 5:2
5 Now He who prepared us for
this very purpose is God, who
gave to us the Spirit as a pledge.
6 Therefore, being always of
good courage, and knowing that
while we are at home in the body
we are absent from the Lord—
7 for we walk by faith, not by
[a]sight— *appearance*
8 we are of good courage, I
say, and [r]prefer rather to be absent
from the body and to be at home
with the Lord. Phil. 1:23
9 Therefore also we have as
our ambition, whether at home or
absent, to be pleasing to Him.
10 For we must all appear before [r]the judgment seat of Christ,
that each one may be recompensed for his deeds in the body,
according to what he has done,
whether good or bad. Eph. 6:8
11 Therefore knowing the fear
of the Lord, we persuade men, but
we are made manifest to God; and
I hope that we are made manifest
also in your consciences.
12 We are not again commending ourselves to you but *are* giving
you an occasion to be proud of us,
that you may have *an answer* for
those who take pride in appearance, and not in heart.
13 For if we [t]are beside ourselves, it is for God; if we are of
sound mind, it is for you. *were*
14 For the love of Christ [r]con-
trols us, having concluded this,
that [r]one died for all, therefore all
died; Acts 18:5 • Rom. 5:15
15 and He died for all, that they
who live should no longer live for
themselves, but for Him who died
and rose again on their behalf.
16 Therefore from now on we
recognize no man according to the
flesh; even though we have known
Christ according to the flesh, yet
now we know *Him thus* no longer.
17 Therefore if any man is in
Christ, *he is* a new creature; the
old things passed away; behold,
new things have come.
18 Now all *these* things are from
God, who reconciled us to Himself
through Christ, and gave us the
ministry of reconciliation,
19 namely, that God was in
Christ reconciling the world to
Himself, not counting their trespasses against them, and [t]He has
[t]committed to us the word of reconciliation. *having • placed in us*
20 Therefore, we are [r]ambassa-
dors for Christ, as though God
were entreating through us; we
beg you on behalf of Christ, be
reconciled to God. Mal. 2:7
21 He made Him who [r]knew no
sin *to be* sin on our behalf, that we
might become the righteousness
of God in Him. Acts 3:14

CHAPTER 6

AND working together *with Him*,
we also urge you not to receive
the grace of God in vain—
2 for He says,

> "AT [r]THE ACCEPTABLE TIME I
> LISTENED TO YOU, Is. 49:8
> AND ON THE DAY OF SALVA-
> TION I HELPED YOU";

behold, now is "THE ACCEPTABLE
TIME," behold, now is "THE DAY OF
SALVATION"—
3 giving no cause for offense in
anything, in order that the ministry be not discredited,

4 but in everything commending ourselves as servants of God, in much endurance, in afflictions, in hardships, in distresses,

5 in beatings, in imprisonments, in tumults, in labors, in sleeplessness, in hunger,

6 in purity, in knowledge, in patience, in kindness, in the Holy Spirit, in genuine love,

7 in [r]the word of truth, in the power of God; by the weapons of righteousness for the right hand and the left, 2 Cor. 2:17; 4:2

8 by glory and dishonor, by evil report and good report; *regarded* as deceivers and yet true;

9 as unknown yet well-known, as dying yet behold, we live; as punished yet not put to death,

10 as [r]sorrowful yet always rejoicing, as poor yet making many rich, as having nothing yet possessing all things. John 16:22

11 Our mouth[t]has spoken freely to you, O Corinthians, our heart is opened wide. *is open to you*

12 You are not restrained by us, but you are restrained in your own [t]affections. *inward parts*

13 Now in a like [r]exchange—I speak as to children—open wide *to us* also. Gal. 4:12

14 Do not be bound together with unbelievers; for what partnership have righteousness and lawlessness, or what fellowship has light with darkness?

15 Or what harmony has Christ with Belial, or what has a believer in common with an unbeliever?

16 Or [r]what agreement has the temple of God with idols? For we are the temple of the living God; just as God said, 1 Cor. 10:21

"I[r] WILL DWELL IN THEM AND
WALK AMONG THEM;
AND I WILL BE THEIR GOD,
AND THEY SHALL BE MY
PEOPLE. Lev. 26:12

17 "Therefore, [r]COME OUT FROM
THEIR MIDST AND BE SEPARATE," says the Lord.
"AND DO NOT TOUCH WHAT IS
UNCLEAN; Rev. 18:4
And I will welcome you.

18 "And[r] I will be a father to
you, 2 Sam. 7:14
And you shall be sons and
daughters to Me,"
Says the Lord Almighty.

CHAPTER 7

THEREFORE, having these promises, beloved, let us cleanse ourselves from all defilement of flesh and spirit, perfecting holiness in the fear of God.

2 [r]Make room for us *in your hearts;* we wronged no one, we corrupted no one, we took advantage of no one. 2 Cor. 6:12f.

3 I do not speak to condemn you; for I have said before that you are in our hearts to die together and to live together.

4 Great is my [r]confidence [t]in you, great is my boasting on your behalf; I am filled with comfort. I am overflowing with joy in all our affliction. 2 Cor. 3:12 • *to*

5 For even when we came into [r]Macedonia our flesh had no rest, but we were [r]afflicted on every side: conflicts without, fears within. Rom. 15:26 • 2 Cor. 4:8

6 But God, who comforts the [a]depressed, comforted us by the coming of Titus; *humble*

7 and not only by his coming, but also by the comfort with which he was comforted in you, as he reported to us your longing, your mourning, your zeal for me; so that I rejoiced even more.

8 For though I caused you sorrow by my letter, I do not regret it; though I did regret it—*for* I see that that letter caused you sorrow, though only for a while—

9 I now rejoice, not that you were made sorrowful, but that you were made sorrowful to *the point of* repentance; for you were made sorrowful according to *the will of* God, in order that you might not suffer loss in anything through us.

10 For the sorrow that is according to *the will of* God produces a [r]repentance without regret, *leading* to salvation; but the sorrow of the world produces death. Acts 11:18

11 For behold what earnestness this very thing, this godly sorrow, has produced in you: what vindication of yourselves, what indignation, what fear, what [r]longing, what zeal, what avenging of wrong! In everything you demonstrated yourselves to be innocent in the matter. 2 Cor. 7:7

12 So although I wrote to you *it was* not for the sake of the offender, nor for the sake of the one offended, but that your earnestness on our behalf might be made known to you in the sight of God.

13 For this reason we have been comforted.

And besides our comfort, we rejoiced even much more for the joy of Titus, because his spirit has been refreshed by you all.

14 For if in anything I have [r]boasted to him about you, I was not put to shame; but as we spoke all things to you in truth, so also our boasting before Titus proved to be *the* truth. 2 Cor. 7:4; 8:24

15 And his [t]affection abounds all the more toward you, as he remembers the obedience of you all, how you received him with fear and trembling. *inward parts*

16 I rejoice that in everything I have confidence in you.

CHAPTER 8

NOW, brethren, we *wish to* make known to you the grace of God which has been given in the churches of Macedonia,

2 that in a great ordeal of affliction their abundance of joy and their deep poverty overflowed in the wealth of their liberality.

3 For I testify that [r]according to their ability, and beyond their ability *they gave* of their own accord, 1 Cor. 16:2; 2 Cor. 8:11

4 begging us with much entreaty for the favor of participation in the support of the saints,

5 and *this,* not as we had [t]expected, but they first [r]gave themselves to the Lord and to us by the will of God. *hoped* • 2 Cor. 8:1

6 Consequently we [r]urged [r]Titus that as he had previously made a beginning, so he would also complete in you this gracious work as well. 2 Cor. 8:17 • 2 Cor. 2:13

7 But just as you [r]abound in everything, in faith and utterance and knowledge and in all earnestness and in the [2]love we inspired

[2] Lit., *love from us in you;* some ancient mss. read *your love for us*

in you, *see* that you abound in this gracious work also. 2 Cor. 9:8

8 I am not speaking *this* as a command, but as proving through the earnestness of others the sincerity of your love also.

9 For you know the grace of our Lord Jesus Christ, that though He was rich, yet for your sake He became poor, that you through His poverty might become rich.

10 And I give *my* opinion in this matter, for this is to your advantage, who were the first to begin a year ago not only to do *this,* but also to desire *to do it.*

11 But now finish [t]doing it also; that just as *there was* the readiness to desire it, so *there may be* also the completion of it by your ability. *the doing*

12 For if the readiness is present, it is acceptable according to what *a man* has, not according to what he does not have.

13 For *this* is not for the ease of others *and* for your affliction, but by way of equality—

14 at this present time your abundance *being a supply* for [r]their want, that their abundance also may become *a supply* for your want, that there may be equality; Acts 4:34; 2 Cor. 9:12

15 as it is written, "HE[r] WHO *gathered* MUCH DID NOT HAVE TOO MUCH, AND HE WHO *gathered* LITTLE HAD NO LACK." Ex. 16:18

16 But thanks be to God, who puts the same earnestness on your behalf in the heart of Titus.

17 For he not only accepted our [r]appeal, but being himself very earnest, he has gone to you of his own accord. 2 Cor. 8:6; 12:18

18 And we have sent along with him the brother whose fame in *the things of* the gospel *has spread* through all the churches;

19 [r]and not only *this,* but he has also been [r]appointed by the churches to travel with us in this gracious work, which is being administered by us for the glory of the Lord Himself, and *to show* our readiness, Rom. 5:3 • Acts 14:23

20 taking precaution that no one should discredit us in our administration of this generous gift;

21 for we [r]have regard for what is honorable, not only in [r]the sight of the Lord, but also in the sight of men. Rom. 12:17 • Prov. 3:4

22 And we have sent with them our brother, whom we have often tested and found diligent in many things, but now even more diligent, because of *his* great confidence in you.

23 As for Titus, *he is* my partner and fellow worker [t]among you; as for our brethren, *they are* [t]messengers of the churches, a glory to Christ. *for you • apostles*

24 Therefore openly before the churches show them the proof of your love and of our [r]reason for boasting about you. 2 Cor. 7:4

CHAPTER 9

FOR it is superfluous for me to write to you about this ministry to the [a]saints; *holy ones*

2 for I know your readiness, of which I [r]boast about you to the Macedonians, *namely,* that Achaia has been prepared since last year, and your zeal has stirred up most of them. 2 Cor. 7:4

3 But I have sent the brethren,

that our [r]boasting about you may
not be made empty in this case,
that, as I was saying, you may be
prepared; 2 Cor. 7:4
4 lest if any [r]Macedonians
come with me and find you unpre-
pared, we (not to speak of you)
should be put to shame by this
confidence. Rom. 15:26
5 So I thought it necessary to
urge the brethren that they would
go on ahead to you and arrange
beforehand your previously promised bountiful gift, that the same
might be ready as a bountiful gift,
and not affected by covetousness.
6 Now this *I say,* he who sows
sparingly shall also reap sparingly; and he who sows bountifully shall also reap bountifully.
7 Let each one *do* just as he
has purposed in his heart; not
grudgingly or under compulsion;
for God loves a cheerful giver.
8 And God is able to make all
grace abound to you, that always
having all sufficiency in everything, you may have an abundance for every good deed;
9 as it is written,

"HE [r]SCATTERED ABROAD, HE
GAVE TO THE POOR,
HIS RIGHTEOUSNESS ABIDES
FOREVER." Ps. 112:9

10 Now He who supplies [r]seed to
the sower and bread for food, will
supply and multiply your seed for
sowing and increase the harvest
of your righteousness; Is. 55:10
11 you will be [r]enriched in
everything for all liberality, which
through us is producing thanksgiving to God. 1 Cor. 1:5
12 For the ministry of this service is not only fully supplying the
needs of the [a]saints, but is also
overflowing through many
thanksgivings to God. *holy ones*
13 Because of the proof given
by this ministry they will glorify
God for *your* obedience to your
confession of the gospel of Christ,
and for the liberality of your contribution to them and to all,
14 while they also, by prayer on
your behalf, yearn for you because of the surpassing grace of
God in you.
15 Thanks be to God for His in-
describable [r]gift! Rom. 5:15f.

CHAPTER 10

NOW I, Paul, myself urge you by
the meekness and gentleness of
Christ—I who am [t]meek when
face to face with you, but bold
toward you when absent! *lowly*
2 I ask that [r]when I am present
I may not be bold with the confidence with which I propose to be
courageous against some, who regard us as if we walked according
to the flesh. 1 Cor. 4:21
3 For though we walk in the
flesh, we do not war [r]according to
the flesh, Rom. 8:4; 2 Cor. 1:17
4 for the [r]weapons of our warfare are not of the flesh, but divinely powerful for the destruction of fortresses. 1 Cor. 9:7
5 *We are* destroying speculations and every lofty thing raised
up against the knowledge of God,
and *we are* taking every thought
captive to the obedience of Christ,
6 and we are ready to punish
all disobedience, whenever your
obedience is complete.
7 You are looking at things as
they are outwardly. If anyone is
confident in himself that he is

Christ's, let him consider this
again within himself, that just as
he is Christ's, so also are we.
8 For even if I should boast
somewhat [a]further about our authority, which the Lord gave for
building you up and not for destroying you, I shall not be put to
shame, *more abundantly*
9 for I do not wish to seem as if
I would terrify you by my letters.
10 For they say, "His letters are
weighty and strong, but his personal presence is unimpressive,
and his speech contemptible."
11 Let such a person consider
this, that what we are in word by
letters when absent, such persons
we are also in deed when present.
12 For we are not bold to class
or compare ourselves with [a]some
of those who [r]commend themselves; but when they measure
themselves by themselves, and
compare themselves with themselves, they are without understanding. *any* • 2 Cor. 3:1
13 But we will not boast beyond
our measure, but within the measure of the sphere which God apportioned to us as a measure, to
reach even as far as you.
14 For we are not overextend-
ing ourselves, as if we did not
reach to you, for [r]we were the first
to come even as far as you in the
gospel of Christ; 1 Cor. 3:6
15 not boasting [r]beyond *our*
measure, *that is,* in other men's labors, but with the hope that as
your faith grows, we shall be,
within our sphere, enlarged even
more by you, 2 Cor. 10:13
16 so as to preach the gospel
even to the regions beyond you,
and not to boast [t]in what has been
accomplished in the sphere of another. *to the things prepared in the*
17 But [r]HE WHO BOASTS, LET HIM
BOAST IN THE LORD. Jer. 9:24
18 For not he who commends
himself is approved, but [r]whom
the Lord commends. Rom. 2:29

CHAPTER 11

I WISH that you would bear with
me in a little foolishness; but indeed you are bearing with me.
2 For I am jealous for you with
a godly jealousy; for I [r]betrothed
you to one husband, that to Christ
I might [r]present you *as* a pure virgin. Hos. 2:19f. • 2 Cor. 4:14
3 But I am afraid, lest as the
serpent deceived Eve by his craftiness, your minds should be led
astray from the simplicity and purity *of devotion* to Christ.
4 For if one comes and
preaches another Jesus whom we
have not preached, or you receive
a different spirit which you have
not received, or a [r]different gospel
which you have not accepted, you
bear *this* beautifully. Gal. 1:6
5 For I consider myself not in
the least inferior to the [a]most eminent apostles. *super-apostles*
6 But even if I am [r]unskilled in
speech, yet I am not *so* in [r]knowl-
edge; in fact, in every way we
have made *this* evident to you in
all things. 1 Cor. 1:17 • Eph. 3:4
7 Or did I commit a sin in humbling myself that you might be exalted, because I preached the gospel of God to you without charge?
8 I robbed other churches, taking wages *from them* to serve you;
9 and when I was present with
you and was in need, I was not a

burden to anyone; for when the
brethren came from Macedonia,
they fully supplied my need, and
in everything I kept myself from
being a burden to you, [t]and will
continue to do so. *and I will keep*
10 As the truth of Christ is in
me, [r]this boasting of mine will not
be stopped in the regions of [r]Acha-
ia. 1 Cor. 9:15 • Acts 18:12
11 Why? Because I do not love
you? God knows *I do!*
12 But what I am doing, I will
continue to do, that I may cut off
opportunity from those who desire an opportunity to be [t]regarded
just as we are in the matter about
which they are boasting. *found*
13 For such men are false apostles, deceitful workers, disguising
themselves as apostles of Christ.
14 And no wonder, for even [r]Sa-
tan disguises himself as an [r]angel
of light. Eph. 6:12 • Col. 1:12
15 Therefore it is not surprising
if his servants also disguise themselves as servants of righteousness; [r]whose end shall be according to their deeds. Rom. 2:6; 3:8
16 [r]Again I say, let no one think
me foolish; but if *you do,* receive
me even as foolish, that I also may
boast a little. 2 Cor. 11:1
17 That which I am speaking, I
am not speaking as the Lord
would, but as in foolishness, in
this confidence of boasting.
18 Since many boast according
to the flesh, I will boast also.
19 For you, being *so* wise, bear
with the foolish gladly.
20 For you bear with anyone if
he [r]enslaves you, if he devours
you, if he takes advantage of you,
if he exalts himself, if he hits you
in the face. 2 Cor. 1:24
21 To *my* shame I *must* say that
we have been weak *by comparison.* But in whatever respect anyone *else* is bold (I speak in foolishness), I am just as bold myself.
22 Are they [r]Hebrews? So am I.
Are they Israelites? So am I. Are
they [t]descendants of Abraham? So
am I. Acts 6:1 • *seed*
23 Are they servants of Christ?
(I speak as if insane) I more so; in
[t]far more labors, in [t]far more imprisonments, beaten times without number, often in danger of
death. *more abundant*
24 Five times I received from
the Jews thirty-nine *lashes.*
25 Three times I was [r]beaten
with rods, once I was [r]stoned,
three times I was shipwrecked, a
night and a day I have spent in the
deep. Acts 16:22 • Acts 14:19
26 *I have been* on frequent journeys, in dangers from rivers, dangers from robbers, dangers from
my [r]countrymen, dangers from the
Gentiles, dangers in the city, dangers in the wilderness, dangers on
the sea, dangers among [r]false
brethren; Acts 9:23 • Gal. 2:4
27 *I have been* in labor and
hardship, [t]through many sleepless
nights, in hunger and thirst, often
without food, in cold and expo-
sure. *often in wakefulness*
28 Apart from *such* [a]external
things, there is the daily pressure
upon me *of* concern for all the
churches. *the things unmentioned*
29 Who is weak without my
being weak? Who is led into sin
without my intense concern?
30 If I have to boast, I will boast
of what pertains to my weakness.
31 The God and Father of the

Lord Jesus, He who is blessed forever, knows that I am not lying.
32 In [r]Damascus the ethnarch
under Aretas the king was guarding the city of the Damascenes in
order to seize me, Acts 9:2
33 and I was let down in a basket through a window in the wall,
and *so* escaped his hands.

CHAPTER 12

BOASTING is necessary, though
it is not profitable; but I will go on
to visions and [r]revelations of the
Lord. 1 Cor. 14:6; 2 Cor. 12:7
2 I know a man in Christ who
fourteen years ago—whether in
the body I do not know, or out of
the body I do not know, God
knows—such a man was caught
up to the third heaven.
3 And I know how such a
man—whether in the body or
apart from the body I do not
know, God knows—
4 was [r]caught up into [r]Paradise,
and heard inexpressible words,
which a man is not permitted to
speak. Ezek. 8:3 • Luke 23:43
5 On behalf of such a man will
I boast; but on my own behalf I
will not boast, except in regard to
my [r]weaknesses. 1 Cor. 2:3
6 For if I do wish to boast I
shall not be foolish, for I shall be
speaking the truth; but I refrain
from this, so that no one may
credit me with more than he sees
in me or hears from me.
7 And because of the surpassing greatness of the revelations,
for this reason, to keep me from
exalting myself, there was given
me a thorn in the flesh, a messenger of Satan to buffet me—to
keep me from exalting myself!
8 Concerning this I entreated
the Lord [r]three times that it might
depart from me. Matt. 26:44
9 And He has said to me, "My
grace is sufficient for you, for
[3]power is perfected in weakness."
Most gladly, therefore, I will
rather [r]boast about my weaknesses, that the power of Christ
may dwell in me. 1 Cor. 2:3
10 Therefore [r]I am well content
with weaknesses, with [a]insults,
with distresses, with persecutions,
with difficulties, for Christ's sake;
for when I am weak, then I am
strong. Rom. 5:3 • *mistreatment*
11 I have become [r]foolish; you
yourselves compelled me. Actually I should have been commended by you, for in no respect
was I inferior to the [a]most eminent
apostles, even though I am a no-
body. 2 Cor. 5:13 • *super-apostles*
12 The signs of a true apostle
were performed among you with
all perseverance, by signs and
wonders and miracles.
13 For in what respect were you
treated as inferior to the rest of
the churches, except that I myself
did not become a burden to you?
Forgive me this wrong!
14 Here for this third time I am
ready to come to you, and I will
not be a burden to you; for I do
not seek what is yours, but you;
for children are not responsible to
save up for *their* parents, but parents for *their* children.
15 And I will [r]most gladly spend
and be expended for your souls. If
I love you the more, am I to be
loved the less? Rom. 9:3

[3]Later mss. read *My power*

16 But be that as it may, I [r]did
not burden you myself; nevertheless, crafty fellow that I am, I took
you in by deceit. 2 Cor. 11:9
17 [r]Certainly I have not taken
advantage of you through any of
those whom I have sent to you,
have I? 2 Cor. 9:5
18 I [r]urged Titus *to go,* and sent
the brother with him. Titus did not
take any advantage of you, did
he? Did we not [t]conduct ourselves
in the same spirit *and walk* in the
same steps? 2 Cor. 8:6 • *walk*
19 All this time you have been
thinking that we are defending
ourselves to you. *Actually,* it is in
the sight of God that we have
been speaking in Christ; and all
for your upbuilding, beloved.
20 For I am afraid that perhaps
[r]when I come I may find you to be
not what I wish and may be found
by you to be not what you wish;
that perhaps *there may be* strife,
jealousy, angry tempers, disputes,
slanders, gossip, arrogance, disturbances; 1 Cor. 4:21
21 I am afraid that when I come
again my God may humiliate me
before you, and I may mourn over
many of those who have sinned in
the past and not repented of the
impurity, immorality and sensuality which they have practiced.

CHAPTER 13

THIS is the third time I am coming to you. EVERY [t]FACT IS TO BE
CONFIRMED BY THE TESTIMONY OF
TWO OR THREE WITNESSES. *word*
2 I have previously said when
present the second time, and
though now absent I say in advance to those who have [r]sinned in
the past and to all the rest as well,
that if I come again, I will not
spare *anyone,* 2 Cor. 12:21
3 since you are seeking for
proof of the Christ who speaks in
me, and who is not weak toward
you, but mighty in you.
4 For indeed He was [r]crucified
because of weakness, yet He lives
[r]because of the power of God. For
we also are weak [4]in Him, yet we
shall live with Him because of the
power of God *directed* toward
you. Phil. 2:7f. • Rom. 1:4
5 Test yourselves *to see* if you
are in the faith; examine yourselves! Or do you not recognize
this about yourselves, that Jesus
Christ is in you—unless indeed
you [t]fail the test? *are unapproved*
6 But I trust that you will realize that we ourselves [t]do not fail
the test. *are not unapproved*
7 Now we pray to God that
you do no wrong; not that we ourselves may appear approved, but
that you may do what is right,
even though we should [t]appear unapproved. *be as*
8 For we can do nothing
against the truth, but *only* for the
truth.
9 For we rejoice when we ourselves are weak but you are
strong; this we also pray for, that
you be [r]made complete. Eph. 4:12
10 For this reason I am writing
these things while absent, in order
that when present [r]I may not use
[r]severity, in accordance with the
authority which the Lord gave me,
for building up and not for tearing
down. 2 Cor. 2:3 • Titus 1:13
11 Finally, brethren, rejoice, [a]be
made complete, be comforted, be

[4]Some early mss. read *with Him*

like-minded, live in peace; and the
God of love and peace shall be
with you. *put yourselves in order*
12 [r]Greet one another with a
holy kiss. Rom. 16:16
13 All the saints greet you.
14 The grace of the Lord Jesus
Christ, and the [r]love of God, and
the fellowship of the Holy Spirit,
be with you all. Rom. 5:5

THE EPISTLE OF PAUL TO THE

GALATIANS

PAUL, [r]an apostle (not *sent* from
men, nor through the agency of
man, but through Jesus Christ,
and God the Father, who raised
Him from the dead), 2 Cor. 1:1
2 and all [r]the brethren who are
with me, to [r]the churches of Galatia: Phil. 4:21 • Acts 16:6
3 [r]Grace to you and peace from
God our Father, and the Lord
Jesus Christ, Rom. 1:7
4 who gave Himself for our
sins, that He might deliver us out
of this present evil age, according
to the will of our God and Father,
5 [r]to whom *be* the glory forevermore. Amen. Rom. 11:36
6 I am amazed that you are so
quickly deserting [r]Him who called
you [t]by the grace of Christ, for a
different gospel; Rom. 8:28 • *in*
7 which is *really* not another;
only there are some who are [r]dis-
turbing you, and want to distort
the gospel of Christ. Acts 15:24
8 But even though we, or an
angel from heaven, should preach
to you a gospel contrary to that
which we have preached to you,
let him be [r]accursed. Rom. 9:3
9 As we [r]have said before, so I
say again now, if any man is
preaching to you a gospel contrary to that which you received,
let him be accursed. Acts 18:23
10 For am I now seeking the favor of men, or of God? Or am I
striving to please men? If I were
still trying to please men, I would
not be a bond-servant of Christ.
11 For [r]I would have you know,
brethren, that the gospel which
was preached by me is not according to man. Rom. 2:16
12 For [r]I neither received it from
man, nor was I taught it, but *I received it* through a revelation of
Jesus Christ. 1 Cor. 11:23
13 For you have heard of my
former manner of life in Judaism,
how I used to persecute the
church of God beyond measure,
and tried to destroy it;
14 and I was advancing in Judaism beyond many of my contem-
poraries among my [t]countrymen,
being more extremely zealous for
my ancestral traditions. *race*
15 But when He who had set me
apart, *even* from my mother's
womb, and [r]called me through His
grace, was pleased Is. 49:1, 5
16 to reveal His Son in me, that
I might preach Him among the
Gentiles, I did not immediately
consult with flesh and blood,

17 [r]nor did I go up to Jerusalem
to those who were apostles before
me; but I went away to Arabia,
and returned once more to [r]Da-
mascus. Acts 9:19-22 • Acts 9:2
18 Then three years later I went
up [r]to Jerusalem to become acquainted with Cephas, and stayed
with him fifteen days. Acts 9:26
19 But I did not see any other of
the apostles except [a]James, the
Lord's brother. *Jacob*
20 (Now in what I am writing to
you, I assure you [r]before God *that*
I am not lying.) Rom. 9:1
21 Then [r]I went into the regions
of Syria and Cilicia. Acts 9:30
22 And I was *still* unknown by
[t]sight to the churches of Judea
which were in Christ; *face*
23 but only, they kept hearing,
"He who once persecuted us is
now preaching [r]the faith which he
once tried to destroy." Acts 6:7
24 And they were glorifying
God [t]because of me. *in me*

CHAPTER 2

THEN after an interval of fourteen years I [r]went up again to Jerusalem with Barnabas, taking Titus
along also. Acts 15:2
2 And it was because of a [r]rev-
elation that I went up; and I submitted to them the [r]gospel which I
preach among the Gentiles, but I
did so in private to those who
were of reputation, for fear that I
might be running, or had run, in
vain. Acts 15:2 • Gal. 1:6
3 But not even Titus who was
with me, though he was a Greek,
was compelled to be circumcised.
4 But *it was* because of the
false brethren who had sneaked in
to spy out our liberty which we
have in Christ Jesus, in order to
bring us into bondage.
5 But we did not yield in subjection to them for even an hour,
so that the truth of the gospel
might remain with you.
6 But from those who were of
high [r]reputation (what they were
makes no difference to me; God
shows no partiality)—well, those
who were of reputation contributed nothing to me. 2 Cor. 11:5
7 But on the contrary, seeing
that I had been entrusted with the
gospel [t]to the uncircumcised, just
as Peter *had been* to the circumcised *of the uncircumcision*
8 (for He who effectually
worked for Peter in *his* apostleship [t]to the circumcised effectually
worked for me also to the Gentiles), *of the uncircumcision*
9 and recognizing the grace
that had been given to me, [a]James
and Cephas and John, who were
reputed to be pillars, gave to me
and Barnabas the right [t]hand of
fellowship, that we might go to
the Gentiles, and they to the circumcised. *Jacob • hands*
10 *They* only *asked* us to remember the poor—the very thing
I also was eager to do.
11 But when Cephas came to
Antioch, I opposed him to his
face, because he [a]stood condemned. *was to be condemned*
12 For prior to the coming of
certain men from James, he used
to eat with the Gentiles; but when
they came, he *began* to withdraw
and hold himself aloof, fearing the
party of the circumcision.

13 And the rest of the Jews joined him in hypocrisy, with the result that even Barnabas was carried away by their hypocrisy.

14 But when I saw that they were not straightforward about [r]the truth of the gospel, I said to Cephas in the presence of all, "If you, being a Jew, live like the Gentiles and not like the Jews, how *is it that* you compel the Gentiles to live like Jews? Gal. 1:6

15 "We *are* [r]Jews by nature, and not [r]sinners from among the Gentiles; Phil. 3:4f. • 1 Sam. 15:18

16 nevertheless knowing that a man is not justified by the works of the Law but through faith in Christ Jesus, even we have believed in Christ Jesus, that we may be justified by faith in Christ, and not by the works of [a]the Law; since by the works of [a]the Law shall no flesh be justified. *law*

17 "But if, while seeking to be justified in Christ, we ourselves have also been found [r]sinners, is Christ then a minister of sin? May it never be! Gal. 2:15

18 "For if I rebuild what I have *once* destroyed, I [r]prove myself to be a transgressor. Rom. 3:5

19 "For through the Law I died to the Law, that I might live to God.

20 "I have been crucified with Christ; and it is no longer I who live, but Christ lives in me; and [a]the *life* which I now live in the flesh I live by faith in the Son of God, who loved me, and delivered Himself up for me. *insofar as I*

21 "I do not nullify the grace of God; for [r]if righteousness *comes* through [a]the Law, then Christ died needlessly." Gal. 3:21 • *law*

CHAPTER 3

[t]YOU foolish Galatians, who has bewitched you, before whose eyes Jesus Christ was publicly portrayed *as* crucified? *O*

2 This is the only thing I want to find out from you: did you receive the Spirit by the works of the Law, or by hearing with faith?

3 Are you so foolish? Having begun by the Spirit, are you now being perfected by the flesh?

4 Did you suffer so many things in vain—[r]if indeed it was in vain? 1 Cor. 15:2

5 Does He then, who provides you with the Spirit and works miracles among you, do it by the works of the Law, or by [t]hearing with faith? *the hearing of faith*

6 [t]Even so Abraham BELIEVED GOD, AND IT WAS RECKONED TO HIM AS RIGHTEOUSNESS. *Just as*

7 Therefore, [t]be sure that it is those who are of faith who are sons of Abraham. *know*

8 And the Scripture, foreseeing that God would justify the [t]Gentiles by faith, preached the gospel beforehand to Abraham, *saying*, "ALL THE NATIONS SHALL BE BLESSED IN YOU." *nations*

9 So then [r]those who are of faith are blessed with Abraham, the believer. Gal. 3:7

10 For as many as are of the works of the Law are under a curse; for it is written, "CURSED IS EVERYONE WHO DOES NOT ABIDE BY ALL THINGS WRITTEN IN THE BOOK OF THE LAW, TO PERFORM THEM."

11 Now that no one is justified [a]by [a]the Law before God is evident; for, "THE RIGHTEOUS MAN SHALL LIVE BY FAITH." *in* • *law*

12 [a]However, the Law is not [a]of faith; on the contrary, "HE WHO PRACTICES THEM SHALL LIVE [a]BY THEM." *And • based on • in*

13 Christ [r]redeemed us from the curse of the Law, having become a curse for us—for it is written, "CURSED IS EVERYONE WHO HANGS ON A [t]TREE"— Gal. 4:5 • *wood*

14 in order that in Christ Jesus the blessing of Abraham might [a]come to the Gentiles, so that we might receive the promise of the Spirit through faith. *occur*

15 Brethren, I speak in terms of human relations: even though it is *only* a man's covenant, yet when it has been ratified, no one sets it aside or adds conditions to it.

16 Now the promises were spoken [r]to Abraham and to his seed. He does not say, "And to seeds," as *referring* to many, but *rather* to one, "And [r]to your seed," that is, Christ. Luke 1:55 • Acts 3:25

17 What I am saying is this: the Law, which came [r]four hundred and thirty years later, does not invalidate a covenant previously ratified by God, so as to nullify the promise. Gen. 15:13f.; Ex. 12:40

18 For if the inheritance is [t]based on law, it is no longer [t]based on a promise; but God has granted it to Abraham by means of a promise. *out of, from*

19 Why the Law then? It was added because of transgressions, having been [r]ordained through angels by the [t]agency of a mediator, until the seed should come to whom the promise had been made. Acts 7:53 • *hand*

20 Now a mediator is not [t]for one *party only*; whereas God is *only* one. *of one*

21 Is the Law then contrary to the promises of God? May it never be! For if a law had been given which was able to impart life, then righteousness would indeed have been based on law.

22 But the Scripture has shut up all men under sin, that the promise by faith in Jesus Christ might be given to those who believe.

23 But before faith came, we were kept in custody under the law, being shut up to the faith which was later to be revealed.

24 Therefore the Law has become our [t]tutor *to lead us* to Christ, that we may be justified by faith. *child-conductor*

25 But now that faith has come, we are no longer under a tutor.

26 For you are all sons of God through faith in Christ Jesus.

27 For all of you who were baptized into Christ have clothed yourselves with Christ.

28 There is neither Jew nor Greek, there is neither slave nor free man, there is [t]neither male nor female; for you are all one in Christ Jesus. *not male and female*

29 And if you belong to Christ, then you are Abraham's offspring, heirs according to promise.

CHAPTER 4

NOW I say, as long as the heir is a [a]child, he does not differ at all from a slave although he is [t]owner of everything, *minor • lord*

2 but he is under guardians and [a]managers until the date set by the father. *stewards*

3 So also we, while we were children, were held [r]in bondage

under the [r]elemental things of the world. Gal. 2:4 • Gal. 4:9

4 But when [r]the fulness of the time came, God sent forth His Son, born of a woman, born under [a]the Law, Mark 1:15 • *law*

5 in order that He might redeem those who were under [a]the Law, that we might receive the adoption as sons. *law*

6 And because you are sons, [r]God has sent forth the Spirit of His Son into our hearts, crying, "Abba! Father!" Acts 16:7

7 Therefore you are no longer a slave, but a son; and if a son, then an heir through God.

8 However at that time, [r]when you did not know God, you were slaves to those which by nature are no gods. 1 Cor. 1:21

9 But now that you have come to know God, or rather to be [r]known by God, how is it that you turn back again to the weak and worthless elemental things, to which you desire to be enslaved all over again? 1 Cor. 8:3

10 You observe days and months and seasons and years.

11 I fear for you, that perhaps I have labored over you in vain.

12 I beg of you, [r]brethren, become as I *am*, for I also *have become* as you *are*. You have done me no wrong; Gal. 6:18

13 but you know that it was because of a [t]bodily illness that I preached the gospel to you the first time; *weakness of the flesh*

14 and that which was a trial to you in my [t]bodily condition you did not despise or loathe, but you received me as an angel of God, as Christ Jesus *Himself*. *flesh*

15 Where then is that sense of blessing you had? For I bear you witness, that if possible, you would have plucked out your eyes and given them to me.

16 Have I therefore become your enemy by [a]telling you the truth? *dealing truthfully with you*

17 They eagerly seek you, not commendably, but they wish to shut you out, in order that you may seek them.

18 But it is good always to be eagerly sought in a commendable manner, and [r]not only when I am present with you. Gal. 4:13f.

19 My children, with whom [r]I am again in labor until Christ is formed in you— 1 Cor. 4:15

20 but I could wish to be present with you now and to change my tone, for [r]I am perplexed about you. 2 Cor. 4:8

21 Tell me, you who want to be under law, do you not [r]listen to the law? Luke 16:29

22 For it is written that Abraham had two sons, [r]one by the bondwoman and [r]one by the free woman. Gen. 16:15 • Gen. 21:2

23 But the son by the bondwoman was born according to the flesh, and the son by the free woman through the promise.

24 This is allegorically speaking: for these *women* are two covenants, one *proceeding* from Mount Sinai bearing children who are to be slaves; she is Hagar.

25 Now this Hagar is Mount Sinai in Arabia, and corresponds to the present Jerusalem, for she is in slavery with her children.

26 But the Jerusalem above is free; [t]she is our mother. *which*

27 For it is written,
"REJOICE,[r] BARREN WOMAN
WHO DOES NOT BEAR;
BREAK FORTH AND SHOUT,
YOU WHO ARE NOT IN LA-
BOR;
FOR MORE ARE THE CHIL-
DREN OF THE DESOLATE
THAN OF THE ONE WHO HAS
A HUSBAND." Is. 54:1
28 And you brethren, like Isaac,
are children of promise.
29 But as at that time [r]he who
was born according to the flesh
[r]persecuted him *who was born* ac-
cording to the Spirit, so it is now
also. Gal. 4:23 • Gen. 21:9
30 But what does the Scripture
say?
"CAST OUT THE BONDWOMAN
AND HER SON,
FOR THE SON OF THE BOND-
WOMAN SHALL NOT BE AN
HEIR WITH THE SON OF
THE FREE WOMAN."
31 So then, brethren, we are not
children of a bondwoman, but of
the free woman.

CHAPTER 5

IT was for freedom that Christ set
us free; therefore keep standing
firm and do not be subject again
to a [r]yoke of slavery. Acts 15:10
2 Behold I, Paul, say to you
that if you receive circumcision,
Christ will be of no benefit to you.
3 And I [r]testify again to every
man who receives circumcision,
that he is under obligation to keep
the whole Law. Luke 16:28
4 You have been severed from
Christ, you who[a]are seeking to be
justified by law; you have fallen
from grace. *would be*
5 For we through the Spirit, by
faith, are [r]waiting for the hope of
righteousness. Rom. 8:23
6 For in [r]Christ Jesus neither
circumcision nor uncircumcision
means anything, but faith working through love. Gal. 3:26
7 You were [r]running well; who
hindered you from obeying the
truth? Gal. 2:2
8 This persuasion *did* not *come*
from Him who calls you.
9 [r]A little leaven leavens the
whole lump *of dough.* 1 Cor. 5:6
10 I have confidence [t]in you in
the Lord, that you will adopt no
other view; but the one who is dis-
turbing you shall bear his judgment, whoever he is. *toward*
11 But I, brethren, if I still
preach circumcision, why am I
still [r]persecuted? Then [r]the stumbling block of the cross has been
abolished. Gal. 4:29 • Rom. 9:33
12 Would that those who are
troubling you would even[a]mutilate
themselves. *cut themselves off*
13 For you were called to [r]free-
dom, brethren; only *do* not *turn*
your freedom into an opportunity
for the flesh, but through love
serve one another. Gal. 5:1
14 For [r]the whole Law is fulfilled
in one word, in the *statement,*
"YOU SHALL LOVE YOUR NEIGHBOR
AS YOURSELF." Matt. 7:12
15 But if you bite and devour
one another, take care lest you be
consumed by one another.
16 But I say, [r]walk by the Spirit,
and you will not carry out the desire of the flesh. Rom. 8:4
17 For the flesh [t]sets its desire
against the Spirit, and the Spirit
against the flesh; for these are in
opposition to one another, so that

you may not do the things that you [t]please. *lusts against • wish*

18 But if you are led by the Spirit, you are not under the Law.

19 Now the deeds of the flesh are evident, which are: immorality, impurity, sensuality,

20 idolatry, [r]sorcery, enmities, strife, jealousy, outbursts of anger, disputes, dissensions, [a]factions, Rev. 21:8 • *heresies*

21 envying, drunkenness, carousing, and things like these, of which I forewarn you just as I have forewarned you that those who practice such things shall not inherit the kingdom of God.

22 But the fruit of the Spirit is love, joy, peace, patience, kindness, goodness, faithfulness,

23 gentleness, [r]self-control; against such things [r]there is no law. Acts 24:25 • Gal. 5:18

24 Now those who belong to Christ Jesus have crucified the flesh with its passions and desires.

25 If we live by the Spirit, let us also walk [r]by the Spirit. Gal. 5:16

26 Let us not become [r]boastful, challenging one another, envying one another. Phil. 2:3

CHAPTER 6

BRETHREN, even if a man is caught in any trespass, you who are [r]spiritual, restore such a one in a spirit of gentleness; *each one* looking to yourself, lest you too be tempted. 1 Cor. 2:15

2 Bear one another's burdens, and thus fulfill the law of Christ.

3 For [r]if anyone thinks he is something when he is nothing, he deceives himself. Acts 5:36

4 But let each one [r]examine his own work, and then he will have *reason for* [r]boasting in regard to himself alone, and not in regard to another. 1 Cor. 11:28 • Phil. 1:26

5 For [r]each one shall bear his own load. Prov. 9:12

6 And let the one who is taught the word share all good things with him who teaches.

7 Do not be deceived, God is not mocked; for whatever a man sows, this he will also reap.

8 For the one who sows to his own flesh shall from the flesh reap [r]corruption, but the one who sows to the Spirit shall from the Spirit reap eternal life. 1 Cor. 15:42

9 And [r]let us not lose heart in doing good, for in due time we shall reap if we [r]do not grow weary. 2 Cor. 4:1 • Matt. 10:22

10 So then, while we have opportunity, let us do good to all men, and especially to those who are of the household of the faith.

11 See with what large letters I [a]am writing to you [r]with my own hand. *have written* • 1 Cor. 16:21

12 Those who desire to make a good showing in the flesh try to compel you to be circumcised, simply that they may not be persecuted for the cross of Christ.

13 For those who [1]are circumcised do not even keep [a]the Law themselves, but they desire to have you circumcised, that they may boast in your flesh. *law*

14 But may it never be that I should boast, except in the cross of our Lord Jesus Christ, through which the world has been crucified to me, and I to the world.

[1]Some ancient mss. read *have been*

15 For neither is circumcision anything, nor uncircumcision, but a new [a]creation. *creature*

16 And those who will [a]walk by this rule, peace and mercy *be* upon them, and upon the [r]Israel of God. *follow this rule* • Rom. 9:6

17 From now on let no one cause trouble for me, for I bear on my body the [r]brand-marks of Jesus. Is. 44:5; Ezek. 9:4

18 The grace of our Lord Jesus Christ be [r]with your spirit, brethren. Amen. 2 Tim. 4:22

THE EPISTLE OF PAUL TO THE

EPHESIANS

PAUL, an apostle of Christ Jesus [t]by the will of God, to the saints who are [1]at Ephesus, and *who are* faithful in Christ Jesus: *through*

2 [r]Grace to you and peace from God our Father and the Lord Jesus Christ. Rom. 1:7

3 [r]Blessed *be* the God and Father of our Lord Jesus Christ, who has blessed us with every spiritual blessing in [r]the heavenly *places* in Christ, 2 Cor. 1:3 • Eph. 1:20

4 just as He chose us in Him before the foundation of the world, that we should be holy and blameless before [2]Him. In love

5 He [r]predestined us to adoption as sons through Jesus Christ to Himself, according to the kind intention of His will, Acts 13:48

6 to the praise of the glory of His grace, which He freely bestowed on us in the Beloved.

7 In [t]Him we have redemption through His blood, the forgiveness of our trespasses, according to the riches of His grace, *whom*

8 which He lavished upon us. In all wisdom and insight

[1]Some ancient mss. do not contain *at Ephesus* [2]Or, *Him, in love.*

9 He [t]made known to us the mystery of His will, according to His kind intention which He purposed in Him *making known*

10 with a view to an administration [t]suitable to the fulness of the times, *that is,* the summing up of all things in Christ, things [t]in the heavens and things upon the earth. In Him *of* • *upon*

11 [t]also we have obtained an inheritance, having been predestined according to His purpose who works all things after the counsel of His will, *in whom also*

12 to the end that we who were the first to hope in [3]Christ should be to the praise of His glory.

13 In [t]Him, you also, after listening to [r]the message of truth, the gospel of your salvation—having [t]also believed, you were [r]sealed in Him with the Holy Spirit of promise, *whom* • Acts 13:26 • John 3:33

14 who is given as a pledge of our inheritance, with a view to the redemption of *God's own* possession, to the praise of His glory.

15 For this reason I too, having heard of the faith in the Lord

[3]I.e., the Messiah

Jesus which *exists* among you,
and [4]your love for all the saints,
16 do not cease giving thanks
for you, [r]while making mention *of*
you in my prayers; Rom. 1:9
17 that the God of our Lord
Jesus Christ, the Father of glory,
may give to you a spirit of wisdom
and of revelation in the [a]knowl-
edge of Him. *true knowledge*
18 *I pray that* the eyes of your
heart [t]may be enlightened, so that
you may know what is the hope of
His calling, what are the riches of
the glory of His inheritance in the
[a]saints, *being* · *holy ones*
19 and what is the surpassing
greatness of His power toward us
who believe. [r]*These are* in accordance with the working of the
strength of His might Eph. 3:7
20 which He brought about in
Christ, when He raised Him from
the dead, and seated Him at His
right hand in the heavenly *places*,
21 far above [r]all rule and authority and power and dominion, and
every [r]name that is named, not
only in this age, but also in the one
to come. Eph. 3:10 · Phil. 2:9
22 And He [r]put all things in subjection under His feet, and gave
Him as [r]head over all things to the
church, Ps. 8:6 · 1 Cor. 11:3
23 which is His body, the fulness of Him who fills all in all.

CHAPTER 2

AND you [t]were dead in your trespasses and sins, *being*
2 in which you formerly
walked according to the [t]course of
this world, according to the prince
of the power of the air, of the
spirit that is now working in the
sons of disobedience. *age*
3 Among them we too all formerly lived in the lusts of our
flesh, [t]indulging the desires of the
flesh and of the [t]mind, and were by
nature children of wrath, even as
the rest. *doing* · *thoughts*
4 But God, being [r]rich in mercy,
because of His great love with
which He loved us, Eph. 1:7
5 even when we were [r]dead in
our transgressions, made us alive
together [5]with Christ (by grace
you have been saved), Eph. 2:1
6 and raised us up with Him,
and seated us with Him in the
heavenly *places*, in Christ Jesus,
7 in order that in the ages to
come He might show the surpassing riches of His grace in kindness
toward us in Christ Jesus.
8 For by grace you have been
saved through faith; and that not
of yourselves, *it is* the gift of God;
9 [r]not as a result of works, that
no one should boast. Titus 3:5
10 For we are His workman-
ship, [r]created in [r]Christ Jesus for
good works, which God prepared
beforehand, that we should walk
in them. Eph. 2:15 · Eph. 1:1
11 Therefore remember, that
formerly you, the Gentiles in the
flesh, who are called "Uncircumcision" by the so-called "Circumcision," *which is* performed in the
flesh by human hands—
12 *remember* that you were at
that time separate from Christ,
excluded from the commonwealth
of Israel, and strangers to the covenants of promise, having no hope
and without God in the world.

[4]Many ancient mss. do not contain *your love*

[5]Some ancient mss. read *in Christ*

13 But now in [r]Christ Jesus you
who formerly were far off [t]have
been brought near [a]by the blood of
Christ. Eph. 1:1 • *became* • *in*
14 For He Himself is [r]our peace,
who made both *groups into* one,
and broke down the barrier of the
dividing wall, Is. 9:6; Eph. 2:15
15 by abolishing in His flesh the
enmity, *which is* the Law of commandments *contained* in ordinances, that in Himself He might
[t]make the two into one new man,
thus establishing peace, *create*
16 and might reconcile them
both in one body to God through
the cross, [a]by it having put to
death the enmity. *in Himself*
17 AND [r]HE CAME AND PREACHED
PEACE TO YOU WHO WERE FAR
AWAY, AND PEACE TO THOSE WHO
WERE NEAR; Is. 57:19
18 for through Him we both
have [r]our access in one Spirit to
the Father. Rom. 5:2
19 So then you are no longer
strangers and aliens, but you are
fellow citizens with the saints,
and are of God's household,
20 having been built upon the
foundation of the apostles and
prophets, Christ Jesus Himself
being the corner *stone*,
21 in whom the whole building,
being fitted together is growing
into a holy temple in the Lord;
22 in whom you also are being
[r]built together into a dwelling of
God in the Spirit. 1 Cor. 3:9, 16

CHAPTER 3

FOR this reason I, Paul, [r]the prisoner of Christ Jesus for the sake
of you Gentiles— Acts 23:18
2 if indeed you have heard of
the stewardship of God's grace
which was given to me for you;
3 that by revelation there was
made known to me the mystery,
as I wrote before in brief.
4 [t]And by referring to this,
when you read you can understand my insight into the mystery
of Christ, *To which, when you read*
5 which in other generations
was not made known to the sons
of men, as it has now been revealed to His holy apostles and
prophets [a]in the Spirit; *by*
6 *to be specific*, that the Gentiles are fellow heirs and fellow
members of the body, and fellow
partakers of the promise in Christ
Jesus through the gospel,
7 of which I was made a [r]minis-
ter, according to the gift of [r]God's
grace which was given to me according to the working of His
power. 1 Cor. 3:5 • Acts 9:15
8 To me, the very least of all
saints, this grace was given, to
preach to the Gentiles the unfathomable riches of Christ,
9 and to bring to light what is
the administration of the mystery
which for ages has been hidden in
God, who created all things;
10 in order that the manifold
[r]wisdom of God might now be
made known through the church
to the rulers and the authorities in
the heavenly *places*. 1 Cor. 2:7
11 *This was* in accordance with
the eternal purpose which He carried out in Christ Jesus our Lord,
12 in whom we have boldness
and [t]confident access through faith
in Him. *access in confidence*
13 Therefore I ask [a]you not to
lose heart at my tribulations on

your behalf, [t]for they are your glory. *that I may not lose • which are*
14 For this reason, I bow my
knees before the Father,
15 from whom [a]every family in
heaven and on earth derives its
name, *the whole*
16 that He would grant you, according to [r]the riches of His glory,
to be [r]strengthened with power
through His Spirit in the inner
man; Eph. 1:18 • 1 Cor. 16:13
17 so that [r]Christ may dwell in
your hearts through faith; *and*
that you, being rooted and
grounded in love, John 14:23
18 may be able to comprehend
with [r]all the saints what is [r]the
breadth and length and height and
depth, Eph. 1:15 • Job 11:8f.
19 and to know the love of
Christ which [r]surpasses knowledge, that you may be filled up to
all the fulness of God. Phil. 4:7
20 Now to Him who is able to
do exceeding abundantly beyond
all that we ask or think, according
to the power that works within us,
21 to Him *be* the glory in the
church and in Christ Jesus to all
generations [t]forever and ever.
Amen. *of the age of the ages*

CHAPTER 4

I, THEREFORE, the prisoner of
the Lord, entreat you to walk in a
manner worthy of the calling with
which you have been called,
2 with all humility and gentleness, with patience, showing forbearance to one another in love,
3 being diligent to preserve the
unity of the Spirit in the [r]bond of
peace. Col. 3:14f.
4 *There is* one body and one
Spirit, just as also you were called
in one hope of your calling;
5 one Lord, one faith, one baptism,
6 one God and Father of all
[r]who is over all and through all and
in all. Rom. 11:36; Col. 1:16
7 But to each one of us [r]grace
was given according to the measure of Christ's gift. Eph. 3:2
8 Therefore [a]it says, *He*
"WHEN [r] HE ASCENDED ON
HIGH, Ps. 68:18
HE [r]LED CAPTIVE A HOST OF
CAPTIVES, Judg. 5:12
AND HE GAVE GIFTS TO
MEN."
9 (Now this *expression,* "He
ascended," what does it mean except that He also had descended
into the lower parts of the earth?
10 He who descended is Himself also He who ascended [r]far
above all the heavens, that He
might fill all things.) Eph. 1:20f.
11 And He [r]gave some *as* apostles, and some *as* prophets, and
some *as* evangelists, and some *as*
pastors and teachers, Eph. 4:8
12 for the equipping of the
[a]saints for the work of service, to
the building up of [r]the body of
Christ; *holy ones* • 1 Cor. 12:27
13 until we all attain to the
unity of the faith, and of the
knowledge of the Son of God, to a
mature man, to the measure of the
stature [t]which belongs to the fulness of Christ. *of the fulness*
14 As a result, we are no longer
to be children, tossed here and
there by waves, and carried about
by every wind of doctrine, by the
trickery of men, by craftiness in
deceitful scheming;
15 but speaking the truth in

love, we [t]are to grow up in all *as-*
pects into Him, who is the head,
even Christ, *may grow up*
16 from whom the whole body,
being fitted and held together by
that which every joint supplies,
according to the proper working
of each individual part, causes the
growth of the body for the building up of itself [r]in love. Eph. 1:4
17 This I say therefore, and affirm together with the Lord, [r]that
you walk no longer just as the
Gentiles also walk, in the futility
of their mind, Eph. 2:2; 4:22
18 being darkened in their understanding, excluded from the
life of God, because of the ignorance that is in them, because of
the hardness of their heart;
19 and they, having [r]become cal-
lous, have given themselves over
to sensuality, for the practice of
every kind of impurity with
greediness. 1 Tim. 4:2
20 But you did not [r]learn Christ
in this way, Matt. 11:29
21 if indeed you [r]have heard Him
and have been taught in Him, just
as truth is in Jesus, Rom. 10:14
22 that, in reference to your former manner of life, you lay aside
the [r]old [t]self, which is being corrupted in accordance with the
lusts of deceit, Rom. 6:6 • *man*
23 and that you be renewed in
the spirit of your mind,
24 and put on the new [t]self,
which in *the likeness of* God has
been created in righteousness and
holiness of the truth. *man*
25 Therefore, laying aside falsehood, SPEAK TRUTH, EACH ONE *of*
you, WITH HIS NEIGHBOR, for we
are members of one another.
26 [r]BE ANGRY, AND *yet* DO NOT
SIN; do not let the sun go down on
your anger, Ps. 4:4
27 and do not [r]give the devil [t]an
opportunity. James 4:7 • *a place*
28 Let him who steals steal no
longer; but rather [r]let him labor,
performing with his own hands
what is good, in order that he may
have *something* to share with him
who has need. Acts 20:35
29 Let no [t]unwholesome word
proceed from your mouth, but
only such *a word* as is good for
edification according to the need
of the moment, that it may give
grace to those who hear. *rotten*
30 And do not grieve the Holy
Spirit of God, by whom you were
sealed for the day of redemption.
31 Let all bitterness and wrath
and anger and clamor and slander
be [r]put away from you, along with
all [r]malice. Eph. 4:22 • 1 Pet. 2:1
32 And [r]be kind to one another,
tender-hearted, forgiving each
other, just as God in Christ also
has forgiven [6]you. 1 Cor. 13:4

CHAPTER 5

THEREFORE be imitators of
God, as beloved children;
2 and walk in love, just as
Christ also loved [6]you, and gave
Himself up for us, an offering and
a sacrifice to God [t]as a fragrant
aroma. *for an odor of fragrance*
3 But do not let immorality [t]or
any impurity or greed even be
named among you, as is proper
among [a]saints; *and all • holy ones*
4 and *there must be no* filthiness and silly talk, or coarse jesting, which are not fitting, but
rather giving of thanks.

[6]Some ancient mss. read *us*

5 For this you know with certainty, that no immoral or impure
person or covetous man, who is
an idolater, has an inheritance in
the kingdom of Christ and God.
6 Let no one deceive you with
empty words, for because of these
things the wrath of God comes
upon the sons of disobedience.
7 Therefore do not be [r]partak-
ers with them; Eph. 3:6
8 for you were formerly darkness, but now you are light in the
Lord; walk as children of light
9 (for [r]the fruit of the light *con-*
sists in all goodness and righteousness and truth), Gal. 5:22
10 [t]trying to learn what is pleasing to the Lord. *proving what*
11 And do not participate in the
unfruitful deeds of darkness, but
instead even expose them;
12 for it is disgraceful even to
speak of the things which are
done by them in secret.
13 But all things become visible
when they are [a]exposed by the
light, for everything that becomes
visible is light. *reproved*
14 For this reason [a]it says,
"Awake,[r] sleeper,
And arise from [r]the dead,
And Christ will shine on
you." *He* • Is. 26:19 • Eph. 2:1
15 Therefore [t]be careful how
you [r]walk, not as unwise men, but
as wise, *look carefully* • Eph. 5:2
16 making the most of your
time, because the days are evil.
17 So then do not be foolish, but
[r]understand what the will of the
Lord is. Rom. 12:2; Col. 1:9
18 And do not get drunk with
wine, for that is dissipation, but
be filled with the Spirit,
19 speaking to one another in
psalms and hymns and spiritual
songs, singing and making melody
with your heart to the Lord;
20 always giving thanks for all
things in the name of our Lord
Jesus Christ to [t]God, even the Father; *the God and Father*
21 and be subject to one another in the fear of Christ.
22 Wives, *be subject* to your
own husbands, as to the Lord.
23 For the husband is the head
of the wife, as Christ also is the
head of the church, He Himself
being the Savior of the body.
24 But as the church is subject
to Christ, so also the wives *ought*
to be to their husbands in everything.
25 [r]Husbands, love your wives,
just as Christ also loved the
church and [r]gave Himself up for
her; Eph. 5:28, 33 • Eph. 5:2
26 that He might sanctify her,
having cleansed her by the washing of water with the word,
27 that He might present to
Himself the church in all her glory, having no spot or wrinkle or
any such thing; but that she
should be holy and blameless.
28 So husbands ought also to
[r]love their own wives as their own
bodies. He who loves his own wife
loves himself; Eph. 5:25, 33
29 for no one ever hated his
own flesh, but nourishes and cherishes it, just as Christ also *does*
the church,
30 because we are [r]members of
His [r]body. 1 Cor. 6:15 • Eph. 1:23
31 [r]FOR THIS CAUSE A MAN SHALL
LEAVE HIS FATHER AND MOTHER,
AND SHALL CLEAVE TO HIS WIFE;

AND THE TWO SHALL BECOME ONE
FLESH. Gen. 2:24; Matt. 19:5
32 This mystery is great; but I
am speaking with reference to
Christ and the church.
33 Nevertheless let each individual among you also [r]love his
own wife even as himself; and *let*
the wife *see to it* that she [t]respect
her husband. 1 Pet. 3:7 • *fear*

CHAPTER 6

CHILDREN, obey your parents
in the Lord, for this is right.
2 HONOR YOUR FATHER AND
MOTHER (which is the first commandment with a promise),
3 THAT IT MAY BE WELL WITH
YOU, AND THAT YOU MAY LIVE
LONG ON THE EARTH.
4 And, [r]fathers, do not provoke
your children to anger; but bring
them up in the discipline and instruction of the Lord. Col. 3:21
5 Slaves, be obedient to those
who are your masters according
to the flesh, with [r]fear and trembling, in the sincerity of your
heart, as to Christ; 1 Cor. 2:3
6 not [t]by way of eyeservice, as
men-pleasers, but as slaves of
Christ, doing the will of God from
the [t]heart. *according to* • *soul*
7 With good will [t]render service, [r]as to the Lord, and not to
men, *rendering* • Col. 3:23
8 knowing that whatever good
thing each one does, this he will
receive back from the Lord,
[r]whether slave or free. Col. 3:11
9 And, masters, do the same
things to them, and [r]give up threatening, knowing that [r]both their
Master and yours is in heaven,
and there is no partiality with
Him. Lev. 25:43 • Job 31:13ff.

10 Finally, [r]be strong in the
Lord, and in [r]the strength of His
might. 1 Cor. 16:13 • Eph. 1:19
11 Put on the full armor of God,
that you may be able to stand firm
against the schemes of the devil.
12 For our struggle is not
against [t]flesh and blood, but
against the rulers, against the
powers, against the world forces
of this darkness, against the spiritual *forces* of wickedness in the
heavenly *places*. *blood and flesh*
13 Therefore, take up the full armor of God, that you may be able
to resist in the evil day, and having done everything, to stand firm.
14 Stand firm therefore, HAVING
GIRDED YOUR LOINS WITH TRUTH,
and HAVING PUT ON THE BREAST-
PLATE OF RIGHTEOUSNESS,
15 and having [r]shod YOUR FEET
WITH THE PREPARATION OF THE
GOSPEL OF PEACE; Is. 52:7
16 in addition to all, taking up
the shield of faith with which you
will be able to extinguish all the
flaming missiles of the evil *one*.
17 And take THE HELMET OF SAL-
VATION, and the sword of the
Spirit, which is the word of God.
18 With all prayer and petition
[t]pray at all times in the Spirit, and
with this in view, be on the alert
with all perseverance and petition
for all the saints, *praying*
19 and [r]*pray* on my behalf, that
utterance may be given to me in
the opening of my mouth, to make
known with boldness the mystery
of the gospel, Col. 4:3
20 for which I am an [r]ambassa-
dor in [t]chains; that [7]in *proclaiming*

[7]Some ancient mss. read *I may speak it boldly*

it I may speak boldly, as I ought to
speak. 2 Cor. 5:20 · *a chain*
21 But that you also may know
about my circumstances, how I
am doing, [r]Tychicus, the beloved
brother and faithful minister in
the Lord, will make everything
known to you. Acts 20:4
22 And I have sent him to you
for this very purpose, so that you
may know about us, and that he
may comfort your hearts.
23 Peace be to the brethren, and
love with faith, from God the Father and the Lord Jesus Christ.
24 Grace be with all those who
love our Lord Jesus Christ [t]with *a*
love incorruptible. *in corruption*

THE EPISTLE OF PAUL TO THE

PHILIPPIANS

PAUL and Timothy, bond-servants of Christ Jesus, to all the
[a]saints in Christ Jesus who are in
Philippi, including the overseers
and deacons: *holy ones*
2 [r]Grace to you and peace from
God our Father and the Lord
Jesus Christ. Rom. 1:7
3 [r]I thank my God in all my remembrance of you, Rom. 1:8
4 always offering prayer with
joy in my every prayer for you all,
5 in view of your [r]participation
in the [r]gospel from the first day until now. Acts 2:42 · Phil. 1:7
6 *For I am* confident of this
very thing, that He who began a
good work in you will perfect it
until the day of Christ Jesus.
7 For it is only right for me to
feel this way about you all, because I have you in my heart,
since both in my [t]imprisonment
and in the defense and confirma-
tion of the gospel, you all are partakers of grace with me. *bonds*
8 For God is my witness, how I
long for you all with the [t]affection
of Christ Jesus. *inward parts*
9 And this I pray, that [r]your
love may abound still more and
more in real knowledge and all
discernment, 1 Thess. 3:12
10 so that you may approve the
things that are excellent, in order
to be sincere and blameless [t]until
the day of Christ; *for*
11 having been filled with the
fruit of righteousness which
comes through Jesus Christ, to the
glory and praise of God.
12 Now I want you to know,
brethren, that my circumstances
have turned out for the greater
progress of the gospel,
13 so that my [t]imprisonment in
the cause of Christ has become
well known throughout the whole
[1]praetorian guard and to [r]everyone
else, *bonds* · Acts 28:30
14 and that most of the brethren, trusting in the Lord because
of my [t]imprisonment, have far
more courage to speak the word
of God without fear. *bonds*
15 [r]Some, to be sure, are preaching Christ even from envy and

[1] Or, *governor's palace*

strife, but some also from good
will; 2 Cor. 11:13
16 [2]the latter *do it* out of love,
knowing that I am appointed for
the defense of the gospel;
17 the former proclaim Christ
out of selfish ambition, [t]rather
than from pure motives, thinking
to cause me distress in my [t]impris-
onment. *not sincerely • bonds*
18 What then? Only that in every way, whether in pretense or in
truth, Christ is proclaimed; and in
this I rejoice, yes, and I will rejoice.
19 For I know that this shall
turn out for my deliverance
through your prayers and the provision of the Spirit of Jesus Christ,
20 according to my [r]earnest expectation and hope, that I shall
not be put to shame in anything,
but *that* with all boldness, Christ
shall even now, as always, be exalted in my body, whether by life
or by death. Rom. 8:19
21 For to me, [r]to live is Christ,
and to die is gain. Gal. 2:20
22 But if *I am* to live *on* in the
flesh, this *will mean* fruitful labor
for me; and I do not know [t]which
to choose. *what I shall choose*
23 But I am hard-pressed from
both *directions,* having the desire
to depart and be with Christ, for
that is very much better;
24 yet to remain on in the flesh
is more necessary for your sake.
25 And convinced of this, I
know that I shall remain and continue with you all for your progress and joy in the faith,
26 so that your [r]proud confidence in me may abound in Christ

[2]Some later mss. reverse the order of vv. 16 and 17

Jesus through my coming to you
again. 2 Cor. 5:12; 7:4; Phil. 2:16
27 Only conduct yourselves in a
manner worthy of the gospel of
Christ; so that whether I come
and see you or remain absent, I
may hear of you that you are
standing firm in one spirit, with
one [t]mind striving together for the
faith of the gospel; *soul*
28 in no way alarmed by *your*
opponents—which is a [r]sign of destruction for them, but of salvation for you, and that *too,* from
God. 2 Thess. 1:5
29 For to you it has been
granted for Christ's sake, not only
to believe in Him, but also to [r]suf-
fer for His sake, Acts 14:22
30 experiencing the same [r]con-
flict which you saw in me, and
now hear *to be* in me. Col. 1:29

CHAPTER 2

If therefore there is any encouragement in Christ, if there is any
consolation of love, if there is any
fellowship of the Spirit, if any affection and compassion,
2 make my joy complete by
being of the same mind, maintain-
ing the same love, united in spirit,
intent on one purpose.
3 Do nothing from [a]selfishness
or empty conceit, but with humility of mind let each of you regard
one another as more important
than himself; *contentiousness*
4 do not *merely* look out for
your own personal interests, but
also for the interests of others.
5 Have this attitude [a]in yourselves which was also in [r]Christ
Jesus, *among* • Phil. 1:1
6 who, although He [r]existed in

the [r]form of God, did not regard equality with God a thing to be grasped, John 1:1 • 2 Cor. 4:4

7 but [3]emptied Himself, taking the form of a bond-servant, *and* being made in the likeness of men.

8 And being found in appearance as a man, [r]He humbled Himself by becoming obedient to the point of death, even [r]death [t]on a cross. 2 Cor. 8:9 • Heb. 12:2 • *of*

9 [r]Therefore also God highly exalted Him, and bestowed on Him [r]the name which is above every name, Heb. 1:9 • Eph. 1:21

10 that at the name of Jesus [r]EVERY KNEE SHOULD BOW, of those who are in heaven, and on earth, and under the earth, Is. 45:23

11 and that every tongue should confess that Jesus Christ is Lord, to the glory of God the Father.

12 So then, my beloved, [r]just as you have always obeyed, not as in my presence only, but now much more in my absence, work out your [r]salvation with fear and trembling; Phil. 1:5, 6 • Heb. 5:9

13 for it is God who is at work in you, both to will and to work [r]for *His* good pleasure. Eph. 1:5

14 Do all things without [r]grumbling or disputing; 1 Cor. 10:10

15 that you may [a]prove yourselves to be blameless and innocent, children of God above reproach in the midst of a crooked and perverse generation, among whom you [a]appear as lights in the world, *become • shine*

16 holding fast the word of life, so that *in the day of Christ I* may have cause to glory because I did not run in vain nor toil in vain.

17 But even if I am being [r]poured out as a drink offering upon the sacrifice and service of your faith, I rejoice and share my joy with you all. 2 Tim. 4:6

18 And you too, *I urge you,* rejoice in the same way and share your joy with me.

19 But I hope in the Lord Jesus to send Timothy to you shortly, so that I also may be encouraged when I learn of your condition.

20 For I have no one *else* of kindred spirit who will genuinely be concerned for your welfare.

21 For they all [r]seek after their own interests, not those of Christ Jesus. 1 Cor. 10:24; 13:5

22 But you know of his proven worth that he served with me in the furtherance of the gospel like a child *serving* his father.

23 [r]Therefore I hope to send him immediately, as soon as I see how things go with me; Phil. 2:19

24 and [r]I trust in the Lord that I myself also shall be coming shortly. Phil. 1:25

25 But I thought it necessary to send to you Epaphroditus, my brother and fellow worker and fellow soldier, who is also your messenger and minister to my need;

26 because he was longing [4]for you all and was distressed because you had heard that he was sick.

27 For indeed he was sick to the point of death, but God had mercy on him, and not on him only but also on me, lest I should have sorrow upon sorrow.

28 Therefore I have sent him all the more eagerly in order that

[3]I.e., laid aside His privileges

[4]Some ancient mss. read *to see you all*

when you see him again you may rejoice and I may be less concerned *about you.*

29 Therefore receive him in the Lord with all joy, and hold men like him in high regard;

30 because he came close to death for the work of Christ, risking his life to complete what was deficient in your service to me.

CHAPTER 3

FINALLY, my brethren, rejoice in the Lord. To write the same things *again* is no trouble to me, and it is a safeguard for you.

2 Beware of the dogs, beware of the evil workers, beware of the [t]false circumcision; *mutilation*

3 for we are the *true* circumcision, who worship in the Spirit of God and glory in Christ Jesus and put no confidence in the flesh,

4 although I myself might have confidence even in the flesh. If anyone else has a mind to put confidence in the flesh, I far more:

5 circumcised the eighth day, of the nation of Israel, of the tribe of Benjamin, a Hebrew of Hebrews; as to the Law, a Pharisee;

6 as to zeal, a [r]persecutor of the church; as to the [r]righteousness which is in the Law, found blameless. Acts 8:3 • Phil. 3:9

7 But [r]whatever things were gain to me, those things I have counted as loss for the sake of Christ. Luke 14:33

8 More than that, I count all things to be loss in view of the surpassing value of [t]knowing Christ Jesus my Lord, for whom I have suffered the loss of all things, and count them but rubbish in order that I may gain Christ, *the knowledge of*

9 and may be found in Him, not having [r]a righteousness of my own derived from *the* Law, but that which is through faith in Christ, [r]the righteousness which *comes* from God on the basis of faith, Rom. 10:5 • Rom. 9:30

10 that I may know Him, and the power of His resurrection and the fellowship of His sufferings, being conformed to His death;

11 in order that I may attain to the resurrection from the dead.

12 Not that I have already obtained *it,* or have already become perfect, but I press on [t]in order that I may lay hold of that for which also I was laid hold of by Christ Jesus. *if I may even*

13 Brethren, I do not regard myself as having laid hold of *it* yet; but one thing *I do:* [r]forgetting what *lies* behind and reaching forward to what *lies* ahead, Luke 9:62

14 I [r]press on toward the goal for the prize of the upward call of God in Christ Jesus. 1 Cor. 9:24

15 Let us therefore, as many as are [a]perfect, have this attitude; and if in anything you have a [r]different attitude, God will reveal that also to you; *mature* • Gal. 5:10

16 however, let us keep [r]living by that same *standard* to which we have attained. Gal. 6:16

17 Brethren, [r]join in following my example, and observe those who walk according to the pattern you have in us. 1 Cor. 4:16

18 For many walk, of whom I often told you, and now tell you even weeping, *that they are* enemies of the cross of Christ,

19 whose end is destruction,

whose god is *their* appetite, and *whose* glory is in their shame, who set their minds on earthly things.

20 For our [t]citizenship is in heaven, from which also we eagerly wait for a Savior, the Lord Jesus Christ; *commonwealth*

21 who will transform[a]the body of our humble state into conformity with the body of His glory, by the exertion of the power that He has even to subject all things to Himself. *our lowly body*

CHAPTER 4

THEREFORE, my beloved brethren [t]whom I long *to see*, my joy and crown, so stand firm in the Lord, my beloved. *and longed for*

2 I urge Euodia and I urge Syntyche to[a]live in harmony in the Lord. *be of the same mind*

3 Indeed, true comrade, I ask you also to help these women who have shared my struggle in *the cause of* the gospel, together with Clement also, and the rest of my [r]fellow workers, whose names are in the book of life. Phil. 2:25

4 Rejoice in the Lord always; again I will say, rejoice!

5 Let your forbearing *spirit* be known to all men. [r]The Lord is [a]near. Heb. 10:37 • *at hand*

6 [r]Be anxious for nothing, but in everything by [r]prayer and supplication with thanksgiving let your requests be made known to God. Matt. 6:25 • Eph. 6:18

7 And the peace of God, which surpasses all [t]comprehension, shall *guard your hearts* and your minds in Christ Jesus. *mind*

8 Finally, brethren, whatever is true, whatever is honorable, whatever is right, whatever is pure, whatever is lovely, whatever is[a]of good repute, if there is any excellence and if anything worthy of praise, let your mind dwell on these things. *attractive*

9 The things you have learned and received and heard and seen [r]in me, practice these things; and [r]the God of peace shall be with you. Phil. 3:17 • Rom. 15:33

10 But I rejoiced in the Lord greatly, that now at last you have revived your concern for me; indeed, you were concerned *before*, but you lacked opportunity.

11 Not that I speak from want; for I have learned to be content in whatever circumstances I am.

12 I know how to get along with humble means, and I also know how to live in prosperity; in any and every circumstance I have learned the secret of being filled and going hungry, both of having abundance and suffering need.

13 I can do all things [t]through Him who strengthens me. *in*

14 Nevertheless, you have done well to[r]share *with me* in my affliction. Heb. 10:33; Rev. 1:9

15 And you yourselves also know, Philippians, that at the[t]first preaching of the gospel, after I departed from [r]Macedonia, no church shared with me in the matter of giving and receiving but you alone; *beginning of* • Rom. 15:26

16 for even in[r]Thessalonica you sent *a gift* more than once for my needs. Acts 17:1; 1 Thess. 2:9

17 Not that I seek the gift itself, but I seek for the [t]profit which increases to your account. *fruit*

18 But I have received every-

thing in full, and have an abundance; I am [t]amply supplied, having received from Epaphroditus
what you have sent, a fragrant
aroma, an acceptable sacrifice,
well-pleasing to God. *made full*
19 And my God shall supply all
your needs according to His
riches in glory in Christ Jesus.
20 Now to our God and Father
be the glory [t]forever and ever.
Amen. *to the ages of the ages*
21 Greet every [a]saint in Christ
Jesus. The brethren who are with
me greet you. *holy one*
22 [r]All the [r]saints greet you, especially those of Caesar's household. 2 Cor. 13:13 • Acts 9:13
23 The grace of the Lord Jesus
Christ be with your spirit.

THE EPISTLE OF PAUL TO THE
COLOSSIANS

PAUL, an apostle of Jesus Christ
[t]by the will of God, and Timothy
[t]our brother, *through • the*
2 to the [a]saints and faithful
brethren in Christ *who are* at Co-
lossae: Grace to you and peace
from God our Father. *holy ones*
3 We give thanks to God, the
Father of our Lord Jesus Christ,
praying always for you,
4 since we heard of your faith
in Christ Jesus and the love which
you have for all the saints;
5 because of the hope laid up
for you in [t]heaven, of which you
previously heard in the word of
truth, the gospel, *the heavens*
6 which has come to you, just
as [a]in all the world also it is constantly bearing fruit and increasing, even as *it has been doing* in
you also since the day you heard
of it and understood the grace of
God in truth; *it is in the world*
7 just as you learned *it* from
Epaphras, our beloved fellow
bond-servant, who is a faithful
servant of Christ on [1]our behalf,
8 and he also informed us of
your love in the Spirit.
9 For this reason also, since
the day we heard *of it*, we have
not ceased to pray for you and to
ask that you may be filled with the
knowledge of His will in all spiritual wisdom and understanding,
10 so that you may walk in a
manner worthy of the Lord, to
please *Him* in all respects, bearing
fruit in every good work and increasing in the knowledge of God;
11 strengthened with all power,
according to His glorious might,
for the attaining of all steadfastness and patience; joyously
12 giving thanks to the Father,
who has qualified us [t]to share in
the inheritance of the saints in
light. *unto the portion of*
13 For He delivered us from the
[t]domain of darkness, and trans-

[1] Some later mss. read *your*

ferred us to the kingdom of His beloved Son, *authority*

14 in whom we have redemption, the forgiveness of sins.

15 And He is the[r]image of the [r]invisible God, the first-born of all creation. 2 Cor. 4:4 • John 1:18

16 For[a]by Him all things were created, *both* in the heavens and on earth, visible and invisible, whether thrones or dominions or rulers or authorities—[r]all things have been created[a]by Him and for Him. *in* • John 1:3 • *through*

17 And He[a]is before all things, and in Him all things hold together. *has existed prior to*

18 He is also head of the body, the church; and He is the beginning, the first-born from the dead; so that He Himself might come to have first place in everything.

19 For it was[r]the *Father's* good pleasure for all the fulness to dwell in Him, Eph. 1:5

20 and through Him[r]to reconcile all things to Himself, having made peace through the blood of His cross; through Him, *I say*, whether things on earth or things in [t]heaven. Eph. 2:16 • *the heavens*

21 And although you were formerly alienated and hostile in mind, *engaged* in evil deeds,

22 yet He has now[r]reconciled you in His fleshly body through death, in order to present you before Him holy and blameless and beyond reproach— 2 Cor. 5:18

23 if indeed you continue in the faith firmly established and steadfast, and *not moved* away from the hope of the gospel that you have heard, which was proclaimed in all creation under heaven, and of which I, Paul,[t]was made a minister. *became*

24 Now I rejoice in my sufferings for your sake, and in my flesh I do my share on behalf of His body (which is the church) in filling up that which is lacking[t]in Christ's afflictions. *of*

25 Of *this church* I[t]was made a minister according to the stewardship from God bestowed on me for your benefit, that I might fully carry out the *preaching of* the word of God, *became*

26 *that is,* the mystery which has been hidden from the *past* ages and generations; but has now been manifested to His saints,

27 to whom[r]God willed to make known what is the riches of the glory of this mystery among the Gentiles, which is Christ in you, the hope of glory. Matt. 13:11

28 And we proclaim Him, admonishing every man and teaching every man[t]with all wisdom, that we may present every man complete in Christ. *in*

29 And for this purpose also I labor, striving according to His [t]power, which[t]mightily works within me. *working* • *in power*

CHAPTER 2

FOR I want you to know how great a struggle I have on your behalf, and for those who are at Laodicea, and for all those who have not personally seen my face,

2 that their hearts may be encouraged, having been knit together in love, and *attaining* to all the wealth[t]that comes from the full assurance of understanding, *resulting* in a true knowledge of

God's mystery, *that is,* Christ
Himself, *of the full assurance*
3 in whom are hidden all [r]the
treasures of wisdom and knowledge. Is. 11:2; Rom. 11:33
4 I say this in order that no one
may delude you with [r]persuasive
argument. Rom. 16:18
5 For even though I am absent
in body, nevertheless I am with
you in spirit, rejoicing [t]to see your
good discipline and the stability of
your faith in Christ. *and seeing*
6 As you therefore have received Christ Jesus the Lord, *so*
[a]walk in Him, *lead your life*
7 having been firmly [r]rooted
and now being built up in Him
and established [2]in your faith, just
as you were instructed, *and* overflowing with gratitude. Eph. 3:17
8 See to it that no one takes
you captive through [r]philosophy
and empty deception, according
to the tradition of men, according
to the elementary principles of the
world, [t]rather than according to
Christ. Eph. 5:6 • *and not*
9 For in Him all the fulness of
Deity dwells in bodily form,
10 and in Him you have been
made complete, and He is the
head over all rule and authority;
11 and in Him you were also circumcised with a circumcision
made without hands, in the removal of the body of the flesh by
the circumcision of Christ;
12 having been buried with Him
in baptism, in which you were
also raised up with Him through
faith in the working of God, who
raised Him from the dead.
13 And when you were [r]dead [a]in
your transgressions and the uncir-

[2]Or, *by*

cumcision of your flesh, He made
you alive together with Him, having forgiven us all our transgressions, Eph. 2:1 • *by reason of*
14 having canceled out [r]the certificate of debt consisting of decrees against us *and* which was
hostile to us; and He has taken it
out of the way, having nailed it to
the cross. Eph. 2:15
15 When He had disarmed the
rulers and authorities, He made a
public display of them, having tri-
umphed over them through Him.
16 Therefore let no one act as
your judge in regard to food or
drink or in respect to a festival or
a new moon or a Sabbath day—
17 things which are a *mere*
shadow of what is to come; but
the substance belongs to Christ.
18 Let no one keep defrauding
you of your prize by delighting in
self-abasement and the worship of
the angels, taking his stand on *vi-*
sions he has seen, inflated without
cause by his fleshly mind,
19 and not holding fast to the
head, from whom the entire body,
being supplied and held together
by the joints and ligaments, grows
with a growth which is from God.
20 If you have died with Christ
[t]to the elementary principles of the
world, why, as if you were living
in the world, do you submit yourself to decrees, such as, *from*
21 "Do not handle, do not taste,
do not touch!"
22 (which all *refer to* things destined to perish with the using)—in
accordance with the commandments and teachings of men?
23 These are matters which
have, to be sure, the appearance
of wisdom in [a]self-made religion

and self-abasement and severe
treatment of the body, *but are* of
no value against fleshly indul-
gence. *delight in religiousness*

CHAPTER 3

IF then you have been raised up
with Christ, keep seeking the
things above, where Christ is,
seated at the right hand of God.
2 [a]Set your mind on the things
above, not on the things that are
on earth. *Be intent on*
3 For you have died and your
life is hidden with Christ in God.
4 When Christ, who is our life,
is revealed, then you also will be
revealed with Him in glory.
5 Therefore consider the members of your earthly body as dead
to [t]immorality, impurity, passion,
evil desire, and greed, which
amounts to idolatry. *fornication*
6 For it is on account of these
things that [r]the wrath of God will
come[3], Rom. 1:18; Eph. 5:6
7 and [r]in them you also once
walked, when you were living in
them. Eph. 2:2
8 But now you also, [r]put them
all aside: anger, wrath, malice,
slander, *and* abusive speech from
your mouth. Eph. 4:22
9 Do not lie to one another,
since you laid aside the old [t]self
with its *evil* practices, *man*
10 and have put on the new self
who is being renewed to a true
knowledge according to the image
of the One who created him
11 —*a renewal* in which [r]there is
no distinction between Greek and
Jew, [r]circumcised and uncircumcised, barbarian, Scythian, slave
and freeman, but Christ is all, and
in all. Rom. 10:12 • 1 Cor. 7:19
12 And so, as those who have
been [r]chosen of God, holy and beloved, put on a heart of compassion, kindness, humility, gentleness and patience; Luke 18:7
13 bearing with one another,
and [r]forgiving each other, whoever
has a complaint against anyone;
just as the Lord forgave you, so
also should you. Rom. 15:7
14 And beyond all these things
put on love, which is [r]the perfect
bond of unity. Eph. 4:3
15 And let the peace of Christ
rule in your hearts, to which [t]in-
deed you were called in one body;
and be thankful. *also*
16 Let [r]the word of [4]Christ richly
dwell within you, [a]with all wisdom
teaching and admonishing one another with psalms *and* hymns *and*
spiritual songs, singing [t]with
thankfulness in your hearts to
God. Rom. 10:17 • *in* • *in His grace*
17 And whatever you do in
word or deed, *do* all in the name
of the Lord Jesus, giving thanks
through Him to God the Father.
18 Wives, be subject to your
husbands, as is fitting in the Lord.
19 [r]Husbands, love your wives,
and do not be embittered against
them. Eph. 5:25; 1 Pet. 3:7
20 Children, be obedient to your
parents in all things, for this is
well-pleasing [t]to the Lord. *in*
21 [r]Fathers, do not [5]exasperate
your children, that they may not
lose heart. Eph. 6:4
22 Slaves, in all things obey
those who are your masters [t]on

[3] Some early mss. add *upon the sons of disobedience*

[4] Some mss. read *the Lord;* others read *God*

[5] Some early mss. read *provoke to anger*

earth, not with external service,
as those who *merely* please men,
but with sincerity of heart, fearing
the Lord. *according to the flesh*
23 Whatever you do, do your
work heartily, as for the Lord
[t]rather than for men; *and not*
24 knowing that from the Lord
you will receive the reward of[r]the
inheritance. It is the Lord Christ
whom you serve. Acts 20:32
25 For[r]he who does wrong will
receive the consequences of the
wrong which he has done, and
that without partiality. Eph. 6:8

CHAPTER 4

MASTERS, grant to your slaves
justice and fairness, knowing that
you too have a Master in heaven.
2 [r]Devote yourselves to prayer,
keeping alert in it with *an attitude*
of thanksgiving; Acts 1:14
3 praying at the same time[r]for
us as well, that God may open up
to us a door for the word, so that
we may speak forth the mystery
of Christ, for which I have also
been imprisoned; Eph. 6:19
4 in order that I may make it
clear in the way I ought to speak.
5 Conduct yourselves with
wisdom toward outsiders, making
the most of the opportunity.
6 Let your speech always be
[a]with grace, seasoned, *as it were,*
with[r]salt, so that you may know
how you should respond to each
person. *gracious* • Mark 9:50
7 As to all my affairs, [r]Tychi-
cus, *our* beloved brother and
faithful servant and fellow bond-
servant in the Lord, will bring you
information. Acts 20:4
8 For I have sent him to you
for this very purpose, that you
may know *about* our circumstances and that he may [r]encour-
age your hearts; Col. 2:2
9 [t]and with him Onesimus, *our*
faithful and beloved brother, who
is one of your *number.* They will
inform you about the whole situation here. *along with Onesimus*
10 Aristarchus, my fellow prisoner, sends you his greetings; and
also Barnabas' cousin Mark
(about whom you received [a]in-
structions: if he comes to you,
welcome him); *orders*
11 and *also* Jesus who is called
Justus; these are the only[r]fellow
workers for the kingdom of God
who are from the circumcision;
and they have proved to be an encouragement to me. Rom. 16:3
12 Epaphras, who is one of your
number, a bondslave of Jesus
Christ, sends you his greetings, always laboring earnestly for you in
his prayers, that you may[a]stand
perfect and fully assured in all the
will of God. *stand firm*
13 For I bear him witness that
he has[a]a deep concern for you and
for those who are in Laodicea and
Hierapolis. *much toil* or *great pain*
14 Luke, the beloved physician,
sends you his greetings, and *also*
[r]Demas. 2 Tim. 4:10; Philem. 24
15 Greet the brethren who are
in Laodicea and also [6]Nympha and
the church that is in her house.
16 And when this letter is read
among you, have it also read in
the church of the Laodiceans; and
you, for your part read my letter
that is coming from Laodicea.

[6]Or, *Nymphas* (masc.)

17 And say to [r]Archippus, "Take
heed to the ministry which you
have received in the Lord, that
you may fulfill it." Philem. 2

18 I, Paul, [r]write this greeting
with my own hand. Remember
my [t]imprisonment. Grace be with
you. 1 Cor. 16:21 • *bonds*

THE FIRST EPISTLE OF PAUL TO THE

THESSALONIANS

PAUL and [r]Silvanus and [r]Timothy
to the church of the Thessalonians
in God the Father and the Lord
Jesus Christ: Grace to you and
peace. 2 Cor. 1:19 • Acts 16:1
2 We give thanks to God always for all of you, making mention *of you* in our prayers;
3 constantly bearing in mind
your work of faith and labor of
love and steadfastness of hope [t]in
our Lord Jesus Christ in the presence of our God and Father, *of*
4 knowing, brethren beloved
by God, *His* choice of you;
5 for our [r]gospel did not come
to you in word only, but also in
power and in the Holy Spirit and
with full conviction; just as you
know what kind of men we
[t]proved to be among you for your
sake. 1 Cor. 9:14 • *became*
6 You also became [r]imitators of
us and of the Lord, [r]having received the word in much tribulation with the joy of the Holy
Spirit, 1 Cor. 4:16 • Acts 17:5-10
7 so that you became an example to all the believers in [r]Macedo-
nia and in Achaia. Rom. 15:26
8 *For the word* of the Lord has
sounded forth from you, not only
in Macedonia and Achaia, but also
in every place your faith toward
God has gone forth, so that we
have no need to say anything.
9 For they themselves report
about us what kind of a [t]reception
we had with you, and how you
turned to God from idols to serve
a living and true God, *entrance*
10 and to wait for His Son from
heaven, whom He raised from the
dead, *that is* Jesus, who delivers
us from the wrath to come.

CHAPTER 2

FOR you yourselves know, brethren, that our [t]coming to you was
not in vain, *entrance*
2 but after we had already suffered and been mistreated in Philippi, as you know, we had the
boldness in our God to speak to
you the gospel of God amid much
[a]opposition. *struggle, conflict*
3 For our exhortation does not
come from error or impurity or [t]by
way of deceit; *in deceit*
4 but just as we have been approved by God to be entrusted
with the gospel, so we speak, not
as pleasing men but God, who [a]ex-
amines our hearts. *approves*
5 For we never came [t]with flattering speech, as you know, nor
with a pretext for greed—God is
witness— *in a word of flattery*

6 nor did we seek glory from men, either from you or from others, even though as apostles of Christ we might have[a] asserted our authority. *been burdensome*

7 But we[t] proved to be [1]gentle among you, as a nursing *mother* [a]tenderly cares for her own children. *became gentle • cherishes*

8 Having thus a fond affection for you, we were well-pleased to impart to you not only the gospel of God but also our own[a] lives, because you had become[t] very dear to us. *souls • beloved*

9 For you recall, brethren, our labor and hardship, *how* working night and day so as not to be a burden to any of you, we proclaimed to you the gospel of God.

10 You are witnesses, and *so is* God, how devoutly and uprightly and blamelessly we [t]behaved toward you believers; *became*

11 just as you know how we *were* exhorting and encouraging and imploring each one of you as a father *would* his own children,

12 so that you may [r]walk in a manner worthy of the God who [r]calls you into His own kingdom and glory. Eph. 4:1 • Rom. 8:28

13 And for this reason we also constantly [r]thank God that when you received from us the word of God's message, you accepted *it* not *as* the word of men, but *for* what it really is, the word of God, which also performs its work in you who believe. Rom. 1:8

14 For you, brethren, became [r]imitators of the churches of God in Christ Jesus that are in Judea, for you also endured the same sufferings at the hands of your own countrymen, even as they *did* from the Jews, 1 Thess. 1:6

15 who both killed the Lord Jesus and the prophets, and drove us out. [t]They are not pleasing to God, but hostile to all men, *and*

16 hindering us from speaking to the Gentiles[r] that they might be saved; with the result that they always fill up the measure of their sins. But wrath has come upon them [2]to the utmost. 1 Cor. 10:33

17 But we, brethren, having been bereft of you for a short while—in [t]person, not in spirit—were all the more eager with great desire to see your face. *face*

18 For we wanted to come to you—I, Paul, more than once—and *yet* Satan thwarted us.

19 For who is our hope or joy or crown of exultation? Is it not even you, in the presence of our Lord Jesus at His[a] coming? *presence*

20 For you are [r]our glory and joy. 2 Cor. 1:14

CHAPTER 3

THEREFORE[r] when we could endure *it* no longer, we thought it best to be left behind at [r]Athens alone; 1 Thess. 3:5 • Acts 17:15f.

2 and we sent [r]Timothy, our brother and God's fellow worker in the gospel of Christ, to strengthen and encourage you as to your faith, 2 Cor. 1:1; Col. 1:1

3 so that no man may be [a]disturbed by these afflictions; for you yourselves know that we have been destined for this. *deceived*

4 For indeed when we were with you, we *kept* telling you in advance that we were going to

[1] Some ancient mss. read *babes*

[2] Or, *forever;* or, *altogether*

suffer affliction; [t]and so it came to pass, [t]as you know. *just as* · *and*

5 For this reason, when I could endure *it* no longer, I also sent to [a]find out about your faith, for fear that the tempter might have tempted you, and our labor should be in vain. *to know, to ascertain*

6 But now that [r]Timothy has come to us from you, and has brought us good news of [r]your faith and love, and that you always think kindly of us, longing to see us just as we also long to see you, Acts 18:5 · 1 Thess. 1:3

7 for this reason, brethren, in all our distress and affliction we were comforted about you through your faith;

8 for now we *really* live, if you stand firm in the Lord.

9 For what thanks can we render to God for you in return for all the joy with which we rejoice before our God on your account,

10 as we night and day keep praying most earnestly that we may see your face, and may complete what is lacking in your faith?

11 Now may [r]our God and Father Himself and Jesus our Lord direct our way to you; Gal. 1:4

12 and may the Lord cause you to increase and [r]abound in love for one another, and for all men, just as we also *do* for you; Phil. 1:9

13 so that He may establish your hearts unblamable in holiness before our God and Father at the [a]coming of our Lord Jesus with all His saints. *presence*

CHAPTER 4

FINALLY then, brethren, we request and exhort you in the Lord Jesus, that, as you received from us *instruction* as to how you ought to walk and please God (just as you actually do [3]walk), that you may excel still more.

2 For you know what commandments we gave you [4]by *the authority of* the Lord Jesus.

3 For this is the will of God, your sanctification; *that is,* that you [r]abstain from [a]sexual immorality; 1 Cor. 6:18 · *fornication*

4 that each of you know how to [a]possess his own [5]vessel in sanctification and honor, *acquire*

5 not in lustful passion, like the Gentiles who do not know God;

6 *and* that no man transgress and [r]defraud his brother in the matter because the Lord is *the* avenger in all these things, just as we also told you before and solemnly warned *you.* 1 Cor. 6:8

7 For [r]God has not called us for the purpose of impurity, but in sanctification. 1 Pet. 1:15

8 Consequently, he who rejects *this* is not rejecting man but the God who [r]gives His Holy Spirit to you. Rom. 5:5; 2 Cor. 1:22

9 Now as to the [r]love of the brethren, you have no need for *anyone* to write to you, for you yourselves are taught by God to love one another; John 13:34

10 for indeed you do practice it toward all the brethren who are in all Macedonia. But we urge you, brethren, to excel still more,

11 and to make it your ambition [r]to lead a quiet life and attend to your own business and work with

[3]Or, *conduct yourselves*
[4]Lit., *through the Lord*
[5]I.e., body; or possibly, wife

your hands, just as we commanded you; 2 Thess. 3:12
12 so that you may [t]behave
properly toward outsiders and not
be in any need. *walk*
13 But[r]we do not want you to be
uninformed, brethren, about those
who[r]are asleep, that you may not
grieve, as do the rest who have no
hope. Rom. 1:13 • Acts 7:60
14 For if we believe that Jesus
died and rose again, even so God
will bring with Him those who
have fallen asleep in Jesus.
15 For this we say to you by the
word of the Lord, that we who are
alive, and remain until the coming
of the Lord, shall not precede
those who have fallen asleep.
16 For the Lord Himself will descend from heaven with a shout,
with the voice of *the* archangel,
and with the trumpet of God; and
the dead in Christ shall rise first.
17 Then we who are alive and
remain shall be caught up together with them in the clouds to
meet the Lord in the air, and thus
we shall always be with the Lord.
18 Therefore comfort one another with these words.

CHAPTER 5

NOW as to the[r]times and the
epochs, brethren, you[r]have no
need of anything to be written to
you. Acts 1:7 • 1 Thess. 4:9
2 For you yourselves know full
well that the day of the Lord will
come just like a thief in the night.
3 While they are saying,
"Peace[r]and safety!" then destruction [t]will come upon them suddenly like birth pangs upon a
woman with child; and they shall
not escape. Jer. 6:14 • *is at hand*
4 But you, brethren, are not in
darkness, that the day should
overtake you like a thief;
5 for you are all sons of light
and sons of day. We are not of
night nor of darkness;
6 so then let us not sleep as
[t]others do, but let us be alert and
[6]sober. *the remaining ones*
7 For those who sleep do their
sleeping at night, and those who
get drunk get drunk at night.
8 But since we are of *the* day,
let us be [6]sober, having put on the
breastplate of faith and love, and
as a helmet, the hope of salvation.
9 For God has not destined us
for[r]wrath, but for obtaining salvation through our Lord Jesus
Christ, 1 Thess. 1:10
10 who died for us, that whether
we are awake or asleep, we may
live together with Him.
11 Therefore encourage one another, and build up one another,
just as you also are doing.
12 But we request of you, brethren, that you appreciate those
who diligently labor among you,
and have charge over you in the
Lord and give you instruction,
13 and that you esteem them
very highly in love because of
their work.[r]Live in peace with one
another. Mark 9:50
14 And we urge you, brethren,
admonish the unruly, encourage
[r]the fainthearted, help the weak,
be patient with all men. Is. 35:4
15 See that no one repays another with evil for evil, but always
seek after that which is good for
one another and for all men.

[6]Or, *self-controlled*

16 [r]Rejoice always; Phil. 4:4

17 pray without ceasing;

18 in everything [r]give thanks; for this is God's will for you in Christ Jesus. Eph. 5:20

19 Do not quench the Spirit;

20 do not despise [r]prophetic [7]utterances. Acts 13:1; 1 Cor. 14:31

21 But [r]examine everything *carefully*; [r]hold fast to that which is good; 1 John 4:1 • Gal. 6:10

22 abstain from every [8]form of evil.

23 Now [r]may the God of peace Himself sanctify you entirely; and may your spirit and soul and body be preserved complete, without blame at the coming of our Lord Jesus Christ. Rom. 15:33

24 Faithful is He who calls you, and He also will bring it to pass.

25 Brethren, pray for us[9].

26 [r]Greet all the brethren with a holy kiss. Rom. 16:16

27 I adjure you by the Lord to [r]have this letter read to all the [r]brethren. Col. 4:16 • Acts 1:15

28 [r]The grace of our Lord Jesus Christ be with you. Rom. 16:20

[7]Or, *gifts* [8]Or, *appearance*

[9]Some mss. add *also*

THE SECOND EPISTLE OF PAUL TO THE

THESSALONIANS

PAUL and Silvanus and Timothy to the [r]church of the Thessalonians in God our Father and the Lord Jesus Christ: Acts 17:1

2 [r]Grace to you and peace from God the Father and the Lord Jesus Christ. Rom. 1:7

3 We ought always to give thanks to God for you, brethren, as is *only* fitting, because your faith is greatly enlarged, and the love of each one of you toward one another grows *ever* greater;

4 therefore, we ourselves speak proudly of you among the churches of God for your perseverance and faith in the midst of all your persecutions and afflictions which you endure.

5 *This is* a [r]plain indication of God's righteous judgment so that you may be considered worthy of the kingdom of God, for which indeed you are suffering. Phil. 1:28

6 [t]For after all it is *only* just for God to repay with affliction those who afflict you, *If indeed*

7 and *to give* relief to you who are afflicted and to us as well when the Lord Jesus shall be revealed from heaven with His mighty angels in flaming fire,

8 dealing out retribution to those who [r]do not know God and to those who do not obey the gospel of our Lord Jesus. Gal. 4:8

9 And these will pay the penalty of eternal destruction, away from the presence of the Lord and from the glory of His power,

10 when He comes to be glorified in His [a]saints on that day, and to be marveled at among all who

have believed—for our testimony
to you was believed. *holy ones*
11 To this end also we [r]pray for
you always that our God may
[a]count you worthy of your calling,
and fulfill every desire for goodness and the work of faith with
power; Col. 1:9 · *make*
12 in order that the [r]name of our
Lord Jesus may be glorified in
you, and you in Him, according to
the grace of our God and the Lord
Jesus Christ. Is. 24:15; 66:5

CHAPTER 2

NOW we request you, brethren,
with regard to the [a]coming of our
Lord Jesus Christ, and our gathering together to Him, *presence*
2 that you may not be quickly
shaken from your [t]composure or
be disturbed either by a spirit or a
[t]message or a letter as if from us,
to the effect that the day of the
Lord has come. *mind · word*
3 Let no one in any way deceive you, for *it will not come* unless the [1]apostasy comes first, and
the man of lawlessness is revealed, the son of destruction,
4 who opposes and exalts himself above every so-called god or
object of worship, so that he takes
his seat in the temple of God, dis-
playing himself as being God.
5 Do you not remember that
while I was still with you, I was
telling you these things?
6 And you know what re-
strains him now, so that in his
time he may be revealed.
7 For the mystery of lawlessness is already at work; only he
who now restrains *will do so* until
he is taken out of the way.
8 And then that lawless one
will be revealed whom the Lord
will slay with the breath of His
mouth and bring to an end by the
appearance of His coming;
9 *that is,* the one whose [a]com-
ing is in accord with the activity
of Satan, with all power and signs
and false wonders, *presence*
10 and with all the deception of
wickedness for those who perish,
because they did not receive the
love of the truth so as to be saved.
11 And for this reason God [t]will
send upon them a deluding influence so that they might believe
[a]what is false, *sends · the lie*
12 in order that they all may be
[a]judged who did not believe the
truth, but [a]took pleasure in wickedness. *condemned · approved*
13 But we should always give
thanks to God for you, [r]brethren
beloved by the Lord, because God
has chosen you [2]from the beginning for salvation [t]through sanctification [t]by the Spirit and faith in
the truth. 1 Thess. 1:4 · *in* · *of*
14 And it was for this He called
you through our gospel, [t]that you
may gain the glory of our Lord
Jesus Christ. *to the gaining of*
15 So then, brethren, stand firm
and hold to the [r]traditions which
you were taught, whether by word
of mouth or by letter from us.
16 Now may our Lord Jesus
Christ [r]Himself and God our Father, who has loved us and given
us eternal comfort and good hope
by grace, 1 Thess. 3:11

[1] Or, *falling away* from the faith

[2] Some ancient mss. read *first fruits*

17 comfort and [r]strengthen your hearts in every good work and word. 2 Thess. 3:3

CHAPTER 3

FINALLY, brethren, pray for us that the word of the Lord may [t]spread rapidly and be glorified, just as *it did* also with you; *run*

2 and that we may be delivered from [t]perverse and evil men; for not all have faith. *improper*

3 But the Lord is faithful, and [t]He will strengthen and protect you from the evil *one.* *will*

4 And we have [r]confidence in the Lord concerning you, that you are doing and will continue to do what we command. 2 Cor. 2:3

5 And may the Lord [r]direct your hearts into the love of God and into the steadfastness of Christ. 1 Thess. 3:11

6 Now we command you, brethren, in the name of our Lord Jesus Christ, that you keep aloof from every brother who [t]leads an unruly life and not according to the tradition which you received from us. *walks disorderly*

7 For you yourselves know how you ought to [t]follow our example, because we did not act in an undisciplined manner among you, *imitate us*

8 nor did we eat [t]anyone's bread [t]without paying for it, but with labor and hardship we *kept* working night and day so that we might not be a burden to any of you; *from anyone • freely*

9 not because we do not have [r]the right *to this,* but in order to offer ourselves as a model for you, that you might [t]follow our example. 1 Cor. 9:4ff. • *imitate us*

10 For even [r]when we were with you, we used to give you this order: if anyone will not work, neither let him eat. 1 Thess. 3:4

11 For we hear that some among you are leading an undisciplined life, doing no work at all, but acting like busybodies.

12 Now such persons we command and exhort in the Lord Jesus Christ to work in quiet fashion and eat their own bread.

13 But as for you, brethren, do not grow weary of doing good.

14 And if anyone does not obey our [t]instruction in this letter, take special note of that man and do not associate with him, so that he may be put to shame. *word*

15 And *yet* do not regard him as an enemy, but [a]admonish him as a brother. *keep admonishing*

16 Now may the Lord of peace Himself continually grant you peace in every [t]circumstance. The Lord be with you all! *way*

17 I, Paul, write this greeting with my own hand, and this is a distinguishing mark in every letter; this is the way I write.

18 The grace of our Lord Jesus Christ be with you all.

THE FIRST EPISTLE OF PAUL TO

TIMOTHY

PAUL, an apostle of Christ Jesus
according to the commandment of
God our Savior, and of Christ
Jesus, *who is* our hope;
2 to[r]Timothy, *my* true child in
the faith: Grace, mercy *and* peace
from God the Father and Christ
Jesus our Lord. Acts 16:1
3 As I urged you upon my departure for Macedonia, [t]remain on
at Ephesus, in order that you may
instruct certain men not to teach
strange doctrines, ***to remain***
4 nor to pay attention to myths
and endless genealogies, which
give rise to mere speculation
rather than *furthering* the administration of God which is by faith.
5 But the goal of our [t]instruc-
tion is love from a pure heart and
a good conscience and a sincere
faith. ***commandment***
6 For some men, straying from
these things, have turned aside to
[r]fruitless discussion, Titus 1:10
7 wanting to be teachers of the
Law, even though they do not understand either what they are saying or the matters about which
they make confident assertions.
8 But we know that the Law is
good, if one uses it lawfully,
9 realizing the fact that law is
not made for a righteous man, but
for those who are lawless and rebellious, for the ungodly and sinners, for the unholy and profane,
for those who kill their fathers or
mothers, for murderers
10 and immoral men and homosexuals and kidnappers and liars
and perjurers, and whatever else
is contrary to sound teaching,
11 according to the glorious
gospel of the blessed God, with
which I have been entrusted.
12 I thank Christ Jesus our
Lord, who has strengthened me,
because He considered me faithful, putting me into service;
13 even though I was formerly a
blasphemer and a [r]persecutor and
a violent aggressor. And yet I was
shown mercy, because I acted ig-
norantly in unbelief; Acts 8:3
14 and the [r]grace of our Lord
was more than abundant, with the
faith and love which are *found* in
Christ Jesus. Rom. 5:20
15 It is a trustworthy statement,
deserving full acceptance, that
[r]Christ Jesus came into the world
to save sinners, among whom I
am foremost *of all*. Mark 2:17
16 And yet for this reason I
found mercy, in order that in me
as the foremost, Jesus Christ
might demonstrate His perfect patience, as an example for those
[t]who would believe in Him for
eternal life. ***destined to***
17 Now to the[r]King [t]eternal, im-
mortal, invisible, the only God, *be*
honor and glory forever and ever.
Amen. Rev. 15:3 • ***of the ages***
18 This [r]command I entrust to
you, Timothy, my [t]son, in accordance with the prophecies previously made concerning you, that
by them you may fight the good
fight, 1 Tim. 1:5 • ***child***
19 keeping faith and a good

conscience, which some have rejected and suffered shipwreck in regard to[t]their faith. *the*

20 Among these are Hymenaeus and Alexander, whom I have delivered over to Satan, so that they may be taught not to blaspheme.

CHAPTER 2

FIRST of all, then, I urge that[r]entreaties *and* prayers, petitions *and* thanksgivings, be made on behalf of all men, Eph. 6:18

2 [r]for kings and all who are in authority, in order that we may lead a tranquil and quiet life in all godliness and dignity. Ezra 6:10

3 This is good and acceptable in the sight of God our Savior,

4 who desires all men to be saved and to come to the[a]knowledge of the truth. *recognition*

5 For there is one God, *and* one mediator also between God and men, *the* man Christ Jesus,

6 who gave Himself as a ransom for all, the testimony *borne* at [t]the proper time. *its own times*

7 And for this I was appointed a[a]preacher and [r]an apostle (I am telling the truth, I am not lying) as a teacher of the Gentiles in faith and truth. *herald* • 1 Cor. 9:1

8 Therefore[r]I want the men[r]in every place to pray, lifting up holy hands, without wrath and dissension. Phil. 1:12 • John 4:21

9 Likewise, *I want* women to adorn themselves with proper clothing, modestly and discreetly, not with braided hair and gold or pearls or costly garments;

10 but rather by means of good works, as befits women making a claim to godliness.

11 Let a woman quietly receive instruction with entire submissiveness.

12 But I do not allow a woman to teach or exercise authority over a man, but to remain quiet.

13 For it was Adam who was first created, *and* then Eve.

14 And *it was* not Adam *who* was deceived, but [r]the woman being quite deceived, fell into transgression. Gen. 3:6, 13

15 But *women* shall be [t]preserved through the bearing of children if they continue in faith and love and sanctity with[a]self-restraint. *saved* • *discretion*

CHAPTER 3

IT is a trustworthy statement: if any man aspires to the office of [a]overseer, it is a fine work he desires *to do*. *bishop*

2 [t]An overseer, then, must be above reproach, [r]the husband of one wife, temperate, prudent, respectable, hospitable, able to teach, *The* • Luke 2:36f.

3 not addicted to wine or pugnacious, but gentle, uncontentious, free from the love of money.

4 *He must be* one who [r]manages his own household well, keeping his children under control with all dignity 1 Tim. 3:12

5 (but if a man does not know how to manage his own household, how will he take care of[r]the church of God?); 1 Cor. 10:32

6 *and* not a new convert, lest he become [r]conceited and fall into the condemnation[t]incurred by the devil. 1 Tim. 6:4 • *of the devil*

7 And he must have a good reputation with[r]those outside *the*

church, so that he may not fall
into reproach and the snare of the
devil. Mark 4:11
8 Deacons likewise *must be*
men of dignity, not double-
tongued, [t]or addicted to much
wine or fond of sordid gain, *not*
9 *but* holding to the mystery of
the faith with a clear conscience.
10 And let these also first be
tested; then let them serve as deacons if they are beyond reproach.
11 Women *must* likewise *be*
dignified, [r]not malicious gossips,
but [r]temperate, faithful in all
things. 2 Tim. 3:3 • 1 Tim. 3:2
12 Let deacons be husbands of
only one wife, *and*[t]good managers
of *their* children and their own
households. *managing well*
13 For those who have served
well as deacons [r]obtain for themselves a [t]high standing and great
confidence in the faith that is in
Christ Jesus. Matt. 25:21 • *good*
14 I am writing these things to
you, hoping to come to you before
long;
15 but in case I am delayed, *I
write* so that you may know how
one ought to conduct himself in
the household of God, which is the
church of the living God, the pillar
and support of the truth.
16 And by common confession
great is the mystery of godliness:

[1]He who was [r]revealed in the flesh, John 1:14
Was [a]vindicated [a]in the Spirit, *justified • by*
Beheld by angels,
[r]Proclaimed among the nations, Rom. 16:26
Believed on in the world,
Taken up in glory.

[1]Some later mss. read *God*

CHAPTER 4

BUT [r]the Spirit explicitly says
that in later times some will fall
away from the faith, paying attention to deceitful spirits and doctrines of demons, John 16:13
2 by means of the hypocrisy of
liars seared in their own conscience as with a branding iron,
3 *men* who forbid marriage
and advocate abstaining from
foods, which God has created to
be gratefully shared in by those
who believe and know the truth.
4 For [r]everything created by
God is good, and nothing is to be
rejected, if it is received with
gratitude; 1 Cor. 10:26
5 for it is sanctified by means
of the word of God and prayer.
6 In pointing out these things
to the brethren, you will be a good
servant of Christ Jesus, *constantly* nourished on the words of
the faith and of the sound doctrine
which you have been following.
7 But have nothing to do with
[r]worldly fables fit only for old
women. On the other hand, discipline yourself for the purpose of
godliness; 1 Tim. 1:9
8 for bodily discipline is only
of little profit, but godliness is
profitable for all things, since it
holds promise for the present life
and *also* for the *life* to come.
9 It is a trustworthy statement
deserving full acceptance.
10 For it is for this we labor and
strive, because we have fixed [r]our
hope on [r]the living God, who is the
Savior of all men, especially of believers. 2 Cor. 1:10 • 1 Tim. 3:15
11 [r]Prescribe and teach these
things. 1 Tim. 5:7; 6:2

12 Let no one look down on
your youthfulness, but *rather* in
speech, conduct, love, faith *and*
purity, show yourself an example
[a]of those who believe. *to*
13 Until I come, give attention
to the *public* reading *of Scripture,*
to exhortation and teaching.
14 Do not neglect the spiritual
gift within you, which was bestowed upon you through pro-
phetic utterance with the laying
on of hands by the presbytery.
15 Take pains with these things;
be *absorbed* in them, so that your
progress may be evident to all.
16 Pay close attention to yourself and to your teaching; perse-
vere in these things; for as you do
this you will [r]insure salvation both
for yourself and for those who
hear you. 1 Cor. 1:21

CHAPTER 5

DO not sharply rebuke an [r]older
man, *but rather* appeal to him as a
father, *to* [r]the younger men as
brothers, Titus 2:2 · Titus 2:6
2 the older women as mothers,
and the younger women as sisters, in all purity.
3 Honor widows who are [r]wid-
ows indeed; Acts 6:1; 9:39, 41
4 but if any widow has children or grandchildren, [r]let them
first learn to practice piety in regard to their own family, and to
make some return to their parents; for this is acceptable in the
sight of God. Eph. 6:2
5 Now she who is a [r]widow indeed, and who has been left alone
has fixed her hope on God, and
continues in entreaties and
prayers night and day. Acts 6:1
6 But she who [r]gives herself to
wanton pleasure is dead even
while she lives. James 5:5
7 [a]Prescribe these things as
well, so that they may be above
reproach. *Keep commanding*
8 But if anyone does not provide for his own, and especially
for those of his household, he has
[r]denied the faith, and is worse than
an unbeliever. 2 Tim. 2:12
9 Let a widow be [r]put on the
list only if she is not less than
sixty years old, *having been* the
wife of one man, 1 Tim. 5:16
10 having a reputation for good
works; *and* if she has brought up
children, if she has shown hospitality to strangers, if she has
washed the [a]saints' feet, if she has
assisted those in distress, *and* if
she has devoted herself to every
good work. *holy ones*
11 But refuse *to put* younger
widows *on the list*, for when they
feel sensual desires in disregard of
Christ, they want to get married,
12 *thus* incurring condemnation, because they have set aside
their previous [l]pledge. *faith*
13 And at the same time they
also learn *to be* idle, as they go
around from house to house; and
not merely idle, but also gossips
and busybodies, talking about
things not proper *to mention.*
14 Therefore, I want younger
widows to get married, bear children, keep house, *and* give the
enemy no occasion for reproach;
15 for some have already turned
aside to follow Satan.
16 If any woman who is a believer [r]has *dependent* widows, let
her [r]assist them, and let not the

church be burdened, so that it
may assist those who are widows
indeed. 1 Tim. 5:4 • 1 Tim. 5:10
17 Let the elders who rule well
be considered worthy of double
honor, especially those who work
hard at preaching and teaching.
18 For the Scripture says, "YOU
SHALL NOT MUZZLE THE OX WHILE
HE IS THRESHING," and "The laborer is worthy of his wages."
19 Do not receive an accusation
against an elder except on the basis of two or three witnesses.
20 Those who continue in sin,
[r]rebuke in the presence of all, [r]so
that the rest also may be fearful *of*
sinning. Gal. 2:14 • 2 Cor. 7:11
21 [r]I solemnly charge you in the
presence of God and of Christ
Jesus and of *His* chosen angels, to
maintain these *principles* without
bias, doing nothing in a *spirit of*
partiality. Luke 9:26; 1 Tim. 6:13
22 Do not lay hands upon anyone *too* hastily and thus share *re-*
sponsibility for the sins of others;
keep yourself [t]free from sin. *pure*
23 No longer drink water *exclu-*
sively, but [r]use a little wine for the
sake of your stomach and your
frequent ailments. 1 Tim. 3:8
24 The sins of some men are
quite evident, going before them
to judgment; for others, their *sins*
[r]follow after. Rev. 14:13
25 Likewise also, deeds that are
good are quite evident, and [r]those
which are otherwise cannot be
concealed. Prov. 10:9

CHAPTER 6

LET all who are under the yoke
as slaves regard their own masters as worthy of all honor so that
the name of God and *our* doctrine
may not be spoken against.
2 And let those who have believers as their masters not be dis-
respectful to them because they
are brethren, but let them serve
them all the more, because those
who partake of the benefit are believers and beloved. Teach and
preach these *principles.*
3 If anyone advocates a different doctrine, and does not agree
with sound words, those of our
Lord Jesus Christ, and with the
doctrine conforming to godliness,
4 he is conceited *and* understands nothing; but he has a mor-
bid interest in controversial questions and disputes about words,
out of which arise envy, strife,
abusive language, evil suspicions,
5 and constant friction between [r]men of depraved mind and
deprived of the truth, who suppose that [a]godliness is a means of
gain. 2 Tim. 3:8 • *religion*
6 But godliness *actually* is a
means of great gain, when accompanied by contentment.
7 For we have brought nothing
into the world, [2]so we cannot take
anything out of it either.
8 And if we [r]have food and covering, with these we shall be content. Prov. 30:8
9 But those who want to get
rich fall into temptation and a
snare and many foolish and harmful desires which plunge men into
ruin and destruction.
10 For the love of money is a
root of all sorts of evil, and some
by longing for it have wandered

[2]Later mss. read *it is clear that*

away from the faith, and pierced
themselves with many a pang.
11 But flee from these things,
you man of God; and pursue righteousness, godliness, faith, love,
perseverance *and* gentleness.
12 Fight the good fight of faith;
take hold of the eternal life to
which you were called, and you
made the good confession in the
presence of many witnesses.
13 I charge you in the presence
of God, who gives life to all
things, and of [r]Christ Jesus, who
testified the good confession before Pontius Pilate, Gal. 3:26
14 that you keep the commandment without stain or reproach
until the [r]appearing of our Lord
Jesus Christ, 2 Thess. 2:8
15 which He will bring about at
the proper time—He who is the
blessed and only Sovereign, the
King of kings and Lord of lords;
16 who alone possesses immortality and dwells in unapproach-
able light; whom no man has seen
or can see. To Him *be* honor and
eternal dominion! Amen.
17 Instruct those who are rich
in [r]this present world not to be
conceited or to fix their hope on
the uncertainty of riches, but on
God, who richly supplies us with
all things to enjoy. Matt. 12:32
18 *Instruct them* to do good, to
be rich in good [a]works, to be generous and ready to share, *deeds*
19 storing up for themselves the
treasure of a good foundation for
the future, so that they may take
hold of that which is life indeed.
20 O Timothy, guard what has
been entrusted to you, avoiding
worldly *and* empty chatter *and*
the opposing arguments of what is
falsely called "knowledge"—
21 which some have professed
and thus gone astray [t]from the
faith. *concerning*
Grace be with you.

THE SECOND EPISTLE OF PAUL TO

TIMOTHY

PAUL, an apostle of Christ Jesus
by the will of God, according to
the promise of life in Christ Jesus,
2 to [r]Timothy, my beloved [t]son:
Grace, mercy *and* peace from God
the Father and Christ Jesus our
Lord. Acts 16:1 • *child*
3 I thank God, whom I serve
with a clear conscience the way
my forefathers did, as I constantly
remember you in my [a]prayers
night and day, *petitions*
4 longing to see you, [r]even as I
recall your tears, so that I may be
filled with joy. Acts 20:37
5 For I am mindful of the sincere faith within you, which first
dwelt in your grandmother Lois,
and your mother Eunice, and I am
sure that *it is* in you as well.
6 And for this reason I remind
you to kindle afresh the gift of
God which is in you through the
laying on of my hands.

7 For God has not given us a
[r]spirit of timidity, but of power and
love and discipline. John 14:27
8 Therefore do not be ashamed
of the testimony of our Lord, or of
me His prisoner; but join with *me*
in suffering for the gospel according to the power of God,
9 who has [r]saved us, and called
us with a holy calling, not according to our works, but according to
His own purpose and grace which
was granted us in Christ Jesus
from all eternity, Rom. 11:14
10 but [r]now has been revealed
by the [r]appearing of our Savior
Christ Jesus, who abolished
death, and brought life and immortality to light through the gospel, Rom. 16:26 • 2 Thess. 2:8
11 [r]for which I was appointed a
preacher and an apostle and a
teacher. 1 Tim. 2:7
12 For this reason I also suffer
these things, but I am not
ashamed; for I know whom I have
believed and I am convinced that
He is able to guard what I have
entrusted to Him until that day.
13 [a]Retain the standard of sound
words which you have heard from
me, in the faith and love which are
in Christ Jesus. *Hold the example*
14 Guard, through the Holy
Spirit who [r]dwells in us, the [t]trea-
sure which has been entrusted to
you. Rom. 8:9 • *good deposit*
15 You are aware of the fact
that all who are in Asia turned
away from me, among whom are
Phygelus and Hermogenes.
16 The Lord grant mercy to the
house of Onesiphorus for he often
refreshed me, and was not
ashamed of my [t]chains; *chain*
17 but when he was in Rome, he
eagerly searched for me, and
found me—
18 the Lord grant to him to find
mercy from the Lord on [r]that
day—and you know very well
what services he rendered at [r]Eph-
esus. 1 Cor. 1:8 • Acts 18:19

CHAPTER 2

YOU therefore, my son, be strong
in the grace that is in Christ Jesus.
2 And the things which you
have heard from me in the presence of many witnesses, these entrust to faithful men, who will be
able to teach others also.
3 Suffer hardship with *me*, as a
good soldier of Christ Jesus.
4 No soldier in active service
[r]entangles himself in the affairs of
everyday life, so that he may
please the one who enlisted him
as a soldier. 2 Pet. 2:20
5 And also if anyone competes
as an athlete, he [t]does not win the
prize unless he competes according to the rules. *is not crowned*
6 [r]The hard-working farmer
ought to be the first to receive his
share of the crops. 1 Cor. 9:10
7 Consider what I say, for the
Lord will give you understanding
in everything.
8 Remember Jesus Christ, ris-
en from the dead, descendant of
David, according to my gospel,
9 [t]for which I [r]suffer hardship
even to imprisonment as a criminal; but the word of God is not imprisoned. *in which* • 2 Tim. 1:8
10 For this reason [r]I endure all
things for [r]the sake of those who
are chosen, that they also may obtain the salvation which is in

Christ Jesus *and* with *it* eternal
glory. Col. 1:24 • Luke 18:7
11 It is a trustworthy statement:
For if we died with Him, we
shall also live with Him;
12 If we endure, we shall also
reign with Him;
If we [t]deny Him, He also
will deny us; *shall deny*
13 If we are faithless, He remains faithful; for He
cannot deny Himself.
14 Remind *them* of these things,
and solemnly [r]charge *them* in the
presence of God not to [r]wrangle
about words, which is useless,
and leads to the ruin of the hearers. 1 Tim. 5:21 • 1 Tim. 6:4
15 Be diligent to [r]present yourself approved to God as a workman who does not need to be
ashamed, handling accurately the
word of truth. Rom. 6:13
16 But [r]avoid worldly *and* empty
chatter, for it will lead to further
ungodliness, Titus 3:9
17 and their [t]talk will spread like
[1]gangrene. Among them are Hymenaeus and Philetus, *word*
18 *men* who have gone astray
from the truth saying that [r]the resurrection has already taken place,
and thus they upset [r]the faith of
some. 1 Cor. 15:12 • 1 Tim. 1:19
19 Nevertheless, the firm foundation of God stands, having this
seal, "The Lord knows those who
are His," and, "Let everyone who
names the name of the Lord abstain from wickedness."
20 Now in a large house there
are not only gold and silver vessels, but also vessels of wood and
of earthenware, and some to hon-
or and some to dishonor.

[1]Or, *cancer*

21 Therefore, if a man cleanses
himself from [r]these *things*, he will
be a vessel for honor, sanctified,
useful to the Master, prepared for
every good work. 1 Tim. 6:11
22 Now flee from youthful lusts,
and pursue righteousness, faith,
love *and* peace, with those who
call on the Lord from a pure heart.
23 But refuse foolish and ignorant speculations, knowing that
they produce [t]quarrels. *fightings*
24 And [r]the Lord's bond-servant
must not be quarrelsome, but be
kind to all, able to teach, patient
when wronged, 1 Tim. 3:3
25 with gentleness correcting
those who are in opposition, [r]if
perhaps God may grant them repentance leading to the knowledge of the truth, Acts 8:22
26 and they may come to their
senses *and escape* from the snare
of the devil, having been held captive by him to do his will.

CHAPTER 3

BUT realize this, that in the last
days difficult times will come.
2 For men will be lovers of
self, lovers of money, boastful, arrogant, revilers, disobedient to
parents, ungrateful, unholy,
3 unloving, irreconcilable, malicious gossips, without self-control, brutal, haters of good,
4 treacherous, [r]reckless, conceited, lovers of pleasure rather
than lovers of God; Acts 19:36
5 holding to a form of [a]godli-
ness, although they have [r]denied
its power; and avoid such men as
these. *religion* • 1 Tim. 5:8
6 For among them are those
who [a]enter into households and

captivate weak women weighed down with sins, led on by various impulses, *creep into*

7 always learning and never able to come to the[a]knowledge of the truth. *recognition*

8 And just as [r]Jannes and Jambres opposed Moses, so these *men* also oppose the truth, men of depraved mind, rejected as regards the faith. Ex. 7:11

9 But they will not make further progress; for their folly will be obvious to all, [r]as also that of those *two* came to be. Ex. 7:11

10 But you followed my teaching, conduct, purpose, faith, patience, love, perseverance,

11 persecutions, *and* [r]sufferings, such as happened to me at Antioch, at Iconium *and* at Lystra; what persecutions I endured, and out of them all [r]the Lord delivered me! 2 Cor. 1:5, 7 • Rom. 15:31

12 And indeed, all who desire to live godly in Christ Jesus [r]will be persecuted. John 15:20

13 But evil men and impostors will proceed *from bad* to worse, deceiving and being deceived.

14 You, however, [r]continue in the things you have learned and become convinced of, knowing from whom you have learned *them*; 2 Tim. 1:13; Titus 1:9

15 and that [r]from childhood you have known [r]the sacred writings which are able to give you the wisdom that leads to salvation through faith which is in Christ Jesus. 2 Tim. 1:5 • John 5:47

16 [2]All Scripture is inspired by God and profitable for teaching, for reproof, for correction, for training in righteousness;

17 that [r]the man of God may be adequate, equipped for every good work. 1 Tim. 6:11

CHAPTER 4

I SOLEMNLY charge *you* in the presence of God and of Christ Jesus, who is to judge the living and the dead, and by His appearing and His kingdom:

2 preach the word; be ready in season *and* out of season; reprove, rebuke, exhort, with [t]great patience and instruction. *all*

3 For the time will come when they will not endure sound doctrine; but *wanting* to have their ears tickled, they will accumulate for themselves teachers in accordance to their own desires;

4 and [r]will turn away their ears from the truth, and will turn aside to myths. 2 Thess. 2:11

5 But you, [r]be sober in all things, endure hardship, do the work of an [r]evangelist, fulfill your ministry. 1 Pet. 1:13 • Acts 21:8

6 For I am already being [r]poured out as a drink offering, and the time of [r]my departure has come. Phil. 2:17 • Phil. 1:23

7 I have fought the good fight, I have finished [r]the course, I have kept the faith; Acts 20:24

8 in the future there [r]is laid up for me the crown of righteousness, which the Lord, the righteous Judge, will award to me on that day; and not only to me, but also to all who have loved His appearing. Col. 1:5; 1 Pet. 1:4

9 [r]Make every effort to come to me soon; 2 Tim. 1:4; 4:21

[2]Or possibly, *Every Scripture inspired by God is also profitable*

10 for[r]Demas, having loved this
present [a]world, has deserted me
and gone to Thessalonica; Cres-
cens *has gone* to Galatia, Titus to
Dalmatia. Col. 4:14 • *age*
11 Only Luke is with me. Pick
up Mark and bring him with you,
for he is useful to me for service.
12 But[r]Tychicus I have sent to
[r]Ephesus. Acts 20:4 • Acts 18:19
13 When you come bring the
cloak which I left at[r]Troas with
Carpus, and the books, especially
the parchments. Acts 16:8
14 Alexander the coppersmith
did me much harm; the Lord will
repay him according to his deeds.
15 Be on guard against him
yourself, for he vigorously opposed our[t]teaching. *words*
16 At my first defense no one
supported me, but all deserted
me;[r]may it not be counted against
them. Acts 7:60; 1 Cor. 13:5
17 But the Lord stood with me,
and strengthened me, in order
that through me the proclamation
might[a]be fully accomplished, and
that all the Gentiles might hear;
and I was delivered out of the
lion's mouth. *be fulfilled*
18 The Lord will deliver me
from every evil deed, and will
bring me safely to His heavenly
kingdom; to[t]Him *be* the glory forever and ever. Amen. *Whom*
19 Greet Prisca and Aquila, and
the household of Onesiphorus.
20 Erastus remained at[r]Corinth,
but[r]Trophimus I left sick at Miletus. Acts 18:1 • Acts 20:4; 21:29
21 Make every effort to come
before winter. Eubulus greets you,
also Pudens and Linus and Clau-
dia and all the brethren.
22 The Lord be with your spirit.
[r]Grace be with you. Col. 4:18

THE EPISTLE OF PAUL TO

TITUS

PAUL, a bond-servant of God,
and an apostle of Jesus Christ, for
the faith of those chosen of God
and the knowledge of the truth
which is according to godliness,
2 in[r]the hope of eternal life,
which God, who cannot lie, promised long ages ago, 2 Tim. 1:1
3 but at the proper time manifested, *even* His word, in the proclamation with which I was entrusted according to the
commandment of God our Savior;
4 to Titus, my true child[t]in a
common faith: Grace and peace
from God the Father and Christ
Jesus our Savior. *according to*
5 For this reason I left you in
Crete, that you might set in order
what remains, and appoint elders
in every city as I directed you,
6 namely,[r]if any man be above
reproach, the [r]husband of one
wife, having children who believe,
not accused of dissipation or rebellion. Titus 1:6-8 • 1 Tim. 3:2

7 For the [a]overseer must be above reproach as [r]God's steward, not self-willed, not quick-tempered, not addicted to wine, not pugnacious, not fond of sordid gain, *bishop* • 1 Cor. 4:1

8 but [r]hospitable, loving what is good, sensible, just, devout, self-controlled, 1 Tim. 3:2

9 holding fast the faithful word which is in accordance with the teaching, that he may be able both to exhort in sound doctrine and to refute those who contradict.

10 For there are many [r]rebellious men, empty talkers and deceivers, especially [r]those of the circumcision, Titus 1:6 • Acts 11:2

11 who must be silenced because they are upsetting [r]whole families, teaching things they should not *teach*, for the sake of sordid gain. 1 Tim. 5:4

12 One of themselves, a prophet of their own, said, "Cretans [r]are always liars, evil beasts, lazy gluttons." Acts 2:11; 27:7

13 This testimony is true. For this cause [r]reprove them severely that they may be [r]sound in the faith, 1 Tim. 5:20 • Titus 2:2

14 not paying attention to Jewish [r]myths and [r]commandments of men who turn away from the truth. 1 Tim. 1:4 • Col. 2:22

15 To the pure, all things are pure; but to those who are defiled and unbelieving, nothing is pure, but both their [r]mind and their conscience are defiled. 1 Tim. 6:5

16 They profess to know God, but by *their* deeds they deny *Him*, being detestable and disobedient, and worthless for any good deed.

CHAPTER 2

BUT as for you, speak the things which are fitting for [r]sound doctrine. Titus 1:9

2 Older men are to be temperate, dignified, sensible, sound in faith, in love, in perseverance.

3 Older women likewise are to be reverent in their behavior, [r]not malicious gossips, nor [r]enslaved to much wine, teaching what is good, 1 Tim. 3:11 • 1 Tim. 3:8

4 that they may encourage the young women to love their husbands, to love their children,

5 *to be* sensible, pure, workers at home, kind, being subject to their own husbands, that the word of God may not be dishonored.

6 Likewise urge [r]the young men to be sensible; 1 Tim. 5:1

7 in all things show yourself to be an example of good deeds, *with* purity in doctrine, dignified,

8 sound *in* speech which is beyond reproach, in order [r]that the opponent may be put to shame, having nothing bad to say about us. 2 Thess. 3:14; 1 Pet. 2:12

9 Urge bondslaves to be subject to their own masters in everything, to be well-pleasing, not [t]argumentative, *contradicting*

10 not pilfering, but showing all good faith that they may adorn the doctrine of [r]God our Savior in every respect. Titus 1:3

11 For the grace of God has appeared, [a]bringing salvation to all men, *to all men, bringing*

12 instructing us to deny ungodliness and worldly desires and to live sensibly, righteously and godly in the present age,

13 looking for the blessed hope and the appearing of the glory of [a]our great God and Savior, Christ Jesus; *the great God and our Savior*

14 who gave Himself for us, that He might redeem us from every lawless deed and purify for Himself a people for His own possession, zealous for good deeds.

15 These things speak and exhort and reprove with all authority. Let no one disregard you.

CHAPTER 3

REMIND them [r]to be subject to rulers, to authorities, to be obedient, to be [r]ready for every good deed, Rom. 13:1 • 2 Tim. 2:21

2 to malign no one, to be uncontentious, gentle, showing every consideration for all men.

3 For we also once were foolish ourselves, [r]disobedient, deceived, enslaved to various lusts and pleasures, spending our life in malice and envy, hateful, hating one another. Titus 1:16

4 But when the [r]kindness of God our Savior and *His* love for mankind appeared, Rom. 2:4

5 He saved us, not on the basis of deeds which we have done in righteousness, but [r]according to His mercy, by the washing of regeneration and renewing by the Holy Spirit, Eph. 2:4; 1 Pet. 1:3

6 [r]whom He poured out upon us [r]richly through Jesus Christ our Savior, Rom. 5:5 • Rom. 2:4

7 that being justified by His grace we might be made heirs according to *the* hope of eternal life.

8 This is a trustworthy statement; and concerning these things I want you to speak confidently, so that those who have believed God may be careful to engage in good deeds. These things are good and profitable for men.

9 But [r]shun [r]foolish controversies and genealogies and strife and disputes about the Law; for they are unprofitable and worthless. 2 Tim. 2:16 • 1 Tim. 1:4

10 Reject a factious man after a first and second warning,

11 knowing that such a man is [r]perverted and is sinning, being self-condemned. Titus 1:14

12 When I send Artemas or [r]Tychicus to you, make every effort to come to me at Nicopolis, for I have decided to spend the winter there. Acts 20:4

13 Diligently help Zenas the [r]lawyer and [r]Apollos on their way so that nothing is lacking for them. Matt. 22:35 • Acts 18:24

14 And let our *people* also learn to engage in good [a]deeds to meet pressing needs, that they may not be unfruitful. *occupations*

15 All who are with me greet you. Greet those who love us [r]in *the* faith. 1 Tim. 1:2

Grace be with you all.

THE EPISTLE OF PAUL TO

PHILEMON

PAUL, [r]a prisoner of Christ Jesus,
and Timothy [t]our brother, to Phile-
mon our beloved *brother* and fellow worker, Eph. 3:1 • *the*
2 and to Apphia our sister, and
to Archippus our fellow soldier,
and to the church in your house:
3 [r]Grace to you and peace from
God our Father and the Lord
Jesus Christ. Rom. 1:7
4 [r]I thank my God always,
making mention of you in my
prayers, Rom. 1:8f.
5 because I hear of your love,
and of the faith which you have
toward the Lord Jesus, and
toward all the [a]saints; *holy ones*
6 *and I pray* that the fellowship of your faith may become effective [1]through the knowledge of
every good thing which is in [2]you
[t]for Christ's sake. *toward Christ*
7 For I have come to have
much joy and comfort in your
love, because the hearts of the
[a]saints have been refreshed
through you, brother. *holy ones*
8 Therefore, though I have
enough confidence in Christ to order you *to do* that which is proper,
9 yet for love's sake I rather
appeal *to you*—since I am such a
person as Paul, the aged, and now
also a prisoner of Christ Jesus—
10 I appeal to you for my child,
whom I have begotten in my [t]im-
prisonment, [3]Onesimus, *bonds*
11 who formerly was useless to
you, but now is useful both to you
and to me.
12 And I have sent him back to
you in person, that is, *sending* my
very heart,
13 whom I wished to keep with
me, that in your behalf he might
minister to me in my [t]imprison-
ment for the gospel; *bonds*
14 but without your consent I
did not want to do anything, that
your goodness should [r]not be as it
were by compulsion, but of your
own free will. 2 Cor. 9:7
15 For perhaps [r]he was for this
reason parted *from you* for a
while, that you should have him
back forever, Gen. 45:5, 8
16 no longer as a slave, but
more than a slave, a beloved
brother, especially to me, but how
much more to you, both [r]in the
flesh and in the Lord. Eph. 6:5
17 If then you regard me a partner, accept him as *you would* me.
18 But if he has wronged you in
any way, or owes you anything,
charge that to my account;
19 I, Paul, am writing this with
my own hand, I will repay it [r](lest I
should [t]mention to you that you
owe to me even your own self as
well). 2 Cor. 9:4 • *say*
20 Yes, brother, let me benefit
from you in the Lord; [r]refresh my
heart in Christ. Philem. 7
21 [r]Having confidence in your
obedience, I write to you, since I
know that you will do even more
than what I say. 2 Cor. 2:3
22 And at the same time also

[1]Or, *in* [2]Some ancient mss. read *us*
[3]I.e., useful

prepare me a lodging; for I hope
that through your prayers I shall
be given to you. Acts 28:23
23 Epaphras, my fellow prisoner in Christ Jesus, greets you,

24 *as do* Mark, Aristarchus, De-
mas, Luke, my fellow workers.
25 The grace of the Lord Jesus
Christ be with your spirit.[4]

[4] Some ancient mss. add *Amen*

THE EPISTLE TO THE HEBREWS

GOD, after He spoke long ago to
the fathers in the prophets in
many portions and in many ways,
2 in these last days has spoken
to us in *His* Son, whom He appointed heir of all things, through
whom also He made the world.
3 And He is the radiance of His
glory and the exact representation
of His nature, and upholds all
things by the word of His power.
When He had made purification of
sins, He sat down at the right
hand of the Majesty on high;
4 having become as much better than the angels, as He has inherited a more excellent name
than they. Eph. 1:21; Phil. 2:9
5 For to which of the angels
did He ever say,

"THOU ART MY SON,
TODAY I HAVE BEGOTTEN
THEE"? Ps. 2:7

And again,

"I WILL BE A FATHER TO HIM,
AND HE SHALL BE A SON TO
ME"? 2 Sam. 7:14

6 And when He again brings
the first-born into the world, He
says, *the inhabited earth*

"AND LET ALL THE ANGELS OF
GOD WORSHIP HIM."

7 And of the angels He says,

"WHO MAKES HIS ANGELS
WINDS, Ps. 104:4
AND HIS MINISTERS A FLAME
OF FIRE."

8 But of the Son *He says,*

"THY THRONE, O GOD, IS FOR-
EVER AND EVER, Ps. 45:6
AND THE RIGHTEOUS SCEP-
TER IS THE SCEPTER OF
[1]HIS KINGDOM.
9 "THOU HAST LOVED RIGHT-
EOUSNESS AND HATED
LAWLESSNESS; Ps. 45:7
THEREFORE GOD, THY GOD,
HATH ANOINTED THEE
WITH THE OIL OF GLADNESS
ABOVE THY COMPANIONS."

10 And,

"THOU, LORD, IN THE BEGIN-
NING DIDST LAY THE
FOUNDATION OF THE
EARTH, Ps. 102:25
AND THE HEAVENS ARE THE
WORKS OF THY HANDS;
11 THEY WILL PERISH, BUT
THOU REMAINEST;
AND THEY ALL WILL BECOME
OLD AS A GARMENT,
12 AND AS A MANTLE THOU
WILT ROLL THEM UP;

[1] Some mss. read *Thy*

AS A GARMENT THEY WILL
ALSO BE CHANGED.
BUT THOU ART THE SAME,
AND THY YEARS WILL NOT
COME TO AN END."
13 But to which of the angels
has He ever said,
"SIT[r] AT MY RIGHT HAND,
[r]UNTIL I MAKE THINE EN-
EMIES Ps. 110:1 • Josh. 10:24
A FOOTSTOOL FOR THY
FEET"?
14 Are they not all [r]ministering
spirits, sent out to render service
for the sake of those who will in-
herit salvation? Ps. 103:20f.

CHAPTER 2

FOR this reason we must pay
much closer attention to what we
have heard, lest [r]we drift away
from it. Prov. 3:21
2 For if the word [r]spoken
through angels proved [a]unalter-
able, and every transgression and
disobedience received a just recompense, Heb. 1:1 • *steadfast*
3 how shall we escape if we
neglect so great a salvation? [t]After
it was at the first spoken through
the Lord, it was confirmed to us
by those who heard, *Which was*
4 God also bearing witness
with them, both by signs and wonders and by various miracles and
by [t]gifts of the Holy Spirit according to His own will. *distributions*
5 For He did not subject to angels the world to come, concerning which we are speaking.
6 But one has testified [r]some-
where, saying,
"WHAT[r] IS MAN, THAT THOU
REMEMBEREST HIM?
OR THE SON OF MAN, THAT
THOU ART CONCERNED
ABOUT HIM? Heb. 4:4 • Ps. 8:4
7 "THOU[r] HAST MADE HIM[a] FOR A
LITTLE WHILE LOWER
THAN THE ANGELS; Ps. 8:5, 6
THOU HAST CROWNED HIM
WITH GLORY AND HONOR,
[2]AND HAST APPOINTED HIM
OVER THE WORKS OF THY
HANDS; *a little lower*
8 [r]THOU HAST PUT ALL THINGS
IN SUBJECTION UNDER HIS
FEET." Ps. 8:6
For in subjecting all things to him,
He left nothing that is not subject
to him. But now we do not yet see
all things subjected to him.
9 But we do see Him who has
been made for a little while lower
than the angels, *namely,* Jesus,
because of the suffering of death
crowned with glory and honor,
that by the grace of God He might
taste death for everyone.
10 For it was fitting for Him, for
whom are all things, and through
whom are all things, in bringing
many sons to glory, to [r]perfect the
[a]author of their salvation through
sufferings. Heb. 5:9 • *leader*
11 For both He who sanctifies
and those who are [a]sanctified are
all from one *Father;* for which reason He is not ashamed to call
them brethren, *being sanctified*
12 saying,
"I[r] WILL PROCLAIM THY NAME
TO MY BRETHREN, Ps. 22:22
IN THE MIDST OF THE [t]CON-
GREGATION I WILL SING
THY PRAISE." *church*
13 And again,
"I[r] WILL PUT MY TRUST IN
HIM." Is. 8:17

[2] Some ancient mss. do not contain *And . . . hands*

And again,
"BEHOLD,ʳ I AND THE CHIL-
DREN WHOM GOD HAS GIV-
EN ME." Is. 8:18
14 Since then the children share
in flesh and blood, He Himself
likewise also partook of the same,
that through death He might render powerless him who had the
power of death, that is, the devil;
15 and might deliver those who
through fear of death were subject to slavery all their lives.
16 For assuredly He does not
give help to angels, but He gives
help to the ˡdescendant of Abraham. *seed*
17 Therefore, He ˡhad to be
made like His brethren in all
things, that He might become a
merciful and faithful high priest in
things pertaining to God, to make
propitiation for the sins of the
people. *was obligated to be*
18 For since He Himself was
tempted in that which He has suffered, He is able to come to the
aid of those who are tempted.

CHAPTER 3

THEREFORE, holy brethren,
partakers of a heavenly calling,
consider Jesus, the Apostle and
High Priest of our confession.
2 ˡHe was faithful to Him who
appointed Him, as Moses also was
in all His house. *Being faithful*
3 ʳFor He has been counted
worthy of more glory than Moses,
by just so much as the builder of
the house has more honor than
the house. 2 Cor. 3:7-11
4 For every house is built by
someone, but the builder of all
things is God.
5 Now Moses was faithful in
all His house as a servant, for a
testimony of those things which
were to be spoken later;
6 but Christ *was faithful* as ʳa
Son over His house whose house
we are, if we hold fast our confidence and the boast of our hope
firm until the end. Heb. 1:2
7 Therefore, just as ʳthe Holy
Spirit says, Acts 28:25; Heb. 9:8
"TODAYʳ IF YOU HEAR HIS
VOICE, Ps. 95:7
8 ʳDO NOT HARDEN YOUR
HEARTS AS WHEN THEY
PROVOKED ME, Ps. 95:8
AS IN THE DAY OF TRIAL IN
THE WILDERNESS,
9 WHERE YOUR FATHERS
TRIED *Me* BY TESTING *Me*,
AND SAW MY WORKS FOR
ʳFORTY YEARS. Acts 7:36
10 "THEREFOREʳ I WAS ANGRY
WITH THIS GENERATION,
AND SAID, 'THEY ALWAYS
GO ASTRAY IN THEIR
HEART; Ps. 95:10
AND THEY DID NOT KNOW
MY WAYS';
11 ʳAS I SWORE IN MY WRATH,
'THEY SHALL NOT ENTER MY
REST.'" Ps. 95:11
12 Take care, brethren, lest
there should be in any one of you
an evil, unbelieving heart, in falling away from the living God.
13 But ʳencourage one another
day after day, as long as it is *still*
called "Today," lest any one of
you be hardened by the deceitfulness of sin. Heb. 10:24f.
14 For we have become partakers of Christ, ʳif we hold fast the
beginning of our assurance firm
until the end; Heb. 3:6

15 while it is said,
"TODAY[r] IF YOU HEAR HIS VOICE, Ps. 95:7f.
DO NOT HARDEN YOUR HEARTS, AS WHEN THEY PROVOKED ME."
16 For who[r] provoked *Him* when
they had heard? Indeed,[r] did not all
those who came out of Egypt *led*
by Moses? Jer. 32:29 • Num. 14:2
17 And with whom was He angry for forty years? Was it not
with those who sinned, whose
bodies fell in the wilderness?
18 And to whom did He swear
[r]that they should not enter His
rest, but to those who were disobedient? Num. 14:23
19 And *so* we see that they were
not able to enter because of [r]unbe-
lief. John 3:18, 36; Rom. 11:23

CHAPTER 4

THEREFORE, let us fear lest,
while a promise remains of entering His rest, any one of you should
seem to have come short of it.
2 For indeed we have had good
news preached to us, just as they
also; but[r] the word[t] they heard did
not profit them, because it was
not united by faith in those who
heard. Rom. 10:17 • *of hearing*
3 [3]For we who have believed
enter that rest, just as He has said,
"AS[r] I SWORE IN MY WRATH,
THEY SHALL NOT ENTER MY REST," Ps. 95:11
although His works were finished
from the foundation of the world.
4 For He has thus said[r] somewhere concerning the seventh
day, "AND[r] GOD RESTED ON THE
SEVENTH DAY FROM ALL HIS WORKS"; Heb. 2:6 • Gen. 2:2
5 and again in this *passage*,
"THEY[r] SHALL NOT ENTER MY REST." Ps. 95:11; Heb. 3:11
6 Since therefore it remains for
some to enter it, and those who
formerly had good news preached
to them failed to enter because of
[r]disobedience, Heb. 3:18; 4:11
7 He again fixes a certain day,
"Today," saying [a]through David
after so long a time just [r]as has
been said before, *in* • Heb. 3:7f.
"TODAY[r] IF YOU HEAR HIS VOICE, Ps. 95:7f.
DO NOT HARDEN YOUR HEARTS."
8 For if Joshua had given them
rest, He would not have spoken of
another day after that.
9 There remains therefore a
Sabbath rest for the people of
God.
10 For the one who has entered
His rest has himself also [r]rested
from his works, as[r] God did from
His. Rev. 14:13 • Gen. 2:2
11 Let us therefore be diligent
to enter that rest, lest anyone fall
through *following* the same[r] example of disobedience. 2 Pet. 2:6
12 For the word of God is living
and active and sharper than any
two-edged sword, and piercing as
far as the division of soul and
spirit, of both joints and marrow,
and able to judge the thoughts
and intentions of the heart.
13 And there is no creature hidden from His sight, but all things
are open and laid bare to the eyes
of Him with whom we have to do.
14 Since then we have a great
[r]high priest who has passed
through the heavens, Jesus the

[3] Some ancient mss. read *Therefore*

Son of God, let us hold fast our confession. Heb. 2:17

15 For we do not have a high priest who cannot sympathize with our weaknesses, but one who has been tempted in all things as *we are, yet* without sin.

16 Let us therefore [r]draw near with [r]confidence to the throne of grace, that we may receive mercy and may find grace to help in time of need. Heb. 7:19 • Heb. 3:6

CHAPTER 5

FOR every high priest [r]taken from among men is appointed on behalf of men in things pertaining to God, in order to offer both gifts and sacrifices for sins; Ex. 28:1

2 [t]he can deal gently with the [r]ignorant and misguided, since he himself also is beset with weakness; *being able to* • Eph. 4:18

3 and because of it he is obligated to offer *sacrifices* [r]for sins, [r]as for the people, so also for himself. 1 Cor. 15:3 • Lev. 9:7

4 And [r]no one takes the honor to himself, but *receives it* when he is called by God, even [r]as Aaron was. Num. 16:40 • Ex. 28:1

5 So also Christ [r]did not glorify Himself so as to become a high priest, but He who said to Him,

"THOU ART MY SON,
TODAY I HAVE BEGOTTEN
THEE"; John 8:54

6 just as He says also in another *passage*,

"THOU ART A PRIEST FOREVER
ACCORDING TO THE ORDER
OF MELCHIZEDEK."

7 In the days of His flesh, He offered up both prayers and supplications with loud crying and tears to the One [r]able to save Him from death, and He was heard because of His piety. Mark 14:36

8 Although He was [r]a Son, He learned obedience from the things which He suffered. Heb. 1:2

9 And having been made [r]perfect, He became to all those who obey Him the source of eternal salvation, Heb. 2:10

10 being designated by God as [r]a high priest according to the order of Melchizedek. Heb. 2:17; 5:5

11 Concerning [4]him we have much to say, and *it is* hard to explain, since you have become dull of hearing.

12 For though [t]by this time you ought to be teachers, you have need again for someone to teach you the elementary principles of the oracles of God, and you have come to need milk and not solid food. *because of the time*

13 For everyone who partakes *only* of milk is not accustomed to the word of righteousness, for he is a [r]babe. 1 Cor. 3:1; 14:20

14 But solid food is for [r]the mature, who because of practice have their senses trained to discern good and evil. 1 Cor. 2:6

CHAPTER 6

THEREFORE leaving the elementary teaching about the Christ, let us press on to [a]maturity, not laying again a foundation of repentance from dead works and of faith toward God, *perfection*

2 of [r]instruction about washings, and laying on of hands, and the resurrection of the dead, and eternal judgment. John 3:25

[4] Or, *Him;* or, *this*

3 And this we shall do,[r]if God
permits. Acts 18:21
4 For in the case of those who
have once been [r]enlightened and
have tasted of the heavenly gift
and have been made partakers of
the Holy Spirit, 2 Cor. 4:4, 6
5 and [r]have tasted the good
word of God and the powers of
the age to come, 1 Pet. 2:3
6 and *then* have fallen away, it
is impossible to renew them again
to repentance, since they again
crucify to themselves the Son of
God, and put Him to open shame.
7 For ground that drinks the
rain which often[t]falls upon it and
brings forth vegetation useful to
those [r]for whose sake it is also
tilled, receives a blessing from
God; *comes* • 2 Tim. 2:6
8 but if it yields thorns and
thistles, it is worthless and close
[t]to being cursed, and it ends up
being burned. *to a curse*
9 But, beloved, we are convinced of better things concerning
you, and things that [a]accompany
salvation, though we are speaking
in this way. *belong to*
10 For God is not unjust so as to
forget your work and the love
which you have shown toward His
name, in having ministered and in
still ministering to the saints.
11 And we desire that each one
of you show the same diligence[t]so
as to realize the full assurance of
hope until the end, *to the full*
12 that you may not be sluggish,
but [r]imitators of those who
through faith and patience inherit
the promises. Heb. 13:7
13 For [r]when God made the
promise to Abraham, since He
could swear by no one greater, He
swore by Himself, Gal. 3:15, 18
14 saying, "I[r]WILL SURELY BLESS
YOU, AND I WILL SURELY MULTIPLY
YOU." Gen. 22:17
15 And thus, having patiently
waited, he obtained the promise.
16 For men swear by one
greater *than themselves*, and with
them an oath *given* as confirma-
tion is an end of every dispute.
17 [a]In the same way God, desiring even more to show to the heirs
of the promise the unchangeable-
ness of His purpose, interposed
with an oath, *Therefore God*
18 in order that by two un-
changeable things, in which it is
impossible for God to lie, we may
have strong encouragement, we
who have fled for refuge in laying
hold of the hope set before us.
19 This hope we have as an anchor of the soul, a *hope* both sure
and steadfast and one which enters[a]within the veil, *inside*
20 where Jesus has entered as a
forerunner for us, having become
a high priest forever according to
the order of Melchizedek.

CHAPTER 7

FOR this Melchizedek, king of
Salem, priest of the Most High
God, who met Abraham as he was
returning from the slaughter of
the kings and blessed him,
2 to whom also Abraham apportioned a tenth part of all *the
spoils*, was first of all, by the
translation *of his name*, king of
righteousness, and then also king
of Salem, which is king of peace.
3 Without father, without
mother, [r]without genealogy, hav-

ing neither beginning of days nor
end of life, but made like[r]the Son
of God, he abides a priest perpetually. Heb. 7:6 • Matt. 4:3
4 Now observe how great this
man was to whom Abraham, the
[r]patriarch, gave a tenth of the
choicest spoils. Acts 2:29; 7:8f.
5 And those indeed of the sons
of Levi who receive the priest's office have commandment [t]in the
Law to collect a tenth from the
people, that is, from their brethren, although these are descended
from Abraham. *according to*
6 But the one[r]whose genealogy
is not traced from them collected
[a]a tenth from Abraham, and
blessed the one who had the
promises. Heb. 7:3 • *tithes*
7 But without any dispute the
lesser is blessed by the greater.
8 And in this case mortal men
receive tithes, but in that case one
receives them, of whom it is witnessed that he lives on.
9 And, so to speak, through
Abraham even Levi, who received
tithes, paid tithes,
10 for he was still in the loins of
his father when Melchizedek met
him.
11 Now if perfection was
through the Levitical priesthood
(for on the basis of it[r]the people
received the Law), what further
need *was there* for another priest
to arise[r]according to the order of
Melchizedek, and not be designated according to the order of
Aaron? Heb. 9:6 • Heb. 5:6
12 For when the priesthood is
changed, of necessity there takes
place a change of law also.
13 For the one concerning
whom these things are spoken belongs to another tribe, from which
no one has officiated at the altar.
14 For it is evident that our
Lord[t]was[r]descended from Judah,
a tribe with reference to which
Moses spoke nothing concerning
priests. *rose from* • Num. 24:17
15 And this is clearer still, if another priest arises according to
the likeness of Melchizedek,
16 who has become *such* not on
the basis of a law of physical requirement, but according to the
power of an indestructible life.
17 For it is witnessed *of Him*,
"THOU ART A PRIEST FOREVER
ACCORDING TO THE ORDER
OF MELCHIZEDEK."
18 For, on the one hand, there is
a setting aside of a former commandment[r]because of its weakness and uselessness Rom. 8:3
19 (for[r]the Law made nothing
perfect), and on the other hand
there is a bringing in of a better
hope, through which we draw
near to God. Acts 13:39
20 And inasmuch as *it was* not
without an oath
21 (for they indeed became
priests without an oath, but He
with an oath through the One who
said to Him,
"THE LORD HAS SWORN
AND[r]WILL NOT CHANGE HIS
MIND, Num. 23:19
'THOU ART A PRIEST [r]FOR-
EVER' "); Heb. 7:23f., 28
22 so much the more also Jesus
has become the[r]guarantee of a
better covenant. Ps. 119:122
23 And the *former* priests, on
the one hand, existed in greater
numbers, because they were prevented by death from continuing,
24 but He, on the other hand,

because He abides forever, holds His priesthood permanently.

25 Hence, also, He is able to save[a] forever those who draw near to God through Him, since He always lives to make intercession for them. *completely*

26 For it was fitting that we should have such a [r]high priest, holy, innocent, undefiled, separated from sinners and exalted above the heavens; Heb. 2:17

27 who does not need daily, like those high priests, to offer up sacrifices, first for His own sins, and then for the *sins* of the people, because this He did once for all when He offered up Himself.

28 For the Law appoints men as high priests [r]who are weak, but the word of the oath, which came after the Law, *appoints* a Son, made perfect forever. Heb. 5:2

CHAPTER 8

NOW the main point in what has been said *is this*: we have such a [r]high priest, who has taken His seat at the right hand of the throne of the [r]Majesty in the heavens, Col. 3:1 • Ps. 110:1

2 a minister [a]in the sanctuary, and [a]in the true tabernacle, which the Lord pitched, not man. *of*

3 For every [r]high priest is appointed to offer both gifts and sacrifices; hence it is necessary that this *high priest* also have something to offer. Heb. 2:17

4 Now if He were on earth, He would not be a priest at all, since there are those who [r]offer the gifts according to the Law; Heb. 5:1

5 who serve a copy and shadow of the heavenly things, just as Moses [t]was warned *by God* when he was about to erect the [a]tabernacle; for, "SEE," He says, "THAT YOU MAKE all things ACCORDING TO THE PATTERN WHICH WAS SHOWN YOU ON THE MOUNTAIN." *is* • *sacred tent*

6 But now He has obtained a more excellent ministry, by as much as He is also the mediator of a better covenant, which has been enacted on better promises.

7 For [r]if that first *covenant* had been faultless, there would have been no occasion sought for a second. Heb. 7:11

8 For finding fault with them, He says,

"BEHOLD, DAYS ARE COMING, SAYS THE LORD,
[t]WHEN I WILL EFFECT [r]A NEW COVENANT *And* • Luke 22:20
WITH THE HOUSE OF ISRAEL AND WITH THE HOUSE OF JUDAH;
9 [r]NOT LIKE THE COVENANT WHICH I MADE WITH THEIR FATHERS Ex. 19:5
ON THE DAY WHEN I TOOK THEM BY THE HAND
TO LEAD THEM OUT OF THE LAND OF EGYPT;
FOR THEY DID NOT CONTINUE IN MY COVENANT,
AND I DID NOT CARE FOR THEM, SAYS THE LORD.
10 "FOR [r]THIS IS THE COVENANT THAT I WILL MAKE WITH THE HOUSE OF ISRAEL
AFTER THOSE DAYS, SAYS THE LORD:
I WILL PUT MY LAWS INTO THEIR MINDS,
AND I WILL WRITE THEM [r]UPON THEIR HEARTS.

AND I WILL BE THEIR GOD,
AND THEY SHALL BE MY
PEOPLE. Jer. 31:33 • 2 Cor. 3:3
11 "AND[r] THEY SHALL NOT TEACH
EVERYONE HIS FELLOW
CITIZEN, Jer. 31:34
AND EVERYONE HIS
BROTHER, SAYING, 'KNOW
THE LORD,'
FOR ALL SHALL KNOW ME,
FROM THE LEAST TO THE
GREATEST OF THEM.
12 "FOR I WILL BE MERCIFUL TO
THEIR INIQUITIES,
AND I WILL REMEMBER
THEIR SINS NO MORE."
13 [a]When He said, "A new *cov-*
enant," He has made the first ob-
solete. But whatever is becoming
obsolete and growing old is ready
to disappear. *In His saying*

CHAPTER 9

NOW even the first *covenant* had
[r]regulations of divine worship and
the earthly sanctuary. Heb. 9:10
2 For there was a [a]tabernacle
prepared, the [t]outer one, in which
were the lampstand and the table
and the sacred bread; this is called
the holy place. *sacred tent • first*
3 And behind the second veil,
there was a tabernacle which is
called the Holy of Holies,
4 having a golden [a]altar of incense and[r] the ark of the covenant
covered on all sides with gold, in
which *was* a golden jar holding
the manna, and Aaron's rod which
budded, and the tables of the covenant. *censer* • Ex. 25:10ff.; 37:1ff.
5 And above it *were* the cherubim of glory overshadowing the
mercy seat; but of these things we
cannot now speak in detail.
6 Now when these things have
been thus prepared, the priests
are continually entering the [t]outer
[a]tabernacle, performing the divine
worship, *first • sacred tent*
7 but into the second only the
high priest *enters*, once a year, not
without *taking* blood, which he offers for himself and for the [t]sins of
the people committed in ignorance. *ignorance of the people*
8 The Holy Spirit *is* signifying
this, [r]that the way into the holy
place has not yet been disclosed,
while the [t]outer tabernacle is still
standing, John 14:6 • *first*
9 which *is* a symbol for the
present time. Accordingly [r]both
gifts and sacrifices are offered
which cannot make the worshiper
perfect in conscience, Heb. 5:1
10 since they *relate* only to food
and drink and various washings,
regulations for the body imposed
until a time of reformation.
11 But when Christ appeared *as*
a high priest of the good things [5]to
come, *He entered* through the
greater and more perfect tabernacle, not made with hands, that is
to say, not of this creation;
12 and not through the blood of
goats and calves, but through His
own blood, He entered the holy
place once for all,[a]having obtained
eternal redemption. *obtaining*
13 For if[r] the blood of goats and
bulls and the ashes of a heifer
sprinkling those who have been
defiled, sanctify for the [t]cleansing
of the flesh, Lev. 16:15 • *purity*
14 how much more will the
blood of Christ, who through the
eternal Spirit offered Himself
without blemish to God, cleanse

[5]Some ancient mss. read *that have come*

your conscience from dead works
to serve the living God?
15 And for this reason[r]He is the
[r]mediator of a new covenant, in order that since a death has taken
place for the redemption of the
transgressions that were *committed* under the first covenant, those
who have been called may receive
the promise of the eternal inheritance. Rom. 3:24 • 1 Tim. 2:5
16 For where a covenant is,
there must of necessity be the
death of the one who made it.
17 For a covenant is valid *only*
when[f]men are dead, [6]for it is never
in force while the one who made it
lives. *over the dead*
18 Therefore even the first *covenant* was not inaugurated without blood.
19 For when every commandment had been[r]spoken by Moses
to all the people according to the
Law, he took the blood of the
calves and the goats, with water
and scarlet wool and hyssop, and
sprinkled both the book itself and
all the people, Heb. 1:1
20 saying, "THIS[r] IS THE BLOOD
OF THE COVENANT WHICH GOD
COMMANDED YOU." Ex. 24:8
21 And in the same way he
sprinkled both the[a]tabernacle and
all the vessels of the ministry with
the blood. *sacred tent*
22 And according to the[a]Law,
one may almost *say*, all things are
cleansed with blood, and without
shedding of blood there is no forgiveness. *Law, almost all things*
23 Therefore it was necessary
for the[r]copies of the things in the
heavens to be cleansed with these,
but [r]the heavenly things themselves with better sacrifices than
these. Heb. 8:5
24 For Christ did not enter a
holy place made with hands, a
mere copy of the true one, but into
heaven itself, now to appear in the
presence of God for us;
25 nor was it that He should offer Himself often, as the high
priest enters the holy place year
by year with blood not his own.
26 Otherwise, He would have
needed to suffer often since the
foundation of the world; but now
once at the consummation of the
ages He has been manifested to
put away sin[a]by the sacrifice of
Himself. *by His sacrifice*
27 And inasmuch as it is appointed for men to die once and
after this *comes* judgment,
28 so Christ also, having been
[r]offered once to[r] bear the sins of
many, shall appear a second time
for salvation without *reference to*
sin, to those who eagerly await
Him. Heb. 7:27 • Is. 53:12

CHAPTER 10

FOR the Law, since it has *only* a
shadow of the good things to
come *and* not the very form of
things, [7]can never by the same
sacrifices year by year, which
they offer continually, make perfect those who draw near.
2 Otherwise, would they not
have ceased to be offered, because
the worshipers, having once been
cleansed, would no longer have
had consciousness of sins?
3 But in those *sacrifices* there
is a reminder of sins year by year.

[6]Some ancient mss. read *for is it then . . . lives?*

[7]Some ancient mss. read *they can*

4 For it is [r]impossible for the
blood of bulls and goats to take
away sins. Heb. 10:1,11
5 Therefore, when He comes
into the world, He says,
"SACRIFICE AND OFFERING
THOU HAST NOT DESIRED,
BUT A BODY THOU HAST PRE-
PARED FOR ME;
6 [r]IN WHOLE BURNT OFFERINGS
AND *sacrifices* FOR SIN
THOU HAST TAKEN NO
PLEASURE. Ps. 40:6
7 "THEN[r] I SAID, 'BEHOLD, I
HAVE COME Ps. 40:7, 8
(IN THE ROLL OF THE BOOK IT
IS WRITTEN OF ME)
TO DO THY WILL, O GOD.'"
8 After saying above, "SACRI-
FICES[r] AND OFFERINGS AND WHOLE
BURNT OFFERINGS AND *sacrifices*
FOR SIN THOU HAST NOT DESIRED,
NOR HAST THOU TAKEN PLEASURE
in them" (which are offered according to the Law), Ps. 40:6
9 then He said, "BEHOLD,[r] I
HAVE COME TO DO THY WILL." He
takes away the first in order to establish the second. Ps. 40:7, 8
10 By [t]this will we have been
[r]sanctified through the offering of
the body of Jesus Christ once for
all. *which* • John 17:19
11 And every priest stands daily
ministering and offering time after time the same sacrifices,
which can never take away sins;
12 but He, having offered one
sacrifice for sins for all time, SAT
DOWN AT THE RIGHT HAND OF GOD,
13 waiting from that time onward UNTIL HIS ENEMIES BE MADE
A FOOTSTOOL FOR HIS FEET.
14 For by one offering He has
perfected for all time those who
are [a]sanctified. *being sanctified*

15 And [r]the Holy Spirit also
bears witness to us; for after saying, Heb. 3:7
16 "THIS[r] IS THE COVENANT THAT
I WILL MAKE WITH THEM
AFTER THOSE DAYS, SAYS
THE LORD: Jer. 31:33
I WILL PUT MY LAWS UPON
THEIR HEART,
AND UPON THEIR MIND I
WILL WRITE THEM,"
He then says,
17 "AND THEIR SINS AND THEIR
LAWLESS DEEDS
I WILL REMEMBER NO MORE."
18 Now where there is forgiveness of these things, there is no
longer *any* offering for sin.
19 Since therefore, brethren, we
have confidence to enter the holy
place by the blood of Jesus,
20 by a new and living way
which He inaugurated for us
through the veil, that is, His flesh,
21 and since *we have* a great
priest over the house of God,
22 let us [r]draw near with a [t]sin-
cere heart in [r]full assurance of
faith, having our hearts sprinkled
clean from an evil conscience and
our bodies washed with pure water. Heb. 7:19 • *true* • Heb. 6:11
23 Let us hold fast the [r]confes-
sion of our [r]hope without wavering, for He who promised is faithful; Heb. 3:1 • Heb. 3:6
24 and let us consider how [r]to
stimulate one another to love and
good deeds, Heb. 13:1
25 not forsaking our own [r]as-
sembling together, as is the habit
of some, but encouraging *one another*; and all the more, as you see
the day drawing near. Acts 2:42
26 For if we go on sinning will-
fully after receiving the knowl-

edge of the truth, there no longer
remains a sacrifice for sins,
27 but a certain terrifying expectation of judgment, and THE
FURY OF A FIRE WHICH WILL CON-
SUME THE ADVERSARIES.
28 [r]Anyone who has set aside
the Law of Moses dies without
mercy on *the testimony of* two or
three witnesses. Deut. 17:2-6
29 How much severer punishment do you think he will deserve
who has trampled under foot the
Son of God, and has regarded as
unclean the blood of the covenant
by which he was sanctified, and
has insulted the Spirit of grace?
30 For we know Him who said,
"VENGEANCE[r] IS MINE, I WILL RE-
PAY." And again, "THE LORD WILL
JUDGE HIS PEOPLE." Deut. 32:35
31 It is a terrifying thing to fall
into the hands of the living God.
32 But remember the former
days, [t]when, after being enlightened, you endured a great conflict
of sufferings, *in which*
33 partly, by being[r] made a public spectacle through reproaches
and tribulations, and partly by becoming sharers with those who
were so treated. 1 Cor. 4:9
34 For you[r] showed sympathy to
the prisoners, and accepted joyfully the seizure of your property,
knowing that you have for yourselves a better possession and an
abiding one. Heb. 13:3
35 Therefore, do not throw
away your [r]confidence, which has
a great reward. Heb. 10:19
36 For you have need of endurance, so that when you have done
the will of God, you may receive
[t]what was promised. *the promise*
37 [r]FOR YET IN A VERY LITTLE
WHILE, Hab. 2:3
[r]HE WHO IS COMING WILL
COME, AND WILL NOT DE-
LAY. Matt. 11:3
38 [r]BUT MY RIGHTEOUS ONE
SHALL LIVE BY FAITH;
AND IF HE SHRINKS BACK,
MY SOUL HAS NO PLEA-
SURE IN HIM. Hab. 2:4
39 But we are not of those who
shrink back to destruction, but of
those who have faith to the [a]pre-
serving of the soul. *possessing*

CHAPTER 11

NOW faith is the [a]assurance of
things hoped for, the conviction of
things not seen. *substance*
2 For by it the [r]men of old
gained approval. Heb. 1:1
3 By faith we understand that
the [t]worlds were prepared by the
word of God, so that what is seen
[r]was not made out of things which
are visible. *ages* • Rom. 4:17
4 By faith [r]Abel offered to God
a better sacrifice than Cain,
through which he obtained the
testimony that he was righteous,
God testifying about his gifts, and
through [t]faith, though he is dead,
he still speaks. Gen. 4:4 • *it*
5 By faith Enoch was taken up
so that he should not see death;
AND HE WAS NOT FOUND BECAUSE
GOD TOOK HIM UP; for he obtained
the witness that before his being
taken up he was pleasing to God.
6 And without faith it is impossible to please *Him*, for he who
[r]comes to God must believe that
He is, and *that* He is a rewarder of
those who seek Him. Heb. 7:19
7 By faith Noah, being warned

by God about things not yet seen, [t]in reverence prepared an ark for the salvation of his household, by which he condemned the world, and became an heir of the righteousness which is according to faith. *having become reverent*

8 By faith [r]Abraham, when he was called, obeyed by going out to a place which he was to [r]receive for an inheritance; and he went out, not knowing where he was going. Gen. 12:1-4 • Gen. 12:7

9 By faith he lived as an alien in [r]the land of promise, as in a foreign *land*, dwelling in tents with Isaac and Jacob, fellow heirs of the same promise; Acts 7:5

10 for he was looking for the city which has foundations, whose architect and builder is God.

11 By faith even [r]Sarah herself received ability to conceive, even beyond the proper time of life, since she considered Him faithful who had promised; Gen. 17:19

12 therefore, also, there was born of one man, and him as good as dead [t]at that, *as many descendants* AS THE STARS OF HEAVEN IN NUMBER, AND INNUMERABLE AS THE SAND WHICH IS BY THE SEASHORE. *in these things*

13 All these died in faith, without receiving the promises, but having seen them and having welcomed them from a distance, and having confessed that they were strangers and exiles on the earth.

14 For those who say such things make it clear that they are seeking a country of their own.

15 And indeed if they had been thinking of that *country* from which they went out, they would have had opportunity to return.

16 But as it is, they desire a better *country*, that is a heavenly one. Therefore God is not [t]ashamed to be called their God; for He has prepared a city for them. *ashamed of them, to be*

17 By faith [r]Abraham, when he was tested, offered up Isaac; and he who had [r]received the promises was offering up his only begotten *son;* Gen. 22:1-10 • Heb. 11:13

18 *it was he* to whom it was said, "IN ISAAC YOUR [t]DESCENDANTS SHALL BE CALLED." *seed*

19 [t]He considered that God is able to raise *men* even from the dead; from which he also received him back as a type. *Considering*

20 By faith [r]Isaac blessed Jacob and Esau, even regarding things to come. Gen. 27:27-29, 39f.

21 By faith Jacob, as he was dying, blessed each of the sons of Joseph, and worshiped, *leaning* on the top of his staff.

22 By faith Joseph, when he was dying, made mention of the exodus of the sons of Israel, and gave orders concerning his bones.

23 By faith Moses, when he was born, was hidden for three months by his parents, because they saw he was a beautiful child; and they were not afraid of the king's edict.

24 By faith Moses, when he had grown up, refused to be called the son of Pharaoh's daughter;

25 choosing rather to [r]endure ill-treatment with the people of God, than to enjoy the passing pleasures of sin; Heb. 11:37

26 considering the reproach of Christ greater riches than the treasures of Egypt; for he was looking to the [r]reward. Heb. 2:2

27 By faith he [r]left Egypt, not

[r]fearing the wrath of the king; for
he endured, as seeing Him who is
unseen. Ex. 2:15 • Ex. 2:14
28 By faith he kept the Passover
and the sprinkling of the blood, so
that he who destroyed the first-
born might not touch them.
29 By faith they passed through
the Red Sea as though *they were*
passing through dry land; and the
Egyptians, when they attempted
it, were [t]drowned. *swallowed up*
30 By faith the walls of Jericho
fell down, after they had been encircled for seven days.
31 By faith Rahab the harlot did
not perish along with those who
were disobedient, after she had
welcomed the spies in peace.
32 And what more shall I say?
For time will fail me if I tell of
Gideon, Barak, Samson, Jephthah,
of [r]David and Samuel and the
prophets, 1 Sam. 16:1, 13
33 who by faith conquered kingdoms, performed *acts of* righteousness, obtained promises, [r]shut
the mouths of lions, Judg. 14:6
34 quenched the power of fire,
[r]escaped the edge of the sword,
from weakness were made strong,
became mighty in war, put foreign
armies to flight. Ex. 18:4
35 Women received *back* their
dead by resurrection; and others
were tortured, not accepting their
release, in order that they might
obtain a better resurrection;
36 and others experienced
mockings and scourgings, yes,
also chains and imprisonment.
37 They were stoned, they were
sawn in two, [8]they were tempted,
they were put to death with the
sword; they went about in sheep-
skins, in goatskins, being destitute, afflicted, ill-treated
38 (*men* of whom the world was
not worthy), wandering in deserts
and mountains and caves and
holes [t]in the ground. *of*
39 And all these, having gained
approval through their faith, did
not receive what was promised,
40 because God had [a]provided
something better for us, so that
apart from us they should not be
made perfect. *foreseen*

CHAPTER 12

THEREFORE, since we have so
great a cloud of witnesses surrounding us, let us also [r]lay aside
every encumbrance, and the sin
which so easily entangles us, and
let us run with endurance the race
that is set before us, Eph. 4:22
2 [t]fixing our eyes on Jesus, the
author and perfecter of faith, who
for the joy set before Him endured
the cross, despising the shame,
and has sat down at the right hand
of the throne of God. *looking to*
3 For consider Him who has
endured such hostility by sinners
against Himself, so that you may
not grow weary and lose heart.
4 You have not yet resisted to
the point of shedding blood in
your striving against sin;
5 and you have forgotten the
exhortation which is addressed to
you as sons,

"MY [r] SON, DO NOT REGARD
LIGHTLY THE DISCIPLINE
OF THE LORD, Job 5:17
NOR FAINT WHEN YOU ARE
REPROVED BY HIM;

[8]Some mss. do not contain *they were tempted*

6 FOR THOSE WHOM THE LORD
LOVES HE DISCIPLINES,
AND HE SCOURGES EVERY
SON WHOM HE RECEIVES."

7 It is for discipline that you endure; [r]God deals with you as with sons; for what son is there whom *his* father does not discipline? Deut. 8:5; 2 Sam. 7:14

8 But if you are without discipline, of which all have become partakers, then you are illegitimate children and not sons.

9 Furthermore, we had earthly fathers to discipline us, and we respected them; shall we not much rather be subject to the Father of [a]spirits, and live? *our spirits*

10 For they [t]disciplined us for a short time as seemed best to them, but He disciplines us for *our* good, [r]that we may share His holiness. *were disciplining* • 2 Pet. 1:4

11 All discipline [r]for the moment seems not to be joyful, but sorrowful; yet to those who have been trained by it, afterwards it yields the [r]peaceful fruit of righteousness. 1 Pet. 1:6 • Is. 32:17

12 Therefore, [r]strengthen the hands that are weak and the knees that are feeble, Is. 35:3

13 and make straight paths for your feet, so that *the limb* which is lame may not be put out of joint, but rather be healed.

14 Pursue peace with all men, and the sanctification without which no one will see the Lord.

15 See to it that no one [r]comes short of the grace of God; that no [r]root of bitterness springing up causes trouble, and by it many be defiled; 2 Cor. 6:1 • Deut. 29:18

16 that *there be* no [r]immoral or [r]godless person like Esau, who sold his own birthright for a *single* meal. Heb. 13:4 • 1 Tim. 1:9

17 For you know that even afterwards, [r]when he desired to inherit the blessing, he was rejected, for he found no place for repentance, though he sought for it with tears. Gen. 27:30-40

18 For you have not come to *a mountain* that may be touched and to a blazing fire, and to darkness and gloom and whirlwind,

19 and to the blast of a trumpet and the sound of words which *sound was such that* those who heard begged that no further word should be spoken to them.

20 For they could not bear the command, "IF [r] EVEN A BEAST TOUCHES THE MOUNTAIN, IT WILL BE STONED." Ex. 19:12f.

21 And so terrible was the sight, *that* Moses said, "I [r]AM FULL OF FEAR and trembling." Deut. 9:19

22 But [r]you have come to Mount Zion and to the city of the living God, the heavenly Jerusalem, and to myriads of angels, Rev. 14:1

23 to the general assembly and church of the first-born who are enrolled in heaven, and to God, the Judge of all, and to the spirits of righteous men made perfect,

24 and to Jesus, the mediator of a new covenant, and to the sprinkled blood, which speaks better than *the blood* of Abel.

25 See to it that you do not refuse Him who is speaking. For if those did not escape when they refused him who warned *them* on earth, much [t]less *shall* we *escape* who turn away from Him who *warns* from heaven. *more*

26 And His voice shook the earth then, but now He has prom-

ised, saying, "YET ONCE MORE I
WILL SHAKE NOT ONLY THE EARTH,
BUT ALSO THE HEAVEN."
27 And this *expression*, "Yet
once more," denotes the removing
of those things which can be
shaken, as of created things, in order that those things which cannot be shaken may remain.
28 Therefore, since we receive a
[r]kingdom which cannot be shaken,
let us [t]show gratitude, by which
we may offer to God an acceptable service with reverence and
awe; Dan. 2:44 • *have*
29 for [r]our God is a consuming
fire. Deut. 4:24; 9:3; Is. 33:14

CHAPTER 13

LET [r]love of the brethren continue. Rom. 12:10; 1 Thess. 4:9
2 Do not neglect to [r]show hospitality to strangers, for by this
some have entertained angels
without knowing it. 1 Pet. 4:9
3 [r]Remember [r]the prisoners, as
though in prison with them, and
those who are ill-treated, since
you yourselves also are in the
body. Col. 4:18 • Matt. 25:36
4 *Let* marriage *be held* in honor
among all, and let the *marriage*
bed *be* undefiled; for fornicators
and adulterers God will judge.
5 Let your character be [r]free
from the love of money, being
content with what you have; for
He Himself has said, "I WILL NEV-
ER DESERT YOU, NOR WILL I EVER
FORSAKE YOU," Eph. 5:3
6 so that we confidently say,
"THE [r] LORD IS MY HELPER, I
WILL NOT BE AFRAID.
WHAT SHALL MAN DO TO
ME?" Ps. 118:6
7 Remember those who led
you, who spoke the word of God
to you; and considering the [a]result
of their conduct, imitate their
faith. *end of their life*
8 Jesus Christ *is* the same yesterday and today, *yes* and forever.
9 Do not be carried away by
varied and strange teachings; for
it is good for the heart to [r]be
strengthened by grace, not by
foods, through which those who
[t]were thus occupied were not
benefited. 2 Cor. 1:21 • *walked*
10 We have an altar, from
which those who serve the tabernacle have no right to eat.
11 For [r]the bodies of those animals whose blood is brought into
the holy place by the high priest
as an offering for sin, are burned
outside the camp. Ex. 29:14
12 Therefore Jesus also, [r]that He
might sanctify the people [r]through
His own blood, suffered outside
the gate. Eph. 5:26 • Heb. 9:12
13 Hence, let us go out to Him
outside the camp, [r]bearing His reproach. Luke 9:23; Heb. 11:26
14 For here we do not have a
lasting city, but we are seeking
the city which is to come.
15 Through Him then, let us
continually offer up a sacrifice of
praise to God, that is, the fruit of
lips that give thanks to His name.
16 And do not neglect doing
good and sharing; for with such
sacrifices God is pleased.
17 Obey your leaders, and submit *to them*; for they keep watch
over your souls, as those who will
give an account. [t]Let them do this
with joy and not with grief, for
this would be unprofitable for
you. *in order that they may do this*
18 Pray for us, for we are sure

that we have a [r]good conscience,
desiring to conduct ourselves hon-
orably in all things. Acts 24:16
19 And I urge *you* all the more
to do this, [r]that I may be restored
to you the sooner. Philem. 22
20 Now the God of peace, who
brought up from the dead the
great Shepherd of the sheep
through the blood of the eternal
covenant, *even* Jesus our Lord,
21 equip you in every good
thing to do His will, working in us
that which is pleasing in His sight,
through Jesus Christ, to whom *be*
the glory forever and ever. Amen.
22 But I urge you, brethren,
[a]bear with [t]this word of exhortation, for I have written to you
briefly. *listen to* • *the*
23 Take notice that [r]our brother
Timothy has been released, with
whom, if he comes soon, I shall
see you. Acts 16:1; Col. 1:1
24 Greet all of your leaders and
all the [a]saints. Those from [r]Italy
greet you. *holy ones* • Acts 18:2
25 Grace be with you all.

THE EPISTLE OF

JAMES

[a]JAMES, a bond-servant of God
and of the Lord Jesus Christ, to
the twelve tribes who are dispersed abroad, greetings. *Jacob*
2 Consider it all joy, my brethren, when you encounter [r]various
[a]trials, 1 Pet. 1:6 • *temptations*
3 knowing that the testing of
your faith produces endurance.
4 And let endurance have *its*
perfect [t]result, that you may be
[a]perfect and complete, lacking in
nothing. *work* • *mature*
5 But if any of you lacks wisdom, let him ask of God, who
gives to all men generously and
[t]without reproach, and it will be
given to him. *does not reproach*
6 But let him ask in faith without any doubting, for the one who
doubts is like the surf of the sea
driven and tossed by the wind.
7 For let not that man expect
that he will receive anything from
the Lord,
8 *being* a double-minded man,
unstable in all his ways.
9 [r]But let the brother of humble
circumstances glory in his high
position; Luke 14:11
10 and *let* the rich man *glory* in
his humiliation, because like flow-
ering grass he will pass away.
11 For the sun rises with [t]a
scorching wind, and [r]withers the
grass; and its flower falls off, and
the beauty of its appearance is destroyed; so too the rich man in the
midst of his pursuits will fade
away. *the* • Ps. 102:4, 11
12 Blessed is a man who perse-
veres under trial; for once he has
been approved, he will receive the
crown of life, which *the Lord* has
promised to those who love Him.
13 Let no one say when he is
tempted, "I [r]am being tempted [t]by

God"; for God cannot be tempted by evil, and He Himself does not tempt anyone. Gen. 22:1 • *from*

14 But each one is tempted when he is carried away and enticed by his own lust.

15 Then [r]when lust has conceived, it gives birth to sin; and when sin is accomplished, it brings forth death. Job 15:35

16 Do not be deceived,[r] my beloved brethren. Acts 1:15

17 Every good thing bestowed and every perfect gift is from above, coming down from the Father of lights, with whom there is no variation, or shifting shadow.

18 In the exercise of His will He brought us forth by the word of truth, so that we might be,[t] as it were, the first fruits among His creatures. *a certain first fruits*

19 [1]*This*[r] you know, my beloved brethren. But let everyone be quick to hear, slow to speak *and* slow to anger; 1 John 2:21

20 for the anger of man does not achieve the righteousness of God.

21 Therefore putting aside all filthiness and *all* that remains of wickedness, in [a]humility receive the word implanted, which is able to save your souls. *gentleness*

22 But prove yourselves doers of the word, and not merely hearers who delude themselves.

23 For if anyone is a hearer of the word and not a doer, he is like a man who looks at his [t]natural face in a mirror; *nature*

24 for *once* he has looked at himself and gone away,[t] he has immediately forgotten what kind of person he was. *and he*

25 But one who looks intently at the perfect law, the *law* of liberty, and abides by it, not having become a forgetful hearer but an effectual doer, this man shall be blessed in what he does.

26 If anyone thinks himself to be religious, and yet does not [r]bridle his tongue but deceives his *own* heart, this man's religion is worthless. Ps. 39:1; 141:3

27 This is pure and undefiled religion in the sight of *our* God and Father, to visit orphans and widows in their distress, *and* to keep oneself unstained by the world.

[1]Or, *Know* this

CHAPTER 2

MY brethren, [r]do not hold your faith in our glorious Lord Jesus Christ with *an attitude of* personal favoritism. Heb. 12:2

2 For if a man comes into your [a]assembly with a gold ring and dressed in [a]fine clothes, and there also comes in a poor man in dirty clothes, *synagogue* • *bright*

3 and you pay special attention to the one who is wearing the fine clothes, and say, "You sit here in a good place," and you say to the poor man, "You stand over there, or sit down by my footstool,"

4 have you not made distinctions among yourselves, and become judges with evil motives?

5 Listen, my beloved brethren: did not God choose the poor of this world *to be* rich in faith and heirs of the kingdom which He promised to those who love Him?

6 But you have dishonored the poor man. Is it not the rich who oppress you and [t]personally drag you into court? *they themselves*

7 [r]Do they not blaspheme the

fair name by which you have been
called? Acts 11:26; 1 Pet. 4:16

8 If, however, you are fulfilling
the [a]royal law, according to the
Scripture, "YOU SHALL LOVE YOUR
NEIGHBOR AS YOURSELF," you are
doing well. *law of* our King

9 But if you [r]show partiality,
you are committing sin *and* are
convicted by the [a]law as transgressors. Acts 10:34; James 2:1 • *Law*

10 For whoever keeps the whole
law and yet stumbles in one *point*,
he has become guilty of all.

11 For He who said, "DO NOT
COMMIT ADULTERY," also said, "DO
NOT COMMIT MURDER." Now if you
do not commit adultery, but do
commit murder, you have become
a transgressor of the [a]law. *Law*

12 So speak and so act, as those
who are to be judged by [r]*the* law of
liberty. James 1:25

13 For [r]judgment *will be* merci-
less to one who has shown no
mercy; mercy [t]triumphs over judgment. Matt. 5:7 • *boasts against*

14 What use is it, [r]my brethren,
if a man says he has faith, but he
has no works? Can [t]that faith save
him? James 1:16 • *the*

15 [r]If a brother or sister is without clothing and in need of daily
food, Matt. 25:35f.; Luke 3:11

16 and one of you says to them,
"Go in peace, be warmed and be
filled," and yet you do not give
them what is necessary for *their*
body, what use is that?

17 Even so faith, if it has no
works, is dead, *being* by itself.

18 But someone [t]may *well* say,
"You have faith, and I have
works; show me your faith without the works, and I will show you
my faith by my works." *will*

19 You believe that [2]God is one.
[r]You do well; the demons also believe, and shudder. James 2:8

20 But are you willing to recognize, you foolish fellow, that faith
without works is useless?

21 [r]Was not Abraham our father
justified by works, when he offered up Isaac his son on the altar? Gen. 22:9, 10, 12, 16-18

22 You see that faith was working with his works, and as a result
of the works, faith was perfected;

23 and the Scripture was ful-
filled which says, "AND [r]ABRAHAM
BELIEVED GOD, AND IT WAS RECK-
ONED TO HIM AS RIGHTEOUSNESS,"
and he was called [r]the friend of
God. Gen. 15:6 • 2 Chr. 20:7

24 You see that a man is justified by works, and not by faith
alone.

25 And in the same way was not
[r]Rahab the harlot also justified by
works, when she received the
messengers and sent them out by
another way? Heb. 11:31

26 For just as the body without
the spirit is dead, so also [r]faith
without works is dead. Gal. 5:6

CHAPTER 3

LET not many *of you* become
teachers, [r]my brethren, knowing
that as such we shall incur a
stricter judgment. James 1:16

2 For we all stumble in many
ways. If anyone does not stumble
in [t]what he says, he is a perfect
man, able to bridle the whole
body as well. *word*

3 Now [r]if we put the bits into
the horses' mouths so that they

[2]Or, *there is one God*

may obey us, we direct their entire body as well. Ps. 32:9
4 Behold, the ships also,
though they are so great and are
driven by strong winds, are still
directed by a very small rudder,
wherever the inclination of the pilot desires.
5 So also the tongue is a small
part of the body, and *yet* it[r]boasts
of great things. Behold, how great
a forest is set aflame by such a
small fire! Ps. 12:3f.; 73:8f.
6 And the tongue is a fire, the
very world of iniquity; the tongue
is set among our members as that
which defiles the entire body, and
sets on fire the course of *our* life,
and is set on fire by hell.
7 For every species of beasts
and birds, of reptiles and creatures of the sea, is tamed, and has
been tamed by the human race.
8 But no one can tame the
tongue; *it is* a restless evil *and* full
of [r]deadly poison. Ps. 140:3
9 With it we bless [r]*our* Lord
and Father; and with it we curse
men, who have been made in the
likeness of God; James 1:27
10 from the same mouth come
both blessing and cursing. My
brethren, these things ought not
to be this way.
11 Does a fountain send out
from the same opening *both*[t]fresh
and bitter *water*? *sweet*
12 [r]Can a fig tree, my brethren,
produce olives, or a vine produce
figs? Neither *can* salt water produce fresh. Matt. 7:16
13 Who among you is wise and
understanding? Let him show by
his good behavior his deeds in the
gentleness of wisdom.
14 But if you have bitter jealousy and[a]selfish ambition in your
heart, do not be arrogant and *so*
lie against the truth. *strife*
15 This wisdom is not that
which comes down from above,
but is earthly, natural, demonic.
16 For where jealousy and selfish ambition exist, there is disorder and every evil thing.
17 But the wisdom from above
is first pure, then peaceable, gentle,[a]reasonable, full of mercy and
good fruits, unwavering, without
hypocrisy. *willing to yield*
18 And the seed whose fruit is
righteousness is sown in peace[a]by
those who make peace. *for*

CHAPTER 4

WHAT is the source of quarrels
and conflicts among you? Is not
the source your pleasures that
wage war in your members?
2 You lust and do not have; *so*
you commit murder. And you are
envious and cannot obtain; *so* you
fight and quarrel. You do not have
because you do not ask.
3 You ask and do not receive,
because you ask[t]with wrong motives, so that you may spend *it*[t]on
your pleasures. *wickedly • in*
4 You[r]adulteresses, do you not
know that friendship with the
world is hostility toward God?
Therefore whoever wishes to be a
friend of the world makes himself
an enemy of God. Jer. 2:2
5 Or do you think that the
Scripture speaks to no purpose:
"[3]He [t]jealously desires the Spirit

[3]Or, *The Spirit which He has made to dwell in us jealously desires us*

which He has made to dwell in
us"? *desires to jealousy*
6 But He gives a greater grace.
Therefore *it* says, "GOD IS OP-
POSED TO THE PROUD, BUT GIVES
GRACE TO THE HUMBLE."
7 [r]Submit therefore to God.[r]Re-
sist the devil and he will flee from
you. 1 Pet. 5:6 • Eph. 4:27
8 Draw near to God and He
will draw near to you. [r]Cleanse
your hands, you sinners; and [r]pu-
rify your hearts, you double-
minded. Job 17:9 • Jer. 4:14
9 [r]Be miserable and mourn and
weep; let your laughter be turned
into mourning, and your joy to
gloom. Neh. 8:9; Prov. 14:13
10 [r]Humble yourselves in the
presence of the Lord, and He will
exalt you. Job 5:11; Ezek. 21:26
11 Do not speak against one another, brethren. He who speaks
against a brother, or judges his
brother, speaks against the law,
and judges the law; but if you
judge the law, you are not a doer
of the law, but a judge *of it.*
12 There is *only* one Lawgiver
and Judge, the One who is able to
save and to destroy; but who are
you who judge your neighbor?
13 Come now, you who say,
"Today or tomorrow, we shall go
to such and such a city, and spend
a year there and engage in business and make a profit."
14 [t]Yet you do not know what
your life will be like tomorrow.
[r]You are *just* a vapor that appears
for a little while and then vanishes
away. *Who do not* • Job 7:7
15 Instead, *you ought* to say, "If[r]
the Lord wills, we shall live and
also do this or that." Acts 18:21
16 But as it is, you boast in your
[a]arrogance; [r]all such boasting is
evil. *pretensions* • 1 Cor. 5:6
17 Therefore, to one who knows
the [a]right thing to do, and does not
do it, to him it is sin. *good*

CHAPTER 5

COME now, [r]you rich, weep and
howl for your miseries which are
coming upon you. Luke 6:24
2 [r]Your riches have rotted and
your garments have become
moth-eaten. Job 13:28; Is. 50:9
3 Your gold and your silver
have rusted; and their rust will be
a witness against you and will
consume your flesh like fire. It is
in the last days that you have
stored up your treasure!
4 Behold,[r]the pay of the laborers who mowed your fields, *and*
which has been withheld by you,
cries out *against you;* and the outcry of those who did the harvesting has reached the ears of the
Lord of Sabaoth. Lev. 19:13
5 You have lived luxuriously
on the earth and led a life of wanton pleasure; you have fattened
your hearts in a day of slaughter.
6 You have condemned and
[a]put to death the righteous *man;* he
does not resist you. *murdered*
7 Be patient, therefore, brethren, until the coming of the Lord.
Behold, the farmer waits for the
precious produce of the soil, being
patient about it, until [a]it gets the
early and late rains. *he*
8 You too be patient;
strengthen your hearts, for the
coming of the Lord is at hand.
9 Do not [t]complain, brethren,
against one another, that you

yourselves may not be judged; behold, the Judge is standing [t]right at
the [t]door. *groan · before · doors*
10 As an example, [r]brethren, of
suffering and patience, take the
prophets who spoke in the name
of the Lord. James 4:11; 5:7, 9
11 Behold, we count those
blessed who endured. You have
heard of the endurance of Job and
have seen the outcome of the
Lord's dealings, that the Lord is
full of compassion and *is* merciful.
12 But above all, [r]my brethren,
do not swear, either by heaven or
by earth or with any other oath;
but let your yes be yes, and your
no, no; so that you may not fall
under judgment. James 1:16
13 Is anyone among you suffering? Let him pray. Is anyone
cheerful? Let him sing praises.
14 Is anyone among you sick?
Let him call for [r]the elders of the
church, and let them pray over
him, anointing him with oil in the
name of the Lord; Acts 11:30
15 and the prayer [t]offered in
faith will [4]restore the one who is
sick, and the Lord will raise him
up, and if he has committed sins,
they will be forgiven him. *of*
16 Therefore, [r]confess your sins
to one another, and pray for one
another, so that you may be
healed. The effective [t]prayer of a
righteous man can accomplish
much. Matt. 3:6 · *supplication*
17 Elijah was a man with a nature like ours, and he prayed earnestly that it might not rain; and it
did not rain on the earth for three
years and six months.
18 And he prayed again, and the
[t]sky poured rain, and the earth
produced its fruit. *heaven*
19 My brethren, [r]if any among
you strays from the truth, and one
turns him back, Matt. 18:15
20 let him know that he who
turns a sinner from the error of his
way will save his soul from death,
and will cover a multitude of sins.

[4]Or, *save*

THE FIRST EPISTLE OF

PETER

PETER, an apostle of Jesus
Christ, to those who reside as
aliens, scattered throughout Pontus, Galatia, Cappadocia, Asia,
and Bithynia, who are chosen
2 according to the [r]foreknowl-
edge of God the Father, by the
sanctifying work of the Spirit,
that you may obey Jesus Christ
and be sprinkled with His blood:
May grace and peace be yours in
fullest measure. Rom. 8:29
3 Blessed be the God and Father of our Lord Jesus Christ, who
according to His great mercy has
caused us to be born again to a
living hope through the resurrection of Jesus Christ from the dead,
4 to *obtain* an inheritance
which is imperishable and undefiled and will not fade away, reserved in heaven for you,
5 who are [r]protected by the
power of God through faith for a

salvation ready to be revealed in
the last time. John 10:28
6 In this you greatly rejoice,
even though now for a little while,
if necessary, you have been distressed by various trials,
7 that the proof of your faith,
being more precious than gold
which is perishable, even though
tested by fire, may be found to result in praise and glory and honor
at the revelation of Jesus Christ;
8 and though you have not
seen Him, you love Him, and
though you do not see Him now,
but believe in Him, you greatly rejoice with joy inexpressible and
[t]full of glory, *glorified*
9 obtaining as [r]the outcome of
your faith the salvation of [1]your
souls. Rom. 6:22
10 As to this salvation, the
prophets who prophesied of the
grace that *would come* to you
made careful search and inquiry,
11 [t]seeking to know what person
or time the Spirit of Christ within
them was indicating as He predicted the sufferings of Christ and
the glories to follow. *inquiring*
12 It was revealed to them that
they were not serving themselves,
but you, in these things which
now have been announced to you
through those who preached the
gospel to you by the Holy Spirit
sent from heaven—things into
which angels long to look.
13 Therefore, gird your minds
for action, keep sober *in spirit,* fix
your hope completely on the
grace to be brought to you at the
revelation of Jesus Christ.
14 As [t]obedient children, do not
be conformed to the former lusts
which were yours in your ignorance, *children of obedience*
15 but like the Holy One who
called you,[a] be holy yourselves also
in all *your* behavior; *become*
16 because it is written, "You
SHALL BE HOLY, FOR I AM HOLY."
17 And if you address as Father
the One who impartially judges
according to each man's work,
conduct yourselves in fear during
the time of your stay *upon earth;*
18 knowing that you were not
[a]redeemed with perishable things
like silver or gold from your futile
way of life inherited from your
forefathers, *ransomed*
19 but with precious blood, as
of a lamb unblemished and spotless, *the blood* of Christ.
20 For He was foreknown before the foundation of the world,
but has appeared in these last
times for the sake of you
21 who through Him are [r]believ-
ers in God, who raised Him from
the dead and [r]gave Him glory, so
that your faith and hope are in
God. Rom. 4:24 • Heb. 2:9
22 Since you have [r]in obedience
to the truth purified your souls for
a [t]sincere love of the brethren, fervently love one another from [2]the
heart, 1 Pet. 1:2 • *unhypocritical*
23 for you have been [r]born again
[r]not of seed which is perishable
but imperishable, *that is,* through
the living and abiding word of
God. John 3:3 • John 1:13
24 For,

"ALL FLESH IS LIKE GRASS,
AND ALL ITS GLORY LIKE THE
FLOWER OF GRASS.
THE GRASS WITHERS,
AND THE FLOWER FALLS OFF,

[1]Some ancient mss. do not contain *your*

[2]Some mss. read *a clean heart*

25 BUT THE WORD OF THE LORD
ABIDES FOREVER."
And this is [r]the word which was
preached to you. Heb. 6:5

CHAPTER 2

THEREFORE, putting aside all
malice and all guile and hypocrisy
and envy and all slander,
2 like newborn babes, long for
the [a]pure milk of the word, that by
it you may grow in respect to salvation, *unadulterated*
3 if you have [r]tasted the kindness of the Lord. Heb. 6:5
4 And coming to Him as to a
living stone, [r]rejected by men, but
[t]choice and precious in the sight of
God, 1 Pet. 2:7 • *chosen*
5 you also, as living stones, are
being built up as a spiritual house
for a holy priesthood, to offer up
spiritual sacrifices acceptable to
God through Jesus Christ.
6 For *this* is contained in [a]Scrip-
ture: *a scripture*

"BEHOLD [r] I LAY IN ZION A
CHOICE STONE, A PRECIOUS
CORNER *stone*, Is. 28:16
AND HE WHO BELIEVES IN
[a]HIM SHALL NOT BE DISAP-
POINTED." *it*

7 This precious value, then, is
for you who believe. But for those
who disbelieve,

"THE [r] STONE WHICH THE
BUILDERS REJECTED,
THIS BECAME THE VERY COR-
NER *stone*," Ps. 118:22

8 and,

"A STONE OF STUMBLING AND
A ROCK OF OFFENSE";

[r]for they stumble because they are
disobedient to the word, and to
this *doom* they were also appointed. 1 Cor. 1:23
9 But you are [r]A CHOSEN RACE, A
royal PRIESTHOOD, A HOLY NATION,
A PEOPLE FOR *God's* OWN POSSES-
SION, that you may proclaim the
excellencies of Him who has
called you out of darkness into
His marvelous light; Is. 43:20f.
10 [r]for you once were NOT A PEO-
PLE, but now you are THE PEOPLE
OF GOD; you had NOT RECEIVED
MERCY, but now you have RE-
CEIVED MERCY. Hos. 1:10; 2:23
11 Beloved, [r]I urge you as aliens
and strangers to abstain from
fleshly lusts, which wage war
against the soul. Rom. 12:1
12 Keep your behavior excellent
among the Gentiles, so that in the
thing in which they slander you as
evildoers, they may [a]on account of
your good deeds, as they observe
them, glorify God in the day of
[3]visitation. *as a result of*
13 [r]Submit yourselves for the
Lord's sake to every human insti-
tution, whether to a king as the
one in authority, Rom. 13:1
14 or to governors as sent [t]by
him [r]for the punishment of evildoers and the praise of those who
do right. *through* • Rom. 13:4
15 For [r]such is the will of God
that by doing right you may silence the ignorance of foolish
men. 1 Pet. 3:17
16 *Act* as [r]free men, and do not
use your freedom as a covering
for evil, but *use it* as bondslaves of
God. John 8:32; James 1:25
17 Honor all men; love the
brotherhood, fear God, honor the
[a]king. *emperor*

[3]I.e., Christ's coming again in judgment

18 Servants, be submissive to
your masters with all respect, not
only to those who are good and
gentle, but also to those who are
[a]unreasonable. *perverse*
19 For this *finds*[a]favor, if for the
sake of conscience toward God a
man bears up under sorrows
when suffering unjustly. *grace*
20 For what credit is there if,
when you sin and are harshly
treated, you endure it with patience? But if[r]when you do what is
right and suffer *for it* you patiently endure it, this *finds* favor
with God. 1 Pet. 3:17
21 For[r]you have been called for
this purpose,[r]since Christ also suffered for you, leaving you an example for you to follow in His
steps, Acts 14:22 • 1 Pet. 3:18
22 WHO[r]COMMITTED NO SIN, NOR
WAS ANY DECEIT FOUND IN HIS
MOUTH; Is. 53:9; 2 Cor. 5:21
23 [t]and while being reviled, He
did not revile in return; while suffering, He uttered no threats, but
kept entrusting *Himself* to Him
who judges righteously; *who*
24 and He Himself bore our sins
in His body on the[t]cross, that we
might die to[t]sin and live to righteousness; for by His wounds you
were healed. *wood • sins*
25 For you were continually
straying like sheep, but now you
have returned to the Shepherd
and Guardian of your souls.

CHAPTER 3

IN the same way, you wives,[r]be
submissive to your own husbands
so that even if any *of them* are disobedient to the word, they may be
won without a word by the behavior of their wives, Eph. 5:22
2 as they observe your chaste
and respectful behavior.
3 [r]And let not your adornment
be *merely* external—braiding the
hair, and wearing gold jewelry, or
putting on dresses; Is. 3:18ff.
4 but *let it be*[r]the hidden person of the heart, with the imperishable quality of a gentle and
quiet spirit, which is precious in
the sight of God. Rom. 7:22
5 For in this way in former
times the holy women also,[r]who
hoped in God, used to adorn
themselves, being submissive to
their own husbands. 1 Pet. 1:3
6 Thus Sarah obeyed Abra-
ham, calling him lord, and you
have become her children if you
do what is right without being
frightened by any fear.
7 [r]You husbands likewise, live
with your wives in an understanding way, as with a weaker vessel,
since she is a woman; and grant
her honor as a fellow heir of the
grace of life, so that your prayers
may not be hindered. Eph. 5:25
8 To sum up, let all be harmo-
nious, sympathetic, brotherly,
kindhearted, and humble in spirit;
9 not returning evil for evil, or
insult for insult, but giving a
blessing instead; for you were
called for the very purpose that
you might inherit a blessing.
10 For,
"LET[r] HIM WHO MEANS TO
LOVE LIFE AND SEE GOOD
DAYS Ps. 34:12, 13
REFRAIN HIS TONGUE FROM
EVIL AND HIS LIPS FROM
SPEAKING GUILE.

11 "AND[r] LET HIM TURN AWAY
FROM EVIL AND DO GOOD;
LET HIM SEEK PEACE AND
PURSUE IT. Ps. 34:14
12 "FOR[r] THE EYES OF THE LORD
ARE UPON THE RIGHTEOUS,
AND HIS EARS ATTEND TO
THEIR PRAYER, Ps. 34:15, 16
BUT THE FACE OF THE LORD
IS AGAINST THOSE WHO DO
EVIL."
13 And[r] who is there to harm
you if you prove zealous for what
is good? Prov. 16:7
14 But even if you should suffer
for the sake of righteousness, *you
are* blessed. [r]AND DO NOT FEAR
THEIR [t]INTIMIDATION, AND DO NOT
BE TROUBLED, 1 Pet. 3:6 • *fear*
15 but [4]sanctify Christ as Lord
in your hearts, always *being* ready
to make a defense to everyone
who asks you to give an account
for the hope that is in you, yet
with gentleness and reverence;
16 [t]and keep a good conscience
so that in the thing in which you
are slandered, those who revile
your good behavior in Christ may
be put to shame. *having a good*
17 For it is better, if [t]God should
will it so, that you suffer for doing
what is right rather than for doing
what is wrong. *the will of God*
18 For [r]Christ also died for sins
once for all, *the* just for *the* unjust,
in order that He might bring us to
God, having been put to death in
the flesh, but made alive in the
[a]spirit; 1 Pet. 2:21 • *Spirit*
19 in[a] which also He went and
made proclamation to the spirits
now in prison, *whom*
20 who once were disobedient,
when the [r]patience of God kept
waiting in the days of Noah, during the construction of the ark, in
which a few, that is, [r]eight persons, were brought safely through
the water. Rom. 2:4 • Gen. 8:18
21 And corresponding to that,
baptism now saves you—[r]not the
removal of dirt from the flesh, but
an appeal to God for a good conscience—through the resurrection
of Jesus Christ, Heb. 9:14
22 who is at the right hand of
God, [r]having gone into heaven, [r]af-
ter angels and authorities and
powers had been subjected to
Him. Heb. 4:14 • Heb. 1:6

CHAPTER 4

THEREFORE, since Christ has
[5]suffered in the flesh, arm yourselves also with the same purpose,
because he who has suffered in
the flesh has ceased from sin,
2 so as to live [r]the rest of the
time in the flesh no longer for the
lusts of men, but for the [r]will of
God. 1 Pet. 1:14 • Mark 3:35
3 For [r]the time already past is
sufficient *for you* to have carried
out the desire of the Gentiles, having pursued a course of sensuality, lusts, drunkenness, carousals,
drinking parties and [t]abominable
idolatries. 1 Cor. 12:2 • *lawless*
4 And in *all* this, they are surprised that you do not run with
them into the same excess of dissipation, and they malign *you*;
5 but they shall give account to
Him who is ready to judge [r]the living and the dead. Acts 10:42
6 For the gospel has for this
purpose been preached even to
those who are dead, that though

[4]I.e., set apart

[5]I.e., suffered death

they are judged in the flesh as
men, they may live in the spirit according to *the will of* God.
7 The end of all things [t]is at
hand; therefore, be of sound judgment and sober *spirit* for the purpose of prayer. *has come near*
8 Above all, keep fervent in
your love for one another, because
love covers a multitude of sins.
9 Be hospitable to one another
without [r]complaint. Phil. 2:14
10 As each one has received a
special gift, employ it in serving
one another, as good stewards of
the manifold grace of God.
11 Whoever speaks, *let him*
speak, as it were, the [r]utterances
of God; whoever serves, *let him*
do so as [t]by the strength which
God supplies; so that in all things
God may be glorified through
Jesus Christ, to whom belongs the
glory and dominion forever and
ever. Amen. Acts 7:38 • *from*
12 Beloved, do not be surprised
at the fiery ordeal among you,
which comes upon you for your
testing, as though some strange
thing were happening to you;
13 but to the degree that you
share the sufferings of Christ,
keep on rejoicing; so that also at
the revelation of His glory, you
may rejoice with exultation.
14 If you are reviled [t]for the
name of Christ, you are blessed,
because the Spirit of glory and of
God rests upon you. *in*
15 By no means [r]let any of you
suffer as a murderer, or thief, or
evildoer, or a [r]troublesome med-
dler; 1 Pet. 2:19f. • 1 Thess. 4:11
16 but if *anyone suffers* as a
[r]Christian, let him not feel
ashamed, but in that name let him
glorify God. Acts 5:41; 28:22
17 For *it is* time for judgment to
begin with the household of God;
and if *it begins* with us first, what
will be the outcome for those who
do not obey the gospel of God?
18 AND IF IT IS WITH DIFFICULTY
THAT THE RIGHTEOUS IS SAVED,
WHAT WILL BECOME OF THE GOD-
LESS MAN AND THE SINNER?
19 Therefore, let those also who
suffer according to the will of God
entrust their souls to a faithful
Creator in doing what is right.

CHAPTER 5

THEREFORE, I exhort the elders
among you, as *your* fellow elder
and witness of the sufferings of
Christ, and a partaker also of the
glory that is to be revealed,
2 shepherd [r]the flock of God
among you, exercising oversight
not under compulsion, but voluntarily, according to *the will of*
God; and not for sordid gain, but
with eagerness; John 21:16
3 nor yet as lording it over
[t]those allotted to your charge, but
[a]proving to be examples to the
flock. *the allotments* • *becoming*
4 And when the Chief Shepherd appears, you will receive the
unfading [t]crown of glory. *wreath*
5 You younger men, likewise,
be subject to your elders; and all
of you, clothe yourselves with humility toward one another, for
GOD IS OPPOSED TO THE PROUD,
BUT GIVES GRACE TO THE HUMBLE.
6 [r]Humble yourselves, therefore, under the mighty hand of
God, that He may exalt you at the
proper time, Matt. 23:12

7 casting all your anxiety upon Him, because He cares for you.

8 Be of sober *spirit,* be on the alert. Your adversary, the devil, prowls about like a roaring lion, seeking someone to devour.

9 But resist him,[r]firm in *your* faith, knowing that the same experiences of suffering are being accomplished by your brethren who are in the world. Col. 2:5

10 And after you have suffered [r]for a little while, the God of all grace, who called you to His eternal glory in Christ, will Himself perfect, confirm, strengthen *and* establish you. 1 Pet. 1:6

11 [r]To Him *be* dominion forever and ever. Amen. Rom. 11:36

12 Through Silvanus, our faithful brother [r](for so I regard *him*),[r]I have written to you briefly, exhorting and testifying that this is the true grace of God. Stand firm in it! *(as I consider)* • Heb. 13:22

13 [6]She who is in Babylon, chosen together with you, sends you greetings, and *so does* my son, [r]Mark. Acts 12:12, 25; 15:37, 39

14 [r]Greet one another with a kiss of love.

[r]Peace be to you all who are in Christ. Rom. 16:16 • Eph. 6:23

[6]Some mss. read *The church which*

THE SECOND EPISTLE OF PETER

SIMON PETER, a bond-servant and apostle of Jesus Christ, to those who have received a faith of the same [a]kind as ours, [a]by the righteousness of our God and Savior, Jesus Christ: *value* • *in*

2 Grace and peace be multiplied to you in the knowledge of God and of Jesus our Lord;

3 seeing that His divine power has granted to us everything pertaining to life and godliness, through the true knowledge of Him who called us by His own glory and [a]excellence. *virtue*

4 For by these He has granted to us His precious and magnificent [r]promises, in order that by them you might become partakers of *the* divine nature, having escaped the corruption that is in the world by lust. 2 Pet. 3:9, 13

5 Now for this very reason also, applying all diligence, in your faith supply moral [a]excellence, and in *your* moral excellence, knowledge; *virtue*

6 and in *your* knowledge, [r]self-control, and in *your* self-control, perseverance, and in *your* perseverance, godliness; Acts 24:25

7 and in *your* godliness,[r]brotherly kindness, and in *your* brotherly kindness, love. Rom. 12:10

8 For if these *qualities* are yours and are increasing, they render you neither useless nor unfruitful in the true knowledge of our Lord Jesus Christ.

[1]Most early mss. read *Simeon*

9 For he who lacks these *quali-*
ties is [r]blind *or* short-sighted, having forgotten *his* purification from
his former sins. 1 John 2:11
10 Therefore, brethren, be all
the more diligent to make certain
about His [r]calling and [r]choosing
you; for as long as you practice
these things, you will never stumble; Matt. 22:14 • 1 Thess. 1:4
11 for in this way the entrance
into the eternal kingdom of our
Lord and Savior Jesus Christ will
be abundantly supplied to you.
12 Therefore, [r]I shall always be
ready to remind you of these
things, even though you *already*
know *them*, and have been established in the truth which is present with *you*. Phil. 3:1
13 And I consider it [r]right, as
long as I am in [r]this *earthly* dwelling, to stir you up by way of reminder, Phil. 1:7 • 2 Pet. 1:14
14 knowing that the laying
aside of my *earthly* dwelling is im-
minent, as also our Lord Jesus
Christ has made clear to me.
15 And I will also be diligent
that at any time after my [r]depar-
ture you may be able to call these
things to mind. Luke 9:31
16 For we did not follow clev-
erly devised [r]tales when we made
known to you the [r]power and coming of our Lord Jesus Christ, but
we were eyewitnesses of His majesty. 1 Tim. 1:4 • Mark 13:26
17 For when He received honor
and glory from God the Father,
such an utterance as this was
made to Him by the Majestic Glory, "This is My beloved Son with
whom I am well-pleased"—
18 and we ourselves heard this
[t]utterance made from heaven
when we were with Him on the
holy mountain. *voice borne*
19 And *so* we have the prophet-
ic word *made* more sure, to which
you do well to pay attention as to
a lamp shining in a dark place, until the day dawns and the morning
star arises in your hearts.
20 But know this first of all, that
no prophecy of Scripture is *a mat-*
ter of one's own interpretation,
21 for [r]no prophecy was ever
made by an act of human will, but
men moved by the Holy Spirit
spoke from God. Jer. 23:26

CHAPTER 2

BUT [r]false prophets also arose
among the people, just as there
will also be false teachers among
you, who will secretly introduce
destructive heresies, even denying
the Master who bought them,
bringing swift destruction upon
themselves. Deut. 13:1ff.
2 And many will follow their
[r]sensuality, and because of them
[r]the way of the truth will be ma-
ligned; Jude 4 • Acts 16:17
3 and in *their* [r]greed they will
[r]exploit you with false words; their
judgment from long ago is not
idle, and their destruction is not
asleep. 1 Tim. 6:5 • 2 Cor. 2:17
4 For [r]if God did not spare angels when they sinned, but cast
them into hell and committed
them to pits of darkness, reserved
for judgment; Jude 6
5 and did not spare [r]the ancient
world, but preserved Noah, a
[a]preacher of righteousness, with
seven others, when He brought a
flood upon the world of the ungodly; Ezek. 26:20 • *herald*

6 and *if* He [r]condemned the
cities of Sodom and Gomorrah to
destruction by reducing *them* to
ashes, having made them an example to those who would live ungodly thereafter; Gen. 19:24
7 and if He rescued righteous
Lot, oppressed by the sensual conduct of unprincipled men
8 (for by what he saw and
heard *that* righteous man, while
living among them, felt *his* righteous soul tormented day after day
with *their* lawless deeds),
9 *then* the Lord knows how to
rescue the godly from [a]temptation,
and to keep the unrighteous under
punishment for the [r]day of judgment, *trial* • Jude 6
10 and especially those who in-
dulge the flesh in *its* corrupt desires and despise authority. Dar-
ing, self-willed, they do not
tremble when they revile angelic
majesties,
11 [r]whereas angels who are
greater in might and power do not
bring a reviling judgment against
them before the Lord. Jude 9
12 But these, like unreasoning
animals, born as creatures of instinct to be captured and killed,
reviling where they have no
knowledge, will in [t]the destruction
of those creatures also be destroyed, *their destruction also*
13 suffering wrong as the wages
of doing wrong. They count it a
pleasure to revel in the daytime.
They are stains and blemishes,
reveling in their [2]deceptions, as
they carouse with you,
14 having eyes full of adultery
and that never cease from sin, [r]en-

[2] Some ancient mss. read *love feasts,* (cf. Jude 12)

ticing [r]unstable souls, having a
heart trained in greed, accursed
children; 2 Pet. 2:18 • James 1:8
15 forsaking [r]the right way they
have gone astray, having followed
the way of Balaam, the *son* of
Beor, who loved the wages of unrighteousness, Acts 13:10
16 but he received a rebuke for
his own transgression; [r]*for* a dumb
donkey, speaking with a voice of a
man, restrained the madness of
the prophet. Num. 22:21, 23, 28
17 These are [r]springs without
water, and mists driven by a
storm, for whom the black darkness has been reserved. Jude 12
18 For speaking out [r]arrogant
words of vanity they entice by
fleshly desires, by sensuality,
those who barely escape from the
ones who live in error, Jude 16
19 promising them freedom
while they themselves are slaves
of corruption; for [r]by what a man
is overcome, by this he is enslaved. John 8:34; Rom. 6:16
20 For if after they have [r]es-
caped the defilements of the
world by [r]the knowledge of the
Lord and Savior Jesus Christ, they
are again entangled in them and
are overcome, the last state has
become worse for them than the
first. 2 Pet. 2:18 • 2 Pet. 1:2
21 For it would be better for
them not to have known the way
of righteousness, than having
known it, to turn away from [r]the
holy commandment [r]delivered to
them. Gal. 6:2 • Jude 3
22 It has happened to them according to the true proverb, "A
DOG RETURNS TO ITS OWN VOMIT,"
and, "A sow, after washing, *re-*
turns to wallowing in the mire."

CHAPTER 3

THIS is now,[r]beloved, the second
letter I am writing to you in which
I am stirring up your sincere mind
by way of reminder, 1 Pet. 2:11
2 that you should remember
the words spoken beforehand by
the holy prophets and the commandment of the Lord and Savior
spoken by your apostles.
3 Know this first of all, that[r]in
the last days mockers will come
with *their* mocking, following after their own lusts, 1 Tim. 4:1
4 and saying, "Where[r] is the
promise of His coming? For *ever*
since the fathers fell asleep, all
continues just as it was from the
beginning of creation." Is. 5:19
5 For when they maintain this,
it escapes their notice that by the
word of God *the* heavens existed
long ago and *the* earth was
formed out of water and by water,
6 through which[r]the world at
that time was destroyed, being
flooded with water. 2 Pet. 2:5
7 But[r]the present heavens and
earth by His word are being reserved for fire, kept for the day of
judgment and destruction of ungodly men. 2 Pet. 3:10, 12
8 But do not let this one *fact*
escape your notice,[r]beloved, that
with the Lord one day is as a thousand years, and[r]a thousand years
as one day. 2 Pet. 3:1 • Ps. 90:4
9 The Lord is not slow about
His promise, as some count slow-
ness, but is patient toward you,
not wishing for any to perish but
for all to come to repentance.
10 But[r]the day of the Lord will
come like a thief, in which[r] the
heavens will pass away with a
roar and the elements will be destroyed with intense heat, and the
earth and its works will be
[3]burned up. 1 Cor. 1:8 • Is. 34:4
11 Since all these things are to
be destroyed in this way, what
sort of people ought you to be in
holy conduct and godliness,
12 looking for and hastening the
coming of the day of God, on account of which[r]the heavens will
be destroyed by burning, and the
[r]elements will melt with intense
heat! 2 Pet. 3:7, 10 • Is. 24:19
13 But according to His[r]promise
we are looking for new heavens
and a new earth, in which righteousness dwells. Is. 65:17
14 Therefore, beloved, since
you look for these things, be diligent to be found by Him in peace,
spotless and blameless,
15 and regard the patience of
our Lord *to be* salvation; just as
also our beloved brother Paul, according to the wisdom given him,
wrote to you,
16 as also in all *his* letters,
speaking in them of these things,
in which are some things hard to
understand, which the untaught
and unstable distort, as *they do*
also the rest of the Scriptures, to
their own destruction.
17 You therefore, [r]beloved,
knowing this beforehand, be on
your guard lest, being carried
away by the error of unprincipled
men, you fall from your own
steadfastness, 2 Pet. 3:1
18 but grow in the grace and
[r]knowledge of our Lord and Savior
Jesus Christ. To Him *be* the glory,
both now and to the day of eternity. Amen. 2 Pet. 1:2

[3]Some ancient mss. read *discovered*

THE FIRST EPISTLE OF

JOHN

WHAT was from the beginning,
what we have heard, what we
have seen with our eyes, what we
beheld and our hands handled,
concerning the Word of Life—
2 and the life was manifested,
and we have seen and bear witness and proclaim to you the eternal life, which was with the Father and was manifested to us—
3 what we have[r]seen and heard
we proclaim to you also, that you
also may have fellowship with us;
and indeed our fellowship is with
the Father, and with His Son
Jesus Christ. John 19:35
4 And [r]these things we write,
so that our[r]joy may be made complete. 1 John 2:1 • John 3:29
5 And[r]this is the message we
have heard from Him and announce to you, that [r]God is light,
and in Him there is no darkness at
all. John 1:19 • James 1:17
6 If we say that we have fellowship with Him and *yet* walk in
the darkness, we [r]lie and do not
practice the truth; John 8:55
7 but if we walk in the light as
He Himself is in the light, we have
fellowship with one another, and
the blood of Jesus His Son
cleanses us from all sin.
8 [r]If we say that we have no sin,
we are deceiving ourselves, and
the truth is not in us. Job 15:14
9 If we confess our sins, He is
faithful and righteous to forgive
us our sins and[r]to cleanse us from
all unrighteousness. Heb. 9:14
10 If we say that we have not
sinned, we make Him a liar, and
His word is not in us.

CHAPTER 2

MY little children, I am writing
these things to you that you may
not sin. And if anyone sins, we
have an [1]Advocate with the Father, Jesus Christ the righteous;
2 and He Himself is the[a]propi-
tiation for our sins; and not for
ours only, but also for *those of* the
whole world. *satisfaction*
3 And by this we know that we
have come to know Him, if we
keep His commandments.
4 The one who says, "I have
come to know Him," and does not
keep His commandments, is a liar,
and the truth is not in him;
5 but whoever[r]keeps His word,
in him the love of God has truly
been perfected. By this we know
that we are in Him: John 14:23
6 the one who says he abides
in Him ought himself to walk in
the same manner as He walked.
7 [r]Beloved, I am not writing a
new commandment to you, but an
old commandment which you
have had from the beginning; the
old commandment is the word
which you have heard. Heb. 6:9
8 [t]On the other hand, I am writing[r]a new commandment to you,
which is true in Him and in you,
because the darkness is passing
away, and the true light is already
shining. *Again* • John 13:34

[1]Gr., *Paracletos*, one called alongside to help

9 The one who says he is in the light and *yet* hates his brother is in the darkness until now.

10 [r]The one who loves his brother abides in the light and there is no cause for stumbling in him. John 11:9; 1 John 2:10, 11

11 But the one who [r]hates his brother is in the darkness and [r]walks in the darkness, and does not know where he is going because the darkness has blinded his eyes. 1 John 2:9 • John 12:35

12 I am writing to you, little children, because your sins are forgiven you for His name's sake.

13 I am writing to you, fathers, because you know Him [r]who has been from the beginning. I am writing to you, young men, because [r]you have overcome the evil one. I have written to you, children, because you know the Father. 1 John 1:1 • John 16:33

14 I have written to you, fathers, because you know Him who has been from the beginning. I have written to you, young men, because you are strong, and the word of God abides in you, and you have overcome the evil one.

15 Do not love [r]the world, nor the things in the world. If anyone loves the world, the love of the Father is not in him. Rom. 12:2

16 For all that is in the world, [r]the lust of the flesh and the lust of the eyes and the boastful pride of life, is not from the Father, but is from the world. Rom. 13:14

17 And [r]the world is passing away, and *also* its lusts; but the one who does the will of God abides forever. 1 Cor. 7:31

18 Children, it is the last hour; and just as you heard that antichrist is coming, even now many antichrists have arisen; from this we know that it is the last hour.

19 They went out from us, but they were not *really* of us; for if they had been of us, they would have remained with us; but *they went out,* in order that it might be shown that they all are not of us.

20 [t]But you have an [r]anointing from the Holy One, and you all know. *And* • 2 Cor. 1:21

21 I have not written to you because you do not know the truth, but because you do know it, and because no lie is of the truth.

22 Who is the liar but [r]the one who denies that Jesus is the Christ? This is [r]the antichrist, the one who denies the Father and the Son. 2 John 7 • 1 John 2:18

23 [r]Whoever denies the Son does not have the Father; the one who confesses the Son has the Father also. John 8:19; 16:3; 17:3

24 As for you, let that abide in you which you heard [r]from the beginning. If what you heard from the beginning abides in you, you also will abide in the Son and in the Father. 1 John 2:7

25 And this is the promise which He Himself [t]made to us: eternal life. *promised us*

26 These things I have written to you concerning those who are trying to deceive you.

27 And as for you, the anointing which you received from Him abides in you, and you have no need for anyone to teach you; but as His anointing teaches you about all things, and is true and is not a lie, and just as it has taught you, you abide in Him.

28 And now, [r]little children,

abide in Him, so that when He appears, we may have confidence
and not shrink away from Him in
shame at His coming. 1 John 2:1
29 If you know that He is righteous, you know that everyone also
who practices righteousness is
[a]born of Him. *begotten*

CHAPTER 3

SEE how great a love the Father
has bestowed upon us, that we
should be called children of God;
and *such* we are. For this reason
the world does not know us, because it did not know Him.
2 Beloved, now we are children of God, and it has not appeared as yet what we shall be.
We know that, when He appears,
we shall be like Him, because we
shall see Him just as He is.
3 And everyone who has this
hope *fixed* on Him purifies himself, just as He is pure.
4 Everyone who practices sin
also practices lawlessness; and [r]sin
is lawlessness. Rom. 4:15
5 And you know that He appeared in order to take away sins;
and in Him there is no sin.
6 No one who abides in Him
sins; no one who sins has seen
Him or [a]knows Him. *has known*
7 Little children, let no one [r]de-
ceive you; the one who practices
righteousness is righteous, just as
He is righteous; 1 John 2:26
8 the one who practices sin is
of the devil; for the devil [t]has
sinned from the beginning. The
Son of God appeared for this purpose, that He might destroy the
works of the devil. *sins*
9 No one who is born of God
practices sin, because His seed
abides in him; and he cannot sin,
because he is born of God.
10 By this the [r]children of God
and the children of the devil are
obvious: anyone who does not
practice righteousness is not of
God, nor the one who does not
love his brother. John 1:12
11 For this is the message
[r]which you have heard from the
beginning, that we should love
one another; 1 John 2:7
12 not as Cain, *who* was of the
evil one, and slew his brother.
And for what reason did he slay
him? Because his deeds were evil,
and his brother's were righteous.
13 Do not marvel, brethren, if
[r]the world hates you. John 15:18
14 We know that we have
passed out of death into life, because we love the brethren. He
who does not love abides in death.
15 Everyone who hates his
brother is a murderer; and you
know that no murderer has eternal life abiding in him.
16 We know love by this, that
[r]He laid down His life for us; and
we ought to lay down our lives for
the brethren. John 10:11; 15:13
17 But whoever has the world's
goods, and beholds his brother in
need and closes his [t]heart [t]against
him, how does the love of God
abide in him? *inward parts • from*
18 Little children, let us not love
with word or with tongue, but in
deed and [r]truth. 2 John 1
19 We shall know by this that
we are of the truth, and shall assure our heart before Him,
20 in whatever our heart condemns us; for God is greater than
our heart, and knows all things.

21 Beloved, if our heart does not
condemn us, we have confidence
[t]before God; *toward*
22 and [r]whatever we ask we receive from Him, because we [r]keep
His commandments and do the
things that are pleasing in His
sight. Job 22:26f. • 1 John 2:3
23 And this is His commandment, that we [a]believe in the name
of His Son Jesus Christ, and love
one another, just as He commanded us. *believe the name*
24 And the one who keeps His
commandments abides in Him,
and He in him. And we know by
this that He abides in us, by the
Spirit whom He has given us.

CHAPTER 4

BELOVED, do not believe every
spirit, but test the spirits to see
whether they are from God; because many false prophets have
gone out into the world.
2 By this you know the Spirit
of God: [r]every spirit that confesses
that Jesus Christ has come in the
flesh is from God; 1 Cor. 12:3
3 and every spirit that [r]does not
confess Jesus is not from God;
and this is the *spirit* of the antichrist, of which you have heard
that it is coming, and now it is already in the world. 1 John 2:22
4 You are from God, little children, and have overcome them;
because greater is He who is in
you than he who is in the world.
5 [r]They are from the world;
therefore they speak *as* from the
world, and the world listens to
them. John 15:19; 17:14, 16
6 We are from God; he who
knows God listens to us; he who is
not from God does not listen to us.
By this we know the spirit of truth
and the spirit of error.
7 Beloved, let us love one another, for love is from God; and
everyone who loves is [a]born of God
and knows God. *begotten*
8 The one who does not love
does not know God, for [r]God is
love. 1 John 4:7, 16
9 By this the love of God was
manifested [a]in us, that God has
sent His only begotten Son into
the world so that we might live
through Him. *in our case*
10 In this is love, [r]not that we
loved God, but that He loved us
and sent His Son *to be* the propitiation for our sins. 1 John 4:19
11 Beloved, if God so loved us,
we also ought to love one another.
12 No one has beheld God at
any time; if we love one another,
God abides in us, and His [r]love is
perfected in us. 1 John 2:5
13 [r]By this we know that we
abide in Him and He in us, because He has given us of His
Spirit. Rom. 8:9; 1 John 3:24
14 And we have beheld and
[r]bear witness that the Father has
sent the Son *to be* the Savior of
the world. John 15:27
15 Whoever confesses that
Jesus is the Son of God, God
abides in him, and he in God.
16 And we have come to know
and have believed the love which
God has for us. God is love, and
the one who abides in love abides
in God, and God abides in him.
17 By this, [r]love is perfected
with us, that we may have confidence in the day of judgment; because as He is, so also are we in
this world. 1 John 2:5; 4:12

18 There is no fear in love; but perfect love casts out fear, because fear [t]involves punishment, and the one who fears is not perfected in love. *has*

19 [r]We love, because He first loved us. 1 John 4:10

20 If someone says, "I love God," and [r]hates his brother, he is a liar; for the one who does not love his brother whom he has seen, cannot love God whom he has not seen. 1 John 2:9, 11

21 And [r]this commandment we have from Him, that the one who loves God should love his brother also. Lev. 19:18

CHAPTER 5

WHOEVER believes that Jesus is the [2]Christ is born of God; and whoever loves the Father loves the *child* born of Him.

2 By this we know that [r]we love the children of God, when we love God and [t]observe His commandments. 1 John 3:14 • *do*

3 For [r]this is the love of God, that we keep His commandments; and His commandments are not burdensome. John 14:15

4 For whatever is [a]born of God overcomes the world; and this is the victory that has overcome the world—our faith. *begotten*

5 And who is the one who overcomes the world, but he who [r]believes that Jesus is the Son of God? 1 John 4:15; 5:1

6 This is the one who came by water and blood, Jesus Christ; not [t]with the water only, but [t]with the water and [t]with the blood. *in*

7 And it is [r]the Spirit who bears witness, because the Spirit is the truth. Matt. 3:16f.; John 15:26

8 For there are three that bear witness, [3]the Spirit and the water and the blood; and the three are [t]in agreement. *for the one thing*

9 If we receive the witness of men, the witness of God is greater; for the witness of God is this, that [r]He has borne witness concerning His Son. Matt. 3:17

10 The one who believes in the Son of God [r]has the witness in himself; the one who does not believe God has made Him a liar, because he has not believed in the witness that God has borne concerning His Son. Rom. 8:16

11 And the witness is this, that God has given us eternal life, and [r]this life is in His Son. John 1:4

12 He who has the Son has the life; he who does not have the Son of God does not have the life.

13 These things I have written to you who [r]believe in the name of the Son of God, in order that you may know that you have eternal life. 1 John 3:23

14 And this is the confidence which we have [t]before Him, that, if we ask anything according to His will, He hears us. *toward*

15 And if we know that He hears us *in* whatever we ask, we know that we have the requests which we have asked from Him.

16 If anyone sees his brother [t]committing a sin not *leading* to death, he shall ask and *God* will for him give life to those who commit sin not *leading* to death.

[2] I.e., Messiah

[3] A few late mss. read *in heaven; the Father, the Word, and the Holy Spirit, and these three are one. And there are three that bear witness on earth, the Spirit*

There is a sin *leading* to death; I
do not say that he should make request for this. *sinning*
17 All unrighteousness is sin,
and there is a sin not *leading* to
death. 1 John 3:4 • 1 John 2:1f.
18 We know that no one who is
born of God sins; but He who was
born of God keeps him and the
evil one does not touch him.
19 We know that we are of God,
and the whole world lies in *the*
power of the evil one. Gal. 1:4
20 And we know that the Son of
God has come, and has given us
understanding, in order that we
might know Him who is true, and
we are in Him who is true, in His
Son Jesus Christ. This is the true
God and eternal life. Rev. 3:7
21 Little children, guard yourselves from idols. 1 Cor. 10:7, 14

THE SECOND EPISTLE OF

JOHN

THE elder to the chosen lady and
her children, whom I love in truth;
and not only I, but also all who
know the truth, Rom. 16:13
2 for the sake of the truth
which abides in us and will be
with us forever: 2 Pet. 1:12
3 Grace, mercy *and* peace will
be with us, from God the Father
and from Jesus Christ, the Son of
the Father, in truth and love.
4 I was very glad to find *some*
of your children walking in truth,
just as we have received commandment *to do* from the Father.
5 And now I ask you, lady, not
as writing to you a new commandment, but the one which we
have had from the beginning, that
we love one another.
6 And this is love, that we
walk according to His commandments. This is the commandment,
just as you have heard from the
beginning, that you should walk in
it. 1 John 2:5 • 1 John 2:24
7 For many deceivers have
gone out into the world, those
who do not acknowledge Jesus
Christ *as* coming in the flesh. This
is the deceiver and the antichrist.
8 Watch yourselves, that you
might not lose what we have accomplished, but that you may receive a full reward. 1 Cor. 3:8
9 Anyone who goes too far and
does not abide in the teaching of
Christ, does not have God; the one
who abides in the teaching, he has
both the Father and the Son.
10 If anyone comes to you and
does not bring this teaching, do
not receive him into *your* house,
and do not give him a greeting;
11 for the one who gives him a
greeting participates in his evil
deeds. Eph. 5:11; 1 Tim. 5:22
12 Having many things to write
to you, I do not want to *do so* with
paper and ink; but I hope to come
to you and speak face to face, that
your joy may be made full.
13 The children of your chosen
sister greet you. 2 John 1

THE THIRD EPISTLE OF

JOHN

THE elder to the beloved Gaius,
whom I love in truth. 2 John 1
2 Beloved, I pray that in all respects you may prosper and be in
good health, just as your soul
prospers.
3 For I was very glad when
brethren came and bore witness
to your truth, *that is,* how you are
walking in truth. 2 John 4
4 I have no greater joy than
this, to hear of my children walking in the truth. 1 Cor. 4:14f.
5 Beloved, you are acting
faithfully in whatever you accomplish for the brethren, and especially *when they are* strangers;
6 and they bear witness to
your love before the church; and
you will do well to send them on
their way in a manner worthy of
God. Acts 15:3 • 1 Thess. 2:12
7 For they went out for the
sake of the Name, accepting nothing from the Gentiles. Acts 5:41
8 Therefore we ought to support such men, that we may be
fellow workers with the truth.
9 I wrote something to the
church; but Diotrephes, who loves
to be first among them, does not
accept what we say. *us*
10 For this reason, if I come, I
will call attention to his deeds
which he does, unjustly accusing
us with wicked words; and not
satisfied with this, neither does he
himself receive the brethren, and
he forbids those who desire *to do
so,* and puts *them* out of the
church. 2 John 12 • 2 John 10
11 Beloved, do not imitate what
is evil, but what is good. The one
who does good is of God; the one
who does evil has not seen God.
12 Demetrius has received a
good testimony from everyone,
and from the truth itself; and we
also bear witness, and you know
that our witness is true.
13 I had many things to write to
you, but I am not willing to write
them to you with pen and ink;
14 but I hope to see you shortly,
and we shall speak face to face.
Peace *be* to you. The friends greet
you. Greet the friends by name.

THE EPISTLE OF

JUDE

JUDE, a [r]bond-servant of Jesus
Christ, and brother of [a]James, to
those who are the called, beloved
in God the Father, and kept for
Jesus Christ: Rom. 1:1 • *Jacob*
2 May mercy and peace and
love be multiplied to you.
3 Beloved, while I was making
every effort to write you about our
common salvation, I felt the necessity to write to you appealing
that you contend earnestly for the
faith which was once for all delivered to the [a]saints. *holy ones*
4 For certain persons have
[r]crept in unnoticed, those who
were long beforehand [a]marked out
for this condemnation, ungodly
persons who turn the grace of our
God into licentiousness and deny
our only Master and Lord, Jesus
Christ. Gal. 2:4 • *written about*
5 Now I desire to remind you,
though you know all things once
for all, that [1]the Lord, [r]after saving
a people out of the land of Egypt,
subsequently destroyed those
who did not believe. Ex. 12:51
6 And angels who did not keep
their own domain, but abandoned
their proper abode, He has kept in
eternal bonds under darkness for
the judgment of the great day.
7 Just as [r]Sodom and Gomorrah and the cities around them,
since they in the same way as
these indulged in gross immorality and went after strange flesh,
are exhibited as an example, in
undergoing the punishment of
eternal fire. Gen. 19:24f.
8 Yet in the same manner
these men, also by dreaming, defile the flesh, and reject authority,
and revile angelic majesties.
9 But Michael the archangel,
when he disputed with the devil
and argued about the body of
Moses, did not dare pronounce
against him a railing judgment,
but said, "The Lord rebuke you."
10 But these men revile the
things which they do not understand; and [r]the things which they
know by instinct, like unreasoning
animals, by these things they are
[t]destroyed. Phil. 3:19 • *corrupted*
11 Woe to them! For they have
gone the way of Cain, and for pay
they have rushed headlong into
the error of Balaam, and perished
in the rebellion of Korah.
12 These men are those who are
hidden reefs in your love feasts
when they feast with you without
fear, caring for themselves; clouds
without water, carried along by
winds; autumn trees without fruit,
[t]doubly dead, uprooted; *twice*
13 wild waves of the sea, casting up their own shame like foam;
wandering stars, for whom the
[t]black darkness has been reserved
forever. *blackness of darkness*
14 And about these also Enoch,
in the seventh *generation* from
Adam, prophesied, saying, "Behold, the Lord came with many
thousands of His holy ones,

[1] Some ancient mss. read *Jesus*

15 to execute judgment upon
all, and to convict all the ungodly
of all their ungodly deeds which
they have done in an ungodly
way, and of all the harsh things
which [r]ungodly sinners have spoken against Him." 1 Tim. 1:9
16 These are grumblers, finding
fault, following after their *own*
lusts; they speak arrogantly, flattering people [r]for the sake of *gaining an* advantage. 2 Pet. 2:3
17 But you, beloved, ought to
remember the words that were
spoken beforehand by the apostles of our Lord Jesus Christ,
18 that they were saying to you,
"In[r] the last time there shall be
mockers, following after their
own ungodly lusts." Acts 20:29
19 These are the ones who
cause divisions, worldly-minded,
[t]devoid of the Spirit. *not having*
20 But you, beloved, building
yourselves up on your most holy
faith; praying in the Holy Spirit;
21 keep yourselves in the love
of God, [r]waiting anxiously for the
mercy of our Lord Jesus Christ to
eternal life. Titus 2:13; Heb. 9:28
22 And have mercy on some,
who are doubting;
23 save others, snatching them
out of the fire; and on some have
mercy with fear, hating even the
garment polluted by the flesh.
24 Now to Him who is able to
keep you from stumbling, and to
[r]make you stand in the presence of
His glory blameless with [r]great
joy, 2 Cor. 4:14 • 1 Pet. 4:13
25 to the only God our Savior,
through Jesus Christ our Lord, *be*
glory, majesty, dominion and authority, before all time and now
and [t]forever. Amen. *to all the ages*

THE REVELATION TO JOHN

THE Revelation of Jesus Christ,
which [r]God gave Him to show to
His bond-servants, the things
which must shortly take place;
and He sent and [a]communicated *it*
by His angel to His [b]bond-servant
John, John 17:8 • *signified*
2 who bore witness to [r]the
word of God and to [r]the testimony
of Jesus Christ, *even* to all that he
saw. Rev. 1:9 • 1 Cor. 1:6
3 Blessed is he who reads and
those who hear the words of the
prophecy, and [a]heed the things
which are written in it; [r]for the
time is near. *keep* • Rev. 3:11
4 John to the seven churches
that are in [r]Asia: [r]Grace to you and
peace, from Him who is and who
was and who is to come; and from
the seven Spirits who are before
His throne; Acts 2:9 • Rom. 1:7
5 and from Jesus Christ, [r]the
faithful witness, the first-born of
the dead, and the ruler of the
kings of the earth. To Him who
loves us, and released us from our
sins [a]by His blood, Is. 55:4 • *in*

6 and He has made us *to be* a kingdom, priests to His God and Father; to Him *be* the glory and the dominion forever and ever. Amen. *God and His Father*

7 BEHOLD, HE IS COMING WITH THE CLOUDS, and every eye will see Him, even those who pierced Him; and all the tribes of the earth will mourn over Him. Even so. Amen. John 19:37 · Luke 23:28

8 "I am the Alpha and the Omega," says the Lord God, "who is and who was and who is to come, the Almighty." Is. 41:4

9 I, John, your brother and fellow partaker in the tribulation and kingdom and perseverance *which are* in Jesus, was on the island called Patmos, because of the word of God and the testimony of Jesus. Acts 1:15 · *steadfastness*

10 I was [1]in the Spirit on the Lord's day, and I heard behind me a loud voice like *the sound* of a trumpet, Acts 20:7 · Rev. 4:1

11 saying, "Write in a book what you see, and send *it* to the seven churches: to Ephesus and to Smyrna and to Pergamum and to Thyatira and to Sardis and to Philadelphia and to Laodicea."

12 And I turned to see the voice that was speaking with me. And having turned I saw seven golden lampstands; Ex. 25:37; 37:23

13 and in the middle of the lampstands one like [2]a son of man, clothed in a robe reaching to the feet, and girded across His breast with a golden girdle. Rev. 2:1

14 And His head and His hair were white like white wool, like snow; and His eyes were like a flame of fire; Dan. 7:9

[1]Or, *in spirit* [2]Or, *the Son of Man*

15 and His feet *were* like burnished bronze, when it has been caused to glow in a furnace, and His voice *was* like the sound of many waters. Ezek. 1:7

16 And in His right hand He held seven stars; and out of His mouth came a sharp two-edged sword; and His face was like the sun shining in its strength.

17 And when I saw Him, I fell at His feet as a dead man. And He laid His right hand upon me, saying, "Do not be afraid; I am the first and the last, Dan. 8:17

18 and the living One; and I was dead, and behold, I am alive forevermore, and I have the keys of death and of Hades. *became*

19 "Write therefore the things which you have seen, and the things which are, and the things which shall take place after these things. Rev. 1:12-16 · Rev. 4:1

20 "As for the mystery of the seven stars which you saw in My right hand, and the seven golden lampstands: the seven stars are the angels of the seven churches, and the seven lampstands are the seven churches. Rom. 11:25

CHAPTER 2

"TO the angel of the church in Ephesus write:

The One who holds the seven stars in His right hand, the One who walks among the seven golden lampstands, says this:

2 'I know your deeds and your toil and perseverance, and that you cannot endure evil men, and you put to the test those who call themselves apostles, and they are not, and you found them *to be* false; *steadfastness* · John 6:6

3 and you have perseverance
and have endured for My name's
sake, and have not grown weary.
4 'But I have *this* against you,
that you have left your first love.
5 'Remember therefore from
where you have fallen, and repent
and do the deeds you did at first;
or else I am coming to you, and
will remove your lampstand out of
its place—unless you repent.
6 'Yet this you do have, that
you hate the deeds of the Nicolaitans, which I also hate.
7 'He who has an ear, let him
hear what the Spirit says to the
churches. To him who overcomes,
I will grant to eat of the tree of
life, which is in the Paradise of
God.' Rev. 2:11, 17 • Gen. 2:9
8 'And to the angel of the
church in Smyrna write:
The first and the last, who was
dead, and has come to life, says
this: Is. 44:6; 48:12 • *became*
9 'I know your tribulation and
your poverty (but you are rich),
and the blasphemy by those who
say they are Jews and are not, but
are a synagogue of Satan.
10 'Do not fear what you are
about to suffer. Behold, the devil
is about to cast some of you into
prison, that you may be tested,
and you will have tribulation ten
days. Be faithful until death, and I
will give you the crown of life.
11 'He who has an ear, let him
hear what the Spirit says to the
churches. He who overcomes
shall not be hurt by the second
death.' Rev. 2:7 • Rev. 20:6, 14
12 'And to the angel of the
church in Pergamum write:
The One who has the sharp
two-edged sword says this:
13 'I know where you dwell,
where Satan's throne is; and you
hold fast My name, and did not
deny My faith, even in the days of
Antipas, My witness, My faithful
one, who was killed among you,
where Satan dwells. Matt. 4:10
14 'But I have a few things
against you, because you have
there some who hold the teaching
of Balaam, who kept teaching Balak to put a stumbling block before the sons of Israel, to eat
things sacrificed to idols, and to
commit *acts of* immorality.
15 'Thus you also have some
who in the same way hold the
teaching of the Nicolaitans.
16 'Repent therefore; or else I
am coming to you quickly, and I
will make war against them with
the sword of My mouth.
17 'He who has an ear, let him
hear what the Spirit says to the
churches. To him who overcomes,
to him I will give *some* of the hidden manna, and I will give him a
white stone, and a new name written on the stone which no one
knows but he who receives it.'
18 'And to the angel of the
church in Thyatira write:
The Son of God, who has eyes
like a flame of fire, and His feet
are like burnished bronze, says
this: Rev. 1:11; 2:24 • *His eyes*
19 'I know your deeds, and your
love and faith and service and perseverance, and that your deeds of
late are greater than at first.
20 'But I have *this* against you,
that you tolerate the woman Jezebel, who calls herself a prophetess, and she teaches and leads My
bond-servants astray, so that they

commit *acts of* immorality and
eat things sacrificed to idols.
21 'And I gave her time to repent; and she does not want to repent of her immorality.
22 'Behold, I will cast her upon a
bed *of sickness*, and those who
commit adultery with her into
great tribulation, unless they repent of [3]her deeds. *I cast · into*
23 'And I will kill her children
with pestilence; and all the
churches will know that I am He
who searches the minds and
hearts; and I will give to each one
of you according to your deeds.
24 'But I say to you, the rest who
are in Thyatira, who do not hold
this teaching, who have not
known the deep things of Satan,
as they call them—I place no other burden on you. Rev. 2:18
25 'Nevertheless what you have,
hold fast until I come. Rev. 3:11
26 'And he who overcomes, and
he who keeps My deeds until the
end, TO HIM I WILL GIVE AUTHOR-
ITY OVER THE NATIONS; *Gentiles*
27 AND HE SHALL RULE THEM
WITH A ROD OF IRON, AS THE VES-
SELS OF THE POTTER ARE BROKEN
TO PIECES, as I also have received
authority from My Father;
28 and I will give him the morning star.
29 'He who has an ear, let him
hear what the Spirit says to the
churches.' Rev. 2:7

CHAPTER 3

"AND to the angel of the church
in Sardis write:
He who has the seven Spirits of
God, and the seven stars, says
this: 'I know your deeds, that you
have a name that you are alive,
but you are dead. Rev. 1:4
2 'Wake up, and strengthen the
things that remain, which were
about to die; for I have not found
your deeds completed in the sight
of My God.
3 'Remember therefore what
you have received and heard; and
keep *it*, and repent. If therefore
you will not wake up, I will come
like a thief, and you will not know
at what hour I will come upon
you. Rev. 2:5 · *how*
4 'But you have a few people in
Sardis who have not soiled their
garments; and they will walk with
Me in white; for they are worthy.
5 'He who overcomes shall thus
be clothed in white garments; and
I will not erase his name from the
book of life, and I will confess his
name before My Father, and before His angels. Rev. 3:4
6 'He who has an ear, let him
hear what the Spirit says to the
churches.' Rev. 2:7
7 "And to the angel of the
church in Philadelphia write:
He who is holy, who is true,
who has the key of David, who
opens and no one will shut, and
who shuts and no one opens, says
this: Rev. 1:11 · Rev. 6:10
8 'I know your [4]deeds. Behold, I
have put before you an open door
which no one can shut, because
you have a little power, and have
kept My word, and have not denied My name. Acts 14:27
9 'Behold, I will cause *those* of
the synagogue of Satan, who say
that they are Jews, and are not,
but lie—behold, I will make them

[3]Some mss. read *their*

[4]Or, *deeds (behold . . . shut), that you*

to come and bow down at your
feet, and to know that I have
loved you. *give • before*
10 'Because you have kept the
word of My perseverance, I also
will keep you from the hour of
testing, that *hour* which is about
to come upon the whole world, to
test those who dwell upon the
earth. *inhabited earth • tempt*
11 'I am coming quickly; hold
fast what you have, in order that
no one take your crown.
12 'He who overcomes, I will
make him a pillar in the temple of
My God, and he will not go out
from it anymore; and I will write
upon him the name of My God,
and the name of the city of My
God, the new Jerusalem, which
comes down out of heaven from
My God, and My new name.
13 'He who has an ear, let him
hear what the Spirit says to the
churches.' Rev. 3:6
14 "And to the angel of the
church in Laodicea write:
The Amen, the faithful and true
Witness, the [5]Beginning of the creation of God, says this:
15 'I know your deeds, that you
are neither cold nor hot; I would
that you were cold or hot.
16 'So because you are luke-
warm, and neither hot nor cold, I
will spit you out of My mouth.
17 'Because you say, "I am rich,
and have become wealthy, and
have need of nothing," and you do
not know that you are wretched
and miserable and poor and blind
and naked, Hos. 12:8; Zech. 11:5
18 I advise you to buy from Me
gold refined by fire, that you may
become rich, and white garments,
that you may clothe yourself, and
that the shame of your nakedness
may not be revealed; and eyesalve
to anoint your eyes, that you may
see. Is. 55:1 • 1 Pet. 1:7
19 'Those whom I love, I reprove
and discipline; be zealous therefore, and repent. Rev. 2:5
20 'Behold, I stand at the door
and knock; if anyone hears My
voice and opens the door, I will
come in to him, and will dine with
him, and he with Me. John 10:3
21 'He who overcomes, I will
grant to him to sit down with Me
on My throne, as I also overcame
and sat down with My Father on
His throne. Matt. 19:28
22 'He who has an ear, let him
hear what the Spirit says to the
churches.' " Rev. 2:7

CHAPTER 4

AFTER these things I looked, and
behold, a door *standing* open in
heaven, and the first voice which I
had heard, like *the sound* of a
trumpet speaking with me, said,
"Come up here, and I will show
you what must take place after
these things." *saying*
2 Immediately I was [6]in the
Spirit; and behold, a throne was
standing in heaven, and One sitting on the throne. Is. 6:1
3 And He who was sitting *was*
like a jasper stone and a sardius in
appearance; and *there was* a rainbow around the throne, like an
emerald in appearance. *halo*
4 And around the throne *were*
twenty-four thrones; and upon the
thrones *I saw* twenty-four elders
sitting, clothed in white garments,

[5]I.e., origin or source

[6]Or, *in spirit*

and golden crowns on their heads.
5 And from the throne proceed
[r]flashes of lightning and sounds
and peals of thunder. And *there*
were seven lamps of fire burning
before the throne, which are the
seven Spirits of God; Ex. 19:16
6 and before the throne *there*
was, as it were, a [r]sea of glass like
crystal; and in the center and
[r]around the throne, four living
creatures full of eyes in front and
behind. Ezek. 1:22 • Rev. 4:4
7 [r]And the first creature *was*
like a lion, and the second creature like a calf, and the third creature had a face like that of a man,
and the fourth creature *was* like a
flying eagle. Ezek. 1:10; 10:14
8 And the [r]four living creatures,
each one of them having six
wings, are full of eyes around and
within; and day and night they do
not cease to say, Ezek. 1:5

"HOLY, HOLY, HOLY, *is* THE
LORD GOD, THE ALMIGHTY,
who was and who is and
who is to come."

9 And when the living creatures give glory and honor and
thanks to Him who [r]sits on the
throne, to [r]Him who lives forever
and ever, Ps. 47:8 • Dan. 4:34
10 the [r]twenty-four elders will
fall down before Him who sits on
the throne, and will worship Him
who lives forever and ever, and
will cast their crowns before the
throne, saying, Rev. 4:4
11 "Worthy art Thou, our Lord
and our God, to receive glory and honor and power; for
Thou [r]didst create all things,
and because of Thy will
they [t]existed, and were created." Acts 14:15 • *were*

CHAPTER 5

AND I saw in the right hand of
Him who sat on the throne a book
written inside and on the back,
sealed up with seven seals.
2 And I saw a strong angel proclaiming with a loud voice, "Who
is worthy to open the [a]book and to
break its seals?" *scroll*
3 And no one [r]in heaven, or on
the earth, or under the earth, was
able to open the [a]book, or to look
into it. Phil. 2:10 • *scroll*
4 And I *began* to weep greatly,
because no one was found worthy
to open the book, or to look into it;
5 and one of the elders *said to
me, "Stop weeping; behold, the
Lion that is from the tribe of Judah, the Root of David, has overcome so as to open the [a]book and
its seven seals." *scroll*
6 And I saw [7]between the
throne (with the four living creatures) and [r]the elders a Lamb
standing, as if slain, having seven
horns and seven eyes, which are
the seven Spirits of God, sent out
into all the earth. Rev. 4:4
7 And He came, and He took [r]*it*
out of the right hand of Him who
sat on the throne. Rev. 5:1
8 And when He had taken the
[a]book, the four living creatures and
the twenty-four elders fell down
before the Lamb, having each one
a harp, and golden bowls full of
incense, which are the prayers of
the [a]saints. *scroll* • *holy ones*
9 And they *sang a [r]new song,
saying, Ps. 33:3; 40:3; 98:1

"Worthy art Thou to take the
[a]book, and to break its seals;

[7]Lit., *in the middle of the throne and of the four living creatures, and in the middle of the elders*

for Thou wast slain, and
didst purchase for God with
Thy blood *men* from every
tribe and tongue and people
and nation. *scroll*
10 "And Thou hast made them
to be a kingdom and priests
to our God; and they will
reign upon the earth."
11 And I looked, and I heard the
voice of many angels around the
throne and the living creatures
and the elders; and the number of
them was myriads of myriads,
and thousands of thousands,
12 saying with a loud voice,
"Worthy[r] is the Lamb that
was slain to receive power
and riches and wisdom and
might and honor and glory
and blessing." Rev. 1:6
13 And [r]every created thing
which is in heaven and on the
earth and under the earth and on
the sea, and all things in them. I
heard saying,
"To Him who [r]sits on the
throne, and to the Lamb, *be*
blessing and honor and glory and dominion forever
and ever." Phil. 2:10 • Rev. 5:1
14 And the four living creatures
kept saying, "Amen." And the elders fell down and worshiped.

CHAPTER 6

AND I saw when the [r]Lamb broke
one of the [r]seven seals, and I heard
one of the four living creatures
saying as with a voice of thunder,
"Come." John 1:29 • Rev. 5:1
2 And I looked, and behold, a
white horse, and he who sat on it
had a bow; and a crown was given
to him; and he went out [r]conquer-
ing, and to conquer. Rev. 3:21
3 And when He broke the second seal, I heard the second living
creature saying, "Come."
4 And another, a red horse,
went out; and to him who sat on
it, it was granted to take peace
from the earth, and that *men*
should slay one another; and a
great sword was given to him.
5 And when He broke the third
seal, I heard the [r]third living creature saying, "Come." And I
looked, and behold, a black horse;
and he who sat on it had a pair of
scales in his hand. Rev. 4:7
6 And I heard as it were a
voice in the center of the [r]four living creatures saying, "A [8]quart of
wheat for a [9]denarius, and three
quarts of barley for a denarius;
and [r]do not harm the oil and the
wine." Rev. 4:6f. • Rev. 7:3
7 And when He broke the
fourth seal, I heard the voice of
the [r]fourth living creature saying,
"Come." Rev. 4:7
8 And I looked, and behold, an
[a]ashen horse; and he who sat on it
had the name Death; and Hades
was following with him. And authority was given to them over a
fourth of the earth, to kill with
sword and with famine and with
[a]pestilence and by the wild beasts
of the earth. *sickly pale • death*
9 And when He broke the fifth
seal, I saw underneath the altar
the souls of those who had been
slain because of the word of God,
and because of the testimony
which they had maintained;

[8]Gr., *choenix;* i.e., a dry measure almost equal to a quart
[9]The denarius was equivalent to one day's wage

10 and they cried out with a
loud voice, saying, "How ʳlong, O
ᵃLord, holy and true, wilt Thou refrain from judging and avenging
our blood on those who dwell on
the earth?" Zech. 1:12 • *Master*
11 And there was given to each
of them a white robe; and they
were told that they should rest for
a little while longer, until *the
number of* their fellow servants
and their brethren who were to be
killed even as they had been,
should be completed also.
12 And I looked when He broke
the sixth seal, and there was a
great ʳearthquake; and the sun became black as sackcloth *made* of
hair, and the whole moon became
like blood; Matt. 24:7; Rev. 8:5
13 and ʳthe stars of the sky fell
to the earth, as a fig tree casts its
unripe figs when shaken by a
great wind. Matt. 24:29
14 And the sky was split apart
like a scroll when it is rolled up;
and every mountain and island
were moved out of their places.
15 And ʳthe kings of the earth
and the great men and the [10]com-
manders and the rich and the
strong and every slave and free
man, hid themselves in the caves
and among the rocks of the mountains; Is. 2:10f., 19, 21; 24:21
16 and they *said to the mountains and to the rocks, "Fall on us
and hide us from the presence of
Him who sits on the throne, and
from the wrath of the Lamb;
17 for ʳthe great day of their
wrath has come; and ʳwho is able
to stand?" Is. 63:4 • Ps. 76:7

[10]I.e., chiliarchs, in command of one thousand troops

CHAPTER 7

AFTER this I saw ʳfour angels
standing at the four corners of the
earth, holding back the four winds
of the earth, so that no wind
should blow on the earth or on the
sea or on any tree. Rev. 9:14
2 And I saw another angel ascending ʳfrom the rising of the sun,
having the ʳseal of the living God;
and he cried out with a loud voice
to the four angels to whom it was
granted to harm the earth and the
sea, Is. 41:2 • Rev. 7:3
3 saying, "Do not harm the
earth or the sea or the trees, until
we have sealed the bond-servants
of our God on their foreheads."
4 And I heard the ʳnumber of
those who were sealed, one hundred and forty-four thousand
sealed from every tribe of the sons
of Israel: Rev. 9:16
5 from the tribe of Judah,
twelve thousand *were* sealed,
from the tribe of Reuben twelve
thousand, from the tribe of Gad
twelve thousand,
6 from the tribe of Asher
twelve thousand, from the tribe of
Naphtali twelve thousand, from
the tribe of Manasseh twelve
thousand,
7 from the tribe of Simeon
twelve thousand, from the tribe of
Levi twelve thousand, from the
tribe of Issachar twelve thousand,
8 from the tribe of Zebulun
twelve thousand, from the tribe of
Joseph twelve thousand, from the
tribe of Benjamin, twelve thousand *were* sealed.
9 After these things I looked,
and behold, a great multitude,
which no one could count, from

[r]every nation and *all* tribes and peoples and tongues, standing [r]before the throne and before the Lamb, clothed in white robes, and palm branches *were* in their hands; Rev. 5:9 • Rev. 7:15

10 and they cry out with a loud voice, saying,

"**S**alvation to our God who sits on the throne, and to the Lamb."

11 And all the angels were standing [r]around the throne and *around* the elders and the four living creatures; and they fell on their faces before the throne and worshiped God, Rev. 4:4

12 saying,

"**A**men, blessing and glory and wisdom and thanksgiving and honor and power and might, *be* to our God forever and ever. Amen."

13 And one of the elders [r]answered, saying to me, "These who are clothed in the white robes, who are they, and from where have they come?" Acts 3:12

14 And I [t]said to him, "My lord, you know." And he said to me, "These are the ones who come out of the great tribulation, and they have washed their robes and made them white in the blood of the Lamb. *have said*

15 "For this reason, they are [r]before the throne of God; and they serve Him day and night in His [a]temple; and He who sits on the throne shall spread His tabernacle over them. Rev. 7:9 • *sanctuary*

16 "They [r]shall hunger no more, neither thirst anymore; neither shall the sun [t]beat down on them, nor any heat; Ps. 121:5f. • *fall*

17 for the Lamb in the center of the throne shall be their shepherd, and shall guide them to springs of the water of life; and God shall wipe every tear from their eyes."

CHAPTER 8

AND when He broke the [r]seventh seal, there was silence in heaven for about half an hour. Rev. 5:1

2 And I saw the seven angels who stand before God; and seven trumpets were given to them.

3 And another angel came and stood at the altar, holding a golden censer; and much incense was given to him, that he might [t]add it to the prayers of all the saints upon the golden altar which was before the throne. *give*

4 And the smoke of the incense, [a]with the prayers of the saints, went up before God out of the angel's hand. *for*

5 And the angel took the censer; and he filled it with the fire of the altar and threw it to the earth; and there followed peals of thunder and sounds and flashes of lightning and an earthquake.

6 And the seven angels who had the seven trumpets prepared themselves to sound them.

7 And the first sounded, and there came hail and fire, mixed with blood, and they were thrown to the earth; and a third of the earth was burned up, and a third of the trees were burned up, and all the green grass was burned up.

8 And the second angel sounded, and *something* like a great mountain burning with fire was thrown into the sea; and a third of the sea became blood;

9 and a third of the creatures, which were in the sea [t]and had life,

died; and a third of the ships were
destroyed. *those which had*
10 And the third angel sounded,
and a great star[r]fell from heaven,
burning like a torch, and it fell on
a third of the rivers and on the
springs of waters; Is. 14:12
11 and the name of the star is
called Wormwood; and a[r]third of
the waters became [r]wormwood;
and many men died from the waters, because they were made bitter. Zech. 13:8, 9 • Jer. 9:15
12 And the fourth angel
sounded, and a third of the sun
and a third of the moon and a
third of the stars were smitten, so
that a third of them might be
darkened and the day might not
shine for a third of it, and the
night in the same way.
13 And I looked, and I heard an
eagle flying in midheaven, saying
with a loud voice, "Woe, woe,
woe, to those who dwell on the
earth, because of the remaining
blasts of the trumpet of the three
angels who are about to sound!"

CHAPTER 9

AND the fifth angel sounded, and
I saw a star from heaven which
had fallen to the earth; and the
key of the[t]bottomless pit was giv-
en to him. *shaft of the abyss*
2 And he opened the bottom-
less pit; and[r]smoke went up out of
the pit, like the smoke of a great
furnace; and[r]the sun and the air
were darkened by the smoke of
the pit. Gen. 19:28 • Joel 2:2, 10
3 And out of the smoke came
forth[r]locusts[t]upon the earth; and
power was given them, as the
scorpions of the earth have
power. Ex. 10:12-15 • *into*
4 And they were told that they
should not[r]hurt the[r]grass of the
earth, nor any green thing, nor
any tree, but only the men who do
not have the seal of God on their
foreheads. Rev. 6:6 • Rev. 8:7
5 And they were not permitted
to kill[t]anyone, but to torment for
five months; and their torment
was like the torment of a scorpion
when it stings a man. *them*
6 And in those days[r]men will
seek death and will not find it; and
they will long to die and death
flees from them. Job 3:21; 7:15
7 And the appearance of the
locusts was like horses prepared
for battle; and on their heads, as it
were, crowns like gold, and their
faces were like the faces of men.
8 And they had hair like the
hair of women, and their teeth
were like *the teeth* of lions.
9 And they had breastplates
like breastplates of iron; and the
[r]sound of their wings was like the
sound of chariots, of many horses
rushing to battle. Jer. 47:3
10 And they have tails like[r]scor-
pions, and stings; and in their[r]tails
is their power to hurt men for five
months. Ezek. 2:6 • Rev. 9:19
11 They have as king over them,
the angel of the abyss; his name in
Hebrew is [11]Abaddon, and in the
Greek he has the name Apollyon.
12 [r]The first woe is past; behold,
two woes are still coming after
these things. Rev. 8:13; 11:14
13 And the sixth angel sounded,
and I heard[t]a voice from the [12]four

[11] I.e., destruction
[12] Some ancient mss. do not contain *four*

horns of the [r]golden altar which is before God, *one voice* • Rev. 8:3

14 one saying to the sixth angel who had the trumpet, "Release the four angels who are bound at the great river Euphrates."

15 And the four angels, who had been prepared for the hour and day and month and year, were released, so that they might kill a third of [t]mankind. *men*

16 And the number of the armies of the horsemen was [r]two hundred million; I heard the number of them. Rev. 5:11

17 And [t]this is how I saw in the vision the horses and those who sat on them: *the riders* had breastplates *the color* of fire and of hyacinth and of brimstone; and the heads of the horses are like the heads of lions; and out of their mouths proceed fire and smoke and brimstone. *thus I saw*

18 A third of [t]mankind was killed by these three plagues, by the fire and the smoke and the [a]brimstone, which proceeded out of their mouths. *men* • *sulphur*

19 For the power of the horses is in their mouths and in their tails; for their tails are like serpents and have heads; and with them they do harm.

20 And the rest of mankind, who were not killed by these plagues, did not repent of the works of their hands, so as not to worship demons, and the idols of gold and of silver and of brass and of stone and of wood, which can neither see nor hear nor walk;

21 and they [r]did not repent of their murders nor of their sorceries nor of their immorality nor of their thefts. Rev. 9:20

CHAPTER 10

AND I saw another [r]strong angel coming down out of heaven, clothed with a cloud; and the rainbow was upon his head, and his face was like the sun, and his feet like pillars of fire; Rev. 5:2

2 and he had in his hand a little book which was open. And he placed his right foot on the sea and his left on the land;

3 and he cried out with a loud voice, [r]as when a lion roars; and when he had cried out, the seven peals of thunder [a]uttered their voices. Is. 31:4 • *spoke*

4 And when the seven peals of thunder had spoken, I was about to write; and I heard [r]a voice from heaven saying, "Seal [r]up the things which the seven peals of thunder have spoken, and do not write them." Rev. 10:8 • Dan. 8:26

5 And the angel whom I saw standing on the sea and on the land [r]lifted up his right hand to heaven, Deut. 32:40; Dan. 12:7

6 and swore by Him who lives forever and ever, WHO CREATED HEAVEN AND THE THINGS IN IT, AND THE EARTH AND THE THINGS IN IT, AND THE SEA AND THE THINGS IN IT, that there shall be delay no longer,

7 but in the days of the voice of the seventh angel, when he is about to sound, then the mystery of God is finished, as He preached to His servants the prophets.

8 And the voice which I heard from heaven, *I heard* again speaking with me, and saying, "Go, take the [a]book which is open in the hand of the angel who stands on the sea and on the land." *scroll*

9 And I went to the angel, tell-

ing him to give me the little book. And he *said to me, "Take it, and eat it; and it will make your stomach bitter, but in your mouth it will be sweet as honey."

10 And I took the little book out of the angel's hand and ate it, and it was in my mouth sweet as honey; and when I had eaten it, my stomach was made bitter.

11 And [r]they *said to me, "You must prophesy again concerning many peoples and nations and tongues and kings." Rev. 11:1

CHAPTER 11

AND there was given me a [t]measuring rod like a staff; and someone said, "Rise and measure the temple of God, and the altar, and those who worship in it. *reed*

2 "And [t]leave out the court which is outside the temple, and do not measure it, for it has been given to the nations; and they will tread under foot the holy city for forty-two months. *throw out*

3 "And I will grant *authority* to my two witnesses, and they will prophesy for twelve hundred and sixty days, clothed in sackcloth."

4 These are the two olive trees and the two lampstands that stand before the Lord of the earth.

5 And if anyone desires to harm them, [r]fire proceeds out of their mouth and devours their enemies; and if anyone would desire to harm them, in this manner he must be killed. 2 Kin. 1:10-12

6 These have the power to [r]shut up the sky, in order that rain may not fall during [r]the days of their prophesying; and they have power over the waters to turn them into blood, and to smite the earth with every plague, as often as they desire. Luke 4:25 • Rev. 11:3

7 And when they have finished their testimony, the beast that comes up out of the abyss will make war with them, and overcome them and kill them.

8 And their dead [13]bodies *will lie* in the street of the [r]great city which [14]mystically is called Sodom and Egypt, where also their Lord was crucified. Rev. 14:8

9 And those from [r]the peoples and tribes and tongues and nations *will* look at their dead [13]bodies for three and a half days, and will not permit their dead bodies to be laid in a tomb. Rev. 5:9

10 And those who dwell on the earth *will* rejoice over them and make merry; and they will send gifts to one another, because these two prophets tormented those who dwell on the earth.

11 And after the three and a half days the breath of life from God came into them, and they stood on their feet; and great fear fell upon those who were beholding them.

12 And they heard a loud voice from heaven saying to them, "Come up here." And they went up into heaven in the cloud, and their enemies beheld them.

13 And in that hour there was a great [r]earthquake, and a tenth of the city fell; and seven thousand people were killed in the earthquake, and the rest were terrified and [r]gave glory to the God of heaven. Rev. 6:12 • John 9:24

[13] Some ancient mss. read *body*
[14] Lit., *spiritually*

14 The second [r]woe is past; behold, the third woe is coming quickly. Rev. 8:13; 9:12

15 And the seventh angel sounded; and there arose loud voices in heaven, saying,

"The kingdom of the world has become *the kingdom* of our Lord, and of His [15]Christ; and He will reign forever and ever."

16 And the twenty-four elders, who [r]sit on their thrones before God, fell on their faces and worshiped God, Matt. 19:28

17 saying,

"We give Thee thanks, O Lord God, the Almighty, who art and who wast, because Thou hast taken Thy great power and [t]hast begun to reign. *didst reign*

18 "And [r]the nations were enraged, and Thy wrath came, and the time *came* for the dead to be judged, and *the time* to give their reward to Thy bond-servants the prophets and to the [a]saints and to those who fear Thy name, the small and the great, and to destroy those who destroy the earth." Ps. 2:1 • *holy ones*

19 And the [a]temple of God which is in heaven was opened; and the ark of His covenant appeared in His [a]temple, and there were flashes of lightning and sounds and peals of thunder and an earthquake and a great [t]hailstorm. *sanctuary* • *hail*

CHAPTER 12

AND a great [r]sign appeared [r]in heaven: a woman clothed with the sun, and the moon under her feet, and on her head a crown of twelve stars; Rev. 12:3 • Rev. 11:19

2 and she was with child; and she *cried out, being in labor and in pain to give birth.

3 And [r]another sign appeared in heaven: and behold, a great red dragon having seven heads and ten horns, and on his heads *were* seven diadems. Rev. 12:1; 15:1

4 And his tail *swept away a [r]third of the stars of heaven, and threw them to the earth. And the dragon stood before the woman who was about to give birth, so that when she gave birth he might devour her child. Rev. 8:7, 12

5 And she gave birth to a son, a male *child*, who is to [a]rule all the [a]nations with a rod of iron; and her child was caught up to God and to His throne. *shepherd* • *Gentiles*

6 And the woman fled into the wilderness where she *had a place prepared by God, so that there she might be nourished for one thousand two hundred and sixty days.

7 And there was war in heaven, [r]Michael and his angels waging war with the [r]dragon. And the dragon and his angels waged war, Jude 9 • Rev. 12:3

8 and they were not strong enough, and there was no longer a place found for them in heaven.

9 And the great dragon was thrown down, the serpent of old who is called the devil and Satan, who deceives the whole [t]world; he was thrown down to the earth, and his angels were thrown down with him. *inhabited earth*

10 And I heard [r]a loud voice in heaven, saying,

"Now the salvation, and the

[15]I.e., Messiah

power, and the kingdom of our
God and the authority of His
Christ have come, for the accuser
of our brethren has been thrown
down, who accuses them before
our God day and night. Rev. 11:15
11 "And they overcame him because of the blood of the Lamb
and because of the word of their
testimony, and they did not love
their life even to death.
12 "For this reason, [r]rejoice, O
heavens and you who [a]dwell in
them. Woe to the earth and the
sea, because the devil has come
down to you, having great wrath,
knowing that he has *only* a short
time." Ps. 96:11 • *tabernacle*
13 And when the dragon saw
that he was thrown down to the
earth, he persecuted the woman
who gave birth to the male *child*.
14 And the two wings of the
great eagle were given to the
woman, in order that she might fly
into the wilderness to her place,
where she *was nourished for a
time and times and half a time,
from the presence of the serpent.
15 And the [r]serpent [t]poured water like a river out of his mouth
after the woman, so that he might
cause her to be swept away with
the flood. Gen. 3:1 • *threw*
16 And the earth helped the
woman, and the earth opened its
mouth and drank up the river
which the dragon [t]poured out of
his mouth. *threw*
17 And the dragon was enraged
with the woman, and went off to
[r]make war with the rest of her offspring, who keep the commandments of God and hold to the testimony of Jesus. Rev. 11:7

CHAPTER 13

AND he stood on the sand of the
[t]seashore. *sea*
And I saw a beast coming up
out of the sea, having ten horns
and seven heads, and on his horns
were ten diadems, and on his
heads *were* blasphemous names.
2 And the beast which I saw
was [r]like a leopard, and his feet
were *like those* of [r]a bear, and his
mouth like the mouth of a lion.
And the dragon gave him his
power and his throne and great
authority. Dan. 7:6 • Dan. 7:5
3 And *I saw* one of his heads as
if it had been [t]slain, and his fatal
wound was healed. And the whole
earth was amazed *and followed*
after the beast; *smitten to death*
4 and they worshiped the
dragon, because he gave his authority to the beast; and they worshiped the beast, saying, "Who [r]is
like the beast, and who is able to
wage war with him?" Is. 46:5
5 And there was given to him a
mouth speaking [t]arrogant words
and blasphemies; and authority to
[t]act for forty-two months was giv-
en to him. *great things* • *do*
6 And he opened his mouth in
blasphemies against God, to blaspheme His name and His tabernacle, *that is*, [r]those who [a]dwell in
heaven. Rev. 7:15 • *tabernacle*
7 And it was given to him to
[r]make war with the [a]saints and to
overcome them; and authority
over every tribe and people and
tongue and nation was given to
him. Dan. 7:21 • *holy ones*
8 And all who dwell on the
earth will worship him, *everyone*

whose name has not been [16]written from the foundation of the world in the book of life of the Lamb who has been slain.

9 [r]If anyone has an ear, let him hear. Rev. 2:7

10 If anyone [17]*is destined* for captivity, to captivity he goes; if anyone kills with the sword, with the sword he must be killed. Here is the[a]perseverance and the faith of the saints. *steadfastness*

11 And I saw another beast coming up out of the earth; and he [r]had two horns like a lamb, and he spoke as a dragon. *was having*

12 And he [r]exercises all the authority of the first beast in his presence. And he makes the earth and those who dwell in it to worship the first beast, whose fatal wound was healed. Rev. 13:4

13 And he performs great signs, so that he even makes [r]fire come down out of heaven to the earth in the presence of men. Rev. 11:5

14 And he deceives those who dwell on the earth because of the signs which it was given him to perform in the presence of the beast, telling those who dwell on the earth to make an image to the beast who *had the wound of the sword and has come to life.

15 And there was given to him to give breath to the image of the beast, that the image of the beast might even [18]speak and cause as many as do not worship the image of the beast to be killed.

16 And he causes all, the small and the great, and the rich and the poor, and the free men and the slaves, to be given a mark on their right hand, or on their forehead,

17 and *he provides* that no one should be able to buy or to sell, except the one who has the [r]mark, *either* the name of the beast or the number of his name. Gal. 6:17

18 Here is wisdom. Let him who has understanding calculate the number of the beast, for the number is that of a man; and his number is [19]six hundred and sixty-six.

CHAPTER 14

AND I looked, and behold, the Lamb *was* standing on Mount Zion, and with Him one hundred and forty-four thousand, having His name and the name of His Father written on their foreheads.

2 And I heard a voice from heaven, like the sound of many waters and like the sound of loud thunder, and the voice which I heard *was* like *the sound* of harpists playing on their harps.

3 And they *sang a new song before the throne and before the four living creatures and the elders; and no one could learn the song except the one hundred and forty-four thousand who had been purchased from the earth.

4 These are the ones who have not been defiled with women, for they [20]have kept themselves chaste. These *are* the ones who [r]follow the Lamb wherever He goes. These have been purchased from among men as first fruits to God and to the Lamb. Rev. 3:4

[16]Or, *written in the book . . . slain from the foundation of the world*
[17]Or, leads *into captivity*
[18]Some ancient mss. read *speak, and he will cause*

[19]Some mss. read 616 [20]Lit., *are chaste men*

5 And no lie was found in their
mouth; they are blameless.
6 And I saw another angel
flying in [r]midheaven, having an
eternal gospel to preach to those
who[t]live on the earth, and to every nation and tribe and tongue
and people; Rev. 8:13 • *sit*
7 and he said with a loud voice,
"Fear God, and give Him glory,
because the hour of His judgment
has come; and worship Him who
made the heaven and the earth
and sea and springs of waters."
8 And another angel, a second
one, followed, saying, "Fallen,
fallen is Babylon the great, she
who has made all the nations
drink of the wine of the[a]passion of
her immorality." *wrath*
9 And another angel, a third
one, followed them, saying with a
loud voice, "If anyone [r]worships
the beast and his image, and receives a mark on his forehead or
upon his hand, Rev. 13:12
10 he also will drink of the wine
of the wrath of God, which is
mixed in full strength in the cup of
His anger; and he will be tormented with fire and brimstone in
the presence of the holy angels
and in the presence of the Lamb.
11 "And the smoke of their torment goes up forever and ever;
and they have no rest day and
night, those who worship the
beast and his image, and whoever
receives the mark of his name."
12 Here is the perseverance of
the saints who keep the commandments of God and[t]their faith
in Jesus. *the faith of*
13 And I heard a voice from
heaven, saying, "Write, 'Blessed[r]
are the dead who die in the Lord
from now on!' " "Yes," says the
Spirit, "that they may rest from
their labors, for their deeds follow
with them." Rev. 20:6
14 And I looked, and behold, a
[r]white cloud, and sitting on the
cloud *was* one[r]like [21]a son of man,
having a golden crown on His
head, and a sharp sickle in His
hand. Matt. 17:5 • Dan. 7:13
15 And another angel came out
of the temple, crying out with a
loud voice to Him who sat on the
cloud, "Put[t] in your sickle and
reap, because the hour to reap has
come, because the harvest of the
earth is ripe." *Send forth*
16 And He who sat on the cloud
[t]swung His sickle over the earth;
and the earth was reaped. *cast*
17 And another angel came out
of the temple which is in heaven,
and he also had a sharp sickle.
18 And another angel, the one
who has power over fire, came out
from the altar; and he called with
a loud voice to him who had the
sharp sickle, saying, "Put in your
sharp sickle, and gather the clusters[t]from the vine of the earth, because her grapes are ripe." *of*
19 And the angel [t]swung his
sickle to the earth, and gathered
the clusters from the vine of the
earth, and threw them into [r]the
great wine press of the wrath of
God. *cast* • Is. 63:2f.
20 And the wine press was trodden outside the city, and blood
came out from the wine press, up
to the horses' bridles, for a distance of [22]two hundred miles.

[21] Or, *the Son of Man*
[22] Lit., *sixteen hundred stadia.* A stadion was about six hundred feet.

CHAPTER 15

AND I saw another sign in
heaven, great and marvelous,
seven angels who had [r]seven
plagues, *which are* [r]the last, because in them the wrath of God is
finished. Lev. 26:21 • Rev. 9:20
2 And I saw, as it were, a [r]sea
of glass mixed with fire, and those
who had come off victorious from
the beast and from his image and
from the number of his name,
standing on the sea of glass, holding harps of God. Rev. 4:6
3 And they *sang the [r]song of
Moses the bond-servant of God
and the [r]song of the Lamb, saying,
"Great and marvelous are
Thy works, Ex. 15:1ff.
O Lord God, the Almighty;
Righteous and true are Thy
ways, Rev. 5:9f., 12f.
Thou King of the [23]nations.
4 "Who will not fear, O Lord,
and glorify Thy name?
For Thou alone art holy;
For [r]ALL THE NATIONS WILL
COME AND WORSHIP BE-
FORE THEE, Ps. 86:9
For Thy righteous acts have
been revealed."
5 After these things I looked,
and [r]the [a]temple of the tabernacle
of testimony in heaven was
opened, Rev. 11:19 • *sanctuary*
6 and the [r]seven angels who
had the seven plagues came out of
the [a]temple, clothed in [24]linen,
clean *and* bright, and girded
around their breasts with golden
girdles. Rev. 15:1 • *sanctuary*
7 And one of the [r]four living
creatures gave to the [r]seven angels
seven golden bowls full of the
wrath of God, who lives forever
and ever. Rev. 4:6 • Rev. 15:1
8 And the [a]temple was filled
with smoke from the glory of God
and from His power; and no one
was able to enter the [a]temple until
the seven plagues of the seven angels were finished. *sanctuary*

CHAPTER 16

AND I heard a loud voice from
the [a]temple, saying to the seven
angels, "Go and pour out the
seven bowls of the wrath of God
into the earth." *sanctuary*
2 And the first *angel* went and
poured out his bowl into the earth;
and it became a loathsome and
malignant sore upon the men who
had the mark of the beast and
who worshiped his image.
3 And the second *angel* poured
out his bowl [r]into the sea, and it
became blood like *that* of a dead
man; and every living [25]thing in the
sea died. Ex. 7:17-21; Rev. 8:8f.
4 And the third *angel* poured
out his bowl into the [r]rivers and
the springs of waters; and [26]they
became blood. Rev. 8:10
5 And I heard the angel of the
waters saying, "Righteous[r] art
Thou, who art and who wast, O
Holy One, because Thou didst
judge these things; John 17:25
6 for they poured out the blood
of saints and prophets, and Thou
hast given them blood to drink.
They [t]deserve it." *are worthy*
7 And I heard [r]the altar saying,

[23] Some ancient mss. read *ages*
[24] Some mss. read *stone*
[25] Lit., *soul*. Some ancient mss. read *thing, the things in the sea.*
[26] Some ancient mss. read *it became*

"Yes, O ʳLord God, the Almighty,
true and righteous are Thy judgments." Rev. 6:9 • Rev. 1:8
8 And the fourth *angel* poured
out his bowl upon ʳthe sun; ʳand it
was given to it to scorch men with
fire. Rev. 6:12 • Rev. 14:18
9 And men were scorched with
ᵗfierce heat; and they ʳblasphemed
the name of God who has the
power over these plagues; and
they did not repent, so as to give
Him glory. *great* • Rev. 16:11, 21
10 And the fifth *angel* poured
out his bowl upon the throne of
the beast; and his kingdom became darkened; and they gnawed
their tongues because of pain,
11 and they blasphemed the
God of heaven because of their
pains and their sores; and they did
not repent of their deeds.
12 And the sixth *angel* poured
out his bowl upon the ʳgreat river,
the Euphrates; and its water was
dried up, that the way might be
prepared for the kings from the
ᵗeast. Rev. 9:14 • *rising of the sun*
13 And I saw *coming* out of the
mouth of the dragon and out of
the mouth of the beast and out of
the mouth of the false prophet,
three unclean spirits like frogs;
14 for they are spirits of demons, performing signs, which go
out to the kings of the whole
ᵗworld, to gather them together for
the war of the great day of God,
the Almighty. *inhabited earth*
15 ("Behold, I am coming like a
thief. Blessed is the one who stays
awake and keeps his garments,
lest he walk about naked and ᵗmen
see his shame.") *they*
16 And they gathered them together to the place which in Hebrew is called [27]Har-Magedon.
17 And the seventh *angel*
poured out his bowl upon ʳthe air;
and a loud voice came out of the
ᵃtemple from the throne, saying,
"It is done." Eph. 2:2 • *sanctuary*
18 And there were flashes of
lightning and sounds and peals of
thunder; and there was a great
earthquake, such as there had not
been since man came to be upon
the earth, so great an earthquake
was it, and so mighty.
19 And the great city was split
into three parts, and the cities of
the nations fell. And Babylon the
great was remembered before
God, to give her the cup of the
wine of His fierce wrath.
20 And ʳevery island fled away,
and the mountains were not
found. Rev. 6:14; 20:11
21 And huge hailstones, about
[28]one hundred pounds each, *came
down from heaven upon men; and
men blasphemed God because of
the plague of the hail, because its
plague *was extremely severe.

CHAPTER 17

AND one of the ʳseven angels who
had the seven bowls came and
spoke with me, saying, "Come
here, I shall show you the judgment of the great harlot who sits
on many waters, Rev. 15:1
2 with whom the kings of the
earth committed *acts of* immorality, and those who dwell on the
earth were made drunk with the
wine of her immorality."
3 And he carried me away [29]in

[27] Some authorities read *Armageddon*
[28] Lit., *the weight of a talent* [29] Or, *in spirit*

the Spirit into a wilderness; and I
saw a woman sitting on a scarlet
beast, full of blasphemous names,
having seven heads and ten horns.
4 And the woman was clothed
in purple and scarlet, and [t]adorned
with gold and precious [t]stones and
pearls, having in her hand a gold
cup full of abominations and of
the unclean things of her immorality, *gilded • stone*
5 and upon her forehead a
name *was* written, a [r]mystery,
"BABYLON THE GREAT, THE
MOTHER OF HARLOTS AND OF
THE ABOMINATIONS OF THE
EARTH." 2 Thess. 2:7; Rev. 1:20
6 And I saw the woman drunk
with the blood of the saints, and
with the blood of the witnesses of
Jesus. And when I saw her, I wondered [t]greatly. *with great wonder*
7 And the angel said to me,
"Why [t]do you wonder? I shall tell
you the mystery of the woman
and of the beast that carries her,
which has the seven heads and the
ten horns. *have you wondered*
8 "The beast that you saw was
and is not, and is about to [r]come
up out of the [r]abyss and [30]to go to
destruction. And those who dwell
on the earth will wonder, whose
name has not been written in the
book of life from the foundation of
the world, when they see the
beast, that he was and is not and
will come. Rev. 11:7 • Rev. 9:1
9 "Here is the mind which has
wisdom. The [r]seven heads are
seven mountains on which the
woman sits, Rev. 17:3
10 and they are seven kings; five
have fallen, one is, the other has
not yet come; and when he comes,
he must remain a little while.
11 "And the beast which was and
is not, is himself also an eighth,
and is *one* of the seven, and he
[r]goes to destruction. Rev. 13:10
12 "And the ten horns which you
saw are ten kings, who have not
yet received a kingdom, but they
receive authority as kings with
the beast for one hour.
13 "These have one [a]purpose and
they give their power and authority to the beast. *mind*
14 "These will wage war against
the Lamb, and the Lamb will overcome them, because He is Lord of
lords and King of kings, and those
who are with Him *are the* called
and chosen and faithful."
15 And he *said to me, "The
waters which you saw where the
harlot sits, are peoples and multitudes and nations and tongues.
16 "And the [r]ten horns which you
saw, and the beast, these will hate
the harlot and will make her [r]deso-
late and naked, and will eat her
flesh and will burn her up with
fire. Rev. 17:12 • Rev. 18:17, 19
17 "For [r]God has put it in their
hearts to execute His [a]purpose by
having a common purpose, and by
giving their kingdom to the beast,
until the words of God should be
fulfilled. 2 Cor. 8:16 • *mind*
18 "And the woman whom you
saw is the great city, which reigns
over the kings of the earth."

CHAPTER 18

AFTER these things I saw another [r]angel coming down from
heaven, having great authority,

[30] Some ancient mss. read *he goes*

and the earth was illumined with his glory. Rev. 17:1, 7

2 And he cried out with a mighty voice, saying, "Fallen, fallen is Babylon the great! And she has become a dwelling place of demons and a prison of every unclean spirit, and a prison of every unclean and hateful bird.

3 "For all the nations [31]have drunk of the wine of the [t]passion of her immorality, and the kings of the earth have committed *acts of* immorality with her, and the merchants of the earth have become rich by the [t]wealth of her sensuality." *wrath* • *power*

4 And I heard another voice from heaven, saying, "Come[r] out of her, my people, that you may not participate in her sins and that you may not receive of her plagues; Is. 52:11; Jer. 50:8

5 for her sins have piled up as high as heaven, and God has remembered her iniquities.

6 "Pay her back even as she has paid, and [t]give back *to her* double according to her deeds; in the cup which she has mixed, mix twice as much for her. *double* to her

7 "To the degree that she glorified herself and lived [a]sensuously, to the same degree give her torment and mourning; for she says in her heart, 'I SIT *as* A QUEEN AND I AM NOT A WIDOW, and will never see mourning.' *luxuriously*

8 "For this reason in one day her plagues will come, [a]pestilence and mourning and famine, and she will be [r]burned up with fire; for the Lord God who judges her is strong. *death* • Rev. 17:16

9 "And [r]the kings of the earth, who committed *acts of* immorality and lived [a]sensuously with her, will weep and lament over her when they see the smoke of her burning, Rev. 17:2 • *luxuriously*

10 standing at a distance because of the fear of her torment, saying, 'Woe, woe, [r]the great city, Babylon, the strong city! For in [r]one hour your judgment has come.' Rev. 11:8 • Rev. 17:12

11 "And the [r]merchants of the earth weep and mourn over her, because no one buys their cargoes any more; Ezek. 27:9-25

12 cargoes of gold and silver and precious [t]stones and pearls and fine linen and purple and silk and scarlet, and every *kind of* citron wood and every article of ivory and every article *made* from very costly wood and [a]bronze and iron and marble, *stone* • *brass*

13 and cinnamon and spice and incense and perfume and frankincense and wine and olive oil and fine flour and wheat and cattle and sheep, and *cargoes* of horses and chariots and [t]slaves and [t]human lives. *bodies* • *souls of men*

14 "And the fruit you long for has gone from you, and all things that were luxurious and splendid have passed away from you and *men* will no longer find them.

15 "The [r]merchants of these things, who became rich from her, will stand at a distance because of the fear of her torment, weeping and mourning, Rev. 18:3

16 saying, 'Woe, woe, the great city, she who was clothed in fine linen and purple and scarlet, and [t]adorned with gold and precious stones and pearls; *gilded*

[31] Many ancient mss. read *have fallen by*

17 for in [r]one hour such great
wealth has been laid waste!' And
every shipmaster and every pas-
senger and sailor, and as many as
make their living by the sea, stood
at a distance, Rev. 18:10
18 and were [r]crying out as they
[r]saw the smoke of her burning,
saying, 'What *city* is like the great
city?' Ezek. 27:30 • Rev. 18:9
19 "And they threw dust on their
heads and were crying out, weeping and mourning, saying, 'Woe,
woe, the great city, in which all
who had ships at sea became rich
by her [t]wealth, for in one hour she
has been laid waste!' *costliness*
20 "Rejoice over her, O heaven,
and you saints and apostles and
prophets, because God has [t]pro-
nounced judgment for you against
her." *judged your judgment of her*
21 And a strong angel took up a
stone like a great millstone and
threw it into the sea, saying,
"Thus will Babylon, the great city,
be thrown down with violence,
and will not be found any longer.
22 "And [r]the sound of harpists
and musicians and flute-players
and trumpeters will not be heard
in you any longer; and no craftsman of any craft will be found in
you any longer; and the [r]sound of a
mill will not be heard in you any
longer; Is. 24:8 • Eccl. 12:4
23 and the light of a lamp will
not shine in you any longer; and
the voice of the bridegroom and
bride will not be heard in you any
longer; for your merchants were
the great men of the earth, because all the nations were deceived by your sorcery.
24 "And in her was found the
blood of prophets and of [a]saints
and of all who have been slain on
the earth." *holy ones*

CHAPTER 19

AFTER these things I heard, as it
were, a loud voice of a great multitude in heaven, saying,
"Hallelujah! Salvation and glory
and power belong to our God;
2 BECAUSE HIS JUDGMENTS ARE
TRUE AND RIGHTEOUS; for He has
judged the great harlot who was
corrupting the earth with her immorality, and HE HAS AVENGED
THE BLOOD OF HIS BOND-SERVANTS
[t]ON HER." *from her hand*
3 And a second time they said,
"Hallelujah![r] HER SMOKE RISES UP
FOREVER AND EVER." Ps. 104:35
4 And the [r]twenty-four elders
and the four living creatures fell
down and worshiped God who sits
on the throne saying, "Amen. Hallelujah!" Rev. 4:4, 10
5 And a voice came from the
throne, saying,
"Give praise to our God, all you
His bond-servants, you who fear
Him, the small and the great."
6 And I heard, as it were, the
voice of a great multitude and as
the sound of many waters and as
the sound of mighty peals of thunder, saying,
"Hallelujah! For the Lord our
God, the Almighty, reigns.
7 "Let us rejoice and be glad
and [r]give the glory to Him, for the
marriage of the Lamb has come
and His [t]bride has made herself
ready." Rev. 11:13 • *wife*
8 And it was given to her to
clothe herself in fine linen, bright

and clean; for the fine linen is the righteous acts of the saints.

9 And he *said to me, "Write, 'Blessed are those who are invited to the marriage supper of the Lamb.' " And he *said to me, "These are true words of God."

10 And I fell at his feet to worship him. And he *said to me, "Do not do that; I am a fellow servant of yours and your brethren who hold the testimony of Jesus; worship God. For the testimony of Jesus is the spirit of prophecy."

11 And I saw heaven opened; and behold, a white horse, and He who sat upon it *is* called Faithful and True; and in [r]righteousness He judges and wages war. Is. 11:4

12 And His eyes *are* a flame of fire, and upon His head *are* many diadems; and He has a name written *upon Him* which no one knows except Himself.

13 And *He is* clothed with a robe dipped in blood; and His name is called The Word of God.

14 And the armies which are in heaven, clothed in [r]fine linen, white *and* clean, were following Him on white horses. Rev. 19:8

15 And [r]from His mouth comes a sharp sword, so that with it He may smite the nations; and He will [a]rule them with a rod of iron; and He treads the wine press of the fierce wrath of God, the Almighty. Rev. 1:16 • *shepherd*

16 And on His robe and on His thigh He has [r]a name written, "KING OF KINGS, AND LORD OF LORDS." Rev. 2:17; 19:12

17 And I saw [t]an angel standing in the sun; and he cried out with a loud voice, saying to [r]all the birds which fly in [r]midheaven, "Come, assemble for the great supper of God; *one* • Rev. 19:21 • Rev. 8:13

18 in order that you may [r]eat the flesh of kings and the flesh of [32]commanders and the flesh of mighty men and the flesh of horses and of those who sit on them and the flesh of all men, both free men and slaves, and small and great." Ezek. 39:18-20

19 And I saw the beast and the kings of the earth and their armies, assembled to make war against Him who sat upon the horse, and against His army.

20 And the beast was seized, and with him the false prophet who performed the signs in his presence, by which he deceived those who had received the mark of the beast and those who worshiped his image; these two were thrown alive into the lake of fire which burns with brimstone.

21 And the rest were killed with the sword which [r]came from the mouth of Him who sat upon the horse, and all the birds were filled with their flesh. Rev. 19:15

CHAPTER 20

AND I saw [r]an angel coming down from heaven, having the key of the abyss and a great chain [t]in his hand. Rev. 10:1 • *upon*

2 And he laid hold of the dragon, the serpent of old, who is the devil and Satan, and bound him for a thousand years,

3 and threw him into the abyss, and shut *it* and sealed *it* over him, so that he should not deceive the nations any longer, until the thousand years were com-

[32]I.e., chiliarchs, in command of one thousand troops

pleted; after these things he must
be released for a short time.
4 And I saw thrones, and they
sat upon them, and judgment was
given to them. And I *saw* the souls
of those who had been beheaded
because of the testimony of Jesus
and because of the word of God,
and those who had not worshiped
the beast or his image, and had
not received the mark upon their
forehead and upon their hand; and
they came to life and reigned with
Christ for a thousand years.
5 The rest of the dead did not
come to life until the thousand
years were completed.[r] This is the
first resurrection. Luke 14:14
6 Blessed and holy is the one
who has a part in the first resurrection; over these the [r]second
death has no power, but they will
be priests of God and of Christ
and will reign with Him for a
thousand years. Rev. 2:11; 20:14
7 And when the thousand
years are completed, Satan will be
released from his prison,
8 and will come out to deceive
the nations which are in the four
corners of the earth, Gog and Magog, to gather them together for
the war; the number of them is
like the sand of the seashore.
9 And they came up on the
[t]broad plain of the earth and surrounded the camp of the saints
and the beloved city, and fire
came down from heaven and devoured them. *breadth of the earth*
10 And the devil who deceived
them was thrown into the lake of
fire and brimstone, where the
beast and the false prophet are
also; and they will be tormented
day and night forever and ever.
11 And I saw a great white
throne and Him who sat upon it,
from whose [t]presence earth and
heaven fled away, and no place
was found for them. *face*
12 And I saw the dead, the great
and the small, standing before the
throne, and books were opened;
and another book was opened,
which is *the book* of life; and the
dead were judged from the things
which were written in the books,
according to their deeds.
13 And the sea gave up the dead
which were in it, and [r]death and
Hades gave up the dead which
were in them; and they were
judged, every one *of them* according to their deeds. 1 Cor. 15:26
14 And death and Hades were
thrown into the lake of fire. This is
the second death, the lake of fire.
15 And if [t]anyone's name was
not found written in [r]the book of
life, he was thrown into the lake
of fire. *anyone was* • Rev. 3:5

CHAPTER 21

AND I saw a new heaven and a
new earth; for the first heaven and
the first earth passed away, and
there is no longer *any* sea.
2 And I saw the holy city, new
Jerusalem, coming down out of
heaven from God, made ready as
a bride adorned for her husband.
3 And I heard a loud voice
from the throne, saying, "Behold,
the tabernacle of God is among
men, and He shall [a]dwell among
them, and they shall be His people, and God Himself shall be
among them,[33] *tabernacle*
4 and He shall [r]wipe away ev-

[33] Some ancient mss. add, and be *their God*

ery tear from their eyes; and there
shall no longer be *any* death; there
shall no longer be *any* mourning,
or crying, or pain; the first things
have passed away." Is. 25:8
5 And [r]He who sits on the
throne said, "Behold, I am making
all things new." And He *said,
"Write, for these words are faithful and true." Rev. 4:9; 20:11
6 And He said to me, "It is
done. I am the Alpha and the
Omega, the beginning and the
end. I will give to the one who
thirsts from the spring of the water of life without cost.
7 "He who overcomes shall inherit these things, and I will be his
God and he will be My son.
8 "But for the cowardly and unbelieving and abominable and
murderers and immoral persons
and sorcerers and idolaters and all
liars, their part *will be* in the lake
that burns with fire and brimstone, which is the second death."
9 And one of the seven angels
who had the seven bowls full of
the seven last plagues, came and
spoke with me, saying, "Come
here, I shall show you the bride,
the wife of the Lamb."
10 And he carried me away [34]in
the Spirit to a great and high
mountain, and showed me the
holy city, Jerusalem, coming
down out of heaven from God,
11 having [r]the glory of God. Her
[t]brilliance was like a very costly
stone, as a stone of crystal-clear
jasper. Is. 60:1f. • *luminary*
12 [t]It had a great and high wall,
with twelve gates, and at the
gates twelve angels; and names
were written on them, which are
those of the twelve tribes of the
sons of Israel. *having*
13 *There were* three gates on the
east and three gates on the north
and three gates on the south and
three gates on the west.
14 And the wall of the city had
twelve foundation stones, and on
them *were* the twelve names of
the twelve apostles of the Lamb.
15 And the one who spoke with
me had a [t]gold measuring rod to
measure the city, and its gates
and its wall. *measure, a gold reed*
16 And the city is laid out as a
square, and its length is as great
as the width; and he measured the
city with the [t]rod, [35]fifteen hundred
miles; its length and width and
height are equal. *reed*
17 And he measured its wall,
[36]seventy-two yards, *according to*
human measurements, which are
also angelic *measurements.*
18 And the material of the wall
was jasper; and the city was pure
gold, like [t]clear glass. *pure*
19 The foundation stones of the
city wall were adorned with every
kind of precious stone. The first
foundation stone was jasper; the
second, sapphire; the third, chal-
cedony; the fourth, emerald;
20 the fifth, sardonyx; the sixth,
[r]sardius; the seventh, chrysolite;
the eighth, beryl; the ninth, topaz;
the tenth, chrysoprase; the eleventh, jacinth; the twelfth, amethyst. Rev. 4:3
21 And the twelve gates were
twelve pearls; each one of the
gates was a single pearl. And the

[34]Or, *in spirit*

[35]Lit., *twelve thousand stadia;* a stadion was about 600 ft.

[36]Lit., *one hundred forty-four cubits*

street of the city was pure gold,
like transparent [r]glass. Rev. 4:6
22 And I saw no temple in it, for
the Lord God, the Almighty, and
the Lamb, are its temple.
23 And the city [r]has no need of
the sun or of the moon to shine
upon it, for [r]the glory of God has
illumined it, and its lamp *is* the
Lamb. Is. 24:23 • Rev. 21:11
24 And the nations shall walk
by its light, and the kings of the
earth shall bring their glory into it.
25 And in the daytime (for there
shall be no night there) its gates
[r]shall never be closed; Is. 60:11
26 and [r]they shall bring the glory
and the honor of the nations into
it; Ps. 72:10f.; Is. 49:23; 60:16
27 and nothing unclean and no
one who practices abomination
and lying, shall ever come into it,
but only those whose names are
written in the Lamb's book of life.

CHAPTER 22

AND [r]he showed me a river of the
water of life, [t]clear as crystal, coming from the throne of God and of
[37]the Lamb, Rev. 1:1 • *bright*
2 in the middle of [r]its street.
And [r]on either side of the river was
the tree of life, bearing twelve
[38]*kinds of* fruit, yielding its fruit
every month; and the leaves of the
tree were for the healing of the nations. Rev. 21:21 • Ezek. 47:12
3 And [r]there shall no longer be
any curse; and [r]the throne of God
and of the Lamb shall be in it, and
His bond-servants shall serve
Him; Zech. 14:11 • Rev. 21:3
4 and they shall [r]see His face,
and His [r]name *shall be* on their
foreheads. Ps. 17:15 • Rev. 14:1
5 And there shall no longer be
any night; and they shall not have
need of the light of a lamp nor the
light of the sun, because the Lord
God shall illumine them; and they
shall reign forever and ever.
6 And [r]he said to me, "These [r]
words are faithful and true"; and
the Lord, the God of the spirits of
the prophets, sent His angel to
show to His bond-servants the
things which must shortly take
place. Rev. 1:1 • Rev. 19:9
7 "And behold, [r]I am coming
quickly. Blessed is he who [a]heeds
the words of the prophecy of this
book." Rev. 1:3 • *keeps*
8 And I, John, am the one who
heard and saw these things. And
when I heard and saw, I fell down
to worship at the feet of the angel
who showed me these things.
9 And [r]he *said to me, "Do not
do that; I am a fellow servant of
yours and of your brethren the
prophets and of those who [a]heed
the words of this book; worship
God." Rev. 19:10 • *keep*
10 And he *said to me, "Do not
seal up the words of the prophecy
of this book, for the time is near.
11 "Let [r]the one who does wrong,
still do wrong; and let the one who
is filthy, still be filthy; and let the
one who is righteous, still practice
righteousness; and let the one
who is holy, still keep himself
holy." Ezek. 3:27; Dan. 12:10
12 "Behold, I am coming quickly,
and My reward *is* with Me, to render to every man [t]according to
what he has done.
13 "I am the Alpha and the

[37]Or, *the Lamb. In the middle of its street, and on either side of the river, was*
[38]Or, crops of *fruit*

Omega, the first and the last, the
beginning and the end."
14 Blessed are those who[r]wash
their robes, that they may have
the right to[r]the tree of life, and
may enter by the gates into the
city. Rev. 7:14 • Gen. 2:9
15 Outside are the[r]dogs and the
sorcerers and the immoral persons and the murderers and the
idolaters, and everyone who loves
and practices lying. Matt. 7:6
16 "I, Jesus, have sent My angel
to testify to you these things[a]for
the churches. I am the root and
the offspring of David, the bright
morning star." *concerning*
17 And the[r]Spirit and the bride
say, "Come." And let the one who
hears say, "Come." And let the
one who is thirsty come; let the
one who wishes take the water of
life without cost. Rev. 2:7
18 I testify to everyone who
hears[r]the words of the prophecy
of this book: if anyone[r]adds to
them, God shall add to him the
plagues which are written in this
book; Rev. 22:7 • Deut. 4:2
19 and if anyone takes away
from the[r]words of the book of this
prophecy, God shall take away his
part from the tree of life and[t]from
the holy city, which are written in
this book. Rev. 22:7 • *out of*
20 He who[r]testifies to these
things says, "Yes,[r]I am coming
quickly." Amen. Come, Lord
Jesus. Rev. 1:2 • Rev. 22:7
21[r]The grace of the Lord Jesus
be with [39]all. Amen. Rom. 16:20

[39]Some ancient mss. read *the saints*

Illustrated

DICTIONARY - CONCORDANCE

to the

NEW AMERICAN STANDARD BIBLE

Nashville, Tennessee

CONC

"All Biblical quotations are from the New American Standard Bible and are reprinted with the permission of the Lockman Foundation."

A

Aa•ron′ The older brother of Moses (Ex. 6:20; 7:7); the spokesman for Moses ((Ex.7:1); brings on plagues with his rod (Ex. 7:10–8:17); from him are descended the class of priests in Israel (Ex. 29:9); he makes atonement and stops a plague (Num. 16:41-50); his rod blossoms (Num. 17:1-11); his death (Num. 20:22-29).

a•base′ to humble, to lower in position.
Ezek. 21:26, **a** that which is high

a•bated′ decreased, made to become less, reduced.
Gen. 8:8, water was **a**
Deut. 34:7, his vigor **a**

Ab′ba Aramaic term, borrowed from children's language, meaning father.
Mark 14:36, saying, **A**! Father
Rom. 8:15, by which we cry out, **A**! Father
Gal. 4:6, crying, **A**! Father

Ab′don A town in the territory of Asher assigned, with its environs, to the Levites of the Gershon family (Josh. 21:27-30). It is perhaps to be identified with Khirbet Abdeh, 10 mi. NNE of Acre.

A′bel Son of Adam; murdered by his brother Cain (Gen. 4:2). He is described as righteous (Matt. 23:35; 1 John 3:12). He stands at the head of the heroes of faith (Heb. 11:4).

ab•hor′ to despise, detest, or loathe.
Prov. 24:24, nations will **a** him
Rom. 12:9, **A** what is evil

A•bi′a•thar A priest in the time of David (1 Sam. 23:9).

Ab′i•e′zer A descendant of Manasseh, the son of Joseph, who settled on the west side of the Jordan (Josh. 17:2; 1 Chr. 7:18) and is probably the same as "Iezer," a contraction of Abiezer, the son of Gilead (Num. 26:30).

Ab′i•gail The wife of Nabal, a rich man of Maon in Judah, and after Nabal's death, a wife of David, to whom, at Hebron, she bore his second son, Chileab (2 Sam. 3:3, called Daniel in 1 Chr. 3:1).

A•bi′hu The second of the four sons of Aaron and Elisheba (Ex. 6:23; Num. 3:2; 26:60; 1 Chr. 6:3; 24:1). When Moses ascended Mount Sinai, Aaron, Nadab, and Abihu, with seventy elders, went part of the way up Sinai with him at the command of the Lord "and they saw the God of Israel" (Ex. 24:1, 9, 10).

A•bi′jah 1. The seventh son of Becher, the son of Benjamin (1 Chr. 7:8). 2. The second son of Samuel who, along with his older brother Joel, was appointed by his father to be a judge in Beersheba (1 Sam. 8:2).

A•bim′e•lech A family surname applied to Philistine rulers as Pharaoh, Agag and Jabin were also applied by the Egyptians, Amalekites, and Canaanites respectively. This title is used of three different persons in the Old Testament: one during Abraham's time (Gen. 20:2), one during Isaac's time (Gen. 26), and during David's days (Ps. 34, title).

A•bi′shai The oldest son of David's sister Zeruiah, and the brother of Joab and Asahel (2 Sam. 2:18).

A•bish′u•a 1. Great grandson of Aaron, son of Phineas, and ancestor of Ezra the scribe (1 Chr. 6:4, 5, 50; Ezra 7:5). 2. Son of Bela and grandson of Benjamin (1 Chr. 8:1-4).

Ab′ner Commander of the Israelite army under Saul (1 Sam. 14:50; 17:55; 26:5); murdered by Joab (2 Sam. 3:27).

a•bode′ the place where one lives, habitation, residence.
Jer. 31:23, **a** of righteousness
Jude 6, their proper **a**
John 14:23, and make Our **a** with him

a•bom′i•na•ble detestable, rejected, disgusting.
Jer. 44:4, do not do this **a** thing
Ezek. 16:25, made your beauty **a**
1 Pet. 4:3, drinking parties and **a** idolatries

a•bom′i•na•tion a detestable thing, an object of disgust.
Ex. 8:26, an **a** to the Egyptians
Prov. 3:32, an **a** to the Lord
Dan. 12:11, the **a** of desolation

a•bound′ to excel, multiply, or be plentiful.
Prov. 28:20, A faithful man will **a** with blessings
Dan. 4:1, May your peace **a**
Rom. 15:13, that you may **a** in hope

A′bra•ham Israel's first great patriarch or leader. Through faith in God's promise to make of him a great nation, he is led from Ur to Canaan (Gen. 11:31–15:7). God makes a covenant with him (Gen. 15:7-21); an angel of God promises that Sarah shall give birth to a son (Gen. 18:10); God tests Abraham's faith (Gen. 22:1-19). He stands as the father of all the faithful (Gal. 3:7).

Ab'sa•lom Son of David and Maacah (2 Sam. 3:3); turned the people against his father (2 Sam. 15:1-18); was defeated and then slain by Joab, to the great sorrow of David (2 Sam. 18:9-15, 32, 33).

ab•stain' to depart, separate oneself from, or refrain from.
Acts 15:20, that they **a** from things
1 Thess. 5:22, **a** from every form of evil

a•bun'dance a surplus, or plenteous supply
Gen. 41:34, seven years of **a**
Ps. 52:7, the **a** of his riches
Ps. 72:7, And **a** of peace till
Matt. 13:12, and he shall have an **a**
Rom. 5:17, receive the **a** of grace

a•byss' deep, depth, pit.
Luke 8:31, depart into the **a**
Rev. 11:7, the beast that comes up out of the **a**
Rev. 17:8, come up out of the **a**
Rev. 20:1, having the key of the **a**
Rev. 20:3, threw him into the **a**

ac•cept'a•ble worthy of being accepted, favorable, pleasing.
Ps. 69:13, at an **a** time
Rom. 15:31, may prove **a** to the saints
Phil. 4:18, an **a** sacrifice
1 Tim. 2:3, good and **a** in the sight

ac•curs'ed under a curse.
Josh. 6:18, make the camp of Israel **a**
Matt. 25:41, Depart from Me, **a** ones
Rom. 9:3, wish that I myself were **a**
1 Cor. 12:3, no one . . . says, Jesus is **a**
Gal. 1:8, let him be **a**

A•cha'ia The Roman province which included all of the Peloponnesus, much of central Greece and the Cyclades. The name is used to refer to the province or its inhabitants (Acts 18:27; Rom. 15:26; 1 Cor. 16:15).

A'chan The descendant of Judah through Zerah (Josh. 7:1). He was stoned to death for violating the "ban" during the conquest of Jericho (Josh. 7:1-26). Achan stole 200 shekels of silver, a Babylonian garment and a wedge of gold weighing 50 shekels and hid them in the earthen floor of his tent (Josh. 7:21).

Ach'bor 1. The father of Baal-hanan, an Edomite king *(Gen. 36:38; 39; 1 Chr. 1:49)*. 2. Son of Micaiah (2 Kin. 22:12) and father of Elnathan (Jer. 26:22). Josiah commanded him to go with some others to consult Huldah the prophetess concerning the newly discovered book of the law (2 Kin. 22:12, 14; 2 Chr. 34:20, called Abdon).

A'chish A king of Gath to whom David went for refuge when fleeing from Saul, after he had received the bread of the Presence as food for his men and the swords of Goliath from Ahimelech the priest. When the servants of Achish disclosed who David was, David pretended he was insane and so escaped to Adullam (1 Sam. 21:10-22:1).

A'chor The valley in which Achan and his family were stoned to death because Achan had taken a beautiful mantle of Shinar, 200 shekels of silver, and a fifty shekel bar of gold from Jericho when no booty was to be taken. Because Achan's sin brought trouble to Israel by the defeat at Ai, the place was named the valley of Achor (Josh. 7:24, 26).

ac•knowl'edge to confess, admit or recognize as true.
Prov. 3:6, In all your ways **a** Him
Acts 23:8, Pharisees **a** them all
Rom. 1:28, see fit to **a** God

ac•quit' to free from charge of wrongdoing.
Job 10:14, wouldst not **a** me of my guilt
Ps. 19:12, **A** me of hidden faults

Ad'am Mankind; the proper name of the first created man, the antitype of Jesus Christ; occasionally man in contrast to woman (Gen. 2:22).

ad•ders' belonging to serpents, vipers, or snakes.
Is. 59:5, They hatch **a** eggs

Adder

ad•jure' to implore or charge as under oath.
1 Kin. 22:16, many times must I **a**
Matt. 26:63, I **a** You by the living God
Acts 19:13, I **a** you by Jesus

ad•mon'ish to warn of a fault.
Acts 20:31, cease to **a** each one
Rom. 15:14, able also to **a** one another

1 Cor. 4:14, to **a** you as my . . . children
1 Thess. 5:14, **a** the unruly

Ad'o•ni'jah The fourth son born to David in Hebron by Haggith (2 Sam. 3:4; 1 Chr. 3:1, 2). He is famous for making an unsuccessful bid for the throne when he presumed himself to be the oldest heir-apparent after the death of his two older brothers Amnon and Absalom, and apparently the death of the third also (Chileab, David's son by Abigail, concerning which the record is silent, 1 Kin. 1 and 2).

A•dul'lam A Canaanite town, situated on the route via Azegah and Soko, that controlled one of the principal passes into the hill-country of Judah from the northern Shephelah (Josh. 12:7-15).

a•dul'ter•ess a woman who commits adultery; strange woman.
Prov. 6:26, an **a** hunts for the precious life
Prov. 22:14, mouth of an **a**

a•dul'ter•y unlawful intercourse.
Ex. 20:14, You shall not commit **a**
Matt. 5:28, has committed **a**
Luke 18:20, Do not commit **a**
2 Pet. 2:14, having eyes full of **a**

ad'ver•sar•y opponent, foe, or enemy.
Ex. 23:22, an **a** to your **a-es**
1 Kin. 11:14, raised up an **a**
1 Cor. 16:9, and there are many **a-es**
Heb. 10:27, which will consume the **a-es**
1 Pet. 5:8, Your **a**, the devil

ad•ver'si•ty condition of suffering or affliction.
Deut. 30:15, death and **a**
Job 2:10, not accept **a**
Ps. 10:6, I shall not be in **a**
Ps. 94:13, relief from the days of **a**
Prov. 17:17, is born for **a**

ad'vo•cate one who pleads the cause of another.
Job 16:19, my **a** is on high
1 John 2:1, we have an **A** with the Father

af•flict' to cause suffering or anguish.
Deut. 26:6, Egyptians . . . **a-ed** us
Ps. 82:3, justice to the **a-ed** and destitute
Ps. 147:6, LORD supports the **a-ed**
Is. 61:1, bring good news to the **a-ed**
2 Cor. 4:8, *we are* **a-ed** in every way

af•flic'tion a condition of misery, oppression or distress.
Deut. 16:3, the bread of **a**
Job 36:15, delivers the afflicted in their **a**
Ps. 25:18, Look upon my **a**
Mark 5:29, she was healed of her **a**
2 Thess. 1:6, repay with **a** those who afflict you

A'gag A name or perhaps a title like Pharaoh belonging to an Amalekite king; one mentioned by Balaam in Num. 24:7 and another by Saul in 1 Sam. 15:8, 9, 20, 32, 33. It appears that Haman was surnamed Agag also (Esth. 3:1).

age world, generations, elder.
1 Chr. 23:1, Now when David reached old **a**
Job 12:12, Wisdom is with **a-d** men
Matt. 12:32, this **a**, or in the **a** to come
Luke 16:8, sons of this **a** are more shrewd
John 9:21, he is of **a**, he shall speak

A•hi'kam A prominent man in the reign of King Josiah and the following decades (2 Kin. 22:12, 14; 25:22; 2 Chr. 34:20; Jer. 26:24; 39:14; 40:5–41:18; 43:6).

A•hi'lud The father of Jehoshaphat, a "recorder" during the reigns of David and Solomon (2 Sam. 8:16; 20:24; 1 Kin. 4:3; 1 Chr. 18:15), and probably also of Baana, one of Solomon's commissariat officers (1 Kin. 4:12).

A•ho'hite A term used by the descendants of Ahoah. The term is always used in connection with military heroes in David's time: Dodo (1 Chr. 11:12), Zalmon (2 Sam. 23:28), Ilai (1 Chr. 11:29).

Ai A town in central Palestine. A study of references to Ai in both early Hebrew and Greek versions indicates a persistent relationship of Ai with Jericho, Jerusalem and Bethel. This seems to establish the location of Ai in the region of these three cities. Ai laid east of Bethel (Gen. 12:8). "Joshua sent men from Jericho to Ai . . . east of Bethel" (Josh. 7:2).

Ai'ja•lon A town on a hill overlooking the valley of Aijalon between Jericho and the Mediterranean Sea and known as Yalo in modern times. Some remains of the town from about 2000 B.C. have been found at Tell el-Qoq'a. The town is mentioned in the 14th and 15th century B.C. Amarna letters as Aialuna (Josh. 10:12).

al'ien stranger, foreigner.
Deut. 10:19, show your love for the **a**
Deut. 14:21, **a** who is in your town
2 Sam. 1:13, the son of an **a**
Acts 7:6, **a-s** in a foreign land
Eph. 2:19, no longer strangers and **a-s**

al·li'ance to bind, join together, or unite.
1 Kin. 3:1, Solomon . . . marriage **a** with Pharaoh
Dan. 11:23, after an **a** is made

al·lot' to distribute by lot or in shares.
Job 7:3, I **a-ed** months of vanity
Rom. 12:3, as God has **a-ed** to each a measure of faith

al'mond a small tree of the rose family with flowers and young fruit resembling those of the peach.
Ex. 25:33, shaped like **a** blossoms
Jer. 1:11, I see a rod of an **a** tree

alms money or goods given to the poor in charity.
Matt. 6:2, therefore you give **a**
Matt. 6:4, your **a** may be in secret
Acts 10:2, gave many **a**
Acts 24:17, I came to bring **a**

al'oes an aromatic substance, probably an aromatic wood, such as white sandalwood, from which was made incense and perfume.
Ps. 45:8, fragrant with myrrh and **a**
John 19:39, bringing a mixture of myrrh and **a**

Aloes

Almond tree and blossoms

al'tar an elevated place.
Gen. 8:20, built an **a** to the LORD
Ps. 43:4, I will go to the **a**
Ezek. 6:4, your **a-s** will become desolate
Matt. 5:23, your offering at the **a**
Rev. 9:13, four horns of the golden **a**

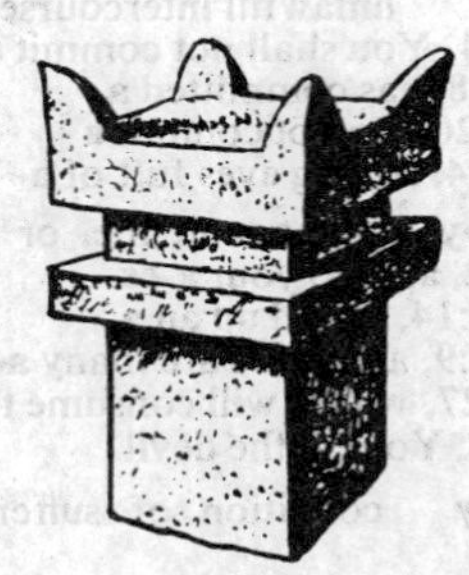

Altar

Am'a·lek One of the sons of Eliphaz and a grandson of Esau (Gen. 36:15, 16; 1 Chr. 1:36). He was born to Eliphaz by his concubine Timna (Gen. 36:12); was one of the tribal chiefs of Edom (Gen. 36:16).

Am'al'ek·ites An ancient marauding people in the South of Canaan and the Negev who were fierce enemies of Israel particularly in the earlier part of her history (Judg. 6:3, 33; 1 Sam. 30:1, 2).

a·mass' heap, to gather up or collect for oneself.
Ps. 39:6, He **a-es** *riches*

A'men' verily; so let it be.
Num. 5:22, the woman shall say, **A.A.**
Ps. 41:13; 72:19; 89:52, **A** and **A**
Matt. 6:13, the glory, forever. **A.**
Rev. 3:14, The **A**, the faithful and true

Amm'i•el 1. Son of Gemalli, of the tribe of Dan; one of the twelve spies sent by Moses into Canaan (Num. 13:12, 16). 2. The father of Machir, in whose house Mephibosheth was hidden from David (2 Sam. 9:4, 5). Machir later befriended David (2 Sam. 17:27-29).

Am•min'a•dab The father of Nahshon, a prince in Judah (Num. 1:7; 2:3; 7:12, 17; 10:14). He was also the father of Elisheba, the wife of Aaron (Ex. 6: 23), and a descendant of Perez, Judah's son (Gen. 38:29; 46:12), and the ancestor of David (Ruth 4:19, 20) as the New Testament also affirms in the two genealogical lists (Matt. 1:4 and Luke 3:33) of Jesus.

Am'non Eldest son of David by Ahinoam, the Jezreelitess (2 Sam. 3:2; 1 Chr. 3:1). He dishonored his half-sister Tamar and was, therefore, slain by her brother Absalom (2 Sam. 13).

A'moz The father of the prophet Isaiah (2 Kin. 19:2; Is. 1:1).

Am'ram A Levite, son of Kohath, the husband of Jochebed, and father of Moses, Aaron, and Miriam (Ex. 6:18, 20; Num. 3:19; 26:59; 1 Chr. 6:3). The Amramites, descended from him, had special duties in the wilderness Tabernacle.

A'nak The hero of the Anakim which was a tribe inhabiting Palestine in pre-Israelite times. Without the article, Anak appears in Hebrew in Num. 13:33; Deut. 9:2, but with the article in Num. 13:22, 28; Joshua 15:13, 14; 21:11; and Judg. 1:20, which seems to be a collective term equal to the plural form, the Anakim.

An'drew The brother of Simon Peter and one of the first disciples of Jesus. Although a native Palestinian Jew, Andrew bore a good Greek name. He was the son of Jona (Matt. 16:17) or John (John 1:42; 21:15-17), whose home was in Bethsaida in Galilee (John 1:44); 12:21). Doubtless Andrew, as a native of Galilee, where life was strongly influenced by Gentile culture, spoke Greek as well as Aramaic.

an'guish distress or pain of body or mind.
Ps. 55:4, heart is in **a**
Is. 30:6, land of distress and **a**
Jer. 6:24, **A** has seized us

a•noint' to pour or rub oil or ointment on.
Ex. 28:41, you shall **a** them
Ps. 23:5, **a-ed** my head with oil
Matt. 6:17, fast, **a** your head
Mark 14:8, she has **a-ed** My body
Mark 16:1, they might come and **a** Him

an'ti•christ' against Christ, or instead of.
1 John 2:18, **a** is coming
1 John 2:22, This is the **a**
1 John 4:3, the spirit of the **a**
2 John 7, the deceiver and the **a**

anx'ious worry, concern, thought.
Matt. 6:25, do not be **a** for your life
Matt 10:19, **a** about how or what you will speak
Mark 13:11, do not be **a** beforehand about what
Luke 12:26, why are you **a** about other
Phil. 4:6, Be **a** for nothing

A•poll'os A gifted, scholarly, zealous preacher in the early Christian church (Acts 18:24-19:1; 1 Cor. 1:12; 3:4-6, 22; 4:6; 16:12; Titus 3:13). Apollos was a Jew, "a native of Alexandria," and he became a disciple of John the Baptist (Acts 18:24-28).

a•pos'ta•sy backsliding, faithlessness.
Jer. 8:5, Turned away in continuous **a**
Hos. 14:4, I will heal their **a**
2 Thess. 2:3, unless the **a** comes first

a•pos'tle one sent out.
Matt. 10:2, names of the twelve **a-s**
Rom. 1:1, called *as* an **a**
Rom. 11:13, **a** of the Gentiles
Eph. 4:11, He gave some as **a-s**

ap•pall' astound, amaze, astonish.
Job 17:8, upright shall be **a-ed**
Ps. 40:15, Let those be **a-ed** because of their shame
Ps. 143:4, My heart is **a-ed** within me
Ezek. 4:17, they will be **a-ed**
Dan. 4:19, Daniel . . . was **a-ed**

ap•point' name, select or designate.
Num. 3:10, you shall **a** Aaron
1 Chr. 17:9, I will **a** a place for My people
Jon. 1:17, **a-ed** a great fish to swallow
Mark 3:14, He **a-ed** twelve, that they
Heb. 9:27, **a-ed** for men to die

ap•por'tion distribute, divide, assign.
Josh. 13:7, **a** this land for an
Job 21:17, Does God **a** destruction
2 Cor. 10:13, sphere which God **a-ed** to us

ap•praise' discern, evaluate, judge.
1 Cor. 2:14, they are spiritually **a-d**

Aq'ui•la A Jew, born in Pontus, who with his wife Priscilla, lived for a time at Rome, but had to leave that city when the emperor Claudius commanded all Jews to depart (Acts 18:1-3).

Ar A city east of the Dead Sea. Numbers 21:15 and 28 indicate that Ar is near the Arnon River.

Ar'a•bah When the word is used with the definite article, as it most frequently is, it refers to the great rift valley running south from the Sea of Galilee including the Jordan Valley and the Dead Sea and extending all the way to the Gulf of Aqabah. As such, it forms a major geographical area of the land of the Bible and certainly the most important feature of the relief of the land (Deut. 1:1; Josh. 18:18).

Ar'ad A city in the NE Negeb some seventeen miles south of Hebron and about the same distance west of Masada (Num. 21:1; 33:40; Josh. 12:14; Judg. 1:16).

Ar'am The name of Syria and its people (2 Kin. 6:8; Is. 7:8).

Ar'a•rat 1. A mountainous country north of Assyria (Jer. 51:27). 2. The mountain which Noah's ark came to rest upon in the Old Testament (Gen. 8:4).

Ar'ba The ancestor of the Anakim and the greatest hero of that race. In the Book of Joshua he is described as "the greatest man among the Anakim" (Josh. 14:15) and "the father of Anak" (15:13; 21:11). He was the founder of the city named for him, on the site of which Hebron was built (21:11).

arch'an•gel a chief angel.
1 Thess. 4:16, with the voice of the **a**
Jude 9, the **a**, when he disputed

Ar'chite A clan mentioned in connection with the allotment of the descendants of Joseph (Josh. 16:2; 2 Sam. 15:32; 16:16; 1 Chr. 27:33).

Ar'i•ma•the'a The native town of Joseph of Arimathea, a member of the Sanhedrin who, after the Crucifixion, obtained the body of Jesus and placed it in his own unused tomb (Matt. 27:57-60; Mark 15:43; Luke 23:50-53; John 19:38).

Ar•is•tar'chus A Thessalonian Christian who was a close companion of Paul (Acts 19:29; 20:4; 27:2; Col. 4:10).

ark a chest, box, or vessel.
Gen. 6:14, an **a** of gopher wood
Ex. 37:1, made the **a** of acacia wood
Matt. 24:38, Noah entered the **a**
Heb. 9:4, **a** of the covenant
Rev. 11:19, the **a** of His covenant

Ark of the Covenant

Ar'non A river, now dried to a wadi, beginning in the hills of northern Arabia and flowing some twenty miles westward to enter the Dead Sea opposite En-gedi (Num. 21:13, 14).

Ar'pad The name of a province and its chief city located in the northern region of Syria near the city of Hamath (2 Kin. 18:34; Is. 37:13).

ar•ray' adorn, clothe.
Judg. 20:20, men . . . **a-ed** for battle
Matt. 6:30, God so **a-s** the grass

A'sa The name of the third King of Judah after the division, and of a Levite of the time of the Exile (1 Kin. 15:9-24; 1 Chr. 9:16).

Ash'dod One of the five important Philistine cities, located on or near the Mediterranean Sea (1 Sam. 5:1; 6:17).

Ash'er The eighth son of Jacob (Gen. 30:9-13; 35:26).

A•sher'ah A wooden symbol of a female deity. The goddess of the sea and the consort of El (Judg. 6:25-30, 1 Kin. 15:13).

Ash'ke•lon An ancient Canaanite city situated on the Mediterranean sea coast about midway between Ashdod and Gaza (Jer. 25:20; 47:5).

Ash'to•reth, Ash'to•roth (pl.) Fertility goddess. It is a title and, strictly speaking, not a name, usually found in the sense of "my lady," "my goddess" (Judg. 2:13; 1 Sam. 31:10; 1 Kin. 11:5).

A'sia The richest and best endowed part of the great Roman province (Acts 2:9; 19:10; 1 Pet. 1:1).

as•sem'bly band, congregation, convocation.
Ex 12:16, you shall have a holy **a**
Ps. 1:5, in the **a** of the righteous

Ashtoreth

Joel 1:14; 2:15, Proclaim a solemn **a**
Acts 19:39, in the lawful **a**
Heb. 12:23, to the general **a** and church

Assh'ur Name of the son of Shem, borne also by the patron deity, people, and capital city of Assyria (Gen. 10:22; 1 Chr. 1:17).

Ass'ir A Levite; son of Korah (Ex. 6:24; 1 Chr. 6:22).

As•syr'i•a One of the ancient kingdoms of Mesopotamia; its chief city was Nineveh (Gen. 10:11; 2 Kin. 15:19).

a•tone'ment reconciliation, amends made for an injury or wrong.
Ex. 30:15, make **a** for yourselves
Lev. 23:27; 25:9, the day of **a**
2 Sam. 21:3, how can I make **a**

au'thor one who originates or gives existence.
Heb. 2:10, the **a** of their salvation
Heb. 12:2, the **a** and perfecter of faith

a•vail' profit, benefit, advantage.
Jer. 7:8, deceptive words to no **a**

a•venge' vengeance, revenge.
1 Sam. 24:12, may the LORD **a** me
Jer. 5:9, 29, Shall I not **a** Myself
2 Cor. 7:11, what zeal, what **a-ing** of wrong

awe fear, reverence.
Ps. 33:8, inhabitants . . . in **a** of Him
Ps. 119:161, stands in **a** of Thy words
Heb. 12:28, with reverence and **a**

awe'some fearful, inspiring reverence.
Gen. 28:17, How **a** is this place
Ex. 15:11, **A** in praises
Judg. 13:6, angel of God, very **a**
Neh. 1:5, the great and **a** God
Job 37:22, Around God is **a** majesty

A•ze'kah A Palestinian town which existed from before 1300 B. C. through Byzantine times (Josh. 10:10, 11; 15:35; 1 Sam. 17:1).

A'zel A son of Eleasah; a descendant of Jonathan, son of King Saul (1 Chr. 8:37; 9:43).

B

Baal A word meaning owner, master, lord or husband. It appears infrequently in the Old Testament as a personal name (1 Chr. 5:5; 8:30; 9:36). Generally, it designates the Canaanite deity (Num. 25:3; Judg. 10:6; 1 Sam. 7:4).

One representation of Baal

Baal-ha'nan 1. A king of Moab who ruled after Shaul (Gen. 36:38). 2. A servant of David who was in charge of David's olive and sycamore trees in the lowlands (Shephelah) (1 Chr. 27:28). He was a Gederite.

Baal of Pe'or The god worshiped in Moab by Israel at the instigation of Balaam while the Israelites were encamped at Shittim (Num. 25:1-9).

Ba'a•sha Third king of the northern kingdom, 909–886 B. C. and founder of its second dynasty (1 Kin. 15:19, 21, 22, 27, 28).

babe immature, a baby or infant.
Ps. 8:2, infants and nursing **b-s**
Matt. 11:25, reveal . . . to **b-s**
1 Cor. 3:1, to **b-s** in Christ
Heb. 5:13, for he is a **b**
1 Pet. 2:2, like newborn **b-s**

Bab'y•lon Capital of the land of Babylonia, South Iraq, from which the land takes its name (2 Kin. 25:27; Is. 13:19; Dan. 4:30).

back'bit'ing slanders or speaks spitefully.
Prov. 25:23, a **b** tongue

back'slid'er one who abandons the faith and practice of a religion previously followed.
Prov. 14:14, **b** in heart will have his fill
Jer. 49:4, O **b-ing** daughter

Ba•hur'im A village near the Mount of Olives on the road from Jerusalem to the Jordan (2 Sam. 16:5; 17:18; 1 Kin. 2:8).

Ba'laam Soothsayer from Mesopotamia secured by Balak to curse Israel (Num. 22:5, 7-10, 12-14).

Ba'lak Son of Zippor; king of Moab when Israel emerged from the wilderness to enter Canaan (Num. 22:2; Josh. 24:9; Judg. 11:25).

bal'ance scale, figurative weighing device for determining outcome of events.
Lev. 19:36, shall have just **b-s**
Ps. 62:9, In the **b-s** they go up
Prov. 11:1, A false **b** is an abomination to the Lord
Prov. 16:11, A just **b** and scales belonging to the LORD
Is. 40:12, weighed the mountains in a **b**

balm fragrant ointment or oil.
Gen. 37:25, **b** and myrrh
Gen. 43:11, a little **b** and . . . honey
Jer. 8:22, no **b** in Gilead
Jer. 51:8, Bring **b** for her pain
Ezek. 27:17, with . . . **b** they paid

band bond, chain, fetter.
Ex. 27:10, their **b-s** shall be of silver
Ex. 28:8, skillfully woven **b**
Judg. 8:26, the neck **b-s**
Ps. 107:14, broke their **b-s** apart
Is. 58:6, undo the **b-s** of the yoke

ban'ish to send away, dismiss.
2 Sam. 14:13, his **b-ed** one
2 Sam. 14:14, **b-ed** one may not be cast out
Ezra 7:26, for **b-ment**

bap'tism the rite of washing, a Christian sacrament.
Matt. 21:25; Mark 11:30; Luke 7:29, **b** of John
Mark 1:4; Luke 3:3; Acts 13:24; 19:4, **b** of repentance
Luke 12:50, I have a **b** to undergo
Rom. 6:4, buried with Him through **b**
Eph. 4:5, one Lord, one faith, one **b**

Ba•rab'bas The criminal whom the crowd, in response to Pilate's offer, chose for release instead of Jesus (Matt. 27:15-26).

Bar'ak Son of Abinoam of Kedesh-naphtali (Judg. 4:1-24).

bar•bar'i•an a member of a people with a civilization regarded as primitive.
Rom. 1:14, and to **b-s**
1 Cor. 14:11, be a **b**

Bar'na•bas A noted member of the early Jerusalem church and an active missionary to the Gentiles; he was Paul's companion on several of his journeys (Acts 4:36; 13:1–14:28).

bar'ren unfruitful, incapable of producing offspring.
Gen. 11:30, Sarai was **b**
Ex. 23:26, no one miscarrying or **b**
Job 24:21, wrongs the **b** woman
Is. 54:1, O **b** one
Luke 1:36, who was called **b**

Bar'uch Son of Neriah and brother of Seraiah. A devoted friend of Jeremiah (Jer. 32:12; 36:10).

Bash'an The fertile tract of country on the east side of the upper Jordan, adjacent to the Sea of Galilee (Deut. 3:4; Josh. 9:10).

bath a Hebrew unit of liquid measure.
1 Kin. 7:26, hold two thousand **b-s**
2 Chr. 2:10, 20,000 **b-s** of oil
Ezra 7:22, 100 **b-s** of wine
Is. 5:10, one **b** of wine

Bath•she'ba The wife of Uriah the Hittite, a soldier in David's army (2 Sam. 11:3). She is the woman with whom David so shamefully sinned and who, after the removal of her husband, became the wife of David and the mother of Solomon (2 Sam. 11:3, 4; 12:24; 1 Kin. 1:11).

beam a log or piece of timber, metal, or stone.
2 Kin. 6:2, take from there a **b**
Ps. 104:3, **b-s** of His upper chambers

Be'bai An Israelite family that returned with Ezra to Jerusalem (Ezra 2: 11; 8:11; 10:28).

Be'cher 1. A son of Benjamin (Gen. 46:21). 2. A son of Ephraim (Num. 26:35).

be•come' to come or grow to be.
Ps. 33:1, Praise is **b-ing** to the upright
Luke 2:40, Child . . . to grow and **b** strong

bed pallet, a place to rest or sleep.
2 Kin. 4:10, set a **b** for him there
Job 7:13, My **b** will comfort me
Ps. 63:6, remember Thee on my **b**
Is. 28:20, The **b** is too short
Matt. 9:6, Rise, take up your **b**

Be•el'ze•bul A name applied to Jesus by the Jewish leaders (Matt. 10:25; Mark 3:22).

Be•e'roth One of the four cities involved in the Gibeonite treaty (Josh. 9:17; 18:25).

Beer•she'ba A town in the Judean Negev district (Gen. 21:28-31).

be•fall' happen, to come to pass.
Gen. 44:29, harm **b-s** him
Gen. 49:1, what shall **b** you
Deut. 31:29, evil will **b** you
Ps. 91:10, No evil will **b** you

be•fit' proper, worthy.
Ps. 93:5, Holiness **b-s** Thy house
1 Tim. 2:10, as **b-s** women making a claim to godliness

be•got'ten to become the father of; to father.
Job 38:28, who has **b** the drops of dew
Ps. 2:7, Today I have **b** Thee
Philem. 10, whom I have **b**

be•hold' look upon, gaze at.
Num. 24:17, I **b** him
Ps. 37:37, **b** the upright
Matt. 18:10, angels . . . **b** the face of My father
John 17:24, that they may **b** My glory
2 Cor. 3:18, **b-ing** as in a mirror

Bel•shaz'zar The Chaldean ruler at the time of the capture of Babylon by Darius the Mede (Dan. 5:30; 7:1).

Bel'te•shaz'zar A Babylonian name ascribed to Daniel (Dan. 1:7; 2:26).

Be•na'iah A popular name, particularly among the Levites (2 Sam. 23:20, 21; 1 Chr. 11:22, 23).

Ben-ha'dad The name of three kings of Syria (1 Kin. 15:18; 20:1-34; 2 Kin. 13:22-25).

Ben'ja•min The youngest of Jacob's twelve sons, and the full brother of Joseph (Gen. 35:16-20).

Be'or 1. The father of Bela (Gen. 36:32; 1 Chr. 1:43). 2. The father of the seer Balaam (Num. 22:5; 24:3, 15).

be•reave' to take away or deprive of something.
Gen. 27:45, Why should I be **b-d** of you
Gen. 42:36, **b-d** me of my children
Lev. 26:22, beasts . . . shall **b** you
Jer. 15:7, I will **b** them
Ezek. 36:12, never again **b** them

be•siege' to hem in with armed forces.
Deut. 20:19, When you **b** a city
2 Sam. 11:1, and **b-d** Rabbah
1 Kin. 16:17, they **b-d** Tirzah
Is. 1:8, like a **b-d** city
Ezek. 6:12, he who remains and is **b-d**

be•stow' grant, to present as a gift or honor.
Ex. 32:29, He may **b** a blessing upon you
1 Chr. 29:25, **b-ed** on him royal majesty
1 Cor. 12:23, we **b** more abundant honor
1 John 3:1, love the Father has **b-ed** upon us

Beth'a•ny A village about two miles southeast of Jerusalem (Mark 11:1; John 11:18).

Beth-a'ven "Village of evil." The location is said to be west of Michmash (1 Sam. 13:5; 14:23).

Beth'el A town twelve miles north of Jerusalem designated as the modern village of Beitin (Gen. 28:19; 31:13).

Beth-hor'on The name means "house of caves" and is the name of two towns located ten and twelve miles northwest of Jerusalem (Josh. 10:10-13).

Beth'le•hem A town in Judah famous as the "city of David" and as the birthplace of Jesus (Matt. 2:5, 6; John 7:42).

Beth•sa'i•da A town on the north shore of the Sea of Galilee (John 1:44; 12:21).

Beth-she'an A city and important stronghold in the Valley of Jalud, near the junction of the Valley of Jezreel with the Jordan Valley (Josh. 17:11; Judg. 1:27).

Beth-shem'esh A place name, apparently applied to towns where a shrine to the sun (-god) was consecrated in pre-Israelite times (Josh. 19:38; Judg. 1:33).

Be•thu'el 1. The last named son of Nahor, brother of Abraham (Gen. 22:

22; 24:15). 2. A town of Simeon (1 Chr. 4:30).

be•troth′ to promise in marriage.
Jer. 2:2, love of your **b-als**
Hos. 2:19, 20, I will **b** you to Me
Matt. 1:18, Mary had been **b-ed** to Joseph
2 Cor. 11:2, I **b-ed** you to one husband

Bez′a•lel The chief artisan and foundryman of the Tabernacle (Ex. 31:2; 35:30).

Be′zer 1. A Levitical city in the region of Reuben (Josh. 21:36). 2. A son of Zophah of the house of Asher (1 Chr. 7:37).

bier a portable framework on which a coffin or corpse is placed.
2 Sam. 3:31, David walked behind the **b**

Big′vai 1. The head of a family that returned from Babylon with Zerubbabel (Ezra 2:2; Neh. 7:7). 2. A man who signed the covenant with Nehemiah (Neh. 10:16).

Bil′hah 1. A slave girl given by Laban to Rachel (Gen. 29:29). 2. A city in the territory of Simeon (1 Chr. 4:29).

birth′right′ any rights that a person has by birth.
Gen. 25:31, First sell me your **b**
Gen. 27:36, Jacob . . . took away my **b**
Heb. 12:16, sold his own **b** for a single meal

blas•pheme′ spoke in an irreverent manner.
Is. 52:5, My name is continually **b-d**
Matt. 9:3, This *fellow* **b-s**
Matt. 26:65, He has **b-d**
Mark 3:29, **b-s** against the Holy Spirit
Acts 26:11, force them to **b**

blem′ish spot, flaw, defect.
Song 4:7, there is no **b** in you
Ezek. 43:22, goat without **b** for a sin offering
Ezek. 46:4, six lambs without **b**
Heb. 9:14, offered Himself **b**

blood the vital fluid circulating through the body.
Lev. 17:11 life of the flesh is in the **b**
Acts 20:28, He purchased with His own **b**
Rom. 3:25, a propitiation in His **b**
Eph. 1:7, redemption through His **b**
Heb. 9:22, shedding of **b** there is no forgiveness

Bo′az A *wealthy* farmer of Bethlehem, the kinsman of Elimelech and Naomi and the great-grandfather of David (Ruth 2:1-23; 3:2-7; 4:1-21).

bois′ter•ous clamor; loud, noisy, and unrestrained.
Prov. 9:13, woman of folly is **b**

bond′-ser′vant one bound to serve without wages.
Luke 2:29, let Thy **b** depart
Rom. 1:1, Paul, a **b** of Christ Jesus
Phil. 1:1, Paul and Timothy, **b-s** of Christ
Titus 1:1, Paul, a **b** of God
2 Pet. 1:1, a **b** and apostle of Jesus Christ

booths temporary stalls for the sale of goods, as at market places.
Gen. 33:17, Jacob made **b** for his livestock
Lev. 23:42, 43, live in **b-s**

boo′ty a rich gain or prize taken from an enemy (as in time of war).
Num. 31:32, **b** that remained
Is. 53.12, He will divide the **b**
Jer. 38:2, have his *own* life as **b**
Jer. 49:32, their cattle for **b**

bos′om breast; the center or heart.
Ps. 35:13, prayer kept returning to my **b**
Prov. 6:27, fire in his **b**
Is. 40:11, carry *them* in His **b**
Luke 16:22, carried . . . to Abraham's **b**
John 1:18, in the **b** of the Father

bough a large branch of a tree.
Gen. 49:22, A fruitful **b** by a spring
Lev. 23:40, **b-s** of leafy trees
Ps. 80:10, cedars of God with its **b-s**
Is. 17:6, on the topmost **b**
Ezek. 31.6, birds . . . nested in its **b-s**

boun′ty something that is given generously.
1 Kin. 10:13, according to his royal **b**

bram′ble briar, prickly shrub or bush.
Judg. 9:14, trees said to the **b**
Judg. 9:15, fire come out from the **b**

brand torch; a mark indicating identity or ownership.
Zech. 3:2, **b** plucked from the fire
1 Tim. 4:2, as with a **b-ing** iron

bray to make a loud, harsh sound.
Job 6:5, wild donkey **b** over *his* grass

breach a breaking or being broken.
Ex. 22:9, **b** of trust
Judg. 21:15, LORD had made a **b** in . . . Israel
1 Kin. 11:27, closed up the **b**
Job 16:14, breaks through me with **b** after **b**

Amos 9:11, wall up its **b-es**

breast'piece a piece of armor for the breast.
Ex. 25:7, stones . . . for the **b**
Ex. 28:15, a **b** of judgment
Ex. 39:8, he made the **b** . . . of gold

breast'plate a piece of armor to cover the breast and chest.
Neh. 4:16, the bows, and the **b-s**
Is. 59:17, put on righteousness like a **b**
Eph. 6:14, put on the **b** of righteousness
1 Thess. 5:8, put on the **b** of faith and love
Rev. 9:9, **b-s** like **b-s** of iron

bri'dle guard, control; a harness for an animal.
2 Kin. 19:28, My **b** in your lips
Prov. 26:3, a **b** for the donkey
James 1:26, not **b** his tongue

brim'stone a former name for sulfur.
Gen. 19:24, **b** and fire from the Lord
Is. 30:33, like a torrent of **b**
Rev. 9:17, of fire . . . and of **b**
Rev. 14:10, tormented with fire and **b**
Rev. 19:20, fire which burns with **b**

bris'tle to rise and stand stiffly erect.
Job 4:15, hair . . . **b-d** up

brood a group of birds or fowl hatched at one time and cared for together.
Matt. 3:7, You **b** of vipers, who warned you
Luke 13:34, a hen *gathers* her **b**

bud a sprout of a plant not yet fully grown or developed.
Num. 17:8, rod . . . put forth **b-s**
Is. 18:5, as soon as the **b** blossoms

buf'fet beat, struggle, contend.
2 Cor. 12:7, to **b** me

bul'rush•es a tall plant found in water and wet land.
Is. 19:7, **b** by the Nile

burnt of'fer•ing a symbolic way of conveying sacrifice and commitment to God.
Gen. 22:7, lamb for the **b**
Ps. 40:6, **B** and sin offering Thou has not required
Jer. 6:20, **b-s** are not acceptable
Hos. 6:6, knowledge of God rather than **b-s**
Mark 12:33, more than all **b-s** and sacrifices

bush'el a unit of measure.
Amos 8:5, make the **b** smaller

by'word' a word or phrase frequently used.
1 Kin. 9:7, Israel will become . . . a **b** among all peoples
2 Chr. 7:20, a **b** among all peoples
Job 17:6, a **b** of the people
Job 30:9, become a **b** to them
Ps. 44:14, **b** among the nations

C

Cae'sar Was a surname of the Julian family, whose most eminent member was Gaius Julius Caesar, the great soldier, statesman, orator and author. Caesar thus became the dynastic name of all the emperors down to Hadrian (Matt. 22:17, 21).

Caes'a•re'a Port of Rome on the Palestine coast, sixty-five miles from Jerusalem (Acts 12:19; 23:33).

Ca'ia•phas The official high priest during the ministry and trial of Jesus (Matt. 26:3, 57).

Cain The eldest son of Adam and Eve, a farmer by occupation. He became a symbol of evil in that he did not exhibit faith in God's revelation (Gen. 4:1; 4:9-16).

ca•lam'ity destruction, dire distress.
2 Sam. 22:19, in the day of my **c**
Job 21:17, **c** fall on them
Job 31:23, **c** from God is a terror
Prov. 1:27, **c** comes on like a whirlwind
Prov. 24:16, the wicked stumble in *time of* **c**

Ca'leb One of the spies sent to survey the land of Canaan (Num. 13; 14).

call'ing summoning; bringing together.
Is. 1:13, the **c** of assemblies
Rom. 11:29, gifts and the **c** of God
2 Tim. 1:9, called us with a holy **c**
Heb. 3:1, partakers of a heavenly **c**

cam'el a one-humped or, less often, two-humped animal used in the Near and Middle East for travel. It can go without water for several days, and its flat feet make it capable of traveling over sand. In Biblical times, trade caravan travel across the deserts was commonplace.
1 Sam. 30:17, men who rode on **c-s** and fled.
Is. 30:6, their treasures on **c-s' humps**

Camels

Ca′naan The land west of Jordan occupied by the Israelites (Acts 7:11; 13:19).

Ca′naan•ite The term is used in a few passages in the Old Testament to denote "trader," or "merchant" (Deut. 20:17; Judg. 1:1, 28).

Ca•per′na•um A city on the northwest shore of the Sea of Galilee which served as Jesus' Galilean home base (Matt. 4:13-16; Luke 4:31).

car′cass corpse, dead body of an animal.
Gen. 15:11, birds of prey came down upon the **c-es**
Judg. 14:8, **c** of the lion

Car′mel A very ancient town in the mountains of Judah (Josh. 15:55; Jer. 46:18).

Car′mi 1. The father of Achan and the son of Zabdi (Josh. 7:1, 18). 2. A son of Reuben who came to Egypt with Jacob (Gen. 46:9).

ca•rouse′ to participate in a lively drinking party.
Rom. 13:13, not in **c-ing** and drunkenness
Gal. 5:21, **c-ing,** and things like these

cas′sia the bark of certain tropical evergreen trees, used like a cinnamon.
Ex. 30:24, of **c** five hundred
Ps. 45:8, garments are fragrant with . . . aloes and **c**
Ezek. 27:19, **c** . . . among your merchandise

cen′ser a container in which incense is burned.
Ezek. 8:11, with his **c** in his hand
Rev. 8:3, a golden **c**
Rev. 8:5, angel took the **c**

cen′sus the act of counting the people and evaluating their property for taxation.
Luke 2:1, a **c** . . . of all the inhabited earth
Acts 5:37, rose up in the days of the **c**

chaff threshed or winnowed husks of wheat or other grain.
Ps. 1:4, they are like **c**
Matt. 3:12, He will burn up the **c**

chal•ced′o•ny a kind of quartz with the luster of wax, variously colored.
Rev. 21:19, the third, **c**

Chal•de′ans The inhabitants of a district in South Babylonia (later applied to a dynasty which controlled all Babylonia) (Gen. 11:31; Is. 13:19; Dan. 1:4).

char′i•ot a horse-drawn, two-wheeled cart used in ancient times for war, racing, and parades.
Gen. 46:29, prepared his **c**
2 Kin. 2:11, a **c** of fire
Ps. 20:7, Some *boast* in **c-s**
Ps. 104:3, makes the clouds his **c**
Acts 8:28, sitting in his **c** . . . reading

Assyrian relief of a royal chariot

charm′er babbler; one who pleases or fascinates.
Ps. 58:5, the voice of **c-s**
Eccl. 10:11, no profit for the **c**

chaste pure in thought and act.
1 Pet. 3:2, **c** and respectful behavior
Rev. 14:4, they have kept themselves **c**

chas′ten discipline, punish.
Ps. 38:1, **c** me not
Ps. 94:12, whom Thou dost **c**
Is. 53:5, **c-ing** for our well-being

Che′mosh The name of the national god of Moab (1 Kin. 11:7, 33).

Che•na′a•nah The father of Zedekiah, the false prophet who predicted victory for Ahab at the battle of Ramoth-Gilead (1 Kin. 22:11, 24; 2 Chr. 18:10, 23).

Chen′a•ni•ah A chief Levite at the bringing of the Ark from Obed-edom's house to Jerusalem (1 Chr. 15:22, 27).

Christ The title literally means "The Anointed One." The Messiah which denoted the anointed king of Israel (Matt. 16:16; 26:63; John 1:41).

Chris'tian The followers and believers of Christ's teachings (Acts 11:26; 26:28; 1 Pet. 4:16).

Ci·li'cia A region in the southeast of Asia; the birthplace of Paul (Acts 21:39; 22:3; 23:34).

cir'cum·cise to cut off all or part of the foreskin.
Gen. 17:10, every male . . . shall be **c-d**
Deut. 30:6, God will **c** your heart
Luke 1:59, came to **c** the child
Phil. 3:5, **c-d** the eighth day
Col. 2:11, in Him you were also **c-d**

cis'tern a receptacle for holding water or other liquid.
Prov. 5:15, water from your own **c**
Eccl. 12:6, wheel at the **c** is crushed
Jer. 2:13, hew for themselves **c-s**
Jer. 38:6, cast him into the **c**

clam'or a loud outcry or shouting.
Eph. 4:31, anger and **c**

cloak a loose outer garment.
Ruth 3:15, Give me the **c** . . . on you
Is. 3:7, neither bread nor **c**
Matt. 9:20, the fringe of His **c**
Acts 12:8, Wrap your **c** around you
2 Tim. 4:13, bring the **c**

cock the male of the chicken; rooster.
Matt. 26:34, 75, before a **c** crows
Mark 13:35, at **c**-crowing, or in the morning.

com'fort·er helper; one who soothes in time of grief or fear.
Job 16:2, Sorry **c-s** are you all
Ps. 69:20, looked for . . . **c-s**, but I found none
Nah. 3:7, Where will I seek **c-s** for you

com·mis'sion an authorization to perform certain duties or to take on certain powers.
Acts 26:12, authority and **c** of . . . priests

com·mit' entrust, practice, wrought.
Ex. 20:14, You shall not **c** adultery
Ps. 31:5, Into Thy hand I **c** my spirit
Ps. 37:5, **C** your way to the Lord
Luke 23:46, into Thy hands I **c** My spirit
John 8:34, everyone who **c-s** sin

com·pan'ion a person who accompanies or associates with another.
Ex. 2:13, Why are you striking your **c**
Job 30:29, a **c** of ostriches
Prov. 13:20, **c** of fools will suffer
Eccl. 4:10, lift up his **c**
Heb. 1:9, oil of gladness above Thy **c-s**

com·pas'sion the deep feeling of sharing the suffering of another and giving aid, support, or showing mercy.
Ex. 33:19, **c** on whom I will show **c**
Ps. 72:13, **c** on the poor and needy
Ps. 103:13, father has **c** on *his* children
Ps. 111:4, Lord is gracious and **c-ate**
Col. 3:12, put on a heart of **c**

com·pel' to force to yield or submit.
Luke 14:23, **c** *them* to come in
2 Cor. 12:11, you yourselves **c-led** me
Gal. 2:14, you **c** the Gentiles

com·pla'cen·cy a feeling of contentment; self-satisfaction.
Prov. 1:32, **c** of fools shall destroy them

com·pre·hend' to grasp mentally; understand or know.
Job 37:5, things . . . cannot **c**
John 1:5, darkness did not **c** it

con·cil'i·ate to overcome the distrust of; to win over.
1 Cor. 4:13, slandered, we try to **c**

con·dem·na'tion the act of condemning; severe reproof; strong censure.
Matt. 23:14, receive greater **c**
Luke 23:40, same sentence of **c**
Rom. 3:8, Their **c** is just
Rom. 8:1, no **c** for those who are in
Rom. 13:2, **c** upon themselves

con'duit a pipe or channel for conveying fluids.
2 Kin. 18:17, the **c** of the upper pool
2 Kin. 20:20, the pool and the **c**
Is. 7:3, end of the **c**

con·fir·ma'tion a confirming or being confirmed.
Phil. 1:7, defense and **c** of the gospel
Heb. 6:16, an oath *given* as **c** is an end

con'gre·ga'tion an assembly of a group.
Ex. 12:3, Speak to all the **c**
Ps. 82:1, His stand in His own **c**
Ps. 149:1, **c** of the godly ones

con'se·crate to sanctify; to set apart as something sacred.
Ex. 28:41, ordain them and **c** them
Lev. 11:44, **C** yourselves
Num. 6:11, **c** his head
1 Sam. 21:4, there is **c-d** bread
Matt. 12:4, they ate **c-d** bread

con·strain' persuade, urge.
Job 32:18, spirit within me **c-s** me

con'sum·ma'tion completion; fulfillment.
Heb. 9:26, at the **c**

con·trite' humbled by guilt and repentant for one's sins.
Ps. 51:17, broken and a **c** heart
Is. 66:2, humble and **c** of spirit

con·ver'sion a change from lack of faith to religious belief.
Acts 15:3, **c** of the Gentiles

cor'ban a gift offered to God.
Mark 7:11, have been helped by is **C**

coun'te·nance the expression of the face.
Gen. 4:6, why has your **c** fallen
Num. 6:26, The Lord lift up His **c**
Ps. 4:6; 89:15, light of Thy **c**

cov'e·nant a binding agreement made by two or more individuals.
Gen. 6:18, I will establish My **c**
2 Kin. 23:2, book of the **c**
Luke 22:20, This cup . . . is the new **c**
Heb. 7:22, Jesus . . . guarantee of a better **c**
Rev. 11:19, the ark of His **c**

cov'et to desire that which belongs to another.
Ex. 20:17, You shall not **c**
Mic. 2:2, They **c** fields
Mark 7:22, deeds of **c-ing** *and* wickedness
Acts 20:33, have **c-ed** no one's silver
Rom. 7:8, produced in me **c-ing** of every kind

cres'cent shaped like the moon in its first or last quarter.
Is. 3:18, will take away . . . **c** ornaments

cro'cus any of a large group of plants of the iris family.
Is. 35:1, blossom; Like the **c**

cru'ci·fix'ion a crucifying or being crucified.
Matt. 26:2, delivered up for **c**

cul'ti·vate' to prepare and use land for growing crops.
Gen. 2:5, no man to **c** the ground
Gen. 2:15, put him into the garden . . . to **c** it
2 Sam. 9:10, shall **c** the land for him
Ps. 37:3, Dwell in the land and **c** faithfulness
Ezek. 36:9, you shall be **c-ed** and sown

cum'min a small plant of the carrot family.
Is. 28:25, sow dill and scatter **c**
Is. 28:27, cartwheel driven over **c**
Matt. 23:23, and dill and **c**

cup'bear'er a person who fills and serves the wine cups as in a king's palace.
Gen. 40:1, the **c** and the baker
Gen. 41:9, the chief **c** spoke
1 Kin. 10:5; 2 Chr. 9:4, his **c-s**
Neh. 1:11, the **c** to the king

Cup

curds the part of milk which has thickened as a result of souring.
Judg. 5:25, she brought him **c**
Is. 7:15, 22, eat **c** and honey

Cush 1. The eldest son of Ham and the grandson of Noah (Gen. 10:6-8). 2. A land lying in the south of Egypt (Is. 11:11).

Cush'i used as a proper name and as a designation of nationality. 1. The great-grandfather of Jehudi (Jer. 36:14). 2. The father of the prophet Zephaniah (Zeph. 1:1).

cym'bal either of a pair of slightly concave plates of brass, used in orchestras or bands.
2 Sam. 6:5, castanets and **c-s**
1 Chr. 15:16; 16:5, loud-sounding **c-s**
Ps. 150:5, Praise Him with loud **c-s**
1 Cor. 13:1, noisy gong or a clanging **c**

Cy'prus A large island in the northeast corner of the Mediterranean Sea (Acts 11:19, 20; 13:4; 15:39).

Cy'rus More precisely, Cyrus II, the great founder of the Achaemenid Persian empire, which continued for two centuries to the time of Alexander the Great (Is. 44:28; 45:1-7).

D

Da'gon The chief god of the Philistines (Judg. 16:23; 1 Sam. 5:3-7).

dain'ty delicious and choice; delicately pretty or lovely.
Gen. 49:20, he shall yield royal **d-ies**
Jer. 6:2, **d** one, the daughter of Zion

Da·mas'cus The well-known city northeast of Mt. Hermon (Gen. 15:2; 2 Kin. 8:7).

Dan A city of the northern extremity of ancient Israel (Gen. 14:14; Judg. 20:1).

Dan, Tribe of Dan was one of the so-called "lost tribes" which were carried away by the Assyrians and disappeared (Ex. 31:6; Num. 1:39).

Dan'iel 1. The celebrated Jewish prophet from the tribe of Judah (Dan. 1:3-21). 2. The second son of David (1 Chr. 3:1; Ezek. 28:3).

Da•ri'us It is the name of two Persian kings mentioned in Haggai, Zechariah, Ezra, and Nehemiah (Ezra 4:5; 6:15).

Da'than Dathan with two other Reubenites joined the Levite Korah in leading a rebellion of 250 chosen men against the leadership of Moses and Aaron (Num. 16:1, 12, 24, 25, 27).

Da'vid The son of Jesse of Bethlehem and second king of Israel (Ruth 4:18-22).

daz'zle to shine brilliantly.
Song 5:10, My beloved is **d-ing**
Luke 24:4, men . . . in **d-ing** apparel

de•ceit' the act or practice of deceiving.
Ps. 10:7, mouth is full of curses and **d** and oppression
Ps. 55:23, Men of bloodshed and **d** will not live

de•ceit'ful false or not honest.
Ps. 17:1, prayer, which is not from **d** lips
Ps. 26:4, I do not sit with **d** men
Ps. 120:3, You **d** tongue
Prov. 12:5, counsels of the wicked are **d**
Prov. 31:30, Charm is **d** and beauty is vain
2 Cor. 11:13, false apostles, **d** workers

de•ceit'ful•ness not trustworthy, dishonest.
Matt. 13:22; Mark 4:19, **d** of riches

de•cep'tive deceiving or meant to deceive.
Mic. 6:11, a bag of **d** weights

De'dan 1. The son of Raamah, son of Cush, the son of Ham (Gen. 10:7). 2. The grandson of Abraham by Keturah. His father was Jokshan (Gen. 25:3; 1 Chr. 1:32).

ded'i•cate' to devote to the worship of a divine being.
Ex. 32:29, **D** yourselves today to the Lord
Judg. 17:3, wholly **d** the silver
1 Kin. 7:51, Solomon brought in the things **d-d**
1 Kin. 8:63, sons of Israel **d-d** the house of the LORD
1 Chr. 26:27, They **d-d** part of the spoil

de•fi'cient lacking in some necessary quality or element.
Dan. 5:27, and found **d**

de•file' to make unclean or impure.
Neh. 13:29, they have **d-d** the priesthood
Ps. 79:1, **d-d** Thy holy temple
Titus 1:15, to those who are **d-d** . . . nothing is pure
James 3:6, that which **d-s** the entire body
Jude 8, these men, also by dreaming, **d** the flesh

de•gen'er•ate having sunk below a former or normal condition.
Jer. 2:21, **d** shoots of a foreign vine

de'i•ty divine nature.
Col. 2:9, fulness of **D** . . . bodily form

De•la'iah When Baruch read Jeremiah's scroll, Delaiah was one of all the princes who heard, referred to the king and one of three who urged him not to burn the inspired prophecy (Jer. 36:12, 25).

de•lude' to mislead.
2 Thess. 2:11, God will send . . . a **d-ing** influence

de'mon an evil spirit.
Matt. 8:31, **d-s** *began* to entreat Him
Mark 3:15, authority to cast out the **d-s**
1 Cor. 10:20, sacrifice to **d-s**
James 2:19, **d-s** also believe, and shudder
James 3:15, is earthly, natural, **d-ic**

de•nounce' to inform against.
Jer. 20:10, **D** *him;* yes, let us **d** him

de•ride' mock, scoff, sneer.
Ps. 119:51, utterly **d** me

de•ri'sion laughingstock, shame.
Ex. 32:25, a **d** among their enemies
Ps. 44:13, a **d** to those around us
Jer. 20:8, reproach and **d** all day long
Ezek. 23:32, laughed at and held in **d**
Hos. 7:16, their **d** in the land

des'o•late showing the effects of abandonment and neglect.
Lev. 26:31, make your sanctuaries **d**
Is. 54:1, sons of the **d** one
Joel 2:3, a **d** wilderness behind them
Zech. 7:14, land is **d-d** behind them
Matt. 23:38, your house is being left to you **d**

des'o•la'tion the condition of being desolated.
Jer. 25:9; Ezek. 35:9, an everlasting **d**
Jer. 32:43, a **d**, without man or beast
Dan. 9:26, there will be war; **d-s** are determined
Zeph. 1:15, day of destruction and **d**

Luke 21:20, Jerusalem . . . **d** is at hand

de•spond'en•cy the state of being discouraged or disheartened.
Ex. 6:9, on account of *their* **d**

des'ti•tute lacking something needed or desirable.
Ps. 102:17, regarded the prayer of the **d**
Ezek. 32:15, the land is **d**
Heb. 11:37, being **d,** afflicted, ill-treated

de•test' despise, loathe.
Deut. 7:26, shall utterly **d** it
Jer. 4:1, put away your **d-ed** things
Amos 6:8, I **d** his citadels

de•test'a•ble arousing intense dislike.
Deut. 14:3, eat any **d** thing
Job 15:16, one who is **d** and corrupt
Is. 66:17, swine's flesh, **d** things
Jer. 16:18, their **d** idols
Luke 16:15, is **d** in the sight of God

dev'as•tate' to bring to ruin.
Nah. 2:2, have **d-d** them
Nah. 3:7, Nineveh is **d-d**

dev'as•ta'tion the action of devastating.
Ps. 12:5, the **d** of the afflicted

devil The personage of Satan. A spirtual being which is hostile to both God and man (Matt. 4:8-11; Heb. 2:14; Rev. 2:10).

de'vi•ous not straightforward; tricky.
Prov. 4:24, put **d** lips far from you

de•vour' to seize and destroy.
2 Sam. 2:26, Shall the sword **d** forever
Zeph. 1:18; 3:8, all the earth will be **d-ed**
Luke 15:30, son of yours . . . has **d-ed** your wealth
Gal. 5:15, if you bite and **d** one another

de•vout' God-fearing and devoted.
Luke 2:25, Simeon . . . righteous and **d**
Acts 2:5; 8:2, **d** men
Acts 10:1, 2, centurion . . . a **d** man
Acts 13:50, the **d** women
Acts 22:12, who was **d** by . . . the Law

di'a•dem' a headband worn as a badge of royalty.
Is. 28:5, a glorious **d**
Is. 62:3, a royal **d**

Di'bon 1. A Judean town toward the south, inhabited in the time of Nehemiah by members of the tribe of Judah (Neh. 11:25). 2. A city in Moab, east of the Dead Sea, north of the Arnon River (*Num. 21:30; 32:3*).

dil'i•gence the attention and care legally expected or required of a person.
Ezra 6:12, carried out with all **d**
Prov. 4:23, Watch over your heart with all **d**
Rom. 12:11, not lagging behind in **d**

dil'i•gent careful, eager, thorough.
Prov. 11:27, **d-ly** seeks good seeks favor
Eph. 4:3, **d** to preserve the unity
2 Tim. 2:15, Be **d** to present yourself approved
Heb. 4:11, Let us therefore be **d**

di•min'ish to become gradually less.
Lev. 25:16, you shall **d** its price
Ezek. 16:27, and **d-ed** your rations

dirge a funeral hymn.
Jer. 9:10, of the wilderness a **d**
Matt. 11:17, we sang a **d**

dis•cern' appraise, analyze, recognize.
Deut. 32:29, they would **d** their future
1 Kin. 3:9, **d** between good and evil
Prov. 8:5, **d** prudence . . . **d** wisdom
Matt. 16:3, **d** the appearance of the sky
Heb. 5:14, senses trained to **d** good and evil

dis•cern'ing revealing insight and understanding.
Gen. 41:33, a man **d** and wise
Deut. 1:13, Choose wise and **d**
1 Kin. 3:12, a wise and **d** heart
Prov. 16:21, wise in heart will be called **d**

dis•cern'ment the quality of being able to grasp and comprehend.
1 Sam. 25:33, blessed be your **d**
1 Kin. 3:11, **d** to understand justice
Ps. 119:66, Teach me good **d**
Is. 27:11, not a people of **d**

dis•cre'tion understanding, wisdom.
1 Chr. 22:12, LORD give you **d**
Prov. 11:22, beautiful woman who lacks **d**

dis•dain' treat with scorn.
1 Sam. 17:42, he **d-ed** him (David)
Job 30:1, Whose fathers I **d-ed**

Di'shan The leader of a clan of the Horites descended from Seir (Gen. 36:20-30; 1 Chr. 1:38-42).

Di'shon 1. A chief of the Horites and fifth son of Seir (Gen. 36:21, 26, 30). 2. A son of the Horite chief Anah, and grandson of Seir (Gen. 36:25).

dis•may' to deprive of courage; to fill with bewilderment.
Deut. 1:21, Do not fear or be **d-ed**
1 Sam. 17:11, they were **d-ed** and greatly afraid
Job 41:22, **d** leaps before him

Jer. 8:21, **d** has taken hold of me
Obad. 9, mighty men will be **d-ed**

dis•perse′ to scatter.
Esth. 3:8, people scattered and **d-ed**
Is. 11:12, gather the **d-d** of Judah
Ezek. 20:23, **d** them among the lands
Ezek. 36:19, **d-ed** throughout the lands
Zeph. 3:10, My **d-d** ones

dis•per′sion a dispersing or being dispersed.
Jer. 25:34, your **d-s** have come
John 7:35, the **D** among the Greeks

dis•pos•sess′ to deprive of the possession of land, house, etc.
Num. 14:12, smite them . . . and **d** them
Deut. 7:17, nations . . . how can I **d** them

dis•sen′sion disagreement and quarrelling.
Acts 15:2, Paul and Barnabas had great **d** . . . with them
Acts 23:7, a **d** between the Pharisees and Sadducees
Rom. 16:17, keep your eye on those who cause **d-s**
1 Tim. 2:8, without wrath and **d**

dis•si•pa′tion a scattering or being scattered.
Eph. 5:18, wine, for that is **d**
Titus 1:6, not accused of **d** or rebellion

dis•till′ to let fall or precipitate in drops.
Deut. 32:2, My speech **d** as the dew
Job 36:27, They **d** rain from the mist

div′i•na′tion the act or practice of trying to foretell the future or the unknown by occult means.
Num. 22:7, *fees* for **d** in their hand
Jer. 14:14, false vision, **d**, futility
Ezek. 13:6, They see falsehood and lying **d**
Ezek. 13:9, utter lying **d-s**
Acts 16:16, having a spirit of **d**

Do′do The grandfather of Judge Tola of Issachar (Judg. 10:1; 2 Sam. 23:9).

Do′eg The name of one of Saul's herdsmen (1 Sam. 21:7; 22:9).

do•main′ a territory over which dominion is exercised.
Luke 4:6, all this **d** and its glory
Col. 1:13, He delivered us from the **d** of darkness
Jude 6, angels who did not keep their own **d**

do•min′ion supreme authority; absolute ownership.
Ps. 103:22, In all places of His **d**
Zech. 9:10, His **d** will be from sea to sea
Eph. 1:21, power and **d**
Col. 1:16, thrones or **d-s** or rulers
1 Pet. 4:11, belongs the glory and **d** forever

Dor A fortified city on the coast of Palestine south of Mount Carmel eight miles north of Caesarea (Josh. 11:2; 1 Chr. 7:29).

drought a prolonged period of dryness.
Job. 24:19, **D** and heat
Jer. 14:1, in regard to the **d**

dwell abide, remain, live.
Ps. 23:6, will **d** in the house of the LORD
Prov. 3:33, He blesses the **d-ing** of the righteous
Luke 16:9, receive you into the eternal **d-ings**
Eph. 3:17, Christ may **d** in your hearts through faith
Col. 1:19, for all the fulness to **d** in Him

dwelt lived or settled.
Ps. 107:10, those who **d** in darkness
Jer. 50:39, never again be inhabited Or **d** in

dwin′dle to become steadily less.
Prov. 13:11, wealth . . . by fraud **d-s**

E

earth′en made of earth.
Jer. 19:1, a potter's **e-ware** jar
Lam. 4:2, regarded as **e** jars
2 Cor. 4:7, have this treasure in **e** vessels

E′bal 1. Several characters in the Old Testament descended from Hurrian or Edomite parentage (Gen. 36:23). 2. Name of a mountain in Ephraim (Deut. 27:4-26).

E′ber Name of an ancestor of Abraham and of four minor individuals in the Old Testament (Gen. 10:21; 1 Chr. 1:19).

E′den The first habitation of our first parents (Gen. 2:8-14).

e′dict an official public order having the force of law.
Ezra 6:11, violates this **e**

ed•i•fi•ca′tion moral or spiritual instruction or improvement.
Rom. 15:2, please his neighbor . . . to his **e**
1 Cor. 14:3, speaks to men for **e**
1 Cor. 14:26, all things be done for **e**

ed′i•fy′ to instruct or to improve spiritually.
1 Cor. 8:1, but love **e-ies**
1 Cor. 10:23, lawful, but not all things **e**
1 Cor. 14:5, church may receive **e-ing**

E′dom 1. The land of the descendants of Esau (Gen. 32:3, 21). 2. A name of Esau, given in memory of his having sold his birthright for red pottage (Gen. 25:30).

Ed′re•i Town name. 1. A residence city of Og, King of Bashan (Deut. 1:4; 3:10; Josh. 12:4; 13:12). 2. A fortified city allotted to Naphtali, near Kedesh in Upper Galilee (Josh. 19:37).

ef•fem′i•nate having or showing qualities generally attributed to women, as weakness, delicacy, etc.
1 Cor. 6:9, Do not be deceived . . . nor **e**

Eg′lon An obese Moabite King, who early in the Judges period occupied territory west of Jordan near Jericho (Judg. 3:12-20).

E′gypt In the northeast corner of Africa, the Nile delta and valley, with their flanking deserts, from the Mediterranean Sea to the first cataract in antiquity, to the second cataract in modern times (Gen. 15:18; Matt. 2:13, 14, 15).

E′hud A Benjaminite name designating the son of Gera (Judg. 3:15-30).

Ek′ron The northern most part of the five major Philistine cities and its inhabitants (Josh. 13:3; 1 Sam. 5:10).

E′lah Fourth king of Israel, son of Baasha of Issachar (1 Kin. 16:8-14).

E′lam The Biblical designation of a people and a country in the southern area of the Iranian plateau in the Zagros mountains (Gen. 10:22; 1 Chr. 1:17).

el′ders the firstborn to succeed as the headship of his father's house; an ordained official of the church.
1 Sam. 15:30, before the **e** of my people
Matt. 15:2, tradition of the **e**
Acts 15:2, the apostles and **e**
1 Tim. 5:17, Let the **e** who rule well

el′e•ment any of the four substances —earth, air, fire, water.
Gal. 4:3, **e-al** things of the world
2 Pet. 3:10, **e-s** will be destroyed

E′li 1. The form of the *divine* name. *"My God, my God,* why hast thou forsaken me?" (Matt. 27:46). Thy cry of the dying Messiah in the passion narrative refers to the mystery of Christ's two natures. 2. A high priest of the family of Ithamar. He also was active as a judge of Israel (1 Sam. 1:9; 1 Kin. 2:27).

E•li′a•saph 1. A son of Deuel (Reuel) and a leader of the tribe of Gad (Num. 1:14; 2:14; 7:42-47). 2. A descendant of Gershon of the tribe of Levi (Num. 3: 24).

E•li′el meaning—"My God is God." The name of nine or perhaps ten different men in the Old Testament (1 Chr. 6:34; 11:47).

E•li′jah The famous 9th century prophet who served in the northern kingdom in the reigns of Ahab and his son Ahaziah (Mal. 4:5; Matt. 16:14; 17:11, 12; Luke 9:33; John 1:21).

E′lim The second recorded stopping place of the Israelites on their journey from the Red Sea to Sinai (Ex. 15:27; 16:1).

El′i•phaz 1. An Edomite from Teman and friend of Job (Job 42:7). 2. A son of Esau, by Adah one of his wives (Gen. 36:4).

E•li′sha A prophet, the successor of Elijah (1 Kin. 19:16; Luke 4:27).

E•li′shah A son of Javan and progenitor of the Japhetic nation which bears his name (Gen. 10:4; 1 Chr. 1:7; Ezek. 27:7).

E•liz′a•beth The wife of the priest Zechariah, and the mother of John the Baptist (Luke 1:5-66).

E•li′zur Son of Shedeur; a chief of the tribe of Reuben (Num. 1:5; 2:10; 7: 30, 35).

El•na′than 1. Elnathan of Jerusalem, the grandfather of King Jehoiachin (2 Kin. 24:8). 2. Several other Elnathan's are mentioned among the Levites who were described as "leading men" and "men of insight" in the days of Ezra (Ezra 8:15, 16).

el′o•quent fluent expression, full of words.
Ex. 4:10, never been **e**
Acts 18:24, Jew named Apollos . . . an **e** man

e•lude′ to avoid or escape.
John 10:39, He **e-d** their grasp

em•bit′ter•ed to make bitter or more bitter.
Ps. 73:21 When my heart was **e**
Acts 14:2, **e** them against the brethren

em·broi'der to form with needlework.
Ex. 35:35, work . . . of an **e-er**
Ezek. 16:10, clothed you with **e-ed** cloth
Ezek. 16:13, your dress was of . . . **e-ed** cloth
Ezek. 27:7, sail was of fine **e-ed** linen
Ezek. 27:16, 24, **e-ed** work

em'i·nent standing above others in some quality or position.
2 Cor. 11:5, inferior to the most **e** apostles

E'nan Father of Ahira, who, as military leader of the tribe of Naphtali at the time of the wilderness wanderings, assisted in the Sinai census and brought the tribal offering (Num. 1:15; 2:29; 7:78).

en·camp' to make, and stay in, a camp.
Ps. 27:3, host **e** against me
Ps. 34:7, angel of the Lord **e-s** around
Ps. 53:5, him who **e-ed** against you
Jer. 50:29, **E** against her on every side

en·cum'brance to weigh down.
Heb. 12:1, also lay aside every **e**

en·dow' to provide.
Gen. 30:20, God has **e-ed** me
2 Chr. 2:13, man, **e-ed** with understanding

en·dur'ance the ability to withstand hardship.
James 1:4, let **e** have *its* perfect result
James 5:11, **e** of Job

en'mi·ty typically mutual hatred.
Gen. 3:15, put **e** Between you
Luke 23:12, at **e** with each other
Eph. 2:15, abolishing in His flesh the **e**
Eph. 2:16, by it having put to death the **e**

E'noch 1. The son of Cain for whom the first city which Cain built was named (Gen. 4:17, 18). 2. He lived 365 years, and he walked with God (Gen. 5:18-24).

E'nosh Son of Seth and the grandson of Adam; an ancestor of Christ (Gen. 4: 26; 5:6-11).

en·rage' to fill with anger.
Prov. 6:34, jealousy **e-s** a man
Matt. 2:16, Herod . . . became very **e-d**

en·tice' to draw on by arousing hope or desire.
2 Chr. 18:19, Who will **e** Ahab
Prov. 1:10, if sinners **e** you
James 1:14, **e-d** by his own lust
2 Pet. 2:14, **e-ing** unstable souls
2 Pet. 2:18, they **e** by fleshly desires

en·treat' to make an earnest request.
Matt. 8:34, they **e-ed** Him to depart from their region
Mark 5:10, he *began* to **e** Him earnestly
2 Cor. 5:20, as though God were **e-ing** through us
Eph. 4:1, I therefore . . . **e** you to walk
1 Tim. 2:1, I urge that **e-es** *and* prayers

E·phe'sians An Epistle of the Apostle Paul to the Christians of Ephesus.

Eph'e·sus The city of Ephesus lay at the mouth of the Cayster, between the Koressos Range and the sea, on the western coast of Asia Minor (Acts 18:19; 19:17).

E'phra·im The younger of two sons born to Joseph in Egypt (Gen. 41:50-52).

E'phra·im, Mount The hill country in central Palestine occupied by the tribe of Ephraim, rather than a single mountain (Josh. 17:15; Judg. 3:27; 1 Sam. 1:1).

E'phron The Hittite from whom Abraham purchased a burial place for Sarah his wife (Gen. 23:8; 49:29).

eq'ui·ty equal, uprightness, straight.
Ps. 17:2, Let Thine eyes look with **e**
Ps. 98:9, judge . . . the peoples with **e**
Prov. 1:3, Righteousness, justice, and **e**
Prov. 2:9, discern righteousness . . . And **e**

err to make a mistake.
Ps. 95:10, people who **e**

E'sau Son of Isaac and Rebekah, and elder twin brother of Jacob (Gen. 25:29-34).

Esh'te·mo'a A Judean town in the southern hill country of Judah (Josh. 21: 14; 1 Sam. 30:28).

es·teem' to set a high value on.
Ps. 119:128, I **e** right . . . precepts
1 Thess. 5:13, you **e** them very highly in love

Es'ther A Benjamite girl, whose name is immortalized in the book that bears her name (Esth. 2:5-7).

es·trange' to remove from customary environment or associations.
Job 19:13, acquaintances . . . **e-d** from me
Ps. 58:3, The wicked are **e-d** from the womb
Ezek. 14:5, hearts . . . **e-d** from Me

E'tam A town between Bethlehem and Tekoa, which Rehoboam fortified after the secession of the ten northern tribes (1 Chr. 4:32; 2 Chr. 11:6).

e·ter′nal everlasting and forever.
Matt. 19:16, I may obtain **e** life
Mark 10:17; Luke 10:25, what . . . to inherit **e** life
John 3:36, who believes in the Son has **e** life
Rom. 6:23, free gift of God is **e** life
1 Pet. 5:10, called you to His **e** glory in Christ

E′thi·o′pi·a The Biblical Ethiopia is Nubia, in southernmost Egypt and the North Sudan, not the modern Ethiopia (also called Abyssinia). Often associated with Egypt in the Bible (Ps. 68:31; Ezek. 30:4, 5).

eu′nuch a castrated man placed in charge of a harem.
Esth. 1:10, seven **e-s** who served
Is. 56:3, Neither let the **e** say
Matt. 19:12, **e-s** for . . . the kingdom of heaven
Acts 8:27, there was an Ethiopian **e**

Eu·phra′tes The longest river of Western Asia (Gen. 2:14; Josh. 1:4).

e·van′gel·ist one who announces good news; one who preaches the gospel.
Acts 21:8, Philip the **e**
Eph. 4:11, He gave some . . . *as* **e-s**
2 Tim. 4:5, do the work of an **e**

Eve The name given by Adam to the first woman because she was the mother of all living (Gen. 3:20; 2 Cor. 11:3).

ev′i·dence something that furnishes proof; testimony.
Deut. 17:6, the **e** of two witnesses

ex·alt′ to raise in rank, power or character.
Ps. 46:10, I will be **e-ed** in the earth
Ps. 108:5, Be **e-ed,** O God, above the heavens
Luke 1:46, My soul **e-s** the Lord
Phil. 1:20, Christ shall . . . be **e-ed** in my body
Phil. 2:9, God highly **e-ed** Him

ex·as′per·ate′ to make angry.
Col. 3:21, do not **e** your children

ex·hort′ to urge earnestly by advice, warning, etc.
Acts 2:40, many other words . . . **e-ing** them
2 Tim. 4:2, **e,** with great patience
Titus 1:9, able both to **e** in sound doctrine
Titus 2:15, **e** and reprove
1 Pet. 5:12, **e-ing** and testifying

ex′hor·ta′tion the act of making an urgent appeal.
Luke 3:18, with many other **e-s**
Acts 20:2, given them much **e**
Rom. 12:8, he who exhorts, in his **e**
Heb. 13:22, this word of **e**

ex′ile a prolonged, often enforced, living away from one's country or community.
2 Sam. 15:19, a foreigner and also an **e**
Is. 51:14, The **e** will soon be set free

ex′or·cists ones who perform exorcism to drive out evil spirits.
Acts 19:13, some of the Jewish **e**

ex·pe′di·ent suitable for achieving a particular end.
John 11:50, **e** for you that one
John 18:14, it was **e** for one man to die

ex·plic′it clearly stated.
1 Tim. 4:1, Spirit **e-ly** says

ex·tol′ to praise highly.
Ex. 15:2, will **e** Him
Ps. 30:1; 145:1, I will **e** Thee

ex·tor′tion the act or practice of obtaining from a person by force or illegal power.
Jer. 22:17, practicing oppression and **e**

ex·tor′tion·er a person guilty of extortion.
Is. 16:4, **e** has come to an end

ex′ul·ta′tion extreme joy.
1 Thess. 2:19, or joy or crown of **e**

E·zek′iel One of the major prophets. He was the son of Buzi, and a priest of the family of Zadok (Ezek. 1:3; 24:24).

Ez′ra The ancestor of Jehozadak, a priest and prominent postexilic leader (Ezra 7:6; Neh. 8:1-8).

F

fa′bles a legendary story of supernatural happenings.
1 Tim. 4:7, worldly **f** fit only for old women

faith firm belief and complete confidence.
Hab. 2:4, the righteous will live by his **f**
Matt. 17:20, **f** as a mustard seed
Eph. 2:8, by grace . . . through **f**
James 1:3, testing of your **f** produces endurance
Jude 20, building . . . on your most holy **f**

faith′ful steadfast in affection or allegiance.
Ps. 31:23, The LORD preserves the **f**
Eph. 1:1, *who are* **f** in Christ Jesus
1 Thess. 5:24, **F** is He who calls you
Heb. 10:23, He who promised is **f**
Rev. 2:10, Be **f** until death

false'hood an untrue statement.
Ps. 24:4, lifted up his soul to **f**
Ps. 119:163, I hate and despise **f**
Prov. 20:17, Bread obtained by **f** is sweet
Jer. 14:14, prophesying **f** in My name
Eph. 4:25, laying aside **f**

fam'ine an extreme scarcity of food.
Ps. 33:19, keep them alive in **f**
Matt. 24:7, there will be **f-s** and earthquakes
Mark 13:8, will *also* be **f-s**
Luke 15:14, a severe **f** occurred in that country
Rom. 8:35, or **f**, or nakedness, or peril

fam'ish to suffer severely from hunger.
Gen. 41:55, Egypt was **f-ed**

fast to abstain from food and drink for a long or short period.
Joel 1:14, Consecrate a **f**
Matt. 4:2, after He had **f-ed** forty days
Matt. 6:16, whenever you **f**, do not . . . as the hypocrites
Matt. 6:17, when you **f**, anoint your head
Acts 13:3, when they had **f-ed** and prayed

fast'ing going hungry, observed as a sign of mourning for sin.
Esth. 4:3, with **f**, weeping, and wailing
Ps. 35:13, I humbled my soul with **f**
Ps. 109:24, weak from **f**
Matt. 6:16, 18, seen **f** by men
Luke 2:37, serving . . . with **f-s** and prayers

Feast of Booths The feast fell on the fifteenth of the seventh month, five days after the Day of Atonement, and occupied seven days (Lev. 23:33-43; Deut. 16:13-16; John 7:2).

Feast of Passover The Passover commemorated the final plague in Egypt in which the firstborn of Egyptians died, but the Israelites were spared by the blood on the doorpost (Ex. 34:25; Luke 2:41; John 13:1).

Feast of Weeks This one day festival is named from the fact that its date is set by counting from the sabbath of Passover to the morrow after the seventh sabbath (Deut. 16:9-12).

fee'ble indicating weakness.
Gen. 30:42, when the flock was **f**
Neh. 4:2, What are these **f** Jews doing
Job 4:4, you have strengthened **f** knees
Is. 35:3, strengthen the **f**
Heb. 12:12, strengthen . . . the knees that are **f**

fel'low•ship' the state of being a fellow or associate.
Ps. 55:14, had sweet **f** together
2 Cor. 6:14, What **f** has light with darkness
2 Cor. 13:14, **f** of the Holy Spirit
Gal. 2:9, right hand of **f**
1 John 1:3, our **f** is with the Father

fer'vent hot; burning; glowing.
Acts 18:25, being **f** in spirit
Rom. 12:11, **f** in spirit, serving
1 Pet. 4:8, keep **f** in your love

fet'ter a chain or shackle for the feet; to put fetters on
2 Sam. 3:34, nor your feet in **f-s**
Job 36:8, they are bound in **f-s**
Ps. 2:3, let us tear their **f-s** apart
Ps. 105:18, afflicted his feet with **f-s**
Prov. 7:22, as one in **f-s**

fig'ur•a•tive representing by means of a figure or symbol.
1 Cor. 4:6, I have **f-ly** applied to myself

filth something that tends to corrupt or defile.
Is. 4:4, LORD has washed away the **f**
Is. 64:6, deeds are like a **f-y** garment
James 1:21, putting aside all **f-iness**

fire'pan a vessel used for carrying live coals.
Ex. 27:3, its forks and its **f-s**
Lev. 16:12, take a **f** full of coals

flask a container (bottle) often somewhat narrowed toward the outlet and often fitted with a closure.
1 Sam. 10:1, Samuel took the **f** of oil
2 King. 9:1, take this **f** of oil
Matt. 25:4, took oil in **f-s**

flax a slender, erect plant with delicate blue flowers and narrow leaves.
Ex. 9:31, **f** and the barley were ruined
Judg. 15:14, his arms were as **f**
Ezek. 40:3, with a line of **f**

fleece the wool covering a sheep or similar animal.
Judg. 6:37, dew on the **f** only
Job 31:20, warmed with the **f**

flint a hard stone that produces a spark when struck by steel.
Ex. 4:25, Zipporah took a **f**
Deut. 8:15, out of the rock of **f**
Zech. 7:12, made their hearts like **f**

flog to beat with a strap or whip.
Mark 13:9, you will be **f-ed**

flu'ent·ly able to write or speak easily, smoothly, and expressively.
Ex. 4:14, he speaks **f**

foe an enemy in war.
1 Chr. 21:12, swept away before your **f-s**
Esth. 7:6, A **f** and an enemy

fol'ly lack of good sense.
Judg. 19:23, do not commit this act of **f**
Prov. 14:18, The naive inherit **f**
Prov. 15:2, mouth of fools spouts **f**
Prov. 15:21, **F** is joy to him
Prov. 24:9, devising of **f** is sin

for·bear'ance the act of refraining from.
Prov. 25:15, By **f** a ruler may be persuaded
Rom. 3:25, in the **f** of God
Eph. 4:2, showing **f** to one another

for·bid' to hinder or prevent.
1 Sam. 26:11, The Lord **f** that I should
1 Kin. 21:3, The Lord **f** me that I should
1 Cor. 14:39, do not **f** to speak in tongues

for'eign alien in character; strange.
Gen. 35:2, Put away the **f** gods
Ex. 2:22, a sojourner in a **f** land
1 Kin. 11:1, Solomon loved many **f** women
Ezra 10:2, have married **f** women
Ps. 137:4, LORD's song in a **f** land

fore'most' in the first place.
Matt. 22:38, great and **f** commandment
Mark 12:28, commandment is the **f** of all
1 Tim. 1:15, among whom I am **f** *of all*

for'feit to lose or lose the right to by some error or crime.
Ezra 10:8, his possessions should be **f-ed**
Dan. 1:10, make me **f** my head to the king

for'ni·ca'tion human sexual intercourse other than between a man and his wife.
Matt. 15:19, murders, adulteries, **f-s**
John 8:41, We are not born of **f**
Acts 15:20, from **f** and from what is strangled

for·sake' to quit or leave entirely.
Josh. 1:5, not fail you or **f** you
2 Chr. 15:2, **f** Him, He will **f** you
Prov. 1:8, do not **f** your mother's teaching
Prov. 9:6, **F** *your* folly and live
Is. 55:7, Let the wicked **f** his way

for'ti·fi·ca'tion something that defends or strengthens.
Is. 25:12, unassailable **f-s** of

foun·da'tion the basis upon which something stands or is supported.
Ps. 89:14; 97:2, Righteousness and justice are the **f**
Luke 6:48, laid a **f** upon the rock
Rom. 15:20, upon another man's **f**
2 Tim. 2:19, the firm **f** of God stands
Heb. 6:1, a **f** of repentance

frank'in·cense' a gum resin from various Asiatic and East African trees, burned as incense.
Ex. 30:34, spices with pure **f**
1 Chr. 9:29, the wine and the oil and the **f**
Song 4:6, And to the hill of **f**

fraud an act of deceiving or misrepresenting.
Acts 13:10, full of all deceit and **f**

frus'trate to cause to have no effect.
Ezra 4:5, against them to **f** their counsel
Job 5:12, He **f-s** the plotting of the shrewd
Prov. 15:22, without consultation, plans are **f-d**
Is. 14:27, who can **f** it

fu'gi·tive fleeing or having fled.
Judg. 12:4, You are **f-s** of Ephraim
Is. 15:5, His **f-s** are as far as Zoar
Is. 52:12, Nor will you go as **f-s**

fu'ry intense, disordered, and often destructive rage.
Gen. 27:44, until your brother's **f** subsides
Ps. 2:5, terrify them in His **f**
Ezek. 19:12, it was plucked up in **f**

fur'rows narrow grooves made in the ground by a plow.
Job 31:38, its **f** weep together
Ps. 65:10, Thou dost water its **f**
Ps. 129:3, They lengthened their **f**

fu'tile serving no useful purpose.
1 Sam. 12:21, **f** things . . . because they are **f**
Rom. 1:21, **f** in their speculations

G

Ga'bri·el The name of a supernatural messenger seen by Daniel in his vision (Dan. 8:16; 9:21; Luke 1:19, 26).

Gad A son of Jacob and his descendants, the tribe of Gad (Gen. 30:10, 11; 35:26; 46:16).

Ga·lat'ia It signifies the kingdom of Galatia in the northern part of the inner plateau of Asia Minor (1 Cor. 16:1; Gal. 1:2).

Gal'i'lee The geographical area in Palestine bounded on the north by the

Litani (Leontes) River, the west by the Mediterranean Sea to Mt. Carmel, the south by the northern edge of the plain of Esdraelon, and on the east by the Jordan valley and the Sea of Galilee (2 Kin. 15:29; 1 Chr. 6:76).

gall something bitter or distasteful.
Ps. 69:21, They also gave me **g** for my food
Matt. 27:34, wine . . . mingled with **g**
Acts 8:23, you are in the **g** of bitterness

Ga•ma'li•el 1. A chief of the tribe of Manasseh who was chosen to aid in the wilderness census (Num. 1:10; 2:20; 7:54, 59). 2. Also a famous Jewish sage mentioned twice in the Acts (Acts 5:34; 22:3).

gan'grene death or decay of tissue in a part of the body.
2 Tim. 2:17, will spread like **g**

gar'ner a grain bin or barn.
Ps. 144:13, *Let* our **g-s** be full

gar'ri•son a military post.
1 Sam. 10:5, where the Philistine **g** is
1 Sam. 14:12, men of the **g** hailed Jonathan
1 Chr. 18:13, Then he put **g-s** in Edom

Ga'za The town was an important Philistine city. It was of great importance to the caravans. It was vital in any military campaign to hold this city as a rest area to or from the desert (Josh. 15:47; Judg. 1:18).

Ge'ba A city of Benjamin. Saul and Jonathan encamped there when the Philistines were at Michmash (Josh. 21:17; 1 Sam. 13:16; 1 Chr. 8:6).

Ge•ha'zi The young servant of the prophet Elisha (2 King. 4:8-37).

gen'e•al'o•gy an account of the descent of a person or family.
1 Chr. 4:33, they have their **g**
Neh. 7:5, the book of the **g**
Heb. 7:3, Without father, without mother, without **g**

Gen'tile a person of a non-Jewish nation or of non-Jewish faith.
Matt. 6:7, as the **G-s** do
Acts 14:2, stirred the minds of the **G-s**

Ger'a A favorite personal name among the people of the tribe of Benjamin from patriarchal times (Gen. 46:21; Judg. 3:15; 2 Sam. 16:5).

Ger'ar A town and district south of Gaza and southwest of the southern border of Canaan near the Mediterranean Sea (Gen. 10:19; 20:1; 26:1, 6, 17, 20, 26; 2 Chr. 14:13, 14).

Ger'shom Moses' oldest son (Ex. 2:22; 18:3).

Ger'shon The oldest son of Levi (Gen. 46:11; Ex. 6:16; Num. 3:17).

Gesh'ur A country east of Jordan (2 Sam. 13:38; 14:23; 1 Chr. 3:2).

Gesh'u•rites A people near Sinai, whose land was not taken originally by the Israelite forces at the time of the conquest (Deut. 3:14; Josh. 13:2; 1 Sam. 27:8).

Geth•sem'a•ne A "plot of ground" which was east of Jerusalem across the Kidron Valley on the Mount of Olives (Matt. 26:36; Mark 14:32).

Ge'zer A major city of the northern Shephelah (Josh. 10:33; Judg. 1:29; 1 Chr. 20:4).

Gib'e•on The chief city of the Hivites who tricked Israel into an alliance to avoid being massacred (Josh. 11:19; 1 Kin. 3:4; 1 Chr. 14:16).

Gib'e•on•ites The inhabitants of the city of Gibeon (2 Sam. 21:1-9).

Gid'e•on The son of Joash, the Abiezrite, a judge of Israel who with 300 men routed the Midianites (Judg. chaps. 6-8).

Gid'e•o'ni The father of Abidan, the leader of the tribe of Benjamin in the wilderness wanderings (Num. 1:11; 2:22).

Gi'hon The more important of the two springs that supplied water to Jerusalem in Old Testament times (2 Chr. 32:30; 33:14).

Gil•bo'a, Mount A mountain or range of mountains, about eight miles long and from three to five miles wide, lying to the east of the Plain of Esdraelon, on the border between Samaria and Galilee (1 Sam. 31:1, 8; 2 Sam. 1:21).

Gil'e•ad A mountainous region east of Jordan (Gen. 37:25; Num. 32:1).

Gil'gal The name of several towns of uncertain location. The most important was Joshua's encampment near Jordan which later became a religious center (Josh. 4:19, 20; 5:2-9).

glean to collect the remaining grain from a field.
Lev. 19:10, Nor shall you **g** your vineyard

Ruth 2:8, Do not go to **g** in another field
Ruth 2:15, When she rose to **g**

glo′ri•fy to bestow honor, praise, or admiration.
Ps. 86:12, will **g** Thy name forever
Matt. 5:16, **g** your Father who is in heaven
John 12:28, Father **g** Thy name
John 16:14, He shall **g** Me
1 Cor. 6:20, **g** God in your body

glut′ton one who eats too much.
Deut. 21:20, he is a **g** and a drunkard
Prov. 23:21, the **g** will come to poverty

goad a sharp-pointed stick used in driving oxen.
Eccl. 12:11, words of wise men are like **g-s**
Acts 26:14, hard for you to kick against the **g-s**

god′li•ness devoted to God.
1 Tim. 2:2, in all **g** and dignity
1 Tim. 3:16, great is the mystery of **g**
1 Tim. 4:8, but **g** is profitable
2 Tim. 3:5, holding to a form of **g**
2 Pet. 1:7, **g**, brotherly kindness

Gog 1. A son of Joel, from the tribe of Reuben (1 Chr. 5:4). 2. The ruler of Magog, called the prince of Meshech and Tubal (Ezek. 38:2; 39:1-16).

Gol′go•tha The Aramaic name of the place near Jerusalem where Christ was crucified (Matt. 27:33; Mark 15:22; John 19:17).

Go•li′ath A Gittite warrior during the reign of Saul. David felled the giant with a stone shot from a sling, and he cut off the giant's head with Goliath's own sword (1 Sam. 17).

Go•mor′rah A city located in the Valley of Siddim, south of the Dead Sea (Gen. 10:19; 18:20; 19:24-28; Matt. 10:15).

gos′pel the teachings of Jesus and the apostles.
Matt. 4:23, the **g** of the kingdom
Mark 16:15, preach the **g** to all
Rom. 1:16. I am not ashamed of the **g**
Gal. 1:7, distort the **g** of Christ
Col. 1:23, from the hope of the **g**

gos′sip one who chatters idly or repeats rumors about others.
Rom. 1:29, *they are* **g-s**
2 Cor. 12:20, **g**, arrogance, disturbances

grace *unmerited favor coming from God.*
Ps. 45:2, **G** is poured upon Thy lips
Luke 2:40, the **g** of God was upon Him
Rom. 1:5, through whom we have received **g**
Rom. 16:20, The **g** of our Lord Jesus be with you
2 Cor. 12:9, My **g** is sufficient

grass′hop•per a plant-eating insect having the hind legs adapted for leaping and sometimes engaging in migratory flights in which whole regions may be stripped of vegetation.
Lev. 11:22, and the **g** in its kinds
Eccl. 12:5, the **g** drags himself along

Grasshopper

grat′i•tude the state of being grateful.
1 Tim. 4:4, is received with **g**

Greek a native of ancient or modern Greece.
Acts 16:1, his father was a **G**
Rom. 2:9, also of the **G**
1 Cor. 12:13, baptized . . . whether Jews or **G-s**
Gal. 3:28, There is neither Jew nor **G**

grieve afflict with deep sorrow.
Gen. 6:6, He was **g-d** in His heart
Is. 63:10, And **g-d** His Holy Spirit
Matt. 26:38, My soul is deeply **g-d**
Mark 3:5, **g-d** at their hardness of heart
Eph. 4:30, do not **g** the Holy Spirit of God

grope to feel or search about blindly or uncertainly.
Deut. 28:29, You shall **g** at noon
Job 12:25, They **g** in darkness
Is. 59:10, We **g** along the wall
Acts 17:27, perhaps they might **g** for Him

grudge to envy a person because of his possession or enjoyment.
Lev. 19:18, You shall not take vengeance, nor bear any **g**
Mark 6:19, a **g** against him

guar′an•tor a person who makes or gives a guaranty or guarantee.
Job 17:3, Who . . . will be my **g**

guard′i•an one who has the care of the person or property of another.
2 King. 10:5, **g-s** of *the children*
Is. 49:23, kings will be your **g-s**
Gal. 4:2, under **g-s** and managers
1 Pet. 2:25, Shepherd and **G** of your souls

guile deceitful; cunning.
John 1:47, in whom is no **g**
1 Pet. 2:1, all malice and all **g**

guilt the act or state of having done a wrong or committed an offense.
Num. 5:31, man shall be free from **g**
Deut. 25:2, stripes according to his **g**
Luke 23:22, found in Him no **g** *demanding* death
1 Cor. 11:27, **g-y** of the body and the blood
James 2:10, he has become **g-y** of all

Gu'ni 1. The second son of Naphtali and grandson of Jacob (Gen. 46:24). 2. A member of the tribe of Gad who settled in Gilead (1 Chr. 5:15, 16).

H

hab'i·ta'tion the act of inhabiting or dwelling.
Ps. 26:8, I love the **h** of Thy house
Ps. 71:3, Be Thou to me a rock of **h**
Ps. 132:13, He has desired it for His **h**
Is. 63:15, Thy holy and glorious **h**
Acts 17:26, the boundaries of their **h**

Ha'dad A son of Ishmael (Gen. 25: 15).

Had'ad·e'zer Son of Rehob and King of Zobah, in Syria (2 Sam. 8:3).

Ha'des the place of the dead (Matt. 11:23; 16:18; Luke 10:15; Acts 2:27; Rev. 1:18).

Ha'gar An Egyptian maid of Sarah (Gen. 16:1-3).

Hag'ga·i A prophet of the Lord to the Jews in 520 B. C. (Ezra 5:1-2; 6:14; Hag. 1:1).

Hag'gith One of David's wives, the mother of Adonijah (2 Sam. 3:4; 1 Kin. 1:5).

hal'le·lu'jah used chiefly as an exclamation in songs of praise or thanks.
Rev. 19:1, 3, 4, 6, saying **H**

hal'lowed made holy; regarded as holy; sacred.
Matt. 6:9; Luke 11:2, **H** be Thy name

Ham The youngest son of Noah (Gen. 5:32; 6:10; 9:24).

Ha'man The great enemy of the Jews in the days of Esther (Esth. 3:1; 7:10; 9:7-10).

Ha'math One of the most ancient surviving cities on this earth, located in upper Syria on the Orontes river (2 Sam. 8:9; 1 Kin. 8:65).

Ham'me·da'tha Father of Haman (Esth. 3:1).

Ha'mor Father of Shechem who criminally assaulted Dinah, a daughter of Jacob, as a result of which both father and son were killed in revenge by her brothers Simeon and Levi (Gen. 34:1-31).

hand'breadth any of various lengths from about 2½ to 4 inches based on the width of a hand.
Ex. 25:25, a rim of a **h**
1 Kin. 7:26; 2 Chr. 4:5, it was a **h** thick
Ps. 39:5, Thou has made my days *as* **h-s**
Ezek. 40:5, a cubit and a **h**

hand'maid a personal maid or female servant.
Ps. 86:16; 116:16, the son of Thy **h**

Han'nah One of the two wives of Elkanah. She became the mother of the prophet Samuel (1 Sam. ch. 1).

Ha'noch 1. A son of Midian, and a descendant of Abraham by Keturah (Gen. 25:4; 1 Chr. 1:33). 2. A son of Reuben and founder of a tribal family, Hanochites (Gen. 46:9; Ex. 6:14; Num. 26:5).

Ha'nun A king of the Ammonites, son and successor of David's friend Nahash (2 Sam. 10:1; 1 Chr. 19).

Ha'ran 1. A son of Terah, and brother of Abraham (Gen. 11:28). 2. A Gershonite Levite, son of Shimei (1 Chr. 23:9).

ha·rass' to worry or annoy with repeated attacks.
Deut. 2:9, Do not **h** Moab

Ha'rim 1. A priest assigned to the third course in David's time (1 Chr. 24: 8). 2. Founder of a nonpriestly family, members of which returned from Babylon with Zerubbabel (Ezra 2:32).

har'lot a woman of loose morals.
Josh. 6:17, Rahab the **h**
Prov. 7:10, Dressed as a **h**
Is. 23:17, her **h's** wages
Matt. 21:31, **h-s** will get into the kingdom
Luke 15:30, devoured your wealth with **h-s**

har'mo·ny agreement, as in opinions, manners, or interests; accord; tranquility.
2 Cor. 6:15, what **h** has Christ with

harp a musical instrument having many strings of graded length stretched across an open triangular frame with a

curving top and played by plucking with the fingers.
1 Sam. 16:23, David would take the **h** and play it with his hand

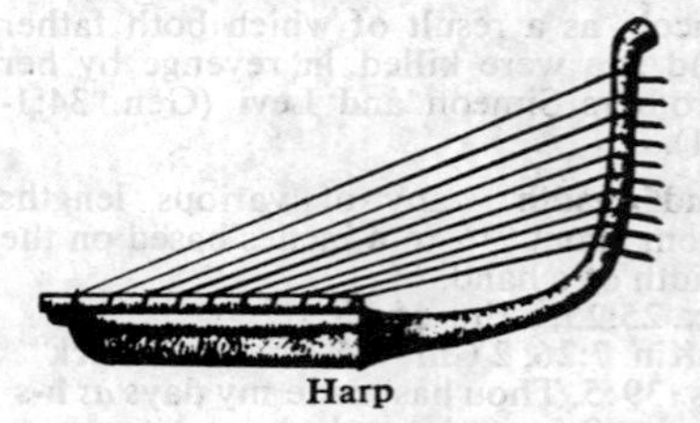
Harp

har'row a farming set with disks or teeth used to break up the soil.
Job 39:10, will he **h** the valleys

har'ry to worry; to torment.
Job 18:11, terrors . . . **h** him at every step

Ha'shum Founder of a family, members of which returned from Babylon with Zerubbabel (Ezra 2:19; 10:33; Neh. 7:22; 8:4).

hate to dislike intensely; to detest.
Ps. 81:15, Those who **h** the Lord
Ps. 97:10, **H** evil, you love the Lord
Eccl. 3:8, A time to love, and a time to **h**
Luke 6:27, do good to those who **h** you
John 15:23, He who **h-s** Me **h-s** My Father

haugh'ty proud and scornful; arrogant.
2 Sam. 22:28, Thine eyes are on the **h**
Ps. 131:1, or my eyes **h**
Prov. 16:18, **h** spirit before stumbling
Zeph. 3:11, never again be **h**
Rom. 12:16, do not be **h** in mind

haunt a place visited again and again.
Is. 34:13, also be a **h** of jackals

ha'ven a harbor; a port; a place of shelter or refuge.
Gen. 49:13, a **h** for ships
Ps. 107:30, to their desired **h**

Hav'i·lah A land encompassed by the river Pishon which flowed from a source in the Garden of Eden (Gen. 2:11, 12).

Haz'a·el A high official of Ben-hadad, King of Syria (1 Kin. 19:15; 2 Kin. 8:7-15).

Ha·ze'roth An encamping ground of the Israelites in the wilderness between Kibroth-hattaavah and Paran (Num. 11:35; 12:16; Deut. 1:1).

He'brew 1. According to Biblical history, the Hebrews were men from the other side of the Euphrates (Gen. 12:5 with 14:13). 2. The language spoken by the Hebrews (John 5:2; Acts21:40).

He'bron 1. One of the oldest cities of the world, and one which has had several names at different times. It is located 19 miles southwest of Jerusalem on the main road to Beersheba (Josh. 10:36; 15:54). 2. A Levite, son of Kohath, and founder of a tribal family (Ex. 6:18; 1 Chr. 6:2).

heir a person who inherits or is entitled to inherit property.
Gen. 15:3, one born in my house is my **h**
Jer. 49:1, has he no **h-s**
Rom. 8:17, **h-s** also, **h-s** of God
Gal. 4:7, an **h** through God
James 2:5, **h-s** of the kingdom

He'lez 1. David's captain for the 7th month and also a mighty man of David (1 Chr. 27:10; 2 Sam. 23:26). 2. A man of Judah, descended from Hezron (1 Chr. 2:39).

Hell The real existence of Hell is irrefutably taught in Scripture as both a place of the wicked dead and a condition of retribution for unredeemed man (Matt. 18:9; Mark 9:43; 2 Pet. 2:4).

He'lon Father of Eliab, leader of Zebulun (Num. 1:9; 2:7; 7:24; 10:16).

hem the edge, border, or margin of a garment.
Ex. 28:33, you shall make on its **h**
Ex. 28:34, on the **h** of the robe

He'man 1. A man from the tribe of Judah whose reputation for wisdom was high in Solomon's reign (1 Kin. 4:31; 1 Chr. 2:6). 2. A singer in David's reign, a son of Joel, a grandson of the prophet Samuel (1 Chr. 6:33; 15:17).

hem'or·rhage any discharge of blood from the blood vessels; usually caused by injury.
Matt. 9:20, a woman . . . suffering from a **h**
Mark 5:25; Luke 8:43, had a **h** for twelve years

her'i·tage something that is passed on from one's ancestors; inheritance; birthright.
Job 20:29, **h** decreed to him by God
Ps. 16:6, my **h** is beautiful
Ps. 135:12, He gave their land as a **h**
Ps. 136:22, a **h** to Israel
Is. 49:8, inherit the desolate **h-s**

Her'mon The mountain that marks the southern terminus of the Anti-Lebanon range (Deut. 3:8, 9; 1 Chr. 5:23; Ps. 89:12).

Her'od The name of several rulers over Palestine and the adjacent regions or portions of them (Matt. 2:1; 14:1; Acts 12:1).

Hesh'bon The city of Sihon, the Amorite king, but apparently taken originally from the Moabites (Num. 21:25-30, 34).

Heth The great-grandson of Noah through Ham and Canaan (Gen. 10:15; 1 Chr. 1:13).

Hez'e•ki'ah King of Judah for 29 years. His story is told in 2 Kin. 18-20; 2 Chr. 29-32; Is. 36-39.

Hez'ron 1. A grandson of Judah (Gen. 46:12). 2. A son of Reuben (Gen. 46:9).

hin'der to keep back or behind; to hamper or restrain.
Matt. 19:14, do not **h** them from coming to Me
Mark 9:39, But Jesus said, Do not **h** him
Luke 18:16, stop **h-ing** them
Gal. 5:7, who **h-ed** you from obeying
1 Pet. 3:7, your prayers may not be **h-ed**

hin'drance a person or thing that prevents or stands in the way of forward progress.
1 Cor. 9:12, cause no **h** to the gospel

Hin'nom (Valley of) A valley at Jerusalem, near the Gate of Potsherds (Jer. 7:31-34).

Hi'ram King of Tyre in the reigns of David and of Solomon, with both of whom he was on friendly terms (2 Sam. 5:11; 1 Kin. 5:1; 9:10-13).

Hit'tites 1. The native non-Indo-European people who lived in central Anatolia (2 King. 7:6). 2. The Nesians who lived around the capital of Hattushash (Gen. 15:20; Ex. 3:8; Deut. 7:1; Josh. 3:10).

Hi'vites One of the races of Canaan before the conquest of the country by the Hebrews (Gen. 10:17; Ex. 3:17; Josh. 9:1).

hoard to lay up; to store away.
Amos 3:10, **h** up violence and devastation

ho'li•ness the quality or state of being saintly, godly, or pious.
Ps. 93:5, **H** befits Thy house
Is. 35:8, be called the highway of **h**
2 Cor. 7:1, perfecting **h** in the fear of God
1 Thess. 3:13, hearts unblameable in **h**
Heb. 12:10, we may share His **h**

Ho'ly Spir'it the active presence of God in human life making the third person of the Trinity.
Matt. 3:11, baptize you with the **H**
Luke 12:12, **H** will teach you
John 20:22, Receive the **H**
Eph. 4:30, do not grieve the **H** of God
1 Thess. 4:8, God who gives His **H** to you

home'stead an ancestral home; a house and adjoining land which is occupied by a family.
Luke 11:21, guards his own **h**

hope the desire for something that a person believes can be obtained or expects.
Job 13:15, I will **h** in Him
Rom. 4:18, **h** against **h** he believed
1 Cor. 13:7, **h-s** all things
1 Cor. 13:13, now abide faith, **h,** love
Titus 3:7, *the* **h** of eternal life

Hoph'ni A son of Eli (1 Sam. 2:22–4:22).

Hor 1. A mountain on the border of the Edomite country, where Aaron died and was buried (Num. 20:22-29). 2. A mountain on the north boundary of Palestine, between the Mediterranean Sea and the entrance of Hamath (Num. 34:7, 8).

Ho'reb The mount of God in the peninsula of Sinai where the law was given to Israel (Ex. 3:1; Deut. 1:2).

Hor'mah The town Zephath called Hormah after its destruction (Num. 14:45; Deut. 1:44).

Ho'sah 1. A gatekeeper in the time of David (1 Chr. 16:38; 26:10). 2. A village on the frontier of Asher (Josh. 19:29).

hu•mil'i•ate to lower the pride or self-respect of; to humble.
2 Cor. 12:21, my God may **h** me before you

hu•mil'i•ty freedom from pride; meekness.
Prov. 15:33, before honor *comes* **h**
Prov. 22:4, The reward of **h**
Phil. 2:3, with **h** of mind
Col. 3:12, put on a heart of . . . **h**
1 Pet. 5:5, clothe yourselves with **h**

Hu'shai One of David's two leading counselors (2 Sam. 15:32-37; 17:5-16).

Hu′shath·ite An inhabitant of Hushan (2 Sam. 21:18; 23:27).

hy·poc′ri·sy the act or practice of pretending to be what one is not, or to feel what one does not feel.
Matt. 23:28, you are full of **h**
Rom. 12:9, Let love be without **h**
1 Tim. 4:2, by means of the **h** of liars
James 3:17, wisdom from above . . . without **h**

hyp′o·crite a person who pretends to be something other than he is or better than he really is.
Matt. 6:2, as the **h-s** do
Matt. 6:5, you are not to be as the **h-s**
Matt. 7:5, You **h**, first take the log
Matt. 22:18, Why are you testing Me, you **h-s**
Luke 12:56, You **h-s**! You know how to analyze

I

I·co′ni·um A city of Asia Minor. Paul and Barnabus visited it on the first missionary journey both going and returning (Acts 13:51; 2 Tim. 3:11).

i·dol′ an image of a god made or used as an object of worship.
Ex. 20:4, make for yourself an **i**
Lev. 19:4, Do not turn to **i-s**
Acts 15:20, abstain from . . . **i-s**
1 John 5:21, guard yourselves from **i-s**

Idol

Ik′kesh Father of David's commander and mighty man Ira (2 Sam. 23:26; 1 Chr. 11:28; 27:9).

il·le·git′i·mate born of a father and mother who are not married.
Deut. 23:2, No one of **i** birth
Heb. 12:8, you are **i** children

il·lu′mine to light up; to make light; to supply with light.
Ps. 18:28, God **i-s** my darkness

Im′mer A descendant of Aaron (Ezra 10:20; Neh. 3:29).

im·mo·ral′i·ty the condition of being wicked, lewd; wickedness.
Matt. 19:9, except for **i**
1 Cor. 6:18, Flee **i**
1 Thess. 4:3, abstain from sexual **i**
Rev. 2:20, they commit *acts of* **i**
Rev. 17:2, the wine of her **i**

im·mor·tal′i·ty endless life; eternal existence.
1 Cor. 15:53, mortal . . . put on **i**
1 Tim. 6:16, who alone possesses **i**
2 Tim. 1:10, brought life and **i**

im·pel′ to drive or urge on; to force.
Mark 1:12, the Spirit **i-ed** Him

im·per′ish·a·ble undying; indestructible ble.
1 Cor. 9:25, perishable wreath, but we an **i**
1 Cor. 15:52, the dead will be raised **i**
1 Pet. 1:4, an inheritance *which is* **i**

im·pet′u·ous impulsive; violent and hasty in action.
Hab. 1:6, Chaldeans, That fierce and **i** people

im′pro·vise to make, invent, arrange offhand without previous preparation.
Amos 6:5, Who **i** to the sound of the harp

in·cite′ to urge or stir to action.
Luke 23:14, one who **i-s** the people

in·de·struc′ti·ble strong and lasting; not able to be destroyed.
Heb. 7:16, power of an **i** life

in·fir′mi·ties weaknesses; frailties, state of being infirm, insecure.
Matt. 8:17, Himself took our **i**

in·iq′ui·ty great injustice; wickedness.
Deut. 5:9, visiting the **i** of the fathers
Ps. 25:11, Pardon my **i**, for it is great
Ps. 51:9, blot out all my **i-es**
Is. 53:5, He was crushed for our **i-es**
James 3:6, tongue is . . . world of **i**

in·junc′tion an order not to do something; a command.
Dan. 6:7, king should . . . enforce an **i**
Dan. 6:8, O king, establish the **i**

in·sig·nif′i·cant not important; not meaningful.
2 Sam. 7:19, **i** in Thine eyes
Job 8:7, your beginning was **i**
Job 40:4, Behold, I am **i**
Acts 21:39, citizen of no **i** city

in'so·lence contemptuous or insulting behavior.
1 Sam. 17:28, I know your **i**

in·teg'ri·ty moral soundness; honesty; purity.
Gen. 20:5, In the **i** of my heart
Ps. 15:2, He who walks with **i**
Ps. 26:1, have walked in my **i**
Prov. 10:9, who walks in **i** walks securely
Prov. 20:7, righteous man who walks in his **i**

in·ter·cede' to beg or plead in behalf of another; to act as a go-between.
1 Sam. 2:25, who can **i** for him
Is. 53:12, **i-d** for the transgressors
Rom. 8:26, the Spirit Himself **i-s** for us

in·ter·ces'sion prayer, petition or entreaty in favor of another.
Heb. 7:25, He always lives to make **i** for them

in·val'i·date to weaken or destroy the effect or value of; to nullify.
Matt. 15:6, you **i-d** the word of God
Mark 7:13, *thus* **i-ing** the word of God

I'ra 1. Priest or chief minister to David (2 Sam. 20:26). 2. One of David's mighty men, son of Ikkesh (2 Sam. 23:26; 1 Chr. 11:28).

ir·rev'er·ence a lack of respect or honor.
2 Sam. 6:7, struck him down . . . for his **i**

I'saac The son of Abraham and Sarah (Gen. 21:3-5).

I·sa'iah A prophet of Judah. The son of Amoz (Is. 1:1; 7:3; 20:1, 2).

Is·car'i·ot A designation of Judas the traitor (Matt. 10:4; Luke 6:16); it was used to distinguish him from the other apostle called Judas (Acts 1:13, 16).

Ish'-bo'sheth One of Saul's younger sons (2 Sam. 2:8-10).

Ish'ma·el 1. The son of Abraham by Hagar the Egyptian maid (Gen. 16:3-16). 2. A son of Nethaniah, who belonged to the royal seed of Judah (2 Kin. 25:25; Jer. 40:7).

Is'ra·el 1. The whole body of the descendants of Jacob at any one time (Gen. 32:32; 36:31). 2. The tribes that acted independently of Judah (Israel is frequently used to denote the 10 tribes) (2 Sam. 2:10; 5:1-5).

Is'sa·char 1. The 9th son of Jacob and the 5th by Leah (Gen. 30:17, 18; 35:23). 2. A Levite, appointed gatekeeper in David's reign (1 Chr. 26:15).

Ith'a·mar The youngest son of Aaron (Ex. 6:23; 1 Chr. 6:3; 24:1).

It'ta·i 1. A son of Ribai. He was one of David's mighty men (2 Sam. 23:29). 2. The commander of 600 men, who followed David from the Philistine city of Gath (2 Sam. 15:18-22).

Iz'har A Levite, son of Kohath, and founder of a tribal family (Ex. 6:18; Num. 3:19; 1 Chr. 6:18; 23:12).

J

Ja'besh Father of King Shallum (2 Kin. 15:10-14).

Ja'besh-gil'e·ad A town of Gilead 20 miles south of the Sea of Galilee (1 Sam. 31:11-13; 1 Chr. 10:11, 12).

Ja'bin 1. A Canaanite, King of Hazor (Josh. 11:1). 2. Another King of Canaan who reigned at Hazor (Judg. 4:2).

Ja'chin 1. A son of Simeon, and founder of a tribal family, the Jachinites (Gen. 46:10; Ex. 6:15). 2. A descendant of Aaron (1 Chr. 24:6-17).

jack'al a doglike wild animal that feeds on dead flesh and small animals.
Job 30:29, a brother to **j-s**
Jer. 9:11, Jerusalem . . . haunt of **j-s**

Ja'cob 1. A son of Isaac and Rebekah, a twin with Esau (Gen. 25:21-26). 2. The father of Joseph, the husband of Mary (Matt. 1:15).

Ja'el The wife of Heber the Kenite (Judg. 4:17, 18).

Ja'haz A place in the tableland of Moab where Sihon, king of the Amorites, was defeated by the Israelites (Num. 21:23; Deut. 2:32; Judg. 11:20).

James 1. Brother of the apostle John, one of the earliest disciples (Matt. 17:1; Mark 3:17). 2. One of the apostles (Matt. 10:3; Luke 6:15). 3. The Lord's brother (Matt. 13:55; Mark 6:3). 4. The father of the apostle Judas (Luke 6:16; Acts 1:13).

Ja'min 1. A son of Simeon and founder of a tribal family, the Jaminites (Gen. 46:10; Ex. 6:15). 2. A man of Judah, a son of Ram, family of Jerahmeel (1 Chr. 2:27).

Ja'pheth A son of Noah (Gen. 6:10; 10:1, 2).

Ja·phi'a 1. A king of Lachish, defeated, captured, and executed by Joshua

(Josh. 10:3-27). 2. A son of David, born at Jerusalem (2 Sam. 5:13-15).

Ja'red Son of Mahalalel and father of Enoch (Gen. 5:16; 1 Chr. 1:2; Luke 3: 37).

Jar'muth 1. A town in the lowland, whose king was defeated, captured, and slain by Joshua (Josh. 10:3-27). 2. A town of Issachar, assigned to the Gershonite Levites (Josh. 21:28, 29).

Ja'son A Christian, a kinsman of Paul (Acts 17:5-9; Rom. 16:21).

Ja'van A region settled by descendants of Japheth (Ezek. 27:13-19).

jav'e•lin a light spear.
Josh. 8:18, Stretch out the **j**
Job 41:29, at the rattling of the **j**

Ja'zer A city east of Jordan in Gilead (2 Sam. 24:5; 1 Chr. 26:31).

Je'bus The city later known as Jerusalem (Judg. 19:10; 1 Chr. 11:4, 5).

Jeb'u•site The name of a tribe of Canaan before the conquest of the country by the Hebrews (Gen. 10:16; Ex. 3: 8).

Jec'o•ni'ah A son of Jehoiakin, and king of Judah (1 Chr. 3:16; Jer. 24:1).

Je•du'thun 1. A Levite, one of the three chief singers in the time of David (1 Chr. 16:41; Neh. 11:17). 2. Father of Obed-edom (1 Chr. 16:38).

Je•hoi'a•kim A son of King Josiah by his wife Zebidah (2 Kin. 23:34-36).

Je•ho'ram 1. Son of Ahab and king of Israel (2 Kin. 3:1). 2. Son of Jehoshaphat and king of Judah (2 Kin. 8:16).

jeop'ar•dize to expose to the danger of death, loss, or injury.
Ruth 4:6, **j** my own inheritance

Je•phun'neh Father of Caleb, the representative spy from the tribe of Judah (Num. 13:6).

Jer'e•mi'ah One of the greatest Hebrew prophets (Jer. 1:6-10; 38:1-6).

Jer'i•cho An important city situated in the Valley of the Jordan (Josh. 2:1; 2 Sam. 10:5).

Jer'o•bo'am 1. An Ephraimite who founded the kingdom of the ten tribes (1 Kin. 11:26-35). 2. The son of Joash, king of Israel, and his successor on the *throne of the ten tribes* (2 Kin. 14:23-28).

Je•ru'sa•lem The royal city, the capital of the only kingdom God has (thus far) established among men (1 Kin. 14: 21; Ps. 68:29; 147:2).

Je•shi'mon 1. A wilderness at the northeast end of the Dead Sea (1 Sam. 23:19, 24). 2. A wilderness to the north of the hill Hachilah and to Maon (1 Sam. 23:19; 26:1).

Jes'se He was father of 8 sons, the youngest of whom was David (1 Sam. 17:12; 1 Chr. 2:13-15).

Jes'us Christ Our Lord was named Jesus in accordance with the directions of the angel to Joseph and Mary (Matt. 1:21; Luke 1:31).

Jeth'ro A priest of Midian and Moses' father-in-law (Ex. 3:1; 4:18; 18: 1, 2, 5).

Jew One belonging to the tribe or to the kingdom of Judah (2 Kin. 25:25; Esth. 2:5; 3:4; Jer. 34:9; Zech. 8:23).

Jez'e•bel Daughter of Ethbaal, king of the Sidonians, and queen of Ahab, king of Israel (1 Kin. 16:31; 21:7).

Jez're•el A fortified town in the territory of Issachar (Josh. 19:17-18).

Jez're•el•ite A person from Jezreel (1 Kin. 21:1, 4; 2 Kin. 9:21).

Jo'ab 1. Son of Seraiah and descendant of Kenaz (1 Chr. 4:13-14). 2. A son of Zeruiah (David's half-sister) (2 Sam. 17:25; 1 Chr. 2:16).

Job The main character of the canonical book which bears his name (Job 1:1-5). The uniqueness of the Book of Job derives from the depth and thoroughness with which it deals with subjects of human suffering and theodicy (Job chapters 1-42).

John (the apostle)...A son of Zebedee, and brother of James (Matt. 4:21; Acts 12:1, 2

John (son of Zechariah) (John the Baptist) The immediate forerunner of Jesus, whose way he was sent to prepare (Luke 1:5-17).

John Mark. Mark the Evangelist (Mark, however, was only the surname) (Acts 12:12, 25).

Joi'a•da 1. A son of Paseah, who helped to repair the Old Gate of Jerusalem (Neh. 3:6). 2. A high priest, great-grandson of Jeshua (Neh. 12:10).

Jok'tan A person or rather tribe descended from Shem through Eber and from which 13 tribes of Arabia sprang (Gen. 10:25-32; 1 Chr. 1:19-23).

Jon'a•dab 1. Son of David's brother Shimeah (2 Sam. 13:3). 2. A son of Rechab, the Kenite (Jer. 35:6-10).

Jo'nah A prophet of Israel, a son of Amittai and a citizen of Gath-hepher in Galilee (2 Kin. 14:25; Jon. 1:1).

Jop'pa An ancient walled town assigned to Dan (Josh. 19:40-46; 2 Chr. 2:16).

Jor'dan The most important river in Palestine (Gen. 13:8-11; 32:10).

Jo'seph (son of Jacob) The 11th of Jacob's 12 sons, and the elder son of Rachel (Gen. 30:22-24).

Jo'seph (husband of Mary) A descendant of David (Luke 2:4-5, 16); he was a carpenter (Matt. 13:55); and was assisted in his work by the young man Jesus (Mark 6:3).

Jo•si'ah 1. Son and successor of Amon as king of Judah (2 Chr. 34:1-7). 2. A son of Zephaniah (Zech. 6:10).

Joz'a•dak Father of Jeshua, the high priest (Ezra 3:2, 8).

Ju'das Is•car'i•ot Son of Simon Iscariot, and the disciple who betrayed his divine Lord (John 6:71; 12:4).

Ju•de'a A geographical term first introduced in the Bible to designate a province of the Persian Empire (Matt. 2:1, 5, 22; 3:1; Mark 1:5).

judg'ment the power of deciding wisely
Ps. 19:9, **j-s** of the Lord are true
John 5:30, judge; and My **j** is just
2 Pet. 3:7, kept for the day of **j**
1 John 4:17, confidence in the day of **j**
Rev. 18:20, God has pronounced **j** for you

jus'tice just or righteous action, management, or treatment.
Job 8:3, Does God pervert **j**
Ps. 89:14, Righteousness and **j** are the
Prov. 28:5, Evil men do not understand **j**
Amos. 5:24, let **j** roll down like waters
Mic. 6:8, to do **j**, to love kindness

jus'ti•fy to prove or show to be just, right, or reasonable.
Gen. 44:16, how can we **j** ourselves
Ps. 51:4, Thou art **j-ed**
Luke 10:29, wishing to **j** himself
Rom. 8:33, God is the one who **j-es**

K

Ka'desh A fountain, city or town, and wilderness on the south frontier of Judah and of Palestine (Num. 20:16; Josh. 15:3; Ps. 29:8).

Kad'mi•el A Levite, head of a tribal house, who returned from Babylon with Zerubbabel (Ezra 2:40; Neh. 7:43; 12:8).

Ka•re'ah Father of the captains Johanan and Jonathan (2 Kin. 25:23; Jer. 40:8).

Ke'dar A tribe descended from Ishmael (Gen. 25:13; Is. 42:11; Ezek. 27:21).

Ke•i'lah 1. A town in the lowland of Judah (Josh. 15:44). 2. The father of Keilah the Germite is listed among the descendants of Caleb (1 Chr. 4:19).

Ke'nite A tribe of which a branch dwelt in Canaan or vicinity in the time of Abraham (Gen. 15:19; Num. 24:20-22).

Kib'roth-hat•ta'a•vah A place in the Sinaitic peninsula, between Mt. Sinai and Hazeroth, where the Israelites were buried who were slain by a plague for lusting after the fleshpots of Egypt (Num. 11:34; Deut. 9:22).

Kid'ron A valley that separates Jerusalem from the Mount of Olives and had to be crossed by those going from the city to Bethany or Jericho (2 Sam. 15:23; John 18:1).

king'dom a realm or region in which something is dominant.
Ps. 22:28, For the **k** is the LORD's
Ps. 145:13, Thy **k** is an everlasting **k**
Matt. 6:10, Thy **k** come. Thy will be done
Matt. 26:29, in My Father's **k**
2 Tim. 4:18, bring me safely to His heavenly **k**

Kir'iath-ar'ba An old name for the city of Hebron (Gen. 23:2; Josh. 14:15; Judg. 1:10).

Kir'iath-je'a•rim A town belonging to the hill country of the tribe of Judah (Josh. 15:60; Judg. 18:12).

Kish 1. A Benjaminite, son of Jeiel (1 Chr. 8:30). 2. A Benjaminite, father of King Saul and son of Abiel (1 Sam. 9:1, 2).

Ki'shon The most important river of Palestine next to the Jordan (Judg. 5:19-21; Ps. 83:9).

knowl'edge the fact of knowing something with familiarity gained through experience or association.
Gen. 2:9, tree of the **k** of good and evil
Prov. 10:14, Wise men store up **k**

1 Cor. 15:34, some have no **k** of God
Eph. 3:19, love of Christ which surpasses **k**
2 Pet. 3:18, grow in the grace and **k** of our Lord

Ko'hath A son of Levi and founder of the great Kohathite family (Gen. 46:11; Ex. 6:16, 18).

L

La'a·dah A man of Judah, family of Shelah. He was the father of the inhabitants of Mareshan (1 Chr. 4:21).

La'ban 1. Son of Bethuel and grandson of Nahor, Abraham's brother (Gen. 24:29). 2. An unidentified place in the Sinaitic Peninsula (Deut. 1:1).

La'chish A fortified city in the lowland of Judah (Josh. 15:39; 2 Chr. 11:9).

lair the bed of a wild beast.
Job 38:40, lie in wait in *their* **l**

la·ment' to express or feel sorrow for or about; to mourn greatly.
Luke 8:52, weeping and **l-ing** for her
Luke 23:27, women . . . mourning and **l-ing**
Rev. 18:9, kings . . . will weep and **l**

lamp'stand the lampstand in the Tabernacle consisted of a base and a shaft with six branches, beaten out of solid gold, and it supported seven lamps. Pure olive oil was used in the lamps, and the light burned from evening to morning.
Ex. 25:31, make a **l** of pure gold.
Rev. 2:5, will remove your **l** out of its place

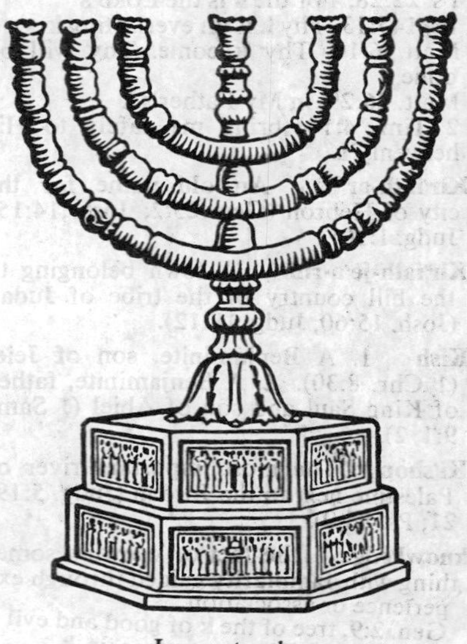
Lampstand

lap'is la'zu·li a semiprecious stone of a deep blue color.
Ezek. 28:13, The **l,** the turquoise

lat'tice a structure of thin strips of wood or metal crossed to form a network, usually on doors or windows.
Judg. 5:28, she looked . . . through the **l**
2 Kin. 1:2, Ahaziah fell through the **l**
Song 2:9, He is peering through the **l**
Is. 60:8, like the doves to their **l-s**

Le'ah The elder daughter of Laban. She was less attractive than her younger sister Rachel (Gen. 29:16, 17).

leav'en a substance that makes dough or batter rise and become light while being cooked.
Matt. 13:33, kingdom of heaven is like **l**
Matt. 16:6, beware of the **l** of the Pharisees
Luke 13:21, It is like **l**
1 Cor. 5:6, a little **l l-s** the whole lump
1 Cor. 5:7, Clean out the old **l**

Leb'a·non A snowclad mountain range extending in a northeasterly direction for 100 miles along the Syrian coast, from Tyre to Arvad, and the country which bears its name (2 Kin. 19:23; Is. 60:13; Hos. 14:5, 6, 7).

lep'er a person who has the disease of leprosy which causes sores and loss of hair.
2 Chr. 26:21, King Uzziah was a **l**
Matt. 8:2, a **l** came to Him
Matt. 10:8, cleanse *the* **l-s**
Matt. 11:5, *the* **l-s** are cleansed
Mark 14:3, the home of Simon the **l**

Le'vi Third son of Jacob and Leah (Gen. 29:34; 46:11; Ex. 6:16).

Le'vites The descendants of Levi, the son of Jacob (Gen. 29:30-34; Num. 3:6); the men of the tribe of Levi were charged with the care of the tabernacle (Num. 1:50-53; 2 Sam. 15:24; 1 Chr. 6:48).

lev'y a collection, as of taxes, by legal authority.
Num. 31:28, **l** a tax for the Lord
1 Kin. 5:13, King Solomon **l-ied** forced *laborers*
2 Chr. 24:6, the **l** *fixed* by Moses

li·ba'tion the pouring out of a liquid,

as wine, in honor of a god; the liquid poured out.
Gen. 35:14, poured out a **l**

Lib'nah 1. An encampment of the Israelites in the wilderness (Num. 33: 20). 2. A city in the lowland between Makkedah and Lachish (Josh. 10:29; 2 Kin. 23:31).

Lib'ni 1. Son of Gershon, and grandson of Levi (Ex. 6:17; Num. 3:18). 2. A Levite, family of Merari, house of Mahli (1 Chr. 6:29).

loathe to dislike greatly; to detest.
Ps. 95:10, I **l-d** *that* generation
Amos 6:8, I **l** the arrogance

loath'some causing loathing; disgusting.
Gen. 46:34, every shepherd is *l* to the Egyptians
Job 6:7, are like **l** food to me

lo'custs These insects are often referred to, and under 9 different names: (1) *Arbeh,* generally and rightly translated "locust." The record of the 8th plague in Egypt gives a true account of a typical severe invasion of locusts; an east wind brought them from the other side of the isthmus of Suez, and a west wind hurled them back into the Red Sea, where they perished. They are placed among the clean creatures (Nah. 3:17).
(2) *Sal'am,* occurring once only, and translated "devastating locust." The word seems to have the same root as *sela,* which means rock; hence we may think of certain species of grasshoppers, which delight in basking on sun-exposed rocks, and translate the word "rock locust" (Lev. 11:22).
(3) *Chargol,* in the vernacular, these are called katydids or long-horned grasshoppers (Num. 13:33).
(4) *Chagab,* generally used for and translated "grasshoppers," many of which are smaller than locusts (Is. 40:22).
(5) *Gazam,* translated in KJV "palmerworm," is interpreted either as the locust in its larval stage or as the larva of butterflies or moths. "Palmerworm" should not apply to locusts (Joel 2:25).
(6) *Yelek,* very difficult to interpret, the more so since there is no evidence that the different authors meant the same creature. It is translated "creeping locust." Etymologically, the word means a creature that licks up the grass. It is evidently intended to express some insect pest (Nah. 3:15).
(7) *Tzelatzal,* the word *tzelatzal* means a tinkling, musical instrument, and is hence applied to a creature able to produce musical sounds. Thus the author may have used it as the name of one of the crickets, the chirping notes of which are frequently loud enough to be heard at some distance, or for the well-known cicada, which is found in abundance all around the Mediterranean (Deut. 28:42).
(8) *Gob* appears several times, and is translated "locust"; it cannot be referred to any particular kind (Amos 7:1).
(9) *Chasil,* generally mentioned together with the locust, and therefore believed to signify the locust in its larval stage. But in some versions it is translated "caterpillar" (Is. 33:4).

Egyptian locust

loins the upper and lower abdominal regions and the region about the hips.
Ex. 12:11, *with* your **l** girded
2 Kin. 4:29, Gird up your **l**

loom a frame for weaving together threads or yarns into cloth.
Judg. 16:14, pulled out the pin of the **l**

Lot Son of Haran, Abraham's brother (Gen. 11:31; 12:5; 13:1).

Lo'tan A tribe of the Horites, dwelling in Mt. Seir (Gen. 36:20).

love (v.) to have or show warm affection for.
Lev. 19:18, you shall **l** your neighbor as yourself
Deut. 6:5, **l** the Lord your God with all
Prov. 17:17, A friend **l-s** at all times
Luke 6:27, **l** your enemies
John 3:16, God so **l-d** the world

love (n.) the feeling experienced when one is strongly attached or deeply devoted to another.
John 13:35, if you have **l** for one another
1 Cor. 13:1, If I . . . do not have **l**
Gal. 5:13, through **l** serve one another
1 Tim. 6:10, **l** of money is a root of . . . evil
2 Pet. 1:7, brotherly kindness . . . *Christian* **l**

loy'al·ty fidelity in thought and act, as to a friend, cause, ideal, or custom.
2 Sam. 16:17, your **l** to your friend
Prov. 20:6, a man proclaims his own **l**

lurk to stay in or about a place secretly.
Prov. 7:12, And **l-s** by every corner

lust a longing or intense desire.
Matt. 5:28, looks on a woman to **l** for her
Rom. 13:14, no provision . . . regard to *its* **l-s**
James 4:2, You **l** and do not have
1 John 2:16, **l** of the flesh . . . **l** of the eyes
Jude 16, following after their *own* **l-s**

Luz 1. A Canaanite town (Gen. 28:19; 35:6). 2. A town in the Hittite country (Judg. 1:22-26).

lyre a stringed musical instrument of the harp family.
Gen. 4:21, those who play the **l**
Ps. 57:8, Awake, harp and **l**
Is. 5:12, *accompanied* by **l**

M

Mac•e•do′ni•a The first European country which was visited by the apostles. Paul was there twice (Acts chapters 16 and 20).

Ma′chi A Gadite, the father of Geuel, whom Moses sent to spy out the land (Num. 13:15).

Ma′chir 1. The oldest son of Manasseh (Josh. 17:1) who even had children born to him during the lifetime of Joseph, his grandfather (Gen. 50:23). 2. A descendant of Machi, son of Ammiel. He took care of the lame son of Jonathan until provision was made for him by David's care (2 Sam. 9:4, 5).

Mach•pe′lah The name of the plot of ground in Hebron containing the cave which Abraham bought from Ephron for a family sepulchre (Gen. 23:9). It became the burying place of Abraham and Sarah, Isaac and Rebekah, Jacob and Leah. This cave is known as the oldest burial place in the world (Gen. 49:30; 50:13).

Mag•da•le′ne A word used to designate a woman named Mary who was relieved of "seven devils" by Christ and became his devoted disciple (Matt. 27:56; Luke 8:2, 3; John 20:1).

ma′gi wise men.
Matt. 2:1, **m** from the east arrived
Matt. 2:7, Herod secretly called the **m**
Matt. 2:16, been tricked by the **m**

mag′ni•tude greatness, as in size or extent, bigness.
Jer. 13:22, the **m** of your iniquity

Ma′gog 1. The second son of Japheth (Gen. 10:2; 1 Chr. 1:5). 2. The descendants of Magog and their land, Scythia, in the North of Asia and Europe (Ezek. 38:2; 39:6).

Ma•hal′a•lel 1. Son of Kenan, grandson of Seth (Gen. 5:12-17). 2. One whose descendants dwelt in Jerusalem after the captivity (Neh. 11:4).

Ma•ha•na′im A town east of Jordan, so named by Jacob (Gen. 32:2; Josh. 13:26; 21:38).

Mah′li 1. Son of Merari, son of Levi (Ex. 6:19; Num. 3:20; Ezra 8:18). 2. Son of Mushi, son of Merari (1 Chr. 6:47; 23:23; 24:30).

maj′es•ty royal dignity or authority.
Ps. 93:1, He is clothed with **m**
Is. 53:2, no *stately* form or **m**
Heb. 1:3, right hand of the **M** on high
Jude 25, glory, **m**, dominion and authority

mal′ice ill will; strong desire that another suffer or be unhappy.
Matt. 22:18, Jesus perceived their **m**
1 Cor. 5:8, nor with the leaven of **m**
Eph. 4:31, along with all **m**
Col. 3:8, put them all aside: anger, wrath, **m**
1 Pet. 2:1, putting aside all **m**

ma•lign′ to speak evil of; to slander; to defame.
Titus 3:2, to **m** no one

Mam′re 1. A place two miles north of Hebron, with oaks. Here Abraham dwelt, and entertained angels (Gen. 13:18; 18:1). 2. An Amorite, confederate with Abraham (Gen. 14:13, 24).

man′i•fold many and varied; including different kinds.
Eph. 3:10, the **m** wisdom of God
1 Pet. 4:10, the **m** grace of God

man′kind the human race.
2 Chr. 6:18, will God indeed dwell with **m**
Job 4:17, Can **m** be just before God

Ma′on 1. A city and wilderness in Judah, seven miles southeast of Hebron (Josh. 15:55; 1 Sam. 25:2). 2. A descendant of Caleb, son of Hezron (1 Chr. 2:42-45).

Ma′rah The first camp of Israel on the east of the Red Sea (Ex. 15:23; Num. 33:8, 9).

Ma•re′shah 1. A fortified city in the plain of Judah (Josh. 15:44; 2 Chr. 11:8;

14:9, 10). 2. The father of Hebron (1 Chr. 2:42).

Mark 1. The surname of John, the cousin of Barnabas, the companion of Paul. He accompanied Paul and Barnabas on their first missionary journey (Col. 4:10). 2. A son or disciple of Peter, said to have written the second Gospel (1 Pet. 5:13).

mar'riage the mutual relation of husband and wife.
Matt. 22:30, marry, nor are given in **m**
Heb. 13:4, *Let* **m** *be held* in honor
Rev. 19:7, **m** of the Lamb has come

Mas'kil Possibly, contemplative, or didactic, or skillful poem (Ps. 32; 42; 44; 45).

Mas'sah a place, also called Meribah, in the wilderness where the people murmured for the want of water.
Ex. 17:7, he named the place **M** and Meribah
Deut. 6:16, as you tested Him at **M**
Ps. 95:8, in the day of **M**

Me•de'ba A plain and city in Reuben, southeast of Heshbon Num. 21:30; Josh. 13:9).

Medes The inhabitants of Media, a rude and uncultivated race (2 Kin. 17:6; 18:11; Is. 13:17).

me'di•a•tor a person or group that acts as a go-between in a dispute in order to arrange a peaceful settlement.
Gal. 3:19, by the agency of a **m**
Gal. 3:20, a **m** is not for one *party*
1 Tim. 2:5, one **m** also between God and men
Heb. 8:6, **m** of a better covenant
Heb. 12:24, to Jesus, the **m** of a new covenant

Me•gid'do One of the royal cities of the Canaanites, whose king was conquered by Joshua (Josh. 12:21; Judg. 1:27).

Men'a•hem An Israelite who rebelled against Shallum, king of Israel, killed him, and reigned in his stead (2 Kin. 15:14-22).

Me•ra'ri The third and youngest son of Levi (Gen. 46:11; Ex. 6:16, 19).

Mer'ib-ba'al Son of Jonathan, son of Saul (1 Chr. 8:34; 9:40).

Me'shach The name given to Mishael, one of Daniel's companions. He was thrown into a fiery furnace together with Shadrach and Abednego, by the command of Nebuchadnezzar, but came out unhurt (Dan. 1:7; 2:49; 3:12-30).

Mes•si'ah Name applied by Daniel to the Redeemer who was to come. It has the same meaning in Hebrew as "Christ" has in Greek (Dan. 9:25, 26; John 1:41).

Me•thu'se•lah Son of Enoch and grandfather of Noah. He was the longest lived man of all ages. He died at the age of 969 years (Gen. 5:21-27; 1 Chr. 1:3).

Mi'chal The younger daughter of King Saul; she became David's wife (1 Sam. 14:49; 18:20; 19:11).

Mich'mas A place to which some belonged who returned with Zerubbabel (Ezra 2:27; Neh. 7:31).

Mid'i•an 1. A son of Abraham by Keturah (Gen. 25:2, 4). 2. His descendants and their land beyond the Jordan, in Edom (Ex. 2:15, 16; 3:1; 4:19; 18:1).

Mikh'tam The name of a particular kind of Psalm, occurs only in the titles of Psalms chapters 16, and 56 through 60.

Mil'cah Daughter of Haran, Abraham's brother. She became wife of Nahor, and mother of Bethuel (Gen. 11:29; 24:15).

Mil'lo 1. The fortress of Shechem, all the occupants or garrison joined in proclaiming Abimelech their king (Judg. 9:6, 20). 2. A part of a fortress in Jerusalem, enlarged by David and Solomon, and where Joash was slain (2 Sam. 5:9; 1 Kin. 9:15; 2 Kin. 12:20).

min'is•ter to serve; to attend; to render aid.
Ex. 28:43, they approach the altar to **m**

Mint

2 Chr. 31:2, to **m** and to give thanks
Is. 61:6, **m-s** of our God
Rom. 15:16, to be a **m** of Christ Jesus
Eph. 3:7, I was made a **m**

mint an herb, the oil of which was used as a condiment and as medicine. Several species are found in Palestine. The Pharisees required the tithing even of mint, but neglected law and justice, mercy and faith.
Matt. 23:23, you tithe **m** and dill
Luke 11:42, you pay tithe of **m**

mir'a•cle an extraordinary event or effect taken to be a manifestation of the supernatural power of God.
Ex. 34:10, Before all your people I will perform **m-s**
Matt. 11:21, if the **m-s** had occurred
Mark 6:5, He could do no **m** there
Acts 4:16, a noteworthy **m** has taken place

Mir'i•am Daughter of Amram, and the sister of Moses and Aaron. She watched the ark of bulrushes in which the infant Moses was hidden away, and when the daughter of Pharaoh discovered it, Miriam artfully arranged for her mother to nurse the child (Ex. 15:20; Num 20:1; 1 Chr. 6:3).

mis•car'riage loss of a child through premature birth.
Ex. 21:22, so that she has a **m**
Job 3:16, like a **m** which is discarded

mis•giv'ing a fear that something bad is going to happen; a feeling of mistrust or doubt.
Acts 10:20, accompany them without **m-s**
Acts 11:12, go with them without **m-s**

Mo'ab 1. Descendant of Lot and his daughter (Gen. 19:37). 2. The descendants of Moab, and the land in which they lived (Gen. 36:35; Ex. 15:15).

Mo'ab•ites Descendants of Moab, son of Lot (Deut. 23:3; Neh. 13:1).

mock to laugh at scornfully; to ridicule.
Job 30:1, those younger than I **m** me
Prov. 14:9, Fools **m** at sin
Prov. 20:1, Wine is a **m-er**
Matt. 20:19, to **m** and scourge and . . . *Him*
Gal. 6:7, God is not **m-ed**

mode a manner of doing something; a *method*; a way.
Judg. 13:12, shall be the boy's **m** of life

Mo'lech A god of the Ammonites. Human sacrifices, especially children, were offered to it (2 Kin. 23:10; Jer. 32:35).

mon'grel of a mixed breed or race.
Zech. 9:6, a **m** race

mor'als concerned with what is right and wrong in human behavior.
1 Cor. 15:33, Bad company corrupts good **m**

Mor'de•cai 1. A chief man that returned from Babylon with Zerubbabel (Ezra 2:2; Neh. 7:7). 2. A Benjaminite, cousin, and guardian of Esther (Esth. 2:5-8).

Mo'ses The youngest child of Amram and Jochebed, of the tribe of Levi (Ex. 6:16-20). At the age of eighty, Moses received the divine commission to deliver his people from their bondage (Ex. 3:3-10).

Mount of Olives A ridge, 3000 feet high and two miles long, overlooking Jerusalem on the east. It is so near to the walls of Jerusalem that nearly every street in that city can easily be seen from its summit (Matt. 21:1; Mark 11:1).

mourn to grieve; to feel or show sorrow.
Is. 61:2, To comfort all who **m**
Jer. 15:5, who will **m** for you
Matt. 5:4, Blessed are those who **m**
Luke 6:25, for you shall **m** and weep
James 4:9, laughter be turned into **m-ing**

mul'ti•tude a crowd; a great number of persons or things.
Gen. 17:4, father of a **m** of nations
Matt. 14:15, send the **m-s** away
Luke 23:27, following Him a great **m**
James 5:20, cover a **m** of sins
1 Pet. 4:8, love covers a **m** of sins

myrrh an aromatic gum resin with a bitter slightly pungent taste obtained from a tree.

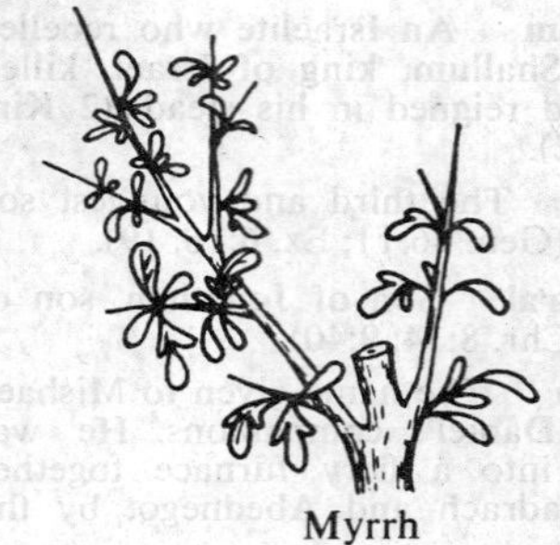
Myrrh

Gen. 43:11, aromatic gum and **m**
Ps. 45:8, garments are fragrant with **m**
Song 5:13, Dripping with liquid **m**
Matt. 2:11, frankincense and **m**
John 19:39, mixture of **m** and aloes

N

Na'bal A rich and wicked man of Maon. He refused, in the most insulting manner, to aid David, who had protected him from robbers. David undertook to destroy him and his property (1 Sam. 25:2-39).

Na'both A Jezreelite, of the tribe of Issachar, whom Jezebel, wife of Ahab, caused to be put to death to obtain his vineyard (1 Kin. 21:1-19).

Na'hor 1. A son of Serug, and grandfather of Abraham (Gen. 11:24, 25). 2. Son of Terah, brother of Abraham (Gen. 11:26-29; Josh. 24:2).

Nah'shon Son of Amminadab, and prince of Judah in the days of Moses (Num. 1:7; 2:3; 7:12).

Na'ioth A place in Ramah, on Mount Ephraim, where Samuel dwelt (1 Sam. 19:18-23; 20:1).

Na•o'mi Wife of Elimelech, mother of Mahlon and Chilion, and the mother-in-law of Ruth (Ruth 1:2, 22; 2:1; 3:1).

Naph'ta•li 1. Sixth son of Jacob, and second of Bilhah, Rachel's maid (Gen. 30:8; 35:25). 2. His descendants (also called Nephthalim) and their territory, which lay in Galilee (Josh. 19:32; 20:7).

na'tion the union of people connected by ties of blood, a common language, or common religion.
Ps. 33:12, Blessed is the **n** whose God
Prov. 14:34, Righteousness exalts a **n**
Is. 2:4, **N** will not lift up sword against **n**
Matt. 24:7, **n** will rise against **n**
Acts 2:5, devout men, from every **n**

Naz'a•rene A native of Nazareth (Matt. 2:23; Acts 3:6).

Naz'a•reth A city in lower Galilee, 70 miles north of Jerusalem. It was the home of Jesus from His childhood until He commenced His public ministry and was rejected by His own townsmen (Matt. 2:22, 23; Luke 1:26; John 1:45).

Naz'i•rite A person, male or female, who was specially consecrated to God (Num. 6:2; Judg. 13:4, 5).

Ne'bat Father of Jeroboam, who rebelled against Rehoboam, became the first king of the ten tribes of Israel, and set up the two golden calves at Bethel and Dan (1 Kin. 12:2; 16:26; 21:22; 22:52).

Neb'u•chad•nez'zar The greatest of the kings of Babylon (2 Kin. 24:10-16; Dan. 1:1-4).

ne•glect' to treat as though of no importance; to fail to notice.
Matt. 6:16, they **n** their appearance
Luke 15:29, I have never **n-ed** a command
1 Tim. 4:14, Do not **n** the spiritual gift
Heb. 2:3, if we **n** so great a salvation
Heb. 13:2, Do not **n** to show hospitality

neg'li•gence failure to attend to something under one's charge; an instance of carelessness.
Dan. 6:4, no **n** or corruption was *to be*

Ner A Benjaminite, grandfather of Saul, the first king of Israel (1 Chr. 8:33; 9:39).

Ne•toph'a•thite An inhabitant of Netophah (2 Sam. 23:28, 29; 2 Kin. 25:23; 1 Chr. 11:30).

Nim'rod Son of Cush, son of Ham (Gen. 10:8, 9; 1 Chr. 1:10).

Nim'shi Grandfather or father of Jehu, who smote Joram, son of Ahab, and reigned in his stead over Israel (1 Kin. 19:16; 2 Kin. 9:2; 2 Chr. 22:7).

No'ah Son of Lamech, and father of Shem, Ham, and Japheth. He was preserved, with his family, in the ark from the flood which destroyed the remainder of the human race. His history is given in Genesis chapters 5-9.

nul'li•fy to make of no value or importance; to destroy; to annul.
Rom. 3:3, unbelief will not **n**
Gal. 2:21, I do not **n** the grace of God
Gal. 3:17, so as to **n** the promise

O

o•be'di•ence willingness to carry out orders of someone or to mind.
Rom. 16:26, to **o** of faith
2 Cor. 10:5, to the **o** of Christ
Heb. 5:8, He learned **o** from the things

ob'li•gate to bind legally or morally.
Matt. 23:16, whoever swears by the gold . . . **o-d**

ob•li•ga'tion the binding power of a promise or contract; something a person

is expected or feels is necessary to do to repay.
Num. 32:22, be free of **o** toward the LORD
Rom. 1:14, I am under **o** both to Greeks
Rom. 8:12, we are under **o,** not to the flesh
Gal. 5:3, he is under **o** to keep the whole Law

ob•scure' not clearly understood; not noticeable; inconspicuous; humble.
Prov. 22:29, He will not stand before **o** men
Luke 23:45, the sun being **o-d**

ob•so•lete' no longer in use; out of date.
Heb. 8:13, He has made the first **o**

Och'ran Father of Pagiel, an Asherite whom Moses chose to number the people (Num. 1:13; 2:27; 7:72; 10:26).

O'ded 1. Father of the prophet Azariah, who encouraged Asa, king of Judah (2 Chr. 15:1, 8). 2. A prophet in Samaria who obtained the release of the captives of Judah (2 Chr. 28:9).

od'i•ous causing hatred or strong dislike; worthy of hatred.
Gen. 34:30, making me **o** among the inhabitants
Ex. 5:21, made us **o** in Pharaoh's sight
1 Sam. 13:4, Israel had become **o** to the Philistines

of'fer•ing a sacrifice ceremonially offered as a part of worship.
Gen. 4:4, Lord had regard for Abel and for his **o**
Lev. 4:29, he shall lay his hand on the head of the sin **o**

Sin offering

off'spring a descendant of a person or animal.
Deut. 28:53, eat the **o** of your own body
Is. 65:9, I will bring forth **o** from Jacob
John 7:42, comes from the **o** of David

O'nam 1. Second son of Shobal, son of Seir (Gen. 36:23; 1 Chr. 1:40). 2. A son of Jerahmeel (1 Chr. 2:26, 28).

O'nan Second son of Judah, by daughter of Shuah the Canaanite. He was punished by premature death for frustrating the purpose of the law requiring him to raise up offspring by the wife of his deceased brother (Gen. 38:4, 8, 9; Num. 26:19; 1 Chr. 2:3).

O'phel A part of ancient Jerusalem, on the east of Zion (2 Chr. 27:3; Neh. 3:26; 11:21).

O'phir 1. The eleventh named of the thirteen sons of Joktan, son of Eber, great-grandson of Shem (Gen. 10:26-29). 2. A famous gold region visited by the ships of Solomon and the Phoenicians. It produced the purest and most precious gold then known (Job 22:24; 28:16; Ps. 45:9).

o•pin'ion a view, judgment, or appraisal formed in the mind about a particular matter.
Job 32:17, I also will tell my **o**
1 Cor. 7:25, I give an **o**
2 Cor. 8:10, give *my* **o** in this matter

op•por•tune' suitable; timely.
Mark 14:11, betray Him at an **o** time

op•press' to weigh down; to burden in spirit as if with weight.
Lev. 19:13, You shall not **o** your neighbor
Hos. 12:7, He loves to **o**
Acts 10:38, healing all who were **o-ed**
James 2:6, Is it not the rich who **o** you

or•dain' to appoint, order or decide upon; to make a person a minister or priest by special ceremony.
Ex. 29:9, So you shall **o** Aaron
Ps. 8:3, Thou hast **o-ed**
Acts 7:53, as **o-ed** by angels

or'di•nance a prescribed usage, practice or ceremony.
Job 38:33, the **o-s** of the heavens
Rom. 13:2, opposed the **o** of God
Eph. 2:15, Law of commandments *contained* in **o-s**

Or'nan A Jebusite prince, by whose threshing floor the angel of the Lord stood (1 Chr. 21:15; 21:18-28).

ought to be bound or obligated by duty or conscience.
Gen. 20:9, things that **o** not to be done
John 4:20, place where men **o** to worship

Heb. 5:12, you **o** to be teachers
James 3:10, these things **o** not to be

o'ver•seer a person whose business is to manage or supervise something.
Phil. 1:1, including the **o-s** and deacons
1 Tim. 3:1, aspires to the office of **o**
Titus 1:7, **o** must be above reproach

o•ver•whelm' to bear down upon so as to crush or destroy; to overpower.
Ex. 17:13, Joshua **o-ed** Amalek
Ps. 55:5, horror has **o-ed** me
Ps. 142:3, When my spirit was **o-ed**
Ps. 143:4, my spirit is **o-ed** within me

P

pact an agreement; a compact.
Is. 28:15, we have made a **p**

Pad'dan-ar'am The plains of Mesopotamia. It was to this country that Abraham sent his servant to obtain a wife for Isaac (Gen. 25:20; 28:2; 31:18).

Pa'gi•el A son of Ochran, and head of the tribe of Asher, chosen to number the people (Num. 1:13; 2:27).

pal'ate the roof of the mouth.
Job 29:10, their tongue stuck to their **p**

palm a simple stem and a terminal crown of large pinnate or fan-shaped leaves.
Neh. 8:15, bring . . . **p** branches
Is. 9:14, Both **p** branch and bulrush

Palm tree

Pam•phyl'i•a A province in the south of Asia Minor. Visitors from Pamphylia were at Jerusalem on the day of Pentecost (Acts 2:10); and this province was twice visited by Paul (Acts 13:13; 14:24; 15:38).

pa•py'rus a substance like paper made from the pith of this plant and used to write on.
Is. 18:2, in **p** vessels

The papyrus, or paper reed

par'a•pet a low wall or railing at the edge of a roof, platform or bridge.
Deut. 22:8, a **p** for your roof

par•ta'kers ones who take part or a share of something.
Eph. 5:7, do not be **p** with them
Heb. 3:1, **p** of a heavenly calling
Heb. 3:14, **p** of Christ
Heb. 6:4, **p** of the Holy Spirit
2 Pet. 1:4, **p** of *the* divine nature

par•tic'i•pate to have a share in common with others; to share; to take part.
Eph. 5:11, do not **p** in the unfruitful deeds

Pass'over an annual Jewish feast commemorating the sparing, or passing over, of the Hebrews in Egypt when God

killed the firstborn children of the Egyptians.
Ex. 12:11, it is the LORD's **P**
Matt. 26:17, prepare for You to eat the **P**
Luke 22:15, desired to eat this **P**
John 18:39, release someone for you at the **P**
1 Cor. 5:7, Christ our **P** also has been sacrificed

pas'tor a spiritual overseer; a clergyman of a local church.
Eph. 4:11, some *as* **p-s** and teachers

pa'tience the quality of being constant, without haste, showing calm self control.
Matt. 18:26, Have **p** with me
2 Cor. 6:6, in **p**, in kindness
Col. 1:11, steadfastness and **p**
2 Tim. 4:2, with great **p** and instruction

Paul The apostle to the Gentiles whose original name was Saul (Acts 13:9, 42; 28:16; 2 Pet. 3:15).

peck the fourth part of a bushel; a large quantity.
Matt. 13:33, hid in three **p-s** of meal

Pe•dah'zur The father of Gamaliel, the chief of Manasseh chosen to number the people (Num. 1:10; 2:20; 7:54).

Pe'kah Son of Remaliah, and an officer of Pekahiah, king of Israel, against whom he conspired and reigned in his stead, and who was himself slain by Hoshea (2 Kin 15:25-37; 2 Chr. 28:6; Is. 7:1).

Pe'leg A son of Eber, of the family of Shem, in whose days the earth was divided (Gen. 10:25; 11:16-19).

pen'al•ty punishment for a crime or offense.
2 Thess. 1:9, pay the **p** of eternal destruction

Pen'u•el A place on the Jabbok River, east of the Jordan, where Jacob wrestled with the angel (Gen. 32:24-32).

per•di'tion utter loss of the soul; eternal damnation.
John 17:12, the son of **p**

Per'ez Elder son of Judah by Tamar his daughter-in-law, and father of Hezron and Hamul (Gen. 38:29; 46:12; Num. 26:20, 21, Ruth 4:12).

per•fec'ter one who made something ideal, without fault or flaw.
Heb. 12:2, author and **p** of faith

per'ju•ry false swearing; conscious violation of one's oath to tell the truth.
Zech. 8:17, do not love **p**

per•pet'u•al lasting forever; eternal; constant.
Ex. 40:15, qualify them for a **p** priesthood
Num. 25:13, a **p** priesthood
Ps. 9:6, an end in **p** ruins
Jer. 15:18, Why has my pain been **p**
Heb. 7:3, abides a priest **p-ly**

per'se•cute to pursue in order to harm or destroy; to harass or cause to suffer.
Matt. 5:11, when *men* revile you, and **p** you
Matt. 5:44, pray for those who **p** you
Matt. 10:23, they **p** you in this city, flee
John 15:20, If they **p-d** Me, they will also **p** you
Acts 9:4, Saul, why are you **p-ing** Me

per•se•ver'ance steadfastness; persistance.
Rom. 2:7, by **p** in doing good
Rom. 5:3, tribulation brings about **p**
Rom. 15:4, **p** and the encouragement of the Scriptures
2 Thess. 1:4, for your **p** and faith

per•se•vere' to keep at something in spite of difficulties, opposition, or discouragement.
Rom. 12:12, hope, **p-ing** in tribulation
James 1:12, Blessed is a man who **p-s** under trial

Per'sia The last of the four great Asiatic empires, anciently called Elam (2 Chr. 36:20; Ezek. 27:10; Dan. 8:20).

per•vert' to turn away from the right or true course; to lead astray.
Deut. 16:19, **p-s** the words of the righteous
2 Sam. 22:27, with the **p-ed**
Job 8:3, Does God **p** justice
Prov. 10:31, the **p-ed** tongue

Pe'ter, Si'mon Brother of Andrew and son of Jona (or Johanan). He was given the name "Peter" by Christ when He called him to the apostleship (Matt. 16:18; John 1:42). His early apostolic work is recorded in the first part of Acts, chapters 1 through 12 and 15.

Pha'raoh The national or official title of the Egyptian kings of the old native dynasties (Gen. 12:15-20; 37:36; Ex. 1:11; 2:15; 3:10).

Pha'raoh Ne'co A king of Egypt who fought against Nabopolassar, king of Assyria, slew King Josiah at Megiddo, bound Jehoahaz at Riblah, and made Eliakim, his brother, king in his stead (2 Kin. 23:29-35).

Phar'i•see The largest of the three or four Jewish sects noted for their self-conceit and long prayers. In the time of Christ, they formed the most powerful party among the Jews, both in politics and in religion (Matt. 23:23-33).

Phi•lip'pi A chief city in Macedonia. The first place in Greece to receive the Gospel. Paul visited the city twice. Paul and Silas were thrown into prison at Philippi, but were miraculously released, and the jailor and his family were converted (Acts 16:12-40; 20:6).

Philis'ti•a The seacoast on the west of Dan and Simeon (Ex. 15:14; Ps. 60:8; 87:4; 108:9).

pi'e•ty dutifulness in religion; loyal devotion.
Acts 3:12, by our own power or **p**
1 Tim. 5:4, practice **p** in regard

Pi'late The surname of the fifth Roman procurator of Judea, who after attempting to set Jesus free, gave Him up to be crucified (Matt. 27:2-65; Luke 3:1; 23:1-25; Acts 3:13).

pil'lage the act of looting or plundering.
Is. 17:14, the lot of those who **p** us
Nah. 3:1, city, . . . full of lies *and* **p**

Pi•ra'thon•ite An inhabitant of Pirathon (Judg. 12:13; 2 Sam. 23:30).

Pis'gah The highest point of, or another name for Mount Nebo in the land of Moab (Num. 23:14; Deut. 34:1-5).

pit'y a feeling of sympathy and sorrow for the sufferings or distress of others; compassion.
Ex. 2:6, she had **p** on him
Deut. 7:16, your eye shall not **p** them
Job 19:21, **P** me, **p** me, O you my friends

plague anything that causes much trouble or suffering; a contagious disease.
Gen. 12:17, struck Pharaoh and his house with great **p-s**
Rev. 16:21, the **p** of the hail
Rev. 21:9, the seven last **p-s**

pledge a promise or agreement to do something.
Prov. 22:26, among those who give **p-s**
2 Cor. 1:22, the Spirit in our hearts as a **p**
2 Cor. 5:5, gave to us the Spirit as a **p**
Eph. 1:14, given as a **p** of our inheritance
1 Tim. 5:12, set aside their previous **p**

plow to turn, break up or work the soil in preparing a seedbed.
Deut. 22:10, You shall not **p** with an ox
Luke 17:7, having a slave **p-ing** or tending sheep

Plowing with cattle, and with a camel

plum'age the entire clothing of feathers of a bird.
Job 39:13, pinion and **p** of love

plun'der (n.) anything taken by robbery or force.
Judg. 5:19, They took no **p** in silver
Hab. 2:7, You will become **p** for them
Zeph. 1:13, their wealth will become **p**

plun'der (v.) to rob, especially openly and by force.
Jer. 50:10, All who **p** her will have enough
Hos. 13:15, It will **p** his treasury
Matt. 12:29, he will **p** his house

pov'er•ty the condition of being poor; want; need.
Prov. 23:21, glutton will come to **p**
Prov. 30:8, neither **p** nor riches
2 Cor. 8:9, through His **p**

prae•to'ri•an guard The duty of which was to guard the imperial palace and its occupant, the emperor (Phil. 1:13).

Prae•to'ri•um the headquarters of the Roman governor.
Matt. 27:27, soldiers . . . took Jesus into the **P**
Mark 15:16, took Him . . . into the palace (that is, the **P**)
John 18:28, led Jesus . . . into the **P**
John 18:33, Pilate . . . entered . . . into the **P**

pray to ask earnestly of God.

Is. 45:20, And **p** to a god who cannot save
Matt. 5:44, **p** for those who persecute
Matt. 14:23, mountain by Himself to **p**
1 Cor. 11:13, for a woman to **p** to God
1 Thess. 5:17, **p** without ceasing

pray′er a request, an entreaty to God.
Ps. 55:1, Give ear to my **p**, O God
Is. 56:7, called a house of **p**
Luke 6:12, whole night in **p**
Acts 3:1, the hour of **p**
Rom. 12:12, devoted to **p**

preach to urge publicly; to advocate; to deliver a sermon.
Matt. 4:17, that time Jesus began to **p**
Mark 16:15, **p** the gospel to all
Luke 4:43, **p** the kingdom of God
Acts 13:32, we **p** to you the good news of the promise
1 Cor. 1:23, we **p** Christ crucified

preach′er a person who preaches; especially a minister.
Eccl. 1:1, words of the **P**
Rom. 10:14, how shall they hear without a **p**
1 Tim. 2:7, I was appointed a **p**
2 Pet. 2:5, Noah, a **p** of righteousness

pre•cede′ to be or go before, as in position, rank, or time.
1 Thess. 4:15, **p** those who have fallen asleep

pre′cept a guiding principle; any principle or instruction taken as a rule of action or behavior.
Ps. 19:8, **p-s** of the LORD are right

pre•de•ter′mine to settle or arrange beforehand.
Acts 2:23, **p-d** plan and foreknowledge of God

pre•em′i•nent very outstanding; superior.
Gen. 49:3, **P** in dignity and **p** in

pres′er•va′tion safekeeping; a keeping of something from injury or decay.
Acts 27:34, food . . . for your **p**

pre•sume′ to act or behave boldly without reason for doing so.
Esth. 7:5, who would **p** to do thus
Rom. 15:18, I will not **p** to speak

pre•sump′tion something that is believed to be so but not proved.
Prov. 13:10, Through **p** comes nothing

prev′a•lent generally or extensively existing; occurring often.
Eccl. 6:1, an evil . . . it is **p**

prey an animal hunted or killed by another animal for food; a victim.
Gen. 49:9, From the **p**, my son, you have gone up
Job 4:11, lion perishes for lack of **p**
Ps. 76:4, than the mountains of **p**
Ezek. 22:25, roaring lion tearing the **p**

priest a person who has the authority to conduct religious rites.
Gen. 14:18, **p** of God Most High
Ex. 19:6, shall be to Me a kingdom of **p-s**
1 Sam. 2:35, raise up for Myself a faithful **p**
Heb. 2:17, faithful high **p**
Heb. 3:1, High **P** of our confession

prin•ci•pal′i•ties territories ruled by a prince or one giving a prince his title.
Rom. 8:38, nor **p** . . . nor powers

pri•va′tion the state of being deprived of something that is needed; lack a necessity; want.
Is. 30:20, given you bread of **p**

pro•con′sul a governor or military commander in ancient Roman provinces.
Acts 13:7, who was with the **p**
Acts 18:12, Gallio was **p** of Achaia
Acts 19:38, courts are in session and **p-s** are *available*

pro•fane′ to violate or treat with irreverence, abuse, or contempt.
Ex. 31:14, Everyone who **p-s** it . . . put to death
Lev. 20:3, to **p** My holy name
Ezek. 23:38, have **p-d** My sabbaths
1 Tim. 1:9, law . . . for the unholy and **p**

prom′i•nence the fact or condition of being well-known; leading; outstanding.
Acts 13:50, devout women of **p**

prom′i•nent attracting attention; well-known; conspicuous.
Mark 15:43, Joseph . . . **p** member
Acts 25:23, the **p** men of the city

prom•is•cu′i•ty sexual behavior not restricted to one sexual partner.
Rom. 13:13, not in sexual **p** and sensuality

proph′e•cy the foretelling of the future.
Dan. 9:24, seal up the vision and **p**
1 Cor. 13:2, if I have *the gift* of **p**
2 Pet. 1:21, no **p** was ever made by . . . human will
Rev. 19:10, testimony . . . is the spirit of **p**

proph′e•sy to utter with or as if with divine inspiration.
1 Sam. 10:11, he **p-ed** now with the prophets

Is. 30:10, not **p** to us what is right
Matt. 7:22, did we not **p** in Your name
Matt. 26:68, **P** to us, You Christ
1 Cor. 13:9, know in part, and we **p** in part

proph'et a person inspired by God to speak for Him.
Matt. 1:22, spoken . . . through the **p**
Matt. 2:5, it has been written by the **p**
Luke 4:24, no **p** is welcome in his home town
John 4:19, perceive that You are a **p**
1 Cor. 14:37, If any one thinks he is a **p**

pro'pi•tia'tion the act of appeasing the wrath and conciliating the favor of an offended person.
Rom. 3:25, God displayed publicly as a **p**
1 John 2:2, He Himself is the **p** for our sins

pros'e•lyte a new convert; one won over to another religion.
Matt. 23:15, make one **p**
Acts 2:10, both Jews and **p-s**
Acts 13:43, God-fearing **p-s** followed Paul

pros•per'i•ty the state of being successful.
Ezra 9:12, never seek . . . their **p**
Job 21:13, spend their days in **p**
Ps. 25:13, His soul will abide in **p**
Ps. 73:3, saw the **p** of the wicked
Acts 19:25, our **p** depends upon this business

pros'ti•tute a woman who offers herself for immoral sexual relations for money.
Deut. 23:17, shall be a cult **p**
Hos. 4:14, offer sacrifices with temple **p**

pros'trate lying flat and outstretched with face to the ground.
2 Sam. 9:6, fell on his face and **p-d** himself
2 Sam. 15:5, man came near to **p** himself
2 Sam. 16:4, I **p** myself
Job 14:10, man dies and lies **p**

prov'erb a well-known maxim; an adage.
Deut. 28:37, you shall become a horror, a **p**
1 Kin. 4:32, He also spoke 3,000 **p-s**
1 Kin. 9:7, Israel will become a **p** and a byword
Jer. 24:9, as a reproach and a **p**
2 Pet. 2:22, according to the true **p**

pro•vi'sion a store or stock of food.
Josh. 9:5, bread of their **p** was dry
Ps. 132:15, abundantly bless her **p**
Rom. 13:14, make no **p** for the flesh

pro•voke' to arouse to action of feeling; to stir up.
2 Chr. 25:19, why should you **p** trouble
Job 12:6, those who **p** God
Prov. 20:2, who **p-s** him to anger
1 Cor. 13:5, is not **p-d**
Eph. 6:4, do not **p** your children to anger

prow the forward end or part of a ship.
Acts 27:41, the **p** stuck fast and remained

pru'dent wise and careful in action or judgment.
Prov. 12:16, **p** man conceals dishonor
Prov. 19:14, a **p** wife is from the LORD
Jer. 49:7, good counsel been lost to the **p**

psalms sacred songs or poems.
Ps. 95:2, shout joyfully to Him with **p**
Luke 20:42, David . . . says in the book of **P**
Luke 24:44, the **P** must be fulfilled
Eph. 5:19, speaking to one another in **p**
Col. 3:16, admonishing one another with **p**

pug•na'cious quarrelsome; fond of fighting.
1 Tim. 3:3, addicted to wine or **p**

pul'ver•ize to smash to pieces; to demolish.
Mic. 4:13, That you may **p** many peoples

purge to cleanse; to purify; to free from sin or guilt.
2 Chr. 34:3, he began to **p** Judah
Ezek. 20:38, I shall **p** from you
Dan. 11:35, in order to refine, **p**
Dan. 12:10, Many will be **p-d,** purified

Q

quake to shake, vibrate, or quiver.
Judg. 5:4, The earth **q-d,** the heavens
Judg. 5:5, The mountains **q-d**
Ps. 60:2, Thou hast made the land **q**
Nah. 1:5, Mountains **q** because of Him

quar'rel a disagreement; a cause to be defended.
Ex. 17:2, Why do you **q** with me
Ex. 21:18, if men have a **q**
Prov. 20:3, any fool will **q**
1 Cor. 1:11, there are **q-s** among you
James 4:1, source of **q-s** and conflicts

quench to put out, as a fire; to subdue.
Ps. 104:11, wild donkeys **q** their thirst.
Song 8:7, Many waters cannot **q** love
1 Thess. 5:19, Do not **q** the Spirit

quilt a bed covering made of two pieces of material, with a filling of wool, cotton, or down, stitched together.
1 Sam. 19:13, put a **q** of goats' *hair*

quo'ta the part or share, forming a definite proportion of the whole.
Ex. 5:18, deliver the **q** of bricks

R

Ra'a•mah 1. Fourth, in order named, of the sons of Cush, son of Ham (Gen. 10:7; 1 Chr. 1:9). 2. A country named after Raamah (Ezek. 27:22).

Rab'bah Chief city of Ammon, 22 miles east of Jordan (Deut. 3:11; Josh. 13:25; 2 Sam. 11:1).

Rab'bi A title given by the Jews to the teachers of their law (Matt. 26:25; Mark 9:5; John 1:38).

Rab•sha'keh An officer of Sennacherib, king of Assyria, in the days of Hezekiah (2 Kin. 18:17; Is. 36:2).

ra'ca An expression of contempt or reproach (Matt. 5:22).

Ra'chel The younger daughter of Laban. She became the favorite wife of Jacob, to whom she bore Joseph and Benjamin. Her history is recorded in Genesis chapters 29-35.

ra'di•ance brilliance, vivid brightness.
Heb. 1:3, **r** of His glory

Ra'hab 1. A poetic and symbolic name for Egypt (Ps. 87:4; 89:10; Is. 51:9). 2. A woman in Jericho who received and concealed the two spies (Josh. 2:1, 3; 6:17; Heb. 11:31; James 2:25).

rai'ment clothing, garments.
Is. 63:3, I stained all My **r**

Ra'moth-gil'e•ad One of the most important cities of Gad; a city of refuge (1 Kin. 4:13; 2 Kin. 8:28; 9:1; 2 Chr. 22:5).

ram'part a broad embankment around a place; a banner.
2 Sam. 20:15, it stood by the **r**
Ps. 48:13, Consider her **r-s**
Is. 26:1, He sets up walls and **r-s**
Lam. 2:8, caused **r** and wall to lament
Nah. 3:8, Whose **r** *was* the sea

ran'som the act of delivering from sin or its penalty.
Ex. 30:12, give a **r** for himself
Prov. 6:35, He will not accept any **r**
Matt. 20:28, give His life a **r** for many
1 Tim. 2:6, gave Himself as a **r** for all

ra'tion an allowance of provisions; an allotment.
Dan. 1:5, king appointed for them a daily **r**
Luke 12:42, give them their **r-s**

rav'age to lay waste; to plunder; to destroy.
Gen. 41:30, famine will **r** the land
1 Sam. 6:5, mice that **r** the land
1 Chr. 20:1, Joab led out the army and **r-d**
Acts 8:3, **r-ing** the church

ra•vine' a depression worn out by running water; a deep gorge.
Luke 3:5, Every **r** shall be filled up
John 18:1, over the **r** of the Kidron

Re•bek'ah Daughter of Bethuel, nephew of Abraham. She became wife of Isaac, and mother of Esau and Jacob (Gen. 22:23; 24:15-67).

re•bel'lion an uprising; a revolt; open resistance to authority.
1 Sam. 24:11, no evil or **r** in my hands
Job 13:23, Make known to me my **r**
Jude 11, perished in the **r** of Korah

re•bel'lious inclined to resist or disobey authority.
Ex. 23:21, do not be **r** toward him
Deut. 9:7, **r** against the Lord
Ps. 78:8, A stubborn and **r** generation
Jer. 5:23, a stubborn and **r** heart
1 Tim. 1:9, those who are lawless and **r**

re•buke' to scold or criticize severely.
Matt. 8:26, **r-d** the winds and
Matt. 17:18, Jesus **r-d** him, and the demon
Mark 9:25, **r-d** the unclean spirit
Luke 4:39, He **r-d** the fever, and it left
1 Tim. 5:1, not sharply **r** an older man

re•cep'tion a party, especially one where guests are formally welcomed.
Luke 5:29, Levi gave a big **r** for Him
Luke 14:13, you give a **r**

reck'less heedless; careless; rash.
Judg. 9:4, hired worthless and **r** fellows
2 Tim. 3:4, treacherous, **r** . . . lovers of pleasure

reck'on to consider; to regard; to depend.
Num. 18:27, offering shall be **r-ed**
Rom. 4:4, his wage is not **r-ed**
Rom. 4:6, God **r-s** righteousness

rec'om•pense payment; return; reward.
Ps. 28:4, Repay them their **r**
Ps. 94:2, Render **r** to the proud
Jer. 51:6, He is going to render **r**
Heb. 2:2, received a just **r**

rec'on•cile to make friendly again; to make to agree.
Matt. 5:24, be **r-d** to your brother
1 Cor. 7:11, be **r-d** to her husband
2 Cor. 5:20, be **r-d** to God
Eph. 2:16, **r** them both in one body
Col. 1:20, **r** all things to Himself

rec•on•cil•i•a'tion settlement or explanation of differences.
Rom. 5:11, we have now received the **r**
2 Cor. 5:18, gave us the ministry of **r**
2 Cor. 5:19, committed to us the word of **r**

Red Sea The sea between Egypt and Arabia. The Red Sea derives its peculiar interest from the miracle of God in dividing its waters, so the children of Israel might escape from Pharaoh (Ex. 13:18; Num. 14:25).

re•deem' to liberate or rescue, as from bondage.
Ex. 6:6, **r** you with an outstretched arm
Ruth 4:4, If you will **r** *it*
Ps. 26:11, **R** me, and be gracious
Ps. 49:15, God will **r** my soul
Gal. 3:13, **r-ed** us from the curse

Re•deem'er Jesus Christ.
Job 19:25, know that my **R** lives
Ps. 19:14, my rock and my **R**
Is. 63:16, our Father, Our **R**
Jer. 50:34, Their **R** is strong

re•demp'tion a ransom; a rescue; a deliverance; salvation.
Ps. 130:7, with Him is abundant **r**
Luke 21:28, your **r** is drawing near
Rom. 3:24, **r** which is in Christ Jesus
Eph. 1:7, **r** through His blood
Eph. 4:30, sealed for the day of **r**

reef a ridge of rocks or sand at or near the surface of the water.
Jude 12, hidden **r-s** in your love feasts

re•fine' to become free from impurities; to improve or perfect.
Job 28:1, where they **r** gold
Ps. 12:6, silver . . . **r-d** seven times
Zech. 13:9, **R** them as silver
Rev. 3:18, gold **r-d** by fire

re•frain' to hold oneself back from doing or saying something.
Ex. 23:5, you shall **r** from leaving it
Job 30:10, they do not **r** from spitting
1 Cor. 9:6, right to **r** from working
2 Cor. 12:6, I **r** *from this*
1 Pet. 3:10, **R** his tongue from evil

ref'uge shelter or protection, as from danger or distress.
Judg. 9:15, come and take **r** in my shade
2 Sam. 22:3, God, my rock, in whom I take **r**
Ps. 46:1, God is our **r** and strength
Is. 17:10, remembered the rock of your **r**
Is. 33:16, His **r** will be the impregnable rock

re•fute' to prove to be false.
Job 32:12, no one who **r-d** Job
Titus 1:9, **r** those who contradict

Re•ho•bo'am Son and successor of Solomon. The ten tribes of Israel, under Jeroboam, revolted from him (1 Kin. 11:43; chapters 12, 14; 15:6).

re•joice' to give joy to; to gladden.
Prov. 5:18, **r** in the wife of your youth
Matt. 2:10, they **r-d** exceedingly
Matt. 5:12, **R**, and be glad

Re'kem A king of Midian, slain by Phinehas when in the plains of Moab (Num. 31:8; Josh. 13:21).

re•mem'brance the act of recollecting, keeping in mind so as to give attention to.
Eccl. 1:11, no **r** of earlier things
Is. 26:14, wiped out all **r** of them
Mal. 3:16, a book of **r** was written
Luke 22:19, do this in **r** of Me
1 Cor. 11:25, drink *it,* in **r** of Me

rem'nant that which remains or is left over.
Deut. 3:11, the **r** of the Rephaim
Jer. 6:9, glean as the vine the **r** of Israel
Jer. 23:3, I Myself shall gather the **r**
Mal. 2:15, who has a **r** of the Spirit
Rom. 11:5, **r** according to *God's* gracious choice

re•mote' out of the way; secluded; far off in place or time.
Neh. 1:9, most **r** part of the heavens

rend to tear apart with force; to split.
1 Kin. 19:11, strong wind was **r-ing** the mountains
Is. 64:1, Thou wouldst **r** the heavens
Joel 2:13, And **r** your heart

re•pent' to turn from sin and dedicate oneself to the amendment of one's life.
Job 42:6, **r** in dust and ashes
Matt. 3:2, **R**, for the kingdom of
Mark 1:15, **r** and believe in the gospel
Mark 6:12, preached that *men* should **r**
Acts 26:20, **r** and turn to God

re•pent'ance a feeling of regret or sorrow for sin and turning from that sin to a better way of life.
Mark 1:4, a baptism of **r**
Luke 24:47, **r** for forgiveness of sins
2 Cor. 7:10, God produces a **r** without regret
Heb. 6:1, laying . . . foundation of **r**
2 Pet. 3:9, all to come to **r**

Reph'a·im 1. A race dwelling around the south of Jerusalem (Gen. 14:5; 15:20). 2. A valley southwest of Jerusalem and north of Bethlehem was the boundary between Judah and Benjamin (Josh. 15:8; 2 Sam. 5:18, 22).

Reph'i·dim The last camp of the Israelites before reaching Sinai. It was here the people murmured for water, and Moses, striking a rock by divine command, supplied their need (Ex. 17:1-6; Num. 33:14).

re·proach' a cause for shame; censure; a rebuke.
Jer. 29:18. a hissing, and a **r**
Ezek. 5:14. a **r** among the nations
Matt. 11:20, He began to **r** the cities
Titus 2:8, speech which is beyond **r**
Heb. 11:26, considering the **r** of Christ

rep'ro·bate a complete scoundrel; unworthy, unacceptable person.
Ps. 15:4, a **r** is despised

re·prove' to scold; to censure.
Job 5:17, the man whom God **r-s**
Prov. 3:12, whom the LORD loves He **r-s**
Matt. 18:15, **r** him in private
2 Tim. 4:2, **r**, rebuke, exhort, with . . . patience
Rev. 3:19, I love, I **r** and discipline

rep·u·ta'tion the character of a person as seen or judged by people in general.
Acts 6:3, seven men of good **r**
1 Tim. 5:10, having a **r** for good works

re·pute' the state of being favorably known, spoken of, or esteemed.
Phil. 4:8, whatever is of good **r**

res'o·lute·ly firmly; steadfastly; not to be moved from one's purpose.
1 Chr. 28:7, **r** performs My
Luke 9:51, He **r** set His face to go

res·ti·tu'tion the restoring of anything to its rightful owner.
Lev. 6:5, he shall make **r** for it
2 Sam. 12:6, make **r** for the lamb

res·ur·rec'tion the rising from the dead.
Matt. 22:23, say there is no **r**
Luke 14:14, at the **r** of the righteous
Luke 20:36, being sons of the **r**
Acts 24:21, For the **r** of the dead
1 Pet. 1:3, living hope through the **r**

ret·ri·bu'tion something given in payment for an offense; punishment.
Deut. 32:35, Vengeance is Mine, and **r**
Hos. 9:7, days of **r** have come
Rom. 11:9, stumbling block and a **r**

Re'u A son of Peleg, the fourth from Shem, and father of Serug (Gen. 11:18-21; 1 Chr. 1:25).

Reu'ben 1. The eldest son of Jacob and Leah (Gen. 29:32). 2. This name is frequently applied to the tribe descended from Reuben (Num. 1:5; Deut. 27:13).

rev'el to be gay and noisy.
2 Pet. 2:13, to **r** in the daytime

rev·e·la'tion a revealing to others of something previously unknown to them; a disclosure.
Rom. 16:25, the **r** of the mystery
1 Cor. 1:7, awaiting eagerly the **r**
Gal. 1:12, through a **r** of Jesus Christ
Gal. 2:2, because of a **r** that I went up
Eph. 1:17, spirit of wisdom and of **r**

re·venge' desire to return evil for evil.
Jer. 20:10, take our **r** on him
Ezek. 25:15, Philistines have acted in **r**
Rom. 12:19, Never take your own **r**

re·vere' to honor and respect.
Lev. 19:30, **r** My sanctuary
Zeph. 3:7, Surely you will **r** Me

rev'er·ence honor and respect mixed with love and awe.
Job 15:4, you do away with **r**
Ps. 2:11, Worship the LORD with **r**
Ps. 5:7, bow in **r** for Thee
Heb. 11:7, in **r** prepared an ark
Heb. 12:28, service with **r** and awe

re·vile' to subject to abuse by loud scolding.
Ps. 74:10, will the adversary **r**
Acts 23:4, Do you **r** God's high priest
1 Cor. 4:12, when we are **r-d**, we bless
1 Pet. 2:23, being **r-d**, He did not **r**

Re'zin 1. The last king of Aram, in the days of Jotham (2 Kin. 15:37; Is. 7:1, 4, 8). 2. One of the Nethinim whose descendants returned from Babylon with Zerubbabel (Ezra 2:48; Neh. 7:50).

Rib'lah A city in the northeastern part of Canaan (Num. 34:11; 2 Kin. 23:33).

right'eous·ness moral good; justice.
Ps. 97:6, heavens declare His **r**
Jer. 23:6, The LORD our **r**
Dan. 12:3, lead the many to **r**
Matt. 5:6, hunger and thirst for **r**
1 Tim. 6:11, pursue **r**

rogue a dishonest person; a scamp; a cheat.
Is. 32:5, **r** be spoken of *as* generous

Ro'mans A people named for their chief city, Rome (John 11:48; Acts 16:21; 22:25-27).

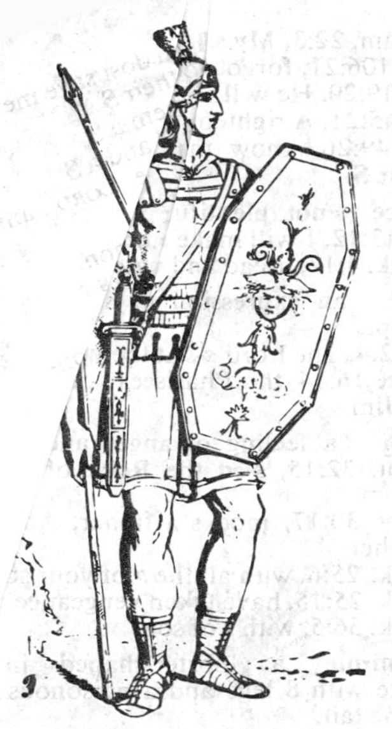
Roman soldier

Rome The capital of Italy (Acts 2: 10; 18:2; 28:16; Rom. 1:7; 2 Tim. 1:17).

route to arrange and direct the course or procedure of.
Judg. 4:15, Lord **r-d** Sisera
2 Sam. 22:15, Lightning, and **r-d** them
Ps. 18:14, flashes in abundance, and **r-d** them

ruth'less having no pity; cruel; showing no mercy.
Job 15:20, stored up for the **r**
Is. 25:3, Cities of **r** nations
Ezek. 28:7, most **r** of the nations

S

Sab'bath the divinely instituted day of rest, ordained for all men.
Ex. 20:8, Remember the **s** day
Lev. 25:8, count off seven **s-s** of years
Matt. 12:8, is Lord of the **S**
Mark 2:27, **S** was made for man
Mark 3:4, on the **S** to do good

sa'cred set apart in honor of someone, or a god; holy.
2 Kin. 12:18, Jehoash . . . took all the **s** things
2 Tim. 3:15, have known the **s** writings

sac'ri•fice the act or ceremony of making an offering to God, especially on an altar.
Ps. 51:17, **s-s** of God are a broken spirit
Rom. 12:1, bodies a living and holy **s**
1 Cor. 10:20, they **s** to demons
Phil. 4:18, an acceptable **s**, well-pleasing
Heb. 9:26, put away sin by the **s** of Himself

Sad'du•cees A sect of the Jews, who, in the time of Christ, were a small but powerful sect, very wealthy and in high position (Matt. 22:23; Acts 23:8).

saint one set apart for the service of God; the word is used by Paul as applying to all Christians.
Rom. 1:7, called *as* **s-s**
Rom. 8:27, He intercedes for the **s-s**
1 Cor. 6:2, **s-s** will judge the world
Eph. 2:19, fellow citizens with the **s-s**
Phil. 1:1, all the **s-s** in Christ Jesus

Sal'mon The father of Boaz, husband of Ruth, and great-grandfather of Jesse, father of David (Ruth 4:20, 21; Matt. 1:4, 5).

sal•va'tion the saving of a person from sin.
Ps. 27:1, LORD is my light and my **s**
Is. 59:17, helmet of **s** on His head
Luke 2:30, my eyes have seen Thy **s**
Acts 16:17, proclaiming to you the way of **s**
1 Thess. 5:9, obtaining **s** through our Lord

Sa•ma'ri•a 1. A hill and city in Ephraim, the capital of the ten tribes of Israel, 42 miles north of Jerusalem (1 Kin. 16:24; 2 Kin. 1:2). 2. The territory or kingdom of the Samaritans (2 Kin. 17:24-41).

Sa•mar'i•tans The inhabitants of the central province of Palestine, or Ephraim. They would hold no fellowship with the Jews, yet many of them gladly received the Gospel (Matt. 10:5; Luke 9:52).

Sam'son A Danite, son of Manoah. His great strength enabled him to kill a lion, thirty Philistines, to break the strongest bands, to smite 1,000 men, to carry off the gates of Gaza, and at last to pull down the house of Dagon (Judges chapters 14-16).

Sam'u•el A Levite, son of Elkanah and Hannah. The last of the judges and the first of the prophets (after Moses). The events of his life are recorded in 1 Samuel beginning with 1:20.

San•bal'lat A Horonite, an enemy of the Jews who opposed Nehemiah (Neh. 2:10; 4:1; 13:28).

sanc'ti•fy to set apart as sacred, to consecrate.
Lev. 22:32, I am the LORD who **s-es**
John 10:36, whom the Father **s-ed**
John 17:17, **S** them in the truth
Rom. 15:16, **s-ed** by the Holy Spirit
1 Thess. 5:23, God of peace . . . **s** you entirely

sanc'ti•ty holiness or saintliness.
1 Tim. 2:15, faith and love and **s**

sanc'tu•ary a holy or sacred place.
Ex. 25:8, let them construct a **s** for Me
Lev. 19:30, revere My **s**; I am the LORD
Ps. 150:1, Praise God in His **s**
Is. 60:13, beautify the place of My **s**
Heb. 8:2, a minister in the **s**

san'dal a sole of leather fastened to the foot by a strap.
Song 7:1, beautiful are your feet in **s-s**
Mark 6:9, but to wear **s-s**

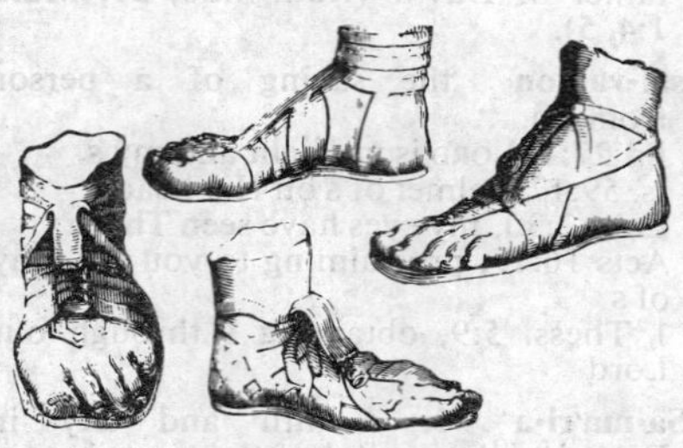

Sandals

Sa'tan the evil spirit that tempts men to sin, the Devil.
Matt. 16:23, Get behind Me, **S**
Mark 1:13, forty days being tempted by **S**
Luke 10:18, watching **S** fall from heaven
Acts 5:3, why has **S** filled your heart
Rom. 16:20, crush **S** under your feet

sa'ti•ate to fill beyond natural desire.
Is. 34:5, My sword is **s-d**
Jer. 46:10, sword will devour and be **s-d**

sa'tyr a forest god (demon) in Greek mythology, having a horse's or goat's ears and tail, and given to boisterous pleasures.
2 Chr. 11:15, he set up priests . . . for the **s-s**

Saul 1. A Benjaminite, son of Kish, and the first king of Israel (1 Sam. 9:3; 11:15). 2. The original name of Paul, an apostle of Jesus (Acts 7:58; 8:1, 3; *9:1)*.

Sav'ior one who saves from ruin or danger.
2 Sam. 22:3, My **s**, Thou dost save me
Ps. 106:21, forgot God their **S**
Is. 19:20, He will send [illegible] **S**
Is. 45:21, A righteous God and a **S**
Is. 49:26, know that I, the LORD, am your **S**

scarce not plentiful; unco[illegible]
Is. 13:12, I will make mortal [illegible]
Ezek. 4:17, bread and water wi[illegible]

scoff an expression of scorn [illegible] tempt.
Ps. 2:4, The Lord **s-s** at them
Luke 16:14, the Pharisees . . . were [illegible] at Him

scorn a feeling of anger and disgu[illegible]
Deut. 32:15, **s-ed** the Rock of his sal vation
Prov. 30:17, mocks a father, And **s-s** a mother
Ezek. 25:6, with all the **s** of your soul
Ezek. 25:15, have taken vengeance with **s**
Ezek. 36:5, with **s** of soul

scor'pi•on a lobster-shaped invertebrate with 8 legs and a poisonous sting in the tail.
Luke 11:12, he will not give him a **s**
Rev. 9:5, like the torment of a **s** when it stings

Scorpion

scourge to whip; to lash; to flog.
Job 5:21, hidden from the **s** of the tongue
Matt. 10:17, **s** you in their synagogues
Matt. 20:19, mock and **s** and crucify *Him*
Heb. 12:6, **s-s** every son whom He receives

scribe a person who copies writing; an official writer acting usually as a clerk.
Matt. 2:4, chief priests and **s-s** of the people

Matt. 23:13, woe to you, **s-s** and Pharisees
Mark 1:22, authority, and not as **s-s**
Mark 12:38, Beware of the **s-s**
1 Cor. 1:20, Where is the **s**

Scrip'ture(s) the books of the Old and New Testament, or of either of them.
Matt. 21:42, Did you never read in the **S-s**
Luke 4:21, Today this **S** has been fulfilled
John 20:9, they did not understand the **S**
Rom. 4:3, For what does the **S** say
2 Tim. 3:16, All **S** is inspired by God

scroll a roll of paper or parchment, especially one on which something is written or engraved.
Jer. 36:2, Take a **s** and write
Ezek. 3:1, eat this **s**, and go
Zech. 5:1, behold, *there was* a flying **s**

se•cu'ri•ty the state of being secure.
Judg. 18:7, living in **s**

Se'ir 1. A hilly region south of the Dead Sea (Gen. 14:6; Deut. 2:12). 2. The grandfather of Hori, ancestor of the Horites (Gen. 36:20, 21; 1 Chr. 1:38).

self-con•trol' control of one's own feelings or acts.
Acts 24:25, righteousness, **s** . . . judgment
Gal. 5:23, gentleness, **s**

self'ish taking care of one's own interests without regard for those of others.
Phil. 2:3, Do nothing from **s-ness**
James 3:14, 16, jealousy and **s** ambition

sense'less stupid; meaningless; silly.
Ps. 49:10, stupid and the **s** alike perish
Ps. 92:6, **s** man has no knowledge

sen•su•al'i•ty the quality or state of satisfying or pleasing the senses.
Mark 7:22, deceit, **s**, envy, slander
2 Cor. 12:21, **s** which they have practiced
Eph. 4:19, given themselves over to **s**
Rev. 18:3, rich by the wealth of her **s**

sen'tence a decision or judgment.
2 Kin. 25:6, he passed **s** on him
Eccl. 8:11, **s** against an evil deed
Matt. 23:33, escape the **s** of hell
Luke 23:24, Pilate pronounced **s**

ser'pent a snake, especially a large snake.
Gen. 3:1, Now the **s** was more crafty
Num. 21:9, Moses made a bronze **s**
Ps. 58:4, venom of a **s**
2 Cor. 11:3, lest as the **s** deceived Eve
Rev. 12:9, the **s** of old who is called the devil

Seth A son of Adam and Eve, born after the death of Abel (Gen. 4:25, 26; 5:3-8).

shack'les something that confines the legs or arms so as to prevent their free motion.
Mark 5:4, the **s** broken in pieces

shame a painful feeling of guilt caused by having done something wrong, improper or immodest.
Is. 54:4, you will not be put to **s**
Zeph. 3:5, the unjust knows no **s**
Acts 5:41, worthy to suffer **s**
2 Cor. 4:2, things hidden because of **s**
Phil. 3:19, glory is in their **s**

Sham'mah 1. A son of Reuel, son of Esau (Gen. 36:13; 1 Chr. 1:37). 2. Third son of Jesse, father of David (1 Sam. 16:9; 17:13).

Shar'on 1. The west of Ephraim and Manasseh, noted for its rich pastures and vegetation (1 Chr. 27:29; Is. 33:9). 2. A plain or city east of Jordan, in Gad (1 Chr. 5:16).

She•al'ti•el Father of Zerubbabel, who led the Jews back from their exile in Babylon (Ezra 3:2, 8; 5:2).

Sheb'na 1. The scribe or secretary of King Hezekiah (Is. 36:3). 2. The treasurer over the house who was to be replaced by Eliakim, son of Hilkiah (Is. 22:15).

Shed'e•ur A Reubenite, father of Elizur, chosen to assist in numbering the people in the days of Moses (Num. 1:5; 2:10; 10:18).

shek'els an ancient unit of weight or money.
Gen. 23:16, four hundred **s** of silver
Josh. 7:21, two hundred **s** of silver
2 Sam. 24:24, threshing floor and the oxen for fifty **s**
Zech. 11:12, weighed out thirty **s**

Shekel of the sanctuary

She'lah Son of Arpachshad, grandson of Shem, and father of Eber (Gen. 10:24; 11:12-15).

She'lah Youngest son of Judah, by the daughter of Shua, the Canaanite (Gen. 38:5; 46:12; Num. 26:20).

She•lu'mi•el The son of Zurishaddai, and a chief of Simeon appointed to assist Moses in numbering the people (Num. 1:6; 2:12; 7:36).

She'ol another name for Hell.
Deut. 32:22, burns to the lowest part of **S**
Job 17:13, look for **S** as my home
Ps. 16:10, not abandon my soul to **S**
Amos 9:2, Though they dig into **S**
Jon. 2:2, help from the depth of **S**

shep'herd (n.) a pastor; one who guards as a shepherd guards his sheep.
Ps. 23:1, The LORD is my **s**
Is. 40:11, Like a **s** He will tend His flock
Zech. 11:16, I am going to raise up a **s**
Matt. 9:36, like sheep without a **s**
John 10:11, I am the good **s**

shep'herd (v.) to herd, lead, or drive as one does sheep; the care and feeding of.
Ps. 78:72, he **s-ed** them
Matt. 2:6, who will **s** My people
John 21:16, **S** My sheep
Acts 20:28, to **s** the church of God
1 Pet. 5:2, **s** the flock of God

Sher•e•bi'ah A priest of the family of Mahli the Merarite. He assisted Ezra in reading the law to the people (Ezra 8:18; Neh. 8:7).

Shi'nar Babylonia in its fullest extent. Its chief cities were Babylon, Erech, Accad, and Calneh (Gen. 10:10; Is. 11:11; Dan. 1:2).

Shi'shak King of the twenty-second Bubastic dynasty in Egypt. He protected Jeroboam against Solomon (1 Kin. 11:40; 14:25; 2 Chr. 12:2).

Shit'tim A place in Moab, east of the Dead Sea, whence Joshua sent forth spies (Num. 25:1; Josh. 2:1).

Sho'bab 1. A son of David born after he became king of Israel (2 Sam. 5:14; 1 Chr. 3:5). 2. A son of Caleb, son of Hezron (1 Chr. 2:18).

shrewd sharp-witted, keen, and clever.
2 Sam. 13:3, Jonadab was a very **s** man
Job 5:13, wise by their own **s-ness**
Matt. 10:16, be **s** as serpents
Luke 16:8, sons of this age are more **s**

shrine A word used to designate small models of the temple of Diana, containing an image of the goddess (Ezek. 16:24; Acts 19:24).

Shu'ah A son of Abraham and Keturah (Gen. 25:2; 1 Chr. 1:32).

Shu'hite Descendant of Shuah, son of Keturah (Job 2:11; 8:1; 42:9).

shun to avoid deliberately.
Eccl. 3:5, time to **s** embracing

Shu'nam•mite Female inhabitant of Shunem (1 Kin. 1:3; 2:17).

Shur A desert reaching from the east border of Egypt as far as the habitations of Amalek and Ishmael (Gen. 16:7; 20:1; Ex. 15:22).

sick'le an agricultural tool with a sharp, curved metal blade and a short handle.
Deut. 16:9, put the **s** to the standing grain
Joel 3:13, Put in the **s** . . . harvest is ripe
Rev. 14:15, Put in your **s** and reap

Si'don 1. The eldest son of Canaan, son of Ham (Gen. 10:15). 2. The city founded by Sidon. It was once visited by Jesus and some of its inhabitants went to hear His preaching (Matt. 15:21; Mark 3:8).

si'lence the state of keeping or being silent.
Ps. 62:1, My soul *waits* in **s** for God
Titus 1:11, who must be **s-d**
Rev. 8:1, there was **s** in heaven

sin a breaking of God's law or will.
Ps. 51:3, my **s** is ever before me
Prov. 14:9, Fools mock at **s**
Is. 1:18, your **s-s** are as scarlet
Matt. 1:21, save His people from their **s-s**
1 Cor. 15:56, sting of death is **s**

sin'ner one who sins, especially habitually or without repentance.
Ps. 1:1, stand in the path of **s-s**
Matt. 9:10, tax-gatherers and **s-s**
Mark 2:17, to call *the* righteous, but **s-s**
Luke 15:7, *more* joy in heaven over one **s**
Luke 18:13, be merciful to me, the **s**

Si'on The peak of Mount Hermon (Deut. 4:48).

sit'u•at•ed located, placed or fixed.
Ps. 144:15, people who are so **s**
Nah. 3:8, was **s** by the waters of the Nile

slan'der a statement tending to injure the reputation of another and deliberately made with this intention.
Ps. 15:3, He does not **s**
Prov. 30:10, Do not **s** a slave to his master

1 Cor. 4:13, when we are **s-ed,** we try to conciliate
2 Cor. 12:20, disputes, **s-s,** gossip
Eph. 4:31, and **s** be put away from you

slaugh'ter the butchering of animals for sacrifice or for food.
Ps. 44:22, as sheep to be **s-ed**
Is. 53:7, lamb that is led to **s**
Rom. 8:36, as sheep to be **s-ed**
James 5:5, in a day of **s**

slave a person who is owned by another and can be sold at his master's will.
Ex. 23:12, son of your female **s**
Prov. 22:7, borrower *becomes* the lender's **s**
Matt. 25:21, Well done . . . faithful **s**
1 Cor. 7:21, Were you called while a **s**
Gal. 4:7, no longer a **s**, but a son

slay to kill.
Job 5:2, vexation **s-s** the foolish man
Job 13:15, Though He **s** me, I will hope
Ps. 34:21, Evil shall **s** the wicked
2 Thess. 2:8, the Lord will **s** with the breath of

sledge a machine used in threshing grain; a strong, heavy vehicle with or without runners used for carrying heavy loads.
Is. 28:27, threshed with a threshing **s**
Is. 41:15, a new, sharp threshing **s**

slew past tense of slay; killed.
2 Chr. 22:8, ministering to Ahaziah, and **s** them
Matt. 2:16, **s** all the male children

sling an instrument for throwing stones that consists of a short strap with strings fastened to its ends and is whirled round to discharge its missile by centrifugal force.
1 Sam. 17:40, his **s** was in his hand
1 Sam. 17:50, prevailed over the Philistine with a **s** and a stone

sloth'ful lazy; sluggish.
Prov. 12:27, **s** man does not roast his prey

slum'ber to sleep.
Job 33:15, they **s** in their beds
Ps. 121:3, who keeps you will not **s**
Ps. 132:4, **s** to my eyelids
Prov. 6:10, A little sleep, a little **s**
Is. 5:27, None **s-s** or sleeps

smelt to melt or fuse, as ore, usually in order to separate the metal.
Job 28:2, from rock copper is **s-ed**
Is. 1:25, **s** away from your dross as with lye

sneer to smile with a contemptuous expression.
Luke 23:35, the rulers were **s-ing**

So'dom A city on the shore of the Dead Sea, destroyed in the days of Abraham and Lot (Gen. 10:19; 13:12, 13; 19:1-29; Luke 17:29).

so'journ to dwell temporarily.
Gen. 26:3, **S** in this land
Ex. 12:48, if a stranger **s-s** with you
2 Kin. 8:1, **s** wherever you can **s**
Ezek. 20:38, land where they **s**

so'journ•er a foreigner or alien who is in the act of a temporary stay.
Ex. 2:22, I have been a **s** in a foreign land
Ex. 12:45, A **s** or a hired servant
Ps. 39:12, A **s** like all my fathers

Sol'o•mon The tenth and last son of David, second by Bathsheba, and the third king of Israel. He was noted for his wisdom, and also for his great wealth (1 Kings chapters 1-11).

sor'did filthy and dirty.
Titus 1:11, for the sake of **s** gain

A sling

spec•u•la'tions to give thought or meditation; questions.
Rom. 1:21, futile in their **s**
2 Cor. 10:5, *We are* destroying **s**
2 Tim. 2:23, foolish and ignorant **s**

spelt an inferior kind of wheat.
Ezek. 4:9, beans, lentils, millet and **s**

spir'it a force within man which moves his body with life, energy and power; the soul.
Ps. 31:5, Into Thy hand I commit my s
Eccl. 12:7, the s will return to God
Matt. 5:3, Blessed are the poor in s
Mark 14:38, s is willing, but
Acts 18:25, being fervent in s

splen'dor brilliance or magnificence and glory.
Ps. 8:1, hast displayed Thy s
Ps. 96:6, **S** and majesty are before Him
Ezek. 16:14, it was perfect because of My s
Ezek. 27:10, they set forth your s

spurned to kick aside; rejected with contempt.
Deut. 32:19, the LORD saw *this* and s *them*
Ps. 10:13, Why has the wicked s God
Ps. 107:11, s the counsel of the Most High
Prov. 1:30, They s all my reproof

squan'dered spent foolishly or wasted.
Luke 15:13, s his estate

sta·bil'i·ty the quality or condition of being stable.
Is. 33:6, He shall be the s of your times
Col. 2:5, s of your faith

stat'ure the natural height of a person.
1 Sam. 16:7, the height of his s
1 Chr. 11:23, an Egyptian, a man of *great* s
Luke 2:52, increasing in wisdom and s
Luke 19:3, he was small in s

stat'ute a man-made law.
Gen. 26:5, My **s-s** and My laws
Ex. 29:9, priesthood by a perpetual s
Lev. 18:5, you shall keep My **s-s**
Ps. 119:12, Teach me Thy **s-s**
Mal. 3:7, turned aside from My **s-s**

stead'fast firmly established.
Job. 11:15, you would be s
Ps. 51:10, renew a s spirit within me
Ps. 57:7, My heart is **s,** O God
Ps. 112:7, His heart is **s,** trusting

stealth sly or underhanded action.
2 Sam. 19:3, people went by s
Matt. 26:4, seize Jesus by s
Mark 14:1, to seize Him by s

stew'ard a manager of a large home or estate.
Gen. 43:19, near to Joseph's house s
Luke 12:42, faithful and sensible s
1 Cor. 4:1, **s-s** of the mysteries of God
1 Cor. 4:2, it is required of **s-s**

stew'ard·ship the office, duties, and obligations of a steward.
Luke 16:2, an account of your s
1 Cor. 9:17, I have a s entrusted to me
Eph. 3:2, the s of God's grace
Col. 1:25, according to the s from God

stink'weed any of various strong-scented plants.
Job 31:40, And s instead of barley

straight·for'ward spoken frankly and openly.
Gal. 2:14, not s about the truth

strait narrow; strict.
1 Sam. 13:6, they were in a s

stra·te'gic of or relating to strategy.
Mark 6:21, a s day came when Herod

stray to wander away from.
Prov. 7:25, not s into her paths
James 5:19, any among you **s-s** from the truth
1 Pet. 2:25, **s-ing** like sheep

strength'en to make or become stronger
1 Sam. 30:6, David **s-ed** himself
Is. 35:3, s the feeble
Luke 22:32, s your brothers
2 Thess. 2:17, s your hearts in every
1 Pet. 5:10, confirm, s *and* establish you

strike to injure or destroy.
Ex. 7:17, I will s the water
Ex. 12:12, s down all the first-born
Ps. 91:12, s your foot
Matt. 26:31, I will s down the shepherd
Acts 23:3, God is going to s you

strong'hold a fortified place.
2 Sam. 5:9, David lived in the s
1 Chr. 11:5, David captured the s of Zion
Ps. 9:9, s in times of trouble
Ps. 59:9, For God is my **s**
Ps. 94:22, the LORD has been my s

stum'bling block something that makes one stumble; a hindrance.
Ezek. 18:30, not become a **s**
Matt. 16:23, Satan! You are a s to Me
Matt. 18:7, Woe . . . because of *its* **s-s**
Gal. 5:11, the s of the cross

stu'por a condition in which the senses or feelings are dulled.
Rom. 11:8, gave them a spirit of s

sub'mis·sive inclined or willing to submit to others; yielding.
1 Tim. 2:11, instruction with . . . **s-ness**
1 Pet. 2:18, be s to your masters
1 Pet. 3:1, be s to your own husbands

sub·sid'ed to become quiet or to grow less.
Gen. 8:1, and the water s
Judg. 8:3, their anger . . . s

suf·fi'cient enough; as much as is needed.
Ex. 36:7, material they had was **s**
Lev. 25:47, means of a stranger . . . becomes **s**
John 6:7, denarii worth of bread is not **s**
2 Cor. 12:9, My grace is **s** for you

su·pe·ri·or'i·ty the quality or state of being superior.
1 Cor. 2:1, not come with **s** of speech

sup·plants' to take another's place, as by force or trickery.
Prov. 30:23, maidservant . . . **s** her mistress

sup·pli·ca'tion the act of supplicating; earnest, urgent, humble entreaty.
Ex. 9:28, Make **s** to the LORD
Ps. 28:2, Hear the voice of my **s-s**
Dan. 9:3, seek *Him by* prayer and **s-s**

sur·mise' to infer without proof; to guess.
Acts 27:27, sailors *began* to **s**

Su'sa A city in Elam, on the river Ulai, the seat of the Persian government (Neh. 1:1; Esth. 1:2; Dan. 8:2).

swin'dler one who gets money or property by fraud or deceit.
Luke 18:11, not like other people: **s-s**
1 Cor. 5:11, a drunkard, or a **s**
1 Cor. 6:10, nor **s-s**, shall inherit

syn'a·gogue a Jewish house of worship.
Matt. 6:2, the **s-s** and in the streets
Matt. 6:5, pray in the **s-s** and on
Matt. 12:9, He went into their **s**
Matt. 13:54, teaching them in their **s**
John 16:2, make you outcasts from the **s**

Syr'i·a A country along the east coast of the Mediterranean and extending far inland. It comprehended most of the regions known in the Old Testament times as Canaan and Aram (Luke 2:2; Acts 15:41).

Syr'i·an One of the Syrian race, or an inhabitant of Syria (Luke 4:27).

T

Ta'a·nach A royal city of the Canaanites, west of the Jordan. It was captured by Joshua (Josh. 12:21; 17:11; Judg. 1:27; 1 Kin. 4:12).

tab'er·na·cle a tent; a structure of wood hung with curtains, used in worship by the Jews in their wanderings under Moses.
Ex. 26:1, **t** with ten curtains
Matt. 17:4, make three **t-s** here
Rev. 21:3, **t** of God is among men

Ta'bor An isolated mountain near the plains of Jezreel, six miles southeast of Nazareth, in the midst of Galilee (Josh. 19:22; Ps. 89:12; Jer. 46:18).

Tah'pen·es Queen of Pharaoh, king of Egypt, in the days of Solomon (1 Kin. 11:19, 20).

Tal'mai 1. A son of Anak, in Hebron, in the days of Joshua (Num. 13:22; Josh. 15:14). 2. A king of Geshur, and father of Maacah, one of David's wives (2 Sam. 3:3; 13:37).

Tal'mon A Levite in Jerusalem in the day of Ezra (1 Chr. 9:17; Ezra 2:42).

Tar'sus The birthplace of Paul the apostle (Acts 9:11, 30; 11:25).

taunt to tease with insults or to ridicule and mock.
Deut. 28:37, a **t** among all the people
Job 30:9, now I have become their **t**
Is. 14:4, you will take up this **t**
Jer. 24:9, a **t** and a curse in all places
Mic. 2:4, take up against you a **t**

tax-gath'er·er one who gathers or collects the taxes.
Matt. 5:46, even the **t-s** do the same
Matt. 10:3, Matthew the **t**
Luke 18:13, **t**, standing some distance away

Te·ko'a 1. A city in Judah, six miles southeast of Bethlehem, and twelve miles south of Jerusalem (2 Sam. 14:2, 4, 9). 2. A descendant of Hezron, grandson of Judah (1 Chr. 2:24; 4:5).

Te'ma 1. A son of Ishmael, and his posterity at the Persian Gulf (Gen. 25:15; 1 Chr. 1:30). 2. A city on the north of Arabia, near the desert of Syria (Job 6:19, Is. 21:14, Jer. 25:23).

tem'per a disposition or frame of mind; calmness and self-control; or a state of anger.
Prov. 29:11, A fool . . . loses his **t**

tem'per·ate showing self-control and restraint.
1 Tim. 3:2, the husband of one wife, **t**,
Titus 2:2, Older men are to be **t**

tem'pest a high wind, especially with rain, snow or hail.
Job 9:17, He bruises me with a **t**
Ps. 55:8, From the stormy winds *and* **t**
Is. 28:2, a **t** of destruction
Amos 1:14, a storm on the day of **t**

tem'ple a building for worship.
2 Sam. 22:7, from His **t** He heard my voice
Ps. 11:4, LORD is in His holy **t**

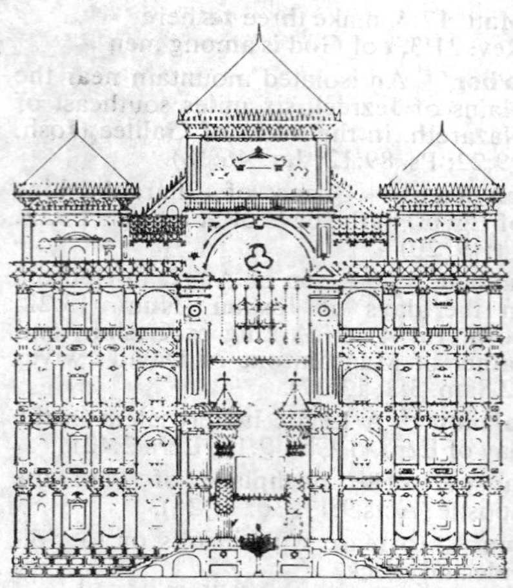

Solomon's temple, front view, after Schick (1896)

Is. 6:4, **t** was filling with smoke
Matt. 12:6, something greater than the **t**
Luke 23:45, veil of the **t** was torn

temp·ta′tion a tempting or a being tempted.
Matt. 6:13, do not lead us into **t**
Matt. 26:41, you may not enter into **t**
Luke 8:13, time of **t** fall away
1 Cor. 10:13, No **t** has overtaken you
2 Pet. 2:9, rescue the godly from **t**

Te′rah Son of Nahor, and father of Abraham (Gen. 11:24-28; Josh. 24:2).

Ter′a·phim Small images resembling the human figure and regarding as household gods (2 Kin. 23:24).

tes′ti·fy to make a solemn statement of what is personally known or believed to be true.
Lev. 5:1, public adjuration to **t**
Acts 2:40, many other words he . . . **t-ed**
Acts 20:24, to **t** solemnly of the gospel
Acts 26:22, **t-ing** both to small and great

tes′ti·mo′ny an open profession or declaration, as of one's religious faith.
Num. 35:30, **t** of one witness
Ps. 19:7, **t** of the Lord is sure
Matt. 8:4, the offering . . . for a **t**
Luke 22:71, need do we have of **t**
John 8:17, the **t** of two men is true
1 Cor. 1:6, **t** concerning Christ was confirmed

thanks·giv′ing the act of giving thanks, especially to God by form of prayer expressing gratitude.
Ps. 26:7, with the voice of **t**
Ps. 95:2, before His presence with **t**
Ps. 100:4, Enter His gates with **t**
Phil. 4:6, supplication with **t**

this′tle a tall, prickly herb with spiny-margined leaves and tight heads of yellowish and purplish flowers.
Is. 34:13, Nettles and **t-s** in its fortified cities
Hos. 10:8, Thorn and **t** will grow on their altars
Matt. 7:16, figs from **t-s**

Thom′as One of the twelve apostles of Jesus, and called also Didymus (Matt. 10:3; Mark 3:18; John 20:24-29).

thrash to go over again and again.
Judg. 8:7, **t** your bodies with the thorns

thresh to beat out grain from straw.
Deut. 25:4, while he is **t-ing**
2 Sam. 24:21, To buy the **t-ing** floor
1 Chr. 21:20, Ornan was **t-ing** wheat
Is. 21:10, O my **t-ed** *people*

thresh′old the sill of a door or an entrance.
Judg. 19:27, with her hands on the **t**
1 Sam. 5:5, on the **t** of Dagon
1 Kin. 14:17, entering the **t** of the house
Ps. 84:10, stand at the **t** of the house
Ezek. 9:3, **t** of the temple

thrive to succeed by hand work, thrift and good management.
Job 8:16, He **t-s** before the sun

throng a great number assembled together; a crowd.
Ps. 55:14, in the house of God in the **t**
Luke 6:17, a great **t** of people

thwart to oppose or baffle, as a purpose.
2 Sam. 15:34, you can **t** the counsel
2 Sam. 17:14, ordained to **t** the good counsel
1 Thess. 2:18, Satan **t-ed** us

tid′ings a piece of news; a message.
Ps. 112:7, He will not fear evil **t**
Rom. 10:15, bring glad **t** of good things

Tim′nah A city in Judah, between Ekron and Beth-shemesh (Josh. 15:10; 2 Chr. 28:18).

Tim′o·thy A favorite disciple of Paul, first mentioned in Acts, where he is described as the son of a Greek, by a Jewish mother (Acts 16:1; 17:14; 2 Tim. 1:2).

Tish′bite An inhabitant of Tisbeh (Tesheb), supposed to have been in Gilead (1 Kin. 17:1; 21:17, 28).

tithe a tenth part of one's income paid as a contribution to church or charity.
Lev. 27:30, all the **t** of the land
Num. 18:26, take from . . . Israel the **t**
Num. 18:28, offering to the LORD from your **t-s**
Matt. 23:23, you **t** mint and dill
Luke 11:42, you pay **t** of mint and rue

Ti'tus A Greek disciple who accompanied Paul in several of his journeys (Gal. 2:1; 2 Tim. 4:10; Titus 1:4).

To•gar'mah A son of Gomer, son of Japheth (Gen. 10:3; 1 Chr. 1:6).

tomb a grave.
Is. 22:16, you have hewn a **t** for
John 11:17, been in the **t** four days
John 19:41, in the garden a new **t**, in which
John 20:11, standing outside the **t** weeping
Rev. 11:9, bodies to be laid in a **t**

To'pheth A place in the valley of Hinnom where human sacrifices were offered to Molech and the dead bodies buried or consumed (2 Kin. 23:10; Jer. 7:31).

tor•ment' to distress with intense physical suffering or mental anguish.
Job 19:2, How long will you **t** me
Luke 8:28, do not **t** me
Luke 16:23, Hades . . . being in **t**
Luke 16:28, to this place of **t**
Rev. 9:5, **t** was like the **t** of a scorpion

tot'ter to shake, tremble, or rock as if about to fall.
Ps. 62:3, like a **t-ing** fence
Is. 24:20, it **t-s** like a shack
Is. 28:7, They **t** *when rendering* judgment

tram'ple to tramp or tread heavily so as to bruise, crush, or injure.
Job 9:8, **t-s** down the waves
Ps. 91:13, you will **t** down
Prov. 25:26, *Like* a **t-d** spring
Hab. 3:12, didst **t** the nations
Matt. 7:6, they **t** them under their feet

tran•scribe' to write a copy of.
Prov. 25:1, proverbs . . . king of Judah **t-d**

trans•form' to change in outward appearance.
Rom. 12:2, **t-ed** by the renewing of
Phil. 3:21, who will **t** the body

trans•gress' to sin; to break the law.
Num. 14:41, Why then are you **t-ing**
Josh. 7:11, they have also **t-ed**
Jer. 2:8, rulers also **t-ed**
Ezek. 20:38, those who **t** against me
Matt. 15:2, Your disciples **t** the tradition

trans•gres'sion a violation of a law; a sin.
Job 14:17, My **t** is sealed up
Job 33:9, pure, without **t**
Ps. 32:1, he whose **t** is forgiven
Matt. 6:14, forgive men for their **t-s**
Col. 2:13, forgiven us all our **t-s**

treach'er•ous guilty of faithless behavior toward someone or something one is supposed to aid.
2 Sam. 18:13, if I had dealt **t-ly** against his life
Prov. 2:22, the **t** will be uprooted
Prov. 13:15, way of the **t** is hard
Is. 21:2, The **t** one still deals **t-ly**

tres'pass to go beyond what is lawful, just, or right.
Gal. 6:1, if a man is caught in any **t**
Eph. 2:1, dead in your **t-s** and sins

tribe a group of people who believe themselves to come from a common stock and who act as a unit, often under a chief.
Gen. 49:28, these are the twelve **t-s**
Num. 1:4, a man of each **t**
Ps. 122:4, even the **t-s** of the LORD
Matt. 24:30, all the **t-s** of the earth
Luke 22:30, judging the twelve **t-s**

trib•u•la'tion distress caused by trouble or sorrow.
Matt. 24:21, will be a great **t**
John 16:33, world you have **t**
Rom. 5:3, **t** brings about perseverance
Rom. 12:12, persevering in **t**
Eph. 3:13, not to lose heart at my **t-s**

tri•bu'nal the seat of a judge.
Acts 25:10, standing before Caesar's **t**

trib'ute a payment made by one ruler or nation to another to show submission or to secure peace or protection.
Deut. 16:10, a **t** of a freewill offering
1 Chr. 18:2, servants to David, bringing **t**
2 Chr. 17:11, silver as **t** to Jehoshaphat
Ezra 7:24, impose tax, **t** or toll
Esth. 10:1, King Ahasuerus laid a **t**

tri'umph a state of joy or exultation for a success or victory.
Ex. 32:18, sound of the cry of **t**
Ps. 41:11, shout in **t** over me
2 Cor. 2:14, leads us in His **t**

trust'wor•thy worthy of trust.
Prov. 20:6, who can find a **t** man
1 Tim. 3:1; 4:9, It is a **t** statement

truth sincerity and honesty in character, action, and speech.
1 Kin. 2:4, walk before Me in **t**
Ps. 119:160, Thy word is **t**
Prov. 3:3, not let kindness and **t** leave you
John 8:32, **t** shall make you free
Gal. 2:5, **t** of the gospel might remain

tu'nic an undergarment worn by the ancient Romans, reaching to or below the knees and girdled at the waist.
Gen. 37:3, he made him a varicolored **t**
Lev. 16:4, put on the holy linen **t**
Matt. 10:10, or even two **t-s**
Luke 9:3, have two **t-s** apiece

tur'ban an Eastern headdress for men, consisting of a cap with a scarf wound around it.
Ex. 28:4, a **t** and a sash
Lev. 16:4, attired with the linen **t**
Job 29:14, like a robe and a **t**
Ezek. 21:26, Remove the **t**

tur'moil an utterly confused or extremely agitated state or condition.
Prov. 15:16, great treasure and **t** with it
Jer. 50:34, **t** to the inhabitants

Tych'i•cus A believer in Asia Minor who accompanied Paul to Jerusalem when he left Greece (Eph. 6:21; Col. 4:7; 2 Tim. 4:12; Titus 3:12).

Tyre (Ty'rus) A city in the center of Phoenicia on the coast of the Mediterranean Sea. Paul visited it and spent seven days there (Josh. 19:29; 2 Sam. 5:11; Neh. 13:16; Matt. 11:22; Acts 21:3, 4).

U

U'lai A river surrounding Susa, falling into the Euphrates below its junction with the Tigris (Dan. 8:2, 16).

um'pire a person selected to give a decision on a disputed question.
Job 9:33, There is no **u** between us

un•ap•proach'a•ble not accessible; not easily approached.
1 Tim. 6:16, dwells in **u** light

un•a•ware' not noticing; ignorant.
Ps. 35:8, destruction come upon him **u-s**
Rom. 1:13, do not want you to be **u**

un•be•lief' doubt; skepticism; absence of belief.
Mark 9:24, help *me in* my **u**
Rom. 11:23, continue in their **u**

un•be•liev'er a doubter; one who does not believe.
Luke 12:46, a place with the **u-s**
1 Cor. 14:23, ungifted men or **u-s**
2 Cor. 6:14, bound together with **u-s**
2 Cor. 6:15, believer in common with an **u**
1 Tim. 5:8, worse than an **u**

un•blem'ished without mark or flaw or anything that would make it imperfect.
Num. 19:2, an **unb-ed** red heifer
1 Pet. 1:19, **u** and spotless

un•ceas'ing not ending; without stopping.
Rom. 9:2, sorrow and **u** grief

un'cle Brother of a parent (Lev. 10:4; 1 Sam. 10:14-16).

un•de•filed' without filth, corrupt, or dishonor.
Heb. 7:26, holy, innocent, **u**
Heb. 13:4, *marriage* bed *be* **u**
James 1:27, pure and **u** religion

un•der•stand'ing knowledge and ability to apply judgment; intelligence.
Prov. 2:2, Incline your heart to **u**
Jer. 10:12, by His **u** He has stretched
Matt. 15:16, Are you still lacking in **u**
Eph. 4:18, being darkened in their **u**
2 Tim. 2:7, Lord will give you **u**

un•dis'ci•plined not trained in self-control or obedience.
2 Thess. 3:7, not act in an **u** manner
2 Thess. 3:11, leading an **u** life

un•faith'ful not believing in; without trust or confidence.
2 Chr. 29:6, our fathers have been **u**
2 Chr. 30:7, who were **u** to the LORD God
Ezra 10:2, **u** to our God

un•fath'om•a•ble not able to be measured.
Rom. 11:33, How . . . **u** His ways

un•fruit'ful not bearing fruit or offspring.
2 Kin. 2:19, water is bad, and the land is **u**
Matt. 13:22, and it becomes **u**
1 Cor. 14:14, my mind is **u**
Eph. 5:11, **u** deeds of darkness
2 Pet. 1:8, neither useless nor **u** in the true knowledge

un•god'ly wicked; sinful; not godly.
Ps. 43:1, against an **u** nation
Rom. 5:6, Christ died for the **u**
Titus 2:12, to deny **u-ness**
Jude 18, after their own **u** lusts

un•ho'ly profane; wicked.
Acts 10:15, no *longer* consider **u**
1 Tim. 1:9, for the **u** and profane
2 Tim. 3:2, disobedient to parents, ungrateful, **u**

un•in•ten'tion•al•ly not done purposely.
Lev. 4:2, If a person sins **u**
Lev. 5:15, acts unfaithfully and sins **u**
Num. 15:27, one person sins **u**
Deut. 4:42, who **u** slew his neighbor
Josh. 20:9, whoever kills any person **u**

un•just' not fair or impartial; not lawful or right.
Prov. 29:27, **u** man is abominable
Jer. 17:11, makes a fortune, but **u-ly**
Heb. 6:10, God is not **u** so as to forget
1 Pet. 3:18, *the* just for *the* **u**

un•lov'ing without feeling or showing love; not affectionate.
Rom. 1:31, untrustworthy, **u**
2 Tim. 3:3, **u**, irreconcilable

un•prof'it•a•ble not yielding or bringing gain; not useful or beneficial.
Titus 3:9, they are **u** and worthless
Heb. 13:17, this would be **u** for you

un•quench'a•ble not able to be put out or subdued.
Matt. 3:12, burn . . . chaff with **u** fire
Mark 9:43, into the **u** fire
Luke 3:17, burn up the chaff with **u** fire

un•righ'teous wicked; sinful.
Is. 55:7, the **u** man his thoughts
Matt. 5:45, rain on *the* righteous and *the* **u**
Rom. 3:5, God who inflicts *wrath is not* **u**
1 Cor. 6:9, **u** shall not inherit the kingdom
2 Pet. 2:9, keep the **u** under punishment

un•ru'ly not yielding easily to rule or restraint; uncontrollable.
1 Thess. 5:14, admonish the **u**
2 Thess. 3:6, who leads an **u** life

un'wor'thy not deserving; not having excellence or worth.
Gen. 32:10, **u** of all the lovingkindness
Luke 17:10, We are **u** slaves
Acts 13:46, judge yourselves **u**

up•hold' to support; to sustain; to hold up.
Ps. 119:117, **U** me that I may be safe
Is. 41:10, I will **u** you
Is. 41:13, God, who **u-s** your right hand
Is. 42:1, My Servant, whom I **u**
Is. 63:5, there was no one to **u**

up'right morally straight or correct; erect.
Deut. 32:4, Righteous and **u** is He
Prov. 4:11, led you in **u** paths
Eccl. 7:29, God made men **u**
Mic. 7:2, is no **u** *person* among men
Acts 14:10, Stand **u** on your feet

up'right•ness trustworthiness, justness.
Deut. 9:5, the **u** of your heart
1 Kin. 3:6, **u** of heart toward Thee
1 Chr. 29:17, delightest in **u**
Prov. 17:26, strike the noble for *their* **u**
Mal. 2:6, with Me in peace and **u**

up'roar a great disturbance and noise.
1 Kin. 1:41, city making such an **u**
Ps. 2:1, Why are the nations in an **u**
Is. 13:4, sound of the **u** of kingdoms
Acts 17:5, set the city in an **u**
Acts 20:1, after the **u** had ceased

up•root' to get completely rid of; to pull up by the roots.
Job 19:10, has **u-ed** my hope
Dan. 11:4, his sovereignty will be **u-ed**
Luke 17:6, Be **u-ed** and be planted
Jude 12, without fruit, doubly dead, **u-ed**

Ur'banus A Christian at Rome to whom Paul sent salutation (Rom. 16:9).

U'ri•el 1. A Kohathite, son of Tahath (1 Chr. 6:24; 15:5). 2. Father of Micaiah, one of Rehoboam's wives (2 Chr. 13:2).

u•sur'i•ous asking or taking an excessively high rate of interest for the use of money.
Lev. 25:36, not take **u** interest from him

ut'most farthest away; most distant; highest or greatest possible.
Gen. 49:26, Up to the **u** bound
1 Thess. 2:16, wrath has come . . . to the **u**

ut'ter•ance an expressing in speech; a statement.
Luke 21:15, give you **u** and wisdom
Acts 2:4, Spirit was giving them **u**
2 Cor. 8:7, in faith and **u** and knowledge
Eph. 6:19, **u** may be given to me

U'zai Father of Palal, who repaired part of the wall of Jerusalem (Neh. 3:25).

U'zal The sixth son of Joktan, of the family of Shem, who settled in South Arabia (Gen. 10:27; 1 Chr. 1:21).

Uz•zi'a An Ashterathite, one of David's valiant men (1 Chr. 11:44).

Uz'zi•el•ites Descendants of Uzziel, son of Kohath (Num. 3:27; 1 Chr. 26:23).

V

va'grant an idle wanderer; a tramp.
Gen. 4:12, a **v** and a wanderer
Gen. 4:14, I shall be a **v**

vain worthless; futile.
Ex. 20:7, take the name of the Lord your God in **v**
Ps. 2:1, peoples devising a **v** thing
Prov. 12:11, he who pursues **v** *things*
Matt. 15:9, in **v** do they worship Me
I Cor. 15:14, then our preaching is **v**

Va•i•za'tha The tenth son of Haman, in the days of Esther and Ahasuerus. He was hanged with his father and brothers (Esth. 9:9, 14).

Valley Gate A gate in the wall of Jerusalem (2 Chr. 26:9; Neh. 2:13; 3:13).

valley of A'chor Near Jericho (Josh. 7:24-26; 15:7; Is. 65:10).

valley of Ba'ca Near Jerusalem (Ps. 84:6).

Valley of Be•ra'cah West of Tekoa (2 Chr. 20:26).

valley of de•ci'sion In the vicinity of Jerusalem (Joel 3:14).

valley of Jer'i•cho Between Jericho and the Dead Sea (Deut. 34:3).

Valley of Salt At the south end of the Salt (Dead) Sea (2 Sam. 8:13; 2 Kin. 14:7).

valley of vi'sion Symbolic name for the lower part of Jerusalem (Is. 22:1, 5).

val•u•a'tion an appraisal; the act of evaluating.
Lev. 5:15, according to your **v** in silver
Lev. 27:25, Every **v** of yours
Num. 18:16, redeem them, by your **v**
2 Kin. 23:35, each according to his **v**

van'i•ty that which is vain, empty, or useless.
2 Kin. 17:15, they followed **v**
Prov. 22:8, sows iniquity will reap **v**
Eccl. 1:2, **V** of **v-es!** All is **v**
2 Pet. 2:18, arrogant *words* of **v**

var'i•col•ored having many various colors.
Gen. 37:3, made him a **v** tunic
Gen. 37:23, the **v** tunic that was on him
Gen. 37:32, they sent the **v** tunic

Vash'ti A queen whom Esther succeeded (Esth. 1:9; 2:1, 4, 17).

vast very great in extent, size, number, quantity, or amount.
Is. 22:18, *To be cast* into a **v** country

vault an arched structure forming a ceiling or roof.
Job 22:14, walks on the **v** of heaven

ven'geance revenge; punishment in return for an injury or offense.
Lev. 19:18, You shall not take **v**
Deut. 32:35, **V** is Mine
Ps. 94:1, O LORD, God of **v**
Is. 34:8, the LORD has a day of **v**
Heb. 10:30, **V** is Mine

ven'om the poison that certain animals transmit by biting or stinging.
Deut. 32:24, **v** of crawling things
Deut. 32:33, wine is the **v** of serpents
Job 20:14, the **v** of cobras
Ps. 58:4, They have **v** like the **v** of a serpent

vex•a'tion a feeling of impatience; annoyance; irritation.
Job 5:2, For **v** slays the foolish man
Ps. 10:14, beheld mischief and **v**
Prov. 12:16, fool's **v** is known

vic'to•ry the overcoming of an opponent; a conquest.
2 Sam. 23:10, Lord brought . . . great **v**
2 Kin. 5:1, had given **v** to Aram
1 Chr. 11:14, the Lord saved them by a great **v**
Ps. 98:1, holy arm have gained the **v**
1 John 5:4, **v** that has overcome the world

vin'di•cate to defend as true, correct, or honest; to sustain; to justify.
Ps. 82:3, **V** the weak and fatherless
Is. 50:8, He who **v-s** Me is near
Ezek. 36:23, I will **v** the holiness
Matt. 11:19, wisdom is **v-d** by her deeds
1 Tim. 3:16, Was **v-d** in the Spirit

vine'yard a field of grapevines.
Gen. 9:20, Noah . . . planted a **v**
Lev. 19:10, nor shall you glean your **v**
Jer. 12:10, Many shepherds have ruined My **v**
Matt. 20:4, You too go into the **v**
1 Cor. 9:7, Who plants a **v**, and does not eat

vi'o•lence the use of force in a way that harms a person or thing.
Gen. 6:11, earth was filled with **v**
Ps. 55:9, **v** and strife in the city
Prov. 4:17, drink the wine of **v**
Is. 53:9, He has done no **v**
Matt. 11:12, kingdom of heaven suffers **v**

vi'per any poisonous snake having a hollow or pit between the eye and the nostril.
Is. 14:29, a **v** will come out
Is. 30:6, lioness and lion, **v** and flying serpent

Matt. 3:7, You brood of **v-s**
Acts 28:3, a **v** came out because of the heat

vir'gin a maiden; a girl or woman who has not had sexual intercourse.
Gen. 24:16, girl was very beautiful, a **v**
Jer. 31:4, you shall be rebuilt, O **v** of Israel!
Matt. 1:23, **v** shall be with child
Matt. 1:25, kept her a **v**
1 Cor. 7:28, if a **v** should marry

vi'sion something that is seen otherwise than by ordinary sight, as in a dream.
Prov. 29:18, Where there is no **v**
Is. 22:1, concerning the valley of **v**
Joel 2:28, young men will see **v-s**
Hab. 2:2, Record the **v** And inscribe it
Matt. 17:9, Tell the **v** to no one

void an empty space; to make of no effect or nullify.
Gen. 1:2, earth was formless and **v**
Jer. 19:7, make **v** the counsel
Rom. 4:14, faith is made **v**

vo'tive given in accordance with a vow or from a feeling of reverence.
Lev. 7:16, his offering is a **v**

vow a solemn promise, especially to God.
Gen. 28:20, Jacob made a **v**
Judg. 11:30, Jephthah made a **v**
2 Sam. 15:7, let me go and pay my **v**
Eccl. 5:5, It is better that you should not **v**
Acts 18:18, he was keeping a **v**

vul'ture a large bird of prey with a naked head; a greedy, ruthless person who preys on others.
Lev. 11:13, not to be eaten: the eagle and the **v**
Matt. 24:28, the **v-s** will gather
Luke 17:37, will the **v-s** be gathered

W

wail to grieve over; to lament for.
Esth. 4:3, fasting, weeping, and **w-ing**
Is. 13:6, **W**, for the day of the Lord
Jer. 9:19, voice of **w-ing** is heard
Mic. 1:8, I must lament and **w**
Mark 5:38, loudly weeping and **w-ing**

waist'band a band fitting around the waist, as on trousers or a skirt.
Jer. 13:1, Go and buy . . . a linen **w**

war fight; strife; struggle; conflict.
Gen. 14:2, they made **w** with Bera
Ex. 13:17, when they see **w**
Josh. 11:23, the land had rest from **w**
2 Cor. 10:3, do not **w** according to the flesh
James 4:1, pleasures that wage **w** in your members

war•club a club-shaped implement used as a weapon.
Jer. 51:20, You are My **w**

war'fare violent or persistent conflict.
2 Sam. 17:8, father is an expert in **w**
Is. 40:2, her **w** has ended
2 Cor. 10:4, weapons of our **w** are not

war'rior a soldier, especially one of long experience in war.
Ex. 15:3, The LORD is a **w**
2 Chr. 32:21, destroyed every mighty **w**
Job 16:14, He runs at me like a **w**
Is. 9:5, every boot of the booted **w**
Is. 42:13, go forth like a **w**

wa'ter•less lacking or destitute of water; dry.
Matt. 12:43, unclean spirit . . . passes through **w**

weak'ness lack of strength; a fault or defect.
1 Cor. 1:25, **w** of God is stronger than
1 Cor. 15:43, it is sown in **w**
2 Cor. 12:9, power is perfected in **w**
2 Cor. 13:4, crucified because of **w**
Heb. 11:34, from **w** were made strong

wealth large possessions; riches; property.
Deut. 8:18, giving you power to make **w**
Prov. 3:9, Honor the LORD from your **w**
Is. 45:3, hidden **w** of secret places
2 Cor. 8:2, **w** of their liberality
Rev. 18:19, became rich by her **w**

whelp one of the young of a dog or of a beast of prey; a puppy, a cub.
Gen. 49:9, Judah is a lion's **w**
Deut. 33:22, Dan is a lion's **w**

whirl'wind a violent windstorm that swirls in the air in a rapid rising column.
2 Kin. 2:1, Elijah by a **w** to
Ps. 58:9, sweep them away with a **w**
Prov. 1:27, calamity comes on . . . **w**
Jer. 4:13, his chariots like the **w**
Hos. 8:7, they reap the **w**

wick'ed morally bad; evil in character, conduct or principle.
Ps. 1:1, not walk in the counsel of the **w**
Prov. 4:19, way of the **w** is like darkness
Prov. 13:9, lamp of the **w** goes out
Is. 53:9, His grave . . . with **w** men
Acts 24:15, both the righteous and the **w**

wick'ed•ness the state of being evil or morally bad.
Gen. 6:5, the **w** of man was great
Prov. 4:17, they eat the bread of **w**

Is. 9:18, **w** burns like a fire
Acts 8:22, repent of this **w** of yours
Eph. 6:12, spiritual *forces* of **w** in the heavenly

wield to exert one's authority by means of influence.
Judg. 5:14, those who **w** the staff of office

wil'der•ness an uncultivated and uninhabited region.
Deut. 29:5, forty years in the **w**
Is. 35:6, waters will break forth in the **w**
Matt. 24:26, Behold, He is in the **w**
Mark 1:13, He was in the **w** forty days
John 6:31, Our fathers ate the manna in the **w**

wine'skin a bag made from the skin of an animal and is used for holding wine.
Josh. 9:13, **w-s** which we filled
Job 32:19, Like new **w-s** it is
Ps. 119:83, like a **w** in the smoke
Mark 2:22, new wine into fresh **w-s**
Luke 5:37, no one puts new wine into old **w-s**

win'now to blow or fan the chaff from threshed grain.
Is. 30:24, which has been **w-ed** with shovel
Is. 41:16, You will **w** them

wis'dom knowledge and the ability to utilize it to benefit oneself and others.
Ex. 28:3, endowed with the spirit of **w**
Ps. 51:6, make me know **w**
Mic. 6:9, it is sound **w** to fear Thy name
Matt. 11:19, **w** is vindicated by her deeds
2 Tim. 3:15, **w** that leads to salvation

with'er to become or cause to become dry or shriveled; to fade.
Ps. 1:3, leaf does not **w**
Ps. 102:11, I **w** away like grass
Jer. 8:13, the leaf shall **w**
Matt. 13:6, had no root, they **w-ed**
James 1:11, **w-s** the grass

wit'ness testimony; proof; evidence.
Ex. 20:16, shall not bear false **w**
Job 21:29, do you not recognize their **w**
John 21:24, we know that his **w** is true
Heb. 10:15, Holy Spirit also bears **w**
Rev. 1:5, Christ, the faithful **w**

woe sorrow; grief; misfortune; affliction.
Job 10:15, If I am wicked, **w** to me!
Is. 6:5, **W** is me, for I am ruined
Jer. 44:11, set My face against you for **w**
Mark 14:21, **w** to that man by whom
Rev. 18:10, **W**,**w**, the great city

womb an organ of female mammals in which the young are formed and nourished till birth.
Gen. 25:23, Two nations are in your **w**
Ex. 13:2, first offspring of every **w**
Job 1:21, Naked . . . from my mother's **w**
Luke 1:41, baby leaped in her **w**
Acts 3:2, lame from his mother's **w**

won'der something extraordinary; a marvel.
1 Chr. 16:9, Speak of all His **w-s**
Job 37:14, consider the **w-s** of God
Ps. 9:1, I will tell of all Thy **w-s**
Is. 9:6, name will be called **W-ful** Counselor
Rom. 15:19, power of signs and **w-s**

won'drous that is to be marveled at; wonderful; marvelous.
Job 9:10, **w** works
Ps. 17:7, **W-ly** show Thy lovingkindness
Ps. 71:17, I still declare Thy **w** deeds
Ps. 75:1, Men declare Thy **w** works
Ps. 86:10, Thou art great and doest **w** deeds

work'man one who works especially at manual or industrial labor.
Ex. 38:23, an engraver and a skillful **w**
Eph. 2:10, For we are His **w-ship**
2 Tim. 2:15, approved to God as a **w**

world the universe; creation.
1 Chr. 16:30, **w** is firmly established
Job 34:13, laid *on Him* the whole **w**
Matt. 5:14, You are the light of the **w**
John 3:16, God so loved the **w**
Acts 17:6, men who have upset the **w**

worm'wood any of several bitter-tasting herbs used as a tonic.
Deut. 29:18, poisonous fruit and **w**
Prov. 5:4, she is bitter as **w**
Jer. 23:15, feed them **w**
Amos 5:7, turn justice into **w**
Rev. 8:11, star is called **W**

wor'ship to pay divine honors to; to adore.
Ps. 2:11, **W** the LORD with reverence
Ps. 29:2, **W** the LORD in holy array
John 4:22, we **w** that which we know
Phil. 3:3, **w** in the Spirit of God
Rev. 4:10, **w** Him who lives forever

worth'less having no worth; without value.
Prov. 16:27, A **w** man
Is. 5:2, it produced *only* **w** ones
Matt. 25:30, cast out the **w** slave
Titus 1:16, **w** for any good deed
James 1:26, this man's religion is **w**

wran'gle to dispute angrily; to argue.
2 Tim. 2:14, not to **w** about words

wrath violent anger; rage.
Ps. 6:1, Nor chasten me in Thy **w**
Matt. 3:7, flee from the **w** to come
Rom. 3:5, God who inflicts **w** is not unrighteous
Col. 3:6, **w** of God will come
1 Thess. 5:9, has not destined us for **w**

wrong'do•er a person who does wrong; especially moral wrong.
Ps. 71:4, the **w** and
Acts 25:11, If then I am a **w**

wrought formed; fashioned; ornamented.
Num. 31:51, all kinds of **w** articles
Ps. 31:19, Thou hast **w** for those
Ps. 139:15, skillfully **w** in the depths
John 3:21, been **w** in God

Y

yearn to be filled with longing; to feel pity or sympathy.
Ps. 84:2, longed and even **y-ed**

yield to produce; to give or grant; to surrender.
Ps. 1:3, Which **y-s** its fruit in
Ps. 67:6, earth has **y-ed** its produce
Heb. 12:11, **y-s** the peaceful fruit

yoke a bar or frame of wood fitting over the necks of two animals, as oxen, and holding them together for drawing a plow or a load; it is frequently used in the Bible to denote servitude or oppression.
Gen. 27:40, you shall break his **y**
Matt. 11:29, Take My **y** upon you
Matt. 11:30, For My **y** is easy
Gal. 5:1, to a **y** of slavery
1 Tim. 6:1, under the **y** as slaves

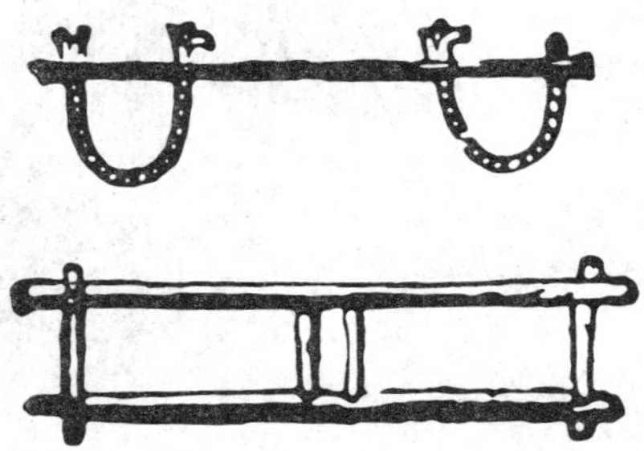

Yokes

Z

Zach•a•ri'as (Zechariah) 1. The son of Berechiah whom the Jews stoned for rebuking them (Matt. 23:35; Luke 11:51). 2. Father of John the Baptist (Luke 1:5).

Zal•mun'na A king of Midian defeated and slain by Gideon (Judg. 8:5-21; Ps. 83:11).

Za•no'ah 1. A city in the west of the plain of Judah (Josh. 15:34; Neh. 3:13). 2. A city on the east of the hill country of Judah (Josh. 15:56).

zeal eagerness in pursuing any course or object; fervor.
2 Kin. 10:16, see my **z** for the LORD
Ps. 119:139, My **z** has consumed me
Rom. 10:2, have a **z** for God
2 Cor. 7:7, your **z** for me
2 Cor. 7:11, what longing, what **z**

zeal'ous full of ardent and active interest.
1 Kin. 19:10, very **z** for the LORD
Acts 21:20, all **z** for the Law
1 Cor. 14:12, **z** of spiritual *gifts*
Titus 2:14, **z** for good deeds
Rev. 3:19, be **z** therefore, and repent

Ze'bah A king of Midian defeated and slain by Gideon (Judg. 8:5-21; Ps. 83:11).

Zeb'e•dee Husband of Salome, and father of James and John, two of the apostles of Jesus (Matt. 4:21; 20:20; 27:56).

Ze•bo'iim One of the five cities in the Valley of Siddim, destroyed with Sodom and Gomorrah (Gen. 10:19; Deut. 29:23; Hos. 11:8).

Ze'bul An officer of Abimelech, and governor of Shechem (Judg. 9:28, 30, 36, 38).

Zeb'u•lun Tenth son of Jacob, and the founder of the tribe Zebulun (Gen. 30:20; 35:23; 46:14; 49:13).

Zech•a•ri'ah 1. Son and successor of Jeroboam, king of Israel (2 Kin. 14:29); 15:8, 11). 2. Father of Abi, wife of Ahaz and mother of Hezekiah, kings of Judah (2 Kin. 18:2).

Zeeb A prince of Midian defeated and slain by Gideon (Judg. 7:25; Ps. 83:11).

Ze•loph'e•had Grandson of Gilead, son of Manasseh. He died in the wilderness, leaving five daughters but no sons. A law was then established giving females the right of inheritance (Num. 26:33; 27:1; 36:2-11).

Ze'phath A city in Simeon, at the south border of Edom, and in Judah (Judg. 1:17).

Zera'hites Descendants of Zerah, son of Judah (Josh. 7:17; 1 Chr. 27:11).

Ze•rub'ba•bel A descendant of David, an ancestor of Jesus, and the leader of the first band of Jews that returned to Palestine from the captivity in Babylon (1 Chr. 3:19; Ezra 3:2, 8; Zech. 4:6-10).

Ze•ru'iah A daughter of Jesse, father of David (1 Sam. 26:6; 2 Sam. 2:13; 3:39).

Zu•ri•shad'dai Father of Shelumiel, a chief of Simeon chosen to aid Moses in the numbering of the people (Num. 1:6; 2:12; 7:36; 10:19).

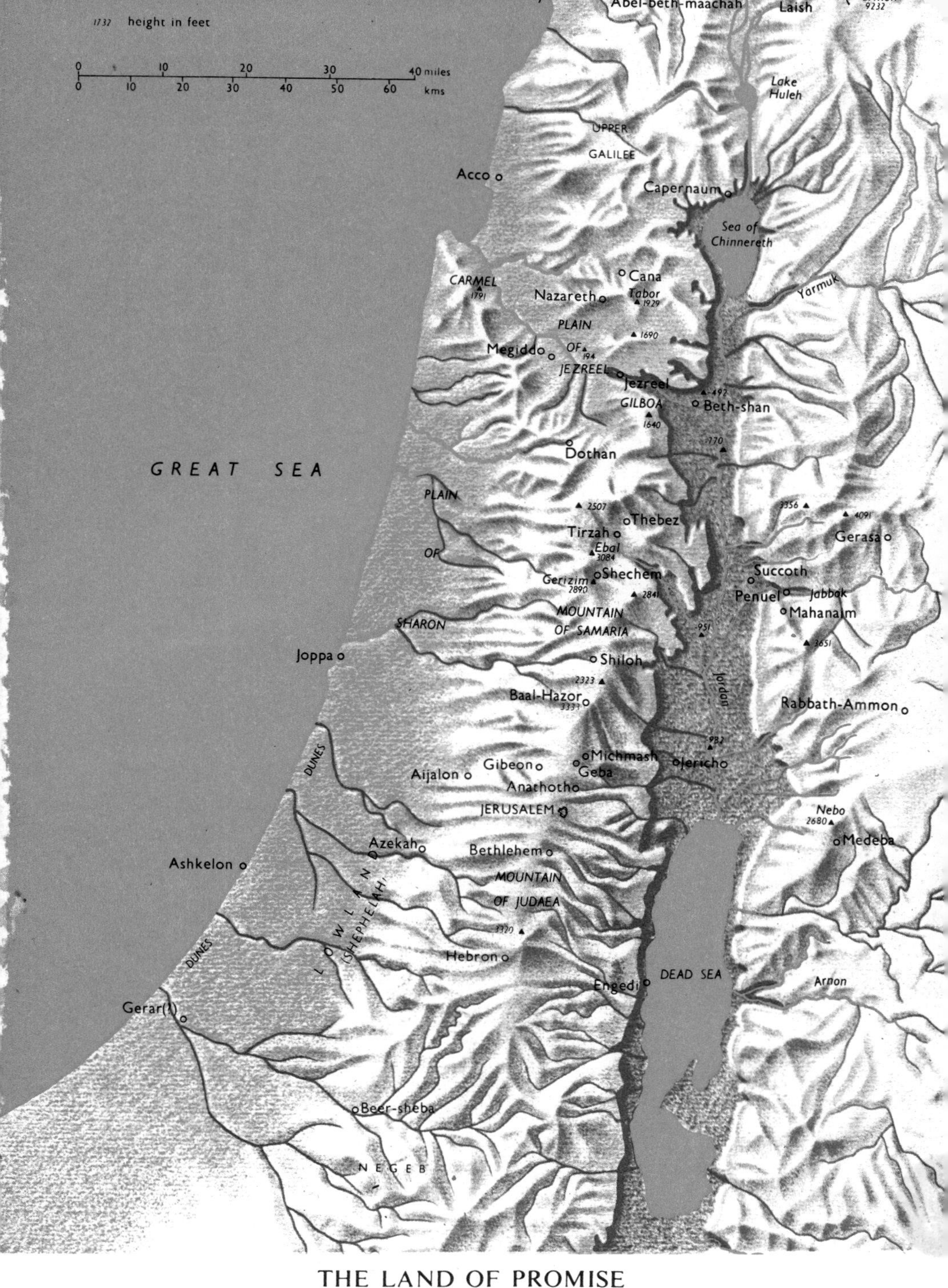

THE LAND OF PROMISE

THE ANCIENT NEAR EAST (1500 TO 600 B.C.)

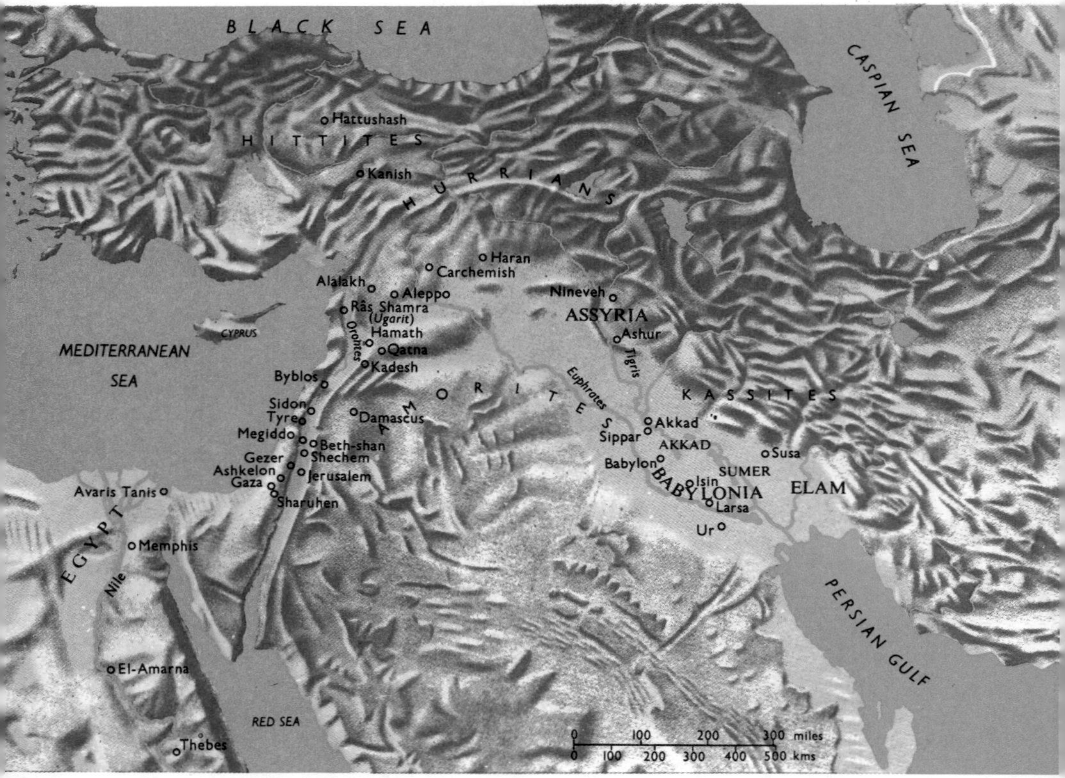

BLACK SEA
CASPIAN SEA
Hattushash
HITTITES
Kanish
HURRIANS
Haran
Carchemish
Alalakh
Aleppo
Nineveh
Râs Shamra
(Ugarit)
ASSYRIA
CYPRUS
Orontes
Hamath
Ashur
Qatna
MEDITERRANEAN
SEA
Kadesh
Tigris
Byblos
Euphrates
AMORITES
KASSITES
Sidon
Tyre
Damascus
Akkad
Megiddo
Sippar
Beth-shan
AKKAD
Shechem
Susa
Gezer
Babylon
Ashkelon
Jerusalem
SUMER
Gaza
Isin
Avaris Tanis
BABYLONIA
ELAM
Sharuhen
Larsa
Ur
EGYPT
Memphis
Nile
PERSIAN GULF
El-Amarna
RED SEA
Thebes
0 100 200 300 miles
0 100 200 300 400 500 kms

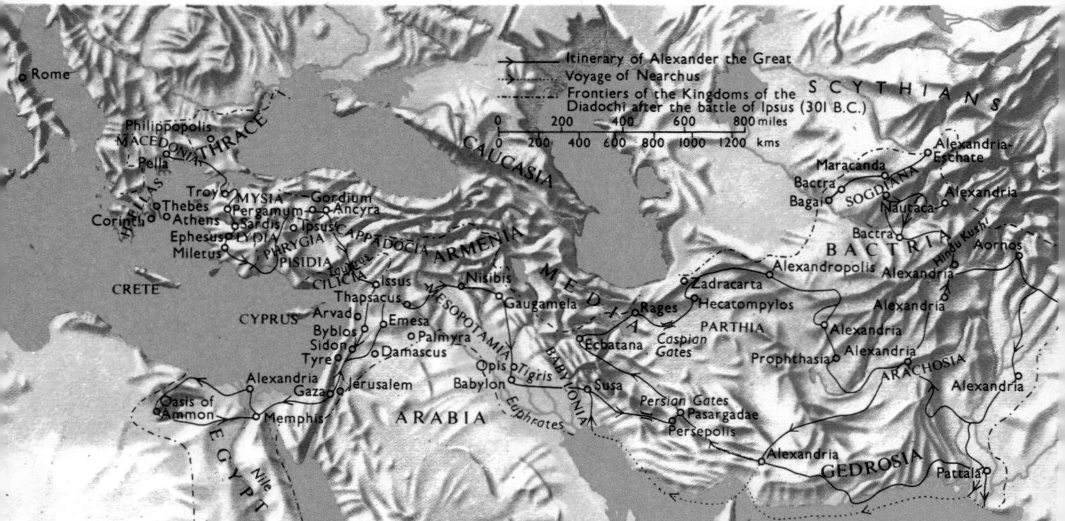

Itinerary of Alexander the Great
Voyage of Nearchus
Frontiers of the Kingdoms of the Diadochi after the battle of Ipsus (301 B.C.)
0 200 400 600 800 miles
0 200 400 600 800 1000 1200 kms

Rome
SCYTHIANS
Philippopolis
MACEDONIA
THRACE
Pella
CAUCASIA
Alexandria-Eschate
Maracanda
SOGDIANA
Bactra
Bagai
Alexandria
Nautaca
Troy
MYSIA
Gordium
HELLAS
Thebes
Pergamum
Ancyra
Corinth
Athens
Sardis
Ipsus
CAPPADOCIA
Ephesus
LYDIA
Bactra
BACTRIA
Hindu Kush
Aornos
ARMENIA
PHRYGIA
Miletus
PISIDIA
Alexandropolis
Alexandria
MEDIA
Taurus
Nisibis
CILICIA
Issus
Zadracarta
CRETE
Thapsacus
Gaugamela
Rages
Hecatompylos
Alexandria
MESOPOTAMIA
PARTHIA
Arvad
CYPRUS
Emesa
Alexandria
Byblos
Palmyra
Ecbatana
Caspian Gates
Sidon
Alexandria
Prophthasia
Tyre
Damascus
BABYLONIA
Opis
Tigris
ARACHOSIA
Alexandria
Babylon
Alexandria
Jerusalem
Susa
Gaza
Persian Gates
Oasis of Ammon
Pasargadae
Memphis
ARABIA
Euphrates
Persepolis
EGYPT
Alexandria
Nile
GEDROSIA
Pattala

THE EMPIRE OF ALEXANDER

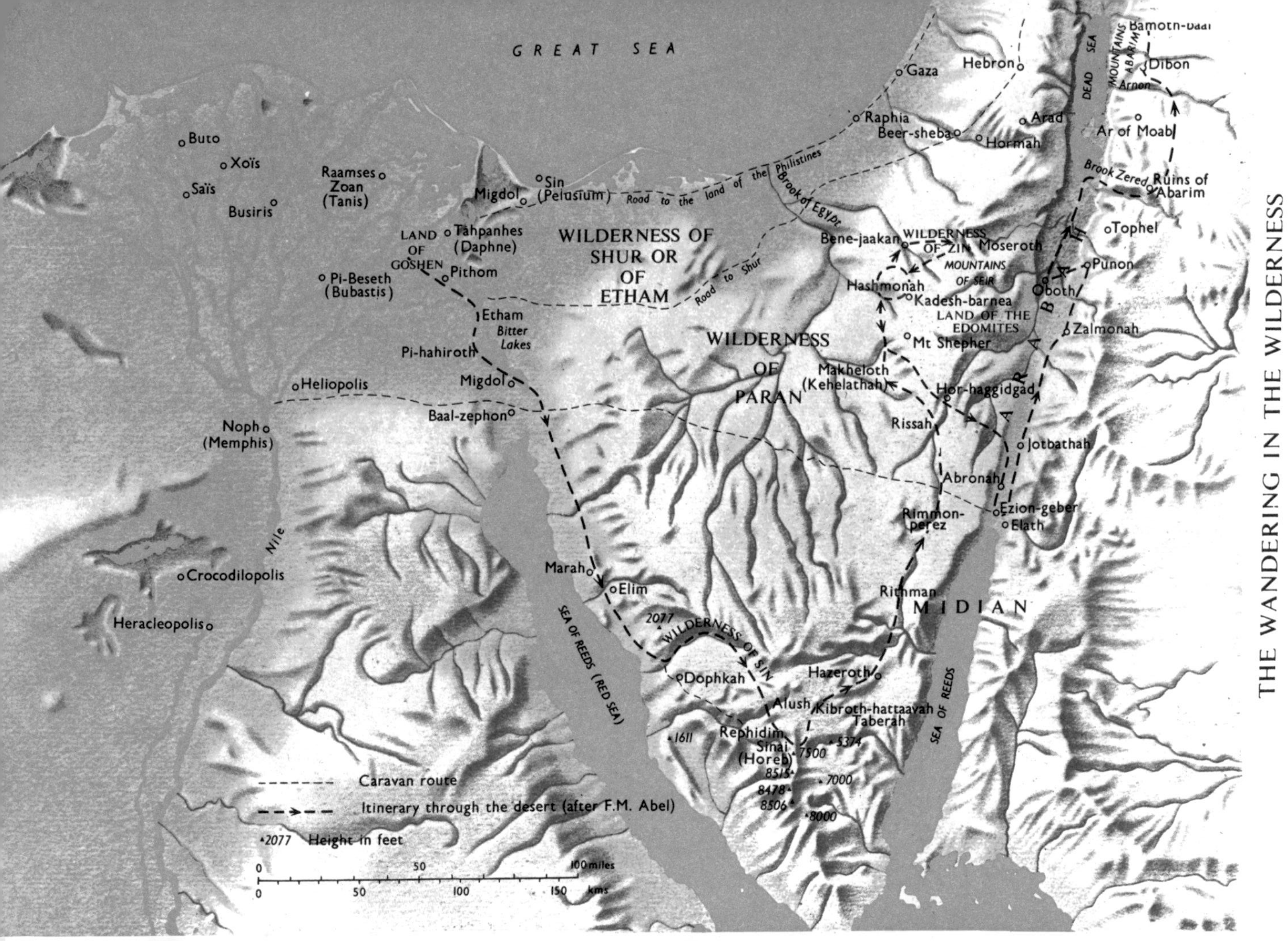

THE WANDERING IN THE WILDERNESS

THE SETTLEMENT IN CANAAN

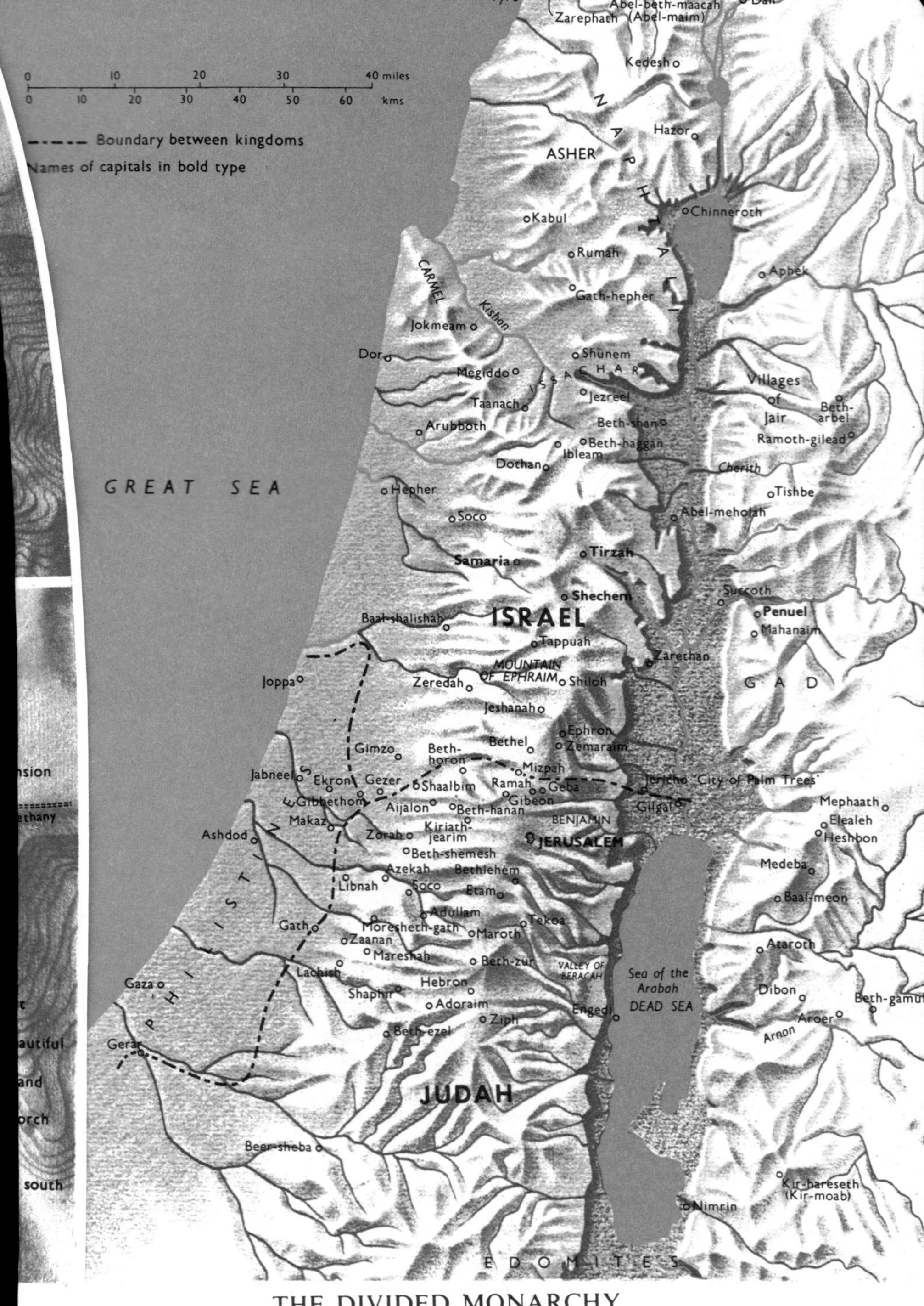

THE DIVIDED MONARCHY

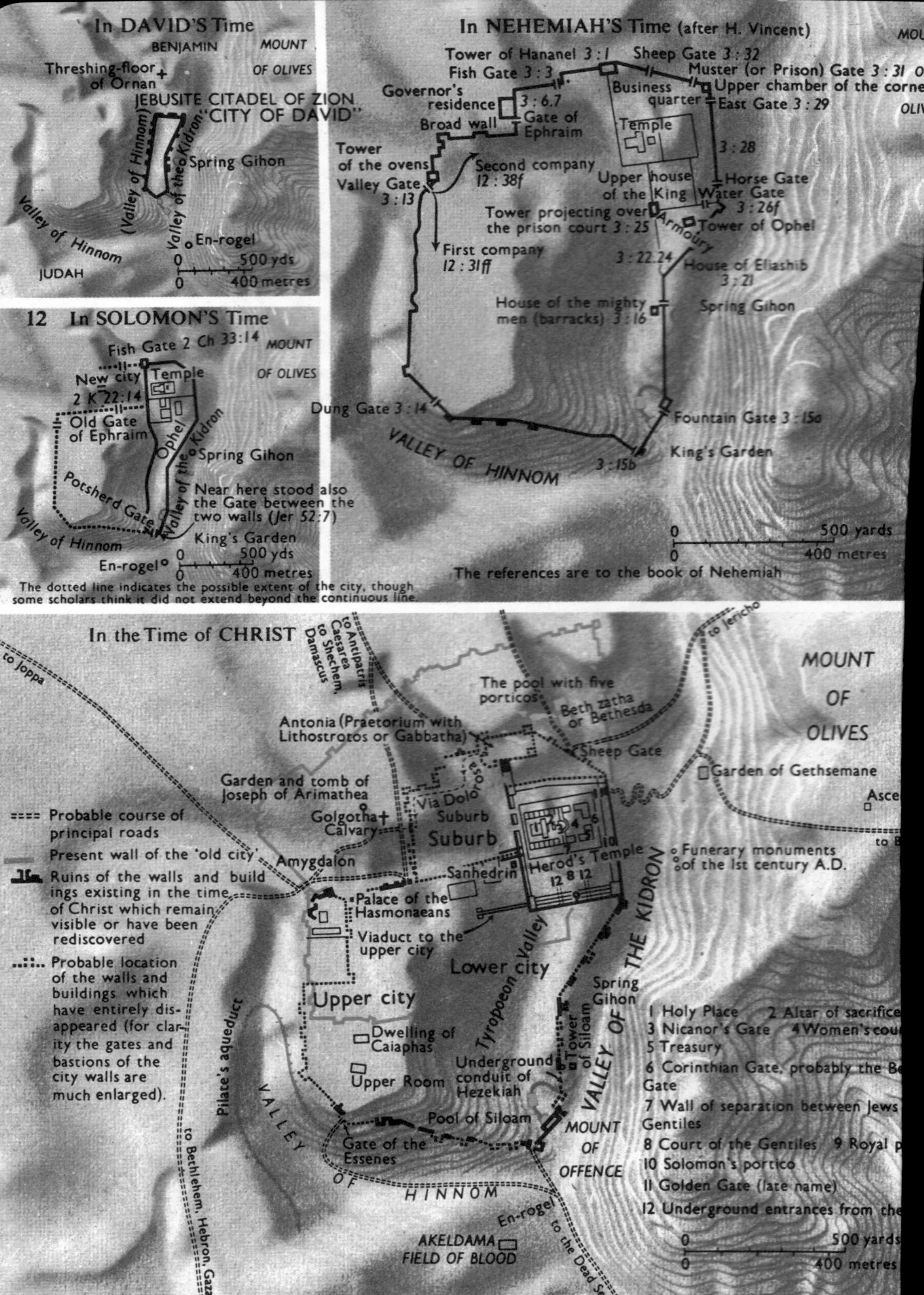
In DAVID'S Time
BENJAMIN
MOUNT OF OLIVES
Threshing-floor of Ornan
JEBUSITE CITADEL OF ZION "CITY OF DAVID"
(Valley of Hinnom)
Valley of the Kidron
Spring Gihon
Valley of Hinnom
En-rogel
JUDAH
0 500 yds
0 400 metres
12 In SOLOMON'S Time
Fish Gate 2 Ch 33:14
MOUNT OF OLIVES
New city 2 K 22:14
Temple
Old Gate of Ephraim
Ophel
Valley of the Kidron
Spring Gihon
Potsherd Gate
Near here stood also the Gate between the two walls (Jer 52:7)
Valley of Hinnom
King's Garden
En-rogel
0 500 yds
0 400 metres
The dotted line indicates the possible extent of the city, though some scholars think it did not extend beyond the continuous line.
In NEHEMIAH'S Time (after H. Vincent)
MOUNT OF OLIVES
Tower of Hananel 3:1
Sheep Gate 3:32
Fish Gate 3:3
Muster (or Prison) Gate 3:31
Governor's residence
3:6.7
Business quarter
Upper chamber of the corner
East Gate 3:29
Gate of Ephraim
Broad wall
Temple
Tower of the ovens
3:28
Second company 12:38f
Valley Gate 3:13
Upper house of the King
Horse Gate
Water Gate 3:26f
Tower projecting over the prison court 3:25
Armoury
Tower of Ophel
First company 12:31ff
3:22.24
House of Eliashib 3:21
House of the mighty men (barracks) 3:16
Spring Gihon
Dung Gate 3:14
Fountain Gate 3:15a
VALLEY OF HINNOM
3:15b
King's Garden
0 500 yards
0 400 metres
The references are to the book of Nehemiah
In the Time of CHRIST
to Joppa
to Antipatris Caesarea
to Shechem, Damascus
to Jericho
MOUNT OF OLIVES
The pool with five porticos
Beth zatha or Bethesda
Antonia (Praetorium with Lithostrotos or Gabbatha)
Sheep Gate
Garden of Gethsemane
Garden and tomb of Joseph of Arimathea
Via Dolorosa
Asce
Golgotha Calvary
Suburb
Suburb
to B
Amygdalon
Sanhedrin
Herod's Temple
Funerary monuments of the 1st century A.D.
Palace of the Hasmonaeans
Viaduct to the upper city
Tyropoeon Valley
VALLEY OF THE KIDRON
Lower city
Spring Gihon
Upper city
Tower of Siloam
Dwelling of Caiaphas
Upper Room
Underground conduit of Hezekiah
Pilate's aqueduct
Pool of Siloam
MOUNT OF OFFENCE
Gate of the Essenes
VALLEY OF HINNOM
En-rogel
AKELDAMA FIELD OF BLOOD
to Bethlehem, Hebron, Gaza
to the Dead Sea
==== Probable course of principal roads
Present wall of the 'old city'
Ruins of the walls and buildings existing in the time of Christ which remain visible or have been rediscovered
Probable location of the walls and buildings which have entirely disappeared (for clarity the gates and bastions of the city walls are much enlarged).
1 Holy Place
2 Altar of sacrifice
3 Nicanor's Gate
4 Women's cou
5 Treasury
6 Corinthian Gate, probably the Be
Gate
7 Wall of separation between Jews
Gentiles
8 Court of the Gentiles
9 Royal p
10 Solomon's portico
11 Golden Gate (late name)
12 Underground entrances from the
0 500 yards
0 400 metres

JERUSALEM

PALESTINE IN NEW TESTAMENT TIMES

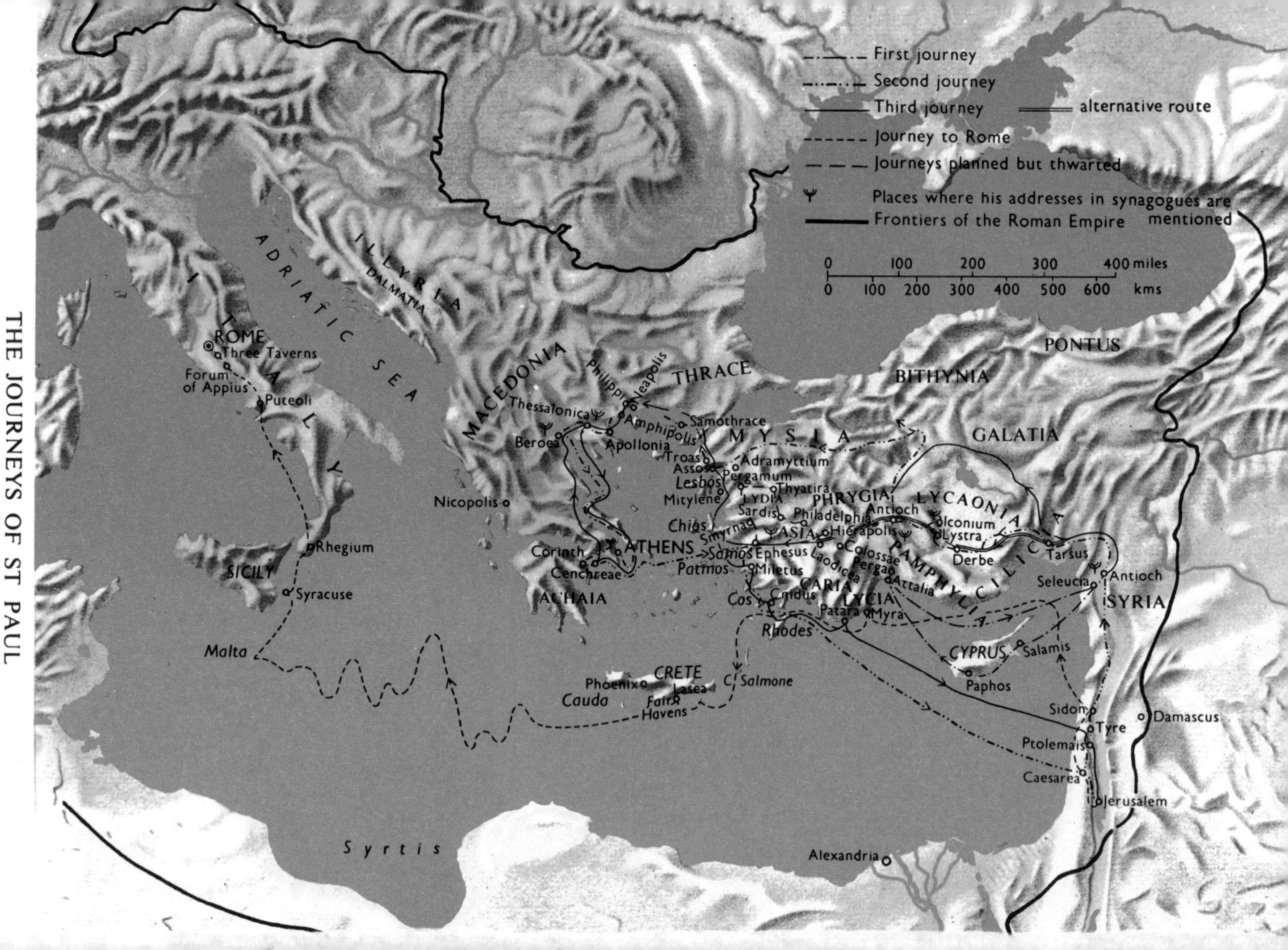

THE JOURNEYS OF ST PAUL

▶ ETERNAL SECURITY ▶
ROM 8:28-30
JOHN 10:27-29
EPH 1:13